FEATURES AND BENEFITS
Pre-Algebra ©2005

See page(s):

Curriculum and Instructional Design
... presents a coherent curriculum that effectively organizes and integrates important mathematical ideas.
- Chapters are grouped by units to bring depth to algebra concepts. — iii
- Most lessons are divided into two related objectives to allow teachers flexibility in presenting the lesson. — 98

Student Support
... is provided throughout the text to help all students succeed in algebra.
- Foldables™ Study Organizers help students actively organize key concepts and create their own review materials. — 199
- Key Concept and Concept Summary boxes help students identify main concepts. — 345, 377
- Study Tips in the margins help students understand new material. — 66, 82
- Homework Help in the margin of the exercise sets links homework exercises to corresponding examples within the lesson. — 78

Reading / Writing In Mathematics
... strategies and activities are essential for student success in mathematics.
- Reading Math Tips help clarify mathematical terms. — 75, 80
- Reading Mathematics pages help students learn to read effectively in mathematics and make connections to everyday meanings of terms. — 127, 225
- Practice in vocabulary usage in each lesson and at the end of each chapter builds reading and writing skills. — 138, 254
- Writing in Math exercises require students to summarize what they have learned in the lesson. — 173

Daily Intervention
... opportunities are provided throughout the program.
- Prerequisite Skills at the beginning of each chapter and in each lesson assess student readiness. — 97, 204
- The Student Handbook contains review and practice of prerequisite skills. — 705–725
- Daily Intervention features provide suggestions for addressing various learning styles and helping students who are having difficulty. — 59, 129
- A variety of Online Study Tools are readily accessible to students. — xxii

Test Preparation and Assessment
... provides targeted practice for local, state, and national tests.
- Standardized Test Practice questions appear in each lesson. — 285
- Standardized Test Practice Examples help students learn how to approach test questions. — 171
- Two pages of Standardized Test Practice at the end of each chapter include multiple-choice, short-response/grid-in, and extended response questions. — 260–261, 488–489
- Preparing for Standardized Tests includes examples and practice to help students become better test takers. — 771–788
- Interactive Standardized Test Practice is available in the Online Study Tools. — xxii

Staff Development
... features are available to assist new teachers and those teaching outside of their primary subject area.
- Mathematical Connections and Background provides an overview of the mathematics in the chapter and links to prior knowledge and future topics. — 4C, 4D
- Building on Prior Knowledge links what students have previously learned to the content of the current lesson. — 58
- Tips for New Teachers provide helpful suggestions for classroom management, teaching techniques, and assessment. — 268, 391

"Sticky Notes" in Chapter I provide a "walk-through" of key features. pp. 4-53

Education Partnership
... strengthens the relevance of applications and projects.
- USA TODAY Snapshots(provide current topics and data in graphs, charts, and tables and enhance the unit WebQuest projects. — 3, 289

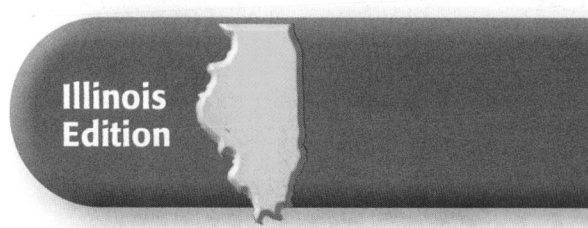
Illinois
Edition

Pre-Algebra

Teacher Wraparound Edition

State Insect
Monarch Butterfly

Contents

Glencoe

ISBN: 0-07-869359-4 *(Illinois Student Edition)*   0-07-869361-6 *(Illinois Teacher Wraparound Edition)*

1 2 3 4 5 6 7 8 9 10   043/127   12 11 10 09 08 07 06 05

Illinois Teacher Advisory Board

Photo Credits: IL1 CORBIS, **IL2** Andre Jenny/Alamy, **IL5** Getty Images

Illinois Vietnam Memorial in Springfield

Illinois Mathematics Assessment Framework, Grade 8, Correlated to *Glencoe Pre-Algebra**

Lessons in which the objectives are a primary focus are indicated in **bold**.

Assessment Objective	Student Edition Lesson(s)
STATE GOAL 6 NUMBER SENSE	
Standard 6A–Representations and Ordering	
6.8.01	Read, write, and recognize equivalent representations of integer powers of 10.	**4-8**
6.8.02	Read, write, recognize, model, and interpret integers, including translating numerical expressions.	**1-2, 2-1**
6.8.03	Recognize, translate between, and apply multiple representations of rational numbers (decimals, fractions, mixed numbers, percents, and roots).	**5-1, 5-2, 6-4**
6.8.04	Use scientific notation to represent numbers and solve problems.	**4-8**
6.8.05	Represent repeated factors using exponents.	**4-2, RM4**, 4-6, 4-7
6.8.06	Order and compare rational numbers.	**2-1, 4-5**, 5-1, 5-2, PS5
6.8.07	Identify and locate rational and irrational numbers (e.g., π, $\sqrt{2}$, $\sqrt{5}$) on a number line.	**2-1, 9-1**
6.8.08	Solve problems involving descriptions of numbers, including characteristics and relationships (e.g., exponents, roots, prime/composite, prime factorization, greatest common factor, least common multiple).	**RM2, 4-1, 4-3, 4-4, RM5, 5-6**, 5-6F, 9-2
Standards 6B, 6C–Computation, Operations, Estimation, and Properties	
6.8.09	Solve problems and number sentences involving addition, subtraction, multiplication, and division using rational numbers, exponents, and roots.	1-1, **2-2P, 2-2, 2-3, 2-4, 2-5, 4-2**, 4-5, **5-3, 5-4, 5-5, 5-7, 9-1, 9-5P, 9-5, 9-7, 9-8**, PS1, PS2, PS3, PS4, PS8, PS10
6.8.10	Identify and apply order of operations to simplify numeric expressions involving integers (including exponents and roots), fractions, and decimals.	**1-2**
6.8.11	Identify and apply the following properties of operations with rational numbers: • the commutative and associative properties for addition and multiplication; • the distributive property; • the additive and multiplicative identity properties; • the additive and multiplicative inverse properties; and • the multiplicative property of zero.	**1-4, 3-1**, 5-4
6.8.12	Describe the effect of multiplying and dividing by numbers, including the effect of multiplying or dividing a rational number by: • a number less than zero; • zero; • a number between zero and one; and • a number greater than one.	**5-3, 5-4**
6.8.13	Select, use, and justify appropriate operations, methods, and tools to compute or estimate with rational numbers. Verify solutions and determine the reasonableness of results.	6-6, 9-1, **9-5F**, PS7, PS9, PS11, PS12
6.8.14	Estimate the square or cube root of a number less than 1,000 between two whole numbers (e.g., $\sqrt[3]{200}$ is between 5 and 6).	**9-1, 9-5F**
Standard 6D–Ratios, Proportions, and Percents	
6.8.15	Use ratios to describe problem situations.	**6-1, RM6, 9-8P, 9-8**
6.8.16	Use proportional reasoning to model and solve problems.	**6-2, 6-2F, 6-5**, 9-8F
6.8.17	Read, write, recognize, model, and interpret percents, including those less than 1% and greater than 100%.	**6-4, 6-5P, 6-6**

P = Preview Lesson, F = Follow-Up Lesson, RM = Reading Math Lesson, PS = Prerequisite Skill Appendix (pp. 706–723)

*For a correlation of the Illinois Mathematics Assessment Framework, Grade 7, to *Glencoe Pre-Algebra*, visit www.il.pre-alg.com.

	Assessment Objective	Student Edition Lesson(s)
6.8.18	Solve number sentences and problems involving fractions, decimals, and percents (e.g., percent increase and decrease, interest rates, tax, discounts, tips).	**6-4, 6-5, 6-6, 6-7, 6-7F, 6-8**

STATE GOAL 7 MEASUREMENT

Standards 7A, 7B, 7C–Units, Tools, Estimation, and Applications

7.8.01	Select and use appropriate standard units and tools to solve measurement problems, including measurements of polygons and circles.	1-7P, **9-3, 9-5F, 11-7**
7.8.02	Solve problems involving perimeter/circumference and area of polygons, circles, and composite figures using diagrams, models, and grids or by measuring or using given formulas (may include sketching a figure from its description).	**3-7F, 10-5P, 10-5, 10-7, 10-8**
7.8.03	Compare and estimate length (including perimeter/circumference), area, volume, weight/mass, and angles (0° to 360°) using referents.	**RM9, RM11, 11-7**
7.8.04	Solve problems involving the volume or surface area of a right rectangular prism, right circular cylinder, or composite shape using an appropriate formula or strategy.	**11-2P, 11-2, 11-4, 11-6**
7.8.05	Solve problems involving unit conversions within the same measurement system for length, weight/mass, capacity, square units, and measures expressed as rates (e.g., converting feet/second to yards/minute).	PS13, PS14
7.8.06	Solve problems involving scale drawings, maps, and indirect measurement (e.g., determining the height of a building by comparing its known shadow length to the known height and shadow length of another object).	**6-3, 9-5P, 9-5, 9-7, 9-8P, 9-8, 9-8F**

STATE GOAL 8 ALGEBRA

Standard 8A–Representations, Patterns, and Expressions

8.8.01	Analyze, extend, and create sequences or linear functions, and determine algebraic expressions to describe the nth term of a sequence.	1-1, **5-10**
8.8.02	Write an expression using variables to represent unknown quantities.	**RM1, 1-3, 3-2**
8.8.03	Simplify algebraic expressions.	**3-2**
8.8.04	Recognize and generate equivalent forms of algebraic expressions.	1-3
8.8.05	Evaluate or simplify algebraic expressions with one or more rational variable values (e.g., $3a^2 - b$ for $a = 3$ and $b = 7$).	**1-3,** 1-3F, **3-2**

Standard 8B–Connections Using Tables, Graphs, and Symbols

8.8.06	Recognize, describe, and extend patterns using rate of change.	**8-4P, 8-4, 8-5P, 8-5,** 8-6, 8-6F, 8-7
8.8.07	Represent linear equations and quantitative relationships on a rectangular coordinate system, and interpret the meaning of a specific part of a graph.	1-6, 1-7P, 1-7, **8-2, 8-3, 8-4, 8-5, 8-6, 8-6F**
8.8.08	Translate between different representations (table, written, graphical, or pictorial) of whole number relationships and linear expressions.	1-6, 1-7P, 1-7, **8-1, 8-2,** RM8, **8-3, 8-4, 8-5, 8-6, 8-6F,** 8-7
8.8.09	Interpret the meaning of slope and intercepts in linear situations.	**8-4P, 8-4, 8-5P, 8-5**
8.8.10	Identify, graph, and interpret up to two inequalities with a single variable (including the intersection or union of these inequalities) on a number line.	7-3, 7-4, 7-5, 7-6

Standards 8C, 8D–Writing, Interpreting, and Solving Equations

8.8.11	Represent and analyze problems with linear equations and inequalities.	**1-5, 3-3, 3-4, 3-5, 3-6, 3-7, 6-7, 7-1, 7-2, RM7, 7-3, 7-4, 7-5, 7-6,** 13-5
8.8.12	Solve linear equations and inequalities in one variable over the rational numbers (e.g., $5x + 7 = -13$, $4x - 3 = -7x + 8$, $-2x + 3 > -5$).	**1-5, 3-3 and 3-4P, 3-3, 3-4, 3-5, 3-6,** 3-7, **5-9, 6-7, 7-1P, 7-1, 7-2, 7-3, 7-4, 7-5, 7-6**

P = Preview Lesson, F = Follow-Up Lesson, RM = Reading Math Lesson, PS = Prerequisite Skill Appendix (pp. 706–723)

Assessment Objective	Student Edition Lesson(s)
8.8.13	Solve word problems involving unknown quantities.	1-1, 3-3, 3-4, 3-5, 3-6, **3-7, 6-7,** 7-1, 7-2, 7-3, 7-4, 7-5, 7-6

STATE GOAL 9   GEOMETRY

Standard 9A–Properties of Single Figures and Coordinate Geometry

9.8.01	Solve problems involving two- and three-dimensional shapes.	**9-5,** 10-5, 11-6
9.8.02	Solve problems that require knowledge of triangle and quadrilateral properties (e.g., triangle inequality).	**9-4, 9-5P, 9-5, 10-4**
9.8.03	Find the length of any side of a right triangle using the Pythagorean theorem (whole number solutions).	**9-5P, 9-5**
9.8.04	Identify, describe, and determine the radius, diameter, and circumference of a circle and their relationship to each other and to pi.	**10-7**
9.8.05	Graph points, and identify coordinates of points on the Cartesian coordinate plane (all four quadrants).	**1-6,** 1-7, **2-6**
9.8.06	Represent and identify geometric figures using coordinate geometry, including those resulting from transformations.	**10-3**
9.8.07	Analyze the results of a combination of transformations, and determine a different transformation that could produce the same result.	**10-3, 10-3F**
9.8.08	Identify or analyze relationships of angles formed by intersecting lines (including parallel lines cut by a transversal) and angles formed by radii of a circle.	**10-1**
9.8.09	Solve problems involving vertical, complementary, and supplementary angles.	**10-1**

Standard 9B–Relationships Between and Among Multiple Figures

9.8.10	Identify front, side, and top views of a three-dimensional solid built with cubes.	**11-1P**
9.8.11	Solve problems involving congruent and similar figures.	**9-7, 10-2**
9.8.12	Relate absolute value to distance on the number line.	**2-1**

Standard 9C–Justifications of Conjectures and Conclusions

This standard is not assessed in isolation. Rather, its essence is assessed indirectly through problems that require this type of thinking.

Standard 9D–Trigonometry   *This standard is not assessed on the state assessment until grade 11.*

STATE GOAL 10   DATA ANALYSIS, STATISTICS, AND PROBABILITY

Standards 10A, 10B–Data Analysis and Statistics

10.8.01	Read, interpret (including possible misleading characteristics), and make predictions from data represented in a bar graph, line (dot) plot, Venn diagram (with two or three circles), chart/table, line graph, scatterplot, circle graph, stem-and-leaf plot, or histogram.	**1-7P, 1-7, 1-7F,** 5-8P, 5-8, 9-2, **12-1, 12-3, 12-5,** PS15
10.8.02	Compare and contrast the effectiveness of different representations of the same data.	**12-5**
10.8.03	Create a bar graph, chart/table, line graph, or circle graph and solve a problem using the data in the graph for a given set of data.	**9-3F, 12-1, 12-3, 12-3F, 12-4, 12-4F**
10.8.04	Identify or draw a reasonable approximation of the line of best fit from a set of data or a scatter plot, and use the line to make predictions.	1-7P, 1-7, 1-7F, **8-8**
10.8.05	Analyze and apply measures of central tendency (mode, range, median, and mean) in problem-solving situations.	5-8P, **5-8, 5-8F**

Standard 10C–Probability

10.8.06	Solve problems involving the probability of an event composed of repeated trials, compound events (including independent events), or future events with or without replacement.	**6-9, 6-9F, 12-9**
10.8.07	Represent all possible outcomes (sample space) for simple or compound events (e.g., tables, grids, tree diagrams).	**6-9**
10.8.08	Solve simple problems involving the number of ways objects can be arranged (permutations and combinations).	**12-6, 12-6F, 12-7**

P = Preview Lesson, F = Follow-Up Lesson, RM = Reading Math Lesson, PS = Prerequisite Skill Appendix (pp. 706–723)

How To...
Prepare for the ISAT

Countdown to ISAT

Pages IL8–IL32 of this text include a section called **Countdown to ISAT.** Each page contains 7 problems that are similar to those on the ISAT. You should plan to complete one page each week to help you prepare for the test.

Plan to spend a few minutes each day working on the ISAT problem(s) for that day unless your teacher asks you to do otherwise. If you have difficulty with any problem, you can refer to the lesson that is referenced in parentheses after the problem.

Each week is comprised of an extended response problem, 4 multiple-choice problems, and 2 short constructed response problems as listed below.

Monday	1 extended response
Tuesday	2 multiple choice
Wednesday	2 multiple choice
Thursday	1 short constructed response
Friday	1 short constructed response

Your teacher can provide you with an answer sheet to record your work and your answers for each week. A printable worksheet is also available at il.pre-alg.com. At the end of each week, your teacher may want you to turn in the answer sheet.

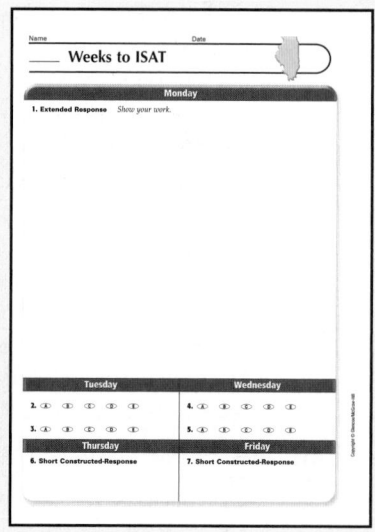

ISAT Workbook, Grade 8

The **Illinois Standards Achievement Test (ISAT) Sample and Practice Test Workbook, Grade 8,** contains a diagnostic test, practice for each Illinois Mathematics Assessment Framework objective, and a sample test.

As you practice and master each objective, you can record your progress in the Student Recording Chart in your workbook.

Your teacher may also ask you to take the sample test at various points throughout the year to see if you're ready to take the real ISAT.

The Countdown to ISAT Answer Sheet master shown above is available in the Teacher's Annotated Edition of this workbook.

Your Textbook

Your textbook contains many opportunities for you to get ready for the ISAT every day. Take advantage of these so you don't need to cram before the test.

- **Each lesson** contains at least two Standardized Test Practice problems. You can use these problems every day to keep your ISAT skills sharp. The **Chapter Practice Test** also includes a Standardized Test Practice problem.

- **Worked-out examples** in each chapter show you step-by-step solutions of Standardized Test Practice problems. Just like the practice problems, these problems model those that appear on the ISAT. **Test-Taking Tips** are also included.

- Two pages of **Standardized Test Practice** are included at the end of each chapter. These problems may cover any of the content up to and including the chapter they follow.

- Pages 771–775 and 780–788 of the **Preparing for Standardized Tests** section of your textbook discusses various strategies for attacking questions like those that appear on the ISAT. Additional practice problems are also provided.

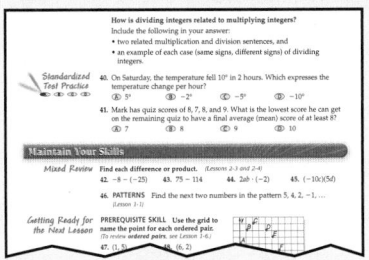

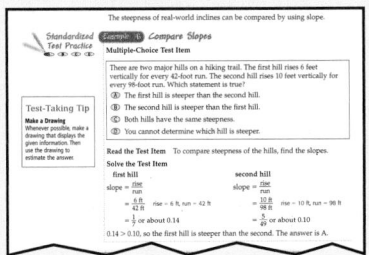

Test-Taking Tips

- ✓ Pace yourself. Don't spend too much time on one problem. You can come back if there is time.

- ✓ Listen to and read the directions carefully.

- ✓ Read each question carefully. It is important that you understand what each question asks.

- ✓ Answer the easy questions first. Then go back and try to answer the more difficult questions.

- ✓ Use logic in more difficult questions. Eliminate as many incorrect answers as you can, then make an educated guess from the remaining answers.

- ✓ Answer every question.

- ✓ Review your work. Check to be sure that you marked only one answer to each question.

- ✓ Be precise in marking your answer document. Check to be sure that the number for the line of circles on your answer document is the same as the number for the question you are answering.

- ✓ Erase completely. If you want to change an answer on your answer document, be sure to erase the unintended mark completely.

25 Weeks to ISAT

Monday

Monday
Extended Response Sample Answers

1A. $7 \div 20 = \$0.35$

1B. $\$250 \div (50 \times 20) = \$0.25$

1C. The price of one case is $280. The price of 49 boxes is 49 × $6 or $294. So, the price of one case is $294 − $280 or $14 less than the price of 49 boxes.

1. **Extended Response Show your work and clearly explain your answer.** The table shows the wholesale prices of Big Bubble Gum. One box holds 20 packs. One case holds 50 boxes. (Lesson 1-1) **See margin.**

   A. What is the price per pack of gum when 12 boxes are purchased?

   B. What is the price per pack when 12 cases are purchased?

   C. How much less is the price of one case than the price of 49 boxes?

Quantity	Price
1–20 boxes	$7/box
21–49 boxes	$6/box
1–5 cases	$280/case
6–10 cases	$260/case
11–20 cases	$250/case
21 or more cases	$230/case

Tuesday

2. **Multiple-Choice** Anderson Lake State Fish and Wildlife Area covers 2,247 acres in west-central Illinois. There are 640 acres in a square mile. Which is the approximate area of the State Fish and Wildlife Area? (Page 720) **A**
   - Ⓐ 3.51 sq mi
   - Ⓑ 3.74 sq mi
   - Ⓒ 3.86 sq mi
   - Ⓓ 3.97 sq mi
   - Ⓔ 4.04 sq mi

3. **Multiple-Choice** A pound of baby greens costs $4.95 per pound and a pound of tomatoes costs $2.49 per pound. Which expression gives the total cost of two pounds of greens and three pounds of tomatoes? (Lesson 1-2) **E**
   - Ⓐ $2 \times \$4.95 \times 3 \times \$2.49$
   - Ⓑ $2 \times \$4.95 + 3 + \$2.49$
   - Ⓒ $2 \times \$4.95 + 3 \div \$2.49$
   - Ⓓ $3 \times \$4.95 + 2 \times \$2.49$
   - Ⓔ $2 \times \$4.95 + 3 \times \$2.49$

Wednesday

4. **Multiple-Choice** Which is the result of evaluating $6a - 5b \div 8$ if $a = 5$ and $b = 16$? (Lesson 1-3) **D**
   - Ⓐ 23
   - Ⓑ 22
   - Ⓒ 21
   - Ⓓ 20
   - Ⓔ 19

5. **Multiple-Choice** Which property is shown by the statement $5 \cdot (xy) = (xy) \cdot 5$? (Lesson 1-4) **B**
   - Ⓐ associative property of multiplication
   - Ⓑ commutative property of multiplication
   - Ⓒ associative property of addition
   - Ⓓ multiplicative identity
   - Ⓔ commutative property of addition

Thursday

6. **Short Constructed-Response** A plant grew five inches in two months to a height of h inches. Write an expression that represents the original height of the plant in inches. (Lesson 1-3) $h - 5$

Friday

7. **Short Constructed-Response** The price to rent a car for one day is given by $P = \$0.15m + \$19.95$, where P is the price and m is the number of miles the car is driven. Find the price P if the car is driven 52 miles. (Lesson 1-5) **$27.75**

Grade 8 Assessment Objectives Addressed

Monday	(1A) 6.8.09 (1B) 6.8.09 (1C) 6.8.09
Tuesday	(2) 7.8.05; (3) 6.8.10
Wednesday	(4) 8.8.05; (5) 6.8.11
Thursday	(6) 8.8.02
Friday	(7) 8.8.11

Monday

1. **Extended Response** Show your work and clearly explain your answer. The price of admission to Santa's Village Amusement Park in East Dundee is $23.50 per person. (Lesson 1-6) **See margin.**

   A. Make a table of ordered pairs in which the x-coordinate represents the number of tickets and the y-coordinate represents the cost of 2, 4, and 6 tickets.

   B. Graph the ordered pairs.

   C. Write an equation that represents the cost of x tickets.

Tuesday

2. **Multiple-Choice** Which is the distance between C and D on the number line? (Lesson 2-1) **D**

   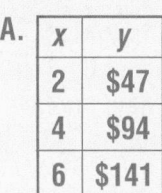

   - Ⓐ 4
   - Ⓑ 5
   - Ⓒ 6
   - Ⓓ 7
   - Ⓔ 8

3. **Multiple-Choice** Drytown lost 17 residents in the past year. The previous population was 204. Which is the new population? (Lesson 2-3) **D**
   - Ⓐ 221
   - Ⓑ 209
   - Ⓒ 193
   - Ⓓ 187
   - Ⓔ 177

Wednesday

4. **Multiple-Choice** Katie had $368 in her bank account before she withdrew $80 with her debit card. Which is the new balance of her account? (Lesson 2-2) **A**
   - Ⓐ $288
   - Ⓑ $328
   - Ⓒ $378
   - Ⓓ $428
   - Ⓔ $448

5. **Multiple-Choice** Which expression is equal to 25? (Lesson 1-2) **B**
   - Ⓐ $77 \div 11 + 15 \times 4$
   - Ⓑ $(98 - 73) \times 3 - 550 \div 11$
   - Ⓒ $75 \div 3 - 10 \times 3$
   - Ⓓ $25 \times 3 - 75 \div 3$
   - Ⓔ $(150 - 75) \div 25 + 23$

Thursday

6. **Short Constructed-Response** Write an integer representing a loss of $10,000 in the stock market. (Lesson 2-1) **−10,000**

Friday

7. **Short Constructed-Response** Simplify $-9s(-3t)(-5)$. (Lesson 2-4) **−135st**

Monday
Extended Response
Sample Answers

1A.

x	y
2	$47
4	$94
6	$141

1B.

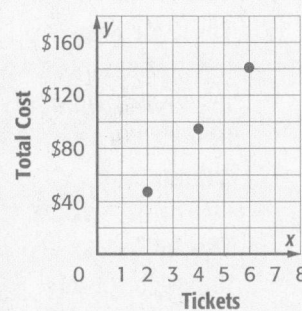

1C. $y = \$23.50x$

Grade 8 Assessment Objectives Addressed

Monday	(1A) 8.8.08 (1B) 8.8.07 (1C) 8.8.08
Tuesday	(2) 9.8.12; (3) 6.8.02
Wednesday	(4) 6.8.02; (5) 6.8.10
Thursday	(6) 6.8.02
Friday	(7) 8.8.03

Countdown
to ISAT

23 Weeks to ISAT

Monday

Monday
Extended Response
Sample Answers

1. **Extended Response Show your work and clearly explain your answer.** A snowman was shrinking at a rate of three inches per day. **See margin.**

   A. Write an integer for the rate of shrinking. (Lesson 2-1)

   B. How many inches shorter was the snowman after four days? (Lesson 2-4)

   C. If the snowman was 42 inches tall on the second day, how tall was the snowman on the seventh day? (Lesson 2-4)

1A. The height is reduced by 3 in. per day, so the integer is −3.

1B. −3(4) = −12, so the snowman was 12 in. shorter.

1C. 7 − 2 or 5 days have passed, so the snowman's height has changed by −3(5) or −15 in. The height on the seventh day was 42 + (−15) or 27 in.

Tuesday	Wednesday

2. **Multiple-Choice** Lake Le-Aqua-Na State Recreation Area in Lena covers 715 acres. The lake covers 40 acres. Which is the number of acres of the park not covered by the lake? (Lesson 2-3) **D**
  Ⓐ 755
  Ⓑ 725
  Ⓒ 685
  Ⓓ 675
  Ⓔ 665
	4. **Multiple-Choice** Which is the distance between −11 and 7 on a number line? (Lesson 2-1) **C**
	  Ⓐ 20
	  Ⓑ 19
	  Ⓒ 18
	  Ⓓ 17
	  Ⓔ 16

3. **Multiple-Choice** Daniel hit a golf ball 270 yards on his first try. On his second try, he hit a ball 15 fewer yards. Which is the distance the second ball traveled? (Lesson 2-2) **B**
  Ⓐ 265 yards
  Ⓑ 255 yards
  Ⓒ 245 yards
  Ⓓ 235 yards
  Ⓔ 225 yards
	5. **Multiple-Choice** At 6:00 A.M., Terrell saw that the outdoor temperature was −13°F. At 2:00 P.M., the temperature was 45°F. Which is the difference in temperature between these two times? (Lesson 2-3) **A**
	  Ⓐ 58°F
	  Ⓑ 57°F
	  Ⓒ 55°F
	  Ⓓ 53°F
	  Ⓔ 48°F

Thursday	Friday
6. **Short Constructed-Response** Evaluate $-18 \div (qp)$ if $q = -3$ and $p = 2$. (Lesson 2-5) **3**	7. **Short Constructed-Response** Name the quadrant in which the point $(3, -2)$ is located. (Lesson 2-6) **IV or 4**

Grade 8 Assessment Objectives Addressed

Monday	(1A) 6.8.02 (1B) 6.8.09 (1C) 6.8.09
Tuesday	(2) 6.8.09; (3) 6.8.02
Wednesday	(4) 9.8.12; (5) 6.8.02
Thursday	(6) 8.8.05
Friday	(7) 9.8.05

22 Weeks to ISAT

Monday

1. **Extended Response** **Show your work and clearly explain your answer.** Raoul won an election for class president by receiving 261 votes, which was 47 more than that of the next highest vote-getter, Caroline. (Lesson 3-3) **See margin.**

   A. Write an equation representing the number of votes V Caroline received using the given information.

   B. Find the number of votes Caroline received.

   C. In all, 516 votes were cast. How many votes were cast for candidates other than Raoul and Caroline?

Tuesday

2. **Multiple-Choice** Suppose you purchase x bottles of orange juice, one less bottle of milk than bottles of orange juice, and twice as many bottles of energy drink as bottles of orange juice. Which expression in simplest form represents the total number of bottles? (Lesson 3-2) **D**
   - Ⓐ $4x + 1$
   - Ⓑ $3x - 1$
   - Ⓒ $3x + 1$
   - Ⓓ $4x - 1$
   - Ⓔ $2x + 2$

3. **Multiple-Choice** The 2004 State Street Thanksgiving Parade in Chicago had 200 high-stepping horses. How many hooves do 200 horses have altogether? (Lesson 2-4) **B**
   - Ⓐ 700
   - Ⓑ 800
   - Ⓒ 900
   - Ⓓ 1,000
   - Ⓔ 1,200

Wednesday

4. **Multiple-Choice** The price for a six-pack of canned lemonade is $3. Which is the price per can? (Lesson 3-4) **E**
   - Ⓐ $0.75
   - Ⓑ $0.65
   - Ⓒ $0.60
   - Ⓓ $0.55
   - Ⓔ $0.50

5. **Multiple-Choice** Which is the solution to $18h - 6 = 30$? (Lesson 3-5) **C**
   - Ⓐ 0
   - Ⓑ 1
   - Ⓒ 2
   - Ⓓ 3
   - Ⓔ 4

Thursday

6. **Short Constructed-Response** Use the Distributive Property to write $7(2x - 3)$ as an equivalent algebraic expression. (Lesson 3-1) **$14x - 21$**

Friday

7. **Short Constructed-Response** Seven more than three times a number is 40. Translate the previous sentence into an equation and solve. (Lesson 3-6) **$3x + 7 = 40$; $x = 11$**

Illinois Pre-Algebra IL11

Monday
Extended Response
Sample Answers

1A. $V + 47 = 261$

1B. $V + 47 - 47 = 261 - 47$ or $V = 214$.

1C. $516 - 261 - 214 = 41$

Grade 8 Assessment Objectives Addressed

Monday	(1A) 8.8.11 (1B) 8.8.12 (1C) 6.8.09
Tuesday	(2) 8.8.03; (3) 6.8.09
Wednesday	(4) 8.8.13; (5) 8.8.12
Thursday	(6) 8.8.04
Friday	(7) 8.8.11

21 Weeks to ISAT

Monday

**Monday
Extended Response
Sample Answers**

1A. $6a - 3(a - 2b + 1) - 4 + b =$
$6a - 3a + 6b - 3 - 4 + b$

1B. $6a - 3a + 6b - 3 - 4 + b =$
$(6a - 3a) + (6b + b) + (-3 - 4) =$
$3a + 7b - 7$

1C. $3(-1) + 7(2) - 7 = -3 + 14 - 7 = 4$

1. **Extended Response Show your work and clearly explain your answer.**
   You are given the expression $6a - 3(a - 2b + 1) - 4 + b$. **See margin.**

   A. Use the Distributive Property to eliminate the parentheses in the expression. (Lesson 3-1)

   B. Collect like terms. Then, write the expression in simplest form. (Lesson 3-2)

   C. Evaluate the expression if $a = -1$ and $b = 2$. (Lesson 2-4)

Tuesday	Wednesday

2. **Multiple-Choice** A cheetah can run 400 feet in 4 seconds. Which is the speed of the cheetah in feet per second? (Lesson 3-7) **C**
   - Ⓐ 96
   - Ⓑ 98
   - Ⓒ 100
   - Ⓓ 102
   - Ⓔ 105

3. **Multiple-Choice** The difference between Chenoa's highest and lowest scoring basketball games is nine points. Her highest score was 15 points. Which was her lowest score? (Lesson 3-3) **D**
   - Ⓐ 3
   - Ⓑ 4
   - Ⓒ 5
   - Ⓓ 6
   - Ⓔ 7

4. **Multiple-Choice** Jamar spent $7 in an arcade. This was $5 less than four times what Sam spent in the arcade. Which equation represents this situation? (Lesson 3-6) **B**
   - Ⓐ $4x + 5 = 7$
   - Ⓑ $4x - 5 = 7$
   - Ⓒ $5x - 4 = 7$
   - Ⓓ $7x + 5 = 4$
   - Ⓔ $5x + 4 = 7$

5. **Multiple-Choice** In 2002, 80,040 tons of sweet corn were produced in Illinois at a price of $93 per ton. Which was the total value of Illinois's sweet corn production in 2002? (Lesson 1-2) **A**
   - Ⓐ $7,443,720
   - Ⓑ $7,443,710
   - Ⓒ $7,434,720
   - Ⓓ $7,433,620
   - Ⓔ $7,413,530

Thursday	Friday

6. **Short Constructed-Response** Gabriela weighs 105 pounds, which is five times what her little sister weighs. Write and solve an equation to find the weight of Gabriela's little sister. (Lesson 3-4) **$5x = 105$ or $x = 21$ lbs**

7. **Short Constructed-Response**
   Solve $\frac{-2k}{5} - 11 = -13$ for k. (Lesson 3-5)
   $k = 5$

Grade 8 Assessment Objectives Addressed

Monday	(1A) 8.8.03 (1B) 8.8.03 (1C) 8.8.05
Tuesday	(2) 8.8.13; (3) 6.8.09
Wednesday	(4) 8.8.11; (5) 6.8.09
Thursday	(6) 8.8.11
Friday	(7) 8.8.12

20 Weeks to ISAT

Monday

1. **Extended Response Show your work and clearly explain your answer.** Use the numbers 252 and 300 to answer the questions. **See margin.**

   A. Find the prime factorization for 252. (Lesson 4-3)

   B. Find the prime factorization for 300. (Lesson 4-3)

   C. Find the greatest common factor of the two numbers. (Lesson 4-4)

Tuesday	Wednesday

2. **Multiple-Choice** Which is the result of evaluating $p^2(q - 2r)^3$ if $p = 2$, $q = -6$, and $r = -2$? (Lesson 4-2) **E**
   - Ⓐ 32
   - Ⓑ 23
   - Ⓒ −12
   - Ⓓ −23
   - Ⓔ −32

3. **Multiple-Choice** Which expression is the simplest form of $\frac{51c^5d^3}{3c^4d}$? (Lesson 4-5) **A**
   - Ⓐ $17cd^2$
   - Ⓑ $17c^2d$
   - Ⓒ $21cd^2$
   - Ⓓ $21c^2d$
   - Ⓔ $14c^2d^2$

4. **Multiple-Choice** Which is the time it would take a spaceship traveling at a speed of 3.5×10^6 meters per second to travel a distance of 1.75×10^8 meters? (Lesson 4-8) **C**
   - Ⓐ 40 seconds
   - Ⓑ 45 seconds
   - Ⓒ 50 seconds
   - Ⓓ 55 seconds
   - Ⓔ 60 seconds

5. **Multiple-Choice** Ticket prices for *La Traviata* at the Peoria Civic Center Theater are shown in the table.

Section	Price
B	$130
I	$100
II	$60
III	$30

   Which is the total price to purchase two tickets for each section? (Lesson 3-1) **B**
   - Ⓐ $960
   - Ⓑ $640
   - Ⓒ $580
   - Ⓓ $420
   - Ⓔ $390

Thursday	Friday

6. **Short Constructed-Response**
   Write $3 \cdot 3 \cdot 3 \cdot 3 \cdot (x + 1) \cdot (x + 1) \cdot (x + 1)$ using exponents. (Lesson 4-2) $3^4(x + 1)^3$

7. **Short Constructed-Response**
   Simplify $15^{-4} \cdot 15^5 \cdot 3^{-3} \cdot 3^2$. (Lesson 4-7) **5**

Illinois Pre-Algebra IL13

Monday
Extended Response
Sample Answers

1A. $252 = 2 \cdot 126 = 2 \cdot 2 \cdot 63 = 2 \cdot 2 \cdot 9 \cdot 7 = 2^2 \cdot 3^2 \cdot 7$

1B. $300 = 2 \cdot 150 = 2 \cdot 2 \cdot 75 = 2 \cdot 2 \cdot 3 \cdot 25 = 2^2 \cdot 3 \cdot 5^2$

1C. The common prime factors are 2, 2, and 3, so the GCF is $2 \cdot 2 \cdot 3$ or 12.

Grade 8 Assessment Objectives Addressed

Monday	(1A) 6.8.08 (1B) 6.8.08 (1C) 6.8.08
Tuesday	(2) 8.8.05; (3) 8.8.03
Wednesday	(4) 6.8.04; (5) 6.8.09
Thursday	(6) 6.8.05
Friday	(7) 6.8.10

Countdown
to ISAT

19 Weeks to ISAT

Monday

1. **Extended Response** **Show your work and clearly explain your answer.** Use the rectangle to answer the questions. **See margin.**
   A. Write an equation for the perimeter of the rectangle. (Lesson 3-2)
   B. Solve for x if the perimeter is 36 meters. (Lesson 3-5)
   C. Find the area of the rectangle. (Lesson 1-3)

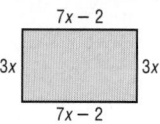

$7x - 2$
$3x$ $3x$
$7x - 2$

Monday
Extended Response
Sample Answers

1A. $P = 3x + (7x - 2)$
$+ 3x + (7x - 2)$
$= 20x - 4$

1B. $20x - 4 = 36$
$20x = 40$
$x = 2$ m

1C. $A = \ell w =$
$(7x - 2)(3x) =$
$(14 - 2)(6) =$
$(12)(6) = 72$ m^2

Tuesday

2. **Multiple-Choice** Which are all of the factors of the number 96? (Lesson 4-1) **B**
   - Ⓐ 1, 2, 4, 6, 8, 12, 16, 24, 48, 96
   - Ⓑ 1, 2, 3, 4, 6, 8, 12, 16, 24, 32, 48, 96
   - Ⓒ 1, 2, 3, 4, 8, 12, 24, 32, 48, 96
   - Ⓓ 1, 2, 3, 4, 6, 8, 12, 16, 24, 33, 48, 96
   - Ⓔ 1, 2, 3, 4, 6, 9, 12, 16, 24, 32, 48, 96

3. **Multiple-Choice** Which is the number of kilometers in 6×10^8 centimeters? (Lesson 4-8) **C**
   - Ⓐ 60
   - Ⓑ 600
   - Ⓒ 6,000
   - Ⓓ 60,000
   - Ⓔ 600,000

Wednesday

4. **Multiple-Choice** Illinois has 186 public use areas, including state parks, memorials, forests, and conservation areas. Combined, these areas cover approximately 250,000 acres. Which is the approximate mean area per public use area? (Lesson 2-5) **A**
   - Ⓐ 1,344 acres
   - Ⓑ 1,433 acres
   - Ⓒ 1,567 acres
   - Ⓓ 1,626 acres
   - Ⓔ 1,812 acres

5. **Multiple-Choice** Which number is prime? (Lesson 4-3) **D**
   - Ⓐ 27
   - Ⓑ 39
   - Ⓒ 49
   - Ⓓ 59
   - Ⓔ 69

Thursday

6. **Short Constructed-Response** Write *one hundred thousand* as a power of 10. (Lesson 4-2) **10^5**

Friday

7. **Short Constructed-Response** Use the Venn diagram to find the greatest common factor of 72 and 84. (Lesson 4-4) **12**

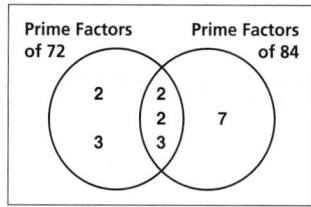

Prime Factors of 72   Prime Factors of 84

2   2   2   7
3   3

Grade 8 Assessment Objectives Addressed

Monday	(1A) 9.8.01 (1B) 8.8.12 (1C) 7.8.02
Tuesday	(2) 6.8.08; (3) 6.8.04
Wednesday	(4) 6.8.09; (5) 6.8.08
Thursday	(6) 6.8.01
Friday	(7) 6.8.08

18 Weeks to ISAT

Monday

1. **Extended Response** **Show your work and clearly explain your answer.** Use the table showing Illinois Corn production to answer the questions. (Lesson 5-8) **See margin.**

   A. Find the mean bushels of corn per acre produced from 1995 through 2002.

   B. Find the median bushels of corn per acre produced from 1995 through 2002.

   C. Find the mode.

Illinois Corn Production	
Year	Bushels per Acre
1995	113
1996	136
1997	129
1998	141
1999	140
2000	151
2001	152
2002	136

Source: http://www.agstats.state.il.us/annual/2003/03021.htm

Tuesday

2. **Multiple-Choice** Which is equivalent to $2\frac{8}{9}$? (Lesson 5-1) **C**
   - Ⓐ $2.\overline{7}$
   - Ⓑ 2.8
   - Ⓒ $2.\overline{8}$
   - Ⓓ 2.895
   - Ⓔ 2.925

3. **Multiple-Choice** Ling needs to divide three-fourths of a pie equally for herself and her five guests. Each slice should be which fraction of a whole pie? (Lesson 5-4) **A**
   - Ⓐ $\frac{1}{8}$ Ⓑ $\frac{1}{7}$ Ⓒ $\frac{1}{6}$ Ⓓ $\frac{1}{5}$ Ⓔ $\frac{1}{4}$

Wednesday

4. **Multiple-Choice** James is putting up a new shelf in his closet. The width of the closet is $49\frac{7}{8}$ inches, and the length of the shelf is 60 inches. Which is the number of inches of the shelf that James must remove so that it will fit? (Lesson 5-7) **B**
   - Ⓐ $9\frac{7}{8}$
   - Ⓑ $10\frac{1}{8}$
   - Ⓒ $10\frac{3}{8}$
   - Ⓓ $10\frac{7}{8}$
   - Ⓔ $11\frac{1}{8}$

5. **Multiple-Choice** Which is the solution to $2\frac{1}{9} - x = \frac{7}{9}$? (Lesson 5-9) **D**
   - Ⓐ $1\frac{2}{3}$ Ⓑ $1\frac{5}{9}$ Ⓒ $1\frac{4}{9}$ Ⓓ $1\frac{1}{3}$ Ⓔ $1\frac{1}{4}$

Thursday

6. **Short Constructed-Response** Replace ● with <, >, or = to make $\frac{13}{16}$ ● 0.8124 a true sentence. (Lesson 5-1) **>**

Friday

7. **Short Constructed-Response** Find the least common multiple of 15 and 11. (Lesson 5-6) **165**

Illinois Pre-Algebra IL15

Monday
Extended Response
Sample Answers

1A. $(113 + 136 + 129 + 141 + 140 + 151 + 152 + 136) \div 8 = 137.25$

1B. Ordered from least to greatest, the data are 113, 129, 136, 136, 140, 141, 151, and 152. The middle two are 136 and 140, so the median is $\frac{136 + 140}{2} = \frac{276}{2}$ or 138.

1C. The only value repeated is 136, so the mode is 136.

Grade 8 Assessment Objectives Addressed	
Monday	(1A) 10.8.05 (1B) 10.8.05 (1C) 10.8.05
Tuesday	(2) 6.8.03; (3) 6.8.09
Wednesday	(4) 6.8.09; (5) 8.8.12
Thursday	(6) 6.8.06
Friday	(7) 6.8.08

17 Weeks to ISAT

Monday

Monday
Extended Response
Sample Answers

1A. $(25 + 35 + x + 54 + 63 + 67) \div 6 = 48$

$25 + 35 + x + 54 + 63 + 67 = 48(6)$

$x + 244 = 288$

$x = 44$

The missing temperature is 44°F.

1B. Since no two known temperatures are the same, and since the temperature for February is 25°F, the missing temperature must be 25°F.

1C. Ordered from least to greatest, the data are 21, 25, 25, 35, 36, 44, 45, 54, 57, 63, 65, and 67. The middle two are 44 and 45, so the median is $\frac{44 + 45}{2} = \frac{89}{2}$ or 44.5°F.

1. **Extended Response** **Show your work and clearly explain your answer.** Use the weather data for Allendale to answer the questions. (Lesson 5-8)

   A. The mean of the average monthly low temperatures from February through July is 48°F. Find the missing temperature for April. **See margin.**

   B. The mode is 25°F. Find the missing temperature for December.

   C. Now that you have all of the monthly average temperatures, find the median.

Allendale Average Monthly Low Temperatures in °F			
Month	Temp.	Month	Temp.
Jan	21	July	67
Feb	25	Aug	65
Mar	35	Sept	57
April	?	Oct	45
May	54	Nov	36
June	63	Dec	?

Source: http://search.weather.yahoo.com/climo/USIL0015_f.html

Tuesday

2. **Multiple-Choice** In a survey, 27 out of 40 people prefer Brand A to Brand B. Which is 27 out of 40 written as a decimal? (Lesson 5-1) **B**
   - Ⓐ 0.65
   - Ⓑ 0.675
   - Ⓒ 0.725
   - Ⓓ 0.75
   - Ⓔ 0.775

3. **Multiple-Choice** What is the simplest form of the product $\frac{56x^3y}{7z^4} \cdot \frac{84zy}{64x}$? (Lesson 5-3) **A**
   - Ⓐ $\frac{21x^2y^2}{2z^3}$
   - Ⓑ $\frac{7x^2y^2}{z^3}$
   - Ⓒ $\frac{21x^2y^2}{2z^2}$
   - Ⓓ $\frac{21xy^2}{22z^3}$
   - Ⓔ $\frac{13x^2y}{3z^3}$

Wednesday

4. **Multiple-Choice** The thickness of a piece of copy paper is 0.097 millimeter. Which fraction of a millimeter is this? (Lesson 5-2) **D**
   - Ⓐ $\frac{97}{1,000,000}$
   - Ⓑ $\frac{97}{100,000}$
   - Ⓒ $\frac{97}{10,000}$
   - Ⓓ $\frac{97}{1,000}$
   - Ⓔ $\frac{97}{100}$

5. **Multiple-Choice** Which is the least common multiple of $28x^2y$ and $70xy$? (Lesson 5-6) **C**
   - Ⓐ $70xy$
   - Ⓑ $14x^2y$
   - Ⓒ $140x^2y$
   - Ⓓ $28x^2y^2$
   - Ⓔ $40xy^2$

Thursday

6. **Short Constructed-Response** Write $-\frac{7}{18} \div \left(-4\frac{2}{3}\right)$ in simplest form. (Lesson 5-4)
   $\frac{1}{12}$

Friday

7. **Short Constructed-Response** State the next term in the sequence.
   312, 285, 258, 231, …
   (Lesson 5-10) **204**

Grade 8 Assessment Objectives Addressed	
Monday	(1A) 10.8.05 (1B) 10.8.05 (1C) 10.8.05
Tuesday	(2) 6.8.03; (3) 8.8.04
Wednesday	(4) 6.8.03; (5) 6.8.08
Thursday	(6) 6.8.09
Friday	(7) 8.8.01

16 Weeks to ISAT

Monday

1. **Extended Response** Show your work and clearly explain your answer. Use the representation of the model of an ant to answer the questions. (Lesson 6-3) **See margin.**

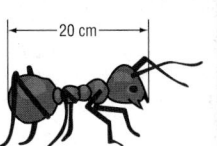
←— 20 cm —→

   A. The scale of the model is 1 cm = 0.4 mm. Find the length of an actual ant.

   B. The model weighs 15 kilograms and the scale is 1 kg = 5 mg. Find the weight of an actual ant.

   C. An actual ant of the size found in Question A can run at a speed of approximately 0.14 miles per hour. If the model were real, about how fast could it run in miles per hour?

Tuesday	Wednesday
2. **Multiple-Choice** Which is the percent of the figure that is shaded? (Lesson 6-4) **D** Ⓐ 24% Ⓑ 28% Ⓒ 32% Ⓓ 36% Ⓔ 40%	4. **Multiple-Choice** Which percent is greater than $\frac{7}{9}$ but less than $\frac{10}{11}$? (Lesson 6-4) **B** Ⓐ 91% Ⓑ 78% Ⓒ 72% Ⓓ 68% Ⓔ 65%
3. **Multiple-Choice** The driving distance from Abingdon to Zion is approximately 245 miles. If you drove from Abingdon to Zion in four hours, which would be your average speed in miles per hour? (Lesson 6-1) **E** Ⓐ 62.25 Ⓑ 62.00 Ⓒ 61.75 Ⓓ 61.50 Ⓔ 61.25	5. **Multiple-Choice** If each strip of staples is made up of 210 staples, which is the number of staples in a box containing 24 strips? (Lesson 6-2) **A** Ⓐ 5,040 Ⓑ 5,032 Ⓒ 5,028 Ⓓ 5,016 Ⓔ 5,008

Thursday	Friday
6. **Short Constructed-Response** Of the students in a classroom, 44% are over five feet four inches tall. If the classroom contains 25 students, how many are over five feet four inches tall? (Lesson 6-5) **11**	7. **Short Constructed-Response** A set of surround-sound speakers are on sale at a 20% discount. If the speakers normally sell for $399.95, what is the sale price? (Lesson 6-7) **$319.96**

Monday
Extended Response
Sample Answers

1A. $\dfrac{x}{20 \text{ cm}} = \dfrac{0.4 \text{ mm}}{1 \text{ cm}}$

$1 \cdot x = 0.4 \cdot 20$

$x = 8 \text{ mm}$

1B. $\dfrac{w}{15 \text{ kg}} = \dfrac{5 \text{ mg}}{1 \text{ kg}}$

$1 \cdot w = 5 \cdot 15$

$w = 75 \text{ mg}$

1C. $\dfrac{1 \text{ cm}}{0.4 \text{ mm}} =$

$\dfrac{10 \text{ mm}}{0.4 \text{ mm}} = \dfrac{100}{4} =$

25, so the model is 25 times the size of the actual ant. Therefore, the speed should be 25 times as fast.

$\dfrac{s}{0.14 \text{ mph}} = \dfrac{25}{1}$

$1 \cdot s = 25 \cdot 0.14$

$s = 3.5 \text{ mph}$

Grade 8 Assessment Objectives Addressed

Monday	(1A) 7.8.06 (1B) 7.8.06 (1C) 7.8.06
Tuesday	(2) 6.8.03; (3) 6.8.15
Wednesday	(4) 6.8.06; (5) 6.8.16
Thursday	(6) 6.8.16
Friday	(7) 6.8.18

15 Weeks to ISAT

Monday

Monday
Extended Response
Sample Answers

1A. $\dfrac{48.0 - 11.0}{11.0} =$

$\dfrac{37.0}{11.0} \approx 3.36$

or 336%

1B. $\dfrac{650{,}000 - 2{,}800{,}000}{2{,}800{,}000}$

$= \dfrac{-2{,}150{,}000}{2{,}800{,}000}$

≈ -0.77 or -77%

1C. 1869: $11.0 \times 2{,}800{,}000 = 30{,}800{,}000$ bushels

2002: $48.0 \times 650{,}000 = 31{,}200{,}000$ bushels

---

1. Extended Response Show your work and clearly explain your answer. Use the wheat production data to answer the questions. Round to the nearest whole number. (Lesson 6-8)

A. Find the percent of change from 1869 to 2002 of the average bushels per acre produced. **See margin.**

B. Find the percent of change from 1869 to 2002 of the number of acres harvested.

C. Find the total number of bushels produced in 1869 and in 2002.

Illinois Wheat Production		
Year	1,000s of Acres Harvested	Average Bushels per Acre
1869	2,800	11.0
1909	2,185	17.3
1959	1,660	26.0
2002	650	48.0

Source: http://www.illinoiswheat.org/about_il_wheat.htm

Tuesday

2. Multiple-Choice Which is the probability that the first spin lands on 4 and the second spin lands on 8? (Lesson 6-9) **B**

Ⓐ $\dfrac{1}{128}$

Ⓑ $\dfrac{1}{64}$

Ⓒ $\dfrac{1}{56}$

Ⓓ $\dfrac{1}{32}$

Ⓔ $\dfrac{1}{28}$

3. Multiple-Choice There are 2.54 centimeters in one inch. Which is the number of centimeters in one foot? (Lesson 6-2) **E**

Ⓐ 15.24
Ⓑ 21.34
Ⓒ 25.60
Ⓓ 28.16
Ⓔ 30.48

Wednesday

4. Multiple-Choice The model of a sailing ship has a scale of 1 inch = 2 feet. Which is the length of the actual ship? (Lesson 6-3) **D**

— 21 in. —

Ⓐ 21 feet
Ⓑ 28 feet
Ⓒ 36 feet
Ⓓ 42 feet
Ⓔ 48 feet

5. Multiple-Choice Three-eighths of the liquid in a recipe is milk. Which percent is this? (Lesson 6-4) **C**

Ⓐ 39.5%
Ⓑ 38.5%
Ⓒ 37.5%
Ⓓ 36.5%
Ⓔ 35.5%

Thursday

6. Short Constructed-Response Which costs less per roll of paper towels, a 3-pack for $3.59 or a 12-pack for $11.76? (Lesson 6-1) **12-pack**

Friday

7. Short Constructed-Response Seventy-three is what percent of 438? (Lesson 6-5) $16\dfrac{2}{3}\%$

Grade 8 Assessment Objectives Addressed

Monday	(1A) 6.8.18 (1B) 6.8.18 (1C) 6.8.18
Tuesday	(2) 10.8.06; (3) 6.8.16
Wednesday	(4) 7.8.06; (5) 6.8.03
Thursday	(6) 6.8.15
Friday	(7) 6.8.17

14 Weeks to ISAT

Monday

1. **Extended Response** Show your work and clearly explain your answer. The data in the table shows the monthly number of new customers for a new business. (Lesson 8-8)

   A. Draw a scatter plot of the data. Let April be $x = 1$. **See margin.**

   B. Draw the line of best fit.

   C. Use the line of best fit to predict the number of new customers in the month of January that follows the month of November given in the table.

New Customers			
Month	Number	Month	Number
April	3	August	10
May	5	September	9
June	5	October	13
July	7	November	14

Tuesday

2. **Multiple-Choice** Which is the solution of $-5x - 3 = x + 21$? (Lesson 7-1) **A**
   - Ⓐ -4
   - Ⓑ -2
   - Ⓒ 0
   - Ⓓ 2
   - Ⓔ 4

3. **Multiple-Choice** Latoya is selling magazine subscriptions. She has sold 57 subscriptions so far. If she sells 150 or more, she will win a new bike. Which is the least number of subscriptions that Latoya must sell to win the prize? (Lesson 7-4) **B**
   - Ⓐ 92
   - Ⓑ 93
   - Ⓒ 94
   - Ⓓ 95
   - Ⓔ 96

Wednesday

4. **Multiple-Choice** Which inequality is graphed on the number line? (Lesson 7-3) **D**

   $-8 \ -7 \ -6 \ -5 \ -4 \ -3 \ -2 \ -1$
   - Ⓐ $x \leq -6$
   - Ⓑ $x > -6$
   - Ⓒ $x \geq -6$
   - Ⓓ $x < -6$
   - Ⓔ $x = -6$

5. **Multiple-Choice** A positive number n is divided by a number greater than zero but less than one. Which is always true about the quotient? (Prerequisite Skill) **C**
   - Ⓐ It is less than n.
   - Ⓑ It is infinite.
   - Ⓒ It is greater than n.
   - Ⓓ It is zero.
   - Ⓔ It is equal to $10n$.

Thursday

6. **Short Constructed-Response** The product of an integer and -3 is greater than 96. Write and solve an inequality to find the integer. (Lesson 7-5) $-3x > 96$ or $x < -32$

Friday

7. **Short Constructed-Response** The percent of the population of Illinois that is female is greater than 51%. Write an inequality for this situation. (Lesson 7-3) $x > 51$, $x > 51\%$, $x > 0.51$, or $x > \dfrac{51}{100}$

Monday
Extended Response
Sample Answers

1A, 1B.

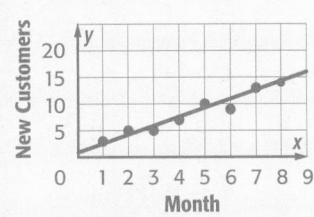

1C. January corresponds with $x = 10$. At $x = 10$, $y = 17$, so the number of new customers in January should be 17.

Grade 8 Assessment Objectives Addressed	
Monday	(1A) 10.8.04 (1B) 10.8.04 (1C) 10.8.04
Tuesday	(2) 8.8.12; (3) 8.8.12
Wednesday	(4) 8.8.10; (5) 6.8.12
Thursday	(6) 8.8.12
Friday	(7) 8.8.11

Monday
Extended Response
Sample Answers

1A. $A = 0.05m + 5$;
$B = 0.09m + 1$

1B. $0.05m + 5 = 0.09m + 1$
$5 - 1 = 0.09m - 0.05m$
$4 = 0.04m$
$m = 100$ min

1C. A: $0.05(45) + 5 = 2.25 + 5 = 7.25$;
B: $0.09(45) + 1 = 4.05 + 1 = 5.05$;

A: $0.05(110) + 5 = 5.5 + 5 = 10.5$;
B: $0.09(110) + 1 = 9.9 + 1 = 10.9$;

Plan B is less expensive for 45 minutes and Plan A is less expensive for 110 minutes.

Thursday
6.

−3−2−1 0 1 2 3 4 5 6

Monday

1. Extended Response Show your work and clearly explain your answer. The costs for two long-distance calling plans are shown in the table. (Lesson 7-1) **See margin.**

Long-Distance Plans		
Plan	Cost per Minute	Monthly Fee
Plan A	$0.05	$5
Plan B	$0.09	$1

A. Write equations that represent the total monthly cost per plan. Let A and B be the total costs for Plans A and B, respectively. Let the number of minutes be m.

B. Set A equal to B and solve for m to find the number of minutes that makes the costs of the plans equal.

C. Which plan is less expensive for 45 minutes of calling time? Which plan is less expensive for 110 minutes of calling time?

Tuesday

2. Multiple-Choice Which is the number of cubic meters in a cubic kilometer? (Lesson 4-8) **D**

- Ⓐ 1×10^6
- Ⓑ 1×10^7
- Ⓒ 1×10^8
- Ⓓ 1×10^9
- Ⓔ 1×10^{10}

3. Multiple-Choice Which is the solution of $3\left(t + \frac{4}{3}\right) = 7(3t - 2)$? (Lesson 7-2) **D**

- Ⓐ 4
- Ⓑ 3
- Ⓒ 2
- Ⓓ 1
- Ⓔ 0

Wednesday

4. Multiple-Choice The fee to have a booth at the Holiday Craft Fair in Bloomingdale is $100. The booth has a square floor plan that is 10 feet on a side. Which is the cost per square foot of booth space? (Lesson 6-1) **A**

- Ⓐ $1.00
- Ⓑ $2.50
- Ⓒ $5.00
- Ⓓ $7.50
- Ⓔ $10.00

5. Multiple-Choice Alberto has 27 cookies to share with his friends. If he gives two cookies to each friend, which is the greatest number of his friends that will receive cookies? (Lesson 7-5) **B**

- Ⓐ 12
- Ⓑ 13
- Ⓒ 14
- Ⓓ 15
- Ⓔ 16

Thursday

6. Short Constructed-Response Graph the compound inequality $x > -2$ and $x < 5$. (Prerequisite Skill) **See margin.**

Friday

7. Short Constructed-Response Solve $7 \leq \frac{2}{15} - k$. (Lesson 7-6) $k \leq -6\frac{13}{15}$

Grade 8 Assessment Objectives Addressed

Monday	(1A) 8.8.11 (1B) 8.8.11 (1C) 8.8.11
Tuesday	(2) 6.8.04; (3) 8.8.12
Wednesday	(4) 6.8.15; (5) 8.8.11
Thursday	(6) 8.8.10
Friday	(7) 8.8.12

12 Weeks to ISAT

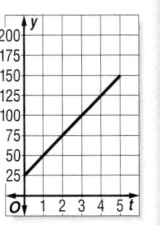

Monday

1. **Extended Response** Show your work and clearly explain your answer. Use the graph to answer the questions. **See margin.**

   A. What is the y-intercept of the graph? (Lesson 8-3)

   B. Find the slope of the graph and write the equation of the graph in slope-intercept form. (Lesson 8-6)

   C. If this graph represents the height y (in feet) above ground at time t (in minutes) of a balloon that is rising at a constant speed, what do the slope and y-intercept mean? (Lesson 8-6)

Tuesday

2. **Multiple-Choice** Which linear equation represents the values in the table? (Lesson 8-2) **E**

x	y
1	5
2	8
3	11
4	14

   Ⓐ $y = -2x + 3$
   Ⓑ $y = -3x + 2$
   Ⓒ $y = 3x - 2$
   Ⓓ $y = 2x + 3$
   Ⓔ $y = 3x + 2$

3. **Multiple-Choice** The speed s at which a rock falls varies directly with the amount of time t that has passed. The rate at which the speed increases is 32 feet per second per second. Which equation models this situation? (Lesson 8-5) **D**

   Ⓐ $t = 32s$
   Ⓑ $s = t + 32$
   Ⓒ $t = s + 32$
   Ⓓ $s = 32t$
   Ⓔ $s = \frac{1}{32}t$

Wednesday

4. **Multiple-Choice** The Bureau County Fair has been held since 1855. In which year will it celebrate its 250th anniversary? (Lesson 2-2) **C**

   Ⓐ 2103
   Ⓑ 2104
   Ⓒ 2105
   Ⓓ 2106
   Ⓔ 2107

5. **Multiple-Choice** Jerold is driving at an average rate of 55 miles per hour. He has already driven 126 miles. Assuming his average speed doesn't change, which is the total number of miles he will have driven in two more hours? (Lesson 8-5) **A**

   Ⓐ 236
   Ⓑ 223
   Ⓒ 212
   Ⓓ 195
   Ⓔ 110

Thursday

6. **Short Constructed-Response** Graph the line with slope -1 and y-intercept 2. (Lesson 8-6) **See margin.**

Friday

7. **Short Constructed-Response** Bottles are filled continuously at a factory. By 10:00 A.M., 4,000 bottles have been filled. By 2:00 P.M., 8,400 have been filled. Let $t = 0$ be 10:00 A.M. and B be the number of bottles filled at time t hours. Write a linear equation in slope-intercept form to represent this situation. (Lesson 8-7)
   $B = 1{,}100t + 4{,}000$

Monday
Extended Response Sample Answers

1A. The y-intercept is 25.

1B. $m = \dfrac{150 - 25}{5 - 0} = \dfrac{125}{5} = 25$;
   $y = 25t + 25$

1C. The slope is the rate that the balloon is rising, 25 feet per minute. The y-intercept is the height of the balloon (25 ft) at $t = 0$, which is when the timer was started.

Thursday

6.
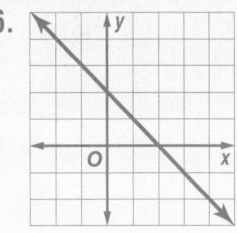

Grade 8 Assessment Objectives Addressed

Monday	(1A) 8.8.09 (1B) 8.8.09 (1C) 8.8.09
Tuesday	(2) 8.8.08; (3) 8.8.08
Wednesday	(4) 6.8.09; (5) 8.8.06
Thursday	(6) 8.8.07
Friday	(7) 8.8.11

Monday
Extended Response
Sample Answers

1A. $\dfrac{\$18}{1 \text{ hr}} = \dfrac{x}{2 \text{ hr}}$

$2 \cdot 18 = x \cdot 1$

$x = \$36$

1B. Tyree earns $36 for two hours of work, and $18 for every hour over the mandatory two hours. The equation is $A = 18h + 36$.

1C.

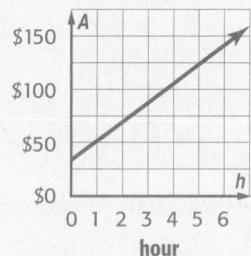

---

11 Weeks to ISAT

Monday

1. **Extended Response** Show your work and clearly explain your answer. Tyree must go to his work whether or not there is any work to be done. After two hours, he can leave if business is slow. His hourly rate of pay is $18 per hour. **See margin.**

   A. What is the least amount Tyree earns in a day? (Lesson 6-2)

   B. Write an equation in slope-intercept form that gives the amount A Tyree earns for h hours of work over the mandatory two hours. (Lesson 8-7)

   C. Graph the equation from Question B. (Lesson 8-6)

Tuesday

2. **Multiple-Choice** From 2002 to 2003, the number of establishments doing business in the Chicago metro area increased by 3,048 for a total of 201,105. Rounded to the nearest hundredth of a percent, which is the percent of change of business establishments from 2002 to 2003? (Lesson 6-8) **D**
   - Ⓐ 1.51%
   - Ⓑ 1.52%
   - Ⓒ 1.53%
   - Ⓓ 1.54%
   - Ⓔ 1.55%

3. **Multiple-Choice** Which is the slope of a line that falls five units for every four units it runs in the positive x-direction? (Lesson 8-4)
   - Ⓐ −1.25
   - Ⓑ −0.8 **A**
   - Ⓒ 0.8
   - Ⓓ 1.25
   - Ⓔ 2.5

Wednesday

4. **Multiple-Choice** A doctor has been tracking the weight loss of one of his patients. Which is the patient's average rate of weight change if 26 pounds were lost in four weeks? (Lesson 8-5) **C**
   - Ⓐ 7.5 pounds per week
   - Ⓑ 6.5 pounds per week
   - Ⓒ −6.5 pounds per week
   - Ⓓ −6.75 pounds per week
   - Ⓔ −7.5 pounds per week

5. **Multiple-Choice** Which is the solution of $-\frac{1}{3}x + 3 = 2x - 6\frac{1}{3}$? (Lesson 7-1) **E**
   - Ⓐ 0 Ⓑ 1 Ⓒ 2 Ⓓ 3 Ⓔ 4

Thursday

6. **Short Constructed-Response** A salesperson sells only one kind of item. The graph shows the profit per day as a function of the number of items sold. What does the y-intercept mean? (Lesson 8-6)

   If no items are sold, the salesperson loses $100.

Friday

7. **Short Constructed-Response** Simplify

$$\frac{x \cdot y \cdot z \cdot 11 \cdot 11 \cdot z \cdot z \cdot z \cdot x \cdot y \cdot x \cdot y \cdot 11}{x \cdot 11 \cdot y \cdot 11 \cdot z}$$

using exponents. (Lesson 4-2) $11x^2y^2z^3$

Grade 8 Assessment Objectives Addressed

Monday	(1A) 6.8.16 (1B) 8.8.07 (1C) 8.8.07
Tuesday	(2) 6.8.18; (3) 8.8.09
Wednesday	(4) 8.8.06; (5) 8.8.12
Thursday	(6) 8.8.09
Friday	(7) 6.8.05

10 Weeks to ISAT

Monday

1. **Extended Response** Show your work and clearly explain your answer. Use the triangle to answer the questions. **See margin.**

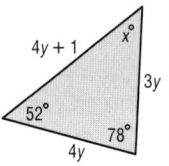

   A. What is the value of x? (Lesson 9-4)

   B. If the perimeter of the triangle is 23 units, what is the value of y? (Lesson 7-2)

   C. If the lengths of only two sides of the triangle were known, could you use the Pythagorean Theorem to find the length of the third? Why or why not? (Lesson 9-5)

Tuesday

2. **Multiple-Choice** Which square root is graphed at A on the number line? (Lesson 9-1) **C**

   ```
   ← + + + + • + + →
    -1  0  1   2 A 3   4
   ```

   Ⓐ $\sqrt{10}$
   Ⓑ $\sqrt{9}$
   Ⓒ $\sqrt{7}$
   Ⓓ $\sqrt{4}$
   Ⓔ $\sqrt{2.5}$

3. **Multiple-Choice** Which is the best whole-number estimate of $\sqrt{253}$? (Lesson 9-1) **E**

   Ⓐ 12 Ⓑ 13 Ⓒ 14 Ⓓ 15 Ⓔ 16

Wednesday

4. **Multiple-Choice** Starting from rest, the time in seconds t it takes for an object to fall d feet is given by $t = \sqrt{d} \div 16$. Which is the number of seconds it takes an object to fall 256 feet? (Lesson 9-2) **D**

   Ⓐ 1 Ⓑ 2 Ⓒ 3 Ⓓ 4 Ⓔ 5

5. **Multiple-Choice** Which statement is *not* true? (Lesson 9-1) **A**

   Ⓐ $11 < \sqrt{120} < 12$
   Ⓑ $10 < \sqrt{110} < 11$
   Ⓒ $13 < \sqrt{170} < 14$
   Ⓓ $12 < \sqrt{145} < 13$
   Ⓔ $14 < \sqrt{209} < 15$

Thursday

6. **Short Constructed-Response** What is the measure of angle ABC? (Lesson 9-3) **120°**

Friday

7. **Short Constructed-Response** Find the distance from Granite City to Mattoon. Round to the nearest mile. (Lesson 9-5)

   107 mi

   Springfield ●Decatur
   68 mi
   82 mi ●Mattoon
   x mi
   Granite City

Monday
Extended Response
Sample Answers

1A. $x° + 52° + 78° = 180°$
$x° = 180° - (52° + 78°)$
$x = 50$

1B. $23 = 4y + 1 + 3y + 4y$
$23 - 1 = y(4 + 3 + 4)$
$22 = 11y$
$y = 2$

1C. No, because none of the interior angles measures 90°.

Grade 8 Assessment Objectives Addressed

Monday	(1A) 9.8.02 (1B) 9.8.02 (1C) 9.8.02
Tuesday	(2) 6.8.07; (3) 6.8.14
Wednesday	(4) 6.8.09; (5) 6.8.14
Thursday	(6) 7.8.03
Friday	(7) 9.8.03

Monday
Extended Response
Sample Answers

1A. Since corresponding angles have the same measure, the triangles are similar.

1B. $\dfrac{x}{8.2 + x} = \dfrac{4}{4 + 8}$

$\dfrac{x}{8.2 + x} = \dfrac{4}{12}$

$12 \cdot x = 4(8.2 + x)$

$12x = 32.8 + 4x$

$8x = 32.8$

$x = 4.1$ m

1C. The length of $\overline{AC}$ has been increased by a factor of $\dfrac{22.5}{15}$ or 1.5. The new perimeter is 1.5 times the old perimeter.

$P = 1.5[(8.2 + 4.1) + (4 + 8) + 15]$

$P = 1.5(12.3 + 12 + 15)$

$P = 1.5(39.3)$

$P = 58.95$ m

---

9 Weeks to ISAT

Monday

1. **Extended Response** **Show your work and clearly explain your answer.** Use the figure to answer the questions. (Lesson 9-7) **See margin.**

A. Are triangles *ABC* and *DBE* similar? Explain.

B. Find *x*.

C. If another triangle is similar to triangle *ABC* and the side corresponding to *AC* is 22.5 m long, what is the perimeter of the triangle?

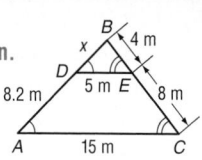

Tuesday

2. **Multiple-Choice** Which is the approximate length of a side of the square? (Lesson 9-1) **C**

166 cm²

- Ⓐ 12.7 cm
- Ⓑ 12.8 cm
- Ⓒ 12.9 cm
- Ⓓ 13.0 cm
- Ⓔ 13.1 cm

3. **Multiple-Choice** Which is the measure of angle *ADB*? (Lesson 9-3) **E**

- Ⓐ 49°
- Ⓑ 46°
- Ⓒ 43°
- Ⓓ 41°
- Ⓔ 39°

Wednesday

4. **Multiple-Choice** Which is the height of the flagpole? (Lesson 9-5) **B**

35 ft

21 ft

- Ⓐ 27 feet
- Ⓑ 28 feet
- Ⓒ 29 feet
- Ⓓ 30 feet
- Ⓔ 31 feet

5. **Multiple-Choice** The Amoco Building in Chicago is 1,136 feet tall. Two Prudential Plaza is a building across the street that is 995 feet tall. If Two Prudential Plaza casts a 199 foot shadow, which is the approximate length of the shadow of the Amoco Building at that same time? (Lesson 9-7) **A**

- Ⓐ 227 feet
- Ⓑ 230 feet
- Ⓒ 232 feet
- Ⓓ 238 feet
- Ⓔ 245 feet

Thursday

6. **Short Constructed-Response** Determine the measures of the angles of a triangle if the measures of the angles are in the ratio 3:4:5. (Lesson 9-4) **45°, 60°, 75°**

Friday

7. **Short Constructed-Response** Are the two triangles similar? (Lesson 9-7) **yes**

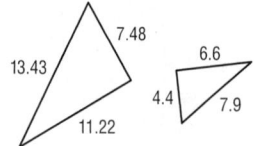

Grade 8 Assessment Objectives Addressed

Monday	(1A) 9.8.11 (1B) 9.8.11 (1C) 9.8.11
Tuesday	(2) 9.8.02; (3) 9.8.01
Wednesday	(4) 9.8.03; (5) 7.8.06
Thursday	(6) 6.8.15
Friday	(7) 9.8.11

Monday

1. **Extended Response** **Show your work and clearly explain your answer.** In the figure, $h \parallel j$ and k is a transversal. (Lesson 10-1) **See margin.**

   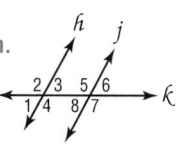

   A. The measure of angle 1 is equal to the measures of which angles?

   B. The measure of angle 2 is 119°. Find the measure of angle 7.

   C. Find the measure of angle 8.

Tuesday

2. **Multiple-Choice** The Illinois State Capitol building in Springfield has a dome with a circular foundation of diameter 92.5 feet. Which is the approximate circumference of the dome's foundation? (Lesson 10-7) **A**

   Ⓐ 291 feet   Ⓑ 322 feet
   Ⓒ 411 feet   Ⓓ 497 feet
   Ⓔ 581 feet

3. **Multiple-Choice** Which transformation is shown? (Lesson 10-3) **D**

   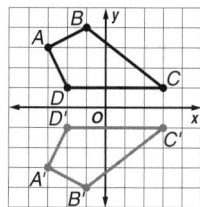

   Ⓐ reflection over the y-axis
   Ⓑ translation 5 units down
   Ⓒ rotation about the origin
   Ⓓ reflection over the x-axis
   Ⓔ translation 8 units down

Wednesday

4. **Multiple-Choice** Which is the value of x? (Lesson 10-4) **B**

   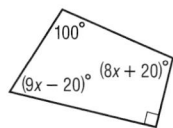

   Ⓐ 8   Ⓑ 10   Ⓒ 11   Ⓓ 12   Ⓔ 14

5. **Multiple-Choice** The area of the triangle is 24.5 square feet. Which is its height h? (Lesson 10-5) **C**

   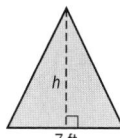

   Ⓐ 6 feet
   Ⓑ 6.5 feet
   Ⓒ 7 feet
   Ⓓ 7.5 feet
   Ⓔ 8 feet

Thursday

6. **Short Constructed-Response** Measure the base b and height h of the trapezoid to the nearest millimeter. (Lesson 10-4)
   $h = 18$ mm, $b = 26$ mm

   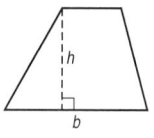

Friday

7. **Short Constructed-Response** Angles M and N are supplementary. The measure of angle M is 73°. Find the measure of angle N. (Lesson 10-1) **107°**

Illinois Pre-Algebra IL25

Monday
Extended Response
Sample Answers

1A. Angles 1 and 3 are vertical angles, so their measures are equal. Angles 1 and 8 are corresponding angles, so their measures are equal. Angles 1 and 6 are alternate exterior angles, so their measures are equal. So angles 3, 6, and 8 have measures equal to that of angle 1.

1B. Angles 2 and 7 are alternate exterior angles, so their measures are equal and the measure of angle 7 is 119°.

1C. Angles 7 and 8 are supplementary, so the measure of angle 8 is 180° − 119° or 61°.

Grade 8 Assessment Objectives Addressed	
Monday	(1A) 9.8.08 (1B) 9.8.08 (1C) 9.8.08
Tuesday	(2) 9.8.04; (3) 9.8.06
Wednesday	(4) 9.8.02; (5) 7.8.02
Thursday	(6) 7.8.01
Friday	(7) 9.8.09

7 Weeks to ISAT

Monday

Monday
Extended Response
Sample Answers

1. **Extended Response Show your work and clearly explain your answer.** Use the figure to answer the questions. **See margin.**

   A. What is the specific name of the figure *ABCD*? (Lesson 10-4)

   B. Graph the 180°-rotation about the origin of *ABCD* and label it *A′B′C′D′*. (Lesson 10-3)

   C. Reflect *A′B′C′D′* over the *y*-axis, then reflect *A″B″C″D″* over the *x*-axis. What do you notice about the location of the figure after the final reflection? (Lesson 10-3)

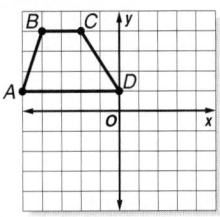

1A. trapezoid

1B.

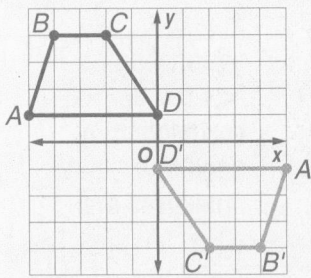

1C.

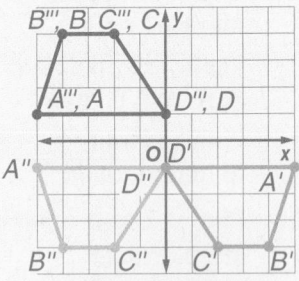

The original and final figures overlap.

Tuesday

2. **Multiple-Choice** A taxi fare *y* can be determined by the equation $y = 3x + 5$, where *x* is the number of miles traveled. What does the slope of the graph of this equation represent? (Lesson 8-6) **B**
   - Ⓐ the distance traveled
   - Ⓑ the cost per mile
   - Ⓒ the initial fee
   - Ⓓ the total cost
   - Ⓔ the distance traveled minus 5

3. **Multiple-Choice** Which is the area of the trapezoid? (Lesson 10-5) **B**

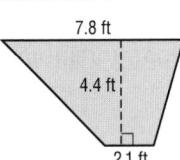

   - Ⓐ 18.28 sq ft
   - Ⓑ 21.78 sq ft
   - Ⓒ 28.94 sq ft
   - Ⓓ 36.36 sq ft
   - Ⓔ 43.56 sq ft

Wednesday

4. **Multiple-Choice** On a hill in Hampshire stands the Purple Martin Tower. This bird tower is 30 feet high and its roof is a regular hexagon. The length of a side of the hexagon is five feet eight inches. Which is the perimeter of the roof in feet? (Lesson 10-6) **D**
   - Ⓐ 22
   - Ⓑ 23
   - Ⓒ 28
   - Ⓓ 34
   - Ⓔ 45

5. **Multiple-Choice** The circumference of a circle is 25π m. Which is its radius? (Lesson 10-7) **C**
   - Ⓐ 25 m
   - Ⓑ 16.5 m
   - Ⓒ 12.5 m
   - Ⓓ 8.5 m
   - Ⓔ 5 m

Thursday

6. **Short Constructed-Response** The circle has an area of 4π cm². Find its diameter *d*. (Lesson 10-7) **d = 4 cm**

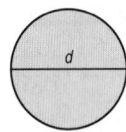

Friday

7. **Short Constructed-Response** The measures of two complementary angles are $(2x - 2)°$ and $\left(\frac{1}{5}x + 4\right)°$. Find *x*. (Lesson 10-1) **x = 40**

Grade 8 Assessment Objectives Addressed

Monday	(1A) 9.8.06 (1B) 9.8.07 (1C) 9.8.07
Tuesday	(2) 8.8.09; (3) 7.8.02
Wednesday	(4) 7.8.02; (5) 9.8.04
Thursday	(6) 7.8.02
Friday	(7) 9.8.09

6 Weeks to ISAT

Monday

1. **Extended Response** Show your work and clearly explain your answer. Use the figure to answer the questions. **See margin.**
   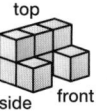
   A. Draw the top, side, and front views of the figure. (Lesson 11-1)
   B. If the edge length of each cube in the figure is 2 cm, what is the volume of each cube? (Lesson 11-2)
   C. What is the volume of the entire figure? (Lesson 11-2)

Tuesday	Wednesday
2. **Multiple-Choice** The Dexter Building in Chicago was erected in 1892. The building has the approximate shape of a rectangular prism. The area of its base is 5,250 square feet and its height is 140 feet. Which is its volume? (Lesson 11-2) Ⓐ 705,000 cu ft **D** Ⓑ 715,000 cu ft Ⓒ 725,000 cu ft Ⓓ 735,000 cu ft Ⓔ 745,000 cu ft	4. **Multiple-Choice** The volume of the square pyramid is 50 cubic inches. Which is the length of a side of its base? (Lesson 11-3) **C** 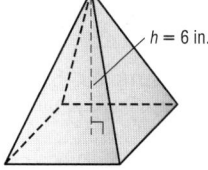 Ⓐ 2 inches Ⓑ 4 inches Ⓒ 5 inches Ⓓ 6 inches Ⓔ 8 inches
3. **Multiple-Choice** The volume of a cylindrical fuel-storage tank is approximately 75.4 m³. Its height is 6 m. Which is its radius? (Lesson 11-2) **B** Ⓐ 1.8 m Ⓑ 2.0 m Ⓒ 2.1 m Ⓓ 2.2 m Ⓔ 2.4 m	5. **Multiple-Choice** A rectangular prism has a height of 4 yards, a width of 3 yards, and a length of 5 yards. If a similar rectangular prism has a volume of 202.5 cubic yards, which are its dimensions in yards? (Lesson 11-6) **A** Ⓐ 6, 4.5, 7.5 Ⓑ 8, 4.5, 3.75 Ⓒ 3, 9, 7.5 Ⓓ 6, 2.25, 15 Ⓔ 12, 4.5, 3.75

Thursday	Friday
6. **Short Constructed-Response** To the nearest centimeter, find the length of the battery. (Lesson 11-7) **5 cm** 	7. **Short Constructed-Response** One cone has height 6 mm and a similar cone has height h. The ratio of the surface area of the first cone to that of the second cone is 9 to 4. Find the height of the second cone. (Lesson 11-6) **4 mm**

Countdown to ISAT

Monday
Extended Response
Sample Answers

1A.
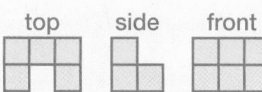

1B. The volume of a cube is $(2 \text{ cm})^3 = 8 \text{ cm}^3$.

1C. There are 8 cubes, so the total volume is $8(8 \text{ cm}^3)$ or 64 cm^3.

Grade 8 Assessment Objectives Addressed

Monday	(1A) 9.8.10 (1B) 7.8.04 (1C) 7.8.04
Tuesday	(2) 7.8.04; (3) 7.8.04
Wednesday	(4) 9.8.01; (5) 9.8.11
Thursday	(6) 7.8.01
Friday	(7) 9.8.11

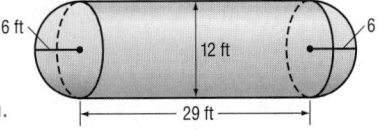

5 Weeks to ISAT

Monday

Monday
Extended Response
Sample Answers

1A. $V_{hemi} = \frac{1}{2}\left(\frac{4}{3}\pi r^3\right)$

$= \frac{2}{3}\pi(6)^3$

$= 144\pi \text{ ft}^3$

1B. $V = \pi r^2 h =$
$\pi(6)^2(29) =$
$1,044\pi \text{ ft}^3$

1C. $V = 2(144\pi) +$
$1,044\pi =$
$1,332\pi \text{ ft}^3$

Thursday

6.

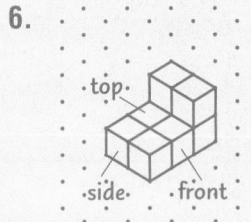

1. **Extended Response Show your work and clearly explain your answer.** The Dresden Nuclear Power Station in Grundy County has a cylindrical reactor vessel with hemispherical ends. A diagram is shown. (Lesson 11-2) **See margin.**

6 ft 12 ft 6 ft 29 ft

   A. The formula for the volume of a sphere is $V = \frac{4}{3}\pi r^3$. Find the volume of one of the hemispherical (half-spherical) ends.
   B. Find the volume of the cylindrical portion of the vessel.
   C. Use your results from Questions A and B to find the total volume of the vessel.

Tuesday

2. **Multiple-Choice** Which shape is represented by the net? (Lesson 11-1) **D**

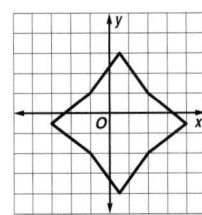

   (A) rectangular prism
   (B) triangular pyramid
   (C) cylinder
   (D) square pyramid
   (E) cone

3. **Multiple-Choice** An octagonal pyramid has height 10 inches and volume 20 cubic inches. Which is its base area in square inches? (Lesson 11-3) **E**
   (A) 2 (B) 4.1 (C) 5.2 (D) 5.6 (E) 6

Wednesday

4. **Multiple-Choice** The triangular prism has a surface area of 108 mm². Which is the value of x? (Lesson 11-4) **B**

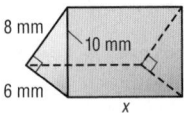
8 mm 10 mm 6 mm x

   (A) 2.0 (B) 2.5 (C) 3.0 (D) 3.5 (E) 4.0

5. **Multiple-Choice** The circumference of the circular ends of a cylinder is 3.8π cm. The height of the cylinder is 6.2 cm. Which is its surface area in square centimeters? (Lesson 11-4) **C**
   (A) 15.39π
   (B) 22.56π
   (C) 30.78π
   (D) 42.88π
   (E) 46.40π

Thursday

6. **Short Constructed-Response** Use isometric dot paper to draw the figure represented by the top, side, and front views. (Lesson 11-1) **See margin.**

top side front

Friday

7. **Short Constructed-Response** The figure is composed of two identical cones. Find its volume to the nearest tenth of a cubic centimeter. (Lesson 11-3) **335.1 cm³**

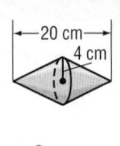
20 cm 4 cm

IL28   *Illinois Pre-Algebra*

Grade 8 Assessment Objectives Addressed

Monday	(1A) 9.8.01 (1B) 7.8.04 (1C) 9.8.01
Tuesday	(2) 9.8.06; (3) 9.8.01
Wednesday	(4) 7.8.04; (5) 7.8.04
Thursday	(6) 9.8.10
Friday	(7) 9.8.01

4 Weeks to ISAT

Monday

1. **Extended Response** Show your work and clearly explain your answer. The University of Illinois Men's Basketball Team's 2003–2004 winning scores are listed in the table. (Lesson 12-1) **See margin.**

   A. How many games did the team win?

   B. To the nearest whole point, what was the mean winning score?

   C. Make a stem-and-leaf plot of the scores.

Winning Scores
94, 93, 75, 84, 85, 74, 71, 75, 80, 85, 88, 80, 67, 51, 79, 75, 65, 66, 78, 66, 81, 64, 71, 74, 72, 92

Source: http://fightingillini.collegesports.com/sports/ m-baskbl/archive/052004aaa.html

Tuesday

2. **Multiple-Choice** Which is the range of the data set? {26, 28, 45, 38, 37, 21, 35, 40, 46} (Lesson 12-2) **A**
   - Ⓐ 25
   - Ⓑ 24
   - Ⓒ 20
   - Ⓓ 19
   - Ⓔ 17

3. **Multiple-Choice** The spinner is spun three times. Which is the probability that it lands on 1, then 2, and then 3 or 4? (Lesson 12-9) **E**

   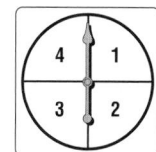

   - Ⓐ $\frac{1}{64}$
   - Ⓑ $\frac{1}{48}$
   - Ⓒ $\frac{1}{42}$
   - Ⓓ $\frac{1}{36}$
   - Ⓔ $\frac{1}{32}$

Wednesday

4. **Multiple-Choice** Six balls, lettered A through F, are lying on a table. Which is the number of ways that four of the six balls can be placed in a row? (Lesson 12-7) **D**
   - Ⓐ 15
   - Ⓑ 60
   - Ⓒ 216
   - Ⓓ 360
   - Ⓔ 480

5. **Multiple-Choice** A vase holds eight flowers, each a different kind. Which is the number of ways that five of the flowers can be chosen to make a new, smaller bouquet? (Lesson 12-7) **B**
   - Ⓐ 28
   - Ⓑ 56
   - Ⓒ 112
   - Ⓓ 3,360
   - Ⓔ 6,720

Thursday

6. **Short Constructed-Response** Cammie is buying a new car. She has narrowed her body color, engine size, and interior color choices to those shown in the table. Draw a tree diagram to find the number of choices she has. (Lesson 12-6) **See margin.**

Body Color	Engine Size	Interior Color
Silver	6-cylinder	Black
Black	8-cylinder	Beige
White		

Friday

7. **Short Constructed-Response** Ten cards are labeled 1 through 10. Two cards are drawn one at a time and without replacement. What is the probability that on the first draw, an even-numbered card is drawn, and on the second draw, an odd-numbered card is drawn? (Lesson 12-9) $\frac{5}{18}$

Grade 8 Assessment Objectives Addressed	
Monday	(1A) 10.8.01 (1B) 10.8.01 (1C) 10.8.01
Tuesday	(2) 10.8.05; (3) 10.8.06
Wednesday	(4) 10.8.08; (5) 10.8.08
Thursday	(6) 10.8.07
Friday	(7) 10.8.06

Monday
Extended Response
Sample Answers

1A. There are 26 winning scores, so the team won 26 games.

1B. (94 + 93 + 75 + 84 + 85 + 74 + 71 + 75 + 80 + 85 + 88 + 80 + 67 + 51 + 79 + 75 + 65 + 66 + 78 + 66 + 81 + 64 + 71 + 74 + 72 + 92) ÷ 26 ≈ 76

1C.

Stem	Leaf
5	1
6	4 5 6 6 7
7	1 1 2 4 4 5 5 5 5 8 9
8	0 0 1 4 5 5 8
9	2 3 4

5 | 1 = 51 points

Thursday

6.

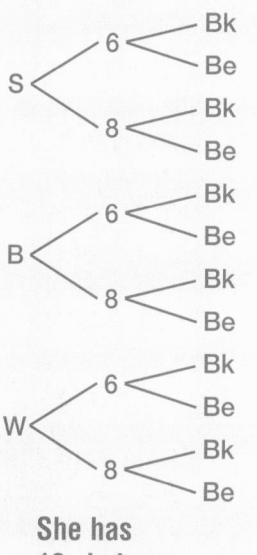

She has 12 choices.

Countdown to
ISAT

3 Weeks to ISAT

Monday

Monday
Extended Response
Sample Answers

1A. Worker Ages

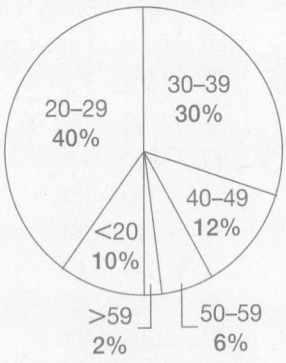

20–29
40%

30–39
30%

<20
10%

40–49
12%

>59
2%

50–59
6%

1B. The circle graph gives the percents of the total, so it compares parts of the data to the whole.

1C. $\dfrac{x}{165} = \dfrac{40}{100}$

$100 \cdot x = 40 \cdot 165$

$100x = 6{,}600$

$x = 66$

It is likely that there are about 66 workers in the 20–29 age range.

Thursday

6. It is not reasonable. She should have rounded to the nearest dollar. The actual amount is
$2.13 + $0.78 + $1.56 + $0.48 + $1.32 + $0.63 = $6.90.

$\dfrac{p}{100} = \dfrac{10}{6.9}$

$6.9 \cdot p = 10 \cdot 100$

$6.9p = 1{,}000$

$p \approx 145\%$

---

1. Extended Response Show your work and clearly explain your answer. The age-ranges of 50 workers chosen at random from a large construction project are shown in the table. (Page 723) **See margin.**

Worker Ages in Years			
Age Range	Workers	Age Range	Workers
< 20	5	40–44	4
20–24	8	45–49	2
25–29	12	50–54	2
30–34	9	55–59	1
35–39	6	> 59	1

A. Make a circle graph of the data. Each section of the graph should represent the percent of workers in each of the following groups: less than 20, 20–29, 30–39, 40–49, 50–59, and over 59.

B. Which representation, table or circle graph, compares parts of the data to the whole?

C. There are 165 workers in all on the project. Use the circle graph to predict the number of workers in the 20–29 age range.

Tuesday

2. Multiple-Choice Which is the interquartile range of the data set? {76, 92, 84, 86, 78, 91, 88, 79, 90, 85} (Lesson 12-2) **B**
ⓐ 10 ⓑ 11 ⓒ 12 ⓓ 13 ⓔ 14

3. Multiple-Choice Illinois is 390 miles long. Which is this distance in yards? (Page 720) **D**
ⓐ 85,800   ⓑ 171,600
ⓒ 343,200   ⓓ 686,400
ⓔ 2,059,200

Wednesday

4. Multiple-Choice Six people arrive at exactly the same time to purchase tickets for a play. Which is the number of ways they can line up in a cue? (Lesson 12-7) **A**
ⓐ 720 ⓑ 360 ⓒ 120 ⓓ 60 ⓔ 1

5. Multiple-Choice Carl must choose three songs to perform. He can select from seven songs. Which is the number of ways three songs can be chosen from seven? (Lesson 12-7) **C**
ⓐ 16 ⓑ 32 ⓒ 35 ⓓ 42 ⓔ 210

Thursday

6. Short Constructed-Response Serena estimated the total amount of money raised from donations of loose change for a charity. Each donation was in an envelope that was labeled with the amount it contained. The amounts were $2.13, $0.78, $1.56, $0.48, $1.32, and $0.63. Serena rounded each amount up to the next dollar to obtain $10. Is this reasonable? Find the actual value of the donations. Then, find the percent $10 is of the actual amount. Round to the nearest percent. (Lesson 6-5) **See margin.**

Friday

7. Short Constructed-Response After viewing the bar graph, Danielle claimed that more than twice as many of her schoolmates prefer dogs to cats. Danielle's classmate Anjelita disagreed. Who was right? (Lesson 12-5) **Anjelita**

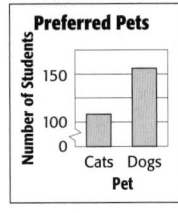

Preferred Pets

Number of Students
150
100
0
Cats   Dogs
Pet

Grade 8 Assessment Objectives Addressed

Monday	(1A) 10.8.03 (1B) 10.8.02 (1C) 10.8.03
Tuesday	(2) 10.8.05; (3) 7.8.05
Wednesday	(4) 10.8.08; (5) 10.8.08
Thursday	(6) 6.8.13
Friday	(7) 10.8.01

2 Weeks to ISAT

Monday

1. **Extended Response** Show your work and clearly explain your answer. The Curt Teich Post Card Archives at the Lake County Museum houses a 1.5-million piece postcard collection. **See margin.**

    A. The length, width, and thickness of a standard postcard are approximately 5.5 inches, 3.5 inches, and 0.01 inch, respectively. Find the volume of a postcard. (Lesson 11-2)

    B. What is the volume of the entire archive? (Lesson 11-2)

    C. If the entire archive was laid out flat, what area would it cover? (Lesson 10-5)

Monday
Extended Response
Sample Answers

1A. $V = (5.5)(3.5)$
$(0.01) = 0.1925$
or $\dfrac{77}{400}$ cu in.

1B. $V = 1,500,000$
$(0.1925) =$
$288,750$ cu in.

1C. $A = 1,500,000$
$(3.5)(5.5) =$
$28,875,000$ sq in.

Tuesday

2. **Multiple-Choice** The length of a rectangle is five more than its width. Which expression represents the area of the rectangle? (Lesson 13-4) **B**
    - Ⓐ $w + 5w$
    - Ⓑ $w(5 + w)$
    - Ⓒ $w + \dfrac{w}{5}$
    - Ⓓ $w^2 + 5$
    - Ⓔ $w^2 - 5w$

3. **Multiple-Choice** The graphs of the equations $y = 2x - 3$ and $y = -3x + 7$ intersect at exactly one point. Which is that point? (Lesson 8-9) **C**
    - Ⓐ $(0, 1)$
    - Ⓑ $(1, 2)$
    - Ⓒ $(2, 1)$
    - Ⓓ $(2, 2)$
    - Ⓔ $(3, 1)$

Wednesday

4. **Multiple-Choice** Which is the value of x? (Lesson 10-1) **A**

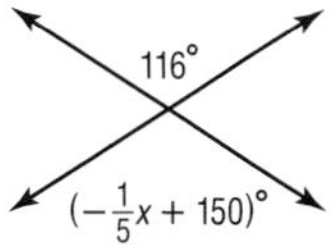

116°
$\left(-\dfrac{1}{5}x + 150\right)°$

   Ⓐ 170 Ⓑ 145 Ⓒ 102 Ⓓ 66 Ⓔ 43

5. **Multiple-Choice** Which pair of transformations gives the result in the graph? (Lesson 10-3) **C**

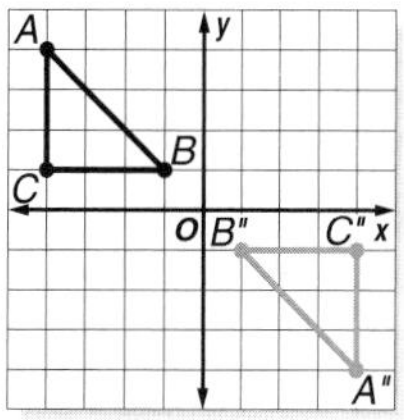

   - Ⓐ translation 5 units down, then 5 units left
   - Ⓑ 90° clockwise rotation about the origin, then reflection over the x-axis
   - Ⓒ reflection over the y-axis, then reflection over the x-axis
   - Ⓓ 270° clockwise rotation about the origin, then reflection over the y-axis
   - Ⓔ reflection over x-axis, then translation 8 units right

Thursday

6. **Short Constructed-Response** Which is the greatest, $\dfrac{17}{5}$, 3.39, or $3\dfrac{19}{50}$? (Lesson 5-1)
   $\dfrac{17}{5}$

Friday

7. **Short Constructed-Response** Simplify $\dfrac{88x^6y^4z^8}{11x^8y^5z^{11}}$ and express the quotient using exponents. (Lesson 4-7) $8x^{-2}y^{-1}z^{-3}$

Grade 8 Assessment Objectives Addressed	
Monday	(1A) 7.8.04 (1B) 7.8.04 (1C) 7.8.02
Tuesday	(2) 8.8.02; (3) 8.8.11
Wednesday	(4) 9.8.09; (5) 9.8.07
Thursday	(6) 6.8.06
Friday	(7) 6.8.05

Monday
Extended Response
Sample Answers

1A. The triangles are similar.
$$\frac{h}{9} = \frac{20}{15}$$
$$15 \cdot h = 20 \cdot 9$$
$$15h = 180$$
$$h = 12 \text{ ft}$$

1B. $\sqrt{15^2 + 20^2} =$

$\sqrt{225 + 400} =$

$\sqrt{625} = 25$ ft

1C. $\sqrt{9^2 + 12^2} =$

$\sqrt{81 + 144} =$

$\sqrt{225} = 15$ ft

1 Week to ISAT

Monday

1. **Extended Response** **Show your work and clearly explain your answer.** A telephone pole that was leaning has been straightened by the wires shown in the diagram. **See margin.**

   A. Find h, the height above the ground where the shorter wire attaches to the pole. (Lesson 9-7)

   B. Find the length of the longer wire. (Lesson 9-5)

   C. Find the length of the shorter wire. (Lesson 9-5)

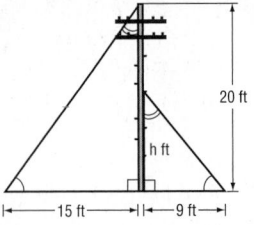

Tuesday

2. **Multiple-Choice** The average number of people per square mile in Illinois is approximately 223. For Nevada, the number is 18. Which is the approximate ratio of people per square mile in Illinois to that in Nevada? (Lesson 6-1) **C**
   - (A) 14:1
   - (B) 13:1
   - (C) 12:1
   - (D) 11:1
   - (E) 10:1

3. **Multiple-Choice** Which number is represented by point B on the number line? (Lesson 9-2) **B**

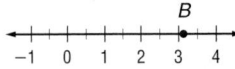

   - (A) 3
   - (B) π
   - (C) $\sqrt{11}$
   - (D) $\sqrt{11.2}$
   - (E) $\sqrt{12}$

Wednesday

4. **Multiple-Choice** Which property is shown by the statement $\frac{7}{x} \cdot \frac{x}{7} = 1$? (Lesson 5-4) **D**
   - (A) associative property of multiplication
   - (B) commutative property of multiplication
   - (C) associative property of addition
   - (D) multiplicative inverse property
   - (E) commutative property of addition

5. **Multiple-Choice** A number n is divided by a number greater than one. Which is always true about the quotient? (Prerequisite Skill) **E**
   - (A) It is less than n.
   - (B) It is zero.
   - (C) It is equal to $-n$.
   - (D) It is greater than n.
   - (E) It is less than $|n|$.

Thursday

6. **Short Constructed-Response** Simplify $(8x^2 - x + 9) - (-8x^2 - 7x - 11)$. (Lesson 13-3) $16x^2 + 6x + 20$

Friday

7. **Short Constructed-Response** Find the sixth term of the sequence. (Lesson 5-10)
$$-800, 100, -\frac{25}{2}, \frac{25}{16}, \cdots$$
$\frac{25}{1,024}$

Grade 8 Assessment Objectives Addressed

Monday	(1A) 9.8.11 (1B) 9.8.03 (1C) 9.8.03
Tuesday	(2) 6.8.15; (3) 6.8.07
Wednesday	(4) 6.8.11; (5) 6.8.12
Thursday	(6) 8.8.03
Friday	(7) 8.8.01

**GLENCOE
MATHEMATICS**

Pre-Algebra

Teacher Wraparound Edition

Malloy   Price

Willard   Sloan

**Glencoe
McGraw-Hill**

New York, New York
Columbus, Ohio
Chicago, Illinois
Peoria, Illinois
Woodland Hills, California

 **Glencoe**

The *McGraw·Hill* Companies

Send all inquiries to:
Glencoe/McGraw-Hill
8787 Orion Place
Columbus, OH 43240

ISBN: 0-07-865108-5 (Student Edition)

ISBN: 0-07-865109-3 (Teacher Edition)

3 4 5 6 7 8 9 10   027/043   12 11 10 09 08 07 06 05

Contents in Brief

Authors

Carol Malloy, Ph.D.
Associate Professor of
   Mathematics Education
University of North Carolina
   at Chapel Hill
Chapel Hill, North Carolina

Jack Price, Ed.D.
Professor Emeritus,
   Mathematics Education
California State Polytechnic
   University
Pomona, California

Teri Willard, Ed.D.
Assistant Professor of
   Mathematics Education
Central Washington
   University
Ellensburg, Washington

**Leon L. "Butch"
Sloan, Ed.D.**
Secondary Mathematics
   Coordinator
Garland ISD
Garland, Texas

Contributing Authors

USA TODAY
   The USA TODAY Snapshots®, created by
USA TODAY®, help students make the connection
between real life and mathematics.

Dinah Zike
Educational Consultant
Dinah-Might Activities, Inc.
San Antonio, Texas

Consultants

Content Consultants

Each of the Content Consultants reviewed every chapter and gave suggestions for improving the effectiveness of the mathematics instruction.

Mathematics Consultants

Rhonda Bailey
Mathematics Consultant
Mathematics by Design
DeSoto, Texas

Gunnar Carlsson, Ph.D.
Professor of Mathematics
Stanford University
Stanford, California

Ralph Cohen, Ph.D.
Professor of Mathematics
Stanford University
Stanford, California

William Leschensky
Former Mathematics Teacher
Glenbard South High School
College of DuPage
Glen Ellyn, Illinois

Yuria Orihuela
Mathematics Supervisor
Miami-Dade County Public Schools
Miami, Florida

Reading Consultants

Nancy Klores Welday
Language Arts Chairperson and
   Reading Resource Teacher
Hialeah-Miami Senior High School
Hialeah, Florida

Lynn T. Havens
Director
Project CRISS
Kalispell, Montana

ELL Consultant

Idania Dorta
Mathematics Educational Specialist
Miami–Dade County Public Schools
Miami, Florida

Teacher Reviewers

Teacher Reviewers

Each Teacher Reviewer reviewed at least two chapters of the Student Edition, giving feedback and suggestions for improving the effectiveness of the mathematics instruction.

Steven L. Arnofsky
Assistant Principal, Supervision
George W. Wingate High School
Brooklyn, New York

James M. Barr, Jr.
Teacher
Sells Middle School
Dublin, Ohio

Fay Bonacorsi
High School Mathematics Teacher
Lafayette High School
Brooklyn, New York

Rose H. Boothe
Subject Area Leader
A.J. Ferrell MST
Tampa, Florida

Diana L. Boyle
Mathematics Teacher, 6–8
Judson Middle School
Salem, Oregon

Beverly Burke
7th Grade Mathematics Teacher
USD 362
LaCygne, Kansas

Barbara A. Cain
Mathematics Teacher
Thomas Jefferson Middle School
Merritt Island, Florida

Rusty Campbell
Mathematics Instructor/Chairperson
North Marion High School
Farmington, West Virginia

Carol Caroff
Mathematics Department
    Chair/Teacher
Solon High School
Solon, Ohio

Vincent Ciraulo
Supervisor of Mathematics
J.P. Stevens High School
Edison, New Jersey

Lisa Cook
Mathematics Teacher
Kaysville Junior High School
Kaysville, Utah

Dianne Coppa
Mathematics Supervisor
Linden School District
Linden, New Jersey

Andrea L. Ellyson
Teacher/Department Chairperson
Great Bridge Middle School
Chesapeake, Virginia

James E. Ewing
7th Grade Pre-Algebra
Hiawatha Middle School
Hiawatha, Kansas

Eve Fingerett
Mathematics Teacher
Mountain Brook Junior High School
Mountain Brook, Alabama

Larry T. Gathers
Mathematics Teacher
Springfield South High School
Springfield, Ohio

Pamela M. Huskey
Mathematics Teacher
Buckingham County Middle School
Dillwyn, Virginia

Donald T. Jobbins
Supervisor of Mathematics
Edison Township Public Schools
Edison, New Jersey

Bonnie Nalesnik Johnston
Academically Gifted Program Facilitator
Valley Springs Middle School
Arden, North Carolina

Michael J. Klein
Math and Science Curriculum Consultant
Warren Consolidated Schools
Warren, Michigan

Thomas Massa
Math Teacher
Los Altos Middle School
Camarillo, California

Jenny L. Miller
Math Teacher
Tuttle Middle School
Crawfordsville, Indiana

Aletha T. Paskett
Mathematics Teacher
Indian Hills Middle School
Sandy, Utah

Mary D. Pistor
Collaborative Peer Teacher
Osborn School District
Phoenix, Arizona

Debra K. Prowse
Mathematics Teacher
Beloit Memorial High School
Beloit, Wisconsin

Carol Read
8th Grade Mathematics Teacher
Legg Middle School
Coldwater, Michigan

Vicki Rentz
Mathematics Teacher
Burnett Middle School
Seffner, Florida

Cherie Rhoades
Mathematics Department Chairperson
Davidson Middle School
Crestview, Florida

Sherri Roberti
TEA/Math Mentor
Beaverton Schools
Beaverton, Oregon

Jack F. Rose, Jr.
Teacher/Department Chairperson
John Winthrop Middle School
Deep River, Connecticut

Sandy Schoff
Math Curriculum Coordinator K–12
Anchorage School District
Anchorage, Alaska

Carol A. Spice
Teacher of Mathematics
Woodlawn Beach Middle School
Gulf Breeze, Florida

Paula Allen Tibbs
Middle School Math
Narrows Elementary/Middle School
Narrows, Virginia

Christine Waddell
Mathematics Department Chair/Teacher
Albion Middle School
Sandy, Utah

Field Test Schools

Glencoe/McGraw-Hill wishes to thank the following schools that field-tested pre-publication manuscript during the 2001–2002 school year. They were instrumental in providing feedback and verifying the effectiveness of this program.

Burnett Middle School
Seffner, Florida

Carwise Middle School
Palm Harbor, Florida

Ft. Zumwalt Middle School
O'Fallon, Missouri

Graham Middle School
Bluefield, Virginia

John F. Kennedy Middle School
Bethpage, New York

McLane Middle School
Brandon, Florida

Martin Middle School
Raleigh, North Carolina

Parkway Southwest Middle School
Ballwin, Missouri

Safety Harbor Middle School
Safety Harbor, Florida

Teacher Handbook

Table of Contents

Designed to be in more

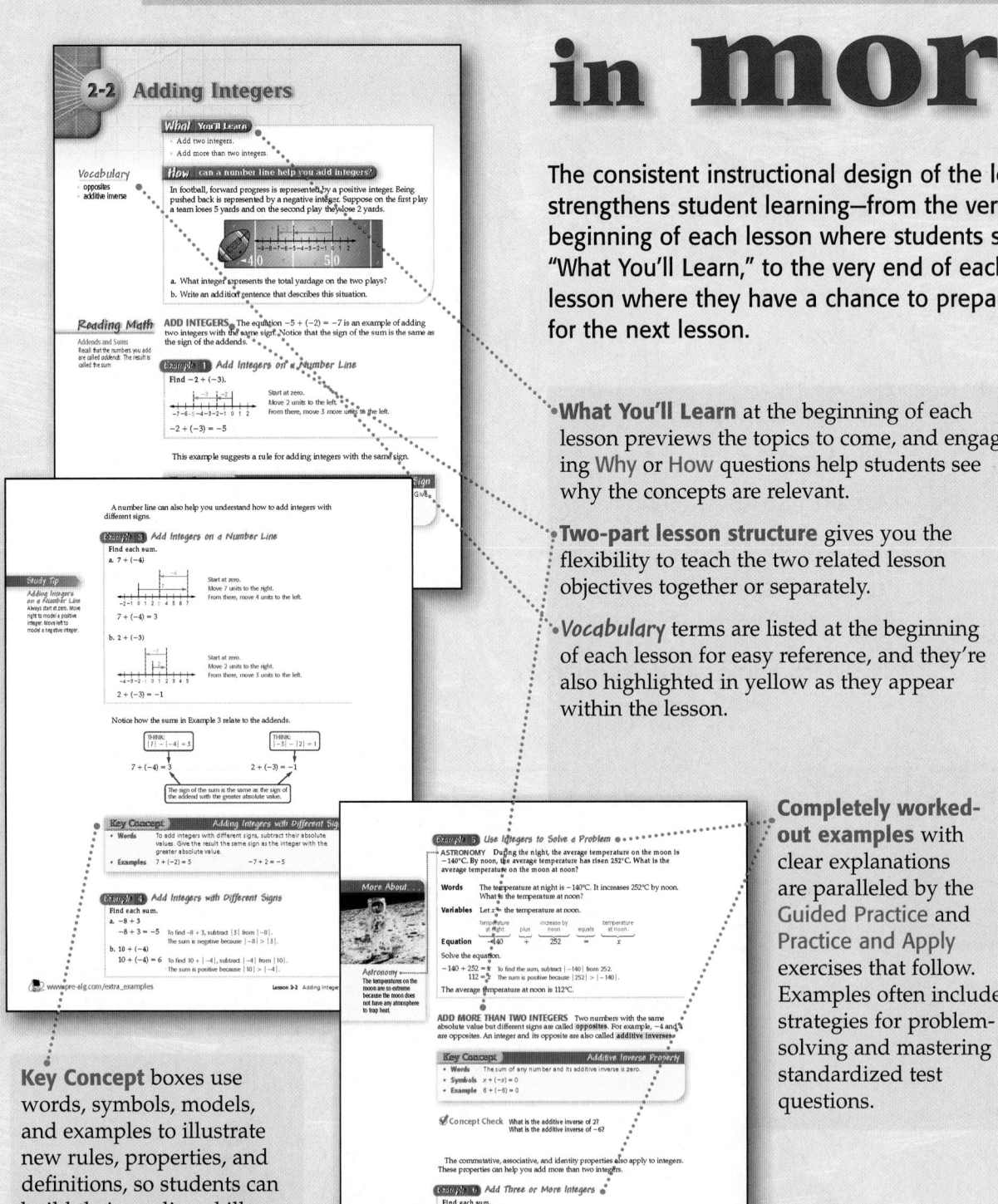

The consistent instructional design of the lessons strengthens student learning—from the very beginning of each lesson where students see "What You'll Learn," to the very end of each lesson where they have a chance to prepare for the next lesson.

•**What You'll Learn** at the beginning of each lesson previews the topics to come, and engaging Why or How questions help students see why the concepts are relevant.

•**Two-part lesson structure** gives you the flexibility to teach the two related lesson objectives together or separately.

•*Vocabulary* terms are listed at the beginning of each lesson for easy reference, and they're also highlighted in yellow as they appear within the lesson.

Completely worked-out examples with clear explanations are paralleled by the Guided Practice and Practice and Apply exercises that follow. Examples often include strategies for problem-solving and mastering standardized test questions.

Key Concept boxes use words, symbols, models, and examples to illustrate new rules, properties, and definitions, so students can build their reading skills as they build their math skills. **Concept Summary** boxes provide a concise overview of key topics.

effective,
ways than one.

Check for Understanding

You can use this portion of exercises in class to ensure that all students understand the concepts.

- *Concept Check* exercises give students opportunities to define, describe, and explain the mathematical concepts they've just learned.

- *Guided Practice* presents a representative sample of the exercises in the Practice and Apply section. A key is provided in the **Teacher Wraparound Edition** that correlates the exercises with appropriate examples.

- *Application* problems give students the opportunity to use the skills they have learned in a real-world setting.

Practice and Apply

- **Skill Exercises** correspond to the Guided Practice exercises and are structured so that students practice the same concepts whether they are assigned odd- or even-numbered problems. Homework Help is provided so students can refer to examples in the lesson as they complete the exercises.

- **Applications** give students frequent opportunities to apply concepts to both real-life and mathematical situations.

- **CRITICAL THINKING** exercises in each lesson require students to explain, make conjectures, and prove mathematical relationships.

- *Standardized Test Practice* questions provide students with ongoing opportunities to sharpen their test-taking skills.
  Ⓐ Ⓑ Ⓒ Ⓓ

Maintain Your Skills

- *Mixed Review* includes spiraled, cumulative exercises from the two previous lessons as well as earlier lessons.

- *Getting Ready for the Next Lesson* exercises give students the chance to preview prerequisite skills for the coming lesson. A reference is provided should students need additional help.

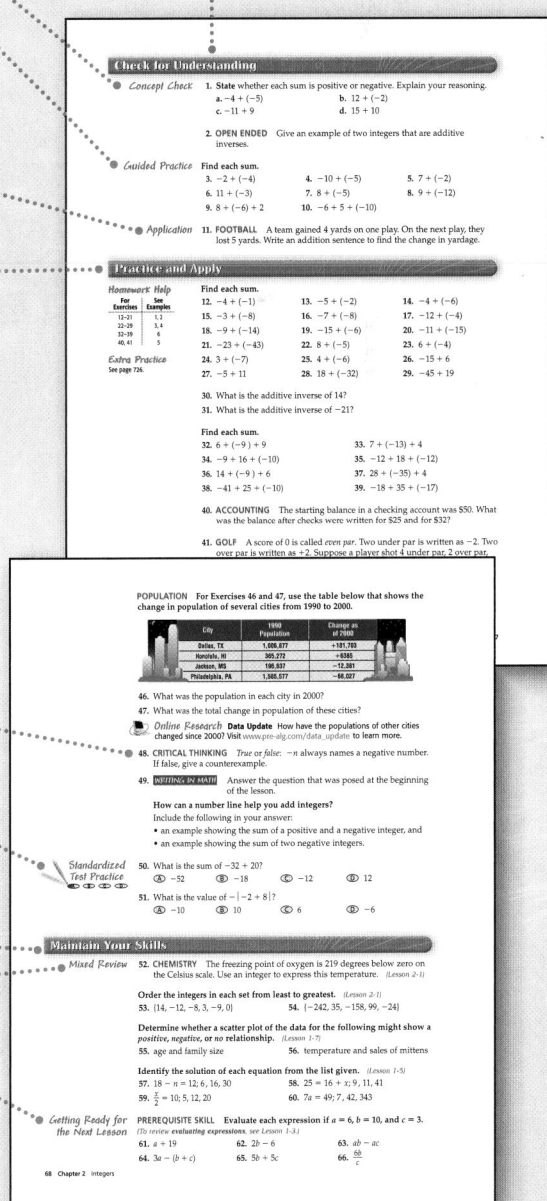

Accomplish more

Glencoe Pre-Algebra provides so many resources for lesson planning and teaching that you can create a complete, customized course in Pre-Algebra quickly...and easily.

This is where you start.

The **Teacher Wraparound Edition** is your key to all of the teaching resources in *Glencoe Pre-Algebra*. In addition to teaching suggestions, additional examples, and answers, the Teacher Wraparound Edition provides a guide for all of the print and software materials available for each lesson.

FAST FILE Chapter Resource Masters contain all of the core supplements you'll need to begin teaching a chapter of *Glencoe Pre-Algebra*. Each chapter booklet features convenient tabs for easy filing.

FAST FILE

- **Vocabulary Builder** helps students locate and define key vocabulary words from the chapter.
- **Study Guide and Intervention** summarizes key concepts and provides practice.
- **Skills Practice** provides ample exercises to help students develop basic computational skills, lesson by lesson.
- **Practice** mimics the computational and verbal problems in each lesson at an average level.
- **Reading to Learn Mathematics** provides students with various reading strategies to master the mathematics presented in each lesson.
- **Enrichment** activities extend students' knowledge and widen their appreciation of how mathematics relates to the world around them.
- **Assessment** options for each chapter include six forms of chapter tests, assessment tasks, quizzes, mid-chapter test, cumulative review, and standardized test practice.

Reading and Writing

WebQuest and Project Resources include teacher notes and answers for the Internet WebQuest projects with teaching notes, as well as other long-term projects that can be used with *Glencoe Pre-Algebra*.

Reading and Writing in the Mathematics Classroom features suggestions and activities for including reading as an integral part of the mathematics curriculum, as well as differentiated approaches to teaching mathematics that promote English learning and inclusion.

Teaching Mathematics with Foldables™ offers guidelines for using Foldables interactive study organizers in your class. The booklet was written by Foldables creator Dinah Zike.

FOLDABLES Study Organizer

Applications

Science and Mathematics Lab Manual includes lab activity masters and teaching suggestions for integrating science into the mathematics classroom.

School-to-Career Masters feature activities showing how mathematics relates to careers.

Graphing Calculator and Spreadsheet Masters include activities to incorporate the TI-83 Plus calculator and spreadsheets into your Pre-Algebra course.

Real-World Transparencies and Masters feature colorful transparencies with accompanying student worksheets to show how mathematics relates to real-world topics.

Investigations for the Special Education Student includes investigations designed for students who are learning disabled, emotionally handicapped, autistic, or students with attention deficit disorder.

than you'd ever imagine

in less time than you'd ever believe

Assessment and Intervention

5-Minute Check Transparencies with Standardized Test Practice include a transparency for each lesson that evaluates what students have learned in the previous lesson. Each transparency also includes a standardized test practice question.

Closing the Gap for Absent Students provides an easy-to-use summary of all the materials you have covered in the chapter in a format that can be posted or distributed to students who have missed class.

DAILY INTERVENTION Guide to Daily Intervention offers suggestions for daily assessment and tips on how to help students succeed.

Prerequisite Skills Workbook: Remediation and Intervention includes worksheets to review the arithmetic skills needed in Pre-Algebra.

Staff Development

Answer Key Transparencies provide answers to Student Edition exercises.

Lesson Planning Guide features a daily resource guide for planning your curriculum, as well as pacing for block scheduling.

Solutions Manual includes completely worked-out solutions for all exercises in the Student Edition.

Using the Internet in the Mathematics Classroom provides guidelines for using the Internet, as well as a guide to additional mathematics resources available on the Internet.

Teaching Pre-Algebra with Manipulatives features activities and teaching suggestions to help you present algebraic concepts with manipulatives and hands-on materials.

Technology Support for Teachers

Glencoe offers many timesaving software products to help you develop creative classroom presentations…fast.

TeacherWorks All-in-One Lesson Planner and Resource Center CD-ROM includes a lesson planner and interactive Teacher Edition, so you can customize lesson plans and reproduce classroom resources quickly and easily, from just about anywhere.

Answer Key Maker software allows you to customize answer keys for your assignments from the Student Edition exercises.

Interactive Chalkboard CD-ROM includes fully worked-out examples, the 5-Minute Check Transparencies, and Your Turn problems in a customizable Microsoft® PowerPoint® format.

And more… Additional technology products and Internet resources for students, teachers, and parents are discussed on pages T6–T13 and T17.

HELP
your students
become fluent

Glencoe Pre-Algebra makes it easy for you to incorporate constructive reading and writing strategies into every class you teach.

Reading Mathematics

Translating Verbal Problems into Equations

An important skill in algebra is translating verbal problems into equations. To do this accurately, analyze the statements until you completely understand the relationships among the given information. Look for key words and phrases.

> Jennifer is 6 years older than Akira. The sum of their ages is 20.

You can explore a problem situation by asking and answering questions.

Questions	Answers
a. Who is older?	a. Jennifer
b. How many years older?	b. 6 years
c. If Akira is *x* years old, how old is Jennifer?	c. $x + 6$
d. What expression represents the phrase *the sum of their ages*?	d. $x + (x + 6)$
e. What equation represents the sentence *the sum of their ages is 20*?	e. $x + (x + 6) = 20$

Reading to Learn

For each verbal problem, answer the related questions.

1. Lucas is 5 inches taller than Tamika, and the sum of their heights is 137 inches.
   a. Who is taller?
   b. How many inches taller?
   c. If *x* represents Tamika's height, how tall is Lucas?
   d. What expression represents *the sum of their heights*?
   e. What equation represents the sentence *the sum of their heights is 137*?

2. There are five times as many students as teachers on the field trip, and the sum of students and teachers is 132.
   a. Are there more students or teachers?
   b. How many times more?
   c. If *x* represents the number of teachers, how many students are there?
   d. What expression represents *the sum of students and teachers*?
   e. What equation represents *the sum of students and teachers is 132*?

Reading Mathematics Translating Verbal Problems into Equations **125**

Reading Mathematics activities help students master new mathematics vocabulary words and develop technical reading skills so they can understand and apply the language of math in their daily lives.

Student Edition

Foldables™ Study Organizers at the beginning of each chapter provide students with tools for organizing what they are reading and studying.

Reading Math Tips appear throughout each chapter, to help students learn and use the language of algebra.

Writing in Math questions in every lesson require students to use critical thinking skills to develop their answers.

Vocabulary terms are listed at the beginning of each lesson and highlighted when defined. The **Vocabulary and Concept Check** in each Study Guide and Review checks students' understanding of the key concepts of the chapter.

Key Concepts are illustrated using Words, Symbols, Models, and Examples, as appropriate. This approach improves reading comprehension by using multiple representations.

Concept Check provides an immediate opportunity to check students' comprehension before progressing to the next part of the lesson.

WebQuest Internet Projects are long-term projects that use problem-based learning to give students the opportunity to develop their research and creative writing skills.

in the Language of MATHEMATICS

Teacher Wraparound Edition

Study Notebook suggestions provide motivational ideas to help students create study notebooks that are thorough and effective.

Skill Check questions require students to describe, write, and explain the mathematical concepts they have learned in each lesson.

Modeling, Speaking, and **Writing** in every lesson require students to summarize what they have learned by responding to open-ended prompts.

ELL Resources highlight features and activities that help English-Language Learners grasp content.

Differentiated Instruction features help students at all points on the learning spectrum develop their reading, writing, and comprehension skills.

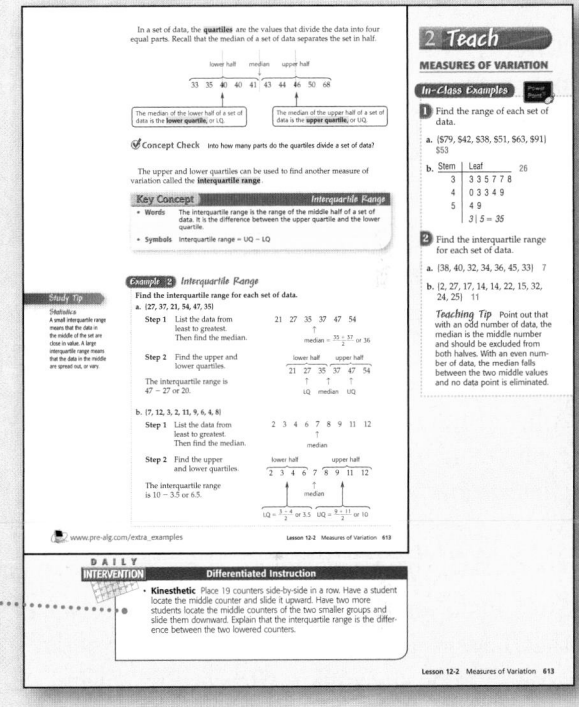

Technology Support

StudentWorks™, Glencoe's backpack solution, includes the entire Student Edition, formatted like the hardbound book, so students can study from just about anywhere—no book required. Students can also print their own lesson worksheet pages and get instant access to interactive web resources.

www.pre-alg.com/vocabulary_review is a Glencoe site that provides online study tools for reviewing the vocabulary of each chapter.

Vocabulary PuzzleMaker software creates crossword, jumble, and word search puzzles using vocabulary lists that you can customize.

Multimedia Applications: Virtual Activities
CD-ROM provides in-depth interactive activities that help students explore the main concepts of each chapter in a real-world setting.

Additional Resources
Chapter Resource Masters

- Vocabulary Builder
- Reading to Learn Mathematics

Teaching Mathematics with Foldables™

Reading and Writing in the Mathematics Classroom

WebQuest and Project Resources

For more information on these products, see pp. T4–T5.

Quick Review Math Handbook: Hot Words, Hot Topics is Glencoe's mathematical handbook for students. The Hot Words section includes a glossary of terms while the Hot Topics section consists of an explanation of key mathematical concepts. An exercise set is also included.

With these TOOLS,
you'll always know

Whether you need daily intervention resources integrated right into the program, or supplemental materials for after school and summer school programs, *Glencoe Pre-Algebra* puts it all right at your fingertips!

Diagnosis

Glencoe's **Diagnostic and Placement Tests** help you identify the key mathematical objectives that students are struggling with so you can make course placement decisions more effectively. A list of intervention resources is provided for each Glencoe program prior to and including *Glencoe Pre-Algebra*.

Prerequisite Skills

Students often struggle in Pre-Algebra because they have not mastered the prerequisite skills needed to be successful. *Glencoe Pre-Algebra* provides several opportunities to check student skills and determine which students need additional review and practice.

- The **Prerequisite Skills** at the beginning of every chapter help students identify and practice the skills they'll need for each new concept.

- Additional **prerequisite skills practice** is provided at the end of each lesson and includes page references to help students get extra review whenever they need it. More prerequisite skill practice appears in the Student Handbook section at the back of the Student Edition.

- The **Prerequisite Skills Workbook** provides extra practice on the basic skills needed for success in Pre-Algebra.

Daily Intervention Opportunities

Guide to Daily Intervention offers suggestions for using Glencoe materials to intercept students who are having difficulties and prescribe a system of reinforcement to promote student success.

The **Chapter Resource Masters** include several types of worksheets that can be used for daily intervention in each lesson. For a description of each worksheet, see page T4.

- **Study Guide and Intervention***
- **Skills Practice***
- **Practice***
- **Reading to Learn Mathematics**

** Each of these types of worksheets is available as a **consumable workbook** in both English and Spanish.*

The **Student Edition** contains additional problems to help students master each lesson before completing the chapter assessment.

- **Extra Practice**, located in the back of the Student Edition, provides additional, immediate practice with the concepts from each lesson.

- **Mixed Problem Solving**, also in the back of the Student Edition, includes numerous verbal problems to help students reinforce their problem-solving skills.

who needs EXTRA HELP.

And you'll be able to *DELIVER* it.

Technology Resources for Intervention

In addition to print resources, Glencoe offers a variety of timesaving technology tools to help students build their math skills more effectively.

Pre-AlgePASS: Tutorial Plus CD-ROM provides an interactive, self-paced tutorial for a complete Pre-Algebra curriculum. The 38 lessons are correlated directly to *Glencoe Pre-Algebra*. Each lesson, or concept, includes a pretest, tutorial, guided practice, and posttest. Students' answers to the pretests automatically determine whether they need the tutorial for each concept, so students can take responsibility for their own learning—without taking teacher time for grading.

Online Study Tools include comprehensive review and intervention tools that are available anytime, anyplace simply by logging on to

www.pre-alg.com.

Additional Teacher Resources

The following materials are available to help you determine which students need intervention and allow you to develop strategies for giving students the help they need. For a description of each feature, see page T5.

- **5-Minute Check Transparencies with Standardized Test Practice**
- **Daily Intervention** features in the Teacher Wraparound Edition
- **Closing the Gap for Absent Students**

Self-check quizzes are available for every lesson, and immediate feedback helps students check their progress and find specific pages and examples in the Student Edition whenever they need extra review. These Online Study Tools also include extra examples, chapter tests, standardized test practice, and vocabulary review.

ALEKS® is an online, intuitive, individualized tutor that students can take anywhere. This artificial intelligence-based system analyzes student answers and targets what the student is prepared to learn next. ALEKS is available by subscription only on the Internet.

www.k12.aleks.com

Give ASSESSMENT

Glencoe Pre-Algebra gives you all the tools you need to prepare students for success – including Standardized Test Practice in each lesson and the powerful ExamView® Pro CD-ROM.

Student Edition

Every lesson contains two Standardized Test Practice questions, and every chapter contains a completely worked-out standardized test example as well as two full pages of Standardized Test Practice with Test-Taking Tips.

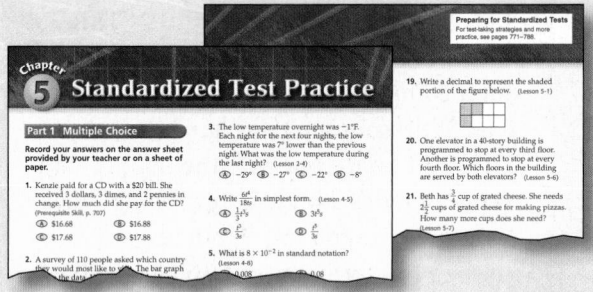

Preparing for Standardized Tests is designed

to help your students become better test-takers. Included are examples and practice for the types of questions and concepts commonly seen on standardized tests.

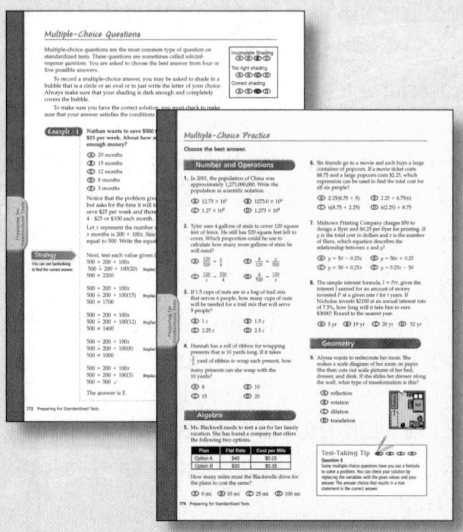

Chapter Study Guide and Review provides

Vocabulary and Concept review—a Glencoe exclusive—and Lesson-by-Lesson Review, all at the point of use for students.

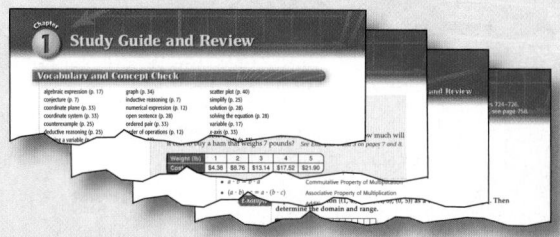

Practice Quizzes (2 per chapter) and a Practice
Test for each chapter provide the variety of practice questions students need to succeed on tests.

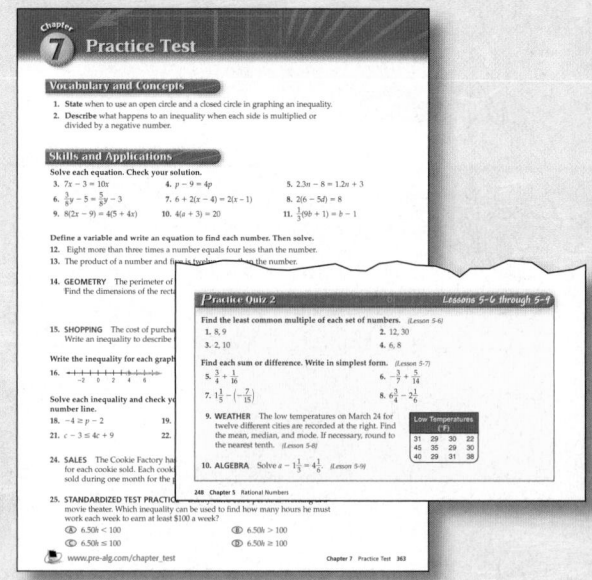

Teacher Wraparound Edition

An **Open-Ended Assessment** activity is provided in each lesson in the margin of the Teacher Wraparound Edition.

the
extra attention
it deserves, without the extra prep time.

Teacher Classroom Resources

5-Minute Check Transparencies with Standardized Test Practice provide full-size transparencies with questions covering the previous lesson or chapter. Standardized Test Practice Questions are also included.

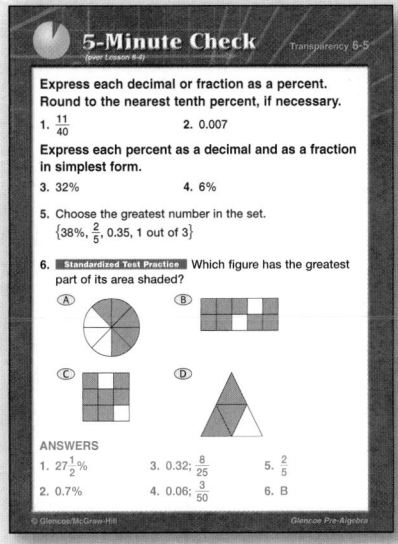

Technology Support

Use the networkable **ExamView® Pro** to:

- Create **multiple versions** of tests.
- Create **modified** tests for *Inclusion* students.
- **Edit** existing questions and **add** your own questions.
- Use built-in **state curriculum correlations** to create tests aligned with state standards.
- Change **English** tests to **Spanish** and vice versa.

MindJogger Videoquizzes present chapter-by-chapter review sessions in a game show format to make review more interesting and active to students…especially great for reluctant readers. Available on VHS or on DVD with Real-Life Math Videos.

Online Study Tools

- Self-Check Quizzes
- Vocabulary Review
- Chapter Test Practice
- Standardized Test Practice

Assessment Options in the Chapter Resource Masters

These assessment resources are available for each chapter in *Glencoe Pre-Algebra*.

- 6 Chapter Tests
- Open-Ended Assessment with Scoring Rubric
- Vocabulary Test and Review
  Glencoe Exclusive!
- 4 Quizzes
- Mid-Chapter Test
- Cumulative Review
- 2-page Standardized Test Practice

Unit Tests, Semester Tests, and a **Final Test** are also available at point of use in the Chapter Resource Masters.

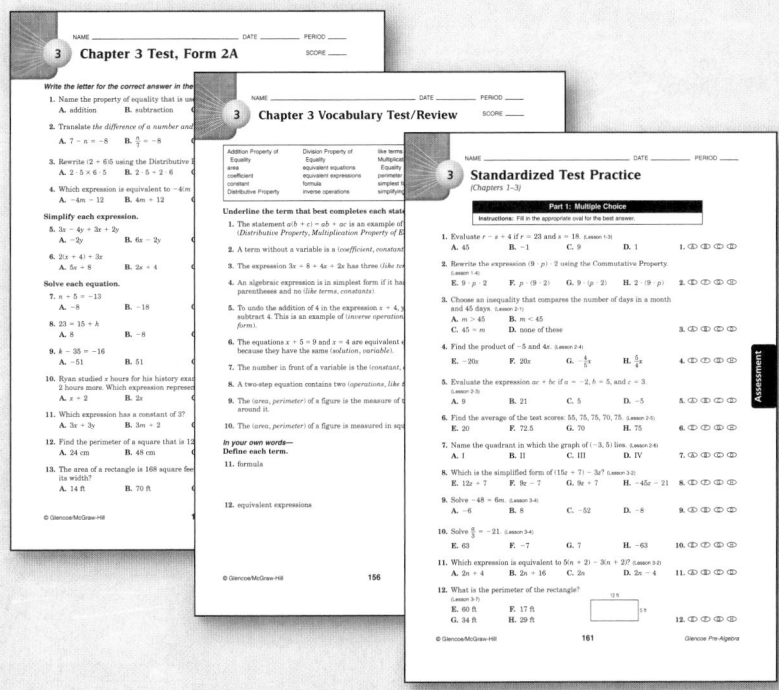

Introducing our new partner

USA TODAY® Education

USA TODAY Snapshots®

This is the same up-to-date data you know so well. But now, in an exclusive partnership with Glencoe/McGraw-Hill, USA TODAY® Education has brought its powerful, one-of-a-kind perspective and dynamic content to the pages of *Glencoe Pre-Algebra*. USA TODAY Snapshots® explode off the page to make Pre-Algebra come alive with current, relevant data.

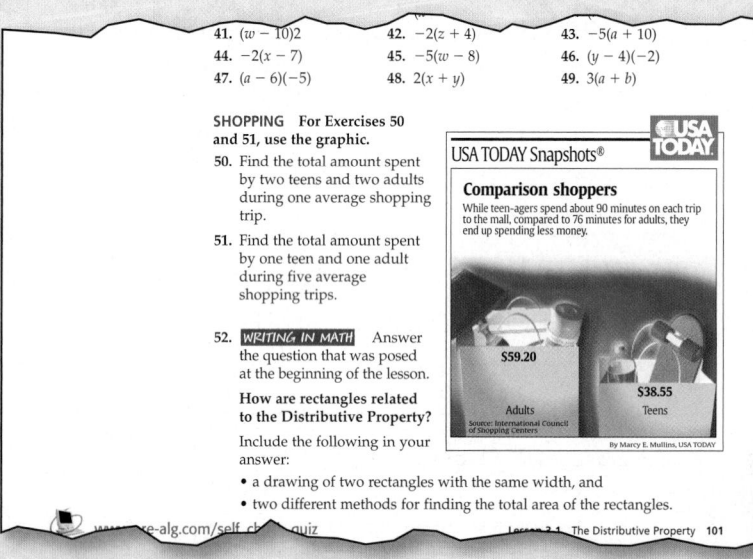

- www.pre-alg.com/usa_today provides additional activities related to the topics presented in the USA TODAY Snapshots®.

- www.education.usatoday.com, USA TODAY® K-12 Education's Web site offers resources and interactive features connected to each day's newspaper. *Experience Today*, USA TODAY®'s daily lesson plan, is available on the site and delivered daily to subscribers. This plan provides instruction for integrating USA TODAY® graphics and key editorial features into your mathematics classroom.

Stay current with additional charts and graphs with USA TODAY®. Log on to www.education.usatoday.com, or call USA TODAY® at (800) 757-TEACH.

WebQuest: Online Projects

www.pre-alg.com/webquest gives students the chance to work through a long-term project to enable them to develop their research, creative writing, and presentation skills.

- WebQuests often utilize USA TODAY Snapshots® or USA TODAY® articles.

- Special features in the Student Edition prompt students to complete each stage of their WebQuest.

- Parents can use the guided instruction to help students become familiar with the Internet in a safe, productive manner.

The INTERNET:
One TOOL.
Endless possibilities.

Many of your students may already be familiar with the Internet, but may not have discovered the full potential of this powerful research tool. With *Glencoe Pre-Algebra*, your students can use the Internet to build their algebra skills. And you can access a wide variety of resources to help you plan classes, extend lessons, even meet professional development requirements.

For Students

Online Study Tools, referenced on the Student Edition pages are keyed specifically to *Glencoe Pre-Algebra*.

- www.pre-alg.com/extra_examples features additional fully worked-out examples.
- www.pre-alg.com/self_check_quiz allows students to check their progress in each lesson.
- www.pre-alg.com/vocabulary_review lets students check their vocabulary comprehension.
- www.pre-alg.com/chapter_test provides additional practice in test taking.
- www.pre-alg.com/standardized_test simulates questions that appear on standardized and proficiency tests.

Other Online Resources

- www.pre-alg.com/webquest offers an online research project.
- www.pre-alg.com/usa_today provides additional activities related to the topics presented in the USA TODAY Snapshots®.
- www.pre-alg.com/data_update features links to updated statistical data presented in exercises.
- www.pre-alg.com/careers offers information about career opportunities.
- www.pre-alg.com/other_calculator_keystrokes provides keystroke instructions for various calculators to accompany graphing calculator activities and exercises in the Student Edition.

For Teachers

Powerful tools to make your job easier

- Classroom Games
- Key Concepts: Mathematical Background and Teaching Notes www.pre-alg.com/key_concepts
- USA TODAY® K-12 Education daily lesson plans
- Sharing Ideas with Other Teachers
- Cool Math Links
- State and National Resources

Staff Development Sites

- NCTM links
- Teaching Today link
- McGraw-Hill Learning Network link
- Cooperative learning suggestions
- Using the Internet in the Mathematics Classroom

For Parents

Help parents get involved with their child's learning

- Parent and Student Study Guide www.pre-alg.com/parent_student
- Involving Parents and Community in the Mathematics Classroom

DISCOVER how a simple sheet of paper can CHANGE the way your students THINK about math... forever.

Students love Foldables™ because they're fun. Teachers love them because they're effective.

Foldables are easy-to-make, three-dimensional interactive graphic organizers that students create out of simple sheets of paper. These unique hands-on tools for learning and reviewing were created exclusively for *Glencoe Pre-Algebra* by teaching specialist Dinah Zike.

Building Prereading Skills

At the beginning of each chapter, students construct one of a variety of Foldables. Each Foldable helps students create an interactive strategy for organizing what they read and observe. As they work through each chapter, students add more detail to their Foldable until they have created a comprehensive, interactive snapshot of the key concepts and vocabulary of the chapter.

Reading and Writing

Each Foldable helps students practice basic reading and writing skills, find and report main ideas, organize information, review key vocabulary terms, and more.

Review and Reinforcement

The completed Foldable is a comprehensive overview of the chapter concepts—perfect for preparing for chapter, unit, and even end-of-course tests.

Assessment

Foldables present an ideal opportunity to probe the depth of your students' understanding of chapter concepts. You'll get detailed feedback on what your students know and what misconceptions they may have.

Staff Development

Teaching Mathematics with Foldables™ equips teachers to extend the use of Foldables in their classrooms by exploring the different Foldable formats and providing suggestions for using them throughout the mathematics curriculum.

Give students control,

so that they leave your classroom with *knowledge and power over their*

own learning.

PROJECT CRISS℠ Study Skill

Project CRISS℠ (**CR**eating **I**ndependence through **S**tudent-owned **S**trategies) is a research-based staff development program created to help students better organize, understand, and retain course information. In short, students receiving the CRISS method of instruction will "LEARN HOW TO LEARN".

CRISS strategies are designed to develop thoughtful and independent readers and learners.

To enhance student learning, CRISS employs several concepts drawn from cognitive psychology.

- Students must be able to integrate new information with prior knowledge.
- Students need to be actively involved in their own learning by discussing, writing, and organizing information.
- Students must self-monitor to identify which strategies are the most effective for their own learning.

These behaviors need to be taught by content teachers to maximize student learning.

CReating Independence Through Student-Owned Strategies

Reading and Writing in Mathematics

Glencoe Pre-Algebra provides numerous opportunities to incorporate reading and writing into the mathematics classroom.

Student Edition
- Foldables™ Study Organizer, p. 5
- Reading Mathematics, p. 11
- Concept Check questions require students to verbalize and write about what they have learned in the lesson. (pp. 6, 7, 9, 12, 14, 17, 19, 23, 24, 26, 30, 34, 36, 40, 41, 42)
- Writing in Math questions in every lesson, pp. 10, 16, 21, 27, 32, 37, 44
- Reading Math, pp. 17, 23, 24, 29
- WebQuest, p. 43

Teacher Wraparound Edition
- Foldables™ Study Organizer, pp. 5, 47
- Study Notebook suggestions, pp. 8, 11, 14, 19, 26, 30, 36, 42
- Speaking activities, pp. 10, 16, 27, 38
- Writing activities, pp. 21, 32, 44
- ELL Resources, pp. 4, 6, 11, 12, 17, 23, 28, 33, 40, 47

For more information on Reading and Writing in Mathematics, see pp. T6–T7.

Additional Resources
- Vocabulary Builder worksheets require students to define and give examples for key vocabulary terms as they progress through the chapter (*Chapter 1 Resource Masters*, pp. vii–viii)
- Reading to Learn Mathematics master for each lesson (*Chapter 1 Resource Masters*, pp. 4, 9, 14, 19, 24, 29, 34)
- *Vocabulary PuzzleMaker* software creates crossword, jumble, and word search puzzles using vocabulary lists that you can customize.
- *Teaching Mathematics with Foldables* provides suggestions for promoting cognition and language.
- *Reading and Writing in the Mathematics Classroom*
- *WebQuest and Project Resources*

PROJECT CRISS Study Skill

Capsule vocabulary is a teaching strategy that helps students verbally review important terms. After students have studied Lesson 1-5, write the properties listed at the right on the chalkboard. Discuss the properties with the class. Divide the class into pairs. Have students talk about the properties with their partners. Each student should make sure his or her partner can explain or give an example of all of the properties. Afterward, have students write a short summary about the properties.

Properties
- Commutative Property of Addition
- Commutative Property of Multiplication
- Associative Property of Addition
- Associative Property of Multiplication
- Additive Identity Property
- Multiplicative Identity Property
- Multiplicative Property of Zero
- Symmetric Property of Equality
- Transitive Property of Equality

CReating **I**ndependence **T**hrough **S**tudent-**O**wned **S**trategies

Chapter 1 The Tools of Algebra

Implementing CRISS Strategies

Project CRISS Study Skills were developed with leaders from Project CRISS to facilitate the teaching of each chapter of *Glencoe Pre-Algebra.* These strategies appear in the interleaf of the Teacher Wraparound Edition.

For more information on project CRISS℠, visit www.projectcriss.com.

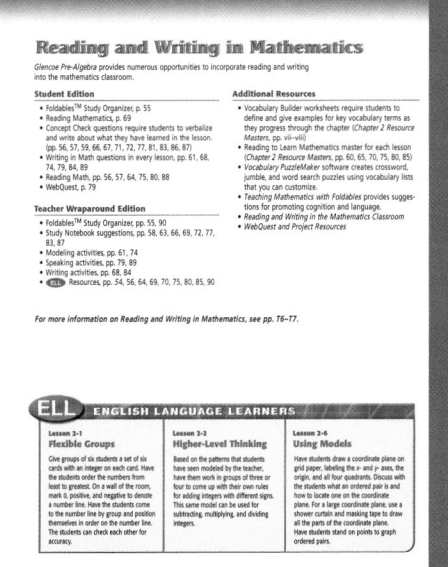

Reading and Writing in Mathematics

Glencoe Pre-Algebra provides numerous opportunities to incorporate reading and writing into the mathematics classroom.

Student Edition
- Foldables™ Study Organizer, p. 55
- Reading Mathematics, p. 69
- Concept Check questions require students to verbalize and write about what they have learned in the lesson. (pp. 56, 57, 59, 66, 67, 71, 72, 77, 81, 83, 86, 87)
- Writing in Math questions in every lesson, pp. 61, 68, 74, 79, 84, 89
- Reading Math, pp. 56, 57, 64, 75, 80, 88
- WebQuest, p. 79

Teacher Wraparound Edition
- Foldables™ Study Organizer, pp. 55, 90
- Study Notebook suggestions, pp. 58, 63, 66, 69, 72, 77, 83, 87
- Modeling activities, pp. 61, 74
- Speaking activities, pp. 79, 89
- Writing activities, pp. 68, 84
- ELL Resources, pp. 54, 56, 64, 69, 70, 75, 80, 85, 90

For more information on Reading and Writing in Mathematics, see pp. T6–T7.

Additional Resources
- Vocabulary Builder worksheets require students to define and give examples for key vocabulary terms as they progress through the chapter (*Chapter 2 Resource Masters*, pp. vii–viii)
- Reading to Learn Mathematics master for each lesson (*Chapter 2 Resource Masters*, pp. 60, 65, 70, 75, 80, 85)
- *Vocabulary PuzzleMaker* software creates crossword, jumble, and word search puzzles using vocabulary lists that you can customize.
- *Teaching Mathematics with Foldables* provides suggestions for promoting cognition and language.
- *Reading and Writing in the Mathematics Classroom*
- *WebQuest and Project Resources*

ELL ENGLISH LANGUAGE LEARNERS

Lesson 2-1
Flexible Groups
Give groups of six students a set of six cards with an integer on each card. Have the students order the numbers from least to greatest. On a wall of the room, mark 0, positive, and negative to denote a number line. Have the students come to the number line by group and position themselves in order on the number line. The students can check each other for accuracy.

Lesson 2-2
Higher-Level Thinking
Based on the patterns that students have seen modeled by the teacher, have them work in groups of three or four to come up with their own rules for adding integers with different signs. This same model can be used for subtracting, multiplying, and dividing integers.

Lesson 2-6
Using Models
Have students draw a coordinate plane on grid paper, labeling the x- and y-axes, the origin, and all four quadrants. Discuss with the students what an ordered pair is and how to locate one on the coordinate plane. For a large coordinate plane, use a shower curtain and masking tape to draw all the parts of the coordinate plane. Have students stand on points to graph ordered pairs.

Chapter 2 Integers

ELL ENGLISH LANGUAGE LEARNERS

English language learners may need specialized help in overcoming a language barrier to learn mathematics. Hands-on activities, modeling, working in flexible groups, and vocabulary building activities are particularly helpful to ELL students. Suggested strategies appear in the interleaf of the Teacher Wraparound Edition.

It's Staff Development,

As professional development continues to take on greater importance for educators across the country, teachers are constantly looking for easy-to-use tools to help them stay abreast of current trends and issues. At Glencoe, we know how valuable your time is, so we've developed a variety of staff development tools to help you meet your district's requirements.

Teacher Wraparound Edition

Mathematical Connections and Background found at the beginning of each chapter gives you an overview of the mathematics skills required in each lesson. Information about prior knowledge as well as future connections lets you see the continuity of instruction.

Building on Prior Knowledge provides you with information that links what students have previously learned to the content of the lesson.

Tips for New Teachers offers helpful suggestions for such things as classroom management, assessment, teaching techniques, and more.

Teaching Tips can be found not only in the margins but also on the reduced student pages at point of use.

Teacher Classroom Resources

Glencoe Mathematics Staff Development Series is a series of publications that allows you to stay current with issues that affect your teaching effectiveness. The series is intended to help you implement new mathematics strategies and enhance your classroom performance.

Available in print

- *Using the Internet in the Mathematics Classroom*
- *Reading and Writing in the Mathematics Classroom*
- *Teaching Mathematics with Foldables™*
- *Teaching Pre-Algebra with Manipulatives*

Available online at
www.math.glencoe.com

- *Graphing Calculators in the Mathematics Classroom*
- *Cooperative Learning in the Mathematics Classroom*
- *Alternative Assessment in the Mathematics Classroom*
- *Involving Parents and the Community in the Mathematics Classroom*

made convenient.

Technology Support

At www.math.glencoe.com, you'll find:

- a Staff Development site that addresses current issues in education.
- a Teacher Forum that allows teachers to discuss issues and ideas with colleagues.
- a State and National Resources site that links to math and math education resources, nationally and by state.

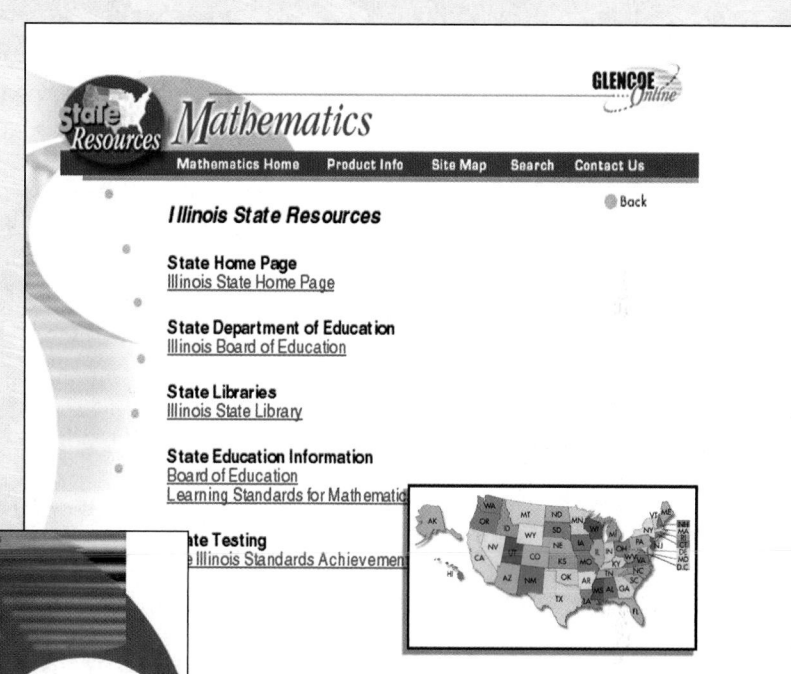

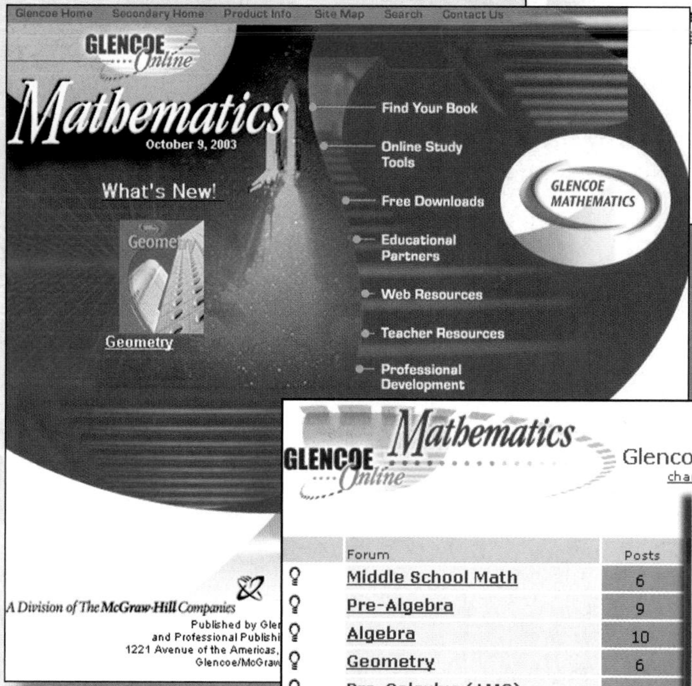

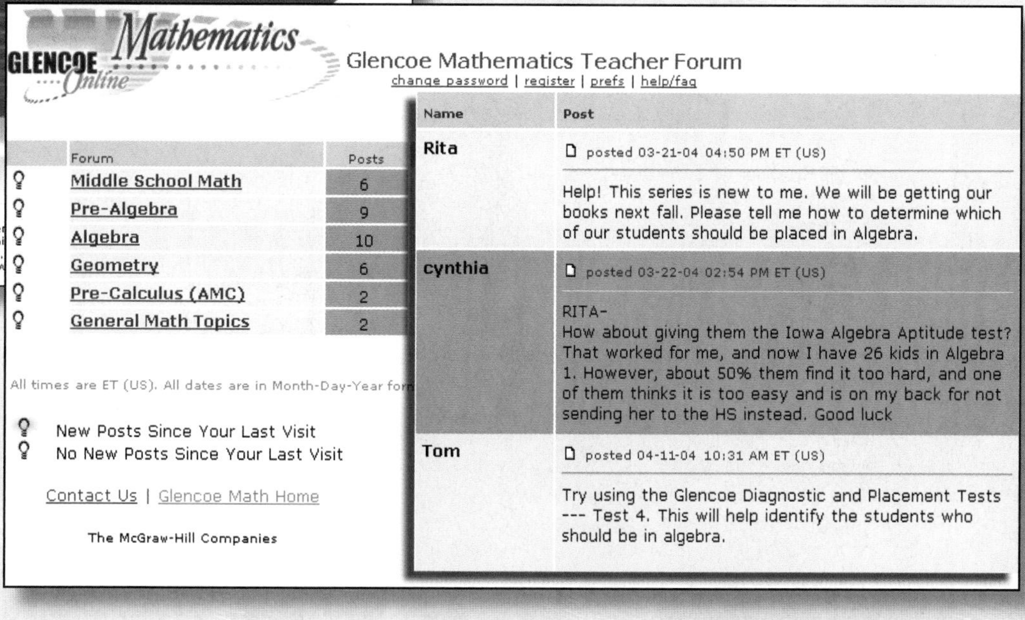

Glencoe Mathematics Programs—
Research-
Based and

Glencoe's mathematics programs are the product of ongoing classroom and educational research activities involving students, teachers, curriculum supervisors, administrators, parents, and college-level mathematics educators, mathematicians, and researchers.

SOUND

Prior to the publication of any Glencoe mathematics program, the following initial research is completed.

- Monitoring of national and state changes and trends such as graduation requirements, standardized test exams, and the latest NCTM and NAEP reports.

- Incorporating the most current and applicable educational research in which reported results show significant improvement on student learning and achievement.

- Analyzing returns from independently contracted mailing and telephone surveys.

- Reviewing all comments and correspondence on appropriate prior editions in terms of specific lessons. This helps Glencoe to build in staff development support, which makes the programs easy to implement from the first day of use.

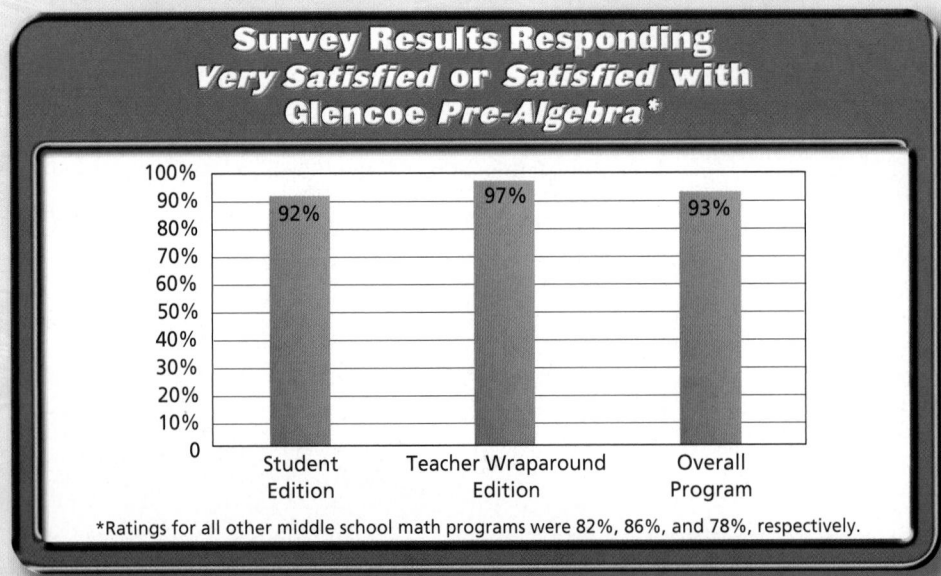

Survey Results Responding Very Satisfied or Satisfied with Glencoe Pre-Algebra*

*Ratings for all other middle school math programs were 82%, 86%, and 78%, respectively.

Source: Middle School Mathematics Longitudinal Survey, 2003

tested to ensure success.

PROVEN

Prior to the publication of *Glencoe Pre-Algebra*, extensive research was conducted using manuscript and pre-publication versions of the program.

- Nationwide discussion groups were conducted, which involved mathematics teachers, department chairpersons, supervisors, and educational learning specialists.
- Face-to-face interviews were carried out with mathematics teachers.
- Reviewers and consultants reviewed *Glencoe Pre-Algebra* manuscripts for accuracy, content development, and thoroughness.
- Before the design of the Student Edition was completed, an independent research company was contracted to organize and conduct blind focus groups with pre-algebra teachers in various cities. The teachers' feedback was used for improvements.
- Follow-up interviews, observations, and surveys of users of Glencoe mathematics programs are continuously conducted and monitored.
- Glencoe conducts Learner Verification Research in which students and teachers use pre-publication manuscript in the classroom. The results, compiled by an independent contractor, for *Glencoe Pre-Algebra* are summarized below.

Top-Line Results
- The research indicates that test scores significantly increased among students using *Glencoe Pre-Algebra*.
- Roughly nine out of ten students earned higher scores after using the Glencoe program.
- The program was equally effective with boys and girls and with minority and non-minority students.
- Overall, the gap between the average pre-test score and a perfect score closed by 53%. Stated differently, on average, scores increased 48% after students used *Glencoe Pre-Algebra*.

EFFECTIVE

What do teachers say? Here are some testimonials from Learner Verification Research teachers.

- *great organization, great examples, and lots of extra practice*
- *program is mathematically correct, challenging, and age appropriate*
- *good balance of practice problems and word problems*
- *program is easy to follow for both teacher and student*
- *abundant resources and technology*

For more details of Glencoe's research, please contact us at www.math.glencoe.com.

Planning Your

Glencoe Pre-Algebra and the accompanying support materials allow you to create a Pre-Algebra course that meets the needs of each class of students. The charts shown on these two pages offer general suggestions for pacing your students through the book for average and advanced levels. Pacing for both standard class periods and block schedule class periods is given. A more detailed pacing chart appears on interleaf page A preceding each chapter in the *Teacher Wraparound Edition.*

The total number of days in each level of pacing is less than the typical 180-day school year and 90-day semester to allow for flexibility in planning due to testing, school cancellation, or shortened class periods.

AVERAGE PACING

Average Pacing is for those students who have a fairly good mathematical preparation for Pre-Algebra. You may want to use one of the six chapter tests provided in the Chapter Resource Masters as a pretest to determine how well your students are prepared for each chapter. If you find that they are well prepared, consider using the Study Guide and Review at the end of the chapter as a one-day lesson and proceed to the next chapter.

If your students are better prepared for Pre-Algebra, you may want to spend less time in the earlier chapters in order to explore Chapter 13.

Modifying Average Pacing for Basic Students

For those students who are less prepared for Pre-Algebra, spend more time on Units 1 and 2 (Chapters 1–6). Unit 5 (Chapters 12–13) may be omitted.

Year-Long Schedule
45–50 minute periods

Grading Period	Chapter	Days
1	1	11
	2	13
	3	12
	4 (through Lesson 4-4)	4
2	4 (Lesson 4-5 to end)	9
	5	14
	6	14
	7 (Lesson 7-1)	3
3	7 (Lesson 7-2 to end)	9
	8	19
	9	15
4	10	14
	11	12
	12	11
optional	13	0
	Total	160

Block Schedule
90 minute periods

Chapter	Days
1	5.5
2	7
3	6
4	7
5	7
6	7
7	6
8	10
9	7
10	7
11	6
12	6.5
13	0
Total	82

Pre-Algebra Course

ADVANCED PACING

Advanced Pacing is for those students who have a strong background in mathematics. These students are often sixth- or seventh-graders taking Pre-Algebra for the first time. In advanced pacing, students spend less time on introductory activities and more on the Follow-Up extension activities. They also cover Chapter 13. One of the six chapter tests provided in the Chapter Resource Masters can be used as a pretest for each chapter.

Year-Long Schedule
45–50 minute periods

Grading Period	Chapter	Days
1	1	11
	2	8
	3	11
	4	12
2	5	15
	6	13
	7	10
3	8	15
	9	15
	10	13
4	11	9
	12	15
	13	13
	Total	160

Block Schedule
90 minute periods

Chapter	Days
1	5.5
2	4
3	5
4	6
5	8
6	7
7	5
8	8
9	7
10	7
11	5
12	8
13	6.5
Total	82

Daily Planning

- A more detailed Suggested Pacing chart appears in the interleaf preceding each chapter in the *Teacher Wraparound Edition.*

- The *Lesson Planning Guide* offers further suggestions for the materials to be covered each day and how to adapt these for Block Scheduling.

- *TeacherWorks: All in One Lesson Planner and Resource Center* CD-ROM enables you to customize an entire course of study to meet your specific needs.

Implementing the NCTM Principles and Standards

In 1989, the National Council of Teachers of Mathematics (NCTM) published their *Curriculum and Evaluation Standards for School Mathematics*, which gave mathematics teachers their first set of goals toward a national mathematics curriculum. Teachers and supervisors have embraced these Standards and developed state standards based on this framework. In 2000, the National Council of Teachers of Mathematics published a revision of these guidelines entitled *NCTM Principles and Standards for School Mathematics*.

NCTM Principles for School Mathematics	Glencoe Pre-Algebra
Equity *Excellence in mathematics education requires equity—high expectations and strong support for all students.*	Glencoe's product line encourages high achievement at every level. Numerous teacher support materials provide activities for **differentiated instruction,** promotion of **reading and writing, pacing** for individual levels of achievement, and **daily intervention.**
Curriculum *A curriculum is more than a collection of activities: it must be coherent, focused on important mathematics, and well articulated across the grades.*	Glencoe authors developed a philosophy and scope and sequence to ensure a continuum of mathematical learning that builds on **prior knowledge** and extends concepts toward more **advanced mathematical thinking.**
Teaching *Effective mathematics teaching requires understanding what students know and need to learn and then challenging and supporting them to learn it well.*	Glencoe offers a plethora of teacher support materials. A comprehensive *Teacher Wraparound Edition* provides **mathematical background,** teaching tips, resource management guidelines, and **tips for new teachers.**
Learning *Students must learn mathematics with understanding, actively building new knowledge from experience and prior knowledge.*	The *Teacher Wraparound Edition* includes instruction on building from prior knowledge with materials in each interleaf and in **Building On Prior Knowledge** features. **Find the Error** and **Unlocking Misconception** teaching tips help to evaluate how students are thinking and learning.
Assessment *Assessment should support the learning of important mathematics and furnish useful information to both teachers and students.*	The **Practice Quizzes** and the **Chapter Practice Test** provide ways for students to check their own progress. Online Study Tools, such as **Self-Check Quizzes,** offer a unique way for students with Internet access to monitor their progress. The assessment tools in the *Chapter Resource Masters* contain different levels and formats for tests, as well as intermediate opportunities for assessment.
Technology *Technology is essential in teaching and learning mathematics; it influences the mathematics that is taught and enhances students' learning.*	The *Student Edition* includes opportunities to utilize graphing calculators and spreadsheets in the exploration of Pre-Algebra concepts. The *Teacher Wraparound Edition* offers teaching tips on using technology. *Graphing Calculator and Spreadsheet Masters* has additional activities. Glencoe's Web site is constantly updated to meet the needs of students and teachers in excelling in mathematics education.

NCTM Standards for School Mathematics

The Standards portion of the *NCTM Principles and Standards for School Mathematics* center upon ten areas of mathematics curriculum development. The number assigned to each standard is for easy reference and is not part of each standard's official title.

Instructional programs from prekindergarten through grade 12 should enable all students to:

1 Numbers and Operations

- Understand numbers, ways of representing numbers, relationships among numbers, and number systems
- Understand the meaning of operations and how they relate to each other
- Compute fluently and make reasonable estimates

Pages: 6-44, 56-84, 98-107, 148-190, 200-236, 238-242, 244-248, 264-315, 340-359, 436-445, 453-482, 506-511, 520-531, 533-543, 563-582, 584-594, 641-657, 674-686

2 Algebra

- Understand patterns, relations, and functions
- Represent and analyze mathematical situations and structures using algebraic symbols
- Use mathematical models to represent and understand quantitative relationships
- Analyze change in various contexts

Pages: 17-21, 40-44, 56-61, 64-89, 98-137, 148-190, 210-231, 237, 244-253, 264-280, 288-292, 298-302, 304-315, 328-359, 368-391, 393-423, 441-445, 453-482, 492-497, 500-504, 513-517, 563-582, 584-588, 669-697

3 Geometry

- Analyze characteristics and properties of two- and three-dimensional geometric shapes and develop mathematical arguments about geometric relationships
- Specify locations and describe spatial relationships using coordinate geometry and other representational systems
- Apply transformations and use symmetry to analyze mathematical situations
- Use visualization, spatial reasoning, and geometric modeling to solve problems

Pages: 85-89, 131-137, 175-179, 210-219, 249-253, 286-287, 304-308, 334-338, 393-397, 447-482, 492-543, 554-594, 673, 682, 687-697

4 Measurement

- Understand measurable attributes of objects and the units, systems, and processes of measurement
- Apply appropriate techniques, tools, and formulas to determine measurements

Pages: 23-27, 169-173, 186-190, 210-219, 238-242, 264-280, 286-287, 386, 392, 436-440, 447-482, 492-504, 512, 518-531, 533-543, 562-594, 673, 682

5 Data Analysis and Probability

- Formulate questions that can be addressed with data and collect, organize, and display relevant data to answer them
- Select and use appropriate statistical methods to analyze data
- Develop and evaluate inferences and predictions that are based on data
- Understand and apply basic concepts of probability

Pages: 40-44, 210-219, 237-243, 275, 303, 309-315, 409-413, 583, 606-657

6 Problem Solving

- Build new mathematical knowledge through problem solving
- Solve problems that arise in mathematics and in other contexts
- Apply and adapt a variety of appropriate strategies to solve problems
- Monitor and reflect on the process of mathematical problem solving

Pages: 6-10, 28-32, 56-89, 98-107, 110-137, 148-185, 200-230, 232-236, 238-253, 270-280, 288-309, 330-338, 345-359, 369-385, 387-391, 393-401, 404-422, 436-440, 447-482, 492-497, 500-504, 513-517, 520-531, 533-543, 556-594, 606-621, 623-628, 635-639, 641-657, 697

7 Reasoning and Proof

- Recognize reasoning and proof as fundamental aspects of mathematics
- Make and investigate mathematical conjectures
- Develop and evaluate mathematical arguments and proofs
- Select and use various types of reasoning and methods of proof

Pages: 137, 148-152, 175-190, 205-209, 220-231, 249-253, 286-292, 368, 386, 392, 402-403, 458-464, 520-525, 533-538, 562, 583, 635-640, 650-657, 673, 697

8 Communication

- Organize and consolidate their mathematical thinking through communication
- Communicate their mathematical thinking coherently and clearly to peers, teachers, and others
- Analyze and evaluate the mathematical thinking and strategies of others
- Use the language of mathematics to express mathematical ideas precisely

Pages: 148-190, 249-253, 275, 288-297, 303, 309-314, 340-349, 404-408, 436-440, 453-481, 492-497, 500-504, 506-517, 520-531, 533-543, 556-561, 563-594, 630-633, 656-657, 682

9 Connections

- Recognize and use connections among mathematical ideas
- Understand how mathematical ideas build on one another to produce a coherent whole
- Recognize and apply mathematics in contexts outside of mathematics

Pages: 98-107, 110-137, 148-190, 249-253, 264-315, 355-359, 392-397, 402-403, 453-457, 471-482, 492-497, 500-504, 506-511, 513-517, 520-531, 533-543, 556-582, 584-594, 612-621, 641-657, 669-697

10 Representation

- Create and use representations to organize, record, and communicate mathematical ideas
- Select, apply, and translate among mathematical representations to solve problems
- Use representations to model and interpret physical, social, and mathematical phenomena

Pages: 56-61, 85-89, 108-109, 137, 148-190, 210-214, 232-236, 264-292, 298-315, 328-329, 368, 374-385, 387-423, 471-481, 520-532, 539-543, 554-561, 563-594, 606-611, 617-640, 669-697

Algebra and Integers

- Introduction **3**
- Follow-Ups **43, 79, 135**
- Culmination **136**

Lesson 1-2, page 15

Prerequisite Skills
- Getting Started **5**
- Getting Ready for the Next Lesson **10, 16, 21, 27, 32, 38**

 **Study Organizer 5**

Reading and Writing Mathematics
- Translating Expressions into Words **11**
- Reading Math Tips **17, 23, 24**
- Writing in Math **10, 16, 21, 27, 32, 37, 44**

Standardized Test Practice
- Multiple Choice **10, 16, 21, 27, 29, 30, 32, 38, 44, 51, 52**
- Short Response/Grid In **53**
- Extended Response **53**

 Snapshots 3, 8, 16

Chapter ❷ Integers 54

Prerequisite Skills

- Getting Started 55
- Getting Ready for the Next Lesson
  61, 68, 74, 79, 84

FOLDABLES™

Study Organizer 55

Reading and Writing Mathematics

- Learning Mathematics Vocabulary 69
- Reading Math Tips 56, 57, 64, 75, 80, 88
- Writing in Math 61, 68, 74, 79, 84, 89

Standardized Test Practice

- Multiple Choice 61, 68, 74, 76, 77, 79, 84, 89, 93, 94
- Short Response/Grid In 95
- Extended Response 95

USA TODAY Snapshots 60

Lesson 2-4, page 78

Chapter ③   Equations   96

Lesson 3-6, page 127

Prerequisite Skills
- Getting Started   97
- Getting Ready for the Next Lesson   102, 107, 114, 119,
                                     124, 130

FOLDABLES Study Organizer   97

Reading and Writing Mathematics
- Translating Verbal Problems into Equations   125
- Reading Math Tips   98, 103
- Writing in Math   101, 106, 114, 119, 123, 130, 136

Standardized Test Practice
- Multiple Choice   102, 107, 112, 113, 114, 119, 124,
                        130, 136, 141, 142
- Short Response/Grid In   124, 143
- Extended Response   143

 Snapshots   101

Chapter 4   Factors and Fractions   146

Lesson 4-8, page 189

Internet Project

- Introduction 145
- Follow-Ups 173, 242, 301
- Culmination 314

Prerequisite Skills

- Getting Started 147
- Getting Ready for the Next Lesson
  152, 157, 163, 168, 173, 179, 185

FOLDABLES

Study Organizer 147

Reading and Writing Mathematics

- Powers 174
- Reading Math Tips 148, 149, 150, 159, 177
- Writing in Math 152, 157, 162, 168, 173, 179, 184, 190

Standardized Test Practice

- Multiple Choice 152, 157, 163, 168, 171, 173, 179, 184, 190, 195, 196
- Short Response/Grid In 197
- Extended Response 197

 Snapshots 145, 156

Chapter ⑤ Rational Numbers

Algebra Activity, page 253

Prerequisite Skills

- Getting Started **199**
- Getting Ready for the Next Lesson **204, 209, 214, 219, 224, 230, 236, 242, 248**

 Study Organizer **199**

Reading and Writing Mathematics

- Factors and Multiples **225**
- Reading Math Tips **200, 205, 206, 215**
- Writing in Math **204, 209, 214, 219, 223, 230, 236, 242, 247, 251**

Standardized Test Practice

- Multiple Choice **204, 209, 214, 219, 224, 230, 236, 240, 241, 242, 247, 252, 259, 260**
- Short Response/Grid In **240, 261**
- Extended Response **261**

 Snapshots **203, 213**

Chapter ⑥ Ratio, Proportion, and Percent 262

Lesson 6-7, page 299

Prerequisite Skills
- Getting Started 263
- Getting Ready for the Next Lesson 268, 274, 280, 285, 292, 297, 302, 308

 **Study Organizer** 263

Reading and Writing Mathematics
- Making Comparisons 269
- Reading Math Tips 281, 300, 311
- Writing in Math 268, 274, 280, 285, 292, 297, 302, 307, 314

Standardized Test Practice
- Multiple Choice 268, 274, 280, 285, 292, 297, 302, 305, 306, 308, 314, 321, 322
- Short Response/Grid In 323
- Extended Response 323

 Snapshots 289, 290, 312, 314

Chapter 7 — Equations and Inequalities — 326

 **Internet Project**

Prerequisite Skills
- Getting Started 327
- Getting Ready for the Next Lesson 333, 338, 344, 349, 354

FOLDABLES™

Study Organizer 327

Reading and Writing Mathematics
- Meanings of *At Most* and *At Least* 339
- Reading Math Tips 341
- Writing in Math 333, 338, 344, 349, 354, 359

Standardized Test Practice
- Multiple Choice 333, 338, 344, 349, 351, 353, 354, 359, 363, 364
- Short Response/Grid In 354, 365
- Extended Response 365

 **Snapshots** 325, 343

Lesson 7-5, page 354

Chapter ⑧ Functions and Graphing 366

Prerequisite Skills

- Getting Started 367
- Getting Ready for the Next Lesson
  373, 379, 385, 391, 397, 401,
  408, 413, 418

FOLDABLES

Study Organizer 367

Reading and Writing Mathematics

- Language of Functions 380
- Reading Math Tips 370, 381, 383
- Writing in Math 373, 379, 385,
  391, 397, 401, 408, 412, 418, 422

Standardized Test Practice

- Multiple Choice 373, 379, 385,
  389, 390, 391, 397, 401, 408,
  413, 418, 422, 429, 430
- Short Response/Grid In 431
- Extended Response 431

Lesson 8-9, page 417

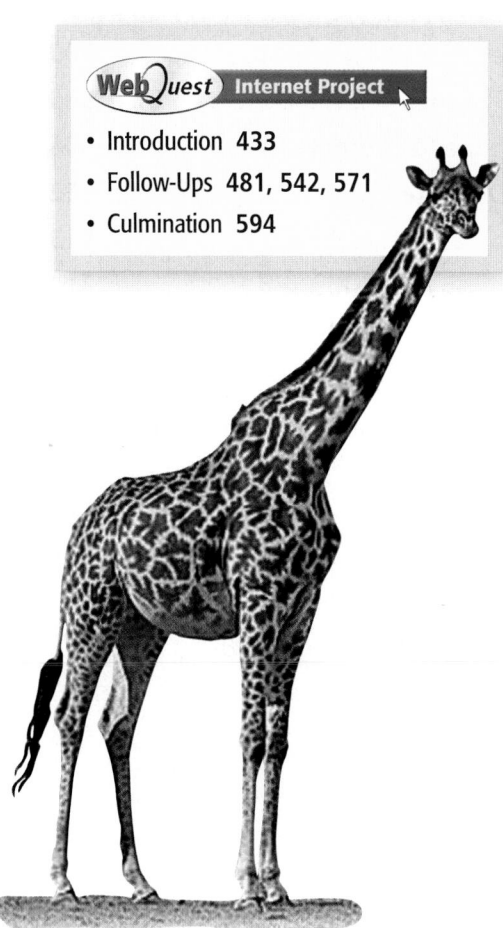

WebQuest Internet Project

Lesson 9-7, page 474

Prerequisite Skills

 **Study Organizer 435**

Reading and Writing Mathematics

Standardized Test Practice

 Snapshots **433, 450**

Chapter 10   Two-Dimensional Figures   490

Prerequisite Skills
- Getting Started 491
- Getting Ready for the Next Lesson
  497, 504, 511, 517, 525, 531, 538

FOLDABLES

Study Organizer 491

Reading and Writing Mathematics
- Learning Mathematics Prefixes 526
- Reading Math Tips 493, 500, 508
- Writing in Math 497, 504, 511, 517, 525, 531, 537, 543

Standardized Test Practice
- Multiple Choice 494, 495, 497, 504, 511, 517, 525, 531, 537, 543, 549, 550
- Short Response/Grid In 517, 531, 537, 551
- Extended Response 551

USA TODAY Snapshots 537

Lesson 10-5, page 524

Chapter ⑪ Three-Dimensional Figures 552

Lesson 11-2, page 564

Extending Algebra to Statistics and Polynomials

Lesson 12-9, page 651

Prerequisite Skills
- Getting Started **605**
- Getting Ready for the Next Lesson **611, 616, 621, 628, 633, 639, 645, 649**

Reading and Writing Mathematics
- Dealing with Bias **634**
- Reading Math Tips **624, 641, 642, 643, 647, 650**
- Writing in Math **610, 616, 621, 627, 633, 639, 645, 649, 654**

 **Study Organizer 605**

Standardized Test Practice
- Multiple Choice **611, 616, 621, 627, 633, 639, 645, 647, 648, 649, 655, 663, 664**
- Short Response/Grid In **665**
- Extended Response **665**

 Snapshots 603, 610, 649, 654

Chapter ⑬ Polynomials and Nonlinear Functions 666

FOLDABLES™

Study Organizer 667

Reading and Writing Mathematics

Standardized Test Practice

 Snapshots 690

Student Handbook

Skills

Reference

Lesson 13-2, page 675

Need extra help or information? Log on to math.glencoe.com or any of the Web addresses to learn more.

Online Study Tools

- www.pre-alg.com/extra_examples shows you additional worked-out examples that mimic the ones in your book.

- www.pre-alg.com/self_check_quiz provides you with a self-checking practice quiz for each lesson.

- www.pre-alg.com/vocabulary_review lets you check your understanding of the terms and definitions used in each chapter.

- www.pre-alg.com/chapter_test allows you to take a self-checking test before the actual test.

- www.pre-alg.com/standardized_test is another way to brush up on your standardized test-taking skills.

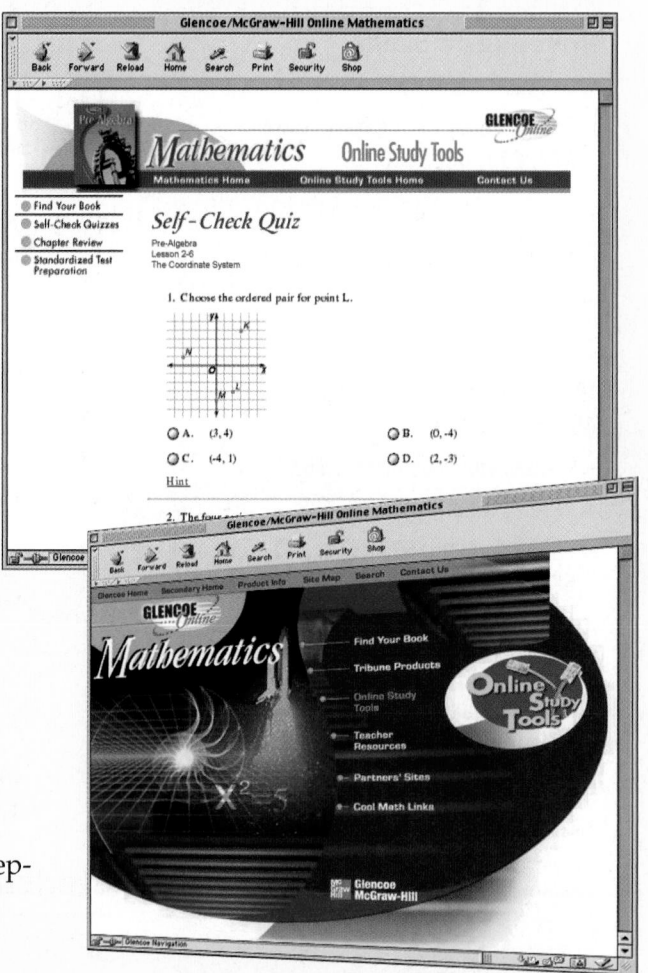

Research Options

- www.pre-alg.com/webquest walks you step-by-step through a long-term project using the Web. One WebQuest for each unit is explored using the mathematics from that unit.

- www.pre-alg.com/usa_today provides activities related to the concept of the lesson as well as up-to-date Snapshot data.

- www.pre-alg.com/careers links you to additional information about interesting careers.

- www.pre-alg.com/data_update links you to the most current data available for subjects such as basketball and family.

Calculator Help

- www.pre-alg.com/other_calculator_keystrokes provides you with keystrokes other than the TI-83 Plus used in your textbook.

Get Started

To help you learn how to use your math book, use the Scavenger Hunt at www.pre-alg.com.

FOLDABLES™

A Handy Way to Help You Study

As easy as 1-2-3! Just fold and you are ready to go! Each chapter provides you with a different Foldable that's easy to create. It's a fun way to organize what you learn and a great study tool.

FOLDABLES™ Study Organizer

Properties Make this Foldable to help you organize your notes. Add definitions and examples to it as you learn new properties throughout the year. Begin with eight half-sheets of plain paper.

Step 1 Fold and Cut

Fold a half sheet of paper in half. Cut a 1" tab along the left edge through one thickness.

Step 2 Glue and Label

Glue the 1" tab down. Write the name of the property on the front tab.

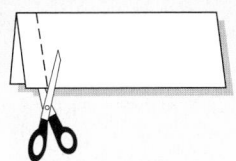

Distributive Property

Step 3 Label

Write the property in words and symbols under the tab.

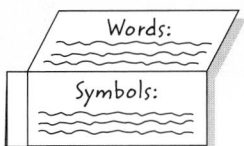

Words:

Symbols:

Step 4 Repeat and Staple

Repeat Steps 1-3 for the remaining sheets of paper. Staple together to form a booklet.

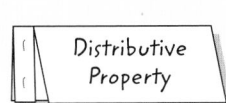

Distributive Property

Foldables can be found on the following pages: 5, 55, 97, 147, 199, 263, 327, 367, 435, 491, 553, 605, and 667.

1

Introduction

In this unit, students will learn about the basic tools of algebra, including variables, integers, and equations. They will use a four-step plan to solve problems, translate verbal phrases and expressions into algebraic expressions, and use mathematical properties and the order of operations. They will compare and order integers and perform operations with integers. Students will evaluate and simplify algebraic expressions and write and solve two-step equations.

Students will use a coordinate plane to locate and graph ordered pairs and represent algebraic relationships.

Assessment Options

Unit 1 Test Pages 163–164 of the *Chapter 3 Resource Masters* may be used as a test or review for Unit 1. This assessment contains both multiple-choice and short answer items.

 **ExamView® Pro**
This CD-ROM can be used to create additional unit tests and review worksheets.

Yearly Progress Pro

An online, research-based instructional, assessment, and intervention tool that provides specific feedback on student mastery of state and national standards, instant remediation, and a data management system to track performance. For more information, contact

mhdigitallearning.com.

Algebra and Integers

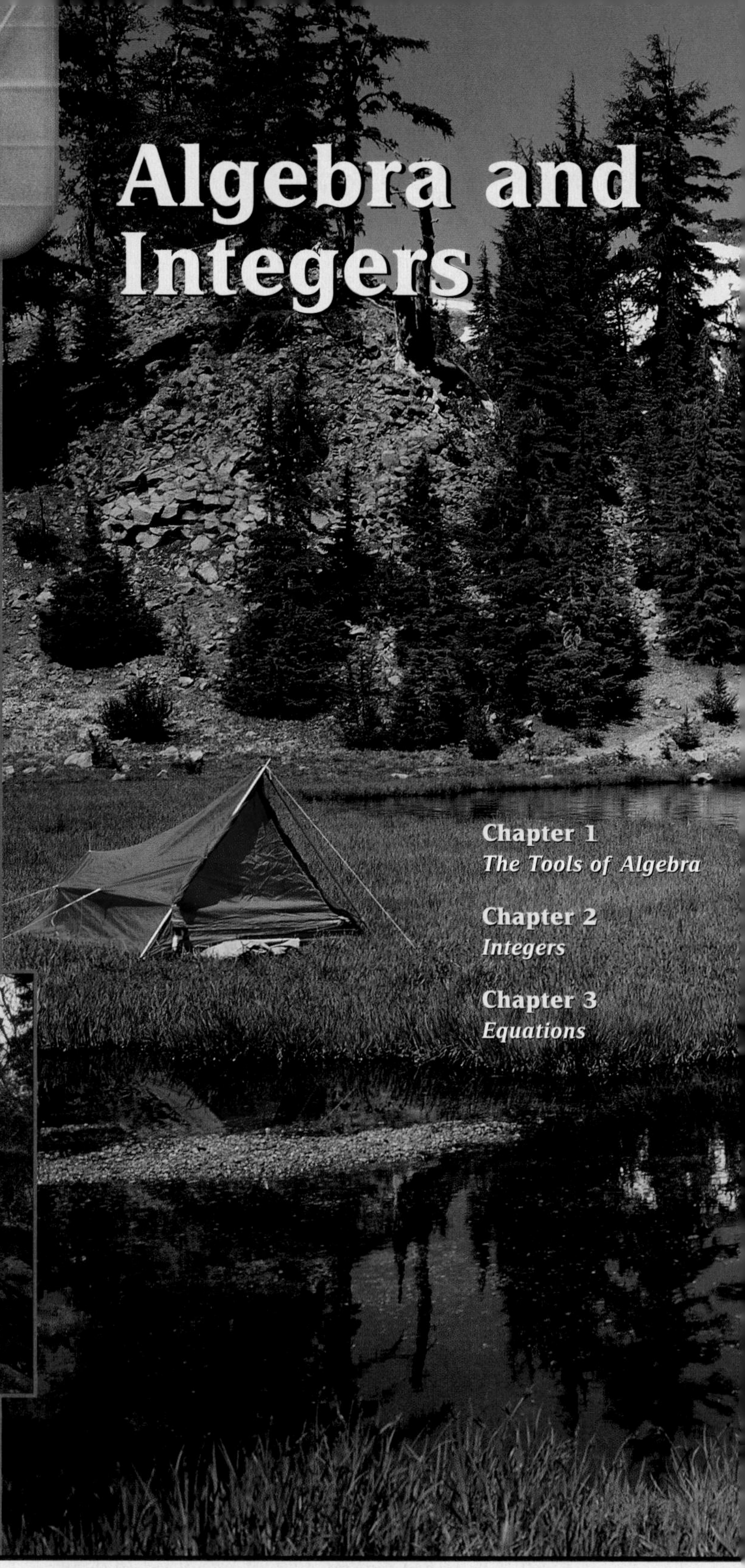

The word *algebra* comes from the Arabic word *al-jebr*, which was part of the title of a book about equations and how to solve them. In this unit, you will lay the foundation for your study of algebra by learning about the language of algebra, its properties, and methods of solving equations.

Chapter 1
The Tools of Algebra

Chapter 2
Integers

Chapter 3
Equations

Real-Life Math Videos

What's Math Got to Do With It? Real-Life Math Videos engage students showing them how math is used in everyday situations. Use Video 1 with this unit.

WebQuest Internet Project

Vacation Travelers Include More Families

"Taking the kids with you is increasingly popular among Americans, according to a travel report that predicts an expanding era of kid-friendly attractions and services." **Source:** *USA TODAY*, November 17, 1999

In this project, you will be exploring how graphs and formulas can help you plan a family vacation.

Log on to www.pre-alg.com/webquest. Begin your WebQuest by reading the Task.

Then continue working on your WebQuest as you study Unit 1.

Lesson	1-7	2-4	3-7
Page	43	79	135

USA TODAY Snapshots®

Spouses are top travel partners

Spouses	58%
Children/grandchildren	34%
Friends	18%
Other family members	14%
Solo	13%
Group tour	8%

Source: Travel Industry Association of America

By Cindy Hall and Sam Ward, USA TODAY

Unit 1 Algebra and Integers **3**

Teaching Suggestions

Have students study the USA TODAY Snapshot®.

• Ask them how the bars on the graphic represent visually the percents written next to them. **The larger the percent is, the longer the bar is.**

• What is the least popular form of travel among Americans? **group travel**

• Point out to students that in their WebQuest they will be using algebraic tools to figure the best vacation destination at the best cost.

Additional USA TODAY Snapshots® appearing in Unit 1:

Chapter 1 Baseball stadium seating (p. 8)

Going places in 2020 (p. 16)

Chapter 2 Lowest temperatures in the USA (p. 60)

Chapter 3 Comparison shoppers (p. 101)

WebQuest Internet Project

Problem-Based Learning A WebQuest is an online project in which students do research on the Internet, gather data, and make presentations using word processing, graphing, page-making, or presentation software. In each chapter, students advance to the next step in their WebQuest. At the end of Chapter 3, the project culminates with a presentation of their findings.

Teaching suggestions and sample answers are available in the *WebQuest and Project Resources.*

The Tools of Algebra
Chapter Overview and Pacing

Year-long pacing: pages T20–T21.

LESSON OBJECTIVES	PACING (days)			
	Regular		Block	
	Basic/ Average	Advanced	Basic/ Average	Advanced
1-1 Using a Problem-Solving Plan *(pp. 6–10)* • Use a four-step plan to solve problems. • Choose an appropriate method of computation.	1	1	0.5	0.5
1-2 Numbers and Expressions *(pp. 12–16)* • Use the order of operations to evaluate expressions. • Translate verbal phrases into numerical expressions.	1	1	0.5	0.5
1-3 Variables and Expressions *(pp. 17–22)* • Evaluate expressions containing variables. • Translate verbal phrases into algebraic expressions. *Follow-Up:* Use a spreadsheet to explore algebraic expressions.	1	2 (with 1-3 Follow-Up)	0.5	1 (with 1-3 Follow-Up)
1-4 Properties *(pp. 23–27)* • Identify and use properties of addition and multiplication. • Use properties of addition and multiplication to simplify algebraic expressions.	1	1	0.5	0.5
1-5 Variables and Equations *(pp. 28–32)* • Identify and solve open sentences. • Translate verbal sentences into equations.	2	1	1	0.5
1-6 Ordered Pairs and Relations *(pp. 33–38)* • Use ordered pairs to locate points. • Use tables and graphs to represent relations.	1	1	0.5	0.5
1-7 Scatter Plots *(pp. 39–46)* *Preview:* Use a scatter plot to investigate the relationship between two sets of data, height and arm span. • Construct scatter plots. • Interpret scatter plots. *Follow-Up:* Describe how a graphing calculator can help create a scatter plot.	2 (with 1-7 Preview)	2 (with 1-7 Follow-Up)	1 (with 1-7 Preview)	1 (with 1-7 Follow-Up)
Study Guide and **Practice Test** *(pp. 47–51)* **Standardized Test Practice** *(pp. 52–53)*	1	1	0.5	0.5
Chapter Assessment	1	1	0.5	0.5
TOTAL	**11**	**11**	**5.5**	**5.5**

*An electronic version of this chapter is available on **StudentWorks™**. This backpack solution CD-ROM allows students instant access to the Student Edition, lesson worksheet pages, and web resources.*

Chapter Resource Manager

CHAPTER 1 RESOURCE MASTERS

Study Guide and Intervention	Practice (Skills and Average)	Reading to Learn Mathematics	Enrichment	Assessment	Prerequisite Skills Workbook	Applications*	Parent and Student Study Guide Workbook	5-Minute Check Transparencies	Interactive Chalkboard	Pre-AlgePASS: Tutorial Plus (lessons)	Materials
1	2–3	4	5		1–8		1	1-1	1-1		
6	7–8	9	10	51	5–12		2	1-2	1-2	1	
11	12–13	14	15		5–12	GCS 19 SC 1	3	1-3	1-3	2	*Follow-Up:* spreadsheet software
16	17–18	19	20	51, 53	5–10		4	1-4	1-4		
21	22–23	24	25		5–10	SC 2 SM 1	5	1-5	1-5		
26	27–28	29	30	52			6	1-6	1-6		
31	32–33	34	35	52		GCS 20	7	1-7	1-7		*Preview:* graph paper, centimeter ruler *Follow-Up:* graphing calculator
				37–50 54–56							

* *Key to Abbreviations:* GCS = Graphing Calculator and Spreadsheet Masters
SC = School-to-Career Masters
SM = Science and Mathematics Lab Manual

ELL Study Guide and Intervention, Skills Practice, Practice, and Parent and Student Study Guide Workbooks are also available in Spanish.

Mathematical Connections and Background

Continuity of Instruction

Prior Knowledge

Prior to studying Pre-Algebra, students should have a basic knowledge of properties of operations, such as the Distributive Property. Students should be familiar with expressing variables as symbols and mathematical relationships using equations. They also should be able to represent and analyze patterns using words, tables, and graphs.

This Chapter

This chapter reinforces and extends the skills learned prior to beginning the Pre-Algebra course and lays the foundation for the studies of algebra, geometry, and statistics in the rest of the book. Students will learn to solve problems, to evaluate expressions, and to use variables and expressions when solving real-world problems.

Future Connections

The tools of algebra learned in this chapter will be used throughout students' math studies in both high school and college. The graphing techniques they learn are also used in geometry, statistics, and other disciplines such as science and social studies.

1-1 Using a Problem-Solving Plan

One method of problem solving is a four-step plan:

1. *Explore* the problem to see what information exists and what needs to be found out.
2. *Plan* the strategy to be used to solve the problem and estimate the answer.
3. *Solve* the problem using the plan.
4. *Examine* the answer to see whether it is reasonable and close to the estimate. If not, use another strategy to solve the problem.

Another problem-solving method, called inductive reasoning, uses a conjecture based on a pattern of examples or past events. When solving a problem, it is important to choose an appropriate method of computation. Depending on the problem, you will want to estimate, use a calculator, or use paper and pencil.

1-2 Numbers and Expressions

When evaluating an expression, find its numerical value using the accepted order of operations:

Step 1 Simplify the expressions inside grouping symbols.
Step 2 Do all multiplications and/or divisions from left to right.
Step 3 Do all additions and/or subtractions from left to right.

An important aspect of translating verbal expressions to numerical ones is the awareness of vocabulary that has mathematical meanings. Develop a list of words and their mathematical translations.

1-3 Variables and Expressions

Algebra is a language of symbols. A variable is a placeholder for any value. Any letter, such as x, can be used as a variable. An expression such as $x + 2$ is an algebraic expression because it contains sums and/or products of variables and numbers. Usually, mathematicians avoid the use of i and e for variables because they have other mathematical meanings ($i = \sqrt{-1}$, e is used with natural logarithms).

To evaluate an algebraic expression, replace the variable or variables with known values—demonstrating the Substitution Property of Equality—and then use the order of operations. Translate verbal phrases into algebraic expressions by first defining a variable: choose a variable and a quantity for the variable to represent. Algebraic expressions can be used to represent real-world situations.

1-4 Properties

In algebra, properties are statements that are true for any numbers. For example, the expression $3 + 8 = 8 + 3$ because each expression equals 11. This illustrates the Commutative Property of Addition. Likewise, $3 \cdot 8 = 8 \cdot 3$ illustrates the Commutative Property of Multiplication.

When evaluating expressions, it is often helpful to group or *associate* the numbers. The Associative Property says that the way in which numbers are grouped when added or multiplied does not change the sum or product.

The following properties are also true:

Additive Identity Property: When 0 is added to any number, the sum is the number.

Multiplicative Identity Property: When any number is multiplied by 1, the product is the number.

Multiplicative Property of Zero: When any number is multiplied by 0, the product is 0.

You can use the properties of numbers to find sums and products mentally. Look for sums or products that end in zero. You also can use the Associative or Commutative Properties to simplify expressions.

1-5 Variables and Equations

A mathematical sentence that contains an equals sign (=) is called an equation. An equation that contains a variable is an open sentence. An open sentence is neither true nor false. When the variable in an open sentence is replaced with a number, you can determine whether the sentence is true or false. A value for the variable that makes an equation true is called a solution. For $x + 7 = 19$, the solution is 12. The process of finding a solution is called solving the equation.

Two properties of equality are the Symmetric Property and the Transitive Property.

Symmetric: If one quantity equals a second quantity, then the second quantity also equals the first. That is, if $a = b$, then $b = a$.

Transitive: If one quantity equals a second quantity and the second quantity equals a third quantity, then the first equals the third. This means if $a = b$ and $b = c$, then $a = c$.

1-6 Ordered Pairs and Relations

The Cartesian coordinate system is used to locate points. The coordinate system is formed by two perpen-dicular number lines that intersect at their zero points. An ordered pair of numbers is used to locate any point on a coordinate plane. The first number is called the x-coordinate or abscissa, and tells how far left or right of the origin the point is located. The second number is called the y-coordinate or ordinate, and tells how far up or down from the origin the point is located.

A set of ordered pairs such as $\{(1, 2), (2, 4), (3, 0), (4, 5)\}$ is a relation. The domain of the relation is the set of x-coordinates. The range of the relation is the set of y-coordinates. A relation can be shown as a set of ordered pairs, as a table, or as a graph.

1-7 Scatter Plots

A scatter plot is a graph that shows the relation-ship between two sets of data. In a scatter plot, two sets of data are graphed as ordered pairs on a coordinate system. Two sets of data can have a positive relation-ship (as x increases, y increases), a negative relationship (as x increases, y decreases), or no relationship (no obvious pattern is shown). Scatter plots can be used to spot trends, draw conclusions, and make predictions.

Quick Review Math Handbook

Hot Words includes a glossary of terms while Hot Topics consists of explanations of key mathematical concepts with exercises to test comprehension. This valuable resource can be used as a reference in the classroom or for home study.

Lesson	Hot Topics Section	Lesson	Hot Topics Section
GS 1	1.5	1-5	1.2, 6.1, 6.2, 6.3, 6.4, 6.7
1-1	1.1	1-6	1.5, 6.7
1-2	1.3, 1.5, 3.4	1-7P	4.3
1-3P	6.1, 6.2, 6.3	1-7	4.3
1-3	1.5, 6.1, 6.2, 6.3	1-7F	4.3
1-4	1.2, 1.5		

GS = Getting started, P = Preview, F = Follow-Up

 Additional mathematical information and teaching notes are available at www.pre-alg.com/key_concepts.

DAILY INTERVENTION and Assessment

Key to Abbreviations:
TWE = Teacher Wraparound Edition; CRM = Chapter Resource Masters

Type	Student Edition	Teacher Resources	Technology/Internet
INTERVENTION Ongoing	Prerequisite Skills, pp. 5, 10, 16, 21, 27, 32, 38 Practice Quiz 1, p. 21 Practice Quiz 2, p. 32	5-Minute Check Transparencies *Prerequisite Skills Workbook*, pp. 1–8, 5–12 Quizzes, *CRM*, pp. 51–52 Mid-Chapter Test, *CRM*, p. 53 Study Guide and Intervention, *CRM*, pp. 1, 6, 11, 16, 21, 26, 31	Pre-AlgePASS: Tutorial Plus, Lessons 1 and 2 www.pre-alg.com/self_check_quiz www.pre-alg.com/extra_examples
Mixed Review	pp. 16, 21, 27, 32, 38, 44	Cumulative Review, *CRM*, p. 54	
Error Analysis	Find the Error, pp. 14, 26	Find the Error, *TWE*, pp. 14, 26	
Standardized Test Practice	pp. 10, 16, 21, 27, 29, 30, 32, 38, 44, 52–53	*TWE*, pp. 52–53 Standardized Test Practice, *CRM*, pp. 55–56	Standardized Test Practice CD-ROM www.pre-alg.com/standardized_test
ASSESSMENT Open-Ended Assessment	Writing in Math, pp. 10, 16, 21, 27, 32, 37, 44 Open Ended, pp. 9, 14, 19, 26, 30, 36, 42 Standardized Test, p. 53	Speaking: *TWE*, pp. 10, 16, 27, 38 Writing: *TWE*, pp. 21, 32, 44 Open-Ended Assessment, *CRM*, p. 49	
Chapter Assessment	Study Guide, pp. 47–50 Practice Test, p. 51	Multiple-Choice Tests (Forms 1, 2A, 2B), *CRM*, pp. 37–42 Free-Response Tests (Forms 2C, 2D, 3), *CRM*, pp. 43–48 Vocabulary Test/Review, *CRM*, p. 50	ExamView®Pro (see below) MindJogger Videoquizzes www.pre-alg.com/vocabulary_review www.pre-alg.com/chapter_test

Yearly ProgressPro

For more information on Yearly ProgressPro, see p. 2.

Pre-Algebra Lesson	Yearly ProgressPro Skill Lesson(s)
1-1	Plan for Problem Solving
1-2	Evaluate Algebraic Expressions
1-3	Evaluate Algebraic Expressions
1-4	Commutative/Associative Properties of Addition Properties of Multiplication
1-5	Writing Expressions and Equations
1-6	Coordinate Locations: Level 3
1-7	Scatter Plots

ExamView® Pro

Use the networkable **ExamView® Pro** to:
- Create **multiple versions** of tests.
- Create **modified** tests for *Inclusion* students.
- **Edit** existing questions and **add** your own questions
- Use built-in **state curriculum correlations** to create tests aligned with state standards.
- Change **English** tests to **Spanish** and vice versa.

For more information on Intervention and Assessment, see pp. T8–T11.

Reading and Writing in Mathematics

Glencoe Pre-Algebra provides numerous opportunities to incorporate reading and writing into the mathematics classroom.

Student Edition

- Foldables™ Study Organizer, p. 5
- Reading Mathematics, p. 11
- Concept Check questions require students to verbalize and write about what they have learned in the lesson. (pp. 6, 7, 9, 12, 14, 17, 19, 23, 24, 26, 30, 34, 36, 40, 41, 42)
- Writing in Math questions in every lesson, pp. 10, 16, 21, 27, 32, 37, 44
- Reading Math, pp. 17, 23, 24, 29
- WebQuest, p. 43

Teacher Wraparound Edition

- Foldables™ Study Organizer, pp. 5, 47
- Study Notebook suggestions, pp. 8, 11, 14, 19, 26, 30, 36, 42
- Speaking activities, pp. 10, 16, 27, 38
- Writing activities, pp. 21, 32, 44
- **ELL** Resources, pp. 4, 6, 11, 12, 17, 23, 28, 33, 40, 47

Additional Resources

- Vocabulary Builder worksheets require students to define and give examples for key vocabulary terms as they progress through the chapter (*Chapter 1 Resource Masters*, pp. vii–viii)
- Reading to Learn Mathematics master for each lesson (*Chapter 1 Resource Masters*, pp. 4, 9, 14, 19, 24, 29, 34)
- *Vocabulary PuzzleMaker* software creates crossword, jumble, and word search puzzles using vocabulary lists that you can customize.
- *Teaching Mathematics with Foldables* provides suggestions for promoting cognition and language.
- *Reading and Writing in the Mathematics Classroom*
- *WebQuest and Project Resources*

For more information on Reading and Writing in Mathematics, see pp. T6–T7.

PROJECT CRISS℠ Study Skill

Capsule vocabulary is a teaching strategy that helps students verbally review important terms. After students have studied Lesson 1-5, write the properties listed at the right on the chalkboard. Discuss the properties with the class. Divide the class into pairs. Have students talk about the properties with their partners. Each student should make sure his or her partner can explain or give an example of all of the properties. Afterward, have students write a short summary about the properties.

Properties
- Commutative Property of Addition
- Commutative Property of Multiplication
- Associative Property of Addition
- Associative Property of Multiplication
- Additive Identity Property
- Multiplicative Identity Property
- Multiplicative Property of Zero
- Symmetric Property of Equality
- Transitive Property of Equality

CReating **I**ndependence **T**hrough **S**tudent-**O**wned **S**trategies

What You'll Learn

Have students read over the list of objectives and make a list of any words with which they are not familiar.

Why It's Important

Point out to students that this is only one of many reasons why each objective is important. Others are provided in the introduction to each lesson.

The chart below correlates the objectives for each lesson to the NCTM Standards 2000. There is also space for you to reference your state and/or local objectives.

Lesson	NCTM Standards	Local Objectives
1-1	1, 6	
1-2	1	
1-3	1, 2	
1-3 Follow-Up	1, 2	
1-4	1, 4	
1-5	1, 6	
1-6	1	
1-7 Preview	1, 2, 5	
1-7	1, 2, 5	
1-7 Follow-Up	1, 2, 5	

Key to NCTM Standards:

1=Number & Operations, 2=Algebra, 3=Geometry, 4=Measurement, 5=Data Analysis & Probability, 6=Problem Solving, 7=Reasoning & Proof, 8=Communication, 9=Connections, 10=Representation

What You'll Learn

- **Lesson 1-1** Use a four-step plan to solve problems and choose the appropriate method of computation.
- **Lessons 1-2 and 1-3** Translate verbal phrases into numerical expressions and evaluate expressions.
- **Lesson 1-4** Identify and use properties of addition and multiplication.
- **Lesson 1-5** Write and solve simple equations.
- **Lesson 1-6** Locate points and represent relations.
- **Lesson 1-7** Construct and interpret scatter plots.

Key Vocabulary

- order of operations (p. 12)
- variable (p. 17)
- algebraic expression (p. 17)
- ordered pair (p. 33)
- relation (p. 35)

Why It's Important

Algebra is important because it can be used to show relationships among variables and numbers. You can use algebra to describe how fast something grows. For example, the growth rate of bamboo can be described using variables. *You will find the growth rate of bamboo in Lesson 1-6.*

Vocabulary Builder   ELL

The Key Vocabulary list introduces students to some of the main vocabulary terms included in this chapter. For a more thorough vocabulary list with pronunciations of new words, give students the Vocabulary Builder worksheets found on pages vii and viii of the *Chapter 1 Resource Masters*. Encourage them to complete the definition of each term as they progress through the chapter. You may suggest that they add these sheets to their study notebooks for future reference when studying for the Chapter 1 test.

Getting Started

▶ **Prerequisite Skills** To be successful in this chapter, you'll need to master these skills and be able to apply them in problem-solving situations. Review these skills before beginning Chapter 1.

For Lesson 1-1   **Add and Subtract Decimals**

Find each sum or difference. *(For review, see page 713.)*

1. $6.6 + 8.2$ **14.8**   **2.** $4.7 + 8.5$ **13.2**   **3.** $5.4 - 2.3$ **3.1**

4. $8.6 - 4.9$ **3.7**   **5.** $2.65 + 0.3$ **2.95**   **6.** $1.08 + 1.2$ **2.28**

7. $4.25 - 0.7$ **3.55**   **8.** $4.3 - 2.89$ **1.41**   **9.** $9.06 - 1.18$ **7.88**

For Lessons 1-1 through 1-5   **Estimate with Whole Numbers**

Estimate each sum, difference, product, or quotient.

10. $1800 + 285$ **2300**   **11.** $328 + 879$ **1200**   **12.** $22,431 - 13,183$ **10,000**

13. $659 - 536$ **120**   **14.** 68×12 **700**   **15.** 189×89 **20,000**

16. $3845 \div 82$ **50**   **17.** $21,789 \div 97$ **220**   **18.** $\$1951 \div 49$ **\$40**

10–18. Sample answers are given.

For Lessons 1-1 through 1-5   **Estimate with Decimals**

Estimate each sum, difference, product, or quotient. *(For review, see pages 712 and 714.)*

19. $8.8 + 5.3$ **14**   **20.** $47.2 + 9.75$ **57**   **21.** $\$7.34 - \$2.16$ **\$5**

22. $83.6 - 75.32$ **9**   **23.** 4.2×29.3 **120**   **24.** $18.8(5.3)$ **100**

25. $7.8 \div 2.3$ **4**   **26.** $54 \div 9.1$ **6**   **27.** $21.3 \div 1.7$ **10**

19–27. Sample answers are given.

FOLDABLES™
Study Organizer

Problem Solving Make this Foldable to help you organize your notes. Begin with a sheet of unlined paper.

Step 1 **Fold**

Fold the short sides so they meet in the middle.

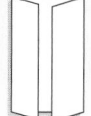

Step 2 **Fold Again**

Fold the top to the bottom.

Step 3 **Cut**

Unfold. Cut along the second fold to make four tabs.

Step 4 **Label**

Label each of the tabs as shown.

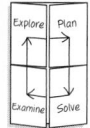

Reading and Writing As you read and study the chapter, you can write examples of each problem-solving step under the tabs.

This section provides a review of the basic concepts needed before beginning Chapter 1. Page references are included for additional student help.

Additional review is provided in the *Prerequisite Skills Workbook,* pages 1–12.

Prerequisite Skills in the Getting Ready for the Next Lesson section at the end of each lesson reviews a skill needed in the next lesson.

For Lesson	Prerequisite Skill
1-2	Round to Nearest Whole Number (p. 10)
1-3	Finding Sums (p. 16)
1-4	Finding Differences (p. 21)
1-5	Finding Products (p. 27)
1-6	Evaluating Expressions (p. 32)
1-7	Finding Quotients (p. 38)

Each chapter opens with Prerequisite Skills practice for lessons in the chapter. More Prerequisite Skill practice can be found at the end of each lesson.

Foldables™ are a unique way to enhance students' study skills. Encourage students to add to their Foldable as they work through the chapter, and use it to review for their chapter test.

FOLDABLES™
Study Organizer

For more information about Foldables, see *Teaching Mathematics with Foldables.*

Sequencing of Steps Under each tab of the Foldable, have students describe that step in detail and include examples of questions they might ask themselves during problem solving. Students can demonstrate their understanding and use of this problem-solving process by writing a problem under the explore tab, and using their Foldable to record how they plan, solve, and examine to reach a solution.

1 Focus

Mathematical Background notes are available for this lesson on page 4C.

Why is it helpful to use a problem-solving plan to solve problems?

The opening activity questions are repeated on page 4 of the *Chapter 1 Resource Masters.*

Reading to Learn Mathematics, p. 4 ELL

Pre-Activity *Why is it helpful to use a problem-solving plan to solve problems?*

Do the activity at the top of page 6 in your textbook. Write your answers below.

a. Find a pattern in the costs. The cost increases by $0.21 for each additional ounce.

b. How can you determine the cost to mail a 6-ounce letter? Add $0.21 to 1.18.

c. Suppose you were asked to find the cost of mailing a letter that weighs 8 ounces. What steps would you take to solve the problem? Sample answer: extend the pattern.

Reading the Lesson 1–2. See students' work.

Write a definition and give an example of each new vocabulary word or phrase.

Vocabulary	Definition	Example
1. conjecture		
2. inductive reasoning		

3. What is the next term: 3, 6, 12, 24 . . .? Explain. 48. Each number is two times the one before it, and 2 x 24 = 48.

4. Complete this sentence. In the ___examine___ step of the four-step problem-solving plan, you check the reasonableness of your answer.

Helping You Remember

5. Explain why each step of the four-step plan is important. Students' answers will vary. Accept all reasonable answers.

Teaching Tip Encourage students to verbalize and write answers to the questions giving as many different explanations as possible.

What You'll Learn

• Use a four-step plan to solve problems.

• Choose an appropriate method of computation.

Vocabulary
• conjecture
• inductive reasoning

Why is it helpful to use a problem-solving plan to solve problems?

The table shows the first-class mail rates in 2004.

Weight (oz)	Cost
1	$0.37
2	$0.60
3	$0.83
4	$1.06
5	$1.29

Source: www.ups.com

a. The cost increases by $0.23 for each additional ounce.
b. Add $0.23 to $1.29.
c. Sample answer: extend the pattern.

a. Find a pattern in the costs.

b. How can you determine the cost to mail a 6-ounce letter?

c. Suppose you were asked to find the cost of mailing a letter that weighs 8 ounces. What steps would you take to solve the problem?

FOUR-STEP PROBLEM-SOLVING PLAN It is often helpful to have an organized plan to solve math problems. The following four steps can be used to solve any math problem.

1. **Explore**
   • Read the problem quickly to gain a general understanding of it.
   • Ask, "What facts do I know?" "What do I need to find out?"
   • Ask, "Is there enough information to solve the problem? Is there extra information?"

2. **Plan**
   • Reread the problem to identify relevant facts.
   • Determine how the facts relate to each other.
   • Make a plan to solve the problem.
   • Estimate the answer.

3. **Solve**
   • Use your plan to solve the problem.
   • If your plan does not work, revise it or make a new plan.

4. **Examine**
   • Reread the problem.
   • Ask, "Is my answer reasonable and close to my estimate?"
   • Ask, "Does my answer make sense?"
   • If not, solve the problem another way.

Study Tip

Problem-Solving Strategies

Here are a few strategies you will use to solve problems in this book.
• Look for a pattern.
• Solve a simpler problem.
• Guess and check.
• Draw a diagram.
• Make a table or chart.
• Work backward.
• Make a list.

☑ **Concept Check** Which step involves estimating the answer? Plan

---

Resource Manager

📂 **Workbooks and Reproducible Masters**

Chapter 1 Resource Masters
• Study Guide and Intervention, p. 1
• Skills Practice, p. 2
• Practice, p. 3
• Reading to Learn Mathematics, p. 4
• Enrichment, p. 5

Parent and Student Study Guide Workbook, p. 1
Prerequisite Skills Workbook, pp. 1–8

 Transparencies
5-Minute Check Transparency 1-1
Answer Key Transparencies

💿 **Technology**
Interactive Chalkboard

Example 1 — Use the Four-Step Problem-Solving Plan

POSTAL SERVICE Refer to page 6. How much would it cost to mail a 9-ounce letter first class?

Explore The table shows the weight of a letter and the respective cost to mail it first class. We need to find how much it will cost to mail a 9-ounce letter.

Plan Use the information in the table to solve the problem. Look for a pattern in the costs. Extend the pattern to find the cost for a 9-ounce letter.

Solve First, find the pattern.

Weight (oz)	1	2	3	4	5
Cost	$0.37	$0.60	$0.83	$1.06	$1.29

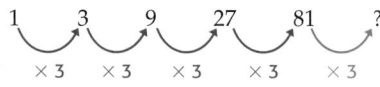

Each consecutive cost increases by $0.23. Next, extend the pattern.

Weight (oz)	5	6	7	8	9
Cost	$1.29	$1.52	$1.75	$1.98	$2.21

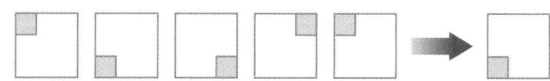

It would cost $2.21 to mail a 9-ounce letter.

Examine It costs $0.37 for the first ounce and $0.23 for each additional ounce. To mail a 9-ounce letter, it would cost $0.37 for the first ounce and $8 \times \$0.23$ or $1.84 for the eight additional ounces. Since $0.37 + $1.84 = $2.21, the answer is correct.

A **conjecture** is an educated guess. When you make a conjecture based on a pattern of examples or past events, you are using **inductive reasoning**. In mathematics, you will use inductive reasoning to solve problems.

Example 2 — Use Inductive Reasoning

a. Find the next term in 1, 3, 9, 27, 81, ….

$$1 \xrightarrow{\times 3} 3 \xrightarrow{\times 3} 9 \xrightarrow{\times 3} 27 \xrightarrow{\times 3} 81 \xrightarrow{\times 3} ?$$

Assuming the pattern continues, the next term is 81×3 or 243.

b. Draw the next figure in the pattern.

In the pattern, the shaded square moves counterclockwise. Assuming the pattern continues, the shaded square will be positioned at the bottom left of the figure.

✓ Concept Check What type of reasoning is used when you make a conclusion based on a pattern? **inductive**

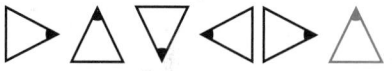

Study Notebook

Have students—
- add the definitions/examples of the vocabulary terms to their Vocabulary Builder worksheets for Chapter 1.
- copy the four-step problem-solving plan and write a brief explanation of each step.
- include any other item(s) that they find helpful in mastering the skills in this lesson.

Study Notebook tips offer suggestions for helping your students keep notes they can use to study this chapter.

About the Exercises . . .

Organization by Objective
- **Four Step Problem-Solving Plan:** 9–26
- **Choose the Method of Computation:** 21–26

Odd/Even Assignments
Exercises 9–20 are structured so that students practice the same concepts whether they are assigned odd or even problems.

Assignment Guide

Basic: 9, 10, 11–15 odd, 19–25 odd, 27–36

Average: 9, 10, 11–25 odd, 27–36

Advanced: 12–26 even, 27–30 (Optional: 31–36)

CHOOSE THE METHOD OF COMPUTATION Choosing the method of computation is also an important step in solving problems. Use the diagram below to help you decide which method is most appropriate.

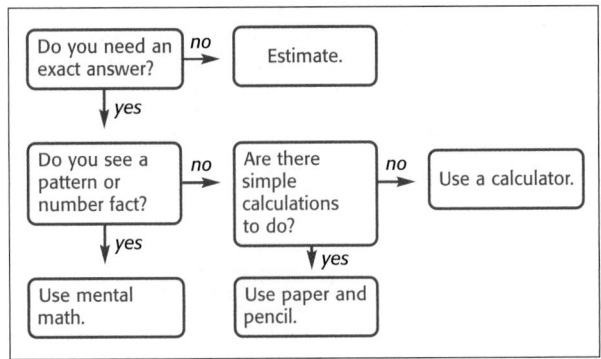

Log on for:
- Updated data
- More activities on Using a Problem-Solving Plan
www.pre-alg.com/usa_today

Glencoe's exclusive partnership with USA TODAY® provides actual USA TODAY Snapshots® that illustrate mathematical concepts.

Example 3 *Choose the Method of Computation*

TRAVEL The graph shows the seating capacity of certain baseball stadiums in the United States. About how many more seats does Comerica Park have than Fenway Park?

USA TODAY Snapshots®

Fenway has baseball's fewest seats
Boston's Fenway Park, opened in 1912, is Major League Baseball's oldest and smallest stadium, with a capacity of 33,871. Baseball's smallest stadiums in terms of capacity:

Fenway Park (Boston) 33,871
Wrigley Field (Chicago) 38,902
Comerica Park (Detroit) 40,000
Kauffman Stadium (Kansas City) 40,625
Pacific Bell Park (San Francisco) 40,800

Source: Major League Baseball
By Ellen J. Horrow and Bob Laird, USA TODAY

Explore You know the seating capacities of Comerica Park and Fenway Park. You need to find how many more seats Comerica Park has than Fenway Park.

Plan The question uses the word *about*, so an exact answer is not needed. We can solve the problem using estimation. Estimate the amount of seats for each park. Then subtract.

Solve Comerica Park: $40,000 \rightarrow 40,000$
Fenway Park: $33,871 \rightarrow 34,000$ Round to the nearest thousand.
$40,000 - 34,000 = 6000$ Subtract 34,000 from 40,000.

So, Comerica Park has about 6000 more seats than Fenway Park.

Examine Since $34,000 + 6000 = 40,000$, the answer makes sense.

DAILY
INTERVENTION   **Differentiated Instruction**

- **Visual/Spatial** Give the students toothpicks to build the following models.

Ask students to build the models, then write down the number of toothpicks used to build each model. Finally, students should determine the number of toothpicks needed to build the tenth model. **21**

Check for Understanding

Concept Check

1. See margin.

1. **Tell** when it is appropriate to solve a problem using estimation.

2. **OPEN ENDED** Write a list of numbers in which four is added to get each succeeding term. **Sample answer: 0, 4, 8, 12, …**

Guided Practice

GUIDED PRACTICE KEY	
Exercises	Examples
4–7	2
3, 8	1, 3

3. **TIME** The ferry schedule at the right shows that the ferry departs at regular intervals. Use the four-step plan to find the earliest time a passenger can catch the ferry if he/she cannot leave until 1:30 P.M. **1:33 P.M.**

South Bass Island Ferry Schedule

Departures	Arrivals
8:45 A.M.	9:
9:33 A.M.	1
10:21 A.M.	
11:09 A.M.	

Find the next term in each list.

4. 10, 20, 30, 40, 50, … **60**

5. 37, 33, 29, 25, 21, … **17**

6. 12, 17, 22, 27, 32, … **37**

7. 3, 12, 48, 192, 768, … **3072**

Application

8. **MONEY** In 1999, the average U.S. household spent $12,057 on housing, $1891 on entertainment, $5031 on food, and $7011 on transportation. How much was spent on food each month? Round to the nearest cent. **Source:** Bureau of Labor Statistics **$419.25**

★ indicates increased difficulty

Practice and Apply

Homework Help	
For Exercises	See Examples
9, 10	1
11–20	2
21–26	3

Extra Practice
See page 724.

9. **178 beats per min**

HEALTH For Exercises 9 and 10, use the table that gives the approximate heart rate a person should maintain while exercising at 85% intensity.

Age	20	25	30	35	40	45
Heart Rate (beats/min)	174	170	166	162	158	154

9. Assume the pattern continues. Use the four-step plan to find the heart rate a 15-year-old should maintain while exercising at this intensity.

10. What heart rate should a 55-year old maintain while exercising at this intensity? **146 beats per min**

Find the next term in each list.

11. 2, 5, 8, 11, 14, … **17**

12. 4, 8, 12, 16, 20, … **24**

13. 0, 5, 10, 15, 20, … **25**

14. 2, 6, 18, 54, 162, … **486**

15. 54, 50, 46, 42, 38, … **34**

16. 67, 61, 55, 49, 43, … **37**

★17. 2, 5, 9, 14, 20, … **27**

★18. 3, 5, 9, 15, 23, … **33**

GEOMETRY Draw the next figure in each pattern. 19–20. See margin.

19.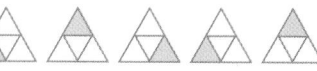

20.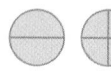

21. **MONEY** Ryan needs to save $125 for a ski trip. He has $68 in his bank. He receives $15 for an allowance and earns $20 delivering newspapers and $16 shoveling snow. Does he have enough money for the trip? Explain. **See margin.**

 www.pre-alg.com/self_check_quiz

Lesson 1-1 Using a Problem-Solving Plan **9**

Answers

1. **When an exact answer is not needed.**

19.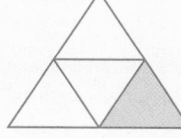

20.

21. **Since $68 + $15 + $20 + $16 = $119, Ryan does not have enough money for the ski trip.**

Lesson 1-1 Using a Problem-Solving Plan **9**

Open-Ended Assessment

Speaking Ask pairs of students to work through a given problem. Have each pair make a poster or transparency showing how they used the four-step problem-solving process. Have each pair present the results of their problem to the class.

New teachers, or teachers new to teaching mathematics, may especially appreciate the Tips for New Teachers.

Tips for New Teachers

Problem Solving Working through a four-step plan with students may take time. Some students find it difficult to plan the solution. You will want to model this process, encourage a variety of strategies, and work with students to estimate solutions. The problem-solving process will need to be reinforced frequently as you encounter new topics throughout the year.

Getting Ready for Lesson 1-2

BASIC SKILL Exercises 31–36 should be used to determine students' abilities to round decimal numbers to the nearest whole number. You may want to review rules for rounding before assigning these exercises.

---

22. **MONEY** Using eight coins, how can you make change for 65 cents that will not make change for a quarter? **2 quarters, 1 dime, 5 pennies**

23. **TRANSPORTATION** A car traveled 280 miles at 55 mph. About how many hours did it take for the car to reach its destination? **about 5 h**

24. **CANDY** A gourmet jelly bean company can produce 100,000 pounds of jelly beans a day. One ounce of these jelly beans contains 100 Calories. If there are 800 jelly beans in a pound, how many jelly beans can be produced in a day? **80,000,000 jelly beans**

25. **MEDICINE** The number of different types of transplants that were performed in the United States in 1999 are shown in the table. About how many transplants were performed?

25. Sample answer: about 21,800 transplants

More About. . .

Candy
In 1981, $3\frac{1}{2}$ tons of red, blue, and white jelly beans were sent to the Presidential Inaugural Ceremonies for Ronald Reagan.
Source: www.jellybelly.com

Transplant	Number
heart	2185
liver	4698
kidney	12,483
heart-lung	49
lung	885
pancreas	363
intestine	70
kidney-pancreas	946

Source: *The World Almanac*

★ 26. **COMMUNICATION** A telephone tree is set up so that every person calls three other people. Anita needs to tell her co-workers about a time change for a meeting. Suppose it takes 2 minutes to call 3 people. In 10 minutes, how many people will know about the change of time? **364 people**

27. **CRITICAL THINKING** Think of a 1 to 9 multiplication table.
 a. Are there more odd or more even products? How can you determine the answer without counting? **a–b. See margin.**
 b. Is this different from a 1 to 9 addition facts table?

28. WRITING IN MATH Answer the question that was posed at the beginning of the lesson. **See margin.**

 Why is it helpful to use a problem-solving plan to solve problems?
 Include the following in your answer:
 • an explanation of the importance of performing each step of the four-step problem-solving plan, and
 • an explanation of why it is beneficial to estimate the answer in the *Plan* step.

Standardized Test Practice
Ⓐ Ⓑ Ⓒ Ⓓ

29. Find the next figure in the pattern shown below. **B**

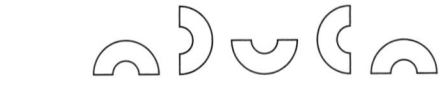

 Ⓐ   Ⓑ 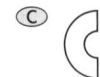 Ⓒ  Ⓓ

30. A wagon manufacturing plant in Chicago, Illinois, can produce 8000 wagons a day at top production. Which of the following is a reasonable amount of wagons that can be produced in a year? **C**
 Ⓐ 24,000 Ⓑ 240,000 Ⓒ 2,400,000 Ⓓ 240,000,000

Getting Ready for the Next Lesson
BASIC SKILL Round each number to the nearest whole number.
31. 2.8 **3**
32. 5.2 **5**
33. 35.4 **35**
34. 49.6 **50**
35. 109.3 **109**
36. 999.9 **1000**

Answers

27a. There are more even products; Since any even number multiplied by any number is even, and only an odd number multiplied by an odd number is odd, there are more even products in the table. There are about 3 times as many evens as odds.

27b. Yes; In the addition table, there is only one more even number than odd.

28. Sample answer: A problem-solving plan helps you to be organized in solving a math problem. Answers should include the following.

• It is important to perform each step. This enables you to understand the problem and its solution.

• By estimating the answer, you will know if your answer is reasonable.

Translating Expressions Into Words

Translating numerical expressions into verbal phrases is an important skill in algebra. Key words and phrases play an essential role in this skill.

The following table lists some words and phrases that suggest addition, subtraction, multiplication, and division.

Addition	Subtraction	Multiplication	Division
plus	minus	times	divided
sum	difference	product	quotient
more than	less than	multiplied	per
increased by	subtract	each	rate
in all	decreased by	of	ratio
	less	factors	separate

Reading Mathematics features help students learn and use the language of mathematics.

A few examples of how to write an expression as a verbal phrase are shown.

Expression	Key Word	Verbal Phrase
5×8	times	5 times 8
$2 + 4$	sum	the sum of 2 and 4
$16 \div 2$	quotient	the quotient of 16 and 2
$8 - 6$	less than	6 less than 8
2×5	product	the product of 2 and 5
$5 - 2$	less	5 less 2

Reading to Learn

1. Refer to the table above. Write a different verbal phrase for each expression.

1. Sample answer: the product of 5 and 8; 2 plus 4; 16 divided by 2; the difference of 8 and 6; 2 times 5; 2 less than 5

Choose the letter of the phrase that best matches each expression.

2. $9 - 3$ c   **a.** the sum of 3 and 9

3. $3 \div 9$ e   **b.** the quotient of 9 and 3

4. $9 \cdot 3$ d   **c.** 3 less than 9

5. $3 + 9$ a   **d.** 9 multiplied by 3

6. $9 \div 3$ b   **e.** 3 divided by 9

11. 12 divided by 3; the quotient of 12 and 3

Write two verbal phrases for each expression. For Exercises 7–14, sample answers are given.

7. $5 + 1$ 5 plus 1; the sum of 5 and 1   **8.** $8 + 6$ the sum of 8 and 6; 6 more than 8

9. 9×5 9 times 5; the product of 9 and 5   **10.** $2(4)$ 2 multiplied by 4; 2 times 4

11. $12 \div 3$ **12.** $\frac{20}{4}$ 20 divided by 4; the quotient of 20 and 4

13. $8 - 7$ 8 decreased by 7; 7 less than 8   **14.** $11 - 5$ 11 minus 5; the difference of 11 and 5

Reading Mathematics Translating Expressions Into Words **11**

Getting Started

Before using this page, ask students to brainstorm any words or phrases they can think of that mean "add." Write the suggestions on the board. Repeat this activity for the words subtract, multiply, and divide.

Teach

- Ask students to look up the words *add, subtract, multiply,* and *divide* in a dictionary or thesaurus to further identify words or phrases that may be added to the list on the page. They can also investigate the origins of the words. Students can then practice translating numerical phrases into verbal phrases.
- Emphasize the difference between *decrease* and *decreased by,* and *less* and *less than.*

Assess

Study Notebook

Ask students to summarize what they have learned about translating expressions into words.

ELL English Language Learners may benefit from writing key concepts from this activity in their Study Notebooks in their native language and then in English.

ELL notations throughout the chapter indicate items that can assist English-Language Learners.

1 Focus

5-Minute Check Transparency 1-2 Use as a quiz or review of Lesson 1-1.

Mathematical Background notes are available for this lesson on page 4C.

Why do we need to agree on an order of operations?

The opening activity questions are repeated on page 9 of the *Chapter 1 Resource Masters*.

Reading to Learn Mathematics, p. 9   ELL

Pre-Activity *Why do we need to agree on an order of operations?*

Do the activity at the top of page 12 in your textbook. Write your answers below.

a. Study the expressions and their respective values. For each expression, tell the order in which the calculator performed the operations. For 1 + 2 × 5, multiplication then addition; for 8 − 4 ÷ 2, division then subtraction; for 10 ÷ 5 + 14 × 2, division, multiplication, then addition.

b. For each expression, does the calculator perform the operations in order from left to right? no

c. Based on your answer to parts **a** and **b**, find the value of each expression below. Check your answer with a scientific calculator.
   12 − 3 × 2 6   16 ÷ 4 − 2 2   18 + 6 − 8 ÷ 2 × 3 12

d. Make a conjecture as to the order in which a scientific calculator performs operations. Sample answer: Multiplication and division first in the order they appear and then addition and subtraction in the order they appear. The calculator performs multiplication and division before addition and subtraction.

Reading the Lesson   1–3. See students' work.

Write a definition and give an example of each new vocabulary word or phrase.

Vocabulary	Definition	Example
1. numerical expression		
2. evaluate		
3. order of operations		

4. In the boxes below, write three different expressions using two operations that each have a value of 6. Sample answers are given.

$\boxed{2}\,\boxed{+}\,\boxed{2}\,\boxed{\times}\,\boxed{2}=6$ $\boxed{4}\,\boxed{\times}\,\boxed{4}\,\boxed{-}\,\boxed{4}=6$ $\boxed{10}\,\boxed{-}\,\boxed{2}\,\boxed{-}\,\boxed{2}=6$

Helping You Remember

5. A mnemonic device helps you remember something. Create your own mnemonic device to remember the order of operations. For example, list the operations in order, use the first letter of each operation and create a phrase with words starting with the same letters. Grouping symbols, Multiplication and Division, Addition and Subtraction phrase: Give Me Dessert After Supper

Teaching Tip You may want to demonstrate a calculation using both a scientific calculator and a four-function calculator to show that one calculator uses the order of operations and the other does not.

Resource Manager

📂 Workbooks and Reproducible Masters

Chapter 1 Resource Masters
- Study Guide and Intervention, p. 6
- Skills Practice, p. 7
- Practice, p. 8
- Reading to Learn Mathematics, p. 9
- Enrichment, p. 10
- Assessment, p. 51

Parent and Student Study Guide Workbook, p. 2
Prerequisite Skills Workbook, pp. 5–12

📺 Transparencies
5-Minute Check Transparency 1-2
Answer Key Transparencies

💿 Technology
Interactive Chalkboard
Pre-AlgePASS: Tutorial Plus, Lesson 1

Vocabulary
- numerical expression
- evaluate
- order of operations

a. For 1 + 2 × 5, multiplication then addition; for 8 − 4 ÷ 2, division then subtraction; for 10 ÷ 5 + 14 × 2, division, multiplication, then addition.

TEACHING TIP
Nonscientific calculators do not follow the order of operations.

d. Sample answer: Multiplication and division first in the order they appear and then addition and subtraction in the order they appear.

Study Tip

Grouping Symbols
Grouping symbols include:
- parentheses ( ),
- brackets [ ], and
- fraction bars, as in $\frac{6+4}{2}$, which means (6 + 4) ÷ 2.

What You'll Learn
- Use the order of operations to evaluate expressions.
- Translate verbal phrases into numerical expressions.

Why do we need to agree on an order of operations?

Scientific calculators are programmed to find the value of an expression in a certain order.

Expression	$1 + 2 \times 5$	$8 - 4 \div 2$	$10 \div 5 + 14 \times 2$
Value	11	6	30

a. Study the expressions and their respective values. For each expression, tell the order in which the calculator performed the operations.

b. For each expression, does the calculator perform the operations in order from left to right? **no**

c. Based on your answer to parts **a** and **b**, find the value of each expression below. Check your answer with a scientific calculator.
   $12 - 3 \times 2$ **6** $16 \div 4 - 2$ **2** $18 + 6 - 8 \div 2 \times 3$ **12**

d. **Make a conjecture** as to the order in which a scientific calculator performs operations.

ORDER OF OPERATIONS Expressions like $1 + 2 \times 5$ and $10 \div 5 + 14 \div 2$ are **numerical expressions**. Numerical expressions contain a combination of numbers and operations such as addition, subtraction, multiplication, and division.

When you **evaluate** an expression, you find its numerical value. To avoid confusion, mathematicians have agreed upon the following **order of operations**.

Concept Summary   Order of Operations

Step 1	Simplify the expressions inside grouping symbols.
Step 2	Do all multiplications and/or divisions from left to right.
Step 3	Do all additions and/or subtractions from left to right.

Numerical expressions have only one value. Consider $6 + 4 \times 3$.

$$6 + 4 \times 3 = 6 + 12$$
$$= 18$$
Multiply, then add.

$$6 + 4 \times 3 = 10 \times 3$$
$$= 30$$
Add, then multiply.

Which is the correct value, 18 or 30? Using the order of operations, the correct value of $6 + 4 \times 3$ is 18.

✓ **Concept Check** Which operation should you perform first to evaluate $10 - 2 + 3$? **subtraction**

Example 1 Evaluate Expressions

Find the value of each expression.

a. $3 + 4 \times 5$

$3 + 4 \times 5 = 3 + 20$ Multiply 4 and 5.

$ = 23$ Add 3 and 20.

b. $18 \div 3 \times 2$

$18 \div 3 \times 2 = 6 \times 2$ Divide 18 by 3.

$ = 12$ Multiply 6 and 2.

c. $6(2 + 9) - 3 \cdot 8$

$6(2 + 9) - 3 \cdot 8 = 6(11) - 3 \cdot 8$ Evaluate $(2 + 9)$ first.

$ = 66 - 3 \cdot 8$ $6(11)$ means 6×11.

$ = 66 - 24$ $3 \cdot 8$ means 3 times 8.

$ = 42$ Subtract 24 from 66.

d. $4[(15 - 9) + 8(2)]$

$4[(15 - 9) + 8(2)] = 4[6 + 8(2)]$ Evaluate $(15 - 9)$.

$ = 4(6 + 16)$ Multiply 8 and 2.

$ = 4(22)$ Add 6 and 16.

$ = 88$ Multiply 4 and 22.

e. $\dfrac{53 + 15}{17 - 13}$

$\dfrac{53 + 15}{17 - 13} = (53 + 15) \div (17 - 13)$ Rewrite as a division expression.

$\phantom{\dfrac{53 + 15}{17 - 13}} = 68 \div 4$ Evaluate $53 + 15$ and $17 - 13$.

$\phantom{\dfrac{53 + 15}{17 - 13}} = 17$ Divide 68 by 4.

Study Tip

Multiplication and Division Notation
A raised dot or parentheses represents multiplication. A fraction bar represents division.

TRANSLATE VERBAL PHRASES INTO NUMERICAL EXPRESSIONS

You have learned to translate numerical expressions into verbal phrases. It is often necessary to translate verbal phrases into numerical expressions.

Example 2 Translate Phrases into Expressions

Write a numerical expression for each verbal phrase.

a. the product of eight and seven

Phrase	the product of eight and seven
Key Word	product
Expression	8×7

b. the difference of nine and three

Phrase	the difference of nine and three
Key Word	difference
Expression	$9 - 3$

Study Tip

Differences and Quotients
In this book, *the difference of 9 and 3* means to start with 9 and subtract 3, so the expression is $9 - 3$. Similarly, *the quotient of 9 and 3* means to start with 9 and divide by 3, so the expression is $9 \div 3$.

 www.pre-alg.com/extra_examples   **Lesson 1-2** Numbers and Expressions   **13**

ORDER OF OPERATIONS

In-Class Example Power Point®

1 Find the value of each expression.

a. $6 + 8 \times 2$ **22**

b. $24 \div 8 \times 3$ **9**

c. $5(4 + 6) - 7 \cdot 7$ **1**

d. $3[(18 - 6) + 2(4)]$ **60**

e. $\dfrac{(49 + 31)}{(19 - 14)}$ **16**

Teaching Tip In Example 1e, you may want to show the division as a fraction to be simplified.

TRANSLATE VERBAL PHRASES INTO NUMERICAL EXPRESSIONS

In-Class Examples Power Point®

Teaching Tip Students may benefit from practicing verbal expressions orally.

2 Write a numerical expression for each verbal phrase.

a. the quotient of eighteen and six   **$18 \div 6$**

b. the sum of nine and five   **$9 + 5$**

3 **EARNINGS** Madison earns an allowance of $5 per week. She also earns $4 per hour babysitting, and usually babysits 6 hours each week. Write and evaluate an expression for the total amount of money she earns in one week.   **$5 + 4 \times 6$; $29**

DAILY
INTERVENTION   Differentiated Instruction

- **Logical** Some students find simplifying complicated expressions intimidating. To help students visualize the step-by-step process of simplifying, ask them to make a mobile. At the top, place an expression requiring several steps to simplify. From this expression, hang a card showing one simplification. Continue hanging cards showing the next simplification until the value is reached at the bottom.

Study Notebook

Have students—
• add the definitions/examples of the vocabulary terms to their Vocabulary Builder worksheets for Chapter 1.
• include any other item(s) that they find helpful in mastering the skills in this lesson.

About the Exercises . . .

Organization by Objective
• **Order of Operations:** 13–30, 40, 42, 48
• **Translate Verbal Phrases into Numerical Expressions:** 31–39, 41, 47

Odd/Even Assignments

Exercises 13–38 are structured so that students practice the same concepts whether they are assigned odd or even problems.

Assignment Guide

Basic: 13–23 odd, 29–35 odd, 39–42, 43, 45, 51–65

Average: 13–37 odd, 39–42, 43, 45, 51–65

Advanced: 14–38 even, 44, 46–61 (Optional: 62–65)

D A I L Y
INTERVENTION **FIND THE ERROR**
Remind students that multiplication and division are performed in order from left to right. Multiplication is *not* automatically performed before division.

Answer

3. Emily; she followed the order of operations and divided first.

Example 3 *Use an Expression to Solve a Problem*

TRANSPORTATION A taxicab company charges a fare of $4 for the first mile and $2 for each additional mile. Write and then evaluate an expression to find the fare for a 10-mile trip.

TEACHING TIP
Be sure to explain why the number 9 is used. After the first mile of a 10-mile trip, there are 9 additional miles.

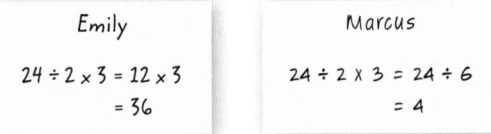

Words	$4 for the first mile	and	$2 for each additional mile
Expression	4	+	2×9

$$4 + 2 \times 9 = 4 + 18 \quad \text{Multiply.}$$
$$= 22 \quad \text{Add.}$$

The fare for a 10-mile trip is $22.

Check for Understanding

Concept Check

1. Sample answer: $(8 - 3) \cdot 2$
2. No; the value of $2 \times 4 + 3$ is 11 and the value of $2 \times (4 + 3)$ is 14.

1. **OPEN ENDED** Give an example of an expression involving multiplication and subtraction, in which you would subtract first.

2. **Tell** whether $2 \times 4 + 3$ and $2 \times (4 + 3)$ have the same value. Explain.

3. **FIND THE ERROR** Emily and Marcus are evaluating $24 \div 2 \times 3$.

Emily
$24 \div 2 \times 3 = 12 \times 3$
$= 36$

Marcus
$24 \div 2 \times 3 = 24 \div 6$
$= 4$

Who is correct? Explain your reasoning. **See margin.**

Guided Practice

GUIDED PRACTICE KEY

Exercises	Examples
4–9	1
10, 11	2
12	3

Name the operation that should be performed first. Then find the value of each expression.

4. $3 \cdot 6 - 4$ $\times$; 14
5. $32 - 24 \div 2$ $\div$; 20
6. $5(8) + 7$ $\times$; 47
7. $6(15 - 4)$ $-$; 66
8. $\dfrac{10 - 4}{1 + 2}$ $-$ or $\div$; 2
9. $11 + 56 \div (2 \cdot 7)$ $\times$; 15

Write a numerical expression for each verbal phrase.

10. the quotient of fifteen and five $15 \div 5$
11. the difference of twelve and nine $12 - 9$

Application

12. **MUSIC** Hector purchased 3 CDs for $13 each and 2 cassette tapes for $9 each. Write and then evaluate an expression for the total cost of the merchandise. $(3 \times 13) + (2 \times 9)$; $57

★ indicates increased difficulty

Practice and Apply

Homework Help

For Exercises	See Examples
13–28	1
31–38	2
39–42, 47, 48	3

Extra Practice
See page 724.

Find the value of each expression.

13. $2 \cdot 6 - 8$ **4**
14. $12 - 3 \times 3$ **3**
15. $12 \div 3 + 21$ **25**
16. $9 + 18 \div 3$ **15**
17. $8 + 5(6)$ **38**
18. $4(7) - 11$ **17**
19. $\dfrac{15 + 9}{32 - 20}$ **2**
20. $\dfrac{45 - 18}{9 \div 3}$ **9**
21. $11(6 - 1)$ **55**
22. $(9 - 7) \cdot 13$ **26**
23. $56 \div (7 \cdot 2) \times 6$ **24**
24. $75 \div (7 + 8) - 3$ **2**
★ 25. $2[5(11 - 3)] - 16$ **64**
★ 26. $5[4 + (12 - 4) \div 2]$ **40**
★ 27. $9[(22 - 17) + 5(1 + 2)]$ **180**
★ 28. $10[9(2 + 4) - 6 \cdot 2]$ **420**

USA TODAY Education

Online Lesson Plans

USA TODAY's Education Online site offers resources and interactive features connected to each day's newspaper. *Experience TODAY*, USA TODAY's daily lesson plan, is available on the site and delivered daily to subscribers. This plan provides instruction for integrating USA TODAY graphics and key editorial features into your mathematics classroom. Log on to **www.education.usatoday.com**

29. Find the value of *six added to the product of four and eleven*. 50

30. What is the value of *sixty divided by the sum of two and ten*? 5

Write a numerical expression for each verbal phrase.

31. six minus three $6 - 3$

32. seven increased by two $7 + 2$

33. nine multiplied by five 9×5

34. eleven more than fifteen $15 + 11$

35. twenty-four divided by six $24 \div 6$

36. four less than eighteen $18 - 4$

★ **37.** the cost of 3 notebooks at \$6 each $3 \times \$6$

★ **38.** the total amount of CDs if Erika has 4 and Roberto has 5 $4 + 5$

GARDENING For Exercises 39 and 40, use the following information.
A bag of potting soil sells for \$2, and a bag of fertilizer sells for \$13.

39. Write an expression for the total cost of 4 bags of soil and 2 bags of fertilizer. $(4 \times 2) + (2 \times 13)$

40. What is the total cost of the gardening supplies? \$34

TRAVEL For Exercises 41 and 42, use the following information.
Miko is packing for a trip. The total weight of her luggage cannot exceed 200 pounds. She has 3 suitcases that weigh 57 pounds each and 2 sport bags that weigh 12 pounds each. **41.** $(3 \times 57) + (2 \times 12)$

41. Write an expression for the total weight of the luggage.

42. Is Miko's luggage within the 200-pound limit? Explain.
$(3 \times 57) + (2 \times 12)$ is 195. So, Miko's luggage is within the limit.

Copy each sentence. Then insert parentheses to make each sentence true.

43. $61 - 15 + 3 = 43$

44. $12 \times 3 \div 1 + 2 = 12$

45. $56 \div 2 + 6 - 4 = 3$

46. $5 + 2 \cdot 9 - 3 = 42$

43–46. See margin.

FOOTBALL For Exercises 47 and 48, use the table and the following information. **47.** $(50 \times 25) + (7 \times 24) + (4 \times 22) + (3 \times 16)$
A national poll ranks college football teams using votes from sports reporters. Each vote is worth a certain number of points. Suppose The Ohio State University receives 50 first-place votes, 7 second-place votes, 4 fourth-place votes, and 3 tenth-place votes.

Number of Points for Each Vote	
Vote	Points
1st place	25
2nd place	24
3rd place	23
4th place	22
5th place	21
⋮	⋮
25th place	1

★ **47.** Write an expression for the number of points that Ohio State receives.

★ **48.** Find the total number of points. 1554

PUBLISHING For Exercises 49 and 50, use the following information.
An ISBN number is used to identify a published book. To determine if an ISBN number is correct, multiply each of the numbers in order by 10, 9, 8, 7, and so on. If the sum of the products can be divided by 11, with no remainder, the number is correct. **49–50.** See margin.

★ **49.** Find the ISBN number on the back cover of this book.

★ **50.** Is the number correct? Explain why or why not.

Football
The Ohio State University Buckeyes ended the 2002 season ranked No. 1 in NCAA Division I-A college football with a 14–0 record.
Source: www.espn.com

Answers

43. $61 - (15 + 3) = 43$

44. $12 \times 3 \div (1 + 2) = 12$

45. $56 \div (2 + 6) - 4 = 3$

46. $(5 + 2) \cdot (9 - 3) = 42$

49. 0-07-825200-8

50. Yes; the total of the expression is 165, and 165 can be divided by 11 with no remainder.

$(0 \cdot 10) + (0 \cdot 9) + (7 \cdot 8) + (8 \cdot 7) + (2 \cdot 6) + (5 \cdot 5) + (2 \cdot 4) + (0 \cdot 3) + (0 \cdot 2) + (8 \cdot 1)$

Open-Ended Assessment

Speaking Show students the expression $3 + 4 \times 5 - 2$. Ask them to give two different verbal phrases for this expression. Then evaluate the expression, explaining their reasoning.

Getting Ready for Lesson 1-3

BASIC SKILL In Lesson 1-3, students will continue to evaluate expressions using addition, subtraction, multiplication, and division. Exercises 62–65 practice the basic skill of finding a sum.

Assessment Options

Quiz (Lessons 1-1 and 1-2) is available on p. 51 of the *Chapter 1 Resource Masters*.

Assessment Options lists the quizzes and tests that are available in the Chapter Resource Masters.

Answer

52. Sample answer: We need to agree on an order of operations so that each expression has one unique value. Answers should include the following.

- When evaluating a numerical expression, simplify any expressions inside grouping symbols. Then do all multiplication and/or division in order from left to right. Then do all addition and/or subtraction from left to right.

- When the order of operations is not followed, an incorrect value for the expression may result.

51. Sample answer:
$111 - (1 + 1 + 1) \times (11 + 1)$

51. CRITICAL THINKING Suppose only the 1,  and ENTER keys on a calculator are working. How can you get a result of 75 if you are only allowed to push these keys fewer than 20 times?

52. **WRITING IN MATH** Answer the question that was posed at the beginning of the lesson. **See margin.**

Why do we need to agree on an order of operations?

Include the following in your answer:

- an explanation of how the order operations are performed, and
- an explanation of what will happen to the value of an expression if the order of operations are not followed.

Standardized Test Practice
Ⓐ Ⓑ Ⓒ Ⓓ

53. Which expression has a value of 18? **C**

- Ⓐ $2[2(6 - 3)] + 5$
- Ⓑ $27 \div 3 + (12 - 4)$
- Ⓒ $(9 \times 3) - 63 \div 7$
- Ⓓ $6(3 + 2) \div (9 - 7)$

54. Identify the expression that represents *the quotient of ten and two.* **B**

- Ⓐ $2 \div 10$
- Ⓑ $\frac{10}{2}$
- Ⓒ 10×2
- Ⓓ $10 - 2$

Maintain Your Skills

Mixed Review **Find the next term in each list.** *(Lesson 1-1)*

55. 2, 4, 8, 16, 32, ... **64**

56. 45, 42, 39, 36, 33, ... **30**

57. 1, 3, 6, 10, 15, 21, ... **28**

58. 15, 18, 22, 25, 29, ... **32**

Solve each problem. *(Lesson 1-1)*

59. BUSINESS Mrs. Lewis is a sales associate for a computer company. She receives a salary, plus a bonus for any computer package she sells. Find Mrs. Lewis' bonus if she sells 16 computer packages. **$275**

Packages	Bonus
2	$100
4	$125
6	$150
8	$175

60. TRAVEL The graph shows the projected number of travelers for 2020. How many more people will travel to the United States than to Spain? **31 million**

61. Sample answer: about 26 compact cars

61. SPACE SHUTTLE The space shuttle can carry a payload of about 65,000 pounds. If a compact car weighs about 2450 pounds, about how many compact cars can the space shuttle carry?

Getting Ready for the Next Lesson

63. 126

BASIC SKILL Find each sum.

62. $18 + 34$ **52**

63. $85 + 41$

64. $342 + 50$ **392**

65. $535 + 28$ **563**

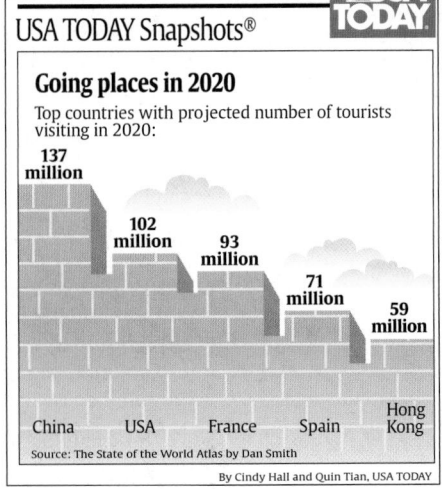

USA TODAY Snapshots®

Going places in 2020
Top countries with projected number of tourists visiting in 2020:

- China: 137 million
- USA: 102 million
- France: 93 million
- Spain: 71 million
- Hong Kong: 59 million

Source: The State of the World Atlas by Dan Smith

By Cindy Hall and Quin Tian, USA TODAY

*The **Resource Manager** lists all of the resources available for the lesson, including workbooks, blackline masters, transparencies, and technology.*

1-3 Variables and Expressions

What You'll Learn

- Evaluate expressions containing variables.
- Translate verbal phrases into algebraic expressions.

Vocabulary

- variable
- algebraic expression
- defining a variable

How are variables used to show relationships?

A baby-sitter earns $5 per hour. The table shows several possibilities for number of hours and earnings.

Number of Hours	Money Earned
2	5 · 2 or 10
5	5 · 5 or 25
8	5 · 8 or 40
11	5 · 11 or 55
h	?

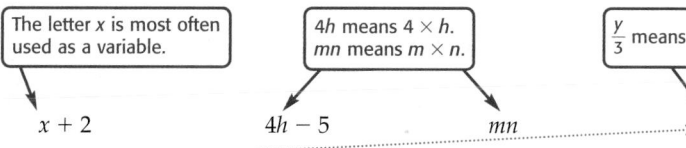

a. Suppose the baby-sitter worked 10 hours. How much would he or she earn? **$50**

b. What is the relationship between the number of hours and the money earned? **The amount earned is five times the number of hours.**

c. If h represents *any number of hours*, what expression could you write to represent the amount of money earned? **$5h$**

Reading Math

Variable
Root Word: Vary
The word *variable* means *likely to change or vary.*

EVALUATE EXPRESSIONS Algebra is a language of symbols. One symbol that is frequently used is a variable. A **variable** is a placeholder for any value. As shown above, h represents some *unknown number of hours*.

Any letter can be used as a variable. Notice the special notation for multiplication and division with variables.

| The letter x is most often used as a variable. | $4h$ means $4 \times h$. mn means $m \times n$. | $\dfrac{y}{3}$ means $y \div 3$. |

$$x + 2 \qquad 4h - 5 \qquad mn \qquad \frac{y}{3}$$

An expression like $x + 2$ is an **algebraic expression** because it contains sums and/or products of variables and numbers.

TEACHING TIP

The expression $\dfrac{y}{3}$ is an algebraic expression because it can be written as $\dfrac{1}{3}y$.

✓ **Concept Check** *True or false:* $2x$ is an example of an algebraic expression. Explain your reasoning. **True; it is a combination of 2, x, and multiplication.**

To evaluate an algebraic expression, replace the variable or variables with known values and then use the order of operations.

Example 1 Evaluate Expressions

Evaluate $x + y - 9$ if $x = 15$ and $y = 26$.

$$\begin{aligned} x + y - 9 &= 15 + 26 - 9 && \text{Replace } x \text{ with 15 and } y \text{ with 26.} \\ &= 41 - 9 && \text{Add 15 and 26.} \\ &= 32 && \text{Subtract 9 from 41.} \end{aligned}$$

Lesson 1-3 Variables and Expressions **17**

---

1 Focus

5-Minute Check Transparency 1-3 Use as a quiz or review of Lesson 1-2.

Mathematical Background notes are available for this lesson on page 4C.

How are variables used to show relationships?

The opening activity questions are repeated on page 14 of the *Chapter 1 Resource Masters*.

Reading to Learn Mathematics, p. 14 **ELL**

Pre-Activity *How are variables used to show relationships?*

Do the activity at the top of page 17 in your textbook. Write your answers below.

a. Suppose the baby-sitter worked 10 hours. How much would he or she earn? $50

b. What is the relationship between the number of hours and the money earned? The amount earned is five times the number of hours.

c. If h represents *any number of hours*, what expression could you write to represent the amount of money earned? $5h$

Reading the Lesson 1-3. See students' work.

Write a definition and give an example of each new vocabulary word or phrase.

Vocabulary	Definition	Example
1. variable		
2. algebraic expression		
3. defining a variable		

4. Name three things that make an algebraic expression. variables, numbers, and operations

5. Why do you think replacing a variable with a number is called the Substitution Property of Equality? If two quantities are equal, then one can be substituted, or replaced, for the other.

Helping You Remember

6. *Variable* is a word used in everyday English.

a. Find the definition of *variable* in the dictionary. Write the definition. able or apt to vary; subject to variation or changes

b. Explain how the English definition can help you remember how *variable* is used in mathematics. See students' answers.

Resource Manager

Workbooks and Reproducible Masters

Chapter 1 Resource Masters
- Study Guide and Intervention, p. 11
- Skills Practice, p. 12
- Practice, p. 13
- Reading to Learn Mathematics, p. 14
- Enrichment, p. 15

Graphing Calculator and Spreadsheet Masters, p. 19
Parent and Student Study Guide Workbook, p. 3
Prerequisite Skills Workbook, pp. 5–12
School-to-Career Masters, p. 1

Transparencies

5-Minute Check Transparency 1-3
Answer Key Transparencies

Technology

Interactive Chalkboard
Pre-AlgePASS: Tutorial Plus, Lesson 2

2 Teach

EVALUATE EXPRESSIONS

In-Class Examples Power Point®

1 Evaluate $x - y + 6$ if $x = 27$ and $y = 12$.   **21**

Teaching Tip Make sure students remember that $4x$ means 4 times x. So if $x = 3$, $4x = 12$, not 43.

2 Evaluate each expression if $x = 3$, $y = 4$, and $z = 7$.

a. $6y - 4x$ **12**

b. $\dfrac{(z - x)}{y}$ **1**

c. $5z + (x + 4y) - 15$ **39**

TRANSLATE VERBAL PHRASES

In-Class Examples Power Point®

3 Translate each phrase into an algebraic expression.

a. 35 more than the number of tickets sold $t + 35$

b. the difference of six times a number and 10 $6n - 10$

4 East Middle School sold tickets for a school play. The price of an adult ticket was $3, and the price of a student ticket was $1.

a. Write an expression that can be used to find the total amount of money collected.
$3a + 1s$

b. Suppose 70 adult tickets and 85 students tickets were sold. How much money was collected?   **$295**

Replacing a variable with a number demonstrates the **Substitution Property of Equality**.

Key Concept — *Substitution Property of Equality*

- **Words**   If two quantities are equal, then one quantity can be replaced by the other.

- **Symbols**   For all numbers a and b, if $a = b$, then a may be replaced by b.

> **Key Concept** boxes highlight definitions, formulas, and other important ideas. Multiple representations—words, symbols, examples, models—reach students of all learning styles.

Example 2 *Evaluate Expressions*

Evaluate each expression if $k = 2$, $m = 7$, and $n = 4$.

a. $6m - 3k$

$\begin{aligned} 6m - 3k &= 6(7) - 3(2) && \text{Replace } m \text{ with 7 and } k \text{ with 2.} \\ &= 42 - 6 && \text{Multiply.} \\ &= 36 && \text{Subtract.} \end{aligned}$

b. $\dfrac{mn}{2}$

$\begin{aligned} \dfrac{mn}{2} &= mn \div 2 && \text{Rewrite as a division expression.} \\ &= (7 \cdot 4) \div 2 && \text{Replace } m \text{ with 7 and } n \text{ with 4.} \\ &= 28 \div 2 && \text{Multiply.} \\ &= 14 && \text{Divide.} \end{aligned}$

c. $n + (k + 5m)$

$\begin{aligned} n + (k + 5m) &= 4 + (2 + 5 \cdot 7) && \text{Replace } n \text{ with 4, } k \text{ with 2, and } m \text{ with 7.} \\ &= 4 + (2 + 35) && \text{Multiply 5 and 7.} \\ &= 4 + 37 && \text{Add 2 and 35.} \\ &= 41 && \text{Add 4 and 37.} \end{aligned}$

TRANSLATE VERBAL PHRASES   The first step in translating verbal phrases into algebraic expressions is to choose a variable and a quantity for the variable to represent. This is called **defining a variable**.

Example 3 *Translate Verbal Phrases into Expressions*

Translate each phrase into an algebraic expression.

a. twelve points more than the Dolphins scored

Words	twelve points more than the Dolphins scored
Variable	Let p represent the points the Dolphins scored.

	twelve points	more than	the Dolphins scored	
Expression	12	+	p	The expression is $p + 12$.

b. four times a number decreased by 6

Words	four times a number decreased by 6
Variable	Let n represent the number.

	four times a number	decreased by	six	
Expression	$4n$	−	6	The expression is $4n - 6$.

> **Study Tip**
>
> *Look Back*
> To review **key words and phrases**, see p. 11.

DAILY
INTERVENTION   **Differentiated Instruction**

- **Logical** Make a set of expression cards with numbers, operation symbols, and variables. Put one character on each card. Some students will hold number cards, some will hold operation symbol cards, and others will hold variable cards. Ask four or five students at a time to line up, making an expression using their cards. Have students with numbers interchange places with students who have variables, and so on, to create many different combinations and expressions.

Algebraic expressions can be used to represent real-world situations.

Example 4 *Use an Expression to Solve a Problem*

SOCCER The Johnstown Soccer League ranks each team in their league using points. A team gets three points for a win and one point for a tie.

a. Write an expression that can be used to find the total number of points a team receives.

Words	three points for a win and one point for a tie
Variables	Let w = number of wins and t = number of ties.

$$\overbrace{\text{three points for a win}}^{} \quad \text{and} \quad \overbrace{\text{one point for a tie}}^{}$$

Expression $\quad\quad 3w \quad\quad\quad + \quad\quad 1t$

The expression $3w + 1t$ can be used to find the total number of points a team will receive.

b. Suppose in one season, the North Rockets had 17 wins and 4 ties. How many points did they receive?

$$\begin{aligned} 3w + 1t &= 3(17) + 1(4) && \text{Replace } w \text{ with 17 and } t \text{ with 4.} \\ &= 51 + 4 && \text{Multiply.} \\ &= 55 && \text{Add.} \end{aligned}$$

The North Rockets received 55 points.

Check for Understanding

Concept Check

1. Sample answer: $7n$ and $3x - 1$; $2 + 3$ and 3×8

1. OPEN ENDED Give two examples of an algebraic expression and two examples of expressions that are *not* algebraic.

2. Define *variable.* A variable is a placeholder for a number.

3. Write an expression that is the same as $4cd$. Sample answer: $4 \times c \times d$

Guided Practice

ALGEBRA Evaluate each expression if $a = 5$, $b = 12$, and $c = 4$.

GUIDED PRACTICE KEY	
Exercises	Examples
4–7	1, 2
8–11	3
12	4

4. $b + 6$ **18**
5. $18 - 3c$ **6**
6. $\dfrac{2b}{8}$ **3**
7. $5a - (b - c)$ **17**

ALGEBRA Translate each phrase into an algebraic expression.

8. eight more than the amount Kira saved $s + 8$

9. five goals less than the Pirates scored $g - 5$

10. the quotient of a number and four, minus five $k \div 4 - 5$

11. seven increased by the quotient of a number and eight $7 + n \div 8$

Application

12. SPACE Due to gravity, objects weigh three times as much on Earth as they do on Mercury.

a. Suppose the weight of an object on Mercury is w. Write an expression for the object's weight on Earth. **$3w$**

b. How much would an object weigh on Earth if it weighs 25 pounds on Mercury? **75 lb**

www.pre-alg.com/extra_examples

Study Notebook

Have students—
• add the definitions/examples of the vocabulary terms to their Vocabulary Builder worksheets for Chapter 1.
• record the different ways to show multiplication and division in algebraic expressions.
• include any other item(s) that they find helpful in mastering the skills in this lesson.

About the Exercises . . .
Organization by Objective
• **Evaluate Expressions:** 13–32, 43–44, 50
• **Translate Verbal Phrases:** 33–42, 48, 49

Odd/Even Assignments
Exercises 13–44 are structured so that students practice the same concepts whether they are assigned odd or even problems.

Alert! Exercises 8–11 and 33–42 can have different variables from given answers.

Assignment Guide
Basic: 13–29 odd, 31, 32, 33–39 odd, 45, 47, 51–62
Average: 13–29 odd, 31, 32, 33–47 odd, 51–62
Advanced: 14–30 even, 34–48 even, 49–58 (Optional: 59–62)
All: Practice Quiz 1 (1–5)

Study Guide and Intervention, p. 11

An **algebraic expression** is a combination of variables, numbers, and at least one operation. To evaluate an algebraic expression, replace the variable(s) with numbers and follow the order of operations.

Example 1 ALGEBRA Evaluate each expression if $r = 6$ and $s = 2$.

a. $8s - 2r$
$8s - 2r = 8 \cdot 2 - 2 \cdot 6$ Replace r with 6 and s with 2.
$= 16 - 12$ Multiply.
$= 4$ Subtract.

b. $3(r + s)$
$3(r + s) = 3(2 + 6)$ Replace r with 6 and s with 2.
$= 3 \cdot 8$ Evaluate the parentheses.
$= 24$ Multiply.

Example 2 FOOTBALL Teams earn three points for field goals and six points for touchdowns.

a. Assuming no other points, write an expression for a team's total points.

Words   three points for field goals and six points for touchdowns
Variables   Let f = number of field goals and t = number of touchdowns.
Expression $3f + 6t$

The total points for the team is $3f + 6t$.

b. Find the total score if a team scored two field goals and three touchdowns.

$3f + 6t = 3 \cdot 2 + 6 \cdot 3$ Replace f with 2 and t with 3.
$= 6 + 18$ Multiply.
$= 24$ Add.

The team scored a total of 24 points.

Exercises

ALGEBRA Evaluate each expression if $x = 10$, $y = 5$, and $z = 1$.

1. $x + y - z$ 14
2. $\frac{x}{y}$ 2
3. $2x + 4z$ 24
4. $xy + z$ 51
5. $\frac{6y}{10z}$ 3
6. $x(2 + z)$ 30
7. $x - 2y$ 0
8. $\frac{(x + y)}{z}$ 15

Translate each phrase into an algebraic expression.

9. eight inches taller than Mycala's height $h + 8$
10. twelve more than four times a number $4n + 12$
11. the difference of sixty and a number $60 - n$
12. three times the number of tickets sold $3t$

Skills Practice, p. 12 and Practice, p. 13 (shown)

ALGEBRA Evaluate each expression if $x = 12$, $y = 20$, and $z = 4$.

1. $x + y + z$ 36
2. $4x - y$ 28
3. $3x + 2y$ 76
4. $y - 3z$ 8
5. $x + y + z$ 17
6. $yz + x$ 92
7. $(y - x) + (y - z)$ 24
8. $\frac{y}{z} + \frac{x}{z}$ 8
9. $\frac{5x}{3y}$ 1
10. $z(y - x) + 4z$ 48

ALGEBRA Evaluate each expression if $a = 3$, $b = 6$, $c = 5$, and $d = 9$.

11. $a + b + c + d$ 23
12. $\frac{(a + b + c)}{2}$ 7
13. $ab + bc$ 48
14. $6d - c \cdot c$ 29
15. $3(a + b + c)$ 42
16. $\frac{100}{5c}$ 4
17. abc 90
18. $10(6c - 3d)$ 30
19. $\frac{2(a + b)}{6(b - c)}$ 3
20. $4[(d - a) + c]$ 44

ALGEBRA Translate each phrase into an algebraic expression.

21. six times a number minus eleven $6n - 11$
22. the product of eight hundred and a number $800n$
23. the quotient of thirty and ten times a number $30 \div (10n)$
24. five times the sum of three and some number $5(3 + n)$
25. half the distance to the school. $\frac{c}{2}$
26. RECYCLING In order to encourage recycling, the city is offering five cents for every pound of newspapers collected, twenty-five cents per pound for cans and ten cents per pound for glass bottles or jars.

a. Write an expression for the total amount earned from recycling. $5n + 25c + 10b$
b. If Chen brings in ten pounds of newspapers, eight pounds of cans, and two pounds of glass, how much will he receive? $2.70

Enrichment, p. 15

Hypatia

Hypatia, pronounced *hi PAY sha*, was the first woman to be mentioned in the history of mathematics. Born about A.D. 370, Hypatia lived in Alexandria and served as a professor at the famous Library of Alexandria. Hypatia wrote important commentaries on the works of mathematician Appollonius and the scientist Ptolemy. She also excelled in the fields of astronomy, medicine, and philosophy.

Egypt was in great political turmoil during Hypatia's lifetime. Because of her influence among scholars of the day, Hypatia became the target of criticism from those who equated science with paganism. In A.D. 415, she was murdered by an angry mob. Soon after her death, the library was destroyed and the Dark Ages began. The serious study of mathematics was limited for the next 500 years.

One of the things Hypatia studied was the relationship between number patterns and geometry. Investigate the geometric patterns below.

Triangular Numbers

Square Numbers

1. Draw the fifth and sixth figures in the pattern of triangular numbers. Then write the first six triangular numbers.   See students' drawings. 1, 3, 6, 10, 15, 21
2. Draw the fifth and sixth figures in the patterns of square numbers. Then write the first six square numbers.   See students' drawings. 1, 4, 9, 16, 25, 36
3. Draw the first four pentagonal and hexagonal numbers.   See students' work.
4. Use counters or drawings to determine if there is a number that is both square and triangular.   Sample answer: 36

Practice and Apply

Homework Help

For Exercises	See Examples
13–32, 43, 44	1, 2
33–42	3
48–50	4

Extra Practice
See page 724.

ALGEBRA   Evaluate each expression if $x = 7$, $y = 3$, and $z = 9$.

13. $z + 2$ 11
14. $5 + x$ 12
15. $2 + 4z$ 38
16. $15 - 2x$ 1
17. $\frac{6y}{z}$ 2
18. $\frac{9x}{y}$ 21
19. $\frac{xy}{3} + 2$ 9
20. $10 - \frac{xz}{9}$ 3
21. $4z - 3y$ 27
22. $3x - 2y$ 15
23. $2x + 3z + 5y$ 56
24. $5z - 3x - 2y$ 18
25. $7z - (y + x)$ 53
26. $(8y + 5) - 2z$ 11
27. $3y + (7z - 4x)$ 44
28. $6x - (z - 2y) + 15$ 54
29. $2x + (4z - 13) - 5$ 32
30. $(9 - 3y) + 4z - 5$ 31

SCIENCE   For Exercises 31 and 32, use the following information.

The number of times a cricket chirps can be used to estimate the temperature in degrees Fahrenheit. Use $c \div 4 + 37$ where c is the number of chirps in one minute.

31. Find the approximate temperature if a cricket chirps 136 times in a minute.   71° F
32. What is the temperature if a cricket chirps 100 times in a minute?   62° F

ALGEBRA   Translate each phrase into an algebraic expression.

33. Mark's salary plus a $200 bonus $s + \$200$
34. three more than the number of cakes baked $c + 3$
35. six feet shorter than the mountain's height $h - 6$
36. two seconds faster than Sarah's time $t + 2$
37. five times a number, minus four $5q - 4$
38. seven less than a number times eight $8n - 7$
39. nine more than a number divided by six $n \div 6 + 9$
40. the quotient of eight and twice a number $8 \div 2b$
★ 41. the difference of seventeen and four times a number $17 - 4w$
★ 42. three times the product of twenty-five and a number $3(25 \times n)$

★ 43. Evaluate $\frac{10mn}{3p - 3}$ if $m = 6$, $n = 3$, and $p = 7$.   10

★ 44. What is the value of $\frac{3(4a - 3b)}{b - 4}$ if $a = 6$ and $b = 7$?   3

ALGEBRA   Write an algebraic expression that represents the relationship in each table.   45. $x + 3$ 46. $5n$ 47. $p - 4$

45.

Age Now	Age in Three Years
10	13
12	15
15	18
20	23
x	■

46.

Number of Items	Total Cost
5	25
6	30
8	40
10	50
n	■

47.

Regular Price	Sale Price
$12	8
$15	11
$18	14
$24	20
$p	■

There is a Study Guide and Intervention, Skills Practice, Practice, Reading to Learn Mathematics, and Enrichment Master for every lesson in the Student Edition. These masters can be found in the Chapter Resource Masters.

48. BUSINESS Cornet Cable charges $32.50 a month for basic cable television. Each premium channel selected costs an additional $4.95 per month. Write an expression to find the cost of a month of cable service. $32.50 + 4.95c$

SALES For Exercises 49 and 50, use the following information.
The selling price of a sweater is the cost plus the markup minus the discount.

49. Write an expression to show the selling price s of a sweater. Use c for cost, m for markup, and d for discount. $s = c + m - d$

50. Suppose the cost of a sweater is $25, the markup is $20, and the discount is $6. What is the selling price of the sweater? **$39**

51. CRITICAL THINKING What value of t makes the expressions $6t$, $t + 5$, and $2t + 4$ equal? **1**

52. WRITING IN MATH   Answer the question that was posed at the beginning of the lesson. **See margin.**

How are variables used to show relationships?

Include the following in your answer:
- an explanation of variables and what they represent, and
- an example showing how variables are used to show relationships.

Standardized Test Practice
Ⓐ Ⓑ Ⓒ Ⓓ

53. If the value of $c + 5$ is 18, what is the value of c? **D**
Ⓐ 3   Ⓑ 8   Ⓒ 7   Ⓓ 13

54. Which expression represents *four less than twice a number*? **B**
Ⓐ $4n - 2$ Ⓑ $2n - 4$ Ⓒ $4(2 + n)$ Ⓓ $2n + 4$

Maintain Your Skills

Mixed Review   **Find the value of each expression.** *(Lesson 1-2)*

55. $3 + (6 \times 2) - 8$ **7**   **56.** $5(16 - 5 \times 3)$ **5**   **57.** $36 \div (9 \cdot 2) + 7$ **9**

58. FOOD The table shows the amount in pounds of certain types of pasta sold in a recent year. About how many million pounds of these types of pasta were sold? *(Lesson 1-1)*
Sample answer: about 660 million lb

Pasta	Amount (millions)
Spaghetti	308
Elbow	121
Noodles	70
Twirl	52
Penne	51
Lasagna	35
Fettuccine	24

Source: *National Pasta Association*

Getting Ready for the Next Lesson   **BASIC SKILL   Find each difference.**

59. $53 - 17$ **36**   **60.** $97 - 28$ **69**   **61.** $104 - 82$ **22**   **62.** $152 - 123$ **29**

Practice Quiz 1   Lessons 1-1 through 1-3

1. What is the next term in the list 4, 5, 7, 10, …? *(Lesson 1-1)* **14**

Find the value of each expression. *(Lesson 1-2)*

2. $28 \div 4 \times 2$ **14**   **3.** $7(3 + 10) - 2 \cdot 6$ **79**   **4.** $3[6(12 - 3)] - 17$ **145**

5. Evaluate $7x - 3y$ if $x = 4$ and $y = 2$. *(Lesson 1-3)* **22**

 www.pre-alg.com/self_check_quiz

Answer

52. Expressions show relationships, and the variables in the relationships are placeholders for numbers. Answers should include the following.

- Variables are placeholders that are represented by letters.
- For example, $x + y = 2$. This shows that the sum of two numbers is equal to 2.

Lesson 1-3 Variables and Expressions   **21**

---

4 Assess

Open-Ended Assessment

Writing Ask students to write an algebraic expression involving two variables and two or more operations. They can then assign values to the variables and evaluate them, showing how the result was determined.

Each lesson ends with Open-Ended Assessment strategies for closing the lesson. These include writing, modeling, and speaking.

Getting Ready for Lesson 1-4

BASIC SKILL Lesson 1-4 continues to utilize algebraic expressions as properties are introduced. Exercises 59–62 practice the basic skill of finding differences. The algebraic expressions can involve all four operations, including subtraction.

Assessment Options

Practice Quiz 1 The quiz provides students with a brief review of the concepts and skills in Lessons 1-1 through 1-3. Lesson numbers are given to the right of exercises or instruction lines so students can review concepts not yet mastered.

A Follow-Up of Lesson 1-3

Getting Started

Objective Use a spreadsheet to explore algebraic expressions.

Materials
spreadsheet application

Teaching Tip Before starting this activity, you may want to familiarize students with the layout of a spreadsheet. Provide students with a copy of a blank spreadsheet template from p. 2 of the *Graphing Calculator and Spreadsheet Masters*. Ask them to locate specific cells.

Teaching Tip Review the formulas that appear in each B cell of the spreadsheet in the Example so that students understand what they mean.

Teach

• Before students enter each spreadsheet command, you may want them to guess what will happen and how the page will look.
• You may want students to work in pairs to discuss their ideas and help each other troubleshoot any problems they may have getting used to the software.

Assess

In **Exercises 6–8**, students should:

• discover that using any type of number in the example problem gives a result of 3.
• verify with algebra tiles that the result of the example problem is 3 unit tiles.
• extend their thinking about expressions and spreadsheets to create their own example problem.

Expressions and Spreadsheets

One of the most common computer applications is a spreadsheet program. A **spreadsheet** is a table that performs calculations. It is organized into boxes called **cells**, which are named by a letter and a number. In the spreadsheet below, cell B1 is highlighted.

An advantage of using a spreadsheet is that values in the spreadsheet are recalculated when a number is changed. You can use a spreadsheet to investigate patterns in data.

Example

Here's a mind-reading trick! Think of a number. Then double it, add six, divide by two, and subtract the original number. What is the result?

You can use a spreadsheet to test different numbers. Suppose we start with the number 10.

	A	B	C
1	Think of a number.	10	10
2	Double it.	2*B1	20
3	Add 6.	B2+6	26
4	Divide by 2.	B3/2	13
5	Subtract the original number.	B4-B1	3
6			

Mind-Reading Trick

Sheet1 / Sheet2 / Sheet3

Ready

> The spreadsheet takes the value in B1, doubles it, and enters the value in B2. Note the * is the symbol for multiplication.

> The spreadsheet takes the value in B3, divides by 2, and enters the value in B4. Note that / is the symbol for division.

The result is 3.

Exercises

To change information in a spreadsheet, move the cursor to the cell you want to access and click the mouse. Then type in the information and press Enter. Find the result when each value is entered in B1.

1. 6 **3**   **2.** 8 **3**   **3.** 25 **3**   **4.** 100 **3**   **5.** 1500 **3**

Make a Conjecture

6. What is the result if a decimal is entered in B1? a negative number? **3, 3**

7. Explain why the result is always 3. **See margin.**

8. Make up your own mind-reading trick. Enter it into a spreadsheet to show that it works. **See margin.**

Answers

7. Let *x* represent the number. When you double the number the result is 2*x*. Adding 6 you get 2*x* + 6. Dividing by 2, *x* + 3 results. Subtracting the original number, you get 3. Thus, regardless of what *x* represents, the result is always 3.

8. Sample answer: Think of a number. Double it, add 4, divide by 2, and subtract the original number. The result is always 2.

1-4 Properties

What You'll Learn

- Identify and use properties of addition and multiplication.
- Use properties of addition and multiplication to simplify algebraic expressions.

Vocabulary
- properties
- counterexample
- simplify
- deductive reasoning

How are real-life situations commutative?

Abraham Lincoln delivered the Gettysburg Address more than 130 years ago. The table lists the number of words in certain historic documents.

Historical Document	Words
Preamble to The U.S. Constitution	52
Mayflower Compact	196
Atlantic Charter	375
Gettysburg Address (Nicolay Version)	238

Source: U.S. Historical Documents Archive

a. Suppose you read the Preamble to The U.S. Constitution first and then the Gettysburg Address. Write an expression for the total number of words read. **52 + 238**

b. Suppose you read the Gettysburg Address first and then the Preamble to the U.S. Constitution. Write an expression for the total number of words read. **238 + 52**

       c. 290; 290; The values are the same.

c. Find the value of each expression. What do you observe?

d. Does it matter in which order you add any two numbers? Why or why not? **no; the result is always the same**

PROPERTIES OF ADDITION AND MULTIPLICATION In algebra, **properties** are statements that are true for any numbers. For example, the expressions $3 + 8$ and $8 + 3$ have the same value, 11. This illustrates the **Commutative Property of Addition**. Likewise, $3 \cdot 8$ and $8 \cdot 3$ have the same value, 24. This illustrates the **Commutative Property of Multiplication**.

Reading Math

Commutative

Root Word: Commute
The everyday meaning of the word *commute* means *to change or exchange.*

Key Concept — Commutative Property of Addition

- **Words** The order in which numbers are added does not change the sum.
- **Symbols** For any numbers a and b, $a + b = b + a$.
- **Example** $2 + 3 = 3 + 2$
  $5 = 5$

Commutative Property of Multiplication

- **Words** The order in which numbers are multiplied does not change the product.
- **Symbols** For any numbers a and b, $a \cdot b = b \cdot a$.
- **Example** $2 \cdot 3 = 3 \cdot 2$
  $6 = 6$

✓ **Concept Check** Write an example that shows the Commutative Property of Multiplication. **Sample answer: $4 \cdot 5 = 5 \cdot 4$**

1-4 Lesson Notes

1 Focus

 5-Minute Check Transparency 1-4 Use as a quiz or review of Lesson 1-3.

Mathematical Background notes are available for this lesson on page 4D.

How are real-life situations commutative?

The opening activity questions are repeated on page 19 of the *Chapter 1 Resource Masters*.

Reading to Learn Mathematics, p. 19 — ELL

Pre-Activity *How are real-life situations commutative?*

Do the activity at the top of page 23 in your textbook. Write your answers below.

a. Suppose you read the Preamble to the U.S. Constitution first and then the Gettysburg Address. Write an expression for the total number of words read. **52 + 238**

b. Suppose you read the Gettysburg Address first and then the Preamble to the U.S. Constitution. Write an expression for the total number of words read. **238 + 52**

c. Find the value of each expression. What do you observe? **290; The values are the same.**

d. Does it matter in which order you add any two numbers? Why or why not? **no; The result is always the same.**

Reading the Lesson 1–4. See students' work.

Write a definition and give an example of each new vocabulary word or phrase.

Vocabulary	Definition	Example
1. properties		
2. counterexample		
3. simplify		
4. deductive reasoning		

Helping You Remember

5. Tell what a counterexample is in your own words. Tell how it is used in mathematics and why it is important. **A counterexample is an example that shows a statement is false. It is used in mathematics to disprove ideas or conjectures. If a counterexample is found for a conjecture, then it must be false and there is no need to try and prove the statement true.**

Resource Manager

Workbooks and Reproducible Masters

Chapter 1 Resource Masters
- Study Guide and Intervention, p. 16
- Skills Practice, p. 17
- Practice, p. 18
- Reading to Learn Mathematics, p. 19
- Enrichment, p. 20
- Assessment pp. 51, 53

Parent and Student Study Guide Workbook, p. 4
Prerequisite Skills Workbook, pp. 5–10

 Transparencies
5-Minute Check Transparency 1-4
Answer Key Transparencies

 Technology
Interactive Chalkboard

PROPERTIES OF ADDITION AND MULTIPLICATION

In-Class Examples

 Power Point®

1 Name the property shown by each statement.

a. $3 \cdot 10 \cdot 2 = 3 \cdot 2 \cdot 10$
Commutative Property ($\times$)

b. $(2 + 5) + m = 2 + (5 + m)$
Associative Property ($+$)

c. $17 \cdot 1 = 17$ **Multiplicative Identity**

Teaching Tip To help students remember the identity properties, remind them that adding 0 to any number or multiplying any number by 1 maintains the number's identity.

2 Find $(18 \cdot 20) \cdot 5$ mentally.
$18 \cdot (20 \cdot 5) = 18 \cdot 100 = 1800$

Teaching Tip When using properties to do computations mentally, it may be helpful to review compatible numbers with students.

3 State whether the following conjecture is true or false. If false, provide a counter-example.

Division of whole numbers is commutative.

False; $12 \div 6 \neq 6 \div 12$

SIMPLIFY ALGEBRAIC EXPRESSIONS

In-Class Example

 Power Point®

4 Simplify each expression.

a. $5 \cdot (3 \cdot r)$ **$15r$**

b. $12 + (x + 18)$ **$30 + x$**

Reading Math

Associative
Root Word: Associate
The word *associate* means *to join together, connect, or combine.*

TEACHING TIP
The order of operations tells you to simplify the expression in parentheses first.

When evaluating expressions, it is often helpful to group or *associate* the numbers. The **Associative Property** says that the way in which numbers are grouped when added or multiplied does not change the sum or the product.

Key Concept — **Associative Property of Addition**

- **Words**   The way in which numbers are grouped when added does not change the sum.

- **Symbols**   For any numbers a, b, and c,
  $(a + b) + c = a + (b + c)$.

- **Example** $(5 + 8) + 2 = 5 + (8 + 2)$
  $13 + 2 = 5 + 10$
  $15 = 15$

Associative Property of Multiplication

- **Words**   The way in which numbers are grouped when multiplied does not change the product.

- **Symbols**   For any numbers a, b, and c,
  $(a \cdot b) \cdot c = a \cdot (b \cdot c)$.

- **Example** $(4 \cdot 6) \cdot 3 = 4 \cdot (6 \cdot 3)$
  $24 \cdot 3 = 4 \cdot 18$
  $72 = 72$

✓ **Concept Check**   Write an example showing the Associative Property of Addition.
Sample answer: $4 + (1 + 3) = (4 + 1) + 3$

The following properties are also true.

TEACHING TIP
The Multiplicative Identity Property allows you to write $1x$ as x.

Key Concept — **Properties of Numbers**

Property	Words	Symbols	Examples
Additive Identity	When 0 is added to any number, the sum is the number.	For any number a, $a + 0 = 0 + a = a$.	$5 + 0 = 5$ $0 + 9 = 9$
Multiplicative Identity	When any number is multiplied by 1, the product is the number.	For any number a, $a \cdot 1 = 1 \cdot a = a$.	$7 \cdot 1 = 7$ $1 \cdot 6 = 6$
Multiplicative Property of Zero	When any number is multiplied by 0, the product is 0.	For any number a, $a \cdot 0 = 0 \cdot a = 0$.	$4 \cdot 0 = 0$ $0 \cdot 2 = 0$

Example 1 **Identify Properties**

Name the property shown by each statement.

a. $3 + 7 + 9 = 7 + 3 + 9$

The order of the numbers changed. This is the Commutative Property of Addition.

b. $(a \cdot 6) \cdot 5 = a \cdot (6 \cdot 5)$

The grouping of the numbers and variables changed. This is the Associative Property of Multiplication.

c. $0 \cdot 12 = 0$

The number was multiplied by zero. This is the Multiplicative Property of Zero.

In-Class Examples, which are included for every example in the Student Edition, exactly parallel the examples in the text. Teaching Tips about the examples in the Student Edition are included where appropriate.

You can use the properties of numbers to find sums and products mentally. Look for sums or products that end in zero.

Example 2 *Mental Math*

Find $4 \cdot (25 \cdot 11)$ mentally.

Group 4 and 25 together because $4 \cdot 25 = 100$. It is easy to multiply by 100 mentally.

$$4 \cdot (25 \cdot 11) = (4 \cdot 25) \cdot 11 \quad \text{Associative Property of Addition}$$
$$= 100 \cdot 11 \quad \text{Multiply 4 and 25 mentally.}$$
$$= 1100 \quad \text{Multiply 100 and 11 mentally.}$$

Study Tip

Counterexample
You can disprove a statement by finding only one counterexample.

You may wonder whether these properties apply to subtraction. One way to find out is to look for a counterexample. A **counterexample** is an example that shows a conjecture is not true.

Example 3 *Find a Counterexample*

State whether the following conjecture is *true* or *false*. If false, provide a counterexample.

Subtraction of whole numbers is associative.

Write two subtraction expressions using the Associative Property, and then check to see whether they are equal.

$$9 - (5 - 3) \stackrel{?}{=} (9 - 5) - 3 \quad \text{State the conjecture.}$$
$$9 - 2 \stackrel{?}{=} 4 - 3 \quad \text{Simplify within the parentheses.}$$
$$7 \neq 1 \quad \text{Subtract.}$$

We found a counterexample. That is, $9 - (5 - 3) \neq (9 - 5) - 3$. So, subtraction is *not* associative. The conjecture is false.

SIMPLIFY ALGEBRAIC EXPRESSIONS To **simplify** algebraic expressions means to write them in a simpler form. You can use the Associative or Commutative Properties to simplify expressions.

Example 4 *Simplify Algebraic Expressions*

Simplify each expression.

a. $(k + 2) + 7$

$$(k + 2) + 7 = k + (2 + 7) \quad \text{Associative Property of Addition}$$
$$= k + 9 \quad \text{Substitution Property of Equality; } 2 + 7 = 9$$

b. $5 \cdot (d \cdot 9)$

$$5 \cdot (d \cdot 9) = 5 \cdot (9 \cdot d) \quad \text{Commutative Property of Multiplication}$$
$$= (5 \cdot 9)d \quad \text{Associative Property of Multiplication}$$
$$= 45d \quad \text{Substitution Property of Equality; } 5 \cdot 9 = 45$$

Study Tip

Inductive Reasoning
In inductive reasoning, conclusions are made based on past events or patterns.

Notice that each step in Example 4 was justified by a property. The process of using facts, properties, or rules to justify reasoning or reach valid conclusions is called **deductive reasoning**.

 www.pre-alg.com/extra_examples

Study Guide and Intervention, p. 16

In algebra, there are certain statements called **properties** that are true for any numbers.

Property	Explanations	Example
Commutative Property of Addition	$a + b = b + a$	$6 + 3 = 3 + 6$ $9 = 9$
Commutative Property of Multiplication	$a \cdot b = b \cdot a$	$4 \cdot 5 = 5 \cdot 4$ $20 = 20$
Associative Property of Addition	$(a + b) + c = a + (b + c)$	$(3 + 4) + 7 = 3 + (4 + 7)$ $14 = 14$
Associative Property of Multiplication	$(a \cdot b) \cdot c = a \cdot (b \cdot c)$	$(2 \cdot 5) \cdot 8 = 2 \cdot (5 \cdot 8)$ $80 = 80$
Additive Identity	$a + 0 = 0 + a = a$	$10 + 0 = 0 + 10 = 10$
Multiplicative Identity	$a \cdot 1 = 1 \cdot a = a$	$5 \cdot 1 = 1 \cdot 5 = 5$
Multiplicative Property of Zero	$a \cdot 0 = 0 \cdot a = 0$	$15 \cdot 0 = 0 \cdot 15 = 0$

Example Simplify $3 \cdot (x \cdot 5)$.

$3 \cdot (x \cdot 5) = 3 \cdot (5 \cdot x)$ Commutative Property of Multiplication
$= (3 \cdot 5) \cdot x$ Associative Property of Multiplication
$= 15 \cdot x$ Multiply 3 and 5.

Exercises

Name the property shown by each statement.

1. $75 + 25 = 25 + 75$
Commutative Property of Addition

2. $2 \cdot (3 \cdot 4) = (2 \cdot 3) \cdot 4$
Associative Property of Multiplication

3. $14 \cdot 1 = 14$
Multiplicative Identity

4. $p \cdot 0 = 0$
Multiplicative Property of Zero

5. $6 + (5 + m) = (6 + 5) + m$
Associative Property of Addition

6. $2(6) = 6(2)$
Commutative Property of Multiplication

Simplify each expression.

7. $24 + (x + 6)$ $30 + x$

8. $3 \cdot (4a)$ $12a$

9. $9 + (12 + c)$ $21 + c$

10. $13d \cdot 0$ 0

Skills Practice, p. 17 and Practice, p. 18 (shown)

Name the property shown by each statement.

1. $55 + 6 = 6 + 55$ Commutative Property of Addition

2. $6 \cdot 7 = 7 \cdot 6$ Commutative Property of Multiplication

3. $(x + 3) + y = x + (3 + y)$ Associative Property of Addition

4. $1 \cdot mp = mp$ Multiplicative Identity

5. $9 + (5 + 35) = (9 + 5) + 35$ Associative Property of Addition

6. $67 + 0 = 67$ Additive Identity

7. $7x \cdot 0 = 0$ Multiplicative Property of Zero

8. $4(3 \cdot z) = (4 \cdot 3)z$ Associative Property of Multiplication

Find each sum or product mentally.

9. $18 + 17 + 22$ 57

10. $12 + 15 + 8 + 5$ 40

11. $60 \cdot 4 \cdot 2$ 480

12. $49 \cdot 0 \cdot 16$ 0

13. $2 \cdot 157 \cdot 5$ 1570

14. $14 + 25 + 16$ 55

ALGEBRA Simplify each expression.

15. $(m + 11) + 19$ $m + 30$

16. $(9 \cdot b) \cdot 10$ $90 \cdot b$

17. $19 + (v + 8)$ $27 + v$

18. $(28 + 12) + x$ $40 + x$

19. $8s \cdot 0$ 0

20. $4 \cdot (r \cdot 5)$ $20r$

21. GEOMETRY The volume of a box is given by $V = \ell \cdot w \cdot h$ where ℓ = length, w = width, and h = height. Find the volume of a box if length is 25 cm, width is 13 cm, and height is 4 cm. $V = 25$ cm $\cdot 13$ cm $\cdot 4$ cm $= 25$ cm $\cdot 4$ cm $\cdot 13$ cm $= 1300$ cm³

22. SCHOOL In math class each assignment is worth 20 points. David got 17, 20, 19, and 13 points on his last four assignments. How many points did David score altogether? $17 + 20 + 19 + 13 = 17 + 13 + 20 + 19 = 69$ points

23. *True or false*: Multiplying any number by one produces the original number. Explain. True. The Multiplicative Identity states that any number times one is the original number.

Enrichment, p. 20

Algebraic Proof

Axioms are statements assumed to be true without being proven. They are used in the proofs of theorems. The following properties are examples of algebraic axioms. Abbreviations for these properties are used in the examples below.

Commutative Property of Addition (CPA)   Addition Property of Equality (APE)
Associative Property of Addition (APA)   Substitution Property of Equality (SPE)
Subtraction Property of Equality (SubPE)   Additive Identity Property (AIP)

Example 1 Prove: $a + (b + c) = c + (a + b)$

Statement	Reason
$a + (b + c) = (a + b) + c$	APA
$= c + (a + b)$	CPA

Example 2 Prove: $5 + (x + 2) = 7 + x$

Statement	Reason
$5 + (x + 2) = 5 + (2 + x)$	CPA
$= (5 + 2) + x$	APA
$= 7 + x$	SPE

Write the reason for each statement.

1. Prove: $(9 + 6) + (x + 3) = x + 18$

Statement	Reason
$(9 + 6) + (x + 3) = 15 + (x + 3)$	a. SPE
$= (15 + x) + 3$	b. APA
$= (x + 15) + 3$	c. CPA
$= x + (15 + 3)$	d. APA
$= x + 18$	e. SPE

Prove each of the following. Identify a reason for each statement.

2. $9 + (x + 4) = 13 + x$
$9 + (x + 4) = 9 + (4 + x)$ CPA
$= (9 + 4) + x$ APA
$= 13 + x$ SPE

3. $5 + (x + 11) = x + (10 + 6)$
$5 + (x + 11) = (x + 11) + 5$ CPA
$= x + (11 + 5)$ APA
$= x + 16$ SPE
$= x + (10 + 6)$ SPE

DAILY INTERVENTION

Differentiated Instruction

• **Interpersonal** Give students a mathematical conjecture (see Example 3). Ask them to work with a partner. One student tries to list examples to support the conjecture, the other student tries to list counterexamples. The pair will use their findings to determine whether the conjecture is true or false.

Have students—
- add the definitions/examples of the vocabulary terms to their Vocabulary Builder worksheets for Chapter 1.
- write down each property and a corresponding example.
- include any other item(s) that they find helpful in mastering the skills in this lesson.

Daily Intervention notes help you help students when they need it most.

DAILY
INTERVENTION **FIND THE ERROR**
You may need to discuss with students that Carlos's problem involves both addition and multiplication so the Associative Property does not apply.

About the Exercises . . .
Organization by Objective
- **Properties of Addition and Multiplication:** 14–25
- **Simplify Algebraic Expressions:** 26–34, 39–47

Odd/Even Assignments
Exercises 14–34 and 39–47 are structured so that students practice the same concepts whether they are assigned odd or even problems.

Assignment Guide
Basic: 15–21 odd, 27–45 odd, 48–65
Average: 15–47 odd, 48–65
Advanced: 14–46 even, 48–59 (Optional: 60–65)

Check for Understanding

Concept Check 1. **OPEN ENDED** Write a numerical sentence that illustrates the Commutative Property of Multiplication. **Sample answer: $3 \cdot 4 = 4 \cdot 3$**

2. **Tell** the difference between the Commutative and Associative Properties.

3. **FIND THE ERROR** Kimberly and Carlos are using the Associative Properties of Addition and Multiplication to rewrite expressions.

Kimberly	Carlos
$(4 + 3) + 6 = 4 + (3 + 6)$	$(2 + 7) \cdot 5 = 2 + (7 \cdot 5)$

Who is correct? Explain your reasoning. **2–3. See margin.**

Guided Practice

GUIDED PRACTICE KEY	
Exercises	Examples
4–6, 13	1
7–9	2
10	3
11, 12	4

Name the property shown by each statement.

4. $7 + 5 = 5 + 7$ **Comm. (+)**
5. $8 + 0 = 8$ **Identity (+)**
6. $8 \cdot 4 \cdot 13 = 4 \cdot 8 \cdot 13$ **Comm. (×)**

Find each sum or product mentally.

7. $13 + 8 + 7$ **28**
8. $6 \cdot 9 \cdot 5$ **270**
9. $8 + 11 + 22 + 4$ **45**

10. State whether the conjecture *division of whole numbers is commutative* is *true* or *false*. If false, provide a counterexample. **False, $4 \div 2 \neq 2 \div 4$.**

ALGEBRA **Simplify each expression.**

11. $6 + (n + 7)$ **$n + 13$**
12. $(3 \cdot w) \cdot 9$ **$27w$**

Application 13. **SHOPPING** Denyce purchased a pair of jeans for $26, a T-shirt for $12, and a pair of socks for $4. What is the total cost of the items? Explain how the Commutative Property of Addition can be used to find the total. **See margin.**

★ indicates increased difficulty

Practice and Apply

Homework Help	
For Exercises	See Examples
14–25	1
26–34	2
35–37	3
39–47	4
Extra Practice See page 725.	

Name the property shown by each statement. **14–25. See margin.**

14. $5 \cdot 3 = 3 \cdot 5$
15. $1 \cdot 4 = 4$
16. $6 \cdot 2 \cdot 0 = 0$
17. $12 \cdot 8 = 8 \cdot 12$
18. $0 + 13 = 13 + 0$
19. $(4 + 5) + 15 = 4 + (5 + 15)$
20. $1h = h$
21. $7k + 0 = 7k$
★ 22. $(5 + x) + 6 = 5 + (x + 6)$
★ 23. $4(mn) = (4m)(n)$
★ 24. $9(gh) = (9g)h$
★ 25. $(3a + b) + 2c = 2c + (3a + b)$

Find each sum or product mentally.

26. $11 + 8 + 19$ **38**
27. $17 + 5 + 33$ **55**
28. $15 \cdot 0 \cdot 2$ **0**
29. $5 + 18 + 15 + 2$ **40**
30. $2 \cdot 7 \cdot 30$ **420**
31. $11 \cdot 9 \cdot 10$ **990**
32. $23 + 3 + 17 + 7$ **50**
33. $125 \cdot 4 \cdot 0$ **0**
★ 34. $16 + 57 + 94 + 33$ **200**

State whether each conjecture is *true* or *false*. If false, provide a counterexample. **35–37. See margin.**

35. Division of whole numbers is associative.
36. The sum of two whole numbers is always greater than either addend.
37. Subtraction of whole numbers is commutative.

Answers

2. The Commutative Property states that the order in which numbers are added or multiplied does not change the sum or product. The Associative Property states that the way numbers are grouped when added or multiplied does not change the sum or product.

3. Kimberly; the Associative Property only holds true if all numbers are added or all numbers are multiplied, not a combination of the two.

38. SCIENCE In chemistry, water is used to dilute acid. Since pouring water into acid could cause spattering and burns, it's important to pour the acid into the water. Is combining acid and water commutative? Explain. **See margin.**

ALGEBRA Simplify each expression.

39. $(m + 8) + 4$ **m + 12**   **40.** $(17 + p) + 9$ **p + 26**   **41.** $15 + (12 + a)$ **a + 27**

42. $21 + (k + 16)$ **k + 37**   **43.** $6 \cdot (y \cdot 2)$ **12y**   **44.** $7 \cdot (d \cdot 4)$ **28d**

45. $(6 \cdot c) \cdot 8$ **48c**   **46.** $(3 \cdot w) \cdot 5$ **15w**   ★**47.** $25s(3)$ **75s**

48. CRITICAL THINKING The **Closure Property** states that because the sum or product of two whole numbers (0, 1, 2, 3, …) is also a whole number, the set of whole numbers is *closed* under addition and multiplication. Tell whether the set of whole numbers is closed under subtraction and division. If not, give counterexamples. **See margin.**

49. WRITING IN MATH Answer the question that was posed at the beginning of the lesson. **See pp. 53A–53B.**

How are real-life situations commutative?

Include the following in your answer:

• an example of a real-life situation that is commutative,
• an example of a real-life situation that is not commutative, and
• an explanation of why each situation is or is not commutative.

50. The statement $e + (f + g) = (f + g) + e$ is an example of which property of addition? **A**

   Ⓐ Commutative   Ⓑ Associative
   Ⓒ Identity   Ⓓ Substitution

51. Rewrite the expression $(7 \cdot m) \cdot 8$ using the Associative Property. **B**

   Ⓐ $(8 \cdot 7) \cdot m$ Ⓑ $7 \cdot (m \cdot 8)$
   Ⓒ $8 \cdot (7 \cdot m)$ Ⓓ $7 \cdot m \cdot 8$

Maintain Your Skills

Mixed Review **ALGEBRA** Evaluate each expression if $a = 6$, $b = 4$, and $c = 5$. *(Lesson 1-3)*

52. $a + c - b$ **7**   **53.** $8a - 3b$ **36**   **54.** $4a - (b + c)$ **15**

55. Translate the phrase *the difference of w and 12* into an algebraic expression. *(Lesson 1-3)* **w − 12**

Find the value of each expression. *(Lesson 1-2)*

56. $7 - 2 \times 3$ **1**   **57.** $21 \div 3 \times 5$ **35**   **58.** $4 \cdot (8 + 9) + 6$ **74**

59. Find the next two terms in the list 0, 1, 3, 6, 10, … *(Lesson 1-1)* **15, 21**

Getting Ready for the Next Lesson **BASIC SKILL** Find each product.

60. 48×5 **240**   **61.** 8×37 **296**   **62.** 16×12 **192**

63. 25×42 **1050**   **64.** 106×13 **1378**   **65.** 59×127 **7493**

Answers

13. $42; To find the total cost, add the three costs together. Since the order in which the costs are added does not matter, the Commutative Property of Addition holds true and makes the addition easier. By adding 4 and 26, the result is 30, and 30 + 12 is 42.

14. Commutative Property ($\times$)
15. Multiplicative Identity
16. Multiplicative Property of Zero
17. Commutative Property ($\times$)
18. Commutative Property ($+$)
19. Associative Property ($+$)

4 Assess

Open-Ended Assessment

Speaking Ask students to summarize at least two ways in which properties can help them perform tasks in mathematics. The explanation should include examples, and should identify which properties are used.

Getting Ready for Lesson 1-5

BASIC SKILL Lesson 1-5 presents variables and equations. A number next to a variable means multiply that variable by the number. Exercises 60–65 should be used to determine your students' familiarity with multiplication.

Assessment Options

Quiz (Lessons 1-3 and 1-4) is available on p. 51 of the *Chapter 1 Resource Masters*.

Mid-Chapter Test (Lessons 1-1 through 1-4) is available on p. 53 of the *Chapter 1 Resource Masters*.

Answers

20. Multiplicative Identity
21. Additive Identity
22. Associative Property ($+$)
23. Associative Property ($\times$)
24. Associative Property ($\times$)
25. Commutative Property ($+$)
35. false; $(100 \div 10) \div 2 \neq 100 \div (10 \div 2)$
36. false; $2 + 0 = 2$ and 2 is not greater than 2.
37. false; $9 - 3 = 3 - 9$
38. No; The acid can be poured into the water, but the water cannot be poured into the acid.
48. The set of whole numbers is not closed under subtraction and division. $2 - 3 = -1$ and -1 is not a whole number. $1 \div 2 = 0.5$ and 0.5 is not a whole number.

1-5 Variables and Equations

1 Focus

5-Minute Check Transparency 1-5 Use as a quiz or review of Lesson 1-4.

Mathematical Background notes are available for this lesson on page 4D.

How is solving an open sentence similar to evaluating an expression?

The opening activity questions are repeated on page 24 of the *Chapter 1 Resource Masters*.

Reading to Learn Mathematics, p. 24   ELL

Pre-Activity How is solving an open sentence similar to evaluating an expression?

Do the activity at the top of page 28 in your textbook. Write your answers below.

  a. If Rebecca is *x* years old, what expression represents Emilio's age?
    x + 7

  b. What two expressions are equal? *x* + 7 and 19

  c. If Emilio is 19, how old is Rebecca? 12

Reading the Lesson   1–4. See students' work.

Write a definition and give an example of each new vocabulary word or phrase.

Vocabulary	Definition	Example
1. equation		
2. open sentence		
3. solution		
4. solving the equation		

5. Complete this sentence. When the ___variable___ in an open sentence is replaced with a number, you can determine whether the sentence is true or false.

6. Consider *x* − 4 = 6. Find a value for *x* that makes the sentence true and another value that makes it false. If *x* = 10, the sentence is true; If *x* is any other value, the sentence is false.

Helping You Remember

7. Explain how an open sentence is different from an algebraic expression. An open sentence is an equation that contains a variable. Therefore, an open sentence has an equal sign. An algebraic expression does not.

What You'll Learn

- Identify and solve open sentences.
- Translate verbal sentences into equations.

Vocabulary
- equation
- open sentence
- solution
- solving the equation

How is solving an open sentence similar to evaluating an expression?

Emilio is seven years older than his sister Rebecca. **a.** *x* + 7

a. If Rebecca is *x* years old, what expression represents Emilio's age?

Suppose Emilio is 19 years old. You can write a mathematical sentence that shows two expressions are equal.

Words   Emilio's age is 19.

Symbols $x + 7 = 19$

b. What two expressions are equal? *x* + 7 and 19

c. If Emilio is 19, how old is Rebecca? 12

EQUATIONS AND OPEN SENTENCES
A mathematical sentence that contains an equals sign (=) is called an **equation**. A few examples are shown.

$$5 + 9 = 14 \qquad 2(6) - 3 = 9 \qquad x + 7 = 19 \qquad 2m - 1 = 13$$

An equation that contains a variable is an **open sentence**. An open sentence is neither true nor false. When the variable in an open sentence is replaced with a number, you can determine whether the sentence is true or false.

Study Tip

Symbols
The symbol ≠ means *is not equal to*.

$x + 7 = 19$
$11 + 7 \stackrel{?}{=} 19$ Replace *x* with 11.
$18 \neq 19$ false

When *x* = 11, this sentence is false.

$x + 7 = 19$
$12 + 7 \stackrel{?}{=} 19$ Replace *x* with 12.
$19 = 19$ true

When *x* = 12, this sentence is true.

A value for the variable that makes an equation true is called a **solution**. For $x + 7 = 19$, the solution is 12. The process of finding a solution is called **solving the equation**.

Example 1 Solve an Equation

Find the solution of $12 - m = 8$. Is it 2, 4, or 7?

Replace *m* with each value.

Value for *m*	12 − *m* = 8	True or False?
2	$12 - 2 \stackrel{?}{=} 8$	false
4	$12 - 4 \stackrel{?}{=} 8$	true ✓
7	$12 - 7 \stackrel{?}{=} 8$	false

Therefore, the solution of $12 - m = 8$ is 4.

Resource Manager

 Workbooks and Reproducible Masters

Chapter 1 Resource Masters
- Study Guide and Intervention, p. 21
- Skills Practice, p. 22
- Practice, p. 23
- Reading to Learn Mathematics, p. 24
- Enrichment, p. 25

Parent and Student Study Guide Workbook, p. 5
Prerequisite Skills Workbook, pp. 5–10
School-to-Career Masters, p. 2
Science and Mathematics Lab Manual, pp. 1–4

 Transparencies
5-Minute Check Transparency 1-5
Answer Key Transparencies

Technology
Interactive Chalkboard

Most standardized tests include questions that ask you to solve equations.

Example 2 *Solve an Equation*

Multiple-Choice Test Item

Which value is the solution of $2x + 1 = 7$?
- Ⓐ 6
- Ⓑ 5
- Ⓒ 4
- Ⓓ 3

Read the Test Item

The *solution* is the value that makes the equation true.

Solve the Test Item Test each value.

$2x + 1 = 7$
$2(6) + 1 = 7$ Replace x with 6.
$13 \neq 7$

$2x + 1 = 7$
$2(5) + 1 = 7$ Replace x with 5.
$11 \neq 7$

$2x + 1 = 7$
$2(4) + 1 = 7$ Replace x with 4.
$9 \neq 7$

$2x + 1 = 7$
$2(3) + 1 = 7$ Replace x with 3.
$7 = 7$ ✓

Since 3 makes the equation true, the answer is D.

> **Test-Taking Tip**
> The strategy of testing each value is called *backsolving*. You can also use this strategy with complex equations.

Example 3 *Solve Simple Equations Mentally*

Solve each equation mentally.

a. $5x = 30$

$5 \cdot 6 = 30$ Think: What number times 5 is 30?
$x = 6$ The solution is 6.

b. $\dfrac{72}{d} = 8$

$\dfrac{72}{9} = 8$ Think: 72 divided by what number is 8?
$d = 9$ The solution is 9.

In Lesson 1-4, you learned that certain properties are true for any number. Two properties of equality are shown below.

Key Concept			*Properties of Equality*
Property	**Words**	**Symbols**	**Example**
Symmetric	If one quantity equals a second quantity, then the second quantity also equals the first.	For any numbers a and b, if $a = b$, then $b = a$.	If $10 = 4 + 6$, then $4 + 6 = 10$.
Transitive	If one quantity equals a second quantity and the second quantity equals a third quantity, then the first equals the third.	For any numbers a, b, and c, if $a = b$ and $b = c$, then $a = c$.	If $3 + 5 = 8$ and $8 = 2(4)$, then $3 + 5 = 2(4)$.

 www.pre-alg.com/extra_examples

DAILY
INTERVENTION

Differentiated Instruction

- **Intrapersonal** Have students write in their journals a number of open sentences using all four operations in their samples. Then for each example they should write a question like that in the text to help them solve mentally ("What number times 2 is 10?"). Ask students to examine their equations and decide which operation is most difficult for them to do mentally. In their journals, they should describe a strategy to help themselves solve such problems more quickly.

---

2 Teach

EQUATIONS AND OPEN SENTENCES

Building on Prior Knowledge

In elementary school, students saw problems like □ + 5 = 8. Remind them that the box was the variable and discuss what processes they used to determine the number to put in the box.

In-Class Examples  Power Point®

1 Find the solution of $44 + p = 53$. Is it 11, 9, or 7?
9

2 **Multiple-Choice Test Item**
Which value is the solution of $4x - 1 = 11$? **C**

A 5 **B** 4 **C** 3 **D** 2

3 Solve each equation mentally.

a. $7x = 56$ **8**

b. $x - 15 = 40$ **55**

4 Name the property of equality shown by each statement.

a. If $3x + 1 = 10$, then $10 = 3x + 1$. **Symmetric Property of Equality**

b. If $z + 6 = 8$ and $8 = 2 + 6$, then $z + 6 = 2 + 6$.
Transitive Property of Equality

 Skills Check
Equations and Open Sentences Show the equation $4x + 1 = 25$. Ask students how they would determine if 5 is a solution. They should then do the problem. Students should explain their method, work through the problem, and state if 5 is the solution. They could even try to find the correct solution if 5 is incorrect. **The solution is not 5. The correct solution is 6.**

TRANSLATE VERBAL SENTENCES INTO EQUATIONS

5 The quotient of a number and four is nine. Find the number. $\frac{n}{4} = 9$; 36

Teaching Tip Emphasize to students that "is" most often translates to "equals" in mathematics problems.

3 Practice/Apply

Study Notebook

Have students—
• add the definitions/examples of the vocabulary terms to their Vocabulary Builder worksheets for Chapter 1.
• include any other item(s) that they find helpful in mastering the skills in this lesson.

About the Exercises . . .
Organization by Objective
• Equations and Open Sentences: 14–23, 26–47, 49, 55
• Translate Verbal Sentences into Equations: 42–48, 54

Odd/Even Assignments
Exercises 14–47 are structured so that students practice the same concepts whether they are assigned odd or even problems.

Assignment Guide
Basic: 15–47 odd, 48, 49, 51, 56–59, 61–73
Average: 15–47 odd, 48, 49, 51, 53, 56–59, 61–73 (Optional: 60)
Advanced: 14–46 even, 50, 52, 54–67 (Optional: 68–73)
All: Practice Quiz 2 (1–5)

Example 4 *Identify Properties of Equality*

Name the property of equality shown by each statement.

a. If $5 = x + 2$, then $x + 2 = 5$.

If $a = b$, then $b = a$. This is the Symmetric Property of Equality.

b. If $y + 8 = 15$ and $15 = 7 + 8$, then $y + 8 = 7 + 8$.

If $a = b$ and $b = c$, then $a = c$. This is the Transitive Property of Equality.

TRANSLATE VERBAL SENTENCES INTO EQUATIONS Just as verbal phrases can be translated into algebraic expressions, verbal sentences can be translated into equations and then solved.

Example 5 *Translate Sentences Into Equations*

The difference of a number and ten is seventeen. Find the number.

Words   The difference of a number and ten is seventeen.

Variables   Let n = the number.   Define the variable.

The difference of a number and ten	is	seventeen.

Equation $n - 10$ $=$ 17

$n - 10 = 17$ Write the equation.

$27 - 10 = 17$ Think: What number minus 10 is 17?

$n = 27$ The solution is 27.

Check for Understanding

Concept Check
1. **OPEN ENDED** Write two different equations whose solutions are 5.
2. **Tell** what it means to *solve an equation*. 1–2. **See margin.**

Guided Practice

ALGEBRA Find the solution of each equation from the list given.

3. $h + 15 = 21$; 5, <u>6</u>, 7

4. $13 - m = 4$; 7, 8, <u>9</u>

ALGEBRA Solve each equation mentally.

5. $a + 8 = 13$ 5

6. $12 - d = 9$ 3

7. $3x = 18$ 6

8. $4 = \frac{36}{t}$ 9

Name the property of equality shown by each statement.

9. If $x + 4 = 9$, then $9 = x + 4$. **Symmetric**

10. If $5 + 7 = 12$ and $12 = 3 \cdot 4$, then $5 + 7 = 3 \cdot 4$. **Transitive**

ALGEBRA Define a variable. Then write an equation and solve.

11. A number increased by 8 is 23. $n + 8 = 23$; 15

12. Twenty-five is 10 less than a number. $25 = d - 10$; 35

13. Find the value that makes $6 = \frac{48}{k}$ true. **C**

Ⓐ 6   Ⓑ 7   Ⓒ 8   Ⓓ 12

GUIDED PRACTICE KEY	
Exercises	Examples
3, 4	1
5–8	3
9, 10	4
11, 12	5
13	2

11. Let n = the number.
12. Let d = the number.

Standardized Test Practice
Ⓐ Ⓑ Ⓒ Ⓓ

Answers

1. Sample answer: $b + 7 = 12$ and $8 - h = 3$
2. To solve an equation, find a value for the variable that makes a true statement.

★ indicates increased difficulty

Homework Help

For Exercises	See Examples
14–23	1
26–41	3
42–49, 54, 55	5
50–53	4

Extra Practice
See page 725.

ALGEBRA Find the solution of each equation from the list given.

14. $c + 12 = 30$; 8, 16, <u>18</u>

15. $g + 17 = 28$; 9, <u>11</u>, 13

16. $23 - m = 14$; 7, <u>9</u>, 11

17. $18 - k = 6$; 8, 10, <u>12</u>

18. $14k = 42$; 2, <u>3</u>, 4

19. $75 = 15n$; 3, 4, <u>5</u>

20. $\frac{51}{z} = 3$; 15, 16, <u>17</u>

21. $\frac{60}{p} = 4$; <u>15</u>, 16, 17

22. What is the solution of $3n + 13 = 25$; 2, 3, <u>4</u>?

23. Find the solution of $7 = 4w - 29$. Is it 8, <u>9</u>, or 10?

Tell whether each sentence is *sometimes, always,* or *never* true.

24. An equation is an open sentence. **sometimes**

25. An open sentence contains a variable. **always**

ALGEBRA Solve each equation mentally.

26. $d + 7 = 12$ **5**   **27.** $19 = 4 + y$ **15**   **28.** $8 + j = 27$ **19**   **29.** $22 + b = 22$ **0**

30. $20 - p = 11$ **9**   **31.** $15 - m = 0$ **15**   **32.** $16 = x - 7$ **23**   **33.** $12 = y - 5$ **17**

34. $7s = 49$ **7**   **35.** $8c = 88$ **11**   **36.** $63 = 9h$ **7**   **37.** $72 = 8w$ **9**

38. $\frac{30}{r} = 3$ **10**   **39.** $\frac{24}{y} = 8$ **3**   **40.** $12 = \frac{36}{p}$ **3**   **41.** $14 = \frac{56}{d}$ **4**

ALGEBRA Define a variable. Then write an equation and solve.

42. The sum of 7 and a number is 23. $7 + k = 23$; **16**

43. A number minus 10 is 27. $h - 10 = 27$; **37**

44. Twenty-four is the product of 8 and a number. $24 = 8a$; **3**

45. The sum of 9 and a number is 36. $9 + w = 36$; **27**

46. The difference of a number and 12 is 54. $z - 12 = 54$; **66**

47. A number times 3 is 45. $3x = 45$; **15**
42–47. See margin for definitions.

MOVIE INDUSTRY For Exercises 48 and 49, use the following information.
Megan purchased movie tickets for herself and two friends. The cost was $24.

48. Define a variable. Then write an equation that can be used to find how much Megan paid for each ticket. **Let c = cost of each ticket; $3c = 24$.**

49. What was the cost of each ticket? **$8**

Name the property of equality shown by each statement.

50. If $2 + 3 = 5$ and $5 = 1 + 4$, then $2 + 3 = 1 + 4$. **Transitive**

51. If $3 + 4 = 7$ then $7 = 3 + 4$. **Symmetric**

★ **52.** If $(1 + 2) + 6 = 9$, then $9 = (1 + 2) + 6$. **Symmetric**

★ **53.** If $m + n = p$, then $p = m + n$. **Symmetric**

HEIGHT For Exercises 54 and 55, use the following information.
Sean grew from a height of 65 inches to a height of 68 inches.

54. Define a variable. Then write an equation that can be used to find the increase in height. **Let h = the increase in height; $65 + h = 68$**

55. How many inches did Sean grow? **3**

 www.pre-alg.com/self_check_quiz

Lesson 1-5 Variables and Equations **31**

More About. . .

Movie Industry
In 1990, the total number of indoor movie screens was about 22,000. Today, there are over 37,000 indoor movie screens and the number keeps rising.
Source: National Association of Theatre Owners

Answers

42. Let k = the number.

43. Let h = the number.

44. Let a = the number.

45. Let w = the number.

46. Let z = the number.

47. Let x = the number.

Every effort is made to show the Answers to exercises (1) on the reduced Student Edition page, or (2) in the margin of the Teacher Wraparound Edition. However, answers that do not fit in either of these places can be found in pages at the end of each chapter.

Lesson 1-5 Variables and Equations **31**

Open-Ended Assessment

Writing Have students prepare a quiz of five questions covering equations, open sentences, and translating verbal sentences. Each question must include instructions and an answer key with complete solutions. The questions can then be exchanged and practiced or collected and a class quiz can be compiled.

Getting Ready for Lesson 1-6

PREREQUISITE SKILL Lesson 1-6 presents ordered pairs and relations, which can often be described by algebraic expressions. Exercises 68–73 review evaluating expressions.

Assessment Options

Practice Quiz 2 The quiz provides students with a brief review of the concepts and skills in Lessons 1-4 and 1-5. Lesson numbers are given to the right of exercises or instruction lines so students can review concepts not yet mastered.

---

56. CRITICAL THINKING Write three different equations in which there is no solution that is a whole number. **See margin.**

57. WRITING IN MATH Answer the question that was posed at the beginning of the lesson. **See margin.**

How is solving an open sentence similar to evaluating an expression?
Include the following in your answer:
- an explanation of how to evaluate an expression, and
- an explanation of what makes an open sentence true.

Standardized Test Practice

58. Find the solution of $9m = 54$. **D**
Ⓐ 4   Ⓑ 7   Ⓒ 5   Ⓓ 6

59. Which value satisfies $2n - 5 = 19$? **B**
Ⓐ 11   Ⓑ 12   Ⓒ 13   Ⓓ 14

Extending the Lesson

60. The table shows equations that have one variable or two variables.

One Variable	Two Variables
$4 + x = 7$	$z + y = 7$
$3t = 24$	$ab = 24$
$s - 5 = 2$	$m - n = 2$

a. Find as many whole number solutions as you can for each equation. **See students' work.**

60b. See margin.

b. **Make a conjecture** about the relationship between the number of variables in equations like the ones above and the number of solutions.

Maintain Your Skills

Mixed Review **Simplify each expression.** *(Lesson 1-4)*
61. $16 + (7 + d)$ **23 + d**   **62.** $(4 \cdot p) \cdot 6$ **24p**

ALGEBRA Translate each phrase into an algebraic expression. *(Lesson 1-3)*
63. ten decreased by a number **10 − n**
64. the sum of three times a number and four **3n + 4**

Find the value of each expression. *(Lesson 1-2)*
65. $3 \cdot 7 - 2(1 + 4)$ **11**   **66.** $3[(17 - 7) - 2(3)]$ **12**

67. What is the next term in $67, 62, 57, 52, 47, ...$? *(Lesson 1-1)* **42**

Getting Ready for the Next Lesson **PREREQUISITE SKILL** Evaluate each expression for the given value.
*(To review **evaluating expressions**, see Lesson 1-5.)*
68. $4x; x = 3$ **12**   **69.** $3m; m = 6$ **18**   **70.** $2d; d = 8$ **16**
71. $5c; c = 10$ **50**   **72.** $8a; a = 9$ **72**   **73.** $6y; y = 15$ **90**

Practice Quiz 2   Lessons 1-4 and 1-5

Name the property shown by each statement. *(Lesson 1-4)*
1. $6 \cdot 1 = 6$ **Identity (×)**   **2.** $9 + 6 = 6 + 9$ **Comm. (+)**

3. Simplify $8 \cdot (h \cdot 3)$. *(Lesson 1-4)* **24h**

4. Find the solution of $2w - 6 = 14$. Is it 8, 10, or 12? *(Lesson 1-4)* **10**

5. Solve $72 = 9x$ mentally. *(Lesson 1-5)* **8**

Answers

56. Sample answer: $4a = 21; 7z = 3; 14 = 5g$

57. Sample answer: Once the variable(s) are replaced in the open sentence, the order of operations is used to find the value of the expression. Answers should include the following.

- To evaluate an expression, replace the variable(s) with the given values, and then find the value of the expression.
- To solve an open sentence, find the value of the variable that makes the sentence true.

60b. For equations like those in the table, an equation with one variable has one unique solution; an equation with more than one variable has more than one solution.

What You'll Learn

- Use ordered pairs to locate points.
- Use tables and graphs to represent relations.

Vocabulary

- coordinate system
- *y*-axis
- coordinate plane
- origin
- *x*-axis
- ordered pair
- *x*-coordinate
- *y*-coordinate
- graph
- relation
- domain
- range

How are ordered pairs used to graph real-life data?

Maria and Hiroshi are playing a game. The player who gets four Xs or Os in a row wins.

1st move Maria places an X at 1 over and 3 up.

2nd move Hiroshi places an O at 2 over and 2 up.

3rd move Maria places an X at 1 over and 1 up.

4th move Hiroshi places an O at 1 over and 2 up.

a. Where should Maria place an X now? Explain your reasoning.

b. Suppose (1, 2) represents 1 over and 2 up. How could you represent 3 over and 2 up? **(3, 2)**

c. How are (5, 1) and (1, 5) different?

d. Where is a good place to put the next O?

e. Work with a partner to finish the game. **See students' work.**

a. Sample answer: 3 over and 2 up; this move would block Hiroshi.

d. See students' work. It depends on where the third X is placed.

c. (5, 1) is 5 over and 1 up; (1, 5) is 1 over and 5 up.

ORDERED PAIRS In mathematics, a **coordinate system** is used to locate points. The coordinate system is formed by the intersection of two number lines that meet at right angles at their zero points.

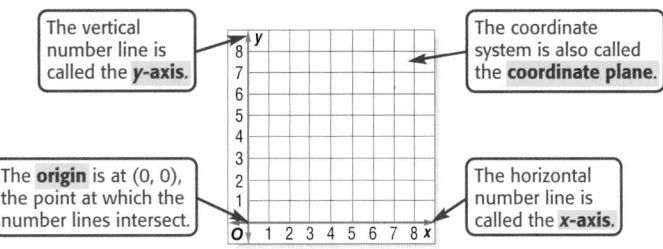

The vertical number line is called the **y-axis**.

The coordinate system is also called the **coordinate plane**.

The **origin** is at (0, 0), the point at which the number lines intersect.

The horizontal number line is called the **x-axis**.

An **ordered pair** of numbers is used to locate any point on a coordinate plane. The first number is called the **x-coordinate**. The second number is called the **y-coordinate**.

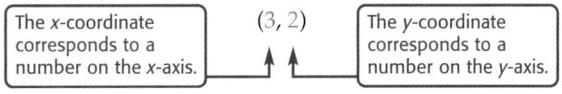

The *x*-coordinate corresponds to a number on the *x*-axis.

(3, 2)

The *y*-coordinate corresponds to a number on the *y*-axis.

1 Focus

5-Minute Check Transparency 1-6 Use as a quiz or review of Lesson 1-5.

Mathematical Background notes are available for this lesson on page 4D.

How are ordered pairs used to graph real-life data?

The opening activity questions are repeated on page 29 of the *Chapter 1 Resource Masters*.

Reading to Learn Mathematics, p. 29 — ELL

Pre-Activity How are ordered pairs used to graph real-life data?

Do the activity at the top of page 33 in your textbook. Write your answers below.

a. Where should Maria place an X now? Explain your reasoning. Sample answer: 3 over and 2 up; this move would block Hiroshi.

b. Suppose (1, 2) represents 1 over and 2 up. How could you represent 3 over and 2 up? (3, 2)

c. How are (5, 1) and (1, 5) different? (5, 1) is 5 over and 1 up; (1, 5) is 1 over and 5 up.

d. Where is a good place to put the next O? It depends on where the next X is placed.

e. Work with a partner to finish the game. See students' work.

Reading the Lesson 1–12. See students' work.

Write a definition and give an example of each new vocabulary word or phrase.

Vocabulary	Definition	Example
1. coordinate system		
2. *y*-axis		
3. coordinate plane		
4. origin		
5. *x*-axis		
6. ordered pair		
7. *x*-coordinate		
8. *y*-coordinate		
9. graph		
10. relation		
11. domain		
12. range		

Teaching Tip Remind students that the starting position is 0, not 1. You must move over a place to reach 1.

Resource Manager

Workbooks and Reproducible Masters

Chapter 1 Resource Masters

- Study Guide and Intervention, p. 26
- Skills Practice, p. 27
- Practice, p. 28
- Reading to Learn Mathematics, p. 29
- Enrichment, p. 30
- Assessment, p. 52

Parent and Student Study Guide Workbook, p. 6

Transparencies

5-Minute Check Transparency 1-6
Answer Key Transparencies

Technology

Interactive Chalkboard

ORDERED PAIRS

1 Graph each ordered pair on a coordinate system.

a. (3, 4)   **b.** (0, 2)

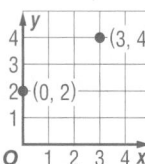

2 Write the ordered pair that names each point.

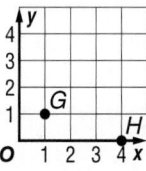

a. G   (1, 1)

b. H   (4, 0)

Study Tip

Coordinate System
You can assume that each unit on the *x*- and *y*-axis represents 1 unit. *Axes* is the plural of *axis*.

Study Tips offer students helpful information about the topics they are studying.

To **graph** an ordered pair, draw a dot at the point that corresponds to the ordered pair. The coordinates are your directions to locate the point.

Example 1 *Graph Ordered Pairs*

Graph each ordered pair on a coordinate system.

a. (4, 1)

Step 1	Start at the origin.
Step 2	Since the *x*-coordinate is 4, move 4 units to the right.
Step 3	Since the *y*-coordinate is 1, move 1 unit up. Draw a dot.

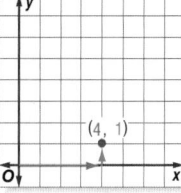

b. (3, 0)

Step 1	Start at the origin.
Step 2	The *x*-coordinate is 3. So, move 3 units to the right.
Step 3	Since the *y*-coordinate is 0, you will not need to move up. Place the dot on the axis.

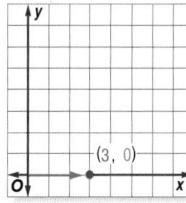

☑ **Concept Check** Where is the graph of (0, 4) located? **4 units up on the *y*-axis**

Sometimes a point on a graph is named by using a letter. To identify its location, you can write the ordered pair that represents the point.

Example 2 *Identify Ordered Pairs*

Write the ordered pair that names each point.

a. *M*

Step 1	Start at the origin.
Step 2	Move right on the *x*-axis to find the *x*-coordinate of point *M*, which is 2.
Step 3	Move up the *y*-axis to find the *y*-coordinate, which is 5.

The ordered pair for point *M* is (2, 5).

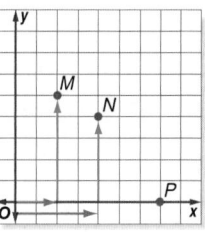

b. *N*

The *x*-coordinate of *N* is 4, and the *y*-coordinate is 4.

The ordered pair for point *N* is (4, 4).

c. *P*

The *x*-coordinate of *P* is 7, and the *y*-coordinate is 0.

The ordered pair for point *P* is (7, 0).

Differentiated Instruction suggestions are keyed to eight commonly-accepted learning styles.

D A I L Y
INTERVENTION   **Differentiated Instruction**

• **Kinesthetic** Use masking tape to mark an *x*-axis and *y*-axis on the floor. Make up cards with ordered pairs. Give each of several students a card and ask them to start at the origin and walk to the location of their point. Make sure they follow the over, up procedure.

RELATIONS A set of ordered pairs such as {(1, 2), (2, 4), (3, 0), (4, 5)} is a **relation**. The **domain** of the relation is the set of *x*-coordinates. The **range** of the relation is the set of *y*-coordinates.

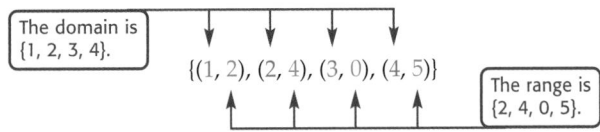

The domain is {1, 2, 3, 4}.

{(1, 2), (2, 4), (3, 0), (4, 5)}

The range is {2, 4, 0, 5}.

A relation can be shown in several ways.

Ordered Pairs	Table		Graph
(1, 2)	**x**	**y**	
(2, 4)	1	2	
(3, 0)	2	4	
(4, 5)	3	0	
	4	5	

Example 3 *Relations as Tables and Graphs*

Express the relation {(0, 0), (2, 1), (1, 3), (5, 2)} as a table and as a graph. Then determine the domain and range.

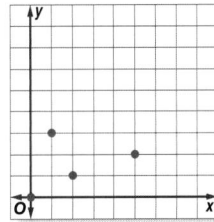

x	y
0	0
2	1
1	3
5	2

The domain is {0, 2, 1, 5}, and the range is {0, 1, 3, 2}.

Example 4 *Apply Relations*

PLANTS Some species of bamboo grow 3 feet in one day.

a. Make a table of ordered pairs in which the *x*-coordinate represents the number of days and the *y*-coordinate represents the amount of growth for 1, 2, 3, and 4 days.

x	y	(x, y)
1	3	(1, 3)
2	6	(2, 6)
3	9	(3, 9)
4	12	(4, 12)

b. Graph the ordered pairs.

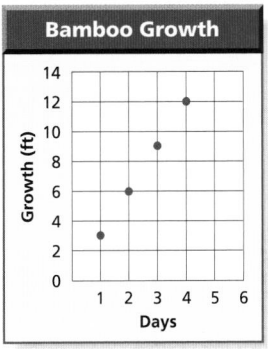

Bamboo Growth

c. Describe the graph.
The points appear to fall in a line.

www.pre-alg.com/extra_examples

Lesson 1-6 Ordered Pairs and Relations **35**

---

3 Express the relation {(1, 4), (2, 2), (3, 0), (0, 2)} as a table and as a graph. Then determine the domain and range. D = {0, 1, 2, 3}, R = {0, 2, 4}

x	y
1	4
2	2
3	0
0	2

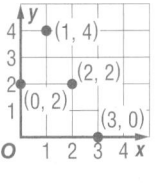

4 **EARNINGS** Austin earns $5 an hour doing yard work. Suppose *x* represents the number of hours Austin works.

a. Make a table of ordered pairs in which the *x*-coordinate represents the hours worked and *y* represents the amount of money Austin earns for 1, 2, 3, 4, and 5 hours of work.

x	y
1	5
2	10
3	15
4	20
5	25

b. Graph the ordered pairs.

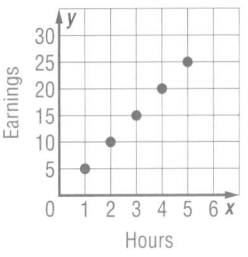

c. Describe the graph. The points fall in a line.

Teacher to Teacher

Rhonda Bailey   Mathematics Consultant, Richardson, TX

"We practice graphing points by playing tic-tac-toe on an overhead-projected coordinate plane. Use two different colors of overhead counters. Students take turns calling out ordered pairs (counters) to be graphed. The first team to get 4 of their counters in a row wins the game. Play the best 2 out of 3."

3 **Practice/Apply**

Study Notebook

Have students—
- add the definitions/examples of the vocabulary terms to their Vocabulary Builder worksheets for Chapter 1.
- draw and label a coordinate plane as shown on page 33.
- include any other item(s) that they find helpful in mastering the skills in this lesson.

About the Exercises . . .

Organization by Objective
- **Ordered Pairs:** 12–24
- **Relations:** 26–42

Odd/Even Assignments
Exercises 12–23 and 31–36 are structured so that students practice the same concepts whether they are assigned odd or even problems.

Assignment Guide

Basic: 13–23 odd, 26–30, 31–35 odd, 37–39, 44, 45, 47, 48, 50–65

Average: 13–25 odd, 26–30, 31–35 odd, 37–39, 44, 45, 47, 48, 50–65 (Optional: 49)

Advanced: 12–24 even, 32–36 even, 40–57 (Optional: 58–65)

Check for Understanding

Concept Check

1. **OPEN ENDED** Give an example of an ordered pair, and identify the x- and y-coordinate. **See margin.**

2. **Name** three ways to represent a relation. **ordered pairs, table, graph**

3. **Define** *domain* and *range*. **See margin.**

Guided Practice

GUIDED PRACTICE KEY	
Exercises	Examples
4, 5	1
6, 7	2
8, 9	3
10, 11	4

Graph each point on a coordinate system.

4. $H(5, 3)$ 5. $D(6, 0)$
4–5. See margin.

Refer to the coordinate system shown at the right. Write the ordered pair that names each point.

6. Q (2, 3)   7. P (6, 5)

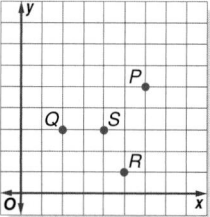

Express each relation as a table and as a graph. Then determine the domain and range. **8–9. See pp. 53A–53B.**

8. {(2, 5), (0, 2), (5, 5)}   9. {(1, 6), (6, 4), (0, 2), (3, 1)}

Application

ENTERTAINMENT For Exercises 10 and 11, use the following information. It costs $4 to buy a student ticket to the movies. **10–11. See pp. 53A–53B.**

10. Make a table of ordered pairs in which the x-coordinate represents the number of student tickets and the y-coordinate represents the cost for 2, 4, and 5 tickets.

11. Graph the ordered pairs (number of tickets, cost).

★ indicates increased difficulty

Practice and Apply

Homework Help	
For Exercises	See Examples
12–17	1
18–23	2
26–30, 37–43	4
31–36	3

Extra Practice
See page 725.

Graph each point on a coordinate system. **12–17. See pp. 53A–53B.**

12. $A(3, 3)$ 13. $D(1, 8)$ 14. $G(2, 7)$
15. $X(7, 2)$ 16. $P(0, 6)$ 17. $N(4, 0)$

Refer to the coordinate system shown at the right. Write the ordered pair that names each point.

18. C (1, 7)   19. J (7, 3)
20. N (0, 4)   21. T (6, 6)
22. Y (2, 1)   23. B (3, 4)

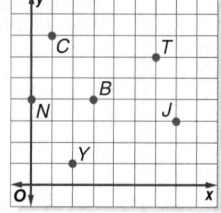

24. What point lies on both the x-axis and y-axis? (0, 0)

★ 25. Where are all of the possible locations for the graph of (x, y) if $y = 0$?, if $x = 0$? **on the x-axis; on the y-axis**

SCIENCE   For Exercises 26 and 27, use the following information. The average speed of a house mouse is 12 feet per second.
Source: *Natural History Magazine*

26. Find the distance traveled in 3, 5, and 7 seconds.

27. Graph the ordered pairs (time, distance). **26–27. See pp. 53A–53B.**

Answers

1. Sample answer: (3, 5); the x-coordinate is 3, and the y-coordinate is 5.

3. The domain of a relation is the set of x-coordinates. The range is the set of y-coordinates.

4.
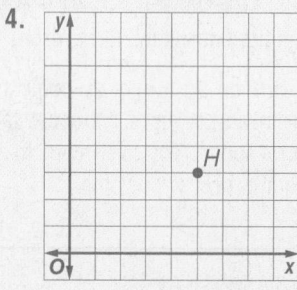

5.
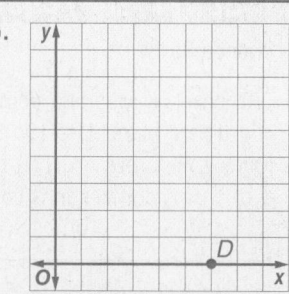

SCIENCE For Exercises 28–30, use the following information.
Keyson is conducting a physics experiment. He drops a tennis ball from a height of 100 centimeters and then records the height after each bounce. The results are shown in the table. 28–30. See pp. 53A–53B.

Bounce	0	1	2	3	4
Height (cm)	100	50	25	13	6

28. Write a set of ordered pairs for the data.

29. Graph the data.

30. How high do you think the ball will bounce on the fifth bounce? Explain.

Express each relation as a table and as a graph. Then determine the domain and range. 31–36. See pp. 53A–53B.

31. {(4, 5), (5, 2), (1, 6)}

32. {(6, 8), (2, 9), (0, 1)}

33. {(7, 0), (3, 2), (4, 4), (5, 1)}

34. {(2, 4), (1, 3), (5, 6), (1, 1)}

35. {(0, 1), (0, 3), (0, 5), (2, 0)}

36. {(4, 3), (3, 4), (1, 2), (2, 1)}

AIR PRESSURE For Exercises 37–39, use the table and the following information.
The air pressure decreases as the distance from Earth increases. The table shows the air pressure for certain distances.

Height (mi)	Pressure (lb/in²)
sea level	14.7
1	10.2
2	6.4
3	4.3
4	2.7
5	1.6

37. (0, 14.7), (1, 10.2), (2, 6.4), (3, 4.3), (4, 2.7), (5, 1.6)

37. Write a set of ordered pairs for the data.

38. Graph the data. See pp. 53A–53B.

39. State the domain and the range of the relation.
domain = {0, 1, 2, 3, 4, 5}; range = {14.7, 10.2, 6.4, 4.3, 2.7, 1.6}

⋯• **SCIENCE** For Exercises 40–43, use the following information and the
★ information at the left. 40–43. See pp. 53A–53B.
Water boils at sea level at 100°C. The boiling point of water decreases about 5°C for every mile above sea level.

40. Make a table that shows the boiling point at sea level and at 1, 2, 3, 4, and 5 miles above sea level.

41. Show the data as a set of ordered pairs.

42. Graph the ordered pairs.

43. At about what temperature does water boil in Albuquerque, New Mexico? in Alpine, Texas? (*Hint*: 1 mile = 5280 feet)

44. CRITICAL THINKING Where are all of the possible locations for the graph of (x, y) if $x = 4$? the vertical line where $x = 4$

45. WRITING IN MATH   Answer the question that was posed at the beginning of the lesson. See margin.

How are ordered pairs used to graph real-life data?

Include the following in your answer:

• an explanation of how an ordered pair identifies a specific point on a graph, and

• an example of a situation where ordered pairs are used to graph data.

www.pre-alg.com/self_check_quiz   Lesson 1-6   Ordered Pairs and Relations   **37**

More About. . .

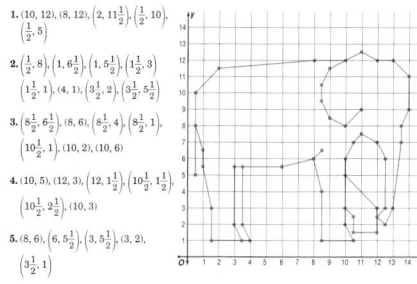

Science •⋯⋯⋯⋯⋯

Albuquerque, New Mexico, is at 7200 feet above sea level. Alpine, Texas, is at 4490 feet above sea level.
Source: *The World Almanac*

Answer

45. Ordered pairs can be used to graph real-life data by expressing the data as ordered pairs and then graphing the ordered pairs. Answers should include the following.

• The *x*- and *y*-coordinate of an ordered pair specifies the point on the graph.

• longitude and latitude lines

Study Guide and Intervention, p. 26

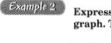
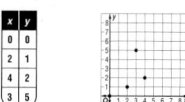

In mathematics, a **coordinate system** is used to locate points. The horizontal number line is called the **x-axis** and the vertical number line is called the **y-axis**. The point where the two axes intersect is the **origin** (0, 0). An **ordered pair** of numbers is used to locate points in the coordinate plane. The point (4, 3) has an **x-coordinate** of 4 and a **y-coordinate** of 3.

Example 1 Graph A(4, 3) on the coordinate system.
Step 1   Start at the origin.
Step 2   Since the x-coordinate is 4, move 4 units to the right.
Step 3   Since the y-coordinate is 3, move 3 units up. Draw a dot.

A set of ordered pairs is called a **relation**. The set of x-coordinates is called the **domain**. The set of y-coordinates is called the **range**.

Example 2 Express the relation {(0, 0), (2, 1), (4, 2), (3, 5)} as a table and as a graph. Then determine the domain and range.

The domain is {0, 2, 4, 3}, and the range is {0, 1, 2, 5}.

Exercises

Graph each point on the coordinate system.

1. A(4,1)   2. B(2,0)
3. C(1,3)   4. D(5,2)
5. E(0,3)   6. F(6,4)

7. Express the relation {(4,6), (0,3), (1,4)} as a table and a graph. Then determine the domain and range.   domain: {4, 0, 1}, range: {6, 3, 4}

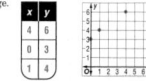

Skills Practice, p. 27 and Practice, p. 28 (shown)

Graph each point on the coordinate system.

1. Q(4, 2)   2. V(3, 7)
3. T(0, 3)   4. B(8, 6)
5. R(5, 0)   6. L(4, 4)

Write the ordered pair that names each point.

7. J (4, 1)   8. X (0, 7)
9. R (2, 2)   10. B (8, 5)
11. K (3, 4)   12. H (8, 0)
13. D (1, 6)   14. N (7, 3)

Express each relation as a table and as a graph. Then determine the domain and range.

15. {(3, 7), (1, 1), (6, 5), (2, 4)}   16. {(0, 2), (4, 6), (3, 7)}

domain = {3, 1, 6, 2}   domain = {0, 4, 3}
range = {7, 1, 5, 4}   range = {2, 6, 7}

17. **GEOMETRY** Graph (2, 1), (2, 4), and (5,1) on the coordinate system.
    a. Connect the points with line segments. What figure is formed?
       a right triangle
    b. Multiply each number in the set of ordered pairs by 2. Graph and connect the new ordered pairs. What figure is formed?
       a right triangle
    c. Compare the two figures you drew. Write a sentence that tells how the figures are the same and how they are different.
       Sample answer: Both figures are right triangles, but one is twice as large as the other.

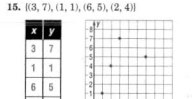
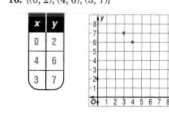
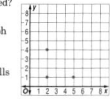

Enrichment, p. 30

The Hidden Animal

Graph the following sets of points. Join successive points by a line segment. Begin a new line segment with each numbered set of ordered pairs. When you finish, you will have a picture of an animal.

1. (10, 12), (8, 12), $\left(2, 11\frac{1}{2}\right)$, $\left(\frac{1}{2}, 10\right)$, $\left(\frac{1}{2}, 5\right)$

2. $\left(\frac{1}{2}, 8\right)$, $\left(1, 6\frac{1}{2}\right)$, $\left(1, 5\frac{1}{2}\right)$, $\left(1\frac{1}{2}, 3\right)$, $\left(1\frac{1}{2}, 1\right)$, (4, 1), $\left(3\frac{1}{2}, 2\right)$, $\left(3\frac{1}{2}, 5\frac{1}{2}\right)$

3. $\left(8\frac{1}{2}, 6\frac{1}{2}\right)$, (8, 6), $\left(8\frac{1}{2}, 4\right)$, $\left(8\frac{1}{2}, 1\right)$, $\left(10\frac{1}{2}, 1\right)$, (10, 2), (10, 6)

4. (10, 5), (12, 3), $\left(12, 1\frac{1}{2}\right)$, $\left(10\frac{1}{2}, 1\frac{1}{2}\right)$, $\left(10\frac{1}{2}, 2\frac{1}{2}\right)$, (10, 3)

5. (8, 6), $\left(6, 5\frac{1}{2}\right)$, $\left(3, 5\frac{1}{2}\right)$, (3, 2), $\left(3\frac{1}{2}, 1\right)$

6. (12, 12), $\left(11, 12\frac{1}{2}\right)$, $\left(9, 11\frac{1}{2}\right)$, $\left(8\frac{1}{2}, 10\frac{1}{2}\right)$, $\left(8\frac{1}{2}, 9\frac{1}{2}\right)$, $\left(9, 8\frac{1}{2}\right)$, (10, 8), (11, 9)

7. (12, 12), (13, 12), (14, 11), (14, 9), $\left(13\frac{1}{2}, 8\right)$, $\left(13\frac{1}{2}, 7\right)$, (13, 3), $\left(12\frac{1}{2}, 2\right)$, $\left(12, 2\frac{1}{2}\right)$, $\left(12\frac{1}{2}, 3\right)$, $\left(12\frac{1}{2}, 6\right)$, (12, 7), $\left(11, 7\frac{1}{2}\right)$, $\left(10\frac{1}{2}, 7\right)$, (10, 6)

8. Suppose you multiply both coordinates of each ordered pair by 2 and graph the resulting pairs on graph paper using the same scale on the axes as for the drawing above. How would the drawings compare?   Each segment in the new figure would be twice as long.

Open-Ended Assessment

Speaking Ask students to explain how to set up a coordinate plane and locate the points of a given relation. Encourage students to use as many vocabulary words from this section of the textbook as possible.

Getting Ready for Lesson 1-7

BASIC SKILL Exercises 58–65 review finding a quotient. These exercises continue to review basic operations necessary for working with algebraic expressions.

Assessment Options

Quiz (Lessons 1-5 and 1-6) is available on p. 52 of the *Chapter 1 Resource Masters*.

Answers

46a.

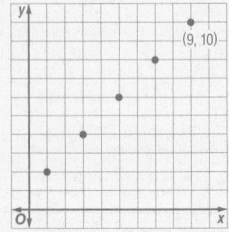

(9, 10)

46b.

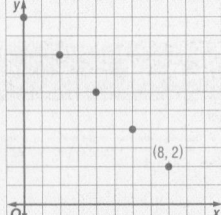

(8, 2)

49a.

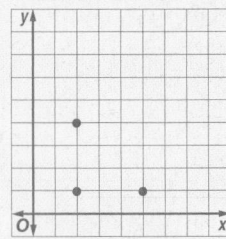

49e. The figures have the same shape but not the same size.

★ **46.** Graph each relation on a coordinate system. Then find the coordinates of another point that follows the pattern in the graph. **46a–b. See margin.**

a.

x	1	3	5	7
y	2	4	6	8

b.

x	0	2	4	6
y	10	8	6	4

Standardized Test Practice
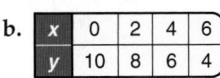

47. State the domain of the relation shown in the graph. **D**

Ⓐ {0, 1, 4, 5, 8}

Ⓑ {A, G, P, S, Z}

Ⓒ {0, 1, 2, 4, 5}

Ⓓ {1, 2, 5, 6, 7}

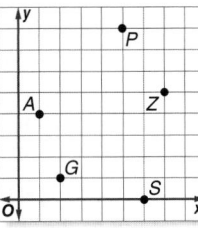

48. What relationship exists between the *x*- and *y*-coordinates of each of the data points shown on the graph? **D**

Ⓐ The *y*-coordinate varies, and the *x*-coordinate is always 4.

Ⓑ The *y*-coordinate is 4 more than the *x*-coordinate.

Ⓒ The sum of the *x*- and *y*-coordinate is always 4.

Ⓓ The *x*-coordinate varies, and the *y*-coordinate is always 4.

Extending the Lesson

49. Draw a coordinate grid. **49b. triangle** **49c. (4, 2), (4, 8), (10, 2)**

a. Graph (2, 1), (2, 4), and (5, 1). **See margin.**

b. Connect the points with line segments. Describe the figure formed.

c. Multiply each coordinate in the set of ordered pairs by 2.

d. Graph the new ordered pairs. Connect the points with line segments. What figure is formed? **triangle**

e. **MAKE A CONJECTURE** How do the figures compare? Write a sentence explaining the similarities and differences of the figures. **See margin.**

Maintain Your Skills

Mixed Review **ALGEBRA** Solve each equation mentally. *(Lesson 1-5)*

50. $a + 6 = 17$ **11**

51. $7t = 42$ **6**

52. $\frac{54}{n} = 6$ **9**

53. Name the property shown by $4 \cdot 1 = 4$. *(Lesson 1-4)* **Multiplicative Identity**

ALGEBRA Evaluate each expression if $a = 5$, $b = 1$, and $c = 3$. *(Lesson 1-3)*

54. $ca - cb$ **12**

55. $5a - 6c$ **7**

Write a numerical expression for each verbal phrase. *(Lesson 1-2)*

56. fifteen less than twenty-one
$21 - 15$

57. the product of ten and thirty
$10 \cdot 30$

Getting Ready for the Next Lesson **BASIC SKILL** Find each quotient.

58. $74 \div 2$ **37**

59. $96 \div 8$ **12**

60. $102 \div 3$ **34**

61. $112 \div 4$ **28**

62. $80 \div 16$ **5**

63. $91 \div 13$ **7**

64. $132 \div 22$ **6**

65. $153 \div 17$ **9**

Algebra Activity

Scatter Plots

Sometimes, it is difficult to determine whether a relationship exists between two sets of data by simply looking at them. To determine whether a relationship exists, we can write the data as a set of ordered pairs and then graph the ordered pairs on a coordinate system.

Collect the Data

Let's investigate whether a relationship exists between height and arm span.

Step 1 Work with a partner. Use a centimeter ruler to measure the length of your partner's height and arm span to the nearest centimeter. Record the data in a table like the one shown.

Name	Height (cm)	Arm Span (cm)

Step 2 Extend the table. Combine your data with that of your classmates.

Step 3 Make a list of ordered pairs in which the *x*-coordinate represents height and the *y*-coordinate represents arm span.

Step 4 Draw a coordinate grid like the one shown and graph the ordered pairs (height, arm span).

Analyze the Data

1. Does there appear to be a trend in the data? If so, describe the trend.
   Yes; as height increases, arm span increases.

Make a Conjecture 2–4. See margin.

2. Estimate the arm span of a person whose height is 60 inches. 72 inches.

3. How does a person's arm span compare to his or her height?

4. Suppose the variable *x* represents height, and the variable *y* represents arm span. Write an expression for arm span.

Extend the Activity

5. Collect and graph data to determine whether a relationship exists between height and shoe length. Explain your results. **See margin.**

Resource Manager

📁 **Teaching Pre-Algebra with Manipulatives**

- p. 1 (master for grid paper)
- p. 22 (rulers)
- p. 33 (student recording sheet)

Glencoe Mathematics Classroom Manipulative Kit

- centimeter rulers
- tape measures

Algebra Activity

Getting Started

Objective Use a scatter plot to investigate the relationship between two sets of data, height and arm span.

Materials
grid paper
centimeter ruler or tape measure

Teach

- Make sure students under-stand how to measure arm span. With arms outstretched, measure the distance from the tips of the middle fingers.
- As students look for trends in the data, ask them to discuss any points that may not follow the trend.

Assess

In **Exercises 1–4**, students should

- discover that height and arm span are somewhat equal.
- make up a problem about how the relationship between height and shoe length can be used by a detective. Then solve the problem.

Answers

2. about 60 inches; about 72 inches

3. A person's arm span is about equal to his/her height.

4. $y = x$

5. See student's work; generally, as height increases, shoe length increases.

1 Focus

Mathematical Background notes are available for this lesson on page 4D.

How can scatter plots help spot trends?

The opening activity questions are repeated on page 34 of the *Chapter 1 Resource Masters*.

Reading to Learn Mathematics, p. 34   ELL

Pre-Activity   *How can scatter plots help spot trends?*

Do the activity at the top of page 40 in your textbook. Write your answers below.

  a. What appears to be the trend in sales of movies on videocassette?
    Sample answer: Consumers are buying less movies on videocassette.

  b. Estimate the number of movies on videocassette sold for 2003.   about 40

Reading the Lesson

Write a definition and give an example of the new vocabulary term.

Vocabulary	Definition	Example
1. scatter plot	See students' work.	

Helping You Remember

2. Scatter plots are used to show relationships.

  a. For a positive relationship, as *x* increases, *y* __increases__ .

  b. For a negative relationship, as *x* increases, *y* __decreases__ .

3. The scatter plot compares the weights and heights of the players on a high school football team.

Heights of Football Players

a. What type of relationship exists, if any?   In general, as the heights of the players increase, so do the weights. The scatter plot shows a positive relationship.

b. Based on the scatter plot, predict the weight of a 5' 5" player who decided to join the team.   approximately 145 pounds

Teaching Tip Make sure students understand how to set up the scale on the axes using equal increments along each axis. The two axes need not have the same scale.

Resource Manager

📁 **Workbooks and Reproducible Masters**

Chapter 1 Resource Masters
• Study Guide and Intervention, p. 31
• Skills Practice, p. 32
• Practice, p. 33
• Reading to Learn Mathematics, p. 34
• Enrichment, p. 35
• Assessment, p. 52

Graphing Calculator and Spreadsheet Masters, pp. 20, 45
Parent and Student Study Guide Workbook, p. 7

📀 **Transparencies**
5-Minute Check Transparency 1-7
Real-World Transparency 1
Answer Key Transparencies

⚙ **Technology**
Interactive Chalkboard

1-7 Scatter Plots

What You'll Learn

• Construct scatter plots.
• Interpret scatter plots.

Vocabulary
• scatter plot

How can scatter plots help spot trends?

Suppose you work in the video department of a home entertainment store. The number of movies on videocassettes you have sold in a five-year period is shown in the graph.

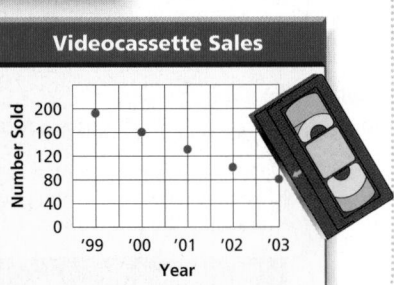

Videocassette Sales

a. What appears to be the trend in sales of movies on videocassette?

b. Estimate the number of movies on videocassette sold for 2005.

a. Sample answer: Consumers are buying less movies on videocassette.
b. about 40

TEACHING TIP
Ask students why they think the sales of videocassettes have fallen.

CONSTRUCT SCATTER PLOTS   A scatter plot is a graph that shows the relationship between two sets of data. In a scatter plot, two sets of data are graphed as ordered pairs on a coordinate system.

Example 1 *Construct a Scatter Plot*

TEST SCORES   The table shows the average SAT math scores from 1993–2002. Make a scatter plot of the data.

Year	'93	'94	'95	'96	'97	'98	'99	'00	'01	'02
Score	503	504	506	508	511	512	511	514	514	516

Source: *The College Board*

Let the horizontal axis, or *x*-axis, represent the year. Let the vertical axis, or *y*-axis, represent the score. Then graph ordered pairs (year, score).

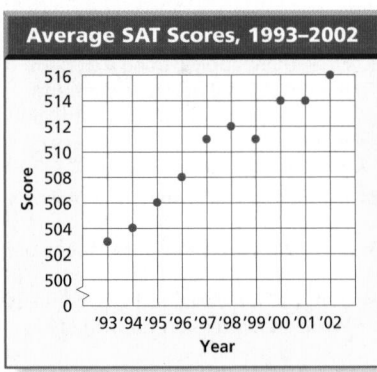

Average SAT Scores, 1993–2002

✓ **Concept Check**   *True* or *false*: A scatter plot represents one set of data. Explain.
False; it shows two sets of data.

INTERPRET SCATTER PLOTS The following scatter plots show the types of relationships or patterns of two sets of data.

Concept Summary — Types of Relationships

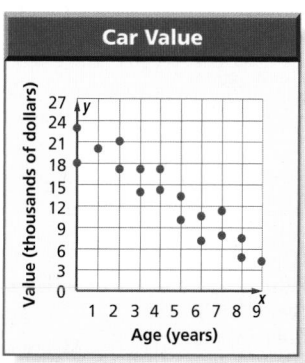

Positive Relationship

As x increases, y increases.

Negative Relationship

As x increases, y decreases.

No Relationship

No obvious pattern.

✓ **Concept Check** What type of relationship is shown on a graph that shows as the values of x increase, the values of y decrease? **negative**

Example 2 Interpret Scatter Plots

Determine whether a scatter plot of the data for the following might show a *positive*, *negative*, or *no* relationship. Explain your answer.

a. age of car and value of car

As the age of a car increases, the value of the car decreases. So, a scatter plot of the data would show a negative relationship.

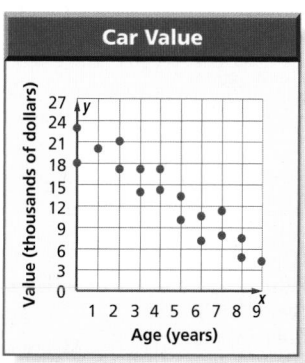

Car Value

b. birth month and birth weight

A person's birth weight is not affected by their birth month. Therefore, a scatter plot of the data would show no relationship.

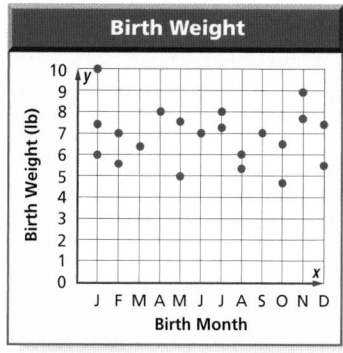

Birth Weight

You can also use scatter plots to spot trends, draw conclusions, and make predictions about the data.

www.pre-alg.com/extra_examples

b. shoe size and math test score
no relationship

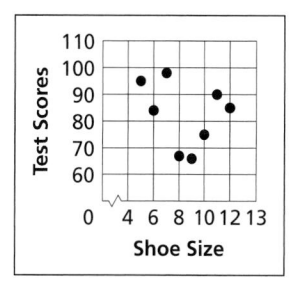

Test Scores / **Shoe Size**

---

2 Teach

CONSTRUCT SCATTER PLOTS

In-Class Example Power Point®

1 The table shows the average cost of a loaf of bread from 1920–2000. Make a scatter plot of the data.

Year	1920	1930	1940	1950	1960
Cents	12	9	8	14	20

Year	1970	1980	1990	2000
Cents	24	52	72	99

Source: *Time Almanac*

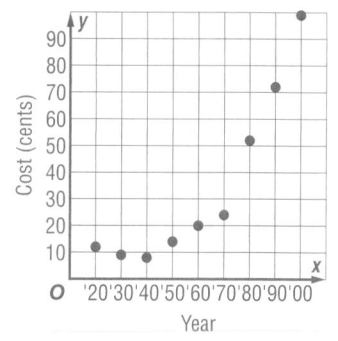

INTERPRET SCATTER PLOTS

In-Class Example Power Point®

2 Determine whether a scatter plot of the data for the following might show a *positive*, *negative* or *no* relationship. Explain your answer.

a. height of basketball player and number of rebounds

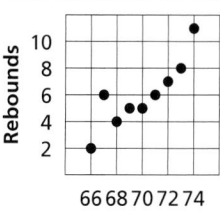

As height increases, number of rebounds increases; positive relationship.

3 The table shows temperatures in degrees Celsius and the corresponding temperatures in Fahrenheit.

°F	32	41	50	59	68	77	86
°C	0	5	10	15	20	25	30

a. Make a scatter plot of the data.

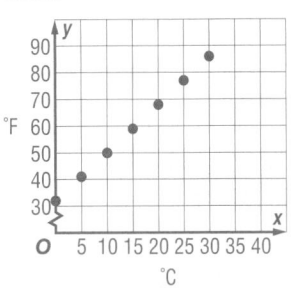

b. Does the scatter plot show a relationship between °C and °F? Explain. **Yes, a positive relationship. As °C increase, so do °F.**

c. Predict the Fahrenheit temperature for 35°C. **about 95°**

3 Practice/Apply

Study Notebook

Have students—
- complete the definition/example for the remaining term on the Vocabulary Builder worksheets for Chapter 1.
- include any other item(s) that they find helpful in mastering the skills in this lesson.

Career Choices

Biologist ••••••••••
Wildlife biologists work in the field of fish and wildlife conservation. Duties may include studying animal populations and monitoring trends of migrating animals.

Online Research
For information about a career as a wildlife biologist, visit: www.pre-alg.com/careers

---

Example 3 *Use Scatter Plots to Make Predictions*

BIOLOGY A biologist recorded the lengths and weights of some largemouth bass. The table shows the results.

Length (in.)	9.2	10.9	12.3	12.0	14.1	15.5	16.4	16.9	17.7	18.4	19.8
Weight (lb)	0.5	0.8	0.9	1.3	1.7	2.2	2.5	3.2	3.6	4.1	4.8

a. Make a scatter plot of the data.

Let the horizontal axis represent length, and let the vertical axis represent weight. Graph the data.

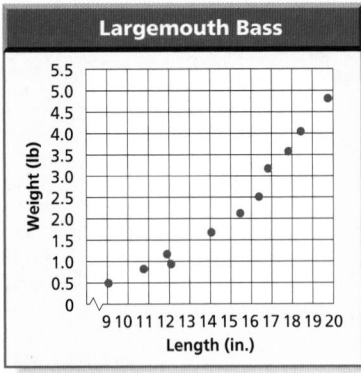

b. Does the scatter plot show a relationship between the length and weight of a largemouth bass? Explain.

As the length of the bass increases, so does its weight. So, the scatter plot shows a positive relationship.

c. Predict the weight of a bass that measures 22 inches.

By looking at the pattern in the graph, we can predict that the weight of a bass measuring 22 inches would be between 5 and 6 pounds.

Check for Understanding

Concept Check

1. Sample answer: make predictions, draw conclusions, spot trends

1. List three ways a scatter plot can be used.

2. OPEN ENDED Draw a scatter plot with ten ordered pairs that show a negative relationship. **See margin.**

3. Name the three types of relationships shown by scatter plots. **negative, positive, and none**

Guided Practice Determine whether a scatter plot of the data for the following might show a *positive*, *negative*, or *no* relationship. Explain your answer. **4–5. See margin.**

4. hours worked and earnings
5. hair color and height

Application

GUIDED PRACTICE KEY	
Exercises	Examples
4, 5	2
6, 7	1, 3

SCHOOL For Exercises 6 and 7, use the table that shows the heights and grade point averages of the students in Mrs. Stanley's class. **6. See pp. 53A–53B.**

6. Make a scatter plot of the data.

7. Does there appear to be a relationship between the scores? Explain. **Since the points appear to be random, there is no relationship.**

Name	Height (in.)	GPA
Jenna	66	3.6
Michael	61	3.2
Laura	59	3.9
Simon	64	2.8
Marcus	61	3.8
Timothy	65	3.1
Brandon	70	2.6
Emily	64	2.2
Eduardo	65	4.0

About the Exercises . . .

Organization by Objective
- **Construct Scatter Plots:** 17
- **Interpret Scatter Plots:** 8–16, 18, 19, 21

Alert! Exercise 20 involves research on the Internet or other reference materials.

Odd/Even Assignments

Exercises 8–13 are structured so that students practice the same concepts whether they are assigned odd or even problems.

Assignment Guide

Basic: 9–13 odd, 14–16, 21–37
Average: 9–13 odd, 17–37
Advanced: 8–12 even, 17–37

Homework Help

For Exercises	See Examples
8–13	2
14–20	1, 3

Extra Practice
See page 726.

Determine whether a scatter plot of the data for the following might show a *positive*, *negative*, or *no* relationship. Explain your answer.

8. size of household and amount of water bill **positive**

9. number of songs on a CD and cost of a CD **no**

10. size of a car's engine and miles per gallon **negative**

11. speed and distance traveled **positive**

12. outside temperature and amount of heating bill **negative**

13. size of a television screen and the number of channels it receives **no**
8–13. See pp. 53A–53B for explanations.

ANIMALS For Exercises 14–16, use the scatter plot shown.

14. Do the data show a *positive*, *negative*, or *no* relationship between the year and the number of bald eagle hatchlings?

15. What appears to be the trend in the number of hatchlings between 1965 and 1972?

16. What appears to be the trend between 1972 and 1985?
The number increases.

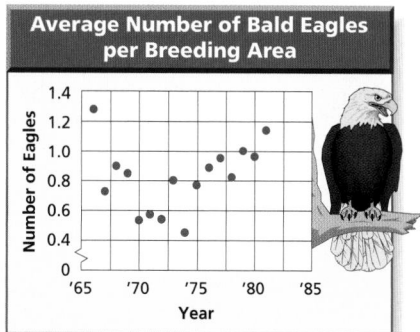

Average Number of Bald Eagles per Breeding Area

Source: CHANCE

14. There is no obvious pattern, so the graph shows no relationship.

15. The number decreases.

 Online Research **Data Update** How has the total number of bald eagle pairs in the United States changed since 1980? Visit www.pre-alg.com/data_update to learn more.

WebQuest

The high and low temperatures for your vacation destinations can be shown in a scatter plot. Visit www.pre-alg.com/webquest to continue work on your WebQuest project.

BASKETBALL For Exercises 17–19, use the following information.
The number of minutes played and the number of field goal attempts for certain players of the Indiana Pacers for the 1999–2000 season is shown below.

Player	Minutes Played	Field Goal Attempts	Player	Minutes Played	Field Goal Attempts
Rose	2978	1196	Best	1691	561
Miller	2987	1041	Jackson	2190	570
Smits	1852	890	Perkins	1620	441
Croshere	1885	653	Mullin	582	187
Davis	2127	602	McKey	634	108

17. Make a scatter plot of the data. **See pp. 53A–53B.**

18. Does the scatter plot show any relationship? If so, is it positive or negative? Explain your reasoning.

19. Suppose a player played 2500 minutes. Predict the number of field goal attempts for that player. **about 800**

20. **RESEARCH** Use the Internet or another source to find two sets of sports statistics that can be shown in a scatter plot. Identify any trends in the data. **See students' work.**

18. Yes; positive; as the number of minutes increases, the number of field goal attempts increases.

 www.pre-alg.com/self_check_quiz

Lesson 1-7 Scatter Plots **43**

Answers (p. 42)

2. Sample answer:

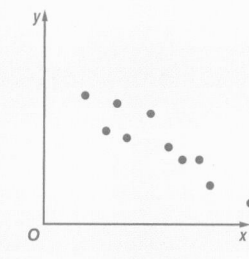

4. Positive; as the number of hours worked increases, so do the earnings.

5. No; hair color is not related to height.

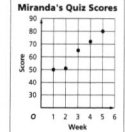
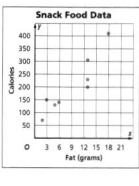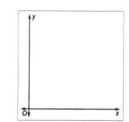
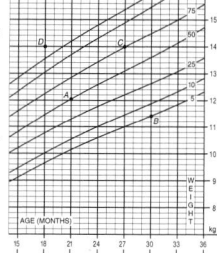
Lesson 1-7 Scatter Plots **43**

Open-Ended Assessment

Writing Provide students with a scatter plot of interesting sports data such as the record 100 m relay times for the last several years. Ask students to write a paragraph describing the graph, any trends or relationships in the data, and any predictions they could make from the past of the future.

Assessment Options

Quiz (Lesson 1-7) is available on p. 52 of the *Chapter 1 Resource Masters.*

Answers

21. Sample answer: Yes; as more emphasis is placed on standardized tests, students will become more comfortable taking the tests, and scores will increase.

22. Sample answer: By studying scatter plots and identifying the type of relationship the scatter plot shows, you can determine trends. Answers should include the following:

    • A positive relationship means that as one set of data increases, the other set also increases. A negative relationship means that as one set of data increases, the other set decreases. No relationship means that one set of data is not related to the other set of data.

    • The amount of money spent and the amount of money saved would be an example of a negative relationship. The number of hours spent studying and test scores would represent a positive relationship. The number of days in a month and the number of rainy days is an example of no relationship.

---

21. **CRITICAL THINKING** Refer to Example 1 on page 40. Do you think the trend in the test scores would continue in the years to come? Explain your reasoning. **See margin.**

22. **WRITING IN MATH** Answer the question that was posed at the beginning of the lesson. **See margin.**

   How can scatter plots help us spot trends?

   Include the following in your answer:
   • definitions of positive relationship, negative relationship, and no relationship, and
   • examples of real-life situations that would represent each type of relationship.

Standardized Test Practice Ⓐ Ⓑ Ⓒ Ⓓ

The scatter plot shows the study time and test scores for the students in Mr. Mock's history class.

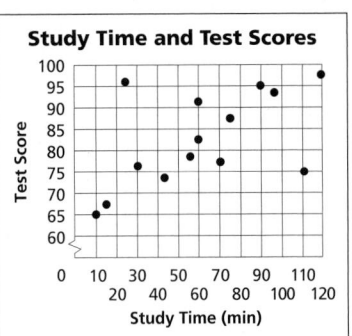

Study Time and Test Scores

23. Based on the results, which of the following is an appropriate score for a student who studies for 1 hour? **C**

   Ⓐ 68   Ⓑ 98
   Ⓒ 87   Ⓓ 72

24. Which of the following is an appropriate score for a student who studies for 1.5 hours? **B**

   Ⓐ 78   Ⓑ 92
   Ⓒ 81   Ⓓ 74

Maintain Your Skills

Mixed Review **Graph each ordered pair on a coordinate system.** *(Lesson 1-6)*

25. $M(3, 2)$ 26. $X(5, 0)$ 27. $K(0, 2)$
25–27. See margin.

Write the ordered pair that names each point. *(Lesson 1-6)*

28. (2, 3) 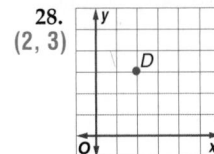   29. (0, 4) 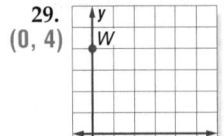   30. (3, 0)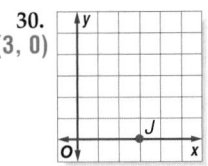

31. Determine the domain and range of the relation {(0, 9), (4, 8), (2, 3), (6, 1)}. *(Lesson 1-6)* domain = {0, 4, 2, 6}; range = {9, 8, 3, 1}

ALGEBRA Solve each equation mentally. *(Lesson 1-5)*

32. $3c = 81$ **27**   33. $15 - x = 8$ **7**   34. $8 = \frac{32}{m}$ **4**

35. **ALGEBRA** Simplify $15 + (b + 3)$. *(Lesson 1-4)* $b + 18$

ALGEBRA Evaluate each expression if $m = 8$ and $y = 6$. *(Lesson 1-3)*

36. $(2m + 3y) - m$ **26**   37. $3m + (y - 2) + 3$ **31**

25. 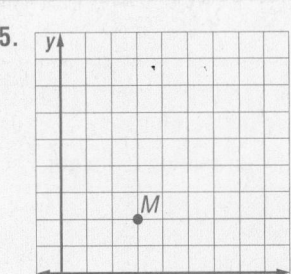   26. 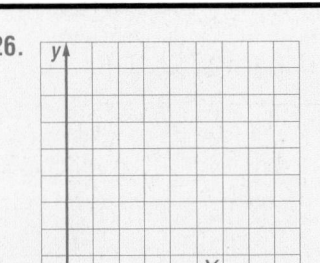   27.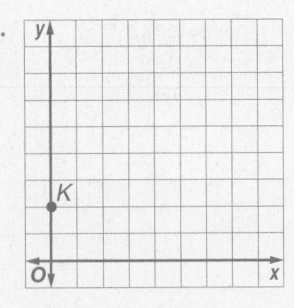

Graphing Calculator Investigation

A Follow-Up of Lesson 1-7

Scatter Plots

You have learned that graphing ordered pairs as a scatter plot on a coordinate plane is one way to make it easier to "see" if there is a relationship. You can use a TI-83 Plus graphing calculator to create scatter plots.

SCIENCE A zoologist studied extinction times (in years) of island birds. The zoologist wanted to see if there was a relationship between the average number of nests and the time needed for each bird to become extinct on the islands. Use the table of data below to make a scatter plot.

Bird Name	Bird Size	Average Number of Nests	Extinction Time
Buzzard	Large	2.0	5.5
Quail	Large	1.0	1.5
Curlew	Large	2.8	3.1
Cuckoo	Large	1.4	2.5
Magpie	Large	4.5	10.0
Swallow	Small	3.8	2.6
Robin	Small	3.3	4.0
Stonechat	Small	3.6	2.4
Blackbird	Small	4.7	3.3
Tree-sparrow	Small	2.2	1.9

Step 1 Enter the data.

- Clear any existing lists.

  KEYSTROKES: STAT ENTER ▲ CLEAR ENTER

- Enter the average number of nests as L1 and extinction times as L2.

  KEYSTROKES: STAT ENTER 2 ENTER 1 ENTER ... 2.2 ENTER ▶ 5.5 ENTER 1.5 ENTER ... 1.9 ENTER

The first data pair is (2, 5.5).

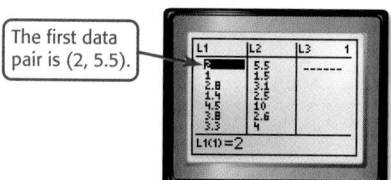

Step 2 Format the graph.

- Turn on the statistical plot.

  KEYSTROKES: 2nd [STAT PLOT] ENTER ENTER

- Select the scatter plot, L1 as the Xlist and L2 as the Ylist.

  KEYSTROKES: ▼ ENTER ▼ 2nd [L1] ENTER 2nd [L2] ENTER

Graphing Calculator Investigation

A Follow-Up of Lesson 1-7

Getting Started

Know Your Calculator Besides creating scatter plots, a graphing calculator can plot statistical data such as histograms, box-and-whisker plots, and other types of displays. The calculator organizes lists of numbers for each type of statistical measure, making it possible to see various displays of a data set.

Teach

- Make sure students have deactivated or cleared out any equations stored in the Y= list before graphing the scatter plot.
- Students should double check that all data have been entered correctly and that each list contains the same number of entries. Only the ordered pairs from the data set should be in L1 and L2.
- Have students complete Exercises 1–9.

Graphing Calculator and Spreadsheet Investigations empower students to use technology tools to solve problems.

Assess

Help students describe how the calculator helps create a scatter plot. Also have them describe any features of the calculator that help them analyze the graph.

Answers

1. The *x*-coordinate represents average number of nests and the *y*-coordinate represents extinction time for each bird.

2. Sample answer: The points seem to be slanting up from left to right. One point seems much higher than the others.

3. Sample answer: Generally, as the number of nests increases, the time it takes to become extinct increases also. There is a positive relationship.

5.

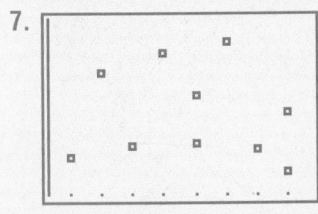

The plot shows larger birds tend to have longer extinction lines.

6.

As *x* increases, *y* increases. There is a positive relationship.

7.

No relationship

8.

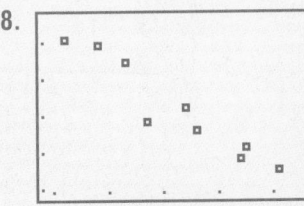

As *x* increases, *y* decreases. There is a negative relationship

---

Step 3 *Graph the data.*

• Display the scatter plot.
  KEYSTROKES: [ZOOM] 9

• Use the [TRACE] feature and the left and right arrow keys to move from one point to another.

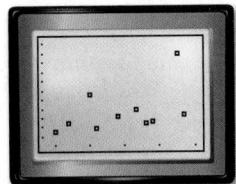

Exercises 1–3. See margin.

1. Press [TRACE]. Use the left and right arrow keys to move from one point to another. What do the coordinates of each data point represent?

2. Describe the scatter plot.

3. Is there a relationship between the average number of nests and extinction times? If so, write a sentence or two that describes the relationship.

4. Are there any differences between the extinction times of large birds versus small birds? **Sample answer: Large birds tend to have longer extinction times.**

5. Separate the data by bird size. Enter average number of nests and extinction times for large birds as lists L1 and L2 and for small birds as lists L3 and L4. Use the graphing calculator to make two scatter plots with different marks for large and small birds. Does your scatter plot agree with your answer in Exercise 4? Explain.

5. See margin for graph. The plot shows larger birds tend to have longer extinction times.

For Exercises 6–8, make a scatter plot for each set of data and describe the relationship, if any, between the *x*- and *y*-values. 6–8. See margin for graphs.

6.

x	y
70	323
80	342
40	244
50	221
30	121
80	399
60	230
60	200
50	215
40	170

As *x* increases, *y* increases. There is a positive relationship.

7.

x	y
8	89
5	32
9	30
10	18
3	26
4	72
10	51
7	34
6	82
7	60

no relationship

8.

x	5.2	5.8	6.3	6.7	7.4	7.6	8.4	8.5	9.1
y	12.1	11.9	11.5	9.8	10.2	9.6	8.8	9.1	8.5

As *x* increases, *y* decreases. There is a negative relationship.

9. **RESEARCH** Find two sets of data on your own. Then determine whether a relationship exists between the data. **Sample data: year vs. 100-meter dash times; year vs. school enrollment.**

Key concepts from the lesson, one or two examples, and several practice problems are included in the Lesson-by-Lesson Review.

Vocabulary and Concept Check

algebraic expression (p. 17)	graph (p. 34)	scatter plot (p. 40)
conjecture (p. 7)	inductive reasoning (p. 7)	simplify (p. 25)
coordinate plane (p. 33)	numerical expression (p. 12)	solution (p. 28)
coordinate system (p. 33)	open sentence (p. 28)	solving the equation (p. 28)
counterexample (p. 25)	ordered pair (p. 33)	variable (p. 17)
deductive reasoning (p. 25)	order of operations (p. 12)	x-axis (p. 33)
defining a variable (p. 18)	origin (p. 33)	x-coordinate (p. 33)
domain (p. 35)	properties (p. 23)	y-axis (p. 33)
equation (p. 28)	range (p. 35)	y-coordinate (p. 33)
evaluate (p. 12)	relation (p. 35)	

Choose the letter of the term that best matches each statement or phrase. Use each letter once.

1. $m + 3n - 4$ **d**
2. to find the value of a numerical expression **b**
3. the set of all y-coordinates of a relation **e**
4. $20 + 12 \div 4 - 1 \times 2$ **a**
5. the set of all x-coordinates of a relation **c**

> a. numerical expression
> b. evaluate
> c. domain
> d. algebraic expression
> e. range

Lesson-by-Lesson Review

1-1 Using a Problem-Solving Plan

See pages 6–10.

Concept Summary
- The four steps of the four-step problem-solving plan are *explore, plan, solve,* and *examine.*
- Some problems can be solved using inductive reasoning.

Example   What is the next term in the list 1, 5, 9, 13, 17, …?

Explore   We know the first five terms. We need to find the next term.

Plan   Use inductive reasoning to determine the next term.

Solve   Each term is 4 more than the previous term.

$$1, \quad 5, \quad 9, \quad 13, \quad 17, \dots$$
$$+4 \quad +4 \quad +4 \quad +4$$

By continuing the pattern, the next term is 17 + 4 or 21.

Examine   Subtract 4 from each term. 21 − 4 = 17, 17 − 4 = 13, 13 − 4 = 9, 9 − 4 = 5, and 5 − 4 = 1. So, the answer is correct.

www.pre-alg.com/vocabulary_review

FOLDABLES™
Study Organizer

For more information about Foldables, see *Teaching Mathematics with Foldables.*

Have students reexamine their Foldables to make sure all examples they have written are correct. Suggest that they refer to their Foldables if needed when working through the Study Guide exercises or preparing for the Chapter Test.

Chapter 1

Study Guide and Review

Vocabulary and Concept Check

- This alphabetical list of vocabulary terms in Chapter 1 includes a page reference where each term was introduced.
- **Assessment** A vocabulary review/test for Chapter 1 is available on p. 50 of the *Chapter 1 Resource Masters.*

Lesson-by-Lesson Review

For each lesson,
- the main ideas are summarized,
- additional examples review concepts, and
- practice exercises are provided.

Vocabulary PuzzleMaker

ELL   The Vocabulary PuzzleMaker software improves students' mathematics vocabulary using four puzzle formats—crossword, scramble, word search using a word list, and word search using clues. Students can work on a computer screen or from a printed handout.

MindJogger Videoquizzes

ELL   MindJogger Videoquizzes provide an alternative review of concepts presented in this chapter. Students work in teams in a game show format to gain points for correct answers. The questions are presented in three rounds.

Round 1 Concepts (5 questions)
Round 2 Skills (4 questions)
Round 3 Problem Solving (4 questions)

Exercises   **Find the next term in each list.**   *See Example 2 on page 7.*

6. 2, 4, 6, 8, 10, ... **12**

7. 5, 8, 11, 14, 17, ... **20**

8. 2, 6, 18, 54, 162, ... **486**

9. 1, 2, 4, 7, 11, 16, ... **22**

10. **FOOD**   The table below shows the cost of various-sized hams. How much will it cost to buy a ham that weighs 7 pounds?   *See Examples 1 and 3 on pages 7 and 8.*

Weight (lb)	1	2	3	4	5	**$30.66**
Cost	$4.38	$8.76	$13.14	$17.52	$21.90	

1-2 Numbers and Expressions

See pages 12–16.

Concept Summary

- When evaluating an expression, follow the order of operations.

  Step 1   Simplify the expressions inside grouping symbols.

  Step 2   Do all multiplications and/or divisions from left to right.

  Step 3   Do all additions and/or subtractions from left to right.

Example   Find the value of $3[(10 - 7) + 2]$.

$$3[(10 - 7) + 2] = 3[3 + 2] \quad \text{Evaluate } (10 - 7).$$
$$= 3[5] \quad \text{Add 3 and 2.}$$
$$= 15 \quad \text{Multiply 3 and 5.}$$

Exercises   **Find the value of each expression.**   *See Example 1 on page 13.*

11. $7 + 3 \cdot 5$ **22**

12. $36 \div 9 - 3$ **1**

13. $5 \cdot (7 - 2) - 9$ **16**

14. $\dfrac{2(17 + 4)}{3}$ **14**

15. $18 \div (7 - 4) + 6$ **12**

16. $4[9 + (1 \cdot 16) - 8]$ **68**

1-3 Variables and Expressions

See pages 17–21.

Concept Summary

- To evaluate an algebraic expression, replace each variable with its known value, and then use the order of operations.

Example   Evaluate $5a + 2$ if $a = 7$.

$$5a + 2 = 5(7) + 2 \quad \text{Replace } a \text{ with 7.}$$
$$= 35 + 2 \quad \text{Multiply 5 and 7.}$$
$$= 37 \quad \text{Add 35 and 2.}$$

Exercises   **ALGEBRA**   **Evaluate each expression if $x = 3$, $y = 8$, and $z = 5$.**
See Examples 1 and 2 on pages 17 and 18.

17. $y + 6$ **14**

18. $17 - 2x$ **11**

19. $z - 3 + y$ **10**

20. $6x - 2z + 7$ **15**

21.  $\dfrac{6y}{x} + 9$ **25**

22. $9x - (y + z)$ **14**

1-4 Properties

See pages 23–27.

Concept Summary

For any numbers a, b, and c:

- $a + b = b + a$ — Commutative Property of Addition
- $(a + b) + c = a + (b + c)$ — Associative Property of Addition
- $a \cdot b = b \cdot a$ — Commutative Property of Multiplication
- $(a \cdot b) \cdot c = a \cdot (b \cdot c)$ — Associative Property of Multiplication
- $a + 0 = 0 + a = a$ — Additive Identity
- $a \cdot 0 = 0 \cdot a = 0$ — Multiplicative Property of Zero
- $a \cdot 1 = 1 \cdot a = a$ — Multiplicative Identity

Example Name the property shown by each statement.

$8 \cdot 1 = 8$	Multiplicative Identity
$(2 + 3) + 6 = 2 + (3 + 6)$	Associative Property of Addition
$1 \cdot 6 \cdot 9 = 6 \cdot 1 \cdot 9$	Commutative Property of Multiplication

Exercises Name the property shown by each statement.
See Example 1 on page 24.

23. $1 + 9 = 9 + 1$ **Comm. (+)**   **24.** $6 + 0 = 6$ **Identity (+)**

25. $15 \times 0 = 0$ **Mult. Zero**   **26.** $(x \cdot 8) \cdot 2 = x \cdot (8 \cdot 2)$ **Assoc. ($\times$)**

1-5 Variables and Equations

See pages 28–32.

Concept Summary

- To solve an equation, find the value for the variable that makes the equation true.

Example Find the solution of $26 = 33 - w$. Is it 5, 6, or 7?

Replace w with each value.

Value for w	$26 = 33 - w$	True or False?
5	$26 \stackrel{?}{=} 33 - 5$	false
6	$26 \stackrel{?}{=} 33 - 6$	false
7	$26 \stackrel{?}{=} 33 - 7$	true $\checkmark$

Therefore, the solution of $26 = 33 - w$ is 7.

ALGEBRA Solve each equation mentally. *See Example 3 on page 29.*

27. $n + 3 = 13$ **10**   **28.** $9 = k - 6$ **15**   **29.** $24 = 7 + g$ **17**

30. $6x = 48$ **8**   **31.** $54 = 9h$ **6**   **32.** $\dfrac{56}{a} = 14$ **4**

Study Guide and Review

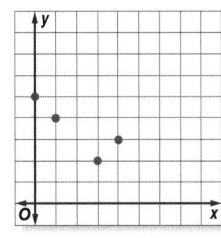

Chapter
1 **For More ...**
• Extra Practice, see pages 724–726.
• Mixed Problem Solving, see page 758.

Answers

33.

x	y
2	3
6	1
7	5

domain: {2, 6, 7};

range: {3, 1, 5}

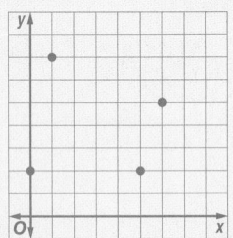

34.

x	y
0	2
1	7
5	2
6	5

domain: {0, 1, 5, 6};

range: {2, 5, 7}

35. Positive; as the height increases, the circumference increases.

36. about 90–95 feet

Answers (p. 51)

2. Simplify the expressions inside grouping symbols. Do all multiplication and/or division in order from left to right. Do all addition and/or subtraction in order from left to right.

17.

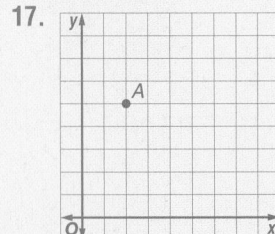

1-6 Ordered Pairs and Relations

See pages 33–38.

Concept Summary

• Ordered pairs are used to graph a point on a coordinate system.
• A relation is a set of ordered pairs. The set of *x*-coordinates is the domain, and the set of *y*-coordinates is the range.

Example Express the relation {(1, 4), (3, 2), (4, 3), (0, 5)} as a table and as a graph. Then determine the domain and range.

x	y
1	4
3	2
4	3
0	5

The domain is {1, 3, 4, 0}, and the range is {4, 2, 3, 5}.

Exercises Express each relation as a table and as a graph. Then determine the domain and range. *See Example 3 on page 35.* **33–34. See margin.**

33. {(2, 3), (6, 1), (7, 5)} **34.** {(0, 2), (1, 7), (5, 2), (6, 5)}

1-7 Scatter Plots

See pages 40–44.

Concept Summary

• A scatter plot is a graph that shows the relationship between two sets of data.

Example The scatter plot shows the approximate heights and circumferences of various giant sequoia trees.

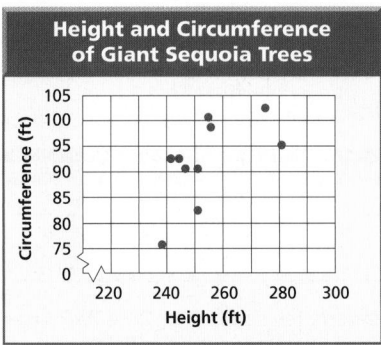

Height and Circumference of Giant Sequoia Trees

35–36. See margin.

Exercises Refer to the scatter plot. *See Example 3 on page 42.*

35. Does the scatter plot show a *positive*, *negative*, or *no* relationship? Explain.
36. Predict the circumference of a 245-foot sequoia. Explain your reasoning.

20.

x	y
8	5
4	3
2	2
6	1

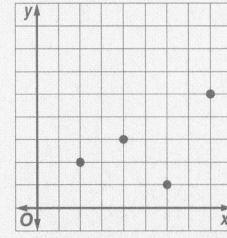

domain: {8, 4, 2, 6}; range: {5, 3, 2, 1}

Vocabulary and Concepts

1. **Write** the steps of the four-step problem-solving plan. **Explore, Plan, Solve, Examine**

2. **List** the order of operations used to find the value of a numerical expression. **See margin.**

Skills and Applications

Find the value of each expression.

3. $24 - 8 \div 2 \cdot 3$ **12**   4. $16 \div 4 + 3(9 - 7)$ **10**   5. $3[18 - 5(7 - 5 + 1)]$ **9**

Write a numerical expression for each verbal phrase.

6. three less than fifteen **15 − 3**   7. twelve increased by seven **12 + 7**

8. the quotient of twelve and six **12 ÷ 6**

ALGEBRA **Evaluate each expression if $a = 7$, $b = 3$, and $c = 5$.**

9. $4a - 3c$ **13**   10. $42 \div [a(c - b)]$ **3**   11. $5c + (a + 2b) - 8$ **30**

12. What property is shown by $(5 \cdot 6) \cdot 8 = 5 \cdot (6 \cdot 8)$? **Assoc. (×)**

ALGEBRA **Simplify each expression.**

13. $9 + (p + 3)$ **$p + 12$**   14. $6 \cdot (7 \cdot k)$ **$42k$**

ALGEBRA **Solve each equation mentally.**

15. $4m = 20$ **5**   16. $16 - a = 9$ **7**

17. Graph $A(2, 5)$ on a coordinate system. **See margin.**

Refer to the coordinate system shown at the right. Write the ordered pair that names each point.

18. C **(3, 0)**   19. D **(1, 3)**

20. Express $\{(8, 5), (4, 3), (2, 2), (6, 1)\}$ as a table and as a graph. Then determine the domain and range. **See margin.**

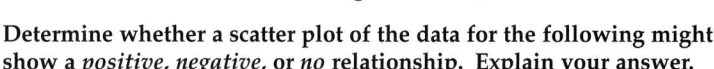

Determine whether a scatter plot of the data for the following might show a *positive*, *negative*, or *no* relationship. Explain your answer.

21. outside temperature and air conditioning bill **positive**

22. number of siblings and height **no**

23. Find the next three terms in the list 3, 5, 9, 15, …. **23, 33, 45**

24. **MONEY** Mrs. Adams rents a car for a week and pays $79 for the first day and $49 for each additional day. Mr. Lowe rents a car for $350 a week. Which was the better deal? Explain.
Renting a car for $350/week was the better deal. It was $23 cheaper.

25. **STANDARDIZED TEST PRACTICE** Katie purchased 6 loaves of bread at the grocery store and paid a total of $12. Which equation can be used to find how much Katie paid for each loaf of bread? **B**

(A) $x + 6 = 12$ (B) $6x = 12$ (C) $x - 6 = 12$ (D) $x \div 6 = 12$

 www.pre-alg.com/chapter_test

Assessment Options

Vocabulary Test A vocabulary review/test for Chapter 1 can be found on p. 50 of the *Chapter 1 Resource Masters.*

Chapter Tests There are six Chapter 1 Tests and an Open-Ended Assessment task available in the *Chapter 1 Resource Masters.*

Chapter 1 Tests			
Form	Type	Level	Pages
1	MC	basic	37–38
2A	MC	average	39–40
2B	MC	average	41–42
2C	FR	average	43–44
2D	FR	average	45–46
3	FR	advanced	47–48

MC = multiple-choice questions
FR = free-response questions

Open-Ended Assessment Performance tasks for Chapter 1 can be found on p. 49 of the *Chapter 1 Resource Masters.* A sample scoring rubric for these tasks appears on p. A25.

**ExamView® PRO**

Use the networkable **ExamView® Pro** to:

- Create **multiple versions** of tests.
- Create **modified** tests for *Inclusion* students.
- **Edit** existing questions and **add** your own questions
- Use built-in **state curriculum correlations** to create tests aligned with state standards.
- Change **English** tests to **Spanish** and vice versa.

Portfolio Suggestion

Introduction Variables are used as placeholders for numbers and quantities that are unknown or can change. Variables, numbers, and at least one operation make up an algebraic expression.

Ask Students to find a problem from their work in this chapter and explain how they used variables to show relationships.

These two pages contain practice questions in the various formats that can be found on the most frequently given standardized tests.

A practice answer sheet for these two pages can be found on page A1 of the *Chapter 1 Resource Masters.*

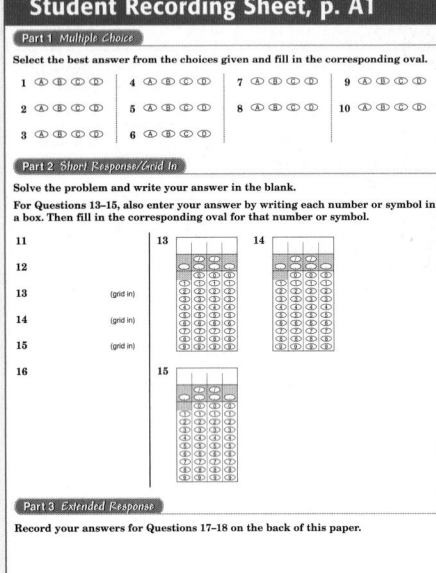

Standardized Test Practice
Student Recording Sheet, p. A1

Additional Practice

See pp. 55–56 of the *Chapter 1 Resource Masters* for additional standardized test practice.

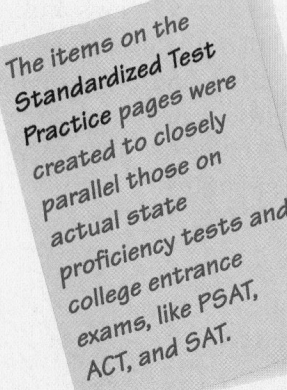

The items on the Standardized Test Practice pages were created to closely parallel those on actual state proficiency tests and college entrance exams, like PSAT, ACT, and SAT.

Part 1 | Multiple Choice

Record your answers on the answer sheet provided by your teacher or on a sheet of paper.

1. Find the next two terms in the pattern 4, 12, 36, 108, ... (Lesson 1-1) **D**

  Ⓐ 116 and 124   Ⓑ 116 and 140
  Ⓒ 324 and 648   Ⓓ 324 and 972

2. Evaluate $2(15 - 3 \cdot 4)$. (Lesson 1-2) **A**

  Ⓐ 6   Ⓑ 16   Ⓒ 18   Ⓓ 96

3. Of the six books in a mystery series, four have 200 pages and two have 300 pages. Which expression represents the total number of pages in the series? (Lesson 1-3) **C**

  Ⓐ $200 + 300$ Ⓑ $6(200 + 300)$
  Ⓒ $4(200) + 2(300)$ Ⓓ $6(200) + 6(300)$

4. The postage for a first-class letter is $0.34 for the first ounce and $0.21 for each additional ounce. Which expression best represents the cost of postage for a letter that weighs 5 ounces? (Lesson 1-3) **D**

  Ⓐ $0.34 + 0.21(5)$ Ⓑ $0.21 + 0.34(4)$
  Ⓒ $0.34(5)$ Ⓓ $0.34 + 0.21(4)$

5. Which property is represented by the equation below? (Lesson 1-4) **C**

$$8 \cdot (5 \cdot 3) = (8 \cdot 5) \cdot 3$$

  Ⓐ Commutative Property of Addition
  Ⓑ Commutative Property of Multiplication
  Ⓒ Associative Property of Multiplication
  Ⓓ Identity Property of Multiplication

6. Which number is the solution of the equation $17 - 2x = 9$? (Lesson 1-5) **B**

  Ⓐ 2   Ⓑ 4   Ⓒ 6   Ⓓ 8

Test-Taking Tip   Ⓐ Ⓑ Ⓒ Ⓓ

Question 6
To solve an equation, you can replace the variable in the equation with the values given in each answer choice. The answer choice that results in a true statement is the correct answer.

---

7. Which sentence does the equation $n + 9 = 15$ represent? (Lesson 1-5) **D**

  Ⓐ A number is the sum of 9 and 15.
  Ⓑ A number decreased by 9 is 15.
  Ⓒ The product of a number and 9 is 15.
  Ⓓ Nine more than a number is 15.

8. What are the coordinates of point P? (Lesson 1-6) **B**

  Ⓐ $(3, 5)$
  Ⓑ $(5, 3)$
  Ⓒ $(3, 3)$
  Ⓓ $(5, 5)$

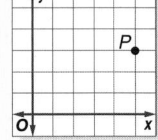

9. Which table shows the set of ordered pairs that represents the points graphed on the grid below? (Lesson 1-6) **C**

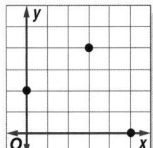

Ⓐ
x	y
2	0
3	4
0	5

Ⓑ
x	y
0	2
4	3
5	0

Ⓒ
x	y
0	2
3	4
5	0

Ⓓ
x	y
2	0
4	3
0	5

10. What type of relationship does the scatter plot below show? (Lesson 1-7) **B**

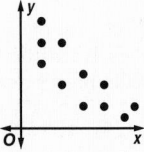

  Ⓐ positive   Ⓑ negative
  Ⓒ associative   Ⓓ none

ExamView® Pro

Special banks of standardized test questions similar to those on the SAT, ACT, TIMSS 8, NAEP 8, and Pre-Algebra End-of-Course tests can be found on this CD-ROM.

Part 2 | Short Response/Grid In

Record your answers on the answer sheet provided by your teacher or on a sheet of paper. **11. Thursday**

11. The graph below shows the number of students absent from school each day of one week. On what day were the fewest students absent? (Prerequisite Skill, p. 722)

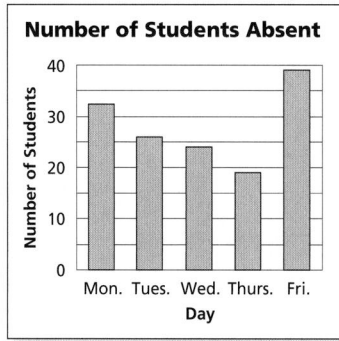

Number of Students Absent

12. The number of Olympic events for women is shown. About how many more events for women were held in 2000 than in 1980? (Prerequisite Skill, p. 722) **about 80**

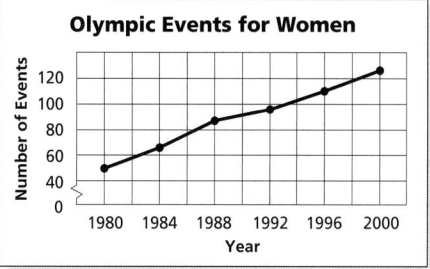

Olympic Events for Women

13. Six tables positioned in a row will be used to display science projects. Each table is 8 feet long. How many yards of fabric are needed to make a banner that will extend from one end of the row of tables to the other? (Lesson 1-1) **16**

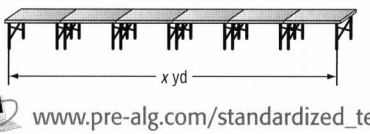

x yd

www.pre-alg.com/standardized_test

14. What is the value of the expression $5 + 4 \times 6 \div 3$? (Lesson 1-2) **13**

15. Evaluate $x(xy + 3)$ if $x = 5$ and $y = 2$. (Lesson 1-3) **65**

16. Write *14 is 12 less than twice the value of x* as an equation. (Lesson 1-5) **$14 = 2x - 12$**

Part 3 | Extended Response

Record your answers on a sheet of paper. Show your work.

17. Kenneth is recording the time it takes him to run various distances. The results are shown. (Lesson 1-6)

Distance (mi)	2	3	5	7	9
Time (min)	13	20	35	53	72

a. Write a set of ordered pairs for the data.
b. Graph the data. **a–c. See margin.**
c. How many minutes do you think it will take Kenneth to run 4 miles? Explain.
d. Predict how far Kenneth will run if he runs for 1 hour. **about 8 mi**

18. The table below shows the results of a survey about the average time that individual students spend studying on weekday evenings. (Lesson 1-7)

Grade	Time (min)	Grade	Time (min)
2	20	6	60
2	15	6	45
2	20	6	55
4	30	6	60
4	20	8	70
4	25	8	80
4	40	8	75
4	30	8	60

a. Make a scatter plot of the data. **See margin.**
b. What are the coordinates of the point that represents the longest time spent on homework? **(8, 80)**
c. Does a relationship exist between grade level and time spent studying? If so, write a sentence to describe the relationship. If not, explain why not. **See margin.**

Chapter 1 Standardized Test Practice **53**

Answers

17a. {(2, 13), (3, 20), (5, 35), (7, 53), (9, 72)}

17b. See graph at right.

17c. About 25–30 minutes because the time it takes to run 4 miles would be between the time it takes to run 3 and 5 miles.

18a. See graph at right.

18c. Yes, there is a positive relationship between grade and time spent on homework. As the grade level increases, the time spent on homework increases.

Evaluating Extended Response Questions

Extended Response questions are graded by using a multilevel rubric that guides you in assessing a student's knowledge of a particular concept.

Goal: Create and interpret a scatter plot of given data.

Sample Scoring Rubric: The following rubric is a sample scoring device. You may wish to add more detail to this sample to meet your individual scoring needs.

Score	Criteria
4	A correct solution that is supported by well-developed, accurate explanations
3	A generally correct solution, but may contain minor flaws in reasoning or computation
2	A partially correct interpretation and/or solution to the problem
1	A correct solution with no supporting evidence or explanation
0	An incorrect solution indicating no mathematical understanding of the concept or task, or no solution is given

17b.

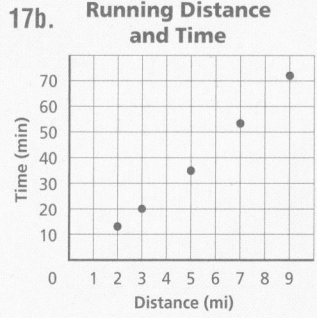

Running Distance and Time

18a.

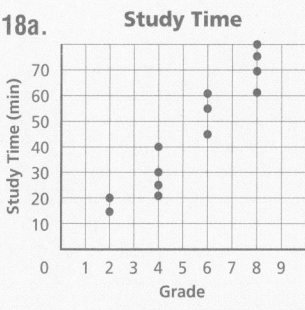

Study Time

Page 27, Lesson 1-4

49. Sample answer: There are many real-life situations in which the order in which things are completed does not matter. For example, you can read the sports page and then the comics, or you can read the comics and then the sports page. No matter the order, both parts of the newspaper will be read. However, some situations are not commutative. For example, when washing clothes, you would add the detergent and then wash the clothes, not wash the clothes and then add the detergent.

Pages 36–37, Lesson 1-6

8.

x	y
2	5
0	2
5	5

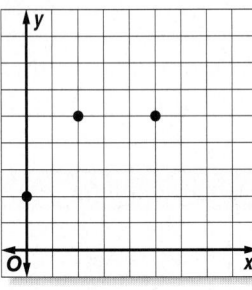

domain = {2, 0, 5};
range = {5, 2}

9.

x	y
1	6
6	4
0	2
3	1

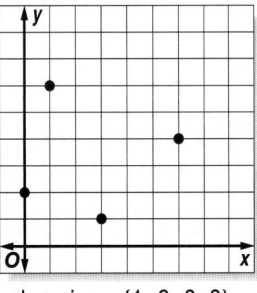

domain = {1, 6, 0, 3};
range = {6, 4, 2, 1}

10.

x	y
2	8
4	16
5	20

11.

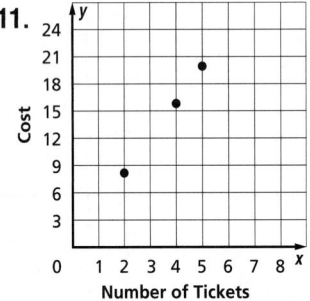

12.

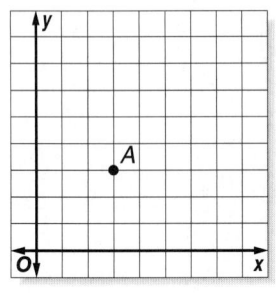

13.

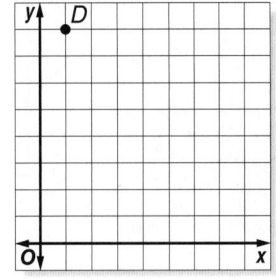

14.

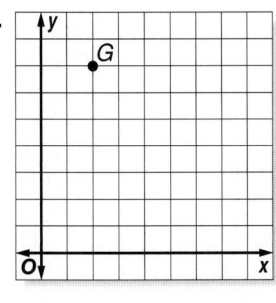

15.

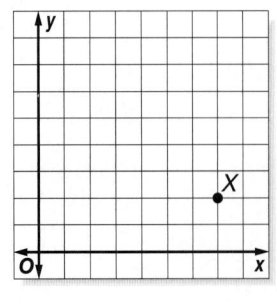

16.

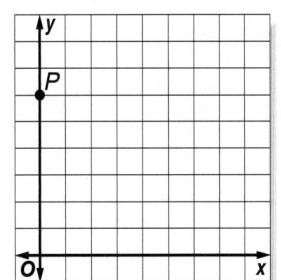

17.

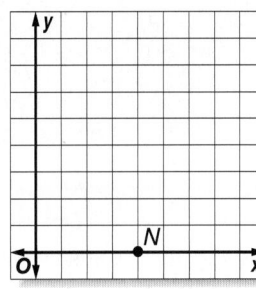

26. 36 ft; 60 ft; 84 ft

27. Speed of a House Mouse

28. (0, 100), (1, 50), (2, 25), (3, 13), (4, 6)

29. Science Experiment

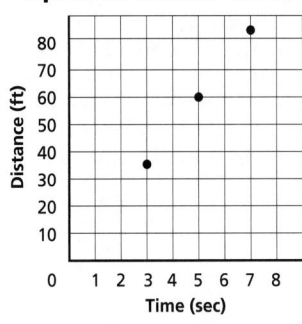

30. The height of each successive bounce is about half of the previous. Since the 4th bounce is 6 cm, the 5th bounce will be about 6 ÷ 2 or 3 cm.

31.

x	y
4	5
5	2
1	6

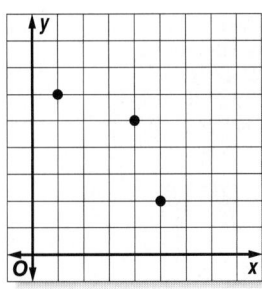

domain = {4, 5, 1}; range = {5, 2, 6}

32.

x	y
6	8
2	9
0	1

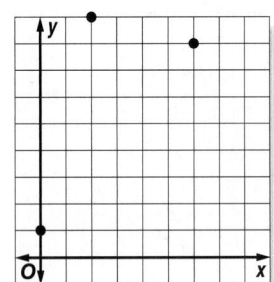

domain = {6, 2, 0}; range = {8, 9, 1}

33.

x	y
7	0
3	2
4	4
5	1

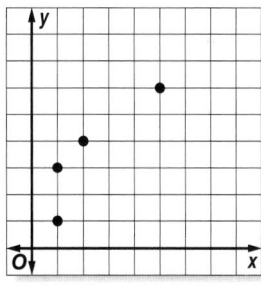

domain = {7, 3, 4, 5}; range = {0, 2, 4, 1}

34.

x	y
2	4
1	3
5	6
1	1

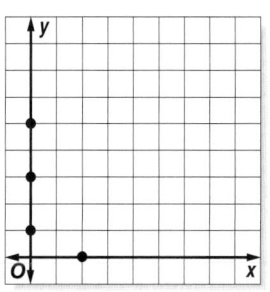

domain = {2, 1, 5}; range = {4, 3, 6, 1}

35.

x	y
0	1
0	3
0	5
2	0

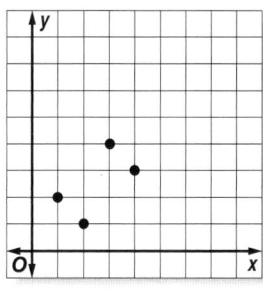

domain = {0, 2}; range = {1, 3, 5, 0}

36.

x	y
4	3
3	4
1	2
2	1

domain = {4, 3, 1, 2}; range = {3, 4, 2, 1}

38.

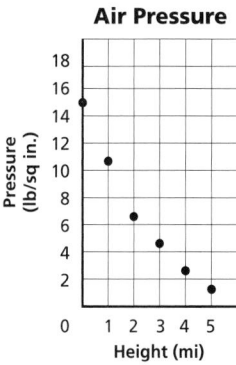

Air Pressure

40.

x	y
0	100
1	95
2	90
3	85
4	80
5	75

41. {(0, 100), (1, 95), (2, 90), (3, 85), (4, 80), (5, 75)}

42. Boiling Point of Water

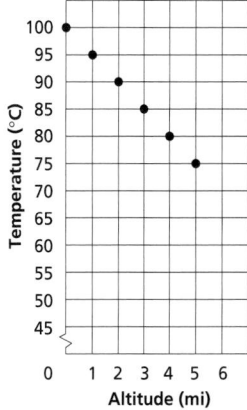

43. about 93°C; about 96°C

Page 42, Lesson 1-7

6.

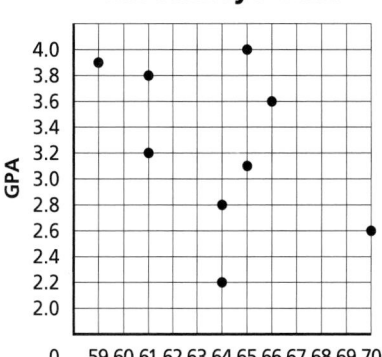

Mr. Stanley's Class

Page 43, Lesson 1-7

8. As a household size increases, the amount of the water bill increases.

9. The number of songs on a CD usually does not affect the cost of the CD.

10. As the size of a car's engine increases, the miles per gallon decrease.

11. As speed increases, distance traveled increases.

12. As the outside temperature increases, the amount of the heating bill decreases.

13. The size of a television screen and the number of channels it receives are not related.

17.

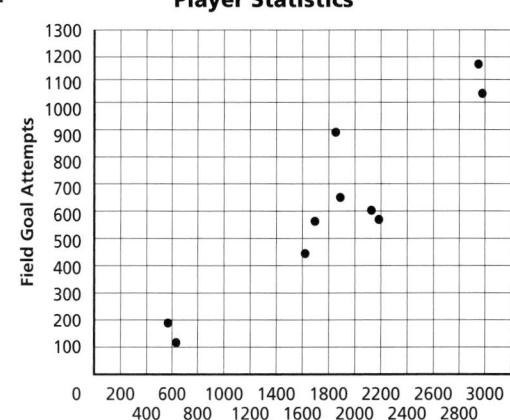

Player Statistics

Chapter 2

Integers
Chapter Overview and Pacing

Year-long pacing: pages T20–T21.

LESSON OBJECTIVES	PACING (days)			
	Regular		Block	
	Basic/Average	Advanced	Basic/Average	Advanced
2-1 Integers and Absolute Value (pp. 56–61) • Compare and order integers. • Find the absolute value of an expression.	2	1	1	0.5
2-2 Adding Integers (pp. 62–68) *Preview:* Model operations with integers with algebra tiles and an integer mat. • Add two integers. • Add more than two integers.	2 (with 2-2 Preview)	1	1.5 (with 2-2 Preview)	0.5
2-3 Subtracting Integers (pp. 70–74) • Subtract integers. • Evaluate expressions containing variables.	2	1	1	0.5
2-4 Multiplying Integers (pp. 75–79) • Multiply integers. • Simplify algebraic expressions.	2	1	1	0.5
2-5 Dividing Integers (pp. 80–84) • Divide integers. • Find the average of a set of data.	2	1	1	0.5
2-6 The Coordinate System (pp. 85–89) • Graph points on a coordinate plane. • Graph algebraic relationships.	1	1	0.5	0.5
Study Guide and **Practice Test** (pp. 90–93) **Standardized Test Practice** (pp. 94–95)	1	1	0.5	0.5
Chapter Assessment	1	1	0.5	0.5
TOTAL	13	8	7	4

*An electronic version of this chapter is available on **StudentWorks**™. This backpack solution CD-ROM allows students instant access to the Student Edition, lesson worksheet pages, and web resources.*

Chapter Resource Manager

Timesaving Tools

TeacherWorks™

All-In-One Planner and Resource Center

See pages T5 and T21.

CHAPTER 2 RESOURCE MASTERS

Study Guide and Intervention	Practice (Skills and Average)	Reading to Learn Mathematics	Enrichment	Assessment	Prerequisite Skills Workbook	Applications*	Parent and Student Study Guide Workbook	5-Minute Check Transparencies	Interactive Chalkboard	Pre-AlgePASS: Tutorial Plus (lessons)	Materials
57	58–59	60	61		1–2, 5–8	SC 3 SM 2	9	2-1	2-1		
62	63–64	65	66	101	5–8		10	2-2	2-2		*Preview:* algebra tiles, integer mat
67	68–69	70	71	101, 103	5–8	SC 4	11	2-3	2-3		
72	73–74	75	76		9–10		12	2-4	2-4		
77	78–79	81	81	102	11–12	GCS 12	13	2-5	2-5	3	
82	83–84	85	86	102		GCS 22	14	2-6	2-6		
				87–100 104–106							

* *Key to Abbreviations:* GCS = Graphing Calculator and Spreadsheet Masters
SC = School-to-Career Masters
SM = Science and Mathematics Lab Manual

ELL Study Guide and Intervention, Skills Practice, Practice, and Parent and Student Study Guide Workbooks are also available in Spanish.

Mathematical Connections and Background

Continuity of Instruction

Prior Knowledge

Students bring their previous experience adding, subtracting, multiplying, and dividing whole numbers, as well as finding patterns, to the study of integers in this chapter. In Chapter 1, students learned to evaluate algebraic expressions. They also learned how to graph points on a coordinate grid.

This Chapter

Students will learn to compare and order integers, find the absolute value of an expression, and find the average of a set of data. They apply the rules for adding, subtracting, multiplying, and dividing integers to evaluating algebraic expressions. Students also use the Cartesian coordinate system to graph points in all four quadrants of the coordinate grid.

Future Connections

The basic rules for adding, subtracting, multiplying, and dividing integers will be used in Chapter 3 as students solve equations. In Chapter 8, students will graph linear equations, systems of linear equations, and linear inequalities on a coordinate plane.

2-1 Integers and Absolute Value

A negative number is a number less than zero. Negative numbers like -8, positive numbers like $+6$, and zero are members of the set of integers. Integers can be represented as points on a number line. This set of integers can be written $\{\ldots, -3, -2, -1, 0, 1, 2, 3, \ldots\}$ where $\ldots$ means "continues indefinitely." When graphing integers, locate the points named by the integers on a number line. The number that corresponds to a point is called the coordinate of that point. The numbers on a number line increase from left to right. This can help determine which of two numbers is greater. Any mathematical sentence containing $<$ (less than) or $>$ (greater than) is called an inequality. An inequality compares numbers or quantities.

In mathematics, when two integers on a number line are on opposite sides of zero, and they are the same distance from zero, they have the same absolute value. The symbol for absolute value is two vertical bars on either side of the number. For example, $|-5| = 5$. Since variables represent numbers, absolute value notation can be used in algebraic expressions involving variables.

2-2 Adding Integers

The equation $-5 + (-2) = -7$ is an example of adding two integers with the same sign. To add integers with the same sign, add their absolute values. The sum takes the same sign as the addends. To add integers with different signs, subtract their absolute values. The sum takes the same sign as the addend with the greater absolute value.

Two numbers with the same absolute value but different signs are called *opposites*. For example, -4 and 4 are opposites. An integer and its opposite are also called *additive inverses*. The Additive Inverse Property says that the sum of any number and its additive inverse is zero. The Commutative, Associative, and Identity Properties also apply to integers. These properties help when adding more than two integers.

2-3 Subtracting Integers

In this lesson, the rules for adding integers are extended to the subtraction of integers. To subtract an integer, add its additive inverse. For example, to find the difference $2 - 5$, add the additive inverse of 5 to 2: $2 + (-5) = -3$. The rule for subtracting integers can be used to solve real-world problems and to evaluate algebraic expressions.

2-4 Multiplying Integers

Since multiplication is repeated addition, $3(-7)$ means that -7 is used as an addend 3 times. By the Commutative Property of Multiplication, $3(-7) = -7(3)$. The product of two integers with different signs is always negative. Students use this fact and the fact that the product of two positive integers is positive to find inductively that the product of two integers with the same sign is positive.

2-5 Dividing Integers

The quotient of two integers can be found by using the related multiplication sentence. For example, the division sentence $-12 \div (-4) = 3$ is related to the multiplication sentence $-4 \times 3 = -12$. Students use examples such as this one, their study of the multiplication of integers in Lesson 2-4, and their prior experience with dividing whole numbers to determine that the quotient of two integers with the same sign is positive. By examining multiplication sentences involving integers with different signs, students learn that the quotient of two integers with different signs is negative.

The division of integers is extended to statistics to find the average, or mean, of a set of data. When finding the mean of a set of numbers, find the sum of the numbers and then divide by the number in the set.

2-6 The Coordinate System

In the Cartesian coordinate system, the y-axis extends above and below the origin and the x-axis extends to the right and left of the origin, which is the point at which the x- and y-axes intersect. Numbers below and to the left of the origin are negative. A point graphed on the coordinate grid is said to have an x-coordinate and a y-coordinate. For example, the point $(1, -2)$, has as its x-coordinate the number 1, and has as its y-coordinate the number -2. This point is graphed by locating the position on the grid that is 1 unit to the right of the origin and 2 units below the origin.

The x-axis and the y-axis separate the coordinate plane into four regions, called *quadrants*. The axes and points located on the axes themselves are not located in any of the quadrants. The quadrants are labeled I to IV, starting in the upper right and proceeding counterclockwise. In quadrant I, both coordinates are positive. In quadrant II, the x-coordinate is negative and the y-coordinate is positive. In quadrant III, both coordinates are negative. In quadrant IV, the x-coordinate is positive and the y-coordinate is negative. A coordinate graph can be used to show algebraic relationships among numbers.

Quick Review Math Handbook

Hot Words includes a glossary of terms while Hot Topics consists of explanations of key mathematical concepts with exercises to test comprehension. This valuable resource can be used as a reference in the classroom or for home study.

Lesson	Hot Topics Section	Lesson	Hot Topics Section
GS 2	6.3, 6.7	2-4	1.5
2-1	1.5	2-5	1.5, 6.7
2-2	1.5, 6.3	2-6	6.7
2-3	1.5		

GS = Getting Started

 Additional mathematical information and teaching notes are available at www.pre-alg.com/key_concepts.

DAILY INTERVENTION and Assessment

Key to Abbreviations:
TWE = Teacher Wraparound Edition; CRM = Chapter Resource Masters

	Type	Student Edition	Teacher Resources	Technology/Internet
INTERVENTION	Ongoing	Prerequisite Skills, pp. 55, 61, 68, 74, 79, 84 Practice Quiz 1, p. 74 Practice Quiz 2, p. 84	5-Minute Check Transparencies *Prerequisite Skills Workbook*, pp. 1–2, 5–12 Quizzes, *CRM*, pp. 101, 102 Mid-Chapter Test, *CRM*, p. 103 Study Guide and Intervention, *CRM*, pp. 57, 62, 67, 72, 77, 82	Pre-AlgePASS: Tutorial Plus, Lesson 3 www.pre-alg.com/self_check_quiz www.pre-alg.com/extra_examples
	Mixed Review	pp. 61, 68, 74, 79, 84, 89	Cumulative Review, *CRM*, p. 104	
	Error Analysis	Find the Error, pp. 72, 87	Find the Error, *TWE*, pp. 72, 87 Unlocking Misconceptions, *TWE*, pp. 58, 65, 82	
	Standardized Test Practice	pp. 61, 68, 74, 76, 77, 79, 84, 89, 94–95	*TWE*, pp. 94–95 Standardized Test Practice, *CRM*, pp. 105–106	Standardized Test Practice CD-ROM www.pre-alg.com/standardized_test
ASSESSMENT	Open-Ended Assessment	Writing in Math, pp. 61, 68, 74, 79, 84, 89 Open Ended, pp. 59, 67, 72, 77, 83, 87 Standardized Test, p. 95	Modeling: *TWE*, pp. 61, 74 Speaking: *TWE*, pp. 79, 89 Writing: *TWE*, pp. 68, 84 Open-Ended Assessment, *CRM*, p. 99	
	Chapter Assessment	Study Guide, pp. 90–92 Practice Test, p. 93	Multiple-Choice Tests (Forms 1, 2A, 2B), *CRM*, pp. 87–92 Free-Response Tests (Forms 2C, 2D, 3), *CRM*, pp. 93–98 Vocabulary Test/Review, *CRM*, p. 100	ExamView® Pro (see below) MindJogger Videoquizzes www.pre-alg.com/vocabulary_review www.pre-alg.com/chapter_test

For more information on Yearly ProgressPro, see p. 2.

Pre-Algebra Lesson	Yearly ProgressPro Skill Lesson(s)
2-1	Writing Integers Absolute Value
2-2	Add Integers
2-3	Subtracting Integers
2-4	Multiply Integers
2-5	Divide Integers
2-6	Coordinate Locations: Level 3

ExamView® Pro

Use the networkable **ExamView® Pro** to:
- Create **multiple versions** of tests.
- Create **modified** tests for *Inclusion* students.
- **Edit** existing questions and **add** your own questions.
- Use built-in **state curriculum correlations** to create tests aligned with state standards.
- Change **English** tests to **Spanish** and vice versa.

For more information on Intervention and Assessment, see pp. T8–T11.

Reading and Writing in Mathematics

Glencoe Pre-Algebra provides numerous opportunities to incorporate reading and writing into the mathematics classroom.

Student Edition

- Foldables™ Study Organizer, p. 55
- Reading Mathematics, p. 69
- Concept Check questions require students to verbalize and write about what they have learned in the lesson. (pp. 56, 57, 59, 66, 67, 71, 72, 77, 81, 83, 86, 87)
- Writing in Math questions in every lesson, pp. 61, 68, 74, 79, 84, 89
- Reading Math, pp. 56, 57, 64, 75, 80, 88
- WebQuest, p. 79

Teacher Wraparound Edition

- Foldables™ Study Organizer, pp. 55, 90
- Study Notebook suggestions, pp. 58, 63, 66, 69, 72, 77, 83, 87
- Modeling activities, pp. 61, 74
- Speaking activities, pp. 79, 89
- Writing activities, pp. 68, 84
- **ELL** Resources, pp. 54, 56, 64, 69, 70, 75, 80, 85, 90

Additional Resources

- Vocabulary Builder worksheets require students to define and give examples for key vocabulary terms as they progress through the chapter (*Chapter 2 Resource Masters*, pp. vii–viii)
- Reading to Learn Mathematics master for each lesson (*Chapter 2 Resource Masters*, pp. 60, 65, 70, 75, 80, 85)
- *Vocabulary PuzzleMaker* software creates crossword, jumble, and word search puzzles using vocabulary lists that you can customize.
- *Teaching Mathematics with Foldables* provides suggestions for promoting cognition and language.
- *Reading and Writing in the Mathematics Classroom*
- *WebQuest and Project Resources*

For more information on Reading and Writing in Mathematics, see pp. T6–T7.

 ENGLISH LANGUAGE LEARNERS

Lesson 2-1
Flexible Groups

Give groups of six students a set of six cards with an integer on each card. Have the students order the numbers from least to greatest. On a wall of the room, mark 0, positive, and negative to denote a number line. Have the students come to the number line by group and position themselves in order on the number line. The students can check each other for accuracy.

Lesson 2-2
Higher-Level Thinking

Based on the patterns that students have seen modeled by the teacher, have them work in groups of three or four to come up with their own rules for adding integers with different signs. This same model can be used for subtracting, multiplying, and dividing integers.

Lesson 2-6
Using Models

Have students draw a coordinate plane on grid paper, labeling the *x*- and *y*- axes, the origin, and all four quadrants. Discuss with the students what an ordered pair is and how to locate one on the coordinate plane. For a large coordinate plane, use a shower curtain and masking tape to draw all the parts of the coordinate plane. Have students stand on points to graph ordered pairs.

What You'll Learn

Have students read over the list of objectives and make a list of any words with which they are not familiar.

Why It's Important

Point out to students that this is only one of many reasons why each objective is important. Others are provided in the introduction to each lesson.

Lesson	NCTM Standards	Local Objectives
2-1	1, 2, 6, 10	
2-2 Preview	1, 6	
2-2	1, 2, 6	
2-3	1, 2, 6	
2-4	1, 2, 6	
2-5	1, 2, 6	
2-6	2, 3, 6, 10	

Key to NCTM Standards:

1=Number & Operations, 2=Algebra, 3=Geometry, 4=Measurement, 5=Data Analysis & Probability, 6=Problem Solving, 7=Reasoning & Proof, 8=Communication, 9=Connections, 10=Representation

Chapter 2 Integers

What You'll Learn

- **Lesson 2-1** Compare and order integers, and find the absolute value of an expression.
- **Lessons 2-2 through 2-5** Add, subtract, multiply, and divide integers.
- **Lessons 2-3 and 2-4** Evaluate and simplify algebraic expressions.
- **Lesson 2-5** Find the average of a set of data.
- **Lesson 2-6** Graph points, and show algebraic relationships on a coordinate plane.

Key Vocabulary

- integer (p. 56)
- inequality (p. 57)
- absolute value (p. 58)
- additive inverse (p. 66)
- quadrants (p. 86)

Why It's Important

In both mathematics and everyday life, there are many situations where integers are used. Some examples include temperatures, sports such as golf and football, and measuring the elevation of points on Earth or the depth below sea level. *You will represent real-world situations with integers in Lesson 2-1.*

Vocabulary Builder

ELL

The Key Vocabulary list introduces students to some of the main vocabulary terms included in this chapter. For a more thorough vocabulary list with pronunciations of new words, give students the Vocabulary Builder worksheets found on pages vii and viii of the *Chapter 2 Resource Masters*. Encourage them to complete the definition of each term as they progress through the chapter. You may suggest that they add these sheets to their study notebooks for future reference when studying for the Chapter 2 test.

Getting Started

Getting Started

▶ **Prerequisite Skills** To be successful in this chapter, you'll need to master these skills and be able to apply them in problem-solving situations. Review these skills before beginning Chapter 2.

For Lesson 2-1   **Evaluate Expressions**

Evaluate each expression if $a = 4$, $b = 10$, and $c = 8$. *(For review, see Lesson 1-3.)*

1. $a + b + c$ **22**   **2.** $bc - ab$ **40**   **3.** $b + ac$ **42**

4. $4c + 3b$ **62**   **5.** $2b - (a + c)$ **8**   **6.** $2c - b + a$ **10**

For Lesson 2-3   **Patterns**

Find the next term in each list. *(For review, see Lesson 1-1.)*

7. 34, 28, 22, 16, 10, …   **4**   **8.** 120, 105, 90, 75, …   **60**

For Lesson 2-6   **Graph Points**

Use the grid to name the point for each ordered pair.
(For review, see Lesson 1-6.)

9. (1, 3)   *T*   **10.** (5, 2)   *L*   **11.** (5, 5)   *V*

12. (3, 4)   *U*   **13.** (0, 2)   *Q*   **14.** (6, 1)   *R*

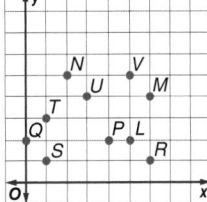

FOLDABLES™ Study Organizer

Operations with Integers Make this Foldable to help you organize your notes. Begin with a piece of graph paper.

Step 1   **Fold in Half**

Fold the graph paper in half lengthwise.

Step 2   **Fold Again in Fourths**

Fold the top to the bottom twice.

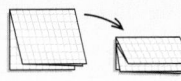

Step 3   **Cut**

Open. Cut along the second fold to make four tabs.

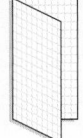

Step 4   **Label**

Fold lengthwise. Draw a number line on the outside. Label each tab as shown.

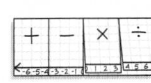

Reading and Writing As you read and study the chapter, write rules and examples for each integer operation under the tabs.

This section provides a review of the basic concepts needed before beginning Chapter 2. Page references are included for additional student help.

Additional review is provided in the *Prerequisite Skills Workbook*, pages 1–2 and 5–12.

Prerequisite Skills in the Getting Ready for the Next Lesson section at the end of each lesson reviews a skill needed in the next lesson.

For Lesson	Prerequisite Skill
2-2	Adding and Subtracting Whole Numbers (p. 61)
2-3	Evaluating Expressions (p. 68)
2-4	Multiplying Whole Numbers (p. 74)
2-5	Dividing Whole Numbers (p. 79)
2-6	Ordered Pairs (p. 84)

FOLDABLES™ Study Organizer

For more information about Foldables, see *Teaching Mathematics with Foldables*.

Reading for Main Ideas and Note Taking Ask students to read and determine the main ideas for each lesson. When searching for the main idea, encourage students to ask themselves, "What is this paragraph or lesson telling me? What is its intent?" After students have determined the main idea, they can also find supporting details or words that give more information about the main idea.

2-1 Integers and Absolute Value

1 Focus

5-Minute Check Transparency 2-1 Use as a quiz or review of Chapter 1.

Mathematical Background notes are available for this lesson on page 54C.

How are integers used to model real-world situations?

The opening activity questions are repeated on page 60 of the *Chapter 2 Resource Masters*.

Reading to Learn Mathematics, p. 60   ELL

Pre-Activity   *How are integers used to model real-world situations?*

Do the activity at the top of page 56 in your textbook. Write your answers below.

  a. What does a value of −7 represent?   7 inches below normal

  b. Which city was farthest from its normal rainfall?   Jackson, MS

  c. How could you represent 5 inches above normal rainfall? +5

Reading the Lesson   1–5. See students' work.

Write a definition and give an example of each new vocabulary word or phrase.

Vocabulary	Definition	Example
1. negative number		
2. integers		
3. coordinate		
4. inequality		
5. absolute value		

Helping You Remember

6. *Absolute* is a word that is used frequently in the English language.

  a. Find the definition of *absolute* in a dictionary. Write the definition that most closely relates to mathematics.   independent of arbitrary standards of measurement

  b. Explain how the English definition can help you remember the meaning of *absolute value* in mathematics.   The absolute value of an integer is independent of the sign of the number.

Vocabulary

- negative number
- integers
- coordinate
- inequality
- absolute value

a. 7 in. below normal

b. Jackson, MS

What You'll Learn

- Compare and order integers.
- Find the absolute value of an expression.

How are integers used to model real-world situations?

The summer of 1999 was unusually dry in parts of the United States. In the graph, a value of −8 represents 8 inches below the normal rainfall.

a. What does a value of −7 represent?

b. Which city was farthest from its normal rainfall?

c. How could you represent 5 inches above normal rainfall? **+5**

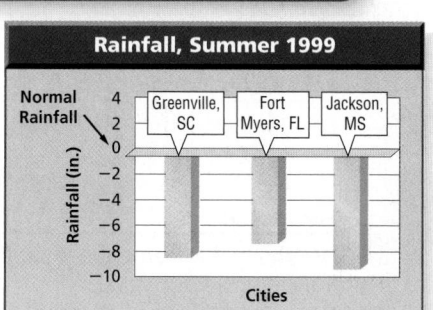

Rainfall, Summer 1999

Reading Math

Integers

Read −8 as *negative 8*. A positive integer like 6 can be written as +6. It is usually written without the + sign, as 6.

TEACHING TIP

Remind students that the arrowheads on the number line indicate that the set of numbers continues indefinitely.

COMPARE AND ORDER INTEGERS   With normal rainfall as the starting point of 0, you can express 8 inches below normal as 0 − 8, or −8. A **negative number** is a number less than zero.

Negative numbers like −8, positive numbers like +6, and zero are members of the set of **integers**. Integers can be represented as points on a number line.

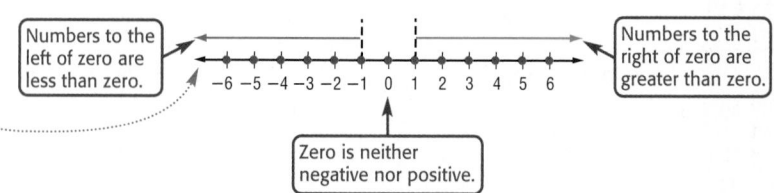

Numbers to the left of zero are less than zero.

Numbers to the right of zero are greater than zero.

Zero is neither negative nor positive.

This set of integers can be written {..., −3, −2, −1, 0, 1, 2, 3, ...} where ... means continues indefinitely.

Example 1 Write Integers for Real-World Situations

Write an integer for each situation.

a. 500 feet below sea level   The integer is −500.

b. a temperature increase of 12°   The integer is +12.

c. a loss of $240   The integer is −240.

 Concept Check   Which integer is neither positive nor negative? **zero**

Resource Manager

📁 Workbooks and Reproducible Masters

Chapter 2 Resource Masters
- Study Guide and Intervention, p. 57
- Skills Practice, p. 58
- Practice, p. 59
- Reading to Learn Mathematics, p. 60
- Enrichment, p. 61

Parent and Student Study Guide Workbook, p. 9
Prerequisite Skills Workbook, pp. 1–2, 5–8
School-to-Career Masters, p. 3
Science and Mathematics Lab Manual, pp. 5–10

Transparencies
5-Minute Check Transparency 2-1
Real-World Transparency 2
Answer Key Transparencies

Technology
Interactive Chalkboard

To graph integers, locate the points named by the integers on a number line. The number that corresponds to a point is called the **coordinate** of that point.

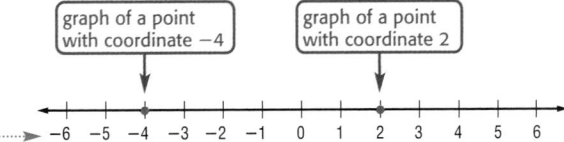

graph of a point with coordinate −4

graph of a point with coordinate 2

Notice that the numbers on a number line increase as you move from left to right. This can help you determine which of two numbers is greater.

Reading Math

Inequality Symbols
Read the symbol < as *is less than*. Read the symbol > as *is greater than*.

Words	−4 is less than 2.	2 is greater than −4.

OR

Symbols	$-4 < 2$	$2 > -4$

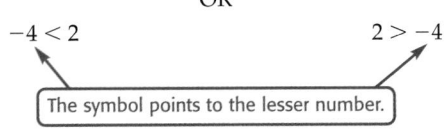

The symbol points to the lesser number.

Any mathematical sentence containing < or > is called an inequality. An **inequality** compares numbers or quantities.

Example 2 Compare Two Integers

Use the integers graphed on the number line below.

$-6\,-5\,-4\,-3\,-2\,-1\ \ 0\ \ 1\ \ 2\ \ 3\ \ 4\ \ 5\ \ 6$

a. Write two inequalities involving −3 and 4.
Since −3 is to the left of 4, write $-3 < 4$.
Since 4 is to the right of −3, write $4 > -3$.

b. Replace the ● with < or > in −5 ● −1 to make a true sentence.
−1 is greater since it lies to the right of −5. So write $-5 < -1$.

Integers are used to compare numbers in many real-world situations.

Example 3 Order Integers

GOLF The top ten fourth round scores of the 2003 LPGA Championship tournament were 0, +1, −4, −2, −1, +4, +2, +3, +5, and −3. Order the scores from least to greatest.

Graph each integer on a number line.

$-5\ \ -4\ \ -3\ \ -2\ \ -1\ \ \ 0\ \ \ 1\ \ \ 2\ \ \ 3\ \ \ 4\ \ \ 5$

Write the numbers as they appear from left to right.
The scores −4, −3, −2, −1, 0, +1, +2, +3, +4, +5 are in order from least to greatest.

✓ **Concept Check** Why is the sentence 5 > 2 an inequality?
It has the > symbol and compares two numbers.

www.pre-alg.com/extra_examples

Lesson 2-1 Integers and Absolute Value **57**

2 Teach

COMPARE AND ORDER INTEGERS

In-Class Examples   Power Point®

Teaching Tip The integers can be described as the natural numbers, their opposites, and zero.

1 Write an integer for each situation.
a. 32 feet under ground −32
b. 8 weeks after birth +8
c. a loss of 6 pounds −6

Teaching Tip You may want to suggest that the < and > symbols "point to the lesser number and open to the greater number."

2 Use the integers graphed on the number line below for each question.

$-4\ \ -2\ \ \ 0\ \ \ 2\ \ \ 4\ \ \ 6\ \ \ 8$

a. Write two inequalities involving 7 and −4.
$7 > -4;\ -4 < 7$

b. Replace the ● with <, >, or = in −2 ● 3 to make a true sentence. <

3 WEATHER The high temperatures for the first seven days of January were −8°, 10°, 2°, −3°, −11°, 0°, and 1°. Order the temperatures from least to greatest.
−11, −8, −3, 0, 1, 2, 10

✓ **Skills Check**

Compare and Order Integers
Order the integers in each set from least to greatest.
a. {2, −7, 0, 1, −3}
{−7, −3, 0, 1, 2}
b. {123, −54, 27, −48, 115}
{−54, −48, 27, 115, 123}

Building on Prior Knowledge

In Chapter 1, students learned how to evaluate algebraic expressions with whole numbers. In Example 5, they will extend this knowledge to evaluate expressions involving integers.

ABSOLUTE VALUE

In-Class Examples

4 Evaluate each expression.

a. $|5|$ **5**

b. $|-8| + |-1|$ **9**

c. $|6| - |-4|$ **2**

Teaching Tip Explain that in expressions such as the one in Example 5, the absolute value symbol cannot be removed from the variables before evaluating the expression.

5 **ALGEBRA** Evaluate the expression $|x| - 8$ if $x = -2$.
−6

3 Practice/Apply

Study Notebook

Have students—

• add the definitions/examples of the vocabulary terms to their Vocabulary Builder worksheets for Chapter 2.

• make a list of words and phrases that indicate positive and negative numbers.

• include any other item(s) that they find helpful in mastering the skills in this lesson.

ABSOLUTE VALUE On the number line, notice that -5 and 5 are on opposite sides of zero, and they are the same distance from zero. In mathematics, we say they have the same **absolute value**, 5.

The symbol for absolute value is two vertical bars on either side of the number.

$$|5| = 5 \quad \text{The absolute value of 5 is 5.}$$
$$|-5| = 5 \quad \text{The absolute value of } -5 \text{ is 5.}$$

Key Concept   **Absolute Value**

• **Words**   The absolute value of a number is the distance the number is from zero on the number line. The absolute value of a number is always greater than or equal to zero.

• **Examples** $|5| = 5$ $|-5| = 5$

Example 4 *Expressions with Absolute Value*

Evaluate each expression.

a. $|-8|$

$$|-8| = 8 \quad \text{The graph of } -8 \text{ is 8 units from 0.}$$

b. $|9| + |-7|$ The absolute value of 9 is 9.
$$|9| + |-7| = 9 + 7 \quad \text{The absolute value of } -7 \text{ is 7.}$$
$$= 16 \quad \text{Simplify.}$$

c. $|-4| - |3|$
$$|-4| - |3| = 4 - 3 \quad |-4| = 4, |3| = 3$$
$$= 1 \quad \text{Simplify.}$$

Study Tip

Common Misconception
It is not always true that the absolute value of a number is the opposite of the number. Remember that absolute value is always positive or zero.

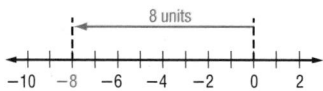

Since variables represent numbers, you can use absolute value notation with algebraic expressions involving variables.

Example 5 *Algebraic Expressions with Absolute Value*

ALGEBRA   Evaluate $|x| - 3$ if $x = -5$.
$$|x| - 3 = |-5| - 3 \quad \text{Replace } x \text{ with } -5.$$
$$= 5 - 3 \quad \text{The absolute value of } -5 \text{ is 5.}$$
$$= 2 \quad \text{Simplify.}$$

58 Chapter 2 Integers

DAILY
INTERVENTION   **Unlocking Misconceptions**

• **Absolute Value** Watch for students who think that the absolute value of a positive number is negative. Remind them that the absolute value of either a positive or negative number represents a distance, and distances are always positive.

Concept Check

1. **Explain** how you would graph -4 on a number line. **See margin.**

2. **OPEN ENDED** Write two inequalities using integers. **See margin.**

3. **Define** *absolute value.* **See margin.**

Guided Practice

GUIDED PRACTICE KEY	
Exercises	Examples
4–6	1
7–12	2
12, 19	3
13–15	4
16–18	5

Write an integer for each situation. Then graph on a number line.

4. 8° below zero -8

5. a 15-yard gain $+15$

4–5. See margin for graphs.

6. Graph the set of integers {0, -3, 6} on a number line. **See margin.**

Write two inequalities using the numbers in each sentence. Use the symbols < or >.

7. $-4°$ is colder than 2°.
$-4 < 2; 2 > -4$

8. -6 is greater than -10.
$-6 > -10; -10 < -6$

Replace each ● with <, >, or = to make a true sentence.

9. -18 ● -8 $<$

10. 0 ● -3 $>$

11. 9 ● -9 $>$

12. Order the integers {28, -6, 0, -2, 5, -52, 115} from least to greatest.
{-52, -6, -2, 0, 5, 28, 115}

Evaluate each expression.

13. $|-10|$ 10

14. $|10| - |-4|$ 6

15. $|16| + |-5|$ 21

ALGEBRA Evaluate each expression if $a = -8$ and $b = 5$.

16. $9 + |a|$ 17

17. $|a| - b$ 3

18. $2|a|$ 16

Application

19. **WEATHER** The table shows the record low temperatures in °F for selected states. Order the temperatures from least to greatest.

State	AL	CA	FL	IN	KY	NY	NC	OK	OR
Temperature	-27	-45	-2	-36	-37	-52	-34	-27	-54

$-54, -52, -45, -37, -36, -34, -27, -27, -2$

★ indicates increased difficulty

Practice and Apply

Homework Help

For Exercises	See Examples
20–25, 66	1
26–43	2
44–47, 67–70	3
48–59	4
60–65	5

Extra Practice
See page 726.

Write an integer for each situation. Then graph on a number line.

20. a bank withdrawal of $100 -100

21. a loss of 6 pounds -6

22. a salary increase of $250 $+250$

23. a gain of 9 yards $+9$

24. 12° above zero $+12$

25. 5 seconds before liftoff -5

20–25. See margin for graphs.

Graph each set of integers on a number line. **26–29. See pp. 95A–95B.**

26. {0, -2, 4}

27. {-3, 1, 2, 5}

28. {-2, -4, -5, -8}

29. {-4, 0, 6, -7, -1}

Write two inequalities using the numbers in each sentence. Use the symbols < or >. 31. $-5 > -10; -10 < -5$

30. 3 meters is taller than 2 meters. $3 > 2; 2 < 3$

31. A temperature of $-5°$F is warmer than a temperature of $-10°$F.

32. 55 miles per hour is slower than 65 miles per hour. $55 < 65; 65 > 55$

Lesson 2-1 Integers and Absolute Value **59**

DAILY INTERVENTION

Differentiated Instruction

- **Auditory/Musical** Bring to class several bars of music in the key of C to distribute to small groups or to individual students. Let middle C correspond to 0 on a number line. Have students plot the notes in the bar of music onto a number line. Let each whole step count as 1; the first F above middle C would equal 3, and the first A before middle C would equal -2. Have students play or sing the music, and then play the notes ordered from least to greatest on the number line.

About the Exercises . . .

Organization by Objective
- **Compare and Order Integers:** 20–47, 66–70
- **Absolute Value:** 48–65

Odd/Even Assignments
Exercises 20–65 are structured so that students practice the same concepts whether they are assigned odd or even problems.

Assignment Guide
Basic: 21–41 odd, 45–57 odd, 61–65 odd, 67–89
Average: 21–65 odd, 67–89
Advanced: 22–66 even, 67–83 (Optional: 84–89)

Answers

1. Draw a number line. Draw a dot at -4.

2. Sample answer: $3 > -2$, $|-5| < |-8|$

3. The absolute value of a number is its distance from 0 on a number line.

4.
-8 -7 -6 -5 -4 -3 -2 -1 0

5.
8 9 10 11 12 13 14 15 16

6.
-3 -2 -1 0 1 2 3 4 5 6

20.
-100 -50 0 50 100

21.
-8 -7 -6 -5 -4 -3 -2 -1 0

22.
0 100 200 300

23.
5 6 7 8 9 10 11 12 13

24.
0 2 4 6 8 10 12 14 16

25.
-8 -7 -6 -5 -4 -3 -2 -1 0

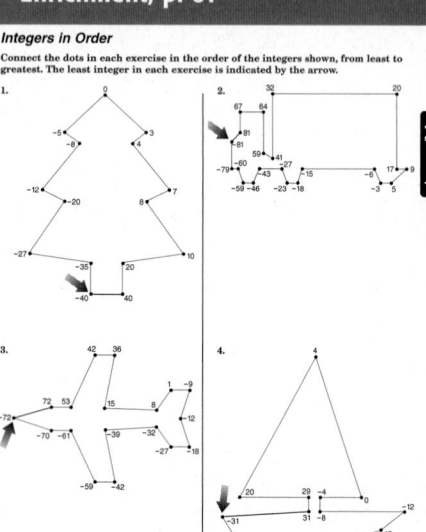
Write two inequalities using the numbers in each sentence. Use the symbols < or >. **33.** 248 < 425; 425 > 248   **34.** −2 < 23; 23 > −2

33. Yesterday's pollen count was 248. Today's count is 425.

34. Yesterday's low temperature was −2°F. The high temperature was 23°F.

35. Water boils at 212°F, and it freezes at 32°F.   212 > 32; 32 < 212

Replace each ● with < , >, or = to make a true sentence.

36. −6 ● −2   <   **37.** −10 ● −13   >   **38.** 0 ● −9   >   **39.** 14 ● 0   >
40. −18 ● 8   <   **41.** 5 ● −23   >   ★**42.** |9| ● |−9| =   ★**43.** |−20| ● |−4| >

Order the integers in each set from least to greatest. **45.** {−15, −4, −2, −1}

44. {5, 0, −8} {−8, 0, 5}   **45.** {−15, −1, −2, −4}
46. {24, 5, −46, 9, 0, −3}   **47.** {98, −57, −60, 38, 188}
{−46, −3, 0, 5, 9, 24}   {−60, −57, 38, 98, 188}

Evaluate each expression.

48. |−15| 15   **49.** |46| 46   **50.** −|20| −20   **51.** −|5| −5
52. |0| 0   **53.** |7| 7   **54.** |−5| + |4| 9   **55.** |0| + |−2| 2
56. |15| − |−1| 14   **57.** |0 + 9| 9   ★**58.** −|−24| −24   ★**59.** −||−6| + |14|| −20

ALGEBRA Evaluate each expression if a = 0, b = 3, and c = −4.

60. 14 + |b| 17   **61.** |c| − a 4   **62.** a + b + |c| 7
63. ab + |−40| 40   **64.** |c| − b 1   **65.** |ab| + b 3

66. GEOGRAPHY The Caribbean Sea has an average depth of 8685 feet below sea level. Use an integer to express this depth. −8685 ft

WEATHER For Exercises 67–70, use the graphic.

67. Graph the temperatures on a number line. **See margin.**

68. Compare the lowest temperature in the United States and the lowest temperature east of the Mississippi using the < symbol. −80 < −54

69. Compare the lowest temperatures of the contiguous 48 states and east of the Mississippi using the > symbol. −54 > −70

70. Write the temperatures in order from greatest to least. −54°, −70°, −80°

71. How many units apart are −4 and 3 on a number line? 7

72. CRITICAL THINKING Consider any two points on the number line where X > Y. Is it *always*, *sometimes*, or *never* true that |X| > |Y|? Explain. **See margin.**

USA TODAY Snapshots®

Lowest temperatures in the USA

Prospect Creek, Alaska Jan. 23, 1971
Rogers Pass, Mont. Jan. 20, 1954
Danbury, Wis. Jan. 24, 1922

−54°
−70°
−80°

Source: National Climatic Data Center

By Marcy E. Mullins, USA TODAY

73. CRITICAL THINKING Consider two numbers *A* and *B* on a number line. Is it *always*, *sometimes*, or *never* true that the distance between *A* and *B* equals the distance between $|A|$ and $|B|$? Explain. **See margin.**

74. WRITING IN MATH   Answer the question that was posed at the beginning of the lesson. **See margin.**

How are integers used to model real-world situations?

Include the following in your answer:
- an explanation of how integers are used to describe rainfall, and
- some situations in the real world where negative numbers are used.

Standardized Test Practice

75. Which of the following describes the absolute value of $-2°$? **B**
- Ⓐ It is the distance from -2 to 2 on a thermometer.
- Ⓑ It is the distance from -2 to 0 on a thermometer.
- Ⓒ It is the actual temperature outside when a thermometer reads $-2°$.
- Ⓓ None of these describes the absolute value of $-2°$.

76. What is the temperature shown on the thermometer at the right? **D**
- Ⓐ 8
- Ⓑ 7
- Ⓒ -7
- Ⓓ -8

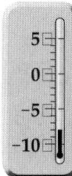

Maintain Your Skills

Mixed Review   **Determine whether a scatter plot of the data for the following might show a *positive*, *negative*, or *no* relationship. Explain your answer.**   *(Lesson 1-7)*

77. height and arm length **positive**   **78.** birth month and weight **none**
77–78. See margin for explanations.

Express each relation as a table and as a list of ordered pairs.   *(Lesson 1-6)*

79–80.
See pp. 95A–95B.

79. 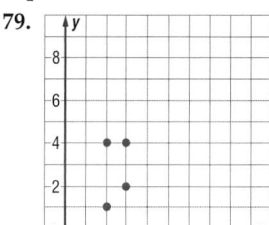   **80.**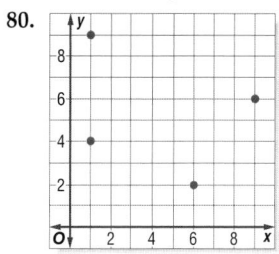

Name the property shown by each statement.   *(Lesson 1-4)*

81. $20 \cdot 18 = 18 \cdot 20$ **Comm. (×)**   **82.** $9 \cdot 8 \cdot 0 = 0$ **Mult. Prop. of 0**   **83.** $3ab = 3ba$ **Comm. (×)**

Getting Ready for the Next Lesson   **BASIC SKILL   Find each sum or difference. 86. 2107**

84. $18 + 29 + 46$ **93**   **85.** $232 + 156$ **388**   **86.** $451 + 629 + 1027$

87. $36 - 19$ **17**   **88.** $479 - 281$ **198**   **89.** $2011 - 962$ **1049**

Lesson 2-1 Integers and Absolute Value   **61**

Answers (p. 60)

67.
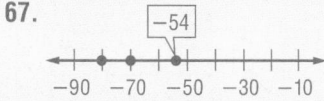

72. Sometimes true; if *X* and *Y* are both negative it will not be true.

73. Sometimes true; if *A* and *B* are both positive, both negative, or one is 0, it is always true. If one number is negative and the other is positive, it is never true.

Algebra Activity

A Preview of Lesson 2-2

Getting Started

Objective Model operations with integers with algebra tiles and an integer mat.

Materials
algebra tiles
integer mat

Teach

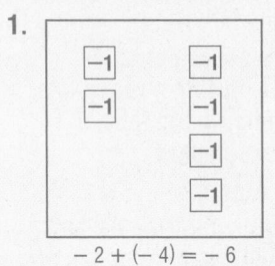

Activity 1

- Encourage students to line their tiles up neatly in side-by-side lines to help them see zero pairs.

Activity 2

- Reproduce the addition table on a transparency. Shade positive integers one color, negative integers another, and the zeros yet another color to make the patterns easier for the class to see. The student recording sheet has this table on it. Students could use colored pencils to do the same color scheme on their own papers.

Answers (p. 63)

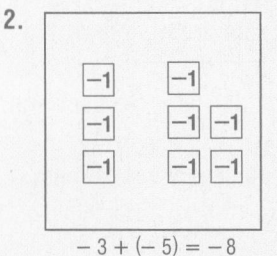

1.

$-2 + (-4) = -6$

Adding Integers

In a set of algebra tiles, $\boxed{1}$ represents the integer 1, and $\boxed{-1}$ represents the integer -1. You can use algebra tiles and an integer mat to model operations with integers.

Activity 1

The following example shows how to find the sum $-3 + (-2)$ using algebra tiles. Remember that addition means *combining*. $-3 + (-2)$ tells you to combine a set of 3 negative tiles with a set of 2 negative tiles.

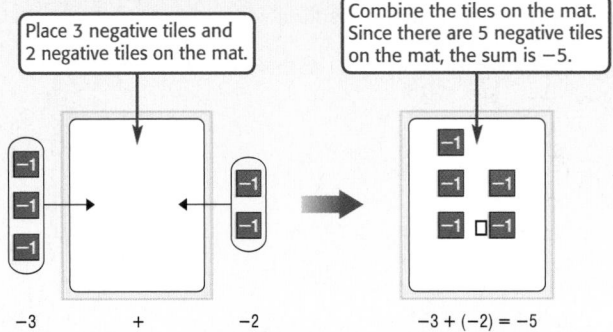

Place 3 negative tiles and 2 negative tiles on the mat.

Combine the tiles on the mat. Since there are 5 negative tiles on the mat, the sum is -5.

$-3 \qquad + \qquad -2 \qquad\qquad -3 + (-2) = -5$

Therefore, $-3 + (-2) = -5$.

There are two important properties to keep in mind when you model operations with integers.

- When one positive tile is paired with one negative tile, the result is called a **zero pair**.
- You can add or remove zero pairs from a mat because removing or adding zero does not change the value of the tiles on the mat.

The following example shows how to find the sum $-4 + 3$.

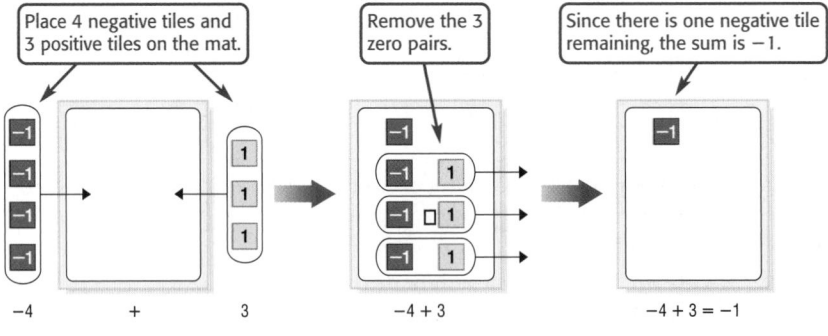

Place 4 negative tiles and 3 positive tiles on the mat.

Remove the 3 zero pairs.

Since there is one negative tile remaining, the sum is -1.

$-4 \qquad + \qquad 3 \qquad\qquad -4 + 3 \qquad\qquad -4 + 3 = -1$

Therefore, $-4 + 3 = -1$.

2.

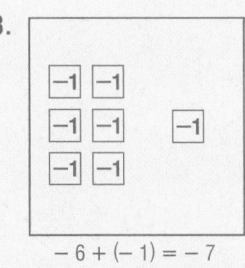

$-3 + (-5) = -8$

3.

$-6 + (-1) = -7$

4.

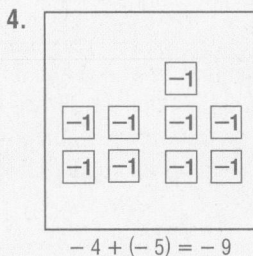

$-4 + (-5) = -9$

5.

$-4 + 2 = -2$

6.

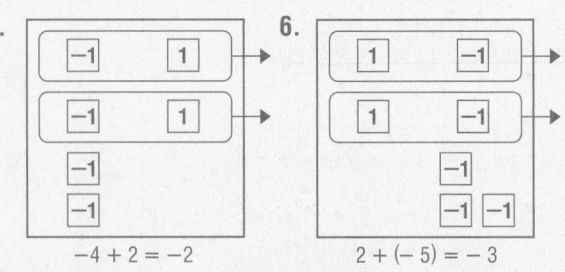

$2 + (-5) = -3$

Model

Use algebra tiles to model and find each sum. 1–8. See margin for models.

1. $-2 + (-4)$ **−6**
2. $-3 + (-5)$ **−8**
3. $-6 + (-1)$ **−7**
4. $-4 + (-5)$ **−9**
5. $-4 + 2$ **−2**
6. $2 + (-5)$ **−3**
7. $-1 + 6$ **5**
8. $4 + (-4)$ **0**

Activity 2

The Addition Table was completed using algebra tiles. In the highlighted portion of the table, the addends are -3 and 1, and the sum is -2. So, $-3 + 1 = -2$. You can use the patterns in the Addition Table to learn more about integers.

Addition Table									
+	**4**	**3**	**2**	**1**	**0**	**−1**	**−2**	**−3**	**−4**
4	8	7	6	5	4	3	2	1	0
3	7	6	5	4	3	2	1	0	−1
2	6	5	4	3	2	1	0	−1	−2
1	5	4	3	2	1	0	−1	−2	−3
0	4	3	2	1	0	−1	−2	−3	−4
−1	3	2	1	0	−1	−2	−3	−4	−5
−2	2	1	0	−1	−2	−3	−4	−5	−6
−3	1	0	−1	−2	−3	−4	−5	−6	−7
−4	0	−1	−2	−3	−4	−5	−6	−7	−8

← addends (top)

sums (right)

addends (bottom-left)

Make a Conjecture

9. Locate all of the positive sums in the table. Describe the addends that result in a positive sum.

10. Locate all of the negative sums in the table. Describe the addends that result in a negative sum.

11. Locate all of the sums that are zero. Describe the addends that result in a sum of zero. **They are additive inverses.**

12. The Identity Property says that when zero is added to any number, the sum is the number. Does it appear that this property is true for addition of integers? If so, write two examples that illustrate the property. If not, give a counterexample. **Yes; see margin for examples.**

13. The Commutative Property says that the order in which numbers are added does not change the sum. Does it appear that this property is true for addition of integers? If so, write two examples that illustrate the property. If not, give a counterexample. **Yes; see margin for examples.**

14. The Associative Property says that the way numbers are grouped when added does not change the sum. Is this property true for addition of integers? If so, write two examples that illustrate the property. If not, give a counterexample.

Algebra Activity Adding Integers **63**

Resource Manager

📁 Teaching Pre-Algebra with Manipulatives

- pp. 7–8 (master for algebra tiles)
- p. 12 (master for integer mat)
- p. 40 (student recording sheet)

Glencoe Mathematics Classroom Manipulative Kit

- algebra tiles
- integer mat

Answers

7.

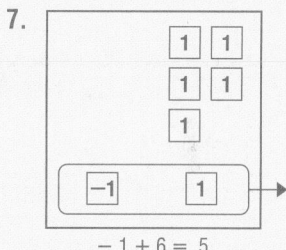

$-1 + 6 = 5$

8.

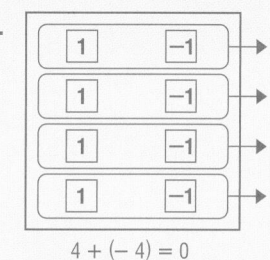

$4 + (-4) = 0$

9. The addends are both +, or one is + and one − with the + addend having the greater absolute value.

10. The addends are both −, or one is + and one − with the − addend having the greater absolute value.

14. Yes; see margin for examples.

12. Sample examples: $-1 + 0 = -1;\ 0 + (-2) = -2$

13. Sample examples: $-1 + 3 = 2$ and $3 + (-1) = 2;\ -2 + (-1) = -3$ and $-1 + (-2) = -3$

14. Sample examples:

$[3 + (-2)] + (-1) = 3 + [(-2) + (-1)]$

$1 + (-1) = 3 + (-3)$

$0 = 0$

and

$[1 + (-2)] + 2 = 1 + [-2 + 2]$

$-1 + 2 = 1 + 0$

$1 = 1$

1 Focus

5-Minute Check Transparency 2-2 Use as a quiz or review of Lesson 2-1.

Mathematical Background notes are available for this lesson on page 54C.

How can a number line help you add integers?

The opening activity questions are repeated on page 65 of the *Chapter 2 Resource Masters*.

Reading to Learn Mathematics, p. 65   ELL

Pre-Activity   *How can a number line help you add integers?*

   Do the activity at the top of page 64 in your textbook. Write your answers below.

   a. What integer represents the total yardage on the two plays? −7

   b. Write an addition sentence that describes this situation.
   −5 + (−2) = −7

Reading the Lesson   1–2. See students' work.
Write a definition and give an example of each new vocabulary word or phrase.

Vocabulary	Definition	Example
1. opposites		
2. additive inverse		

3. Draw a number line model that shows how to find the sum −4 + (−2). Explain your model.

   Start at zero on the number line. Move 4 units to the left because −4 is negative. Then move 2 more units to the left because −2 is negative. Then land on −6, so the sum is −6.

4. The sum of any number and its ___additive inverse___ is zero.

Helping You Remember

5. Suppose that one of your classmates was absent the day you learned how to add integers.

   a. Explain to your classmate how to add two integers with the same sign.
   Add their absolute values. Give the result the same sign as the integers.

   b. Explain to your classmate how to add two integers with different signs.
   Subtract their absolute values. Give the result the same sign as the integer with the greater absolute value.

2-2 Adding Integers

What You'll Learn

- Add two integers.
- Add more than two integers.

Vocabulary
- opposites
- additive inverse

How can a number line help you add integers?

In football, forward progress is represented by a positive integer. Being pushed back is represented by a negative integer. Suppose on the first play a team loses 5 yards and on the second play they lose 2 yards.

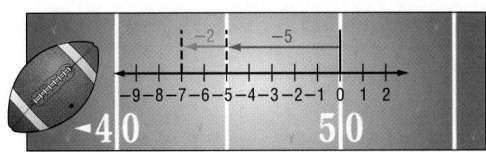

a. What integer represents the total yardage on the two plays? −7

b. Write an addition sentence that describes this situation. −5 + (−2) = −7

Reading Math

Addends and Sums
Recall that the numbers you add are called *addends*. The result is called the *sum*.

> **TEACHING TIP**
> Point out that the length of each arrow on the number line represents the absolute value of the addend.

ADD INTEGERS   The equation −5 + (−2) = −7 is an example of adding two integers with the same sign. Notice that the sign of the sum is the same as the sign of the addends.

Example 1 Add Integers on a Number Line

Find −2 + (−3).

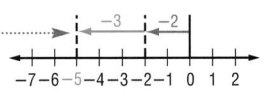

Start at zero.
Move 2 units to the left.
From there, move 3 more units to the left.

−2 + (−3) = −5

This example suggests a rule for adding integers with the same sign.

> **Key Concept**   Adding Integers with the Same Sign
>
> - **Words**   To add integers with the same sign, add their absolute values. Give the result the same sign as the integers.
>
> - **Examples**   −5 + (−2) = −7   6 + 3 = 9

Example 2 Add Integers with the Same Sign

Find −4 + (−5).

−4 + (−5) = −9   Add |−4| and |−5|. Both numbers are negative, so the sum is negative.

Resource Manager

📁 Workbooks and Reproducible Masters

Chapter 2 Resource Masters
- Study Guide and Intervention, p. 62
- Skills Practice, p. 63
- Practice, p. 64
- Reading to Learn Mathematics, p. 65
- Enrichment, p. 66
- Assessment, p. 101

Parent and Student Study Guide
   Workbook, p. 10
Prerequisite Skills Workbook, pp. 5–8

📀 Transparencies
5-Minute Check Transparency 2-2
Answer Key Transparencies

💿 Technology
Interactive Chalkboard

A number line can also help you understand how to add integers with different signs.

Example 3 Add Integers on a Number Line

Find each sum.

a. $7 + (-4)$

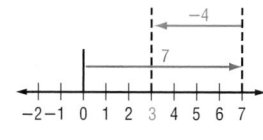

Start at zero.
Move 7 units to the right.
From there, move 4 units to the left.

$7 + (-4) = 3$

b. $2 + (-3)$

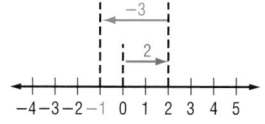

Start at zero.
Move 2 units to the right.
From there, move 3 units to the left.

$2 + (-3) = -1$

Notice how the sums in Example 3 relate to the addends.

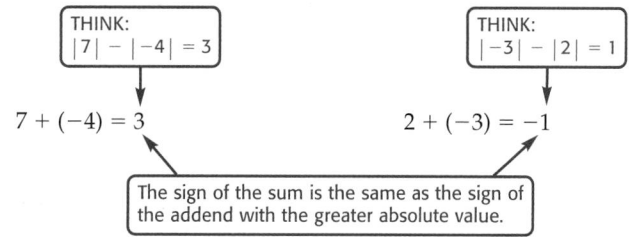

THINK:
$|7| - |-4| = 3$

$7 + (-4) = 3$

THINK:
$|-3| - |2| = 1$

$2 + (-3) = -1$

The sign of the sum is the same as the sign of the addend with the greater absolute value.

Key Concept   Adding Integers with Different Signs

- **Words**   To add integers with different signs, subtract their absolute values. Give the result the same sign as the integer with the greater absolute value.

- **Examples** $7 + (-2) = 5$ $-7 + 2 = -5$

Example 4 Add Integers with Different Signs

Find each sum.

a. $-8 + 3$

   $-8 + 3 = -5$ To find $-8 + 3$, subtract $|3|$ from $|-8|$.
                The sum is negative because $|-8| > |3|$.

b. $10 + (-4)$

   $10 + (-4) = 6$ To find $10 + |-4|$, subtract $|-4|$ from $|10|$.
                The sum is positive because $|10| > |-4|$.

 www.pre-alg.com/extra_examples

Lesson 2-2 Adding Integers   **65**

ADD INTEGERS

In-Class Examples   Power Point®

Teaching Tip Tell students that positive indicates a movement right, and negative is a movement left. When adding a positive integer to a positive or negative integer, move right on the number line. When adding a negative integer to a positive or negative integer, move left on the number line.

1 Find $3 + 4$.   **7**

2 Find $-5 + (-4)$.   **−9**

3 Find each sum.

a. $7 + (-11)$ **−4**

b. $-2 + 9$ **7**

4 Find each sum.

a. $-9 + 10$ **1**

b. $8 + (-15)$ **−7**

✓ Skills Check

Add Integers Find each sum.
a. $5 + (-6)$ **−1**
b. $8 + 5$ **13**
c. $-8 + (-9)$ **−17**
d. $-3 + 9$ **6**
e. $-11 + 5$ **−6**

DAILY
INTERVENTION   **Unlocking Misconceptions**

- **Add Integers** After presenting Example 4, some students may mistakenly assume the sign of the first addend is the sign of the sum. Emphasize that the sum has the same sign of the number that is farthest from 0 on the number line.

In-Class Example *Power Point®*

5 **WEATHER** On February 1, the temperature at dawn was −22°F. By noon it had risen 19 degrees. What was the temperature at noon? **−3°F**

ADD MORE THAN TWO INTEGERS

In-Class Example *Power Point®*

Teaching Tip Have students try using mental math to solve In-Class Example 6a. Working left-to-right, they should add the first two terms, then take that sum and add it to the third term.

6 Find each sum.

a. −8 + (−4) + 8   **−4**

b. 6 + (−3) + (−9) + 2   **−4**

3 Practice/Apply

Study Notebook

Have students—
• add the definitions/examples of the vocabulary terms to their Vocabulary Builder worksheets for Chapter 2.
• write examples for adding two negative integers, adding two positive integers, and adding two integers with different signs.
• include any other item(s) that they find helpful in mastering the skills in this lesson.

Answers (p. 67)

1a. Both addends are negative.

1b. $|12| > |−2|$

1c. $|−11| > |9|$

1d. Both addends are positive.

More About . . .

Astronomy •
The temperatures on the moon are so extreme because the moon does not have any atmosphere to trap heat.

Example 5 *Use Integers to Solve a Problem*

•••• **ASTRONOMY** During the night, the average temperature on the moon is −140°C. By noon, the average temperature has risen 252°C. What is the average temperature on the moon at noon?

Words   The temperature at night is −140°C. It increases 252°C by noon. What is the temperature at noon?

Variables   Let x = the temperature at noon.

Temperature at night	plus	increase by noon	equals	temperature at noon.
Equation −140	+	252	=	x

Solve the equation.

$-140 + 252 = x$ To find the sum, subtract $|−140|$ from 252.
$\quad\quad 112 = x$ The sum is positive because $|252| > |−140|$.

The average temperature at noon is 112°C.

ADD MORE THAN TWO INTEGERS   Two numbers with the same absolute value but different signs are called **opposites**. For example, −4 and 4 are opposites. An integer and its opposite are also called **additive inverses**.

Key Concept   *Additive Inverse Property*

• **Words**   The sum of any number and its additive inverse is zero.
• **Symbols** $x + (−x) = 0$
• **Example** $6 + (−6) = 0$

☑ **Concept Check**   What is the additive inverse of 2? **−2**
What is the additive inverse of −6? **6**

The commutative, associative, and identity properties also apply to integers. These properties can help you add more than two integers.

Example 6 *Add Three or More Integers*

Find each sum.

a. **9 + (− 3) + (−9)**

$9 + (−3) + (−9) = 9 + (−9) + (−3)$ Commutative Property
$\quad\quad\quad\quad\quad\quad = 0 + (−3)$ Additive Inverse Property
$\quad\quad\quad\quad\quad\quad = −3$ Identity Property of Addition

b. **−4 + 6 + (−3) + 9**

$-4 + 6 + (−3) + 9 = −4 + (−3) + 6 + 9$ Commutative Property
$\quad\quad\quad\quad\quad\quad = [−4 + (−3)] + (6 + 9)$ Associative Property
$\quad\quad\quad\quad\quad\quad = −7 + 15 \text{ or } 8$ Simplify.

Study Tip

Adding Mentally
One way to add mentally is to group the positive addends together and the negative addends together. Then add to find the sum. You should also look for addends that are opposites. You can always add in order from left to right.

66 Chapter 2 Integers

DAILY INTERVENTION — Differentiated Instruction

• **Visual/Spatial** To illustrate the concept of opposites on a number line, bring a small unbreakable mirror to class. Draw a number line on a piece of paper and hold the mirror perpendicular to the number line at the zero position. Have students come up a few at a time to observe what happens as a counter is moved along the positive side of a number line. **The counter's opposite value appears on the number line in the mirror, exactly the same distance from zero as the real counter.**

Concept Check

GUIDED PRACTICE KEY

Exercises	Examples
3, 4	1, 2
5–8	3, 4
9, 10	6
11	5

1. **State** whether each sum is positive or negative. Explain your reasoning.
   a. $-4 + (-5)$ **negative**
   b. $12 + (-2)$ **positive**
   c. $-11 + 9$ **negative**
   d. $15 + 10$ **positive**
   1a–d. See margin for explanations.

2. **OPEN ENDED** Give an example of two integers that are additive inverses. **Sample answer: -1 and 1**

Guided Practice

Find each sum.

3. $-2 + (-4)$ **-6**
4. $-10 + (-5)$ **-15**
5. $7 + (-2)$ **5**
6. $11 + (-3)$ **8**
7. $8 + (-5)$ **3**
8. $9 + (-12)$ **-3**
9. $8 + (-6) + 2$ **4**
10. $-6 + 5 + (-10)$ **-11**
11. $4 + (-5) = -1$

Application

11. **FOOTBALL** A team gained 4 yards on one play. On the next play, they lost 5 yards. Write an addition sentence to find the change in yardage.

★ indicates increased difficulty

Practice and Apply

Homework Help

For Exercises	See Examples
12–21	1, 2
22–29	3, 4
32–39	6
40, 41	5

Extra Practice
See page 726.

Find each sum.

12. $-4 + (-1)$ **-5**
13. $-5 + (-2)$ **-7**
14. $-4 + (-6)$ **-10**
15. $-3 + (-8)$ **-11**
16. $-7 + (-8)$ **-15**
17. $-12 + (-4)$ **-16**
18. $-9 + (-14)$ **-23**
19. $-15 + (-6)$ **-21**
20. $-11 + (-15)$ **-26**
21. $-23 + (-43)$ **-66**
22. $8 + (-5)$ **3**
23. $6 + (-4)$ **2**
24. $3 + (-7)$ **-4**
25. $4 + (-6)$ **-2**
26. $-15 + 6$ **-9**
27. $-5 + 11$ **6**
28. $18 + (-32)$ **-14**
29. $-45 + 19$ **-26**

30. What is the additive inverse of 14? **-14**
31. What is the additive inverse of -21? **21**

Find each sum.

32. $6 + (-9) + 9$ **6**
33. $7 + (-13) + 4$ **-2**
34. $-9 + 16 + (-10)$ **-3**
35. $-12 + 18 + (-12)$ **-6**
36. $14 + (-9) + 6$ **11**
37. $28 + (-35) + 4$ **-3**
38. $-41 + 25 + (-10)$ **-26**
39. $-18 + 35 + (-17)$ **0**

TEACHING TIP

Refer students to the Study Tip on page 66 for strategies to use when adding more than two integers.

40. **ACCOUNTING** The starting balance in a checking account was $50. What was the balance after checks were written for $25 and for $32? **$-\$7$**

41. **GOLF** A score of 0 is called *even par*. Two under par is written as -2. Two over par is written as $+2$. Suppose a player shot 4 under par, 2 over par, even par, and 3 under par in four rounds of a tournament. What was the player's final score? **-5**

Find each sum.

★ 42. $|18 + (-13)|$ **5**
★ 43. $|-27 + 19|$ **8**
★ 44. $|-25 + (-12)|$ **37**
★ 45. $|-28 + (-12)|$ **40**

www.pre-alg.com/self_check_quiz

Tips for New Teachers

Intervention If there is any doubt whether your students thoroughly understand the adding of integers, consider spending an extra day on this lesson. Use the Extra Practice on p. 726. You can also use the Study Guide and Intervention masters or the Practice masters in the *Chapter 2 Resource Masters* to reinforce this concept.

Study Guide and Intervention, p. 62

Adding Integers with the Same Sign	Add their absolute values. Give the result the same sign as the integers.

Example 1 Find the sum $-3 + (-4)$.
$-3 + (-4) = -7$ Add $|-3|$ and $|-4|$. Both numbers are negative so the sum is negative.

Adding Integers with Different Signs	Subtract their absolute values. Give the result the same sign as the integer with the greater absolute value.

Example 2 Find each sum.
a. $-5 + 4$
$-5 + 4 = |-5| - |4|$ Subtract $|4|$ from $|-5|$.
$\quad = 5 - 4$ or 1 Simplify.
$\quad = -1$ The sum is negative because $|-5| > |4|$.

b. $6 + (-2)$
$6 + (-2) = |6| - |-2|$ Subtract $|-2|$ from $|6|$.
$\quad = 6 - 2$ or 4 Simplify.
$\quad = 4$ The sum is positive because $|6| > |-2|$.

Exercises

Find each sum.

1. $6 + (-3)$ **3**
2. $-3 + (-5)$ **-8**
3. $7 + (-3)$ **4**
4. $-4 + (-4)$ **-8**
5. $-8 + 5$ **-3**
6. $-12 + (-10)$ **-22**
7. $6 + (-13)$ **-7**
8. $-14 + 4$ **-10**
9. $6 + (-6)$ **0**
10. $-15 + (-5)$ **-20**
11. $-9 + 8$ **-1**
12. $20 + (-8)$ **12**
13. $-19 + (-11)$ **-30**
14. $17 + (-9)$ **8**
15. $-16 + (-5)$ **-21**
16. $-12 + 14$ **2**
17. $9 + (-25)$ **-16**
18. $-36 + 19$ **-17**
19. $7 + (-18)$ **-11**
20. $-12 + (-15)$ **-27**
21. $10 + (-14)$ **-4**
22. $-33 + 19$ **-14**
23. $-20 + (-5)$ **-25**
24. $-12 + (-10)$ **-22**
25. $-15 + 4$ **-11**
26. $-34 + 29$ **-5**
27. $46 + (-32)$ **14**

Skills Practice, p. 63 and Practice, p. 64 (shown)

Find each sum.

1. $-19 + (-7)$ **-26**
2. $-29 + 30$ **1**
3. $-32 + 9$ **-23**
4. $10 + 37$ **47**
5. $34 + 22$ **56**
6. $-16 + (-28)$ **-44**
7. $-4 + (-50)$ **-54**
8. $-12 + (-63)$ **-75**
9. $26 + (-9)$ **17**
10. $-17 + (-23)$ **-40**
11. $12 + (-22)$ **-10**
12. $18 + (-56)$ **-38**
13. $-36 + (-36)$ **-72**
14. $-54 + 45$ **-9**
15. $-34 + 17$ **-17**
16. $-16 + (-24)$ **-40**
17. $70 + (-108)$ **-38**
18. $-52 + 36$ **-16**
19. $-71 + (-86)$ **-157**
20. $-39 + (-40)$ **-79**
21. $25 + 18 + (-23)$ **20**
22. $-65 + (-2) + 9$ **-58**
23. $80 + 15 + (-26)$ **69**
24. $-5 + 4 + (-27)$ **-28**
25. $-29 + 12 + 44$ **27**
26. $-1 + (-8) + (-49)$ **-58**
27. $-16 + (-56) + (-90)$ **-162**
28. $-18 + 13 + (-35)$ **-40**
29. $10 + (-34) + 17$ **-7**
30. $30 + (-9) + 1$ **22**
31. $-24 + 7 + 47$ **30**
32. $51 + (-21) + (-12)$ **18**

33. **TEMPERATURE** At 4:00 A.M., the outside temperature was $-28°$F. By 4:00 P.M. it rose 38 degrees. What was the temperature at 4:00 P.M.? **$+10°$F**

34. **HEALTH** Three friends decided to exercise together four times a week to lose fat and increase muscle mass. While all three were healthier after six weeks, one had lost 5 pounds, another had gained 3 pounds, and one had lost 4 pounds. What was the total number of pounds gained or lost by the three friends? **-6 pounds**

35. **ROLLER COASTERS** The latest thrill ride at a popular theme park takes roller coaster fans on an exciting ride. In the first 20 seconds, it carries its passengers up a 100-meter hill, plunges them 72 meters down, and quickly takes them back up a 48-meter rise. How much higher or lower from the start of the ride are they after these 20 seconds? **76 m higher**

Enrichment, p. 66

Modular Arithmetic

In modular arithmetic, there is a finite set of numbers. An example of a finite set would be the numbers on the face of a clock. No matter how many numbers are added together, the answer will still be one of the twelve numbers found on the face of the clock.

Example 1 In mod 12, $5 + 8 + 2 = 3$.
To find the sum, start at 0. Count 5 units in a clockwise direction, then 8 units, and then 2 units. You should end at the number 3.

Find each sum in mod 12.

1. $6 + 8 + 4$ **6**
2. $7 + 9 + 11 + 5$ **8**
3. $6 + 4 + 11 + 12 + 5$ **2**
4. $1 + 4 + 9 + 11 + 6$ **7**
5. $7 + 10 + 9 + 12 + 10$ **0**
6. $6 + 12 + 5 + 12 + 8 + 12$ **7**
7. $12 + 12 + 12 + 12 + 6$ **6**
8. $4 + 9 + 3 + 7 + 8 + 11 + 5$ **11**
9. $6 + 10 + 7 + 8 + 4 + 3 + 9$ **11**
10. $9 + 2 + 4 + 3 + 10 + 12 + 4 + 11$ **7**

Example 2 In mod 7, $3 + 5 + 2 = 3$.
To find the sum, start at 0. Count 3 units in a clockwise direction, then 5 units, and then 2 units. You should end at the number 3.

Find each sum in mod 7.

11. $2 + 4 + 3$ **2**
12. $5 + 1 + 6 + 3$ **1**
13. $2 + 2 + 4 + 6 + 7$ **0**
14. $5 + 3 + 4 + 6 + 1$ **5**
15. $7 + 7 + 7 + 7 + 5$ **5**
16. $6 + 5 + 1 + 2 + 4$ **4**
17. $4 + 3 + 1 + 5 + 6 + 2$ **0**
18. $4 + 2 + 1 + 6 + 7 + 5 + 4 + 3$ **1**
19. $6 + 5 + 4 + 3 + 2 + 1 + 7 + 6$ **6**
20. $5 + 7 + 4 + 4 + 2 + 6 + 1 + 2$ **3**

21. Can you find a pattern to these exercises? Explain. **Yes; the sum in mod x is the remainder when the sum is divided by x.**

POPULATION For Exercises 46 and 47, use the table below that shows the change in population of several cities from 1990 to 2000.

City	1990 Population	Change as of 2000
Dallas, TX	1,006,877	+181,703
Honolulu, HI	365,272	+6385
Jackson, MS	196,637	−12,381
Philadelphia, PA	1,585,577	−68,027

46. Dallas: 1,188,580; Honolulu: 371,657; Jackson: 184,256; Philadelphia: 1,517,550

46. What was the population in each city in 2000?

47. What was the total change in population of these cities? **+107,680**

Online Research **Data Update** How have the populations of other cities changed since 2000? Visit www.pre-alg.com/data_update to learn more.

48. False; sample counterexample: If $n = -2$, then $-(-2)$ is positive.

48. **CRITICAL THINKING** *True* or *false*: $-n$ always names a negative number. If false, give a counterexample.

49.  Answer the question that was posed at the beginning of the lesson. **See margin.**

How can a number line help you add integers?

Include the following in your answer:
- an example showing the sum of a positive and a negative integer, and
- an example showing the sum of two negative integers.

Standardized Test Practice

50. What is the sum of $-32 + 20$? **C**
- Ⓐ −52
- Ⓑ −18
- Ⓒ −12
- Ⓓ 12

51. What is the value of $-|-2 + 8|$? **D**
- Ⓐ −10
- Ⓑ 10
- Ⓒ 6
- Ⓓ −6

Maintain Your Skills

Mixed Review

52. **CHEMISTRY** The freezing point of oxygen is 219 degrees below zero on the Celsius scale. Use an integer to express this temperature. *(Lesson 2-1)* **−219°C**

Order the integers in each set from least to greatest. *(Lesson 2-1)*

53. $\{14, -12, -8, 3, -9, 0\}$
$\{-12, -9, -8, 0, 3, 14\}$

54. $\{-242, 35, -158, 99, -24\}$
$\{-242, -158, -24, 35, 99\}$

Determine whether a scatter plot of the data for the following might show a *positive*, *negative*, or *no* relationship. *(Lesson 1-7)*

55. age and family size
no relationship

56. temperature and sales of mittens
negative

Identify the solution of each equation from the list given. *(Lesson 1-5)*

57. $18 - n = 12$; <u>6</u>, 16, 30

58. $25 = 16 + x$; <u>9</u>, 11, 41

59. $\frac{x}{2} = 10$; 5, 12, <u>20</u>

60. $7a = 49$; <u>7</u>, 42, 343

Getting Ready for the Next Lesson

PREREQUISITE SKILL Evaluate each expression if $a = 6$, $b = 10$, and $c = 3$.
*(To review **evaluating expressions**, see Lesson 1-3.)*

61. $a + 19$ **25**

62. $2b - 6$ **14**

63. $ab - ac$ **42**

64. $3a - (b + c)$ **5**

65. $5b + 5c$ **65**

66. $\frac{6b}{c}$ **20**

Answer

49. To add integers on a number line, start at 0. Move right to show positive integers and left to show negative integers.

- Sample answer:
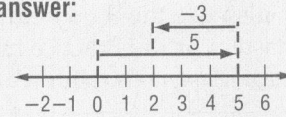

- Sample answer:
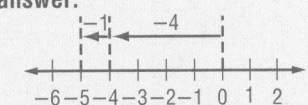

Learning Mathematics Vocabulary

Some words used in mathematics are also used in English and have similar meanings. For example, in mathematics *add* means *to combine*. The meaning in English is *to join or unite*.

Some words are used only in mathematics. For example, *addend* means *a number to be added to another*.

Some words have more than one mathematical meaning. For example, an *inverse* operation *undoes the effect of another operation*, and an additive *inverse* is *a number that when added to a given number gives zero*.

The list below shows some of the mathematics vocabulary used in Chapters 1 and 2.

Vocabulary	Meaning	Examples
algebraic expression	an expression that contains at least one variable and at least one mathematical operation	$2 + x$, $\frac{4}{c}$, $3b$
evaluate	to find the value of an expression	$2 + 5 = 7$
simplify	to find a simpler form of an expression	$3b + 2b = 5b$
integer	a whole number, its inverse, or zero	$-3, 0, 2$
factor	a number that is multiplied by another number	$3(4) = 12$ 3 and 4 are factors.
product	the result of multiplying	$3(4) = 12 \longleftarrow$ product
quotient	the result of dividing two numbers	$\frac{12}{4} = 3 \longleftarrow$ quotient
dividend	the number being divided	$\frac{12}{4} = 3$ dividend
divisor	the number being divided into another number	$\frac{12}{4} = 3$ divisor
coordinate	a number that locates a point	$(5, 2)$

Reading to Learn 1–3. See margin.

1. Name two of the words above that are also used in everyday English. Use the Internet, a dictionary, or another reference to find their everyday definition. How do the everyday definitions relate to the mathematical definitions?

2. Name two words above that are used only in mathematics.

3. Name two words above that have more than one mathematical meaning. List their meanings.

Answers

1. Sample answer: Simplify – make simpler; coordinate – put in the same order

2. Answers should include two of the following: divisor, quotient, integer, algebraic expression.

3. Sample answer: Simplify – also means to simplify a fraction; factor – also means to find the factors of a number.

2-3 Subtracting Integers

1 Focus

Mathematical Background notes are available for this lesson on page 54C.

How are addition and subtraction of integers related?

The opening activity questions are repeated on page 70 of the *Chapter 2 Resource Masters*.

Teaching Tip Point out that the part of the arrow for -8 that extends beyond the arrow for $+5$ represents the difference.

What You'll Learn

- Subtract integers.
- Evaluate expressions containing variables.

How are addition and subtraction of integers related?

You can use a number line to subtract integers. The model below shows how to find $6 - 8$.

Step 1 Start at 0. Move 6 units right to show positive 6.

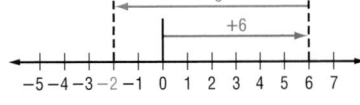

Step 2 From there, move 8 units left to subtract positive 8.

a. What is $6 - 8$? -2

b. What direction do you move to indicate subtracting a positive integer?   **left**

c. What addition sentence is also modeled by the number line above?

c. $6 + (-8) = -2$

SUBTRACT INTEGERS   When you subtract $6 - 8$, as shown on the number line above, the result is the same as adding $6 + (-8)$. When you subtract $-3 - 5$, the result is the same as adding $-3 + (-5)$.

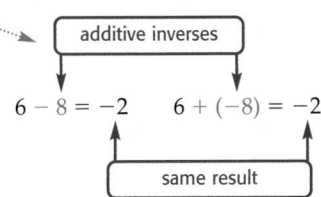

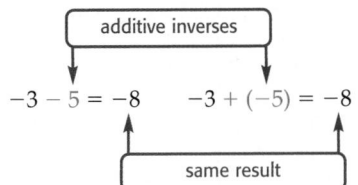

These examples suggest a method for subtracting integers.

Key Concept   Subtracting Integers

- **Words**   To subtract an integer, add its additive inverse.
- **Symbols** $a - b = a + (-b)$
- **Examples** $5 - 9 = 5 + (-9)$ or -4 $-2 - 7 = -2 + (-7)$ or -9

Example 1   Subtract a Positive Integer

Find each difference.

a. $8 - 13$

   $8 - 13 = 8 + (-13)$ To subtract 13, add -13.
            $= -5$ Simplify.

b. $-4 - 10$

   $-4 - 10 = -4 + (-10)$ To subtract 10, add -10.
              $= -14$ Simplify.

Resource Manager

📁 Workbooks and Reproducible Masters

Chapter 2 Resource Masters
- Study Guide and Intervention, p. 67
- Skills Practice, p. 68
- Practice, p. 69
- Reading to Learn Mathematics, p. 70
- Enrichment, p. 71
- Assessment, pp. 101, 103

Parent and Student Study Guide Workbook, p. 11
Prerequisite Skills Workbook, pp. 5–8
School-to-Career Masters, p. 4

Transparencies
5-Minute Check Transparency 2-3
Answer Key Transparencies

🔵 Technology
Interactive Chalkboard

In Example 1, you subtracted a positive integer by adding its additive inverse. Use inductive reasoning to see if the method also applies to subtracting a negative integer.

Study Tip

Look Back
To review **inductive reasoning**, see Lesson 1-1.

Subtracting an Integer	↔	Adding Its Additive Inverse
$2 - 2 = 0$		$2 + (-2) = 0$
$2 - 1 = 1$		$2 + (-1) = 1$
$2 - 0 = 2$		$2 + 0 = 2$
$2 - (-1) = ?$		$2 + 1 = 3$

Continuing the pattern in the first column, $2 - (-1) = 3$. The result is the same as when you add the additive inverse. This suggests that the method also works for subtracting a negative integer.

Example 2 *Subtract a Negative Integer*

Find each difference.

a. $7 - (-3)$

$7 - (-3) = 7 + 3$ To subtract -3, add 3.
$\quad\quad\quad = 10$

b. $-2 - (-4)$

$-2 - (-4) = -2 + 4$ To subtract -4, add 4.
$\quad\quad\quad\quad = 2$

✓ **Concept Check**   How do you find the difference $9 - (-16)$?   **Add 9 and 16.**

Example 3 *Subtract Integers to Solve a Problem*

WEATHER   The table shows the record high and low temperatures recorded in selected states through 1999. What is the range, or difference between the highest and lowest temperatures, for Virginia?

State	Lowest Temp. °F	Highest Temp. °F
Utah	−69	117
Vermont	−50	105
Virginia	−30	110
Washington	−48	118
West Virginia	−37	112
Wisconsin	−54	114
Wyoming	−66	114

Source: *The World Almanac*

Explore   You know the highest and lowest temperatures. You need to find the range for Virginia's temperatures.

Plan   To find the range, or difference, subtract the lowest temperature from the highest temperature.

Solve $110 - (-30) = 110 + 30$ To subtract -30, add 30.
$\quad\quad\quad\quad\quad = 140$ Add 110 and 30.
The range for Virginia is 140°.

Examine   Think of a thermometer. The difference between 110° above zero and 30° below zero must be $110 + 30$ or 140°. The answer appears to be reasonable.

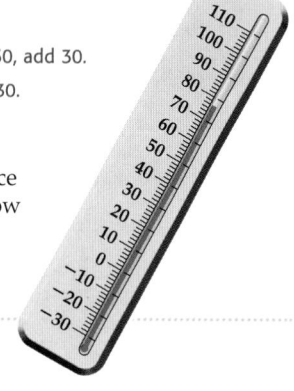

Lesson 2-3 Subtracting Integers   **71**

2 Teach

Building on Prior Knowledge

In Chapter 1, students studied patterns. In this lesson, students will examine patterns in the subtraction of integers.

SUBTRACT INTEGERS

In-Class Examples   Power Point®

1 Find each difference.
a. $9 - 14$ **−5**
b. $-10 - 8$ **−18**

2 Find each difference.
a. $15 - (-4)$ **19**
b. $-10 - (-7)$ **−3**

3 **WEATHER**   Refer to the table in the Student Edition. What is the range for Wyoming?
180°

✓ Skills Check

Subtract Integers Find each difference.
a. $-13 - 9$ **−22**
b. $20 - (-15)$ **35**
c. $-1 - (-10)$ **9**
d. $-16 - (-3)$ **−13**

EVALUATE EXPRESSIONS

In-Class Example   Power Point®

4 a. Evaluate $m - (-2)$ if $m = 4$.   **6**

b. Evaluate $x - y$ if $x = -14$ and $y = -2$.   **−12**

c. Evaluate $p + q - r$ if $p = -11$, $q = 6$, and $r = -12$.   **7**

Teacher to Teacher

Kurt Parchment   Homestead M.S., Homestead, FL

"I use pre-printed response cards (numbers and signs), along with the overhead projector, to guide the whole class through evaluating expressions that involve integers."

Study Notebook

Have students—
- write a paragraph comparing subtraction of integers with addition of integers.
- give samples that illustrate subtraction of integers.
- include any other item(s) that they find helpful in mastering the skills in this lesson.

DAILY

INTERVENTION **FIND THE ERROR**
Help students understand that subtracting −2 is not the same as adding −2, as Reiko's work shows.

About the Exercises . . .

Organization by Objective
- **Subtract Integers:** 14–39, 52–53
- **Evaluate Expressions:** 40–51, 54

Odd/Even Assignments
Exercises 14–53 are structured so that students practice the same concepts whether they are assigned odd or even problems.

Alert! For Exercises 52 and 53, you may wish to have students use a calculator.

Assignment Guide

Basic: 15–33 odd, 39–51 odd, 55–74

Average: 15–51 odd, 52, 53, 55–74

Advanced: 14–50 even, 54–70 (Optional: 71–74)

All: Practice Quiz 1 (1–10)

ALGEBRA CONNECTION

EVALUATE EXPRESSIONS You can use the rule for subtracting integers to evaluate expressions.

Example 4 *Evaluate Algebraic Expressions*

a. Evaluate $x - (-6)$ if $x = 12$.

$$x - (-6) = 12 - (-6) \quad \text{Write the expression. Replace } x \text{ with 12.}$$
$$= 12 + 6 \quad \text{To subtract } -6, \text{ add its additive inverse, 6.}$$
$$= 18 \quad \text{Add 12 and 6.}$$

b. Evaluate $s - t$ if $s = -9$ and $t = -3$.

$$s - t = -9 - (-3) \quad \text{Replace } s \text{ with } -9 \text{ and } t \text{ with } -3.$$
$$= -9 + 3 \quad \text{To subtract } -3, \text{ add 3.}$$
$$= -6 \quad \text{Add } -9 \text{ and 3.}$$

c. Evaluate $a - b + c$ if $a = 15$, $b = 5$, and $c = -8$.

$$a - b + c = 15 - 5 + (-8) \quad \text{Replace } a \text{ with 15, } b \text{ with 5, and } c \text{ with } -8.$$
$$= 10 + (-8) \quad \text{Order of operations}$$
$$= 2 \quad \text{Add 10 and } -8.$$

Concept Check: Find the sum of the first integer and the additive inverse of the second integer.

✓ **Concept Check** How do you subtract integers using additive inverses?

Check for Understanding

Concept Check
1. **OPEN ENDED** Write examples of a positive and a negative integer and their additive inverses. **Sample answer: 5, −5; −9, 9**

2. **FIND THE ERROR** José and Reiko are finding $8 - (-2)$.

José	Reiko
$8 - (-2) = 8 + 2$	$8 - (-2) = 8 + (-2)$
$= 10$	$= 6$

Who is correct? Explain your reasoning. **See margin.**

Guided Practice Find each difference.

GUIDED PRACTICE KEY	
Exercises	Examples
3, 4	1
5–8	2
9–11	4
12, 13	3

3. $8 - 11$ **−3**   4. $-9 - 3$ **−12**   5. $5 - (-4)$ **9**
6. $7 - (-10)$ **17**   7. $-6 - (-4)$ **−2**   8. $-2 - (-8)$ **6**

ALGEBRA Evaluate each expression if $x = 10$, $y = -4$, and $z = -15$.

9. $x - (-10)$ **20**   10. $y - x$ **−14**   11. $x + y - z$ **21**

Application **WEATHER** For Exercises 12 and 13, use the table in Example 3 on page 71.

12. Find the range in temperature for Vermont. **155°**

13. Name a state that has a greater range than Vermont's. **Utah, Washington, Wisconsin, or Wyoming**

Answer

2. José; Reiko added −2 instead of its additive inverse.

Practice and Apply

Homework Help

For Exercises	See Examples
14–21, 30–33	1
22–29, 34–37	2
38, 39	3
40–51	4

Extra Practice
See page 727.

Find each difference.

14. $3 - 8$ **−5**   15. $4 - 5$ **−1**   16. $2 - 9$ **−7**

17. $9 - 12$ **−3**   18. $-3 - 1$ **−4**   19. $-5 - 4$ **−9**

20. $-6 - 7$ **−13**   21. $-4 - 8$ **−12**   22. $6 - (-8)$ **14**

23. $4 - (-6)$ **10**   24. $7 - (-4)$ **11**   25. $9 - (-3)$ **12**

26. $-9 - (-7)$ **−2**   27. $-7 - (-10)$ **3**   28. $-11 - (-12)$ **1**

29. $-16 - (-7)$ **−9**   30. $10 - 24$ **−14**   31. $45 - 59$ **−14**

32. $-27 - 14$ **−41**   33. $-16 - 12$ **−28**   34. $48 - (-50)$ **98**

★ 35. $125 - (-114)$ **239**   ★ 36. $-320 - (-106)$ **−214**   ★ 37. $-2200 - (-3500)$ **1300**

38. **WEATHER** During January, the normal high temperature in Duluth, Minnesota, is 16°F, and the normal low temperature is −2°F. Find the difference between the temperatures. **18°F**

39. **GEOGRAPHY** The highest point in California is Mount Whitney, with an elevation of 14,494 feet. The lowest point is Death Valley, elevation −282 feet. Find the difference in the elevations. **14,776 ft**

ALGEBRA Evaluate each expression if $x = -3$, $y = 8$, and $z = -12$.

40. $y - 10$ **−2**   41. $12 - z$ **24**   42. $3 - x$ **6**

43. $z - 24$ **−36**   44. $x - y$ **−11**   45. $z - x$ **−9**

46. $y - z$ **20**   47. $z - y$ **−20**   48. $x + y - z$ **17**

49. $z - y + x$ **−23**   50. $x - y - z$ **1**   51. $z - y - x$ **−17**

52. **+59; −4242; −1769; −1899; −3039; +68**

PETS For Exercises 52 and 53, use the following table.

52. Describe the change in the number of dogs of each breed registered from Year 1 to Year 2.

53. What was the total change in the number of dogs of these breeds registered from Year 1 to Year 2? **−10,822**

Registration in American Kennel Club		
Breed	Year 1	Year 2
Airedale Terrier	2891	2950
Beagle	53,322	49,080
Chinese Shar-Pei	8614	6845
Chow Chow	6241	4342
Labrador Retriever	157,936	154,897
Pug	21,487	21,555

Source: www.akc.org

54. **BUSINESS** The formula $P = I - E$ is used to find the profit (P) when income (I) and expenses (E) are known. One month a small business has income of $19,592 and expenses of $20,345.

   a. What is the profit for the month? **−$753**

   b. What does a negative profit mean? **expenses > income**

55. **CRITICAL THINKING** Determine whether each statement is *true* or *false*. If false, give a counterexample.

   a. Subtraction of integers is commutative. **False; $3 - 4 \neq 4 - 3$**

   b. Subtraction of integers is associative. **False; $(5 - 2) - 1 \neq 5 - (2 - 1)$**

Career Choices

Veterinarian •••••••••

Veterinarians work with animals to diagnose, treat, and prevent disease, disorders, and injuries.

Online Research
For information about a career as a veterinarian, visit:
www.pre-alg.com/careers

Study Guide and Intervention, p. 67

Subtracting Integers	To subtract an integer, add its additive inverse.

Example 1 Find each difference.

a. $9 - 17$
$9 - 17 = 9 + (-17)$ To subtract 17, add −17.
$= -8$ Simplify.

b. $-7 - 3$
$-7 - 3 = -7 + (-3)$ To subtract 3, add −3.
$= -10$ Simplify.

Example 2 Find each difference.

a. $4 - (-5)$
$4 - (-5) = 4 + 5$ To subtract −5, add +5.
$= 9$ Simplify.

b. $-6 - (-2)$
$-6 - (-2) = -6 + 2$ To subtract −2, add +2.
$= -4$ Simplify.

Exercises

Find each difference.

1. $9 - 16$ −7   2. $7 - 19$ −12   3. $12 - 21$ −9

4. $-5 - 3$ −8   5. $-8 - 9$ −17   6. $-13 - 17$ −30

7. $7 - (-4)$ 11   8. $9 - (-9)$ 18   9. $-11 - (-2)$ −9

10. $-6 - (-9)$ 3   11. $-6 - 4$ −10   12. $-16 - (-20)$ 4

13. $-14 - 4$ −18   14. $8 - (-6)$ 14   15. $-10 - (-6)$ −4

16. $13 - (-17)$ 30   17. $24 - (-16)$ 40   18. $17 - (-9)$ 26

19. $-24 - 8$ −32   20. $18 - (-9)$ 27   21. $26 - 49$ −23

22. $-45 - (-26)$ −19   23. $-15 - (-25)$ 10   24. $29 - (-6)$ 35

Skills Practice, p. 68 and Practice, p. 69 (shown)

Find each difference.

1. $-26 - (-30)$ 4   2. $25 - 32$ −7   3. $-18 - 54$ −72   4. $59 - (-19)$ 78

5. $-41 - (-19)$ −22   6. $-20 - 13$ −33   7. $31 - (-56)$ 87   8. $15 - (-40)$ 55

9. $-32 - 28$ −60   10. $10 - (-23)$ 33   11. $-14 - 64$ −78   12. $-12 - (-36)$ 24

13. $-81 - 4$ −85   14. $9 - 30$ −21   15. $-4 - (-21)$ −23   16. $140 - (-9)$ 149

Evaluate each expression if $a = -11$, $b = 8$, and $c = -6$.

17. $a - 17$ −28   18. $10 - b$ 2   19. $-30 - c$ −24   20. $b - a$ 19

21. $a - b$ −19   22. $c - b$ −14   23. $b - c + a$ 3   24. $b - c - a$ 25

25. $c - a - b$ −3   26. $b + a - c$ 3   27. $b + c - a$ 13   28. $c - a + b$ 13

29. $a - b + c$ −25   30. $b - a + c$ 13   31. $a - b - c$ −13   32. $c + b - a$ 13

33. $c - b + a$ −25   34. $a + b - c$ 3   35. $16 + a + c$ −1   36. $a - b + 14$ −5

37. **ELEVATORS** Linda entered an elevator on floor 9. She rode down 8 floors. Then she rode up 11 floors and got off. What floor was she on when she left the elevator? 12

38. **INVESTMENTS** The NASDAQ lost 36 points on a Monday, but rebounded the next day, gaining 24 points. What was the total change in points? −12 points

39. **OFFICE BUILDINGS** Randi takes the stairs at work whenever possible instead of the elevator. She must climb up 51 steps from her office to get to the accounting department. The human resources department is 34 steps below her office. How many steps are there between human resources and accounting? 85 steps

Enrichment, p. 71

Subtracting in a Finite Number System

To subtract in a finite number system, add a number's additive inverse. The additive inverse of a number in a finite number system is that number which, when added to the first number, results in a sum that is the mod or identity.

Example 1 What is the additive inverse of 4 in mod 7?
$-(4) = 3$ What is added to 4 to equal 7? The answer is 3.
The additive inverse of 4 in mod 7 is 3.

The additive inverses for 1, 2, 3, 5, and 6 are 6, 5, 4, 2, and 1, respectively. In mod 7, subtraction is the same as adding the additive inverse.

Example 2
$3 - 4 = 3 + (-4) = 3 + 3 = 6$ Subtract 4 by adding its additive inverse, 3.
$1 - 6 = 1 + (-6) = 1 + 1 = 2$ Subtract 6 by adding its additive inverse, 1.

Solve each equation in mod 7.

1. $x = 1 - 3$ $x = 1 + 4 = 5$ 2. $5 - 6 = y$ $y = 5 + 1 = 6$ 3. $2 - 5 = z$ $z = 2 + 2 = 4$

4. $q = 6 - 4$ $q = 6 + 3 = 2$ 5. $b = 2 - 6$ $b = 2 + 1 = 3$ 6. $3 - 4 = z$ $z = 3 + 3 = 6$

7. $y = 0 - 4$ $y = 0 + 3 = 3$ 8. $3 - 6 = x$ $x = 3 + 1 = 4$ 9. $4 - 5 = p$ $p = 4 + 2 = 6$

Solve each equation in mod 12.

10. $y = 2 - 9$ $y = 2 + 3 = 5$ 11. $x = 1 - 8$ $x = 1 + 4 = 5$ 12. $3 - 5 = r$ $r = 3 + 7 = 10$

13. $z = 0 - 4$ $z = 0 + 8 = 8$ 14. $q = 4 - 10$ $q = 4 + 2 = 6$ 15. $6 - 11 = p$ $p = 6 + 1 = 7$

16. $5 - 3 = k$ $k = 5 + 9 = 2$ 17. $7 - 11 = z$ $z = 7 + 1 = 8$ 18. $2 - 3 = b$ $b = 2 + 9 = 11$

19. $8 - 10 = r$ $r = 8 + 2 = 10$ 20. $9 - 7 = f$ $f = 9 + 5 = 2$ 21. $4 - 7 = w$ $w = 4 + 5 = 9$

22. $m = 1 - 11$ $m = 1 + 1 = 2$ 23. $z = 3 - 8$ $z = 3 + 4 = 7$ 24. $g = 5 - 9$ $g = 5 + 3 = 8$

DAILY INTERVENTION

Differentiated Instruction

• **Interpersonal** Have students make 4 cards with a different positive integer on each one and 4 other cards with a different negative integer on each. Then have them ask another student to draw 2 cards randomly and subtract the second card from the first card drawn. Students can work in pairs, small groups, or circulate around the room.

Open-Ended Assessment

Modeling Have students use a number line to show how to find the differences $8 - (-3)$ and $-8 - (-3)$.

Getting Ready for Lesson 2-4

PREREQUISITE SKILL Lesson 2-4 presents multiplying integers. Exercises 71–74 should be used to determine your students' familiarity with finding the products of positive integers.

Assessment Options

Practice Quiz 1 The quiz provides students with a brief review of the concepts and skills in Lessons 2-1 through 2-3. Lesson numbers are given to the right of exercises or instruction lines so students can review concepts not yet mastered.

Quiz (Lesson 2-3) is available on p. 101 of the *Chapter 2 Resource Masters*.

Mid-Chapter Test (Lessons 2-1 through 2-3) is available on p. 103 of the *Chapter 2 Resource Masters*.

Answer

56. Addition and subtraction of integers are related because a subtraction problem can be rewritten as an addition problem. Answers should include the following.

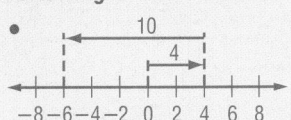

• $4 - 10$ is rewritten as the addition expression $4 + (-10)$.

---

56. **WRITING IN MATH** Answer the question that was posed at the beginning of the lesson. **See margin.**

How are addition and subtraction of integers related?

Include the following in your answer:
• a model that shows how to find the difference $4 - 10$, and
• the expression $4 - 10$ rewritten as an addition expression.

Standardized Test Practice Ⓐ Ⓑ Ⓒ Ⓓ

57. The terms in a pattern are given in the table. What is the value of the 5th term? **A**

Term	1	2	3	4	5
Value	13	8	3	−2	?

Ⓐ −7   Ⓑ −5
Ⓒ 7   Ⓓ 5

58. When 5 is subtracted from a number, the result is −4. What is the number? **B**

Ⓐ 9   Ⓑ 1   Ⓒ −1   Ⓓ −9

Maintain Your Skills

Mixed Review

59. **OCEANOGRAPHY** A submarine at 1300 meters below sea level descends an additional 1150 meters. What integer represents the submarine's position with respect to sea level? *(Lesson 2-2)* **−2450**

60. **ALGEBRA** Evaluate $|b| - |a|$ if $a = 2$ and $b = -4$. *(Lesson 2-1)* **2**

ALGEBRA Solve each equation mentally. *(Lesson 1-5)*

61. $x + 9 = 12$ **3**   62. $18 = w - 2$ **20**   63. $5a = 35$ **7**   64. $\frac{64}{b} = 8$ **8**

ALGEBRA Translate each phrase into an algebraic expression. *(Lesson 1-3)*

65. a number divided by 5 $\frac{x}{5}$ 66. the sum of t and 9 $t + 9$
67. the quotient of eighty-six and b $\frac{86}{b}$ 68. s decreased by 8 $s - 8$

Find the value of each expression. *(Lesson 1-2)*

69. $2 \times (5 + 8) - 6$ **20**   70. $96 \div (6 \times 8) \div 2$ **1**

Getting Ready for the Next Lesson

BASIC SKILL Find each product.

71. $5 \cdot 15$ **75**   72. $8 \cdot 12$ **96**   73. $3 \cdot 5 \cdot 8$ **120**   74. $2 \cdot 7 \cdot 5 \cdot 9$ **630**

Practice Quiz 1   Lessons 2-1 through 2-3

1. **WEATHER** The three states with the lowest recorded temperatures are Alaska at −80°F, Utah at −69°F, and Montana at −70°F. Order the temperatures from least to greatest. *(Lesson 2-1)* **−80, −70, −69**

Find each sum. *(Lesson 2-2)*

2. $-5 + (-15)$ **−20**   3. $-5 + 11$ **6**   4. $-6 + 9 + (-8)$ **−5**

Find each difference. *(Lesson 2-3)*

5. $16 - 23$ **−7**   6. $-15 - 8$ **−23**   7. $25 - (-7)$ **32**

ALGEBRA Evaluate each expression if $x = 5$, $y = -2$, and $z = -3$. *(Lesson 2-3)*

8. $x - y$ **7**   9. $z - 6$ **−9**   10. $x - y - z$ **10**

Multiplying Integers

What You'll Learn

- Multiply integers.
- Simplify algebraic expressions.

How are the signs of factors and products related?

The temperature drops 7°C for each 1 kilometer increase in altitude. A drop of 7°C is represented by -7. So, the temperature change equals the altitude times -7. The table shows the change in temperature for several altitudes.

Altitude (km)	Altitude × Rate of Change	Temperature Change (°C)
1	1(−7)	−7
2	2(−7)	−14
3	3(−7)	−21
...	...	...
11	11(−7)	−77

a. Suppose the altitude is 4 kilometers. Write an expression to find the temperature change. **4(−7)**

b. Use the pattern in the table to find 4(−7). **−28**

1 Focus

5-Minute Check Transparency 2-4 Use as a quiz or review of Lesson 2-3.

Mathematical Background notes are available for this lesson on page 54D.

How are the signs of factors and products related?

The opening activity questions are repeated on page 75 of the *Chapter 2 Resource Masters*.

Reading to Learn Mathematics, p. 75 | ELL

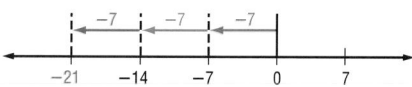

Pre-Activity *How are the signs of factors and products related?*

Do the activity at the top of page 75 in your textbook. Write your answers below.

a. Suppose the altitude is 4 kilometers. Write an expression to find the temperature change. 4(−7)

b. Use the pattern in the table on page 75 to find 4(−7). −28

Reading the Lesson

1. The product of two integers with _____different_____ sign(s) is negative.

2. The product of two integers with _____the same_____ sign(s) is positive.

3. Draw a number line model that shows how to find the product 4(−2). Explain your model.

Start at zero. Move 2 units to the left to show −2. Do this three more times to show that −2, moved 4 times, equals −8.

4. Show how to use a pattern to find (−5)(−1).
(−5)(1) = −5
(−5)(0) = 0 } + 5
(−5)(−1) = 5 } + 5

5. You can use the _____Associative Property of Multiplication_____ when you multiply more than two integers.

Helping You Remember

6. In your own words, describe how to tell the sign of the product of two integers. Sample answer is given. If the two integers have different signs, the product is negative. If the two integers have the same sign, the product is positive.

Reading Math

Parentheses

Recall that a product can be written using parentheses. Read 3(−7) as *3 times negative 7*.

MULTIPLY INTEGERS Multiplication is repeated addition. So, 3(−7) means that −7 is used as an addend 3 times.

$$3(-7) = (-7) + (-7) + (-7)$$
$$= -21$$

By the Commutative Property of Multiplication, 3(−7) = −7(3).

This example suggests the following rule.

Key Concept | Multiplying Two Integers with Different Signs

- **Words** The product of two integers with different signs is negative.
- **Examples** 4(−3) = −12   −3(4) = −12

Example 1 Multiply Integers with Different Signs

Find each product.

a. 5(−6)

5(−6) = −30   The factors have different signs. The product is negative.

b. −4(16)

−4(16) = −64   The factors have different signs. The product is negative.

Resource Manager

Workbooks and Reproducible Masters

Chapter 2 Resource Masters
- Study Guide and Intervention, p. 72
- Skills Practice, p. 73
- Practice, p. 74
- Reading to Learn Mathematics, p. 75
- Enrichment, p. 76

Parent and Student Study Guide Workbook, p. 12
Prerequisite Skills Workbook, pp. 9–10

 Transparencies

5-Minute Check Transparency 2-4
Answer Key Transparencies

 Technology

Interactive Chalkboard

2 Teach

Teaching Tip Use a transparency of a Celsius thermometer with the gradients clearly visible. Prepare cut-outs to represent 7° on the drawing. Place one cut-out on the thermometer. Show how the addition of each subsequent cut-out below the previous one pushes the temperature down by 7°.

MULTIPLY INTEGERS

In-Class Examples Power Point®

1 Find each product.
  a. 8(−12) **−96**
  b. −9(11) **−99**

2 Find −4(−16). **64**

3 Find −7(11)(−2). **154**

Teaching Tip Write several problems multiplying more than two integers on the chalkboard. Vary the number of total factors, as well as the number of negatives and positives. Then group the factors in each problem by pairs and keep multiplying pairs, so students see what is happening with the signs. Lead students to discover the rule that if the number of negative integers is odd, the product is negative, and if the number of negative integers is even, then the product is positive.

4 **Multiple-Choice Test Item**
A student missed only 4 problems on a test, each worth 20 points. What is the total number of points missed? **D**
  A −5 **B** −20 **C** 24 **D** −80

✓ Skills Check

Multiply Integers Find each product.
  a. 21(−6) **−126**
  b. −8(−4) **32**
  c. −10(7) **−70**
  d. −3(−4)(5) **60**
  e. −9(−5)(−2) **−90**

The product of two positive integers is positive. What is the sign of the product of two negative integers? Use a pattern to find (−4)(−2).

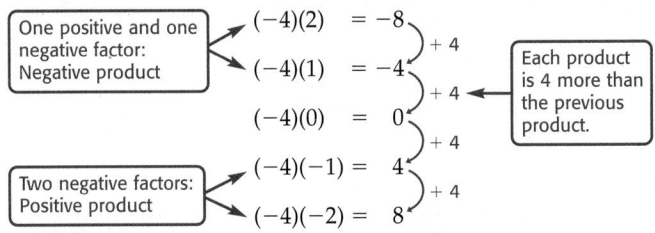

This example suggests the following rule.

Key Concept **Multiplying Two Integers with the Same Sign**
• **Words** The product of two integers with the same sign is positive.
• **Examples** 4(3) = 12   −4(−3) = 12

Example 2 **Multiply Integers with the Same Sign**
Find −6(−12).
  −6(−12) = 72   The two factors have the same sign. The product is positive.

Study Tip

Look Back
To review the **Associative Property**, see Lesson 1-4.

Example 3 **Multiply More Than Two Integers**
Find −4(−5)(−8).
  −4(−5)(−8) = [(−4)(−5)](−8)   Associative Property
            = 20(−8)   (−4)(−5) = 20
            = −160   20(−8) = −160

Standardized Test Practice
Ⓐ Ⓑ Ⓒ Ⓓ

Example 4 **Use Integers to Solve a Problem**
Multiple-Choice Test Item

A glacier was receding at a rate of 300 feet per day. What is the glacier's movement in 5 days?
  Ⓐ 305 feet   Ⓑ −1500 feet   Ⓒ −300 feet   Ⓓ −60 feet

Read the Test Item

The word *receding* means moving backward, so the rate per day is represented by −300. Multiply 5 times −300 to find the movement in 5 days.

Test-Taking Tip
Read the problem. Try to picture the situation. Look for words that suggest mathematical concepts.

Solve the Test Item
  5(−300) = −1500   The product is negative.

The answer is B.

 **Standardized Test Practice**
Ⓐ Ⓑ Ⓒ Ⓓ

Example 4 By understanding that receding means a negative movement, students can immediately eliminate choice A from the answers given. Since the glacier recedes over 300 feet, answers C and D can also be eliminated, leaving choice B.

ALGEBRAIC EXPRESSIONS You can use the rules for multiplying integers to simplify and evaluate algebraic expressions.

Example 5 *Simplify and Evaluate Algebraic Expressions*

a. Simplify −4(9x).

$-4(9x) = (-4 \cdot 9)x$ Associative Property of Multiplication

$\quad\quad = -36x$ Simplify.

b. Simplify −2x(3y).

$-2x(3y) = (-2)(x)(3)(y)$ $-2x = (-2)(x),\ 3y = (3)(y)$

$\quad\quad = (-2 \cdot 3)(x \cdot y)$ Commutative Property of Multiplication

$\quad\quad = -6xy$ $-2 \cdot 3 = -6,\ x \cdot y = xy$

c. Evaluate 4ab if a = 3 and b = −5.

$4ab = 4(3)(-5)$ Replace a with 3 and b with −5.

$\quad = [4(3)](-5)$ Associative Property of Multiplication

$\quad = 12(-5)$ The product of 4 and 3 is positive.

$\quad = -60$ The product of 12 and −5 is negative.

Check for Understanding

Concept Check

1. Write the product that is modeled on the number line below. $3(-5) = -15$

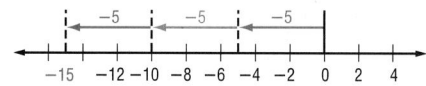

2. State whether each product is positive or negative.

a. $-5 \cdot 8$ **neg.**   b. $6(-4)$ **neg.**   c. $8 \cdot 24$ **pos.**

d. $-9(-7)$ **pos.**   e. $-2(9)(-3)$ **pos.**   f. $-7(-5)(-11)$ **neg.**

3. OPEN ENDED Give an example of three integers whose product is negative. **Sample answer: $(-4)(9)(2)$**

Guided Practice

GUIDED PRACTICE KEY	
Exercises	Examples
4, 5	1
6, 7	2
8, 9	3
10–14	5
15	4

Find each product.

4. $-3 \cdot 8$ **−24**   5. $5(-8)$ **−40**   6. $4 \cdot 30$ **120**

7. $-7(-4)$ **28**   8. $-4(2)(-6)$ **48**   9. $-5(-9)(-12)$ **−540**

ALGEBRA Simplify each expression.

10. $-4 \cdot 3x$ **−12x**   11. $7(-3y)$ **−21y**   12. $-8a(-3b)$ **24ab**

ALGEBRA Evaluate each expression.

13. $-6h$, if $h = -20$ **120**   14. $-4st$, if $s = -9$ and $t = 3$ **108**

Standardized Test Practice
Ⓐ Ⓑ Ⓒ Ⓓ

15. The research submarine *Alvin*, used to locate the wreck of the *Titanic*, descends at a rate of about 100 feet per minute. Which integer describes the distance *Alvin* travels in 5 minutes? **A**

Ⓐ −500 ft   Ⓑ −100 ft   Ⓒ −20 ft   Ⓓ 100 ft

www.pre-alg.com/extra_examples

ALGEBRAIC EXPRESSIONS

In-Class Example **Power Point®**

5 a. Simplify $-7(6k)$. **−42k**

b. Simplify $8a(-5b)$. **−40ab**

c. Evaluate $-3xy$ if $x = -4$ and $y = 9$. **108**

3 Practice/Apply

Study Notebook

Have students—
- write a paragraph about how to multiply integers. They should use examples to illustrate their explanations.
- include any other item(s) that they find helpful in mastering the skills in this lesson.

About the Exercises...

Organization by Objective
- **Multiply Integers:** 16–35, 54–55
- **Algebraic Expressions:** 36–53

Odd/Even Assignments
Exercises 16–55 are structured so that students practice the same concepts whether they are assigned odd or even problems.

Assignment Guide

Basic: 17–53 odd, 54–85

Average: 17–53 odd, 54–85

Advanced: 16–52 even, 54–79 (Optional: 80–85)

 **Tips for New Teachers**

Mental Math Have the class look over Exercises 16–33. Without having them do any calculations, have students tell whether a product will be positive or negative just by examining the signs of the factors.

Study Guide and Intervention, p. 72

Multiplying Integers with Different Signs	The product of two integers with different signs is negative.

Example 1 Find each product.
a. 4(−3)
   4(−3) = −12
b. −8(5)
   −8(5) = −40

Multiplying Integers with the Same Sign	The product of two integers with the same sign is positive.

Example 2 Find each product.
a. 6(6)
   6(6) = 36
b. −7(−4)
   −7(−4) = 28

Example 3 Find 6(−3)(−2).
6(−3)(−2) = [6(−3)](−2)   Use the Associative Property.
= −18(−2)   6(−3) = −18
= 36   −18(−2) = 36

Exercises

Find each product.
1. −5(7) −35
2. 6(−9) −54
3. −10 · 4 −40
4. −12 · −2 24
5. 5(−11) −55
6. −15(−4) 60
7. −14(2) −28
8. 6(14) 84
9. −18 · 2 −36
10. −9(10) −90
11. 12(−6) −72
12. −11(−11) 121
13. −4(−4)(5) 80
14. 6(−7)(2) −84
15. −10(−4)(−6) −240
16. −7(−3)(2) 42
17. −9(4)(2) −72
18. 6(−4)(−12) 288
19. 11(3)(−2) −66
20. −5(−6)(7) 210
21. −3(−4)(−8) −96
22. 22(3)(−3) −198
23. −8(10)(−2) 160
24. −6(5)(−9) 270

Skills Practice, p. 73 and Practice, p. 74 (shown)

Find each product.
1. 8(16) 128
2. −4(17) −68
3. −1(−40) 40
4. −5(−7) 35
5. 0(−54) 0
6. 29(−2) −58
7. −20(−20) 400
8. −31(−4) 124
9. −2(−15)(−6) −180
10. 3(−5)(−8) 120
11. −10(17)(−2) 340
12. −2(−2)(−2) −8
13. 12(10)(5) 600
14. −50(−21)(2) 2100
15. −8(−13)(−25) −2600
16. −5(16)(4) −320

ALGEBRA Simplify each expression.
17. −6r · (12s) −72rs
18. −15 · (9v) −135v
19. 2ab · (−25) −50ab
20. −27y · (−z) 27yz
21. −60m(−2)(−3n) −360mn
22. −9u(−4)(−w) −36uw
23. 29g(0)(−15) 0
24. −b(−12)(11) 132b
25. 19h(−1)(−2s) 38hs
26. −h(−jk) hjk
27. (−1)(−a)(−bc) −abc
28. (−1)(−fg)(−xy) −fgxy

ALGEBRA Evaluate each expression if a = −1, b = −6, and c = 5.
29. −11a 11
30. 4ab 24
31. −8bc 240
32. −10ac 50
33. 15ab 80
34. 12ac −60
35. abc 30
36. −abc −30
37. −11a(−bc) 330
38. 4ab(−8c) −960
39. 9a(−2b)(5c) −2700
40. −3a(−2b)(−c) −180

41. **REAL ESTATE** In Montyville, the value of homes has experienced an annual increase of −2 percent. If the rate continues, what will be the increase over 10 years? −20 percent

42. **RETAIL** The Good Food n' More grocery store loses an average of $210 a day due to breakage, shoplifting, and food expiration. How much money does the store lose on average per 7-day week? −$1470

Enrichment, p. 76

Carpeting

Suppose you want to figure the cost of carpeting a room. Room sizes are usually given in square feet. Carpet prices are usually given in square yards. You need to apply three formulas.

The formula a = ℓw is used to compute the area, a, of a rectangle in square feet.

a (area in square feet) = ℓ (length in feet) · w (width in feet)

The formula for the area in square yards is given below.

A (area in square yards) = a (area in square feet) / 9

The following formula can be used to compute the cost of carpeting.

c (cost) = A (number of square yards) · p (price per square yard)

Example Find the cost of carpeting a room 21 feet long and 15 feet wide if the carpeting costs $7.70 per square yard.

a = ℓ · w
= 21 · 15
= 315 square feet

A = a/9
= 315/9
= 35 square yards

c = A · p
= 35 · $7.70
= $269.50

The cost of carpeting the room is $269.50.

Find the cost of carpeting each room listed in the chart below.

	Room	Length	Width	Price Per Square Yard	Cost Per Room
1.	Living Room	18	24	$17.00	$816
2.	Dining Room	15	15	$22.50	$562.50
3.	Den	12	9	$15.00	$180
4.	Bedroom A	12	18	$18.50	$444
5.	Bedroom B	9	15	$21.00	$315
6.	Bathroom	6	6	$ 8.95	$35.80

7. Find the total carpeting bill. $2353.30

78 Chapter 2 Integers

Practice and Apply

Homework Help

For Exercises	See Examples
16–21	1
22–25	2
26–33	3
34, 35, 54, 55	4
36–53	5

Extra Practice
See page 727.

Find each product.
16. −3 · 4 −12
17. −7 · 6 −42
18. 4(−8) −32
19. 9 · (−8) −72
20. −12 · 3 −36
21. 14(−5) −70
22. 6 · 19 114
23. 4(32) 128
24. −8(−11) 88
25. −15(−3) 45
26. −5(−4)(6) 120
27. 5(−13)(−2) 130
28. −7(−8)(−3) −168
29. −11(−4)(−7) −308
30. −12(−9)(6) 648
31. −6(−8)(11) 528
32. 2(−8)(−9)(10) 1440
33. 4(−7)(−4)(−12) −1344

34. **FLOODS** In 1993, the Mississippi River was so high that it caused the Illinois River to flow backward. If the Illinois River flowed at the rate of −1500 feet per hour, how far would the water travel in 24 hours? −36,000 ft or about −6.8 mi

35. **TEMPERATURE** During a 10-hour period, the temperature in Browning, Montana, changed at a rate of −10°F per hour, starting at 44°F. What was the ending temperature? −56°F

ALGEBRA Simplify each expression.
36. −5 · 7x −35x
37. −8 · 12y −96y
38. 6(−8a) −48a
39. 5(−11b) −55b
40. −7s(−8t) 56st
41. −12m(−9n) 108mn
42. 2ab(3)(−7) −42ab
43. 3x(5y)(−9) −135xy
44. −4(−p)(−q) −4pq
45. −8(−11b)(−c) −88bc
46. 9(−2c)(3d) −54cd
47. −6j(3)(5k) −90jk

ALGEBRA Evaluate each expression.
48. −7n, if n = −4 28
49. 9s, if s = −11 −99
50. ab, if a = 9 and b = 8 72
51. −2xy, if x = −8 and y = 5 80
52. −16cd, if c = 4 and d = −5 320
53. 18gh, if g = −3 and h = 4 −216

More About. . .

Tides •••••••••••••••••••••

It takes about 6 hours for the ocean to move from low to high tide. High tide can change the width of the beach at a rate of −17 feet an hour.

••• **TIDES** For Exercises 54 and 55, use the information below and at the left.
In Wrightsville, North Carolina, during low tide, the beachfront in some places is about 350 feet from the ocean to the homes. At high tide, the water is much closer to the homes. 54. −102 ft

54. What is the change in the width of the beachfront from low to high tide?

55. What is the distance from the ocean to the homes at high tide? 248 ft

56. **CRITICAL THINKING** Write a rule that will help you determine the sign of the product if you are multiplying two or more integers. See margin.

57. **CRITICAL THINKING** Determine whether each statement is *true* or *false*. If false, give a counterexample. If true, give an example.
   a. Multiplication of integers is commutative. True; 3(−5) = −5(3)
   b. Multiplication of integers is associative. True; −2(3 · 5) = (−2 · 3)(5)

Answer

56. If there is an even number of negative numbers being multiplied, the product will be positive. If there is an odd number of negative numbers being multiplied, the product will be negative.

58. WRITING IN MATH Answer the question that was posed at the beginning of the lesson. **See margin.**

How are the signs of factors and products related?

Include the following in your answer:
- a model of $2(-4)$,
- an explanation of why the product of a positive and a negative integer must be negative, and
- a pattern that explains why the product $-3(-3)$ is positive.

Standardized Test Practice

59. The product of two negative integers is— **B**
  (A) always negative.   (B) always positive.
  (C) sometimes negative. (D) never positive.

60. Which values complete the table at the right for $y = -3x$? **D**

x	-2	-1	0	1
y				

  (A) $-6, -3, 0, 3$ (B) $-6, -2, 0, 2$
  (C) $6, 2, 0, -2$ (D) $6, 3, 0, -3$

Maintain Your Skills

Mixed Review **ALGEBRA** Evaluate each expression if $a = -2$, $b = -6$, and $c = 14$.
(Lesson 2-3)

61. $a - c$ **−16**   **62.** $b - a$ **−4**   **63.** $a - b$ **4**

64. $a + b + c$ **6**   **65.** $b - a + c$ **10**   **66.** $a - b - c$ **−10**

67. WEATHER RECORDS The highest recorded temperature in Columbus, Ohio, is 104°F. The lowest recorded temperature is −22°F. What is the difference between the highest and lowest temperatures? *(Lesson 2-3)* **126°F**

Find each sum. *(Lesson 2-2)*

68. $-10 + 8 + 4$ **2**   **69.** $-4 + (-3) + (-7)$ **−14**   **70.** $9 + (-14) + 2$ **−3**

WebQuest

The cost of a trip to a popular amusement park can be determined with integers. Visit www.pre-alg.com/ webquest to continue work on your WebQuest project.

Refer to the coordinate system. Write the ordered pair that names each point. *(Lesson 1-6)*

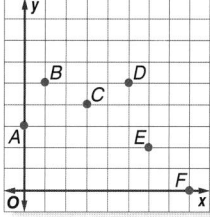

71. E **(6, 2)**   **72.** C **(3, 4)**

73. B **(1, 5)**   **74.** F **(8, 0)**

75. D **(5, 5)**   **76.** A **(0, 3)**

Find each sum or product mentally. *(Lesson 1-4)*

77. $3 \cdot 8 \cdot 20$ **480**   **78.** $8 + 98 + 102$ **208**   **79.** $5 \cdot 11 \cdot 10$ **550**

Getting Ready for the Next Lesson **BASIC SKILL** Find each quotient.

80. $40 \div 8$ **5**   **81.** $90 \div 15$ **6**   **82.** $45 \div 3$ **15**

83. $105 \div 7$ **15**   **84.** $240 \div 6$ **40**   **85.** $96 \div 24$ **4**

DAILY INTERVENTION   **Differentiated Instruction**

- **Logical** On a blank transparency, draw a multiplication table similar to the addition table shown on p. 63. Have students find the products for two positive factors. Then have them find a pattern for the values in the table and extend the pattern to complete the table.

---

4 Assess

Open-Ended Assessment

Speaking Have students explain the difference in rules between addition of integers and multiplication of integers.

Getting Ready for Lesson 2-5

PREREQUISITE SKILL Lesson 2-5 presents the division of integers, for which the students need to know how to divide whole numbers. Exercises 80–85 should be used to determine your students' familiarity with finding quotients.

Answer

58. When you multiply two integers with the same sign, the product is positive; when you multiply two integers with different signs, the product is negative. Answers should include the following.

-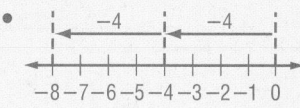

- If the positive integer represents the number of groups made up of the negative integer, the total will be negative.

- $-3 \cdot 2 = -6$
  $-3 \cdot 1 = -3$
  $-3 \cdot 0 = 0$
  $-3 \cdot (-1) = 3$
  $-3 \cdot (-2) = 6$
  $-3 \cdot (-3) = 9$

2-5 Dividing Integers

Mathematical Background notes are available for this lesson on page 54D.

How **is dividing integers related to multiplying integers?**

The opening activity questions are repeated on page 80 of the *Chapter 2 Resources Masters*.

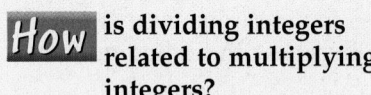

Reading to Learn Mathematics, p. 80 ELL

Pre-Activity *How is dividing integers related to multiplying integers?*

Do the activity at the top of page 80 in your textbook. Write your answers below.

a. How many groups are there? 3

b. What is the quotient of $-12 \div (-4)$? 3

c. What multiplication sentence is also shown on the number line?
$-4 \cdot 3 = -12$

d. Draw a number line and find the quotient $-10 \div (-2)$. 5

Reading the Lesson

Write a definition and give an example of the new vocabulary word.

Vocabulary	Definition	Example
1. average (mean)	See students' work.	

2. The quotient of two integers with ___different___ sign(s) is negative.

3. The quotient of two integers with ___the same___ sign(s) is positive.

4. Draw a number line model that shows how to find the quotient $-9 \div (-3)$. Explain your model.

Start at zero. Move 9 units to the left to show -9. Divide this into three equal segments. Because each segment has 3 units, and because both signs are negative, the quotient is 3.

Helping You Remember

5. You have learned how to divide positive and negative integers. Write one example of each quotient described below. Then find the quotient. Samples are given.

a. dividing a positive integer by a negative integer $14 \div (-2) = -7$

b. dividing a negative integer by a negative integer $-16 \div (-2) = 8$

c. dividing a negative integer by a positive integer $-18 \div 3 = -6$

Vocabulary
- average (mean)

c. $-4 \cdot 3 = -12$

d.
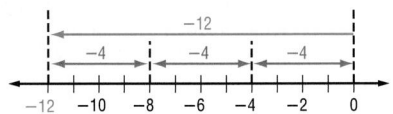

Reading Math

Parts of a Division Sentence

In a division sentence, like $15 \div 5 = 3$, the number you are dividing, 15, is called the *dividend*. The number you are dividing by, 5, is called the *divisor*. The result, 3, is called the *quotient*.

What **You'll Learn**

- Divide integers.
- Find the average of a set of data.

How **is dividing integers related to multiplying integers?**

You can find the quotient $-12 \div (-4)$ using a number line. To find how many groups of -4 there are in -12, show -12 on a number line. Then divide it into groups of -4.

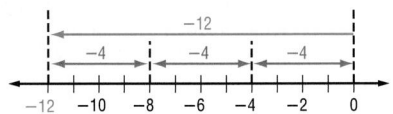

a. How many groups are there? **3**
b. What is the quotient of $-12 \div (-4)$? **3**
c. What multiplication sentence is also shown on the number line?
d. Draw a number line and find the quotient $-10 \div (-2)$. **5**

DIVIDE INTEGERS   You can find the quotient of two integers by using the related multiplication sentence.

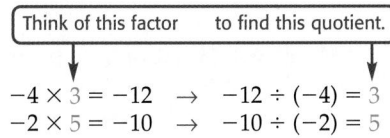

Think of this factor   to find this quotient.

$$-4 \times 3 = -12 \quad \rightarrow \quad -12 \div (-4) = 3$$
$$-2 \times 5 = -10 \quad \rightarrow \quad -10 \div (-2) = 5$$

In the division sentences $-12 \div (-4) = 3$ and $-10 \div (-2) = 5$, notice that the dividends and divisors are both negative. In both cases, the quotient is positive.

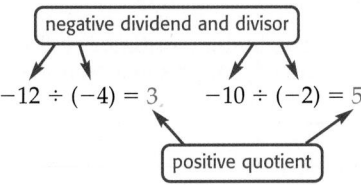

negative dividend and divisor

$$-12 \div (-4) = 3 \qquad -10 \div (-2) = 5$$

positive quotient

You already know that the quotient of two positive integers is positive.

$$12 \div 4 = 3 \qquad 10 \div 2 = 5$$

These and similar examples suggest the following rule for dividing integers with the same sign.

Key Concept   *Dividing Integers with the Same Sign*

- **Words**   The quotient of two integers with the same sign is positive.
- **Examples** $-12 \div (-3) = 4$ $12 \div 3 = 4$

Resource Manager

Workbooks and Reproducible Masters

Chapter 2 Resource Masters
- Study Guide and Intervention, p. 77
- Skills Practice, p. 78
- Practice, p. 79
- Reading to Learn Mathematics, p. 80
- Enrichment, p. 81
- Assessment, p. 102

Graphing Calculator and Spreadsheet Masters, p. 21
Parent and Student Study Guide Workbook, p. 13
Prerequisite Skills Workbook, pp. 11–12

Transparencies
5-Minute Check Transparency 2-5
Answer Key Transparencies

Technology
Interactive Chalkboard
Pre-AlgePASS: Tutorial Plus, Lesson 3

Example 1 Divide Integers with the Same Sign

Find each quotient.

a. $-32 \div (-8)$ The dividend and the divisor have the same sign.

$-32 \div (-8) = 4$ The quotient is positive.

b. $\dfrac{75}{5}$

$\dfrac{75}{5} = 75 \div 5$ The dividend and divisor have the same sign.

$= 15$ The quotient is positive.

What is the sign of the quotient of a positive and a negative integer? Look for a pattern in the following related sentences.

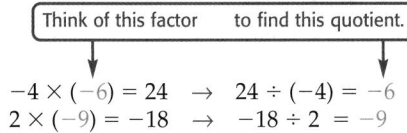

Think of this factor   to find this quotient.

$$-4 \times (-6) = 24 \;\; \rightarrow \;\; 24 \div (-4) = -6$$
$$2 \times (-9) = -18 \;\; \rightarrow \;\; -18 \div 2 = -9$$

Notice that the signs of the dividend and divisor are different. In both cases, the quotient is negative.

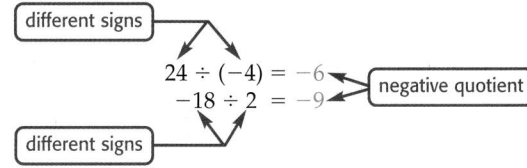

different signs

$$24 \div (-4) = -6$$
$$-18 \div 2 = -9$$

negative quotient

different signs

These and other similar examples suggest the following rule.

> **Key Concept**   *Dividing Integers with Different Signs*
>
> - **Words**   The quotient of two integers with different signs is negative.
> - **Examples** $-12 \div 4 = -3$ $12 \div (-4) = -3$

Concept Check: The sign is positive if the integers have the same sign, and negative if they have different signs.

✓ **Concept Check**   How do you know the sign of the quotient of two integers?

Example 2 Divide Integers with Different Signs

Find each quotient.

a. $-42 \div 3$

$-42 \div 3 = -14$ The signs are different. The quotient is negative.

b. $\dfrac{48}{-6}$

$\dfrac{48}{-6} = 48 \div (-6)$ The signs are different. The quotient is negative.

$= -8$ Simplify.

 www.pre-alg.com/extra_examples   **Lesson 2-5** Dividing Integers   **81**

$$(-12) \div 2 = -6$$
$$(-12) \div 1 = -12$$
$$(-12) \div (-1) = 12$$
$$(-12) \div (-2) = 6$$
$$(-12) \div (-3) = 4$$
$$(-12) \div (-4) = 3$$

2 Teach

DIVIDE INTEGERS

In-Class Examples   Power Point®

1 Find each quotient.

a. $-28 \div (-4)$ 7

b. $\dfrac{96}{8}$ 12

2 Find each quotient.

a. $54 \div (-3)$ -18

b. $\dfrac{-42}{6}$ -7

3 Evaluate $6x \div y$, if $x = -4$ and $y = -8$.   3

✓ Skills Check

Divide Integers Find each quotient.

a. $-18 \div -9$ 2

b. $40 \div (-8)$ -5

c. $-30 \div 6$ -5

d. $60 \div 10$ 6

AVERAGE (MEAN)

In-Class Example   Power Point®

4 **a.** Sam had quiz scores of 89, 98, 96, 97, and 95. Find the average (mean) of his test scores.   95

b. Find the average (mean) of 10, -12, 9, 15, -4, 0, -1, and 7.   3

DAILY INTERVENTION   Differentiated Instruction

- **Kinesthetic** Have students model "average." Write $-7 + 2 + 10 + (-6) + (-9) + (-8)$ on the board. One student holds a sign with "($+$)" on one side and "($-$)" on the other. Then 7 students come up and the sign bearer shows the negative sign. Two students then leave. In order to add 10, after the remaining 5 students sit down, 5 more must come up, and the sign changes to positive. After all the terms are added, the students divide into 6 equal groups to find the average. -3

Dividing Integers with the Same Sign	The quotient of two integers with the same sign is positive.

Example 1 Find each quotient.

a. $14 \div 2$
The dividend and the divisor have the same sign.
$14 \div 2 = 7$ The quotient is positive.

b. $\frac{-25}{-5}$
$\frac{-25}{-5} = -25 \div (-5)$ The dividend and divisor have the same sign.
$= 5$ The quotient is positive.

Dividing Integers with Different Signs	The quotient of two integers with different signs is negative.

Example 2 Find each quotient.

a. $36 \div (-4)$ The signs are different.
$36 \div (-4) = -9$ The quotient is negative.

b. $\frac{-42}{6}$ The signs are different.
$\frac{-42}{6} = -42 \div 6$ The quotient is negative.
$= -7$ Simplify.

Exercises

Find each quotient.

1. $32 \div (-4)$ -8
2. $-18 \div (-2)$ 9
3. $-24 \div 6$ -4
4. $-36 \div (-2)$ 18
5. $50 \div (-5)$ -10
6. $-81 \div (-9)$ 9
7. $-72 \div (-2)$ 36
8. $-45 \div 3$ -15
9. $-60 \div (-12)$ 5
10. $99 \div (-11)$ -9
11. $-200 \div (-4)$ 50
12. $38 \div (-2)$ -19
13. $-144 \div 12$ -12
14. $100 \div (+5)$ -20
15. $-200 \div (-20)$ 10
16. $\frac{-28}{2}$ -14
17. $\frac{36}{-4}$ -9
18. $\frac{-150}{-25}$ 6

Find each quotient.

1. $-44 \div 4$ -11
2. $0 \div (-5)$ 0
3. $-21 \div 21$ -1
4. $32 \div 8$ 4
5. $-17 \div -17$ 1
6. $-49 \div 7$ -7
7. $80 \div -4$ -20
8. $-64 \div -8$ 8
9. $\frac{72}{-9}$ -8
10. $\frac{-100}{-5}$ 20
11. $\frac{-90}{6}$ -15
12. $\frac{360}{12}$ 30
13. $\frac{-400}{-25}$ 16
14. $\frac{-525}{5}$ -105
15. $\frac{84}{-6}$ -14
16. $\frac{215}{5}$ 43

Evaluate each expression if $a = -2$, $b = 5$, and $c = -4$.

17. $-35 \div b$ -7
18. $54 \div a$ -27
19. $-56 \div c$ 14
20. $205 \div b$ 41
21. $\frac{c}{-2}$ 2
22. $\frac{b}{5}$ 1
23. $\frac{2}{a}$ -1
24. $\frac{-4}{c}$ 1
25. $\frac{-28}{c}$ 7
26. $\frac{ac}{-8}$ -1
27. $\frac{bc}{a}$ 10
28. $\frac{250}{ab}$ -25

Find the average (mean) of each group of numbers.

29. 23, 20, 27, 18 22
30. $-8, 9, 4, 0, 2, -1$ 1
31. 17, 21, 4 14
32. $-20, -15, -12, -1, 1, 12, 15, 20$ 0
33. $-7, -3, -9, 0, 21, -2, -14$ -2

34. **TESTS** Miranda earned scores of 84, 91, 95, 78, and 92 on her math tests. Find her average (mean) score. 88

35. **TEMPERATURE** At noon on Friday, the temperature was 0°F. Six hours later the temperature was -18°F. On average, what was the temperature change per hour? -3°F

36. **BUSINESS** The architecture firm of Stuart and Maxwell, Ltd., had monthly profits of $1200, $755, $-450, $210, and $-640 over 5 months. What was the average profit for those months? 215

Cross-Number Puzzle

Use the clues below to complete the following cross-number puzzle. Any negative signs should be placed in the same box as the first digit of the integer.

ACROSS
1. $23 \cdot (-54)$
5. $-56 - 15$
7. $-4283 + 7316$
8. $46.8 \div (-1.3)$
10. $-3840 \div (-96)$
11. $-1.6 \cdot (-2785)$
12. $91.5 \div (-11.5)$
13. $-42 - 679$
15. $50 \cdot (-0.48)$
18. $-53,000 \cdot (-0.001)$
19. $-181 \cdot 5$
21. $-42 + 61$
23. $10 \cdot (-13) \cdot (-19)$
25. $26.1 \div (-0.45)$
26. $-750 \cdot (-0.024)$
27. $-38.56 \div (-0.004)$
28. $-38 - (-54)$
29. $11,260 + (-5210)$

DOWN
1. $-718 + 584$
2. $-0.8 \cdot (-255)$
3. $198 - (-237)$
4. $-118 \div (-0.5)$
5. $-2 \cdot (-22) \cdot (-17)$
6. $-1000 \div -100$
8. $-6.46 \div 0.17$
9. $1547 + (-939)$
13. $-5000 \cdot 0.015$
14. $-832 \cdot (-28)$
15. $-40 \cdot (-20) \cdot (-25)$
16. $-9 \cdot (-5)$
17. $-79 \cdot 3 \cdot 3$
19. $-13,406 + 3661$
20. $-649 + 1535$
22. $46 - (-52)$
24. $-10 \cdot (-46)$
25. $-0.663 \div 0.013$

ALGEBRA CONNECTION

You can use the rules for dividing integers to evaluate algebraic expressions.

Example 3 Evaluate Algebraic Expressions

Evaluate $ab \div (-4)$ if $a = -6$ and $b = -8$.

$ab \div (-4) = -6(-8) \div (-4)$ Replace a with -6 and b with -8.
$= 48 \div (-4)$ The product of -6 and -8 is positive.
$= -12$ The quotient of 48 and -4 is negative.

AVERAGE (MEAN) Division is used in statistics to find the **average**, or **mean**, of a set of data. To find the mean of a set of numbers, find the sum of the numbers and then divide by the number in the set.

Study Tip

Checking Reasonableness
The average must be between the greatest and least numbers in the set. Are the averages in Examples 4a and 4b reasonable?

Example 4 Find the Mean

a. Rachel had test scores of 84, 90, 89, and 93. Find the average (mean) of her test scores.

$\frac{84 + 90 + 89 + 93}{4} = \frac{356}{4}$ Find the sum of the test scores.
Divide by the number of scores.
$= 89$ Simplify.

The average of her test scores is 89.

b. Find the average (mean) of $-2, 8, 5, -9, -12,$ and -2.

$\frac{-2 + 8 + 5 + (-9) + (-12) + (-2)}{6} = \frac{-12}{6}$ Find the sum of the set of integers.
Divide by the number in the set.
$= -2$ Simplify.

The average is -2.

You can refer to the following table to review operations with integers.

Concept Summary — Operations with Integers

Words	Examples
Adding Integers To add integers with the same sign, add their absolute values. Give the result the same sign as the integers.	$-5 + (-4) = -9$ $5 + 4 = 9$
To add integers with different signs, subtract their absolute values. Give the result the same sign as the integer with the greater absolute value.	$-5 + 4 = -1$ $5 + (-4) = 1$
Subtracting Integers To subtract an integer, add its additive inverse.	$5 - 9 = 5 + (-9)$ or -4 $5 - (-9) = 5 + 9$ or 14
Multiplying Integers The product of two integers with the same sign is positive. The product of two integers with different signs is negative.	$5 \cdot 4 = 20$ $-5 \cdot (-4) = 20$ $-5 \cdot 4 = -20$ $5 \cdot (-4) = -20$
Dividing Integers The quotient of two integers with the same sign is positive. The quotient of two integers with different signs is negative.	$20 \div 5 = 4$ $-20 \div (-5) = 4$ $-20 \div 5 = -4$ $20 \div (-5) = -4$

DAILY INTERVENTION

Unlocking Misconceptions

- From the answer in Example 4, students may assume that the average is always a number from the set of data. Use In-Class Example 4b to dispel these wrong assumptions.

Check for Understanding

Concept Check
1. **OPEN ENDED** Write an equation with three integers that illustrates dividing integers with different signs. **See margin.**

2. **Explain** how to find the average of a set of numbers. **See margin.**

Guided Practice

Find each quotient.

GUIDED PRACTICE KEY	
Exercises	Examples
3, 4, 6	1
5, 7, 8	2
9, 10	3
11	4

3. $88 \div 8$ **11**

4. $-20 \div (-5)$ **4**

5. $-18 \div 6$ **−3**

6. $\frac{-36}{-4}$ **9**

7. $\frac{70}{-7}$ **−10**

8. $\frac{-81}{9}$ **−9**

ALGEBRA Evaluate each expression.

9. $x \div 4$, if $x = -52$ **−13**

10. $\frac{s}{t}$, if $s = -45$ and $t = 5$ **−9**

Application
11. **WEATHER** The low temperatures for 7 days in January were $-2, 0, 5, -1, -4, 2,$ and 0. Find the average for the 7-day period. **0**

★ indicates increased difficulty

Practice and Apply

Homework Help	
For Exercises	See Examples
12–17, 24, 25	1
18–23	2
26–31	3
32, 33	4

Extra Practice
See page 727.

Find each quotient.

12. $54 \div 9$ **6**

13. $45 \div 5$ **9**

14. $-27 \div (-3)$ **9**

15. $-64 \div (-8)$ **8**

16. $-72 \div (-9)$ **8**

17. $-60 \div (-6)$ **10**

18. $-77 \div 7$ **−11**

19. $-300 \div 6$ **−50**

20. $480 \div (-12)$ **−40**

★ 21. $\frac{132}{-12}$ **−11**

★ 22. $\frac{175}{-25}$ **−7**

★ 23. $\frac{143}{-13}$ **−11**

24. What is -91 divided by -7? **13**

25. Divide -76 by -4. **19**

ALGEBRA Evaluate each expression.

26. $\frac{x}{-5}$, if $x = 85$ **−17**

27. $\frac{108}{m}$, if $m = -9$ **−12**

28. $\frac{c}{d}$, if $c = -63$ and $d = -7$ **9**

29. $\frac{s}{t}$, if $s = 52$ and $t = -4$ **−13**

30. $xy \div (-3)$ if $x = 9$ and $y = -7$ **21**

31. $ab \div 6$ if $a = -12$ and $b = -8$ **16**

32. **STATISTICS** Find the average (mean) of $4, -8, 9, -3, -7, 10,$ and 2. **1**

33. **BASKETBALL** In their first five games, the Jefferson Middle School basketball team scored 46, 52, 49, 53, and 45 points. What was their average number of points per game? **49 points**

ENERGY For Exercises 34–36, use the information below.

The formula $d = \left| 65 - \frac{h + l}{2} \right|$ can be used to find degree days, where h is the high and l is the low temperature.

34. If Baltimore had a high of 81° and a low of 65°, find the degree days.

35. If Milwaukee had a high of 8° and a low of 0°, find the degree days.

36. **RESEARCH** Use the Internet or another resource to find the high and low temperature for your city for a day in January. Find the degree days. **See students' work.**

www.pre-alg.com/self_check_quiz

Study Notebook

Have students—
• add the definition/example of the vocabulary term to their Vocabulary Builder worksheets for Chapter 2.
• describe how to find the average (mean) and include 2 examples.
• copy the "Concept summary" table into their notebooks, including the examples.
• include any other item(s) that they find helpful in mastering the skills in this lesson.

About the Exercises . . .
Organization by Objective
• **Divide Integers:** 12–31, 34, 35
• **Average (Mean):** 32, 33

Odd/Even Assignments
Exercises 12–35 are structured so that students practice the same concepts whether they are assigned odd or even problems.

Alert! Exercise 36 involves research on the Internet or other reference materials.

Assignment Guide
Basic: 13–19 odd, 25–35 odd, 36–40, 42–50
Average: 13–35 odd, 36–50
Advanced: 12–34 even, 36–46 (Optional: 47–50)
All: Practice Quiz 2 (1–10)

Answers
1. Sample answer: $-16 \div 4 = -4$
2. Find the sum of the numbers. Divide by the number in the set.

Open-Ended Assessment

Writing Have students write a paragraph explaining how they know whether a quotient should be positive or negative. How does this compare with products of multiplication?

Getting Ready for Lesson 2-6

PREREQUISITE SKILL In Lesson 2-6, students need to understand how points are named in ordered pairs in order to graph them. Exercises 47–50 should be used to determine your students' familiarity with ordered pairs.

Assessment Options

Practice Quiz 2 The quiz provides students with a brief review of the concepts and skills in Lessons 2-4 and 2-5. Lesson numbers are given to the right of exercises or instruction lines so students can review concepts not yet mastered.

Quiz (Lessons 2-4 and 2-5) is available on p. 102 of the *Chapter 2 Resource Masters.*

Answers

37. Sample answer: $x = -144$; $y = 12$; $z = -12$

39. Sample answer: When the signs of the integers are the same, both a product and a quotient are positive; when the signs are different, the product and quotient are negative. Answers should include the following.

- Sample answer: $4 \cdot (-6) = -24$ and $-24 \div 4 = -6$; $-3 \cdot 2 = -6$ and $-6 \div (-3) = 2$

- Sample answers: same sign: $-30 \div (-5) = 6$, $30 \div 5 = 6$ different signs: $-24 \div 8 = -3$, $24 \div (-8) = 3$

---

37. **CRITICAL THINKING** Find values for x, y, and z, so that all of the following statements are true. **See margin.**
    - $y > x$, $z < y$, and $x < 0$
    - $z \div 2$ and $z \div 3$ are integers.
    - $x \div z = -z$
    - $x \div y = z$

38. **CRITICAL THINKING** Addition and multiplication are said to be closed for whole numbers, but subtraction and division are not. That is, when you add or multiply any two whole numbers, the result is a whole number. Which operations are closed for integers? **add., subt., and mult.**

39. WRITING IN MATH   Answer the question that was posed at the beginning of the lesson. **See margin.**

    How is dividing integers related to multiplying integers?

    Include the following in your answer:
    - two related multiplication and division sentences, and
    - an example of each case (same signs, different signs) of dividing integers.

 **Standardized Test Practice**
Ⓐ Ⓑ Ⓒ Ⓓ

40. On Saturday, the temperature fell 10° in 2 hours. Which expresses the temperature change per hour? **C**
    Ⓐ 5°   Ⓑ −2°   Ⓒ −5°   Ⓓ −10°

★ 41. Mark has quiz scores of 8, 7, 8, and 9. What is the lowest score he can get on the remaining quiz to have a final average (mean) score of at least 8? **B**
    Ⓐ 7   Ⓑ 8   Ⓒ 9   Ⓓ 10

Maintain Your Skills

Mixed Review   Find each difference or product.   *(Lessons 2-3 and 2-4)* 44. −4*ab*   45. −50*cd*
42. $-8 - (-25)$ **17**   43. $75 - 114$ **−39**   44. $2ab \cdot (-2)$ 45. $(-10c)(5d)$

46. **PATTERNS** Find the next two numbers in the pattern 5, 4, 2, −1, …
    (Lesson 1-1) **−5, −10**

Getting Ready for the Next Lesson   **PREREQUISITE SKILL**   Use the grid to name the point for each ordered pair.
(To review ordered pairs, see Lesson 1-6.)
47. $(1, 5)$ **B**   48. $(6, 2)$ **F**
49. $(4, 5)$ **D**   50. $(0, 3)$ **A**

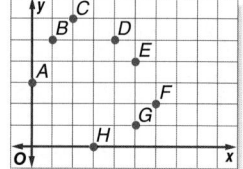

Practice Quiz 2 ⟋⟋ Lessons 2-4 and 2-5

Find each product.   *(Lesson 2-4)*
1. $-12 \cdot 7$ **−84**   2. $-6(-15)$ **90**   3. $-3(-7)(-6)$ **−126**   4. $3(-8)(-5)$ **120**

Find each quotient.   *(Lesson 2-5)*
5. $-124 \div 4$ **−31**   6. $-90 \div (-6)$ **15**   7. $125 \div (-5)$ **−25**   8. $-126 \div (-9)$ **14**

9. Simplify $4x(-5y)$.   *(Lesson 2-4)* **−20xy**

10. Evaluate $-9a$ if $a = -6$.   *(Lesson 2-4)* **54**

What You'll Learn

- Graph points on a coordinate plane.
- Graph algebraic relationships.

Vocabulary
- quadrants

How is a coordinate system used to locate places on Earth?

A GPS, or Global Positioning System, can be used to find a location anywhere on Earth by identifying its latitude and longitude. Several cities are shown on the map below. For example, Sydney, Australia, is located at approximately 30°S, 150°E.

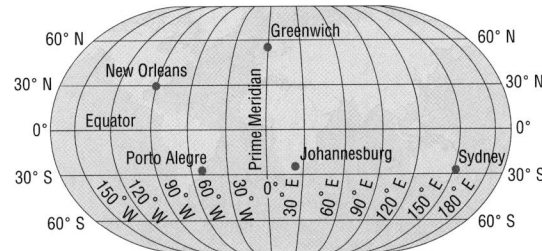

a. Latitude is measured north and south of the equator. What is the latitude of New Orleans? **30°N**

b. Longitude is measured east and west of the prime meridian. What is the longitude of New Orleans? **90°W**

c. What does the location 30°N, 90°W mean?

c. **30° north of the equator; 90° west of the prime meridian**

GRAPH POINTS Latitude and longitude are a kind of coordinate system. The coordinate system you used in Lesson 1-6 can be extended to include points below and to the left of the origin.

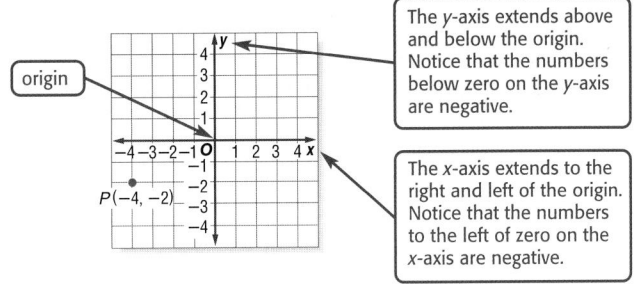

origin

The *y*-axis extends above and below the origin. Notice that the numbers below zero on the *y*-axis are negative.

The *x*-axis extends to the right and left of the origin. Notice that the numbers to the left of zero on the *x*-axis are negative.

TEACHING TIP
Ask: Is (−2, −4) the same point? Locate (−2, −4) on the coordinate system. Emphasize the idea of order in ordered pairs.

Recall that a point graphed on the coordinate system has an *x*-coordinate and a *y*-coordinate. The dot at the ordered pair (−4, −2) is the graph of point *P*.

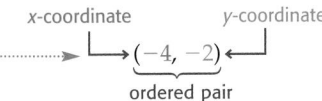

x-coordinate   *y*-coordinate

$(-4, -2)$

ordered pair

---

1 Focus

 5-Minute Check Transparency 2-6 Use as a quiz or review of Lesson 2-5.

Mathematical Background notes are available for this lesson on page 54D.

How is a coordinate system used to locate places on Earth?

The opening activity questions are repeated on page 85 of the *Chapter 2 Resource Masters.*

Reading to Learn Mathematics, p. 85 **ELL**

Pre-Activity *How is a coordinate system used to locate places on Earth?*

Do the activity at the top of page 85 in your textbook. Write your answers below.

a. Latitude is measured north and south of the equator. What is the latitude of New Orleans? 30°N

b. Longitude is measured east and west of the prime meridian. What is the longitude of New Orleans? 90°W

c. What does the location 30°N, 90°W mean?

30° north of the equator; 90° west of the prime meridian

Reading the Lesson

Write a definition and give an example of the new vocabulary word.

Vocabulary	Definition	Example
1. quadrants	See students' work.	

2. A point graphed on the coordinate system has a(n) __x-coordinate__ and a(n) __y-coordinate__ .

3. In which quadrant does the point A(4, −2) lie? IV

Helping You Remember

4. Draw a coordinate grid with points to represent your classroom and where your classmates sit. Explain how to name the locations of your classmates.

Sample answer. Let the center row of desks be the *y*-axis, and the center column of desks be the *x*-axis. Have the front of the class be positive. A student sitting at (3, −22) would be 3 desks to the right of the center desk, and 2 desks behind the center desk.

Resource Manager

Workbooks and Reproducible Masters

Chapter 2 Resource Masters
- Study Guide and Intervention, p. 82
- Skills Practice, p. 83
- Practice, p. 84
- Reading to Learn Mathematics, p. 85
- Enrichment, p. 86
- Assessment, p. 102

Graphing Calculator and Spreadsheet Masters, p. 22
Parent and Student Study Guide Workbook, p. 14

 Transparencies

5-Minute Check Transparency 2-6
Answer Key Transparencies

 Technology

Interactive Chalkboard
Multimedia Applications

2 Teach

Building on Prior Knowledge

Students will apply the same skills for graphing points from Chapter 1 to graph points in all four quadrants.

GRAPH POINTS

Teaching Tip Have students look at the *x*-axis and ask what this represents.   a number line   Ask them to examine the *y*-axis and ask the same question. For those who cannot see that the *y*-axis is a number line, have them rotate their books 90° clockwise and look at the *y*-axis again.

In-Class Examples

 Power Point®

1 Write the ordered pair that names each point.

　a. *P* 　　b. *Q* 　　c. *R*

　(4, −2) 　(−3, −1) 　(2, 0)

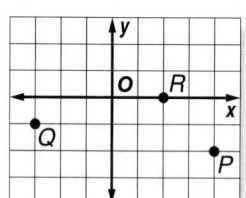

Teaching Tip Just as *x* and *y* are in alphabetical order in the ordered pair (*x*, *y*), so are the directions from the origin that they represent (horizontal, vertical) or (across, up and down).

2 Graph and label each point on a coordinate plane. Then name the quadrant in which each point lies.

　a. *S*(−1, −5)
　　Quadrant III

　b. *U*(−2, 3)
　　Quadrant II

　c. *T*(0, −3)
　　not in any quadrant

 Study Tip

Ordered Pairs
Notice that the axes in an ordered pair (*x*, *y*) are listed in alphabetical order.

Example 1 Write Ordered Pairs

Write the ordered pair that names each point.

　a. *A*

　　The *x*-coordinate is −3.
　　The *y*-coordinate is 2.
　　The ordered pair is (−3, 2).

　b. *B*

　　The *x*-coordinate is 4.
　　The *y*-coordinate is –2.
　　The ordered pair is (4, −2).

　c. *C*

　　The point lies on the *y*-axis, so its *x*-coordinate is 0.
　　The *y*-coordinate is −3. The ordered pair is (0, −3).

The *x*-axis and the *y*-axis separate the coordinate plane into four regions, called **quadrants**. The axes and points on the axes are not located in any of the quadrants.

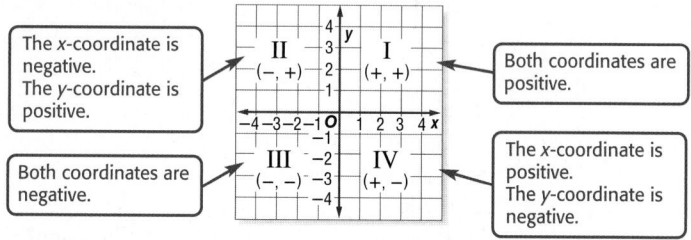

The *x*-coordinate is negative. The *y*-coordinate is positive.

Both coordinates are positive.

Both coordinates are negative.

The *x*-coordinate is positive. The *y*-coordinate is negative.

Example 2 Graph Points and Name Quadrant

Graph and label each point on a coordinate plane. Name the quadrant in which each point lies.

　a. *D*(2, 4)

　　Start at the origin. Move 2 units right.
　　Then move 4 units up and draw a dot.
　　Point *D*(2, 4) is in Quadrant I.

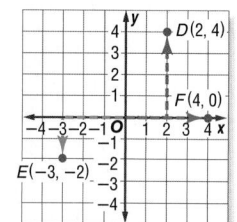

　b. *E*(−3, −2)

　　Start at the origin. Move 3 units left.
　　Then move 2 units down and draw a dot.
　　Point *E*(−3, −2) is in Quadrant III.

　c. *F*(4, 0)

　　Start at the origin. Move 4 units right. Since the *y*-coordinate is 0, the point lies on the *x*-axis. Point *F*(4, 0) is not in any quadrant.

✓ **Concept Check**   What parts of a coordinate graph do not lie in any quadrant?
the two axes

DAILY INTERVENTION

Differentiated Instruction

- **Visual/Spatial** Have students create a line design extending beyond a single quadrant, on a coordinate grid. Have them list each "corner" or vertex of the design as an ordered pair. They should list the ordered pairs in sequence as they progress around the outline of the objects in the designs. Then have them give their ordered lists to their partners to plot on a coordinate grid. As the partners "connect the dots," they will see the designs take shape.

GRAPH ALGEBRAIC RELATIONSHIPS You can use a coordinate graph to show relationships between two numbers.

GRAPH ALGEBRAIC RELATIONSHIPS

Example 3 *Graph an Algebraic Relationship*

The sum of two numbers is 5. If x represents the first number and y represents the second number, make a table of possible values for x and y. Graph the ordered pairs and describe the graph.

First, make a table.
Choose values for x and y that have a sum of 5.

$x + y = 5$		
x	y	(x, y)
2	3	(2, 3)
1	4	(1, 4)
0	5	(0, 5)
−1	6	(−1, 6)
−2	7	(−2, 7)

Then graph the ordered pairs on a coordinate plane.

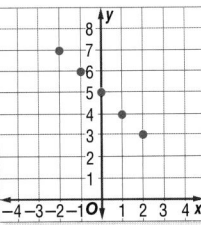

The points on the graph are in a line that slants downward to the right. The line crosses the y-axis at $y = 5$.

3 The difference between two integers is 4. If x represents the first integer and y is subtracted from it, make a table of possible values for x and y. Then graph the ordered pairs and describe the graph.

$x - y = 4$		
x	y	(x, y)
2	−2	(2, −2)
1	−3	(1, −3)
0	−4	(0, −4)
−1	−5	(−1, −5)
−2	−6	(−2, −6)

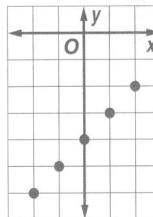

The points on the graph are in a line that slants upward to the right. The line crosses the y-axis at $y = -4$.

Check for Understanding

Concept Check

1. **Explain** why the point (3, 6) is different from the point (6, 3). **See pp. 95A–95B.**

2. **OPEN ENDED** Name two ordered pairs whose graphs are *not* located in one of the four quadrants. **Sample answer: (0, 0), (4, 0)**

3. **FIND THE ERROR** Keisha says that if you interchange the coordinates of any point in Quadrant I, the new point would still be in Quadrant I. Jason says the new point would be in Quadrant 3. Who is correct? Explain your reasoning. **See pp. 95A–95B.**

Guided Practice

Name the ordered pair for each point graphed at the right.

4. A (−4, 5)   5. C (1, 3)

6. G (−3, −2)   7. K (5, −4)

Graph and label each point on a coordinate plane. Name the quadrant in which each point is located.

8. $J(3, -4)$ **IV**   9. $K(-2, 2)$ **II**

10. $L(0, 4)$ **none**   11. $M(-1, -2)$ **III**

GUIDED PRACTICE KEY

Exercises	Examples
4–7	1
8–11	2
12	3

8–11. See pp. 95A–95B for graphs.

Application

12. **ALGEBRA** Make a table of values and graph six ordered integer pairs where $x + y = 3$. Describe the graph. **See pp. 95A–95B.**

 www.pre-alg.com/extra_examples

---

3 Practice/Apply

Study Notebook

Have students—
• complete the definition/example for the remaining term on the Vocabulary Builder Worksheets for Chapter 2.
• include any other item(s) that they find helpful in mastering the skills in this lesson.

DAILY

INTERVENTION **FIND THE ERROR** Have students review the illustration of the quadrants shown on p. 86. Ask them which quadrants, when the ordered pairs defining their points are interchanged, retain the resulting points, and which quadrants do not. **I and III; II and IV**

Study Guide and Intervention, p. 82

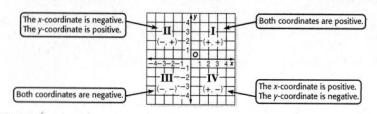

Example

Graph and label each point on a coordinate plane. Name the quadrant in which each point lies.

a. *M*(−2, 5)
Start at the origin. Move 2 units left. Then move 5 units up and draw a dot. Point *M*(−2, 5) is in Quadrant II.

b. *N*(4, −4)
Start at the origin. Move 4 units right. Then move 4 units down and draw a dot. Point *N*(4, −4) is in Quadrant IV.

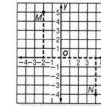

Exercises

Graph and label each point on the coordinate plane. Name the quadrant in which each point is located.

1. *A*(2, 6) I
2. *B*(−1, 4) II
3. *C*(0, −5) none
4. *D*(−4, −3) III
5. *E*(2, 0) none
6. *F*(3, −2) IV
7. *G*(−4, 4) II
8. *H*(2, −5) IV
9. *I*(6, 3) I
10. *J*(−5, −8) III
11. *K*(3, −5) IV
12. *L*(−7, −3) III

Skills Practice, p. 83 and Practice, p. 84 (shown)

Graph and label each point on the coordinate plane. Name the quadrant in which each point is located.

1. *A* (8, 6) I
2. *B* (−8, 6) II
3. *C* (−4, −11) III
4. *D* (3, −6) IV
5. *E* (9, 0) none
6. *F* (−4, 1) II
7. *G* (−10, −10) III
8. *H* (0, −8) none
9. *I* (6, −2) IV
10. *J* (2, 13) I

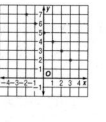

11. **ALGEBRA** Make a table of values and graph six sets of ordered pairs for the equation *y* = 5 − *x*. Describe the graph.

y = 5 − *x*		
x	*y*	(*x*, *y*)
3	2	(3, 2)
2	3	(2, 3)
1	4	(1, 4)
0	5	(0, 5)
−1	6	(−1, 6)
−2	7	(−2, 7)

The points are along a line slanting down to the right, crossing the *y*-axis at 5 and the *x*-axis at 5.

12. **GEOMETRY** On the coordinate plane, draw a rectangle *ABCD* with vertices at *A*(1, 4), *B*(5, 4), *C*(5, 1), and *D*(1, 1). Then graph and describe the new rectangle formed when you subtract 3 from each coordinate of the vertices in rectangle *ABCD*.

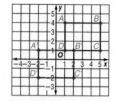

The new rectangle is the same size as rectangle *ABCD* and is shifted to the left 3 units and down 3 units, with vertices at (−2, 1), (2, 1), (2, −2), and (−2, −2).

Enrichment, p. 86

Polar Coordinates

In a rectangular coordinate system, the ordered pair (*x*, *y*) describes the location of a point *x* units from the origin along the *x*-axis and *y* units from the origin along the *y*-axis.

In a polar coordinate system, the ordered pair (*r*, θ) describes the location of a point *r* units from the pole on the ray (vector) whose endpoint is the pole and which forms an angle of θ with the polar axis.

The graph of (2, 30°) is shown on the polar coordinate plane at the right below. Note that the concentric circles indicate the number of units from the pole.

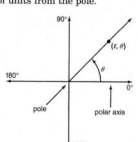

Locate each point on the polar coordinate system below.

1. (3, 45°)
2. (1, 135°)
3. (2½, 60°)
4. (4, 120°)
5. (2, 225°)
6. (3, −30°)
7. (1, −90°)
8. (−2, 30°)

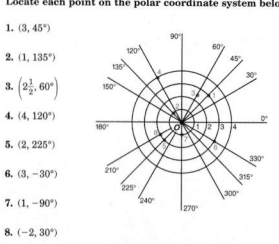

★ indicates increased difficulty

Practice and Apply

Homework Help

For Exercises	See Examples
13–22	1
23–34, 41, 42	2
35–40, 43, 44	3

Extra Practice
See page 728.

Name the ordered pair for each point graphed at the right.

13. *R* (−2, 4)
14. *G* (−4, 2)
15. *M* (4, −2)
16. *B* (1, −4)
17. *V* (2, 2)
18. *H* (4, 3)
19. *U* (0, −2)
20. *W* (3, 0)
21. *A* (−3, −5)
22. *T* (−2, −2)

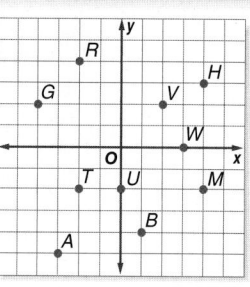

Graph and label each point on a coordinate plane. Name the quadrant in which each point is located. **23–34. See pp. 95A–95B for graphs.**

23. *A*(4, 5) I
24. *K*(−5, 1) II
25. *M*(4, −2) IV
26. *B*(−5, −5) III
27. *S*(2, −5) IV
28. *R*(−3, 5) II
29. *E*(0, 3) none
30. *H*(0, −3) none
31. *G*(5, 0) none
32. *C*(6, −1) IV
33. *D*(0, 0) none
34. *F*(−4, 0) none

ALGEBRA Make a table of values and graph six sets of ordered integer pairs for each equation. Describe the graph. **35–40. See pp. 95A–95B.**

35. *x* + *y* = 5
36. *x* + *y* = −2
37. *y* = 2*x*
38. *y* = −2*x*
39. *y* = *x* + 2
40. *y* = *x* − 1

Graph each point. Then connect the points in alphabetical order and identify the figure. **41–42. See pp. 95A–95B for graphs.**

41. *A*(0, 6), *B*(4, −6), *C*(−6, 2), *D*(6, 2), *E*(−4, −6), *F*(0, 6) **5-point star**

42. *A*(5, 8), *B*(1, 13), *C*(5, 18), *D*(9, 13), *E*(5, 8), *F*(5, 6), *G*(3, 7), *H*(3, 5), *I*(7, 7), *J*(7, 5), *K*(5, 6), *L*(5, 3), *M*(3, 4), *N*(3, 2), *P*(7, 4), *Q*(7, 2), *R*(5, 3), *S*(5, 1) **kite**

★ 43. Graph eight ordered integer pairs where |*x*| > 3. Describe the graph.

★ 44. Graph all ordered integer pairs that satisfy the condition |*x*| < 4 and |*y*| < 3.
43–44. See pp. 95A–95B.

Reading Math

Vertex, Vertices

A *vertex* of a triangle is a point where two sides of a triangle meet. *Vertices* is the plural of *vertex*.

GEOMETRY On a coordinate plane, draw a triangle *ABC* with vertices at *A*(3, 1), *B*(4, 2), and *C*(2, 4). Then graph and describe each new triangle formed in Exercises 45–48. **45–48. See pp. 95A–95B.**

45. Multiply each coordinate of the vertices in triangle *ABC* by 2.

46. Multiply each coordinate of the vertices in triangle *ABC* by −1.

47. Add 2 to each coordinate of the vertices in triangle *ABC*.

48. Subtract 4 from each coordinate of the vertices in triangle *ABC*.

49. **MAPS** Find a map of your school and draw a coordinate grid on the map with the library as the center. Locate the cafeteria, principal's office, your math classroom, gym, counselor's office, and the main entrance on your grid. Write the coordinates of these places. How can you use these points to help visitors find their way around your school?
See students' work.

About the Exercises . . .

Organization by Objective
• **Graph Points:** 13–34, 41, 42, 45–48
• **Graph Algebraic Relationships:** 35–40, 43, 44

Alert! Exercises 8–12 and 23–49 require graph paper.

Odd/Even Assignments
Exercises 13–42 are structured so that students practice the same concepts whether they are assigned odd or even problems.

50. CRITICAL THINKING If the graph of A(x, y) satisfies the given condition, name the quadrant in which point A is located.

   a. $x > 0, y > 0$ **I**   **b.** $x < 0, y < 0$ **III**   **c.** $x < 0, y > 0$ **II**

51. CRITICAL THINKING Graph eight sets of integer coordinates that satisfy $|x| + |y| > 3$. Describe the location of the points. **See margin.**

52.  Answer the question that was posed at the beginning of the lesson. **See margin.**

   How is a coordinate system used to locate places on Earth?

   Include the following in your answer:
- an explanation of how coordinates can describe a location, and
- a description of how latitude and longitude are related to the *x*- and *y*-axes on a coordinate plane. Include what corresponds to the origin on a coordinate plane.

Standardized Test Practice Ⓐ Ⓑ Ⓒ Ⓓ

53. On the coordinate plane at the right, what are the coordinates of the point that shows the location of the library? **D**

   Ⓐ $(4, -2)$ Ⓑ $(-2, -4)$

   Ⓒ $(4, 2)$ Ⓓ $(-4, -2)$

54. On the coordinate plane at the right, what location has coordinates $(5, -2)$? **B**

   Ⓐ Park   Ⓑ School

   Ⓒ Library   Ⓓ Grocery Store

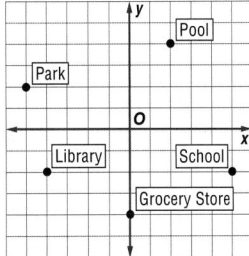

Maintain Your Skills

Mixed Review **Find each quotient.** *(Lesson 2-5)*

  55. $-24 \div 8$ **−3**   **56.** $105 \div (-5)$ **−21**   **57.** $-400 \div (-50)$ **8**

ALGEBRA **Evaluate each expression if** $f = -9$, $g = -6$, **and** $h = 8$. *(Lesson 2-4)*

  58. $-5fg$ **−270**   **59.** $2gh$ **−96**   **60.** $-10fh$ **720**

61. WEATHER In the newspaper, Amad read that the low temperature for the day was expected to be $-5°F$ and the high temperature was expected to be $8°F$. What was the difference in the expected high and low temperature? *(Lesson 2-3)* **13°F**

ALGEBRA **Simplify each expression.** *(Lesson 1-4)*

  62. $(a + 8) + 6$ **$a + 14$**   **63.** $4(6h)$ **24h**   **64.** $(n \cdot 7) \cdot 8$ **56n**

  65. $(b \cdot 9) \cdot 5$ **45b**   **66.** $(16 + 3y) + y$ **$4y + 16$**   **67.** $0(4z)$ **0**

Assignment Guide

Basic: 13–41 odd, 45–48, 50–67

Average: 13–43 odd, 45–48, 50–67

Advanced: 12–44 even, 45–67

---

4 Assess

Open-Ended Assessment

Speaking Give a set of ordered pairs to the class, including at least one point in each quadrant, and have students explain step-by-step how to graph each one.

Assessment Options

Quiz (Lesson 2-6) is available on p. 102 of the *Chapter 2 Resource Masters*.

Answers

51. Sample answer:

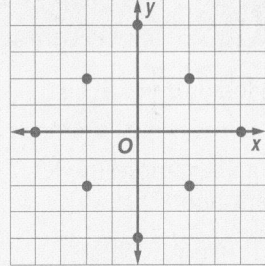

Description: The points lie outside a rhombus defined by (0, 4), (4, 0), (0, −4), and (−4, 0).

52. Latitude and longitude lines are similar to a coordinate system. Answers should include the following.
- Coordinates describe a location by telling how far and in what direction the location is from a given starting point.
- In the latitude and longitude system, longitude is similar to the *x*-coordinate of a point in a coordinate plane. Latitude is similar to the *y*-coordinate. The point where the prime meridian and the equator meet is similar to the origin in the coordinate system.

Vocabulary and Concept Check

- This alphabetical list of vocabulary terms in Chapter 2 includes a page reference where each term was introduced.

- **Assessment** A vocabulary review/test for Chapter 2 is available on p. 100 of the *Chapter 2 Resource Masters*.

Lesson-by-Lesson Review

For each lesson,

- the main ideas are summarized,
- additional examples review concepts, and
- practice exercises are provided.

Vocabulary PuzzleMaker

ELL The Vocabulary PuzzleMaker software improves students' mathematics vocabulary using four puzzle formats—crossword, scramble, word search using a word list, and word search using clues. Students can work on a computer screen or from a printed handout.

MindJogger Videoquizzes

ELL MindJogger Videoquizzes provide an alternative review of concepts presented in this chapter. Students work in teams in a game show format to gain points for correct answers. The questions are presented in three rounds.

Round 1 Concepts (5 questions)
Round 2 Skills (4 questions)
Round 3 Problem Solving (4 questions)

Vocabulary and Concept Check

absolute value (p. 58)	inequality (p. 57)	opposites (p. 66)
additive inverse (p. 66)	integers (p. 56)	quadrants (p. 86)
average (p. 82)	mean (p. 82)	
coordinate (p. 57)	negative number (p. 56)	

Complete each sentence with the correct term. Choose from the list above.

1. A(n) _____ is a number less than zero. **negative number**

2. The four regions separated by the axes on a coordinate plane are called _____. **quadrants**

3. The number that corresponds to a point on the number line is called the _____ of that point. **coordinate**

4. An integer and its opposite are also called _____ of each other. **additive inverses**

5. The set of _____ includes positive whole numbers, their opposites, and zero. **integers**

6. The _____ of a number is the distance the number is from zero on the number line. **absolute value**

7. A(n) _____ is a mathematical sentence containing $<$ or $>$. **inequality**

Lesson-by-Lesson Review

2-1 Integers and Absolute Value

See pages 56–61.

Concept Summary

- Numbers on a number line increase as you move from left to right.
- The absolute value of a number is the distance the number is from zero on the number line.

Examples

1 Replace the ● with $<$, $>$, or $=$ in -3 ● 2 to make a true sentence.

$$-4\ -3\ -2\ -1\ \ 0\ \ 1\ \ 2\ \ 3\ \ 4$$

Since -3 is to the left of 2, write $-3 < 2$.

2 Evaluate $|-4|$.

$$-5\ -4\ -3\ -2\ -1\ \ 0\ \ 1\ \ 2$$

The graph of -4 is 4 units from 0. So, $|-4| = 4$.

Exercises Replace each ● with $<$, $>$, or $=$ to make a true sentence.
See Example 2 on page 57.

8. 8 ● -8 **>** **9.** -3 ● -3 **=** **10.** -2 ● 0 **<** **11.** -12 ● -21 **>**

Evaluate each expression. *See Example 4 on page 58.*

12. $|-32|$ **32** **13.** $|25|$ **25** **14.** $-|15|$ **−15** **15.** $|-8| + |-14|$ **22**

 www.pre-alg.com/vocabulary_review

Study Organizer

For more information about Foldables, see *Teaching Mathematics with Foldables.*

Have students reexamine their Foldables to make sure all examples they have written are correct. Have them refer to their Foldables if needed when working through the Study Guide exercises.

2-2 Adding Integers

See pages 64–68.

Concept Summary

- To add integers with the same sign, add their absolute values. Give the result the same sign as the integers.
- To add integers with different signs, subtract their absolute values. Give the result the same sign as the integer with the greater absolute value.

Examples Find each sum.

1 $-3 + (-4)$

$-3 + (-4) = -7$ The sum is negative.

2 $5 + (-2)$

$5 + (-2) = 3$ The sum is positive.

Exercises Find each sum.   *See Examples 2, 4, and 6 on pages 64–66.*

16. $-6 + (-3)$ **−9**
17. $-4 + (-1)$ **−5**
18. $-2 + 7$ **5**
19. $4 + (-8)$ **−4**
20. $6 + (-9) + (-8)$ **−11**
21. $4 + (-7) + (-3) + (-4)$ **−10**

2-3 Subtracting Integers

See pages 70–74.

Concept Summary

- To subtract an integer, add its additive inverse.

Examples Find each difference.

1 $-5 - 2$

$\begin{aligned} -5 - 2 &= -5 + (-2) \\ &= -7 \end{aligned}$ To subtract 2, add −2.

2 $8 - (-4)$

$\begin{aligned} 8 - (-4) &= 8 + 4 \\ &= 12 \end{aligned}$ To subtract −4, add 4.

Exercises Find each difference.   *See Examples 1 and 2 on pages 70–71.*

22. $4 - 9$ **−5**
23. $-3 - 5$ **−8**
24. $7 - (-2)$ **9**
25. $-1 - (-6)$ **5**
26. $-7 - 8$ **−15**
27. $6 - 10$ **−4**
28. $-3 - (-7)$ **4**
29. $6 - (-3)$ **9**

2-4 Multiplying Integers

See pages 75–79.

Concept Summary

- The product of two integers with different signs is negative.
- The product of two integers with the same sign is positive.

Examples Find each product.

1 $6(-4)$

$6(-4) = -24$ The factors have different signs, so the product is negative.

2 $-8(-2)$

$-8(-2) = 16$ The factors have the same sign, so the product is positive.

Study Guide and Review

Chapter
2 For More ...
- Extra Practice, see pages 726–728.
- Mixed Problem Solving, see page 759.

Answers

40–43.

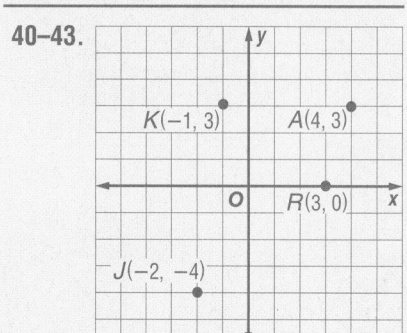

Answers (p. 93)

1. Find the difference of their absolute values. Give the result the sign of the integer having the larger absolute value.

2. Add the additive inverse of the integer being subtracted.

3.

28–30.

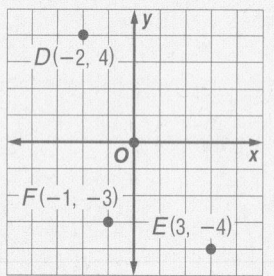

Exercises Find each product. *See Examples 1 and 2 on pages 75–76.*

30. $-9(5)$ **−45**   31. $11(-6)$ **−66**   32. $-4(-7)$ **28**   33. $-3(-16)$ **48**

34. Simplify $-2a(4b)$. *See Example 5 on page 77.* **−8ab**

2-5 Dividing Integers

See pages 80–84.

Concept Summary
- The quotient of two integers with the same sign is positive.
- The quotient of two integers with different signs is negative.

Examples Find each quotient.

1 $-30 \div (-5)$.

$-30 \div (-5) = 6$ The signs are the same, so the quotient is positive.

2 $27 \div (-3)$

$27 \div (-3) = -9$ The signs are different, so the quotient is negative.

Exercises Find each quotient. *See Examples 1 and 2 on page 81.*

35. $-14 \div (-2)$ **7**   36. $-52 \div (-4)$ **13**   37. $-36 \div 9$ **−4**   38. $88 \div (-4)$ **−22**

39. Find the average (mean) of -3, -6, 9, -3, and 13. *See Example 4 on page 82* **2**

2-6 The Coordinate System

See pages 85–89.

Concept Summary
- The x-axis and the y-axis separate the coordinate plane into four quadrants.
- The axes and points on the axes are not located in any of the quadrants.

Examples Graph and label each point on a coordinate plane. Name the quadrant in which each point is located.

1 $F(5, -3)$

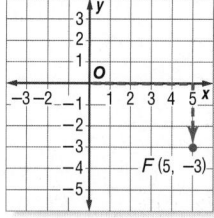

Point $F(5, -3)$ is in quadrant IV.

2 $G(0, 4)$

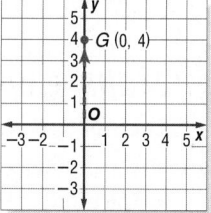

Point $G(0, 4)$ is not in any quadrant.

40–43. See margin for graphs.

Exercises Graph and label each point on a coordinate plane. Name the quadrant in which each point is located. *See Example 2 on page 86.*

40. $A(4, 3)$ **I**   41. $J(-2, -4)$ **III**   42. $K(-1, 3)$ **II**   43. $R(3, 0)$ **none**

Vocabulary and Concepts

1. **Explain** how to add two integers with different signs. See margin.

2. **State** a rule used for subtracting integers. See margin.

3. **Graph** the set of integers $\{-6, 2, -1, 1\}$ on a number line. See margin.

Skills and Applications

Write two inequalities using the numbers in each sentence. Use the symbols < and >.

4. -5 is less than 2. $-5 < 2; 2 > -5$

5. 12 is greater than -15. $12 > -15; -15 < 12$

Replace each ● with <, >, or = to make a true sentence.

6. $-5 ● -3$ <

7. $-5 ● -14$ >

8. $4 ● |-7|$ <

Find each sum or difference.

9. $-4 + (-8)$ -12

10. $-9 + 15$ 6

11. $12 + (-15)$ -3

12. $14 + (-7) + -11$ -4

13. $4 - 13$ -9

14. $8 - (-6)$ 14

15. $-6 - (-10)$ 4

16. $-14 - (-7)$ -7

Find each product or quotient.

17. $6(-8)$ -48

18. $-9(8)$ -72

19. $-7(-5)$ 35

20. $2(-4)(11)$ -88

21. $54 ÷ (-9)$ -6

22. $-64 ÷ (-4)$ 16

23. $-250 ÷ 25$ -10

24. $-144 ÷ (-6)$ 24

ALGEBRA   Evaluate each expression if $a = -5$, $b = 3$, and $c = -10$.

25. $ab - c$ -5

26. $c ÷ a$ 2

27. $4c + |a|$ -35

Graph and label each point on a coordinate plane. Name the quadrant in which each point is located.   28–30. See margin for graphs.

28. $D(-2, 4)$ II

29. $E(3, -4)$ IV

30. $F(-1, -3)$ III

31. **WEATHER**   The table shows the low temperatures during one week in Anchorage, Alaska. Find the average low temperature for the week. $-3°F$

Day	S	M	T	W	T	F	S
Temperature (°F)	-12	3	-7	0	-4	1	-2

32. **SPORTS**   During the first play of the game, the Brownville Tigers football team lost seven yards. On each of the next three plays, an additional four yards were lost. Express the total yards lost at the end of the first four plays as an integer. -19 yd

33. **STANDARDIZED TEST PRACTICE**   Suppose Jason's home represents the origin on a coordinate plane. If Jason leaves his home and walks two miles west and then four miles north, what is the location of his destination as an ordered pair? In which quadrant is his destination? **A**

Ⓐ $(-2, 4)$; II   Ⓑ $(2, 4)$; I   Ⓒ $(-2, -4)$; II   Ⓓ $(4, -2)$; IV

 www.pre-alg.com/chapter_test

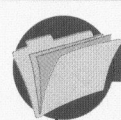

Portfolio Suggestion

Introduction   The rules for operations on integers are fundamental to algebra as they apply to operations on variables as well.

Ask Students to include a summary of the rules for operations on integers. They should organize the information in the way that best suits them, such as in a chart, on a foldable, or in a paragraph.

Assessment Options

Vocabulary Test   A vocabulary review/test for Chapter 2 can be found on p. 100 of the *Chapter 2 Resource Masters*.

Chapter Tests   There are six Chapter 2 Tests and an Open-Ended Assessment task available in the *Chapter 2 Resource Masters*.

Chapter 2 Tests			
Form	Type	Level	Pages
1	MC	basic	87–88
2A	MC	average	89–90
2B	MC	average	91–92
2C	FR	average	93–94
2D	FR	average	95–96
3	FR	advanced	97–98

MC = multiple-choice questions
FR = free-response questions

Open-Ended Assessment
Performance tasks for Chapter 2 can be found on p. 99 of the *Chapter 2 Resource Masters*, along with a sample scoring rubric for these tasks on p. A22.

ExamView® Pro

Use the networkable **ExamView® Pro** to:

• Create **multiple versions** of tests.

• Create **modified** tests for *Inclusion* students.

• **Edit** existing questions and **add** your own questions.

• Use built-in **state curriculum correlations** to create tests aligned with state standards.

• Change **English** tests to **Spanish** and vice versa.

These two pages contain practice questions in the various formats that can be found on the most frequently given standardized tests.

A practice answer sheet for these two pages can be found on page A1 of the *Chapter 2 Resource Masters*.

Standardized Test Practice
Student Recording Sheet, p. A1

Part 1 *Multiple Choice*

Select the best answer from the choices given and fill in the corresponding oval.

1 Ⓐ Ⓑ Ⓒ Ⓓ   4 Ⓐ Ⓑ Ⓒ Ⓓ   7 Ⓐ Ⓑ Ⓒ Ⓓ   9 Ⓐ Ⓑ Ⓒ Ⓓ
2 Ⓐ Ⓑ Ⓒ Ⓓ   5 Ⓐ Ⓑ Ⓒ Ⓓ   8 Ⓐ Ⓑ Ⓒ Ⓓ   10 Ⓐ Ⓑ Ⓒ Ⓓ
3 Ⓐ Ⓑ Ⓒ Ⓓ   6 Ⓐ Ⓑ Ⓒ Ⓓ

Part 2 *Short Response/Grid In*

Solve the problem and write your answer in the blank.

For Questions 11, 12, 14, and 15 also enter your answer by writing each number or symbol in a box. Then fill in the corresponding oval for that number or symbol.

11 _____ (grid in)   11   12
12 _____ (grid in)
13 _____
14 _____ (grid in)
15 _____ (grid in)
16 _____   14   15

Part 3 *Extended Response*

Record your answers for Question 17 on the back of this paper.

Teaching Tip In part 2, only Exercises 10 and 11 could appear as grid-in questions on a standardized test.

Additional Practice

See pp. 105–106 of the *Chapter 2 Resource Masters* for additional standardized test practice.

Part 1 Multiple Choice

Record your answers on the answer sheet provided by your teacher or on a sheet of paper.

1. The table below shows the number of cells present after a certain form of bacteria multiplies for a number of hours. How many cells will be present in five hours? (Lesson 1-1) **C**

Number of Hours	Number of Cells
0	1
1	3
2	9
3	27

Ⓐ 81   Ⓑ 91
Ⓒ 243   Ⓓ 279

2. Suppose your sister has 3 more CDs than you do. Which equation represents the number of CDs that you have? Let y represent your CDs and s represent your sister's CDs. (Lesson 1-5) **B**

Ⓐ $y = s + 3$ Ⓑ $y = s - 3$
Ⓒ $y = 3 - s$ Ⓓ $y = 3s$

3. Which expression represents the greatest integer? (Lesson 1-6) **C**

Ⓐ $|4|$ Ⓑ $|-3|$
Ⓒ $|-8|$ Ⓓ -9

4. The water level of a local lake is normally 0 feet above sea level. In a flood, the water level rose 4 feet above normal. A month later, the water level had gone down 5 feet. Which integer best represents the water level at that time? (Lesson 2-1) **B**

Ⓐ -3 Ⓑ -1
Ⓒ 4 Ⓓ 9

5. What is the sum of -5 and 2? (Lesson 2-2) **B**

Ⓐ -7 Ⓑ -3
Ⓒ 3 Ⓓ 7

6. Find the value of x if $x = 7 - (-3)$. (Lesson 2-3) **D**

Ⓐ -10 Ⓑ -4
Ⓒ 4 Ⓓ 10

7. If $t = -5$, what is the value of the expression $-3t + 7$? (Lesson 2-4) **D**

Ⓐ -8 Ⓑ -6
Ⓒ 8 Ⓓ 22

8. If $a = -2$ and $b = 5$, what is the value of $\frac{b - 13}{a}$? (Lesson 2-5) **D**

Ⓐ -4 Ⓑ -9
Ⓒ 9 Ⓓ 4

For Questions 9 and 10, use the following graph.

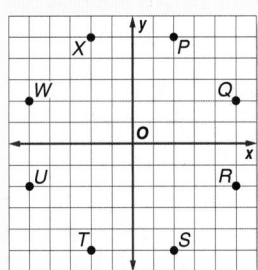

9. Which letter represents the ordered pair $(-2, 5)$? (Lesson 2-6) **B**

Ⓐ R   Ⓑ X
Ⓒ T   Ⓓ W

10. Which ordered pair represents point U? (Lesson 2-6) **C**

Ⓐ $(5, -2)$ Ⓑ $(-2, -5)$
Ⓒ $(-5, -2)$ Ⓓ $(-2, 5)$

ExamView® Pro

Special banks of standardized test questions similar to those on the SAT, ACT, TIMSS 8, NAEP 8, and Pre-Algebra End-of-Course tests can be found on this CD-ROM.

Preparing for Standardized Tests
For test-taking strategies and more
practice, see pages 771–788.

Part 2 Short Response/Grid In

Record your answers on the answer sheet
provided by your teacher or on a sheet of
paper.

1. The bar graph shows the numbers of girls
and boys in each grade at Muir Middle
School. In which grade is the difference
between the number of girls and the number
of boys the greatest?   (Prerequisite Skill, p. 722) **6**

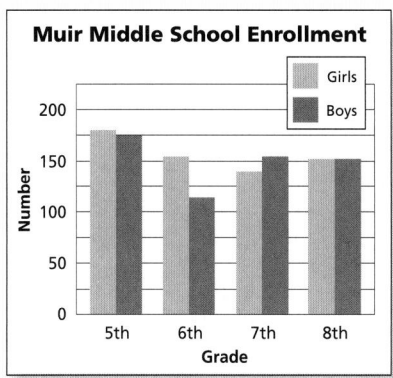

Muir Middle School Enrollment

2. Nine less than a number is 15. Find the
number.   (Lesson 1-5) **24**

3. The Springfield High School football team
gained 7 yards on one play. On the next
play, they lost 11 yards. Write an integer that
represents the net result of these two plays.
(Lesson 2-2) **−4**

4. The low temperature one winter night in
Bismarck, North Dakota, was −15°F. The
next day the high temperature was 3°F. How
many degrees had the temperature risen?
(Lesson 2-3) **18**

5. The table below was used to change values
of x into values of y.

x	$y = x - 7$
6	−1
7	0
8	1

What value of x can be used to obtain
a y-value equal to 5?   (Lesson 2-3) **12**

16. The low temperatures in Minneapolis
during four winter days were +2°F, −7°F,
−12°F, and +9°F. What was the average low
temperature during these four days?
(Lesson 2-5) **−2°F**

Part 3 Extended Response

Record your answers on a sheet of paper.
Show your work.

17. On graph paper, graph the points $A(4, 2)$,
$B(-3, 7)$, and $C(-3, 2)$. Connect the points to
form a triangle.   (Lesson 2-6)

a. Add 6 to the x-coordinate of each
coordinate pair. Graph and connect the
new points to form a new figure. Is the
new figure the same size and shape as the
original triangle? Describe how the size,
shape, and position of the new triangle
relate to the size, shape, and position of
the original triangle. **See margin.**

b. If you add −6 to each original
x-coordinate, and graph and connect the
new points to create a new figure, how
will the position of the new figure relate
to that of the original one? **See margin.**

c. Multiply the y-coordinate of each original
ordered pair by −1. Graph and connect
the new points to form a new figure.
Describe how the size, shape, and
position of the new triangle relate to the
size, shape, and position of the original
triangle. **See margin.**

d. If you multiply each original x-coordinate
by −1, and graph and connect the new
points to create a new figure, how will
the position of the new figure relate to
that of the original one? **See margin.**

Test-Taking Tip   Ⓐ Ⓑ Ⓒ Ⓓ

Question 17
When answering open-ended items on standardized tests,
follow these steps:
1. Read the item carefully.
2. Show all of your work. You may receive points for
   items that are only partially correct.
3. Check your work.

Evaluating Extended Response Questions

Extended Response questions
are graded by using a multilevel
rubric that guides you in assessing a student's knowledge of a
particular concept.

Goal: Graph geometric figures
on a coordinate grid and analyze
the relationships among figures,
points, and mathematical
operations.

Sample Scoring Rubric: The
following rubric is a sample
scoring device. You may wish
to add more detail to this sample
to meet your individual scoring
needs.

Score	Criteria
4	A correct solution that is supported by well-developed, accurate explanations
3	A generally correct solution, but may contain minor flaws in reasoning or computation
2	A partially correct interpretation and/or solution to the problem
1	A correct solution with no supporting evidence or explanation
0	An incorrect solution indicating no mathematical understanding of the concept or task, or no solution is given

Answer

17a–d.

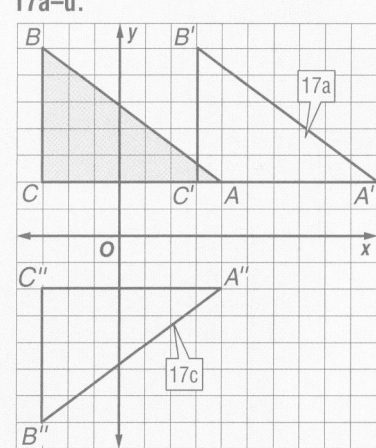

17a. Yes, the new figure is the same size and
shape as the original triangle. The original triangle could be slid (translated)
6 units to the right to create the new
figure.

17b. If −6 were added to each x-coordinate,
the original triangle could be slid 6 units
to the left (or slid −6 units) to create the
new figure.

17c. Yes, the new figure is the same size and
shape as the original triangle. The original triangle could be flipped (reflected)
across the x-axis to create the new
figure.

17d. If you multiplied the x-coordinate of
each original coordinate pair by −1, the
original triangle would be flipped
(reflected) over the y-axis.

Page 59, Lesson 2-1

26.
```
←─┼──┼──●──┼──●──┼──┼──┼──●→
 −4−3−2−1  0  1  2  3  4
```

27.
```
←─●──┼──┼──┼──┼──●──┼──┼──●→
 −3−2−1  0  1  2  3  4  5
```

28.
```
←─┼──●──┼──┼──●──┼──┼──●──┼→
 −8−7−6−5−4−3−2−1  0
```

29.
```
←─┼──●──┼──●──┼──●──┼──●──┼→
 −8−6−4−2  0  2  4  6  8
```

Page 61, Lesson 2-1

79. {(3, 2), (3, 4), (2, 1), (2, 4)} **80.** {(1, 4), (6, 2), (9, 6), (1, 9)}

x	y
3	2
3	4
2	1
2	4

x	y
1	4
6	2
9	6
1	9

Page 87, Lesson 2-6

1. Sample answer: (3, 6) represents a point 3 units to the right and 6 units up from the origin. (6, 3) represents a point 6 units to the right and 3 units up from the origin.

3. Keisha; a point in Quadrant I has two positive coordinates. Interchanging the coordinates will still result in two positive coordinates, and the point will be in Quadrant I.

8–11.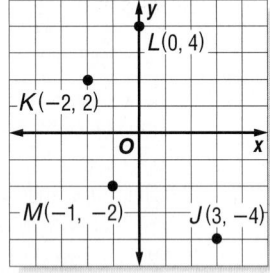

12. Sample answer:

x	y
−2	5
−1	4
0	3
1	2
2	1
3	0

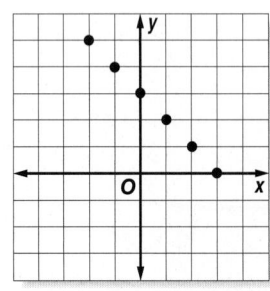

The points are along a diagonal line that crosses the y-axis at y = 3 and the x-axis at x = 3.

23–34.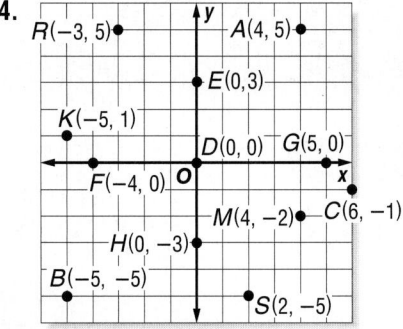

35–40. Sample answers given.

35.

x	y
1	4
2	3
3	2
4	1
5	0
6	−1

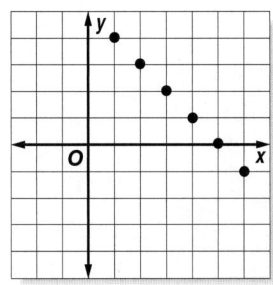

The points are along a line slanting down to the right, crossing the y-axis at 5 and the x-axis at 5.

36.

x	y
−2	0
−1	−1
0	−2
1	−3
2	−4
3	−5

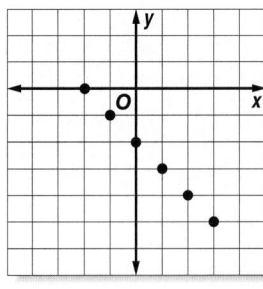

The points are along a line slanting down, crossing the x-axis at −2 and the y-axis at −2.

37.

x	y
−2	−4
−1	−2
0	0
1	2
2	4
3	6

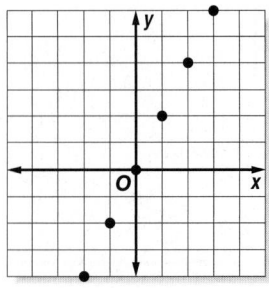

The points are along a line slanting up, through the origin

38.

x	y
−2	4
−1	2
0	0
1	−2
2	−4
3	−6

The points are along a line slanting down, through the origin

39.

x	y
−3	−1
−2	0
−1	1
0	2
1	3
2	4

The points are along a line slanting up, crossing the y-axis at 2 and the x-axis at −2

40.

x	y
−2	−3
−1	−2
0	−1
1	0
2	1
3	2

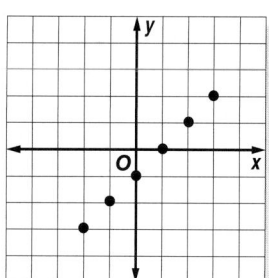

The points are along a line slanting up, crossing the y-axis at −1 and the x-axis at 1

41.

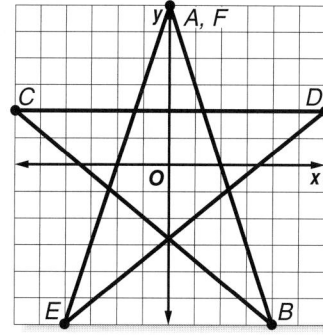

42.

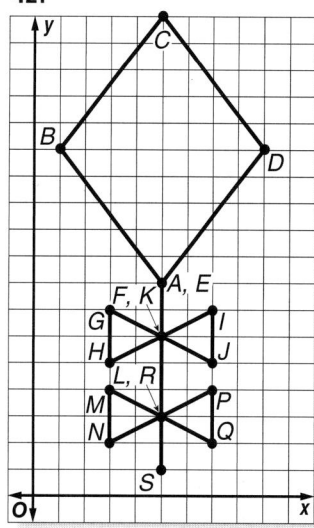

43. Sample answer:

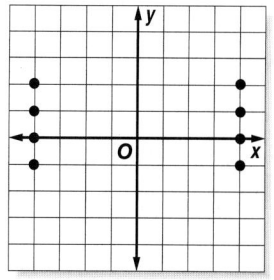

The graph can include any ordered pair in which $x > 3$ or $x < −3$.

44.

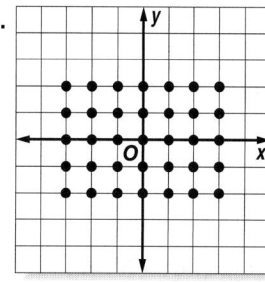

The graph can include any integer pairs where $x > 4$ or $x < −4$.

45.

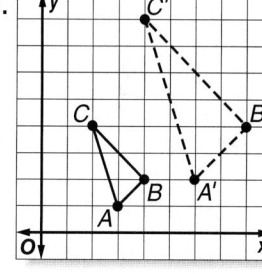

The new triangle is twice the size of the original triangle, and is moved to the right and up.

46.

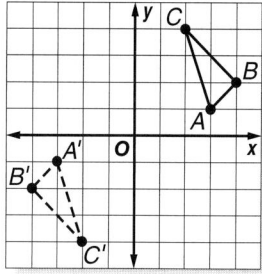

The new triangle is reflected over the x- and y-axes; it is the same size as the original triangle.

47.

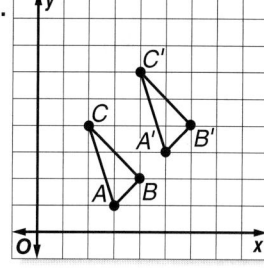

The new triangle is translated right 2 units and up 2 units; it is the same size as the original triangle.

48.

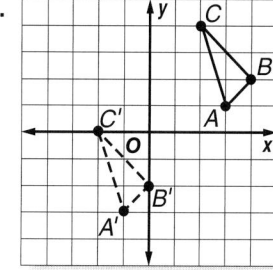

The new triangle is translated left 4 and down 4; it is the same size as the original triangle.

Equations
Chapter Overview and Pacing

Year-long pacing: pages T20–T21.

LESSON OBJECTIVES	PACING (days)			
	Regular		Block	
	Basic/ Average	Advanced	Basic/ Average	Advanced
3-1 The Distributive Property (pp. 98–102) • Use the Distributive Property to write equivalent numerical expressions. • Use the Distributive Property to write equivalent algebraic expressions.	1	1	0.5	0.5
3-2 Simplifying Algebraic Expressions (pp. 103–107) • Use the Distributive Property to simplify algebraic expressions.	1	1	0.5	0.5
3-3 Solving Equations by Adding or Subtracting (pp. 108–114) *Preview:* Solve equations using algebra tiles. • Solve equations by using the Subtraction Property of Equality. • Solve equations by using the Addition Property of Equality.	2 (with 3-3 Preview)	1	1 (with 3-3 Preview)	0.5
3-4 Solving Equations by Multiplying or Dividing (pp. 115–119) • Solve equations by using the Division Property of Equality. • Solve equations by using the Multiplication Property of Equality.	1	1	0.5	0.5
3-5 Solving Two-Step Equations (pp. 120–124) • Solve two-step equations.	2	2	1	0.5
3-6 Writing Two-Step Equations (pp. 126–130) • Write verbal sentences as two-step equations. • Solve verbal problems by writing and solving two-step equations.	2	1	1	0.5
3-7 Using Formulas (pp. 131–137) • Solve problems by using formulas. • Solve problems involving the perimeters and areas of rectangles. *Follow-Up:* Use a spreadsheet to find perimeter and area.	1	2 (with 3-7 Follow-Up)	0.5	1 (with 3-7 Follow-Up)
Study Guide and **Practice Test** (pp. 138–141) **Standardized Test Practice** (pp. 142–143)	1	1	0.5	0.5
Chapter Assessment	1	1	0.5	0.5
TOTAL	12	11	6	5

*An electronic version of this chapter is available on **StudentWorks™**. This backpack solution CD-ROM allows students instant access to the Student Edition, lesson worksheet pages, and web resources.*

Chapter Resource Manager

CHAPTER 3 RESOURCE MASTERS

Study Guide and Intervention	Practice (Skills and Average)	Reading to Learn Mathematics	Enrichment	Assessment	Prerequisite Skills Workbook	Applications*	Parent and Student Study Guide Workbook	5-Minute Check Transparencies	Interactive Chalkboard	Pre-AlgePASS: Tutorial Plus (lessons)	Materials
107	108–109	110	111			9–10		16	3-1	3-1	
112	113–114	115	116		157			17	3-2	3-2	
117	118–119	120	121			5–8	SC 5	18	3-3	3-3	*Preview:* algebra tiles, equation mat
122	123–124	125	126		157, 159	9–12		19	3-4	3-4	4
127	128–129	130	131			21–26	SM 9 GCS 23	20	3-5	3-5	5, 6
132	133–134	135	136		158			21	3-6	3-6	
137	138–139	140	141		158		SC 6 GCS 24	22	3-7	3-7	*Follow-Up:* spreadsheet software
					143–156, 160–162 163–164						

* *Key to Abbreviations:* GCS = Graphing Calculator and Spreadsheet Masters
SC = School-to-Career Masters
SM = Science and Mathematics Lab Manual

 Study Guide and Intervention, Skills Practice, Practice, and Parent and Student Study Guide Workbooks are also available in Spanish.

Continuity of Instruction

Prior Knowledge

Prior to beginning the Pre-Algebra course, students learned addition, subtraction, multiplication, and division of whole numbers. In Chapter 1 they learned to solve equations mentally, to use addition and subtraction properties, and to translate verbal expressions into algebraic expressions. In Chapter 2 students learned addition, subtraction, multiplication, and division of integers.

This Chapter

In this chapter, students will study how to use the Distributive Property to combine like terms in order to simplify algebraic expressions. They solve equations using properties of equality. Students will learn how to write and solve two-step equations and they will use formulas to solve real-world problems such as finding the area and perimeter of rectangles.

Future Connections

Skill in solving equations will be needed in Chapter 6 when students learn to solve proportion and percent problems and in Chapter 7 when they learn to solve inequalities. Solving two-step equations will be extended to include solving equations with variables on each side in Chapter 8. The study of area of rectangles in this chapter forms the basis of the formulas for area of parallelograms, triangles, and trapezoids in Chapter 10.

3-1 The Distributive Property

Two expressions are said to be equivalent if they have the same value. The Distributive Property says that to multiply a number by a sum, multiply each number inside the parentheses by the number outside the parentheses. For example, the expression $3(x - 4) = 3x - 12$. Algebra tiles can be used to demonstrate the Distributive Property by showing that two equivalent algebraic expressions will always have the same value, no matter what variables are used in the expression.

3-2 Simplifying Algebraic Expressions

The Distributive Property can be used to simplify algebraic expressions. When plus or minus signs separate an algebraic expression into parts, each part is a term. The numerical part of a term that contains a variable is called the *coefficient* of the variable. Like terms are terms that contain the same variables, such as $2n$ and $5n$ or $6xy$ and $4xy$. A term without a variable is called a *constant*. Constant terms are also like terms. Rewriting a subtraction expression using addition helps identify the terms of an expression. An algebraic expression is in simplest form if it has no like terms and no parentheses.

3-3 Solving Equations by Adding or Subtracting

Inverse operations often can be used to solve equations. Inverse operations reverse one another. For example, the inverse of the addition of 4 in the expression $x + 4$ is the subtraction of 4. The Addition and Subtraction Properties of Equality say that if you add or subtract the same number from each side of an equation, the two sides remain equal. Two equations are equivalent equations if they have the same solution. When solving an equation, check to be sure that the first and last equations are equivalent. If an equation has a subtraction expression, first rewrite the expression as an addition expression. Then add the additive inverse to each side.

3-4 Solving Equations by Multiplying or Dividing

Multiplication and division are inverse operations of one another. Some equations can be solved by multiplying or dividing each side by the same number. The Division Property of Equality says that when you divide each side of an equation by the same nonzero number, the two sides remain equal. For example, when solving $4x = 20$, $\frac{4x}{4} = \frac{20}{4}$, which simplifies to $x = 5$. The Multiplication Property of Equality says that when you multiply each side of an equation by the same number, the two sides remain equal. For example, when solving $\frac{x}{3} = 5$, $3\left(\frac{x}{3}\right) = 3(5)$, which simplifies to $x = 15$.

3-5 Solving Two-Step Equations

A two-step equation contains two operations. In the equation $2x + 1 = 9$, x is multiplied by 2 and then 1 is added. When solving two-step equations, use inverse operations to undo each operation in reverse order. The equation $2x + 1 = 9$ can be solved in two steps. First, subtract 1 from each side. Second, divide each side by 2. When two-step equations have terms with negative coefficients, rewrite subtraction expressions as addition expressions before solving. Sometimes it also is necessary to combine like terms before solving.

3-6 Writing Two-Step Equations

An equation is a statement that two expressions are equal. The expressions are joined with an equals sign ($=$). Words such as *is, equals,* or *is equal to* can be used when you translate sentences into equations. For example, the sentence "The difference between 3 times some number and 78 is -33" can be expressed by the equation $3n - 78 = -33$.

Many real-world situations can be represented by two-step equations. For example, a savings account may be started with a deposit of $100, and added to at the rate of $25 a month. To show how many months it would take to save $500, you could write the equation $25x + 100 = 500$.

3-7 Using Formulas

A formula is an equation that shows a relationship among certain quantities. A formula usually contains two or more variables. One of the most commonly used formulas shows the relationship between distance, rate (or speed), and time. The distance formula $d = rt$ means that "distance equals the rate multiplied by the time."

Other formulas find geometric quantities. For example, the distance around a geometric figure is called the *perimeter*. One method of finding the perimeter P of a rectangle is to add the measures of the four sides. The formula for the perimeter of a rectangle expresses this as $P = 2(\ell + w)$. Likewise, the measure of the surface enclosed by a figure is its area. The formula for the area of a rectangle is $A = \ell w$.

Quick Review Math Handbook

Hot Words includes a glossary of terms while Hot Topics consists of explanations of key mathematical concepts with exercises to test comprehension. This valuable resource can be used as a reference in the classroom or for home study.

Lesson	Hot Topics Section	Lesson	Hot Topics Section
GS 3	1.5, 6.1	3-4	1.5, 6.4
3-1	1.2, 1.5, 6.2	3-5	6.1, 6.4
3-2	1.2, 1.5, 6.2	3-6	6.1, 6.4
3-3	1.5, 6.4	3-7	6.3, 6.4, 7.4, 7.5

GS = Getting Started

 Additional mathematical information and teaching notes are available at www.pre-alg.com/key_concepts.

DAILY INTERVENTION and Assessment

Key to Abbreviations:
TWE = Teacher Wraparound Edition; CRM = Chapter Resource Masters

	Type	Student Edition	Teacher Resources	Technology/Internet
INTERVENTION	Ongoing	Prerequisite Skills, pp. 97, 102, 107, 114, 119, 124, 130 Practice Quiz 1, p. 107 Practice Quiz 2, p. 130	5-Minute Check Transparencies *Prerequisite Skills Workbook*, pp. 5–12, 21–26 Quizzes, *CRM*, pp. 157, 158 Mid-Chapter Test, *CRM*, p. 159 Study Guide and Intervention, *CRM*, pp. 107, 112, 117, 122, 127, 132, 137	Pre-AlgePASS: Tutorial Plus, Lessons 4, 5, and 6 www.pre-alg.com/self_check_quiz www.pre-alg.com/extra_examples
	Mixed Review	pp. 102, 107, 114, 119, 124, 130, 136	Cumulative Review, *CRM*, p. 160	
	Error Analysis	Find the Error, pp. 100, 105, 128	Find the Error, *TWE*, pp. 100, 105, 128 Unlocking Misconceptions, *TWE*, pp. 104, 116	
ASSESSMENT	Standardized Test Practice	pp. 102, 107, 112, 113, 114, 119, 124, 130, 136, 142–143	*TWE*, pp. 142–143 Standardized Test Practice, *CRM*, pp. 161–162	Standardized Test Practice CD-ROM www.pre-alg.com/standardized_test
	Open-Ended Assessment	Writing in Math, pp. 101, 106, 114, 119, 123, 130, 136 Open Ended, pp. 100, 105, 113, 117, 122, 128, 133 Standardized Test, p. 143	Speaking: *TWE*, pp. 107, 114 Writing: *TWE*, p. 130 Modeling: *TWE*, pp. 102, 119, 124, 136 Open-Ended Assessment, *CRM*, p. 155	
	Chapter Assessment	Study Guide, pp. 138–140 Practice Test, p. 141	Multiple-Choice Tests (Forms 1, 2A, 2B), *CRM*, pp. 143–148 Free-Response Tests (Forms 2C, 2D, 3), *CRM*, pp. 149–154 Vocabulary Test/Review, *CRM*, p. 156	ExamView® Pro (see below) MindJogger Videoquizzes www.pre-alg.com/vocabulary_review www.pre-alg.com/chapter_test

For more information on Yearly ProgressPro, see p. 2.

Pre-Algebra Lesson	Yearly ProgressPro Skill Lesson(s)
3-1	Distributive Property
3-2	Simplifying Algebraic Expressions
3-3	Solving Addition/Subtraction Equations
3-4	Solving Multiplication Equations Solving Equations with Division
3-5	Solving Two-Step Equations
3-6	Writing Two-Step Equations
3-7	Area of Rectangles Perimeters of Rectangles/Squares/Triangles

ExamView® Pro

Use the networkable **ExamView® Pro** to:
- Create **multiple versions** of tests.
- Create **modified** tests for *Inclusion* students.
- **Edit** existing questions and **add** your own questions.
- Use built-in **state curriculum correlations** to create tests aligned with state standards.
- Change **English** tests to **Spanish** and vice versa.

For more information on Intervention and Assessment, see pp. T8–T11.

Reading and Writing in Mathematics

Glencoe Pre-Algebra provides numerous opportunities to incorporate reading and writing into the mathematics classroom.

Student Edition

- Foldables™ Study Organizer, p. 97
- Reading Mathematics, p. 125
- Concept Check questions require students to verbalize and write about what they have learned in the lesson. (pp. 98, 99, 100, 103, 104, 105, 110, 111, 113, 116, 117, 121, 122, 126, 128, 131, 133)
- Writing in Math questions in every lesson, pp. 101, 106, 114, 119, 123, 130, 136
- Reading Math, pp. 98, 103
- WebQuest, pp. 135, 136

Teacher Wraparound Edition

- Foldables™ Study Organizer, pp. 97, 138
- Study Notebook suggestions, pp. 100, 105, 109, 112, 117, 122, 125, 128, 133
- Modeling activities, pp. 102, 119, 124, 136
- Speaking activities, pp. 107, 114
- Writing activities, p. 130
- Differentiated Instruction, (Verbal/ Linguistic), p. 129
-  Resources, pp. 96, 98, 103, 110, 115, 120, 125, 126, 129, 131, 138

Additional Resources

- Vocabulary Builder worksheets require students to define and give examples for key vocabulary terms as they progress through the chapter (*Chapter 3 Resource Masters*, pp. vii–viii)
- Reading to Learn Mathematics master for each lesson (*Chapter 3 Resource Masters*, pp. 110, 115, 120, 125, 130, 135, 140)
- *Vocabulary PuzzleMaker* software creates crossword, jumble, and word search puzzles using vocabulary lists that you can customize.
- *Teaching Mathematics with Foldables* provides suggestions for promoting cognition and language.
- *Reading and Writing in the Mathematics Classroom*
- *WebQuest and Project Resources*

For more information on Reading and Writing in Mathematics, see pp. T6–T7.

ELL ENGLISH LANGUAGE LEARNERS

Lesson 3-1
Flexible Groups

Give groups of students a set of index cards with several examples of the properties mentioned. Students can come to consensus and write the name of the property on the back of each card. Students can add their own mathematical or real-world examples of the properties and explain them in their own words.

Lesson 3-5
Using Modeling

Model solving a two-step equation. For example, to solve $5x + 4 = 29$, first cover the coefficient to show the students the equation $x + 4 = 29$. Ask students how they would solve this equation. Subtract 4 from each side. Now the equation is $5x = 25$. Ask students to solve this equation. Then solve for x. This method allows students to see that two steps are involved and that the addition or subtraction occurs first, followed by the multiplication or division. You may wish to do several examples the same way until students see a pattern and make a conjecture about how to solve two-step equations.

Lesson 3-6
Peer Tutoring

Write the words *addition, subtraction, multiplication,* and *division* on the chalkboard. Have students come to the chalkboard and write words that signify each operation. Allow for spelling/grammatical errors. Help students with the translation between verbal sentences and mathematical sentences by writing a verbal sentence on the chalkboard and highlighting text and translating each piece until they have formed the equation. Have the students then practice with a partner, pairing English Language Learners with bilingual students whenever possible.

What You'll Learn

Have students read over the list of objectives and make a list of any words with which they are not familiar.

Why It's Important

Point out to students that this is only one of many reasons why each objective is important. Others are provided in the introduction to each lesson.

Lesson	NCTM Standards	Local Objectives
3-1	1, 2, 6, 9	
3-2	1, 2, 6, 9	
3-3 and 3-4 Preview	2, 10	
3-3	2, 6, 9	
3-4	2, 6, 9	
3-5	2, 6, 9	
3-6	2, 6, 9	
3-7	2, 3, 6, 9	
3-7 Follow-Up	2, 3, 6, 7, 10	

Key to NCTM Standards:

1=Number & Operations, 2=Algebra, 3=Geometry, 4=Measurement, 5=Data Analysis & Probability, 6=Problem Solving, 7=Reasoning & Proof, 8=Communication, 9=Connections, 10=Representation

Chapter 3 Equations

What You'll Learn

- **Lessons 3-1 and 3-2** Use the Distributive Property to simplify expressions.
- **Lessons 3-3 and 3-4** Solve equations using the Properties of Equality.
- **Lessons 3-5 and 3-6** Write and solve two-step equations.
- **Lesson 3-7** Use formulas to solve real-world and geometry problems.

Key Vocabulary

- equivalent expressions (p. 98)
- coefficient (p. 103)
- constant (p. 103)
- perimeter (p. 132)
- area (p. 132)

Why It's Important

As you continue to study algebra, you will learn how to describe quantitative relationships using variables and equations. For example, the equation $d = rt$ shows the relationship between the variables d (distance), r (rate or speed), and t (time). *You will solve a problem about ballooning in Lesson 3-7.*

Vocabulary Builder

The Key Vocabulary list introduces students to some of the main vocabulary terms included in this chapter. For a more thorough vocabulary list with pronunciations of new words, give students the Vocabulary Builder worksheets found on pages vii and viii of the *Chapter 3 Resource Masters.* Encourage them to complete the definition of each term as they progress through the chapter. You may suggest that they add these sheets to their study notebooks for future reference when studying for the Chapter 3 test.

▶ **Prerequisite Skills** To be successful in this chapter, you'll need to master these skills and be able to apply them in problem-solving situations. Review these skills before beginning Chapter 3.

For Lesson 3-1   Multiply Integers

Find each product.   *(For review, see Lesson 2-4.)*

1. $2(-3)$ **−6**   **2.** $-4(3)$ **−12**   **3.** $-5(-2)$ **10**   **4.** $-4(6)$ **−24**

For Lesson 3-2   Write Addition Expressions

Write each subtraction expression as an addition expression.   *(For review, see Lesson 2-3.)*

5. $5 - 7$ $5 + (-7)$ **6.** $6 - 10$ $6 + (-10)$ **7.** $-5 - 9$ $-5 + (-9)$ **8.** $11 - 10$
$11 + (-10)$

For Lessons 3-3 and 3-5   Add Integers

Find each sum.   *(For review, see Lesson 2-2.)*

9. $6 + (-9)$ **−3**   **10.** $-8 + 4$ **−4**   **11.** $4 + (-4)$ **0**   **12.** $7 + (-10)$ **−3**

For Lesson 3-6   Write Algebraic Expressions

Write an algebraic expression for each verbal expression.   *(For review, see Lesson 1-3.)*

13. five more than twice a number $5 + 2n$ **14.** the difference of a number and 15 $n - 15$

15. three less than a number $n - 3$ **16.** the quotient of a number and 10 $n \div 10$

 **FOLDABLES™**
Study Organizer

Writing and Solving Equations Make this Foldable to help you organize your notes. Begin with four sheets of $8\frac{1}{2}$" × 11" paper.

Step 1 **Stack Pages**	**Step 2** **Roll Up Bottom Edges**
Place 4 sheets of paper $\frac{3}{4}$ inch apart. 	All tabs should be the same size. 

Step 3 **Crease and Staple**	**Step 4** **Label**
Staple along the fold. 	Label the tabs with topics from the chapter. 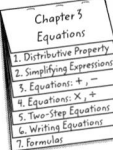

Reading and Writing As you read and study the chapter, record examples under each tab.

This section provides a review of the basic concepts needed before beginning Chapter 3. Page references are included for additional student help.

Additional review is provided in the *Prerequisite Skills Workbook*, pages 5–12 and 21–26.

Prerequisite Skills in the Getting Ready for the Next Lesson section at the end of each lesson reviews a skill needed in the next lesson.

For Lesson	Prerequisite Skill
3-2	Subtraction Expressions (p. 102)
3-3	Adding Integers (p. 107)
3-4	Dividing Integers (p. 114)
3-5	Subtracting Integers (p. 119)
3-6	Algebraic Expressions (p. 124)
3-7	Solving Equations (p. 130)

FOLDABLES™
Study Organizer

For more information about Foldables, see *Teaching Mathematics with Foldables.*

Descriptive Writing and Organizing Data Students use their Foldables to take notes, define terms, record concepts, and write examples. At the end of the appropriate lessons, ask students to write a descriptive paragraph about each method of solution and what equations can be solved that way. Encourage students to see the connectivity of the methods with the operations in the equation. Their writings should help them develop a deeper understanding of the algebraic processes being used.

3-1 The Distributive Property

1 Focus

5-Minute Check Transparency 3-1 Use as a quiz or review of Chapter 2.

Mathematical Background notes are available for this lesson on page 96C.

How are rectangles related to the Distributive Property?

The opening activity questions are repeated on page 110 of the *Chapter 3 Resource Masters*.

Reading to Learn Mathematics, p. 110 — ELL

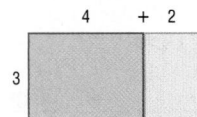

Pre-Activity *How are rectangles related to the Distributive Property?*
Do the activity at the top of page 98 in your textbook. Write your answers below.

a. Draw a 2-by-5 and a 2-by-4 rectangle. Find the total area in two ways.
2 · 5 + 2 · 4 = 10 + 8 or 18;   2(5 + 4) = 2(9) or 18

b. Draw a 4-by-4 and a 4-by-1 rectangle. Find the total area in two ways.
4 · 4 + 4 · 1 = 16 + 4 or 20;   4(4 + 1) = 4(5) or 20

c. Draw any two rectangles that have the same width. Find the total area in two ways.   Sample answer: 3(2 + 2) = 12;
3 · 2 + 3 · 2 = 12

d. What did you notice about the total area in each case?
The areas are equal.

Reading the Lesson
Write a definition and give an example of the new vocabulary term.

	Vocabulary	Definition	Example
1.	equivalent expressions	See students' work.	

2. In rewriting 3(x + 2), which term is "distributed" to the other terms in the expression?   3

Helping You Remember

3. *Distribute* is a word that is used frequently in the English language.

a. Find the definition of *distribute* in a dictionary. Write the definition.
to give out or deliver especially to members of a group

b. Explain how the English definition can help you remember how the word *distributive* relates to mathematics.   The number outside the parentheses is "distributed" to each number inside.

What You'll Learn

- Use the Distributive Property to write equivalent numerical expressions.
- Use the Distributive Property to write equivalent algebraic expressions.

Vocabulary
- equivalent expressions

TEACHING TIP
Remind students how to find the area of a rectangle. They will learn more about the formula for the area of a rectangle in Lesson 3-7.

How are rectangles related to the Distributive Property?

To find the area of a rectangle, multiply the length and width. You can find the total area of the blue and yellow rectangles in two ways.

Method 1
Put them together. Add the lengths, then multiply.

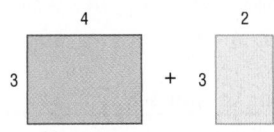

$3(4 + 2) = 3 \cdot 6$ Add.
$= 18$ Multiply.

Method 2
Separate them. Multiply to find each area, then add.

$3 \cdot 4 + 3 \cdot 2 = 12 + 6$ Multiply.
$= 18$ Add.

a. Draw a 2-by-5 and a 2-by-4 rectangle. Find the total area in two ways.

b. Draw a 4-by-4 and a 4-by-1 rectangle. Find the total area in two ways.

c. Draw any two rectangles that have the same width. Find the total area in two ways.   a–c. See margin.

d. What did you notice about the total area in each case?   d. The areas are equal.

DISTRIBUTIVE PROPERTY The expressions $3(4 + 2)$ and $3 \cdot 4 + 3 \cdot 2$ are **equivalent expressions** because they have the same value, 18. This example shows how the **Distributive Property** combines addition and multiplication.

Reading Math

Distributive
Root Word: Distribute
To *distribute* means to deliver to each member of a group.

Key Concept — Distributive Property

- **Words**   To multiply a number by a sum, multiply each number inside the parentheses by the number outside the parentheses.

- **Symbols** $a(b + c) = ab + ac$ $(b + c)a = ba + ca$

- **Examples** $3(4 + 2) = 3 \cdot 4 + 3 \cdot 2$ $(5 + 3)2 = 5 \cdot 2 + 3 \cdot 2$

Concept Check   Name two operations that are combined by the Distributive Property.   multiplication, addition

Resource Manager

Workbooks and Reproducible Masters

Chapter 3 Resource Masters
- Study Guide and Intervention, p. 107
- Skills Practice, p. 108
- Practice, p. 109
- Reading to Learn Mathematics, p. 110
- Enrichment, p. 111

Parent and Student Study Guide Workbook, p. 16
Prerequisite Skills Workbook, pp. 9–10

Transparencies
5-Minute Check Transparency 3-1
Answer Key Transparencies

Technology
Interactive Chalkboard

Example 1 Use the Distributive Property

Use the Distributive Property to write each expression as an equivalent expression. Then evaluate the expression.

a. 2(6 + 4)

$$2(6 + 4) = 2 \cdot 6 + 2 \cdot 4$$
$$= 12 + 8 \quad \text{Multiply.}$$
$$= 20 \quad \text{Add.}$$

b. (8 + 3)5

$$(8 + 3)5 = 8 \cdot 5 + 3 \cdot 5$$
$$= 40 + 15 \quad \text{Multiply.}$$
$$= 55 \quad \text{Add.}$$

Example 2 Use the Distributive Property to Solve a Problem

AMUSEMENT PARKS A one-day pass to an amusement park costs $40. A round-trip bus ticket to the park costs $5.

a. Write two equivalent expressions to find the total cost of a one-day pass and a bus ticket for 15 students.

Method 1 Find the cost for 1 person, then multiply by 15.

$$15(\$40 + \$5)$$
→ cost for 1 person

Method 2 Find the cost of 15 passes and 15 tickets. Then add.

$$15(\$40) + 15(\$5)$$
cost of 15 passes ←   → cost of 15 tickets

b. Find the total cost.

Evaluate either expression to find the total cost.

$$15(\$40 + 5) = 15(\$40) + 15(\$5) \quad \text{Distributive Property}$$
$$= \$600 + \$75 \quad \text{Multiply.}$$
$$= \$675 \quad \text{Add.}$$

The total cost is $675.

CHECK You can check your results by evaluating 15($45).

More About. . .

Amusement Parks

Attendance at U.S. amusement parks increased 22% in the 1990s. In 1999, over 300 million people attended these parks.

Source: *International Association of Amusement Parks and Attractions*

ALGEBRA CONNECTION

TEACHING TIP

Ask students to evaluate 2(x + 3) and 2x + 6 for different values of x to convince them the expressions are equivalent.

ALGEBRAIC EXPRESSIONS You can also model the Distributive Property by using algebra tiles.

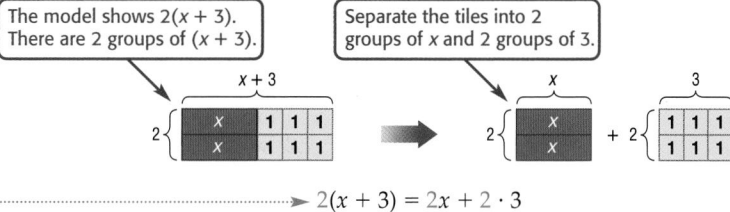

The model shows 2(x + 3). There are 2 groups of (x + 3).

Separate the tiles into 2 groups of x and 2 groups of 3.

$$2(x + 3) = 2x + 2 \cdot 3$$
$$= 2x + 6$$

The expressions $2(x + 3)$ and $2x + 6$ are equivalent expressions because no matter what x is, these expressions have the same value.

✓ **Concept Check** Are $3(x + 1)$ and $3x + 1$ equivalent expressions? Explain.
No; if $x = 1$, $3(x + 1) = 6$ and $3x + 1 = 4$.

www.pre-alg.com/extra_examples

DISTRIBUTIVE PROPERTY

In-Class Examples   Power Point®

1 Use the Distributive Property to write each expression as an equivalent expression. Then evaluate the expression.

a. $4(5 + 8)$ $4 \cdot 5 + 4 \cdot 8$; 52

b. $(6 + 9)2$ $6 \cdot 2 + 9 \cdot 2$; 30

2 **RECREATION** North Country Rivers of York, Maine, offers one-day white-water rafting trips on the Kennebec River. The trip costs $69 per person, and wet suits are $15 each.

a. Write two equivalent expressions to find the total cost of one trip for a family of four if each person uses a wet suit. $4(69 + 15)$; $4 \cdot 69 + 4 \cdot 15$

b. Find the total cost. $336

ALGEBRAIC EXPRESSIONS

In-Class Examples   Power Point®

3 Use the Distributive Property to write each expression as an equivalent algebraic expression.

a. $2(x + 4)$ $2x + 8$

b. $(y + 3)6$ $6y + 18$

Teaching Tip Watch for students who miss steps when working Example 4. Have them do a few problems, writing out the explanation for each step as in the Example.

4 Use the Distributive Property to write each expression as an equivalent algebraic expression.

a. $4(x - 2)$ $4x - 8$

b. $-2(n - 3)$ $-2n + 6$

Building on Prior Knowledge

In Chapter 2, students studied operations with integers. These skills will be used in Lesson 3-1.

Study Notebook

Have students—

- add the definition/example of the vocabulary term to their Vocabulary Builder worksheets for Chapter 3.
- use the Distributive Property to show examples of equivalent expressions.
- give an example of the Distributive Property. Use arrows to show which numbers or variables are multiplied.
- include any other item(s) that they find helpful in mastering the skills in this lesson.

DAILY

INTERVENTION FIND THE ERROR Have students replace x with 8 in $3(x + 2)$, $3x + 2$, and $3x + 6$ to determine which is correct. Then ask what the error is. **Julia forgot to multiply the second number by 3.**

About the Exercises . . .

Organization by Objective
- **Distributive Property:** 12–25, 50, 51
- **Algebraic Expressions:** 26–49

Odd/Even Assignments
Exercises 12–51 are structured so that students practice the same concepts whether they are assigned odd or even problems.

Assignment Guide

Basic: 13–21 odd, 25–47 odd, 51–55, 64–77

Average: 13–51 odd, 52–55, 64–77 (Optional: 56–63)

Advanced: 12–52 even, 53–71 (Optional: 72–77)

TEACHING TIP
You may want to point out that when students replace $3 \cdot 1$ with 3, they are using the Substitution Property.

Example 3 Simplify Algebraic Expressions

Use the Distributive Property to write each expression as an equivalent algebraic expression.

a. $3(x + 1)$

$3(x + 1) = 3x + 3 \cdot 1$
$= 3x + 3$ Simplify.

b. $(y + 4)5$

$(y + 4)5 = y \cdot 5 + 4 \cdot 5$
$= 5y + 20$ Simplify.

Study Tip

Look Back
To review **subtraction expressions,** see Lesson 2-3.

Example 4 Simplify Expressions with Subtraction

Use the Distributive Property to write each expression as an equivalent algebraic expression.

a. $2(x - 1)$

$2(x - 1) = 2[x + (-1)]$ Rewrite $x - 1$ as $x + (-1)$.
$= 2x + 2(-1)$ Distributive Property
$= 2x + (-2)$ Simplify.
$= 2x - 2$ Definition of subtraction

b. $-3(n - 5)$

$-3(n - 5) = -3[n + (-5)]$ Rewrite $n - 5$ as $n + (-5)$.
$= -3n + (-3)(-5)$ Distributive Property
$= -3n + 15$ Simplify.

Check for Understanding

Concept Check

2. Catelyn; each number inside the parentheses should be multiplied by 3.

1. OPEN ENDED Write an equation using three integers that is an example of the Distributive Property. **Sample answer:** $2(3 + 4) = 2 \cdot 3 + 2 \cdot 4$

2. FIND THE ERROR Julia and Catelyn are using the Distributive Property to simplify $3(x + 2)$. Who is correct? Explain your reasoning.

Julia	Catelyn
$3(x + 2) = 3x + 2$	$3(x + 2) = 3x + 6$

Guided Practice

GUIDED PRACTICE KEY	
Exercises	Examples
3–5	1
6–9	3, 4
10, 11	2

Use the Distributive Property to write each expression as an equivalent expression. Then evaluate it.

3. $5(7 + 8)$
$5 \cdot 7 + 5 \cdot 8, 75$

4. $2(9 + 1)$
$2 \cdot 9 + 2 \cdot 1, 20$

5. $(2 + 4)6$
$2 \cdot 6 + 4 \cdot 6, 36$

ALGEBRA Use the Distributive Property to write each expression as an equivalent algebraic expression.

6. $4(x + 3)$
$4x + 12$

7. $(n + 2)3$
$3n + 6$

8. $8(y - 2)$
$8y - 16$

9. $-6(x - 5)$
$-6x + 30$

Application

MONEY For Exercises 10 and 11, use the following information.
Suppose you work in a grocery store 4 hours on Friday and 5 hours on Saturday. You earn $6.25 an hour.

10. $6.25(4 + 5)$, $6.25(4) + $6.25(5)

10. Write two different expressions to find your wages.

11. Find the total wages for that weekend. **$56.25**

DAILY

INTERVENTION | **Differentiated Instruction**

- **Visual/Spatial** Have students write the equations shown in the definition of the Distributive Property in the Key Concept box on page 98. Then have them use colored pencils or markers to color each number or variable in an equation using the same unique color each time it appears. Have students describe the pattern shown by the colors and use the Distributive Property to explain the pattern.

Practice and Apply

Homework Help

For Exercises	See Examples
12–23	1
24–25	2
26–33	3
34–47	4

Extra Practice
See page 728.

Use the Distributive Property to write each expression as an equivalent expression. Then evaluate it. 12–23. See pp. 143A–143B.

12. $2(6 + 1)$ **13.** $5(7 + 3)$ **14.** $(4 + 6)9$

15. $(4 + 3)3$ **16.** $(9 + 2)4$ **17.** $(8 + 8)2$

18. $7(3 - 2)$ **19.** $6(8 - 5)$ **20.** $-5(8 - 4)$

21. $-3(9 - 2)$ ★ **22.** $(8 - 4)(-2)$ ★ **23.** $(10 - 3)(-5)$

24. MOVIES One movie ticket costs $7, and one small bag of popcorn costs $3. Write two equivalent expressions for the total cost of four movie tickets and four bags of popcorn. Then find the cost.
$4(\$7 + \$3)$, $4(\$7) + 4(\$3)$; $40

25. SPORTS A volleyball uniform costs $15 for the shirt, $10 for the pants, and $8 for the socks. Write two equivalent expressions for the total cost of 12 uniforms. Then find the cost.
$12(\$15 + \$10 + \$8)$, $12(\$15) + 12(\$10) + 12(\$8)$; $396

ALGEBRA Use the Distributive Property to write each expression as an equivalent algebraic expression. 26–49. See pp. 143A–143B.

26. $2(x + 3)$ **27.** $5(y + 6)$ **28.** $3(n + 1)$

29. $7(y + 8)$ **30.** $(x + 3)4$ **31.** $(y + 2)10$

32. $(3 + y)6$ **33.** $(2 + x)5$ **34.** $3(x - 2)$

35. $9(m - 2)$ **36.** $8(z - 3)$ **37.** $15(s - 3)$

38. $(r - 5)6$ **39.** $(x - 3)12$ **40.** $(t - 4)5$

41. $(w - 10)2$ **42.** $-2(z + 4)$ **43.** $-5(a + 10)$

44. $-2(x - 7)$ **45.** $-5(w - 8)$ **46.** $(y - 4)(-2)$

47. $(a - 6)(-5)$ ★ **48.** $2(x + y)$ ★ **49.** $3(a + b)$

SHOPPING For Exercises 50 and 51, use the graphic.

50. Find the total amount spent by two teens and two adults during one average shopping trip. $195.50

51. Find the total amount spent by one teen and one adult during five average shopping trips. $488.75

52. WRITING IN MATH Answer the question that was posed at the beginning of the lesson.

How are rectangles related to the Distributive Property?

Include the following in your answer: See pp. 143A–143B.
• a drawing of two rectangles with the same width, and
• two different methods for finding the total area of the rectangles.

USA TODAY Snapshots®

Comparison shoppers

While teen-agers spend about 90 minutes on each trip to the mall, compared to 76 minutes for adults, they end up spending less money.

$59.20 Adults
$38.55 Teens

Source: International Council of Shopping Centers
By Marcy E. Mullins, USA TODAY

www.pre-alg.com/self_check_quiz

Online Lesson Plans

USA TODAY's Education Online site offers resources and interactive features connected to each day's newspaper. *Experience TODAY*, USA TODAY's daily lesson plan, is available on the site and delivered daily to subscribers. This plan provides instruction for integrating USA TODAY graphics and key editorial features into your mathematics classroom. Log on to **www.education.usatoday.com**

Open-Ended Assessment
Modeling Ask students to use algebra tiles or draw a model to explain the Distributive Property to another student.

Getting Ready
for Lesson 3-2
PREREQUISITE SKILL In Lesson 3-2, students use the Distributive Property to simplify algebraic expressions involving addition and subtraction of integers. Exercises 72–77 should be used to determine your students' familiarity with writing a subtraction expression as an addition expression.

Answer
64a.

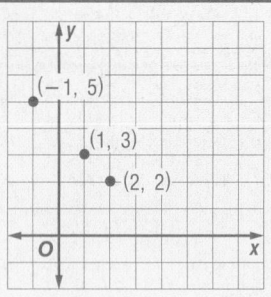

53. **CRITICAL THINKING** Is $3 + (x \cdot y) = (3 + x) \cdot (3 + y)$ a true statement? If so, explain your reasoning. If not, give a counterexample.
No; $3 + (4 \cdot 5) = 23$, $(3 + 4)(3 + 5) = 56$

Standardized Test Practice
Ⓐ Ⓑ Ⓒ Ⓓ

54. One ticket to a baseball game costs t dollars. A soft drink costs s dollars. Which expression represents the total cost of a ticket and soft drink for p people? **D**
Ⓐ pst Ⓑ $p + (ts)$ Ⓒ $t(p + s)$ Ⓓ $p(t + s)$

55. Which equation is always true? **C**
Ⓐ $5(a + b) = 5a + b$ Ⓑ $5(ab) = (5a)(5b)$
Ⓒ $5(a + b) = 5(b + a)$ Ⓓ $5(a + 0) = 5a + 5$

Extending the Lesson
MENTAL MATH The Distributive Property allows you to find certain products mentally. Replace one factor with the sum of a number and a multiple of ten. Then apply the Distributive Property.

Example Find $15 \cdot 12$ mentally.

$$15 \cdot 12 = 15(10 + 2)$$ Think: 12 is 10 + 2.
$$= 15 \cdot 10 + 15 \cdot 2$$ Distributive Property
$$= 150 + 30$$ Multiply mentally.
$$= 180$$ Add mentally.

56. $7(10 + 4) = 98$
57. $8(20 + 3) = 184$
58. $9(30 + 2) = 288$
59. $16(10 + 1) = 176$
60. $14(10 + 2) = 168$
61. $9(100 + 3) = 927$
62. $11(100 + 2) = 1122$
63. $12(1000 + 4) = 12,048$

Rewrite each product so it is easy to compute mentally. Then find the product.
56. $7 \cdot 14$ 57. $8 \cdot 23$ 58. $9 \cdot 32$ 59. $16 \cdot 11$
60. $14 \cdot 12$ 61. $9 \cdot 103$ 62. $11 \cdot 102$ 63. $12 \cdot 1004$

Maintain Your Skills

Mixed Review
64. The table shows several solutions of the equation $x + y = 4$. *(Lesson 2-6)* **a. See margin.**
    a. Graph the ordered pairs on a coordinate plane.
    b. Describe the graph. **The points are in a straight line.**

$x + y = 4$		
x	y	(x, y)
-1	5	$(-1, 5)$
1	3	$(1, 3)$
2	2	$(2, 2)$

65. **ALGEBRA** Evaluate $\dfrac{-4y}{x}$ if $x = 2$ and $y = -3$. *(Lesson 2-5)* **6**

ALGEBRA Find the solution of each equation if the replacement set is {**1, 2, 3, 4, 5**}. *(Lesson 1-5)*
66. $2n + 3 = 9$ **3**   67. $3n - 4 = 8$ **4**   68. $4x - 9 = -5$ **1**

Find the next three terms in each pattern. *(Lesson 1-1)*
69. $5, 9, 13, 17, \ldots$ 70. $20, 22, 26, 32, \ldots$ 71. $5, 10, 20, 40, \ldots$
    21, 25, 29   **40, 50, 62**   **80, 160, 320**

Getting Ready for the Next Lesson
PREREQUISITE SKILL Write each subtraction expression as an addition expression. *(To review subtraction expressions, see Lesson 2-3.)*
72. $5 - 3$ **$5 + (-3)$**   73. $-8 - 4$ **$-8 + (-4)$**   74. $10 - 14$ **$10 + (-14)$**
75. $3 - 9$ **$3 + (-9)$**   76. $-2 - (-5)$ **$-2 + 5$**   77. $-7 - 10$ **$-7 + (-10)$**

Interactive Chalkboard
PowerPoint® Presentations

This CD-ROM is a customizable Microsoft® Power-Point® presentation that includes:
• Step-by-step, dynamic solutions of each In-Class Example from the Teacher Wraparound Edition
• Additional, Your Turn exercises for each example
• The 5-Minute Check Transparencies
• Hot links to Glencoe Online Study Tools

Simplifying Algebraic Expressions

What You'll Learn

* Use the Distributive Property to simplify algebraic expressions.

How can you use algebra tiles to simplify an algebraic expression?

You can use algebra tiles to represent expressions. You can also sort algebra tiles by their shapes and group them.

The drawing on the left represents the expression $2x + 3 + 3x + 1$. On the right, the algebra tiles have been sorted and combined.

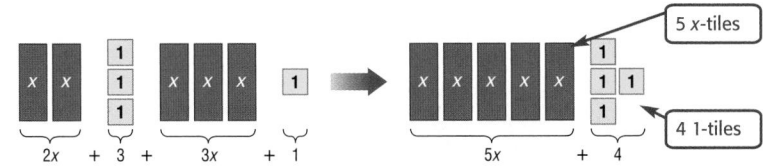

5 x-tiles

4 1-tiles

$2x + 3 + 3x + 1$ $5x + 4$

Therefore, $2x + 3 + 3x + 1 = 5x + 4$.

Model each expression with algebra tiles or a drawing. Then sort them by shape and write an expression represented by the tiles.

a. $3x + 2 + 4x + 3$ $7x + 5$

b. $2x + 5 + x$ $3x + 5$

c. $4x + 5 + 3$ $4x + 8$

d. $x + 2x + 4x$ $7x$

Vocabulary
* term
* coefficient
* like terms
* constant
* simplest form
* simplifying an expression

SIMPLIFY EXPRESSIONS When plus or minus signs separate an algebraic expression into parts, each part is a **term**. The numerical part of a term that contains a variable is called the **coefficient** of the variable.

TEACHING TIP
If an expression has no plus or minus signs, the entire expression is a term.

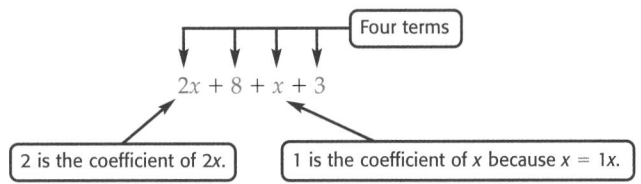

Four terms

$2x + 8 + x + 3$

2 is the coefficient of 2x.

1 is the coefficient of x because x = 1x.

Reading Math
Constant
Everyday Meaning: unchanging
Math Meaning: fixed value in an expression

Like terms are terms that contain the same variables, such as $2n$ and $5n$ or $6xy$ and $4xy$. A term without a variable is called a **constant**. Constant terms are also like terms.

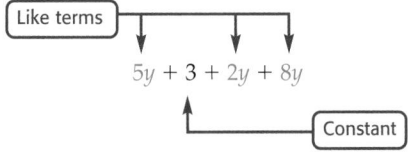

Like terms

$5y + 3 + 2y + 8y$

Constant

✓ **Concept Check** Are 5x and 5y like terms? Explain. No; they contain different variables.

---

1 Focus

5-Minute Check Transparency 3-2 Use as a quiz or review of Lesson 3-1.

Mathematical Background notes are available for this lesson on page 96C.

How can you use algebra tiles to simplify an algebraic expression?

The opening activity questions are repeated on page 115 of the *Chapter 3 Resource Masters*.

Reading to Learn Mathematics, p. 115 ELL

Pre-Activity How can you use algebra tiles to simplify an algebraic expression?

Do the activity at the top of page 103 in your textbook. Write your answers below.

a. $3x + 2 + 4x + 3$ 7x + 5

b. $2x + 5 + x$ 3x + 5

c. $4x + 5 + 3$ 4x + 8

d. x + 2x + 4x 7x

Reading the Lesson 1–6. See students' work.

Write a definition and give an example of each new vocabulary word or phrase.

Vocabulary	Definition	Example
1. term		
2. coefficient		
3. like terms		
4. constant		
5. simplest form		
6. simplifying an expression		

7. Is 2(r + 1) in simplest form? Explain. No; the expression contains parentheses.

Helping You Remember

8. *Constant* is a word used in everyday English as well as in mathematics.
   a. Find the definition of *constant* in a dictionary. Write the definition. something invariable or unchanging
   b. Explain how the English definition can help you remember how *constant* is used in mathematics. In mathematics, because a constant has no variable, its value is not subject to change.

Resource Manager

📂 Workbooks and Reproducible Masters

Chapter 3 Resource Masters
* Study Guide and Intervention, p. 112
* Skills Practice, p. 113
* Practice, p. 114
* Reading to Learn Mathematics, p. 115
* Enrichment, p. 116
* Assessment, p. 157

Parent and Student Study Guide Workbook, p. 17

📺 Transparencies
5-Minute Check Transparency 3-2
Answer Key Transparencies

💿 Technology
Interactive Chalkboard

SIMPLIFY EXPRESSIONS

In-Class Examples Power Point®

1 Identify the terms, like terms, coefficients, and constants in the expression $4x - x + 2y - 3$. terms: $4x$, $-x$, $2y$, -3; coefficients: 4, -1, 2; like terms: $4x$, $-x$; constant: -3

Teaching Tip Remind students that the order of the addends does not affect the sum.

2 Simplify each expression.

a. $5x + 4x$ $9x$

b. $8n + 4 + 4n$ $12n + 4$

c. $6x + 4 - 5x - 7$ $x - 3$

d. $-y + 2(x + 3y)$ $2x + 5y$

3 **WORK** You and a friend worked in the school store last week. You worked 4 hours more than your friend. Write an expression in simplest form that represents the total number of hours you both worked. $2h + 4$, where h is the number of hours your friend worked

✓ Skills Check
Simplify Expressions
Simplify each expression.
a. $2x + 5x$ $7x$
b. $2x - 2(y + 5x)$ $-8x - 2y$
c. $3x + 7(5 - x)$ $-4x + 35$

Rewriting a subtraction expression using addition will help you identify the terms of an expression.

Example 1 *Identify Parts of Expressions*

Identify the terms, like terms, coefficients, and constants in the expression $3x - 4x + y - 2$.

$$3x - 4x + y - 2 = 3x + (-4x) + y + (-2) \quad \text{Definition of subtraction}$$
$$= 3x + (-4x) + 1y + (-2) \quad \text{Identity Property}$$

The terms are $3x$, $-4x$, y, and -2. The like terms are $3x$ and $-4x$.

The coefficients are 3, -4, and 1. The constant is -2.

An algebraic expression is in **simplest form** if it has no like terms and no parentheses. When you use the Distributive Property to combine like terms, you are **simplifying the expression**.

Example 2 *Simplify Algebraic Expressions*

Simplify each expression.

a. $2x + 8x$

$2x$ and $8x$ are like terms.
$$2x + 8x = (2 + 8)x \quad \text{Distributive Property}$$
$$= 10x \quad \text{Simplify.}$$

b. $6n + 3 + 2n$

$6n$ and $2n$ are like terms.
$$6n + 3 + 2n = 6n + 2n + 3 \quad \text{Commutative Property}$$
$$= (6 + 2)n + 3 \quad \text{Distributive Property}$$
$$= 8n + 3 \quad \text{Simplify.}$$

c. $3x - 5 - 8x + 6$

$3x$ and $-8x$ are like terms. -5 and 6 are also like terms.
$$3x - 5 - 8x + 6 = 3x + (-5) + (-8x) + 6 \quad \text{Definition of subtraction}$$
$$= 3x + (-8x) + (-5) + 6 \quad \text{Commutative Property}$$
$$= [3 + (-8)]x + (-5) + 6 \quad \text{Distributive Property}$$
$$= -5x + 1 \quad \text{Simplify.}$$

d. $m + 3(n + 4m)$

$$m + 3(n + 4m) = m + 3n + 3(4m) \quad \text{Distributive Property}$$
$$= m + 3n + 12m \quad \text{Associative Property}$$
$$= 1m + 3n + 12m \quad \text{Identity Property}$$
$$= 1m + 12m + 3n \quad \text{Commutative Property}$$
$$= (1 + 12)m + 3n \quad \text{Distributive Property}$$
$$= 13m + 3n \quad \text{Simplify.}$$

Study Tip

Equivalent Expressions
To check whether $2x + 8x$ and $10x$ are equivalent expressions, substitute any value for x and see whether the expressions have the same value.

TEACHING TIP
Substituting one value for x does not *guarantee* that the expressions are equivalent. But if the expressions do *not* have the same value, you'll know that the expressions are *not* equivalent.

TEACHING TIP
When students understand that $m = 1 \cdot m$, have them try to perform this step mentally.

✓ Concept Check Expressions like $4(x - 3)$, $4x - 12$, and $x + 3x - 12$ are equivalent expressions. Which is in simplest form? $4x - 12$

DAILY INTERVENTION   **Unlocking Misconceptions**

- **Simplify Expressions** When expressions include coefficients of 1, students may forget to include all of the terms. For example, they may mistakenly simplify $5n + n$ as $5n$, forgetting about the unwritten 1 before the second n. Have them first rewrite the expression as $5n + 1n$ before combining like terms.

Example 3 *Translate Verbal Phrases into Expressions*

BASEBALL CARDS Suppose you and your brother collect baseball cards. He has 15 more cards in his collection than you have. Write an expression in simplest form that represents the total number of cards in both collections.

Words   You have some cards. Your brother has 15 more.

Variables Let x = number of cards you have.

Let $x + 15$ = number of cards your brother has.

Expression To find the total, add the expressions.

$x + (x + 15) = (x + x) + 15$	Associative Property
$= (1x + 1x) + 15$	Identity Property
$= (1 + 1)x + 15$	Distributive Property
$= 2x + 15$	Simplify.

The expression $2x + 15$ represents the total number of cards, where x is the number of cards you have.

Check for Understanding

Concept Check

2. Sample answer: $4x + 5y - 1$

1. Define *like terms*. **terms that contain the same variable or are constants**

2. **OPEN ENDED** Write an expression containing three terms that is in simplest form. One of the terms should be a constant.

3. **FIND THE ERROR** Koko and John are simplifying the expression $5x - 4 + x + 2$.

Koko	John
$5x - 4 + x + 2 =$	$5x - 4 + x + 2 =$
$6x - 2$	$5x - 2$

Who is correct? Explain your reasoning. **Koko; $5x + x = 6x$, not $5x$.**

Guided Practice

GUIDED PRACTICE KEY	
Exercises	Examples
4–6	1
7–15	2
16	3

Identify the terms, like terms, coefficients, and constants in each expression. **4–6. See margin.**

4. $4x + 3 + 5x + y$ 5. $2m - n + 6m$ 6. $4y - 2x - 7$

Simplify each expression. **9. $7c + 12$ 12. $-2x + 3$**

7. $6a + 2a$ **$8a$**   8. $x + 9x + 3$ **$10x + 3$**   9. $6c + 4 + c + 8$

10. $7m - 2m$ **$5m$**   11. $9y + 8 - 8$ **$9y$**   12. $2x - 5 - 4x + 8$

13. $5 - 3(y + 7)$ **$-3y - 16$** 14. $3x + 2y + 4y$ 15. $x + 3(x + 4y)$
                                            $3x + 6y$ **$4x + 12y$**

Application

16. **MONEY** You have saved some money. Your friend has saved $20 more than you. Write an expression in simplest form that represents the total amount of money you and your friend have saved. **$2x + 20$**

 www.pre-alg.com/extra_examples

Lesson 3-2 Simplifying Algebraic Expressions **105**

DAILY INTERVENTION
Differentiated Instruction

- **Kinesthetic** Have students work in groups to model combining like terms. Call out an everyday school item, such as "pencil." Each student in the group then places the pencils in his or her possession in a pile on the table or desk. Then the group writes an expression to show, for example, that each person in turn had 4, 3, 1, and 0 pencils: $4p + 3p + 1p + 0$. Finally, the group simplifies the expression: $8p$.

---

3 Practice/Apply

Study Notebook

Have students—
- add the definitions/examples of the vocabulary terms to their Vocabulary Builder worksheets for Chapter 3.
- write a checklist for the things to look for when simplifying expressions.
- include any other item(s) that they find helpful in mastering the skills in this lesson.

DAILY INTERVENTION **FIND THE ERROR**

Ask students why John made the error and how they would teach him to add the x-term in such expressions.

About the Exercises . . .

Odd/Even Assignments
Exercises 17–55 are structured so that students practice the same concepts whether they are assigned odd or even problems.

Assignment Guide

Basic: 17–45 odd, 51–55 odd, 56–73

Average: 17–55 odd, 56–73

Advanced: 18–56 even, 57–67 (Optional: 68–73)

All: Quiz 1 (1–5)

Answers

4. terms: $4x$, 3, $5x$, y; like terms: $4x$, $5x$; coefficients: 4, 5, 1; constant: 3

5. terms: $2m$, $-1n$, $6m$; like terms: $2m$, $6m$; coefficients: 2, -1, 6; constant: none

6. terms: $4y$, $-2x$, -7; like terms: none; coefficients: 4, -2; constant: -7

★ indicates increased difficulty

Practice and Apply

Identify the terms, like terms, coefficients, and constants in each expression. 17–22. See margin.

17. $3 + 7x + 3x + x$ 18. $y + 3y + 8y + 2$

19. $2a + 5c - a + 6a$ 20. $5c - 2d + 3d - d$

21. $6m - 2n + 7$ 22. $7x - 3y + 3z - 2$

Simplify each expression. 28. $4 + 3m$ 29. $7y + 9$ 30. $10x + 12$

23. $2x + 5x$ **7x**   24. $7b + 2b$ **9b**   25. $y + 10y$ **11y**

26. $5y + y$ **6y**   27. $2a + 3 + 5a$ **7a + 3**   28. $4 + 2m + m$

29. $2y + 8 + 5y + 1$ 30. $8x + 5 + 7 + 2x$ 31. $5x - 3x$ **2x**

32. $10b - 2b$ **8b**   33. $4y - 5y$ **−y**   34. $r - 3r$ **−2r**

35. $8 + x - 5x$ **−4x + 8**   36. $6x + 4 - 7x$ 37. $8y - 7 + 7$ **8y**

38. $9x + 2 - 2$ **9x**   39. $2x + 3 - 3x + 9$ 40. $5t - 3 - t + 2$

41. $3(b + 2) + 2b$ 42. $5(x + 3) + 8x$ 43. $-3(a + 2) - a$

44. $-2(x + 3) + 2x$ **−6**   45. $4x - 4(2 + x)$ **−8**   46. $8a - 2(a - 7)$

★ 47. $6m + 2n + 10m$ ★ 48. $-2y + x + 3y$ ★ 49. $c + 2(d - 5c)$
     16m + 2n   **x + y**   **−9c + 2d**

For Exercises 50–53, write an expression in simplest form that represents the total amount in each situation.

50. **SCHOOL SUPPLIES** You bought 5 folders that each cost x dollars, a calculator for $45, and a set of pens for $3.   **5x + 48**

51. **SHOPPING** Suppose you buy 3 shirts that each cost s dollars, a pair of shoes for $50, and jeans for $30.   **3s + 80**

52. **BIRTHDAYS** Today is your friend's birthday. She is y years old. Her sister is 5 years younger.   **2y − 5**

53. **BABY-SITTING** Alicia earned d dollars baby-sitting. Her friend earned twice as much. You earned $2 less than Alicia's friend earned.   **5d − 2**

GEOMETRY You can find the perimeter of a geometric figure by adding the measures of its sides. Write an expression in simplest form for the perimeter of each figure.

54.   **12x**
55.   **6x + 2**

56. **WRITING IN MATH** Answer the question that was posed at the beginning of the lesson. See pp. 143A–143B.

How can you use algebra tiles to simplify an algebraic expression?

Include the following in your answer:
- a drawing that shows how to simplify the expression $4x + 2 + 3x + 1$ using algebra tiles,
- a definition of *like terms*, and
- an explanation of how you use the Commutative and Distributive Properties to simplify $4x + 2 + 3x + 1$.

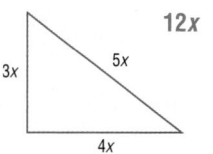

More About...

Baby-sitting

In a recent survey, 10% of students in grades 6–12 reported that most of their spending money came from baby-sitting.

Source: USA WEEKEND

Answers

17. terms: 3, 7x, 3x, x; like terms: 7x, 3x, x; coefficients: 7, 3, 1; constant: 3

18. terms: y, 3y, 8y, 2; like terms: y, 3y, 8y; coefficients: 1, 3, 8; constant: 2

19. terms: 2a, 5c, −1a, 6a; like terms: 2a, −1a, 6a; coefficients: 2, 5, −1, 6; constant: none

20. terms: 5c, −2d, 3d, −1d; like terms: −2d, 3d, -1d; coefficients: 5, −2, 3, −1; constant: none

21. terms: 6m, −2n, 7; like terms: none; coefficients: 6, −2; constant: 7

22. terms: 7x, −3y, 3z, −2; like terms: none; coefficients: 7, −3, 3; constant: −2

57. CRITICAL THINKING You use *deductive reasoning* when you base a conclusion on mathematical rules or properties. Indicate the property that justifies each step that was used to simplify $3(x + 4) + 5(x + 1)$.

a. $3(x + 4) + 5(x + 1) = 3x + 12 + 5x + 5$ Distributive

b. $= 3x + 5x + 12 + 5$ Commutative

c. $= 3x + 5x + 17$ Substitution

d. $= 8x + 17$ Distributive

Standardized Test Practice
Ⓐ Ⓑ Ⓒ Ⓓ

58. Which expression is *not* equivalent to the other three? **C**

Ⓐ $-6(x - 2)$ Ⓑ $x + 12 - 7x$

Ⓒ $-6x - 12$ Ⓓ $-x - 5x + 12$

59. Katie practiced the clarinet for m minutes. Her sister practiced 10 minutes less. Which expression represents the total time they spent practicing? **C**

Ⓐ $m - 10$ Ⓑ $m + 10$ Ⓒ $2m - 10$ Ⓓ $2m + 10$

Maintain Your Skills

Mixed Review   **ALGEBRA** Use the Distributive Property to write each expression as an equivalent expression. *(Lesson 3-1)*

60. $3(a + 5)$ $3a + 15$ **61.** $-2(y + 8)$ $-2y - 16$ **62.** $-3(x - 1)$ $-3x + 3$

63. Name the quadrant in which $P(-5, -6)$ is located. *(Lesson 2-6)*   III

64. CRUISES The table shows the number of people who took a cruise in various years. Make a scatter plot of the data. *(Lesson 1-7)* **See margin.**

People Taking Cruises				
Year	1970	1980	1990	2000
Number (millions)	0.5	1.4	3.6	6.5

Source: Cruise Lines International Association

Evaluate each expression. *(Lesson 1-2)*

65. $2 + 3 \cdot 5$ **17**   **66.** $8 \div 2 \cdot 4$ **16**   **67.** $10 - 2 \cdot 4$ **2**

Getting Ready for the Next Lesson   **PREREQUISITE SKILL** Find each sum. *(To review **adding integers**, see Lesson 2-2.)*

68. $-5 + 4$ **−1**   **69.** $-8 + (-3)$ **−11**   **70.** $10 + (-1)$ **9**

71. $4 + (-9)$ **−5**   **72.** $11 + (-7)$ **4**   **73.** $-4 + (-9)$ **−13**

Practice Quiz 1   Lessons 3-1 and 3-2

Simplify each expression. *(Lessons 3-1 and 3-2)*

1. $6(x + 2)$ $6x + 12$ **2.** $5(x - 7)$ $5x - 35$ **3.** $6y - 4 + y$ $7y - 4$ **4.** $2a + 4(a - 9)$ $6a - 36$

5. SCHOOL You spent m minutes studying on Monday. On Tuesday, you studied 15 more minutes than you did on Monday. Write an expression in simplest form that represents the total amount of time spent studying on Monday and Tuesday. *(Lesson 3-2)* $2m + 15$

---

4 Assess

Open-Ended Assessment

Speaking Have pairs of students take turns challenging each other to simplify algebraic expressions by combining like terms. Have one student state an expression to simplify. Then have the other student state which are the like terms, and then state the simplified expression. Students should then switch roles.

Getting Ready for Lesson 3-3

PREREQUISITE SKILL In Lesson 3-3, students will solve equations by adding or subtracting. Exercises 68–73 should be used to determine your students' familiarity with adding integers.

Assessment Options

Practice Quiz 1 The quiz provides students with a brief review of the concepts and skills in Lessons 3-1 and 3-2. Lesson numbers are given to the right of exercises or instruction lines so students can review concepts not yet mastered.

Quiz (Lessons 3-1 and 3-2) is available on p. 157 of the *Chapter 3 Resource Masters*.

Answer

64. People Taking Cruises

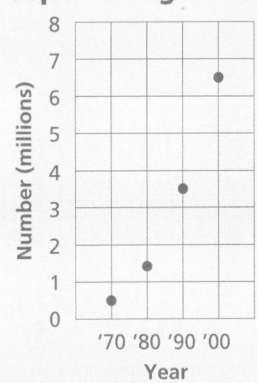

Algebra Activity

Getting Started

Objective Solve equations using algebra tiles.

Materials
algebra tiles
equation mat

Teaching Tip If algebra tiles and an equation mat are unavailable, students could draw the tiles on the chalkboard or an erasable board, or make their own tiles from stiff paper or cardboard.

Teach

Activity 1
• Relate the adding or removing of the same number of tiles to each side of the equation to keeping a scale in balance.

Activity 2
• Remind students that they need to add counters to each side of an equation to make enough zero pairs to leave the x-tile alone on one side of the mat.

Activity 3
• Remind students that they need to match each x-tile with an equal number of counters.

Algebra Activity

Solving Equations Using Algebra Tiles

Activity 1

In a set of algebra tiles, represents the variable x, $\boxed{1}$ represents the integer 1, and $\boxed{-1}$ represents the integer -1. You can use algebra tiles and an equation mat to model equations.

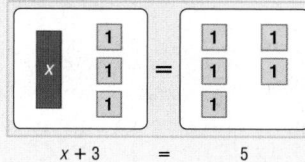 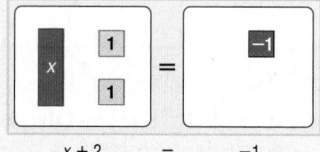

$$x + 3 = 5 \qquad\qquad x + 2 = -1$$

When you solve an equation, you are trying to find the value of x that makes the equation true. The following example shows how to solve $x + 3 = 5$ using algebra tiles.

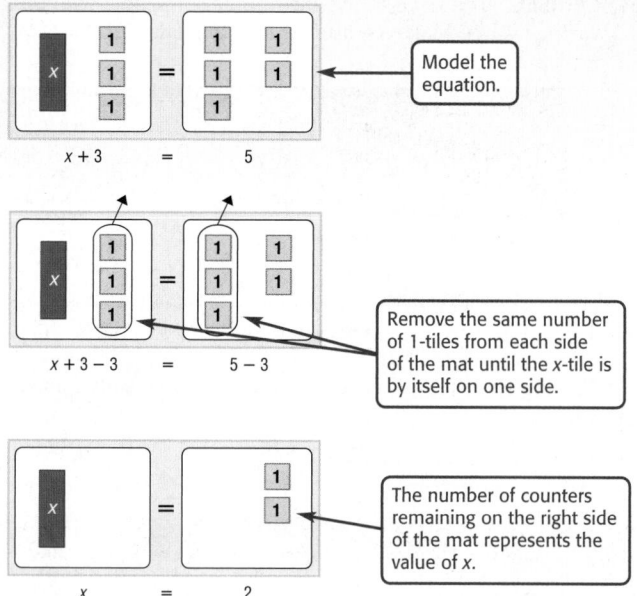

Model the equation.

$$x + 3 = 5$$

Remove the same number of 1-tiles from each side of the mat until the x-tile is by itself on one side.

$$x + 3 - 3 = 5 - 3$$

The number of counters remaining on the right side of the mat represents the value of x.

$$x = 2$$

Therefore, $x = 2$. Since $2 + 3 = 5$, the solution is correct.

Model 1–4. See margin for models.

Use algebra tiles to model and solve each equation.

1. $3 + x = 7$ **4** **2.** $x + 4 = 5$ **1** **3.** $6 = x + 4$ **2** **4.** $5 = 1 + x$ **4**

Resource Manager

📁 **Teaching Pre-Algebra with Manipulatives**

• pp. 7–8 (Master for algebra tiles)
• p. 13 (Master for equation mat)
• p. 51 (student recording sheet)

Glencoe Mathematics Classroom Manipulative Kit

• algebra tiles
• equation mat

Activity 2

Some equations are solved by using zero pairs. You may add or subtract a zero pair from either side of an equation mat without changing its value. The following example shows how to solve $x + 2 = -1$ by using zero pairs.

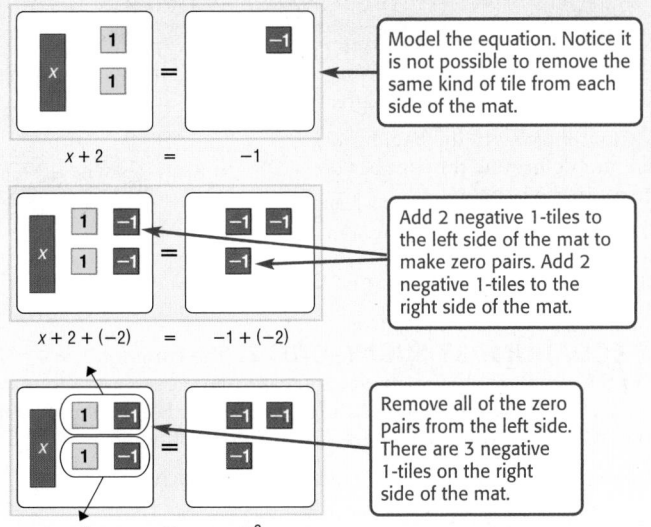

TEACHING TIP

Model the equation. Notice it is not possible to remove the same kind of tile from each side of the mat.

$$x + 2 = -1$$

Add 2 negative 1-tiles to the left side of the mat to make zero pairs. Add 2 negative 1-tiles to the right side of the mat.

$$x + 2 + (-2) = -1 + (-2)$$

Remove all of the zero pairs from the left side. There are 3 negative 1-tiles on the right side of the mat.

$$x = -3$$

Therefore, $x = -3$. Since $-3 + 2 = -1$, the solution is correct.

Model

Use algebra tiles to model and solve each equation. **5–8. See pp. 143A–143B for models.**

5. $x + 2 = -2$ **−4**   **6.** $x - 3 = 2$ **5**   **7.** $0 = x + 3$ **−3**   **8.** $-2 = x + 1$ **−3**

Activity 3

Some equations are modeled using more than one x-tile. The following example shows how to solve $2x = -6$ using algebra tiles.

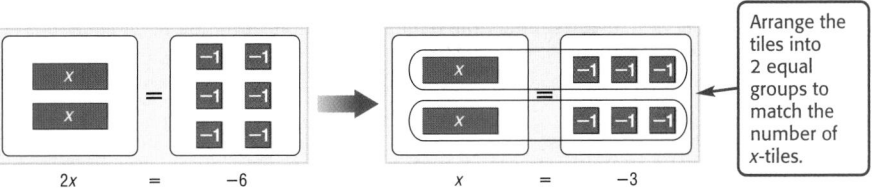

Arrange the tiles into 2 equal groups to match the number of x-tiles.

$$2x = -6 \qquad x = -3$$

Therefore, $x = -3$. Since $2(-3) = -6$, the solution is correct.

Model

Use algebra tiles to model and solve each equation. **9–12. See pp. 143A–143B for models.**

9. $3x = 3$ **1**   **10.** $2x = -8$ **−4**   **11.** $6 = 3x$ **2**   **12.** $-4 = 2x$ **−2**

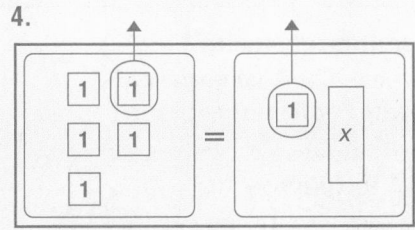
4.

Assess

In **Exercises 1–4,** students should subtract the same number from each side of the equation.

In **Exercises 5–8,** students should add enough counters to each side to make zero pairs with all the counters on the side with the x-tile.

In **Exercises 9–12,** ask students to solve equations by division.

Study Notebook

Have students write how using algebra tiles can help them better understand how to solve equations.

Answers

1.
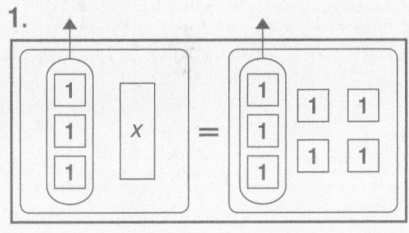

2.
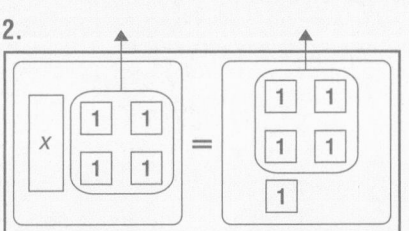

3.
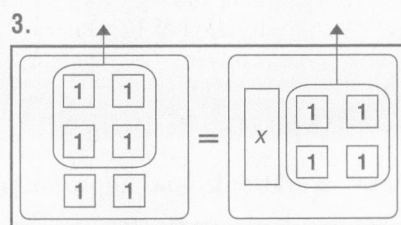

1 Focus

5-Minute Check Transparency 3-3 Use as a quiz or review of Lesson 3-2.

Mathematical Background notes are available for this lesson on page 96C.

How is solving an equation similar to keeping a scale in balance?

The opening activity questions are repeated on page 120 of the *Chapter 3 Resource Masters*.

Reading to Learn Mathematics, p. 120   ELL

Pre-Activity *How is solving an equation similar to keeping a scale in balance?*

Do the activity at the top of page 110 in your textbook. Write your answers below.

a. Without looking in the bag, how can you determine the number of blocks in the bag? Remove 4 blocks from each side. There are 3 blocks left on the right, so there must be 3 blocks in the bag.

b. Explain why your method works. Removing the same number of blocks from each side keeps the scale in balance.

Reading the Lesson 1–2. See students' work.

Write a definition and give an example of each new vocabulary phrase.

Vocabulary	Definition	Example
1. inverse operations		
2. equivalent equations		

3. Are $x - 2 = 8$ and $x = 6$ equivalent equations? Explain. No; they do not have the same solution. The solution of $x - 2 = 8$ is 10, and the solution of $x = 6$ is 6.

Helping You Remember

4. How is adding 2 blocks to each side of a balanced scale like the Addition Property of Equality? Adding 2 blocks to each side keeps the scale in balance. Adding the same number on each side of an equation keeps the two sides of the equation equal.

Teaching Tip Use an overhead projector to model the equation $x + 4 = 7$ using overhead algebra tiles on an equation mat transparency.

Vocabulary
- inverse operation
- equivalent equations

a. Remove 4 blocks from each side. There are 3 blocks left on the right, so there must be 3 blocks in the bag.

What You'll Learn
- Solve equations by using the Subtraction Property of Equality.
- Solve equations by using the Addition Property of Equality.

How is solving an equation similar to keeping a scale in balance?

On the balance below, the paper bag contains a certain number of blocks. (Assume that the paper bag weighs nothing.)

a. Without looking in the bag, how can you determine the number of blocks in the bag?

b. Explain why your method works.

b. Removing the same number of blocks from each side keeps the scale in balance.

SOLVE EQUATIONS BY SUBTRACTING The equation $x + 4 = 7$ is a model of the situation shown above. You can use inverse operations to solve the equation. **Inverse operations** "undo" each other. For example, to undo the addition of 4 in the expression $x + 4$, you would subtract 4.

To solve the equation $x + 4 = 7$, subtract 4 from each side.

$$x + 4 = 7$$
$$x + 4 - 4 = 7 - 4$$
$$x + 0 = 3$$
$$x = 3$$

Subtract 4 from the left side of the equation to isolate the variable.

Subtract 4 from the right side of the equation to keep it balanced.

The solution is 3.

You can use the **Subtraction Property of Equality** to solve any equation like $x + 4 = 7$.

Key Concept *Subtraction Property of Equality*

- **Words** If you subtract the same number from each side of an equation, the two sides remain equal.

- **Symbols** For any numbers a, b, and c, if $a = b$, then $a - c = b - c$.

- **Examples**

$$5 = 5 \qquad\qquad x + 2 = 3$$
$$5 - 3 = 5 - 3 \qquad x + 2 - 2 = 3 - 2$$
$$2 = 2 \qquad\qquad x = 1$$

✓ **Concept Check** Which integer would you subtract from each side of $x + 7 = 20$ to solve the equation? 7

110 Chapter 3 Equations

Resource Manager

 **Workbooks and Reproducible Masters**

Chapter 3 Resource Masters
- Study Guide and Intervention, p. 117
- Skills Practice, p. 118
- Practice, p. 119
- Reading to Learn Mathematics, p. 120
- Enrichment, p. 121

Parent and Student Study Guide Workbook, p. 18
Prerequisite Skills Workbook, pp. 5–8
School-to-Career Masters, p. 5

 **Transparencies**
5-Minute Check Transparency 3-3
Answer Key Transparencies

 **Technology**
Interactive Chalkboard

The equations $x + 4 = 7$ and $x = 3$ are **equivalent equations** because they have the same solution, 3. When you solve an equation, you should always check to be sure that the first and last equations are equivalent.

☑ **Concept Check**   Are $x + 4 = 15$ and $x = 4$ equivalent equations? Explain.
         No; the solution of $x + 4 = 15$ is 11, not 4.

Example 1   *Solve Equations by Subtracting*

Solve $x + 8 = -5$. Check your solution.

$x + 8 = -5$	Write the equation.
$x + 8 - 8 = -5 - 8$	Subtract 8 from each side.
$x + 0 = -13$	$8 - 8 = 0, -5 - 8 = -13$
$x = -13$	Identity Property; $x + 0 = x$

To check your solution, replace x with -13 in the original equation.

CHECK $x + 8 = -5$ Write the equation.

           $-13 + 8 \stackrel{?}{=} -5$ Check to see whether this sentence is true.

                 $-5 = -5 \checkmark$ The sentence is true.

The solution is -13.

Example 2   *Graph the Solutions of an Equation*

Graph the solution of $16 + x = 14$ on a number line.

$16 + x = 14$	Write the equation.
$x + 16 = 14$	Commutative Property; $16 + x = x + 16$
$x + 16 - 16 = 14 - 16$	Subtract 16 from each side.
$x = -2$	Simplify.

The solution is -2. To graph the solution, draw a dot at -2 on a number line.

```
 +--+--●--+--+--+--+--+--+-->
-3 -2 -1  0  1  2  3  4
```

SOLVE EQUATIONS BY ADDING   Some equations can be solved by adding the same number to each side. This property is called the **Addition Property of Equality**.

Key Concept	**Addition Property of Equality**
• **Words**	If you add the same number to each side of an equation, the two sides remain equal.
• **Symbols**	For any numbers a, b, and c, if $a = b$, then $a + c = b + c$.
• **Examples**	$\begin{array}{ll} 6 = 6 & x - 2 = 5 \\ 6 + 3 = 6 + 3 & x - 2 + 2 = 5 + 2 \\ 9 = 9 & x = 7 \end{array}$

☑ Skills Check

Solve Equations by Subtracting or Adding Solve and check each equation.

a. $m - 4 = -5$ -1

b. $r + 7 = -23$ -30

c. $11 = t - 8$ 19

d. $4 = -21 + k$ 25

---

2 Teach

Building on Prior Knowledge

In Chapter 2, students learned how to add and subtract integers. In this lesson, students will use the Addition Property of Equality and the Subtraction Property of Equality with integers to solve equations.

SOLVE EQUATIONS BY SUBTRACTING

In-Class Examples   Power Point®

> *Teaching Tip*   Point out that this method of checking solutions can save time when solving similar problems on standardized tests.

1   Solve $x + 4 = -3$. Check your solution. -7

2   Graph the solution of $x + 8 = 7$ on a number line.

```
 +----●----+----+----+-->
-2   -1    0    1    2
```

SOLVE EQUATIONS BY ADDING

In-Class Examples   Power Point®

3   Solve $y - 3 = -14$. -11

4   **ENTERTAINMENT** Movie *A* earned $225 million at the box office. That is $38 million less than Movie *B* earned. Write and solve an equation to find the amount Movie *B* earned.
$B - 38 = 225$; Movie *B* earned $263 million at the box office.

5   **Multiple-Choice Test Item**
What value of x makes $x - 1 = 8$ a true statement?

   A 9   **B** 7   **C** -7 **D** -9
   A

Study Notebook

Have students—
- add the definitions/examples of the vocabulary terms to their Vocabulary Builder worksheets for Chapter 3.
- explain the Subtraction Property of Equality and the Addition Property of Equality in their own words.
- include any other item(s) that they find helpful in mastering the skills in this lesson.

About the Exercises . . .

Organization by Objective
- **Solve Equations by Subtracting:** 12–19, 28–29
- **Solve Equations by Adding:** 20–27, 30–32

Odd/Even Assignments
Exercises 12–42 are structured so that students practice the same concepts whether they are assigned odd or even problems.

Alert! Exercises 45–47 require access to the Internet or other research materials.

Assignment Guide

Basic: 13–31 odd, 37–45 odd, 46–67

Average: 13–45 odd, 46–67

Advanced: 12–44 even, 45–61 (Optional: 62–67)

If an equation has a subtraction expression, first rewrite the expression as an addition expression. Then add the additive inverse to each side.

Example 3 Solve Equations by Adding

Solve $y - 7 = -25$.

$y - 7 = -25$	Write the equation.
$y + (-7) = -25$	Rewrite $y - 7$ as $y + (-7)$.
$y + (-7) + 7 = -25 + 7$	Add 7 to each side.
$y + 0 = -25 + 7$	Additive Inverse Property; $(-7) + 7 = 0$.
$y = -18$	Identity Property; $y + 0 = y$

The solution is -18. Check your solution.

TEACHING TIP
When students understand that $(-7) + 7 = 0$, you may want them to perform this step mentally.

More About. . .

Aviation •
On December 17, 1903, the Wright brothers made the first flights in a power-driven airplane. Orville's flight covered 120 feet, which was 732 feet shorter than Wilbur's.
Source: www.infoplease.com

Example 4 Use an Equation to Solve a Problem

AVIATION Use the information at the left. Write and solve an equation to find the length of Wilbur Wright's flight.

Words   Orville's flight was 732 feet shorter than Wilbur's.

Variables   Let x = the length of Wilbur's flight.

Orville's flight   was   732 feet shorter than Wilbur's flight.

Equation 120 $=$ $x - 732$

Solve the equation.

$120 = x - 732$	Think of $x - 732$ as $x + (-732)$.
$120 + 732 = x - 732 + 732$	Add 732 to each side.
$852 = x$	Simplify.

Wilbur's flight was 852 feet.

Almost all standardized tests have items involving equations.

Standardized Test Practice
Ⓐ Ⓑ Ⓒ Ⓓ

Example 5 Solve Equations

Multiple-Choice Test Item

What value of x makes $x - 4 = -2$ a true statement?
Ⓐ 6   Ⓑ 2   Ⓒ -2 Ⓓ -6

Read the Test Item   To find the value of x, solve the equation.

Solve the Test Item

$x - 4 = -2$	Write the equation.
$x - 4 + 4 = -2 + 4$	Add 4 to each side.
$x = 2$	Simplify.

The answer is B.

Standardized Test Practice
Ⓐ Ⓑ Ⓒ Ⓓ

Example 5 Tell students to eliminate choices whenever possible. For example, in the equation $x - 4 = -2$, $x - 4$ must be negative, so choice **A** can be eliminated without solving the equation.

Concept Check

1. Addition Property of Equality

1. **Tell** what property you would use to solve $x - 15 = -3$.

2. **OPEN ENDED** Write two equations that are equivalent. Then write two equations that are *not* equivalent. **See pp. 143A–143B.**

Guided Practice

GUIDED PRACTICE KEY	
Exercises	Examples
3–8	1, 3
9, 10	2
11	5

ALGEBRA Solve each equation. Check your solution.

3. $x + 14 = 25$ **11**
4. $w + 4 = -10$ **−14**
5. $16 = y + 20$ **−4**
6. $n - 8 = 5$ **13**
7. $k - 25 = 30$ **55**
8. $r - 4 = -18$ **−14**

ALGEBRA Graph the solution of each equation on a number line.

9. $-8 = x - 6$
10. $y - 3 = -1$ **9–10. See pp. 143A–143B.**

Standardized Test Practice
Ⓐ Ⓑ Ⓒ Ⓓ

11. What value of x makes $x - 10 = -5$ a true statement? **C**
   Ⓐ -5 　 Ⓑ 15 　 Ⓒ 5 　 Ⓓ -15

★ indicates increased difficulty

Homework Help

For Exercises	See Examples
12–32	1, 3
37–42	2
43–47	4

Extra Practice
See page 729.

ALGEBRA Solve each equation. Check your solution.

12. $y + 7 = 21$ **14**
13. $x + 5 = 18$ **13**
14. $m + 10 = -2$ **−12**
15. $x + 5 = -3$ **−8**
16. $a + 10 = -4$ **−14**
17. $t + 6 = -9$ **−15**
18. $y + 8 = 3$ **−5**
19. $9 = 10 + b$ **−1**
20. $k - 6 = 13$ **19**
21. $r - 5 = 10$ **15**
22. $8 = r - 5$ **13**
23. $19 = g - 5$ **24**
24. $x - 6 = -2$ **4**
25. $y - 49 = -13$ **36**
26. $-15 = x - 16$ **1**
27. $-8 = t - 4$ **−4**
28. $23 + y = 14$ **−9**
29. $59 = s + 90$ **−31**
30. $x - 27 = -63$ **−36**
31. $84 = r - 34$ **118**
32. $y - 95 = -18$ **77**

ALGEBRA Write and solve an equation to find each number.

★ 33. The sum of a number and 9 is –2. $n + 9 = -2; -11$

★ 34. The sum of –5 and a number is –15. $-5 + n = -15; -10$

★ 35. The difference of a number and 3 is –6. $n - 3 = -6; -3$

★ 36. When 5 is subtracted from a number, the result is 16. $n - 5 = 16; 21$

ALGEBRA Graph the solution of each equation on a number line.

37. $8 + w = 3$
38. $z - 5 = -8$
39. $8 = x - 2$
40. $9 + x = 12$
41. $-11 = y - 7$
42. $x - (-1) = 0$

37–42. See pp. 143A–143B.

43. **ELECTIONS** In the 2000 presidential election, Indiana had 12 electoral votes. That was 20 votes fewer than the number of electoral votes in Texas. Write and solve an equation to find the number of electoral votes in Texas.
$12 = x - 20; 32$

44. **WEATHER** The difference between the record high and low temperatures in Charlotte, North Carolina, is 109°F. The record low temperature was −5°F. Write and solve an equation to find the record high temperature.
$x - (-5) = 109; 104°$

45. See students' work.
45. **RESEARCH** Use the Internet or another source to find record temperatures in your state. Use the data to write a problem.

 www.pre-alg.com/self_check_quiz 　 **Lesson 3-3** Solving Equations by Adding or Subtracting 　**113**

Step 1	Identify the variable.
Step 2	To isolate the variable, add the same number to or subtract the same number from each side of the equation.
Step 3	Check the solution.

Example 1 Solve $x + 2 = 6$.
$x + 2 = 6$
$x + 2 - 2 = 6 - 2$ 　 Subtract 2 from each side.
$x = 4$
Check: $x + 2 = 6$
$4 + 2 = 6$
$6 = 6$ ✔
The solution is 4.

Example 2 Solve $x - 9 = -13$.
$x - 9 = -13$
$x - 9 + 9 = -13 + 9$ 　 Add 9 to each side.
$x = -4$
Check: $x - 9 = -13$
$-4 - 9 = -13$
$-13 = -13$ ✔
The solution is −4.

Exercises

Solve each equation. Graph the solution of each equation on the number line.

1. $x + 5 = 2$ **−3**
2. $11 + w = 10$ **−1**
3. $k + 3 = -1$ **−4**
4. $m - 2 = 3$ **5**
5. $a - 7 = -5$ **2**
6. $b - 13 = -13$ **0**
7. $-3 + h = -7$ **−4**
8. $-12 = y - 9$ **−3**
9. $2 + r = -3$ **−5**
10. $9 + b = 9$ **0**
11. $7 + k = 10$ **3**
12. $g - 9 = -5$ **4**

Solve each equation. Check your solution.

1. $z + 6 = -5$ 　−11
2. $x - 8 = -3$ 　5
3. $c - 2 = 21$ 　23
4. $v + 9 = 0$ 　−9
5. $q + 10 = -30$ 　−40
6. $w + 15 = 0$ 　−15
7. $z + 12 = -19$ 　−31
8. $b - 11 = 8$ 　19
9. $a - 12 = 0$ 　12
10. $r + 11 = 12$ 　1
11. $p + (-9) = 33$ 　42
12. $n - 16 = -16$ 　0
13. $s + 13 = -5$ 　−18
14. $t - (-15) = 21$ 　6
15. $r - 14 = -23$ 　−9
16. $m + (-3) = 9$ 　12
17. $d - 19 = 1$ 　20
18. $y + 30 = -1$ 　−31
19. $u - 21 = 0$ 　21
20. $k - 18 = 2$ 　20
21. $f - 23 = 23$ 　46
22. $g - 24 = -24$ 　0
23. $h + 35 = 7$ 　−28
24. $j + 40 = 25$ 　−15
25. $x + 3 = -15$ 　−18
26. $c + 22 = -27$ 　−49
27. $v - 18 = -4$ 　14
28. $b - 41 = -30$ 　11
29. $h - 10 = 19$ 　29
30. $y - (-12) = 0$ 　−12
31. $g + 58 = 9$ 　−49
32. $n + 29 = 4$ 　−25
33. $j + (-14) = 1$ 　15
34. $p - 21 = -2$ 　19
35. $k - (-13) = -8$ 　−21
36. $m + 33 = 16$ 　−17

37. **SAVINGS ACCOUNT** Jhumpa has $55 in her savings account. This is $21 more than David. Write and solve an equation to find the amount David has in his savings account. $d + 21 = 55; \$34$

38. **WEATHER** The temperature fell 16° between noon and 3:00 P.M. At 3:00, the temperature was −3°F. Write an equation to determine the temperature at noon. $t - 16 = -3; 13°F$

Creating a Line Design

Connect each pair of equivalent expressions with a straight line segment. Describe the finished design.

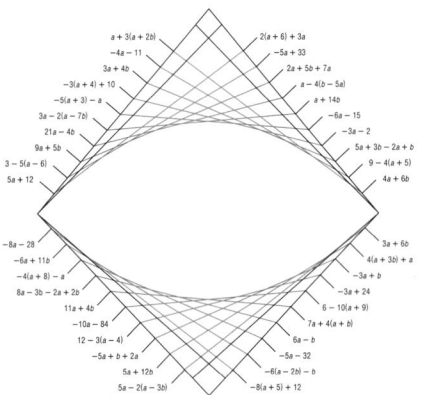

Differentiated Instruction

• **Interpersonal** Have students work with a partner. First, one student writes an equation such as $x + 6 = -2$ or $x - 5 = 8$. Then the other student solves the equation using algebra tiles. The partners should then switch roles and repeat the activity.

Open-Ended Assessment

Speaking Working in pairs, have students take turns presenting one another with simple equations such as $x + 4 = 8$. The second student should state which Property of Equality to use to solve the equation and what the first step would be, for example, "Subtract 4 from each side."

Getting Ready for Lesson 3-4

PREREQUISITE SKILL Lesson 3-4 presents solving equations by multiplying or dividing. Exercises 62–67 should be used to determine your students' familiarity with dividing integers.

Answer

49. When you solve an equation, you perform the same operation on each side so that the two sides remain equal. Answers should include the following.
   - In an equation, both sides are equal. In a balance scale, the weight of the items on both sides are equal.
   - The Addition and Subtraction Properties of Equality allow you to add or subtract the same number from each side of an equation. The two sides of the equation remain equal.

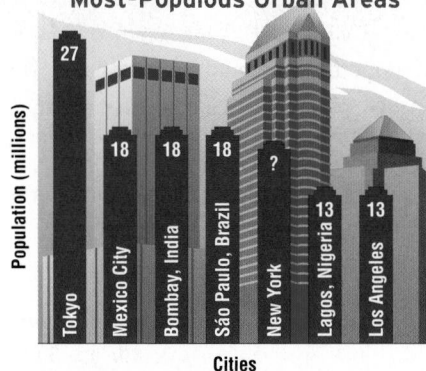

Most-Populous Urban Areas

Source: United Nations

POPULATION For Exercises 46 and 47, use the graph and the following information.
Tokyo's population is 10 million greater than New York's population. Los Angeles' population is 4 million less than New York's population.

46. Write two different equations to find New York's population.

47. Solve the equations.
17 million
46. $27 = x + 10$, $13 = x - 4$

 Online Research **Data Update** How are the populations of these cities related today? Visit www.pre-alg.com/data_update to learn more.

48. **CRITICAL THINKING** Write two equations in which the solution is −5.
Sample answer: $x - 2 = -7$, $x + 2 = -3$

49. **WRITING IN MATH** Answer the question that was posed at the beginning of the lesson. **See margin.**

Why is solving an equation similar to keeping a scale in balance?

Include the following in your answer:
- a comparison of an equation and a balanced scale, and
- an explanation of the Addition and Subtraction Properties of Equality.

Standardized Test Practice

★50. If $x + 4 = -2$, the numerical value of $-3x - 2$ is **B**
(A) −20.   (B) 16.   (C) 4.   (D) −8.

★51. When 7 is subtracted from a number 5 times, the result is 3. What is the number? **C**
(A) 10   (B) −2   (C) 38   (D) 35

Maintain Your Skills

Mixed Review

ALGEBRA Simplify each expression. *(Lessons 3-1 and 3-2)*

52. $-2(x + 5)$ $-2x - 10$
53. $(t + 4)3$ $3t + 12$
54. $-4(x - 2)$ $-4x + 8$
55. $6z - 3 - 10z + 7$ $-4z + 4$
56. $2(x + 6) + 4x$ $6x + 12$
57. $3 - 4(m + 1)$ $-4m - 1$

ALGEBRA What property is shown by each statement? *(Lessons 2-2 and 1-4)*

58. $9a + b = b + 9a$
Commutative (+)
59. $x[y + (-y)] = x(0)$
Additive Inverse
60. $6(3x) = (6 \cdot 3)x$
Associative (×)

61. **ALGEBRA** Evaluate $9a + 4b$ if $a = 8$ and $b = 3$. *(Lesson 1-3)* **84**

Getting Ready for the Next Lesson

PREREQUISITE SKILL Divide. *(To review dividing integers, see Lesson 2-5.)*

62. $-100 \div 10$ **−10**
63. $50 \div (-2)$ **−25**
64. $-49 \div (-7)$ **7**
65. $\dfrac{72}{-8}$ **−9**
66. $\dfrac{-18}{-6}$ **3**
67. $\dfrac{-36}{9}$ **−4**

What You'll Learn

- Solve equations by using the Division Property of Equality.
- Solve equations by using the Multiplication Property of Equality.

How are equations used to find the U.S. value of foreign currency?

In Mexico, about 9 *pesos* can be exchanged for $1 of U.S. currency, as shown in the table.

In general, if we let d represent the number of U.S. dollars and p represent the number of pesos, then $9d = p$.

a. Suppose lunch in Mexico costs 72 pesos. Write an equation to find the cost in U.S. dollars. **$9d = 72$**

b. How can you find the cost in U.S. dollars? **Divide by 9.**

U.S. Value ($)	Number of Pesos
1	9(1) = 9
2	9(2) = 18
3	9(3) = 27
4	9(4) = 36

SOLVE EQUATIONS BY DIVIDING The equation $9x = 72$ is a model of the relationship described above. To undo the multiplication operation in $9x$, you would divide by 9.

To solve the equation $9x = 72$, divide each side by 9.

$$9x = 72$$

Divide the left side of the equation by 9 to undo the multiplication $9 \cdot x$.

$$\frac{9x}{9} = \frac{72}{9}$$

$$1x = 8$$

Divide the right side of the equation by 9 to keep it balanced.

$$x = 8$$

The solution is 8.

You can use the **Division Property of Equality** to solve any equation like $9x = 72$.

Key Concept — Division Property of Equality

- **Words** When you divide each side of an equation by the same nonzero number, the two sides remain equal.

- **Symbols** For any numbers a, b, and c, where $c \neq 0$, then $\frac{a}{c} = \frac{b}{c}$.

- **Examples**

$$14 = 14 \qquad\qquad 3x = -12$$

$$\frac{14}{7} = \frac{14}{7} \qquad\qquad \frac{3x}{3} = \frac{-12}{3}$$

$$2 = 2 \qquad\qquad x = -4$$

Lesson 3-4 Solving Equations by Multiplying or Dividing **115**

2 Teach

SOLVE EQUATIONS BY DIVIDING

 In-Class Examples · Power Point®

1 Solve $7x = -56$. Check your solution and graph it on a number line. $x = -8$;

$$-10 \quad -8 \quad -6 \quad -4 \quad -2$$

2 **HOBBIES** Esteban spent $112 on boxes of baseball cards. If he paid $14 per box, how many boxes of cards did Esteban buy? **8 boxes**

✓ Skills Check

Solve Equations by Dividing
Solve each equation. Check your solution.

a. $8a = -48$ -6

b. $-3b = 27$ -9

c. $12c = -48$ -4

SOLVE EQUATIONS BY MULTIPLYING

In-Class Example · Power Point®

Teaching Tip Ask students to make a rule to identify equations that can be solved by multiplying.

3 Solve $\dfrac{y}{-5} = -12$.   **60**

Example 1   Solve Equations by Dividing

Solve $5x = -30$. Check your solution and graph it on a number line.

$5x = -30$ Write the equation.

$\dfrac{5x}{5} = \dfrac{-30}{5}$ Divide each side by 5 to undo the multiplication in $5 \cdot x$.

$1x = -6$ $5 \div 5 = 1$, $-30 \div 5 = -6$

$x = -6$ Identity Property; $1x = x$

To check your solution, replace x with -6 in the original equation.

CHECK $5x = -30$ Write the equation.

$5(-6) \stackrel{?}{=} -30$ Check to see whether this statement is true.

$-30 = -30 \checkmark$ The statement is true.

The solution is -6.

To graph the solution, draw a dot at -6 on a number line.

$$-7 \quad -6 \quad -5 \quad -4 \quad -3 \quad -2 \quad -1 \quad 0$$

✓ Concept Check   Explain how you could find the value of x in $3x = 18$. **Divide each side by 3.**

Example 2   Use an Equation to Solve a Problem

PARKS It costs $3 per car to use the hiking trails along the Columbia River Highway. If income from the hiking trails totaled $1275 in one day, how many cars entered the park?

Words $3 times the number of cars equals the total.

Variables   Let x represent the number of cars.

The cost per car	times	the number of cars	equals	the total.
Equation $3	$\cdot$	x	$=$	$1275

Solve the equation.

$3x = 1275$ Write the equation.

$\dfrac{3x}{3} = \dfrac{1275}{3}$ Divide each side by 3.

$x = 425$ Simplify.

CHECK $3x = 1275$ Write the equation.

$3(425) \stackrel{?}{=} 1275$ Check to see whether this statement is true.

$1275 = 1275 \checkmark$ The statement is true.

Therefore, 425 cars entered the park.

✓ Concept Check   Suppose it cost $5 per car to use the hiking trails and the total income was $1275. What equation would you solve? $5x = 1275$

More About. . .

Parks
The Columbia River Highway, built in 1913, is a historic route in Oregon that curves around twenty waterfalls through the Cascade Mountains.
Source: *USA TODAY*

DAILY INTERVENTION

Unlocking Misconceptions

- **Solve Equations by Multiplying** Many students mistakenly switch dividends and divisors when solving equations by multiplying. Have them check their answers by substituting the found value into the equation.

SOLVE EQUATIONS BY MULTIPLYING   Some equations can be solved by multiplying each side by the same number. This property is called the **Multiplication Property of Equality**.

> **Key Concept**   **Multiplication Property of Equality**
>
> • **Words**   When you multiply each side of an equation by the same number, the two sides remain equal.
>
> • **Symbols**   For any numbers a, b, and c, if $a = b$, then $ac = bc$.
>
> • **Examples** $8 = 8$ $\frac{x}{6} = 7$
>
> $8(-2) = 8(-2)$ $\left(\frac{x}{6}\right)6 = (7)6$
>
> $-16 = -16$ $x = 42$

Example 3 Solve Equations by Multiplying

Solve $\dfrac{y}{-4} = -9$. Check your solution.

$\dfrac{y}{-4} = -9$ Write the equation.

$\dfrac{y}{-4}(-4) = -9(-4)$ Multiply each side by -4 to undo the division in $\dfrac{y}{-4}$.

$y = 36$ Simplify.

CHECK $\dfrac{y}{-4} = -9$ Write the equation.

$\dfrac{36}{-4} \overset{?}{=} -9$ Check to see whether this statement is true.

$-9 = -9 \checkmark$ The statement is true.

The solution is 36.

Check for Understanding

Concept Check

1. Multiplication Property of Equality
2. Divide each side by -5; $y = 9$.

1. **State** what property you would use to solve $\dfrac{x}{-9} = -36$.

2. **Explain** how to find the value of y in $-5y = -45$.

3. **OPEN ENDED** Write an equation of the form $ax = c$ where a and c are integers and the solution is 4. **Sample answer: $-5x = -20$**

Guided Practice

GUIDED PRACTICE KEY	
Exercises	Examples
4–9	1, 3
10	2

ALGEBRA Solve each equation. Check your solution.

4. $4x = 24$ **6**   5. $-2a = 10$ **-5**   6. $-42 = -7t$ **6**

7. $\dfrac{k}{3} = 9$ **27**   8. $\dfrac{y}{5} = -8$ **-40**   9. $-11 = \dfrac{n}{-6}$ **66**

Application

10. $80x = 4000$; 50 toys

10. **TOYS**   A spiral toy that can bounce down a flight of stairs is made from 80 feet of wire. Write and solve an equation to find how many of these toys can be made from a spool of wire that contains 4000 feet.

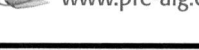 www.pre-alg.com/extra_examples   **Lesson 3-4** Solving Equations by Multiplying or Dividing   **117**

★ indicates increased difficulty

Practice and Apply

Homework Help

For Exercises	See Examples
11–34, 39–44	1, 3
45–48	2

Extra Practice See page 729.

ALGEBRA Solve each equation. Check your solution.

11. $3t = 21$ 7
12. $8x = 72$ 9
13. $-32 = 4y$ -8
14. $5n = -95$ -19
15. $-56 = -7p$ 8
16. $-8j = -64$ 8
17. $\frac{h}{4} = 6$ 24
18. $\frac{c}{9} = 4$ 36
19. $\frac{g}{-2} = -7$ 14
20. $-42 = \frac{x}{-2}$ 84
21. $11 = \frac{b}{-3}$ -33
22. $\frac{h}{-7} = 20$ -140
23. $45 = 5x$ 9
24. $3u = 51$ 17
25. $86 = -2v$ -43
26. $-8a = 144$ -18
27. $\frac{m}{45} = -3$ -135
28. $\frac{d}{3} = -3$ -9
29. $\frac{f}{-13} = -10$ 130
30. $\frac{v}{-11} = -132$ 1452
31. $-116 = -4w$ 29
32. $-68 = -4m$ 17
33. $-21 = \frac{k}{8}$ -168
34. $-56 = \frac{t}{9}$ -504

ALGEBRA Write and solve an equation for each sentence.

★ 35. The product of a number and 6 is -42. $6x = -42;$ -7

★ 36. The product of -7 and a number is -35. $-7x = -35;$ 5

★ 37. The quotient of a number and -4 is 8. $\frac{x}{-4} = 8;$ -32

★ 38. When you divide a number by -5, the result is -2. $\frac{x}{-5} = -2;$ 10

39–44. See margin.

ALGEBRA Graph the solution of each equation on a number line.

39. $48 = -6x$
40. $-32t = 64$
41. $-6r = -18$
42. $-42 = -7x$
43. $\frac{n}{12} = 3$
44. $\frac{y}{-4} = -1$

45. **RANCHING** The largest ranch in the world is in the Australian Outback. It is about 12,000 square miles, which is five times the size of the largest United States ranch. Write and solve an equation to find the size of the largest United States ranch. $12,000 = 5x;$ 2400 mi^2

46. **RANCHING** In the driest part of an Outback ranch, each cow needs about 40 acres for grazing. Write and solve an equation to find how many cows can graze on 720 acres of land. $40x = 720;$ 18 cows

★ 47. **PAINTING** A **person-day** is a unit of measure that represents one person working for one day. A painting contractor estimates that it will take 24 person-days to paint a house. Write and solve an equation to find how many painters the contractor will need to hire to paint the house in 6 days. $6p = 24,$ 4 painters

★ 48. **MEASUREMENT** The chart shows several conversions in the customary system. Write and solve an equation to find each quantity.

a. the number of feet in 132 inches $12f = 132;$ 11 ft

b. the number of yards in 15 feet $3y = 15;$ 5 yd

c. the number of miles in 10,560 feet $5280m = 10,560;$ 2 mi

Customary System (length)
1 mile = 5280 feet
1 mile = 1760 yards
1 yard = 3 feet
1 foot = 12 inches
1 yard = 36 inches

118 Chapter 3 Equations

Answers

39.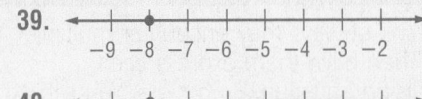

40.

41.

42.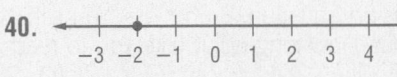

43.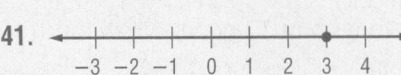

44.

49a. True; one pyramid balances two cubes, so this is the same as adding one cube to each side.
49b. True; one pyramid and one cube balance three cubes, which balance one cylinder.

49. CRITICAL THINKING Suppose that one pyramid balances two cubes and one cylinder balances three cubes. Determine whether each statement is *true* or *false*. Justify your answers.

a. One pyramid and one cube balance three cubes.

b. One pyramid and one cube balance one cylinder.

c. One cylinder and one pyramid balance four cubes.
False; one cylinder and one pyramid balance five cubes.

50. WRITING IN MATH Answer the question that was posed at the beginning of the lesson. **See margin.**

How are equations used to find the U.S. value of foreign currency?

Include the following in your answer:

• the cost in U.S. dollars of a 12-*pound* bus trip in Egypt, if 4 *pounds* can be exchanged for one U.S. dollar, and

• the cost in U.S. dollars of a 3040-*schilling* hotel room in Austria, if 16 *schillings* can be exchanged for one U.S. dollar.

 *Online Research* **Data Update** How many pounds and schillings can be exchanged for a U.S. dollar today? Visit www.pre-alg.com/data_update to learn more.

Standardized Test Practice
Ⓐ Ⓑ Ⓒ Ⓓ

★ **51.** Solve $\frac{mx}{n} = p$ for x. **B**

Ⓐ $x = \frac{m}{pn}$ Ⓑ $x = \frac{pn}{m}$ Ⓒ $x = \frac{p - n}{m}$ Ⓓ $x = pn - m$

52. A number is divided by -6, and the result is 24. What is the original number? **C**

Ⓐ -4 Ⓑ 4   Ⓒ -144 Ⓓ 144

Maintain Your Skills

Mixed Review **ALGEBRA** Solve each equation. *(Lesson 3-3)*

53. $3 + y = 16$ **13**   **54.** $29 = n + 4$ **25**   **55.** $k - 12 = -40$ **−28**

ALGEBRA Simplify each expression. *(Lesson 3-2)*

56. $4x + 7x$ **11x**   **57.** $2y + 6 + 5y$ **7y + 6**   **58.** $3 - 2(y + 4)$ **−2y − 5**

59. ALGEBRA Evaluate $3ab$ if $a = -6$ and $b = 2$. *(Lesson 2-4)* **−36**

60. Replace ● in -14 ● -4 with $<$, $>$, or $=$ to make a true sentence. *(Lesson 2-1)* **<**

Getting Ready for the Next Lesson **PREREQUISITE SKILL** Find each difference.
(To review subtracting integers, see Lesson 2-3.)

61. $8 - (-2)$ **10**   **62.** $-5 - 5$ **−10**   **63.** $-10 - (-8)$ **−2**

64. $-18 - 4$ **−22**   **65.** $-3 - (-5)$ **2**   **66.** $-45 - (-9)$ **−36**

67. $-24 - (-5)$ **−19**   **68.** $-15 - (-15)$ **0**   **69.** $-8 - 19$ **−27**

Open-Ended Assessment

Modeling Have students use algebra tiles and an equation mat to model these equations. Identify which of the equations can be solved by dividing and which can be solved by multiplying. Then solve.

1. $48 = 24m$ dividing; 2

2. $6j = 54$ dividing; 9

3. $\frac{k}{7} = 5$ multiplying; 35

Getting Ready for Lesson 3-5

PREREQUISITE SKILL Lesson 3-5 presents solving two-step equations, in which students will need to know how to subtract integers. Exercises 61–69 should be used to determine your students' familiarity with subtracting integers.

Assessment Options

Quiz (Lessons 3-3 and 3-4) is available on p. 157 of the *Chapter 3 Resource Masters.*

Mid-Chapter Test (Lessons 3-1 through 3-4) is available on p. 159 of the *Chapter 3 Resource Masters.*

Answer

50. Sample answer: You can use the exchange rate to write and solve an equation involving foreign currency. Answers should include the following.

• The equation is $4d = 12$, where d is the number of U.S. dollars. The bus trip costs $3 U.S. dollars.

• The equation is $16d = 3040$, where d is the number of U.S. dollars. The hotel room costs $190 U.S. dollars.

3-5 **Solving Two-Step Equations**

1 Focus

5-Minute Check Transparency 3-5 Use as a quiz or review of Lesson 3-4.

Mathematical Background notes are available for this lesson on page 96D.

How can algebra tiles show the properties of equality?

The opening activity questions are repeated on page 130 of the *Chapter 3 Resource Masters.*

Reading to Learn Mathematics, p. 130   ELL

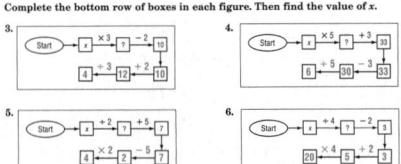

Pre-Activity *How can algebra tiles show the properties of equality?*

Do the activity at the top of page 120 in your textbook. Write your answers below.

a. What property is shown by removing a tile from each side?
   Subtraction Property of Equality

b. What property is shown by separating the tile into two groups?
   Division Property of Equality

c. What is the solution of $2x + 1 = 9$? 4

Reading the Lesson

Write a definition and give an example of the new vocabulary phrase.

Vocabulary	Definition	Example
1. two-step equation	See students' work.	

2. To solve two-step equations, use __inverse operations__ to undo each operation in reverse order.

Helping You Remember

Suppose you start with a number x, multiply it by 2, add three, and the result is 17. The top row of boxes at the right represents the equation $2x + 3 = 17$. To solve the equation, you undo the operations in reverse order. This is shown in the bottom row of boxes.

Complete the bottom row of boxes in each figure. Then find the value of x.

3. [figure]   4. [figure]

5. [figure]   6. [figure]

What You'll Learn

• Solve two-step equations.

How can algebra tiles show the properties of equality?

Vocabulary
• two-step equation

The equation $2x + 1 = 9$, modeled below, can be solved with algebra tiles.

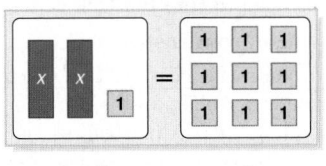

$2x + 1 = 9$

You can use the steps shown at the right to solve the equation.

Step 1   Remove 1 tile from each side of the mat.

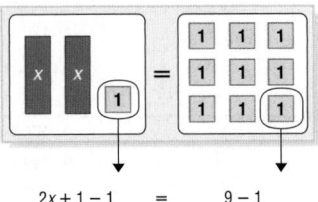

$2x + 1 - 1 = 9 - 1$

Step 2   Separate the remaining tiles into two equal groups.

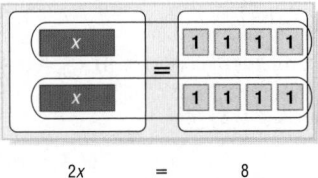

$2x = 8$

a. **Subtraction Property of Equality**
b. **Division Property of Equality**

a. What property is shown by removing a tile from each side?

b. What property is shown by separating the tiles into two groups?

c. What is the solution of $2x + 1 = 9$? **4**

SOLVE TWO-STEP EQUATIONS   A **two-step equation** contains two operations. In the equation $2x + 1 = 9$, x is multiplied by 2 and then 1 is added. To solve two-step equations, use inverse operations to undo each operation in reverse order. You can solve $2x + 1 = 9$ in two steps.

Step 1   First, undo addition.

$$2x + 1 = 9$$
$$2x + 1 - 1 = 9 - 1 \qquad \text{Subtract 1 from each side.}$$
$$2x = 8$$

Step 2   Then, undo multiplication.

$$2x = 8$$
$$\frac{2x}{2} = \frac{8}{2} \qquad \text{Divide each side by 2.}$$
$$x = 4$$

The solution is 4.

Resource Manager

📁 Workbooks and Reproducible Masters

Chapter 3 Resource Masters
• Study Guide and Intervention, p. 127
• Skills Practice, p. 128
• Practice, p. 129
• Reading to Learn Mathematics, p. 130
• Enrichment, p. 131

Graphing Calculator and Spreadsheet Masters, p. 23
Parent and Student Study Guide Workbook, p. 20
Prerequisite Skills Workbook, pp. 21–26
Science and Mathematics Lab Manual, pp. 39–42

📺 Transparencies

5-Minute Check Transparency 3-5
Answer Key Transparencies

💿 Technology

Interactive Chalkboard
Pre-AlgePASS: Tutorial Plus, Lessons 5 and 6

Example 1 Solve Two-Step Equations

a. Solve $5x - 2 = 13$. Check your solution.

$5x - 2 = 13$	Write the equation.
$5x - 2 + 2 = 13 + 2$	Undo subtraction. Add to each side.
$5x = 15$	Simplify.
$\dfrac{5x}{5} = \dfrac{15}{5}$	Undo multiplication. Divide each side by 5.
$x = 3$	Simplify.

CHECK	$5x - 2 = 13$	Write the equation.
	$5(3) - 2 \stackrel{?}{=} 13$	Check to see whether this statement is true.
	$13 = 13 \checkmark$	The statement is true.

The solution is 3.

b. Solve $4 = \dfrac{n}{6} + 11$.

$4 = \dfrac{n}{6} + 11$	Write the equation.
$4 - 11 = \dfrac{n}{6} + 11 - 11$	Undo addition. Subtract 11 from each side.
$-7 = \dfrac{n}{6}$	Simplify.
$6(-7) = 6\left(\dfrac{n}{6}\right)$	Undo division. Multiply each side by 6.
$-42 = n$	Simplify.

The solution is -42. Check your solution.

✓ **Concept Check** Explain how inverse operations can be used to solve a two-step equation. **You undo each operation in reverse order.**

Many real-world situations can be modeled with two-step equations.

Example 2 Use an Equation to Solve a Problem

SALES Mandy bought a DVD player. The sales clerk says that if she pays $80 now, her monthly payments will be $32. The total cost will be $400. Solve $80 + 32x = 400$ to find how many months she will make payments.

$80 + 32x = 400$	Write the equation.
$80 - 80 + 32x = 400 - 80$	Subtract 80 from each side.
$32x = 320$	Simplify.
$\dfrac{32x}{32} = \dfrac{320}{32}$	Divide each side by 32.
$x = 10$	Simplify.

The solution is 10.

Therefore, Mandy will make payments for 10 months.

 www.pre-alg.com/extra_examples

Lesson 3-5 Solving Two-Step Equations **121**

SOLVE TWO-STEP EQUATIONS

In-Class Examples Power Point®

Teaching Tip Use students to model the opening activity equation in front of the classroom. Two students should stand together holding signs labeled with an X. One other student should stand to the left of a chair, representing the equals sign, and nine students should stand to the right of the chair. Then have them act out solving the equation.

Teaching Tip Encourage students to use the acronym SADMP, which stands for Simple As Doing Math Problems and indicates that subtraction and addition are undone first, then division and multiplication, and finally operations within parentheses when solving multi-step equations.

1 **a.** Solve $3x - 4 = 17$. Check your solution. **7**

b. Solve $3 = \dfrac{n}{5} + 8$. **−25**

2 **MEASUREMENT** The formula $F = 1.8C + 32$ can be used to convert Fahrenheit degrees to Celsius degrees. Solve the equation to find the equivalent Celsius temperature for 59°F. **15°C**

Teacher to Teacher

Jack Price Author, Pomona, CA

"It often helps to show how an expression in an equation was 'built' graphically, so you can show how to 'unbuild' it. To solve an equation like $2x + 1 = 13$, you must undo the + 1 first because it is the last thing you built in forming the expression."

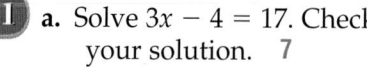

Example: $2x + 1 = 13$

x	→ x
x + x	→ $2x$
x + x + 1	→ $2x + 1$

3 Solve $5 - x = 7$. -2

4 Solve $b - 3b + 8 = 18$. -5

 Skills Check

Solve Two-Step Equations
Solve each equation. Check your
solution.

a. $3y + 4 = 13$ **3**

b. $20 - z = 11$ **9**

c. $3n + n - 4 = 12$ **4**

3 Practice/Apply

Study Notebook

Have students—

• add the definition/example of
the vocabulary term to their
Vocabulary Builder worksheets for
Chapter 3.

• draw models of the equations they
write for Exercise 2.

• include any other item(s) that
they find helpful in mastering the
skills in this lesson.

About the Exercises . . .
Odd/Even Assignments
Exercises 13–48 are structured
so that students practice the
same concepts whether they
are assigned odd or even
problems.

Assignment Guide
Basic: 13–49 odd, 50–74

Average: 13–49 odd, 50–74

Advanced: 14–48 even, 50–69
(Optional: 70–74)

Some two-step equations have terms with negative coefficients.

Example 3 *Equations with Negative Coefficients*

Solve $4 - x = 10$.

$4 - x = 10$	Write the equation.
$4 - 1x = 10$	Identity Property; $x = 1x$
$4 + (-1x) = 10$	Definition of subtraction
$-4 + 4 + (-1x) = -4 + 10$	Add -4 to each side.
$-1x = 6$	Simplify.
$\dfrac{-1x}{-1} = \dfrac{6}{-1}$	Divide each side by -1.
$x = -6$	Simplify.

The solution is -6. Check your solution.

TEACHING TIP
You may want to have
students write the equa-
tion as $(-1x) + 4 = 10$
before adding -4 to each
side.

Sometimes it is necessary to combine like terms before solving.

Example 4 *Combine Like Terms Before Solving*

Solve $m - 5m + 3 = 47$.

$m - 5m + 3 = 47$	Write the equation.
$1m - 5m + 3 = 47$	Identity Property; $m = 1m$
$-4m + 3 = 47$	Combine like terms, $1m$ and $-5m$.
$-4m + 3 - 3 = 47 - 3$	Subtract 3 from each side.
$-4m = 44$	Simplify.
$\dfrac{-4m}{-4} = \dfrac{44}{-4}$	Divide each side by -4.
$m = -11$	Simplify.

The solution is -11. Check your solution.

Study Tip

Mental Computation
You use the Distributive
Property to simplify
$1m - 5m$.
$1m - 5m = (1 - 5)m$
$= -4m$
You can also simplify the
expression mentally.

Check for Understanding

Concept Check

1. You undo the
operations in reverse
order.

1. **Explain** how you can work backward to solve a two-step equation.

2. **OPEN ENDED** Write a two-step equation that could be solved by using
the Addition and Multiplication Properties of Equality.
Sample answer: $\dfrac{x}{2} - 3 = 5$

Guided Practice

GUIDED PRACTICE KEY	
Exercises	Examples
3–8	1
9–11	2, 3
12	4

ALGEBRA Solve each equation. Check your solution.

3. $2x - 7 = 9$ **8**

4. $3t + 5 = 2$ -1

5. $-16 = 6a - 4$ -2

6. $\dfrac{y}{3} + 2 = 10$ **24**

7. $1 + \dfrac{k}{4} = -9$ -40

8. $8 = \dfrac{n}{-7} - 5$ -91

9. $3 - c = 7$ -4

10. $2a - 8a = 24$ -4

11. $8y - 9y + 6 = -4$ **10**

Application

12. **MEDICINE** For Jillian's cough, her doctor says that she should take eight
tablets the first day and then four tablets each day until her prescription
runs out. There are 36 tablets. Solve $8 + 4d = 36$ to find the number of
days she will take four tablets. **7 days**

Homework Help

For Exercises	See Examples
13–34	1
35–38	3
39–46	4
47–49	2

Extra Practice
See page 729.

ALGEBRA Solve each equation. Check your solution.

13. $3x + 1 = 7$ **2**

14. $5x - 4 = 11$ **3**

15. $4h + 6 = 22$ **4**

16. $8n + 3 = -5$ **-1**

17. $37 = 4d + 5$ **8**

18. $9 = 15 + 2p$ **-3**

19. $2n - 5 = 21$ **13**

20. $3j - 9 = 12$ **7**

21. $-1 = 2r - 7$ **3**

22. $12 = 5k - 8$ **4**

23. $10 = 6 + \frac{y}{7}$ **28**

24. $14 = 6 + \frac{n}{5}$ **40**

25. $3 + \frac{t}{2} = 35$ **64**

26. $13 + \frac{p}{3} = -4$ **-51**

27. $\frac{k}{5} - 10 = 3$ **65**

28. $\frac{w}{8} - 4 = -7$ **-24**

29. $8 = \frac{c}{-3} + 15$ **21**

30. $\frac{b}{-4} + 8 = -42$ **200**

ALGEBRA Find each number.

31. Five more than twice a number is 27. Solve $2n + 5 = 27$. **11**

32. Three less than four times a number is -7. Solve $4n - 3 = -7$. **-1**

33. Ten less than the quotient of a number and 2 is 5. Solve $\frac{n}{2} - 10 = 5$. **30**

34. Six more than the quotient of a number and 6 is -3. Solve $\frac{n}{6} + 6 = -3$. **-54**

ALGEBRA Solve each equation. Check your solution.

35. $8 - t = -25$ **33**

36. $3 - y = 13$ **-10**

37. $-5 - b = 8$ **-13**

38. $10 = -9 - x$ **-19**

39. $2w - 4w = -10$ **5**

40. $3x - 5x = 22$ **-11**

41. $x + 4x + 6 = 31$ **5**

42. $5r + 3r - 6 = 10$ **2**

43. $1 - 3y + y = 5$ **-2**

44. $16 = w - 2w + 9$ **-7**

45. $23 = 4t - 7 - t$ **10**

46. $-4 = -a + 8 - 2a$ **4**

47. POOLS There were 640 gallons of water in a 1600-gallon pool. Water is being pumped into the pool at a rate of 320 gallons per hour. Solve $1600 = 320t + 640$ to find how many hours it will take to fill the pool. **3 h**

48. PHONE CALLING CARDS A telephone calling card allows for 25¢ per minute plus a one-time service charge of 75¢. If the total cost of the card is $5, solve $25m + 75 = 500$ to find the number of minutes you can use the card. **17 min**

49. BUSINESS Twelve-year old Aaron O'Leary of Columbus, Ohio, bought old bikes at an auction for $350. He fixed them and sold them for $50 each. He made a $6200 profit. Solve $6200 = 50b - 350$ to determine how many bikes he sold. **131 bikes**

50. WRITING IN MATH Answer the question that was posed at the beginning of the lesson. **See pp. 143A–143B.**

How can algebra tiles show the properties of equality?

Include the following in your answer:
• a drawing that shows how to solve $2x + 3 = 7$ using algebra tiles, and
• a list of the properties of equality that you used to solve $2x + 3 = 7$.

Open-Ended Assessment

Modeling Have students use algebra tiles and an equation mat to solve the following equations.

1. $2x + 6 = 14$ **4**
2. $3x - 5 = -2$ **1**
3. $9 = -4x - 3$ **−3**

*Getting Ready
for Lesson 3-6*

PREREQUISITE SKILL Lesson 3-6 presents writing two-step equations. Exercises 70–74 should be used to determine your students' familiarity with writing algebraic expressions from verbal expressions.

---

51. **CRITICAL THINKING** Write a two-step equation with a variable using the numbers 2, 5, and 8, in which the solution is 2. **$5x - 2 = 8$**

*Standardized
Test Practice*
Ⓐ Ⓑ Ⓒ Ⓓ

52. **GRID IN** The charge to park at an art fair is a flat rate plus a per hour fee. The graph shows the charge for parking for up to 4 hours. If x represents the number of hours and y represents the total charge, what is the charge for parking for 7 hours? **$4.50**

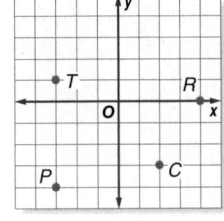

53. A local health club charges an initial fee of $45 for the first month and then a $32 membership fee each month after the first. The table shows the cost to join the health club for up to 6 months.

Months	1	2	3	4	5	6
Cost (dollars)	45	77	109	141	173	205

What is the cost to join the health club for 10 months? **C**

Ⓐ $215 Ⓑ $320 Ⓒ $333 Ⓓ $450

Maintain Your Skills

Mixed Review

ALGEBRA Solve each equation. Check your solution. *(Lessons 3-3 and 3-4)*

54. $5y = 60$ **12**
55. $14 = -2n$ **−7**
56. $\frac{x}{3} = -9$ **−27**
57. $x - 4 = -6$ **−2**
58. $-13 = y + 5$ **−18**
59. $18 = 20 + x$ **−2**

ALGEBRA Simplify each expression. *(Lesson 3-1)*

60. $4(x + 1)$ **$4x + 4$**
61. $-5(y + 3)$ **$-5y - 15$**
62. $3(k - 10)$ **$3k - 30$**
63. $-9(y - 4)$ **$-9y + 36$**
64. $7(a - 2)$ **$7a - 14$**
65. $-8(r - 5)$ **$-8r + 40$**

Name the ordered pair for each point graphed on the coordinate plane at the right. *(Lesson 2-6)*

66. T **$(-3, 1)$**
67. C **$(2, -3)$**
68. R **$(4, 0)$**
69. P **$(-3, -4)$**

*Getting Ready for
the Next Lesson*

PREREQUISITE SKILL Write an algebraic expression for each verbal expression. *(To review algebraic expressions, see Lesson 1-3.)*

70. two times a number less six **$2x - 6$**
71. the quotient of a number and 15 **$x \div 15$**
72. the difference between twice a number and 8 **$2x - 8$**
73. twice a number increased by 10 **$2x + 10$**
74. the sum of $2x$, $7x$, and 4 **$9x + 4$**

DAILY
INTERVENTION   **Differentiated Instruction**

• **Auditory/Musical** Have groups of students each write a two-step equation and then perform solving it for the class. For example, have them sing or shout in unison a catchy phrase for each step in the solution, such as "To each side, add a 2," and "Now it's time to simplify!"

Reading Mathematics

Translating Verbal Problems into Equations

An important skill in algebra is translating verbal problems into equations. To do this accurately, analyze the statements until you completely understand the relationships among the given information. Look for key words and phrases.

> Jennifer is <u>6 years older than</u> Akira. The <u>sum of their ages is 20</u>.

You can explore a problem situation by asking and answering questions.

Questions	Answers
a. Who is older?	**a.** Jennifer
b. How many years older?	**b.** 6 years
c. If Akira is x years old, how old is Jennifer?	**c.** $x + 6$
d. What expression represents the phrase *the sum of their ages*?	**d.** $x + (x + 6)$
e. What equation represents the sentence *the sum of their ages is 20*?	**e.** $x + (x + 6) = 20$

Reading to Learn

For each verbal problem, answer the related questions.

1. Lucas is 5 inches taller than Tamika, and the sum of their heights is 137 inches.
   a. Who is taller? **Lucas**
   b. How many inches taller? **5 inches**
   c. If x represents Tamika's height, how tall is Lucas? **$x + 5$**
   d. What expression represents *the sum of their heights*? **$x + (x + 5)$ or $2x + 5$**
   e. What equation represents the sentence *the sum of their heights is 137*? **$2x + 5 = 137$**

2. There are five times as many students as teachers on the field trip, and the sum of students and teachers is 132.
   a. Are there more students or teachers? **students**
   b. How many times more? **5 times**
   c. If x represents the number of teachers, how many students are there? **$5x$**
   d. What expression represents *the sum of students and teachers*? **$x + 5x$ or $6x$**
   e. What equation represents *the sum of students and teachers is 132*? **$6x = 132$**

Reading Mathematics   Translating Verbal Problems into Equations   **125**

Getting Started

Before teaching this lesson, ask students what languages they speak or have studied other than English. Have them state some words and their equivalent words or phrases in English. Point out that translating from one spoken language to another is similar to translating verbal problems into equations.

Teach

Translating Verbal Problems into Equations
- After reading the Questions and Answers chart, ask students to explain how to find each answer.
- After completing the lesson, ask students to explain how to write an equation for the boxed statement using x to represent Jennifer's age.

Assess

Study Notebook

Ask students to summarize what they have learned about translating verbal problems into equations. Have them include an example.

ELL English Language Learners may benefit from writing key concepts from this activity in their Study Notebooks in their native language and then in English.

3-6 Writing Two-Step Equations

1 Focus

5-Minute Check Transparency 3-6 Use as a quiz or review of Lesson 3-5.

Mathematical Background notes are available for this lesson on page 96D.

How are equations used to solve real-world problems?

The opening activity questions are repeated on page 135 of the *Chapter 3 Resource Masters*.

Reading to Learn Mathematics, p. 135 — ELL

Pre-Activity How are equations used to solve real-world problems?
Do the activity at the top of page 126 in your textbook. Write your answers below.

a. Let *n* represent the number of minutes. Write an expression that represents the cost when your call lasts *n* minutes $4n + 99$

b. Suppose your monthly cost was 299¢. Write and solve an equation to find the number of minutes you used the calling card. $4n + 99 = 299$

c. Why is your equation considered to be a two-step equation?
It has two operations, multiplication and addition.

Reading the Lesson

Refer to Example 3 on page 127. Read the Explore and Plan steps. Then complete the following.

1. Suppose you have already saved $75 and plan to save $5 a week.
   a. Complete the table below.

Week	Amount Saved ($)
0	$5(0) + 75 = $ 75
1	$5(1) + 75 = $ 80
2	$5(2) + 75 = $ 85
3	$5(3) + 75 = $ 90
n	$5(n) + 75 = 5n + 75$

   b. Write an equation that represents how many weeks it will take you to save $100. $5n + 75 = 100$

2. Suppose you have already saved $25 and plan to save $10 each week.
   a. Complete the table below.

Week	Amount Saved ($)
0	$10(0) + 25 = 25$
1	$10(1) + 25 = 35$
2	$10(2) + 25 = 45$
3	$10(3) + 25 = 55$
n	$10(n) + 25 = 10n + 25$

   b. Write an equation that represents how many weeks it will take you to save $175. $10n + 25 = 175$

3-6 Writing Two-Step Equations

What You'll Learn

- Write verbal sentences as two-step equations.
- Solve verbal problems by writing and solving two-step equations.

How are equations used to solve real-world problems?

A phone company advertises that you can call anywhere in the United States for 4¢ per minute plus a monthly fee of 99¢ with their calling card. The table shows how to find your total monthly cost.

Time (minutes)	Monthly Cost (cents)
0	$4(0) + 99 = 99$
5	$4(5) + 99 = 119$
10	$4(10) + 99 = 139$
15	$4(15) + 99 = 159$
20	$4(20) + 99 = 179$

a. $4n + 99$

a. Let *n* represent the number of minutes. Write an expression that represents the cost when your call lasts *n* minutes.

TEACHING TIP
Point out that the monthly cost must be expressed in cents. A monthly cost of $2.99 is 299¢.

b. Suppose your monthly cost was 299¢. Write and solve an equation to find the number of minutes you used the calling card. $4n + 99 = 299$; 50

c. Why is your equation considered to be a two-step equation?

c. It has two operations, multiplication and addition.

WRITE TWO-STEP EQUATIONS   In Chapter 1, you learned how to write verbal phrases as expressions.

Phrase   the sum of 4 times some number and 99

Expression $4n$ $+ 99$

An equation is a statement that two expressions are equal. The expressions are joined with an equals sign. Look for the words *is*, *equals*, or *is equal to* when you translate sentences into equations.

Sentence   The sum of 4 times some number and 99 is 299.

Equation $4n + 99$ $= 299$

Study Tip

Expression
An expression is any combination of numbers and operations.

Example 1 Translate Sentences into Equations

Translate each sentence into an equation.

Sentence	Equation
a. Six more than twice a number is −20.	$2n + 6 = -20$
b. Eighteen is 6 less than four times a number.	$18 = 4n - 6$
c. The quotient of a number and 5, increased by 8, is equal to 14.	$\frac{n}{5} + 8 = 14$

Concept Check: An expression is any combination of numbers and operations; an equation is a statement that two expressions are equal.

✓ **Concept Check**   What is the difference between an expression and an equation?

126   Chapter 3   Equations

Resource Manager

 Workbooks and Reproducible Masters

Chapter 3 Resource Masters
- Study Guide and Intervention, p. 132
- Skills Practice, p. 133
- Practice, p. 134
- Reading to Learn Mathematics, p. 135
- Enrichment, p. 136
- Assessment, p. 158

Parent and Student Study Guide Workbook, p. 21

Transparencies
5-Minute Check Transparency 3-6
Answer Key Transparencies

 Technology

Interactive Chalkboard

Example **2** **Translate and Solve an Equation**

Seven more than three times a number is 31. Find the number.

Words	Seven more than three times a number is 31.

Variables	Let n = the number.

Equation	$3n + 7 = 31$	Write the equation.
	$3n + 7 - 7 = 31 - 7$	Subtract 7 from each side.
	$3n = 24$	Simplify.
	$n = 8$	Mentally divide each side by 3.

Therefore, the number is 8.

TWO-STEP VERBAL PROBLEMS   There are many real-world situations in which you start with a given amount and then increase it at a certain rate. These situations can be represented by two-step equations.

Example **3** **Write and Solve a Two-Step Equation**

• **SCOOTERS**   **Suppose you are saving money to buy a scooter that costs $100. You have already saved $60 and plan to save $5 each week. How many weeks will you need to save?**

Explore	You have already saved $60. You plan to save $5 each week until you have $100.

Plan	Organize the data for the first few weeks in a table. Notice the pattern.

Week	Amount
0	$5(0) + 60 = 60$
1	$5(1) + 60 = 65$
2	$5(2) + 60 = 70$
3	$5(3) + 60 = 75$

Write an equation to represent the situation.

Let x = the number of weeks.

$5 each week for x weeks	plus	amount already saved	equals	$100.
$5x$	$+$	60	$=$	100

Solve	$5x + 60 = 100$	Write the equation.
	$5x + 60 - 60 = 100 - 60$	Subtract 60 from each side.
	$5x = 40$	Simplify.
	$x = 8$	Mentally divide each side by 5.

You need to save $5 each week for 8 weeks.

Examine	If you save $5 each week for 8 weeks, you'll have an additional $40. The answer appears to be reasonable.

www.pre-alg.com/extra_examples

Lesson 3-6 Writing Two-Step Equations **127**

4 **COMMUNITY SERVICE** In a canned food drive, Sam collected 12 more cans than Louise. Together, they collected 128 cans. How many cans did Sam collect? **70**

Study Notebook

Have students—

• list several words or phrases in verbal problems that can be translated into each of the four basic operations.

• write about the process they used to translate verbal problems into equations.

• include any other item(s) that they find helpful in mastering the skills in this lesson.

About the Exercises . . .
Organization by Objective
• Write Two-Step Equations: 8–19
• Two-Step Verbal Problems: 20–23

Odd/Even Assignments
Exercises 8–23 are structured so that students practice the same concepts whether they are assigned odd or even problems.

Assignment Guide
Basic: 9–15 odd, 21, 23, 26–42
Average: 9–25 odd, 26–42
Advanced: 8–24 even, 26–36 (Optional: 37–42)
All: Quiz 2 (1–5)

Study Tip

Alternative Method
Let x = number of U.S. medals. Then $x - 9$ = number of Russian medals.
$x + (x - 9) = 185$
$x = 97$
In this case, x is the number of U.S. medals, 97.

Example 4 *Write and Solve a Two-Step Equation*

OLYMPICS In the 2000 Summer Olympics, the United States won 9 more medals than Russia. Together they won 185 medals. How many medals did the United States win?

Words   Together they won 185 medals.

Variables   Let x = number of medals won by Russia.
Then $x + 9$ = number of medals won by United States.

Equation

$x + (x + 9) = 185$	Write the equation.
$(x + x) + 9 = 185$	Associative Property
$2x + 9 = 185$	Combine like terms.
$2x + 9 - 9 = 185 - 9$	Subtract 9 from each side.
$2x = 176$	Simplify.
$\dfrac{2x}{2} = \dfrac{176}{2}$	Divide each side by 2.
$x = 88$	Simplify.

Since x represents the number of medals won by Russia, Russia won 88 medals. The United States won $88 + 9$ or 97 medals.

Check for Understanding

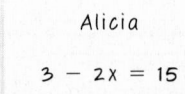

Concept Check

1. **List** three words or phrases in a verbal problem that can be translated into an equals sign in an equation. **is, equals, is equal to**

2. **OPEN ENDED** Write a verbal sentence involving an unknown number and two operations. **Sample answer: Three more than twice a number is 15.**

3. **FIND THE ERROR** Alicia and Ben are translating the following sentence into an equation: *Three less than two times a number is 15.*

GUIDED PRACTICE KEY	
Exercises	Examples
4, 5	1
6	2
7	3

Alicia	Ben
$3 - 2x = 15$	$2x - 3 = 15$

Who is correct? Explain your reasoning. **Ben;** *Three less than* **means that three is subtracted** *from* **a number.**

Guided Practice

Translate each sentence into an equation. Then find each number.

4. Three more than four times a number is 23. **$4n + 3 = 23$, 5**

5. Four less than twice a number is –2. **$2n - 4 = -2$, 1**

Applications

Solve each problem by writing and solving an equation.

6. **METEOROLOGY** Suppose the current temperature is 17°F. It is expected to rise 3°F each hour for the next several hours. In how many hours will the temperature be 32°F? **$17 + 3x = 32$, 5 h**

7. **AGES** Lawana is five years older than her brother Cole. The sum of their ages is 37. How old is Lawana? **$2x + 5 = 37$, 21 yr**

DAILY
INTERVENTION **FIND THE ERROR**
To choose whether Alicia or Ben is correct, translate each mathematical equation back into a verbal sentence without looking at the original sentence. Then compare sentences.

Practice and Apply

Homework Help

For Exercises	See Examples
8–19	1, 2
20, 21	3
22–24	4

Extra Practice
See page 730.

Translate each sentence into an equation. Then find each number.

8. Seven more than twice a number is 17. $2n + 7 = 17, 5$

9. Twenty more than three times a number is -4. $3n + 20 = -4, -8$

10. Four less than three times a number is 20. $3n - 4 = 20, 8$

11. Eight less than ten times a number is 82. $10n - 8 = 82, 9$

12. Ten more than the quotient of a number and -2 is three. $\frac{n}{-2} + 10 = 3, 14$

13. The quotient of a number and -4, less 8, is -42. $\frac{n}{-4} - 8 = -42, 136$

14. The difference between twice a number and 9 is 17. $2n - 9 = 17, 13$

15. The difference between three times a number and 8 is -2. $3n - 8 = -2, 2$

★ 16. If 5 is decreased by 3 times a number, the result is -4. $5 - 3n = -4, 3$

★ 17. If 17 is decreased by twice a number, the result is 5. $17 - 2n = 5, 6$

★ 18. Three times a number plus twice the number plus 1 is -4.

★ 19. Four times a number plus five more than three times the number is 47.
$4n + 3n + 5 = 47, 6$ 18. $3n + 2n + 1 = -4, -1$

Solve each problem by writing and solving an equation.

20. **WILDLIFE** Your friend bought 3 bags of wild bird seed and an $18 bird feeder. Each bag of birdseed costs the same amount. If your friend spent $45, find the cost of one bag of birdseed. $3x + 18 = 45, \$9$

21. **METEOROLOGY** The temperature is 8°F. It is expected to fall 5° each hour for the next several hours. In how many hours will the temperature be -7°F? $8 - 5x = -7, 3$ h

22. **FOOD SERVICE** You and your friend spent a total of $15 for lunch. Your friend's lunch cost $3 more than yours did. How much did you spend for lunch? $2x + 3 = 15, \$6$

23. **POPULATION** By 2020, California is expected to have 2 million more senior citizens than Florida, and the sum of the number of senior citizens in the two states is expected to be 12 million. Find the expected senior citizen population of Florida in 2020. $2x + 2 = 12.$ 5 million people

★ 24. **NATIVE AMERICANS** North Carolina's Native-American population is 22,000 greater than New York's. New York's Native-American population is 187,000 less than Oklahoma's. If the total population of all three is 437,000, find each state's Native-American population. NC: 98,000; NY: 76,000; OK: 263,000

Native-American Populations
(thousands)

California	309
Arizona	256
New Mexico	163
Washington	103
Alaska	100
Texas	96
Michigan	60
Oklahoma	?
New York	?
North Carolina	?

Source: U.S. Census Bureau

www.pre-alg.com/self_check_quiz

Career Choices

Meteorologist
Meteorologists are best known for forecasting the weather. However, they also work in the fields of air pollution, agriculture, and defense.

Online Research
For information about a career as a meteorologist, visit:
www.pre-alg.com/careers

Study Guide and Intervention, p. 132

You can use two-step equations to represent situations in which you start with a given amount and then increase it at a certain rate.

Example **PRINTING:** A laser printer prints 9 pages per minute. Liza refilled the paper tray after it had printed 92 pages. In how many more minutes will there be a total of 245 pages printed?

EXPLORE You know the number of pages printed and the total number of pages to be printed. You need to find the number of minutes required to print the remaining pages.

PLAN Let m = the number of minutes. Write and solve an equation. The remaining pages to print is $9m$.
remaining pages + pages printed = total pages
$9m$ + 92 = 245

SOLVE
$9m + 92 = 245$
$9m + 92 - 92 = 245 - 92$
$9m = 153$
$9m = \frac{153}{9}$
$m = 17$

EXAMINE The remaining 153 pages will print in 17 minutes. Since $245 - 153 = 92$, the answer is correct.

Exercises

Solve each problem by writing and solving an equation.

1. **METEOROLOGY** During one day in 1918, the temperature in Granville, North Dakota, began at $-33°$ and rose for 12 hours. The high temperature was about 51°. About how many degrees per hour did the temperature rise? $-33 + 12d = 51$; about 7 degrees

2. **SAVINGS** John has $825 in his savings account. He has decided to deposit $65 per month until he has a total of $1800. In how many months will this occur? $65m + 825 = 1800$; 15 months

3. **SKYDIVING** A skydiver jumps from an airplane at an altitude of 12,000 feet. After 42 seconds, she reaches 4608 feet and opens her parachute. What was her average velocity during her descent? $12,000 - 42f = 4608$; 176 feet per second

4. **FLOODING** The water level of a creek has risen 4 inches above its flood stage. If it continues to rise steadily at 2 inches per hour, how long will it take for the creek to be 12 inches above its flood stage? $4 + 2h = 12$; 4 hours

Skills Practice, p. 133 and Practice, p. 134 (shown)

Translate each sentence into an equation. Then find each number.

1. Eight less than 7 times a number is -29.
$7n - 8 = -29$; -3

2. Twenty more than twice a number is 52.
$20 + 2n = 52$; 16

3. The difference between three times a number and 11 is 10.
$3n - 11 = 10$; 7

4. One more than the difference between 18 and seven times a number is -9.
$1 + 18 - 7n = -9$; 4

5. Eight times a number plus 6 less than twice the number is 34.
$8n + 2n - 6 = 34$; 4

6. 26 more than the product of a number and 17 is -42.
$17n + 26 = -42$; -4

7. Twelve less than the quotient of a number and 8 is -1.
$\frac{n}{8} - 12 = -1$; 88

Solve each problem by writing and solving an equation.

8. **ANIMAL TRAINING** Last summer, Gary trained 32 more dogs than Zina. Together they trained 126 dogs. How many dogs did Gary train? $g + (g - 32) = 126$; 79 dogs

9. **SALES** Julius sold five times as many computers as Sam sold last year. In total, they sold 78 computers. How many computers did Julius sell? $5s + s = 78$; 65 computers

10. **TRACK** In one season, Ana ran 18 races. This was four fewer races than twice the number of races Kelly ran. How many races did Kelly run? $18 = 2r - 4$; 11 races

11. **BASEBALL** André hit four more home runs than twice the number of home runs Larry hit. Together they hit 10 home runs. How many home runs did André hit? $h + 2h + 4 = 10$; 8 home runs

Enrichment, p. 136

Systems of Equations

A **system of equations** is a set of equations with the same variables. The equations shown below are an example of one kind of system of equations.

$y = x + 2$
$3x - 5 = 16$

The solution of this system must be a pair of numbers, x and y, that make both equations true.

To solve this type of system, first solve the equation that contains only one variable. Then substitute that answer into the second equation and solve for the remaining variable.

Example Solve each system of equations.

a. $y = x + 2$
$3x - 5 = 16$

Solve $3x - 5 = 16$ first.
$3x - 5 = 16$
$3x - 5 + 5 = 16 + 5$
$3x = 21$
$\frac{3x}{3} = \frac{21}{3}$
$x = 7$

Substitute 7 for x in the other equation.
$y = x + 2$
$y = 7 + 2$ or 9
The solution is $x = 7$ and $y = 9$.

b. $4d - 1 = 19$
$c = d - 3$

Solve $4d - 1 = 19$ first.
$4d - 1 = 19$
$4d - 1 + 1 = 19 + 1$
$4d = 20$
$\frac{4d}{4} = \frac{20}{4}$
$d = 5$

Substitute 5 for d in the other equation.
$c = d - 3$
$c = 5 - 3$ or 2
The solution is $c = 2$ and $d = 5$.

Solve each system of equations.

1. $40 - 2t = 10$
$3t = s + 35$
$t = 15, s = 10$

2. $4a + 2b = 22$
$25 = 11a - 8$
$a = 3, b = 5$

3. $82.5 = 1.5s$
$d = 3s + 35$
$s = 55, d = 200$

4. $\frac{m}{5} + 1.5 = 2$
$7m + n = 17.5$
$m = 2.5, n = 0$

5. $6x + \frac{y}{2} = 43$
$22 + 3x = 43$
$x = 7, y = 2$

6. $\frac{c}{5} + p = 4$
$20 = 4p - 3$
$p = 5.75, c = -8.75$

D A I L Y

INTERVENTION **Differentiated Instruction** **ELL**

• **Verbal/Linguistic** Have students make a chart of mathematical expressions and the different phrases they can be translated into. For example, the phrase *is increased by* indicates addition and the phrase *separated into equal parts* indicates division.

Open-Ended Assessment

Writing Have students write a verbal problem that can be solved by the equation $2x - 5 = 19$. **Sample answer: Olga scored five less than twice as many points as Tricia scored in the basketball game. If Tricia scored 19 points, how many did Olga score?**

Intervention
Make sure that students get into the habit of stating what the variable represents. It's the first thing to check if they make an error.

Getting Ready for Lesson 3-7

PREREQUISITE SKILL Lesson 3-7 presents solving problems by using formulas. Exercises 37–42 should be used to determine your students' familiarity with solving equations.

Assessment Options

Practice Quiz 2 The quiz provides students with a brief review of the concepts and skills in Lessons 3-3 through 3-6. Lesson numbers are given to the right of exercises or instruction lines so students can review concepts not yet mastered.

Quiz (Lessons 3-5 and 3-6) is available on p. 158 of the *Chapter 3 Resource Masters*.

---

25. See margin.

★ 25. **WRITE A PROBLEM** The table shows the expected population age 85 or older for certain states in 2020. Use the data to write a problem that can be solved by using a two-step equation.

Population (age 85 or older)	
State	Number (thousands)
CA	809
FL	735
TX	428
NY	418

26. **CRITICAL THINKING** If you begin with an even integer and count by two, you are counting *consecutive even integers*. Write and solve an equation to find two consecutive even integers whose sum is 50. **$2x + 2 = 50$, 24 and 26**

27. **WRITING IN MATH** Answer the question that was posed at the beginning of the lesson. **See margin.**

How are equations used to solve real-world problems?

Include the following in your answer:
- an example that starts with a given amount and increases, and
- an example that involves the sum of two quantities.

Standardized Test Practice
Ⓐ Ⓑ Ⓒ Ⓓ

28. Which verbal expression represents the phrase *three less than five times a number?* **C**
- Ⓐ $3 - 5n$
- Ⓑ $n - 3$
- Ⓒ $5n - 3$
- Ⓓ $5 + n - 3$

29. The Bank of America building in San Francisco is 74 feet shorter than the Transamerica Pyramid. If their combined height is 1632 feet, how tall is the Transamerica Pyramid? **D**
- Ⓐ 41 ft
- Ⓑ 779 ft
- Ⓒ 781 ft
- Ⓓ 853 ft

Maintain Your Skills

Mixed Review **ALGEBRA** Solve each equation. *(Lessons 3-3, 3-4, and 3-5)*

30. $6 - 2x = 10$ **−2**   31. $-4x = -16$ **4**   32. $y - 7 = -3$ **4**

Evaluate each expression if $x = -12$, $y = 4$, and $z = -1$. *(Lesson 2-1)*

33. $|x| - 7$ **5**   34. $|x| + |y|$ **16**   35. $|z| - |x|$ **−11**

36. Name the property shown by $(2 + 6) + 9 = 2 + (6 + 9)$. *(Lesson 1-4)* **Associative Property of Addition**

Getting Ready for the Next Lesson **PREREQUISITE SKILL** Solve each equation. Check your solution.
*(To review **solving equations**, see Lesson 3-4.)*

37. $2x = -8$ **−4**   38. $24 = 6y$ **4**   39. $5w = -25$ **−5**

40. $15s = 75$ **5**   41. $108 = 18x$ **6**   42. $25z = 175$ **7**

Practice Quiz 2   Lessons 3-3 through 3-6

ALGEBRA Solve each equation. *(Lessons 3-3, 3-4, and 3-5)*

1. $4h = -52$ **−13**   2. $\frac{x}{-3} = 4$ **−12**   3. $y - 5 = -23$ **−18**   4. $2v - 11 = -5$ **3**

5. **ALGEBRA** Twenty more than three times a number is 32. Write and solve an equation to find the number. *(Lesson 3-6)* **$3n + 20 = 32$, 4**

Answers

25. Sample answer: By 2020, Texas is expected to have 10,000 more people age 85 or older than New York will have. Together, they are expected to have 846,000 people age 85 or older. Find the expected number of people age 85 or older in New York by 2020.

27. Sample answer: Two-step equations can be used when you start with a certain amount and increase or decrease at a certain rate. Answers should include the following.
- You've been running 15 minutes each day as part of a fitness program. You plan to increase your time by 5 minutes each week.
 After how many weeks do you plan to run 30 minutes each day? ($5w + 15 = 30$; 3 weeks)
- You are three years older than your sister is. Together the sum of your ages is 21. How old is your sister? ($2x + 3 = 21$; 9 years old)

3-7 Using Formulas

What You'll Learn

- Solve problems by using formulas.
- Solve problems involving the perimeters and areas of rectangles.

Vocabulary
- formula
- perimeter
- area

Why are formulas important in math and science?

The top recorded speed of a mallard duck in level flight is 65 miles per hour. You can make a table to record the distances that a mallard could fly at that rate.

a. Write an expression for the distance traveled by a duck in t hours. **65t**

b. What disadvantage is there in showing the data in a table?

c. Describe an easier way to summarize the relationship between the speed, time, and distance.

Speed (mph)	Time (hr)	Distance (mi)
65	1	65
65	2	130
65	3	195
65	t	?

c. Write an equation that relates speed, time, and distance.

TEACHING TIP
Point out that a formula also shows how one quantity can be computed from other quantities.

FORMULAS A **formula** is an equation that shows a relationship among certain quantities. A formula usually contains two or more variables. One of the most commonly-used formulas shows the relationship between distance, rate (or speed), and time.

Words Distance equals the rate multiplied by the time.

Variables Let d = distance, r = rate, and t = time.

Equation $d = rt$

Example 1 Use the Distance Formula

SCIENCE What is the rate in miles per hour of a dolphin that travels 120 miles in 4 hours?

$d = rt$ Write the formula.

$120 = r \cdot 4$ Replace d with 120 and t with 4.

$\dfrac{120}{4} = \dfrac{r \cdot 4}{4}$ Divide each side by 4.

$30 = r$ Simplify.

The dolphin travels at a rate of 30 miles per hour.

✓ **Concept Check** Name an advantage of using a formula to show a relationship among quantities. A formula is a concise way to describe a relationship among quantities.

Lesson 3-7 Using Formulas **131**

3-7 Lesson Notes

1 Focus

 5-Minute Check Transparency 3-7 Use as a quiz or review of Lesson 3-6.

Mathematical Background notes are available for this lesson on page 96D.

Why are formulas important in math and science?

The opening activity questions are repeated on page 140 of the *Chapter 3 Resource Masters*.

Reading to Learn Mathematics, p. 140   **ELL**

Pre-Activity Why are formulas important in math and science?
Do the activity at the top of page 131 in your textbook. Write your answers below.

a. Write an expression for the distance traveled by a duck in t hours. 65t

b. What disadvantage is there in showing the data in a table? You cannot show all of the possible relationships in a table.

c. Describe an easier way to summarize the relationship between the speed, time, and distance. Write an equation that relates speed, time, and distance.

Reading the Lesson 1–3. See students' work.
Write a definition and give an example of each new vocabulary word.

Vocabulary	Definition	Example
1. formula		
2. perimeter		
3. area		

Helping You Remember

4. The word *perimeter* is composed of the prefix *peri-* and the suffix *-meter*.

a. Find the definitions of *peri-* and *-meter* in a dictionary. Write their definitions. Enclosing or surrounding; means for measuring

b. Find two other words in a dictionary that begin with the prefix *peri-*. Write their definitions. Sample answers: peripheral: of, relating to, or being the outer part of the field of vision; pericardium: the membrane that encloses the heart of vertebrates

c. Explain how your definitions can help you remember how perimeter is used in mathematics. The definitions relate to the outer edge of something, just as perimeter is a measure of the distance around a figure.

Teaching Tip Ask students to list formulas they have used in the past. Ask what each is used for. Discuss the importance of formulas in real-world situations.

Resource Manager

📁 **Workbooks and Reproducible Masters**

Chapter 3 Resource Masters
- Study Guide and Intervention, p. 137
- Skills Practice, p. 138
- Practice, p. 139
- Reading to Learn Mathematics, p. 140
- Enrichment, p. 141
- Assessment, p. 158

Graphing Calculator and Spreadsheet Masters, p. 24
Parent and Student Study Guide Workbook, p. 22
School-to-Career Masters, p. 6

 Transparencies
5-Minute Check Transparency 3-7
Answer Key Transparencies

💿 **Technology**
Interactive Chalkboard

FORMULAS

Teaching Tip In the example below, have students identify which parts of the distance formula correspond to each number in the problem. 135 mi = d; 3 h = t

1 **TRAVEL** If you travel 135 miles in 3 hours, what is your average speed in miles per hour? **45 mph**

PERIMETER AND AREA

2 Find the perimeter of the rectangle.

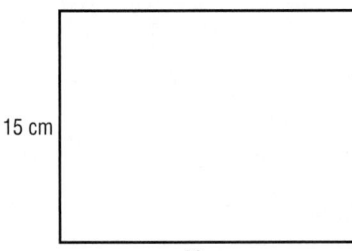

15 cm

20 cm

70 cm

Teaching Tip Have students sketch a rectangle and label what is known on the rectangle. In the example below, two opposing sides each measure 9 feet, and the other two sides have the same length, ℓ. This will help students write the equation $P = 2\ell + 2(9)$.

3 The perimeter of a rectangle is 60 feet. Its width is 9 feet. Find its length. **21 ft**

PERIMETER AND AREA The distance around a geometric figure is called the **perimeter**. One method of finding the perimeter P of a rectangle is to add the measures of the four sides.

> **Key Concept** **Perimeter of a Rectangle**
>
> - **Words** The perimeter of a rectangle is twice the sum of the length and width.
>
> - **Symbols** $P = \ell + \ell + w + w$
> $P = 2\ell + 2w$ or $2(\ell + w)$
>
> - **Model**
> ℓ
> w

Study Tip

Common Misconception
Although the length of a rectangle is usually greater than the width, it does not matter which side you choose to be the length.

Example 2 *Find the Perimeter of a Rectangle*

Find the perimeter of the rectangle.

$P = 2(\ell + w)$ — Write the formula.
$P = 2(11 + 5)$ — Replace ℓ with 11 and w with 5.
$P = 2(16)$ — Add 11 and 5.
$P = 32$ — Simplify.

11 in.
5 in.

The perimeter is 32 inches.

Example 3 *Find a Missing Length*

The perimeter of a rectangle is 28 meters. Its width is 8 meters. Find the length.

$P = 2(\ell + w)$ — Write the formula.
$P = 2\ell + 2w$ — Distributive Property
$28 = 2\ell + 2(8)$ — Replace P with 28 and w with 8.
$28 = 2\ell + 16$ — Simplify.
$28 - 16 = 2\ell + 16 - 16$ — Subtract 16 from each side.
$12 = 2\ell$ — Simplify.
$6 = \ell$ — Mentally divide each side by 2.

The length is 6 meters.

The measure of the surface enclosed by a figure is its **area**.

> **Key Concept** **Area of a Rectangle**
>
> - **Words** The area of a rectangle is the product of the length and width.
> - **Symbols** $A = \ell w$
>
> - **Model**
> ℓ
> w

Example 4 — Find the Area of a Rectangle

Find the area of a rectangle with length 15 meters and width 7 meters.

$A = \ell w$ Write the formula.

$A = 15 \cdot 7$ Replace ℓ with 15 and w with 7.

$A = 105$ Simplify.

The area is 105 square meters.

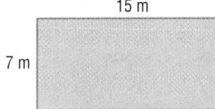
15 m
7 m

Example 5 — Find a Missing Width

The area of a rectangle is 45 square feet. Its length is 9 feet. Find its width.

$A = \ell w$ Write the formula.

$45 = 9w$ Replace A with 45 and ℓ with 9.

$5 = w$ Mentally divide each side by 9.

The width is 5 feet.

✓**Concept Check**   Which is measured in square units, area or perimeter? **area**

Check for Understanding

Concept Check   **1. Write** the formula that shows the relationship among distance, rate, and time. $d = rt$

2. See margin.   **2. Explain** the difference between the perimeter and area of a rectangle.

3. OPEN ENDED   Draw and label a rectangle that has a perimeter of 18 inches. **See margin.**

Guided Practice   **GEOMETRY**   Find the perimeter and area of each rectangle.

GUIDED PRACTICE KEY	
Exercises	Examples
4–6	2, 3
7, 8	3, 5
9	1

4.
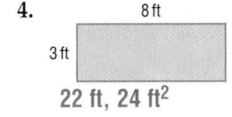
8 ft
3 ft
22 ft, 24 ft²

5.
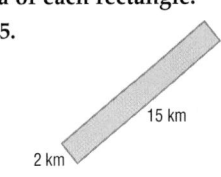
15 km
2 km
34 km, 30 km²

6. a rectangle with length 15 feet and width 6 feet **42 ft, 90 ft²**

GEOMETRY   Find the missing dimension in each rectangle.

7.
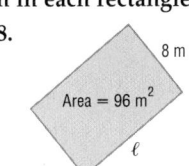
12 in.
w
Perimeter = 32 in.
4 in.

8.
8 m
Area = 96 m²
ℓ
12 m

Application   **9. MILITARY**   How long will it take an Air Force jet fighter to fly 5200 miles at 650 miles per hour? **8 h**

www.pre-alg.com/extra_examples   **Lesson 3-7** Using Formulas   **133**

Answers

2. Perimeter is the measure of the distance around a rectangle; area is the measure of the surface the perimeter encloses.

3. Sample answer:

5 in.
4 in.

Answers (p. 135)

37.

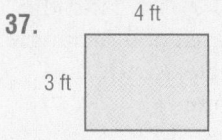

38.

39.

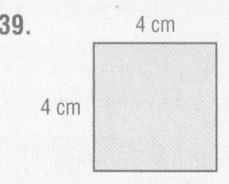

40.

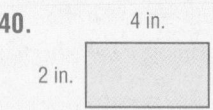

Answer (Differentiated Instruction)

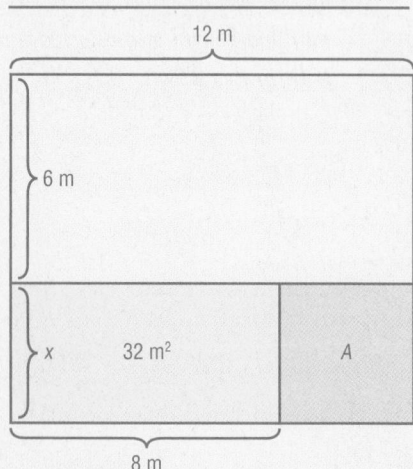

$x = 4$ m, $A = 16$ m^2, $P = 44$ m

★ indicates increased difficulty

Practice and Apply

10. TRAVEL Find the distance traveled by driving at 55 miles per hour for 3 hours. **165 mi**

11. BALLOONING What is the rate, in miles per hour, of a balloon that travels 60 miles in 4 hours? **15 mph**

GEOMETRY Find the perimeter and area of each rectangle.

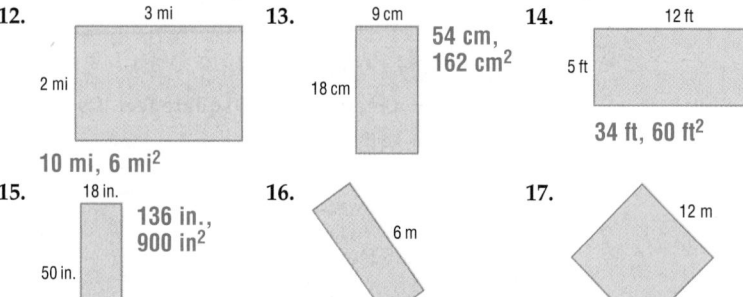

12. 3 mi, 2 mi **10 mi, 6 mi²**

13. 9 cm, 18 cm **54 cm, 162 cm²**

14. 12 ft, 5 ft **34 ft, 60 ft²**

15. 18 in., 50 in. **136 in., 900 in²**

16. 6 m, 17 m **46 m, 102 m²**

17. 12 m, 12 m **17. 48 m, 144 m²**

18. a rectangle that is 38 meters long and 10 meters wide **96 m, 380 m²**

19. a square that is 5 meters on each side **20 m, 25 m²**

GEOMETRY Find the missing dimension in each rectangle.

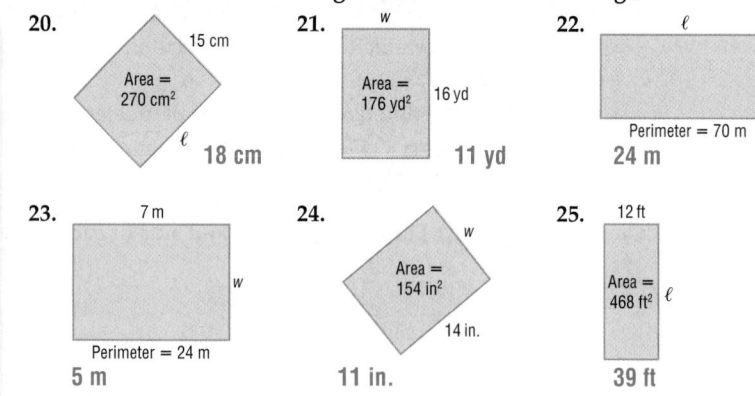

20. Area = 270 cm², 15 cm, ℓ **18 cm**

21. w, Area = 176 yd², 16 yd **11 yd**

22. ℓ, 11 m, Perimeter = 70 m **24 m**

23. 7 m, w, Perimeter = 24 m **5 m**

24. Area = 154 in², w, 14 in. **11 in.**

25. 12 ft, Area = 468 ft², ℓ **39 ft**

26. GEOMETRY The perimeter of a rectangle is 46 centimeters. Its width is 5 centimeters. Find the length. **18 cm**

27. GEOMETRY The area of a rectangle is 323 square yards. Its length is 17 yards. Find the width. **19 yd**

28. COMMUNITY SERVICE Each participant in a community garden is allotted a rectangular plot that measures 18 feet by 45 feet. How much fencing is needed to enclose each plot? **126 ft**

29. SOCCER Find the perimeter and area of the soccer field described at the left. **390 yd, 9000 yd²**

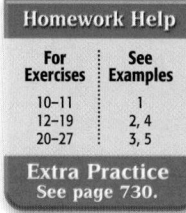

WebQuest

Using a formula can help you find the cost of a vacation. Visit www.pre-alg.com/webquest to continue work on your WebQuest project.

For Exercises 30 and 31, translate each sentence into a formula.

30. **SALES** The sale price of an item s is equal to the list price ℓ minus the discount d. $s = \ell - d$

31. **GEOMETRY** In a circle, the diameter d is twice the length of the radius r. $d = 2r$

32. **RUNNING** The *stride rate* r of a runner is the number of strides n that he or she takes divided by the amount of time t, or $r = \frac{n}{t}$. The best runners usually have the greatest stride rate. Use the table to determine which runner has the greater stride rate. **A**

Runner	Number of Strides	Time (s)
A	20	5
B	30	10

LANDSCAPING For Exercises 33 and 34, use the figure at the right.

33. What is the area of the lawn?

34. Suppose your family wants to fertilize the lawn that is shown. If one bag of fertilizer covers 2500 square feet, how many bags of fertilizer should you buy? **2 bags**

33. 4300 ft²

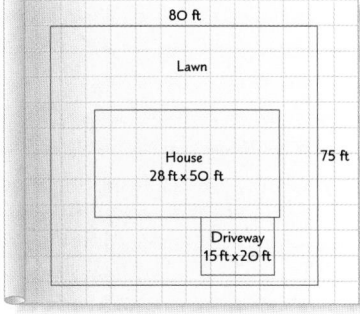

★ **BICYCLING** For Exercises 35 and 36, use following information.
American Lance Armstrong won the 2000 Tour De France, completing the 2178-mile race in 92 hours 33 minutes 8 seconds.

35. Find Armstrong's average rate in miles per hour for the race. **≈ 23.5 mph**

36. Armstrong also won the 1999 Tour de France. He completed the 2213-mile race in 91 hours 32 minutes 16 seconds. Without calculating, determine which race was completed with a faster average speed. Explain. **1999; he traveled a greater distance in less time.**

★ **GEOMETRY** Draw and label the dimensions of each rectangle whose perimeter and area are given. **37–40. See margin.**

37. $P = 14$ ft, $A = 12$ ft²
38. $P = 16$ m, $A = 12$ m²
39. $P = 16$ cm, $A = 16$ cm²
40. $P = 12$ in., $A = 8$ in²

41. **CRITICAL THINKING** Is it *sometimes*, *always*, or *never* true that the perimeter of a rectangle is numerically greater than its area? Give an example. **See margin.**

42. **CRITICAL THINKING** An airplane flying at a rate of 500 miles per hour leaves Los Angeles. One-half hour later, a second airplane leaves Los Angeles in the same direction flying at a rate of 600 miles per hour. How long will it take the second airplane to overtake the first? **2.5 h**

Answer

41. Sometimes; a 3-inch by 4-inch rectangle has a perimeter of 14 inches and an area of 12 square inches; a 6-inch by 8-inch rectangle has a perimeter of 28 inches and an area of 48 square inches.

Study Guide and Intervention, p. 137

The formula $d = rt$ relates distance d, rate r, and time t, traveled.

Example 1 Find the distance traveled if you drive at 40 miles per hour for 3 hours.
$d = rt$
$d = 40 \times 3$ Replace r with 40 and t with 3.
$d = 120$ The distance traveled is 120 miles.

The formula $P = 2(\ell + w)$ relates perimeter P, length ℓ, and width w for a rectangle.
The formula $A = \ell w$ relates area A, length ℓ, and width w for a rectangle.

Example 2 Find the perimeter and area of a rectangle with length 7 feet and width 2 feet.

$P = 2(\ell + w)$ $A = \ell \cdot w$
$P = 2(7 + 2)$ $A = 7 \cdot 2$
$P = 2(9)$ $A = 14$
$P = 18$ The area is 14 square feet.
The perimeter is 18 feet.

Exercises

1. **TRAIN TRAVEL** How far does a train travel in 12 hours at 48 miles per hour? 576 miles

2. **TRAVEL** How long does it take a car traveling 40 miles per hour to go 200 miles? 5 hours

3. **BICYCLING** What is the rate, in miles per hour, of a bicyclist who travels 56 miles in 4 hours? 14 miles per hour

4. **RACING** How long will it take a driver to finish a 980-mile rally race at 70 miles per hour? 14 hours

Find the perimeter and area of each rectangle.

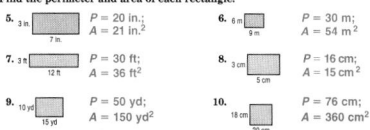

5. $P = 20$ in.; $A = 21$ in.²
6. $P = 30$ m; $A = 54$ m²
7. $P = 30$ ft; $A = 36$ ft²
8. $P = 16$ cm; $A = 15$ cm²
9. $P = 50$ yd; $A = 150$ yd²
10. $P = 76$ cm; $A = 360$ cm²

Skills Practice, p. 138 and Practice, p. 139 (shown)

1. **AIR TRAVEL** What is the rate, in miles per hour, of a plane that travels 1680 miles in 3 hours? 560 mph

2. **TRAVEL** A train is traveling at 54 miles per hour. How long will it take to go 378 miles? 7 h

3. **SWIMMING** What is the rate, in feet per second, of a swimmer who crosses a 164-foot-long pool in 41 seconds? 4 ft/sec

4. **BALLOONING** A balloon is caught in a wind traveling at 25 feet per second. If the wind is constant, how long will it take the balloon to travel 1000 feet? 40 seconds

Find the perimeter and area of each rectangle.

5. 58 cm; area: 210 cm²
6. 88 yd; area: 484 yd²
7. 230 mi; area: 3294 mi²
8. 192 m; area: 2304 m²

9. a rectangle that is 92 meters long and 18 meters wide 220 m; area: 1656 m²

10. a rectangle that is 30 inches long and 29 inches wide 118 in; area: 870 in²

Find the missing dimension in each rectangle.

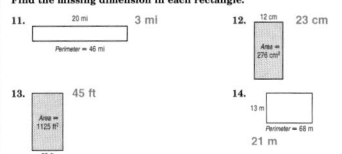

11. 3 mi
12. 23 cm
13. 45 ft
14. 21 m

15. **GEOMETRY** The area of a rectangle is 1260 square inches. Its length is 36 inches. Find the width. 35 in.

Enrichment, p. 141

Mathematics and Social Studies

Since the discovery that Earth is round, people have been fascinated with the prospect of making ever faster trips around the world. Ferdinand Magellan's ship *Victoria* set sail on September 20, 1519, and completed the first voyage around the world about three years later on September 6, 1522. With more consistent modes of transportation came new records in circling Earth.

Solve each problem by finding the average speed it took to circle Earth. Use 24,900 miles to approximate the distance around Earth.

1. **DIRIGIBLE** In 1929, Graf Zeppelin made the first round-the-world dirigible flight in 21 days, 8 hours on the *LZ127*. What was the Zeppelin's average speed in miles per hour? about 48.6 mph

2. **AIRPLANE** Air Force bomber *Lucky Lady II* made the first nonstop flight around the world in 1949. The flight took 94 hours. What was the average speed of the *Lucky Lady II* on that trip? about 264.9 mph

3. **SPACESHIP** In 1961, Yuri Gagarin and Bherman Titov of Russia each circled Earth in a little over an hour and 45 minutes. At what speed must one travel to circle Earth at its surface in an hour and a half? 14,228.6 mph

AIRCRAFT In Exercises 4–6, assume that each aircraft travels at a constant rate. Use 24,900 miles as the distance traveled. How long would it take each aircraft to circle Earth?

4. a commercial plane of the 1930s traveling at 168 mph about 148.2 hours

5. a Boeing 707 cruising at 640 mph about 38.9 hours

6. a Concorde flying at 1450 mph about 17.2 hours

7. **BALLOONING** Jules Verne wrote about circling Earth in a hot air balloon in his novel *Around the World in Eighty Days* (1873). Suppose it were possible for a hot air balloon to circle Earth in 80 days. What would be the average speed in miles per hour? about 13.0 mph

Modeling Cut out rectangles of various sizes and shapes and give one to each student. Then have the students find the perimeters of their rectangles by measuring the sides with a ruler and applying the formulas for perimeter and area.

Assessment Options

Quiz (Lesson 3-7) is available on p. 158 of the *Chapter 3 Resource Masters*.

Answer

43. Formulas are important in math and science because they summarize the relationships among quantities. Answers should include the following.
   - Sample answer: The formula to find acceleration is $a = \dfrac{v_f - v_i}{t}$ where v_f is the final velocity and v_i is the initial velocity.
   - You can find the acceleration of an automobile with this formula.

53a. {(1870, 14), (1881, 600), (1910, 1000), (2000, 1500)}
53b. domain: {1870, 1881, 1910, 2000}, range: {14, 600, 1000, 1500}

43.  **WRITING IN MATH**   Answer the question that was posed at the beginning of the lesson. **See margin.**

Why are formulas important in math and science?

Include the following in your answer:
- an example of a formula from math or science that you have used, and
- an explanation of how you used the formula.

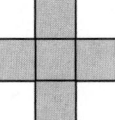

Standardized Test Practice
Ⓐ Ⓑ Ⓒ Ⓓ

★ 44. The formula $d = rt$ can be rewritten as $\dfrac{d}{t} = r$. How is the rate affected if the time t increases and the distance d remains the same? **B**
   - Ⓐ It increases.
   - Ⓑ It decreases.
   - Ⓒ It remains the same.
   - Ⓓ There is not enough information.

45. The area of each square in the figure is 16 square units. Find the perimeter. **C**
   - Ⓐ 16 units
   - Ⓑ 32 units
   - Ⓒ 48 units
   - Ⓓ 64 units

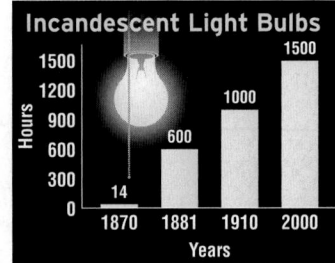

Maintain Your Skills

Mixed Review
46. Eight more than five times a number is 78. Find the number.   *(Lesson 3-6)*
   14

ALGEBRA   Solve each equation. Check your solution.
(Lessons 3-3, 3-4, and 3-5)
47. $-5x + 8 = 53$ **−9**   48. $4y = -24$ **−6**   49. $m + 5 = -3$ **−8**

ALGEBRA   Simplify each expression.   *(Lesson 3-2)*
50. $3y + 5 - 2y$ **$y + 5$**   51. $9 + x - 5x$ **$-4x + 9$**   52. $3(r + 2) + 6r$ **$9r + 6$**

53. **LIGHT BULBS**   The table shows the average life of an incandescent bulb for selected years.   *(Lesson 1-6)*
   a. Write a set of ordered pairs for the data.
   b. State the domain and the range of the relation.

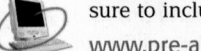
WebQuest **Internet Project**

Vacation Travelers Include More Families
It's time to complete your Internet project. Use the information and data you have gathered about the costs of lodging, transportation, and entertainment for each of the vacations. Prepare a brochure or Web page to present your project. Be sure to include graphs and/or tables in the presentation.
www.pre-alg.com/webquest

Spreadsheet Investigation

A Follow-Up of Lesson 3-7

Perimeter and Area

A spreadsheet allows you to use formulas to investigate problems. When you change a numerical value in a cell, the spreadsheet recalculates the formula and automatically updates the results.

Example

Suppose a gardener wants to enclose a rectangular garden using part of a wall as one side and 20 feet of fencing for the other three sides. What are the dimensions of the largest garden she can enclose?

If w represents the length of each side attached to the wall, $20 - 2w$ represents the length of the side opposite the wall. These values are listed in column B. The areas are listed in column C.

Garden Dimensions

	A	B	C
1	Length of Fence	20	
2	Length of Side Attached to Wall	Length of Side Opposite Wall	Area
3	1	18	18
4	2	16	32
5	3	14	42
6	4	12	48
7	5	10	50
8	6	8	48
9	7	6	42
10	8	4	32
11	9	2	18
12			

Sheet1 / Sheet2

> The spreadsheet evaluates the formula $B1 - 2 \times A3$.

> The spreadsheet evaluates the formula $A9 \times B9$.

The greatest possible area is 50 square feet. It occurs when the length of each side attached to the wall is 5 feet, and the length of the side opposite the wall is 10 feet.

Exercises

1. What is the area if the length of the side attached to the wall is 10 feet? 11 feet? **0, −22**

2. Are the answers to Exercise 1 reasonable? Explain. **No; area cannot be zero or a negative number.**

3. Suppose you want to find the greatest area that you can enclose with 30 feet of fencing. Which cell should you modify to solve this problem? **B1**

4. Use a spreadsheet to find the dimensions of the greatest area you can enclose with 40 feet, 50 feet, and 60 feet of fencing. **10 ft by 20 ft; 12.5 ft by 25 ft; 15 ft by 30 ft**

5. **MAKE A CONJECTURE** Use any pattern you may have observed in your answers to Exercise 4 to find the dimensions of the greatest area you can enclose with 100 feet of fencing. Explain. **25 ft by 50 ft; the opposite wall is twice the attached wall.**

Getting Started

Before students turn to this page in class, present the Example problem on a transparency. Ask a few students to sketch out some possible dimensions for the garden as described in the Example. Then ask for a formula to represent the garden's possible dimensions.

Teach

- Explain to students that spreadsheet programs use column letters and row numbers to designate the location of cells, and that these designations are used as variables in spreadsheet formulas. To reinforce this, point to a few cells, one at a time, and have the class call out the cells' "names."

- If students need to review using formulas to solve problems, have them revisit Lesson 3-7.

Assess

Have students complete Exercises 1–5. If any students have difficulty with Exercise 3, have them sketch or cut out the dimensions on paper. You may wish to have students discuss Exercise 5 in small groups.

Chapter 3 Study Guide and Review

Vocabulary and Concept Check

- This alphabetical list of vocabulary terms in Chapter 3 includes a page reference where each term was introduced.

- **Assessment** A vocabulary review/test for Chapter 3 is available on p. 156 of the *Chapter 3 Resource Masters.*

Lesson-by-Lesson Review

For each lesson,
- the main ideas are summarized,
- additional examples review concepts, and
- practice exercises are provided.

Vocabulary PuzzleMaker

ELL The Vocabulary PuzzleMaker software improves students' mathematics vocabulary using four puzzle formats—crossword, scramble, word search using a word list, and word search using clues. Students can work on a computer screen or from a printed handout.

MindJogger Videoquizzes

ELL MindJogger Videoquizzes provide an alternative review of concepts presented in this chapter. Students work in teams in a game show format to gain points for correct answers. The questions are presented in three rounds.

Round 1 Concepts (5 questions)
Round 2 Skills (4 questions)
Round 3 Problem Solving (4 questions)

Vocabulary and Concept Check

area (p. 132)	inverse operations (p. 110)	Properties of Equality
coefficient (p. 103)	like terms (p. 103)	Multiplication (p. 117)
constant (p. 103)	perimeter (p. 132)	Subtraction (p. 110)
Distributive Property (p. 98)	Properties of Equality	simplest form (p. 104)
equivalent equations (p. 111)	Addition (p. 111)	simplifying an expression (p. 104)
equivalent expression (p. 98)	Division (p. 115)	term (p. 103)
formula (p. 131)		two-step equation (p. 120)

Complete each sentence with the correct term.

1. Terms that contain the same variables are called _____ . **like terms**

2. The _____ of a geometric figure is the measure of the distance around it. **perimeter**

3. The _____ states that when you multiply each side of an equation by the same number, the two sides remain equal. **Multiplication Property (=)**

4. The equations $x + 3 = 8$ and $x = 5$ are _____ because they have the same solution. **equivalent**

5. You could use the _____ Property to rewrite $9(t - 2)$ as $9t - 18$. **Distributive**

6. In the term $4b$, 4 is the _____ of the expression. **coefficient**

7. The solution of $2y + 5 = 13$ is a _____ of a point on a number line. **coordinate**

8. The measure of the surface enclosed by a geometric figure is its _____ . **area**

9. In the expression $10x + 6$, the number 6 is the _____ term. **constant**

10. Addition and subtraction are _____ because they "undo" each other.

10. inverse operations

Lesson-by-Lesson Review

3-1 *The Distributive Property*

See pages 98–102.

Concept Summary
- The Distributive Property combines addition and multiplication.
- For any numbers a, b, and c, $a(b + c) = ab + ac$ and $(b + c)a = ba + ca$.

Example **Use the Distributive Property to rewrite $2(t - 3)$.**

$2(t - 3) = 2[(t + (-3)]$	Rewrite $t - 3$ as $t + (-3)$.
$= 2t + 2(-3)$	Distributive Property
$= 2t + (-6)$	Simplify.
$= 2t - 6$	Definition of subtraction

11. $3h + 18$ 12. $7x + 14$
13. $-5k - 5$ 14. $-2a - 16$
15. $9t - 45$ 16. $7x - 21$
17. $-2b + 8$ 18. $-6y + 18$

Exercises **Use the Distributive Property to rewrite each expression.**
See Examples 3 and 4 on page 100.

11. $3(h + 6)$ 12. $7(x + 2)$ 13. $-5(k + 1)$ 14. $-2(a + 8)$
15. $(t - 5)9$ 16. $(x - 3)7$ 17. $-2(b - 4)$ 18. $-6(y - 3)$

 www.pre-alg.com/vocabulary_review

Study Organizer

For more information about Foldables, see *Teaching Mathematics with Foldables.*

Have students review their Foldables to be sure they have included notes on every lesson in this chapter.

Encourage students to refer to their Foldables while completing the Study Guide and Review and to use them in preparing for the Chapter Test.

3-2 Simplifying Algebraic Expressions

See pages
103–107.

Concept Summary

- Simplest form means no like terms and no parentheses.

Example

Simplify $9x + 3 - 7x$.

$$9x + 3 - 7x = 9x + 3 + (-7x) \quad \text{Definition of subtraction}$$
$$= 9x + (-7x) + 3 \quad \text{Commutative Property}$$
$$= [9 + (-7)]x + 3 \quad \text{Distributive Property}$$
$$= 2x + 3 \quad \text{Simplify.}$$

Exercises **Simplify each expression.** *See Example 2 on page 104.*

19. $4a + 5a$ **20.** $3x + 7 + x$ **21.** $8(n - 1) - 10n$ **22.** $6w + 2(w + 9)$

$9a$ $4x + 7$ $-2n - 8$ $8w + 18$

3-3 Solving Equations by Adding or Subtracting

See pages
110–114.

Concept Summary

- When you add or subtract the same number from each side of an equation, the two sides remain equal.

Examples

1 Solve $x + 3 = 7$.

$$x + 3 = 7$$
$$x + 3 - 3 = 7 - 3 \quad \text{Subtract 3 from each side.}$$
$$x = 4$$

2 Solve $y - 5 = -2$.

$$y - 5 = -2$$
$$y - 5 + 5 = -2 + 5 \quad \text{Add 5 to each side.}$$
$$y = 3$$

Exercises **Solve each equation.** *See Examples 1 and 3 on pages 111 and 112.*

23. $t + 5 = 8$ **3**   **24.** $12 = x + 4$ **8**   **25.** $k - 1 = 4$ **5**   **26.** $-7 = n - 6$ **−1**

3-4 Solving Equations by Multiplying or Dividing

See pages
115–119.

Concept Summary

- When you multiply or divide each side of an equation by the same nonzero number, the two sides remain equal.

Examples

1 Solve $-5x = -30$.

$$-5x = -30 \quad \text{Write the equation.}$$
$$\frac{-5x}{-5} = \frac{-30}{-5} \quad \text{Divide each side by −5.}$$
$$x = 6 \quad \text{Simplify.}$$

2 Solve $\dfrac{a}{-8} = 3$.

$$\frac{a}{-8} = 3 \quad \text{Write the equation.}$$
$$-8\left(\frac{a}{-8}\right) = -8(3) \quad \text{Multiply each side by −8.}$$
$$a = -24 \quad \text{Simplify.}$$

Exercises **Solve each equation.** *See Examples 1 and 3 on pages 116 and 117.*

27. $6n = 48$ **8**   **28.** $-3x = 30$ **−10**   **29.** $\dfrac{t}{2} = -9$ **−18**   **30.** $\dfrac{r}{-5} = -2$ **10**

Study Guide and Review

Chapter 3 For More ...
• Extra Practice, see pages 728–730.
• Mixed Problem Solving, see page 760.

3-5 Solving Two-Step Equations

See pages 120–124.

Concept Summary

• To solve a two-step equation undo operations in reverse order.

Example Solve $6k - 4 = 14$.

$$6k - 4 = 14 \quad \text{Write the equation.}$$
$$6k - 4 + 4 = 14 + 4 \quad \text{Undo subtraction. Add 4 to each side.}$$
$$6k = 18 \quad \text{Simplify.}$$
$$k = 3 \quad \text{Mentally divide each side by 6.}$$

Exercises Solve each equation. *See Examples 1, 3, and 4 on pages 121 and 122.*

31. $6 + 2y = 8$ **1** **32.** $3n - 5 = -17$ **33.** $\frac{t}{3} + 4 = 2$ **-6** **34.** $\frac{c}{9} - 3 = 2$ **45**

-4

3-6 Writing Two-Step Equations

See pages 126–130.

Concept Summary

• The words *is*, *equals*, or *is equal to*, can be translated into an equals sign.

Example Seven less than three times a number is -22. Find the number.

$$3n - 7 = -22 \quad \text{Write the equation.}$$
$$3n - 7 + 7 = -22 + 7 \quad \text{Add 7 to each side.}$$
$$3n = -15 \quad \text{Simplify.}$$
$$n = -5 \quad \text{Mentally divide each side by 3.}$$

Exercises Translate the sentence into an equation. Then find the number.
See Examples 1 and 2 on pages 126 and 127.

35. Three more than twice n is 53. **36.** Four times x minus 16 is 52.

$2n + 3 = 53; 25$ $4x - 16 = 52; 17$

3-7 Using Formulas

See pages 131–136.

Concept Summary

• Perimeter of a rectangle: $P = 2(\ell + w)$ • Area of a rectangle: $A = \ell w$

Example Find the perimeter and area of a 14-meter by 6-meter rectangle.

$P = 2(\ell + w)$ Formula for perimeter	$A = \ell w$ Formula for area
$P = 2(14 + 6)$ $\ell = 14$ and $w = 6$.	$A = 14 \cdot 6$ $\ell = 14$ and $w = 6$.
$P = 40$ Simplify.	$A = 84$ Simplify.

Exercises Find the perimeter and area of each rectangle whose dimensions are given. *See Examples 2 and 4 on pages 132 and 133.*

37. 8 feet by 9 feet **34 ft, 72 ft²** **38.** 5 meters by 15 meters **40 m, 75 m²**

Answers (p. 141)

1. Sample answer: like terms—$2x$ and $3x$, not like terms—$5y$ and 2.

2. To multiply a number by a sum, multiply the number outside the parentheses by each number inside the parentheses.

Chapter 3 Practice Test

Vocabulary and Concepts

1. **OPEN ENDED** Give an example of two terms that are like terms and two terms that are *not* like terms. **See margin.**
2. **State** the Distributive Property in your own words. **See margin.**
3. **Explain** the difference between perimeter and area. **Perimeter is the distance around a figure; area is a measure of the surface the perimeter encloses.**

Skills and Applications

Simplify each expression.

4. $9x + 5 - x + 3$ **$8x + 8$**
5. $-3(a - 8)$ **$-3a + 24$**
6. $10(y + 3) - 4y$ **$6y + 30$**

Solve each equation. Check your solution.

7. $19 = f + 5$ **14**
8. $-15 + z = 3$ **18**
9. $x - 7 = 16$ **23**
10. $g - 9 = -10$ **-1**
11. $-8y = 72$ **-9**
12. $\frac{n}{-30} = -6$ **180**
13. $25 = 2d - 9$ **17**
14. $4w - 18 = -34$ **-4**
15. $6v + 10 = -62$ **-12**
16. $-7 = \frac{d}{-5} + 1$ **40**
17. $7 - x = 18$ **-11**
18. $b - 7b + 6 = -30$ **6**

Translate each sentence into an equation. Then find each number.

19. The quotient of a number and 8, decreased by 17 is -15. **$\frac{n}{8} - 17 = -15$, 16**
20. Five less than 3 times a number is 25. **$3n - 5 = 25$, 10**

Find the perimeter and area of each rectangle.

21.
48 m
20 m
136m, 960 m²

22.
100 yd
75 yd
350 yd, 7500 yd²

23. **ENTERTAINMENT** Suppose you pay $15 per hour to go horseback riding. You ride 2 hours today and plan to ride 4 more hours this weekend.
    a. Write two different expressions to find the total cost of horseback riding.
    b. Find the total cost. **$90**
    23a. $15(2 + 4)$, $15 \cdot 2 + 15 \cdot 4$

24. **HEIGHT** Todd is 5 inches taller than his brother. The sum of their heights is 139 inches. Find Todd's height. **72 in.**

25. **STANDARDIZED TEST PRACTICE** A carpet store advertises 16 square yards of carpeting for $300, which includes the $60 installation charge. Which equation could be used to determine the cost of one square yard of carpet x? **D**
    (A) $16x = 300$
    (B) $x + 60 = 300$
    (C) $60x + 16 = 300$
    (D) $16x + 60 = 300$

 www.pre-alg.com/chapter_test

Portfolio Suggestion

Introduction Equations are used to solve many different types of problems. Sometimes special types of equations called formulas are used.

Ask Students to find a problem from their work in this chapter and explain how they used an equation or formula to solve it.

Assessment Options

Vocabulary Test A vocabulary review/test for Chapter 3 can be found on p. 156 of the *Chapter 3 Resource Masters*.

Chapter Tests There are six Chapter 3 Tests and an Open-Ended Assessment task available in the *Chapter 3 Resource Masters*.

Chapter 3 Tests			
Form	Type	Level	Pages
1	MC	basic	143–144
2A	MC	average	145–146
2B	MC	average	147–148
2C	FR	average	149–150
2D	FR	average	151–152
3	FR	advanced	153–154

MC = multiple-choice questions
FR = free-response questions

Open-Ended Assessment Performance tasks for Chapter 3 can be found on p. 155 of the *Chapter 3 Resource Masters*, along with a sample scoring rubric for these tasks on p. A25.

Unit 1 Test/Review Pages 163–164 of the *Chapter 3 Resource Masters* provide a cumulative review of Unit 1, which can be used as a Unit Review or a Unit Test.

 ExamView® Pro

Use the networkable **ExamView® Pro** to:

- Create **multiple versions** of tests.
- Create **modified** tests for *Inclusion* students.
- **Edit** existing questions and **add** your own questions.
- Use built-in **state curriculum correlations** to create tests aligned with state standards.
- Change **English** tests to **Spanish** and vice versa.

These two pages contain practice questions in the various formats that can be found on the most frequently given standardized tests.

A practice answer sheet for these two pages can be found on page A1 of the *Chapter 3 Resource Masters*.

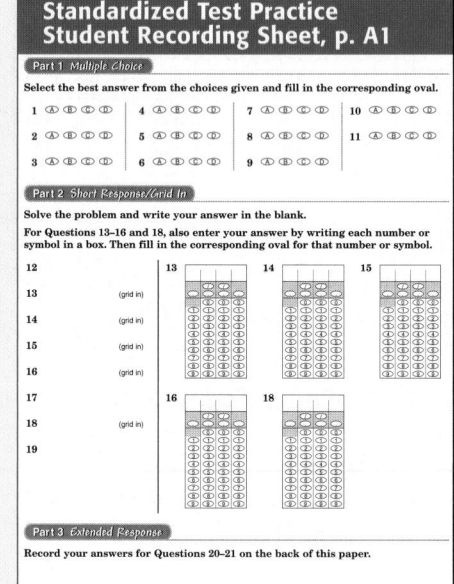

Standardized Test Practice
Student Recording Sheet, p. A1

Part 1 Multiple Choice

Select the best answer from the choices given and fill in the corresponding oval.

Part 2 Short Response/Grid In

Solve the problem and write your answer in the blank.

For Questions 13–16 and 18, also enter your answer by writing each number or symbol in a box. Then fill in the corresponding oval for that number or symbol.

Part 3 Extended Response

Record your answers for Questions 20–21 on the back of this paper.

Additional Practice

See pp. 161–162 of the *Chapter 3 Resource Masters* for additional standardized test practice.

Part 1 Multiple Choice

Record your answers on the answer sheet provided by your teacher or on a sheet of paper.

1. Ms. Bauer notices that her car's gas tank is nearly empty. Gasoline costs $1.59 a gallon. *About* how many gallons can she buy with a $20 bill? (Prerequisite Skills, p. 714) **C**
   (A) 10
   (B) 30
   (C) 12
   (D) 20

2. Which is equivalent to $3 \times 8 - 6 \div 2$? (Lesson 1-2) **D**
   (A) 3
   (B) 9
   (C) 13
   (D) 21

3. Which statement illustrates the Commutative Property of Multiplication? (Lesson 1-4) **B**
   (A) $5 + w + 8 = 5 + 8 + w$
   (B) $5 \cdot w \cdot 8 = 5 \cdot 8 \cdot w$
   (C) $(5 \cdot w) \cdot 8 = 5 \cdot (w \cdot 8)$
   (D) $(5 + w) + 8 = 5 + (w + 8)$

4. Which point on the graph below represents the ordered pair $(4, 3)$? (Lesson 1-6) **B**

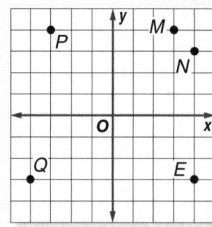

   (A) M   (B) N   (C) P   (D) Q

5. The temperature at 6:00 A.M. was $-5°F$. What was the temperature at 8:00 A.M. if it had risen 7 degrees? (Lesson 2-2) **A**
   (A) 2°F
   (B) $-2°F$
   (C) 12°F
   (D) $-12°F$

6. Suppose points at (x, y) are graphed using the values in the table. Which statement is true about the graphs? (Lesson 2-6) **B**

x	y
−1	5
−3	10
−5	6

   (A) The graphs are located in Quadrant I.
   (B) The graphs are located in Quadrant II.
   (C) The graphs are located in Quadrant III.
   (D) The graphs are located in Quadrant IV.

7. Which expression is equivalent to $5 \times 3 + 5 \times 12$? (Lesson 3-1) **C**
   (A) $5 \times 8 \times 12$ (B) $3 + (5 \times 12)$
   (C) $5 \times (3 + 12)$ (D) $5 + (3 \times 12)$

8. Simplify $x - 4(x + 3)$. (Lesson 3-2) **B**
   (A) $5x + 12$
   (B) $-3x - 12$
   (C) $-3x + 12$
   (D) $5x - 12$

9. Solve $y - (-4) = 6 - 8$. (Lesson 3-3) **A**
   (A) -6 (B) -2
   (C) 2   (D) 6

10. Mr. Samuels is a car sales associate. He makes a salary of $400 per week. He also earns a bonus of $100 for each car he sells. Which equation represents the total amount of money Mr. Samuels earns in a week when he sells n cars? (Lesson 3-6) **C**
   (A) $T = 400n + 100$
   (B) $T = n(100 + 400)$
   (C) $T = 100n + 400$
   (D) $T = 400 + 100 + n$

11. Tiffany's Gift Shop has fixed monthly expenses, E, of $1850. If the owner wants to make a profit, P, of $4000 next month, how many dollars in sales, S, does the shop need to earn? Use the formula $P = S - E$. (Lesson 3-7) **C**
   (A) 2150   (B) 4000
   (C) 5850   (D) 7400

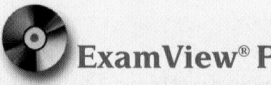

ExamView® Pro

Special banks of standardized test questions similar to those on the SAT, ACT, TIMSS 8, NAEP 8, and Pre-Algebra End-of-Course tests can be found on this CD-ROM.

Preparing for Standardized Tests
For test-taking strategies and more
practice, see pages 771–788.

Test-Taking Tip ⒶⒷⒸⒹ
Question 15
This problem does not include a drawing. Make one. Your drawing will help you see how to solve the problem.

Part 2 Short Response/Grid In

Record your answers on the answer sheet provided by your teacher or on a sheet of paper.

12. The charge to enter a nature preserve is a flat amount per vehicle plus a fee for each person in the vehicle. The table shows the charge for vehicles holding up to 4 people.

Number of People	Charge (dollars)
1	1.50
2	2.00
3	2.50
4	3.00

What is the charge, in dollars, for a vehicle holding 8 people? (Lesson 1-1) **$5**

13. Evaluate $-2(-8 + 5)$. (Lesson 1-2) **6**

14. Last week, the stock market rose 10 points in two days. What number expresses the average change in the stock market per day? (Lesson 2-1) **5**

15. The ordered pairs $(-7, -2)$, $(-3, 5)$, and $(-3, -2)$ are coordinates of three of the vertices of a rectangle. What is the y-coordinate of the ordered pair that represents the fourth vertex? (Lesson 2-6) **5**

16. What value of x makes $x - 4 = -2$ a true statement? (Lesson 3-3) **2**

17. Cara filled her car's gas tank with 15 gallons of gas. Her car usually gets 24 miles per gallon. How many miles can she drive using 15 gallons of gas? (Lesson 3-7) **360 mi**

 www.pre-alg.com/standardized_test

18. A mail-order greeting card company charges $3 for each box of greeting cards plus a handling charge of $2 per order. How many boxes of cards can you order from this company if you want to spend $26? (Lesson 3-6) **8**

19. Mr. Ruiz owns a health club and is planning to increase the floor area of the weight room. In the figure below, the rectangle with the solid border represents the floor area of the existing room, and the rectangle with the dashed border represents the floor area to be added. What will be the length, in feet, of the new weight room? (Lesson 3-7) **30 ft**

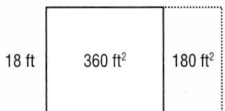

18 ft   360 ft²   180 ft²

Part 3 Extended Response

Record your answers on a sheet of paper. Show your work.

20. The overnight low in Fargo, North Dakota, was $-14°F$. The high the next day was $6°F$. (Lesson 3-3)

a. Draw a number line to represent the increase in temperature. **See margin.**

b. How many degrees did the temperature rise from the low to the high? **20°F**

c. Explain how the concept of absolute value relates to this question. **See margin.**

21. In a school basketball game, each field goal is worth 2 points, and each free throw is worth 1 point. Josh heard the Springdale Stars scored a total of 63 points in their last game. Soledad says that they made a total of 12 free throws in that game. (Lesson 3-6)

a. Write an equation to represent the total points scored p. Use f for the number of free throws and g for the number of field goals. **$f + 2g = p$**

b. Can both Josh and Soledad be correct? Explain. **No; a team can't score half of a basket.**

Evaluating Extended Response Questions

Extended Response questions are graded by using a multilevel rubric that guides you in assessing a student's knowledge of a particular concept.

Goal: Use knowledge of integers and algebraic equations to solve real-world problems.

Sample Scoring Rubric: The following rubric is a sample scoring device. You may wish to add more detail to this sample to meet your individual scoring needs.

Score	Criteria
4	A correct solution that is supported by well-developed, accurate explanations
3	A generally correct solution, but may contain minor flaws in reasoning or computation
2	A partially correct interpretation and/or solution to the problem
1	A correct solution with no supporting evidence or explanation
0	An incorrect solution indicating no mathematical understanding of the concept or task, or no solution is given

Answers

20a.

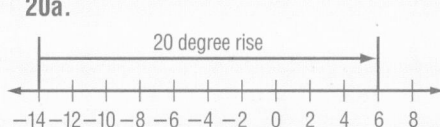

20 degree rise

−14 −12 −10 −8 −6 −4 −2 0 2 4 6 8

20c. The increase from the low temperature to 0° is the absolute value of the low temperature. The increase from 0° to the high temperature is the absolute value of the high temperature. The total increase can be found by adding the absolute values of the two temperatures. $|-14| + |6| = 20$.

Page 101, Lesson 3-1

12. $2 \cdot 6 + 2 \cdot 1, 14$

13. $5 \cdot 7 + 5 \cdot 3, 50$

14. $4 \cdot 9 + 6 \cdot 9, 90$

15. $4 \cdot 3 + 3 \cdot 3, 21$

16. $9 \cdot 4 + 2 \cdot 4, 44$

17. $8 \cdot 2 + 8 \cdot 2, 32$

18. $7 \cdot 3 + 7(-2), 7$

19. $6 \cdot 8 + 6(-5), 18$

20. $-5 \cdot 8 + (-5)(-4), -20$

21. $-3 \cdot 9 + (-3)(-2), -21$

22. $8(-2) - 4(-2), -8$

23. $10(-5) - 3(-5), -35$

26. $2x + 6$

27. $5y + 30$

28. $3n + 3$

29. $7y + 56$

30. $4x + 12$

31. $10y + 20$

32. $18 + 6y$

33. $10 + 5x$

34. $3x - 6$

35. $9m - 18$

36. $8z - 24$

37. $15s - 45$

38. $6r - 30$

39. $12x - 36$

40. $5t - 20$

41. $2w - 20$

42. $-2z - 8$

43. $-5a - 50$

44. $-2x + 14$

45. $-5w + 40$

46. $-2y + 8$

47. $-5a + 30$

48. $2x + 2y$

49. $3a + 3b$

52. Sample answer: You can compute the area of two rectangles with the same width in two ways. You can put them together and multiply to find the total area or find each area separately and then add to find the total. The Distributive Property states that the expressions $a(b + c)$, and $ab + ac$ are equivalent.

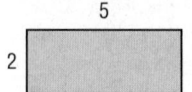   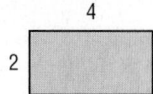

• $2(5 + 4) = 18; 2 \cdot 5 + 2 \cdot 4 = 18$

Page 106, Lesson 3-2

56. Sample answer: You can use algebra tiles to simplify an algebraic expression by grouping the tiles with the same size and shape together.

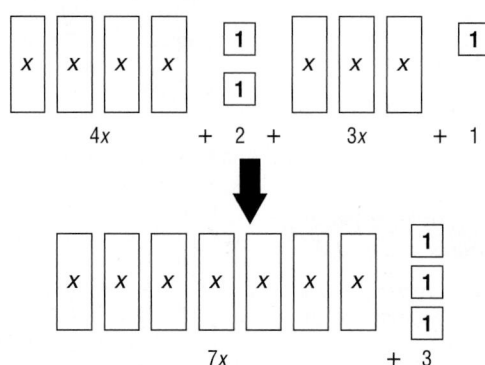

• *Like terms* are terms that have the same variable(s) or are constants.

• You use the Commutative Property when you change the order of 2 and $3x$. You use the Distributive Property when you write $4x + 3x$ as $7x$.

Page 109, Algebra Activity

5.

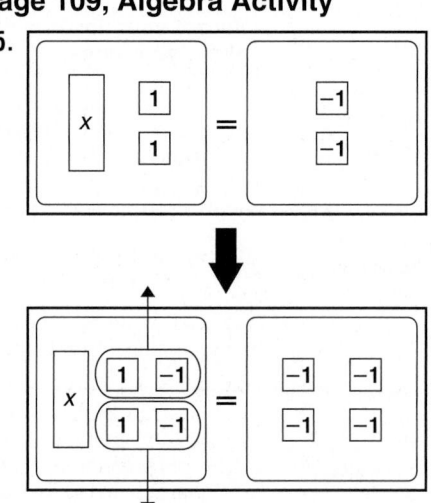

6.

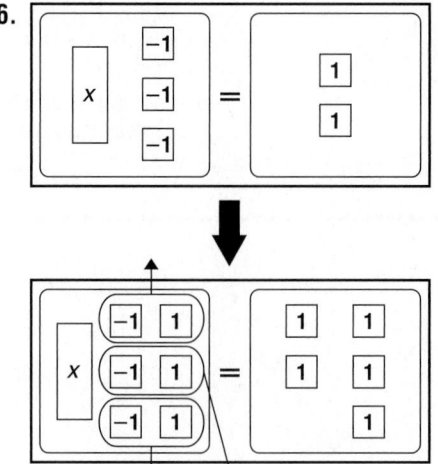

7.

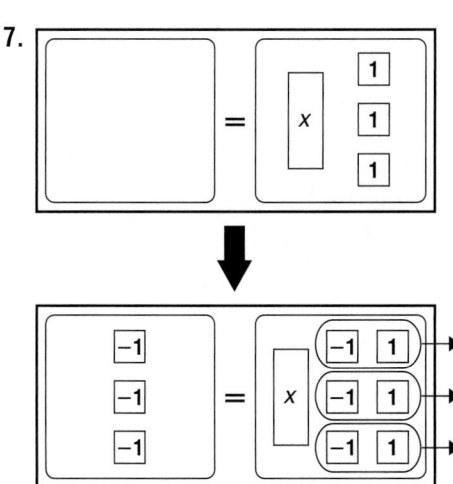

8.

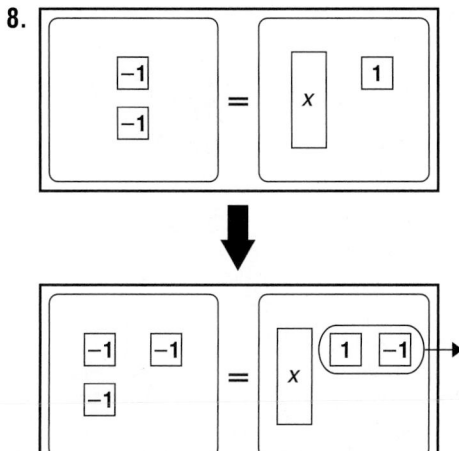

9.

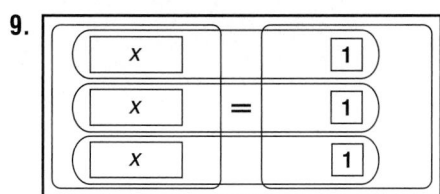

10.

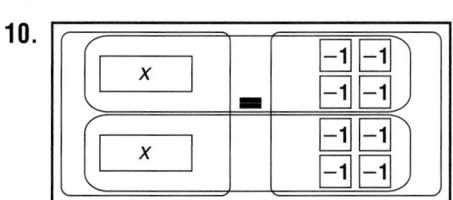

11.

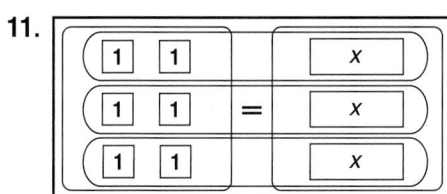

12.

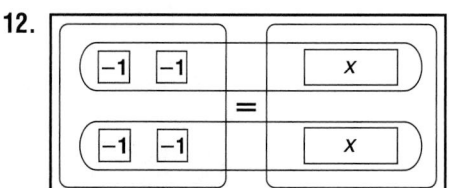

Page 113, Lesson 3-3

2. Sample answer: equivalent—$x + 3 = 5$, $x = 2$; not equivalent—$x + 5 = 2$, $x + 1 = 5$

9.
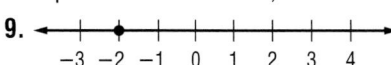

10.

37.

38.

39.

40.

41.

42.

Page 123, Lesson 3-5

50. Sample answer: You can add or remove tiles from each side of a mat. This models the Addition and Subtraction Properties of Equality. Also, separating tiles into groups models the Division Property of Equality.

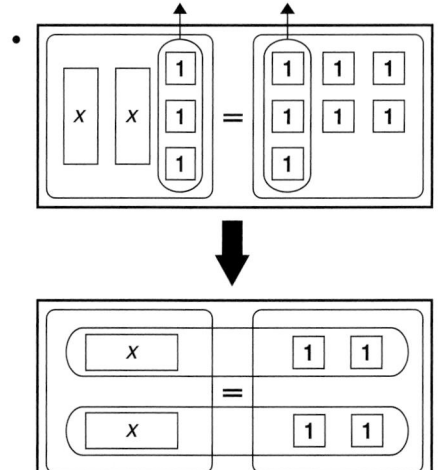

- Subtraction Property of Equality, Division Property of Equality

UNIT
2

Algebra and Rational Numbers

Introduction

In this unit, students explore rational numbers. They will learn to use prime factorization and greatest common factor to solve real-world problems and simplify algebraic equations.

Students will examine exponents, multiply and divide monomials, and use scientific notation. Students will also compute and solve equations with rational numbers. They will use measures of central tendency. Students will apply ratios and proportions to problems involving fractions, decimals, and percents. Students will use percent equations, calculate percent of change, and make predictions based on probability.

Assessment Options

Unit 2 Test Pages 365–366 of the *Chapter 6 Resource Masters* may be used as a test or review for Unit 2. This assessment contains both multiple-choice and short answer items.

ExamView® Pro

This CD-ROM can be used to create additional unit tests and review worksheets.

Yearly Progress Pro

An online, research-based instructional, assessment, and intervention tool that provides specific feedback on student mastery of state and national standards, instant remediation, and a data management system to track performance. For more information, contact mhdigitallearning.com.

Most of the numbers you encounter in the real world are *rational numbers*—fractions, decimals, and percents. In this unit, you will build on your foundation of algebra so that it includes rational numbers.

Chapter 4
Factors and Fractions

Chapter 5
Rational Numbers

Chapter 6
Ratio, Proportion, and Percent

144 Unit 2 Algebra and Rational Numbers

Real-Life Math Videos

What's Math Got to Do With It? Real-Life Math Videos engage students showing them how math is used in everyday situations. Use Video 1 with this unit.

Teaching Suggestions

Have students study the USA TODAY Snapshot®.

- Ask them whether the survey data are based on the use of mean, median, or mode.
  mean

- How much does the average teenager spend per week on fast food? **$12.18**

- Students eat 7 percent of their meals at fast-food restaurants. What does 1 percent of their meals represent in dollars? **$1,814,285,714**

Additional USA TODAY Snapshots® appearing in Unit 2:

Chapter 4 Our daily time behind the wheel (p. 156)

Chapter 5 Favorite subjects (p. 203)

Discussing school at home (p. 213)

Chapter 6 Number of threatened species in USA (p. 289)

Kids don't enjoy cleaning their rooms (p. 290)

Monster cookies (p. 312)

Chocolate cravings (p. 314)

WebQuest Internet Project

Kids Gobbling Empty Calories

"Teens are eating 150 more calories a day in snacks than they did two decades ago. And kids of all ages are munching on more of the richer goodies between meals than children did in the past."

Source: *USA TODAY,* April 30, 2001

In this project, you will be exploring how rational numbers are related to nutrition.

 Log on to www.pre-alg.com/webquest. Begin your WebQuest by reading the Task.

Then continue working on your WebQuest as you study Unit 2.

Lesson	4-5	5-8	6-7
Page	173	242	301

USA TODAY Snapshots®

Teen fuel
Kids ages 12-17 eat an average of 7% of their meals at fast-food restaurants, spending $12.7 billion a year. Teens and fast food:

Fast-food visits per week	2.13
Average spent per visit	$5.72
Favorite order	Hamburger (46%)
Time of day	5-8 p.m. (38%)

Source: David Michaelson & Associates for Channel One Network

By Anne R. Carey and Jerry Mosemak, USA TODAY

WebQuest Internet Project

Problem-Based Learning A WebQuest is an online project in which students do research on the Internet, gather data, and make presentations using word processing, graphing, page-making, or presentation software. In each chapter, students advance to the next step in their WebQuest. At the end of Chapter 6, the project culminates with a presentation of their findings.

Teaching suggestions and sample answers are available in the *WebQuest and Project Resources.*

Chapter 4

Factors and Fractions
Chapter Overview and Pacing

Year-long pacing: pages T20–T21.

LESSON OBJECTIVES	PACING (days)			
	Regular		Block	
	Basic/ Average	Advanced	Basic/ Average	Advanced
4-1 Factors and Monomials (pp. 148–152) • Determine whether one number is a factor of another. • Determine whether an expression is a monomial.	1	1	0.5	0.5
4-2 Powers and Exponents (pp. 153–158) • Write expressions using exponents. • Evaluate expressions containing exponents. *Follow-Up:* Investigate writing numerals in base 2.	1	2 (with 4-2 Follow-Up)	0.5	1 (with 4-2 Follow-Up)
4-3 Prime Factorization (pp. 159–163) • Write the prime factorizations of composite numbers. • Factor monomials.	1	1	0.5	0.5
4-4 Greatest Common Factor (GCF) (pp. 164–168) • Find the greatest common factor of two or more numbers or monomials. • Use the Distributive Property to factor algebraic expressions.	1	1	0.5	0.5
4-5 Simplifying Algebraic Fractions (pp. 169–173) • Simplify fractions using the GCF. • Simplify algebraic fractions.	2	1	1	0.5
4-6 Multiplying and Dividing Monomials (pp. 175–180) • Multiply monomials. • Divide monomials. *Follow-Up:* Model and investigate radioactive half-lives.	2	2 (with 4-6 Follow-Up)	1.5	1 (with 4-6 Follow-Up)
4-7 Negative Exponents (pp. 181–185) • Write expressions using negative exponents. • Evaluate numerical expressions containing negative exponents.	2	1	1	0.5
4-8 Scientific Notation (pp. 186–190) • Express numbers in standard form and in scientific notation. • Compare and order numbers written in scientific notation.	1	1	0.5	0.5
Study Guide and **Practice Test** (pp. 191–195) **Standardized Test Practice** (pp. 196–197)	1	1	0.5	0.5
Chapter Assessment	1	1	0.5	0.5
TOTAL	**13**	**12**	**7**	**6**

*An electronic version of this chapter is available on **StudentWorks**™. This backpack solution CD-ROM allows students instant access to the Student Edition, lesson worksheet pages, and web resources.*

Chapter Resource Manager

Timesaving Tools

TeacherWorks™

All-In-One Planner and Resource Center

See pages T5 and T21.

CHAPTER 4 RESOURCE MASTERS

Study Guide and Intervention	Practice (Skills and Average)	Reading to Learn Mathematics	Enrichment	Assessment	Prerequisite Skills Workbook	Applications*	Parent and Student Study Guide Workbook	5-Minute Check Transparencies	Interactive Chalkboard	Pre-AlgePASS: Tutorial Plus (lessons)	Materials
165	166–167	168	169		13–14	GCS 26	24	4-1	4-1		
170	171–172	173	174	219		SC 7 GCS 25	25	4-2	4-2		*Follow-Up:* grid paper
175	176–177	178	179		13–14		26	4-3	4-3		
180	181–182	183	184	219, 221			27	4-4	4-4	7	
185	186–187	188	189				28	4-5	4-5		
190	191–192	193	194	220		SC 8	29	4-6	4-6		*Follow-Up:* 50 pennies, grid paper, shoebox with lid
195	196–197	198	199				30	4-7	4-7		
200	201–202	203	204	220	33–36		31	4-8	4-8	8	
				205–218 222–224							

* *Key to Abbreviations:* GCS = Graphing Calculator and Spreadsheet Masters
SC = School-to-Career Masters
SM = Science and Mathematics Lab Manual

ELL Study Guide and Intervention, Skills Practice, Practice, and Parent and Student Study Guide Workbooks are also available in Spanish.

Mathematical Connections and Background

Continuity of Instruction

Prior Knowledge

In Chapter 3, students learned to simplify algebraic expressions. They solved equations by adding, subtracting, multiplying, or dividing. They also learned to apply equations to real-world problems and to write and solve two-step equations. Students used formulas to find the perimeter and area of rectangles and squares.

This Chapter

Students examine factors and monomials. They learn to evaluate expressions containing powers and exponents. They use greatest common factor to simplify expressions and algebraic fractions. They also learn to multiply and divide monomials and express numbers using positive and negative exponents and scientific notation.

Future Connections

Prime factorization, greatest common factor, powers, exponents, and multiplying and dividing monomials are important elements of algebraic manipulation in Pre-Algebra and Algebra I. Powers, exponents, and scientific notation are utilized in various sciences, including astronomy, chemistry, physics, archaeology, and geology.

4-1 Factors and Monomials

Two or more numbers that are multiplied to form a product are called factors. Divisibility rules can be used to determine whether 2, 3, 5, 6, or 10 are factors of a given number. Divisibility rules can be used to solve real-world problems and to identify factors suitable for simplifying equations.

A monomial is a number, a variable, or a product of numbers and/or variables. So, $3abc$ is a monomial, but $6 + 4n$ is not because it involves addition.

4-2 Powers and Exponents

An expression such as $3 \cdot 3 \cdot 3 \cdot 3$ can be written as a power. A power has two parts, a base and an exponent. The base is the number that is multiplied (3). The exponent tells how many times the base is used as a factor (4 times). Thus, $3 \cdot 3 \cdot 3 \cdot 3$ can be written as 3^4. Numbers and variables can be written using exponents. For example, $8 \cdot 8 \cdot 8 \cdot m \cdot m \cdot m \cdot m \cdot m$ can be expressed as $8^3 m^5$. Exponents also can be used with place value to express numbers in expanded form. Using this method, 1462 can be written as $(1 \times 10^3) + (4 \times 10^2) + (6 \times 10^1) + (2 \times 10^0)$.

4-3 Prime Factorization

A prime number is a whole number that has exactly two factors, 1 and itself. A composite number is a whole number that has more than two factors. Zero and 1 are neither prime nor composite. When a composite number is expressed as the product of prime factors, it is called the prime factorization of the number. The prime factorization of 40 is $2 \cdot 2 \cdot 2 \cdot 5$ or $2^3 \cdot 5$, each factor being a prime number.

A monomial also may be factored. The monomial $27ab^3$ is factored as $3 \cdot 3 \cdot 3 \cdot a \cdot b \cdot b \cdot b$.

4-4 Greatest Common Factor (GCF)

Often numbers have some of the same factors. The greatest number that is a factor of two or more numbers is called the greatest common factor (GCF). There are two methods to find the GCF. One way is to list the factors of the numbers and identify the largest factor they have in common. The other method uses prime factorization to express each number as the product of prime factors. The GCF is then found by multiplying the common prime factors.

4-5 Simplifying Algebraic Fractions

A fraction is in simplest form when the GCF of the numerator and the denominator is 1. One way to write a fraction in simplest form is to write the prime factorization of the numerator and the denominator and then divide each by the GCF. For example, $\frac{12}{76}$ can be reduced to simplest form by factoring the numerator ($12 = 2 \cdot 2 \cdot 3$) and the denominator ($76 = 2 \cdot 2 \cdot 19$) and then dividing each by the GCF (in this case, $2 \cdot 2$). The resulting fraction, $\frac{3}{19}$, is in simplest form. Note that the value of the fraction remains the same; it just is expressed with simpler numbers.

4-6 Multiplying and Dividing Monomials

The rule for multiplying monomials is the same as that for multiplying powers with the same base: the base remains the same and the exponents are added. Thus, $6^3 \cdot 6^4$ equals 6^7, and $b^2 \cdot b^7$ equals b^9. This rule also can be used with the Commutative and Associative Properties. For example, $(-3m^3)(5m^5)$ can be expressed as $(-3 \cdot 5)(m^5 \cdot m^3)$ or $-15m^8$. Powers and monomials with the same base may be divided by subtracting their exponents.

4-7 Negative Exponents

Very small numbers can be expressed using negative exponents. For example, $\frac{1}{625}$ can be written as 5^{-4}. A negative power indicates that the base is the denominator of a fraction. One way to write a fraction as an equivalent expression with negative exponents is to use prime factorization. The fraction $\frac{1}{32}$ can be expressed as $\frac{1}{2} \cdot \frac{1}{2} \cdot \frac{1}{2} \cdot \frac{1}{2} \cdot \frac{1}{2} = \frac{1}{2^5}$ or 2^{-5}. Negative exponents often are used in science to express small numbers, usually as a power of 10. In this way, $\frac{1}{100,000}$ can be written as 10^{-5}.

Algebraic expressions containing negative exponents also can be written as fractions and then evaluated. For example, if $w = 3$, then $w^{-3} = \frac{1}{w^3}$ or $\frac{1}{27}$. While positive exponents are a notation for repeated multiplication, a negative exponent can be thought of as the reciprocal of the number expressed, or as repeated division. For example, $3^{-6} = \frac{1}{3^6} = \frac{1}{3} \cdot \frac{1}{3} \cdot \frac{1}{3} \cdot \frac{1}{3} \cdot \frac{1}{3} \cdot \frac{1}{3}$.

$$a^1 \cdot a^{-1} = a^0 \qquad \text{Product of powers}$$
$$a \cdot a^{-1} = 1 \qquad \text{Definition of } a^1 \text{ and } a^0$$
$$a^{-1} = \frac{1}{a} \qquad \text{Divide each side by } a.$$

So, $a^{-n} = \underbrace{\frac{1}{a} \cdot \frac{1}{a} \cdot \frac{1}{a} \dots \frac{1}{a}}_{n \text{ factors}}$ where $a \neq 0$.

$$= \frac{1}{a^n}$$

4-8 Scientific Notation

When dealing with very large numbers like 1,500,000 or very small numbers like 0.000015, it is helpful to keep track of the place value by writing the numbers in scientific notation. Powers of 10 with positive exponents are used with a decimal to express large numbers. The exponent represents the number of places the decimal point is to be moved to the right. So, 528,000 is written in scientific notation as 5.28×10^5. Powers of 10 with negative exponents are used to express small numbers. The exponent represents the number of places the decimal point is to be moved to the left. The number 0.00047 is expressed as 4.7×10^{-4}. Numbers can be converted between standard form and scientific notation. Scientific notation is used in all the sciences.

Quick Review Math Handbook

Hot Words includes a glossary of terms while Hot Topics consists of explanations of key mathematical concepts with exercises to test comprehension. This valuable resource can be used as a reference in the classroom or for home study.

Lesson	Hot Topics Section	Lesson	Hot Topics Section
GS 4	2.6, 6.2, 6.3	4-5	2.1, 6.2
4-1	1.4, 1.5	4-6	2.1, 2.9
4-2	1.4, 3.1, 3.4	4-7	2.6, 3.3
4-3	1.2, 1.4, 6.1	4-8	3.3
4-4	1.4, 8.2		

GS = Getting Started

 Additional mathematical information and teaching notes are available at www.pre-alg.com/key_concepts.

DAILY
INTERVENTION and Assessment

Key to Abbreviations:
TWE = Teacher Wraparound Edition; CRM = Chapter Resource Masters

Type	Student Edition	Teacher Resources	Technology/Internet
INTERVENTION			
Ongoing	Prerequisite Skills, pp. 147, 152, 157, 163, 168, 173, 179, 185 Practice Quiz 1, p. 163 Practice Quiz 2, p. 185	5-Minute Check Transparencies *Prerequisite Skills Workbook*, pp. 13–14, 33–36 Quizzes, *CRM*, pp. 219, 220 Mid-Chapter Test, *CRM*, p. 221 Study Guide and Intervention, *CRM*, pp. 165, 170, 175, 180, 185, 190, 195, 200	Pre-AlgePASS: Tutorial Plus, Lessons 7 and 8 www.pre-alg.com/self_check_quiz www.pre-alg.com/extra_examples
Mixed Review	pp. 152, 157, 163, 168, 173, 179, 185, 190	Cumulative Review, *CRM*, p. 222	
Error Analysis	Find the Error, pp. 161, 166	Find the Error, *TWE*, pp. 161, 166	
Standardized Test Practice	pp. 152, 157, 163, 168, 171, 173, 179, 184, 190, 196–197	*TWE*, pp. 196–197 Standardized Test Practice, *CRM*, pp. 223–224	Standardized Test Practice CD-ROM www.pre-alg.com/standardized_test
ASSESSMENT			
Open-Ended Assessment	Writing in Math, pp. 152, 157, 162, 168, 173, 179, 184, 190 Open Ended, pp. 150, 155, 161, 166, 171, 177, 183, 188 Standardized Test, p. 197	Speaking: *TWE*, pp. 157, 185, 190 Writing: *TWE*, pp. 168, 173, 179 Modeling: *TWE*, pp. 152, 163 Open-Ended Assessment, *CRM*, p. 217	
Chapter Assessment	Study Guide, pp. 191–194 Practice Test, p. 195	Multiple-Choice Tests (Forms 1, 2A, 2B), *CRM*, pp. 205–210 Free-Response Tests (Forms 2C, 2D, 3), *CRM*, pp. 211–216 Vocabulary Test/Review, *CRM*, p. 218	ExamView® Pro (see below) MindJogger Videoquizzes www.pre-alg.com/vocabulary_review www.pre-alg.com/chapter_test

For more information on Yearly ProgressPro, see p. 144.

Pre-Algebra Lesson	Yearly ProgressPro Skill Lesson
4-1	Divide Integers
4-2	Evaluate Expressions with Exponents: Level 3
4-3	Prime Factorization with Algebraic Expressions
4-4	Greatest Common Factor with Algebraic Expressions
4-5	Prime Factorization with Algebraic Expressions
4-6	Multiplying and Dividing Monomials
4-7	Negative Exponents
4-8	Scientific Notation: Level 1

ExamView® Pro

Use the networkable **ExamView® Pro** to:
- Create **multiple versions** of tests.
- Create **modified** tests for *Inclusion* students.
- **Edit** existing questions and **add** your own questions.
- Use built-in **state curriculum correlations** to create tests aligned with state standards.
- Change **English** tests to **Spanish** and vice versa.

For more information on Intervention and Assessment, see pp. T8–T11.

Reading and Writing in Mathematics

Glencoe Pre-Algebra provides numerous opportunities to incorporate reading and writing into the mathematics classroom.

Student Edition

- Foldables™ Study Organizer, p. 147
- Reading Mathematics, p. 174
- Concept Check questions require students to verbalize and write about what they have learned in the lesson. (pp. 148, 150, 154, 155, 160, 161, 166, 170, 171, 176, 177, 182, 183, 186, 188)
- Writing in Math questions in every lesson, pp. 152, 157, 162, 168, 173, 179, 184, 190
- Reading Math, pp. 148, 149, 150, 159, 177
- WebQuest, p. 173

Teacher Wraparound Edition

- Foldables™ Study Organizer, pp. 147, 191
- Study Notebook suggestions, pp. 150, 155, 158, 161, 166, 171, 174, 178, 183, 188
- Modeling activities, pp. 152, 163
- Speaking activities, pp. 157, 185, 190
- Writing activities, pp. 168, 173, 179
- Differentiated Instruction (Verbal/Linguistic), p. 155
- **ELL** Resources, pp. 148, 153, 159, 164, 169, 175, 181, 186, 191

Additional Resources

- Vocabulary Builder worksheets require students to define and give examples for key vocabulary terms as they progress through the chapter (*Chapter 4 Resource Masters,* pp. vii–viii)
- Reading to Learn Mathematics master for each lesson (*Chapter 4 Resource Masters,* pp. 168, 173, 178, 183, 188, 193, 198, 203)
- *Vocabulary PuzzleMaker* software creates crossword, jumble, and word search puzzles using vocabulary lists that you can customize.
- *Teaching Mathematics with Foldables* provides suggestions for promoting cognition and language.
- *Reading and Writing in the Mathematics Classroom*
- *WebQuest and Project Resources*

For more information on Reading and Writing in Mathematics, see pp. T6–T7.

PROJECT CRISS℠ Study Skill

A problem-solution graphic structure can be used by students to develop a step-by-step plan for solving a problem. Students begin by writing details of the problem. Next, they write the steps that are necessary to solve the problem. Finally, they solve the problem and write out their result.

The graphic structure at the right applies the four-step plan presented in Chapter 1 to solving a problem containing an exponent. Have students develop a similar structure to solve factorization problems and other types of problems they encounter in this chapter.

Problem

Evaluate the expression $5x^3$ if $x = -2$.

Steps to Solution

Step	Result
1. Explore	1. The exponent means that -2 is used as a factor 3 times
2. Plan	2. Replace x with -2.
3. Solve	3. $5x^3 = 5(-2)^3$ $= 5(-8)$ $= -40$
4. Examine	4. $5(-2)^3 = -40$ is a reasonable answer.

End Result

$5(-2)^3 = -40$

CReating Independence Through Student-Owned Strategies

Factors and Fractions

What You'll Learn

Have students read over the list of objectives and make a list of any words with which they are not familiar.

Why It's Important

Point out to students that this is only one of many reasons why each objective is important. Others are provided in the introduction to each lesson.

What You'll Learn

- **Lessons 4-1, 4-3, and 4-6** Identify, factor, multiply, and divide monomials.
- **Lessons 4-2 and 4-7** Evaluate expressions containing exponents.
- **Lesson 4-4** Factor algebraic expressions by finding the GCF.
- **Lesson 4-5** Simplify fractions using the GCF.
- **Lesson 4-8** Write numbers in scientific notation.

Key Vocabulary

- factors (p. 148)
- monomial (p. 150)
- power (p. 153)
- prime factorization (p. 160)
- scientific notation (p. 186)

Why It's Important

Fractions can be used to analyze and compare real-world data. For example, does a hummingbird or a tiger eat more, in relation to its size? You can use fractions to find the answer. *You will compare eating habits of these and other animals in Lesson 4-5.*

Lesson	NCTM Standards	Local Objectives
4-1	1, 2, 6, 7, 8, 9, 10	
4-2	1, 2, 6, 8, 9, 10	
4-2 Follow-Up	1, 6, 7, 8, 9, 10	
4-3	1, 2, 6, 8, 9, 10	
4-4	1, 2, 6, 8, 9, 10	
4-5	1, 2, 4, 6, 8, 9, 10	
4-6	1, 2, 3, 6, 7, 8, 9, 10	
4-6 Follow-Up	1, 4, 5, 6, 7, 8, 9, 10	
4-7	1, 2, 6, 7, 8, 9, 10	
4-8	1, 2, 4, 7, 8, 9, 10	

Key to NCTM Standards:

1=Number & Operations, 2=Algebra, 3=Geometry, 4=Measurement, 5=Data Analysis & Probability, 6=Problem Solving, 7=Reasoning & Proof, 8=Communication, 9=Connections, 10=Representation

Vocabulary Builder

The Key Vocabulary list introduces students to some of the main vocabulary terms included in this chapter. For a more thorough vocabulary list with pronunciations of new words, give students the Vocabulary Builder worksheets found on pages vii and viii of the *Chapter 4 Resource Masters*. Encourage them to complete the definition of each term as they progress through the chapter. You may suggest that they add these sheets to their study notebooks for future reference when studying for the Chapter 4 test.

► **Prerequisite Skills** To be successful in this chapter, you'll need to master these skills and be able to apply them in problem-solving situations. Review these skills before beginning Chapter 4.

For Lesson 4-1   Distributive Property

Simplify. *(For review, see Lesson 3-1.)*

1. $2(x + 1)$ $2x + 2$ **2.** $3(n - 1)$ $3n - 3$ **3.** $-2(k + 8)$ $-2k - 16$ **4.** $-4(x - 5)$ $-4x + 20$

5. $6(2c + 4)$ **6.** $5(-3s + t)$ **7.** $7(a + b)$ $7a + 7b$ **8.** $9(b - 2c)$
$12c + 24$ $-15s + 5t$ $9b - 18c$

For Lesson 4-2   Order of Operations

Evaluate each expression if $x = 2$, $y = 5$, and $z = -1$. *(For review, see Lesson 1-3.)*

9. $x + 12$ **14**   **10.** $z + (-5)$ -6 **11.** $4y + 8$ **28**   **12.** $10 + 3z$ **7**

13. $(2 + y)9$ **63**   **14.** $6(x - 4)$ -12 **15.** $3xy$ **30**   **16.** $2z + y$ **3**

For Lesson 4-8   Product of Decimals

Find each product. *(For review, see page 715.)*

17. $4.5 \cdot 10$ **45**   **18.** $3.26 \cdot 100$ **326**   **19.** $0.1 \cdot 780$ **78**   **20.** $15 \cdot 0.01$ **0.15**

21. $3.9 \cdot 0.1$ **0.39**   **22.** $63.2 \cdot 0.1$ **6.32**   **23.** $0.01 \cdot 0.5$ **0.005**   **24.** $301.8 \cdot 0.001$
                                                                                               0.3018

 **FOLDABLES™ Study Organizer**

Factors and Monomials Make this Foldable to help you organize your notes. Begin with four sheets of notebook paper.

Step 1 **Fold**

Fold four sheets of notebook paper in half from top to bottom.

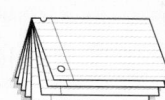

Step 2 **Cut and Staple**

Cut along the fold. Staple the eight half-sheets together to form a booklet.

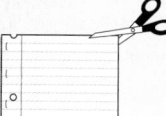

Step 3 **Cut Tabs into Margin**

Make the top tab 2 lines wide, the next tab 4 lines wide, and so on.

Step 4 **Label**

Label each of the tabs with the lesson number and title.

Reading and Writing As you read and study the chapter, write notes and examples on each page.

This section provides a review of the basic concepts needed before beginning Chapter 4. Page references are included for additional student help.

Additional review is provided in the *Prerequisite Skills Workbook*, pages 13–14, and 33–36.

Prerequisite Skills in the Getting Ready for the Next Lesson section at the end of each lesson reviews a skill needed in the next lesson.

For Lesson	Prerequisite Skill
4-2	Multiplying Integers (p. 152)
4-3	Factoring (p. 157)
4-4	Distributive Property (p. 163)
4-5	Converting Measurements (p. 168)
4-6	Properties of Multiplication (p. 173)
4-7	Evaluating Expressions (p. 179)
4-8	Multiplying Decimals (p. 185)

FOLDABLES™ Study Organizer

For more information about Foldables, see *Teaching Mathematics with Foldables.*

Organization of Data: Write a Summary After students make their Foldables, have them label the side tabs to correspond to the eight lessons in this chapter. Students use their Foldables to take notes, define terms, record concepts, and write examples. At the end of each lesson, ask students to write a summary of the lesson, or write in their own words what the lesson was about. Summaries are useful for condensing data.

1 Focus

Mathematical Background notes are available for this lesson on page 146C.

How are side lengths of rectangles related to factors?

The opening activity questions are repeated on page 168 of the *Chapter 4 Resource Masters*.

Reading to Learn Mathematics, p. 168 — ELL

Pre-Activity How are side lengths of rectangles related to factors?

Do the activity at the top of page 148 in your textbook. Write your answers below.

a. Use grid paper to draw as many other rectangles as possible with an area of 36 square units. Label the length and width of each rectangle.
Students should draw rectangles with dimensions 1 × 36, 2 × 18, 3 × 12, and 6 × 6.

b. Did you draw a rectangle with a length of 5 units? Why or why not?
No, if the length were 5, there is no whole number width that would give an area of 36.

c. List all of the pairs of whole numbers whose product is 36. Compare this list to the lengths and widths of all the rectangles that have an area of 36 square units. What do you observe? 1 and 36, 2 and 18, 3 and 12, 4 and 9, 6 and 6; they are the same.

d. Predict the number of rectangles that can be drawn with an area of 64 square units. Explain how you can predict without actually drawing them. 4 rectangles; find the factor pairs whose product is 64: 1 × 64, 2 × 32, 4 × 16, 8 × 8.

Reading the Lesson 1–3. See students' work.

Write a definition and give an example of each new vocabulary word.

Vocabulary	Definition	Example
1. factors		
2. divisible		
3. monomial		

4. Is the expression 2x − 1 a monomial? Explain. 2x − 1 is not a monomial because it is the difference of two terms.

Helping You Remember

5. Explain in your own words how to determine whether an expression is a monomial. Sample answer: A monomial is a number, a variable, or the product of numbers and/or variables.

Teaching Tip Point out that all measurements are whole number quantities.

What You'll Learn

- Determine whether one number is a factor of another.
- Determine whether an expression is a monomial.

Vocabulary

- factors
- divisible
- monomial

a. Students should draw rectangles with dimensions 1 × 36, 2 × 18, 3 × 12, and 6 × 6.

b. No, if the length were 5, there is no whole number width that would give an area of 36.

c. 1 and 36, 2 and 18, 3 and 12, 4 and 9, 6 and 6; they are the same.

d. 4 rectangles; find factor pairs whose product is 64: 1 × 64, 2 × 32, 4 × 16, 8 × 8.

How are side lengths of rectangles related to factors?

The rectangle at the right has an area of 9 · 4 or 36 square units.

a. Use grid paper to draw as many other rectangles as possible with an area of 36 square units. Label the length and width of each rectangle.

b. Did you draw a rectangle with a length of 5 units? Why or why not?

c. List all of the pairs of whole numbers whose product is 36. Compare this list to the lengths and widths of all the rectangles that have an area of 36 square units. What do you observe?

d. Predict the number of rectangles that can be drawn with an area of 64 square units. Explain how you can predict without drawing.

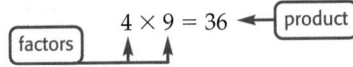

Area = 36 units²

FIND FACTORS Two or more numbers that are multiplied to form a product are called **factors**.

$$4 \times 9 = 36 \longleftarrow \text{product}$$

So, 4 and 9 are factors of 36 because they each divide 36 with a remainder of 0. We can say that 36 is **divisible** by 4 and 9. However, 5 is not a factor of 36 because $36 \div 5 = 7$ with a remainder of 1.

Sometimes you can test for divisibility mentally. The following rules can help you determine whether a number is divisible by 2, 3, 5, 6, or 10.

Reading Math

Even and Odd Numbers

A number that is divisible by 2 is called an *even number*. A number that is not divisible by 2 is called an *odd number*.

Concept Summary		Divisibility Rules
A number is divisible by:	Examples	Reasons
• 2 if the ones digit is divisible by 2.	54 →	4 is divisible by 2.
• 3 if the sum of its digits is divisible by 3.	72 →	7 + 2 = 9, and 9 is divisible by 3.
• 5 if the ones digit is 0 or 5.	65 →	The ones digit is 5.
• 6 if the number is divisible by 2 and 3.	48 →	48 is divisible by 2 and 3.
• 10 if the ones digit is 0.	120 →	The ones digit is 0.

✓ **Concept Check** Is 51 divisible by 3? Why or why not?
Yes; 5 + 1 = 6, and 6 is divisible by 3.

Resource Manager

 Workbooks and Reproducible Masters

Chapter 4 Resource Masters
- Study Guide and Intervention, p. 165
- Skills Practice, p. 166
- Practice, p. 167
- Reading to Learn Mathematics, p. 168
- Enrichment, p. 169

Parent and Student Study Guide Workbook, p. 24
Prerequisite Skills Workbook, pp. 13–14

Transparencies
5-Minute Check Transparency 4-1
Answer Key Transparencies

 Technology
Interactive Chalkboard

Example 1 Use Divisibility Rules

Determine whether 138 is divisible by 2, 3, 5, 6, or 10.

Number	Divisible?	Reason
2	yes	The ones digit is 8, and 8 is divisible by 2.
3	yes	The sum of the digits is $1 + 3 + 8$ or 12, and 12 is divisible by 3.
5	no	The ones digit is 8, not 0 or 5.
6	yes	138 is divisible by 2 and 3.
10	no	The ones digit is not 0.

So, 138 is divisible by 2, 3, and 6.

More About. . .

Weddings
On average, it costs four times more to book reception sites in Los Angeles than in the Midwest.
Source: newschannel5.
webpoint.com/wedding

Example 2 Use Divisibility Rules to Solve a Problem

WEDDINGS A bride must choose whether to seat 5, 6, or 10 people per table at her reception. If there are 192 guests and she wants all the tables to be full, which should she choose?

Seats Per Table	Yes/No	Reason
5	no	The ones digit of 192 does not end in 0 or 5, so 192 is not divisible by 5. There would be empty seats.
6	yes	192 is divisible by 2 and 3, so it is also divisible by 6. Therefore, all the tables would be full.
10	no	The ones digit of 192 does not end in 0, so 192 is not divisible by 10. There would be empty seats.

The bride should choose tables that seat 6 people.

You can also use the rules for divisibility to find the factors of a number.

Example 3 Find Factors of a Number

Reading Math

Divisible/Factor
The following statements mean the same thing.
- 72 is divisible by 2.
- 2 is a factor of 72.

List all the factors of 72.
Use the divisibility rules to determine whether 72 is divisible by 2, 3, 5, and so on. Then use division to find other factors of 72.

Number	72 Divisible by Number?	Factor Pairs
1	yes	$1 \cdot 72$
2	yes	$2 \cdot 36$
3	yes	$3 \cdot 24$
4	yes	$4 \cdot 18$
5	no	—
6	yes	$6 \cdot 12$
7	no	—
8	yes	$8 \cdot 9$
9	yes	$9 \cdot 8$

Use division to find the other factor in each factor pair.
$72 \div 2 = 36$

You can stop finding factors when the numbers start repeating.

So, the factors of 72 are 1, 2, 3, 4, 6, 8, 9, 12, 18, 24, 36, and 72.

www.pre-alg.com/extra_examples

Lesson 4-1 Factors and Monomials **149**

Interactive Chalkboard
PowerPoint® Presentations

This CD-ROM is a customizable Microsoft® Power-Point® presentation that includes:
- Step-by-step, dynamic solutions of each In-Class Example from the Teacher Wraparound Edition
- Additional, Your Turn exercises for each example
- The 5-Minute Check Transparencies
- Hot links to Glencoe Online Study Tools

---

2 Teach

FIND FACTORS

Teaching Tip Point out that a number is divisible by 9 if the sum of the digits is divisible by 9.

In-Class Examples Power Point®

1 Determine whether 435 is divisible by 2, 3, 5, 6, or 10.
435 is divisible by 3 and 5.

2 Sonya is running for student council president. She wants to give out campaign flyers with a pen to each student in the school. She can buy "Vote for Sonya" pens in packages of 5, 6, or 10. If there are 306 students in the school and she wants no pens left over, which size packages should she buy?
She should buy pens in packages of 6.

3 List all the factors of 64.
1, 2, 4, 8, 16, 32, 64

MONOMIALS

In-Class Example Power Point®

Teaching Tip An expression that is not a monomial may simplify to two or more terms. When simplifying expressions, you may need to review the Distributive Property.

4 Determine whether each expression is a monomial.

a. $4(n + 3)$ This expression is not a monomial because in its simplest form, $4n + 12$, it involves two terms that are added.

b. $\dfrac{x}{3}$ This expression is a monomial because it is the product of a rational number and a variable.

3 Practice/Apply

About the Exercises . . .

Organization by Objective
- **Find Factors:** 16–35, 48–55
- **Monomials:** 36–47

Odd/Even Assignments
Exercises 16–53 are structured so that students practice the same concepts whether they are assigned odd or even problems.

Alert! Exercise 3 requires a calculator. Exercise 51 involves research on the Internet or other reference materials.

Assignment Guide

Basic: 17–25 odd, 29–47 odd, 48, 49, 56–72

Average: 17–47 odd, 50, 51, 53, 56–72

Advanced: 16–46 even, 50–66 (Optional: 67–72)

Answer

1. Use the rules for divisibility to determine whether 18,450 is divisible by both 2 and 3. If it is, then the number is also divisible by 6 and there is no remainder.

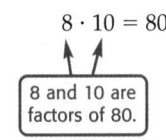

ALGEBRA CONNECTION

MONOMIALS A number such as 80 or an expression such as $8x$ is called a monomial. A **monomial** is a number, a variable, or a product of numbers and/or variables.

$$8 \cdot 10 = 80 \qquad\qquad 8 \cdot x = 8x$$

8 and 10 are factors of 80.

8 and x are factors of $8x$.

Monomials		Not Monomials	
4	a number	$2 + x$	two terms are added
y	a variable	$5c - 6$	one term is subtracted from another term
$-2rs$	the product of a number and variables	$3(a + b)$	two terms are added $3(a + b) = 3a + 3b$

Reading Math

Monomial

The prefix *mono* means one. A monomial is an expression with one term.

TEACHING TIP

Clarify that a monomial is the product of variables and rational numbers and may have a number as a denominator, but not a variable. For example, $\frac{x}{2}$ is a monomial, but $\frac{2}{x}$ is not.

✓ **Concept Check** Explain why $7q \cdot n$ is a monomial, but $7q + n$ is not.
$7q \cdot n$ is a product; $7q + n$ is the sum of two terms.

Before you determine whether an expression is a monomial, be sure the expression is in simplest form.

Example 4 *Identify Monomials*

Determine whether each expression is a monomial.

a. $2(x - 3)$

$2(x - 3) = 2x + 2(-3)$ Distributive Property
$\qquad\qquad = 2x - 6$ Simplify.

This expression is not a monomial because it has two terms involving subtraction.

b. $-48xyz$

This expression is a monomial because it is the product of integers and variables.

Check for Understanding

Concept Check

2. No; 132 is divisible by 3, but 125 is not.

GUIDED PRACTICE KEY	
Exercises	Examples
4–7	1
8–10	3
11–14	4
15	2

1. **Explain** how you can mentally determine whether there is a remainder when 18,450 is divided by 6. **See margin.**

2. **Determine** whether 3 is a common factor of 125 and 132. Explain.

3. **OPEN ENDED** Use mental math, paper and pencil, or a calculator to find at least one number that satisfies each condition.
   a. a 3-digit number that is divisible by 2, 3, and 6 **102**   b. **1035**
   b. a 4-digit number that is divisible by 3 and 5, but is not divisible by 10.
   c. a 3-digit number that is not divisible by 2, 3, 5, or 10 **343**
   3a–c. Sample answers are given.

Guided Practice

Use divisibility rules to determine whether each number is divisible by 2, 3, 5, 6, or 10.

4. 51 **3**   5. 146 **2**   6. 876 **2, 3, 6**   7. 3050 **2, 5, 10**

DAILY INTERVENTION

Differentiated Instruction

- **Logical** Try the following game. Give each pair of students a hundreds chart and a calculator (optional). Have students take turns crossing one number off the chart until each student has crossed off 5 numbers. Each student should use a different color pencil or pen for this activity. Then have students find all factors of the numbers they selected. The winner is the student who compiled the most factors overall. Repeat the activity with the winner compiling the least number of factors overall.

List all the factors of each number. **9.** 1, 2, 4, 5, 8, 10, 16, 20, 40, 80

8. 203 1, 7, 29, 203   **9.** 80   **10.** 115 1, 5, 23, 115

ALGEBRA Determine whether each expression is a monomial. Explain why or why not. 11–14. See margin for explanations.

11. 38 yes   **12.** $2n - 2$ no   **13.** $5(x + y)$ no   **14.** $17(4)k$ yes

Application **15. CALENDARS** Years that are divisible by 4, called *leap years*, are 366 days long. Also, years ending in "00" that are divisible by 400 are leap years. Use the rule given below to determine whether 2000, 2004, 2015, 2018, 2022, and 2032 are leap years. **2000, 2004, and 2032 are leap years.**

> If the last two digits form a number that is divisible by 4, then the number is divisible by 4.

★ indicates increased difficulty

Practice and Apply

Homework Help

For Exercises	See Examples
16–27	1
28–35	3
36–47	4
48–51	2

Extra Practice
See page 730.

Use divisibility rules to determine whether each number is divisible by 2, 3, 5, 6, or 10. **19.** 2, 3, 5, 6, 10

16. 39 3   **17.** 135 3, 5   **18.** 82 2   **19.** 120

20. 250 2, 5, 10   **21.** 118 2   **22.** 378 2, 3, 6   **23.** 955 5

24. 5010   **25.** 684   ★ **26.** 10,523   ★ **27.** 24,640
2, 3, 5, 6, 10   2, 3, 6   none   2, 5, 10

List all the factors of each number. 28–35. See margin.

28. 75   **29.** 114   **30.** 57   **31.** 65

32. 90   **33.** 124   **34.** 102   **35.** 135

ALGEBRA Determine whether each expression is a monomial. Explain why or why not. 36–47. See p. 197A for explanations.

36. m yes   **37.** 110 yes   **38.** $s + t$ no   **39.** $g - h$ no

40. $-12 + 12x$ no   **41.** $3c + 6$ no   **42.** $7(a + 1)$ no   **43.** $4(2t - 1)$ no

44. $4b$ yes   **45.** $10(-t)$ yes   **46.** $-25abc$ yes   **47.** $8j(4k)$ yes

MUSIC For Exercises 48 and 49, use the following information.
The band has 72 students who will march during halftime of the football game. For one drill, they need to march in rows with the same number of students in each row. 48–49. See p. 197A.

48. Can the whole band be arranged in rows of 7? Explain.

49. How many different ways could students be arranged? Describe the arrangements.

HISTORY For Exercises 50 and 51, use the following information.
★ Each star on the U.S. flag represents a state. As states joined the Union, the rectangular arrangement of the stars changed. 50–51. See p. 197A.

50. Use the information at the left to make a conjecture about how you think the stars of the flag were arranged in 1912 and in 1959.

51. Research What is the correct arrangement of stars on the U.S. flag? Explain why the arrangement is not rectangular.

More About...

History
In 1912, when there were 48 states, the stars of the flag were arranged in equal rows. In 1959, after Alaska joined the Union, a new arrangement was proposed.
Source: www.usflag.org

www.pre-alg.com/self_check_quiz   **Lesson 4-1** Factors and Monomials **151**

Answers

11. a number

12. one term is subtracted from another term

13. two terms are added

14. the product of numbers and a variable

28. 1, 3, 5, 15, 25, 75

29. 1, 2, 3, 6, 19, 38, 57, 114

30. 1, 3, 19, 57

31. 1, 5, 13, 65

32. 1, 2, 3, 5, 6, 9, 10, 15, 18, 30, 45, 90

33. 1, 2, 4, 31, 62, 124

34. 1, 2, 3, 6, 17, 34, 51, 102

35. 1, 3, 5, 9, 15, 27, 45, 135

Lesson 4-1 Factors and Monomials **151**

Open-Ended Assessment
Modeling Have students work in pairs using 42 rainbow or centimeter cubes. Students will use these blocks to model the factors of 42. Show students that one row of 42 blocks is the same thing as two rows of 21 blocks, because both use 42 blocks. Have students model all of the factors of 42 in this way.

Getting Ready for Lesson 4-2

PREREQUISITE SKILL Lesson 4-2 presents powers and exponents. To evaluate a power, students must be able to find products of integers. Exercises 67–72 should be used to determine your students' familiarity with multiplying integers.

Answers

52. If a number is divisible by 3 and by 2, then it is also divisible by 6. If a number is divisible by 3, but not divisible by 2, then it is not divisible by 6.

53. A number that has 10 as a factor is divisible by $2 \cdot 5$, so it is always divisible by 5.

54. A number that has a factor of 10 is divisible by $2 \cdot 5$. Since such a number is divisible by 2, it must be even.

57. The side lengths or dimensions of a rectangle are factors of the number that is the area of the rectangle. Answers should include the following.

- A rectangle with dimensions and area labeled; for example, a 4×5 rectangle would have length 5 units, width 4 units, and area 20 square units.

- Factors are numbers that are multiplied to form a product. The dimensions of a rectangle are factor pairs of the area since they are multiplied to form the area.

Determine whether each statement is *sometimes*, *always*, or *never* true. Explain your reasoning. 52–54. See margin for explanations.

★ 52. A number that is divisible by 3 is also divisible by 6. **sometimes**

★ 53. A number that has 10 as a factor is not divisible by 5. **never**

★ 54. A number that has a factor of 10 is an even number. **always**

★ 55. **MONEY** The homecoming committee can spend $144 on refreshments for the dance. Soft drinks cost $6 per case, and cookies cost $4 per bag.
  a. How many cases of soft drinks can they buy with $144? **24 cases**
  b. How many bags of cookies can they buy with $144? **36 bags**
  c. Suppose they want to buy approximately the same amounts of soft drinks and cookies. How many of each could they buy with $144?

55c. Sample answers:
12 cases, 18 bags;
14 cases, 15 bags;
16 cases, 12 bags

56. **CRITICAL THINKING** Write a number that satisfies each set of conditions.
  a. the greatest three-digit number that is not divisible by 2, 3, or 10 **997**
  b. the least three-digit number that is not divisible by 2, 3, 5, or 10 **101**

57. WRITING IN MATH Answer the question that was posed at the beginning of the lesson. See margin.

  How are side lengths of rectangles related to factors?
  Include the following in your answer:
  - a drawing of a rectangle with its dimensions and area labeled, and
  - a definition of *factors* and a description of the relationship between rectangle dimensions and factor pairs of a number.

Standardized Test Practice

58. Which number is divisible by 3? **B**
  Ⓐ 133　　Ⓑ 444　　Ⓒ 53　　Ⓓ 250

59. Determine which expression is *not* a monomial. **C**
  Ⓐ 6d　　Ⓑ $6d \cdot 5$　　Ⓒ $6d - 5$　　Ⓓ 5

Maintain Your Skills

Mixed Review **GEOMETRY** Find the perimeter and area of each rectangle. *(Lesson 3-7)*

60.
3.5 m
4.9 m
16.8 m, 17.15 m²

61.
5 in.
12 in.
34 in., 60 in²

ALGEBRA Translate each sentence into an equation. Then find each number. *(Lesson 3-6)*

62. Eight more than twice a number is -16. $2n + 8 = -16; -12$

63. Two less than 5 times a number equals 3. $5n - 2 = 3; 1$

ALGEBRA Solve each equation. Check your solution. *(Lesson 3-5)*

64. $2x - 1 = 9$ **5**　　65. $14 = 8 + 3n$ **2**　　66. $7 + \frac{k}{5} = -1$ **−40**

Getting Ready for the Next Lesson **PREREQUISITE SKILL** Find each product.
(To review multiplying integers, see Lesson 2-4.)

67. $4 \cdot 4 \cdot 4$ **64**　　68. $10 \cdot 10 \cdot 10 \cdot 10$ **10,000** 69. $(-3)(-3)(-3)$ **−27**

70. $(-2)(-2)(-2)(-2)$ **16** 71. $8 \cdot 8 \cdot 6 \cdot 6$ **2304**　　72. $(2)(2)(-5)(-5)(-5)$ **−500**

Powers and Exponents

What You'll Learn

- Write expressions using exponents.
- Evaluate expressions containing exponents.

Why are exponents important in comparing computer data?

Computer data are measured in small units called *bytes*. These units are based on factors of 2.

a. Write 16 as a product of factors of 2. How many factors are there?

b. How many factors of 2 form the product 128?

c. One megabyte is 1024 kilobytes. How many factors of 2 form the product 1024?

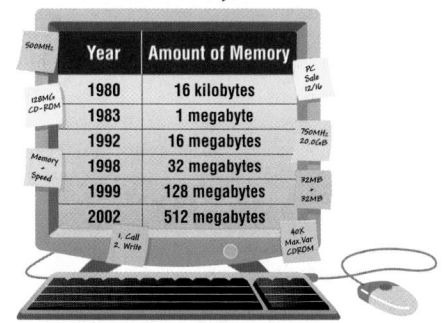

Personal Computers

Year	Amount of Memory
1980	16 kilobytes
1983	1 megabyte
1992	16 megabytes
1998	32 megabytes
1999	128 megabytes
2002	512 megabytes

Source: www.islandnet.com

Vocabulary
- base
- exponent
- power
- standard form
- expanded form

a. $2 \times 2 \times 2 \times 2$; 4 factors

b. 7 factors

c. 10 factors

EXPONENTS An expression like $2 \times 2 \times 2 \times 2$ can be written as a power. A power has two parts, a base and an exponent. The expression $2 \times 2 \times 2 \times 2$ can be written as 2^4.

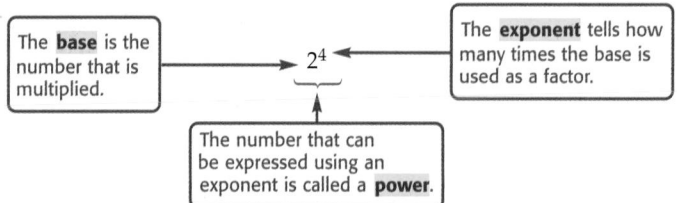

The **base** is the number that is multiplied.

2^4

The **exponent** tells how many times the base is used as a factor.

The number that can be expressed using an exponent is called a **power**.

The table below shows how to write and read powers with positive exponents.

Study Tip

First Power

When a number is raised to the first power, the exponent is usually omitted. So 2^1 is written as 2.

Powers	Words	Repeated Factors
2^1	2 to the first power	2
2^2	2 to the second power or 2 squared	$2 \cdot 2$
2^3	2 to the third power or 2 cubed	$2 \cdot 2 \cdot 2$
2^4	2 to the fourth power or 2 to the fourth	$2 \cdot 2 \cdot 2 \cdot 2$
$\vdots$	$\vdots$	
2^n	2 to the nth power or 2 to the nth	$\underbrace{2 \cdot 2 \cdot 2 \cdot \ldots \cdot 2}_{n \text{ factors}}$

Any number, except 0, raised to the zero power is defined to be 1.

$$1^0 = 1 \qquad 2^0 = 1 \qquad 3^0 = 1 \qquad 4^0 = 1 \qquad 5^0 = 1 \qquad x^0 = 1, x \neq 0$$

1 Focus

5-Minute Check Transparency 4-2 Use as a quiz or review of Lesson 4-1.

Mathematical Background notes are available for this lesson on page 146C.

Why are exponents important in comparing computer data?

The opening activity questions are repeated on page 173 of the *Chapter 4 Resource Masters*.

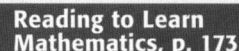

Reading to Learn Mathematics, p. 173 ELL

A **prime number** is a whole number that has exactly two factors, 1 and itself. A **composite number** is a whole number that has more than two factors. Zero and 1 are neither prime nor composite.

Example 1 Determine whether 29 is prime or composite.

Find the factors of 29.

$29 = 1 \cdot 29$

The only factors of 29 are 1 and 29, therefore 29 is a prime number.

Any composite number can be written as a product of prime numbers. A factor tree can be used to find the prime factorization.

Example 2 Find the prime factorization of 48.

48 is the number to be factored.

Find any pair of whole number factors of 48.

Continue to factor any number that is not prime.

The factor tree is complete when there is a row of prime numbers.

The prime factorization of 48 is $2 \cdot 2 \cdot 2 \cdot 3$ or $2^4 \cdot 3$.

In algebra, monomials can be factored as a product of prime numbers and variables with no exponent greater than 1. So, $8x^2$ factors as $2 \cdot 2 \cdot 2 \cdot x \cdot x$.

Exercises

Determine whether each number is *prime* or *composite*.

1. 27 composite 2. 151 prime
3. 77 composite 4. 25 composite

Write the prime factorization for each number. Use exponents for repeated factors.

5. 16 2^4 6. 45 $3^2 \cdot 5$
7. 78 $2 \cdot 3 \cdot 13$ 8. 70 $2 \cdot 5 \cdot 7$

Factor each monomial.

9. $6m^3$ $2 \cdot 3 \cdot m \cdot m \cdot m$ 10. $-20xy^2$ $-1 \cdot 2 \cdot 2 \cdot 5 \cdot x \cdot y \cdot y$
11. $a^2b^2c^3$ $a \cdot a \cdot b \cdot b \cdot c \cdot c \cdot c$ 12. $25h$ $5 \cdot 5 \cdot h$

Teaching Tip Emphasize to students that 2^4 is not $2 \cdot 4$, but $2^4 = 2 \cdot 2 \cdot 2 \cdot 2$ or 16.

Resource Manager

Workbooks and Reproducible Masters

Chapter 4 Resource Masters
- Study Guide and Intervention, p. 170
- Skills Practice, p. 171
- Practice, p. 172
- Reading to Learn Mathematics, p. 173
- Enrichment, p. 174
- Assessment, p. 219

Graphing Calculator and Spreadsheet Masters, p. 25
Parent and Student Study Guide Workbook, p. 25
School-to-Career Masters, p. 7

 Transparencies

5-Minute Check Transparency 4-2
Answer Key Transparencies

 Technology

Interactive Chalkboard

Building on Prior Knowledge

In Chapter 1, students learned order of operations. In this lesson they will add a step to the order that involves evaluating exponents.

EXPONENTS

In-Class Examples | Power Point®

1 Write each expression using exponents.

a. $6 \cdot 6 \cdot 6 \cdot 6$ 6^4

b. p p^1

c. $(-1)(-1)(-1)$ $(-1)^3$

d. $(5x + 1)(5x + 1)$ $(5x + 1)^2$

e. $\frac{1}{2} \cdot x \cdot x \cdot x \cdot x \cdot y \cdot y \cdot y$

$\frac{1}{2}x^4y^3$

2 Express 235,016 in expanded form. $235{,}016 = (2 \times 10^5) + (3 \times 10^4) + (5 \times 10^3) + (0 \times 10^2) + (1 \times 10^1) + (6 \times 10^0)$

✓ Skills Check

Exponents Ask students to explain the meaning of

a. $(23)^5$ b. $2a^3$ c. $(2a)^3$

EVALUATE EXPRESSIONS

In-Class Example | Power Point®

3 Evaluate each expression.

a. 4^2 16

b. $r^3 - 3$ if $r = -2$ -11

c. $x(y + 2)^2$ if $x = 2$ and $y = -2$ 0

Teaching Tip Emphasize that the value of x^5 increases more rapidly than $5x$ when evaluated for positive numbers. Substitute values to verify this.

Example 1 Write Expressions Using Exponents

Write each expression using exponents.

a. $3 \cdot 3 \cdot 3 \cdot 3 \cdot 3$

The base is 3. It is a factor 5 times, so the exponent is 5.
$3 \cdot 3 \cdot 3 \cdot 3 \cdot 3 = 3^5$

b. $t \cdot t \cdot t \cdot t$

The base is t. It is a factor 4 times, so the exponent is 4.
$t \cdot t \cdot t \cdot t = t^4$

c. $(-9)(-9)$

The base is -9. It is a factor 2 times, so the exponent is 2.
$(-9)(-9) = (-9)^2$

d. $(x + 1)(x + 1)(x + 1)$

The base is $x + 1$. It is a factor 3 times, so the exponent is 3.
$(x + 1)(x + 1)(x + 1) = (x + 1)^3$

e. $7 \cdot a \cdot a \cdot a \cdot b \cdot b$

First, group the factors with like bases. Then, write using exponents.
$7 \cdot a \cdot a \cdot a \cdot b \cdot b = 7 \cdot (a \cdot a \cdot a) \cdot (b \cdot b)$
$= 7a^3b^2$ $a \cdot a \cdot a = a^3$ and $b \cdot b = b^2$

Study Tip

Common Misconception
$(-9)^2$ is not the same as -9^2.
$-9^2 = -1 \cdot 9^2$

✓ **Concept Check** How would you write *ten to the fourth* using an exponent? 10^4

TEACHING TIP

Numbers written using exponents are in *exponential form*.

The number 13,548 is in **standard form** because it does not contain exponents. You can use place value and exponents to express a number in **expanded form**.

Example 2 Use Exponents in Expanded Form

Express 13,048 in expanded form.

Step 1 Use place value to write the value of each digit in the number.

$13{,}048 = 10{,}000 + 3000 + 0 + 40 + 8$
$= (1 \times 10{,}000) + (3 \times 1000) + (0 \times 100) + (4 \times 10) + (8 \times 1)$

Step 2 Write each place value as a power of 10 using exponents.

$13{,}048 = (1 \times 10^4) + (3 \times 10^3) + (0 \times 10^2) + (4 \times 10^1) + (8 \times 10^0)$

Recall that $10^0 = 1$.

EVALUATE EXPRESSIONS Since powers are forms of multiplication, they need to be included in the rules for order of operations.

Concept Summary		Order of Operations	
	Words		**Example**
Step 1	Simplify the expressions inside grouping symbols. Start with the innermost grouping symbols.		$(3 + 4)^2 + 5 \cdot 2 = 7^2 + 5 \cdot 2$
Step 2	Evaluate all powers.		$= 49 + 5 \cdot 2$
Step 3	Do all multiplications or divisions in order from left to right.		$= 49 + 10$
Step 4	Do all additions or subtractions in order from left to right.		$= 59$

Teacher to Teacher

Jenny L. Miller   Tuttle M.S., Crawfordsville, IN

"Students have trouble understanding the effect a power has on a number. I have my students use blocks to build visual images of powers such as 2^1, 2^2, 2^3, and so on."

Follow the order of operations to evaluate algebraic expressions.

Example 3 Evaluate Expressions

Evaluate each expression.

a. 2^3

$$2^3 = 2 \cdot 2 \cdot 2 \quad \text{2 is a factor 3 times.}$$
$$= 8 \qquad\quad \text{Multiply.}$$

b. $y^2 + 5$ if $y = -3$

$$y^2 + 5 = (-3)^2 + 5 \qquad \text{Replace } y \text{ with } -3.$$
$$= (-3)(-3) + 5 \qquad -3 \text{ is a factor two times.}$$
$$= 9 + 5 \qquad\qquad \text{Multiply.}$$
$$= 14 \qquad\qquad\quad \text{Add.}$$

c. $3(x + y)^4$ if $x = -2$ and $y = 1$

$$3(x + y)^4 = 3(-2 + 1)^4 \qquad \text{Replace } x \text{ with } -2 \text{ and } y \text{ with } 1.$$
$$= 3(-1)^4 \qquad\qquad \text{Simplify the expression inside the parentheses.}$$
$$= 3(1) \qquad\qquad\quad \text{Evaluate } (-1)^4.$$
$$= 3 \qquad\qquad\qquad \text{Simplify.}$$

Check for Understanding

Concept Check

1. Sample answer:
2^5, x^5
2–3. See margin.

1. **OPEN ENDED** Use exponents to write a numerical expression and an algebraic expression in which the base is a factor 5 times.

2. **Explain** how the expression *6 cubed* is repeated multiplication.

3. **Make a conjecture** about the value of 1^n and the value of $(-1)^n$ for any value of n. Explain.

Guided Practice

Write each expression using exponents.

GUIDED PRACTICE KEY	
Exercises	Examples
4–6, 11	1
7	2
8–10	3

4. $n \cdot n \cdot n$ n^3

5. $7 \cdot 7$ 7^2

6. $3 \cdot 3 \cdot x \cdot x \cdot x \cdot x$ $3^2 x^4$

7. Express 2695 in expanded form. $(2 \times 10^3) + (6 \times 10^2) + (9 \times 10^1) + (5 \times 10^0)$

ALGEBRA Evaluate each expression.

8. 2^4 16

9. $x^3 - 3$ if $x = -2$ −11

10. $5(y - 1)^2$ if $y = 4$ 45

Application

11. **SOUND** Fireworks can easily reach a sound of 169 decibels, which can be dangerous if prolonged. Write this number using exponents and a smaller base. 13^2

★ indicates increased difficulty

Practice and Apply

Write each expression using exponents. 15. $(-8)^4$ 20. $a^2 b^4$ 23. $9(p + 1)^2$

12. $4 \cdot 4 \cdot 4 \cdot 4 \cdot 4 \cdot 4$ 4^6

13. 6 6^1

14. $(-5)(-5)(-5)$ $(-5)^3$

15. $(-8)(-8)(-8)(-8)$

16. $k \cdot k$ k^2

17. $(-t)(-t)(-t)$ $(-t)^3$

18. $(r \cdot r)(r \cdot r)$ r^4

19. $m \cdot m \cdot m \cdot m$ m^4

20. $a \cdot a \cdot b \cdot b \cdot b \cdot b$

21. $2 \cdot x \cdot x \cdot y \cdot y$ $2x^2y^2$

22. $7 \cdot 7 \cdot 7 \cdot n \cdot n \cdot n \cdot n$ $7^3 n^4$

23. $9 \cdot (p + 1) \cdot (p + 1)$

25. $(8 \times 10^2) + (0 \times 10^1) + (3 \times 10^0)$
26. $(6 \times 10^3) + (9 \times 10^2) + (9 \times 10^1) + (4 \times 10^0)$
27. $(2 \times 10^4) + (3 \times 10^3) + (7 \times 10^2) + (8 \times 10^1) + (1 \times 10^0)$

Express each number in expanded form.   24. $(4 \times 10^2) + (5 \times 10^1) + (2 \times 10^0)$

24. 452   25. 803   26. 6994   27. 23,781

ALGEBRA Evaluate each expression if $a = 2$, $b = 4$, and $c = -3$.

28. 7^2 49
29. 10^3 1000
30. $(-9)^3$ -729
31. $(-2)^5$ -32
32. b^4 256
33. c^4 81
34. $5a^4$ 80
35. ac^3 -54
36. $b^0 - 10$ -9
37. $c^2 + a^2$ 13
★ 38. $3a + b^3$ 70
★ 39. $a^2 + 3a - 1$ 9
★ 40. $b^2 - 2b + 6$ 14
★ 41. $3(b - 1)^4$ 243
★ 42. $2(3c + 7)^2$ 8

43. **TRAVEL** Write each number in the graphic as a power. $81 = 9^2$ or 3^4, $64 = 8^2$ or 4^3 or 2^6

44. Write *7 cubed times x squared* as repeated multiplication. $7 \cdot 7 \cdot 7 \cdot x \cdot x$

45. Write *negative eight, cubed* using exponents, as a product of repeated factors, and in standard form. $(-8)^3$; $(-8)(-8)(-8)$; -512

46. Without using a calculator, order 96, 96^2, 96^{10}, 96^5, and 96^0 from least to greatest. Explain your reasoning.   **See margin.**

47. **NUMBER THEORY** Explain whether the square of any nonzero number is *sometimes*, *always*, or *never* a positive number.   **Always; the product of two negative numbers is always positive.**

48. **BIOLOGY** A man burns approximately 121 Calories by standing for an hour. A woman burns approximately 100 Calories per hour when standing. Write each of these numbers as a power with an exponent other than 1. $121 = 11^2$; $100 = 10^2$

HISTORY For Exercises 49–51, use the following information.

★ In an ancient Chinese tradition, a chef stretches and folds dough to make long, thin noodles called *so*. After the first fold, he makes 2 noodles. He stretches and folds it a second time to make 4 noodles. Each time he repeats this process, the number of noodles doubles.

49. Use exponents to express the number of noodles after each of the first five folds. 2^1, 2^2, 2^3, 2^4, 2^5

50. Legendary chefs have completed as many as thirteen folds. How many noodles is this? $2^{13} = 8192$ noodles

51. If the noodles are laid end to end and each noodle is 5 feet long, after how many of these folds will the length be more than a mile?   **See margin.**

Replace each ● with $<$, $>$, or $=$ to make a true statement.

52. 3^7 ● 7^3 $>$
53. 2^4 ● 4^2 $=$
54. 6^3 ● 4^4 $<$

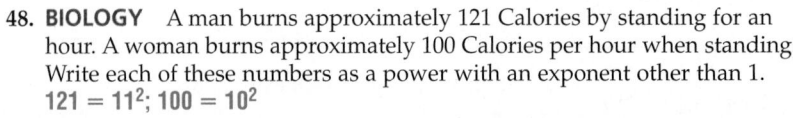

USA TODAY Snapshots®

Our daily time behind the wheel

Men   81 minutes

Women   64 minutes

Source: Federal Highway Administration, American Automobile Manufacturers Association

By Anne R. Carey and Marcy E. Mullins, USA TODAY

Answers

46. 96^0, 96, 96^2, 96^5, 96^{10}; As the exponents increase, the additional factors of 96, and therefore the values of the expressions, increase. Since $96^0 = 1$, it has the least value.

51. After 10 folds, the noodles are $5(2^{10}) = 5(1024)$ or 5120 feet long, which is slightly less than a mile. So, after 11 folds the length of the noodles will be greater than a mile.

GEOMETRY For Exercises 55–57, use the cube below.

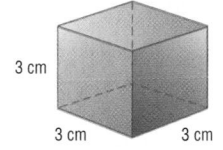

55. The *surface area* of a cube is the sum of the areas of the faces. Use exponents to write an expression for the surface area of the cube. $6 \cdot 3^2$ cm^2

3 cm

3 cm   3 cm

56. The *volume* of a cube, or the amount of space that it occupies, is the product of the length, width, and height. Use exponents to write an expression for the volume of the cube. 3^3 cm^3

57. If you double the length of each edge of the cube, are the surface area and volume also doubled? Explain.

57. No; the surface area is multiplied by 4. The volume is multiplied by 8.

58. **CRITICAL THINKING** Suppose the length of a side of a square is n units and the length of an edge of a cube is n units.

  a. If all the side lengths of a square are doubled, are the perimeter and the area of the square doubled? Explain.

  b. If all the side lengths of a square are tripled, show that the area of the new square is 9 times the area of the original square.

  c. If all the edge lengths of a cube are tripled, show that the volume of the new cube is 27 times the volume of the original cube.

58a. The perimeter is doubled and the area is four times the area of the original square.
58b. original area: n^2, new area: $(3n)^2$ or $9n^2$
58c. original volume: n^3, new volume: $(3n)^3$ or $27n^3$

59. WRITING IN MATH   Answer the question that was posed at the beginning of the lesson. **See margin.**

   Why are exponents important in comparing computer data?

   Include the following in your answer:
   • an explanation of how factors of 2 describe computer memory, and
   • a sentence explaining the advantage of using exponents.

 Online Research **Data Update** How many megabytes of memory are common today? Visit www.pre-alg.com/data_update to learn more.

Standardized Test Practice
Ⓐ Ⓑ Ⓒ Ⓓ

60. Write *ten million* as a power of ten. **C**

   Ⓐ 10^5 Ⓑ 10^6 Ⓒ 10^7 Ⓓ 10^8

61. What value of x will make $256 = 2^x$ true? **B**

   Ⓐ 7   Ⓑ 8   Ⓒ 9   Ⓓ 128

Maintain Your Skills

State whether each number is divisible by 2, 3, 5, 6, or 10. *(Lesson 4-1)*

62. 128 **2**   63. 370 **2, 5, 10**   64. 945 **3, 5**

65. **METEOROLOGY** A tornado travels 300 miles in 2 hours. Use the formula $d = rt$ to find the tornado's speed in miles per hour. *(Lesson 3-7)* **150 mph**

ALGEBRA Solve each equation. Check your solution. *(Lesson 3-5)*

66. $2x + 1 = 7$ **3**   67. $16 = 5k - 4$ **4**   68. $\frac{n}{3} + 8 = 6$ **−6**

69. **ALGEBRA** Simplify $4(y + 2) - y$. *(Lesson 3-2)* **$3y + 8$**

PREREQUISITE SKILL List all the factors for each number.
*(To review **factoring**, see Lesson 4-1.)*

70. 11 **1, 11**   71. 5 **1, 5**   72. 9 **1, 3, 9**

73. 16 **1, 2, 4, 8, 16**   74. 19 **1, 19**   75. 35 **1, 5, 7, 35**

www.pre-alg.com/self_check_quiz

Getting Started

Objective Investigate writing numerals in base 2.

Materials
paper and pencil
grid paper

Teach

- If students find base 2 difficult, try using sticks (or toothpicks) to represent the numbers. If you have 13 toothpicks, ask what is the largest base 2 bundle you could make. Since you could make 1 bundle of 8, you have 5 left. Now make 1 bundle of 4 and 1 bundle of 1. Thus, $(1 \times 8) + (1 \times 4) + (0 \times 2) + (1 \times 1) = 1101_2$.

Assess

After completing **Exercises 1–7**, students should be able to write any base 10 number in another base using the rules for place value.

Study Notebook

You may wish to have students summarize this activity and what they learned from it.

Answers

7. Sample answer: Write 314 in

   base 4.

1	0	3	2	2
256	64	16	4	1

   $314 = 10322_4$

8. Sample answer: Write 5123 in

   base 8.

1	2	0	0	3
4096	512	64	8	1

   $5123 = 12003_8$

Algebra Activity

Base 2

Activity

A computer contains a large number of tiny electronic switches that can be turned ON or OFF. The digits 0 and 1, also called *bits*, are the alphabet of computer language. This **binary** language uses a **base two** system of numbers.

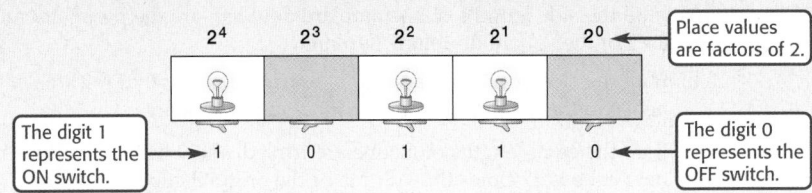

Place values are factors of 2.

The digit 1 represents the ON switch.

The digit 0 represents the OFF switch.

$$10110_2 = (1 \times 2^4) + (0 \times 2^3) + (1 \times 2^2) + (1 \times 2^1) + (0 \times 2^0)$$
$$= 16 + 0 + 4 + 2 + 0$$
$$= 22$$

So, $10110_2 = 22_{10}$ or 22.

You can also reverse the process and express base ten numbers as equivalent numbers in base two.

Express the decimal number 13 as a number in base two.

Step 1 Make a base 2 place-value chart. Find the greatest factor of 2 that is less than 13. Place a 1 in that place value.

	1			
16	8	4	2	1

Step 2 Subtract $13 - 8 = 5$. Now find the greatest factor of 2 that is less than 5. Place a 1 in that place value.

	1	1		
16	8	4	2	1

Step 3 Subtract $5 - 4 = 1$. Place a 1 in that place value.

Step 4 There are no factors of 2 left, so place a 0 in any unfilled spaces.

	1	1	0	1
16	8	4	2	1

So, 13 in the base 10 system is equal to 1101 in the base 2 system. Or, $13 = 1101_2$.

TEACHING TIP

Base 10 numbers are called *decimal* numbers. Base 2 numbers are called *binary* numbers.

Exercises

1. Express 1011_2 as an equivalent number in base 10. **11**

Express each base 10 number as an equivalent number in base 2.

2. 6 **110_2**   3. 9 **1001_2**   4. 15 **1111_2**   5. 21 **10101_2**

Extend the Activity

6. The first five place values for base 5 are shown. Any digit from 0 to 4 can be used to write a base 5 number. Write 179 in base 5. **1204_5**

625	125	25	5	1

7. **OPEN ENDED**   Write 314 as an equivalent number in a base other than 2, 5, or 10. Include a place-value chart. **See margin.**

8. **OPEN ENDED**   Choose a base 10 number and write it as an equivalent number in base 8. Include a place-value chart. **See margin.**

Resource Manager

📁 *Teaching Pre-Algebra with Manipulatives*

- p. 1 (master for grid paper)
- p. 60 (student recording sheet)

Prime Factorization

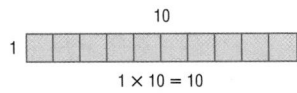 **What** You'll Learn

- Write the prime factorizations of composite numbers.
- Factor monomials.

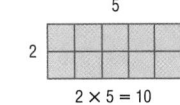 **How** can models be used to determine whether numbers are prime?

Vocabulary
- prime number
- composite number
- prime factorization
- factor tree
- factor

There are two ways that 10 can be expressed as the product of whole numbers. This can be shown by using 10 squares to form rectangles.

$$10$$
$$1 \times 10 = 10$$

$$5$$
$$2 \times 5 = 10$$

a. Use grid paper to draw as many different rectangular arrangements of 2, 3, 4, 5, 6, 7, 8, and 9 squares as possible. See students' work.

b. Which numbers of squares can be arranged in more than one way?

c. Which numbers of squares can only be arranged one way? 2, 3, 5, 7

d. What do the rectangles in part **c** have in common? Explain.

b. 4, 6, 8, 9
d. They all have a width of 1 because no other pair of factors can be found.

Reading Math

Composite
Everyday Meaning: materials that are made up of many substances
Math Meaning: numbers having many factors

PRIME NUMBERS AND COMPOSITE NUMBERS A **prime number** is a whole number that has exactly two factors, 1 and itself. A **composite number** is a whole number that has more than two factors. Zero and 1 are neither prime nor composite.

Whole Numbers	Factors	Number of Factors
2	1, 2	2
3	1, 3	2
5	1, 5	2
7	1, 7	2
4	1, 2, 4	3
6	1, 2, 3, 6	4
8	1, 2, 4, 8	4
9	1, 3, 9	3
0	all numbers	infinite
1	1	1

Prime Numbers — 2, 3, 5, 7
Composite Numbers — 4, 6, 8, 9
Neither Prime nor Composite — 0, 1

Example 1 *Identify Numbers as Prime or Composite*

a. Determine whether 19 is prime or composite.

Find factors of 19 by listing the whole number pairs whose product is 19.

$$19 = 1 \times 19$$

The number 19 has only two factors. Therefore, 19 is a prime number.

---

1 Focus

5-Minute Check Transparency 4-3 Use as a quiz or review of Lesson 4-2.

Mathematical Background notes are available for this lesson on page 146C.

How can models be used to determine whether numbers are prime?

The opening activity questions are repeated on page 178 of the *Chapter 4 Resource Masters.*

Reading to Learn Mathematics, p. 178 ELL

Pre-Activity How can models be used to determine whether numbers are prime?
Do the activity at the top of page 159 in your textbook. Write your answers below.

a. Use grid paper to draw as many different rectangular arrangements of 2, 3, 4, 5, 6, 7, 8, and 9 squares as possible. See students' answers.

b. Which numbers of squares can be arranged in more than one way? 4, 6, 8, 9

c. Which numbers of squares can only be arranged one way? 2, 3, 5, 7

d. What do all rectangles that you listed in part **c** have in common? Explain. They all have a width of 1 because no other pair of factors can be found.

Reading the Lesson 1–5. See students' work.

Write a definition and give an example of each new vocabulary word or phrase.

Vocabulary	Definition	Example
1. composite number		
2. factor		
3. factor tree		
4. prime factorization		
5. prime number		

Helping You Remember

6. *Composite* is a word used in everyday English.
   a. Find the definition of *composite* in the dictionary. Write the definition. made up of distinct parts
   b. Explain how the English definition can help you remember how composite is used in mathematics. Sample answer: Composite numbers are made up of many distinct parts, or factors.

Resource Manager

Workbooks and Reproducible Masters

Chapter 4 Resource Masters
- Study Guide and Intervention, p. 175
- Skills Practice, p. 176
- Practice, p. 177
- Reading to Learn Mathematics, p. 178
- Enrichment, p. 179

Graphing Calculator and Spreadsheet Masters, p. 26
Parent and Student Study Guide Workbook, p. 26
Prerequisite Skills Workbook, pp. 13–14

 Transparencies
5-Minute Check Transparency 4-3
Answer Key Transparencies

 Technology
Interactive Chalkboard

PRIME NUMBERS AND COMPOSITE NUMBERS

In-Class Examples

1 Determine whether each number is prime or composite.

a. 31   The number 31 has only two factors. Therefore, 31 is a prime number.

b. 36   The factors of 36 are 1, 2, 3, 4, 6, 9, 12, 18, and 36. Since there are more than two factors, the number is composite.

2 Write the prime factorization of 56. $2^3 \cdot 7$

Teaching Tip Make sure students carry any prime numbers down to the bottom of the factor tree. Otherwise, they may lose track of these factors.

✓ Skills Check

Prime Factorization Ask students to describe the similarities and differences between two factor trees made for the same number.

FACTOR MONOMIALS

In-Class Example

3 Factor each monomial.

a. $16p^2q^4$ $2 \cdot 2 \cdot 2 \cdot 2 \cdot p \cdot p \cdot q \cdot q \cdot q \cdot q$

b. $-21x^2y$ $-1 \cdot 3 \cdot 7 \cdot x \cdot x \cdot y$

Study Tip

Mental Math
To determine whether a number is prime or composite, you can mentally use the rules for divisibility rather than listing factors.

TEACHING TIP
Emphasize that factors are natural numbers.

Study Tip

Commutative
The order of the factors does not matter because the operation of multiplication is commutative.

---

b. Determine whether 28 is prime or composite.

Find factors of 28 by listing the whole number pairs whose product is 28.

$28 = 1 \times 28$
$28 = 2 \times 14$
$28 = 4 \times 7$

The factors of 28 are 1, 2, 4, 7, 14, and 28. Since the number has more than two factors, it is composite.

When a composite number is expressed as the product of prime factors, it is called the **prime factorization** of the number. One way to find the prime factorization of a number is to use a **factor tree**.

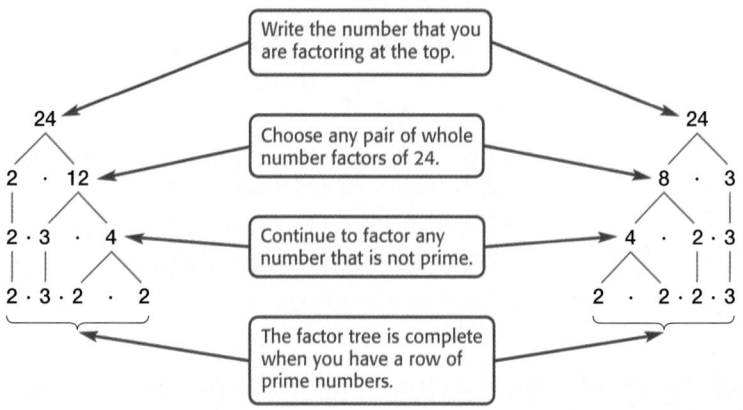

Both trees give the same prime factors, except in different orders. There is exactly one prime factorization of 24. The prime factorization of 24 is $2 \cdot 2 \cdot 2 \cdot 3$ or $2^3 \cdot 3$.

✓ **Concept Check** Could a different factor tree have been used to write the prime factorization of 24? If so, would the result be the same? **Yes, the first factor pair could have been 4 · 6.**

Example **2** *Write Prime Factorization*

Write the prime factorization of 36.

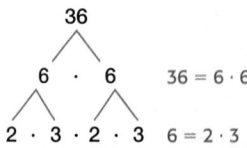

The factorization is complete because 2 and 3 are prime numbers. The prime factorization of 36 is $2 \cdot 2 \cdot 3 \cdot 3$ or $2^2 \cdot 3^2$.

Teacher to Teacher

Butch Sloan   Garland ISD, Garland, TX

"Another way to factor is to use what we call the L method. To find the factors of 210, you divide by a prime factor and write the quotient underneath. Then divide the quotient by another prime factor, and so on until the result is 1. This method transfers well to two or more numbers and finding the GCF and LCM later in this chapter."

2	210
3	105
5	35
7	7
	1

You can also use a strategy involving division called the *cake method* to find a prime factorization. The prime factorization of 210 is shown below using the cake method.

Step 1
Begin with the smallest prime that is a factor of 210, in this case, 2. Divide 210 by 2.

$$2\overline{)210} \atop 105$$

→

Step 2
Divide the quotient 105 by the smallest possible prime factor, 3.

$$3\overline{)105} \atop 35 \atop 2\overline{)210}$$

→

Step 3
Repeat until the quotient is prime.

$$5\overline{)35} \atop 3\overline{)105} \atop 2\overline{)210} \atop 7$$

The prime factorization of 210 is $2 \cdot 3 \cdot 5 \cdot 7$. Multiply to check the result.

FACTOR MONOMIALS To **factor** a number means to write it as a product of its factors. A monomial can also be factored as a product of prime numbers and variables with no exponent greater than 1. Negative coefficients can be factored using -1 as a factor.

Example 3 *Factor Monomials*

Factor each monomial.

a. $8ab^2$
$$8ab^2 = 2 \cdot 2 \cdot 2 \cdot a \cdot b^2 \qquad 8 = 2 \cdot 2 \cdot 2$$
$$= 2 \cdot 2 \cdot 2 \cdot a \cdot b \cdot b \qquad a \cdot b^2 = a \cdot b \cdot b$$

b. $-30x^3y$
$$-30x^3y = -1 \cdot 2 \cdot 3 \cdot 5 \cdot x^3 \cdot y \qquad -30 = -1 \cdot 2 \cdot 3 \cdot 5$$
$$= -1 \cdot 2 \cdot 3 \cdot 5 \cdot x \cdot x \cdot x \cdot y \qquad x^3 \cdot y = x \cdot x \cdot x \cdot y$$

Check for Understanding

Concept Check
1. A prime number has exactly two factors: 1 and itself. A composite number has more than two factors.

1. **Explain** the difference between a prime and composite number.

2. **OPEN ENDED** Write a 2-digit number with prime factors that include 2 and 3. Sample answer: 12

3. **FIND THE ERROR** Cassidy and Francisca each factored 88.

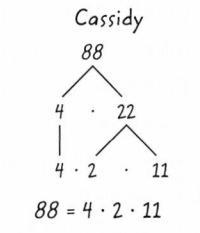

Cassidy

88

4 · 22

4 · 2 · 11

$88 = 4 \cdot 2 \cdot 11$

Francisca

$$2\overline{)22} \atop 2\overline{)44} \atop 2\overline{)88} \atop 11$$

$88 = 2 \cdot 2 \cdot 2 \cdot 11$

Who is correct? Explain your reasoning. Francisca; 4 is not prime.

www.pre-alg.com/extra_examples

Lesson 4-3 Prime Factorization **161**

Study Guide and Intervention, p. 175

A **prime number** is a whole number that has exactly two factors, 1 and itself. A **composite number** is a whole number that has more than two factors. Zero and 1 are neither prime nor composite.

Example 1 Determine whether 29 is prime or composite.

Find the factors of 29.

$29 = 1 \cdot 29$

The only factors of 29 are 1 and 29, therefore 29 is a prime number.

Any composite number can be written as a product of prime numbers. A factor tree can be used to find the prime factorization.

Example 2 Find the prime factorization of 48.

48 is the number to be factored.

Find any pair of whole number factors of 48.

Continue to factor any number that is not prime.

The factor tree is complete when there is a row of prime numbers.

The prime factorization of 48 is $2 \cdot 2 \cdot 2 \cdot 2 \cdot 3$ or $2^4 \cdot 3$.

In algebra, monomials can be factored as a product of prime numbers and variables with no exponent greater than 1. So, $8x^2$ factors as $2 \cdot 2 \cdot 2 \cdot x \cdot x$.

Exercises

Determine whether each number is *prime or composite*.

1. 27 composite
2. 151 prime
3. 77 composite
4. 25 composite

Write the prime factorization for each number. Use exponents for repeated factors.

5. 16 2^4
6. 45 $3^2 \cdot 5$
7. 78 $2 \cdot 3 \cdot 13$
8. 70 $2 \cdot 5 \cdot 7$

Factor each monomial.

9. $6m^3$ $2 \cdot 3 \cdot m \cdot m \cdot m$
10. $-20xy^2$ $-1 \cdot 2 \cdot 2 \cdot 5 \cdot x \cdot y \cdot y$
11. $a^2b^2c^3$ $a \cdot a \cdot b \cdot b \cdot c \cdot c \cdot c$
12. $25h$ $5 \cdot 5 \cdot h$

Skills Practice, p. 176 and Practice, p. 177 (shown)

Determine whether each number is *prime or composite*.

1. 11 prime
2. 63 composite
3. 73 prime
4. 75 composite
5. 49 composite
6. 69 composite
7. 53 prime
8. 83 prime

Write the prime factorization of each number. Use exponents for repeated factors.

9. 33 $3 \cdot 11$
10. 24 $2^3 \cdot 3$
11. 72 $2^3 \cdot 3^2$
12. 276 $2^2 \cdot 3 \cdot 23$
13. 85 $5 \cdot 17$
14. 1024 2^{10}
15. 95 $5 \cdot 19$
16. 200 $2^3 \cdot 5^2$
17. 243 3^5
18. 735 $3 \cdot 5 \cdot 7^2$

Factor each monomial.

19. $35v$ $5 \cdot 7 \cdot v$
20. $49c^2$ $7 \cdot 7 \cdot c \cdot c$
21. $-14b^3$ $-1 \cdot 2 \cdot 7 \cdot b \cdot b \cdot b$
22. $-81h^2$ $-1 \cdot 3 \cdot 3 \cdot 3 \cdot 3 \cdot h \cdot h$
23. $33wz$ $3 \cdot 11 \cdot w \cdot z$
24. $-56ghj$ $-1 \cdot 2 \cdot 2 \cdot 2 \cdot 7 \cdot g \cdot h \cdot j$

25. **NUMBER THEORY** *Twin primes* are a pair of consecutive odd primes, which differ by 2. For example, 3 and 5 are twin primes. Find the twin primes less than 100. (*Hint:* There are 8 pairs of twins less than 100.) 3, 5; 5, 7; 11, 13; 17, 19; 29, 31; 41, 43; 59, 61; 71, 73

Enrichment, p. 179

Prime Pyramid

A **prime number** is a whole number that has exactly two factors—itself and 1. The pyramid below is called a *prime pyramid*. Each row begins with 1 and ends with the number of that row. So, row 2 begins with 1 and ends with 2, row 3 begins with 1 and ends with 3, and so on. In each row, the numbers from 1 to the row number are arranged such that the sum of any two adjacent numbers is a prime number.

For example, look at row 4:

- It must contain the numbers 1, 2, 3, and 4.
- It must begin with 1 and end with 4.
- The sum of adjacent pairs must be a prime number:
  $1 + 2 = 3, 2 + 3 = 5, 3 + 4 = 7$

```
          1   2
        1   2   3
      1   2   3   4
    1   4   3   2   5
  1   4   3   2   5   6
1   4   3   2   5   6   7
1   2   3   4   7   6   5   8
1   2   3   4   7   6   5   8   9
1   2   3   4   7   6   5   8   9   10
1   4   3   2   5   6   7   10  9   8   11
1   4   3   2   5   6   7   10  9   8   11  12
```

1. Complete the pyramid by filling in the missing numbers.

2. Extend the pyramid to row 13.
   1, 4, 3, 2, 5, 6, 7, 10, 9, 8, 11, 12, 13

3. Explain the patterns you see in the completed pyramid.
   Sample answer: Each row alternates odd and even numbers. Multiples of 3 form diagonals that are constant.

Guided Practice

GUIDED PRACTICE KEY	
Exercises	Examples
4–6, 13	1
7–9	2
10–12	3

Determine whether each number is *prime* or *composite*.

4. 7 prime
5. 23 prime
6. 15 composite

Write the prime factorization of each number. Use exponents for repeated factors.

7. 18 $2 \cdot 3^2$
8. 39 $3 \cdot 13$
9. 50 $2 \cdot 5^2$

ALGEBRA Factor each monomial.

10. $4c^2$ $2 \cdot 2 \cdot c \cdot c$
11. $5a^2b$ $5 \cdot a \cdot a \cdot b$
12. $-70xyz$ $-1 \cdot 2 \cdot 5 \cdot 7 \cdot x \cdot y \cdot z$

Application

13. **NUMBER THEORY** One mathematical conjecture that is unproved states that there are infinitely many *twin primes*. Twin primes are prime numbers that differ by 2, such as 3 and 5. List all the twin primes that are less than 50. 3 and 5, 5 and 7, 11 and 13, 17 and 19, 29 and 31, 41 and 43

★ indicates increased difficulty

Practice and Apply

Homework Help	
For Exercises	See Examples
14–21	1
22–29	2
30–41	3

Extra Practice
See page 731.

Determine whether each number is *prime* or *composite*.

14. 21 composite
15. 33 composite
16. 23 prime
17. 70 composite
18. 17 prime
19. 51 composite
20. 43 prime
21. 31 prime

Write the prime factorization of each number. Use exponents for repeated factors.

22. 26 $2 \cdot 13$
23. 81 3^4
24. 66 $2 \cdot 3 \cdot 11$
25. 63 $3^2 \cdot 7$
26. 56 $2^3 \cdot 7$
27. 100 $2^2 \cdot 5^2$
28. 392 $2^3 \cdot 7^2$
29. 110 $2 \cdot 5 \cdot 11$

ALGEBRA Factor each monomial. 30–41. See margin.

30. $14w$
31. $9t^2$
32. $-7c^2$
33. $-25z^3$
34. $20st$
35. $-38mnp$
36. $28x^2y$
37. $21gh^3$
38. $13q^2r^2$
★ 39. $64n^3$
★ 40. $-75ab^2$
★ 41. $-120r^2st$

42. Is the value of $n^2 - n + 41$ prime or composite if $n = 3$? prime

43. **OPEN ENDED** Write a monomial whose factors include -1, 5, and x.
Sample answer: $-25x$

44. **TECHNOLOGY** *Mersenne primes* are prime numbers in the form $2^n - 1$. In 2001, a computer programmer used special software to discover the largest prime number so far, $2^{13,466,917} - 1$. Write the prime factorization of each number, or write *prime* if the number is a Mersenne prime.

a. $2^5 - 1$ prime
b. $2^6 - 1$ $3^2 \cdot 7$
c. $2^7 - 1$ prime
d. $2^8 - 1$ $3 \cdot 5 \cdot 17$

45. **WRITING IN MATH** Answer the question that was posed at the beginning of the lesson. See margin.

How can models be used to determine whether numbers are prime?

Include the following in your answer:

- the number of rectangles that can be drawn to represent prime and composite numbers, and
- an explanation of how one model can show that a number is *not* prime.

Answers

30. $2 \cdot 7 \cdot w$
31. $3 \cdot 3 \cdot t \cdot t$
32. $-1 \cdot 7 \cdot c \cdot c$
33. $-1 \cdot 5 \cdot 5 \cdot z \cdot z \cdot z$
34. $2 \cdot 2 \cdot 5 \cdot s \cdot t$
35. $-1 \cdot 2 \cdot 19 \cdot m \cdot n \cdot p$
36. $2 \cdot 2 \cdot 7 \cdot x \cdot x \cdot y$
37. $3 \cdot 7 \cdot g \cdot h \cdot h \cdot h$
38. $13 \cdot q \cdot q \cdot r \cdot r$
39. $2 \cdot 2 \cdot 2 \cdot 2 \cdot 2 \cdot 2 \cdot n \cdot n \cdot n$
40. $-1 \cdot 3 \cdot 5 \cdot 5 \cdot a \cdot b \cdot b$
41. $-1 \cdot 2 \cdot 2 \cdot 2 \cdot 3 \cdot 5 \cdot r \cdot r \cdot s \cdot t \cdot t \cdot t$

46. **CRITICAL THINKING** Find the prime factors of these numbers that are divisible by 12: 12, 60, 84, 132, and 180. Then, write a rule to determine when a number is divisible by 12. See margin.

Standardized Test Practice

47. Which table of values represents the following rule? C
Add the input number to the square of the input number.

Ⓐ

Input (x)	Output (y)
0	1
2	3
4	5

Ⓑ

Input (x)	Output (y)
1	1
2	6
4	8

Ⓒ

Input (x)	Output (y)
1	2
2	6
4	20

Ⓓ

Input (x)	Output (y)
1	2
2	4
4	8

48. Determine which number is *not* a prime factor of 70. D

Ⓐ 2 Ⓑ 5 Ⓒ 7 Ⓓ 10

Maintain Your Skills

Mixed Review

49. Write $(-5)\cdot(-5)\cdot(-5)\cdot h\cdot h\cdot k$ using exponents. *(Lesson 4-2)* $(-5)^3h^2k$

Determine whether each expression is a monomial. *(Lesson 4-1)*

50. $14cd$ yes 51. -5 yes 52. $x - y$ no 53. $3(1 + 3r)$ no

ALGEBRA **Solve each equation. Check your solution.** *(Lesson 3-4)*

54. $\frac{n}{8} = -4$ -32 55. $2x = -18$ -9 56. $30 = 6n$ 5 57. $-7 = \frac{y}{4}$ -28

Getting Ready for the Next Lesson

PREREQUISITE SKILL **Use the Distributive Property to rewrite each expression.** *(To review the* ***Distributive Property****, see Lesson 3-1.)*

58. $2(n + 4)$ $2n + 8$ 59. $5(x - 7)$ $5x - 35$ 60. $-3(t + 4)$ $-3t - 12$

61. $(a + 6)10$ $10a + 60$ 62. $(b - 3)(-2)$ $-2b + 6$ 63. $8(9 - y)$ $72 - 8y$

Practice Quiz 1 — *Lessons 4-1 through 4-3*

Use divisibility rules to determine whether each number is divisible by 2, 3, 5, 6, or 10. *(Lesson 4-1)*

1. 105 3, 5 2. 270 2, 3, 5, 6, 10 3. 511 none 4. 1368 2, 3, 6

5. **ALGEBRA** Evaluate $b^2 - 4ac$ if $a = -1$, $b = 5$, and $c = 3$. *(Lesson 4-2)* 37

6. **LITERATURE** In a story, a knight received a reward for slaying a dragon. He received 1 cent on the first day, 2 cents on the second day, 4 cents on the third day, and so on, continuing to double the amount for 30 days. *(Lesson 4-2)*
   a. Express his reward on each of the first three days as a power of 2. $2^0, 2^1, 2^2$
   b. Express his reward on the 8th day as a power of 2. Then evaluate. $2^7 = 128$ cents

Factor each monomial. *(Lesson 4-3)*

7. $77x$ $7\cdot 11\cdot x$ 8. $18st$ $2\cdot 3\cdot 3\cdot s\cdot t$ 9. $-23n^3$ $-1\cdot 23\cdot n\cdot n\cdot n$ 10. $30cd^2$ $2\cdot 3\cdot 5\cdot c\cdot d\cdot d$

www.pre-alg.com/self_check_quiz

4 Assess

Open-Ended Assessment

Modeling Have students find the prime factorization of a number using index cards and string. At the top of the model, place the index card with the number written on it. Have students use cards to write the whole number factors for the number until they have expressed the prime factors. Then, make a factor tree by attaching the factor cards to the original number with the string.

Getting Ready for Lesson 4-4

PREREQUISITE SKILL Lesson 4-4 presents the greatest common factor. Finding the greatest common factor of two terms of an algebraic expression requires the Distributive Property. Exercises 58–63 should be used to determine your students' familiarity with using the Distributive Property.

Answer

46. $12 = 2^2\cdot 3$
$60 = 2^2\cdot 3\cdot 5$
$84 = 2^2\cdot 3\cdot 7$
$132 = 2^2\cdot 3\cdot 11$
$180 = 2^2\cdot 3^2\cdot 5$
Sample answer: A number is divisible by 12 if the number is divisible by 3 and 4.

Answer (p.162)

45. The number of rectangles that can be modeled to represent a number indicate whether the number is prime or composite. Answers should include the following.
- If a number is prime, then only one rectangle can be drawn to represent the number. If a number is composite, then more than one rectangle can be drawn to represent the number.
- If a model has a length or width of 1, then the number may be prime or composite. If a model does not have a length or width of 1, then the number must be composite.

1 Focus

5-Minute Check Transparency 4-4 Use as a quiz or review of Lesson 4-3.

Mathematical Background notes are available for this lesson on page 146C.

How can a diagram be used to find the greatest common factor?

The opening activity questions are repeated on page 183 of the *Chapter 4 Resource Masters.*

Reading to Learn Mathematics, p. 183 — ELL

Pre-Activity *How can a diagram be used to find the greatest common factor?*

Do the activity at the top of page 164 in your textbook. Write your answers below.

a. Which numbers are in both circles? 2, 2

b. Find the product of the numbers that are in both circles. 4

c. Is the product also a factor of 12 and 20? yes

d. Make a Venn diagram showing the prime factors of 16 and 28. Then use it to find the common factors of the numbers. 2, 2

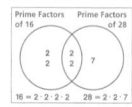

$16 = 2 \cdot 2 \cdot 2 \cdot 2 \qquad 28 = 2 \cdot 2 \cdot 7$

Reading the Lesson 1–2. See students' work.
Write a definition and give an example of each new vocabulary word or phrase.

Vocabulary	Definition	Example
1. Venn diagram		
2. greatest common factor		

Helping You Remember

3. Summarize in your own words how to find the greatest common factor of two numbers using each method.

a. prime factorization Write the prime factorization of each number, then look for the prime factors common to both numbers. The greatest common factor is the product of the common factors.

b. lists of factors Make a list of all factors of both numbers. The largest factor that is in both lists is the greatest common factor.

c. a Venn diagram Make a Venn diagram with the prime factors of each number in a circle. The GCF is the product of the factors in the overlapping section of the diagram.

Vocabulary
- Venn diagram
- greatest common factor

Study Tip

Choosing a Method
To find the GCF of two or more numbers, it is easier to
- list the factors if the numbers are small, or
- use prime factorization if the numbers are large.

What You'll Learn
- Find the greatest common factor of two or more numbers or monomials.
- Use the Distributive Property to factor algebraic expressions.

How can a diagram be used to find the greatest common factor?

A **Venn diagram** shows the relationships among sets of numbers or objects by using overlapping circles in a rectangle.

The Venn diagram at the right shows the prime factors of 12 and 20. The common prime factors are in both circles.

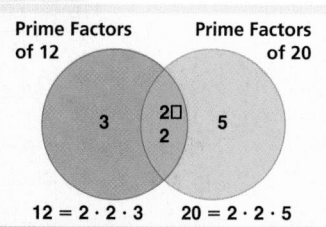

Prime Factors of 12   Prime Factors of 20

3   2 2   5

$12 = 2 \cdot 2 \cdot 3 \qquad 20 = 2 \cdot 2 \cdot 5$

a. Which numbers are in both circles? **2, 2**

b. Find the product of the numbers that are in both circles. **4**

c. Is the product also a factor of 12 and 20? **yes**

d. Make a Venn diagram showing the prime factors of 16 and 28. Then use it to find the common factors of the numbers. **See margin.**

GREATEST COMMON FACTOR Often, numbers have some of the same factors. The greatest number that is a factor of two or more numbers is called the **greatest common factor (GCF)**. Below are two ways to find the GCF of 12 and 20.

Example 1 *Find the GCF*

Find the GCF of 12 and 20.

Method 1 List the factors.

factors of 12: 1, 2, 3, ④ 6, 12 ◄— Common factors of 12 and 20: 1, 2, 4
factors of 20: 1, 2, ④ 5, 10, 20 ◄—

The greatest common factor of 12 and 20 is 4.

Method 2 Use prime factorization.

$12 = ②\cdot②\cdot 3$ ◄— Common prime factors
$20 = ②\cdot②\cdot 5$ of 12 and 20: 2, 2

The GCF is the product of the common prime factors.
$2 \cdot 2 = 4$

Again, the GCF of 12 and 20 is 4.

Resource Manager

📂 Workbooks and Reproducible Masters

Chapter 4 Resource Masters
- Study Guide and Intervention, p. 180
- Skills Practice, p. 181
- Practice, p. 182
- Reading to Learn Mathematics, p. 183
- Enrichment, p. 184
- Assessment, pp. 219, 221

Parent and Student Study Guide Workbook, p. 27

📺 Transparencies
5-Minute Check Transparency 4-4
Answer Key Transparencies

💿 Technology
Interactive Chalkboard
Pre-AlgePASS: Tutorial Plus, Lesson 7

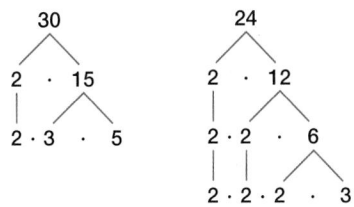 **Example 2** *Find the GCF*

Find the GCF of each set of numbers.

a. 30, 24

First, factor each number completely. Then circle the common factors.

```
      30              24
     /  \            /  \
    2 · 15          2 · 12
        / \             / \
       2 · 3 · 5       2 · 2 · 6
                           / \
                      2 · 2 · 2 · 3
```

Study Tip

Writing Prime Factors
Try to line up the common prime factors so that it is easier to circle them.

$30 = \boxed{2} \cdot \boxed{3} \cdot 5$ The common prime
$24 = \boxed{2} \cdot 2 \cdot 2 \cdot \boxed{3}$ factors are 2 and 3.

The GCF of 30 and 24 is $2 \cdot 3$ or 6.

b. 54, 36, 45

$54 = 2 \cdot \boxed{3} \cdot \boxed{3} \cdot 3$ The common
$36 = 2 \cdot 2 \cdot \boxed{3} \cdot \boxed{3}$ prime factors
$45 = \boxed{3} \cdot \boxed{3} \cdot 5$ are 3 and 3.

The GCF is $3 \cdot 3$ or 9.

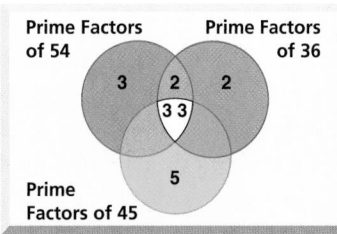

Prime Factors of 54   **Prime Factors of 36**
3 2 2
3 3
5
Prime Factors of 45

More About. . .

Track and Field
In some events such as sprints and the long jump, if the wind speed is greater than 2 meters per second, then the time or mark cannot be considered for record purposes.
Source: www.encarta.msn.com

Example 3 *Use the GCF to Solve Problems*

TRACK AND FIELD There are 208 boys and 240 girls participating in a field day competition.

a. What is the greatest number of teams that can be formed if each team has the same number of girls and each team has the same number of boys?

Find the GCF of 208 and 240.

$208 = \boxed{2} \cdot \boxed{2} \cdot \boxed{2} \cdot \boxed{2} \cdot 13$ The common prime factors
$240 = \boxed{2} \cdot \boxed{2} \cdot \boxed{2} \cdot \boxed{2} \cdot 3 \cdot 5$ are 2, 2, 2, and 2.

The greatest common factor of 208 and 240 is $2 \cdot 2 \cdot 2 \cdot 2$ or 16. So, 16 teams can be formed.

b. How many boys and girls will be on each team?

$208 \div 16 = 13$
$240 \div 16 = 15$

So, each team will have 13 boys and 15 girls.

 www.pre-alg.com/extra_examples   **Lesson 4-4** Greatest Common Factor (GCF) **165**

DAILY INTERVENTION   **Differentiated Instruction**

- **Visual/Spatial** Give students rectangles cut from grid paper. Their task is to cut the rectangle into equal squares with no material left. Discuss their results. What is the connection between the sizes of squares and the length and width of the original rectangle? Students should discover that a side on a square will be a factor of the length and width. The side of the largest square will give the GCF of the length and width.

Study Notebook

Have students—
- add the definitions/examples of the vocabulary terms to their Vocabulary Builder worksheets for Chapter 4.
- write down examples of each method for finding greatest common factors.
- include any other item(s) that they find helpful in mastering the skills in this lesson.

DAILY
INTERVENTION **FIND THE ERROR**
Some students have difficulty identifying common prime factors when the factors are written with exponents. Students may benefit from writing prime factorizations without exponents until they learn to pick out common factors.

About the Exercises . . .
Organization by Objective
- **Greatest Common Factor:** 17–43, 53–55
- **Factor Algebraic Expressions:** 44–52

Odd/Even Assignments
Exercises 17–42 and 44–52 are structured so that students practice the same concepts whether they are assigned odd or even problems.

Assignment Guide
Basic: 17–37 odd, 45–49 odd, 53, 55, 57–60, 67–81

Average: 17–55 odd, 57–60, 67–81 (Optional: 61–66)

Advanced: 18–56 even, 57–75 (Optional: 76–81)

ALGEBRA CONNECTION

FACTOR ALGEBRAIC EXPRESSIONS You can also find the GCF of two or more monomials by finding the product of their common prime factors.

Example 4 Find the GCF of Monomials

Find the GCF of $16xy^2$ and $30xy$.
Completely factor each expression.

$$16xy^2 = \boxed{2} \cdot 2 \cdot 2 \cdot 2 \cdot \boxed{x} \cdot \boxed{y} \cdot y$$
$$30xy = \boxed{2} \cdot 3 \cdot 5 \cdot \boxed{x} \cdot \boxed{y}$$
Circle the common factors.

The GCF of $16xy^2$ and $30xy$ is $2 \cdot x \cdot y$ or $2xy$.

Study Tip

Look Back
To review the **Distributive Property**, see Lesson 3-1.

In Lesson 3-1, you used the Distributive Property to rewrite $2(x + 3)$ as $2x + 6$. You can also use this property to factor an algebraic expression such as $2x + 6$.

Example 5 Factor Expressions

Factor $2x + 6$.
First, find the GCF of $2x$ and 6.

$$2x = \boxed{2} \cdot x$$
$$6 = \boxed{2} \cdot 3 \qquad \text{The GCF is 2.}$$

Now write each term as a product of the GCF and its remaining factors.
$$2x + 6 = 2(x) + 2(3)$$
$$= 2(x + 3) \qquad \text{Distributive Property}$$
So, $2x + 6 = 2(x + 3)$.

✓ Concept Check Which property allows you to factor $3x + 9$?
Distributive Property

Check for Understanding

Concept Check

2. Sample answer: 12 and 24
3. Jack; the common prime factors of the expressions are 2 and 11, so the GCF is $2 \cdot 11$ or 22.

1. **Explain** how to find the greatest common factor of two or more numbers. **See margin.**

2. **OPEN ENDED** Name two different numbers whose GCF is 12.

3. **FIND THE ERROR** Christina and Jack both found the GCF of $2 \cdot 3^2 \cdot 11$ and $2^3 \cdot 5 \cdot 11$.

Christina
$$2 \cdot 3^2 \cdot \boxed{11}$$
$$2^3 \cdot 5 \cdot \boxed{11}$$
GCF = 11

Jack
$$\boxed{2} \cdot 3^2 \cdot \boxed{11}$$
$$\boxed{2} \cdot 2 \cdot 2 \cdot 5 \cdot \boxed{11}$$
GCF = $2 \cdot 11$ or 22

Who is correct? Explain your reasoning.

Answer

1. Sample answer: Find the prime factorization of each number. Multiply the factors that are common to both.

Guided Practice

GUIDED PRACTICE KEY

Exercises	Examples
4–10	1, 2
11, 12	4
13–15	5
16	3

Find the GCF of each set of numbers or monomials.

4. 6, 8 **2**
5. 21, 45 **3**
6. 16, 56 **8**

7. 28, 42 **14**
8. 7, 30 **1**
9. 108, 144 **36**

10. 12, 24, 36 **12**
11. $14n, 42n^2$ **14n**
12. $36a^3b, 56ab^2$ **4ab**

Factor each expression.

13. $3n + 9$ **3(n + 3)**
14. $t^2 + 4t$ **t(t + 4)**
15. $15 + 20x$ **5(3 + 4x)**

Application

16. PARADES In the parade, 36 members of the color guard are to march in front of 120 members of the high school marching band. Both groups are to have the same number of students in each row. Find the greatest number of students in each row. **12 students**

★ indicates increased difficulty

Practice and Apply

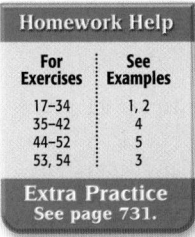

Homework Help

For Exercises	See Examples
17–34	1, 2
35–42	4
44–52	5
53, 54	3

Extra Practice
See page 731.

Find the GCF of each set of numbers or monomials.

17. 12, 8 **4**
18. 3, 9 **3**
19. 24, 40 **8**

20. 21, 14 **7**
21. 20, 30 **10**
22. 12, 18 **6**

23. 18, 45 **9**
24. 22, 21 **1**
25. 16, 40 **8**

26. 42, 56 **14**
27. 30, 35 **5**
28. 12, 60 **12**

29. 116, 100 **4**
30. 135, 315 **45**
31. 9, 15, 24 **3**

32. 20, 21, 25 **1**
33. 20, 28, 36 **4**
34. 66, 90, 150 **6**

35. $12x, 40x^2$ **4x**
36. $18, 45mn$ **9**
37. $4st, 10s$ **2s**

38. $5ab, 6b^2$ **b**
★ **39.** $14b, 56b^2$ **14b**
★ **40.** $30a^3b^2, 24a^2b$ **$6a^2b$**

★ **41.** What is the greatest common factor of $32mn^2$, $16n$, and $12n^3$? **4n**

★ **42.** Name the GCF of $15v^2$, $70vw$, and $36w^2$. **1**

★ **43.** Name two monomials whose GCF is $2x$. **Sample answer: $2x, 6x^2$**

Factor each expression.

44. $2x + 8$ **2(x + 4)**
45. $3r + 12$ **3(r + 4)**
46. $8 + 32a$ **8(1 + 4a)**

47. $6 + 3y$ **3(2 + y)**
48. $9 + 3t$ **3(3 + t)**
49. $14 + 21c$ **7(2 + 3c)**

★ **50.** $k^2 + 5k$ **k(k + 5)**
★ **51.** $4y - 16$ **4(y - 4)**
★ **52.** $5n - 10$ **5(n - 2)**

53. PATTERNS Consider the pattern 7, 14, 21, 28, 35, … . **a. See margin.**
   a. Find the GCF of the terms in the pattern. Explain how you know.
   b. Write the next two terms in the pattern. **42, 49**

54. CARPENTRY Tamika is helping her father make shelves to store her sports equipment in the garage. How many shelves measuring 12 inches by 16 inches can be cut from a 48-inch by 72-inch piece of plywood so that there is no waste? **18 shelves**

55. DESIGN Lauren is covering the surface of an end table with equal-sized ceramic tiles. The table is 30 inches long and 24 inches wide.
   a. What is the largest square tile that Lauren can use and not have to cut any tiles? **6-in. squares**
   b. How many tiles will Lauren need? **20 tiles**

  www.pre-alg.com/self_check_quiz

Lesson 4-4 Greatest Common Factor (GCF) **167**

Answer

53a. 7; Sample answer:

7   14   21   28   35
↓   ↓   ↓   ↓   ↓
7(1) 7(2) 7(3) 7(4) 7(5)

The terms increase by a factor of 7.

Open-Ended Assessment

Writing Have students write a paragraph relating any two of the following ideas—use of Venn diagrams, finding greatest common factors, and applying the Distributive Property.

Getting Ready for Lesson 4-5

PREREQUISITE SKILL Lesson 4-5 presents simplifying fractions. Students will also determine what fraction one measurement is of another. Exercises 76–81 should be used to determine your students' familiarity with converting measurements.

Assessment Options

Quiz (Lessons 4-3 and 4-4) is available on p. 219 of the *Chapter 4 Resource Masters.*

Mid-Chapter Test (Lessons 4-1 through 4-4) is available on p. 221 of the *Chapter 4 Resource Masters.*

★ **56. HISTORY** *The Nine Chapters on the Mathematical Art* is a Chinese math book written during the first century. It describes a procedure for finding the greatest common factors. Follow each step below to find the GCF of 86 and 110. **b. 86 − 24 = 62**

  a. Subtract the lesser number, *a*, from the greater number, *b*. **24**

  b. If the result in part **a** is a factor of both numbers, it is the GCF. If the result is not a factor of both numbers, subtract the result from *a* or subtract *a* from the result so that the difference is a positive number.

  c. Continue subtracting and checking the results until you find a number that is a factor of both numbers. **2**

57. CRITICAL THINKING Can the GCF of a set of numbers be equal to one of the numbers? Give an example or a counterexample to support your answer. **Yes; the GCF of 2 and 8 is 2.**

58. WRITING IN MATH   Answer the question that was posed at the beginning of the lesson. **See margin.**

How can a diagram be used to find the greatest common factor?

Include the following in your answer:
- a description of how a Venn diagram can be used to display the prime factorization of two or more numbers, and
- the part of a Venn diagram that is used to find the greatest common factor.

Standardized Test Practice

59. Write $6y + 21$ in factored form. **D**

  Ⓐ $6(y + 3)$ Ⓑ $2(3y + 7)$ Ⓒ $3(y + 7)$ Ⓓ $3(2y + 7)$

60. Find the GCF of $42x^2y$ and $38xy^2$. **C**

  Ⓐ $2x^2y$ Ⓑ $3xy$ Ⓒ $2xy$ Ⓓ $6x^2y^2$

Extending the Lesson   Two numbers are **relatively prime** if their only common factor is 1. Determine whether the numbers in each pair are relatively prime. Write *yes* or *no*.

61. 7 and 8 **yes**   **62.** 13 and 11 **yes**   **63.** 27 and 18 **no**

64. 20 and 25 **no**   **65.** 22 and 23 **yes**   **66.** 8 and 12 **no**

Maintain Your Skills

Mixed Review   **ALGEBRA**   Factor each monomial. *(Lesson 4-3)*

70. $2 \cdot 11 \cdot a \cdot b \cdot b \cdot b$ **67.** $9n$ $3 \cdot 3 \cdot n$ **68.** $15x^2$ **69.** $-5jk$ **70.** $22ab^3$

                                        $3 \cdot 5 \cdot x \cdot x$ $-1 \cdot 5 \cdot j \cdot k$

71. ALGEBRA   Evaluate $7x^2 + y^3$ if $x = -2$ and $y = 4$. *(Lesson 4-2)* **92**

Find each quotient. *(Lesson 2-5)*

72. $69 \div 23$ **3**   **73.** $48 \div (-8)$ **−6**   **74.** $-24 \div (-12)$ **2**   **75.** $-50 \div 5$ **−10**

Getting Ready for the Next Lesson   **PREREQUISITE SKILL**   Find each equivalent measure. *(To review **converting measurements**, see pages 718–721.)*

76. 1 ft = _?_ in. **12**   **77.** 1 yd = _?_ in. **36**   **78.** 1 lb = _?_ oz **16**

79. 1 day = _?_ h **24**   **80.** 1 m = _?_ cm **100**   **81.** 1 kg = _?_ g **1000**

Answer

58. A Venn diagram can be used to display the prime factorizations of two or more numbers. Answers should include the following.
- Each circle in a Venn diagram represents a number. The prime factors of each number are listed inside its circle. The overlapping part(s) of the circles contain the common prime factors.
- The overlapping area in the Venn diagram is used to find the greatest common factor. Multiply the numbers found in this area.

Simplifying Algebraic Fractions

What You'll Learn

- Simplify fractions using the GCF.
- Simplify algebraic fractions.

Vocabulary
- simplest form
- algebraic fraction

How are simplified fractions useful in representing measurements?

You can use a fraction to compare a *part* of something to a *whole*. The figures below show what part 15 minutes is of 1 hour.

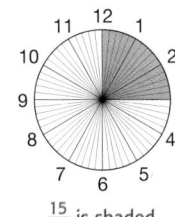
$\frac{15}{60}$ is shaded.

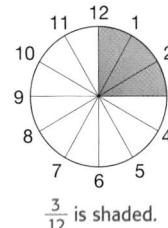
$\frac{3}{12}$ is shaded.

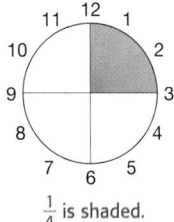
$\frac{1}{4}$ is shaded.

a. Are the three fractions equivalent? Explain your reasoning.

b. Which figure is divided into the least number of parts? **the third figure**

c. Which fraction would you say is written in simplest form? Why?

a. Yes; the same portion of each circle is shaded.

c. $\frac{1}{4}$; The shaded part is not divided into smaller parts.

SIMPLIFY NUMERICAL FRACTIONS
A fraction is in **simplest form** when the GCF of the numerator and the denominator is 1.

Fractions in Simplest Form	Fractions *not* in Simplest Form
$\frac{1}{4}, \frac{1}{3}, \frac{3}{4}, \frac{17}{50}$	$\frac{3}{12}, \frac{15}{60}, \frac{6}{8}, \frac{5}{20}$

One way to write a fraction in simplest form is to write the prime factorization of the numerator and the denominator. Then divide the numerator and denominator by the GCF.

Study Tip

Use a Venn Diagram To simplify fractions, let one circle in a Venn diagram represent the numerator and let another circle represent the denominator. The number or product of numbers in the intersection is the GCF.

Example 1 Simplify Fractions

Write $\frac{9}{12}$ in simplest form.

$9 = 3 \cdot \boxed{3}$ Factor the numerator.
$12 = 2 \cdot 2 \cdot \boxed{3}$ Factor the denominator.

The GCF of 9 and 12 is 3.

$\frac{9}{12} = \frac{9 \div 3}{12 \div 3}$ Divide the numerator and the denominator by the GCF.

$= \frac{3}{4}$ Simplest form

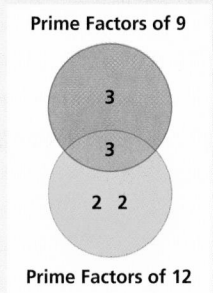
Prime Factors of 9
3
3
2 2
Prime Factors of 12

Workbooks and Reproducible Masters

Chapter 4 Resource Masters
- Study Guide and Intervention, p. 185
- Skills Practice, p. 186
- Practice, p. 187
- Reading to Learn Mathematics, p. 188
- Enrichment, p. 189

Parent and Student Study Guide Workbook, p. 28

---

1 Focus

5-Minute Check Transparency 4-5 Use as a quiz or review of Lesson 4-4.

Mathematical Background notes are available for this lesson on page 146D.

How are simplified fractions useful in representing measurements?

The opening activity questions are repeated on page 188 of the *Chapter 4 Resource Masters.*

 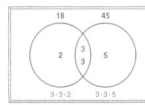

Resource Manager

 Transparencies

5-Minute Check Transparency 4-5
Answer Key Transparencies

 Technology

Interactive Chalkboard
Multimedia Applications

SIMPLIFY NUMERICAL FRACTIONS

In-Class Examples Power Point®

1 Write $\frac{16}{24}$ in simplest form.
$\frac{2}{3}$

2 Write $\frac{72}{120}$ in simplest form.
$\frac{3}{5}$

3 250 pounds is what part of 1 ton? **There are 2000 pounds in 1 ton, so $\frac{250}{2000} = \frac{1}{8}$.**

Teaching Tip You can have students multiply the numerator and denominator of the simplified fraction by the GCF. The result should be the original fraction. This is often helpful when checking work.

SIMPLIFY ALGEBRAIC FRACTIONS

In-Class Examples Power Point®

4 Simplify $\frac{20m^3n^2}{65mn}$. $\frac{4m^2n}{13}$

5 **Multiple-Choice Test Item**

Which fraction is $\frac{x^3y^2}{x^2y^3}$

written in simplest form? **C**

A $\frac{y}{x}$

B $\frac{y^2}{x^2}$

C $\frac{x}{y}$

D $\frac{x^2}{y^2}$

The division in Example 1 can be represented in another way.

TEACHING TIP
This method is sometimes called *canceling*.

$$\frac{9}{12} = \frac{\overset{1}{\cancel{3}} \cdot 3}{2 \cdot 2 \cdot \underset{1}{\cancel{3}}}$$ The slashes mean that the numerator and the denominator are both divided by the GCF, 3.

$$= \frac{3}{2 \cdot 2} \text{ or } \frac{3}{4}$$ Simplify.

Example 2 *Simplify Fractions*

TEACHING TIP
Emphasize that if a common factor other than the GCF is used to simplify a fraction, the resulting fraction will not be in simplest form.

Write $\frac{15}{60}$ in simplest form.

$$\frac{15}{60} = \frac{\overset{1}{\cancel{3}} \cdot \overset{1}{\cancel{5}}}{2 \cdot 2 \cdot \underset{1}{\cancel{3}} \cdot \underset{1}{\cancel{5}}}$$ Divide the numerator and denominator by the GCF, $3 \cdot 5$.

$$= \frac{1}{4}$$ Simplify.

✓ **Concept Check** How do you know when a fraction is in simplest form? **The GCF of the numerator and the denominator is 1.**

Simplifying fractions is a useful tool in measurement.

Example 3 *Simplify Fractions in Measurement*

MEASUREMENT **Eighty-eight feet is what part of 1 mile?**

There are 5280 feet in 1 mile. Write the fraction $\frac{88}{5280}$ in simplest form.

Study Tip

Alternative Method
You can also divide the numerator and denominator by common factors until the fraction is in simplest form.
$$\frac{88}{5280} = \frac{44}{2640}$$
$$= \frac{22}{1320}$$
$$= \frac{11}{660} \text{ or } \frac{1}{60}$$

$$\frac{88}{5280} = \frac{\overset{1}{\cancel{2}} \cdot \overset{1}{\cancel{2}} \cdot \overset{1}{\cancel{2}} \cdot \overset{1}{\cancel{11}}}{\underset{1}{\cancel{2}} \cdot \underset{1}{\cancel{2}} \cdot \underset{1}{\cancel{2}} \cdot 2 \cdot 2 \cdot 3 \cdot 5 \cdot \underset{1}{\cancel{11}}}$$ Divide the numerator and denominator by the GCF, $2 \cdot 2 \cdot 2 \cdot 11$.

$$= \frac{1}{60}$$ Simplify.

So, 88 feet is $\frac{1}{60}$ of a mile.

ALGEBRA CONNECTION

SIMPLIFY ALGEBRAIC FRACTIONS A fraction with variables in the numerator or denominator is called an **algebraic fraction**. Algebraic fractions can also be written in simplest form.

Example 4 *Simplify Algebraic Fractions*

Simplify $\frac{21x^2y}{35xy}$.

$$\frac{21x^2y}{35xy} = \frac{3 \cdot \overset{1}{\cancel{7}} \cdot \overset{1}{\cancel{x}} \cdot x \cdot \overset{1}{\cancel{y}}}{5 \cdot \underset{1}{\cancel{7}} \cdot \underset{1}{\cancel{x}} \cdot \underset{1}{\cancel{y}}}$$ Divide the numerator and denominator by the GCF, $7 \cdot x \cdot y$.

$$= \frac{3x}{5}$$ Simplify.

D A I L Y
INTERVENTION | **Differentiated Instruction**

- **Intrapersonal** Have students evaluate how well they understand each example. Have them make a list of questions that they have about the examples that they do not understand completely. Use the Guided Practice or the Study Guide master to reteach any concept that they have identified as a weakness.

Example 5 Simplify Algebraic Fractions

Multiple-Choice Test Item

Which fraction is $\dfrac{abc^3}{a^2b}$ written in simplest form?

Ⓐ $\dfrac{bc^3}{a}$　　Ⓑ $\dfrac{bc^2}{a}$　　Ⓒ $\dfrac{c^3}{a}$　　Ⓓ $\dfrac{c^2}{a}$

Read the Test Item *In simplest form* means that the GCF of the numerator and the denominator is 1.

Solve the Test Item

$$\frac{abc^3}{a^2b} = \frac{ab\!\!\!/\,c^3}{a^2b\!\!\!/}$$

Without factoring, you can see that the variable b will not appear in the simplified fraction. That eliminates choices A and B.

$$\frac{abc^3}{a^2b} = \frac{\overset{1}{a} \cdot \overset{1}{b} \cdot c \cdot c \cdot c}{\underset{1}{a} \cdot a \cdot \underset{1}{b}} \qquad \text{Factor.}$$

$$= \frac{c^3}{a} \qquad \text{Multiply.}$$

The answer is C.

Check for Understanding

Concept Check
1. **Explain** what it means to express a fraction in simplest form.
   The GCF of the numerator and denominator is 1.

2. **OPEN ENDED** Write examples of a numerical fraction and an algebraic fraction in simplest form and examples of a numerical fraction and an algebraic fraction not in simplest form. **See margin.**

Guided Practice

Write each fraction in simplest form. If the fraction is already in simplest form, write *simplified*.

GUIDED PRACTICE KEY	
Exercises	Examples
3–7	1, 2
8–11	4
12	3
13	5

3. $\dfrac{2}{14}$　$\dfrac{1}{7}$　　4. $\dfrac{9}{15}$　$\dfrac{3}{5}$　　5. $\dfrac{5}{11}$ simp.　　6. $\dfrac{25}{40}$　$\dfrac{5}{8}$　　7. $\dfrac{64}{68}$　$\dfrac{16}{17}$

ALGEBRA Simplify each fraction. If the fraction is already in simplest form, write *simplified*.

8. $\dfrac{x}{x^3}$　$\dfrac{1}{x^2}$　　9. $\dfrac{8a^2}{16a}$　$\dfrac{a}{2}$　　10. $\dfrac{12c}{15d}$　$\dfrac{4c}{5d}$　　11. $\dfrac{24}{5k}$ simp.

12. **MEASUREMENT** Nine inches is what part of 1 yard? $\dfrac{1}{4}$

13. Which fraction is $\dfrac{25mn}{65n}$ written in simplest form? **B**

Ⓐ $\dfrac{2m}{6}$　　Ⓑ $\dfrac{5m}{13}$　　Ⓒ $\dfrac{5m}{13n}$　　Ⓓ $\dfrac{25mn}{65}$

www.pre-alg.com/extra_examples　　　　Lesson 4-5 Simplifying Algebraic Fractions　**171**

Study Notebook

Have students—
- add the definitions/examples of the vocabulary terms to their Vocabulary Builder worksheets for Chapter 4.
- record several measurement conversions for use with application problems. For example 1 mile = 5280 feet; 3 feet = 1 yard; 2000 pound = 1 ton, etc.
- include a fully worked example of simplifying an algebraic fraction.

Answer

2. Sample answer: $\dfrac{2}{3}$ and $\dfrac{x}{4}$ are in simplest form; $\dfrac{2}{4}$ and $\dfrac{3n}{n^2}$ are not in simplest form.

About the Exercises . . .

Organization by Objective
- Simplify Numerical Fractions: 14–29, 42–49
- Simplify Algebraic Fractions: 30–41

Odd/Even Assignments
Exercises 14–28 and 30–43 are structured so that students practice the same concepts whether they are assigned odd or even problems.

Assignment Guide
Basic: 15–25 odd, 29–39 odd, 43, 45, 47–68
Average: 15–45 odd, 47–68
Advanced: 14–46 even, 47–64 (Optional: 65–68)

Example 5 After eliminating choices A and B, have students look at the original expression. Note that there is no factor of c in the denominator, so the answer will contain c^3 in the numerator. Of the remaining choices, only C meets this criterion.

Practice and Apply

Write each fraction in simplest form. If the fraction is already in simplest form, write *simplified*.

14. $\frac{3}{18}$ $\frac{1}{6}$ 15. $\frac{10}{12}$ $\frac{5}{6}$ 16. $\frac{15}{21}$ $\frac{5}{7}$ 17. $\frac{8}{36}$ $\frac{2}{9}$ 18. $\frac{17}{20}$ simp.
19. $\frac{18}{44}$ $\frac{9}{22}$ 20. $\frac{16}{64}$ $\frac{1}{4}$ 21. $\frac{30}{37}$ simp. 22. $\frac{34}{38}$ $\frac{17}{19}$ 23. $\frac{17}{51}$ $\frac{1}{3}$
24. $\frac{51}{60}$ $\frac{17}{20}$ 25. $\frac{25}{60}$ $\frac{5}{12}$ 26. $\frac{36}{96}$ $\frac{3}{8}$ ★27. $\frac{133}{140}$ $\frac{19}{20}$ ★28. $\frac{765}{2023}$ $\frac{45}{119}$

29. **AIRCRAFT** A model of Lindbergh's *Spirit of St. Louis* has a wingspan of 18 inches. The wingspan of the actual airplane is 46 feet. Write a fraction in simplest form comparing the wingspan of the model and the wingspan of the actual airplane. (*Hint:* convert 46 feet to inches.) $\frac{3}{92}$

ALGEBRA Simplify each fraction. If the fraction is already in simplest form, write *simplified*.

30. $\frac{a}{a^4}$ $\frac{1}{a^3}$ 31. $\frac{y^3}{y}$ $\frac{y^2}{1}$ or y^2 32. $\frac{12m}{15m}$ $\frac{4}{5}$ 33. $\frac{40d}{42d}$ $\frac{20}{21}$
34. $\frac{4k}{19m}$ simp. 35. $\frac{8t}{64t^2}$ $\frac{1}{8t}$ 36. $\frac{16n}{18n^2p}$ $\frac{8}{9np}$ 37. $\frac{28z^3}{16z}$ $\frac{7z^2}{4}$
38. $\frac{6r}{15rs}$ $\frac{2}{5s}$ 39. $\frac{12cd}{19e}$ simp. 40. $\frac{30x^2}{51xy}$ $\frac{10x}{17y}$ ★41. $\frac{17g^2h}{51g}$ $\frac{gh}{3}$

42. **MEASUREMENT** Fifteen hours is what part of one day? $\frac{5}{8}$

43. **MEASUREMENT** Ninety-six centimeters is what part of a meter? $\frac{24}{25}$

44. **MEASUREMENT** Twelve ounces is what part of a pound? (*Hint*: 1 lb = 16 oz) $\frac{3}{4}$

45. **MUSIC** Musical notes C and A sound harmonious together because of their *frequencies*, or vibrations. The fraction that is formed by the two frequencies can be simplified, as shown below.

$$\frac{C}{A} = \frac{264}{440} \text{ or } \frac{3}{5}$$

When a fraction formed by two frequencies *cannot* be simplified, the notes sound like noise. Determine whether each pair of notes would sound harmonious together. Explain why or why not.

a. E and A   b. D and F   c. first C and last C
a–c. See margin.

Note	Frequency (hz)
C	264
D	294
E	330
F	349
G	392
A	440
B	494
C	528

46. **ANIMALS** The table shows the average amount of food each animal can eat in a day and its average weight. What fraction of its weight can each animal eat per day?
elephant, $\frac{1}{20}$; hummingbird, $\frac{2}{3}$; polar bear, $\frac{1}{60}$; tiger, $\frac{1}{25}$

Animal	Daily Amount of Food	Weight of Animal
elephant	450 lb	9000 lb
hummingbird	2 g	3 g
polar bear	25 lb	1500 lb
tiger	20 lb	500 lb

Source: *Animals as Our Companions, Wildlife Fact File*

Answer

45a. yes; $\frac{330}{440} = \frac{3}{4}$

45b. No; $\frac{294}{349}$ cannot be simplified.

45c. yes; $\frac{264}{528} = \frac{1}{2}$

MONEY For Exercises 47–49, use the graph to write each fraction in simplest form.

47. the fraction of a dollar that students in Japan save $\frac{31}{50}$

48. the fraction of a dollar that students in the U.S. save $\frac{21}{100}$

49. a fraction showing the amount of a dollar that students in the U.S. save compared to students in France $\frac{7}{10}$

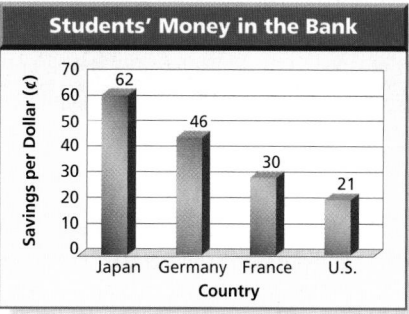

Students' Money in the Bank

50. **CRITICAL THINKING** Is it true that $\frac{23}{53} = \frac{2\!\!\!/3}{5\!\!\!/3}$ or $\frac{2}{5}$? Explain. No, $23 \neq 2 \cdot 3$ and $53 \neq 5 \cdot 3$.

51. **WRITING IN MATH** Answer the question that was posed at the beginning of the lesson. **See margin.**

How are simplified fractions useful in representing measurements?

Include the following in your answer:
- an explanation of how measurements represent parts of a whole, and
- examples of fractions that represent measurements.

Standardized Test Practice
Ⓐ Ⓑ Ⓒ Ⓓ

52. Which fraction represents the shaded area written in simplest form? **B**

　Ⓐ $\frac{9}{30}$　　Ⓑ $\frac{3}{10}$　　Ⓒ $\frac{6}{20}$　　Ⓓ $\frac{30}{100}$

53. Write $\frac{15ab}{25b^2}$ in simplest form. **A**

　Ⓐ $\frac{3a}{5b}$　　Ⓑ $\frac{15a}{25b}$　　Ⓒ $\frac{3ab}{5}$　　Ⓓ $\frac{15a}{25b^2}$

Maintain Your Skills

Mixed Review Find the greatest common factor of each set of numbers or monomials. *(Lesson 4-4)*

54. 9, 15 **3**　　55. 4, 12, 10 **2**　　56. $40x^2$, $16x$ **8x**　　57. $25a$, $30b$ **5**

Determine whether each number is *prime* or *composite*. *(Lesson 4-3)*

58. 13 **prime**　　59. 34 **comp.**　　60. 99 **comp.**　　61. 79 **prime**

ALGEBRA Solve each equation. Check your solution. *(Lesson 3-3)*

62. $t - 18 = 24$ **42**　　63. $30 = 3 + y$ **27**　　64. $-7 = x + 11$ **−18**

Getting Ready for the Next Lesson **PREREQUISITE SKILL** For each expression, use parentheses to group the numbers together and to group the powers with like bases together. *(To review **properties of multiplication**, see Lesson 1-4.)* 68. $(5 \cdot 2)(n^3 \cdot n)(p \cdot p)$

Example: $a \cdot 4 \cdot a^3 \cdot 2 = (4 \cdot 2)(a \cdot a^3)$

65. $6 \cdot 7 \cdot k^3$ **$(6 \cdot 7)(k^3)$**　　66. $s \cdot t^2 \cdot s \cdot t$ **$(s \cdot s)(t^2 \cdot t)$**

67. $3 \cdot x^4 \cdot (-5) \cdot x^2$ **$(3 \cdot -5)(x^4 \cdot x^2)$**　　68. $5 \cdot n^3 \cdot p \cdot 2 \cdot n \cdot p$

Answer

51. Fractions represent parts of a whole. So, measurements that contain parts of units can be represented using fractions. Answers should include the following.
- Measurements can be given as parts of a whole because smaller units make up larger units. For example, inches make up feet.
- Twelve inches equals 1 foot. So, 3 inches equals $\frac{3}{12}$ or $\frac{1}{4}$ foot.

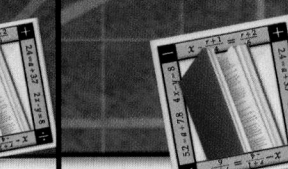
Powers

The phrase *the quantity* is used to indicate parentheses when reading expressions. Recall that an exponent indicates the number of times that the base is used as a factor. Suppose you are to write each of the following in symbols.

Words	Symbols	Examples (Let $x = 2$.)
three times x squared	$3x^2$	$3x^2 = 3 \cdot 2^2$ $= 3 \cdot 4$ Evaluate 2^2. $= 12$ Multiply $3 \cdot 4$.
three times x the quantity squared	$(3x)^2$	$(3x)^2 = (3 \cdot 2)^2$ $= 6^2$ Evaluate $3 \cdot 2$. $= 36$ Square 6.

In the expression $(3x)^2$, parentheses are used to show that $3x$ is used as a factor twice.

$$(3x)^2 = (3x)(3x)$$

The quantity can also be used to describe division of monomials.

Words	Symbols	Examples (Let $x = 2$.)
eight divided by x squared	$\dfrac{8}{x^2}$	$\dfrac{8}{x^2} = \dfrac{8}{2^2}$ $= \dfrac{8}{4}$ Evaluate 2^2. $= 2$ Divide $8 \div 4$.
eight divided by x the quantity squared	$\left(\dfrac{8}{x}\right)^2$	$\left(\dfrac{8}{x}\right)^2 = \left(\dfrac{8}{2}\right)^2$ $= 4^2$ Evaluate $8 \div 2$. $= 16$ Square 4.

Reading to Learn

State how you would read each expression. 1–10. See margin.

1. $4a^2$ **2.** $(10x)^5$ **3.** $\dfrac{5}{n^3}$ **4.** $\left(\dfrac{4}{r}\right)^2$ **5.** $(m + n)^3$

6. $(a - b)^4$ **7.** $a - b^4$ **8.** $\dfrac{a}{b^4}$ **9.** $(4c^2)^3$ **10.** $\left(\dfrac{8}{c^2}\right)^3$

Determine whether each pair of expressions is equivalent. Write *yes* or *no*.

11. $4ab^5$ and $4(ab)^5$ **no**   **12.** $(2x)^3$ and $8x^3$ **yes**   **13.** $(mn)^4$ and $m^4 \cdot n^4$ **yes**

14. c^3d^3 and cd^3 **no**   **15.** $\dfrac{x}{y^2}$ and $\left(\dfrac{x}{y}\right)^2$ **no**   **16.** $\dfrac{n^2}{r^2}$ and $\left(\dfrac{n}{r}\right)^2$ **yes**

174 Chapter 4 Factors and Fractions

Answers

1–10. Sample answers are given.

1. four times *a* squared

2. ten times *x* the quantity to the fifth power

3. five divided by *n* cubed

4. four divided by *r* the quantity squared

5. the sum of *m* and *n* the quantity cubed

6. *a* minus *b* the quantity to the fourth power

7. *a* minus *b* to the fourth power

8. *a* divided by *b* to the fourth power

9. four times *c* squared the quantity cubed

10. eight divided by *c* squared the quantity cubed

Multiplying and Dividing Monomials

What You'll Learn

- Multiply monomials.
- Divide monomials.

How are powers of monomials useful in comparing earthquake magnitudes?

For each increase on the Richter scale, an earthquake's vibrations, or *seismic waves*, are 10 times greater. So, an earthquake of magnitude 4 has seismic waves that are 10 times greater than that of a magnitude 3.

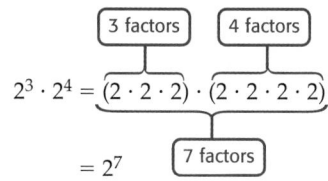

Richter Scale	Times Greater than Magnitude 3 Earthquake	Written Using Powers
4	10	10^1
5	$10 \times 10 = 100$	$10^1 \times 10^1 = 10^2$
6	$10 \times 100 = 1000$	$10^1 \times 10^2 = 10^3$
7	$10 \times 1000 = 10,000$	$10^1 \times 10^3 = 10^4$
8	$10 \times 10,000 = 100,000$	$10^1 \times 10^4 = 10^5$

a. The exponents of the factors are added to get the exponent of each product.

b. Sample answer: Add the exponents.

a. Examine the exponents of the factors and the exponents of the products in the last column. What do you observe?

b. Make a conjecture about a rule for determining the exponent of the product when you multiply powers with the same base. Test your rule by multiplying $2^2 \cdot 2^4$ using a calculator.

MULTIPLY MONOMIALS Recall that exponents are used to show repeated multiplication. You can use the definition of exponent to help find a rule for multiplying powers with the same base.

$$2^3 \cdot 2^4 = \underbrace{(2 \cdot 2 \cdot 2)}_{\text{3 factors}} \cdot \underbrace{(2 \cdot 2 \cdot 2 \cdot 2)}_{\text{4 factors}}$$

$$= 2^7 \quad \text{7 factors}$$

Notice the sum of the original exponents and the exponent in the final product. This relationship is stated in the following rule.

Study Tip

Common Misconception
When multiplying powers, do not multiply the bases. $3^2 \cdot 3^4 = 3^6$, not 9^6

Key Concept — Product of Powers

- **Words** You can multiply powers with the same base by adding their exponents.
- **Symbols** $a^m \cdot a^n = a^{m+n}$
- **Example** $3^2 \cdot 3^4 = 3^{2+4}$ or 3^6

Lesson 4-6 Multiplying and Dividing Monomials **175**

---

1 Focus

5-Minute Check Transparency 4-6 Use as a quiz or review of Lesson 4-5.

Mathematical Background notes are available for this lesson on page 146D.

How are powers of monomials useful in comparing earthquake magnitudes?

The opening activity questions are repeated on page 193 of the *Chapter 4 Resource Masters*.

Reading to Learn Mathematics, p. 193   ELL

Pre-Activity *How are powers of monomials useful in comparing earthquake magnitudes?*

Do the activity at the top of page 175 in your textbook. Write your answers below.

a. Examine the exponents of the factors and the exponents of the products in the last column. What do you observe? The exponents of the factors are added to get the exponent of the product.

b. Make a conjecture about a rule for determining the exponent of the product when you multiply powers with the same base. Test your rule by multiplying $2^2 \cdot 2^4$ using a calculator. Sample answer: Add the exponents.

Reading the Lesson

1. When multiplying powers with like bases, __add__ the exponents.
2. When dividing powers with like bases, __subtract__ the exponents.
3. Write a division expression whose quotient is 7^2. Sample answer: $\frac{7^3}{7}$
4. Write a multiplication expression whose product is v^5. Sample answer: $v^2 \cdot v^3$
5. Find each product.
   a. $4 \cdot 4^3$ 4^4 **b.** $y^7 \cdot y^5$ y^{12}
   c. $(-2x^2)(5x^2)$ $-10x^4$ **d.** $-3r^2 \cdot r$ $-3r^3$
6. Find each quotient.
   a. $\frac{7^4}{7^2}$ 7^2 **b.** $\frac{v^9}{v^3}$ v^6
   c. $\frac{6^7}{6^6}$ 6^1 or 6 **d.** $\frac{a^2b^2}{b^2}$ a^2

Helping You Remember

7. Explain how dividing powers is related to simplifying fractions. Provide an example as part of your explanation. Sample answer: When dividing powers with like bases, subtracting the exponents is equivalent to simplifying fractions. For example, $3^4 \div 3^2 = 3^{4-2}$ or 3^2 by the Quotient of Powers rule. When simplifying $\frac{3^4}{3^2}$, divide the numerator and denominator by the GCF, 3^2, to get $\frac{3^2}{1}$ or 3^2.

Resource Manager

Workbooks and Reproducible Masters

Chapter 4 Resource Masters
- Study Guide and Intervention, p. 190
- Skills Practice, p. 191
- Practice, p. 192
- Reading to Learn Mathematics, p. 193
- Enrichment, p. 194
- Assessment, p. 220

Parent and Student Study Guide Workbook, p. 29
School-to-Career Masters, p. 8

Transparencies
5-Minute Check Transparency 4-6
Answer Key Transparencies

Technology
Interactive Chalkboard

Teaching Tip Students may be tempted to multiply exponents when multiplying monomials. Be sure to emphasize that we add the exponents because we want to know how many times each factor is used.

MULTIPLY MONOMIALS

In-Class Examples

1 Find $3^4 \cdot 3^6$. 3^{10}

2 Find each product.

a. $y^4 \cdot y$ y^5

b. $(3p^4)(-2p^3)$ $-6p^7$

Teaching Tip Some students will benefit initially from writing out all factors until they understand why exponents are added.

3 Find each quotient.

a. $\dfrac{8^{11}}{8^5}$ 8^6

b. $\dfrac{x^{12}}{x}$ x^{11}

4 FOLDING PAPER If you fold a sheet of paper in half, you have a thickness of 2 sheets. Folding again, you have a thickness of 4 sheets. Continue folding in half and recording the thickness. How many times thicker is a sheet that has been folded 4 times than a sheet that has not been folded?

$\dfrac{2^4}{2^0} = 2^{4-0}$ or 16 times

Example 1 Multiply Powers

Find $7^3 \cdot 7$.

$$7^3 \cdot 7 = 7^3 \cdot 7^1 \qquad 7 = 7^1$$
$$= 7^{3+1} \qquad \text{The common base is 7.}$$
$$= 7^4 \qquad \text{Add the exponents.}$$

CHECK $7^3 \cdot 7 = (7 \cdot 7 \cdot 7)(7)$
$$= 7 \cdot 7 \cdot 7 \cdot 7 \text{ or } 7^4 \checkmark$$

✓ **Concept Check** Can you simplify $2^3 \cdot 3^3$ using the Product of Powers rule? Explain. **No; the bases are different.**

ALGEBRA CONNECTION

Monomials can also be multiplied using the rule for the product of powers.

Example 2 Multiply Monomials

Find each product.

a. $x^5 \cdot x^2$

$$x^5 \cdot x^2 = x^{5+2} \qquad \text{The common base is } x.$$
$$= x^7 \qquad \text{Add the exponents.}$$

Study Tip

Look Back
To review the **Commutative and Associative Properties of Multiplication,** see Lesson 1-4.

b. $(-4n^3)(2n^6)$

$$(-4n^3)(2n^6) = (-4 \cdot 2)(n^3 \cdot n^6) \qquad \text{Use the Commutative and Associative Properties.}$$
$$= (-8)(n^{3+6}) \qquad \text{The common base is } n.$$
$$= -8n^9 \qquad \text{Add the exponents.}$$

DIVIDE MONOMIALS You can also write a rule for finding quotients of powers.

$$\frac{2^6}{2^1} = \frac{2 \cdot 2 \cdot 2 \cdot 2 \cdot 2 \cdot 2}{2} \quad \boxed{\text{6 factors}} \quad \boxed{\text{1 factor}}$$

$$= \frac{2 \cdot 2 \cdot 2 \cdot 2 \cdot 2 \cdot \overset{1}{\cancel{2}}}{\underset{1}{\cancel{2}}} \qquad \text{Divide the numerator and the denominator by the GCF, 2.}$$

$$= 2^5 \quad \boxed{\text{5 factors}} \quad \text{Simplify.}$$

Compare the difference between the original exponents and the exponent in the final quotient. This relationship is stated in the following rule.

Key Concept *Quotient of Powers*

- **Words** You can divide powers with the same base by subtracting their exponents.

- **Symbols** $\dfrac{a^m}{a^n} = a^{m-n}$, where $a \neq 0$

- **Example** $\dfrac{4^5}{4^2} = 4^{5-2}$ or 4^3

DAILY INTERVENTION

Differentiated Instruction

- **Auditory/Musical** The phrase *Please Excuse My Dear Aunt Sally* indicates the correct order of operations: Parentheses, Exponents, Multiplication, Division, Addition, Subtraction. Challenge students to create a catchy phrase, rhyme, or rap that articulates the rules for multiplying and dividing monomials with powers. Share ideas with the class.

Example 3 *Divide Powers*

Find each quotient.

a. $\dfrac{5^7}{5^4}$

$\dfrac{5^7}{5^4} = 5^{7-4}$ The common base is 5.

$= 5^3$ Subtract the exponents.

b. $\dfrac{y^5}{y^3}$

$\dfrac{y^5}{y^3} = y^{5-3}$ The common base is y.

$= y^2$ Subtract the exponents.

☑ **Concept Check** Can you simplify $\dfrac{x^7}{y^2}$ using the Quotient of Powers rule? Why or why not? **No; the bases are different.**

Example 4 *Divide Powers to Solve a Problem*

Reading Math

How Many/How Much

How many times faster indicates that division is to be used to solve the problem. If the question had said *how much faster*, then subtraction $(10^9 - 10^8)$ would have been used to solve the problem.

COMPUTERS The table compares the processing speeds of a specific type of computer in 1993 and in 1999. Find how many times faster the computer was in 1999 than in 1993.

Write a division expression to compare the speeds.

$\dfrac{10^9}{10^8} = 10^{9-8}$ Subtract the exponents.

$= 10^1$ or 10 Simplify.

So, the computer was 10 times faster in 1999 than in 1993.

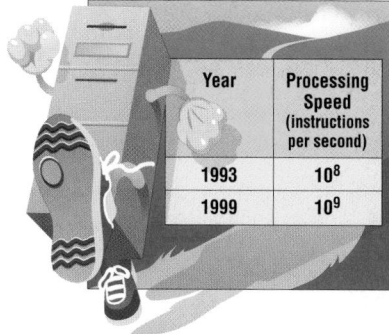

Year	Processing Speed (instructions per second)
1993	10^8
1999	10^9

Source: *The Intel Microprocessor Quick Reference Guide*

Check for Understanding

Concept Check

GUIDED PRACTICE KEY	
Exercises	Examples
4–7	1, 2
8–11	3
12	4

1. **State** whether you could use the Product of Powers rule, Quotient of Powers rule, or neither to find $m^5 \cdot n^4$. Explain.
   Neither; the factors have different bases.

2. **Explain** whether $4^8 \cdot 4^6$ and $4^4 \cdot 4^{10}$ are equivalent expressions.
   Yes; they both equal 4^{14}.

3. **OPEN ENDED** Write a multiplication expression whose product is 5^3.
   Sample answer: $5 \cdot 5^2 = 5^3$

Guided Practice Find each product or quotient. Express using exponents.
7. $-12x^5$

4. $9^3 \cdot 9^2$ 9^5

5. $a \cdot a^5$ a^6

6. $(n^4)(n^4)$ n^8

7. $-3x^2(4x^3)$

8. $\dfrac{3^8}{3^5}$ 3^3

9. $\dfrac{10^5}{10^3}$ 10^2

10. $\dfrac{x^3}{x}$ x^2

11. $\dfrac{a^{10}}{a^6}$ a^4

Application

12. **EARTHQUAKES** In 2000, an earthquake measuring 8 on the Richter scale struck Indonesia. Two months later, an earthquake of magnitude 5 struck northern California. How many times greater were the seismic waves in Indonesia than in California? (*Hint:* Let 10^8 and 10^5 represent the earthquakes, respectively.) **10^3 or 1000 times greater**

www.pre-alg.com/extra_examples

Lesson 4-6 Multiplying and Dividing Monomials **177**

Study Guide and Intervention, p. 190

When multiplying powers with the same base, add the exponents.

Symbols	Example
$a^m \cdot a^n = a^{m+n}$	$4^2 \cdot 4^5 = 4^{2+5}$ or 4^7

When dividing powers with the same base, subtract the exponents.

Symbols	Example
$\dfrac{a^m}{a^n} = a^{m-n}$, where $a \neq 0$	$\dfrac{5^8}{5^2} = 5^{8-2}$ or 5^4

Example 1 Find $2a^2(3a)$. Express your answer using exponents.

$2a^2(3a) = (2 \cdot 3)(a^2 \cdot a)$ Use the Commutative and Associative Properties.

$= (6)(a^{2+1})$ The common base is a.

$= 6a^3$ Add the exponents.

Example 2 Find $\dfrac{(-8)^4}{(-8)^2}$. Express your answer using exponents.

$\dfrac{(-8)^4}{(-8)^2} = (-8)^{4-2}$ The common base is -8.

$= (-8)^2$ Subtract the exponents.

Exercises

Find each product or quotient. Express your answer using exponents.

1. $4^7 \cdot 4^6$ 4^{13}
2. $v^5 \cdot v^4$ v^9
3. $(f^3)(f^9)$ f^{12}
4. $22^5 \cdot 22^5$ 22^{10}
5. $7h(5h^3)$ $35h^4$
6. $-10x^2(7x^3)$ $-70x^5$
7. $\dfrac{7^5}{7^2}$ 7^3
8. $\dfrac{1^8}{1^6}$ 1^2
9. $\dfrac{(-12)^3}{(-12)^3}$ $(-12)^0$ or 1
10. $3^8 \cdot 3^3$ 3^{11}
11. $\dfrac{c^{20}}{c^{13}}$ c^7
12. $\dfrac{(-p)^{18}}{(-p)^{12}}$ $(-p)^6$
13. $-7u^5(-6u^5)$ $42u^{11}$
14. $\dfrac{2u^3}{2w}$ w^2
15. $-5m^3(4m^6)$ $-20m^9$
16. the product of two cubed and two squared 2^5
17. the quotient of six to the eighth power and six squared 6^6

Skills Practice, p. 191 and Practice, p. 192 (shown)

Find each product or quotient. Express your answer using exponents.

1. $4^2 \cdot 4^3$ 4^5
2. $9^8 \cdot 9^6$ 9^{14}
3. $7^4 \cdot 7^2$ 7^6
4. $13^2 \cdot 13^4$ 13^6
5. $(-8)^5(-8)^3$ $(-8)^8$
6. $(-21)^9(-21)^5$ $(-21)^{14}$
7. $t^9 \cdot t^3$ t^{12}
8. $h^4 \cdot h^{13}$ h^{17}
9. $(m^6)(m^6)$ m^{12}
10. $(u^{11})(u^{10})$ u^{21}
11. $(-r)^7(-r)^{20}$ $(-r)^{27}$
12. $(-w)(-w)^9$ $(-w)^{10}$
13. $4d^5 \cdot 8d^6$ $32d^{11}$
14. $7j^{50} \cdot 6j^{50}$ $42j^{100}$
15. $-5b^9 \cdot 6b^2$ $-30b^{11}$
16. $12^1 \cdot 12^2$ 12^3
17. $\dfrac{6^{11}}{6^3}$ 6^8
18. $\dfrac{15^3}{15^2}$ 15^1 or 15
19. $\dfrac{9^8}{9^7}$ 9^2
20. $\dfrac{18^4}{18^4}$ 18^0 or 1
21. $\dfrac{(-7)^6}{(-7)^5}$ $(-7)^1$ or -7
22. $\dfrac{95^{21}}{95^{18}}$ 95^3
23. $\dfrac{t^{30}}{t^{20}}$ v^{10}
24. $\dfrac{n^{19}}{n^{11}}$ n^8
25. the product of five cubed and five to the fourth power 5^7
26. the quotient of eighteen to the ninth power and eighteen squared 18^7
27. the product of z cubed and z squared z^6
28. the quotient of x to the fifth power and x cubed x^2
29. **SOUND** Decibels are units used to measure sound. The softest sound that can be heard is rated as 0 decibels (or a relative loudness of 1). Ordinary conversation is rated at about 60 decibels (or a relative loudness of 10^6). A rock concert is rated at about 120 decibels (or a relative loudness of 10^{12}). How many times greater is the relative loudness of a rock concert than the relative loudness of ordinary conversation? 10^6 or 1,000,000 times

Enrichment, p. 194

Dividing Powers with Different Bases

Some powers with different bases can be divided. First, you must be able to write both as powers of the same base. An example is shown below.

$\dfrac{2^5}{8^2} = \dfrac{2^5}{(2^3)^2}$ To find the power of a power, multiply the exponents.

$= \dfrac{2^5}{2^6}$

$= 2^{-1}$ or $\dfrac{1}{2}$

This method could not have been used to divide $\dfrac{2^5}{9^2}$, since 9 cannot be written as a power of 2 using integers.

Simplify each fraction using the method shown above. Express the solution without exponents.

1. $\dfrac{8^2}{2^2}$ 16
2. $\dfrac{16^4}{8^3}$ 128
3. $\dfrac{9^3}{3^3}$ 27
4. $\dfrac{81^4}{3^4}$ 531,441
5. $\dfrac{3^9}{81^2}$ 3
6. $\dfrac{32^4}{16^4}$ 16
7. $\dfrac{125^2}{25^3}$ 1
8. $\dfrac{6^6}{216^2}$ 1
9. $\dfrac{10^6}{1000^3}$ 0.001
10. $\dfrac{64^3}{8^5}$ 8
11. $\dfrac{27^5}{9^4}$ 2187
12. $\dfrac{343^3}{7^5}$ 2401

Lesson 4-6 Multiplying and Dividing Monomials **177**

3 Practice/Apply

Study Notebook

Have students—

- copy the rules for multiplying and dividing monomials, including an example of each.
- include any other item(s) that they find helpful in mastering the skills in this lesson.

About the Exercises . . .

Organization by Objective
- **Multiplying Monomials:** 13–24, 37, 39
- **Dividing Monomials:** 25–36, 38, 41–44

Odd/Even Assignments
Exercises 13–40 are structured so that students practice the same concepts whether they are assigned odd or even problems.

Assignment Guide

Basic: 13–21 odd, 25–31 odd, 37, 45, 46, 50–69

Average: 13–39 odd, 45–47, 50–69

Advanced: 14–40 even, 41–44, 47–63 (Optional: 64–69)

★ indicates increased difficulty

Practice and Apply

Homework Help

For Exercises	See Examples
13–24	1, 2
25–36	3
41–44	4

Extra Practice
See page 732.

24. $-20x^4y^3$
31. $(-2)^1$ or -2

Find each product or quotient. Express using exponents. 23. $8a^3b^{10}$

13. $3^3 \cdot 3^2$ 3^5
14. $6 \cdot 6^7$ 6^8
15. $d^4 \cdot d^6$ d^{10}
16. $10^4 \cdot 10^3$ 10^7

17. $n^8 \cdot n$ n^9
18. $t^2 \cdot t^4$ t^6
19. $9^4 \cdot 9^5$ 9^9
20. $a^6 \cdot a^6$ a^{12}

21. $2y \cdot 9y^4$ $18y^5$
22. $(5r^3)(4r^4)$ $20r^7$
★ 23. $ab^5 \cdot 8a^2b^5$
★ 24. $10x^3y \cdot (-2xy^2)$

25. $\frac{5^5}{5^2}$ 5^3
26. $\frac{8^4}{8^3}$ 8^1 or 8
27. $b^6 \div b^3$ b^3
28. $10^{10} \div 10^2$ 10^8

29. $\frac{m^{20}}{m^8}$ m^{12}
30. $\frac{a^8}{a^8}$ a^0 or 1
31. $\frac{(-2)^6}{(-2)^5}$
32. $\frac{(-x)^5}{(-x)}$ $(-x)^4$

★ 33. $\frac{n^3(n^5)}{n^2}$ n^6
★ 34. $\frac{s^7}{s \cdot s^2}$ s^4
★ 35. $\left(\frac{k^3}{k}\right)\left(\frac{m^2}{m}\right)$ k^2m
★ 36. $\left(\frac{15}{5}\right)\left(\frac{n^9}{n}\right)$ $3n^8$

37. the product of nine to the fourth power and nine cubed 9^7

38. the quotient of k to the fifth power and k squared k^3

★ 39. What is the product of 7^3, 7^5, and 7? 7^9

★ 40. Find $a^4 \cdot a^6 \div a^2$. a^8

TEACHING TIP
In multiplication or division exercises, students may actually multiply or divide exponents rather than add or subtract them. Review the rules with students.

CHEMISTRY For Exercises 41–43, use the following information.
★ The pH of a solution describes its acidity. Neutral water has a pH of 7. Each one-unit *decrease* in the pH means that the solution is 10 times more acidic. For example, a pH of 4 is 10 times more acidic than a pH of 5.

41. Suppose the pH of a lake is 5 due to acid rain. How much more acidic is the lake than neutral water? 10^2 or 100 times

42. Use the information at the left to find how much more acidic vinegar is than baking soda. 10^6 or $1,000,000$ times

43. Cola is 10^4 times more acidic than neutral water. What is the pH value of cola? **3**

★ 44. **LIFE SCIENCE** When bacteria reproduce, they split so that one cell becomes two. The number of cells after t cycles of reproduction is 2^t.
   a. *E. coli* reproduce very quickly, about every 15 minutes. If there are 100 *E. coli* in a dish now, how many will there be in 30 minutes? **400**
   b. How many times more *E. coli* are there in a population after 3 hours than there were after 1 hour? **256 times more**

GEOMETRY For Exercises 45 and 46, use the information in the figures.

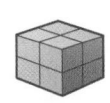

45. How many times greater is the length of the edge of the larger cube than the smaller one? **2 times**

46. How many times greater is the volume of the larger cube than the smaller one? 2^3 or 8 times

Volume = 2^3 cubic units

Volume = 2^6 cubic units

★ **Find each missing exponent.**

47. $(4^\bullet)(4^3) = 4^{11}$ **8**

48. $\frac{t^\bullet}{t^2} = t^{14}$ **16**

49. $\frac{13^5}{13^\bullet} = 1$ **5**

More About. . .

Chemistry
The pH values of different kitchen items are shown below.

Item	pH
lemon juice	2
vinegar	3
tomatoes	4
baking soda	9

Source: *Biology*, Raven

50. CRITICAL THINKING Use the laws of exponents to show why the value of *any* nonzero number raised to the zero power equals 1. **See margin.**

51. WRITING IN MATH Answer the question that was posed at the beginning of the lesson. **See margin.**

How are powers of monomials useful in comparing earthquake magnitudes?

Include the following in your answer:
- a description of the Richter scale, and
- a comparison of two earthquakes of different magnitudes by using the Quotient of Powers rule.

52. Multiply $7xy$ and $x^{14}z$. **A**

   Ⓐ $7x^{15}yz$ Ⓑ $7x^{15}y$ Ⓒ $7x^{13}yz$ Ⓓ $x^{15}yz$

53. Find the quotient $a^5 \div a$. **B**

   Ⓐ a^5 Ⓑ a^4 Ⓒ a^6 Ⓓ a

Maintain Your Skills

Mixed Review Write each fraction in simplest form. If the fraction is already in simplest form, write *simplified*. *(Lesson 4-5)*

54. $\frac{12}{40}$ $\frac{3}{10}$ **55.** $\frac{20}{53}$ simplified   **56.** $\frac{8n^2}{32n}$ $\frac{n}{4}$ **57.** $\frac{6x^3}{4x^2y}$ $\frac{3x}{2y}$

Find the greatest common factor of each set of numbers or monomials.
(Lesson 4-4)

58. 36, 4 **4**   **59.** 18, 28 **2**   **60.** 42, 54 **6**   **61.** $9a, 10a^3$ **a**

62. Evaluate $|a| - |b| \cdot |c|$ if $a = -16$, $b = 2$, and $c = 3$. *(Lesson 2-1)* **10**

63. ENERGY The graph shows the high temperature and the maximum amount of electricity that was used during each of fifteen summer days. Do the data show a *positive*, *negative*, or *no* relationship? Explain.
(Lesson 1-7)
Positive; as the high temperature increases, the amount of electricity that is used also increases.

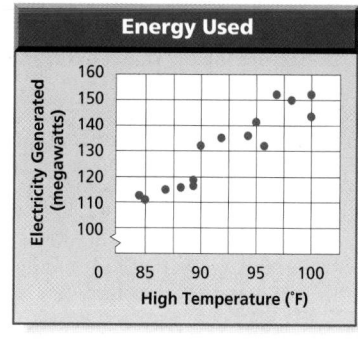

Getting Ready for the Next Lesson **PREREQUISITE SKILL** Evaluate each expression if $x = 10$, $y = -5$, and $z = 4$. Write as a fraction in simplest form.
(To review evaluating expressions, see Lesson 1-3.)

64. $\frac{1}{x}$ $\frac{1}{10}$ **65.** $\frac{y}{50}$ $-\frac{1}{10}$ **66.** $\frac{z}{100}$ $\frac{1}{25}$

67. $\frac{1}{zy}$ $-\frac{1}{20}$ **68.** $\frac{1}{x \cdot x}$ $\frac{1}{100}$ **69.** $\frac{1}{(z)(z)(z)}$ $\frac{1}{64}$

Answers

50. Sample answer: By the law of exponents,
$\frac{a^n}{a^n} = a^{n-n}$ or a^0 for $a \neq 0$.
Since $\frac{a^n}{a^n} = 1$, then $a^0 = 1$. So, any number raised to the zero power must equal 1. Or, $a^0 \cdot a^m = a^{0+m}$ or a^m. Therefore, by the Identity Property of Multiplication, a^0 must equal 1.

51. Each level on the Richter scale is 10 times greater than the previous level. So, powers of 10 can be used to compare earthquake magnitudes. Answers should include the following.
- On the Richter scale, each whole-number increase represents a 10-fold increase in the magnitude of seismic waves.
- An earthquake of magnitude 7 is 10^5 times greater than an earthquake of magnitude 2 because $10^7 \div 10^2 = 10^{7-2}$ or 10^5.

Getting Started

Objective Model and investigate radioactive half-lives.

Materials
50 pennies   grid paper
shoebox with lid   pencil

Teach

- Ask students to predict how many pennies will remain after each half-life. Discuss discrepancies between their predictions and the actual number of pennies.
- Combine everyone's data to make a classroom data set. How does the classroom data fit the anticipated result?

Assess

In **Exercises 1–2,** students should create a scatter plot and describe the relationship between the number of half-lives and number of pennies.

In **Exercises 3–4,** students should relate the expressions to the experiment.

Answer

1. Sample answer:

Number of Half-Lives	Number of Pennies That Remain
1	27
2	14
3	6
4	3
5	1

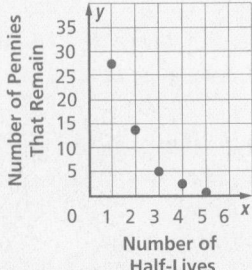

Algebra Activity

A Half-Life Simulation

A radioactive material such as uranium decomposes or decays in a regular manner best described as a *half-life*. A half-life is the time it takes for half of the atoms in the sample to decay.

Collect the Data

Step 1 Place 50 pennies heads up in a shoebox. Put the lid on the box and shake it up and down one time. This simulates one half-life.

Step 2 Open the lid of the box and remove all the pennies that are now tails up. In a table like the one at the right, record the number of pennies that remain.

Step 3 Put the lid back on the box and again shake the box up and down one time. This represents another half-life.

Step 4 Open the lid. Remove all the tails up pennies. Count the pennies that remain.

Step 5 Repeat the half-life of decay simulation until less than five pennies remain in the shoebox.

Number of Half-Lives	Number of Pennies That Remain
1	
2	
3	
4	
5	

Analyze the Data

1. On grid paper, draw a coordinate grid in which the *x*-axis represents the number of half-lives and the *y*-axis represents the number of pennies that remain. Plot the points (number of half-lives, number of remaining pennies) from your table. **See margin.**

2. Describe the graph of the data. **Points descend from left to right in a curve.**

After each half-life, you expect to remove about one-half of the pennies. So, you expect about one-half to remain. The expressions at the right represent the average number of pennies that remain if you start with 50, after one, two, and three half-lives.

one half-life:	$50\left(\frac{1}{2}\right) = 50\left(\frac{1}{2}\right)^1$
two half-lives:	$50\left(\frac{1}{2}\right)\left(\frac{1}{2}\right) = 50\left(\frac{1}{2}\right)^2$
three half-lives:	$50\left(\frac{1}{2}\right)\left(\frac{1}{2}\right)\left(\frac{1}{2}\right) = 50\left(\frac{1}{2}\right)^3$

Make a Conjecture 3. 6.25 or about 6 pennies; see students' work.

3. Use the expressions to predict how many pennies remain after three half-lives. Compare this number to the number in the table above. Explain any differences.

4. Suppose you started with 1000 pennies. Predict how many pennies would remain after three half-lives. **125 pennies**

Resource Manager

📁 *Teaching Pre-Algebra with Manipulatives*
- p. 1 (master for grid paper)
- p. 63 (student recording sheet)

Negative Exponents

What You'll Learn

- Write expressions using negative exponents.
- Evaluate numerical expressions containing negative exponents.

How do negative exponents represent repeated division?

Copy the table at the right.

a. The exponents decrease by 1.

a. Describe the pattern of the powers in the first column. Continue the pattern by writing the next two powers in the table.

b. Each number is divided by 2.

b. Describe the pattern of values in the second column. Then complete the second column.

c. See students' work.

c. Verify that the powers you wrote in part **a** are equal to the values that you found in part **b**.

d. Determine how 3^{-1} should be defined. $\frac{1}{3}$

Power	Value
2^6	64
2^5	32
2^4	16
2^3	8
2^2	4
2^1	2
? 2^0	? 1
? 2^{-1}	? $\frac{1}{2}$

ALGEBRA CONNECTION

NEGATIVE EXPONENTS Extending the pattern at the right shows that 2^{-1} can be defined as $\frac{1}{2}$.

You can apply the Quotient of Powers rule and the definition of a power to $\frac{x^3}{x^5}$ and write a general rule about negative powers.

$$2^2 = 4$$
$$\Big\downarrow \div 2$$
$$2^1 = 2$$
$$\Big\downarrow \div 2$$
$$2^0 = 1$$
$$\Big\downarrow \div 2$$
$$2^{-1} = \frac{1}{2}$$

Method 1 Quotient of Powers

$$\frac{x^3}{x^5} = x^{3-5}$$
$$= x^{-2}$$

Method 2 Definition of Power

$$\frac{x^3}{x^5} = \frac{\overset{1}{\cancel{x}} \cdot \overset{1}{\cancel{x}} \cdot \overset{1}{\cancel{x}}}{\underset{1}{\cancel{x}} \cdot \underset{1}{\cancel{x}} \cdot \underset{1}{\cancel{x}} \cdot x \cdot x}$$
$$= \frac{1}{x \cdot x}$$
$$= \frac{1}{x^2}$$

Since $\frac{x^3}{x^5}$ cannot have two different values, you can conclude that $x^{-2} = \frac{1}{x^2}$. This suggests the following definition.

Key Concept — Negative Exponents

- **Symbols** $a^{-n} = \frac{1}{a^n}$, for $a \neq 0$ and any integer n

- **Example** $5^{-4} = \frac{1}{5^4}$

4-7 Lesson Notes

1 Focus

 5-Minute Check Transparency 4-7 Use as a quiz or review of Lesson 4-6.

Mathematical Background notes are available for this lesson on page 146D.

How do negative exponents represent repeated division?

The opening activity questions are repeated on page 198 of the *Chapter 4 Resource Masters*.

Reading to Learn Mathematics, p. 198   ELL

Pre-Activity *How do negative exponents represent repeated division?*

Do the activity at the top of page 181 in your textbook. Write your answers below.

  a. Describe the pattern of powers in the first column. Continue the pattern by writing the next two powers in the table. The exponents decrease by 1; 2^0, 2^{-1}.

  b. Describe the pattern of values in the second column. Then complete the second column. Each number is divided by 2; 1, $\frac{1}{2}$.

  c. Verify that the powers you wrote in part **a** are equal to the values that you found in part **b**. See students' work.

  d. Determine how 3^{-1} should be defined. $\frac{1}{3}$

Reading the Lesson

1. Explain the value of 5^{-3} using a pattern. Sample answer: The value in each row is the previous value divided by 5, so 5^{-3} is $\frac{1}{125}$.

Power	Value
5^1	5
5^0	1
5^{-1}	$\frac{1}{5}$
5^{-2}	$\frac{1}{25}$
5^{-3}	$\frac{1}{125}$

2. Using what you know about the Quotient of Powers rule, fill in the missing number. $5^{-3} = \frac{?}{5^5}$, $5^{-3} = \frac{5^2}{5^5}$

Helping You Remember

3. Are $-x^2$ and x^{-2} equivalent? Explain. Sample answer: No; let $x = 3$. $-3^2 = -9$, but $3^{-2} = \frac{1}{3^2} = \frac{1}{9}$.

Resource Manager

Workbooks and Reproducible Masters

Chapter 4 Resource Masters
- Study Guide and Intervention, p. 195
- Skills Practice, p. 196
- Practice, p. 197
- Reading to Learn Mathematics, p. 198
- Enrichment, p. 199

Parent and Student Study Guide Workbook, p. 30

 Transparencies

5-Minute Check Transparency 4-7
Answer Key Transparencies

 Technology

Interactive Chalkboard

NEGATIVE EXPONENTS

In-Class Examples

1 Write each expression using a positive exponent.

a. 3^{-4} $\dfrac{1}{3^4}$

b. m^{-2} $\dfrac{1}{m^2}$

2 Write $\dfrac{1}{125}$ as an expression using a negative exponent.
5^{-3}

3 An atom is an incredibly small unit of matter. The smallest atom has a diameter of approximately $\dfrac{1}{10}$th of a nanometer, or 0.0000000001 meter. Write the decimal as a fraction and as a power of 10.

$$\dfrac{1}{10,000,000,000} = \dfrac{1}{10^{10}} = 10^{-10}$$

Teaching Tip Remind students that saying a decimal properly will automatically give the fraction. So, 0.001 is 1 one thousandth or $\dfrac{1}{1000}$.

EVALUATE EXPRESSIONS

In-Class Example

4 Evaluate r^{-2} if $r = -4$. $\dfrac{1}{16}$

Example 1 **Use Positive Exponents**

Write each expression using a positive exponent.

a. 6^{-2}

$6^{-2} = \dfrac{1}{6^2}$ Definition of negative exponent

b. x^{-5}

$x^{-5} = \dfrac{1}{x^5}$ Definition of negative exponent

One way to write a fraction as an equivalent expression with negative exponents is to use prime factorization.

Example 2 **Use Negative Exponents**

Write $\dfrac{1}{9}$ as an expression using a negative exponent.

$\dfrac{1}{9} = \dfrac{1}{3 \cdot 3}$ Find the prime factorization of 9.

$= \dfrac{1}{3^2}$ Definition of exponent

$= 3^{-2}$ Definition of negative exponent

✓ **Concept Check** How can $\dfrac{1}{9}$ be written as an expression with a negative exponent other than 3^{-2}? 9^{-1}

Negative exponents are often used in science when dealing with very small numbers. Usually the number is a power of ten.

Example 3 **Use Exponents to Solve a Problem**

WATER A molecule of water contains two hydrogen atoms and one oxygen atom. A hydrogen atom is only 0.00000001 centimeter in diameter. Write the decimal as a fraction and as a power of ten.

The digit 1 is in the 100-millionths place.

$0.00000001 = \dfrac{1}{100,000,000}$ Write the decimal as a fraction.

$= \dfrac{1}{10^8}$ $100,000,000 = 10^8$

$= 10^{-8}$ Definition of negative exponent

More About . . .

Water
A single drop of water contains about 10^{20} molecules.
Source: www.composite.about.com

EVALUATE EXPRESSIONS Algebraic expressions containing negative exponents can be written using positive exponents and evaluated.

Example 4 **Algebraic Expressions with Negative Exponents**

Evaluate n^{-3} if $n = 2$.

$n^{-3} = 2^{-3}$ Replace n with 2.

$= \dfrac{1}{2^3}$ Definition of negative exponent

$= \dfrac{1}{8}$ Find 2^3.

TEACHING TIP
Remind students that the negative exponent in n^{-3} does not change the sign of the expression.

182   **Chapter 4** Factors and Fractions

DAILY INTERVENTION — **Differentiated Instruction**

- **Intrapersonal** To insure that students understand the difference between negative numbers and numbers with negative exponents, have them write a paragraph about each of these in their Math Study Notebooks. Check their explanations to make sure each student has described the difference successfully.

Check for Understanding

Concept Check

1-2. See margin.

1. **OPEN ENDED** Write a convincing argument that $3^0 = 1$ using the fact that $3^4 = 81$, $3^3 = 27$, $3^2 = 9$, and $3^1 = 3$.

2. Order 8^{-8}, 8^3 and 8^0 from greatest to least. Explain your reasoning.

Guided Practice

GUIDED PRACTICE KEY	
Exercises	Examples
3–6	1
7–10	2
11, 12	4
13	3

Write each expression using a positive exponent.

3. 5^{-2} $\dfrac{1}{5^2}$

4. $(-7)^{-1}$ $\dfrac{1}{(-7)^1}$ or $\dfrac{1}{-7}$

5. t^{-6} $\dfrac{1}{t^6}$

6. n^{-2} $\dfrac{1}{n^2}$

Write each fraction as an expression using a negative exponent other than -1.

7. $\dfrac{1}{3^4}$ 3^{-4}

8. $\dfrac{1}{9^2}$ 9^{-2}

9. $\dfrac{1}{49}$ 7^{-2}

10. $\dfrac{1}{8}$ 2^{-3}

ALGEBRA Evaluate each expression if $a = 2$ and $b = -3$.

11. a^{-5} $\dfrac{1}{32}$

12. $(ab)^{-2}$ $\dfrac{1}{36}$

Application

13. **MEASUREMENT** A unit of measure called a *micron* equals 0.001 millimeter. Write this number using a negative exponent. 10^{-3}

★ indicates increased difficulty

Practice and Apply

Homework Help

For Exercises	See Examples
14–27	1
28–35	2
36–39	3
40–43	4

Extra Practice
See page 732.

Write each expression using a positive exponent.

14. 4^{-1} $\dfrac{1}{4^1}$ or $\dfrac{1}{4}$

15. 5^{-3} $\dfrac{1}{5^3}$

16. $(-6)^{-2}$ $\dfrac{1}{(-6)^2}$

17. $(-3)^{-3}$ $\dfrac{1}{(-3)^3}$

18. 3^{-5} $\dfrac{1}{3^5}$

19. 10^{-4} $\dfrac{1}{10^4}$

20. p^{-1} $\dfrac{1}{p^1}$ or $\dfrac{1}{p}$

21. a^{-10} $\dfrac{1}{a^{10}}$

22. d^{-3} $\dfrac{1}{d^3}$

23. q^{-4} $\dfrac{1}{q^4}$

★ 24. $2s^{-5}$ $2\left(\dfrac{1}{s^5}\right)$

★ 25. $\dfrac{1}{x^{-2}}$ x^2

For Exercises 26 and 27, write each expression using a positive exponent. Then write as a decimal.

26. A snowflake weighs 10^{-6} gram. $\dfrac{1}{10^6}$; **0.000001**

27. A small bird uses 5^{-4} Joules of energy to sing a song. $\dfrac{1}{5^4}$; **0.0016**

Write each fraction as an expression using a negative exponent other than -1.

28. $\dfrac{1}{9^4}$ 9^{-4}

29. $\dfrac{1}{5^5}$ 5^{-5}

30. $\dfrac{1}{8^3}$ 8^{-3}

31. $\dfrac{1}{13^2}$ 13^{-2}

32. $\dfrac{1}{100}$ 10^{-2}

33. $\dfrac{1}{81}$ 9^{-2}

★ 34. $\dfrac{1}{27}$ 3^{-3}

★ 35. $\dfrac{1}{16}$ 2^{-4} or 4^{-2}

Write each decimal using a negative exponent.

36. 0.1 10^{-1}

37. 0.01 10^{-2} or 100^{-1}

38. 0.0001 10^{-4} or 100^{-2}

39. 0.00001 10^{-5}

ALGEBRA Evaluate each expression if $w = -2$, $x = 3$, and $y = -1$.

40. x^{-4} $\dfrac{1}{81}$

41. w^{-7} $-\dfrac{1}{128}$

42. 8^w $\dfrac{1}{64}$

★ 43. $(xy)^{-6}$ $\dfrac{1}{729}$

20. $\dfrac{1}{p^1}$ or $\dfrac{1}{p}$

www.pre-alg.com/self_check_quiz

Lesson 4-7 Negative Exponents **183**

---

3 Practice/Apply

Study Notebook

Have students—
* copy the rule for negative exponents. (See key concept in the box on p. 181.)
* include any other item(s) that they find helpful in mastering the skills in this lesson.

About the Exercises . . .

Organization by Objective
* **Negative Exponents:** 14–39
* **Evaluate Expressions:** 40–43

Odd/Even Assignments
Exercises 14–43 and 45–52 are structured so that students practice the same concepts whether they are assigned odd or even problems.

Assignment Guide

Basic: 15–23 odd, 27–33 odd, 37–41 odd, 45, 53–56, 61–74

Average: 15–53 odd, 54–56, 61–74 (Optional: 57–60)

Advanced: 14–52 even, 53–68 (Optional: 69–74)

All: Practice Quiz 2 (1–10)

Answers

1. To get each successive power, divide the previous power by 3. Therefore, $3^0 = 3 \div 3$ or 1.

2. 8^3, 8^0, 8^{-8}; Sample answer: 8^3 is the greatest because its exponent is positive. 8^0 is next because it equals 1. The expression 8^{-8} is a fraction less than 1.

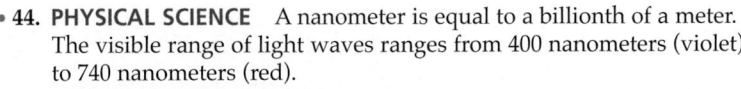

44. **PHYSICAL SCIENCE** A nanometer is equal to a billionth of a meter. The visible range of light waves ranges from 400 nanometers (violet) to 740 nanometers (red).

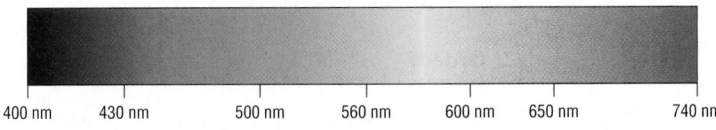

400 nm   430 nm   500 nm   560 nm   600 nm   650 nm   740 nm

a. Write one billionth of a meter as a fraction and with a negative exponent.

b. Use the information at the left to express the greatest wavelength of an X ray in meters. Write the expression using a negative exponent. 10^{-8} m

a. $\frac{1}{1,000,000,000}$ m; 10^{-9} m

More About...

Physical Science
The wavelengths of X rays are between 1 and 10 nanometers.
Source: *Biology*, Raven

45. **ANIMALS** A common flea 2^{-4} inch long can jump about 2^3 inches high. How many times its body size can a flea jump? **128 times**

★ 46. **MEDICINE** Which type of molecule in the table has a greater mass? How many times greater is it than the other type? **penicillin; 10^5 times greater**

Molecule	Mass (kg)
penicillin	10^{-18}
insulin	10^{-23}

Use the Product of Power and Quotient of Power rules to simplify each expression.

★ 47. $x^{-2} \cdot x^{-3}$ x^{-5} ★ 48. $r^{-5} \cdot r^9$ r^4 ★ 49. $\frac{x^4}{x^7}$ x^{-3}

★ 50. $\frac{y^6}{y^{-10}}$ y^{16} ★ 51. $\frac{a^4 b^{-4}}{ab^{-2}}$ $a^3 b^{-2}$ or $\frac{a^3}{b^2}$ ★ 52. $\frac{36 s^3 t^5}{12 s^6 t^{-3}}$ $3s^{-3}t^8$ or $\frac{3t^8}{s^3}$

53. **CRITICAL THINKING** Using what you learned about exponents, is $(x^3)^{-2} = (x^{-2})^3$? Why or why not? **Yes; see margin for explanation.**

54. **WRITING IN MATH** Answer the question that was posed at the beginning of the lesson. **See margin.**

How do negative exponents represent repeated division?

Include the following in your answer:

- an example of a power containing a negative exponent written in fraction form, and
- a discussion about whether the value of a fraction such as $\frac{1}{2^n}$ increases or decreases as the value of n increases.

Standardized Test Practice

55. Which is 15^{-5} written as a fraction? **C**

(A) $\frac{1}{5^5}$ (B) $\frac{1}{15}$

(C) $\frac{1}{15^5}$ (D) $-\frac{1}{15^5}$

56. One square millimeter equals $\underline{}$ square centimeter(s). (*Hint*: 1 cm = 10 mm) **B**

(A) 10^{-1} (B) 10^{-2}

(C) 10^{-3} (D) 10^3

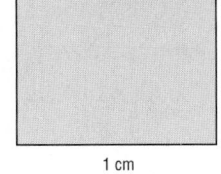

1 mm   1 mm   1 cm   1 cm

Answer

53. $(x^3)^{-2} = \frac{1}{(x^3)^2}$ $(x^{-2})^3 = (x^{-2})(x^{-2})(x^{-2})$

     $= \frac{1}{x^3 \cdot x^3}$ or $\frac{1}{x^6}$ $= x^{-6}$ or $\frac{1}{x^6}$

Extending
the Lesson
58. $(2 \times 10^{-1}) +$
(4×10^{-2})
59. $(1 \times 10^{-1}) +$
$(7 \times 10^{-2}) +$
(3×10^{-3})

Numbers less than 1 can also be expressed in expanded form.

Example: $0.568 = 0.5 + 0.06 + 0.008$
$$= (5 \times 10^{-1}) + (6 \times 10^{-2}) + (8 \times 10^{-3})$$

Express each number in expanded form.

57. 0.9 9×10^{-1} 58. 0.24   59. 0.173   60. 0.5875

60. $(5 \times 10^{-1}) + (8 \times 10^{-2}) + (7 \times 10^{-3}) + (5 \times 10^{-4})$

Maintain Your Skills

Mixed Review   Find each product or quotient. Express your answer using exponents.
(Lesson 4-6)

61. $3^6 \cdot 3$ 3^7

62. $x^2 \cdot x^4$ x^6

63. $\dfrac{5^5}{5^2}$ 5^3

64. **ALGEBRA**   Write $\dfrac{16n^3}{8n}$ in simplest form.   *(Lesson 4-5)* $2n^2$

ALGEBRA   Use the Distributive Property to rewrite each expression.   *(Lesson 3-1)*

65. $8(y + 6)$ $8y + 48$

66. $(9 + k)(-2)$ $-18 - 2k$ 67. $(n - 3)5$ $5n - 15$

68. Write the ordered pair that names point P.   *(Lesson 2-6)* $(1, -4)$

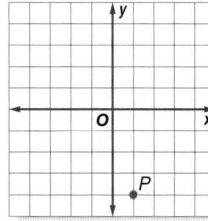

Getting Ready for   **PREREQUISITE SKILL**   Find each product.
the Next Lesson   *(To review multiplying decimals, see page 715.)*

69. 7.2×100 **720**

70. 1.6×1000 **1600**

71. 4.05×10 **40.5**

72. 3.8×0.01 **0.038**

73. 5.0×0.0001 **0.0005**

74. 9.24×0.1 **0.924**

Practice Quiz 2   Lessons 4-4 through 4-7

Find the GCF of each set of numbers or monomials.   *(Lesson 4-4)*

1. 15, 20 **5**

2. 24, 30 **6**

3. $2ab, 6a^2$ **2a**

Write each fraction in simplest form.   *(Lesson 4-5)*

4. **SCHOOL**   What fraction of days were you absent from school this nine-week period if you were absent twice out of 44 days? $\dfrac{1}{22}$

5. **COMMUNICATION**   What fraction of E-mail messages did you respond to, if you responded to 6 out of a total of 15 messages? $\dfrac{2}{5}$

ALGEBRA   Find each product or quotient. Express using exponents.   *(Lesson 4-6)*

6. $4^2 \cdot 4^4$ 4^6

7. $(n^4)(-2n^3)$ $-2n^7$

8. $\dfrac{q^9}{q^4}$ q^5

9. **ALGEBRA**   Write b^{-6} as an expression using a positive exponent.   *(Lesson 4-7)* $\dfrac{1}{b^6}$

10. **ALGEBRA**   Evaluate x^{-5} if $x = -2$.   *(Lesson 4-7)* $-\dfrac{1}{32}$

Answer (p.184)

54. Exponents are used to represent repeated factors in a multiplication. If the exponent is a negative number, then the repeated factors act as repeated divisors in the denominator. Answers should include the following.
- $4^{-2} = \dfrac{1}{4^2} = \dfrac{1}{4 \cdot 4}$ or $\dfrac{1}{16}$

- In 2^{-3}, the negative sign indicates that the factor 2 is repeated three times in the denominator, or 1 is divided by 2 three times. So, $2^{-3} = \dfrac{1}{2 \cdot 2 \cdot 2}$. If the exponent were -4, then 1 would be divided by 2 four times, and so on. So, as the value of n increases, the value of $\dfrac{1}{2^n}$ decreases.

Open-Ended Assessment

Speaking   Have students explain how to simplify an expression with negative exponents using the rules for multiplying monomials. For example, $2x^{-2} \cdot 3x$ could be simplified. Then ask students to evaluate the expression if $x = 3$.

Getting Ready
for Lesson 4-8

PREREQUISITE SKILL   Lesson 4-8 presents scientific notation, which expresses numbers as the product of a number and a power of 10. Exercises 69–74 should be used to determine your students' familiarity with multiplying by powers of 10.

Assessment Options

Practice Quiz 2   The quiz provides students with a brief review of the concepts and skills in Lessons 4-4 through 4-7. Lesson numbers are given to the right of exercises or instruction lines so students can review concepts not yet mastered.

1 Focus

5-Minute Check Transparency 4-8 Use as a quiz or review of Lesson 4-7.

Mathematical Background notes are available for this lesson on page 146D.

Why *is scientific notation an important tool in comparing real-world data?*

The opening activity questions are repeated on page 203 of the *Chapter 4 Resource Masters.*

Reading to Learn Mathematics, p. 203   **ELL**

Pre-Activity *Why is scientific notation an important tool in comparing real-world data?*

Do the activity at the top of page 186 in your textbook. Write your answers below.

a. Write the track length in millimeters. 5,000,000 mm

b. Write the track width in millimeters. (1 micron = 0.001 millimeter) 0.0005 mm

Reading the Lesson

Write a definition and give an example of the new vocabulary phrase.

Vocabulary	Definition	Example
1. slope intercept form	See students' work.	

2. To multiply by a power of 10, move the decimal point to the __right__ if the exponent is positive.

3. Which is larger, -2.1×10^4 or -2.1×10^{-4}? Explain. -2.1×10^{-4} is larger, since the numbers are negative and it is closer to zero.

Helping You Remember

4. Explain how to express each number in scientific notation.

a. a number greater than 1 Place the decimal point after the first nonzero digit, then multiply by the appropriate positive power of 10.

b. a number less than one Place the decimal point after the first nonzero digit, then multiply by the appropriate negative power of 10.

c. the number 1 Place the decimal point after the 1, then multiply by 10^0 (1.0×10^0).

Vocabulary
- scientific notation

b. 0.0005 mm

TEACHING TIP

Emphasize the difference between scientific notation and standard form. Students should feel comfortable with the terminology.

Study Tip

Powers of Ten
To multiply by a power of 10,
- move the decimal point to the right if the exponent is positive, and
- move the decimal point to the left if the exponent is negative.

In each case, the exponent tells you how many places to move the decimal point.

What You'll Learn

- Express numbers in standard form and in scientific notation.
- Compare and order numbers written in scientific notation.

Why is scientific notation an important tool in comparing real-world data?

A compact disc or CD has a single spiral track that stores data. It circles from the inside of the disc to the outside. If the track were stretched out in a straight line, it would be 0.5 micron wide and over 5000 meters long.

Track Length	Track Width
5000 meters	0.5 micron

a. Write the track length in millimeters. **5,000,000 mm**

b. Write the track width in millimeters. (1 micron = 0.001 millimeter.)

SCIENTIFIC NOTATION When you deal with very large numbers like 5,000,000 or very small numbers like 0.0005, it is difficult to keep track of the place value. Numbers such as these can be written in **scientific notation**.

Key Concept   Scientific Notation

- **Words** A number is expressed in scientific notation when it is written as the product of a factor and a power of 10. The factor must be greater than or equal to 1 and less than 10.

- **Symbols** $a \times 10^n$, where $1 \le a < 10$ and n is an integer

- **Examples** $5,000,000 = 5.0 \times 10^6$ $0.0005 = 5.0 \times 10^{-4}$

✓ Concept Check Is 13.0×10^2 written in scientific notation? Why or why not?
No; 13.0 is not a factor between 1 and 10. It should be 1.3×10^3.

You can express numbers that are in scientific notation in standard form.

Example 1 Express Numbers in Standard Form

Express each number in standard form.

a. 3.78×10^6

$3.78 \times 10^6 = 3.78 \times 1,000,000$ $10^6 = 1,000,000$

$= 3,780,000$ Move the decimal point 6 places to the right.

b. 5.1×10^{-5}

$5.1 \times 10^{-5} = 5.1 \times 0.00001$ $10^{-5} = 0.00001$

$= 0.000051$ Move the decimal point 5 places to the left.

186 Chapter 4 Factors and Fractions

Resource Manager

📁 Workbooks and Reproducible Masters

Chapter 4 Resource Masters
- Study Guide and Intervention, p. 200
- Skills Practice, p. 201
- Practice, p. 202
- Reading to Learn Mathematics, p. 203
- Enrichment, p. 204
- Assessment, p. 220

Parent and Student Study Guide Workbook, p. 31
Prerequisite Skills Workbook, pp. 33–36

 Transparencies
5-Minute Check Transparency 4-8
Real-World Transparency 4
Answer Key Transparencies

 Technology
Interactive Chalkboard
Pre-AlgePASS: Tutorial Plus, Lesson 8

To write a number in scientific notation, place the decimal point after the first nonzero digit. Then find the power of 10.

Example 2 *Express Numbers in Scientific Notation*

Express each number in scientific notation.

a. 60,000,000

$$60,\!000,\!000 = 6.0 \times 10,\!000,\!000 \quad \text{The decimal point moves 7 places.}$$
$$= 6.0 \times 10^7 \quad \text{The exponent is positive.}$$

b. 32,800

$$32,\!800 = 3.28 \times 10,\!000 \quad \text{The decimal point moves 4 places.}$$
$$= 3.28 \times 10^4 \quad \text{The exponent is positive.}$$

c. 0.0049

$$0.0049 = 4.9 \times 0.001 \quad \text{The decimal point moves 3 places.}$$
$$= 4.9 \times 10^{-3} \quad \text{The exponent is negative.}$$

People who make comparisons or compute with extremely large or extremely small numbers use scientific notation.

Example 3 *Use Scientific Notation to Solve a Problem*

SPACE The table shows the planets and their distances from the Sun. Light travels 300,000 kilometers per second. Estimate how long it takes light to travel from the Sun to Pluto. (*Hint:* Recall that
$$\text{distance} = \text{rate} \times \text{time.})$$

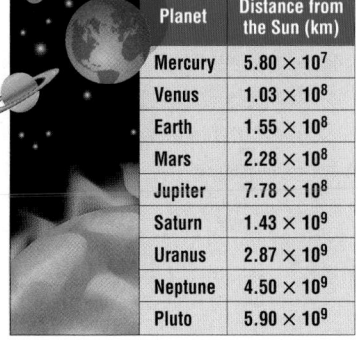

Planet	Distance from the Sun (km)
Mercury	5.80×10^7
Venus	1.03×10^8
Earth	1.55×10^8
Mars	2.28×10^8
Jupiter	7.78×10^8
Saturn	1.43×10^9
Uranus	2.87×10^9
Neptune	4.50×10^9
Pluto	5.90×10^9

Explore You know that the distance from the Sun to Pluto is 5.90×10^9 kilometers and that the speed of light is 300,000 kilometers per second.

Plan To find the time, solve the equation $d = rt$. Since you are estimating, round the distance 5.90×10^9 to 6.0×10^9. Write the rate 300,000 as 3.0×10^5.

Solve
$$d = rt \quad \text{Write the formula.}$$
$$6.0 \times 10^9 = (3.0 \times 10^5)t \quad \text{Replace } d \text{ with } 6.0 \times 10^9 \text{ and } r \text{ with } 3.0 \times 10^5.$$
$$\frac{6.0 \times 10^9}{3.0 \times 10^5} \approx \frac{(3.0 \times 10^5)t}{3.0 \times 10^5} \quad \text{Divide each side by } 3.0 \times 10^5.$$
$$2.0 \times 10^4 \approx t \quad \text{Divide 6.0 by 3.0 and } 10^9 \text{ by } 10^5.$$

So, it would take about 2.0×10^4 seconds or about 6 hours for light to travel from the Sun to Pluto.

Examine Use estimation to check the reasonableness of these results.

www.pre-alg.com/extra_examples

SCIENTIFIC NOTATION

In-Class Examples Power Point®

1 Express each number in standard form.

a. 4.395×10^4 **43,950**

b. 6.79×10^{-6} **0.00000679**

2 Express each number in scientific notation.

a. 800,000 **8.0×10^5**

b. 1,320,000 **1.32×10^6**

c. 0.0119 **1.19×10^{-2}**

3 **SPACE** Use the table in Example 3 in the textbook. Estimate how many times farther Pluto is from the Sun than Mercury is from the Sun. **Pluto is about 100 times farther from the Sun than Mercury.**

Teaching Tip Emphasize to students that using scientific notation instead of standard form requires them to use the rules for multiplying and dividing monomials. Since the numbers are typically very large or small, estimation is often encouraged.

COMPARE AND ORDER NUMBERS

In-Class Example Power Point®

4 **SPACE** The diameters of Mercury, Saturn, and Pluto are 4.9×10^3 km, 1.2×10^5 km, and 2.3×10^3 km, respectively. List the planets in order of increasing diameter. **Pluto, Mercury, Saturn**

DAILY
INTERVENTION

Differentiated Instruction

• **Naturalist** Have students research the sizes of very small or very large quantities in nature. Have them illustrate these and write the quantities in scientific notation.

Have students—

• complete the definitions/examples for the remaining terms on the Vocabulary Builder worksheets for Chapter 4.

• copy the rules for writing numbers in scientific notation from p. 186.

• include any other item(s) that they find helpful in mastering the skills in this lesson.

About the Exercises . . .

Organization by Objective
• **Scientific Notation:** 12–34
• **Compare and Order Numbers:** 35–41

Odd/Even Assignments
Exercises 12–33, 35–40, 42–45, and 47–48 are structured so that students practice the same concepts whether they are assigned odd or even problems.

Alert! Exercises 44–46 require a scientific calculator.

Assignment Guide

Basic: 13–41 odd, 49–59
Average: 13–45 odd, 49–59
Advanced: 12–46 even, 47–59

Answers

1. Sample answer: Numbers that are greater than 1 can be expressed as the product of a factor and a positive power of 10. So, these numbers are written in scientific notation using positive exponents. Numbers between 0 and 1 cannot be expressed as the product of a factor and a whole number power of 10, so they are written in scientific notation using negative exponents.

COMPARE AND ORDER NUMBERS   To compare and order numbers in scientific notation, first compare the exponents. With positive numbers, any number with a greater exponent is greater. If the exponents are the same, compare the factors.

Example 4 *Compare Numbers in Scientific Notation*

SPACE   Refer to the table in Example 3. Order Mars, Jupiter, Mercury, and Saturn from least to greatest distance from the Sun.

First, order the numbers according to their exponents. Then, order the numbers with the same exponent by comparing the factors.

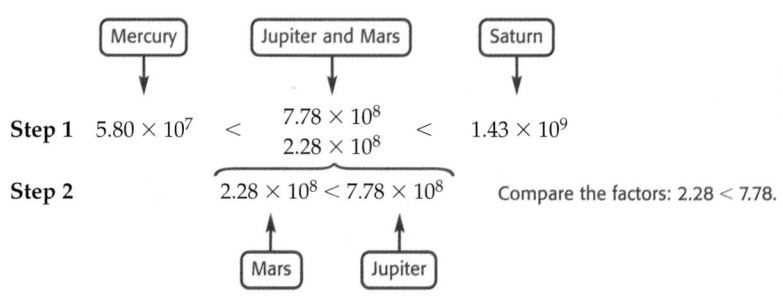

So, the order is Mercury, Mars, Jupiter, and Saturn.

Check for Understanding

Concept Check
1–2. See margin.

1. **Explain** the relationship between a number in standard form and the sign of the exponent when the number is written in scientific notation.

2. **OPEN ENDED**   Write a number in standard form and then write the number in scientific notation, explaining each step that you used.

Guided Practice

GUIDED PRACTICE KEY	
Exercises	Examples
3–5	1
6–9	2
10	3
11	4

Express each number in standard form.

3. 3.08×10^{-4} **0.000308**   4. 1.4×10^2 **140**   5. 8.495×10^5 **849,500**

Express each number in scientific notation.

6. 80,000,000 8.0×10^7 7. 697,000 6.97×10^5 8. 0.059 5.9×10^{-2}

9. the diameter of a spider's thread, 0.001 inch 1.0×10^{-3}

Applications

10. **SPACE**   Refer to the table in Example 3 on page 187. To the nearest second, how long does it take light to travel from the Sun to Earth? **517 s**

11. **SPACE**   Rank the planets in the table at the right by diameter, from least to greatest.
Mars, Venus, Earth

Planet	Diameter (km)
Earth	1.276×10^4
Mars	6.790×10^3
Venus	1.208×10^4

2. Sample answer: 312 is in standard form. First, move the decimal point in 312 two places to the left, 3.12×100. Next, write 100 using a positive exponent, 3.12×10^2.

Practice and Apply

Homework Help

For Exercises	See Examples
12–20	1
21–33	2
34	3
39–41	4

Extra Practice
See page 733.

Express each number in standard form. 15. 0.005689

12. 4.24×10^2 **424**   13. 5.72×10^4 **57,200**   14. 3.347×10^{-1} **0.3347**

15. 5.689×10^{-3} 16. 6.1×10^4 **61,000**   17. 9.01×10^{-2} **0.0901**

18. 1.399×10^5 **139,900**   19. 2.505×10^3 **2505**   20. 1.5×10^{-4} **0.00015**

Express each number in scientific notation. 30. 3.1×10^{-4}

21. $2,000,000$ 2.0×10^6 22. $499,000$ 4.99×10^5 23. 0.006 6.0×10^{-3}

24. 0.0125 1.25×10^{-2} 25. $50,000,000$ 5.0×10^7 26. $39,560$ 3.956×10^4

27. $5,894,000$ 5.894×10^6 28. 0.000078 7.8×10^{-5} 29. 0.000425 4.25×10^{-4}

30. The flow rate of some Antarctic glaciers is 0.00031 mile per hour.

31. Humans blink about 6.25 million times a year. 6.25×10^6

32. The number of possible ways that a player can play the first four moves in a chess game is 3 billion. 3.0×10^9

33. A particle of dust floating in the air weighs 0.000000753 gram. 7.53×10^{-7}

34. **SPACE** Refer to the table in Example 3 on page 187. To the nearest second, how long does it take light to travel from the Sun to Venus? 343 s

Choose the greater number in each pair.

35. $\underline{2.3 \times 10^5}$, 1.7×10^5 36. $\underline{1.8 \times 10^3}$, 1.9×10^{-1}

37. 5.2×10^2, $\underline{5000}$ 38. 0.012, $\underline{1.6 \times 10^{-1}}$

39. **OCEANS** Rank the oceans in the table at the right by area from least to greatest. **Arctic, Indian, Atlantic, Pacific**

Ocean	Area (sq mi)
Arctic	5.44×10^6
Atlantic	3.18×10^7
Indian	2.89×10^7
Pacific	6.40×10^7

40. petameter, gigameter, kilometer, nanometer, picometer, attometer

40. **MEASUREMENT** The table at the right shows the values of different prefixes that are used in the metric system. Write the units attometer, gigameter, kilometer, nanometer, petameter, and picometer in order from greatest to least measure.

Metric Measures	
Prefix	Meaning
atto	10^{-18}
giga	10^9
kilo	10^3
nano	10^{-9}
peta	10^{15}
pico	10^{-12}

41. Order 6.1×10^4, 6100, 6.1×10^{-5}, 0.0061, and 6.1×10^{-2} from least to greatest. 6.1×10^{-5}, 0.0061, 6.1×10^{-2}, 6100, 6.1×10^4

★ 42. Write $(6 \times 10^0) + (4 \times 10^{-3}) + (3 \times 10^{-5})$ in standard form. 6.00403

★ 43. Write $(4 \times 10^4) + (8 \times 10^3) + (3 \times 10^2) + (9 \times 10^1) + (6 \times 10^0)$ in standard form. 48,396

44. 2.0×10^6; 2,000,000
45. 2.52×10^5; 252,000
46. 1.6575×10^{-5}; 0.000016575

Convert the numbers in each expression to scientific notation. Then evaluate the expression. Express in scientific notation and in decimal notation.

★ 44. $\dfrac{20,000}{0.01}$ ★ 45. $\dfrac{(420,000)(0.015)}{0.025}$ ★ 46. $\dfrac{(0.078)(8.5)}{0.16(250,000)}$

Open-Ended Assessment

Speaking Have students explain orally how to convert a number in standard form to scientific notation and vice versa.

Assessment Options

Quiz (Lessons 4-7 and 4-8) is available on p. 220 of the *Chapter 4 Resource Masters*.

Answers

47. Bezymianny; Santa Maria; Agung; Mount St. Helens tied with Hekla 1947; Hekla, 1970; Ngauruhoe

50. Scientific notation is a shorthand way of writing very large or very small numbers. Answers should include the following.

- Examples of data that can be written in scientific notation, such as the surface area of planets and the diameter of atoms.

- Scientific notation is useful because you can compare quantities by simply looking at the exponent of the power of 10, rather than counting decimal places.

PHYSICAL SCIENCE For Exercises 47 and 48, use the graph.

The graph shows the maximum amounts of lava in cubic meters per second that erupted from seven volcanoes in the last century.

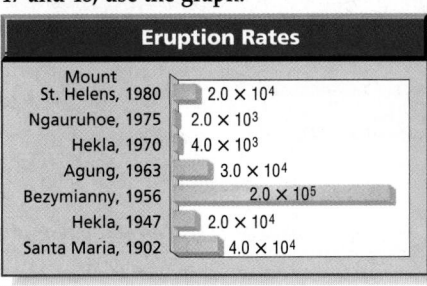

Eruption Rates

Mount St. Helens, 1980	2.0×10^4
Ngauruhoe, 1975	2.0×10^3
Hekla, 1970	4.0×10^3
Agung, 1963	3.0×10^4
Bezymianny, 1956	2.0×10^5
Hekla, 1947	2.0×10^4
Santa Maria, 1902	4.0×10^4

Source: University of Alaska

47. Rank the volcanoes in order from greatest to least eruption rate. **See margin.**

48. How many times larger was the Santa Maria eruption than the Mount St. Helens eruptions? **2 times**

 Online Research **Data Update** How do the eruption rates of other volcanoes compare with those in the graph? Visit www.pre-alg.com/data_update to learn more.

49. **CRITICAL THINKING** In standard form, $3.14 \times 10^{-4} = 0.000314$, and $3.14 \times 10^4 = 31,400$. What is 3.14×10^0 in standard form? **3.14**

50. WRITING IN MATH Answer the question that was posed at the beginning of the lesson. **See margin.**

Why is scientific notation an important tool in comparing real-world data?

Include the following in your answer:
- some real-world data that is written in scientific notation, and
- the advantages of using scientific notation to compare data.

 *Standardized Test Practice*

51. If the bodies of water in the table are ordered from least to greatest area, which would be third in the list? **B**

(A) Lake Huron (B) Lake Victoria

(C) Red Sea (D) Great Salt Lake

Body of Water	Area (km²)
Lake Huron	5.7×10^4
Lake Victoria	6.9×10^4
Red Sea	4.4×10^5
Great Salt Lake	4.7×10^3

52. Which is 5.80×10^{-4} written in standard form? **D**

(A) 58,000 (B) 5800 (C) 0.58 (D) 0.00058

Maintain Your Skills

Mixed Review **ALGEBRA** Evaluate each expression if $s = -2$ and $t = 3$. *(Lesson 4-7)*

53. t^{-4} $\dfrac{1}{81}$

54. s^{-5} $-\dfrac{1}{32}$

55. 7^s $\dfrac{1}{49}$

ALGEBRA Find each product or quotient. Express using exponents.
(Lesson 4-6)

56. $4^4 \cdot 4^7$ 4^{11}

57. $3a^2 \cdot 5a^2$ $15a^4$

58. $c^5 \div c^2$ c^3

59. **BUSINESS** Online Book Distributors add a $2.50 shipping and handling charge to the total price of every order. If the cost of books in an order is c, write an expression for the total cost. *(Lesson 1-3)* $c + \$2.50$

Study Guide and Review

Chapter
4
Study Guide and Review

Vocabulary and Concept Check

algebraic fraction (p. 170)	exponent (p. 153)	power (p. 153)
base (p. 153)	factor (p. 161)	prime factorization (p. 160)
base two (p. 158)	factors (p. 148)	prime number (p. 159)
binary (p. 158)	factor tree (p. 160)	scientific notation (p. 186)
composite number (p. 159)	greatest common factor (GCF)	simplest form (p. 169)
divisible (p. 148)	(p. 164)	standard form (p. 154)
expanded form (p. 154)	monomial (p. 150)	Venn diagram (p. 164)

Determine whether each statement is *true* or *false*. If false, replace the underlined word or number to make a true statement. 4. false; product

1. A <u>prime number</u> is a whole number that has exactly two factors, 1 and itself. true

2. Numbers expressed using exponents are called <u>powers</u>. true

3. The number 7 is a <u>factor</u> of 49 because it divides 49 with a remainder of zero. true

4. A monomial is a number, a variable, or a <u>sum</u> of numbers and/or variables.

5. The number 64 is a <u>composite number</u>. true

6. The number 9,536 is written in <u>standard form</u>. true

7. To write a fraction in simplest form, divide the numerator and the denominator by the <u>GCF</u>. true

8. A fraction is in simplest form when the GCF of the numerator and the denominator is <u>2</u>. false; 1

Lesson-by-Lesson Review

4-1 Factors and Monomials

See pages 148–152.

Concept Summary

- Numbers that are multiplied to form a product are called factors.

Example Determine whether 102 is divisible by 2, 3, 5, 6, or 10.
  2: Yes, the ones digit is divisible by 2.
  3: Yes, the sum of the digits is 3, and 3 is divisible by 3.
  5: No, the ones digit is not 0 or 5.
  6: Yes, the number is divisible by 2 and by 3.
  10: No, the ones digit is not 0.

Exercises Use divisibility rules to determine whether each number is divisible by 2, 3, 5, 6, or 10. *See Example 1 on page 149.*

  9. 111 3   10. 405 3, 5   11. 635 5   12. 863 none
  13. 582 2, 3, 6   14. 2124 2, 3, 6   15. 700 2, 5, 10   16. 4200 2, 3, 5, 6, 10

Vocabulary and Concept Check

- This alphabetical list of vocabulary terms in Chapter 4 includes a page reference where each term was introduced.

- **Assessment** A vocabulary review/test for Chapter 4 is available on p. 218 of the *Chapter 4 Resource Masters*.

Lesson-by-Lesson Review

For each lesson,
- the main ideas are summarized,
- additional examples review concepts, and
- practice exercises are provided.

Vocabulary PuzzleMaker

ELL The Vocabulary PuzzleMaker software improves students' mathematics vocabulary using four puzzle formats—crossword, scramble, word search using a word list, and word search using clues. Students can work on a computer screen or from a printed handout.

MindJogger Videoquizzes

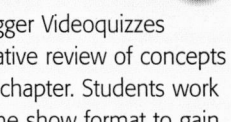

ELL MindJogger Videoquizzes provide an alternative review of concepts presented in this chapter. Students work in teams in a game show format to gain points for correct answers. The questions are presented in three rounds.

Round 1 Concepts (5 questions)
Round 2 Skills (4 questions)
Round 3 Problem Solving (4 questions)

Have students reread the lesson notes and summaries they wrote in their Foldables. Ask them to highlight the ideas they consider most difficult.

Encourage students to refer to their Foldables while completing the Study Guide and Review and to use them in preparing for the Chapter Test.

4-2 Powers and Exponents

See pages 153–157.

Concept Summary

- An exponent is a shorthand way of writing repeated multiplication.
- A number can be written in expanded form by using exponents.
- Follow the order of operations to evaluate algebraic expressions containing exponents.

Example Evaluate $4(a + 2)^3$ if $a = -5$.

$$4(a + 2)^3 = 4(-5 + 2)^3 \quad \text{Replace } a \text{ with } -5.$$
$$= 4(-3)^3 \quad \text{Simplify the expression inside the parentheses.}$$
$$= 4(-27) \quad \text{Evaluate } (-3)^3.$$
$$= -108 \quad \text{Simplify.}$$

Exercises Evaluate each expression if $x = -3$, $y = 4$, and $z = -2$.
See Example 3 on page 155.

17. 3^3 **27**
18. 10^4 **10,000**
19. $(-5)^2$ **25**
20. y^3 **64**
21. $10x^2$ **90**
22. xy^3 **−192**
23. $7y^0z^4$ **112**
24. $2(3z + 4)^5$ **−64**

4-3 Prime Factorization

See pages 159–163.

Concept Summary

- A prime number is a whole number that has exactly two factors, 1 and itself.
- A composite number is a whole number that has more than two factors.

Example Write the prime factorization of 40.

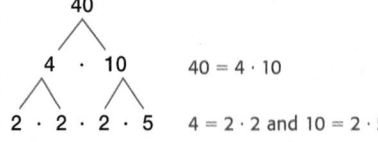

$$40 = 4 \cdot 10$$
$$4 = 2 \cdot 2 \text{ and } 10 = 2 \cdot 5$$

The prime factorization of 40 is $2 \cdot 2 \cdot 2 \cdot 5$ or $2^3 \cdot 5$.

Example Factor $9s^3t^2$.

$$9s^3t^2 = 3 \cdot 3 \cdot s^3 \cdot t^2 \qquad 9 = 3 \cdot 3$$
$$= 3 \cdot 3 \cdot s \cdot s \cdot s \cdot t \cdot t \quad s^3 \cdot t^2 = s \cdot s \cdot s \cdot t \cdot t$$

Exercises Write the prime factorization of each number. Use exponents for repeated factors. *See Example 2 on page 160.*

25. 45 $3^2 \cdot 5$
26. 55 $5 \cdot 11$
27. 68 $2^2 \cdot 17$
28. 200 $2^3 \cdot 5^2$

30. $-1 \cdot 3 \cdot 5 \cdot n \cdot n$

Factor each monomial. *See Example 3 on page 161.* 31. $2 \cdot 13 \cdot p \cdot p \cdot p$

29. $49k$ $7 \cdot 7 \cdot k$
30. $-15n^2$
31. $26p^3$
32. $10a^2b$ $2 \cdot 5 \cdot a \cdot a \cdot b$

4-4 Greatest Common Factor (GCF)

See pages 164–168.

Concept Summary

- The greatest number or monomial that is a factor of two or more numbers or monomials is the GCF.
- The Distributive Property can be used to factor algebraic expressions.

Examples

1 Find the GCF of $12a^2$ and $15ab$.

$12a^2 = 2 \cdot 2 \cdot \boxed{3} \cdot \boxed{a} \cdot a$

$15ab = \boxed{3} \cdot 5 \cdot \boxed{a} \cdot b$ The GCF of $12a^2$ and $15ab$ is $3 \cdot a$ or $3a$.

2 Factor $4n + 8$.

Step 1   Find the GCF of $4n$ and 8.

$4n = \boxed{2} \cdot \boxed{2} \cdot n$

$8 = \boxed{2} \cdot \boxed{2} \cdot 2$ The GCF is $2 \cdot 2$ or 4.

Step 2   Write the product of the GCF and its remaining factors.

$4n + 8 = 4(n) + 4(2)$ Rewrite each term using the GCF.

$ = 4(n + 2)$ Distributive Property

Exercises   Find the GCF of each set of numbers or monomials.
See Examples 2 and 4 on pages 165 and 166.

33. 6, 48 **6**   **34.** 16, 24 **8**   **35.** $4n, 5n^2$ **n**   **36.** $20c^3d, 12cd$ **$4cd$**

Factor each expression.   *See Example 5 on page 166.*

37. $2t + 20$ **$2(t + 10)$**   **38.** $3x + 24$ **$3(x + 8)$**   **39.** $30 + 4n$ **$2(15 + 2n)$**

4-5 Simplifying Algebraic Fractions

See pages 169–173.

Concept Summary

- Algebraic fractions can be written in simplest form by dividing the numerator and the denominator by the GCF.

Example   Simplify $\dfrac{8np}{18n^2}$.

$\dfrac{8np}{18n^2} = \dfrac{\overset{1}{\cancel{2}} \cdot 2 \cdot 2 \cdot \overset{1}{\cancel{n}} \cdot p}{\underset{1}{\cancel{2}} \cdot 3 \cdot 3 \cdot \underset{1}{\cancel{n}} \cdot n}$ Divide the numerator and the denominator by the GCF, $2 \cdot n$.

$\phantom{\dfrac{8np}{18n^2}} = \dfrac{4p}{9n}$ Simplify.

Exercises   Write each fraction in simplest form. If the fraction is already in simplest form, write *simplified*.   *See Examples 2 and 4 on page 170.*

40. $\dfrac{6}{21}$ **$\dfrac{2}{7}$**   **41.** $\dfrac{24}{40}$ **$\dfrac{3}{5}$**   **42.** $\dfrac{15}{16}$ **simplified**   **43.** $\dfrac{30}{51}$ **$\dfrac{10}{17}$**

44. $\dfrac{st}{t^4}$ **$\dfrac{s}{t^3}$**   **45.** $\dfrac{23x}{32y}$ **simplified**   **46.** $\dfrac{9mn}{18n^2}$ **$\dfrac{m}{2n}$**   **47.** $\dfrac{15ac^2}{24ab}$ **$\dfrac{5c^2}{8b}$**

Study Guide and Review

Chapter
4 For More ...   • Extra Practice, see pages 730–733.
• Mixed Problem Solving, see page 761.

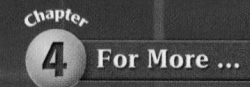

Additional Answers (p. 195)

1. A number is divisible by: 2 if the ones digit is even; 3 if the sum of its digits is divisible by 3; 5 if the ones digit is 0 or 5; 6 if the number is divisible by 2 and 3; 10 if the ones digit is 0.

2. A prime number has only two factors, 1 and the number itself. A composite number has more than two factors.

4-6 Multiplying and Dividing Monomials

See pages 175–179.

Concept Summary

• Powers with the same base can be multiplied by adding their exponents.
• Powers with the same base can be divided by subtracting their exponents.

Examples 1 Find $x^3 \cdot x^2$.

$$x^3 \cdot x^2 = x^{3+2} \quad \text{The common base is } x.$$
$$= x^5 \quad \text{Add the exponents.}$$

2 Find $\frac{4^5}{4^3}$.

$$\frac{4^5}{4^3} = 4^{5-3} \quad \text{The common base is 4.}$$
$$= 4^2 \quad \text{Subtract the exponents.}$$

Exercises Find each product or quotient. Express using exponents.
See Examples 1–3 on pages 176 and 177.

48. $8^4 \cdot 8^5$ 8^9 49. $c \cdot c^3$ c^4 50. $\frac{3^7}{3^2}$ 3^5 51. $\frac{r^{11}}{r^9}$ r^2 52. $7x \cdot 2x^6$ $14x^7$

4-7 Negative Exponents

See pages 181–185.

Concept Summary

• For $a \neq 0$ and any integer n, $a^{-n} = \frac{1}{a^n}$.

Example Write 3^{-4} as an expression using a positive exponent.

$$3^{-4} = \frac{1}{3^4} \quad \text{Definition of negative exponent}$$

Exercises Write each expression using a positive exponent.
See Example 1 on page 182. 54. $\frac{1}{10^1}$ or $\frac{1}{10}$

53. 7^{-2} $\frac{1}{7^2}$ 54. 10^{-1} 55. b^{-4} $\frac{1}{b^4}$ 56. t^{-8} $\frac{1}{t^8}$ 57. $(-4)^{-3}$ $\frac{1}{(-4)^3}$

4-8 Scientific Notation

See pages 186–190.

Concept Summary

• A number in scientific notation contains a factor and a power of 10.

Examples 1 Express 3.5×10^{-2} in standard form.

$$3.5 \times 10^{-2} = 3.5 \times 0.01 \quad 10^{-2} = 0.01$$
$$= 0.035 \quad \text{Move the decimal point 2 places to the left.}$$

2 Express 269,000 in scientific notation.

$$269{,}000 = 2.69 \times 100{,}000 \quad \text{The decimal point moves 5 places.}$$
$$= 2.69 \times 10^5 \quad \text{The exponent is positive.}$$

Exercises Express each number in standard form.   *See Example 1 on page 186.*

58. 6.1×10^2 610   59. 2.9×10^{-3} 0.0029   60. 1.85×10^{-2} 0.0185   61. 7.045×10^4 70,450

Express each number in scientific notation.   *See Example 2 on page 187.*

62. 1200   63. 0.008   64. 0.000319   65. 45,710,000
    1.2×10^3 8.0×10^{-3} 3.19×10^{-4} 4.571×10^7

Vocabulary and Concepts

1. **Explain** how to use the divisibility rules to determine whether a number is divisible by 2, 3, 5, 6, or 10. **1–2. See margin.**
2. **Explain** the difference between a prime number and a composite number.
3. **OPEN ENDED** Write an algebraic fraction that is in simplest form.
   Sample answer: $\frac{x}{2}$

Skills and Applications

Determine whether each expression is a monomial. Explain why or why not.

4. $6xyz$ **yes; product of a number and variables**   5. $-2m + 9$ **no; sum of two terms**

Write each expression using exponents.

6. $3 \cdot 3 \cdot 3 \cdot 3$ **3^4**

7. $-2 \cdot -2 \cdot -2 \cdot a \cdot a \cdot a \cdot a$
   $(-2)^3 a^4$

Factor each expression.

8. $12r^2$ **$2 \cdot 2 \cdot 3 \cdot r \cdot r$**   9. $50xy^2$ **$2 \cdot 5 \cdot 5 \cdot x \cdot y \cdot y$**   10. $7 + 21p$ **$7(1 + 3p)$**

Find the GCF of each set of numbers or monomials.

11. $70, 28$ **14**   12. $36, 90, 180$ **18**   13. $12a^3b, 40ab^4$ **$4ab$**

Write each fraction in simplest form. If the fraction is already in simplest form, write *simplified*.

14. $\frac{57}{95}$ **$\frac{3}{5}$**   15. $\frac{240}{360}$ **$\frac{2}{3}$**   16. $\frac{56m^3n}{32mn}$ **$\frac{7m^2}{4}$**

Find each product or quotient. Express using exponents.

17. $5^3 \cdot 5^6$ **5^9**   18. $(4x^7)(-6x^3)$ **$-24x^{10}$**   19. $w^9 \div w^5$ **w^4**

Write each expression using a positive exponent.

20. 4^{-2} **$\frac{1}{4^2}$**   21. t^{-6} **$\frac{1}{t^6}$**   22. $(yz)^{-3}$ **$\frac{1}{(yz)^3}$**

Write each number in standard form.

23. 9.0×10^{-2} **0.09**   24. 5.206×10^{-3} **0.005206**   25. 3.71×10^4 **37,100**

Write each number in scientific notation.

26. $345,000$ **3.45×10^5**   27. $1,680,000$ **1.68×10^6**   28. 0.00072 **7.2×10^{-4}**

29. **BAKING** A recipe for butter cookies requires 12 tablespoons of sugar for every 16 tablespoons of flour. Write this as a fraction in simplest form. **$\frac{3}{4}$**

30. **STANDARDIZED TEST PRACTICE** Earth is approximately 93 million miles away from the Sun. Express this distance in scientific notation. **A**
    Ⓐ 9.3×10^7 mi   Ⓑ 9.3×10^6 mi
    Ⓒ 93×10^6 mi   Ⓓ $93,000,000$ mi

 www.pre-alg.com/chapter_test

Assessment Options

Vocabulary Test A vocabulary review/test for Chapter 4 can be found on p. 218 of the *Chapter 4 Resource Masters.*

Chapter Tests There are six Chapter 4 Tests and an Open-Ended Assessment task available in the *Chapter 4 Resource Masters.*

Chapter 4 Tests			
Form	**Type**	**Level**	**Pages**
1	MC	basic	205–206
2A	MC	average	207–208
2B	MC	average	209–210
2C	FR	average	211–212
2D	FR	average	213–214
3	FR	advanced	215–216

MC = multiple-choice questions
FR = free-response questions

Open-Ended Assessment
Performance tasks for Chapter 4 can be found on p. 217 of the *Chapter 4 Resource Masters.* A sample scoring rubric for these tasks appears on p. A27.

 ExamView® Pro

Use the networkable **ExamView® Pro** to:
- Create **multiple versions** of tests.
- Create **modified** tests for *Inclusion* students.
- **Edit** existing questions and **add** your own questions.
- Use built-in **state curriculum correlations** to create tests aligned with state standards.
- Change **English** tests to **Spanish** and vice versa.

Portfolio Suggestion

Introduction In mathematics, many quantities are expressed as fractions. Some fractions may be very large or very small. Other fractions may be algebraic.

Ask Students to locate one numerical and one algebraic fraction in Chapter 4. Write a portfolio entry that explains how factors and related concepts such as divisibility are used to write the fractions in simplest form.

These two pages contain practice questions in the various formats that can be found on the most frequently given standardized tests.

A practice answer sheet for these two pages can be found on page A1 of the *Chapter 4 Resource Masters*.

Standardized Test Practice
Student Recording Sheet, p. A1

Part 1 *Multiple Choice*

Select the best answer from the choices given and fill in the corresponding oval.

1 Ⓐ Ⓑ Ⓒ Ⓓ   4 Ⓐ Ⓑ Ⓒ Ⓓ   7 Ⓐ Ⓑ Ⓒ Ⓓ   10 Ⓐ Ⓑ Ⓒ Ⓓ
2 Ⓐ Ⓑ Ⓒ Ⓓ   5 Ⓐ Ⓑ Ⓒ Ⓓ   8 Ⓐ Ⓑ Ⓒ Ⓓ   11 Ⓐ Ⓑ Ⓒ Ⓓ
3 Ⓐ Ⓑ Ⓒ Ⓓ   6 Ⓐ Ⓑ Ⓒ Ⓓ   9 Ⓐ Ⓑ Ⓒ Ⓓ

Part 2 *Short Response/Grid In*

Solve the problem and write your answer in the blank.

For Questions 15, 17, and 19, also enter your answer by writing each number or symbol in a box. Then fill in the corresponding oval for that number or symbol.

12 _____   15   17   19
13 _____
14 _____
15 _____ (grid in)
16 _____
17 _____ (grid in)
18 _____
19 _____ (grid in)
20 _____
21 _____

Part 3 *Extended Response*

Record your answers for Question 22 on the back of this paper.

Additional Practice

See pp. 223–224 of the *Chapter 4 Resource Masters* for additional standardized test practice.

Part 1 Multiple Choice

Record your answers on the answer sheet provided by your teacher or on a sheet of paper.

1. Andy has 7 fewer computer games than Ling. Carlos has twice as many computer games as Andy. If Ling has x computer games, which of these represents the number of computer games that Carlos has? (Lesson 1-3) **D**

   Ⓐ $7 - 2x$ Ⓑ $x - 7$

   Ⓒ $2x - 7$ Ⓓ $2(x - 7)$

2. Which of the following statements is *false*, when r, s, and t are different integers? (Lesson 1-4) **D**

   Ⓐ $(rs)t = r(st)$ Ⓑ $r + s = s + r$

   Ⓒ $rs = sr$ Ⓓ $r - s = s - r$

3. The low temperatures during the past five days are given in the table. Find the average (mean) of the temperatures. (Lesson 2-5) **B**

Day	1	2	3	4	5
Temperature (°F)	−2	0	4	5	4

   Ⓐ 3°F   Ⓑ 2.2°F   Ⓒ 13°F   Ⓓ 2.75°F

4. Which coordinates are most likely to be the coordinates of point P? (Lesson 2-6) **A**

   Ⓐ $(-13, 7)$

   Ⓑ $(7, -13)$

   Ⓒ $(13, 7)$

   Ⓓ $(7, 13)$

Test-Taking Tip Ⓐ Ⓑ Ⓒ Ⓓ

Question 2
When a multiple-choice question asks you to verify statements that include variables, you can substitute numbers into the variables to determine which statements are true and which are false.

5. Solve $3n - 6 = -39$ for n. (Lesson 3-5) **B**

   Ⓐ -15 Ⓑ -11
   Ⓒ 11 Ⓓ 15

6. For every order purchased from an Internet bookstore, the shipping and handling charges include a base fee of $5 plus a fee of $3 per item purchased in the order. Which equation represents the shipping and handling charge for ordering n items? (Lesson 3-6) **D**

   Ⓐ $S = 5(3n)$ Ⓑ $S = 3n - 5$

   Ⓒ $S = 5 + \dfrac{3}{n}$ Ⓓ $S = 5 + 3n$

7. The area of the rectangle below is 18 square units. Use the formula $A = \ell w$ to find its width. (Lesson 3-7) **C**

   Ⓐ $\dfrac{1}{3}$ unit

   Ⓑ 2 units

   Ⓒ 3 units

   Ⓓ 12 units   6 units

8. Write the prime factorization of 84. (Lesson 4-3) **D**

   Ⓐ $2 \cdot 3 \cdot 7$

   Ⓑ $4 \cdot 21$

   Ⓒ $3 \cdot 4 \cdot 7$

   Ⓓ $2 \cdot 2 \cdot 3 \cdot 7$

9. What is the greatest common factor of 28 and 42? (Lesson 4-4) **C**

   Ⓐ 2   Ⓑ 7

   Ⓒ 14   Ⓓ 28

10. Write 3^{-3} as a fraction. (Lesson 4-7) **C**

   Ⓐ $-\dfrac{1}{9}$ Ⓑ $-\dfrac{1}{27}$

   Ⓒ $\dfrac{1}{27}$ Ⓓ $\dfrac{1}{9}$

11. Asia is the largest continent. It has an area of 17,400,000 square miles. What is 17,400,000 expressed in scientific notation? (Lesson 4-8) **B**

   Ⓐ 174×10^5 Ⓑ 1.74×10^7

   Ⓒ 174×10^7 Ⓓ 1.74×10^8

ExamView® Pro

Special banks of standardized test questions similar to those on the SAT, ACT, TIMSS 8, NAEP 8, and Pre-Algebra End-of-Course tests can be found on this CD-ROM.

Part 2 | Short Response/Grid In

Record your answers on the answer sheet provided by your teacher or on a sheet of paper.

12. A health club charges an initial fee of $60 for the first month, and then a $28 membership fee each month after the first month, as shown in the table. What is the total membership cost for 9 months? (Lesson 1-1) **$284**

Number of Months	Total Cost ($)
1	60
2	88
3	116
4	144
5	172

13. The temperature in Concord at 5 P.M. was -3 degrees. By midnight, the temperature had dropped 9 degrees. What was the temperature at midnight? (Lesson 2-3) **-12 or -12 degrees**

14. A skating rink charges $2.00 to rent a pair of skates and $1.50 per hour of skating. Jeff wants to spend no more than $8.00 and he needs to rent skates. How many hours can he skate? (Lesson 3-5) **4 h**

15. At a birthday party, Maka gave 30 gel pens to her friends as prizes. Everyone got at least 1 gel pen. Six friends got just 1 gel pen each, 4 friends got 3 gel pens each for winning games, and the rest of the friends got 2 gel pens each. How many friends got 2 gel pens? (Lesson 3-6) **6**

16. A table 8 feet long and 2 feet wide is to be covered for the school bake sale. If organizers want the covering to hang down 1 foot on each side, what is the area of the covering that they need? (Lesson 3-7) **40 square feet**

17. What is the least 3-digit number that is divisible by 3 and 5? (Lesson 4-1) **105**

18. Write $10 \cdot 10 \cdot 10 \cdot 10$ using an exponent. (Lesson 4-2) **10^4**

19. Find the greatest common factor of 18, 44, and 12. (Lesson 4-4) **2**

www.pre-alg.com/standardized_test

20. Write $\frac{1}{5 \cdot 5 \cdot 5}$ using a negative exponent. (Lesson 4-7) **5^{-3}**

21. The Milky Way galaxy is made up of about 200 billion stars, including the Sun. Write this number in scientific notation. (Lesson 4-8) **2.0×10^{11}**

Part 3 | Extended Response

Record your answers on a sheet of paper. Show your work.

22. Chandra plans to order CDs from an Internet shopping site. She finds that the CD prices are the same at three different sites, but that the shipping costs vary. The shipping costs include a fee per order, plus an additional fee for each item in the order, as shown in the table below. (Lesson 3-6) **a–c. See margin.**

| Company | Shipping Cost | |
	Per Order	Per Item
CDBargains	$4.00	$1.00
WebShopper	$6.00	$3.00
EverythingStore	$2.50	$1.50

a. For each company, write an equation that represents the shipping cost. In each of your three equations, use S to represent the shipping cost and n to represent the number of items purchased.

b. If Chandra orders 2 CDs, which company will charge the least for shipping? Use the equations you wrote and show your work.

c. If Chandra orders 10 CDs, which company will charge the least for shipping? Use the equations you wrote and show your work.

d. For what number of CDs do both CDBargains and EverythingStore charge the same amount for shipping and handling costs? **3 CDs**

Evaluating Extended Response Questions

Extended Response questions are graded by using a multilevel rubric that guides you in assessing a student's knowledge of a particular concept.

Goal: Use mathematical equations to solve a realistic word problem.

Sample Scoring Rubric: The following rubric is a sample scoring device. You may wish to add more detail to this sample to meet your individual scoring needs.

Score	Criteria
4	A correct solution that is supported by well-developed, accurate explanations
3	A generally correct solution, but may contain minor flaws in reasoning or computation
2	A partially correct interpretation and/or solution to the problem
1	A correct solution with no supporting evidence or explanation
0	An incorrect solution indicating no mathematical understanding of the concept or task, or no solution is given

Answer

22a. CDBargains $S = 4 + n$

WebShopper $S = 6 + 3n$

EverythingStore $S = 2.5 + 1.5n$

22b. Let $n = 2$.

CD Bargains $S = 4 + 2$ or $6

WebShopper $S = 6 + 3(2)$ or $12

EverythingStore $S = 2.5 + 1.5(2)$ or $5.50; EverythingStore has the least shipping cost.

22c. Let $n = 10$.

CD Bargains $S = 4 + 10$ or $14

WebShopper $S = 6 + 3(10)$ or $36

EverythingStore $S = 2.5 + 1.5(10)$ or $17.50; CD Bargains has the least shipping cost.

Page 151, Lesson 4-1

36. a variable
37. a number
38. two terms are added
39. one term is subtracted from another term
40. two terms are added
41. two terms are added
42. two terms are added
43. one term is subtracted from another term
44. the product of a number and a variable
45. the product of a number and a variable
46. the product of a number and variables
47. the product of numbers and variables
48. No; 72 is not divisible by 7.
49. 6 ways; 1×72, 2×36, 3×24, 4×18, 6×12, 8×9
50. 1912, a 6-by-8 arrangement; 1959, a 7-by-7 arrangement
51. Alternating rows of a flag contain 6 stars and 5 stars, respectively. 50 is not divisible by a number that would make the arrangement of stars in an appropriate-sized rectangle.

Chapter 5 Rational Numbers
Chapter Overview and Pacing

*An electronic version of this chapter is available on **StudentWorks**™. This backpack solution CD-ROM allows students instant access to the Student Edition, lesson worksheet pages, and web resources.*

Year-long pacing: pages T20–T21.

LESSON OBJECTIVES	PACING (days)			
	Regular		Block	
	Basic/ Average	Advanced	Basic/ Average	Advanced
5-1 Writing Fractions as Decimals (pp. 200–204) • Write fractions as terminating or repeating decimals. • Compare fractions and decimals.	1	1	0.5	0.5
5-2 Rational Numbers (pp. 205–209) • Write rational numbers as fractiions. • Identify and classify rational numbers.	1	1	0.5	0.5
5-3 Multiplying Rational Numbers (pp. 210–214) • Multiply fractions. • Use dimensional analysis to solve problems.	1	1	0.5	0.5
5-4 Dividing Rational Numbers (pp. 215–219) • Divide fractions using multiplicative inverses. • Use dimensional analysis to solve problems.	1	1	0.5	0.5
5-5 Adding and Subtracting Like Fractions (pp. 220–224) • Add like fractions. • Subtract like fractions.	1	1	0.5	0.5
5-6 Least Common Multiple (pp. 226–231) • Find the least common multiple of two or more numbers. • Find the least common denominator of two or more fractions. *Follow-Up:* Participate in a strategic game utilizing factors and multiples.	2 (with 5-6 Follow-Up)	2 (with 5-6 Follow-Up)	1	1.5 (with 5-6 Follow-Up)
5-7 Adding and Subtracting Unlike Fractions (pp. 232–236) • Add unlike fractions. • Subtract unlike fractions.	1	1	0.5	0.5
5-8 Measures of Central Tendency (pp. 237–243) *Preview:* Determine a number that best represents or describes a set of data. • Use the mean, median, and mode as measures of central tendency. • Analyze data using mean, median, and mode. *Follow-Up:* Describe how a graphing calculator can be used to store data in a list.	2 (with 5-8 Preview)	2 (with 5-8 Follow-Up)	1	1.5 (with 5-8 Follow-Up)
5-9 Solving Equations with Rational Numbers (pp. 244–248) • Solve equations containing rational numbers.	1	1	0.5	0.5
5-10 Arithmetic and Geometric Sequences (pp. 249–253) • Find the terms of arithmetic sequences. • Find the terms of geometric sequences. *Follow-Up:* Become familiar with the Fibonacci Sequence.	1	2 (with 5-10 Follow-Up)	0.5	0.5
Study Guide and **Practice Test** (pp. 254–259) **Standardized Test Practice** (pp. 260–261)	1	1	0.5	0.5
Chapter Assessment	1	1	0.5	0.5
TOTAL	**14**	**15**	**7**	**8**

Chapter Resource Manager

Timesaving Tools
TeacherWorks™
All-In-One Planner and Resource Center
See pages T5 and T21.

CHAPTER 5 RESOURCE MASTERS

Study Guide and Intervention	Practice (Skills and Average)	Reading to Learn Mathematics	Enrichment	Assessment	Prerequisite Skills Workbook	Applications*	Parent and Student Study Guide Workbook	5-Minute Check Transparencies	Interactive Chalkboard	Pre-AlgePASS: Tutorial Plus (lessons)	Materials
225	226–227	228	229		15–18	GCS 28	33	5-1	5-1		
230	231–232	233	234			SC 9	34	5-2	5-2		
235	236–237	238	239	289		SM 3	35	5-3	5-3		
240	241–242	243	244			SC 10	36	5-4	5-4		
245	246–247	248	249	289, 291	37–44		37	5-5	5-5		
250	251–252	253	254				38	5-6	5-6		*Follow-Up:* hundreds chart, colored markers
255	256–257	258	259		37–44	GCS 27	39	5-7	5-7		
260	261–262	263	264	290	19–22, 29–30		40	5-8	5-8	9	*Preview:* weather data, graph or data table/newspaper, small box of raisins *Follow-Up:* graphing calculator
265	266–267	268	269		21–24, 27–28, 31–32, 47–62		41	5-9	5-9		
270	271–272	273	274	290	1–2, 45–48		42	5-10	5-10	10, 11	*Follow-Up:* artichoke, pinecone, pineapple, or sunflower, markers
				275–288 292–298							

Key to Abbreviations: GCS = Graphing Calculator and Spreadsheet Masters
SC = School-to-Career Masters
SM = Science and Mathematics Lab Manual

ELL Study Guide and Intervention, Skills Practice, Practice, and Parent and Student Study Guide Workbooks are also available in Spanish.

Mathematical Connections and Background

Continuity of Instruction

Prior Knowledge

In the previous chapter, students examined factors and monomials and learned to evaluate expressions containing powers and exponents. They learned to simplify expressions and algebraic fractions using greatest common factor. They also multiplied and divided monomials and expressed numbers using positive and negative integers and exponents.

This Chapter

Students will explore rational numbers, learning to multiply and divide fractions and add and subtract like and unlike fractions. They will also learn to convert fractions to decimals, factor numbers, and determine least common multiple (LCM). They will examine measures of central tendency. Students will learn to solve equations and identify sequences.

Future Connections

The study of rational numbers is essential for real-world problem solving and lays the groundwork for future classwork in algebra, business mathematics, and number theory. Measures of central tendency are important in statistical analysis and research sciences. Arithmetic and geometric sequences are used to develop formulas in higher mathematics.

5-1 Writing Fractions as Decimals

Any fraction $\frac{a}{b}$, where $b \neq 0$, can be written as a decimal by dividing the numerator by the denominator. So, $\frac{a}{b} = a \div b$. If the division ends, or terminates, when the remainder is zero, the decimal is a terminating decimal. Not all fractions can be written as terminating decimals. Some have a repeating decimal. A bar indicates that the decimal repeats forever. For example, the fraction $\frac{4}{9}$ can be converted to a repeating decimal, $0.\overline{4}$.

5-2 Rational Numbers

A number that can be written as a fraction is called a rational number. Terminating and repeating decimals are rational numbers because both can be written as fractions. Decimals that are neither terminating nor repeating are called irrational numbers because they cannot be written as fractions. Terminating decimals can be converted to fractions by placing the number (without the decimal point) in the numerator. Count the number of places to the right of the decimal point and in the denominator, place a 1 followed by a number of zeros equal to the number of places that you counted. The fraction can then be reduced to simplest form.

5-3 Multiplying Rational Numbers

To multiply fractions (rational numbers), multiply the numerators and multiply the denominators. If the fractions have common factors in the numerators and denominators, they can be simplified before multiplication. If one of the fractions is negative, then the product will be negative. Mixed numbers can be multiplied in the same manner, after first being renamed as improper fractions. A fraction that contains one or more variables in the numerator or the denominator is called an algebraic fraction. Algebraic fractions may be multiplied using the same method described above.

5-4 Dividing Rational Numbers

Rational numbers have all of the properties of whole numbers and integers. Another property is shown by $\frac{7}{4} \cdot \frac{4}{7} = 1$. Two numbers whose product is 1 are called multiplicative inverses or reciprocals. To divide by a fraction (rational number), multiply by its multiplicative inverse. When dividing by a mixed number, first rename the number as an improper fraction, and then multiply by its multiplicative inverse. This process of multiplying by a number's reciprocal can also be used when dividing algebraic fractions and in dimensional analysis.

5-5 Adding and Subtracting Like Fractions

Fractions with the same denominator are called like fractions. To add like fractions, add the numerators and write the sum over the denominator. To add mixed numbers with like fractions, add the whole numbers and fractions separately, adding the numerators of the fractions, then simplifying if necessary. The rule for subtracting fractions with like denominators is similar to the rule for addition. The numerators can be subtracted and the difference written over the denominator. Mixed numbers are written as improper fractions before subtracting. These same rules apply to adding or subtracting like algebraic fractions.

5-6 Least Common Multiple

A multiple of a number is a product of that number and a whole number. Sometimes different numbers have some of the same multiples. These are called common multiples. The smallest of the nonzero common multiples is called the least common multiple (LCM). When numbers are large, an easy way of finding the least common multiple is to use prime factorization. The LCM is the smallest product that contains the prime factors of each number.

5-7 Adding and Subtracting Unlike Fractions

Fractions with different denominators are called unlike fractions. The LCM of the denominators is used to rename the fractions with a common denominator. After a common denominator is found, the numerators can then be added or subtracted. To add mixed numbers with unlike fractions, rename the mixed numbers as improper fractions. Then find a common denominator, add the numerators, and simplify the answer.

5-8 Measures of Central Tendency

It is often helpful to use one or more numbers to represent a whole set of data. These numbers are measures of central tendency. The mean is the sum of the data divided by the number of items in the data set. The median is the middle number of the ordered data (or the mean of the two middle numbers). The mode is the number or numbers that occur most often. These measures allow data to be analyzed.

5-9 Solving Equations with Rational Numbers

Rational number equations can be solved using the same method used to solve integer equations, by applying opposite operations to each side of the equation. Addition, subtraction, multiplication, and division (reciprocal) can be used. For example, to solve $4.9 = b + 8.5$, subtract 8.5 from each side to get $b = -3.6$. The skill of solving equations with rational numbers may be applied to many real-world problems.

5-10 Arithmetic and Geometric Sequences

A sequence is an ordered list of numbers. An arithmetic sequence is a sequence in which the difference between any two consecutive terms is the same. A geometric sequence is a sequence in which the quotient of any two consecutive terms is the same. The next term in a geometric sequence can be found by multiplying the previous term by the same number. So, the sequence $7, 3, -1, -5$ is arithmetic because the difference between the terms is the same number, -4. The sequence $2, -4, 8, -16$ is geometric because the quotient of any two consecutive numbers is the same, -2.

Quick Review Math Handbook

Hot Words includes a glossary of terms while Hot Topics consists of explanations of key mathematical concepts with exercises to test comprehension. This valuable resource can be used as a reference in the classroom or for home study.

Lesson	Hot Topics Section	Lesson	Hot Topics Section
5-1	2.1, 2.9	5-5, 5-6	1.4, 2.3
5-2	2.1, 2.2, 2.4	5-7	1.5, 2.3
5-3	1.4, 2.4	5-8	2.6, 4.4
5-4	2.1, 2.4	5-9	1.5, 6.4

 Additional mathematical information and teaching notes are available at www.pre-alg.com/key_concepts.

Chapter 5

DAILY INTERVENTION and Assessment

Key to Abbreviations:
TWE = Teacher Wraparound Edition; CRM = Chapter Resource Masters

	Type	Student Edition	Teacher Resources	Technology/Internet
INTERVENTION	Ongoing	Prerequisite Skills, pp. 199, 204, 209, 214, 219, 224, 230, 236, 242, 248 Practice Quiz 1, p. 224 Practice Quiz 2, p. 248	5-Minute Check Transparencies *Prerequisite Skills Workbook*, pp. 1–2, 15–24, 27–32, 37–62 Quizzes, *CRM*, pp. 289, 290 Mid-Chapter Test, *CRM*, p. 291 Study Guide and Intervention, *CRM*, pp. 225, 230, 235, 240, 245, 250, 255, 260, 265, 270	Pre-AlgePASS: Tutorial Plus, Lessons 9,10, and 11 www.pre-alg.com/self_check_quiz www.pre-alg.com/extra_examples
	Mixed Review	pp. 204, 209, 214, 219, 224, 230, 236, 242, 248, 252	Cumulative Review, *CRM*, p. 292	
	Error Analysis	Find the Error, pp. 212, 222, 234, 246	Find the Error, *TWE*, pp. 212, 222, 234, 246 Unlocking Misconceptions, *TWE*, p. 211	
ASSESSMENT	Standardized Test Practice	pp. 204, 209, 214, 219, 224, 230, 236, 240, 241, 242, 247, 252, 260–261	*TWE*, pp. 260–261 Standardized Test Practice, *CRM*, pp. 293–294	Standardized Test Practice CD-ROM www.pre-alg.com/standardized_test
	Open-Ended Assessment	Writing in Math, pp. 204, 209, 214, 219, 223, 230, 236, 242, 247, 251 Open Ended, pp. 202, 207, 212, 217, 222, 228, 234, 241, 246, 251 Standardized Test, p. 261	Speaking: *TWE*, pp. 209, 224, 248 Writing: *TWE*, pp. 204, 219, 230, 242 Modeling: *TWE*, pp. 214, 236, 252 Open-Ended Assessment, *CRM*, p. 287	
	Chapter Assessment	Study Guide, pp. 254–258 Practice Test, p. 259	Multiple-Choice Tests (Forms 1, 2A, 2B), *CRM*, pp. 275–280 Free-Response Tests (Forms 2C, 2D, 3), *CRM*, pp. 281–286 Vocabulary Test/Review, *CRM*, p. 288	ExamView® Pro (see below) MindJogger Videoquizzes www.pre-alg.com/vocabulary_review www.pre-alg.com/chapter_test

For more information on Yearly ProgressPro, see p. 144.

Pre-Algebra Lesson	Yearly ProgressPro Skill Lesson
5-1	Compare/Order Positive and Negative Rational Numbers
5-2	Fraction/Decimal/Percent Conversions: Level 2
5-3	Multiply Fractions
5-4	Divide Fractions
5-5	Add/Subtract Fractions with Like Denominatiors: Level 3
5-6	Least Common Multiple: Level 2
5-7	Add/Subtract Fractions with Unlike Denominators: Level 3
5-8	Mean; Median; Mode: Level 2
5-9	Solve One-Step Equations with Rational Numbers
5-10	Sequences

ExamView® Pro

Use the networkable **ExamView® Pro** to:
- Create **multiple versions** of tests.
- Create **modified** tests for *Inclusion* students.
- **Edit** existing questions and **add** your own questions.
- Use built-in **state curriculum correlations** to create tests aligned with state standards.
- Change **English** tests to **Spanish** and vice versa.

For more information on Intervention and Assessment, see pp. T8–T11.

Reading and Writing in Mathematics

Glencoe Pre-Algebra provides numerous opportunities to incorporate reading and writing into the mathematics classroom.

Student Edition

- Foldables™ Study Organizer, p. 199
- Reading Mathematics, p. 225
- Concept Check questions require students to verbalize and write about what they have learned in the lesson. (pp. 201, 202, 205, 207, 212, 216, 217, 221, 222, 227, 228, 232, 239, 241, 245, 246, 250, 251)
- Writing in Math questions in every lesson, pp. 204, 209, 214, 219, 223, 230, 236, 242, 247, 251
- Reading Math, pp. 200, 205
- WebQuest, p. 242

Teacher Wraparound Edition

- Foldables™ Study Organizer, pp. 199, 254
- Study Notebook suggestions, pp. 202, 207, 212, 217, 222, 225, 228, 231, 234, 237, 240, 246, 251, 253
- Modeling activities, pp. 214, 236, 252
- Speaking activities, pp. 209, 224, 248
- Writing activities, pp. 204, 219, 230, 242
- Differentiated Instruction (Verbal/Linguistic), p. 228
- **ELL** Resources, pp. 198, 200, 205, 210, 215, 220, 225, 226, 232, 238, 244, 249, 254

Additional Resources

- Vocabulary Builder worksheets require students to define and give examples for key vocabulary terms as they progress through the chapter (*Chapter 5 Resource Masters*, pp. vii–viii)
- Reading to Learn Mathematics master for each lesson (*Chapter 5 Resource Masters*, pp. 228, 233, 238, 243, 248, 253, 258, 263, 268, 273)
- *Vocabulary PuzzleMaker* software creates crossword, jumble, and word search puzzles using vocabulary lists that you can customize.
- *Teaching Mathematics with Foldables* provides suggestions for promoting cognition and language.
- *Reading and Writing in the Mathematics Classroom*
- *WebQuest and Project Resources*

For more information on Reading and Writing in Mathematics, see pp. T6–T7.

 **ENGLISH LANGUAGE LEARNERS**

Lesson 5-1
Using Manipulatives

Give each group of students a bag with fraction cards inside. Have one student draw a card and find a decimal equivalent for the fraction using a calculator. Make sure students know how to input the numbers into the calculator. Have students write down the answer from the calculator and ask them what they notice. Have the students categorize the quotients as terminating or repeating decimals.

Lesson 5-4
Reading and Writing

Write the term *reciprocal* on the chalkboard and give students examples of how to find the reciprocal of a number. Be sure to include finding reciprocals of whole numbers as well as fractions.

Lesson 5-9
Building on Prior Knowledge

Students who know how to solve equations involving intergers oftern have trouble solving equations with rational numbers because of the more complex computations. In order to help them with this transition, have students solve an equation with whole numbers, than with integers, and then integrate the rational numbers. When students need to perform an operation with the rational numbers, take the operation out of the problem or equation, perform it and then let the variable equal the answer.

What You'll Learn

Have students read over the list of objectives and make a list of any words with which they are not familiar.

Why It's Important

Point out to students that this is only one of many reasons why each objective is important. Others are provided in the introduction to each lesson.

Lesson	NCTM Standards	Local Objectives
5-1	1, 6	
5-2	1, 6, 7	
5-3	1–6, 10	
5-4	1–6	
5-5	1, 2, 6, 7	
5-6	1, 2, 6, 7	
5-6 Follow-Up	1, 2, 7	
5-7	1, 6, 10	
5-8 Preview	2, 5	
5-8	1, 4, 5, 6	
5-8 Follow-Up	5, 6	
5-9	1, 2, 6	
5-10	2, 3, 6–9	
5-10 Follow-Up	2, 3, 6–9	

Key to NCTM Standards:

1=Number & Operations, 2=Algebra,
3=Geometry, 4=Measurement,
5=Data Analysis & Probability, 6=Problem
Solving, 7=Reasoning & Proof,
8=Communication, 9=Connections,
10=Representation

What You'll Learn

- **Lessons 5-1 and 5-2** Write fractions as decimals and write decimals as fractions.
- **Lessons 5-3, 5-4, 5-5, and 5-7** Add, subtract, multiply, and divide rational numbers.
- **Lessons 5-6 and 5-9** Use the least common denominator to compare fractions and to solve equations.
- **Lesson 5-8** Use the mean, median, and mode to analyze data.
- **Lesson 5-10** Find the terms of arithmetic and geometric sequences.

Key Vocabulary

- rational number (p. 205)
- algebraic fraction (p. 211)
- multiplicative inverse (p. 215)
- measures of central tendency (p. 238)
- sequence (p. 249)

Why It's Important

Rational numbers are the numbers used most often in the real world. They include fractions, decimals, and integers. Understanding rational numbers is important in understanding and analyzing real-world occurrences, such as changes in barometric pressure during a storm. *You will compare the barometric pressure before and after a storm in Lesson 5-9.*

Vocabulary Builder
ELL

The Key Vocabulary list introduces students to some of the main vocabulary terms included in this chapter. For a more thorough vocabulary list with pronunciations of new words, give students the Vocabulary Builder worksheets found on pages vii and viii of the *Chapter 5 Resource Masters*. Encourage them to complete the definition of each term as they progress through the chapter. You may suggest that they add these sheets to their study notebooks for future reference when studying for the Chapter 5 test.

Getting Started

Getting Started

▶ **Prerequisite Skills** To be successful in this chapter, you'll need to master these skills and be able to apply them in problem-solving situations. Review these skills before beginning Chapter 5.

For Lessons 5-1 through 5-4   **Multiply and Divide Integers**

Find each product or quotient. If necessary, round to the nearest tenth.

(For review, see Lessons 2-4 and 2-5.)

1. $3 \div 5$ **0.6**   **2.** $-1 \div 8$ **-0.1**   **3.** $2 \cdot 17$ **34**

4. $-12 \cdot 3$ **-36**   **5.** $-2 \div (-9)$ **0.2**   **6.** $-4(-6)$ **24**

7. $5(-15)$ **-75**   **8.** $4 \div (-15)$ **-0.3**   **9.** $-24 \div 14$ **-1.7**

For Lesson 5-5   **Simplify Fractions Using the GCF**

Write each fraction in simplest form. If the fraction is already in simplest form, write *simplified*. *(For review, see Lesson 4-5.)*

10. $\frac{5}{40}$ $\frac{1}{8}$ **11.** $\frac{12}{20}$ $\frac{3}{5}$ **12.** $\frac{14}{39}$ simplified   **13.** $\frac{36}{50}$ $\frac{18}{25}$

For Lessons 5-8 through 5-10   **Add and Subtract Integers**

Find each sum or difference. *(For review, see Lessons 2-2 and 2-3.)*

14. $4 + (-9)$ **-5**   **15.** $-10 + 16$ **6**   **16.** $20 - 12$ **8**   **17.** $19 - 32$ **-13**

18. $7 + (-5)$ **2**   **19.** $26 - 11$ **15**   **20.** $(-3) + (-8)$ **-11**   **21.** $-1 - (-10)$ **9**

Study Organizer

Rational Numbers Make this Foldable to help you organize your notes. Begin with three sheets of $8\frac{1}{2}$" by 11" paper.

Step 1 **Fold and Cut Two Sheets**

Fold each sheet in half from top to bottom. Cut along the fold from the edges to the margin.

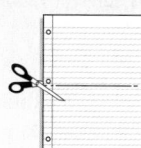

Step 2 **Fold and Cut the Other Sheet**

Fold in half from top to bottom. Cut along fold between the margins.

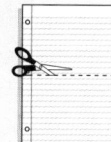

Step 3 **Fold**

Insert the first two sheets through the third sheet and align the folds.

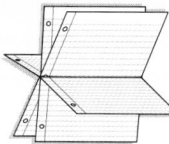

Step 4 **Label**

Label each page with a lesson number and title. Write the chapter title on the front.

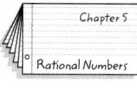
Chapter 5
Rational Numbers

Reading and Writing As you read and study the chapter, fill the journal with notes, diagrams, and examples for rational numbers.

This section provides a review of the basic concepts needed before beginning Chapter 5. Page references are included for additional student help.

Additional review is provided in the *Prerequisite Skills Workbook*, pages 1–2, 15–24, 27–32, and 37–62.

Prerequisite Skills in the Getting Ready for the Next Lesson section at the end of each lesson reviews a skill needed in the next lesson.

For Lesson	Prerequisite Skill
5-2	Simplifying Fractions (p. 204)
5-3	Estimating Products (p. 209)
5-4	GCF of Monomials (p. 214)
5-5	Simplifying Fractions (p. 219)
5-6	Prime Factorization (p. 224)
5-7	Estimating with Fractions (p. 230)
5-8	Adding Integers (p. 236)
5-9	Dividing Decimals (p. 242)
5-10	Dividing Integers (p. 248)

FOLDABLES™
Study Organizer

For more information about Foldables, see *Teaching Mathematics with Foldables*.

Journal Writing Have students write about rational numbers. For example, they might compare fractions and decimals in writing, or they might rename decimals as fractions. Math journals can also be used to record the direction and progress of learning, to describe positive and negative experiences during learning, to write about personal associations and experiences during learning, and to list examples of ways in which new knowledge has or will be used in their daily life.

1 Focus

5-Minute Check Transparency 5-1 Use as a quiz or review of Chapter 4.

Mathematical Background notes are available for this lesson on page 198C.

How were fractions used to determine the size of the first coins?

The opening activity questions are repeated on page 228 of the *Chapter 5 Resource Masters*.

Reading to Learn Mathematics, p. 228 ELL

Pre-Activity *How were fractions used to determine the size of the first coins?*

Do the activity at the top of page 200 in your textbook. Write your answers below.

a. A half dollar contained half the silver of a silver dollar. What was it worth? $0.50

b. Write the decimal value of each coin in the table. $0.25, $0.10, $0.05

c. Order the fractions in the table from least to greatest. (*Hint*: Use the values of the coins.) $\frac{1}{20}, \frac{1}{10}, \frac{1}{4}$

Reading the Lesson 1–5. See students' work.

Write a definition and give an example of each new vocabulary word or phrase.

Vocabulary	Definition	Example
1. terminating decimal		
2. mixed number		
3. repeating decimal		
4. bar notation		
5. period		

Helping You Remember

6. Describe in your own words how to determine whether a fraction is written as a terminating or a repeating decimal. Sample answer: When dividing, a terminating decimal will eventually produce a remainder of 0.

What You'll Learn

- Write fractions as terminating or repeating decimals.
- Compare fractions and decimals.

Vocabulary
- terminating decimal
- mixed number
- repeating decimal
- bar notation
- period

How were fractions used to determine the size of the first coins?

In the 18th century, a silver dollar contained $1 worth of silver. The sizes of all other coins were based on this coin.

a. A half dollar contained half the silver of a silver dollar. What was it worth? **$0.50**

b. Write the decimal value of each coin in the table. **$0.25, $0.10, $0.05**

c. Order the fractions in the table from least to greatest. (*Hint*: Use the values of the coins.)

Coin	Fraction of Silver of $1 Coin
quarter-dollar (quarter)	$\frac{1}{4}$
10-cent (dime)	$\frac{1}{10}$
half-dime* (nickel)	$\frac{1}{20}$

* In 1866, nickels were enlarged for convenience

c. $\frac{1}{20}, \frac{1}{10}, \frac{1}{4}$

Reading Math

Terminating
Everyday Meaning: bringing to an end
Math Meaning: a decimal whose digits end

WRITE FRACTIONS AS DECIMALS Any fraction $\frac{a}{b}$, where $b \neq 0$, can be written as a decimal by dividing the numerator by the denominator. So, $\frac{a}{b} = a \div b$. If the division ends, or terminates, when the remainder is zero, the decimal is a **terminating decimal**.

Example 1 Write a Fraction as a Terminating Decimal

Write $\frac{3}{8}$ as a decimal.

Method 1 Use paper and pencil.

$$\begin{array}{r} 0.375 \\ 8)\overline{3.000} \\ \underline{-24} \\ 60 \\ \underline{-56} \\ 40 \\ \underline{-40} \\ 0 \end{array}$$

Division ends when the remainder is 0.

0.375 is a terminating decimal.

Method 2 Use a calculator.

3 ÷ 8 [ENTER] .375

$\frac{3}{8} = 0.375$

A **mixed number** such as $3\frac{1}{2}$ is the sum of a whole number and a fraction. Mixed numbers can also be written as decimals.

Resource Manager

📁 Workbooks and Reproducible Masters

Chapter 5 Resource Masters
- Study Guide and Intervention, p. 225
- Skills Practice, p. 226
- Practice, p. 227
- Reading to Learn Mathematics, p. 228
- Enrichment, p. 229

Graphing Calculator and Spreadsheet Masters, p. 28
Parent and Student Study Guide Workbook, p. 33
Prerequisite Skills Workbook, pp. 15–18

Transparencies

5-Minute Check Transparency 5-1
Answer Key Transparencies

Technology

Interactive Chalkboard

Example 2 Write a Mixed Number as a Decimal

Write $3\frac{1}{2}$ as a decimal.

$$3\frac{1}{2} = 3 + \frac{1}{2} \quad \text{Write as the sum of an integer and a fraction.}$$
$$= 3 + 0.5 \quad \frac{1}{2} = 0.5$$
$$= 3.5 \quad \text{Add.}$$

Not all fractions can be written as terminating decimals.

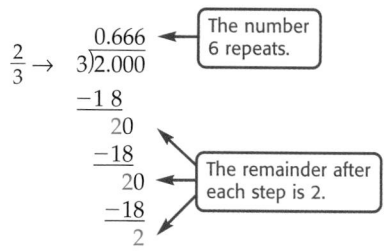

$$\frac{2}{3} \rightarrow 3\overline{)2.000}$$

The number 6 repeats.

The remainder after each step is 2.

CHECK 2 ÷ 3 ENTER .6666666667 ✓ The last digit is rounded.

So, $\frac{2}{3} = 0.6666666666\ldots$. This decimal is called a **repeating decimal**. You can use **bar notation** to indicate that the 6 repeats forever.

$$0.6666666666\ldots = 0.\overline{6} \quad \text{The digit 6 repeats, so place a bar over the 6.}$$

The **period** of a repeating decimal is the digit or digits that repeat. So, the period of $0.\overline{6}$ is 6.

Decimal	Bar Notation	Period
0.13131313…	$0.\overline{13}$	13
6.855555…	$6.8\overline{5}$	5
19.1724724…	$19.1\overline{724}$	724

✓ **Concept Check** Is $0.\overline{75}$ a terminating or a repeating decimal? Explain.
Repeating; the digits 75 repeat.

Example 3 Write Fractions as Repeating Decimals

a. Write $-\frac{6}{11}$ as a decimal.

$$-\frac{6}{11} \rightarrow 11\overline{)6.0000\ldots}\ 0.5454\ldots \quad \text{The digits 54 repeat.}$$

So, $-\frac{6}{11} = -0.\overline{54}$.

b. Write $\frac{2}{15}$ as a decimal.

$$\frac{2}{15} \rightarrow 15\overline{)2.0000\ldots}\ 0.1333\ldots \quad \text{The digit 3 repeats.}$$

So, $\frac{2}{15} = 0.1\overline{3}$.

Study Notebook

Have students—

- add the definitions/examples of the vocabulary terms to their Vocabulary Builder worksheets for Chapter 5.
- write a list of commonly used fractions and their decimal equivalents. These may be memorized for convenience. Students should also include an example of expressing a fraction as a decimal using division.
- include any other item(s) that they find helpful in mastering the skills in this lesson.

About the Exercises . . .
Organization by Objective
- **Write Fractions as Decimals:** 13–30
- **Compare Fractions and Decimals:** 31–44

Odd/Even Assignments
Exercises 13–30 and 32–44 are structured so that students practice the same concepts whether they are assigned odd or even problems.

Assignment Guide
Basic: 13–39 odd, 46–73
Average: 13–45 odd, 46–73
Advanced: 14–44 even, 45–65 (Optional: 66–73)

Answer
2. $0.5 = 0.50$ and $0.\overline{5} = 0.55...; 0.\overline{5}$ is greater because in the hundredths place, $5 > 0$.

COMPARE FRACTIONS AND DECIMALS It may be easier to compare numbers when they are written as decimals.

Example 4 Compare Fractions and Decimals

Replace ● with $<$, $>$, or $=$ to make $\frac{3}{5}$ ● 0.75 a true sentence.

$\frac{3}{5}$ ● 0.75   Write the sentence.

0.6 ● 0.75   Write $\frac{3}{5}$ as a decimal.

0.6 $<$ 0.75   In the tenths place, $6 < 7$.

On a number line, 0.6 is to the left of 0.75, so $\frac{3}{5} < 0.75$.

Example 5 Compare Fractions to Solve a Problem

BREAKFAST   In a survey of students, $\frac{13}{20}$ of the boys and $\frac{17}{25}$ of the girls make their own breakfast. Of those surveyed, do a greater fraction of boys or girls make their own breakfast?

Write the fractions as decimals and then compare the decimals.

boys: $\frac{13}{20} = 0.65$

girls: $\frac{17}{25} = 0.68$

On a number line, 0.65 is to the left of 0.68. Since $0.65 < 0.68$, $\frac{13}{20} < \frac{17}{25}$. So, a greater fraction of girls make their own breakfast.

Check for Understanding

Concept Check
1. Sample answer: write the fractions as decimals and then compare.

1. **Describe** the steps you should take to order $\frac{5}{8}$, 0.8, and $\frac{3}{5}$.
2. **Explain** how 0.5 and $0.\overline{5}$ are different. Which is greater? **See margin.**
3. **OPEN ENDED**   Give an example of a repeating decimal whose period is 14. **Sample answer: $0.\overline{14}$**

Guided Practice

GUIDED PRACTICE KEY	
Exercises	Examples
4, 5	1, 2
6, 7	3
8–11	4
12	5

Write each fraction or mixed number as a decimal. Use a bar to show a repeating decimal.

4. $\frac{7}{8}$ **0.875**   5. $2\frac{2}{25}$ **2.08**   6. $-\frac{5}{9}$ **$-0.\overline{5}$**   7. $\frac{4}{15}$ **$0.2\overline{6}$**

Replace each ● with $<$, $>$, or $=$ to make a true sentence.

8. $\frac{9}{10}$ ● 0.90 **$=$**   9. 0.3 ● $\frac{1}{3}$ **$<$**   10. $\frac{1}{4}$ ● $\frac{1}{3}$ **$<$**   11. $-\frac{3}{4}$ ● $-\frac{7}{8}$ **$>$**

Application
12. **TRUCKS**   Of all the passenger trucks sold each year in the United States, $\frac{1}{5}$ are pickups and 0.17 are SUVs. Are more SUVs or pickups sold? Explain.   **Source:** U.S. Department of Energy, EPA **Pickups; $\frac{1}{5} = 0.2$, and $0.2 > 0.17$.**

DAILY
INTERVENTION   **Differentiated Instruction**

- **Kinesthetic**   Give each student a large index card with a fraction or mixed number on one side. Each student should rewrite the number as a decimal on the back side of the card. Then have students line up in the front of the classroom in order from least value to greatest value.

★ indicates increased difficulty

Practice and Apply

Homework Help

For Exercises	See Examples
13–20	1, 2
21–28	3
32–43	4
46, 47	5

Extra Practice
See page 733.

Write each fraction or mixed number as a decimal. Use a bar to show a repeating decimal.

13. $\frac{1}{5}$ 0.2

14. $\frac{3}{20}$ 0.15

15. $\frac{8}{25}$ 0.32

16. $-\frac{5}{8}$ -0.625

17. $7\frac{3}{10}$ 7.3

18. $1\frac{1}{2}$ 1.5

19. $5\frac{1}{8}$ 5.125

20. $-3\frac{3}{4}$ -3.75

21. $\frac{1}{9}$ $0.\overline{1}$

22. $-\frac{2}{9}$ $-0.\overline{2}$

23. $-\frac{5}{11}$ $-0.\overline{45}$

24. $\frac{4}{11}$ $0.\overline{36}$

25. $\frac{1}{6}$ $0.1\overline{6}$

26. $\frac{7}{15}$ $0.4\overline{6}$

27. $\frac{5}{16}$ 0.3125

★ 28. $\frac{7}{12}$ $0.58\overline{3}$

29. **ANIMALS** A marlin can swim $\frac{5}{6}$ mile in one minute. Write $\frac{5}{6}$ as a decimal rounded to the nearest hundredth. 0.83

30. **COMPUTERS** In a survey, 17 students out of 20 said they use a home PC as a reference source for school projects. Write 17 out of 20 as a decimal.
Source: NPD Online Research 0.85

31. Order $\frac{7}{8}$, 0.8, and $\frac{7}{9}$ from least to greatest. $\frac{7}{9}$, 0.8, $\frac{7}{8}$

Replace each ● with <, >, or = to make a true sentence.

32. 0.3 ● $\frac{1}{4}$ >

33. $\frac{5}{8}$ ● 0.65 <

34. $\frac{2}{5}$ ● 0.4 =

35. $\frac{1}{3}$ ● $\frac{1}{2}$ <

36. $\frac{1}{5}$ ● $0.\overline{5}$ <

37. $1\frac{1}{20}$ ● 1.01 >

38. $\frac{7}{8}$ ● $\frac{8}{9}$ <

39. $3\frac{4}{9}$ ● $3.\overline{4}$ =

40. 6.18 ● $6\frac{1}{5}$ <

★ 41. -0.75 ● $-\frac{7}{9}$ >

★ 42. $0.3\overline{4}$ ● $\frac{34}{99}$ >

★ 43. $-2\frac{1}{12}$ ● -2.09 >

44. On a number line, would $\frac{11}{15}$ be graphed to the right or to the left of $\frac{3}{4}$? Explain. To the left; $\frac{11}{15} = 0.7\overline{3}$ and $\frac{3}{4} = 0.75$; since $0.7\overline{3} < 0.75$, $\frac{11}{15} < \frac{3}{4}$.

★ 45. Find a terminating and a repeating decimal between $\frac{1}{6}$ and $\frac{8}{9}$. Explain how you found them. See margin.

SCHOOL For Exercises 46 and 47, use the graphic at the right and the information below.

28% = 0.28	21% = 0.21
16% = 0.16	15% = 0.15
13% = 0.13	5% = 0.05

46. More than; $\frac{1}{4} = 0.25$ and $0.28 > 0.25$.

46. Did more or less than one-fourth of the students surveyed choose math as their favorite subject? Explain.

47. This is greater than those who chose English in the survey because $\frac{1}{7} ≈ 0.14$, and $0.14 > 0.13$.

47. Suppose $\frac{1}{7}$ of the students in your class choose English as their favorite subject. How does this compare to the results of the survey? Explain.

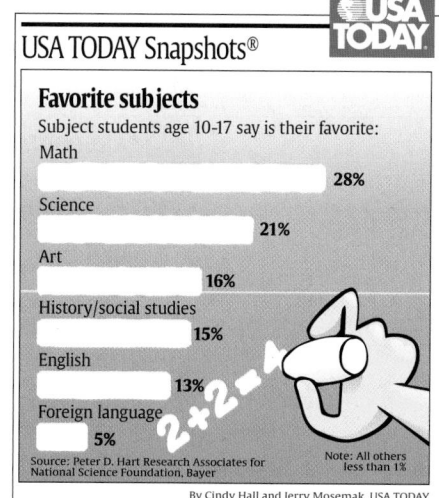

USA TODAY Snapshots®

Favorite subjects
Subject students age 10-17 say is their favorite:

Math — 28%
Science — 21%
Art — 16%
History/social studies — 15%
English — 13%
Foreign language — 5%

Note: All others less than 1%

Source: Peter D. Hart Research Associates for National Science Foundation, Bayer

By Cindy Hall and Jerry Mosemak, USA TODAY

www.pre-alg.com/self_check_quiz

Lesson 5-1 Writing Fractions as Decimals 203

Answer

45. Sample answer: 0.7 and $0.\overline{7}$; $\frac{1}{6} = 0.1\overline{6}$ and $\frac{8}{9} = 0.\overline{8}$; 0.7 and $0.\overline{7}$ are both greater than $0.1\overline{6}$ and less than $0.\overline{8}$.

Study Guide and Intervention, p. 225

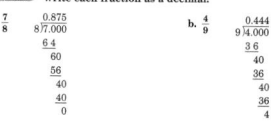

Fractions can be written as decimals by dividing the numerator by the denominator. If the division ends, or terminates, when the remainder is 0, it is a terminating decimal. If the decimal number repeats without end, it is a repeating decimal.

Example 1 Write each fraction as a decimal.

a. $\frac{7}{8}$

$$8\overline{)7.000}$$
0.875
64
60
56
40
40
0

0.875 is a terminating decimal.

b. $\frac{4}{9}$

$$9\overline{)4.000}$$
0.444
36
40
36
40
36
4

0.4... or $0.\overline{4}$ is a repeating decimal.

It may be easier to compare numbers if they are written as decimals.

Example 2 Replace ● with <, >, or = to make $\frac{3}{8}$ ● 0.28 a true sentence.

$\frac{3}{8} = 0.375$, so $\frac{3}{8}$ ● 0.28 can be written as 0.375 ● 0.28. Since $0.375 > 0.28$, $\frac{3}{8} > 0.28$.

Exercises

Write each fraction or mixed number as a decimal. Use a bar to show a repeating decimal.

1. $\frac{7}{20}$ 0.35
2. $\frac{2}{11}$ $0.\overline{18}$
3. $\frac{5}{6}$ $0.8\overline{3}$
4. $\frac{5}{6}$ $0.8\overline{3}$
5. $\frac{6}{25}$ 0.24
6. $\frac{5}{20}$ 0.25
7. $8\frac{3}{5}$ 8.6
8. $3\frac{7}{25}$ 3.28
9. $\frac{4}{15}$ $0.2\overline{6}$
10. $\frac{12}{32}$ 0.375
11. $-6\frac{9}{10}$ -6.9
12. $1\frac{5}{11}$ $1.\overline{45}$

Replace each ● with <, >, or = to make a true sentence.

13. $\frac{5}{8}$ ● $\frac{6}{5}$ <
14. $1\frac{4}{5}$ ● 1.8 =
15. $-2\frac{7}{12}$ ● $-2\frac{4}{5}$ >
16. 5.09 ● $5\frac{1}{2}$ <
17. 9.3 ● $\frac{28}{3}$ <
18. $\frac{28}{20}$ ● $\frac{31}{23}$ >

Skills Practice, p. 226 and Practice, p. 227 (shown)

Write each fraction or mixed number as a decimal. Use a bar to show a repeating decimal.

1. $\frac{3}{5}$ 0.6
2. $\frac{1}{8}$ 0.125
3. $\frac{9}{11}$ $0.\overline{81}$
4. $-\frac{3}{16}$ -0.1875
5. $\frac{3}{40}$ 0.075
6. $\frac{8}{11}$ $0.\overline{72}$
7. $\frac{5}{12}$ $0.41\overline{6}$
8. $\frac{1}{3}$ $0.\overline{3}$
9. $\frac{7}{9}$ $0.\overline{7}$
10. $-\frac{11}{15}$ $-0.7\overline{3}$
11. $-\frac{12}{16}$ -0.75
12. $\frac{13}{60}$ $0.21\overline{6}$
13. $\frac{1}{45}$ $0.0\overline{2}$
14. $-\frac{5}{24}$ $-0.208\overline{3}$
15. $\frac{13}{20}$ 0.65
16. $\frac{17}{18}$ $0.9\overline{4}$
17. $-11\frac{1}{4}$ -11.25
18. $23\frac{5}{11}$ $23.\overline{45}$
19. $-18\frac{2}{3}$ $-18.\overline{6}$
20. $5\frac{7}{8}$ 5.875

Replace each ● with <, >, or = to make a true sentence.

21. $-\frac{13}{2}$ ● -6.4 <
22. $\frac{6}{7}$ ● $\frac{5}{6}$ >
23. -0.75 ● $-\frac{15}{20}$ =
24. $-4\frac{3}{8}$ ● -4.40 >
25. $\frac{7}{8}$ ● $\frac{8}{9}$ <
26. $-\frac{33}{100}$ ● $-0.\overline{3}$ >

27. Order $\frac{4}{9}$, $\frac{444}{1000}$, and 0.4 from least to greatest. 0.4, $\frac{444}{1000}$, $\frac{4}{9}$

28. Order $-\frac{8}{9}$, $-\frac{8}{10}$, and $-0.\overline{80}$ from least to greatest. $-\frac{8}{9}$, -0.80, $-\frac{8}{10}$

29. **OPINION** In a school survey, 787 out of 1000 students preferred hip-hop music to techno. Is this figure more or less than $\frac{7}{9}$ of those surveyed? Explain.

More; $\frac{787}{1000} = 0.787$ and $\frac{7}{9} = 0.\overline{7}$, so $\frac{787}{1000}$ is greater than $\frac{7}{9}$.

Enrichment, p. 229

GCF, LCM, and Ladders

When two or more numbers have common factors, the greatest of these is called the **greatest common factor (GCF)**. When two or more numbers have nonzero common multiples, the least of these is called the **least common multiple (LCM)** of the numbers. A method of determining the GCF and LCM for two or more numbers is the ladder.

Example Find the GCF and LCM of 24 and 36.

6	24	36	Find any number that will divide into both numbers.
2	4	6	Both 24 and 36 can be divided evenly by 6.
1	2	3	Continue to choose divisors until the only remaining divisor is 1.
	2	3	

To find the GCF, multiply all the divisors.
$6 \cdot 2 \cdot 1 = 12$ The GCF is 12.

To find the LCM, multiply the GCF and the numbers remaining on the bottom of the ladder.
$12 \cdot 2 \cdot 3 = 72$ The LCM is 72.

Find the GCF and LCM for each pair of numbers by using a ladder. The numbers used as divisors may vary.

1. 18, 27 GCF: 9 LCM: 54
2. 24, 42 GCF: 6 LCM: 168
3. 44, 66 GCF: 22 LCM: 132
4. 36, 81 GCF: 9 LCM: 324
5. 42, 48 GCF: 6 LCM: 336
6. 100, 125 GCF: 25 LCM: 500
7. 64, 72 GCF: 8 LCM: 576
8. 90, 150 GCF: 30 LCM: 450
9. 250, 300 GCF: 50 LCM: 1500

Open-Ended Assessment

Writing Have students write three fractions. They should express each as a decimal, explain whether they are terminating or repeating, then order them. Encourage students to utilize as many math terms as possible in their explanations.

Getting Ready for Lesson 5-2

PREREQUISITE SKILL Lesson 5-2 presents rational numbers. Students will need to be able to write rational numbers as fractions. Exercises 66–73 should be used to determine your students' familiarity with simplifying fractions.

Answers

48a. $2 = 2, 3 = 3, 4 = 2^2, 5 = 5,$
$6 = 2 \cdot 3, 8 = 2^3, 9 = 3^2,$
$10 = 2 \cdot 5, 12 = 2^2 \cdot 3,$
$15 = 3 \cdot 5, 20 = 2^2 \cdot 5$

48b. $\frac{1}{2} = 0.5, \frac{1}{3} = 0.\overline{3}, \frac{1}{4} = 0.25,$

$\frac{1}{5} = 0.2, \frac{1}{6} = 0.1\overline{6}, \frac{1}{8} = 0.125,$

$\frac{1}{9} = 0.\overline{1}, \frac{1}{10} = 0.1, \frac{1}{12} = 0.083\overline{3},$

$\frac{1}{15} = 0.0\overline{6}, \frac{1}{20} = 0.05$

48c. Sample answer: Fractions whose denominators have only 2 or 5 as prime factors are terminating decimals. Fractions whose denominators have 3 as a prime factor are repeating decimals.

49. All coins were made with a fraction of silver that was contained in a silver dollar. Answers should include the following.
   - A quarter had one-fourth the amount of silver as a silver dollar, a dime had one-tenth the amount, and a nickel had one-twentieth the amount.
   - It is easier to perform arithmetic operations using decimals rather than using fractions.

---

48. **CRITICAL THINKING** a–c. See margin.
   a. Write the prime factorization of each denominator in the fractions listed below.
   $$\frac{1}{2}, \frac{1}{3}, \frac{1}{4}, \frac{1}{5}, \frac{1}{6}, \frac{1}{8}, \frac{1}{9}, \frac{1}{10}, \frac{1}{12}, \frac{1}{15}, \frac{1}{20}$$
   b. Write the decimal equivalent of each fraction.
   c. **Make a conjecture** relating prime factors of denominators and the decimal equivalents of fractions.

49.  Answer the question that was posed at the beginning of the lesson. **See margin.**

   How were fractions used to determine the size of the first coins?
   Include the following in your answer:
   - a description of the first coins, and
   - an explanation of why decimals rather than fractions are used in money exchange today.

Standardized Test Practice
Ⓐ Ⓑ Ⓒ Ⓓ

50. Which decimal is equivalent to $\frac{1}{100}$? **B**
   Ⓐ 0.001   Ⓑ 0.01   Ⓒ 0.1   Ⓓ $0.\overline{1}$

51. Write the shaded portion of the figure at the right as a decimal. **D**
   Ⓐ 0.6   Ⓑ $0.\overline{6}$
   Ⓒ 0.63   Ⓓ $0.6\overline{3}$

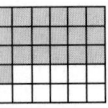

Maintain Your Skills

Mixed Review **Write each number in scientific notation.** *(Lesson 4-8)*
52. 854,000,000   53. 0.077   54. 0.00016   55. 925,000
   8.54×10^8 7.7×10^{-2} 1.6×10^{-4} 9.25×10^5

Write each expression using a positive exponent. *(Lesson 4-7)*
56. 10^{-5} $\frac{1}{10^5}$ 57. $(-2)^{-7}$ $\frac{1}{(-2)^7}$ 58. x^{-4} $\frac{1}{x^4}$ 59. y^{-3} $\frac{1}{y^3}$

60. **ALGEBRA** Write $(a \cdot a \cdot a)(a \cdot a)$ using an exponent. *(Lesson 4-2)* a^5

61. **TRANSPORTATION** A car can travel an average of 464 miles on one tank of gas. If the tank holds 16 gallons of gasoline, how many miles per gallon does it get? *(Lesson 3-7)* **29**

ALGEBRA Solve each equation. Check your solution. *(Lesson 3-4)*
62. $4n = 32$ **8**   63. $-64 = 2t$ **−32**
64. $\frac{a}{5} = -9$ **−45**   65. $-8 = \frac{x}{-7}$ **56**

Getting Ready for the Next Lesson **PREREQUISITE SKILL** Simplify each fraction.
(To review simplifying fractions, see Lesson 4-5.)
66. $\frac{4}{30}$ $\frac{2}{15}$ 67. $\frac{5}{65}$ $\frac{1}{13}$ 68. $\frac{36}{60}$ $\frac{3}{5}$ 69. $\frac{12}{18}$ $\frac{2}{3}$

70. $\frac{21}{24}$ $\frac{7}{8}$ 71. $\frac{16}{28}$ $\frac{4}{7}$ 72. $\frac{32}{48}$ $\frac{2}{3}$ 73. $\frac{125}{1000}$ $\frac{1}{8}$

5-2 Rational Numbers

What You'll Learn

- Write rational numbers as fractions.
- Identify and classify rational numbers.

How are rational numbers related to other sets of numbers?

Vocabulary
- rational number

The solution of $2x = 4$ is 2. It is a member of the set of *natural numbers* N = {1, 2, 3, …}.

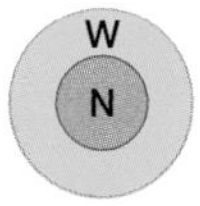

The solution of $x + 3 = 3$ is 0. It is a member of the set of *whole numbers* W = {0, 1, 2, 3, …}.

The solution of $x + 5 = 2$ is -3. It is a member of the set of *integers* I = {…, −3, −2, −1, 0, 1, 2, 3, …}.

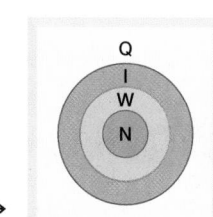

The solution of $2x = 3$ is $\frac{3}{2}$, which is neither a natural number, a whole number, nor an integer. It is a member of the set of *rational numbers* Q.

Rational numbers include fractions and decimals as well as natural numbers, whole numbers, and integers.

a. Is 7 a natural number? a whole number? an integer? yes; yes; yes
b. How do you know that 7 is also a rational number?
c. Is every natural number a rational number? Is every rational number a natural number? Give an explanation or a counterexample to support your answers.

b. The set of rational numbers includes natural numbers, whole numbers, and integers.
c. Yes; any natural number can be written as a fraction with a denominator of 1. No; $\frac{8}{9}$ is rational, but it is not a natural number.

Reading Math

Rational
Root Word: Ratio
A *ratio* is the comparison of two quantities by division. Recall that $\frac{a}{b} = a \div b$, where $b \neq 0$.

WRITE RATIONAL NUMBERS AS FRACTIONS A number that can be written as a fraction is called a **rational number**. Some examples of rational numbers are shown below.

$$0.75 = \frac{3}{4} \qquad -0.\overline{3} = -\frac{1}{3} \qquad 28 = \frac{28}{1} \qquad 1\frac{1}{4} = \frac{5}{4}$$

Example 1 Write Mixed Numbers and Integers as Fractions

a. Write $5\frac{2}{3}$ as a fraction.

$5\frac{2}{3} = \frac{17}{3}$ Write $5\frac{2}{3}$ as an improper fraction.

b. Write -3 as a fraction.

$-3 = \frac{-3}{1}$ or $-\frac{3}{1}$

Concept Check Explain why any integer n is a rational number.
It can be written as a fraction $\frac{n}{1}$.

5-2 Lesson Notes

1 Focus

5-Minute Check Transparency 5-2 Use as a quiz or review of Lesson 5-1.

Mathematical Background notes are available for this lesson on page 198C.

How are rational numbers related to other sets of numbers?

The opening activity questions are repeated on page 233 of the *Chapter 5 Resource Masters*.

Reading to Learn Mathematics, p. 233 ELL

Pre-Activity *How are rational numbers related to other sets of numbers?*

Do the activity at the top of page 205 in your textbook. Write your answers below.

a. Is 7 a natural number? a whole number? an integer?
yes; yes; yes

b. How do you know that 7 is also a rational number?
The set of rational numbers includes natural numbers, whole numbers, and integers.

c. Is every natural number a rational number? Is every rational number a natural number? Give an explanation or a counterexample to support your answers. Yes; any natural number can be written as a fraction with a denominator of 1. No; $\frac{8}{9}$ is rational, but it is not a natural number.

Reading the Lesson

Write a definition and give an example of the new vocabulary term.

	Vocabulary	Definition	Example
1.	rational number	See students' work.	

2. Terminating decimals can be written as fractions with a denominator of 10, 100, 1000, and so on.

3. A number such as π is called irrational because it cannot be written as a fraction.

4. Is -3 a rational number? Explain. Yes, any integer is a rational number.

Helping You Remember

5. *Irrational* is a word that is used in everyday English.
   a. Find the definition of *irrational* in the dictionary. Write the definition.
   not endowed with reason or understanding
   b. Explain how the English definition can help you remember how irrational and rational are used in mathematics. The decimal form of an irrational number has no repeating pattern or terminating features, whereas rational numbers do.

Resource Manager

Workbooks and Reproducible Masters

Chapter 5 Resource Masters
- Study Guide and Intervention, p. 230
- Skills Practice, p. 231
- Practice, p. 232
- Reading to Learn Mathematics, p. 233
- Enrichment, p. 234

Parent and Student Study Guide Workbook, p. 34
School-to-Career Masters, p. 9

Transparencies
5-Minute Check Transparency 5-2
Answer Key Transparencies

Technology
Interactive Chalkboard

WRITE RATIONAL NUMBERS AS FRACTIONS

In-Class Examples Power Point®

1 a. Write $-4\frac{3}{8}$ as a fraction.

$-\frac{35}{8}$

b. Write 10 as a fraction. $\frac{10}{1}$

2 Write each decimal as a fraction or mixed number in simplest form.

a. 0.26 $\frac{13}{50}$

b. 2.875 $2\frac{7}{8}$

3 Write $0.\overline{39}$ as a fraction in simplest form. $\frac{13}{33}$

Teaching Tip Remind students that reading a decimal number properly gives a fraction, so 0.12 is 12 hundredths or $\frac{12}{100}$.

✓ Skills Check

Write Rational Numbers as Fractions Ask students to explain whether each of the following is a rational number. If so, how do you express the decimals as fractions?

a. 0.125   b. $0.\overline{125}$

IDENTIFY AND CLASSIFY RATIONAL NUMBERS

In-Class Example Power Point®

4 Identify all sets to which each number belongs.

a. 15   whole number, integer, and rational

b. $\frac{1}{8}$ rational

c. 0.30303030 . . .   rational

Terminating decimals are rational numbers because they can be written as a fraction with a denominator of 10, 100, 1000, and so on.

Example 2 **Write Terminating Decimals as Fractions**

Write each decimal as a fraction or mixed number in simplest form.

a. 0.48

$0.48 = \frac{48}{100}$ 0.48 is 48 hundredths.

$= \frac{12}{25}$ Simplify. The GCF of 48 and 100 is 4.

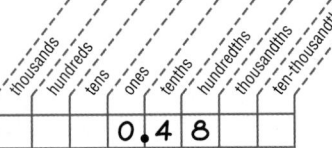

b. 6.375

$6.375 = 6\frac{375}{1000}$ 6.375 is 6 and 375 thousandths.

$= 6\frac{3}{8}$ Simplify. The GCF of 375 and 1000 is 125.

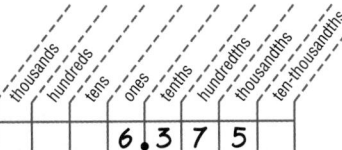

Reading Math

Decimals
Use the word *and* to represent the decimal point.
- Read 0.375 as three hundred seventy-five thousandths.
- Read 300.075 as three hundred *and* seventy-five thousandths.

Any repeating decimal can be written as a fraction, so repeating decimals are also rational numbers.

Study Tip

Repeating Decimals
When *two* digits repeat, multiply each side by 100. Then subtract N from $100N$ to eliminate the repeating part.

Example 3 **Write Repeating Decimals as Fractions**

Write $0.\overline{8}$ as a fraction in simplest form.

$N = 0.888\ldots$ Let N represent the number.

$10N = 10(0.888\ldots)$ Multiply each side by 10 because one digit repeats.
$10N = 8.888\ldots$

Subtract N from $10N$ to eliminate the repeating part, 0.888... .

$10N = 8.888\ldots$
$\underline{-(N = 0.888\ldots)}$
$9N = 8$ $10N - N = 10N - 1N$ or $9N$

$\frac{9N}{9} = \frac{8}{9}$ Divide each side by 9.

$N = \frac{8}{9}$ Simplify.

Therefore, $0.\overline{8} = \frac{8}{9}$.

CHECK 8 ÷ 9 [ENTER] .8888888889 ✓

IDENTIFY AND CLASSIFY RATIONAL NUMBERS All rational numbers can be written as terminating or repeating decimals. Decimals that are neither terminating nor repeating, such as the numbers below, are called *irrational* because they cannot be written as fractions. *You will learn more about irrational numbers in Chapter 9.*

$\pi = 3.141592654\ldots$ → The digits do not repeat.

$4.232232223\ldots$ → The same block of digits do not repeat.

Teacher to Teacher

Teri Willard   Mathematics Consultant, Belgrade, MT

"I like for students to see the patterns that develop in the rational numbers before simplifying. For example, $0.\overline{2} = \frac{2}{9}$, $0.\overline{35} = \frac{35}{99}$, $0.\overline{625} = \frac{625}{999}$, and $0.\overline{7123} = \frac{7123}{9999}$. The number of 9s in the denominator is the same as the number of repeated digits."

The following model can help you classify rational numbers.

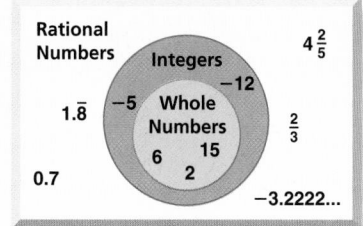
Example 4 Classify Numbers

Identify all sets to which each number belongs.

a. -6

-6 is an integer and a rational number.

b. $2\frac{4}{5}$

Because $2\frac{4}{5} = \frac{14}{5}$, it is a rational number. It is neither a whole number nor an integer.

c. $0.914114111\ldots$

This is a nonterminating, nonrepeating decimal. So, it is not a rational number.

Check for Understanding

Concept Check

1. any number that can be written as a fraction

1. **Define** *rational number* in your own words.

2. **OPEN ENDED** Give an example of a number that is not rational. Explain why it is not rational. **See margin.**

Guided Practice

Write each number as a fraction.

3. $-2\frac{1}{3}$ $-\frac{7}{3}$ 4. $10\frac{10}{1}$

Write each decimal as a fraction or mixed number in simplest form.

5. 0.8 $\frac{4}{5}$ 6. 6.35 $6\frac{7}{20}$ 7. $-0.\overline{7}$ $-\frac{7}{9}$ 8. $0.\overline{45}$ $\frac{5}{11}$

Identify all sets to which each number belongs.

9. -5 I, Q   10. 6.05 Q

GUIDED PRACTICE KEY	
Exercises	Examples
3, 4	1
5, 6, 11	2
7, 8	3
9, 10	4

Application

11. **MEASUREMENT** A *micron* is a unit of measure that is approximately 0.000039 inch. Express this as a fraction. $\frac{39}{1,000,000}$

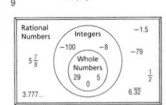

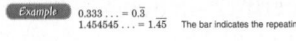

Study Guide and Intervention, p. 230

A number that can be written as a fraction is called a rational number. Mixed numbers, integers, and many decimals can be written as fractions. Only decimals that terminate or repeat can be written as fractions. Other decimal numbers such as $\pi = 3.141592654...$ are infinite and nonrepeating. They are called irrational numbers.

Example Write each number as a fraction.

a. $3\frac{2}{5}$
$3\frac{2}{5} = \frac{17}{5}$ Write the mixed number as an improper fraction.

b. -7
$-7 = \frac{-7}{1}$ The denominator is 1.

c. 0.14
0.14 is 14 hundredths.
$0.14 = \frac{14}{100}$ or $\frac{7}{50}$ Simplify.

d. $0.\overline{5}$
$0.\overline{5} = 0.555...$
$N = 0.555...$ Let N represent the number.
$10N = 5.555...$ Multiply each side by 10 because one digit repeats.
$10N = 5.555...$
$\underline{-(N = 0.555...)}$ Subtract N from 10N.
$9N = 5$
$\frac{9N}{9} = \frac{5}{9}$ Divide each side by 9.
$N = \frac{5}{9}$ Simplify.

The diagram at the right illustrates the relationships among whole numbers, integers, and rational numbers.

Exercises

Write each number as a fraction.

1. $1\frac{1}{5}$ $\frac{6}{5}$
2. -2 $-\frac{2}{1}$
3. 0.7 $\frac{7}{10}$
4. 0.32 $\frac{8}{25}$
5. $-0.\overline{1}$ $-\frac{1}{9}$
6. $0.\overline{49}$ $\frac{49}{99}$

Identify all sets to which each number belongs (N = natural numbers, W = whole numbers, I = integers, Q = rational numbers).

7. -12 I, Q
8. 8.5 Q
9. 582 W, N, Q

Skills Practice, p. 231 and Practice, p. 232 (shown)

Write each number as a fraction.

1. 29 $\frac{29}{1}$
2. 0 $\frac{0}{1}$
3. $3\frac{7}{8}$ $\frac{31}{8}$
4. -47 $\frac{-47}{1}$
5. $-5\frac{6}{7}$ $-\frac{41}{7}$
6. $4\frac{3}{20}$ $\frac{83}{20}$
7. $-7\frac{2}{15}$ $-\frac{107}{15}$
8. $10\frac{2}{9}$ $\frac{92}{9}$

Write each decimal as a fraction or mixed number in simplest form.

9. 0.32 $\frac{8}{25}$
10. 0.42 $\frac{21}{50}$
11. $0.\overline{8}$ $\frac{8}{9}$
12. $-6.\overline{3}$ $-6\frac{1}{3}$
13. 0.91 $\frac{91}{100}$
14. 17.875 $17\frac{7}{8}$
15. $-0.666...$ $-\frac{2}{3}$
16. 0.07 $\frac{7}{100}$
17. $9.\overline{7}$ $9\frac{7}{9}$
18. 7.75 $7\frac{3}{4}$
19. 0.525 $\frac{21}{40}$
20. -8.26 $-8\frac{13}{50}$
21. $6.\overline{5}$ $6\frac{5}{9}$
22. -4.12 $-4\frac{3}{25}$
23. 13.006 $13\frac{3}{500}$
24. $3.\overline{34}$ $3\frac{34}{99}$

Identify all sets to which each number belongs (N = natural numbers, W = whole numbers, I = integers, Q = rational numbers).

25. 15 W, N, I, Q
26. $-3.\overline{8}$ Q
27. -5.075 Q
28. $\frac{50}{25}$ W, N, I, Q
29. π not rational
30. $-\frac{4}{2}$ I, Q

31. **BOTANY** The smallest flowering plant is the flowering aquatic duckweed found in Australia. It is 0.0236 inch long and 0.0129 inch wide. Write these dimensions as fractions in simplest form.
$\frac{59}{2500}$ in. long and $\frac{129}{10,000}$ in. wide

Enrichment, p. 234

Irrational Numbers

Decimals in which a digit or group of digits repeats are called **repeating decimals**.

Example $0.333... = 0.\overline{3}$
$1.454545... = 1.\overline{45}$ The bar indicates the repeating digit or digits.

Decimals in which only a 0 repeats are called terminating decimals.

Example $0.5000... = 0.5$
$42.19500... = 42.195$

Consider the decimal 0.757757775 .... It does not terminate in zero nor does it have a group of digits that repeat. Numbers that are represented by nonterminating, nonrepeating decimals are irrational numbers.

Example $\pi = 3.14159...$
$\sqrt{5} = 2.236068...$

Determine whether each decimal is repeating or nonrepeating.

1. 0.373373337... nonrepeating
2. 24.15971597... repeating
3. 5.71571571... repeating
4. 0.5795579555... nonrepeating
5. 8.3121121112... nonrepeating

Name the next three digits in the following irrational numbers.

6. 0.13141516... 171
7. 0.96796679666... 796

Name an irrational number between each pair of numbers. Answers will vary. Sample answers given.

8. 6.7 and 6.8 6.7121221222...
9. 17.3 and 17.4 17.353553555...
10. 0.1231233 ... and 0.1231134111 ... 0.1231152552555...
11. 2.333 ... and 2.444 ... 2.43344333444...

Find each sum.

12. 0.232232223... + 0.323323332... 0.555555555... or $0.\overline{5}$
13. 0.131131113... + 0.868868886... 0.999999999... or $0.\overline{9}$

208 Chapter 5 Rational Numbers

★ indicates increased difficulty

Practice and Apply

Homework Help

For Exercises	See Examples
12–15	1
16–21, 28–33	2
22–27	3
34–41	4

Extra Practice See page 733.

Write each number as a fraction.

12. $5\frac{2}{3}$ $\frac{17}{3}$
13. $-1\frac{4}{7}$ $-\frac{11}{7}$
14. -21 $-\frac{21}{1}$
15. 60 $\frac{60}{1}$

Write each decimal as a fraction or mixed number in simplest form.

16. 0.4 $\frac{2}{5}$
17. 0.09 $\frac{9}{100}$
18. 5.22 $5\frac{11}{50}$
19. 1.68 $1\frac{17}{25}$
20. 0.625 $\frac{5}{8}$
21. 8.004 $8\frac{1}{250}$
22. $0.\overline{2}$ $\frac{2}{9}$
23. $-0.333...$ $-\frac{1}{3}$
24. $4.\overline{5}$ $4\frac{5}{9}$
25. $5.\overline{6}$ $5\frac{2}{3}$
★ 26. $0.\overline{32}$ $\frac{32}{99}$
★ 27. $2.\overline{25}$ $2\frac{25}{99}$

28. **WHITE HOUSE** The White House covers an area of 0.028 square mile. What fraction of a square mile is this? $\frac{7}{250}$

29. **RECYCLING** In 1999, 0.06 of all recycled newspapers were used to make tissues. What fraction is this? $\frac{3}{50}$

GEOGRAPHY Africa makes up $\frac{1}{5}$ of all the land on Earth. Use the table to find the fraction of Earth's land that is made up by other continents. Write each fraction in simplest form.

30. Antarctica $\frac{19}{200}$
31. Asia $\frac{59}{200}$
32. Europe $\frac{7}{100}$
33. North America $\frac{4}{25}$

Continent	Decimal Portion of Earth's Land
Antarctica	0.095
Asia	0.295
Europe	0.07
North America	0.16

Source: *Incredible Comparisons*

Identify all sets to which each number belongs.

34. 4 N, W, I, Q
35. -7 I, Q
36. $-2\frac{5}{8}$ Q
37. $\frac{6}{3}$ N, W, I, Q
38. 15.8 Q
39. 9.0202020... Q
40. 1.2345... not rational
41. 30.151151115... not rational

42. Write 125 thousandths as a fraction in simplest form. $\frac{1}{8}$

★ 43. Express *two hundred and nineteen hundredths* as a fraction or mixed number in simplest form. $200\frac{19}{100}$

Determine whether each statement is *sometimes, always,* or *never* true. Explain by giving an example or a counterexample.

44. An integer is a rational number. always
45. A rational number is an integer. sometimes
46. A whole number is not a rational number. never
44–46. See margin for explanations.

47. **MANUFACTURING** A garbage bag has a thickness of 0.8 mil. This is 0.0008 inch. What fraction of an inch is this? $\frac{1}{1250}$ in.

48. **GEOMETRY** Pi (π) to six decimal places has a value of 3.141592. Pi is often estimated as $\frac{22}{7}$. Is the estimate for π greater than or less than the actual value of π? Explain. greater than; $\frac{22}{7} \approx 3.142857 > 3.141592$

208 Chapter 5 Rational Numbers

More About...

Recycling

The portions of recycled newspapers used for other purposes are shown below.
Newsprint: 0.34
Exported for recycling: 0.22
Paperboard: 0.17
Other products: 0.18

Source: American Forest and Paper Association, Newspaper Association of America

---

Answers

44. Every integer can be written as a fraction with 1 as the denominator; $5 = \frac{5}{1}$, so 5 is a rational number.

45. $\frac{1}{2}$ and 2 are both rational numbers, but only 2 is an integer.

46. Every whole number can be written as a fraction with 1 as the denominator. 3 is a whole number and $3 = \frac{3}{1}$, so it is a rational number.

★ **49. MACHINERY** Will a steel peg 2.37 inches in diameter fit in a $2\frac{3}{8}$-inch diameter hole? How do you know? **Yes;** $2\frac{3}{8} = 2.375$ **and** $2.375 > 2.37$.

50. CRITICAL THINKING Show that 0.999… = 1. **See margin.**

51. **WRITING IN MATH** Answer the question that was posed at the beginning of the lesson. **See margin.**

How are rational numbers related to other sets of numbers?

Include the following in your answer:
- examples of numbers that belong to more than one set, and
- examples of numbers that are only rational.

Standardized Test Practice
Ⓐ Ⓑ Ⓒ Ⓓ

52. There are infinitely many __?__ between S and T on the number line. **A**

   Ⓐ rational numbers   Ⓑ integers

   Ⓒ whole numbers   Ⓓ natural numbers

53. Express 0.56 as a fraction in simplest form. **C**

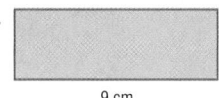

   Ⓐ $\frac{56}{100}$ Ⓑ $\frac{28}{50}$ Ⓒ $\frac{14}{25}$ Ⓓ $\frac{7}{12}$

Maintain Your Skills

Mixed Review Write each fraction or mixed number as a decimal. Use a bar to show a repeating decimal. *(Lesson 5-1)*

54. $\frac{2}{5}$ **0.4**   **55.** $-7\frac{4}{5}$ **−7.8**   **56.** $-\frac{13}{20}$ **−0.65**   **57.** $2\frac{5}{9}$ $2.\overline{5}$

Write each number in standard form. *(Lesson 4-8)*

58. 2×10^3 **2000**   **59.** 3.05×10^6 **60.** 7.4×10^{-4} **61.** 1.681×10^{-2}
                      3,050,000   **0.00074**   **0.01681**

62. ALGEBRA Write $\frac{12n^2}{3an}$ in simplest form. *(Lesson 4-5)* $\frac{4n}{a}$

63. Use place value and exponents to express 483 in expanded form. *(Lesson 4-2)*
$(4 \times 10^2) + (8 \times 10^1) + (3 \times 10^0)$

Find the perimeter and area of each rectangle. *(Lesson 3-7)*

64.   **46 in.; 112 in²** **65.**   **24 cm;**
                                           3 cm **27 cm²**
          7 in.

          16 in.   9 cm

Use the Distributive Property to rewrite each expression. *(Lesson 3-1)*

66. $3(5 + 9)$ **67.** $(8 + 1)2$ **68.** $6(b - 5)$ **69.** $(x + 4)7$
   $3 \cdot 5 + 3 \cdot 9$ $8 \cdot 2 + 1 \cdot 2$ $6b - 30$ $7x + 28$

Getting Ready for the Next Lesson **PREREQUISITE SKILL** Estimate each product.
(To review estimating products, see page 717.) **70–75. Sample answers are given.**

Example: $-3\frac{1}{4} \cdot 5\frac{7}{8} \approx -3 \cdot 6$ or -18 **71.** $-5 \cdot 4 = -20$

70. $1\frac{2}{3} \cdot 4\frac{1}{8}$ $2 \cdot 4 = 8$ **71.** $-5\frac{2}{5} \cdot 3\frac{4}{5}$ **72.** $2\frac{1}{4} \cdot 2\frac{1}{9}$ $2 \cdot 2 = 4$

73. $6\frac{7}{8} \cdot 1\frac{9}{10}$ $7 \cdot 2 = 14$ **74.** $9\frac{1}{8} \cdot \left(-4\frac{3}{4}\right)$ **75.** $15\frac{5}{7} \cdot 2\frac{1}{3}$ $16 \cdot 2 = 32$
                                   $9 \cdot (-5) = -45$

www.pre-alg.com/self_check_quiz   **Lesson 5-2** Rational Numbers **209**

Open-Ended Assessment

Speaking Have students explain how to express terminating and repeating decimals as fractions. They can pair off and explain their reasoning to a partner or engage in a whole class discussion. Each student should practice explaining until the listener understands the thinking.

Getting Ready for Lesson 5-3

PREREQUISITE SKILL Lesson 5-3 presents multiplication with rational numbers. Estimating products is a useful skill for this lesson. Exercises 70–75 should be used to determine your students' familiarity with estimating products of mixed numbers.

Answers

50. Let $N = 0.999…$ and let $10N = 9.999….$

$10N = 9.999…$
$- (N = 0.999…)$
$\overline{9N = 9}$

$\frac{9N}{9} = \frac{9}{9}$

$N = 1$

51. The set of rational numbers includes the set of natural numbers, whole numbers, and integers. In the same way, natural numbers are part of the set of whole numbers and the set of whole numbers is part of the set of integers. Answers should include the following.
- The number 5 belongs to the set of natural numbers, whole numbers, integers, and rational numbers.
- The number $\frac{1}{2}$ belongs only to the set of rational numbers.

1 Focus

 5-Minute Check Transparency 5-3 Use as a quiz or review of Lesson 5-2.

Mathematical Background notes are available for this lesson on page 198C.

How is multiplying fractions related to areas of rectangles?

The opening activity questions are repeated on page 238 of the *Chapter 5 Resource Masters.*

Reading to Learn Mathematics, p. 238 — ELL

Pre-Activity How is multiplying fractions related to areas of rectangles?
Do the activity at the top of page 210 in your textbook. Write your answers below.

a. The overlapping green area represents the product $\frac{2}{3}$ and $\frac{3}{4}$. What is the product? $\frac{6}{12}$ or $\frac{1}{2}$

Use an area model to find each product.

b. $\frac{1}{2} \cdot \frac{1}{3}$ $\frac{1}{6}$ c. $\frac{3}{5} \cdot \frac{1}{4}$ $\frac{3}{20}$ d. $\frac{3}{4} \cdot \frac{1}{3}$ $\frac{3}{12}$ or $\frac{1}{4}$

e. What is the relationship between the numerators and denominators of the factors and the numerator and denominator of the product? The numerator of the product equals the product of the numerators of the factors. The denominator of the product equals the product of the denominators of the factors.

Reading the Lesson 1–2. See students' work.

Write a definition and give an example of each new vocabulary phrase.

Vocabulary	Definition	Example
1. algebraic fraction		
2. dimensional analysis		

3. Draw a model that shows $\frac{2}{5} \cdot \frac{3}{4}$.

$\frac{6}{20}$ or $\frac{3}{10}$

Helping You Remember

4. Compare the process of multiplying numerical fractions and algebraic fractions. The process of multiplying numerical fractions and algebraic fractions is the same. The only difference is that algebraic fractions contain variables.

What You'll Learn

- Multiply fractions.
- Use dimensional analysis to solve problems.

Vocabulary
- dimensional analysis

How is multiplying fractions related to areas of rectangles?

To find $\frac{2}{3} \cdot \frac{3}{4}$, think of using an area model to find $\frac{2}{3}$ of $\frac{3}{4}$.

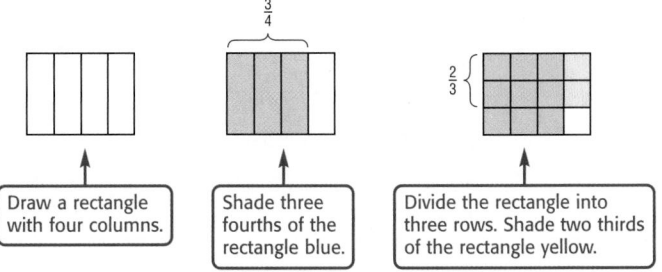

| Draw a rectangle with four columns. | Shade three fourths of the rectangle blue. | Divide the rectangle into three rows. Shade two thirds of the rectangle yellow. |

a. The overlapping green area represents the product of $\frac{2}{3}$ and $\frac{3}{4}$. What is the product? $\frac{6}{12}$ or $\frac{1}{2}$

Use an area model to find each product.

b. $\frac{1}{2} \cdot \frac{1}{3}$ $\frac{1}{6}$ c. $\frac{3}{5} \cdot \frac{1}{4}$ $\frac{3}{20}$ d. $\frac{3}{4} \cdot \frac{1}{3}$ $\frac{3}{12}$ or $\frac{1}{4}$

e. What is the relationship between the numerators and denominators of the factors and the numerator and denominator of the product?

e. The numerator of the product equals the product of the numerators of the factors. The denominator of the product equals the product of the denominators of the factors.

MULTIPLY FRACTIONS These and other similar models suggest the following rule for multiplying fractions.

Key Concept — Multiplying Fractions

- **Words** To multiply fractions, multiply the numerators and multiply the denominators.
- **Symbols** $\frac{a}{b} \cdot \frac{c}{d} = \frac{a \cdot c}{b \cdot d}$, where $b, d \neq 0$
- **Example** $\frac{1}{3} \cdot \frac{2}{5} = \frac{1 \cdot 2}{3 \cdot 5}$ or $\frac{2}{15}$

Example 1 Multiply Fractions

Find $\frac{2}{3} \cdot \frac{3}{4}$. Write the product in simplest form.

$\frac{2}{3} \cdot \frac{3}{4} = \frac{2 \cdot 3}{3 \cdot 4}$ ← Multiply the numerators.
← Multiply the denominators.

$= \frac{6}{12}$ or $\frac{1}{2}$ Simplify. The GCF of 6 and 12 is 6.

Study Tip

Look Back
To review **GCF**, see Lesson 4-4.

Resource Manager

 Workbooks and Reproducible Masters

Chapter 5 Resource Masters
- Study Guide and Intervention, p. 235
- Skills Practice, p. 236
- Practice, p. 237
- Reading to Learn Mathematics, p. 238
- Enrichment, p. 239
- Assessment, p. 289

Parent and Student Study Guide Workbook, p. 35
Science and Mathematics Lab Manual, pp. 11–14

 Transparencies
5-Minute Check Transparency 5-3
Answer Key Transparencies

Technology
Interactive Chalkboard

If the fractions have common factors in the numerators and denominators, you can simplify before you multiply.

Example 2 Simplify Before Multiplying

Find $\frac{4}{7} \cdot \frac{1}{6}$. Write the product in simplest form.

$$\frac{4}{7} \cdot \frac{1}{6} = \frac{\overset{2}{\cancel{4}}}{7} \cdot \frac{1}{\underset{3}{\cancel{6}}} \qquad \text{Divide 4 and 6 by their GCF, 2.}$$

$$= \frac{2 \cdot 1}{7 \cdot 3} \qquad \text{Multiply the numerators and multiply the denominators.}$$

$$= \frac{2}{21} \qquad \text{Simplify.}$$

Study Tip

Negative Fractions
$-\frac{5}{12}$ can be written as $\frac{-5}{12}$ or as $\frac{5}{-12}$.

Example 3 Multiply Negative Fractions

Find $-\frac{5}{12} \cdot \frac{3}{8}$. Write the product in simplest form.

$$-\frac{5}{12} \cdot \frac{3}{8} = \frac{-5}{\underset{4}{\cancel{12}}} \cdot \frac{\overset{1}{\cancel{3}}}{8} \qquad \text{Divide 3 and 12 by their GCF, 3.}$$

$$= \frac{-5 \cdot 1}{4 \cdot 8} \qquad \text{Multiply the numerators and multiply the denominators.}$$

$$= -\frac{5}{32} \qquad \text{Simplify.}$$

Example 4 Multiply Mixed Numbers

Find $1\frac{2}{5} \cdot 2\frac{1}{2}$. Write the product in simplest form.   Estimate: $1 \cdot 3 = 3$

$$1\frac{2}{5} \cdot 2\frac{1}{2} = \frac{7}{5} \cdot \frac{5}{2} \qquad \text{Rename } 1\frac{2}{5} \text{ as } \frac{7}{5} \text{ and rename } 2\frac{1}{2} \text{ as } \frac{5}{2}.$$

$$= \frac{7}{\underset{1}{\cancel{5}}} \cdot \frac{\overset{1}{\cancel{5}}}{2} \qquad \text{Divide by the GCF, 5.}$$

$$= \frac{7 \cdot 1}{1 \cdot 2} \qquad \text{Multiply.}$$

$$= \frac{7}{2} \text{ or } 3\frac{1}{2} \qquad \text{Simplify.}$$

ALGEBRA CONNECTION

TEACHING TIP
In this text, assume the denominator in an algebraic fraction is not equal to zero.

Algebraic fractions are multiplied in the same manner as numeric fractions.

Example 5 Multiply Algebraic Fractions

Find $\frac{2a}{b} \cdot \frac{b^2}{d}$. Write the product in simplest form.

$$\frac{2a}{b} \cdot \frac{b^2}{d} = \frac{2a}{\cancel{b}} \cdot \frac{\overset{1}{\cancel{b}} \cdot b}{d} \qquad \text{The GCF of } b \text{ and } b^2 \text{ is } b.$$

$$= \frac{2ab}{d} \qquad \text{Simplify.}$$

 www.pre-alg.com/extra_examples   **Lesson 5-3** Multiplying Rational Numbers   **211**

D A I L Y
INTERVENTION   **Unlocking Misconceptions**

- From Example 3, students may think that the negative sign in a fraction always goes with the numerator. Point out that $-\frac{5}{12} = \frac{-5}{12} = \frac{5}{-12}$, but NOT $\frac{-5}{-12}$.

- Point out that dimensional analysis is not just a math skill but one used in science classes such as chemistry and physics.

---

2 Teach

MULTIPLY FRACTIONS

In-Class Examples Power Point®

1 Find $\frac{2}{5} \cdot \frac{5}{8}$. Write the product in simplest form.
$\frac{1}{4}$

2 Find $\frac{8}{9} \cdot \frac{5}{6}$. Write the product in simplest form.
$\frac{20}{27}$

3 Find $-\frac{1}{4} \cdot \frac{2}{7}$. Write the product in simplest form.
$-\frac{1}{14}$

4 Find $1\frac{1}{2} \cdot 3\frac{2}{3}$. Write the product in simplest form.
$\frac{11}{2}$ or $5\frac{1}{2}$

5 Find $\frac{3p^2}{q} \cdot \frac{q^2}{r}$. Write the product in simplest form.
$\frac{3p^2 q}{r}$

✓ Skills Check

Multiply Fractions Ask students to find $\frac{4}{9} \cdot \frac{3}{8}$ two ways: simplify before multiplying and simplify after multiplying. Which do they prefer? Why?

DIMENSIONAL ANALYSIS

In-Class Example Power Point®

6 **RUNNING TRACK** The track at Cole's school is $\frac{1}{4}$ mile around. If Cole runs one lap in two minutes, how far (in miles) does he run in 30 minutes? $3\frac{3}{4}$ miles

Study Notebook

Have students—
- add the definitions/examples of the vocabulary terms to their Vocabulary Builder worksheets for Chapter 5.
- include any other item(s) that they find helpful in mastering the skills in this lesson.

DAILY INTERVENTION **FIND THE ERROR**
If students are having difficulty with Exercise 2, remind them that the numerator and denominator must be simplified by the same factor. You may want to show them that $\frac{18}{24} \neq \frac{9}{4}$ by expressing each fraction as a decimal.

About the Exercises . . .

Organization by Objective
- **Multiply Fractions:** 13–33, 38–45
- **Dimensional Analysis:** 34–37, 49–52

Odd/Even Assignments
Exercises 13–33 are structured so that students practice the same concepts whether they are assigned odd or even problems.

Assignment Guide

Basic: 13–41 odd, 45, 47, 53–56, 60–74

Average: 13–51 odd, 53–56, 60–74 (Optional: 57–59)

Advanced: 14–52 even, 53–68 (Optional: 69–74)

Answer

2. Terrence; Marie incorrectly divided the 18 in the numerator of the second fraction.

DIMENSIONAL ANALYSIS **Dimensional analysis** is the process of including units of measurement when you compute. You can use dimensional analysis to check whether your answers are reasonable.

Example 6 Use Dimensional Analysis

SPACE TRAVEL The landing speed of the space shuttle is about 216 miles per hour. How far does the shuttle travel in $\frac{1}{3}$ hour during landing?

Words	Distance equals the rate multiplied by the time.
Variables	Let d = distance, r = rate, and t = time.
Formula	

$d = rt$ Write the formula.

$d = 216$ miles per hour $\cdot \frac{1}{3}$ hour Include the units.

$= \dfrac{\overset{72}{\cancel{216} \text{ miles}}}{1 \text{ hour}} \cdot \dfrac{1}{\underset{1}{\cancel{3}}} \text{ hour}$ Divide by the common factors and units.

$= 72$ miles Simplify.

The space shuttle travels 72 miles in $\frac{1}{3}$ hour during landing.

CHECK The problem asks for the distance. When you divide the common units, the answer is expressed in miles. So, the answer is reasonable.

✓ **Concept Check** What is the final unit when you multiply feet per second by seconds? **feet**

Check for Understanding

Concept Check

1. **OPEN ENDED** Choose two rational numbers whose product is a number between 0 and 1. **Sample answer:** $\frac{1}{2}, \frac{1}{3}$

2. **FIND THE ERROR** Terrence and Marie are finding $\frac{5}{24} \cdot \frac{18}{25}$.

Terrence
$\dfrac{\overset{1}{\cancel{5}}}{\underset{4}{\cancel{24}}} \cdot \dfrac{\overset{3}{\cancel{18}}}{\underset{5}{\cancel{25}}} = \dfrac{3}{20}$

Marie
$\dfrac{\overset{1}{\cancel{5}}}{\underset{4}{\cancel{24}}} \cdot \dfrac{\overset{9}{\cancel{18}}}{\underset{5}{\cancel{25}}} = \dfrac{9}{20}$

Who is correct? Explain your reasoning. **See margin.**

Guided Practice

GUIDED PRACTICE KEY	
Exercises	Examples
3–6	1–3
7, 8	4
9–11	5
12	6

Find each product. Write in simplest form.

3. $\frac{1}{4} \cdot \frac{3}{5}$ $\frac{3}{20}$

4. $\frac{1}{2}\left(-\frac{5}{6}\right)$ $-\frac{5}{12}$

5. $-\frac{2}{3}\left(-\frac{5}{6}\right)$ $\frac{5}{9}$

6. $7\left(\frac{8}{21}\right)$ $2\frac{2}{3}$

7. $3\frac{1}{4} \cdot \frac{2}{11}$ $\frac{13}{22}$

8. $-5\frac{1}{3} \cdot 3\frac{3}{8}$ -18

ALGEBRA **Find each product. Write in simplest form.**

9. $\frac{2}{x} \cdot \frac{3x}{7}$ $\frac{6}{7}$

10. $\frac{a}{b} \cdot \frac{5b}{c}$ $\frac{5a}{c}$

11. $\frac{4t}{9r} \cdot \frac{18r}{t^2}$ $\frac{8}{t}$

Application

12. **TRAVEL** A car travels 65 miles per hour for $3\frac{1}{2}$ hours. What is the distance traveled? Use the formula $d = rt$ and show how you can divide by the common units. $d = 65 \frac{\text{mi}}{\text{h}} \cdot \frac{7}{2} \text{h}$ or $227\frac{1}{2}$ mi

---

DAILY INTERVENTION **Differentiated Instruction**

- **Intrapersonal** Ask students to extend the area model for multiplying fractions to multiplying a mixed number by a proper fraction, such as $4\frac{3}{5} \cdot \frac{2}{3}$. In their Math Journals, have students draw 5 rectangles, divide into fifths, and shade $4\frac{3}{5}$; divide each rectangle into thirds and shade two-thirds of each; state what the overlapping areas represent.

Practice and Apply

Homework Help

For Exercises	See Examples
13–24	1–3
25–33	4
37–42	5
47–50	6

Extra Practice
See page 734.

Find each product. Write in simplest form.

13. $\frac{6}{7} \cdot \frac{2}{7}$ $\frac{12}{49}$

14. $\frac{4}{9} \cdot \frac{2}{3}$ $\frac{8}{27}$

15. $\frac{1}{5}\left(-\frac{1}{8}\right)$ $-\frac{1}{40}$

16. $-\frac{3}{4} \cdot \frac{3}{5}$ $-\frac{9}{20}$

17. $\frac{5}{9} \cdot \frac{8}{25}$ $\frac{8}{45}$

18. $-\frac{1}{2}\left(-\frac{2}{7}\right)$ $\frac{1}{7}$

19. $\frac{2}{5} \cdot \frac{5}{6}$ $\frac{1}{3}$

20. $\frac{8}{9} \cdot \frac{27}{28}$ $\frac{6}{7}$

21. $\frac{3}{4}\left(-\frac{1}{3}\right)$ $-\frac{1}{4}$

22. $-\frac{7}{8} \cdot \frac{2}{5}$ $-\frac{7}{20}$

23. $\frac{3}{5} \cdot \frac{15}{24}$ $\frac{3}{8}$

24. $\frac{3}{32} \cdot \frac{24}{39}$ $\frac{3}{52}$

25. $2 \cdot \frac{7}{12}$ $1\frac{1}{6}$

26. $\frac{6}{15}(-3)$ $-1\frac{1}{5}$

27. $6\frac{2}{3} \cdot \frac{1}{2}$ $3\frac{1}{3}$

28. $\frac{5}{12} \cdot 3\frac{1}{9}$ $1\frac{8}{27}$

29. $2\frac{2}{6} \cdot 6\frac{2}{7}$ $14\frac{2}{3}$

30. $3\frac{1}{3} \cdot 2\frac{5}{8}$ $8\frac{3}{4}$

31. $-6\frac{2}{3}\left(-1\frac{1}{2}\right)$ 10

32. $1\frac{3}{7}\left(-9\frac{4}{5}\right)$ -14

33. $-1\frac{1}{4} \cdot 3\frac{5}{9}$ $-4\frac{4}{9}$

MEASUREMENT   Complete.

34. ___?___ feet = $\frac{5}{6}$ mile   **4400**
(*Hint:* 1 mile = 5280 feet)

35. ___?___ ounces = $\frac{3}{8}$ pound   **6**
(*Hint:* 1 pound = 16 ounces)

36. $\frac{2}{3}$ hour = ___?___ minutes   **40**

37. $\frac{3}{4}$ yard = ___?___ inches   **27**

ALGEBRA   Find each product. Write in simplest form.

38. $\frac{4a}{5} \cdot \frac{3}{a}$ $2\frac{2}{5}$

39. $\frac{3x}{y} \cdot \frac{9y}{x}$ 27

40. $\frac{12}{jk} \cdot \frac{3k}{4}$ $\frac{9}{j}$

41. $\frac{8}{c} \cdot \frac{c^2}{11}$ $\frac{8c}{11}$

42. $\frac{n}{18} \cdot \frac{6}{n^4}$ $\frac{1}{3n^3}$

★43. $\frac{x}{2z} \cdot \frac{2z^3}{3}$ $\frac{xz^2}{3}$

44. **ALGEBRA**   Evaluate x^2 if $x = -\frac{1}{2}$. $\frac{1}{4}$

45. **ALGEBRA**   Evaluate $(xy)^2$ if $x = \frac{3}{4}$ and $y = -\frac{4}{5}$. $\frac{9}{25}$

SCHOOL   For Exercises 46 and 47, use the graphic at the right.

46. Five-eighths of an eighth grade class are boys. Predict approximately what fraction of the eighth graders are boys who talk about school at home. $\left(Hint: 40\% = \frac{2}{5}\right)$ $\frac{1}{4}$

47. In a 12th grade class, five-ninths of the students are girls. Predict about what fraction of twelfth graders are girls who talk about school at home. $\left(Hint: 33\% = \frac{33}{100}\right)$ $\frac{11}{60}$

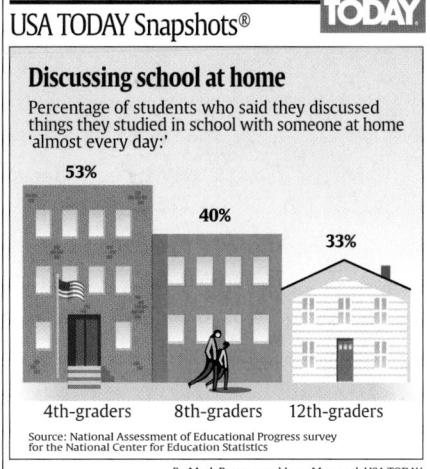

USA TODAY Snapshots®

Discussing school at home

Percentage of students who said they discussed things they studied in school with someone at home 'almost every day:'

53%   40%   33%

4th-graders   8th-graders   12th-graders

Source: National Assessment of Educational Progress survey for the National Center for Education Statistics

By Mark Pearson and Jerry Mosemak, USA TODAY

48. **GARDENING**   Jamal's lawn is $\frac{2}{3}$ of an acre. If $7\frac{1}{2}$ bags of fertilizer are needed for 1 acre, how much will he need to fertilize his lawn?   **5 bags**

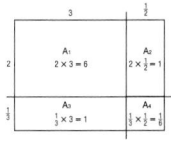

Study Guide and Intervention, p. 235

To multiply fractions, multiply the numerators and multiply the denominators. So $\frac{a}{b} \cdot \frac{c}{d} = \frac{ac}{bd}$, where b, $d \neq 0$. The fractions may be simplified either before or after multiplying.

Example   **Find each product. Write in simplest form.**

a. $\frac{8}{15} \cdot \frac{5}{7}$

$\frac{8}{15} \cdot \frac{5}{7} = \frac{8}{\overset{3}{\cancel{15}}} \cdot \frac{\overset{1}{\cancel{5}}}{7}$ Divide 5 and 15 by their GCF, 5.

$= \frac{8 \cdot 1}{3 \cdot 7}$ Multiply.

$= \frac{8}{21}$ Simplify.

b. $7\frac{1}{2} \cdot 2\frac{2}{3}$

$7\frac{1}{2} \cdot 2\frac{2}{3} = \frac{15}{2} \cdot \frac{8}{3}$ Rename mixed numbers as improper fractions.

$= \frac{\overset{5}{\cancel{15}}}{\underset{1}{\cancel{2}}} \cdot \frac{\overset{4}{\cancel{8}}}{\underset{1}{\cancel{3}}}$ Divide 15 and 3 by 3, and 8 and 2 by 2.

$= \frac{5 \cdot 4}{1 \cdot 1}$ Multiply.

$= \frac{20}{1}$ or 20   Simplify.

Exercises

Find each product. Write in simplest form.

1. $\frac{1}{2} \cdot \frac{3}{5}$ $\frac{3}{10}$

2. $-\frac{8}{9} \cdot \frac{5}{16}$ $-\frac{5}{18}$

3. $\frac{4}{5} \cdot \frac{5}{2}$ 2

4. $\frac{3}{10} \cdot \left(-\frac{1}{4}\right)$ $-\frac{3}{40}$

5. $\frac{7}{9} \cdot \frac{11}{20}$ $\frac{77}{180}$

6. $\frac{2}{5} \cdot (-5)$ -2

7. $-4\frac{4}{5} \cdot 1\frac{1}{8}$ $-5\frac{2}{5}$

8. $1\frac{5}{9} \cdot 10\frac{1}{2}$ 18

9. $-2\frac{1}{8} \cdot \left(-4\frac{4}{7}\right)$ $9\frac{5}{7}$

10. $\frac{5x}{y} \cdot \frac{y^3}{z^2}$ $\frac{5xy^2}{z^2}$

Skills Practice, p. 236 and Practice, p. 237 (shown)

Find each product. Write in simplest form.

1. $\frac{3}{4} \cdot \frac{2}{3}$ $\frac{1}{2}$

2. $\frac{3}{7} \cdot \frac{21}{39}$ $\frac{3}{13}$

3. $-\frac{3}{4} \cdot \frac{10}{27}$ $-\frac{5}{18}$

4. $\frac{11}{14} \cdot \frac{7}{33}$ $\frac{1}{6}$

5. $-\frac{18}{24} \cdot \frac{3}{4}$ $-\frac{9}{16}$

6. $\frac{9}{10} \cdot \frac{20}{21}$ $\frac{6}{7}$

7. $-50 \cdot \frac{3}{1000}$ $-\frac{3}{20}$

8. $\frac{16}{17}\left(-\frac{5}{8}\right)$ $-\frac{10}{17}$

9. $-\frac{1}{2} \cdot \left(-\frac{20}{27}\right)$ $\frac{10}{27}$

10. $-\frac{14}{15}\left(-\frac{15}{28}\right)$ $\frac{1}{3}$

11. $4\frac{4}{7} \cdot 9\frac{1}{3}$ $42\frac{2}{3}$

12. $-2\frac{14}{25} \cdot 4\frac{3}{8}$ $-11\frac{1}{5}$

13. $4\frac{1}{8} \cdot \left(-1\frac{5}{11}\right)$ -6

14. $-5 \cdot \frac{17}{25}$ $-3\frac{2}{5}$

15. $2\frac{9}{10} \cdot \frac{1}{5}$ $3\frac{12}{25}$

16. $\frac{6m}{13} \cdot \frac{2}{mn}$ $\frac{12}{13n}$

17. $\frac{p}{3} \cdot \frac{p}{q}$ $\frac{p^2}{3q}$

18. $\frac{2u}{v} \cdot \frac{3}{u}$ $\frac{6}{v^2}$

19. $\frac{4x}{3y} \cdot \frac{9y}{2x}$ 6

20. $\frac{2a}{c} \cdot \frac{c}{2d}$ $\frac{ac}{bd}$

21. $\frac{rs}{9t} \cdot \frac{3}{s^2} \cdot \frac{r}{3st}$

22. $2x \cdot \frac{1}{4x^2}$ $\frac{1}{2x}$

23. $\frac{x^2}{4y} \cdot \frac{16y^2}{3x}$ $\frac{4xy}{3}$

24. $\frac{2}{r} \cdot \frac{3}{r}$ $\frac{6}{r^2}$

25. **WEIGHTS**   How many ounces are in $3\frac{3}{4}$ pounds?   60 oz

26. **FOOTBALL**   The total length of 17.6 football fields equals 1 mile. How long is a mile? (*Hint:* length of a football field = 100 yd)   1760 yd or 5280 ft

27. **AIRPLANES**   The fastest airliner, the Concorde, has the capability of cruising at speeds of up to 1450 mph. While cruising at this top speed, how far would the Concorde travel in $2\frac{1}{2}$ hours?   3625 mi

---

Enrichment, p. 239

Visualizing the Distributive Property

The Distributive Property can be used to demonstrate the product of two mixed numbers. The product of $3\frac{1}{2} \times 2\frac{1}{3}$ is modeled by the rectangle below. Each factor has been rewritten as a sum of a whole number and a fraction, thus creating four rectangles in the area model.

Find the area of each rectangle.

$A_1 = 2 \times 3$ or 6

$A_2 = 2 \times \frac{1}{2}$ or 1

$A_3 = \frac{1}{3} \times 3$ or 1

$A_4 = \frac{1}{3} \times \frac{1}{2}$ or $\frac{1}{6}$

Find the sum of the areas.

$A = 6 + 1 + 1 + \frac{1}{6}$ or $8\frac{1}{6}$

Therefore, $3\frac{1}{2} \times 2\frac{1}{3} = 8\frac{1}{6}$.

For each product, model the factors as the lengths of the sides of a rectangle and find the product.

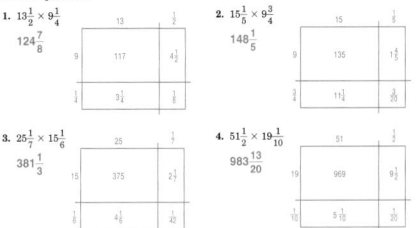

1. $13\frac{1}{2} \times 9\frac{1}{4}$ $124\frac{7}{8}$

2. $15\frac{1}{5} \times 9\frac{3}{4}$ $148\frac{1}{5}$

3. $25\frac{1}{7} \times 15\frac{1}{6}$ $381\frac{1}{3}$

4. $51\frac{1}{4} \times 19\frac{1}{10}$ $983\frac{13}{20}$

Open-Ended Assessment

Modeling Ask students to use an area model to show $\frac{7}{8} \cdot \frac{4}{5}$. Verify the result by multiplying. Students should explain the process of simplifying their answers.

Getting Ready for Lesson 5-4

PREREQUISITE SKILL Lesson 5-4 presents division of rational numbers. Exercises 69–74 should be used to determine your students' familiarity with finding greatest common factors, which is used in simplifying answers.

Assessment Options

Quiz (Lessons 5-1 through 5-3) is available on p. 289 of the *Chapter 5 Resource Masters*.

Answer

54. Fractions can be used to represent parts of rectangles. The product of the fractions equals a portion of the rectangle's area. Answers should include the following.

- A rectangle that is divided into rows and columns; one fraction represents the fraction of columns that are shaded and another fraction represents the fraction of rows that are shaded.

- The product of the fractions is the overlapping shaded area.

More About...

Converting Measures

In 1998, a Mars probe was lost because scientists did not convert a customary measure of force to a metric measure.

Source: *Newsday*

CONVERTING MEASURES Use dimensional analysis and the fractions in the table to find each missing measure.

★ **49.** 5 inches = __?__ centimeters **12.7**

★ **50.** 10 kilometers = __?__ miles **6.2**

★ **51.** 26.3 centimeters = __?__ inches **10.257**

★ **52.** $8\frac{2}{3}$ square feet = __?__ square meters **0.78**

Conversion Factors	
Customary → Metric	Metric → Customary
$\frac{2.54 \text{ cm}}{1 \text{ in.}}$	$\frac{0.39 \text{ in.}}{1 \text{ cm}}$
$\frac{1.61 \text{ km}}{1 \text{ mi}}$	$\frac{0.62 \text{ mi}}{1 \text{ km}}$
$\frac{0.09 \text{ m}^2}{1 \text{ ft}^2}$	$\frac{10.76 \text{ ft}^2}{1 \text{ m}^2}$

53. CRITICAL THINKING Use the digits 3, 4, 5, 6, 8, and 9 to make true sentences. **a–b. Sample answers are given.**

a. $\frac{\square}{\square} \times \frac{\square}{\square} = \frac{6}{5}$ $\frac{8}{4} \times \frac{3}{5}$

b. $\frac{\square}{\square} \times \frac{\square}{\square} = \frac{5}{8}$ $\frac{3}{4} \times \frac{5}{6}$

54. **WRITING IN MATH** Answer the question that was posed at the beginning of the lesson. **See margin.**

How is multiplying fractions related to areas of rectangles?

Include the following in your answer:

- an area model of a multiplication problem involving fractions, and
- an explanation of how rectangles can be used to show multiplication of fractions.

Standardized Test Practice
Ⓐ Ⓑ Ⓒ Ⓓ

55. The product of $\frac{8}{15}$ and $\frac{3}{8}$ is a number **A**

Ⓐ between 0 and 1. Ⓑ between 1 and 2.

Ⓒ between 2 and 3. Ⓓ greater than 3.

56. What is the equivalent length of a chain that is 52 feet long? **C**

Ⓐ 4 yards 5 feet Ⓑ 4.5 yards

Ⓒ 17 yards 1 foot Ⓓ 17.1 yards

Extending the Lesson

Evaluate each expression if $n = 2$ and $p = -4$.

57. $5n^{-3}$ $\frac{5}{8}$

58. $7 \cdot 3^p$ $\frac{7}{81}$

59. $13n^{-1}p^{-2}$ $\frac{13}{32}$

Maintain Your Skills

Mixed Review

Write each decimal as a fraction or mixed number in simplest form. *(Lesson 5-2)*

60. 0.18 $\frac{9}{50}$

61. −0.2 $-\frac{1}{5}$

62. 3.04 $3\frac{1}{25}$

63. $0.\overline{7}$ $\frac{7}{9}$

Write each fraction or mixed number as a decimal. Use a bar to show a repeating decimal. *(Lesson 5-1)*

64. $\frac{17}{20}$ **0.85**

65. $\frac{1}{6}$ $0.1\overline{6}$

66. $2\frac{2}{11}$ $2.\overline{18}$

67. $-4\frac{7}{8}$ **−4.875**

68. ALGEBRA What is the product of x^2 and x^4? *(Lesson 4-6)* x^6

Getting Ready for the Next Lesson

PREREQUISITE SKILL Find the GCF of each pair of monomials.
*(To review the **GCF of monomials**, see Lesson 4-4.)*

69. 8n, 16n **8n**

70. 5ab, 8b **b**

71. 12t, 10t **2t**

72. 2rs, 3rs **rs**

73. 9k, 27 **9**

74. $4p^2$, 6p **2p**

Dividing Rational Numbers

What You'll Learn

- Divide fractions using multiplicative inverses.
- Use dimensional analysis to solve problems.

Vocabulary
- multiplicative inverses
- reciprocals

How is dividing by a fraction related to multiplying?

The model shows $4 \div \frac{1}{3}$. Each of the 4 circles is divided into $\frac{1}{3}$-sections.

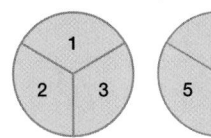 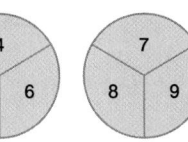 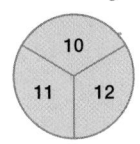

There are twelve $\frac{1}{3}$-sections, so $4 \div \frac{1}{3} = 12$. Another way to find the number of sections is $4 \times 3 = 12$.

Use a model to find each quotient. Then write a related multiplication problem. c. $12; 3 \times 4 = 12$

a. $2 \div \frac{1}{3}$ $6; 2 \times 3 = 6$ b. $4 \div \frac{1}{2}$ $8; 4 \times 2 = 8$ c. $3 \div \frac{1}{4}$

d. **Make a conjecture** about how dividing by a fraction is related to multiplying.

d. Dividing by a fraction with 1 in the numerator is the same as multiplying by the number that is in the denominator.

DIVIDE FRACTIONS
Rational numbers have all of the properties of whole numbers and integers. Another property is shown by $\frac{1}{3} \cdot \frac{3}{1} = 1$. Two numbers whose product is 1 are called **multiplicative inverses** or **reciprocals**.

Study Tip

Reading Math
Multiplicative inverse and reciprocal are different terms for the same concept. They may be used interchangeably.

> **Key Concept** — *Inverse Property of Multiplication*
>
> - **Words** The product of a number and its multiplicative inverse is 1.
> - **Symbols** For every number $\frac{a}{b}$, where $a, b \neq 0$,
>   there is exactly one number $\frac{b}{a}$ such that $\frac{a}{b} \cdot \frac{b}{a} = 1$.
> - **Example** $\frac{3}{4}$ and $\frac{4}{3}$ are multiplicative inverses because $\frac{3}{4} \cdot \frac{4}{3} = 1$.

Example 1 Find Multiplicative Inverses

Find the multiplicative inverse of each number.

a. $-\frac{3}{8}$

$-\frac{3}{8}\left(-\frac{8}{3}\right) = 1$ The product is 1.

The multiplicative inverse or reciprocal of $-\frac{3}{8}$ is $-\frac{8}{3}$.

b. $2\frac{1}{5}$

$2\frac{1}{5} = \frac{11}{5}$ Write as an improper fraction.

$\frac{11}{5} \cdot \frac{5}{11} = 1$ The product is 1.

The reciprocal of $2\frac{1}{5}$ is $\frac{5}{11}$.

Lesson 5-4 Dividing Rational Numbers **215**

---

1 Focus

5-Minute Check Transparency 5-4 Use as a quiz or review of Lesson 5-3.

Mathematical Background notes are available for this lesson on page 198C.

How is dividing by a fraction related to multiplying?

The opening activity questions are repeated on page 243 of the *Chapter 5 Resource Masters.*

Reading to Learn Mathematics, p. 243   ELL

Pre-Activity   *How is dividing by a fraction related to multiplying?*

Do the activity at the top of page 215 in your textbook. Write your answers below. Use a model to find each quotient. Then write a related multiplication problem.

a. $2 \div \frac{1}{3}$ 6; 2 × 3 = 6

b. $4 \div \frac{1}{2}$ 8; 4 × 2 = 8

c. $3 \div \frac{1}{4}$ 12; 3 × 4 = 12

d. Make a conjecture about how dividing by a fraction is related to multiplying.   Dividing by a fraction with 1 in the numerator is the same as multiplying by the number that is in the denominator.

Reading the Lesson   1–2. See students' work.

Write a definition and give an example of each new vocabulary word or phrase.

Vocabulary	Definition	Example
1. multiplicative inverses		
2. reciprocals		

Helping You Remember

3. Explain in your own words how to relate dividing rational numbers to multiplication. Give an example.   Sample answer: Dividing by a fraction is equivalent to multiplying by its reciprocal. $8 \div 4 = \frac{8}{1} \cdot \frac{1}{4}; \frac{2}{5} \div \frac{3}{5} = \frac{2}{5} \cdot \frac{5}{3}$

Teaching Tip Remind students that for any numbers a, b, c ($b \neq 0$), $a \div b = c$ if and only if $b \cdot c = a$. For example, $10 \div 5 = 2$ since $2 \cdot 5 = 10$.

Resource Manager

Workbooks and Reproducible Masters

Chapter 5 Resource Masters
- Study Guide and Intervention, p. 240
- Skills Practice, p. 241
- Practice, p. 242
- Reading to Learn Mathematics, p. 243
- Enrichment, p. 244

Parent and Student Study Guide Workbook, p. 36
School-to-Career Masters, p. 10

Transparencies
5-Minute Check Transparency 5-4
Real-World Transparency 5
Answer Key Transparencies

Technology
Interactive Chalkboard

DIVIDE FRACTIONS

In-Class Examples Power Point®

1 Find the multiplicative inverse of each number.

a. $\frac{6}{7}$ $\frac{7}{6}$

b. $3\frac{2}{5}$ $\frac{5}{17}$

2 Find $\frac{4}{5} \div \frac{3}{10}$. Write the quotient in simplest form.

$\frac{8}{3}$ or $2\frac{2}{3}$

3 Find $\frac{5}{6} \div 3$. Write the quotient in simplest form.

$\frac{5}{18}$

Teaching Tip Encourage students to check their answers using multiplication. In Example 3, $\frac{5}{8} \div 6 = \frac{5}{48}$; $\frac{5}{48} \cdot 6 = \frac{5}{8}$.

4 Find $4\frac{2}{3} \div -3\frac{1}{9}$. Write the quotient in simplest form.

$-\frac{3}{2}$ or $-1\frac{1}{2}$

5 Find $\frac{5x}{8y} \div \frac{10}{16y}$. Write the quotient in simplest form. *x*

✓ Skills Check

Divide Fractions Have students explain how to divide by an algebraic fraction. Then ask them to discuss the similarities and differences between dividing by an algebraic fraction and dividing by a numerical fraction.

Dividing by 2 is the same as multiplying by $\frac{1}{2}$, its multiplicative inverse. This is true for any rational number.

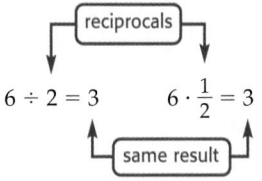

reciprocals

$6 \div 2 = 3$ $6 \cdot \frac{1}{2} = 3$

same result

Key Concept — Dividing Fractions

- **Words**   To divide by a fraction, multiply by its multiplicative inverse.
- **Symbols** $\frac{a}{b} \div \frac{c}{d} = \frac{a}{b} \cdot \frac{d}{c}$, where $b, c, d \neq 0$
- **Example** $\frac{1}{4} \div \frac{5}{7} = \frac{1}{4} \cdot \frac{7}{5}$ or $\frac{7}{20}$

Concept Check: No; 0 does not have a reciprocal because the product of 0 and any number is 0.

✓ **Concept Check**   Does every rational number have a multiplicative inverse? Explain.

Example 2 Divide by a Fraction

Find $\frac{1}{3} \div \frac{5}{9}$. Write the quotient in simplest form.

$\frac{1}{3} \div \frac{5}{9} = \frac{1}{3} \cdot \frac{9}{5}$ Multiply by the multiplicative inverse of $\frac{5}{9}$, $\frac{9}{5}$.

$= \frac{1}{\overset{1}{3}} \cdot \frac{\overset{3}{9}}{5}$ Divide 3 and 9 by their GCF, 3.

$= \frac{3}{5}$ Simplify.

Study Tip

Dividing By a Whole Number
When dividing by a whole number, always rename it as an improper fraction first. Then multiply by its reciprocal.

Example 3 Divide by a Whole Number

Find $\frac{5}{8} \div 6$. Write the quotient in simplest form.

$\frac{5}{8} \div 6 = \frac{5}{8} \div \frac{6}{1}$ Write 6 as $\frac{6}{1}$.

$= \frac{5}{8} \cdot \frac{1}{6}$ Multiply by the multiplicative inverse of $\frac{6}{1}$, $\frac{1}{6}$.

$= \frac{5}{48}$ Multiply the numerators and multiply the denominators.

TEACHING TIP

You may want to encourage students to write the negative sign with the numerator so that it does not get left out in the final answer.

$\frac{-15}{2}$

Example 4 Divide by a Mixed Number

Find $-7\frac{1}{2} \div 2\frac{1}{10}$. Write the quotient in simplest form.

$-7\frac{1}{2} \div 2\frac{1}{10} = -\frac{15}{2} \div \frac{21}{10}$ Rename the mixed numbers as improper fractions.

$= -\frac{15}{2} \cdot \frac{10}{21}$ Multiply by the multiplicative inverse of $\frac{21}{10}$, $\frac{10}{21}$.

$= -\frac{\overset{5}{15}}{\overset{1}{2}} \cdot \frac{\overset{5}{10}}{\overset{7}{21}}$ Divide out common factors.

$= -\frac{25}{7}$ or $-3\frac{4}{7}$ Simplify.

You can divide algebraic fractions in the same way that you divide numerical fractions.

Example 5 Divide by an Algebraic Fraction

Find $\frac{3xy}{4} \div \frac{2x}{8}$. Write the quotient in simplest form.

$\frac{3xy}{4} \div \frac{2x}{8} = \frac{3xy}{4} \cdot \frac{8}{2x}$ Multiply by the multiplicative inverse of $\frac{2x}{8}$, $\frac{8}{2x}$.

$= \frac{3xy}{\underset{1}{4}} \cdot \frac{\overset{2}{8}}{\underset{1}{2x}}$ Divide out common factors.

$= \frac{6y}{2}$ or $3y$ Simplify.

DIMENSIONAL ANALYSIS   Dimensional analysis is a useful way to examine the solution of division problems.

Example 6 Use Dimensional Analysis

CHEERLEADING   How many cheerleading uniforms can be made with $22\frac{3}{4}$ yards of fabric if each uniform requires $\frac{7}{8}$-yard?

To find how many uniforms, divide $22\frac{3}{4}$ by $\frac{7}{8}$.

$22\frac{3}{4} \div \frac{7}{8} = 22\frac{3}{4} \cdot \frac{8}{7}$ Multiply by the reciprocal of $\frac{7}{8}$, $\frac{8}{7}$.

$= \frac{91}{4} \cdot \frac{8}{7}$ Write $22\frac{3}{4}$ as an improper fraction.

$= \frac{\overset{13}{91}}{\underset{1}{4}} \cdot \frac{\overset{2}{8}}{\underset{1}{7}}$ Divide out common factors.

$= 26$ Simplify.

So, 26 uniforms can be made.

CHECK   Use dimensional analysis to examine the units.

$$\text{yards} \div \frac{\text{yards}}{\text{uniform}} = \text{yards} \cdot \frac{\text{uniform}}{\text{yards}} \qquad \text{Divide out the units.}$$
$$= \text{uniform} \qquad \text{Simplify.}$$

The result is expressed as uniforms. This agrees with your answer of 26 uniforms.

More About. . .

Cheerleading
In the 1930s, both men and women cheerleaders began wearing cheerleading uniforms.
Source: www.umn.edu

TEACHING TIP
In Example 6, point out that students could also include the units when solving the problem. Stress that the reciprocal of $\frac{\text{yards}}{\text{uniform}}$ is $\frac{\text{uniform}}{\text{yards}}$.

Check for Understanding

Concept Check   1. **Explain** how reciprocals are used in division of fractions.
   Dividing by a fraction is the same as multiplying by its reciprocal.
2. **OPEN ENDED**   Write a division expression that can be simplified by using the multiplicative inverse $\frac{7}{5}$. Sample answer: $14 \div \frac{5}{7}$

DAILY
INTERVENTION   **Differentiated Instruction**

• **Interpersonal** Have students work in pairs. Each student makes up a division of fractions problem and works out the solution. Then the partners trade problems. They compare results and the methods they used.

DIMENSIONAL ANALYSIS

In-Class Example   Power Point®

6 **TRAVEL** How many gallons of gas are needed to travel $78\frac{3}{4}$ miles if a car gets $25\frac{1}{2}$ miles per gallon? $\frac{105}{34}$ or $3\frac{3}{34}$ gallons

Teaching Tip Dimensional analysis, examining the units, can help students set up the problem correctly. The values in the problem must be divided so that the correct unit remains.

3 Practice/Apply

Study Notebook

Have students—
• add the definitions/examples of the vocabulary terms to their Vocabulary Builder worksheets for Chapter 5.
• include any other item(s) that they find helpful in mastering the skills in this lesson.

About the Exercises . . .

Organization by Objective
• **Divide Fractions:** 16–45, 48–49
• **Dimensional Analysis:** 46–47, 50–51

Odd/Even Assignments
Exercises 16–51 are structured so that students practice the same concepts whether they are assigned odd or even problems.

Assignment Guide

Basic: 17–43 odd, 51–74
Average: 17–51 odd, 52–74
Advanced: 16–50 even, 52–65 (Optional: 66–74)

218 Chapter 5 Rational Numbers

Guided Practice Find the multiplicative inverse of each number.

3. $\frac{4}{5}$ $\frac{5}{4}$

4. -16 $-\frac{1}{16}$

5. $3\frac{1}{8}$ $\frac{8}{25}$

Find each quotient. Write in simplest form.

6. $\frac{1}{2} \div \frac{6}{7}$ $\frac{7}{12}$

7. $-\frac{2}{3} \div \left(-\frac{5}{6}\right)$ $\frac{4}{5}$

8. $\frac{7}{9} \div \frac{2}{3}$ $1\frac{1}{6}$

9. $7\frac{1}{3} \div 5$ $1\frac{7}{15}$

10. $-\frac{8}{9} \div 3\frac{1}{5}$ $-\frac{5}{18}$

11. $2\frac{1}{6} \div \left(-1\frac{1}{5}\right)$ $-1\frac{29}{36}$

ALGEBRA Find each quotient. Write in simplest form.

12. $\frac{14}{n} \div \frac{1}{n}$ 14

13. $\frac{ab}{4} \div \frac{b}{6}$ $\frac{3a}{2}$

14. $\frac{x^2}{5} \div \frac{ax}{2}$ $\frac{2x}{5a}$

Application 15. **CARPENTRY** How many boards, each 2 feet 8 inches long, can be cut from a board 16 feet long if there is no waste? **6 boards**

★ indicates increased difficulty

Practice and Apply

Find the multiplicative inverse of each number.

16. $\frac{6}{11}$ $\frac{11}{6}$

17. $-\frac{1}{5}$ $-\frac{5}{1}$ or -5

18. -7 $-\frac{1}{7}$

19. 24 $\frac{1}{24}$

20. $5\frac{1}{4}$ $\frac{4}{21}$

21. $-3\frac{2}{9}$ $-\frac{9}{29}$

Find each quotient. Write in simplest form.

22. $\frac{1}{4} \div \frac{3}{5}$ $\frac{5}{12}$

23. $\frac{2}{9} \div \frac{1}{4}$ $\frac{8}{9}$

24. $-\frac{1}{2} \div \frac{5}{6}$ $-\frac{3}{5}$

25. $\frac{6}{11} \div \left(-\frac{4}{5}\right)$ $-\frac{15}{22}$

26. $\frac{8}{9} \div \frac{4}{3}$ $\frac{2}{3}$

27. $\frac{7}{8} \div \frac{14}{15}$ $\frac{15}{16}$

28. $\frac{3}{4} \div \frac{3}{4}$ 1

29. $\frac{2}{9} \div \left(-\frac{2}{9}\right)$ -1

30. $\frac{3}{5} \div \frac{5}{9}$ $1\frac{2}{25}$

31. $\frac{3}{10} \div \frac{1}{5}$ $1\frac{1}{2}$

32. $12 \div \frac{4}{9}$ 27

33. $-8 \div \frac{4}{5}$ -10

34. $-\frac{5}{8} \div (-4)$ $\frac{5}{32}$

35. $6\frac{2}{3} \div 5$ $1\frac{1}{3}$

36. $-1\frac{1}{9} \div \frac{2}{3}$ $-1\frac{2}{3}$

37. $-\frac{2}{3} \div \left(-\frac{1}{3}\right)$ 2

38. $3\frac{3}{10} \div 1\frac{5}{6}$ $1\frac{4}{5}$

39. $7\frac{1}{2} \div \left(-1\frac{1}{5}\right)$ $-6\frac{1}{4}$

ALGEBRA Find each quotient. Write in simplest form.

40. $\frac{a}{7} \div \frac{a}{42}$ 6

41. $\frac{10}{3x} \div \frac{5}{2x}$ $\frac{4}{3}$

42. $\frac{c}{8} \div \frac{cd}{5}$ $\frac{5}{8d}$

43. $\frac{5s}{t} \div \frac{6rs}{t}$ $\frac{5}{6r}$

44. $\frac{k^3}{9} \div \frac{k}{24}$ $\frac{8k^2}{3}$

★ 45. $\frac{2s}{t^2} \div \frac{st^3}{8}$ $\frac{16}{t^5}$

46. **COOKING** How many $\frac{1}{4}$-pound hamburgers can be made from $2\frac{3}{4}$ pounds of ground beef? **11 hamburgers**

★ 47. **SEWING** How many 9-inch ribbons can be cut from $1\frac{1}{2}$ yards of ribbon? **6 ribbons**

ALGEBRA Evaluate each expression.

48. $m \div n$ if $m = -\frac{8}{9}$ and $n = \frac{7}{18}$ $-2\frac{2}{7}$

★ 49. $r^2 \div s^2$ if $r = -\frac{3}{4}$ and $s = 1\frac{1}{3}$ $\frac{81}{256}$

For Exercises 50 and 51, solve each problem. Then check your answer using dimensional analysis.

50. **TRAVEL** How long would it take a train traveling 80 miles per hour to go 280 miles? **3.5 h**

51. **FOOD** The average young American woman drinks $1\frac{1}{2}$ cans of cola each day. At this rate, in how many days would it take to drink a total of 12 cans? **Source:** U.S. Department of Agriculture **8 days**

52. **CRITICAL THINKING** **b. The quotient increases.**
a. Divide $\frac{3}{4}$ by $\frac{1}{2}, \frac{1}{4}, \frac{1}{8}$, and $\frac{1}{12}$. $1\frac{1}{2}$, **3, 6, 9**
b. What happens to the quotient as the value of the divisor decreases?
c. **Make a conjecture** about the quotient when you divide $\frac{3}{4}$ by fractions that increase in value. Test your conjecture. **The quotient decreases.**

53. **WRITING IN MATH** Answer the question that was posed at the beginning of the lesson. **See margin.**

How is dividing by a fraction related to multiplying?
Include the following in your answer:
• a model of a whole number divided by a fraction, and
• an explanation of how division of fractions is related to multiplication.

54. Carla baby-sits for $2\frac{1}{4}$ hours and earns \$11.25. What is her rate? **D**
Ⓐ \$4.00/h Ⓑ \$5.50/h Ⓒ \$4.50/h Ⓓ \$5.00/h

55. What is $\frac{3}{10}$ divided by $1\frac{4}{5}$? **C**
Ⓐ $\frac{1}{2}$ Ⓑ $\frac{3}{8}$ Ⓒ $\frac{1}{6}$ Ⓓ $\frac{27}{50}$

Maintain Your Skills

Mixed Review Find each product. Write in simplest form. *(Lesson 5-3)* 59. $-\frac{10}{21}$
56. $\frac{3}{5} \cdot \frac{1}{3}$ $\frac{1}{5}$
57. $\frac{2}{9} \cdot \frac{15}{16}$ $\frac{5}{24}$
58. $2\frac{4}{5} \cdot \frac{3}{8}$ $1\frac{1}{20}$
59. $-\frac{5}{12} \cdot 1\frac{1}{7}$

Identify all sets to which each number belongs. *(Lesson 5-2)*
60. 16 **N, W, I, Q**
61. $-2.8888\ldots$ **Q**
62. $0.\overline{9}$ **Q**
63. $5.121221222\ldots$ **not rational**

64. Write the prime factorization of 150. Use exponents for repeated factors. *(Lesson 4-3)* $2 \cdot 3 \cdot 5^2$

65. **ALGEBRA** Solve $3x - 5 = 16$. *(Lesson 3-5)* **7**

Getting Ready for the Next Lesson **PREREQUISITE SKILL** Write each improper fraction as a mixed number in simplest form. *(To review simplifying fractions, see Lesson 4-5.)*
66. $\frac{9}{4}$ $2\frac{1}{4}$
67. $\frac{8}{7}$ $1\frac{1}{7}$
68. $\frac{17}{2}$ $8\frac{1}{2}$
69. $\frac{25}{4}$ $6\frac{1}{4}$
70. $\frac{24}{5}$ $4\frac{4}{5}$
71. $\frac{22}{6}$ $3\frac{2}{3}$
72. $\frac{15}{6}$ $2\frac{1}{2}$
73. $\frac{30}{18}$ $1\frac{2}{3}$
74. $\frac{18}{15}$ $1\frac{1}{5}$

Open-Ended Assessment
Writing Have students write an outline describing a procedure to divide fractions. Students should include at least one example to illustrate their ideas.

Getting Ready for Lesson 5-5
PREREQUISITE SKILL Lesson 5-5 presents adding and subtracting like fractions. Exercises 66–74 should be used to determine your students' familiarity with simplifying fractions.

Answer

53. Dividing by a fraction is the same as multiplying by its reciprocal. Answers should include the following.
• For example, a model of two circles, each divided into four sections, represents $2 \div \frac{1}{4}$. Since there are 8 sections, $2 \div \frac{1}{4} = 8$.
• Division of fractions and multiplication of fractions are inverse operations. So, $2 \div \frac{1}{4}$ equals $2 \cdot 4$ or 8.

1 Focus

5-Minute Check Transparency 5-5 Use as a quiz or review of Lesson 5-4.

Mathematical Background notes are available for this lesson on page 198D.

Why are fractions important when taking measurements?

The opening activity questions are repeated on page 248 of the *Chapter 5 Resource Masters*.

a. $\frac{4}{8}$ or $\frac{1}{2}$ in.

b. $\frac{7}{8}$ in.

c. $\frac{8}{8}$ or 1 in.

d. $\frac{3}{8}$ in.

Reading to Learn Mathematics, p. 248   ELL

Pre-Activity *Why are fractions important when taking measurements?*

Do the activity at the top of page 220 in your textbook. Write your answers below. Use a ruler to find each measure.

a. $\frac{1}{8}$ in. + $\frac{3}{8}$ in. $\frac{4}{8}$ or $\frac{1}{2}$ in.

b. $\frac{3}{8}$ in. + $\frac{4}{8}$ in. $\frac{7}{8}$ in.

c. $\frac{4}{8}$ in. + $\frac{4}{8}$ in. $\frac{8}{8}$ or 1 in.

d. $\frac{6}{8}$ in. − $\frac{3}{8}$ in. $\frac{3}{8}$ in.

Reading the Lesson

1. Like fractions have like __denominators__.

2. Find two fractions whose sum is $\frac{7}{8}$. Sample answer: $\frac{3}{8}, \frac{4}{8}$

3. Find two fractions whose difference is $\frac{2}{7}$. Sample answer: $\frac{6}{7}, \frac{4}{7}$

4. To add or subtract like fractions, you __add or subtract__ the numerators and keep the __denominators__ the same.

5. Explain how to use a ruler to add $\frac{3}{8} + \frac{7}{8}$.
Sample answer: Starting at zero, count over $\frac{3}{8}$ inch. Continue counting for an additional $\frac{7}{8}$ inch. The ending location is $1\frac{2}{8}$ or $1\frac{1}{4}$ inches.

Helping You Remember

6. Sketch a model to show each sum or difference.

a. $\frac{3}{10} + \frac{6}{10}$ $\frac{3}{10} + \frac{6}{10} = \frac{9}{10}$

b. $\frac{6}{7} - \frac{3}{7}$ $\frac{6}{7} - \frac{3}{7} = \frac{3}{7}$

Adding and Subtracting Like Fractions

5-5

What You'll Learn

- Add like fractions.
- Subtract like fractions.

Why are fractions important when taking measurements?

Measures of different parts of an insect are shown in the diagram. The sum of the parts is $\frac{6}{8}$ inch. Use a ruler to find each measure.

a. $\frac{1}{8}$ in. + $\frac{3}{8}$ in.

b. $\frac{3}{8}$ in. + $\frac{4}{8}$ in.

c. $\frac{4}{8}$ in. + $\frac{4}{8}$ in.

d. $\frac{6}{8}$ in. − $\frac{3}{8}$ in.

ADD LIKE FRACTIONS   Fractions with the same denominator are called *like fractions*. The rule for adding like fractions is stated below.

Key Concept   *Adding Like Fractions*

- **Words**   To add fractions with like denominators, add the numerators and write the sum over the denominator.

- **Symbols** $\frac{a}{c} + \frac{b}{c} = \frac{a+b}{c}$, where $c \neq 0$

- **Example** $\frac{1}{5} + \frac{2}{5} = \frac{1+2}{5}$ or $\frac{3}{5}$

Example 1 Add Fractions

Find $\frac{3}{7} + \frac{5}{7}$. Write the sum in simplest form.   **Estimate:** $0 + 1 = 1$

$\frac{3}{7} + \frac{5}{7} = \frac{3+5}{7}$ The denominators are the same. Add the numerators.

$= \frac{8}{7}$ or $1\frac{1}{7}$ Simplify and rename as a mixed number.

Study Tip

Alternative Method
You can also stack the mixed numbers vertically to find the sum.

$6\frac{5}{8}$

$+1\frac{1}{8}$

$\overline{7\frac{6}{8}}$ or $7\frac{3}{4}$

Example 2 Add Mixed Numbers

Find $6\frac{5}{8} + 1\frac{1}{8}$. Write the sum in simplest form.   **Estimate:** $7 + 1 = 8$

$6\frac{5}{8} + 1\frac{1}{8} = (6 + 1) + \left(\frac{5}{8} + \frac{1}{8}\right)$ Add the whole numbers and fractions separately.

$= 7 + \frac{5+1}{8}$ Add the numerators.

$= 7\frac{6}{8}$ or $7\frac{3}{4}$ Simplify.

Resource Manager

Workbooks and Reproducible Masters

Chapter 5 Resource Masters
- Study Guide and Intervention, p. 245
- Skills Practice, p. 246
- Practice, p. 247
- Reading to Learn Mathematics, p. 248
- Enrichment, p. 249
- Assessment, pp. 289, 291

Parent and Student Study Guide Workbook, p. 37
Prerequisite Skills Workbook, pp. 37–44

Transparencies
5-Minute Check Transparency 5-5
Answer Key Transparencies

Technology
Interactive Chalkboard

SUBTRACT LIKE FRACTIONS The rule for subtracting fractions with like denominators is similar to the rule for addition.

> **Key Concept** — Subtracting Like Fractions
>
> - **Words** To subtract fractions with like denominators, subtract the numerators and write the difference over the denominator.
> - **Symbols** $\frac{a}{c} - \frac{b}{c} = \frac{a-b}{c}$, where $c \neq 0$
> - **Example** $\frac{5}{7} - \frac{1}{7} = \frac{5-1}{7}$ or $\frac{4}{7}$

Concept Check: It is the same, except the numerators are subtracted rather than added.

✓ **Concept Check** How is the rule for subtracting fractions with like denominators similar to the rule for adding fractions with like denominators?

Example 3 Subtract Fractions

Find $\frac{9}{20} - \frac{13}{20}$. Write the difference in simplest form. **Estimate:** $\frac{1}{2} - 1 = -\frac{1}{2}$

$\frac{9}{20} - \frac{13}{20} = \frac{9-13}{20}$ The denominators are the same. Subtract the numerators.

$= \frac{-4}{20}$ or $-\frac{1}{5}$ Simplify.

You can write the mixed numbers as improper fractions before adding or subtracting.

Example 4 Subtract Mixed Numbers

Evaluate $a - b$ if $a = 9\frac{1}{6}$ and $b = 5\frac{2}{6}$. **Estimate:** $9 - 5 = 4$

$a - b = 9\frac{1}{6} - 5\frac{2}{6}$ Replace a with $9\frac{1}{6}$ and b with $5\frac{2}{6}$.

$= \frac{55}{6} - \frac{32}{6}$ Write the mixed numbers as improper fractions.

$= \frac{23}{6}$ Subtract the numerators.

$= 3\frac{5}{6}$ Simplify.

 **ALGEBRA CONNECTION**

You can use the same rules for adding or subtracting like algebraic fractions as you did for adding or subtracting like numerical fractions.

Example 5 Add Algebraic Fractions

Find $\frac{n}{8} + \frac{5n}{8}$. Write the sum in simplest form.

$\frac{n}{8} + \frac{5n}{8} = \frac{n + 5n}{8}$ The denominators are the same. Add the numerators.

$= \frac{6n}{8}$ Add the numerators.

$= \frac{3n}{4}$ Simplify.

 www.pre-alg.com/extra_examples   **Lesson 5-5** Adding and Subtracting Like Fractions **221**

---

2 Teach

ADD LIKE FRACTIONS

In-Class Examples Power Point®

1 Find $\frac{3}{4} + \frac{3}{4}$. Write the sum in simplest form. $1\frac{1}{2}$

2 Find $3\frac{4}{9} + 8\frac{2}{9}$. Write the sum in simplest form. $11\frac{2}{3}$

Teaching Tip Remind students that Example 2 illustrates the Commutative and Associative Properties of Addition.

SUBTRACT LIKE FRACTIONS

In-Class Examples Power Point®

Teaching Tip Emphasize that rules for adding and subtracting integers are used when numerators are added or subtracted.

3 Find $\frac{11}{12} - \frac{5}{12}$. Write the difference in simplest form. $\frac{1}{2}$

4 **ALGEBRA** Evaluate $r - q$ if $r = 7\frac{3}{5}$ and $q = 9\frac{1}{5}$. $-\frac{8}{5}$ or $-1\frac{3}{5}$

5 **ALGEBRA** Find $\frac{5}{2b} + \frac{3}{2b}$. Write the sum in simplest form. $\frac{4}{b}$

Teaching Tip Point out to students that expressing mixed numbers as improper fractions will help them make the transition to adding algebraic fractions.

✓ **Skills Check**

Add and Subtract Like Fractions Write each answer in simplest form.

a. $\frac{4}{9} + \frac{5}{9}$ 1   **b.** $3\frac{1}{4} - 2\frac{3}{4}$ $\frac{1}{2}$

c. $2\frac{5}{14} + 3\frac{3}{14}$ $5\frac{4}{7}$

DAILY
INTERVENTION **FIND THE ERROR**
If students are having difficulty with negative numbers, suggest that they keep negative signs with the numerators. Emphasize that if the rest of the work is correct, the answer will be incorrect if the negative sign is omitted.

About the Exercises . . .
Odd/Even Assignments
Exercises 15–46 are structured so that students practice the same concepts whether they are assigned odd or even problems.

Assignment Guide
Basic: 15–31 odd, 35–45 odd, 48–65
Average: 15–47 odd, 48–65
Advanced: 16–46 even, 47–59 (Optional: 60–65)
All: Practice Quiz 1 (1–10)

Answer
1.
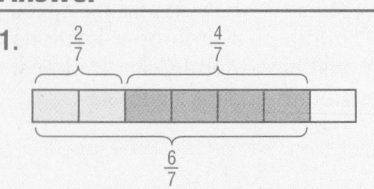

Check for Understanding

Concept Check 1. **Draw** a model to show the sum $\frac{2}{7} + \frac{4}{7}$. **See margin.**

2. **OPEN ENDED** Write a subtraction expression in which the difference of two fractions is $\frac{18}{25}$. **Sample answer:** $\frac{19}{25} - \frac{1}{25}$

3. **FIND THE ERROR** Kayla and Ethan are adding $-2\frac{1}{8}$ and $-4\frac{3}{8}$.

Kayla
$$-2\frac{1}{8} + \left(-4\frac{3}{8}\right) = -\frac{17}{8} + \left(-\frac{35}{8}\right)$$
$$= -\frac{52}{8} \text{ or } -6\frac{1}{2}$$

Ethan
$$-2\frac{1}{8} + \left(-4\frac{3}{8}\right) = \frac{17}{8} + \left(-\frac{35}{8}\right)$$
$$= -\frac{18}{8} \text{ or } -2\frac{1}{4}$$

Who is correct? Explain your reasoning.
Kayla; Ethan incorrectly left out the negative sign on the first term.

GUIDED PRACTICE KEY

Exercises	Examples
4–9, 14	1–3
10	4
11–13	5

Guided Practice Find each sum or difference. Write in simplest form.

4. $\frac{1}{7} + \frac{5}{7}$ $\frac{6}{7}$

5. $\frac{11}{14} - \frac{3}{14}$ $\frac{4}{7}$

6. $\frac{3}{10} + \frac{3}{10}$ $\frac{3}{5}$

7. $-\frac{1}{8} - \frac{5}{8}$ $-\frac{3}{4}$

8. $-2\frac{4}{5} + \left(-\frac{2}{5}\right)$ $-3\frac{1}{5}$

9. $7\frac{1}{8} - \left(-1\frac{3}{8}\right)$ $8\frac{1}{2}$

10. **ALGEBRA** Evaluate $x + y$ if $x = 2\frac{4}{9}$ and $y = 8\frac{7}{9}$. $11\frac{2}{9}$

TEACHING TIP
Remind students that answers to application problems should be given in simplest form.

ALGEBRA Find each sum or difference. Write in simplest form.

11. $\frac{6r}{11} + \frac{2r}{11}$ $\frac{8r}{11}$

12. $\frac{19}{a} - \frac{12}{a}, a \neq 0$ $\frac{7}{a}$

13. $\frac{5}{3x} - \frac{6}{3x}, x \neq 0$ $-\frac{1}{3x}$

Application 14. **MEASUREMENT** Hoai was $62\frac{1}{8}$ inches tall at the end of school in June. He was $63\frac{7}{8}$ inches tall in September. How much did he grow during the summer? $1\frac{3}{4}$ in.

★ indicates increased difficulty

Practice and Apply

Homework Help

For Exercises	See Examples
15–24	1–3
25–38, 45, 46	4
39–44	5

Extra Practice
See page 734.

Find each sum or difference. Write in simplest form.

15. $\frac{2}{5} + \frac{1}{5}$ $\frac{3}{5}$

16. $\frac{10}{11} - \frac{8}{11}$ $\frac{2}{11}$

17. $\frac{17}{18} - \frac{5}{18}$ $\frac{2}{3}$

18. $\frac{3}{10} + \frac{7}{10}$ 1

19. $\frac{1}{12} + \left(-\frac{7}{12}\right)$ $-\frac{1}{2}$

20. $\frac{9}{20} - \left(-\frac{7}{20}\right)$ $\frac{4}{5}$

21. $-\frac{3}{4} + \left(-\frac{3}{4}\right)$ $-1\frac{1}{2}$

22. $-\frac{13}{16} + \left(-\frac{9}{16}\right)$ $-1\frac{3}{8}$

23. $-\frac{7}{9} + \frac{5}{9}$ $-\frac{2}{9}$

24. $-\frac{17}{20} + \frac{9}{20}$ $-\frac{2}{5}$

25. $7\frac{2}{5} + 4\frac{2}{5}$ $11\frac{4}{5}$

26. $-4\frac{5}{8} - \frac{3}{8}$ -5

27. $5\frac{7}{9} - \left(-3\frac{5}{9}\right)$ $9\frac{1}{3}$

28. $2\frac{5}{12} + \left(-2\frac{7}{12}\right)$ $-\frac{1}{6}$

29. $2\frac{3}{8} - 1\frac{5}{8}$ $\frac{3}{4}$

30. $8\frac{9}{10} - 6\frac{1}{10}$ $2\frac{4}{5}$

31. $7\frac{4}{7} - 2\frac{5}{7}$ $4\frac{6}{7}$

32. $-8\frac{6}{11} - \left(-2\frac{5}{11}\right)$ $-6\frac{1}{11}$

★33. Find $12\frac{7}{8} - 7\frac{3}{8} + 2\frac{5}{8}$. $8\frac{1}{8}$

★34. Find $5\frac{5}{6} + 3\frac{5}{6} - 2\frac{1}{6}$. $7\frac{1}{2}$

DAILY
INTERVENTION **Differentiated Instruction**

• **Visual/Spatial** Have students use rectangles divided into parts to model addition and subtraction of fractions. Students can draw rectangles on paper (or grid paper), then shade in the fractions to be added or subtracted.

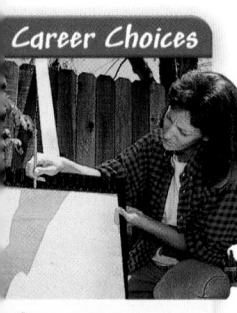
ALGEBRA   Evaluate each expression if $x = \frac{8}{15}$, $y = 2\frac{1}{15}$, and $z = \frac{11}{15}$. Write in simplest form.

35. $x + y$ $2\frac{3}{5}$

36. $z + y$ $2\frac{4}{5}$

37. $z - x$ $1\frac{1}{5}$

38. $y - x$ $1\frac{8}{15}$

ALGEBRA   Find each sum or difference. Write in simplest form.

39. $\frac{x}{8} + \frac{4x}{8}$ $\frac{5x}{8}$

40. $\frac{3r}{10} + \frac{3r}{10}$ $\frac{3r}{5}$

41. $\frac{12}{m} - \frac{9}{m}, m \neq 0$ $\frac{3}{m}$

★ 42. $\frac{10a}{3b} - \frac{7a}{3b}, b \neq 0$ $\frac{a}{b}$

43. $5\frac{4}{7}c - 3\frac{1}{7}c$ $2\frac{3}{7}c$

44. $-2\frac{1}{6}y + 8\frac{5}{6}y$ $6\frac{2}{3}y$

45. **CARPENTRY**   A 5-foot long kitchen countertop is to be installed between two walls that are $54\frac{5}{8}$ inches apart. How much of the countertop must be cut off so that it fits between the walls? $5\frac{3}{8}$ in.

46. **SEWING**   Chumani is making a linen suit. The portion of the pattern envelope that shows the yards of fabric needed for different sizes is shown at the right. If Chumani is making a size 6 jacket and skirt from 45-inch fabric, how much fabric should she buy?
$3\frac{1}{2}$ yd

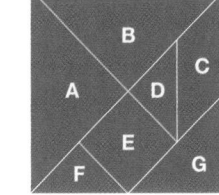

Size	(6	8	10)
JACKET			
45"	$2\frac{5}{8}$	$2\frac{3}{4}$	$2\frac{3}{4}$
60"	2	2	2
SKIRT			
45"	$\frac{7}{8}$	$1\frac{1}{8}$	$1\frac{1}{8}$
60"	$\frac{7}{8}$	$\frac{7}{8}$	$\frac{7}{8}$

★ 47. **GARDENING**   Melanie's flower garden has a perimeter of 25 feet. She plans to add 2 feet 9 inches to the width and 3 feet 9 inches to the length. What is the new perimeter in feet?   **38 ft**

48. **CRITICAL THINKING**   The 7-piece puzzle at the right is called a *tangram*.

48a. $A = \frac{1}{4}$, $B = \frac{1}{4}$,

$C = \frac{1}{8}$, $D = \frac{1}{16}$, $E = \frac{1}{8}$,

$F = \frac{1}{16}$, $G = \frac{1}{8}$

48c. $\frac{2}{16}$ or $\frac{1}{8}$

a. If the value of the entire puzzle is 1, what is the value of each piece?

b. How much is A + B? $\frac{2}{4}$ or $\frac{1}{2}$

c. How much is F + D?

d. How much is C + E? $\frac{2}{8}$ or $\frac{1}{4}$

e. Which pieces each equal the sum of E and G?   **A and B**

49. **WRITING IN MATH**   Answer the question that was posed at the beginning of the lesson.   **See margin.**

Why are fractions important when taking measurements?

Include the following in your answer:
- the fraction of an inch that each mark on a ruler or tape measure represents, and
- some real-world examples in which fractional measures are used.

Answer

49. When you use a ruler or a tape measure, measurements are usually a fraction of an inch. Answers should include the following.

- The marks on a ruler represent $\frac{1}{16}$ of an inch, $\frac{1}{8}$ of an inch, $\frac{1}{4}$ of an inch, and $\frac{1}{2}$ of an inch.

- Fractional measures are used in sewing and construction.

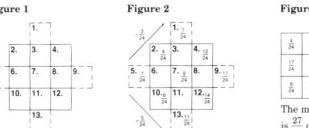
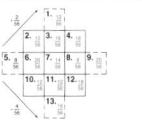

Open-Ended Assessment

Speaking Show students the following diagram:

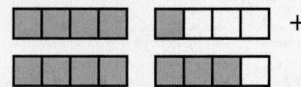

Have them explain the problem shown and tell how to find the sum. They should explain how to give the sum in simplest form. Repeat with several similar examples including subtraction.

Getting Ready for Lesson 5-6

PREREQUISITE SKILL Lesson 5-6 presents least common multiple. Exercises 60–65 should be used to determine your students' familiarity with finding prime factorization, which can be used to find LCM.

Assessment Options

Practice Quiz 1 The quiz provides students with a brief review of the concepts and skills in Lessons 5-1 through 5-5. Lesson numbers are given to the right of exercises or instruction lines so students can review concepts not yet mastered.

Quiz (Lessons 5-4 and 5-5) is available on p. 289 of the *Chapter 5 Resource Masters*.

Mid-Chapter Test (Lessons 5-1 through 5-5) is available on p. 291 of the *Chapter 5 Resource Masters*.

Standardized Test Practice
Ⓐ Ⓑ Ⓒ Ⓓ

50. Find $\frac{13}{20} - \frac{7}{20}$. Write in simplest form. **D**

   Ⓐ $\frac{6}{10}$ Ⓑ $\frac{3}{5}$ Ⓒ $\frac{6}{20}$ Ⓓ $\frac{3}{10}$

51. A piece of wood is $1\frac{9}{16}$ inches thick. A layer of padding $\frac{15}{16}$ inch thick is placed on top. What is the total thickness of the wood and the padding? **A**

   Ⓐ $2\frac{1}{2}$ in.   Ⓑ $1\frac{1}{2}$ in.   Ⓒ $1\frac{24}{16}$ in.   Ⓓ $1\frac{3}{8}$ in.

Maintain Your Skills

Mixed Review   **Find each quotient. Write in simplest form.** *(Lesson 5-4)*

52. $\frac{1}{6} \div \frac{3}{4}$ $\frac{2}{9}$ **53.** $-\frac{5}{8} \div \frac{1}{3}$ $-1\frac{7}{8}$ **54.** $\frac{2}{5} \div 1\frac{1}{2}$ $\frac{4}{15}$

Find each product. Write in simplest form. *(Lesson 5-3)*

55. $\frac{2}{5} \cdot \frac{3}{4}$ $\frac{3}{10}$ **56.** $\frac{1}{6} \cdot \left(-\frac{8}{9}\right)$ $-\frac{4}{27}$ **57.** $\frac{4}{7} \cdot 2\frac{1}{3}$ $1\frac{1}{3}$

58. Find the product of $4y^2$ and $8y^5$. *(Lesson 4-6)* **$32y^7$**

59. GEOMETRY Find the perimeter and area of the rectangle. *(Lesson 3-7)* **42 cm; 90 cm²**

6 cm

15 cm

Getting Ready for the Next Lesson   **PREREQUISITE SKILL** Use exponents to write the prime factorization of each number or monomial. *(To review **prime factorization**, see Lesson 4-3.)*

60. 60 $2^2 \cdot 3 \cdot 5$ **61.** 175 $5^2 \cdot 7$ **62.** 112 $2^4 \cdot 7$

63. $12n$ $2^2 \cdot 3 \cdot n$ **64.** $24s^2$ $2^3 \cdot 3 \cdot s^2$ **65.** $42a^2b$ $2 \cdot 3 \cdot 7 \cdot a^2 \cdot b$

Practice Quiz 1   Lessons 5-1 through 5-5

Write each fraction or mixed number as a decimal. Use a bar to show a repeating decimal. *(Lesson 5-1)*

1. $\frac{4}{25}$ **0.16**   **2.** $-\frac{2}{9}$ **$-0.\overline{2}$**   **3.** $3\frac{1}{8}$ **3.125**

Write each decimal as a fraction or mixed number in simplest form. *(Lesson 5-2)*

4. -6.75 **$-6\frac{3}{4}$**   **5.** 0.12   **$\frac{3}{25}$**   **6.** 0.5555…   **$\frac{5}{9}$**

Simplify each expression. *(Lessons 5-3, 5-4, and 5-5)*

7. $\frac{5}{18} \cdot \frac{4}{15}$ **$\frac{2}{27}$**   **8.** $\frac{7}{8} \div \left(-\frac{1}{4}\right)$ **$-3\frac{1}{2}$**   **9.** $\frac{11}{12} - \frac{6}{12}$ **$\frac{5}{12}$**

10. ALGEBRA Find $6\frac{3}{5}a + 2\frac{4}{5}a$. Write in simplest form. *(Lesson 5-5)* **$9\frac{2}{5}a$**

Reading Mathematics

Factors and Multiples

Many words used in mathematics are also used in everyday language. You can use the everyday meaning of these words to better understand their mathematical meaning. The table shows both meanings of the words *factor* and *multiple*.

Term	Everyday Meaning	Mathematical Meaning
factor	something that contributes to the production of a result • The weather was not a *factor* in the decision. • The type of wood is one *factor* that contributes to the cost of the table.	one of two or more numbers that are multiplied together to form a product
multiple	involving more than one or shared by many • *multiple* births • *multiple* ownership	the product of a quantity and a whole number

Source: *Merriam Webster's Collegiate Dictionary*

When you count by 2, you are listing the multiples of 2. When you count by 3, you are listing the multiples of 3, and so on, as shown in the table below.

Number	Factors	Multiples
2	1, 2	2, 4, 6, 8, …
3	1, 3	3, 6, 9, 12, …
4	1, 2, 4	4, 8, 12, 16, …

Notice that the mathematical meaning of each word is related to the everyday meaning. The word *multiple* means many, and in mathematics, a number has infinitely many multiples.

1. Sample answer: a factor is found by dividing a number; a multiple is found by multiplying a number.

3. Sample answer: words with fact- generally mean make or do, and words with multi- mean many.

Reading to Learn

1. Write your own rule for remembering the difference between *factor* and *multiple*.

2. **RESEARCH** Use the Internet or a dictionary to find the everyday meaning of each word listed below. Compare them to the mathematical meanings of *factor* and *multiple*. Note the similarities and differences. a–c. See margin.

   a. factotum   b. multicultural   c. multimedia

3. Make lists of other words that have the prefixes fact- or multi-. Determine what the words in each list have in common.

Before starting this activity, ask students to count by 2's, 3's, 4's, 5's, and 6's, writing down the numbers. Then have students describe any patterns they see. To see patterns, encourage students to write down at least 10 numbers each time.

Teach

Factors and Multiples Neal and Rayna name numbers related to the number 18. Neal names 1, 2, 3, 6, 9, and 18. Rayna names 18, 36, 54, 72, 90, and 180. Ask students to classify the numbers named by each person. **Neal named factors; Rayna named multiples.**

Assess

Study Notebook

Ask students to look up factor and multiple *in a thesaurus. Have them write the synonyms that relate to the mathematical meanings of the words. Then ask them to summarize what they learned about the words* factor and multiple.

ELL English Language Learners may benefit from writing key concepts from this activity in their Study Notebooks in their native language and then in English.

Sample Answers

2a. A factotum is a person that has many diverse activities or responsibilities. A factotum produces results, just as factors produce products.

2b. Multicultural means many diverse cultures, just as a multiple is one of many numbers that can be formed.

2c. Multimedia means using several media, or multiple media.

5-6 Least Common Multiple

1 Focus

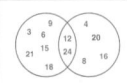 **5-Minute Check Transparency 5-6** Use as a quiz or review of Lesson 5-5.

Mathematical Background notes are available for this lesson on page 198D.

How can you use prime factors to find the least common multiple?

The opening activity questions are repeated on page 253 of the *Chapter 5 Resource Masters*.

Reading to Learn Mathematics, p. 253 **ELL**

Pre-Activity *How can you use prime factors to find the least common multiple?*

Do the activity at the top of page 226 in your textbook. Write your answers below.

  a. List the next three years in which the voter can vote for a president. 2004, 2008, 2012

  b. List the next three years in which the voter can vote for senator. 2006, 2012, 2018

  c. What will be the next year in which the voter has a chance to vote for both a president and a senator? 2012

Reading the Lesson 1–4. See students' work.

Write a definition and give an example of each new vocabulary word or phrase.

Vocabulary	Definition	Example
1. multiple		
2. common multiples		
3. least common multiple (LCM)		
4. least common denominator (LCD)		

5. Find two numbers whose LCM is 24. Sample answer: 6 and 8

6. Find two fractions whose LCD is 2a. Sample answer: $\frac{1}{2}$ and $\frac{1}{a}$

7. Explain what happens if a common multiple is used to find a common denominator, but the multiple is not the LCM. Sample answer: The fractions formed will be equivalent to fractions written with the LCD.

Helping You Remember

8. Use a Venn diagram to show multiples of 3 and multiples of 4. Explain how to use the diagram to find common multiples and the LCM. Sample answer: The overlapping circles show the common multiples. The LCM is the smallest of these numbers.

What You'll Learn

- Find the least common multiple of two or more numbers.
- Find the least common denominator of two or more fractions.

Vocabulary
- multiple
- common multiples
- least common multiple (LCM)
- least common denominator (LCD)

a. 2004, 2008, 2012
b. 2006, 2012, 2018

How can you use prime factors to find the least common multiple?

A voter voted for both president and senator in the year 2000.

a. List the next three years in which the voter can vote for president.

b. List the next three years in which the voter can vote for senator.

c. What will be the next year in which the voter has a chance to vote for both president and senator? 2012

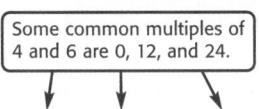

Candidate	Length of Term (years)
President	4
Senator	6

LEAST COMMON MULTIPLE A **multiple** of a number is a product of that number and a whole number.

Sometimes numbers have some of the same multiples. These are called **common multiples**.

Some common multiples of 4 and 6 are 0, 12, and 24.

multiples of 4: 0, 4, 8, 12, 16, 20, 24, 28, …

multiples of 6: 0, 6, 12, 18, 24, 30, 36, 42, …

The least of the *nonzero* common multiples is called the **least common multiple (LCM)**. So, the LCM of 4 and 6 is 12.

When numbers are large, an easier way of finding the least common multiple is to use prime factorization. The LCM is the smallest product that contains the prime factors of each number.

Multiples of 5
$5 \cdot 0 = 0$
$5 \cdot 1 = 5$
$5 \cdot 2 = 10$
$5 \cdot 3 = 15$
⋮   ⋮

Study Tip

Prime Factors
If a prime factor appears in both numbers, use the factor with the greatest exponent.

Example 1 Find the LCM

Find the LCM of 108 and 240.

Number	Prime Factorization	Exponential Form
108	$2 \cdot 2 \cdot 3 \cdot 3 \cdot 3$	$2^2 \cdot 3^3$
240	$2 \cdot 2 \cdot 2 \cdot 2 \cdot 3 \cdot 5$	$2^4 \cdot 3 \cdot 5$

226 Chapter 5 Rational Numbers

Resource Manager

 Workbooks and Reproducible Masters

Chapter 5 Resource Masters
- Study Guide and Intervention, p. 250
- Skills Practice, p. 251
- Practice, p. 252
- Reading to Learn Mathematics, p. 253
- Enrichment, p. 254

Parent and Student Study Guide Workbook, p. 38

 Transparencies
5-Minute Check Transparency 5-6
Answer Key Transparencies

Technology
Interactive Chalkboard
Multimedia Applications

The prime factors of both numbers are 2, 3, and 5. Multiply the greatest power of 2, 3, and 5 appearing in either factorization.

$$LCM = 2^4 \cdot 3^3 \cdot 5$$
$$= 2160$$

So, the LCM of 108 and 240 is 2160.

✅ **Concept Check** What is the LCM of 6 and 12? 12

The LCM of two or more monomials is found in the same way as the LCM of two or more numbers.

Example 2 The LCM of Monomials

Find the LCM of $18xy^2$ and $10y$.

$$18xy^2 = 2 \cdot 3^2 \cdot x \cdot y^2$$
$$10y = 2 \cdot 5 \cdot y$$

$$LCM = 2 \cdot 3^2 \cdot 5 \cdot x \cdot y^2 \quad \text{Multiply the greatest power of each prime factor.}$$
$$= 90xy^2$$

The LCM of $18xy^2$ and $10y$ is $90xy^2$.

LEAST COMMON DENOMINATOR The **least common denominator (LCD)** of two or more fractions is the LCM of the denominators.

Example 3 Find the LCD

Find the LCD of $\frac{5}{9}$ and $\frac{11}{21}$.

$$9 = 3^2 \longleftarrow \boxed{\text{Write the prime factorization of 9 and 21.}}$$
$$21 = 3 \cdot 7 \longleftarrow \boxed{\text{Highlight the greatest power of each prime factor.}}$$

$$LCM = 3^2 \cdot 7 \quad \text{Multiply.}$$
$$= 63$$

The LCD of $\frac{5}{9}$ and $\frac{11}{21}$ is 63.

The LCD for algebraic fractions can also be found.

Example 4 Find the LCD of Algebraic Fractions

Find the LCD of $\frac{5}{12b^2}$ and $\frac{3}{8ab}$.

$$12b^2 = 2^2 \cdot 3 \cdot b^2$$
$$8ab = 2^3 \cdot a \cdot b$$

$$LCM = 2^3 \cdot 3 \cdot a \cdot b^2 \text{ or } 24ab^2$$

Thus, the LCD of $\frac{5}{12b^2}$ and $\frac{3}{8ab}$ is $24ab^2$.

✅ **Concept Check** What is the LCD of $\frac{1}{x^2}$ and $\frac{1}{xy}$? x^2y

 www.pre-alg.com/extra_examples

Lesson 5-6 Least Common Multiple **227**

 ✅ **Skills Check**

Least Common Denominator

Find the LCD of each pair of fractions.

a. $\frac{4}{9}, \frac{7}{12}$ 36

b. $\frac{2}{15n^2}, \frac{5}{18nr^2}$ $90n^2r^2$

2 Teach

Building on Prior Knowledge

In Lesson 4-3, students learned to find the prime factorization of numbers. Prime factorization will be used in this lesson to find least common multiples.

LEAST COMMON MULTIPLE

In-Class Examples

1. Find the LCM of 168 and 180. $2^3 \cdot 3^2 \cdot 5 \cdot 7$ or 2520

2. Find the LCM of $12x^2y^2$ and $6y^3$. $2^2 \cdot 3 \cdot x^2 \cdot y^3$ or $12x^2y^3$

Teaching Tip Encourage students to write their prime factorizations in numerical order. It is easier to look for common factors when determining the LCM.

✅ **Skills Check**

Least Common Multiple

Find the LCM of each pair of numbers or monomials.

a. 12, 20 60

b. $6a^3c, 8abc^2$ $24a^3bc^2$

LEAST COMMON DENOMINATOR

In-Class Examples

3. Find the LCD of $\frac{7}{8}$ and $\frac{13}{20}$. 40

4. **ALGEBRA** Find the LCD of $\frac{9}{36a^2b}$ and $\frac{16}{27ab^2}$. $108a^2b^2$

5. Replace ● with <, >, or = to make $\frac{7}{15}$ ● $\frac{3}{7}$ a true statement. >

Teaching Tip Remind students that multiplying by 1 illustrates the Multiplicative Identity Property. So, $\frac{1}{2} \cdot \frac{4}{4} = \frac{4}{8}$ or $\frac{1}{2}$.

Study Notebook

Have students—

- add the definitions/examples of the vocabulary terms to their Vocabulary Builder worksheets for Chapter 5.
- record an example of finding an LCM two ways—by listing the multiples and by using the prime factorizations of the numbers.
- include any other item(s) that they find helpful in mastering the skills in this lesson.

About the Exercises . . .

Organization by Objective
- **Least Common Multiple:** 16–33
- **Least Common Denominator:** 34–41

Odd/Even Assignments
Exercises 16–54 are structured so that students practice the same concepts whether they are assigned odd or even problems.

Assignment Guide

Basic: 17–25 odd, 31–49 odd, 53, 59–80

Average: 17–57 odd, 59–80

Advanced: 16–54 even, 55–74 (Optional: 75–80)

Answer

1. The LCM involves the common multiples of a set of numbers; the LCD is the LCM of the denominators of two or more fractions.

One way to compare fractions is to write them using the LCD. We can multiply the numerator and the denominator of a fraction by the same number, because it is the same as multiplying the fraction by 1.

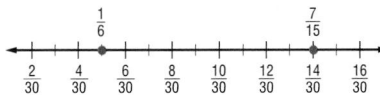 **Example 5 Compare Fractions**

Replace ● with <, >, or = to make $\frac{1}{6}$ ● $\frac{7}{15}$ a true statement.

The LCD of the fractions is $2 \cdot 3 \cdot 5$ or 30. Rewrite the fractions using the LCD and then compare the numerators.

$\frac{1}{6} = \frac{1 \cdot 5}{2 \cdot 3 \cdot 5} = \frac{5}{30}$ Multiply the fraction by $\frac{5}{5}$ to make the denominator 30.

$\frac{7}{15} = \frac{7 \cdot 2}{3 \cdot 5 \cdot 2} = \frac{14}{30}$ Multiply the fraction by $\frac{2}{2}$ to make the denominator 30.

Since $\frac{5}{30} < \frac{14}{30}$, then $\frac{1}{6} < \frac{7}{15}$.

$\frac{1}{6}$ is to the left of $\frac{7}{15}$ on the number line.

Check for Understanding

Concept Check

1. **Compare and contrast** least common multiple (LCM) and least common denominator (LCD). **See margin.**

2. **OPEN ENDED** Write two fractions whose least common denominator (LCD) is 35. **Sample answer:** $\frac{1}{7}$ and $\frac{1}{5}$

Guided Practice

Find the least common multiple (LCM) of each pair of numbers or monomials.

GUIDED PRACTICE KEY	
Exercises	Examples
3–7, 15	1
8	2
9, 10	3
11	4
12–14	5

3. 6, 8 **24**

4. 7, 9 **63**

5. 10, 14 **70**

6. 12, 30 **60**

7. 16, 24 **48**

8. $36ab$, $4b$ **$36ab$**

Find the least common denominator (LCD) of each pair of fractions.

9. $\frac{1}{2}, \frac{3}{8}$ **8**

10. $\frac{2}{3}, \frac{7}{10}$ **30**

11. $\frac{2}{25x}, \frac{13}{20x}$ **$100x$**

Replace each ● with <, >, or = to make a true statement.

12. $\frac{1}{4}$ ● $\frac{3}{16}$ **>**

13. $\frac{10}{45}$ ● $\frac{2}{9}$ **=**

14. $\frac{5}{7}$ ● $\frac{7}{9}$ **<**

Application

15. **CYCLING** The front bicycle gear has 52 teeth and the back gear has 20 teeth. How many revolutions must each gear make for them to align again as shown? (*Hint:* First, find the number of teeth. Then divide to find the final answers.)
front gear: 5; back gear: 13

back gear   front gear

DAILY INTERVENTION

Differentiated Instruction **ELL**

- **Verbal/Linguistic** Give students several pairs of fractions. Ask them to explain how they would find the LCD in each case. Also, ask them to discuss what would happen if they used a common denominator that wasn't the LCD.

Practice and Apply

Homework Help

For Exercises	See Examples
16–29	1
30–33	2
34–39	3
40, 41	4
44–54	5

Extra Practice
See page 735.

Find the least common multiple (LCM) of each set of numbers or monomials.

16. 4, 10 **20** 17. 20, 12 **60** 18. 2, 9 **18**

19. 16, 3 **48** 20. 15, 75 **75** 21. 21, 28 **84**

22. 14, 28 **28** 23. 20, 50 **100** 24. 18, 32 **288**

25. 24, 32 **96** ★ 26. 10, 20, 40 **40** ★ 27. 7, 21, 84 **84**

★ 28. 9, 12, 15 **180** ★ 29. 45, 30, 35 **630** 30. $20c$, $12c$ **$60c$**

31. $16a^2$, $14ab$ **$112a^2b$** 32. $7x$, $12x$ **$84x$** 33. $75n^2$, $25n^4$ **$75n^4$**

Find the least common denominator (LCD) of each pair of fractions.

34. $\frac{1}{4}, \frac{7}{8}$ **8** 35. $\frac{8}{15}, \frac{1}{3}$ **15** 36. $\frac{4}{5}, \frac{1}{2}$ **10** 37. $\frac{2}{5}, \frac{6}{7}$ **35**

38. $\frac{4}{9}, \frac{5}{12}$ **36** 39. $\frac{3}{8}, \frac{5}{6}$ **24** 40. $\frac{1}{3t}, \frac{4}{5t^2}$ **$15t^2$** 41. $\frac{7}{8cd}, \frac{5}{16c^2}$ **$16c^2d$**

42. **PLANETS** The table shows the number of Earth years it takes for some of the planets to revolve around the Sun. Find the least common multiple of the revolution times to determine approximately how often these planets align. **420 yr**

Planet	Revolution Time (Earth Years)
Jupiter	12
Saturn	30
Uranus	84

43. **AUTO RACING** One driver can circle a one-mile track in 30 seconds. Another driver takes 20 seconds. If they both start at the same time, in how many seconds will they be together again at the starting line? **60 s**

Replace each ● with <, > , or = to make a true statement.

44. $\frac{1}{2}$ ● $\frac{5}{12}$ **>** 45. $\frac{7}{9}$ ● $\frac{5}{6}$ **<** 46. $\frac{3}{5}$ ● $\frac{4}{7}$ **>**

47. $\frac{21}{100}$ ● $\frac{1}{5}$ **>** 48. $\frac{17}{34}$ ● $\frac{1}{2}$ **=** 49. $\frac{12}{17}$ ● $\frac{36}{51}$ **=**

50. $\frac{8}{9}$ ● $\frac{19}{21}$ **<** ★ 51. $-\frac{9}{11}$ ● $-\frac{5}{6}$ **>** ★ 52. $-\frac{14}{15}$ ● $-\frac{9}{10}$ **<**

53. **ANIMALS** Of all the endangered species in the world, $\frac{7}{39}$ of the reptiles and $\frac{5}{9}$ of the amphibians are in the United States. Is there a greater fraction of endangered reptiles or amphibians in the U.S.? **amphibians**

 **Data Update** How many endangered species are in the United States today? Visit www.pre-alg.com/data_update to learn more.

54. **TELEPHONES** Eleven out of 20 people in Chicago, Illinois, have cell phones, and $\frac{14}{25}$ of the people in Anchorage, Alaska, have cell phones. In which city do a greater fraction of people have cell phones? **Source:** Polk Research **Anchorage**

★ 55. Find two composite numbers between 10 and 20 whose least common multiple (LCM) is 36. **12 and 18**

www.pre-alg.com/self_check_quiz

Lesson 5-6 Least Common Multiple **229**

More About. . .

Planets •

A spacecraft's launch date depends on planet alignment because the gravitational forces could affect the spacecraft's flight path.
Source: Memphis Space Center

Open-Ended Assessment

Writing Have each student write a five-question quiz that covers the concepts of this lesson. Each student must provide a fully worked answer key. The questions can be used later for review.

Getting Ready for Lesson 5-7

PREREQUISITE SKILL Lesson 5-7 presents adding and subtracting unlike fractions. Estimating an answer before doing the problem will help students see if their answer is reasonable. Exercises 75–80 should be used to determine your students' familiarity with estimating sums of fractions.

Answers

56. Sample answer: the LCM of 2, 4, and 8 is 8, which is one of the numbers. The LCM of 2, 3, and 4 is 12, which is not one of the numbers.

57. Sample answer: 5 and 6 do not contain any factors in common, and the LCM of 5 and 6 is 30.

58. Sample answer: the GCF of 6 and 12 is 6 and the LCM is 12. The GCF of 3 and 5 is 1 and the LCM is 15. In each case, LCM > GCF.

59a. If two numbers are relatively prime, then their LCM is the product of the two numbers. For example, the LCM of 4 and 5 is $2^2 \cdot 5$ or 20; the LCM of 6 and 25 is $2 \cdot 3 \cdot 5^2$ or 150.

59b. Always; the LCM contains all of the factors of both numbers. Therefore, it must contain any common factors.

Determine whether each statement is *sometimes,* *always,* **or** *never* **true. Give an example to support your answer. 56–58. See margin for examples.**

56. The LCM of three numbers is one of the numbers. **sometimes**

57. If two numbers do not contain any factors in common, then the LCM of the two numbers is 1. **never**

58. The LCM of two numbers is greater than the GCF of the numbers. **always**

Study Tip
Relatively Prime
Recall that two numbers that are relatively prime have a GCF of 1.

59. **CRITICAL THINKING** a–b. See margin.
   a. If two numbers are relatively prime, what is their LCM? Give two examples and explain your reasoning.
   b. Determine whether the LCM of two whole numbers is *always,* *sometimes,* or *never* a multiple of the GCF of the same two numbers. Explain.

60. **WRITING IN MATH** Answer the question that was posed at the beginning of the lesson. See margin.

   How can you use prime factors to find the least common multiple?
   Include the following in your answer:
   • a definition of least common multiple, and
   • a description of the steps you take to find the LCM of two or more numbers.

Standardized Test Practice
Ⓐ Ⓑ Ⓒ Ⓓ

61. Find the least common multiple of $12a^2b$ and $9ac$. **B**
   Ⓐ $36a^2b$ Ⓑ $36a^2bc$ Ⓒ $3a^2bc$ Ⓓ $3abc$

62. A $\frac{7}{8}$-inch wrench is too large to tighten a bolt. Of these, which is the next smaller size? **D**
   Ⓐ $\frac{3}{4}$-inch   Ⓑ $\frac{5}{8}$-inch   Ⓒ $\frac{7}{16}$-inch   Ⓓ $\frac{13}{16}$-inch

Maintain Your Skills

Mixed Review

Find each sum or difference. Write in simplest form. *(Lesson 5-5)*

63. $\frac{7}{8} - \frac{3}{8}$ $\frac{1}{2}$ 64. $3\frac{9}{11} - \frac{5}{11}$ $3\frac{4}{11}$ 65. $\frac{13}{14} + \frac{3}{14}$ $1\frac{1}{7}$ 66. $2\frac{5}{6} + 4\frac{1}{6}$ 7

ALGEBRA   Find each quotient. Write in simplest form. *(Lesson 5-4)*

67. $\frac{3}{n} \div \frac{1}{n}$ 3   68. $\frac{x}{8} \div \frac{x}{6}$ $\frac{3}{4}$ 69. $\frac{ac}{5} \div \frac{c}{d}$ $\frac{ad}{5}$ 70. $\frac{6k}{7m} \div \frac{3}{14m}$ 4k

71. **ALGEBRA** Translate *the sum of 7 and two times a number is 11* into an equation. Then find the number. *(Lesson 3-6)* $7 + 2n = 11$; 2

ALGEBRA   Solve each equation. Check your solution. *(Lessons 3-3 and 3-4)*

72. $9 = x - 4$ 13   73. $\frac{a}{-2} = 10$ −20   74. $-5c = -105$ 21

Getting Ready for the Next Lesson

PREREQUISITE SKILL   Estimate each sum.
(To review **estimating with fractions,** *see page 716.)* 75–80. Sample answers are given.

75. $\frac{3}{8} + \frac{3}{4}$ 0 + 1 = 1   76. $\frac{9}{10} + \frac{14}{15}$ 1 + 1 = 2   77. $\frac{4}{7} + 2\frac{1}{5}$ 1 + 2 = 3

78. $5\frac{7}{8} + \frac{2}{3}$ 6 + 1 = 7   79. $8\frac{3}{11} + 7\frac{2}{9}$ 8 + 7 = 15   80. $20\frac{5}{16} + 6\frac{1}{9}$ 20 + 6 = 26

60. The LCM of two or more numbers involves the product of prime factors. Answers should include the following.
   • The LCM of two numbers is the least number into which both of the numbers will divide evenly.
   • Write the prime factorization of each number in exponential form. Multiply each factor the greatest number of times that it appears in either factorization. If the same factors appear in more than one number, multiply the greatest power of the factor that appears.

Algebra Activity

A Follow-Up of Lesson 5-6

Juniper Green

Juniper Green is a game that was invented by a teacher in England.

Getting Ready
This game is for two people, so students should divide into pairs.

Rules of the Game
- The first player selects an even number from the hundreds chart and circles it with a colored marker.
- The next player selects any remaining number that is a factor or multiple of this number and circles it.
- Players continue taking turns circling numbers, as shown below.
- When a player cannot select a number or circles a number incorrectly, then the game is over and the other player wins.

2nd move
Player 2 circles 7 because it is a factor of 42.

1st move
Player 1 circles 42.

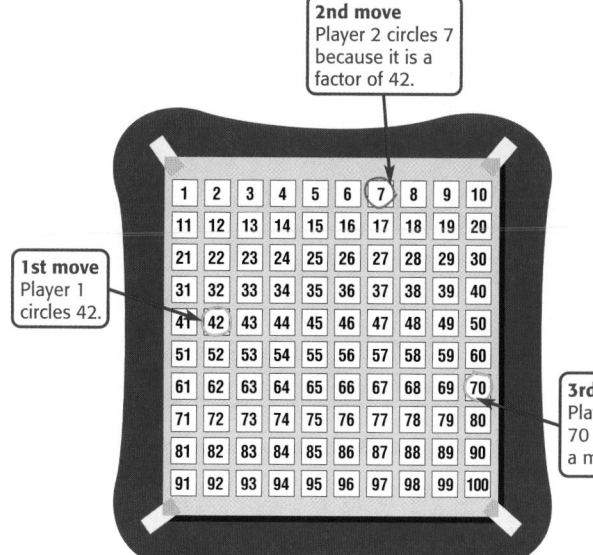

3rd move
Player 1 circles 70 because it is a multiple of 7.

Analyze the Strategies 1–2. See margin.
Play the game several times and then answer the following questions.
1. Why do you think the first player must select an even number? Explain.
2. Describe the kinds of moves that were made just before the game was over.

Answers
1. The first number selected must be even to guarantee that the second player can circle a number; for example, if the first number were 97, there is no factor or multiple on the hundreds chart.
2. Sample answer: finding patterns in the chart

Resource Manager

📁 **Teaching Pre-Algebra with Manipulatives**
- p. 70 (student recording sheet)

Getting Started

Objective Participate in a strategic game utilizing factors and multiples.

Materials
hundreds chart
colored markers

Teach

- Before starting, review briefly factors and multiples. Discuss numbers with many factors as well as prime numbers.
- Remind students to consider the restriction of using only the numbers on the chart and plan their moves accordingly. For example, larger numbers will have no other multiples on the chart.
- Encourage students to reflect on their choices of numbers and try to create a strategy to win. You may want to have a class discussion of their findings.

Assess

In **Exercises 1 and 2,** students should
- reflect on their experience playing the game.
- articulate strategies for winning or playing a competitive game.

Study Notebook

Have students summarize the rules of the game and any strategies for success that they learned.

1 Focus

5-Minute Check Transparency 5-7 Use as a quiz or review of Lesson 5-6.

Mathematical Background notes are available for this lesson on page 198D.

How can the LCM be used to add and subtract fractions with different denominators?

The opening activity questions are repeated on page 258 of the *Chapter 5 Resource Masters.*

Reading to Learn Mathematics, p. 258   **ELL**

Pre-Activity How can the LCM be used to add and subtract fractions with different denominators?

Do the activity at the top of page 232 in your textbook. Write your answers below.

a. What is the LCM of the denominators? 6

b. If you partition the model into six parts, what fraction of the model is shaded? $\frac{5}{6}$

c. How many parts are $\frac{1}{2}$? $\frac{1}{3}$? 3; 2

d. Describe a model that you could use to add $\frac{1}{3}$ and $\frac{1}{4}$. Then use it to find the sum. a figure with 12 parts; $\frac{7}{12}$

Reading the Lesson

1. Fractions with different denominators are called ___unlike fractions___ .

2. To add unlike fractions, you must first find a(n) ___common denominator___ .

3. Name a common denominator of $\frac{3}{5}$ and $\frac{9}{12}$. 60

4. To subtract unlike fractions, you must first find a(n) ___common denominator___ .

5. Monique rewrote $\frac{6}{4} - \frac{1}{3}$ as $\frac{36}{24} - \frac{8}{24}$. Is she correct? Explain.

Monique correctly rewrote the fractions using a common denominator. However, she did not choose the LCD, which is 12. The problem can be finished and simplified correctly.

Helping You Remember

6. Describe two methods that can be used to add $1\frac{1}{2} + 3\frac{2}{3}$. Then find the sum.

Either add the whole numbers separately from the fractions, or write the mixed numbers as improper fractions and then add. In both cases, use a common denominator.

The sum is $5\frac{1}{6}$.

What You'll Learn

- Add unlike fractions.
- Subtract unlike fractions.

How can the LCM be used to add and subtract fractions with different denominators?

The sum $\frac{1}{2} + \frac{1}{3}$ is modeled at the right. We can use the LCM to find the sum.

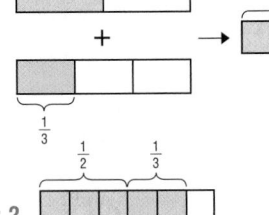

a. What is the LCM of the denominators? **6**

b. If you partition the model into six parts, what fraction of the model is shaded? $\frac{5}{6}$

c. How many parts are $\frac{1}{2}$? $\frac{1}{3}$? **3; 2**

d. Describe a model that you could use to add $\frac{1}{3}$ and $\frac{1}{4}$. Then use it to find the sum. **a figure with 12 parts;** $\frac{7}{12}$

ADD UNLIKE FRACTIONS Fractions with different denominators are called *unlike fractions*. In the activity above, you used the LCM of the denominators to rename the fractions. You can use any common denominator.

Key Concept	*Adding Unlike Fractions*

- **Words** To add fractions with unlike denominators, rename the fractions with a common denominator. Then add and simplify.

- **Example** $\frac{1}{3} + \frac{2}{5} = \frac{1}{3} \cdot \frac{5}{5} + \frac{2}{5} \cdot \frac{3}{3}$

  $= \frac{5}{15} + \frac{6}{15}$ or $\frac{11}{15}$

Example 1 Add Unlike Fractions

Find $\frac{1}{4} + \frac{2}{3}$.

$\frac{1}{4} + \frac{2}{3} = \frac{1}{4} \cdot \frac{3}{3} + \frac{2}{3} \cdot \frac{4}{4}$ Use 4 · 3 or 12 as the common denominator.

$= \frac{3}{12} + \frac{8}{12}$ Rename each fraction with the common denominator.

$= \frac{11}{12}$ Add the numerators.

✓ **Concept Check** Name a common denominator of $\frac{5}{9}$ and $\frac{4}{5}$. 45

Resource Manager

📂 **Workbooks and Reproducible Masters**

Chapter 5 Resource Masters
- Study Guide and Intervention, p. 255
- Skills Practice, p. 256
- Practice, p. 257
- Reading to Learn Mathematics, p. 258
- Enrichment, p. 259

Graphing Calculator and Spreadsheet Masters, p. 27
Parent and Student Study Guide Workbook, p. 39
Prerequisite Skills Workbook, pp. 37–44

💡 **Transparencies**
5-Minute Check Transparency 5-7
Answer Key Transparencies

💿 **Technology**
Interactive Chalkboard

You can rename unlike fractions using any common denominator. However, it is usually simpler to use the least common denominator.

Example 2 Add Fractions

Find $\frac{3}{8} + \frac{7}{12}$. **Estimate:** $\frac{1}{2} + \frac{1}{2} = 1$

$$\frac{3}{8} + \frac{7}{12} = \frac{3}{8} \cdot \frac{3}{3} + \frac{7}{12} \cdot \frac{2}{2} \qquad \text{The LCD is } 2^3 \cdot 3 \text{ or } 24.$$

$$= \frac{9}{24} + \frac{14}{24} \qquad \text{Rename each fraction with the LCD.}$$

$$= \frac{23}{24} \qquad \text{Add the numerators.}$$

Example 3 Add Mixed Numbers

Find $1\frac{2}{9} + \left(-2\frac{1}{3}\right)$. **Write in simplest form.** **Estimate:** $1 + (-2) = -1$

$$1\frac{2}{9} + \left(-2\frac{1}{3}\right) = \frac{11}{9} + \left(-\frac{7}{3}\right) \qquad \text{Write the mixed numbers as improper fractions.}$$

$$= \frac{11}{9} + \left(-\frac{7}{3}\right) \cdot \frac{3}{3} \qquad \text{Rename } -\frac{7}{3} \text{ using the LCD, 9.}$$

$$= \frac{11}{9} + \left(\frac{-21}{9}\right) \qquad \text{Simplify.}$$

$$= \frac{-10}{9} \qquad \text{Add the numerators.}$$

$$= -1\frac{1}{9} \qquad \text{Simplify.}$$

SUBTRACT UNLIKE FRACTIONS The rule for subtracting fractions with unlike denominators is similar to the rule for addition.

Key Concept Subtracting Unlike Fractions

- **Words** To subtract fractions with unlike denominators, rename the fractions with a common denominator. Then subtract and simplify.

- **Example** $\frac{6}{7} - \frac{2}{3} = \frac{6}{7} \cdot \frac{3}{3} - \frac{2}{3} \cdot \frac{7}{7}$

  $= \frac{18}{21} - \frac{14}{21}$ or $\frac{4}{21}$

Example 4 Subtract Fractions

Find $\frac{5}{21} - \frac{6}{7}$.

$$\frac{5}{21} - \frac{6}{7} = \frac{5}{21} - \frac{6}{7} \cdot \frac{3}{3} \qquad \text{The LCD is 21.}$$

$$= \frac{5}{21} - \frac{18}{21} \qquad \text{Rename } \frac{6}{7} \text{ using the LCD.}$$

$$= \frac{-13}{21} \text{ or } -\frac{13}{21} \qquad \text{Subtract the numerators.}$$

 www.pre-alg.com/extra_examples

---

2 Teach

ADD UNLIKE FRACTIONS

In-Class Examples Power Point®

Teaching Tip To emphasize the importance of a common denominator, ask students to find $\frac{1}{2} + \frac{1}{3}$ without referring to a common denominator.

Teaching Tip Another way to rename fractions with the LCD is to divide the LCD by the denominator and multiply that number by the numerator.

1 Find $\frac{3}{4} + \frac{1}{7}$. $\frac{25}{28}$

2 Find $\frac{5}{6} + \frac{3}{10}$. $1\frac{2}{15}$

3 Find $2\frac{1}{8} + \left(-3\frac{2}{3}\right)$. Write in simplest form. $-1\frac{13}{24}$

Teaching Tip Encourage students to write mixed numbers as improper fractions before adding or subtracting. This method produces fewer errors than adding or subtracting the whole numbers and fractions separately.

SUBTRACT UNLIKE FRACTIONS

In-Class Examples Power Point®

4 Find $\frac{9}{16} - \frac{5}{8}$. $-\frac{1}{16}$

5 Find $4\frac{2}{3} - 3\frac{6}{7}$. $\frac{17}{21}$

6 **JOGGING** Juyong jogged three days this week. She jogged $3\frac{1}{2}$ miles, $4\frac{1}{4}$ miles, and $4\frac{1}{10}$ miles. How far did she jog altogether? $11\frac{17}{20}$ miles

---

✓ Skills Check
Add and Subtract Unlike Fractions

a. Have students explain how they would find $4 + 8\frac{5}{12} + 2\frac{1}{3} + \left(21\frac{1}{6}\right)$.

b. Have students explain how they would find $7\frac{1}{9} - 4\frac{5}{6}$.

Study Notebook

Have students—
* record the key concepts for adding and subtracting unlike fractions.
* include any other item(s) that they find helpful in mastering the skills in this lesson.

DAILY INTERVENTION FIND THE ERROR

If students are having difficulty with Exercise 3, remind them they can add the numerators only when there is a common denominator. Estimating the answer before adding will help students understand that Daniel cannot be correct.

About the Exercises . . .

Odd/Even Assignments
Exercises 11–34 are structured so that students practice the same concepts whether they are assigned odd or even problems.

Assignment Guide

Basic: 11–25 odd, 31, 33, 35–39, 43–56

Average: 11–33 odd, 35–39, 43–56 (Optional: 40–42)

Advanced: 12–34 even, 35–52 (Optional: 53–56)

Answers

2. Sample answer: A piece of string $15\frac{3}{4}$ inches long is cut so that it is $2\frac{1}{8}$ inches shorter. How long is the piece of string after it is cut?

3. José; he finds a common denominator by multiplying the denominators. Daniel incorrectly adds the numerators and the denominators of unlike fractions.

Example 5 Subtract Mixed Numbers

Find $6\frac{1}{2} - 4\frac{1}{5}$. Write in simplest form.

$$6\frac{1}{2} - 4\frac{1}{5} = \frac{13}{2} - \frac{21}{5}$$ Write the mixed numbers as improper fractions.

$$= \frac{13}{2} \cdot \frac{5}{5} - \frac{21}{5} \cdot \frac{2}{2}$$ Rename the fractions using the LCD.

$$= \frac{65}{10} - \frac{42}{10}$$ Simplify.

$$= \frac{23}{10} \text{ or } 2\frac{3}{10}$$ Subtract.

Example 6 Use Fractions to Solve a Problem

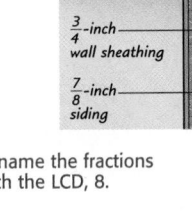

$\frac{5}{8}$-inch drywall

$5\frac{1}{2}$-inch insulation

$\frac{3}{4}$-inch wall sheathing

$\frac{7}{8}$-inch siding

HOUSES The diagram shows a cross-section of an outside wall. How thick is the wall?

Explore You know the measure of each layer of the wall.

Plan Add the measures to find the total thickness of the wall. Estimate your answer.

$$\frac{1}{2} + 5\frac{1}{2} + 1 + 1 = 8$$

Solve $\dfrac{5}{8} + 5\dfrac{1}{2} + \dfrac{3}{4} + \dfrac{7}{8} = \dfrac{5}{8} + 5\dfrac{4}{8} + \dfrac{6}{8} + \dfrac{7}{8}$ Rename the fractions with the LCD, 8.

$$= 5\frac{22}{8}$$ Add the like fractions.

$$= 7\frac{6}{8} \text{ or } 7\frac{3}{4} \text{ in.}$$ Simplify.

The wall is $7\frac{3}{4}$ inches thick.

Examine Since $7\frac{3}{4}$ is close to 8, the answer is reasonable.

Check for Understanding

Concept Check
1. **Describe** the first step in adding or subtracting fractions with unlike denominators. **Find the least common denominator.**

2. **OPEN ENDED** Write a real-world problem that you could solve by subtracting $2\frac{1}{8}$ from $15\frac{3}{4}$. **See margin.**

3. **FIND THE ERROR** José and Daniel are finding $\frac{9}{10} + \frac{7}{12}$.

José	Daniel
$\frac{9}{10} + \frac{7}{12} = \frac{9}{10} \cdot \frac{12}{12} + \frac{7}{12} \cdot \frac{10}{10}$	$\frac{9}{10} + \frac{7}{12} = \frac{9+7}{10+12}$

Who is correct? Explain your reasoning. **See margin.**

DAILY INTERVENTION **Differentiated Instruction**

* **Naturalist** Students often learn best when mathematics is applied to the world around them. Have students examine a log or tree stump and study the growth rings. Have them measure the exact widths of five consecutive rings in inches. Have them total the growth for the five-year period. Are the rings the same width? Explain.

Note: If a tree stump is unavailable, an enlarged picture of the tree rings can be used.

Guided Practice

Find each sum or difference. Write in simplest form.

GUIDED PRACTICE KEY	
Exercises	Examples
4–9	1–5
10	6

4. $\frac{1}{10} + \frac{1}{3}$ $\frac{13}{30}$

5. $-\frac{1}{6} + \frac{7}{18}$ $\frac{2}{9}$

6. $\frac{1}{4} - \frac{2}{3}$ $-\frac{5}{12}$

7. $-\frac{7}{10} - \frac{2}{15}$ $-\frac{5}{6}$

8. $6\frac{4}{5} + \left(-1\frac{3}{4}\right)$ $5\frac{1}{20}$

9. $-9\frac{3}{4} - \left(-5\frac{1}{2}\right)$ $-4\frac{1}{4}$

Application

10. **SEWING** Jessica needs $1\frac{5}{8}$ yards of fabric to make a skirt and $3\frac{1}{2}$ yards to make a coat. How much fabric does she need in all? $5\frac{1}{8}$ yd

★ indicates increased difficulty

Practice and Apply

Homework Help	
For Exercises	See Examples
11–28	1–5
31–34	6

Extra Practice
See page 735.

Find each sum or difference. Write in simplest form.

11. $\frac{3}{5} + \frac{3}{10}$ $\frac{9}{10}$

12. $\frac{9}{26} + \frac{3}{13}$ $\frac{15}{26}$

13. $\frac{3}{7} + \left(-\frac{1}{4}\right)$ $\frac{5}{28}$

14. $-\frac{5}{8} + \left(-\frac{1}{3}\right)$ $-\frac{23}{24}$

15. $\frac{7}{8} - \left(-\frac{3}{16}\right)$ $1\frac{1}{16}$

16. $-\frac{2}{5} - \frac{7}{8}$ $-1\frac{11}{40}$

17. $\frac{3}{4} - \frac{5}{8}$ $\frac{1}{8}$

18. $\frac{5}{7} + \left(-\frac{10}{21}\right)$ $\frac{5}{21}$

19. $-\frac{1}{2} + \frac{3}{8}$ $-\frac{1}{8}$

20. $-\frac{2}{3} + \frac{7}{12}$ $-\frac{1}{12}$

21. $1\frac{2}{5} - \frac{1}{3}$ $1\frac{1}{15}$

22. $\frac{7}{8} + 4\frac{1}{24}$ $4\frac{11}{12}$

23. $-6\frac{2}{3} - \frac{8}{9}$ $-7\frac{5}{9}$

24. $2\frac{16}{30} - \frac{7}{15}$ $2\frac{1}{15}$

25. $-4\frac{1}{6} + \left(-7\frac{11}{18}\right)$ $-11\frac{7}{9}$

26. $3\frac{1}{2} - \left(-7\frac{1}{3}\right)$ $10\frac{5}{6}$

★ 27. $-19\frac{3}{8} - \left(-4\frac{3}{4}\right)$ $-14\frac{5}{8}$

★ 28. $-3\frac{2}{5} - \left(-2\frac{4}{7}\right)$ $-\frac{29}{35}$

★ 29. **ALGEBRA** Evaluate $x - y$ if $x = 4\frac{7}{18}$ and $y = 1\frac{1}{12}$. $3\frac{11}{36}$

★ 30. **ALGEBRA** Solve $\frac{64}{143} - \frac{21}{208} = a$. $\frac{61}{176}$

31. **EARTH SCIENCE** Did you know that water has a greater density than ice? Use the information in the table to find how much more water weighs per cubic foot. $5\frac{3}{5}$ lb

1 Cubic Foot	Weight (lb)
water	$62\frac{1}{2}$
ice	$56\frac{9}{10}$

32. **GRILLING** Use the table to find the fraction of people who grill two, three, or four times per month. $\frac{7}{10}$

33. **PUBLISHING** The length of a page in a yearbook is 10 inches. The top margin is $\frac{1}{2}$ inch, and the bottom margin is $\frac{3}{4}$ inch. What is the length of the page inside the margins? $8\frac{3}{4}$ in.

34. **VOTING** In the class election, Murray received $\frac{1}{3}$ of the votes and Sara received $\frac{2}{5}$ of the votes. Makayla received the rest. What fraction of the votes did Makayla receive? $\frac{4}{15}$

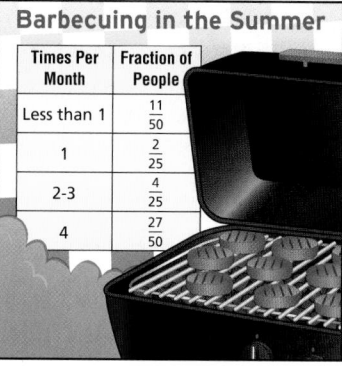

Barbecuing in the Summer

Times Per Month	Fraction of People
Less than 1	$\frac{11}{50}$
1	$\frac{2}{25}$
2-3	$\frac{4}{25}$
4	$\frac{27}{50}$

Source: American Plastics Council

www.pre-alg.com/self_check_quiz

Lesson 5-7 Adding and Subtracting Unlike Fractions 235

Open-Ended Assessment
Modeling Have students model the addition of unlike fractions using the problem of their choice. They may shade in rectangles as shown in the opening activity or use any commercial fraction model. Students should explain their reasoning and then write the corresponding problem using fractions.

Getting Ready
for Lesson 5-8
PREREQUISITE SKILL Lesson 5-8 presents measures of central tendency. Exercises 53–56 should be used to determine your students' familiarity with finding sums of integers. This is a necessary skill when finding the mean.

35. **CRITICAL THINKING** A set of measuring cups has measures of 1 cup, $\frac{3}{4}$ cup, $\frac{1}{2}$ cup, $\frac{1}{3}$ cup, and $\frac{1}{4}$ cup. How could you get $\frac{1}{6}$ cup of milk by using these measures? **See margin.**

36. **CRITICAL THINKING** Do you think the rational numbers are closed under *addition, subtraction, multiplication,* or *division*? Explain. **See margin.**

37. **WRITING IN MATH** Answer the question that was posed at the beginning of the lesson. **See margin.**

   How can the LCM be used to add and subtract fractions with different denominators?

   Include the following in your answer:
   • an example using the LCM, and
   • an explanation of how prime factorization is a helpful way to add and subtract fractions that have different denominators.

Standardized
Test Practice

38. For an art project, Halle needs $11\frac{3}{8}$ inches of red ribbon and $6\frac{7}{9}$ inches of white ribbon. Which is the best estimate for the total amount of ribbon that she needs? **A**
   Ⓐ 18 in.   Ⓑ 26 in.   Ⓒ 10 in.   Ⓓ 8 in.

39. How much less is $\frac{6}{15}$ than $9\frac{1}{2}$? **B**
   Ⓐ $9\frac{27}{30}$ Ⓑ $9\frac{1}{10}$ Ⓒ $1\frac{11}{30}$ Ⓓ $9\frac{3}{10}$

Extending
the Lesson
More than a thousand years ago, the Greeks wrote all fractions as the sum of *unit fractions*. A unit fraction is a fraction that has a numerator of 1, such as $\frac{1}{5}, \frac{1}{7},$ or $\frac{1}{4}$. Express each fraction below as the sum of two different unit fractions. **40–42. Sample answers are given.**

40. $\frac{7}{12}$ $\frac{1}{3} + \frac{1}{4}$ 41. $\frac{3}{5}$ $\frac{1}{2} + \frac{1}{10}$ 42. $\frac{2}{9}$ $\frac{1}{18} + \frac{1}{6}$

Maintain Your Skills

Mixed Review
Find the LCD of each pair of fractions. *(Lesson 5-6)*

43. $\frac{4}{9}, \frac{7}{12}$ **36**   44. $\frac{3}{15t}, \frac{2}{5t}$ **15t**   45. $\frac{1}{3n}, \frac{7}{6n^3}$ **$6n^3$**

Find each sum or difference. Write in simplest form. *(Lesson 5-5)*

46. $\frac{4}{7} + \frac{6}{7}$ $1\frac{3}{7}$ 47. $2\frac{3}{4} + 6\frac{3}{4}$ $9\frac{1}{2}$ 48. $\frac{7}{8} - \frac{5}{8}$ $\frac{1}{4}$

49. $3\frac{2}{5} - \frac{3}{5}$ $2\frac{4}{5}$ 50. $4\frac{1}{6} + 5\frac{5}{6}$ **10**   51. $8 - 6\frac{1}{5}$ $1\frac{4}{5}$

52. Write the prime factorization of 124. *(Lesson 4-3)* $2^2 \cdot 31$

Getting Ready for
the Next Lesson
PREREQUISITE SKILL Find each sum.
*(To review **adding integers**, see Lesson 2-2.)*

53. $24 + (-12) + 15$ **27**   54. $(-2) + 5 + (-3)$ **0**

55. $4 + (-9) + (-9) + 5$ **−9**   56. $-10 + (-9) + (-11) + (-8)$ **−38**

Answers

35. Sample answer: Fill the $\frac{1}{2}$-cup.
   From the $\frac{1}{2}$-cup, fill the $\frac{1}{3}$-cup.
   $\frac{1}{6}$ cup will be left in the $\frac{1}{2}$-cup because $\frac{1}{2} - \frac{1}{3} = \frac{1}{6}$.

36. Rational numbers are closed under addition, subtraction, and multiplication because the sum, difference, or product of two rational numbers is a rational number. They are not closed under division because a rational number divided by zero is undefined.

37. Find the LCM of the denominators. Then rename the fractions as like fractions with the LCM as the denominators. Answers should include the following.
   • For example, the LCM of 4 and 6 is 12. So, $\frac{1}{4} + \frac{5}{6} = \frac{3}{12} + \frac{10}{12} = \frac{13}{12}$ or $1\frac{1}{12}$.

   • Writing the prime factorization of the denominators is the first step in finding the LCM of the denominators, which is the LCD. Then the fractions can be added or subtracted.

Algebra Activity

A Preview of Lesson 5-8

Analyzing Data

Often, it is useful to describe or represent a set of data by using a single number. The table shows the daily maximum temperatures for twenty days during a recent April in Norfolk, Virginia.

One number to describe this data set might be 68. Some reasons for choosing this number are listed below.

- It occurs four times, more often than any other number.
- If the numbers are arranged in order from least to greatest, 68 falls in the center of the data set.

Norfolk, Virginia Maximum Temperatures (nearest °F)			
48	71	61	66
80	83	64	53
54	57	70	68
66	68	68	72
68	76	84	76

There is an equal number of data above and below 68.

48 53 54 57 61 64 66 66 68 68 68 68 70 71 72 76 76 80 83 84

So, if you wanted to describe a typical high temperature for Norfolk during April, you could say 68°F.

Collect the Data

Collect a group of data. Use one of the suggestions below, or use your own method.
- Research data about the weather in your city or in another city, such as temperatures, precipitation, or wind speeds.
- Find a graph or table of data in the newspaper or a magazine. Some examples include financial data, population data, and so on.
- Conduct a survey to gather some data about your classmates.
- Count the number of raisins in a number of small boxes.

Analyze the Data 1–3. See students' work.
1. Choose a number that best describes all of the data in the set.
2. Explain what your number means, and explain which method you used to choose your number.
3. Describe how your number might be useful in real life.

Algebra Activity

A Preview of Lesson 5-8

Getting Started

Objective Determine a number that best represents or describes a set of data.

Possible Materials
weather data from newspaper or Internet
graph or data table from newspaper
small boxes of raisins

Teach

- Before starting this activity, ask students why it is desirable to have a number that describes an entire set of data. Who would use such a number?
- Encourage students to record their data in a chart or table.

Assess

In **Exercises 1–3,** students should
- organize the data in order (usually least to greatest).
- identify the value(s) in the middle.
- look for data that are repeated.

Study Notebook

Have students summarize their activities and write a brief description of the number that best described their data.

Resource Manager

 **Teaching Pre-Algebra with Manipulatives**
- p. 71 (student recording sheet)

5-8 Measures of Central Tendency

1 Focus

5-Minute Check Transparency 5-8 Use as a quiz or review of Lesson 5-7.

Mathematical Background notes are available for this lesson on page 198D.

How are measures of central tendency used in the real world?

The opening activity questions are repeated on page 263 of the *Chapter 5 Resource Masters*.

Reading to Learn Mathematics, p. 263 **ELL**

Pre-Activity *How are measures of central tendency used in the real world?*

Do the activity at the top of page 238 in your textbook. Write your answers below.

a. Which number appears most often? 11

b. If you list the data in order from least to greatest, which number is in the middle? 12

c. What is the sum of all the numbers divided by 28? If necessary, round to the nearest tenth. 13.0

d. If you had to give one number that best represents the winning times, which would you choose? Explain. Sample answer: 11, because it occurs more often than any other number; 12, because it is the middle value in the data set; 13, because it is the sum of the data values divided by the number of values.

Reading the Lesson 1–4. See students' work.

Write a definition and give an example of each new vocabulary word or phrase.

Vocabulary	Definition	Example
1. measures of central tendency		
2. mean		
3. median		
4. mode		

5. How do you find the median if the data have an even number of items?
Find the mean of the two middle numbers.

6. Describe a situation in which no mode exists.
There is no mode if each number occurs once in the set.

7. An extreme value will affect which measure of central tendency the most? mean

Helping You Remember

8. You have learned about mean, median, and mode. In each circle, write three numbers that satisfy the given information. Sample answers are given.

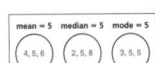
mean = 5   median = 5   mode = 5
4, 5, 6   2, 5, 8   3, 5, 5

5-8 Measures of Central Tendency

What You'll Learn

• Use the mean, median, and mode as measures of central tendency.

• Analyze data using mean, median, and mode.

Vocabulary
• measures of central tendency
• mean
• median
• mode

How are measures of central tendency used in the real world?

The *Iditarod* is a 1150-mile dogsled race across Alaska. The winning times for 1973–2000 are shown in the table.

Winning Times (days)

20	21	15	19	17	15	15
14	12	16	13	13	18	12
11	11	11	11	13	11	11
11	9	9	9	9	10	9

Source: *Anchorage Daily News*

a. Which number appears most often? **11**

b. If you list the data in order from least to greatest, which number is in the middle? **12**

c. What is the sum of all the numbers divided by 28? If necessary, round to the nearest tenth. **13.0**

d. If you had to give one number that best represents the winning times, which would you choose? Explain.

MEAN, MEDIAN, AND MODE When you have a list of numerical data, it is often helpful to use one or more numbers to represent the whole set. These numbers are called **measures of central tendency**. You will study three types.

Key Concept — Measures of Central Tendency

Statistic	Definition
mean	the sum of the data divided by the number of items in the data set
median	the middle number of the ordered data, or the mean of the middle two numbers
mode	the number or numbers that occur most often

Example 1 Find the Mean, Median, and Mode

SPORTS The heights of the players on the girls' basketball team are shown in the chart. Find the mean, median, and mode.

Height of Players (cm)

130	154	148
155	172	153
160	162	140
149	151	150

$$\text{mean} = \frac{\text{sum of heights}}{\text{number of players}}$$

$$= \frac{130 + 154 + 148 + \ldots + 150}{12}$$

$$= \frac{1824}{12} \text{ or } 152$$

The mean height is 152 centimeters.

Resource Manager

 Workbooks and Reproducible Masters

Chapter 5 Resource Masters
• Study Guide and Intervention, p. 260
• Skills Practice, p. 261
• Practice, p. 262
• Reading to Learn Mathematics, p. 263
• Enrichment, p. 264
• Assessment, p. 290

Parent and Student Study Guide Workbook, p. 40
Prerequisite Skills Workbook, pp. 19–22, 29–30

Transparencies
5-Minute Check Transparency 5-8
Answer Key Transparencies

 Technology
Interactive Chalkboard
Pre-AlgePASS: Tutorial Plus, Lesson 9

To find the median, order the numbers from least to greatest.

130, 140, 148, 149, 150, <u>151, 153</u>, 154, 155, 160, 162, 172

$$\frac{151 + 153}{2} = 152 \leftarrow$$ There is an even number of items. Find the mean of the two middle numbers.

The median height is 152.

There is no mode because each number in the set occurs once.

Example 2 Use a Line Plot

HURRICANES The line plot shows the number of Atlantic hurricanes that occurred each year from 1974–2000. Find the mean, median, and mode.

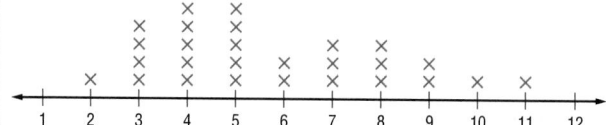

Source: Colorado State/Tropical Prediction Center

$$\text{mean} = \frac{2 + 3(4) + 4(5) + 5(5) + 6(2) + 7(3) + 8(3) + 9(2) + 10 + 11}{27} \approx 5.7$$

There are 27 numbers. So the middle number, which is the median, is the 14th number, or 5.

You can see from the graph that 4 and 5 both occur most often in the data set. So there are two modes, 4 and 5.

✓ Concept Check
If 4 were added to the data set, what would be the new mode?
4 only

A number in a set of data that is much greater or much less than the rest of the data is called an *extreme value*. An extreme value can affect the mean of the data.

Example 3 Find Extreme Values that Affect the Mean

NUTRITION The table shows the number of Calories per serving of each vegetable. Identify an extreme value and describe how it affects the mean.

Vegetable	Calories	Vegetable	Calories
asparagus	14	cauliflower	10
beans	30	celery	17
bell pepper	20	corn	66
broccoli	25	lettuce	9
cabbage	17	spinach	9
carrots	28	zucchini	17

TEACHING TIP
Have students explain whether 66 affects the median.

The data value 66 appears to be an extreme value. Calculate the mean with and without the extreme value to find how it affects the mean.

mean with extreme value

$$\frac{\text{sum of values}}{\text{number of values}} = \frac{262}{12}$$

$$\approx 21.8$$

mean without extreme value

$$\frac{\text{sum of values}}{\text{number of values}} = \frac{196}{11}$$

$$\approx 17.8$$

The extreme value increases the mean by 21.8 − 17.8 or about 4.

www.pre-alg.com/extra_examples

---

2 Teach

MEAN, MEDIAN, AND MODE

In-Class Examples Power Point®

Teaching Tip Make sure students order their data before locating the median and mode. Also, emphasize that more than one mode or no mode are possibilities.

1 **MOVIES** The revenue of the 10 highest grossing movies as of June 2000 are given in the table. Find the mean, median, and mode of the revenues.
mean, $379.8 million; median, $343.5 million; no mode

Top 10 Movie Revenues (millions of $)	
601	330
461	313
431	309
400	306
357	290

Source: World Almanac

2 **OLYMPICS** The line plot below shows the number of gold medals earned by each country that participated in the 1998 Winter Olympic Games in Nagano, Japan. Find the mean, median, and mode for the gold medals won. mean, 2.875; median, 2; mode, 0

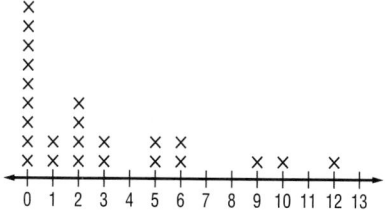

Source: Time Almanac

3 **QUIZ SCORES** The quiz scores for a math class are 8, 7, 6, 10, 8, 8, 9, 8, 7, 9, 8, 0, and 10. Identify an extreme value and describe how it affects the mean. 0; it lowers the mean by about $\frac{2}{3}$.

In-Class Examples Power Point®

4 The table shows the monthly salaries of the employees at two bookstores. Find the mean, median, and mode for each set of data. Based on the averages, which bookstore pays its employees better?

Bob's Books	The Reading Place
1290	1400
1400	1450
1400	1550
1600	1600
3650	2000

Bob's Books: $1868, $1400, $1400; The Reading Place: $1600, $1550, no mode; The Reading Place

5 Jenny's bowling average is 146. Today she bowled 138, 140, and 145. What does she need to score on her fourth game to maintain her average?   at least a 161

---

3 ## Practice/Apply

Study Notebook

Have students—
• add the definitions/examples of the vocabulary terms to their Vocabulary Builder worksheets for Chapter 5.
• include any other item(s) that they find helpful in mastering the skills in this lesson.

TEACHING TIP

Suppose that for this grading period you were to allow students to choose whether you should use the mean, the median, or the mode of their test and quiz scores to determine their grade. Ask them which they would choose and why.

ANALYZE DATA   You can use measures of central tendency to analyze data.

Example 4 *Use Mean, Median, and Mode to Analyze Data*

HOURLY PAY   Compare and contrast the central tendencies of the salaries for the two stores. Based on the averages, which store pays its employees better?

Hourly Salaries ($)	
Sports Superstore	Extreme Sports
7, 24, 7, 6, 8, 8, 8, 6	8, 9, 10, 10, 9, 8, 10, 10

Sports Superstore

mean:
$$= \frac{7 + 24 + 7 + 6 + 8 + 8 + 8 + 6}{8}$$
$$= \$9.25$$

median: 6, 6, 7, 7, 8, 8, 8, 24
$$\frac{7 + 8}{2} \text{ or } \$7.50$$

mode: $8

Extreme Sports

mean:
$$= \frac{8 + 9 + 10 + 10 + 9 + 8 + 10 + 10}{8}$$
$$= \$9.25$$

median: 8, 8, 9, 9, 10, 10, 10, 10
$$\frac{9 + 10}{2} \text{ or } \$9.50$$

mode: $10

The $24 per hour salary at Sports Superstore is an extreme value that increases the mean salary. However, the employees at Extreme Sports are generally better paid, as shown by the higher median and mode salaries.

If you know the value of the mean, you can work backward to find a missing value in the data set.

Standardized Test Practice
Ⓐ Ⓑ Ⓒ Ⓓ

Example 5 *Work Backward*

Grid-In Test Item

Francisca needs an average score of 92 on five quizzes to earn an A. The mean of her first four scores was 91. What is the lowest score that she can receive on the fifth quiz to earn an A?

Read the Test Item   To find the lowest score, write an equation to find the sum of the first four scores. Then write an equation to find the fifth score.

Solve the Test Item

Step 1   Find the sum of the first four scores *x*.

[mean of first four scores] $91 = \frac{x}{4}$ [sum of first four scores]

$(91)4 = \left(\frac{x}{4}\right)4$ Multiply each side by 4.

$364 = x$ Simplify.

Step 2   Find the fifth score *y*.

$\text{mean} = \frac{\text{sum of the first four scores} + \text{fifth score}}{5}$ Write an equation.

$92 = \frac{364 + y}{5}$ Substitution

$460 = 364 + y$ Multiply each side by 5 and simplify.

$96 = y$ Subtract 364 from each side and simplify.

Test-Taking Tip

Substituting   Check that your answer satisfies the conditions of the original problem.

About the Exercises . . .

Organization by Objective
• Mean, Median, and Mode: 10–15
• Analyze Data: 16–18

Odd/Even Assignments
Exercises 10–15 are structured so that students practice the same concepts whether they are assigned odd or even problems.

Assignment Guide

Basic: 11–15 odd, 19–35

Average: 11–17 odd, 19–35

Advanced: 10–16 even, 17–31 (Optional: 32–35)

Check for Understanding

1. **Explain** which measure of central tendency is most affected by an extreme value. **See margin.**

2. **OPEN ENDED** Write a set of data with at least four numbers that has a mean of 8 and a median that is *not* 8. **Sample answer: 4, 7, 9, 10, 10**

Guided Practice

GUIDED PRACTICE KEY	
Exercises	Examples
3, 4, 6	1
5	2
7	3
8	4
9	5

Find the mean, median, and mode for each set of data. If necessary, round to the nearest tenth.

3. 4, 5, 7, 3, 9, 11, 23, 37 **12.4; 8; none**

4. 7.2, 3.6, 9.0, 5.2, 7.2, 6.5, 3.6 **6.0; 6.5; 3.6 and 7.2**

5. **3.6; 3.5; 4**

```
                    ×
        ×   ×   ×       ×
    ×   ×   ×   ×   ×   ×
    ×   ×   ×   ×       ×   ×
  ──┼───┼───┼───┼───┼───┼───┼───┼──
    1   2   3   4   5   6   7   8
```

Application

VACATIONS For Exercises 6–8, use the table. **6. 29.4; 28; 25**

6. Find the mean, median, and mode.

7–8. See margin.

7. Identify any extreme values and describe how they affect the mean.

8. Which statistic would you say best represents the data? Explain.

Standardized Test Practice
Ⓐ Ⓑ Ⓒ Ⓓ

9. Brad's average for five quizzes is 86. If he wants to have an average of 88 for six quizzes, what is the lowest score he can receive on his sixth quiz? **98**

Annual Vacation Days	
Country	Number of Days
Brazil	34
Canada	26
France	37
Germany	35
Italy	42
Japan	25
Korea	25
United Kingdom	28
United States	13

Source: World Tourism Organization

★ indicates increased difficulty

Practice and Apply

Homework Help	
For Exercises	See Examples
10–13	1
14, 15	2
16	3
17, 18	4

Extra Practice
See page 735.

Find the mean, median, and mode for each set of data. If necessary, round to the nearest tenth. 13. 7.6; 7.5; 7.1 and 7.4 15. 4.3; 4.2; 4.1 and 4.2

10. 41, 37, 43, 43, 36 **40; 41; 43**

11. 2, 8, 16, 21, 3, 8, 9, 7, 6 **8.9; 8; 8**

12. 14, 6, 8, 10, 9, 5, 7, 13 **9; 8.5; none**

13. 7.5, 7.1, 7.4, 7.6, 7.4, 9.0, 7.9, 7.1

14. **18.3; 18; 16, 18, and 20**

```
            ×       ×       ×
        ×   ×   ×   ×   ×
        ×   ×   ×   ×   ×   ×
    ──┼───┼───┼───┼───┼───┼───┼───┼──
      15  16  17  18  19  20  21  22
```

15.

```
    ×
    ×       ×
    ×   ×   ×
    ×   ×   ×   ×                   ×
  ──┼───┼───┼───┼───┼───┼───┼───┼──
   4.1 4.2 4.3 4.4 4.5 4.6 4.7 4.8
```

16. **BASKETBALL** Refer to the cartoon at the right. Which measure of central tendency would make opponents believe that the height of the team is much taller than it really is? Explain.

★ 17. **TESTS** Which measure of central tendency best summarizes the test scores shown below? Explain.

97, 99, 95, 89, 99, 100, 87, 85, 89, 92, 96, 95, 60, 97, 85 **See margin.**

Lesson 5-8 Measures of Central Tendency **241**

Sidebar / Answers Margin

16. Mean; the height of the tallest basketball player increases the mean height of the team.

When working with numerical data, it is often helpful to use one or more numbers to represent the whole set. These numbers are called the measures of central tendency. You will study the mean, median, and mode.

Statistic	Definition
mean	sum of the data divided by the number of items in the data set
median	middle number of the ordered data, or the mean of the middle two numbers
mode	number or numbers that occur most often

Example Jason recorded the number of hours he spent watching television each day for a week. Find the mean, median, and mode for the number of hours.

Mon.	Tues.	Wed.	Thurs.	Fri.	Sat.	Sun.
2	3.5	3	0	2.5	6	4

$$\text{mean} = \frac{\text{sum of hours}}{\text{number of days}}$$

$$= \frac{2 + 3.5 + 3 + \ldots + 4}{7}$$

$$= 3 \quad \text{The mean is 3 hours.}$$

To find the median, order the numbers from least to greatest and locate the number in the middle.

0   2   2.5   ③   3.5   4   6   The median is 3 hours.

There is no mode because each number occurs once in the set.

Exercises

Find the mean, median, and mode for each set of data.

1. Maria's test scores
   92, 86, 90, 74, 95, 100, 90, 50 **84.6; 90; 90**

2. Rainfall last week in inches
   0, 0.3, 0, 0.1, 0, 0.5, 0.2 **0.16; 0.1; 0**

3. Resting heart rates of 8 males
   84, 59, 72, 63, 75, 68, 72, 63 **69.5; 70; 72, 63**

Find the mean, median, and mode for each set of data. If necessary, round to the nearest tenth.

1. 4, 6, 12, 5, 8
   7; 6; none

2. 16, 18, 15, 16, 21, 16
   17; 16; 16

3. 55, 46, 50, 42, 39
   46.4; 46; none

4. 17, 16, 13, 17, 17, 10, 10, 13, 10
   13.7; 13; 10, 17

5. 25, 25, 25, 20
   23.8; 25; 25

6. 3.1, 4.5, 4.5, 4.3, 6.0, 3.2
   4.3; 4.4; 4.5

Find the mean, median, and mode for each set of data. If necessary, round to the nearest tenth.

7.
```
        ×
    ×   ×       ×   ×
    ×   ×   ×   ×   ×
  ──┼───┼───┼───┼───┼──
    0   1   2   3   4   5
```
2.3; 2; 2

8.
```
        ×
    ×   ×   ×   ×
    ×   ×   ×   ×   ×
  ──┼───┼───┼───┼───┼───┼──
  10.1 10.2 10.3 10.4 10.5 10.6 10.7
```
10.4; 10.5; 10.2, 10.6

9. **TORNADOES** The table below shows the number of tornadoes reported in the United States from 1980–1990. Find the mean, median, and mode for the number of tornadoes.

Year	1980	1981	1982	1983	1984	1985	1986	1987	1988	1989	1990
Number of Tornadoes	866	783	1046	931	907	684	764	656	702	858	1132

Source: The Universal Almanac

848.1; 858; none

Mean Variation

Mean variation is the average amount by which the data differ from the mean.

Example The mean for the set of data at the right is 17.

12, 16, 27, 16, 14

Find the mean variation as follows.

Step 1 Find the difference between the mean and each item in the set.

17 − 12 = 5
17 − 16 = 1
27 − 17 = 10
17 − 16 = 1
17 − 14 = + 3

Step 2 Add the differences.
20

Step 3 Find the mean of the differences. This is the mean variation.

$$\frac{20}{5} = 4$$

The mean variation is 4.

Find the mean variation for each set of numbers.

1. 100, 250, 200, 175, 300
   The mean is 205.
   205 − 100 = 105
   250 − 205 = 45
   205 − 200 = 5
   205 − 175 = 30
   300 − 205 = 95
   Add the differences above.
   Then, divide by 5.
   The mean variation is **56**.

2. 124, 128, 121, 123
   The mean is 124.
   124 − 124 = 0
   128 − 124 = 4
   124 − 121 = 3
   124 − 123 = 1
   Add the differences above.
   Then, divide by 4.
   The mean variation is **2**.

For each set of data, find the mean and the mean variation.

3. 68, 43, 28, 25 **41; 14.5**

4. 13, 18, 22, 28, 35, 46 **27; $9\frac{1}{3}$**

5. 68, 25, 36, 42, 603, 16, 8, 18
   102; 125.25

6. 79, 81, 85, 80, 78, 86, 84, 83, 75, 88
   81.9; 3.3

Answers

1. Mean; when an extreme value is added to the other data, it can raise or lower the sum, and therefore the mean.

7. Sample answer: 13 could be an extreme value because it is 12 less than the next value. It lowers the mean by 2.1.

8. Sample answer: median, because half the data are less than the median and half are greater than the median.

17. Sample answer: the median, 95, or the modes, 95 and 97, because most students scored higher than mean, which is 91.

Lesson 5-8 Measures of Central Tendency **241**

Open-Ended Assessment

Writing Give students a data set to analyze. They should write a short report of their analysis including use of mean, median, mode, and extreme value.

Getting Ready for Lesson 5-9

PREREQUISITE SKILL Lesson 5-9 presents solving equations with rational numbers. Some problems will require using division of decimals. Exercises 32–35 should be used to determine your students' familiarity with finding quotients of decimals.

Assessment Options

Quiz (Lessons 5-6 through 5-8) is available on p. 290 of the *Chapter 5 Resource Masters*.

Answers

18. Sample answer: The mean is greater than the median because of the high salaries of the top baseball players. These are the extreme values that affect the mean.

19. Sample answer: The median home price would be useful because it is not affected by the cost of the very expensive homes. The cost of half the homes in the county would be greater than the median cost and half would be less.

20. Measures of central tendency are used to describe or represent real-world data. Answers should include the following.
    • Test scores, heights of students, and number of hours worked per week can be described using the mean, median, or mode.
    • Newspaper articles may discuss the average cost of living, the average family size, or the average income for people in a certain age bracket.

★ **18. SALARIES** The graph shows the mean and median salaries of baseball players from 1983 to 2000. Explain why the mean is so much greater than the median. **See margin.**

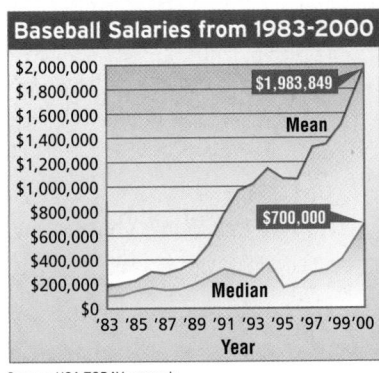

Baseball Salaries from 1983-2000

Source: USA TODAY research

WebQuest

Using measures of central tendency can help you analyze the data from fast-food restaurants. Visit www.pre-alg.com/webquest to continue work on your WebQuest project.

19. CRITICAL THINKING A real estate guide lists the "average" home prices for counties in your state. Do you think the mean, median, or mode would be the most useful average for homebuyers? Explain. **See margin.**

20. WRITING IN MATH Answer the question that was posed at the beginning of the lesson. **See margin.**

How are measures of central tendency used in the real world?

Include the following in your answer:
• examples of real-life data from home or school that can be described using the mean, median, or mode, and
• one or more newspaper articles in which averages are used.

Standardized Test Practice
Ⓐ Ⓑ Ⓒ Ⓓ

21. If 18 were added to the data set below, which statement is true? **C**

16, 14, 22, 16, 16, 18, 15, 25

Ⓐ The mode increases.　　Ⓑ The mean decreases.

Ⓒ The mean increases.　　Ⓓ The median increases.

22. Jonelle's tips as a waitress are shown in the table. On Friday, her tips were $74. Which measure of central tendency will change the *most* as a result? **A**

Ⓐ mean　　　　　　　Ⓑ median

Ⓒ mode　　　　　　　Ⓓ no measure

Day	Tips
Monday	$36
Tuesday	$32
Wednesday	$40
Thursday	$36

Maintain Your Skills

Mixed Review **Find each sum or difference. Write in simplest form.** *(Lesson 5-7)*

23. $9\frac{2}{3} + \frac{1}{6}$ $9\frac{5}{6}$ 　　　**24.** $\frac{7}{8} - \frac{3}{10}$ $\frac{23}{40}$ 　　　**25.** $-2\frac{3}{4} - 1\frac{1}{8}$ $-3\frac{7}{8}$

Replace each ● with <, >, or = to make a true statement. *(Lesson 5-6)*

26. $\frac{1}{2}$ ● $\frac{5}{12}$ > 　　　**27.** $\frac{16}{50}$ ● $\frac{9}{30}$ > 　　　**28.** $\frac{4}{5}$ ● $\frac{48}{60}$ =

ALGEBRA **Solve each equation. Check your solution.** *(Lessons 3-3 and 3-4)*

29. $y - 5 = 13$ **18** 　　　**30.** $10 = 14 + n$ **−4** 　　　**31.** $-4w = 20$ **−5**

Getting Ready for the Next Lesson **PREREQUISITE SKILL** **Find each quotient. If necessary, round to the nearest tenth.** *(To review **dividing decimals**, see page 715.)*

32. $25.6 \div 3$ **8.5** 　　**33.** $37 \div 4.7$ **7.9** 　　**34.** $30.5 \div 11.2$ **2.7** 　　**35.** $46.8 \div 15.6$ **3**

DAILY INTERVENTION

Differentiated Instruction

• **Kinesthetic** Have students use a stack of blocks to represent each number in a data set. To represent the mean, have students "even out" each stack of blocks until each stack is equal. How tall is each stack? Students should try this several times, then write a journal entry, complete with diagrams, describing the averaging process.

Graphing Calculator Investigation

A Follow-Up of Lesson 5-8

Mean and Median

A graphing calculator is able to perform operations on large data sets efficiently. You can use a TI-83 Plus graphing calculator to find the mean and median of a set of data.

Getting Started

Know Your Calculator The graphing calculator will store data in a list. The data will remain in the list until it is deleted.

SURVEYS Fifteen seventh graders were surveyed and asked what was their weekly allowance (in dollars). The results of the survey are shown at the right.

20	10	5	5	10
15	5	10	5	10
5	5	5	5	5

Find the mean and median allowance.

Step 1 *Enter the data.*

• Clear any existing lists.

KEYSTROKES: [STAT] [ENTER] [▲] [CLEAR] [ENTER]

• Enter the allowances as L1.

KEYSTROKES: 20 [ENTER] 10 [ENTER] ... 5 [ENTER]

Step 2 *Find the mean and median.*

• Display a list of statistics for the data.

KEYSTROKES: [STAT] [▶] [ENTER] [ENTER]

The first value, $\bar{x}$, is the mean. →

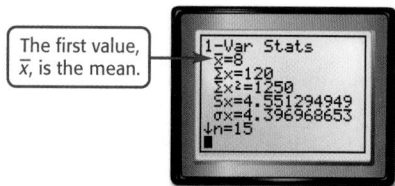

Use the down arrow key to locate "Med." The median allowance is $5 and the mean allowance is $8.

Teach

• If students make an error entering data, simply use the arrow keys within the list to change and correct. To delete an entry completely, use [DEL].

• Have students complete Exercises 1–6.

Assess

Have students describe when the mean best represents the data and when the median best represents the data. Students should be able to provide a list of numbers to illustrate their ideas.

Exercises

Clear list L1 and find the mean and median of each data set. Round decimal answers to the nearest hundredth.

1. 6.4, 5.6, 7.3, 1.2, 5.7, 8.9 **5.85; 6.05**

2. −23, −13, −16, −21, −15, −34, −22 **−20.57; −21**

3. 123, 423, 190, 289, 99, 178, 156, 217, 217 **210.22; 190**

4. 8.4, 2.2, −7.3, −5.3, 6.7, −4.3, 5.1, 1.3, −1.1, −3.2, 2.2, 2.9, 1.4, 68 **5.5; 1.8**

5. Look back at the medians found. When is the median a member of the data set? **See margin.**

6. Refer to Exercise 4. **a–c. See margin.**

   a. Which statistic better represents the data, the mean or median? Explain.

   b. Suppose the number 68 should have been 6.8. Recalculate the mean and median. Is there a significant difference between the first pair of values and the second pair?

   c. When there is an error in one of the data values, which statistic is less likely to be affected? Why?

Answers

5. The median is a term when the number of terms is odd.

6a. Median; 68 in the data set increases the mean so that it does not best represent the data.

6b. 1.13; 1.8; There is a significant difference between the pair of means. The second mean is 4.37 less than the first mean. The median remains the same.

6c. Median; an error can change the mean significantly because it affects the sum of the data. However, the median could remain the same.

Solving Equations with Rational Numbers

1 Focus

 5-Minute Check Transparency 5-9 Use as a quiz or review of Lesson 5-8.

Mathematical Background notes are available for this lesson on page 198D.

How are reciprocals used in solving problems involving music?

The opening activity questions are repeated on page 268 of the *Chapter 5 Resource Masters*.

Reading to Learn Mathematics, p. 268 ELL

Pre-Activity *How are reciprocals used in solving problems involving music?*

Do the activity at the top of page 244 in your textbook. Write your answers below.

a. A guitar string vibrates 440 times per second to produce the A above middle C. Write an equation to find the number of vibrations per second to produce middle C. If you multiply each side by 3, what is the result? $\frac{5}{3}n = 440$; $5n = 1320$

b. How would you solve the second equation you wrote in part **a**? Divide each side by 5.

c. How can you combine the steps in parts **a** and **b** into one step? Multiply each side by $\frac{3}{5}$.

d. How many vibrations per second are needed to produce middle C? 264

Reading the Lesson

1. Dividing by a fraction is the same as multiplying by the ___reciprocal___.

2. Write the first step in solving each equation.

  a. $y - 1.1 = 6.8$ Add 1.1 to each side.

  b. $6 + x = -9$ Subtract 6 from each side.

  c. $\frac{c}{6} = \frac{1}{2}$ Multiply each side by 6.

  d. $-\frac{2}{3}p = -\frac{2}{3}$ Divide each side by $-\frac{2}{3}$ or multiply by $-\frac{3}{2}$.

Helping You Remember

3. You learned to solve equations. Addition equations are solved using subtraction; subtraction equations are solved using addition; multiplication equations are solved using division; division equations are solved using multiplication. In the table below, write three equations that can be solved using the given operations. Be sure to use a variety of rational numbers. Sample answers are given.

Addition	Subtraction	Multiplication	Division
1. $x - 3 = 6$	1. $m + 6 = 11$	1. $\frac{k}{8} = 10$	1. $-6x = 12$
2. $x - 2.5 = 3.6$	2. $3.8 + p = 6$	2. $\frac{q}{1.1} = 9$	2. $\frac{5}{8}a = 16$
3. $t - \frac{1}{2} = \frac{2}{3}$	3. $x + \frac{3}{7} = \frac{9}{14}$	3. $-\frac{v}{6} = \frac{2}{3}$	3. $8.9h = -20$

Teaching Tip You may want students to estimate solutions to the equations before solving.

Resource Manager

📁 Workbooks and Reproducible Masters

Chapter 5 Resource Masters
- Study Guide and Intervention, p. 265
- Skills Practice, p. 266
- Practice, p. 267
- Reading to Learn Mathematics, p. 268
- Enrichment, p. 269

Parent and Student Study Guide Workbook, p. 41
Prerequisite Skills Workbook, pp. 21–24, 27–28, 31–32, 47–62

Transparencies
5-Minute Check Transparency 5-9
Answer Key Transparencies

💿 Technology
Interactive Chalkboard

What You'll Learn

- Solve equations containing rational numbers.

How are reciprocals used in solving problems involving music?

Musical sounds are made by vibrations. If n represents the number of vibrations for middle C, then the approximate vibrations for the other notes going up the scale are given below.

Notes	Middle C	D	E	F	G	A	B	C
Number of Vibrations	n	$\frac{9}{8}n$	$\frac{5}{4}n$	$\frac{4}{3}n$	$\frac{3}{2}n$	$\frac{5}{3}n$	$\frac{15}{8}n$	$\frac{2}{1}n$

a. A guitar string vibrates 440 times per second to produce the A above middle C. Write an equation to find the number of vibrations per second to produce middle C. If you multiply each side by 3, what is the result?

b. How would you solve the second equation you wrote in part **a**?

c. How can you combine the steps in parts **a** and **b** into one step?

d. How many vibrations per second are needed to produce middle C?

SOLVE ADDITION AND SUBTRACTION EQUATIONS You can solve rational number equations the same way you solved equations with integers.

Study Tip

Look Back
To review **solving equations**, see Lessons 3-3 and 3-4.

Example 1 Solve by Using Addition

Solve $2.1 = t - 8.5$. Check your solution.

$2.1 = t - 8.5$	Write the equation.
$2.1 + 8.5 = t - 8.5 + 8.5$	Add 8.5 to each side.
$10.6 = t$	Simplify.

CHECK

$2.1 = t - 8.5$	Write the original equation.
$2.1 \stackrel{?}{=} 10.6 - 8.5$	Replace t with 10.6.
$2.1 = 2.1 \checkmark$	Simplify.

TEACHING TIP

You may want to introduce the use of rational numbers in equations by first solving problems using whole numbers. Then replace whole numbers with decimals and fractions and solve.

Example 2 Solve by Using Subtraction

Solve $x + \frac{3}{5} = \frac{2}{3}$.

$x + \frac{3}{5} = \frac{2}{3}$	Write the equation.
$x + \frac{3}{5} - \frac{3}{5} = \frac{2}{3} - \frac{3}{5}$	Subtract $\frac{3}{5}$ from each side.
$x = \frac{2}{3} - \frac{3}{5}$	Simplify.
$x = \frac{10}{15} - \frac{9}{15}$ or $\frac{1}{15}$	Rename the fractions using the LCD and subtract.

---

a. $\frac{5}{3}n = 440$; $5n = 1320$

b. Divide each side by 5.

c. Multiply each side by $\frac{3}{5}$.

d. 264

Study Tip

Reciprocals
Recall that dividing by a fraction is the same as multiplying by its multiplicative inverse.

SOLVE MULTIPLICATION AND DIVISION EQUATIONS To solve $\frac{1}{2}x = 3$, you can divide each side by $\frac{1}{2}$ or multiply each side by the multiplicative inverse of $\frac{1}{2}$, which is 2.

$$\frac{1}{2}x = 3 \qquad \text{Write the equation.}$$

The product of any number and its multiplicative inverse is 1.

$$2 \cdot \frac{1}{2}x = 2 \cdot 3 \qquad \text{Multiply each side by 2.}$$
$$1x = 6 \qquad \text{Simplify.}$$
$$x = 6$$

Example 3 Solve by Using Division

Solve $-3y = 1.5$. Check your solution.

$$-3y = 1.5 \qquad \text{Write the equation.}$$
$$\frac{-3y}{-3} = \frac{1.5}{-3} \qquad \text{Divide each side by } -3.$$
$$y = -0.5 \qquad \text{Simplify.}$$

CHECK
$$-3y = 1.5 \qquad \text{Write the original equation.}$$
$$-3(-0.5) \stackrel{?}{=} 1.5 \qquad \text{Replace } y \text{ with } -0.5.$$
$$1.5 = 1.5 \checkmark \qquad \text{Simplify.}$$

Example 4 Solve by Using Multiplication

a. Solve $5 = \frac{1}{4}y$. Check your solution.

$$5 = \frac{1}{4}y \qquad \text{Write the equation.}$$
$$4(5) = 4\left(\frac{1}{4}y\right) \qquad \text{Multiply each side by 4.}$$
$$20 = y \qquad \text{Simplify.}$$

CHECK
$$5 = \frac{1}{4}y \qquad \text{Write the original equation.}$$
$$5 \stackrel{?}{=} \frac{1}{4}(20) \qquad \text{Replace } y \text{ with 20.}$$
$$5 = 5 \checkmark \qquad \text{Simplify.}$$

b. Solve $\frac{2}{3}x = 7$. Check your solution.

$$\frac{2}{3}x = 7 \qquad \text{Write the equation.}$$
$$\frac{3}{2}\left(\frac{2}{3}x\right) = \frac{3}{2}(7) \qquad \text{Multiply each side by } \frac{3}{2}.$$
$$x = \frac{21}{2} \qquad \text{Simplify.}$$
$$x = 10\frac{1}{2} \qquad \text{Simplify. Check the solution.}$$

 **Concept Check** What is the first step in solving $\frac{1}{8}r = \frac{1}{4}$?
 Multiply each side by 8.

www.pre-alg.com/extra_examples

SOLVE ADDITION AND SUBTRACTION EQUATIONS

In-Class Examples Power Point®

1 Solve $y - \frac{3}{8} = \frac{3}{4}$. Check your solution. $\frac{9}{8}$ or $1\frac{1}{8}$

2 Solve $m + 8.6 = 11.2$. Check your solution. **2.6**

SOLVE MULTIPLICATION AND DIVISION EQUATIONS

In-Class Examples Power Point®

3 Solve $9a = 3.6$. Check your solution. **0.4**

4 **a.** Solve $8 = \frac{1}{6}x$. Check your solution. **48**

b. Solve $\frac{3}{5}t = -6$. Check your solution. **−10**

Teaching Tip In Example 4a in the text, when multiplying both sides of an equation by 4, some students may need to write 4 as $\frac{4}{1}$ initially.

✓ Skills Check

Solving Equations What needs to be added or subtracted from each side of the equation to solve it?

a. $y + \frac{3}{4} = 3$ subtract $\frac{3}{4}$

b. $x - 5.5 = 2.4$ add 5.5

What needs to be multiplied or divided to solve each equation?

a. $3m = 8.3$ divide by 3

b. $\frac{2}{5}n = 8$ multiply by $\frac{5}{2}$

Study Notebook

Have students—
- record Examples 1–4 to illustrate solving equations using each operation.
- include any other item(s) that they find helpful in mastering the skills in this lesson.

DAILY
INTERVENTION FIND THE ERROR
Have students review Example 3 on page 245. Remind them that the goal is to end up with the variable alone on one side of the equation. When there are decimals in the equation, they need to pay particular attention not to overlook decimal points. 3 is not the same as 0.3.

About the Exercises . . .
Organization by Objective
- **Solve Addition and Subtraction Equations:** 14–27, 37–40
- **Solve Multiplication and Division Equations:** 28–36

Odd/Even Assignments
Exercises 14–40 are structured so that students practice the same concepts whether they are assigned odd or even problems.

Assignment Guide
Basic: 15–43 odd, 46–70
Average: 15–45 odd, 46–70
Advanced: 14–44 even, 45–64 (Optional: 65–70)
All: Practice Quiz 2 (1–10)

Check for Understanding

Concept Check

1. Subtraction Property of Equality

1. **Name** the property of equality that you would use to solve $2 = \frac{3}{4} + x$.

2. **OPEN ENDED** Write an equation that can be solved by multiplying each side by 6. **Sample answer:** $\frac{1}{6}x = 2$

3. **FIND THE ERROR** Grace and Ling are solving $0.3x = 4.5$.

Grace	Ling
$0.3x = 4.5$	$0.3x = 4.5$
$\dfrac{0.3x}{3} = \dfrac{4.5}{3}$	$\dfrac{0.3x}{0.3} = \dfrac{4.5}{0.3}$
$x = 1.5$	$x = 15$

Who is correct? Explain your reasoning. **Ling; dividing 0.3 by 3 does not isolate the variable on one side.**

Guided Practice Solve each equation. Check your solution.

GUIDED PRACTICE KEY	
Exercises	Examples
4–9, 13	1, 2
10–12	3, 4

4. $y + 3.5 = 14.9$ **11.4**

5. $b - 5 = 13.7$ **18.7**

6. $\frac{3}{2} = w + \frac{3}{5}$ **$\frac{9}{10}$**

7. $c - \frac{3}{5} = \frac{5}{6}$ **$1\frac{13}{30}$**

8. $x + \frac{5}{8} = 7\frac{1}{2}$ **$6\frac{7}{8}$**

9. $4\frac{1}{6} = r + 6\frac{1}{4}$ **$-2\frac{1}{12}$**

10. $3.5a = 7$ **2**

11. $-\frac{1}{6}s = 15$ **-90**

12. $9 = \frac{3}{4}g$ **12**

Application

13. **METEOROLOGY** When a storm struck, the barometric pressure was 28.79 inches. Meteorologists said that the storm caused a 0.36-inch drop in pressure. What was the barometric pressure before the storm? **29.15 in.**

★ indicates increased difficulty

Practice and Apply

Homework Help	
For Exercises	See Examples
14–27, 37–40	1, 2
28–36	3, 4

Extra Practice
See page 736.

Solve each equation. Check your solution. 18. **−6.34**

14. $y + 7.2 = 21.9$ **14.7**

15. $4.7 = a + 7.1$ **−2.4**

16. $x - 5.3 = 8.1$ **13.4**

17. $n - 4.72 = 7.52$ **12.24**

18. $t + 3.17 = -3.17$

19. $a - 2.7 = 3.2$ **5.9**

20. $\frac{2}{3} = \frac{1}{8} + b$ **$\frac{13}{24}$**

21. $m + \frac{7}{12} = -\frac{5}{18}$ **$-\frac{31}{36}$**

22. $g + \frac{2}{3} = 2$ **$1\frac{1}{3}$**

23. $7 = \frac{2}{9} + k$ **$6\frac{7}{9}$**

24. $n - \frac{3}{8} = \frac{1}{6}$ **$\frac{13}{24}$**

25. $x - \frac{2}{5} = -\frac{8}{15}$ **$-\frac{2}{15}$**

26. $7\frac{1}{3} = c - \frac{4}{5}$ **$8\frac{2}{15}$**

27. $-2 = \frac{3}{10} + f$ **$-2\frac{3}{10}$**

28. $\frac{7}{9}k = -\frac{5}{12}$ **$-\frac{15}{28}$**

29. $4.1p = 16.4$ **4**

30. $8 = \frac{2}{3}d$ **12**

31. $0.4y = 2$ **5**

32. $\frac{1}{5}t = 9$ **45**

33. $4 = -\frac{1}{8}q$ **−32**

34. $\frac{1}{3}n = \frac{2}{9}$ **$\frac{2}{3}$**

35. $\frac{5}{8} = \frac{1}{2}r$ **$1\frac{1}{4}$**

36. $\frac{2}{3}a = 6$ **9**

37. $b - 1\frac{1}{2} = 4\frac{1}{4}$ **$5\frac{3}{4}$**

38. $7\frac{1}{2} = r - 5\frac{2}{3}$ **$13\frac{1}{6}$**

39. $3\frac{3}{4} + n = 6\frac{5}{8}$ **$2\frac{7}{8}$**

40. $y + 1\frac{1}{3} = 3\frac{1}{18}$ **$1\frac{13}{18}$**

41. **PUBLISHING** A newspaper is $12\frac{1}{4}$ inches wide and 22 inches long. This is $1\frac{1}{4}$ inches narrower and half an inch longer than the old edition. What were the previous dimensions of the newspaper? **$13\frac{1}{2}$ in. by $21\frac{1}{2}$ in.**

Answer (p.247)

47. Equations with fractions can be written to represent the number of vibrations per second for different notes. To solve, multiply each side of the equation by the reciprocal of the fraction. Answers should include the following.

- For example, if n vibrations per second produce middle C, then $\frac{5}{4}n$ vibrations per second produce the note E above middle C.

42. AIRPORTS The graph shows the world's busiest cargo airports. What is the difference in cargo handling between Memphis and Tokyo? **0.73 million or 730,000 metric tons**

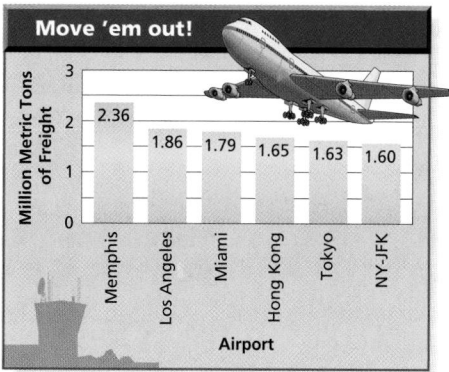

Move 'em out!

Airport	Million Metric Tons of Freight
Memphis	2.36
Los Angeles	1.86
Miami	1.79
Hong Kong	1.65
Tokyo	1.63
NY-JFK	1.60

Source: Airports Council International

43. BUSINESS A store is going out of business. All of the items are marked $\frac{1}{3}$ off the ticketed price. How much would a shirt that was originally priced at $24.99 cost now? **$16.66**

44. COOKING Lucas made $2\frac{1}{2}$ batches of cookies for a bake sale and used $3\frac{3}{4}$ cups of sugar. How much sugar is needed for one batch of cookies? **$1\frac{1}{2}$ c**

★ **45. TRAINS** As a train begins to roll, the cars are "jerked" into motion. Slack is built into the couplings so that the engine does not have to move every car at once. If the slack built into each coupling is 3 inches, how many feet of slack is there between ten freight cars? (*Hint:* Do not include the coupling between the engine and the first car.) **$2\frac{1}{4}$ ft**

46. CRITICAL THINKING The denominator of a fraction is 4 more than the numerator. If both the numerator and denominator are increased by 1, the resulting fraction equals $\frac{1}{2}$. Find the original fraction. **$\frac{3}{7}$**

47. WRITING IN MATH Answer the question that was posed at the beginning of the lesson. **See margin.**

How are reciprocals used in solving problems involving music?

Include the following in your answer:
- an example of how fractions are used to compare musical notes, and
- an explanation of how reciprocals are useful in finding the number of vibrations per second needed to produce certain notes.

48. Find the value of z in $\frac{5}{6}z = \frac{3}{5}$. **A**

Ⓐ $\frac{18}{25}$ Ⓑ $\frac{15}{30}$ Ⓒ $\frac{1}{2}$ Ⓓ $1\frac{7}{18}$

49. The area A of the triangle is $33\frac{3}{4}$ square centimeters. Use the formula $A = \frac{1}{2}bh$ to find the height h of the triangle. **D**

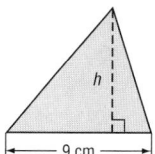

Ⓐ $3\frac{13}{18}$ cm   Ⓑ $6\frac{1}{2}$ cm

Ⓒ $18\frac{13}{18}$ cm   Ⓓ $7\frac{1}{2}$ cm

More About. . .

Airports •••••••••

In 1995, there were 580 million airline passengers. In 2005, there will be an estimated 823 million airline passengers.

Source: Department of Transportation

- The equation $\frac{5}{3}n = 440$ represents the number of vibrations per second to produce middle C. To solve, multiply each side by the reciprocal of $\frac{5}{3}$, $\frac{3}{5}$.

Open-Ended Assessment

Speaking Put students in groups of three. Give each group three equations to solve. After the groups solve the equations, have them present their work to the class. Each student must present one problem. The class and teacher may give feedback. Look for clarity of explanations, correctness of work, and a check of the solution.

Tips for New Teachers

Repetition Some students may require additional time and examples to fully understand solving equations with fractions. You may want to frequently refer to equations involving whole numbers as well as consider spending an extra day on this lesson. Use the Extra Practice on page 736. You can also use the Study Guide and Intervention masters or the Practice masters in the *Chapter 5 Resource Masters* to reinforce this concept.

Getting Ready for Lesson 5-10

PREREQUISITE SKILL Lesson 5-10 presents arithmetic and geometric sequences. Exercises 65–70 should be used to determine your students' familiarity with dividing integers. This skill will be used to find ratios of terms in sequences.

Assessment Options

Practice Quiz 2 The quiz provides students with a brief review of the concepts and skills in Lessons 5-6 through 5-9. Lesson numbers are given to the right of exercises or instruction lines so students can review concepts not yet mastered.

Maintain Your Skills

Mixed Review   Find the mean, median, and mode for each set of data. If necessary, round to the nearest tenth.   *(Lesson 5-8)*   **51. 13; 12; 11 and 12**

50. 2, 8, 5, 18, 3, 5, 6   **6.7; 5; 5**

51. 11, 12, 12, 14, 16, 11, 15

52. 0.9, 0.5, 0.7, 0.4, 0.3, 0.2   **0.5; 0.5; none**

53. 56, 77, 60, 60, 72, 100   **70.8; 66; 60**

Find each sum or difference. Write in simplest form.   *(Lesson 5-7)*

54. $\frac{3}{5} + \frac{1}{3}$ $\frac{14}{15}$

55. $\frac{5}{6} - \frac{1}{8}$ $\frac{17}{24}$

56. $-4\frac{1}{4} - \frac{1}{6}$ $-4\frac{5}{12}$

57. $\frac{5}{9} + \left(-\frac{1}{12}\right)$ $\frac{17}{36}$

58. $-3\frac{3}{4} + \left(-2\frac{1}{8}\right)$ $-5\frac{7}{8}$

59. $8\frac{9}{10} - 1\frac{1}{6}$ $7\frac{11}{15}$

60. ALGEBRA   Evaluate $a - b$ if $a = 9\frac{5}{6}$ and $b = 1\frac{1}{6}$.   *(Lesson 5-5)* $8\frac{2}{3}$

61. HEALTH   According to the National Sleep Foundation, teens should get approximately 9 hours of sleep each day. What fraction of the day is this? Write in simplest form.   *(Lesson 4-5)* $\frac{3}{8}$

ALGEBRA   Solve each equation. Check your solution.   *(Lesson 3-5)*

62. $3t - 6 = 15$ **7**

63. $8 = \frac{k}{-2} + 5$ **−6**

64. $9n - 13n = 4$ **−1**

Getting Ready for the Next Lesson   **PREREQUISITE SKILL**   Divide. If necessary, write as a fraction in simplest form.   *(To review **dividing integers**, see Lesson 2-5.)*

65. $-18 \div 3$ **−6**

66. $24 \div (-2)$ **−12**

67. $-20 \div (-4)$ **5**

68. $-55 \div (-5)$ **11**

69. $-12 \div 36$ $-\frac{1}{3}$

70. $9 \div (-81)$ $-\frac{1}{9}$

Practice Quiz 2   Lessons 5-6 through 5-9

Find the least common multiple of each set of numbers.   *(Lesson 5-6)*

1. 8, 9   **72**

2. 12, 30   **60**

3. 2, 10   **10**

4. 6, 8   **24**

Find each sum or difference. Write in simplest form.   *(Lesson 5-7)*

5. $\frac{3}{4} + \frac{1}{16}$ $\frac{13}{16}$

6. $-\frac{3}{7} + \frac{5}{14}$ $-\frac{1}{14}$

7. $1\frac{1}{5} - \left(-\frac{7}{15}\right)$ $1\frac{2}{3}$

8. $6\frac{3}{4} - 2\frac{1}{6}$ $4\frac{7}{12}$

9. WEATHER   The low temperatures on March 24 for twelve different cities are recorded at the right. Find the mean, median, and mode. If necessary, round to the nearest tenth.   *(Lesson 5-8)*   **32.4; 30.5; 29**

Low Temperatures (°F)			
31	29	30	22
45	35	29	30
40	29	31	38

10. ALGEBRA   Solve $a - 1\frac{1}{3} = 4\frac{1}{6}$.   *(Lesson 5-9)* $5\frac{1}{2}$

Arithmetic and Geometric Sequences

What You'll Learn

- Find the terms of arithmetic sequences.
- Find the terms of geometric sequences.

Vocabulary

- sequence
- arithmetic sequence
- term
- common difference
- geometric sequence
- common ratio

How can sequences be used to make predictions?

The table shows the distance a car moves during the time it takes to apply the brakes and while braking.

a. What is the reaction distance for a car going 70 mph? **70 ft**

b. What is the braking distance for a car going 70 mph? **245 ft**

c. What is the difference in reaction distances for every 10-mph increase in speed? **10 ft**

d. Describe the braking distance as speed increases.

d. Sample answer: The difference increases by 10 feet each time: 25, 35, 45, 55....

Speed (mph)	Reaction Distance (ft)	Braking Distance (ft)
20	20	20
30	30	45
40	40	80
50	50	125
60	60	180

TEACHING TIP

Discuss the pronunciation of arithmetic (ar-ith-met'-ik) when it is used as an adjective rather than a noun.

ARITHMETIC SEQUENCES

A **sequence** is an ordered list of numbers. An **arithmetic sequence** is a sequence in which the difference between any two consecutive terms is the same. So, you can find the next term in the sequence by adding the same number to the previous term.

Each number is called a **term** of the sequence.

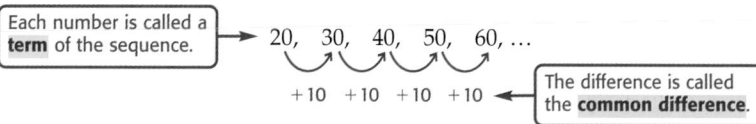

20, 30, 40, 50, 60, ...
+10 +10 +10 +10

The difference is called the **common difference**.

Example 1 Identify an Arithmetic Sequence

State whether the sequence 8, 5, 2, −1, −4, ... is arithmetic. If it is, state the common difference and write the next three terms.

8, 5, 2, −1, −4   Notice that $5 - 8 = -3$, $2 - 5 = -3$, and so on.
−3 −3 −3 −3

The terms have a common difference of −3, so the sequence is arithmetic. Continue the pattern to find the next three terms.

−4, −7, −10, −13
−3 −3 −3

The next three terms of the sequence are −7, −10, and −13.

---

1 Focus

 5-Minute Check Transparency 5-10 Use as a quiz or review of Lesson 5-9.

Mathematical Background notes are available for this lesson on page 198D.

How can sequences be used to make predictions?

The opening activity questions are repeated on page 273 of the *Chapter 5 Resource Masters*.

Reading to Learn Mathematics, p. 273   ELL

Pre-Activity How can sequences be used to make predictions?
Do the activity at the top of page 249 in your textbook. Write your answers below.

a. What is the reaction distance for a car going 70 mph? 70 ft
b. What is the braking distance for a car going 70 mph? 245 ft
c. What is the difference in reaction distances for every 10-mph increase in speed? 10 ft
d. Describe the braking distance as speed increases.
Sample answer: The difference increases by 10 feet each time: 25, 35, 45, 55, ...

Reading the Lesson   1–6. See students' work.

Write a definition and give an example of each new vocabulary word or phrase.

Vocabulary	Definition	Example
1. sequence		
2. arithmetic sequence		
3. term		
4. common difference		
5. geometric sequence		
6. common ratio		

7. What is the common difference in the sequence 8, 17, 26, 35, . . .? 9
8. What is the common ratio in the sequence 1, −2, 4, −8, 16, . . .? −2

Helping You Remember

9. *Sequence* is a word that is used in everyday English.

a. Find the definition of *sequence* in a dictionary. Write the definition. act of following
b. Explain how the English definition can help you remember how *sequence* is used in mathematics. Terms in arithmetic and geometric sequences follow based on a common difference or ratio.

Resource Manager

Workbooks and Reproducible Masters

Chapter 5 Resource Masters
- Study Guide and Intervention, p. 270
- Skills Practice, p. 271
- Practice, p. 272
- Reading to Learn Mathematics, p. 273
- Enrichment, p. 274
- Assessment, p. 290

Parent and Student Study Guide Workbook, p. 42
Prerequisite Skills Workbook, pp. 1–2, 45–48

Transparencies

5-Minute Check Transparency 5-10
Answer Key Transparencies

Technology

Interactive Chalkboard
Pre-AlgePASS: Tutorial Plus, Lessons 10 and 11

ARITHMETIC SEQUENCES

In-Class Examples

1 State whether the sequence −5, −1, 3, 7, 11, . . . is arithmetic. If it is, state the common difference and write the next three terms.
arithmetic; 4; 15, 19, 23

2 State whether the sequence 0, 2, 6, 12, 20, . . . is arithmetic. If it is, state the common difference and write the next three terms.
not arithmetic

Teaching Tip In-class Example 2 does have a pattern that allows you to determine the next three terms: 30, 42, and 56.

GEOMETRIC SEQUENCES

In-Class Example

3 **a.** State whether the sequence 2, 4, 4, 8, 8, 16, 16, . . . is geometric. If it is, state the common ratio and write the next three terms.   **not geometric**

Teaching Tip Note that two ratios alternate throughout the sequence, but it does not meet the definition of geometric.

b. State whether the sequence 27, −9, 3, −1, $\frac{1}{3}$, . . . is geometric. If it is, state the common ratio and write the next three terms.   **geometric;**
$-\frac{1}{3}; -\frac{1}{9}, \frac{1}{27}, -\frac{1}{81}$

Example 2 **Identify an Arithmetic Sequence**

State whether the sequence 1, 2, 4, 7, 11, . . . is arithmetic. If it is, write the next three terms of the sequence.

1, 2, 4, 7, 11   The terms do not have a common difference.
  +1 +2 +3 +4

The sequence is not arithmetic. However, if the pattern continues, the next three differences will be 5, 6, and 7.

11, 16, 22, 29
  +5 +6 +7   The next three terms are 16, 22, and 29.

GEOMETRIC SEQUENCES A **geometric sequence** is a sequence in which the quotient of any two consecutive terms is the same. So, you can find the next term in the sequence by multiplying the previous term by the same number.

1, 4, 16, 64, 256, . . .
  ×4 ×4 ×4 ×4   → The quotient is called the **common ratio**.

TEACHING TIP
Point out that common differences and common ratios may be positive or negative numbers.

☑ **Concept Check** Name the common ratio in the sequence 10, 20, 40, 80, 160, ... **2**

Example 3 **Identify Geometric Sequences**

a. **State whether the sequence −2, 6, −18, 54, . . . is geometric. If it is, state the common ratio and write the next three terms.**

−2, 6, −18, 54   Notice that $6 ÷ (−2) = −3$, $−18 ÷ 6 = −3$, and $54 ÷ (−18) = −3$.
  ×(−3) ×(−3) ×(−3)

The common ratio is −3, so the sequence is geometric. Continue the pattern to find the next three terms.

54, −162, 486, −1458
  ×(−3) ×(−3) ×(−3)   The next three terms are −162, 486, and −1458.

b. **State whether the sequence 20, 10, 5, $\frac{5}{2}$, $\frac{5}{4}$, . . . is geometric. If it is, state the common ratio and write the next three terms.**

20, 10, 5, $\frac{5}{2}$, $\frac{5}{4}$
  ×$\frac{1}{2}$ ×$\frac{1}{2}$ ×$\frac{1}{2}$ ×$\frac{1}{2}$

The common ratio is $\frac{1}{2}$ or 0.5, so the sequence is geometric. Continue the pattern to find the next three terms.

$\frac{5}{4}$, $\frac{5}{8}$, $\frac{5}{16}$, $\frac{5}{32}$
  ×$\frac{1}{2}$ ×$\frac{1}{2}$ ×$\frac{1}{2}$ The next three terms are $\frac{5}{8}$, $\frac{5}{16}$, and $\frac{5}{32}$.

Study Tip

Alternative Method
Multiplying by $\frac{1}{2}$ is the same as dividing by 2, so the following is also true.

20, 10, 5, $\frac{5}{2}$, $\frac{5}{4}$
  ÷2 ÷2 ÷2 ÷2

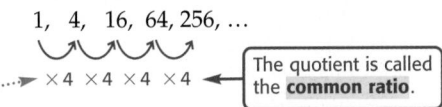

DAILY INTERVENTION   **Differentiated Instruction**

• **Auditory/Musical** Students who relate to music should identify a musical scale and relate it to an arithmetic sequence. Skipping every other note on the scale can also represent an arithmetic sequence. Challenge the students to find a sequence of musical notes to represent a geometric sequence.

Check for Understanding

Concept Check

1. See margin.
2. The terms are decreasing; sample answer: 8, 4, 2, 1; 0.5.

1. **Compare and contrast** arithmetic and geometric sequences.

2. **OPEN ENDED** Describe the terms of a geometric sequence whose common ratio is a fraction or decimal between 0 and 1. Then write four terms of such a sequence and name the common ratio.

Guided Practice

GUIDED PRACTICE KEY	
Exercises	Examples
3–9	1–3

State whether each sequence is *arithmetic, geometric,* or *neither.* If it is arithmetic or geometric, state the common difference or common ratio and write the next three terms of the sequence. **3–8. See margin.**

3. 3, 7, 11, 15, …

4. 1, 3, 9, 27, …

5. 6, 8, 12, 18, …

6. 13, 8, 3, −2, …

7. $3, \frac{8}{3}, \frac{7}{3}, 2, \ldots$

8. $48, 12, 3, \frac{3}{4}, \ldots$

Application

9. **CARS** A new car is worth only about 0.82 of its value from the previous year during the first three years. Approximately how much will a $20,000 car be worth in 3 years? **Source:** www.caprice.com **$11,027.36**

★ indicates increased difficulty

Practice and Apply

Homework Help

For Exercises	See Examples
10–29	1–3

Extra Practice
See page 736.

State whether each sequence is *arithmetic, geometric,* or *neither.* If it is arithmetic or geometric, state the common difference or common ratio and write the next three terms of the sequence. **10–27. See p. 261A.**

10. 2, 5, 8, 11, …

11. −6, 5, 16, 27, …

12. $\frac{1}{2}, 1, 2, 4, \ldots$

13. 2, 6, 18, 54, …

14. 18, 11, 4, −3, …

15. 25, 22, 19, 16, …

16. $4, 1, \frac{1}{4}, \frac{1}{16}, \ldots$

17. $-5, 1, -\frac{1}{5}, \frac{1}{25}, \ldots$

18. $\frac{1}{2}, 1, \frac{3}{2}, 2, \ldots$

19. $0, \frac{1}{6}, \frac{1}{3}, \frac{1}{2}, \ldots$

20. 0.75, 1.5, 2.25, …

21. 4.5, 4.0, 3.5, 3.0, …

22. 11, 14, 19, 26, …

23. 17, 16, 14, 11, …

24. 24, 12, 6, 3, …

★ 25. $18, -6, 2, -\frac{2}{3}, \ldots$

★ 26. 0.1, 0.3, 0.9, 2.7, …

★ 27. $\frac{1}{2}, \frac{1}{4}, \frac{1}{8}, \frac{1}{16}, \ldots$

28. **PHYSICAL SCIENCE** A ball bounces back 0.75 of its height on every bounce. If a ball is dropped from 160 feet, how high does it bounce on the third bounce? **67.5 ft**

29. **TELEPHONE RATES** For an overseas call, WorldTel charges $6 for the first minute and then $3 for each additional minute. **a. See p. 261A.**

   a. Is the cost an arithmetic or geometric sequence? Explain.

   b. How much would a 15-minute call cost? **$48**

30. **CRITICAL THINKING** The sum of four numbers in an arithmetic sequence is 42. What could the numbers be? Give two different examples.
   Sample answer: 9, 10, 11, 12; 6, 9, 12, 15

31. WRITING IN MATH Answer the question that was posed at the beginning of the lesson. **See p. 261A.**

   How can sequences be used to make predictions?

   Include the following in your answer:

   • a discussion of common difference and common ratio, and

   • examples of sequences occurring in nature.

 www.pre-alg.com/self_check_quiz

Study Notebook

Have students—

• complete the definitions/examples for the remaining terms on their Vocabulary Builder worksheets for Chapter 5.

• record examples of sequences that are geometric, arithmetic, and neither. Each example should have a brief explanation.

• include any other item(s) that they find helpful in mastering the skills in this lesson.

About the Exercises . . .

Odd/Even Assignments

Exercises 10–27 are structured so that students practice the same concepts whether they are assigned odd or even problems.

Assignment Guide

Basic: 11–23 odd, 29, 30–33, 36–49

Average: 11–29 odd, 30–33, 36–49 (Optional: 34–35)

Advanced: 10–28 even, 30–49

Answers

1. Arithmetic sequences have a common difference and the terms can be found by adding or subtracting. Geometric sequences have a common ratio and the terms can be found by multiplying or dividing.

3. A; 4; 19, 23, 27

4. G; 3; 81, 243, 729

5. neither

6. A; −5; −7, −12, −17

7. A; $-\frac{1}{3}; \frac{5}{3}, \frac{4}{3}, 1$

8. G; $\frac{1}{4}; \frac{3}{16}, \frac{3}{64}, \frac{3}{256}$

A sequence is an ordered list of numbers. An arithmetic sequence is a sequence in which the difference between any two consecutive terms, called the common difference, is the same. In the sequence 2, 9, 16, 23, 30, . . . , the common difference is 7.
A geometric sequence is a sequence in which the quotient of any two consecutive terms, called the common ratio, is the same. In the sequence 1, −4, 16, −64, 256, . . . , the common ratio is −4.

Example State whether the sequence is *arithmetic, geometric,* or *neither.* If it is arithmetic or geometric, state the common difference or common ratio and write the next three terms of the sequence.

a. 7, 14, 28, 56, 112, . . .

The common ratio is 2, so the sequence is geometric. The next three terms are 112 · 2 or 224, 224 · 2 or 448, and 448 · 2 or 896.

b. 8, 6, 4, 2, 0, −2, . . .

The common difference is −2, so the sequence is arithmetic. The next three terms are −2 + (−2) or −4, −4 + (−2) or −6, and −6 + (−2) or −8.

Exercises

State whether each sequence is *arithmetic, geometric,* or *neither.* If it is arithmetic or geometric, state the common difference or common ratio and write the next three terms.

1. 10, 20, 40, 80, 160, . . .
geometric; 2; 320, 640, 1280

2. 7, 17, 27, 37, 47, . . .
arithmetic; 10; 57, 67, 77

3. 100, 50, 25, $\frac{25}{2}$, $\frac{25}{4}$, . . .
geometric; $\frac{1}{2}$; $\frac{25}{8}$, $\frac{25}{16}$, $\frac{25}{32}$

4. 12, 9, 6, 3, 0, . . .
arithmetic; −3; −3, −6, −9

5. 1, 2, 2, 3, 3, 3, . . .
neither

6. 1, −1, 1, −1, 1, . . .
geometric; −1; −1, 1, −1

7. 2, 3, 4.5, . . .
geometric; 1.5; 6.75, 10.125, 15.1875

8. −21, −10, 1, 12, 23, . . .
arithmetic; 11; 34, 45, 56

9. 1.6, 3.2, 4.8, . . .
arithmetic; 1.6; 6.4, 8, 9.6

10. 4, 12, 36, . . .
geometric; 3; 108, 324, 972

State whether each sequence is *arithmetic, geometric,* or *neither.* If it is arithmetic or geometric, state the common difference or common ratio and write the next three terms of the sequence.

1. 4, 12, 20, 28, 36, . . . arithmetic; 8; 44, 52, 60

2. 1, 1$\frac{1}{3}$, 1$\frac{2}{3}$, 2, 2$\frac{1}{3}$, . . . arithmetic; $\frac{1}{3}$; 2$\frac{2}{3}$, 3, 3$\frac{1}{3}$

3. 10, 11, 13, 16, 20, . . . neither

4. 3, −9, 27, −81, 243, . . . geometric; −3; −729, 2187, −6561

5. 1, 0.5, 0.25, 0.125, 0.0625, . . . geometric; 0.5; 0.03125, 0.015625, 0.0078125

6. 4, −1, −6, −11, −16, . . . arithmetic; −5; −21, −26, −31

7. 0.7, 1.4, 2.8, 5.6, 11.2, . . . geometric; 2; 22.4, 44.8, 89.6

8. 17, 10, 3, −4, −11, . . . arithmetic; −7; −18, −25, −32

9. 1, 0, 2, 0, 3, . . . neither

10. 2, 3$\frac{1}{2}$, 5, 6$\frac{1}{2}$, 8, . . . arithmetic; 1$\frac{1}{2}$; 9$\frac{1}{2}$, 11, 12$\frac{1}{2}$

11. 100, 20, 4, 0.8, 0.16, . . . geometric; 0.2; 0.032, 0.0064, 0.00128

12. 6, 2, $\frac{2}{3}$, $\frac{2}{9}$, $\frac{2}{27}$, . . . geometric; $\frac{1}{3}$; $\frac{2}{81}$, $\frac{2}{243}$, $\frac{2}{729}$

13. −23, −12, −1, 10, 21, . . . arithmetic; 11; 32, 43, 54

14. **DEPRECIATION** A new sport utility vehicle (SUV) costs $25,000. If it depreciates 20% of its value each year, find the value of the vehicle for each of the next five years. $20,000, $16,000, $12,800, $10,240, $8192

Applications of Geometric Sequences

Populations often grow according to a geometric sequence. If the population of a city grows at the rate of 2% per year, then the common ratio, r, is 1.02. To find the population of a city of 100,000 after 5 years of 2% growth, use the formula ar^{n-1}, where r is the common ratio and n is the number of years.

$ar^{n-1} = 100,000\,(1.02)^{5-1}$ $a = 100,000, r = 1.02, n = 5$
$= 100,000\,(1.02)^4$
$\approx 108,243$ So, the city has a population of 108,243 people.

After a few years, a small change in the annual growth rate can cause enormous differences in the population.

Assume that the nation of Grogro had a population of one million in 2000. Using a calculator, find the population of the country in the years 2020, 2070, and 2120 at growth rates of 1%, 3%, and 5% per year. Record your results in the table below.

Growth Rate	Population of Grogro		
	Year		
	2020	2070	2120
1. 1%	1,208,109	1,986,894	3,267,710
2. 3%	1,753,506	7,687,206	33,699,988
3. 5%	2,526,950	28,977,548	332,297,129

Suppose we want to find the total upward distance a bouncing ball has moved. It bounces up 36 inches on the first bounce and $\frac{3}{4}$ times its height on each of five more consecutive bounces.

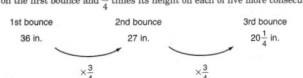

1st bounce 36 in.   2nd bounce 27 in.   3rd bounce 20$\frac{1}{4}$ in.

The distances form the terms of a geometric sequence. We want to find the sum of the distances, or the sum of the six terms in the sequence.

The sum of the terms of a geometric sequence is called a geometric series. The formula for the sum S_n of the first n terms of a geometric series is $S_n = \frac{a - ar^n}{1-r}$, where a = the first term and r = the common ratio (r ≠ 1).

$S_n = \frac{a - ar^n}{1-r}$ Write the formula.

$= \frac{36 - 36\left(\frac{3}{4}\right)^6}{1 - \frac{3}{4}}$ $a = 36, r = \frac{3}{4}, n = 6$

≈ 118.4 So, the ball bounces upward approximately 118.4 inches.

Use the formula above to find each sum. Then check your answer by adding.

4. 5 + 10 + 20 + 40 + 80 155

5. 80 + 240 + 720 + 2160 + 6480 9680

---

32. State the next term in the sequence 56, 48, 40, 32, ... **C**

Ⓐ 20   Ⓑ 22   Ⓒ 24   Ⓓ 28

33. Which statement is true as the side length of a square increases? **A**

Ⓐ The perimeter values form an arithmetic sequence.

Ⓑ The perimeter values form a geometric sequence.

Ⓒ The area values form an arithmetic sequence.

Ⓓ The area values form a geometric sequence.

Side Length	Perimeter	Area
1	4	1
2	8	4
3	12	9
4	16	16
5	20	25

Extending the Lesson In an arithmetic sequence, d represents the common difference, a_1 represents the first term, a_2 represents the second term, and so on. For example, in the sequence 6, 9, 12, 15, 18, 21, . . ., $a_1 = 6$ and $d = 3$.

34. Use the information in the table to write an expression for finding the nth term of an arithmetic sequence. $a_1 + (n-1)d$

Arithmetic Sequence	numbers	6	9	12	15	...	
	symbols	a_1	a_2	a_3	a_4	...	a_n
Expressed in Terms of d and the First Term	numbers	6 + 0(3)	6 + 1(3)	6 + 2(3)	6 + 3(3)	...	6 + (n − 1)(3)
	symbols	$a_1 + 0d$	$a_1 + 1d$	$a_1 + 2d$	$a_1 + 3d$	...	?

35. Use the expression you wrote in Exercise 34 to find the 9th term of an arithmetic sequence if $a_1 = 16$ and $d = 5$. **56**

Maintain Your Skills

Mixed Review

ALGEBRA Solve each equation. Check your solution. *(Lesson 5-9)*

36. $\frac{7}{6} = y + \frac{5}{12}$ $\frac{3}{4}$

37. $k - 4.1 = -9.38$ **−5.28**

38. $40.3 = 6.2x$ **6.5**

39. $\frac{3}{4}b = 7\frac{1}{2}$ **10**

Find the mean, median, and mode for each set of data. If necessary, round to the nearest tenth. *(Lesson 5-8)*

40. 11, 45, 62, 12, 47, 8, 12, 35
29; 23.5; 12

41. 2.3, 3.6, 4.1, 3.6, 2.9, 3.0
3.3; 3.3; 3.6

42. ALGEBRA Find the LCD of $\frac{1}{6a^2}$ and $\frac{5}{9a^3}$. *(Lesson 5-6)* **$18a^3$**

43. HOME REPAIR Cole is installing shelves in his closet. Because of the shape of the closet, the three shelves measure $34\frac{3}{8}$ inches, $33\frac{7}{8}$ inches, and $34\frac{5}{8}$ inches. What length of lumber does he need to buy? *(Lesson 5-5)* **$102\frac{7}{8}$ in.**

Find each product or quotient. Express using exponents. *(Lesson 4-6)*

44. $3^4 \cdot 3^2$ **3^6**

45. $\frac{b^5}{b^2}$ **b^3**

46. $2x^3(5x^2)$ **$10x^5$**

Find the greatest common factor of each set of numbers. *(Lesson 4-4)*

47. 36, 42 **6**

48. 9, 24 **3**

49. 60, 45, 30 **15**

4 Assess

Open-Ended Assessment

Modeling Have students model different sequences using small blocks or number cubes. Include an arithmetic sequence, a geometric sequence, and a sequence that has a pattern other than these.

Assessment Options

Quiz (Lessons 5-9 and 5-10) is available on p. 290 of the *Chapter 5 Resource Masters*.

Fibonacci Sequence

A special sequence that is neither arithmetic nor geometric is called the **Fibonacci sequence**. Each term in the sequence is the sum of the previous two terms, beginning with 1.

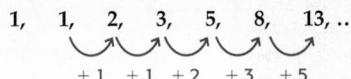

1,   1,   2,   3,   5,   8,   13, ...
        +1 +1 +2 +3 +5

Collect the Data

- Examine an artichoke, a pineapple, a pinecone, or the seeds in the center of a sunflower.
- For each item, count the number of spiral rows and record your data in a table. If possible, count the rows that spiral up from left to right and count the rows that spiral up from right to left. *Note:* It may be helpful to use a marker to keep track of the rows as you are counting.

Analyze the Data 1–3. See p. 261A.

1. What do you notice about the number of rows in each item?

2. Compare your data with the data of the other students. How do they compare?

Make a Conjecture

3. Have a discussion with other students to determine the relationship between the number of rows in sunflowers, pinecones, pineapples, and artichokes and the Fibonacci sequence.

Extend the Activity 5. See p. 261A.

Numbers in an arithmetic sequence have a common difference, and numbers in a geometric sequence have a common ratio. The numbers in a Fibonacci sequence have a different kind of pattern. **4. 1, 1, 2, 3, 5, 8, 13, 21, 34, 55, 89, 144, 233, 377, 610**

4. Write the first fifteen terms in the Fibonacci sequence.

5. Use a calculator to divide each term by the previous term. Make a list of the quotients. If necessary, round to seven decimal places.

6. Describe the pattern in the quotients. **They get increasingly closer to 1.618.**

7. **RESEARCH** Find the definition of the **golden ratio**. What is the relationship between the numbers in the Fibonacci sequence and the golden ratio? **See p. 261A.**

A Follow-Up of Lesson 5-10

Getting Started

Objective Become familiar with the Fibonacci sequence.

Materials
artichoke, pineapple, pinecone, or sunflower, markers

Teach

- Before starting this activity, have students describe the appearance of an artichoke, pineapple, pinecone, and/or sunflower. Have them compare features.
- Encourage students to research other connections to the Fibonacci sequence in nature.
- Direct students to notice some of the patterns of divisibility. For example, every third number is divisible by 2, every fourth by 3, every fifth by 5, every sixth by 8, every seventh by 13, and every eighth by 21.

Assess

In **Exercises 1–3**, students should recognize the number of rows as a number in the Fibonacci sequence.

In **Exercises 4–7**, students explore the connection between the Fibonacci sequence and the golden ratio.

Study Notebook

You may wish to have students summarize this activity and what they learned from it.

Resource Manager

📁 **Teaching Pre-Algebra with Manipulatives**
- p. 79 (student recording sheet)

Chapter 5 Study Guide and Review

Vocabulary and Concept Check

Vocabulary and Concept Check

- This alphabetical list of vocabulary terms in Chapter 5 includes a page reference where each term was introduced.

- **Assessment** A vocabulary review/test for Chapter 5 is available on p. 288 of the *Chapter 5 Resource Masters*.

Lesson-by-Lesson Review

For each lesson,
- the main ideas are summarized,
- additional examples review concepts, and
- practice exercises are provided.

Vocabulary PuzzleMaker

ELL The Vocabulary PuzzleMaker software improves students' mathematics vocabulary using four puzzle formats—crossword, scramble, word search using a word list, and word search using clues. Students can work on a computer screen or from a printed handout.

MindJogger Videoquizzes

ELL MindJogger Videoquizzes provide an alternative review of concepts presented in this chapter. Students work in teams in a game show format to gain points for correct answers. The questions are presented in three rounds.

Round 1 Concepts (5 questions)
Round 2 Skills (4 questions)
Round 3 Problem Solving (4 questions)

arithmetic sequence (p. 249)	least common denominator (LCD) (p. 227)	multiplicative inverse (p. 215)
bar notation (p. 201)	least common multiple (LCM) (p. 226)	period (p. 201)
common difference (p. 249)	mean (p. 238)	rational number (p. 205)
common multiples (p. 226)	measures of central tendency (p. 238)	reciprocals (p. 215)
common ratio (p. 250)	median (p. 238)	repeating decimal (p. 201)
dimensional analysis (p. 212)	mixed number (p. 200)	sequence (p. 249)
Fibonacci sequence (p. 253)	mode (p. 238)	term (p. 249)
geometric sequence (p. 250)	multiple (p. 226)	terminating decimal (p. 200)

Choose the correct term to complete each sentence.

1. A mixed number is an example of a (whole, <u>rational</u>) number.

2. The decimal 0.900 is a (<u>terminating</u>, repeating) decimal.

3. $\frac{x}{15}$ is an example of an (<u>algebraic fraction</u>, integer).

4. The numbers 12, 15, and 18 are (factors, <u>multiples</u>) of 3.

5. To add unlike fractions, rename the fractions using the (<u>LCD</u>, GCF).

6. The product of a number and its multiplicative inverse is (0, <u>1</u>).

7. To divide by a fraction, multiply the number by the (<u>reciprocal</u>, LCD) of the fraction.

8. The (median, <u>mode</u>) is the number that occurs most often in a set of data.

9. A common difference is found between terms in a(n) (<u>arithmetic</u>, geometric) sequence.

Lesson-by-Lesson Review

5-1 Writing Fractions as Decimals

See pages 200–204.

Concept Summary
- Any fraction or mixed number can be written as a terminating or repeating decimal.

Example Write $2\frac{7}{10}$ as a decimal.

$$2\frac{7}{10} = 2 + \frac{7}{10} \qquad \text{Write as the sum of an integer and a fraction.}$$
$$= 2 + 0.7 \text{ or } 2.7 \quad \text{Write } \frac{7}{10} \text{ as a decimal and add.}$$

Exercises Write each fraction or mixed number as a decimal. Use a bar to show a repeating decimal. *See Examples 1–3 on pages 200 and 201.*

10. $\frac{7}{8}$ 0.875 11. $\frac{9}{20}$ 0.45 12. $\frac{2}{3}$ $0.\overline{6}$ 13. $-\frac{7}{15}$ $-0.4\overline{6}$ 14. $8\frac{3}{25}$ 8.12 15. $6\frac{4}{11}$ $6.\overline{36}$

 www.pre-alg.com/vocabulary_review

FOLDABLES Study Organizer

For more information about Foldables, see *Teaching Mathematics with Foldables*.

Have students look through the chapter to make sure they have included notes and examples in their Foldables for each lesson of Chapter 5.

Encourage students to refer to their Foldable journals while completing the Study Guide and Review and to use them in preparing for the Chapter Test.

5-2 Rational Numbers

See pages 205–209.

Concept Summary

- Any number that can be written as a fraction is a rational number.
- Decimals that are terminating or repeating are rational numbers.

Example Write 0.16 as a fraction in simplest form.

$0.16 = \dfrac{16}{100}$ 0.16 is 16 hundredths.

$\quad\;\; = \dfrac{4}{25}$ Simplify. The GCF of 16 and 100 is 4.

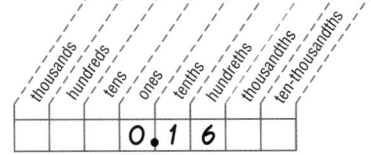

Exercises Write each decimal as a fraction or mixed number in simplest form. *See Examples 2 and 3 on page 206.*

16. 0.23 $\dfrac{23}{100}$

17. 0.6 $\dfrac{3}{5}$

18. −0.05 $-\dfrac{1}{20}$

19. 0.125 $\dfrac{1}{8}$

20. 2.36 $2\dfrac{9}{25}$

21. 4.44 $4\dfrac{11}{25}$

22. −8.002 $-8\dfrac{1}{500}$

23. 0.555... $\dfrac{5}{9}$

24. $0.\overline{3}$ $\dfrac{1}{3}$

25. $1.\overline{7}$ $1\dfrac{7}{9}$

26. $0.\overline{72}$ $\dfrac{8}{11}$

27. $3.\overline{36}$ $3\dfrac{4}{11}$

5-3 Multiplying Rational Numbers

See pages 210–214.

Concept Summary

- To multiply fractions, multiply the numerators and multiply the denominators.
- Dimensional analysis is a useful way to keep track of units while computing.

Example Find $\dfrac{4}{5} \cdot 3\dfrac{1}{3}$. Write the product in simplest form.

$\dfrac{4}{5} \cdot 3\dfrac{1}{3} = \dfrac{4}{5} \cdot \dfrac{10}{3}$ Rename $3\dfrac{1}{3}$ as an improper fraction.

$\quad\quad = \dfrac{4}{\cancel{5}_1} \cdot \dfrac{\cancel{10}^2}{3}$ Divide by the GCF, 5.

$\quad\quad = \dfrac{8}{3}$ or $2\dfrac{2}{3}$ Multiply and then simplify.

Exercises Find each product. Write in simplest form. *See Examples 1–5 on pages 210 and 211.*

28. $\dfrac{2}{3} \cdot \dfrac{1}{8}$ $\dfrac{1}{12}$

29. $-\dfrac{7}{15} \cdot \dfrac{5}{9}$ $-\dfrac{7}{27}$

30. $\dfrac{6}{11} \cdot \dfrac{2}{15}$ $\dfrac{4}{55}$

31. $8 \cdot \dfrac{4}{5}$ $6\dfrac{2}{5}$

32. $-1\dfrac{5}{6} \cdot 9$ $-16\dfrac{1}{2}$

33. $\dfrac{6}{7} \cdot \dfrac{14}{9}$ $1\dfrac{1}{3}$

34. $\dfrac{8}{9} \cdot \dfrac{5}{12}$ $\dfrac{10}{27}$

35. $2\dfrac{1}{4} \cdot \left(-\dfrac{4}{3}\right)$ -3

36. $\dfrac{14}{15} \cdot 3\dfrac{2}{7}$ $3\dfrac{1}{15}$

37. $2\dfrac{5}{6} \cdot 3\dfrac{1}{3}$ $9\dfrac{4}{9}$

38. $\dfrac{ab}{4} \cdot \dfrac{2}{bc}$ $\dfrac{a}{2c}$

39. $\dfrac{x^2}{r} \cdot \dfrac{r}{x}$ x

5-4 Dividing Rational Numbers

See pages 215–219.

Concept Summary

- The product of a number and its multiplicative inverse or reciprocal is 1.
- To divide by a fraction, multiply by its reciprocal.

Example Find $\frac{6}{7} \div \frac{3}{4}$. Write the quotient in simplest form.

$$\frac{6}{7} \div \frac{3}{4} = \frac{\overset{2}{\cancel{6}}}{7} \cdot \frac{4}{\underset{1}{\cancel{3}}} \qquad \text{Multiply by the reciprocal of } \frac{3}{4}, \frac{4}{3}.$$

$$= \frac{8}{7} \text{ or } 1\frac{1}{7} \qquad \text{Multiply and then simplify.}$$

Exercises Find each quotient. Write in simplest form.
See Examples 2–5 on pages 216 and 217.

40. $\frac{4}{9} \div \frac{1}{3}$ $1\frac{1}{3}$ 41. $\frac{2}{5} \div \left(-\frac{1}{15}\right)$ -6 42. $\frac{6}{13} \div \frac{8}{9}$ $\frac{27}{52}$ 43. $5 \div \left(-1\frac{1}{3}\right)$ $-3\frac{3}{4}$

44. $\frac{11}{18} \div 4\frac{1}{2}$ $\frac{11}{81}$ 45. $-3\frac{3}{5} \div \frac{6}{7}$ $-4\frac{1}{5}$ 46. $\frac{n}{8} \div \frac{n}{32}$ 4 47. $\frac{2}{7x} \div \frac{3}{2}$ $\frac{4}{21x}$

5-5 Adding and Subtracting Like Fractions

See pages 220–224.

Concept Summary

- To add like fractions, add the numerators and write the sum over the denominator.
- To subtract like fractions, subtract the numerators and write the sum over the denominator.

Example Find $3\frac{7}{8} + 9\frac{3}{8}$. Write the sum in simplest form.

Estimate: $4 + 9 = 13$

$$3\frac{7}{8} + 9\frac{3}{8} = (3 + 9) + \left(\frac{7}{8} + \frac{3}{8}\right) \qquad \text{Add the whole numbers and fractions separately.}$$

$$= 12 + \frac{7 + 3}{8} \qquad \text{The denominators are the same. Add the numerators.}$$

$$= 12\frac{10}{8} \qquad \text{Simplify.}$$

$$= 13\frac{2}{8} \text{ or } 13\frac{1}{4} \qquad \text{Simplify.}$$

Exercises Find each sum or difference. Write in simplest form.
See Examples 1–3 and 5 on pages 220 and 221.

48. $\frac{5}{18} + \frac{11}{18}$ $\frac{8}{9}$ 49. $\frac{7}{9} + \left(-\frac{2}{9}\right)$ $\frac{5}{9}$ 50. $\frac{19}{20} - \frac{17}{20}$ $\frac{1}{10}$ 51. $1\frac{16}{21} - \frac{9}{21}$ $1\frac{1}{3}$

52. $-\frac{12}{17} + \frac{10}{17}$ $-\frac{2}{17}$ 53. $8\frac{3}{10} - 5\frac{7}{10}$ $2\frac{3}{5}$ 54. $\frac{7t}{15} + \frac{t}{15}$ $\frac{8t}{15}$ 55. $\frac{5}{3x} - \frac{1}{3x}$ $\frac{4}{3x}$

5-6 Least Common Multiple

See pages 226–230.

Concept Summary

- The LCM of two numbers is the least nonzero multiple common to both numbers.
- To compare fractions with unlike denominators, write the fractions using the LCD and compare the numerators.

Example   Replace ● with $<$, $>$, or $=$ to make $\frac{7}{15}$ ● $\frac{5}{9}$ a true statement.

The LCD is $3^2 \cdot 5$ or 45. Rewrite the fractions using the LCD.

$$\frac{7}{15} \cdot \frac{3}{3} = \frac{21}{45} \qquad\qquad \frac{5}{9} \cdot \frac{5}{5} = \frac{25}{45}$$

Since $21 < 25$, $\frac{21}{45} < \frac{25}{45}$. So, $\frac{7}{15} < \frac{5}{9}$.

Exercises   Find the least common multiple (LCM) of each pair of numbers or monomials.   *See Examples 1 and 2 on pages 226 and 227.*

56. 4, 18 **36**   **57.** 24, 20 **120**   **58.** $4a, 6a$ **12a**   **59.** $7c^2, 21c$ **21c²**

Replace each ● with $<$, $>$, or $=$ to make a true statement.
See Example 5 on page 228.

60. $\frac{3}{8}$ ● $\frac{5}{12}$ $<$ **61.** $\frac{2}{9}$ ● $\frac{4}{15}$ $<$ **62.** $\frac{5}{20}$ ● $\frac{1}{4}$ $=$ **63.** $\frac{3}{7}$ ● $\frac{8}{21}$ $>$

5-7 Adding and Subtracting Unlike Fractions

See pages 232–236.

Concept Summary

- To add or subtract fractions with unlike denominators, rename the fractions with the LCD. Then add or subtract.

Example   Find $\frac{7}{9} - \frac{5}{12}$.

$$\frac{7}{9} - \frac{5}{12} = \frac{7}{9} \cdot \frac{4}{4} - \frac{5}{12} \cdot \frac{3}{3} \qquad \text{The LCD is } 3^2 \cdot 2^2 \text{ or 36.}$$

$$= \frac{28}{36} - \frac{15}{36} \qquad \text{Rename the fractions using the LCD.}$$

$$= \frac{13}{36} \qquad \text{Subtract the like fractions.}$$

Exercises   Find each sum or difference. Write in simplest form.
See Examples 2–5 on pages 233 and 234.

64. $\frac{1}{3} + \frac{5}{6}$ $1\frac{1}{6}$ **65.** $\frac{11}{12} + \frac{3}{4}$ $1\frac{2}{3}$ **66.** $\frac{7}{8} - \frac{5}{6}$ $\frac{1}{24}$ **67.** $3\frac{7}{12} - \frac{3}{4}$ $2\frac{5}{6}$

68. $-1\frac{3}{14}$ **68.** $-\frac{3}{7} + \left(-\frac{11}{14}\right)$ **69.** $1\frac{2}{5} - \left(-\frac{1}{3}\right)$ $1\frac{11}{15}$ **70.** $5\frac{1}{2} - 2\frac{2}{3}$ $2\frac{5}{6}$ **71.** $-2\frac{1}{6} + 5\frac{1}{3}$ $3\frac{1}{6}$

Study Guide and Review

Chapter **5** For More ...
• Extra Practice, see pages 733–736.
• Mixed Problem Solving, see page 762

5-8 Measures of Central Tendency

See pages 238–242.

Concept Summary

• The mean, median, and mode can be used to describe sets of data.

Example Find the mean, median, and mode of 8, 4, 2, 2, and 10.

mean: $\dfrac{8 + 4 + 2 + 2 + 10}{5}$ or 5.2   median: 4   mode: 2

Exercises Find the mean, median, and mode for each set of data. If necessary, round to the nearest tenth. *See Example 1 on page 238.*

72. 4, 5, 7, 3, 9, 11, 23, 37 **12.4; 8; none** **73.** 3.6, 7.2, 9.0, 5.2, 7.2, 6.5, 3.6

6.0; 6.5; 3.6 and 7.2

5-9 Solving Equations with Rational Numbers

See pages 244–248.

Concept Summary

• To solve an equation, use inverse operations to isolate the variable.

Example Solve $1.6x = 8$. Check your solution.

$1.6x = 8$	Write the equation.	**CHECK**	$1.6x = 8$	Write the equation.
$\dfrac{1.6x}{1.6} = \dfrac{8}{1.6}$	Divide each side by 1.6.		$1.6(5) \stackrel{?}{=} 8$	Replace x with 5.
$x = 5$	Simplify.		$8 = 8$ ✓	Simplify.

Exercises Solve each equation. Check your solution.
See Examples 1–4 on pages 244 and 245.

74. $\dfrac{1}{2} = a + \dfrac{3}{8}$ $\dfrac{1}{8}$ **75.** $x - 1.5 = 1.75$ **76.** $0.2t = 6$ **30** **77.** $2 = -\dfrac{4}{5}n$ $-2\dfrac{1}{2}$
3.25

5-10 Arithmetic and Geometric Sequences

See pages 249–252.

Concept Summary

• In an arithmetic sequence, the terms have a common difference.
• In a geometric sequence, the terms have a common ratio.

Example State whether −8, −2, 4, 10, 16, ... is *arithmetic, geometric,* or *neither.* If it is arithmetic or geometric, write the next three terms.

−8, −2, 4, 10, 16   The common difference is 6, so the sequence is arithmetic.
$\;\;\;+6\;\;+6\;\;+6\;\;+6$ The next three terms are 16 + 6 or 22, 22 + 6 or 28, and
                    28 + 6 or 34.   **80.** G; $\dfrac{1}{4}, \dfrac{1}{8}, \dfrac{1}{32}, \dfrac{1}{128}$

Exercises State whether each sequence is *arithmetic, geometric,* or *neither.* If it is arithmetic or geometric, state the common difference or common ratio and write the next three terms of the sequence. *See Examples 1–3 on pages 249 and 250.*

78. 4, 9, 14, 19, ... **79.** 1, 3, 9, 27, ... **80.** 32, 8, 2, $\dfrac{1}{2}$, ... **81.** −6, −5, −2, 3, ...
A; 5; 24, 29, 34   **G; 3; 81, 243, 729**   **neither**

Vocabulary and Concepts

1. **State** the difference between a terminating and a repeating decimal. **1–2. See p. 261A.**
2. **Describe** how to add fractions with unlike denominators.
3. **Define** *geometric sequence.* **a sequence in which the quotient of any two consecutive terms is the same**

Skills and Applications

Write each fraction or mixed number as a decimal. Use a bar to show a repeating decimal.

4. $\frac{9}{20}$ **0.45**

5. $-\frac{7}{8}$ **−0.875**

6. $4\frac{2}{9}$ **$4.\overline{2}$**

Write each decimal as a fraction or mixed number in simplest form.

7. 0.24 **$\frac{6}{25}$**

8. 5.06 **$5\frac{3}{50}$**

9. $-2.\overline{3}$ **$-2\frac{1}{3}$**

Replace each ● with <, >, or = to make a true sentence.

10. 0.6 ● $\frac{2}{3}$ **<**

11. $-1\frac{5}{8}$ ● -1.6 **<**

Find the least common denominator (LCD) of each pair of fractions.

12. $\frac{5}{6}, \frac{2}{9}$ **18**

13. $\frac{9}{4a^2}, \frac{2}{3ab}$ **$12a^2b$**

Find each product, quotient, sum, or difference. Write in simplest form.

14. $\frac{5}{8} \cdot \frac{6}{11}$ **$\frac{15}{44}$**

15. $\frac{5}{8} + \frac{1}{8}$ **$\frac{3}{4}$**

16. $\frac{7}{9} \div \frac{4}{15}$ **$2\frac{11}{12}$**

17. $3\frac{5}{6} + 1\frac{2}{9}$ **$5\frac{1}{18}$**

18. $\frac{ab}{9} \div \frac{b}{3}$ **$\frac{a}{3}$**

19. $\frac{11x}{3y} - \frac{8x}{3y}$ **$\frac{x}{y}$**

For Exercises 20 and 21, use the data set {20.5, 18.6, 16.3, 4.8, 19.1, 17.3, 20.5}.

20. Find the mean, median, and mode. If necessary, round to the nearest tenth. **16.7; 18.6; 20.5**
21. Identify an extreme value and describe how it affects the mean. **4.8; It decreases the mean by 2.**

Solve each equation. Check your solution.

22. $x + 4.3 = 9.8$ **5.5**

23. $12 = 0.75x$ **16**

24. $3.1m = 12.4$ **4**

25. $p - \frac{4}{5} = \frac{2}{3}$ **$1\frac{7}{15}$**

26. $-\frac{3}{8} = \frac{5}{3}a$ **$-\frac{9}{40}$**

27. $y - 2\frac{1}{4} = 1\frac{5}{6}$ **$4\frac{1}{12}$**

State whether each sequence is *arithmetic, geometric,* or *neither.* If it is arithmetic or geometric, state the common difference or common ratio and write the next three terms of the sequence. **28. G; 4; 512, 2048, 8192 29. A; −0.6; 3.1, 2.5, 1.9**

28. 2, 8, 32, 128, ...

29. 5.5, 4.9, 4.3, 3.7, ...

30. 1, 2, 4, 7, ... **neither**

31. **TRAVEL** Max drives 6 hours at an average rate of 65 miles per hour. What is the distance Max travels? Use $d = rt$. **390 mi**

32. **SEWING** Allie needs $4\frac{2}{3}$ yards of lace to finish sewing the edges of a blanket. She only has $\frac{3}{4}$ of that amount. How much lace does Allie have? **$3\frac{1}{2}$ yd**

33. **STANDARDIZED TEST PRACTICE** Write the sum of $-6\frac{1}{4}$ and $-9\frac{3}{20}$. **A**

Ⓐ $-15\frac{2}{5}$ Ⓑ $-15\frac{1}{4}$ Ⓒ $-16\frac{2}{5}$ Ⓓ $-3\frac{1}{5}$

Portfolio Suggestion

Introduction In Chapter 5, students converted numbers to different forms, solved equations, performed computations, found measures of central tendency, and examined sequences. This chapter opened up a variety of application problems based on utilizing rational numbers.

Ask Students to write three ways that rational numbers help them relate to the world. For example, data in the newspaper help them become more informed citizens or better consumers.

Assessment Options

Vocabulary Test A vocabulary review/test for Chapter 5 can be found on p. 288 of the *Chapter 5 Resource Masters.*

Chapter Tests There are six Chapter 5 Tests and an Open-Ended Assessment task available in the *Chapter 5 Resource Masters.*

Chapter 5 Tests			
Form	Type	Level	Pages
1	MC	basic	275–276
2A	MC	average	277–278
2B	MC	average	279–280
2C	FR	average	281–282
2D	FR	average	283–284
3	FR	advanced	285–286

MC = multiple-choice questions
FR = free-response questions

Open-Ended Assessment Performance tasks for Chapter 5 can be found on p. 287 of the *Chapter 5 Resource Masters,* along with a sample scoring rubric for these tasks on p. A32.

First Semester Test A test for Chapters 1–5 can be found on pp. 295–298 of the *Chapter 5 Resource Masters.*

 ExamView® Pro

Use the networkable **ExamView® Pro** to:

- Create **multiple versions** of tests.
- Create **modified** tests for *Inclusion* students.
- **Edit** existing questions and **add** your own questions.
- Use built-in **state curriculum correlations** to create tests aligned with state standards.
- Change **English** tests to **Spanish** and vice versa.

Chapter 5 Practice Test **259**

These two pages contain practice questions in the various formats that can be found on the most frequently given standardized tests.

A practice answer sheet for these two pages can be found on page A1 of the *Chapter 5 Resource Masters*.

Standardized Test Practice
Student Recording Sheet, p. A1

Part 1 *Multiple Choice*

Select the best answer from the choices given and fill in the corresponding oval.

1 Ⓐ Ⓑ Ⓒ Ⓓ   4 Ⓐ Ⓑ Ⓒ Ⓓ   7 Ⓐ Ⓑ Ⓒ Ⓓ   9 Ⓐ Ⓑ Ⓒ Ⓓ
2 Ⓐ Ⓑ Ⓒ Ⓓ   5 Ⓐ Ⓑ Ⓒ Ⓓ   8 Ⓐ Ⓑ Ⓒ Ⓓ   10 Ⓐ Ⓑ Ⓒ Ⓓ
3 Ⓐ Ⓑ Ⓒ Ⓓ   6 Ⓐ Ⓑ Ⓒ Ⓓ

Part 2 *Short Response/Grid In*

Solve the problem and write your answer in the blank.

For Questions 11, 13, 19, and 22, also enter your answer by writing each number or symbol in a box. Then fill in the corresponding oval for that number or symbol.

11 (grid in)   11   13
12
13 (grid in)
14
15
16   19   22
17
18
19 (grid in)
20
21
22 (grid in)

Part 3 *Extended Response*

Record your answers for Question 23 on the back of this paper.

Additional Practice

See pp. 293–294 of the *Chapter 5 Resource Masters* for additional standardized test practice.

Part 1 | Multiple Choice

Record your answers on the answer sheet provided by your teacher or on a sheet of paper.

1. Kenzie paid for a CD with a $20 bill. She received 3 dollars, 3 dimes, and 2 pennies in change. How much did she pay for the CD? (Prerequisite Skill, p. 707) **A**

   Ⓐ $16.68   Ⓑ $16.88

   Ⓒ $17.68   Ⓓ $17.88

2. A survey of 110 people asked which country they would most like to visit. The bar graph shows the data. How many people chose Canada, England, or Australia as the country they would most like to visit? (Prerequisite Skill, pp. 722–723) **B**

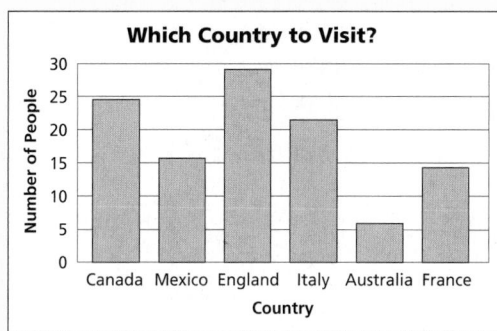

   Ⓐ 52   Ⓑ 58

   Ⓒ 68   Ⓓ 74

Test-Taking Tip

Question 2
When an item includes a graph, scan the graph to see what kind of information it includes and how the information is organized. Don't try to memorize the information. Read each answer choice and compare it with the graph to see if the information in the answer choice is correct. Eliminate any wrong answer choices.

260   Chapter 5   Rational Numbers

3. The low temperature overnight was $-1°F$. Each night for the next four nights, the low temperature was 7° lower than the previous night. What was the low temperature during the last night? (Lesson 2-4) **A**

   Ⓐ $-29°$ Ⓑ $-27°$ Ⓒ $-22°$ Ⓓ $-8°$

4. Write $\frac{6t^4}{18ts}$ in simplest form. (Lesson 4-5) **C**

   Ⓐ $\frac{1}{3}t^3s$ Ⓑ $3t^5s$

   Ⓒ $\frac{t^3}{3s}$ Ⓓ $\frac{t^5}{3s}$

5. What is 8×10^{-2} in standard notation? (Lesson 4-8) **B**

   Ⓐ 0.008   Ⓑ 0.08

   Ⓒ 0.8   Ⓓ 800

6. Add $\frac{2}{3} + \frac{1}{4} + \frac{5}{6}$. (Lesson 5-7) **C**

   Ⓐ $\frac{2}{3}$ Ⓑ $\frac{5}{4}$

   Ⓒ $\frac{7}{4}$ Ⓓ $\frac{11}{6}$

7. Evaluate $\frac{1}{4}(2 - x) - x$ if $x = \frac{1}{2}$. (Lesson 5-7)

   Ⓐ $-\frac{1}{2}$ Ⓑ $-\frac{1}{8}$ Ⓒ $\frac{1}{8}$ Ⓓ $\frac{1}{2}$

8. Antonia read four books that had the following number of pages: 324, 375, 420, 397. What is the mean number of pages in these books? (Lesson 5-8) **B**

   Ⓐ 375   Ⓑ 379

   Ⓒ 380   Ⓓ 386

9. Which sequence is a geometric sequence with a common ratio of 2? (Lesson 5-10) **D**

   Ⓐ $2, -4, 8, -16, …$ Ⓑ $2, 4, 6, 8, 10, …$

   Ⓒ $3, 5, 7, 9, 11, …$ Ⓓ $3, 6, 12, 24, …$

10. State the next three terms in the sequence $128, 32, 8, 2, ….$ (Lesson 5-10) **A**

   Ⓐ $\frac{1}{2}, \frac{1}{8}, \frac{1}{32}$ Ⓑ $\frac{1}{2}, \frac{1}{16}, \frac{1}{32}$

   Ⓒ $\frac{1}{4}, \frac{1}{8}, \frac{1}{16}$ Ⓓ $\frac{1}{4}, \frac{1}{6}, \frac{1}{8}$

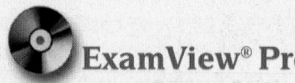

ExamView® Pro

Special banks of standardized test questions similar to those on the SAT, ACT, TIMSS 8, NAEP 8, and Pre-Algebra End-of-Course tests can be found on this CD-ROM.

Preparing for Standardized Tests
For test-taking strategies and more
practice, see pages 771–788.

Part 2 Short Response/Grid In

Record your answers on the answer sheet
provided by your teacher or on a sheet of
paper.

1. Nate is cutting shelves from a board that is
15 feet long. Each shelf is 3 feet 4 inches
long. What is the greatest number of
shelves he can make from the board?
(Prerequisite Skill, pp. 720–721) **4**

2. Write the ordered pair that names point L.
(Lesson 2-6) **(4, −3)**

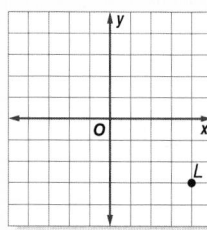

3. Find x if $3x + 4 = 28$. (Lesson 3-5) **8**

4. Write an equation to represent the total
number of Calories t in one box of snack
crackers. The box of crackers contains
8 servings. Each serving has 125 Calories.
(Lesson 3-6) $t = 8 \cdot 125$

5. On Saturday, Juan plans to drive 275 miles
at a rate of 55 miles per hour. How many
hours will his trip take? Use the formula
$d = rt$, where d represents the distance,
r represents rate, and t represents the time.
(Lesson 3-7) **5 h**

6. Write $4^2 \times 5^3$ as a product of prime factors
without using exponents. (Lesson 4-3)
$2 \cdot 2 \cdot 2 \cdot 2 \cdot 5 \cdot 5 \cdot 5$

7. The average American worker spends
44 minutes traveling to and from work
each day. What fraction of the day is this?
(Lesson 4-5) $\dfrac{11}{360}$

8. The Saturn V rocket that took the Apollo
astronauts to the moon weighed 6.526×10^6
pounds at lift-off. Write its weight in
standard notation. (Lesson 4-8) **6,526,000 lb**

www.pre-alg.com/standardized_test

19. Write a decimal to represent the shaded
portion of the figure below. (Lesson 5-1)
.375

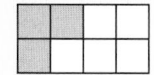

20. One elevator in a 40-story building is
programmed to stop at every third floor.
Another is programmed to stop at every
fourth floor. Which floors in the building
are served by both elevators? (Lesson 5-6)
floor 12, floor 24, floor 36

21. Beth has $\dfrac{3}{4}$ cup of grated cheese. She needs
$2\dfrac{1}{2}$ cups of grated cheese for making pizzas.
How many more cups does she need?
(Lesson 5-7) $1\dfrac{3}{4}$

22. The number of tickets sold for each
performance of the Spring Music Fest are
352, 417, 307, 367, 433, and 419. What is
the median number of tickets sold per
performance? (Lesson 5-8) **392**

Part 3 Extended Response

Record your answers on a sheet of paper.
Show your work. **23a–d. See margin.**

23. During seven regular season games, the
Hawks basketball team scored the points
shown in the table below. (Lesson 5-8)

Game	1	2	3	4	5	6	7
Points	68	60	73	74	64	78	73

a. Find the mean, median, and mode of
these seven scores.

b. During the first playoff game after the
regular season, the Hawks scored only
40 points. Find the mean, median, and
mode of all eight scores.

c. Which of these three measures of central
tendency—mean, median, or mode—
changed the most as a result of the
playoff score? Explain your answer.

d. Does the mean score or the median score
best represent the team's scores for all
eight games? Explain your answer.

Chapter 5 Standardized Test Practice **261**

Evaluating Extended Response Questions

Extended Response questions
are graded by using a multilevel
rubric that guides you in assessing a student's knowledge of a
particular concept.

Goal: Review the measures of
central tendency.

Sample Scoring Rubric: The
following rubric is a sample
scoring device. You may wish to
add more detail to this sample to
meet your individual scoring
needs.

Score	Criteria
4	A correct solution that is supported by well-developed, accurate explanations
3	A generally correct solution, but may contain minor flaws in reasoning or computation
2	A partially correct interpretation and/or solution to the problem
1	A correct solution with no supporting evidence or explanation
0	An incorrect solution indicating no mathematical understanding of the concept or task, or no solution is given

23d. The median best represents the
team's eight scores, because it
is less affected by the playoff
game score, which is much
lower than the other scores.

Answers

23a. mean $= \dfrac{60 + 64 + 68 + 73 + 73 + 74 + 78}{7} = \dfrac{490}{7}$ or **70**

median = **73**, mode = **73**

23b. mean $= \dfrac{490 + 40}{8} = \dfrac{530}{8}$ or **66.25**

median $= \dfrac{68 + 73}{2}$ or **70.5**; mode = **73**

23c. The mean changed the most. To find the difference, subtract
the mean for the 8 scores from the mean for the 7 scores.
Do the same for the medians and the modes.

	7 scores	8 scores	Change
mean	70	66.25	$70 - 66.25 = 3.75$
median	73	70.5	$73 - 70.5 = 2.5$
mode	73	73	$73 - 73 = 0$

Page 251, Lesson 5-10

10. A; 3; 14, 17, 20,

11. A; 11; 38, 49, 60

12. G; 2; 8, 16, 32

13. G; 3; 162, 486, 1458

14. A; -7; -10, -17, -24

15. A; -3; 13, 10, 7

16. G; $\dfrac{1}{4}$, $\dfrac{1}{64}$, $\dfrac{1}{256}$, $\dfrac{1}{1024}$

17. G; $-\dfrac{1}{5}$, $-\dfrac{1}{125}$, $\dfrac{1}{625}$, $-\dfrac{1}{3125}$

18. A; $\dfrac{1}{2}$, $\dfrac{5}{2}$, 3, $\dfrac{7}{2}$

19. A; $\dfrac{1}{6}$, $\dfrac{2}{3}$, $\dfrac{5}{6}$, 1

20. A; 0.75; 3, 3.75, 4.5

21. A; -0.5, 2.5, 2, 1.5

22. neither

23. neither

24. G; $\dfrac{1}{2}$, $\dfrac{3}{2}$, $\dfrac{3}{4}$, $\dfrac{3}{8}$

25. G; $-\dfrac{1}{3}$, $\dfrac{2}{9}$, $-\dfrac{2}{27}$, $\dfrac{2}{81}$

26. G; 3; 8.1, 24.3, 72.9

27. G; $\dfrac{1}{2}$, $\dfrac{1}{32}$, $\dfrac{1}{64}$, $\dfrac{1}{128}$

29a. Arithmetic; the common difference is $3.

31. Find the pattern, continue the sequence, and use the new values to make predictions. Answers should include the following.

- The difference between any two consecutive terms in an arithmetic sequence is the common difference. To find the next value in such a sequence, add the common difference to the last term. The ratio of any two consecutive terms in a geometric sequence is the common ratio. So, to find the next value in such a sequence, multiply the last term by the common ratio.

- Sequences occurring in nature include geysers spouting every few minutes, the arrangement of geese in migration patterns, and ocean tides.

Page 253, Algebra Activity

1. Sample answer: Most of them should be terms of the Fibonacci sequence.

2. Sample answer: Most of them should be terms of the Fibonacci sequence. Some groups may have different numbers based on the size of their object.

3. Sample answer: The number of rows is a term of the Fibonacci sequence.

5. 1, 2, 1.5, 1.6666667, 1.6, 1.625, 1.6153846, 1.6190476, 1.6176471, 1.6181818, 1.6179775, 1.6180556, 1.6180258, 1.6180371

7. The golden ratio is approxiamately 1:1.618. After the first few terms, the ratio of successive numbers in the Fibonacci sequence is the golden ratio.

Page 259, Practice Test

1. The digits of a terminating decimal end and the digits of a repeating decimal continue repeating.

2. Rename the fractions with a common denominator. Then add and simplify.

Notes

Additional Answers for Chapter 5

Chapter 6

Ratio, Proportion, and Percent
Chapter Overview and Pacing

An electronic version of this chapter is available on StudentWorks™. This backpack solution CD-ROM allows students instant access to the Student Edition, lesson worksheet pages, and web resources.

Year-long pacing: pages T20–T21.

LESSON OBJECTIVES	PACING (days)			
	Regular		Block	
	Basic/ Average	Advanced	Basic/ Average	Advanced
6-1 Ratios and Rates *(pp. 264–268)* • Write ratios as fractions in simplest form. • Determine unit rates.	1	1	0.5	0.5
6-2 Using Proportions *(pp. 270–275)* • Solve proportions. • Use proportions to solve real-world problems. *Follow-Up:* Use proportions with the capture-recapture method of counting.	2 (with 6-2 Follow-Up)	2 (with 6-2 Follow-Up)	1	1.5 (with 6-2 Follow-Up)
6-3 Scale Drawings and Models *(pp. 276–280)* • Use scale drawings. • Construct scale drawings.	1	1	0.5	0.5
6-4 Fractions, Decimals, and Percents *(pp. 281–285)* • Express percents as fractions and vice versa. • Express percents as decimals and vice versa.	1	1	0.5	0.5
6-5 Using the Percent Proportion *(pp. 286–292)* *Preview:* Use a percent model to find a percent or a part. • Use the percent proportion to solve problem	2 (with 6-5 Preview)	1	1	0.5
6-6 Finding Percents Mentally *(pp. 293–297)* • Compute mentally with percents. • Estimate with percents.	1	1	0.5	0.5
6-7 Using Percent Equations *(pp. 298–303)* • Solve percent problems using percent equations. • Solve real-life problems involving discount and interest. *Follow-Up:* Find compound interest.	1	2 (with 6-7 Follow-Up)	0.5	1 (with 6-7 Follow-Up)
6-8 Percent of Change *(pp. 304–308)* • Find percent of increase. • Find percent of decrease.	1	1	0.5	0.5
6-9 Probability and Predictions *(pp. 309–315)* *Preview:* Take a survey. • Find the probability of simple events. • Use a sample to predict the actions of a larger group. *Follow-Up:* Describe how the graphing calculator generates random numbers.	2 (with 6-9 Preview)	1	1	0.5
Study Guide and **Practice Test** *(pp. 316–321)* **Standardized Test Practice** *(pp. 322–323)*	1	1	0.5	0.5
Chapter Assessment	1	1	0.5	0.5
TOTAL	14	13	7	7

Chapter Resource Manager

CHAPTER 6 RESOURCE MASTERS

Study Guide and Intervention	Practice (Skills and Average)	Reading to Learn Mathematics	Enrichment	Assessment	Prerequisite Skills Workbook	Applications*	Parent and Student Study Guide Workbook	5-Minute Check Transparencies	Interactive Chalkboard	Pre-AlgePASS: Tutorial Plus (lessons)	Materials
299	300–301	302	303			39–40		44	6-1	6-1	12, 13	
304	305–306	307	308			37–40	SC 11	45	6-2	6-2	14	*Follow-Up:* bag of dried beans, paper bag, permanent marker
309	310–311	312	313	359			GCS 30	46	6-3	6-3		
314	315–316	317	318			15–18		47	6-4	6-4	15	
319	320–321	322	323	359, 361			SM 18	48	6-5	6-5		*Preview:* grid paper
324	325–326	327	328			39–40		49	6-6	6-6		
329	330–331	332	333	360				50	6-7	6-7	16, 17	*Follow-Up:* spreadsheet software
334	335–336	337	338				SC 12 GCS 29	51	6-8	6-8		
339	340–341	342	343	360				52	6-9	6-9	18	*Follow-Up:* graphing calculator
				345–358 362–364 365–366								

* *Key to Abbreviations:* GCS = Graphing Calculator and Spreadsheet Masters, SC = School-to-Career Masters, SM = Science and Mathematics Lab Manual

 **ELL** Study Guide and Intervention, Skills Practice, Practice, and Parent and Student Study Guide Workbooks are also available in Spanish.

Chapter 6 Mathematical Connections and Background

Continuity of Instruction

Prior Knowledge

In Chapter 5, students learned to multiply and divide rational numbers. They also converted fractions to decimals and added and subtracted fractions. They factored numbers and determined least common multiple. They also used measures of central tendency to analyze data. Students solved equations with rational numbers and identified sequences.

This Chapter

Students will examine ratios and rates and use cross products to determine whether two rates form a proportion. They will use ratios and proportions to solve problems, including scale drawings and models. Students will extend their study of ratios to include percent and the conversion of fractions and decimals to percents. Students will also find simple probability.

Future Connections

Ratios, rates, proportions, and percents all relate to the world of business. Ratios and scale drawings and models are used extensively in architecture and engineering. Probability is frequently used in chemistry and physics to predict the orbits of electrons.

6-1 Ratios and Rates

A ratio is a comparison of two numbers by division. If a basketball player makes 8 out of 10 free throws, the ratio would be written as 8 to 10, 8:10, and $\frac{8}{10}$. Ratios are usually written in simplest form. In simplest form, the ratio 8 out of 10 is written as 4 to 5, 4:5, or $\frac{4}{5}$.

A rate is a ratio of two measurements having different kinds of units. When a rate is simplified so that it has a denominator of 1, it is called a unit rate. An example of a unit rate is 9 miles per hour.

6-2 Using Proportions

A proportion is an equation stating that two ratios are equal. For example, $\frac{3}{18} = \frac{13}{78}$ is an example of a proportion. Every proportion has two cross products. In the proportion, $\frac{3}{18} = \frac{13}{78}$, the cross products are $3 \cdot 78$ and $18 \cdot 13$. The cross products of a proportion are equal.

6-3 Scale Drawings and Models

A scale drawing or a scale model is used to represent an object that is too large or too small to be drawn or built at actual size. The ratio of length on a scale drawing or model corresponds to the length of the real object. This ratio is called the scale factor. The lengths and widths of objects of a scale drawing or model are proportional to those of the actual object.

6-4 Fractions, Decimals, and Percents

A percent is a ratio that compares a number to 100. To write a percent as a fraction, express the ratio as a fraction with a denominator of 100. Then simplify, if possible. For example, $76\% = \frac{76}{100}$ or $\frac{19}{25}$. To write a fraction as a percent, write an equivalent fraction with a denominator of 100. For example, $\frac{3}{4} = \frac{75}{100}$ or 75%.

A fraction can be expressed as a percent by first expressing the fraction as a decimal, by dividing the numerator by the denominator, and then converting the decimal to a percent by moving the decimal point two places to the right.

6-5 Using the Percent Proportion

In the percent proportion $\frac{\text{part}}{\text{base}} = \frac{\text{percent}}{100}$, one of the numbers, called the part, is being compared to the whole quantity, called the base. The other ratio is the percent, written as a fraction, whose base is 100. The percent proportion can be used to find a missing part or base.

6-6 Finding Percents Mentally

When working with common percents like 10%, 25%, 40%, and 50%, it may be helpful to use the fraction form of the percent. Percent-fraction equivalents can be useful in solving real-world problems, particularly when dealing with sale prices. To find the percent of each number mentally, convert the percent to its fractional equivalent and then calculate. For example, to find 25% of 40, change 25% to $\frac{1}{4}$; and $\frac{1}{4}$ of 40 is 10.

6-7 Using Percent Equations

The percent equation is an equivalent form of the percent proportion in which the percent is written as a decimal. The percent equation is written as Part = Percent · Base. You can use this equation to find the missing part, percent, or base. The percent equation can also be used to solve problems involving discount and interest. Discount is the amount by which the regular price of an item is reduced. Simple interest is the amount of money paid or earned for the use of money.

6-8 Percent of Change

A percent of change tells the percent an amount has increased or decreased in relation to the original amount. To find the percent of change, write a ratio that compares the amount of change to the original measurement. That is, percent of change = $\frac{\text{amount of change}}{\text{original measurement}}$. Express the ratio as a percent. When an amount increases, the percent of change is a percent of increase. When an amount decreases, the percent of change is a percent of decrease. Percent of change is particularly useful in solving real-world, money-related problems.

6-9 Probability and Predictions

Probability is a ratio that compares the number of favorable outcomes to the number of possible outcomes. Probability is expressed as the ratio $\frac{\text{number of favorable outcomes}}{\text{number of possible outcomes}}$. The probability of an event is always between 0 and 1, inclusive. The closer a probability is to 1, the more likely it is to occur. The set of all possible outcomes is called the sample space. For a number cube, the sample space is {1, 2, 3, 4, 5, 6}, for a coin it is {heads, tails}. There are two types of probabilities. Theoretical probability is what should occur. Experimental probability is what actually occurs when conducting a probability experiment.

Quick Review Math Handbook

Hot Words includes a glossary of terms while Hot Topics consists of explanations of key mathematical concepts with exercises to test comprehension. This valuable resource can be used as a reference in the classroom or for home study.

Lesson	Hot Topics Section	Lesson	Hot Topics Section
GS 6	2.1, 2.6, 8.2	6-5	2.4, 2.9
6-1	6.4, 6.5	6-6	2.8, 6.4
6-2	6.5, 8.2	6-7	2.6, 2.8, 2.9
6-2F	6.5	6-8	2.8, 2.9
6-3	2.1, 6.5	6-9P	4.6
6-4	2.1, 2.8	6-9	4.6
6-5P	2.9	6-9F	4.6

GS = Getting Started, P = Preview, F = Follow-Up

 Additional mathematical information and teaching notes are available at www.pre-alg.com/key_concepts.

DAILY

INTERVENTION and **Assessment**

Key to Abbreviations:
TWE = Teacher Wraparound Edition; CRM = Chapter Resource Masters

Type	Student Edition	Teacher Resources	Technology/Internet
INTERVENTION — Ongoing	Prerequisite Skills, pp. 263, 268, 274, 280, 285, 292, 297, 302, 308 Practice Quiz 1, p. 292 Practice Quiz 2, p. 308	5-Minute Check Transparencies *Prerequisite Skills Workbook*, pp. 15–18, 37–40 Quizzes, *CRM*, pp. 359, 360 Mid-Chapter Test, *CRM*, p. 361 Study Guide and Intervention, *CRM*, pp. 299, 304, 309, 314, 319, 324, 329, 334, 339	Pre-AlgePASS: Tutorial Plus, Lessons 12, 13, 14, 15, 16, 17, and 18 www.pre-alg.com/self_check_quiz www.pre-alg.com/extra_examples
Mixed Review	pp. 268, 274, 280, 285, 292, 297, 302, 308, 314	Cumulative Review, *CRM*, p. 362	
Error Analysis	Find the Error, pp. 278, 291, 306	Find the Error, *TWE*, pp. 278, 290 Unlocking Misconceptions, *TWE*, pp. 267, 306	
Standardized Test Practice	pp. 268, 274, 280, 285, 292, 297, 302, 305, 306, 308, 314, 322–323	*TWE*, pp. 322–323 Standardized Test Practice, *CRM*, pp. 363–364	Standardized Test Practice CD-ROM www.pre-alg.com/standardized_test
ASSESSMENT — Open-Ended Assessment	Writing in Math, pp. 268, 274, 280, 285, 292, 297, 302, 307, 314 Open Ended, pp. 266, 272, 278, 283, 291, 295, 300, 306, 312 Standardized Test, p. 323	Speaking: *TWE*, pp. 274, 285, 314 Writing: *TWE*, pp. 268, 292, 302 Modeling: *TWE*, pp. 280, 297, 308 Open-Ended Assessment, *CRM*, p. 357	
Chapter Assessment	Study Guide, pp. 316–320 Practice Test, p. 321	Multiple-Choice Tests (Forms 1, 2A, 2B), *CRM*, pp. 345–350 Free-Response Tests (Forms 2C, 2D, 3), *CRM*, pp. 351–356 Vocabulary Test/Review, *CRM*, p. 358	ExamView® Pro (see below) MindJogger Videoquizzes www.pre-alg.com/vocabulary_review www.pre-alg.com/chapter_test

For more information on Yearly ProgressPro, see p. 144.

Pre-Algebra Lesson	Yearly ProgressPro Skill Lesson
6-1	Rates
6-2	Solve Proportions
6-3	Scale Models
6-4	Fraction/Decimal/Percent Conversions: Level 2
6-5	Ratios and Percent
6-6	Finding Percents Mentally
6-7	Percent Proportion and Equation
6-8	Percent of Change
6-9	Probability as Fractions: Level 2

ExamView® Pro

Use the networkable **ExamView® Pro** to:
- Create **multiple versions** of tests.
- Create **modified** tests for *Inclusion* students.
- **Edit** existing questions and **add** your own questions.
- Use built-in **state curriculum correlations** to create tests aligned with state standards.
- Change **English** tests to **Spanish** and vice versa.

For more information on Intervention and Assessment, see pp. T8–T11.

Reading and Writing in Mathematics

Glencoe Pre-Algebra provides numerous opportunities to incorporate reading and writing into the mathematics classroom.

Student Edition

- Foldables™ Study Organizer, p. 263
- Reading Mathematics, p. 269
- Concept Check questions require students to verbalize and write about what they have learned in the lesson. (pp. 265, 266, 270, 272, 276, 278, 283, 288, 291, 295, 300, 306, 310, 312)
- Writing in Math questions in every lesson, pp. 268, 274, 280, 285, 292, 297, 302, 307, 314
- Reading Math, pp. 281, 300, 311
- WebQuest, pp. 301, 314

Teacher Wraparound Edition

- Foldables™ Study Organizer, pp. 263, 316
- Study Notebook suggestions, pp. 266, 269, 272, 275, 278, 283, 287, 290, 295, 300, 303, 306, 309, 312
- Modeling activities, pp. 280, 297, 308
- Speaking activities, pp. 274, 285, 314
- Writing activities, pp. 268, 292, 302
- Differentiated Instruction (Verbal/Linguistic), pp. 294, 311
- **ELL** Resources, pp. 262, 264, 269, 270, 276, 281, 288, 293, 294, 298, 304, 310, 311, 316

Additional Resources

- Vocabulary Builder worksheets require students to define and give examples for key vocabulary terms as they progress through the chapter (*Chapter 6 Resource Masters*, pp. vii–viii)
- Reading to Learn Mathematics master for each lesson (*Chapter 6 Resource Masters*, pp. 302, 307, 312, 317, 322, 327, 332, 337, 342)
- *Vocabulary PuzzleMaker* software creates crossword, jumble, and word search puzzles using vocabulary lists that you can customize.
- *Teaching Mathematics with Foldables* provides suggestions for promoting cognition and language.
- *Reading and Writing in the Mathematics Classroom*
- *WebQuest and Project Resources*

For more information on Reading and Writing in Mathematics, see pp. T6–T7.

PROJECT CRISS℠ Study Skill

Sequence maps can help students solve problems as they write out the organized steps. As students work through lessons in Chapter 6, encourage them to draw sequence maps describing problem-solving procedures they are learning.

The sequence map at the right describes how to convert percents to decimals. Have students create their own sequence maps for converting decimals to percents, fractions to percents, and ratios to percents.

Percent

↓

Divide by 100

↓

Remove % symbol

↓

Decimal

CReating **I**ndependence **T**hrough **S**tudent-Owned **S**trategies

Chapter
6 Ratio, Proportion, and Percent

What You'll Learn

Have students read over the list of objectives and make a list of any words with which they are not familiar.

Why It's Important

Point out to students that this is only one of many reasons why each objective is important. Others are provided in the introduction to each lesson.

Lesson	NCTM Standards	Local Objectives
6-1	1, 2, 4, 9, 10	
6-2	1, 2, 4, 6, 9, 10	
6-2 Follow-Up	1,2,4,5,6,8,9,10	
6-3	1, 2, 4, 6, 9, 10	
6-4	1, 9, 10	
6-5 Preview	1, 3, 4, 7, 9, 10	
6-5	1, 2, 6, 7, 8, 9, 10	
6-6	1, 6, 8, 9	
6-7	1, 2, 6, 9, 10	
6-7 Follow-Up	1, 5, 6, 8, 9, 10	
6-8	1, 2, 3, 6, 9, 10	
6-9 Preview	1,2,5,6,8,9,10	
6-9	1, 2, 5, 9, 10	
6-9 Follow-Up	1, 2, 5, 9, 10	

Key to NCTM Standards:

1=Number & Operations, 2=Algebra,
3=Geometry, 4=Measurement,
5=Data Analysis & Probability, 6=Problem
Solving, 7=Reasoning & Proof,
8=Communication, 9=Connections,
10=Representation

Chapter 6 Ratio, Proportion, and Percent

What You'll Learn

- **Lesson 6-1** Write ratios as fractions and find unit rates.
- **Lessons 6-2 and 6-3** Use ratios and proportions to solve problems, including scale drawings.
- **Lesson 6-4** Write decimals and fractions as percents and vice versa.
- **Lessons 6-5, 6-6, 6-7, and 6-8** Estimate and compute with percents.
- **Lesson 6-9** Find simple probability.

Key Vocabulary

- ratio (p. 264)
- rate (p. 265)
- proportion (p. 270)
- percent (p. 281)
- probability (p. 310)

Why It's Important

The concept of proportionality is the foundation of many branches of mathematics, including geometry, statistics, and business math. Proportions can be used to solve real-world problems dealing with scale drawings, indirect measurement, predictions, and money. *You will solve a problem about currency exchange rates in Lesson 6-2.*

Vocabulary Builder   ELL

The Key Vocabulary list introduces students to some of the main vocabulary terms included in this chapter. For a more thorough vocabulary list with pronunciations of new words, give students the Vocabulary Builder worksheets found on pages vii and viii of the *Chapter 6 Resource Masters*. Encourage them to complete the definition of each term as they progress through the chapter. You may suggest that they add these sheets to their study notebooks for future reference when studying for the Chapter 6 test.

▶ **Prerequisite Skills** To be successful in this chapter, you'll need to master these skills and be able to apply them in problem-solving situations. Review these skills before beginning Chapter 6.

For Lesson 6-1   Convert Measurements

Complete each sentence. *(For review, see pages 718–721.)*

1. 2 ft = _?_ in. **24**
2. 4 yd = _?_ ft **12**
3. 2 mi = _?_ ft **10,560**

4. 3 h = _?_ min **180**
5. 8 min = _?_ s **480**
6. 4 lb = _?_ oz **64**

7. 2 T = _?_ lb **4000**
8. 5 gal = _?_ qt **20**
9. 3 pt = _?_ c **6**

10. 3 m = _?_ cm **300**
11. 5.8 m = _?_ cm **580**
12. 2 km = _?_ m **2000**

13. 5 cm = _?_ mm **50**
14. 2.3 L = _?_ mL **2300**
15. 15 kg = _?_ g **15,000**

For Lessons 6-2 and 6-3   Multiply Decimals

Find each product. *(For review, see page 715.)*

16. 7(3.4) **23.8**
17. 6.1(8) **48.8**
18. 2.8×5.9 **16.52**
19. 1.6×8.4 **13.44**

20. 0.8×9.3 **7.44**
21. 0.6(0.3) **0.18**
22. 12.4(3.8) **47.12**
23. 15.2×0.2 **3.04**

For Lesson 6-9   Write Fractions in Simplest Form

Simplify each fraction. If the fraction is already in simplest form, write *simplified*.
(For review, see Lesson 4-5.)

24. $\frac{4}{8}$ $\frac{1}{2}$
25. $\frac{5}{15}$ $\frac{1}{3}$
26. $\frac{6}{10}$ $\frac{3}{5}$
27. $\frac{12}{25}$ simplified

28. $\frac{22}{20}$ $\frac{11}{10}$
29. $\frac{15}{16}$ simplified
30. $\frac{36}{42}$ $\frac{6}{7}$
31. $\frac{36}{48}$ $\frac{3}{4}$

FOLDABLES™
Study Organizer

Fractions, Decimals, and Percents Make this Foldable to help you organize your notes. Begin with a piece of notebook paper.

Step 1 **Fold in Thirds**

Fold in thirds lengthwise.

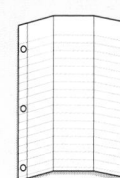

Step 2 **Label**

Draw lines along folds and label as shown.

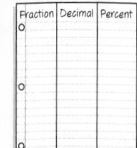

Reading and Writing As you read and study the chapter, complete the table with the commonly-used fraction, decimal, and percent equivalents.

This section provides a review of the basic concepts needed before beginning Chapter 6. Page references are included for additional student help.

Additional review is provided in the *Prerequisite Skills Workbook*, pages 15–18 and 37–40.

Prerequisite Skills in the Getting Ready for the Next Lesson section at the end of each lesson reviews a skill needed in the next lesson.

For Lesson	Prerequisite Skill
6-2	Solving Equations (p. 268)
6-3	Converting Measurements (p. 274)
6-4	Simplest Form (p. 280)
6-5	Proportions (p. 285)
6-6	Multiplying Fractions (p. 292)
6-7	Solving Equations (p. 297)
6-8	Writing Decimals as Percents (p. 302)
6-9	Writing Fractions as Percents (p. 308)

FOLDABLES™
Study Organizer

For more information about Foldables, see *Teaching Mathematics with Foldables.*

Using Charts to Compare and Contrast Students can use their Foldables to take notes, define terms, and record concepts about fractions, decimals, and percentages. Encourage students to record daily examples of how they use fractions, decimals, and percent, such as telling time, making change, eating a whole sandwich, and walking a quarter of a mile. Use the back of the Foldable if necessary.

1 Focus

5-Minute Check Transparency 6-1 Use as a quiz or review of Chapter 5.

Mathematical Background notes are available for this lesson on page 262C.

How are ratios used in paint mixtures?

The opening activity questions are repeated on page 302 of the *Chapter 6 Resource Masters*.

Reading to Learn Mathematics, p. 302 **ELL**

Pre-Activity *How are ratios used in paint mixtures?*

Do the activity at the top of page 264 in your textbook. Write your answers below.

  a. Which combination of paint would you use to make a smaller amount of the same shade of paint? Explain. Combination B; It has the same ratio as the original mixture but in a smaller amount.

  b. Suppose you want to make the same shade of paint as the original mixture. How many parts of yellow paint should you use for each part of blue paint? For each part of blue paint, 2 parts yellow paint should be used.

Reading the Lesson 1–3. See students' work.

Write a definition and give an example of each new vocabulary word or phrase.

Vocabulary	Definition	Example
1. ratio		
2. rate		
3. unit rate		

4. What is the difference between a ratio that compares measurements and a rate? The units of measure in a ratio that compares two measurements must have the same unit of measure. A rate is a comparison of two measurements having different kinds of units.

Helping You Remember

5. The word *rate* is part of the term *unit rate*. Explain how a rate can be written as a unit rate. Simplify the rate so it has a denominator of 1.

Teaching Tip Students can use two-color counters to model ratios in this lesson.

Vocabulary
- ratio
- rate
- unit rate

a. Combination B; It has the same ratio as the original mixture but in a smaller amount.

b. For each part of blue paint, 2 parts yellow paint should be used.

Study Tip

Look Back
To review how to write a fraction in **simplest form**, see Lesson 4-5.

What You'll Learn
- Write ratios as fractions in simplest form.
- Determine unit rates.

How are ratios used in paint mixtures?

The diagram shows a gallon of paint that is made using 2 parts blue paint and 4 parts yellow paint.

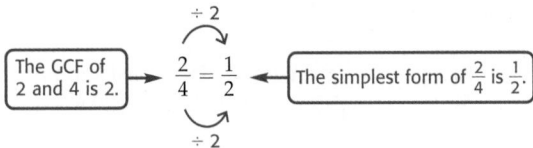

a. Which combination of paint would you use to make a smaller amount of the same shade of paint? Explain.

Combination A   Combination B

b. Suppose you want to make the same shade of paint as the original mixture? How many parts of yellow paint should you use for each part of blue paint?

WRITE RATIOS AS FRACTIONS IN SIMPLEST FORM A **ratio** is a comparison of two numbers by division. If a gallon of paint contains 2 parts blue paint and 4 parts yellow paint, then the ratio comparing the blue paint to the yellow paint can be written as follows.

$$2 \text{ to } 4 \qquad\qquad 2{:}4 \qquad\qquad \frac{2}{4}$$

Recall that a fraction bar represents division. When the first number being compared is less than the second, the ratio is usually written as a fraction in simplest form.

The GCF of 2 and 4 is 2. $\dfrac{2}{4} = \dfrac{1}{2}$ The simplest form of $\frac{2}{4}$ is $\frac{1}{2}$.
$\div 2$

Example 1 Write Ratios as Fractions

Express the ratio 9 goldfish out of 15 fish as a fraction in simplest form.

$$\frac{9}{15} = \frac{3}{5} \qquad \text{Divide the numerator and denominator by the GCF, 3.}$$
$\div 3$

The ratio of goldfish to fish is 3 to 5. This means that for every 5 fish, 3 of them are goldfish.

Resource Manager

📁 Workbooks and Reproducible Masters

Chapter 6 Resource Masters
- Study Guide and Intervention, p. 299
- Skills Practice, p. 300
- Practice, p. 301
- Reading to Learn Mathematics, p. 302
- Enrichment, p. 303

Parent and Student Study Guide Workbook, p. 44
Prerequisite Skills Workbook, pp. 39–40

Transparencies
5-Minute Check Transparency 6-1
Answer Key Transparencies

Technology
Interactive Chalkboard
Pre-AlgePASS: Tutorial Plus, Lessons 12 and 13

When writing a ratio involving measurements, both quantities should have the same unit of measure.

Example 2 Write Ratios as Fractions

Express the ratio *3 feet to 16 inches* as a fraction in simplest form.

3 ft

16 in.

$$\frac{3 \text{ feet}}{16 \text{ inches}} = \frac{36 \text{ inches}}{16 \text{ inches}}$$ Convert 3 feet to inches.

$$= \frac{9 \text{ inches}}{4 \text{ inches}}$$ Divide the numerator and denominator by the GCF, 4.

Written in simplest form, the ratio is 9 to 4.

✓ **Concept Check**   Give an example of a ratio in simplest form.
Sample answer: 2 to 3

FIND UNIT RATES   A **rate** is a ratio of two measurements having different kinds of units. Here are two examples of rates.

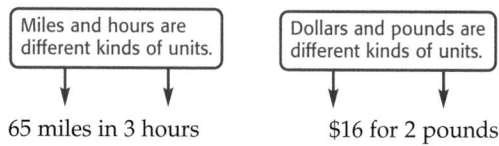

| Miles and hours are different kinds of units. | Dollars and pounds are different kinds of units. |

65 miles in 3 hours $16 for 2 pounds

When a rate is simplified so that it has a denominator of 1, it is called a **unit rate**. An example of a unit rate is $5 per pound, which means $5 per 1 pound.

Example 3 Find Unit Rate

Study Tip

Alternative Method
Another way to find the unit rate is to divide the cost of the package by the number of CDs in the package.

SHOPPING   A package of 20 recordable CDs costs $18, and a package of 30 recordable CDs costs $28. Which package has the lower cost per CD?

Find and compare the unit rates of the packages.

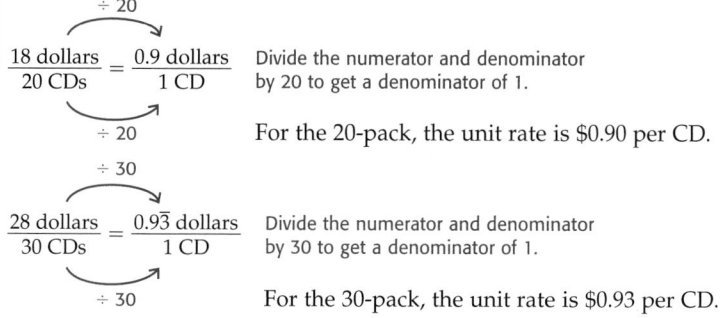

÷ 20

$$\frac{18 \text{ dollars}}{20 \text{ CDs}} = \frac{0.9 \text{ dollars}}{1 \text{ CD}}$$ Divide the numerator and denominator by 20 to get a denominator of 1.

÷ 20   For the 20-pack, the unit rate is $0.90 per CD.

÷ 30

$$\frac{28 \text{ dollars}}{30 \text{ CDs}} = \frac{0.9\overline{3} \text{ dollars}}{1 \text{ CD}}$$ Divide the numerator and denominator by 30 to get a denominator of 1.

÷ 30   For the 30-pack, the unit rate is $0.93 per CD.

So, the package that contains 20 CDs has the lower cost per CD.

Concept Check: Since the ratio does not have a denominator of 1, it is a rate.

✓ **Concept Check**   Is $50 in 3 days a rate or a unit rate? Explain.

www.pre-alg.com/extra_examples   **Lesson 6-1** Ratios and Rates   **265**

2 Teach

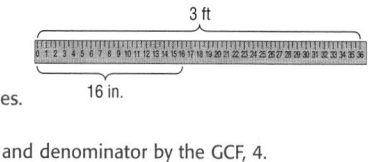

WRITE RATIOS AS FRACTIONS IN SIMPLEST FORM

In-Class Examples   Power Point®

1 Express the ratio *10 roses out of 12 flowers* as a fraction in simplest form. $\frac{5}{6}$

2 Express the ratio *21 inches to 2 yards* as a fraction in simplest form. $\frac{7}{24}$

Teaching Tip   Watch for students who use subtraction instead of division to simplify ratios.

✓ **Skills Check**

Write Ratios as Fractions in Simplest Form   A class consists of 12 girls and 16 boys. Express the ratio of boys to total students as a fraction in simplest form. $\frac{4}{7}$

FIND UNIT RATES

In-Class Example   Power Point®

3 **SHOPPING** A 12-oz bottle of cleaner costs $4.50. A 16-oz bottle of cleaner costs $6.56. Which costs less per ounce? **12-oz bottle. $ 0.38; 16-oz bottle: $ 0.41; The 12-oz bottle costs less.**

Teaching Tip Suggest that students use dimensional analysis to keep them from switching the divisor and dividend when finding unit prices.

Interactive Chalkboard
PowerPoint® Presentations

This CD-ROM is a customizable Microsoft® Power-Point® presentation that includes:

- Step-by-step, dynamic solutions of each In-Class Example from the Teacher Wraparound Edition
- Additional, Your Turn exercises for each example
- The 5-Minute Check Transparencies
- Hot links to Glencoe Online Study Tools

4 **ANIMALS** A snail moved 30 feet in 2 hours. How many inches per minute did the snail move? **3 in./min**

3 Practice/Apply

Study Notebook

Have students—

• add the definitions/examples of the vocabulary terms to their Vocabulary Builder worksheets for Chapter 6.

• write a paragraph describing a situation in which using a unit price would be helpful to them.

• include any other item(s) that they find helpful in mastering the skills in this lesson.

About the Exercises . . .

Organization by Objective
• Write Ratios as Fractions in Simplest Form: 16–27
• Find Unit Rates: 28–37, 46–48

Odd/Even Assignments
Exercises 16–45 are structured so that students practice the same concepts whether they are assigned odd or even problems.

Alert! Exercise 46 involves research on the Internet or other reference materials.

Assignment Guide

Basic: 17–23 odd, 29–33 odd, 37–43 odd, 47–52, 54–70

Average: 17–45 odd, 47–52, 54–70 (Optional: 53)

Advanced: 16–44 even, 47–64 (Optional: 65–70)

To convert a rate such as miles per hour to a rate such as feet per second, you can use dimensional analysis. Recall that this is the process of carrying units throughout a computation.

Example 4 **Convert Rates**

ANIMALS A grizzly bear can run 30 miles in 1 hour. How many feet is this per second?

You need to convert $\frac{30 \text{ mi}}{1 \text{ h}}$ to $\frac{\blacksquare \text{ ft}}{1 \text{ s}}$. There are 5280 feet in 1 mile and 3600 seconds in 1 hour. Write 30 miles per hour as $\frac{30 \text{ mi}}{1 \text{ h}}$.

$$\frac{30 \text{ mi}}{1 \text{ h}} = \frac{30 \text{ mi}}{1 \text{ h}} \cdot \frac{5280 \text{ ft}}{1 \text{ mi}} \div \frac{3600 \text{ s}}{1 \text{ h}}$$ Convert miles to feet and hours to seconds.

$$= \frac{30 \text{ mi}}{1 \text{ h}} \cdot \frac{5280 \text{ ft}}{1 \text{ mi}} \cdot \frac{1 \text{ h}}{3600 \text{ s}}$$ The reciprocal of $\frac{3600 \text{ s}}{1 \text{ h}}$ is $\frac{1 \text{ h}}{3600 \text{ s}}$.

$$= \frac{\overset{1}{30 \text{ mi}}}{1 \text{ h}} \cdot \frac{\overset{44}{5280 \text{ ft}}}{1 \text{ mi}} \cdot \frac{1 \text{ h}}{\underset{120}{3600 \text{ s}}}$$ Divide the common factors and units.

$$= \frac{44 \text{ ft}}{\text{s}}$$ Simplify.

So, 30 miles per hour is equivalent to 44 feet per second.

Check for Understanding

Concept Check 1. **Draw** a diagram in which the ratio of circles to squares is 2:3.

2. **Explain** the difference between ratio and rate. **1–3. See pp. 323A–323B.**

3. **OPEN ENDED** Give an example of a unit rate.

Guided Practice Express each ratio as a fraction in simplest form. **4–11. See pp. 323A–323B.**

GUIDED PRACTICE KEY	
Exercises	Examples
4–7	1, 2
8–11	3
12, 13	4
14, 15	2

4. 4 goals in 10 attempts
5. 15 dimes out of 24 coins
6. 10 inches to 3 feet
7. 5 feet to 5 yards

Express each ratio as a unit rate. Round to the nearest tenth, if necessary.

8. $183 for 4 concert tickets
9. 9 inches of snow in 12 hours
10. 100 feet in 14.5 seconds
11. 254.1 miles on 10.5 gallons

Convert each rate using dimensional analysis.

12. 20 mi/h = ■ ft/min **1760**
13. 16 cm/s = ■ m/h **576**

Application **GEOMETRY** For Exercises 14 and 15, refer to the figure below.

14. Express the ratio of width to length as a fraction in simplest form. $\frac{3}{5}$

15. Suppose the width and length are each increased by 2 centimeters. Will the ratio of the width to length be the same as the ratio of the width to length of the original rectangle? Explain. **No; the ratio will be 2 to 3.**

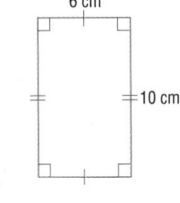

DAILY
INTERVENTION

Differentiated Instruction

• **Visual/Spatial** Have students bring advertisements and coupons from newspapers and magazines. Ask them to explain the different ways ratios are used in the ads or coupons. Then have them work together to make a collage of the ads or coupons. Encourage them to highlight the ratios and to include some math problems based on the ratios.

Practice and Apply

Express each ratio as a fraction in simplest form. 16–35. See pp. 323A–323B.

16. 6 ladybugs out of 27 insects

17. 14 girls to 35 boys

18. 18 cups to 45 cups

19. 12 roses out of 28 flowers

20. 7 cups to 9 pints

21. 9 pounds to 16 tons

22. 11 gallons to 11 quarts

23. 18 miles to 18 yards

★ 24. 15 dollars out of 123 dollars

★ 25. 17 rubies out of 118 gems

★ 26. 155 apples to 75 oranges

★ 27. 321 articles in 107 magazines

Express each ratio as a unit rate. Round to the nearest tenth, if necessary.

28. $3 for 6 cans of tuna

29. $0.99 for 10 pencils

30. 140 miles on 6 gallons

31. 68 meters in 15 seconds

32. 19 yards in 2.5 minutes

33. 25 feet in 3.2 hours

★ 34. 236.7 miles in 4.5 days

★ 35. 331.5 pages in 8.5 weeks

36. **MAGAZINES** Which costs more per issue, an 18-issue subscription for $40.50 or a 12-issue subscription for $33.60? Explain.
36–37. See pp. 323A–323B.

37. **SHOPPING** Determine which is less expensive per can, a 6-pack of soda for $2.20 or a 12-pack of soda for $4.25. Explain.

Convert each rate using dimensional analysis.

38. $45 \text{ mi/h} = \blacksquare \text{ ft/s}$ 66

39. $18 \text{ mi/h} = \blacksquare \text{ ft/s}$ 26.4

40. $26 \text{ cm/s} = \blacksquare \text{ m/min}$ 15.6

41. $32 \text{ cm/s} = \blacksquare \text{ m/min}$ 19.2

42. $2.5 \text{ qt/min} = \blacksquare \text{ gal/h}$ 37.5

43. $4.8 \text{ qt/min} = \blacksquare \text{ gal/h}$ 72

★ 44. $4 \text{ c/min} = \blacksquare \text{ qt/h}$ 60

★ 45. $7 \text{ c/min} = \blacksquare \text{ qt/h}$ 105

46. **POPULATION** Population density is a unit rate that gives the number of people per square mile. Find the population density for each state listed in the table at the right. Round to the nearest whole number. See pp. 323A–323B.

State	Population (2000)	Area (sq mi)
Alaska	626,932	570,374
New York	18,976,457	47,224
Rhode Island	1,048,319	1045
Texas	20,851,820	261,914
Wyoming	493,782	97,105

Source: U.S. Census Bureau

Online Research Data Update How has the population density of the states in the table changed since 2000? Visit www.pre-alg.com/data_update to learn more.

TRAVEL For Exercises 47 and 48, use the following information.
An airplane flew from Boston to Chicago to Denver. The distance from Boston to Chicago was 1015 miles and the distance from Chicago to Denver was 1011 miles. The plane traveled for 3.5 hours and carried 285 passengers.

47. About how fast did the airplane travel? about 579 mi/h

★ 48. Suppose it costs $5685 per hour to operate the airplane. Find the cost per person per hour for the flight. $19.95/per hour

www.pre-alg.com/self_check_quiz

Open-Ended Assessment

Writing Have students express the ratio of toes to elbows in simplest form and explain whether the ratio is a unit ratio.

Motivating Students
Have students look around the room for ratios, such as desks per student, windows to doors, and so forth. Display the representations in the room for the remainder of the chapter.

Getting Ready for Lesson 6-2

PREREQUISITE SKILL Lesson 6-2 presents solving proportions, which requires students to solve equations using the Division Property of Equality. Exercises 65–70 should be used to determine your students' familiarity with solving equations.

Answers

50. Ratios are used in paint mixtures to achieve a desired color by using two or more different colors. Answers should include the following.
    - If you want a darker shade of green, use a ratio in which there is a greater amount of blue paint compared to yellow paint. An example is 3 blue to 4 yellow.
    - If you want a lighter shade of green, use a ratio in which there is a greater amount of yellow paint compared to blue paint. An example is 5 yellow to 2 blue.

---

49. **CRITICAL THINKING** Marty and Spencer each saved money earned from shoveling snow. The ratio of Marty's money to Spencer's money is 3:1. If Marty gives Spencer $3, their ratio will be 1:1. How much money did Marty earn? **$9**

50. **WRITING IN MATH** Answer the question that was posed at the beginning of the lesson. **See margin.**

   How are ratios used in paint mixtures?

   Include the following in your answer:
   - an example of a ratio of blue to yellow paint that would result in a darker shade of green, and
   - an example of a ratio of blue to yellow paint that would result in a lighter shade of green.

Standardized Test Practice

51. Which ratio represents the same relationship as *for every 4 apples, 3 of them are green*? **C**
    - (A) 9:16
    - (B) 3:4
    - (C) 12:9
    - (D) 6:8

52. Joe paid $2.79 for a gallon of milk. Find the cost per quart of milk. **A**
    - (A) $0.70
    - (B) $1.40
    - (C) $0.93
    - (D) $0.55

Extending the Lesson

53. Many objects such as credit cards or phone cards are shaped like golden rectangles. **a–c. See margin.**

    > A *golden rectangle* is a rectangle in which the ratio of the length to the width is approximately 1.618 to 1. This ratio is called the **golden ratio**.

    a. Find three different objects that are close to a golden rectangle. Make a table to display the dimensions and the ratio found in each object.

    b. Describe how each ratio compares to the golden ratio.

    c. **RESEARCH** Use the Internet or another source to find three places where the golden rectangle is used in architecture.

Maintain Your Skills

Mixed Review State whether each sequence is *arithmetic, geometric,* or *neither*. Then state the common difference or common ratio and write the next three terms of the sequence. *(Lesson 5-10)* **54–55. See margin.**

54. −3, 6, −12, 24, …

55. 12.1, 12.4, 12.7, 13, …

ALGEBRA Solve each equation. *(Lesson 5-9)*

56. $3.6 = x - 7.1$ **10.7**

57. $y + \frac{3}{4} = \frac{2}{3} - \frac{1}{12}$

58. $-4.8 = 6z$ **−0.8**

59. $\frac{3}{8}w = 5$ **$13\frac{1}{3}$**

60. Find the quotient of $1\frac{1}{7}$ and $-\frac{4}{7}$. *(Lesson 5-4)* **−2**

Write each number in scientific notation. *(Lesson 4-8)*

61. 52,000,000 **5.2×10^7**

62. 42,240 **4.224×10^4**

63. 0.038 **3.8×10^{-2}**

64. Write $8 \cdot (k + 3) \cdot (k + 3)$ using exponents. *(Lesson 4-2)* **$8(k + 3)^2$**

Getting Ready for the Next Lesson

PREREQUISITE SKILL Solve each equation.
*(To review **solving equations**, see Lesson 3-4.)*

65. $10x = 300$ **30**

66. $25m = 225$ **9**

67. $8k = 320$ **40**

68. $192 = 4t$ **48**

69. $195 = 15w$ **13**

70. $231 = 33n$ **7**

---

53. a. Answers will vary.

    b. The ratios should be close in value.

    c. Sample answer: Pyramid of Khufu in Giza, Egypt; The Taj Mahal in India; The Lincoln Memorial in Washington, D.C.

54. geometric; −2; −48, 96, −192

55. arithmetic; Each term increases by 0.3; 13.3, 13.6, 13.9

Reading Mathematics

Making Comparisons

In mathematics, there are many different ways to compare numbers. Consider the information in the table.

Zoo	Size (acres)	Animals	Species
San Diego	100	4000	800
Houston	55	5000	700
Oakland	100	400	100
Columbus	400	11,000	700

The following types of comparison statements can be used to describe this information.

Difference Comparisons

- The Houston Zoo has 1000 more animals than the San Diego Zoo.
- The Columbus Zoo is 345 acres larger than the Houston Zoo.
- The Oakland Zoo has 700 less species of animals than the San Diego Zoo.

Ratio Comparisons

- The ratio of the size of the San Diego Zoo to the size of the Columbus Zoo is 1:4. So, the San Diego Zoo is one-fourth the size of the Columbus Zoo.
- The ratio of the number of animals at the San Diego Zoo to the number of animals at the Oakland Zoo is 4000:400 or 10:1. So, San Diego Zoo has ten times as many animals as the Oakland Zoo.

Reading to Learn 1–4. See margin.

1. Refer to the zoo information above. Write a difference comparison and a ratio comparison statement that describes the information.

Refer to the information below. Identify each statement as a difference comparison or a ratio comparison.

Florida *The Sunshine State*
Total area: 59,928 sq mi
Land area: 53,937 sq mi
Land forested: 26,478.4 sq mi

Ohio *The Buckeye State*
Total area: 44,828 sq mi
Land area: 40,953 sq mi
Land forested: 12,580.8 sq mi

Source: *The World Almanac*

2. The area of Florida is about 15,000 square miles greater than the area of Ohio.

3. The ratio of the amount of land forested in Ohio to the amount forested in Florida is about 1 to 2.

4. More than one-fourth of the land in Ohio is forested.

Have students use the word "difference" in a sentence. Then show how the word describes a comparison between two things. Do the same for the word "ratio."

Teach

Making Comparisons
Encourage students to associate the word "difference" with subtraction and the words "ratio" and "fraction" with division.

Assess

Study Notebook

Ask students to write two comparison statements, each comparing their height to the height of a 7-foot door. One should be a difference statement; the other should be a ratio statement.

ELL English Language Learners may benefit from writing key concepts from this activity in their Study Notebooks in their native language and then in English.

Answers

1. Sample answer: difference comparison: The Houston Zoo has 6000 fewer animals than the Columbus Zoo; ratio comparison: The ratio of the size of the San Diego Zoo to the Houston Zoo is 100:55 or 20:11. The San Diego Zoo is about twice the size of the Houston Zoo.

2. difference comparison

3. ratio comparison

4. ratio comparison

1 Focus

5-Minute Check Transparency 6-2 Use as a quiz or review of Lesson 6-1.

Mathematical Background notes are available for this lesson on page 262C.

How **are proportions used in recipes?**

The opening activity questions are repeated on page 307 of the *Chapter 6 Resource Masters*.

Reading to Learn Mathematics, p. 307   **ELL**

Pre-Activity *How are proportions used in recipes?*

Do the activity at the top of page 270 in your textbook. Write your answers below.

a. For each of the first four ingredients, write a ratio that compares the number of ounces of each ingredient to the number of ounces of water.

lemonade: $\frac{1}{7}$; grape juice: $\frac{1}{7}$; orange juice: $\frac{1}{7}$; lemon-lime soda: $\frac{10}{21}$

b. Double the recipe. (*Hint:* Multiply each number of ounces by 2.) Then write a ratio for the ounces of each of the first four ingredients to the ounces of water as a fraction in simplest form.

lemonade: $\frac{1}{7}$; grape juice: $\frac{1}{7}$; orange juice: $\frac{1}{7}$; lemon-lime soda: $\frac{10}{21}$

c. Are the ratios in parts **a** and **b** the same? Why or why not?
Yes; each part was multiplied by the same number.

Reading the Lesson   1–2. See students' work.
Write a definition and give an example of each new vocabulary word or phrase.

Vocabulary	Definition	Example
1. proportion		
2. cross products		

3. Do $\frac{3}{5}$ and $\frac{12}{20}$ form a proportion? Explain.   Yes; both cross products are 60.

4. Write a ratio that forms a proportion with $\frac{3}{4}$.   Sample answer: $\frac{9}{12}$

Helping You Remember

5. *Proportion* is a common word in the English language.

  a. Write its definition.   relation of parts to each other or to the whole

  b. How does this definition relate to the one given on page 270 of your textbook?
  A proportion is an equation that states how two ratios relate to each other.

  c. Explain how cross products are used to solve a proportion.   First find the cross products and write an equation to show that they are equal. Then solve the equation.

Teaching Tip Emphasize that adding or subtracting the same number to the numerator and denominator of a fraction changes the ratio.

Resource Manager

📁 Workbooks and Reproducible Masters

Chapter 6 Resource Masters
- Study Guide and Intervention, p. 304
- Skills Practice, p. 305
- Practice, p. 306
- Reading to Learn Mathematics, p. 307
- Enrichment, p. 308

Parent and Student Study Guide Workbook, p. 45
Prerequisite Skills Workbook, pp. 37–40
School-to-Career Masters, p. 11

📺 Transparencies

5–Minute Check Transparency 6-2
Answer Key Transparencies

💿 Technology

Interactive Chalkboard
Pre-AlgePASS: Tutorial Plus, Lesson 14

What **You'll Learn**

- Solve proportions.
- Use proportions to solve real-world problems.

Vocabulary
- proportion
- cross products

a. lemonade: $\frac{1}{7}$;

grape juice: $\frac{1}{7}$;

orange juice: $\frac{1}{7}$;

lemon-lime soda: $\frac{10}{21}$

b. same as part a
c. Yes; each part was multiplied by the same number.

How **are proportions used in recipes?**

For many years, Phyllis Norman was famous in her neighborhood for making her flavorful fruit punch.

Fruit Punch
12 oz frozen lemonade concentrate
12 oz frozen grape juice concentrate
12 oz frozen orange juice concentrate
40 oz lemon-lime soda
84 oz water
Yields: 160 oz of punch

a. For each of the first four ingredients, write a ratio that compares the number of ounces of each ingredient to the number of ounces of water.

b. Double the recipe. Write a ratio for the ounces of each of the first four ingredients to the ounces of water as a fraction in simplest form.

c. Are the ratios in parts **a** and **b** the same? Why or why not?

PROPORTIONS   To solve problems that relate to ratios, you can use a proportion. A **proportion** is a statement of equality of two ratios.

Key Concept   Proportion
- **Words**   A proportion is an equation stating that two ratios are equal.
- **Symbols** $\dfrac{a}{b} = \dfrac{c}{d}$ • **Example** $\dfrac{2}{3} = \dfrac{6}{9}$

Consider the following proportion.

$$\frac{a}{b} = \frac{c}{d}$$

$$\frac{a}{\cancel{b}} \cdot \cancel{b}d = \frac{c}{\cancel{d}} \cdot b\cancel{d} \qquad \text{Multiply each side by } bd \text{ to eliminate the fractions.}$$

$$ad = cb \qquad \text{Simplify.}$$

The products ad and cb are called the **cross products** of a proportion. Every proportion has two cross products.

Study Tip

Properties
When you multiply each side of an equation by bd, you are using the Multiplication Property of Equality.

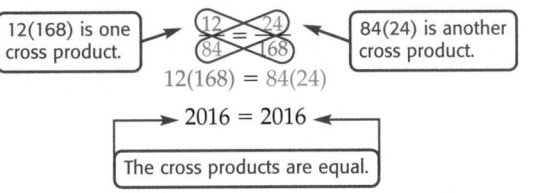

12(168) is one cross product.

84(24) is another cross product.

$$12(168) = 84(24)$$

$$2016 = 2016$$

The cross products are equal.

✓ **Concept Check**   Write a proportion whose cross products are equal to 18.
Sample answer: $\dfrac{2}{6}$ and $\dfrac{3}{9}$

270 **Chapter 6** Ratio, Proportion, and Percent

Cross products can be used to determine whether two ratios form a proportion.

Key Concept — Property of Proportions

- **Words** The cross products of a proportion are equal.
- **Symbols** If $\frac{a}{b} = \frac{c}{d}$, then $ad = bc$. If $ad = bc$, then $\frac{a}{b} = \frac{c}{d}$.

Example 1 Identify Proportions

Determine whether each pair of ratios forms a proportion.

a. $\frac{1}{3}, \frac{3}{9}$

$\frac{1}{3} \stackrel{?}{=} \frac{3}{9}$ Write a proportion.

$1 \cdot 9 \stackrel{?}{=} 3 \cdot 3$ Cross products

$9 = 9$ Simplify.

So, $\frac{1}{3} = \frac{3}{9}$.

b. $\frac{1.2}{4.0}, \frac{2}{5}$

$\frac{1.2}{4.0} \stackrel{?}{=} \frac{2}{5}$ Write a proportion.

$1.2 \cdot 5 \stackrel{?}{=} 4.0 \cdot 2$ Cross products

$6 \neq 8$ Simplify.

So, $\frac{1.2}{4.0} \neq \frac{2}{5}$.

Example 2 Solve Proportions

Solve each proportion.

a. $\frac{a}{25} = \frac{52}{100}$

$\frac{a}{25} = \frac{52}{100}$

$a \cdot 100 = 25 \cdot 52$ Cross products

$100a = 1300$ Multiply.

$\frac{100a}{100} = \frac{1300}{100}$ Divide.

$a = 13$

The solution is 13.

b. $\frac{12.5}{m} = \frac{15}{7.5}$

$\frac{12.5}{m} = \frac{15}{7.5}$

$12.5 \cdot 7.5 = m \cdot 15$ Cross products

$93.75 = 15m$ Multiply.

$\frac{93.75}{15} = \frac{15m}{15}$ Divide.

$6.25 = m$

The solution is 6.25.

Study Tip

Cross Products
When you find cross products, you are *cross multiplying*.

USE PROPORTIONS TO SOLVE REAL-WORLD PROBLEMS   When you solve a problem using a proportion, be sure to compare the quantities in the same order.

Example 3 Use a Proportion to Solve a Problem

FOOD   Refer to the recipe at the beginning of the lesson. How much soda should be used if 16 ounces of each type of juice are used?

Explore   You know how much soda to use for 12 ounces of each type of juice. You need to find how much soda to use for 16 ounces of each type of juice.

Plan   Write and solve a proportion using ratios that compare juice to soda. Let *s* represent the amount of soda to use in the new recipe.

(continued on the next page)

 www.pre-alg.com/extra_examples   **Lesson 6-2**   Using Proportions   **271**

Teacher to Teacher

Barbara Cain   Thomas Jefferson M.S., Merritt Island, FL

"When we multiply a decimal by another number using a multiplication dot in my classroom, we usually put the decimal number in parentheses. This helps to avoid confusion in a handwritten problem with two different uses of the dot."

2 Teach

PROPORTIONS

In-Class Examples    Power Point®

1 Determine whether each pair of ratios forms a proportion.

a. $\frac{2}{3}, \frac{12}{20}$ $\frac{2}{3} \neq \frac{12}{20}$

b. $\frac{0.8}{3.2}, \frac{2}{8}$ $\frac{0.8}{3.2} = \frac{2}{8}$

2 Solve each proportion.

a. $\frac{c}{36} = \frac{9}{15}$ $c = 21.6$

b. $\frac{16}{v} = \frac{4.8}{1.5}$ $v = 5$

Teaching Tip   Frequently remind students to check their answer by substituting it into the original proportion.

✓ Skills Check

Solve Proportions   Ask students how they know which number to divide by after they have written the cross products. **Divide by the coefficient of the variable.**

USE PROPORTIONS TO SOLVE REAL-WORLD PROBLEMS

In-Class Example   Power Point®

3 **ARCHITECTURE** An architect builds a model of a building before the actual building is built. The model is 8 inches tall and the actual building will be 22 feet tall. The model is 20 inches wide. Find the width of the actual building.   **55 ft**

In-Class Example Power Point®

4 **ATTRACTIONS** The Circleville Pumpkin Show in Circleville, Ohio, boasts the world's largest pumpkin pie. The pie weighs 350 pounds and is 5 feet in diameter. Find the diameter of the pie in centimeters if 1 ft = 30.48 cm. **152.4 cm**

---

3 Practice/Apply

Study Notebook

Have students—
- add the definitions/examples of the vocabulary terms to their Vocabulary Builder worksheets for Chapter 6.
- include any other item(s) that they find helpful in mastering the skills in this lesson.

About the Exercises . . .

Organization by Objective
- **Proportions:** 9–31
- **Use Proportions to Solve Real-World Problems:** 32–42, 45

Odd/Even Assignments
Exercises 9–35 are structured so that students practice the same concepts whether they are assigned odd or even problems.

Assignment Guide

Basic: 9–25 odd, 33, 35–37, 39, 41, 43–55

Average: 9–35 odd, 36–37, 39, 41, 43–55

Advanced: 10–34 even, 38–51 (Optional: 52–55)

TEACHING TIP
You can also solve the problem by comparing soda to juice.

$$\frac{\text{soda in original}}{\text{juice in original}} = \frac{\text{soda in new}}{\text{juice in new}}$$

More About . . .

Attractions
The world's largest baseball bat is located in Louisville, Kentucky. It is 120 feet long, has a diameter from 3.5 to 9 feet, and weighs 68,000 pounds.
Source: World's Largest Roadside Attractions

Solve

$$\frac{\text{juice in original recipe}}{\text{soda in original recipe}} = \frac{\text{juice in new recipe}}{\text{soda in new recipe}}$$

$$\frac{12}{40} = \frac{16}{s} \qquad \text{Write a proportion.}$$

$$12 \cdot s = 40 \cdot 16 \qquad \text{Cross products}$$

$$12s = 640 \qquad \text{Multiply.}$$

$$\frac{12s}{12} = \frac{640}{12} \qquad \text{Divide.}$$

$$s = 53\tfrac{1}{3} \qquad \text{Simplify.}$$

$53\tfrac{1}{3}$ ounces of soda should be used.

Examine Check the cross products. Since $12 \cdot 53\tfrac{1}{3} = 640$ and $40 \cdot 16 = 640$, the answer is correct.

Proportions can also be used in measurement problems.

Example 4 *Convert Measurements*

ATTRACTIONS Louisville, Kentucky, is home to the world's largest baseball glove. The glove is 4 feet high, 10 feet long, 9 feet wide, and weighs 15 tons. Find the height of the glove in centimeters if 1 ft = 30.48 cm.

Let x represent the height in centimeters.

customary measurement → $\dfrac{1 \text{ ft}}{30.48 \text{ cm}} = \dfrac{4 \text{ ft}}{x \text{ cm}}$ ← customary measurement
metric measurement →   ← metric measurement

$$1 \cdot x = 30.48 \cdot 4 \qquad \text{Cross products}$$

$$x = 121.92 \qquad \text{Simplify.}$$

The height of the glove is 121.92 centimeters.

Check for Understanding

Concept Check
1. **Define** *proportion*. **1–2. See margin.**

2. **OPEN ENDED** Find two counterexamples for the statement *Two ratios always form a proportion.*

Guided Practice

GUIDED PRACTICE KEY	
Exercises	Examples
3, 4	1
5–7	2
8	3, 4

Determine whether each pair of ratios forms a proportion.

3. $\dfrac{1}{4}, \dfrac{4}{16}$ **yes**

4. $\dfrac{2.1}{3.5}, \dfrac{3}{7}$ **no**

ALGEBRA Solve each proportion.

5. $\dfrac{k}{35} = \dfrac{3}{7}$ **15**

6. $\dfrac{3}{t} = \dfrac{18}{24}$ **4**

7. $\dfrac{10}{8.4} = \dfrac{5}{m}$ **4.2**

Application
8. **PHOTOGRAPHY** A 3″ × 5″ photo is enlarged so that the length of the new photo is 7 inches. Find the width of the new photo. $4\tfrac{1}{5}$ **in.**

272 Chapter 6 Ratio, Proportion, and Percent

Answers

1. A statement of equality of two ratios.

2. Sample answer: $\dfrac{2}{3} = \dfrac{3}{4}; \dfrac{1}{2} = \dfrac{1}{4}$

Practice and Apply

Determine whether each pair of ratios forms a proportion.

9. $\frac{2}{3}, \frac{8}{12}$ yes

10. $\frac{4}{2}, \frac{16}{5}$ no

11. $\frac{1.5}{5.0}, \frac{3}{9}$ no

12. $\frac{18}{2.4}, \frac{15}{2}$ yes

13. $\frac{3.4}{1.6}, \frac{5.1}{2.4}$ yes

14. $\frac{5.3}{15.9}, \frac{2.7}{8.1}$ yes

ALGEBRA Solve each proportion.

15. $\frac{p}{6} = \frac{24}{36}$ 4

16. $\frac{w}{11} = \frac{14}{22}$ 7

17. $\frac{4}{10} = \frac{8}{a}$ 20

18. $\frac{18}{12} = \frac{24}{q}$ 16

19. $\frac{5}{h} = \frac{10}{30}$ 15

20. $\frac{51}{z} = \frac{17}{7}$ 21

21. $\frac{7}{45} = \frac{x}{9}$ 1.4

22. $\frac{2}{15} = \frac{c}{72}$ 9.6

23. $\frac{7}{5} = \frac{10.5}{b}$ 7.5

24. $\frac{16}{7} = \frac{4.8}{h}$ 2.1

25. $\frac{2}{9.4} = \frac{0.2}{v}$ 0.94

26. $\frac{9}{7.2} = \frac{3.5}{k}$ 2.8

★ 27. $\frac{a}{0.28} = \frac{4}{1.4}$ 0.8

★ 28. $\frac{3}{14} = \frac{15}{m-3}$ 73

★ 29. $\frac{16}{x+5} = \frac{4}{5}$ 15

★ 30. Find the value of d that makes $\frac{5.1}{1.7} = \frac{7.5}{d}$ a proportion. 2.5

★ 31. What value of m makes $\frac{6.5}{1.3} = \frac{m}{5.2}$ a proportion? 26

Write a proportion that could be used to solve for each variable. Then solve.

32. 8 pencils in 2 boxes
20 pencils in x boxes $\frac{8}{2} = \frac{20}{x}$; 5

33. 12 glasses in 3 crates
72 glasses in m crates

33. $\frac{12}{3} = \frac{72}{m}$; 18

34. y dollars for 5.4 gallons
14 dollars for 3 gallons
$\frac{y}{5.4} = \frac{14}{3}$; $25.20

35. 5 quarts for $6.25
d quarts for $8.75 $\frac{5}{6.25} = \frac{d}{8.75}$; 7

OLYMPICS For Exercises 36 and 37, use the following information.
There are approximately 3.28 feet in 1 meter.

36. Write a proportion that could be used to find the distance in feet of the 110-meter dash. $\frac{1\text{ m}}{3.28\text{ ft}} = \frac{110\text{ m}}{x\text{ ft}}$

37. What is the distance in feet of the 110-meter dash? about 360.8 ft

38. **PHOTOGRAPHY** Suppose an 8″ × 10″ photo is reduced so that the width of the new photo is 4.5 inches. What is the length of the new photo? $5\frac{5}{8}$ in.

CURRENCY For Exercises 39 and 40, use the following information and the table shown.
The table shows the exchange rates for certain countries compared to the U.S. dollar on a given day.

Country	Rate
United Kingdom	0.667
Egypt	3.481
Australia	1.712
China	8.280

39. What is the cost of an item in U.S. dollars if it costs 14.99 in British pounds? $22.47

40. Find the cost of an item in U.S. dollars if it costs 12.50 in Egyptian pounds. $3.59

 www.pre-alg.com/self_check_quiz

---

DAILY INTERVENTION

Differentiated Instruction

• **Interpersonal** Write ratios on several index cards. Write equivalent ratios on the same number of other index cards. Give one card to each student. Have them look for the equivalent ratio held by another student. Encourage discussion by the students, and ask them to stand in pairs to display their equivalent ratios.

Open-Ended Assessment

Speaking Have students explain to the class how to write and solve a proportion. Be sure they use specific examples.

Tips for New Teachers

Cooperative Learning Allow students to work in pairs or small groups to work the word problems together. Assign roles for students, such as reader, recorder, planner, and presenter.

Getting Ready for Lesson 6-3

PREREQUISITE SKILL Lesson 6-3 uses proportion to solve problems involving scale drawings and models. Exercises 52–55 should be used to determine your students' familiarity with converting measurements.

Answer

44. Proportions can be used in recipes to determine the amount of ingredients needed when increasing or decreasing a recipe. Answers should include the following.

- If you want to increase or decrease a recipe, you can use proportions to find the amounts needed so that the ratios remain the same.

- Adding 10 ounces to each ingredient in the punch recipe will not result in the same flavor because the ingredients are in proportion to each other. By adding the same amount to each ingredient, the ingredients are no longer proportional and the flavor is changed.

---

41. **SNACKS** The Skyway Snack Company makes a snack mix that contains raisins, peanuts, and chocolate pieces. The ingredients are shown at the right. Suppose the company wants to sell a larger-sized bag that contains 6 cups of raisins. How many cups of chocolate pieces and peanuts should be added? **chocolate pieces: 3 c; peanuts: $1\frac{1}{2}$ c**

★ 42. **PAINT** If 1 pint of paint is needed to paint a square that is 5 feet on each side, how many pints must be purchased in order to paint a square that is 9 feet 6 inches on each side? **4 pints**

43. **CRITICAL THINKING** The Property of Proportions states that if $\frac{a}{b} = \frac{c}{d}$, then $ad = bc$. Write two proportions in which the cross products are ad and bc. $\frac{a}{c} = \frac{b}{d}$, $\frac{b}{a} = \frac{d}{c}$, or $\frac{c}{a} = \frac{d}{b}$

44.  Answer the question that was posed at the beginning of the lesson. **See margin.**

How are proportions used in recipes?

Include the following in your answer:

- an explanation telling how proportions can be used to increase or decrease the amount of ingredients needed, and

- an explanation of why adding 10 ounces to each ingredient in the punch recipe will not result in the same flavor of punch.

Standardized Test Practice
Ⓐ Ⓑ Ⓒ Ⓓ

45. Jack is standing next to a flagpole as shown at the right. Jack is 6 feet tall. Which proportion could you use to find the height of the flagpole? **C**

Ⓐ $\frac{3}{6} = \frac{x}{12}$ Ⓑ $\frac{x}{6} = \frac{3}{12}$

Ⓒ $\frac{6}{3} = \frac{x}{12}$ Ⓓ $\frac{3}{x} = \frac{12}{6}$

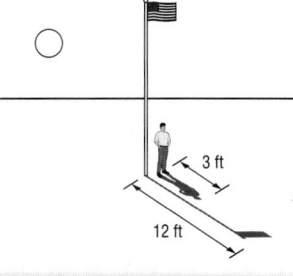

Maintain Your Skills

Mixed Review Express each ratio as a unit rate. Round to the nearest tenth, if necessary. *(Lesson 6-1)*

46. $5 for 4 loaves of bread **$1.25/loaf**   47. 183.4 miles in 3.2 hours **57.3 mph**

48. Find the next three numbers in the sequence 2, 5, 8, 11, 14, ... *(Lesson 5-10)* **17, 20, 23**

ALGEBRA Find each quotient. *(Lesson 5-4)*

49. $\frac{x}{5} \div \frac{x}{20}$ **4**   50. $\frac{3y}{4} \div \frac{5y}{8}$ **$\frac{6}{5}$**   51. $\frac{4z}{w} \div \frac{7yz}{w}$ **$\frac{4}{7y}$**

Getting Ready for the Next Lesson   **PREREQUISITE SKILL** Complete each sentence. *(To review **converting measurements**, see pages 720 and 721.)*

52. 5 feet = ■ inches **60**   53. 8.5 feet = ■ inches **102**

54. 36 inches = ■ feet **3**   55. 78 inches = ■ feet **6.5**

Algebra Activity

Algebra Activity

Capture-Recapture

Scientists often determine the number of fish in a pond, lake, or other body of water by using the *capture-recapture* method. A number of fish are captured, counted, carefully tagged, and returned to their habitat. The tagged fish are counted again and proportions are used to estimate the entire population. In this activity, you will model this estimation technique.

Collect the Data

Step 1 Copy the table below onto a sheet of paper.

Original Number Captured:		
Sample	**Recaptured**	**Tagged**
1		
2		
3		
4		
⋮		
10		
Total		

Step 2 Empty a bag of dried beans into a paper bag.

Step 3 Remove a handful of beans. Using a permanent marker, place an X on each side of each bean. These beans will represent the tagged fish. Record this number at the top of your table as the original number captured. Return the beans to the bag and mix.

Step 4 Remove a second handful of beans without looking. This represents the first sample of recaptured fish. Record the number of beans. Then count and record the number of beans that are tagged. Return the beans to the bag and mix.

Step 5 Repeat Step 4 for samples 2 through 10. Then use the results to find the total number of recaptured fish and the total number of tagged fish.

Analyze the Data

1. Use the following proportion to estimate the number of beans in the bag.

$$\frac{\text{original number captured}}{\text{total number in bag}} = \frac{\text{total number tagged}}{\text{total number recaptured}}$$

2. Count the number of beans in the bag. Compare the estimate to the actual number.
   1–2. Answers will vary. The estimate should be close to the actual number.

Make a Conjecture

3. Why is it a good idea to base a prediction on several samples instead of one sample? Sample answer: More samples leads to an accurate estimate.

4. Why does this method work?

4. Sample answer: The ratio of tagged fish to actual fish should be approximately the same as the ratio of tagged fish to total recaptured fish in the samples.

Resource Manager

📂 *Teaching Pre-Algebra with Manipulatives*
• p. 86 (student recording sheet)

Getting Started

Objective Use proportions with the capture-recapture method of counting.

Materials
bag of dried beans
paper bag
permanent marker

Teach

- Have two students simultaneously use the beans to demonstrate the capture-recapture method to the class. Then have the class compare their results.
- Have two groups of students collect the data in Steps 1–5.
- Divide each group into smaller groups to answer the questions.
- When students get to Exercise 2, have students count the total beans from each original bag of beans.

Assess

In **Exercise 3,** students should explain why several samples give a more accurate result than one sample.

Study Notebook

Ask students to write a paragraph explaining the capture-recapture method. Have them record their results of the activity with the explanation.

6-3 Scale Drawings and Models

1 Focus

5-Minute Check Transparency 6-3 Use as a quiz or review of Lesson 6-2.

Mathematical Background
notes are available for this lesson on page 262C.

How are scale drawings used in everyday life?

The opening activity questions are repeated on page 312 of the *Chapter 6 Resource Masters.*

Reading to Learn Mathematics, p. 312   ELL

Pre-Activity   *How are scale drawings used in everyday life?*

Do the activity at the top of page 276 in your textbook. Write your answers below.

a. Suppose the landscape plans are drawn on graph paper and the side of each square on the paper represents 2 feet. What is the actual width of a rose garden if its width on the drawing is 4 squares long? **8 ft**

b. All maps have a scale. How can the scale help you estimate the distance between cities? Sample answer: Suppose a map has a scale of 0.25 inch = 10 miles, and two towns are 1 inch apart. Since 1 inch is equivalent to four times 0.25 inch, and each of the 0.25 inch equals 10 miles, this tells you that the actual distance is 4 × 10 or 40 miles. Use a proportion. $\frac{0.25}{10} = \frac{1.0}{x}$

Reading the Lesson   1–4. See students' work.

Write a definition and give an example of each new vocabulary word or phrase.

Vocabulary	Definition	Example
1. scale drawing		
2. scale model		
3. scale		
4. scale factor		

Helping You Remember

5. How is a scale different from a scale factor? A scale gives a relationship that can contain different units of measure, while a scale factor is a ratio that uses the same units of measure.

Teaching Tip Show students a map of your state and a map of your town. Compare the scales. Ask students why the scales are different.

Resource Manager

📁 **Workbooks and Reproducible Masters**

Chapter 6 Resource Masters
- Study Guide and Intervention, p. 309
- Skills Practice, p. 310
- Practice, p. 311
- Reading to Learn Mathematics, p. 312
- Enrichment, p. 313
- Assessment, p. 359

Graphing Calculator and Spreadsheet Masters, p. 30
Parent and Student Study Guide Workbook, p. 46

🖳 **Transparencies**
5-Minute Check Transparency 6-3
Answer Key Transparencies

💿 **Technology**
Interactive Chalkboard

6-3 Scale Drawings and Models

What You'll Learn

- Use scale drawings.
- Construct scale drawings.

Vocabulary
- scale drawing
- scale model
- scale
- scale factor

How are scale drawings used in everyday life?

A set of landscape plans and a map are shown.

Designers use blueprints when planning landscapes.

Maps are used to find actual distances between cities.

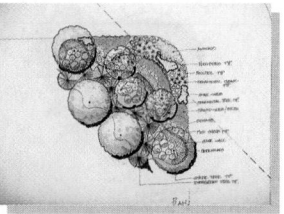

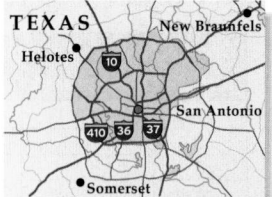

a. Suppose the landscape plans are drawn on graph paper and the side of each square on the paper represents 2 feet. What is the actual width of a rose garden if its width on the drawing is 4 squares long? **8 ft**

b. All maps have a scale. How can the scale help you estimate the distance between cities? **See margin.**

USE SCALE DRAWINGS AND MODELS   A **scale drawing** or a **scale model** is used to represent an object that is too large or too small to be drawn or built at actual size. A few examples are maps, blueprints, model cars, and model airplanes.

Model cars are replicas of actual cars.

Concept Check: to represent an object that is too large or too small to be drawn or built at actual size

✓ **Concept Check**   Why are scale drawings or scale models used?

The **scale** gives the relationship between the measurements on the drawing or model and the measurements of the real object. Consider the following scales.

1 inch = 3 feet   1:24

1 inch represents an actual distance of 3 feet.

1 unit represents an actual distance of 24 units.

Study Tip

Scale Factor
When finding the scale factor, be sure to use the same units of measure.

The ratio of a length on a scale drawing or model to the corresponding length on the real object is called the **scale factor**. Suppose a scale model has a scale of 2 inches = 16 inches. The scale factor is $\frac{2}{16}$ or $\frac{1}{8}$.

The lengths and widths of objects of a scale drawing or model are proportional to the lengths and widths of the actual object.

Example 1 Find Actual Measurements

DESIGN A set of landscape plans shows a flower bed that is 6.5 inches wide. The scale on the plans is 1 inch = 4 feet.

←— 6.5 in. —→

a. What is the width of the actual flower bed?

Let x represent the actual width of the flower bed. Write and solve a proportion.

plan width → $\frac{1 \text{ inch}}{4 \text{ feet}} = \frac{6.5 \text{ inches}}{x \text{ feet}}$ ←— plan width
actual width → ←— actual width

$1 \cdot x = 4 \cdot 6.5$ Find the cross products.

$x = 26$ Simplify.

The actual width of the flower bed is 26 feet.

b. What is the scale factor?

To find the scale factor, write the ratio of 1 inch to 4 feet in simplest form.

$\frac{1 \text{ inch}}{4 \text{ feet}} = \frac{1 \text{ inch}}{48 \text{ inches}}$ Convert 4 feet to inches.

The scale factor is $\frac{1}{48}$. That is, each measurement on the plan is $\frac{1}{48}$ the actual measurement.

Example 2 Determine the Scale

More About . . .

Architecture •·······
The exterior of the Lincoln Memorial features 36 columns that represent the states in the Union when Lincoln died in 1865. Each column is 44 feet high.

Source: www.infoplease.com

ARCHITECTURE The inside of the Lincoln Memorial contains three chambers. The central chamber, which features a marble statue of Abraham Lincoln, has a height of 60 feet. Suppose a scale model of the chamber has a height of 4 inches. What is the scale of the model?

Write the ratio of the height of the model to the actual height of the statue. Then solve a proportion in which the height of the model is 1 inch and the actual height is x feet.

model height → $\frac{4 \text{ inches}}{60 \text{ feet}} = \frac{1 \text{ inch}}{x \text{ feet}}$ ←— model height
actual height → ←— actual height

$4 \cdot x = 60 \cdot 1$ Find the cross products.

$4x = 60$ Simplify.

$\frac{4x}{4} = \frac{60}{4}$ Divide each side by 4.

$x = 15$ Simplify.

So, the scale is 1 inch = 15 feet.

---

2 Teach

USE SCALE DRAWINGS AND MODELS

In-Class Examples   Power Point®

1 **MAP** A map has a scale of 1 inch = 8 miles. Two towns are 3.25 inches apart on the map.

a. What is the actual distance between the two towns? **26 miles**

b. What is the scale factor?
$\frac{1}{506,880}$

2 **MODEL CAR** A model car is 4 inches long. The actual car is 12 feet long. What is the scale of the model?
1 inch = 3 feet

Teaching Tip Ask students to compare scale factor and scale in Examples 1 and 2.

CONSTRUCT SCALE DRAWINGS

In-Class Example   Power Point®

Teaching Tip For Example 3, ask students if the drawing would become larger or smaller if the scale were changed from 0.25 inches = 4 feet to 0.25 inches = 2 feet. **larger**

3 **PATIO DESIGN** Sheila is designing a patio that is 16 feet long and 14 feet wide. Make a scale drawing of the patio. Use a scale of 0.5 inches = 4 feet. **Check students' drawings. The length should be 2 inches and the width should be 1.75 inches.**

✓ Skills Check

Use Scale Drawings and Models Ask students if they can invert the ratios on both sides of the equations and get the same answer. **yes** Ask if it works consistently. **yes** Ask why it works. **The cross products are the same.** Ask if they can invert one ratio and not the other. **no**

DAILY
INTERVENTION **FIND THE ERROR**
If students are having difficulty determining the correct scale, have them find 1 inch and 2 feet on a yardstick. Using the yardstick, they can see how many inches are in 2 feet.

About the Exercises . . .

Organization by Objective
• **Use Scale Drawings and Models:** 8–19
• **Construct Scale Drawings:** 20

Odd/Even Assignments
Exercises 8–19 are structured so that students practice the same concepts whether they are assigned odd or even problems.

Assignment Guide

Basic: 9–21 odd, 22–24, 26–44
Average: 9–19 odd, 21–24, 26–44 (Optional: 25)
Advanced: 8–18 even, 20–36 (Optional: 37–44)

Answers

1. ☐ 1 unit ☐ 3 units

2. Luisa; Since there are 24 inches in 2 feet, the ratio 1:24 is correct.

Career Choices

Interior Designer

Interior designers plan the space and furnish the interiors of places such as homes, offices, restaurants, hotels, hospitals, and even theaters. Creativity and knowledge of computer-aided design software is essential.

Online Research
For information about a career as an interior designer, visit:
www.pre-alg.com/careers

CONSTRUCT SCALE DRAWINGS To construct a scale drawing of an object, use the actual measurements of the object and the scale to which the object is to be drawn.

Example 3 *Construct a Scale Drawing*

INTERIOR DESIGN Antonio is designing a room that is 20 feet long and 12 feet wide. Make a scale drawing of the room. Use a scale of 0.25 inch = 4 feet.

Step 1 Find the measure of the room's length on the drawing. Let x represent the length.

drawing length → $\dfrac{0.25 \text{ inch}}{4 \text{ feet}} = \dfrac{x \text{ inches}}{20 \text{ feet}}$ ← drawing length
actual length → ← actual length

$0.25 \cdot 20 = 4 \cdot x$ Find the cross products.
$5 = 4x$ Simplify.
$1.25 = x$ Divide each side by 4.

On the drawing, the length is 1.25 or $1\frac{1}{4}$ inches.

Step 2 Find the measure of the room's width on the drawing. Let w represent the width.

drawing length → $\dfrac{0.25 \text{ inch}}{4 \text{ feet}} = \dfrac{w \text{ inches}}{12 \text{ feet}}$ ← drawing length
actual length → ← actual length

$0.25 \cdot 12 = 4 \cdot w$ Find the cross products.
$3 = 4w$ Simplify.
$\dfrac{3}{4} = \dfrac{4w}{4}$ Divide each side by 4.
$0.75 = w$ Simplify.

On the drawing, the width is 0.75 or $\frac{3}{4}$ inch.

Step 3 Make the scale drawing. Use $\frac{1}{4}$-inch grid paper. Since $1\frac{1}{4}$ inches = 5 squares and $\frac{3}{4}$ inch = 3 squares, draw a rectangle that is 5 squares by 3 squares.

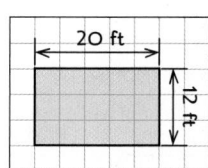

Check for Understanding

Concept Check
1–2. See margin.

1. **OPEN ENDED** Draw two squares in which the ratio of the sides of the first square to the sides of the second square is 1:3.

2. **FIND THE ERROR** Montega and Luisa are rewriting the scale 1 inch = 2 feet in *a*:*b* form.

Montega	Luisa
1:36	1:24

Who is correct? Explain your reasoning.

DAILY
INTERVENTION **Differentiated Instruction**

• **Intrapersonal** Have students find a magazine photo, then have them tape a 0.25-inch grid transparency on top of the picture. Ask students to systematically copy the contents of each grid onto centimeter grid paper. Their drawing will be an enlargement of the original. Encourage them to include both the photo and their drawing in their Math Journals, and ask them whether it helped their understanding of scale and proportions.

Guided Practice

On a map of Pennsylvania, the scale is 1 inch = 20 miles. Find the actual distance for each map distance.

GUIDED PRACTICE KEY

Exercises	Examples
3, 4	1
5, 6	1, 2
7	3

	From	To	Map Distance	
3.	Pittsburgh	Perryopolis	2 inches	40 mi
4.	Johnston	Homer City	$1\frac{3}{4}$ inches	35 mi

Applications

STATUES For Exercises 5 and 6, use the following information.
The Statue of Zeus at Olympia is one of the Seven Wonders of the World. On a scale model of the statue, the height of Zeus is 8 inches. **5. 1 in. = 5 ft**

5. If the actual height of Zeus is 40 feet, what is the scale of the statue?

6. What is the scale factor? $\frac{1}{60}$

7. **DESIGN** An architect is designing a room that is 15 feet long and 10 feet wide. Construct a scale drawing of the room. Use a scale of 0.5 in. = 10 ft. **See margin.**

Practice and Apply

Homework Help

For Exercises	See Examples
8–17	1
18, 19	1, 2
20	3

Extra Practice
See page 737.

On a set of architectural drawings for an office building, the scale is $\frac{1}{2}$ inch = 3 feet. Find the actual length of each room.

	Room	Drawing Distance	
8.	Conference Room	7 inches	42 ft
9.	Lobby	2 inches	12 ft
10.	Mail Room	2.3 inches	13.8 ft
11.	Library	4.1 inches	24.6 ft
12.	Copy Room	2.2 inches	13.2 ft
13.	Storage	1.9 inches	11.4 ft
14.	Exercise Room	$3\frac{3}{4}$ inches	$22\frac{1}{2}$ ft
15.	Cafeteria	$8\frac{1}{4}$ inches	$49\frac{1}{2}$ ft

16. Refer to Exercises 8–15. What is the scale factor? $\frac{1}{72}$

17. What is the scale factor if the scale is 8 inches = 1 foot? $\frac{2}{3}$

18. **ROLLER COASTERS** In a scale model of a roller coaster, the highest hill has a height of 6 inches. If the actual height of the hill is 210 feet, what is the scale of the model? **1 in. = 35 ft**

19. **INSECTS** In an illustration of a honeybee, the length of the bee is 4.8 centimeters. The actual size of the honeybee is 1.2 centimeters. What is the scale of the drawing? **1 cm = 0.25 cm**

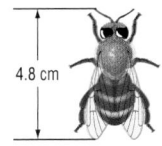
4.8 cm

20. **GARDENS** A garden is 8 feet wide by 16 feet long. Make a scale drawing of the garden that has a scale of $\frac{1}{4}$ in. = 2 ft. **See margin.**

Study Guide and Intervention, p. 309

A **scale** gives the relationship between the measurements on the drawing or model and the measurements of the real object.

Example A map shows a scale of 1 inch = 6 miles. The distance between two places on the map is 4.25 inches. What is the actual distance?

Let x represent the actual distance. Write and solve a proportion.

map width → $\frac{1 \text{ inch}}{6 \text{ miles}} = \frac{4.25 \text{ inches}}{x \text{ miles}}$ ← map width
actual width → ← actual width

$1 \cdot x = 6 \cdot 4.25$ Find the cross products.

$x = 25.5$ Simplify.

The actual distance is 25.5 miles.

Exercises
On a set of architectural drawings for an office building, the scale is 0.25 inch = 5 feet. Find the actual length of each room.

	Room	Drawing Distance	Actual Distance
1.	Lobby	1.6 inches	32 feet
2.	CEO Office	1.35 inches	27 feet
3.	Copy Room	0.55 inch	11 feet
4.	CEO Secretary's Office	0.6 inch	12 feet
5.	Vice President's Office	0.9 inch	18 feet
6.	Library	1.525 inches	30.5 feet
7.	Storage Area	2.1125 inches	42.25 feet
8.	Personal Manager's Office	1.7375 inches	34.75 feet
9.	Manager's Office	0.625 inch	12.5 feet
10.	Mail Room	2.2625 inches	45.25 feet
11.	Boiler Room	3.725 inches	74.5 feet
12.	Conference Room A	2.62 inches	52.4 feet
13.	Conference Room B	0.925 inch	18.5 feet
14.	Cafeteria	2.3 inches	46 feet
15.	Kitchen	2 inches	40 feet

Skills Practice, p. 310 and Practice, p. 311 (shown)

On a map, the scale is 5 centimeters = 2 kilometers. Find the missing distances.

	Location	Map Distance	Actual Distance
1.	Town A to Town B	10 cm	4 km
2.	Town A to Town C	25 cm	10 km
3.	Town A to Town D	14 cm	5.6 km
4.	Town A to Town E	2 cm	0.8 km
5.	Town A to Town F	0.5 cm	0.2 km
6.	Town A to Town G	8 cm	3.2 km
7.	Town A to Town H	0.25 cm	0.1 km
8.	Town A to Town I	6 cm	2.4 km
9.	Town A to Town J	0.1 cm	0.04 km
10.	Town A to Town K	1 cm	0.4 km
11.	Town A to Town L	2.5 cm	1 km
12.	Town A to Town M	1.2 cm	0.48 km

13. Refer to Exercises 1–12. What is the scale factor?
$\frac{5}{200,000}$ or $\frac{1}{40,000}$

14. What is the scale factor if the scale is 15 inches = 1 yard?
$\frac{15}{36}$ or $\frac{5}{12}$

15. **STRUCTURES** A barn is 50 feet wide by 80 feet long. Make a scale drawing of the barn that has a scale of $\frac{1}{2}$ inch = 10 feet. Check students' drawings. The width is 2.5 inches and the length is 4 inches.

16. **PHOTOGRAPHY** A man in a photograph is 1.5 inches in height. If the man is 6 feet tall, what is the scale? 1 inch = 4 feet

Enrichment, p. 313

Direct Variation

If the relationship between two quantities is such that when one quantity increases, the other increases, or when one quantity decreases, the other decreases, the quantities are said to **vary directly**.

Example **MONEY** If 2 loaves of bread cost $1.60, how much will 3 loaves of the same type of bread cost?

The number of loaves and the cost vary directly; that is, as the number of loaves increases, so does the cost.

$\frac{2 \text{ loaves}}{\$1.60} = \frac{3 \text{ loaves}}{x}$ For direct variations, place like quantities directly across from each other in a proportion.

$2x = 4.80$

$x = 2.40$

The cost for 3 loaves of bread is $2.40.

Write a proportion to represent each situation. Then solve.

1. **MONEY** Three gallons of gasoline cost $3.36. How much do 5 gallons cost?
$\frac{3}{3.36} = \frac{5}{x}$; $x = 5.6$; $5.60

2. **DISTANCE** At a rate of 50 mph, a car travels a distance of 600 miles. How far will the car travel at a rate of 40 mph if it is driven the same amount of time?
$\frac{50}{600} = \frac{40}{x}$; $x = 480$; 480 miles

3. **MONEY** If the rent for two weeks is $500, how much rent is paid for 5 weeks?
$\frac{2}{500} = \frac{5}{x}$; $x = 1250$; $1250

4. **MONEY** If 8 newspapers cost $3.20, how much will 6 newspapers cost?
$\frac{8}{3.20} = \frac{6}{x}$; $x = 2.40$; $2.40

5. **WEIGHT** If 9 fully loaded trucks carry a total of 140,400 pounds, how many pounds can 3 trucks carry?
$\frac{9}{140,400} = \frac{3}{x}$; $x = 46,800$;
46,800 pounds

6. **TECHNOLOGY** Twelve floppy disks can hold 16.8 million bytes of data. How many bytes will 20 floppy disks hold?
$\frac{12}{16,800,000} = \frac{20}{x}$; $x = 28,000,000$;
28 million bytes

7. **TECHNOLOGY** If 12 floppy disks hold 16.8 million bytes of data, how many floppy disks are needed to hold 10 million bytes of data?
$\frac{12}{16,800,000} = \frac{x}{10,000,000}$; $x = 7.14$;
8 disks are needed.

8. **HEALTH** There are a total of 2100 Calories in 5 candy bars (all the same kind). How many total Calories are there in 3 dozen of these candy bars?
$\frac{5}{2100} = \frac{36}{x}$; $x = 15,120$;
15,120 Calories

Answers

7.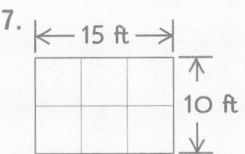
|← 15 ft →|

10 ft

20.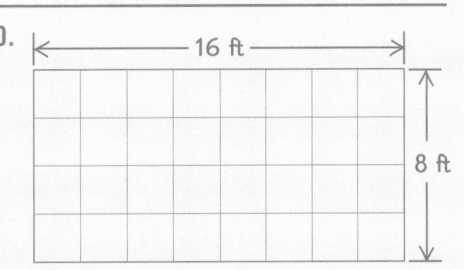
|← 16 ft →|

8 ft

Open-Ended Assessment

Modeling Have students draw a 9-by-15 rectangle on grid paper. Then have them draw a similar rectangle so that the scale factor of the original rectangle to the new rectangle is 3:1. Have them explain how the new rectangle would differ if the scale factor were 1:3. **The new rectangle would be larger.**

Getting Ready for Lesson 6-4

PREREQUISITE SKILL In Lesson 6-4, students will express percents as fractions. Exercises 37–44 should be used to determine your students' familiarity with writing fractions in simplest form.

Assessment Options

Quiz (Lessons 6-1 through 6-3) is available on p. 359 of the *Chapter 6 Resource Masters.*

Answers

21. A scale factor less than 1 means that the drawing or model is drawn smaller than actual size. A scale factor of 1 means that the drawing or model is drawn actual size. A scale factor greater than 1 means the drawing or model is drawn larger than actual size.

22. In everyday life, scale drawings or models are used to represent objects that are too large or too small to be drawn or built at actual size. Answers should include the following.
    • Sample answer: a model airplane, a globe, and a set of blueprints
    • Sample answer: A scale drawing such as a map can help you find actual distance and a scale model such as a replica of a dinosaur can help to see the actual image of a dinosaur.

---

21. **CRITICAL THINKING** What does it mean if the scale factor of a scale drawing or model is less than 1? greater than 1? equal to 1? **See margin.**

22.  Answer the question that was posed at the beginning of the lesson. **See margin.**

    How are scale drawings used in everyday life?

    Include the following in your answer:
    • an example of three kinds of scale drawings or models, and
    • an explanation of how you use scale drawings in your life.

Standardized Test Practice
Ⓐ Ⓑ Ⓒ Ⓓ

23. Which scale has a scale factor of $\frac{1}{18}$? **B**
    Ⓐ 3 in. = 6 ft   Ⓑ 6 in. = 9 ft   Ⓒ 3 in. = 54 ft   Ⓓ 6 in. = 6 ft

24. A model airplane is built using a 1:16 scale. On the model, the length of the wing span is 5.8 feet. What is the actual length of the wing? **C**
    Ⓐ 84.8 ft   Ⓑ 91.6 ft   Ⓒ 92.8 ft   Ⓓ 89.8 ft

Extending the Lesson

25. Two rectangles are shown. The ratio comparing their sides is 1:2.
    a. Write the ratio that compares their perimeters. $\frac{1}{2}$
    b. Write the ratio that compares their areas. $\frac{1}{4}$
    c. Find the perimeter and area of a 3-inch by 5-inch rectangle. Then make a conjecture about the perimeter and area of a 6-inch by 10-inch rectangle. Check by finding the actual perimeter and area. **See margin.**

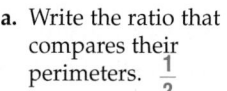
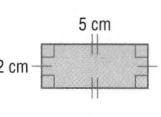
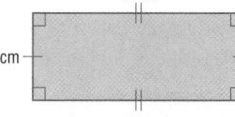

Maintain Your Skills

Mixed Review **Solve each proportion.** *(Lesson 6-2)*

26. $\frac{n}{20} = \frac{15}{50}$ **6**   27. $\frac{14}{32} = \frac{x}{8}$ **3.5**   28. $\frac{3}{2.2} = \frac{7.5}{y}$ **5.5**

Convert each rate using dimensional analysis. *(Lesson 6-1)*

29. 36 cm/s = ■ m/min **21.6**   30. 66 gal/h = ■ qt/min **4.4**

31. Find $1\frac{1}{4} + 4\frac{5}{6}$. Write the answer in simplest form. *(Lesson 5-7)* $6\frac{1}{12}$

ALGEBRA **Find each product or quotient. Express in exponential form.** *(Lesson 4-6)*

32. $4^3 \cdot 4^5$ **4^8**   33. $3t^4 \cdot 6t$ **$18t^5$**   34. $7^{14} \div 7^8$ **7^6**   35. $\frac{24m^5}{18m^2}$ **$\frac{4m^3}{3}$**

36. **ALGEBRA** Find the greatest common factor of $14x^2y$ and $35xy^3$. *(Lesson 4-4)* **$7xy$**

Getting Ready for the Next Lesson **PREREQUISITE SKILL** **Simplify each fraction.**
*(To review **simplest form**, see Lesson 4-5.)*

37. $\frac{5}{100}$ $\frac{1}{20}$ 38. $\frac{25}{100}$ $\frac{1}{4}$ 39. $\frac{40}{100}$ $\frac{2}{5}$ 40. $\frac{52}{100}$ $\frac{13}{25}$

41. $\frac{78}{100}$ $\frac{39}{50}$ 42. $\frac{75}{100}$ $\frac{3}{4}$ 43. $\frac{82}{100}$ $\frac{41}{50}$ 44. $\frac{95}{100}$ $\frac{19}{20}$

25c. The perimeter of a 3-inch by 5-inch rectangle is 16 inches. The area is 15 square inches. For a 6-inch by 10-inch rectangle, the perimeter should be double the 3-inch by 5-inch rectangle. That is, 16 × 2 or 32 inches. The area should be 4 times the area of the 3-inch by 5-inch rectangle. That is, 4 × 15 or 60 square inches. Since the perimeter of the 6-inch by 10-inch rectangle is 32 and its area is 60, the conjecture is true.

Fractions, Decimals, and Percents

What You'll Learn

- Express percents as fractions and vice versa.
- Express percents as decimals and vice versa.

How are percents related to fractions and decimals?

A portion of each figure is shaded.

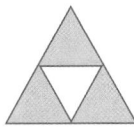 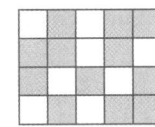 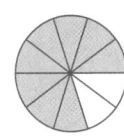

a. Write a ratio that compares the shaded region of each figure to its total region as a fraction in simplest form.

b. Rewrite each fraction using a denominator of 100. $\frac{75}{100}, \frac{60}{100}, \frac{80}{100}$

c. Which figure has the greatest part of its area shaded? **circle**

d. Was it easier to compare the fractions in part **a** or part **b**? Explain.

Vocabulary

- percent

a. $\frac{3}{4}, \frac{3}{5}, \frac{4}{5}$

d. Part b; the fractions have a common denominator.

Reading Math

Percent

Root Word: Cent
There are 100 *cents* in one dollar. *Percent* means *per hundred* or *hundredths*.

PERCENTS AND FRACTIONS A **percent** is a ratio that compares a number to 100. The meaning of 75% is shown at the right. In the figure, 75 out of 100 squares are shaded.

To write a percent as a fraction, express the ratio as a fraction with a denominator of 100. Then simplify if possible. Notice that a percent can be greater than 100% or less than 1%.

Example 1 Percents as Fractions

Express each percent as a fraction in simplest form.

a. **45%**

$$45\% = \frac{45}{100}$$
$$= \frac{9}{20}$$

b. **120%**

$$120\% = \frac{120}{100}$$
$$= \frac{6}{5} \text{ or } 1\frac{1}{5}$$

c. **0.5%**

$$0.5\% = \frac{0.5}{100}$$
$$= \frac{0.5}{100} \cdot \frac{10}{10}$$
$$= \frac{5}{1000} \text{ or } \frac{1}{200}$$

Multiply by $\frac{10}{10}$ to eliminate the decimal in the numerator.

d. $83\frac{1}{3}\%$

$$83\frac{1}{3}\% = \frac{83\frac{1}{3}}{100}$$

The fraction bar indicates division.

$$= 83\frac{1}{3} \div 100$$
$$= \frac{\overset{5}{\cancel{250}}}{3} \cdot \frac{1}{\underset{2}{\cancel{100}}} \text{ or } \frac{5}{6}$$

6-4 **Lesson Notes**

1 Focus

5-Minute Check Transparency 6-4 Use as a quiz or review of Lesson 6-3.

Mathematical Background notes are available for this lesson on page 262C.

How are percents related to fractions and decimals?

The opening activity questions are repeated on page 317 of the *Chapter 6 Resource Masters*.

Reading to Learn Mathematics, p. 317 **ELL**

Pre-Activity *How are percents related to fractions and decimals?*

Do the activity at the top of page 281 in your textbook. Write your answers below.

a. Write a ratio that compares the shaded region of each figure to its total region as a fraction in simplest form. $\frac{3}{4}, \frac{3}{5}, \frac{4}{5}$

b. Rewrite each fraction using a denominator of 100. $\frac{75}{100}, \frac{60}{100}, \frac{80}{100}$

c. Which figure has the greatest part of its area shaded? circle

d. Was it easier to compare the fractions in part **a** or part **b**? Explain. Part b; the fractions have a common denominator.

Reading the Lesson

Write a definition and give an example of the new vocabulary word.

Vocabulary	Definition	Example
1. percent	See students' work.	

2. Shade 50% of each grid below, using three different ways. Be creative. Sample answers are given.

Helping You Remember

3. Percents can be expressed as fractions or decimals and vice versa. Fill in each box below with an example of the process described. Answers will vary.

% → fraction	% → decimal
fraction → %	**decimal → %**

Resource Manager

Transparencies
5-Minute Check Transparency 6-4
Answer Key Transparencies

Technology
Interactive Chalkboard
Pre-AlgePASS: Tutorial Plus, Lesson 15

PERCENTS AND FRACTIONS

In-Class Examples Power Point®

1 Express each percent as a fraction in simplest form.

a. 60% $\frac{3}{5}$

b. 104% $1\frac{1}{25}$

c. 0.3% $\frac{3}{1000}$

d. $56\frac{1}{4}\%$ $\frac{9}{16}$

2 Express each fraction as a percent.

a. $\frac{19}{20}$ 95%

b. $\frac{8}{5}$ 160%

Teaching Tip To express a fraction as a percent, divide 100 by the denominator. Then multiply that number by the numerator to find the percent.

PERCENTS AND DECIMALS

In-Class Examples Power Point®

3 Express each percent as a decimal.

a. 60% 0.6

b. 2% 0.02

c. 658% 6.58

d. 0.4% 0.004

4 Express each decimal as a percent.

a. 0.4 40%

b. 0.05 5%

c. 0.0008 0.08%

d. 7.3 730%

To write a fraction as a percent, write an equivalent fraction with a denominator of 100.

Example 2 *Fractions as Percents*

Express each fraction as a percent.

a. $\frac{4}{5}$

$\frac{4}{5} = \frac{80}{100}$ or 80%

b. $\frac{9}{4}$

$\frac{9}{4} = \frac{225}{100}$ or 225%

PERCENTS AND DECIMALS Remember that *percent* means *per hundred*. In the previous examples, you wrote percents as fractions with 100 in the denominator. Similarly, you can write percents as decimals by dividing by 100.

Key Concept — Percents and Decimals

- To write a percent as a decimal, divide by 100 and remove the percent symbol.
- To write a decimal as a percent, multiply by 100 and add the percent symbol.

Example 3 *Percents as Decimals*

Express each percent as a decimal.

a. 28%

28% = 28%   Divide by 100 and remove the %.
= 0.28

b. 8%

8% = 08%   Divide by 100 and remove the %.
= 0.08

c. 375%

375% = 375%   Divide by 100 and remove the %.
= 3.75

d. 0.5%

0.5% = 00.5%   Divide by 100 and remove the %.
= 0.005

Example 4 *Decimals as Percents*

Express each decimal as a percent.

a. 0.35

0.35 = 0.35   Multiply by 100 and add the %.
= 35%

b. 0.09

0.09 = 0.09   Multiply by 100 and add the %.
= 9%

c. 0.007

0.007 = 0.007   Multiply by 100 and add the %.
= 0.7%

d. 1.49

1.49 = 1.49   Multiply by 100 and add the %.
= 149%

You have expressed fractions as decimals and decimals as percents. Fractions, decimals, and percents are all different names that represent the same number.

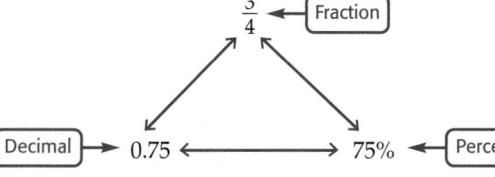

Study Tip

Mental Math
To divide a number by 100, move the decimal point two places to the left. To multiply a number by 100, move the decimal point two places to the right.

D A I L Y
INTERVENTION   **Differentiated Instruction**

- **Logical** Have students make a display or poster showing the following ratios expressed as fractions, decimals, and percents: 1:8, 1:4, 3:8, 1:3, 1:2, 5:8, 2:3, 3:4, 7:8, and 8:8.

You can also express a fraction as a percent by first expressing the fraction as a decimal and then expressing the decimal as a percent.

Example 5 *Fractions as Percents*

Express each fraction as a percent. Round to the nearest tenth percent, if necessary.

a. $\frac{7}{8}$

$\frac{7}{8} = 0.875$

$= 87.5\%$

b. $\frac{2}{3}$

$\frac{2}{3} = 0.6666666\ldots$

$\approx 66.7\%$

c. $\frac{3}{500}$

$\frac{3}{500} = 0.006$

$= 0.6\%$

d. $\frac{15}{7}$

$\frac{15}{7} \approx 2.1428571$

$\approx 214.3\%$

Example 6 *Compare Numbers*

SHOES In a survey, one-fifth of parents said that they buy shoes for their children every 4–5 months while 27% of parents said that they buy shoes twice a year. Which of these groups is larger?

Write one-fifth as a percent. Then compare.

$\frac{1}{5} = 0.20$ or 20%

Since 27% is greater than 20%, the group that said they buy shoes twice a year is larger.

Check for Understanding

Concept Check

1–2. See margin.

1. **Describe** two ways to express a fraction as a percent. Then tell how you know whether a fraction is greater than 100% or less than 1%.

2. **OPEN ENDED** Explain the method you would use to express $64\frac{1}{2}\%$ as a decimal.

Guided Practice

GUIDED PRACTICE KEY	
Exercises	Examples
3–8	1, 3
9–14	2, 4, 5
15	6

Express each percent as a fraction or mixed number in simplest form and as a decimal.

3. 30% $\frac{3}{10}$, 0.3
4. $12\frac{1}{2}\%$ $\frac{1}{8}$, 0.125
5. 125% $1\frac{1}{4}$, 1.25
6. 65% $\frac{13}{20}$, 0.65
7. 135% $1\frac{7}{20}$, 1.35
8. 0.2% $\frac{1}{500}$, 0.002

Express each decimal or fraction as a percent. Round to the nearest tenth percent, if necessary.

9. 0.45 **45%**
10. 1.3 **130%**
11. 0.008 **0.8%**
12. $\frac{1}{4}$ **25%**
13. $\frac{12}{9}$ **133.3%**
14. $\frac{3}{600}$ **0.5%**

Application

15. **MEDIA** In a survey, 55% of those surveyed said that they get the news from their local television station while three-fifths said that they get the news from a daily newspaper. From which source do more people get their news? **daily newspaper**

 www.pre-alg.com/extra_examples

Lesson 6-4 Fractions, Decimals, and Percents **283**

Answers

1. Sample answer: Write an equivalent fraction with a denominator of 100 or express the fraction as a decimal and then express the decimal as a percent. A fraction is greater than 100% if it is greater than 1. It is less than 1% if it is less than $\frac{1}{100}$.

2. Sample answer: Change $64\frac{1}{2}\%$ to 64.5% and then move the decimal point two places to the left and drop the percent sign.

5 Express each fraction as a percent. Round to the nearest tenth percent, if necessary.

a. $\frac{5}{8}$ **62.5%**

b. $\frac{1}{3}$ **33.3%**

c. $\frac{9}{1000}$ **0.9%**

d. $\frac{23}{14}$ **164.3%**

6 **BAKERY** A baker says that 25% of his customers buy only bread and $\frac{2}{5}$ of his customers buy only cookies. Which group is larger?

$\frac{2}{5} = 40\%$ and $40\% > 25\%$. So, the group buying cookies is larger.

3 Practice/Apply

Study Notebook

Have students—
• add the definition/example of the vocabulary term to their Vocabulary Builder worksheets for Chapter 6.
• include any other item(s) that they find helpful in mastering the skills in this lesson.

About the Exercises . . .

Organization by Objective
• Percents and Fractions: 16–27, 34–39
• Percents and Decimals: 28–33

Odd/Even Assignments
Exercises 16–48 are structured so that students practice the same concepts whether they are assigned odd or even problems.

Assignment Guide
Basic: 17–47 odd, 51–71
Average: 17–49 odd, 51–71
Advanced: 16–48 even, 49–65 (Optional: 66–71)

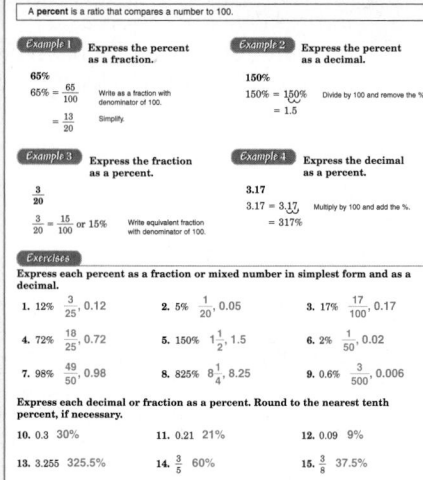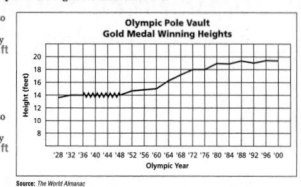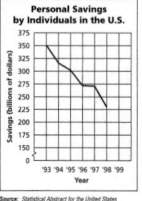
★ indicates increased difficulty

Practice and Apply

Express each percent as a fraction or mixed number in simplest form and as a decimal. 16–27. See margin.
16. 42%
17. 88%
18. $16\frac{2}{3}\%$
19. 87.5%
20. 150%
21. 350%
22. 18%
23. 61%
24. 117%
25. 223%
26. 0.8%
27. 0.53%

Express each decimal or fraction as a percent. Round to the nearest tenth percent, if necessary.
28. 0.51 **51%**
29. 0.09 **9%**
30. 3.21 **321%**
31. 2.7 **270%**
32. 0.0042 **0.42%**
33. 0.0006 **0.06%**
34. $\frac{7}{25}$ **28%**
35. $\frac{9}{40}$ **22.5%**
36. $\frac{10}{3}$ **333.3%**
37. $\frac{14}{8}$ **175%**
38. $\frac{15}{2500}$ **0.6%**
39. $\frac{20}{1200}$ **1.7%**

40. **GEOGRAPHY** Forty-six percent of the world's water is in the Pacific Ocean. What fraction is this? $\frac{23}{50}$

41. **GEOGRAPHY** The Arctic Ocean contains 3.7% of the world's water. What fraction is this? $\frac{37}{1000}$

42. **FOOD** According to a survey, 22% of people said that mustard is their favorite condiment while two-fifths of people said that they prefer ketchup. Which group is larger? Explain. **See pp. 323A–323B.**

Choose the greatest number in each set.
43. $\left\{\frac{2}{5}, \underline{0.45}, 35\%, 3\text{ out of }8\right\}$
44. $\left\{\frac{3}{4}, 0.70, 78\%, \underline{4\text{ out of }5}\right\}$
45. $\left\{\underline{19\%}, \frac{3}{16}, 0.155, 2\text{ to }15\right\}$
46. $\left\{89\%, \frac{10}{11}, 0.884, 12\text{ to }14\right\}$

Write each list of numbers in order from least to greatest.
47. $\frac{2}{3}$, 61%, 0.69 **61%, $\frac{2}{3}$, 0.69**
48. $\frac{2}{7}$, 0.027, 27% **0.027, 27%, $\frac{2}{7}$**

★ **GEOMETRY** For Exercises 49 and 50, use the information and the figure shown.
Suppose that two fifths of the rectangle is shaded.

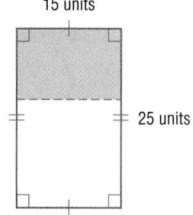

49. Write the decimal that represents the shaded region of the figure. **0.4**

50. What is the area of the shaded region? **150 square units**

51. **CRITICAL THINKING** Find a fraction that satisfies the conditions below. Then write a sentence explaining why you think your fraction is or is not the only solution that satisfies the conditions. **See pp. 323A–323B.**
  • The fraction can be written as a percent greater than 1%.
  • The fraction can be written as a percent less than 50%.
  • The decimal equivalent of the fraction is a terminating decimal.
  • The value of the denominator minus the value of the numerator is 3.

284 Chapter 6 Ratio, Proportion, and Percent

Answers

16. $\frac{21}{50}$, 0.42
19. $\frac{7}{8}$, 0.875
22. $\frac{9}{50}$, 0.18
25. $2\frac{23}{100}$, 2.23

17. $\frac{22}{25}$, 0.88
20. $1\frac{1}{2}$, 1.5
23. $\frac{61}{100}$, 0.61
26. $\frac{1}{125}$, 0.008

18. $\frac{1}{6}$, 0.16$\overline{6}$
21. $3\frac{1}{2}$, 3.5
24. $1\frac{17}{100}$, 1.17
27. $\frac{53}{1000}$, 0.0053

52. CRITICAL THINKING   Explain why percents are rational numbers.
See margin

53. WRITING IN MATH   Answer the question that was posed at the beginning of the lesson. **See margin.**

How are percents related to fractions and decimals?

Include the following in your answer:

- examples of figures in which 25%, 30%, 40%, and 65% of the area is shaded, and
- an explanation of why each percent represents the shaded area.

Standardized Test Practice
Ⓐ Ⓑ Ⓒ Ⓓ

54. Assuming that the regions in each figure are equal, which figure has the greatest part of its area shaded? **D**

Ⓐ 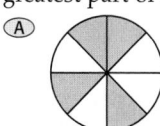   Ⓑ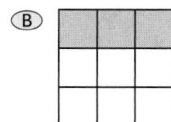

Ⓒ 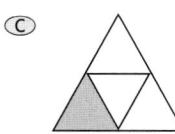   Ⓓ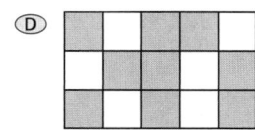

55. According to a survey, 85% of people eat a salad at least once a week. Which ratio represents this portion? **A**

Ⓐ 17 to 20   Ⓑ 13 to 20   Ⓒ 9 to 10   Ⓓ 4 to 5

Maintain Your Skills

Mixed Review   Write the scale factor of each scale.   *(Lesson 6-3)*

56. 3 inches = 18 inches $\frac{1}{6}$ **57.** 2 inches = 2 feet $\frac{1}{12}$

58. ALGEBRA   Find the solution of $\frac{x}{54} = \frac{2}{3}$.   *(Lesson 6-2)*   **36**

Find each product. Write in simplest form.   *(Lesson 5-3)*

59. $\frac{4}{7} \cdot \frac{11}{12}$ $\frac{11}{21}$ **60.** $-\frac{3}{5} \cdot \frac{10}{18}$ $-\frac{1}{3}$ **61.** $4 \cdot \frac{16}{52}$ $1\frac{3}{13}$

62. Write 5.6×10^{-4} in standard form.   *(Lesson 4-8)*   **0.00056**

Determine whether each number is *prime* or *composite*.   *(Lesson 4-3)*

63. 21 **composite**   **64.** 47 **prime**   **65.** 57 **composite**

Getting Ready for the Next Lesson   **PREREQUISITE SKILL**   Solve each proportion.
*(To review **proportions**, see Lesson 6-2.)*

66. $\frac{25}{4} = \frac{x}{100}$ **625**   **67.** $\frac{56}{7} = \frac{y}{100}$ **800**

68. $\frac{75}{8} = \frac{n}{100}$ **937.5**   **69.** $\frac{m}{10} = \frac{9.4}{100}$ **0.94**

70. $\frac{h}{350} = \frac{46}{100}$ **161**   **71.** $\frac{86.4}{k} = \frac{27}{100}$ **320**

4 Assess

Open-Ended Assessment
Speaking   Have students explain how they can compare a percent to a decimal or a fraction to determine which is greater.

Tips for New Teachers   **Intervention**
Many students seek simplified ways to relate fractions, decimals, and percents. For example, students may write $\frac{2}{5}$ as 2.5 or 0.25 instead of 0.4. Use models to show the multiple representations of $2 \div 5$.

Getting Ready for Lesson 6-5
PREREQUISITE SKILL   In Lesson 6-5, students use the percent proportion to solve percent problems. Exercises 66–71 should be used to determine your students' familiarity with solving proportions.

Answers

52. Because they can be expressed in the form $\frac{a}{b}$ where a and b are integers and $b \neq 0$

53. Percents are related to fractions and decimals because they can be expressed as them. Answers should include the following.

$25\% = \frac{1}{4} = 0.25$
25%

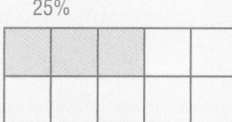
30%
$30\% = \frac{3}{10} = 0.3$

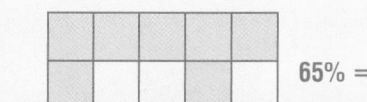
40%
$40\% = \frac{2}{5} = 0.4$

65%
$65\% = \frac{13}{20} = 0.65$

Lesson 6-4   Fractions, Decimals, and Percents.   **285**

Getting Started

Objective Use a percent model to find a percent or a part.

Materials
grid paper

Teach

Activity 1

- Ask one student to demonstrate Exercise 1 on the board. Encourage students to discuss any questions they may have concerning this model.
- Have students draw the percent model on the far right-hand side of the page. Then they can reuse the model by folding the grid paper over the left-hand numbers.
- Have students complete the rest of the page individually or in small groups.

Using a Percent Model

Activity 1

When you see advertisements on television or in magazines, you are often bombarded with many claims. For example, you might hear that four out of five use a certain long-distance phone service. What percent does this represent?

You can find the percent by using a model.

Finding a Percent		
Step 1	**Step 2**	**Step 3**
Draw a 10-unit by 1-unit rectangle on grid paper. Label the units on the right from 0 to 100, because percent is a ratio that compares a number to 100.	On the left side, mark equal units from 0 to 5, because 5 represents the whole quantity. Locate 4 on this scale.	Draw a horizontal line from 4 on the left side to the right side of the model. The number on the right side is the percent. Label the model as shown.

Using the model, you can see that the ratio *4 out of 5* is the same as 80%. So, according to this claim, 80% of people prefer the certain long-distance phone service.

Model 1–10. Exact answers are given. For models, see pp. 323A–323B.
Draw a model and find the percent that is represented by each ratio. If it is not possible to find the exact percent using the model, estimate.

1. 6 out of 10 **60%**
2. 9 out of 10 **90%**
3. 2 out of 5 **40%**
4. 3 out of 4 **75%**
5. 9 out of 20 **45%**
6. 8 out of 50 **16%**
7. 2 out of 8 **25%**
8. 3 out of 8 **37.5%**
9. 2 out of 3 $66\frac{2}{3}\%$
10. 5 out of 9 $55\frac{5}{9}\%$

286 Chapter 6 Ratio, Proportion, and Percent

Resource Manager

📁 *Teaching Pre-Algebra with Manipulatives*
- p. 1 (master for grid paper)
- p. 89 (student recording sheet)

Activity 2

Suppose a store advertises a sale in which all merchandise is 20% off the original price. If the original price of a pair of shoes is $50, how much will you save?

In this case, you know the percent. You need to find what part of the original price you'll save.

You can find the part by using a similar model.

Finding a Part		
Step 1	**Step 2**	**Step 3**
Draw a 10-unit by 1-unit rectangle on grid paper. Label the units on the right from 0 to 100 because percent is a ratio that compares a number to 100.	On the left side, mark equal units from 0 to 50, because 50 represents the whole quantity.	Draw a horizontal line from 20% on the right side to the left side of the model. The number on the left side is the part. Label the model as shown.

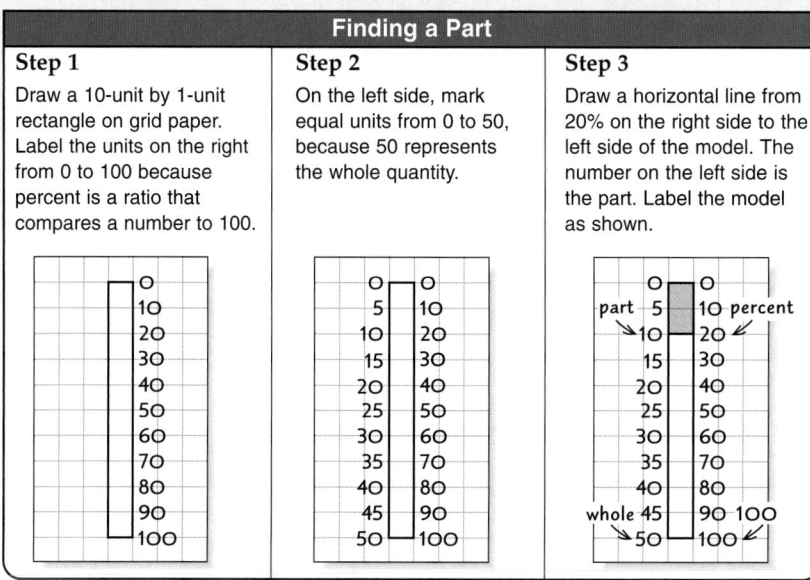

Using the model, you can see that 20% of 50 is 10. So, you will save $10 if you buy the shoes.

Model 11–20. Exact answers are given. For models, see pp. 323A–323B.

Draw a model and find the part that is represented. If it is not possible to find an exact answer from the model, estimate.

11. 10% of 50 **5**   **12.** 60% of 20 **12**

13. 90% of 40 **36**   **14.** 30% of 10 **3**

15. 25% of 20 **5**   **16.** 75% of 40 **30**

17. 5% of 200 **10**   **18.** 85% of 500 **425**

19. $33\frac{1}{3}$% of 12 **4**   **20.** 37.5% of 16 **6**

Activity 2

- Ask one student to demonstrate Exercise 1 on the board. Encourage students to discuss any questions they may have concerning this model.
- Have students complete the rest of the page individually or in pairs.

Assess

In **Exercises 1–10,** students should use a model to write the ratio of two numbers as a percent.

In **Exercises 11–20,** students should use a model to find the part that is represented by a percent.

Study Notebook

Have students record a model for finding the percent represented by the ratio 4 out of 12. Then have students record a model for finding 35% of 80.

1 Focus

🕐 **5-Minute Check Transparency 6-5** Use as a quiz or review of Lesson 6-4.

Mathematical Background notes are available for this lesson on page 262D.

Why are percents important in real-world situations?

The opening activity questions are repeated on page 322 of the *Chapter 6 Resource Masters.*

Reading to Learn Mathematics, p. 322 | **ELL**

Pre-Activity *Why are percents important in real-world situations?*
Do the activity at the top of page 288 in your textbook. Write your answers below.

   a. Write a ratio that compares the amount of copper to the total amount of metal in the outer layer. 3 to 4

   b. Write the ratio as a fraction and as a percent. $\frac{3}{4}$, 75%

Reading the Lesson 1–3. See students' work.

Write a definition and give an example of each new vocabulary word or phrase.

Vocabulary	Definition	Example
1. percent proportion		
2. part		
3. base		

4. In a percent proportion, the percent is always written as a fraction whose denominator is ___100___.

5. What can percent proportions be used to do? solve problems that involve percents

Helping You Remember

6. Fill in the blanks to identify the base, the part, and the percent in the following percent proportion.

   $\frac{\text{Part}}{\text{Base}}\;\frac{13}{20}=\frac{65}{100}\;\text{Percent}$

   What letter do both numerators begin with? p

Vocabulary
- percent proportion
- part
- base

Study Tip

Estimation
Five is a little more than one-half of eight. So, the answer should be a little more than 50%.

What You'll Learn
- Use the percent proportion to solve problems.

Why are percents important in real-world situations?

Have you collected any of the new state quarters?

The quarters are made of a pure copper core and an outer layer that is an alloy of 3 parts copper and 1 part nickel.

  a. Write a ratio that compares the amount of copper to the total amount of metal in the outer layer. **3 to 4**

  b. Write the ratio as a fraction and as a percent. $\frac{3}{4}$, **75%**

USE THE PERCENT PROPORTION In a **percent proportion**, one of the numbers, called the **part**, is being compared to the whole quantity, called the **base**. The other ratio is the percent, written as a fraction, whose base is 100.

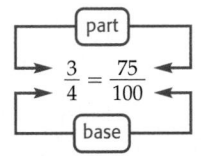

Key Concept   *Percent Proportion*

- **Words** $\dfrac{\text{part}}{\text{base}}=\dfrac{\text{percent}}{100}$

- **Symbols** $\dfrac{a}{b}=\dfrac{p}{100}$, where a is the part, b is the base, and p is the percent.

Example 1 Find the Percent

Five is what percent of 8?

Five is being compared to 8. So, 5 is the part and 8 is the base. Let p represent the percent.

$$\frac{a}{b}=\frac{p}{100}\rightarrow\frac{5}{8}=\frac{p}{100}\qquad\text{Replace }a\text{ with 5 and }b\text{ with 8.}$$

$$5\cdot 100 = 8\cdot p\qquad\text{Find the cross products.}$$

$$500 = 8p\qquad\text{Simplify.}$$

$$\frac{500}{8}=\frac{8p}{8}\qquad\text{Divide each side by 8.}$$

$$62.5 = p\qquad\text{So, 5 is 62.5% of 8.}$$

✓ **Concept Check** In the percent proportion $\frac{15}{20}=\frac{75}{100}$, which number is the base? **20**

Resource Manager

 **Workbooks and Reproducible Masters**

Chapter 6 Resource Masters
- Study Guide and Intervention, p. 319
- Skills Practice, p. 320
- Practice, p. 321
- Reading to Learn Mathematics, p. 322
- Enrichment, p. 323
- Assessment, pp. 359, 361

Parent and Student Study Guide Workbook, p. 48
Science and Mathematics Lab Manual, pp. 83–86

 **Transparencies**
5-Minute Check Transparency 6-5
Answer Key Transparencies

 **Technology**
Interactive Chalkboard

Example 2 Find the Percent

What percent of 4 is 7?

Seven is being compared to 4. So, 7 is the part and 4 is the base. Let p represent the percent.

$$\frac{a}{b} = \frac{p}{100} \rightarrow \frac{7}{4} = \frac{p}{100} \qquad \text{Replace } a \text{ with 7 and } b \text{ with 4.}$$

$$7 \cdot 100 = 4 \cdot p \qquad \text{Find the cross products.}$$

$$700 = 4p \qquad \text{Simplify.}$$

$$\frac{700}{4} = \frac{4p}{4} \qquad \text{Divide each side by 4.}$$

$$175 = p \qquad \text{So, 175\% of 4 is 7.}$$

Example 3 Apply the Percent Proportion

ENVIRONMENT The graphic shows the number of threatened species in the United States. What percent of the total number of threatened species are mammals?

Compare the number of species of mammals, 37, to the total number of threatened species, 443. Let a represent the part, 37, and let b represent the base, 443, in the percent proportion. Let p represent the percent.

$$\frac{a}{b} = \frac{p}{100} \rightarrow \frac{37}{443} = \frac{p}{100}$$

$$37 \cdot 100 = 443 \cdot p$$

$$3700 = 443p \qquad \text{Simplify.}$$

$$\frac{3700}{443} = \frac{443p}{443} \qquad \text{Divide each side by 443.}$$

$$8.4 \approx p \qquad \text{Simplify.}$$

So, about 8.4% of the total number of threatened species are mammals.

USA TODAY Snapshots®

Number of threatened species in USA

Plants 168	Reptiles 27	Birds 55
	Amphibians 25	Mammals 37
	Fish 131	

Source: The International Union for Conservation of Nature and Natural Resources

By Hilary Wasson and Alejandro Gonzalez, USA TODAY

You can also use the percent proportion to find a missing part or base.

Concept Summary — *Types of Percent Problems*

Type	Example	Proportion
Find the Percent	3 is <u>what percent</u> of 4?	$\frac{3}{4} = \frac{p}{100}$
Find the Part	<u>What number</u> is 75% of 4?	$\frac{a}{4} = \frac{75}{100}$
Find the Base	3 is 75% of <u>what number</u>?	$\frac{3}{b} = \frac{75}{100}$

 www.pre-alg.com/extra_examples

Lesson 6-5 Using the Percent Proportion **289**

Study Notebook

Have students—
- add the definitions/examples of the vocabulary terms to their Vocabulary Builder worksheets for Chapter 6.
- include any other item(s) that they find helpful in mastering the skills in this lesson.

DAILY
INTERVENTION **FIND THE ERROR**
If students are having difficulty with determining the correct proportion, have them make and fill in a table like the following.

	actual numbers	percent numbers
parts	(unknown)	35
whole	21	100

Then encourage them to notice that Judie's proportion is the one that resembles the table.

About the Exercises . . .

Odd/Even Assignments
Exercises 9–22 are structured so that students practice the same concepts whether they are assigned odd or even problems.

Alert! Exercise 24 involves research on the Internet or other reference materials.

Assignment Guide

Basic: 9–15 odd, 21, 23, 25–41

Average: 9–23 odd, 25–41

Advanced: 10–26 even, 27–35 (Optional: 36–41)

All: Practice Quiz 1 (1–5)

Example 4 **Find the Part**

What number is 5.5% of 650?

The percent is 5.5, and the base is 650. Let a represent the part.

$\frac{a}{b} = \frac{p}{100} \to \frac{a}{650} = \frac{5.5}{100}$ Replace b with 650 and p with 5.5.

$a \cdot 100 = 650 \cdot 5.5$ Find the cross products.

$100a = 3575$ Simplify.

$a = 35.75$ Mentally divide each side by 100.

So, 5.5% of 650 is 35.75.

USA TODAY **Log on for:**
Education
- Updated data
- More activities on using the percent proportion.
www.pre-alg.com/usa_today

Example 5 **Apply the Percent Proportion**

CHORES Use the graphic to determine how many of the 1074 youths surveyed do not clean their room because there is not enough time.

The total number of youths is 1074. So, 1074 is the base. The percent is 29%.

To find 29% of 1074, let b represent the base, 1074, and let p represent the percent, 29%, in the percent proportion. Let a represent the part.

$\frac{a}{b} = \frac{p}{100} \to \frac{a}{1074} = \frac{29}{100}$

$a \cdot 100 = 1074 \cdot 29$

$100a = 31146$ Simplify.

$a = 311.46$ Mentally divide each side by 100.

So, about 311 youths do not clean their room because there is not enough time.

USA TODAY Snapshots®

Kids don't enjoy cleaning their rooms

When 1,074 youths 19 and under were asked why they don't clean their room more often, these were their responses[1]:

I don't like to — 66%
Not enough time — 29%
I'm too lazy — 28%
The rest of the house is dirty — 6%
No reply — 2%

1 — More than one response allowed

Source: BSMG Worldwide   By Lori Joseph and Sam Ward, USA TODAY

Example 6 **Find the Base**

Fifty-two is 40% of what number?

The percent is 40% and the part is 52. Let b represent the base.

$\frac{a}{b} = \frac{p}{100} \to \frac{52}{b} = \frac{40}{100}$ Replace a with 52 and p with 40.

$52 \cdot 100 = b \cdot 40$ Find the cross products.

$5200 = 40b$ Simplify.

$\frac{5200}{40} = \frac{40b}{40}$ Divide each side by 40.

$130 = b$ Simplify.

So, 52 is 40% of 130.

DAILY
INTERVENTION   **Differentiated Instruction**

- **Visual/Spatial** Have students make and fill in a table to aid them in writing a proportion. For example, to find 90% of 15, the table would look like this:

	actual numbers	percent numbers
parts	(unknown)	90
whole	15	100

Check for Understanding

Concept Check

1-2. See margin.

1. OPEN ENDED Write a proportion that can be used to find the percent scored on an exam that has 50 questions.

2. FIND THE ERROR Judie and Pennie are using a proportion to find what number is 35% of 21. Who is correct? Explain your reasoning.

GUIDED PRACTICE KEY	
Exercises	Examples
3–6	1, 2, 4, 6
7	3
8	5

Judie
$$\frac{n}{21} = \frac{35}{100}$$

Pennie
$$\frac{21}{n} = \frac{35}{100}$$

Guided Practice Use the percent proportion to solve each problem.

3. 16 is what percent of 40? **40%**

4. 21 is 30% of what number? **70**

5. What is 80% of 130? **104**

6. What percent of 5 is 14? **280%**

Applications

7. BOOKS Fifty-four of the 90 books on a shelf are history books. What percent of the books are history books? **60%**

8. CHORES Refer to Example 5 on page 290. How many of the 1074 youths surveyed do not clean their room because they do not like to clean?

★ indicates increased difficulty **about 709**

Practice and Apply

Homework Help	
For Exercises	See Examples
9–20	1, 2, 4, 6
21, 23, 24	3
22, 25	5
Extra Practice See page 738.	

Use the percent proportion to solve each problem. Round to the nearest tenth. **9–20. See margin.**

9. 72 is what percent of 160?

10. 17 is what percent of 85?

11. 36 is 72% of what number?

12. 27 is 90% of what number?

13. What is 44% of 175?

14. What is 84% of 150?

15. 52.2 is what percent of 145?

16. 19.8 is what percent of 36?

★ **17.** 14 is $12\frac{1}{2}$% of what number?

★ **18.** 36 is $8\frac{3}{4}$% of what number?

★ **19.** 7 is what percent of 3500?

★ **20.** What is 0.3% of 750?

21. BIRDS If 12 of the 75 animals in a pet store are parakeets, what percent are parakeets? **16%**

22. FISH Of the fish in an aquarium, 26% are angelfish. If the aquarium contains 50 fish, how many are angelfish? **13**

SCIENCE For Exercises 23 and 24, use the information in the table.

23. What percent of the world's fresh water does the Antarctic Icecap contain? **about 70%**

24. The total volume of the world's fresh and salt water is 326,038,400 mi³. The Antarctic Icecap contains about 2% of the world's total water supply.

24. RESEARCH Use the Internet or another source to find the total volume of the world's fresh and salt water. What percent of the world's total water supply does the Antarctic Icecap contain?

World's Fresh Water Supply	
Source	Volume (mi³)
Freshwater Lakes	30,000
All Rivers	300
Antarctic Icecap	6,300,000
Arctic Icecap and Glaciers	680,000
Water in the Atmosphere	3100
Ground Water	1,000,000
Deep-lying Ground Water	1,000,000
Total	**9,013,400**

Source: Time Almanac

www.pre-alg.com/self_check_quiz

Lesson 6-5 Using the Percent Proportion **291**

Answers

1. $\frac{\text{number correct}}{50} = \frac{\%}{100}$

2. Judie; In the sentence *what number is 35% of 21*, *what number* is the part, 21 is the base, and 35% is the percent. So, to solve the problem, you would use the proportion $\frac{n}{21} = \frac{35}{100}$.

9. 45%
10. 20%
11. 50
12. 30
13. 77
14. 126
15. 36%
16. 55%
17. 112
18. 411.4
19. 0.2%
20. 2.25

Study Guide and Intervention, p. 319

In a **percent proportion**, one of the numbers, called the **part**, is being compared to the whole quantity, called the **base**. The other ratio is the percent, written as a fraction, whose base is 100.

Example 1 Find each percent.

a. Twelve is what percent of 16?

$$\frac{a}{b} = \frac{p}{100} \rightarrow \frac{12}{16} = \frac{p}{100}$$ Replace the variables.
$$12 \cdot 100 = p \cdot 16$$ Find the cross products.
$$1200 = 16p$$ Simplify.
$$75 = p$$ Divide.

So, twelve is 75% of 16.

b. What percent of 8 is 7?

$$\frac{a}{b} = \frac{p}{100} \rightarrow \frac{7}{8} = \frac{p}{100}$$
$$p \cdot 8 = 100 \cdot 7$$
$$700 = 8p$$
$$87.5 = p$$

So, 87.5% of 8 is 7.

Example 2 Find the part or the base.

a. What number is 1.4% of 15?

$$\frac{a}{b} = \frac{p}{100} \rightarrow \frac{a}{15} = \frac{1.4}{100}$$ Replace the variables.
$$a \cdot 100 = 15 \cdot 1.4$$ Find the cross products.
$$100a = 21$$ Simplify.
$$a = 0.21$$ Divide.

So, 0.21 is 1.4% of 15.

b. 225 is 36% of what number?

$$\frac{a}{b} = \frac{p}{100} \rightarrow \frac{225}{b} = \frac{36}{100}$$
$$225 \cdot 36 = 100 \cdot b$$
$$22,500 = 36b$$
$$625 = b$$

So, 225 is 36% of 625.

Exercises

Use the percent proportion to solve each problem. Round to the nearest tenth.

1. 48 is what percent of 52? 92.3%
2. 295 is what percent of 400? 73.8%
3. What percent of 22 is 56? 254.5%
4. What percent of 4 is 15? 375%
5. What is 99% of 840? 831.6
6. What is 4.5% of 38? 1.7
7. What is 16% of 36.2? 5.8
8. 85 is 80% of what number? 106.3
9. 60 is 29% of what number? 206.9
10. 4.5 is 90% of what number? 5

Skills Practice, p. 320 and Practice, p. 321 (shown)

Use the percent proportion to solve each problem. Round to the nearest tenth.

1. 128 is what percent of 640? 20%
2. What percent of 21 is 28? 133.3%
3. 3.4 is what percent of 5? 68%
4. What percent of 930 is 720? 77.4%
5. 15 is what percent of 120? 12.5%
6. What percent of 24 is 21? 87.5%
7. 36 is what percent of 40? 90%
8. What percent of 48 is 0.6? 1.3%
9. 12 is 80% of what number? 15
10. 15 is 4% of what number? 375
11. 33 is 90% of what number? 36.7
12. 0.24 is 36% of what number? 0.7
13. 19 is 10% of what number? 190
14. 49 is 77% of what number? 63.6
15. 42 is 7.5% of what number? 560
16. 65 is 5% of what number? 1300
17. 27.5 is 2% of what number? 1375
18. What is 15.8% of 21? 3.3
19. What is 65% of 441.1? 286.7
20. What is 0.4% of 82? 0.3
21. What is 7% of 329.8? 23.1
22. What is 88% of 1? 0.9
23. What is 35% of 20? 7
24. What is 20% of 35? 7
25. **PAINT** About 42% of a paint mix is white. A painter orders 18 gallons of the paint mix. How much of it is white? 7.56 gallons

Enrichment, p. 323

Percent Puzzle

Solve each problem.

1. 8% of 75 6
2. 16% of 80 12.8
3. 20% of 85 17
4. 17% of 300 51
5. 40% of 170 68
6. 50% of 380 190
7. 75% of 160 120
8. $33\frac{1}{3}$% of 240 80
9. $62\frac{1}{2}$% of 72 45
10. 30% of 180 54
11. $66\frac{2}{3}$% of 210 140
12. 80% of 160 128
13. 110% of 60 66
14. 95% of 300 285
15. 150% of 75 112.5
16. 400% of 50 200

Answers	
6	= F
12.8	= U
17	= R
45	= G
51	= A
54	= T
66	= I
68	= D
80	= N
112.5	= S
120	= Y
128	= P
140	= H
190	= O
200	= E
285	= E

Find the answer to each exercise above and note the letter next to it. Put this letter on the line or lines below that correspond to the exercise number.
HOW MUCH DID THE WORLD'S LARGEST PIZZA WEIGH?

E I G H T E E N
14 13 9 6 10 14 14 8

T H O U S A N D
10 6 16 2 15 4 8 5

S I X   H U N D R E D
15 13 11   6 2 8 5 3 14 5

S I X T Y · F O U R
15 13 11 10 7   1 16 2 3

P O U N D S
12 16 2 8 5 15

Lesson 6-5 Using the Percent Proportion **291**

Open-Ended Assessment

Writing Have students write their own percent problems based on what they see in their own classroom. For example, if 4 out of 20 students are wearing red today, what percent of the students are wearing red? Have them solve their problems, and then trade with another student to solve.

Getting Ready for Lesson 6-6

PREREQUISITE SKILL Lesson 6-6 presents finding percents mentally. It is helpful to use the fraction form of a percent. Exercises 36–41 should be used to determine your students' familiarity with finding products involving fractions.

Assessment Options

Practice Quiz 1 The quiz provides students with a brief review of the concepts and skills in Lessons 6-1 through 6-5. Lesson numbers are given to the right of exercises or instruction lines so students can review concepts not yet mastered.

Quiz (Lessons 6-4 and 6-5) is available on p. 359 of the *Chapter 6 Resource Masters.*

Mid-Chapter Test (Lessons 6-1 through 6-5) is available on p. 361 of the *Chapter 6 Resource Masters.*

Answers

26. Since n is 25% of some number a, and 35% of some number b, we can write $\frac{n}{a} = \frac{25}{100}$ and $\frac{n}{b} = \frac{35}{100}$. By solving for n, we find that $n = \frac{25a}{100}$ and $n = \frac{35b}{100}$. Since $n = n$, we can write $\frac{25a}{100} = \frac{35b}{100}$. Solving for a, $a = \frac{35b}{25} = \frac{7b}{5} = \frac{7}{5}b = 1.4b$ results. So, $a > b$.

---

25. LIFE SCIENCE Carbon constitutes 18.5% of the human body by weight. Determine the amount of carbon contained in a person who weighs 145 pounds. **26.8 lb**

26. CRITICAL THINKING A number n is 25% of some number a and 35% of a number b. Tell the relationship between a and b. Is $a < b$, $a > b$, or is it impossible to determine the relationship? Explain. **See margin.**

27. **WRITING IN MATH** Answer the question that was posed at the beginning of the lesson. **See margin.**

Why are percents important in real-world situations?

Include the following in your answer:
- an example of a real-world situation where percents are used, and
- an explanation of the meaning of the percent in the situation.

Standardized Test Practice
Ⓐ Ⓑ Ⓒ Ⓓ

28. The table shows the number of people in each section of the school chorale. Which section makes up exactly 25% of the chorale? **B**

Ⓐ Tenor   Ⓑ Alto

Ⓒ Soprano   Ⓓ Bass

School Chorale	
Section	**Number**
Soprano	16
Alto	15
Tenor	12
Bass	17

Maintain Your Skills

Mixed Review   Write each percent as a fraction in simplest form. *(Lesson 6-4)*

29. 42% $\frac{21}{50}$ **30.** 56% $\frac{14}{25}$ **31.** 120% $1\frac{1}{5}$

32. MAPS On a map of a state park, the scale is 0.5 inch = 1.5 miles. Find the actual distance from the ranger's station to the beach if the distance on the map is 1.75 inches. *(Lesson 6-3)* **5.25 mi**

Find each sum or difference. Write in simplest form. *(Lesson 5-5)*

33. $\frac{2}{9} + \frac{5}{9}$ $\frac{7}{9}$ **34.** $\frac{11}{12} - \frac{3}{12}$ $\frac{2}{3}$ **35.** $2\frac{5}{8} + \frac{7}{8}$ $3\frac{1}{2}$

Getting Ready for the Next Lesson   **PREREQUISITE SKILL** Find each product.
*(To review **multiplying fractions**, see Lesson 5-3.)*

36. $\frac{1}{2} \times 14$ **7**   **37.** $\frac{1}{4} \times 32$ **8**   **38.** $\frac{1}{5} \times 15$ **3**

39. $\frac{2}{3} \times 9$ **6**   **40.** $\frac{3}{4} \times 16$ **12**   **41.** $\frac{5}{6} \times 30$ **25**

Practice Quiz 1   *Lessons 6-1 through 6-5*

1. Express $3.29 for 24 cans of soda as a unit rate. *(Lesson 6-1)* **$0.14 per can**

2. What value of x makes $\frac{3}{4} = \frac{x}{68}$ a proportion? *(Lesson 6-2)* **51**

3. SCIENCE A scale model of a volcano is 4 feet tall. If the actual height of the volcano is 12,276 feet, what is the scale of the model? *(Lesson 6-3)* **1 ft = 3069 ft**

4. Express 352% as a decimal. *(Lesson 6-4)* **3.52**

5. Use the percent proportion to find 32.5% of 60. *(Lesson 6-5)* **19.5**

---

27. In real-world situations, percents are important because they show how something compares to the whole. Answers should include the following.
- Sample answer: The outer layer of the new state quarters is an alloy of 3 parts copper to 1 part nickel.
- There are 4 parts to the outer layer (copper, copper, copper, nickel). The outer layer is $\frac{3}{4}$ or 75% copper and $\frac{1}{4}$ or 25% nickel.

6-6 Finding Percents Mentally

What You'll Learn

- Compute mentally with percents.
- Estimate with percents.

How is estimation used when determining sale prices?

A sporting goods store is having a sale in which all merchandise is on sale at half off. A few regularly priced items are shown at the right.

a. What is the sale price of each item?
b. What percent represents half off? 50%
c. Suppose the items are on sale for 25% off. Explain how you would determine the sale price.

a. tennis racquet: $34; baseball hat: $7.50; baseball glove: $18.50; football: $22
c. Sample answer: Divide the regular price by 4 and then subtract the result from the original price.

FIND PERCENTS OF A NUMBER MENTALLY When working with common percents like 10%, 25%, 40%, and 50%, it may be helpful to use the fraction form of the percent. A few percent-fraction equivalents are shown.

0%	$12\frac{1}{2}$%	25%	40%	50%	$66\frac{2}{3}$%	75%	$87\frac{1}{2}$%	100%
0	$\frac{1}{8}$	$\frac{1}{4}$	$\frac{2}{5}$	$\frac{1}{2}$	$\frac{2}{3}$	$\frac{3}{4}$	$\frac{7}{8}$	1

Some percents are used more frequently than others. So, it is a good idea to be familiar with these percents and their equivalent fractions.

Concept Summary — *Percent-Fraction Equivalents*

$20\% = \frac{1}{5}$	$10\% = \frac{1}{10}$	$25\% = \frac{1}{4}$	$12\frac{1}{2}\% = \frac{1}{8}$	$16\frac{2}{3}\% = \frac{1}{6}$
$40\% = \frac{2}{5}$	$30\% = \frac{3}{10}$	$50\% = \frac{1}{2}$	$37\frac{1}{2}\% = \frac{3}{8}$	$33\frac{1}{3}\% = \frac{1}{3}$
$60\% = \frac{3}{5}$	$70\% = \frac{7}{10}$	$75\% = \frac{3}{4}$	$62\frac{1}{2}\% = \frac{5}{8}$	$66\frac{2}{3}\% = \frac{2}{3}$
$80\% = \frac{4}{5}$	$90\% = \frac{9}{10}$		$87\frac{1}{2}\% = \frac{7}{8}$	$83\frac{1}{3}\% = \frac{5}{6}$

Example 1 Find Percent of a Number Mentally

Find the percent of each number mentally.

a. 50% of 32

$50\% \text{ of } 32 = \frac{1}{2} \text{ of } 32$ Think: $50\% = \frac{1}{2}$.

$= 16$ Think: $\frac{1}{2}$ of 32 is 16.

So, 50% of 32 is 16.

Study Tip

Look Back
To review **multiplying fractions**, see Lesson 5-3.

6-6 Lesson Notes

1 Focus

5-Minute Check Transparency 6-6 Use as a quiz or review of Lesson 6-5.

Mathematical Background notes are available for this lesson on page 262D.

How is estimation used when determining sale prices?

The opening activity questions are repeated on page 327 of the *Chapter 6 Resource Masters.*

Reading to Learn Mathematics, p. 327 ELL

Pre-Activity *How is estimation used when determining sale prices?*

Do the activity at the top of page 293 in your textbook. Write your answers below.

a. What is the sale price of each item? Tennis racquet: $34; baseball hat: $7.50; baseball glove: $18.50; football: $22
b. What percent represents half off? 50%
c. Suppose the items are on sale for 25% off. Explain how you would determine the sale price. Sample answer: Divide the regular price by 4 and then subtract the result from the original price.

Reading the Lesson

1. Give an example of a real-life situation in which you can estimate with percents. Sample answer: determining the amount of a tip
2. When can you find the percent of a number mentally? when working with common percents like 10%, 25%, 40%, and 50%

Helping You Remember

3. Name the three methods that can be used to estimate with percents. Give an example of each. Examples will vary. See students' work.

Method	Example
Fraction	
1%	
Meaning of Percent	

Teaching Tip Ask students what percent they pay if an item is marked 50% off. 50% Also ask what percent they pay if an item is marked 25% off. 75%

Resource Manager

Workbooks and Reproducible Masters

Chapter 6 Resource Masters
- Study Guide and Intervention, p. 324
- Skills Practice, p. 325
- Practice, p. 326
- Reading to Learn Mathematics, p. 327
- Enrichment, p. 328

Parent and Student Study Guide Workbook, p. 49
Prerequisite Skills Workbook, pp. 39–40

Transparencies

5-Minute Check Transparency 6-6
Answer Key Transparencies

Technology

Interactive Chalkboard

FIND PERCENTS OF A NUMBER MENTALLY

1 Find the percent of each number mentally.

a. 50% of 46   **23**

b. 25% of 88   **22**

c. 70% of 110   **77**

Teaching Tip Encourage students to solve problems mentally by having them work in small groups of similar capabilities. Provide problems one at a time and have students see if they can solve them faster than others in their group.

ESTIMATE WITH PERCENTS

2 **a.** Estimate 22% of 494.   **100**

b. Estimate 63% of 788.   **480**

c. Estimate $\frac{1}{4}$% of 1,219.   **3**

d. Estimate 155% of 38.   **60**

Teaching Tip To help students develop number sense for percents, have them check their estimates by finding the actual amount.

3 **MONEY** A restaurant bill totals $21.35. You want to leave a 15% tip. What is a reasonable amount for the tip?   **$3**

Teaching Tip Depending upon whether both the percent and the number are rounded up or down, the estimate will be too high or too low. Recommend that students round one up and one down whenever possible to find a more reliable estimate.

Find the percent of each number mentally.

b. **25% of 48**

25% of 48 $= \frac{1}{4}$ of 48   Think: 25% $= \frac{1}{4}$.

$= 12$ Think: $\frac{1}{4}$ of 48 is 12.

So, 25% of 48 is 12.

c. **40% of 45**

40% of 45 $= \frac{2}{5}$ of 45   Think: 40% $= \frac{2}{5}$.

$= 18$ Think: $\frac{1}{5}$ of 45 is 9. So, $\frac{2}{5}$ of 45 is 18.

So, 40% of 45 is 18.

ESTIMATE WITH PERCENTS   Sometimes, an exact answer is not needed. In these cases, you can estimate. Consider the following model.

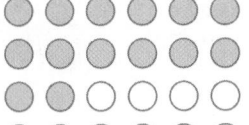

- 14 of the 30 circles are shaded.
- $\frac{14}{30}$ is about $\frac{15}{30}$ or $\frac{1}{2}$.
- $\frac{1}{2} = 50\%$. So, about 50% of the model is shaded.

The table below shows three methods you can use to estimate with percents. For example, let's estimate 22% of 237.

Method	Estimate 22% of 237.
Fraction	22% is a bit more than 20% or $\frac{1}{5}$. 237 is a bit less than 240. So, 22% of 237 is about $\frac{1}{5}$ of 240 or 48. Estimate: 48
1%	22% = 22 × 1% 1% of 237 = 2.37 or about 2. So, 22% of 237 is about 22 × 2 or 44. Estimate: 44
Meaning of Percent	22% means about 20 for every 100 or about 2 for every 10. 237 has 2 hundreds and about 4 tens. (20 × 2) + (2 × 4) = 40 + 8 or 48 Estimate: 48

You can use these methods to estimate the percent of a number.

Example 2 *Estimate Percents*

a. **Estimate 13% of 120.**

13% is about 12.5% or $\frac{1}{8}$.

$\frac{1}{8}$ of 120 is 15.

So, 13% of 120 is about 15.

b. **Estimate 80% of 296.**

80% is equal to $\frac{4}{5}$.

296 is about 300.

$\frac{4}{5}$ of 300 is 240.

So, 80% of 296 is about 240.

Study Tip

Percents
To find 1% of any number, move the decimal point two places to the left.

DAILY INTERVENTION   **Differentiated Instruction**   **ELL**

- **Verbal/Linguistic** Give students one estimate problem at a time. Have them speak their answer as soon as they get it. When students have different estimates, encourage them to compare their strategies and then to explain to the class why the estimates did not match.

c. Estimate $\frac{1}{3}\%$ of 598.

$\frac{1}{3}\% = \frac{1}{3} \times 1\%$. 598 is almost 600.

1% of 600 is 6.

So, $\frac{1}{3}\%$ of 598 is about $\frac{1}{3} \times 6$ or 2.

d. Estimate 118% of 56.

118% means about 120 for every 100 or about 12 for every 10.

56 has about 6 tens.

$12 \times 6 = 72$

So, 118% of 56 is about 72.

Estimating percents is a useful skill in real-life situations.

Example 3 *Use Estimation to Solve a Problem*

MONEY Amelia takes a taxi from the airport to a hotel. The fare is $31.50. Suppose she wants to tip the driver 15%. What would be a reasonable amount of tip for the driver?

$31.50 is about $32.

$15\% = 10\% + 5\%$

10% of $32 is $3.20. *Move the decimal point 1 place to the left.*

5% of $32 is $1.60. *5% is one half of 10%.*

So, 15% is about 3.20 + 1.60 or $4.80.

A reasonable amount for the tip would be $5.

Check for Understanding

Concept Check

1. Explain how to estimate 18% of 216 using the fraction method.

2. Estimate the percent of the figure that is shaded. **1–2. See margin.**

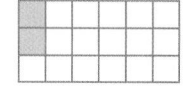

3. OPEN ENDED Tell which method of estimating a percent you prefer. Explain your decision. **See students' work.**

Guided Practice

Find the percent of each number mentally. **4–12. See margin.**

4. 75% of 64

5. 25% of 52

6. $33\frac{1}{3}\%$ of 27

7. 90% of 80

Estimate. Explain which method you used to estimate.

8. 20% of 61

9. 34% of 24

10. $\frac{1}{2}\%$ of 396

11. 152% of 14

Application

12. MONEY Lu Chan wants to leave a tip of 20% on a dinner check of $52.48. About how much should he leave?

www.pre-alg.com/extra_examples

Lesson 6-6 Finding Percents Mentally **295**

Study Notebook

Have students—
• copy the Percent-Fraction Table from page 293.
• copy Exercise 5 in Check for Understanding and explain how to find the percent mentally.
• explain how to estimate 32% of 62.
• include any other item(s) that they find helpful in mastering the skills in this lesson.

About the Exercises . . .

Organization by Objective
• **Find Percents of a Number Mentally:** 13–26
• **Estimate with Percents:** 27–42

Odd/Even Assignments
Exercises 13–35 and 39–42 are structured so that students practice the same concepts whether they are assigned odd or even problems.

Assignment Guide
Basic: 13–35 odd, 39, 43–66
Average: 13–41 odd, 43–66
Advanced: 14–34 even, 36–38, 40, 42, 43–60 (Optional: 61–66)

Answers

1. 18% is about 20% or $\frac{1}{5}$. 216 is about 220. $\frac{1}{5}$ of 220 is 44. So, 18% of 216 is about 44.

2. about 10%

4–12. Sample answers are given.

4. 48

5. 13

6. 9

7. 72

8. 12; fraction method: $\frac{1}{5} \times 60$ or 12

9. 8; fraction method: $\frac{1}{3} \times 24$ or 8

10. 2; 1% method: Since 1% of 396 is about 4, $\frac{1}{2}\%$ of 396 is about $\frac{1}{2}$ of 4 or 2.

11. 21; meaning of percent method: 152% means about 150 for every 100 or about 15 for every 10. 14 has 1 tens. $1 \times 15 = 15$. So, 152% of 14 is about 21.

12. $\frac{1}{5} \times \$50$ or $10

Study Guide and Intervention, p. 324

When working with common percents like 10%, 25%, 40%, and 50%, it may be helpful to use the fraction form of the percent.

Percent-Fraction Equivalents

$20\% = \frac{1}{5}$	$10\% = \frac{1}{10}$	$25\% = \frac{1}{4}$	$12\frac{1}{2}\% = \frac{1}{8}$	$16\frac{2}{3}\% = \frac{1}{6}$
$40\% = \frac{2}{5}$	$30\% = \frac{3}{10}$	$50\% = \frac{1}{2}$	$37\frac{1}{2}\% = \frac{3}{8}$	$33\frac{1}{3}\% = \frac{1}{3}$
$60\% = \frac{3}{5}$	$70\% = \frac{7}{10}$	$75\% = \frac{3}{4}$	$62\frac{1}{2}\% = \frac{5}{8}$	$66\frac{2}{3}\% = \frac{2}{3}$
$80\% = \frac{4}{5}$	$90\% = \frac{9}{10}$	$100\% = 1$	$87\frac{1}{2}\% = \frac{7}{8}$	$83\frac{1}{3}\% = \frac{5}{6}$

Example Find 20% of 35 mentally.

20% of $35 = \frac{1}{5}$ of 35 Think: $20\% = \frac{1}{5}$.

$= 7$ Think: $\frac{1}{5}$ of 35 is 7. So, 20% of 35 is 7.

Exercises

Find the percent of each number mentally.

1. 50% of 6   3
2. 25% of 100   25
3. 60% of 25   15
4. 75% of 28   21
5. $66\frac{2}{3}\%$ of 33   22
6. 150% of 2   3
7. 125% of 4   5
8. 175% of 4   7
9. 10% of 110   11
10. 80% of 20   16
11. 20% of 80   16
12. 20% of 800   160
13. 90% of 600   540
14. 25% of 240   60
15. 50% of 7   3.5
16. 30% of 250   75
17. 60% of 250   150
18. 75% of 1000   750
19. 10% of 900   90
20. 20% of 900   180
21. 40% of 900   360
22. 25% of 360   90
23. 50% of 360   180
24. 75% of 360   270
25. 25% of 56   14
26. $33\frac{1}{3}\%$ of 363   121
27. $16\frac{2}{3}\%$ of 66   11
28. $62\frac{1}{2}\%$ of 32   20
29. $37\frac{1}{2}\%$ of 32   12
30. 200% of 21   42
31. $66\frac{2}{3}\%$ of 54   36
32. 150% of 2222   3333
33. $12\frac{1}{2}\%$ of 720   90
34. 30% of 30   9
35. $66\frac{2}{3}\%$ of 150   100
36. 80% of 1500   1200

Skills Practice, p. 325 and Practice, p. 326 (shown)

Find the percent of each number mentally.

1. 10% of 812   81.2
2. 50% of 1044   522
3. 40% of 25   10
4. 20% of 45   9
5. $62\frac{1}{2}\%$ of 80   50
6. 80% of 15   12
7. 30% of 400   120
8. 75% of 880   660
9. $16\frac{2}{3}\%$ of 72   12
10. $33\frac{1}{3}\%$ of 150   50
11. 60% of 2500   1500
12. $37\frac{1}{2}\%$ of 48   18
13. 25% of 244   61
14. 900% of 3   27
15. 150% of 260   390

Estimate.   16–33. Sample answers are given.

16. 31% of 62 $\frac{3}{10}$ of 60; 18
17. 65% of 83 $\frac{2}{3}$ of 81; 54
18. 87% of 850 $\frac{7}{8}$ of 800; 700
19. 32% of 26 $\frac{1}{3}$ of 27; 9
20. 47% of 213 $\frac{1}{2}$ of 200; 100
21. 22% of 536 $\frac{1}{5}$ of 500; 100
22. 68% of 12 $\frac{2}{3}$ of 12; 8
23. 11% of 29 $\frac{1}{10}$ of 30; 3
24. 78% of 4 $\frac{3}{4}$ of 4; 3
25. 21% of 18 $\frac{1}{5}$ of 20; 4
26. 73% of 91 $\frac{3}{4}$ of 88; 66
27. 8% of 1008 $\frac{1}{10}$ of 1000; 100
28. $\frac{1}{2}\%$ of 381 $\frac{1}{2}$ of 4; 2
29. $\frac{1}{6}\%$ of 567 $\frac{1}{6}$ of 6; 1
30. $\frac{2}{9}\%$ of 856 $\frac{2}{9}$ of 9; 6
31. 210% of 425 2×400; 800
32. 153% of 801 $800 + 400$; 1200
33. 689% of 2981 7×3000; 21,000

34. **MONEY** Last week a waitress made $204 in tips. This week she made 135% of that. How much did she make this week? $275.40

Enrichment, p. 328

Finding the Percent One Number Is of Another

Solve. Use the circle graph.

1. How much money did Eric spend on all the camera equipment? $520

2. What percent of the total cost of the equipment did Eric spend on the camera?   47%

3. What percent of the total cost was spent on the camera case?   6%

4. What percent of the total cost was spent on the flash?   11%

5. What percent of the total cost was spent on the wide-angle lens?   27%

6. What percent of the total cost was spent on the tripod?   9%

7. What percent of the total cost was spent on the camera case, tripod, and flash?   26%

8. The salesperson who sold Eric the equipment earned a $6\frac{1}{2}\%$ commission on the sale. How much was the commission? $33.80

Cost of Eric's Camera Equipment

Camera $244.40
Camera Case $31.20
Tripod $46.80
Flash $57.20
Wide-Angle Lens $140.40

Practice and Apply

Homework Help

For Exercises	See Examples
13–26	1
27–35	2
39, 40	3

Extra Practice
See page 738.

Find the percent of each number mentally. 13–24. See margin.

13. 50% of 28
14. 75% of 16
15. 60% of 55
16. 20% of 105
17. $87\frac{1}{2}\%$ of 56
18. $16\frac{2}{3}\%$ of 42
19. $12\frac{1}{2}\%$ of 32
20. $66\frac{2}{3}\%$ of $24
21. 200% of 45
22. 150% of 54
23. 125% of 300
24. 175% of 200

MONEY For Exercises 25 and 26, use the following information.
In a recent year, the number of $1 bills in circulation in the United States was about 7 billion. 25–26. See margin.

25. Suppose the number of $5 bills in circulation was 25% of the number of $1 bills. About how many $5 bills were in circulation?

26. If the number of $10 bills was 20% of the number of $1 bills, about how many $10 bills were in circulation?

Estimate. Explain which method you used to estimate. 27–34. See margin.

27. 30% of 89
28. 25% of 162
29. 38% of 88
30. 81% of 25
31. $\frac{1}{4}\%$ of 806
32. $\frac{1}{5}\%$ of 40
33. 127% of 64
34. 140% of 95
35. 295% of 145

35. See pp. 323A–323B.

SPACE For Exercises 36–38, refer to the information in the table.

36. Which planet has a radius that measures about 50% of the radius of Mercury? **Pluto**

37. Sample answer: Pluto and Mars, or Neptune and Jupiter

★ 37. Name two planets such that the radius of one planet is about one-third the radius of the other planet.

★ 38. Name two planets such that the mass of one planet is about 330% the mass of the other. **Sample answer: Jupiter and Saturn**

Radius and Mass of Each Planet

Planet	Radius (mi)	Mass
Mercury	1516	0.0553
Venus	3761	0.815
Earth	3960	1.000
Mars	2107	0.107
Jupiter	43,450	317.830
Saturn	36,191	95.160
Uranus	15,763	14.540
Neptune	15,304	17.150
Pluto	707	0.0021

Source: The World Almanac

More About...

Geography
There are four U.S. coastlines. They are the Atlantic, Gulf, Pacific, and Arctic coasts. Most of the coastline is located on the Pacific Ocean. It contains 40,298 miles.
Source: The World Almanac

39. **GEOGRAPHY** The United States has 88,633 miles of shoreline. Of the total amount, 35% is located in Alaska. About how many miles of shoreline are located in Alaska? **See pp. 323A–323B.**

40. **GEOGRAPHY** About 8.5% of the total Pacific coastline is located in California. Use the information at the left to estimate the number of miles of coastline located in California. **See pp. 323A–323B.**

★ 41. **FOOD** A serving of shrimp contains 90 Calories and 7 of those Calories are from fat. About what percent of the Calories are from fat? **about 10%**

★ 42. **FOOD** Fifty-six percent of the Calories in corn chips are from fat. Estimate the number of Calories from fat in a serving of corn chips if one serving contains 160 Calories. **about 80**

296   **Chapter 6** Ratio, Proportion, and Percent

Answers

13–24. Sample answers are given.	17. 49	23. 375
	18. 7	24. 350
13. 14	19. 4	25. $\frac{1}{4} \times 8$ or 2 billion
14. 12	20. 16	
15. 33	21. 90	26. $\frac{1}{5} \times 10$ or 2 billion
16. 21	22. 81	

43. CRITICAL THINKING In an election, 40% of the Democrats and 92.5% of the Republicans voted "yes". Of all of the Democrats and Republicans, 68% voted "yes". Find the ratio of Democrats to Republicans. **7 to 8**

44. WRITING IN MATH Answer the question that was posed at the beginning of the lesson. **See margin.**

How is estimation used when determining sale prices?

Include the following in your answer:
- an example of a situation in which you used estimation to determine the sale price of an item, and
- an example of a real-life situation other than shopping in which you would use estimation with percents.

Standardized Test Practice

45. Which percent is greater than $\frac{3}{5}$ but less than $\frac{2}{3}$? **C**

(A) 68%   (B) 54%   (C) 64%   (D) 38%

46. Choose the best estimate for 26% of 362. **A**

(A) 91   (B) 72   (C) 108   (D) 85

Maintain Your Skills

Mixed Review **Use the percent proportion to solve each problem.** *(Lesson 6-5)*

47. What is 28% of 75? **21**

48. 37.8 is what percent of 84? **45%**

49. FORESTRY The five states with the largest portion of land covered by forests are shown in the graphic. For each state, how many square miles of land are covered by forests? **See margin.**

State	Percent of land covered by forests	Area of state (square miles)
Maine	89.9%	35,387
New Hampshire	88.1%	9351
West Virginia	77.5%	24,231
Vermont	75.7%	9615
Alabama	66.9%	52,423

Source: The Learning Kingdom, Inc.

Express each decimal as a percent. *(Lesson 6-4)*

50. 0.27 **27%**   **51.** 1.6 **160%**   **52.** 0.008 **0.8%**

Express each percent as a decimal. *(Lesson 6-4)*

53. 77% **0.77**   **54.** 8% **0.08**   **55.** 421% **4.21**   **56.** 3.56% **0.0356**

ALGEBRA Solve each equation. Check your solution. *(Lesson 5-9)*

57. $n + 4.7 = 13.6$ **8.9**   **58.** $x + \frac{5}{6} = 2\frac{3}{8}$ **$1\frac{13}{24}$**   **59.** $\frac{3}{7}r = -9$ **−21**

60. GEOMETRY The perimeter of a rectangle is 22 feet. Its length is 7 feet. Find its width. *(Lesson 3-7)* **4 ft**

Getting Ready for the Next Lesson **PREREQUISITE SKILL** Solve each equation. Check your solution.
*(To review **solving equations**, see Lesson 3-4.)*

61. $10a = 5$ **0.5**   **62.** $20m = 4$ **0.2**

63. $60h = 15$ **0.25**   **64.** $28g = 1.4$ **0.05**

65. $80w = 5.6$ **0.07**   **66.** $125n = 15$ **0.12**

4 Assess

Open-Ended Assessment

Modeling Make two sets of cards, one with various percents on them and the other with various numbers on them. Shuffle each deck separately. Have students choose a card from each deck and mentally estimate the product of the amounts on the two cards.

Getting Ready for Lesson 6-7

PREREQUISITE SKILL Lesson 6-7 presents using percent equations to solve percent problems. Exercises 61–66 should be used to determine your students' familiarity with solving equations.

Answers

44. By estimating the cost of an item and estimating the percent of the discount, the sale price can be determined. Answers should include the following.
- Sample answer: Estimating the cost of a book that was on sale for 25% off.
- Sample answer: Estimating the amount of paint needed to paint a room.

49. Maine: 31,813 sq mi; New Hampshire: 8238 sq mi; West Virginia: 18,779 sq mi; Vermont: 7279 sq mi; Alabama: 35,071 sq mi

Answers

27. 27; fraction method: $\frac{3}{10} \times 90$ or 27

28. 40; fraction method: $\frac{1}{4} \times 160$ or 40

29. 36; fraction method: $\frac{2}{5} \times 90$ or 36

30. 20; fraction method: $\frac{4}{5} \times 25$ or 20

31. 2; 1% method: Since 1% of 806 is about 8, $\frac{1}{4}$% of 806 is about $\frac{1}{4}$ of 8 or 2.

32. 0.08; 1% method: Since 1% of 40 is 0.4, $\frac{1}{5}$% of 40 is $\frac{1}{5}$ of 0.4 or 0.08.

33. 78; meaning of percent: 127% means about 130 for every 100 or about 13 for every 10. 64 has 6 tens. $6 \times 13 = 78$. So, 127% of 64 is about 78.

34. 140; meaning of percent: 140% means about 140 for every 100 or about 14 for every 10. 95 has about one 100. $1 \times 140 = 140$. So, 140% of 95 is about 140.

1 Focus

5-Minute Check Transparency 6-7 Use as a quiz or review of Lesson 6-6.

Mathematical Background notes are available for this lesson on page 262D.

How is the percent proportion related to an equation?

The opening activity questions are repeated on page 332 of the *Chapter 6 Resource Masters*.

Reading to Learn Mathematics, p. 332 ELL

Pre-Activity *How is the percent proportion related to an equation?*

Do the activity at the top of page 298 in your textbook. Write your answers below.

a. Use the percent proportion to find the amount of tax on a $35 purchase for each state. AL: $1.40; CT: $2.10; NM: $1.75; TX: $2.19

b. Express each tax rate as a decimal. AL: 0.04; CT: 0.06; NM: 0.05; TX: 0.0625

c. Multiply the decimal form of the tax rate by $35 to find the amount of tax on the $35 purchase for each state. AL: $1.40; CT: $2.10; NM: $1.75; TX: $2.19

d. How are the amounts of tax in parts a and c related? They are the same.

Reading the Lesson 1–3. See students' work.

Write a definition and give an example of each new vocabulary word or phrase.

Vocabulary	Definition	Example
1. percent equation		
2. discount		
3. simple interest		

Helping You Remember

4. The label above each oval represents what is missing from a percent equation. In each oval, write and solve a percent equation to find that missing information. Sample answers are given.

Missing Base	Missing Part	Missing Percent
$54 = 0.72(n)$	$n = 0.36(80)$	$45 = n(125)$
$n = 75$	$n = 28.8$	$n = 36\%$

What You'll Learn

- Solve percent problems using percent equations.
- Solve real-life problems involving discount and interest.

Vocabulary
- percent equation
- discount
- simple interest

How is the percent proportion related to an equation?

As of July 1, 1999, 45 of the 50 U.S. states had a sales tax. The table shows the tax rate for four U.S. states.

a. Use the percent proportion to find the amount of tax on a $35 purchase for each state. **a–c. See margin.**

b. Express each tax rate as a decimal.

c. Multiply the decimal form of the tax rate by $35 to find the amount of tax on the $35 purchase for each state.

d. How are the amounts of tax in parts **a** and **c** related? **They are the same.**

State	Tax Rate (percent)
Alabama	4%
Connecticut	6%
New Mexico	5%
Texas	6.25%

Source: www.taxadmin.org

PERCENT EQUATIONS

The **percent equation** is an equivalent form of the percent proportion in which the percent is written as a decimal.

$$\frac{\text{Part}}{\text{Base}} = \text{Percent}$$ ← The percent is written as a decimal.

$$\frac{\text{Part}}{\text{Base}} \cdot \text{Base} = \text{Percent} \cdot \text{Base}$$ Multiply each side by the base.

$$\text{Part} = \text{Percent} \cdot \text{Base}$$ ← This form is called the percent equation.

Concept Summary		The Percent Equation
Type	**Example**	**Equation**
Missing Part	What number is 75% of 4?	$n = 0.75(4)$
Missing Percent	3 is what percent of 4?	$3 = n(4)$
Missing Base	3 is 75% of what number?	$3 = 0.75n$

Study Tip

Estimation
To determine whether your answer is reasonable, estimate before finding the exact answer.

Example 1 Find the Part

Find 52% of 85. **Estimate:** $\frac{1}{2}$ of 90 is 45.

You know that the base is 85 and the percent is 52%. Let n represent the part.

$n = 0.52(85)$ Write 52% as the decimal 0.52.

$n = 44.2$ Simplify.

So, 52% of 85 is 44.2.

Resource Manager

Workbooks and Reproducible Masters

Chapter 6 Resource Masters
- Study Guide and Intervention, p. 329
- Skills Practice, p. 330
- Practice, p. 331
- Reading to Learn Mathematics, p. 332
- Enrichment, p. 333
- Assessment, p. 360

Parent and Student Study Guide Workbook, p. 50

Transparencies

5-Minute Check Transparency 6-7
Answer Key Transparencies

Technology

Interactive Chalkboard
Pre-AlgePASS: Tutorial Plus, Lessons 16 and 17

Example 2 Find the Percent

28 is what percent of 70?   **Estimate:** $\frac{28}{70} \approx \frac{25}{75}$ or $\frac{1}{3}$, which is $33\frac{1}{3}\%$.

You know that the base is 70 and the part is 28.
Let n represent the percent.

$28 = n(70)$

$\frac{28}{70} = n$ Divide each side by 70.

$0.4 = n$ Simplify.

So, 28 is 40% of 70.   The answer makes sense compared to the estimate.

Example 3 Find the Base

18 is 45% of what number?   **Estimate:** 18 is 50% of 36.

You know that the part is 18 and the percent is 45.
Let n represent the base.

$18 = 0.45n$ Write 45% as the decimal 0.45.

$\frac{18}{0.45} = \frac{0.45n}{0.45}$ Divide each side by 0.45.

$40 = n$ Simplify.

So, 18 is 45% of 40.   The answer is reasonable since it is close to the estimate.

DISCOUNT AND INTEREST   The percent equation can also be used to solve problems involving discount and interest. **Discount** is the amount by which the regular price of an item is reduced.

Example 4 Find Discount

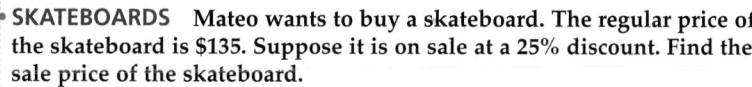

SKATEBOARDS   **Mateo wants to buy a skateboard. The regular price of the skateboard is $135. Suppose it is on sale at a 25% discount. Find the sale price of the skateboard.**

Method 1
First, use the percent equation to find 25% of 135.   **Estimate:** $\frac{1}{4}$ of 140 = 35

Let d represent the discount.
$d = 0.25(135)$ The base is 135 and the percent is 25%.
$d = 33.75$ Simplify.

Then, find the sale price.
$135 - 33.75 = 101.25$ Subtract the discount from the original price.

Method 2
A discount of 25% means the item will cost 100% − 25% or 75% of the original price. Use the percent equation to find 75% of 135.

Let s represent the sale price.
$s = 0.75(135)$ The base is 135 and the percent is 75%.
$s = 101.25$ Simplify.

The sale price of the skateboard will be $101.25.

www.pre-alg.com/extra_examples

Lesson 6-7 Using Percent Equations **299**

---

2 Teach

PERCENT EQUATIONS

Teaching Tip   Discuss how to write an equation for "find 36% of 120." Explain that it helps to rewrite the sentence as "36% of 120 is what?" Then write the equation: $0.36(120) = n$.

In-Class Examples

Teaching Tip   Review changing percents to decimals.

1 Find 38% of 22.   **8.36**

2 19 is what percent of 25?   **76%**

3 84 is 16% of what number?   **525**

DISCOUNT AND INTEREST

In-Class Examples

4 **JEWELRY**   The regular price of a ring is $495. It is on sale at a 20% discount. What is the sale price of the ring?   **$396**

Teaching Tip   Have students work each problem using both methods until they understand each method. Then have them choose the method they prefer.

5 **BANKING**   Suppose you invest $2000 at an annual interest rate of 4.5%. How long will it take for it to earn $495?   **5.5 years**

✓ Skills Check

a. Sandrine invests $500 at 5.5% interest. In two years, how much interest will she earn?   **$55**

b. Ricardo borrows $250 at 9% interest. In six months, how much interest will he pay?   **$11.25**

DAILY
INTERVENTION

Differentiated Instruction

- **Kinesthetic**   Have students play "rock, paper, scissors" by having them randomly make a fist (rock), flatten their hand (paper), or creating cutting scissors with the index and middle fingers. Count the rocks and determine what percent of the students in the class made rocks. Continue playing several rounds, randomly choosing which item should be counted.

Lesson 6-7   Using Percent Equations   **299**

Study Notebook

Have students—

• add the definitions/examples of the vocabulary terms to their Vocabulary Builder worksheets for Chapter 6.

• copy three different exercises from their homework that represent each of the three different types of percent problems. Have them explain how to write an equation for each.

• include any other item(s) that they find helpful in mastering the skills in this lesson.

About the Exercises . . .

Organization by Objective
• **Percent Equations:** 12–27
• **Discount and Interest:** 28–38

Odd/Even Assignments
Exercises 12–41 are structured so that students practice the same concepts whether they are assigned odd or even problems.

Assignment Guide

Basic: 13–23 odd, 29–39 odd, 42–61

Average: 13–41 odd, 42–61

Advanced: 12–40 even, 42–55 (Optional: 56–61)

Tips for New Teachers

Introducing Algebra
Encourage students to write the equations, even if they can work the problems mentally. Emphasize that using equations will become easier with practice and that some problems must be solved by using equations.

Simple interest is the amount of money paid or earned for the use of money. For a savings account, interest is earned. For a credit card, interest is paid. To solve problems involving interest, use the following formula.

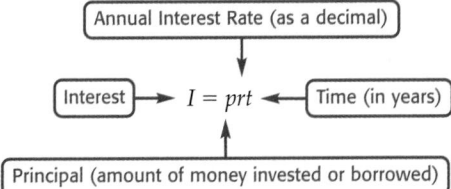

Reading Math

Formulas
The formula $I = prt$ is read *Interest is equal to principal times rate times time.*

☑ **Concept Check** Name a situation where interest is earned and a situation where interest is paid. **Sample answers: checking account; home loan**

Example 5 Apply Simple Interest Formula

BANKING Suppose Miguel invests $1200 at an annual rate of 6.5%. How long will it take until Miguel earns $195?

$I = prt$	Write the simple interest formula.
$195 = 1200(0.065)t$	Replace I with 195, p with 1200, and r with 0.065.
$195 = 78t$	Simplify.
$\dfrac{195}{78} = \dfrac{78t}{78}$	Divide each side by 78.
$2.5 = t$	Simplify.

Miguel will earn $195 in interest in 2.5 years.

Check for Understanding

Concept Check
1. **OPEN ENDED** Give an example of a situation in which using the percent equation would be easier than using the percent proportion.

2. **Define** *discount.* **1–3. See margin.**

3. **Explain** what I, p, r, and t represent in the simple interest formula.

Guided Practice

GUIDED PRACTICE KEY	
Exercises	Examples
4–7	1–3
8, 10	4
9, 11	5

Solve each problem using the percent equation.

4. 15 is what percent of 60? **25%** 　　5. 30 is 60% of what number? **50**

6. What is 20% of 110? **22** 　　　　7. 12 is what percent of 400? **3%**

8. Find the discount for a $268 DVD player that is on sale at 20% off. **$53.60**

9. What is the interest on $8000 that is invested at 6% for $3\frac{1}{2}$ years? Round to the nearest cent. **$1680**

Applications
10. **SHOPPING** A jacket that normally sells for $180 is on sale at a 35% discount. What is the sale price of the jacket? **$117**

11. **BANKING** How long will it take to earn $252 in interest if $2400 is invested at a 7% annual interest rate? **1.5 years**

300 Chapter 6 Ratio, Proportion, and Percent

Answers

1. Use the percent equation in any situation where the rate and base are known.

2. Discount is the amount by which the regular price of an item is reduced.

3. I = interest; p = principal; r = annual interest rate; t = time in years

Practice and Apply

Homework Help

For Exercises	See Examples
12–27, 39	1–3
28–33	4
34–38	5

Extra Practice
See page 738.

Solve each problem using the percent equation. 12–27. See margin.

12. 9 is what percent of 25?

13. 38 is what percent of 40?

14. 48 is 64% of what number?

15. 27 is 54% of what number?

16. Find 12% of 72.

17. Find 42% of 150.

18. 39.2 is what percent of 112?

19. 49.5 is what percent of 132?

20. What is 37.5% of 89?

21. What is 24.2% of 60?

22. 37.5 is what percent of 30?

23. 43.6 is what percent of 20?

★ 24. 1.6 is what percent of 400?

★ 25. 1.35 is what percent of 150?

★ 26. 83.5 is 125% of what number?

★ 27. 17.6 is $133\frac{1}{3}$% of what number?

28. **FOOD** A frozen pizza is on sale at a 25% discount. Find the sale price of the pizza if it normally sells for $4.85. **$3.64**

29. **CALCULATORS** Suppose a calculator is on sale at a 15% discount. If it normally sells for $29.99, what is the sale price? **$25.49**

Find the discount to the nearest cent.

30.  **$16.25**

SALE! 25% off Original Price: $65

31. $85 cordless phone, 20% off **$17**

32. $489 stereo, 15% off **$73.35**

33. 25% off a $74 baseball glove **$18.50**

Find the interest to the nearest cent. 34. **$1010.35**

34.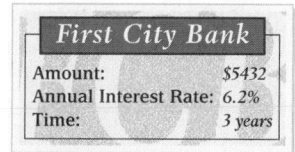

First City Bank
Amount: $5432
Annual Interest Rate: 6.2%
Time: 3 years

35. $4500 at 5.5% for $4\frac{1}{2}$ years **$1113.75**

36. $3680 at 6.75% for $2\frac{1}{4}$ years **$558.90**

37. 5.5% for $1\frac{3}{4}$ years on $2543 **$244.76**

38. **BANKING** What is the annual interest rate if $1600 is invested for 6 years and $456 in interest is earned? **4.75%**

39. **SPORTS** One season, a football team had 7 losses. This was 43.75% of the total games they played. How many games did they play? **16**

WebQuest

The percent equation can help you analyze the nutritional value of food. Visit www.pre-alg.com/webquest to continue work on your WebQuest project.

★ 40. **REAL ESTATE** A **commission** is a fee paid to a salesperson based on a percent of sales. Suppose a real estate agent earns a 3% commission. What commission would be earned for selling the house shown?

New Listing! Two-story home with 4 bedrooms and 2 bathrooms. Price: $130,000

40. $3900

★ 41. **BUSINESS** To make a profit, stores try to sell an item for more than it paid for the item. The increase in price is called the **markup**. Suppose a store purchases paint brushes for $8 each. Find the markup if the brushes are sold for 15% over the price paid for them. **$1.20**

www.pre-alg.com/self_check_quiz

Lesson 6-7 Using Percent Equations **301**

Answers

12. 36%	18. 35%	24. 0.4%
13. 95%	19. 37.5%	25. 0.9%
14. 75	20. 33.375	26. 66.8
15. 50	21. 14.52	27. 13.2
16. 8.64	22. 125%	
17. 63	23. 218%	

Open-Ended Assessment

Writing Have students work in pairs. Each student should write three percent problems, including at least one interest problem and one discount problem. Have them trade problems and check each others' work.

Getting Ready for Lesson 6-8

PREREQUISITE SKILL Lesson 6-8 presents percent of change. Students will need to express decimals as percents. Exercises 56–61 should be used to determine your students' familiarity with writing decimals as percents.

Assessment Options

Quiz (Lessons 6-6 and 6-7) is available on p. 360 of the *Chapter 6 Resource Masters*.

Answers

42. Yes; $n\%$ of $m = \frac{n}{100} \cdot m$ or $\frac{mn}{100}$ and $m\%$ of $n = \frac{m}{100} \cdot n$ or $\frac{mn}{100}$.

43. If you know two of the three values, you can use the percent proportion to solve for the missing value. Answers should include the following.

• To find the amount of tax on an item, you can use the percent proportion or the percent equation.

• For example, the following methods can be used to find 6% tax on $24.99.
Method 1: Percent Proportion
$\frac{x}{24.99} = \frac{6}{100}$
Method 2: Percent Equation
$n = 0.06(24.99)$
Using either method, $x = 1.50$. The amount of tax is $1.50.

46–48. Sample answers are given.

46. 40; fraction method: $\frac{1}{2} \times 80$ or 40

42. CRITICAL THINKING Determine whether $n\%$ of m is always equal to $m\%$ of n. Give examples to support your answer. **See margin.**

43. **WRITING IN MATH** Answer the question that was posed at the beginning of the lesson. **See margin.**

How is the percent proportion related to an equation?

Include the following in your answer:
• an explanation describing two methods for finding the amount of tax on an item, and
• an example of using both methods to find the amount of sales tax on an item.

44. What percent of 320 is 19.2? **C**
Ⓐ 0.6%   Ⓑ 60%   Ⓒ 6%   Ⓓ 0.06%

45. Ryan wants to buy a tent that costs $150 for his camping trip. The tent is on sale at a 30% discount. What will be the sale price of the tent? **B**
Ⓐ 95   Ⓑ 105   Ⓒ 45   Ⓓ 110

Maintain Your Skills

Mixed Review
46–48. See margin.

Estimate. Explain which method you used to estimate. *(Lesson 6-6)*

46. 47% of 84   **47.** 126% of 198   **48.** 9% of 514

Use the percent proportion to solve each problem. *(Lesson 6-5)*

49. What is 55% of 220? **121**   **50.** 50.88 is what percent of 96? **53%**

51. POPULATION The graphic shows the number of stories of certain buildings in Tulsa, Oklahoma. What is the mean of the data? *(Lesson 5-8)* **41**

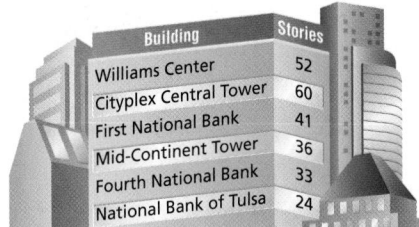

Building	Stories
Williams Center	52
Cityplex Central Tower	60
First National Bank	41
Mid-Continent Tower	36
Fourth National Bank	33
National Bank of Tulsa	24

Source: *The World Almanac*

52. List all the factors of 30. *(Lesson 4-1)* **1, 2, 3, 5, 6, 10, 15, 30**

GEOMETRY **Find the perimeter of each rectangle.** *(Lesson 3-7)*

53. 13 cm, 6 cm **38 cm**   **54.** 25 in., 11 in. **72 in.**

55. ALGEBRA Use the Distributive Property to rewrite $(w - 3)8$. *(Lesson 3-1)*
$8w - 24$

Getting Ready for the Next Lesson

PREREQUISITE SKILL **Write each decimal as a percent.**
*(To review **writing decimals as percents**, see Lesson 6-4.)*

56. 0.58 **58%**   **57.** 0.89 **89%**   **58.** 0.125 **12.5%**

59. 1.56 **156%**   **60.** 2.04 **204%**   **61.** 0.224 **22.4%**

302 **Chapter 6** Ratio, Proportion, and Percent

47. 250; meaning of percent method: 126% means about 125 for every 100 and 12.5 for every 10. 198 has about 2 one-hundreds. $125 \times 2 = 250$. So, 126% of 198 is about 250.

48. 45; 1% method: Since 1% of 514 is about 5, 9% of 514 is 9×5 or about 45.

Spreadsheet Investigation

A Follow-Up of Lesson 6-7

Compound Interest

Simple interest, which you studied in the previous lesson, is paid only on the initial principal of a savings account or a loan. **Compound interest** is paid on the initial principal and on interest earned in the past. You can use a spreadsheet to investigate the impact of compound interest.

SAVINGS **Find the value of a $1000 savings account after five years if the account pays 6% interest compounded semiannually.**

6% interest compounded semiannually means that the interest is paid twice a year, or every 6 months. The interest rate is 6% ÷ 2 or 3%.

The rate is entered as a decimal.

The spreadsheet evaluates the formula A4 × B1.

The interest is added to the principal every 6 months. The spreadsheet evaluates the formula A4 + B4.

	A	B	C	D
1	RATE	0.03		
2				
3	PRINCIPAL	INTEREST	NEW PRINCIPAL	TIME (YR)
4	1000.00	30.00	1030.00	0.5
5	1030.00	30.90	1060.90	1.0
6	1060.90	31.83	1092.73	1.5
7	1092.73	32.78	1125.51	2.0
8	1125.51	33.77	1159.27	2.5
9	1159.27	34.78	1194.05	3.0
10	1194.05	35.82	1229.87	3.5
11	1229.87	36.90	1266.77	4.0
12	1266.77	38.00	1304.77	4.5
13	1304.77	39.14	1343.92	5.0

Sheet1 / Sheet2 / Sh

Edit

The value of the savings account after five years is $1343.92.

1. The simple interest, $300, is $43.92 less than the compound interest.

Model and Analyze

1. Suppose you invest $1000 for five years at 6% simple interest. How does the simple interest compare to the compound interest shown above?

2. Use a spreadsheet to find the amount of money in a savings account if $1000 is invested for five years at 6% interest compounded quarterly. **$1346.86**

3. Suppose you leave $100 in each of three bank accounts paying 5% interest per year. One account pays simple interest, one pays interest compounded semiannually, and one pays interest compounded quarterly. Use a spreadsheet to find the amount of money in each account after three years.
$115.00, $115.97, $116.08

Make a Conjecture

4. How does the amount of interest change if the compounding occurs more frequently? **The amount of interest increases.**

Spreadsheet Investigation

A Follow-Up of Lesson 6-7

Getting Started

Objective Find compound interest.

Materials
spreadsheet software

Teaching Tip Have students work the first two or three rows by hand or with a calculator so they can see how the added interest also earns interest.

Teach

- Have students use the simple interest formula $I = prt$ to help them estimate the compounded interest.

In **Exercises 1–3,** students should:

- use a spreadsheet to compare simple interest to compound interest.
- use a spreadsheet to determine the amount of growth of an account earning compound interest.
- compare different intervals of compound interest.

In **Exercise 4,** students make a conjecture based on different time intervals for the same interest rate and principal.

Assess

- After students have worked Exercises 1–3, ask them how long it would take for an account with an initial amount $75 at 10% compounded semiannually to exceed that of one with $100 at 5% interest compounded semiannually. **6 years**

Study Notebook

Have student print out one of their spreadsheets to keep in their journal. Have them circle and label the interest rate, principal, and elapsed time.

1 Focus

5-Minute Check Transparency 6-8 Use as a quiz or review of Lesson 6-7.

Mathematical Background notes are available for this lesson on page 262D.

How can percents help to describe a change in area?

The opening activity questions are repeated on page 337 of the *Chapter 6 Resource Masters*.

Reading to Learn Mathematics, p. 337 **ELL**

Pre-Activity *How can percents help to describe a change in area?*
Do the activity at the top of page 304 in your textbook. Write your answers below.

Draw each pair of rectangles. Then compare the rectangles. Express the increase as a fraction and as a percent.

a. X: 2 units by 3 units   b. G: 2 units by 5 units
   Y: 2 units by 4 units   H: 2 units by 6 units
   $\frac{1}{3}$ or $33\frac{1}{3}$% $\frac{1}{5}$ or 20%

c. J: 2 units by 4 units   d. P: 2 units by 6 units
   K: 2 units by 5 units   Q: 2 units by 7 units
   $\frac{1}{4}$ or 25% $\frac{1}{6}$ or $16\frac{2}{3}$%

e. For each pair of rectangles, the change in area is 2 square units. Explain why the percent of change is different. The percent of change is different because the area of each original rectangle is different.

Reading the Lesson 1–3. See students' work.
Write a definition and give an example of each new vocabulary phrase.

Vocabulary	Definition	Example
1. percent of change		
2. percent of increase		
3. percent of decrease		

Helping You Remember

4. For a percent of increase, is the percent of change always positive or negative? Why?
Positive; The smaller amount is always subtracted from the larger amount.

5. For a percent of decrease, is the percent of change always positive or negative? Why?
Negative; The larger amount is always subtracted from the smaller amount.

What You'll Learn

- Find percent of increase.
- Find percent of decrease.

How can percents help to describe a change in area?

Suppose the length of rectangle A is increased from 4 units to 5 units.

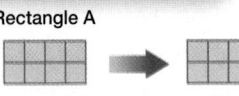

Rectangle A

4 units → 5 units

Rectangle A had an initial area of 8 square units. It increased to 10 square units. This is a change in area of 2 square units. The following ratio shows this relationship.

$$\frac{\text{change in area}}{\text{original area}} = \frac{2}{8} = \frac{1}{4} \text{ or } 25\%$$

This means that, compared to the original area, the new area increased by 25%.

Draw each pair of rectangles. Then compare the rectangles. Express the increase as a fraction and as a percent.

a. X: 2 units by 3 units   **b.** G: 2 units by 5 units
    Y: 2 units by 4 units   H: 2 units by 6 units

c. J: 2 units by 4 units   **d.** P: 2 units by 6 units
    K: 2 units by 5 units   Q: 2 units by 7 units

e. For each pair of rectangles, the change in area is 2 square units. Explain why the percent of change is different.

Vocabulary

- percent of change
- percent of increase
- percent of decrease

a. $\frac{1}{3}$ or $33\frac{1}{3}$%

b. $\frac{1}{5}$ or 20%

c. $\frac{1}{4}$ or 25%

d. $\frac{1}{6}$ or $16\frac{2}{3}$%

e. The percent of change is different because the area of each original rectangle is different.

FIND PERCENT OF INCREASE A **percent of change** tells the percent an amount has increased or decreased in relation to the original amount.

Example 1 *Find Percent of Change*

Find the percent of change from 56 inches to 63 inches.

Step 1 Subtract to find the amount of change.

$63 - 56 = 7$ new measurement − original measurement

Step 2 Write a ratio that compares the amount of change to the original measurement. Express the ratio as a percent.

$$\text{percent of change} = \frac{\text{amount of change}}{\text{original measurement}}$$

$$= \frac{7}{56} \qquad \text{Substitution.}$$

$$= 0.125 \text{ or } 12.5\% \quad \text{Write the decimal as a percent.}$$

The percent of change from 56 inches to 63 inches is 12.5%.

Resource Manager

 Workbooks and Reproducible Masters

Chapter 6 Resource Masters
- Study Guide and Intervention, p. 334
- Skills Practice, p. 335
- Practice, p. 336
- Reading to Learn Mathematics, p. 337
- Enrichment, p. 338

Graphing Calculator and Spreadsheet Masters, p. 29
Parent and Student Study Guide Workbook, p. 51
School-to-Career Masters, p. 12

 **Transparencies**
5-Minute Check Transparency 6-8
Real-World Transparency 6
Answer Key Transparencies

Technology
Interactive Chalkboard

When an amount increases, as in Example 1, the percent of change is a **percent of increase**.

Example 2 Find Percent of Increase

FUEL In 1975, the average price per gallon of gasoline was $0.57. In 2000, the average price per gallon was $1.47. Find the percent of change.

Source: *The World Almanac*

Step 1 Subtract to find the amount of change.

$$1.47 - 0.57 = 0.9 \quad \text{new price} - \text{original price}$$

Step 2 Write a ratio that compares the amount of change to the original price. Express the ratio as a percent.

$$\text{percent of change} = \frac{\text{amount of change}}{\text{original price}}$$

$$= \frac{0.9}{0.57} \qquad \text{Substitution.}$$

$$\approx 1.58 \text{ or } 158\% \quad \text{Write the decimal as a percent.}$$

The percent of change is about 158%. In this case, the percent of change is a percent of increase.

Standardized Test Practice
(A) (B) (C) (D)

Example 3 Find Percent of Increase

Multiple-Choice Test Item

Refer to the table shown. Which county had the greatest percent of increase in population from 1990 to 2000?

(A) Breckinridge (B) Bracken
(C) Calloway (D) Fulton

County	1990	2000
Breckinridge	16,312	18,648
Bracken	7766	8279
Calloway	30,735	34,177
Fulton	8271	7752

Read the Test Item

Percent of increase tells how much the population has increased in relation to 1990.

Solve the Test Item

Use a ratio to find each percent of increase. Then compare the percents.

- **Breckinridge**

  $$\frac{18,648 - 16,312}{16,312} = \frac{2336}{16,312}$$
  $$\approx 0.1432 \text{ or } 14.3\%$$

- **Bracken**

  $$\frac{8279 - 7766}{7766} = \frac{513}{7766}$$
  $$\approx 0.0661 \text{ or } 6.6\%$$

- **Calloway**

  $$\frac{34,177 - 30,735}{30,735} = \frac{3442}{30,735}$$
  $$\approx 0.112 \text{ or } 11.2\%$$

- **Fulton**

  Eliminate this choice because the population decreased.

Breckinridge County had the greatest percent of increase in population from 1990 to 2000. The answer is A.

Test-Taking Tip
If you are unsure of the correct answer, eliminate the choices you know are incorrect. Then consider the remaining choices.

DAILY
INTERVENTION

Differentiated Instruction

- **Kinesthetic** Provide students with one-inch grid paper. Have them cut out a rectangle with a maximum area of 20 square inches. Then have students cut out a larger rectangle. Have them count the squares in each rectangle and find the percent of increase in size.

FIND PERCENT OF INCREASE

In-Class Examples Power Point®

Teaching Tip Have students work several problems using both methods to assure that they understand both before they choose which they prefer.

1 Find the percent of change from 325 to 390.   **20%**

Teaching Tip Have students identify the original amount before computing.

2 **TUITION** In 1965, when John entered college, the tuition per year was $7500. In 2000, when his daughter went to the same school, the tuition was $25,500. Find the percent of change.   **240%**

3 **Multiple-Choice Test Item** In Example 3, which county had the least percent of increase in population from 1990 to 2000?   **B**

A Breckinridge   B Bracken
C Calloway   D Fulton

PERCENT OF DECREASE

In-Class Example Power Point®

4 **CLOTHING** A $110 sweater is on sale for $88. What is the percent of change?   **−20%**

Standardized Test Practice
(A) (B) (C) (D)

Example 3 Point out to students that Fulton can be eliminated immediately, since its population decreased rather than increased. The other choices can be quickly determined by rounding each of the numbers to the nearest thousand before computing. Any two that come too close to determine can then be calculated accurately.

Study Notebook

Have students—
- add the definitions/examples of the vocabulary terms to their Vocabulary Builder worksheets for Chapter 6.
- choose which solving method they prefer and explain why they prefer it.
- include any other item(s) that they find helpful in mastering the skills in this lesson.

About the Exercises . . .

Organization by Objective
- **Percent of Increase:** 10–11, 16–17, 19, 20, 23
- **Percent of Decrease:** 12–15, 18, 21, 22

Odd/Even Assignments
Exercises 9–25 are structured so that students practice the same concepts whether they are assigned odd or even problems.

Alert! Exercise 26 involves research on the Internet or other reference materials.

Assignment Guide

Basic: 11–19 odd, 24–42
Average: 11–23 odd, 24–42
Advanced: 10–22 even, 24–37 (Optional: 38–42)
All: Practice Quiz 2 (1–5)

Answers

1. If the amount increases, it is a percent of increase. If the amount decreases, it is a percent of decrease.

2. Sample answer: a temperature change from 65°F to 50°F.

3. Mark is correct because he divided the difference of the new amount and the original amount by the original amount.

More About. . .

Stock Market •·········
About 20 years ago, only 12.2% of Americans had money invested in the stock market. Today, more than 44% of Americans invest in the stock market.
Source: www.infoplease.com

PERCENT OF DECREASE When the amount decreases, the percent of change is negative. You can state a negative percent of change as a **percent of decrease**.

Example 4 *Find Percent of Decrease*

STOCK MARKET One of the largest stock market drops on Wall Street occurred on October 19, 1987. On this day, the stock market opened at 2246.74 points and closed at 1738.42 points. What was the percent of change?

Step 1 Subtract to find the amount of change.

$$1738.42 - 2246.74 = -508.32 \quad \text{closing points} - \text{opening points}$$

Step 2 Compare the amount of change to the opening points.

$$\text{percent of change} = \frac{\text{amount of change}}{\text{opening points}}$$

$$= \frac{-508.32}{2246.74} \quad \text{Substitution.}$$

$$\approx -0.226 \text{ or } -22.6\% \quad \text{Write the decimal as a percent.}$$

The percent of change is −22.6%. In this case, the percent of change is a percent of decrease.

Check for Understanding

Concept Check

1. **Explain** how you know whether a percent of change is a percent of increase or a percent of decrease. **1–2. See margin.**

2. **OPEN ENDED** Give an example of a percent of decrease.

3. **FIND THE ERROR** Scott and Mark are finding the percent of change when a shirt that costs $15 is on sale for $10.

Scott	Mark
$\frac{10-15}{10} = \frac{-5}{10}$ or −50%	$\frac{10-15}{15} = \frac{-5}{15}$ or $-33\frac{1}{3}\%$

Who is correct? Explain your reasoning. **See margin.**

Guided Practice

Find the percent of change. Round to the nearest tenth, if necessary. Then state whether the percent of change is a *percent of increase* or a *percent of decrease*.

GUIDED PRACTICE KEY	
Exercises	Examples
4–8	1, 2, 4
9	3

4. from $50 to $67 **34%; I**

5. from 45 in. to 18 in. **−60%; D**

6. from 80 cm to 55 cm **−31.3%; D**

7. from $228 to $251 **10.1%; I**

8. **ANIMALS** In 2000, there were 356 endangered species in the U.S. One year later, 367 species were considered endangered. What was the percent of change? **3.1%**

Standardized Test Practice

9. Refer to Example 3 on page 305. Suppose in 10 years, the population of Calloway is 36,851. What will be the percent of change from 1990? **A**

Ⓐ 19.9% Ⓑ 9.8% Ⓒ 10.7% Ⓓ 15.3%

DAILY
INTERVENTION

Unlocking Misconceptions

- **Percent Change** Watch for students who systematically want to divide the greater number into the lesser number. Tell them to always first ask themselves what the original measurement was.

- **Undoing Increases** Students may think that a 20% decrease will "undo" a 20% increase. Have them find a 20% increase of $100. **$120** Then show them that from $120 to $100 is not a 20% change. **The change is about −16.7%.**

Practice and Apply

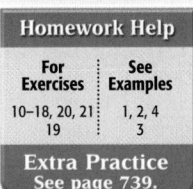

Homework Help

For Exercises	See Examples
10–18, 20, 21	1, 2, 4
19	3

Extra Practice
See page 739.

Find the percent of change. Round to the nearest tenth, if necessary. Then state whether the percent of change is a *percent of increase* or a *percent of decrease*.

10. from 25 cm to 36 cm **44%; I**

11. from $10 to $27 **170%; I**

12. from 68 min to 51 min **−25%; D**

13. from 50 lb to 44 lb **−12%; D**

14. from $135 to $120 **−11.1%; D**

15. from 257 m to 243 m **−5.4%; D**

16. from 365 ft to 421 ft **15.3%; I**

17. from $289 to $762 **164%; I**

18. **WEATHER** Seattle, Washington, receives an average of 6.0 inches of precipitation in December. In March, the average precipitation is 3.8 inches. What is the percent of change in precipitation from December to March? **−36.7%**

19. **POPULATION** In 1990, the population of Alabama was 4,040,587. In 2000, the population was 4,447,100. Find the percent of change from 1990 to 2000. **10.1%**

★ 20. Suppose 36 videos are added to a video collection that has 24 videos. What is the percent of change? **150%**

★ 21. A biology class has 28 students. Four of the students transferred out of the class to take chemistry. Find the percent of change in the number of students in the biology class. **−14.3%**

★ 22. **BUSINESS** A restaurant manager wants to reduce spending on supplies 10% in January and an additional 15% in February. In January, the expenses were $2875. How much should the expenses be at the end of February? **$2199.38**

★ 23. **SCHOOL** Jiliana is using a copy machine to increase the size of a 2-inch by 3-inch picture of a spider. The enlarged picture needs to measure 3 inches by 4.5 inches. **150%**

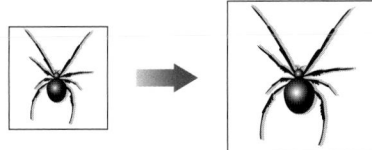

What enlargement setting on the copy machine should she use?

24. **CRITICAL THINKING** Explain why a 10% increase followed by a 10% decrease is less than the original amount if the original amount was positive. **See margin.**

25. **WRITING IN MATH** Answer the question that was posed at the beginning of the lesson. **See margin.**

   How can percents help to describe a change in area?

   Include the following in your answer:

   • an explanation describing how you can tell whether the percent of increase will be greater than 100%, and

   • an example of a model that shows an increase less than 100% and one that shows an increase greater than 100%.

Lesson 6-8 Percent of Change **307**

Answer

24. Suppose *x* represents the original amount. After the increase, it is 1.1*x*. After the decrease, it is 0.9(1.1*x*) or 0.99*x*. Since when *x* is positive, 0.99*x* < *x*, the final amount is less than the original.

25. See p. 308.

Lesson 6-8 Percent of Change **307**

Open-Ended Assessment

Modeling Have students bring to class advertisements from newspapers or magazines that show reduced prices for items. Post some of the ads and have students figure out the percent of change for the prices of the items. Discuss the steps involved, and post the percent changes with the ads.

Getting Ready for Lesson 6-9

PREREQUISITE SKILL In Lesson 6-9, students will use what they have learned about percents and ratios to solve probability problems. Exercises 38–42 should be used to determine your students' familiarity with writing fractions as percents.

Assessment Options

Practice Quiz 2 The quiz provides students with a brief review of the concepts and skills in Lessons 6-6 through 6-8. Lesson numbers are given to the right of exercises or instruction lines so students can review concepts not yet mastered.

Answer (p. 307)

25. The amount by which a rectangle is increased or decreased can be represented by a percent. Answers should include the following.
   - If the size of the new rectangle is greater than the size of the original rectangle, the percent of increase is greater than 100%.

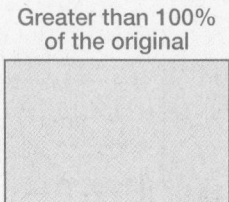

Original Rectangle

Greater than 100% of the original

Less than 100% of the original

---

26. **RESEARCH** Use the Internet or another source to find the population of your town now and ten years ago. What is the percent of change? **See students' work.**

Standardized Test Practice Ⓐ Ⓑ Ⓒ Ⓓ

For Exercises 27 and 28, refer to the information in the table.

27. What percent represents the percent of change in the number of beagles from 1998 to 1999? **D**

   Ⓐ −8.1%   Ⓑ −7.5%

   Ⓒ −9.7%   Ⓓ −8.0%

Kennel Club Registrations		
Breed	**1998**	**1999**
Labrador Retriever	157,936	157,897
Beagle	53,322	49,080
Maltese	18,013	16,358
Golden Retriever	65,681	62,652
Shih Tzu	38,468	34,576
Cocker Spaniel	34,632	29,958
Siberian Husky	21,078	18,106

28. Which breed had the largest percent of decrease? **A**

   Ⓐ Siberian Husky   Ⓑ Cocker Spaniel

   Ⓒ Golden Retriever   Ⓓ Labrador Retriever

Maintain Your Skills

Mixed Review

29. Find the discount to the nearest cent for a television that costs $999 and is on sale at 15% off. *(Lesson 6-7)* **$149.85**

30. Find the interest on $1590 that is invested at 8% for 3 years. Round to the nearest cent. *(Lesson 6-7)* **$381.60**

31. A calendar is on sale at a 10% discount. What is the sale price if it normally sells for $14.95? *(Lesson 6-7)* **$13.46**

Estimate. Explain which method you used to estimate. *(Lesson 6-6)*

32–34. Sample answers are given. See pp. 323A–323B for explanations.

32. 60% of 134 **81**   33. 88% of 72 **63**   34. 123% of 32 **36**

Identify all of the sets to which each number belongs. *(Lesson 5-2)*

35. −8 **integer, rational**   36. $1\frac{1}{4}$ **rational**   37. −5.63 **rational**

Getting Ready for the Next Lesson

PREREQUISITE SKILL Write each fraction as a percent.
(To review writing fractions as percents, see Lesson 6-4.)

38. $\frac{3}{4}$ **75%**   39. $\frac{1}{5}$ **20%**   40. $\frac{2}{3}$ **$66\frac{2}{3}$%**   41. $\frac{5}{6}$ **$83\frac{1}{3}$%**   42. $\frac{3}{8}$ **$37\frac{1}{2}$%**

Practice Quiz 2   Lessons 6-6 through 6-8

Estimate. Explain which method you used to estimate. *(Lesson 6-6)*

1. 42% of 68   2. $66\frac{2}{3}$% of 34 **1–2. See margin.**

3. Find the discount to the nearest cent on a backpack that costs $58 and is on sale at 25% off. *(Lesson 6-7)* **$14.50**

4. Find the interest to the nearest cent on $2500 that is invested at 4% for 2.5 years. *(Lesson 6-7)* **$250**

5. Find the percent of change from $0.95 to $2.45. *(Lesson 6-8)* **158%**

Answers (Practice Quiz 2)

For Exercises 1 and 2, sample answers are given.

1. 28; fraction method: $\frac{2}{5} \times 70$ or 28

2. 22; fraction method: $\frac{2}{3} \times 33$ or 22

Algebra Activity

A Preview of Lesson 6-9

Taking a Survey

The graph shows the results of a survey about what types of stores people in the United States shop at the most. Since it would be impossible to survey everyone in the country, a sample was used. A **sample** is a subgroup or subset of the population.

It is important to obtain a sample that is unbiased. An **unbiased** sample is a sample that is:

- representative of the larger population,
- selected at **random** or without preference, and
- large enough to provide accurate data.

WHERE WE SHOP MOST

- 62.4% Discount stores
- 15.6% National chains
- 22.0% Conventional stores

Source: International Mass Retail Association

To insure an unbiased sample, the following sampling methods may be used.

- **Random**   The sample is selected at random.
- **Systematic**   The sample is selected by using every nth member of the population.
- **Stratified**   The sample is selected by dividing the population into groups.

Model and Analyze 1–6. See pp. 323A–323B.

Tell whether or not each of the following is a random sample. Then provide an explanation describing the strengths and weaknesses of each sample.

Type of Survey	Location of Survey
1. travel preference	mall
2. time spent reading	library
3. favorite football player	Miami Dolphins football game

4. Brad conducted a survey to find out which food people in his community prefer. He surveyed every second person that walked into a certain fast-food restaurant. Identify this type of sampling. Explain how the survey may be biased.

5. Suppose a study shows that teenagers who eat breakfast each day earn higher grades than teenagers who skip breakfast. Tell how you can use the stratified sampling technique to test this claim in your school.

6. Suppose you want to determine where students in your school shop the most.
   a. Formulate a hypothesis about where students shop the most.
   b. Design and conduct a survey using one of the sampling techniques described above.
   c. Organize and display the results of your survey in a chart or graph.
   d. Evaluate your hypothesis by drawing a conclusion based on the survey.

Algebra Activity Taking a Survey **309**

Resource Manager

📂 ***Teaching Pre-Algebra with Manipulatives***

- p. 94 (student recording sheet)

Algebra Activity

A Preview of Lesson 6-9

Getting Started

Objective Take a survey.

Teach

- Personalize this lesson by asking one student what he or she thinks is the favorite song of most students. Ask the class why they should or should not assume that person's choice is correct. Ask what a better sample would be.
- Discuss Exercises 1–3 with the class. Have students explain their answers and suggest alternative locations.
- Have students work in small groups to answer Exercises 4–6.

Assess

In **Exercises 1–5,** students should

- correctly identify an appropriate location for each type of survey.
- understand how surveys can be biased.
- describe an unbiased survey for a particular situation.

In **Exercise 6,** students conduct a survey from its hypothesis to its conclusion. Be sure students use an appropriate sampling technique and use it correctly.

Study Notebook

Have students start a journal page entitled Taking a Survey. They should copy the tables Criteria for an Unbiased Sample and Sampling Techniques. Ask them to summarize the survey they performed, including an evaluation of its strengths and weaknesses.

1 Focus

5-Minute Check Transparency 6-9 Use as a quiz or review of Lesson 6-8.

Mathematical Background notes are available for this lesson on page 262D.

How can probability help you make predictions?

The opening activity questions are repeated on page 342 of the *Chapter 6 Resource Masters*.

Reading to Learn Mathematics, p. 342 — ELL

Pre-Activity *How can probability help you make predictions?*

Do the activity at the top of page 310 in your textbook. Write your answers below.

a. Write the ratio that compares the number of tiles labeled E to the total number of tiles. $\frac{12}{100}$

b. What percent of the tiles are labeled E? 12%

c. What fraction of tiles is this? $\frac{3}{25}$

d. Suppose a player chooses a tile. Is there a better chance of choosing a D or an N? Explain. There is a better chance of choosing an N because there are more of them.

Reading the Lesson 1–6. See students' work.

Write a definition and give an example of each new vocabulary word or phrase.

Vocabulary	Definition	Example
1. outcomes		
2. simple event		
3. probability		
4. sample space		
5. theoretical probability		
6. experimental probability		

Helping You Remember

7. Look up *theoretical* and *experimental* in the dictionary. How can their definitions help you remember the difference between theoretical probability and experimental probability? Theoretical means based on theory or speculation; theoretical probability is what *should* occur. Experimental means based on experience or experiment; experimental probability is what *actually* occurs.

What You'll Learn

- Find the probability of simple events.
- Use a sample to predict the actions of a larger group.

Vocabulary

- outcomes
- simple event
- probability
- sample space
- theoretical probability
- experimental probability

How can probability help you make predictions?

A popular word game is played using 100 letter tiles. The object of the game is to use the tiles to spell words scoring as many points as possible. The table shows the distribution of the tiles.

Letter	Number of Tiles
E	12
A, I	9
O	8
N, R, T	6
D, L, S, U	4
G	3
B, C, F, H, M, P, V, W, Y, blank	2
J, K, Q, X, Z	1

a. Write the ratio that compares the number of tiles labeled E to the total number of tiles. $\frac{12}{100}$

b. What percent of the tiles are labeled E? **12%**

c. What fraction of tiles is this? $\frac{3}{25}$

d. Suppose a player chooses a tile. Is there a better chance of choosing a D or an N? Explain.

d. There is a better chance of choosing an N because there are more of them.

PROBABILITY OF SIMPLE EVENTS In the activity above, there are 27 possible tiles. These results are called **outcomes**. A **simple event** is one outcome or a collection of outcomes. For example, choosing a tile labeled E is a simple event.

You can measure the chances of an event happening with **probability**.

> **Study Tip**
>
> *Probability*
> Each of the outcomes must be equally likely to happen.

Key Concept — Probability

- **Words** The probability of an event is a ratio that compares the number of favorable outcomes to the number of possible outcomes.

- **Symbols** $P(\text{event}) = \dfrac{\text{number of favorable outcomes}}{\text{number of possible outcomes}}$

The probability of an event is always between 0 and 1, inclusive. The closer a probability is to 1, the more likely it is to occur.

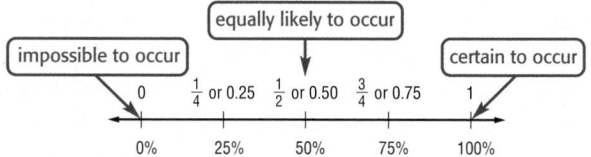

✓ Concept Check Suppose there is a 45% chance that an event occurs. How likely is it that the event will occur? **about equally likely**

310 Chapter 6 Ratio, Proportion, and Percent

Resource Manager

📂 Workbooks and Reproducible Masters

Chapter 6 Resource Masters
- Study Guide and Intervention, p. 339
- Skills Practice, p. 340
- Practice, p. 341
- Reading to Learn Mathematics, p. 342
- Enrichment, p. 343
- Assessment, p. 360

Parent and Student Study Guide Workbook, p. 52

🖥 Transparencies

5-Minute Check Transparency 6-9
Answer Key Transparencies

⚙ Technology

Interactive Chalkboard
Pre-AlgePASS: Tutorial Plus, Lesson 18
Multimedia Applications

Example 1 Find Probability

Suppose a number cube is rolled. What is the probability of rolling a prime number?

There are 3 prime numbers on a number cube: 2, 3, and 5.

There are 6 possible outcomes: 1, 2, 3, 4, 5, and 6.

$$P(\text{prime}) = \frac{\text{number of favorable outcomes}}{\text{number of possible outcomes}}$$

$$= \frac{3}{6} \text{ or } \frac{1}{2}$$

So, the probability of rolling a prime number is $\frac{1}{2}$ or 50%.

Reading Math

P(prime)

P(prime) is read as *the probability of rolling a prime number.*

The set of all possible outcomes is called the **sample space**. For Example 1, the sample space was {1, 2, 3, 4, 5, 6}. When you toss a coin, the sample space is {heads, tails}.

Example 2 Find Probability

Suppose two number cubes are rolled. Find the probability of rolling an even sum.

Make a table showing the sample space when rolling two number cubes.

	1	2	3	4	5	6
1	(1, 1)	(1, 2)	(1, 3)	(1, 4)	(1, 5)	(1, 6)
2	(2, 1)	(2, 2)	(2, 3)	(2, 4)	(2, 5)	(2, 6)
3	(3, 1)	(3, 2)	(3, 3)	(3, 4)	(3, 5)	(3, 6)
4	(4, 1)	(4, 2)	(4, 3)	(4, 4)	(4, 5)	(4, 6)
5	(5, 1)	(5, 2)	(5, 3)	(5, 4)	(5, 5)	(5, 6)
6	(6, 1)	(6, 2)	(6, 3)	(6, 4)	(6, 5)	(6, 6)

There are 18 outcomes in which the sum is even.

So, $P(\text{even sum}) = \frac{18}{36}$ or $\frac{1}{2}$.

This means there is a 50% chance of rolling an even sum.

The probabilities in Examples 1 and 2 are called theoretical probabilities. **Theoretical probability** is what *should* occur. **Experimental probability** is what *actually* occurs when conducting a probability experiment.

Example 3 Find Experimental Probability

The table shows the results of an experiment in which a coin was tossed. Find the experimental probability of tossing a coin and getting tails for this experiment.

Outcome	Tally	Frequency
Heads	JHT JHT IIII	14
Tails	JHT JHT I	11

$$\frac{\text{number of times tails occur}}{\text{number of possible outcomes}} = \frac{11}{14 + 11} \text{ or } \frac{11}{25}$$

The experimental probability of getting tails in this case is $\frac{11}{25}$ or 44%.

2 Teach

Building on Prior Knowledge

In Lesson 4-5, students learned how to simplify fractions. This is a necessary skill when solving problems of probability.

PROBABILITY OF SIMPLE EVENTS

In-Class Examples  Power Point®

1 Suppose a number cube is rolled. What is the probability of rolling a 4 or a 5? $\frac{1}{3}$ or $33\frac{1}{3}$%

2 Suppose two number cubes are rolled. Find the probability of rolling two identical numbers. $\frac{1}{6}$ or $16\frac{2}{3}$%

Teaching Tip Many students require help in organizing information in a table. Draw students' attention to how various tables are organized.

3 Use the table in Example 3 to determine the experimental probability of landing on heads for this experiment. $\frac{14}{25}$ or 56%

USE A SAMPLE TO MAKE PREDICTIONS

In-Class Example Power Point®

4 SPORTS Miss Newman surveyed her class to see which sports they preferred watching. 44% preferred football, 28% basketball, 20% soccer, and 8% tennis. Out of 560 students in the entire school, how many would you expect to say they preferred watching basketball? about 157 students

DAILY

| INTERVENTION | **Differentiated Instruction** | ELL |

- **Verbal/Linguistic** Have students work in small groups and look over Exercises 21 to 26 on page 313. Ask them to discuss how to find the opposite probabilities—*P*(not blue), *P*(not yellow), *P*(green), *P*(not purple), *P*(neither red nor blue), *P*(neither blue nor yellow). Ask them how they might find the opposite probability if they already know the probability. **Subtract it from 100%.**

Study Notebook

Have students—

• complete the definitions/examples for the remaining terms on the Vocabulary Builder worksheets for Chapter 6.

• copy Exercise 11 and write a paragraph explaining how to make the prediction.

• include any other item(s) that they find helpful in mastering the skills in this lesson.

About the Exercises . . .

Organization by Objective
• **Probability of Simple Events:** 12–36
• **Use a Sample to Make Predictions:** 35–37

Odd/Even Assignments
Exercises 12–36 are structured so that students practice the same concepts whether they are assigned odd or even problems.

Assignment Guide

Basic: 13–17 odd, 21–25 odd, 29–37 odd, 38–47

Average: 13–37 odd, 38–47

Advanced: 12–34 even, 35, 36, 38–47

Answers

2. Theoretical probability is what should occur. Experimental probability is what actually occurs.

3. Sample answer: Spinning the spinner as shown and having it land on 4.

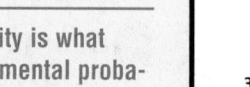

USE A SAMPLE TO MAKE PREDICTIONS You can use an athlete's past performance to predict whether she will get a hit or make a basket. You can also use the results of a survey to predict the actions of a larger group.

USA TODAY Education
Log on for:
• Updated data
• More activities on Making Predictions

www.pre-alg.com/usa_today

Example 4 *Make a Prediction*

FOOD The graph shows the results of a survey. Out of a group of 450 people, how many would you expect to say that they prefer thin mint cookies?

The total number of people is 450. So, 450 is the base. The percent is 26%.

To find 26% of 450, let b represent the base, 450, and let p represent the percent, 26%, in the percent proportion. Let a represent the part.

$$\text{part} \rightarrow \frac{a}{450} = \frac{26}{100} \leftarrow \text{percent}$$
$$\text{base} \rightarrow$$

$$100 \cdot a = 26 \cdot 450$$
$$100a = 11700 \qquad \text{Simplify.}$$
$$a = 117 \qquad \text{Mentally divide each side by 100.}$$

You can expect 117 people to say that they prefer thin mint cookies.

USA TODAY Snapshots®

Monster cookies
Girl Scout cookie sales are an annual tradition from January to March in most of the USA. Last year's best-selling cookies in sales share:

26% Thin Mints
19% Samoas/ Caramel deLites[1]
13% Tagalongs/ Peanut Butter
12% Do-Si-Dos/ Peanut Butter Sandwich[1]
11% Trefoils/ Short-bread

1 – Same cookie with different name depending on baker
Source: Girl Scouts of the U.S.A.
By Anne R. Carey and Quin Tian, USA TODAY

Check for Understanding

Concept Check
1. **Tell** what a probability of 0 means. **The event will not happen.**

2. **Compare and contrast** theoretical and experimental probability.

3. **OPEN ENDED** Give an example of a situation in which the probability of the event is 25%. **2–3. See margin.**

Guided Practice

Ten cards are numbered 1 through 10, and one card is chosen at random. Determine the probability of each outcome. Express each probability as a fraction and as a percent. **4–7. See pp. 323A–323B.**

4. $P(5)$
5. $P(\text{odd})$
6. $P(\text{less than 3})$
7. $P(\text{greater than 6})$

GUIDED PRACTICE KEY

Exercises	Examples
4–7	1
8, 9	2
10	3
11	4

8–9. See pp. 323A–323B.

For Exercises 8 and 9, refer to the table in Example 2 on page 311. Determine each probability. Express each probability as a fraction and as a percent.

8. $P(\text{sum of 2 or 6})$
9. $P(\text{even or odd sum})$

10. Refer to Example 3 on page 311. Find the experimental probability of getting heads for the experiment. $\frac{14}{25}$ or 56%

Application
11. **FOOD** Maresha took a sample from a package of jellybeans and found that 30% of the beans were red. Suppose there are 250 jellybeans in the package. How many can she expect to be red? 75

Online Lesson Plans

USA TODAY Education

USA TODAY's Education Online site offers resources and interactive features connected to each day's newspaper. *Experience TODAY*, USA TODAY's daily lesson plan, is available on the site and delivered daily to subscribers. This plan provides instruction for integrating USA TODAY graphics and key editorial features into your mathematics classroom. Log on to **www.education.usatoday.com**

★ *indicates increased difficulty*

Practice and Apply

Homework Help

For Exercises	See Examples
12–34, 35, 36	1, 2
	3
37	4

Extra Practice
See page 739.

A spinner like the one shown is used in a game. Determine the probability of each outcome if the spinner is equally likely to land on each section. Express each probability as a fraction and as a percent. **12–28. See margin.**

12. $P(8)$

13. $P(\text{red})$

14. $P(\text{even})$

15. $P(\text{prime})$

16. $P(\text{greater than 5})$

17. $P(\text{less than 2})$

★ **18.** $P(\text{blue or 11})$

★ **19.** $P(\text{not yellow})$

20. $P(\text{not red})$

There are 2 red marbles, 4 blue marbles, 7 green marbles, and 5 yellow marbles in a bag. Suppose one marble is selected at random. Find the probability of each outcome. Express each probability as a fraction and as a percent.

21. $P(\text{blue})$

22. $P(\text{yellow})$

23. $P(\text{not green})$

24. $P(\text{purple})$

25. $P(\text{red or blue})$

26. $P(\text{blue or yellow})$

★ **27.** $P(\text{not orange})$

★ **28.** $P(\text{not blue or not red})$

29. What is the probability that a calendar is randomly turned to the month of January or April? $\frac{1}{6}$

30. Find the probability that today is November 31. **0**

Suppose two spinners like the ones shown are spun. Find the probability of each outcome. (*Hint*: Make a table to show the sample space as in Example 2 on page 311.)

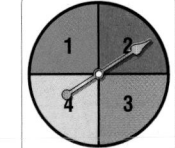 

31. $P(2, 7)$ $\frac{1}{16}$

32. $P(\text{even, even})$ $\frac{1}{4}$

33. $P(\text{sum of 9})$ $\frac{1}{4}$

34. $P(2, \text{greater than 5})$ $\frac{3}{16}$

DRIVING For Exercises 35 and 36, use the following information and the table shown.
The table shows the approximate number of licensed automobile drivers in the United States in a certain year. An automobile company is conducting a telephone survey using a list of licensed drivers.

Age	Drivers (millions)
19 and under	9
20–29	34
30–39	41
40–49	37
50–59	24
60–69	18
70 and over	17
Total	**180**

Source: U.S. Department of Transportation

35. Find the probability that a driver will be 19 years old or younger. Express the answer as a decimal rounded to the nearest hundredth and as a percent. **0.05; 5%**

36. What is the probability that a randomly chosen driver will be 40–49 years old? Write the answer as a decimal rounded to the nearest hundredth and as a percent. **0.21; 21%**

www.pre-alg.com/self_check_quiz

Lesson 6-9 Probability and Predictions **313**

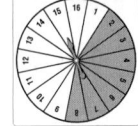
Lesson 6-9 Probability and Predictions **313**

Answers

12. $\frac{1}{8}$; $12\frac{1}{2}\%$

13. $\frac{1}{4}$; 25%

14. $\frac{1}{2}$; 50%

15. $\frac{1}{2}$; 50%

16. $\frac{5}{8}$; $62\frac{1}{2}\%$

17. 0; 0%

18. $\frac{1}{2}$; 50%

19. $\frac{7}{8}$; 87.5%

20. $\frac{3}{4}$; 75%

21. $\frac{2}{9}$; 22.2%

22. $\frac{5}{18}$; 27.8%

23. $\frac{11}{18}$; 61.1%

24. 0; 0%

25. $\frac{1}{3}$; $33\frac{1}{3}\%$

26. $\frac{1}{2}$; 50%

27. 1; 100%

28. $\frac{2}{3}$; $66\frac{2}{3}\%$

Lesson 6-9 Probability and Predictions **313**

Open-Ended Assessment

Speaking Have students explain what each of the following phrases means.

a. 0% chance of rain

b. 50% chance of rain

c. 100% chance of rain

d. 25% chance of guessing a correct answer

e. 80% of guessing incorrectly

Assessment Options

Quiz (Lessons 6-8 and 6-9) is available on p. 360 of the *Chapter 6 Resource Masters.*

Answers

38. No; many of the common two-letter words like *at*, *in*, *of*, and *on* do not contain the letter E.

39. Once the probability or likeliness of something happening is known, then you can use the probability to make a prediction. For example, in football, if you know the number of field goals a player has made in the past, you can use the information to predict the number of field goals he/she will make in upcoming games. Answers should include the following.

- E: $\frac{12}{100}$ or 12%; A, I: $\frac{9}{100}$ or 9%; O: $\frac{8}{100}$ or 8%; N, R, T: $\frac{6}{100}$ or 6%; D, L, S, U: $\frac{4}{100}$ or 4%; G: $\frac{3}{100}$ or 3%; B, C, F, H, M, P, V, W, Y, blank: $\frac{2}{100}$ or 2%; J, K, Q, X, Z: $\frac{1}{100}$ or 1%

- See students' work.

---

37. **FOOD** Refer to the graph. Out of 1200 people, how many would you expect to say they crave chocolate after dinner? **444**

38. See margin.

38. **CRITICAL THINKING** In the English language, 13% of the letters used are E's. Suppose you are guessing the letters in a two-letter word of a puzzle. Would you guess an E? Explain.

39.  **WRITING IN MATH** Answer the question that was posed at the beginning of the lesson.

How can probability help you make predictions?

Include the following in your answer: **See margin.**

- an explanation telling the probability of choosing each letter tile, and
- an example of how you can use probability to make predictions.

USA TODAY Snapshots®

Chocolate cravings
Time of day that adults say they crave chocolate:

Midafternoon **47%**
Evening **42%**
After dinner **37%**
Lunch **21%**
Before bed **18%**
Midmorning **17%**
Middle of the night **10%**
Breakfast **9%**

Source: Yankelovich Partners for the American Boxed Chocolate Manufacturers

By Cindy Hall and Alejandro Gonzalez, USA TODAY

Standardized Test Practice
Ⓐ Ⓑ Ⓒ Ⓓ

40. What is the probability of spinning an even number on the spinner shown? **D**

   Ⓐ $\frac{1}{2}$ Ⓑ $\frac{1}{4}$ Ⓒ $\frac{2}{3}$ Ⓓ $\frac{3}{4}$

 **Maintain Your Skills**

Mixed Review

41. Find the percent of change from 32 feet to 79 feet. Round to the nearest tenth, if necessary. Then state whether the percent of change is a *percent of increase* or a *percent of decrease*. *(Lesson 6-8)* **146.9%; I**

Solve each problem using an equation. Round to the nearest tenth.
(Lesson 6-7)

42. 7 is what percent of 32? **21.9%**   43. What is 28.5% of 84? **23.9**

ALGEBRA Find each product or quotient. Express your answer in exponential form. *(Lesson 4-6)*

44. $7^2 \cdot 7^3$ **7^5**   45. $x^4 \cdot 2x$ **$2x^5$**   46. $\frac{8^{12}}{8^8}$ **8^4**   47. $\frac{36n^4}{14n^2}$ **$\frac{18n^2}{7}$**

WebQuest Internet Project

Kids Gobbling Empty Calories
It is time to complete your project. Use the information and data you have gathered to prepare a brochure or Web page about the nutritional value of fast-food meals. Include the total Calories, grams of fat, and amount of sodium for five meals that a typical student would order from at least three fast-food restaurants.

www.pre-alg.com/webquest

Graphing Calculator Investigation

A Follow-Up of Lesson 6-9

Probability Simulation

A random number generator can simulate a probability experiment. From the simulation, you can calculate experimental probabilities. Repeating a simulation may result in different probabilities since the numbers generated are different each time.

Example **Generate 30 random numbers from 1 to 6, simulating 30 rolls of a number cube.**

- Access the random number generator.
- Enter 1 as a lower bound and 6 as an upper bound for 30 trials.

KEYSTROKES: [MATH] [◄] 5 1 [,] 6 [,] 30 [)] [ENTER]

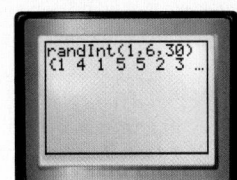

A set of 30 numbers ranging from 1 to 6 appears. Use the right arrow key to see the next number in the set. Record all 30 numbers, as a column, on a separate sheet of paper.

Exercises 1–4. See margin.

1. Record how often each number on the number cube appeared.

   a. Find the experimental probability of each number.

   b. Compare the experimental probabilities with the theoretical probabilities.

2. Repeat the simulation of rolling a number cube 30 times. Record this second set of numbers in a column next to the first set of numbers. Each pair of 30 numbers represents a roll of two number cubes. Find the sum for each of the 30 pairs of rolls.

   a. Find the experimental probability of each sum.

   b. Compare the experimental probability with the theoretical probabilities.

3. Design an experiment to simulate 30 spins of a spinner that has equal sections colored red, white, and blue.

   a. Find the experimental probability of each color.

   b. Compare the experimental probabilities with the theoretical probabilities.

4. Suppose you play a game where there are three containers, each with ten balls numbered 0 to 9. Pick three numbers and then use the random number generator to simulate the game. Score 2 points if one number matches, 16 points if two numbers match, and 32 points if all three numbers match. Note: numbers can appear more than once.

   a. Play the game if the order of your numbers *does not* matter. Total your score for 10 simulations.

   b. Now play the game if the order of the numbers *does* matter. Total your score for 10 simulations.

   c. With which game rules did you score more points?

www.pre-alg.com/other_calculator_keystrokes **Graphing Calculator Investigation** Probability Simulation **315**

A Follow-Up of Lesson 6-9

Getting Started

Know Your Calculator The graphing calculator has the capability of generating random numbers when given an upper limit, a lower limit, and the quantity of numbers to generate.

Teaching Tip To clarify Exercises 4a and 4b, point out to students that in 4a, if you choose the numbers 446 and the simulation shows 564, you score 16 points for picking one 4 and one 6. In 4b, where order does matter, 446 and 564 would be a score of 0 points.

Teach

- Have students duplicate the keystrokes given in the example.
- If students need to review entering numbers in a list, see page 45.

Assess

- Ask students how the graphing calculator helps make simulating a probability an easier task.   **Many numbers can be quickly generated.**
- Ask students why different numbers are generated each time.   **Because the numbers are generated randomly.**

Answers

1–2. See students' answers.

3–4. To use the random number generator, let red = 1, let white = 2, and let blue = 3. See students' answers.

Chapter 6 — Study Guide and Review

Vocabulary and Concept Check

Vocabulary and Concept Check

- This alphabetical list of vocabulary terms in Chapter 6 includes a page reference where each term was introduced.
- **Assessment** A vocabulary review/test for Chapter 6 is available on p. 358 of the *Chapter 6 Resource Masters*

Lesson-by-Lesson Review

For each lesson,
- the main ideas are summarized,
- additional examples review concepts, and
- practice exercises are provided.

Vocabulary PuzzleMaker

ELL The Vocabulary PuzzleMaker software improves students' mathematics vocabulary using four puzzle formats—crossword, scramble, word search using a word list, and word search using clues. Students can work on a computer screen or from a printed handout.

MindJogger Videoquizzes

ELL MindJogger Videoquizzes provide an alternative review of concepts presented in this chapter. Students work in teams in a game show format to gain points for correct answers. The questions are presented in three rounds.

Round 1 Concepts (5 questions)
Round 2 Skills (4 questions)
Round 3 Problem Solving (4 questions)

---

base (p. 288)	percent of decrease (p. 306)	scale (p. 276)
compound interest (p. 303)	percent of increase (p. 305)	scale drawing (p. 276)
cross products (p. 270)	percent proportion (p. 288)	scale factor (p. 277)
discount (p. 299)	probability (p. 310)	scale model (p. 276)
experimental probability (p. 311)	proportion (p. 270)	simple event (p. 310)
outcome (p. 310)	random (p. 309)	simple interest (p. 300)
part (p. 288)	rate (p. 265)	theoretical probability (p. 311)
percent (p. 281)	ratio (p. 264)	unbiased (p. 309)
percent equation (p. 298)	sample (p. 309)	unit rate (p. 265)
percent of change (p. 304)	sample space (p. 311)	

Complete each sentence with the correct term.

1. A statement of equality of two ratios is called a(n) ___proportion___.
2. A(n) ___percent___ is a ratio that compares a number to 100.
3. The ratio of a length on a scale drawing to the corresponding length on the real object is called the ___scale factor___.
4. The set of all possible outcomes is the ___sample space___.
5. _____ is what actually occurs when conducting a probability experiment. **Experimental probability**

Lesson-by-Lesson Review

6-1 Ratios and Rates

See pages 264–268.

Concept Summary
- A ratio is a comparison of two numbers by division.
- A rate is a ratio of two measurements having different units of measure.
- A rate that is simplified so that it has a denominator of 1 is called a unit rate.

Example Express the ratio *2 meters to 35 centimeters* as a fraction in simplest form.

$$\frac{2 \text{ meters}}{35 \text{ centimeters}} = \frac{200 \text{ centimeters}}{35 \text{ centimeters}}$$ Convert 2 meters to centimeters.

$$= \frac{40 \text{ centimeters}}{7 \text{ centimeters}} \text{ or } \frac{40}{7}$$ Divide the numerator and denominator by the GCF, 5.

Exercises Express each ratio as a fraction in simplest form.
See Examples 1 and 2 on pages 264 and 265.

6. 9 students out of 33 students $\frac{3}{11}$
7. 12 hits out of 16 times at bat $\frac{3}{4}$
8. 30 hours to 18 hours $\frac{5}{3}$
9. 5 quarts to 5 gallons $\frac{1}{4}$
10. 10 inches to 4 feet $\frac{5}{24}$
11. 2 tons to 1800 pounds $\frac{20}{9}$

 www.pre-alg.com/vocabulary_review

Study Organizer

For more information about Foldables, see *Teaching Mathematics with Foldables.*

Have students reexamine their Foldables to make sure all their equivalents are correct. Have them refer to their Foldables if needed when working through the Study Guide and Review or preparing for the Chapter Test.

6-2 Using Proportions

See pages 270–274.

Concept Summary

- A proportion is an equation stating two ratios are equal.
- If $\frac{a}{b} = \frac{c}{d}$, then $ad = bc$.

Example Solve $\frac{3}{7} = \frac{15}{x}$.

$$\frac{3}{7} = \frac{15}{x} \qquad \text{Write the proportion.}$$

$$3 \cdot x = 7 \cdot 15 \qquad \text{Cross products}$$

$$3x = 105 \qquad \text{Multiply.}$$

$$\frac{3x}{3} = \frac{105}{3} \qquad \text{Divide each side by 3.}$$

$$x = 35 \qquad \text{The solution is 35.}$$

Exercises Solve each proportion. *See Example 2 on page 271.*

12. $\frac{n}{12} = \frac{4}{3}$ **16**   13. $\frac{21}{x} = \frac{84}{120}$ **30**   14. $\frac{9}{7} = \frac{22.5}{y}$ **17.5**   15. $\frac{5}{7.5} = \frac{0.6}{k}$ **0.9**

6-3 Scale Drawings and Models

See pages 276–280.

Concept Summary

- A scale drawing or a scale model represents an object that is too large or too small to be drawn or built at actual size.
- The ratio of a length on a scale drawing or model to the corresponding length on the real object is called the scale factor.

Example A scale drawing shows a pond that is 1.75 inches long. The scale on the drawing is 0.25 inch = 1 foot. What is the length of the actual pond?

$$\begin{array}{l} \text{drawing length} \rightarrow \\ \text{actual length} \rightarrow \end{array} \quad \frac{0.25 \text{ in.}}{1 \text{ ft}} = \frac{1.75 \text{ in.}}{x \text{ ft}} \quad \begin{array}{l} \leftarrow \text{drawing length} \\ \leftarrow \text{actual length} \end{array}$$

$$0.25 \cdot x = 1 \cdot 1.75 \quad \text{Find the cross products.}$$

$$0.25x = 1.75 \quad \text{Simplify.}$$

$$x = 7 \quad \text{Divide each side by 0.25.}$$

The actual length of the pond is 7 feet.

Exercises On the model of a ship, the scale is 1 inch = 12 feet. Find the actual length of each room. *See Example 1 on page 277.*

	Room	Model Length	
16.	Stateroom	0.9 in.	10.8 ft
17.	Galley	3.8 in.	45.6 ft
18.	Gym	6.0 in.	72 ft

6-4 Fractions, Decimals, and Percents

See pages 281–285.

Concept Summary

- A percent is a ratio that compares a number to 100.
- Fractions, decimals, and percents are all different ways to represent the same number.

Examples

1 Express 60% as a fraction in simplest form and as a decimal.

$$60\% = \frac{60}{100} \text{ or } \frac{3}{5} \qquad 60\% = \underset{\sim}{.60}\% \text{ or } 0.6$$

2 Express 0.38 as a percent.

0.38 = 0.38 or 38%

3 Express $\frac{5}{8}$ as a percent.

$$\frac{5}{8} = 0.625 \text{ or } 62.5\%$$

Exercises   Express each percent as a fraction or mixed number in simplest form and as a decimal.   *See Examples 1 and 3 on pages 281 and 282.*

19. 35% $\frac{7}{20}$; 0.35   **20.** 42% $\frac{21}{50}$; 0.42   **21.** 8% $\frac{2}{25}$; 0.08   **22.** 19% $\frac{19}{100}$; 0.19

23. 120% $1\frac{1}{5}$; 1.2   **24.** 250% $2\frac{1}{2}$; 2.5   **25.** 62.5% $\frac{5}{8}$; 0.625   **26.** 8.8% $\frac{11}{125}$; 0.088

Express each decimal or fraction as a percent. Round to the nearest tenth percent, if necessary.   *See Examples 2, 4, and 5 on pages 282 and 283.*

27. 0.24 24%   **28.** 0.03 3%   **29.** 0.452 45.2%   **30.** 1.9 190%

31. $\frac{2}{5}$ 40%   **32.** $\frac{13}{22}$ 59.1%   **33.** $\frac{6}{80}$ 7.5%   **34.** $\frac{77}{225}$ 34.2%

6-5 Using the Percent Proportion

See pages 288–292.

Concept Summary

- If a is the part, b is the base, and p is the percent, then $\frac{a}{b} = \frac{p}{100}$.

Example   Forty-eight is 32% of what number?

$$\frac{a}{b} = \frac{p}{100} \rightarrow \frac{48}{b} = \frac{32}{100} \qquad \text{Replace } a \text{ with 48 and } p \text{ with 32.}$$

$$48 \cdot 100 = b \cdot 32 \qquad \text{Find the cross products.}$$

$$4800 = 32b \qquad \text{Simplify.}$$

$$150 = b \qquad \text{Divide each side by 32.}$$

So, 48 is 32% of 150.

Exercises   Use the percent proportion to solve each problem.
See Examples 1–6 on pages 288–290.

35. 18 is what percent of 45? 40%   **36.** What percent of 60 is 39? 65%

37. 23 is 92% of what number? 25   **38.** What is 74% of 110? 81.4

39. What is 80% of 62.5? 50   **40.** 36 is 15% of what number? 240

6-6 Finding Percents Mentally

See pages 293–297.

Concept Summary

- When working with common percents like 10%, 20%, 25%, and 50%, it is helpful to use the fraction form of the percent.

Examples

1 Find 20% of $45 mentally.

20% of 45 = $\frac{1}{5}$ of 45   Think: 20% = $\frac{1}{5}$.

   = 9   Think: $\frac{1}{5}$ of 45 is 9.

So, 20% of $45 is $9.

2 Estimate 32% of 150.

32% is about $33\frac{1}{3}$% or $\frac{1}{3}$.

$\frac{1}{3}$ of 150 is 50.

So, 32% of 150 is about 50.

Exercises Find the percent of each number mentally.
See Example 1 on pages 293 and 294.

41. 50% of 86 **43**

42. 20% of 55 **11**

43. 25% of 36 **9**

44. 40% of 75 **30**

45. $33\frac{1}{3}$% of 24 **8**

46. 90% of 60 **54**

Estimate. Explain which method you used to estimate.
See Example 2 on pages 294 and 295. **47–52. See margin.**

47. 48% of 32

48. 67% of 30

49. 20% of 51

50. 25% of 27

51. $\frac{1}{3}$% of 304

52. 147% of 200

6-7 Using Percent Equations

See pages 298–302.

Concept Summary

- The percent equation is an equivalent form of the percent proportion in which the percent is written as a decimal.
- Part = Percent · Base, where percent is in decimal form.

Example

119 is 85% of what number?
The part is 119, and the percent is 85%. Let n represent the base.

$119 = 0.85n$ Write 85% as the decimal 0.85.

$\frac{119}{0.85} = \frac{0.85n}{0.85}$ Divide each side by 0.85.

$140 = n$ So, 119 is 85% of 140.

Exercises Solve each problem using the percent equation.
See Examples 1–3 on pages 298 and 299.

53. 24 is what percent of 50? **48%**

54. 70 is 40% of what number? **175**

55. What is 90% of 105? **94.5**

56. What is 12.5% of 68? **8.5**

57. 56 is 28% of what number? **200**

58. 35.7 is what percent of 17? **210%**

Answers

For Exercises 47–52, sample answers are given.

47. 16; fraction method: $\frac{1}{2} \times 32$ or 16

48. 20; fraction method: $\frac{2}{3} \times 30$ or 20

49. 10; fraction method: $\frac{1}{5} \times 50$ or 10

50. 7; fraction method: $\frac{1}{4} \times 28$ or 7

51. 1; 1% method: Since 1% of 304 is about 3, $\frac{1}{3}$% of 304 is about $\frac{1}{3}$ of 3 or 1.

52. 300; meaning of percent: 147% means about 150 for every 100. 200 has two 100. $150 \times 2 = 300$

6-8 Percent of Change

See pages 304–308.

Concept Summary

- A percent of increase tells how much an amount has increased in relation to the original amount. (The percent will be positive.)
- A percent of decrease tells how much an amount has decreased in relation to the original amount. (The percent will be negative.)

Example Find the percent of change from 36 pounds to 14 pounds.

$$\text{percent of change} = \frac{\text{new weight} - \text{original weight}}{\text{original weight}} \qquad \text{Write the ratio.}$$

$$= \frac{14 - 36}{36} \qquad \text{Substitution}$$

$$= \frac{-22}{36} \qquad \text{Subtraction}$$

$$\approx -0.611 \text{ or } -61.1\% \qquad \text{Simplify.}$$

The percent of decrease is about 61.1%.

Exercises Find the percent of change. Round to the nearest tenth, if necessary. Then state whether each change is a *percent of increase* or a *percent of decrease.* See Examples 1, 2, and 4 on pages 304–306.

59. from 40 ft to 12 ft D; −70%   **60.** from 80 cm to 96 cm I; 20%

61. from 29 min to 54 min I; 86.2%   **62.** from 80 lb to 77 lb D; −3.8%

6-9 Probability and Predictions

See pages 310–314.

Concept Summary

- The probability of an event is a ratio that compares the number of favorable outcomes to the number of possible outcomes.

Example Suppose a number cube is rolled. Find the probability of rolling a 5 or 6.

Favorable outcomes: 5 and 6.
Possible outcomes: 1, 2, 3, 4, 5, and 6.

$$P(5 \text{ or } 6) = \frac{\text{number of favorable outcomes}}{\text{number of possible outcomes}}$$

$$= \frac{2}{6} \text{ or } \frac{1}{3} \qquad \text{So, the probability of rolling a 5 or 6 is } \frac{1}{3} \text{ or } 33\frac{1}{3}\%$$

Exercises There are 2 blue marbles, 5 red marbles, and 8 green marbles in a bag. One marble is selected at random. Find the probability of each outcome. See Examples 1 and 2 on page 311.

63. $P(\text{red})$ $\frac{1}{3}$ **64.** $P(\text{green})$ $\frac{8}{15}$ **65.** $P(\text{blue or green})$ $\frac{2}{3}$

66. $P(\text{not blue})$ $\frac{13}{15}$ **67.** $P(\text{yellow})$ 0   **68.** $P(\text{green, red, or blue})$ 1

320 Chapter 6 Ratio, Proportion, and Percent

Answers (p. 321)

1. A ratio is a comparison of two numbers by division. A rate is a ratio of two measurements having different kinds of units. For example, 2 inches to 24 inches is a ratio, and 2 inches in 3 hours is a rate.

2. To write a fraction as a percent, first write the fraction as a decimal. Then write the decimal as a percent by moving the decimal 2 places to the right and adding the percent symbol.

Vocabulary and Concepts

1. **Explain** the difference between a ratio and a rate. **1–2. See margin.**
2. **Describe** how to express a fraction as a percent.

Skills and Applications

Express each ratio as a fraction in simplest form.

3. 15 girls out of 40 students $\frac{3}{8}$

4. 6 feet to 3 yards $\frac{2}{3}$

Express each ratio as a unit rate. Round to the nearest tenth or cent.

5. 145 miles in 3 hours **48.3 mi/h**

6. $245 for 9 tickets **$27.22 per ticket**

7. Convert 15 miles per hour to x feet per minute. **1320 feet per minute**

8. What value of y makes $\frac{8.4}{y} = \frac{1.2}{1.1}$ a proportion? **7.7**

Express each percent as a fraction or mixed number in simplest form and as a decimal.

9. 36% $\frac{9}{25}$; **0.36**

10. 52% $\frac{13}{25}$; **0.52**

11. 225% $2\frac{1}{4}$; **2.25**

12. 315% $3\frac{3}{20}$; **3.15**

13. 0.6% $\frac{3}{500}$; **0.006**

14. 0.4% $\frac{1}{250}$; **0.004**

Express each decimal or fraction as a percent. Round to the nearest tenth percent, if necessary.

15. 0.47 **47%**

16. 0.025 **2.5%**

17. 5.38 **538%**

18. $\frac{7}{20}$ **35%**

19. $\frac{30}{22}$ **136.4%**

20. $\frac{18}{4000}$ **0.45%**

Use the percent proportion to solve each problem.

21. 36 is what percent of 80? **45%**

22. 35.28 is 63% of what number? **56**

Estimate.

23. 25% of 82 **20**

24. 63% of 77 **48**

25. Find the interest on $2700 that is invested at 4% for $2\frac{1}{2}$ years. **$270**

26. Find the discount for a $135 coat that is on sale at 15% off. **$20.25**

27. Find the percent of change from 175 pounds to 140 pounds. Round to the nearest tenth. **−20%**

28. There are 3 purple balls, 5 orange balls, and 8 yellow balls in a bowl. Suppose one ball is selected at random. Find P(orange). $\frac{5}{16}$

29. **DESIGN** A builder is designing a swimming pool that is 8.5 inches in length on the scale drawing. The scale of the drawing is 1 inch = 6 feet. What is the length of the actual swimming pool? **51 feet**

30. **STANDARDIZED TEST PRACTICE** The table lists the reasons shoppers use online customer service. Out of 350 shoppers who own a computer, how many would you expect to say they use online customer service to track packages? **A**

Reasons	Percent
Track Delivery	54
Product Information	24
Verify Shipping Charges	17
Transaction Help	16

Ⓐ 189　　Ⓑ 84　　Ⓒ 19　　Ⓓ 154

 www.pre-alg.com/chapter_test

---

Assessment Options

Vocabulary Test A vocabulary review/test for Chapter 6 can be found on p. 358 of the *Chapter 6 Resource Masters*.

Chapter Tests There are six Chapter 6 Tests and an Open-Ended Assessment task available in the *Chapter 6 Resource Masters*.

Chapter 6 Tests			
Form	Type	Level	Pages
1	MC	basic	345–346
2A	MC	average	347–348
2B	MC	average	349–350
2C	FR	average	351–352
2D	FR	average	353–354
3	FR	advanced	355–356

MC = multiple-choice questions
FR = free-response questions

Open-Ended Assessment
Performance tasks for Chapter 6 can be found on p. 357 of the *Chapter 6 Resource Masters*, along with a sample scoring rubric for these tasks on p. A30.

Unit 2 Test A unit test/review can be found on pp. 365–366 of the *Chapter 6 Resource Masters*.

 ExamView® Pro

Use the networkable **ExamView® Pro** to:

- Create **multiple versions** of tests.
- Create **modified** tests for *Inclusion* students.
- **Edit** existing questions and **add** your own questions.
- Use built-in **state curriculum correlations** to create tests aligned with state standards.
- Change **English** tests to **Spanish** and vice versa.

Portfolio Suggestion

Introduction Equations are used to solve many different types of problems. Sometimes special types of equations called formulas are used.

Ask Students to find a problem from their work in this chapter and explain how they used an equation or formula to solve it.

These two pages contain practice questions in the various formats that can be found on the most frequently given standardized tests.

A practice answer sheet for these two pages can be found on page A1 of the *Chapter 6 Resource Masters*.

Standardized Test Practice
Student Recording Sheet, p. A1

Part 1 *Multiple Choice*

Select the best answer from the choices given and fill in the corresponding oval.

1 Ⓐ Ⓑ Ⓒ Ⓓ   4 Ⓐ Ⓑ Ⓒ Ⓓ   7 Ⓐ Ⓑ Ⓒ Ⓓ

2 Ⓐ Ⓑ Ⓒ Ⓓ   5 Ⓐ Ⓑ Ⓒ Ⓓ   8 Ⓐ Ⓑ Ⓒ Ⓓ

3 Ⓐ Ⓑ Ⓒ Ⓓ   6 Ⓐ Ⓑ Ⓒ Ⓓ   9 Ⓐ Ⓑ Ⓒ Ⓓ

Part 2 *Short Response/Grid In*

Solve the problem and write your answer in the blank.

For Questions 12, 13, 15, and 17, also enter your answer by writing each number or symbol in a box. Then fill in the corresponding oval for that number or symbol.

10
11
12 (grid in)
13 (grid in)
14
15 (grid in)
16
17 (grid in)

Part 3 *Extended Response*

Record your answers for Questions 18-19 on the back of this paper.

Additional Practice

Additional Standardized Test Practice is available on pp. 363–364 of the *Chapter 6 Resource Masters*.

Part 1 Multiple Choice

Record your answers on the answer sheet provided by your teacher or on a sheet of paper.

1. Evaluate $x - y + z$ if $x = -6$, $y = 9$, and $z = -3$.   (Lesson 2-3) **C**

  Ⓐ 0   Ⓑ -6

  Ⓒ -18 Ⓓ 15

2. Which figure has an area of 192 cm²? (Lesson 3-7) **D**

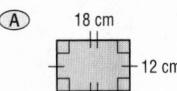
Ⓐ 18 cm, 12 cm

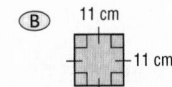
Ⓑ 11 cm, 11 cm

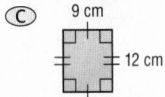
Ⓒ 9 cm, 12 cm

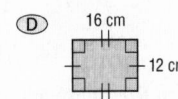
Ⓓ 16 cm, 12 cm

3. Which expression is *not* a monomial? (Lesson 4-1) **C**

  Ⓐ $5(-y)$ Ⓑ $8k$

  Ⓒ $m - n$ Ⓓ $2x(-3y)$

4. Which fraction represents the ratio *8 apples to 36 pieces of fruit* in simplest form? (Lesson 6-1) **C**

  Ⓐ $\frac{1}{4}$ Ⓑ $\frac{4}{9}$

  Ⓒ $\frac{2}{9}$ Ⓓ $\frac{1}{6}$

5. The ratio of girls to boys in a class is 5 to 4. Suppose there are 27 students in the class. How many of the students are girls? (Lesson 6-2) **B**

  Ⓐ 40   Ⓑ 15

  Ⓒ 12   Ⓓ 9

6. A scale model of an airplane has a width of 13.5 inches. The scale of the model is 1 inch = 8 feet. What is the width of the actual airplane?   (Lesson 6-3) **B**

  Ⓐ 110 ft   Ⓑ 108 ft

  Ⓒ 104 ft   Ⓓ 115 ft

---

7. Randy, Eduardo, and Kelli took a quiz. For every 50 questions on the quiz, Randy answered 47 correctly. Eduardo answered 91% of the questions correctly. For every 10 questions on the quiz, Kelli answered 9 correctly. Who had the highest score? **A**

  Ⓐ Randy   Ⓑ Eduardo

  Ⓒ Kelli   Ⓓ all the same

8. The graph shows the amount of canned food collected by the 9th grade classes at Hilltop High School.

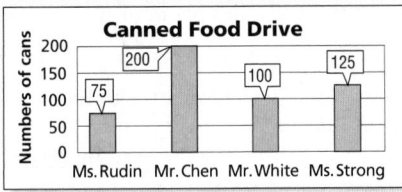

Canned Food Drive — Numbers of cans: Ms. Rudin 75, Mr. Chen 200, Mr. White 100, Ms. Strong 125

Of the total amount of cans collected, what percent did Mr. Chen's class collect? (Lesson 6-4) **C**

  Ⓐ 25%   Ⓑ 33%   Ⓒ 40%   Ⓓ 50%

9. The table shows the average salaries in each of the four major sports for the 1990–91 and 2000–01 seasons.   (Lesson 6-8)

Sport	1990–91	2000–01
Hockey	$271,000	$1,400,000
Basketball	823,000	3,530,000
Football	430,000	1,200,000
Baseball	597,537	2,260,000

Source: *USA TODAY*

Which sport had a percent of increase in average salary of about 325%? **B**

  Ⓐ Hockey   Ⓑ Basketball

  Ⓒ Football   Ⓓ Baseball

Test-Taking Tip

Question 8
To find what percent of the cans a class collected, you will first need to find the total number of cans collected by all of the 9th grade classes.

ExamView® Pro

Special banks of standardized test questions similar to those on the SAT, ACT, TIMSS 8, NAEP 8, and Pre-Algebra End-of-Course tests can be found on this CD-ROM.

Part 2 Short Response/Grid In

Record your answers on the answer sheet provided by your teacher or on a sheet of paper.

0. Ana earns $6.80 per hour when she works on weekdays. She earns twice that amount per hour when she works on weekends. If Ana worked 4 hours on Tuesday, 4 hours on Thursday, and 5 hours on Saturday, then how much did she earn?
(Prerequisite Skill, p. 713) **$122.40**

1. Juan and Julia decided to eat lunch at The Sub Shop. Juan ordered a veggie sub, lemonade, and a cookie. Julia ordered a ham sub, milk, and a cookie. What was the total cost of Juan and Julia's lunch?   (Prerequisite Skill, p. 713) **$11.15**

Item	Cost
Veggie Sub	$3.89
Turkey Sub	$3.79
Ham Sub	$3.49
Soda	$1.25
Lemonade	$1.00
Milk	$0.79
Cookie	$0.99

2. What number should replace X in this pattern?
(Lesson 4-2) **256**

$$4^0 = 1$$
$$4^1 = 4$$
$$4^2 = 16$$
$$4^3 = 64$$
$$4^4 = X$$

3. Find the value of m in $\frac{3}{8}m = \frac{1}{4}$.   (Lesson 5-9) **2/3**

4. Nakayla purchased a package of 8 hamburger buns for $1.49. What is the ratio of the cost per hamburger bun? Round to the nearest penny.   (Lesson 6-1)
$0.19 per hamburger bun

5. What is 40% of 70?   (Lesson 6-5) **28**

6. Cameron purchased the portable stereo shown. About how much money did he save?   (Lesson 6-7) **$21**

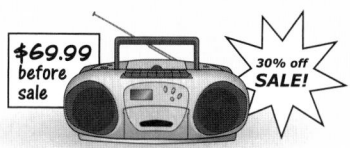

$69.99 before sale

30% off SALE!

17. If you spin the spinner shown at the right, what is the probability that the arrow will stop at an even number?
(Lesson 6-9) **3/8**

Part 3 Extended Response

Record your answers on a sheet of paper. Show your work.

18. An electronics store is having a sale on certain models of televisions. Mr. Castillo would like to buy a television that is on sale. This television normally costs $679.
(Lesson 6-7) **c. $271.60**

Last Year's Models
40% off
Wednesday Only
Take an additional
10% off
Television Sale!

a. What price, not including tax, will Mr. Castillo pay if he buys the television on Saturday? **$407.40**

b. What price, not including tax, will Mr. Castillo pay if he buys the television on Wednesday? **$339.50**

c. How much money will Mr. Castillo save if he buys the television on a Saturday?

19. The graph shows the number of domain registrations for the years 1997–2000.

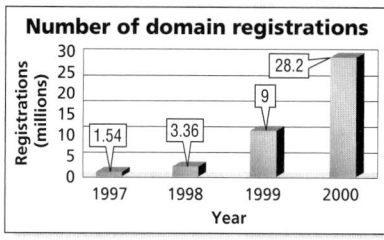

Number of domain registrations

Source: Network Solutions (VeriSign)

Write a few sentences describing the percent of change in the number of domain registrations from one year to the next.
(Lesson 6-8) **See margin.**

Answer

19. From 1997 to 1998, the percent of change was 118%, from 1998 to 1999, the percent of change was 168%, and from 1999 to 2000, the percent of change was 213%.

Evaluating Extended Response Questions

Extended Response questions are graded by using a multilevel rubric that guides you in assessing a student's knowledge of a particular concept.

Goal: Review ratios, proportions, and percents.

Sample Scoring Rubric: The following rubric is a sample scoring device. You may wish to add more detail to this sample to meet your individual scoring needs.

Score	Criteria
4	A correct solution that is supported by well-developed, accurate explanations
3	A generally correct solution, but may contain minor flaws in reasoning or computation
2	A partially correct interpretation and/or solution to the problem
1	A correct solution with no supporting evidence or explanation
0	An incorrect solution indicating no mathematical understanding of the concept or task, or no solution is given

Page 266, Lesson 6-1

1. ○○□□□

2. A ratio is a comparison of two numbers by division. A rate is a ratio of two measurements having different units of measure.

3. Sample answer: $12 per person

4. $\frac{2}{5}$ **5.** $\frac{5}{8}$ **6.** $\frac{5}{18}$ **7.** $\frac{1}{3}$

8. $45.75/ticket

9. 0.75 inches/hour

10. 6.9 feet/second

11. 24.2 miles/gallon

Page 267, Lesson 6-1

16. $\frac{2}{9}$ **17.** $\frac{2}{5}$ **18.** $\frac{2}{5}$ **19.** $\frac{3}{7}$

20. $\frac{7}{18}$ **21.** $\frac{9}{32,000}$ **22.** $\frac{4}{1}$ **23.** $\frac{1760}{1}$

24. $\frac{5}{41}$ **25.** $\frac{17}{118}$ **26.** $\frac{31}{15}$ **27.** $\frac{3}{1}$

28. $0.50/can

29. 0.10 cents/pencil

30. 23.3 mi/gal

31. 4.5 m/sec

32. 7.6 yd/min

33. 7.8 ft/h

34. 52.6 mi/day

35. 39 pages/week

36. Since the 12-issue subscription costs $2.80 per issue, and the 18-issue subscription costs $2.25 per issue, the 12-issue subscription costs more per issue.

37. The 6-pack of soda costs $0.37 per can. The 12-pack of soda costs $0.35 per can. So, the 12-pack is less expensive.

46. Alaska: 1 person/sq mi; New York: 402/people/sq mi; Rhode Island: 1003 people/sq mi; Texas: 80 people/sq mi; Wyoming: 5 people/sq mi

Page 284, Lesson 6-4

42. Since $\frac{2}{5} = 40\%$, and 40% is greater than 22%, the group that said they prefer ketchup is larger.

51. There are only two possibilities that satisfy the conditions, $\frac{1}{4}$ and $\frac{2}{5}$. See students' explanations.

Pages 286–287, Algebra Activity

1. 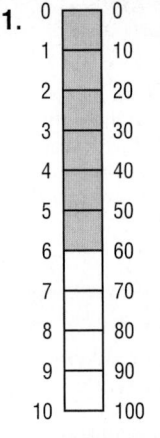 **2.** 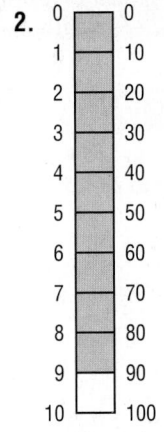 **3.**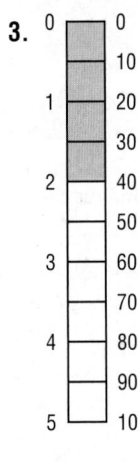

4. 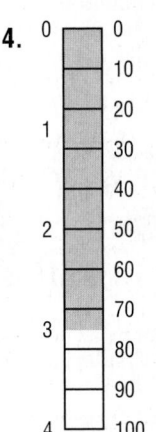 **5.** 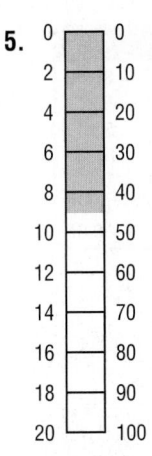 **6.**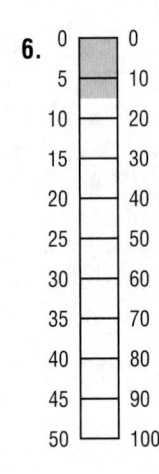

7. 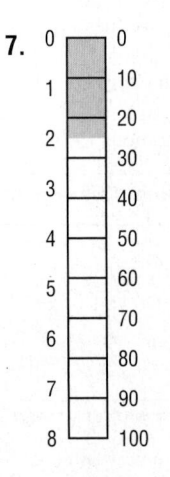 **8.** 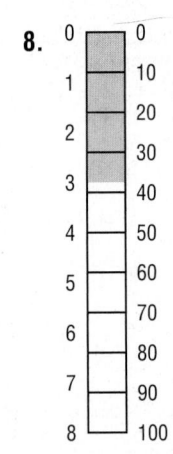 **9.**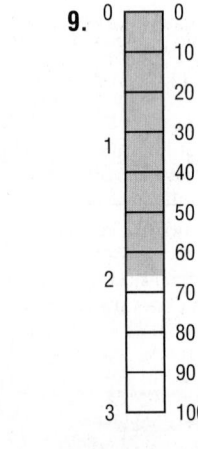

10. 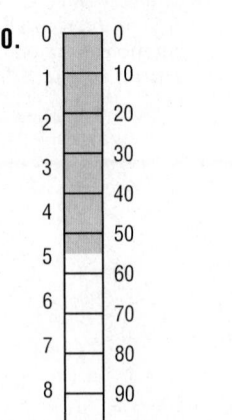 **11.** 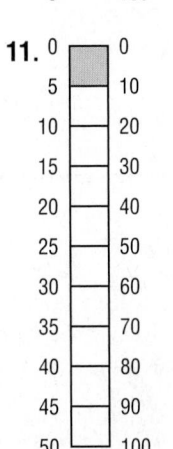 **12.**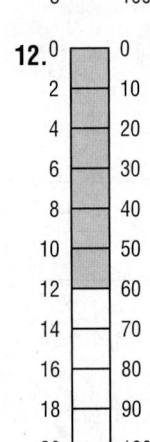

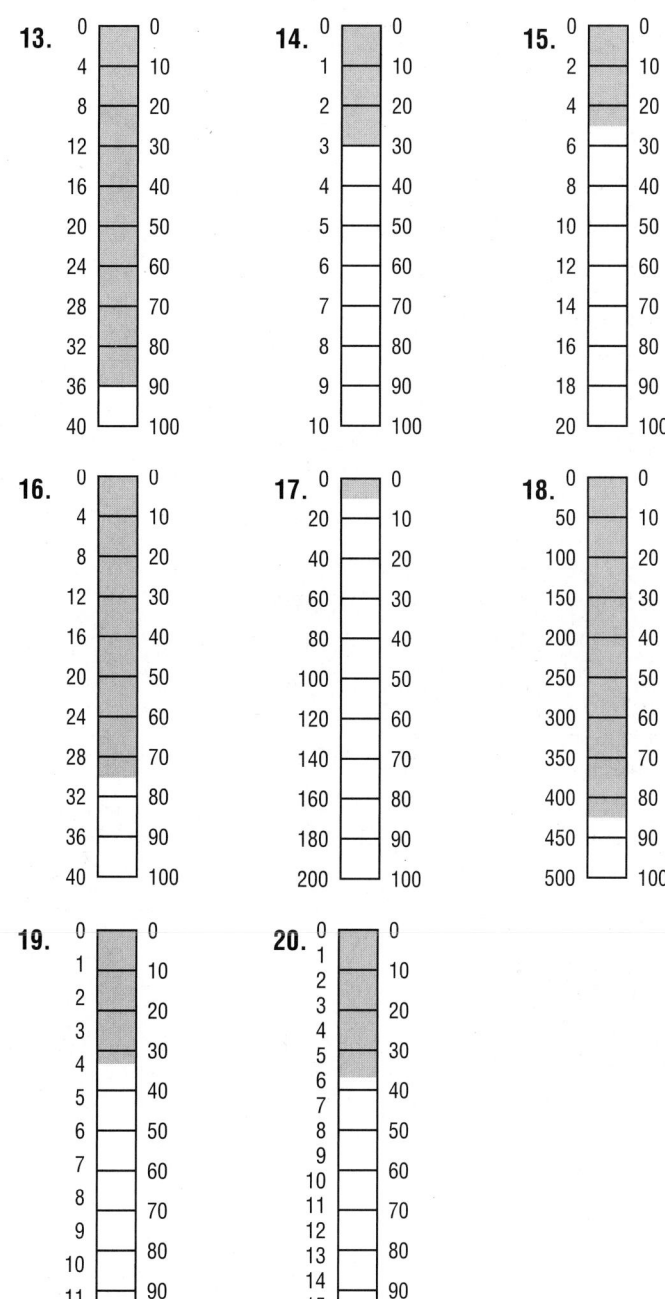

13. **14.** **15.** **16.** **17.** **18.** **19.** **20.**

35. 450; meaning of percent: 295% means about 300 for every 100 or about 30 for every 10. 145 has one 100 and about 5 tens. $(300 \times 1) + (30 \times 5) = 300 + 150$ or 450.

39. Sample answer: $\frac{1}{3} \times 90,000$ or 30,000 miles

40. Sample answer: $\frac{1}{10} \times 40,000$ or 4000 miles

Page 308, Lesson 6-8

32. Sample answer: 81; fraction method: $\frac{3}{5} \times 135$ or 81

33. Sample answer: 63; fraction method: $\frac{9}{10} \times 70$ or 63

34. Sample answer: 36; meaning of percent: 123% means about 123 for every 100 or about 12 for every 10. 32 has 3 tens. $3 \times 12 = 36$. So, 123% of 32 is about 36.

Page 309, Algebra Activity

1. Yes; strength: large enough population

2. no; weakness: the people in a library may read more often than others.

3. no; weakness: many of the fans may be Dolphin fans

4. systematic; people may prefer the restaurant

5. Find the percent of students in each grade that eat breakfast.

6a–d. See students' work.

Page 312, Lesson 6-9

4. $\frac{1}{10}$; 10%

5. $\frac{1}{2}$; 50%

6. $\frac{1}{5}$; 20%

7. $\frac{2}{5}$; 40%

8. $\frac{1}{6}$; $16\frac{2}{3}$%

9. 1; 100%

Additional Answers for Chapter 6

Linear Equations, Inequalities, and Functions

Introduction

In this unit, students will learn about linear equations, inequalities, functions, and graphing. They will analyze data to discover whether a linear relationship exists. They will learn that inequalities can help describe relationships between mathematical expressions.

Students will analyze how equations and graphs are used to describe mathematical relationships. They will expand their knowledge in the use of *x*- and *y*-intercepts, slope, and rate of change.

Assessment Options

 **Unit 3 Test** Pages 487–488 of the *Chapter 8 Resource Masters* may be used as a test or review for Unit 3. This assessment contains both multiple-choice and short answer items.

ExamView® Pro

This CD-ROM can be used to create additional unit tests and review worksheets.

 Yearly Progress Pro

An online, research-based instructional, assessment, and intervention tool that provides specific feedback on student mastery of state and national standards, instant remediation, and a data management system to track performance. For more information, contact

mhdigitallearning.com.

Your study of algebra includes more than just solving equations. Many real-world situations can be modeled by equations and their graphs. In this unit, you will learn about functions and graphs.

Chapter 7
Equations and Inequalities

Chapter 8
Functions and Graphing

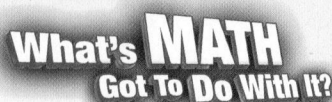 What's **MATH** Got To Do With It?

Real-Life Math Videos

What's Math Got to Do With It? Real-Life Math Videos engage students showing them how math is used in everyday situations. Use Video 2 with this unit.

Just for Fun

What do you like to do in your spare time—shop at the mall, attend a baseball or football game, go to the movies, ride the rides at an amusement park, or hike in the great outdoors?

In this project, you will be exploring how equations, functions, and graphs can help you examine how people spend their leisure time.

 Log on to www.pre-alg.com/webquest. Begin your WebQuest by reading the Task.

Then continue working on your WebQuest as you study Unit 3.

Lesson	7-1	8-8
Page	333	411

USA TODAY Snapshots®

What fans pay after ticket
An average fan at a Major League Baseball game spends $15.40 on parking, food, drinks and souvenirs in addition to the $15 ticket price.

MLB   NBA   NHL   NFL

$15.40 $18.20 $18.25 $19.00

Source: *American Demographics*, Team Marketing Report

By Anne R. Carey and Marcy E. Mullins, USA TODAY

Unit 3 Linear Equations, Inequalities, and Functions **325**

Teaching Suggestions

Have students study the USA TODAY Snapshot®.

• Which sport has the most expensive ticket price? **football**

• Ask students whether it is possible to represent these data in a graph. If so, how would they represent the data? **not possible to graph on a coordinate plane**

• Point out to students that in their WebQuest they will be analyzing other statistics describing how people spend their leisure time.

Additional USA TODAY Snapshot® appearing in Unit 3:

Chapter 7 High school homework time (p. 343)

WebQuest Internet Project

Problem-Based Learning A WebQuest is an online project in which students do research on the Internet, gather data, and make presentations using word processing, graphing, page-making, or presentation software. In each chapter, students advance to the next step in their WebQuest. At the end of Chapter 8, the project culminates with a presentation of their findings.

Teaching suggestions and sample answers are available in the *WebQuest and Project Resources*.

Equations and Inequalities
Chapter Overview and Pacing

Year-long pacing: pages T20–T21.

LESSON OBJECTIVES	PACING (days)			
	Regular		Block	
	Basic/ Average	Advanced	Basic/ Average	Advanced
7-1 Solving Equations with Variables on Each Side *(pp. 328–333)* ***Preview:*** *Use algebra tiles and an equation mat to solve equations with variables on each side.* • Solve equations with variables on each side.	3 (with 7-1 Preview)	2	1.5 (with 7-1 Preview)	1
7-2 Solving Equations with Grouping Symbols *(pp. 334–338)* • Solve equations that involve grouping symbols. • Identify equations that have no solution or an infinite number of solutions.	2	1	1	0.5
7-3 Inequalities *(pp. 340–344)* • Write inequalities. • Graph inequalities.	1	1	0.5	0.5
7-4 Solving Inequalities by Adding or Subtracting *(pp. 345–349)* • Solve inequalities by using the Addition and Subtraction Properties of Inequality.	1	1	0.5	0.5
7-5 Solving Inequalities by Multiplying or Dividing *(pp. 350–354)* • Solve inequalities by multiplying or dividing by a positive number. • Solve inequalities by multiplying or dividing by a negative number.	2	2	1	1
7-6 Solving Multi-Step Inequalities *(pp. 355–359)* • Solve inequalities that involve more than one operation.	1	1	0.5	0.5
Study Guide and **Practice Test** *(pp. 360–363)* **Standardized Test Practice** *(pp. 364–365)*	1	1	0.5	0.5
Chapter Assessment	1	1	0.5	0.5
TOTAL	12	10	6	5

*An electronic version of this chapter is available on **StudentWorks**™. This backpack solution CD-ROM allows students instant access to the Student Edition, lesson worksheet pages, and web resources.*

Chapter Resource Manager

CHAPTER 7 RESOURCE MASTERS

Study Guide and Intervention	Practice (Skills and Average)	Reading to Learn Mathematics	Enrichment	Assessment	Prerequisite Skills Workbook	Applications*	Parent and Student Study Guide Workbook	5-Minute Check Transparencies	Interactive Chalkboard	Pre-AlgePASS: Tutorial Plus (lessons)	Materials
367	368–369	370	371				54	7-1	7-1		
372	373–374	375	376	411			55	7-2	7-2	19	
377	378–379	380	381	411, 413	1–2	GCS 32	56	7-3	7-3	20	
382	383–384	385	386		1–2, 21–24, 55–62	SC 13	57	7-4	7-4		
387	388–389	390	391	412	1–2, 27–28, 31–32, 47–54		58	7-5	7-5		
392	393–394	395	396	412	1–2	SC 14 GCS 31	59	7-6	7-6	21	
				397–410 414–416							

Key to Abbreviations: GCS = Graphing Calculator and Spreadsheet Masters
SC = School-to-Career Masters
SM = Science and Mathematics Lab Manual

ELL Study Guide and Intervention, Skills Practice, Practice, and Parent and Student Study Guide Workbooks are also available in Spanish.

Continuity of Instruction

Prior Knowledge

Students solved basic one- and two-step equations in Chapter 3. In Chapter 4, students learned about rational numbers, including fractions, decimals, and integers. In Chapter 5, students learned about adding, subtracting, multiplying, and dividing rational numbers. In Chapter 6, students learned to solve proportions.

This Chapter

Students expand their skill in solving equations to solving equations with variables on each side. They solve equations involving grouping symbols by using the Distributive Property. Students write and graph inequalities and learn to solve inequalities by using properties of inequality. Finally, they solve inequalities involving more than one operation.

Future Connections

Students will solve systems of linear equations and linear inequalities in Chapter 8. In Chapter 9, they will solve equations by finding square roots and will find dimensions of triangles by solving equations involving the Pythagorean Theorem, proportions, and trigonometric ratios. In Chapters 10 and 11, students will solve equations to find missing values in two- and three-dimensional figures.

7-1 Solving Equations with Variables on Each Side

To solve equations with variables on each side, use the Addition or Subtraction Property of Equality, which was introduced in Lesson 3-3, to write an equivalent equation with the variables on one side of the equation. Then solve the equation. For example, to solve $3x - 8 = 5x$, subtract $3x$ from each side to get $-8 = 2x$, then divide each side by 2 to find that $x = -4$.

7-2 Solving Equations with Grouping Symbols

Equations often contain grouping symbols such as parentheses or brackets. The first step in solving these equations is to use the Distributive Property to remove the grouping symbols.

Some equations have no solution. That is, there is no value of the variable that results in a true sentence. For such an equation, the solution set is called the null or empty set, and is represented by the symbol $\varnothing$ or {}. Other equations may have every number as the solution. An equation that is true for every value of the variable is called an identity.

7-3 Inequalities

A mathematical sentence that contains the symbols < (less than), > (greater than), ≤ (less than or equal to), or ≥ (greater than or equal to) is called an inequality. For example, the statement that it is legal to drive 55 miles per hour or slower on a stretch of highway can be shown by the sentence $s \le 55$. Inequalities with variables are called open sentences. When a variable is replaced with a number, the inequality may be true or false.

The solutions of inequalities can be graphed on a number line. For example, if the solution of an inequality is $x < 5$, start an arrow at 5 on the number line and continue the arrow left to show all values less than 5 as the solution. Put an open circle at 5 to show that the point 5 is *not* included in the graph. Use a closed circle when graphing solutions that are greater than or equal to, or less than or equal to, a number.

7-4 Solving Inequalities by Adding or Subtracting

Solving an inequality means finding values for the variable that make the inequality true. Some inequalities can be solved by using the Addition and Subtraction Properties of Inequalities. These properties say that when you add or subtract the same number from each side of an inequality, the inequality remains true. For example, if you add 5 to each side of the inequality $3 < 6$, the resulting inequality $8 < 11$ is also true. Adding or subtracting the same number from each side of an inequality does not affect the inequality sign. Since the solutions to an inequality include all rational numbers satisfying it, inequalities have an infinite number of solutions.

7-5 Solving Inequalities by Multiplying or Dividing

Some inequalities can be solved by using the Multiplication and Division Properties of Inequalities. These properties say that when multiplying or dividing each side of an inequality by the same positive number, the inequality remains true. In such cases, the inequality symbol does not change. When multiplying or dividing each side of an inequality by a negative number, the inequality symbol must be reversed. For example, when dividing each side of the inequality $-4 \geq -8$ by -2, the inequality sign must be changed to $\leq$ for the resulting inequality, $2 \leq 4$, to be true.

7-6 Solving Multi-Step Inequalities

When solving inequalities that involve more than one operation, work backward to undo the operations, just as when solving multi-step equations. Remember to reverse the inequality symbol if you multiply or divide each side of an inequality by a negative number. Use the Distributive Property to begin simplifying inequalities that contain grouping symbols.

Quick Review Math Handbook

Hot Words includes a glossary of terms while Hot Topics consists of explanations of key mathematical concepts with exercises to test comprehension. This valuable resource can be used as a reference in the classroom or for home study.

Lesson	Hot Topics Section	Lesson	Hot Topics Section
GS 7	1.5, 6.4	7-4	6.4, 6.6
7-1	6.2, 6.4	7-5	6.4, 6.6
7-2	6.3, 6.4	7-6	6.6
7-3	6.4, 6.6		

GS = Getting Started

 Additional mathematical information and teaching notes are available at www.pre-alg.com/key_concepts.

DAILY INTERVENTION and Assessment

Key to Abbreviations:
TWE = Teacher Wraparound Edition; CRM = Chapter Resource Masters

	Type	Student Edition	Teacher Resources	Technology/Internet
INTERVENTION	Ongoing	Prerequisite Skills, pp. 327, 333, 338, 344, 349, 354 Practice Quiz 1, p. 338 Practice Quiz 2, p. 354	5-Minute Check Transparencies *Prerequisite Skills Workbook*, pp. 1–2, 21–24, 27–28, 31–32, 47–62 Quizzes, *CRM*, pp. 411, 412 Mid-Chapter Test, *CRM*, p. 413 Study Guide and Intervention, *CRM*, p. 367, 372, 377, 382, 387, 392	Pre-AlgePASS: Tutorial Plus, Lessons 19, 20, and 21 www.pre-alg.com/ self_check_quiz www.pre-alg.com/ extra_examples
	Mixed Review	pp. 333, 338, 344, 349, 354, 359	Cumulative Review, *CRM*, p. 414	
	Error Analysis	Find the Error, pp. 347, 353, 357	Find the Error, *TWE*, pp. 353, 357 Unlocking Misconceptions, *TWE*, pp. 335, 357	
	Standardized Test Practice	pp. 333, 338, 344, 349, 351, 353, 354, 359, 364–365	*TWE*, pp. 364–365 Standardized Test Practice, *CRM*, pp. 415–416	Standardized Test Practice CD-ROM www.pre-alg.com/ standardized_test
ASSESSMENT	Open-Ended Assessment	Writing in Math, pp. 333, 338, 344, 349, 354, 359 Open Ended, pp. 332, 336, 342, 347, 353, 357 Standardized Test, p. 365	Speaking: *TWE*, pp. 354, 359 Writing: *TWE*, pp. 344, 349 Modeling: *TWE*, pp. 332, 338 Open-Ended Assessment, *CRM*, p. 409	
	Chapter Assessment	Study Guide, pp. 360–362 Practice Test, p. 363	Multiple-Choice Tests (Forms 1, 2A, 2B), *CRM*, pp. 397–402 Free-Response Tests (Forms 2C, 2D, 3), *CRM*, pp. 403–408 Vocabulary Test/Review, *CRM*, p. 410	ExamView® Pro (see below) MindJogger Videoquizzes www.pre-alg.com/ vocabulary_review www.pre-alg.com/chapter_test

For more information on Yearly ProgressPro, see p. 324.

Pre-Algebra Lesson	Yearly ProgressPro Skill Lesson
7-1	Solving Equations with Variables on Each Side
7-2	Solving Equations with Variables on Each Side
7-3	Inequalities
7-4	Solve Simple Inequalities
7-5	Solve Simple Inequalities
7-6	Problem Solving with Inequalities

ExamView® Pro

Use the networkable **ExamView® Pro** to:
- Create **multiple versions** of tests.
- Create **modified** tests for *Inclusion* students.
- **Edit** existing questions and **add** your own questions.
- Use built-in **state curriculum correlations** to create tests aligned with state standards.
- Change **English** tests to **Spanish** and vice versa.

For more information on Intervention and Assessment, see pp. T8–T11.

Reading and Writing in Mathematics

Glencoe Pre-Algebra provides numerous opportunities to incorporate reading and writing into the mathematics classroom.

Student Edition

- Foldables™ Study Organizer, p. 327
- Reading Mathematics, p. 339
- Concept Check questions require students to verbalize and write about what they have learned in the lesson. (pp. 330, 332, 335, 336, 342, 345, 346, 347, 352, 353, 356, 357)
- Writing in Math questions in every lesson, pp. 333, 338, 344, 349, 354, 359
- Reading Math, p. 341
- WebQuest, p. 333

Teacher Wraparound Edition

- Foldables™ Study Organizer, pp. 327, 360
- Study Notebook suggestions, pp. 329, 332, 336, 339, 342, 347, 352, 357
- Modeling activities, pp. 332, 338
- Speaking activities, pp. 354, 359
- Writing activities, pp. 344, 349
- Differentiated Instruction (Verbal/Linguistic), p. 331
- **ELL** Resources, pp. 326, 330, 331, 334, 339, 340, 345, 350, 355, 360

Additional Resources

- Vocabulary Builder worksheets require students to define and give examples for key vocabulary terms as they progress through the chapter (*Chapter 7 Resource Masters,* pp. vii–viii)
- Reading to Learn Mathematics master for each lesson (*Chapter 7 Resource Masters,* pp. 370, 375, 380, 385, 390, 395)
- *Vocabulary PuzzleMaker* software creates crossword, jumble, and word search puzzles using vocabulary lists that you can customize.
- *Teaching Mathematics with Foldables* provides suggestions for promoting cognition and language.
- *Reading and Writing in the Mathematics Classroom*
- *WebQuest and Project Resources*

For more information on Reading and Writing in Mathematics, see pp. T6–T7.

PROJECT CRISS℠ Study Skill

Before beginning this chapter, demonstrate how students can use two-column notes like those for solving equations shown at the right. Explain that the left column should contain each of the topics presented in the chapter. The right column should include short summaries of the steps needed to solve the problems.

Students may also wish to include other notes about the topics that they feel are helpful.

Topic	Notes
Solving equations with variables on each side	1. combine like terms 2. can use the Distributive Property 3. place all variable terms on one side 4. solve for unknown

CReating **I**ndependence **T**hrough **S**tudent-**O**wned **S**trategies

What You'll Learn

Have students read over the list of objectives and make a list of any words with which they are not familiar.

Why It's Important

Point out to students that this is only one of many reasons why each objective is important. Others are provided in the introduction to each lesson.

What You'll Learn

- **Lessons 7-1 and 7-2** Solve equations with variables on each side and with grouping symbols.
- **Lesson 7-3** Write and graph inequalities.
- **Lessons 7-4 and 7-5** Solve inequalities using the Properties of Inequalities.
- **Lesson 7-6** Solve multi-step inequalities.

Key Vocabulary

- null or **empty set** (p. 336)
- **identity** (p. 336)
- **inequality** (p. 340)

Why It's Important

An equation is a statement that two expressions are equal. Sometimes, you want to know when one expression is greater or less than another. This kind of statement is an inequality. For example, you can solve an inequality to determine a healthy backpack weight. *You will solve problems involving backpacking in Lesson 7-6.*

326   Chapter 7   Equations and Inequalities

Lesson	NCTM Standards	Local Objectives
7-1 Preview	2, 10	
7-1	2, 6	
7-2	2, 3, 6	
7-3	1, 2, 8	
7-4	1, 2, 6, 8	
7-5	1, 2, 6	
7-6	1, 2, 6, 9	

Key to NCTM Standards:

1=Number & Operations, 2=Algebra, 3=Geometry, 4=Measurement, 5=Data Analysis & Probability, 6=Problem Solving, 7=Reasoning & Proof, 8=Communication, 9=Connections, 10=Representation

Vocabulary Builder   ELL

The Key Vocabulary list introduces students to some of the main vocabulary terms included in this chapter. For a more thorough vocabulary list with pronunciations of new words, give students the Vocabulary Builder worksheets found on pages vii and viii of the *Chapter 7 Resource Masters*. Encourage them to complete the definition of each term as they progress through the chapter. You may suggest that they add these sheets to their study notebooks for future reference when studying for the Chapter 7 test.

▶ **Prerequisite Skills** To be successful in this chapter, you'll need to master these skills and be able to apply them in problem-solving situations. Review these skills before beginning Chapter 7.

For Lesson 7-1   **Solve Two-Step Equations**

Solve each equation. Check your solution. *(For review, see Lesson 3-5.)*

1. $2x + 5 = 13$ **4**   **2.** $4n - 3 = 5$ **2**   **3.** $16 = 8 + \dfrac{d}{3}$ **24**   **4.** $\dfrac{c}{-4} + 3 = -9$ **48**

For Lesson 7-4   **Add and Subtract Integers**

Find each sum or difference. *(For review, see Lessons 2-2 and 2-3.)*

5. $-28 + (-16)$ **−44**   **6.** $17 + (-25)$ **−8**   **7.** $-13 + 24$ **11**

8. $36 + (-18)$ **18**   **9.** $31 - 48$ **−17**   **10.** $-16 - 7$ **−23**

11. $4 - (-12)$ **16**   **12.** $-23 - (-29)$ **6**   **13.** $-19 - (-5)$ **−14**

For Lesson 7-5   **Multiply and Divide Integers**

Find each product or quotient. *(For review, see Lessons 2-4 and 2-5.)*

14. $-6(8)$ **−48**   **15.** $-3 \cdot 5$ **−15**   **16.** $-6(-25)$ **150**

17. $2(-4)(-9)$ **72**   **18.** $64 \div (-32)$ **−2**   **19.** $-15 \div 3$ **−5**

20. $-12 \div (-3)$ **4**   **21.** $-6 \div (-6)$ **1**   **22.** $24 \div (-2)$ **−12**

 **FOLDABLES™** **Study Organizer**

Equations and Inequalities Make this Foldable to help you organize your notes. Begin with a plain sheet of $8\frac{1}{2}"$ by $11"$ paper.

Step 1   **Fold in Half**

Fold in half lengthwise.

Step 2   **Fold in Sixths**

Fold in thirds and then fold each third in half.

Step 3   **Cut**

Open. Cut one side along the folds to make tabs.

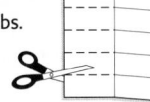

Step 4   **Label**

Label each tab with a lesson number as shown.

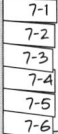

| 7-1 |
| 7-2 |
| 7-3 |
| 7-4 |
| 7-5 |
| 7-6 |

Reading and Writing As you read and study the chapter, write notes and examples under each tab.

This section provides a review of the basic concepts needed before beginning Chapter 7. Page references are included for additional student help.

Additional review is provided in the *Prerequisite Skills Workbook*, pages 1–2, 21–24, 27–28, 31–32, and 47–62.

Prerequisite Skills in the Getting Ready for the Next Lesson section at the end of each lesson reviews a skill needed in the next lesson.

For Lesson	Prerequisite Skill
7-2	Using the Distributive Property (p. 333)
7-3	Evaluating Expressions (p. 338)
7-4	Solving Equations (p. 344)
7-5	Solving Equations (p. 349)
7-6	Solving Two-Step Equations (p. 354)

FOLDABLES™ **Study Organizer**

For more information about Foldables, see *Teaching Mathematics with Foldables.*

Questioning Skills Before beginning each lesson, ask students to look through the lesson and write one question that they have about what they have seen. Write the question on the front of the corresponding lesson tab. As students study the lesson, have them record the answer to their question under the tab and other questions that arise. Self-questioning is a strategy that helps students stay focused during reading, writing, and skills practice.

Getting Started

Objective Use algebra tiles and an equation mat to solve equations with variables on each side.

Materials
algebra tiles
equation mat

Teaching Tip Model Activity 1 on an overhead with an equation mat and algebra tiles.

Teach

- Show students how algebra tiles are both added or both removed to maintain balance on each side of the equation.
- Also show students examples where they don't end up with just one *x*-tile on the side.

Answers

1.
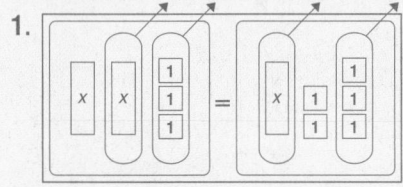

2.
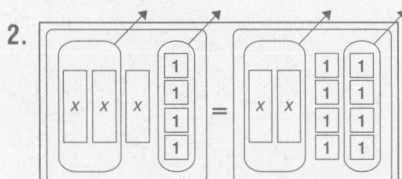

3.
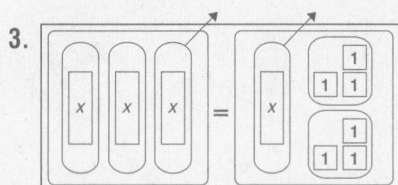

4.
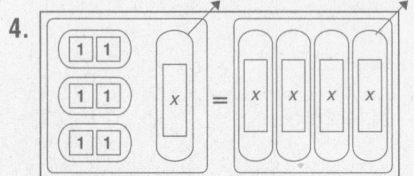

Algebra Activity
A Preview of Lesson 7-1

Equations with Variables on Each Side

In Chapter 3, you used algebra tiles and an equation mat to solve equations in which the variable was on only one side of the equation. You can use algebra tiles and an equation mat to solve equations with variables on each side of the equation.

Activity 1

The following example shows how to solve $x + 3 = 2x + 1$ using algebra tiles.

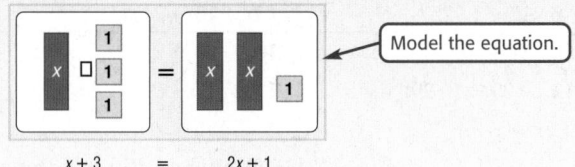

Model the equation.

$x + 3 = 2x + 1$

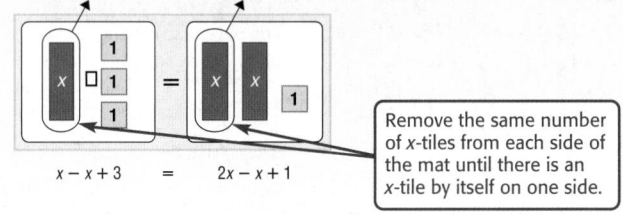

Remove the same number of *x*-tiles from each side of the mat until there is an *x*-tile by itself on one side.

$x - x + 3 = 2x - x + 1$

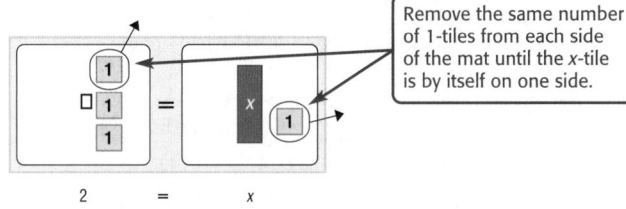

Remove the same number of 1-tiles from each side of the mat until the *x*-tile is by itself on one side.

$2 = x$

There are two 1-tiles on the left side of the mat and one *x*-tile on the right side. Therefore, $x = 2$. Since $2 + 3 = 2(2) + 1$, the solution is correct.

Model

Use algebra tiles to model and solve each equation. 1–6. See margin for models.

1. $2x + 3 = x + 5$ **2** **2.** $3x + 4 = 2x + 8$ **4** **3.** $3x = x + 6$ **3**

4. $6 + x = 4x$ **2** **5.** $2x - 4 = x - 6$ **−2** **6.** $5x - 1 = 4x - 5$ **−4**

Analyze 8. The value of *x* is the same on each side of the mat.

7. Which property of equality allows you to remove a 1-tile from each side of the mat? **subtraction**

8. Explain why you can remove an *x*-tile from each side of the mat.

328 Chapter 7 Equations and Inequalities

Resource Manager

📁 *Teaching Pre-Algebra with Manipulatives*
- pp. 7–8 (masters for algebra tiles)
- p. 13 (master for equation mat)
- p. 99 (student recording sheet)

Glencoe Mathematics Classroom Manipulative Kit
- algebra tiles
- equation mat

Activity 2

Some equations are solved by using zero pairs. Remember, you may add or subtract a zero pair from either side of an equation mat without changing its value. The following example shows how to solve $2x + 1 = x - 5$.

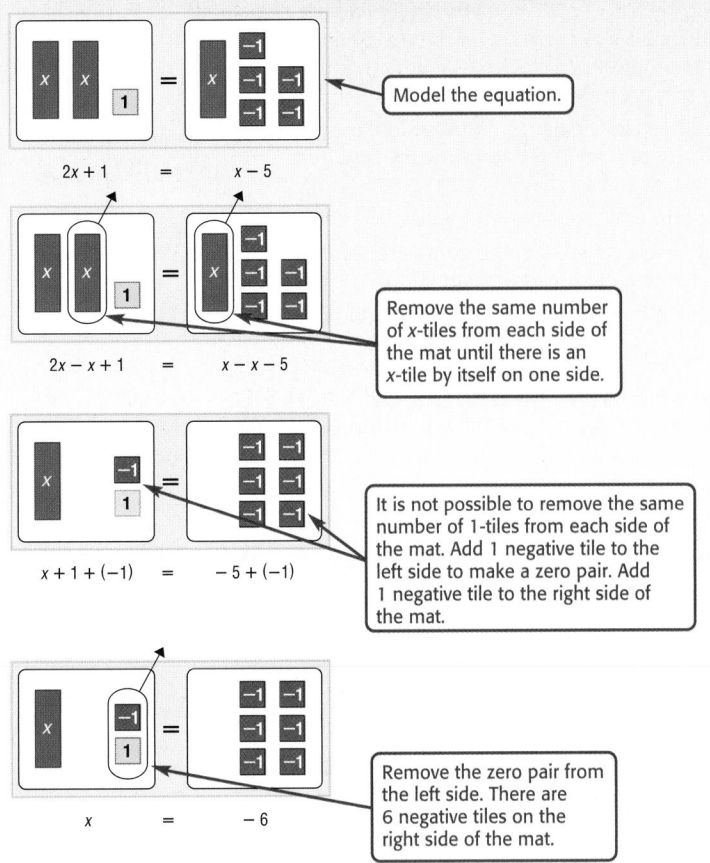

$$2x + 1 = x - 5$$

Model the equation.

$$2x - x + 1 = x - x - 5$$

Remove the same number of x-tiles from each side of the mat until there is an x-tile by itself on one side.

$$x + 1 + (-1) = -5 + (-1)$$

It is not possible to remove the same number of 1-tiles from each side of the mat. Add 1 negative tile to the left side to make a zero pair. Add 1 negative tile to the right side of the mat.

$$x = -6$$

Remove the zero pair from the left side. There are 6 negative tiles on the right side of the mat.

Therefore, $x = -6$. Since $2(-6) + 1 = -6 - 5$, the solution is correct.

Model

Use algebra tiles to model and solve each equation. **9–14. See pp. 365A–365B for models.**

9. $2x + 3 = x - 5$ **−8**
10. $3x - 2 = x + 6$ **4**
11. $x - 1 = 3x + 7$ **−4**
12. $x + 6 = 2x - 3$ **9**
13. $2x + 4 = 3x - 2$ **6**
14. $4x - 1 = 2x + 5$ **3**

Analyze

15. Does it matter whether you remove x-tiles or 1-tiles first? Explain. **See margin.**

16. Explain how you could use models to solve $-2x + 5 = -x - 2$. **See margin.**

Algebra Activity   Equations with Variables on Each Side   **329**

 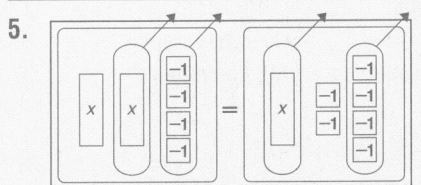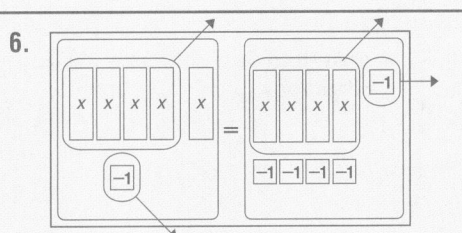
Assess

In **Exercises 1–6** and **9–14,** students should
- correctly model equations using equation mats and algebra tiles.
- manipulate algebra tiles to solve equations.
- use zero pairs, one positive counter, and one negative counter when solving equations.

In **Exercises 15–16,** have students model both scenarios—removing x-tiles first, or removing 1-tiles first.

Study Notebook

You may wish to have students summarize this activity and what they learned from it.

15. You can remove either tile first. But it is a good idea to remove the 1-tile first, because you are using the work backward strategy.

16. Add two 1-tiles to each side. Then add 2 x-tiles to each side. So, $x = 7$.

1 Focus

5-Minute Check Transparency 7-1 Use as a quiz or review of Chapter 6.

Mathematical Background notes are available for this lesson on page 326C.

How **is solving equations with variables on each side like solving equations with variables on one side?**

The opening activity questions are repeated on page 370 of the *Chapter 7 Resource Masters.*

Reading to Learn Mathematics, p. 370 — ELL

Pre-Activity *How is solving equations with variables on each side like solving equations with variables on one side?*

Do the activity at the top of page 330 in your textbook. Write your answers below.

a. The two sides balance. Without looking in a bag, how can you determine the number of blocks in each bag? Sample answer: Remove one bag from each side. Then remove 3 blocks from each side. There must be 2 blocks in each bag.

b. Explain why your method works. Removing the same thing from each side keeps the scale in balance.

c. Suppose x represents the number of blocks in the bag. Write an equation that is modeled by the balance. $2x + 3 = x + 5$

d. Explain how you could solve the equation. Subtract x from each side. Then subtract 3 from each side.

Reading the Lesson

Describe in words each step shown for solving the following equation.

1. $2x + 4 = 4x - 8$ — Write the equation.
2. $2x - 2x + 4 = 4x - 2x - 8$ — Subtract $2x$ from each side.
3. $4 = 2x - 8$ — Simplify.
4. $4 + 8 = 2x - 8 + 8$ — Add 8 to each side.
5. $12 = 2x$ — Simplify.
6. $\frac{12}{2} = \frac{2x}{2}$ — Divide each side by 2.
7. $6 = x$ — Simplify.

Helping You Remember

8. Write out an equation like that shown above ($2x + 4 = 4x - 8$), along with all the steps needed to solve the equation. Exchange equations with a partner. Then each of you should explain verbally why each step in solving the equation was carried out, for example, "2x was subtracted from each side to eliminate the variable on the left side." Students should be able to describe correctly why each step in the solution process is necessary.

---

a. Sample answer: Remove one bag from each side. Then remove 3 blocks from each side. There must be 2 blocks in each bag.
b. Removing the same thing from each side keeps the scale in balance.

Study Tip

Look Back
To review **Addition and Subtraction Properties of Equality,** see Lesson 3-3.

What **You'll Learn**

- Solve equations with variables on each side.

How **is solving equations with variables on each side like solving equations with variables on one side?**

On the balance at the right, each bag contains the same number of blocks. (Assume that the paper bag weighs nothing.)

a. The two sides balance. Without looking in a bag, how can you determine the number of blocks in each bag?

b. Explain why your method works.

c. Suppose x represents the number of blocks in the bag. Write an equation that is modeled by the balance. $2x + 3 = x + 5$

d. Explain how you could solve the equation.

d. Subtract x from each side. Then subtract 3 from each side.

EQUATIONS WITH VARIABLES ON EACH SIDE To solve equations with variables on each side, use the Addition or Subtraction Property of Equality to write an equivalent equation with the variables on one side. Then solve the equation.

Example 1 *Equations with Variables on Each Side*

Solve $2x + 3 = 3x$. Check your solution.

$2x + 3 = 3x$	Write the equation.
$2x - 2x + 3 = 3x - 2x$	Subtract $2x$ from each side.
$3 = x$	Simplify.

Subtract $2x$ from the left side of the equation to isolate the variable.

Subtract $2x$ from the right side of the equation to keep it balanced.

To check your solution, replace x with 3 in the original equation.

CHECK	$2x + 3 = 3x$	Write the equation.
	$2(3) + 3 \stackrel{?}{=} 3(3)$	Replace x with 3.
	$6 + 3 \stackrel{?}{=} 9$	Check to see whether this statement is true.
	$9 = 9 \checkmark$	The statement is true.

The solution is 3.

✓ **Concept Check** What property allows you to add the same quantity to each side of an equation? **Addition Property of Equality**

Resource Manager

 Workbooks and Reproducible Masters

Chapter 7 Resource Masters
- Study Guide and Intervention, p. 367
- Skills Practice, p. 368
- Practice, p. 369
- Reading to Learn Mathematics, p. 370
- Enrichment, p. 371

Parent and Student Study Guide Workbook, p. 54

Transparencies
5-Minute Check Transparency 7-1
Answer Key Transparencies

 Technology

Interactive Chalkboard
Multimedia Applications

Example 2 *Equations with Variables on Each Side*

a. **Solve $5x + 4 = 3x - 2$. Check your solution.**

$5x + 4 = 3x - 2$	Write the equation.
$5x - 3x + 4 = 3x - 3x - 2$	Subtract $3x$ from each side.
$2x + 4 = -2$	Simplify.
$2x + 4 - 4 = -2 - 4$	Subtract 4 from each side.
$2x = -6$	Simplify.
$x = -3$	Mentally divide each side by 2.

TEACHING TIP
Point out that this step eliminates the variable on the right side.

This step eliminates the constant term on the left side.

CHECK

$5x + 4 = 3x - 2$	Write the equation.
$5(-3) + 4 \stackrel{?}{=} 3(-3) - 2$	Is this statement true?
$-11 = -11 \checkmark$	The solution checks.

The solution is -3.

b. **Solve $2.4 + a = 2.5a - 4.5$.**

$2.4 + a = 2.5a - 4.5$	Write the equation.
$2.4 + a - a = 2.5a - a - 4.5$	Subtract a from each side.
$2.4 = 1.5a - 4.5$	Simplify.
$2.4 + 4.5 = 1.5a - 4.5 + 4.5$	Add 4.5 to each side.
$6.9 = 1.5a$	Simplify.
$\dfrac{6.9}{1.5} = \dfrac{1.5a}{1.5}$	Divide each side by 1.5.
$4.6 = a$	Check your solution.

The solution is 4.6.

You can use equations with variables on each side to solve problems.

Example 3 *Use an Equation to Solve a Problem*

VIDEOS A video store has two membership plans. Under plan A, a yearly membership costs $30 plus $1.50 for each rental. Under plan B, the yearly membership costs $12 plus $3 for each rental. What number of rentals results in the same yearly cost?

Let v represent the number of videos rented.

Words	$30 plus $1.50 for each video	$12 plus $3 for each video
Variables	$30 + 1.50v$	$12 + 3v$

Equation	$30 + 1.50v = 12 + 3v$	Write an equation.
	$30 + 1.5v - 1.5v = 12 + 3v - 1.5v$	Subtract $1.5v$ from each side.
	$30 = 12 + 1.5v$	Simplify.
	$30 - 12 = 12 - 12 + 1.5v$	Subtract 12 from each side.
	$18 = 1.5v$	Simplify.
	$\dfrac{18}{1.5} = \dfrac{1.5v}{1.5}$	Divide each side by 1.5.
	$12 = v$	Simplify.

The yearly cost is the same for 12 rentals.

More About. . .

Videos
In 1980, only 1% of American households owned a VCR. Today, more than 80% do.
Source: Statistical Abstracts

---

2 Teach

Building on Prior Knowledge

In Chapter 3, students learned to solve two-step equations. In this lesson, students learn to solve more complex equations with variables on each side.

EQUATIONS WITH VARIABLES ON EACH SIDE

In-Class Examples Power Point®

1 Solve $5x + 12 = 2x$. Check your solution. -4

2 a. Solve $7x + 3 = 2x + 23$.   4

   b. Solve $1.7 + a = 2.5a - 4.9$.   4.4

Teaching Tip You can show the solutions for the Example problems by using a graphing calculator. Graph each side of a problem as separate equations in y_1 and y_2. The x-coordinate of their intersection point is the solution to the problem.

3 **CAR RENTAL** A car rental agency has two plans. Under plan A, a car rents for $80 plus $20 each day. Under plan B, a car rents for $120 plus $15 each day. What number of days results in the same cost?   The cost is the same for 8 days.

Teaching Tip You may want to investigate the scenario of Example 3 by having students observe the patterns of renting 1 day, renting 2 days, renting 3 days, etc.

D A I L Y
INTERVENTION   **Differentiated Instruction**   **ELL**

- **Verbal/Linguistic** On cards, have students write an equation that requires several steps to solve, such as $8c + 16 = 4c - 4$. Then, on separate cards or slips of paper, have them write out in words each step necessary to solve the equation, for example, "Subtract $4c$ from each side." Students should shuffle the cards, exchange sets with a partner, and place the cards in the correct order and determine a solution.

Study Notebook

Have students—

- write out a simple equation with variables on both sides and list the steps to solve the equation.
- include any other item(s) that they find helpful in mastering the skills in this lesson.

About the Exercises . . .

Odd/Even Assignments
Exercises 10–35 are structured so that students practice the same concepts whether they are assigned odd or even problems.

Assignment Guide

Basic: 11–29 odd, 35, 37–40, 42–53

Average: 11–35 odd, 37–40, 42–53 (Optional: 41)

Advanced: 10–36 even, 37–47 (Optional: 48–53)

4 Assess

Open-Ended Assessment

Modeling Have students create balances and use blocks and paper bags to develop problems similar to the one at the beginning of the lesson.

Getting Ready for Lesson 7-2

PREREQUISITE SKILL Lesson 7-2 presents solving equations with grouping symbols. Exercises 48–53 should be used to determine your students' familiarity with using the Distributive Property to rewrite algebraic expressions.

Check for Understanding

Concept Check

GUIDED PRACTICE KEY	
Exercises	Examples
3–8	1, 2
9	3

1. **Name** the property of equality that allows you to subtract the same quantity from each side of an equation. **Subt. Prop. of Equality**

2. **OPEN ENDED** Write an example of an equation with variables on each side. State the steps you would use to isolate the variable. **See margin.**

Guided Practice

Solve each equation. Check your solution.

3. $4x - 8 = 5x$ **−8**
4. $12x = 2x + 40$ **4**
5. $4x - 1 = 3x + 2$ **3**
6. $4k + 24 = 6k - 10$ **17**
7. $n + 0.4 = -n + 1$ **0.3**
8. $3.1w + 5 = 0.8 + w$ **−2**

Application

9. **CAR RENTAL** Suppose you can rent a car from ABC Auto for either $25 a day plus $0.45 a mile or for $40 a day plus $0.25 a mile. What number of miles results in the same cost for one day? **75 miles**

★ indicates increased difficulty

Practice and Apply

Homework Help

For Exercises	See Examples
10–27, 30–33	1, 2
28, 29, 34–36	3

Extra Practice
See page 739.

Solve each equation. Check your solution.

10. $4x + 9 = 7x$ **3**
11. $6a = 26 + 4a$ **13**
12. $3y + 16 = 5y$ **8**
13. $n - 14 = 3n$ **−7**
14. $8 - 3c = 2c - 2$ **2**
15. $3 - 4b = 10b + 10$ **−0.5**
16. $7d - 13 = 3d + 7$ **5**
17. $2f - 6 = 7f + 24$ **−6**
18. $-s + 4 = 7s - 3$ **0.875**
19. $4a - 2 = 7a - 6$ $\frac{4}{3}$
20. $12n - 24 = -14n + 28$ **2**
21. $13y - 18 = -5y + 36$ **3**
22. $12 + 1.5a = 3a$ **8**
23. $12.6 - x = 2x$ **4.2**
24. $2b + 6.2 = 13.2 - 8b$ **0.7**
25. $3c + 4.5 = 7.2 - 6c$ **0.3**
26. $12.4y + 14 = 6y - 2$ **−2.5**
27. $4.3n - 1.6 = 2.3n + 5.2$ **3.4**

Define a variable and write an equation to find each number. Then solve.

28. Twice a number is 220 less than six times the number. What is the number? $2x = 6x - 220$; **55**

29. Fourteen less than three times a number equals the number. What is the number? $3y - 14 = y$; **7**

Solve each equation. Check your solution.

★30. $\frac{4}{5}y - 8 = \frac{2}{5}y + 16$ **60**
★31. $\frac{3}{4}k + 16 = 2 - \frac{1}{8}k$ **−16**
★32. $\frac{x}{0.4} = 2x + 1.2$ **2.4**
★33. $\frac{1}{3}b + 8 = \frac{1}{2}b - 4$ **72**

34. **GEOGRAPHY** The coastline of California is 46 miles longer than twice the length of Louisiana's coastline. It is also 443 miles longer than Louisiana's coastline. Find the lengths of the coastlines of California and Louisiana. **CA: 840 mi; LA: 397 mi**

35. **CELLULAR PHONES** One cellular phone carrier charges $29.75 a month plus $0.15 a minute for local calls. Another carrier charges $19.95 a month and $0.29 a minute for local calls. For how many minutes is the cost of the plans the same? **70 min**

332 **Chapter 7** Equations and Inequalities

Answers

2. Sample answer: $3x + 4 = 2x - 8$; subtract $2x$ from each side, subtract 4 from each side.

38. In both cases, the goal is to isolate the variable. Answers should include the following.
- Sample equations: variables on both sides: $-2x - 8 = 4x - 2$, variables on one side: $3x + 2 = 8$
- They are alike because the goal is to isolate the variable. However, in equations with variables on both sides, you have to add or subtract variables from each side as well as constant terms.

★ **36.** An empty bucket is put under two faucets. If one faucet is turned on alone, the bucket fills in 6 minutes. If the other faucet is turned on alone, the bucket fills in 4 minutes. If both are turned on, how many seconds will it take to fill the bucket? **144 s**

37. CRITICAL THINKING Three times the quantity $y + 7$ equals four times the quantity $y - 2$. What value of y makes the sentence true? **29**

38. WRITING IN MATH Answer the question that was posed at the beginning of the lesson. **See margin.**

How is solving equations with variables on each side like solving equations with variables on one side?

Include the following in your answer:
- examples of an equation with variables on each side and an equation with the variable on one side, and
- an explanation of how they are alike and how they are different.

Standardized Test Practice
Ⓐ Ⓑ Ⓒ Ⓓ

39. Shoe World offers Olivia a temporary job during her spring break. The manager gives her a choice as to how she wants to be paid, but she must decide before she starts working. The choices are shown below.

	Pay per Hour	Pay for Each Dollar of Shoe Sales
Plan 1	$3	15¢
Plan 2	$4	10¢

Which equation shows what Olivia's sales would need to be in one hour to earn the same amount under either plan? **A**

Ⓐ $3 + 0.15s = 4 + 0.10s$ 　　Ⓑ $3s + 0.15 = 4s + 0.10$

Ⓒ $3 + 0.10s = 4 + 0.15s$ 　　Ⓓ $3(s + 0.15) = 4(s + 0.10)$

40. What is the solution of $3x - 1 = x + 3$? **B**

Ⓐ 1　　　Ⓑ 2　　　Ⓒ 3　　　Ⓓ 4

Extending the Lesson
★ **41. WEATHER** The formula $F = \frac{9}{5}C + 32$ is used for finding the Fahrenheit temperature when a Celsius temperature is known. Find the temperature where the Celsius and Fahrenheit scales are the same. **−40°**

Maintain Your Skills

Mixed Review
42. PROBABILITY What is the probability of randomly choosing the letter T from the letters in PITTSBURGH? *(Lesson 6-9)* **20%**

43. Find the percent of increase from $80 to $90. *(Lesson 6-8)* **12.5%**

ALGEBRA Solve each problem using an equation. *(Lesson 6-7)*

44. 14 is what percent of 20? **70%**　　**45.** Find 36% of 18. **6.48**

46. 1.5 is 30% of what number? **5**　　**47.** Find 140% of 50. **70**

Getting Ready for the Next Lesson
PREREQUISITE SKILL Use the Distributive Property to rewrite each expression as an equivalent algebraic expression.
(To review the Distributive Property, see Lesson 3-1.) **52. $-32k + 18.4$**

48. $4(x - 8)$ **$4x - 32$**　　**49.** $3(2a + 9)$ **$6a + 27$**　　**50.** $5(12 - x)$ **$60 - 5x$**

51. $2(1.2c + 14)$ **$2.4c + 28$**　　**52.** $8(-4k + 2.3)$　　**53.** $\frac{1}{2}(n - 9)$ **$\frac{1}{2}n - \frac{9}{2}$**

The trends in attendance at various sporting events can be represented by equations. Visit www.pre-alg.com/webquest to continue work on your WebQuest project.

Teacher to Teacher

Jack F. Rose, Jr.　　**John Winthrop M.S., Deep River, CT**

"I like to use a graphing calculator to show how to solve equations with variables on each side. For an equation like $30 + 1.50v = 12 + 3v$, enter the expression $30 + 1.50X = 12 + 3X$ in the Y= list. The equals sign can be found in the TEST menu. Use the TABLE feature to observe the values for X and Y1. A Y1 value of 1 identifies the values of x for which the equation is true."

1 Focus

5-Minute Check Transparency 7-2 Use as a quiz or review of Lesson 7-1.

Mathematical Background notes are available for this lesson on page 326C.

Why is the Distributive Property important in solving equations?

The opening activity questions are repeated on page 375 of the *Chapter 7 Resource Masters.*

Reading to Learn Mathematics, p. 375 — ELL

Pre-Activity *Why is the Distributive Property important in solving equations?*

Do the activity at the top of page 334 in your textbook. Write your answers below.

a. What does *t* represent? the time Josh travels

b. Why is Maria's time shown as *t* − 1?
She left 1 h later than Josh.

c. Write an equation that represents the time when Maria catches up to Josh. (*Hint:* They will have traveled the same distance.)
$2t = 10(t − 1)$

Reading the Lesson 1–2. See students' work.

Write a definition and give an example of each new vocabulary word or phrase.

Vocabulary	Definition	Example
1. null or empty set		
2. identity		

3. If an equation results in a sentence that is never true, the solution set
is the null or empty set .

4. When an equation results in an identity, the solution set
is all numbers .

5. To solve an equation containing grouping symbols, you must first use
the Distributive Property .

6. For a rectangle, two times the length plus two times the width equals
the perimeter .

Helping You Remember

7. Explain in a paragraph why solving a geometry problem, like that in Example 2 in your text, requires the use of the Distributive Property. You may wish to sketch a figure and assign values to the sides to aid your explanation. Sample answer: To find the perimeter, you must add together two times the width and two times the length. Since the length is given as an expression, such as 3x + 2, you must multiply the expression by 2, 2(3x + 2), therefore requiring the use of the Distributive Property.

Vocabulary
- null or empty set
- identity

a. the time Josh travels

Study Tip

Look Back
To review the **Distributive Property**, see Lesson 3-1.

What You'll Learn

- Solve equations that involve grouping symbols.
- Identify equations that have no solution or an infinite number of solutions.

Why is the Distributive Property important in solving equations?

Josh starts walking at a rate of 2 mph. One hour later, his sister Maria starts on the same path on her bike, riding at 10 mph.

The table shows expressions for the distance each has traveled after a given time.

	Rate (mph)	Time (hours)	Distance (miles)
Josh	2	t	$2t$
Maria	10	$t-1$	$10(t-1)$

a. What does *t* represent?

b. Why is Maria's time shown as $t − 1$? She left 1 h later than Josh.

c. Write an equation that represents the time when Maria catches up to Josh. (*Hint:* They will have traveled the same distance.) $2t = 10(t − 1)$

SOLVE EQUATIONS WITH GROUPING SYMBOLS To find how many hours it takes Maria to catch up to Josh, you can solve the equation $2t = 10(t − 1)$. First, use the Distributive Property to remove the grouping symbols.

Example 1 Solve Equations with Parentheses

a. **Solve the equation $2t = 10(t − 1)$. Check your solution.**

$2t = 10(t − 1)$	Write the equation.
$2t = 10(t) − 10(1)$	Use the Distributive Property.
$2t = 10t − 10$	Simplify.
$2t − 10t = 10t − 10t − 10$	Subtract 10t from each side.
$−8t = −10$	Simplify.
$\dfrac{−8t}{−8} = \dfrac{−10}{−8}$	Divide each side by −8.
$t = \dfrac{5}{4}$ or $1\dfrac{1}{4}$	Simplify.

CHECK Josh traveled $\dfrac{2 \text{ miles}}{\text{hour}} \cdot \dfrac{5 \text{ hour}}{4}$ or $2\dfrac{1}{2}$ miles.

Maria traveled one hour less than Josh. She traveled

$\dfrac{10 \text{ miles}}{\text{hour}} \cdot \dfrac{1 \text{ hour}}{4}$ or $2\dfrac{1}{2}$ miles.

Therefore, Maria caught up to Josh in $\dfrac{1}{4}$ hour, or 15 minutes.

Resource Manager

📁 Workbooks and Reproducible Masters

Chapter 7 Resource Masters
- Study Guide and Intervention, p. 372
- Skills Practice, p. 373
- Practice, p. 374
- Reading to Learn Mathematics, p. 375
- Enrichment, p. 376
- Assessment, p. 411

Parent and Student Study Guide Workbook, p. 55

Transparencies
5-Minute Check Transparency 7-2
Real-World Transparency 7
Answer Key Transparencies

Technology
Interactive Chalkboard
Pre-AlgePASS: Tutorial Plus, Lesson 19

b. Solve $5(a - 4) = 3(a + 1.5)$.

$5(a - 4) = 3(a + 1.5)$	Write the equation.
$5a - 20 = 3a + 4.5$	Use the Distributive Property.
$5a - 20 + 20 = 3a + 4.5 + 20$	Add 20 to each side.
$5a = 3a + 24.5$	Simplify.
$5a - 3a = 3a - 3a + 24.5$	Subtract $3a$ from each side.
$2a = 24.5$	Simplify.
$\dfrac{2a}{2} = \dfrac{24.5}{2}$	Divide each side by 2.
$a = 12.25$	Simplify.

The solution is 12.25. Check your solution.

Study Tip

Alternative Method
You can also solve the equation by subtracting $3a$ from each side first, then adding 20 to each side.

✓ **Concept Check** What property do you use to remove the grouping symbols from the equation $2(8 - a) = 4(a + 9)$? **Distributive Property**

Sometimes a geometric figure is described in terms of only one of its dimensions. To find the dimensions, you may have to solve an equation that contains grouping symbols.

Example 2 *Use an Equation to Solve a Problem*

GEOMETRY The perimeter of a rectangle is 46 inches. Find the dimensions if the length is 5 inches greater than twice the width.

Words The length is 5 inches greater than twice the width. The perimeter is 46 inches.

Variables Let w = the width.
Let $2w + 5$ = the length.

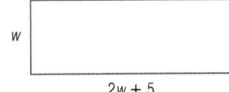

$2w + 5$

Study Tip

Look Back
To review **perimeter of a rectangle**, see Lesson 3-7.

Equation $\underbrace{2 \text{ times length}}_{2(2w + 5)} + \underbrace{2 \text{ times width}}_{2w} = \underbrace{\text{perimeter}}_{46}$

Solve $2(2w + 5) + 2w = 46$.

$2(2w + 5) + 2w = 46$	Write the equation.
$4w + 10 + 2w = 46$	Use the Distributive Property.
$6w + 10 = 46$	Simplify.
$6w + 10 - 10 = 46 - 10$	Subtract 10 from each side.
$6w = 36$	Simplify.
$w = 6$	Mentally divide each side by 6.

Evaluate $2w + 5$ to find the length.

$2(6) + 5 = 12 + 5$ or 17   Replace w with 6.

CHECK Add the lengths of the four sides.
$6 + 17 + 6 + 17 = 46$ ✓

The width is 6 inches. The length is 17 inches.

SOLVE EQUATIONS WITH GROUPING SYMBOLS

In-Class Examples   Power Point®

1 a. Solve the equation $3h = 5(h - 2)$. Check your solution. **$h = 5$**

b. Solve $6(b - 2) = 3(b + 8.5)$. **$b = 12.5$**

2 GEOMETRY The perimeter of a rectangle is 36 inches. Find the dimensions if the length is 2 inches greater than three times the width. **$w = 4$ in., $\ell = 14$ in.**

Teaching Tip Have students make drawings whenever they do problems related to geometric figures.

✓ **Skills Check**

Solve Equations with Grouping Symbols The perimeter of a rectangle is 74 mm. Find the dimensions if the length is 2 mm greater than six times the width. **$w = 5$ mm, $\ell = 32$ mm**

Interactive Chalkboard
PowerPoint®
Presentations

This CD-ROM is a customizable Microsoft® Power-Point® presentation that includes:

- Step-by-step, dynamic solutions of each In-Class Example from the Teacher Wraparound Edition
- Additional, Your Turn exercises for each example
- The 5-Minute Check Transparencies
- Hot links to Glencoe Online Study Tools

DAILY
INTERVENTION **Unlocking Misconceptions**

- **No Solution** When the variable term drops out of an equation, students may assume there is no solution. Remind them to evaluate the statement that remains. If it is not a true statement, then there is no solution. There will never be a variable in the final step of an equation with no solution. However, if the statement is true, the equation has an infinite number of solutions.

3 Practice/Apply

Study Notebook

Have students—

• add the definitions/examples of the vocabulary terms to their Vocabulary Builder worksheets for Chapter 7.

• copy the rectangle from Example 2 and write notes on how to solve for its dimensions.

• include any other item(s) that they find helpful in mastering the skills in this lesson.

About the Exercises . . .

Organization by Objective
• Solve Equations that Involve Grouping Symbols: 10–29
• Identify Equations that Have No Solution or an Infinite Number of Solutions: 20–23, 26–27

Odd/Even Assignments
Exercises 10–33 are structured so that students practice the same concepts whether they are assigned odd or even problems.

Assignment Guide

Basic: 11–25 odd, 31–35 odd, 38–56
Average: 11–37 odd, 38–56
Advanced: 10–36 even, 37–50 (Optional: 51–56)
All: Practice Quiz 1 (1–5)

NO SOLUTION OR ALL NUMBERS AS SOLUTIONS Some equations have *no* solution. That is, no value of the variable results in a true sentence. The solution set is the **null** or **empty set**, shown by the symbol $\varnothing$ or {}.

Example 3 No Solution

Solve $3x + \frac{1}{3} = 3x - \frac{1}{2}$.

$3x + \frac{1}{3} = 3x - \frac{1}{2}$ Write the equation.

$3x - 3x + \frac{1}{3} = 3x - 3x - \frac{1}{2}$ Subtract 3x from each side.

$\frac{1}{3} = -\frac{1}{2}$ Simplify.

The sentence $\frac{1}{3} = -\frac{1}{2}$ is *never* true. So, the solution set is $\varnothing$.

Other equations may have every number as the solution. An equation that is true for every value of the variable is called an **identity**.

Example 4 All Numbers as Solutions

Solve $2(2x - 1) + 6 = 4x + 4$.

$2(2x - 1) + 6 = 4x + 4$ Write the equation.

$4x - 2 + 6 = 4x + 4$ Use the Distributive Property.

$4x + 4 = 4x + 4$ Simplify.

$4x + 4 - 4 = 4x + 4 - 4$ Subtract 4 from each side.

$4x = 4x$ Simplify.

$x = x$ Mentally divide each side by 4.

The sentence $x = x$ is *always* true. The solution set is all numbers.

Check for Understanding

Concept Check

1. **List** the steps you would take to solve the equation $2x + 3 = 4(x - 1)$. See margin.

2. **OPEN ENDED** Give an example of an equation that has no solution and an equation that is an identity. **Sample answer: $3x + 2 = 3x + 1$ has no solution; $2x + 4 = 2(x + 2)$ is an identity.**

Guided Practice

GUIDED PRACTICE KEY

Exercises	Examples
3–6	1
7, 8	3, 4
9	2

Solve each equation. Check your solution.

3. $3(a - 5) = 18$ **11**

4. $32 = 4(x + 9)$ **−1**

5. $2(d + 6) = 3d - 1$ **13**

6. $6(n - 3) = 4(n + 2.1)$ **13.2**

7. $12 - h = -h + 3$ **$\varnothing$**

8. $3(2g + 4) = 6(g + 2)$ **all numbers**

Application

9. **GEOMETRY** The perimeter of a rectangle is 20 feet. The width is 4 feet less than the length. Find the dimensions of the rectangle. Then find its area. **$\ell = 7$ ft; $w = 3$ ft; $A = 21$ ft²**

DAILY INTERVENTION

Differentiated Instruction

• **Logical** Have students write equations that are identities by working in reverse order. Students should begin with $x = x$, then multiply or divide the variable by a number, followed by several more operations until a complete equation is achieved. A grouping symbol (parentheses) that requires the use of the Distributive Property should be included.

Practice and Apply

Homework Help

For Exercises	See Examples
10–19, 24, 25, 28, 29	1
20–23, 26, 27 30–33	3, 4 2

Extra Practice
See page 740.

Solve each equation. Check your solution.

10. $3(g - 3) = 6$ **5**

11. $3(x + 1) = 21$ **6**

12. $5(2c + 7) = 80$ **4.5**

13. $6(3d + 5) = 75$ **2.5**

14. $3(a - 3) = 2(a + 4)$ **17**

15. $3(s + 22) = 4(s + 12)$ **18**

16. $4(x - 2) = 3(1.5 + x)$ **12.5**

17. $3(a - 1) = 4(a - 1.5)$ **3**

18. $2(3.5n + 6) = 2.5n - 2$ **−3.$\overline{1}$**

19. $4.2x - 9 = 3(1.2x + 4)$ **35**

20. $4(f + 3) + 5 = 17 + 4f$ **all numbers**

21. $3n + 4 = 5(n + 2) - 2n$ **∅**

23. all numbers

22. $8y - 3 = 5(y - 1) + 3y$ **∅**

23. $2(x - 5) = 4x - 2(x + 5)$

24. $\frac{1}{2}(2n - 5) = 4n - 1$ **−0.5**

25. $y - 2 = \frac{1}{3}(y + 6)$ **6**

26. all numbers

★ 26. $-3(4b - 10) = \frac{1}{2}(-24b + 60)$

★ 27. $\frac{3}{4}a + 4 = \frac{1}{4}(3a + 16)$ **all numbers**

★ 28. $\frac{d}{0.4} = 2d + 1.24$ **2.48**

★ 29. $\frac{a - 6}{12} = \frac{a - 2}{4}$ **0**

Find the dimensions of each rectangle. The perimeter is given.

30. $P = 460$ ft

31. $P = 440$ yd

32. $P = 11$ m

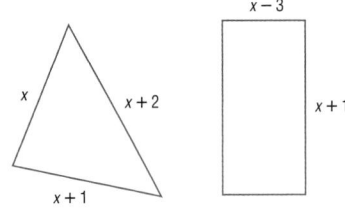

w

$w + 30$
100 ft by 130 ft

w

$3w - 60$
70 yd by 150 yd

w

$2w - 2$
2.5 m by 3 m

33. **GEOMETRY** The perimeter of a rectangle is 32 feet. Find the dimensions if the length is 4 feet longer than three times the width. Then find the area of the rectangle. **w: 3 ft; ℓ: 13 ft; A: 39 ft²**

34. **NUMBER THEORY** Three times the sum of three consecutive integers is 72. What are the integers? **7, 8, 9**

35. **GEOMETRY** The triangle and the rectangle have the same perimeter. Find the dimensions of each figure. Then find the perimeter. **triangle: 7, 8, 9; rectangle, 4, 8; perimeter: 24**

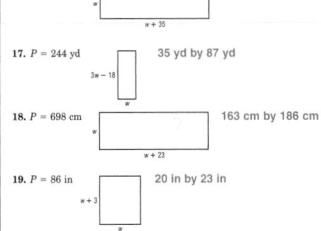

x, $x + 2$, $x + 1$, $x - 3$, $x + 1$

36. **BASKETBALL** Camilla has three times as many points as Lynn. Lynn has five more points than Kim. Camilla, Lynn, and Kim combined have twice as many points as Jasmine. If Jasmine has 25 points, how many points does each of the other three girls have? **Kim: 6, Lynn: 11, Camilla: 33**

37. **DECORATING** Suppose a rectangular room measures 15 feet long by 12 feet wide by 7 feet high and has two windows and two doors. Use the information at the left to find how many gallons of paint are needed to paint the room using two coats of paint. **2 gal**

More About. . .

Decorating • • • • • • • • • •

A gallon of paint covers about 350 square feet. Estimate the square footage by multiplying the combined wall lengths by wall height and subtracting 15 square feet for each window and door.

Source: *The Family Handyman Magazine Presents Handy Hints for Home, Yard, and Workshop*

Answer (p. 336)

1. Multiply 4 times $(x - 1)$. Subtract $2x$ from each side. Add 4 to each side. Divide each side by 2.

Study Guide and Intervention, p. 372

Equations with grouping symbols can be solved by first using the Distributive Property to remove the grouping symbols.

Example 1 Solve the equation $2(6m - 1) = 8m$. Check your solution.

$2(6m - 1) = 8m$ Write the equation.

$12m - 2 = 8m$ Apply the Distributive Property.

$12m - 12m - 2 = 8m - 12m$ Subtract $12m$ from each side.

$-2 = -4m$ Simplify.

$\frac{-2}{-4} = \frac{-4m}{-4}$ Divide each side by -4.

$\frac{1}{2} = m$ Simplify.

CHECK

$2(6m - 1) = 8m$

$2\left(6\left(\frac{1}{2}\right) - 1\right) \stackrel{?}{=} 8\left(\frac{1}{2}\right)$ Replace m with $\frac{1}{2}$.

$2(3 - 1) \stackrel{?}{=} 4$ Simplify.

$4 = 4$ ✓   The solution checks.

Some equations have no solution. The solution set is the **null** or **empty set**. Other equations have every number as a solution. Such an equation is called an **identity**.

Example 2 Solve each equation.

a. $2(x - 1) = 4 + 2x$
$-2x - 2 = 4 + 2x$
$2x - 2x - 2 = 4 + 2x - 2x$
$-2 = 4$
The solution set is Ø.

b. $-2(x - 1) = 2 - 2x$
$-2x + 2 = 2 - 2x$
$-2x + 2 - 2 = 2 - 2 - 2x$
$-2x = -2x$
$x = x$
The solution set is all real numbers.

Exercises

Solve each equation. Check your solution.

1. $8(g - 3) = 24$ $g = 6$
2. $5(x + 3) = 25$ $x = 2$
3. $7(2c - 5) = 7$ $c = 3$
4. $2(3d + 7) = 5 + 6d$ Ø

5. $2(s + 11) = 5(s + 2)$ $s = 4$
6. $7y - 1 = 2(y + 3) - 2$ $y = 1$
7. $2(f + 3) - 2 = 8 + 2f$ Ø

8. $2(x - 2) + 3 = 2x - 1$ all numbers
9. $1 + 2(b + 6) = 5(b - 1)$ $b = 6$
10. $2x - 5 = 3(x + 3)$ $x = -14$

Skills Practice, p. 373 and Practice, p. 374 (shown)

Solve each equation. Check your solution.

1. $4(j - 7) = 12$ 10
2. $5(2k + 10) = 40$ −1
3. $7(2p + 3) - 8 = 6p + 29$ 2
4. $7(g - 4) = 3$ $4\frac{3}{7}$
5. $3(4c + 5) = 24$ 0.75
6. $2(a - 1) = 3(a + 1)$ −5
7. $3(x - 3) = 5(1.5 + x)$ −8.25
8. $2(1.5m + 3) = 3.5m - 1$ 14
9. $a - \frac{5}{10} = 2a - \frac{3}{5}$ 0.1
10. $2.2x - 5 = 2(1.4x + 3)$ −18.3
11. $\frac{d}{0.2} = 3d + 2.1$ 1.05
12. $5n + 3 = 2(n + 2) - 3n$ $\frac{1}{6}$
13. $\frac{3}{2}a + 2 = \frac{1}{3}(4a + 1)$ $2\frac{1}{2}$
14. $y - 7 = \frac{1}{4}(y + 2)$ 10
15. $5(f + 2) = 9 + 5f$ Ø

Find the dimensions of each rectangle. The perimeter is given.

16. $P = 122$ m   13 m by 48 m $w + 35$

17. $P = 244$ yd   35 yd by 87 yd $3w - 18$

18. $P = 698$ cm   163 cm by 186 cm $w + 23$

19. $P = 86$ in   20 in by 23 in $w + 3$

20. **GEOMETRY** The perimeter of a rectangle is 80 feet. Find the dimensions if the length is 5 feet longer than four times the width. Then find the area of the rectangle. $w = 7$ ft, $\ell = 33$ ft; $A = 231$ ft²

21. **NUMBER THEORY** Five times the sum of three consecutive integers is 150. What are the integers?   9, 10, 11

Enrichment, p. 376

Sonya Vasilievna Kovalesky

Sonya Vasilievna Kovalevsky (1850–1891), a Russian mathematician, achieved a good education and a successful career despite the disadvantage at that time of being female. Discover her accomplishments by working the problems at the bottom of the page. Then if you find your answer in the chart, circle the fact in that square. Each circled fact is a true statement about Kovalevsky's life.

SONYA VASILIEVNA KOVALEVSKY (1850–1891)

She was denied an education in Russia.	She was married just so the European universities would allow her to attend higher education classes.	Upon receiving her doctorate, she was offered several professional appointments all over Europe.
$\frac{1}{4}$	3	156
Sonya was a Russian mathematician and physicist.	She wrote a play that was produced in Moscow.	Sonya was born in Poland and became a well-known mathematician and novelist.
33	10	−5
She became a Lecturer and later Professor of Higher Mathematics in Stockholm.	She began her formal study at the Naval Academy in St. Petersburg.	She was taught privately by renowned mathematician Karl Weierstrass in Berlin.
$-\frac{1}{2}$	6	$\frac{1}{2}$

1. $2z - 8 = 12$ 10
2. $28 = 11x - 5$ 3
3. $n - 12 = 54 - n$ 33
4. $3x + 8 = 5x - 6$ 7
5. $6 + 2s = 7$ $\frac{1}{2}$
6. $\frac{x}{9} - 3 = 17$ 180
7. $9 - (2a + 6) = -9$ 6
8. $x + 6 = 5 - x$ $-\frac{1}{2}$
9. $x + 3(2x - 1) = 4(2x + 1)$ −7

Open-Ended Assessment

Modeling Have students draw a generic rectangle. Then on separate slips of paper, they can write various expressions for the length of a side (using the width, w) and various values for the perimeter. Students can then use the rectangles and slips of paper to present problems to one another.

Getting Ready for Lesson 7-3

PREREQUISITE SKILL Lesson 7-3 presents inequalities in which students evaluate expressions to determine whether a given number is a solution. Exercises 51–56 should be used to determine your students' familiarity with evaluating expressions.

Assessment Options

Practice Quiz 1 The quiz provides students with a brief review of the concepts and skills in Lessons 7-1 and 7-2. Lesson numbers are given to the right of exercises or instruction lines so students can review concepts not yet mastered.

Quiz (Lessons 7-1 and 7-2) is available on p. 411 of the *Chapter 7 Resource Masters*.

38. CRITICAL THINKING An apple costs the same as 2 oranges. Together, an orange and a banana cost 10¢ more than an apple. Two oranges cost 15¢ more than a banana. What is the cost for one of each fruit? **apple: 50¢, banana: 35¢; orange: 25¢**

39. `WRITING IN MATH` Answer the question that was posed at the beginning of the lesson. **See margin.**

Why is the Distributive Property important in solving equations?

Include the following in your answer:
- a definition of the Distributive Property, and
- a description of its use in solving equations.

Standardized Test Practice
Ⓐ Ⓑ Ⓒ Ⓓ

40. Which equation is equivalent to $2(3x - 1) = 10 + 2x$? **C**

Ⓐ $8x - 2 = 10$ Ⓑ $6x = 11 + 2x$

Ⓒ $4x - 2 = 10$ Ⓓ $6x - 1 = 10 + 2x$

41. Car X leaves Northtown traveling at a steady rate of 55 mph. Car Y leaves 1 hour later following Car X, traveling at a steady rate of 60 mph. Which equation can be used to determine how long after Car X leaves Car Y will catch up? **D**

Ⓐ $55x = 60x - 1$ Ⓑ $55x = 60x$

Ⓒ $60x = 55(x - 1)$ Ⓓ $55x = 60(x - 1)$

Maintain Your Skills

Mixed Review **ALGEBRA** Solve each equation. Check your solution. *(Lesson 7-1)*

42. $4x = 2x + 5$ **2.5** **43.** $3x + 5 = 7 - 2x$ **0.4** **44.** $1.5x + 9 = 3x - 3$ **8**

45. PROBABILITY Find the probability of choosing a girl's name at random from 20 girls' names and 30 boys' names. *(Lesson 6-9)* **40%**

Write each fraction as a decimal. Use a bar to show a repeating decimal. *(Lesson 5-1)*

46. $\frac{4}{10}$ **0.4** **47.** $\frac{3}{8}$ **0.375** **48.** $-\frac{1}{3}$ **$-0.\overline{3}$** **49.** $3\frac{6}{25}$ **3.24** **50.** $4\frac{5}{11}$ **$4.\overline{45}$**

Getting Ready for the Next Lesson **PREREQUISITE SKILL** Evaluate each expression.
*(To review **evaluating expressions**, see Lesson 1-3.)*

51. $x - 12, x = 5$ **-7** **52.** $b + 11, b = -15$ **-4** **53.** $4a, a = -6$ **-24**

54. $2t + 8, t = -3$ **2** **55.** $\frac{24}{c}, c = -3$ **-8** **56.** $\frac{3x}{4} + 2, x = 6$ **6.5**

Practice Quiz 1
Lessons 7-1 and 7-2

Define a variable and write an equation. Then solve. *(Lesson 7-1)*

1. Twice a number is 150 less than 5 times the number. What is the number? **$2x = 5x - 150$; 50**

Solve each equation. Check your solution. *(Lessons 7-1 and 7-2)*

2. $6y + 42 = 4y$ **-21** **3.** $7m - 12 = 2.5m + 2$ **$3.\overline{1}$**

4. $8(p - 4) = 2(2p + 1)$ **8.5** **5.** $b + 2(b + 5) = 3(b - 1) + 13$ **all numbers**

Answer

39. Sample answer: Many equations include grouping symbols. You must use the Distributive Property to correctly solve the equation. Answers should include the following.

- The Distributive Property states that $a(b + c) = ab + ac$.

- You use the Distributive Property to remove the grouping symbols when you are solving equations.

Reading Mathematics

Meanings of At Most and At Least

The phrases *at most* and *at least* are used in mathematics. In order to use them correctly, you need to understand their meanings.

Phrase	Meaning	Mathematical Symbol
at most	• no more than • less than or equal to	$\leq$
at least	• no less than • greater than or equal to	$\geq$

Here is an example of one common use of each phrase, its meaning, and a mathematical expression for the situation.

Verbal Expression	You can spend *at most* $20.
Meaning	You can spend $20 or any amount less than $20.
Mathematical Expression	$s \leq 20$, where s represents the amount you spend.

Verbal Expression	A person must be *at least* 18 to vote.
Meaning	A person who is 18 years old or any age older than 18 may vote.
Mathematical Expression	$a \geq 18$, where a represents age.

Notice that the word *or* is part of the meaning in each case.

Reading to Learn

1. Write your own rule for remembering the meanings of *at most* and *at least*.
Sample answer: at <u>m</u>ost—no <u>m</u>ore than; at <u>l</u>east—no <u>l</u>ess than

For each expression, write the meaning. Then write a mathematical expression using $\leq$ or $\geq$. 2–5. See margin for meanings.

2. You need to earn at least $50 to help pay for a class trip. $e \geq 50$

3. The sum of two numbers is at most 6. $a + b \leq 6$

4. You want to drive at least 250 miles each day. $m \geq 250$

5. You want to hike 4 hours each day at most. $h \leq 4$

Getting Started

Have students write the following on index cards: $\leq$, $\geq$, *at most, at least, no more than, less than or equal to, no less than,* and *greater than or equal to*. In pairs, have students match the cards that are equivalent in meaning.

Teach

At Most/At Least Ask students to write inequalities on index cards such as $x \geq 4$. Then have students use their index cards from the exercise above to describe the inequality. In groups, students can switch their inequalities and quiz one another.

Assess

Study Notebook

Ask students to summarize what they have learned about mathematical and verbal expressions.

ELL English Language Learners may benefit from writing key concepts from this activity in their Study Notebooks in their native language and then in English.

Sample Answers

2. You must earn $50 or more than $50.

3. The sum is 6 or less than 6.

4. You drive 250 miles or more.

5. You will hike 4 hours or less than 4 hours.

1 Focus

5-Minute Check Transparency 7-3 Use as a quiz or review of Lesson 7-2.

Mathematical Background notes are available for this lesson on page 326C.

How can inequalities help you describe relationships?

The opening activity questions are repeated on page 380 of the *Chapter 7 Resource Masters*.

Reading to Learn Mathematics, p. 380 **ELL**

Pre-Activity *How can inequalities help you describe relationships?*

Do the activity at the top of page 340 in your textbook. Write your answers below.

　a. Name three ages of children who can eat free at the restaurant. Does a child who is 6 years old eat free?　Sample ages: 3, 4, 5; no

　b. Name three heights of children who can ride the ride at the amusement park. Can a child who is 40 inches tall ride?　Sample heights: 42 in., 43 in., 44 in., no

　c. Name three speeds that are legal. Is a driver who is traveling at 35 mph driving at a legal speed?　Sample speeds: 25 mph, 30 mph, 35 mph; yes

Reading the Lesson

Write a definition and give an example of the new vocabulary word.

Vocabulary	Definition	Example
1. inequality	See students' work.	

For each of the following phrases, write in the blank the corresponding inequality symbol. Use $<$, $>$, $\leq$, or $\geq$.

2. is greater than　$>$　　3. is less than or equal to　$\leq$

4. is at least　$\geq$　　5. is no less than　$\geq$

6. exceeds　$>$　　7. is less than　$<$

8. is more than　$>$　　9. is at most　$\leq$

Helping You Remember

10. The word *inequality* is composed of the prefix *in-* and the base word *equality*.

　a. Find the definitions of *in-* and *equality* in a dictionary. Write their definitions. not, without; of the same size or value

　b. Explain how the definitions can help you remember how *inequality* is used in mathematics. Since *in-* means "not" and *equality* means "same size," *inequality* means not the same size, or not equal in value.

Teaching Tip Have students make their own poster or sign and write an inequality to match it.

What You'll Learn

- Write inequalities.
- Graph inequalities.

Vocabulary
- inequality

How can inequalities help you describe relationships?

Children under 6 eat free.

If your age is less than 6, you eat free.

MUST BE OVER 40 INCHES TALL TO RIDE.

If your height is more than 40 inches, you can ride.

Speed Limit 35

A speed of 35 or less is legal.

　a. Name three ages of children who can eat free at the restaurant. Does a child who is 6 years old eat free? **Sample ages: 3, 4, 5; no**

　b. Name three heights of children who can ride the ride at the amusement park. Can a child who is 40 inches tall ride?

　c. Name three speeds that are legal. Is a driver who is traveling at 35 mph driving at a legal speed? **Sample speeds: 25 mph, 30 mph, 35 mph; yes**

WRITE INEQUALITIES A mathematical sentence that contains $<$ or $>$ is called an **inequality**.

Example **Write Inequalities with $<$ or $>$**

Write an inequality for each sentence.

　a. **Your age is less than 6 years.**

　　Variable　Let a represent age.

　　Inequality　$a < 6$

　b. **Your height is greater than 40 inches.**

　　Variable　Let h represent height.

　　Inequality　$h > 40$

Some inequalities contain $\leq$ or $\geq$ symbols.

Example **Write Inequalities with $\leq$ or $\geq$**

Write an inequality for each sentence.

　a. **Your speed is less than or equal to 35 miles per hour.**

　　Variable　Let s represent speed.

　　Inequality　$s \leq 35$

Resource Manager

📁 Workbooks and Reproducible Masters

Chapter 7 Resource Masters
- Study Guide and Intervention, p. 377
- Skills Practice, p. 378
- Practice, p. 379
- Reading to Learn Mathematics, p. 380
- Enrichment, p. 381
- Assessment, pp. 411, 413

Graphing Calculator and Spreadsheet Masters, p. 32
Parent and Student Study Guide Workbook, p. 56
Prerequisite Skills Workbook, pp. 1–2

📺 Transparencies
5-Minute Check Transparency 7-3
Answer Key Transparencies

💿 Technology
Interactive Chalkboard
Pre-AlgePASS: Tutorial Plus, Lesson 20

b. Your speed is greater than or equal to 55 miles per hour.

Variable   Let s represent speed.

Inequality $s \geq 55$

The table below shows some common verbal phrases and the corresponding mathematical inequalities.

Concept Summary			Inequalities
<	>	≤	≥
• is less than • is fewer than	• is greater than • is more than • exceeds	• is less than or equal to • is no more than • is at most	• is greater than or equal to • is no less than • is at least

Example 3   *Use an Inequality*

NUTRITION   A food can be labeled low fat only if it has no more than 3 grams of fat per serving. Write an inequality to describe low fat foods.

Words   Grams of fat per serving is no more than 3.

Variable   Let f = number of grams of fat per serving.

Inequality f $\leq$ 3

The inequality is $f \leq 3$.

Inequalities with variables are open sentences. When the variable in an open sentence is replaced with a number, the inequality may be true or false.

Example 4   *Determine Truth of an Inequality*

For the given value, state whether each inequality is *true* or *false*.

a. $s - 7 < 5$, $s = 14$

    $s - 7 < 5$ Write the inequality.

    $14 - 7 \overset{?}{<} 5$ Replace s with 14.

    $7 \not< 5$ Simplify.

This sentence is false.

b. $12 \geq \frac{a}{2} + 2$, $a = 20$

    $12 \geq \frac{a}{2} + 2$ Write the inequality.

    $12 \overset{?}{\geq} \frac{20}{2} + 2$ Replace a with 20.

    $12 \overset{?}{\geq} 10 + 2$ Simplify.

    $12 \geq 12$ Simplify.

Although the inequality $12 > 12$ is false, the equation $12 = 12$ is true.

Therefore, this sentence is true.

In-Class Examples   Power Point®

1 Write an inequality for each sentence.

a. Your age is less than 19 years. $a < 19$

b. Your height is greater than 52 inches. $h > 52$

2 Write an inequality for each sentence.

a. Your speed is less than or equal to 62. $s \leq 62$

b. Your speed is greater than or equal to 42. $s \geq 42$

Teaching Tip   Students may still confuse the $<$ and $>$ symbols. Remind them that the symbol always points to the lesser value. You may also use the elementary reminder that the symbol is like an open mouth and always opens toward the greater value.

3 **AIR POLLUTION** To meet a certain air quality standard, an automobile must have a fuel efficiency of not less than 27.5 miles per gallon. Write an inequality to describe this situation. $e \geq 27.5$

Teaching Tip   Remind students that "2 is greater than x" and "x is less than 2" are equivalent statements. The variable can be on either side of the equation—the direction of the inequality simply changes.

4 For the given value, state whether each inequality is *true* or *false*.

a. $s - 9 < 4$, $s = 6$
This sentence is true.

b. $14 \leq \frac{a}{3} + 1$, $a = 36$
This sentence is false.

GRAPH INEQUALITIES

In-Class Examples

Power Point®

5 Graph each inequality.

a. $x > 10$

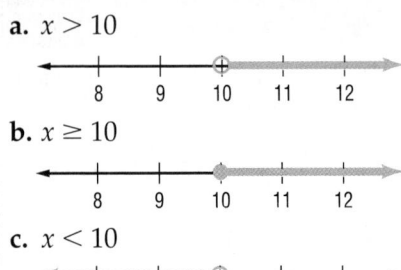

b. $x \geq 10$

c. $x < 10$

d. $x \leq 10$

6 Write the inequality for the graph. $x \geq -38$

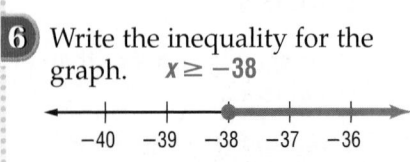

3 Practice/Apply

About the Exercises . . .

Organization by Objective
- **Write Inequalities:** 13–22
- **Graph Inequalities:** 23–40

Odd/Even Assignments
Exercises 13–42 are structured so that students practice the same concepts whether they are assigned odd or even problems.

Assignment Guide
Basic: 13–43 odd, 45–48, 50–62
Average: 13–43 odd, 45–48, 50–62 (Optional: 49)
Advanced: 14–44 even, 45–56 (Optional: 57–62)

GRAPH INEQUALITIES Inequalities can be graphed on a number line. The graph helps you visualize the values that make the inequality true.

Example 5 Graph Inequalities

Graph each inequality on a number line.

a. $x > 4$

b. $x \geq 4$

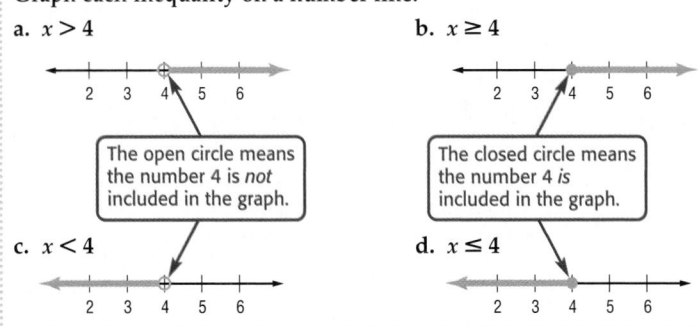

The open circle means the number 4 is *not* included in the graph.

The closed circle means the number 4 *is* included in the graph.

c. $x < 4$

d. $x \leq 4$

Example 6 Write an Inequality

Write the inequality for the graph.

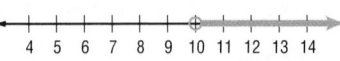

An open circle is on 10, so the point 10 is *not* included in the graph. The arrow points to the right, so the graph includes all numbers greater than 10. The inequality is $x > 10$.

✓ **Concept Check** What symbols are used to write inequalities and what does each symbol mean? $<$ (less than), $>$ (greater than), $\leq$ (less than or equal to), $\geq$ (greater than or equal to)

Check for Understanding

Concept Check

1. **Explain** why a number line graph is a good way to represent an inequality. 1–2. pp. 365A–365B.

2. **OPEN ENDED** Write four examples of inequalities using each of the symbols $<$, $>$, $\leq$, and $\geq$. Tell the meaning of each inequality.

Guided Practice

GUIDED PRACTICE KEY	
Exercises	Examples
3, 4	1, 2
5, 6	4
7–9	5
10, 11	6
12	3

Write an inequality for each sentence.

3. A number increased by 14 is at least 25. $n + 14 \geq 25$

4. Five times some number is less than 65. $5n < 65$

ALGEBRA For the given value, state whether the inequality is *true* or *false*.

5. $n + 4 > 6$, $n = 12$ **true**

6. $34 \leq 4r$, $r = 8$ **false**

Graph each inequality on a number line. 7–9. See pp. 365A–365B.

7. $n > 3$

8. $p \leq 5$

9. $x < 7$

Write the inequality for each graph. 10. $x < 11$ 11. $x \geq -20$

10.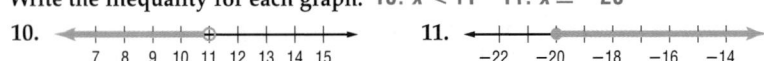

11.

Study Notebook

Have students—

- add the definition/example of the vocabulary term to their Vocabulary Builder worksheets for Chapter 7.
- include any other item(s) that they find helpful in mastering the skills in this lesson.

Application **12. SAFETY** The elevators in an office building have been approved for a maximum load of 3600 pounds. Write an inequality to describe a safe load. $m \le 3600$

★ indicates increased difficulty

Practice and Apply

Homework Help

For Exercises	See Examples
13–16	1, 2
17–22	4
23–34	5
35–40	6
41–43	3

Extra Practice
See page 740.

Write an inequality for each sentence.

13. More than 18,000 fans attended the Kings' opening hockey game at the Staples Center in Los Angeles. $f > 18{,}000$

14. Kyle's earnings at $15 per hour were no more than $60. $15h \le 60$

15. The 10-km race time of 86 minutes was at least twice as long as the winner's time. $86 \ge 2w$

16. A savings account decreased by $75 is now less than $500. $s - 75 < 500$

ALGEBRA For the given value, state whether each inequality is *true* or *false.*

17. $18 - x > 4$, $x = 12$ true

18. $14 + n < 23$, $n = 8$ true

19. $5k > 35$, $k = 7$ false

20. $16 \le 3c$, $c = 8$ true

21. $\dfrac{x}{3} \ge 2$, $x = 9$ true

22. $\dfrac{14}{c} < 7$, $c = 2$ false

Graph each inequality on a number line. 23–34. See pp. 365A–365D.

23. $a > 4$ **24.** $x > 6$ **25.** $n < 11$ **26.** $x < 5$

27. $t \ge 9$ **28.** $b \ge 8$ **29.** $d \le 5$ **30.** $w \le 8$

31. $x > -4$ **32.** $n \ge -3$ **33.** $x \le -5$ **34.** $x < -2$

Write the inequality for each graph. 35. $x > 13$ 36. $x \ge -8$ 37. $x \le -3$

35.
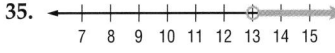

36.
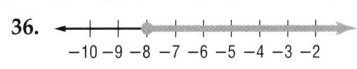

37.
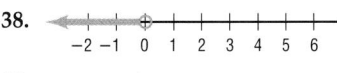

38.
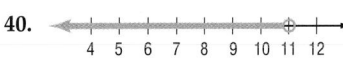

38. $x < 0$

39.

40.

39. $x \ge -32$
40. $x < 11$

HOMEWORK For Exercises 41 and 42, use the graphic.

41. Inali spends at least an hour more than the average time spent by boys on homework each week. Write an inequality for Inali's homework time. $m \ge 6.4$

42. Anna usually spends no more than the average time spent by girls on homework each week. Write an inequality to represent Anna's homework time. $j \le 6.8$

USA TODAY Snapshots®

High school homework time

Students ages 14-18 say they spent a weekly average 6.1 hours on homework last school year, down from 6.6 in 1996-97. Weekly average hours reported by these groups:

Male	Female	Public school student	Private school student	Caucasian	African-American	Other race/ethnicity
5.4	6.8	5.5	10.2	5.8	6.9	8.3

Source: The State of Our Nation's Youth 1998-1999, Horatio Alger Association

By Cindy Hall and Sam Ward, USA TODAY

Writing Have students search newspapers or magazines for graphs that can be used to write inequality statements. They can exchange graphs and inequalities with other students to check.

Getting Ready for Lesson 7-4

PREREQUISITE SKILL Lesson 7-4 presents solving inequalities by adding or subtracting. Exercises 57–62 should be used to determine your students' familiarity with solving equations by adding or subtracting.

Assessment Options

Quiz (Lesson 7-3) is available on p. 411 of the *Chapter 7 Resource Masters.*

Mid-Chapter Test (Lessons 7-1 through 7-3) is available on p. 413 of the *Chapter 7 Resource Masters.*

Answers

45. Symmetric: If $a < b$, then $b < a$; not true. Sample counter-example: $4 < 5$, but $5 \not< 4$. Transitive: If $a < b$ and $b < c$, then $a < c$; true.

46. Inequalities describe numbers that are greater than or less than a given number. Answers should include the following.
- Sample answer: My brother's age is less than (<) my age. My age is less than or equal to (≤) the ages of the other students in my class. My house is more than 2 miles (>) from school. I drink at least 2 (≥) glasses of milk each day.
- Sample answer: My brother is younger than I am. The other students are my age or older. I live farther than 2 miles from school. I drink 2 or more glasses of milk each day.

More About...

Sports •

Almost twice as many boys play high school football as basketball, but basketball is offered at more high schools.

Source: National Association of State High School Associations

Standardized Test Practice
Ⓐ Ⓑ Ⓒ Ⓓ

Extending the Lesson ★

Getting Ready for the Next Lesson

---

43. SPORTS There are more than 30,000 high school basketball and track programs in the United States. If there are 14,600 track programs, write and solve an inequality to determine the number of basketball programs. $b + 14{,}600 > 30{,}000$; $b > 15{,}400$

★ **44.** Find a value for x that satisfies the inequality $0.6 < x < 0.75$. **Sample answer: 0.7**

45. CRITICAL THINKING In Chapter 1, you studied the Symmetric and Transitive Properties of Equality. Restate these properties using inequalities. Are the properties true for inequalities? If a property is not true, give a counterexample. **See margin.**

46. [WRITING IN MATH] Answer the question that was posed at the beginning of the lesson. **See margin.**

How can inequalities help you describe relationships?

Include the following in your answer:
- real-life examples using the four inequality symbols, and
- an explanation of the relationships described by each inequality.

47. Which inequality represents *a number decreased by 2 is at most 8*? **B**
Ⓐ $n - 2$
Ⓑ $n - 2 \le 8$
Ⓒ $n - 2 \ge 8$
Ⓓ $n - 2 > 8$

48. Which of the following is an inequality? **A**
Ⓐ $4 \le x + 2$
Ⓑ $x + 4 = 3$
Ⓒ $x + 5 + y$
Ⓓ $x - y$

★ **49.** Graph the solutions for each compound inequality. **See margin.**
a. $y < -2$ or $y > 3$. (*Hint:* In a sentence, *or* means either part is true.)
b. $y \ge 0$ and $y \le 5$ (*Hint:* In a sentence, *and* means both parts must be true.)

Maintain Your Skills

Mixed Review **ALGEBRA** Solve each equation. Check your solution. *(Lesson 7-2)*

50. $2(3 + x) = 14$ **4**
51. $63 = 9(2y - 3)$ **5**
52. $3(n - 1) = 1.5(n + 2)$ **4**

53. ALGEBRA Four times a number minus 6 is equal to the sum of 3 times the number and 2. Define a variable and write an equation to find the number. *(Lesson 7-1)* $4n - 6 = 3n + 2$; 8

State whether each sequence is *arithmetic, geometric,* or *neither.* Then write the next three terms of each sequence. *(Lesson 5-10)*

54. $-4, -1, 2, 5, \ldots$ **A: 8, 11, 14**
55. $-1, 2, -4, 8, \ldots$ **G: −16, 32, −64**
56. $1, 2, 4, 7, \ldots$ **N: 11, 16, 22**

PREREQUISITE SKILL Solve each equation. *(To review solving equations, see Lesson 3-3.)*

57. $x + 19 = 32$ **13**
58. $a + 7 = -3$ **−10**
59. $26 + c = 19$ **−7**
60. $44 - c = 26$ **18**
61. $y - 9.7 = 10.1$ **19.8**
62. $r - 1.6 = -0.6$ **1**

---

49. a.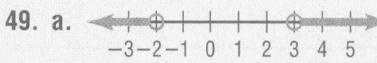

b.

Solving Inequalities by Adding or Subtracting

What You'll Learn

- Solve inequalities by using the Addition and Subtraction Properties of Inequality.

How is solving an inequality similar to solving an equation?

On the balance at the right, the paper bag may contain some blocks.

The blocks and bag on the scale model an inequality because the two sides are not equal.

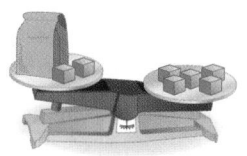

$x + 2 < 5$

The model shows the inequality $x + 2 < 5$. The side with the bag and 2 blocks weighs less than the side with 5 blocks.

a. How many blocks would be in the bag if the left side balanced the right side? (Assume that the paper bag weighs nothing.) **3**

b. Explain how you determined your answer to part **a.**

c. What numbers of blocks can be in the bag to make the left side weigh *less than* the right side? **0, 1, or 2**

d. Write an inequality to represent your answer to part **c.** $x < 3$

b. Sample answer: Remove 2 blocks from each side. There are 3 blocks remaining on the right, so there must be 3 blocks in the bag.

SOLVE INEQUALITIES BY ADDING OR SUBTRACTING Solving an inequality means finding values for the variable that make the inequality true. In the example above, any number less than 3 is a solution. The solution is written as the inequality $x < 3$.

You can solve inequalities by using the Addition and Subtraction Properties of Inequalities.

Key Concept — Addition and Subtraction Properties

- **Words** — When you add or subtract the same number from each side of an inequality, the inequality remains true.

- **Symbols** — For all numbers a, b, and c,
  1. if $a > b$, then $a + c > b + c$ and $a - c > b - c$.
  2. if $a < b$, then $a + c < b + c$ and $a - c < b - c$.

- **Examples**

$2 < 4$	$6 > 3$
$2 + 3 < 4 + 3$	$6 - 4 > 3 - 4$
$5 < 7$	$2 > -1$

These properties are also true for $a \geq b$ and $a \leq b$.

✓ Concept Check How are these properties similar to the Properties of Equality? **See margin.**

Study Tip

Inequalities
When you add or subtract any number from each side of an inequality, the inequality symbol remains the same.

---

1 Focus

 5-Minute Check Transparency 7-4 Use as a quiz or review of Lesson 7-3.

Mathematical Background notes are available for this lesson on page 326D.

How is solving an inequality similar to solving an equation?

The opening activity questions are repeated on page 385 of the *Chapter 7 Resource Masters.*

Reading to Learn Mathematics, p. 385 — ELL

Pre-Activity *How is solving an inequality similar to solving an equation?*

Do the activity at the top of page 345 in your textbook. Write your answers below.

  a. How many blocks would be in the bag if the left side balanced the right side? (Assume that the paper bag weighs nothing.) 3

  b. Explain how you determined your answer to part **a.** Sample answer: Remove 2 blocks from each side. There are 3 blocks remaining on the right, so there must be 3 blocks in the bag.

  c. What numbers of blocks can be in the bag to make the left side weigh *less than* the right side? 0, 1, or 2

  d. Write an inequality to represent your answer to part **c.** $x < 3$

Reading the Lesson

1. Describe the Addition Property of Inequality and give an example of a problem that requires its use. When you add the same number to each side of an inequality, the inequality remains true. Students' examples will vary.

2. Describe the Subtraction Property of Inequality and give an example of a problem that requires its use. When you subtract the same number from each side of an inequality, the inequality remains true. Students' examples will vary.

3. Is 6 a solution for the inequality $17 + x > 23$? Explain. No; the solution is $x > 6$, so 6 will not work.

Helping You Remember

4. In each box below, write three inequalities that can be solved by using the given property. Include at least one negative integer in each box. Sample answers are given.

Addition Property of Inequality	Subtraction Property of Inequality
$x - 4 > 10$	$x + 1 < 2$
$y - 2 \leq -3$	$y + 5 \geq 10$
$z - 8 \geq 2$	$z + 2 > -4$

Concept Check answer appears on next page.

Resource Manager

Workbooks and Reproducible Masters

Chapter 7 Resource Masters
- Study Guide and Intervention, p. 382
- Skills Practice, p. 383
- Practice, p. 384
- Reading to Learn Mathematics, p. 385
- Enrichment, p. 386

Parent and Student Study Guide Workbook, p. 57
Prerequisite Skills Workbook, pp. 1–2, 21–24, 55–62
School-to-Career Masters, p. 13

 Transparencies
5-Minute Check Transparency 7-4
Answer Key Transparencies

Technology
Interactive Chalkboard

2 Teach

Building on Prior Knowledge

In Chapter 2, students reviewed adding and subtracting integers. In this lesson, they will use addition and subtraction to solve inequalities.

SOLVE INEQUALITIES BY ADDING OR SUBTRACTING

In-Class Examples

1 Solve $y + 5 > 11$. Check your solution. $y > 6$

Teaching Tip Another way to check the solution is to see whether 7 is a solution of the equation $x + 3 = 10$. Then try a number greater than 7 and compare the sum to the original equation to determine whether the solution is greater than or less than 7.

2 Solve $-21 \geq d - 8$. Check your solution. $-13 \geq d$ or $d \leq -13$

3 Solve $h - 1\frac{1}{2} < 5$. Graph the solution on a number line.
$h < 6\frac{1}{2}$

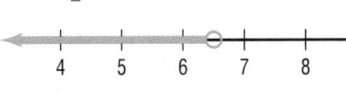

✓ Skills Check

Solve Inequalities by Adding or Subtracting Solve $f + 3\frac{1}{2} > 3$. Graph the solution on a number line. $f > -\frac{1}{2}$

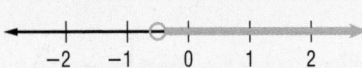

Study Tip

Checking Solutions
Try a number less than 7 to show that it is *not* a solution.

TEACHING TIP
Ask students whether 7 is included in the solution.

TEACHING TIP
Remind students that an open circle means the number is not included in the solution.

Example 1 Solve an Inequality Using Subtraction

Solve $x + 3 > 10$. Check your solution.

$x + 3 > 10$	Write the inequality.
$x + 3 - 3 > 10 - 3$	Subtract 3 from each side.
$x > 7$	Simplify.

To check your solution, try any number greater than 7.

CHECK $x + 3 > 10$ Write the inequality.
$8 + 3 \overset{?}{>} 10$ Replace x with 8.
$11 > 10$ ✓   This statement is true.

Any number greater than 7 will make the statement true. Therefore, the solution is $x > 7$.

Example 2 Solve an Inequality Using Addition

Solve $-6 \geq n - 5$. Check your solution.

$-6 \geq n - 5$	Write the inequality.
$-6 + 5 \geq n - 5 + 5$	Add 5 to each side.
$-1 \geq n$	Simplify.

CHECK   You can check your result by replacing n in the original inequality with a number less than or equal to -1.

The solution is $-1 \geq n$ or $n \leq -1$.

Example 3 Graph Solutions of Inequalities

Solve $a + \frac{1}{2} < 2$. Graph the solution on a number line.

$a + \frac{1}{2} < 2$	Write the inequality.
$a + \frac{1}{2} - \frac{1}{2} < 2 - \frac{1}{2}$	Subtract $\frac{1}{2}$ from each side.
$a < \frac{4}{2} - \frac{1}{2}$	Rename 2 as a fraction with a denominator of 2.
$a < \frac{3}{2}$ or $1\frac{1}{2}$	Simplify.

The solution is $a < 1\frac{1}{2}$.   Check your solution.

Graph the solution.

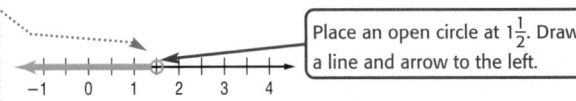

Place an open circle at $1\frac{1}{2}$. Draw a line and arrow to the left.

✓ Concept Check   Does an inequality have only one solution? Explain.
No; there are infinite solutions.

Answer (Concept Check, p. 345)

Sample answer: For both equalities and inequalities, adding or subtracting the same number from each side does not change the truth of the statement.

Example 4 *Use an Inequality to Solve a Problem*

STATE FAIRS Antonio has $18 to ride go-carts and play games at the State Fair. If the go-carts cost $5.50, what is the most he can spend on games?

Explore We need to find the greatest amount of money Antonio can spend on games.

Plan Let x represent the amount Antonio can spend on games. Write an inequality to represent the problem. Recall that *at most* means *less than or equal to*.

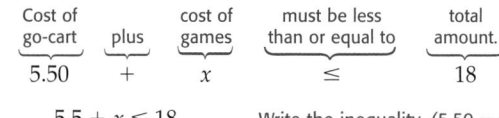

Cost of go-cart	plus	cost of games	must be less than or equal to	total amount.
5.50	+	x	≤	18

Solve

$5.5 + x \le 18$ Write the inequality. (5.50 = 5.5)

$5.5 - 5.5 + x \le 18 - 5.5$ Subtract 5.5 from each side.

$x \le 12.5$ Simplify.

Examine Check by choosing an amount less than or equal to $12.50, say, $10. Then Antonio would spend $5.50 + $10 or $15.50 in all. Since $15.50 < $18, the answer is reasonable.

So, the most Antonio can spend on games is $12.50.

In-Class Example **Power Point®**

4 **BOWLING** Katya has $12 to take to the bowling alley. If the shoe rental costs $3.75, what is the most she can spend on games and snacks? **Katya can spend no more than $8.25 on games and snacks.**

Teaching Tip Remind students that the expression "no more than" means less than or equal to, which is symbolized by ≤.

3 Practice/Apply

Study Notebook

Have students—
• write an example of an inequality and list the steps needed to solve the inequality by adding or subtracting.
• include any other item(s) that they find helpful in mastering the skills in this lesson.

Check for Understanding

Concept Check

1. Use addition to undo subtraction; use subtraction to undo addition.

1. **Explain** when you would use addition and when you would use subtraction to solve an inequality.

2. **FIND THE ERROR** Dylan and Jada are using the statement *a minus three is greater than or equal to 15* to find values of *a*. **See margin.**

Dylan	Jada
$a - 3 \ge 15$	$a - 3 = 15$
$a - 3 + 3 \ge 15 + 3$	$a - 3 + 3 = 15 + 3$
$a \ge 18$	$a = 18$

Who is correct? Explain your reasoning.

3. **OPEN ENDED** Make up a problem whose solution is graphed below. **See margin.**

Guided Practice

GUIDED PRACTICE KEY	
Exercises	Examples
4–6	1
7–9	2
10, 11	3
12	4

Solve each inequality. Check your solution.

4. $x + 3 < 8$ $x < 5$ **5.** $14 + y \ge 7$ $y \ge -7$ **6.** $-13 \ge 9 + b$ $b \le -22$

7. $a - 5 > 6$ $a > 11$ **8.** $c - (-2) \le 3$ $c \le 1$ **9.** $-5 < t - 2$ $t > -3$

Solve each inequality. Then graph the solution on a number line.

10. $h + 4 > 4$ $h > 0$ **11.** $x - 6 \le 4$ $x \le 10$

10–11. See pp. 365A–365D for graphs.

Application **12.** **SAVINGS** Chris is saving money for a ski trip. He has $62.50, but his goal is to save at least $100. What is the least amount Chris needs to save to reach his goal? **$37.50**

About the Exercises . . .
Odd/Even Assignments
Exercises 13–46 are structured so that students practice the same concepts whether they are assigned odd or even problems.

Alert! A follow-up activity for Exercise 44 involves research on the Internet or other reference materials.

Assignment Guide
Basic: 13–45 odd, 47–70
Average: 13–45 odd, 47–70
Advanced: 14–46 even, 47–64 (Optional: 65–70)

Answers

2. Sample answer: Dylan; both solutions include 18, but the solution to the inequality also includes numbers greater than 18.

3. Sample answer: Joanna works part-time at a clothing store. Part-time workers must work fewer than 30 hours a week. If Joanna has already worked 8 hours this week, how many hours can she still work?

Practice and Apply

31–42. See pp. 365A–365D for graphs.

37. $m \geq 27$

Solve each inequality. Check your solution. 18. $n > 37$ 24. $d \geq -25$

13. $p + 7 < 9$ $p < 2$
14. $t + 6 > -3$ $t > -9$
15. $-14 \geq 8 + b$ $b \leq -22$
16. $16 > -11 + k$ $k < 27$
17. $3 \geq -2 + y$ $y \leq 5$
18. $25 < n + (-12)$
19. $r - 5 \leq 2$ $r \leq 7$
20. $a - 6 < 13$ $a < 19$
21. $j - 8 \leq -12$ $j \leq -4$
22. $-8 > h - 1$ $h < -7$
23. $22 > w - (-16)$ $w < 6$
24. $-30 \leq d + (-5)$
25. $1 + y \leq 2.4$ $y \leq 1.4$
26. $2.9 < c + 7$ $c > -4.1$
27. $f + (-4) \geq 1.4$ $f \geq 5.4$
28. $z + (-2) > -3.8$
    $z > -1.8$
29. $b - \frac{3}{4} < 2\frac{1}{2}$ $b < 3\frac{1}{4}$
30. $g - 1\frac{2}{3} > 2\frac{1}{6}$ $g > 3\frac{5}{6}$

Solve each inequality. Then graph the solution on a number line. 36. $a \leq -27$

31. $n + 4 < 9$ $n < 5$
32. $t + 7 > 12$ $t > 5$
33. $p + (-5) > -3$ $p > 2$
34. $-3 + z > 2$ $z > 5$
35. $-13 \geq x - 8$ $x \leq -5$
36. $-32 \geq a + (-5)$
37. $33 \leq m - (-6)$
38. $k + 9 \geq -21$ $k \geq -30$
39. $1\frac{1}{4} + b < 3$ $b < 1\frac{3}{4}$
40. $3 \leq \frac{1}{2} + a$ $a \geq 2\frac{1}{2}$
41. $4 \geq s - \frac{2}{3}$ $s \leq 4\frac{2}{3}$
42. $-\frac{3}{4} < w - 1$ $w > \frac{1}{4}$

43. **TRANSPORTATION** A certain minivan has a maximum carrying capacity of 1100 pounds. If the luggage weighs 120 pounds, what is the maximum weight allowable for passengers? **980 lb**

44. **BIOLOGY** Female killer whales usually weigh more than 3000 pounds and are up to 19 feet long. Suppose a female whale is 12 feet long. Write and solve an inequality to find how much longer the whale could grow. **Source:** www.seaworld.org $12 + y \leq 19$; the whale could grow as much as 7 feet.

 Online Research Data Update Are there any whales in the world that are heavier or longer than the killer whale? Visit www.pre-alg.com/data_update to learn more.

WEATHER For Exercises 45 and 46, use the diagram below.

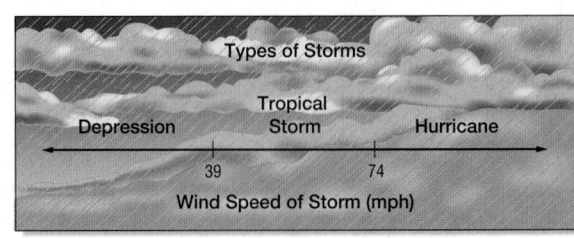

Types of Storms

Depression | Tropical Storm | Hurricane

39 | 74

Wind Speed of Storm (mph)

45. A hurricane has winds that are at least 74 miles per hour. Suppose a tropical storm has winds that are 42 miles per hour. Write and solve an inequality to find how much the winds must increase before the storm becomes a hurricane. $42 + x \geq 74$; $x \geq 32$; at least 32 mph

46. A *major storm* has wind speeds that are at least 110 miles per hour. Write and solve an inequality that describes how much greater these wind speeds are than the slowest hurricane. $74 + y \geq 110$; $y \geq 36$; at least 36 mph

47. **CRITICAL THINKING** Is it *always, sometimes,* or *never* true that $x - 1 < x$? Explain your answer. **Always; subtracting x gives $-1 < 0$, which is always true.**

48. WRITING IN MATH   Answer the question that was posed at the beginning of the lesson. **See margin.**

How is solving an inequality similar to solving an equation?

Include the following in your answer:

• a description of what would happen if 3 blocks were removed from each side of the scale modeled at the right, and,

• a sentence that compares removing 3 blocks from each side of a scale and subtracting 3 from each side of an inequality.

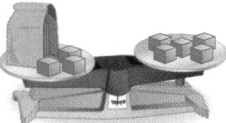

$x + 3 > 5$

*Standardized
Test Practice*
Ⓐ Ⓑ Ⓒ Ⓓ

49. Which inequality represents a temperature that is equal to or less than 42°? **C**

  Ⓐ $t \geq 42$ Ⓑ $t > 42$ Ⓒ $t \leq 42$ Ⓓ $t < 42$

50. Trevor has $25 to spend on a T-shirt and shorts for gym class. The shorts cost $14. Based on the inequality $14 + t \leq 25$, where t represents the cost of the T-shirt, what is the most Trevor can spend on the T-shirt? **C**

  Ⓐ $9   Ⓑ $10.99   Ⓒ $11   Ⓓ $11.50

Maintain Your Skills

Mixed Review   **ALGEBRA**   For the given value, state whether each inequality is *true* or *false*.
(Lesson 7-3)

51. $x - 5 > 4, x = 9$ **F**   **52.** $9 + a \leq 3, a = -7$ **T**

53. $\frac{x}{2} \geq 8, x = 4$ **F**   **54.** $6n < -4, n = -1$ **T**

55. **GEOMETRY**   The perimeter of a rectangle is 24 centimeters. Find the dimensions if the length is 3 more than twice the width.   *(Lesson 7-2)*
3 cm, 9 cm

56. **GEOMETRY**   Find the perimeter and area of the rectangle at the right.
(Lesson 3-7) **P = 54 cm; A = 152 cm²**

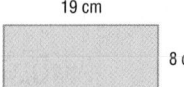

19 cm

8 cm

ALGEBRA   Use the Distributive Property to rewrite each expression.
(Lesson 3-1)

57. $4(2 + 8)$ **8 + 32**   **58.** $-2(n + 6)$ **−2n − 12**

59. $5(x - 3.5)$ **5x − 17.5**   **60.** $(9 - d)(-3c)$ **−27c + 3cd**

Find each difference.   *(Lesson 2-3)*

61. $-15 - (-12)$ **−3**   **62.** $8 - (-5)$ **13**

63. $-9 - 6$ **−15**   **64.** $27 - 45$ **−18**

*Getting Ready for
the Next Lesson*   **PREREQUISITE SKILL**   Solve each equation.
*(To review **solving equations**, see Lesson 3-4.)*

65. $-7x = 14$ **−2**   **66.** $-3y = -27$ **9**

67. $5x = -20$ **−4**   **68.** $\frac{d}{-3} = -6$ **18**

69. $\frac{c}{-4} = 12$ **−48**   **70.** $\frac{a}{2} = -8$ **−16**

Open-Ended Assessment

Writing Have students write a number of inequalities that must be solved by adding or subtracting and graph the solutions on number lines. Students should then recopy their inequalities without the inequality signs. They should present the number lines and the incomplete inequalities to a partner. Partners must fill in the correct inequality signs.

*Getting Ready
for Lesson 7-5*

PREREQUISITE SKILL Lesson 7-5 presents solving inequalities by multiplying or dividing. Exercises 65–70 should be used to determine your students' familiarity with solving equations using multiplication and division.

Answer

---

48. Solving an inequality is similar to solving an equation because when you add or subtract the same thing on each side, the inequality remains true. Sample answers should include the following.

• If you subtract 3 blocks from each side, the balance will stay the same.

• Subtracting 3 blocks from each side of the scale is like subtracting 3 from each side of an inequality—the inequality remains true.

1 Focus

7-5 Solving Inequalities by Multiplying or Dividing

5-Minute Check Transparency 7-5 Use as a quiz or review of Lesson 7-4.

Mathematical Background notes are available for this lesson on page 326D.

How are inequalities used in studying space?

The opening activity questions are repeated on page 390 of the *Chapter 7 Resource Masters.*

Reading to Learn Mathematics, p. 390   ELL

Pre-Activity *How are inequalities used in studying space?*

Do the activity at the top of page 350 in your textbook. Write your answers below.

a. Divide each side of the inequality $300 > 50$ by 2. Is the inequality still true? Explain by using an inequality. yes; $150 > 25$

b. Would the weight of 5 astronauts be greater on Pluto or on Earth? Explain by using an inequality. Earth; $300 > 67$, so $5(300) > 5(67)$.

Reading the Lesson

1. Describe the Multiplication Property of Inequality for both positive and negative numbers and give an example of a problem for each type of number. When you multiply each side of an inequality by the same positive number, the inequality remains true. When you multiply each side of an inequality by the same negative number, the inequality sign must be reversed for the inequality to remain true. Students' examples will vary.

2. Describe the Division Property of Inequality for both positive and negative numbers and give an example of a problem for each type of number. When you divide each side of an inequality by the same positive number, the inequality remains true. When you divide each side of an inequality by the same negative number, the inequality sign must be reversed for the inequality to remain true. Students' examples will vary.

Helping You Remember

3. In the boxes below, write examples of inequalities in which the sign does and does not reverse. Write at least three examples in each box. Sample answers are given.

Inequalities in Which the Sign Does Not Reverse	Inequalities in Which the Sign Reverses
$\frac{x}{4} \le 5$	$9 < -3x$
$3y \ge 3$	$25 \le \frac{y}{-9}$
$\frac{z}{2} < -4$	$-3z \ge -4$

What You'll Learn

- Solve inequalities by multiplying or dividing by a positive number.
- Solve inequalities by multiplying or dividing by a negative number.

How are inequalities used in studying space?

An astronaut in a space suit weighs about 300 pounds on Earth, but only 50 pounds on the moon because of weaker gravity.

$$\underbrace{300}_{\substack{\text{weight} \\ \text{on Earth}}} > \underbrace{50}_{\substack{\text{weight} \\ \text{on moon}}}$$

Location	Weight of Astronaut (lb)
Earth	300
Moon	50
Pluto	67
Mars	113
Neptune	407
Jupiter	796

If the astronaut and space suit each weighed half as much, would the inequality still be true? That is, would the astronaut's weight still be greater on Earth?

a. Divide each side of the inequality $300 > 50$ by 2. Is the inequality still true? Explain by using an inequality. **yes; $150 > 25$**

b. Would the weight of 5 astronauts be greater on Pluto or on Earth? Explain by using an inequality. **Earth; $300 > 67$, so $5(300) > 5(67)$.**

MULTIPLY OR DIVIDE BY A POSITIVE NUMBER   The application above demonstrates how you can solve inequalities by using the Multiplication and Division Properties of Inequalities.

Study Tip

Positive Number
The inequality $c > 0$ means that c is a positive number.

Key Concept — Multiplication and Division Properties

- **Words** When you multiply or divide each side of an inequality by the same positive number, the inequality remains true.

- **Symbols** For all numbers a, b, and c, where $c > 0$,

  1. if $a > b$, then $ac > bc$ and $\dfrac{a}{c} > \dfrac{b}{c}$.

  2. if $a < b$, then $ac < bc$ and $\dfrac{a}{c} < \dfrac{b}{c}$.

- **Examples**

  $2 < 6$ $3 > -9$

  $4(2) < 4(6)$ $\dfrac{3}{3} > \dfrac{-9}{3}$

  $8 < 24$ $1 > -3$

These properties are also true for $a \ge b$ and $a \le b$.

Resource Manager

📂 Workbooks and Reproducible Masters

Chapter 7 Resource Masters
- Study Guide and Intervention, p. 387
- Skills Practice, p. 388
- Practice, p. 389
- Reading to Learn Mathematics, p. 390
- Enrichment, p. 391
- Assessment, p. 412

Parent and Student Study Guide Workbook, p. 58
Prerequisite Skills Workbook, pp. 1–2, 27–28, 31–32, 47–54

Transparencies
5-Minute Check Transparency 7-5
Answer Key Transparencies

Technology
Interactive Chalkboard

Example 1 — Multiply or Divide by a Positive Number

a. Solve $8x \leq 40$. Check your solution.

$8x \leq 40$ Write the inequality.

$\dfrac{8x}{8} \leq \dfrac{40}{8}$ Divide each side by 8.

$x \leq 5$ Simplify.

The solution is $x \leq 5$. You can check this solution by substituting 5 or a number less than 5 into the inequality.

b. Solve $\dfrac{d}{2} > 7$. Check your solution.

$\dfrac{d}{2} > 7$ Write the inequality.

$2\left(\dfrac{d}{2}\right) > 2(7)$ Multiply each side by 2.

$d > 14$ Simplify.

The solution is $d > 14$. You can check this solution by substituting a number greater than 14 into the inequality.

Standardized Test Practice
Ⓐ Ⓑ Ⓒ Ⓓ

Example 2 — Write an Inequality

Multiple-Choice Test Item

> Ling earns \$8 per hour in the summer working at the zoo. Which inequality can be used to find how many hours he must work in a week to earn at least \$120?
>
> Ⓐ $8x < 120$ Ⓑ $8x \leq 120$ Ⓒ $8x > 120$ Ⓓ $8x \geq 120$

Test-Taking Tip
Before taking a standardized test, review the meanings of phrases like *at least* and *at most*.

Read the Test Item

You are to write an inequality to represent a real-world problem.

Solve the Test Item

Let x represent the number of hours worked.

Amount earned per hour	times	number of hours	is at least	amount earned each week.
8	·	x	$\geq$	120

The answer is D.

MULTIPLY OR DIVIDE BY A NEGATIVE NUMBER
What happens when each side of an inequality is multiplied or divided by a negative number?

$-6 < 11$	$10 > 5$
$-1(-6) \overset{?}{<} -1(11)$ Multiply each side by -1.	$\dfrac{10}{-5} \overset{?}{>} \dfrac{5}{-5}$ Divide each side by -5.
$6 \overset{?}{<} -11$ This inequality is false.	$-2 \overset{?}{>} -1$ This inequality is false.

 www.pre-alg.com/extra_examples

Lesson 7-5 Solving Inequalities by Multiplying or Dividing   **351**

Standardized Test Practice
Ⓐ Ⓑ Ⓒ Ⓓ

Example 2 Point out to students that *at least* and *at most* are common phrases that appear on standardized tests. Having a good understanding of these phrases will help students more quickly recognize the type of inequality sign required for the problem.

---

2 Teach

Building on Prior Knowledge

In Chapter 2, students reviewed multiplying and dividing integers. In this lesson, students will solve inequalities using multiplication and division.

MULTIPLY OR DIVIDE BY A POSITIVE NUMBER

In-Class Examples Power Point®

1
  a. Solve $9x \leq 54$. Check your solution. $x \leq 6$

  b. Solve $\dfrac{d}{9} > 4$. Check your solution. $d > 36$

2   **Multiple-Choice Test Item**
Martha earns \$9 per hour working for a fast food restaurant. Which inequality can be used to find how many hours she must work in a week to earn at least \$243?

  A $9x < 243$

  B $9x \geq 243$

  C $9x > 243$

  D $9x \leq 243$ **B**

MULTIPLY OR DIVIDE BY A NEGATIVE NUMBER

In-Class Example Power Point®

3   Solve each inequality and check your solution. Then graph the solution on a number line.

  a. $\dfrac{x}{-5} \geq 7$ $x \leq -35$

     −37   −36   −35   −34   −33

  b. $-9x < -27$ $x > 3$

     1   2   3   4   5

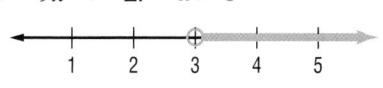

About the Exercises . . .

Organization by Objective
- **Solve Inequalities by Multiplying or Dividing by a Positive Number:** 14–21, 32–33, 38–39
- **Solve Inequalities by Multiplying or Dividing by a Negative Number:** 22–31, 34–37

Odd/Even Assignments

Exercises 14–39 are structured so that students practice the same concepts whether they are assigned odd or even problems.

Assignment Guide

Basic: 15–39 odd, 40–57

Average: 15–39 odd, 40–57

Advanced: 14–38 even, 40–51 (Optional: 52–57)

All: Practice Quiz 2 (1–10)

The inequalities $6 < -11$ and $-2 > -1$ are both false. However, they would both be true if the inequality symbols were reversed. That is, change $<$ to $>$ and change $>$ to $<$.

$$6 > -11 \quad \text{true} \qquad -2 < -1 \quad \text{true}$$

This investigation suggests the following properties.

Study Tip

Negative Number
The inequality $c < 0$ means that c is a negative number.

> **Key Concept** — **Multiplication and Division Properties**
>
> - **Words** — When you multiply or divide each side of an inequality by the same negative number, the inequality symbol must be reversed for the inequality to remain true.
>
> - **Symbols** — For all numbers a, b, and c, where $c < 0$,
>   1. if $a > b$, then $ac < bc$ and $\dfrac{a}{c} < \dfrac{b}{c}$.
>   2. if $a < b$, then $ac > bc$ and $\dfrac{a}{c} > \dfrac{b}{c}$.
>
> - **Examples**
>
> $7 > 1$
> $-2(7) < -2(1)$ Reverse the symbols.
> $-14 < -2$
>
> $-4 < 16$
> $\dfrac{-4}{-4} > \dfrac{16}{-4}$
> $1 > -4$

These properties are also true for $a \geq b$ and $a \leq b$.

✓ **Concept Check** — Explain why it is necessary to reverse the symbol when you multiply each side of an inequality by a negative number.
The inequality symbol must be reversed to keep the inequality true.

Example 3 *Multiply or Divide by a Negative Number*

Solve each inequality and check your solution. Then graph the solution on a number line.

a. $\dfrac{x}{-3} \leq 4$

$\dfrac{x}{-3} \leq 4$ Write the inequality.

$-3\left(\dfrac{x}{-3}\right) \geq -3(4)$ Multiply each side by -3 and reverse the symbol.

$x \geq -12$ Check this result.

CHECK You can check your result by replacing x in the original inequality with a number greater than -12.

Graph the solution, $x \geq -12$.

b. $-7x > -56$

$-7x > -56$ Write the inequality.

$\dfrac{-7x}{-7} < \dfrac{-56}{-7}$ Divide each side by -7 and reverse the symbol.

$x < 8$ Check this result.

Graph the solution, $x < 8$.

DAILY INTERVENTION

Differentiated Instruction

- **Kinesthetic** Using cardboard, glue, toothpicks or wire, scissors, and any other necessary materials, have students create a board with a flipping (reversing) inequality sign to which numbers/terms can be attached to model various inequalities. As students carry out the operations necessary to solve an inequality, they can replace the numbers/terms to show each step and flip the inequality sign to face the correct way.

Concept Check

1. **List** the steps you would use to solve $\frac{y}{-12} < 6$. **See margin.**

2. **OPEN ENDED** Write an inequality that can be solved using the Division Property of Inequality, where the inequality symbol is *not* reversed. **Sample answer: $3x < 24$**

3. **FIND THE ERROR** Brittany and Tamika each solved $-45 \geq 9k$.

Brittany	Tamika
$-45 \geq 9k$	$-45 \geq 9k$
$\dfrac{-45}{9} \leq \dfrac{9k}{9}$	$\dfrac{-45}{9} \geq \dfrac{9k}{9}$
$-5 \leq k$	$-5 \geq k$

Who is correct? Explain your reasoning. **See margin.**

Guided Practice

Solve each inequality and check your solution. Then graph the solution on a number line. **4–12. See pp. 365A–365D for graphs.**

GUIDED PRACTICE KEY	
Exercises	Examples
4, 5, 7	1
6, 8–12	3
13	2

4. $2x < 8$ $x < 4$
5. $3x \geq -6$ $x \geq -2$
6. $-4t > -20$ $t < 5$
7. $\frac{a}{5} > 10$ $a > 50$
8. $-8 > \frac{k}{-0.4}$ $k > 3.2$
9. $\frac{m}{-7} \leq 1.2$ $m \geq -8.4$
10. $-\frac{s}{3} \leq -3.5$ $s \geq 10.5$
11. $36 \geq -\frac{1}{2}y$ $y \geq -72$
12. $-273 \geq -13z$ $z \geq 21$

Standardized Test Practice

13. **EARNINGS** Julia delivers pizzas on weekends. Her average tip is $1.50 for each pizza that she delivers. How many pizzas must she deliver to earn at least $20 in tips? **C**

Ⓐ 10   Ⓑ 13   Ⓒ 14   Ⓓ 20

Practice and Apply

Homework Help	
For Exercises	See Examples
14–21, 32, 33	1
22–31, 34–37	3
42, 43	2

Extra Practice
See page 741.

Solve each inequality and check your solution. Then graph the solution on a number line. **14–37. See pp. 365A–365D for graphs.**

14. $4x < 4$ $x < 1$
15. $7y > 63$ $y > 9$
16. $13a \geq -26$ $a \geq -2$
17. $-15 \leq 5b$ $b \geq -3$
18. $144 < 12d$ $d > 12$
19. $15 \geq 3t$ $t \leq 5$
20. $\frac{p}{6} > 5$ $p > 30$
21. $7 \geq \frac{h}{14}$ $h \leq 98$
22. $-3m > -33$ $m < 11$
23. $-8z \leq -24$ $z \geq 3$
24. $18 > -2g$ $g > -9$
25. $-8 \leq -4w$ $w \leq 2$
26. $6 > \frac{x}{-7}$ $x > -42$
27. $\frac{r}{-2} < -2$ $r > 4$
28. $\frac{y}{-3} < -7$ $y > 21$
29. $\frac{k}{-2} < 9$ $k > -18$
30. $-6a > -78$ $a < 13$
31. $-25t \leq 400$ $t \geq -16$
32. $\frac{y}{4} \geq 2.4$ $y \geq 9.6$
33. $\frac{n}{5} \leq 0.8$ $n \leq 4$
34. $-5 \leq \frac{c}{-4.5}$ $c \leq 22.5$
35. $-19 > \frac{y}{-0.3}$ $y > 5.7$
36. $-\frac{1}{3}x \geq -9$ $x \leq 27$
37. $-36 < -\frac{1}{2}b$ $b < 72$

38. **SOCCER** Tomás wants to spend less than $100 for a new soccer ball and shoes. The ball costs $24. **a. $24 + s < 100$**

a. Write an inequality to represent the amount left for shoes.

b. What amount can he spend on shoes? **less than $76**

 www.pre-alg.com/self_check_quiz

Lesson 7-5 Solving Inequalities by Multiplying or Dividing **353**

Answers

1. Multiply each side by −12 and reverse the inequality symbol.

3. Tamika is correct. She divided each side of the inequality by 9. Since 9 is a positive number, she did not reverse the inequality symbol.

DAILY
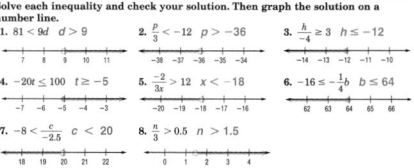
INTERVENTION FIND THE ERROR
Students may incorrectly assume that the inequality sign must be reversed whenever an inequality contains a negative number.

Study Guide and Intervention, p. 387

Use the Multiplication and Division Properties of Inequalities to solve inequalities. When you multiply or divide each side of an inequality by a positive number, the inequality remains true. The direction of the inequality sign does not change.

Example 1 Solve $8x \geq 72$. Check your solution.

$8x \geq 72$ Write the inequality.
$\frac{8x}{8} \geq \frac{72}{8}$ Divide each side by 8.
$x \geq 9$ Simplify.

The solution is $x \geq 9$. You can check this solution by substituting 9 or a number greater than 9 into the inequality.

For an inequality to remain true when multiplying or dividing each side of the inequality by a negative number, however, you must reverse the direction of the inequality symbol.

Example 2 Solve $\frac{y}{-12} < 4$ and check your solution. Then graph the solution on a number line.

$\frac{y}{-12} < 4$ Write the inequality.
$-12\left(\frac{y}{-12}\right) > -12(4)$ Multiply each side by −12 and reverse the symbol.
$y > -48$ Check the result.
Graph the solution, $y > -48$.

Exercises

Solve each inequality and check your solution. Then graph the solution on a number line.

1. $81 < 9d$ $d > 9$
2. $\frac{p}{3} < -12$ $p > -36$
3. $\frac{h}{-4} \geq 3$ $h \leq -12$
4. $-20t \leq 100$ $t \geq -5$
5. $\frac{-2}{3x} > 12$ $x < -18$
6. $-16 \leq -\frac{1}{4}b$ $b \leq 64$
7. $-8 < \frac{c}{-2.5}$ $c < 20$
8. $\frac{n}{3} > 0.5$ $n > 1.5$

Skills Practice, p. 388 and Practice, p. 389 (shown)

Solve each inequality and check your solution. Then graph the solution on a number line.

1. $9x > 18$ $x > 2$
2. $10d \leq 80$ $d \leq 8$
3. $25 \leq 5c$ $c \geq 5$
4. $\frac{t}{13} > 3$ $t > 39$
5. $24 \geq \frac{g}{-4}$ $g \geq -96$
6. $-78 > 6h$ $h < -13$
7. $\frac{f}{-6} < -12$ $f > 60$
8. $100 \geq -4s$ $s \geq -25$
9. $\frac{p}{-36} < 6$ $p > -216$
10. $-4 > \frac{c}{-3.5}$ $c > 14$
11. $-24 < \frac{1}{2b}$ $b > -48$
12. $-3 \leq \frac{c}{-1.5}$ $c \leq 4.5$

13. **DISCOUNTS** To qualify for a store discount, Jorge's soccer team must spend at least $560 for new jerseys. The team needs 20 jerseys.
   a. Write an inequality to represent how much the team should spend on each jersey to qualify for the discount. $20p \geq 560$
   b. How much should the team spend for each jersey? $p \geq 28

14. **POLITICS** Mi-Ling wants to mail at least 850 fliers encouraging voters to vote for the upcoming school levy. She has five days to get them all in the mail.
   a. Write an inequality to represent how many fliers Mi-Ling must mail every day. $5f \geq 850$
   b. How many fliers should Mi-Ling mail each day? $f \geq 170$

Enrichment, p. 391

Hidden Word

In each group of five inequalities, only two have the same solution set. For each group, write the solution of each inequality and then circle the letters of the two inequalities having the same solution set. After completing all four groups, use the circled letters to form a one-word answer to the question at the bottom of the page.

GROUP 1
Ⓔ $3x < 30$ B. $-3x < -30$ F. $-30 > 3x$ Ⓓ $-30 < -3x$ D. $-3x < 30$
$x < 10$ $x > 10$ $-10 > x$ $10 > x$ $x > -10$

GROUP 2
M. $\frac{x}{-5} \leq -2$ N. $\frac{-x}{5} \leq 2$ Ⓦ $\frac{x}{-5} \leq -2$ Ⓡ $\frac{x}{5} \leq -5$ R. $\frac{-x}{5} < -2$
$x \leq -10$ $x \geq -10$ $x \geq 10$ $x \geq 10$ $x > 10$

GROUP 3
Q. $\frac{3x}{2} < 0$ K. $0 \leq -12x$ L. $\frac{-1}{x} \leq 0$ Ⓛ $0.73x \geq 0$ Ⓐ $0 \geq -912x$
$x < 0$ $0 \geq x$ $x > 0$ $x \geq 0$ $0 \leq x$

GROUP 4
L. $200 > 0.05x$ Ⓐ $0.05x < 20$ D. $\frac{1}{5}x > 20$ E. $200 > 5x$ Ⓔ $\frac{x}{0.1} < 4000$
$4000 > x$ $x < 400$ $x > 100$ $40 > x$ $x < 400$

Unscramble the circled letters to find the name of the first of the original 13 colonies to ratify the U.S. Constitution. Delaware

Open-Ended Assessment

Speaking Have students describe what should happen to an inequality symbol when the inequality is multiplied or divided by a positive and a negative number.

Tips for New Teachers

Intervention If there is any doubt whether your students thoroughly understand multiplying or dividing inequalities by negative numbers, consider spending an extra day on this lesson. Use the Extra Practice on pp. 388 and 389. You can also use the Study Guide and Intervention masters or the Practice masters in the *Chapter 7 Resource Masters* to reinforce this concept.

Getting Ready for Lesson 7-6

PREREQUISITE SKILL Lesson 7-6 presents solving multi-step inequalities. Exercises 52–57 should be used to determine your students' familiarity with solving two-step equations.

Assessment Options

Practice Quiz 2 The quiz provides students with a brief review of the concepts and skills in Lessons 7-3 through 7-5. Lesson numbers are given to the right of exercises or instruction lines so students can review concepts not yet mastered.

Quiz (Lessons 7-4 and 7-5) is available on p. 412 of the *Chapter 7 Resource Masters*.

---

39. **SWIMMING** Nicole swims 40 meters per minute, and she wants to swim at least 2000 meters this morning. **a. $40m \geq 2000$**
    a. Write an inequality to represent how long she should swim.
    b. How many minutes should she swim? **at least 50 min**

40. **CRITICAL THINKING** The product of an integer and -7 is less than -84. Find the least integer that meets this condition. **13**

41. WRITING IN MATH   Answer the following question that was posed at the beginning of the lesson. **See margin.**

    How are inequalities used in studying space?
    Include the following in your answer:
    • inequalities comparing the weight of two astronauts on Mars and on the moon, and
    • an explanation of how the Multiplication and Division Properties of Inequality can be used to compare planets' gravities.

Standardized Test Practice

42. Which number is *not* a possible length of the rectangle if the area is less than 36 square inches? **D**

    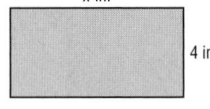

    (A) 6   (B) 7
    (C) 8   (D) 9

43. **GRID IN** Jessica is putting water into a 20-gallon fish tank using a 2-quart pitcher. How many pitchers of water will she need to fill the tank? **40**

Maintain Your Skills

Mixed Review   **ALGEBRA**   Solve each inequality. Check your solution. *(Lesson 7-4)*

44. $-4 + x > 23$ $x > 27$ 45. $c + 18 \leq -2$ $c \leq -20$ 46. $6 > n - 10$ $n < 16$

47. Write an inequality for *2 times a number is at most 14*. *(Lesson 7-3)* $2n \leq 14$

Find each product. Write in simplest form.   *(Lesson 5-3)*

48. $\frac{1}{8} \cdot \frac{3}{4}$ $\frac{3}{32}$ 49. $-\frac{3}{7} \cdot \frac{5}{9}$ $-\frac{5}{21}$ 50. $2\frac{1}{2} \cdot \left(-\frac{5}{6}\right)$ $-2\frac{1}{12}$ 51. $\frac{ab}{2} \cdot \frac{4}{bc}$ $\frac{2a}{c}$

Getting Ready for the Next Lesson   **PREREQUISITE SKILL**   **ALGEBRA**   Solve each equation.
*(To review **two-step equations**, see Lesson 3-5.)*

52. $2x + 3 = 9$ **3**   53. $5a - 6 = 14$ **4**   54. $3n - 8 = -26$ **−6**
55. $\frac{t}{3} + 5 = 2$ **−9**   56. $\frac{c}{4} - 1 = 4$ **20**   57. $\frac{d}{2} + 3 = 19$ **32**

Practice Quiz 2   *Lessons 7-3 through 7-5*

Graph each inequality on a number line.   *(Lesson 7-3)* **1–2. See margin.**
1. $x < -3$ 2. $y \geq 5$

Solve each inequality. Check your solution.   *(Lessons 7-4 and 7-5)*
3. $a - 26 \leq 14$ $a \leq 40$ 4. $46 + k > -8$ $k > -54$ 5. $115 \leq -9 + n$ $n \geq 124$ 6. $2.5 > 5r$ $r < 0.5$
7. $\frac{r}{5} < -45$ $r < -225$ 8. $-\frac{s}{8} < -80$ $s > 640$ 9. $-12g \geq -84$ $g \leq 7$ 10. $5w \geq -2$ $w \geq -0.4$

Answer

41. Inequalities can be used to compare the weights of objects on different planets. Answers should include the following.
    • Comparing the weight of an astronaut in a space suit on Mars to the same astronaut on the moon: 113 > 50.
    • If you multiply or divide the astronaut's weight by the same number, the

inequality comparing the weights on different planets would still be true.

Answers (Practice Quiz 2)

1.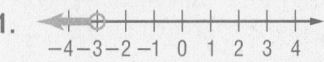

2.

What You'll Learn

- Solve inequalities that involve more than one operation.

How are multi-step inequalities used in backpacking?

Nearly 10 million Americans go backpacking each year. According to a fitness magazine, to avoid injury, three times the weight of your backpack and its contents should be less than your body weight.

a. Write an inequality that represents the relationship between body weight and a safe total backpack and contents weight. $3(p + c) < b$

b. Suppose you weigh 120 pounds and your empty backpack weighs 5 pounds. Write an inequality that represents the maximum weight you can safely carry in the backpack. $3(5 + c) < 120$

INEQUALITIES WITH MORE THAN ONE OPERATION Some inequalities involve more than one operation. To solve the inequality, work backward to undo the operations, just as you did in solving multi-step equations.

Example 1 Solve a Two-Step Inequality

Solve $6x + 15 > 9$ and check your solution. Graph the solution on a number line.

$6x + 15 > 9$	Write the inequality.
$6x + 15 - 15 > 9 - 15$	Subtract 15 from each side.
$6x > -6$	Simplify.
$x > -1$	Mentally divide each side by 6.

To check your solution, try 0, a number greater than -1.

CHECK	$6x + 15 > 9$	Write the inequality.
	$6(0) + 15 > 9$	Replace x with 0.
	$0 + 15 > 9$	Simplify.
	$15 > 9$ ✓	The solution checks.

Graph the solution, $x > -1$.

Study Tip

Common Misconception
Do not reverse the inequality sign just because there is a negative sign in the inequality. Only reverse the sign when you multiply or divide by a negative number.

---

1 Focus

5-Minute Check Transparency 7-6 Use as a quiz or review of Lesson 7-5.

Mathematical Background notes are available for this lesson on page 326D.

How are multi-step inequalities used in backpacking?

The opening activity questions are repeated on page 395 of the *Chapter 7 Resource Masters*.

Reading to Learn Mathematics, p. 395   **ELL**

Pre-Activity *How are multi-step inequalities used in backpacking?*

Do the activity at the top of page 355 in your textbook. Write your answers below.

a. Write an inequality that represents the relationship between body weight and a safe total backpack and contents weight.
$3(p + c) < b$

b. Suppose you weigh 120 pounds and your empty backpack weighs 5 pounds. Write an inequality that represents the maximum weight you can safely carry in the backpack. $3(5 + c) < 120$

Reading the Lesson

Fill in the blank with the term or phrase that best completes each statement.

1. Solving multi-step inequalities is much like solving multi-step ___equations___ .

2. To solve a multi-step inequality, you should work ___backward___ to undo the operations.

3. The first step in solving an inequality that contains parentheses is to ___use the Distributive Property___ .

4. Remember to ___reverse___ the inequality symbol when multiplying or dividing both sides of the inequality by a negative number.

5. To check the solution $x > 14$, you should try a number ___greater___ than 14 in the original inequality.

Helping You Remember

6. Fill in the flow chart for solving an inequality such as $-4(d + 2) \geq -8d - 32$ using the steps listed below. Write the letter of the correct step in the appropriate box on the flow chart.
   a. Multiply or divide both sides by the coefficient of the variable
   b. Use the Distributive Property
   c. Add or subtract a term with the variable from both sides
   d. Reverse the inequality sign if necessary
   e. Add or subtract a constant term from both sides

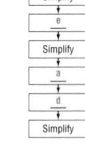

Resource Manager

Workbooks and Reproducible Masters

Chapter 7 Resource Masters
- Study Guide and Intervention, p. 392
- Skills Practice, p. 393
- Practice, p. 394
- Reading to Learn Mathematics, p. 395
- Enrichment, p. 396
- Assessment, p. 412

Graphing Calculator and Spreadsheet Masters, p. 31
Parent and Student Study Guide Workbook, p. 59
Prerequisite Skills Workbook, pp. 1–2
School-to-Career Masters, p. 14

 Transparencies

5-Minute Check Transparency 7-6
Answer Key Transparencies

 Technology

Interactive Chalkboard
Pre-AlgePASS: Tutorial Plus, Lesson 21

INEQUALITIES WITH MORE THAN ONE OPERATION

In-Class Examples

1 Solve $5x + 13 > 83$ and check your solution. Graph the solution on a number line. $x > 14$

number line from 12 to 16, open circle at 14

2 Solve $7 - 4a \leq 23 - 2a$ and check your solution. Graph the solution on a number line. $a \geq -8$

number line from −10 to −6, closed circle at −8

3 A person weighing 213 pounds has a 10-pound backpack. Refer to the application at the beginning of page 355 in the student text. What is the maximum weight for the contents of the pack?   **The weight of the contents should be less than 61 pounds.**

Teaching Tip   Remind students that $4 > a$ is the same as $a < 4$.

✓ Skills Check

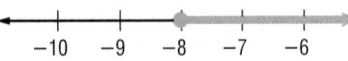

Inequalities with More than One Operation Solve $-4(h - 3) \leq 32$ and check your solution. $h \geq -5$

More About...

Backpacking
One of the most popular treks for backpackers is Yosemite National Park in California's High Sierra. It is possible to hike there for two weeks and never see a road!

Source: www.gorp.com

Remember that you must reverse the inequality symbol if you multiply or divide each side of an inequality by a negative number.

Example 2 **Reverse the Inequality Symbol**

Solve $10 - 3a \leq 25 + 2a$ and check your solution. Graph the solution on a number line.

$10 - 3a \leq 25 + 2a$	Write the inequality.
$10 - 3a - 2a \leq 25 + 2a - 2a$	Subtract $2a$ from each side.
$10 - 5a \leq 25$	Simplify.
$10 - 10 - 5a \leq 25 - 10$	Subtract 10 from each side.
$-5a \leq 15$	Simplify.
$\dfrac{-5a}{-5} \geq \dfrac{15}{-5}$	Divide each side by −5 and change ≤ to ≥
$a \geq -3$	Simplify.

Reverse the inequality in this step. →

CHECK

$10 - 3a \leq 25 + 2a$	Try −2, a number greater than −3.
$10 - 3(-2) \overset{?}{\leq} 25 + 2(-2)$	Replace a with −2.
$10 + 6 \overset{?}{\leq} 25 - 4$	Simplify.
$16 \leq 21 \checkmark$	The solution checks.

Graph the solution, $a \geq -3$.

number line from −5 to 5, closed circle at −3

When inequalities contain grouping symbols, you can use the Distributive Property to begin simplifying the inequality.

Example 3 **Inequalities with Grouping Symbols**

BACKPACKING   A person weighing 126 pounds has a 6-pound backpack. Refer to the application at the beginning of page 355. What is the maximum weight for the contents of the pack?

Let c represent the weight of the contents of the pack.

Words	3	times	weight of pack and contents	should be less than	body weight.
Inequality	3	·	$(6 + c)$	<	126

Solve the inequality.

$3(6 + c) < 126$	Write the inequality.
$18 + 3c < 126$	Use the Distributive Property.
$18 + 3c - 18 < 126 - 18$	Subtract 18 from each side.
$3c < 108$	Simplify.
$\dfrac{3c}{3} < \dfrac{108}{3}$	Divide each side by 3.
$c < 36$	Simplify.

The weight of the contents should be less than 36 pounds.

✓ **Concept Check**   **Undo the operations in reverse order.** How do you solve an inequality with more than one operation?

DAILY
INTERVENTION   **Differentiated Instruction**

- **Intrapersonal** Have students make a journal entry that includes the steps in solving a multi-step inequality, what they find most difficult about solving such problems, any hints they have learned to aid them, and what they need to do or practice to become more proficient at solving such inequalities.

Check for Understanding

1. **OPEN ENDED** Explain how to check the solution of an inequality.

2. **Write** an inequality for the model at the right. Then solve the inequality.
$2x + 3 < 7$; $x < 2$

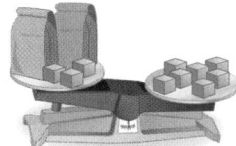

3. **FIND THE ERROR** Jerome and Ryan are beginning to solve $2(2y + 3) > y + 1$.

Jerome	Ryan
$2(2y + 3) > y + 1$	$2(2y + 3) > y + 1$
$4y + 6 > y + 1$	$4y + 3 > y + 1$

Who is correct? Explain your reasoning. **See margin.**

Guided Practice

Solve each inequality and check your solution. Then graph the solution on a number line. 4–11. See pp. 365A–365D for graphs.

GUIDED PRACTICE KEY	
Exercises	Examples
4–6, 12	1
7–9	2
10, 11	3

4. $3x + 4 \leq 31$ $x \leq 9$
5. $2n + 5 > 11 - n$ $n > 2$
6. $y + 1 \geq 4y + 4$ $y \leq -1$
7. $16 - 2c < 14$ $c > 1$
8. $-6.1n \geq 3.9n + 5$ $n \leq -0.5$
9. $-4 \leq \frac{x}{4} - 6$ $x \geq 8$
10. $-3(b - 1) > 18$ $b < -5$
11. $\frac{1}{2}(2d + 3) < -8$ $d < -9\frac{1}{2}$

Application

12. **MONEY** Dante's telephone company charges $10 a month plus $0.05 for every minute or part of a minute. Dante wants his monthly bill to be under $30. What is the greatest number of minutes he can talk? **399 min**

★ indicates increased difficulty

Practice and Apply

Homework Help	
For Exercises	See Examples
13–18, 25, 26	1
19, 20, 27, 28	2
21–24, 29, 30, 33–36	3

Extra Practice
See page 741.

Solve each inequality and check your solution. Then graph the solution on a number line. 13–28. See pp. 365A–365D for graphs.

13. $2x + 8 > 24$ $x > 8$
14. $3y - 1 \leq 5$ $y \leq 2$
15. $3 + 4c > -13$ $c > -4$
16. $9 + 2p \leq 15$ $p \leq 3$
17. $3x - 2 > 10 - x$ $x > 3$
18. $c - 1 < 3c + 5$ $c > -3$
19. $4 - 3k \leq 19$ $k \geq -5$
20. $16 - 4n > 20$ $n < -1$
21. $2(n + 3) < -4$ $n < -5$
22. $2(d + 1) > 16$ $d > 7$
23. $8 + 3b \leq 2(9 - b)$ $b \leq 2$
24. $\frac{m}{2} + 9 \geq 5$ $m \geq -8$
25. $2 + 0.3y \geq 11$ $y \geq 30$
26. $0.5a - 1.4 \leq 2.1$ $a \leq 7$
27. $\frac{1}{2}(6 - c) > 5$ $c < -4$
28. $\frac{2}{3}(9 - x) < 3$ $x > 4.5$

29. Four times a number less 6 is greater than two times the same number plus 8. For what number or numbers is this true? $n > 7$

30. One-half of the sum of a number and 6 is less than 25. What is the number? $n < 44$

 www.pre-alg.com/self_check_quiz

D A I L Y
INTERVENTION **Unlocking Misconceptions**

• **Solving Inequalities with Fractions** When solving inequalities with fractions, it is common for students to take only one approach to problem solving. Have students solve problems like those in Exercises 35 and 36 by finding least common denominators, by multiplying each side of the equation by the least common denominator, and by cross multiplication.

Study Notebook

Have students—
• write out several examples of inequalities that require two steps to solve and label each step with the operation being undone.
• include any other item(s) that they find helpful in mastering the skills in this lesson.

D A I L Y
INTERVENTION **FIND THE ERROR**
If students are having difficulty with solving inequalities that contain grouping symbols, discuss and practice using the Distributive Property.

About the Exercises . . .
Odd/Even Assignments
Exercises 13–40 are structured so that students practice the same concepts whether they are assigned odd or even problems.

Assignment Guide
Basic: 13–33 odd, 37, 39, 43, 45–48, 50–63
Average: 13–43 odd, 45–48, 50–63 (Optional: 49)
Advanced: 14–44 even, 45–63

Answers

1. Check the solution by replacing the variable with a number in the solution. If the inequality is true, the solution checks.

3. Jerome is correct. By the Distributive Property $2(2y + 3) = 4y + 6$ not $4y + 3$.

Solve each inequality and check your solution. Graph the solution on a number line. **31–36. See margin for graphs.**

31. $1.3n + 6.7 \geq 3.1n - 1.4$ $n \leq 4.5$
32. $-5a + 3 > 3a + 23$ $a < -2.5$
33. $-5(t + 4) \geq 3(t - 4)$ $t \leq -1$
34. $8x - (x - 5) > x + 17$ $x > 2$
★ 35. $\frac{c + 8}{4} < \frac{5 - c}{9}$ $c < -4$
★ 36. $\frac{2(n + 1)}{7} \geq \frac{n + 4}{5}$ $n \geq 6$

For Exercises 37–40, write and solve an inequality.

37. **CANDY** You buy some candy bars at $0.55 each and one newspaper for $0.35. How many candy bars can you buy with $2?
    $0.55c + 0.35 \leq 2$; 3 candy bars

38. **SCHOOL** Nate has scores of 85, 91, 89, and 93 on four tests. What is the least number of points he can get on the fifth test to have an average of at least 90? $(85 + 91 + 89 + 93 + p) \div 5 \geq 90$; 92 points

39. **SALES** You earn $2.00 for every magazine subscription you sell plus a salary of $10 each week. How many subscriptions do you need to sell each week to earn at least $40 each week? $2s + 10 \geq 40$, 15 subscriptions

40. **REAL ESTATE** A real estate agent receives a monthly salary of $1500 plus a 4% commission on every home sold. For what amount of monthly sales will the agent earn at least $5000? $1500 + 0.04s \geq 5000$; $87,500

★ 41. **CAR RENTAL** The costs for renting a car from Able Car Rental and from Baker Car Rental are shown in the table. For what mileage does Baker have the better deal? Use the inequality $30 + 0.05x > 20 + 0.10x$. Explain why this inequality works.
    $x < 200$; See margin for explanation.

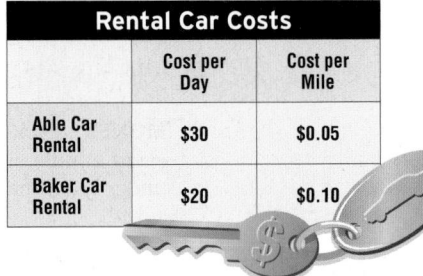

Rental Car Costs		
	Cost per Day	Cost per Mile
Able Car Rental	$30	$0.05
Baker Car Rental	$20	$0.10

42. **HIKING** You hike along the Appalachian Trail at 3 miles per hour. You stop for one hour for lunch. You want to walk at least 18 miles. How many hours should you expect to spend on the trail? **at least 7 h**

43. **PHONE SERVICES** Miko was asked by FoneCom to sign up for their service at $15 per month plus $0.10 per minute. Miko currently has BestPhone service at $20 per month plus $0.05 per minute. Miko figures that her monthly bill would be more with FoneCom. For how many minutes per month does she use the phone? **more than 100 minutes**

★ 44. **FUND-RAISERS** The Booster Club sells football programs for $1 each. The costs to make the programs are $60 for page layout plus $0.20 for printing each program. If they print 400 programs, how many programs must the Club sell to make at least $200 profit? **at least 340**

45. **CRITICAL THINKING** Assume that k is an integer. Solve the inequality $10 - 2|k| > 4$. $k < 3$ and $k > -3$, or $k = \{-2, -1, 0, 1, 2\}$

358   **Chapter 7** Equations and Inequalities

Answers

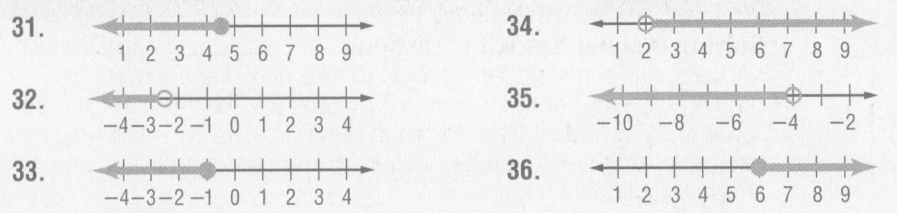

31.
32.
33.
34.
35.
36.

46. **WRITING IN MATH** Answer the question that was posed at the beginning of the lesson. **See margin.**

How are multi-step inequalities used in backpacking?

Include the following in your answer:
- an explanation of what multi-step inequalities are, and
- a solution of the inequality you wrote for part **b** on page 355.

47. Which inequality represents *five more than twice a number is less than ten?* **D**

Ⓐ $(5 + 2)n < 10$ Ⓑ $2n - 5 < 10$

Ⓒ $10 < 2n + 5$ Ⓓ $5 + 2n < 10$

48. Enola's scores on the first five science tests are shown in the table. Which inequality represents the score she must receive on the sixth test to have an average score of more than 88? **D**

Test	Score
1	85
2	84
3	90
4	95
5	88

Ⓐ $s \geq 86$ Ⓑ $s \leq 88$

Ⓒ $s < 88$ Ⓓ $s > 86$

Extending ★ **49.** The sum of three times a number and 5 lies between −10 and 8. Solve
the Lesson the *compound inequality* $-10 < 3x + 5 < 8$ to find the solution(s). (*Hint:* Any operation must be done to all three parts of the inequality.)
$-5 < x < 1$

Maintain Your Skills

Mixed Review **ALGEBRA** Solve each inequality. Check your solution. *(Lessons 7-4 and 7-5)*

50. $20 < -9 + k$ $k > 29$ **51.** $22 \leq -15 + y$ $y \geq 37$

52. $6x < -27$ $x < -4.5$ **53.** $-5n \geq -25$ $n \leq 5$

54. $\dfrac{n}{-4} \leq -11$ $n \geq 44$ **55.** $\dfrac{a}{-3} > 6.2$ $a < -18.6$

56. If 12 of the 20 students in a class are boys, what percent are boys? *(Lesson 6-5)* **60%**

57. Write $\dfrac{1}{200}$ as a percent. *(Lesson 6-4)* **0.5%**

Express each ratio as a unit rate. *(Lesson 6-1)*

58. $5 for 2 loaves of bread **$2.50 a loaf**   **59.** 200 miles on 12 gallons **16.$\overline{6}$ mpg**

60. 24 meters in 4 seconds
6 meters per second

61. 9 monthly issues for $11.25
$1.25 an issue

GEOMETRY **Find the missing dimension in each rectangle.** *(Lesson 3-7)*

62. 18.4 ft   **6.4 ft**   **63.** ℓ **6 m**

w   5.1 m   Area = 30.6 m²

Perimeter = 49.6 ft

Lesson 7-6 Solving Multi-Step Inequalities   **359**

Answers

41. Sample explanation: The inequality finds at what mileage Able's charge is greater than Baker's charge.

46. Multi-step inequalities are used to find the amount of weight a certain person can carry in proportion to that person's body weight. Answers should include the following.
- Multi-step inequalities are inequalities that involve more than one operation.
- $c < 35$

Chapter 7 — Study Guide and Review

Vocabulary and Concept Check

- This alphabetical list of vocabulary terms in Chapter 7 includes a page reference where each term was introduced.

- **Assessment** A vocabulary review/test for Chapter 7 is available on p. 410 of the *Chapter 7 Resource Masters*.

Lesson-by-Lesson Review

For each lesson,
- the main ideas are summarized,
- additional examples review concepts, and
- practice exercises are provided.

Vocabulary PuzzleMaker

ELL The Vocabulary PuzzleMaker software improves students' mathematics vocabulary using four puzzle formats—crossword, scramble, word search using a word list, and word search using clues. Students can work on a computer screen or from a printed handout.

MindJogger Videoquizzes

ELL MindJogger Videoquizzes provide an alternative review of concepts presented in this chapter. Students work in teams in a game show format to gain points for correct answers. The questions are presented in three rounds.

Round 1 Concepts (5 questions)
Round 2 Skills (4 questions)
Round 3 Problem Solving (4 questions)

Vocabulary and Concept Check

identity (p. 336)   inequality (p. 340)   null or empty set (p. 336)

Determine whether each statement is *true* or *false*. If false, replace the underlined word or number to make a true statement. 3. false; identity   4. false; Multiplication

1. When an equation has no solution, the solution set is the <u>null set</u>. **true**
2. The inequality $n + 8 - 8 \geq 14 - 8$ demonstrates the <u>Subtraction</u> Property of Inequality. **true**
3. An equation that is true for every value of the variable is called an <u>inequality</u>.
4. The inequality $\frac{x}{4}(4) < 7(4)$ demonstrates the <u>Division</u> Property of Inequality.
5. A mathematical sentence that contains $<$ or $>$ is called an <u>empty set</u>. **false; inequality**
6. When the final result in solving an equation is $5 = -8$, the solution set is the <u>null set</u>. **true**
7. When the final result in solving an equation is $x = x$, the solution set is <u>all numbers</u>. **true**
8. To solve $3(x + 5) = 10$, use the <u>Distributive Property</u> to remove the parentheses. **true**
9. The symbol $\geq$ means <u>is less than or equal to</u>. **false; is greater than or equal to**
10. A closed circle on a number line indicates that the point <u>is included</u> in the solution set for the inequality. **true**

Lesson-by-Lesson Review

7-1 *Solving Equations with Variables on Each Side*

See pages 330–333.

Concept Summary
- Use the Addition or Subtraction Property of Equality to isolate the variables on one side of an equation.

Example   **Solve $7x = 3x - 12$.**

$7x = 3x - 12$	Write the equation.
$7x - 3x = 3x - 3x - 12$	Subtract $3x$ from each side.
$4x = -12$	Simplify.
$x = -3$	Mentally divide each side by 4.

Exercises   **Solve each equation. Check your solution.**
See Example 1 on page 330. 17. −1

11. $2a + 9 = 5a$ **3**   12. $x - 4 = 3x$ **−2**   13. $3y - 8 = y$ **4**
14. $19t = 26 + 6t$ **2**   15. $2 + 7n = 8 + n$ **1**   16. $5 + 6t = 10t - 7$ **3**
17. $-r + 4.2 = 8.8r + 14$ 18. $12 + 1.5x = 9x$ **1.6**   19. $5b - 1 = 2.5b - 4$ **−1.2**

 www.pre-alg.com/vocabulary_review

Study Organizer

For more information about Foldables, see *Teaching Mathematics with Foldables.*

Have students review their Foldables and reexamine the questions they wrote for each lesson. They should also reexamine the answers they recorded under each lesson's tab. Have them refer to their Foldables as they prepare for the Chapter Test.

7-2 Solving Equations with Grouping Symbols

See pages 334–338.

Concept Summary

- Use the Distributive Property to remove the grouping symbols.

Example **Solve $2(x + 3) = 15$.**

$2(x + 3) = 15$	Write the equation.
$2x + 6 = 15$	Use the Distributive Property.
$2x = 9$	Subtract 6 from each side and simplify.
$x = 4.5$	Divide each side by 2 and simplify.

Exercises Solve each equation. *See Examples 1–4 on pages 334–336.* **25. all numbers**

20. $4(k + 1) = 16$ **3**   **21.** $2(n - 5) = 8$ **9**   **22.** $11 + 2q = 2(q + 4)$ $\varnothing$

23. $\frac{1}{2}(t + 8) = \frac{3}{4}t$ **16**   **24.** $4(x + 2.5) = 3(7 + x)$ **11**   **25.** $3(x + 1) - 5 = 3x - 2$

7-3 Inequalities

See pages 340–344.

Concept Summary

- An inequality is a mathematical sentence that contains $<$, $>$, $\le$, or $\ge$.

Example **State whether $n + 11 < 14$ is *true* or *false* for $n = 5$.**

$n + 11 < 14$	Write the inequality.
$5 + 11 \overset{?}{<} 14$	Replace n with 5.
$16 \not< 14$	Simplify. The sentence is false.

Exercises For the given value, state whether each inequality is *true* or *false*.
See Example 4 on page 341.

26. $x + 4 > 9$, $x = 12$ **true**   **27.** $15 \le 5n$, $n = 3$ **true**   **28.** $3n + 1 \ge 14$, $n = 4$ **false**

7-4 Solving Inequalities by Adding or Subtracting

See pages 345–349.

Concept Summary

- Solving an inequality means finding values for the variable that make the inequality true.

Example **Solve $x - 7 < 3$. Graph the solution on a number line.**

$x - 7 < 3$	Write the inequality.
$x - 7 + 7 < 3 + 7$	Add 7 to each side.
$x < 10$	Simplify.

Exercises Solve each inequality. Graph the solution on a number line.
See Examples 1 and 2 on page 346. **29–31. See margin for graphs.**

29. $b - 9 \ge 8$ $b \ge 17$ **30.** $x + 4.8 \le 2$ $x \le -2.8$ **31.** $t + \frac{1}{2} < 4$ $t < 3\frac{1}{2}$

Answers

29.

30.

31.

Study Guide and Review

Chapter **7** For More ...
• Extra Practice, see pages 739–741.
• Mixed Problem Solving, see page 764

Answers

32.

20 22 24 26 28

33.
-1 0 1 2 3 4 5 6 7 8 9

34.
2   4   6   8   10   12

35.
-12 -10 -8 -6 -4

36.
-40 -38 -36 -34 -32

37.
-4 -2   0   2   4   6

Answers (p. 363)

1. An open circle is used when the inequality symbol is $<$ or $>$; a closed circle is used when the inequality symbol is $\leq$ or $\geq$.

2. When an inequality is multiplied or divided by a negative number, the direction of the inequality symbol is reversed.

18.
-4 -3 -2 -1 0 1 2 3 4

19.
1 2 3 4 5 6 7 8 9

20.
10   30   50   70   90

21.
-10 -8 -6 -4 -2

22.
-4 -3 -2 -1 0 1 2 3 4

23.
-20 -18 -16 -14 -12

See pages 350–354.

7-5 Solving Inequalities by Multiplying or Dividing

Concept Summary

• When you multiply or divide each side of an inequality by a positive number, the inequality symbol remains the same.

• When you multiply or divide each side of an inequality by a negative number, the inequality symbol must be reversed.

Examples

1 Solve $\frac{a}{3} > 2$. Graph the solution on a number line.

$\frac{a}{3} > 2$ Write the inequality.

$3\left(\frac{a}{3}\right) > 3(2)$ Multiply each side by 3.

$a > 6$ Simplify.

2   4   6   8   10

The solution is $a > 6$.

2 Solve $-2n \geq 26$. Graph the solution on a number line.

$-2n \geq 26$ Write the inequality.

$\frac{-2n}{-2} \leq \frac{26}{-2}$ Divide each side by -2 and reverse the symbol.

$n \leq -13$ Simplify.

-18 -16 -14 -12 -10

The solution is $n \leq -13$.

Exercises Solve each inequality. Graph the solution on a number line.
See Examples 1 and 3 on pages 351 and 352. **32–37. See margin for graphs.**

32. $\frac{n}{4} < 6$ $n < 24$ **33.** $\frac{k}{1.7} \leq 3$ $k \leq 5.1$ **34.** $0.5x > 3.2$ $x > 6.4$

35. $-56 \geq 8y$ $y \leq -7$ **36.** $9 > \frac{x}{-4}$ $x > -36$ **37.** $-\frac{5}{6}a \leq 2$ $a \geq -2\frac{2}{5}$

See pages 355–359.

7-6 Solving Multi-Step Inequalities

Concept Summary

• To solve an inequality that involves more than one operation, work backward to undo the operations.

Example

Solve $4t + 7 < -5$.

$4t + 7 < -5$ Write the inequality.

$4t + 7 - 7 < -5 - 7$ Subtract 7 from each side.

$4t < -12$ Simplify.

$t < -3$ Mentally divide each side by 4.   The solution is $t < -3$.

Exercises Solve each inequality. *See Examples 1 and 2 on pages 355 and 356.*

38. $2x - 3 > 19$ $x > 11$ **39.** $5n + 4 \leq 24$ $n \leq 4$ **40.** $6 \geq \frac{r}{7} + 1$ $r \leq 35$

41. $\frac{t}{-2} + 15 < 21$ $t > -12$ **42.** $3(a + 8.4) > 30$ $a > 1.6$ **43.** $\frac{1}{4} + 2b < 13 + 5b$ $b > -4\frac{1}{4}$

Vocabulary and Concepts

1. **State** when to use an open circle and a closed circle in graphing an inequality. **See margin.**
2. **Describe** what happens to an inequality when each side is multiplied or divided by a negative number. **See margin.**

Skills and Applications

Solve each equation. Check your solution.

3. $7x - 3 = 10x$ **−1**
4. $p - 9 = 4p$ **−3**
5. $2.3n - 8 = 1.2n + 3$ **10**
6. $\frac{3}{8}y - 5 = \frac{5}{8}y - 3$ **−8**
7. $6 + 2(x - 4) = 2(x - 1)$ **all numbers**
8. $2(6 - 5d) = 8$ **0.4**
9. $8(2x - 9) = 4(5 + 4x)$ **∅**
10. $4(a + 3) = 20$ **2**
11. $\frac{1}{3}(9b + 1) = b - 1$ **$-\frac{2}{3}$**

Define a variable and write an equation to find each number. Then solve.

12. Eight more than three times a number equals four less than the number. **$3x + 8 = x - 4; -6$**
13. The product of a number and five is twelve more than the number. **$5x = x + 12; 3$**

14. **GEOMETRY** The perimeter of the rectangle is 22 feet. Find the dimensions of the rectangle. **2.5 ft by 8.5 ft**

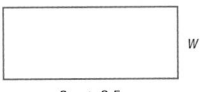
$2w + 3.5$
w

15. **SHOPPING** The cost of purchasing four shirts is at least $120. Write an inequality to describe this situation. **$4s \geq 120$**

Write the inequality for each graph.

16. ![number line] $x > 4$

17. ![number line] $x \leq -1$

Solve each inequality and check your solution. Then graph the solution on a number line. 18–23. See margin for graphs.

18. $-4 \geq p - 2$ **$p \leq -2$**
19. $3x \geq 15$ **$x \geq 5$**
20. $-42 < -0.6x$ **$x < 70$**
21. $c - 3 \leq 4c + 9$ **$c \geq -4$**
22. $7(3 - 2b) > 5b + 2$ **$b < 1$**
23. $\frac{1}{2}(a + 4) > \frac{1}{4}(a - 8)$ **$a > -16$**

24. **SALES** The Cookie Factory has a fixed cost of $300 per month plus $0.45 for each cookie sold. Each cookie sells for $0.95. How many cookies must be sold during one month for the profit to be at least $100? **at least 800 cookies**

25. **STANDARDIZED TEST PRACTICE** Danny earns $6.50 per hour working at a movie theater. Which inequality can be used to find how many hours he must work each week to earn at least $100 a week? **D**

   Ⓐ $6.50h < 100$
   Ⓑ $6.50h > 100$
   Ⓒ $6.50h \leq 100$
   Ⓓ $6.50h \geq 100$

Chapter
7 Practice Test

Assessment Options

Vocabulary Test A vocabulary review/test for Chapter 7 can be found on p. 410 of the *Chapter 7 Resource Masters.*

Chapter Tests There are six Chapter 7 Tests and an Open-Ended Assessment task available in the *Chapter 7 Resource Masters.*

Chapter 7 Tests			
Form	Type	Level	Pages
1	MC	basic	397–398
2A	MC	average	399–400
2B	MC	average	401–402
2C	FR	average	403–404
2D	FR	average	405–406
3	FR	advanced	407–408

MC = multiple-choice questions
FR = free-response questions

Open-Ended Assessment
Performance tasks for Chapter 7 can be found on p. 409 of the *Chapter 7 Resource Masters.* A sample scoring rubric for these tasks appears on p. A22.

 ExamView® Pro

Use the networkable **ExamView® Pro** to:

- Create **multiple versions** of tests.
- Create **modified** tests for *Inclusion* students.
- **Edit** existing questions and **add** your own questions.
- Use built-in **state curriculum correlations** to create tests aligned with state standards.
- Change **English** tests to **Spanish** and vice versa.

Portfolio Suggestion

Introduction The ability to translate words into equations or inequalities is an important skill that applies mathematics to real-life situations. This chapter featured word problems that required increasingly more complex equations/inequalities to solve.

Ask Students to choose their favorite word problem from the chapter and place it in their portfolio. They should attach a note explaining why it is their favorite.

These two pages contain practice questions in the various formats that can be found on the most frequently given standardized tests.

A practice answer sheet for these two pages can be found on page A1 of the *Chapter 7 Resource Masters*.

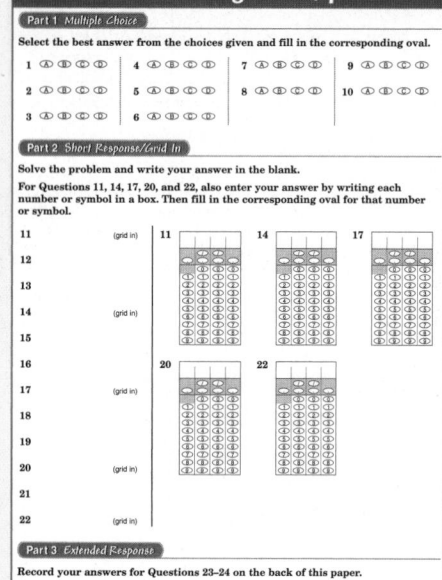

Standardized Test Practice
Student Recording Sheet, p. A1

Additional Practice

See pp. 415–416 of the *Chapter 7 Resource Masters* for additional standardized test practice.

Part 1 Multiple Choice

Record your answers on the answer sheet provided by your teacher or on a sheet of paper.

1. A delivery service calculates the cost c of shipping a package with the equation $c = 0.30w + 6$, where w is the weight of the package in pounds. Your package weighs at least 8 pounds. What is the lowest possible cost to ship your package? (Lesson 3-7) **B**

   Ⓐ $6.30
   Ⓑ $8.40
   Ⓒ $14.30
   Ⓓ $30.00

2. The school band traveled on two buses with 36 students on each bus. At a lunch stop, two-thirds of the students on the first bus ate at Hamburger Haven, and the others ate at Taco Time. Three-fourths of the students on the second bus ate at Hamburger Haven. How many students in all ate at Hamburger Haven? (Lesson 5-3) **C**

   Ⓐ 24
   Ⓑ 48
   Ⓒ 51
   Ⓓ 102

3. Shanté earned $360 last summer. She spent $\frac{5}{9}$ of her earnings. How much money did she have left? (Lesson 5-3) **B**

   Ⓐ $40
   Ⓑ $160
   Ⓒ $200
   Ⓓ $320

4. While exercising, Luke's heart is beating at 170 beats per minute. If he maintains this rate, about how many times will his heart beat in one hour? (Lesson 6-1) **C**

   Ⓐ 1000
   Ⓑ 5000
   Ⓒ 10,000
   Ⓓ 100,000

Test-Taking Tip
Questions 9 and 10
When an item requires you to solve an equation or inequality, plug in your solution to the original problem in order to check your answer.

5. Which of the circles has approximately the same fractional part shaded as that of the rectangle below? (Lesson 6-4) **C**

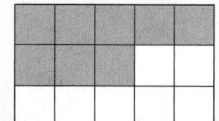

   Ⓐ Ⓑ Ⓒ Ⓓ

6. Which of the following statements is true? (Lesson 6-4) **D**

   Ⓐ $0.4 > 40\%$
   Ⓑ $0.04 = 40\%$
   Ⓒ $40\% \leq 0.04$
   Ⓓ $40\% > 0.04$

7. A survey at the MegaMall showed that 15% of visitors attend a movie while at the mall. If 8700 people are at the mall, how many of these visitors are likely to attend a movie there? (Lesson 6-7) **C**

   Ⓐ 580
   Ⓑ 870
   Ⓒ 1305
   Ⓓ 5800

8. Last year there were 1536 students at Cortéz Middle School. This year there are 5% more students. *About* how many students attend Cortéz this year? (Lesson 6-9) **B**

   Ⓐ 1550
   Ⓑ 1600
   Ⓒ 1650
   Ⓓ 1700

9. If $5(x + 2) = 40$, what is the value of x? (Lesson 7-2) **B**

   Ⓐ 4
   Ⓑ 6
   Ⓒ 8
   Ⓓ 10

10. Which of the following inequalities is equivalent to $\frac{x}{3} < 5$? (Lesson 7-5) **D**

   Ⓐ $x < \frac{5}{3}$
   Ⓑ $x < 2$
   Ⓒ $x > 2$
   Ⓓ $x < 15$

ExamView® Pro

Special banks of standardized test questions similar to those on the SAT, ACT, TIMSS 8, NAEP 8, and Pre-Algebra End-of-Course tests can be found on this CD-ROM.

Part 2 | Short Response/Grid In

Record your answers on the answer sheet provided by your teacher or on a sheet of paper.

11. What is the value of $16 + 18 \div 2 \times 3$? (Lesson 1-2) **43**

12. In 5 days, the stock market fell 25 points. What integer expresses the average change in the stock market per day? (Lesson 2-5) **−5**

13. Write $\dfrac{1}{5 \times 5 \times 5 \times 5}$ using a negative exponent. (Lesson 4-7) **5^{-4}**

14. Find $\dfrac{5}{12} - \dfrac{3}{8}$. (Lesson 5-4) **1/24**

15. The high temperatures for five days in April are shown in the table below. What was the median high temperature? (Lesson 5-8) **53°**

High Temperatures	
Monday	45°
Tuesday	62°
Wednesday	57°
Thursday	41°
Friday	53°

16. To mix a certain color of paint, Alexis combines 5 liters of white paint, 2 liters of red paint, and 1 liter of blue paint. What is the ratio of white paint to the total amount of paint? (Lesson 6-1) **5:8**

17. A box contains 42 pencils. Some are yellow, some are red, some are white, and some are black. If the probability of randomly selecting a red pencil is $\dfrac{3}{7}$, how many red pencils are in the box? (Lesson 6-2) **18**

18. A city received a federal grant of $350 million to build a light-rail system which actually cost $625 million. What percent of the total cost was paid for with the Federal grant? Round to the nearest percent. (Lesson 6-7) **56%**

 www.pre-alg.com/standardized_test

19. A leather jacket is on sale for 40% off the original price. The sale price is $64 less than the original price. What was the original price of the jacket? (Lesson 6-8) **$160**

20. Find x if $8x - 12 = 5x + 6$. (Lesson 7-1) **6**

21. Find the width w of the rectangle below if its perimeter is 88 meters. (Lesson 7-2) **8 m**

$$5w - 4$$

w ☐

22. Dakota earns $8 per hour working at a landscaping company and wants to earn at least $1200 this summer. What is the minimum number of hours he will have to work? (Lesson 7-5) **150**

Part 3 | Extended Response

Record your answers on a sheet of paper. Show your work.

23. At a post office, a customer bought an equal number of the following stamps: 1¢, 22¢, and 34¢. She also mailed a package that required $2.80 in postage. The total bill was $14. (Lesson 3-6) **a–d. See margin.**

   a. Write an equation that describes this situation.

   b. What does the variable in your equation represent?

   c. Solve the equation. Show your work.

   d. Write a sentence describing what the solution represents.

24. A magazine publisher collected data on subscription renewals and found that each year 3 out of 50 subscribers do *not* renew. The magazine currently has 24,000 subscribers. (Lesson 6-6)

   a. What percent of subscribers do *not* renew their subscriptions? **6%**

   b. What percent of subscribers per year do renew their subscriptions? **94%**

   c. How many subscribers will likely renew their subscriptions this year? **22,560**

Evaluating Extended Response Questions

Extended Response questions are graded by using a multilevel rubric that guides you in assessing a student's knowledge of a particular concept.

Goal: Solve problems using equations/percentages.

Sample Scoring Rubric: The following rubric is a sample scoring device. You may wish to add more detail to this sample to meet your individual scoring needs.

Score	Criteria
4	A correct solution that is supported by well-developed, accurate explanations
3	A generally correct solution, but may contain minor flaws in reasoning or computation
2	A partially correct interpretation and/or solution to the problem
1	A correct solution with no supporting evidence or explanation
0	An incorrect solution indicating no mathematical understanding of the concept or task, or no solution is given

Answer

23a. $0.01x + 0.22x + 0.34x + 2.80 = 14$
23b. the number of each kind of stamp

23c.
$$0.01x + 0.22x + 0.34x + 2.80 = 14.20$$
$$(0.01 + 0.22 + 0.34)x + 2.80 = 14.20$$
$$0.57x + 2.80 = 14.20$$
$$0.57x + 2.80 - 2.80 = 14.20 - 2.80$$
$$0.57x = 11.40$$
$$\frac{0.57x}{0.57} = \frac{11.40}{0.57}$$
$$x = 20$$

23d. The customer bought 20 of each kind of stamp.

9.

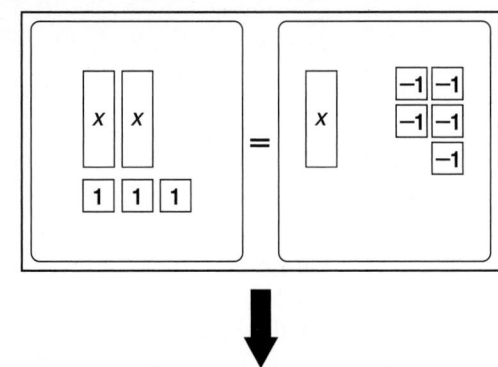

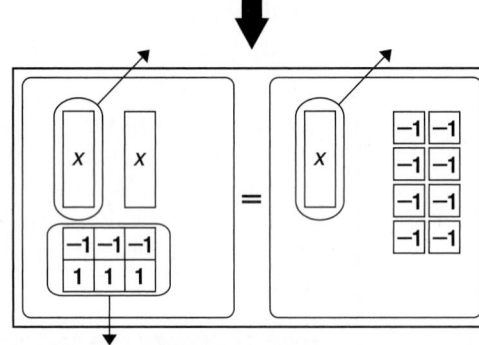

10.

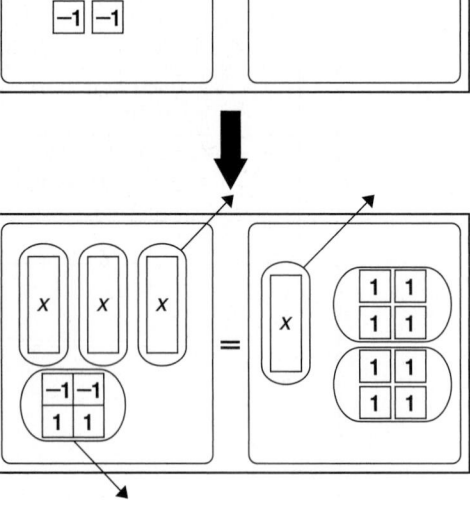

11.

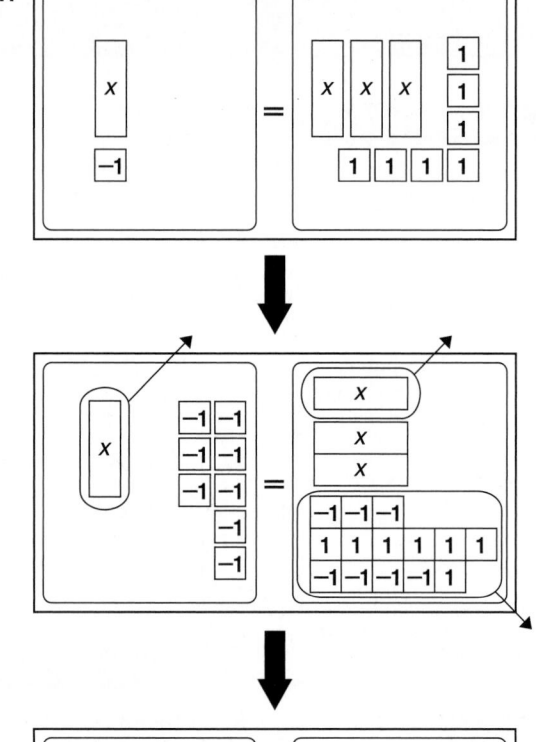

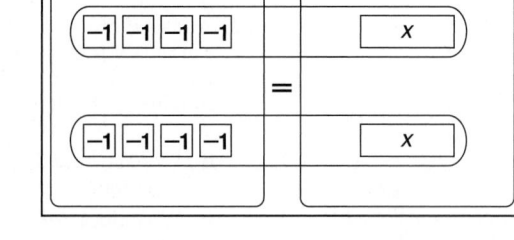

12.

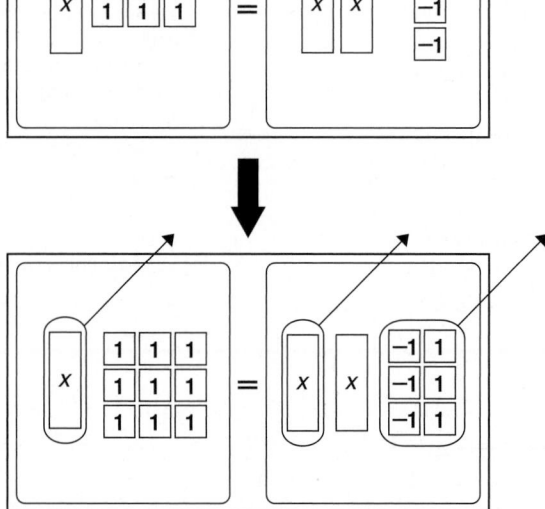

13.

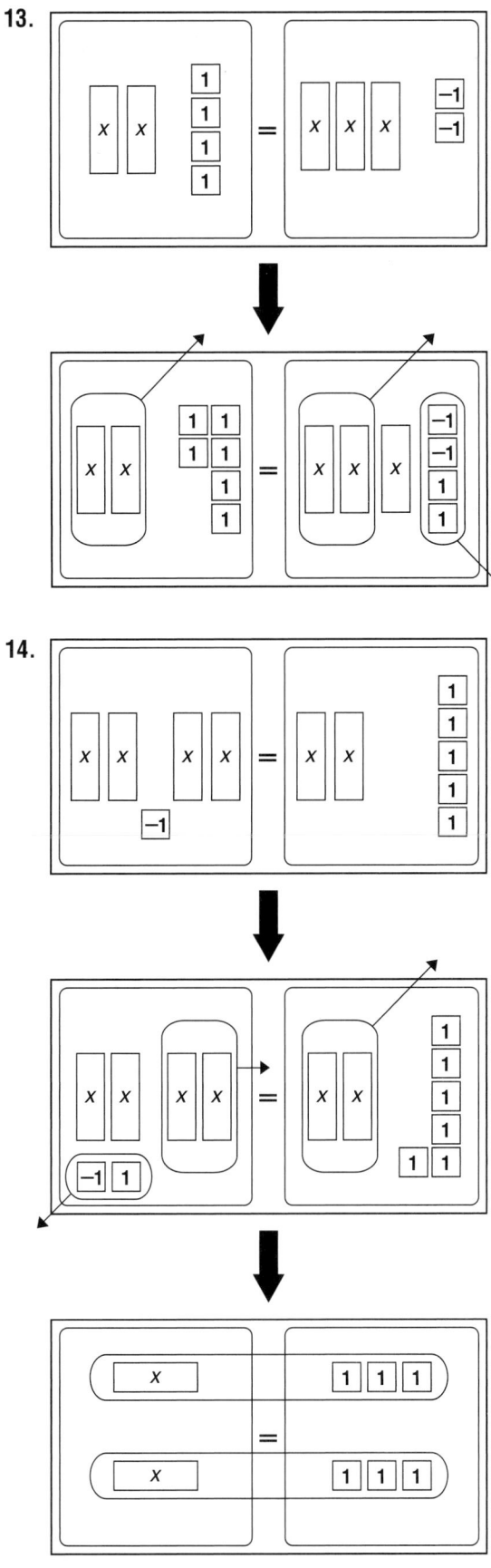

14.

1. A number line graph can represent all numbers greater or less than a given number.

2. Sample answer: $x < 9$ means that the value of x is less than 9; $x > 9$ means that the value of x is greater than 9; $x \leq 9$ means that the value of x is 9 or less; $x \geq 9$ means that the value of x is 9 or greater.

7.
```
←+++++⊕+++→
 −2 −1 0 1 2 3 4 5 6
```

8.
```
←━━━━━━●+→
 −2 −1 0 1 2 3 4 5 6
```

9.
```
←━━━━━⊕++→
 1 2 3 4 5 6 7 8 9
```

Page 343, Lesson 7-3

23.
```
←+++++⊕━━→
 −1 0 1 2 3 4 5 6 7
```

24.
```
←+++⊕━━━━→
 3 4 5 6 7 8 9 10 11
```

25.
```
←━━━━━━⊕+→
 4 5 6 7 8 9 10 11 12
```

26.
```
←━━━━━━━⊕+→
 −2 −1 0 1 2 3 4 5 6
```

27.
```
←++●━━━━━→
 6 7 8 9 10 11 12 13 14
```

28.
```
←+●━━━━━━→
 6 7 8 9 10 11 12 13 14
```

29.
```
←━━━━━━●++→
 −2 −1 0 1 2 3 4 5 6
```

30.
```
←━━━━━●++→
 2 3 4 5 6 7 8 9 10
```

31.
```
←++⊕━━━━━→
 −6−5−4−3−2−1 0 1 2
```

32.
```
←++●━━━━━→
 −6−5−4−3−2−1 0 1 2
```

33.
```
←━━━●++++++→
 −8−7−6−5−4−3−2−1 0
```

34.
```
←━━━━⊕+++→
 −6−5−4−3−2−1 0 1 2
```

Page 347, Lesson 7-4

10.
```
←+++++⊕━━→
 −4−3−2−1 0 1 2 3 4
```

11.
```
←━━━●++++++→
 7 8 9 10 11 12 13 14 15
```

Page 348, Lesson 7-4

31. 1 2 3 4 5 6 7 8 9

32. 1 2 3 4 5 6 7 8 9

33. 1 2 3 4 5 6 7 8 9

34. 1 2 3 4 5 6 7 8 9

35. −7 −6 −5 −4 −3 −2 −1 0 1

36. −30 −28 −26 −24 −22

37. 23 25 27 29 31

38. −31 −29 −27 −25 −23

39. 0 $\frac{1}{2}$ 1 $1\frac{1}{2}$ 2

40. 0 1 2 3 4

41. 3 4 5

42. 0 $\frac{1}{2}$ 1 $1\frac{1}{2}$ 2

Page 353, Lesson 7-5

4. 1 2 3 4 5 6 7 8 9

5. −4 −3 −2 −1 0 1 2 3 4

6. 1 2 3 4 5 6 7 8 9

7. 10 30 50 70 90

8. 3 3.2 3.4 3.6 3.8

9. −9 −8.6 −8.2 −7.8 −7.4

10. 9 10 11 12 13

11. −80 −76 −72 −68 −64

12. 20 22 24 26 28

14. −4 −3 −2 −1 0 1 2 3 4

15. 5 6 7 8 9 10 11 12 13

16. −4 −3 −2 −1 0 1 2 3 4

17. −4 −3 −2 −1 0 1 2 3 4

18. 0 4 8 12 16

19. 1 2 3 4 5 6 7 8 9

20. 10 30 50 70 90

21. 90 94 98 102 106

22. 10 12 14 16 18

23. 1 2 3 4 5 6 7 8 9

24. −10 −8 −6 −4 −2

25. −4 −3 −2 −1 0 1 2 3 4

26. −50 −46 −42 −38 −34

27. 1 2 3 4 5 6 7 8 9

28. 16 18 20 22 24

29. −20 −18 −16 −14 −12

30. 10 12 14 16 18

31. −20 −18 −16 −14 −12

32. 9.0 9.2 9.4 9.6 9.8

33. 1 2 3 4 5 6 7 8 9

34.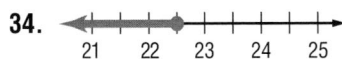
21　22　23　24　25

35.
5　5.2　5.4　5.6　5.8

36.
25　27　29　31　33

37.
70　74　78　82　86

Page 357, Lesson 7-6

4.
5　6　7　8　9　10　11　12　13

5.
1　2　3　4　5　6　7　8　9

6.
−4 −3 −2 −1　0　1　2　3　4

7.
−4 −3 −2 −1　0　1　2　3　4

8.
−1　0　1　2　3

9.
1　2　3　4　5　6　7　8　9

10.
−7 −6 −5 −4 −3 −2 −1　0　1

11.
−10　−9　−8　−7　−6

13.
1　2　3　4　5　6　7　8　9

14.
−4 −3 −2 −1　0　1　2　3　4

15.
−4 −3 −2 −1　0　1　2　3　4

16.
−4 −3 −2 −1　0　1　2　3　4

17.
−4 −3 −2 −1　0　1　2　3　4

18.
−4 −3 −2 −1　0　1　2　3　4

19.
−7 −6 −5 −4 −3 −2 −1　0　1

20.
−4 −3 −2 −1　0　1　2　3　4

21.
−7 −6 −5 −4 −3 −2 −1　0　1

22.
1　2　3　4　5　6　7　8　9

23.
−4 −3 −2 −1　0　1　2　3　4

24.
−10　−8　−6　−4　−2

25.
10　30　50　70　90

26.
1　2　3　4　5　6　7　8　9

27.
−10　−8　−6　−4　−2

28.
1　2　3　4　5　6　7　8　9

Chapter 8
Functions and Graphing
Chapter Overview and Pacing

An electronic version of this chapter is available on **StudentWorks™**. This backpack solution CD-ROM allows students instant access to the Student Edition, lesson worksheet pages, and web resources.

Year-long pacing: pages T20–T21.

LESSON OBJECTIVES

	PACING (days)			
	Regular		**Block**	
	Basic/ Average	Advanced	Basic/ Average	Advanced
8-1 Functions (pp. 368–373) *Preview:* Explore the relationship between sets of numbers by making a function machine. • Determine whether relations are functions. • Use functions to describe relationships between two quantities.	2 (with 8-1 Preview)	1	1 (with 8-1 Preview)	0.5
8-2 Linear Equations in Two Variables (pp. 374–379) *Preview:* Demonstrate an understanding of the relationship between domain and range. • Solve linear equations with two variables. • Graph linear equations using ordered pairs.	2 (with 8-2 Preview)	1	1 (with 8-2 Preview)	0.5
8-3 Graphing Linear Equations Using Intercepts (pp. 381–385) • Find the *x*- and *y*-intercepts of graphs. • Graph linear equations using the *x*- and *y*-intercepts.	1	1	0.5	0.5
8-4 Slope (pp. 386–391) *Preview:* Explore slope by examining how fast an object rolls down various hills. • Find the slope of a line.	2 (with 8-4 Preview)	1	1 (with 8-4 Preview)	0.5
8-5 Rate of Change (pp. 392–397) *Preview:* Explore the relationship between slope and rate of change by comparing heights of water levels in a glass. • Find rates of change. • Solve problems involving direct variation.	2 (with 8-5 Preview)	1	1 (with 8-5 Preview)	0.5
8-6 Slope-Intercept Form (pp. 398–403) • Determine slopes and *y*-intercepts of lines. • Graph linear equations using the slope and *y*-intercept. *Follow-Up:* Use a graphing calculator to investigate families of graphs.	2	2 (with 8-6 Follow-Up)	1	1 (with 8-6 Follow-Up)
8-7 Writing Linear Equations (pp. 404–408) • Write equations given the slope and *y*-intercept, a graph, a table, or two points.	1	1	0.5	0.5
8-8 Best-Fit Lines (pp. 409–413) • Draw best-fit lines for sets of data. • Use best-fit lines to make predictions about data.	2	1	1	0.5
8-9 Solving Systems of Equations (pp. 414–418) • Solve systems of linear equations by graphing. • Solve systems of linear equations by substitution.	2	2	1.5	1
8-10 Graphing Inequalities (pp. 419–423) • Graph linear inequalities. • Describe solutions of linear inequalities. *Follow-Up:* Use a graphing calculator to investigate graphs of inequalities.	1	2 (with 8-10 Follow-Up)	0.5	1.5 (with 8-10 Follow-Up)
Study Guide and **Practice Test** (pp. 424–429) **Standardized Test Practice** (pp. 430–431)	1	1	0.5	0.5
Chapter Assessment	1	1	0.5	0.5
TOTAL	19	15	10	8

Chapter Resource Manager

CHAPTER 8 RESOURCE MASTERS

Study Guide and Intervention	Practice (Skills and Average)	Reading to Learn Mathematics	Enrichment	Assessment	Prerequisite Skills Workbook	Applications*	Parent and Student Study Guide Workbook	5-Minute Check Transparencies	Interactive Chalkboard	Pre-AlgePASS: Tutorial Plus (lessons)	Materials
417	418–419	420	421				61	8-1	8-1	22	*Preview:* 3 x 5 index cards, scissors
422	423–424	425	426				62	8-2	8-2		
427	428–429	430	431	481		SM 4	63	8-3	8-3		
432	433–434	435	436				64	8-4	8-4	23	*Preview:* posterboard, tape, book, ruler, toy car
437	438–439	440	441	481, 483		GCS 34 SC 15	65	8-5	8-5		*Preview:* grid paper, water, beaker, metric ruler, tablespoon, $\frac{1}{8}$-cup measuring cup
442	443–444	445	446				66	8-6	8-6	24	*Follow-Up:* graphing calculator
447	448–449	450	451				67	8-7	8-7		
452	453–454	455	456	482			68	8-8	8-8		
457	458–459	460	461			GCS 33	69	8-9	8-9		
462	463–464	465	466	482	1–2	SC 16	70	8-10	8-10	25	*Follow-Up:* graphing calculator
				467–480, 484–488							

* *Key to Abbreviations:* GCS = Graphing Calculator and Spreadsheet Masters, SC = School-to-Career Masters, SM = Science and Mathematics Lab Manual

 ELL Study Guide and Intervention, Skills Practice, Practice, and Parent and Student Study Guide Workbooks are also available in Spanish.

Mathematical Connections and Background

Continuity of Instruction

Prior Knowledge

Students studied relations in Chapter 1, including ordered pairs and how to determine the domain and range of a relation. Then in Chapter 2 they learned about the Cartesian coordinate system and how to locate points on a coordinate plane. In Chapter 7, students learned to write, solve, and graph inequalities.

This Chapter

Students will learn that a function is a special type of relation and that a linear equation is one of many ways to represent a function. They will learn to write linear equations and use them to solve real-world problems such as those involving rate of change. Students also will learn to graph linear equations and inequalities. They will use best-fit lines to predict data.

Future Connections

Students will study functions further in Chapter 13, examining linear and nonlinear functions. In particular, they will learn to graph quadratic and cubic functions on a coordinate plane. Graphing functions and inequalities is a skill that students will use in future mathematics courses and in engineering fields.

8-1 Functions

A function is a special relation in which each member of the domain is paired with exactly one member in the range. Functions may be represented using ordered pairs, tables, or graphs. One way to determine whether a relation is a function is to use the vertical line test. Using an object to represent a vertical line, move the object from left to right across the graph. If, for each value of x in the domain, the object passes through no more than one point on the graph, then the graph represents a function.

8-2 Linear Equations in Two Variables

In a linear equation in two variables, such as $y = x - 3$, the variables appear in separate terms and neither variable contains an exponent other than 1. The graphs of all linear equations are straight lines. All points on a line are solutions of the equation that is graphed.

8-3 Graphing Linear Equations Using Intercepts

Sets of data can be either discrete or continuous. Discrete data have a finite number of possible values, such as books or people. Continuous data usually are associated with physical measurements. In mathematics, an intercept is the point where a line crosses a coordinate axis. In graphing a linear equation, you can find, plot, and connect the points where the graph crosses the x- and y-axes.

8-4 Slope

Slope is the ratio of the rise, or vertical change, to the run, or horizontal change of a line: slope $= \frac{\text{rise}}{\text{run}}$. Slope ($m$) is the same for any two points on a straight line and can be found by using the coordinates of any two points on a line: $m = \frac{y_2 - y_1}{x_2 - x_1}$, where $x_2 \neq x_1$.

8-5 Rate of Change

A change in one quantity with respect to another quantity is called the rate of change. Rates of change can be described using slope:

$$\text{slope} = \frac{\text{change in } y}{\text{change in } x}.$$

You can find rates of change from an equation, a table of values, or a graph.

A special type of linear equation that describes rate of change is called a direct variation. The graph of a direct variation always passes through the origin and represents a proportional situation. In the equation $y = kx$, k is called the constant of variation. It is the slope, or rate of change. As x increases in value, y increases or decreases at a constant rate k, or y varies directly with x. Another way to say this is that y is directly proportional to x. The direct variation $y = kx$ also can be written as $k = \frac{y}{x}$. In this form, you can see that the ratio of y to x is the same for any corresponding values of y and x.

8-6 Slope-Intercept Form

Equations written as $y = mx + b$, where m is the slope and b is the y-intercept, are linear equations in slope-intercept form. For example, the graph of $y = 5x - 6$ is a line that has a slope of 5 and crosses the y-axis at $(0, -6)$. Sometimes you must first write an equation in slope-intercept form before finding the slope and y-intercept. For example, the equation $2x + 3y = 15$ can be expressed in slope-intercept form by subtracting $2x$ from each side and then dividing by 3: $y = -\frac{2}{3}x + 5$, revealing a slope of $-\frac{2}{3}$ and a y-intercept of 5.

8-7 Writing Linear Equations

If you know the slope and y-intercept, you can write the equation of a line by substituting these values in $y = mx + b$. For example, if a line has a slope of 2 and a y-intercept of 3, its equation can be expressed as $y = 2x + 3$. You can also use the graph of a line to write an equation. Locate the y-intercept and choose another point on the line. Find the slope between the two points. Then write the equation for the line.

You also can write an equation for a line if you know the coordinates of two points on the line by using the definition of slope: $m = \frac{y_2 - y_1}{x_2 - x_1}$.

8-8 Best-Fit Lines

When real-life data are collected, the points graphed usually do not form a straight line, but they may approximate a linear relationship. A best-fit line is a line that lies very close to most of the data points. It can be used to predict data. You also can use the equation of the best-fit line to make predictions.

8-9 Solving Systems of Equations

Two equations together are called a system of equations. The solution of a system is the ordered pair that is a solution of both equations. The system of equations can have one solution, no solution, or infinitely many solutions. One method for solving is to graph the equations on the same coordinate plane. The coordinates of the point where the graphs intersect is the solution. A more accurate way to solve a system of equations is by using a method called substitution. Write both equations in terms of y. Replace y in the first equation with the right side of the second equation.

8-10 Graphing Inequalities

To graph an inequality, first graph the related equation, which is the boundary. All points in the shaded region are solutions of the inequality. If an inequality contains the symbol $\leq$ or $\geq$, then use a solid line to indicate that the boundary is included in the graph. If an inequality contains the symbol $<$ or $>$, then use a dashed line to indicate that the boundary is not included in the graph.

Quick Review Math Handbook

Hot Words includes a glossary of terms while Hot Topics consists of explanations of key mathematical concepts with exercises to test comprehension. This valuable resource can be used as a reference in the classroom or for home study.

Lesson	Hot Topics Section	Lesson	Hot Topics Section
GS 8	6.4, 6.6, 6.7	8-5	6.4, 6.8
8-1	6.3, 6.8	8-6	1.3, 6.2, 6.8
8-2	6.7, 6.8	8-7	4.3, 6.7, 6.8
8-3	1.5, 2.3, 2.6, 6.8	8-8	4.3, 6.4
8-4	6.4, 6.8	8-10	6.6

GS = Getting Started

 Additional mathematical information and teaching notes are available at www.pre-alg.com/key_concepts.

DAILY INTERVENTION and Assessment

Key to Abbreviations:
TWE = Teacher Wraparound Edition; CRM = Chapter Resource Masters

	Type	Student Edition	Teacher Resources	Technology/Internet
INTERVENTION	Ongoing	Prerequisite Skills, pp. 367, 373, 379, 385, 391, 397, 401, 408, 413, 418 Practice Quiz 1, p. 397 Practice Quiz 2, p. 418	5-Minute Check Transparencies *Prerequisite Skills Workbook*, pp. 1–2 Quizzes, *CRM*, pp. 481, 482 Mid-Chapter Test, *CRM*, p. 483 Study Guide and Intervention, *CRM*, pp. 417, 422, 427, 432, 437, 442, 447, 452, 457, 462	Pre-AlgePASS: Tutorial Plus, Lessons 22, 23, 24, and 25 www.pre-alg.com/ self_check_quiz www.pre-alg.com/ extra_examples
	Mixed Review	pp. 373, 379, 385, 391, 397, 401, 408, 413, 418, 422	Cumulative Review, *CRM*, p. 484	
	Error Analysis	Find the Error, pp. 389, 395, 400	Find the Error, *TWE*, pp. 389, 395 Unlocking Misconceptions, *TWE*, p. 371, 394, 399, 406 Tips for New Teachers, *TWE*, p. 408	
	Standardized Test Practice	pp. 373, 379, 385, 389, 390, 391, 397, 401, 408, 413, 418, 422, 430–431	*TWE*, pp. 430–431 Standardized Test Practice, *CRM*, pp. 485–486	Standardized Test Practice CD-ROM www.pre-alg.com/ standardized_test
ASSESSMENT	Open-Ended Assessment	Writing in Math, pp. 373, 379, 385, 391, 397, 401, 408, 412, 418, 422 Open Ended, pp. 371, 377, 384, 389, 395, 400, 407, 410, 416, 421 Standardized Test, p. 431	Speaking: *TWE*, pp. 373, 413, 422 Writing: *TWE*, pp. 379, 401, 408 Modeling: *TWE*, pp. 385, 391, 397, 418 Open-Ended Assessment, *CRM*, p. 479	
	Chapter Assessment	Study Guide, pp. 424–428 Practice Test, p. 429	Multiple-Choice Tests (Forms 1, 2A, 2B), *CRM*, pp. 467–472 Free-Response Tests (Forms 2C, 2D, 3), *CRM*, pp. 473–478 Vocabulary Test/Review, *CRM*, p. 480	ExamView® Pro (see below) MindJogger Videoquizzes www.pre-alg.com/ vocabulary_review www.pre-alg.com/chapter_test

For more information on Yearly ProgressPro, see p. 324.

Pre-Algebra Lesson(s)	Yearly ProgressPro Skill Lesson
8-1	Functions
8-2	Functions and Equations
8-3	Graphing Linear Equations
8-4	Slope: Level 1
8-5	Rate of Change
8-6, 8-7	Slope-Intercept Form
8-8	Scatter Plots
8-9	Graphing Systems of Equations
8-10	Graphing Inequalities

ExamView® Pro

Use the networkable **ExamView® Pro** to:
- Create **multiple versions** of tests.
- Create **modified** tests for *Inclusion* students.
- **Edit** existing questions and **add** your own questions.
- Use built-in **state curriculum correlations** to create tests aligned with state standards.
- Change **English** tests to **Spanish** and vice versa.

For more information on Intervention and Assessment, see pp. T8–T11.

Reading and Writing in Mathematics

Glencoe Pre-Algebra provides numerous opportunities to incorporate reading and writing into the mathematics classroom.

Student Edition

- Foldables™ Study Organizer, p. 367
- Reading Mathematics, p. 380
- Concept Check questions require students to verbalize and write about what they have learned in the lesson. (pp. 370, 371, 376, 377, 381, 384, 387, 389, 395, 398, 400, 407, 410, 414, 416, 420, 421)
- Writing in Math questions in every lesson, pp. 373, 379, 385, 391, 397, 401, 408, 412, 418, 422
- Reading Math, pp. 370, 381, 383
- WebQuest, pp. 411, 422

Teacher Wraparound Edition

- Foldables™ Study Organizer, pp. 367, 424
- Study Notebook suggestions, pp. 368, 371, 378, 380, 384, 386, 389, 392, 395, 401, 406, 411, 416, 420
- Modeling activities, pp. 385, 391, 397, 418
- Speaking activities, pp. 373, 413, 422
- Writing activities, pp. 379, 401, 408
- Differentiated Instruction (Verbal/Linguistic), pp. 412, 415
-  Resources, pp. 366, 369, 375, 380, 381, 387, 393, 398, 404, 409, 412, 415, 419, 424

Additional Resources

- Vocabulary Builder worksheets require students to define and give examples for key vocabulary terms as they progress through the chapter (*Chapter 8 Resource Masters*, pp. vii–viii)
- Reading to Learn Mathematics master for each lesson (*Chapter 8 Resource Masters*, pp. 420, 425, 430, 435, 440, 445, 450, 455, 460, 465)
- *Vocabulary PuzzleMaker* software creates crossword, jumble, and word search puzzles using vocabulary lists that you can customize.
- *Teaching Mathematics with Foldables* provides suggestions for promoting cognition and language.
- *Reading and Writing in the Mathematics Classroom*
- *WebQuest and Project Resources*

For more information on Reading and Writing in Mathematics, see pp. T6–T7.

ELL ENGLISH LANGUAGE LEARNERS

Lesson 8-1
Building on Prior Knowledge

Give students an example of evaluating an expression. For example, $3x - 6$, where $x = 5$.

$$3x - 6 = 3(5) - 6$$
$$= 15 - 6$$
$$= 9$$

Then show students the concept of evaluating a function for a specified value. Have the students note the similarities in the procedures.

Lesson 8-4
Using Technology

Have pairs of students use a graphing calculator. Show the students how to input ordered pairs using the list function of the calculator. Once the calculator has graphed the data, ask students what they noticed about the points. Use the connected graph feature to see what is formed when the points on the graph are connected. Ask students to write the linear equation and tell the slope and y-intercept of the equation.

Lesson 8-8
Using Multisensory Activities

To determine a line of best fit, bring in a box of spaghetti. Have students graph a set of data and use the spaghetti to model the line of best fit. Using the spaghetti helps students determine a positive or negative relationship for the given values. Once they have agreed on a best line for a set of data, the group can find the slope and y-intercept for the line.

What You'll Learn

- **Lesson 8-1** Use functions to describe relationships between two quantities.
- **Lessons 8-2, 8-3, 8-6, and 8-7** Graph and write linear equations using ordered pairs, the *x*- and *y*-intercepts, and slope and *y*-intercept.
- **Lessons 8-4 and 8-5** Find slopes of lines and use slope to describe rates of change.
- **Lesson 8-8** Draw and use best-fit lines to make predictions about data.
- **Lessons 8-9 and 8-10** Solve systems of linear equations and linear inequalities.

Key Vocabulary

- function (p. 369)
- linear equation (p. 375)
- slope (p. 387)
- rate of change (p. 393)
- system of equations (p. 414)

Why It's Important

You can often use functions to represent real-world data. For example, the winning times in Olympic swimming events can be shown in a scatter plot. You can then use the data points to write an equation representing the relationship between the year and the winning times. *You will use a function in Lesson 8-8 to predict the winning time in the women's 800-meter freestyle event for the 2008 Olympics.*

Lesson	NCTM Standards	Local Objectives
8-1 Preview	2, 7, 10	
8-1	2, 6	
8-2 Preview	2, 6, 10	
8-2	2, 6, 10	
8-3	2, 6, 10	
8-4 Preview	2, 4, 7	
8-4	2, 6, 10	
8-5 Preview	4, 7, 9, 10	
8-5	2, 3, 6, 9, 10	
8-6	2, 6, 10	
8-6 Follow-Up	2, 7, 9, 10	
8-7	2, 6, 8, 10	
8-8	2, 5, 6, 10	
8-9	2, 6, 10	
8-10	2, 6, 10	
8-10 Follow-Up	2, 10	

Key to NCTM Standards:

1=Number & Operations, 2=Algebra,
3=Geometry, 4=Measurement,
5=Data Analysis & Probability, 6=Problem Solving, 7=Reasoning & Proof,
8=Communication, 9=Connections,
10=Representation

Vocabulary Builder

The Key Vocabulary list introduces students to some of the main vocabulary terms included in this chapter. For a more thorough vocabulary list with pronunciations of new words, give students the Vocabulary Builder worksheets found on pages vii and viii of the *Chapter 8 Resource Masters*. Encourage them to complete the definition of each term as they progress through the chapter. You may suggest that they add these sheets to their study notebooks for future reference when studying for the Chapter 8 test.

Getting Started

Prerequisite Skills   To be successful in this chapter, you'll need to master these skills and be able to apply them in problem-solving situations. Review these skills before beginning Chapter 8.

For Lesson 8-1
Relations

Express each relation as a table. Then determine the domain and range.
(For review, see Lesson 1-6.) **1–5. See pp. 431A–431H.**

1. $\{(0, 4), (-3, 3)\}$ **2.** $\{(-5, 11), (2, 1)\}$ **3.** $\{(6, 8), (7, 10), (8, 12)\}$

4. $\{(1, -9), (5, 12), (-3, -10)\}$ **5.** $\{(-8, 5), (7, -1), (6, 1), (1, -2)\}$

For Lesson 8-3
The Coordinate System

Use the coordinate grid to name the point for each ordered pair.   *(For review, see Lesson 2-6.)*

6. $(-3, 0)$ *C*

7. $(3, -2)$ *E*

8. $(-4, -2)$ *D*

9. $(0, 4)$ *A*

10. $(4, 6)$ *B*

11. $(4, 0)$ *F*

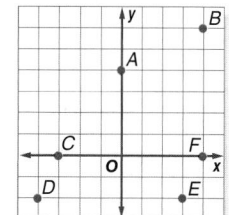

For Lesson 8-10
Inequalities

For the given value, state whether the inequality is *true* or *false*.   *(For review, see Lesson 7-3.)*

12. $8y \geq 25,\ y = 4$ **true**   **13.** $18 < t + 12,\ t = 10$ **true**   **14.** $n - 15 > 7,\ n = 20$ **false**

15. $5 \geq 2x + 3,\ x = 1$ **true**   **16.** $12 \leq \frac{2}{3}n,\ n = 9$ **false**   **17.** $\frac{1}{2}x - 5 < 0,\ x = 8$ **true**

Functions   Make this Foldable to help you organize your notes. Begin with an 11" × 17" sheet of paper.

Step 1 Fold

Fold the short sides so they meet in the middle.

Step 2 Fold Again

Fold the top to the bottom.

Step 3 Cut

Open. Cut along the second fold to make four tabs. Staple a sheet of grid paper inside.

Step 4 Label

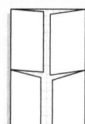

Add axes as shown. Label the quadrants on the tabs.

Reading and Writing   As you read and study the chapter, draw examples of functions on the grid paper and write notes under the tabs.

This section provides a review of the basic concepts needed before beginning Chapter 8. Page references are included for additional student help.

Additional review is provided in the *Prerequisite Skills Workbook*, pages 1–2.

Prerequisite Skills in the Getting Ready for the Next Lesson section at the end of each lesson reviews a skill needed in the next lesson.

For Lesson	Prerequisite Skill
8-2	Evaluate Expressions (p. 373)
8-3	Substitution (p. 379)
8-4	Subtract Integers (p. 385)
8-5	Substitution (p. 391)
8-6	Solve Equations for a Variable (p. 397)
8-7	Order of Operations (p. 401)
8-8	Scatter Plots (p. 408)
8-9	Substitution (p. 413)
8-10	Inequalities (p. 418)

Note Taking and Organizing Data   Note taking is a skill that is based upon listening or reading for main ideas and then recording those ideas for future reference. Under the tabs of their Foldables, have students take notes about what they need to know about functions and graphs. Encourage students to apply these concepts by drawing examples of functions on the front of each tab, and writing about them under the tabs.

For more information about Foldables, see *Teaching Mathematics with Foldables.*

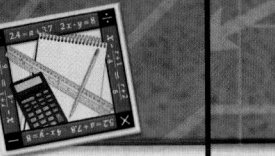

Getting Started

Objective Explore the relationship between sets of numbers by making a function machine.

Materials
3-by-5-inch index cards
scissors

Teaching Tip The concept of a function machine can be observed using a graphing calculator. Enter the rule into the Y= list letting X represent any number. Use TABLE to view the results.

Teach

- Have a sample function machine on hand to show students who might have difficulty visualizing the final product.
- Some students may wish to glue the sides of another index card to the back of the front card and cut the inside card slightly narrower. This will make it possible to hold the function machine up with one hand while using the other hand to write.

Assess

In **Exercises 1–5**, students should come to understand clearly how data entered into the function become output.

In **Exercise 6**, students should demonstrate an ease with using function machines.

Study Notebook

You may wish to have students summarize this activity and what they learned from it.

Input and Output

In a *function*, there is a relationship between two quantities or sets of numbers. You start with an input value, apply a function rule of one or more operations, and get an output value. In this way, each input is assigned exactly one output.

Collect the Data

Step 1 To make a *function machine*, draw three squares in the middle of a 3-by-5-inch index card, shown here in blue.

Step 2 Cut out the square on the left and the square on the right. Label the left "window" INPUT and the right "window" OUTPUT.

Step 3 Write a rule such as "× 2 + 3" in the center square.

Step 4 On another index card, list the integers from −5 to 4 in a column close to the left edge.

Step 5 Place the function machine over the number column so that −5 is in the left window.

Step 6 Apply the rule to the input number. The output is −5 × 2 + 3, or −7. Write −7 in the right window.
1. −5, −3, −1, 1, 3, 5, 7, 9, 11

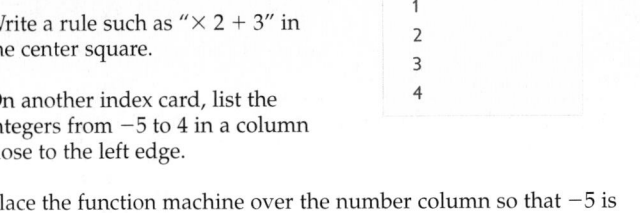

Make a Conjecture

1. Slide the function machine down so that the input is −4. Find the output and write the number in the right window. Continue this process for the remaining inputs.

2. Suppose x represents the input and y represents the output. Write an algebraic equation that represents what the function machine does. $y = 2x + 3$

3. Explain how you could find the input if you are given a rule and the corresponding output. **Write an equation and work backward to solve for the input value.**

4. Determine whether the following statement is *true* or *false*. Explain.

   The input values depend on the output values.

5. Write an equation that describes the relationship between the input value x and output value y in each table.

Input	Output
−1	−2
0	0
1	2
3	6

$y = 2x$

Input	Output
−2	2
−1	3
0	4
1	5

$y = x + 4$

Extend the Activity

6. Write your own rule and use it to make a table of inputs and outputs. Exchange your table of values with another student. Use the table to determine each other's rule. **See pp. 431A–431H.**   **4. False; the output values depend on the input values**

Resource Manager

📁 *Teaching Pre-Algebra with Manipulatives*
- p. 105 (student recording sheet)

Glencoe Mathematics Classroom Manipulative Kit
- scissors

What You'll Learn

- Determine whether relations are functions.
- Use functions to describe relationships between two quantities.

How can the relationship between actual temperatures and windchill temperatures be a function?

Vocabulary
- function
- vertical line test

a–c. See margin.

The table compares actual temperatures and windchill temperatures when the wind is blowing at 10 miles per hour.

a. On grid paper, graph the temperatures as ordered pairs (actual, windchill).

b. Describe the relationship between the two temperature scales.

c. When the actual temperature is −20°F, which is the best estimate for the windchill temperature: −46°F, −28°F, or 0°F? Explain.

Actual Temperature (°F)	Windchill Temperature (°F)
−10	−34
0	−22
10	−9
20	3

Source: *The World Almanac*

RELATIONS AND FUNCTIONS Recall that a relation is a set of ordered pairs. A **function** is a special relation in which each member of the domain is paired with *exactly* one member in the range.

Relation	Diagram	Is the Relation a Function?
{(−10, −34), (0, −22), (10, −9), (20, 3)}	domain (*x*) range (*y*) −10 → −34 0 → −22 10 → −9 20 → 3	Yes, because each domain value is paired with exactly one range value.
{(−10, −34), (−10, −22), (10, −9), (20, 3)}	domain (*x*) range (*y*) −10 → −34 ↗ −22 10 → −9 20 → 3	No, because −10 in the domain is paired with two range values, −34 and −22.

Since functions are relations, they can be represented using ordered pairs, tables, or graphs.

Example 1 Ordered Pairs and Tables as Functions

Determine whether each relation is a function. Explain.

a. {(−3, 1), (−2, 4), (−1, 7), (0, 10), (1, 13)}

This relation is a function because each element of the domain is paired with exactly one element of the range.

b.

x	5	3	2	0	−4	−6
y	1	3	1	3	−2	2

This is a function because for each element of the domain, there is only one corresponding element in the range.

www.pre-alg.com/extra_examples

RELATIONS AND FUNCTIONS

In-Class Examples

1 Determine whether each relation is a function. Explain.

a. $\{(-3, -3), (-1, -1), (0, 0), (-1, 1), (3, 3)\}$ **No; −1 in the domain is paired with −1 and 1 in the range.**

b.

x	7	6	5	2	−3	−6
y	2	4	6	4	2	−2

Yes; each x value is paired with only one y value.

2 Determine whether the graph is a function. Explain.

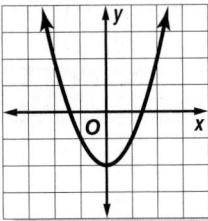

Yes; it passes the vertical line test.

DESCRIBE RELATIONSHIPS

In-Class Example

3 **BUSINESS** The table shows the number of boxes made.

Number of Hours	Number of Boxes
0	0
10	3000
20	6000
30	9000

a. Do these data represent a function? Explain.   **Yes; for each 10 hours, only one amount of boxes is made.**

b. Describe how box production is related to hours of operation.   **As hours increase, the number of boxes produced increases.**

Reading Math

Function

Everyday Meaning: a relationship in which one quality or trait depends on another. Height is a function of age.

Math Meaning: a relationship in which a range value depends on a domain value. *y* is a function of *x*.

Another way to determine whether a relation is a function is to use the **vertical line test**. Use a pencil or straightedge to represent a vertical line.

Place the pencil at the left of the graph. Move it to the right across the graph. If, for each value of *x* in the domain, it passes through no more than one point on the graph, then the graph represents a function.

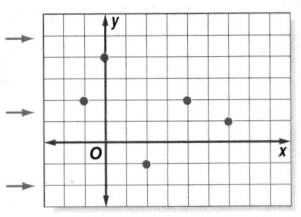

Example 2   Use a Graph to Identify Functions

Determine whether the graph at the right is a function. Explain your answer.

The graph represents a relation that is *not* a function because it does not pass the vertical line test. By examining the graph, you can see that when $x = 2$, there are three different y values.

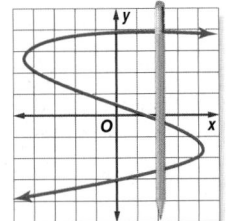

DESCRIBE RELATIONSHIPS   A function describes the relationship between two quantities such as time and distance. For example, the distance you travel on a bike depends on how long you ride the bike. In other words, *distance is a function of time.*

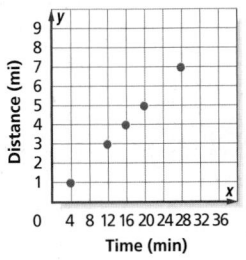

Example 3   Use a Function to Describe Data

SCUBA DIVING   The table shows the water pressure as a scuba diver descends.

a. Do these data represent a function? Explain.

This relation is a function because at each depth, there is only one measure of pressure.

b. Describe how water pressure is related to depth.

Water pressure depends on the depth. As the depth increases, the pressure increases.

Depth (ft)	Water Pressure (lb/ft³)
0	0
1	62.4
2	124.8
3	187.2
4	249.6
5	312.0

Source: www.infoplease.com

More About. . .

Scuba Diving

To prevent decompression sickness, or the "bends," it is recommended that divers ascend to the surface no faster than 30 feet per minute.

Source: www.mtsinai.org

✓ **Concept Check**   In Example 3, what is the domain and what is the range?
The depth values are the domain, the water pressure values are the range.

Interactive Chalkboard
PowerPoint® Presentations

This CD-ROM is a customizable Microsoft® Power-Point® presentation that includes:

- Step-by-step, dynamic solutions of each In-Class Example from the Teacher Wraparound Edition
- Additional, Your Turn exercises for each example
- The 5-Minute Check Transparencies
- Hot links to Glencoe Online Study Tools

Concept Check

1. **Describe** three ways to represent a function. Show an example of each.

2. **Describe** two methods for determining whether a relation is a function.

3. **OPEN ENDED** Draw the graph of a relation that is not a function. Explain why it is not a function.
1–3. See pp. 431A–431H.

Guided Practice

Determine whether each relation is a function. Explain.

4. {(13, 5), (−4, 12), (6, 0), (13, 10)} No; 13 is paired with 5 and 10.

5. {(9.2, 7), (9.4, 11), (9.5, 9.5), (9.8, 8)}

5. Yes; each *x* value is paired with only one *y* value.

6.
Domain	Range
−3	3
−1	−2
0	5
1	−4
2	3

6. Yes; each domain value is paired with only one range value.

7.
x	y
5	4
2	8
−7	9
2	12
5	14

No; 5 is paired with 4 and 14.

8.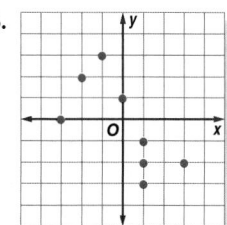

8. No; a vertical line passes through more than one point.

9.

9. Yes; any vertical line passes through no more than one point of the graph.

Application

WEATHER For Exercises 10 and 11, use the table that shows how various wind speeds affect the actual temperature of 30°F.

10. Do the data represent a function? Explain.

10. Yes; each wind speed is paired with only one windchill temperature.

11. Describe how windchill temperatures are related to wind speed.
As wind speed increases, the windchill temperature decreases.

Wind Speed (mph)	Windchill Temperature (°F)
0	30
10	16
20	4
30	−2
40	−5

Source: *The World Almanac*

Practice and Apply

Determine whether each relation is a function. Explain. 12–17. See margin.

12. {(−1, 6), (4, 2), (2, 36), (1, 6)}

13. {(−2, 3), (4, 7), (24, −6), (5, 4)}

14. {(9, 18), (0, 36), (6, 21), (6, 22)}

15. {(5, −4), (−2, 3), (5, −1), (2, 3)}

16.
Domain	Range
−4	−2
−2	1
0	2
3	1

17.
Domain	Range
−1	5
−2	5
−2	1
−6	1

3 Practice/Apply

Study Notebook

Have students—
• add the definitions/examples of the vocabulary terms to their Vocabulary Builder worksheets for Chapter 8.
• include a graph of a function and a graph that is not a function with accompanying explanations of the vertical line test.
• include any other item(s) that they find helpful in mastering the skills in this lesson.

About the Exercises . . .

Organization by Objective
• **Relations and Functions:** 12–24, 26, 28, 30–31
• **Describe Relationships:** 25, 27, 29

Odd/Even Assignments
Exercises 12–31 are structured so that students practice the same concepts whether they are assigned odd or even problems.

Assignment Guide

Basic: 13–23 odd, 24–29, 31–52

Average: 13–23 odd, 24–29, 31–52

Advanced: 12–22 even, 24–29, 30–46 (Optional: 47–52)

Answers

12. Yes; each *x* value is paired with only one *y* value.

13. Yes; each *x* value is paired with only one *y* value.

14. No; 6 in the domain is paired with 21 and 22 in the range.

15. No; 5 in the domain is paired with −4 and −1 in the range.

16. Yes; each domain value is paired with only one range value.

17. No; −2 in the domain is paired with 5 and 1 in the range.

DAILY

Unlocking Misconceptions

• **Relations and Functions**
Students may mistakenly think that each value in the domain *and* range must be paired with only one value. Stress that only the values in the domain of a function must have unique range values. It might be helpful to show students a table such as the one above.

x	1	2	3	−1	−2	−3
y	1	4	9	1	4	9

Study Guide and Intervention, p. 417

Function	A special relation in which each member of the domain is paired with exactly one member in the range.
Vertical Line Test	Move a pencil or straightedge from left to right across the graph of a relation. • If it passes through no more than one point on the graph, the graph represents a function. • If it passes through more than one point on the graph, the graph does not represent a function.

Since functions are relations, they can be represented using ordered pairs, tables, or graphs.

Example Determine whether each relation is a function. Explain.

a. {(−10, −34), (0, −22), (10, −9), (20, 3)}

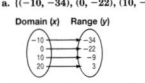

Because each element in the domain is paired with only one value in the range, this is a function.

b.
	−10	−10	10	20
	−34	−22	−9	3

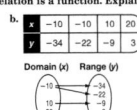

Because −10 in the domain is paired with −34 and −22 in the range, this is not a function.

Exercises

Determine whether each relation is a function. Explain.

1. {(−5, 2), (3, −3), (1, 7), (3, 0)}
No; 3 in the domain is paired with −3 and 0 in the range.

2. {(2, 7), (−5, 20), (−10, 20), (−2, 10), (1, 20)}
Yes; each x value is paired with only one y value.

3.
x	1	−3	8	−8	20
y	2	6	6	5	11

Yes; each x value is paired with only one y value.

4.
x	8	1	−5	1	−10
y	−2	3	7	7	13

No; 1 in the domain is paired with 3 and 7 in the range.

Skills Practice, p. 418 and Practice, p. 419 (shown)

Determine whether each relation is a function. Explain.

1. {(4, −5), (0, −9), (1, 0), (7, 0)}
Yes; each x value is paired with only one y value.

2. {(5, −12), (−1, −2), (8, −5), (4, −2), (3, −5)}
Yes; each x value is paired with only one y value.

3. {(−2, −3), (6, −8), (4, 2), (6, −5), (2, −5)}
No; 6 in the domain is paired with −8 and −5 in the range.

4. {(5, 2), (−2, 15), (−7, 15), (1, 5), (4, 15), (−7, 2)}
No; −7 in the domain is paired with 15 and 2 in the range.

5.
x	4	−5	11	−5	23
y	−3	1	1	0	6

No; −5 in the domain is paired with 1 and 0 in the range.

6.
x	7	14	11	−10	−1
y	−3	−9	−4	−3	15

Yes; each x value is paired with only one y value.

7.
x	−3.0	3.5	4.1	−3.0	3.4
y	4.2	3.7	−3.8	3.7	4.0

No; −3.0 in the domain is paired with 4.2 and 3.7 in the range.

8.
x	11	4	−2	4	−7
y	−7	−2	2	2	6

No; 4 in the domain is paired with −2 and 2 in the range.

EMPLOYMENT For Exercises 9–12, use the table, which shows the percent of employed men and women in the U.S. labor force every five years from 1980 to 2000.

Year	Men (% of male population)	Women (% of female population)
1980	77.4	51.5
1985	76.3	54.5
1990	76.4	57.5
1995	75.0	58.9
2000	78.9	67.3

Source: U.S. Census Bureau

9. Is the relation (year, percent of men) a function? Explain. Yes; each year is paired with only one value for the percent of employed men.

10. Describe how the percent of employed men is related to the year. The number of employed men varies each year, but is around 76 percent of the male population.

11. Is the relation (year, percent of women) a function? Explain. Yes; each year is paired with only one value for the percent of employed women.

12. Describe how the percent of employed women is related to the year. As the years progress, the percent of employed women increases.

Enrichment, p. 421

Emmy Noether

Emmy Noether (1882–1935) was a German mathematician and a leading figure in modern abstract algebra. Her contributions helped change the role of women in German universities and advanced the mathematical progress of the time. Noether fought and overcame rules that once prevented her from becoming a faculty member. Her most notable work pertains to linear transformations of non-commutative algebras and their structures.

A linear equation is an example of a **transformation**, unless it is the equation for a vertical line. In a transformation, a given rule transforms each number in one set, the **domain**, into one and only one number in another set, the **range**. In graphing linear equations, the domain is usually the set of real numbers and the range is either the set of real numbers or a subset of the real numbers. Each value of x is transformed into some value of y.

Transformation f is shown in the diagram below. The transformation takes each element of the domain {1, 2, 3} and adds 1 to produce the corresponding value in the range. Functional notation is used to show the rule f(x) = x + 1.

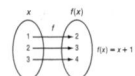

Use functional notation to write the rule for each transformation.

1.

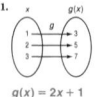

g(x) = 2x + 1

2.

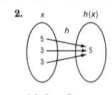

h(x) = 5

3. What do you think is a **non-commutative** algebra?
a + b ≠ b + a for some a, b ∈ R

4. Explain whether the diagram below shows a transformation.

No, the number 4 corresponds to more than one value in the range.

Determine whether each relation is a function. Explain.

18–23. See margin.

18.
x	y
−7	2
0	4
11	6
11	8
0	10

19.
x	y
14	5
15	10
16	15
17	20
18	25

20.

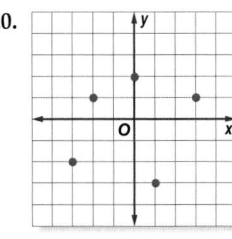

21.

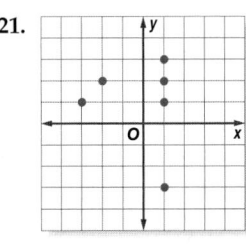

22.

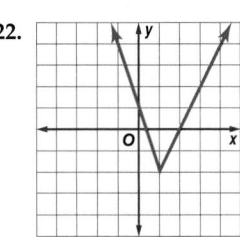

23.

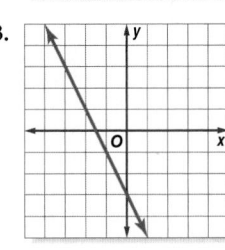

Study Tip

Trends

There may be general trends in sets of data. However, not every data point may follow the trend exactly.

FARMING For Exercises 24–27, use the table that shows the number and size of farms in the United States every decade from 1950 to 2000. 24–26. See margin.

24. Is the relation (year, number of farms) a function? Explain.

25. Describe how the number of farms is related to the year.

26. Is the relation (year, average size of farms) a function? Explain.

27. Describe how the average size of farms is related to the year. Generally, as the years progress, the size of farms increases. An exception is in the year 2000.

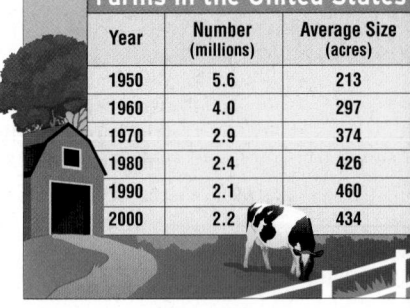

Farms in the United States

Year	Number (millions)	Average Size (acres)
1950	5.6	213
1960	4.0	297
1970	2.9	374
1980	2.4	426
1990	2.1	460
2000	2.2	434

Source: The Wall Street Journal Almanac

MEASUREMENTS For Exercises 28 and 29, use the data in the table.

28. Do the data represent a function? Explain.

29. Is there any relation between foot length and height? Explain. Generally, as foot length increases, height increases.

Name	Foot Length (cm)	Height (cm)
Rosa	24	163
Tanner	28	182
Enrico	25	163
Jahad	24	168
Abbi	22	150
Cory	26	172

28. No; 24 in the domain is paired with 163 and 168 in the range.

Tell whether each statement is *always*, *sometimes*, or *never* true. Explain.

30. A function is a relation.

31. A relation is a function. 30–31. See margin.

Answers

18. No; the x value 0 is paired with y values 4 and 10; the x value 11 is paired with y values 6 and 8.

19. Yes; each x value is paired with only one y value.

20. Yes; any vertical line passes through no more than one point of the graph.

21. No; a vertical line passes through more than one point.

22. Yes; any vertical line passes through no more than one point of the graph.

23. Yes; any vertical line passes through no more than one point of the graph.

2b. Sometimes; the inverse of {(1, 5), (2, 10)} is also a function, but the inverse of {(1, 5), (2, 5)} is not a function.

32. CRITICAL THINKING The *inverse* of any relation is obtained by switching the coordinates in each ordered pair of the relation.

a. Determine whether the inverse of the relation {(4, 0), (5, 1), (6, 2), (6, 3)} is a function. **yes**

b. Is the inverse of a function *always*, *sometimes*, or *never* a function? Give an example to explain your reasoning.

33.  Answer the question that was posed at the beginning of the lesson. **See pp. 431A–431H.**

How can the relationship between actual temperatures and windchill temperatures be a function?

Include the following in your answer:
• an explanation of how actual temperatures and windchill temperatures are related for a given wind speed, and
• a discussion about whether an actual temperature can ever have two corresponding windchill temperatures when the wind speed remains the same.

Standardized Test Practice
Ⓐ Ⓑ Ⓒ Ⓓ

34. The relation {(2, 11), (−9, 8), (14, 1), (5, 5)} is *not* a function when which ordered pair is added to the set? **D**

Ⓐ (8, −9)　　Ⓑ (6, 11)　　Ⓒ (0, 0)　　Ⓓ (2, 18)

35. Which statement is true about the data in the table? **A**

Ⓐ The data represent a function.

Ⓑ The data do not represent a function.

Ⓒ As the value of *x* increases, the value of *y* increases.

Ⓓ A graph of the data would not pass the vertical line test.

x	y
−4	−4
2	16
5	8
10	−4
12	15

Maintain Your Skills

Mixed Review **Solve each inequality. Check your solution.** *(Lessons 7-5 and 7-6)*

36. $4y > 24$　$y > 6$　　**37.** $\frac{a}{3} < -7$　$a < -21$　　**38.** $18 \geq -2k$　$k \geq -9$

39. $2x + 5 < 17$　$x < 6$　　**40.** $2t - 3 \geq 1.4t + 6$　　**41.** $12r - 4 > 7 + 12r$　∅
$t \geq 15$

Solve each problem by using the percent equation. *(Lesson 6-7)*

42. 10 is what percent of 50? **20%**　　**43.** What is 15% of 120? **18**

44. Find 95% of 256. **243.2**　　**45.** 46.5 is 62% of what number? **75**

46. State whether the sequence 120, 100, 80, 60, … is *arithmetic*, *geometric*, or *neither*. Then write the next three terms of the sequence. *(Lesson 5-10)*
arithmetic; 40, 20, 0

Getting Ready for the Next Lesson **PREREQUISITE SKILL** Evaluate each expression if $x = 4$ and $y = -1$.
(To review evaluating expressions, see Lesson 1-3.)

47. $3x + 1$　**13**　　**48.** $2y$　**−2**　　**49.** $y + 6$　**5**

50. $-5x$　**−20**　　**51.** $2x - 8$　**0**　　**52.** $3y - 4$　**−7**

Lesson 8-1 Functions　**373**

---

4 Assess

Open-Ended Assessment

Speaking Have students explain how to determine whether a function is a relation.

Connections Show students how functions are like many everyday machines by choosing one or a few such items to bring to class. For example, a toaster receives bread as input and produces toast as output. Other machines include a label maker, a shredder, and a laminator.

Getting Ready for Lesson 8-2

PREREQUISITE SKILL Lesson 8-2 presents linear equations in two variables for which they will choose a value for *x* and find the corresponding value for *y*. Exercises 47–52 should be used to determine your students' familiarity with evaluating expressions.

Answers (p. 372)

24. Yes; each year is only paired with one value for the number of farms.

25. Generally, as the years progress, the number of farms decreases. An exception is in the year 2000.

26. Yes; each year is paired with only one value for the average size of farms.

30. Always; every function can be written as a set of ordered pairs.

31. Sometimes; a relation that has a member of the domain paired with more than one member in the range is not a function.

Graphing Calculator Investigation

A Preview of Lesson 8-2

Getting Started

Know Your Calculator If after pressing $\boxed{Y=}$ you see something other than a Y= list, the calculator is set for a different mode. To change the mode to graph functions, press $\boxed{\text{MODE}}$ and use the arrow keys to highlight FUNC in the fourth row. Press $\boxed{\text{ENTER}}$ and try entering values into the Y= list again.

Table Setup Because you will be entering all values for the domain, you do not need to adjust the values after **TblStart=** and **ΔTbl=**.

Teach

- The far right column in the table is for Y2 values. Ask students what would be true if the X values resulted in Y1 and Y2 values. **The equation in the Y= list would not be a function.**
- Have students complete Exercises 1–3.

Assess

Students should demonstrate an understanding of the relationship between the domain and the range.

Teaching Tip If graphing calculators are unavailable, have students work this activity later in the chapter by computing the range values by hand.

Function Tables

You can use a TI-83 Plus graphing calculator to create function tables. By entering a function and the domain values, you can find the corresponding range values.

Use a function table to find the range of $y = 3n + 1$ if the domain is $\{-5, -2, 0, 0.5, 4\}$.

Step 1 *Enter the function.*

- The graphing calculator uses X for the domain values and Y for the range values. So, $Y = 3X + 1$ represents $y = 3n + 1$.
- Enter $Y = 3X + 1$ in the Y= list.
  KEYSTROKES: $\boxed{Y=}$ 3 $\boxed{X,T,\theta,n}$ $\boxed{+}$ 1

Step 2 *Format the table.*

- Use TBLSET to select *Ask* for the independent variable and *Auto* for the dependent variable. Then you can enter any value for the domain.
  KEYSTROKES: $\boxed{\text{2nd}}$ [TBLSET]
  $\boxed{\text{ENTER}}$ ▼ $\boxed{\text{ENTER}}$

Step 3 *Find the range by entering the domain values.*

- Access the table.
  KEYSTROKES: $\boxed{\text{2nd}}$ [TABLE]

- Enter the domain values.
  KEYSTROKES: -5 $\boxed{\text{ENTER}}$ -2 $\boxed{\text{ENTER}}$ ... 4 $\boxed{\text{ENTER}}$

The range is $\{-14, -5, 1, 2.5, 13\}$.

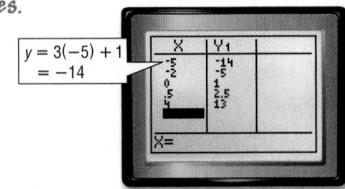

$$y = 3(-5) + 1 = -14$$

Exercises **1b. As X increases by 1 unit, Y decreases by 2 units.**

Use the TABLE option on a graphing calculator to complete each exercise.

1. Consider the function $f(x) = -2x + 4$ and the domain values $\{-2, -1, 0, 1, 2\}$.
   a. Use a function table to find the range values. **{8, 6, 4, 2, 0}**
   b. Describe the relationship between the X and Y values.
   c. If X is less than -2, would the value for Y be greater or less than 8? Explain. **See pp. 431A–431H.**

2. Suppose you are using the formula $d = rt$ to find the distance d a car travels for the times t in hours given by $\{0, 1, 3.5, 10\}$.
   a. If the rate is 60 miles per hour, what function should be entered in the Y= list? **Y = 60X**
   b. Make a function table for the given domain. **See pp. 431A–431H.**
   c. Between which two times in the domain does the car travel 150 miles? **1 h and 3.5 h**
   d. Describe how a function table can be used to better estimate the time it takes to drive 150 miles. **See pp. 431A–431H.**

3. Serena is buying one packet of pencils for $1.50 and a number of fancy folders x for $0.40 each. The total cost y is given by $y = 1.50 + 0.40x$.
   a. Use a function table to find the total cost if Serena buys 1, 2, 3, 4, and 12 folders. **$1.90, $2.30, $2.70, $3.10, $6.30**
   b. Suppose plain folders cost $0.25 each. Enter $y = 1.50 + 0.25x$ in the Y= list as Y2. How much does Serena save if she buys pencils and 12 plain folders rather than pencils and 12 fancy folders? **$1.80**

374 Chapter 8 Functions and Graphing

 www.pre-alg.com/other_calculator_keystroke

Tips for New Teachers

Independence Discourage students from becoming totally dependent on their calculators. Many values can be easily calculated mentally. Calculators should be used only when hand calculation is too tedious or is unfeasible.

What You'll Learn

- Solve linear equations with two variables.
- Graph linear equations using ordered pairs.

How can linear equations represent a function?

Peaches cost $1.50 per can.

a. Complete the table to find the cost of 2, 3, and 4 cans of peaches.

b. On grid paper, graph the ordered pairs (number, cost). Then draw a line through the points. **See margin.**

c. Write an equation representing the relationship between number of cans x and cost y. $y = 1.5x$ or $1.50x$

Number of Cans (x)	1.50x	Cost (y)
1	1.50(1)	1.50
2	1.50(2)	3.00
3	1.50(3)	4.50
4	1.50(4)	6.00

Study Tip

Input and Output
The variable for the input is called the **independent variable** because it can be any number. The variable for the output is called the **dependent variable** because it *depends* on the input value.

SOLUTIONS OF EQUATIONS Functions can be represented in words, in a table, as ordered pairs, with a graph, and with an equation.

An equation such as $y = 1.50x$ is called a linear equation. A **linear equation** in two variables is an equation in which the variables appear in separate terms and neither variable contains an exponent other than 1.

Solutions of a linear equation are ordered pairs that make the equation true. One way to find solutions is to make a table. Consider the equation $y = -x + 8$.

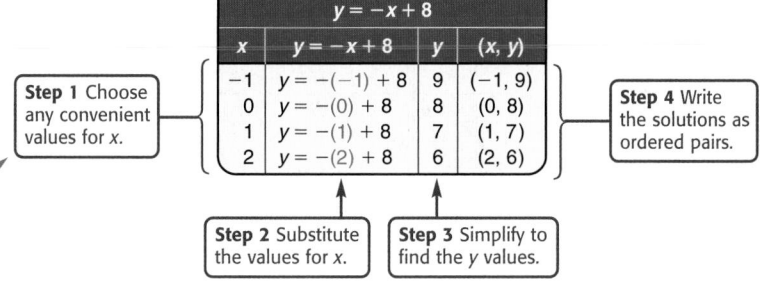

		$y = -x + 8$		
	x	$y = -x + 8$	y	(x, y)
	-1	$y = -(-1) + 8$	9	$(-1, 9)$
	0	$y = -(0) + 8$	8	$(0, 8)$
	1	$y = -(1) + 8$	7	$(1, 7)$
	2	$y = -(2) + 8$	6	$(2, 6)$

Step 1 Choose any convenient values for x.

Step 4 Write the solutions as ordered pairs.

Step 2 Substitute the values for x.

Step 3 Simplify to find the y values.

TEACHING TIP

Be sure students understand that any rational numbers may be chosen for x, but integers are usually most convenient.

So, four solutions of $y = -x + 8$ are $(-1, 9)$, $(0, 8)$, $(1, 7)$, and $(2, 6)$.

Example 1 Find Solutions

Find four solutions of $y = 2x - 1$.

Choose four values for x. Then substitute each value into the equation and solve for y.

Four solutions are $(0, -1)$, $(1, 1)$, $(2, 3)$, and $(3, 5)$.

x	$y = 2x - 1$	y	(x, y)
0	$y = 2(0) - 1$	-1	$(0, -1)$
1	$y = 2(1) - 1$	1	$(1, 1)$
2	$y = 2(2) - 1$	3	$(2, 3)$
3	$y = 2(3) - 1$	5	$(3, 5)$

---

1 Focus

5-Minute Check Transparency 8-2 Use as a quiz or review of Lesson 8-1.

Mathematical Background notes are available for this lesson on page 366C.

How can linear equations represent a function?

The opening activity questions are repeated on page 425 of the *Chapter 8 Resource Masters*.

Reading to Learn Mathematics, p. 425 **ELL**

Pre-Activity *How can linear equations represent a function?*
Do the activity at the top of page 375 in your textbook. Write your answers below.

a. Complete the table to find the cost of 2, 3, and 4 cans of peaches.

b. On grid paper, graph the ordered pairs (number, cost). Then draw a line through the points.

Number of Cans (x)	1.50x	Cost (y)
1	1.50(1)	1.50
2	1.50(2)	3.00
3	1.50(3)	4.50
4	1.50(4)	6.00

c. Write an equation representing the relationship between number of cans x and cost y. $y = 1.5x$ or $1.50x$

Reading the Lesson

Write a definition and give an example of the new vocabulary phrase.

Vocabulary	Definition	Example
1. linear equation	See students' work.	

2. Determine whether each equation below is linear or nonlinear and explain why.
 a. $y = x + 1$ Linear; the variables appear in separate terms, and neither variable contains an exponent other than 1.
 b. $y = x^2 + 1$ Nonlinear; the variable x has an exponent of 2.
 c. $xy = 4$ Nonlinear; the variables appear in the same term.

3. Solutions of a linear equation are ___ordered pairs___ that make the equation true.

Helping You Remember

4. Work with one of your classmates translating linear equations into English. First, each of you should write a linear equation. Then trade equations and take turns reading the equations in everyday words. Second, each of you should describe a line in terms of its x and y values. Write sentences and translate them into linear equations. Sample answer: $x - y = 10$; The value of y subtracted from the value of x is 10.

Resource Manager

Workbooks and Reproducible Masters

Chapter 8 Resource Masters
- Study Guide and Intervention, p. 422
- Skills Practice, p. 423
- Practice, p. 424
- Reading to Learn Mathematics, p. 425
- Enrichment, p. 426

Parent and Student Study Guide Workbook, p. 62

 Transparencies
5-Minute Check Transparency 8-2
Answer Key Transparencies

 Technology
Interactive Chalkboard
Multimedia Applications

SOLUTIONS OF EQUATIONS

In-Class Examples

1 Find four solutions of
$y = 4x + 3$.   **Sample answer:**
(0, 3), (1, 7), (2, 11), and (3, 15)

Teaching Tip Because
Example 2 asks for a number
of real items, positive integers
should be chosen for sample
x values.

2 **BUSINESS** At a local software company, Level 1
employees *x* earn $48,000,
and level 2 employees *y* earn
$24,000. Find four solutions
of $48{,}000x + 24{,}000y =$
$216{,}000$ to determine how
many employees at each
level the company can hire
for $216,000.   **Sample answer:**
(0, 9), (1, 7), (2, 5), (3, 3)
0 Level 1, 9 Level 2
1 Level 1, 7 Level 2
2 Level 1, 5 Level 2
3 Level 1, 3 Level 2

GRAPH LINEAR EQUATIONS

In-Class Example

3 Graph $y = x - 3$ by plotting
ordered pairs.

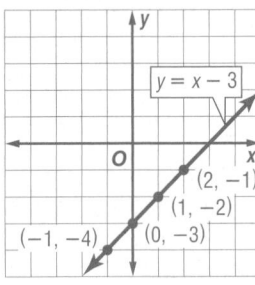

Sometimes it is necessary to first rewrite an equation by solving for *y*.

Example 2 **Solve an Equation for y**

SHOPPING Fancy goldfish *x* cost $3, and regular goldfish *y* cost $1. Find
four solutions of $3x + y = 8$ to determine how many of each type of fish
Tyler can buy for $8.

First, rewrite the equation by solving for *y*.

$$3x + y = 8 \qquad \text{Write the equation.}$$
$$3x + y - 3x = 8 - 3x \qquad \text{Subtract } 3x \text{ from each side.}$$
$$y = 8 - 3x \qquad \text{Simplify.}$$

Choose four *x* values and substitute them
into $y = 8 - 3x$. Four solutions are (0, 8),
(1, 5), (2, 2), and (3, −1).

x	y = 8 − 3x	y	(x, y)
0	$y = 8 - 3(0)$	8	(0, 8)
1	$y = 8 - 3(1)$	5	(1, 5)
2	$y = 8 - 3(2)$	2	(2, 2)
3	$y = 8 - 3(3)$	−1	(3, −1)

(0, 8) → He can buy 0 fancy goldfish
and 8 regular goldfish.

(1, 5) → He can buy 1 fancy goldfish
and 5 regular goldfish.

(2, 2) → He can buy 2 fancy goldfish and 2 regular goldfish.

(3, −1) → This solution does not make sense, because there cannot be a
negative number of goldfish.

Study Tip

Choosing x Values
It is often convenient to
choose 0 as an *x* value to
find a value for *y*.

✓ **Concept Check**   Write the solution of $3x + y = 10$ if $x = 2$. **(2, 4)**

GRAPH LINEAR EQUATIONS   A linear equation can also be represented
by a graph. Study the graphs shown below.

Linear Equations

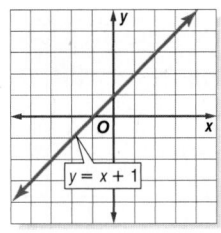
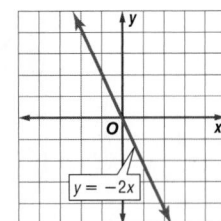
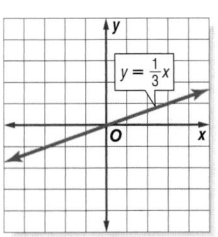

Nonlinear Equations

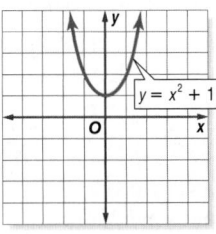
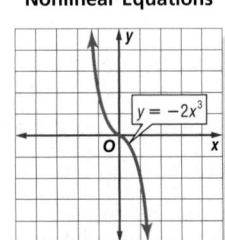
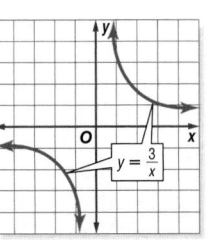

Notice that graphs of the linear equations are straight lines. This is true for
all linear equations and is the reason they are called "linear." The coordinates
of all points on a line are solutions to the equation.

376 Chapter 8 Functions and Graphing

D A I L Y
INTERVENTION   **Differentiated Instruction**

• **Auditory/Musical** Bring several passages of sheet music to class.
Include scales, melodic strings of notes, and passages with chords.
Have students tell which passages are similar to functions and which
ones are dissimilar.   **Sample answer: scales resemble linear functions;**
melodic passages have one unique *y* value for each beat, *x*. Passages
with chords do not resemble functions because for each beat, *x*, there
is more than one note, *y*.

To graph a linear equation, find ordered pair solutions, plot the corresponding points, and draw a line through them. It is best to find at least three points.

Example 3 Graph a Linear Equation

Graph $y = x + 1$ by plotting ordered pairs.

First, find ordered pair solutions. Four solutions are $(-1, 0)$, $(0, 1)$, $(1, 2)$, and $(2, 3)$.

x	$y = x + 1$	y	(x, y)
-1	$y = -1 + 1$	0	$(-1, 0)$
0	$y = 0 + 1$	1	$(0, 1)$
1	$y = 1 + 1$	2	$(1, 2)$
2	$y = 2 + 1$	3	$(2, 3)$

Plot these ordered pairs and draw a line through them. Note that the ordered pair for any point on this line is a solution of $y = x + 1$. The line is a complete graph of the function.

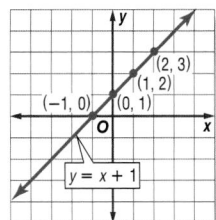

CHECK It appears from the graph that $(-2, -1)$ is also a solution. Check this by substitution.

$y = x + 1$ Write the equation.

$-1 \overset{?}{=} -2 + 1$ Replace x with -2 and y with -1.

$-1 = -1$ ✓   Simplify.

A linear equation is one of many ways to represent a function.

Concept Summary   *Representing Functions*

- **Words**   The value of y is 3 less than the corresponding value of x.

- **Table**

x	y
0	-3
1	-2
2	-1
3	0

- **Graph**

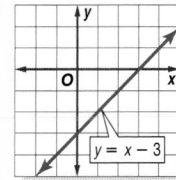

- **Ordered Pairs** $(0, -3)$, $(1, -2)$, $(2, -1)$, $(3, 0)$

- **Equation** $y = x - 3$

Check for Understanding

Concept Check

1. **Explain** why a linear equation has infinitely many solutions. See margin.

2. **OPEN ENDED** Write a linear equation that has $(-2, 4)$ as a solution.

2. Sample answer: $y = x + 6$

Guided Practice

3. Copy and complete the table. Use the results to write four solutions of $y = x + 5$. Write the solutions as ordered pairs. $(-3, 2)$, $(-1, 4)$, $(0, 5)$, $(1, 6)$

x	$x + 5$	y
-3	$-3 + 5$	2
-1	$-1 + 5$	4
0	$0 + 5$	5
1	$1 + 5$	6

Answer

1. Sample answer: Infinitely many values can be substituted for x, or the domain.

Answers (p. 378)

4. Sample answer: $(-1, 7)$, $(0, 8)$, $(1, 9)$, $(2, 10)$

5. Sample answer: $(-1, -4)$, $(0, 0)$, $(1, 4)$, $(2, 8)$

6. Sample answer: $(-1, -9)$, $(0, -7)$, $(1, -5)$, $(2, -3)$

7. Sample answer: $(-1, 1)$, $(0, 6)$, $(1, 11)$, $(2, 16)$

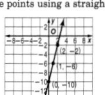
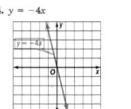 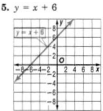 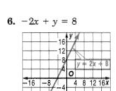
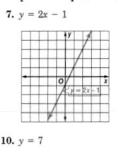 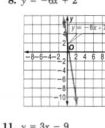 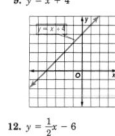
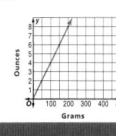 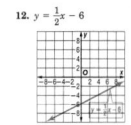

Study Notebook

Have students—

- add the definition/example of the vocabulary term to their Vocabulary Builder worksheets for Chapter 8.
- copy the four steps for finding solutions of equations from p. 375. Illustrate them with an equation.
- include any other item(s) that they find helpful in mastering the skills in this lesson.

About the Exercises . . .

Organization by Objective
- **Solutions of Equations:** 12–25
- **Graph Linear Equations:** 30–41

Odd/Even Assignments
Exercises 12–41 and 45–50 are structured so that students practice the same concepts whether they are assigned odd or even problems.

Alert! Exercises 8–10, 30–41, and 43 require graph paper.

Assignment Guide

Basic: 13–23 odd, 27, 31–37 odd, 42–51 odd, 52–65

Average: 13–41 odd, 42–44, 45–51 odd, 52–65

Advanced: 12–42 even, 43, 44–50 even, 51–61 (Optional: 62–65)

GUIDED PRACTICE KEY	
Exercises	**Examples**
4–7	1
8–10	3
11	2

Find four solutions of each equation. Write the solutions as ordered pairs.

4. $y = x + 8$ **5.** $y = 4x$ **6.** $y = 2x - 7$ **7.** $-5x + y = 6$

4–7. See p. 377 margin.

Graph each equation by plotting ordered pairs. **8–10. See margin.**

8. $y = x + 3$ **9.** $y = 2x - 1$ **10.** $x + y = 5$

Application

11. SCIENCE The distance y in miles that light travels in x seconds is given by $y = 186,000x$. Find two solutions of this equation and describe what they mean. **See margin.**

★ **indicates increased difficulty**

Practice and Apply

Homework Help	
For Exercises	**See Examples**
12–25	1
26–29	2
30–41	3

Extra Practice
See page 742.

Copy and complete each table. Use the results to write four solutions of the given equation. Write the solutions as ordered pairs.

12. $y = x - 9$

x	x − 9	y
−1	−1 − 9	−10
0	0 − 9	−9
4	4 − 9	−5
7	7 − 9	−2

(−1, −10), (0, −9), (4, −5), (7, −2)

13. $y = 2x + 6$

x	2x + 6	y
−4	2(−4) + 6	−2
0	2(0) + 6	6
2	2(2) + 6	10
4	2(4) + 6	14

(−4, −2), (0, 6), (2, 10), (4, 14)

Find four solutions of each equation. Write the solutions as ordered pairs.

14. $y = x + 2$ **15.** $y = x - 7$ **16.** $y = 3x$ **17.** $y = -5x$

18. $y = 2x - 3$ **19.** $y = 3x + 1$ **20.** $x + y = 9$ **21.** $x + y = -6$

22. $4x + y = 2$ **23.** $3x - y = 10$ ★ **24.** $y = 8$ ★ **25.** $x = -1$

14–25. See margin.

MEASUREMENT The equation $y = 0.62x$ describes the approximate number of miles y in x kilometers.

26. Describe what the solution (8, 4.96) means. **8 km ≈ 4.96 mi**

27. About how many miles is a 10-kilometer race? **6.2 mi**

HEALTH During a workout, a target heart rate y in beats per minute is represented by $y = 0.7(220 - x)$, where x is a person's age.

★ **28.** Compare target heart rates of people 20 years old and 50 years old.

★ **29.** In which quadrant(s) would the graph of $y = 0.7(220 - x)$ make sense? Explain your reasoning. **28–29. See margin.**

Graph each equation by plotting ordered pairs. **30–41. See pp. 431A–431H.**

30. $y = x + 2$ **31.** $y = x + 5$ **32.** $y = x - 4$ **33.** $y = -x - 6$

34. $y = -2x + 2$ **35.** $y = 3x - 4$ **36.** $x + y = 1$ **37.** $x - y = 6$

38. $2x + y = 5$ ★ **39.** $3x - y = 7$ ★ **40.** $x = 2$ ★ **41.** $y = -3$

GEOMETRY For Exercises 42–44, use the following information.
The formula for the perimeter of a square with sides s units long is $P = 4s$.

42. Find three ordered pairs that satisfy this condition. **42–44. See margin.**

43. Draw the graph that contains these points.

44. Why do negative values of s make no sense?

Answers

8.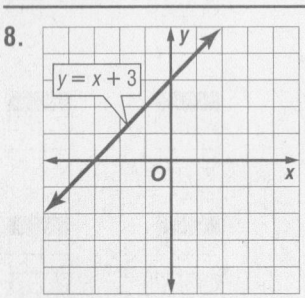

9.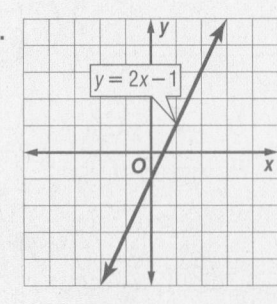

10.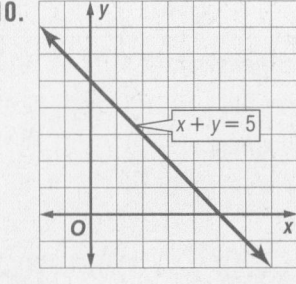

11. Sample answer:
(1, 186,000) means that light travels 186,000 miles in 1 second. (2, 372,000) means that light travels 372,000 miles in 2 seconds.

Determine whether each relation or equation is linear. Explain.

45.

x	y
−1	−2
0	0
1	2
2	4

46.

x	y
−1	1
0	0
1	1
2	4

47.

x	y
−1	−1
0	−1
1	−1
2	−1

48. $3x + y = 20$

49. $y = x^2$

50. $y = 5$

51. **CRITICAL THINKING** Compare and contrast the functions shown in the tables. (*Hint:* Compare the change in values for each column.) See pp. 431A–431H.

x	y
−1	−2
0	0
1	2
2	4

x	y
−1	1
0	0
1	1
2	4

52. **WRITING IN MATH** Answer the question that was posed at the beginning of the lesson. See pp. 431A–431H.

How can linear equations represent a function?

Include the following in your answer:
- a description of four ways that you can represent a function, and
- an example of a linear equation that could be used to determine the cost of x pounds of bananas that are $0.49 per pound.

Standardized Test Practice
Ⓐ Ⓑ Ⓒ Ⓓ

53. Identify the equation that represents the data in the table. **B**

x	y
−2	11
0	5
1	2
3	−4

 Ⓐ $y = x + 5$ Ⓑ $y = -3x + 5$

 Ⓒ $y = -5x + 1$ Ⓓ $y = x + 13$

54. The graph of $2x - y = 4$ goes through which pair of points? **C**

 Ⓐ $P(-2, -3), Q(0, 2)$ Ⓑ $P(-2, -1), Q(2, -3)$

 Ⓒ $P(1, -2), Q(3, 2)$ Ⓓ $P(-3, 2), Q(0, -4)$

Maintain Your Skills

Mixed Review
55–58. See pp. 431A–431H.

Determine whether each relation is a function. Explain. *(Lesson 8-1)*

55. $\{(2, 3), (3, 4), (4, 5), (5, 6)\}$ 56. $\{(0, 6), (-3, 9), (4, 9), (-2, 1)\}$

57. $\{(11, 8), (13, -2), (11, 21)\}$ 58. $\{(-0.1, 5), (0, 10), (-0.1, -5)\}$

Solve each inequality and check your solution. Graph the solution on a number line. *(Lesson 7-6)* 59–60. See pp. 431A–431H for graphs.

59. $3x + 4 < 16$ $x < 4$ 60. $9 - 2d \le 23$ $d \ge -7$

61. Evaluate $a \div b$ if $a = \frac{4}{7}$ and $b = \frac{2}{3}$. *(Lesson 5-4)* $\frac{6}{7}$

Getting Ready for the Next Lesson

PREREQUISITE SKILL In each equation, find the value of y when $x = 0$. *(To review substitution, see Lesson 1-5.)*

62. $y = 5x - 3$ −3   63. $-x + y = 3$ 3

64. $x + 2y = 12$ 6   65. $4x - 5y = -20$ 4

14–25. Sample answers are given.

14. $(-1, 1), (0, 2), (1, 3), (2, 4)$

15. $(-1, -8), (0, -7), (1, -6), (2, -5)$

16. $(-1, -3), (0, 0), (1, 3), (2, 6)$

17. $(-1, 5), (0, 0), (1, -5), (2, -10)$

18. $(-1, -5), (0, -3), (1, -1), (2, 1)$

19. $(-1, -2), (0, 1), (1, 4), (2, 7)$

20. $(-1, 10), (0, 9), (1, 8), (2, 7)$

21. $(-1, -5), (0, -6), (1, -7), (2, -8)$

22. $(-1, 6), (0, 2), (1, -2), (2, -6)$

23. $(-1, -13), (0, -10), (1, -7), (2, -4)$

24. $(-1, 8), (0, 8), (1, 8), (2, 8)$

25. $(-1, 0), (-1, 1), (-1, 2), (-1, 3)$

Answers (p. 378)

28. 140 beats per minute; 119 beats per minute

29. Quadrant I; a person cannot have a negative age or heart rate.

42. Sample answer: (1, 4), (2, 8), (3, 12)

43.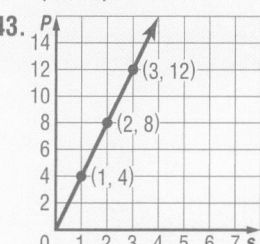

44. Length cannot have a negative value.

Getting Started

Remind students of the function machines they made at the beginning of the chapter. Have them think of the middle box of the function machine as the function f. The input x goes into the function f as shown by x being enclosed by parentheses. The output then comes out as $f(x)$.

Teach

Functional Notation Point out that when functions are graphed, the functional notation for the range is used to designate the y-axis. For example, when graphing $f(x) = x + 2$, the y-axis is marked on the graph as $f(x)$ instead of as y.

Assess

Study Notebook

Have students write a paragraph explaining in their own words the meaning of the notation $f(x) = 2x - 3$.

ELL English Language Learners may benefit from writing key concepts from this activity in their Study Notebooks in their native language and then in English.

Language of Functions

Equations that are functions can be written in a form called *functional notation*, as shown below.

equation	functional notation
$y = 4x + 10$	$f(x) = 4x + 10$

Read $f(x)$ as f of x.

TEACHING TIP
Explain that $f(x)$ can also be read as f at x. This makes the concept of functions easier for students to understand.

So, $f(x)$ is simply another name for y. Letters other than f are also used for names of functions. For example, $g(x) = 2x$ and $h(x) = -x + 6$ are also written in functional notation.

In a function, x represents the domain values, and $f(x)$ represents the range values.

$$\underset{\downarrow}{\text{range}} \quad \underset{\downarrow}{\text{domain}}$$
$$f(x) = 4x + 10$$

$f(3)$ represents the element in the range that corresponds to the element 3 in the domain. To find $f(3)$, substitute 3 for x in the function and simplify.

Read $f(3)$ as f of 3.

$f(x) = 4x + 10$ Write the function.
$f(3) = 4(3) + 10$ Replace x with 3.
$f(3) = 12 + 10$ or 22   Simplify.

So, the functional value of f for $x = 3$ is 22.

Reading to Learn

1. **RESEARCH** Use the Internet or a dictionary to find the everyday meaning of the word *function*. Write a sentence describing how the everyday meaning relates to the mathematical meaning. **See margin.**

2. Write your own rule for remembering how the domain and the range are represented using functional notation. **Sample answer: x represents the domain; y represents the range.**

3. Copy and complete the table below.

x	$f(x) = 3x + 5$	$f(x)$
0	$f(0) = 3(0) + 5$	5
1	$f(1) = 3(1) + 5$	8
2	$f(2) = 3(2) + 5$	11
3	$f(3) = 3(3) + 5$	14

4. If $f(x) = 4x - 1$, find each value.
   a. $f(2)$ **7**
   b. $f(-3)$ **−13**
   c. $f\left(\frac{1}{2}\right)$ **1**

5. Find the value of x if $f(x) = -2x + 5$ and the value of $f(x)$ is -7. **6**

Answer

1. Sample answer: One meaning of the word *function* is purpose. In mathematics, the purpose of a function is to assign each value of the domain exactly one range value.

Graphing Linear Equations Using Intercepts

What You'll Learn

- Find the *x*- and *y*-intercepts of graphs.
- Graph linear equations using the *x*- and *y*-intercepts.

Vocabulary

- *x*-intercept
- *y*-intercept

How can intercepts be used to represent real-life information?

The relationship between the temperature in degrees Fahrenheit *F* and the temperature in degrees Celsius *C* is given by the equation $F = \frac{9}{5}C + 32$. This equation is graphed at the right.

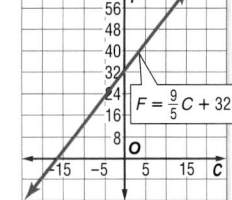

a. Write the ordered pair for the point where the graph intersects the *y*-axis. What does this point represent?

b. Write the ordered pair for the point where the graph intersects the *x*-axis. What does this point represent?

a. (0, 32); a temperature of 0°C equals 32°F.

b. (−18, 0); a temperature of approximately −18°C equals 0°F.

Reading Math

Intercept

Everyday Meaning: to interrupt or cut off

Math Meaning: the point where a coordinate axis crosses a line

FIND INTERCEPTS The **x-intercept** is the *x*-coordinate of a point where a graph crosses the *x*-axis. The *y*-coordinate of this point is 0.

The **y-intercept** is the *y*-coordinate of a point where a graph crosses the *y*-axis. The *x*-coordinate of this point is 0.

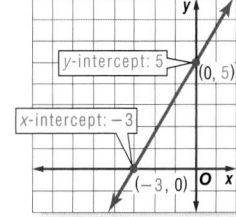

Example 1 Find Intercepts From Graphs

State the *x*-intercept and the *y*-intercept of each line.

a.

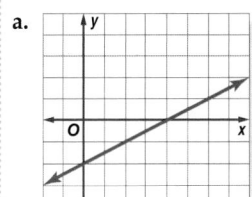

b.

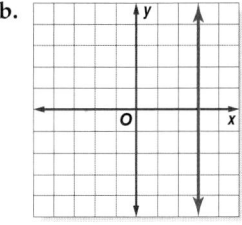

The graph crosses the *x*-axis at (4, 0). The *x*-intercept is 4. The graph crosses the *y*-axis at (0, −2). The *y*-intercept is −2.

The graph crosses the *x*-axis at (3, 0). The *x*-intercept is 3. The graph does not cross the *y*-axis. There is no *y*-intercept.

✓ Concept Check A graph passes through a point at (0, −10). Is −10 an *x*-intercept or a *y*-intercept? *y*-intercept

Lesson 8-3 Graphing Linear Equations Using Intercepts **381**

1 Focus

5-Minute Check Transparency 8-3 Use as a quiz or review of Lesson 8-2.

Mathematical Background notes are available for this lesson on page 366C.

How can intercepts be used to represent real-life information?

The opening activity questions are repeated on page 430 of the *Chapter 8 Resource Masters*.

Reading to Learn Mathematics, p. 430 ELL

Pre-Activity   How can intercepts be used to represent real-life information?
Do the activity at the top of page 381 in your textbook. Write your answers below.

    a. Write the ordered pair for the point where the graph intersects the *y*-axis. What does this point represent? (0, 32); a temperature of 0°C equals 32°F.

    b. Write the ordered pair for the point where the graph intersects the *x*-axis. What does this point represent? (−18, 0); a temperature of approximately −18°C equals 0°F.

Reading the Lesson   1–2. See students' work.
Write a definition and give an example of each new vocabulary word.

Vocabulary	Definition	Example
1. *x*-intercept		
2. *y*-intercept		

3. The *y*-coordinate of the *x*-intercept is 0.
The *x*-coordinate of the *y*-intercept is 0.

4. Draw a model on the coordinate grid that shows how to graph a line using the *x*-intercept and the *y*-intercept of a line. Explain your model.

Sample answer: The *x*-intercept is 5, which means that one point of the graph is at (5, 0). The *y*-intercept is 3, which means that another point of the graph is at (0, 3). Graph both points on the grid and draw a line through them.

5. Is a line with no *x*-intercept vertical or horizontal? Explain.   Horizontal; if a line has no *x*-intercept, the line will never cross the *x*-axis. Therefore, the line must be parallel to the *x*-axis.

Helping You Remember

6. The word *intercept* has many synonyms in English. Look up *intercept* in a thesaurus and find one or two synonyms that help you remember the mathematical meaning of the word. Explain your selection.   Sample answer: cut off; The *y*-intercept is where the *y*-axis cuts off the line; the *x*-intercept is where the *x*-axis cuts off the line.

Resource Manager

Workbooks and Reproducible Masters

Chapter 8 Resource Masters
- Study Guide and Intervention, p. 427
- Skills Practice, p. 428
- Practice, p. 429
- Reading to Learn Mathematics, p. 430
- Enrichment, p. 431
- Assessment, p. 481

Parent and Student Study Guide Workbook, p. 63
Science and Mathematics Lab Manual, pp. 15–20

Transparencies
5-Minute Check Transparency 8-3
Answer Key Transparencies

Technology
Interactive Chalkboard

2 Teach

FIND INTERCEPTS

1 State the x-intercept and the y-intercept of each line.

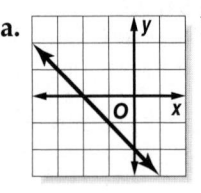

a.   b.

−2; −2   none; 2

2 Find the x-intercept and the y-intercept for the graph of $x + 2y = 4$.   4; 2

GRAPH EQUATIONS

3 Graph $y = 3x - 6$ using the x- and y-intercepts.

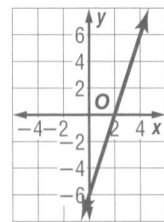

4 **HOME REPAIR** Renata Jones has $300 for home repairs. A plumber charges her $50 an hour. The equation $y = -50x + 300$ represents the amount of money left in her budget after x number of plumbing hours.

a. Use the intercepts to graph the equation.

Home Repair Budget

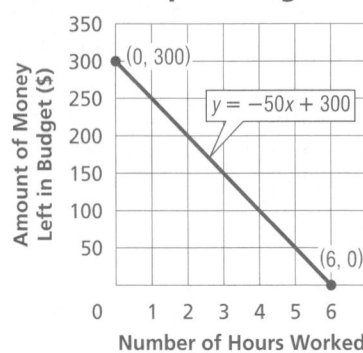

You can also find the x-intercept and the y-intercept from an equation of a line.

> **Key Concept**   **Intercepts of Lines**
>
> - To find the x-intercept, let $y = 0$ in the equation and solve for x.
> - To find the y-intercept, let $x = 0$ in the equation and solve for y.

Example 2 **Find Intercepts from Equations**

Find the x-intercept and the y-intercept for the graph of $y = x - 6$.

To find the x-intercept, let $y = 0$.	To find the y-intercept, let $x = 0$.
$y = x - 6$ Write the equation.	$y = x - 6$ Write the equation.
$0 = x - 6$ Replace y with 0.	$y = 0 - 6$ Replace x with 0.
$6 = x$ Simplify.	$y = -6$ Simplify.
The x-intercept is 6. So, the graph crosses the x-axis at (6, 0).	The y-intercept is −6. So, the graph crosses the y-axis at (0, −6).

GRAPH EQUATIONS   You can use the x- and y-intercepts to graph equations of lines.

In Example 2, we determined that the graph of $y = x - 6$ passes through (6, 0) and (0, −6). To draw the graph, plot these points and draw a line through them.

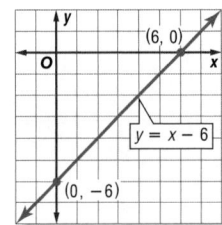

Example 3 **Use Intercepts to Graph Equations**

Graph $x + 2y = 4$ using the x- and y-intercepts.

Step 1
Find the x-intercept.

$x + 2y = 4$ Write the equation.
$x + 2(0) = 4$ Let $y = 0$.
$x = 4$ Simplify.

The x-intercept is 4, so the graph passes through (4, 0).

Step 2
Find the y-intercept.

$x + 2y = 4$ Write the equation.
$0 + 2y = 4$ Let $x = 0$.
$y = 2$ Divide each side by 2.

The y-intercept is 2, so the graph passes through (0, 2).

Step 3
Graph the points at (4, 0) and (0, 2) and draw a line through them.

CHECK   Choose some other point on the line and determine whether its ordered pair is a solution of $x + 2y = 4$.

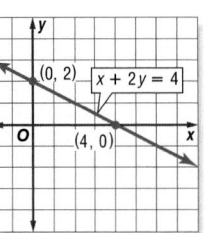

> **Study Tip**
>
> *Graphing Shortcuts*
> The ordered pairs of any two solutions can be used to graph a linear equation. However, it is often easiest to find the intercepts.

b. Describe what the intercepts mean.   The y-intercept shows how much money Renata has in her budget before any work is done. The x-intercept means that she can afford only 6 hours of plumbing repair.

More About . . .

Earth Science •·······
The temperature of the air is about 3°F cooler for every 1000 feet increase in altitude.
Source: www.hot-air-balloons.com

TEACHING TIP
Point out to students that when real-life data are represented by a linear function, the intercepts of the graph of the function often reveal useful information.

Example 4 Intercepts of Real-World Data

•··· **EARTH SCIENCE** Suppose you take a hot-air balloon ride on a day when the temperature is 24°C at sea level. The equation $y = -6.6x + 24$ represents the temperature at x kilometers above sea level.

a. Use the intercepts to graph the equation.

Step 1 Find the x-intercept.

$y = -6.6x + 24$ Write the equation.
$0 = -6.6x + 24$ Replace y with 0.
$0 - 24 = -6.6x + 24 - 24$ Subtract 24 from each side.
$\dfrac{-24}{-6.6} = \dfrac{-6.6x}{-6.6}$ Divide each side by -6.6.
$3.6 \approx x$ The x-intercept is approximately 3.6.

Step 2 Find the y-intercept.

$y = -6.6x + 24$ Write the equation.
$y = -6.6(0) + 24$ Replace x with 0.
$y = 24$ The y-intercept is 24.

Step 3 Plot the points with coordinates (3.6, 0) and (0, 24). Then draw a line through the points.

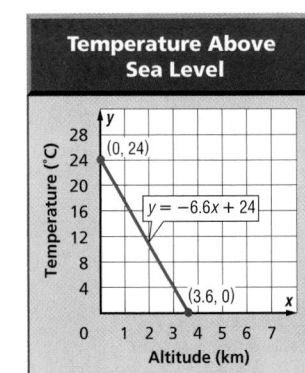

b. Describe what the intercepts mean.

The x-intercept 3.6 means that when the hot-air balloon is 3.6 kilometers above sea level, the temperature is 0°C. The y-intercept 24 means that the temperature at sea level is 24°C.

Some linear equations have just one variable. Their graphs are horizontal or vertical lines.

Example 5 Horizontal and Vertical Lines

Graph each equation using the x- and y-intercepts.

Reading Math

• $y = 3$ can be read for all x, $y = 3$.
• $x = -2$ can be read for all y, $x = -2$.

a. $y = 3$

Note that $y = 3$ is the same as $0x + y = 3$. The y-intercept is 3, and there is no x-intercept.

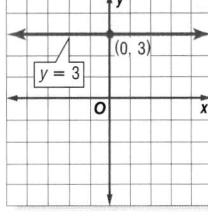

b. $x = -2$

Note that $x = -2$ is the same as $x + 0y = -2$. The x-intercept is -2, and there is no y-intercept.

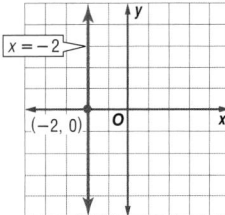

www.pre-alg.com/extra_examples   Lesson 8-3 Graphing Linear Equations Using Intercepts **383**

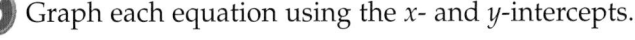

5 Graph each equation using the x- and y-intercepts.

a. $y = -4$

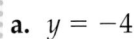
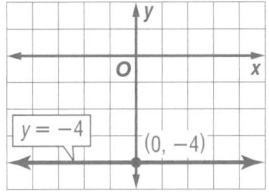

b. $x = 5$

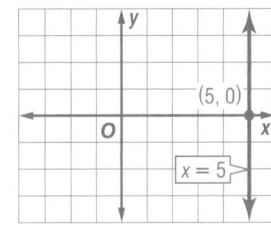

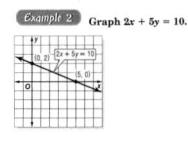
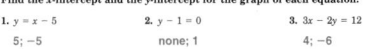

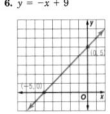
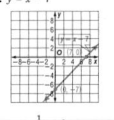
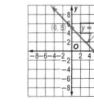
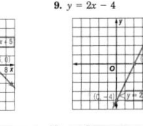

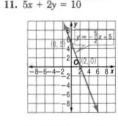
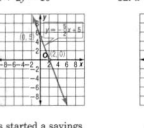
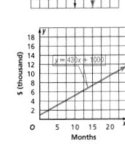
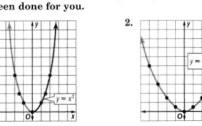
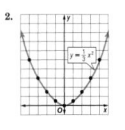
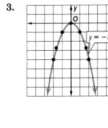
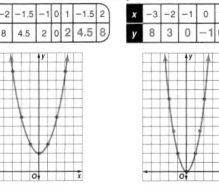
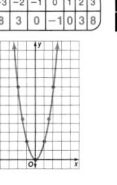
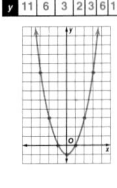

Study Notebook

Have students—
- add the definitions/examples of the vocabulary terms to their Vocabulary Builder worksheets for Chapter 8.
- copy the Key Concept box and add a graph for each item.
- include any other item(s) that they find helpful in mastering the skills in this lesson.

About the Exercises . . .

Organization by Objective
- Find Intercepts: 12–24, 36
- Graph Equations: 25–35

Odd/Even Assignments
Exercises 12–35 are structured so that students practice the same concepts whether they are assigned odd or even problems.

Alert! Exercises 8–11, 25–35, 37, and 38 require graph paper.

Assignment Guide

Basic: 13–31 odd, 35, 37–53
Average: 13–37 odd, 38–53
Advanced: 12–36 even, 37–49 (Optional: 50–53)

Answers

1. To find the *x*-intercept, let $y = 0$ and solve for *x*. To find the *y*-intercept, let $x = 0$ and solve for *y*.

2. Sample answer:

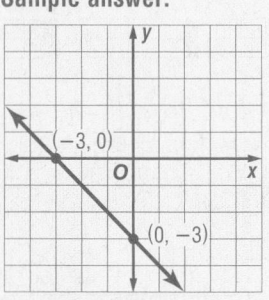

Check for Understanding

Concept Check

1–2. See margin.

1. **Explain** how to find the *x*- and *y*-intercepts of a line given its equation.

2. **OPEN ENDED** Sketch the graph of a function whose *x*- and *y*-intercepts are both negative. Label the intercepts.

Guided Practice

State the *x*-intercept and the *y*-intercept of each line.

GUIDED PRACTICE KEY	
Exercises	Examples
3, 4	1
5–7	2
8–10	3, 5
11	4

3. 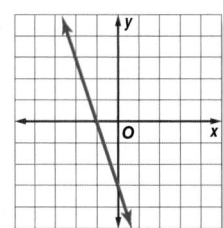 −1; −3

4. 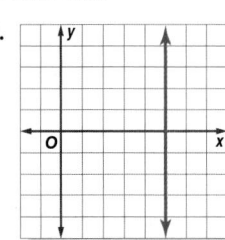 5; none

Find the *x*-intercept and the *y*-intercept for the graph of each equation.

5. $y = x + 4$ −4; 4
6. $y = 7$ none; 7
7. $2x + 3y = 6$ 3; 2

Graph each equation using the *x*- and *y*-intercepts. 8–10. See margin.

8. $y = x + 1$
9. $x - 2y = 6$
10. $x = -1$

Application

11. **BUSINESS** A lawn mowing service charges a base fee of $3, plus $6 per hour for labor. This can be represented by $y = 6x + 3$, where *y* is the total cost and *x* is the number of hours. Graph this equation and explain what the *y*-intercept represents. See pp. 431A–431H.

★ indicates increased difficulty

Practice and Apply

Homework Help	
For Exercises	See Examples
12–15	1
16–24	2
25–33	3, 5
34, 35	4

Extra Practice
See page 742.

State the *x*-intercept and the *y*-intercept of each line.

12. 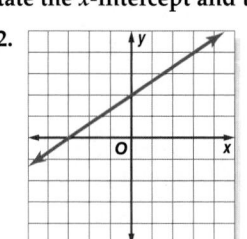 −3; 2

13. 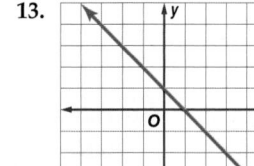 1; 1

14. 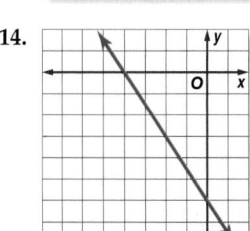 −4; −6

15. 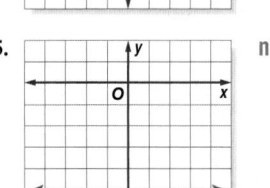 none; −5

Find the *x*-intercept and the *y*-intercept for the graph of each equation.

16. $y = x - 1$ 1; −1
17. $y = x + 5$ −5; 5
18. $x = 9$ 9; none
19. $y + 4 = 0$ none; −4
20. $y = 2x + 10$ −5; 10
21. $x - 2y = 8$ 8; −4
22. $y = -3x - 12$ −4; −12
23. $4x + 5y = 20$ 5; 4
★24. $6x + 7y = 12$ 2; $\frac{12}{7}$

Answers

8.
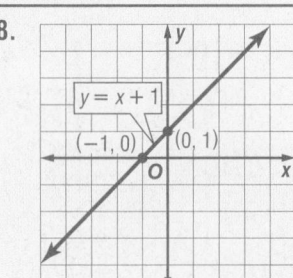

9.
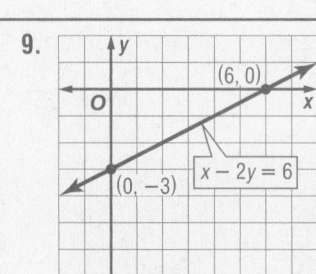

10.
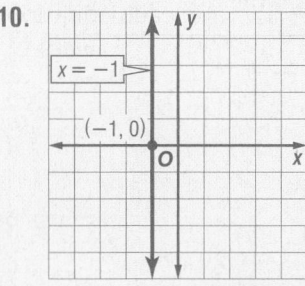

25–33. See pp.
431A–431H.

Graph each equation using the *x*- and *y*-intercepts.

25. $y = x + 2$ **26.** $y = x - 3$ **27.** $x + y = 4$

28. $y = 5x + 5$ **29.** $y = -2x + 4$ **30.** $x + 2y = -6$

31. $y = -2$ **32.** $x - 3 = 0$ ★ **33.** $3x + 6y = 18$

TEACHING TIP
Discuss the difference between continuous and discrete sets of data. For example, temperature is continuous; books and people are discrete.

34. CATERING For a luncheon, a caterer charges $8 per person, plus a setup fee of $24. The total cost of the luncheon *y* can be represented by $y = 8x + 24$, where *x* is the number of people. Graph the equation and explain what the *y*-intercept represents. **See margin.**

35. MONEY Jasmine has $18 to buy books at the library used book sale. Paperback books cost $3 each. The equation $y = 18 - 3x$ represents the amount of money she has left over if she buys *x* paperback books. Graph the equation and describe what the intercepts represent. **See margin.**

36. 25; 25; They represent one dimension when the other dimension is 0, which is impossible for a rectangle.

★ **36. GEOMETRY** The perimeter of a rectangle is 50 centimeters. This can be given by the equation $50 = 2\ell + 2w$, where ℓ is the length and *w* is the width. Name the *x*- and *y*-intercepts of the equation and explain what they mean.

37. CRITICAL THINKING Explain why you cannot graph $y = 2x$ by using intercepts only. Then draw the graph. **See pp. 431A–431H.**

38. WRITING IN MATH Answer the question that was posed at the beginning of the lesson. **See pp. 431A–431H.**

How can intercepts be used to represent real-life information?

Include the following in your answer:
- a graph showing a decrease in temperature, with the *x*-axis representing time and the *y*-axis representing temperature, and
- an explanation of what the intercepts mean.

Standardized Test Practice
Ⓐ Ⓑ Ⓒ Ⓓ

39. What is the *x*-intercept of the graph of $y = 8x - 32$? **B**
Ⓐ −4   Ⓑ 4   Ⓒ −32   Ⓓ 32

40. The graph of which equation does *not* have a *y*-intercept of 3? **C**
Ⓐ $2x + 3y = 9$ Ⓑ $4x + y = 3$ Ⓒ $x + 3y = 6$ Ⓓ $x - 2y = -6$

Maintain Your Skills

Mixed Review
41–43. See margin for sample answers.

Find four solutions of each equation. *(Lesson 8-2)*

41. $y = 2x + 7$ **42.** $y = -3x + 1$ **43.** $4x - y = -5$

Determine whether each relation is a function. *(Lesson 8-1)*

44. {(2, 12), (4, −5), (−3, −4), (11, 0)} **yes**

45. {(−4.2, 17), (−4.3, 16), (−4.3, 15), (−4.3, 14)} **no**

Solve each inequality. *(Lesson 7-4)*

46. $y + 3 < 5$ **y < 2**   **47.** $-2 + n > 10$ **n > 12**   **48.** $7 \le x + 8$ **x ≥ −1**

49. Express 0.028 as a percent. *(Lesson 6-4)* **2.8%**

Getting Ready for the Next Lesson

PREREQUISITE SKILL Subtract. *(To review subtracting integers, see Lesson 2-3.)*

50. $-11 - 13$ **−24** **51.** $15 - 31$ **−16** **52.** $-26 - (-26)$ **0** **53.** $9 - (-16)$ **25**

DAILY **INTERVENTION**

Differentiated Instruction

- **Visual/Spatial** Bring in weather reports clipped from the newspaper showing temperatures in both Fahrenheit and Celsius degrees. A page of temperatures in different cities around the world would work well. Make a large graph on the chalkboard similar to the one in the opening activity. Have each student plot a city's Fahrenheit and Celsius temperatures on the graph. After all the points have been plotted, ask the class what the graph looks like. **a straight line; a function**

4 Assess

Open-Ended Assessment
Modeling Have students list the steps necessary to graph a linear equation using the *x*- and *y*-intercepts.

Getting Ready for Lesson 8-4

PREREQUISITE SKILL In Lesson 8-4, students will subtract *x* and *y* values to find slope. Exercises 50–53 should be used to determine your students' familiarity with subtracting integers.

Assessment Options

Quiz (Lessons 8-1 through 8-3) is available on p. 481 of the *Chapter 8 Resource Masters*.

Answers

34.

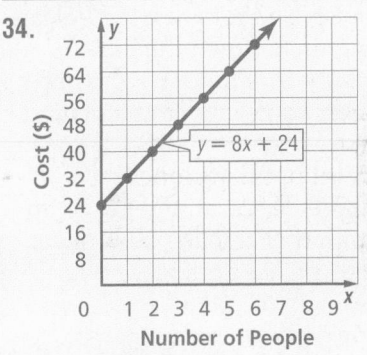

The *y*-intercept 24 represents the setup fee.

35.

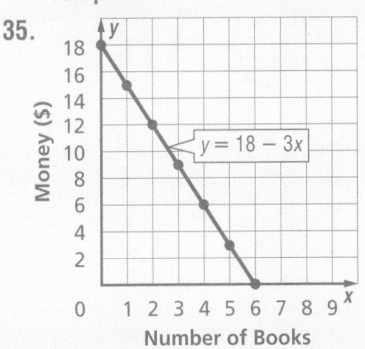

The *x*-intercept 6 represents the number of books she can buy with no money left over. The *y*-intercept 18 represents the money she has before she buys any books.

41. (−1, 5), (0, 7), (1, 9), (2, 11)

42. (−1, 4), (0, 1), (1, −2), (2, −5)

43. (−1, 1), (0, 5), (1, 9), (2, 13)

Algebra Activity

Getting Started

Objective Explore slope by examining how fast an object rolls down various hills.

Materials
posterboard or wooden board
tape
books
ruler
toy car

Teach

- Use smaller toy cars that are not carried beyond the length of the room by their weight. Also, be sure that students do not push the cars when releasing them down the hill.
- Watch for students who need reassurance while calculating slope.
- Point out that slope is expressed as an integer or an improper fraction, and never as a mixed number.

Assess

In **Exercises 1–3,** students should discover the relationship between slope and distance traveled.

In **Exercise 4,** students need not predict the exact distance the car will travel but should accurately predict whether it will travel farther on the new hill.

Study Notebook

You may wish to have students summarize this activity and what they learned from it.

It's All Downhill

The steepness, or *slope*, of a hill can be described by a ratio.

$$\text{slope} = \frac{\text{vertical change}}{\text{horizontal change}} \begin{array}{l} \leftarrow \text{height} \\ \leftarrow \text{length} \end{array}$$

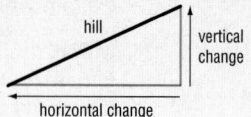

Collect the Data

Step 1 Use posterboard or a wooden board, tape, and three or more books to make a "hill."

Step 2 Measure the height y and length x of the hill to the nearest $\frac{1}{2}$ inch or $\frac{1}{4}$ inch. Record the measurements in a table like the one below.

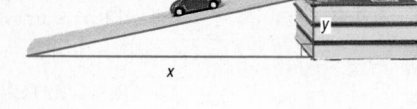

Hill	Height y (in.)	Length x (in.)	Car Distance (in.)	Slope $\frac{y}{x}$
1				
2				
3				

Step 3 Place a toy car at the top of the hill and let it roll down. Measure the distance from the bottom of the ramp to the back of the car when it stops. Record the distance in the table.

Step 4 For the second hill, increase the height by adding one or two more books. Roll the car down and measure the distance it rolls. Record the dimensions of the hill and the distance in the table.

Step 5 Take away two or three books so that hill 3 has the least height. Roll the car down and measure the distance it rolls. Record the dimensions of the hill and the distance in the table.

Step 6 Find the slopes of hills 1, 2, and 3 and record the values in the table.

Analyze the Data   1. slope increased   2. slope decreased

1. How did the slope change when the height increased and the length decreased?

2. How did the slope change when the height decreased and the length increased?

3. **MAKE A CONJECTURE** On which hill would a toy car roll the farthest—a hill with slope $\frac{18}{25}$ or $\frac{25}{18}$? Explain by describing the relationship between slope and distance traveled. $\frac{25}{18}$ because it is greater than $\frac{18}{25}$; the greater the slope, the farther the toy car traveled.

4. The car will travel farther if the slope is greater than the other slopes and less far if the slope is less than the other slopes.

Extend the Activity

4. Make a fourth hill. Find its slope and predict the distance a toy car will go when it rolls down the hill. Test your prediction by rolling a car down the hill.

Resource Manager

📁 ***Teaching Pre-Algebra with Manipulatives***
- p. 22 (master for rulers)
- p. 106 (student recording sheet)

Glencoe Mathematics Classroom Manipulative Kit
- rulers

What You'll Learn

- Find the slope of a line.

How is slope used to describe roller coasters?

Vocabulary
- slope

Some roller coasters can make you feel heavier than a shuttle astronaut feels on liftoff. This is because the speed and steepness of the hills increase the effects of gravity.

56 ft

42 ft

a. Use the roller coaster to write the ratio $\frac{height}{length}$ in simplest form. $\frac{4}{3}$

b. Find the ratio of a hill that has the same length but is 14 feet higher than the hill above. Is this hill steeper or less steep than the original? $\frac{5}{3}$; steeper

---

TEACHING TIP

Encourage students to orally relate the *x* value, or domain, with a move to the right or left and the *y* value, or range, with a move up or down.

SLOPE **Slope** describes the steepness of a line. It is the ratio of the *rise*, or the vertical change, to the *run*, or the horizontal change.

$$\text{slope} = \frac{\text{rise}}{\text{run}} \quad \leftarrow \text{vertical change}$$
$$\quad\quad\quad\quad\quad\quad\quad \leftarrow \text{horizontal change}$$
$$= \frac{4}{3}$$

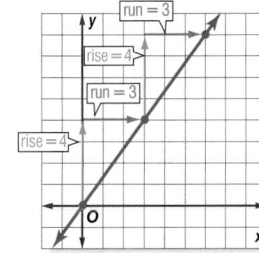

Note that the slope is the same for any two points on a straight line.

Example 1 Use Rise and Run to Find Slope

Find the slope of a road that rises 25 feet for every horizontal change of 80 feet.

$$\text{slope} = \frac{\text{rise}}{\text{run}} \quad \text{Write the formula.}$$

$$= \frac{25 \text{ ft}}{80 \text{ ft}} \quad \text{rise} = 25 \text{ ft, run} = 80 \text{ ft}$$

$$= \frac{5}{16} \quad \text{Simplify.}$$

The slope of the road is $\frac{5}{16}$ or 0.3125.

25 ft

80 ft

✓ **Concept Check** What is the slope of a ramp that rises 2 inches for every horizontal change of 24 inches? $\frac{1}{12}$

---

1 Focus

5-Minute Check Transparency 8-4 Use as a quiz or review of Lesson 8-3.

Mathematical Background notes are available for this lesson on page 366C.

How is slope used to describe roller coasters?

The opening activity questions are repeated on page 435 of the *Chapter 8 Resource Masters.*

Reading to Learn Mathematics, p. 435 **ELL**

Pre-Activity *How is slope used to describe roller coasters?*

Do the activity at the top of page 387 in your textbook. Write your answers below.

a. Use the roller coaster to write the ratio $\frac{height}{length}$ in simplest form. $\frac{4}{3}$

b. Find the ratio of a hill that has the same length but is 14 feet higher than the hill on page 387. Is this hill steeper or less steep than the original? $\frac{5}{3}$; steeper

Reading the Lesson

Write a definition and give an example of the new vocabulary word.

Vocabulary	Definition	Example
1. slope	See students' work.	

Complete each sentence.

2. Slope is __the same__ for any two points on the line.

3. A line that slopes downward from left to right has a __negative__ slope.

4. A line that slopes upward from left to right has a __positive__ slope.

5. A horizontal line has a __zero__ slope.

6. The slope of a vertical line is __undefined__.

Helping You Remember

7. For each graph, draw a line with the given slope.

  a. Positive   b. Negative   c. Zero   d. Undefined

See students' graphs.

Resource Manager

Workbooks and Reproducible Masters

Chapter 8 Resource Masters
- Study Guide and Intervention, p. 432
- Skills Practice, p. 433
- Practice, p. 434
- Reading to Learn Mathematics, p. 435
- Enrichment, p. 436

Parent and Student Study Guide Workbook, p. 64

Transparencies

5-Minute Check Transparency 8-4
Answer Key Transparencies

Technology

Interactive Chalkboard
Pre-AlgePASS: Tutorial Plus, Lesson 23

SLOPE

1 Find the slope of a hill that rises 30 feet for every horizontal change of 150 feet. $\frac{1}{5}$

2 Find the slope of the line.

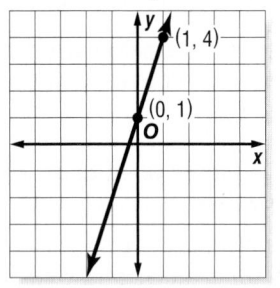

3

3 Find the slope of the line.

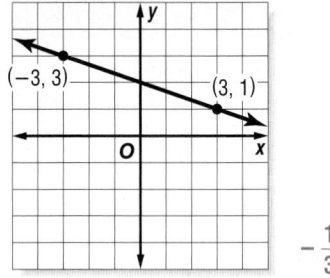

$-\frac{1}{3}$

Teaching Tip Point out that mental math should be sufficient to find the answer to Example 4.

4 Find the slope of the line.

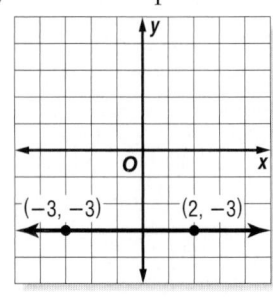

0

Study Tip

Choosing Points
• Any two points on a line can be chosen as (x_1, y_1) and (x_2, y_2).
• The coordinates of both points must be used in the same order.

Check: In Example 2, let $(x_1, y_1) = (5, 3)$ and let $(x_2, y_2) = (2, 2)$, then find the slope.

You can also find the slope by using the coordinates of any two points on a line.

Key Concept | **Slope**

• **Words** The slope m of a line passing through points at (x_1, y_1) and (x_2, y_2) is the ratio of the difference in y-coordinates to the corresponding difference in x-coordinates.

• **Model**

• **Symbols** $m = \dfrac{y_2 - y_1}{x_2 - x_1}$, where $x_2 \neq x_1$

The slope of a line may be positive, negative, zero, or undefined.

Example 2 *Positive Slope*

Find the slope of the line.

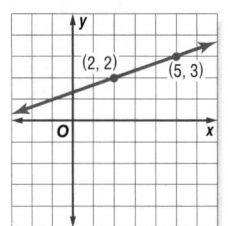

$m = \dfrac{y_2 - y_1}{x_2 - x_1}$ Definition of slope

$m = \dfrac{3 - 2}{5 - 2}$ $(x_1, y_1) = (2, 2),$
             $(x_2, y_2) = (5, 3)$

$m = \dfrac{1}{3}$

The slope is $\dfrac{1}{3}$.

Example 3 *Negative Slope*

Find the slope of the line.

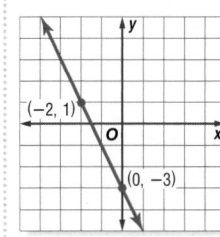

$m = \dfrac{y_2 - y_1}{x_2 - x_1}$ Definition of slope

$m = \dfrac{-3 - 1}{0 - (-2)}$ $(x_1, y_1) = (-2, 1),$
               $(x_2, y_2) = (0, -3)$

$m = \dfrac{-4}{2}$ or -2

The slope is -2.

Example 4 *Zero Slope*

Find the slope of the line.

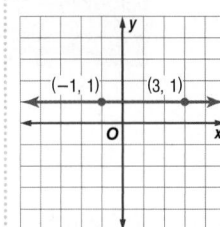

$m = \dfrac{y_2 - y_1}{x_2 - x_1}$ Definition of slope

$m = \dfrac{1 - 1}{3 - (-1)}$ $(x_1, y_1) = (-1, 1),$
               $(x_2, y_2) = (3, 1)$

$m = \dfrac{0}{4}$ or 0

The slope is 0.

D A I L Y
INTERVENTION | **Differentiated Instruction**

• **Naturalist** Have students collect data on the slant of several tree branches. They should consider the point where a branch connects with the trunk to be the origin. Then they should measure the rise and the run. They can number the branches and organize the data in a chart. Then, back in the classroom, they can graph the branches and label them on the graph.

Example 5 *Undefined Slope*

Find the slope of the line.

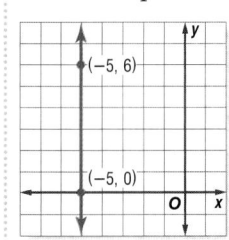

$m = \dfrac{y_2 - y_1}{x_2 - x_1}$ Definition of slope

$m = \dfrac{0 - 6}{-5 - (-5)}$ $(x_1, y_1) = (-5, 6)$, $(x_2, y_2) = (-5, 0)$

$m = \dfrac{6}{0}$

Division by 0 is undefined. So, the slope is undefined.

The steepness of real-world inclines can be compared by using slope.

Example 6 *Compare Slopes*

Multiple-Choice Test Item

There are two major hills on a hiking trail. The first hill rises 6 feet vertically for every 42-foot run. The second hill rises 10 feet vertically for every 98-foot run. Which statement is true?

Ⓐ The first hill is steeper than the second hill.

Ⓑ The second hill is steeper than the first hill.

Ⓒ Both hills have the same steepness.

Ⓓ You cannot determine which hill is steeper.

Test-Taking Tip

Make a Drawing
Whenever possible, make a drawing that displays the given information. Then use the drawing to estimate the answer.

Read the Test Item To compare steepness of the hills, find the slopes.

Solve the Test Item

first hill

$\text{slope} = \dfrac{\text{rise}}{\text{run}}$

$= \dfrac{6 \text{ ft}}{42 \text{ ft}}$ rise = 6 ft, run = 42 ft

$= \dfrac{1}{7}$ or about 0.14

second hill

$\text{slope} = \dfrac{\text{rise}}{\text{run}}$

$= \dfrac{10 \text{ ft}}{98 \text{ ft}}$ rise = 10 ft, run = 98 ft

$= \dfrac{5}{49}$ or about 0.10

$0.14 > 0.10$, so the first hill is steeper than the second. The answer is A.

Check for Understanding

Concept Check

1. **Describe** your own method for remembering whether a horizontal line has 0 slope or an undefined slope.

2. **OPEN ENDED** Draw a line whose slope is $-\dfrac{1}{4}$. **See margin.**

3. **FIND THE ERROR** Mike and Chloe are finding the slope of the line that passes through $Q(-2, 8)$ and $R(11, 7)$.

Mike
$m = \dfrac{8 - 7}{-2 - 11}$

Chloe
$m = \dfrac{7 - 8}{11 - 2}$

Who is correct? Explain your reasoning.

1. Sample answer: horizontals do not rise, so slope $= \dfrac{\text{rise}}{\text{run}} = \dfrac{0}{\text{run}}$ or 0.

3. Mike; Chloe should have subtracted -2 from 11 in the denominator.

 www.pre-alg.com/extra_examples

Answer

2. Sample answer:

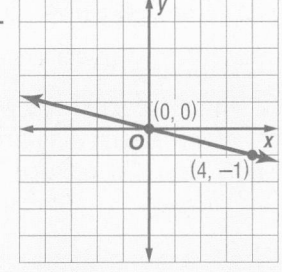

DAILY
INTERVENTION FIND THE ERROR
If students are having difficulty keeping their signs straight, have them write down each step of the slope calculation and use parentheses to separate negative signs from minus signs.

---

5 Find the slope of the line.

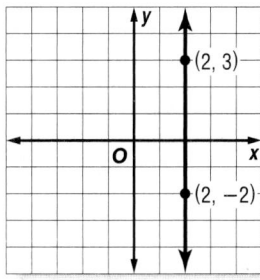

undefined

6 **Multiple-Choice Test Item**
Two highway routes connect City A and City B. The first route rises 4 yards vertically for every 30-mile stretch. The second route rises 8 yards vertically for every 70-mile stretch. Which statement is true?   **A**

A The first route is steeper than the second route.

B The second route is steeper than the first route.

C Both routes have the same steepness.

D You cannot determine which route is steeper.

---

3 Practice/Apply

Study Notebook

Have students—
• add the definition/example of the vocabulary term to their Vocabulary Builder worksheets for Chapter 8.
• include a sample equation, graph, and slope for each of the following: positive slope, negative slope, zero slope, and undefined slope.
• include any other item(s) that they find helpful in mastering the skills in this lesson.

Study Guide and Intervention, p. 432

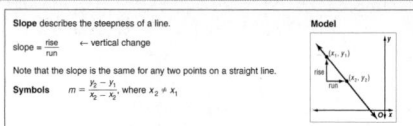

Slope describes the steepness of a line.

slope = $\frac{\text{rise}}{\text{run}}$ ← vertical change

Note that the slope is the same for any two points on a straight line.

Symbols $m = \frac{y_2 - y_1}{x_2 - x_2}$, where $x_2 \neq x_1$

Model

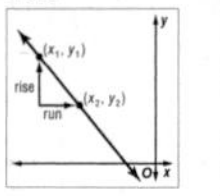

Example **Find the slope of the line.**

$m = \frac{y_2 - y_1}{x_2 - x_1}$ Definition of slope

$m = \frac{4 - 1}{9 - 5}$ $(x_1, y_1) = (5, 1)$, $(x_2, y_2) = (9, 4)$

$m = \frac{3}{4}$

The slope is $\frac{3}{4}$.

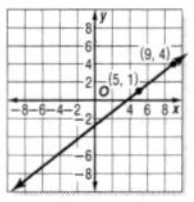

Exercises

Find the slope of each line.

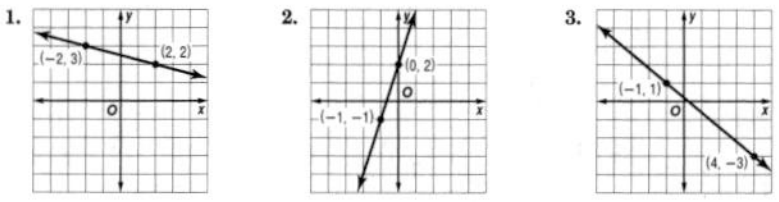

1. $-\frac{1}{4}$
2. 3
3. $-\frac{4}{5}$

Find the slope of the line that passes through each pair of points.

4. $A(2, 2), B(-5, 4)$ $-\frac{2}{7}$
5. $L(5, 5), M(4, 2)$ 3
6. $R(7, -4), S(7, 3)$ undefined

Skills Practice, p. 433 and Practice, p. 434 (shown)

Find the slope of each line.

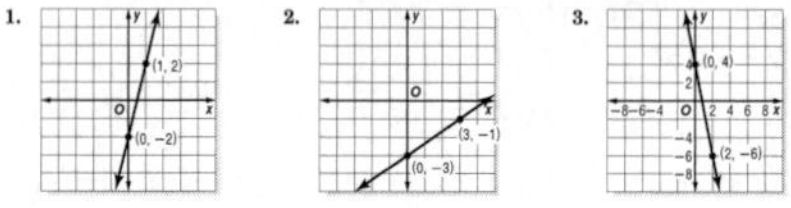

1. 4
2. $\frac{2}{3}$
3. −5

Find the slope of the line that passes through each pair of points.

4. $A(-10, 6), B(-5, 8)$ $\frac{2}{5}$
5. $C(7, -3), D(11, -4)$ $-\frac{1}{4}$
6. $E(5, 2), F(12, -3)$ $-\frac{5}{7}$
7. $G(-15, 7), H(-10, 6)$ $-\frac{1}{5}$
8. $J(13, 0), K(-3, -12)$ $\frac{3}{4}$
9. $L(-5, 3), M(-4, 9)$ 6
10. $P(12, 2), Q(18, -2)$ $-\frac{2}{3}$
11. $R(-2, -3), S(-2, -5)$ undefined
12. $T(-13, 8), U(21, 8)$ 0
13. **CAKES** A wedding cake measures 2 feet high in the center and the diameter of the bottom tier is 12 inches. What is the slope of the cake? 4
14. **INSECTS** One particularly large ant hill found in 1997 measured 40 inches wide at the base and 18 inches high. What was the slope of the ant hill? $\frac{9}{10}$
15. **ARCHAEOLOGY** Today, the Great Pyramid at Giza near Cairo, Egypt, stands 137 meters tall, coming to a point. Its base is a square with each side measuring 230 meters wide. What is the slope of the pyramid? $\frac{137}{115}$
16. **BUSINESS** One warehouse uses 8-foot long ramps to load its forklifts onto the flat beds of trucks for hauling. If the bed of a truck is 2 feet above the ground and the ramp is secured to the truck at its end, what is the slope of the ramp while in operation? $\frac{1}{4}$

Enrichment, p. 436

Investments

The graph below represents two different investments. Line *A* represents an initial investment of $30,000 at a bank paying passbook-savings interest. Line *B* represents an initial investment of $5000 in a profitable mutual fund with dividends reinvested and capital gains accepted in shares. By deriving the equation, $y = mx + b$, for *A* and *B*, a projection of the future can be made.

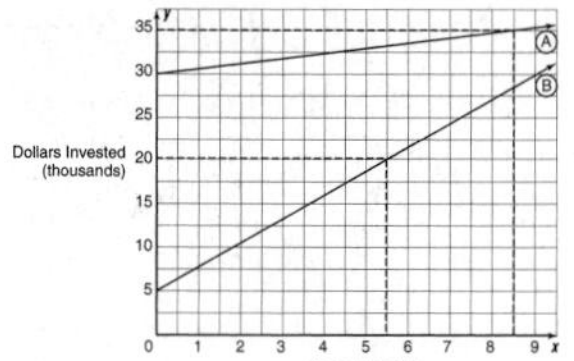

Solve.

1. The *y*-intercept, *b*, is the initial investment. Find *b* for each of the following.
   a. line *A* 30,000 b. line *B* 5000
2. The slope of the line, *m*, is the rate of return. Find *m* for each of the following.
   a. line *A* $\frac{35{,}000 - 30{,}000}{8.5 - 0} \approx 588$ b. line *B* $\frac{20{,}000 - 5000}{5.5 - 0} \approx 2727$
3. What are the equations of each of the following lines?
   a. line *A* $y = 588x + 30{,}000$ b. line *B* $y = 2727x + 5000$

Answer each of the following, assuming that the growth of each investment continues in the same pattern.

4. What will be the value of the mutual fund after the 11th year?
   $y = 2727(11) + 5000 = \$34{,}997$
5. What will be the value of the bank account after the 11th year?
   $y = 588(11) + 30{,}000 = \$36{,}468$
6. When will the mutual fund and the bank account be of equal value?
   $588x + 30{,}000 = 2727x + 5000 \rightarrow x \approx 11.7$ years
7. In the long term, which investment has the greater payoff? mutual fund

Guided Practice

GUIDED PRACTICE KEY	
Exercises	Examples
4	1
5–10	2–5
11	6

4. Find the slope of a line that decreases 24 centimeters vertically for every 30-centimeter horizontal increase. $-\frac{4}{5}$

Find the slope of each line.

5. 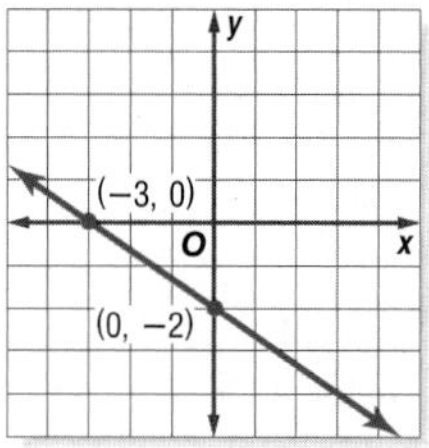

$-\frac{2}{3}$

6. 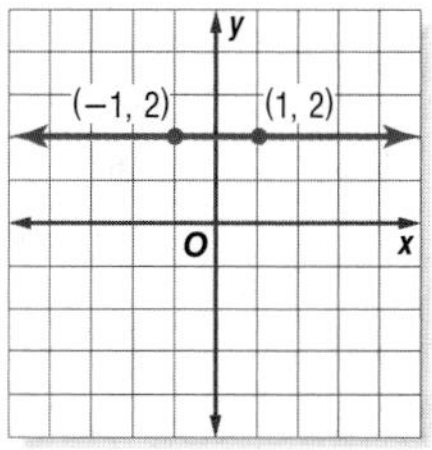

0

Find the slope of the line that passes through each pair of points.

7. $A(3, 4), B(4, 6)$ **2**
8. $J(-8, 0), K(-8, 10)$ **undefined**
9. $P(7, -1), Q(9, -1)$ **0**
10. $C(-6, -4), D(-8, -3)$ $-\frac{1}{2}$

Standardized Test Practice

11. Which bike ramp is the steepest? **B**

    Ⓐ 1
    Ⓑ 2
    Ⓒ 3
    Ⓓ 4

Bike Ramp	Height (ft)	Length (ft)
1	6	8
2	10	4
3	5	3
4	8	4

★ **indicates increased difficulty**

Practice and Apply

Homework Help

For Exercises	See Examples
12, 13	1
14–25	2–5
26, 27	6

Extra Practice
See page 742.

12. **CARPENTRY** In a stairway, the slope of the handrail is the ratio of the riser to the tread. If the tread is 12 inches long and the riser is 8 inches long, find the slope. $\frac{2}{3}$
13. **HOME REPAIR** The bottom of a ladder is placed 4 feet away from a house and it reaches a height of 16 feet on the side of the house. What is the slope of the ladder? **4**

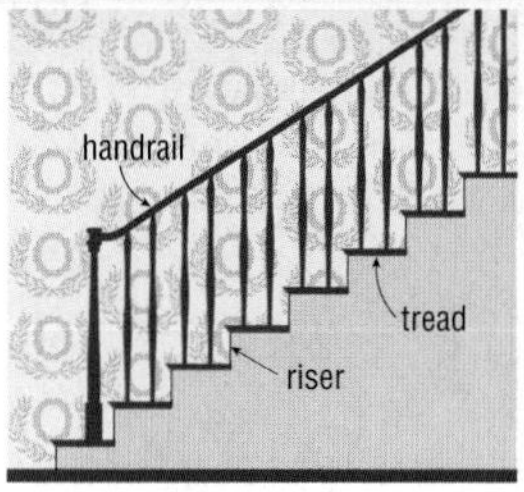

Find the slope of each line.

14. 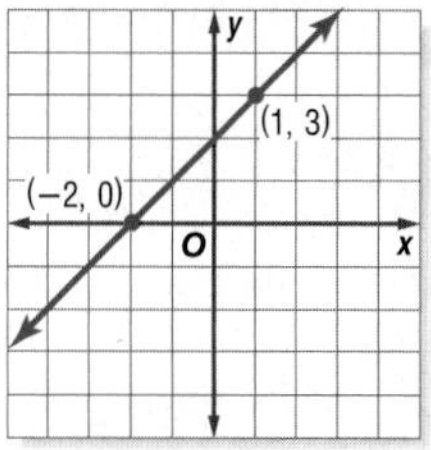

1

15. 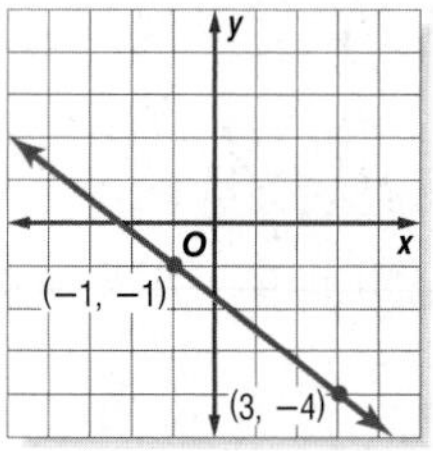

$-\frac{3}{4}$

16. 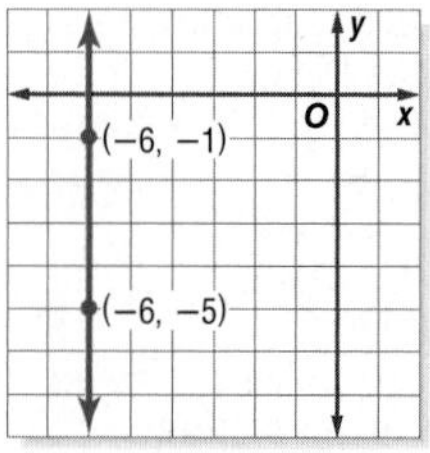

undefined

17. 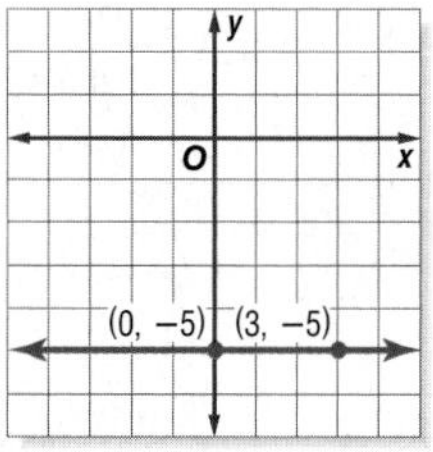

0

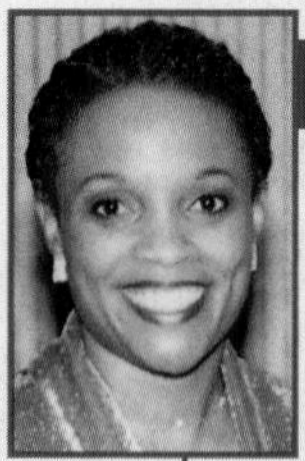

Teacher to Teacher

Rhonda Bailey Mathematics Consultant, Richardson, TX

"I like for my students to use 1-inch grid paper and a game piece to allow students to 'move-out' a slope. Have them move toward the right and toward the left to understand what slope means. The experience of moving in the direction of the slope really becomes concrete when experienced in this manner."

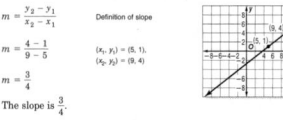

Find the slope of the line that passes through each pair of points. 20. $-\dfrac{5}{8}$

23. undefined

18. $A(1, -3), B(5, 4)$ $\dfrac{7}{4}$ 19. $Y(4, -3), Z(5, -2)$ **1** 20. $D(5, -1), E(-3, 4)$

21. $J(-3, 6), K(-5, 9)$ $-\dfrac{3}{2}$ 22. $N(2, 6), P(-1, 6)$ **0** 23. $S(-9, -4), T(-9, 8)$

★ 24. $F(0, 1.6), G(0.5, 2.1)$ **1**   ★ 25. $W\left(3\dfrac{1}{2}, 5\dfrac{1}{4}\right), X\left(2\dfrac{1}{2}, 6\right)$ $-\dfrac{3}{4}$

ENTERTAINMENT For Exercises 26 and 27, use the graph.

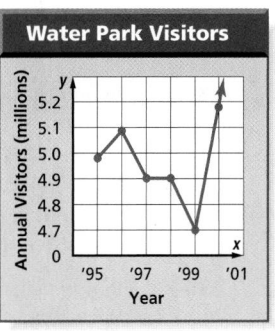

Water Park Visitors

Source: Amusement Business

★ 26. Which section of the graph shows the greatest increase in attendance? Describe the slope. **'99-'00; steep positive slope**

27. It decreased; negative slope.

★ 27. What happened to the attendance at the water park from 1996–1997? Describe the slope of this part of the graph.

28. $\dfrac{b}{a}$; the slope is the y-coordinate of C divided by the x-coordinate of C.

28. **CRITICAL THINKING** The graph of a line goes through the origin $(0, 0)$ and $C(a, b)$. State the slope of this line and explain how it relates to the coordinates of point C.

29. [WRITING IN MATH] Answer the question that was posed at the beginning of the lesson. **See margin.**

How is slope used to describe roller coasters?

Include the following in your answer:
- a description of slope, and
- an explanation of how changes in rise or run affect the steepness of a roller coaster.

Standardized Test Practice
Ⓐ Ⓑ Ⓒ Ⓓ

30. Identify the graph that has a positive slope. **D**

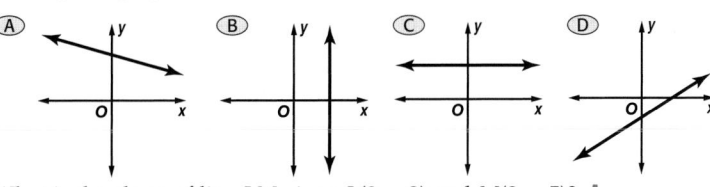

31. What is the slope of line LM given $L(9, -2)$ and $M(3, -5)$? **A**

Ⓐ $\dfrac{1}{2}$ Ⓑ $-\dfrac{1}{2}$ Ⓒ 5 Ⓓ $-\dfrac{1}{3}$

Maintain Your Skills

Mixed Review **Find the x-intercept and the y-intercept for the graph of each equation.**
(Lesson 8-3)

32. $y = x + 8$ $-8; 8$ 33. $y = -3x + 6$ $2; 6$ 34. $4x - y = 12$ $3; -12$

36. $(-1, 3), (0, 0),$ $(1, -3), (2, -6)$

37. $(-1, 8), (0, 7),$ $(1, 6), (2, 5)$

Find four solutions of each equation. Write the solutions as ordered pairs.
(Lesson 8-2) 35. $(-1, 3), (0, 5), (1, 7), (2, 9)$ 35–37. Sample answers are given.

35. $y = 2x + 5$ 36. $y = -3x$ 37. $x + y = 7$

Getting Ready for the Next Lesson **PREREQUISITE SKILL** Rewrite $y = kx$ by replacing k with each given value.
*(To review **substitution**, see Lesson 1-3.)*

38. $k = 5$ $y = 5x$ 39. $k = -2$ 40. $k = 0.25$ 41. $k = \dfrac{1}{3}$ $y = \dfrac{1}{3}x$

$y = -2x$ $y = 0.25x$

Answer

29. Slope can be used to describe the steepness of roller coaster hills. Answers should include the following.
- Slope is the steepness of a line or incline. It is the ratio of the rise to the run.

- An increase in rise with no change in run makes a roller coaster hill steeper. An increase in run with no change in rise makes a roller coaster less steep.

About the Exercises . . .
Odd/Even Assignments
Exercises 12–27 are structured so that students practice the same concepts whether they are assigned odd or even problems.

Assignment Guide
Basic: 13–23 odd, 28–41
Average: 13–27 odd, 28–41
Advanced: 12–26 even, 28–37 (Optional: 38–41)

4 Assess

Open-Ended Assessment
Modeling Have students work in pairs using a length of string or yarn to model slope. Each student should hold one end of the string to the forehead while his or her partner tapes the other end to a spot on the floor. Each pair should then measure rise and run and calculate the slope of the string.

Tips for New Teachers

Cooperative Learning This lesson presents a good opportunity for students to work cooperatively. Set up flash cards with the coordinates of a point written on each. Have students work in two teams to calculate slopes quickly and accurately. Two members of a team draw a card each and find the slope. Make sure all students get a fair number of turns.

Getting Ready for Lesson 8-5

PREREQUISITE SKILL Lesson 8-5 presents rates of change, in which they must explore values for x and y. Exercises 38–41 should be used to determine your students' familiarity with substituting for variables.

Algebra Activity

Getting Started

Objective Explore the relationship between slope and rate of change by comparing heights of water levels in a glass.

Materials
grid paper
water
beaker
metric ruler
tablespoon
$\frac{1}{8}$-cup measuring cup

Teach

• Use narrow beakers so that removing a tablespoon of water will cause a noticeable drop in water level.
• Have students use different colors for tablespoons as for cups in the table and on the graph.

Assess

In **Exercises 1–7**, students should make the connection between steepness of slope and rate of change.

In **Exercise 8**, students should demonstrate a clear understanding of rate of change. While **a** has a constant rate of change, **b**'s rate of change increases gradually, and **c** experiences an abrupt shift from a constant rate of change to a gradually increasing rate of change.

Study Notebook

You may wish to have students summarize this activity and what they learned from it.

Algebra Activity

Slope and Rate of Change

In this activity, you will investigate the relationship between slope and rate of change.

Collect the Data

Step 1 On grid paper, make a coordinate grid of the first quadrant. Label the *x*-axis *Number of Measures* and label the *y*-axis *Height of Water (cm)*.

Step 2 Pour water into a drinking glass or a beaker so that it is more than half full.

Step 3 Use a ruler to find the initial height of the water and record the measurement in a table.

Step 4 Remove a tablespoon of water from the glass or beaker and record the new height in your table.

Step 5 Repeat Step 4 so that you have six measures.

Step 6 Fill the glass or beaker again so that it has the same initial height as in Step 3.

Step 7 Repeat Steps 4 and 5, using a $\frac{1}{8}$-cup measuring cup.

Analyze the Data 2. Line 2 has a steeper negative slope.

1. On the coordinate grid, graph the ordered pairs (number of measures, height of water) for each set of data. Draw a line through each set of points. Label the lines 1 and 2, respectively. **See students' work.**

2. Compare the steepness of the two graphs. Which has a steeper slope?

3. What does the height of the water depend on? **number of measures removed**

4. What happens as the number of measures increases? **The height of water decreases.**

5. Did you empty the glass at a faster rate using a tablespoon or a $\frac{1}{8}$-cup? Explain. **See pp. 431A–431H.**

Make a Conjecture

6. Describe the relationship between slope and the rate at which the glass was emptied. **The steeper the slope, the faster the rate.**

7. What would a graph look like if you emptied a glass using a teaspoon? a $\frac{1}{4}$ cup? Explain. **See pp. 431A–431H.**

Extend the Activity

8. Water is emptied at a constant rate from containers shaped like the ones shown below. Draw a graph of the water level in each of the containers as a function of time. **a–c. See pp. 431A–431H.**

a. 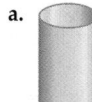   b. 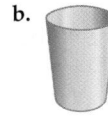   c.

Resource Manager

📁 *Teaching Pre-Algebra with Manipulatives*
• p. 1 (master for grid paper)
• p. 22 (master for rulers)
• p. 108 (student recording sheet)

Glencoe Mathematics Classroom Manipulative Kit
• rulers
• measuring cups

Rate of Change

Vocabulary
- rate of change
- direct variation
- constant of variation

What You'll Learn
- Find rates of change.
- Solve problems involving direct variation.

How are slope and speed related?

A car traveling 55 miles per hour goes 110 miles in 2 hours, 165 miles in 3 hours, and 220 miles in 4 hours, as shown.

a. For every 1-hour increase in time, what is the change in distance? **55 mi**

b. Find the slope of the line. **55**

c. **Make a conjecture** about the relationship between slope of the line and speed of the car.

c. Slope is equal to the speed of the car.

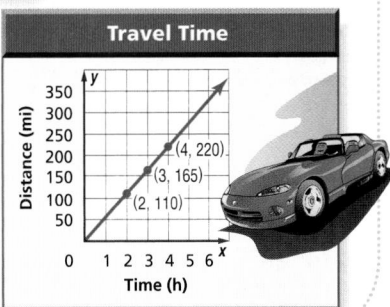

Travel Time

RATE OF CHANGE

A change in one quantity with respect to another quantity is called the **rate of change**. Rates of change can be described using slope.

$$\text{slope} = \frac{\text{change in } y}{\text{change in } x}$$

$$= \frac{55 \text{ mi}}{1 \text{ h}} \text{ or } 55 \text{ mi/h}$$

The slope of the line is the speed of the car.

Time (h)	Distance (mi)
x	**y**
2	110
3	165
4	220
5	275

+1) +55
+1) +55
+1) +55

Each time x increases by 1, y increases by 55.

You can find rates of change from an equation, a table of values, or a graph.

Example 1 Find a Rate of Change

TECHNOLOGY The graph shows the expected growth of subscribers to satellite radio for the first five years that it is introduced. Find the expected rate of change from Year 2 to Year 5.

rate of change = slope

$$= \frac{y_2 - y_1}{x_2 - x_1} \qquad \text{Definition of slope}$$

$$= \frac{21.0 - 3.4}{5 - 2} \qquad \begin{array}{l}\leftarrow \text{change in subscribers} \\ \leftarrow \text{change in time}\end{array}$$

$$\approx 5.9 \qquad \text{Simplify.}$$

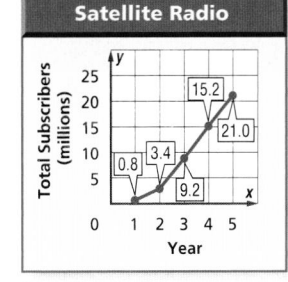

Satellite Radio

Source: The Yankee Group

So, the expected rate of change in satellite radio subscribers is an increase of about 5.9 million people per year.

TEACHING TIP

Students can identify a rate of increase by stating "increase" or by using a positive number. In the same way, they can identify a rate of decrease by stating "decrease" or by using a negative number.

1 Focus

 5-Minute Check Transparency 8-5 Use as a quiz or review of Lesson 8-4.

Mathematical Background notes are available for this lesson on page 366C.

How are slope and speed related?

The opening activity questions are repeated on page 440 of the *Chapter 8 Resource Masters*.

Reading to Learn Mathematics, p. 440 **ELL**

Pre-Activity *How are slope and speed related?*

Do the activity at the top of page 393 in your textbook. Write your answers below.

a. For every 1-hour increase in time, what is the change in distance? 55 mi

b. Find the slope of the line. 55

c. Make a conjecture about the relationship between slope of the line and speed of the car. Slope is equal to the speed of the car.

Reading the Lesson 1–3. See students' work.

Write a definition and give an example of each new vocabulary phrase.

Vocabulary	Definition	Example
1. rate of change		
2. direct variation		
3. constant of variation		

Complete each sentence.

4. Rates of change can be described using ___slope___ .

5. Direct variation is a special type of ___linear___ equation.

Helping You Remember

6. The word *ratio* comes from the Latin word meaning rate and can also mean proportion or relation. Direct variation is often called direct proportion. Look up *ratio* in the dictionary. Then use this information to explain the relationship between rate of change and direct variation. Sample answers: The rate of change is the ratio of the change in one quantity to the change in another quantity. If the ratio is direct, or proportional, then both quantities vary at the same, or constant, rate. Either they both increase at the same rate or they both decrease at the same rate.

Teaching Tip Students will need graph paper in this lesson.

Resource Manager

Workbooks and Reproducible Masters

Chapter 8 Resource Masters
- Study Guide and Intervention, p. 437
- Skills Practice, p. 438
- Practice, p. 439
- Reading to Learn Mathematics, p. 440
- Enrichment, p. 441
- Assessment, pp. 481, 483

Graphing Calculator and Spreadsheet Masters, p. 34
Parent and Student Study Guide Workbook, p. 65
School-to-Career Masters, p. 15

 Transparencies

5-Minute Check Transparency 8-5
Answer Key Transparencies

Technology

Interactive Chalkboard

RATE OF CHANGE

1 **SCHOOL** The graph shows Jadon's quiz scores for the first five weeks after he joined a study group. Find the rate of change from Week 2 to Week 5.

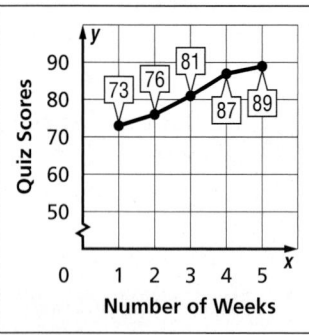

about 4.3 points per week

2 **INCOME** The table shows the yearly incomes of two families. Compare the rates of change.

Year	Income ($)	
	Millers	**Joneses**
2001	49,000	50,000
2002	51,000	52,000
2003	52,500	54,500
2004	55,000	57,000

The income of the Joneses increases at a faster rate than the income of the Millers.

DIRECT VARIATION

3 Suppose y varies directly with x and $y = 6$ when $x = 54$. Write an equation relating x and y. $y = \frac{1}{9}x$

The steepness of slopes is also important in describing rates of change.

Example 2 Compare Rates of Change

GEOMETRY The table shows how the perimeters of an equilateral triangle and a square change as side lengths increase. Compare the rates of change.

Side Length x	Perimeter y	
	Triangle	**Square**
0	0	0
2	6	8
4	12	16

triangle rate of change $= \dfrac{\text{change in } y}{\text{change in } x}$

$= \dfrac{6}{2}$ or 3   For each side length increase of 2, the perimeter increases by 6.

square rate of change $= \dfrac{\text{change in } y}{\text{change in } x}$

$= \dfrac{8}{2}$ or 4   For each side length increase of 2, the perimeter increases by 8.

The perimeter of a square increases at a faster rate than the perimeter of a triangle. A steeper slope on the graph indicates a greater rate of change for the square.

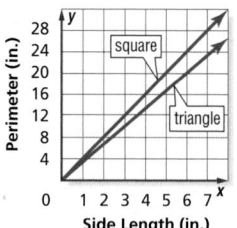

Study Tip
Slopes
• Positive slopes represent a rate of increase.
• Negative slopes represent a rate of decrease.
• Steeper slopes represent greater rates of change.
• Less steep slopes represent a smaller rate of change.

DIRECT VARIATION   A special type of linear equation that describes rate of change is called a **direct variation**. The graph of a direct variation always passes through the origin and represents a proportional situation.

Key Concept   Direct Variation

• **Words**   A direct variation is a relationship such that as x increases in value, y increases or decreases at a constant rate k.

• **Model**
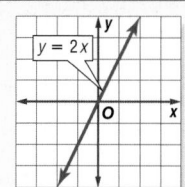

• **Symbols** $y = kx$, where $k \neq 0$

• **Example** $y = 2x$

In the equation $y = kx$, k is called the **constant of variation**. It is the slope, or rate of change. We say that y *varies directly with* x.

Example 3 Write a Direct Variation Equation

Suppose y varies directly with x and $y = -6$ when $x = 2$. Write an equation relating x and y.

Step 1 Find the value of k.

$y = kx$ Direct variation
$-6 = k(2)$ Replace y with -6 and x with 2.
$-3 = k$ Simplify.

Step 2 Use k to write an equation

$y = kx$ Direct variation
$y = -3x$ Replace k with -3.

So, a direct variation equation that relates x and y is $y = -3x$.

D A I L Y
INTERVENTION   **Unlocking Misconceptions**

• **Slope** In Example 1, students might assume that the slope is the same for any two points. However, they should realize that a line graph is actually composed of many line segments, each with its own distinct slope.

• **Rates** Remind students that the denominator is always 1 with rates. They should write rates as decimals rather than fractions.

The direct variation $y = kx$ can be written as $k = \frac{y}{x}$. In this form, you can see that the ratio of y to x is the same for any corresponding values of y and x.

Example 4 Use Direct Variation to Solve Problems

POOLS The height of the water as a pool is being filled is recorded in the table below.

a. **Write an equation that relates time and height.**

Step 1 Find the ratio of y to x for each recorded time. These are shown in the third column of the table. The ratios are approximately equal to 0.4.

Time (min)	Height (in.)	$k = \dfrac{y}{x}$
x	y	
5	2.0	0.40
10	3.75	0.38
15	5.5	0.37
20	7.5	0.38

Step 2 Write an equation.

$y = kx$ Direct variation
$y = 0.4x$ Replace k with 0.4.

So, a direct variation equation that relates the time x and the height of the water y is $y = 0.4x$.

> To the nearest tenth, $k \approx 0.4$.

b. **Predict how long it will take to fill the pool to a height of 48 inches.**

$y = 0.4x$ Write the direct variation equation.
$48 = 0.4x$ Replace y with 48.
$120 = x$ Divide each side by 0.4.

It will take about 120 minutes, or 2 hours to fill the pool.

More About. . .

Pools

The Johnson Space Center in Houston, Texas, has a 6.2 million gallon pool used to train astronauts for space flight. It is 202 feet long, 102 feet wide, and 40 feet deep.
Source: www.jsc.nasa.gov

Check for Understanding

Concept Check
1. **Describe** how slope, rate of change, and constant of variation are related by using $y = 60x$ as a model. **See margin.**

2. **OPEN ENDED** Draw a line that shows a 2-unit increase in y for every 1-unit increase in x. State the rate of change.

2. See pp. 431A–431H for graph; rate of change = 2.

3. Justin; any linear function, including direct variations, has a rate of change.

3. **FIND THE ERROR** Justin and Carlos are determining how to find rate of change from the equation $y = 4x + 5$.

Justin
The rate of change is the slope of its graph.

Carlos
There is no rate of change because the equation is not a direct variation.

Who is correct? Explain your reasoning.

Guided Practice

Find the rate of change for each linear function. 5. increase of $12 per hour

GUIDED PRACTICE KEY	
Exercises	Examples
4, 5	1, 2
6, 7	3
8	4

4.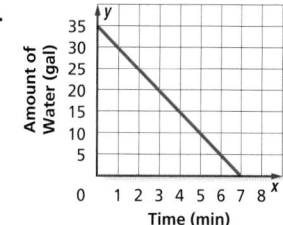

decrease of 5 gal/min

5.
Time (h)	Wage ($)
x	y
0	0
1	12
2	24
3	36

www.pre-alg.com/extra_examples

In-Class Example Power Point®

4. **LANDSCAPING** The depth of a wide hole for a back-yard pond as it is being dug is recorded in the table.

Time (min)	Hole Depth (in.)
x	y
10	8
20	15
30	24
40	31

a. Write an equation that relates time and hole depth. $y = 0.8x$

b. Predict how long it will take to dig to a depth of 36 inches. **45 min**

3 Practice/Apply

Study Notebook

Have students—
• add the definitions/examples of the vocabulary terms to their Vocabulary Builder worksheets for Chapter 8.
• include their answers to Exercise 1.
• include any other item(s) that they find helpful in mastering the skills in this lesson.

DAILY
INTERVENTION **FIND THE ERROR**
Have students compare the definition of *slope* on p. 387 with the definition of *rate of change* on p. 393.

Answer

1. The slope is 60, the rate of change is 60 units for every 1 unit, and the constant of variation is 60.

DAILY
INTERVENTION **Differentiated Instruction**

• **Kinesthetic** Have students experience rate of change first hand. Ask them to choose a physical activity to repeat several times and measure according to performance. For example, how many stomach crunches can they do per minute over 5 minutes? What is the rate of change from the first minute to the fifth minute?

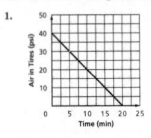

Rate of Change	A change in one quantity with respect to another quantity	slope = $\frac{\text{change in } y}{\text{change in } x}$
Direct Variation	A special type of linear equation that describes rate of change	$y = kx$, where $k \neq 0$
	x and y both increase or both decrease at the same rate—y varies directly with x.	
	Slope, or rate of change, k, is called the constant of variation.	

Example 1 Find the rate of change for the linear function represented in the table.

rate of change = slope
$= \frac{\text{change in } y}{\text{change in } x}$
$= \frac{2}{1}$ or 2   For each time increase of 1h, the temperature increases by 2°C.

| Time (h) | x | 0 | 1 | 2 | 3 |
| Temperature (°C) | y | 0 | 2 | 4 | 6 |

Example 2 Write an equation relating x and y from Example 1.

Step 1 Find the value of k.
$y = kx$ Direct variation
$2 = k(1)$ Replace y with 2 and x with 1.
$2 = k$ Simplify.

Step 2 Use k to write an equation.
$y = kx$ Direct variation
$y = 2x$ Replace k with 2.

Exercises

1. Find the rate of change for the linear function. increase of 500 mph

| Time (h) | x | 0 | 2 | 4 | 6 |
| Distance Flown (mi) | y | 0 | 1000 | 2000 | 3000 |

Suppose y varies directly with x. Write an equation relating x and y.

2. $y = 14$ when $x = 7$
$y = 2x$

3. $y = 3$ when $x = 5$
$y = \frac{3}{5}x$

4. $y = 2$ when $x = -4$
$y = -\frac{1}{2}x$

Skills Practice, p. 438 and Practice, p. 439 (shown)

Find the rate of change for each linear function.

1.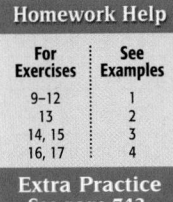

2.
Time (h)	Distance (km)
x	y
0	0
5	510
10	1020
15	1530

decrease of 2 psi/min   increase of 102 km/h

Suppose y varies directly with x. Write an equation relating x and y.

3. $y = -6$ when $x = -2$
$y = 3x$

4. $y = -27$ when $x = 9$
$y = -3x$

5. $y = 4$ when $x = 16$
$y = \frac{1}{4}x$

6. $y = 10$ when $x = 2$
$y = 5x$

7. $y = -42$ when $x = 7$
$y = -6x$

8. $y = 3$ when $x = 36$
$y = \frac{1}{12}x$

9. $y = 4.5$ when $x = -9$
$y = -0.5x$

10. $y = 11$ when $x = 33$
$y = \frac{1}{3}x$

11. $y = 25$ when $x = -5$
$y = -5x$

12. $y = 63$ when $x = 7$
$y = 9x$

13. $y = 48$ when $x = -4$
$y = -12x$

14. $y = 26$ when $x = 13$
$y = 2x$

TRAFFIC MANAGEMENT For Exercises 15 and 16, use the following information.

San Diego reserves express lanes on the freeways for the use of carpoolers. In order to increase traffic flow during rush hours, other drivers may use the express lanes for a fee. The toll varies directly with the number of cars on the road. The table shows a sample of possible tolls.

Toll ($)	Traffic Volume (vehicles/h)
1.00	521
2.00	1042
3.00	1563
4.00	2084

15. Write an equation that relates the toll x and traffic volume y.
$y = 521x$

16. Predict the number of vehicles at a peak time if the toll increases to $6.00. 3126 vehicles/h

17. **OFFICE SUPPLIES** The cost of paper varies directly with the number of reams of paper purchased. If 2 reams cost $9.60, find the cost of 41 reams. $196.80

Enrichment, p. 441

Fibonacci Sequence

The first fifteen terms of the **Fibonacci sequence** are shown below.

1, 1, 2, 3, 5, 8, 13, 21, 34, 55, 89, 144, 233, 377, 610

In addition to the fact that each term is the sum of the two previous terms, there are other interesting relationships.

Complete.

1. Find the sum of the first four terms. 7
2. Find the sum of the first five terms. 12
3. Find the sum of the first six terms. 20
4. What is the relationship between the sums and terms in the sequence? The sum is one less than the Fibonacci number after the next Fibonacci number.
5. Use your answer from Exercise 4 above to predict the sum of the first 10 terms, and of the first 12 terms. Check your answers by finding the sums. 143, 376
6. Divide each of the first 15 terms by 4. Make a list of the remainders. What pattern do you see in the remainder sequence? 1, 1, 2, 3, 1, 0, 1, 1, 2, 3, 1, 0, 1, 1, 2; The six digits 1, 1, 2, 3, 1, 0 repeat.
7. The sums of the squares of consecutive terms of the Fibonacci sequence are shown below. Complete the next three lines of this pattern.

$1^2 + 1^2 = 1 \times 2$
$1^2 + 1^2 + 2^2 = 2 \times 3$
$1^2 + 1^2 + 2^2 + 3^2 = 3 \times 5$
$1^2 + 1^2 + 2^2 + 3^2 + 5^2 = 5 \times 8$
$1^2 + 1^2 + 2^2 + 3^2 + 5^2 + 8^2 = 8 \times 13$
$1^2 + 1^2 + 2^2 + 3^2 + 5^2 + 8^2 + 13^2 = 13 \times 21$
$1^2 + 1^2 + 2^2 + 3^2 + 5^2 + 8^2 + 13^2 + 21^2 = 21 \times 34$

Suppose y varies directly with x. Write an equation relating x and y.

6. $y = 5$ when $x = -15$ $y = -\frac{1}{3}x$

7. $y = 24$ when $x = 4$ $y = 6x$

Application

8. **PHYSICAL SCIENCE** The length of a spring varies directly with the amount of weight attached to it. When a 25-gram weight is attached, a spring stretches to 8 centimeters. **a.** $y = 0.32x$ **b.** 19.2 cm

a. Write a direct variation equation relating the weight x and the length y.

b. Estimate the length of a spring that has a 60-gram weight attached.

★ indicates increased difficulty

Practice and Apply

Homework Help

For Exercises	See Examples
9–12	1
13	2
14, 15	3
16, 17	4

Extra Practice See page 743.

Find the rate of change for each linear function.

9. 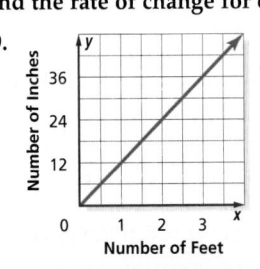 increase of 12 in./ft

10. 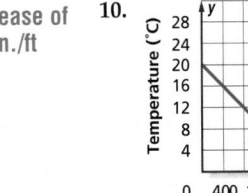 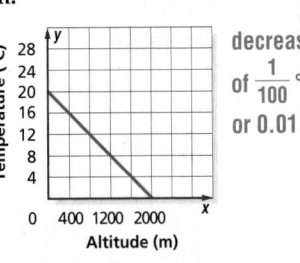 decreas of $\frac{1}{100}$° or 0.01

11.
Time (min)	Temperature (°F)
x	y
0	58
1	56
2	54
3	52

decrease of 2°F/min

12.
Time (h)	Distance (mi)
x	y
0.0	0
0.5	25
1.5	75
3.0	150

increase of 50 mi/h

★ 13. **ENDANGERED SPECIES** The graph shows the populations of California condors in the wild and in captivity. **See margin.**

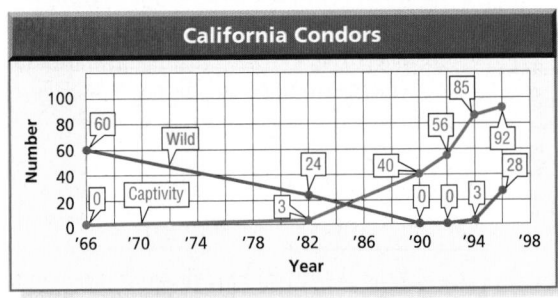

California Condors

Source: Los Angeles Zoo

Write several sentences that describe how the populations have changed since 1966. Include the rate of change for several key intervals.

 Online Research **Data Update** What has happened to the condor population since 1996? Visit www.pre-alg.com/data_update to learn more.

Suppose y varies directly with x. Write an equation relating x and y.

14. $y = 8$ when $x = 4$ $y = 2x$

15. $y = -30$ when $x = 6$ $y = -5x$

16. $y = 9$ when $x = 24$ $y = \frac{3}{8}x$

17. $y = 7.5$ when $x = 10$ $y = 0.75x$

Answer

13. Sample answer: The population of wild condors decreased from 1966 to 1990. Then the population increased from 1990 to 1996. The population of condors in captivity increased slowly from 1966 to 1982, then increased more rapidly from 1982 to 1996.

Interval	Rate of Change (number per year)	
	Condors in the Wild	Condors in Captivity
1966–1982	−2.25	0.1875
1982–1990	−3	4.625
1990–1992	0	8
1992–1994	1.5	14.5
1994–1996	12.5	3.5

18. FOOD COSTS The cost of cheese varies directly with the number of pounds bought. If 2 pounds cost $8.40, find the cost of 3.5 pounds.

19. CONVERTING MEASUREMENTS The number of centimeters in a measure varies directly as the number of inches. Write a direct variation equation that could be used to convert inches to centimeters. $y = 2.54x$

Measure in Inches x	Measure in Centimeters y
1	2.54
2	5.08
3	7.62

20. CRITICAL THINKING Describe the rate of change for a graph that is a horizontal line and a graph that is a vertical line. **See pp. 431A–431H.**

21. WRITING IN MATH Answer the question that was posed at the beginning of the lesson. **See pp. 431A–431H.**

How are slope and speed related?

Include the following in your answer:
- a drawing of a graph showing distance versus time, and
- an explanation of how slope changes when speed changes.

Standardized
Test Practice

22. A graph showing an increase in sales over time would have a(n) **A**
- Ⓐ positive slope.
- Ⓑ negative slope.
- Ⓒ undefined slope.
- Ⓓ slope of 0.

23. Choose an equation that does *not* represent a direct variation. **B**
- Ⓐ $y = x$
- Ⓑ $y = 1$
- Ⓒ $y = -5x$
- Ⓓ $y = 0.9x$

Maintain Your Skills

Mixed Review **Find the slope of the line that passes through each pair of points.** *(Lesson 8-4)*

24. $Q(-4, 4)$, $R(3, 5)$ $\frac{1}{7}$ **25.** $A(2, 6)$, $B(-1, 0)$ **2**

Graph each equation using the x- and y-intercepts. *(Lesson 8-3)*

26–28. See pp.
431A–431H.

26. $y = x + 5$ **27.** $y = -x + 1$ **28.** $2x + y = 4$

29. Estimate 20% of 72. *(Lesson 6-6)* **14**

Getting Ready for the Next Lesson **PREREQUISITE SKILL** Solve each equation for y.
*(To review **solving equations for a variable**, see Lesson 8-2.)* **32.** $y = 2 + \frac{1}{5}x$

30. $x + y = 6$ $y = 6 - x$ **31.** $3x + y = 1$ $y = 1 - 3x$ **32.** $-x + 5y = 10$

Practice Quiz 1   Lessons 8-1 through 8-5

Determine whether each relation is a function. Explain. *(Lesson 8-1)*

1. $\{(0, 5), (1, 2), (1, -3), (2, 4)\}$
No; 1 is paired with 2 and −3.

2. $\{(-6, 3.5), (-3, 4.0), (0, 4.5), (3, 5.0)\}$
Yes; each x value is paired with only one y value.

Graph each equation using ordered pairs. *(Lesson 8-2)*

3. $y = x - 4$

4. $y = 2x + 3$ **3–4. See margin.**

Find the x-intercept and the y-intercept for the graph of each equation. *(Lesson 8-3)*

5. $y = x + 9$ $-9; 9$ **6.** $x + 2y = 12$ $12; 6$ **7.** $4x - 5y = 20$ $5; -4$

Find the slope of the line that passes through each pair of points. *(Lessons 8-4 and 8-5)*

8. $(1, 4), (0, 0)$ **4**   **9.** $(-2, 4), (3, -6)$ -2 **10.** $(0, 2), (5, 2)$ **0**

Answers (Practice Quiz 1)

3.
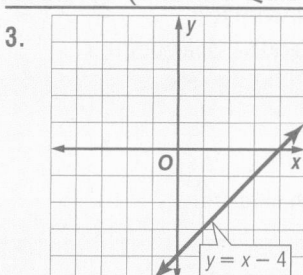

4.
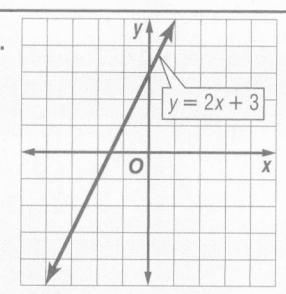

4 Assess

Open-Ended Assessment

Modeling Have students measure the outside temperature during class every day for a week. Ask them to find the rate of change in temperatures.

Getting Ready for Lesson 8-6

PREREQUISITE SKILL In Lesson 8-6 students rewrite equations in slope-intercept form ($y = mx + b$). Exercises 30–32 should be used to determine your students' familiarity with solving equations for a given variable.

Assessment Options

Practice Quiz 1 The quiz provides students with a brief review of the concepts and skills in Lessons 8-1 through 8-5. Lesson numbers are given to the right of exercises or instruction lines so students can review concepts not yet mastered.

Quiz (Lessons 8-4 and 8-5) is available on p. 481 of the *Chapter 8 Resource Masters*.

Mid-Chapter Test (Lessons 8-1 through 8-5) is available on p. 483 of the *Chapter 8 Resource Masters*.

About the Exercises . . .
Organization by Objective
- **Rate of Change:** 9–13
- **Direct Variation:** 14–19

Odd/Even Assignments
Exercises 9–12 and 14–19 are structured so that students practice the same concepts whether they are assigned odd or even problems.

Assignment Guide
Basic: 9, 11, 15–19 odd, 20–32
Average: 9–19 odd, 20–32
Advanced: 10–18 even, 20–29 (Optional: 30–32)
All: Practice Quiz 1 (1–10)

8-6 Lesson Notes

1 Focus

8-6 Slope-Intercept Form

5-Minute Check Transparency 8-6 Use as a quiz or review of Lesson 8-5.

Mathematical Background notes are available for this lesson on page 366D.

How can knowing the slope and *y*-intercept help you graph an equation?

The opening activity questions are repeated on page 445 of the *Chapter 8 Resource Masters*.

Reading to Learn Mathematics, p. 445 **ELL**

Pre-Activity How can knowing the slope and y-intercept help you graph an equation?

Do the activity at the top of page 398 in your textbook. Write your answers below.

a. On the same coordinate plane, use ordered pairs or intercepts to graph each equation in a different color.

b. Find the slope and the y-intercept of each line. Complete the table.

Equation	Slope	y-Intercept
$y = 2x + 1$	2	1
$y = \frac{1}{3}x - 3$	$\frac{1}{3}$	-3
$y = -2x + 1$	-2	1

c. Compare each equation with the value of its slope and y-intercept. What do you notice? The slope is the coefficient of x, the y-intercept is the constant.

Reading the Lesson

Write a definition and give an example of the new vocabulary phrase.

Vocabulary	Definition	Example
1. slope-intercept form	See students' work.	

2. Sometimes you must solve an equation for ___y___ before you can write the equation in slope-intercept form.

3. Explain why $y = mx + b$ is called the slope-intercept form. The form $y = mx + b$ describes a line according to its slope, m, and its y-intercept, b.

Helping You Remember

4. Mathematicians debate the origin of the slope-intercept form of a line, particularly the use of m to represent slope. Make up a mnemonic phrase to help you remember the slope-intercept form. Sample answer: y is the m(ountain slope) times x plus the b(all intercepted on the y-yardline).

8-6 Slope-Intercept Form

What You'll Learn

- Determine slopes and *y*-intercepts of lines.
- Graph linear equations using the slope and *y*-intercept.

Vocabulary
- slope-intercept form

How can knowing the slope and *y*-intercept help you graph an equation?

Copy the table.

a. On the same coordinate plane, use ordered pairs or intercepts to graph each equation in a different color. **See margin.**

b. Find the slope and the *y*-intercept of each line. Complete the table.

Equation	Slope	y-intercept
$y = 2x + 1$	2	1
$y = \frac{1}{3}x - 3$	$\frac{1}{3}$	-3
$y = -2x + 1$	-2	1

c. The slope is the coefficient of *x*; the *y*-intercept is the constant.

c. Compare each equation with the value of its slope and *y*-intercept. What do you notice?

SLOPE AND *y*-INTERCEPT

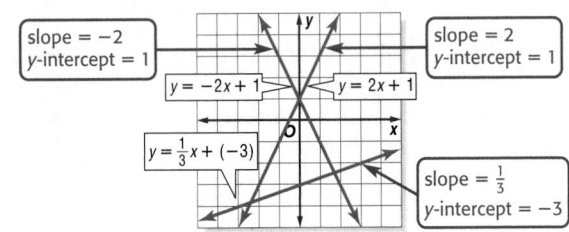

All the equations above are written in the form $y = mx + b$, where *m* is the slope and *b* is the *y*-intercept. This is called **slope-intercept form**.

$$y = mx + b$$

slope ⎯⎺⎺⎺⎼ ⎽⎺⎺⎺⎼ *y*-intercept

Study Tip

Different Forms
Both equations below are written in slope-intercept form.
$$y = x + (-2)$$
$$y = x - 2$$

Example 1 Find the Slope and *y*-Intercept

State the slope and the *y*-intercept of the graph of $y = \frac{3}{5}x - 7$.

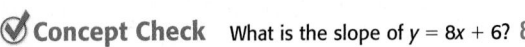

$y = \frac{3}{5}x - 7$ Write the original equation.

$y = \frac{3}{5}x + (-7)$ Write the equation in the form $y = mx + b$.

$y = mx + b$ $m = \frac{3}{5}, b = -7$

The slope of the graph is $\frac{3}{5}$, and the *y*-intercept is -7.

✓ **Concept Check** What is the slope of $y = 8x + 6$? **8**

Resource Manager

📁 Workbooks and Reproducible Masters

Chapter 8 Resource Masters
- Study Guide and Intervention, p. 442
- Skills Practice, p. 443
- Practice, p. 444
- Reading to Learn Mathematics, p. 445
- Enrichment, p. 446

Parent and Student Study Guide Workbook, p. 66

📀 Transparencies
5-Minute Check Transparency 8-6
Answer Key Transparencies

📀 Technology
Interactive Chalkboard
Pre-AlgePASS: Tutorial Plus, Lesson 24

Sometimes you must first write an equation in slope-intercept form before finding the slope and y-intercept.

Example 2 Write an Equation in Slope-Intercept Form

State the slope and the y-intercept of the graph of $5x + y = 3$.

$$5x + y = 3 \qquad \text{Write the original equation.}$$
$$5x + y - 5x = 3 - 5x \qquad \text{Subtract } 5x \text{ from each side.}$$
$$y = -5x + 3 \qquad \text{Write the equation in slope-intercept form.}$$
$$y = \quad mx + b \qquad m = -5, b = 3$$

The slope of the graph is -5, and the y-intercept is 3.

TEACHING TIP

Explain to students that there are two ways to interpret a negative slope. Both give the same result.

• $\dfrac{-1}{2}$ means go down 1 unit and right 2 units.

• $\dfrac{1}{-2}$ means go up 1 unit and left 2 units.

GRAPH EQUATIONS You can use the slope-intercept form of an equation to easily graph a line.

Example 3 Graph an Equation

Graph $y = -\dfrac{1}{2}x - 4$ using the slope and y-intercept.

Step 1 Find the slope and y-intercept.

$$\text{slope} = -\dfrac{1}{2} \qquad y\text{-intercept} = -4$$

Step 2 Graph the y-intercept point at $(0, -4)$.

Step 3 Write the slope $-\dfrac{1}{2}$ as $\dfrac{-1}{2}$. Use it to locate a second point on the line.

$$m = \dfrac{-1}{2} \quad \begin{array}{l} \leftarrow \text{change in } y\text{: down 1 unit} \\ \leftarrow \text{change in } x\text{: right 2 units} \end{array}$$

Another point on the line is at $(2, -5)$.

Step 4 Draw a line through the two points.

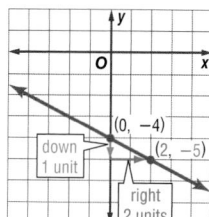

down 1 unit
right 2 units
$(0, -4)$
$(2, -5)$

Career Choices

Business Owner

Business owners must understand the factors that affect cost and profit. Graphs are a useful way for them to display this information.

Online Research
For information about a career as a business owner, visit: www.pre-alg.com/careers

Example 4 Graph an Equation to Solve a Problem

BUSINESS A T-shirt company charges a design fee of $24 for a pattern and then sells the shirts for $12 each. The total cost y can be represented by the equation $y = 12x + 24$, where x represents the number of T-shirts.

a. Graph the equation.

First, find the slope and the y-intercept.

slope = 12
y-intercept = 24

Plot the point at $(0, 24)$. Then go up 12 and right 1. Connect these points.

b. Describe what the y-intercept and the slope represent.

The y-intercept 24 represents the design fee. The slope 12 represents the cost per T-shirt, which is the rate of change.

Cost ($)
Number of T-Shirts
$(0, 24)$

www.pre-alg.com/extra_examples

SLOPE AND Y-INTERCEPT

In-Class Examples Power Point®

1 State the slope and the y-intercept of the graph of $y = \dfrac{1}{2}x + 3$. $\dfrac{1}{2}$; 3

2 State the slope and the y-intercept of the graph of $-4x + 5y = -10$. $\dfrac{4}{5}$; -2

GRAPH EQUATIONS

In-Class Examples Power Point®

3 Graph $3x + y = 9$ using the slope and y-intercept.

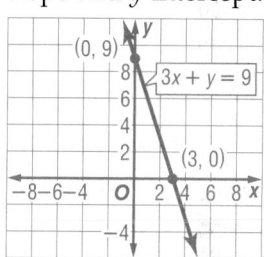

$(0, 9)$
$3x + y = 9$
$(3, 0)$

4 **BAKING** A school group making cookies for a bake sale spends $75 on ingredients and then sells the cookies for $5 a dozen. The amount earned y can be represented by the equation $y = 5x - 75$, where x equals the number of dozens sold.

a. Graph the equation.

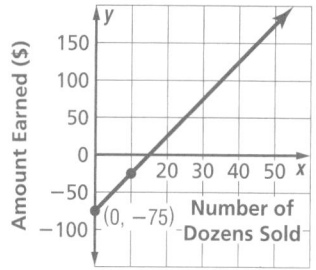

Amount Earned ($)
Number of Dozens Sold
$(0, -75)$

b. Describe what the y-intercept and the slope represent. **The y-intercept -75 represents the cost of the ingredients. Slope 5 represents the dollars earned per dozen cookies.**

DAILY INTERVENTION

Unlocking Misconceptions

• **Discrete Solutions** Students might assume that every point on the graph in Example 4 is a solution for the problem. Emphasize that the equation represents a set of points in which the solutions to the real-world problem exist. A true graph of the real-world situation would only have points where x is a whole number.

Study Guide and Intervention, p. 442

The **slope-intercept form** of a line makes it easy to graph the line:
$y = mx + b$ **Example:** $y = 3x + 2$
slope $= m$ slope $= 3$
y-intercept $= b$ y-intercept $= 2$

Example   Graph $y = -4x - 3$ using the slope and y-intercept.

Step 1 Find the slope and y-intercept.
slope $= -4$ y-intercept $= -3$

Step 2 Graph the y-intercept point at $(0, -3)$.

Step 3 Write the slope -4 as $\frac{-4}{1}$. Use the slope to locate a second point on the line.
$m = \frac{-4}{1}$ change in y: down 4 units
              change in x: right 1 unit

Step 4 Draw a line through the two points.

Step 5 Check by locating another point on the line and substituting the coordinates into the original equation.

Exercises

Given the slope and y-intercept, graph each line.

1. slope $= 4$,   2. slope $= 6$,   3. slope $= -\frac{1}{4}$,
y-intercept $= -1$ y-intercept $= 4$ y-intercept $= 5$

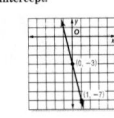

Graph each equation using the slope and y-intercept.

4. $y = 3x - 2$ 5. $y = \frac{2}{3}x + 3$ 6. $y = 5x - 3$

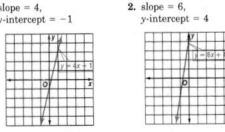 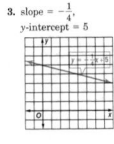

Skills Practice, p. 443 and Practice, p. 444 (shown)

Given the slope and y-intercept, graph each line.

1. slope $= \frac{3}{4}$,   2. slope $= \frac{5}{6}$,   3. slope $= 1$,
y-intercept $= -3$ y-intercept $= 1$ y-intercept $= 5$

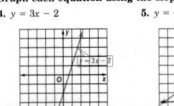 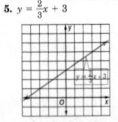 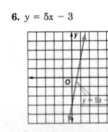

Graph each equation using the slope and y-intercept.

4. $y = -\frac{1}{2}x - 4$ 5. $y = x - 4$ 6. $y = -6x + 3$

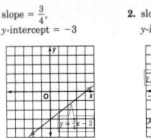 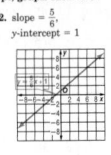 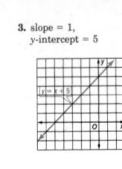

EXERCISE For Exercises 7 and 8, use the following information.
A person weighing 150 pounds burns about 320 Calories per hour walking at a moderate pace. Suppose that the same person burns an average of 1500 Calories per day through basic activities. The total Calories y burned by that person can be represented by the equation $y = 320x + 1500$, where x represents the number of hours spent walking.

7. Graph the equation using the slope and y-intercept.

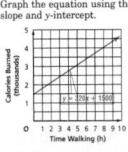

8. State the slope and y-intercept of the graph of the equation and describe what they represent. **The y-intercept 1500 represents the number of Calories burned without exercising. The slope 320 represents the number of Calories burned per hour when walking.**

Enrichment, p. 446

Translations and Reflections

The lines on graph paper can help you draw slide images of figures.

1. Graph $\triangle ABC$ with vertices $A(1, 1)$, $B(-3, 4)$, and $C(-3, -4)$. Draw $\triangle A'B'C'$, the translation image of $\triangle ABC$, where the slide is 3 units to the right. Name the coordinates of the image of each vertex.
$A'(4, 1)$, $B'(0, 4)$, $C'(0, -4)$

2. Draw $\triangle JKL$ with vertices $J(-4, 3)$, $K(0, 2)$, and $L(-2, 0)$. Let $\triangle J'K'L'$ be the image of $\triangle JKL$ under a slide of 4 units to the right and then a slide of 3 units up. Graph $\triangle J'K'L'$. Name the coordinates of the vertices of $\triangle J'K'L'$.
$J'(0, 6)$, $K'(4, 5)$, $L'(2, 3)$

3. Draw $\overline{A'B'}$, the image formed by reflecting $\overline{AB}$ over the y-axis. Then draw $\overline{A''B''}$, the image formed by reflecting $\overline{A'B'}$ over the x-axis. What are the coordinates of A'' and B''? What is the relationship between the coordinates of the endpoints of $\overline{AB}$ and those of $\overline{A''B''}$?

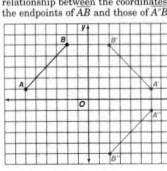

4. Draw $\overline{P'Q'}$, the reflection image of $\overline{PQ}$ over the y-axis. Draw $\overline{P''Q''}$, the reflection image of $\overline{P'Q'}$ over the x-axis. Find the slopes of $\overline{PQ}$, $\overline{P'Q'}$, and $\overline{P''Q''}$. What is the relationship between the slopes of $\overline{PQ}$ and $\overline{P''Q''}$?

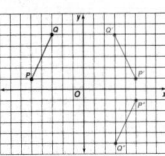

$A''(6, -1)$, $B''(2, -5)$; The coordinates of A'' and B'' have the opposite signs of A and B.

Slope of $\overline{PQ} = 2$; slope of $\overline{P'Q'} = -2$; slope of $\overline{P''Q''} = 2$; They are the same.

Check for Understanding

Concept Check

1. **State** the value that tells you how many units to go up or down from the y-intercept if the slope of a line is $\frac{a}{b}$. **a**

2. **OPEN ENDED**   Draw the graph of a line that has a y-intercept but no x-intercept. What is the slope of the line? **See pp. 431A–431H for graph; slope $= 0$.**

3. **FIND THE ERROR**   Carmen and Alex are finding the slope and y-intercept of $x + 2y = 8$. **Alex; the equation in slope-intercept form is $y = -\frac{1}{2}x + 4$.**

> Carmen
>
> slope $= 2$
>
> y-intercept $= 8$

> Alex
>
> slope $= -\frac{1}{2}$
>
> y-intercept $= 4$

Who is correct? Explain your reasoning.

Guided Practice   State the slope and the y-intercept for the graph of each equation.

GUIDED PRACTICE KEY	
Exercises	Examples
4–6	1, 2
7–9	3
10, 11	4

4. $y = x + 8$ **1; 8**   5. $x + y = 0$ **−1; 0**   6. $x + 3y = 6$ **$-\frac{1}{3}$; 2**

Graph each equation using the slope and y-intercept. **7–9. See pp. 431A–431H.**

7. $y = \frac{1}{4}x + 1$ 8. $3x + y = 2$ 9. $x - 2y = 4$

Application   **BUSINESS**   Mrs. Allison charges $25 for a basic cake that serves 12 people. A larger cake costs an additional $1.50 per serving. The total cost can be given by $y = 1.5x + 25$, where x represents the number of additional slices.

10. Graph the equation. **See pp. 431A–431H.**

11. Explain what the y-intercept and the slope represent.
The y-intercept 25 represents the charge for a basic cake. Slope 1.5 represents the cost per additional slice.

★ indicates increased difficulty

Practice and Apply

Homework Help	
For Exercises	See Examples
12–17	1, 2
18–31	3
32–34	4

Extra Practice
See page 743.

20–31. See pp. 431A–431H.

State the slope and the y-intercept for the graph of each equation.

12. $y = x + 2$ **1; 2**   13. $y = 2x - 4$ **2; −4**

14. $x + y = -3$ **−1; −3**   15. $2x + y = -3$ **−2; −3**

16. $5x + 4y = 20$ **$-\frac{5}{4}$; 5**   17. $y = 4$ **0; 4**

Graph each line with the given slope and y-intercept.

18. slope $= 3$, y-intercept $= 1$ 19. slope $= -\frac{3}{2}$, y-intercept $= -1$

18–19. See pp. 431A–431H.

Graph each equation using the slope and y-intercept.

20. $y = x + 5$ 21. $y = -x + 6$

22. $y = 2x - 3$ 23. $y = \frac{3}{4}x + 2$

24. $x + y = -3$ 25. $x + y = 0$

26. $-2x + y = -1$ 27. $5x + y = -3$

★ 28. $x - 3y = -6$ ★ 29. $2x + 3y = 12$

★ 30. $3x + 4y = 12$ ★ 31. $y = -3$

400   **Chapter 8** Functions and Graphing

HANG GLIDING For Exercises 32–34, use the following information.
The altitude in feet y of a hang glider who is slowly landing can be given by $y = 300 - 50x$, where x represents the time in minutes.

★ **32.** Graph the equation using the slope and y-intercept. **See pp.431A–431H.**

★ **33.** State the slope and y-intercept of the graph of the equation and describe what they represent. **See margin.**

★ **34.** Name the x-intercept and describe what it represents.
6; the time in minutes that it takes the glider to land

35. CRITICAL THINKING What is the x-intercept of the graph of $y = mx + b$? Explain how you know. $-\dfrac{b}{m}$. **Replace y with 0 in $y = mx + b$ and solve for x.**

36. WRITING IN MATH Answer the question that was posed at the beginning of the lesson. **See margin.**

How can knowing the slope and y-intercept help you graph an equation?

Include the following in your answer:
- a description of how the slope-intercept form of an equation gives information, and
- an explanation of how you could write an equation for a line if you know the slope and y-intercept.

37. Which is $2x + 3y = 6$ written in slope-intercept form? **B**

Ⓐ $y = -\dfrac{2}{3}x - 2$ Ⓑ $y = -\dfrac{2}{3}x + 2$

Ⓒ $y = -\dfrac{3}{2}x + 2$ Ⓓ $y = \dfrac{3}{2}x - 2$

38. What is the slope and y-intercept of the graph of $-x + 2y = 6$? **D**

Ⓐ $-\dfrac{1}{2}, 1$ Ⓑ $1, 6$

Ⓒ $1, 3$ Ⓓ $\dfrac{1}{2}, 3$

Maintain Your Skills

Mixed Review Suppose y varies directly with x. Write an equation relating x and y for each pair of values. *(Lesson 8-5)*

39. $y = -36$ when $x = 9$ $y = -4x$ **40.** $y = 5$ when $x = 25$ $y = \dfrac{1}{5}x$

Find the slope of the line that passes through each pair of points.
(Lesson 8-4)

41. $A(3, 1), B(6, 7)$ **2** **42.** $J(-2, 5), K(8, 5)$ **0** **43.** $Q(2, 4), R(0, -4)$ **4**

44. Solve $4(r - 3) = 8$. *(Lesson 7-2)* **5**

45. Six times a number is 28 more than twice the number. Write an equation and find the number. *(Lesson 7-1)* $6x = 2x + 28; 7$

Getting Ready for the Next Lesson **PREREQUISITE SKILL** Simplify. *(To review order of operations, see Lesson 1-2.)*

46. $2(18) - 1$ **35** **47.** $(-2 - 4) \div 10$ $-\dfrac{3}{5}$

48. $-1(6) + 8$ **2** **49.** $5 - 8(-3)$ **29**

50. $(9 + 6) \div 3$ **5** **51.** $3 - (-2)(4)$ **11**

Answers

33. slope $= -50$, the descent in feet per minute; y-intercept $= 300$, initial altitude

36. Graph the y-intercept point. Then use the slope to locate a second point on the line. Draw a line through the two points. Answers should include the following.

- When an equation is written in slope-intercept form $y = mx + b$, the slope is m and the y-intercept is b.
- To write an equation of a line, substitute the known values for m and b in $y = mx + b$.

Study Notebook

Have students—
- add the definition/example of the vocabulary term to their Vocabulary Builder worksheets for Chapter 8.
- include any other item(s) that they find helpful in mastering the skills in this lesson.

About the Exercises . . .
Organization by Objective
- **Slope and y-Intercept:** 12–27
- **Graph Equations:** 18–32

Odd/Even Assignments
Exercises 12–31 are structured so that students practice the same concepts whether they are assigned odd or even problems.

Alert! Exercises 2, 7–10, and 18–32 require graph paper.

Assignment Guide
Basic: 13–27 odd, 35–51
Average: 13–35 odd, 36–51
Advanced: 12–34 even, 35–45 (Optional: 46–51)

Open-Ended Assessment
Writing Have students explain how to graph linear equations using slope and y-intercept.

Getting Ready for Lesson 8-7

PREREQUISITE SKILL Lesson 8-7 presents writing linear functions and evaluating them for given values. Exercises 46–51 should be used to determine students' familiarity with order of operations when evaluating expressions.

Know Your Calculator The graphing calculator has the ability to make the graphs appear differently on screen. The symbol before each Y= entry shows how the line will appear. Use the arrow keys to highlight a symbol repeatedly until a thin slanted line appears.

Standard Viewing Window
Pressing ZOOM 6 selects the standard viewing window.

Entering Multiple Functions To enter a new function while keeping the previously entered function, be sure to use the down arrow to enter the new function on a different line.

- If students find that TRACE shows r and θ values instead of x and y values, have them enter 2nd [Format] and highlight RectGC in the first line.

- Have students complete Exercises 1–13.

Families of Graphs

A graphing calculator is a valuable tool when investigating characteristics of linear functions. Before graphing, you must create a viewing window that shows both the x- and y-intercepts of the graph of a function.

You can use the standard viewing window $[-10, 10]$ scl: 1 by $[-10, 10]$ scl: 1 or set your own minimum and maximum values for the axes and the scale factor by using the WINDOW option.

You can use a TI-83 Plus graphing calculator to enter several functions and graph them at the same time on the same screen. This is useful when studying a **family of graphs**. A family of linear graphs is related by having the same slope or the same y-intercept.

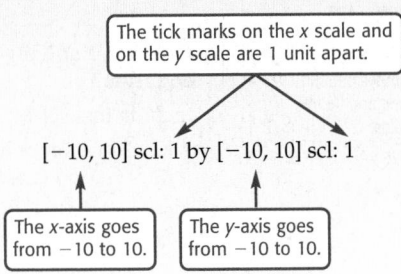

The tick marks on the x scale and on the y scale are 1 unit apart.

$[-10, 10]$ scl: 1 by $[-10, 10]$ scl: 1

The x-axis goes from -10 to 10.

The y-axis goes from -10 to 10.

Graph $y = 3x - 2$ and $y = 3x + 4$ in the standard viewing window and describe how the graphs are related.

Step 1 Graph $y = 3x + 4$ in the standard viewing window.

- Clear any existing equations from the Y= list.
  KEYSTROKES: Y= CLEAR

- Enter the equation and graph.
  KEYSTROKES: Y= 3 X,T,θ,n + 4 ZOOM 6

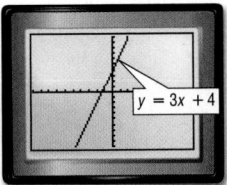

$y = 3x + 4$

Step 2 Graph $y = 3x - 2$.

- Enter the function $y = 3x - 2$ as Y2 with $y = 3x + 4$ already existing as Y1.
  KEYSTROKES: Y= 3 X,T,θ,n − 2

- Graph both functions in the standard viewing window.
  KEYSTROKES: ZOOM 6

The first function graphed is Y1 or $y = 3x + 4$. The second function graphed is Y2 or $y = 3x - 2$. Press TRACE . Move along each function using the right and left arrow keys. Move from one function to another using the up and down arrow keys. The graphs have the same slope, 3, but different y-intercepts at 4 and -2.

www.pre-alg.com/other_calculator_keystroke

Exercises

Graph $y = 2x - 5$, $y = 2x - 1$, and $y = 2x + 7$.

1. Compare and contrast the graphs. **They all have the same slope, different *y*-intercepts.**

2. How does adding or subtracting a constant c from a linear function affect its graph? **It shifts the graph vertically c units.**

3. Write an equation of a line whose graph is parallel to $y = 3x - 5$, but is shifted up 7 units. **$y = 3x + 2$**

4. Write an equation of the line that is parallel to $y = 3x - 5$ and passes through the origin. **$y = 3x$**

5. Four functions with a slope of 1 are graphed in the standard viewing window, as shown at the right. Write an equation for each, beginning with the left-most graph.
   $y = x + 6$, $y = x$, $y = x - 4$, $y = x - 7$

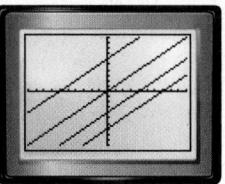

Clear all functions from the Y= menu and graph $y = \frac{1}{3}x$, $y = \frac{3}{4}x$, $y = x$, and $y = 4x$ in the standard viewing window. 6. See margin.

6. How does the steepness of a line change as the coefficient for x increases?

7. Without graphing, determine whether the graph of $y = 0.4x$ or the graph of $y = 1.4x$ has a steeper slope. Explain. **$y = 1.4x$, because $1.4 > 0.4$**

Clear all functions from the Y= menu and graph $y = -4x$ and $y = 4x$.

8. How are these two graphs different? **8–11. See margin.**

9. How does the sign of the coefficient of x affect the slope of a line?

10. Clear Y2. Then with $y = -4x$ as Y1, enter $y = -x$ as Y2 and $y = -\frac{1}{2}x$ as Y3.

   Graph the functions and draw the three graphs on grid paper. How does the steepness of the line change as the absolute value of the coefficient of x increases?

11. The graphs of $y = 3x + 1$, $y = \frac{1}{2}x + 1$, and $y = -x + 1$ are shown at the right. Draw the graphs on the same coordinate grid and label each graph with its equation.

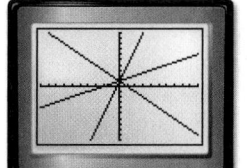

12. Describe the similarities and differences between the graph of $y = 2x - 3$ and the graph of each equation listed below.
   a. $y = 2x + 3$ **a–c. See margin.**
   b. $y = -2x - 3$
   c. $y = 0.5x + 3$

13. Write an equation of a line whose graph lies between the graphs of $y = -3x$ and $y = -6x$. **Sample answer: $y = -4x$**

Answers

6. As the coefficient of x increases, the line becomes steeper.

8. The graphs have opposite slopes; the graph of $y = -4x$ falls from left to right and the graph of $y = 4x$ rises from left to right.

9. If the coefficient is negative, the graph has a negative slope. If the coefficient is positive, the graph has a positive slope.

10. As the absolute value of the coefficient of x increases, the line becomes steeper.

Assess

Have students work individually using their graphing calculators to answer Exercises 12 and 13. Students should be able to operate the calculator with enough ease to be able to concentrate on the concept of families of functions.

Answers

11.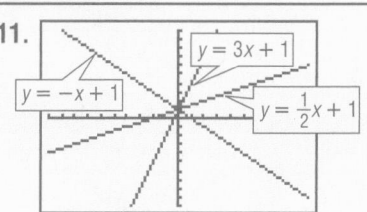

12a. same slope, different *y*-intercepts

12b. Same *y*-intercepts, opposite slopes; $y = 2x - 3$ slopes up from left to right and $y = -2x - 3$ slopes down from left to right.

12c. The graph of $y = 0.5x + 3$ is less steep and has a different *y*-intercept.

8-7 # Writing Linear Equations

1 Focus

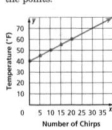 **5-Minute Check Transparency 8-7** Use as a quiz or review of Lesson 8-6.

Mathematical Background notes are available for this lesson on page 366D.

How can you model data with a linear equation?

The opening activity questions are repeated on page 450 of the *Chapter 8 Resource Masters.*

Reading to Learn Mathematics, p. 450 | ELL

Pre-Activity | *How can you model data with a linear equation?*

Do the activity at the top of page 404 in your textbook. Write your answers below.

a. Graph the ordered pairs (chirps, temperature). Draw a line through the points.

b. Find the slope and the y-intercept of the line. What do these values represent? Slope = 1 represents the rate of change, 1 degree for every 1 chirp; y-intercept = 40 represents the temperature at which the crickets are not chirping.

c. Write an equation in the form y = mx + b for the line then translate the equation into a sentence. y = x + 40; The temperature equals the number of chirps in 15 seconds plus 40.

Reading the Lesson

1. Explain how you can use the following information to write the slope-intercept form of a line.

a. graph of a line Find the y-intercept. From that point, count how many units up or down and how many units left or right to another point. The slope is the ratio of the rise over the run. Then substitute the slope and the y-intercept into the slope-intercept form.

b. two points on a line Substitute the coordinates of two points on the line into the definition of slope. Then use the slope and one of the points to find the y-intercept. Substitute the slope and the point's coordinates into slope-intercept form. Then substitute the slope and the y-intercept into the slope-intercept form.

c. a table of values Use the table to identify the coordinates of two points on the line. Then substitute the coordinates of the two points on the line into the definition of slope. Then use the slope and one of the points to find the y-intercept. Substitute the slope and the point's coordinates into slope-intercept form. Then substitute the slope and the y-intercept into the slope-intercept form.

What You'll Learn

- Write equations given the slope and y-intercept, a graph, a table, or two points.

How can you model data with a linear equation?

You can determine the approximate outside temperature by counting the chirps of crickets, as shown in the table.

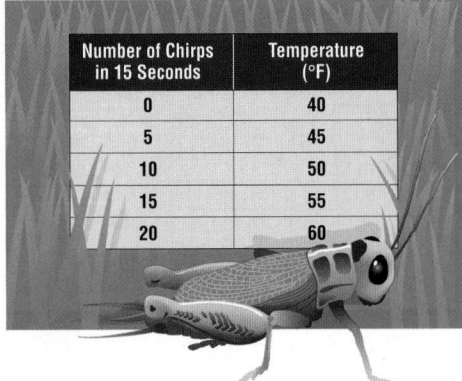

Number of Chirps in 15 Seconds	Temperature (°F)
0	40
5	45
10	50
15	55
20	60

a–b. See margin.

a. Graph the ordered pairs (chirps, temperature). Draw a line through the points.

b. Find the slope and the y-intercept of the line. What do these values represent?

c. *y = x + 40*; The temperature equals the number of chirps in 15 seconds plus 40.

c. Write an equation in the form $y = mx + b$ for the line. Then translate the equation into a sentence.

WRITE EQUATIONS There are many different methods for writing linear equations. If you know the slope and y-intercept, you can write the equation of a line by substituting these values in $y = mx + b$.

Example **1** *Write Equations From Slope and y-Intercept*

Write an equation in slope-intercept form for each line.

a. slope = 4, y-intercept = −8

$$y = mx + b \quad \text{Slope-intercept form}$$
$$y = 4x + (−8) \quad \text{Replace } m \text{ with 4 and } b \text{ with } −8.$$
$$y = 4x − 8 \quad \text{Simplify.}$$

b. slope = 0, y-intercept = 5

$$y = mx + b \quad \text{Slope-intercept form}$$
$$y = 0x + 5 \quad \text{Replace } m \text{ with 0 and } b \text{ with 5.}$$
$$y = 5 \quad \text{Simplify.}$$

c. slope = $-\frac{1}{2}$, y-intercept = 0

$$y = mx + b \quad \text{Slope-intercept form}$$
$$y = -\frac{1}{2}x + 0 \quad \text{Replace } m \text{ with } -\frac{1}{2} \text{ and } b \text{ with 0.}$$
$$y = -\frac{1}{2}x \quad \text{Simplify.}$$

Resource Manager

📁 **Workbooks and Reproducible Masters**

Chapter 8 Resource Masters
- Study Guide and Intervention, p. 447
- Skills Practice, p. 448
- Practice, p. 449
- Reading to Learn Mathematics, p. 450
- Enrichment, p. 451

Parent and Student Study Guide Workbook, p. 67

 Transparencies
5-Minute Check Transparency 8-7
Answer Key Transparencies

 Technology
Interactive Chalkboard

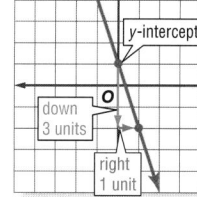
You can also write equations from a graph.

Example 2 *Write an Equation From a Graph*

Write an equation in slope-intercept form for the line graphed.

The *y*-intercept is 1. From (0, 1), you can go down 3 units and right 1 unit to another point on the line. So, the slope is $\frac{-3}{1}$, or -3.

$y = mx + b$ Slope-intercept form
$y = -3x + 1$ Replace *m* with -3 and *b* with 1.

In Lesson 8-3, you explored the relationship between altitude and temperature. You can write an equation for this relationship and use it to make predictions.

Example 3 *Write an Equation to Solve a Problem*

EARTH SCIENCE   On a summer day, the temperature at altitude 0, or sea level, is 30°C. The temperature decreases 2°C for every 305 meters increase in altitude.

a. Write an equation to show the relationship between altitude *x* and temperature *y*.

Words   Temperature decreases 2°C for every 305 meters increase in altitude.

Variables   Let *x* = the altitude and let *y* = the temperature.

Equations   Use $m = \frac{\text{change in } y}{\text{change in } x}$ and $y = mx + b$.

Step 1
Find the slope *m*.

$m = \dfrac{\text{change in } y}{\text{change in } x}$ ← change in temperature
   ← change in altitude

$= \dfrac{-2}{305}$ ← decrease of -2°C
   ← increase of 305 m

≈ -0.007 Simplify.

Step 2
Find the *y*-intercept *b*.

$(x, y) = $ (altitude, temperature)
   $= (0, b)$

When the altitude is 0, or sea level, the temperature is 30°C. So, the *y*-intercept is 30.

Step 3
Write the equation.

$y = mx + b$ Slope-intercept form
$y = -0.007x + 30$ Replace *m* with -0.007 and *b* with 30.

So, the equation that represents this situation is $y = -0.007x + 30$.

b. Predict the temperature for an altitude of 2000 meters.

$y = -0.007x + 30$ Write the equation.
$y = -0.007(2000) + 30$ Replace *x* with 2000.
$y \approx 16$ Simplify.

So, at an altitude of 2000 meters, the temperature is about 16°C.

WRITE EQUATIONS

In-Class Examples Power Point®

1 Write an equation in slope-intercept form for each line.

a. slope $= -\dfrac{1}{4}$, *y*-intercept $= 7$
$y = -\dfrac{1}{4}x + 7$

b. slope $= 0$, *y*-intercept $= -3$
$y = -3$

c. slope $= 2$, *y*-intercept $= 0$
$y = 2x$

2 Write an equation in slope-intercept form for the line graphed.

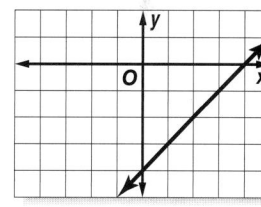

$y = x + (-4)$ or $y = x - 4$

3 **BUSINESS** The owners of the Good Times Eatery surveyed their customers to find out where they lived. They learned that for each 5-mile radius from their restaurant, 30 fewer people visited them. They had 150 patrons in the area immediately surrounding the diner.

a. Write an equation to show the relationship between miles *x* and customers *y*.
$y = -6x + 150$

b. Predict the number of customers who lived 20 miles away.   **30**

4 Write an equation for the line that passes through $(7, 0)$ and $(6, 3)$.
$y = -3x + 21$

5 Use the table of values to write an equation in slope-intercept form.
$y = -6x + 4$

x	y
-2	16
-1	10
0	4
1	-2

3 Practice/Apply

Study Notebook

Have students—
- copy Example 4 into their notebooks and illustrate the equation with a graph.
- include any other item(s) that they find helpful in mastering the skills in this lesson.

About the Exercises . . .

Odd/Even Assignments
Exercises 11–30 are structured so that students practice the same concepts whether they are assigned odd or even problems.

Assignment Guide
Basic: 11–29 odd, 33–41
Average: 11–33 odd, 34–41
Advanced: 12–32 even, 33–40
(Optional: 41)

You can also write an equation for a line if you know the coordinates of two points on a line.

Example 4 *Write an Equation Given Two Points*

Write an equation for the line that passes through $(-2, 5)$ and $(2, 1)$.

Step 1 Find the slope m.

$m = \dfrac{y_2 - y_1}{x_2 - x_1}$ Definition of slope

$m = \dfrac{5 - 1}{-2 - 2}$ or -1 $(x_1, y_1) = (-2, 5)$, $(x_2, y_2) = (2, 1)$

Step 2 Find the y-intercept b. Use the slope and the coordinates of either point.

$y = mx + b$ Slope-intercept form
$5 = -1(-2) + b$ Replace (x, y) with $(-2, 5)$ and m with -1.
$3 = b$ Simplify.

Step 3 Substitute the slope and y-intercept.

$y = mx + b$ Slope-intercept form
$y = -1x + 3$ Replace m with -1 and b with 3.
$y = -x + 3$ Simplify.

Example 5 *Write an Equation From a Table*

Use the table of values to write an equation in slope-intercept form.

x	y
-5	6
5	-2
10	-6
15	-10

Step 1 Find the slope m. Use the coordinates of any two points.

$m = \dfrac{y_2 - y_1}{x_2 - x_1}$ Definition of slope

$m = \dfrac{-2 - 6}{5 - (-5)}$ or $-\dfrac{4}{5}$ $(x_1, y_1) = (-5, 6)$, $(x_2, y_2) = (5, -2)$

Study Tip

Alternate Strategy
If a table includes the y-intercept, simply use this value and the slope to write an equation.

x	y
-5	6
0	2

y-intercept = 2

Step 2 Find the y-intercept b. Use the slope and the coordinates of any point.

$y = mx + b$ Slope-intercept form
$6 = -\dfrac{4}{5}(-5) + b$ Replace (x, y) with $(-5, 6)$ and m with $-\dfrac{4}{5}$.
$2 = b$ Simplify.

Step 3 Substitute the slope and y-intercept.

$y = mx + b$ Slope-intercept form
$y = -\dfrac{4}{5}x + 2$ Replace m with $-\dfrac{4}{5}$ and b with 2.

CHECK $y = -\dfrac{4}{5}x + 2$ Write the equation.

$-10 \overset{?}{=} -\dfrac{4}{5}(15) + 2$ Replace (x, y) with the coordinates of another point, $(15, -10)$.
$-10 = -10 \checkmark$ Simplify.

406 Chapter 8 Functions and Graphing

DAILY INTERVENTION

Unlocking Misconceptions

- **Use Two Points on the Line** Some students may mistakenly believe that they must choose points in a particular order, such as left to right, or such that the smaller number is subtracted from the larger number. Demonstrate that any arrangement of any two points on the line will result in the same equation in slope-intercept form. Switch the position of the points in Example 4 and find the equation.

Concept Check

1. **Explain** how to write the equation of a line if you are given a graph.

1–2. See margin.

2. **OPEN ENDED** Choose a slope and y-intercept. Then graph the line.

Guided Practice

Write an equation in slope-intercept form for each line. 4. $y = -7$

GUIDED PRACTICE KEY	
Exercises	Examples
3, 4	1
5, 6	2
7, 8	4
9	5
10	3

3. slope = $\frac{1}{2}$, y-intercept = 1 $y = \frac{1}{2}x + 1$ 4. slope = 0, y-intercept = -7

5. 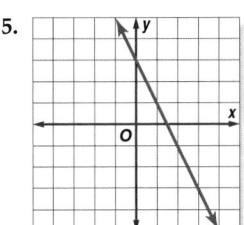 $y = -2x + 3$ 6. 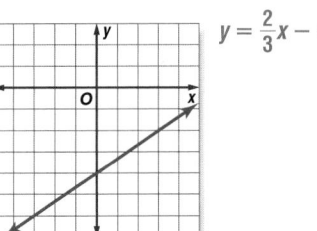 $y = \frac{2}{3}x - 4$

Write an equation in slope-intercept form for the line passing through each pair of points.

7. (2, 2) and (4, 3) $y = \frac{1}{2}x + 1$

8. (3, −4) and (−1, 4) $y = -2x + 2$

9. $y = \frac{3}{4}x - 1$

9. Write an equation in slope-intercept form to represent the table of values.

x	−4	0	4	8
y	−4	−1	2	5

Application

10. **PICNICS** It costs $50 plus $10 per hour to rent a park pavilion.

   a. Write an equation in slope-intercept form that shows the cost y for renting the pavilion for x hours. $y = 10x + 50$

   b. Find the cost of renting the pavilion for 8 hours. $130

★ indicates increased difficulty

Practice and Apply

Homework Help	
For Exercises	See Examples
11–16	1
17–22	2
23–28	4
29, 30	5
31–33	3

Extra Practice
See page 743.

Write an equation in slope-intercept form for each line. 12. $y = -4x + 1$

11. slope = 2, y-intercept = 6 $y = 2x + 6$ 12. slope = −4, y-intercept = 1

13. slope = 0, y-intercept = 5 $y = 5$ 14. slope = 1, y-intercept = −2

15. slope = $-\frac{1}{3}$, y-intercept = 8 16. slope = $\frac{2}{5}$, y-intercept = 0 $y = \frac{2}{5}x$

14. $y = x - 2$

15. $y = -\frac{1}{3}x + 8$

17. $y = 2x + 3$

18. $y = -x + 6$

19. $y = -2.5$

20. $y = 4x - 5$

21. $y = -\frac{1}{2}x$

22. $y = \frac{1}{4}x + 2$

17. 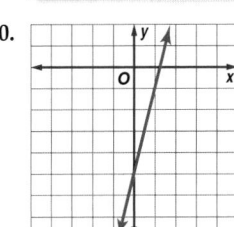 18. 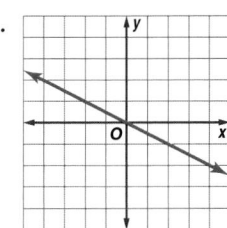 19.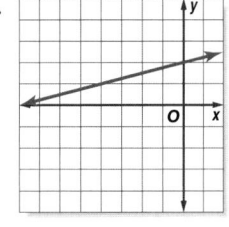

20. 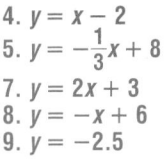 21. 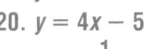 22.

Answers

1. Sample answer: Find the y-intercept b and another point on the line. Use the points to determine the slope m. Then substitute these values in $y = mx + b$ and write the equation.

2. Sample answer: State the slope and y-intercept. Include a graph whose y-intercept point and another point on the line are both labeled. Show how the slope was used to graph the line.

Study Guide and Intervention, p. 447

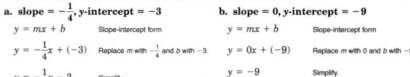

If you know the slope and y-intercept, you can write the equation of a line by substituting these values in $y = mx + b$.

Example 1

Write an equation in slope-intercept form for each line.

a. slope = $-\frac{1}{4}$, y-intercept = -3
   $y = mx + b$ Slope-intercept form
   $y = -\frac{1}{4}x + (-3)$ Replace m with $-\frac{1}{4}$ and b with -3.
   $y = -\frac{1}{4}x - 3$ Simplify.

b. slope = 0, y-intercept = -9
   $y = mx + b$ Slope-intercept form
   $y = 0x + (-9)$ Replace m with 0 and b with -9.
   $y = -9$ Simplify.

Example 2

Write an equation in slope-intercept form for the line passing through $(-4, 4)$ and $(2, 7)$.

Step 1 Find the slope m.
   $m = \frac{y_2 - y_1}{x_2 - x_1}$ Definition of slope
   $m = \frac{7 - 4}{2 - (-4)}$ or $\frac{1}{2}$ $(x_1, y_1) = (-4, 4)$, $(x_2, y_2) = (2, 7)$

Step 2 Find the y-intercept b. Use the slope and the coordinates of either point.
   $y = mx + b$ Slope-intercept form
   $4 = \frac{1}{2}(-4) + b$ Replace (x, y) with $(-4, 4)$ and m with $\frac{1}{2}$.
   $6 = b$ Simplify.

An equation is $y = \frac{1}{2}x + 6$.

Exercises

Write an equation in slope-intercept form for each line.

1. slope = 1, y-intercept = 2 $y = x + 2$
2. slope = $-\frac{3}{4}$, y-intercept = -5 $y = -\frac{3}{4}x - 5$
3. slope = 0, y-intercept = -3 $y = -3$

Write an equation in slope-intercept form for the line passing through each pair of points.

4. (6, 2) and (3, 1) $y = \frac{1}{3}x$
5. (8, 8) and (−4, 5) $y = \frac{1}{4}x + 6$
6. (7, −3) and (−5, −3) $y = -3$

Skills Practice, p. 448 and Practice, p. 449 (shown)

Write an equation in slope-intercept form for each line.

1. slope = 3, y-intercept = −2 $y = 3x - 2$
2. slope = 0, y-intercept = 7 $y = 7$
3. 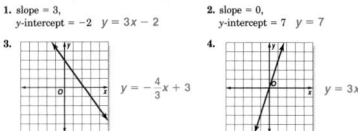 $y = -\frac{4}{3}x + 3$
4. $y = 3x$

Write an equation in slope-intercept form for the line passing through each pair of points.

5. (9, 0) and (6, −1) $y = \frac{1}{3}x - 3$
6. (8, 6) and (−8, 2) $y = \frac{1}{4}x + 4$
7. (7, −5) and (−4, −5) $y = -5$
8. (2, 7) and (−1, 4) $y = x + 5$
9. (4, 4) and (−8, 10) $y = -\frac{1}{2}x + 6$
10. (0, 2) and (−3, 14) $y = -4x + 2$

BUSINESS For Exercises 11 and 12, use the following information.
Flourishing Flowers charges $125 plus $60 for each standard floral arrangement to deliver and set up flowers for a banquet.

11. Write an equation in slope-intercept form that shows the cost y for flowers for x number of arrangements. $y = 60x + 125$

12. Find the cost of providing 20 floral arrangements. $1325

INSULATION For Exercises 13 and 14, use the following information.
Renata González wants to increase the energy efficiency of her house by adding to the insulation previously installed. The better a material protects against heat loss, the higher its R-value, or resistance to heat flow. The table shows the R-value of fiberglass blanket insulation per inch of thickness. The existing insulation in Renata's attic has an R-value of 10.

R-value	Thickness (in.)
0.0	0
3.2	1
6.4	2
9.6	3

Source: Oak Ridge National Laboratory

13. Write an equation in slope-intercept form that shows the total R-value y in the attic if she adds x number of inches of additional insulation. $y = 3.2x + 10$

14. Estimate the total R-value in the attic if she adds 6 inches of insulation. 29.2

Enrichment, p. 451

Problem Solving: Gathering Data

When investors decide to buy or sell stock, they usually base their decisions on data. They read stock market reports, investigate companies they are interested in, and look at economic trends. This activity focuses on reading stock market reports.

To read a stock market report, you need to become familiar with the terms that are used, the facts and figures that are published in the newspaper, and the methods used to keep track of the stocks.

Many newspapers print stock reports such as the New York Stock Exchange (NYSE) report. The final entry for each stock is a fraction or mixed number that is positive (indicating a gain in value) or negative (indicating a loss).

Find the New York Stock Exchange (NYSE) report in the business section of your local Sunday newspaper. Using just those stocks that begin with A, B, or C, tally the number of stocks that had each of the gains and losses listed below.

+2 points or more		+1.00		−.12		−1.12	
+1.87		+.87		−.25		−1.25	
+1.75		+.75		−.37		−1.37	
+1.62		+.62		−.50		−1.50	
+1.50		+.50		−.62		−1.62	
+1.37		+.37		−.75		−1.75	
+1.25		+.25		−.87		−1.87	
+1.12		+.12		−1.00		−2 points or more	
+1.12		No change					

1–5. Answers will vary.

1. Did more stocks gain in value or lose value?
2. How did the market do as a whole?
3. How did the newspapers describe the trading this week?
4. Make a scatterplot that shows how two specific stocks change over the period of one week. Use their daily closing prices.
5. Is there any relationship between the two stocks you chose? Explain why or why not.

4 Assess

Open-Ended Assessment

Writing Have students write a paragraph comparing the methods for writing linear functions shown in Example 2 and Example 4. Suggest that they use the same pair of points with both methods. **Students should note that both methods use two points and the concept of rise over run.**

Tips for New Teachers

Intervention If there is any doubt whether your students thoroughly understand writing linear functions, consider spending an extra day on this lesson. Use the Extra Practice on p. 743. You can also use the Study Guide and Intervention masters or the Practice masters in the *Chapter 8 Resource Masters* to reinforce this concept.

Getting Ready for Lesson 8-8

PREREQUISITE SKILL Lesson 8-8 presents best-fit lines drawn on scatter plots. Exercise 41 should be used to determine your students' familiarity with scatter plots.

Answers

31. $y = 1088x$; The speed of sound is 1088 feet per second.

34. Write the data as ordered pairs and graph the points. Then draw a line through the points. Find the slope and y-intercept of the line and substitute the values in $y = mx + b$. Answers should include the following.

- The y-intercept is the y value in the table when the corresponding x value is 0. Use two pairs of x- and y-coordinates in the table to find the slope.

---

23. $y = x + 1$
24. $y = -\frac{1}{2}x + 1$
25. $y = -x$
26. $y = \frac{3}{2}x - 4$

More About . . .

Sound

Coyotes communicate by using different barks and howls. Because of the way in which sound travels, a coyote is usually not in the area from which the sound seems to be coming.

Source: www.livingdesert.org

Standardized Test Practice
Ⓐ Ⓑ Ⓒ Ⓓ

Write an equation in slope-intercept form for the line passing through each pair of points.

23. $(-2, -1)$ and $(1, 2)$ 24. $(-4, 3)$ and $(4, -1)$ 25. $(0, 0)$ and $(-1, 1)$
26. $(4, 2)$ and $(-8, -16)$ 27. $(8, 7)$ and $(-9, 7)$ 28. $(5, -6)$ and $(3, 2)$
   $y = 7$ $y = -4x + 14$

Write an equation in slope-intercept form for each table of values.

29.

x	−1	0	1	2
y	−7	−3	1	5

$y = 4x - 3$

30.

x	−3	−1	1	3
y	7	5	3	1

$y = -x + 4$

SOUND For Exercises 31 and 32, use the table that shows the distance that sound travels through dry air at 0°C.

Time(s) x	Distance (ft) y
0	0
1	1088
2	2176
3	3264

31. See margin.

★ 31. Write an equation in slope-intercept form to represent the data in the table. Describe what the slope means.

★ 32. Estimate the number of miles that sound travels through dry air in one minute. **12.4 mi**

33. **CRITICAL THINKING** A CD player has a pre-sale price of c. Kim buys it at a 30% discount and pays 6% sales tax. After a few months, she sells it for d, which was 50% of what she paid originally.

   a. Express d as a function of c. $d = 0.5(0.7c \times 1.06)$ or $d = 0.371c$
   b. How much did Kim sell it for if the pre-sale price was $50? **$18.55**

34. **WRITING IN MATH** Answer the question that was posed at the beginning of the lesson. **See margin.**

   How can you model data with a linear equation?
   Include the following in your answer:
   • an explanation of how to find the y-intercept and slope by using a table.

35. Which equation is of a line that passes through $(2, -2)$ and $(0, 2)$? **C**
   Ⓐ $y = -3x$ Ⓑ $y = -2x + 3$ Ⓒ $y = -2x + 2$ Ⓓ $y = -3x + 2$

36. Which equation represents the table of values? **C**
   Ⓐ $y = -2x + 4$ Ⓑ $y = 2x + 6$
   Ⓒ $y = -\frac{1}{2}x + 4$ Ⓓ $y = -x - 6$

x	−4	−8	−12	−16
y	6	8	10	12

Maintain Your Skills

Mixed Review

State the slope and the y-intercept for the graph of each equation.
(Lesson 8-6)

37. $y = 6x + 7$ **6; 7**   38. $y = -x + 4$ **−1; 4**   39. $-3x + y = -2$ **3; −2**

40. Suppose y varies directly as x and $y = 14$ when $x = 35$. Write an equation relating x and y. *(Lesson 8-5)* $y = \frac{2}{5}x$

Getting Ready for the Next Lesson

PREREQUISITE SKILL *(To review scatter plots, see Lesson 1-7.)*

41. State whether a scatter plot containing the following set of points would show a *positive*, *negative*, or *no* relationship.
   $(0, 15), (2, 20), (4, 36), (5, 44), (4, 32), (3, 30), (6, 50)$ **positive**

What You'll Learn

- Draw best-fit lines for sets of data.
- Use best-fit lines to make predictions about data.

Vocabulary
- best-fit line

How can a line be used to predict life expectancy for future generations?

The scatter plot shows the number of years people in the United States are expected to live, according to the year they were born.

a. Use the line drawn through the points to predict the life expectancy of a person born in 2010. **83**

b. What are some limitations in using a line to predict life expectancy? **See margin.**

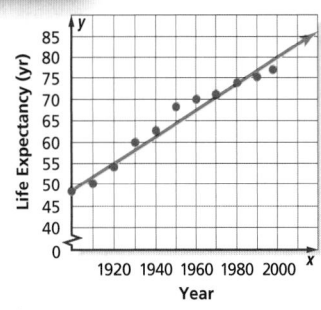

Source: *The World Almanac*

Study Tip

Estimation
Drawing a best-fit line using the method in this lesson is an estimation. Therefore, it is possible to draw different lines to approximate the same data.

BEST-FIT LINES When real-life data are collected, the points graphed usually do not form a straight line, but may approximate a linear relationship. A best-fit line can be used to show such a relationship. A **best-fit line** is a line that is very close to most of the data points.

Example 1 Make Predictions from a Best-Fit Line

MONEY The table shows the changes in the minimum wage since 1980.

TEACHING TIP

Explain to students that lines of best fit can be calculated using sophisticated statistical methods, rather than the visual estimations used in this lesson.

a. Make a scatter plot and draw a best-fit line for the data.

Draw a line that best fits the data.

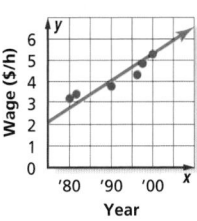

Year	Wage ($/h)
1980	3.10
1981	3.35
1990	3.80
1996	4.25
1997	4.75
2000	5.15

b. Use the best-fit line to predict the minimum wage for the year 2010.

Extend the line so that you can find the y value for an x value of 2010. The y value for 2010 is about 6.4. So, a prediction for the minimum wage in 2010 is approximately $6.40.

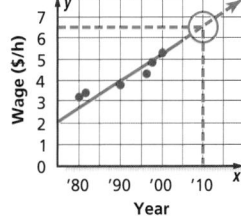

---

1 Focus

5-Minute Check Transparency 8-8 Use as a quiz or review of Lesson 8-7.

Mathematical Background notes are available for this lesson on page 366D.

How can a line be used to predict life expectancy for future generations?

The opening activity questions are repeated on page 455 of the *Chapter 8 Resource Masters.*

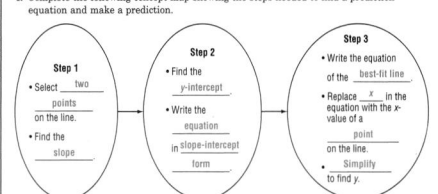

Reading to Learn Mathematics, p. 455 ELL

Pre-Activity How can a line be used to predict life expectancy for future generations?

Do the activity at the top of page 409 in your textbook. Write your answers below.

a. Use the line drawn through the points to predict the life expectancy of a person born in 2010. **83**

b. What are some limitations in using a line to predict life expectancy? Sample answer: Medical improvements could change the accuracy of the model. Also, the line continues to go up, but people's ages will not increase forever.

Reading the Lesson

Write a definition and give an example of the new vocabulary phrase.

Vocabulary	Definition	Example
1. slope intercept form	See students' work.	

2. A best-fit line can be used when the data points approximate a ___linear___ relationship.

3. Explain what a prediction equation is. A prediction equation is an equation of a best-fit line used to tell what course the data will likely take in the future.

Helping You Remember

4. Complete the following concept map showing the steps needed to find a prediction equation and make a prediction.

Resource Manager

Workbooks and Reproducible Masters

Chapter 8 Resource Masters
- Study Guide and Intervention, p. 452
- Skills Practice, p. 453
- Practice, p. 454
- Reading to Learn Mathematics, p. 455
- Enrichment, p. 456
- Assessment, p. 482

Parent and Student Study Guide Workbook, p. 68

Transparencies
5-Minute Check Transparency 8-8
Real-World Transparency 8
Answer Key Transparencies

Technology
Interactive Chalkboard

BEST-FIT LINES

In-Class Example Power Point®

1 **AGRICULTURE** The table shows the amount of land in U. S. farms from 1980 to 2000.

Year	Land (million acres)
1980	1039
1985	1012
1990	986
1995	963
2000	943

Source: U.S. Department of Agriculture

a. Make a scatter plot and draw a best-fit line for the data.

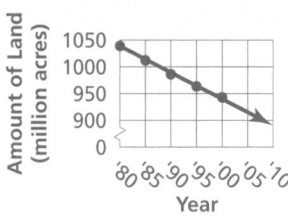

b. Use the best-fit line to predict the amount of land in the year 2010. **about 892 million acres**

PREDICTION EQUATIONS

In-Class Example Power Point®

2 **AGRICULTURE** The scatter plot shows the number of milk cow operations in New Mexico from 1975 to 1995.

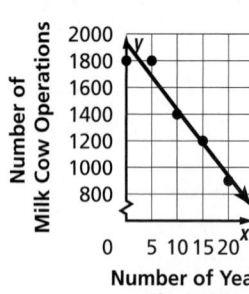

Source: U.S. Department of Agriculture

a. Write an equation in slope-intercept form for the best-fit line.
$y = -48x + 1920$

b. Predict the number of milk cow operations in the year 2005. **about 480**

PREDICTION EQUATIONS You can also make predictions from the equation of a best-fit line.

Example 2 **Make Predictions from an Equation**

SWIMMING The scatter plot shows the winning Olympic times in the women's 800-meter freestyle event from 1968 through 2000.

TEACHING TIP
If you extend the best-fit line, it will cross the x-axis, making the winning time 0 seconds. This is not possible and shows one limitation of using a model to predict real-world situations.

a. Write an equation in slope-intercept form for the best-fit line.

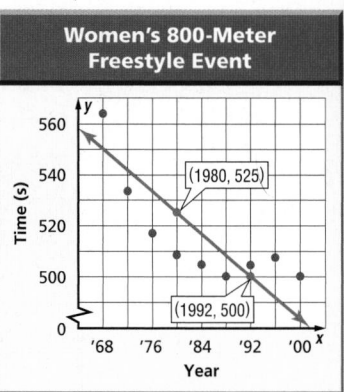

Women's 800-Meter Freestyle Event

Step 1

First, select two points on the line and find the slope. Notice that the two points on the best-fit line are not original data points. We have chosen (1980, 525) and (1992, 500).

$m = \dfrac{y_2 - y_1}{x_2 - x_1}$ Definition of slope

$= \dfrac{525 - 500}{1980 - 1992}$ $(x_1, y_1) = (1992, 500)$, $(x_2, y_2) = (1980, 525)$

≈ -2.1 Simplify.

Step 2

Next, find the y-intercept.

$y = mx + b$ Slope-intercept form

$525 = -2.1(1980) + b$ Replace (x, y) with (1980, 525) and m with -2.1.

$4683 \approx b$ Simplify.

Step 3

Write the equation.

$y = mx + b$ Slope-intercept form

$y = -2.1x + 4683$ Replace m with -2.1 and b with 4683.

b. Predict the winning time in the women's 800-meter freestyle event in the year 2008.

$y = -2.1x + 4683$ Write the equation of the best-fit line.

$y = -2.1(2008) + 4683$ Replace x with 2008.

$y \approx 466.2$ Simplify.

A prediction for the winning time in the year 2008 is approximately 466.2 seconds or 7 minutes, 46.2 seconds.

Check for Understanding

Concept Check
1–2. See margin.

1. **Explain** how to use a best-fit line to make a prediction.

2. **OPEN ENDED** Make a scatter plot with at least ten points that appear to be somewhat linear. Draw two different lines that could approximate the data.

Guided Practice

GUIDED PRACTICE KEY

Exercises	Examples
3, 4	1
5, 6	2

TECHNOLOGY For Exercises 3 and 4, use the table that shows the number of U.S. households with Internet access. 3. See margin.

3. Make a scatter plot and draw a best-fit line.

4. Use the best-fit line to predict the number of U.S. households that will have Internet access in 2005. **Sample answer: 65 million**

Year	Number of Households (millions)
1995	9.4
1996	14.7
1997	21.3
1998	27.3
1999	32.7
2000	36.0

Source: Wall Street Journal Almanac

Application

SPENDING For Exercises 5 and 6, use the best-fit line that shows the billions of dollars spent by travelers in the United States.

5. Write an equation in slope-intercept form for the best-fit line. $y = 20x + 320$

6. Use the equation to predict how much money travelers will spend in 2008. **$620 billion**

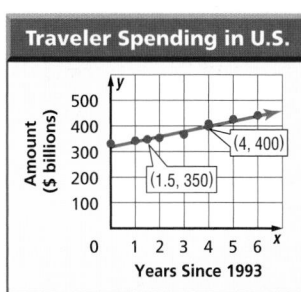

Traveler Spending in U.S.

★ indicates increased difficulty

Practice and Apply

Homework Help

For Exercises	See Examples
7, 8, 12, 13	1
9–11, 14–17	2

Extra Practice
See page 744.

ENTERTAINMENT For Exercises 7 and 8, use the table that shows movie attendance in the United States. 7. See pp. 431A–431H.

7. Make a scatter plot and draw a best-fit line.

8. Use the best-fit line to predict movie attendance in 2005. **Sample answer: 1700 million**

Year	Attendance (millions)
1993	1244
1994	1292
1995	1263
1996	1339
1997	1388
1998	1475
1999	1460

Source: Wall Street Journal Almanac

10. Sample answer: $y = -0.0006x + 27$; -9; this is not reasonable because barometric pressure cannot be negative.

11. No, the equation gives a negative value for barometric pressure, which is not possible. Also, the data in the scatter plot do not appear to be linear.

PRESSURE For Exercises 9–11, use the table that shows the approximate barometric pressure at various altitudes.

9. Make a scatter plot of the data and draw a best-fit line. See pp. 431A–431H.

★ 10. Write an equation for the best-fit line and use it to estimate the barometric pressure at 60,000 feet. Is the estimation reasonable? Explain.

★ 11. Do you think that a line is the best model for this data? Explain.

Altitude (ft)	Barometric Pressure (in. mercury)
0	30
5000	25
10,000	21
20,000	14
30,000	9
40,000	6
50,000	3

Source: New York Public Library Science Desk Reference

www.pre-alg.com/self_check_quiz

Answers (p. 410)

1. Sample answer: Use a ruler to extend the line so that it passes through the *x* value for which you want to predict. Locate the *x* value on the line and determine the corresponding *y* value. Or, write an equation for the best-fit line and substitute the desired value of *x* to find the corresponding value of *y*.

2. Sample answer:

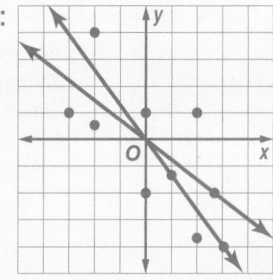

Study Notebook

Have students—

• add the definition/example of the vocabulary term to their Vocabulary Builder worksheets for Chapter 8.

• copy Exercises 3 and 4, including the answers, into their notebooks.

• include any other item(s) that they find helpful in mastering the skills in this lesson.

About the Exercises . . .

Organization by Objective
• Best-Fit Lines: 7, 9, 12, 14
• Prediction Equations: 8, 10–11, 13, 15–17

Odd/Even Assignments
Exercises 7–10 and 12–17 are structured so that students practice the same concepts whether they are assigned odd or even problems.

Alert! Exercises 2, 3, 7, 9, 12, and 14 require graph paper.

Assignment Guide
Basic: 7, 9, 12, 13, 15, 17–42
Average: 7–11 odd, 12, 13, 15, 17–42
Advanced: 8–12 even, 13, 14–18 even, 20–36 (Optional: 37–42)

Answer

3. Sample answer:

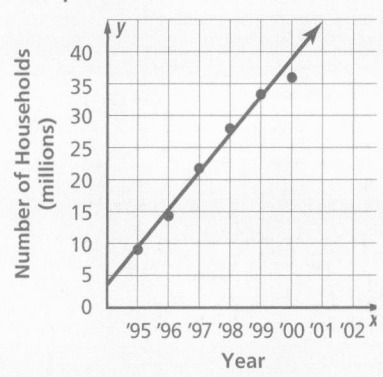

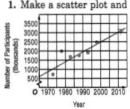
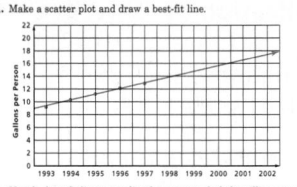
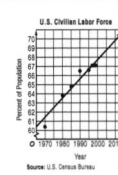
16. Sample answer:
$y = -1.33x + 127.8$

•**POLE VAULTING** For Exercises 12 and 13, use the table that shows the men's winning Olympic pole vault heights to the nearest inch.

Year	Height (in.)
1976	217
1980	228
1984	226
1988	232
1992	228
1996	233
2000	232

Source: *The World Almanac*

12. Make a scatter plot and draw a best-fit line. **See pp. 431A–431H.**

13. Use the best-fit line to predict the winning pole vault height in the 2008 Olympics. **Sample answer: 238 in.**

EARTH SCIENCE For Exercises 14–17, use the table that shows the latitude and the average temperature in July for five cities in the United States.

City	Latitude (°N)	Average July High Temperature (°F)
Chicago, IL	41	73
Dallas, TX	32	85
Denver, CO	39	74
New York, NY	40	77
Duluth, MN	46	66

Source: *The World Almanac*

14. Make a scatter plot of the data and draw a best-fit line. **See pp. 431A–431H.**

15. Describe the relationship between latitude and temperature shown by the graph. **As latitude increases, temperature decreases.**

★ 16. Write an equation for the best-fit line you drew in Exercise 14.

17. Use your equation to estimate the average July temperature for a location with latitude 50° north. **Sample answer: 61.3°F**

18. **CRITICAL THINKING** The table at the right shows the percent of public schools in the United States with Internet access. Suppose you use (Year, Percent of Schools) to write a linear equation describing the data. Then you use (Years Since 1996, Percent of Schools) to write an equation. Is the slope or y-intercept of the graphs of the equations the same? Explain. **See margin.**

Year	Years Since 1996	Percent of Schools
1996	0	65
1997	1	78
1998	2	89
1999	3	95
2000	4	98

Source: National Center for Education Statistics

19. **WRITING IN MATH** Answer the question that was posed at the beginning of the lesson. **See margin.**

How can a line be used to predict life expectancy for future generations?

Include the following in your answer:
• a description of a best-fit line, and
• an explanation of how lines can represent sets of data that are not exactly linear.

412 Chapter 8 Functions and Graphing

20. Use the best-fit line at the right to predict the value of y when $x = 7$. **B**

    (A) 4   (B) 6

    (C) 0   (D) 7

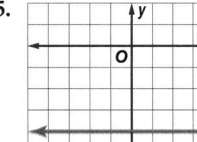

21. Choose the correct statement about best-fit lines. **A**

    (A) A best-fit line is close to most of the data points.

    (B) A best-fit line describes the exact coordinates of each point in the data set.

    (C) A best-fit line always has a positive slope.

    (D) A best-fit line must go through at least two of the data points.

Maintain Your Skills

Mixed Review

22. $y = 3x + 5$
23. $y = -2x + 2$

Write an equation in slope-intercept form for each line. *(Lesson 8-7)*

22. slope $= 3$, y-intercept $= 5$ **23.** slope $= -2$, y-intercept $= 2$

24. 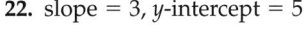   **25.**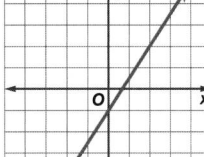

$y = \frac{3}{2}x - 1$ $y = -4$

Graph each equation using the slope and y-intercept. *(Lesson 8-6)*

26. $y = x - 2$ **27.** $y = -x + 3$ **28.** $y = \frac{1}{2}x$

26–28. See margin.

Solve each inequality and check your solution. *(Lesson 7-6)* **31.** $d > -\frac{3}{2}$

29. $3n - 11 \leq 10$ **30.** $8(x + 1) < 16$ **31.** $5d + 2 > d - 4$

    $n \leq 7$ $x < 1$

32. SCHOOL Zach has no more than twelve days to complete his science project. Write an inequality to represent this sentence. *(Lesson 7-3)* $d \leq 12$

Solve each proportion. *(Lesson 6-2)*

33. $\frac{a}{3} = \frac{16}{24}$ **2**   **34.** $\frac{5}{10} = \frac{15}{x}$ **30**   **35.** $\frac{2}{16} = \frac{n}{36}$ **4.5**

36. Evaluate xy if $x = \frac{8}{9}$ and $y = \frac{12}{30}$. Write in simplest form. *(Lesson 5-3)* $\frac{16}{45}$

Getting Ready for the Next Lesson

PREREQUISITE SKILL Find the value of y in each equation by substituting the given value of x. *(To review substitution, see Lesson 1-2.)*

37. $y = x + 1; x = 2$ **3**   **38.** $y = x + 5; x = -1$ **4**

39. $y = x - 4; x = 3$ **−1**   **40.** $x + y = 2; x = 0$ **2**

41. $x + y = -1; x = 1$ **−2**   **42.** $x + y = 0; x = 4$ **−4**

Answers

26. 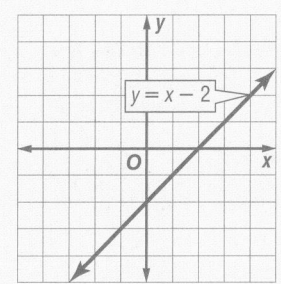   **27.** 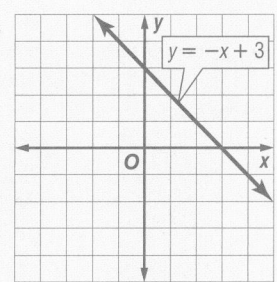   **28.**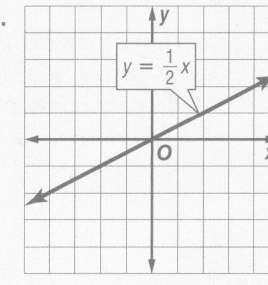

8-9 Solving Systems of Equations

1 Focus

5-Minute Check Transparency 8-9 Use as a quiz or review of Lesson 8-8.

Mathematical Background notes are available for this lesson on page 366D.

How can a system of equations be used to compare data?

The opening activity questions are repeated on page 460 of the *Chapter 8 Resource Masters*.

Reading to Learn Mathematics, p. 460   ELL

Pre-Activity *How can a system of equations be used to compare data?*

Do the activity at the top of page 414 in your textbook. Write your answers below.

a. Write an equation to represent the income from each job. Let y equal the salary and let x equal the number of hours worked. (*Hint*: Income = hourly rate · number of hours worked + bonus.)
$y = 10x + 50$ and $y = 15x$

b. Graph both equations on the same coordinate plane.

c. What are the coordinates of the point where the two lines meet? What does this point represent? (10, 150); In 10 hours, the salary will be the same for both jobs, $150.

Reading the Lesson 1–2. See students' work.

Write a definition and give an example of each new vocabulary word or phrase.

Vocabulary	Definition	Example
1. system of equations		
2. substitution		

3. The __solution__ of a system of equations is the coordinates of the point where the graphs of the equations __intersect__.

4. If two equations have the same graph, there are __infinitely many__ solutions to that system of equations.

Helping You Remember

5. Review the Study Tip on page 415 in your textbook. Complete each section of the chart with the number of solutions and an explanation, model, or logical proof for the situation. Sample answers are given.

Different Slopes	Same Slope, Different y-Intercepts	Same Slope, Same y-Intercept
Exactly one solution; if two lines have different slopes, they will meet at one point even if that point is far beyond the scope of the graph. Because both lines are straight, they will only meet once.	No solution; if two lines have the same slope but different y-intercepts, they are parallel lines. By definition, the two lines will never meet.	Infinitely many solutions; if two lines have the same slope and the same y-intercept, then they have the same graph. Any point on the graph satisfies both equations.

What You'll Learn

• Solve systems of linear equations by graphing.

• Solve systems of linear equations by substitution.

Vocabulary
• system of equations
• substitution

Study Tip

Matrices
Another way to organize the data displayed in this table is with a *matrix*. To learn more about matrices, see page 705.

c. (10, 150); For 10 hours worked, the salary is the same for both jobs, $150.

How can a system of equations be used to compare data?

Yolanda is offered two summer jobs, as shown in the table.

a. Write an equation to represent the income from each job. Let y equal the salary and let x equal the number of hours worked. (*Hint*: Income = hourly rate · number of hours worked + bonus.) $y = 10x + 50$ and $y = 15x$

b. Graph both equations on the same coordinate plane. **See margin.**

c. What are the coordinates of the point where the two lines meet? What does this point represent?

Job	Hourly Rate	Bonus
A	$10	$50
B	$15	$0

SOLVE SYSTEMS BY GRAPHING The equations $y = 10x + 50$ and $y = 15x$ together are called a **system of equations**. The solution of this system is the ordered pair that is a solution of both equations, (10, 150).

$$y = 10x + 50$$
$$150 \stackrel{?}{=} 10(10) + 50$$
$$150 = 150 \checkmark$$

Replace (x, y) with (10, 150).

$$y = 15x$$
$$150 \stackrel{?}{=} 15(10)$$
$$150 = 150 \checkmark$$

One method for solving a system of equations is to graph the equations on the same coordinate plane. The coordinates of the point where the graphs intersect is the solution of the system of equations.

Example 1 *Solve by Graphing*

Solve the system of equations by graphing.

$$y = -x$$
$$y = x + 2$$

The graphs appear to intersect at $(-1, 1)$. Check this estimate by substituting the coordinates into each equation.

CHECK

$$y = -x \qquad\qquad y = x + 2$$
$$1 \stackrel{?}{=} -(-1) \qquad 1 \stackrel{?}{=} -1 + 2$$
$$1 = 1 \checkmark \qquad\qquad 1 = 1 \checkmark$$

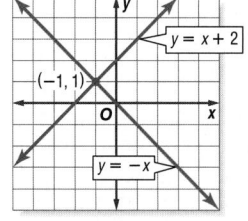

The solution of the system of equations is $(-1, 1)$.

✓ **Concept Check** Is (0, 0) a solution of the system of equations in Example 1? Explain. No; (0, 0) is a solution of the first equation, but not the second.

Resource Manager

📁 Workbooks and Reproducible Masters

Chapter 8 Resource Masters
• Study Guide and Intervention, p. 457
• Skills Practice, p. 458
• Practice, p. 459
• Reading to Learn Mathematics, p. 460
• Enrichment, p. 461

Graphing Calculator and Spreadsheet Masters, p. 33
Parent and Student Study Guide Workbook, p. 69

📺 Transparencies

5-Minute Check Transparency 8-9
Answer Key Transparencies

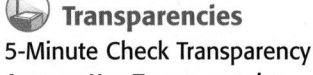

💿 Technology

Interactive Chalkboard

Example 2 *One Solution*

ENTERTAINMENT Video Planet offers two rental plans.

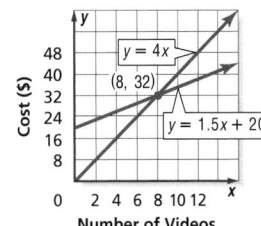

Plan	Rental Fee Per Video	Annual Fee
A	$4.00	$0
B	$1.50	$20

a. How many videos would Walt need to rent in a year for the plans to cost the same?

Explore You know the rental fee per video and the annual fee.

Plan Write an equation to represent each plan, and then graph the equations to find the solution.

Solve Let x = number of videos rented and let y = the total cost.

	total cost		rental fee times number of videos		annual fee
Plan A	y	=	$4x$	+	0
Plan B	y	=	$1.50x$	+	20

The graph of the system shows the solution is (8, 32). This means that if Walt rents 8 videos in a year, the plans cost the same, $32.

Examine Check by substituting (8, 32) into both equations in the system.

b. Which plan would cost less if Walt rents 12 videos in a year?

For $x = 12$, the line representing Plan B has a smaller y value. So, Plan B would cost less.

Example 3 *No Solution*

Solve the system of equations by graphing.

$y = 2x + 4$
$y = 2x - 1$

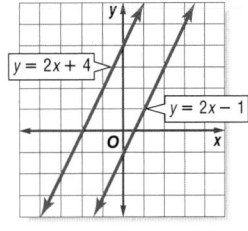

The graphs appear to be parallel lines. Since there is no coordinate pair that is a solution to both equations, there is no solution of this system of equations.

Example 4 *Infinitely Many Solutions*

Solve the system of equations by graphing.

$2y = x + 6$
$y = \frac{1}{2}x + 3$

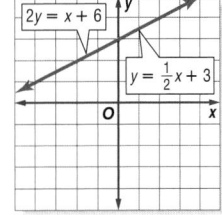

Both equations have the same graph. Any ordered pair on the graph will satisfy both equations. Therefore, there are infinitely many solutions of this system of equations.

www.pre-alg.com/extra_examples   Lesson 8-9 Solving Systems of Equations **415**

SOLVE SYSTEMS BY GRAPHING

In-Class Examples   Power Point®

1 Solve the system of equations by graphing.

$y = x - 1$ **(1, 0)**
$y = 2x - 2$

2 **ENTERTAINMENT** One CD club, A, charges members a $25.00 annual fee. After that, CDs cost $5.00 each. Another CD club, B, has no annual fee and sells its members CDs for $7.50 each.

a. How many CDs would you need to buy in a year for the clubs to cost the same?   **10**

b. Which club would be a better deal for a customer buying 20 CDs in a year?   **Club A**

Teaching Tip Ask students whether it is safe to say that any two equations with the same slopes will never meet. **No; they must also have different *y*-intercepts in order to never meet.**

3 Solve the system of equations by graphing.

$y = \frac{1}{3}x - 5$ **no solution**
$y = \frac{1}{3}x + 2$

4 Solve the system of equations by graphing.

$y = \frac{3}{4}x + 6$
$4y - 3x = 24$

infinitely many solutions

DAILY
INTERVENTION   Differentiated Instruction   ELL

• **Verbal/Linguistic** Point out that systems of linear equations often are used in business to maximize profits. In such situations, the point at which two lines intersect is called a *break-even point*. At this point, the money invested is returned; after this point, everything is profit. For example, a book publisher may find that it must sell 120,000 copies of a novel before it will show a profit. Have students write a paragraph relating what they have learned in this lesson to this concept.

In-Class Example
Power Point®

5 Solve the system of equations by substitution.

$y = 3x - 4$ (2, 2)

$y = 2$

---

3 Practice/Apply

Study Notebook

Have students—
- add the definitions/examples of the vocabulary terms to their Vocabulary Builder worksheets for Chapter 8.
- copy the Study Tip from p. 415 into their notebooks.
- include any other item(s) that they find helpful in mastering the skills in this lesson.

About the Exercises . . .

Organization by Objective
- Solve Systems by Graphing: 9–17
- Solve Systems by Substitution: 18–26

Odd/Even Assignments
Exercises 9–10 and 12–26 are structured so that students practice the same concepts whether they are assigned odd or even problems.

Alert! Exercises 2, 4, 5, and 12–17 require graph paper.

Assignment Guide
Basic: 9–21 odd, 24–40
Average: 9–23 odd, 24–40
Advanced: 10–24 even, 25–34 (Optional: 35–40)
All: Practice Quiz 2 (1–10)

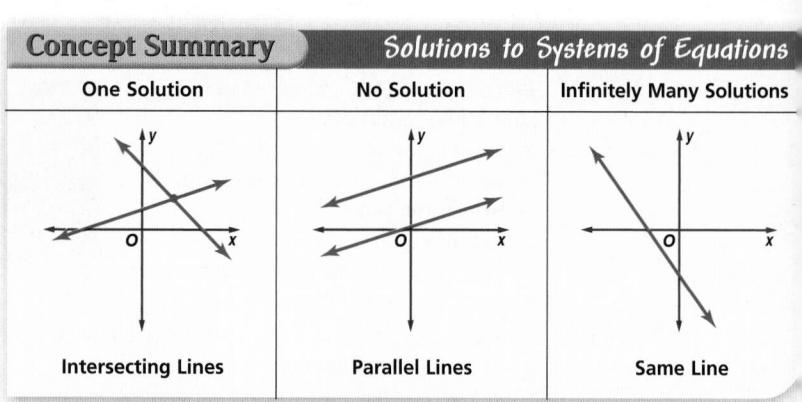

Concept Summary — Solutions to Systems of Equations

One Solution	No Solution	Infinitely Many Solutions
Intersecting Lines	Parallel Lines	Same Line

SOLVE SYSTEMS BY SUBSTITUTION A more accurate way to solve a system of equations is by using a method called **substitution**.

Example 5 *Solve by Substitution*

Solve the system of equations by substitution.

$y = x + 5$

$y = 3$

Since y must have the same value in both equations, you can replace y with 3 in the first equation.

$y = x + 5$ Write the first equation.

$3 = x + 5$ Replace y with 3.

$-2 = x$ Solve for x.

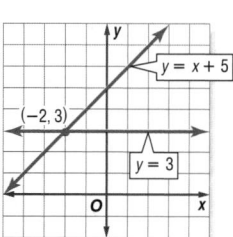

The solution of this system of equations is $(-2, 3)$. You can check the solution by graphing. The graphs appear to intersect at $(-2, 3)$, so the solution is correct.

Check for Understanding

Concept Check

1. See margin.

1. **Explain** what is meant by a system of equations and describe its solution.

2. **OPEN ENDED** Draw a graph of a system of equations that has one solution, a system that has no solution, and a system that has infinitely many solutions. **See margin.**

Guided Practice

3. State the solution of the system of equations graphed at the right. $(-5, -4)$

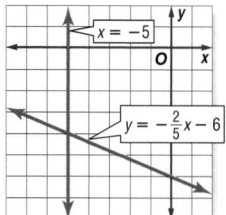

GUIDED PRACTICE KEY	
Exercises	Examples
3–5	1, 3, 4
6, 7	5
8	2

4–5. See pp. 431A–431H for graphs.

Solve each system of equations by graphing.

4. $y = 2x + 1$ (0, 1)
   $y = -x + 1$

5. $x + y = 4$ no
   $x + y = 2$ solution

Solve each system of equations by substitution.

6. $y = 3x - 4$ (0, −4)
   $x = 0$

7. $x + y = 8$ (2, 6)
   $y = 6$

Answers

1. Sample answer: A group of two or more equations form a system of equations. The solution is the ordered pair that satisfies all the equations in the system. If the equations are graphed, the solution is the coordinates of the point where the graphs intersect. The system has infinitely many solutions if the equations are the same and the graphs coincide.

2. Sample answers are shown at the right.

Application

8. $2x + 2y = 40$ and $y = 7$; 13 ft

8. **GEOMETRY** The perimeter of a garden is 40 feet. If the width y equals 7 feet, write and solve a system of equations to find the length of the garden.

★ indicates increased difficulty

Practice and Apply

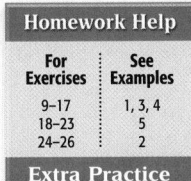

Homework Help

For Exercises	See Examples
9–17	1, 3, 4
18–23	5
24–26	2

Extra Practice
See page 744.

State the solution of each system of equations.

9.
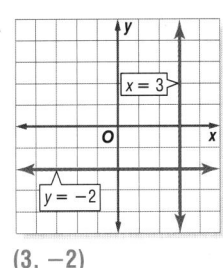
$(3, -2)$

10.
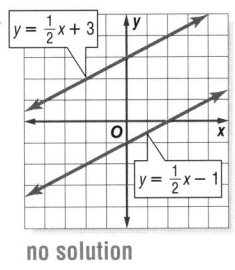
no solution

11.
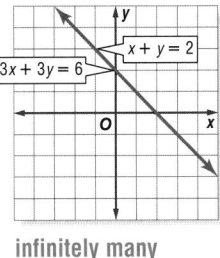
infinitely many

12–17. See pp. 431A–431H for graphs.

Solve each system of equations by graphing.

12. $y = -x$ $(-1, 1)$
$y = x + 2$

13. $x + y = 6$ $(3, 3)$
$y = x$

14. $2x + y = 1$ no solution
$y = -2x + 5$

15. $y = \frac{2}{3}x$ infinitely many
$2x - 3y = 0$

16. $x + y = -4$ $(-4, 0)$
$x - y = -4$

17. $y = -\frac{1}{2}x + 3$
$y = -2x$ $(-2, 4)$

Solve each system of equations by substitution.

18. $y = x + 1$ $(3, 4)$
$x = 3$

19. $y = x + 2$ $(-2, 0)$
$y = 0$

20. $y = 2x + 7$ $(-6, -5)$
$y = -5$

21. $x + y = 6$ $(-4, 10)$
$x = -4$

★ 22. $2x + 3y = 5$ $(1, 1)$
$y = x$

★ 23. $x + y = 9$ $(3, 6)$
$y = 2x$

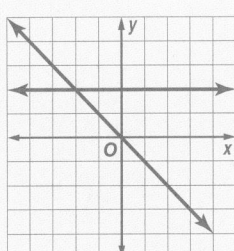

More About. . .

Snowboards

In 1998, snowboarding became an Olympic event in Nagano, Japan, with a giant slalom and halfpipe competition.
Source: www.snowboarding.about.com

SNOWBOARDS For Exercises 24–26, use the following information and the table.
Two Internet sites sell a snowboard for the same price, but have different shipping charges. 24. $y = 5 + x$ and $y = 2 + 1.5x$

Shipping Charges

Internet Site	Base Fee	Charge per Pound
A	$5.00	$1.00
B	$2.00	$1.50

24. Write a system of equations that represents the shipping charges y for x pounds. (*Hint:* Shipping charge = base fee + charge per pound · number of pounds.)

25. Solve the system of equations. Explain what the solution means.

26. If the snowboard weighs 8 pounds, which Internet site would be less expensive? Explain. site A; $13.00 < $14.00

25. $(6, 11)$; an order of 6 pounds will cost the same, $11.00, for both sites.

27. **CRITICAL THINKING** Two runners A and B are 50 meters apart and running at the same rate along the same path. a–b. See pp. 431A–431H.

a. If their rates continue, will the second runner ever catch up to the first? Draw a graph to explain why or why not.

b. Draw a graph that represents the second runner catching up to the first. What is different about the two graphs that you drew?

 www.pre-alg.com/self_check_quiz

Lesson 8-9 Solving Systems of Equations **417**

one solution
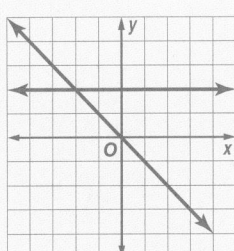

no solution
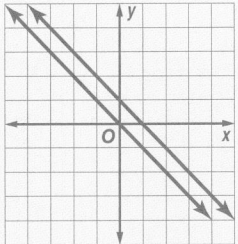

infinitely many solutions
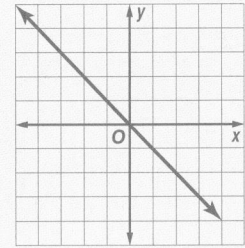

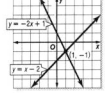
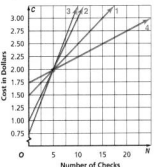
Lesson 8-9 Solving Systems of Equations **417**

Open-Ended Assessment

Modeling Have students use a geoboard and rubber bands to model the three situations shown in the Concept Summary box on p. 416.

Getting Ready for Lesson 8-10

PREREQUISITE SKILL The concept of graphing inequalities is presented in Lesson 8-10. Exercises 35–40 should be used to determine your students' familiarity with solving inequalities.

Assessment Options

Practice Quiz 2 The quiz provides students with a brief review of the concepts and skills in Lessons 8-6 through 8-9. Lesson numbers are given to the right of exercises or instruction lines so students can review concepts not yet mastered.

Answer

28. Each set of data can be represented by an equation. All the equations in the system can be graphed and analyzed to compare the data. Answers should include the following.
    - Equations can be used to represent incomes of different employees, where y represents income, m is the hourly rate, x is the number hours, and b is the bonus.
    - A solution (x, y) represents a situation in which the number of hours worked and the income is the same for all the employees.

---

28. **WRITING IN MATH** Answer the question that was posed at the beginning of the lesson. **See margin.**

    How can a system of equations be used to compare data?

    Include the following in your answer:
    - a situation that can be modeled by a system of equations, and
    - an explanation of what a solution to such a system of equations means.

Standardized Test Practice
Ⓐ Ⓑ Ⓒ Ⓓ

29. Which system of equations represents the following verbal description? **C**
    The sum of two numbers is 6. The second number is three times greater than the first number.

    Ⓐ $x + y = 6$ Ⓑ $y = x + 6$ Ⓒ $x + y = 6$ Ⓓ $x - y = 6$
    　　$x = 3 + y$ 　　$y = x + 3$ 　　$y = 3x$ 　　$y = -3x$

30. Which equation, together with $x + y = 1$, forms a system that has a solution of $(-3, 4)$? **C**

    Ⓐ $y = x$ Ⓑ $x - y = 1$ Ⓒ $y = x + 7$ Ⓓ $-3x + 4y = 1$

Maintain Your Skills

Mixed Review

31. **SALES** Ice cream sales increase as the temperature outside increases. Describe the slope of a best-fit line that represents this situation. *(Lesson 8-8)*
    positive slope

    Write an equation in slope-intercept form for the line passing through each pair of points. *(Lesson 8-7)*

34. $y = \frac{1}{4}x - 2$

32. $(0, 1)$ and $(3, 7)$ 33. $(-2, 6)$ and $(1, -3)$ 34. $(8, 0)$ and $(-8, -4)$
    $y = 2x + 1$ 　　$y = -3x$

Getting Ready for the Next Lesson

PREREQUISITE SKILL State whether each number is a solution of the given inequality. *(To review **inequalities**, see Lesson 7-3.)*

35. $1 < x + 3$; 0 **yes**   36. $9 > t - 5$; 1 **yes**   37. $2y \geq 2$; -1 **no**

38. $14 < 6 - n$; 0 **no**   39. $35 > 12 + k$; 12 **yes**   40. $5n + 1 \leq 0$; -2 **yes**

Practice Quiz 2
Lessons 8-6 through 8-9

State the slope and the y-intercept for the graph of each equation. *(Lesson 8-6)*

1. $y = -x + 8$ **-1; 8**   2. $y = 3x - 5$ **3; -5**   3. $x + 2y = 6$ **$-\frac{1}{2}$; 3**

Write an equation in slope-intercept form for each line. *(Lesson 8-7)*

4. slope = 6 **$y = 6x - 7$**   5. slope = 0 **$y = 1$**   6. slope = 1 **$y = x$**
   y-intercept = -7 　y-intercept = 1   　y-intercept = 0

7. **STATISTICS** The table shows the average age of the Women's U.S. Olympic track and field team. Make a scatter plot of the data and draw a best-fit line. *(Lesson 8-8)* **See margin.**

Year	1984	1988	1992	1996	2000
Average Age	24.6	25.0	27.3	28.7	29.2

Source: *Sports Illustrated*

Solve each system of equations by substitution. *(Lesson 8-9)*

8. $y = x - 1$ **(3, 2)**   9. $y = x + 5$ **(0, 5)**   10. $y = 2x + 4$ **$(-4, -4)$**
   $y = 2$ 　$x = 0$ 　$y = -4$

Answer (Practice Quiz 2)

7. Sample answer:

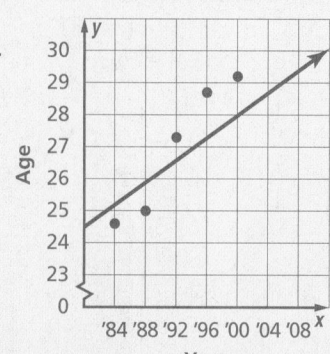

Graphing Inequalities

What You'll Learn

- Graph linear inequalities.
- Describe solutions of linear inequalities.

Vocabulary
- boundary
- half plane

How can shaded regions on a graph model inequalities?

Refer to the graph at the right.

a. Substitute $(-4, 2)$ and $(3, 1)$ in $y > 2x + 1$. Which ordered pair makes the inequality true? **(-4, 2)**

b. Substitute $(-4, 2)$ and $(3, 1)$ in $y < 2x + 1$. Which ordered pair makes the inequality true? **(3, 1)**

c. Which area represents the solution of $y < 2x + 1$? **shaded area**

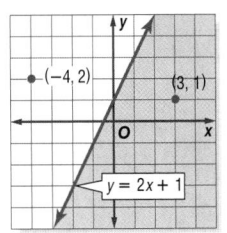

GRAPH INEQUALITIES

To graph an inequality such as $y > 2x - 3$, first graph the related equation $y = 2x - 3$. This is the **boundary**.

- If the inequality contains the symbol $\leq$ or $\geq$, then use a solid line to indicate that the boundary is included in the graph.
- If the inequality contains the symbol $<$ or $>$, then use a dashed line to indicate that the boundary is not included in the graph.

Next, test any point above or below the line to determine which region is the solution. It is easy to test $(0, 0)$.

$$y > 2x - 3 \qquad \text{Write the inequality.}$$
$$0 \overset{?}{>} 2(0) - 3 \qquad \text{Replace } x \text{ with 0 and } y \text{ with 0.}$$
$$0 > -3 \checkmark \qquad \text{Simplify.}$$

Since $0 > -3$ is true, $(0, 0)$ is a solution of $y > 2x - 3$. Shade the region that contains the solution. This region is called a **half plane**. All points in this region are solutions of the inequality.

Example 1 Graph Inequalities

a. Graph $y < -x + 1$.

Graph $y = -x + 1$. Draw a dashed line since the boundary is not part of the graph.

Test $(0, 0)$: $\quad y < -x + 1$
$$0 \overset{?}{<} -0 + 1 \qquad \text{Replace } (x, y) \text{ with } (0, 0).$$
$$0 < 1 \checkmark$$

Thus, the graph is all points in the region below the boundary.

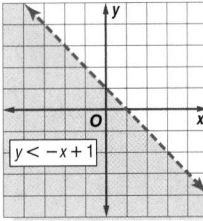

---

1 Focus

5-Minute Check Transparency 8-10 Use as a quiz or review of Lesson 8-9.

Mathematical Background notes are available for this lesson on page 366D.

How can shaded regions on a graph model inequalities?

The opening activity questions are repeated on page 465 of the *Chapter 8 Resource Masters.*

Reading to Learn Mathematics, p. 465 **ELL**

Pre-Activity How can shaded regions on a graph model inequalities?

Do the activity at the top of page 419 in your textbook. Write your answers below.

a. Substitute $(-4, 2)$ and $(3, 1)$ in $y > 2x + 1$. Which ordered pair makes the inequality true? $(-4, 2)$

b. Substitute $(-4, 2)$ and $(3, 1)$ in $y < 2x + 1$. Which ordered pair makes the inequality true? $(3, 1)$

c. Which area represents the solution of $y < 2x + 1$? shaded area

Reading the Lesson 1–2. See students' work.

Write a definition and give an example of each new vocabulary word or phrase.

Vocabulary	Definition	Example
1. boundary		
2. half plane		

3. If an inequality contains $\geq$ or $\leq$, then use a __solid__ line to indicate that the boundary __is__ included in the graph.

4. If an inequality contains $>$ or $<$, then use a __dashed__ line to indicate that the boundary __is not__ included in the graph.

Helping You Remember

5. Suppose that for the next seven days, you can have either an apple or an orange with your lunch. Graph all possible solutions on a coordinate grid. Assume that each day you have exactly one whole fruit.

Then suppose that you have a total of 3.5 apples and 2.5 oranges during the seven days. Plot this solution point on the grid and shade the region containing this point. What advantages does graphing the inequality have over graphing just the points? Graphing the inequality makes it possible to show a more complex situation, including the possibility of having part of a fruit or no fruit at all on some days.

Resource Manager

Workbooks and Reproducible Masters

Chapter 8 Resource Masters
- Study Guide and Intervention, p. 462
- Skills Practice, p. 463
- Practice, p. 464
- Reading to Learn Mathematics, p. 465
- Enrichment, p. 466
- Assessment, p. 482

Parent and Student Study Guide Workbook, p. 70
Prerequisite Skills Workbook, pp. 1–2
School-to-Career Masters, p. 16

Transparencies

5-Minute Check Transparency 8-10
Answer Key Transparencies

Technology

Interactive Chalkboard
Pre-AlgePASS: Tutorial Plus, Lesson 25

GRAPH INEQUALITIES

In-Class Example Power Point®

1 a. Graph $y > 3x - 3$.

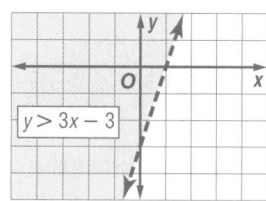

$y > 3x - 3$

b. Graph $y \le -\dfrac{1}{4}x$.

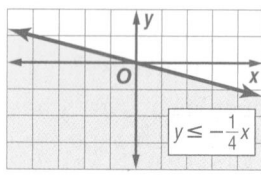

$y \le -\dfrac{1}{4}x$

FIND SOLUTIONS

In-Class Example Power Point®

2 BAKING Terrence needs 3 cups of flour to make a batch of cookies and 5 cups to make a loaf of bread. He has 30 cups of flour. How many batches of cookies and loaves of bread can he bake?
Sample answer:
0 batches of cookies, 6 loaves
4 batches of cookies, 3 loaves
5 batches of cookies, 3 loaves
7 batches of cookies, 1 loaf

3 Practice/Apply

Study Notebook

Have students—
• complete the definitions/examples for the remaining terms on the Vocabulary Builder worksheets for Chapter 8.
• include any other item(s) that they find helpful in mastering the skills in this lesson.

---

b. Graph $y \ge 2x + 2$.

Graph $y = 2x + 2$. Draw a solid line since the boundary is part of the graph.

Test (0, 0):
$$y \ge 2x + 2$$
$$0 \overset{?}{\ge} 2(0) + 2 \quad \text{Replace } (x, y) \text{ with } (0, 0).$$
$$0 \ge 2 \quad \text{not true.}$$

(0, 0) is not a solution, so shade the other half plane.

CHECK Test an ordered pair in the other half plane.

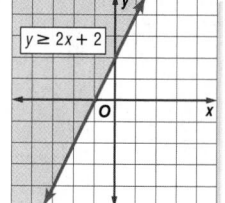

$y \ge 2x + 2$

✔ **Concept Check** Is (0, 2) a solution of $y \ge 2x + 2$? Explain.
Yes; (0, 2) lies on the boundary, which is included in the solution.

FIND SOLUTIONS You can write and graph inequalities to solve real-world problems. In some cases, you may have to solve the inequality for y first and then graph the inequality.

Example 2 *Write and Graph an Inequality to Solve a Problem*

SCHOOL Nathan has at most 30 minutes to complete his math and science homework. How much time can he spend on each?

Step 1 Write an inequality.

Let x represent the time spent doing math homework and let y represent the time spent doing science homework.

Minutes doing math	plus	minutes doing science	is at most	30 minutes.
x	$+$	y	$\le$	30

Step 2 Graph the inequality.

To graph the inequality, first solve for y.

$x + y \le 30$ Write the inequality.
$y \le -x + 30$ Subtract x from each side.

Graph $y \le -x + 30$ as a solid line since the boundary is part of the graph. The origin is part of the graph since $0 \le -0 + 30$. Thus, the coordinates of all points in the shaded region are possible solutions.

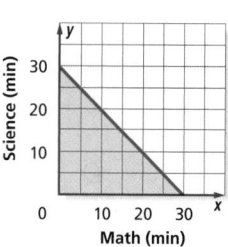

$(10, 20) = 10$ minutes on math, 20 minutes on science

$(15, 15) = 15$ minutes on math, 15 minutes on science

$(10, 15) = 10$ minutes on math, 15 minutes on science

$(30, 0) = 30$ minutes on math, 0 minutes on science

Note that the solutions are only in the first quadrant because negative values of time do not make sense.

Study Tip

Common Misconception
You may think that only whole number solutions are possible. Points in the shaded region such as (10.5, 18.5) are also solutions.

DAILY INTERVENTION **Differentiated Instruction**

• **Visual/Spatial** Scott sells tapes for $6 and CDs for $12. How many of each can he sell and still collect at least $144? Let tapes $= x$ and CDs $= y$. Graph $6x + 12y = 144$. Have each student graph a point that produces an answer greater than or equal to 144 on the same grid on the chalkboard or with stickers on poster board. Ask students what the graph would look like if infinitely many solution points were graphed. **a solid line with a shaded plane above and to the right of the line**

Concept Check

1. **Write** an inequality that describes the graph at the right. $y < -x + 3$

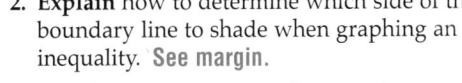

2. **Explain** how to determine which side of the boundary line to shade when graphing an inequality. **See margin.**

3a–b. Sample answers are given.
3a. (0, −1), (1, 0), (2, 1)
3b. (0, 0), (1, 1), (2, 2)

3. **List** three solutions of each inequality.
   a. $y < x$ b. $y \geq x - 3$

4. **OPEN ENDED** Write an inequality that has (1, 4) as a solution. **Sample answer:** $x + y < 6$

Guided Practice

Graph each inequality. **5–7. See pp. 431A–431H.**

5. $y > x - 1$ 6. $y \leq 2$ 7. $y \geq -3x + 2$

Application

ENTERTAINMENT For Exercises 8 and 9, use the following information. Adult passes for World Waterpark are $25, and children's passes are $15. A company is buying tickets for its employees and wants to spend no more than $630.

GUIDED PRACTICE KEY	
Exercises	Examples
5–7	1
8, 9	2

8. Write an inequality to represent this situation. $25x + 15y \leq 630$

9. Graph the inequality and use the graph to determine three possible combinations of tickets that the company could buy. **See pp. 431A–431H.**

Homework Help

For Exercises	See Examples
10–21	1
22–32	2

Extra Practice
See page 744.

Graph each inequality. **10–21. See pp. 431A–431H.**

10. $y \geq x$ 11. $y < x$ 12. $y < 1$

13. $y \geq -3$ 14. $y > x - 1$ 15. $y \leq x + 4$

16. $y \leq -x$ 17. $y \geq 0$ 18. $y > 2x + 3$

19. $y < 2x - 4$ 20. $y < \frac{1}{2}x + 2$ 21. $y \geq -\frac{1}{3}x - 1$

BUSINESS For Exercises 22–26, use the following information.
For a certain business to be successful, its monthly sales y must be at least $3000 greater than its monthly costs x.

22. Write an inequality to represent this situation. $y \geq x + 3000$

23. Graph the inequality. **See margin.**

24. Do points above or below the boundary line indicate a successful business? Explain how you know.

25. Would negative numbers make sense in this problem? Explain.

26. List two solutions. **Sample answer:** (1000, 5000), (4000, 7000)

24. Above the line; (1000, 5000) is a solution of $y \geq x + 3000$.

25. No; the number of sales and the costs cannot be negative.

Study Tip

Solutions
In Exercise 29, only whole-number solutions make sense since there cannot be parts of baskets.

CRAFTS For Exercises 27–29, use the following information.
Celia can make a small basket in 10 minutes and a large basket in 25 minutes. This month, she has no more than 24 hours to make these baskets for an upcoming craft fair.

27. Write an inequality to represent this situation. $10x + 25y \leq 1440$

28. Graph the inequality. **See margin.**

29. Use the graph to determine how many of each type of basket that she could make this month. List three possibilities. **See margin.**

 www.pre-alg.com/self_check_quiz

Answer

2. Sample answer: Choose a test point not on the boundary line and substitute its coordinates in the inequality. If the result is true, shade that side of the boundary. If the result is false, shade the other side of the boundary.

23, 28, 29. See p. 422.

Reading Tip To help students read inequality symbols correctly, suggest that they think of the < and > symbols as microscopes. Each symbol takes what is on the small, pointed end and magnifies it, moving it to the open end. The symbols ≤ and ≥ are similar, but include the bottom part of the equal sign, to mean *less than or equal to* and *greater than or equal to.*

To graph a linear inequality, first graph the **boundary**. Test any point to determine which region is the solution, or **half plane**. Shade this region. You can also use inequalities to solve real-world problems.

Example

GARDENING Marisol has 10 square feet in her garden for planting squash and peppers. How many square feet can she plant of each?

Squash	plus	peppers	is at most	10 square feet
x	+	y	≤	10

$x + y \leq 10$ Write the inequality

$y \leq -x + 10$ Subtract x from each side.

Graph $y \leq -x + 10$ as a solid line since the boundary is part of the graph. The origin is part of the graph since $0 \leq -0 + 10$. Thus, the coordinates of all points in the shaded region are possible solutions.

(7, 3) = 7 square feet of squash, 3 square feet of peppers
(4, 6) = 4 square feet of squash, 6 square feet of peppers
(2, 7) = 2 square feet of squash, 7 square feet of peppers

Exercises

LEISURE Use the following information for Exercises 1–3.
Fred and Roya have $500 to spend on ballroom dancing classes. Each foxtrot class costs $16 per couple and each salsa lesson costs $20 per couple.

1. Write an inequality to represent this situation. $16x + 20y \leq 500$

2. Graph the inequality.

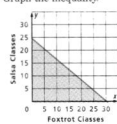

3. Use the graph to determine how many of each type of dance class Fred and Roya can take. **Sample answers:** (5 foxtrot, 21 salsa) (10 foxtrot, 17 salsa), (15 foxtrot, 10 salsa)

Graph each inequality.

1. $y > -x - 5$ 2. $y \leq 2$ 3. $y \geq x + 6$

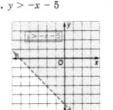 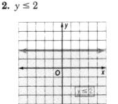 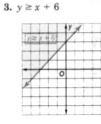

DRIVING For Exercises 4–6, use the following information.
Sarah needs to spend at least 90 hours driving in order to qualify to take a driver's test. She can either drive with a licensed instructor or her parent or guardian.

4. Write an inequality to represent this situation. $x + y \geq 90$

5. Graph the inequality.

6. Use the graph to determine how many hours Sarah can drive with an instructor or a parent. **Sample answers:** (10 instructor, 90 parent), (20 instructor, 80 parent), (30 instructor, 90 parent)

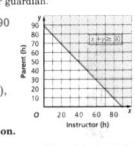

READING For Exercises 7–9, use the following information.
Jai joined a reading club for the summer. He pledged to read more than 200 points worth of reading material. Books count 10 points each while other materials such as magazines, poems, or short stories count 2 points each.

7. Write an inequality to represent this situation.
$10x + 2y > 200$

8. Graph the inequality.

9. Use the graph to determine how many books and how many pieces of other material Jai needs to read to meet his commitment. **Sample answers:** (30 books, 0 other), (10 books, 70 other), (20 books, 10 other)

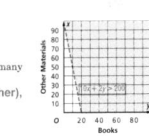

Graphing Systems of Inequalities

Suppose you are given the following system of inequalities.

$y \geq x + 2$
$y \leq -2x - 1$

The solution of this system is the set of all ordered pairs that satisfy both inequalities. To find the solution, graph each inequality. The intersection of the graphs represents the solution.

The graphs of the equations $y = x + 2$ and $y = -2x - 1$ are the boundaries of each region. The solution of the system is the region that contains ordered pairs that are solution of *both* inequalities.

For example, (−6, 2) is a solution of the system. Check by substituting the coordinates into each inequality.

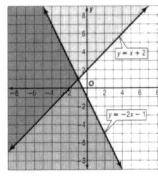

Solve each system by graphing. State one solution of each system.
1–6. Sample solutions are given.

1. $y \geq 2x + 1$ 2. $y < -2$ 3. $y \geq x - 3$
   $y \leq -x + 1$ $y - x > 1$ $y \geq -x - 1$

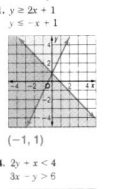 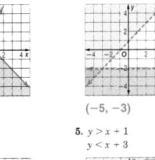 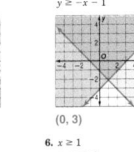

(−1, 1)   (−5, −3)   (0, 3)

4. $2y + x < 4$ 5. $y > x + 1$ 6. $x \geq 1$
   $3x - y > 6$ $y < x + 3$ $y \leq x \leq 3$

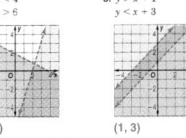

(3, −4)   (1, 3)   (2, −1)

Organization by Objective
• **Graph Solutions:** 10–23
• **Find Solutions:** 24–32

Odd/Even Assignments
Exercises 10–25 and 27–32 are structured so that students practice the same concepts whether they are assigned odd or even problems.

Alert! Exercises 5–7, 9–21, 23, and 28 require graph paper.

Assignment Guide
Basic: 11–21 odd, 22–43
Average: 11–21 odd, 22–43
Advanced: 10–20 even, 22–43

4 Assess

Open-Ended Assessment

Speaking Have one student write an inequality, another student translate it into words, and the two work together to graph it.

Assessment Options
Quiz (Lessons 8-9 and 8-10) is available on p. 482 of the *Chapter 8 Resource Masters.*

Answers (pp. 421–422)

23.
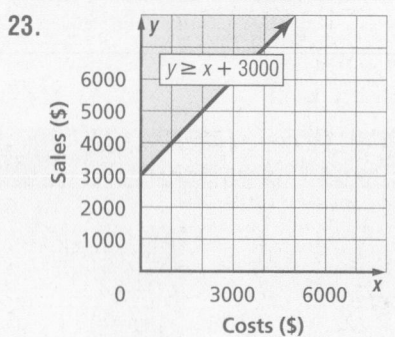

28.
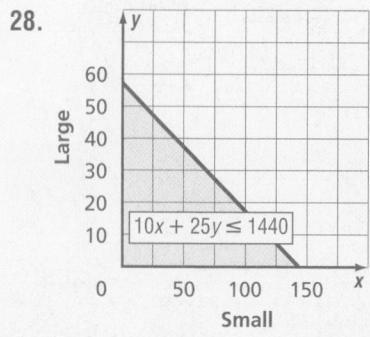

More About. . .

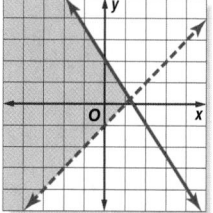

Rafting •
More than 25 whitewater rafting companies are located on the American River in California. A typical fee is $125 per person per day.
Source: www.rafting-whitewater.com

RAFTING For Exercises 30–32, use the following information.
Collin's Rent-a-Raft rents Super Rafts for $100 per day and Econo Rafts for $40 per day. He wants to receive at least $1500 per day renting out the rafts.

30. Write an inequality to represent this situation. $100x + 40y \geq 1500$

31. Graph the inequality. **See pp. 431A–431H.**

32. Determine how many of each type of raft that Collin could rent out each day in order to receive at least $1500. List three possibilities. **See margin.**

33. **CRITICAL THINKING** The solution of a *system of inequalities* is the set of all ordered pairs that satisfies *both* inequalities.
   a. Write a system of inequalities for the graph at the right. $y > x - 1, y \leq -\frac{3}{2}x + 2$
   b. List three solutions of the system.
      Sample answers: $(0, 2)$, $(-1, 2)$, $(-3, -2)$

34. **WRITING IN MATH** Answer the question that was posed at the beginning of the lesson. **See margin.**

   How can shaded regions on a graph model inequalities?
   Include the following in your answer:
   • a description of which points in the graph are solutions of the inequality.

Standardized Test Practice

35. Determine which ordered pair is a solution of $y - 8 > x$. **C**
   Ⓐ $(0, 2)$ Ⓑ $(2, 5)$ Ⓒ $(-9, 0)$ Ⓓ $(1, 4)$

36. Which inequality does *not* have the boundary included in its graph? **A**
   Ⓐ $y > x$ Ⓑ $y \leq 1$ Ⓒ $y \geq x + 5$ Ⓓ $y \geq 0$

Maintain Your Skills

Mixed Review
37–39. See pp. 431A–431H for graphs.

40. Sample answer: Make a scatter plot of the data and draw a best-fit line. Then use the line to make a prediction.

Solve each system of equations by graphing. *(Lesson 8-9)*

37. $y = x + 3$ **(0, 3)**
    $x = 0$

38. $y = -x + 2$ **(−1, 3)**
    $y = x + 4$

39. $y = -2x - 1$ **(2, −5)**
    $y = -x - 3$

40. Explain how you can make predictions from a set of ordered-pair data. *(Lesson 8-8)*

Write each fraction or mixed number as a decimal. Use a bar to show a repeating decimal. *(Lesson 5-1)*

41. $\frac{2}{5}$ **0.4**

42. $3\frac{7}{10}$ **3.7**

43. $-\frac{5}{9}$ **$-0.\overline{5}$**

WebQuest **Internet Project**

Just for Fun
It is time to complete your project. Use the information and data you have gathered about recreational activities to prepare a Web page or poster. Be sure to include a scatter plot and a prediction for each activity.

www.pre-alg.com/webquest

---

29. Sample answer: 25 small, 45 large; 50 small, 30 large; 100 small, 10 large

32. Sample answer: 5 Super, 30 Econo; 10 Super, 15 Econo; 15 Super, 5 Econo

34. To model an inequality, graph the related equation and choose a point not on the line. If the inequality is true when the coordinates of the point are substituted, then that region is shaded.

If the inequality is false, then the region on the other side of the line is shaded. Answers should include the following.

• Any point in the shaded region is a solution of the inequality.

Graphing Calculator Investigation

A Follow-Up of Lesson 8-10

Graphing Inequalities

You can use a TI-83 Plus graphing calculator to investigate the graphs of inequalities. Since the graphing calculator only shades between two functions, enter a lower boundary as well as an upper boundary for each inequality.

Graph two different inequalities on your graphing calculator.

 Step 1 Graph $y \leq -x + 4$.

- Clear all functions from the **Y=** list.
  KEYSTROKES: [Y=] [CLEAR]

- Graph $y \leq -x + 4$ in the standard window.
  KEYSTROKES: [2nd] [DRAW] 7 [(−)] 10 [,]
  [(−)] [X,T,θ,n] [+] 4 [)]
  [ENTER]

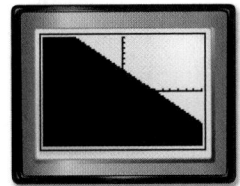

Ymin or -10 is used as the lower boundary and $y = -x + 4$ as the upper boundary. All ordered pairs in the shaded region satisfy the inequality $y \leq -x + 4$.

Step 2 Graph $y \geq -x + 4$.

- Clear the current drawing displayed.
  KEYSTROKES: [2nd] [DRAW] [ENTER]

- Graph $y \geq -x + 4$ in the standard window.
  KEYSTROKES: [2nd] [DRAW] 7 [(−)]
  [X,T,θ,n] [+] 4 [,] 10 [)]
  [ENTER]

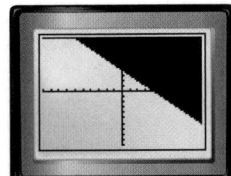

In this case, the lower boundary is $y = -x + 4$. The upper boundary is **Ymax** or 10. All ordered pairs in the shaded region satisfy the inequality $y \geq -x + 4$.

Exercises **2b. lower bound: $-2x - 6$; upper bound: Ymax or 10**

1. Compare and contrast the two graphs shown above. **See margin.**

2. **a.** Graph $y \geq -2x - 6$ in the standard viewing window. Draw the graph on grid paper. **See margin.**

   b. What functions do you enter as the lower and upper boundaries?

   c. Use the graph to name four solutions of the inequality.
   Sample answer: (0, 0), (1, 5), (−1, 4), (−2, 2)

Use a graphing calculator to graph each inequality. Draw each graph on grid paper. 3–10. See pp. 431A–431H.

3. $y \leq x - 3$	**4.** $y \leq -1$	**5.** $x + y \geq 6$	**6.** $y \geq 3x$
7. $y \leq 0$	**8.** $y + 3 \leq -x$	**9.** $x + y \leq 5$	**10.** $2y - x \geq 2$

www.pre-alg.com/other_calculator_keystrokes
Graphing Calculator Investigation Graphing Inequalities **423**

Getting Started

Know Your Calculator The **DRAW** menu on the graphing calculator has many interesting capabilities that students may wish to experiment with. Before beginning this Investigation, students should clear existing drawings by pressing [2nd] [DRAW] 1 [ENTER] . Before using ClrDraw, drawings can be stored with StorePic in the **DRAW STO** menu.

Teach

- Point out that students must have in mind where the shading should fall before graphing an inequality. You may wish to write several inequalities on the chalkboard and have the class call out where the shading should go.
- Have students complete Exercises 1–10.

Assess

Ask students to name several solutions that satisfy the inequalities in Exercises 3–10.

Answers

1. The graphs have the same boundary line, but opposite sides of the line are shaded.

2a.

Vocabulary and Concept Check

- This alphabetical list of vocabulary terms in Chapter 8 includes a page reference where each term was introduced.

- **Assessment** A vocabulary review/test for Chapter 8 is available on p. 480 of the *Chapter 8 Resource Masters*.

Lesson-by-Lesson Review

For each lesson,

- the main ideas are summarized,
- additional examples review concepts, and
- practice exercises are provided.

Vocabulary PuzzleMaker

ELL The Vocabulary PuzzleMaker software improves students' mathematics vocabulary using four puzzle formats—crossword, scramble, word search using a word list, and word search using clues. Students can work on a computer screen or from a printed handout.

MindJogger Videoquizzes

ELL MindJogger Videoquizzes provide an alternative review of concepts presented in this chapter. Students work in teams in a game show format to gain points for correct answers. The questions are presented in three rounds.

Round 1 Concepts (5 questions)
Round 2 Skills (4 questions)
Round 3 Problem Solving (4 questions)

Vocabulary and Concept Check

best-fit line (p. 409)	half plane (p. 419)	system of equations (p. 414)
boundary (p. 419)	linear equation (p. 375)	vertical line test (p. 370)
constant of variation (p. 394)	rate of change (p. 393)	x-intercept (p. 381)
direct variation (p. 394)	slope (p. 387)	y-intercept (p. 381)
family of graphs (p. 402)	slope-intercept form (p. 398)	
function (p. 369)	substitution (p. 416)	

Choose the letter of the term that best matches each statement or phrase.

1. a relation in which each member of the domain is paired with exactly one member of the range **d**
2. in a graph of an inequality, the line of the related equation **b**
3. a value that describes the steepness of a line **h**
4. a group of two or more equations **j**
5. can be drawn through data points to approximate a linear relationship **a**
6. a change in one quantity with respect to another quantity **g**
7. a graph of this is a straight line **f**
8. one type of method for solving systems of equations **i**
9. a linear equation that describes rate of change **c**
10. in the graph of an inequality, the region that contains all solutions **e**

a.	best-fit line
b.	boundary
c.	direct variation
d.	function
e.	half plane
f.	linear equation
g.	rate of change
h.	slope
i.	substitution
j.	system of equations

Lesson-by-Lesson Review

8-1 Functions

See pages 369–373.

Concept Summary

- In a function, each member in the domain is paired with exactly one member in the range.

Example **Determine whether {(−9, 2), (1, 5), (1, 10)} is a function. Explain.**

domain (x)   range (y)

−9 ⟶ 2
1 ⟶ 5
 ⟶ 10

This relation is not a function because 1 in the domain is paired with two range values, 5 and 10.

Exercises **Determine whether each relation is a function. Explain.**
See Example 1 on page 369. **11–14. See margin for explanations.**

11. {(1, 12), (−4, 3), (6, 36), (10, 6)} **yes** 12. {(11.8, −9), (10.4, −2), (11.8, 3.8)} **no**
13. {(0, 0), (2, 2), (3, 3), (4, 4)} **yes**   14. {(−0.5, 1.2), (3, 1.2), (2, 36)} **yes**

 www.pre-alg.com/vocabulary_review

FOLDABLES™

Study Organizer

For more information about Foldables, see *Teaching Mathematics with Foldables*.

Have students review the notes they have taken under the tabs of their Foldables, as well as any examples they have drawn. If any of the notes are hard for them to understand, they should review the lessons covering those topics and revise their notes.

Encourage students to refer to their Foldables while completing the Study Guide and Review and to use them in preparing for the Chapter Test.

8-2 Linear Equations in Two Variables

See pages 375–379.

Concept Summary

- A solution of a linear equation is an ordered pair that makes the equation true.
- To graph a linear equation, plot points and draw a line through them.

Example   **Graph $y = -x + 2$ by plotting ordered pairs.**

Find ordered pair solutions. Then plot and connect the points.

x	−x + 2	y	(x, y)
0	−0 + 2	2	(0, 2)
1	−1 + 2	1	(1, 1)
2	−2 + 2	0	(2, 0)
3	−3 + 2	−1	(3, −1)

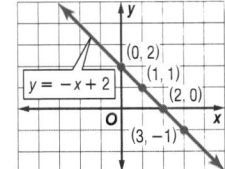

Exercises   **Graph each equation by plotting ordered pairs.**

See Example 3 on page 377. **15–22. See margin.**

15. $y = x + 4$ **16.** $y = x - 2$ **17.** $y = -x$ **18.** $y = 2x$

19. $y = 3x + 2$ **20.** $y = -2x - 4$ **21.** $x + y = 4$ **22.** $x - y = -3$

8-3 Graphing Linear Equations Using Intercepts

See pages 381–385.

Concept Summary

- To graph a linear equation, you can find and plot the points where the graph crosses the x-axis and the y-axis. Then connect the points.

Example   **Graph $-3x + y = 3$ using the x- and y-intercepts.**

$-3x + y = 3$
$-3x + 0 = 3$
$ x = -1$ The x-intercept is −1.

$-3x + y = 3$
$-3(0) + y = 3$
$ y = 3$ The y-intercept is 3.

Graph the points at $(-1, 0)$ and $(0, 3)$ and draw a line through them.

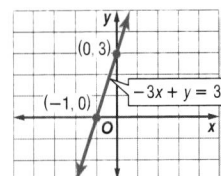

Exercises   **Graph each equation using the x- and y-intercepts.**

See Example 3 on page 382. **23–30. See pp. 426–427.**

23. $y = x + 2$ **24.** $y = x + 6$ **25.** $y = -x - 3$ **26.** $y = x - 1$

27. $x = -4$ **28.** $y = 5$ **29.** $x + y = -2$ **30.** $3x + y = 6$

Answers

16.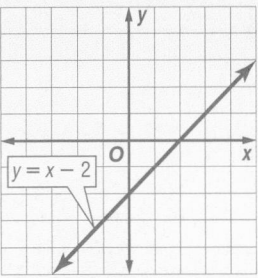

17.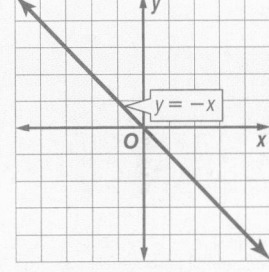

18.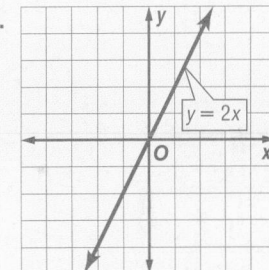

19.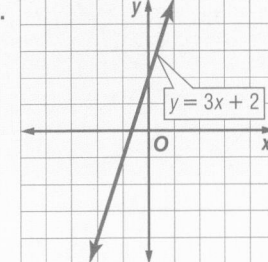

20.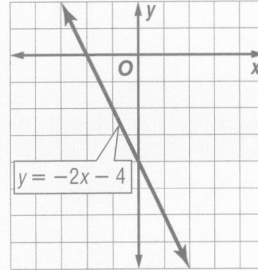

(continued on the next page)

Answers (pp. 424–425)

11. Yes; each x value is paired with only one y value.

12. No; 11.8 in the domain is paired with −9 and 3.8 in the range.

13. Yes; each x value is paired with only one y value.

14. Yes; each x value is paired with only one y value.

15.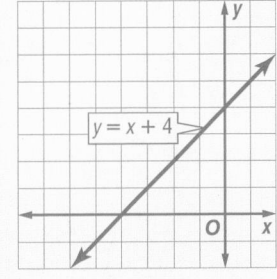

Answers (p. 425)

21.
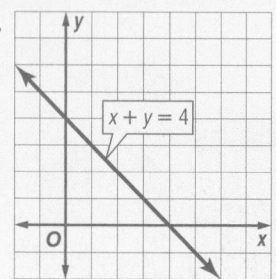

22.
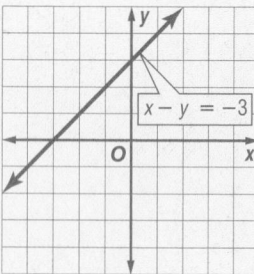

23.
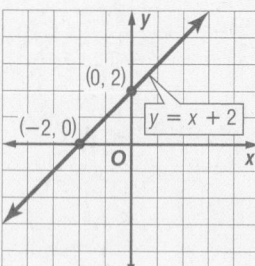

24.
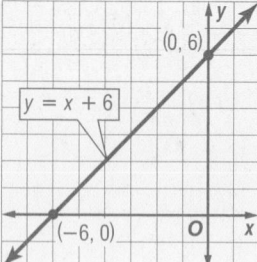

25.
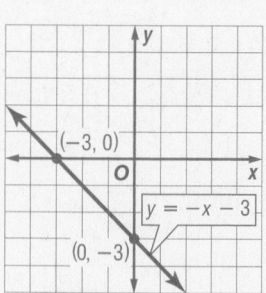

8-4 Slope

See pages 387–391.

Concept Summary

- Slope is the ratio of the *rise*, or the vertical change, to the *run*, or the horizontal change.

Example Find the slope of the line that passes through $A(0, 6)$, $B(4, -2)$.

$m = \dfrac{y_2 - y_1}{x_2 - x_1}$ Definition of slope

$m = \dfrac{-2 - 6}{4 - 0}$ $(x_1, y_1) = (0, 6),$ $(x_2, y_2) = (4, -2)$

$m = \dfrac{-8}{4}$ or -2 The slope is -2.

Exercises Find the slope of the line that passes through each pair of points.
See Examples 2–5 on pages 388 and 389.

31. $J(3, 4)$, $K(4, 5)$ **1**   **32.** $C(2, 8)$, $D(6, 7)$ $-\dfrac{1}{4}$ **33.** $R(7, 3)$, $B(-1, -4)$ $\dfrac{7}{8}$

34. $Q(2, 10)$, $B(4, 6)$ **-2**   **35.** $X(-1, 5)$, $Y(-1, 9)$ **36.** $S(0, 8)$, $T(-3, 8)$ **0**

undefined

8-5 Rate of Change

See pages 393–397.

Concept Summary

- A change in one quantity with respect to another quantity is called the rate of change.
- Slope can be used to describe rates of change.

Example Find the rate of change in population from 1990 to 2000 for Oakland, California, using the graph.

Year	Population (1000s)
x	y
1990	372
2000	400

rate of change $= \dfrac{y_2 - y_1}{x_2 - x_1}$ Definition of slope

$= \dfrac{400 - 372}{2000 - 1990}$ ← change in population
← change in time

$= 2.8$ Simplify.

So, the rate of change in population was an increase of about 2.8 thousand, or 2800 people per year.

Exercises Find the rate of change for the linear function represented in each table. *See Example 1 on page 393.* **37.** inc. of 8 m/s **38.** dec. of 2°F/h

37.

Time (s)	Distance (m)
x	y
0	0
1	8
2	16

38.

Time (h)	Temperature (°F)
x	y
1	45
2	43
3	41

26.
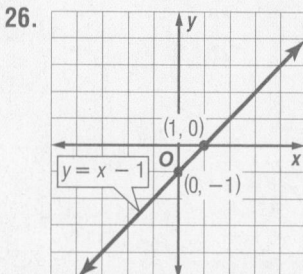

27.
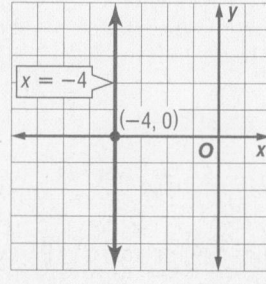

28.
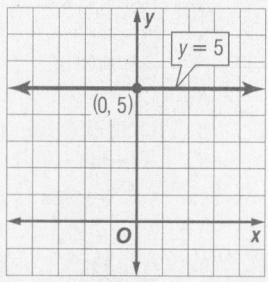

8-6 Slope-Intercept Form

See pages 398–401.

Concept Summary

- In the slope-intercept form $y = mx + b$, m is the slope and b is the y-intercept.

Example State the slope and the y-intercept of the graph of $y = -2x + 3$.

The slope of the graph is -2, and the y-intercept is 3.

Exercises Graph each equation using the slope and y-intercept.
See Example 3 on page 399. **39–42. See margin.**

39. $y = x + 4$ **40.** $y = -2x + 1$ **41.** $y = \frac{1}{3}x - 2$ **42.** $x + y = -5$

8-7 Writing Linear Equations

See pages 404–408.

Concept Summary

- You can write a linear equation by using the slope and y-intercept, two points on a line, a graph, a table, or a verbal description.

Example Write an equation in slope-intercept form for the line having slope 4 and y-intercept -2.

$y = mx + b$ Slope-intercept form
$y = 4x + (-2)$ Replace m with 4 and b with -2.
$y = 4x - 2$ Simplify.

Exercises Write an equation in slope-intercept form for each line.
See Example 1 on page 404. **43.** $y = -x + 3$

43. slope $= -1$, y-intercept $= 3$ **44.** slope $= 6$, y-intercept $= -3$ $y = 6x - 3$

8-8 Best-Fit Lines

See pages 409–413.

Concept Summary

- A best-fit line can be used to approximate data.

Example Draw a best-fit line through the scatter plot.

Draw a line that is close to as many data points as possible.

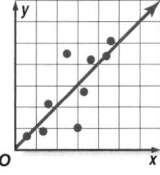

Exercises The table shows the attendance for an annual art festival. See Example 1 on page 409.

45. Make a scatter plot and draw a best-fit line. **See margin.**

46. Use the best-fit line to predict art festival attendance in 2008. **Sample answer: 3600**

Year	Attendance
2000	2500
2001	2650
2002	2910
2003	3050

Answers

39.

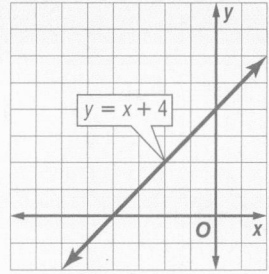

40.

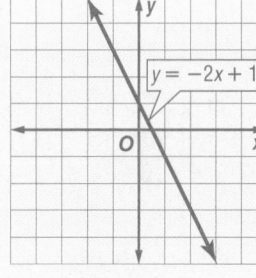

41.

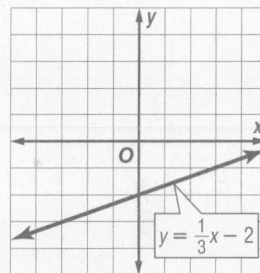

42.

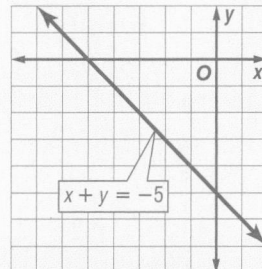

45. Sample answer:

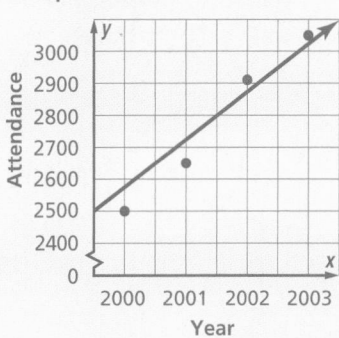

29.

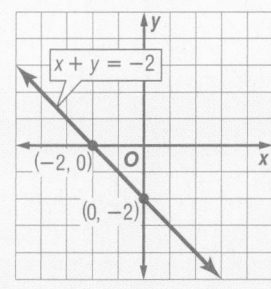

30.

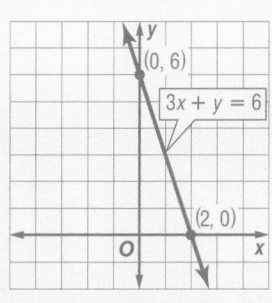

Study Guide and Review

Chapter
8 For More ...

• Extra Practice, see pages 741–744.
• Mixed Problem Solving, see page 765.

Answers

47.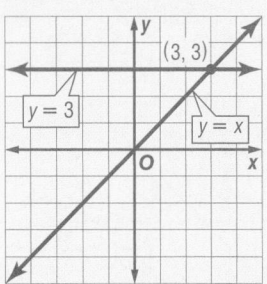

48.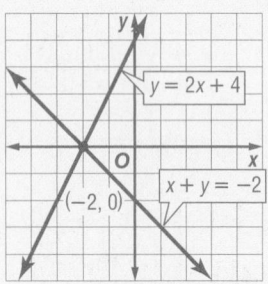

49.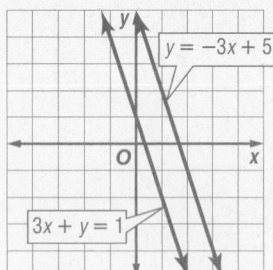

53.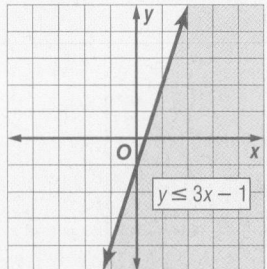

54.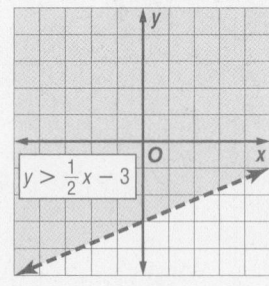

8-9 Solving Systems of Equations

See pages 414–418.

Concept Summary

• The solution of a system of equations is the ordered pair that satisfies all equations in the system.

Examples

1 Solve the system of equations by graphing.

$$y = x$$
$$y = -x + 2$$

The graphs appear to intersect at (1, 1). The solution of the system of equations is (1, 1).

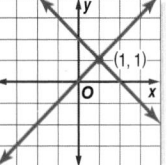

2 Solve the system $y = x - 1$ and $y = 3$ by substitution.

$y = x - 1$ Write the first equation.
$3 = x - 1$ Replace y with 3.
$4 = x$ Solve for x.

The solution of this system of equations is (4, 3). Check by graphing.

Exercises Solve each system of equations by graphing.
See Examples 1–4 on pages 414 and 415. **47–49. See margin for graphs.**

47. $y = x$ **(3, 3)**
$y = 3$

48. $y = 2x + 4$ **(−2, 0)**
$x + y = -2$

49. $3x + y = 1$ **no solution**
$y = -3x + 5$

Solve each system of equations by substitution. *See Example 5 on page 416.*

50. $y = x + 6$ **(−7, −1)**
$y = -1$

51. $y = x$ **(4, 4)**
$x = 4$

52. $y = 2x - 3$ $\left(\dfrac{3}{2}, 0\right)$
$y = 0$

8-10 Graphing Inequalities

See pages 419–422.

Concept Summary

• To graph an inequality, first graph the related equation, which is the boundary.

• All points in the shaded region are solutions of the inequality.

Example Graph $y < x + 2$.

Graph $y = x + 2$. Draw a dashed line since the boundary is not part of the graph.
Test a point in the original inequality and shade the appropriate region. **53–56. See margin.**

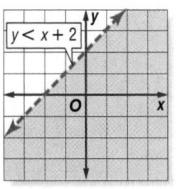

Exercises Graph each inequality. *See Example 1 on pages 419 and 420.*

53. $y \leq 3x - 1$ 　**54.** $y > \dfrac{1}{2}x - 3$ 　**55.** $y \geq -x + 4$ 　**56.** $y < -2x$

428 Chapter 8 Functions and Graphing

55.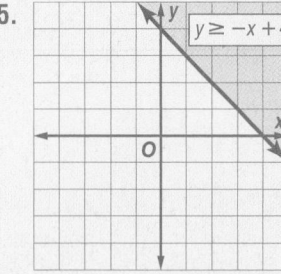

56.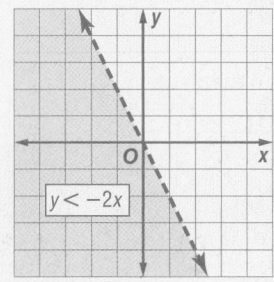

Vocabulary and Concepts

1. **Describe** how to find the x-intercept and the y-intercept of a linear equation. **1–2. See pp. 431A–431H.**

2. **State** how to choose which half plane to shade when graphing an inequality.

3. **OPEN ENDED** Write a system of equations and explain what the solution is.
Sample answer: $y = x$ and $y = -x + 2$; the solution $(1, 1)$ is a solution of both equations.

Skills and Applications

Determine whether each relation is a function. Explain. **4–5. See pp. 431A–431H for explanations.**

4. $\{(-3, 4), (2, 9), (4, -1), (-3, 6)\}$ **no**   5. $\{(1, 2), (4, -6), (-3, 5), (6, 2)\}$ **yes**

Graph each equation by plotting ordered pairs. **6–7. See pp. 431A–431H.**

6. $y = 2x + 1$ 7. $3x + y = 4$

Find the x-intercept and y-intercept for the graph of each equation.
Then, graph the equation using the x- and y-intercepts. **8–9. See pp. 431A–431H for graphs.**

8. $y = x + 3$ **−3; 3**   9. $2x - y = 4$ **2; −4**

Find the slope of the line that passes through each pair of points.

10. $A(2, 5), B(4, 11)$ **3**   11. $C(-4, 5), D(6, -3)$ $-\dfrac{4}{5}$

12. Find the rate of change for the linear function represented in the table.
increase \$5.50/h

Hours Worked	1	2	3	4
Money Earned ($)	5.50	11.00	16.50	22.00

State the slope and y-intercept for the graph of each equation. Then,
graph each equation using the slope and y-intercept. **13–14. See pp. 431A–431H for graphs.**

13. $y = \dfrac{2}{3}x - 4$ $\dfrac{2}{3}$**; −4**   14. $2x + 4y = 12$ $-\dfrac{1}{2}$**; 3**

15. Write an equation in slope-intercept form for the line with a slope of $\dfrac{3}{8}$ and y-intercept $= -2$. $y = \dfrac{3}{8}x - 2$

16. Solve the system of equations $2x - y = 4$ and $4x + y = 2$. **(1, −2)**

17. Graph $y > 2x - 1$. **See pp. 431A–431H.**

GARDENING For Exercises 18 and 19, use the table at the right and
the information below.
The full-grown height of a tomato plant and the number of tomatoes it
bears are recorded for five tomato plants. **18. See pp. 431A–431H.**

Height (in.)	Number of Tomatoes
27	12
33	18
19	9
40	16
31	15

18. Make a scatter plot of the data and draw a best-fit line.

19. Use the best-fit line to predict the number of tomatoes a
43-inch tomato plant will bear. **Sample answer: 20**

20. **STANDARDIZED TEST PRACTICE** Which is a solution of $y \geq -2x + 5$? **D**

   Ⓐ $(1, -7)$ Ⓑ $(1, -3)$ Ⓒ $(-1, 3)$ Ⓓ $(-1, 7)$

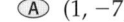 www.pre-alg.com/chapter_test

Chapter 8 Practice Test **429**

Portfolio Suggestion

Introduction Linear equations and their graphs often can be used to
solve real-world problems. Being able to recognize the various ways in
which lines can be represented will help you solve many problems more
quickly.

Ask Students to choose a line to represent in their portfolios. Show its
equation in slope-intercept form, its x- and y-intercepts, a table of values
showing selected points on the line, and a graph of the line.

Assessment Options

Vocabulary Test A vocabulary
review/test for Chapter 8 can be
found on p. 480 of the *Chapter 8
Resource Masters*.

Chapter Tests There are six
Chapter 8 Tests and an Open-
Ended Assessment task available
in the *Chapter 8 Resource Masters*.

Chapter 8 Tests			
Form	Type	Level	Pages
1	MC	basic	467–468
2A	MC	average	469–470
2B	MC	average	471–472
2C	FR	average	473–474
2D	FR	average	475–476
3	FR	advanced	477–478

MC = multiple-choice questions
FR = free-response questions

Open-Ended Assessment
Performance tasks for Chapter 8
can be found on p. 479 of the
Chapter 8 Resource Masters. A
sample scoring rubric for these
tasks appears on p. A32.

Unit Test for Unit 3 is available
on pp. 487–488 of the *Chapter 8
Resource Masters*.

 ExamView® Pro

Use the networkable
ExamView® Pro to:

• Create **multiple versions** of
tests.

• Create **modified** tests for
Inclusion students.

• **Edit** existing questions and
add your own questions.

• Use built-in **state curriculum
correlations** to create tests
aligned with state standards.

• Change **English** tests to
Spanish and vice versa.

These two pages contain practice questions in the various formats that can be found on the most frequently given standardized tests.

A practice answer sheet for these two pages can be found on page A1 of the *Chapter 8 Resource Masters*.

Standardized Test Practice
Student Recording Sheet, p. A1

Part 1 Multiple Choice

Select the best answer from the choices given and fill in the corresponding oval.

1 Ⓐ Ⓑ Ⓒ Ⓓ   4 Ⓐ Ⓑ Ⓒ Ⓓ   7 Ⓐ Ⓑ Ⓒ Ⓓ   9 Ⓐ Ⓑ Ⓒ Ⓓ
2 Ⓐ Ⓑ Ⓒ Ⓓ   5 Ⓐ Ⓑ Ⓒ Ⓓ   8 Ⓐ Ⓑ Ⓒ Ⓓ   10 Ⓐ Ⓑ Ⓒ Ⓓ
3 Ⓐ Ⓑ Ⓒ Ⓓ   6 Ⓐ Ⓑ Ⓒ Ⓓ

Part 2 Short Response/Grid In

Solve the problem and write your answer in the blank.

For Questions 12, 15, and 19, also enter your answer by writing each number or symbol in a box. Then fill in the corresponding oval for that number or symbol.

11 _____   12 [grid]   15 [grid]   19 [grid]
12 _____ (grid in)
13 _____
14 _____
15 _____ (grid in)
16 _____
17 _____
18 _____
19 _____ (grid in)
20 _____

Part 3 Extended Response

Record your answers for Question 21 on the back of this paper.

Additional Practice

See pp. 485–486 of the *Chapter 8 Resource Masters* for additional standardized test practice.

Part 1 Multiple Choice

Record your answers on the answer sheet provided by your teacher or on a sheet of paper.

1. A wooden rod is 5.5 feet long. If you cut the rod into 10 equal pieces, how many inches long will each piece be? (Prerequisite Skill, p. 715) **C**
   Ⓐ 0.55 in.   Ⓑ 5.5 in.
   Ⓒ 6.6 in.   Ⓓ 66 in.

2. Which of the following is a true statement? (Lesson 2-1) **D**
   Ⓐ $\frac{9}{3} < \frac{3}{9}$ Ⓑ $-\frac{3}{9} < -\frac{9}{3}$
   Ⓒ $-\frac{9}{3} > \frac{3}{9}$ Ⓓ $-\frac{3}{9} > -\frac{9}{3}$

3. You roll a cube that has 2 blue sides, 2 yellow sides, and 2 red sides. What is the probability that a yellow side will face upwards when the cube stops rolling? (Lesson 6-9) **B**
   Ⓐ $\frac{1}{6}$ Ⓑ $\frac{1}{3}$
   Ⓒ $\frac{1}{2}$ Ⓓ $\frac{2}{3}$

4. Luis used 3 quarts of paint to cover 175 square feet of wall. He now wants to paint 700 square feet in another room. Which proportion could he use to calculate how many quarts of paint he should buy? (Lesson 6-3) **D**
   Ⓐ $\frac{175}{700} = \frac{x}{3}$ Ⓑ $\frac{3}{700} = \frac{175}{x}$
   Ⓒ $\frac{700}{3} = \frac{175}{x}$ Ⓓ $\frac{3}{175} = \frac{x}{700}$

Test-Taking Tip Ⓐ Ⓑ Ⓒ Ⓓ
Question 1
Pay attention to units of measurement, such as inches, feet, grams, and kilograms. A problem may require you to convert units; for example, you may be told the length of an object in feet and need to find the length of that object in inches.

5. A shampoo maker offered a special bottle with 30% more shampoo than the original bottle. If the original bottle held 12 ounces of shampoo, how many ounces did the special bottle hold? (Lesson 6-7) **C**
   Ⓐ 3.6   Ⓑ 12.3   Ⓒ 15.6   Ⓓ 16

6. The graph shows the materials in a town's garbage collection. If the week's garbage collection totals 6000 pounds, how many pounds of garbage are *not* paper? (Lesson 6-7) **B**

   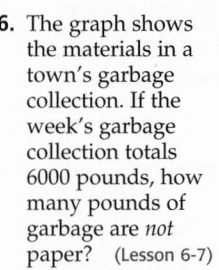
   Garbage Contents
   16% Yard waste
   37% Paper
   25% Glass, metal, plastic
   15% Other
   7% Food waste

   Ⓐ 2220   Ⓑ 3780   Ⓒ 5630   Ⓓ 5963

7. The sum of an integer and the next greater integer is more than 51. Which of these could be the integer? (Lesson 7-6) **D**
   Ⓐ 23   Ⓑ 24   Ⓒ 25   Ⓓ 26

8. The table represents a function between x and y. What is the missing number in the table? (Lesson 8-1) **B**
   Ⓐ 4   Ⓑ 5
   Ⓒ 6   Ⓓ 7

x	y
1	3
2	■
4	9
6	13

9. Which equation is represented by the graph? (Lesson 8-7) **B**
   Ⓐ $y = 2x - 4$
   Ⓑ $y = 2x + 8$
   Ⓒ $y = \frac{1}{2}x - 8$
   Ⓓ $y = \frac{1}{2}x + 4$

   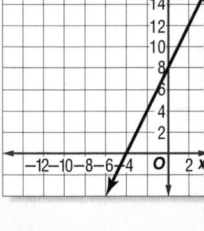

10. Which ordered pair is the solution of this system of equations? (Lesson 8-9) **C**
    $$2x + 3y = 7$$
    $$3x - 3y = 18$$
    Ⓐ (25, 1)   Ⓑ (2, 1)
    Ⓒ (5, −1)   Ⓓ (7, 1)

ExamView® Pro
Special banks of standardized test questions similar to those on the SAT, ACT, TIMSS 8, NAEP 8, and Pre-Algebra End-of-Course tests can be found on this CD-ROM.

Part 2 Short Response/Grid In

Record your answers on the answer sheet provided by your teacher or on a sheet of paper.

11. The graph shows the shipping charges per order, based on the number of items shipped in the order. What is the shipping charge for an order with 4 items? (Prerequisite Skill, pp. 722–723) **$13**

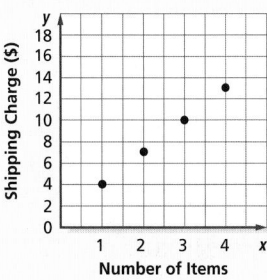

Number of Items

12. The length of a rectangle is 8 centimeters, and its perimeter is 24 centimeters. What is the area of the rectangle in square centimeters? (Lesson 3-5) **32**

13. Write the statement *y is 5 more than one half the value of x* as an equation. (Lesson 3-6)
$y = \frac{1}{2}x + 5$

14. Write the number 0.09357 in scientific notation. Round your answer to two decimal places. (Lesson 4-8) 9.36×10^{-2}

15. If $y = -\frac{3}{2}$, what is the value of x in $y = 4x - 3$? (Lesson 5-8) **3/8**

16. Write $\frac{3}{5}$ as a percent. (Lesson 6-4) **60%**

17. In a diving competition, the diver in first place has a total score of 345.4. Ming has scored 68.2, 68.9, 67.5, and 71.7 for her first four dives and has one more dive remaining. Write an inequality to show the score x that Ming must receive on her fifth dive in order to overtake the diver in first place. (Lesson 7-4) $x > 69.1$

www.pre-alg.com/standardized_test

18. Ms. Vang drove at 30 mph for 30 minutes and at 56 mph for one hour and fifteen minutes. How far did she travel? (Lesson 8-5) **85 miles**

19. What is the slope of the line that contains (0, 4) and (2, 5)? (Lesson 8-6) **1/2**

20. Find the solution of the system of equations graphed below. (Lesson 8-9) **(4, 5)**

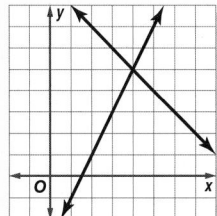

Part 3 Extended Response

Record your answers on a sheet of paper. Show your work. 21a, b, d. See margin.

21. Krishnan is considering three plans for cellular phone service. The plans each offer the same services for different monthly fees and different costs per minute. (Lesson 8-6)

Plan	Monthly Fee	Cost per Minute
X	$0	$0.24
Y	$15.95	$0.08
Z	$25.95	$0.04

a. For each plan, write an equation that shows the total monthly cost c for m minutes of calls.

b. What is the cost of each plan if Krishnan uses 100 minutes per month?

c. Which plan costs the least if Krishnan uses 100 minutes per month? **Plan Y**

d. What is the cost of each plan if Krishnan uses 300 minutes per month?

e. Which plan costs the least if Krishnan uses 300 minutes per month? **Plan Z**

Chapter 8 Standardized Test Practice **431**

Evaluating Extended Response Questions

Extended Response questions are graded by using a multilevel rubric that guides you in assessing a student's knowledge of a particular concept.

Goal: Analyze the given data to determine the best cellular phone service plan.

Sample Scoring Rubric: The following rubric is a sample scoring device. You may wish to add more detail to this sample to meet your individual scoring needs.

Score	Criteria
4	A correct solution that is supported by well-developed, accurate explanations
3	A generally correct solution, but may contain minor flaws in reasoning or computation
2	A partially correct interpretation and/or solution to the problem
1	A correct solution with no supporting evidence or explanation
0	An incorrect solution indicating no mathematical understanding of the concept or task, or no solution is given

Answer

21a. X: $c = 0 + 0.24m$
     Y: $c = 15.95 + 0.08m$
     Z: $c = 25.95 + 0.04m$

21b. X: $c = 0.24(100) = \$24.00$
     Y: $c = 15.95 + 0.08(100) = \$23.95$
     Z: $c = 25.95 + 0.04(100) = \$29.95$

21d. X: $c = 0.24(300) = \$72.00$
     Y: $c = 15.95 + 0.08(300) = \$39.95$
     Z: $c = 25.95 + 0.04(300) = \$37.95$

Page 367, Getting Started

1.

x	y
0	4
−3	3

domain = {0, −3};
range = {4, 3}

2.

x	y
−5	11
2	1

domain = {−5, 2};
range = {11, 1}

3.

x	y
6	8
7	10
8	12

domain = {6, 7, 8};
range = {8, 10, 12}

4.

x	y
1	−9
5	12
−3	−10

domain = {1, 5, −3};
range = {−9, 12, −10}

5.

x	y
−8	5
7	−1
6	1
1	−2

domain = {−8, 7, 6, 1};
range = {5, −1, 1, −2}

Page 368, Algebra Activity

6. Sample answer:

Input	Output
−5	−9
−4	−7
−3	−5
−2	−3
−1	−1
0	1
1	3
2	5
3	7
4	9

rule: × 2 + 1

Page 371, Lesson 8-1

1. Sample answer: a set of ordered pairs: {(1, 2), (4, 3), (−2, −1), (−3, 3)}

x	y
1	2
4	3
−2	−1
−3	3

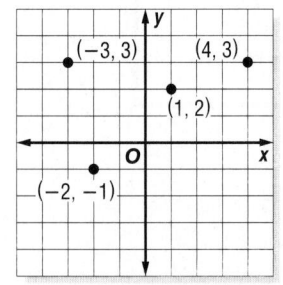

2. Sample answer: Check that each domain value is paired with only one range value or use the vertical line test.

3. Sample answer: This graph does not represent a function because when *x* equals 1, there are two *y* values, 0 and 2.

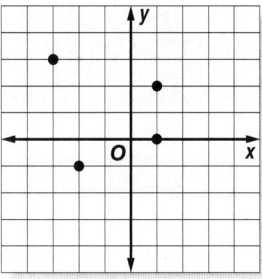

Page 373, Lesson 8-1

33. For a given wind speed, there is only one windchill temperature for each actual temperature. So, the relationship between actual temperatures and windchill temperatures is a function. Answers should include the following.

- For a given wind speed, as the actual temperature increases, the windchill temperature increases.
- Since the relationship between actual temperatures and windchill temperatures is a function, there cannot be two different windchill temperatures for the same actual temperature when the wind speed remains the same.

Page 374, Graphing Calculator Investigation

1c. Greater than 8; the pattern of the range values indicates that if the domain value decreases by 1, then the range value increases by 2.

2b.

Time	Distance
x	y
0	0
1	60
3.5	210
10	600

2d. Sample answer: Input X values between 1 and 3.5 until you get a Y value closer to 150.

Page 378, Lesson 8-2

30.

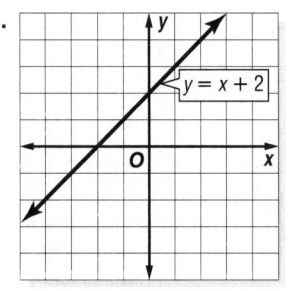

$y = x + 2$

31.

$y = x + 5$

32.

$y = x − 4$

33.

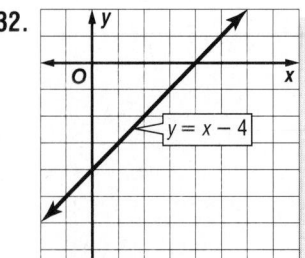

$y = −x − 6$

34.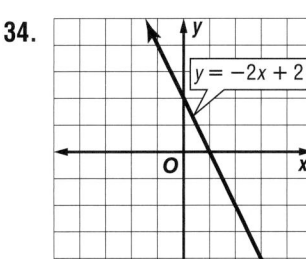

35.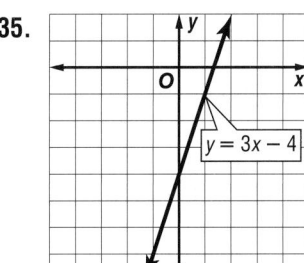

36.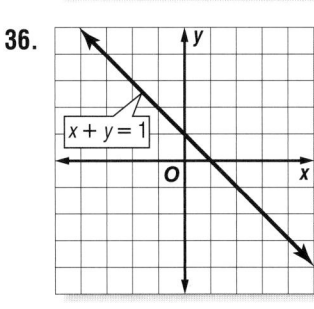

37.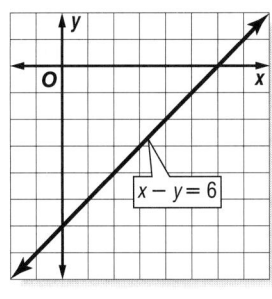

38.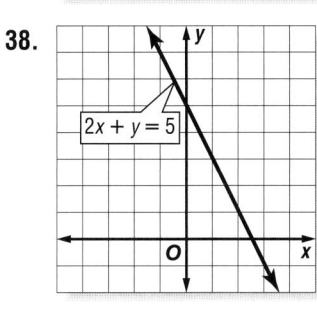

39.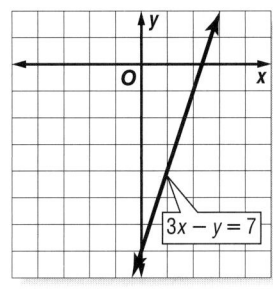

40.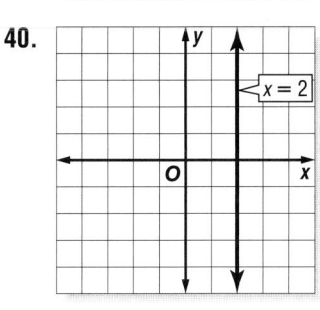

41.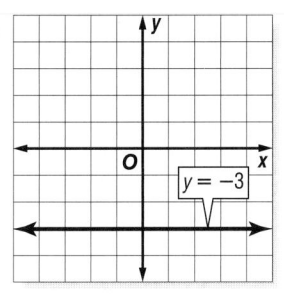

Page 379, Lesson 8-2

51. Sample answer: In the first table, as the x values increase by 1, the y values increase by 2. In the second table, as the x values increase by 1, the y values do not change by a constant amount.

52. Linear equations use variables to show the relationship between the domain values and the range values of a function. Answers should include the following.

- Functions can be represented using a table, a graph, a verbal description, or an equation.
- The equation $y = 0.49x$ represents the cost of x pounds of bananas at $0.49 per pound.

55. Yes; each x value is paired with only one y value.

56. Yes; each x value is paired with only one y value.

57. No; 11 in the domain is paired with 8 and 21 in the range.

58. No; -0.1 in the domain is paired with 5 and -5 in the range.

59.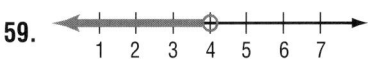

60.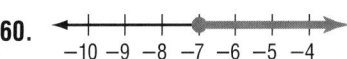

Page 384, Lesson 8-3

11.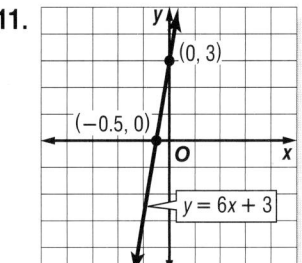

The y-intercept 3 represents the base fee of $3.

Page 385, Lesson 8-3

25.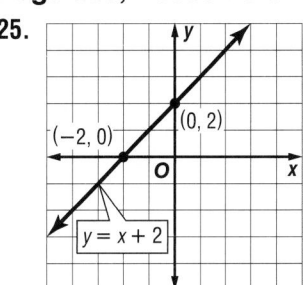

26.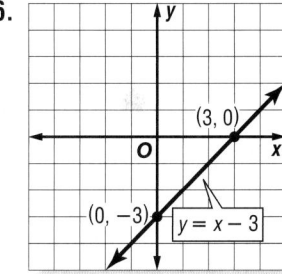

27.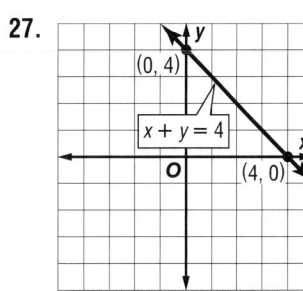

28.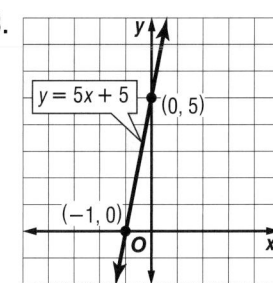

29.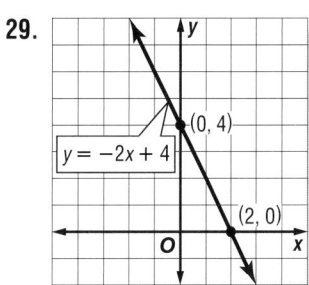

30.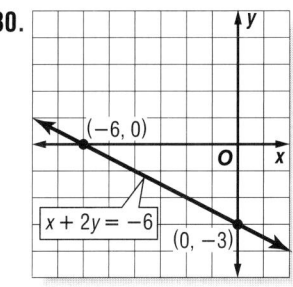

31.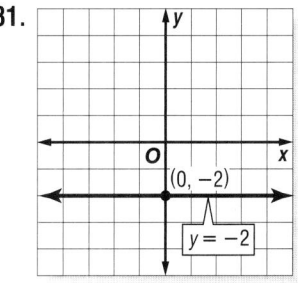

32.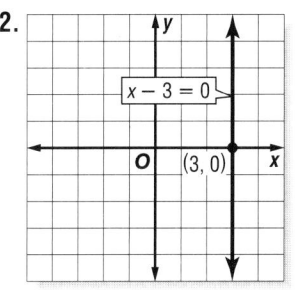

33.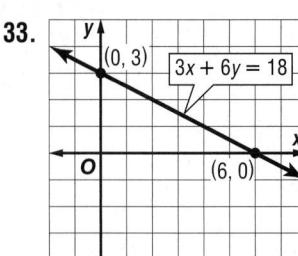

37. The *x*- and *y*-intercept are both 0. Therefore, the line passes through the origin. Since two points are needed to graph a line, $y = 2x$ cannot be graphed using only the intercepts.

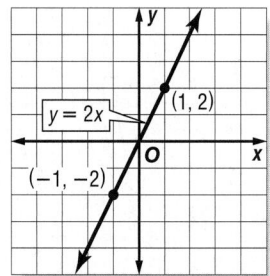

38. The intercepts can be used to show values at time 0, temperature 0, and so on. Answers should include the following.
- Sample graph:
- The *x*-intercept 5 means that after 5 hours the temperature is 0°F. The *y*-intercept 30 means that at time 0, the temperature was 30°F.

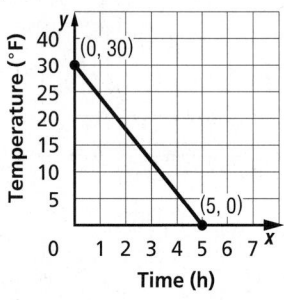

Page 392, Algebra Activity

5. Using a $\frac{1}{8}$ cup; the cup is larger than the tablespoon, so it emptied the glass at a faster rate.

7. Sample answer: teaspoon: slope is less steep than the other graphs because the rate of emptying the glass is slower; $\frac{1}{4}$ cup: steeper slope than the other graphs because the rate of emptying the glass is faster.

8a. 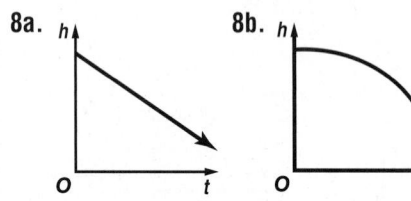   **8b.** 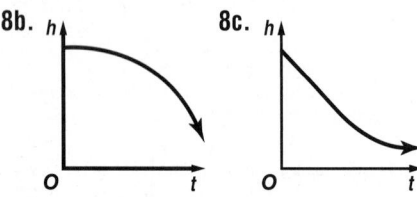   **8c.**

Page 395, Lesson 8-5

2. Sample answer:

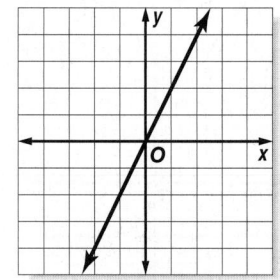

Page 397, Lesson 8-5

20. A horizontal line represents a zero rate of change because there is no change in *y*. A vertical line represents no passage of time, so a rate of change does not make sense.

21. A line representing the relationship between time and distance has a slope that is equal to the speed. Answers should include the following.
- Sample drawing:

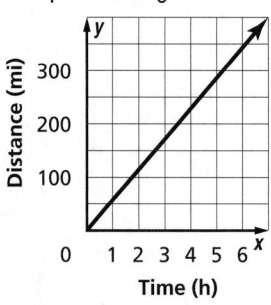

- As speed increases, the slope of the graph becomes steeper.

26. 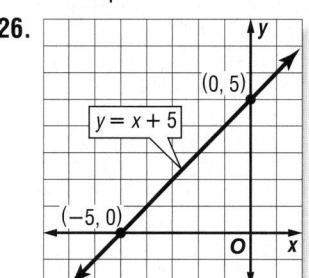   **27.**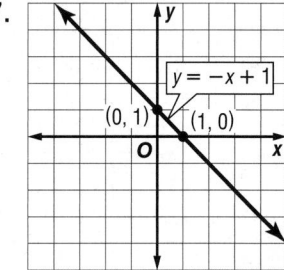

28.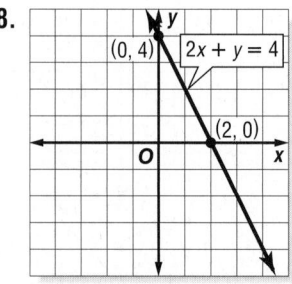

Page 400, Lesson 8-6

2. Sample answer: **7.**

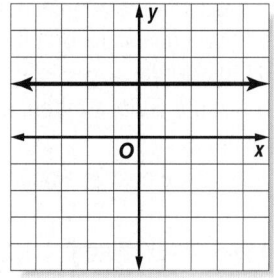   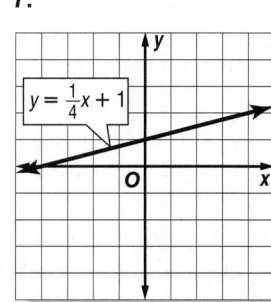

8.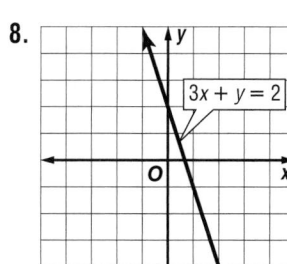
$3x + y = 2$

9.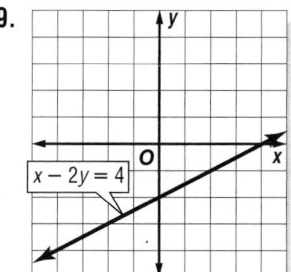
$x - 2y = 4$

10.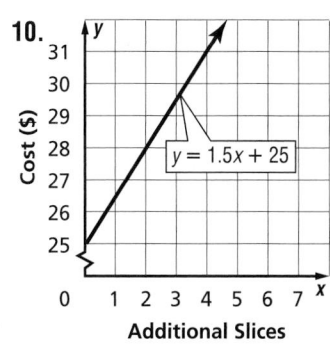
$y = 1.5x + 25$

18.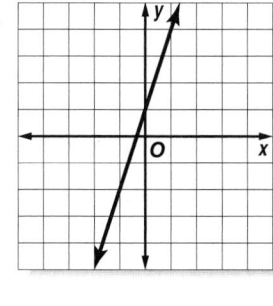

19.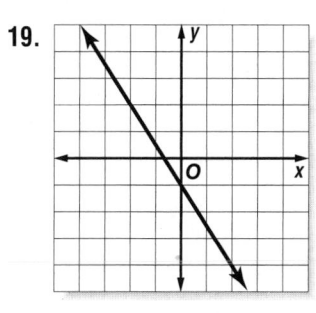

20.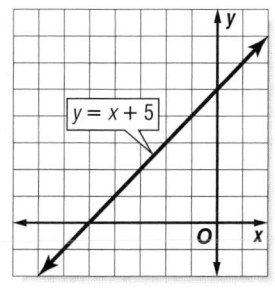
$y = x + 5$

21.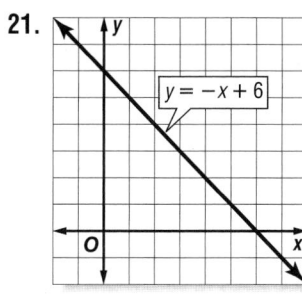
$y = -x + 6$

22.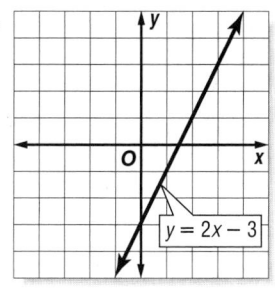
$y = 2x - 3$

23.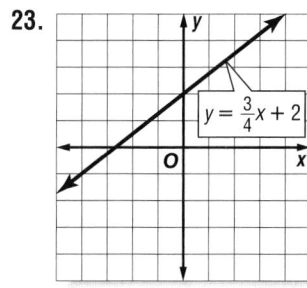
$y = \frac{3}{4}x + 2$

24.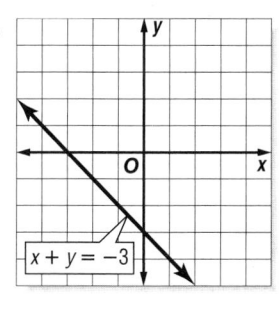
$x + y = -3$

25.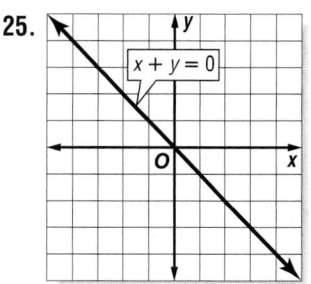
$x + y = 0$

26.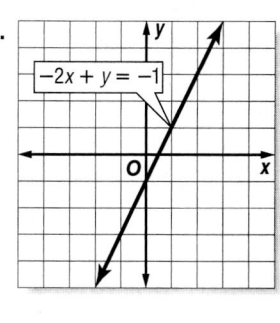
$-2x + y = -1$

27.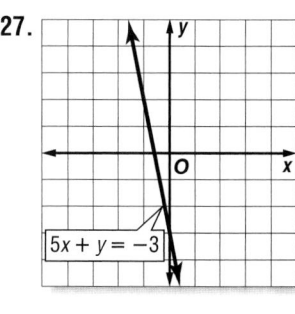
$5x + y = -3$

28.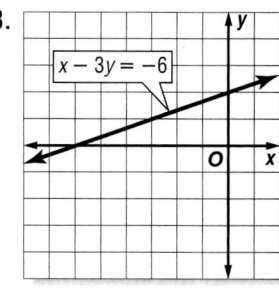
$x - 3y = -6$

29.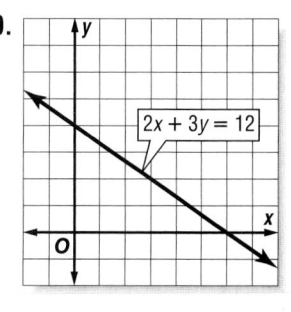
$2x + 3y = 12$

30.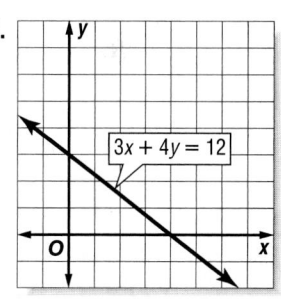
$3x + 4y = 12$

31.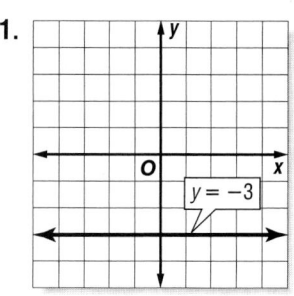
$y = -3$

Page 401, Lesson 8-6

32.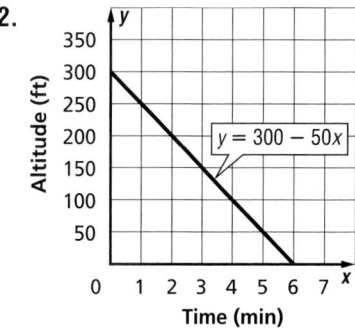
$y = 300 - 50x$

Page 411, Lesson 8-8

7.

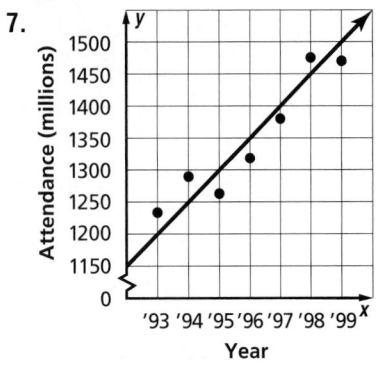

9.

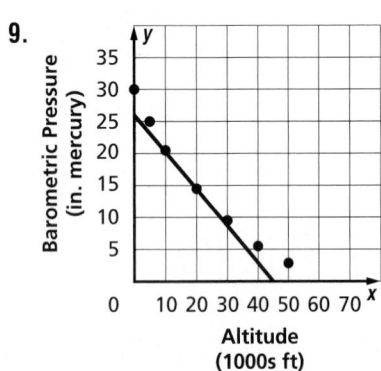

Page 412, Lesson 8-8

12. Sample answer:

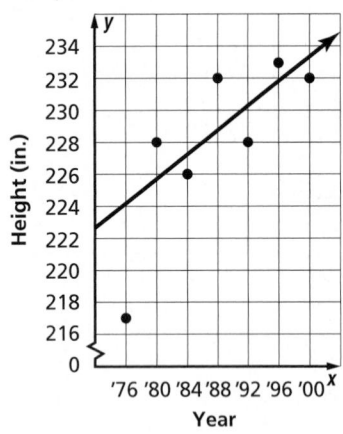

14.

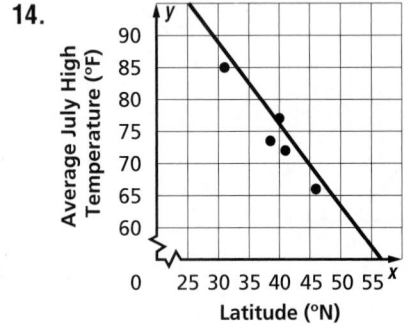

Page 416, Lesson 8-9

4.

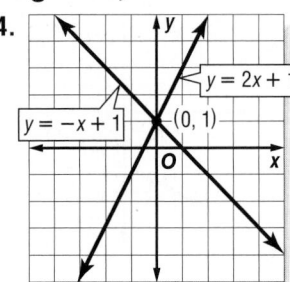

5.

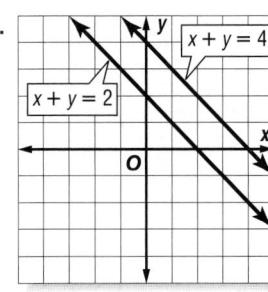

Page 417, Lesson 8-9

12.

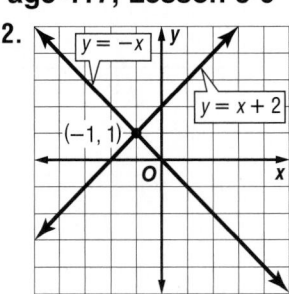

13.

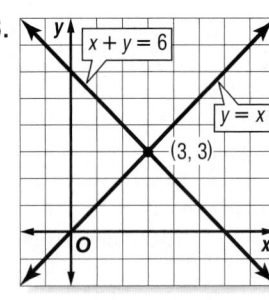

14.

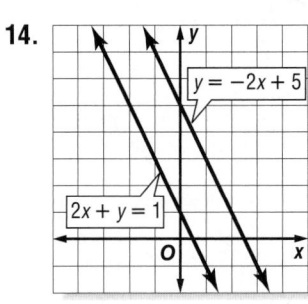

15.

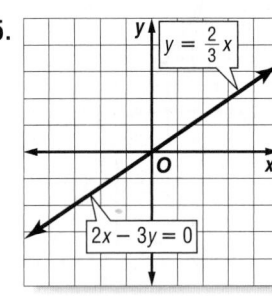

16.

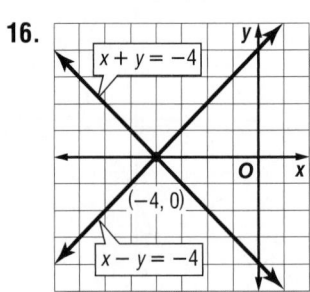

17.

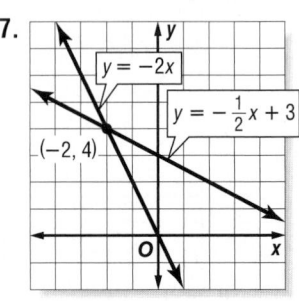

27a. Sample answer:

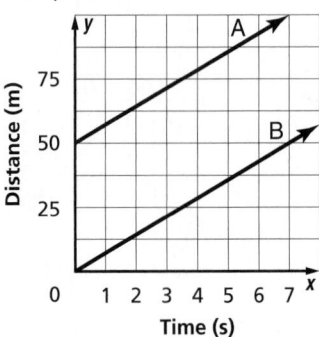

No; since slope represents rate, the slopes of the graphs are the same. Therefore, the runners will never meet.

27b. Sample answer:

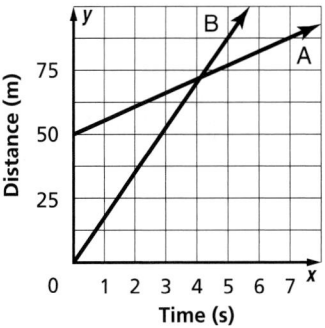

The line representing runner B has a steeper slope than the line representing runner A. The intersection point represents the time and distance at which runner B catches up to runner A.

Page 421, Lesson 8-10

5.

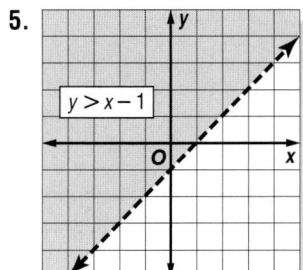

$y > x - 1$

6.

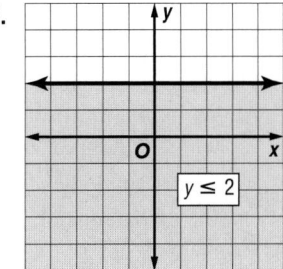

$y \leq 2$

7.

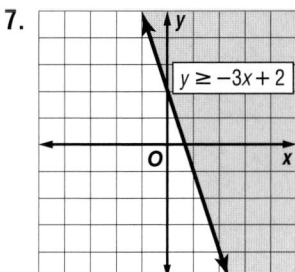

$y \geq -3x + 2$

9.

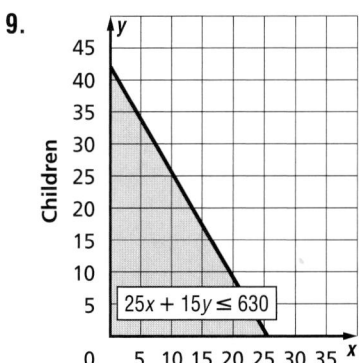

$25x + 15y \leq 630$

Sample answer: 5 adults, 30 children; 10 adults, 22 children; 15 adults, 15 children

10.

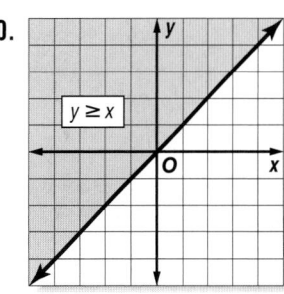

$y \geq x$

11.

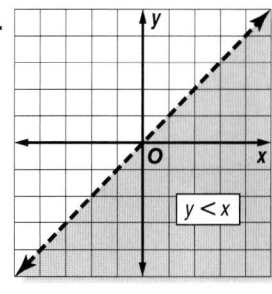

$y < x$

12.

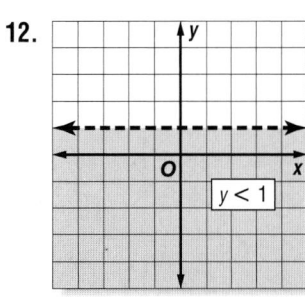

$y < 1$

13.

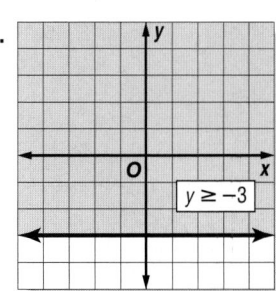

$y \geq -3$

14.

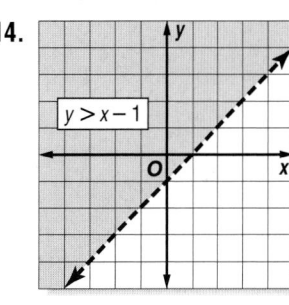

$y > x - 1$

15.

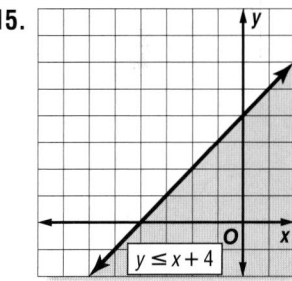

$y \leq x + 4$

16.

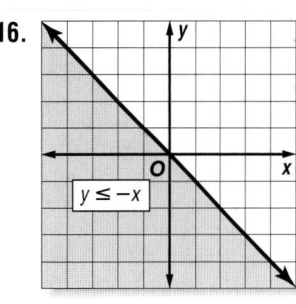

$y \leq -x$

17.

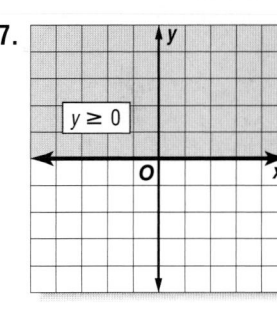

$y \geq 0$

18.

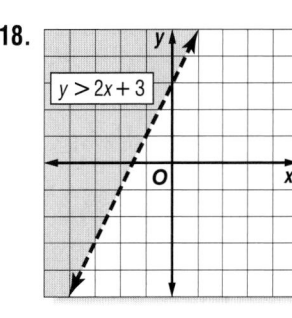

$y > 2x + 3$

19.

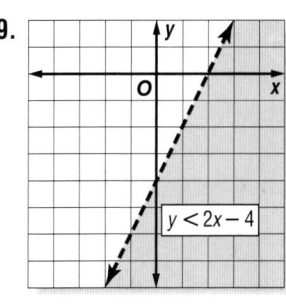

$y < 2x - 4$

20.

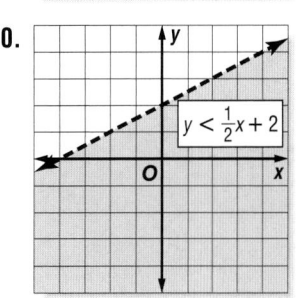

$y < \frac{1}{2}x + 2$

21.

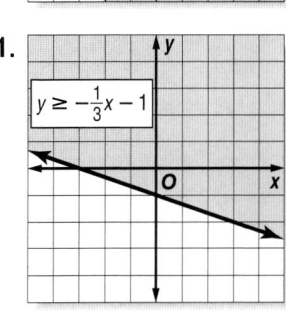

$y \geq -\frac{1}{3}x - 1$

Page 422, Lesson 8-10

31.

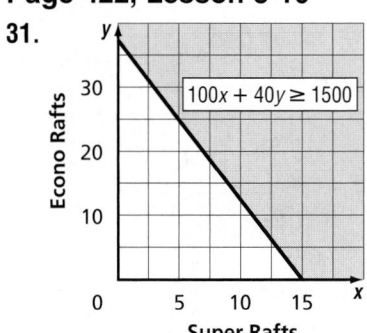

37.

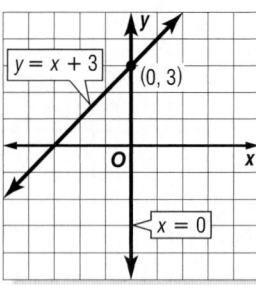

38.

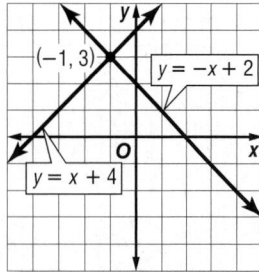

39.

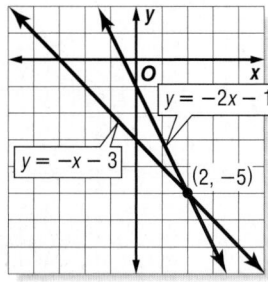

Page 423, Graphing Calculator Investigation

3.

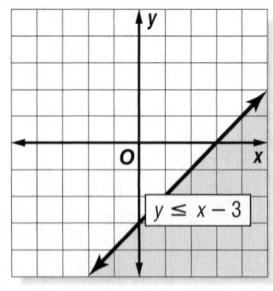

4.

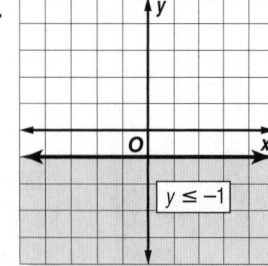

5.

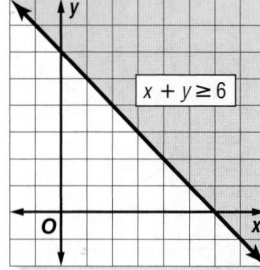

6.

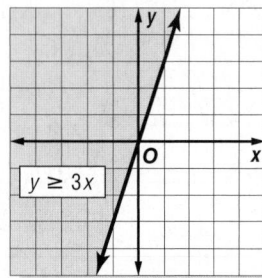

7.

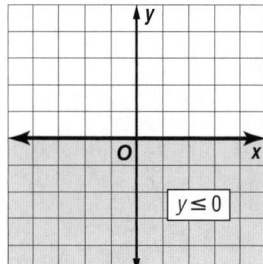

8.

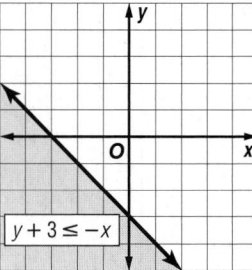

9.

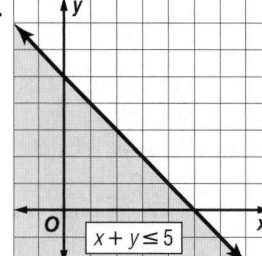

10.

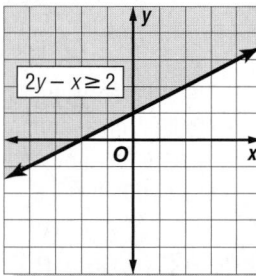

Page 429, Practice Test

1. To find the x-intercept, let $y = 0$ in the equation and solve for x. To find the y-intercept, let $x = 0$ in the equation and solve for y.

2. Choose a point above or below the boundary line and substitute its coordinates in the inequality. If the result is true, shade that side of the boundary. If the result is false, shade the other side of the boundary.

4. -3 in the domain is paired with 4 and 6 in the range.

5. Each x value is paired with only one y value.

6.

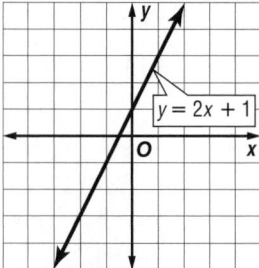

7.

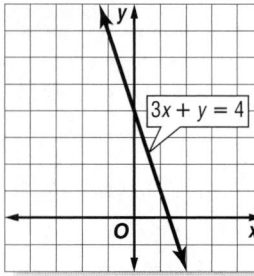

8.

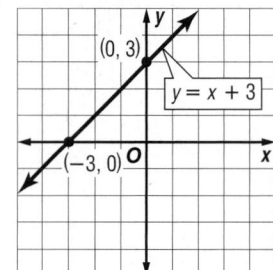

9.

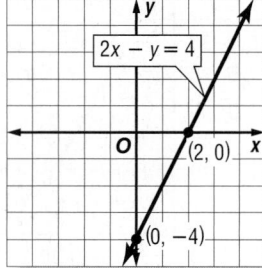

13.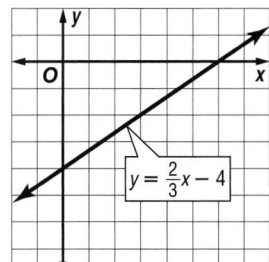

$y = \frac{2}{3}x - 4$

14.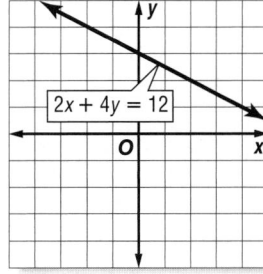

$2x + 4y = 12$

17.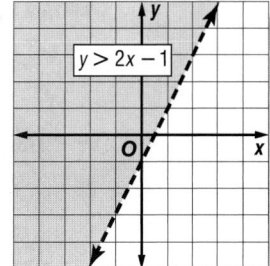

$y > 2x - 1$

18.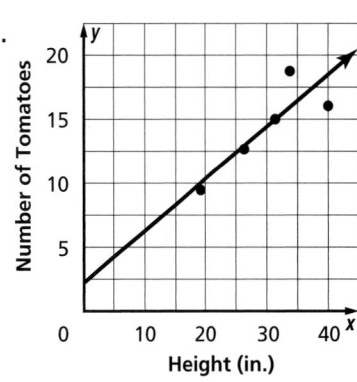

UNIT 4

Applying Algebra to Geometry

Introduction

In this unit, students will examine square roots, and the real number system. They will classify angles and triangles, and explore the Pythagorean Theorem, the Distance Formula, Midpoint Formula, and the properties of similar figures. Students will also use trigonometric ratios to solve problems. In addition, students will classify, find the angle measures, and find the area of various polygons. Students will examine the circumference and area of circles. Additionally, they will find the volume and surface area of three-dimensional objects, and use precision and significant digits to describe measurements.

Although they may seem like different subjects, algebra and geometry are closely related. In this unit, you will use algebra to solve geometry problems.

Chapter 9
Real Numbers and Right Triangles

Chapter 10
Two-Dimensional Figures

Chapter 11
Three-Dimensional Figures

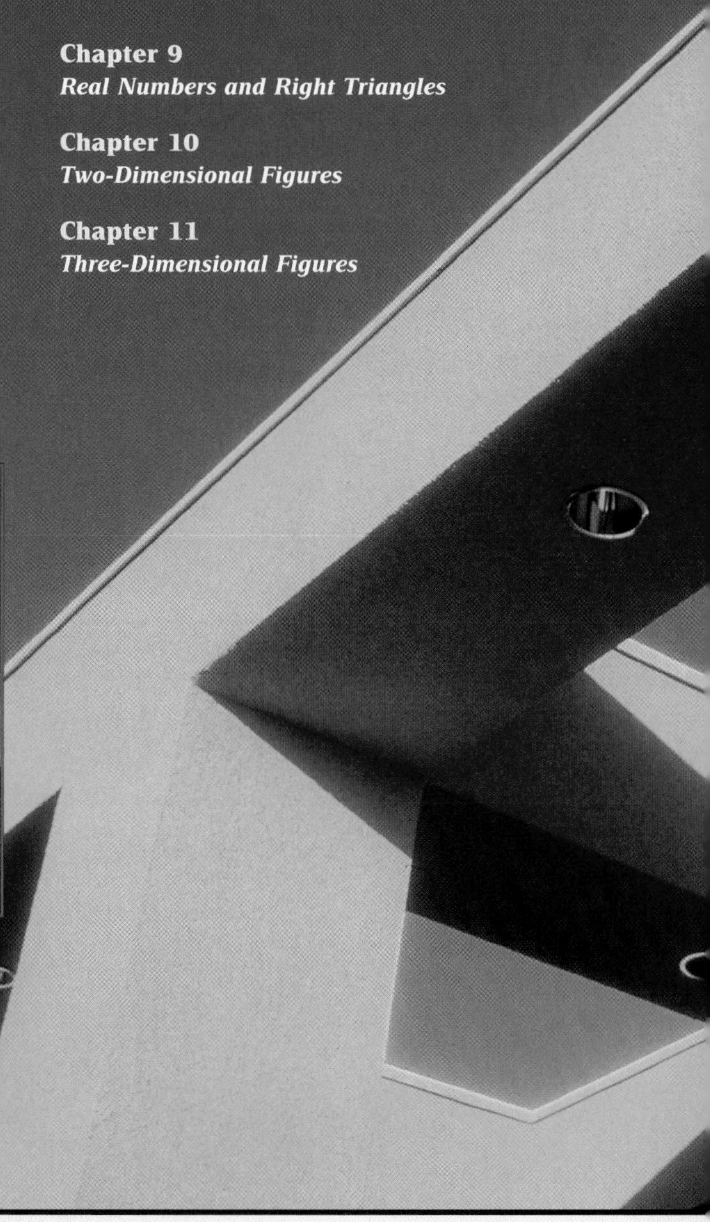

Assessment Options

Unit 4 Test Pages 665–666 of the *Chapter 11 Resource Masters* may be used as a test or review for Unit 4. This assessment contains both multiple-choice and short answer items.

ExamView® Pro

This CD-ROM can be used to create additional unit tests and review worksheets.

An online, research-based instructional, assessment, and intervention tool that provides specific feedback on student mastery of state and national standards, instant remediation, and a data management system to track performance. For more information, contact mhdigitallearning.com.

Real-Life Math Videos
What's Math Got to Do With It? Real-Life Math Videos engage students showing them how math is used in everyday situations. Use Video 3 with this unit.

What's MATH Got To Do With It?

Able to Leap Tall Buildings

The building with the tallest rooftop is the Sears Tower in Chicago, with a height of 1450 feet. However, the tallest building is the Petronas Twin Towers in Kuala Lumpur, Malaysia, whose architectural spires rise to 1483 feet.

In this project, you will be exploring how geometry and algebra can help you describe unusual or large structures of the world.

Log on to www.pre-alg.com/webquest.
Begin your WebQuest by reading the Task.

Then continue working on your WebQuest as you study Unit 4.

Lesson	9-8	10-8	11-3
Page	481	542	571

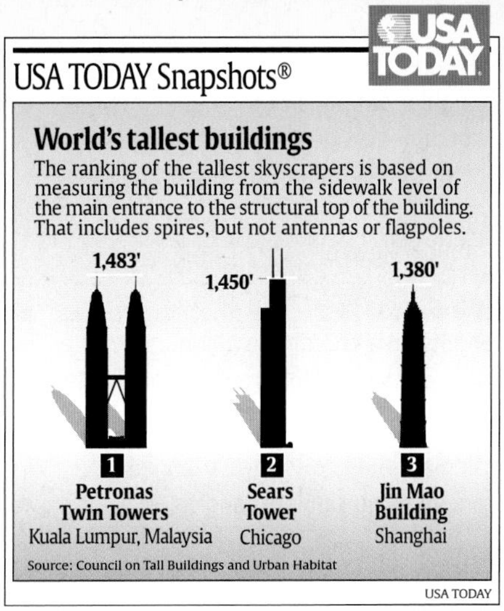

USA TODAY Snapshots®

World's tallest buildings

The ranking of the tallest skyscrapers is based on measuring the building from the sidewalk level of the main entrance to the structural top of the building. That includes spires, but not antennas or flagpoles.

1,483'
1,450'
1,380'

1 Petronas Twin Towers
Kuala Lumpur, Malaysia

2 Sears Tower
Chicago

3 Jin Mao Building
Shanghai

Source: Council on Tall Buildings and Urban Habitat

USA TODAY

Unit 4 Applying Algebra to Geometry 433

WebQuest Internet Project

Problem-Based Learning A WebQuest is an online project in which students do research on the Internet, gather data, and make presentations using word processing, graphing, page-making, or presentation software. In each chapter, students advance to the next step in their WebQuest. At the end of Chapter 11, the project culminates with a presentation of their findings.

Teaching suggestions and sample answers are available in the *WebQuest and Project Resources*.

Real Numbers and Right Triangles
Chapter Overview and Pacing

Year-long pacing: pages T20–T21.

LESSON OBJECTIVES	PACING (days)			
	Regular		Block	
	Basic/ Average	Advanced	Basic/ Average	Advanced
9-1 Squares and Square Roots (pp. 436–440) • Find squares and square roots. • Estimate square roots.	1	1	0.5	0.5
9-2 The Real Number System (pp. 441–442) • Identify and compare numbers in the real number system. • Solve equations by finding square roots.	1	1	0.5	0.5
9-3 Angles (pp. 447–452) • Measure and draw angles. • Classify angles as acute, right, obtuse, or straight. *Follow-Up:* Graph the results of a probability experiment in a circle graph.	1	2 (with 9-3 Follow-Up)	0.5	0.5 (with 9-3 Follow-Up)
9-4 Triangles (pp. 453–457) • Find the missing angle measure of a triangle. • Classify triangles by angles and by sides.	1	1	0.5	0.5
9-5 The Pythagorean Theorem (pp. 458–465) *Preview:* Find the area of figures using rectangular dot paper. • Use the Pythagorean Theorem to find the length of a side of a right triangle. • Use the converse of the Pythagorean Theorem to determine whether a triangle is a right triangle. *Follow-Up:* Graph irrational numbers on a number line.	3 (with 9-5 Preview)	2 (with 9-5 Follow-Up)	1	1 (with 9-5 Follow-Up)
9-6 The Distance and Midpoint Formulas (pp. 466–470) • Use the Distance Formula to determine lengths on a coordinate plane. • Use the Midpoint Formula to find the midpoint of a line segment on the coordinate plane.	2	2	1	1
9-7 Similar Triangles and Indirect Measurement (pp. 471–475) • Identify corresponding parts and find missing measures of similar triangles. • Solve problems involving indirect measurement using similar triangles.	1	1	0.5	0.5
9-8 Sine, Cosine, and Tangent Ratios (pp. 476–482) *Preview:* Discover the special relationship among right triangles and their sides. • Find sine, cosine, and tangent ratios. • Solve problems by using the trigonometric ratios. *Follow-Up:* Use a graphing calculator to find angle measures in a right triangle	3 (with 9-8 Preview	3 (with 9-8 Follow-Up)	1.5 (with 9-8 Preview	1.5 (with 9-8 Follow-Up)
Study Guide and **Practice Test** (pp. 483–487) **Standardized Test Practice** (pp. 488–489)	1	1	0.5	0.5
Chapter Assessment	1	1	0.5	0.5
TOTAL	15	15	7	7

*An electronic version of this chapter is available on **StudentWorks™**. This backpack solution CD-ROM allows students instant access to the Student Edition, lesson worksheet pages, and web resources.*

Chapter Resource Manager

Timesaving Tools
TeacherWorks™
All-In-One Planner and Resource Center
See pages T5 and T21.

CHAPTER 9 RESOURCE MASTERS

Study Guide and Intervention	Practice (Skills and Average)	Reading to Learn Mathematics	Enrichment	Assessment	Prerequisite Skills Workbook	Applications*	Parent and Student Study Guide Workbook	5-Minute Check Transparencies	Interactive Chalkboard	Pre-AlgePASS: Tutorial Plus (lessons)	Materials
489	490–491	492	493				72	9-1	9-1	26	
494	495–496	497	498	543		GCS 35	73	9-2	9-2		
499	500–501	502	503				74	9-3	9-3		*Follow-Up:* spreadsheet software
504	505–506	507	508	543, 545			75	9-4	9-4		
509	510–511	512	513			SC 17	76	9-5	9-5	27, 28	*Preview:* rectangular dot paper *Follow-Up:* grid paper, compass
514	515–516	517	518	544			77	9-6	9-6		
519	520–521	522	523			SC 18	78	9-7	9-7	29	
524	525–526	527	528	544		GCS 36	79	9-8	9-8	30	*Preview:* metric ruler, protractor, calculator *Follow-Up:* graphing calculator
				529–542, 546–548							

* *Key to Abbreviations:* GCS = Graphing Calculator and Spreadsheet Masters, SC = School-to-Career Masters, SM = Science and Mathematics Lab Manual

ELL Study Guide and Intervention, Skills Practice, Practice, and Parent and Student Study Guide Workbooks are also available in Spanish.

Chapter 9 Mathematical Connections and Background

Continuity of Instruction

Prior Knowledge

In Chapter 7, students learned to solve equations with variables on each side of the equation. They also learned to write and graph inequalities, and to solve multi–step inequalities. In Chapter 8, students wrote and graphed equations, found slopes of lines, and used slope to describe rates of change. Students also learned to use best–fit lines to make predictions.

This Chapter

Students learn to use squares and square roots, classify angles and triangles, and find missing angle measurements in triangles. They use the Pythagorean Theorem to explore right triangles, and study the Distance and Midpoint Formulas. Students also identify and use properties of similar figures. In addition, they learn to use trigonometric ratios to solve problems.

Future Connections

The properties of right triangles are the basis for the study of trigonometry, which is related to geometry. Trigonometry was developed to calculate distances and angles in various fields such as cartography, astronomy, and surveying. The Distance Formula and Midpoint Formula will be used in Calculus.

9-1 Squares and Square Roots

The square root of a number is one of two equal factors of a number. Every positive number has a positive and a negative square root. For example, since $8 \cdot 8 = 64$, 8 is a square root of 64. Since $(-8) \cdot (-8) = 64$, -8 is a square root of 64. The notation $\sqrt{}$ indicates the positive square root, $-\sqrt{}$ indicates the negative square root, and $\pm\sqrt{}$ indicates both square roots. For example, $\sqrt{81} = 9$, $-\sqrt{49} = -7$, and $\pm\sqrt{4} = \pm 2$. A negative number has no real square root because the square root of a number is never negative. That is, $\sqrt{-32}$ is not possible.

9-2 The Real Number System

The real number system is made up of the sets of rational and irrational numbers. Rational numbers are numbers that can be written in the form $\frac{a}{b}$ where a and b are integers and $b \neq 0$. Examples are 0.45, $\frac{1}{4}$, and $\sqrt{0.36}$. Irrational numbers are non–repeating or non–terminating decimals. Examples are $\sqrt{71}$, π, and $0.020020002....$

9-3 Angles

Two rays that have the same endpoint form an angle. The common endpoint is called the vertex, and the two rays that make up the angle are called the sides of the angle. The most common unit of measure for angles is the degree. Protractors can be used to measure angles or to draw an angle of a given measure.

Angles can be classified by their degree measure. Acute angles have measures less than 90° but greater than 0°. Obtuse angles have measures greater than 90° but less than 180°. Right angles have measures of 90°.

9-4 Triangles

A triangle is a figure formed by three line segments that intersect only at their endpoints. The sum of the measures of the angles of a triangle is 180°.

Triangles can be classified by their angles. An acute triangle contains all acute angles. An obtuse triangle has one obtuse angle. A right triangle has one right angle.

Triangles also can be classified by their sides. A scalene triangle has no congruent sides. An isosceles triangle has at least two sides congruent. An equilateral triangle has all sides congruent.

9-5 The Pythagorean Theorem

In a right triangle, the sides that are adjacent to the right angle are called the legs. The side opposite the right angle is the hypotenuse.

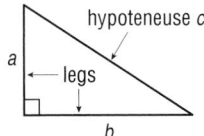

The Pythagorean Theorem describes the relationship between the lengths of the legs and the hypotenuse c. It states that if a triangle is a right triangle, then the square of the length of the hypotenuse is equal to the sum of the squares of the lengths of the legs. In symbols, $c^2 = a^2 + b^2$.

9-6 The Distance and Midpoint Formulas

The Distance Formula can be used to find the length of a segment on a coordinate plane. It states that the distance d between two points with coordinates (x_1, y_1) and (x_2, y_2) is given by

$$d = \sqrt{(x_2 - x_1)^2 + (y_2 - y_1)^2}.$$

On a line segment, the point that is halfway between the endpoints is called the midpoint. To find the midpoint of a segment on a coordinate plane, you can use the Midpoint Formula. This formula states that on a coordinate plane, the coordinates of the midpoint of a segment whose endpoints have coordinates at (x_1, y_1) and (x_2, y_2) are given by $\left(\dfrac{x_1 + x_2}{2}, \dfrac{y_1 + y_2}{2}\right)$.

9-7 Similar Triangles and Indirect Measurement

Triangles that have the same shape but not necessarily the same dimensions are similar triangles. Similar triangles have corresponding angles and sides. Arcs are used to show congruent angles.

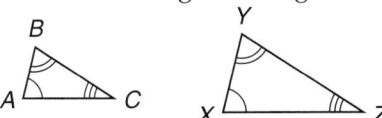

If two triangles are similar, then the corresponding angles have the same measure, and the corresponding sides are proportional. Therefore, to determine the measures of the sides of similar triangles when some measures are known, proportions can be used.

9-8 Sine, Cosine, and Tangent Ratios

Trigonometry is the study of the properties of triangles. A trigonometric ratio is a ratio of the lengths of two sides of a right triangle. The most common trigonometric ratios are the sine, cosine, and tangent ratios. These ratios are abbreviated as sin, cos, and tan, respectively. Consider the right triangle shown.

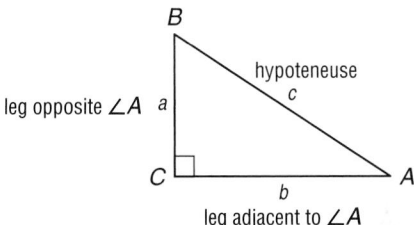

If $\angle A$ is an acute angle of a right triangle, then

$$\sin \angle A = \frac{\text{measure of leg opposite } \angle A}{\text{measure of hypotenuse}},$$

$$\cos \angle A = \frac{\text{measure of leg adjacent to } \angle A}{\text{measure of hypotenuse}}, \text{ and}$$

$$\tan \angle A = \frac{\text{measure of leg opposite } \angle A}{\text{measure of leg adjacent to } \angle A}.$$

Quick Review Math Handbook

Hot Words includes a glossary of terms while Hot Topics consists of explanations of key mathematical concepts with exercises to test comprehension. This valuable resource can be used as a reference in the classroom or for home study.

Lesson	Hot Topics Section	Lesson	Hot Topics Section
9-1	3.1, 3.2	9-6	6.5
9-3	6.4, 7.1, 7.2	9-7	8.6
9-4	3.1, 3.4, 6.2, 7.1	9-8	7.10
9-5	3.1, 3.4, 6.2, 7.9		

 Additional mathematical information and teaching notes are available at www.pre-alg.com/key_concepts.

DAILY INTERVENTION and Assessment

Key to Abbreviations:
TWE = Teacher Wraparound Edition; CRM = Chapter Resource Masters

Type	Student Edition	Teacher Resources	Technology/Internet
INTERVENTION			
Ongoing	Prerequisite Skills, p. 435, 440, 445, 451, 457, 464, 470, 475 Practice Quiz 1, p. 451 Practice Quiz 2, p. 470	5-Minute Check Transparencies Quizzes, *CRM*, pp. 543, 544 Mid-Chapter Test, *CRM*, p. 545 Study Guide and Intervention, *CRM*, pp. 489, 494, 499, 504, 509, 514, 519, 524	Pre-AlgePASS: Tutorial Plus, Lessons 26, 27, 28, 29, and 30 www.pre-alg.com/self_check_quiz www.pre-alg.com/extra_examples
Mixed Review	pp. 440, 445, 451, 457, 464, 470, 475, 481	Cumulative Review, *CRM*, p. 546	
Error Analysis	Find the Error, pp. 462, 479	Find the Error, *TWE*, pp. 462, 479 Unlocking Misconceptions, *TWE*, pp. 437, 448, 455, 472, 478 Tips for New Teachers, *TWE*, pp. 451, 464	
Standardized Test Practice	pp. 440, 445, 451, 457, 461, 462, 464, 470, 475, 481, 488–489	*TWE*, pp. 488–489 Standardized Test Practice, *CRM*, pp. 547–548	Standardized Test Practice CD-ROM www.pre-alg.com/standardized_test
ASSESSMENT			
Open-Ended Assessment	Writing in Math, pp. 440, 445, 451, 457, 464, 469, 475, 481 Open Ended, pp. 438, 443, 449, 455, 462, 468, 473, 479 Standardized Test, p. 489	Speaking: *TWE*, pp. 440, 464 Writing: *TWE*, pp. 445, 475, 481 Modeling: *TWE*, pp. 451, 457, 470 Open-Ended Assessment, *CRM*, p. 479	
Chapter Assessment	Study Guide, pp. 483–486 Practice Test, p. 487	Multiple Choice Tests (Forms 1, 2A, 2B), *CRM*, pp. 529–534 Free-Response Tests (Forms 2C, 2D, 3), *CRM*, pp. 535–540 Vocabulary Test/Review, *CRM*, p. 542	ExamView® Pro (see below) MindJogger Videoquizzes www.pre-alg.com/vocabulary_review www.pre-alg.com/chapter_test

For more information on Yearly ProgressPro, see p. 432.

Pre-Algebra Lesson	Yearly ProgressPro Skill Lesson(s)
9-1	Square Roots
9-2	Classify Real Numbers
9-3	Types of Angles: Level 2
9-4	Types of Triangles
9-5	Pythagorean Theorem
9-6	Distance on the Coordinate Plane
9-7	Similar Figures Indirect measurement
9-8	Trigonometric Ratios

ExamView® Pro

Use the networkable **ExamView® Pro** to:
- Create **multiple versions** of tests.
- Create **modified** tests for *Inclusion* students.
- **Edit** existing questions and **add** your own questions.
- Use built-in **state curriculum correlations** to create tests aligned with state standards.
- Change **English** tests to **Spanish** and vice versa.

For more information on Intervention and Assessment, see pp. T8–T11.

Reading and Writing in Mathematics

Glencoe Pre-Algebra provides numerous opportunities to incorporate reading and writing into the mathematics classroom.

Student Edition

- Foldables™ Study Organizer, p. 435
- Reading Mathematics, p. 446
- Concept Check questions require students to verbalize and write about what they have learned in the lesson. (pp. 437, 438, 441, 443, 449, 455, 461, 462, 466, 468, 472, 473, 479)
- Writing in Math questions in every lesson, pp. 440, 445, 451, 457, 464, 469, 475, 481
- Reading Math, pp. 437, 448, 453, 471, 472, 477
- WebQuest, p. 481

Teacher Wraparound Edition

- Foldables™ Study Organizer, pp. 435, 483
- Study Notebook suggestions, pp. 438, 443, 446, 449, 452, 455, 459, 462, 465, 468, 473, 476, 479
- Modeling activities, pp. 451, 457, 470
- Speaking activities, pp. 440, 464
- Writing activities, pp. 445, 475, 481
- Differentiated Instruction (Verbal/Linguistic), p. 442
- **ELL** Resources, pp. 434, 436, 441, 442, 446, 447, 453, 460, 466, 471, 477, 483

For more information on Reading and Writing in Mathematics, see pp. T6–T7.

Additional Resources

- Vocabulary Builder worksheets require students to define and give examples for key vocabulary terms as they progress through the chapter (*Chapter 9 Resource Masters*, pp. vii–viii)
- Reading to Learn Mathematics master for each lesson (*Chapter 9 Resource Masters*, pp. 492, 497, 502, 507, 512, 517, 522, 527)
- *Vocabulary PuzzleMaker* software creates crossword, jumble, and word search puzzles using vocabulary lists that you can customize.
- *Teaching Mathematics with Foldables* provides suggestions for promoting cognition and language.
- *Reading and Writing in the Mathematics Classroom*
- *WebQuest and Project Resources*

PROJECT CRISS℠ Study Skill

Producing an accurate, detailed written summary can help students' understanding of new material. Demonstrate the summarization process using the example at the right for Lesson 9-1. Begin by having students notice lesson titles, boldface words, and illustrations. Next, have them read the lesson. Then summarize it on the chalkboard as shown. Finally, students should write a summary, in their own words, based on the notes.

Have students work through this process individually or in cooperative groups for the remaining lessons in Chapter 9.

Lesson 9-1

- The square of a number is the product of the number and itself.
  Example: $3^2 = 9$
- Perfect squares are squares of whole numbers.
  Example: 25 is a perfect square with factors 5, 5
- Square roots are the factors multiplied to form perfect squares.
- A radical sign indicates the positive square root of a number.

CReating **I**ndependence **T**hrough **S**tudent-**O**wned **S**trategies

What You'll Learn

Have students read over the list of objectives and make a list of any words with which they are not familiar.

Why It's Important

Point out to students that this is only one of many reasons why each objective is important. Others are provided in the introduction to each lesson.

Lesson	NCTM Standards	Local Objectives
9-1	1, 4, 6, 8	
9-2	1, 2	
9-3	3, 4, 6	
9-3 Follow-Up	3, 4, 6	
9-4	1, 2, 3, 4, 6, 8, 9	
9-5 Preview	1, 2, 3, 4, 6, 7, 8	
9-5	1, 2, 3, 4, 6, 7, 8	
9-5 Follow-Up	1, 2, 3, 4, 6, 8	
9-6	1, 2, 3, 4, 6, 8	
9-7	1, 2, 3, 4, 6, 8, 9, 10	
9-8 Preview	1, 2, 3, 4, 6, 8, 9, 10	
9-8	1, 2, 3, 4, 6, 8, 9, 10	
9-8 Follow-Up	1, 2, 3, 4, 6, 9	

Key to NCTM Standards:

1=Number & Operations, 2=Algebra,
3=Geometry, 4=Measurement,
5=Data Analysis & Probability, 6=Problem
Solving, 7=Reasoning & Proof,
8=Communication, 9=Connections,
10=Representation

What You'll Learn

- **Lessons 9-1 and 9-2** Find and use squares and square roots and identify numbers in the real number system.
- **Lessons 9-3 and 9-4** Classify angles and triangles and find the missing angle measure of a triangle.
- **Lessons 9-5 and 9-6** Use the Pythagorean Theorem, the Distance Formula, and the Midpoint Formula.
- **Lesson 9-7** Identify and use properties of similar figures.
- **Lesson 9-8** Use trigonometric ratios to solve problems.

Key Vocabulary

- angle (p. 447)
- triangle (p. 453)
- Pythagorean Theorem (p. 460)
- similar triangles (p. 471)
- trigonometric ratios (p. 477)

Why It's Important

All of the numbers we use on a daily basis are real numbers. Formulas that contain real numbers can be used to solve real-world problems dealing with distance. For example, if you know the height of a lighthouse, you can use a formula to determine how far you can see from the top of the lighthouse. *You will solve a problem about lighthouses in Lesson 9-1.*

Vocabulary Builder

ELL

The Key Vocabulary list introduces students to some of the main vocabulary terms included in this chapter. For a more thorough vocabulary list with pronunciations of new words, give students the Vocabulary Builder worksheets found on pages vii and viii of the *Chapter 9 Resource Masters*. Encourage them to complete the definition of each term as they progress through the chapter. You may suggest that they add these sheets to their study notebooks for future reference when studying for the Chapter 9 test.

▶ **Prerequisite Skills** To be successful in this chapter, you'll need to master these skills and be able to apply them in problem-solving situations. Review these skills before beginning Chapter 9.

For Lesson 9-2   **Compare Decimals**

Replace each ● with $<$, $>$, or $=$ to make a true statement.   *(For review, see page 710.)*

1. $3.2 ● 3.5$ $<$ **2.** $7.8 ● 7.7$ $>$ **3.** $5.13 ● 5.16$ $<$ **4.** $4.92 ● 4.89$ $>$

5. $2.62 ● 2.6$ $>$ **6.** $3.4 ● 3.41$ $<$ **7.** $0.07 ● 0.7$ $<$ **8.** $1.16 ● 1.06$ $>$

For Lessons 9-4 and 9-7   **Solve Equations by Dividing**

ALGEBRA Solve each equation.   *(For review, see Lesson 3-4.)*

9. $3x = 24$ **8**   **10.** $7y = 49$ **7**   **11.** $120 = 2n$ **60**   **12.** $54 = 6a$ **9**

13. $90 = 10m$ **9**   **14.** $144 = 12m$ **12**   **15.** $15d = 165$ **11**   **16.** $182 = 14w$ **13**

For Lesson 9-6   **Exponents**

Find the value of each expression.   *(For review, see Lesson 4-2.)*

17. $(3 - 1)^2 + (4 - 2)^2$ **8**   **18.** $(5 - 2)^2 + (6 - 3)^2$ **18**   **19.** $(4 - 7)^2 + (3 - 8)^2$ **34**

20. $(8 - 2)^2 + (3 - 9)^2$ **72**   **21.** $(2 - 6)^2 + [(-8) - 1]^2$ **97** **22.** $(-7 - 2)^2 + [3 - (-4)]^2$

                                                                                  130

 **Study Organizer**

Right Triangles Make this Foldable to help you organize your notes. Begin with three plain sheets of $8\frac{1}{2}$" by 11" paper.

Step 1 **Fold**

Fold to make a triangle. Cut off the extra paper.

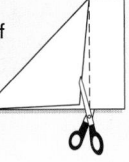

Step 2 **Repeat**

Repeat Step 1 twice. You have three squares.

Step 3 **Stack and Staple**

Stack the three squares and staple along the fold.

Step 4 **Label**

Label each section with a lesson number.

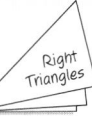

Right Triangles

Reading and Writing As you read and study the chapter, fill the pages with examples, diagrams, and formulas.

This section provides a review of the basic concepts needed before beginning Chapter 9. Page references are included for additional student help.

Prerequisite Skills in the Getting Ready for the Next Lesson section at the end of each lesson reviews a skill needed in the next lesson.

For Lesson	Prerequisite Skill
9-2	Rational Numbers (p. 440)
9-3	Drawing Angles (p. 445)
9-4	Solving Two-Step Equations (p. 451)
9-5	Exponents (p. 457)
9-6	Order of Operations/Exponents (p. 464)
9-7	Proportions (p. 470)
9-8	Writing Fractions as Decimals (p. 475)

FOLDABLES ™
Study Organizer

For more information about Foldables, see *Teaching Mathematics with Foldables.*

Use of Visuals, Captions, and Labels On the pages of their Foldable journals, students take notes, define terms, sketch diagrams, and write formulas. Have students design one or more visuals (graph, diagram, picture, chart) per lesson that present the information introduced in a concise, easy-to-study format. Encourage students to clearly label their visuals and write captions when needed.

9-1 Squares and Square Roots

5-Minute Check Transparency 9-1 Use as a quiz or review of Chapter 8.

Mathematical Background notes are available for this lesson on page 434C.

How are square roots related to factors?

The opening activity questions are repeated on page 492 of the *Chapter 9 Resource Masters*.

Reading to Learn Mathematics, p. 492 **ELL**

Pre-Activity How are square roots related to factors?

Do the activity at the top of page 436 in your textbook. Write your answers below.

a. Describe the difference between the first four and the last four values of x.
The first four are whole numbers and the last four are not.

b. Explain how you found an exact answer for the first four values of x.
To find an exact answer, determine what number times itself is equal to each value of x.

c. How did you find an estimate for the last four values of x?
Choose a decimal value that, when multiplied by itself, is approximately equal to the value of x.

Reading the Lesson 1–3. See students' work.

Write a definition and give an example of each new vocabulary word or phrase.

Vocabulary	Definition	Example
1. perfect square		
2. square root		
3. radical sign		

Helping You Remember

4. For each number in the table, tell whether it has a real square root and explain why or why not. Then indicate if the number is a perfect square and explain.

	Real Square Root ?	Perfect Square ?
26	Yes; positive number	No; not the square of a whole number
−81	No; negative number	
256	Yes; positive number	Yes; square of 16
1444	Yes; positive number	Yes; square of 38
−5	No; negative number	

Teaching Tip The positive or nonnegative square root is also called the principal square root. The symbol $\sqrt{x}$ indicates the principal square root of x.

What You'll Learn

- Find squares and square roots.
- Estimate square roots.

Vocabulary

- perfect square
- square root
- radical sign

How are square roots related to factors?

Values of x^2 are shown in the second column in the table. Guess and check to find the value of x that corresponds to x^2. If you cannot find an exact answer, estimate with decimals to the nearest tenth to find an approximate answer.

x	x^2
5	25
7	49
13	169
15	225
2.8	8
3.5	12
8.1	65
10.5	110

a. Describe the difference between the first four and the last four values of x.

b. Explain how you found an exact answer for the first four values of x.

c. How did you find an estimate for the last four values of x?

SQUARES AND SQUARE ROOTS Numbers like 25, 49, 169, and 225 are **perfect squares** because they are squares of whole numbers.

5×5 or 5^2 7×7 or 7^2 13×13 or 13^2 15×15 or 15^2

  ↓   ↓   ↓   ↓

  25   49   169   225

A **square root** of a number is one of two equal factors of the number. Every positive number has a positive square root and a negative square root. A negative number like −9 has no real square root because the square of a number is never negative.

Key Concept — Square Root

- **Words**   A square root of a number is one of its two equal factors.
- **Symbols**   If $x^2 = y$, then x is a square root of y.
- **Examples**   Since $5 \cdot 5$ or $5^2 = 25$, 5 is a square root of 25.
  Since $(-5) \cdot (-5)$ or $(-5)^2 = 25$, −5 is a square root of 25.

A **radical sign**, $\sqrt{}$, is used to indicate the square root.

Example 1 Find Square Roots

Find each square root.

a. $\sqrt{36}$ $\sqrt{36}$ indicates the *positive* square root of 36.
Since $6^2 = 36$, $\sqrt{36} = 6$.

436 Chapter 9 Real Numbers and Right Triangles

Resource Manager

Workbooks and Reproducible Masters

Chapter 9 Resource Masters
- Study Guide and Intervention, p. 489
- Skills Practice, p. 490
- Practice, p. 491
- Reading to Learn Mathematics, p. 492
- Enrichment, p. 493

Parent and Student Study Guide Workbook, p. 72

Transparencies

5-Minute Check Transparency 9-1
Answer Key Transparencies

Technology

Interactive Chalkboard
Pre-AlgePASS: Tutorial Plus, Lesson 26

Reading Math

Plus or Minus Symbol
The notation $\pm\sqrt{9}$ is read *plus or minus the square root of 9*.

b. $-\sqrt{81}$ $-\sqrt{81}$ indicates the *negative* square root of 81.

Since $9^2 = 81$, $-\sqrt{81} = -9$.

c. $\pm\sqrt{9}$ $\pm\sqrt{9}$ indicates *both* square roots of 9.

Since $3^2 = 9$, $\sqrt{9} = 3$ and $-\sqrt{9} = -3$.

✓ **Concept Check**   What does the radical sign indicate? **the square root**

You can use a calculator to find an approximate square root of a number that is not a perfect square. The decimal portion of these square roots goes on forever.

Example 2 *Calculate Square Roots*

Use a calculator to find each square root to the nearest tenth.

a. $\sqrt{10}$

[2nd] [√] 10 [ENTER]   3.16227766   Use a calculator.

$\sqrt{10} \approx 3.2$ Round to the nearest tenth.

CHECK   Since $(3)^2 = 9$, the answer is reasonable. ✓

Reading Math

Approximately Equal To Symbol
The symbol $\approx$ is read *is approximately equal to*.

b. $-\sqrt{27}$

[2nd] [√] 27 [ENTER]   5.19615242   Use a calculator.

$-\sqrt{27} \approx -5.2$ Round to the nearest tenth.

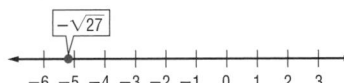

CHECK   Since $(-5)^2 = 25$, the answer is reasonable. ✓

ESTIMATE SQUARE ROOTS   You can also estimate square roots without using a calculator.

Example 3 *Estimate Square Roots*

Estimate each square root to the nearest whole number.

a. $\sqrt{38}$

Find the two perfect squares closest to 38. To do this, list some perfect squares.

$$1, 4, 9, 16, 25, 36, 49, \ldots$$

36 and 49 are closest to 38.

$36 < 38 < 49$ 38 is between 36 and 49.

$\sqrt{36} < \sqrt{38} < \sqrt{49}$ $\sqrt{38}$ is between $\sqrt{36}$ and $\sqrt{49}$.

$6 < \sqrt{38} < 7$ $\sqrt{36} = 6$ and $\sqrt{49} = 7$.

Since 38 is closer to 36 than 49, the best whole number estimate for $\sqrt{38}$ is 6.

www.pre-alg.com/extra_examples

---

2 Teach

SQUARES AND SQUARE ROOTS

In-Class Examples   Power Point®

1 Find each square root.

a. $\sqrt{64}$ **8**

b. $-\sqrt{121}$ **−11**

c. $\pm\sqrt{4}$ **+2 and −2**

Teaching Tip   Remind students to check the sign of their answer.

Teaching Tip   Discuss with students why the square of a number is never negative.

2 Use a calculator to find each square root to the nearest tenth.

a. $\sqrt{23}$ **4.8**

b. $-\sqrt{46}$ **−6.8**

ESTIMATE SQUARE ROOTS

In-Class Example   Power Point®

3 Estimate each square root to the nearest whole number.

a. $\sqrt{22}$ **5**

b. $-\sqrt{319}$ **−18**

Interactive Chalkboard
PowerPoint® Presentations

This CD-ROM is a customizable Microsoft® Power-Point® presentation that includes:

- Step-by-step, dynamic solutions of each In-Class Example from the Teacher Wraparound Edition
- Additional, Your Turn exercises for each example
- The 5-Minute Check Transparencies
- Hot links to Glencoe Online Study Tools

DAILY INTERVENTION

Unlocking Misconceptions

- **Squares and Square Roots**   Students may confuse $-\sqrt{16}$ and $\sqrt{-16}$ and believe the answer for both to be −4. Explain the difference and demonstrate why the square root of a negative number does not exist.

4 **LANDMARKS** The observation deck at the Seattle Space Needle is 520 feet above the ground. On a clear day, about how far could a tourist on the deck see? Round to the nearest tenth.
27.8 mi

3 Practice/Apply

Study Notebook

Have students—

• add the definitions/examples of the vocabulary terms to their Vocabulary Builder worksheets for Chapter 9.

• include any other item(s) that they find helpful in mastering the skills in this lesson.

About the Exercises . . .

Organization by Objective
• **Squares and Square Roots:** 12–33
• **Estimate Square Roots:** 34–46

Odd/Even Assignments
Exercises 12–33, 35–48, 49–50, and 52–55 are structured so that students practice the same concepts whether they are assigned odd or even problems.

Assignment Guide

Basic: 13–19 odd, 25–31 odd, 35–41 odd, 47–51 odd, 57–60, 64–80

Average: 13–55 odd, 57–60, 64–80 (Optional: 61–63)

Advanced: 12–56 even, 57–74 (Optional: 75–80)

---

b. $-\sqrt{175}$

Find the two perfect squares closest to 175. List some perfect squares.

..., 100, 121, 144, 169, 196, ...

⌐ 169 and 196 are closest to 175.

$-196 < -175 < -169$ -175 is between -196 and -169.
$-\sqrt{196} < -\sqrt{175} < -\sqrt{169}$ $-\sqrt{175}$ is between $-\sqrt{196}$ and $-\sqrt{169}$.
$-14 < -\sqrt{175} < -13$ $-\sqrt{196} = -14$ and $-\sqrt{169} = -13$.

Since -175 is closer to -169 than -196, the best whole number estimate for $-\sqrt{175}$ is -13.   **CHECK** $-\sqrt{175} \approx -13.2$ ✓

More About . . .

Science •·············
To estimate how far you can see from a point above the horizon, you can use the formula $D = 1.22 \times \sqrt{A}$ where D is the distance in miles and A is the altitude, or height, in feet.

Many formulas used in real-world applications involve square roots.

Example 4 *Use Square Roots to Solve a Problem*

• **SCIENCE**   Use the information at the left. The light on Cape Hatteras Lighthouse in North Carolina is 208 feet high. On a clear day, from about what distance on the ocean is the light visible? Round to the nearest tenth.

$D = 1.22 \times \sqrt{A}$ Write the formula.
 $= 1.22 \times \sqrt{208}$ Replace A with 208.
 $\approx 1.22 \times 14.42$ Evaluate the square root first.
 ≈ 17.5924 Multiply.

On a clear day, the light will be visible from about 17.6 miles.

Check for Understanding

Concept Check
1–3. See margin.

1. **Explain** why every positive number has two square roots.

2. **List** three numbers between 200 and 325 that are perfect squares.

3. **OPEN ENDED**   Write a problem in which the negative square root is not an integer. Then graph the square root.

Guided Practice

Find each square root, if possible.

4. $\sqrt{49}$ **7**   5. $-\sqrt{64}$ **−8**   6. $\sqrt{-36}$ **not possible**

GUIDED PRACTICE KEY	
Exercises	Examples
4–6	1
7, 8	2
9, 10	3
11	4

Use a calculator to find each square root to the nearest tenth.

7. $\sqrt{15}$ **3.9**   8. $-\sqrt{32}$ **−5.7**

Estimate each square root to the nearest whole number. Do not use a calculator.

9. $\sqrt{66}$ **8**   10. $-\sqrt{103}$ **−10**

Application   11. **SKYSCRAPERS**   Refer to Example 4. Ryan is standing in the observation area of the Sears Tower in Chicago. About how far can he see on a clear day if the deck is 1353 feet above the ground? **44.9 mi**

D A I L Y
INTERVENTION   **Differentiated Instruction**

• **Intrapersonal**   Have students write in their journals some examples of when and why squares and square roots are used. Have them ask their science teacher how squares are used in science and include the answer in their entries.

★ indicates increased difficulty

Homework Help	
For Exercises	**See Examples**
12–23	1
24–33	2
34–46	3
47, 48	4

Extra Practice
See page 745.

Find each square root, if possible. 16, 17. not possible

12. $\sqrt{16}$ 4   13. $\sqrt{36}$ 6   14. $-\sqrt{1}$ −1   15. $-\sqrt{25}$ −5

16. $\sqrt{-4}$ 17. $\sqrt{-49}$ 18. $\sqrt{100}$ 10   19. $\sqrt{196}$ 14

★ 20. $\pm\sqrt{256}$ ★ 21. $\pm\sqrt{324}$ ★ 22. $\sqrt{0.81}$ 0.9   ★ 23. $\sqrt{2.25}$ 1.5
    16, −16   18, −18

Use a calculator to find each square root to the nearest tenth. 31. −1.7

24. $\sqrt{15}$ 3.9   25. $\sqrt{56}$ 7.5   26. $-\sqrt{43}$ −6.6   27. $-\sqrt{86}$ −9.3

28. $\sqrt{180}$ 13.4   29. $\sqrt{250}$ 15.8   30. $-\sqrt{0.75}$ −0.9   31. $-\sqrt{3.05}$

★ 32. Find the negative square root of 1000 to the nearest tenth. −31.6

★ 33. If $x = \sqrt{5000}$, what is the value of x to the nearest tenth? 70.7

34. The number $\sqrt{54}$ lies between which two consecutive whole numbers? Do not use a calculator. 7 and 8

Estimate each square root to the nearest whole number. Do not use a calculator.

35. $\sqrt{79}$ 9   36. $\sqrt{95}$ 10   37. $-\sqrt{54}$ −7   38. $-\sqrt{125}$ −11

39. $\sqrt{200}$ 14   40. $\sqrt{396}$ 20   41. $-\sqrt{280}$ −17   42. $-\sqrt{490}$ −22

★ 43. $-\sqrt{5.25}$ −2   ★ 44. $-\sqrt{17.3}$ −4   ★ 45. $\sqrt{38.75}$ 6   ★ 46. $\sqrt{140.57}$ 12

ROLLER COASTERS For Exercises 47–48, use the table shown and refer to Example 4 on page 438.

47. On a clear day, how far can a person see from the top hill of the Vortex? 14.8 mi

48. How far can a person see on a clear day from the top hill of the Titan? 19.5 mi

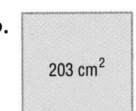

Coaster	Maximum Height (ft)
Double Loop	95
The Villain	120
Mean Streak	161
Raptor	137
The Beast	110
Vortex	148
Titan	255
Shockwave	116

Source: Roller Coaster Database

 **Online Research Data Update**
How far can you see from the top of the tallest roller coaster in the United States? Visit www.pre-alg.com/data_update to learn more.

Complete Exercises 49 and 50 without the help of a calculator.

49–50. See margin for explanations.

49. Which is greater, $\sqrt{65}$ or 9? Explain your reasoning. 9

50. Which is less, 11 or $\sqrt{120}$? Explain your reasoning. $\sqrt{120}$

51. **GEOMETRY** The area of each square is given. Estimate the length of a side of each square to the nearest tenth. Then find its approximate perimeter.

a. 109 in² — 10.4 in.; 41.6 in.

b. 203 cm² — 14.2 cm; 56.8 cm

c. 70 m² — 8.4 m; 33.6 m

Simplify.

★ 52. $2 + \sqrt{81} \times 3$ 29   ★ 53. $\sqrt{256} \div 8 \times 5$ 10

★ 54. $(9 - \sqrt{36}) + (16 - \sqrt{100})$ 9   ★ 55. $(\sqrt{1} + 7) \div (\sqrt{121} - 7)$ 2

Find each square root, if possible.

1. $\sqrt{100}$ 10   2. $\sqrt{144}$ 12   3. $\sqrt{-36}$ not possible

4. $\sqrt{121}$ 11   5. $\sqrt{-148}$ not possible   6. $-\sqrt{4}$ −2

7. $-\sqrt{9}$ −3   8. $\sqrt{-49}$ −7   9. $\sqrt{256}$ 16

10. $\sqrt{529}$ 23   11. $\sqrt{361}$ 19   12. $-\sqrt{196}$ −14

Use a calculator to find each square root to the nearest tenth.

13. $-\sqrt{2.25}$ −1.5   14. $\sqrt{38}$ 6.2   15. $\sqrt{249}$ 15.8

16. $\sqrt{131}$ 11.4   17. $\sqrt{7}$ 2.6   18. $\sqrt{52}$ 7.2

19. $\sqrt{168}$ 13.0   20. $\sqrt{499}$ 22.3   21. $-\sqrt{217}$ −14.7

22. $\pm\sqrt{218}$ ±14.8   23. $\pm\sqrt{42}$ ±6.5   24. $\pm\sqrt{94}$ ±9.7

25. $\pm\sqrt{50}$ ±7.1   26. $\pm\sqrt{137}$ ±11.7   27. $\pm\sqrt{208}$ ±14.4

28. Find the negative square root of 840 to the nearest tenth. −29.0

29. If $x^2 = 476$, what is the value of x to the nearest tenth? 21.8

30. The number $\sqrt{22}$ lies between which two consecutive whole numbers? Do not use a calculator. 4 and 5

Estimate each square root to the nearest whole number. Do not use a calculator.

31. $\sqrt{76}$ 9   32. $\sqrt{123}$ 11   33. $\sqrt{300}$ 17

34. $\sqrt{90}$ 9   35. $\sqrt{19}$ 4   36. $\sqrt{248}$ 16

37. **GEOMETRY** A square tarpaulin covering a softball field has an area of 441 m². What is the length of one side of the tarpaulin? 21 m

38. **MONUMENTS** Refer to Example 4 on page 438 of your textbook. The highest observation deck on the Eiffel Tower in Paris is about 899 feet above the ground. About how far could a visitor see on a clear day? about 36.6 mi

Roots
The symbol $\sqrt{\ }$ indicates a square root. By placing a number in the upper left, the symbol can be changed to indicate higher roots.

$\sqrt[3]{8} = 2$ because $2^3 = 8$
$\sqrt[4]{81} = 3$ because $3^4 = 81$
$\sqrt[5]{100,000} = 10$ because $10^5 = 100,000$

Find each of the following.

1. $\sqrt[3]{125}$ 5   2. $\sqrt[4]{16}$ 2   3. $\sqrt[5]{1}$ 1

4. $\sqrt[3]{27}$ 3   5. $\sqrt[5]{32}$ 2   6. $\sqrt[3]{64}$ 4

7. $\sqrt[3]{1000}$ 10   8. $\sqrt[3]{216}$ 6   9. $\sqrt[6]{1,000,000}$ 10

10. $\sqrt[3]{1,000,000}$ 100   11. $\sqrt[4]{256}$ 4   12. $\sqrt[3]{729}$ 9

13. $\sqrt[6]{64}$ 2   14. $\sqrt[4]{625}$ 5   15. $\sqrt[5]{243}$ 3

Answers

1. A positive number squared results in a positive number, and a negative number squared results in a positive number.

2. Sample answer: 225, 256, 324

3. Sample answer: $-\sqrt{1.69}$

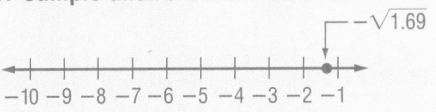

49. 9; Since $64 < 65 < 81$, $\sqrt{64} < \sqrt{65} < \sqrt{81}$. Thus, it follows that $8 < \sqrt{65} < 9$. So, 9 is greater than $\sqrt{65}$.

50. $\sqrt{120}$; Since $100 < 120 < 121$, $\sqrt{100} < \sqrt{120} < \sqrt{121}$. Thus, it follows that $10 < \sqrt{120} < 11$. So, $\sqrt{120}$ is less than 11.

Open-Ended Assessment

Speaking Write all the perfect squares between 1 and 400 on the chalkboard. Then have students take turns explaining how to estimate square roots of numbers provided by you or other students.

Tips for New Teachers

Assessment When having students estimate, make sure they are not using their calculators. You may wish to have students work in pairs so they can discuss developing estimates and check each other's work.

Getting Ready for Lesson 9-2

PREREQUISITE SKILL Lesson 9-2 presents the real number system. The real number system is composed of rational and irrational numbers. Exercises 75–80 should be used to determine your students' familiarity with rational numbers.

Answers

57. Sample answer: A number that has a rational square root will have an ending digit of 0, 1, 4, 5, 6, or 9. The last digit is the ending digit in one of the squares from 1–100. There are just six ending digits.

58. Square roots are related to factors in that if a number is a perfect square, the square root of the number is a factor of the number. Answers should include the following.
- Sample answer: 121
- Sample answer: 120

---

56. **GEOMETRY** Find the perimeter of a square that has an area of $\sqrt{2080}$ square meters. Round to the nearest tenth. **about 182.4 m**

57. **CRITICAL THINKING** What are the possibilities for the ending digit of a number that has a whole number square root? Explain your reasoning. **See margin.**

58. **WRITING IN MATH** Answer the question that was posed at the beginning of the lesson. **See margin.**

How are square roots related to factors?

Include the following in your answer:
- an example of a number between 100 and 200 whose square root is a whole number, and
- an example of a number between 100 and 200 whose square root is a decimal that does not terminate.

Standardized Test Practice

59. Which statement is *not* true? **D**
- Ⓐ $6 < \sqrt{39} < 7$
- Ⓑ $9 < \sqrt{89} < 10$
- Ⓒ $-7 > -\sqrt{56} > -8$
- Ⓓ $-4 < -\sqrt{17} < -5$

60. Choose the expression that is a rational number. **A**
- Ⓐ $-\sqrt{361}$
- Ⓑ $\sqrt{125}$
- Ⓒ $\sqrt{200}$
- Ⓓ $\sqrt{325}$

Extending the Lesson

61. Sample answer: addition and subtraction

61. Squaring a number and finding the square root of a number are *inverse operations*. That is, one operation undoes the other operation. Name another pair of inverse operations.

62. Use inverse operations to evaluate each expression.
a. $(\sqrt{64})^2$ **64**
b. $(\sqrt{100})^2$ **100**
c. $(\sqrt{169})^2$ **169**

63. Use the pattern from Exercise 62 to find $(\sqrt{a})^2$. **a**

Maintain Your Skills

Mixed Review **ALGEBRA** Graph each inequality. *(Lesson 8-10)* **64–66. See pp. 489A–489B.**

64. $y > x - 2$
65. $y < -4$
66. $y \geq 2x + 3$

ALGEBRA Solve each system of equations by substitution. *(Lesson 8-9)*

67. $y = x + 2$
$x = 5$ **(5, 7)**
68. $y = x + 3$
$y = 0$ **(−3, 0)**
69. $y = 2x + 5$
$y = -3$ **(−4, −3)**

70. Determine whether the relation (4, −1), (3, 5), (−4, 1), (4, 2) is a function. Explain. *(Lesson 8-1)* **No, because 4 is paired with −1 and 2.**

71. Suppose a number cube is rolled. What is the probability of rolling a 4 or a prime number? *(Lesson 6-9)* $\frac{2}{3}$

Solve each proportion. *(Lesson 6-2)*

72. $\frac{n}{9} = \frac{15}{27}$ **5**
73. $\frac{4}{b} = \frac{16}{36}$ **9**
74. $\frac{7}{8.4} = \frac{0.5}{x}$ **0.6**

Getting Ready for the Next Lesson **PREREQUISITE SKILL** Explain why each number is a rational number. *(To review rational numbers, see Lesson 5-2.)* **75–80. See margin.**

75. $\frac{10}{2}$
76. $1\frac{1}{2}$
77. 0.75
78. $0.\overline{8}$
79. 6
80. -7

---

75. It can be written as a fraction.

76. It can be written as $\frac{3}{2}$.

77. It can be written as $\frac{3}{4}$.

78. It can be written as $\frac{8}{9}$.

79. It can be written as $\frac{6}{1}$.

80. It can be written as $-\frac{7}{1}$.

The Real Number System

What You'll Learn

- Identify and compare numbers in the real number system.
- Solve equations by finding square roots.

How can squares have lengths that are not rational numbers?

In this activity, you will find the length of a side of a square that has an area of 2 square units.

Vocabulary
- irrational numbers
- real numbers

a. The small square at the right has an area of 1 square unit. Find the area of the shaded triangle.

a. $\frac{1}{2}$ units²

b. Suppose eight triangles are arranged as shown. What shape is formed by the shaded triangles? **square**

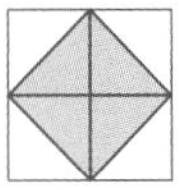

c. Find the total area of the four shaded triangles.

c. 2 square units

d. What number represents the length of the side of the shaded square? $\sqrt{2}$

IDENTIFY AND COMPARE REAL NUMBERS
In Lesson 5-2, you learned that *rational numbers* can be written as fractions. A few examples of rational numbers are listed below.

$$-6 \qquad 8\frac{2}{5} \qquad 0.05 \qquad -2.6 \qquad 5.\overline{3} \qquad -8.12121212\ldots \qquad \sqrt{16}$$

Not all numbers are rational numbers. A few examples of numbers that are *not* rational are shown below. These numbers are not repeating or terminating decimals. They are called **irrational numbers**.

$$0.101001000100001\ldots \qquad \sqrt{2} = 1.414213562\ldots \qquad \pi = 3.14159\ldots$$

Key Concept — Irrational Number

An irrational number is a number that cannot be expressed as $\frac{a}{b}$, where a and b are integers and b does not equal 0.

☑ **Concept Check** *True or False?* All square roots are irrational numbers. **False**

The set of rational numbers and the set of irrational numbers together make up the set of **real numbers**. The Venn diagram at the right shows the relationship among the real numbers.

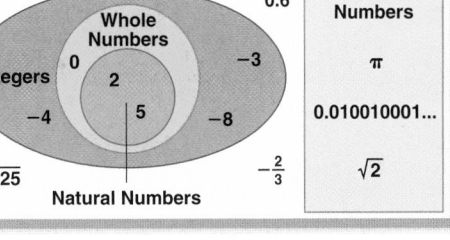

Real Numbers

Rational Numbers: $\frac{1}{3}$, $0.\overline{2}$, 0.6, -3, -8, $-\frac{2}{3}$

Whole Numbers: 0, 2, 5

Integers: -4

Natural Numbers

$\sqrt{0.25}$

Irrational Numbers: π, $0.010010001\ldots$, $\sqrt{2}$

---

1 Focus

5-Minute Check Transparency 9-2 Use as a quiz or review of Lesson 9-1.

Mathematical Background notes are available for this lesson on page 434C.

How can squares have lengths that are not rational numbers?

The opening activity questions are repeated on page 497 of the *Chapter 9 Resource Masters*.

Reading to Learn Mathematics, p. 497 ELL

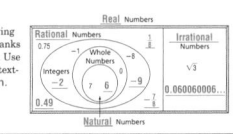

Pre-Activity How can squares have lengths that are not rational numbers?

Do the activity at the top of page 441 in your textbook. Write your answers below.

a. The small square at the right has an area of 1 square unit. Find the area of the shaded triangle. $\frac{1}{2}$ units²

b. Suppose eight triangles are arranged as shown. What shape is formed by the shaded triangles? square

c. Find the total area of the four shaded triangles. 2 square units

d. What number represents the length of the side of the shaded square? $\sqrt{2}$

Reading the Lesson 1–2. See students' work.

Write a definition and give an example of each new vocabulary word or phrase.

Vocabulary	Definition	Example
1. irrational numbers		
2. real numbers		

Choose the correct term to complete each sentence.

3. Numbers with decimals that are not repeating or terminating (are, are not) irrational numbers.

4. All square roots (are, are not) irrational numbers.

5. Irrational numbers (are, are not) real numbers.

Helping You Remember

6. Fill in the missing terms on the following diagram. Then fill in the remaining blanks with examples of each type of number. Use numbers different than those in your textbook. Sample examples are given.

Teaching Tip Review repeating decimals and terminating decimals with students.

Resource Manager

Workbooks and Reproducible Masters

Chapter 9 Resource Masters
- Study Guide and Intervention, p. 494
- Skills Practice, p. 495
- Practice, p. 496
- Reading to Learn Mathematics, p. 497
- Enrichment, p. 498
- Assessment, p. 543

Graphing Calculator and Spreadsheet Masters, p. 35
Parent and Student Study Guide Workbook, p. 73

 Transparencies
5-Minute Check Transparency 9-2
Answer Key Transparencies

 Technology
Interactive Chalkboard

IDENTIFY AND COMPARE REAL NUMBERS

In-Class Examples Power Point®

1 Name all of the sets of numbers to which each real number belongs.

a. 17   natural number, whole number, integer, rational number

b. $-\dfrac{72}{6}$ integer, rational number

c. $\sqrt{225}$ natural number, whole number, integer, rational number

d. $0.2\overline{46}$ rational number

e. $\sqrt{52}$ irrational number

Teaching Tip In Example 2, make sure students rewrite each number into the same format before comparing.

2 a. Replace ● with <, >, or = to make $\sqrt{125}$ ● $11\dfrac{7}{8}$ a true statement.   <

b. Order $6\dfrac{1}{4}$, $\sqrt{38}$, $6.\overline{5}$, and $\sqrt{36}$ from least to greatest.
$\sqrt{36}$, $\sqrt{38}$, $6\dfrac{1}{4}$, $6.\overline{5}$

Example 1 *Classify Real Numbers*

Name all of the sets of numbers to which each real number belongs.

a. 9   This number is a natural number, a whole number, an integer, and a rational number.

b. $0.\overline{3}$ This repeating decimal is a rational number because it is equivalent to $\dfrac{1}{3}$. $1 \div 3 = 0.33333\ldots$

c. $\sqrt{67}$ $\sqrt{67} = 8.185352772\ldots$ It is not the square root of a perfect square so it is irrational.

d. $-\dfrac{28}{4}$ Since $-\dfrac{28}{4} = -7$, this number is an integer and a rational number.

e. $-\sqrt{121}$ Since $-\sqrt{121} = -11$, this number is an integer and a rational number.

Concept Summary **Classification of Numbers**

Example	Natural	Whole	Integer	Rational	Irrational	Real
0		✓	✓	✓		✓
4	✓	✓	✓	✓		✓
−7			✓	✓		✓
$\sqrt{25}$	✓	✓	✓	✓		✓
$\sqrt{41}$					✓	✓
$\dfrac{3}{4}$				✓		✓
0.121212...				✓		✓
0.010110111...					✓	✓

Example 2 *Compare Real Numbers on a Number Line*

a. **Replace ● with <, >, or = to make $\sqrt{34}$ ● $5\dfrac{3}{8}$ a true statement.**

Express each number as a decimal. Then graph the numbers.

$\sqrt{34} = 5.830951895\ldots$

$5\dfrac{3}{8} = 5.375$

Since $\sqrt{34}$ is to the right of $5\dfrac{3}{8}$, $\sqrt{34} > 5\dfrac{3}{8}$.

b. **Order $4\dfrac{1}{2}$, $\sqrt{17}$, $4.\overline{4}$, and $\sqrt{16}$ from least to greatest.**

Express each number as a decimal. Then compare the decimals.

$4\dfrac{1}{2} = 4.5$

$\sqrt{17} = 4.123105626\ldots$

$4.\overline{4} = 4.444444444\ldots$

$\sqrt{16} = 4$

From least to greatest, the order is $\sqrt{16}$, $\sqrt{17}$, $4.\overline{4}$, $4\dfrac{1}{2}$.

Study Tip

Look Back
To review **comparing fractions and decimals**, see Lesson 5-1.

DAILY INTERVENTION **Differentiated Instruction** **ELL**

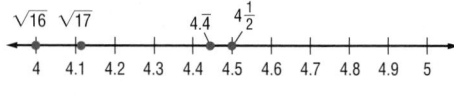

- **Verbal/Linguistic** Have teams of students find real-world examples for each type of number in the real number system. Then have students present their findings to the rest of the class. Encourage students to find unique examples. For example, the bus has four tires. Four is a natural number.

SOLVE EQUATIONS BY FINDING SQUARE ROOTS Some equations have irrational number solutions. You can solve some of these equations by taking the square root of each side.

Example 3 Solve Equations

Solve each equation. Round to the nearest tenth, if necessary.

a. $x^2 = 64$

$$x^2 = 64 \qquad \text{Write the equation.}$$
$$\sqrt{x^2} = \sqrt{64} \qquad \text{Take the square root of each side.}$$
$$x = \sqrt{64} \text{ or } x = -\sqrt{64} \qquad \text{Find the positive and negative square root.}$$
$$x = 8 \text{ or } x = -8$$

The solutions are 8 and −8.

b. $n^2 = 85$

$$n^2 = 85 \qquad \text{Write the equation.}$$
$$\sqrt{n^2} = \sqrt{85} \qquad \text{Take the square root of each side.}$$
$$n = \sqrt{85} \text{ or } n = -\sqrt{85} \qquad \text{Find the positive and negative square root.}$$
$$n \approx 9.2 \text{ or } n \approx -9.2 \qquad \text{Use a calculator.}$$

The solutions are 9.2 and −9.2.

Check for Understanding

Concept Check

1. **Explain** the difference between a rational and irrational number. **See margin.**
2. **OPEN ENDED** Give an example of a number that is an integer and a rational number. **Sample answer:** $-\sqrt{25}$

Guided Practice

Name all of the sets of numbers to which each real number belongs. Let N = natural numbers, W = whole numbers, Z = integers, Q = rational numbers, and I = irrational numbers.

3. 7 N, W, Z, Q	**4.** 0.5555... Q	**5.** $-\frac{3}{4}$ Q	**6.** $\sqrt{12}$ I

GUIDED PRACTICE KEY

Exercises	Examples
3–6	1
7–9	2
10–12	3

Replace each ● with <, >, or = to make a true statement.

7. $6\frac{4}{5}$ ● $\sqrt{48}$ <

8. $-\sqrt{74}$ ● $-8.\overline{4}$ <

9. Order $3.\overline{7}, 3\frac{3}{5}, \sqrt{13}, \frac{10}{3}$ from least to greatest. $\frac{10}{3}, 3\frac{3}{5}, \sqrt{13}, 3.\overline{7}$

ALGEBRA Solve each equation. Round to the nearest tenth, if necessary.

10. $y^2 = 25$ 5, −5

11. $m^2 = 74$ 8.6, −8.6

Application

12. **GEOMETRY** To find the radius r of a circle, you can use the formula $r = \sqrt{\dfrac{A}{\pi}}$ where A is the area of the circle. To the nearest tenth, find the radius of a circle that has an area of 40 square feet. **3.6 ft**

Answer

1. Whereas rational numbers can be expressed in the form $\frac{a}{b}$, where a and b are integers and b does not equal 0, irrational numbers cannot.

In-Class Example Power Point®

3 Solve each equation. Round to the nearest tenth, if necessary.

a. $w^2 = 169$ $w = 13$ or $w = -13$

b. $r^2 = 50$ $r \approx 7.1$ or $r \approx -7.1$

3 Practice/Apply

Study Notebook

Have students—
• add the definitions/examples of the vocabulary terms to their Vocabulary Builder worksheets for Chapter 9.
• include any other item(s) that they find helpful in mastering the skills in this lesson.

About the Exercises . . .

Organization by Objective
• **Identify and Compare Real Numbers** : 13–44
• **Solve Equations by Finding Square Roots:** 45–61

Odd/Even Assignments
Exercises 13–58 and 60–61 are structured so that students practice the same concepts whether they are assigned odd or even problems.

Assignment Guide

Basic: 13–55 odd, 61, 62–65, 69–84

Average: 13–61 odd, 62–65, 69–84 (Optional: 66–68)

Advanced: 14–60 even, 62–78 (Optional: 79–84)

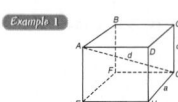
★ indicates increased difficulty

Practice and Apply

Name all of the sets of numbers to which each real number belongs. Let N = natural numbers, W = whole numbers, Z = integers, Q = rational numbers, and I = irrational numbers.

13. 8 N, W, Z, Q
14. 4 N, W, Z, Q
15. $\frac{2}{5}$ Q
16. $\frac{1}{2}$ Q
17. $0.\overline{2}$ Q
18. 0.131313... Q
19. $\sqrt{10}$ I
20. $\sqrt{32}$ I
21. 1.247896... I
22. 6.182576... I
23. $-\frac{24}{8}$ Z, Q
24. $-\frac{56}{8}$ Z, Q
25. 2.8 Q
26. 7.6 Q
27. $-\sqrt{64}$ Z, Q
28. $-\sqrt{100}$ Z, Q

Determine whether each statement is *sometimes*, *always*, or *never* true.

29. A whole number is an integer. always
30. An irrational number is a negative integer. never
31. A repeating decimal is a real number. always
32. An integer is a whole number. sometimes

Replace each ● with <, >, or = to make a true statement.

33. $5\frac{1}{4}$ ● $\sqrt{26}$ >
34. $\sqrt{80}$ ● 9.2 <
35. −3.3 ● $-\sqrt{10}$ <
36. $-\sqrt{18}$ ● $-4\frac{3}{8}$ >
37. $1\frac{1}{2}$ ● $\sqrt{2.25}$ =
38. $-\sqrt{6.25}$ ● $-\frac{5}{2}$ =

Order each set of numbers from least to greatest. 39–42. See margin.

39. $5\frac{1}{4}$, $2.\overline{1}$, $\sqrt{4}$, $\frac{6}{5}$
40. $4.\overline{23}$, $4\frac{2}{3}$, $\sqrt{18}$, $\sqrt{16}$
41. −10, −1.05, $-\sqrt{105}$, $-10\frac{1}{2}$
42. $-\sqrt{14}$, $-4\frac{1}{10}$, −3.8, $-\frac{17}{4}$

Give a counterexample for each statement.

43. All square roots are irrational numbers. **Sample answer:** $\sqrt{4}$ and $\sqrt{49}$
44. All rational numbers are integers. **Sample answer:** $\frac{1}{2}$ and −4.5

45–56. See margin.

ALGEBRA Solve each equation. Round to the nearest tenth, if necessary.

45. $a^2 = 49$
46. $d^2 = 81$
47. $y^2 = 22$
48. $p^2 = 63$
49. $144 = w^2$
50. $289 = m^2$
51. $127 = b^2$
52. $300 = h^2$
53. $x^2 = 1.69$
54. $0.0016 = q^2$
55. $n^2 = 3.56$
56. $0.0058 = k^2$

★ 57. If $(-a)^2 = 144$, what is the value of a? 12 or −12

★ 58. What is the value of x to the nearest tenth if $x^2 - 4^2 = \sqrt{15^2}$? 5.6 or −5.6

★ 59. Find the value of m if $\sqrt{256} = m^2$. 4 or −4

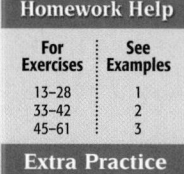
● 60. WEATHER Use the information at the left. Suppose a thunderstorm is 7 miles wide. How long will the storm last? about 1.3 h

61. FLOORING A square room has an area of 324 square feet. The homeowners plan to cover the floor with 6-inch square tiles. How many tiles will be in each row on the floor? 36

Answers

39. $\frac{6}{5}$, $\sqrt{4}$, $2.\overline{1}$, $5\frac{1}{4}$
40. $\sqrt{16}$, $4.\overline{23}$, $\sqrt{18}$, $4\frac{2}{3}$
41. $-10\frac{1}{2}$, $-\sqrt{105}$, −10, −1.05
42. $-\frac{17}{4}$, $-4\frac{1}{10}$, −3.8, $-\sqrt{14}$
45. 7, −7
46. 9, −9
47. 4.7, −4.7
48. 7.9, −7.9
49. 12, −12
50. 17, −17
51. 11.3, −11.3
52. 17.3, −17.3
53. 1.3, −1.3
54. 0.04, −0.04
55. 1.9, −1.9
56. 0.1, −0.1

62. CRITICAL THINKING   Tell whether the product of a rational number like 8 and an irrational number like 0.101001000… is rational or irrational. Explain your reasoning. **Irrational; see students' explanations.**

63. **WRITING IN MATH**   Answer the question that was posed at the beginning of the lesson. **See margin.**

How can squares have lengths that are not rational numbers?

Include the following in your answer:
- an example of a square whose side length is irrational, and
- an example of a square that has a rational side length.

Standardized Test Practice
Ⓐ Ⓑ Ⓒ Ⓓ

64. Which number can *only* be classified as a rational number? **A**

Ⓐ $\frac{1}{2}$ Ⓑ $\sqrt{2}$ Ⓒ -2 Ⓓ 2

65. Which statement is *not* true? **B**

Ⓐ All integers are rational numbers.

Ⓑ Every whole number is a natural number.

Ⓒ All natural numbers are integers.

Ⓓ Every real number is either a rational or irrational number.

Extending the Lesson

66. Heron's formula states that if the measures of the sides of a triangle are a, b, and c, the area $A = \sqrt{s(s-a)(s-b)(s-c)}$, where s is one-half the perimeter. Find the area of the triangle at the right. Round to the nearest tenth, if necessary. **14.5 m²**

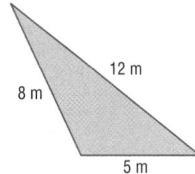

12 m
8 m
5 m

67. Find the area of a triangle whose sides measure 65 feet, 82 feet, and 95 feet. **2621.2 ft²**

68. Make a Conjecture   Is the area of any triangle always a rational number? Support your answer with an example. **See margin.**

Maintain Your Skills

Mixed Review   **Estimate each square root to the nearest whole number.** *(Lesson 9-1)*

69. $\sqrt{54}$ **7**   **70.** $-\sqrt{126}$ **−11**   **71.** $\sqrt{8.67}$ **3**

ALGEBRA   **List three solutions of each inequality.** *(Lesson 8-10)*

72. Sample answer: (0, −2), (1, −3), (2, −4)

73. Sample answer: (0, 5), (1, 6), (−6, 2)

74. Sample answer: (0, −3), (1, −2), (2, −3)

72. $y < -x$ **73.** $y \geq x + 5$ **74.** $y \leq x - 3$

ALGEBRA   **Solve each inequality.** *(Lesson 7-6)*

75. $3x + 2 > 17$ $x > 5$ **76.** $-2y + 9 \leq 3$ $y \geq 3$

Express each ratio as a unit rate. Round to the nearest tenth, if necessary. *(Lesson 6-1)*

77. $8 for 15 cupcakes **$0.53/cupcake**

78. 120 miles on 4.3 gallons **27.9 mi/gal**

Getting Ready for the Next Lesson   **BASIC SKILL**   Use a ruler or straightedge to draw a diagram that shows how the hands on a clock appear at each time. **79–84. See margin.**

79. 3:00   **80.** 9:15   **81.** 10:00

82. 2:30   **83.** 7:45   **84.** 8:05

---

63. If a square has an area that is not a perfect square, the lengths of the sides will be irrational. Answers should include the following.

- Area = 56 in²
- Area = 64 in²

68. No, because triangles can have dimensions that are irrational numbers. Thus, the area will be irrational. For example, a triangle with a base of 2 inches and a height of $\sqrt{3}$ inches has an area of $\frac{1}{2} \cdot 2 \cdot \sqrt{3}$ or $\sqrt{3}$ square inches.

---

4 Assess

Open-Ended Assessment

Writing Have students write a paragraph explaining how to compare and order a group of numbers that are in different formats.

Getting Ready for Lesson 9-3

BASIC SKILL Lesson 9-3 presents angles. Students will need to be able to draw angles of various degrees. Exercises 79–84 should be used to determine your students' familiarity with drawing angles.

Quiz (Lessons 9-1 and 9-2) is available on p. 543 of the *Chapter 9 Resource Masters.*

Answers

79.

3:00

80.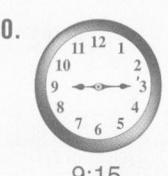

9:15

81.

10:00

82.

2:30

83.

7:45

84.

8:05

Lesson 9-2 Squares and Square Roots **445**

Getting Started

Ask students what the word *line* can mean. Besides its geometrical definition, they may mention "policy," "business," or "a series of objects." Then have students read the meanings of *ray*. Discuss how a ray and a line are related.

Teach

Discuss how a point, rays, and degrees are combined to make angles. Make sure students understand that the arrowhead on a ray represents that the ray continues on into infinity.

Alert! Exercises 2 and 3 involve research on the Internet or other reference materials.

Assess

Study Notebook

Ask students to describe how the everyday meaning of one of the terms relates to its mathematical meaning.

ELL English Language Learners may benefit from writing key concepts from this activity in their Study Notebooks in their native language and then in English.

Learning Geometry Vocabulary

Many of the words used in geometry are commonly used in everyday language. The everyday meanings of these words can be used to understand their mathematical meaning better.

The table below shows the meanings of some geometry terms you will use throughout this chapter.

Term	Everyday Meaning	Mathematical Meaning
ray	any of the thin lines, or beams, of light that appear to come from a bright source • a *ray* of light	a part of a line that extends from a point indefinitely in one direction
degree	extent, amount, or relative intensity • third *degree* burns	a common unit of measure for angles
acute	characterized by sharpness or severity • an *acute* pain	an angle with a measure that is greater than 0° and less than 90°
obtuse	not producing a sharp impression • an *obtuse* statement	an angle with a measure that is greater than 90° but less than 180°

Source: Merriam Webster's Collegiate Dictionary

Reading to Learn

1. Write a sentence using each term listed above. Be sure to use the everyday meaning of the term. **See margin.**

2. **RESEARCH** Use the Internet or a dictionary to find the everyday meaning of each term listed below. Compare them to their mathematical meaning. Note any similarities and/or differences. **See students' work.**
   a. midpoint   b. converse   c. indirect

3. **RESEARCH** Use the Internet or dictionary to determine which of the following words are used only in mathematics. **equilateral, scalene, isosceles**
   vertex   equilateral   similar   scalene   side   isosceles

446   Chapter 9   Real Numbers and Right Triangles

Answer

1. Sample answer: *ray*: A ray of sunshine appeared through a cloud. *degree*: Today's temperature is 10 degrees colder than yesterday's temperature. *acute*: Neena is experiencing acute stomach pains.
obtuse: His answer to the question was vague and obtuse.

What You'll Learn

- Measure and draw angles.
- Classify angles as acute, right, obtuse, or straight.

Vocabulary

point
ray
line
angle
vertex
side
degree
protractor
acute angle
right angle
obtuse angle
straight angle

How are angles used in circle graphs?

The graph shows how voters prefer to vote.

a. Which method did half of the voters prefer? **in booths**

b. Suppose 100 voters were surveyed. How many more voters preferred to vote in booths than on the Internet? **26**

c. Each section of the graph shows an *angle*. A *straight angle* resembles a line. Which section shows a straight angle? **in booths**

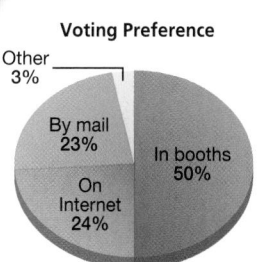

Voting Preference

Other 3%
By mail 23%
In booths 50%
On Internet 24%

Source: Princeton Survey Research

MEASURE AND DRAW ANGLES

The center of a circle represents a **point**. A point is a specific location in space with no size or shape.

Points are named using capital letters.

A point is represented by a dot.

In the circle below, notice how the sides of each section begin at the center and extend in one direction. These are examples of **rays**. A **line** is a never-ending straight path extending in two directions.

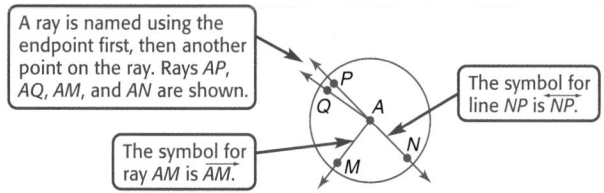

A ray is named using the endpoint first, then another point on the ray. Rays *AP*, *AQ*, *AM*, and *AN* are shown.

The symbol for line *NP* is $\overleftrightarrow{NP}$.

The symbol for ray *AM* is $\overrightarrow{AM}$.

Two rays that have the same endpoint form an **angle**. The common endpoint is called the **vertex**, and the two rays that make up the angle are called the **sides** of the angle.

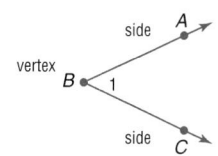

The symbol ∠ represents angle. There are several ways to name the angle shown above.

Study Tip

Angles
To name an angle using only the vertex or a number, no other angles can share the vertex of the angle being named.

- Use the vertex and a point from each side. ∠ABC or ∠CBA
  The vertex is always the middle letter.

- Use the vertex only. ∠B

- Use a number. ∠1

---

1 Focus

5-Minute Check Transparency 9-3 Use as a quiz or review of Lesson 9-2.

Mathematical Background notes are available for this lesson on page 434C.

How are angles used in circle graphs?

The opening activity questions are repeated on page 502 of the *Chapter 9 Resource Masters*.

Reading to Learn Mathematics, p. 502 **ELL**

Pre-Activity *How are angles used in circle graphs?*

Do the activity at the top of page 447 in your textbook. Write your answers below.

a. Which method did half of the voters prefer? in booths

b. Suppose 100 voters were surveyed. How many more voters preferred to vote in booths than on the Internet? 26

c. Each section of the graph shows an angle. A straight angle resembles a line. Which section shows a straight angle? in booths

Reading the Lesson 1–12. See students' work.

Write a definition and give an example of each new vocabulary word or phrase.

Vocabulary	Definition	Example
1. point		
2. ray		
3. line		
4. angle		
5. vertex		
6. side		
7. degree		
8. protractor		
9. acute angle		
10. right angle		
11. obtuse angle		
12. straight angle		

Helping You Remember

13. Label the parts of the angles below and classify each as *acute, right, obtuse,* or *straight*.

Teaching Tip You may want students to copy ∠QAP, ∠QAM, ∠MAP, ∠PAN, ∠QAN, and ∠MAN separately so they can visualize each angle without distractions.

Resource Manager

Workbooks and Reproducible Masters

Chapter 9 Resource Masters
- Study Guide and Intervention, p. 499
- Skills Practice, p. 500
- Practice, p. 501
- Reading to Learn Mathematics, p. 502
- Enrichment, p. 503

Parent and Student Study Guide Workbook, p. 74

Transparencies
5-Minute Check Transparency 9-3
Answer Key Transparencies

Technology
Interactive Chalkboard

2 Teach

MEASURE AND DRAW ANGLES

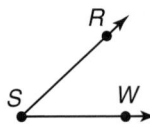
In-Class Examples — Power Point®

1 a. Use a protractor to measure ∠RSW. **42°**

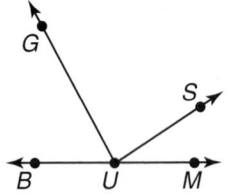

b. Find the measures of ∠GUM, ∠SUM, and ∠BUG.

$m\angle GUM = 120°$ $m\angle SUM = 32°$
$m\angle BUG = 60°$

2 Draw ∠R having a measure of 145°.

145°
R

Teaching Tip Make sure students understand why the numbers on a protractor go in two directions.

CLASSIFY ANGLES

In-Class Example — Power Point®

3 Classify each angle as *acute, obtuse, right,* or *straight.*

a.
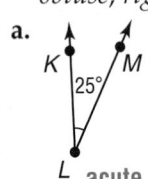
K M
25°
L **acute**

b.
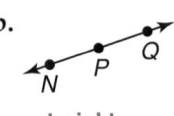
N P Q
straight

c.
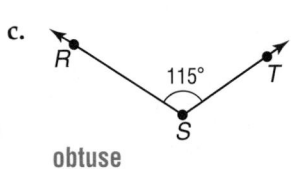
R 115° T
S
obtuse

The most common unit of measure for angles is the **degree**. A circle can be separated into 360 arcs of the same length. An angle has a measurement of one degree if its vertex is at the center of the circle and the sides contain the endpoints of one of the 360 equal arcs.

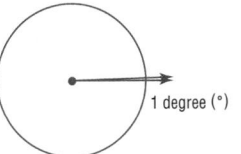
1 degree (°)

You can use a **protractor** to measure angles.

Example 1 Measure Angles

a. Use a protractor to measure ∠CDE.

Step 1 Place the center point of the protractor's base on vertex D. Align the straight side with side $\overrightarrow{DE}$ so that the marker for 0° is on the ray.

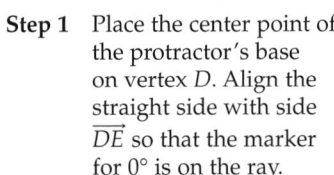

Step 2 Use the scale that begins with 0° at $\overrightarrow{DE}$. Read where the other side of the angle, $\overrightarrow{DC}$, crosses this scale.

The measure of angle CDE is 120°. Using symbols, $m\angle CDE = 120°$.

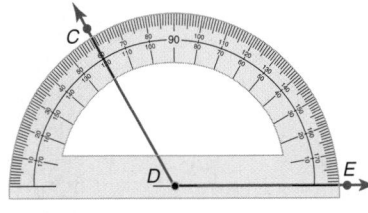

Reading Math

Angle Measure
Read $m\angle CDE = 120°$ as the measure of angle CDE is 120 degrees.

b. Find the measures of ∠KXN, ∠MXN, and ∠JXK.

$m\angle KXN = 135°$
$\overline{XN}$ is at 0° on the right.

$m\angle MXN = 70°$
$\overline{XN}$ is at 0° on the right.

$m\angle JXK = 45°$
$\overline{XJ}$ is at 0° on the left.

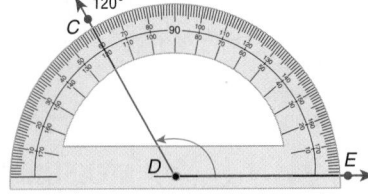

Protractors can also be used to draw an angle of a given measure.

Example 2 Draw Angles

Draw ∠X having a measure of 85°.

Step 1 Draw a ray with endpoint X.

X

Step 2 Place the center point of the protractor on X. Align the mark labeled 0 with the ray.

Step 3 Use the scale that begins with 0. Locate the mark labeled 85. Then draw the other side of the angle.

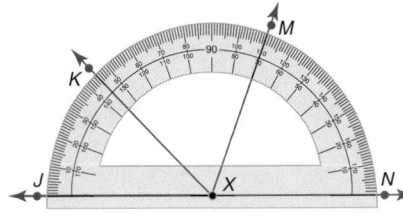
85°
X

DAILY
INTERVENTION

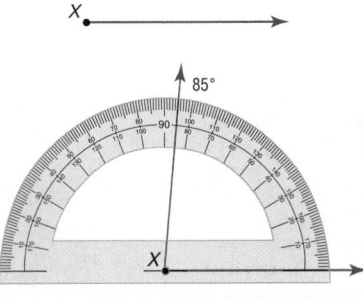

Unlocking Misconceptions

- **Measure and Draw Angles** Students may see angles in which neither of the rays is set at 0° and misjudge the measure of the angle, not recognizing a right angle or believing the measure to be greater than it is. If students are having trouble measuring an angle, encourage them to rotate the illustration clockwise until a ray lines up at 0°.

CLASSIFY ANGLES Angles can be classified by their degree measure.

Key Concept — Types of Angles

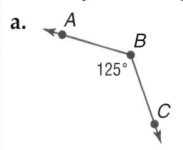 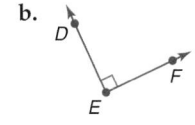 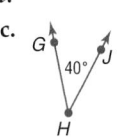

Acute Angle	Right Angle	Obtuse Angle	Straight Angle
$0° < m\angle A < 90°$	$m\angle A = 90°$	$90° < m\angle A < 180°$	$m\angle A = 180°$

This symbol is used to indicate a right angle.

Example 3 Classify Angles

Classify each angle as *acute*, *obtuse*, *right*, or *straight*.

a.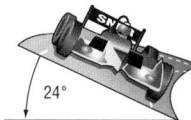

$m\angle ABC > 90°$.
So, $\angle ABC$ is obtuse.

b.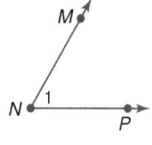

$m\angle DEF = 90°$.
So, $\angle DEF$ is right.

c.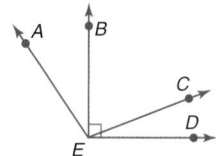

$m\angle GHJ < 90°$.
So, $\angle GHJ$ is acute.

Example 4 Use Angles to Solve a Problem

RACING The diagram shows the angle of the track at a corner of the Texas Motor Speedway in Fort Worth, Texas. Classify this angle.

Since 24° is greater than 0° and less than 90°, the angle is acute.

24°

Check for Understanding

Concept Check
1. **Name** the vertex and sides of the angle shown. Then name the angle in four ways. **1–2. See pp. 489A–489B.**

2. **OPEN ENDED** Draw an obtuse angle.

M
N 1
P

Guided Practice

Use a protractor to find the measure of each angle. Then classify each angle as *acute*, *obtuse*, *right*, or *straight*.

3. $\angle CED$ **20°; acute**   4. $\angle BED$ **90°; right**

5. $\angle CEB$ **70°; acute**   6. $\angle AED$ **125°; obtuse**

A   B
C
D
E

GUIDED PRACTICE KEY	
Exercises	Examples
3–6	1, 3
7, 8	2, 3
9	4

Use a protractor to draw an angle having each measurement. Then classify each angle as *acute*, *obtuse*, *right*, or *straight*. **7–8. See pp. 489A–489B for graphs.**

7. 55° **acute**   8. 140° **obtuse**

Application
9. **TIME** What type of angle is formed by the hands on a clock at 6:00?
straight angle

www.pre-alg.com/extra_examples

3 Practice/Apply

★ indicates increased difficulty

Practice and Apply

Use a protractor to find the measure of each angle. Then classify each angle as *acute, obtuse, right,* **or** *straight.*

10. ∠XZY   11. ∠SZT
12. ∠SZY   13. ∠UZX
14. ∠TZW   15. ∠XZT
16. ∠UZV   17. ∠WZU

10. 30°; acute
11. 15°; acute
12. 180°; straight
13. 85°; acute
14. 105°; obtuse
15. 135°; obtuse
16. 25°; acute
17. 60°; acute

Use a protractor to find the measure of each angle.

18.  45°   19. 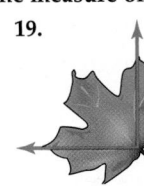 90°   20. 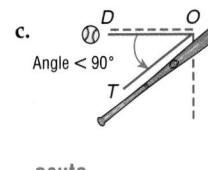 60°

Use a protractor to draw an angle having each measurement. Then classify each angle as *acute, obtuse, right,* **or** *straight.* 21–23. See margin.

21. 40°   22. 70°   23. 65°   24. 85°   25. 95°
26. 110°   27. 155°   28. 140°   ★29. 38°   ★30. 127°

24–30. See pp. 489A–489B.

31. **BASEBALL** If you swing the bat too early or too late, the ball will probably go foul. The best way to hit the ball is at a right angle. Classify each angle shown.

a.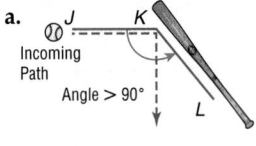
Incoming Path
Angle > 90°
obtuse

b.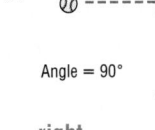
Angle = 90°
right

c. Angle < 90°
acute

FITNESS For Exercises 32–34, use the graphic.

32. Classify each angle in the circle graph as *acute, obtuse, right,* or *straight.*

33. Find the measure of each angle of the circle graph.

32–33. See pp. 489A–489B.

34. Suppose 500 adults were surveyed. How many would you expect to exercise moderately? **145**

35. **CRITICAL THINKING** In twelve hours, how many times do the hands of a clock form a right angle? **24**

USA TODAY Snapshots®

Regular fitness activities

Nearly half of adults say they exercise regularly during an average week. Type of exercise they do:

Moderate (walking, yoga) 29%
Light (house-cleaning, gardening, golfing) 20%
Intense (aerobics, running, swimming, biking) 19%
No standard routine (take stairs instead of elevator) 13%
Don't exercise on a regular basis 19%

Source: Opinion Research Corp. for TOPS (Take Off Pounds Sensibly)
By Cindy Hall and Dave Merrill, USA TODAY

---

36. WRITING IN MATH Answer the question that was posed at the beginning of the lesson. **See margin.**

How are angles used in circle graphs?

Include the following in your answer:
- a classification of the angles in each section of the circle graph shown at the beginning of the lesson, and
- a range of percents that can be represented by an acute angle and an obtuse angle.

37. Which angle is an obtuse angle? **C**

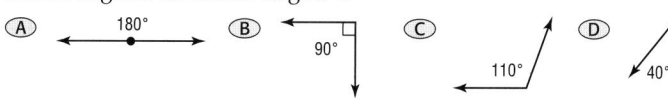

38. Which of the following is closest to the measure of ∠XYZ? **A**

Ⓐ 45°
Ⓑ 55°
Ⓒ 135°
Ⓓ 145°

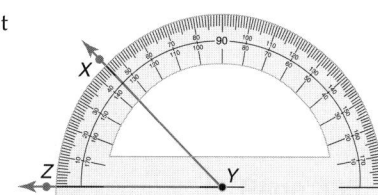

Maintain Your Skills

Mixed Review Name all of the sets of numbers to which each real number belongs. Let N = natural numbers, W = whole numbers, Z = integers, Q = rational numbers, and I = irrational numbers. *(Lesson 9-2)*

39. −5 **Z, Q**   **40.** $0.\overline{4}$ **Q**   **41.** $\sqrt{63}$ **I**   **42.** 7.4 **Q**

Estimate each square root to the nearest whole number. *(Lesson 9-1)*

43. $\sqrt{18}$ **4**   **44.** $\sqrt{79}$ **9**

45. Translate the sentence *A number decreased by seven is at least twenty-two.* *(Lesson 7-3)* $x - 7 \geq 22$

Getting Ready for the Next Lesson **PREREQUISITE SKILL** Solve each equation.
(To review solving two-step equations, see Lesson 3-5.)

46. $18 + 57 + x = 180$ **105**   **47.** $x + 27 + 54 = 180$ **99**   **48.** $85 + x + 24 = 180$ **71**

49. $x + x + x = 180$ **60**   **50.** $2x + 3x + 4x = 180$ **20**   **51.** $2x + 3x + 5x = 180$ **18**

Practice Quiz 1   *Lessons 9-1 through 9-3*

Find each square root, if possible. *(Lesson 9-1)*

1. $\sqrt{36}$ **6**   **2.** $-\sqrt{169}$ **−13**

3. ALGEBRA Solve $m^2 = 68$ to the nearest tenth. *(Lesson 9-2)* **8.2, −8.2**

Classify each angle measure as *acute, obtuse, right,* or *straight.* *(Lesson 9-3)*

4. 83° **acute**   **5.** 115° **obtuse**

Answers (p. 450)

21.

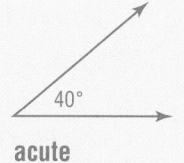

40°

acute

22.

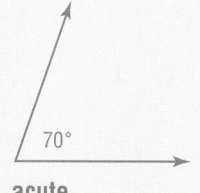

70°

acute

23.

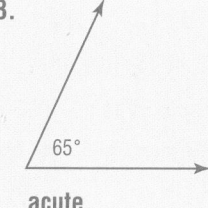

65°

acute

---

4 Assess

Open-Ended Assessment

Modeling Have students find examples of different types of angles in pictures from magazines and create a poster with the angles clearly measured and labeled.

Tips for New Teachers

Intervention Check with each student to make sure they understand how to use a protractor correctly. Have each student draw a specific angle and then measure another angle to demonstrate their proficiency.

Getting Ready for Lesson 9-4

PREREQUISITE SKILL Lesson 9-4 presents triangles. Students will be asked to find angle measures using algebraic equations. Exercises 46–51 should be used to determine your students' familiarity with solving equations.

Assessment Options

Practice Quiz 1 The quiz provides students with a brief review of the concepts and skills in Lessons 9-1 through 9-3. Lesson numbers are given to the right of exercises or instruction lines so students can review concepts not yet mastered.

Answer

36. The sides of each section on a circle graph represent an angle. Answers should include the following.
- In booths: 180°; On Internet: about 86°; By mail: about 83°; Other: about 11°
- $0 < p < 25$; $25 < p < 50$

Spreadsheet Investigation

A Follow-Up of Lesson 9-3

Getting Started

Objective Graph the results of a probability experiment in a circle graph.

Materials
spreadsheet software

Teaching Tip After reading the example, ask students what different methods are used for keeping track of frequency data. Discuss why a spreadsheet would be an easy way to organize frequency data.

Teach

• Remind students that the sum of their totals for each color should equal the number of spins performed.
• Be careful that only the totals are used when selecting the data to be included in the graph. The totals are at the top of the spreadsheet so that trials can be added without inserting rows.

Assess

For Exercise 4, discuss with students why the experimental number must be high to match the theoretical number. Make sure they understand that using a spreadsheet simplifies the work because it makes it easier to add more data and create a new circle graph.

Study Notebook

Have students print their graph to keep in their journal. Have them include a paragraph describing the experiment as they carried it out.

Circle Graphs and Spreadsheets

In the following example, you will learn how to use a computer spreadsheet program to graph the results of a probability experiment in a circle graph.

Example

The spinner like the one shown at the right was spun 20 times each for two trials. The data are shown below. Use a spreadsheet to make a circle graph of the results.

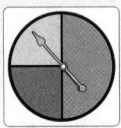

Step 1 Enter the data in a spreadsheet as shown.

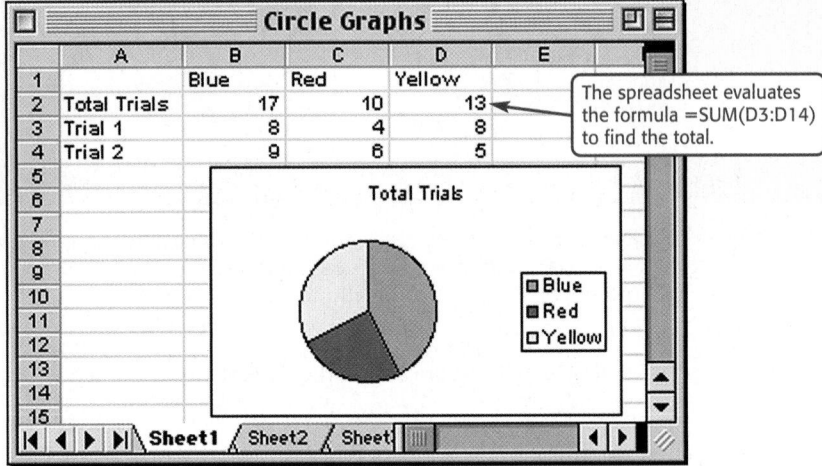

The spreadsheet evaluates the formula =SUM(D3:D14) to find the total.

Step 2 Select the data to be included in your graph. Then use the graph tool to create the graph. The spreadsheet will allow you to add titles, change colors, and so on.

Exercises

1. Describe the results you would theoretically expect for one trial of 20 spins. Explain your reasoning. **See margin.**

2. Make a spinner like the one shown above. Collect data for five trials of 20 spins each. Use a spreadsheet program to create a circle graph of the data. **See students' work.**

3. A **central angle** is an angle whose vertex is the center of a circle and whose sides intersect the circle. After 100 spins, what kind of central angle would you theoretically expect for each section of the circle graph? Explain. **See margin.**

4. Predict how many trials of the experiment are required to match the theoretical results. Test your prediction. **See students' work.**

5. When the theoretical results match the experimental results, what is true about the circle graph and the spinner? **They look the same.**

452 Chapter 9 Real Numbers and Right Triangles

Answers

1. $P(\text{Blue}) = \frac{1}{2}$, so you would expect $\frac{1}{2}$ of 20 or 10 Blue. $P(\text{Yellow}) = \frac{1}{4}$, so you would expect $\frac{1}{4}$ of 20 or 5 Yellow. Similarly, you would expect 5 Red.

3. The central angle for the Blue section should be a straight angle because $\frac{1}{2}$ of 360° is 180°. The central angle for the Red or Yellow section should be a right angle because $\frac{1}{4}$ of 360° is 90°.

9-4 Triangles

What You'll Learn

- Find the missing angle measure of a triangle.
- Classify triangles by angles and by sides.

Vocabulary

- line segment
- triangle
- vertex
- acute triangle
- obtuse triangle
- right triangle
- congruent
- scalene triangle
- isosceles triangle
- equilateral triangle

How do the angles of a triangle relate to each other?

There is a relationship among the measures of the angles of a triangle.

a. Use a straightedge to draw a triangle on a piece of paper. Then cut out the triangle and label the vertices X, Y, and Z. **a–d. See students' work.**

b. Fold the triangle as shown so that point Z lies on side XY as shown. Label $\angle Z$ as $\angle 2$.

c. Fold again so point X meets the vertex of $\angle 2$. Label $\angle X$ as $\angle 1$.

d. Fold so point Y meets the vertex of $\angle 2$. Label $\angle Y$ as $\angle 3$.

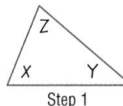 Step 1  Step 2 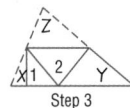 Step 3 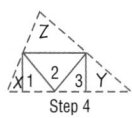 Step 4

e. **Make a Conjecture** about the sum of the measures of $\angle 1$, $\angle 2$, and $\angle 3$. Explain your reasoning. **The sum of the measures is 180°.**

ANGLE MEASURES OF A TRIANGLE A **line segment** is part of a line containing two endpoints and all of the points between them. A **triangle** is a figure formed by three line segments that intersect only at their endpoints.

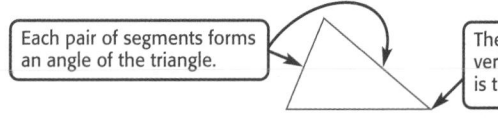

Each pair of segments forms an angle of the triangle.

The **vertex** of each angle is a vertex of the triangle. Vertices is the plural of vertex.

Triangles are named by the letters at their vertices. Triangle XYZ, written $\triangle XYZ$, is shown.

Reading Math

Line Segment
The symbol for line segment XY is $\overline{XY}$.

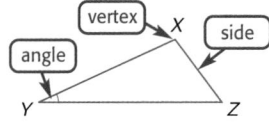

The sides are $\overline{XY}$, $\overline{YZ}$, and $\overline{XZ}$.
The vertices are X, Y, and Z.
The angles are $\angle X$, $\angle Y$, and $\angle Z$.

The activity above suggests the following relationship about the angles of any triangle.

Key Concept — Angles of a Triangle

- **Words** The sum of the measures of the angles of a triangle is 180°.
- **Model**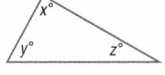
- **Symbols** $x + y + z = 180$

Lesson 9-4 Triangles **453**

9-4 Lesson Notes

1 Focus

5-Minute Check Transparency 9-4 Use as a quiz or review of Lesson 9-3.

Mathematical Background notes are available for this lesson on page 434C.

How do the angles of a triangle relate to each other?

The opening activity questions are repeated on page 507 of the *Chapter 9 Resource Masters*.

Reading to Learn Mathematics, p. 507 — ELL

Pre-Activity How do the angles of a triangle relate to each other?

Do the activity at the top of page 453 in your textbook. Write your answers below. **a–d. See students' work.**

a. Use a straightedge to draw a triangle on a piece of paper. Then cut out the triangle and label the vertices X, Y, and Z.

b. Fold the triangle as shown so that point Z lies on side XY as shown. Label $\angle Z$ as $\angle 2$.

c. Fold again so point X meets the vertex of $\angle 2$. Label $\angle X$ as $\angle 1$.

d. Fold so point Y meets the vertex of $\angle 2$. Label $\angle Y$ as $\angle 3$.

e. Make a conjecture about the sum of the measures of $\angle 1$, $\angle 2$, and $\angle 3$. Explain your reasoning. **The sum of the measures is 180°.**

Reading the Lesson 1–10. See students' work.

Write a definition and give an example of each new vocabulary word or phrase.

Vocabulary	Definition	Example
1. line segment		
2. vertex		
3. acute triangle		
4. obtuse triangle		
5. right triangle		
6. congruent		
7. scalene triangle		
8. isosceles triangle		
9. equilateral triangle		

Helping You Remember

10. Describe an obtuse, scalene triangle. **a triangle with one obtuse angle and no congruent sides**

11. Describe an equilateral triangle. **all angles and sides are congruent**

Teaching Tip Remind students that in step **b** of the opening activity, the fold should be parallel to the bottom of the figure.

Resource Manager

Workbooks and Reproducible Masters

Chapter 9 Resource Masters
- Study Guide and Intervention, p. 504
- Skills Practice, p. 505
- Practice, p. 506
- Reading to Learn Mathematics, p. 507
- Enrichment, p. 508
- Assessment, pp. 543, 545

Parent and Student Study Guide Workbook, p. 75

Transparencies

5-Minute Check Transparency 9-4
Answer Key Transparencies

Technology

Interactive Chalkboard

Building on Prior Knowledge

In Lesson 3-4, students solved equations by dividing. In this lesson, they will need to divide when using ratios to solve for angle measures.

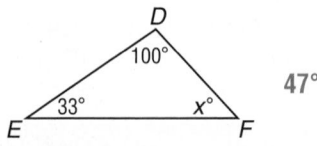

ANGLE MEASURES OF A TRIANGLE

 **In-Class Examples** | Power Point®

1 Find the value of x in $\triangle DEF$.

47°

2 **ALGEBRA** The measures of the angles of a certain triangle are in the ratio 2:3:5. What are the measures of the angles? **36°, 54°, 90°**

Teaching Tip Tell students it is important that the sum of their three answers is 180. For example, 10, 40, and 70 are three numbers in the ratio 1:4:7. However, they don't add to 180, so they can't represent the measures of the angles of one triangle.

CLASSIFY TRIANGLES

 In-Class Example | Power Point®

3 Classify each triangle by its angles and by its sides.

a.

acute equilateral

b.

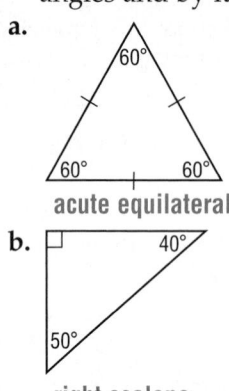

right scalene

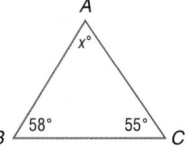 **Example 1** *Find Angle Measures*

Find the value of x in $\triangle ABC$.

$m\angle A + m\angle B + m\angle C = 180$	The sum of the measures is 180.
$x + 58 + 55 = 180$	Replace $m\angle B$ with 58 and $m\angle C$ with 55.
$x + 113 = 180$	Simplify.
$x + 113 - 113 = 180 - 113$	Subtract 113 from each side.
$x = 67$	

The measure of $\angle A$ is 67°.

The relationships of the angles in a triangle can be represented using algebra.

Example 2 *Use Ratios to Find Angle Measures*

ALGEBRA The measures of the angles of a certain triangle are in the ratio 1:4:7. What are the measures of the angles?

Words The measures of the angles are in the ratio 1:4:7.

Variables Let x represent the measure of one angle, $4x$ the measure of a second angle, and $7x$ the measure of the third angle.

Equation
$x + 4x + 7x = 180$	The sum of the measures is 180.
$12x = 180$	Combine like terms.
$\dfrac{12x}{12} = \dfrac{180}{12}$	Divide each side by 12.
$x = 15$	Simplify.

Since $x = 15$, $4x = 4(15)$ or 60, and $7x = 7(15)$ or 105. The measures of the angles are 15°, 60°, and 105°.
CHECK $15 + 60 + 105 = 180$. So, the answer is correct. ✓

CLASSIFY TRIANGLES Triangles can be classified by their angles. All triangles have at least two acute angles. The third angle is either acute, obtuse, or right.

Study Tip

Equiangular
In an *equiangular* triangle, all angles have the same measure, 60°.

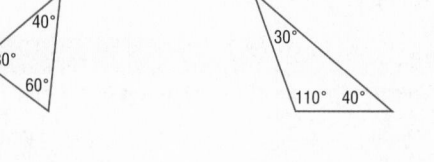

Key Concept		*Classify Triangles by their Angles*
Acute Triangle	**Obtuse Triangle**	**Right Triangle**

| all acute angles | one obtuse angle | one right angle |

DAILY INTERVENTION

Differentiated Instruction

- **Visual/Spatial** Have students cut out a triangle and color each of its three corners, putting a heavy dot near each vertex. Then have students cut or tear the triangle into three pieces so that each vertex is on a separate piece. Tell students to arrange the pieces so that the vertices are all on the same location and so that the sides of the angles create adjacent angles. Ask what figure is formed by the outer sides of the outer two angles. **a straight line** What kind of angle is formed by all three pieces and what is its measure? **a straight angle; 180°**

Triangles can also be classified by their sides. **Congruent** sides have the same length.

Key Concept	Classify Triangles by their Sides

Scalene Triangle	Isosceles Triangle	Equilateral Triangle
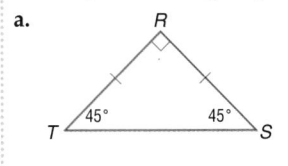		
no congruent sides	at least two sides congruent	all sides congruent

Example 3 Classify Triangles

Classify each triangle by its angles and by its sides.

a.
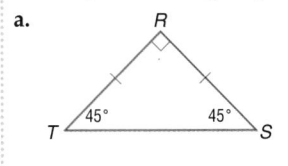

Angles
△RST has a right angle.

Sides
△RST has two congruent sides.
So, △RST is a right isosceles triangle.

b.
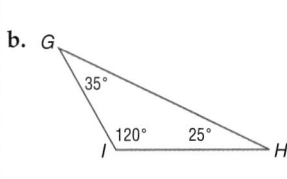

Angles
△GHI has one obtuse angle.

Sides
△GHI has no two sides that are congruent.
So, △GHI is an obtuse scalene triangle.

Check for Understanding

Concept Check

2. Sample answer: yield sign

7. right isosceles
8. obtuse scalene
9. acute isosceles

1. **Compare** an isosceles triangle and an equilateral triangle. **See margin.**

2. **Name** a real-world object that is an equilateral triangle.

3. **OPEN ENDED** Draw an obtuse isosceles triangle. **See margin.**

Guided Practice

GUIDED PRACTICE KEY	
Exercises	Examples
4–6	1
7–9	3
10	2

Find the value of *x* in each triangle. Then classify each triangle as *acute*, *right*, or *obtuse*.

4. 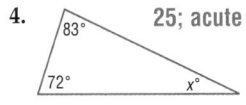 **25; acute**

5. 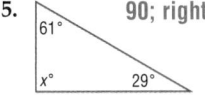 **90; right**

6. 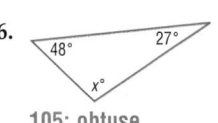 **105; obtuse**

Classify each indicated triangle by its angles and by its sides.

7.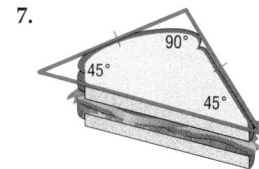

8.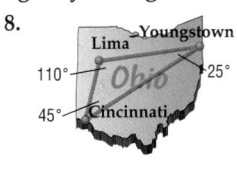

9.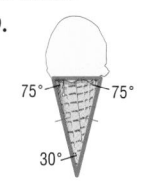

Application

10. **ALGEBRA** Triangle *EFG* has angles whose measures are in the ratio 2:4:9. What are the measures of the angles? **24°, 48°, 108°**

DAILY

INTERVENTION **Unlocking Misconceptions**

- **Classify Triangles** Students may be confused by the fact that all triangles, including right and obtuse triangles, contain acute angles. Tell students to look carefully for right and obtuse angles before they classify a triangle.

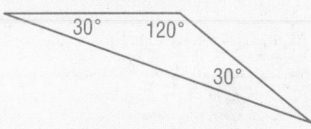

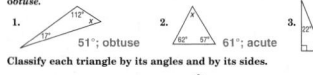
 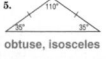 
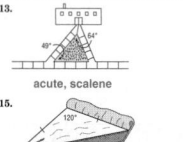 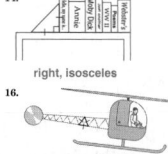
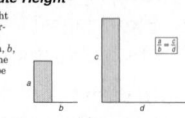
★ indicates increased difficulty

Practice and Apply

Homework Help

For Exercises	See Examples
11–16	1
17, 18	2
19–24	3

Extra Practice
See page 746.

Find the value of *x* in each triangle. Then classify each triangle as *acute, right,* or *obtuse.*

11.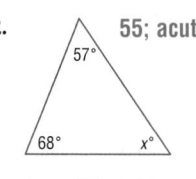
27; right

12.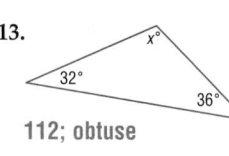
55; acute

13.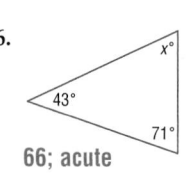
112; obtuse

14. 102; obtuse

15. 90; right

16. 66; acute

17. **ALGEBRA** The measures of the angles of a triangle are in the ratio 1:3:5. What is the measure of each angle? 20°, 60°, 100°

18. **ALGEBRA** Determine the measures of the angles of △*ABC* if the measures of the angles are in the ratio 7:7:22. 35°, 35°, 110°

19–24. See margin.

Classify each indicated triangle by its angles and by its sides.

19.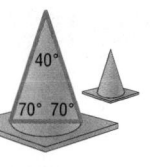

20.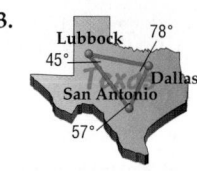

21.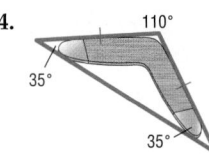

22.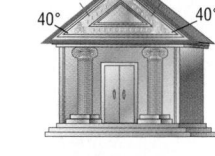

23.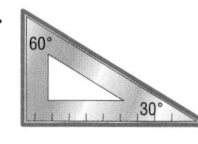

24.

Determine whether each statement is *sometimes, always,* or *never* true.

25. Equilateral triangles are isosceles triangles. always

26. Isosceles triangles are equilateral triangles. sometimes

Estimate the measure of the angles in each triangle. Then classify each triangle as *acute, right,* or *obtuse.*

27. obtuse   28. right   29. acute

Sketch each triangle. If it is not possible to sketch the triangle, write *not possible.* 30–33. See margin.

★ 30. acute scalene

★ 31. right equilateral

★ 32. obtuse and *not* scalene

★ 33. obtuse equilateral

Billiards •·············

According to the rules of billiards, each ball must weigh 5.5 to 6.0 ounces and have a diameter of $2\frac{1}{4}$ inches.

Source: www.bca-pool.com

Answers

19. acute equilateral
20. obtuse isosceles
21. right scalene
22. acute isosceles
23. acute scalene
24. obtuse isosceles

30.

31. not possible

32.

33. not possible

ALGEBRA Find the measures of the angles in each triangle.

★ 34.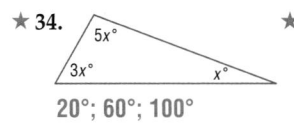
20°; 60°; 100°

★ 35.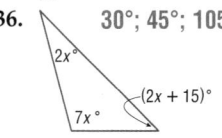
45°; 50°; 85°

★ 36. 30°; 45°; 105°
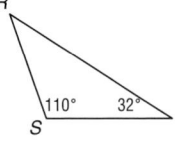

37. **CRITICAL THINKING** Numbers that can be represented by a triangular arrangement of dots are called *triangular numbers*. The first three triangular numbers are 1, 3, and 6. Find the next three triangular numbers. **10, 15, 21**

38. WRITING IN MATH Answer the question that was posed at the beginning of the lesson. **See margin.**

How do the angles of a triangle relate to each other?

Include the following in your answer:
• an explanation telling why the sum of the angles is 180°, and
• drawings of two triangles with their angles labeled.

39. Refer to the figure shown. What is the measure of ∠R? **B**
   Ⓐ 28°   Ⓑ 38°
   Ⓒ 48°   Ⓓ 180°
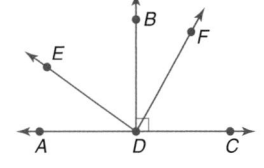

40. The measures of the angles of a triangle are 30°, 90°, and 60°. Which triangle most likely has these angle measures? **C**
   Ⓐ   Ⓑ   Ⓒ 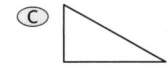   Ⓓ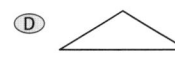

Maintain Your Skills

Mixed Review

Use a protractor to find the measure of each angle. Then classify each angle as *acute, obtuse, right,* or *straight*.
(Lesson 9-3) **41. 180°; straight**

41. ∠ADC   42. ∠ADE **35°; acute**
43. ∠CDE   44. ∠EDF
145°; obtuse   **85°; acute**

ALGEBRA Solve each equation. Round to the nearest tenth, if necessary.
(Lesson 9-2)
45. $m^2 = 81$ **9, −9**   46. $196 = y^2$ **14, −14**   47. $84 = p^2$ **9.2, −9.2**

48. Twenty-six is 25% of what number? *(Lesson 6-5)* **104**

Getting Ready for the Next Lesson

PREREQUISITE SKILL Find the value of each expression.
(To review exponents, see Lesson 4-2.)
49. 12^2 **144**   50. 15^2 **225**   51. 18^2 **324**
52. 24^2 **576**   53. 27^2 **729**   54. 31^2 **961**

Open-Ended Assessment

Modeling Give students state maps, tacks, and string and have them find groups of three towns that, when connected with straight lines, form acute triangles, obtuse triangles, and if possible, right triangles.

Getting Ready for Lesson 9-5

PREREQUISITE SKILL Lesson 9-5 presents the Pythagorean Theorem, which requires the use of squares and square roots. Exercises 49–54 should be used to determine your students' familiarity with squaring numbers.

Quiz (Lessons 9-3 and 9-4) is available on p. 543 of the *Chapter 9 Resource Masters.*

Mid-Chapter Test (Lessons 9-1 through 9-4) is available on p. 545 of the *Chapter 9 Resource Masters.*

Answer

38. The angles of a triangle have a sum of 180°. Answers should include the following.
   • The angles of a triangle can be folded to form a straight angle. Since the measure of a straight angle is 180°, the sum of the angles of a triangle is 180°.
   • Sample answer:

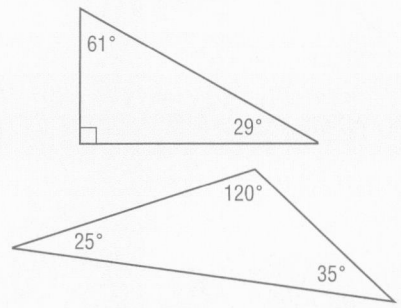

Getting Started

Objective Find the area of figures using rectangular dot paper.

Materials
rectangular dot paper

Teach

Activity 1
- You may need to review formulas for area.
- Students may use colored pencils to organize the smaller regions.
- Students could carefully cut the figures out and then cut the figures into smaller regions. They could then reassemble the pieces onto dot paper to determine the total area.

Activity 2
- Explain to students that the hypotenuse is always designated as side "c."

Algebra Activity
A Preview of Lesson 9-5

The Pythagorean Theorem

Activity 1

To find the area of certain geometric figures, dot paper can be used. Consider the following examples.

Find the area of each shaded region if each square  represents one square unit.

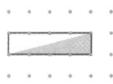

$A = \frac{1}{2}(1)$ or $\frac{1}{2}$ unit^2 $A = \frac{1}{2}(2)$ or 1 unit^2 $A = \frac{1}{2}(4)$ or 2 units^2

The area of other figures can be found by first separating the figure into smaller regions and then finding the sum of the areas of the smaller regions.

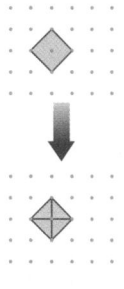   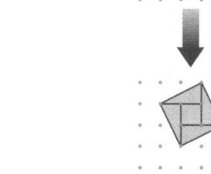   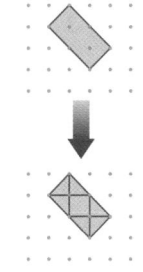

$A = 2$ units^2 $A = 5$ units^2 $A = 4$ units^2

Model

Find the area of each figure.

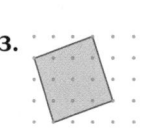

1. 8 units^2 2. 6 units^2

3. 10 units^2 4. 17 units^2

458   Chapter 9   Real Numbers and Right Triangles

Resource Manager

📁 *Teaching Pre-Algebra with Manipulatives*
- p. 15 (rectangular dot paper)
- p. 115 (student recording sheet)

Glencoe Mathematics Classroom Manipulative Kit
- rectangular dot paper

Activity 2

Let's investigate the relationship that exists among the sides of a right triangle. In each diagram shown, notice how a square is attached to each side of a right triangle.

Triangle 1

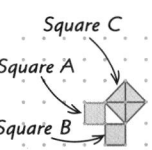

Square C
Square A
Square B

Triangle 2

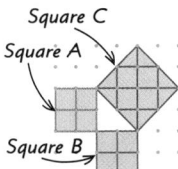

Square C
Square A
Square B

Triangle 3

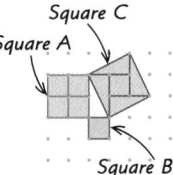

Square C
Square A
Square B

Triangle 4

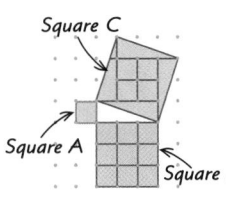

Square C
Square A
Square B

Triangle 5

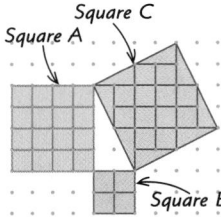

Square C
Square A
Square B

Copy the table. Then find the area of each square that is attached to the triangle. Record the results in your table.

Triangle	Area of Square A (units²)	Area of Square B (units²)	Area of Square C (units²)
1	1	1	2
2	4	4	8
3	4	1	5
4	1	9	10
5	16	4	20

Exercises   **5. The sum of the areas of squares A and B is equal to the area of square C.**

5. Refer to your table. How does the sum of the areas of square A and square B compare to the area of square C?

6. Refer to the diagram shown at the right. If the lengths of the sides of a right triangle are whole numbers such that $a^2 + b^2 = c^2$, the numbers a, b, and c are called a **Pythagorean Triple**. Tell whether each set of numbers is a Pythagorean Triple. Explain why or why not. **See margin for explanations.**

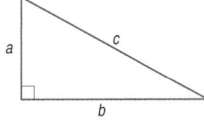

a. 3, 4, 5 **yes**   b. 5, 7, 9 **no**   c. 6, 9, 12 **no**   d. 7, 24, 25 **yes**

7. Write two different sets of numbers that are a Pythagorean Triple.
   Sample answer: 10, 24, 26 and 12, 16, 20

Algebra Activity   The Pythagorean Theorem   **459**

1 Focus

**5-Minute Check
Transparency 9-5** Use as a
quiz or review of Lesson 9-4.

Mathematical Background
notes are available for this lesson
on page 434D.

How do the sides of a right
triangle relate to each
other?

The opening activity questions
are repeated on page 512 of the
Chapter 9 Resource Masters.

Reading to Learn Mathematics, p. 512 — ELL

Pre-Activity How do the sides of a right triangle relate to each other?

Do the activity at the top of page 460 in your textbook. Write your answers below.

a. Find the area of each square.   9 units²; 16 units²; 25 units²

b. What relationship exists among the areas of the squares?   The area of the large square is equal to the sum of the areas of the two smaller squares.

c. Draw three squares with sides 5, 12, and 13 units so that they form a right triangle. What relationship exists among the areas of these squares?   The area of the large square is equal to the sum of the areas of the two smaller squares.

Reading the Lesson 1–5. See students' work.

Write a definition and give an example of the new vocabulary word or phrase.

Vocabulary	Definition	Example
1. legs		
2. hypotenuse		
3. Pythagorean Theorem		
4. solving a right triangle		
5. converse		

Helping You Remember

6. Write out in words the steps for solving the right triangle shown.

$c^2 = a^2 + b^2$	Pythagorean Theorem
$22^2 = a^2 + 20^2$	Replace c with 22 and b with 20.
$484 = a^2 + 400$	Evaluate 22^2 and 20^2.
$484 - 400 = a^2 + 400 - 400$	Subtract 400 from each side.
$84 = a^2$	Simplify.
$\sqrt{84} = \sqrt{a^2}$	Take the square root of each side.
$a \approx 9.2$	The length of the leg is about 9.2 units.

9-5 The Pythagorean Theorem

What You'll Learn

- Use the Pythagorean Theorem to find the length of a side of a right triangle.
- Use the converse of the Pythagorean Theorem to determine whether a triangle is a right triangle.

Vocabulary

- legs
- hypotenuse
- Pythagorean Theorem
- solving a right triangle
- converse

a. 9 units², 16 units², 25 units²
b. The area of the large square is equal to the sum of the areas of the two smaller squares.

Study Tip

Hypotenuse
The hypotenuse is the longest side of a triangle.

How do the sides of a right triangle relate to each other?

In the diagram, three squares with
sides 3, 4, and 5 units are used to form
a right triangle.

a. Find the area of each square.

b. What relationship exists among the
areas of the squares?

c. Draw three squares with sides 5, 12,
and 13 units so that they form a right
triangle. What relationship exists among
the areas of these squares?

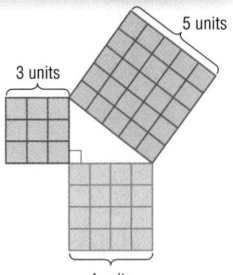

c. The area of the large square is equal to the sum of the areas of the two smaller squares.

THE PYTHAGOREAN THEOREM In a right
triangle, the sides that are adjacent to the right angle
are called the **legs**. The side opposite the right angle
is the **hypotenuse**.

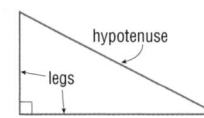

The **Pythagorean Theorem** describes the relationship between the lengths
of the legs and the hypotenuse. This theorem is true for *any* right triangle.

Key Concept — Pythagorean Theorem

- **Words**   If a triangle is a right triangle, then the square of the length of
  the hypotenuse is equal to the sum of the squares of the lengths
  of the legs.

- **Model**

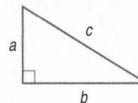

- **Symbols** $c^2 = a^2 + b^2$
- **Example** $5^2 = 3^2 + 4^2$
  $25 = 9 + 16$
  $25 = 25$

Example 1 Find the Length of the Hypotenuse

Find the length of the hypotenuse of the right triangle.

$c^2 = a^2 + b^2$	Pythagorean Theorem
$c^2 = 12^2 + 16^2$	Replace a with 12 and b with 16.
$c^2 = 144 + 256$	Evaluate 12^2 and 16^2.
$c^2 = 400$	Add 144 and 256.
$\sqrt{c^2} = \sqrt{400}$	Take the square root of each side.
$c = 20$	The length of the hypotenuse is 20 feet.

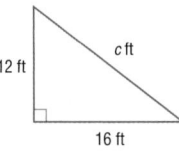

Resource Manager

📁 Workbooks and Reproducible Masters

Chapter 9 Resource Masters
- Study Guide and Intervention, p. 509
- Skills Practice, p. 510
- Practice, p. 511
- Reading to Learn Mathematics, p. 512
- Enrichment, p. 513

**Parent and Student Study Guide
Workbook,** p. 76
School-to-Career Masters, p. 17

💡 Transparencies

5-Minute Check Transparency 9-5
Real-World Transparency 9
Answer Key Transparencies

💿 Technology

Interactive Chalkboard
Pre-AlgePASS: Tutorial Plus, Lessons 27, 28
Multimedia Applications

☑ Concept Check Which side of a right triangle is the hypotenuse?
The side across from the right angle.

If you know the lengths of two sides of a right triangle, you can use the Pythagorean Theorem to find the length of the third side. This is called **solving a right triangle**.

Example 2 *Solve a Right Triangle*

Find the length of the leg of the right triangle.

$$c^2 = a^2 + b^2 \qquad \text{Pythagorean Theorem}$$
$$14^2 = a^2 + 10^2 \qquad \text{Replace } c \text{ with 14 and } b \text{ with 10.}$$
$$196 = a^2 + 100 \qquad \text{Evaluate } 14^2 \text{ and } 10^2.$$
$$196 - 100 = a^2 + 100 - 100 \qquad \text{Subtract 100 from each side.}$$
$$96 = a^2 \qquad \text{Simplify.}$$
$$\sqrt{96} = \sqrt{a^2} \qquad \text{Take the square root of each side.}$$

2nd [√] 96 ENTER 9.797958971

The length of the leg is about 9.8 centimeters.

Standardized tests often contain questions involving the Pythagorean Theorem.

Standardized Test Practice

Example 3 *Use the Pythagorean Theorem*

Multiple-Choice Test Item

> A painter positions a 20-foot ladder against a house so that the base of the ladder is 4 feet from the house. About how high does the ladder reach on the side of the house?
>
> Ⓐ 17.9 ft   Ⓑ 18.0 ft   Ⓒ 19.6 ft   Ⓓ 20.4 ft

Read the Test Item

Make a drawing to illustrate the problem. The ladder, ground, and side of the house form a right triangle.

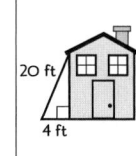

Test-Taking Tip
To help visualize the problem, it may be helpful to draw a diagram that represents the situation.

Solve the Test Item

Use the Pythagorean Theorem to find how high the ladder reaches on the side of the house.

$$c^2 = a^2 + b^2 \qquad \text{Pythagorean Theorem}$$
$$20^2 = 4^2 + b^2 \qquad \text{Replace } c \text{ with 20 and } a \text{ with 4.}$$
$$400 = 16 + b^2 \qquad \text{Evaluate } 20^2 \text{ and } 4^2.$$
$$400 - 16 = 16 + b^2 - 16 \qquad \text{Subtract 16 from each side.}$$
$$384 = b^2 \qquad \text{Simplify.}$$
$$\sqrt{384} = \sqrt{b^2} \qquad \text{Take the square root of each side.}$$
$$19.6 \approx b \qquad \text{Round to the nearest tenth.}$$

The ladder reaches about 19.6 feet on the side of the house. The answer is C.

www.pre-alg.com/extra_examples

Lesson 9-5 The Pythagorean Theorem **461**

THE PYTHAGOREAN THEOREM

In-Class Examples 〔Power Point®〕

1 Find the length of the hypotenuse of the right triangle. **29 ft**

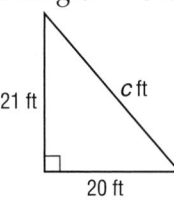

2 Find the length of the leg of the right triangle. **≈7.5 m**

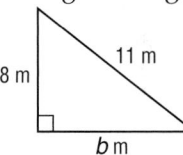

Teaching Tip Make sure students recognize that *a* and *b* always represent the legs, and *c* always represents the hypotenuse when solving a triangle with the Pythagorean Theorem.

3 **Multiple-Choice Test Item**
A building is 10 feet tall. A ladder is positioned against the building so that the base of the ladder is 3 feet from the building. How long is the ladder? **B**

A 12.4 ft   B 10.4 ft

C 10.0 ft   D 14.9 ft

Standardized Test Practice

Example 3 Point out to students that they should draw a simple picture and label the triangle, including the right angle, for such test items. Then solve for the missing side.

Lesson 9-5 The Pythagorean Theorem **461**

4 The measures of three sides of a triangle are given. Determine whether each triangle is a right triangle.

a. 48 ft, 60 ft, 78 ft **no**

b. 24 cm, 70 cm, 74 cm **yes**

3 Practice/Apply

Study Notebook

Have students—
- add the definitions/examples of the vocabulary terms to their Vocabulary Builder worksheets for Chapter 9.
- draw a right triangle, label the parts, and show how the Pythagorean Theorem applies to the triangle.
- include any other item(s) that they find helpful in mastering the skills in this lesson.

About the Exercises . . .

Organization by Objective
- The Pythagorean Theorem: 10–27
- Converse of the Pythagorean Theorem: 28–33

Odd/Even Assignments
Exercises 10–33 are structured so that students practice the same concepts whether they are assigned odd or even problems.

Assignment Guide

Basic: 11, 13, 17–21 odd, 27–31 odd, 37–40, 44–52

Average: 11–33 odd, 34, 35, 37–40, 44–52 (Optional: 41–43)

Advanced: 10–32 even, 34–49 (Optional: 50–52)

CONVERSE OF THE PYTHAGOREAN THEOREM The Pythagorean Theorem is written in *if-then* form. If you reverse the statements after *if* and *then*, you have formed the **converse** of the Pythagorean Theorem.

Pythagorean Theorem If a triangle is a right triangle, then $c^2 = a^2 + b^2$.

Converse If $c^2 = a^2 + b^2$, then a triangle is a right triangle.

You can use the converse to determine whether a triangle is a right triangle.

Example 4 Identify a Right Triangle

The measures of three sides of a triangle are given. Determine whether each triangle is a right triangle.

a. 9 m, 12 m, 15 m

$c^2 = a^2 + b^2$
$15^2 \stackrel{?}{=} 9^2 + 12^2$
$225 \stackrel{?}{=} 81 + 144$
$225 = 225$

The triangle is a right triangle.

b. 6 in., 7 in., 12 in.

$c^2 = a^2 + b^2$
$12^2 \stackrel{?}{=} 6^2 + 7^2$
$144 \stackrel{?}{=} 36 + 49$
$144 \neq 85$

The triangle is *not* a right triangle.

Check for Understanding

Concept Check

1. **OPEN ENDED** State the measures of three sides that could form a right triangle. **Sample answer: 8, 15, 17**

2. See margin.

2. **FIND THE ERROR** Marcus and Allyson are finding the missing measure of the right triangle shown. Who is correct? Explain your reasoning.

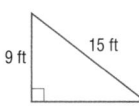

Marcus
$c^2 = a^2 + b^2$
$15^2 = 9^2 + b^2$
$12 = b$

Allyson
$c^2 = a^2 + b^2$
$c^2 = 9^2 + 15^2$
$c \approx 17.5$

(triangle: 9 ft, 15 ft)

Guided Practice

Find the length of the hypotenuse in each right triangle. Round to the nearest tenth, if necessary.

GUIDED PRACTICE KEY	
Exercises	**Examples**
3, 4	1
5, 6	2
7, 8	4
9	3

3. **25** (triangle: 15 m, 20 m, c m)

4. **13.4** (triangle: 12 ft, 6 ft, c ft)

If c is the measure of the hypotenuse, find each missing measure. Round to the nearest tenth, if necessary.

5. $a = 8, b = ?, c = 17$ **15**

6. $a = ?, b = 24, c = 25$ **7**

The lengths of three sides of a triangle are given. Determine whether each triangle is a right triangle.

7. 5 cm, 7 cm, 8 cm **no**

8. 10 ft, 24 ft, 26 ft **yes**

Standardized Test Practice

9. Kendra is flying a kite. The length of the kite string is 55 feet and she is positioned 40 feet away from beneath the kite. About how high is the kite? **B**

Ⓐ 33.1 ft Ⓑ 37.7 ft Ⓒ 56.2 ft Ⓓ 68.0 ft

DAILY
INTERVENTION FIND THE ERROR
If students are having difficulty with determining which side of the triangle is a, b, or c, have them draw a few right triangles using a ruler. Remind them that c is always the longest side.

Answer

2. Marcus; Allyson incorrectly substitutes 15 for b in the equation. Since the side measuring 15 units is opposite the right angle, it is a hypotenuse. So, 15 should be substituted for c in the equation.

★ indicates increased difficulty

Homework Help

For Exercises	See Examples
10–15	1
16, 17	3
18–27	2
28–33	4

Extra Practice
See page 736.

Find the length of the hypotenuse in each right triangle. Round to the nearest tenth, if necessary.

10. 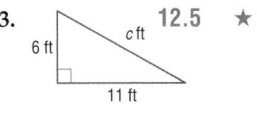 **10**

11. 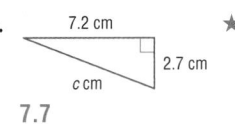 **26**

12. 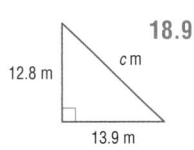 **10.3**

13. 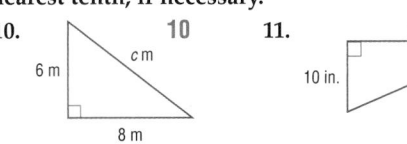 **12.5**

★ 14. 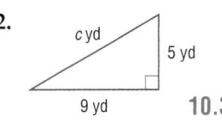 **7.7**

★ 15. **18.9**

16. **GYMNASTICS** The floor exercise mat measures 40 feet by 40 feet. Find the measure of the diagonal. **about 56.6 ft**

17. **TELEVISION** The size of a television set is determined by the length of the diagonal of the screen. If a 35-inch television screen is 26 inches long, what is its height to the nearest inch? **23 in.**

If c is the measure of the hypotenuse, find each missing measure. Round to the nearest tenth, if necessary.

18. $a = 9, b = ?, c = 41$ **40**

19. $a = ?, b = 35, c = 37$ **12**

20. $a = ?, b = 12, c = 19$ **14.7**

21. $a = 7, b = ?, c = 14$ **12.1**

★ 22. $a = 27, b = ?, c = 61$ **54.7**

★ 23. $a = ?, b = 73, c = 82$ **37.3**

★ 24. $a = ?, b = \sqrt{123}, c = 22$ **19**

★ 25. $a = \sqrt{177}, b = ?, c = 31$ **28**

Find each missing measure to the nearest tenth.

26. 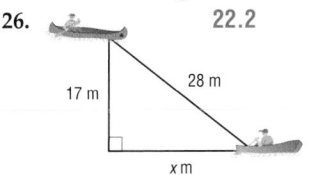 **22.2**

27. 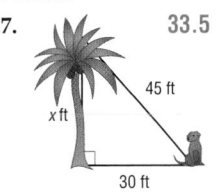 **33.5**

More About...

Gymnastics
The floor exercise mat is a square of plywood covered by a 2-inch padding and mounted on 4" springs.
Source: The Gymnastics Place!

The lengths of three sides of a triangle are given. Determine whether each triangle is a right triangle.

28. $a = 5, b = 8, c = 9$ **no**

29. $a = 16, b = 30, c = 34$ **yes**

30. $a = 18, b = 24, c = 30$ **yes**

31. $a = 24, b = 28, c = 32$ **no**

★ 32. $a = \sqrt{21}, b = 6, c = \sqrt{57}$ **yes**

★ 33. $a = 11, b = \sqrt{55}, c = \sqrt{177}$ **no**

ART For Exercises 34 and 35, use the plasterwork design shown.

34. If the sides of the square measures 6 inches, what is the length of $\overline{AB}$? **about 8.5 in.**

★ 35. What is the perimeter of the design if $\overline{AB}$ measures $\sqrt{128}$? (*Hint:* Use the guess-and-check strategy.) **32 in.**

DAILY INTERVENTION

Differentiated Instruction

- **Auditory/Musical** Have students split into groups to create jingles to help commit Pythagorean triples and the Pythagorean Theorem to memory. **Sample jingles:** *a* times *a*, plus *b* times *b*, will always come to *c* times *c*. Sides 3, 4, and long side 5, make the Theorem come alive.

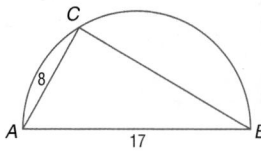

4 Assess

Open-Ended Assessment

Speaking Have students take turns giving one another problems to solve on the chalkboard. Problems could be finding a hypotenuse or leg or determining whether three measures indicate a right triangle. The student at the chalkboard should draw a sketch and explain the steps for solving.

Getting Ready for Lesson 9-6

PREREQUISITE SKILL Lesson 9-6 presents the distance and midpoint formulas. The order of operations must be followed to successfully use these formulas. Exercises 50–52 should be used to determine your students' familiarity with order of operations and exponents.

Answer

37. There is enough information to find the lengths of the legs. Since the right triangle is an isosceles right triangle, we know that the lengths of the legs are equal. So, in the Pythagorean Theorem, we can say that $a = b$. In addition, we know that $c = 8$.

$c^2 = a^2 + b^2$	Pythagorean Theorem
$8^2 = a^2 + a^2$	$a = b$ and $c = 8$
$8^2 = 2a^2$	Add a^2 and a^2.
$64 = 2a^2$	Evaluate 8^2.
$\dfrac{64}{2} = \dfrac{2a^2}{2}$	Divide each side by 2.
$32 = a^2$	Simplify.
$\sqrt{32} = a$	Take the square root of each side.

So, if a triangle is an isosceles right triangle and the hypotenuse is 8 inches, the length of each leg is $\sqrt{32}$ inches or about 5.7 inches.

---

36. GEOMETRY All angles *inscribed* in a semicircle are right angles. In the figure at the right, ∠*ACB* is an inscribed right angle. If the length of $\overline{AB}$ is 17 and the length of $\overline{AC}$ is 8, find the length of $\overline{BC}$. **15**

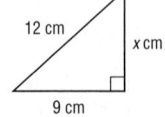

37. CRITICAL THINKING The hypotenuse of an isosceles right triangle is 8 inches. Is there enough information to find the length of the legs? If so, find the length of the legs. If not, explain why not. **See margin.**

38. WRITING IN MATH   Answer the question that was posed at the beginning of the lesson. **See pp. 489A–489B.**

How do the sides of a right triangle relate to each other?

Include the following in your answer:
- a right triangle with the legs and hypotenuse labeled, and
- an example of a set of numbers that represents the measures of the lengths of the legs and hypotenuse of a right triangle.

Standardized Test Practice

39. Which numbers represent the measures of the sides of a right triangle? **D**
- Ⓐ 3, 3, 6
- Ⓑ 3, 4, 7
- Ⓒ 5, 7, 12
- Ⓓ 6, 8, 10

40. Which is the best estimate for the value of *x*? **B**
- Ⓐ 5.0
- Ⓑ 7.9
- Ⓒ 8.3
- Ⓓ 16.0

Extending the Lesson

GEOMETRY In the *rectangular prism* shown, $\overline{BD}$ is the diagonal of the base, and $\overline{FD}$ is the diagonal of the prism. **41. 17 units**

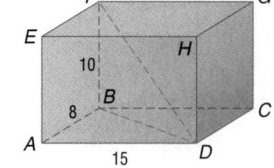

41. Find the measure of the diagonal of the base.

42. What is the measure of the diagonal of the prism to the nearest tenth? **19.7 units**

43. MODELING Measure the dimensions of a shoebox and use the dimensions to calculate the length of the diagonal of the box. Then use a piece of string and a ruler to check your calculation. **See students' work.**

Maintain Your Skills

Mixed Review   Find the value of *x* in each triangle. Then classify each triangle as *acute, right,* or *obtuse.* *(Lesson 9-4)*

44. **101; obtuse**   **45.** **90; right**   **46.** **78; acute**

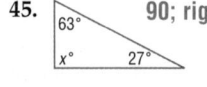

47. Use a protractor to draw an angle having a measure of 115°. *(Lesson 9-3)* **See students' work.**

ALGEBRA Solve each inequality. *(Lesson 7-4)*

48. $x + 4 < 12$ $x < 8$ **49.** $-15 \le n - 6$ $n \ge -9$

Getting Ready for the Next Lesson   **PREREQUISITE SKILL** Simplify each expression.
(To review order of operations and exponents, see Lessons 1-2 and 4-2.)

50. $(2 + 6)^2 + (-5 + 6)^2$ **65** **51.** $(-4 + 3)^2 + (0 - 2)^2$ **5** **52.** $[3 + (-1)]^2 + (8 - 4)^2$ **20**

Tips for New Teachers

Intervention You may want to have students complete Exercises 1–9 in pairs. Check for questions before having them complete the assignment independently.

Graphing Irrational Numbers

In Lesson 2-1, you learned to graph integers on a number line. Irrational numbers can also be graphed on a number line. Consider the irrational number $\sqrt{53}$. To graph $\sqrt{53}$, construct a right triangle whose hypotenuse measures $\sqrt{53}$ units.

Step 1 Find two numbers whose squares have a sum of 53. Since $53 = 49 + 4$ or $7^2 + 2^2$, one pair that will work is 7 and 2. These numbers will be the lengths of the legs of the right triangle.

Step 2 Draw the right triangle
- First, draw a number line on grid paper.

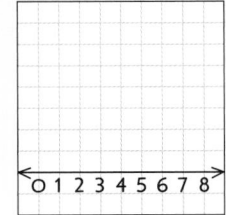

- Next, draw a right triangle whose legs measure 7 units and 2 units. Notice that this triangle can be drawn in two ways. Either way is correct.

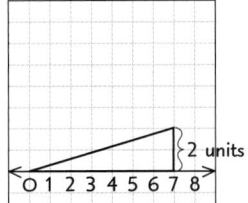
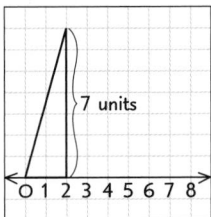

Step 3 Graph $\sqrt{53}$.
- Open your compass to the length of the hypotenuse.
- With the tip of the compass at 0, draw an arc that intersects the number line at point B.
- The distance from 0 to B is $\sqrt{53}$ units. From the graph, $\sqrt{53} \approx 7.3$.

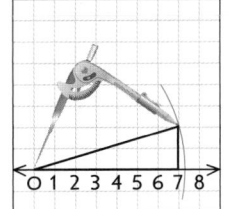
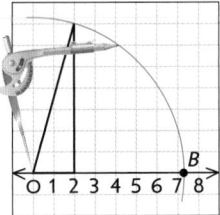

Model and Analyze

Use a compass and grid paper to graph each irrational number on a number line. 1–6. See pp. 489A–489B.

1. $\sqrt{5}$ **2.** $\sqrt{20}$ **3.** $\sqrt{45}$ **4.** $\sqrt{97}$

5. Describe two different ways to graph $\sqrt{34}$.

6. Explain how the graph of $\sqrt{2}$ can be used to locate the graph of $\sqrt{3}$.

Algebra Activity   Graphing Irrational Numbers   **465**

Getting Started

Objective Graph irrational numbers on a number line.

Materials
grid paper
compass

Teach

- This method is an alternative means of finding the square root of a number.
- Discuss with students why the orientation of the triangle is not important.

Assess

In **Exercises 1–4**, students should:
- check their answers with a calculator.
- compare their work to see if they chose the same triangles to work the problems.

For **Exercises 5–6,** have students work in small groups. Discuss as a class how groups arrived at their answers.

Study Notebook

Have students summarize the procedure in this activity and provide another example.

Resource Manager

📁 Teaching Pre-Algebra with Manipulatives
- p. 1 (master for grid paper)
- p. 117 (student recording sheet)

Glencoe Mathematics Classroom Manipulative Kit
- compass

1 Focus

Mathematical Background
notes are available for this lesson on page 434D.

How is the Distance Formula related to the Pythagorean Theorem?

The opening activity questions are repeated on page 517 of the *Chapter 9 Resource Masters*.

Reading to Learn Mathematics, p. 517 | ELL

Pre-Activity *How is the Distance Formula related to the Pythagorean Theorem?*

Do the activity at the top of page 466 in your textbook. Write your answers below.

a. Name the coordinates of *P*. (3, 3)

b. Find the distance between *M* and *P*. 7 units

c. Find the distance between *N* and *P*. 3 units

d. Classify △*MNP*. right

e. What theorem can be used to find the distance between *M* and *N*? Pythagorean Theorem

f. Find the distance between *M* and *N*. $\sqrt{58}$ units

Reading the Lesson   1–3. See students' work.

Write a definition and give an example of each new vocabulary word or phrase.

Vocabulary	Definition	Example
1. Distance Formula		
2. midpoint		
3. Midpoint Formula		

4. The distance formula is based on the   Pythagorean Theorem   .

5. To determine the midpoint, you must know the coordinates of the   endpoints   of the line segment.

Helping You Remember

6. Describe in a paragraph how you would find the perimeter of △*STU* shown below. Write out any formulas that must be used.

To find the perimeter of the triangle, you must use the Distance Formula ($d = \sqrt{(x_2 - x_1)^2 + (y_2 - y_1)^2}$) to find the length of each side. Once you have found the lengths of all three sides, add the lengths to find the perimeter.

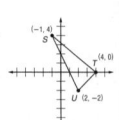

What You'll Learn

- Use the Distance Formula to determine lengths on a coordinate plane.
- Use the Midpoint Formula to find the midpoint of a line segment on the coordinate plane.

Vocabulary
- Distance Formula
- midpoint
- Midpoint Formula

e. Pythagorean Theorem

How is the Distance Formula related to the Pythagorean Theorem?

The graph of points $N(3, 0)$ and $M(-4, 3)$ is shown. A horizontal segment is drawn from M, and a vertical segment is drawn from N. The intersection is labeled P.

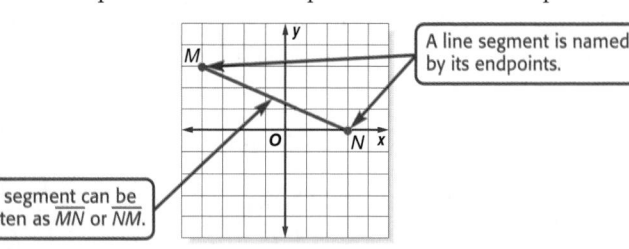

a. Name the coordinates of P. **(3, 3)**

b. Find the distance between M and P. **7 units**

c. Find the distance between N and P. **3 units**

d. Classify $\triangle MNP$. **right**

e. What theorem can be used to find the distance between M and N?

f. Find the distance between M and N. $\sqrt{58}$ **units**

THE DISTANCE FORMULA   Recall that a line segment is a part of a line. It contains two endpoints and all of the points between the endpoints.

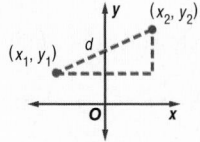
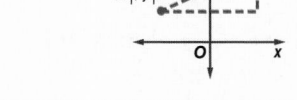

A line segment is named by its endpoints.

The segment can be written as $\overline{MN}$ or $\overline{NM}$.

To find the length of a segment on a coordinate plane, you can use the **Distance Formula**, which is based on the Pythagorean Theorem.

Study Tip

Look Back
To review the notation (x_1, y_1) and (x_2, y_2), see Lesson 8-4.

Key Concept   *Distance Formula*

- **Words**   The distance d between two points with coordinates (x_1, y_1) and (x_2, y_2), is given by $d = \sqrt{(x_2 - x_1)^2 + (y_2 - y_1)^2}$.

- **Model**

✓ Concept Check   How is a line segment named? **by its endpoints**

Resource Manager

📂 **Workbooks and Reproducible Masters**

Chapter 9 Resource Masters
- Study Guide and Intervention, p. 514
- Skills Practice, p. 515
- Practice, p. 516
- Reading to Learn Mathematics, p. 517
- Enrichment, p. 518
- Assessment, p. 544

Parent and Student Study Guide Workbook, p. 77

Transparencies
5-Minute Check Transparency 9-6
Answer Key Transparencies

Technology
Interactive Chalkboard

Example 1 *Use the Distance Formula*

Find the distance between $G(-3, 1)$ and $H(2, -4)$. Round to the nearest tenth, if necessary.

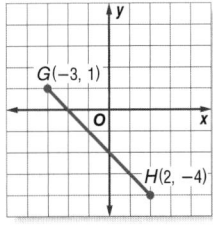

Use the Distance Formula.

$$d = \sqrt{(x_2 - x_1)^2 + (y_2 - y_1)^2} \qquad \text{Distance Formula}$$

$$GH = \sqrt{[2 - (-3)]^2 + (-4 - 1)^2} \qquad (x_1, y_1) = (-3, 1), (x_2, y_2) = (2, -4)$$

$$GH = \sqrt{(5)^2 + (-5)^2} \qquad \text{Simplify.}$$

$$GH = \sqrt{25 + 25} \qquad \text{Evaluate } 5^2 \text{ and } (-5)^2.$$

$$GH = \sqrt{50} \qquad \text{Add 25 and 25.}$$

$$GH \approx 7.1 \qquad \text{Take the square root.}$$

The distance between points G and H is about 7.1 units.

Study Tip

Substitution
You can use either point as (x_1, y_1). The distance will be the same.

The Distance Formula can be used to solve geometry problems.

Example 2 *Use the Distance Formula to Solve a Problem*

GEOMETRY Find the perimeter of $\triangle ABC$ to the nearest tenth.

First, use the Distance Formula to find the length of each side of the triangle.

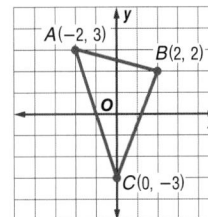

Side $\overline{AB}$: $A(-2, 3)$, $B(2, 2)$

$$d = \sqrt{(x_2 - x_1)^2 + (y_2 - y_1)^2}$$

$$AB = \sqrt{[2 - (-2)]^2 + (2 - 3)^2}$$

$$AB = \sqrt{(4)^2 + (-1)^2}$$

$$AB = \sqrt{16 + 1}$$

$$AB = \sqrt{17}$$

Side $\overline{BC}$: $B(2, 2)$, $C(0, -3)$

$$d = \sqrt{(x_2 - x_1)^2 + (y_2 - y_1)^2}$$

$$BC = \sqrt{[0 - 2]^2 + (-3 - 2)^2}$$

$$BC = \sqrt{(-2)^2 + (-5)^2}$$

$$BC = \sqrt{4 + 25}$$

$$BC = \sqrt{29}$$

Side $\overline{CA}$: $C(0, -3)$, $A(-2, 3)$

$$d = \sqrt{(x_2 - x_1)^2 + (y_2 - y_1)^2}$$

$$CA = \sqrt{[-2 - 0]^2 + (3 - (-3))^2}$$

$$CA = \sqrt{(-2)^2 + (6)^2}$$

$$CA = \sqrt{4 + 36}$$

$$CA = \sqrt{40}$$

Study Tip

Common Misconception
To find the sum of square roots, do *not* add the numbers inside the square root symbols.

$\sqrt{17} + \sqrt{29} + \sqrt{40} \neq \sqrt{86}$

Then add the lengths of the sides to find the perimeter.

$$\sqrt{17} + \sqrt{29} + \sqrt{40} \approx 4.123 + 5.385 + 6.325$$

$$\approx 15.833$$

The perimeter is about 15.8 units.

 www.pre-alg.com/extra_examples

Lesson 9-6 The Distance and Midpoint Formulas **467**

2 Teach

Building on Prior Knowledge

In Lesson 4-2, students studied exponents. In this lesson, students must use exponents when using the Distance Formula.

THE DISTANCE FORMULA

In-Class Examples

1 Find the distance between $M(8, 4)$ and $N(-6, -2)$. Round to the nearest tenth, if necessary. **15.2**

Teaching Tip Point out to students that, given two points, it is always possible to make them the endpoints of the hypotenuse of a right triangle.

2 **GEOMETRY** Find the perimeter of $\triangle XYZ$ to the nearest tenth. **15.8**

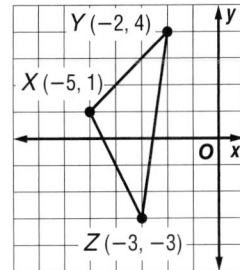

Teaching Tip You may need to remind students that they must find the distance for all three line segments to determine perimeter.

DAILY INTERVENTION

Differentiated Instruction

- **Kinesthetic** Using masking tape, lay out a grid on the floor in the gymnasium or classroom. Mark the origin and axes with different colored tape. Have each student choose a spot on the grid and determine its coordinates. Then have students find the distance between themselves and three other classmates. Use ropes marked off in grid units to check the answers.

THE MIDPOINT FORMULA

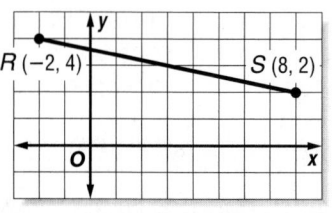
THE MIDPOINT FORMULA   On a line segment, the point that is halfway between the endpoints is called the **midpoint**.

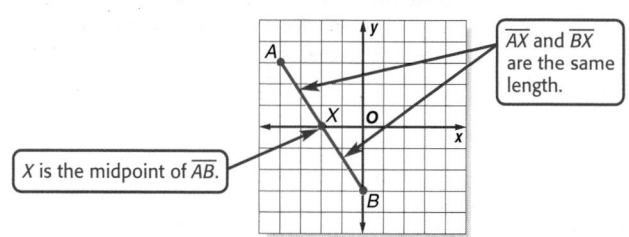

$\overline{AX}$ and $\overline{BX}$ are the same length.

X is the midpoint of $\overline{AB}$.

To find the midpoint of a segment on a coordinate plane, you can use the **Midpoint Formula**.

Key Concept — Midpoint Formula

- **Words**   On a coordinate plane, the coordinates of the midpoint of a segment whose endpoints have coordinates at (x_1, y_1) and (x_2, y_2) are given by $\left(\dfrac{x_1 + x_2}{2}, \dfrac{y_1 + y_2}{2}\right)$.

- **Model**

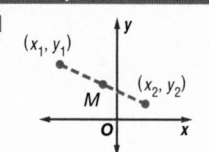

Example 3   Use the Midpoint Formula

Find the coordinates of the midpoint of $\overline{CD}$.

$$\text{midpoint} = \left(\frac{x_1 + x_2}{2}, \frac{y_1 + y_2}{2}\right) \quad \text{Midpoint Formula}$$

$$= \left(\frac{-2 + 4}{2}, \frac{-3 + 3}{2}\right) \quad \text{Substitution}$$

$$= (1, 0) \quad \text{Simplify.}$$

The coordinates of the midpoint of $\overline{CD}$ are (1, 0).

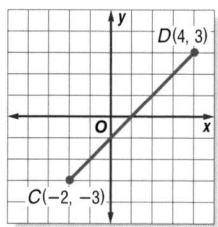

Check for Understanding

Concept Check

1. **Define** *midpoint*. the point halfway between two endpoints
2. **Explain** the Distance Formula in your own words. **2–3. See margin.**
3. **OPEN ENDED**   Draw any line segment on a coordinate system. Then find the midpoint of the segment.

Guided Practice

Find the distance between each pair of points. Round to the nearest tenth, if necessary.

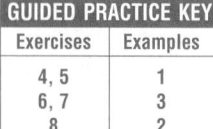

GUIDED PRACTICE KEY	
Exercises	Examples
4, 5	1
6, 7	3
8	2

4. $A(-1, 3)$, $B(8, -6)$ **12.7**   5. $M(4, -2)$, $N(-6, -7)$ **11.2**

The coordinates of the endpoints of a segment are given. Find the coordinates of the midpoint of each segment.

6. $B(4, 1)$, $C(-2, 5)$ **(1, 3)**   7. $R(3, -6)$, $S(1, -4)$ **(2, -5)**

Application

8. **GEOMETRY**   Triangle EFG has vertices $E(1, 4)$, $F(-3, 0)$, and $G(4, -1)$. Find the perimeter of $\triangle EFG$ to the nearest tenth. **18.6**

Answers

2. Sample answer: To find the distance between any two points with coordinates (x_1, y_1) and (x_2, y_2), first find the difference between x_2 and x_1, and the difference between y_2 and y_1. Then square each difference and take the square root of the sum of the squares.

3. Sample answer: The coordinates of the midpoint of $\overline{AB}$ are $\left(-\frac{1}{2}, 0\right)$.

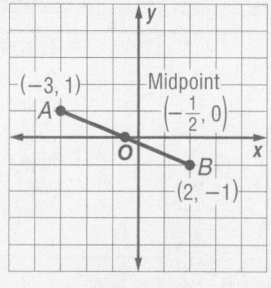

Practice and Apply

Homework Help

For Exercises	See Examples
9–16	1
17, 18	2
19–28	3

Extra Practice
See page 746.

Find the distance between each pair of points. Round to the nearest tenth, if necessary.

9. $J(5, -4)$, $K(-1, 3)$ **9.2**

10. $C(-7, 2)$, $D(6, -4)$ **14.3**

11. $E(-1, -2)$, $F(9, -4)$ **10.2**

12. $V(8, -5)$, $W(-3, -5)$ **11**

13. $S(-9, 0)$, $T(6, -7)$ **16.6**

14. $M(0, 0)$, $N(-7, -8)$ **10.6**

★15. $Q\left(5\frac{1}{4}, 3\right)$, $R\left(2, 6\frac{1}{2}\right)$ **4.8**

★16. $A\left(-2\frac{1}{2}, 0\right)$, $B\left(-8\frac{3}{4}, -6\frac{1}{4}\right)$ **8.8**

GEOMETRY Find the perimeter of each figure.

17. 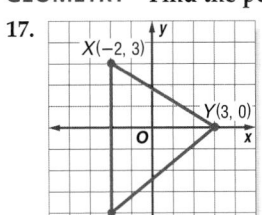 **19.2**

18. 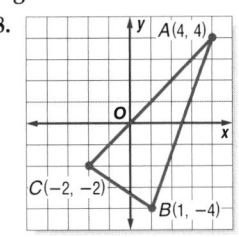 **20.6**

The coordinates of the endpoints of a segment are given. Find the coordinates of the midpoint of each segment.

19. 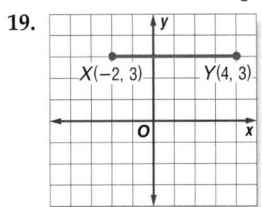 **(1, 3)**

20. 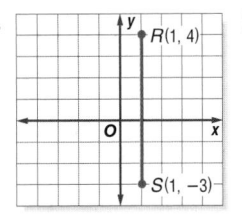 **$\left(1, \frac{1}{2}\right)$**

21. $A(6, 1)$, $B(2, -5)$ **(4, −2)**

22. $J(-3, 5)$, $K(7, 9)$ **(2, 7)**

23. $M(-1, -3)$, $N(5, 7)$ **(2, 2)**

24. $C(-4, 9)$, $D(6, -5)$ **(1, 2)**

25. $T(10, -3)$, $U(-4, -5)$ **(3, −4)**

26. $P(6, 11)$, $Q(-4, -3)$ **(1, 4)**

★27. $F(15, -4)$, $G(8, -6)$ **$\left(11\frac{1}{2}, -5\right)$**

★28. $E(-12, -5)$, $F(-3, -4)$

28. $\left(-7\frac{1}{2}, -4\frac{1}{2}\right)$

29. Yes; $\overline{PM}$ and $\overline{MN}$ have equal measures.

29. **GEOMETRY** Determine whether $\triangle MNP$ with vertices $M(3, -1)$, $N(-3, 2)$, and $P(6, 5)$ is isosceles. Explain your reasoning.

30. Yes; none of the measures of the sides are equal.

30. **GEOMETRY** Is $\triangle ABC$ with vertices $A(8, 4)$, $B(-2, 7)$, and $C(0, 9)$ a scalene triangle? Explain.

31. **CRITICAL THINKING** Suppose $C(8, -9)$ is the midpoint of $\overline{AB}$ and the coordinates of B are $(18, -21)$. What are the coordinates of A? **(−2, 3)**

32. **WRITING IN MATH** Answer the question that was posed at the beginning of the lesson. See p. 470 margin.

How is the Distance Formula related to the Pythagorean Theorem?

Include the following in your answer:
- a drawing showing how to use the Pythagorean Theorem to find the distance between two points on the coordinate system, and
- a comparison of the expressions $(x_2 - x_1)$ and $(y_2 - y_1)$ with the length of the legs of a right triangle.

 www.pre-alg.com/self_check_quiz   **Lesson 9-6** The Distance and Midpoint Formulas   **469**

Study Guide and Intervention, p. 514

Distance and Midpoint Formulas On a coordinate plane, the distance d between two points with coordinates (x_1, y_1) and (x_2, y_2) is given by $d = \sqrt{(x_2 - x_1)^2 + (y_2 - y_1)^2}$. The midpoint of a line segment whose endpoints are (x_1, y_1) and (x_2, y_2) is given by $\left(\frac{x_1 + x_2}{2}, \frac{y_1 + y_2}{2}\right)$.

Example Find the distance between $M(8, 1)$ and $N(-2, 3)$. Round to the nearest tenth, if necessary. Then find the coordinates of the midpoint of $\overline{MN}$.

$d = \sqrt{(x_2 - x_1)^2 + (y_2 - y_1)^2}$ Distance Formula
$MN = \sqrt{(8 - (-2))^2 + (1 - 3)^2}$ $(x_1, y_1) = (2, 3), (x_2, y_2) = (8, 1)$
$MN = \sqrt{(10)^2 + (-2)^2}$ Simplify.
$MN = \sqrt{100 + 4}$ Evaluate 10^2 and $(-2)^2$.
$MN = \sqrt{104}$ Add 100 and 4.
$MN = 10.2$ Take the square root.
The distance between points M and N is about 10.2 units.
midpoint $= \left(\frac{x_1 + x_2}{2}, \frac{y_1 + y_2}{2}\right)$ Midpoint Formula
$= \left(\frac{8 + (-2)}{2}, \frac{1 + 3}{2}\right)$ Substitution
$= (3, 2)$ Simplify.
The coordinates of the midpoint of $\overline{MN}$ are (3, 2).

Exercises

Find the distance between each pair of points. Round the nearest tenth, if necessary.

1. $A(3, 1), B(2, 5)$ 4.1
2. $C(-2, -4), D(3, 7)$ 12.1
3. $E(5, -3), F(4, 2)$ 5.1
4. $G(-6, 5), H(-4, -3)$ 8.2
5. $I(-4, -3), J(4, 4)$ 10.6
6. $K(5, 0), L(-2, 1)$ 7.1
7. $M(2, 1), N(6, 5)$ 5.7
8. $O(0, 0), P(-5, 6)$ 7.8

The coordinates of the endpoints of a segment are given. Find the coordinates of the midpoint of each segment.

9. $Q(3, 5), R(4, 2)$ (3.5, 3.5)
10. $S(-6, -4), T(-5, 6)$ (−5.5, 1)
11. $U(2, 1), V(4, 4)$ (3, 2.5)
12. $W(5, 1), X(-2, -1)$ (1.5, 0)
13. $Y(-5, -3), Z(2, 5)$ (−1.5, 1)
14. $A(8, -1), B(3, -1)$ (5.5, −1)
15. $C(0, 0), D(2, 4)$ (1, 2)
15. $E(-5, 3), F(4, 7)$ (−0.5, 5)

Skills Practice, p. 515 and Practice, p. 516 (shown)

Find the distance between each pair of points. Round to the nearest tenth, if necessary.

1. $A(5, 2), B(3, 4)$ 2.8
2. $C(-2, -4), D(1, 3)$ 7.6
3. $E(-3, 4), F(-2, 1)$ 3.2
4. $G(0, 0), H(-7, 8)$ 10.6
5. $R(-4, -8), S(2, -3)$ 7.8
6. $G(9, 9), H(-9, -9)$ 25.5
7. $M(1, 1), N(-10, -10)$ 15.6
8. $P(1\frac{1}{2}, 3), Q(5, 6\frac{1}{4})$ 4.8
9. $R(7, 4\frac{1}{2}), S(6\frac{1}{2}, 3\frac{1}{4})$ 1.3
10. $T(-3\frac{1}{2}, -4\frac{1}{4}), U(5\frac{1}{2}, 1\frac{1}{2})$ 10.7

GEOMETRY Find the perimeter of each figure.

11. 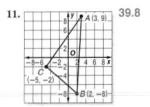 39.8
12. 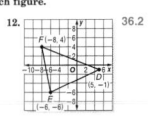 36.2

The coordinates of the endpoints of a segment are given. Find the coordinates of the midpoint of each segment.

13. $A(5, 1), B(-4, -3)$ (0.5, −1)
14. $V(4, 6), W(-8, -12)$ (−2, −3)
15. $C(-2, -4), D(-5, 6)$ (−3.5, 1)
16. $X(1, -7), Y(-1, 7)$ (0, 0)
17. $E(5, -3), F(-7, 8)$ (−1, 2.5)
18. $A(8, 8), B(-8, -8)$ (0, 0)
19. $G(0, 6), H(12, -12)$ (6, −3)
20. $C(-4, -6), D(-5, 14)$ (−4.5, 4)
21. $P(-7, 2), Q(8, 9)$ (0.5, 5.5)
22. $J(-12, -3), K(4, 7)$ (−4, 2)

23. Determine whether $\triangle XYZ$ with vertices $X(3, 4), Y(2, -3)$, and $Z(-5, -2)$ is isosceles. Explain your answer. Yes; XY and YZ equal 7.1 units.

24. Is $\triangle DEF$ with vertices $D(1, 4), E(6, 2), F(-1, 3)$ a scalene triangle? Explain. Yes; none of measures of the sides are equal.

Enrichment, p. 518

Coordinate Proof

Recall that the midpoint of a line segment is the point that separates the segment into two congruent segments. Use this justification of the x-coordinate of the midpoint formula by beginning with $\triangle RST$. The midpoint is $M(x, y)$, and the distance between R and S is 2 units. Therefore, the distance between R and midpoint M is 1 unit.

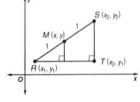

Write the reason for each statement.

1. Prove: $x = \frac{(x_1 + x_2)}{2}$

Statement	Reason
a. $\frac{1}{2} = \frac{x - x_1}{x_2 - x_1}$	a. Given (due to similar triangles)
b. $2(x - x_1) = 1(x_2 - x_1)$	b. Cross Products
c. $2x - 2x_1 = x_2 - x_1$	c. Distributive Prop.
d. $2x - 2x_1 + 2x_1 = x_2 - x_1 + 2x_1$	d. Add. Prop. Equality
e. $2x = x_2 + x_1$	e. Simplify
f. $2x = x_1 + x_2$	f. Comm. Prop. Add.
g. $x = \frac{x_1 + x_2}{2}$	g. Div. Prop. Equality

Use Problem 1 as an example to justify the y-coordinate of the midpoint.

2. Prove: $y = \frac{(y_1 + y_2)}{2}$

Statement	Reason
a. $\frac{1}{2} = \frac{y - y_1}{y_2 - y_1}$	a. Given (due to similar triangles)
b. $2(y - y_1) = 1(y_2 - y_1)$	b. Cross Products
c. $2y - 2y_1 = y_2 - y_1$	c. Distributive Prop.
d. $2y - 2y_1 + 2y_1 = y_2 - y_1 + 2y_1$	d. Add. Prop. Equality
e. $2y = y_2 + y_1$	e. Simplify
f. $2y = y_1 + y_2$	f. Comm. Prop. Add.
g. $y = \frac{y_1 + y_2}{2}$	g. Div. Prop. Equality

Open-Ended Assessment

Modeling Have students mark a piece of paper in units equal to the size of their grid paper. Have them use this paper to check their distance and midpoint answers.

Getting Ready for Lesson 9-7

PREREQUISITE SKILL Lesson 9-7 presents similar triangles and indirect measurement. Proportions are used to find missing measurements. Exercises 43–48 should be used to determine your students' familiarity with proportions.

Assessment Options

Practice Quiz 2 The quiz provides students with a brief review of the concepts and skills in Lessons 9-4 through 9-6. Lesson numbers are given to the right of exercises or instruction lines so students can review concepts not yet mastered.

Quiz (Lessons 9-5 and 9-6) is available on p. 544 of the *Chapter 9 Resource Masters*.

Answer (p. 469)

32. Both the Distance Formula and the Pythagorean Theorem can be used to find the distance between any two points on the coordinate system. Answers should include the following.

- First, use the two points. Draw vertical and horizontal lines so that a right triangle is formed. Then determine the lengths of the legs. Replace the lengths of the legs in the Pythagorean Theorem to determine the length of the hypotenuse.

33. What are the coordinates of the midpoint of the line segment with endpoints $H(-2, 0)$ and $G(8, 6)$? **C**

  Ⓐ $(-1, 7)$ Ⓑ $(5, 3)$ Ⓒ $(3, 3)$ Ⓓ $(2, 2)$

34. Which expression shows how to find the distance between points $M(-5, -3)$ and $N(2, 3)$? **B**

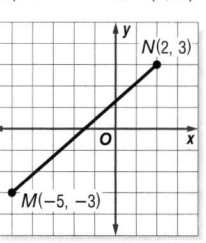

  Ⓐ $\sqrt{(2-5)^2 + (3-3)^2}$

  Ⓑ $\sqrt{[2-(-5)]^2 + [3-(-3)]^2}$

  Ⓒ $\sqrt{[2-(-5)]^2 + (3-3)^2}$

  Ⓓ $\sqrt{(3-2)^2 + [-3-(-5)]^2}$

Maintain Your Skills

Mixed Review **Find the length of the hypotenuse in each right triangle. Round to the nearest tenth, if necessary.** *(Lesson 9-5)*

35. 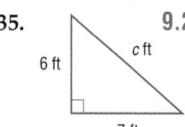 **9.2**   **36.** 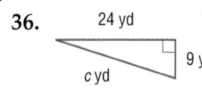 **25.6**   **37.** 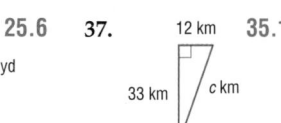 **35.1**

38. The measures of the angles of a triangle are in the ratio 1:4:5. Find the measure of each angle. *(Lesson 9-4)* **18°, 72°, 90°**

ALGEBRA State the slope and the y-intercept for the graph of each equation. *(Lesson 8-6)*

39. $y = 2x + 1$ **2, 1**   **40.** $x + y = -4$ **−1, −4**   **41.** $4x + y = -6$ **−4, −6**

42. What number is 56% of 85? *(Lesson 6-7)* **47.6**

Getting Ready for the Next Lesson **PREREQUISITE SKILL** Solve each proportion.
*(To review **proportions**, see Lesson 6-2.)*

43. $\dfrac{4}{16} = \dfrac{7}{x}$ **28**   **44.** $\dfrac{a}{15} = \dfrac{12}{60}$ **3**   **45.** $\dfrac{84}{m} = \dfrac{52}{13}$ **21**

46. $\dfrac{2.8}{h} = \dfrac{4.2}{12}$ **8**   **47.** $\dfrac{3.4}{85} = \dfrac{2.36}{n}$ **59**   **48.** $\dfrac{k}{5.5} = \dfrac{111}{15}$ **40.7**

Practice Quiz 2   *Lessons 9-4 through 9-6*

Classify each triangle by its angles and by its sides. *(Lesson 9-4)*

1. 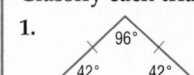 **obtuse isosceles**   **2.** 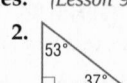 **right scalene**

3. The lengths of three sides of a triangle are 34 meters, 30 meters, and 16 meters. Is the triangle a right triangle? Explain. *(Lesson 9-5)* **Yes; $34^2 = 30^2 + 16^2$**

4. Find the distance between $A(-4, -1)$ and $B(7, -9)$ to the nearest tenth. *(Lesson 9-6)* **13.6**

5. The coordinates of the endpoints of $\overline{MN}$ are $M(-2, 3)$ and $N(0, 7)$. What are the coordinates of the midpoint of $\overline{MN}$? *(Lesson 9-6)* **$(-1, 5)$**

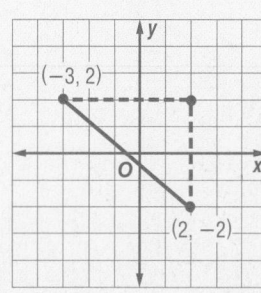

Pythagorean Theorem
$$c^2 = a^2 + b^2$$
$$c^2 = 5^2 + 4^2$$
$$c^2 = 25 + 16$$
$$c^2 = 41$$
$$c \approx 6.4$$

- The value of $(x_2 - x_1)$ and $(y_2 - y_1)$ equals the lengths of a right triangle.

9-7 Similar Triangles and Indirect Measurement

What You'll Learn

- Identify corresponding parts and find missing measures of similar triangles.
- Solve problems involving indirect measurement using similar triangles.

How can similar triangles be used to create patterns?

The triangle at the right is called *Sierpinski's triangle*. The triangle is made up of various equilateral triangles. The following activity investigates patterns similar to the ones in Sierpinski's triangle.

Step 1 On dot paper, draw a right triangle whose legs measures 8 and 16 units. Find the measure of each angle.

Step 2 Count to find the midpoint of each side of the triangle. Then connect the midpoints of each side.

Step 3 Shade the middle triangle.

Step 4 Repeat this process with each non-shaded triangle. Your triangles will resemble those shown below.

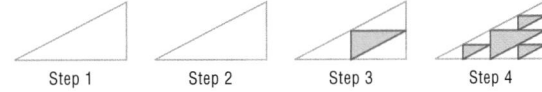

Step 1   Step 2   Step 3   Step 4

a. Compare the measures of the angles of each non-shaded triangle to the original triangle. **They are the same.**

b. They are shorter. **b.** How do the lengths of the legs of the triangles compare?

Vocabulary
- similar triangles
- indirect measurement

CORRESPONDING PARTS

Triangles that have the same shape but not necessarily the same size are called **similar triangles**. In the figure below, △ABC is similar to △XYZ. This is written as △ABC ~ △XYZ.

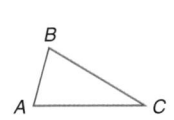 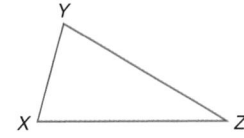

Reading Math

Similar Symbol
The symbol ~ is read *is similar to.*

Similar triangles have corresponding angles and corresponding sides. Arcs are used to show congruent angles.

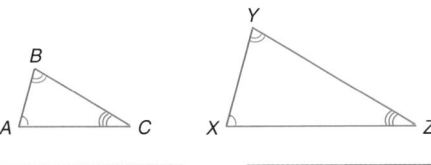

Corresponding Angles
$\angle A \leftrightarrow \angle X$ $\angle B \leftrightarrow \angle Y$ $\angle C \leftrightarrow \angle Z$

Corresponding Sides
$\overline{AB} \leftrightarrow \overline{XY}$ $\overline{BC} \leftrightarrow \overline{YZ}$ $\overline{AC} \leftrightarrow \overline{XZ}$

Lesson 9-7 Similar Triangles and Indirect Measurement **471**

9-7 Lesson Notes

1 Focus

5-Minute Check Transparency 9-7 Use as a quiz or review of Lesson 9-6.

Mathematical Background notes are available for this lesson on page 434D.

How can similar triangles be used to create patterns?

The opening activity questions are repeated on page 522 of the *Chapter 9 Resource Masters*.

Reading to Learn Mathematics, p. 522 ELL

Pre-Activity How can similar triangles be used to create patterns?

Do the activity at the top of page 471 in your textbook. Write your answers below.

a. Compare the measures of the angles of each non-shaded triangle to the original triangle. They are the same.

b. How do the lengths of the legs of the triangles compare? They are shorter.

Reading the Lesson 1–2. See students' work.

Write a definition and give an example of each new vocabulary word or phrase.

Vocabulary	Definition	Example
1. similar triangles		
2. indirect measurement		

3. The symbol ~ means (is uneven, <u>is similar to</u>).

4. Indirect measurement uses the properties of (<u>similar triangles</u>, midpoints) to find measurements that are difficult to measure directly.

Helping You Remember

5. *Similar* is a word that is used in everyday English.

a. Find the definition of *similar* in a dictionary. Write the definition. related in appearance or nature; alike though not identical

b. Explain how the definition can help you remember how *similar* is used in mathematics. Similar triangles have angles that are the same and sides that, though not identical, are proportional.

Teaching Tip Explain to students that if a triangle were enlarged or reduced on a copier, similar triangles would be created.

Resource Manager

Workbooks and Reproducible Masters

Chapter 9 Resource Masters
- Study Guide and Intervention, p. 519
- Skills Practice, p. 520
- Practice, p. 521
- Reading to Learn Mathematics, p. 522
- Enrichment, p. 523

Parent and Student Study Guide Workbook, p. 78
School-to-Career Masters, p. 18

Transparencies
5-Minute Check Transparency 9-7
Answer Key Transparencies

Technology
Interactive Chalkboard
Pre-AlgePASS: Tutorial Plus, Lesson 29

2 Teach

CORRESPONDING PARTS

In-Class Example

Power Point®

1 If $\triangle RUN \sim \triangle CAB$, what is the value of x? **20**

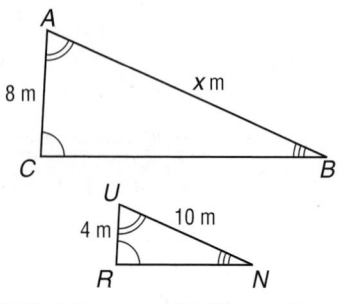

INDIRECT MEASUREMENT

In-Class Example

Power Point®

2 **MAPS** A surveyor wants to find the distance RS across the lake. He constructs $\triangle PQT$ similar to $\triangle PRS$ and measures the distances as shown. What is the distance across the lake? **28.8 m**

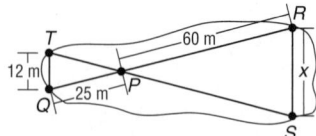

Teaching Tip Discuss with students when this type of measurement may be useful. Ask for examples from your neighborhood or area when indirect measurement might be used.

Reading Math

Segment Measure
The symbol AB means *the measure of segment AB.*

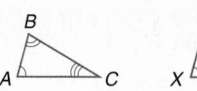

☑ **Concept Check** Define similar triangles.

The following properties are true for similar triangles.

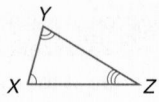

> **Key Concept** ▸ *Corresponding Parts of Similar Triangles*
>
> - **Words** If two triangles are similar, then
>   - the corresponding angles have the same measure, and
>   - the corresponding sides are proportional.
>
> - **Model**
>
> - **Symbols** $\angle A \cong \angle X$, $\angle B \cong \angle Y$, $\angle C \cong \angle Z$ and $\dfrac{AB}{XY} = \dfrac{BC}{YZ} = \dfrac{AC}{XZ}$

You can use proportions to determine the measures of the sides of similar triangles when some measures are known.

Example 1 Find Measures of Similar Triangles

If $\triangle JKM \sim \triangle RST$, what is the value of x?

The corresponding sides are proportional.

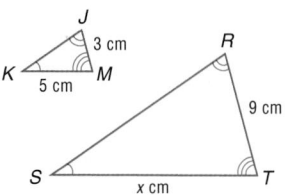

$$\frac{JM}{RT} = \frac{KM}{ST} \quad \text{Write a proportion.}$$

$$\frac{3}{9} = \frac{5}{x} \quad \begin{array}{l}\text{Replace } JM \text{ with 3, } RT \text{ with 9,}\\ KM \text{ with 5, and } ST \text{ with } x.\end{array}$$

$$3 \cdot x = 9 \cdot 5 \quad \text{Find the cross products.}$$

$$3x = 45 \quad \text{Simplify.}$$

$$x = 15 \quad \text{Mentally divide each side by 3.}$$

The value of x is 15.

INDIRECT MEASUREMENT The properties of similar triangles can be used to find measurements that are difficult to measure directly. This kind of measurement is called **indirect measurement**.

Example 2 Use Indirect Measurement

MAPS In the figure, $\triangle ABE \sim \triangle DCE$. Find the distance across the lake.

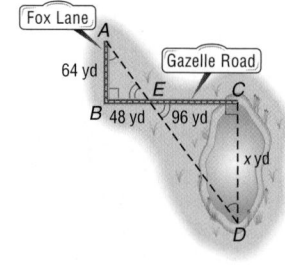

$$\frac{EC}{EB} = \frac{CD}{BA} \quad \text{Write a proportion.}$$

$$\frac{96}{48} = \frac{x}{64} \quad \begin{array}{l}\text{Replace } EC \text{ with 96, } EB \text{ with 48,}\\ CD \text{ with } x, \text{ and } BA \text{ with 64.}\end{array}$$

$$96 \cdot 64 = 48 \cdot x \quad \text{Find the cross products.}$$

$$6144 = 48x \quad \text{Multiply.}$$

$$128 = x \quad \text{Divide each side by 48.}$$

The distance across the lake is 128 yards.

472 Chapter 9 Real Numbers and Right Triangles

D A I L Y
INTERVENTION   **Unlocking Misconceptions**

- **Indirect Measurement** When looking at an illustration like that in Example 2 in the text, students may not recognize the similar triangles because of their orientation. If students are having difficulty, encourage them to copy the illustration, then cut the triangles apart and rotate them until the corresponding angles align. This should allow students to recognize the corresponding sides and set up a correct proportion.

The properties of similar triangles can be used to determine missing measures in shadow problems. This is called *shadow reckoning*.

Example 3 Use Shadow Reckoning

LANDMARKS Suppose the Space Needle in Seattle, Washington, casts a 220-foot shadow at the same time a nearby tourist casts a 2-foot shadow. If the tourist is 5.5 feet tall, how tall is the Space Needle?

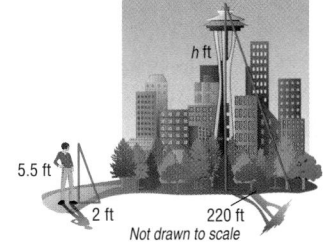

5.5 ft   2 ft   220 ft
Not drawn to scale

Explore You know the lengths of the shadows and the height of the tourist. You need to find the Space Needle's height.

Plan Write and solve a proportion.

Solve

tourist's height → $\dfrac{5.5}{h} = \dfrac{2}{220}$ ← tourist's shadow
Space Needle's height →   ← Space Needle's shadow

$5.5 \cdot 220 = h \cdot 2$ Find the cross products.

$1210 = 2h$ Multiply.

$605 = h$ Mentally divide each side by 2.

The height of the Space Needle is 605 feet.

Examine The tourist's height is a little less than 3 times the length of his or her shadow. The space needle should be a little less than 3 times its shadow, or $3 \cdot 220$, which is 660 feet. So, 605 is reasonable.

Check for Understanding

Concept Check

1. **OPEN ENDED** Draw two similar triangles and label the vertices. Then write a proportion that compares the corresponding sides. 1–2. See pp. 489A–489B.

2. **Explain** indirect measurement in your own words.

Guided Practice In Exercises 3 and 4, the triangles are similar. Write a proportion to find each missing measure. Then find the value of *x*. 3–4. See pp. 489A–489B.

GUIDED PRACTICE KEY	
Exercises	Examples
3, 4	1
5	2
6	3

3.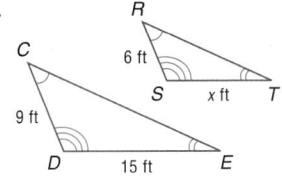

4.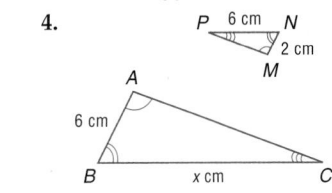

Applications

5. **MAPS** In the figure, $\triangle ABC \sim \triangle EDC$. Find the distance from Austintown to North Jackson. **6 km**

North Jackson   Austintown
Deerfield   Ellsworth
x km   2 km   6 km   18 km

6. **SHADOWS** At the same time a 10-foot flagpole casts an 8-foot shadow, a nearby tree casts a 40-foot shadow. How tall is the tree? **50 ft**

www.pre-alg.com/extra_examples

Lesson 9-7 Similar Triangles and Indirect Measurement **473**

3 Practice/Apply

About the Exercises . . .

Organization by Objective
• **Corresponding Parts:** 7–12
• **Indirect Measurement:** 15–18

Odd/Even Assignments
Exercises 7–18 are structured so that students practice the same concepts whether they are assigned odd or even problems.

Assignment Guide

Basic: 7, 9, 13–17 odd, 19–35
Average: 7–17 odd, 19–35
Advanced: 8–18 even, 19–31 (Optional: 32–35)

Study Guide and Intervention, p. 519

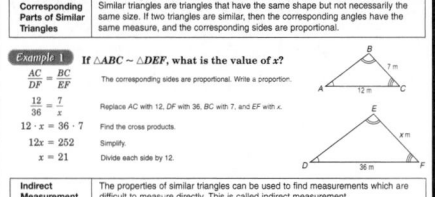

Corresponding Parts of Similar Triangles	Similar triangles are triangles that have the same shape but not necessarily the same size. If two triangles are similar, then the corresponding angles have the same measure, and the corresponding sides are proportional.

Example 1 If $\triangle ABC \sim \triangle DEF$, what is the value of x?

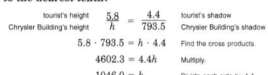

$\dfrac{AC}{DF} = \dfrac{BC}{EF}$ The corresponding sides are proportional. Write a proportion.

$\dfrac{12}{36} = \dfrac{7}{x}$ Replace AC with 12, DF with 36, BC with 7, and EF with x.

$12 \cdot x = 36 \cdot 7$ Find the cross products.

$12x = 252$ Simplify.

$x = 21$ Divide each side by 12.

Indirect Measurement	The properties of similar triangles can be used to find measurements which are difficult to measure directly. This is called indirect measurement.

Example 2 The Chrysler Building in New York casts a 793.5 foot shadow the same time a 5.8 foot tourist casts a 4.4 foot shadow. How tall is the Chrysler Building to the nearest tenth?

tourist's height $\dfrac{5.8}{h} = \dfrac{4.4}{793.5}$ tourist's shadow
Chrysler Building's height   Chrysler Building's shadow

$5.8 \cdot 793.5 = h \cdot 4.4$ Find the cross products.

$4602.3 = 4.4h$ Multiply.

$1046.0 = h$ Divide each side by 4.4.

The height of the Chrysler Building is 1046 feet.

Exercises

The triangles are similar. Write a proportion and find the value of x.

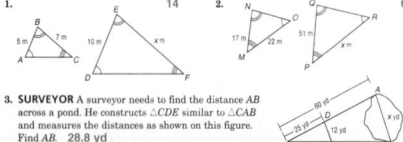

1.   14   2.   66

3. **SURVEYOR** A surveyor needs to find the distance AB across a pond. He constructs $\triangle CDE$ similar to $\triangle CAB$ and measures the distances as shown on this figure. Find AB. **28.8 yd**

Skills Practice, p. 520 and Practice, p. 521 (shown)

In Exercises 1–10, the triangles are similar. Write a proportion to find each missing measure. Then find the value of x.

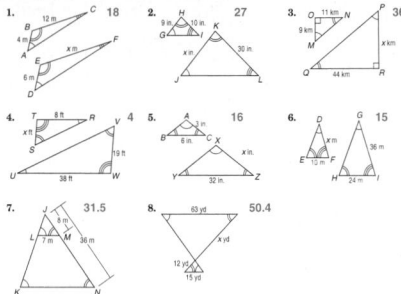

1.   18   2.   27   3.   36

4.   4   5.   16   6.   15

7.   31.5   8.   50.4

For Exercises 9–12, write a proportion. Then determine the missing measure.

9. **CHIMNEYS** A 6-ft observer casts a 4-ft shadow at the same time the chimney on the Ohio Power Company casts an 804-foot shadow. How tall is the chimney?
$\dfrac{6 \text{ ft}}{4 \text{ ft}} = \dfrac{x \text{ ft}}{804 \text{ ft}}$; 1206 ft

10. **BUILDINGS** The May Road Apartments in Hong Kong cast a 90-meter shadow at the same time a 1.5-meter tall tenant casts a 0.75-meter shadow. How tall is the apartment building? $\dfrac{1.5 \text{ m}}{0.75 \text{ m}} = \dfrac{x \text{ m}}{90 \text{ m}}$; 180 meters

11. **WORLD RECORDS** The world's tallest man lived from 1918 to 1940. He cast a 4-foot $5\frac{1}{2}$-inch shadow when a 3-foot pole cast a 3-foot shadow. How tall was he? $\dfrac{x \text{ in.}}{53.5 \text{ in.}} = \dfrac{72 \text{ in.}}{36 \text{ in.}}$; 8 feet 11 inches

12. **SHADOWS** A man casts a 14-foot shadow. A 4-foot child casts a 9-foot 4-inch shadow at the same time. How tall is the man? $\dfrac{x \text{ in.}}{168 \text{ in.}} = \dfrac{48 \text{ in.}}{112 \text{ in.}}$; 6 feet

Enrichment, p. 523

Constant Rate of Change

In Chapter 8 you learned how to calculate the slope m of a line by using the ratio $\dfrac{rise}{run}$ between any two points on the line. You may have wondered why it does not matter which two points you pick. Now that you have worked with similar triangles, it is possible to justify why all slopes on a line are the same.

Points A, B, C, and D lie on the same line. We will show that the slope is the same when using points A and B as it is when using points C and D.

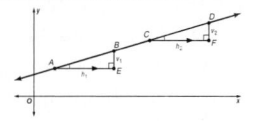

Write the reason for each statement.

1. Prove: $\dfrac{v_1}{h_1} = \dfrac{v_2}{h_2}$

Statement	Reason
a. $\overline{AE} \parallel \overline{CF}$	a. Definition of Horizontal Lines
b. $\angle A \cong \angle C$	b. Corresponding $-s$
c. $\angle E \cong \angle F$	c. All Right $-s \cong$
d. $\triangle ABE \sim \triangle CDF$	d. AA Similarity
e. $\dfrac{v_1}{v_2} = \dfrac{h_1}{h_2}$	e. Def. Similar Triangles
f. $v_1 \cdot h_2 = h_1 \cdot v_2$	f. Cross Products
g. $\dfrac{v_1 \cdot h_2}{h_1 \cdot h_2} = \dfrac{h_1 \cdot v_2}{h_1 \cdot h_2}$	g. Div. Prop. Equality
h. $\dfrac{v_1}{h_1} = \dfrac{v_2}{h_2}$	h. Simplify

Since $\dfrac{rise}{run_1} = \dfrac{rise}{run_2}$, any two points on a line can be used to calculate the slope.

Practice and Apply

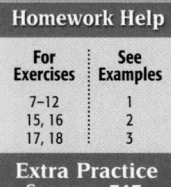

Homework Help

For Exercises	See Examples
7–12	1
15, 16	2
17, 18	3

Extra Practice
See page 747.

In Exercises 7–12, the triangles are similar. Write a proportion to find each missing measure. Then find the value of x. **7–12. See margin.**

7.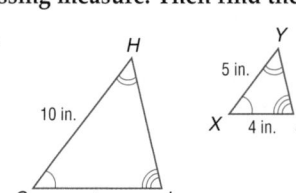
5 in.   10 in.   4 in. x in.

8.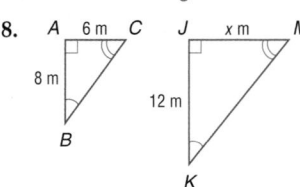
6 m   8 m x m   12 m

9.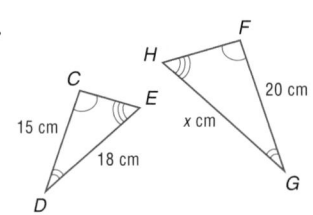
15 cm   18 cm   20 cm x cm

10.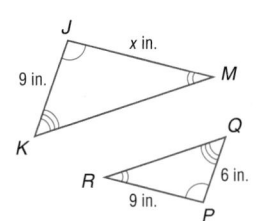
x in.   9 in.   6 in.   9 in.

★ 11.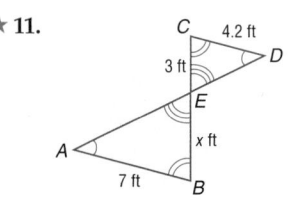
4.2 ft   3 ft x ft   7 ft

★ 12.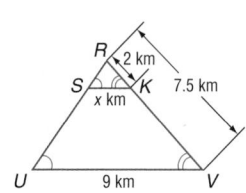
2 km x km   7.5 km   9 km

Determine whether each statement is *sometimes*, *always*, **or** *never* **true.**

13. The measures of corresponding angles in similar triangles are the same. **always**

14. Similar triangles have the same shape and the same size. **sometimes**

In Exercises 15 and 16, the triangles are similar.

15. **PARKS** How far is the pavilion from the log cabin? **68 yd**

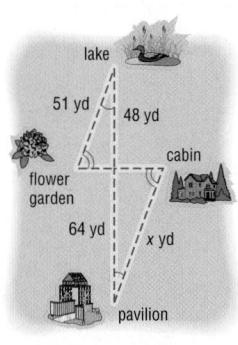
lake   51 yd   48 yd   cabin   flower garden   64 yd x yd   pavilion

16. **ZOO** How far are the gorillas from the cheetahs? **105 m**

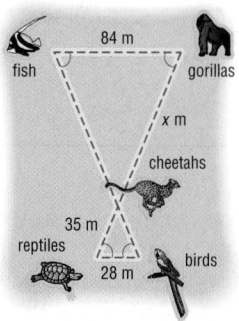
84 m   fish   gorillas x m   cheetahs   35 m   reptiles   28 m   birds

For Exercises 17 and 18, write a proportion. Then determine the missing measure.

17. **ANIMALS** At the same time a baby giraffe casts a 3.2-foot shadow, a 15-foot adult giraffe casts an 8-foot shadow. How tall is the baby giraffe? **6 ft**

Answers

7. $\dfrac{x}{4} = \dfrac{10}{5}$; 8

8. $\dfrac{x}{6} = \dfrac{12}{8}$; 9

9. $\dfrac{x}{18} = \dfrac{20}{15}$; 24

10. $\dfrac{x}{9} = \dfrac{9}{6}$; 13.5

11. $\dfrac{x}{3} = \dfrac{7}{4.2}$; 5

12. $\dfrac{x}{9} = \dfrac{2}{7.5}$; 2.4

18. RIDES Suppose a roller coaster casts a shadow of 31.5 feet. At the same time, a nearby Ferris wheel casts a 19-foot shadow. If the roller coaster is 126 feet tall, how tall is the Ferris wheel? **76 ft**

19. No; triangles *ABC* and *DEF* are not similar since corresponding sides are not proportional.

19. CRITICAL THINKING Triangle *ABC* has side lengths 3 cm, 5 cm, and 6 cm. Triangle *DEF* has side lengths 4 cm, 6 cm, and 8 cm. Determine whether $\triangle ABC \sim \triangle DEF$. Explain.

20. WRITING IN MATH Answer the question that was posed at the beginning of the lesson. **See margin.**

How can similar triangles be used to create patterns?

Include the following in your answer:

• an explanation telling how Sierpinski's triangle relates to similarity, and
• an example of the pattern formed when Steps 1–4 are performed on an acute scalene triangle.

21. The triangles shown are similar. Find the length of $\overline{JM}$ to the nearest tenth. **A**

  Ⓐ 3.7   Ⓑ 3.9
  Ⓒ 4.1   Ⓓ 8.3

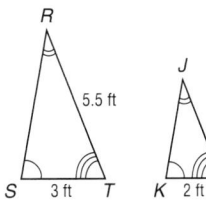

22. On the coordinate system, $\triangle MNP$ and two coordinates for $\triangle RST$ are shown. Which coordinate for point *T* will make $\triangle MNP$ and $\triangle RST$ similar triangles? **B**

  Ⓐ $T(3, 1)$ Ⓑ $T(1, -1)$
  Ⓒ $T(1, 2)$ Ⓓ $T(1, 1)$

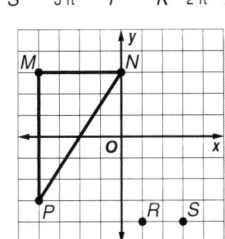

Maintain Your Skills

Mixed Review Find the distance between each pair of points. Round to the nearest tenth, if necessary. *(Lesson 9-6)*

23. $S(2, 3)$, $T(0, 6)$ **3.6**   **24.** $E(-1, 1)$, $F(3, -2)$ **5**   **25.** $W(4, -6)$, $V(-3, -5)$ **7.1**

If *c* is the measure of the hypotenuse, find each missing measure. Round to the nearest tenth, if necessary. *(Lesson 9-5)*

26. $a = 8$, $b = ?$, $c = 34$ **33.0**   **27.** $a = ?$, $b = 27$, $c = 82$ **77.4**

28. ALGEBRA Write an equation for the line that passes through points at $(1, -1)$ and $(-2, 11)$. *(Lesson 8-7)* $y = -4x + 3$

Write each percent as a fraction in simplest form. *(Lesson 6-4)*

29. 25% $\frac{1}{4}$ **30.** $87\frac{1}{2}$% $\frac{7}{8}$ **31.** 150% $1\frac{1}{2}$

Getting Ready for the Next Lesson **PREREQUISITE SKILL** Express each fraction as a decimal. Round to four decimal places, if necessary. *(To review writing fractions as decimals, see Lesson 5-1.)*

32. $\frac{12}{16}$ **0.75**   **33.** $\frac{10}{14}$ **0.7143**   **34.** $\frac{20}{25}$ **0.8**   **35.** $\frac{9}{40}$ **0.225**

---

4 Assess

Open-Ended Assessment

Writing Have students write instructions for finding height or length using similar triangles. Their example can involve shadow reckoning or another type of similar triangles problem.

Getting Ready for Lesson 9-8

PREREQUISITE SKILL Lesson 9-8 presents trigonometric ratios. Ratios involving the sides of triangles are used to find a trigonometric value. Exercises 32–35 should be used to determine your students' familiarity with expressing fractions as decimals.

Answer

20. By increasing or decreasing the size of similar triangles, patterns can be formed. Answers should include the following.

• All of the triangles used in Sierpinski's triangle are similar.

• Sample answer:

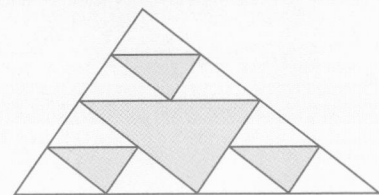

Teacher to Teacher

Andrea L. Ellyson   Great Bridge M.S., Chesapeake, VA

"My students often have trouble identifying corresponding parts when working with proportions. Have students use patty paper or tracing paper to trace each pair of similar triangles. Cut them apart and rotate or flip them so that the corresponding angles and sides are more easily identified. This visualization really helps students set up the proportions correctly."

Algebra Activity

Algebra Activity

A Preview of Lesson 9-8

Getting Started

Objective Discover the special relationship among right triangles and their sides.

Materials
metric ruler
protractor
calculator

Teach

- Make sure students measure their angles accurately.
- You may want to have students work in pairs and check each other's work.

Assess

In **Exercises 1–3**, students should
- make a new table for each triangle drawn.
- test their conjecture.

Study Notebook

You may wish to have students summarize this activity and what they learned from it.

Answers

1. See students' work.

2. The ratios of the sides of any 30°-60°-90° triangle are about 0.50, 0.875, and 1.75.

3. See students' work. The ratios of the sides of any 45°-45°-90° triangle are about 0.71, 0.71, and 1.00.

Ratios in Right Triangles

In the following activity, you will discover the special relationship among right triangles and their sides.

In any right triangle, the side **opposite** an angle is the side that is not part of the angle. In the triangle shown,
- side a is opposite $\angle A$,
- side b is opposite $\angle B$, and
- side c is opposite $\angle C$.

The side that is not opposite an angle and not the hypotenuse is called the **adjacent** side. In $\triangle ABC$,
- side b is adjacent to $\angle A$,
- side a is adjacent to $\angle B$, and
- sides a and b are adjacent to $\angle C$.

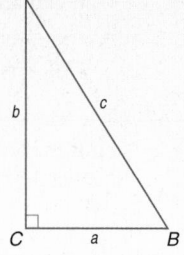

Step 1 Copy the table shown.

Step 2 Draw right triangle XYZ in which $m\angle X = 30°$, $m\angle Y = 60°$, and $m\angle Z = 90°$.

Step 3 Find the length to the nearest millimeter of the leg opposite the angle that measures 30°. Record the length.

Step 4 Find the length of the leg adjacent to the 30° angle. Record the length.

	30° angle	60° angle
Length (mm) of opposite leg		
Length (mm) of adjacent leg		
Length (mm) of hypotenuse		
Ratio 1		
Ratio 2		
Ratio 3		

Step 5 Find the length of the hypotenuse. Record the length.

Step 6 Using the measurements and a calculator, find each of the following ratios to the nearest hundredth. Record the results.

$$\text{Ratio 1} = \frac{\text{opposite leg}}{\text{hypotenuse}} \quad \text{Ratio 2} = \frac{\text{adjacent leg}}{\text{hypotenuse}} \quad \text{Ratio 3} = \frac{\text{opposite leg}}{\text{adjacent leg}}$$

Step 7 Repeat the procedure for the 60° angle. Record the results.

Model and Analyze 1–3. See margin.

1. Draw another 30°-60°-90° triangle with side lengths that are different than the one drawn in the activity. Then find the ratios for the 30° angle and the 60° angle.

2. **Make a conjecture** about the ratio of the sides of any 30°-60°-90° triangle.

3. Repeat the activity with a triangle whose angles measure 45°, 45°, and 90°.

476 Chapter 9 Real Numbers and Right Triangles

Resource Manager

Teaching Pre-Algebra with Manipulatives
- p. 21 (master for protractors)
- p. 22 (master for rulers)
- p. 120 (student recording sheet)

Glencoe Mathematics Classroom Manipulative Kit
- metric ruler
- protractor

Sine, Cosine, and Tangent Ratios

What You'll Learn

- Find sine, cosine, and tangent ratios.
- Solve problems by using the trigonometric ratios.

Vocabulary

- trigonometry
- trigonometric ratio
- sine
- cosine
- tangent

How are ratios in right triangles used in the real world?

In parasailing, a towrope is used to attach the parachute to the boat.

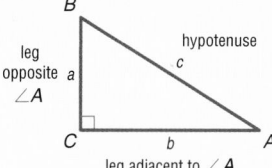

a. What type of triangle do the towrope, water, and height of the person above the water form? **right**

b. Name the hypotenuse of the triangle. $\overline{AC}$

c. What type of angle do the towrope and the water form? **acute**

d. Which side is opposite this angle? $\overline{AB}$

e. Other than the hypotenuse, name the side adjacent to this angle. $\overline{BC}$

FIND TRIGONOMETRIC RATIOS   **Trigonometry** is the study of the properties of triangles. The word trigonometry means *angle measure*. A **trigonometric ratio** is a ratio of the lengths of two sides of a right triangle.

The most common trigonometric ratios are the **sine**, **cosine**, and **tangent** ratios. These ratios are abbreviated as *sin*, *cos*, and *tan*, respectively.

Key Concept — Trigonometric Ratios

- **Words**   If $\angle A$ is an acute angle of a right triangle,

$$\sin \angle A = \frac{\text{measure of leg opposite } \angle A}{\text{measure of hypotenuse}},$$

$$\cos \angle A = \frac{\text{measure of leg adjacent to } \angle A}{\text{measure of hypotenuse}}, \text{ and}$$

$$\tan \angle A = \frac{\text{measure of leg opposite } \angle A}{\text{measure of leg adjacent to } \angle A}.$$

- **Model**

  leg opposite $\angle A$, a ; hypotenuse c ; leg adjacent to $\angle A$, b

- **Symbols** $\sin A = \dfrac{a}{c}$

  $\cos A = \dfrac{b}{c}$

  $\tan A = \dfrac{a}{b}$

Reading Math

Trigonometry Terms
The notation sin A is read *the sine of angle A*. The notation cos A is read *the cosine of angle A*. The notation tan A is read *the tangent of angle A*.

All right triangles that have the same measure for $\angle A$ are similar. So, the value of the trigonometric ratio depends only on the measure of $\angle A$, not the size of the triangle. The trigonometric ratios are the same for angle A no matter what the size of the triangle.

Lesson 9-8   Sine, Cosine, and Tangent Ratios   **477**

---

1 Focus

5-Minute Check Transparency 9-8   Use as a quiz or review of Lesson 9-7.

Mathematical Background notes are available for this lesson on page 434D.

How are ratios in right triangles used in the real world?

The opening activity questions are repeated on page 527 of the *Chapter 9 Resource Masters*.

Reading to Learn Mathematics, p. 527   **ELL**

Pre-Activity   How are ratios in right triangles used in the real world?

Do the activity at the top of page 477 in your textbook. Write your answers below.

a. What type of triangle do the towrope, water, and height of the person above the water form?   right

b. Name the hypotenuse of the triangle. $\overline{AC}$

c. What type of angle do the towrope and the water form?   acute

d. Which side is opposite this angle? $\overline{AB}$

e. Other than the hypotenuse, name the side adjacent to this angle. $\overline{BC}$

Reading the Lesson   1–5. See students' work.

Write a definition and give an example of each new vocabulary word or phrase.

Vocabulary	Definition	Example
1. trigonometry		
2. trigonometric ratio		
3. sine		
4. cosine		
5. tangent		

Decide whether each statement is true or false.

6. Trigonometric ratios can be used with acute and obtuse angles.   false

7. The value of the trigonometric ratio does not depend on the size of the triangle.   true

8. To determine tangent, you must know the measure of the hypotenuse.   false

Helping You Remember

9. Develop a rhyme, abbreviation, or other memory device to help you remember the trigonometric ratios.   Sample answer: SOH-CAH-TOA

Resource Manager

Workbooks and Reproducible Masters

Chapter 9 Resource Masters
- Study Guide and Intervention, p. 524
- Skills Practice, p. 525
- Practice, p. 526
- Reading to Learn Mathematics, p. 527
- Enrichment, p. 528
- Assessment, p. 544

Graphing Calculator and Spreadsheet Masters, p. 36
Parent and Student Study Guide Workbook, p. 79

Transparencies

5-Minute Check Transparency 9-8
Answer Key Transparencies

Technology

Interactive Chalkboard
Pre-AlgePASS: Tutorial Plus, Lesson 30

FIND TRIGONOMETRIC RATIOS

1 Find sin A, cos A, and tan A.

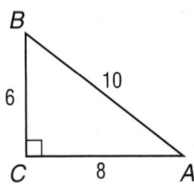

sin $A = 0.6$; cos $A = 0.8$;
tan $A = 0.75$

2 Find each value to the nearest ten thousandth.

a. sin 19°   **0.3256**

b. cos 51°   **0.6293**

c. tan 24°   **0.4452**

Teaching Tip Show students a table of trigonometric ratios and discuss how it is used.

APPLY TRIGONOMETRIC RATIOS

3 Find the missing measure. Round to the nearest tenth.
36.9

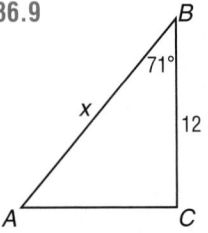

4 **ARCHITECTURE** A tourist visiting the Petronas Towers in Kuala Lumpur, Malaysia, stands 261 feet away from their base. She looks at the top at an angle of 80° with the ground. How tall are the Towers?   **1480.2 ft**

Rounding
When written as decimals, trigonometric ratios are often rounded to four decimal places.

Example 1 Find Trigonometric Ratios

Find sin P, cos P, and tan P.

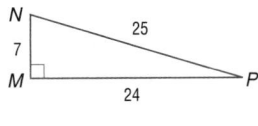

$$\sin P = \frac{\text{measure of leg opposite } \angle P}{\text{measure of hypotenuse}}$$

$$= \frac{7}{25} \text{ or } 0.28$$

$$\cos P = \frac{\text{measure of leg adjacent to } \angle P}{\text{measure of hypotenuse}}$$

$$= \frac{24}{25} \text{ or } 0.96$$

$$\tan P = \frac{\text{measure of leg opposite } \angle P}{\text{measure of leg adjacent to } \angle P}$$

$$= \frac{7}{24} \text{ or } 0.2917$$

You can use a calculator or a table of trigonometric ratios to find the sine, cosine, or tangent ratio for an angle with a given degree measure. Be sure that your calculator is in *degree* mode.

Example 2 Use a Calculator to Find Trigonometric Ratios

Find each value to the nearest ten thousandth.

a. sin 42°

[SIN] 42 [ENTER] 0.669130606
So, sin 42° is about 0.6691.

b. cos 65°

[COS] 65 [ENTER] 0.422618262
So, cos 65° is about 0.4226.

c. tan 78°

[TAN] 78 [ENTER] 4.704630109
So, tan 78° is about 4.7046.

APPLY TRIGONOMETRIC RATIOS   Trigonometric ratios can be used to find missing measures in a right triangle if the measure of an acute angle and the length of one side of the triangle are known.

Example 3 Use Trigonometric Ratios

Find the missing measure. Round to the nearest tenth.

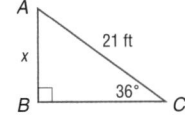

The measures of an acute angle and the hypotenuse are known. You need to find the measure of the side opposite the angle. Use the sine ratio.

$$\sin \angle C = \frac{\text{measure of leg opposite to } \angle C}{\text{measure of hypotenuse}} \quad \text{Write the sine ratio.}$$

$$\sin 36° = \frac{x}{21} \quad \text{Substitution}$$

$$21(\sin 36°) = 21 \cdot \frac{x}{21} \quad \text{Multiply each side by 21.}$$

21 [×] [SIN] 36 [ENTER] 12.3434903

$$12.3 \approx x \quad \text{Simplify.}$$

The measure of the side opposite the acute angle is about 12.3 feet.

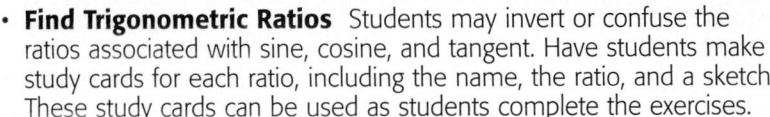

D A I L Y
INTERVENTION   **Unlocking Misconceptions**

- **Find Trigonometric Ratios** Students may invert or confuse the ratios associated with sine, cosine, and tangent. Have students make study cards for each ratio, including the name, the ratio, and a sketch. These study cards can be used as students complete the exercises.

Example 4 — Use Trigonometric Ratios to Solve a Problem

ARCHITECTURE The Leaning Tower of Pisa in Pisa, Italy, tilts about 5.2° from vertical. If the tower is 55 meters tall, how far has its top shifted from its original position?

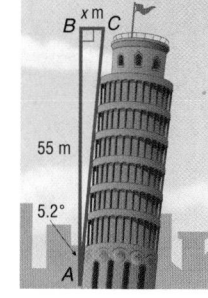

Use the tangent ratio.

$$\tan \angle A = \frac{\text{measure of leg opposite } \angle A}{\text{measure of leg adjacent to } \angle A}$$ Write the tangent ratio.

$$\tan 5.2° = \frac{x}{55}$$ Substitution

$$55(\tan 5.2°) = 55 \cdot \frac{x}{55}$$ Multiply each side by 55.

$$55 \;\boxed{\times}\; \boxed{\text{TAN}}\; 5.2 \;\boxed{\text{ENTER}}\; 5.00539211$$

$$5.0 \approx x$$ Simplify.

The top of the tower has shifted about 5.0 meters from its original position.

Check for Understanding

Concept Check

1–2. See margin.

1. **OPEN ENDED** Compare and contrast the sine, cosine, and tangent ratios.

2. **FIND THE ERROR** Susan and Tadeo are finding the height of the hill.

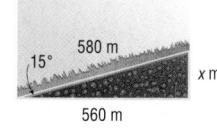

Susan
$$\sin 15° = \frac{x}{580}$$
$$580(\sin 15°) = x$$
$$150 \approx x$$

Tadeo
$$\sin 15° = \frac{x}{560}$$
$$560(\sin 15°) = x$$
$$145 \approx x$$

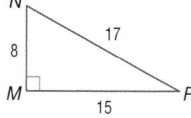

Who is correct? Explain your reasoning.

Guided Practice

GUIDED PRACTICE KEY	
Exercises	Examples
3–5	1
6–8	2
9–11	3
12	4

Find each sine, cosine, or tangent. Round to four decimal places, if necessary.

3. sin N **0.8824**

4. cos N **0.4706**

5. tan N **1.875**

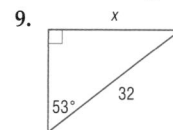

Use a calculator to find each value to the nearest ten thousandth.

6. sin 52° **0.7880**   7. cos 19° **0.9455**   8. tan 76° **4.0108**

For each triangle, find each missing measure to the nearest tenth.

9. **25.6**   10. **26.2**   11. **7.8**

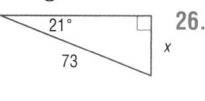

Application

12. **RECREATION** Miranda is flying a kite on a 50-yard string, which makes a 50° angle with the ground. How high above the ground is the kite? **38.3 yd**

Answers

1. The sine ratio compares the measure of the leg opposite the angle to the measure of the hypotenuse. The cosine ratio compares the measure of the leg adjacent to the angle to the measure of the hypotenuse. The tangent ratio compares the measure of the leg opposite the angle to the measure of the leg adjacent to the angle.

2. Susan; The sine ratio is the ratio of the opposite side to the hypotenuse. The length of the side opposite the 15° angle is x m. The length of the hypotenuse is 580 m.
So, $\sin 15° = \frac{x}{580}$.

---

3 Practice/Apply

Study Notebook

Have students—
- complete the definitions/examples for the remaining terms on the Vocabulary Builder worksheets for Chapter 9.
- draw a right triangle, label its sides and angles, and write out in symbols the formulas for sine, cosine, and tangent for one of the angles.
- include any other item(s) that they find helpful in mastering the skills in this lesson.

About the Exercises . . .

Organization by Objective
- Find Trigonometric Ratios: 13–26
- Apply Trigonometric Ratios: 27–32, 33–36, 37–39

Odd/Even Assignments
Exercises 13–32 are structured so that students practice the same concepts whether they are assigned odd or even problems.

Assignment Guide

Basic: 13–17 odd, 21–35 odd, 40–52

Average: 13–39 odd, 40–52

Advanced: 14–38 even, 40–52

DAILY INTERVENTION FIND THE ERROR If students are having difficulty recognizing which side is the hypotenuse when setting up trigonometric ratios, remind them that the hypotenuse is always the longest side of the triangle. Tell them to carefully observe the triangle when substituting values in the sine and cosine formulas.

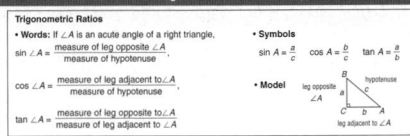
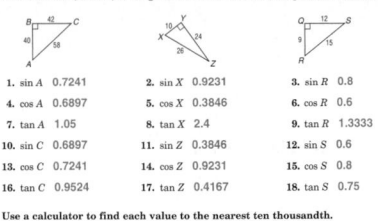
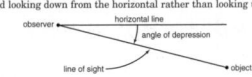
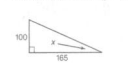
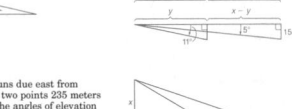
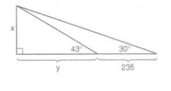
★ indicates increased difficulty

Practice and Apply

Find each sine, cosine, or tangent. Round to four decimal places, if necessary.

13. sin N **0.9231**   14. sin K **0.3846**
15. cos C **0.7241**   16. cos A **0.6897**
17. tan N **2.4**   18. tan C **0.9524**

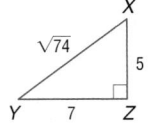

★ 19. Triangle RST is shown. Find sin R, cos R, and tan R.   **0.8944; 0.4472; 2.0**

★ 20. For △XYZ, what is the value of sin X, cos X, and tan X?   **0.8137; 0.5812; 1.**

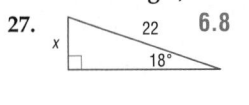 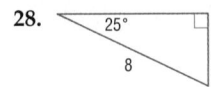

Use a calculator to find each value to the nearest ten thousandth.

21. sin 6° **0.1045**   22. sin 51° **0.7771**   23. cos 31° **0.8572**
24. cos 87° **0.0523**   25. tan 12° **0.2126**   26. tan 66° **2.2460**

For each triangle, find each missing measure to the nearest tenth.

27. **6.8**   28. **3.4**   29. **24.9**

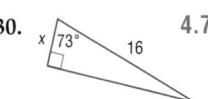 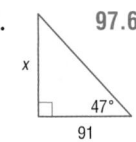 

30. **4.7**   31. **97.6**   32. **24.4**

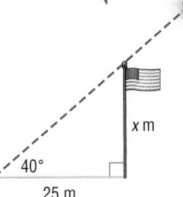

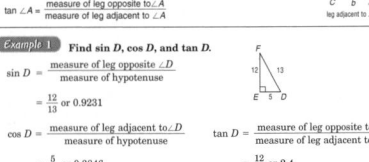
33. **SHADOWS** An *angle of elevation* is formed by a horizontal line and a line of sight above it. A flagpole casts a shadow 25 meters long when the angle of elevation of the Sun is 40°. How tall is the flagpole? **about 21 m**

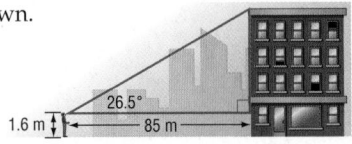

34. **SAFETY** The angle that a wheelchair ramp forms with the ground should not exceed 6°. What is the height of the ramp if it is 20 feet long? Round to the nearest tenth. **2.1 ft**

35. **BUILDINGS** Refer to the diagram shown. What is the height of the building? **about 44 m**

36. **CIVIL ENGINEERING** An exit ramp makes a 17° angle with the highway. Suppose the length of the ramp is 210 yards. What is the length of the base of the ramp? Round to the nearest tenth. **200.8 yd**

Find each measure. Round to the nearest tenth.

★ 37.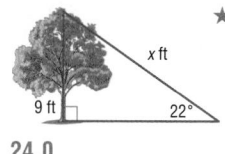
x ft
9 ft
22°
24.0

★ 38.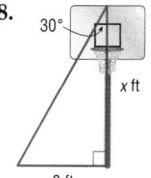
30°
x ft
8 ft
13.9

★ 39.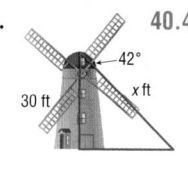
42°
30 ft
x ft
40.4

WebQuest

Trigonometric ratios are used to solve problems about the height of structures. Visit www.pre-alg.com/webquest to continue work on your WebQuest project.

CRITICAL THINKING
For Exercises 40–42, refer to the 45°-45°-90° and 30°-60°-90° triangles shown.

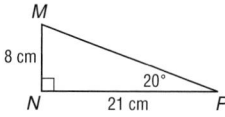
45° √2
1
45°
1

60° 2
1
30°
√3

40. Complete the table shown. Round to four decimal places, if necessary.

x	30°	45°	60°
sin x	0.5	0.7071	0.866
cos x	0.866	0.7071	0.5
tan x	0.5774	1	1.7321

41. Write a few sentences describing the similarities among the resulting sine and cosine values. **See margin.**

42. Which angle measure has the same sine and cosine ratio? **45°**

43. **WRITING IN MATH** Answer the question that was posed at the beginning of the lesson. **See margin.**

How are ratios in right triangles used in the real world?

Include the following in your answer:
- an explanation of two different methods for finding the measures of the lengths of the sides of a right triangle, and
- a drawing of a real-world situation that involves the sine ratio, with the calculations and solution included.

Standardized Test Practice
Ⓐ Ⓑ Ⓒ Ⓓ

44. If the measure of the hypotenuse of a right triangle is 5 feet and $m\angle B = 58°$, what is the measure of the leg adjacent to $\angle B$? **D**

Ⓐ 4.2402 Ⓑ 8.0017 Ⓒ 0.1060 Ⓓ 2.6496

45. Find the value of tan P to the nearest tenth. **C**

M
8 cm
N
21 cm
20°
P

Ⓐ 2.6 Ⓑ 0.5
Ⓒ 0.4 Ⓓ 0.1

Maintain Your Skills

Mixed Review

46. At the same time a 40-foot silo casts a 22-foot shadow, a fence casts a 3.3-foot shadow. Find the height of the fence. *(Lesson 9-7)* **6 ft**

The coordinates of the endpoints of a segment are given. Find the coordinates of the midpoint of each segment. *(Lesson 9-6)*

47. $\left(1\frac{1}{2}, \frac{1}{2}\right)$ 47. A(3, −4), C(0, 5)   48. M(−2, 1), N(6, −9)   49. R(−3, 0), S(−3, −8)
48. (2, −4)
49. (−3, −4)

ALGEBRA Solve each inequality. *(Lesson 7-5)*

50. $5m < 5$ $m < 1$ 51. $\frac{a}{-2} > 3$ $a < -6$ 52. $-4x \geq -16$ $x \leq 4$

---

4 Assess

Open-Ended Assessment
Writing Have students write a paragraph explaining how knowing the angle between an observer on the ground and the top of a flagpole and the distance between the observer and flagpole will allow them to find the flagpole's height.

Tips for New Teachers

Small-Group Management
If you are having students work in groups of three to four, make sure each student has an assigned task or part of a problem. Students should have specific responsibilities to keep them involved and on-task.

Assessment Options
Quiz (Lessons 9-7 and 9-8) is available on p. 544 of the *Chapter 9 Resource Masters.*

Answers

41. sin 45° = cos 45°; sin 60° = cos 30°; sin 30° = cos 60°

43. To find heights of buildings. Answers should include the following.
- If two of the three measures of the sides of a right triangle are known, you can use the Pythagorean Theorem to find the measure of the third side. If the measure of an acute angle and the length of one side of a right triangle are known, trigonometric ratios can be used to find the missing measures.

6°
19 ft
x ft

$$\sin 6° = \frac{x}{19}$$
$$19(\sin 6°) = x \quad 2.0 \approx x$$

The height of the ramp is about 2 feet.

Getting Started

Know Your Calculator The graphing calculator has two functions assigned to each key. The additional function is accessed by pressing **2nd** first. The **flashing up arrow** icon will appear on your screen. This method must be used to solve for angles in a right triangle when only measures of the sides are provided.

Teach

- Have students write out each ratio before solving. As students work the exercises, their calculators should be in the degree, not radian, mode.
- Remind students that they can check their answers by adding the angle measures. The sum of the two acute angles should equal 90.
- Remind students that sin⁻¹ means the inverse sine function, not the value of sine raised to the negative one power.
- Have students complete Exercises 1–3.

Assess

- Have students make up a problem and exchange with another student. Make sure they check their answers.
- Ask students what ratio they would use to solve a problem if the measures of the two sides and not the hypotenuse were given. **tangent**

Finding Angles of a Right Triangle

A calculator can be used to find the measure of an acute angle of a right triangle if you know the measures of two sides of the triangle.

Example

The end of an exit ramp from an interstate highway is 22 feet higher than the highway. If the ramp is 630 feet long, what angle does it make with the highway?

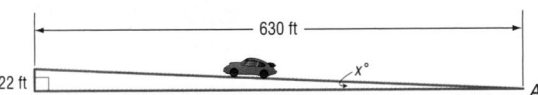

Step 1 Determine which trigonometric ratio is needed to solve the problem. Since you know the measure of the leg opposite $\angle A$ and the hypotenuse, use the sine ratio.

Step 2 Write the ratio.

$$\sin \angle A = \frac{\text{opposite}}{\text{hypotenuse}} \quad \text{Sine Ratio}$$

$$\sin \angle A = \frac{22}{630} \quad \text{Substitution}$$

Step 3 Use a calculator to find the measure of $\angle A$. The SIN⁻¹ function will find the angle measure, given the value of its sine.

2nd [SIN⁻¹] 22 **÷** 630 **ENTER** 2.001211869

To the nearest degree, the measure of $\angle A$ is 2°.

Exercises

Use a calculator to find the measure of each acute angle. Round to the nearest degree.

1.

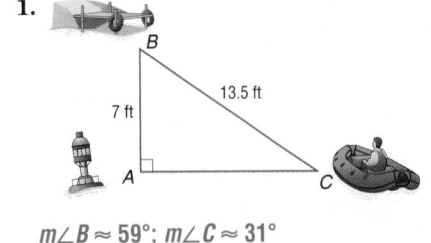

$m\angle B \approx 59°$; $m\angle C \approx 31°$

2.

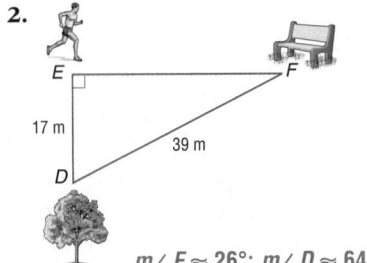

$m\angle F \approx 26°$; $m\angle D \approx 64°$

3. A flower garden is located 46 meters due west of an elm tree. A fountain is located 19 meters due south of the same elm tree. What are the measures of the angles formed by these three park features? **22°, 68°, 90°**

 www.pre-alg.com/other_calculator_keystrokes

Study Guide and Review

Vocabulary and Concept Check

acute angle (p. 449)	line (p. 447)	right triangle (p. 454)
acute triangle (p. 454)	line segment (p. 453)	scalene triangle (p. 455)
angle (p. 447)	midpoint (p. 468)	sides (p. 447)
congruent (p. 455)	Midpoint Formula (p. 468)	similar triangles (p. 471)
converse (p. 462)	obtuse angle (p. 449)	sine (p. 477)
cosine (p. 477)	obtuse triangle (p. 454)	solving a right triangle (p. 461)
degree (p. 448)	perfect square (p. 436)	square root (p. 436)
Distance Formula (p. 466)	point (p. 447)	straight angle (p. 449)
equilateral triangle (p. 455)	protractor (p. 448)	tangent (p. 477)
hypotenuse (p. 460)	Pythagorean Theorem (p. 460)	triangle (p. 453)
indirect measurement (p. 472)	radical sign (p. 436)	trigonometric ratio (p. 477)
irrational numbers (p. 441)	ray (p. 447)	trigonometry (p. 477)
isosceles triangle (p. 455)	real numbers (p. 441)	vertex (pp. 447, 453)
legs (p. 460)	right angle (p. 449)	

Complete each sentence with the correct term. Choose from the list above.

1. The set of rational numbers and the set of irrational numbers make up the set of __?__. **real numbers**

2. A(n) __?__ measures between 0° and 90°. **acute angle**

3. A(n) __?__ triangle has one angle with a measurement greater than 90°. **obtuse**

4. A(n) __?__ has all sides congruent. **equilateral triangle**

5. In a right triangle, the side opposite the right angle is the __?__. **hypotenuse**

6. Triangles that have the same shape but not necessarily the same size are called __?__. **similar triangles**

7. A(n) __?__ is a ratio of the lengths of two sides of a right triangle. **trigonometric ratio**

8. A(n) __?__ is a part of a line that extends indefinitely in one direction. **ray**

Lesson-by-Lesson Review

9-1 Squares and Square Roots

See pages 436–440.

Concept Summary
- The square root of a number is one of two equal factors of the number.

Example Find the square root of $-\sqrt{49}$.

$-\sqrt{49}$ indicates the *negative* square root of 49. Since $7^2 = 49$, $-\sqrt{49} = -7$.

Exercises Find each square root, if possible. *See Example 1 on page 436.*

9. $\sqrt{36}$ **6**   10. $\sqrt{100}$ **10**   11. $-\sqrt{81}$ **−9**

12. $\pm\sqrt{121}$ **±11**   13. $\sqrt{-25}$ **not possible**   14. $-\sqrt{225}$ **−15**

Vocabulary and Concept Check

- This alphabetical list of vocabulary terms in Chapter 9 includes a page reference where each term was introduced.

- **Assessment** A vocabulary review/test for Chapter 9 is available on p. 542 of the *Chapter 9 Resource Masters*.

Lesson-by-Lesson Review

For each lesson,
- the main ideas are summarized,
- additional examples review concepts, and
- practice exercises are provided.

Vocabulary PuzzleMaker

ELL The Vocabulary PuzzleMaker software improves students' mathematics vocabulary using four puzzle formats—crossword, scramble, word search using a word list, and word search using clues. Students can work on a computer screen or from a printed handout.

MindJogger Videoquizzes

ELL MindJogger Videoquizzes provide an alternative review of concepts presented in this chapter. Students work in teams in a game show format to gain points for correct answers. The questions are presented in three rounds.

Round 1 Concepts (5 questions)
Round 2 Skills (4 questions)
Round 3 Problem Solving (4 questions)

FOLDABLES™
Study Organizer

For more information about Foldables, see *Teaching Mathematics with Foldables*.

Have students review their Foldables to be sure they have included visuals for every lesson in this chapter.

Encourage students to refer to their Foldables while completing the Study Guide and Review and to use them in preparing for the Chapter Test.

9-2 The Real Number System

See pages 441–445.

Concept Summary

- Numbers that cannot be written as terminating or repeating decimals are called irrational numbers.
- The set of rational numbers and the set of irrational numbers together make up the set of real numbers.

Example   Solve $x^2 = 72$. Round to the nearest tenth.

$$x^2 = 72$$ Write the equation.

$$\sqrt{x^2} = \sqrt{72}$$ Take the square root of each side.

$$x = \sqrt{72} \text{ or } x = -\sqrt{72}$$ Find the positive and negative square root.

$$x \approx 8.5 \text{ or } x \approx -8.5$$

Exercises   Solve each equation. Round to the nearest tenth, if necessary.

See Example 3 on page 443.   **16.** 6.2, −6.2   **17.** 1.2, −1.2

15. $n^2 = 81$ 9, −9   **16.** $t^2 = 38$ **17.** $y^2 = 1.44$ **18.** $7.5 = r^2$ 2.7, −2.7

9-3 Angles

See pages 447–451.

Concept Summary

- An acute angle has a measure between 0° and 90°.
- A right angle measures 90°.
- An obtuse angle has a measure between 90° and 180°.
- A straight angle measures 180°.

Example   Use a protractor to find the measure of $\angle ABC$. Then classify the angle as *acute*, *obtuse*, *right*, or *straight*.

$\angle ABC$ appears to be acute. So, its measure should be between 0° and 90°.

$m\angle ABC = 65°$

Since $m\angle ABC < 90°$, $\angle ABC$ is acute.

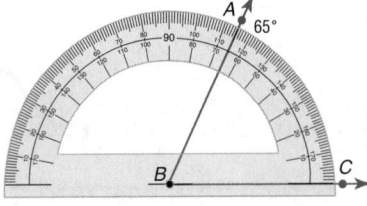

Exercises   Use a protractor to find the measure of each angle. Then classify each angle as *acute*, *obtuse*, *right*, or *straight*.

See Examples 1 and 3 on pages 448 and 449.

19. 90°; right   **20.** 115°; obtuse   **21.** 35°; acute

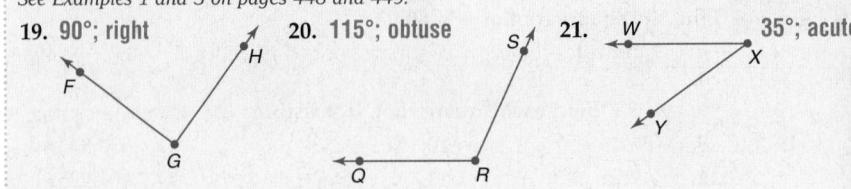

9-4 Triangles

See pages 453–457.

Concept Summary

- Triangles can be classified by their angles as acute, obtuse, or right and by their sides as scalene, isosceles, or equilateral.

Example Classify the triangle by its angles and by its sides.

$\triangle HJK$ has all acute angles and two congruent sides. So, $\triangle HJK$ is an acute isosceles triangle.

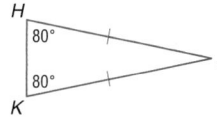

Exercises Classify each triangle by its angles and by its sides. *See Example 3 on page 455.* **22. acute equilateral**

22.
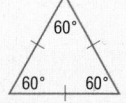

23.
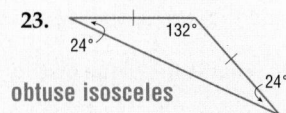
obtuse isosceles

24.
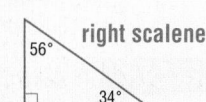
right scalene

9-5 The Pythagorean Theorem

See pages 460–464.

Concept Summary

- Pythagorean Theorem: $c^2 = a^2 + b^2$

Example Find the missing measure of the right triangle.

$c^2 = a^2 + b^2$	Pythagorean Theorem
$22^2 = 9^2 + b^2$	Replace c with 22 and a with 9.
$403 = b^2$	Simplify; subtract 81 from each side.
$20.1 \approx b$	Take the square root of each side.

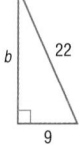

Exercises If c is the measure of the hypotenuse, find each missing measure. Round to the nearest tenth, if necessary. *See Example 2 on page 461.* **25. 13.7**

25. $a = 6, b = ?, c = 15$ **26.** $a = ?, b = 2, c = 7$ **6.7** **27.** $a = 18, b = ?, c = 24$ **15.9**

9-6 The Distance and Midpoint Formulas

See pages 466–470.

Concept Summary

- Distance Formula: $d = \sqrt{(x_2 - x_1)^2 + (y_2 - y_1)^2}$
- Midpoint Formula: $\left(\dfrac{x_1 + x_2}{2}, \dfrac{y_1 + y_2}{2}\right)$

Example Find the distance between $A(-4, 0)$ and $B(2, 5)$.

$d = \sqrt{(x_2 - x_1)^2 + (y_2 - y_1)^2}$	Distance Formula
$d = \sqrt{[2 - (-4)]^2 + (5 - 0)^2}$	$(x_1, y_1) = (-4, 0), (x_2, y_2) = (2, 5).$

$d \approx 7.8$ The distance between points A and B is about 7.8 units.

Study Guide and Review

Chapter 9 For More ...
• Extra Practice, see pages 745–747.
• Mixed Problem Solving, see page 766.

Exercises Find the distance between each pair of points. Round to the nearest tenth, if necessary. *See Example 1 on page 467.*

28. $J(0, 9)$, $K(2, 7)$ **2.8**   **29.** $A(-5, 1)$, $B(3, 6)$ **9.4**   **30.** $W(8, -4)$, $Y(3, 3)$ **8.6**

The coordinates of the endpoints of a segment are given. Find the coordinates of the midpoint of each segment. *See Example 3 on page 468.*

31. $M(8, 0)$, $N(-2, 10)$ **32.** $C(5, 9)$, $D(-7, 3)$ **33.** $Q(-6, 4)$, $R(6, -8)$

31. (3, 5) **32.** (−1, 6) **33.** (0, −2)

9-7 Similar Triangles and Indirect Measurement

See pages 471–475.

Concept Summary

• If two triangles are similar, then the corresponding angles have the same measure, and the corresponding sides are proportional.

Example If $\triangle ABC \sim \triangle KLM$, what is the value of x?

$\dfrac{AC}{KM} = \dfrac{BC}{LM}$ Write a proportion.

$\dfrac{x}{3} = \dfrac{2}{4}$ Substitution

$x = 1.5$ Find cross products and simplify.

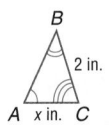 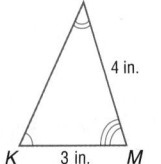

Exercises In Exercises 34 and 35, the triangles are similar. Write a proportion to find each missing measure. Then find the value of x. *See Example 1 on page 472.*

34. 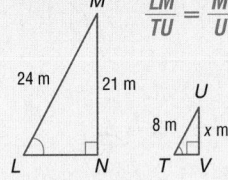 $\dfrac{LM}{TU} = \dfrac{MN}{UV}$; **7**

35. 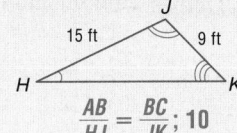 $\dfrac{AB}{HJ} = \dfrac{BC}{JK}$; **10**

9-8 Sine, Cosine, and Tangent Ratios

See pages 477–481.

Concept Summary

• Trigonometric ratios compare the lengths of two sides of a right triangle.

Example Find cos S.

$\cos S = \dfrac{15}{25}$ or 0.6

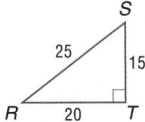

Exercises Find each sine, cosine, or tangent in $\triangle RST$ above. Round to four decimal places, if necessary. *See Example 1 on page 478.*

36. $\sin R$ **0.6**   **37.** $\tan S$ **1.3333**   **38.** $\tan R$ **0.75**

Practice Test

Vocabulary and Concepts

1. **OPEN ENDED** Give an example of a whole number, a natural number, an irrational number, a rational number, and an integer. **Sample answer: 1; 5; $\sqrt{27}$; $\frac{5}{8}$; −6**

2. Explain how to classify a triangle by its angles and by its sides. **See margin.**

Skills and Applications

Find each square root, if possible.

3. $\sqrt{81}$ **9**

4. $-\sqrt{121}$ **−11**

5. $\pm\sqrt{49}$ **−7, 7**

6. Without using a calculator, estimate $-\sqrt{42}$ to the nearest integer. **−6**

ALGEBRA Solve each equation. Round to the nearest tenth, if necessary.

7. $x^2 = 100$ **10, −10**

8. $w^2 = 38$ **6.2, −6.2**

9. Use a protractor to measure $\angle CAB$. Then classify the angle as *acute*, *obtuse*, *right*, or *straight*. **65°; acute**

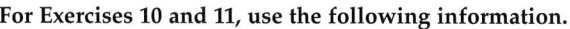

For Exercises 10 and 11, use the following information.
In $\triangle MNP$, $m\angle N = 87°$ and $m\angle P = 32°$.

10. Find the measure of $\angle M$. **61°**

11. Classify $\triangle MNP$ by its angles and by its sides. **acute scalene**

If c is the measure of the hypotenuse, find each missing measure. Round to the nearest tenth, if necessary.

12. $a = 6, b = 8, c = ?$ **10**

13. $a = 15, b = ?, c = 32$ **28.3**

14. **HIKING** Brandon hikes 7 miles south and 4 miles west. How far is he from the starting point of his hike? Round to the nearest tenth. **8.1 m**

15. Find the distance between $A(3, 8)$ and $B(-5, 2)$. Then find the coordinates of the midpoint of $\overline{AB}$. **10; (−1, 5)**

16. **PARKS** In the map of the park, the triangles are similar. Find the distance to the nearest tenth from the playground to the swimming pool. **62.5 ft**

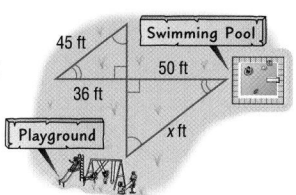

Find each sine, cosine, or tangent. Round to four decimal places, if necessary.

17. $\sin P$ **0.9231**

18. $\tan M$ **0.4167**

19. $\cos P$ **0.3846**

20. **STANDARDIZED TEST PRACTICE** Which statement is true? **C**

Ⓐ $4 < \sqrt{10} < 3$

Ⓑ $-6 > -\sqrt{28} > -5$

Ⓒ $-7 > -\sqrt{59} > -8$

Ⓓ $7 < \sqrt{47} < 6$

Portfolio Suggestion

Introduction Trigonometric ratios can be used to find the measure of a side or an acute angle of a right triangle. The ratios are used with the sine, cosine, and tangent functions.

Ask Students to find examples of each trigonometric function in their homework. Students should write a description of how to use them to solve problems and include these descriptions in their portfolios.

Practice Test

Assessment Options

Vocabulary Test A vocabulary review/test for Chapter 9 can be found on p. 542 of the *Chapter 9 Resource Masters*.

Chapter Tests There are six Chapter 9 Tests and an Open-Ended Assessment task available in the *Chapter 9 Resource Masters*.

Chapter 9 Tests			
Form	Type	Level	Pages
1	MC	basic	529–530
2A	MC	average	531–532
2B	MC	average	533–534
2C	FR	average	535–536
2D	FR	average	537–538
3	FR	advanced	539–540

MC = multiple-choice questions
FR = free-response questions

Open-Ended Assessment
Performance tasks for Chapter 9 can be found on p. 541 of the *Chapter 9 Resource Masters*, along with a sample scoring rubric for these tasks on p. A27.

ExamView® Pro

Use the networkable **ExamView® Pro** to:

- Create **multiple versions** of tests.
- Create **modified** tests for *Inclusion* students.
- **Edit** existing questions and **add** your own questions.
- Use built-in **state curriculum correlations** to create tests aligned with state standards.
- Change **English** tests to **Spanish** and vice versa.

Answer

2. To classify a triangle by its angles and sides, first determine whether the triangle is acute, right, or obtuse. Then determine whether the triangle is scalene, isosceles, or equilateral.

These two pages contain practice questions in the various formats that can be found on the most frequently given standardized tests.

A practice answer sheet for these two pages can be found on page A1 of the *Chapter 9 Resource Masters*.

Standardized Test Practice
Student Recording Sheet, p. A1

Part 1 *Multiple Choice*

Select the best answer from the choices given and fill in the corresponding oval.

1 Ⓐ Ⓑ Ⓒ Ⓓ   4 Ⓐ Ⓑ Ⓒ Ⓓ   7 Ⓐ Ⓑ Ⓒ Ⓓ   10 Ⓐ Ⓑ Ⓒ Ⓓ
2 Ⓐ Ⓑ Ⓒ Ⓓ   5 Ⓐ Ⓑ Ⓒ Ⓓ   8 Ⓐ Ⓑ Ⓒ Ⓓ   11 Ⓐ Ⓑ Ⓒ Ⓓ
3 Ⓐ Ⓑ Ⓒ Ⓓ   6 Ⓐ Ⓑ Ⓒ Ⓓ   9 Ⓐ Ⓑ Ⓒ Ⓓ

Part 2 *Short Response/Grid In*

Solve the problem and write your answer in the blank.

For Questions 12, 14, 16–17, and 20, also enter your answer by writing each number or symbol in a box. Then fill in the corresponding oval for that number or symbol.

12 (grid in)
13
14 (grid in)
15
16 (grid in)
17 (grid in)
18
19
20 (grid in)
21
22
23

Part 3 *Extended Response*

Record your answers for Question 24 on the back of this paper.

Additional Practice

See pp. 547–548 of the *Chapter 9 Resource Masters* for additional standardized test practice.

Part 1 Multiple Choice

Record your answers on the answer sheet provided by your teacher or on a sheet of paper.

1. When *m* and *n* are any two numbers, which of the following statements is true?   (Lesson 1-4) **D**
   Ⓐ $m \cdot 0 = n$ Ⓑ $m \cdot n = n$
   Ⓒ $n \cdot 1 = m$ Ⓓ $m + n = n + m$

2. How many units apart are the numbers −8 and 5 on a number line?   (Lesson 2-1) **A**
   Ⓐ 13   Ⓑ 3
   Ⓒ 14   Ⓓ 10

3. Find the length of a rectangle having a width of 9 feet and an area of 54 square feet.
   (Lesson 3-7) **B**
   Ⓐ 9 ft   Ⓑ 6 ft
   Ⓒ 10 ft   Ⓓ 18 ft

4. Which of the following results in a negative number?   (Lessons 4-2 and 4-7) **A**
   Ⓐ $(-2)^5$ Ⓑ $(5)^{-3}$
   Ⓒ $-5 \cdot (-2)^5$ Ⓓ $(-3)^{-2} \cdot 5$

5. What is the value of *x* if $\frac{1}{2} + x = \frac{5}{6}$?
   (Lesson 5-7) **D**
   Ⓐ $\frac{1}{4}$ Ⓑ $\frac{2}{5}$
   Ⓒ $\frac{2}{3}$ Ⓓ $\frac{1}{3}$

6. Elisa purchased two books that cost $15.95 and $6.95. The sales tax on the books was 6%. If she gave the sales clerk $25, then how much change did she receive?   (Lesson 6-9) **B**
   Ⓐ $0.27   Ⓑ $0.73
   Ⓒ $1.73   Ⓓ $2.10

7. What is the value of *t* in $2s - t = s + 3t$ if $s = \frac{1}{2}$?   (Lesson 7-1) **A**
   Ⓐ $\frac{1}{8}$ Ⓑ $\frac{1}{4}$
   Ⓒ $\frac{1}{2}$ Ⓓ $\frac{3}{8}$

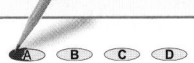

Test-Taking Tip   Ⓐ Ⓑ Ⓒ Ⓓ
Question 9
You can tell if a line has a negative or positive slope by looking at its graph. A line with a negative slope will slant down from left to right. A line with a positive slope will slant up from left to right.

8. The relation shown in the table is a function. Find the value of *y* when *x* = 5.   (Lesson 8-2) **C**
   Ⓐ 13   Ⓑ 14
   Ⓒ 17   Ⓓ 18

x	y
0	2
1	5
2	8
3	11

9. Which graph shows a line with a slope of −2?   (Lesson 8-6) **D**

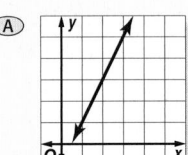

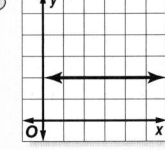
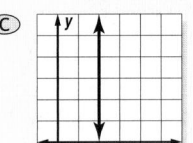
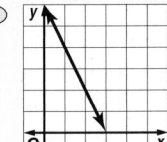

10. Which point on the number line shown is closest to $\sqrt{7}$?   (Lesson 9-1) **B**

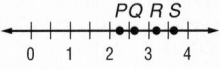

   Ⓐ point P   Ⓑ point Q
   Ⓒ point R   Ⓓ point S

11. Triangles *ABC* and *DEF* are similar triangles. What is the measure of side *AB*?   (Lesson 9-5)

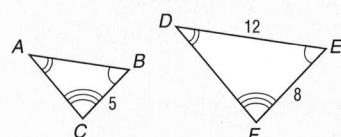

   Ⓐ 3.33   Ⓑ 5.0   Ⓒ 6.5   Ⓓ 7.5

 ExamView® Pro

Special banks of standardized test questions similar to those on the SAT, ACT, TIMSS 8, NAEP 8, and Pre-Algebra End-of-Course tests can be found on this CD-ROM.

Preparing for Standardized Tests
For test-taking strategies and more
practice, see pages 771–788.

Part 2 Short Response/Grid In

Record your answers on the answer sheet
provided by your teacher or on a sheet of
paper.

2. When 8 is added to a number three times,
the result is 27. Find the number.
(Lesson 3-3) **3**

3. Order the numbers 1.4×10^{-5}, 4.0×10^2,
and 1.04×10^{-2} from least to greatest.
(Lesson 4-8) 1.4×10^{-5}, 1.04×10^{-2}, 4.0×10^2

4. A conveyor belt moves at a rate of 6 miles
in 4 hours. How many feet per minute
does this conveyor belt move? (*Hint:*
1 mile = 5280 feet) (Lesson 6-1) **132**

5. Write $\frac{11}{14}$ as a percent, and round to the
nearest tenth. (Lesson 6-4) **78.6%**

6. If you spin the arrow on the spinner below,
what is the probability that the arrow will
land on an even number? (Lesson 6-9) **1/2**

7. What is the least value of x in $y \leq 4x - 3$ if
$y = 9$? (Lesson 7-6) **3**

8. Write *y is less than one-half the value of x* as a
mathematical statement. (Lesson 7-7) $y < \frac{1}{2}x$

9. What is the slope of the line shown?
(Lesson 8-4) $-\frac{2}{3}$

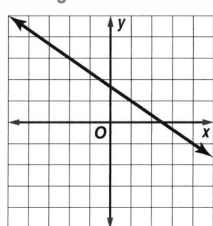

10. Find the positive square root of 196.
(Lesson 9-1) **14**

www.pre-alg.com/standardized_test

21. What type of angle is formed by the minute
hand and hour hand when the time on the
clock is 3:35? (Lesson 9-3) **obtuse**

22. What is the
measure of $\angle X$?
(Lesson 9-4) **68°**

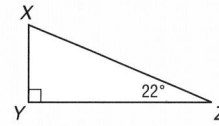

23. Find the distance between $A(-5, 4)$ and
$B(6, -3)$ to the nearest tenth. (Lesson 9-6)
13.0 units

Part 3 Extended Response

Record your answers on a sheet of paper.
Show your work.

24. The walls of a house usually meet to form a
right angle. You can use string to determine
whether two walls meet at a right angle.

a. Copy the diagram shown below. Then
illustrate the following situation. **See margin.**

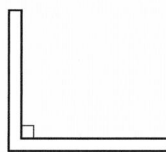

From a corner of the house, a 6-foot
long piece of string is extended along
one side of the wall, parallel to the floor.
From the same corner, an 8-foot long
piece of string is extended along the
other wall, parallel to the floor.

b. If the walls of the house meet at a right
angle, then what is the distance between
the ends of the two pieces of string? **10 feet**

c. Draw an example of a situation where
two walls of a house meet at an angle
whose measure is greater than the
measure of a right angle. **See margin.**

d. Suppose the length of the walls in part c
are the same length as the walls in part
a, and that the 6-foot and 8-foot pieces of
string are extended from the same
corner. Do you think the distance
between the two ends will be the same
as in part **b**? Explain your reasoning. **See margin.**

Chapter 9 Standardized Test Practice **489**

Evaluating Extended Response Questions

Extended Response questions
are graded by using a multilevel
rubric that guides you in assessing a student's knowledge of a
particular concept.

Goal: Form a right triangle given
the lengths of the two sides.

Sample Scoring Rubric: The
following rubric is a sample
scoring device. You may wish to
add more detail to this sample to
meet your individual scoring
needs.

Score	Criteria
4	A correct solution that is supported by well-developed, accurate explanations
3	A generally correct solution, but may contain minor flaws in reasoning or computation
2	A partially correct interpretation and/or solution to the problem
1	A correct solution with no supporting evidence or explanation
0	An incorrect solution indicating no mathematical understanding of the concept or task, or no solution is given

Answer

24a.

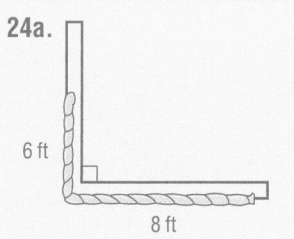

24c.

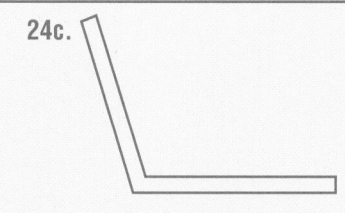

24d. No; If the measure of
the angle between the
walls is greater than
90°, then the length of
the side opposite it will
be greater than the side
opposite the 90° angle.

Page 440, Lesson 9-1

64.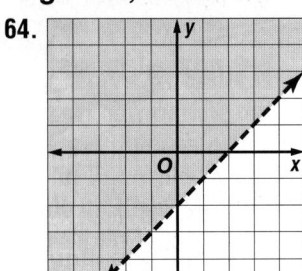

65.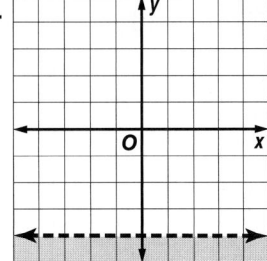

66.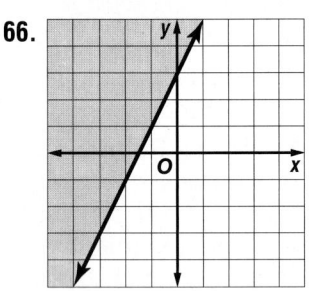

Page 449, Lesson 9-3

1. N; $\overrightarrow{NM}$, $\overrightarrow{NP}$; $\angle 1$, $\angle MNP$, $\angle PNM$, $\angle N$

2. Sample answer:

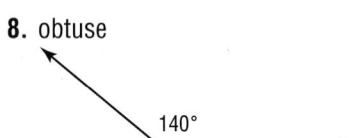

130°

7. acute

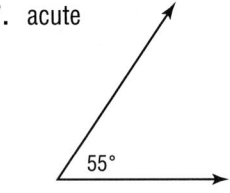

55°

8. obtuse

140°

Page 450, Lesson 9-3

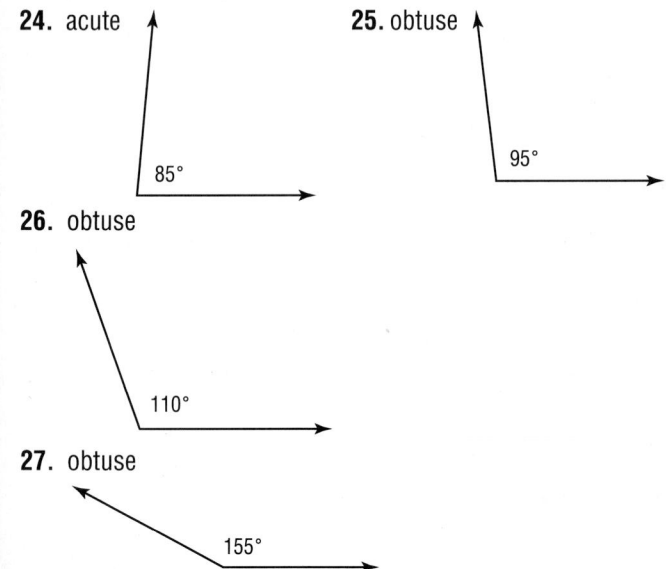

24. acute

85°

25. obtuse

95°

26. obtuse

110°

27. obtuse

155°

28. obtuse

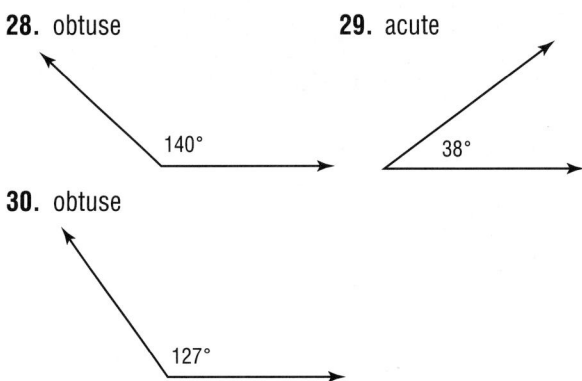

140°

29. acute

38°

30. obtuse

127°

32. Moderate: obtuse; all other angles: acute

33. Intense: about 68°; Moderate: about 104°; Light: 72°; No standard routine: about 47°; Don't exercise regularly: about 68°

Page 464, Lesson 9-5

38. The sum of the squares of the lengths of the legs is equal to the square of the length of the hypotenuse. Answers should include the following.

-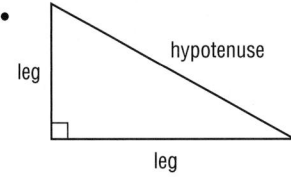

  leg, hypotenuse, leg

- An example of a set of numbers that represents the measures of the lengths of the legs and hypotenuse of a right triangle is 15, 20, 25.

Page 465, Algebra Activity

1.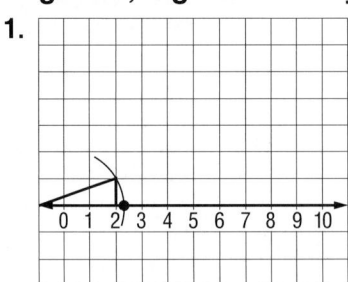

2.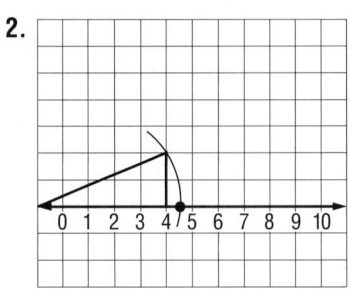

3.

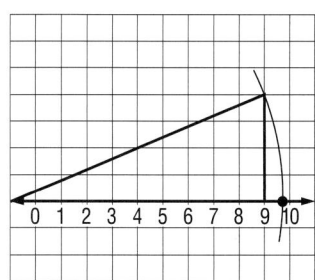

4.

5. Sample answer: First, find two numbers whose square roots have a sum of 34. Since $3^2 + 5^2 = 34$, draw a right triangle with legs 3 units and 5 units long. Then, open the compass to the length of the hypotenuse. With the tip of the compass at 0, draw an arc that intersects the number line.

6. Sample answer: Since $(\sqrt{2})^2 + 1^2 = 3$, use $\sqrt{2}$ as one leg of a right triangle and 1 unit as the other leg. Then follow the procedure in the activity to locate the graph of $\sqrt{3}$.

Page 473, Lesson 9-7

1. Sample answer:

corresponding sides:
$$\frac{AB}{XY} = \frac{BC}{YZ} = \frac{AC}{XZ}$$

2. Sample answer: A method used to find measurements that are difficult to measure directly.

3. $\frac{x}{15} = \frac{6}{9}$; 10

4. $\frac{x}{6} = \frac{6}{2}$; 18

Two-Dimensional Figures
Chapter Overview and Pacing

Year-long pacing: pages T20–T21.

LESSON OBJECTIVES

	PACING (days)			
	Regular		**Block**	
	Basic/Average	Advanced	Basic/Average	Advanced
10-1 Line and Angle Relationships (pp. 492–499) • Identify the relationships of angles formed by two parallel lines and a transversal. • Identify the relationships of vertical, adjacent, complementary, and supplementary angles. *Follow-Up:* Construct congruent line segments and angles and perpendicular bisectors and angle bisectors.	2	2	1	1
10-2 Congruent Triangles (pp. 500–504) • Identify congruent triangles and corresponding parts of congruent triangles.	1	1	0.5	0.5
10-3 Transformations on the Coordinate Plane (pp. 505–512) *Preview:* Introduce three types of symmetry. • Draw translations, rotations, and reflections on a coordinate plane. *Follow-Up:* Investigate dilations, which alter the size of a figure.	3 (with 10-3 Preview)	2 (with 10-3 Follow-Up)	1.5 (with 10-3 Preview)	1.5 (with 10-3 Follow-Up)
10-4 Quadrilaterals (pp. 513–517) • Find the missing angles measures of a quadrilateral. • Classify quadrilaterals.	1	1	0.5	0.5
10-5 Area: Parallelograms, Triangles, and Trapezoids (pp. 518–525) *Preview:* Use geoboards to find the area of figures. • Find area of parallelograms. • Find the areas of triangles and trapezoids.	2	1	1	0.5
10-6 Polygons (pp. 527–532) • Classify polygons. • Determine the sum of the measures of the interior and exterior angles of a polygon. *Follow-Up:* Create tessellations using transformations.	1	2 (with 10-6 Follow-Up)	0.5	1 (with 10-6 Follow-Up)
10-7 Circumference and Area: Circles (pp. 533–538) • Find circumference of circles. • Find area of circles.	1	1	0.5	0.5
10-8 Area: Irregular Figures (pp. 539–543) • Find area of irregular figures.	1	1	0.5	0.5
Study Guide and **Practice Test** (pp. 544–549) **Standardized Test Practice** (pp. 550–551)	1	1	0.5	0.5
Chapter Assessment	1	1	0.5	0.5
TOTAL	14	13	7	7

*An electronic version of this chapter is available on **StudentWorks™**. This backpack solution CD-ROM allows students instant access to the Student Edition, lesson worksheet pages, and web resources.*

Chapter Resource Manager

Timesaving Tools

TeacherWorks™
All-In-One Planner
and Resource Center
See pages T5 and T21.

CHAPTER 10 RESOURCE MASTERS

Study Guide and Intervention	Practice (Skills and Average)	Reading to Learn Mathematics	Enrichment	Assessment	Prerequisite Skills Workbook	Applications*	Parent and Student Study Guide Workbook	5-Minute Check Transparencies	Interactive Chalkboard	Pre-AlgePASS: Tutorial Plus (lessons)	Materials
549	550–551	552	553				81	10-1	10-1	31	*Follow-Up:* compass
554	555–556	557	558	603			82	10-2	10-2	32	
559	560–561	562	563			GCS 37	83	10-3	10-3	33	*Preview:* tracing paper (optional) *Follow-Up:* grid paper, protractor, ruler
564	565–566	567	568	603, 605			84	10-4	10-4		
569	570–571	572	573			SC 19 GCS 38	85	10-5	10-5		*Preview:* geoboards, geobands
574	575–576	577	578	604			86	10-6	10-6		*Follow-Up:* light cardboard (optional)
579	580–581	582	583			SC 20	87	10-7	10-7		
584	585–586	587	588	604		SM 5	88	10-8	10-8	34	
				589–602, 606–608							

* *Key to Abbreviations:* GCS = Graphing Calculator and Spreadsheet Masters
SC = School-to-Career Masters
SM = Science and Mathematics Lab Manual

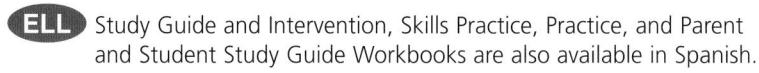 **ELL** Study Guide and Intervention, Skills Practice, Practice, and Parent and Student Study Guide Workbooks are also available in Spanish.

Chapter 10 Mathematical Connections and Background

Continuity of Instruction

Prior Knowledge

In Chapter 9, students explored real numbers and right triangles, and classified angles and triangles. They used squares and square roots, and the Pythagorean Theorem to examine right triangles. Students also learned to use trigonometric ratios to find the missing measures of right triangles. In addition, the Distance and Midpoint Formulas were also examined.

This Chapter

Students will identify the relationships of parallel and intersecting lines, and the properties of congruent triangles. They will also identify and draw transformations, and classify and find angle measures of polygons. Students will also find the area of polygons and irregular figures. In addition, students will learn to find the circumference and area of circles.

Future Connections

Parallel and intersecting lines is a key concept that is also covered in algebra. The properties of triangles are the focus of geometry and trigonometry, as in the classification and measurement of angles. The area of polygons and circles will also be explored in geometry, and can be used in house design and landscaping.

10-1 Line and Angle Relationships

Two lines in a plane that never intersect are called parallel lines. When two parallel lines are intersected by a third line, called a transveral, eight angles are formed. Of these angles, corresponding angles are congruent, as are alternate interior angles and alternate exterior angles.

When two lines intersect, the form two pairs of opposite, congruent angles called vertical angles. When two angles have the same vertex and share a common side, they are adjacent angles. If the sum of the measures of two angles is 90°, the angles are complementary. If the sum of two angles is 180°, the angles are supplementary.

10-2 Congruent Triangles

Figures that have the same size and shape are congruent. The parts of congruent triangles that match are called corresponding parts. Congruence statements are used to identify corresponding parts of congruent triangles. When writing a congruence statement, the letters must be written so that corresponding vertices appear in the same order. Corresponding parts can be used to find the measures of angles and sides in a figure that is congruent to a figure with known measures.

10-3 Transformations on the Coordinate Plane

A transformation is a movement of a geometric figure. There are three types of transformations. In a translation, a figure is slid from one position to another without turning it. Every point of the original figure is moved the same distance and in the same direction. In a reflection, a figure is flipped over a line to form a mirror image. Every point of the original figure has a corresponding point on the other side of the line of symmetry. In a rotation, a figure is turned around a fixed point. A figure may be rotated 90° clockwise, 90° counterclockwise, or 180°.

10-4 Quadrilaterals

A quadrilateral is a closed figure with four sides and four vertices. The segments of a quadrilateral intersect only at their endpoints. Quadrilaterals can be separated into two triangles. Since the sum of the interior angles of all triangles totals 180°, the measures of the interior angles of a quadrilateral equal 360°. Quadrilaterals are classified according to their characteristics, and include trapezoids, parallelograms, rectangles, squares, and rhombuses.

10-5 Area: Parallelograms, Triangles, and Trapezoids

The area A of a parallelogram can be found by multiplying the measures of the base b and the height h. That is, $A = b \cdot h$.

The area of a triangle can be found by multiplying the measures of the base and height, and dividing the result by 2. In symbols, we write $A = \frac{1}{2}b \cdot h$. Any side of the triangle can be used as a base.

To find the area of a trapezoid, find the sum of the bases and then multiply the sum by one-half times the base. The formula can be written as $A = \frac{1}{2}h(a + b)$.

10-6 Polygons

A polygon is a simple, closed figure formed by three or more line segments. The line segments meet only at their endpoints. The points of intersection are called vertices, and the line segments are called sides. Polygons are classified by the number of sides they have.

The diagonals of a polygon divide the polygon into triangles. The number of triangles formed is two less than the number of sides. To find the sum of the measures of the interior angles of any polygon, multiply the number of triangles within a polygon by 180. That is, if n equals number of sides, then $(n - 2)\,180$ gives the sum of the measures of the polygon's interior angles.

10-7 Cirumference and Area: Circles

A circle is the set of all points in a plane that are the same distance from a given point. The distance across the circle through the center point is called the diameter. The distance from the center to any point on the circle is called the radius. The circumference is the distance around the circle. The ratio of the circumference of a circle to its diameter is always equal to 3.1415926. The Greek letter π (pi) represents this number. The circumference C of a circle is equal to its diameter d times π, or 2 times its radius times π. In symbols, this is written as $C = \pi d$, or $C = 2\pi r$. The area A of a circle is equal to π times the square of its radius. In symbols, this is written as $A = \pi r^2$.

10-8 Area: Irregular Figures

Irregular figures are figures that are composed of polygons of various shapes and sizes. To find the area of an irregular figure, separate the irregular figure into figures whose areas you do know how to find. The area of each polygon can then be determined. The sum of these areas provides the area of the irregular figure. Many real-world situations involve finding the area of an irregular figure.

Quick Review Math Handbook

Hot Words includes a glossary of terms while Hot Topics consists of explanations of key mathematical concepts with exercises to test comprehension. This valuable resource can be used as a reference in the classroom or for home study.

Lesson	Hot Topics Section	Lesson	Hot Topics Section
GS 10	2.3, 2.6, 6.4	10-4	2.6, 7.2
10-1	7.1, 9.3	10-5P	7.5
10-1F	7.1	10-5	1.3, 7.5
10-2	6.7, 7.1	10-6	7.2
10-3P	7.3	10-6F	7.3
10-3	6.4, 7.3	10-7	2.6, 7.8

GS = Getting Started, P = Preview, F = Follow-Up

 Additional mathematical information and teaching notes are available at www.pre-alg.com/key_concepts.

Chapter 10

DAILY INTERVENTION and Assessment

Key to Abbreviations:
TWE = Teacher Wraparound Edition; CRM = Chapter Resource Masters

INTERVENTION

Type	Student Edition	Teacher Resources	Technology/Internet
Ongoing	Prerequisite Skills, pp. 491, 497, 504, 511, 517, 525, 531, 538 Practice Quiz 1, p. 517 Practice Quiz 2, p. 538	5-Minute Check Transparencies Quizzes, *CRM*, pp. 603, 604 Mid-Chapter Test, *CRM*, p. 605 Study Guide and Intervention, *CRM*, pp. 549, 554, 559, 564, 574, 579, 584	Pre-AlgePASS: Tutorial Plus, Lessons 31, 32, 33, and 34 www.pre-alg.com/self_check_quiz www.pre-alg.com/extra_examples
Mixed Review	pp. 497, 504, 511, 517, 525, 531, 538, 543	Cumulative Review, *CRM*, p. 606	
Error Analysis	Find the Error, p. 536	Find the Error, *TWE*, p. 536 Unlocking Misconceptions, *TWE*, pp. 493, 501, 534 Tips for New Teachers, *TWE*, p. 511	
Standardized Test Practice	pp. 494, 495, 497, 504, 511, 517, 525, 531, 537, 543, 550–551	*TWE*, pp. 550–551 Standardized Test Practice, *CRM*, pp. 607–608	Standardized Test Practice CD-ROM www.pre-alg.com/standardized_test

ASSESSMENT

Type	Student Edition	Teacher Resources	Technology/Internet
Open-Ended Assessment	Writing in Math, pp. 497, 504, 511, 517, 525, 531, 537, 543 Open Ended, pp. 495, 502, 509, 515, 523, 529, 535, 541 Standardized Test, p. 551	Speaking: *TWE*, pp. 504, 511 Writing: *TWE*, pp. 525, 538 Modeling: *TWE*, pp. 497, 517, 531, 543 Open-Ended Assessment, *CRM*, p. 601	
Chapter Assessment	Study Guide, pp. 544–548 Practice Test, p. 549	Multiple-Choice Tests (Forms 1, 2A, 2B), *CRM*, pp. 589–594 Free-Response Tests (Forms 2C, 2D, 3), *CRM*, pp. 595–600 Vocabulary Test/Review, *CRM*, p. 602	ExamView® Pro (see below) MindJogger Videoquizzes www.pre-alg.com/vocabulary_review www.pre-alg.com/chapter_test

For more information on Yearly ProgressPro, see p. 432.

Pre-Algebra Lesson	Yearly ProgressPro Skill Lesson(s)
10-1	Line and Angle Relationships
10-2	Congruent Polygons
10-3	Reflections; Translations; Rotations
10-4	Classifying Quadrilaterals
10-5	Area of Parallelograms Area of Triangles and Trapezoids
10-6	Congruent Polygons
10-7	Area of Circles Circumference of Circles
10-8	Area of Complex Figures

ExamView® Pro

Use the networkable **ExamView® Pro** to:
- Create **multiple versions** of tests.
- Create **modified** tests for *Inclusion* students.
- **Edit** existing questions and **add** your own questions.
- Use built-in **state curriculum correlations** to create tests aligned with state standards.
- Change **English** tests to **Spanish** and vice versa.

For more information on Intervention and Assessment, see pp. T8–T11.

Reading and Writing in Mathematics

Glencoe Pre-Algebra provides numerous opportunities to incorporate reading and writing into the mathematics classroom.

Student Edition

- Foldables™ Study Organizer, p. 491
- Reading Mathematics, p. 526
- Concept Check questions require students to verbalize and write about what they have learned in the lesson. (pp. 493, 495, 500, 502, 509, 513, 515, 521, 523, 527, 529, 534, 535, 540, 541)
- Writing in Math questions in every lesson, pp. 497, 504, 511, 517, 525, 531, 537, 543
- Reading Math, pp. 493, 500, 508
- WebQuest, p. 542

Teacher Wraparound Edition

- Foldables™ Study Organizer, pp. 491, 544
- Study Notebook suggestions, pp. 495, 499, 502, 505, 509, 512, 515, 519, 523, 526, 529, 532, 535, 541
- Modeling activities, pp. 497, 517, 531, 543
- Speaking activities, pp. 504, 511
- Writing activities, pp. 525, 538
- Differentiated Instruction (Verbal/Linguistic), p. 508
-  Resources, pp. 490, 492, 500, 506, 508, 513, 520, 526, 527, 533, 539, 544

Additional Resources

- Vocabulary Builder worksheets require students to define and give examples for key vocabulary terms as they progress through the chapter (*Chapter 10 Resource Masters*, pp. vii–viii)
- Reading to Learn Mathematics master for each lesson (*Chapter 10 Resource Masters*, pp. 552, 557, 562, 567, 572, 577, 582, 587)
- *Vocabulary PuzzleMaker* software creates crossword, jumble, and word search puzzles using vocabulary lists that you can customize.
- *Teaching Mathematics with Foldables* provides suggestions for promoting cognition and language.
- *Reading and Writing in the Mathematics Classroom*
- *WebQuest and Project Resources*

For more information on Reading and Writing in Mathematics, see pp. T6–T7.

ELL ENGLISH LANGUAGE LEARNERS

Lesson 10-2
Using Manipulatives

Give each group of students sets of shapes and have them categorize them as *similar* or *congruent*. It is important to emphasize that shapes that are congruent are also similar, but they may be similar and not congruent.

Lesson 10-3
Language Experience Approach to Illustrations

Write the words *transformation* and *translation* on the chalkboard. Ask students what these words have in common. Underline the prefix *trans* and have students look this up in a dictionary or on the Internet. They will find that trans means "across". This will help students to remember that they are moving an object or polygon across a plane.

Lesson 10-5
Reading and Writing

Allow students time to work in pairs to do the Concept Check and Writing in Math exercises. This enables English Language Learners to express themselves in English and to express what they have learned. By allowing students to express themselves, you are permitting the opportunity to practice the language, writing skills, and understanding of the topic.

What You'll Learn

Have students read over the list of objectives and make a list of any words with which they are not familiar.

Why It's Important

Point out to students that this is only one of many reasons why each objective is important. Others are provided in the introduction to each lesson.

Lesson	NCTM Standards	Local Objectives
10-1	2, 3, 4, 6, 8, 9	
10-1 Follow-Up	3, 4	
10-2	2, 3, 4, 6, 8, 9	
10-3 Preview	3	
10-3	1, 3, 8, 9	
10-3 Follow-Up	3, 4, 8	
10-4	2, 3, 6, 8, 9	
10-5 Preview	3, 4	
10-5	1, 3, 4, 6, 7, 8, 9, 10	
10-6	1, 3, 4, 6, 8, 9, 10	
10-6 Follow-Up	3, 10	
10-7	1, 3, 4, 6, 7, 8, 9	
10-8	1, 3, 4, 6, 8, 9, 10	

Key to NCTM Standards:

1=Number & Operations, 2=Algebra, 3=Geometry, 4=Measurement, 5=Data Analysis & Probability, 6=Problem Solving, 7=Reasoning & Proof, 8=Communication, 9=Connections, 10=Representation

Chapter 10 Two-Dimensional Figures

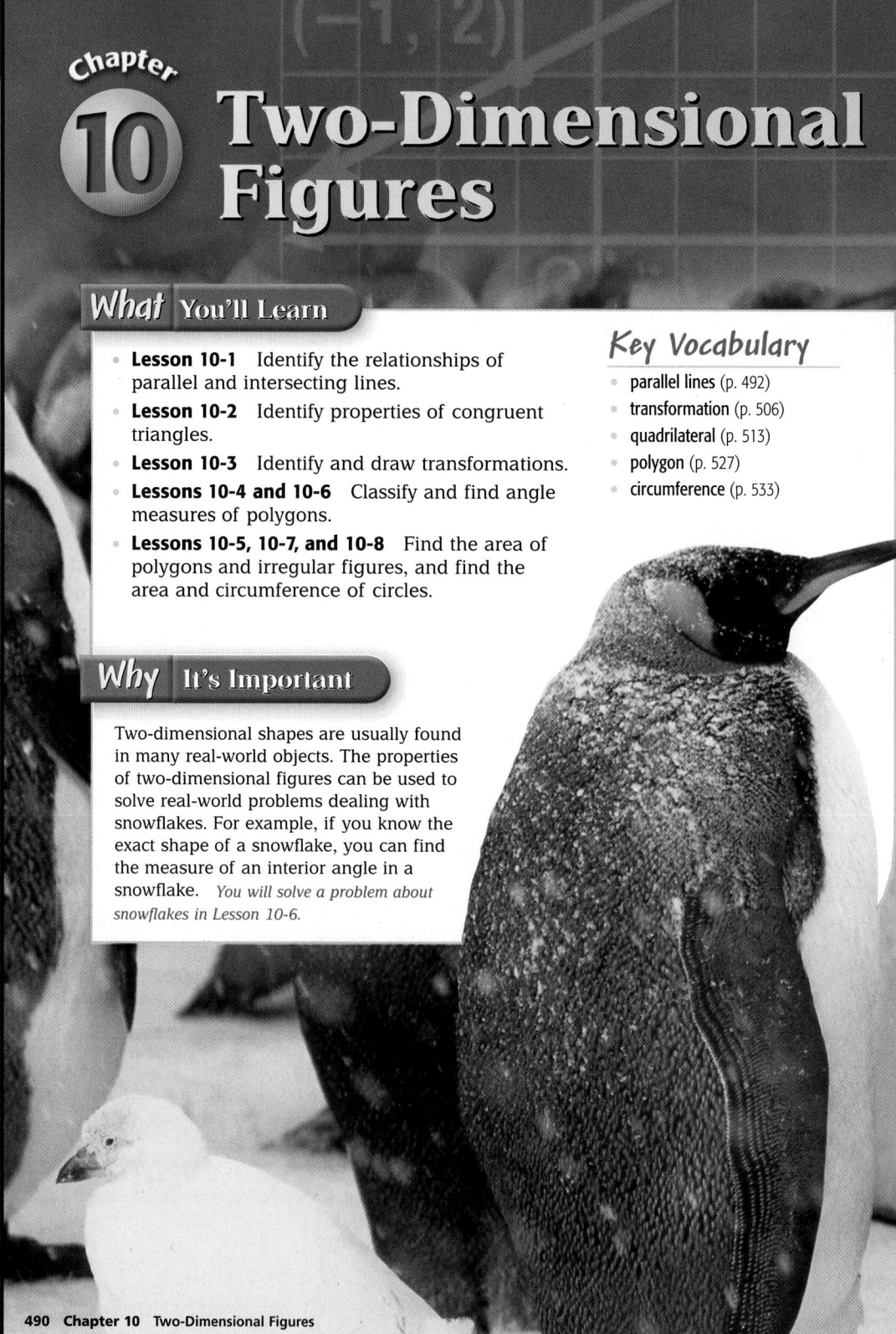

What You'll Learn

- **Lesson 10-1** Identify the relationships of parallel and intersecting lines.
- **Lesson 10-2** Identify properties of congruent triangles.
- **Lesson 10-3** Identify and draw transformations.
- **Lessons 10-4 and 10-6** Classify and find angle measures of polygons.
- **Lessons 10-5, 10-7, and 10-8** Find the area of polygons and irregular figures, and find the area and circumference of circles.

Key Vocabulary

- parallel lines (p. 492)
- transformation (p. 506)
- quadrilateral (p. 513)
- polygon (p. 527)
- circumference (p. 533)

Why It's Important

Two-dimensional shapes are usually found in many real-world objects. The properties of two-dimensional figures can be used to solve real-world problems dealing with snowflakes. For example, if you know the exact shape of a snowflake, you can find the measure of an interior angle in a snowflake. *You will solve a problem about snowflakes in Lesson 10-6.*

Vocabulary Builder
ELL

The Key Vocabulary list introduces students to some of the main vocabulary terms included in this chapter. For a more thorough vocabulary list with pronunciations of new words, give students the Vocabulary Builder worksheets found on pages vii and viii of the *Chapter 10 Resource Masters.* Encourage them to complete the definition of each term as they progress through the chapter. You may suggest that they add these sheets to their study notebooks for future reference when studying for the Chapter 10 test.

▶ **Prerequisite Skills** To be successful in this chapter, you'll need to master these skills and be able to apply them in problem-solving situations. Review these skills before beginning Chapter 10.

For Lessons 10-1 and 10-4   Solve Equations

Solve each equation. *(For review, see Lessons 3-3 and 3-5.)*

1. $x + 46 = 90$ **44** **2.** $x + 35 = 180$ **145** **3.** $2x - 12 = 90$ **51** **4.** $3x - 24 = 180$ **68**

5. $2x + 34 = 90$ **28** **6.** $4x + 44 = 180$ **34** **7.** $5x + 165 = 360$ **39** **8.** $4x + 184 = 360$ **44**

For Lessons 10-5, 10-7, and 10-8   Multiply Decimals

Find each product. Round to the nearest tenth, if necessary. *(For review, see page 715.)*

9. $(5.5)(8)$ **44** **10.** $(7.5)(3.4)$ **25.5** **11.** $(6.3)(11.4)$ **71.8** **12.** $\frac{1}{2}(8)(2.5)$ **10**

13. $\frac{1}{2}(4.3)(5.8)$ **12.5** **14.** $(3.14)(7)$ **22.0** **15.** $(2)(3.14)(1.7)$ **10.7** **16.** $2(3.1)(3.14)$ **19.5**

For Lesson 10-5   Add Mixed Numbers

Find each sum. *(For review, see Lesson 5-7.)*

17. $5\frac{1}{2} + 4\frac{2}{3}$ $10\frac{1}{6}$ **18.** $2\frac{1}{3} + 3\frac{3}{4}$ $6\frac{1}{12}$ **19.** $1\frac{3}{8} + 2\frac{1}{2}$ $3\frac{7}{8}$ **20.** $6\frac{1}{4} + 1\frac{5}{6}$ $8\frac{1}{12}$

21. $3\frac{5}{8} + 1\frac{3}{4}$ $5\frac{3}{8}$ **22.** $2\frac{3}{5} + 4\frac{7}{10}$ $7\frac{3}{10}$ **23.** $2\frac{2}{3} + 3\frac{5}{9}$ $6\frac{2}{9}$ **24.** $5\frac{2}{3} + 3\frac{4}{5}$ $9\frac{7}{15}$

FOLDABLES™
Study Organizer

Polygons Make this Foldable to help you organize your notes. Begin with four plain sheets of $8\frac{1}{2}$" by 11" paper, eight index cards, and glue.

Step 1 Fold

Fold a sheet of paper in half widthwise.

Step 2 Open and Fold Again

Open and fold the bottom to form a pocket. Glue edges.

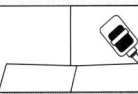

Step 3 Repeat Steps 1 and 2

Repeat three times. Then glue all four pieces together to form a booklet.

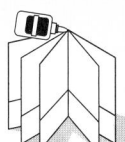

Step 4 Label

Label each pocket. Place an index card in each pocket

Reading and Writing As you read and study the chapter, write the name of a two-dimensional figure on each index card, draw a diagram, and write a definition or describe the characteristics of each figure.

This section provides a review of the basic concepts needed before beginning Chapter 10. Page references are included for additional student help.

Prerequisite Skills in the Getting Ready for the Next Lesson section at the end of each lesson reviews a skill needed in the next lesson.

For Lesson	Prerequisite Skill
10-2	Angles (p. 497)
10-3	The Coordinate System (p. 504)
10-4	Solving Equations (p. 511)
10-5	Multiplying Decimals (p. 517)
10-6	Order of Operations (p. 525)
10-7	Rounding Decimals (p. 531)
10-8	Adding Decimals (p. 538)

Tips for New Teachers

Visualizing Geometry is a visual form of mathematics. Make models or posters of concepts presented in this chapter to help students visualize what they are learning.

FOLDABLES™
Study Organizer

For more information about Foldables, see *Teaching Mathematics with Foldables.*

Organization of Data Students will need 3" × 5" index cards or sheets of notebook paper cut into quarter sections. Each card can become a flashcard study tool. With each lesson, use the study cards to take notes, solve equations, record and define vocabulary words, and explain concepts. Use the cards to summarize concepts needed for the Chapter Test.

10-1 Line and Angle Relationships

1 Focus

5-Minute Check Transparency 10-1 Use as a quiz or review of Chapter 9.

Mathematical Background notes are available for this lesson on page 490C.

How are parallel lines and angles related?

The opening activity questions are repeated on page 552 of the *Chapter 10 Resource Masters*.

Reading to Learn Mathematics, p. 552 **ELL**

Pre-Activity How are parallel lines and angles related?

Do the activity at the top of page 492 in your textbook. Write your answers below.

a. Trace two of the horizontal lines on a sheet of notebook paper. Then draw another line that intersects the horizontal lines. See students' work.

b. Label the angles as shown. See students' work.

c. Find the measure of each angle. Sample answer: $m\angle 1 = 110°$, $m\angle 2 = 70°$, $m\angle 3 = 110°$, $m\angle 4 = 70°$, $m\angle 5 = 110°$, $m\angle 6 = 70°$, $m\angle 7 = 110°$, $m\angle 8 = 70°$

d. What do you notice about the measures of the angles? There are just two different measures.

e. Which angles have the same measure? Sample answer: The angles across from each other; the angles in the same position on each of the horizontal lines; the angles on opposite sides inside the horizontal lines; the angles on opposite sides above and below the parallel lines

f. What do you notice about the measures of the angles that share a side? Their sum is 180°.

Reading the Lesson 1–12. See students' work.

Write a definition and give an example of each new vocabulary word or phrase.

Vocabulary	Definition	Example
1. parallel lines		
2. transversal		
3. interior angles		
4. exterior angles		
5. alternate interior angles		
6. alternate exterior angles		
7. corresponding angles		
8. vertical angles		
9. adjacent angles		
10. complementary angles		
11. supplementary angles		
12. perpendicular lines		

Teaching Tip Help students find parallel lines in the classroom. For example, the opposite edges of a doorway are parallel.

Vocabulary

- parallel lines
- transversal
- interior angles
- exterior angles
- alternate interior angles
- alternate exterior angles
- corresponding angles
- vertical angles
- adjacent angles
- complementary angles
- supplementary angles
- perpendicular lines

Study Tip

Parallel Lines
Arrowheads are often used in figures to indicate parallel lines.

What You'll Learn

- Identify the relationships of angles formed by two parallel lines and a transversal.
- Identify the relationships of vertical, adjacent, complementary, and supplementary angles.

How are parallel lines and angles related?

Let's investigate what happens when two horizontal lines are intersected by a third line. **a–f. See margin.**

a. Trace two of the horizontal lines on a sheet of notebook paper. Then draw another line that intersects the horizontal lines.

b. Label the angles as shown.

c. Find the measure of each angle.

d. What do you notice about the measures of the angles?

e. Which angles have the same measure?

f. What do you notice about the measures of the angles that share a side?

PARALLEL LINES AND A TRANSVERSAL In geometry, two lines in a plane that never intersect are **parallel lines**.

Lines m and n are parallel. Using symbols, $m \parallel n$.

Parallel lines have no point of intersection.

When two parallel lines are intersected by a third line called a **transversal**, eight angles are formed.

Key Concept — *Names of Special Angles*

The eight angles formed by parallel lines and a transversal have special names.

- **Interior angles** lie inside the parallel lines.
  $\angle 3$, $\angle 4$, $\angle 5$, $\angle 6$

- **Exterior angles** lie outside the parallel lines.
  $\angle 1$, $\angle 2$, $\angle 7$, $\angle 8$

- **Alternate interior angles** are on opposite sides of the transversal and inside the parallel lines.
  $\angle 3$ and $\angle 5$, $\angle 4$ and $\angle 6$

- **Alternate exterior angles** are on opposite sides of the transversal and outside the parallel lines.
  $\angle 1$ and $\angle 7$, $\angle 2$ and $\angle 8$

- **Corresponding angles** are in the same position on the parallel lines in relation to the transversal.
  $\angle 1$ and $\angle 5$, $\angle 2$ and $\angle 6$, $\angle 3$ and $\angle 7$, $\angle 4$ and $\angle 8$

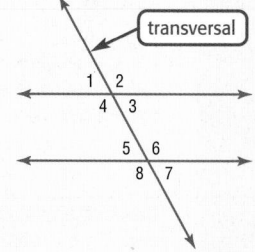

Resource Manager

Workbooks and Reproducible Masters

Chapter 10 Resource Masters
- Study Guide and Intervention, p. 549
- Skills Practice, p. 550
- Practice, p. 551
- Reading to Learn Mathematics, p. 552
- Enrichment, p. 553

Parent and Student Study Guide Workbook, p. 81

 Transparencies
5-Minute Check Transparency 10-1
Answer Key Transparencies

 Technology
Interactive Chalkboard
Pre-AlgePASS: Tutorial Plus, Lesson 31

In Lesson 9-4, you learned that line segments are congruent if they have the same measure. Similarly, angles are congruent if they have the same measure.

Key Concept — Parallel Lines Cut by a Transversal

If two parallel lines are cut by a transversal, then the following pairs of angles are congruent.
- Corresponding angles are congruent.
- Alternate interior angles are congruent.
- Alternate exterior angles are congruent.

✓ **Concept Check** How many angles are formed when two parallel lines are intersected by a transversal? **8**

Example 1 — Find Measures of Angles

In the figure at the right, $m \parallel n$ and t is a transversal. If $m\angle 1 = 68°$, find $m\angle 5$ and $m\angle 6$.

Since $\angle 1$ and $\angle 5$ are corresponding angles, they are congruent. So, $m\angle 5 = 68°$.

Since $\angle 1$ and $\angle 6$ are alternate exterior angles, they are congruent. So $m\angle 6 = 68°$.

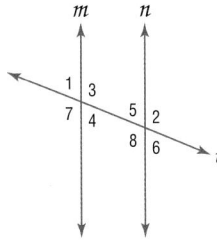

INTERSECTING LINES AND ANGLES Other pairs of angles have special relationships. When two lines intersect, they form two pairs of opposite angles called **vertical angles**. Vertical angles are congruent. The symbol for *is congruent to* is $\cong$.

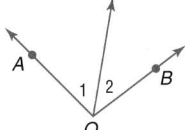

$\angle 1$ and $\angle 2$ are vertical angles.
$\angle 1 \cong \angle 2$

$\angle 3$ and $\angle 4$ are vertical angles.
$\angle 3 \cong \angle 4$

When two angles have the same vertex, share a common side, and do not overlap, they are **adjacent angles**.

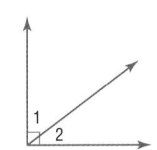

$\angle 1$ and $\angle 2$ are adjacent angles.

$m\angle AOB = m\angle 1 + m\angle 2$

If the sum of the measures of two angles is 90°, the angles are **complementary**.

$m\angle 1 = 50°, m\angle 2 = 40°$
$m\angle 1 + m\angle 2 = 90°$

$m\angle 3 = 60°, m\angle 4 = 30°$
$m\angle 3 + m\angle 4 = 90°$

www.pre-alg.com/extra_examples

Lesson 10-1 Line and Angle Relationships **493**

INTERSECTING LINES AND ANGLES

In-Class Examples Power Point®

2 **Multiple-Choice Test Item**
If $m\angle D = 53°$ and $\angle D$ and $\angle E$ are complementary, what is $m\angle E$? **B**

A 53°   **B** 37°

C 127°   **D** 7°

Teaching Tip In Example 3, make sure students realize that when they have found the value of *x*, this is not the answer to the problem. They must use that value to calculate the angle measures.

3 **ALGEBRA** Angles *PQR* and *STU* are supplementary. If $m\angle PQR = x - 15$ and $m\angle STU = x - 65$, find the measure of each angle.
$m\angle PQR = 115°$, $m\angle STU = 65°$

4 **TRANSPORTATION** A road crosses railroad tracks at an angle as shown.

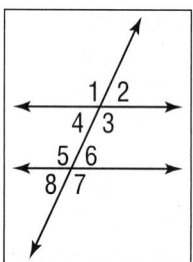

If $m\angle 1 = 131°$, find $m\angle 6$ and $m\angle 5$. $m\angle 6 = 49°$ and $m\angle 5 = 131°$

If the sum of the measures of two angles is 180°, the angles are **supplementary**.

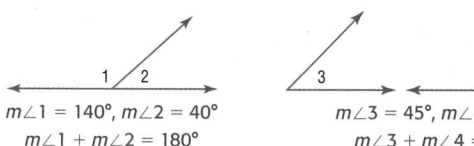

$m\angle 1 = 140°, m\angle 2 = 40°$ $m\angle 3 = 45°, m\angle 4 = 135°$
$m\angle 1 + m\angle 2 = 180°$ $m\angle 3 + m\angle 4 = 180°$

Lines that intersect to form a right angle are **perpendicular lines**.

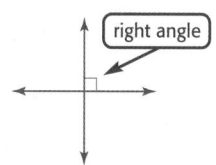
right angle

Standardized Test Practice
(A) (B) (C) (D)

Example 2 **Find a Missing Angle Measure**

Multiple-Choice Test Item

If $m\angle B = 87°$ and $\angle A$ and $\angle B$ are supplementary, what is $m\angle A$?

(A) 3°   (B) 87°

(C) 93°   (D) 95°

Read the Test Item
Since $\angle A$ and $\angle B$ are supplementary, $m\angle A + m\angle B = 180°$.

Solve the Test Item

$m\angle A + m\angle B = 180°$	Supplementary angles
$m\angle A + 87° = 180°$	Replace $m\angle B$ with 87°.
$m\angle A + 87° - 87° = 180° - 87°$	Subtract 87 from each side.
$m\angle A = 93°$	

The answer is C.

Test-Taking Tip
It is a good idea to review definitions of key terms, such as supplementary, before taking the test.

Example 3 **Find Measures of Angles**

ALGEBRA Angles *ABC* and *FGH* are complementary. If $m\angle ABC = x + 8$ and $m\angle FGH = x - 10$, find the measure of each angle.

Step 1 Find the value of *x*.

$m\angle ABC + m\angle FGH = 90°$	Complementary angles
$(x + 8) + (x - 10) = 90°$	Substitution
$2x - 2 = 90°$	Combine like terms.
$2x = 92°$	Add 2 to each side.
$x = 46°$	Divide each side by 2.

Step 2 Replace *x* with 46 to find the measure of each angle.

$m\angle ABC = x + 8$ $m\angle FGH = x - 10$
$\quad\quad\quad = 46 + 8$ or 54 $\quad\quad\quad = 46 - 10$ or 36

So, $m\angle ABC = 54°$ and $m\angle FGH = 36°$.

Study Tip

Checking Reasonableness of Results
To check your answer, add to see if the sum of the measures of the angles is 90. Since 54 + 36 = 90, the answer is correct.

Standardized Test Practice
(A) (B) (C) (D)

Example 2 Point out to students that they must distinguish between supplementary, complementary, and congruent angles to answer this question. Answer choice A identifies a complementary angle, and choice B a congruent one. The diagram is very helpful in reminding students that the sum of the measures of supplementary angles is 180°. This will enable them to arrive at the correct answer, choice C.

Example 4 Apply Angle Relationships

SAFETY A lifeguard chair is shown. If $m\angle 1 = 105°$, find $m\angle 4$ and $m\angle 6$.

Since $\angle 1$ and $\angle 4$ are vertical angles, they are congruent. So, $m\angle 4 = 105°$.

Since $\angle 6$ and $\angle 1$ are supplementary, the sum of their measures is 180°.

$180 - 105 = 75$. So, $m\angle 6 = 75°$.

Concept Summary — Line and Angle Relationships

Parallel Lines	Perpendicular Lines	Vertical Angles
$a \parallel b$	$m \perp n$	$\angle 1 \cong \angle 3$ $\angle 2 \cong \angle 4$
Adjacent Angles	**Complementary Angles**	**Supplementary Angles**
$m\angle ABC = m\angle 1 + m\angle 2$	$m\angle 1 + m\angle 2 = 90°$	$m\angle 1 + m\angle 2 = 180°$

Check for Understanding

Concept Check
1–2. See margin.

1. **Explain** the difference between complementary and supplementary angles.

2. **OPEN ENDED** Draw a pair of adjacent, supplementary angles.

Guided Practice

In the figure at the right, $\ell \parallel m$ and k is a transversal. If $m\angle 1 = 56°$, find the measure of each angle.

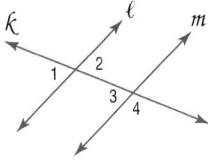

GUIDED PRACTICE KEY	
Exercises	Examples
3–5	1, 4
6, 7, 9	2
8	3

3. $\angle 2$ **56°**   4. $\angle 3$ **56°**   5. $\angle 4$ **124°**

Find the value of x in each figure.

6.  **140**

7. 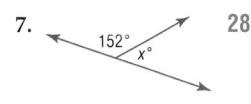 **28**

8. **ALGEBRA** If $m\angle N = 3x$ and $m\angle M = 2x$ and $\angle M$ and $\angle N$ are supplementary, what is the measure of each angle? **108°; 72°**

Standardized Test Practice

9. If $m\angle B = 26°$ and $\angle A$ and $\angle B$ are complementary, what is $m\angle A$? **D**
   (A) 154°   (B) 90°   (C) 26°   (D) 64°

Teacher to Teacher

Diana L. Boyle   Judson M.S., Salem, OR

"The concept summary on this page provides another opportunity to use Foldables. Make a foldable study organizer out of five sheets of paper that are cut halfway down the middle and interlocked to form a book. Have students copy each type of geometry figure presented in this chart on a seperate page and list the pertinent information below the figure"

Study Guide and Intervention, p. 549

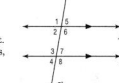

Names of Special Angles

Interior angles lie inside the parallel lines.	∠3, ∠4, ∠5, ∠6
Exterior angles lie outside the parallel lines.	∠1, ∠2, ∠7, ∠8
Alternate interior angles are on opposite sides of the transversal and inside the parallel lines.	∠3, and ∠5, ∠4 and ∠6
Alternate exterior angles are on opposite sides of the transversal and outside the parallel lines.	∠1 and ∠7, ∠2, and ∠8
Corresponding angles are in the same position on the parallel lines in relation to the transversal.	∠1 and ∠5, ∠2 and ∠6, ∠3 and ∠7, ∠4 and ∠8

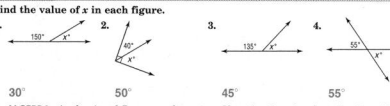

Line and Angle Relationships

Parallel Lines	Perpendicular Lines	Vertical Angles	Adjacent Angles	Complementary Angles	Supplementary Angles

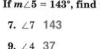

Example In the figure, $f \parallel n$ and v is a transversal.
If $m\angle 3 = 100°$, find $m\angle 1$ and $m\angle 6$.

Since ∠1 and ∠3 are corresponding angles, they are congruent.
So, $m\angle 1 = 100°$. Since ∠3 and ∠6 are alternate interior angles,
they are congruent. So, $m\angle 6 = 100°$.

Exercises

Find the value of x in each figure.

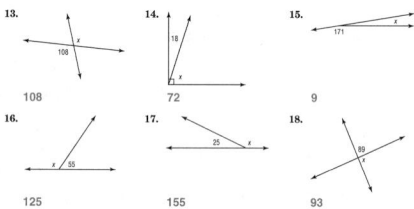

1. 30° 2. 50° 3. 45° 4. 55°

5. **ALGEBRA** Angles A and B are complementary. If $m\angle A = 3x - 8$ and $m\angle B = 5x + 10$, what is the measure of each angle? 25°; 65°

6. **ALGEBRA** Angles Q and R are supplementary. If $m\angle Q = 4x + 9$ and $m\angle R = 8x + 3$, what is the measure of each angle? 65°; 115°

Skills Practice, p. 550 and Practice, p. 551 (shown)

In the figure at the right, $m \parallel n$ and r is a transversal.
If $m\angle 2 = 45°$, find the measure of each angle.

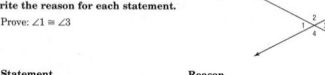

1. ∠4 135 2. ∠5 135
3. ∠7 45   4. ∠8 135
5. ∠6 45   6. ∠3 45

In the figure at the right, $d \parallel e$ and a is a transversal.
If $m\angle 5 = 143°$, find the measure of each angle.

7. ∠7 143   8. ∠6 143
9. ∠4 37   10. ∠2 37
11. ∠1 37   12. ∠8 143

Find the value of x in each figure.

13. 108 14. 72 15. 9

16. 125 17. 155 18. 93

19. Angles Q and R are complementary. Find $m\angle R$ if $m\angle Q = 24°$. 66

20. Find $m\angle J$ if $m\angle K = 29°$ and ∠J and ∠K are supplementary. 151

21. The measures of angles A and B are equal and complementary. What is the measure of each angle? 45

22. **ALGEBRA** Angles G and H are complementary. If $m\angle G = 3x + 6$ and $m\angle H = 2x - 11$, what is the measure of each angle? $m\angle G = 63$; $m\angle H = 27$

Enrichment, p. 553

Geometric Proof

Use definitions and theorems for angle congruence to complete the proofs.

Write the reason for each statement.

1. Prove: ∠1 ≅ ∠3

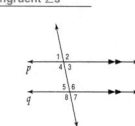

Statement	Reason
a. ∠1 and ∠3 are vertical angles.	a. Given
b. $m\angle 1 + m\angle 2 = 180°$; $m\angle 3 + m\angle 2 = 180°$	b. Def. Supp. ∠s
c. $m\angle 1 = 180° - m\angle 2$; $m\angle 3 = 180° - m\angle 2$	c. Subtr. Prop. Equality
d. $m\angle 1 = m\angle 3$	d. Substitution
e. ∠1 ≅ ∠3	e. Def. Congruent ∠s

2. Prove: $m\angle 3 ≅ m\angle 7$

Statement	Reason
a. Line p is parallel to line q.	a. Given
b. $m\angle 3 ≅ m\angle 5$	b. Alternate Interior ∠s
c. $m\angle 5 ≅ m\angle 7$	c. Vertical ∠s ≅
d. $m\angle 3 ≅ m\angle 7$	d. Substitution

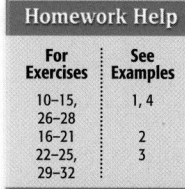

Practice and Apply

Homework Help

For Exercises	See Examples
10–15, 26–28	1, 4
16–21	2
22–25, 29–32	3

Extra Practice
See page 747.

In the figure at the right, $g \parallel h$ and t is a transversal.
If $m\angle 4 = 53°$, find the measure of each angle.

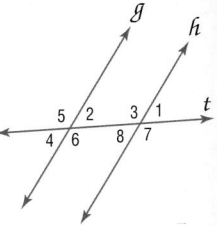

10. ∠1 53°   11. ∠5 127°
12. ∠7 127°   13. ∠8 53°
14. ∠2 53°   15. ∠3 127°

Find the value of x in each figure.

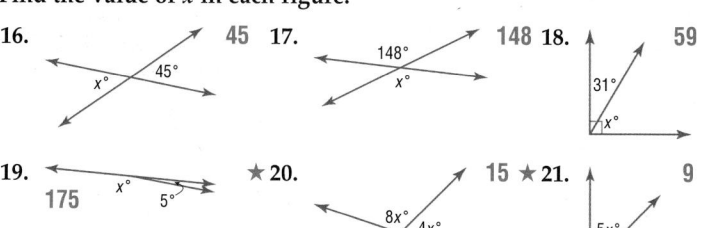

16. 45   17. 148   18. 59

19. 175   ★ 20. 15   ★ 21. 9

22. Find $m\angle A$ if $m\angle B = 17°$ and ∠A and ∠B are complementary. 73°

23. Angles P and Q are supplementary. Find $m\angle P$ if $m\angle Q = 139°$. 41°

24. **ALGEBRA** Angles J and K are complementary. If $m\angle J = x - 9$ and $m\angle K = x + 5$, what is the measure of each angle? 38°; 52°

★ 25. **ALGEBRA** Find $m\angle E$ if ∠E and ∠F are supplementary, $m\angle E = 2x + 15$, and $m\angle F = 5x - 38$. 73°

26. **SAFETY** Refer to Example 4 on page 495. Find the measure of angles ∠2, ∠3, ∠5, ∠7, and ∠8. 105°; 105°; 75°; 75°; 75°

CONSTRUCTION For Exercises 27 and 28, use the following information and the diagram shown.

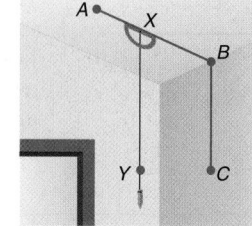

To measure the angle between a sloped ceiling and a wall, a carpenter uses a plumb line (a string with a weight attached).

27. If $m\angle YXB = 68°$, what is $m\angle XBC$? 112°

28. What type of angles are ∠YXB and ∠XBC? supplementary angles

ALGEBRA In the figure at the right, $m \parallel \ell$ and t is a transversal. Find the value of x for each of the following.

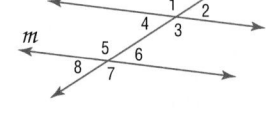

29. $m\angle 2 = 2x + 3$ and $m\angle 4 = 4x - 7$ 5

30. $m\angle 8 = 4x - 32$ and $m\angle 5 = 5x + 50$ 18

31. $m\angle 7 = 10x + 15$ and $m\angle 3 = 7x + 42$ 9

★ 32. **ALGEBRA** The measure of the supplement of an angle is 15° less than four times the measure of the complement. Find the measure of the angle. 55°

DAILY INTERVENTION — Differentiated Instruction

- **Kinesthetic** Using masking tape, set up two parallel lines and a transversal on the floor in a large open space. Separate the class into eight groups and have each group stand in one of the eight angles. Give angle 1 a measure. Have the other seven groups determine their measure and what relationship they have to angle 1. Repeat for all eight angles.

33. CRITICAL THINKING Suppose two parallel lines are cut by a transversal. How are the interior angles on the same side of the transversal related? **See margin.**

34.  Answer the question that was posed at the beginning of the lesson. **See margin.**

How are parallel lines and angles related?

Include the following in your answer:
- a drawing of parallel lines intersected by a transversal, and
- a list of the congruent and supplementary angles.

For Exercises 35 and 36, use the diagram.

35. The upper rail is parallel to the lower rail. What is the measure of the angle formed by the upper rail and the first vertical post? **A**

Ⓐ 135°   Ⓑ 100°

Ⓒ 90°   Ⓓ 45°

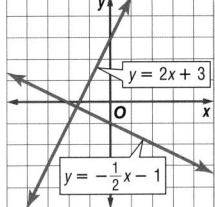

36. What is the measure of the angle formed by the second vertical post and the lower rail? **C**

Ⓐ 100°   Ⓑ 135°   Ⓒ 45°   Ⓓ 90°

Extending the Lesson

37–39. See margin.

For Exercises 37–39, use the pairs of graphs shown at the right.

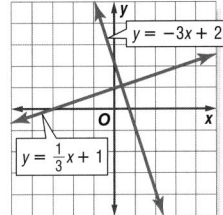

37. How are each pair of graphs related?

38. What seems to be true about the slopes of the graphs?

39. Make a conjecture about the slopes of the graphs of perpendicular lines.

Maintain Your Skills

Mixed Review **Use a calculator to find each value to the nearest ten thousandth.**
(Lesson 9-8)

40. cos 21° **0.9336**   **41.** sin 63° **0.8910**   **42.** tan 38° **0.7813**

43. If △ABC ~ △DEF, what is the value of x? *(Lesson 9-7)* **7.5**

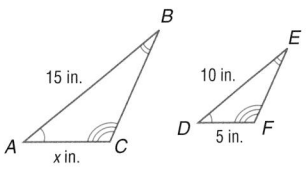

Simplify each expression. *(Lesson 3-2)*

44. $6a + (-18)a$ **$-12a$**

45. $-5m + (-4)m$ **$-9m$**

Getting Ready for the Next Lesson **PREREQUISITE SKILL Use a protractor to draw an angle having each measurement.** *(To review **angles**, see Lesson 9-3.)* **46–50. See margin.**

46. 20°   **47.** 45°   **48.** 65°   **49.** 145°   **50.** 170°

 www.pre-alg.com/self_check_quiz

Answers

46.

48.

49.

47.

50.

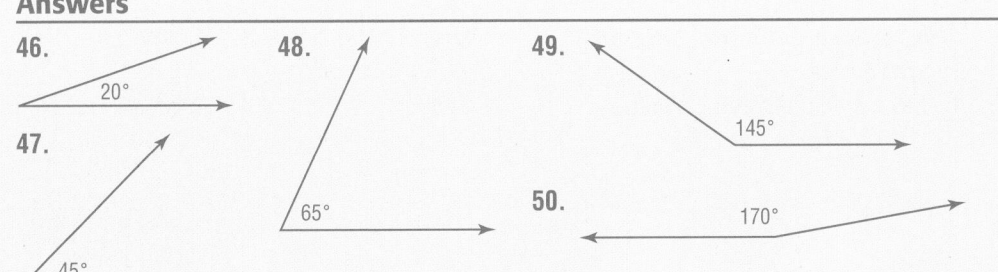

Open-Ended Assessment

Modeling Have students draw two parallel lines and a transversal on a piece of paper. Then give them one of the angle measures and have them fill in the measures of the other angles.

Getting Ready for Lesson 10-2

PREREQUISITE SKILL Lesson 10-2 presents congruent triangles. Congruent triangles have congruent corresponding angles. Exercises 46–50 should be used to determine your students' familiarity with drawing angles.

Answers

33. They are supplementary.

34. Angles and parallel lines are related in that when two parallel lines are cut by a transversal, angles are formed. Answers should include the following.

-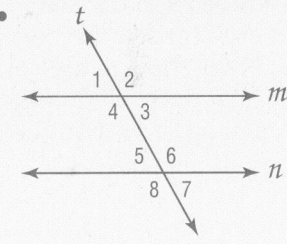

- congruent angles: ∠1, ∠3, ∠5, ∠7 and ∠2, ∠4, ∠6, ∠8

  supplementary angles: ∠1 and ∠2, ∠1 and ∠4, ∠3 and ∠4, ∠2 and ∠3, ∠5 and ∠6, ∠6 and ∠7, ∠8 and ∠7, ∠5 and ∠8, ∠1 and ∠6, ∠4 and ∠7, ∠2 and ∠5, ∠3 and ∠8, ∠3 and ∠6, ∠2 and ∠7, ∠4 and ∠5, ∠1 and ∠8

37. Sample answer: Both graphs intersect to form right angles.

38. They are negative reciprocals of each other.

39. Sample answer: The slopes of the graphs of perpendicular lines are negative reciprocals of each other.

Algebra Activity

A Follow-Up of Lesson 10-1

Getting Started

Objective Construct congruent line segments and angles and perpendicular bisectors and angle bisectors.

Materials
compass

Teaching Tip Make sure students know how to use a compass.

Teach

- Students may benefit from taping their paper to a piece of cardboard. Have them poke the tip of the compass into the cardboard to keep it from slipping.
- Point out that the letters used in the copied figure are totally arbitrary.
- Ask students to try to explain why each construction is valid. Encourage them to use colored pencils to draw other segments that may help them in their explanations.

Constructions

Activity 1 Construct a line segment congruent to a given line segment.

Step 1

Draw $\overline{AB}$. Then use a straightedge to draw $\overrightarrow{GH}$ so it is longer than $\overline{AB}$.

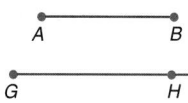

Step 2

Place the tip of the compass at A and the pencil tip at B.

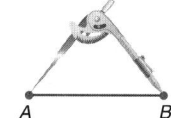

Step 3

Using this setting, place the tip at G. Draw an arc to intersect $\overrightarrow{GH}$. Label the intersection J. $\overline{GJ} \cong \overline{AB}$.

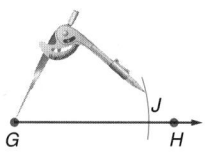

Activity 2 Construct an angle congruent to a given angle.

Step 1

Draw $\angle DEF$. Then use a straightedge to draw $\overrightarrow{JK}$.

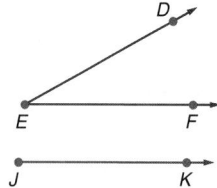

Step 2

Place the tip of the compass at E. Draw an arc to intersect both sides of $\angle DEF$ to locate points X and Y.

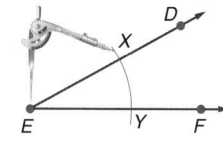

Step 3

Using this setting, place the compass at point J. Draw an arc to intersect $\overrightarrow{JK}$. Label the intersection A.

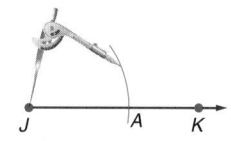

Step 4

Place the point of the compass on X and adjust so that the pencil tip is on Y.

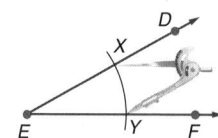

Step 5

Using this setting, place the compass at A and draw an arc to intersect the arc drawn in Step 3. Label the intersection M.

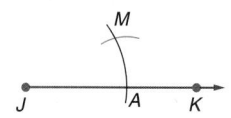

Step 6

Draw $\overrightarrow{JM}$. $\angle MJK \cong \angle DEF$.

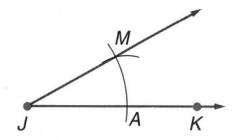

Model and Analyze 1–2. See students' work.

1. Draw a line segment. Construct a line segment congruent to the one drawn.

2. Draw an angle. Construct an angle congruent to the one drawn.

498 Chapter 10 Two-Dimensional Figures

Resource Manager

📁 **Teaching Pre-Algebra with Manipulatives**
- p. 126 (student recording sheet)

Glencoe Mathematics Classroom Manipulative Kit
- compass

Activity 3   Construct the perpendicular bisector of a line segment.

Step 1

Draw $\overline{XY}$. Then place the compass at point X. Use a setting greater than one half of $\overline{XY}$. Draw an arc above and below $\overline{XY}$.

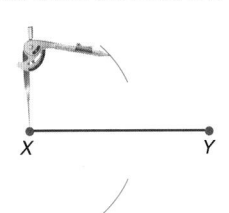

Step 2

Using this setting, place the compass at point Y. Draw an arc above and below $\overline{XY}$ as shown.

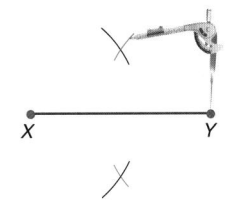

Step 3

Use a straightedge to align the two intersections. Draw a segment that intersects $\overline{XY}$. Label the intersection M.

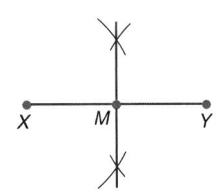

Activity 4   Construct the bisector of an angle.

Step 1

Draw $\angle MNP$. Then place the compass at point N and draw an arc that intersects both sides of the angle. Label the intersections X and Y.

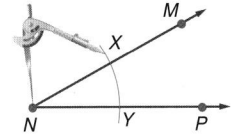

Step 2

With the compass at point X, draw an arc in the interior of $\angle N$. Using this setting, place the compass at point Y. Draw another arc. Label the intersection Q.

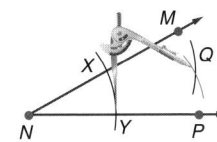

Step 3

Draw $\overrightarrow{NQ}$. $\overrightarrow{NQ}$ is the bisector of $\angle MNP$.

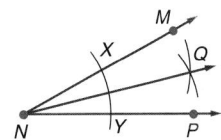

Model and Analyze

3. In Activity 3, use a ruler to measure $\overline{XM}$ and $\overline{MY}$. This construction *bisects* a segment. What do you think *bisects* means? **to divide into two equal parts**

4. Draw a line segment. Construct the perpendicular bisector of the segment. **See students' work.**

5. In Activity 4, what is true about the measures of $\angle MNQ$ and $\angle QNP$? **They are the same.**

6. Why do we say $\overrightarrow{NQ}$ is the bisector of $\angle MNP$? **$\overrightarrow{NQ}$ divides $\angle MNP$ into two equal angles.**

Tips for New Teachers

Safety Tip
There are safety compasses available that do not have sharp points. If using this type of compass, have students practice drawing arcs with them before attempting constructions.

Assess

In **Exercises 1–6**, students construct congruent line segments, congruent angles, perpendicular bisectors of line segments, and bisectors of angles. Ask them to conjecture how a landscape architect might use these skills.

Study Notebook

You may wish to have students summarize this activity and what they learned from it.

5-Minute Check Transparency 10-2 Use as a quiz or review of Lesson 10-1.

Mathematical Background
notes are available for this lesson on page 490C.

Where are congruent triangles present in nature?

The opening activity questions are repeated on page 557 of the *Chapter 10 Resource Masters*.

Reading to Learn Mathematics, p. 557   ELL

Pre-Activity   *Where are congruent triangles present in nature?*

Do the activity at the top of page 500 in your textbook. Write your answers below.

a. Trace the triangles shown in your textbook onto a sheet of paper. Then label the triangles. See students' work.

b. Measure and then compare the lengths of the sides of the triangles. $AB = DF$, $AC = DE$, $BC = FE$

c. Measure the angles of each triangle. How do the angles compare? $m\angle A = m\angle D$, $m\angle B = m\angle F$, $m\angle C = m\angle E$

d. Make a conjecture about the triangles. Since the angles have the same measures and the sides have the same length, the triangles have the same size and shape.

Reading the Lesson 1–2. See students' work.

Write a definition and give an example of each new vocabulary word or phrase.

Vocabulary	Definition	Example
1. congruent		
2. corresponding parts		

Helping You Remember

3. Below are two congruent triangles. Name the corresponding parts and complete the congruence statement.

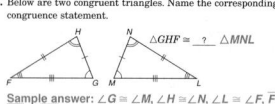

$\triangle GHF \cong$ __?__ $\triangle MNL$

Sample answer: $\angle G \cong \angle M$, $\angle H \cong \angle N$, $\angle L \cong \angle F$, $\overline{FG} \cong \overline{ML}$, $\overline{FH} \cong \overline{LN}$, $\overline{HG} \cong \overline{NM}$

Vocabulary
- congruent
- corresponding parts

a. See students' work.
b. $AB = DF$, $AC = DE$, $BC = FE$
c. $m\angle A = m\angle D$, $m\angle B = m\angle F$, $m\angle C = m\angle E$
d. Since the angles have the same measures and the sides have the same length, the triangles have the same size and shape.

Reading Math

Corresponding
Everyday Meaning: *matching*
Math Meaning: *having the same position*

What You'll Learn
- Identify congruent triangles and corresponding parts of congruent triangles.

Where are congruent triangles present in nature?

Ivy is a type of climbing plant. Most ivy leaves have five major veins. In the photo shown, the veins outlined form two triangles.

a. Trace the triangles shown at the right onto a sheet of paper. Then label the triangles.
b. Measure and then compare the lengths of the sides of the triangles.
c. Measure the angles of each triangle. How do the angles compare?
d. Make a conjecture about the triangles.

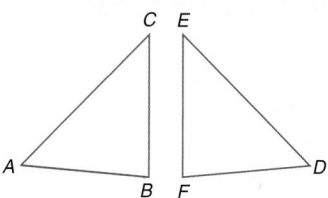

CONGRUENT TRIANGLES   Figures that have the same size and shape are **congruent**. The parts of congruent triangles that "match" are **corresponding parts**.

Key Concept   Corresponding Parts of Congruent Triangles

- **Words**   If two triangles are congruent, their corresponding sides are congruent and their corresponding angles are congruent.

- **Model**

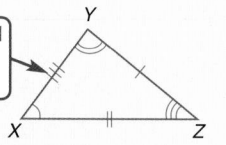

Slash marks are used to indicate which *sides* are congruent.

Arcs are used to indicate which *angles* are congruent.

- **Symbols**   Congruent Angles: $\angle X \cong \angle P$, $\angle Y \cong \angle Q$, $\angle Z \cong \angle R$
  Congruent Sides: $\overline{XY} \cong \overline{PQ}$, $\overline{YZ} \cong \overline{QR}$, $\overline{XZ} \cong \overline{PR}$

Concept Check   What is true about the corresponding angles and sides of congruent triangles? They are congruent.

Resource Manager

Workbooks and Reproducible Masters

Chapter 10 Resource Masters
- Study Guide and Intervention, p. 554
- Skills Practice, p. 555
- Practice, p. 556
- Reading to Learn Mathematics, p. 557
- Enrichment, p. 558
- Assessment, p. 603

Parent and Student Study Guide Workbook, p. 82

Transparencies
5-Minute Check Transparency 10-2
Answer Key Transparencies

Technology
Interactive Chalkboard
Pre-AlgePASS: Tutorial Plus, Lesson 32

When writing a congruence statement, the letters must be written so that corresponding vertices appear in the same order. For example, for the diagram below, write $\triangle FGH \cong \triangle JKM$.

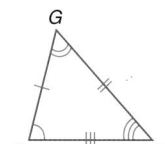 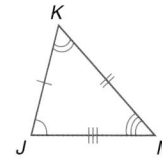

$\triangle FGH \cong \triangle JKM$

Vertex F corresponds to vertex J.
Vertex G corresponds to vertex K.
Vertex H corresponds to vertex M.

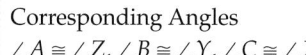 **Example 1** Name Corresponding Parts

Name the corresponding parts in the congruent triangles shown. Then complete the congruence statement.

Corresponding Angles
$\angle A \cong \angle Z$, $\angle B \cong \angle Y$, $\angle C \cong \angle X$

Corresponding Sides
$\overline{AB} \cong \overline{ZY}$, $\overline{BC} \cong \overline{YX}$, $\overline{CA} \cong \overline{XZ}$

$\triangle ABC \cong$ _?_

One congruence statement is $\triangle ABC \cong \triangle ZYX$.

Congruence statements can be used to identify corresponding parts of congruent triangles.

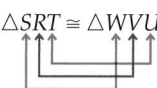 **Example 2** Use Congruence Statements

If $\triangle SRT \cong \triangle WVU$, complete each congruence statement.

$\angle S \cong$ _?_ $\angle U \cong$ _?_ $\angle R \cong$ _?_

$\overline{WV} \cong$ _?_ $\overline{RT} \cong$ _?_ $\overline{ST} \cong$ _?_

Explore   You know the congruence statement. You need to find the corresponding parts.

Plan   Use the order of the vertices in $\triangle SRT \cong \triangle WVU$ to identify the corresponding parts.

Solve $\triangle SRT \cong \triangle WVU$ $\angle S$ corresponds to $\angle W$ so $\angle S \cong \angle W$.
      $\angle R$ corresponds to $\angle V$ so $\angle R \cong \angle V$.
      $\angle T$ corresponds to $\angle U$ so $\angle T \cong \angle U$.
S corresponds to W, and R corresponds to V so $\overline{SR} \cong \overline{WV}$.
R corresponds to V, and T corresponds to U so $\overline{RT} \cong \overline{VU}$.
S corresponds to W, and T corresponds to U so $\overline{ST} \cong \overline{WU}$.

Examine   Draw the triangles, using arcs and slash marks to show the congruent angles and sides.

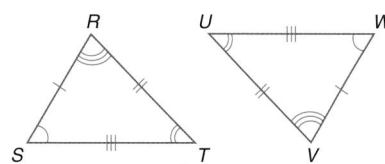

---

2 Teach

CONGRUENT TRIANGLES

Teaching Tip Remind students that angles are congruent when their measures are equal, and line segments are congruent when their lengths are equal.

In-Class Examples Power Point®

1 Name the corresponding parts in the congruent triangles shown. Then complete the congruence statement.

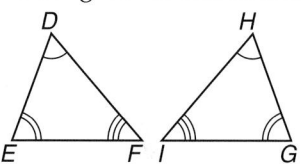

$\angle D \cong \angle H$, $\angle E \cong \angle G$, $\angle F \cong \angle I$; $\overline{DE} \cong \overline{HG}$, $\overline{DF} \cong \overline{HI}$, $\overline{EF} \cong \overline{GI}$; $\triangle HGI \cong \triangle DEF$

Teaching Tip Have students write other triangle congruence statements so they recognize how to match up the vertices if the original triangle is not named in alphabetical order.

Teaching Tip For Example 2, encourage students to draw the triangles and mark the congruent parts before completing the congruence statements.

2 If $\triangle MNO \cong \triangle QPR$, complete each congruence statement.

$\angle M \cong$ _?_ $\angle P \cong$ _?_ $\angle O \cong$ _?_

$\overline{QP} \cong$ _?_ $\overline{NO} \cong$ _?_ $\overline{MO} \cong$ _?_

$\angle M \cong \angle Q$, $\angle P \cong \angle N$, $\angle O \cong \angle R$; $\overline{QP} \cong \overline{MN}$, $\overline{NO} \cong \overline{PR}$, $\overline{MO} \cong \overline{QR}$

In-Class Example

3 **CONSTRUCTION** A brace is used to support a tabletop. In the figure, $\triangle ABC \cong \triangle DEF$.

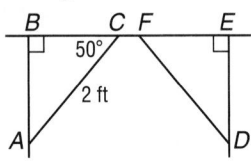

a. What is the measure of $\angle F$? **50°**

b. What is the length of $\overline{DF}$? **2 ft**

---

3 Practice/Apply

Study Notebook

Have students—
• add the definitions/examples of the vocabulary terms to their Vocabulary Builder worksheets for Chapter 10.
• draw a set of congruent triangles and write congruence statements for them.
• include any other item(s) that they find helpful in mastering the skills in this lesson.

About the Exercises . . .

Odd/Even Assignments
Exercises 10–15 and 18–28 are structured so that students practice the same concepts whether they are assigned odd or even problems.

Assignment Guide

Basic: 11–33 odd, 34–49

Average: 11–33 odd, 34–49

Advanced: 10–32 even, 34–43 (Optional: 44–49)

You can use corresponding parts to find the measures of angles and sides in a figure that is congruent to a figure with known measures.

Example 3 **Find Missing Measures**

LANDSCAPING A brace is used to support a tree and help it to grow straight. In the figure, $\triangle TRS \cong \triangle ERS$.

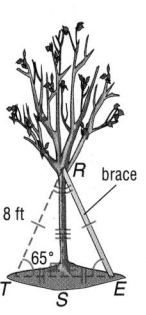

a. At what angle is the brace placed against the ground?

$\angle E$ and $\angle T$ are corresponding angles. So, they are congruent. Since $m\angle T = 65°$, $m\angle E = 65°$.

The brace is placed at a 65° angle with the ground.

b. What is the length of the brace?

$\overline{RE}$ corresponds to $\overline{RT}$. So, $\overline{RE}$ and $\overline{RT}$ are congruent. Since $RT = 8$ feet, $RE = 8$ feet.

The length of the brace is 8 feet.

Check for Understanding

Concept Check

1. **Explain** when two figures are congruent.

2. **OPEN ENDED** Draw and label a pair of congruent triangles. Be sure to mark the corresponding parts. **1–2. See pp. 551A–551B.**

Guided Practice

For each pair of congruent triangles, name the corresponding parts. Then complete the congruence statement. **3–4. See pp. 551A–551B.**

GUIDED PRACTICE KEY	
Exercises	Examples
3, 4	1
5–8	2
9	3

3.
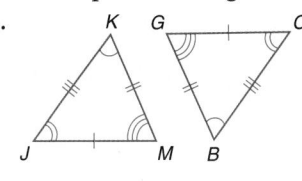

$\triangle KMJ \cong$ ___?___

4.
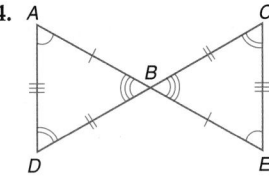

$\triangle CBE \cong$ ___?___

Complete each congruence statement if $\triangle DKJ \cong \triangle NAM$.

5. $\angle J \cong$ ___?___ $\angle M$ 6. $\angle A \cong$ ___?___ $\angle K$ 7. $\overline{JD} \cong$ ___?___ $\overline{MN}$ 8. $\overline{AN} \cong$ ___?___   8. $\overline{KD}$

Application

9. **TOWERS** A tower that supports high voltage power lines is shown at the right. In the tower, $\triangle ETC \cong \triangle YRC$. What is the length of $\overline{RC}$ if $EC = 10$ feet and $TC = 15$ feet? **15 ft**

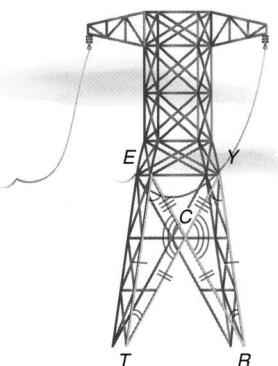

DAILY INTERVENTION

Differentiated Instruction

• **Visual/Spatial** Have students use compasses to create congruent triangles. Then have students cut out the triangles and lay one triangle on top of the other to verify that they match. Have students indicate the congruent sides and angles.

Practice and Apply

For each pair of congruent triangles, name the corresponding parts.
Then complete the congruence statement. 10–13. See margin.

10.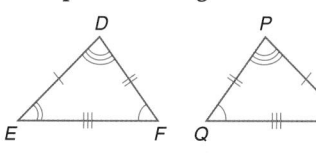

$\triangle DFE \cong$ ___?___

11.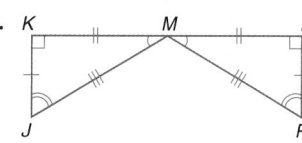

$\triangle KJM \cong$ ___?___

12.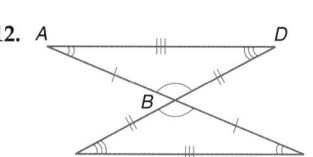

$\triangle DBA \cong$ ___?___

13.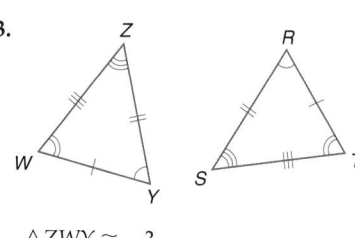

$\triangle ZWY \cong$ ___?___

Tell whether each statement is *sometimes*, *always*, or *never* true.

14. If two triangles are congruent, then the perimeters are equal. **always**

15. If the perimeters of two triangles are equal, then the triangles are congruent. **sometimes**

•ARCHITECTURE   For Exercises
16 and 17, use the diagram of the
roof truss at the right and the fact
that $\triangle TRU \cong \triangle SRU$.

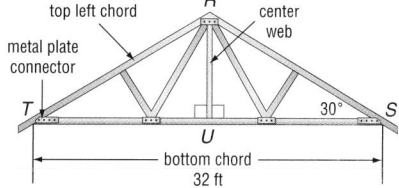

16. Find the distance from the left
metal plate connector to the
center web. **16 ft**

17. What is the measure of the angle formed by the top left chord and the
bottom chord? **30°**

Complete each congruence statement if $\triangle FHG \cong \triangle CBD$ and
$\triangle KMA \cong \triangle PRQ$.

18. $\angle G \cong$ ___?___ $\angle D$

19. $\angle C \cong$ ___?___ $\angle F$

20. $\angle M \cong \angle$ ___?___ $\angle R$

21. $\angle Q \cong$ ___?___ $\angle A$

22. $\overline{HG} \cong$ ___?___ $\overline{BD}$

23. $\overline{BC} \cong$ ___?___ $\overline{HF}$

24. $\overline{DC} \cong$ ___?___ $\overline{GF}$

25. $\overline{GF} \cong$ ___?___ $\overline{DC}$

★ 26. $\angle GFH \cong \angle$ ___?___ $\angle DCB$

Find the value of x for each pair of congruent triangles.

27. 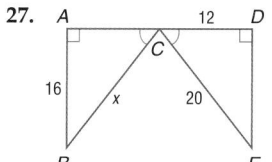 **20**

28. **18**

Answers

10. $\angle D \cong \angle P$, $\angle F \cong \angle Q$, $\angle E \cong \angle R$,
$\overline{DF} \cong \overline{PQ}$, $\overline{FE} \cong \overline{QR}$, $\overline{DE} \cong \overline{PR}$; $\triangle PQR$

11. $\angle K \cong \angle N$, $\angle J \cong \angle P$, $\angle M \cong \angle M$,
$\overline{KJ} \cong \overline{NP}$, $\overline{JM} \cong \overline{PM}$, $\overline{KM} \cong \overline{NM}$; $\triangle NPM$

12. $\angle D \cong \angle E$, $\angle B \cong \angle B$, $\angle A \cong \angle C$,
$\overline{DB} \cong \overline{EB}$, $\overline{BA} \cong \overline{BC}$, $\overline{DA} \cong \overline{EC}$; $\triangle EBC$

13. $\angle Z \cong \angle S$, $\angle W \cong \angle T$, $\angle Y \cong \angle R$,
$\overline{ZW} \cong \overline{ST}$, $\overline{WY} \cong \overline{TR}$, $\overline{ZY} \cong \overline{SR}$; $\triangle STR$

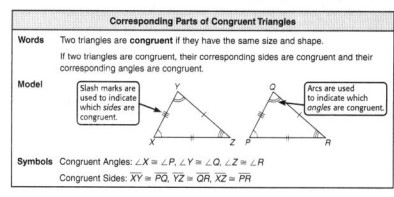
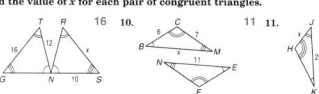 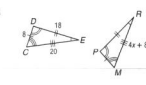
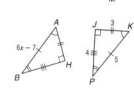
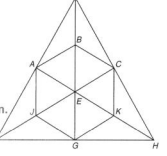
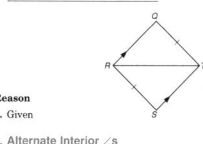

Open-Ended Assessment

Speaking Divide students into groups of four. Have each student take a turn describing corresponding parts of congruent triangles. Students should also describe one real-world example of corresponding triangles.

Getting Ready for Lesson 10-3

PREREQUISITE SKILL Lesson 10-3 presents transformations on the coordinate plane. Exercises 44–49 should be used to determine your students' familiarity with graphing points on a coordinate plane.

Assessment Options

Quiz (Lessons 10-1 and 10-2) is available on p. 603 of the *Chapter 10 Resource Masters.*

---

29. ALGEBRA If $\triangle ABC \cong \triangle XYZ$, what is the value of x? **6**

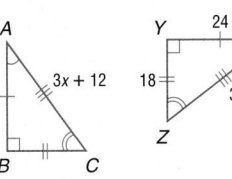
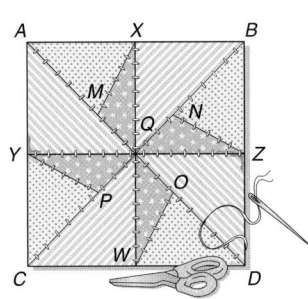

For Exercises 30–33, sample answers are given.

QUILTS For Exercises 30–33, use the quilt pattern shown at the left. Name a triangle that appears to be congruent to each triangle listed.

30. $\triangle XBQ$ $\triangle WCQ$ **31.** $\triangle YQP$ $\triangle ZQN$

32. $\triangle DWO$ $\triangle CYP$ **33.** $\triangle ZQN$ $\triangle WQO$

34. $\triangle ABH \cong \triangle IJG$; $\triangle ACG \cong \triangle IEF$

34. CRITICAL THINKING In the figure at the right, there are two pairs of congruent triangles. Write a congruence statement for each pair.

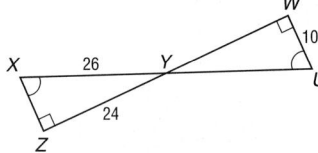

35. **WRITING IN MATH**   Answer the question that was posed at the beginning of the lesson. **See margin.**

Where are congruent triangles present in nature?

Include the following in your answer:
- a definition of congruent triangles, and
- two examples of objects in nature that contain congruent triangles.

Standardized Test Practice
Ⓐ Ⓑ Ⓒ Ⓓ

36. Which of the following must be true if $\triangle ACD \cong \triangle EHF$? **D**

Ⓐ $\angle C \cong \angle E$ Ⓑ $\overline{CA} \cong \overline{HF}$ Ⓒ $\overline{DC} \cong \overline{EF}$ Ⓓ $\angle CAD \cong \angle HEF$

37. Find the measure of $\overline{UY}$ if $\triangle XYZ \cong \triangle UYW$. **D**

Ⓐ 10   Ⓑ 20
Ⓒ 24   Ⓓ 26

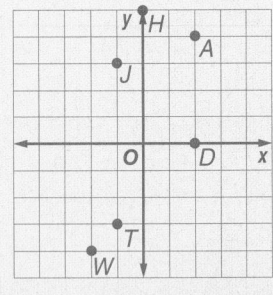

Maintain Your Skills

Mixed Review

38. 51°

38. Angles P and Q are supplementary. Find $m\angle P$ if $m\angle Q = 129°$. *(Lesson 10-1)*

Use a calculator to find each value to the nearest ten-thousandth. *(Lesson 9-8)*

39. $\cos 83°$ **0.1219**   **40.** $\sin 39.7°$ **0.6388**   **41.** $\tan 49.2°$ **1.1585**

42. Name the multiplicative inverse of $2\frac{1}{2}$. *(Lesson 5-4)* $\frac{2}{5}$

43. ALGEBRA Solve $-5a - 6 = 24$. *(Lesson 3-5)* **−6**

Getting Ready for the Next Lesson

PREREQUISITE SKILL   Graph each point on a coordinate system. *(To review the coordinate system, see Lesson 2-6.)* **44–49. See margin.**

44. $A(2, 4)$ **45.** $J(-1, 3)$ **46.** $H(0, 5)$

47. $D(2, 0)$ **48.** $W(-2, -4)$ **49.** $T(-1, -3)$

Answers

35. Congruent triangles can be found on objects in nature like leaves and animals. Answers should include the following.
- Congruent triangles are triangles with the same angle measures and the same side lengths.

- Sample answer: A bird's wings when extended are an example of congruent angles. Another example of congruent angles would be the wings of a butterfly.

44–49.

Algebra Activity

A Preview of Lesson 10-3

Symmetry

Activity 1

Trace the outline of the butterfly shown. Then draw a line down the center of the butterfly. Notice how the two halves match. When this happens, a figure is said to have **line symmetry** and the line is called a *line of symmetry*. A figure that has line symmetry has **bilateral symmetry**.

Analyze

Determine whether each figure has line symmetry. If it does, trace the figure, and draw all lines of symmetry. If not, write *none*. **1, 3. See pp. 551A–551B.**

1.

2.  none

3.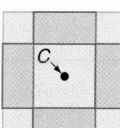

Activity 2

Copy the figure at the right. Then cut out the figure. Next, rotate the figure 90°, 180°, and 270°, about point C. What do you notice about the appearance of the figure in each rotation? **It looks exactly as it did in the original figure.**

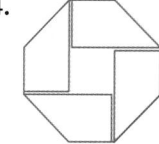

Any figure that can be turned or rotated less than 360° about a fixed point so that the figure looks exactly as it does in its original position has **rotational** or **turn symmetry**.

Analyze 7. Sample answer: capital letter H, yield sign, square

Determine whether each figure has rotational symmetry. Write *yes* **or** *no*.

4. yes

5.  yes

6. 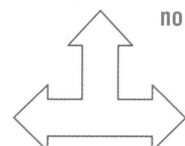 no

7. Name three objects that have both line symmetry and rotational symmetry.

Resource Manager

📁 ***Teaching Pre-Algebra with Manipulatives***

• p. 128 (student recording sheet)

Algebra Activity

A Preview of Lesson 10-3

Getting Started

Objective Introduce three types of symmetry.

Materials
tracing paper (optional)

Teaching Tip Allow students to trace the figures onto paper and fold the paper to check for lines of symmetry. They may have to hold the paper up to the light to see through it.

Teach

• Line symmetry can also be introduced by using a mirror. Place the mirror on a figure so that the mirror is perpendicular to the page. If the image formed matches the original figure, the mirror is on a line of symmetry. For example, have students check the butterfly by placing the mirror along the middle of the body. The new image should match the original figure. Now check the starfish, the letter J, and the snowflake.

Assess

Ask students how symmetry might apply to the life sciences. Have them find pictures of animals that have bilateral symmetry and pictures of animals that have rotational symmetry.

Study Notebook

You may wish to have students summarize this activity and what they learned from it.

10-3 Transformations on the Coordinate Plane

1 Focus

5-Minute Check Transparency 10-3 Use as a quiz or review of Lesson 10-2.

Mathematical Background notes are available for this lesson on page 490C.

How **are transformations involved in recreational activities?**

The opening activity questions are repeated on page 562 of the *Chapter 10 Resource Masters*.

Reading to Learn Mathematics, p. 562 — ELL

Pre-Activity *How are transformations involved in recreational activities?*

Do the activity at the top of page 506 in your textbook. Write your answers below.

a. Describe the motion involved in making a 180° turn on a skateboard.
Sample answer: The skateboard lands in the opposite direction from where it started.

b. Describe the motion that is used when swinging on a swing.
Sample answer: a back-and-forth motion

c. What type of motion does a scooter display when moving?
Sample answer: A scooter moves from one position to another position.

Reading the Lesson 1–5. See students' work.

Write a definition and give an example of each new vocabulary word or phrase.

Vocabulary	Definition	Example
1. transformation		
2. translation		
3. reflection		
4. line of symmetry		
5. rotation		

Helping You Remember

6. Complete the diagrams below by filling in each blank with one of the vocabulary words or phrases.

A movement of a geometric figure is called a ___transformation___.

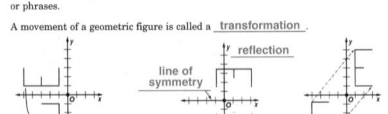

Vocabulary

- transformation
- translation
- reflection
- line of symmetry
- rotation

a. Sample answer: The skateboard lands on an opposite position from where it started.
b. Sample answer: a back-and-forth motion
c. Sample answer: A scooter moves from one position to another position.

What You'll Learn

- Draw translations, rotations, and reflections on a coordinate plane.

How **are transformations involved in recreational activities?**

The physical motions used in recreational activities such as skateboarding, swinging, or riding a scooter, are related to mathematics.

a. Describe the motion involved in making a 180° turn on a skateboard.
b. Describe the motion that is used when swinging on a swing.
c. What type of motion does a scooter display when moving?

TRANSFORMATIONS A movement of a geometric figure is a **transformation**. Three types of transformations are shown below.

- In a **translation**, you slide a figure from one position to another without turning it. Translations are also called *slides*.

Translation

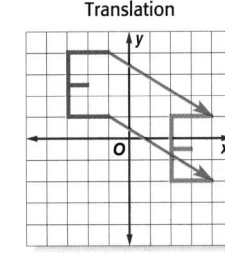

- In a **reflection**, you flip a figure over a line. The figures are mirror images of each other. Reflections are also called *flips*. The line is called a **line of symmetry**.

Reflection

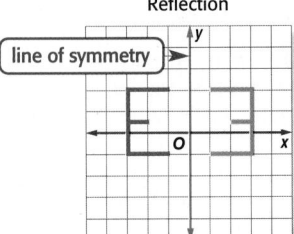

- In a **rotation**, you turn the figure around a fixed point. Rotations are also called *turns*.

Rotation

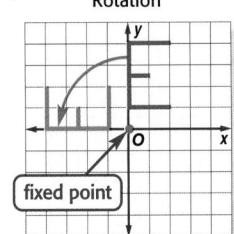

fixed point

Resource Manager

Workbooks and Reproducible Masters

Chapter 10 Resource Masters
- Study Guide and Intervention, p. 559
- Skills Practice, p. 560
- Practice, p. 561
- Reading to Learn Mathematics, p. 562
- Enrichment, p. 563

Graphing Calculator and Spreadsheet Masters, p. 37
Parent and Student Study Guide Workbook, p. 83

Transparencies

5-Minute Check Transparency 10-3
Answer Key Transparencies

Technology

Interactive Chalkboard
Pre-AlgePASS: Tutorial Plus, Lesson 33

When translating a figure, every point of the original figure is moved the same distance and in the same direction.

Translation
4 units left

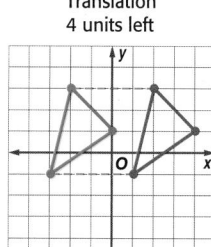

Translation
5 units down

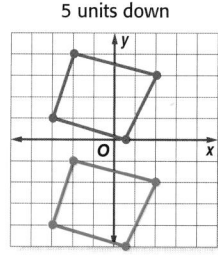

Translation
6 units right, 3 units up

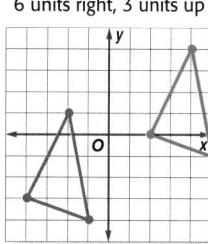

The following steps can be used to translate a point in the coordinate plane.

Key Concept   *Translation*

Step 1   Describe the translation using an ordered pair.

Step 2   Add the coordinates of the ordered pair to the coordinates of the original point.

Example 1   *Translation in a Coordinate Plane*

The vertices of △MNP are M(4, −2), N(0, 2), and P(5, 2). Graph the triangle and the image of △MNP after a translation 5 units left and 3 units up.

This translation can be written as the ordered pair (−5, 3). To find the coordinates of the translated image, add −5 to each x-coordinate and add 3 to each y-coordinate.

vertex		5 left, 3 up		translation
$M(4, -2)$	+	$(-5, 3)$	→	$M'(-1, 1)$
$N(0, 2)$	+	$(-5, 3)$	→	$N'(-5, 5)$
$P(5, 2)$	+	$(-5, 3)$	→	$P'(0, 5)$

The coordinates of the vertices of △M′N′P′ are M′(−1, 1), N′(−5, 5), and P′(0, 5).

When reflecting a figure, every point of the original figure has a corresponding point on the other side of the line of symmetry.

Reflection
over the **x**-axis

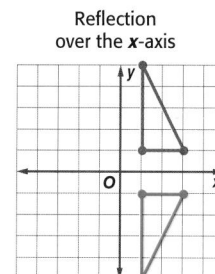

Reflection
over the **y**-axis

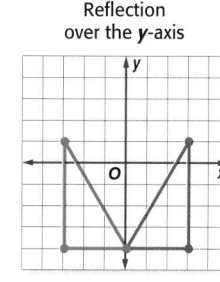

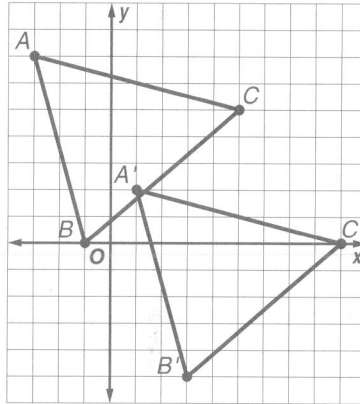

In-Class Example

2 The vertices of a figure are $M(-8, 6)$, $N(5, 9)$, $O(2, 1)$, and $P(-10, 3)$. Graph the figure and the image of the figure after a reflection over the y-axis.

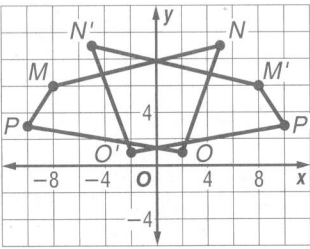

Teaching Tip Point out to students that a translation simply slides the figure to a new location and only requires addition to calculate the new vertices. Rotations and reflections change the way the figure is facing, and for these kinds of transformations, calculating the new vertices requires multiplication by -1.

Answers (p. 509)

1. The figure is moved 5 units to the right and 2 units down.

2. Sample answer:

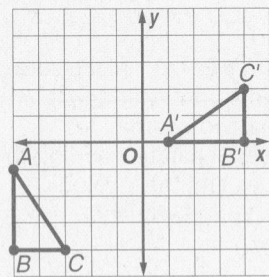

The following rules can be used to reflect a point over the x- or y-axis.

Key Concept Reflection

- To reflect a point over the x-axis, use the same x-coordinate and multiply the y-coordinate by -1.

- To reflect a point over the y-axis, use the same y-coordinate and multiply the x-coordinate by -1.

Example 2 *Reflection in a Coordinate Plane*

The vertices of the figure below are $A(-2, 3)$, $B(0, 5)$, $C(3, 1)$, and $D(3, 3)$. Graph the figure and the image of the figure after a reflection over the x-axis.

To find the coordinates of the vertices of the image after a reflection over the x-axis, use the same x-coordinate and multiply the y-coordinate by -1.

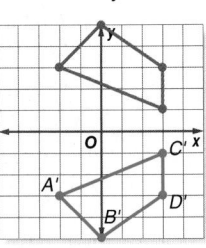

vertex				reflection
$A(-2, 3)$	$\rightarrow$	$(-2, -1 \cdot 3)$	$\rightarrow$	$A'(-2, -3)$
$B(0, 5)$	$\rightarrow$	$(0, -1 \cdot 5)$	$\rightarrow$	$B'(0, -5)$
$C(3, 1)$	$\rightarrow$	$(3, -1 \cdot 1)$	$\rightarrow$	$C'(3, -1)$
$D(3, 3)$	$\rightarrow$	$(3, -1 \cdot 3)$	$\rightarrow$	$D'(3, -3)$

The coordinates of the vertices of the reflected figure are $A'(-2, -3)$, $B'(0, -5)$, $C'(3, -1)$, and $D'(3, -3)$.

The diagrams below show three of the ways a figure can be rotated.

Reading Math

clockwise
The word clockwise refers to *the direction in which the hands of a clock rotate.*

counterclockwise
The word counterclockwise refers to *the direction opposite to that in which the hands of a clock rotate.*

Rotation of 90° clockwise

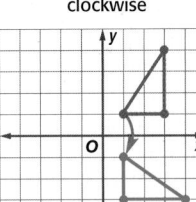

Rotation of 90° counterclockwise

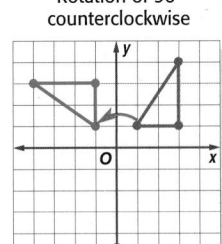

Rotation of 180°

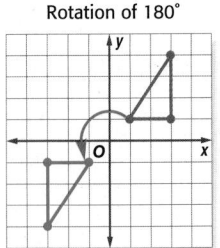

You can use these rules to rotate a figure 90° clockwise, 90° counterclockwise, or 180° about the origin.

Key Concept Rotation

- To rotate a figure 90° clockwise about the origin, switch the coordinates of each point and then multiply the new second coordinate by -1.

- To rotate a figure 90° counterclockwise about the origin, switch the coordinates of each point and then multiply the new first coordinate by -1.

- To rotate a figure 180° about the origin, multiply both coordinates of each point by -1.

DAILY INTERVENTION **Differentiated Instruction** **ELL**

- **Verbal/Linguistic** Have students write descriptions of transformations in real-world situations. Encourage them to bring in pictures or models of what they are describing.

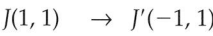 **Example 3** *Rotations in a Coordinate Plane*

A figure has vertices $J(1, 1)$, $K(4, 1)$, $M(1, 2)$, $N(4, 2)$, and $P(3, 4)$. Graph the figure and the image of the figure after a rotation of 90° counterclockwise.

To rotate the figure, switch the coordinates of each vertex and multiply the first by -1.

$J(1, 1) \rightarrow J'(-1, 1)$ $N(4, 2) \rightarrow N'(-2, 4)$

$K(4, 1) \rightarrow K'(-1, 4)$ $P(3, 4) \rightarrow P'(-4, 3)$

$M(1, 2) \rightarrow M'(-2, 1)$

The coordinates of the vertices of the rotated figure are $J'(-1, 1)$, $K'(-1, 4)$, $M'(-2, 1)$, $N'(-2, 4)$, and $P'(-4, 3)$.

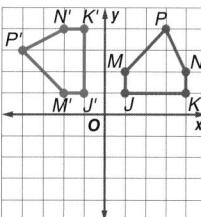

Check for Understanding

Concept Check

1–2. See margin.

1. **Write** a sentence to describe a figure that is translated by $(5, -2)$.

2. **OPEN ENDED**   Draw a triangle on grid paper. Then draw the image of the triangle after it is moved 5 units right and then rotated counterclockwise 90°.

Guided Practice

GUIDED PRACTICE KEY	
Exercises	Examples
3	1
4	2
5	3
6	1–3

3. Rectangle *RSTU* is shown at the right. Graph the image of the rectangle after a translation 4 units right and 2 units down. **See margin.**

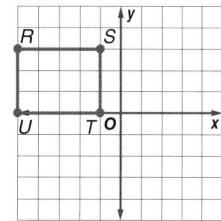

4. Suppose the figure graphed is reflected over the *y*-axis. Find the coordinates of the vertices after the reflection.
W' (4, 3), X' (1, 5), Y' (3, −1), Z' (1,−2)

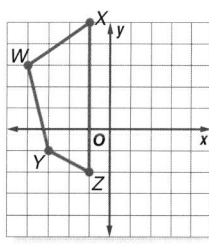

5. Triangle *ABC* is shown. Graph the image of △*ABC* after a rotation of 90° counterclockwise. **See margin.**

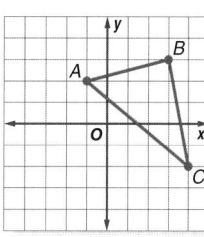

Application

6. **ART**   Identify the type of transformation that is shown below. translation or reflection

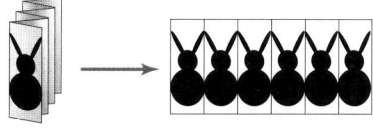

Lesson 10-3   Transformations on the Coordinate Plane   **509**

Answers

3.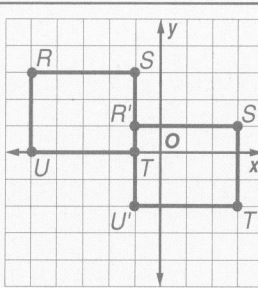

5.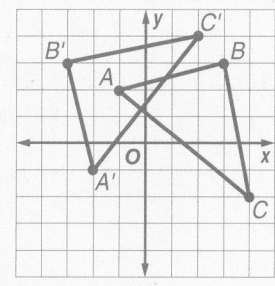

In-Class Example

3 A figure has vertices $A(-4, 5)$, $B(-2, 4)$, $C(-1, 2)$, $D(-3, 1)$, and $E(-5, 3)$. Graph the figure and the image of the figure after a rotation of 180°.

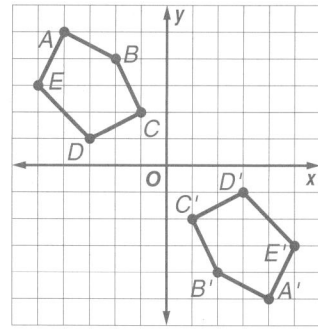

3 Practice/Apply

Study Notebook

Have students—

• add the definitions/examples of the vocabulary terms to their Vocabulary Builder worksheets for Chapter 10.

• include any other item(s) that they find helpful in mastering the skills in this lesson.

About the Exercises . . .

Odd/Even Assignments
Exercises 7–10, 11–14, 15, 17, and 25–56 are structured so that students practice the same concepts whether they are assigned odd or even problems.

Assignment Guide

Basic: 7, 11, 15–23 odd, 24–40

Average: 7–23 odd, 24–40

Advanced: 8–22 even, 24–34 (Optional: 35–40)

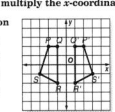
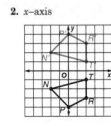 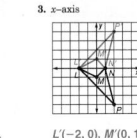
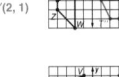
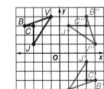
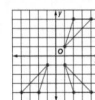 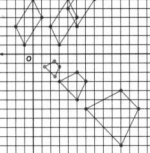
★ indicates increased difficulty

Practice and Apply

Find the coordinates of the vertices of each figure after the given translation. Then graph the translation image. **7–10. See margin.**

7. (2, 3)   8. (−4, 3)   ★9. $\left(5, 2\frac{1}{2}\right)$

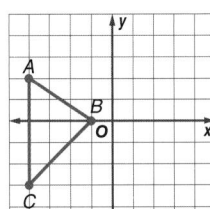 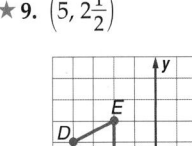

10. The vertices of a figure are *D*(1, 2), *E*(1, 4), *F*(−1, 2), *G*(−4, 4). Graph the image of the figure after a translation 4 units down.

Find the coordinates of the vertices of each figure after a reflection over the given axis. Then graph the reflection image. **11–14. See pp. 551A–551B.**

11. *x*-axis   12. *y*-axis   ★13. *x*-axis

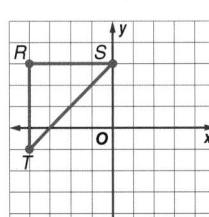 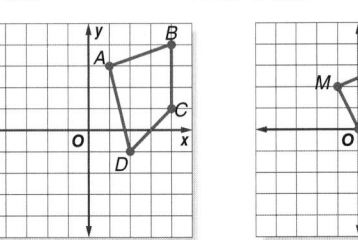

14. The vertices of a figure are *W*(−3, −3), *X*(0, −4), *Y*(4, −2), and *Z*(2, −1). Graph the image of its reflection over the *y*-axis.

For Exercises 15–17, use the graph shown.

15. Graph the image of the figure after a rotation of 90° counterclockwise.

16. Find the coordinates of the vertices of the figure after a 180° rotation.

17. Graph the image of the figure after a rotation of 90° clockwise.

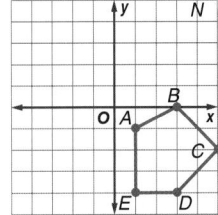

15, 17. See pp. 551A–551B.

16. *A'*(−1, 1), *B'*(−3, 0), *C'*(−5, 2), *D'*(−3, 4), *E'*(−1, 4)

Identify each transformation as a *translation*, a *reflection*, or a *rotation*.

18.   19.   20.

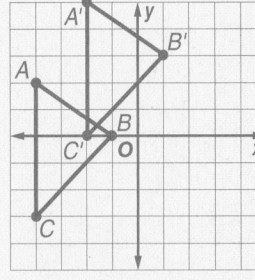 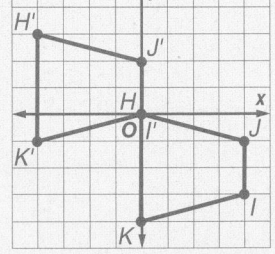

18. rotation
19. translation
20. reflection

21. Give a counterexample for the following statement. *The image of a figure's reflection is never the same as the image of its translation.* **See pp. 551A–551B.**

Answers

7. *A'*(−2, 5),
   B'(1, 3),
   C'(−2, 0)

8. *H'*(−4, 3),
   I'(0, 0),
   J'(0, 2),
   K'(−4, −1)

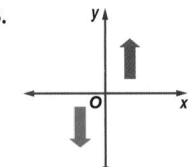 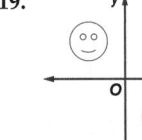 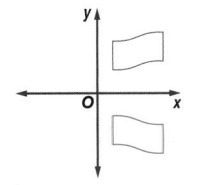

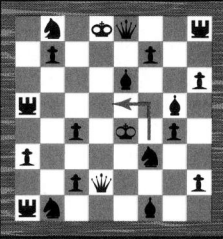

More About...

Games

In chess, each player has 16 game pieces, or chessmen. There are two rooks, two knights, two bishops, a queen, a king, and eight pawns.
Source: www.infoplease.com

22. GAMES What type of transformation is used when moving a knight in a game of chess? **translation**

23. MIRRORS Which transformation exists when you look into a mirror? **reflection**

24. CRITICAL THINKING After a rotation of 90° counterclockwise, the coordinates of the vertices of the image of $\triangle ABC$ are $A'(3, 2)$, $B'(0, 4)$, and $C'(5, 5)$. What were the coordinates of the vertices before the rotation? **See margin.**

25. [WRITING IN MATH] Answer the question that was posed at the beginning of the lesson. **See margin.**

How are the transformations involved in recreational activities?

Include the following in your answer:
- an explanation describing each type of transformation, and
- an explanation telling the type of transformation each recreational activity represents.

Standardized Test Practice
Ⓐ Ⓑ Ⓒ Ⓓ

For Exercises 26 and 27, suppose the figure shown is translated 4 units to the left and 3 units down.

26. Which point is *not* a vertex of the translated image? **B**
- Ⓐ $(-2, -3)$
- Ⓑ $(-4, -3)$
- Ⓒ $(-3, -1)$
- Ⓓ $(-2, 1)$

27. Which statement best describes this translation? **C**
- Ⓐ $(x, y) \rightarrow (x + 4, y + 3)$
- Ⓑ $(x, y) \rightarrow (x - 4, y + 3)$
- Ⓒ $(x, y) \rightarrow (x - 4, y - 3)$
- Ⓓ $(x, y) \rightarrow (x + 4, y - 3)$

Maintain Your Skills

Mixed Review

Complete each congruence statement if $\triangle ABC \cong \triangle DEF$. *(Lesson 10-2)*

28. $\angle D \cong \underline{\ ?\ }$ $\angle A$

29. $\overline{AC} \cong \underline{\ ?\ }$ $\overline{DF}$

30. $\overline{DE} \cong \underline{\ ?\ }$ $\overline{AB}$

Find the value of x in each figure. *(Lesson 10-1)*

31. 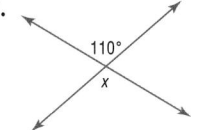 **110°**

110° / x

32. 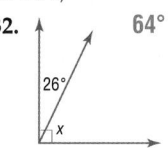 **64°**

26° / x

33. ALGEBRA Solve $x - 3.4 \geq 6.2$. Graph the solution on a number line. *(Lesson 7-4)* $x \geq 9.6$; **See margin for graph.**

34. Evaluate $|-4| - |3|$. *(Lesson 2-1)* **1**

Getting Ready for the Next Lesson

PREREQUISITE SKILL Solve each equation.
*(To review **solving two-step equations**, see Lesson 3-5.)*

35. $2x + 134 = 360$ **113**

36. $3x + 54 = 360$ **102**

37. $5x + 125 = 360$ **47**

38. $4x + 92 = 360$ **67**

39. $2x + 148 = 360$ **106**

40. $6x + 102 = 360$ **43**

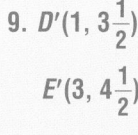

www.pre-alg.com/self_check_quiz

---

9. $D'(1, 3\frac{1}{2})$,

$E'(3, 4\frac{1}{2})$,

$G'(1, -1\frac{1}{2})$,

$F'(3, -\frac{1}{2})$

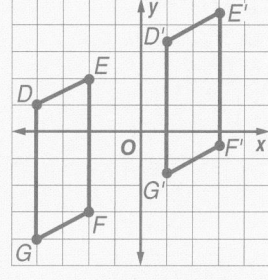

10.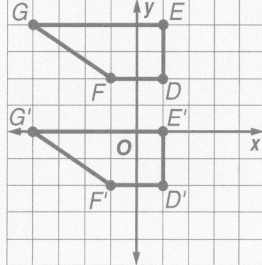

Open-Ended Assessment

Speaking Have pairs of students take turns talking each other through a transformation exercise.

Tips for New Teachers

Intervention If there is any doubt whether your students thoroughly understand transformations, consider spending an extra day on this lesson. Use the Extra Practice on p. 748. You can also use the Study Guide and Intervention masters or the Practice masters in the *Chapter 10 Resource Masters* to reinforce this concept.

Getting Ready for Lesson 10-4

PREREQUISITE SKILL Lesson 10-4 presents quadrilaterals. Exercises 35–40 should be used to determine your students' familiarity with solving equations.

Answers

24. $A(2, -3)$, $B(4, 0)$, $C(5, -5)$

25. Since many of the movements used in recreational activities involve rotating, sliding, and flipping, they are examples of transformations. Answers should include the following.

- A translation is a slide, a reflection is a mirror-image, and a rotation is a turn.
- Sample answer: the swing represents a rotation, the scooter represents a translation, and the skateboard represents reflection.

33.

7.0   8.0   9.0   10.0

Algebra Activity

A Follow-Up of Lesson 10-3

Getting Started

Objective Investigate dilations, which alter the size of a figure.

Materials
grid paper, protractor, ruler

Teaching Tip Have students look up the definition of dilation in a dictionary, then predict what will happen to the figures.

Teach

• Review the term *scale factor*, presented in Chapter 6.
• Show students examples of figures enlarged on the copy machine. These are dilations.
• Compare dilations to the transformations in Lesson 10-3.
• Be sure students understand that a dilation can either enlarge (scale factor >1) or reduce (scale factor <1) the image.

Assess

In **Exercises 1–6**, students should recognize that the corresponding angles are equal, and that ratios of corresponding sides are equal. Ask students what relationship exists between *ABCD* and *A'B'C'D'*. **They are similar.**

In **Exercises 7–9**, students need to multiply both coordinates of each vertex by the given scale factor to find the dilation image.

Ask students what they think would happen if the scale factor were negative. **It would enlarge or reduce in the opposite direction.**

Study Notebook

You may wish to have students summarize this activity and what they learned from it.

Dilations

In this activity, you will investigate **dilations**, which alter the size of a figure.

Collect the Data

Step 1 Draw and label a polygon on a coordinate plane. Trapezoid *ABCD* is shown.

Step 2 Suppose the scale factor is 2. Multiply the coordinates of each vertex by 2.
$A(-1, 2) \rightarrow A'(-2, 4)$ $B(0, 3) \rightarrow B'(0, 6)$
$C(4, 1) \rightarrow C'(8, 2)$ $D(2, -1) \rightarrow D'(4, -2)$

Step 3 Draw the new trapezoid.

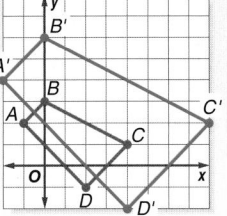

Analyze the Data 1–6. See pp. 551A–551B.

1. Use a protractor to measure the angles in each trapezoid. How do they compare?
2. Use a ruler to measure the sides of each trapezoid. How do they compare?
3. What ratio compares the measures of the corresponding sides?
4. Repeat the activity by multiplying the coordinates of trapezoid *ABCD* by $\frac{1}{2}$. Are the results the same? Explain.

Make a Conjecture

5. Explain how you know whether a dilation is a reduction or an enlargement.
6. Explain the difference between dilations and the other types of transformations.

Extend the Activity

Find the coordinates of the dilation image for the given scale factor, and graph the dilation image. 7–9. See pp. 551A–551B.

7. 3   **8.** $\frac{1}{4}$ **9.** $1\frac{1}{2}$

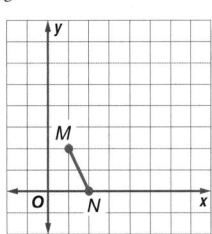 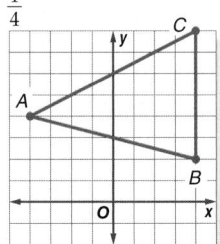 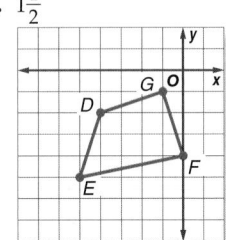

Identify each transformation as a *translation*, *rotation*, *reflection*, or *dilation*.

10.   **11.**   **12.**

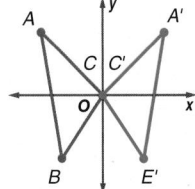 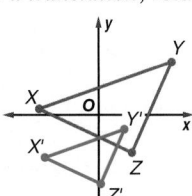 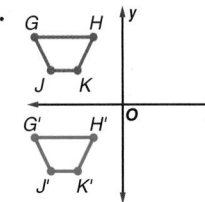

10. reflection
11. dilation
12. translation

Resource Manager

📂 ***Teaching Pre-Algebra with Manipulatives***
• p. 1 (master for grid paper)
• p. 21 (master for protractors)
• p. 22 (master for rulers)
• p. 129 (student recording sheet)

Glencoe Mathematics Classroom Manipulative Kit
• protractor
• ruler

What You'll Learn

- Find the missing angle measures of a quadrilateral.
- Classify quadrilaterals.

How are quadrilaterals used in design?

Geometric figures are often used to create various designs. The design of a brick walkway is shown at the right. Notice how the walkway is formed using different-shaped bricks to create circles.

a. Describe the bricks that are used to create the smallest circles.

b. Describe how the shape of the bricks change as the circles get larger.

Vocabulary
- quadrilateral

a. squares, rectangles, trapezoids
b. Sample answer: The center of the circle is one square brick. The first row contains small trapezoids. The next four rows contain larger trapezoids. The next three rows contain trapezoids and squares that alternate.

QUADRILATERALS Squares, rectangles, and trapezoids are examples of quadrilaterals. A **quadrilateral** is a closed figure with four sides and four vertices. The segments that make up a quadrilateral intersect only at their endpoints.

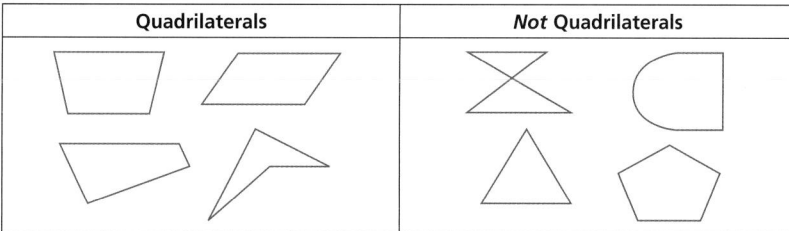

Quadrilaterals	*Not* Quadrilaterals

As with triangles, a quadrilateral can be named by its vertices. The quadrilateral below can be named quadrilateral *ABCD*.

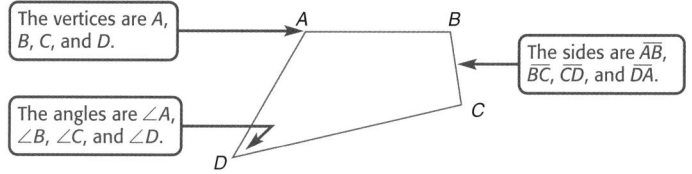

The vertices are *A*, *B*, *C*, and *D*.

The sides are $\overline{AB}$, $\overline{BC}$, $\overline{CD}$, and $\overline{DA}$.

The angles are $\angle A$, $\angle B$, $\angle C$, and $\angle D$.

Study Tip

Naming Quadrilaterals
When you name a quadrilateral, you can begin at any vertex. However, it is important to name vertices in order.

The quadrilateral shown above has many names. For example, it can also be named quadrilateral *BCDA*, quadrilateral *DABC*, or quadrilateral *CBAD*.

✓ **Concept Check** How many vertices does a quadrilateral have? **4**

Lesson 10-4 Quadrilaterals **513**

---

1 Focus

5-Minute Check Transparency 10-4 Use as a quiz or review of Lesson 10-3.

Mathematical Background notes are available for this lesson on page 490C.

How are quadrilaterals used in design?

The opening activity questions are repeated on page 567 of the *Chapter 10 Resource Masters*.

Reading to Learn Mathematics, p. 567 ELL

Pre-Activity *How are quadrilaterals used in design?*

Do the activity at the top of page 513 in your textbook. Write your answers below.

a. Describe the bricks that are used to create the smallest circles. squares, rectangles, trapezoids

b. Describe how the shape of the bricks changes as the circles get larger. Sample answer: The center of the circle is one square brick. The first row contains small trapezoids. The next four rows contain larger trapezoids. The next three rows contain trapezoids and squares that alternate.

Reading the Lesson

Write a definition and give an example of the new vocabulary word.

	Vocabulary	Definition	Example
1.	quadrilateral	See students' work.	

After each description, write the correct word from the list.

trapezoid   rhombus   parallelogram   square   rectangle

2. a parallelogram with four right angles   rectangle

3. a parallelogram with both pairs of opposite sides parallel and congruent   parallelogram

4. a parallelogram with four congruent sides and four right angles   square

5. a parallelogram with one pair of opposite sides parallel   trapezoid

6. a parallelogram with four congruent sides   rhombus

Helping You Remember

7. The sum of the measures of the angles of a quadrilateral is 360°. Identify the quadrilaterals below and find the missing angle measure.

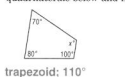 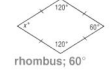 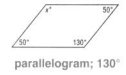

trapezoid; 110°   rhombus; 60°   parallelogram; 130°

Teaching Tip Point out to students that *quad* means four, so a *quadrilateral* must have four vertices and four sides.

Resource Manager

Workbooks and Reproducible Masters

Chapter 10 Resource Masters
- Study Guide and Intervention, p. 564
- Skills Practice, p. 565
- Practice, p. 566
- Reading to Learn Mathematics, p. 567
- Enrichment, p. 568
- Assessment, pp. 603, 605

Parent and Student Study Guide Workbook, p. 84

Transparencies
5-Minute Check Transparency 10-4
Answer Key Transparencies

Technology
Interactive Chalkboard

2 Teach

QUADRILATERALS

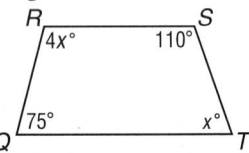
CLASSIFY QUADRILATERALS

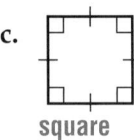
A quadrilateral can be separated into two triangles. Since the sum of the measures of the angles of a triangle is 180°, the sum of the measures of the angles of a quadrilateral is 2(180°) or 360°.

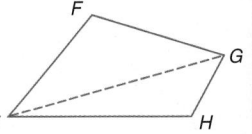

Key Concept — **Angles of a Quadrilateral**

The sum of the measures of the angles of a quadrilateral is 360°.

Example 1 **Find Angle Measures**

ALGEBRA Find the value of x. Then find each missing angle measure.

Words The sum of the measures of the angles is 360°.

Variable Let $m\angle A$, $m\angle B$, $m\angle C$, and $m\angle D$ represent the measures of the angles.

Equation

$m\angle A + m\angle B + m\angle C + m\angle D = 360$	Angles of a quadrilateral
$88 + 62 + 2x + x = 360$	Substitution
$3x + 150 = 360$	Combine like terms.
$3x + 150 - 150 = 360 - 150$	Subtract 150 from each side.
$3x = 210$	Simplify.
$x = 70$	

The value of x is 70. So, $m\angle D = 70°$ and $m\angle C = 2(70)$ or 140°.

CLASSIFY QUADRILATERALS The diagram below shows how quadrilaterals are related. Notice that it goes from the most general quadrilateral to the most specific.

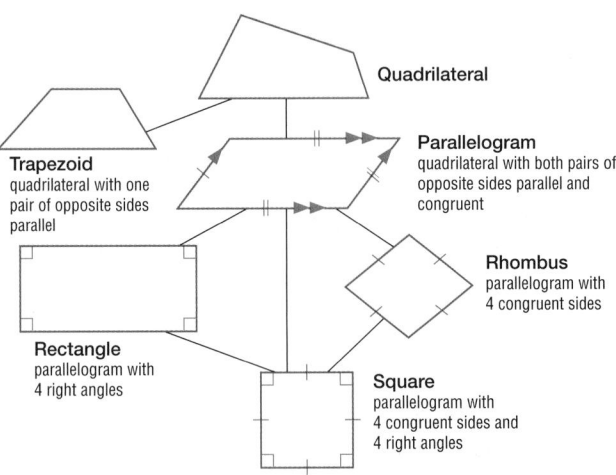

The best description of a quadrilateral is the one that is the most specific.

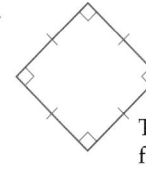
Example 2 *Classify Quadrilaterals*

Classify each quadrilateral using the name that best describes it.

a.

The quadrilateral has four congruent sides and four right angles. It is a square.

b.

The quadrilateral has opposite sides parallel and opposite sides congruent. It is a parallelogram.

c. **ART** Classify the quadrilaterals that are outlined in the painting at the right.

Each of the quadrilaterals has four right angles, but the four sides are not congruent. The quadrilaterals are rectangles.

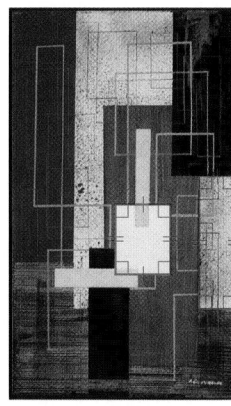

Irene Rice Periera. *Untitled.* 1951

Check for Understanding

Concept Check

1. **OPEN ENDED** Give a real-world example of a quadrilateral, a parallelogram, a rhombus, and a square. **1–2. See margin.**

2. **Describe** the characteristics of a rectangle and draw an example of one.

Guided Practice

ALGEBRA Find the value of x. Then find the missing angle measures.

GUIDED PRACTICE KEY	
Exercises	Examples
3, 4	1
5–7	2

3. 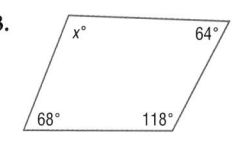 **110; 110°**

4. 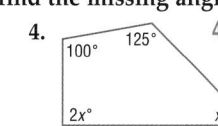 **45; 45°; 90°**

Classify each quadrilateral using the name that *best* describes it.

5. 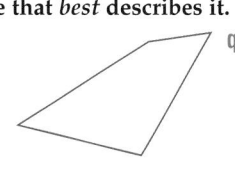 **rectangle**

6. **quadrilateral**

Application

7. **SPORTS** Classify the quadrilaterals that are found on the scoring region of a shuffleboard court.
trapezoids, parallelograms

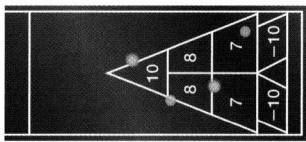

www.pre-alg.com/extra_examples

Answers

1. Sample answer: A textbook is an example of a quadrilateral; the tiles in a shuffle-board scoring region are examples of parallelograms; a "dead end" road sign is an example of a rhombus; and a floppy disk is an example of a square.

2. A rectangle has four sides, four right angles, opposite sides parallel, and opposite sides congruent.

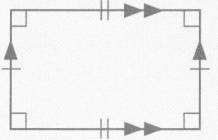

Study Notebook

Have students—

• add the definitions/examples of the vocabulary terms to their Vocabulary Builder worksheets for Chapter 10.

• copy the chart showing how quadrilaterals are related.

• include any other item(s) that they find helpful in mastering the skills in this lesson.

About the Exercises . . .

Organization by Objective
• Quadrilaterals: 8–13
• Classify Quadrilaterals: 16–22, 27–28

Odd/Even Assignments
Exercises 8–21 and 23–28 are structured so that students practice the same concepts whether they are assigned odd or even problems.

Alert! Exercise 33 requires graph paper.

Assignment Guide
Basic: 9, 11, 15–25 odd, 29–40
Average: 9–27 odd, 29–40
Advanced: 8–28 even, 29–36 (Optional: 37–40)
All: Practice Quiz 1 (1–5)

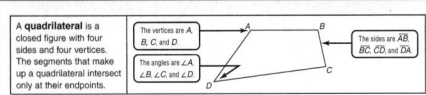
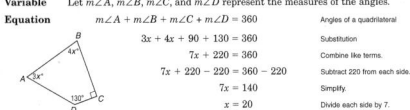
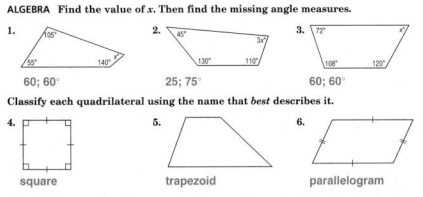
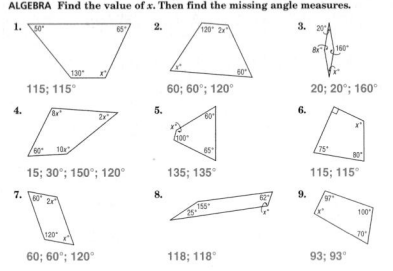
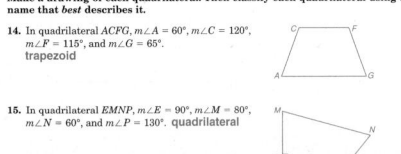
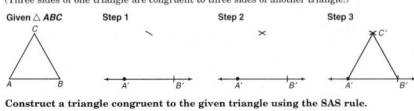
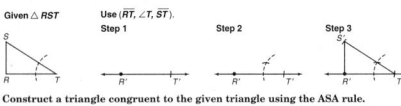
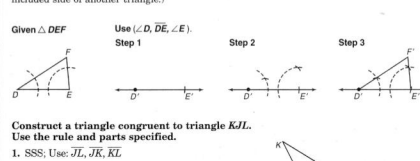
★ indicates increased difficulty

Practice and Apply

ALGEBRA Find the value of x. Then find the missing angle measures.

8. 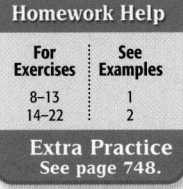 71; 71°

9.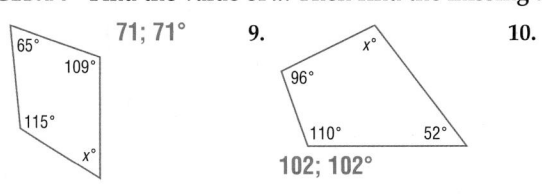

10. 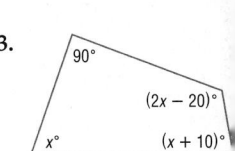 28; 28°; 84°

9. 102; 102°

11.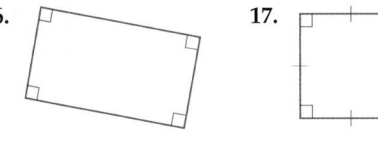

★ 12.

★ 13.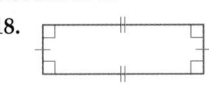

11. 60; 60°; 60°; 120°
12. 55; 55°; 60°; 110°
13. 70; 70°; 80°; 120°

14. **COOKING** Name an item found in a kitchen that is rectangular in shape. Explain why the item is a rectangle. 14–15. See margin.

15. **GAMES** Identify a board game that is played on a board that is shaped like a square. Explain why the board is a square.

Classify each quadrilateral using the name that *best* describes it.

16. 17. 18.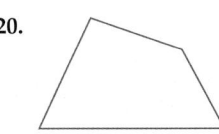

16. rectangle
17. square
18. rectangle
19. parallelogram
20. quadrilateral
21. rhombus

19. 20. 21.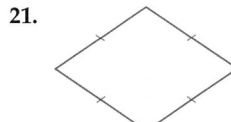

22. **ART** The abstract painting is an example of how shape and color are used in art. Write a few sentences describing the geometric shapes used by the artist. **See margin.**

Elizabeth Murray. *Painter's Progress*, 1981

Tell whether each statement is *sometimes*, *always*, or *never* true.

23. A square is a rhombus. always

24. A parallelogram is a rectangle. sometimes

25. A rectangle is a square. sometimes

26. A parallelogram is a quadrilateral. always

Make a drawing of each quadrilateral. Then classify each quadrilateral using the name that *best* describes it. 27–28. See margin.

★ 27. In quadrilateral JKLM, $m\angle J = 90°$, $m\angle K = 50°$, $m\angle L = 90°$, and $m\angle M = 130°$.

★ 28. In quadrilateral CDEF, $\overline{CD}$ and $\overline{EF}$ are parallel, and $\overline{CF}$ and $\overline{DE}$ are parallel. Angle C is not congruent to $\angle D$.

Answers

14. Sample answer: A baking sheet; it is a rectangle because it is a parallelogram with 4 right angles.

15. Sample answer: A chessboard; it is a square because it is a parallelogram with 4 congruent sides and 4 right angles.

22. Sample answer: The artist used triangles, quadrilaterals, and a few shapes having five and six sides. Some of the quadrilaterals are trapezoids.

27. See students' drawings; quadrilateral

28. See students' drawings; parallelogram

29. CRITICAL THINKING An *equilateral* figure is one in which all sides have the same measure. An *equiangular* figure is one in which all angles have the same measure. **a–b. See margin.**

  a. Is it possible for a quadrilateral to be equilateral without being equiangular? If so, explain with a drawing.

  b. Is it possible for a quadrilateral to be equiangular without being equilateral? If so, explain with a drawing.

30. WRITING IN MATH Answer the question that was posed at the beginning of the lesson. **See margin.**

How are quadrilaterals used in design?

Include the following in your answer:
  • an example of a real-world design that contains quadrilaterals, and
  • an explanation of the figures used in the design.

Standardized Test Practice
Ⓐ Ⓑ Ⓒ Ⓓ

31. Which figure is a rhombus? **B**

Ⓐ 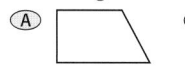 Ⓑ 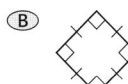 Ⓒ 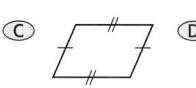 Ⓓ

32. GRID IN Find the value of x in the figure at the right. **147**

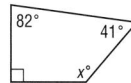

Maintain Your Skills

Mixed Review

33. A figure has vertices $D(1, 2)$, $E(1, 4)$, $F(-4, 4)$, and $G(-2, 2)$. Graph the figure and its image after a translation 4 units down. *(Lesson 10-3)* **See margin.**

Complete each congruence statement if $\triangle AKM \cong \triangle NDQ$. *(Lesson 10-2)*

34. $\angle K \cong$ ___?___ $\angle D$ **35.** $\overline{QN} \cong$ ___?___ $\overline{MA}$

36. Find the discount for a $45 shirt that is on sale for 20% off. *(Lesson 6-7)* **$9**

Getting Ready for the Next Lesson

PREREQUISITE SKILL Find each product.
*(To review **multiplying decimals**, see page 715.)*

37. $(3)(4.8)$ **14.4**   **38.** $(5.4)(6)$ **32.4**   **39.** $(9.2)(3.1)$ **28.52**   **40.** $(10.5)(5.7)$ **59.85**

Practice Quiz 1   *Lessons 10-1 through 10-4*

1. Angle A and $\angle B$ are complementary. Find $m\angle A$ if $m\angle B = 55°$. *(Lesson 10-1)* **35°**

2. Suppose $\triangle ABC \cong \triangle DEF$. Which angle is congruent to $\angle D$? *(Lesson 10-2)* **$\angle A$**

3. $\triangle QRS$ has vertices $Q(3, 3)$, $R(5, 6)$, and $S(7, 3)$. Find the coordinates for the vertices of the triangle after the figure is reflected over the x-axis. *(Lesson 10-3)*
  $Q'(3, -3)$, $R'(5, -6)$, $S'(7, -3)$

ALGEBRA Find the value of x. Then find the missing angle measures. *(Lesson 10-4)*

4. 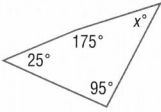 **65; 65°**   **5.** 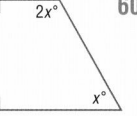 **60; 60°; 120°**

29a. Yes; a rhombus is equilateral but may not be equiangular.

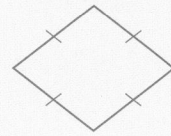

29b. Yes; a rectangle is equiangular but may not be equilateral.

30. Many designs contain patterns formed by using shapes such as quadrilaterals. Answers should include the following.

  • Sample answer: Many quilt designs contain quadrilaterals. One such example is shown.

  • The quadrilaterals used are trapezoids, squares, and parallelograms.

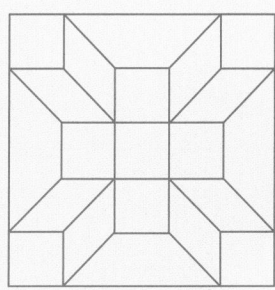

---

4 Assess

Open-Ended Assessment

Modeling Have students use sticks or pipe cleaners to form different quadrilaterals. They can use pieces of yarn to mark any congruent angles or sides.

Getting Ready for Lesson 10-5

PREREQUISITE SKILL In Lesson 10-5, students find the areas of two-dimensional figures. This requires multiplying measures, some of which may be decimals. Exercises 37–40 should be used to determine your students' familiarity with multiplying decimals.

Assessment Options

Practice Quiz 1 The quiz provides students with a brief review of the concepts and skills in Lessons 10-1 through 10-4. Lesson numbers are given to the right of exercises or instruction lines so students can review concepts not yet mastered.

Quiz (Lessons 10-3 and 10-4) is available on p. 603 of the *Chapter 10 Resource Masters*.

Mid-Chapter Test (Lessons 10-1 through 10-4) is available on p. 605 of the *Chapter 10 Resource Masters*.

Answer

33.

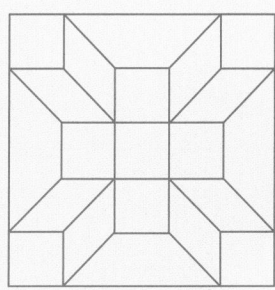

A Preview of Lesson 10-5

Getting Started

Objective Use geoboards to find the area of figures.

Materials
geoboards
geobands

Teaching Tip Have students practice making different-sized figures before starting the exercises.

Teach

- If you don't have geoboards, you can use dot paper or graph paper.
- Discuss with students if they can generalize from Activity 2 how to develop an equation for finding the area of a triangle.

Area and Geoboards

Activity 1

One square on a geoboard has an area of one square unit.

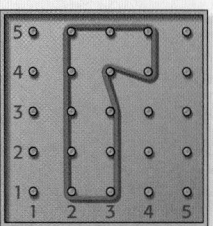 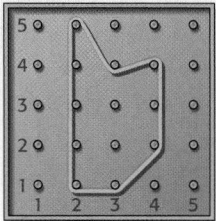 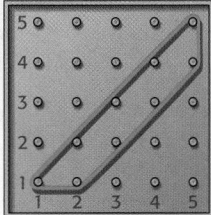

The area is about
5 square units.

The area is about
6 square units.

The area is
3.5 square units.

Model and Analyze 1. 11 sq units   2. about 4 sq units   3. about 5.5 sq units

Find the area of each figure. Estimate, if necessary.

1. 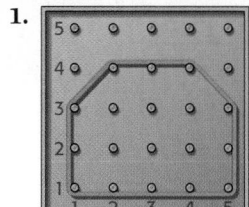 2. 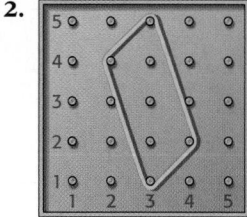 3.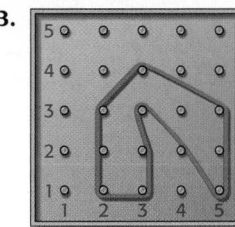

4. Explain how you found the area of each figure in Exercises 1–3.

5. Make a figure on the geoboard. Ask a classmate to find the area of the figure. **See students' work**
   4. Sample answer: count whole-squares and half-squares.

Activity 2

The following example shows how to find the area of a right triangle on a geoboard.

Step 1 First, make another triangle so that the two triangles form a rectangle.

Step 2 Then find the area of the rectangle.

Step 3 Next, divide by 2 to find the area of each triangle.
The area of the rectangle is 6 square units. So, the area of each triangle is 3 square units.

518 **Chapter 10** Two-Dimensional Figures

Resource Manager

📁 *Teaching Pre-Algebra with Manipulatives*
- p. 132 (student recording sheet)

Glencoe Mathematics Classroom Manipulative Kit
- geoboards
- geobands

Model and Analyze 9–10. See students' work.
Find the area of each triangle. 6. 3 sq units   7. 6 sq units   8. 4 sq units

6. 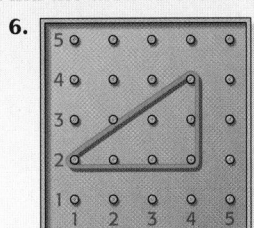   **7.** 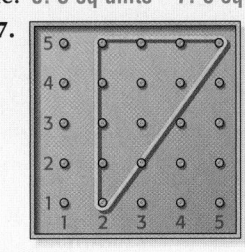   **8.**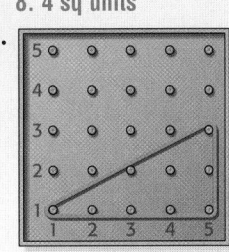

9. Make a right triangle on your geoboard. Find its area using this method.

10. Write a few sentences explaining how you found the area of the triangle.

Activity 3

Another way to find the area of a figure on a geoboard is to build a rectangle around the figure. Consider the following example.

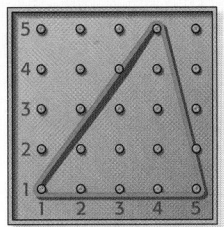

Step 1 Make the triangle shown on a geoboard.

Step 2 Build a rectangle around the triangle.

Step 3 Subtract to find the area of the original triangle.

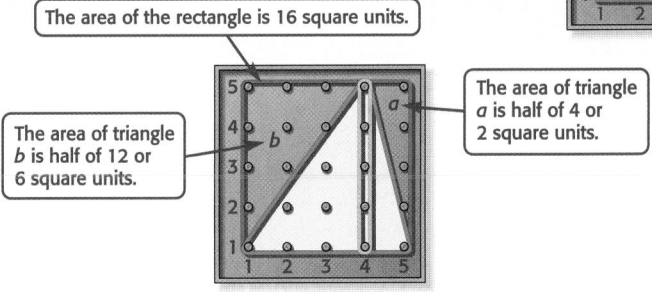

The area of the rectangle is 16 square units.

The area of triangle *a* is half of 4 or 2 square units.

The area of triangle *b* is half of 12 or 6 square units.

The area of the original triangle is 16 − 2 − 6 or 8 square units.

Model and Analyze 11. 4.5 sq units   12. 6 sq units   13. 4 sq units
Find the area of each figure by building a rectangle around the figure.

11. 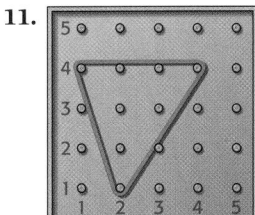   **12.** 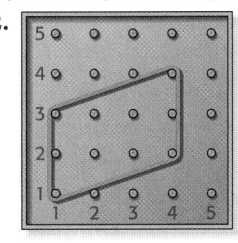   **13.**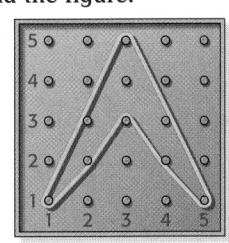

14. Make a figure on your geoboard. Find the area using this method. **See students' work.**

Algebra Activity Area and Geoboards **519**

In **Exercises 1–5,** students should count squares to find the area of the figure.

In **Exercises 6–10,** students use a rectangle to find the area of a right triangle.

In **Exercises 11–14,** build a rectangle and subtract to find the area of the figure.

Study Notebook

You may wish to have students summarize this activity and what they learned from it.

10-5 **Area: Parallelograms, Triangles, and Trapezoids**

1 Focus

5-Minute Check
Transparency 10-5 Use as a quiz or review of Lesson 10-4.

Mathematical Background
notes are available for this lesson on page 490D.

How is the area of a parallelogram related to the area of a rectangle?

The opening activity questions are repeated on page 572 of the *Chapter 10 Resource Masters*.

Reading to Learn Mathematics, p. 572   ELL

Pre-Activity	*How is the area of a parallelogram related to the area of a rectangle?*
	Do the activity at the top of page 520 in your textbook. Write your answers below.
	a. What figure is formed? parallelogram
	b. Compare the area of the rectangle to the area of the parallelogram. They are the same.
	c. What parts of a rectangle and parallelogram determine their area? height and base

Reading the Lesson   1–2. See students' work.
Write a definition and give an example of each new vocabulary word.

Vocabulary	Definition	Example
1. base		
2. altitude		

Helping You Remember

3. Below are three figures and three formulas for finding area. Match the formula with the correct figure and find its area.

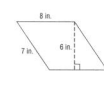

$A = \frac{1}{2}h(a + b)$ $A = bh$ $A = \frac{1}{2}bh$

Formula: $A = \frac{1}{2}bh$ Formula: $A = bh$ Formula: $A = \frac{1}{2}h(a + b)$
Area: 52.5 cm²   Area: 48 in²   Area: 45.5 ft²

Teaching Tip Show students the similarities and differences between trapezoids and parallelograms.

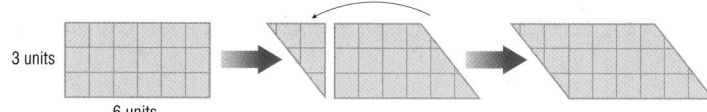

What You'll Learn

- Find area of parallelograms.
- Find the areas of triangles and trapezoids.

Vocabulary
- base
- altitude

How is the area of a parallelogram related to the area of a rectangle?

The area of a rectangle can be found by multiplying the length and width. The rectangle shown below has an area of 3×6 or 18 square units.

Suppose a triangle is cut from one side of the rectangle and moved to the other side. **b. They are the same.   c. height and base**

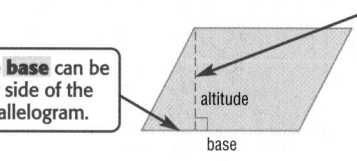

3 units

6 units

a. What figure is formed? **parallelogram**

b. Compare the area of the rectangle to the area of the parallelogram.

c. What parts of a rectangle and parallelogram determine their area?

AREAS OF PARALLELOGRAMS   The area of a parallelogram can be found by multiplying the measures of the base and the height.

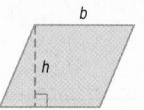

The **base** can be any side of the parallelogram.

altitude

base

The *height* is the length of an **altitude**, a line segment perpendicular to the bases with endpoints on the base and the side opposite the base.

Key Concept   Area of a Parallelogram

- **Words**   If a parallelogram has a base of b units and a height of h units, then the area A is bh square units.

- **Symbols** $A = bh$

- **Model**

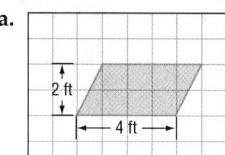

Example 1   Find Areas of Parallelograms

Find the area of each parallelogram.

a.

2 ft

4 ft

The base is 4 feet. The height is 2 feet.

$A = bh$ Area of a parallelogram
$A = 4 \cdot 2$ Replace b with 4 and h with 2.
$A = 8$ Multiply.

The area is 8 square feet.

Resource Manager

📂 Workbooks and Reproducible Masters

Chapter 10 Resource Masters
- Study Guide and Intervention, p. 569
- Skills Practice, p. 570
- Practice, p. 571
- Reading to Learn Mathematics, p. 572
- Enrichment, p. 573

Graphing Calculator and Spreadsheet Masters, p. 38
Parent and Student Study Guide Workbook, p. 85
School-to-Career Masters, p. 19

📺 Transparencies
5-Minute Check Transparency 10-5
Answer Key Transparencies

💿 Technology
Interactive Chalkboard

b.

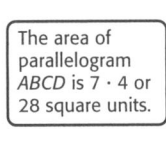

The base is 5.9 centimeters. The height is 7.5 centimeters.

$A = bh$ Area of a parallelogram

$A = (5.9)(7.5)$ Replace b with 5.9 and h with 7.5.

$A = 44.25$ Multiply.

The area is 44.25 square centimeters.

AREA OF TRIANGLES AND TRAPEZOIDS   A diagonal of a parallelogram separates the parallelogram into two congruent triangles. The area of each triangle is one-half the area of the parallelogram.

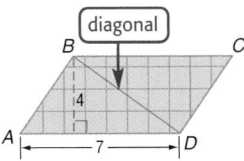

The area of parallelogram *ABCD* is 7 · 4 or 28 square units.

The area of triangle *ABD* is $\frac{1}{2}$ · 28 or 14 square units.

Using the formula for the area of a parallelogram, we can find the formula for the area of a triangle.

> **Key Concept**   *Area of a Triangle*
>
> - **Words**   If a triangle has a base of b units and a height of h units, then the area A is $\frac{1}{2}bh$ square units.
>
> - **Symbols** $A = \frac{1}{2}bh$ • **Model**
>
>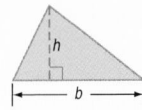

✓ **Concept Check**   The area of a triangle is one half of the area of what figure with the same height and base? **parallelogram**

As with parallelograms, any side of a triangle can be used as a base. The height is the length of a corresponding altitude.

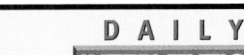

Study Tip

Altitudes
An altitude can be outside the triangle.

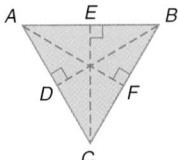

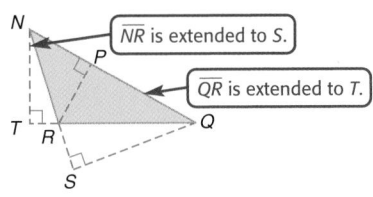

$\overline{NR}$ is extended to S.

$\overline{QR}$ is extended to T.

base	$\overline{AC}$	$\overline{AB}$	$\overline{BC}$
altitude	$\overline{BD}$	$\overline{CE}$	$\overline{AF}$

base	$\overline{NQ}$	$\overline{NR}$	$\overline{QR}$
altitude	$\overline{RP}$	$\overline{QS}$	$\overline{NT}$

✓ **Concept Check**   Which side of a triangle can be used as the base? **any side**

Building on Prior Knowledge

In Lesson 5-7, students learned to add mixed numbers. In this lesson, students will add mixed numbers when calculating the area of a trapezoid.

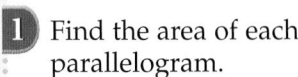

2 Teach

AREAS OF PARALLELOGRAMS

In-Class Example   Power Point®

1   Find the area of each parallelogram.

a.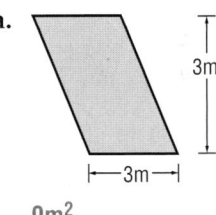

$9m^2$

b.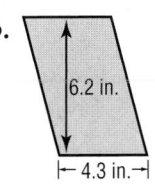

26.66 in^2

Teaching Tip   Make sure students include the correct units with their answers.

DAILY

| **INTERVENTION** |

Differentiated Instruction

- **Kinesthetic**   Have students model a rectangle on grid paper using toothpicks with a small amount of modeling clay at the vertices. Have them determine the area of the figure. Then modify the rectangle to form a parallelogram with the same side lengths. Determine the area of the figure. Repeat for other sizes of rectangles.

AREAS OF TRIANGLES AND TRAPEZOIDS

2 Find the area of each triangle.

a.
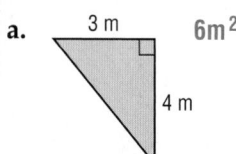
3 m
4 m
6 m²

b.
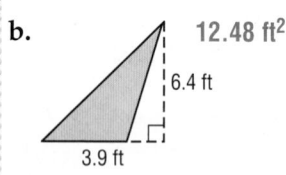
12.48 ft²
6.4 ft
3.9 ft

3 Find the area of the trapezoid. **$38\frac{1}{4}$ m²**

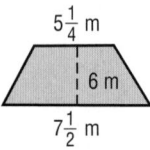
$5\frac{1}{4}$ m
6 m
$7\frac{1}{2}$ m

4 **PAINTING** A wall that needs to be painted is 16 feet wide and 9 feet tall. There is a doorway that is 3 feet by 8 feet and a window that is 6 feet by $5\frac{1}{2}$ feet. What is the area to be painted?
87 ft²

Teaching Tip If students are having trouble understanding the formula for the area of a trapezoid, have them try the following exercise. Ask them to draw a trapezoid on a piece of paper and cut it out. They should then cut the trapezoid horizontally in half. Next, cut a right triangle from one end of the upper half of the trapezoid. Now, students should arrange the three pieces into a long rectangle whose area is $\frac{1}{2}h(b_1 + b_2)$.

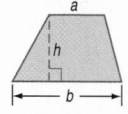
cut here
h
$\frac{1}{2}h$
b_1
$b_1 + b_2$

Study Tip

Alternative Method
Multiplication is commutative and associative. So you can also find $\frac{1}{2}$ of 6 first and then multiply by 5.

Example 2 *Find Areas of Triangles*

Find the area of each triangle.

a.
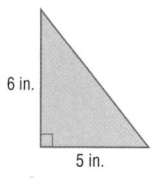
6 in.
5 in.

The base is 5 inches. The height is 6 inches.

$A = \frac{1}{2}bh$	Area of a triangle
$A = \frac{1}{2}(5)(6)$	Replace b with 5 and h with 6.
$A = \frac{1}{2}(30)$	Multiply. $5 \times 6 = 30$
$A = 15$	The area of the triangle is 15 square inches.

b.
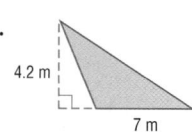
4.2 m
7 m

The base is 7 meters. The height is 4.2 meters.

$A = \frac{1}{2}bh$	Area of a triangle
$A = \frac{1}{2}(7)(4.2)$	Replace b with 7 and h with 4.2.
$A = \frac{1}{2}(29.4)$	Multiply. $7 \times 4.2 = 29.4$
$A = 14.7$	The area of the triangle is 14.7 square meters.

A trapezoid has two bases. The height of a trapezoid is the distance between the bases. A trapezoid can be separated into two triangles.

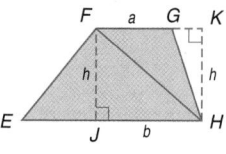

The triangles are $\triangle FGH$ and $\triangle EFH$.
The measure of a base of $\triangle FGH$ is a units.
The measure of a base of $\triangle EFH$ is b units.
The altitudes of the triangles, $\overline{FJ}$ and $\overline{HK}$, are congruent. Both are h units long.

$$\text{area of trapezoid } EFGH = \underbrace{\text{area of } \triangle FGH}_{} + \underbrace{\text{area of } \triangle EFH}_{}$$
$$= \underbrace{\frac{1}{2}ah}_{} + \underbrace{\frac{1}{2}bh}_{}$$
$$= \frac{1}{2}h(a + b) \quad \text{Distributive Property}$$

Key Concept
Area of a Trapezoid

- **Words** If a trapezoid has bases of a units and b units and a height of h units, then the area A of the trapezoid is $\frac{1}{2}h(a + b)$ square units.

- **Symbols** $A = \frac{1}{2}h(a + b)$

- **Model**
a
h
b

Example 3 *Find Area of a Trapezoid*

Find the area of the trapezoid.

The height is 4 inches.

The bases are $6\frac{1}{2}$ inches and $3\frac{1}{4}$ inches.

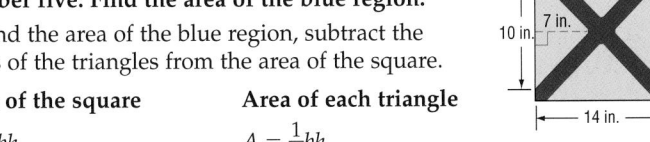

$A = \frac{1}{2}h(a + b)$ Area of a trapezoid

$A = \frac{1}{2} \cdot 4\left(6\frac{1}{2} + 3\frac{1}{4}\right)$ Replace h with 4, a with $6\frac{1}{2}$ and b with $3\frac{1}{4}$.

$A = \frac{1}{2} \cdot 4 \cdot 9\frac{3}{4}$ $6\frac{1}{2} + 3\frac{1}{4} = 9\frac{3}{4}$

$A = \frac{1}{2} \cdot \frac{\cancel{4}}{1} \cdot \frac{39}{\cancel{4}}$ Divide out the common factors.

$A = \frac{39}{2}$ or $19\frac{1}{2}$ The area of the trapezoid is $19\frac{1}{2}$ square inches.

Study Tip

Look Back
To review **multiplying fractions**, see Lesson 5-3.

Example 4 *Use Area to Solve a Problem*

FLAGS The signal flag shown represents the number five. Find the area of the blue region.

To find the area of the blue region, subtract the areas of the triangles from the area of the square.

Area of the square	Area of each triangle
$A = bh$	$A = \frac{1}{2}bh$
$A = 14 \cdot 14$	$A = \frac{1}{2} \cdot 10 \cdot 7$
$A = 196$	$A = 35$ $\frac{1}{2} \cdot 10 = 5, 5 \cdot 7 = 35$

The total area of the triangles is 4(35) or 140 square inches. So, the area of the blue region is 196 − 140 or 56 square inches.

Check for Understanding

Concept Check
1. **OPEN ENDED** Draw and label a parallelogram that has an area of 24 square inches. **1–2. See margin.**

2. **Define** an *altitude* of a triangle and draw an example.

Guided Practice

Find the area of each figure.

GUIDED PRACTICE KEY	
Exercises	Examples
3–5	1–3
6	4

3. **8 ft²**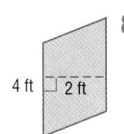

4. **8.1 cm²**

5. 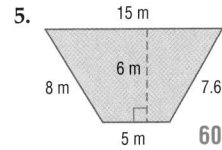 **60 m²**

Application
6. **FLAGS** The flag shown at the right is the international signal for the number three. Find the area of the red region. **48 in²**

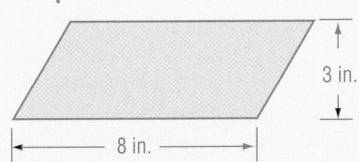

Answers

1. **Sample answer:**

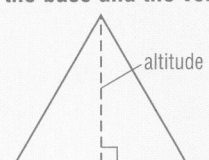

2. The altitude of a triangle is a line segment perpendicular to the base with endpoints on the base and the vertex opposite the base.

---

3 Practice/Apply

Study Notebook

Have students—
• add the definitions/examples of the vocabulary terms to their Vocabulary Builder worksheets for Chapter 10.
• include an example of each figure and how to determine its area.
• include any other item(s) that they find helpful in mastering the skills in this lesson.

About the Exercises . . .

Organization by Objective
• Areas of Parallelograms: 7, 8, 15, 18, 19, 21, 23, 24, 26
• Areas of Triangles and Trapezoids: 9–14, 16–17, 20–24, 27–29

Odd/Even Assignments
Exercises 7–20 are structured so that students practice the same concepts whether they are assigned odd or even problems.

Alert! Exercise 36 requires graph paper.

Assignment Guide
Basic: 7–19 odd, 27, 30–43
Average: 7–23 odd, 24, 25, 27, 29, 30–43
Advanced: 8–22 even, 24–26, 28, 30–39 (Optional: 40–43)

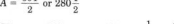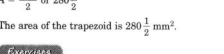
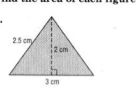 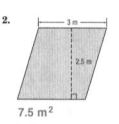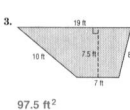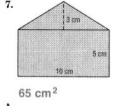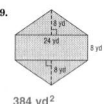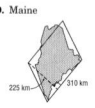
 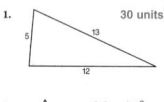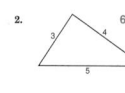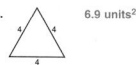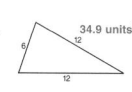
★ indicates increased difficulty

Practice and Apply

Find the area of each figure.

7. 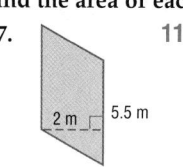   **11 m²**   8. 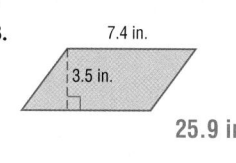   **25.9 in²**   9. 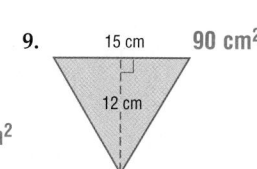   **90 cm²**

10. **21.6 in²** 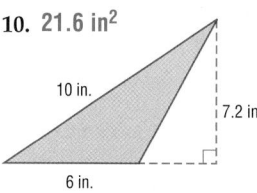   11. 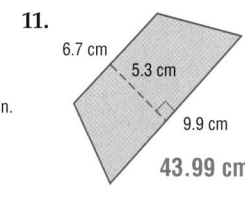   **43.99 cm²**   12. 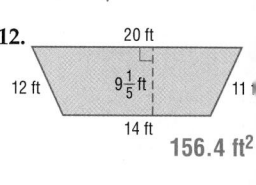   **156.4 ft²**

Find the area of each figure described.

13. triangle: base, 8 in.; height, 7 in. **28 in²**

14. trapezoid: height, 2 cm; bases, 3 cm, 6 cm **9 cm²**

15. parallelogram: base, 3.8 yd; height, 6 yd **22.8 yd²**

16. triangle: base, 9 ft; height, 3.2 ft **14.4 ft²**

17. trapezoid: height, 3.5 m; bases, 10 m and 11 m **36.75 m²**

18. parallelogram: base, 5.6 km; height, 4.5 km **25.2 km²**

···• **GEOGRAPHY** For Exercises 19 and 20, use the approximate measurements to estimate the area of each state.

19. 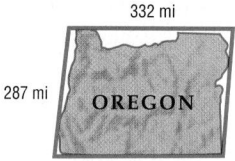   **about 95,284 mi²**   20. 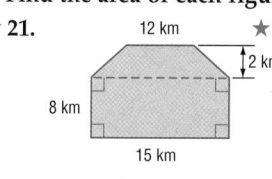   **about 51,113 mi²**

Find the area of each figure.

★ 21. **147 km²**   ★ 22. **48 m²**   ★ 23. 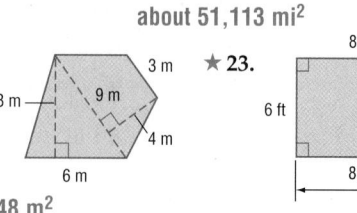   **57 ft²**

★ **LAWNCARE** For Exercises 24 and 25, use the diagram shown and the following information.
Mrs. Malone plans to fertilize her lawn. The fertilizer she will be using indicates that one bag fertilizes 2000 square feet.

24. Find the area of the lawn. **9270 ft²**

25. How many bags of fertilizer should she buy? **5 bags**

Answers (p. 525)

30. $A = \frac{1}{2}h(a + b)$; In a triangle, one "base" = 0, so $A = \frac{1}{2}h(0 + b)$, then $A = \frac{1}{2}hb$ or $A = \frac{1}{2}bh$. In a parallelogram, the bases are congruent so $a = b$. Thus, $A = \frac{1}{2}h(b + b)$ or $A = \frac{1}{2}h(2b)$, then $A = bh$.

31. The area of a parallelogram is found by multiplying the base and the height of the parallelogram. The area of a rectangle is found by multiplying the length and the width of the rectangle. Since in a parallelogram, the base is the length of the parallelogram, and the height is the width of the parallelogram, both

26. Find the base of a parallelogram with a height of 9.2 meters and an area of 36.8 square meters. **4 m**

27. Suppose a triangle has an area of 20 square inches and a base of 2.5 inches. What is the measure of the height? **16 in.**

28. A trapezoid has an area of 54 square feet. What is the measure of the height if the bases measure 16 feet and 8 feet? **4.5 ft**

★ **29. REAL ESTATE** The McLaughlins plan to build a house on the lot shown. If an acre is 43,560 square feet, what percent of an acre is the land? **24.5%**

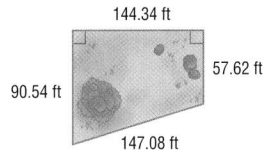

144.34 ft
57.62 ft
90.54 ft
147.08 ft

30. CRITICAL THINKING Explain how the formula for the area of a trapezoid can be used to find the formulas for the areas of parallelograms and triangles. **See margin.**

31. WRITING IN MATH Answer the question that was posed at the beginning of the lesson. **See margin.**

How is the area of a parallelogram related to the area of a rectangle?

Include the following in your answer:

• an explanation telling the similarities and differences between a rectangle and a parallelogram, and

• a diagram that shows how the area of a parallelogram is related to the area of a rectangle.

Standardized Test Practice
Ⓐ Ⓑ Ⓒ Ⓓ

32. Which figure does *not* have an area of 48 square meters? **C**

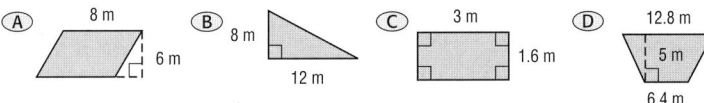

Ⓐ 8 m / 6 m   Ⓑ 8 m / 12 m   Ⓒ 3 m / 1.6 m   Ⓓ 12.8 m / 5 m / 6.4 m

33. Square X has an area of 9 square feet. The sides of square Y are twice as long as the sides of square X. Find the area of square Y. **B**

Ⓐ 18 ft² 　 Ⓑ 36 ft² 　 Ⓒ 9 ft² 　 Ⓓ 6 ft²

Maintain Your Skills

Mixed Review **Find the value of x. Then find the missing angle measures.** *(Lesson 10-4)*

34. 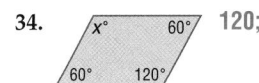 **120; 120°**

x° 60°
60° 120°

35. **24; 24°; 96°**

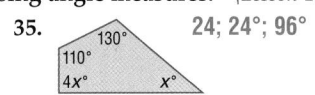

130°
110°
4x°　x°

36. Triangle MNP has vertices M(−1, 1), N(5, 4), and P(4, 1). Graph the image of △MNP after a translation 3 units left and 4 units down. *(Lesson 10-3)* **See margin.**

Find the percent of each number mentally. *(Lesson 6-6)*

37. 25% of 120 **30** 　　 **38.** 75% of 160 **120** 　　 **39.** 40% of 65 **26**

Getting Ready for the Next Lesson **PREREQUISITE SKILL** **Simplify each expression.**
(To review order of operations, see Lesson 1-2).

40. (5 − 2)180 **540** 　 **41.** (7 − 2)180 **900** 　 **42.** (10 − 2)180 **1440** 　 **43.** (9 − 2)180 **1260**

4 Assess

Open-Ended Assessment

Writing Have students write an exercise that has to be solved using area. They should then trade exercises with a partner and solve.

Getting Ready for Lesson 10-6

PREREQUISITE SKILL Lesson 10-6 presents polygons. To find the measure of the interior angles of a polygon requires evaluating a formula that involves multiple operations. Exercises 40–43 should be used to determine your students' familiarity with order of operations.

Answer

36.

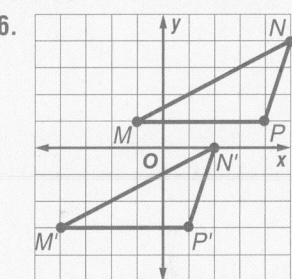

(bottom margin)

areas are found by multiplying the length and the width. Answers should include the following.

• Parallelograms and rectangles are similar in that they are quadrilaterals with opposite sides parallel and opposite sides congruent. They are different in that rectangles always have 4 right angles.

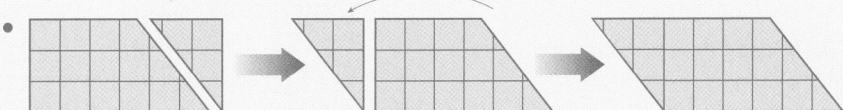

Reading Mathematics

Getting Started

Show students pictures of a bicycle, biped, tripod, quad-runner (four wheel bike), the Pentagon, and an octopus. Discuss where the names came from and how they describe the objects.

Teach

Word Origins Explain to students that you often can tell what a word means by breaking it down into parts. Use the word *equiangular* as an example. By dividing the word into *equi-* (equal) and *angular,* students can see that it refers to something with equal angles.

Assess

Study Notebook

Ask students to write a familiar word for each prefix that will help them remember what the prefix means.

ELL English Language Learners may benefit from writing key concepts from this activity in their Study Notebooks in their native language and then in English.

Learning Mathematics Prefixes

The table shows some of the prefixes that are used in mathematics. These prefixes are also used in everyday language. In order to use each prefix correctly, you need to understand its meaning.

Prefix	Meaning	Everyday Words	Meaning
quad-	four	quadrennial quadruple quadruplet quadriceps	happening every four years a sum four times as great as another one of four offspring born at one birth a muscle with four points of origin
pent-	five	Pentagon pentagram pentathlon pentad	headquarters of the Department of Defense a five-pointed star a five-event athletic contest a group of five
hex-	six	hexapod hexagonal hexastich hexangular	having six feet having six sides a poem of six lines having six angles
hept-	seven	heptad heptagonal heptarchy heptastich	a group of seven having seven sides a government by seven rulers a poem of seven lines
oct-	eight	octopus octet octan octennial	a type of mollusk having eight arms a musical composition for eight instruments occurring every eight days lasting eight years
dec-	ten	decade decameter decathlon decare	a period of ten years ten meters a ten-event athletic contest a metric unit of area equal to 10 acres

Reading to Learn   1. See margin.

1. Refer to the table above. For each prefix listed, choose one of the everyday words listed and write a sentence that contains the word.

2. **RESEARCH**   Use the Internet, a dictionary, or another reference source to find a mathematical term that contains each of the prefixes listed. Write the definition of each term. 2–3. See pp. 551A–551B

3. **RESEARCH**   Use the Internet, a dictionary, or another reference source to find a different word that contains each prefix. Then define the term.

526   Chapter 10   Two-Dimensional Figures

Answer

1. **Sample answer: quad:** A leap day is a quadrennial event.

    pent: Many military personnel work at the Pentagon.

    hex: An insect is an example of a hexapod.

    hept: Heptarchy was the name given to the seven kingdoms of England during the 7th and 8th centuries.

    oct: The giant octopus found in the Pacific Ocean may have a diameter greater than 30 feet.

    dec: Dan O'Brien is the current world record holder in the decathlon with 8891 points.

What You'll Learn

- Classify polygons.
- Determine the sum of the measures of the interior and exterior angles of a polygon.

Vocabulary
- polygon
- diagonal
- interior angles
- regular polygon

How are polygons used in tessellations?

The tiled patterns below are called *regular tessellations*. Notice how the figures repeat to form patterns that contain no gaps or overlaps.

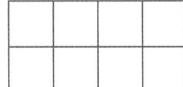  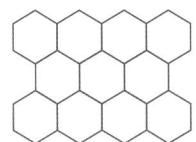

a. square, triangle, hexagon

a. Which figure is used to create each tessellation?

b. Refer to the diagram at the right. What is the sum of the measures of the angles that surround the vertex? **360**

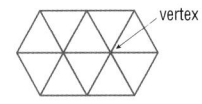
vertex

c. Yes; for each tessellation shown, the sum of the measures of the angles that surround a vertex is 360°.

c. Does the sum in part **b** hold true for the square tessellation? Explain.

d. Make a conjecture about the sum of the measures of the angles that surround a vertex in the hexagon tessellation. **The sum is 360°.**

CLASSIFY POLYGONS

A **polygon** is a simple, closed figure formed by three or more line segments. The figures below are examples of polygons.

The line segments meet only at their endpoints.

The line segments are called *sides*.

The points of intersection are called *vertices*.

The following figures are *not* polygons.

 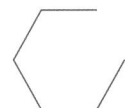 

This is not a polygon because it has a curved side.

This is not a polygon because it is an open figure.

This is not a polygon because the sides overlap.

Concept Check:
Sample answer:

☑ **Concept Check** Sketch a different figure that is *not* a polygon.

---

1 Focus

5-Minute Check Transparency 10-6 Use as a quiz or review of Lesson 10-5.

Mathematical Background notes are available for this lesson on page 490D.

How are polygons used in tessellations?

The opening activity questions are repeated on page 577 of the *Chapter 10 Resource Masters*.

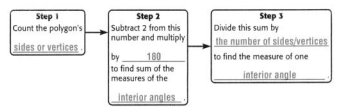

Reading to Learn Mathematics, p. 577 **ELL**

Pre-Activity How are polygons used in tessellations?

Do the activity at the top of page 527 in your textbook. Write your answers below.

a. Which figure is used to create each tessellation?
square, triangle, hexagon

b. Refer to the diagram in your textbook. What is the sum of the measures of the angles that surround the vertex? 360°

c. Does the sum in part **b** hold true for the square tessellation? Explain.
Yes; for each tessellation shown, the sum of the measures of the angles that surround a vertex is 360°.

d. Make a conjecture about the sum of the measures of the angles that surround a vertex in the hexagon tessellation. The sum is 360°.

Reading the Lesson 1–4. See students' work.

Write a definition and give an example of each new vocabulary word or phrase.

Vocabulary	Definition	Example
1. polygon		
2. diagonal		
3. interior angles		
4. regular polygon		

Helping You Remember

5. Complete the following concept map of how to find the sum of the measures of the interior angles of a regular polygon (all sides and angles are congruent) and how to find the measure of one interior angle.

Resource Manager

📁 **Workbooks and Reproducible Masters**

Chapter 10 Resource Masters
- Study Guide and Intervention, p. 574
- Skills Practice, p. 575
- Practice, p. 576
- Reading to Learn Mathematics, p. 577
- Enrichment, p. 578
- Assessment, p. 604

Parent and Student Study Guide Workbook, p. 86

🖥 **Transparencies**
5-Minute Check Transparency 10-6
Answer Key Transparencies

💿 **Technology**
Interactive Chalkboard

CLASSIFY POLYGONS

1 Classify each polygon.

a.

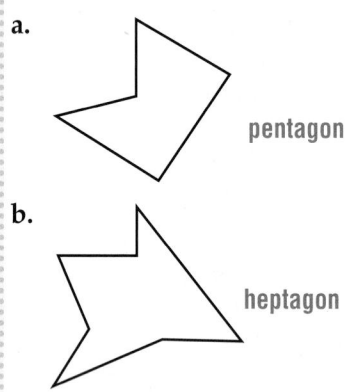

pentagon

b.

heptagon

MEASURES OF THE ANGLES OF A POLYGON

Teaching Tip You may want to give students copies of various polygons and ask them to determine the diagonals from one vertex and the number of triangles formed before presenting the information in the student text.

2 Find the sum of the measures of the interior angles of a quadrilateral. **360°**

Teaching Tip Remind students that the sum of the measures of the interior angles of a triangle is 180° (Chapter 9).

Study Tip

n-gon
A polygon with *n* sides is called an *n*-gon. For example, an octagon can also be called an 8-gon.

Polygons can be classified by the number of sides they have.

Number of Sides	Name of Polygon	Number of Sides	Name of Polygon
3	triangle	7	heptagon
4	quadrilateral	8	octagon
5	pentagon	9	nonagon
6	hexagon	10	decagon

Example 1 *Classify Polygons*

Classify each polygon.

a.

The polygon has 8 sides. It is an octagon.

b.

The polygon has 6 sides. It is a hexagon.

MEASURES OF THE ANGLES OF A POLYGON A **diagonal** is a line segment in a polygon that joins two nonconsecutive vertices. In the diagram below, all possible diagonals from one vertex are shown.

quadrilateral   pentagon   hexagon   heptagon   octagon

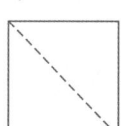 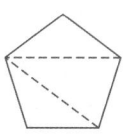 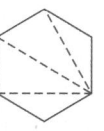 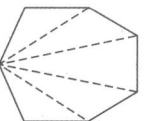 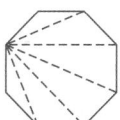

	Quadrilateral	Pentagon	Hexagon	Heptagon	Octagon
Sides	4	5	6	7	8
Diagonals	1	2	3	4	5
Triangles	2	3	4	5	6

Notice that the number of triangles is 2 less than the number of sides.

You can use the property of the sum of the measures of the angles of a triangle to find the sum of the measures of the interior angles of any polygon. An **interior angle** is an angle inside a polygon.

Key Concept   *Interior Angles of a Polygon*

If a polygon has *n* sides, then $n - 2$ triangles are formed. The sum of the degree measures of the interior angles of the polygon is $(n - 2)180$.

Example 2 *Measures of Interior Angles*

Find the sum of the measures of the interior angles of a heptagon.

A heptagon has 7 sides. Therefore, $n = 7$.

$(n - 2)180 = (7 - 2)180$ Replace *n* with 7.

$\quad\quad\quad\quad = 5(180)$ or 900 Simplify.

The sum of the measures of the interior angles of a heptagon is 900°.

D A I L Y
INTERVENTION   **Differentiated Instruction**

• **Visual/Spatial** Have students design their own tessellations. Encourage them to use a variety of regular polygons. Then have them cut the shapes out of colored paper and adhere them to a backing to make a mosaic. Students should include descriptions of the polygons they used in their tessellations.

A **regular polygon** is a polygon that is *equilateral* (all sides are congruent) and *equiangular* (all angles are congruent). Since the angles of a regular polygon are congruent, their measures are equal.

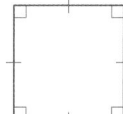 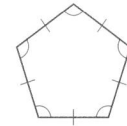 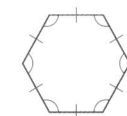 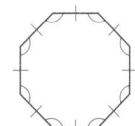

More About . . .

•Snow •

nowflakes are also called
now crystals. It is said
at no two snowflakes
re alike. They differ from
ach other in size, lacy
ructure, and surface
arkings.
ource: www.infoplease.com

Example 3 Find Angle Measure of a Regular Polygon

SNOW Snowflakes are some of the most beautiful objects in nature. Notice how they are regular and hexagonal in shape. What is the measure of one interior angle in a snowflake?

Step 1 Find the sum of the measures of the angles.

A hexagon has 6 sides. Therefore, $n = 6$.

$(n - 2)180 = (6 - 2)180$ Replace n with 6.

$= 4(180)$ or 720 Simplify.

The sum of the measures of the interior angles is 720°.

Step 2 Divide the sum by 6 to find the measure of one angle.

$720 \div 6 = 120$

So, the measure of one interior angle in a snowflake is 120°.

Check for Understanding

Concept Check
–3. See margin.

1. **OPEN ENDED** Draw a polygon that is both equiangular and equilateral.

2. **Draw** examples of a pentagon, hexagon, heptagon, octagon, nonagon, and decagon.

3. **Explain** the relationship between the number of sides in a polygon and the number of triangles formed by each of the diagonals.

Guided Practice

Classify each polygon. Then determine whether it appears to be *regular* or *not regular*.

GUIDED PRACTICE KEY	
Exercises	Examples
4, 5, 8	1
6	2
7	3

4.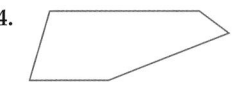

pentagon; not regular

5. 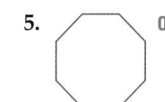   octagon; regular

6. Find the sum of the measures of the interior angles of a nonagon. **1260°**

7. What is the measure of each interior angle of a regular heptagon? Round to the nearest tenth. **128.6°**

Application

8. **TESSELLATIONS** Identify the polygons that are used to create the tessellation shown at the right. **square, hexagon, 12-gon**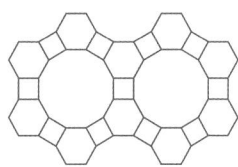

www.pre-alg.com/extra_examples

Answers

1.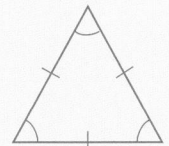

2. **Answers may vary. See students' work.**

3. **The number of triangles is 2 less than the number of sides.**

3 **TRAFFIC SIGNS** A stop sign is a regular octagon. What is the measure of one interior angle in a stop sign? **135°**

3 Practice/Apply

Study Notebook

Have students—

• add the definitions/examples of the vocabulary terms to their Vocabulary Builder worksheets for Chapter 10.

• draw six different polygons, showing how each one can be divided into n–2 triangles.

• include any other item(s) that they find helpful in mastering the skills in this lesson.

About the Exercises . . .

Organization by Objective
• Classify Polygons: 9–14, 21, 29, 30
• **Measures of the Angles of a Polygon:** 15–20, 23–28

Odd/Even Assignments
Exercises 9–20, 23–30, and 32–33 are structured so that students practice the same concepts whether they are assigned odd or even problems.

Alert! Exercise 22 requires research on the Internet or another source. Exercises 50–53 require a scientific calculator.

Assignment Guide

Basic: 9–17 odd, 21–25 odd, 29, 33–37, 44–53

Average: 9–33 odd, 34–37, 44–53 (Optional: 38–43)

Advanced: 10–32 even, 34–49 (Optional: 50–53)

Lesson 10-6 Polygons **529**

Study Guide and Intervention, p. 574

A **polygon** is a simple, closed figure formed by three or more line segments. The line segments, called *sides*, meet only at their endpoints. The points of intersection are called *vertices*. Polygons can be classified by the number of sides they have.

A **diagonal** is a line segment in a polygon that joins two nonconsecutive vertices, forming triangles. You can use the property of the sum of the measures of the angles of a triangle to find the sum of the measures of the interior angles of any polygon. An **interior angle** is an angle inside a polygon.

Number of Sides	Name of Polygon
3	triangle
4	quadrilateral
5	pentagon
6	hexagon
7	heptagon
8	octagon
9	nonagon
10	decagon

If a polygon has n sides, then $n - 2$ triangles are formed. The sum of the degree measures of the interior angles of the polygon is $(n - 2)180$.

A regular polygon is a polygon that is *equilateral* (all sides are congruent) and *equiangular* (all angles are congruent). Since the angles of a regular polygon are congruent, their measures are equal.

Example Find the measure of one interior angle of a regular 20-gon.

Step 1 A 20-gon has 20 sides. Therefore, $n = 20$.

$(n - 2)180 = (20 - 2)180$ Replace n with 20.

$= 18(180)$ or 3240 Simplify.

The sum of the measures of the interior angles is $3240°$.

Step 2 Divide the sum by 20 to find the measure of one angle.

$3240 \div 20 = 162$

So, the measure of one interior angle in a regular 20-gon is $162°$.

Exercises

Classify each polygon. Then determine whether it appears to be *regular* or *not regular*.

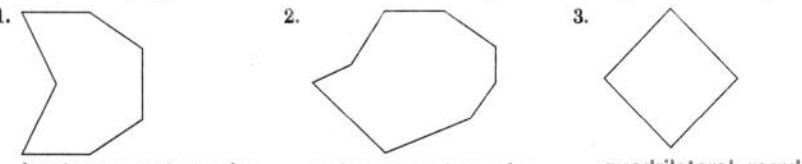

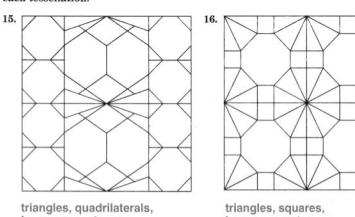

1. heptagon; not regular   2. octagon; not regular   3. quadrilateral; regular

Find the sum of the measures of the interior angles of each polygon.

4. quadrilateral 360°   5. nonagon 1260°   6. heptagon 900°   7. 12-gon 1800°

Skills Practice, p. 575 and Practice, p. 576 (shown)

Find the sum of the measures of the interior angles of each polygon.

1. quadrilateral 360°   2. decagon 1440°   3. 12-gon 1800°
4. heptagon 900°   5. pentagon 540°   6. hexagon 720°
7. 25-gon 4140°   8. 100-gon 17,640°

Find the measure of an interior angle of each polygon.

9. regular nonagon 140°   10. regular octagon 135°   11. regular hexagon 120°
12. regular 12-gon 150°   13. regular quadrilateral 90°   14. regular decagon 144°

TESSELLATIONS For Exercises 15 and 16, identify the polygons used to create each tessellation.

15. 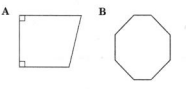   16.

triangles, quadrilaterals, hexagons, octagons

triangles, squares, hexagons, octagons

17. Which figure best represents a regular polygon? D

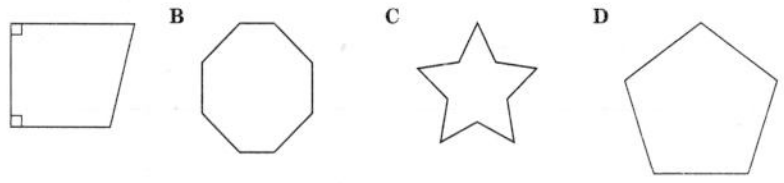

Enrichment, p. 578

Polygons and Diagonals

A **diagonal** of a polygon is any segment that connects two nonconsecutive vertices of the polygon. In each of the following polygons, all possible diagonals are drawn.

Examples

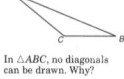
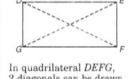
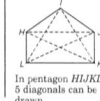

In $\triangle ABC$, no diagonals can be drawn. Why?

In quadrilateral *DEFG*, 2 diagonals can be drawn.

In pentagon *HIJKL*, 5 diagonals can be drawn.

Complete the chart below and try to find a pattern that will help you answer the questions that follow.

	Polygons	Number of Sides	Number of Diagonals From One Vertex	Total Number of Diagonals
	triangle	3	0	0
	quadrilateral	4	1	2
	pentagon	5	2	5
1.	hexagon	6	3	9
2.	heptagon	7	4	14
3.	octagon	8	5	20
4.	nonagon	9	6	27
5.	decagon	10	7	35

Find the total number of diagonals that can be drawn in a polygon with the given number of sides.

6. 6 9   7. 7 14   8. 8 20   9. 9 27
10. 10 35   11. 11 44   12. 12 54   13. 15 90
14. 20 170   15. 50 1175   16. 75 2700   17. n $\frac{n^2 - 3n}{2}$

530 Chapter 10 Two-Dimensional Figures

★ indicates increased difficulty

Practice and Apply

Homework Help

For Exercises	See Examples
9–14, 21 29, 30	1
15–20	2
23–28	3

Extra Practice See page 749.

Classify each polygon. Then determine whether it appears to be *regular* or *not regular*. 9–14. See margin.

9.    10. 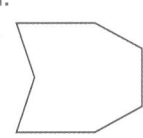   11.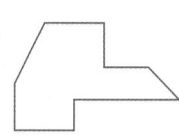

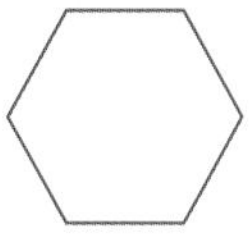

12. 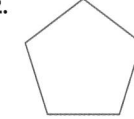   13.    14.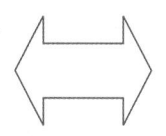

Find the sum of the measures of the interior angles of each polygon.

15. pentagon 540°   16. octagon 1080°   17. decagon 1440°
18. hexagon 720°   ★ 19. 18-gon 2880°   ★ 20. 23-gon 3780°

ART For Exercises 21 and 22, use the painting shown.

21. List five polygons used in the painting.

22. **RESEARCH** The title of the painting mentions the music symbol, *clef*. Use the Internet or another source to find a drawing of a clef. Is a clef a polygon? Explain.

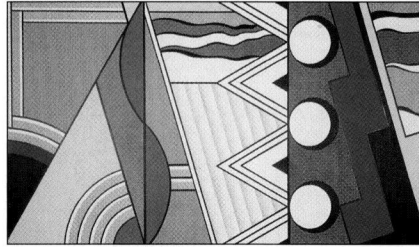

Roy Lichtenstein. *Modern Painting with Clef.* 1967

21. Sample answer: hexagon, triangle, decagon, quadrilateral, and pentagon

22. No, it is not a polygon since it has curved sides.

Find the measure of an interior angle of each polygon.

23. regular nonagon 140°   24. regular pentagon 108°   25. regular octagon 135
26. regular decagon 144°   ★ 27. regular 12-gon 150°   ★ 28. regular 25-gon 165.6°

TESSELLATIONS For Exercises 29 and 30, identify the polygons used to create each tessellation.

29. 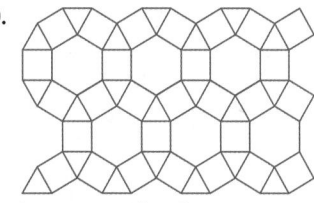   30.

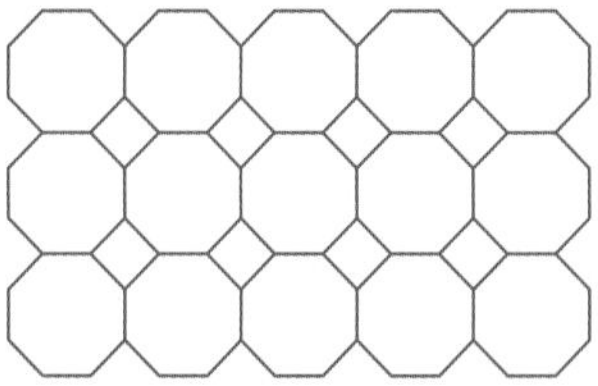

octagons, squares

hexagons, triangles, squares

★ 31. **ART** Refer to Exercise 8 on page 529. The tessellation design contains regular polygons. Find the perimeter of the design if the measure of the sides of the 12-gon is 5 centimeters. 180 cm

32. What is the perimeter of a regular pentagon with sides 4.2 feet long? 21 ft

33. Find the perimeter of a regular nonagon having sides $6\frac{1}{2}$ inches long. 58.5 in.

530 Chapter 10 Two-Dimensional Figures

Answers

9. hexagon; regular
10. heptagon; not regular
11. nonagon; not regular
12. pentagon; regular
13. decagon; not regular
14. decagon; not regular

34. CRITICAL THINKING Copy the dot pattern shown at the right. Then without lifting your pencil from the paper, draw four line segments that connect all of the points. **See margin.**

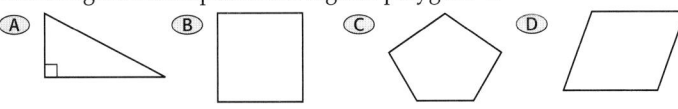

35. WRITING IN MATH Answer the question that was posed at the beginning of the lesson. **See margin.**

How are polygons used in tessellations?

Include the following in your answer:
- an example of a tessellation in which the pattern is formed using only one type of polygon, and
- an example of a tessellation in which the pattern is formed using more than one polygon.

Standardized Test Practice
Ⓐ Ⓑ Ⓒ Ⓓ

36. 60°

36. GRID IN The measure of one angle of a regular polygon with n sides is $\frac{180(n-2)}{n}$. What is the measure of an interior angle in a regular triangle?

37. Which figure best represents a regular polygon? **B**

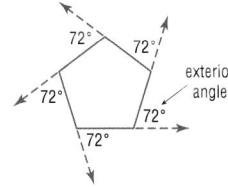

ⓐ   ⓑ   ⓒ   ⓓ

Extending the Lesson   **EXTERIOR ANGLES** When a side of a polygon is extended, an **exterior angle** is formed.

> In any polygon, the sum of the measures of the exterior angles, one at each vertex, is 360.

72° 72°
72° exterior angle
72°
72°

Find the measure of each exterior angle of each regular polygon.

38. regular octagon **45°**   **39.** regular triangle **120°**   **40.** regular nonagon **40°**

41. regular hexagon **60°**   **42.** regular decagon **36°**   **43.** regular 12-gon **30°**

Maintain Your Skills

Mixed Review   **Find the area of each figure described.** *(Lesson 10-5)*

44. triangle: base, 9 in.; height, 6 in. **27 in²**

45. trapezoid: height, 3 cm; bases, 4 cm, 8 cm **18 cm²**

Classify each quadrilateral using the name that *best* describes it. *(Lesson 10-4)*

46. rhombus   **47.** quadrilateral   **48.** rectangle

49. ALGEBRA Simplify $4.6x + 2.5x + 9.3x$. *(Lesson 3-2)* **16.4x**

Getting Ready for the Next Lesson   **PREREQUISITE SKILL** Use a calculator to find each product. Round to the nearest tenth. *(To review rounding decimals, see page 711.)*

50. $\pi \cdot 4.3$ **13.5**   **51.** $2 \cdot \pi \cdot 5.4$ **33.9**   **52.** $\pi \cdot 4^2$ **50.3**   **53.** $\pi(2.4)^2$ **18.1**

Open-Ended Assessment

Modeling Have students find examples of polygons in their homes. Have them bring pictures or sketches of the various objects to present to the class. Encourage students to be creative in recognizing polygons in common places.

Getting Ready for Lesson 10-7

PREREQUISITE SKILL Lesson 10-7 presents the formulas for circumference and area of a circle. These formulas involve π. Use Exercises 50–53 to determine your students' familiarity with evaluating expressions involving π.

Quiz (Lessons 10-5 and 10-6) is available on p. 604 of the *Chapter 10 Resource Masters*.

Sample Answers

34.

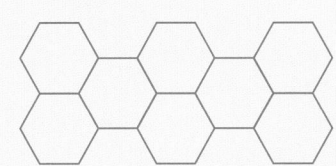

35. In tessellations, polygons are fit together to create a pattern such that there are no gaps or spaces. Answers should include the following.

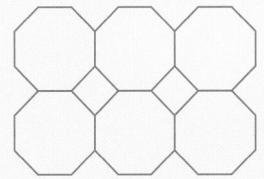

Getting Started

Objective Create tessellations using transformations.

Materials
While no special materials are needed for this activity, you may want students to use light cardboard to create each tessellation pattern unit for easier tracing.

Teaching Tip Students may want to cut figures out to make the tessellations. Have them cut out the section to be translated and tape it into position to create the pattern piece.

Teach

- Have students use colored pencils to keep track of the patterns.
- Show examples of artwork using tessellations, such as an Escher print.

Assess

In **Exercises 1–3**, students should practice making translations so that the tessellation has an even fit and discuss other pairs of figures that can be used to create tessellations.

In **Exercises 4–6**, students should make sure their rotations are done evenly so their tessellations maintain a consistent pattern.

Study Notebook

You may wish to have students summarize this activity and what they learned from it.

Algebra Activity

Tessellations

A tessellation is a pattern of repeating figures that fit together with no overlapping or empty spaces. Tessellations can be formed using transformations.

Activity 1   **Create a tessellation using a translation.**

Step 1   Draw a square. Then draw a triangle inside the top of the square as shown.

Step 2   Translate or slide the triangle from the top to the bottom of the square.

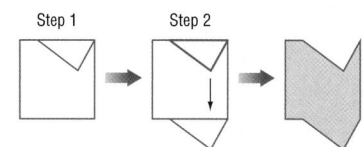

Step 3   Repeat this pattern unit to create a tessellation.

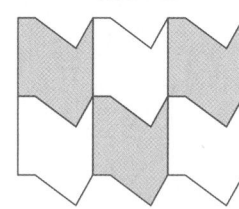

It is sometimes helpful to complete one pattern, cut it out, and trace it for the other pattern units.

Activity 2   **Create a tessellation using a rotation.**

Step 1   Draw an equilateral triangle. Then draw another triangle inside the left side of the triangle as shown below.

Step 2   Rotate the triangle so you can trace the change on the side as indicated.

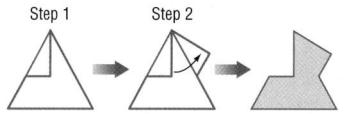

Step 3   Repeat this pattern unit to create a tessellation.

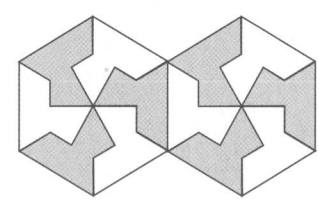

Model 1–6. See pp. 551A–551B.

Use a translation to create a tessellation for each pattern unit shown.

1. 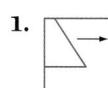   **2.**   **3.**

Use a rotation to create a tessellation for each pattern unit shown.

4. 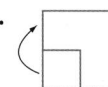   **5.**    **6.**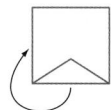

7. Make a tessellation that involves a translation, a rotation, or a combination of the two.
See students' work.

532 Chapter 10 Two-Dimensional Figures

Resource Manager

📁 **Teaching Pre-Algebra with Manipulatives**
- p. 135 (student recording sheet)

10-7 **Lesson Notes**

What You'll Learn

- Find circumference of circles.
- Find area of circles.

Vocabulary

- circle
- diameter
- center
- circumference
- radius
- π (pi)

a–b. See students' work.
c. The results are about 3.

How are circumference and diameter related?

Coins, paper plates, cookies, and CDs are all examples of objects that are circular in shape.

a. Collect three different-sized circular objects. Then copy the table shown.

b. Using a tape measure, measure each distance below to the nearest millimeter. Record your results.

- the distance across the circular object through its center (*d*)
- the distance around each circular object (*C*)

c. For each object, find the ratio $\frac{C}{d}$. Record the results in the table.

Object	*d*	*C*	$\frac{C}{d}$
1			
2			
3			

CIRCUMFERENCE OF CIRCLES
A **circle** is the set of all points in a plane that are the same distance from a given point.

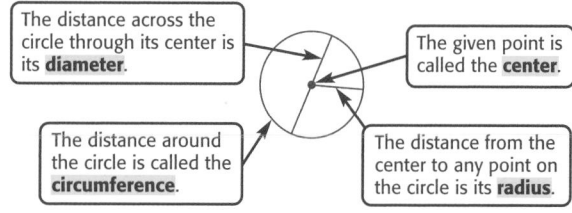

The distance across the circle through its center is its **diameter**.

The given point is called the **center**.

The distance around the circle is called the **circumference**.

The distance from the center to any point on the circle is its **radius**.

The relationship you discovered in the activity above is true for all circles. The ratio of the circumference of a circle to its diameter is always equal to 3.1415926… The Greek letter **π (pi)** stands for this number. Using this ratio, you can derive a formula for the circumference of a circle.

Study Tip

Although π is an irrational number, 3.14 and $\frac{22}{7}$ are generally accepted approximations for π.

$$\frac{C}{d} = \pi \qquad \text{The ratio of the circumference to the diameter equals pi.}$$

$$\frac{C}{d} \cdot d = \pi \cdot d \qquad \text{Multiply each side by } d.$$

$$C = \pi d \qquad \text{Simplify.}$$

Key Concept   *Circumference of a Circle*

- **Words** The circumference of a circle is equal to its diameter times π, or 2 times its radius times π.

- **Model**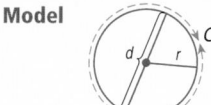

- **Symbols** $C = \pi d$ or $C = 2\pi r$

---

1 *Focus*

5-Minute Check Transparency 10-7 Use as a quiz or review of Lesson 10-6.

Mathematical Background notes are available for this lesson on page 490D.

How are circumference and diameter related?

The opening activity questions are repeated on page 582 of the *Chapter 10 Resource Masters*.

Reading to Learn Mathematics, p. 582 **ELL**

| Pre-Activity | *How are circumference and diameter related?* |

Do the activity at the top of page 533 in your textbook. Write your answers below.

a. Collect three different-sized circular objects. Then copy the table shown. **See students' work.**

b. Using a tape measure, measure each distance below to the nearest millimeter. Record your results.

- the distance across the circular object through its center (*d*)
- the distance around each circular object (*C*) **See students' work.**

c. For each object, find the ratio $\frac{C}{d}$. Record the results in the table. **The results are about 3.**

Reading the Lesson 1–6. See students' work.

Write a definition and give an example of each new vocabulary word.

Vocabulary	Definition	Example
1. circle		
2. diameter		
3. center		
4. circumference		
5. radius		
6. π (pi)		

Helping You Remember

7. Study the circle at the right, label each part, then find the circle's circumference and area (round to the nearest tenth).

formula for circumference: $C = \pi d$ or $2\pi r$

formula for area: $A = \pi r^2$

circumference: 15.7 cm

area: 19.6 cm²

Teaching Tip Remind students that pi is a constant, not a variable. Also remind them to use π on their calculator and round the answer after calculating.

Resource Manager

Workbooks and Reproducible Masters

Chapter 10 Resource Masters
- Study Guide and Intervention, p. 579
- Skills Practice, p. 580
- Practice, p. 581
- Reading to Learn Mathematics, p. 582
- Enrichment, p. 583

Parent and Student Study Guide Workbook, p. 87
School-to-Career Masters, p. 20

Transparencies

5-Minute Check Transparency 10-7
Answer Key Transparencies

Technology

Interactive Chalkboard
Multimedia Applications

2 Teach

CIRCUMFERENCE OF CIRCLES

1 Find the circumference of each circle to the nearest tenth.

a.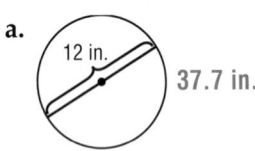

12 in. 37.7 in.

b.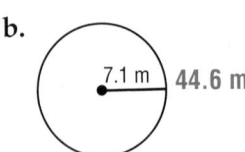

7.1 m 44.6 m

2 **LANDSCAPING** A landscaper has a tree whose roots form a ball-shaped bulb with a circumference of about 110 inches. How wide will the landscaper have to dig the hole in order to plant the tree? **at least 35 in.**

Teaching Tip Make sure students keep track of whether they are using the radius or diameter.

Study Tip

Calculating with π
Unless otherwise specified, use a calculator to evaluate expressions involving π and then follow any instructions regarding rounding.

Study Tip

Estimation
To estimate the circumference of a circle, multiply the diameter by 3.

✓ **Concept Check** Which term describes the distance from the center of a circle to any point on the circle? **radius**

Example 1 Find the Circumference of a Circle

Find the circumference of each circle to the nearest tenth.

a.

5 cm

$C = \pi d$ Circumference of a circle
$C = \pi \cdot 5$ Replace d with 5.
$C = 5\pi$ Simplify. This is the *exact* circumference.

To estimate the circumference, use a calculator.

5 ⊠ 2nd [π] ENTER 15.70796327

The circumference is about 15.7 centimeters.

b.

3.2 ft

$C = 2\pi r$ Circumference of a circle
$C = 2 \cdot \pi \cdot 3.2$ Replace r with 3.2.
$C \approx 20.1$ Simplify. Use a calculator.

The circumference is about 20.1 feet.

Many situations involve circumference and diameter of circles.

Example 2 Use Circumference to Solve a Problem

TREES A tree in Madison's yard was damaged in a storm. She wants to replace the tree with another whose trunk is the same size as the original tree. Suppose the circumference of the original tree was 14 inches. What should be the diameter of the replacement tree?

Explore You know the circumference of the original tree. You need to know the diameter of the new tree.

Plan Use the formula for the circumference of a circle to find the diameter.

Solve
$C = \pi d$ Circumference of a circle
$14 = \pi \cdot d$ Replace C with 14.
$\dfrac{14}{\pi} = d$ Divide each side by π.
$4.5 \approx d$ Simplify. Use a calculator.

The diameter of the tree should be about 4.5 inches.

Examine Check the reasonableness of the solution by replacing d with 4.5 in $C = \pi d$.

$C = \pi d$ Circumference of a circle
$C = \pi \cdot 4.5$ Replace d with 4.5.
$C \approx 14.1$ Simplify. Use a calculator.

The solution is reasonable.

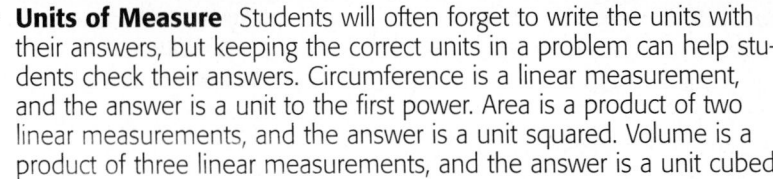

DAILY
INTERVENTION

Unlocking Misconceptions

- **Units of Measure** Students will often forget to write the units with their answers, but keeping the correct units in a problem can help students check their answers. Circumference is a linear measurement, and the answer is a unit to the first power. Area is a product of two linear measurements, and the answer is a unit squared. Volume is a product of three linear measurements, and the answer is a unit cubed.

AREAS OF CIRCLES A circle can be separated into parts as shown below. The parts can then be arranged to form a figure that resembles a parallelogram.

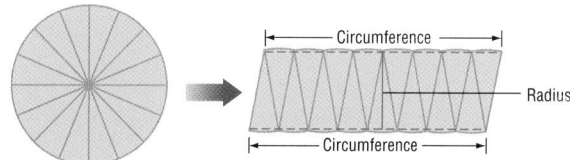

Since the circle has an area that is relatively close to the area of the figure, you can use the formula for the area of a parallelogram to find the area of a circle.

$A = bh$ Area of a parallelogram

$A = \left(\frac{1}{2} \times C\right) r$ The base of the parallelogram is one-half the circumference, and the radius is the height.

$A = \left(\frac{1}{2} \times 2\pi r\right) r$ Replace C with $2\pi r$.

$A = \pi \times r \times r$ Simplify.

$A = \pi r^2$ Replace $r \times r$ with r^2.

Study Tip

Look Back
review **exponents**, see Lesson 4-2.

Key Concept   Area of a Circle

- **Words**   The area of a circle is equal to π times the square of its radius.

- **Symbols** $A = \pi r^2$

- **Model**

Study Tip

Estimation
To estimate the area of a circle, square the radius and then multiply by 3.

Example 3   Find Areas of Circles

Find the area of each circle. Round to the nearest tenth.

a.
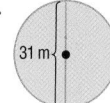
6 in.

$A = \pi r^2$ Area of a circle
$A = \pi \cdot 6^2$ Replace r with 6.
$A = \pi \cdot 36$ Evaluate 6^2.
$A \approx 113.1$ Use a calculator.

The area is about 113.1 square inches.

b.
31 m

$A = \pi r^2$ Area of a circle
$A = \pi \cdot (15.5)^2$ Replace r with 15.5.
$A = \pi \cdot 240.25$ Evaluate $(15.5)^2$.
$A \approx 754.8$ Use a calculator.

The area is about 754.8 square meters.

Check for Understanding

Concept Check

1. **Tell** how to find the circumference of a circle if you know the measure of the radius. **Multiply 2 times π times the radius.**

2. **OPEN ENDED** Draw and label a circle that has an area between 5 and 8 square units. **See margin.**

In-Class Example Power Point®

Teaching Tip You may want students to actually do the development of the circumference as an activity.

3 Find the area of each circle. Round to the nearest tenth.

a.
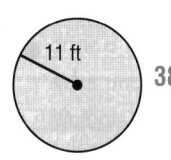
11 ft   380.1 ft²

b.
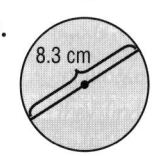
8.3 cm   54.1 cm²

3 Practice/Apply

Study Notebook

Have students—
- add the definitions/examples of the vocabulary terms to their Vocabulary Builder worksheets for Chapter 10.
- include sketches depicting diameter and radius, along with the formulas for circumference and area of circles.
- include any other item(s) that they find helpful in mastering the skills in this lesson.

Answer

2. Sample answer:

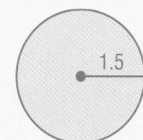
1.5

About the Exercises . . .

Organization by Objective

- **Circumference of Circles:** 10–21, 24, 25, 27, 29, 34
- **Areas of Circles:** 10–19, 22–23, 26, 28, 30–33

Odd/Even Assignments

Exercises 10–29 are structured so that students practice the same concepts whether they are assigned odd or even problems.

Assignment Guide

Basic: 11, 13, 17, 19, 25–31 odd, 32, 33, 35–38, 48–56

Average: 11–31 odd, 32, 33, 35–38, 48–56 (Optional: 39–47)

Advanced: 10–32 even, 33–53 (Optional: 54–56)

All: Practice Quiz 2 (1–5)

DAILY INTERVENTION **FIND THE ERROR** If students are having difficulty with the problem, have them diagram the circle. Ask them to label both the diameter ($d = 7$ units) and the radius ($r = 3.5$ units) of this circle.

Answer

3. Mark; since the diameter of the circle is 7 units, its radius is 3.5 units. Thus, the area of the circle is π $(3.5)^2$ or 38.5 square units.

Answer (p. 537)

34.

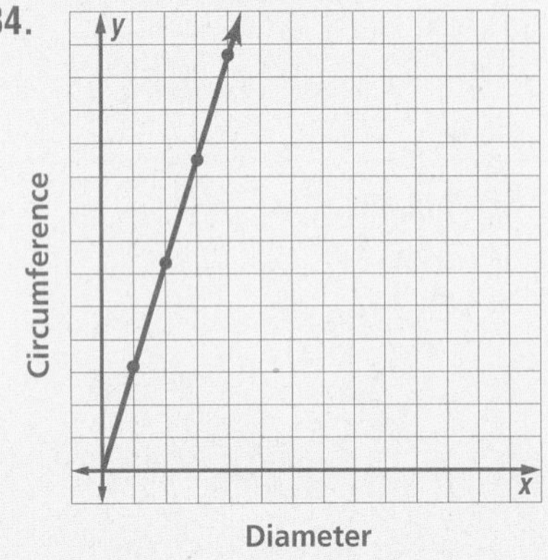

3. **FIND THE ERROR** Dario and Mark are finding the area of a circle with diameter 7. **See margin.**

Dario	Mark
$A \approx 153.9$ units^2	$A \approx 38.5$ units^2

Who is correct? Explain your reasoning.

Guided Practice

GUIDED PRACTICE KEY	
Exercises	Examples
4–9	1–3

Find the circumference and area of each circle. Round to the nearest tenth.

4. 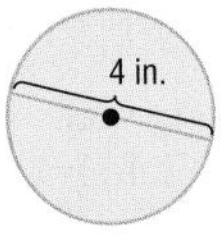

12.6 in; 12.6 in^2

5. 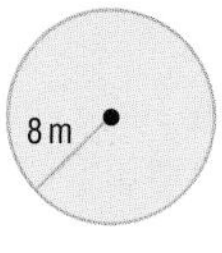

50.3 m; 201.1 m^2

6. 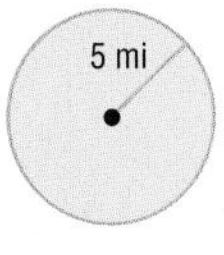

31.4 mi; 78.5 mi^2

7. The radius is 1.3 kilometers. **8.2 km; 5.3 km^2**

8. The diameter is 6.1 centimeters. **19.2 cm; 29.2 cm^2**

Application

9. **MUSIC** During a football game, a marching band can be heard within a radius of 1.7 miles. What is the area of the neighborhood that can hear the band? **about 9.1 mi^2**

★ indicates increased difficulty

Practice and Apply

Homework Help	
For Exercises	See Examples
10–19, 24, 26–35	1, 3
20–23, 25	2

Extra Practice
See page 749.

Find the circumference and area of each circle. Round to the nearest tenth.

10. 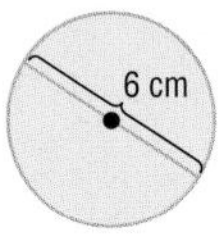

18.8 cm; 28.3 cm^2

11. 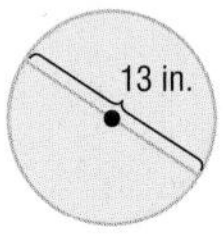

40.8 in.; 132.7 in^2

12. 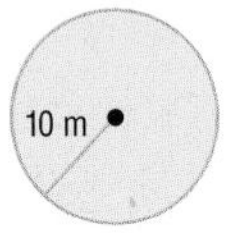

62.8 m; 314.2 m

13. 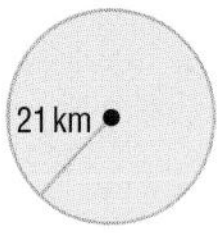

131.9 km; 1385.4 km^2

★ 14. 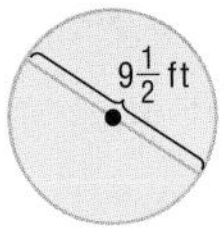

29.8 ft; 70.9 ft^2

★ 15. 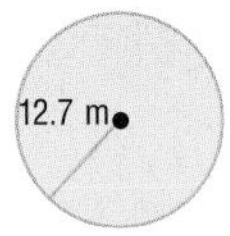

79.8 m; 506.7 m

16. 28.3 m; 63.6 m^2
17. 22.9 cm; 41.9 cm^2
18. 24.5 ft; 47.8 ft^2
19. 96.6 in; 742.6 in^2

16. The radius is 4.5 meters.

17. The diameter is 7.3 centimeters.

18. The diameter is $7\frac{4}{5}$ feet.

19. The radius is $15\frac{3}{8}$ inches.

★ 20. What is the diameter of a circle if its circumference is 25.8 inches? Round to the nearest tenth. **8.2 in.**

★ 21. Find the radius of a circle if its circumference is 9.2 meters. Round to the nearest tenth. **1.5 m**

★ 22. Find the radius of a circle if its area is 254.5 square inches. **9 in.**

★ 23. What is the diameter of a circle if its area is 132.7 square meters? **13 cm**

24. **BICYCLES** If a bicycle tire has a diameter of 27 inches, what is the distance the bicycle will travel in 10 rotations of the tire? **848.2 in.**

25. **SCIENCE** The circumference of Earth is about 25,000 miles. What is the distance to the center of Earth? **about 3979 mi**

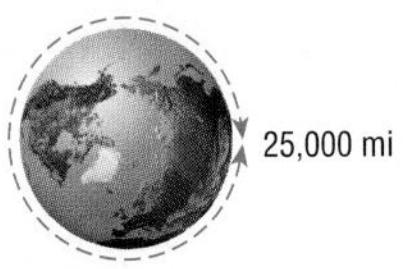

DAILY INTERVENTION **Differentiated Instruction**

- **Intrapersonal** Ask students to choose a hobby or sport that they enjoy. They should then find a circle related to that activity and determine the circumference, area, diameter, and radius of the circle. For example, a basketball player might calculate the diameter of a basketball. He or she could then compare the diameter of the ball to the diameter of the hoop. Ask students to record any insights into their activity in their Math Journals.

Match each circle described in the column on the left with its corresponding measurement in the column on the right.

26. radius: 4 units c
27. diameter: 7 units d
28. diameter: 3 units b
29. radius: 6 units a

    a. circumference: 37.7 units
    b. area: 7.1 units^2
    c. area: 50.3 units^2
    d. circumference: 22.0 units

30. **MONUMENTS**   The Stonehenge monument in England is enclosed within a circular ditch that has a diameter of 300 feet. Find the area within the ditch to the nearest tenth. **70,685.8 ft^2**

31. **HISTORY**   The dome of the Roman Pantheon has a diameter of 42.7 meters. Use the information at the left to find about how many times more area the Astrodome covers than the Pantheon. **about 26 times**

FOOD   For Exercises 32 and 33, use the following information and the graphic shown at the right.
Suppose the circle graph is redrawn onto a poster board so that the diameter of the graph is 9 inches.

32. How much space on the poster board will the circle graph cover? **63.6 in^2**

33. How much of the total space will each section of the graph cover?
**are safe: 25.4 in^2;
are unsafe: 24.2 in^2;
don't know: 14.0 in^2**

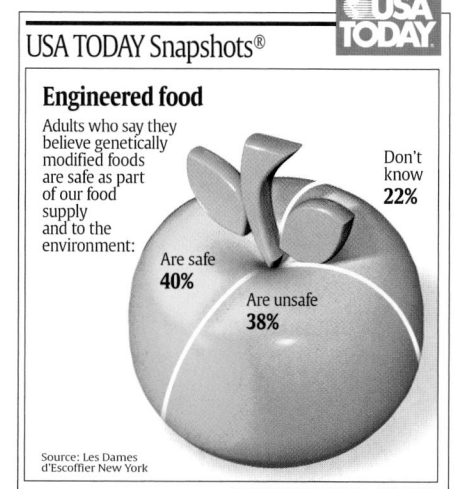

USA TODAY Snapshots®

Engineered food

Adults who say they believe genetically modified foods are safe as part of our food supply and to the environment:

Don't know **22%**

Are safe **40%**

Are unsafe **38%**

Source: Les Dames d'Escoffier New York

By Cindy Hall and Quin Tian, USA TODAY

★ 34. **FUNCTIONS**   Graph the circumference of a circle as a function of the diameter. Use values of *d* like 1, 2, 3, 4, and so on. What is the slope of this graph? (*Hint:* To review **slope**, see Lesson 8-4.) **See margin for graph; π.**

35. **CRITICAL THINKING**   The numerical value of the area of a circle is twice the numerical value of the circumference. What is the radius of the circle? (*Hint*: Use a chart of values for radius, circumference, and area.) **4**

36. **WRITING IN MATH**   Answer the question that was posed at the beginning of the lesson. **See margin.**

How are circumference and diameter related?

Include the following in your answer:
- the ratio of the circumference to the diameter, and
- an explanation describing what happens to the circumference as the diameter increases or decreases.

37. The diameter of a circle is 8 units. What is the area of the circle if the diameter is doubled? **C**

    (A) 50.3 units^2 (B) 100.5 units^2 (C) 201.1 units^2 (D) 804.2 units^2

38. **GRID IN**   The circumference of a circle is 18.8 meters. What is its area to the nearest tenth? **28.1 m^2**

Right sidebar

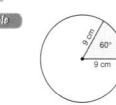 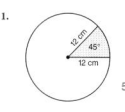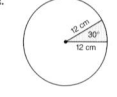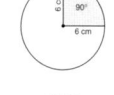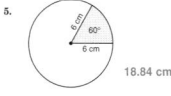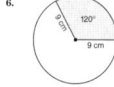

Answer

36. The circumference of a circle is about 3 times its diameter. Answers should include the following.
- Since the circumference is about 3 times the diameter, the ratio describing the relationship would be about 3 to 1.
- As the diameter increases, the circumference increases. As the diameter decreases, the circumference decreases.

Open-Ended Assessment

Writing Have students write a paragraph explaining how to find the circumference and area of a circle when given the radius of the circle and when given the diameter of the circle.

Getting Ready for Lesson 10-8

PREREQUISITE SKILL In Lesson 10-8, students find the areas of irregular figures. This requires students to add and subtract areas that may be expressed as decimals. Use Exercises 54–56 to determine your students' familiarity with adding decimals.

Assessment Options

Practice Quiz 2 The quiz provides students with a brief review of the concepts and skills in Lessons 10-5 through 10-7. Lesson numbers are given to the right of exercises or instruction lines so students can review concepts not yet mastered.

Extending the Lesson

CENTRAL ANGLES A **central angle** is an angle whose vertex is the center of the circle. It separates a circle into a *major arc* and a *minor arc*. An **inscribed angle** has its vertex on the circle and sides that are chords. A **chord** is a segment of a circle whose endpoints are on the circle.

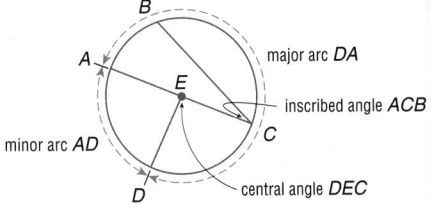

- The degree measure of a minor arc is the degree measure of the central angle.
- The measure of an inscribed angle equals one-half the measure of its intercepted arc.
- The degree measure of a major arc is 360 minus the degree measure of the central angle.

Refer to the diagram shown. Find the measures of the following angles and arcs.

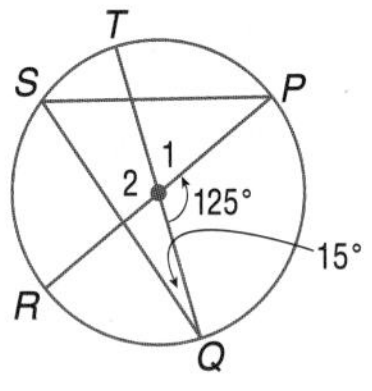

39. minor arc PQ **125°**   40. $\angle 1$ **55°**
41. major arc QP **235°**   42. $\angle 2$ **125°**
43. minor TR **125°**   44. minor RQ **55°**
45. $\angle PSQ$ **62.5°**   ★ 46. minor SR **95°**
47. List three chords of the circle. **Sample answer:** $\overline{SP}$, $\overline{SQ}$, $\overline{RP}$

Maintain Your Skills

Mixed Review **Find the measure of an interior angle of each polygon.** *(Lesson 10-6)*
48. regular hexagon **120°** 49. regular decagon **144°** 50. regular octagon **135°**

Find the area of each figure described. *(Lesson 10-5)*
51. trapezoid: height, 2 m; bases, 20 m and 18 m **38 m²**
52. parallelogram: base, 6 km; height, 8 km **48 km²**
53. **ALGEBRA** Solve $2x - 7 > 5x + 14$. *(Lesson 7-6)* $x < -7$

Getting Ready for the Next Lesson **PREREQUISITE SKILL** **Find each sum.** *(To review **adding decimals**, see page 713.)*
54. $200 + 43.9$ **243.9**   55. $23.6 + 126.9$ **150.5**   56. $345.14 + 23.8$ **368.94**

Practice Quiz 2   Lessons 10-5 through 10-7

Find the area of each figure. *(Lesson 10-5)*

1. **112.86 cm²**
2. 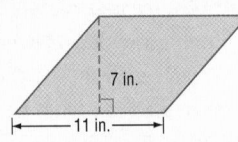 **77 in²**
3. 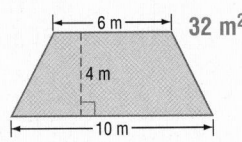 **32 m²**

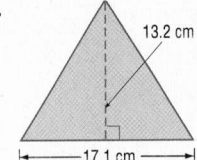

4. Find the sum of the measures of the interior angles of a 15-gon. *(Lesson 10-6)* **2340°**
5. A circle has a radius of 4.7 inches. Find the circumference and area to the nearest tenth. *(Lesson 10-7)* **29.5 in.; 69.4 in²**

Area: Irregular Figures

What You'll Learn

- Find area of irregular figures.

How can polygons help to find the area of an irregular figure?

California is the most populous state in the United States. It ranks third among the U.S. states in area.
Source: www.infoplease.com

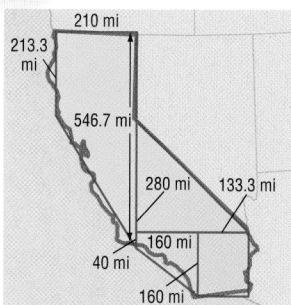

In the diagram, the area of California is separated into polygons.

a. Identify the polygons.

b. Explain how polygons can be used to estimate the total land area.

c. What is the area of each region?

d. What is the total area? 158,190 sq mi

, two trapezoids, triangle, and a ectangle

. Add the areas to nd the total area.

. large trapezoid: 9,800 sq mi; triangle: 1,062 sq mi; small apezoid: 16,000 sq i; rectangle: 1,328 sq mi

AREA OF IRREGULAR FIGURES

So far in this chapter, we have discussed the following area formulas.

Triangle
$A = \frac{1}{2}bh$

Trapezoid
$A = \frac{1}{2}h(a + b)$

Parallelogram
$A = bh$

Circle
$A = \pi r^2$

These formulas can be used to help you find the area of irregular figures. Some examples of irregular figures are shown.

IDAHO

To find the area of an irregular figure, separate the irregular figure into figures whose areas you know how to find.

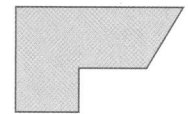 parallelogram

half of a circle or semicircle

triangle

trapezoid

rectangle

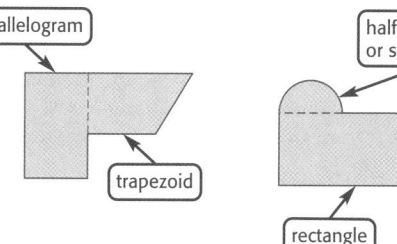

rectangle

IDAHO

rectangle

tudy Tip

regular Figures
ere can be more than e way to separate an egular figure. For ample, another way to parate the first figure at e right is shown below.

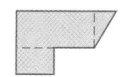

10-8 Lesson Notes

1 Focus

5-Minute Check Transparency 10-8 Use as a quiz or review of Lesson 10-7.

Mathematical Background notes are available for this lesson on page 490D.

How can polygons help to find the area of an irregular figure?

The opening activity questions are repeated on page 587 of the *Chapter 10 Resource Masters*.

Reading to Learn Mathematics, p. 587   ELL

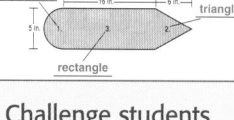

Pre-Activity *How can polygons help to find the area of an irregular figure?*

Do the activity at the top of page 539 in your textbook. Write your answers below.

In the diagram, the area of California is separated into polygons.

a. Identify the polygons. two trapezoids, a triangle, and a rectangle

b. Explain how polygons can be used to estimate the total land area. Add the areas to find the total area.

c. What is the area of each region? large trapezoid: 79,800 sq mi; triangle: 41,062 sq mi; small trapezoid: 16,000 sq mi; rectangle: 21,328 sq mi

d. What is the total area? 158,190 sq mi

Reading the Lesson

Complete the following statements by filling in the blanks with the following words or symbols.

triangle $A = \frac{1}{2}h(a + b)$ separating   formula $A = bh$
trapezoid $A = \pi r^2$ area   irregular figure

1. The area of a(n) irregular figure can be determined by separating the figure into simple polygons.

2. Each separate polygon has a specific formula to determine its area. For a circle, it's $A = \pi r^2$, while $A = \frac{1}{2}bh$ works for a triangle .

3. To find the area of a parallelogram, the formula $A = bh$ should be applied.

4. A(n) trapezoid , on the other hand, requires the formula $A = \frac{1}{2}h(a + b)$.

5. To find the area of the whole figure, the areas of the polygons are added together.

Helping You Remember

6. Study the figure below, identify the separate polygons, find the area of each polygon, and find the area of the entire figure. Round to the nearest tenth.

area of polygon 1: 9.8 in²
area of polygon 2: 15 in²
area of polygon 3: 80 in²
total area of figure: 104.8 in²

Teaching Tip Challenge students to find examples of both regular and irregular figures around the classroom.

Resource Manager

Workbooks and Reproducible Masters

Chapter 10 Resource Masters
- Study Guide and Intervention, p. 584
- Skills Practice, p. 585
- Practice, p. 586
- Reading to Learn Mathematics, p. 587
- Enrichment, p. 588
- Assessment, p. 604

Parent and Student Study Guide Workbook, p. 88
Science and Mathematics Lab Manual, pp. 21–26

Transparencies

5-Minute Check Transparency 10-8
Real-World Transparency 10
Answer Key Transparencies

Technology

Interactive Chalkboard
Pre-AlgePASS: Tutorial Plus, Lesson 34

AREA OF IRREGULAR FIGURES

1 Find the area of the figure to the nearest tenth.

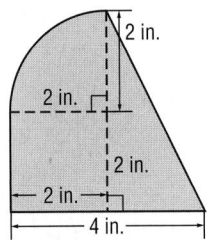

11.1 in²

Teaching Tip Encourage students to look carefully at the irregular figure and separate it into the simplest possible areas before doing their calculations.

Answer (Concept Check)

Sample answer: triangle

$(A = \frac{1}{2} bh)$, paralleogram

$(A = bh)$, circle

$(A = \pi r^2)$

✓ **Concept Check** Name three area formulas that can be used to find the area o an irregular figure. **See margin.**

Example 1 **Find Area of Irregular Figures**

Find the area of the figure to the nearest tenth.

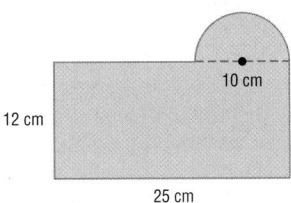

Explore You know the dimensions of the figure. You need to find its area.

Plan Solve a simpler problem. First, separate the figure into a parallelogram and a semicircle. Then find the sum of the areas of the figures.

Estimate: The area of the entire figure should be a little greater than the area of the rectangle. One estimate is 10×25 or 250.

Solve Area of Parallelogram

$A = bh$ Area of a parallelogram

$A = 25 \cdot 12$ Replace b with 25 and h with 12.

$A = 300$ Simplify.

Area of Semicircle

$A = \frac{1}{2}\pi r^2$ Area of a semicircle

$A = \frac{1}{2} \cdot \pi \cdot 5^2$ Replace r with 5.

$A \approx 39.3$ Simplify.

The area of the figure is $300 + 39.3$ or about 339.3 square centimeters.

Examine Check the reasonableness of the solution by solving the problem another way. Separate the figure into two rectangles and a semicircle.

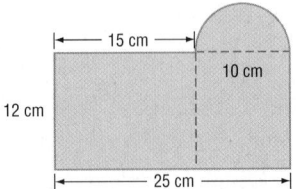

The area of one rectangle is $10 \cdot 12$ or 120 square centimeters, the area of the other rectangle is $12 \cdot 15$ or 180 square centimeters, and the area of the semicircle remains 39.3 square centimeters.

$120 + 180 + 39.3 = 339.3$

So, the answer is correct.

Differentiated Instruction

- **Interpersonal** Have students work in pairs or teams. Assign each team one of the fifty states or a Canadian province. Team members should decide what regular figures they might use to estimate the area for the state or province. If you have simple outline maps with scales, students can estimate the area and check against real totals. Have teams share their strategies with the class.

Many real-world situations involve finding the area of an irregular figure.

Example 2 Use Area of Irregular Figures

LANDSCAPE DESIGN Suppose one bag of mulch covers an area of about 9 square feet. How many bags of mulch will be needed to cover the flower garden?

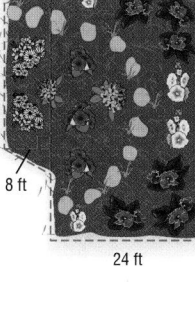

Step 1 Find the area of the flower garden.

Area of rectangle

$A = bh$	Area of a rectangle
$A = 24 \cdot 38$	Replace b with 24 and h with 38.
$A = 912$	Simplify.

Area of parallelogram

$A = bh$	Area of a parallelogram
$A = 28 \cdot 8$	Replace b with 28 and h with 8.
$A = 224$	Simplify.

The area of the garden is $912 + 224$ or 1136 square feet.

Step 2 Find the number of bags of mulch needed.

$$1136 \div 9 \approx 126.2$$

So, 127 bags of mulch will be needed.

In-Class Example Power Point®

2 CARPETING Carpeting costs $2 per square foot. How much will it cost to carpet the area shown?

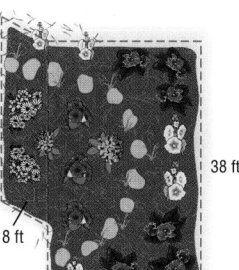
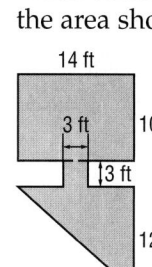

$466

Teaching Tip Encourage students to look carefully at the irregular figure and separate it into the simplest possible areas before doing their calculations.

Check for Understanding

Concept Check
1. **OPEN ENDED** Draw two examples of irregular figures.

2. **Write** the steps you would use to find the area of the irregular figure shown at the right. **1–2. See margin.**

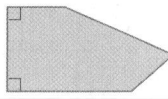

Guided Practice Find the area of each figure. Round to the nearest tenth.

GUIDED PRACTICE KEY	
Exercises	Examples
3, 4	1
5, 6	2

3. 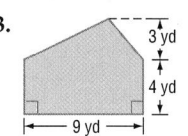 49.5 yd²

4. 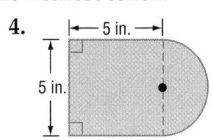 34.8 in²

Application

HOME IMPROVEMENT For Exercises 5 and 6, use the diagram shown and the following information.
The Slavens are planning to stain their wood deck. One gallon of stain costs $19.95 and covers approximately 200 square feet.

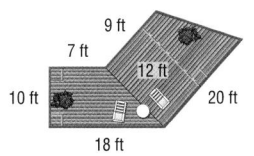

5. Suppose the Slavens need to apply only one coat of stain. How many gallons of stain will they need to buy? **2**

6. Find the total cost of the stain, not including tax. **$39.90**

 www.pre-alg.com/extra_examples

Lesson 10-8 Area: Irregular Figures **541**

---

3 Practice/Apply

Study Notebook

Have students—
• identify an irregular figure and describe in a paragraph how they might find its area.
• include any other item(s) that they find helpful in mastering the skills in this lesson.

About the Exercises . . .
Odd/Even Assignments
Exercises 7–17 are structured so that students practice the same concepts whether they are assigned odd or even problems.

Alert! Exercise 23 involves research on the Internet or other reference materials.

Assignment Guide
Basic: 7, 9, 15, 19, 21–35
Average: 7–19 odd, 21–35
Advanced: 8–20 even, 21–35

Sample Answers

1.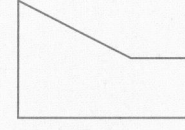

2. First, separate the figure into a rectangle and two triangles. Then find the area of each of the figures. Then find the sum of their areas.

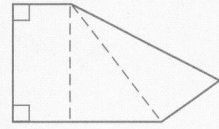

Study Guide and Intervention, p. 584

To find the area of an irregular figure, separate the irregular figure into figures whose area you know how to find. Use the area formulas you have learned in this chapter.

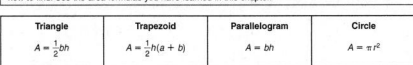

Example Find the area of each figure. Round to the nearest tenth, if necessary.

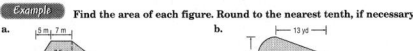

Exercises

Find the area of each figure. Round to the nearest tenth, if necessary.

1. What is the area of a figure formed using a rectangle with a base of 10 yards and a height of 4 yards and two semicircles, one with a radius of 5 yards and the other a radius of 2 yards? **85.6 yd²**

2. Find the area of a figure formed using a square with sides of 9 centimeters and three attached triangles with heights of 6 centimeters. **162 cm²**

Find the area of each shaded region. Round to the nearest tenth. (*Hint:* Find the total area and subtract the non-shaded area.)

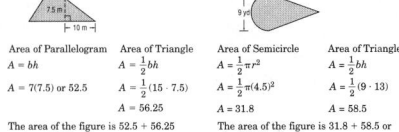

3. **6.9cm²** 4. **110.8in²** 5. **169 m²**

Skills Practice, p. 585 and Practice, p. 586 (shown)

Find the area of each figure to the nearest tenth, if necessary.

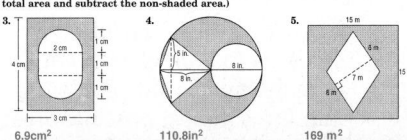

1. **180 mm²** 2. **9.2 cm²** 3. **73.1 in²** 4. **100.4 yd²**

5. **8.4 m²** 6. **46.3 ft²** 7. **156.8 in²** 8. **147.0 m²**

9. What is the area of a figure formed using a square with sides of 15 centimeters and four attached semicircles? **578.4 cm²**

10. Find the area of a figure formed using a parallelogram with a base of 10 yards and a height of 12 yards and two triangles with bases of 10 yards and heights of 5 yards. **170 yd²**

Find the area of each shaded area. Round to the nearest tenth, if necessary. (*Hint:* Find the total area and subtract the non-shaded area.)

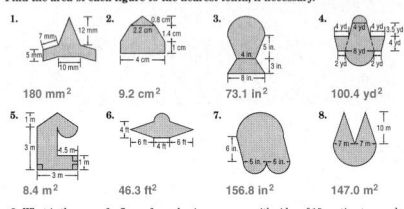

11. **468.2 in²** 12. **17.5 ft²** 13. **6.6 cm²**

14. **HISTORY** What is the area of the track in the Circus Maximus as represented below? The center barrier was named the *spina*. **48,307.9 yd²**

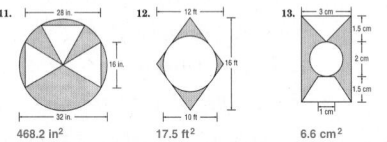

Enrichment, p. 588

Area of a Regular Polygon

The area of a regular polygon is equal to one-half the product of the **apothem** and the **perimeter**. The apothem is the distance from the center of the polygon to a side. The perimeter is the sum of the lengths of all of the sides.

Example

$A = \frac{1}{2}ap$ $a = 13.8, p = 100$

$= \frac{1}{2}(13.8) \cdot (100)$

$= 690$ in²

Find the area of each regular polygon.

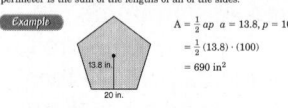

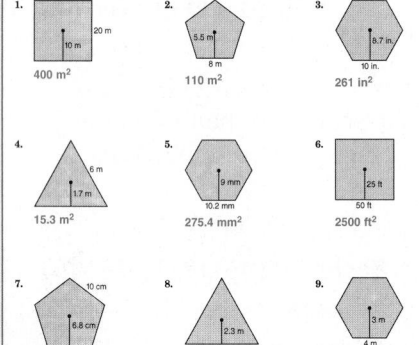

1. **400 m²** 2. **110 m²** 3. **261 in²**
4. **15.3 m²** 5. **275.4 mm²** 6. **2500 ft²**
7. **170 cm²** 8. **27.6 m²** 9. **36 m²**

Practice and Apply

Homework Help

For Exercises	See Examples
7–15	1
19–22	2

Extra Practice See page 750.

Find the area of each figure to the nearest tenth, if necessary.

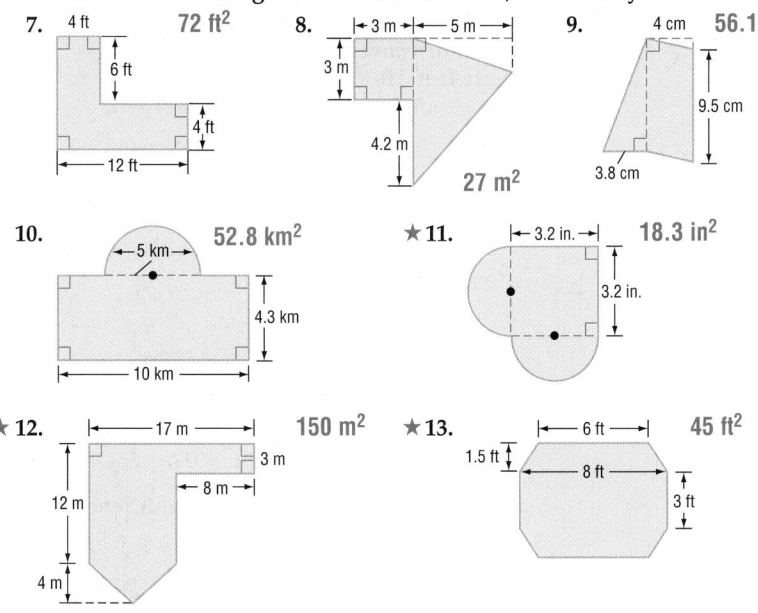

7. **72 ft²** 8. **27 m²** 9. **56.1 cm²**

10. **52.8 km²** ★11. **18.3 in²**

★12. **150 m²** ★13. **45 ft²**

14. What is the area of a figure that is formed using a square with sides 8 meters and a semicircle with a diameter of 5.6 meters? **76.3 m²**

15. Find the area of a figure formed using a rectangle with base 3.5 yards and height 2.8 yards and a semicircle with radius 7 yards. **86.8 yd²**

Find the area of each shaded region. Round to the nearest tenth, if necessary. (*Hint:* Find the total area and subtract the non-shaded area.)

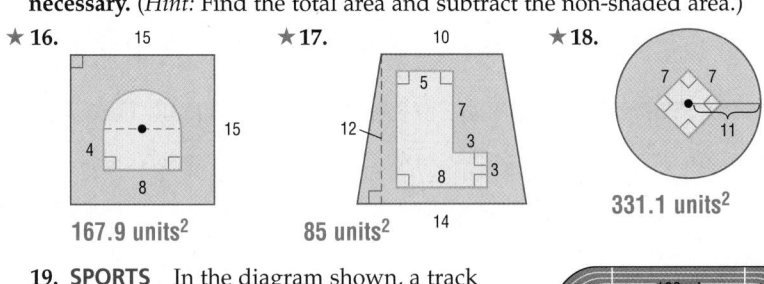

★16. **167.9 units²** ★17. **85 units²** ★18. **331.1 units²**

19. **SPORTS** In the diagram shown, a track surrounds a football field. To the nearest tenth, what is the area of the grass region inside the track? **6963.5 yd²**

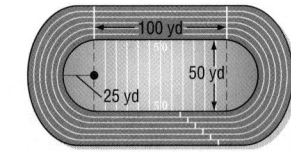

20. **WALKWAYS** A sidewalk forms a 3-foot wide border with the grass as shown. Find the area of the sidewalk. **108 ft²**

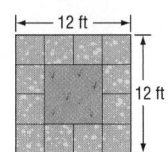

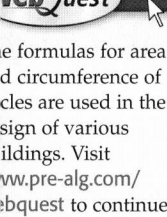

GEOGRAPHY For Exercises 21–23, use the diagram shown at the right.

21. Tell how you would separate the irregular figure into polygons to find its area.

22. Use your method to find the total land area of Oklahoma.

23. **RESEARCH** Use the Internet or another source to find the actual total land area of Oklahoma. **21–23. See margin.**

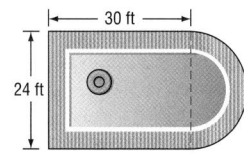

Online Research **Data Update** How can you use irregular figures to estimate the total land area of your state? Visit www.pre-alg.com/data_update to learn more.

24. **CRITICAL THINKING** In the diagram, a patio that is 4 feet wide surrounds a swimming pool. What is the area of the patio? **429.7 ft²**

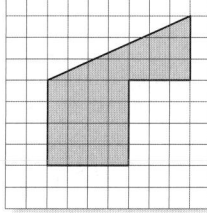

25. **WRITING IN MATH** Answer the question that was posed at the beginning of the lesson. **See margin.**

How can polygons help to find the area of an irregular figure?

Include the following in your answer:
- an example of an irregular figure, and
- an explanation as to how the figure can be separated to find its area.

Standardized Test Practice
(A) (B) (C) (D)

For Exercises 26 and 27, refer to the diagram shown. Suppose 1 square unit equals 5 square feet.

26. What is the area of the figure? **C**
  (A) 26.5 ft²   (B) 34.5 ft²
  (C) 132.5 ft²   (D) 185 ft²

27. What is the area of the nonshaded region? **C**
  (A) 73.5 ft²   (B) 140.5 ft²
  (C) 367.5 ft²   (D) 473.5 ft²

Maintain Your Skills

Mixed Review Find the circumference and area of each circle. Round to the nearest tenth.
(Lesson 10-7)

28. The wheel on a game show has a diameter of 8.5 feet. **26.7 ft, 56.7 ft²**

29. The radius is 7 centimeters.   30. The diameter is 19 inches.
  44.0 cm, 153.9 cm²   **59.7 in., 283.5 in²**

Find the sum of the measures of the interior angles of each polygon.
(Lesson 10-6)

31. pentagon **540°**   32. quadrilateral **360°**   33. octagon **1080°**

34. Draw an angle that measures 35°. *(Lesson 9-3)* **See margin.**

35. Simplify $(4x)(-6y)$. *(Lesson 3-2)* **−24xy**

---

4 Assess

Open-Ended Assessment

Modeling Have students cut out an irregular figure. Then have them cut the figure into smaller figures for which they can find the area. Then use these areas to determine the area of the irregular figure.

Assessment Options

Quiz (Lessons 10-7 and 10-8) is available on p. 604 of the *Chapter 10 Resource Masters.*

Answers

21. Sample answer: Separate the area into a rectangle and a trapezoid.

22. Sample answer: 62,500 mi²

23. 68,679 mi²

25. You can use polygons to find the area of an irregular figure by finding the area of each individual polygon and then finding the total area of the irregular figure. Answers should include the following.

-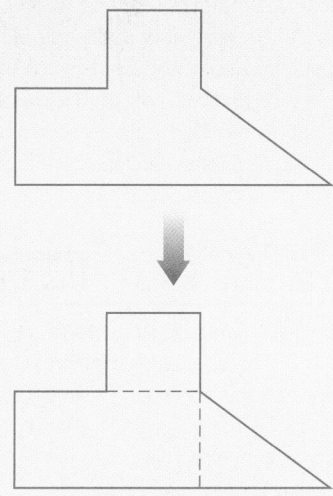

- To find the area of the irregular figure shown above, the figure can be separated into two rectangles and a triangle.

34.

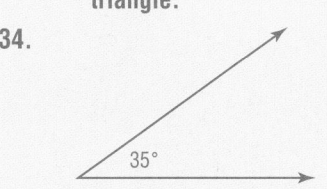

Chapter 10 Study Guide and Review

Vocabulary and Concept Check

- This alphabetical list of vocabulary terms in Chapter 10 includes a page reference where each term was introduced.
- **Assessment** A vocabulary review/test for Chapter 10 is available on p. 602 of the *Chapter 10 Resource Masters*.

Lesson-by-Lesson Review

For each lesson,
- the main ideas are summarized,
- additional examples review concepts, and
- practice exercises are provided.

Vocabulary PuzzleMaker

ELL The Vocabulary PuzzleMaker software improves students' mathematics vocabulary using four puzzle formats—crossword, scramble, word search using a word list, and word search using clues. Students can work on a computer screen or from a printed handout.

MindJogger Videoquizzes

ELL MindJogger Videoquizzes provide an alternative review of concepts presented in this chapter. Students work in teams in a game show format to gain points for correct answers. The questions are presented in three rounds.

Round 1 Concepts (5 questions)
Round 2 Skills (4 questions)
Round 3 Problem Solving (4 questions)

Vocabulary and Concept Check

adjacent angles (p. 493)	diameter (p. 533)	regular polygon (p. 529)
alternate exterior angles (p. 492)	dilation (p. 512)	rhombus (p. 514)
alternate interior angles (p. 492)	exterior angles (p. 492, 531)	rotation (p. 506)
altitude (p. 520)	interior angles (pp. 492, 528)	rotational symmetry (p. 505)
base (p. 520)	line symmetry (p. 505)	supplementary (p. 494)
bilateral symmetry (p. 505)	line of symmetry (pp. 505, 506)	tessellation (p. 532)
center (p. 533)	parallel lines (p. 492)	transformation (p. 506)
circle (p. 533)	parallelogram (p. 514)	translation (p. 506)
circumference (p. 533)	perpendicular lines (p. 494)	transversal (p. 492)
complementary (p. 493)	pi (p. 533)	trapezoid (p. 514)
congruent (p. 500)	polygon (p. 527)	turn symmetry (p. 505)
corresponding angles (p. 492)	quadrilateral (p. 513)	vertical angles (p. 493)
corresponding parts (p. 500)	radius (p. 533)	
diagonal (p. 528)	reflection (p. 506)	

Choose the correct term to complete each sentence.

1. Two angles are (complementary, <u>supplementary</u>) if the sum of their measures is 180°.
2. A (<u>rhombus</u>, trapezoid) has four congruent sides.
3. In congruent triangles, the (<u>corresponding angles</u>, adjacent angles) are congruent.
4. In a (<u>rotation</u>, translation), a figure is turned around a fixed point.
5. A polygon in which all sides are congruent is called (equiangular, <u>equilateral</u>).

Lesson-by-Lesson Review

10-1 Angle Relationships

See pages 492–497.

Concept Summary

- When two parallel lines are cut by a transversal, the corresponding angles, the alternate interior angles, and the alternate exterior angles are congruent.
- Two angles are complementary if the sum of their measures is 90°.
- Two angles are supplementary if the sum of their measures is 180°.

Example In the figure at the right, $\ell \parallel m$ and t is a transversal. If $m\angle 1 = 109°$, find $m\angle 7$.

Since $\angle 1$ and $\angle 7$ are alternate exterior angles, they are congruent. So, $m\angle 7 = 109°$.

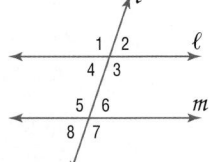

Exercises Use the figure shown to find the measure of each angle. *See Example 1 on page 493.*

6. $\angle 5$ **109°** 7. $\angle 3$ **109°** 8. $\angle 2$ **71°** 9. $\angle 6$ **71°**

FOLDABLES™ Study Organizer

For more information about Foldables, see *Teaching Mathematics with Foldables.*

Have students reexamine their Foldables to make sure all the information they have included about two-dimensional figures is correct. Suggest that they refer to their Foldables if needed when working through the Study Guide exercises.

10-2 Congruent Triangles

See pages 500–504.

Concept Summary

- Figures that have the same size and shape are congruent.
- The corresponding parts of congruent triangles are congruent.

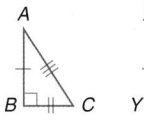

$\triangle ABC = \triangle XYZ$

Example Use $\triangle ABC$ and $\triangle XYZ$ above to complete each congruence statement.

$\angle B \cong$ _?_ $\overline{YZ} \cong$ _?_

B corresponds to Y, so $\angle B \cong \angle Y$.

$\overline{YZ}$ corresponds to $\overline{BC}$, so $\overline{YZ} \cong \overline{BC}$.

Exercises Complete each congruence statement if $\triangle FGH \cong \triangle QRS$.
See Example 2 on page 501.

10. $\angle F \cong$ _?_ $\angle Q$ 11. $\angle S \cong$ _?_ $\angle H$ 12. $\angle R \cong$ _?_ $\angle G$
13. $\overline{GH} \cong$ _?_ $\overline{RS}$ 14. $\overline{HF} \cong$ _?_ $\overline{SQ}$ 15. $\overline{RQ} \cong$ _?_ $\overline{GF}$

10-3 Transformations on the Coordinate Plane

See pages 506–511.

Concept Summary

- Three types of transformations are translations, reflections, and rotations.

Examples

1 The vertices of $\triangle JKL$ are $J(1, 2)$, $K(3, 2)$, and $L(1, -1)$. Graph the triangle and its image after a translation 3 units left and 2 units up.

This translation can be written as $(-3, 2)$.

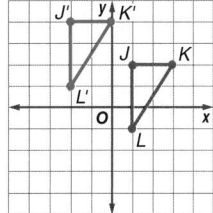

vertex	3 left, 2 up		translation
$J(1, 2)$	$+$ $(-3, 2)$	$\rightarrow$	$J'(-2, 4)$
$K(3, 2)$	$+$ $(-3, 2)$	$\rightarrow$	$K'(0, 4)$
$L(1, -1)$	$+$ $(-3, 2)$	$\rightarrow$	$L'(-2, 1)$

2 The vertices of figure $ABCD$ are $A(1, -3)$, $B(4, -3)$, $C(1, -1)$, and $D(-2, -1)$. Graph the figure and its image after a reflection over the x-axis.

Use the same x-coordinate and multiply the y-coordinate by -1.

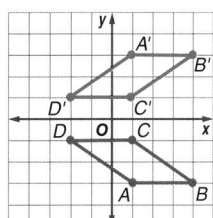

vertex			reflection
$A(1, -3)$	$\rightarrow$	$(1, -3 \cdot -1)$	$\rightarrow$ $A'(1, 3)$
$B(4, -3)$	$\rightarrow$	$(4, -3 \cdot -1)$	$\rightarrow$ $B'(4, 3)$
$C(1, -1)$	$\rightarrow$	$(1, -1 \cdot -1)$	$\rightarrow$ $C'(1, 1)$
$D(-2, -1)$	$\rightarrow$	$(-2, -1 \cdot -1)$	$\rightarrow$ $D'(-2, 1)$

Answers

16.

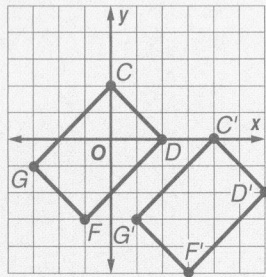

17.

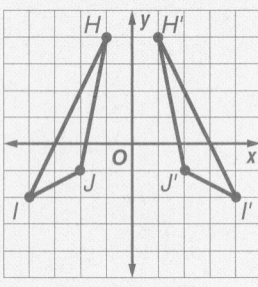

18.

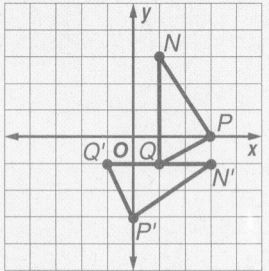

Example 3 **A triangle has vertices** $T(-2, 0)$, $W(-4, -2)$, **and** $Z(-3, -4)$. **Graph the triangle and its image after a rotation of 180° about the origin.**

Multiply both coordinates of each point by -1.

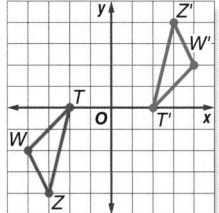

vertex		rotation
$T(-2, 0)$	$\rightarrow$	$T'(2, 0)$
$W(-4, -2)$	$\rightarrow$	$W'(4, 2)$
$Z(-3, -4)$	$\rightarrow$	$Z'(3, 4)$

Exercises **Graph each figure and its image.**
See Examples 1–3 on pages 507–509. **16–18. See margin.**

16. The vertices of a rectangle are $C(0, 2)$, $D(2, 0)$, $F(-1, -3)$, and $G(-3, -1)$. The rectangle is translated 4 units right and two units down.

17. The vertices of a triangle are $H(-1, 4)$, $I(-4, -2)$, and $J(-2, -1)$. The triangle is reflected over the y-axis.

18. A triangle has vertices $N(1, 3)$, $P(3, 0)$, and $Q(1, -1)$. The triangle is rotated 90° clockwise.

10-4 Quadrilaterals

See pages 513–517.

Concept Summary

- The sum of the angle measures of a quadrilateral is 360°.
- A trapezoid, parallelogram, rhombus, square, and rectangle are examples of quadrilaterals.

Example **Find the value of** x. **Then find the missing angle measures.**

$$x + 2x + 96 + 87 = 360 \quad \text{Angles of a quadrilateral}$$
$$3x + 183 = 360 \quad \text{Combine like terms.}$$
$$3x = 177 \quad \text{Simplify.}$$
$$x = 59 \quad \text{Divide each side by 3.}$$

The value of x is 59. So, the missing angle measures are 59° and 2(59) or 118°

Exercises **Find the value of** x. **Then find the missing angle measures.**
See Example 1 on page 514. **20. 64; 64°; 128°**

19.
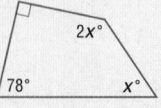
112; 112°

20.
2x°

21.
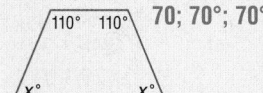
70; 70°; 70°

10-5 Area: Parallelograms, Triangles, and Trapezoids

See pages 520–525.

Concept Summary

- Area of a parallelogram: $A = bh$
- Area of a triangle: $A = \frac{1}{2}bh$
- Area of a trapezoid: $A = \frac{1}{2}h(a + b)$

Example   Find the area of the trapezoid.

$A = \frac{1}{2}h(a + b)$ Area of a trapezoid

$A = \frac{1}{2}(1.8)(2 + 5)$ Substitution

$A = \frac{1}{2} \cdot 1.8 \cdot 7$ Add 2 and 5.

$A = 6.3$ The area of the trapezoid is 6.3 square centimeters.

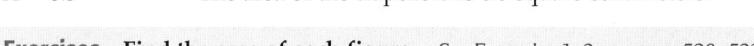

Exercises   Find the area of each figure.   *See Examples 1–3 on pages 520–523.*

22.   117 in²   23.   11 yd²   24.   42.47 m²

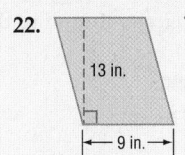 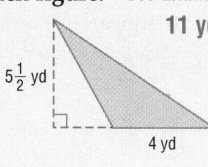 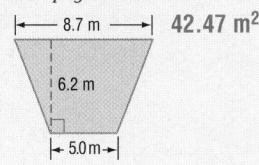

10-6 Polygons

See pages 527–531.

Concept Summary

- Polygons can be classified by the number of sides they have.
- If a polygon has n sides, then the sum of the degree measures of the interior angles of the polygon is $(n - 2)180$.

Example   Classify the polygon. Then find the sum of the measures of the interior angles.

The polygon has 5 sides. It is a pentagon.

$(n - 2)180 = (5 - 2)180$ Replace n with 5.

$= 3(180)$ or 540   Simplify.

The sum of the measures of the angles is 540.

Exercises   Classify each polygon. Then find the sum of the measures of the interior angles.   *See Examples 1 and 2 on page 528.*

25.   26.   heptagon; 900°   27.   decagon; 1440°

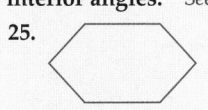  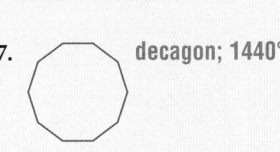

hexagon; 720°

Study Guide and Review

Chapter
10 For More …
• Extra Practice, see pages 747–750.
• Mixed Problem Solving, see page

Answers (p. 549)

1a.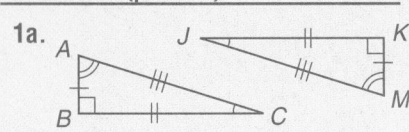

1b.

1c.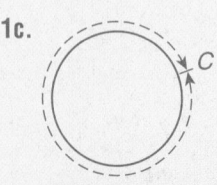

2. Whereas the sum of complementary angles is 90°, the sum of supplementary angles is 180°.

10.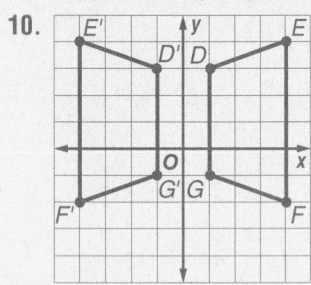

D' (−1, 3); E' (−4, 4); F' (−4, −2); G' (−1, −1)

11.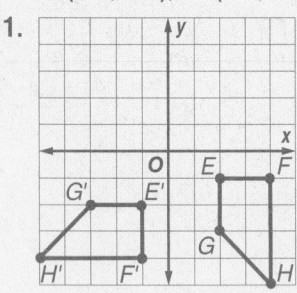

E' (−1, −2); F' (−1, −4); G' (−3, −2); H' (−5, −4)

10-7 Circumference and Area: Circles

See pages 533–538.

Concept Summary

• The circumference C of a circle with radius r is given by $C = 2\pi r$.
• The area A of a circle with radius r is given by $A = \pi r^2$.

Example Find the circumference and area of the circle. Round to the nearest tenth.

15 m

$C = 2\pi r$	Circumference of a circle
$C = 2 \cdot \pi \cdot 7.5$	Replace r with 7.5.
$C \approx 47.1$	The circumference is about 47.1 inches.

$A = \pi r^2$	Area of a circle
$A = \pi \cdot 7.5^2$	Replace r with 7.5.
$A = \pi \cdot 56.25$	Evaluate 7.5^2.
$A \approx 176.7$	The area is about 176.7 square meters.

Exercises Find the circumference and area of each circle. Round to the nearest tenth. *See Examples 1 and 3 on pages 534 and 535.*

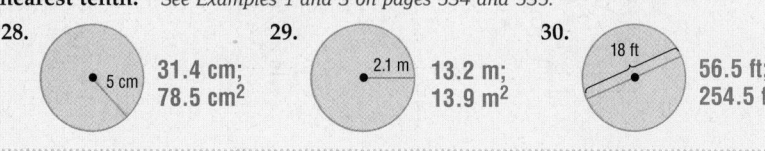

28. 5 cm   31.4 cm; 78.5 cm²

29. 2.1 m   13.2 m; 13.9 m²

30. 18 ft   56.5 ft; 254.5 ft²

10-8 Area: Irregular Figures

See pages 539–543.

Concept Summary

• To find the area of an irregular figure, separate the irregular figure into figures whose areas you know how to find.

Example Find the area of the figure.

5 cm
3 cm
3 cm

Area of Parallelogram	Area of Square
$A = bh$	$A = s^2$
$A = 3(5)$ or 15	$A = 3^2$ or 9

The area of the figure is 15 + 9 or 24 square centimeters.

Exercises Find the area of each figure. Round to the nearest tenth, if necessary. *See Example 1 on page 540.*

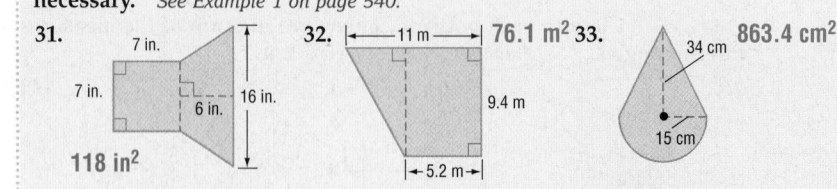

31. 7 in. 7 in. 6 in. 16 in.   118 in²

32. 11 m 9.4 m 5.2 m   76.1 m²

33. 34 cm 15 cm   863.4 cm²

Vocabulary and Concepts

1. **Draw** and label a diagram that represents each of the following. **1–2. See margin.**
   a. congruent triangles   b. quadrilateral   c. circumference
2. **Compare and contrast** complementary and supplementary angles.

Skills and Applications

In the figure at the right, $a \parallel b$, and c is a transversal. If $m\angle 5 = 58°$, find the measure of each angle.

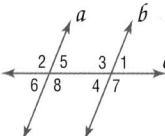

3. $\angle 6$ **58°**   4. $\angle 7$ **122°**   5. $\angle 4$ **58°**   6. $\angle 3$ **122°**

Complete each congruence statement if $\triangle MNO \cong \triangle PRS$.

7. $\angle P \cong$? $\angle M$ 8. $\overline{RS} \cong$? $\overline{NO}$ 9. $\angle MNO \cong$? $\angle PRS$

Find the coordinates of the vertices of each figure after the given transformation. Then graph the transformation image. 10–11. See margin.

10. reflection over the y-axis

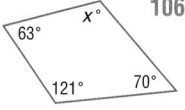

11. rotation of 90° clockwise

ALGEBRA   **Find the value of x. Then find the missing angle measure.**

12. **106°**

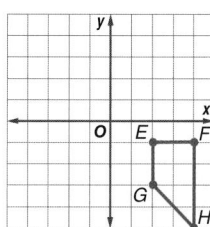

13. **83°; 72°; 165°**

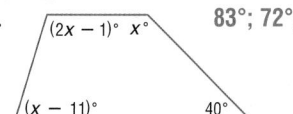

Find the area of each figure described.

14. triangle: base, 21 ft.; height, 16 ft **168 ft²**
15. parallelogram: base, 7 ft; height, 2.5 ft **17.5 ft²**

Classify each polygon. Find the sum of the measures of the interior angles.

16. **hexagon; 720°**

17. **octagon; 1080°**

Find the area and circumference of each circle. Round to the nearest tenth.

18. The radius is 3 miles. **28.3 mi²; 18.8 mi**
19. The diameter is 10 inches. **78.5 in²; 31.4 in.**

20. **STANDARDIZED TEST PRACTICE**   What is the diameter of a circle if its circumference is 54.8 meters? Round to the nearest tenth. **C**
      (A) 8.7 m   (B) 15.6 m   (C) 17.4 m   (D) 34.9 m

www.pre-alg.com/chapter_test

Portfolio Suggestion

Introduction   When finding the area of an irregular figure, there may be multiple ways to divide the figure.

Ask Students   to pick an irregular figure from their work in this chapter and show at least two ways of subdividing it. Compare the ways based on number of formulas needed. Have them place their drawings and comparisons in their portfolios.

Assessment Options

Vocabulary Test   A vocabulary review/test for Chapter 10 can be found on p. 602 of the *Chapter 10 Resource Masters*.

Chapter Tests   There are six Chapter 10 Tests and an Open-Ended Assessment task available in the *Chapter 10 Resource Masters*.

Chapter 10 Tests			
Form	Type	Level	Pages
1	MC	basic	589–590
2A	MC	average	591–592
2B	MC	average	593–594
2C	FR	average	595–596
2D	FR	average	597–598
3	FR	advanced	599–600

MC = multiple-choice questions
FR = free-response questions

Open-Ended Assessment
Performance tasks for Chapter 10 can be found on p. 601 of the *Chapter 10 Resource Masters*, along with a sample scoring rubric for these tasks on p. A27.

ExamView® Pro

Use the networkable **ExamView® Pro** to:

- Create **multiple versions** of tests.
- Create **modified** tests for *Inclusion* students.
- **Edit** existing questions and **add** your own questions.
- Use built-in **state curriculum correlations** to create tests aligned with state standards.
- Change **English** tests to **Spanish** and vice versa.

These two pages contain practice questions in the various formats that can be found on the most frequently given standardized tests.

A practice answer sheet for these two pages can be found on page A1 of the *Chapter 10 Resource Masters*.

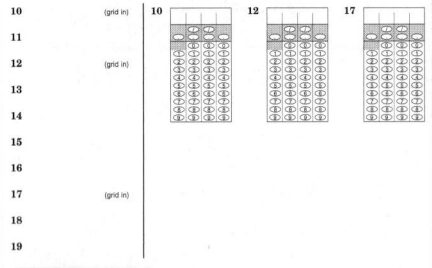

Standardized Test Practice Student Recording Sheet, p. A1

Additional Practice

See pp. 607–608 of the *Chapter 10 Resource Masters* for additional standardized test practice.

Part 1 Multiple Choice

Record your answers on the answer sheet provided by your teacher or on a sheet of paper.

1. Which expression is equivalent to $\frac{5^5}{5^3}$? (Lessons 4-2 and 4-7) **B**

   (A) 5^{-2} (B) 5^2 (C) 5^8 (D) 5^{15}

2. The rectangles shown below are similar. Which proportion can be used to find x? (Lesson 6-2) **D**

   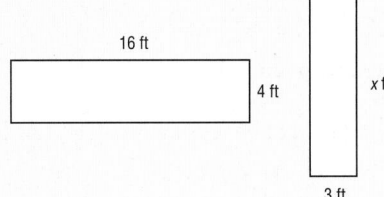

   (A) $\frac{x}{3} = \frac{4}{16}$ (B) $\frac{3}{16} = \frac{4}{x}$

   (C) $\frac{16}{3} = \frac{x}{4}$ (D) $\frac{16}{4} = \frac{x}{3}$

3. Suppose 2% of the containers made by a manufacturer are defective. If 750 of the containers are inspected, how many can be expected *not* to be defective? (Lesson 6-9) **C**

   (A) 150   (B) 730   (C) 735   (D) 748

4. Lawanda plans to paint each side of a cube either white or blue so that when the cube is tossed, the probability that the cube will land on a blue side is $\frac{1}{3}$. How many sides of the cube should she paint blue? (Lesson 6-9) **B**

   (A) 1   (B) 2   (C) 3   (D) 4

5. In the spreadsheet below, a formula applied to the values in columns A and B results in the values in column C. What is the formula? (Lesson 8-1) **B**

   (A) $C = A - B$

   (B) $C = A - 2B$

   (C) $C = A + B$

   (D) $C = A + 2B$

	A	B	C
1	4	0	4
2	5	1	3
3	6	2	2
4	7	3	1

6. Triangle *ABC* is a right triangle. What is the length of the hypotenuse? (Lesson 9-5) **C**

   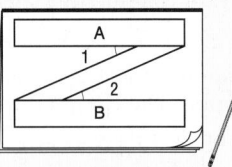

   (A) 12 units

   (B) 32 units

   (C) 60 units

   (D) 84 units

7. A graphic artist has designed the logo shown below. If rectangles A and B are parallel, then which statement is true? (Lesson 10-1) **A**

   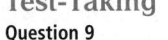

   (A) $m\angle 1 - m\angle 2 = 0°$

   (B) $m\angle 1 - m\angle 2 = 45°$

   (C) $m\angle 1 + m\angle 2 = 90°$

   (D) $m\angle 1 + m\angle 2 = 180°$

8. In quadrilateral *ABCD*, $m\angle A = 100°$, $m\angle B = 100°$, and $m\angle C = 90°$. Find $m\angle D$. (Lesson 10-4) **A**

   (A) $70°$ (B) $85°$ (C) $90°$ (D) $170°$

9. Refer to the figure shown. What is the best estimate of the area of the circle inscribed in the square? (Lesson 10-7) **A**

   (A) 7 in²   (B) 9 in²

   (C) 19 in²   (D) 28 in²

   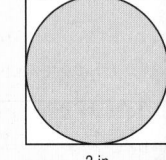

   3 in.

Test-Taking Tip   (A) (B) (C) (D)

Question 9
Most standardized tests include any necessary formulas in the test booklet. It helps to be familiar with formulas such as the area of a rectangle and the circumference of a circle, but use any formulas that are given to you.

ExamView® Pro

Special banks of standardized test questions similar to those on the SAT, ACT, TIMSS 8, NAEP 8, and Pre-Algebra End-of-Course tests can be found on this CD-ROM.

Part 2 | Short Response/Grid In

Record your answers on the answer sheet provided by your teacher or on a sheet of paper.

10. If $x = 3$, what is the value of $\frac{14x + 6}{5x - 3}$?
(Lesson 1-2) **4**

11. Refer to the data set shown.

    20 20 21 22 24 24 24 26

    Which is greater, the median or the mode?
    (Lesson 5-8) **mode**

12. A magazine asked 512 students who use computers if they use e-mail. About 83% of the students said that they use e-mail. About how many of these students use e-mail? (Lesson 6-9) **425**

13. Gracia is finding three consecutive whole numbers whose sum is 78. She uses the equation $n + (n + 1) + (n + 2) = 78$. What expression represents the greatest of the three numbers? (Lesson 7-2) **$n + 2$**

14. Solve $4x + 7 < 39$. (Lesson 7-6) **$x < 8$**

15. What is the slope of the line represented by the equation $3x + y = 5$? (Lesson 8-4) **−3**

16. Find the coordinates of the vertices for quadrilateral $WXYZ$ after a translation of $(-2, -1)$. (Lesson 10-3) **See margin.**

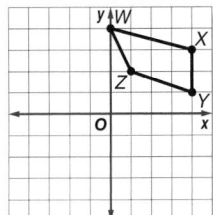

17. These two triangles are congruent. What is the value of x? (Lesson 9-4) **40**

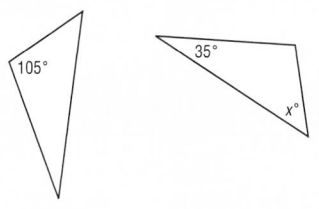

18. What name *best* classifies this quadrilateral?
(Lesson 10-4) **rhombus**

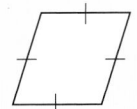

19. The diagram shows a kitchen counter with an area cut out for a sink. What is the area of the counter top?
(Lesson 10-8) **42 ft²**

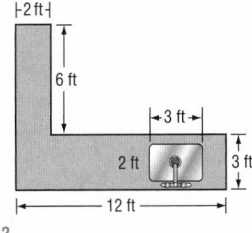

Part 3 | Extended Response

Record your answers on a sheet of paper. Show your work.

20. Triangle JKM is shown.
(Lesson 10-3)

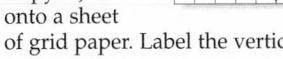

a. What are the coordinates of the vertices of $\triangle JKM$?

b. Copy $\triangle JKM$ onto a sheet of grid paper. Label the vertices.

c. Graph the image of $\triangle JKM$ after a translation 2 units left and 3 units down. Label the translated image $\triangle J'K'M'$.

d. Graph the image of $\triangle J'K'M'$ after a reflection over the y-axis. Label the reflection of $\triangle J'K'M'$ as $\triangle J''K''M''$.

e. On another sheet of grid paper, graph $\triangle JKM$. Then graph $\triangle JKM$ after a reflection over the y-axis. Label the reflection $\triangle J'K'M'$.

f. Graph the image of the reflection in part **e** after a translation 2 units right and 3 units down. Label the translated image $\triangle J''K''M''$.

g. Tell whether the image of $\triangle J''K''M''$ in part **d** is the same as the image of $\triangle J''K''M''$ in part **e**. Explain why or why not. **a–g. See margin.**

Chapter 10 Standardized Test Practice **551**

Evaluating Extended Response Questions

Extended Response questions are graded by using a multilevel rubric that guides you in assessing a student's knowledge of a particular concept.

Goal: Identify the coordinates and vertices of a triangle/Carry out a series of translations and reflections with a triangular figure.

Sample Scoring Rubric: The following rubric is a sample scoring device. You may wish to add more detail to this sample to meet your individual scoring needs.

Score	Criteria
4	A correct solution that is supported by well-developed, accurate explanations
3	A generally correct solution, but may contain minor flaws in reasoning or computation
2	A partially correct interpretation and/or solution to the problem
1	A correct solution with no supporting evidence or explanation
0	An incorrect solution indicating no mathematical understanding of the concept or task, or no solution is given

Answers

16. $W'(-2, 3)$, $X'(2, 2)$, $Y'(2, 0)$, $Z'(-1, 1)$

20a. $J(-3, 4)$, $K(-2, 1)$, $M(-1, 2)$

20b–d.

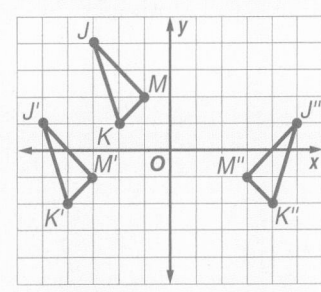

20e–f.

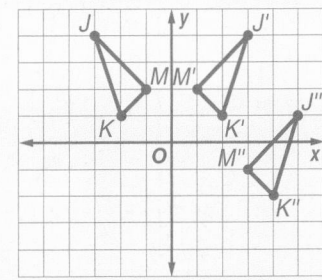

20g. The two images are the same because the order in which these operations are performed does not matter. Thus, the result is the same.

Page 502, Lesson 10-2

1. They have the same size and shape.

2.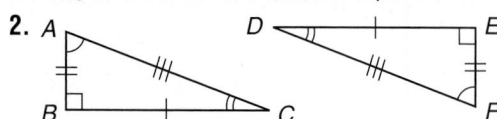

3. $\angle J \cong \angle C$, $\angle K \cong \angle B$, $\angle M \cong \angle G$, $\overline{KM} \cong \overline{BG}$, $\overline{MJ} \cong \overline{GC}$, $\overline{KJ} \cong \overline{BC}$; $\triangle BGC$

4. $\angle C \cong \angle D$, $\angle B \cong \angle B$, $\angle E \cong \angle A$, $\overline{CB} \cong \overline{DB}$, $\overline{BE} \cong \overline{BA}$, $\overline{CE} \cong \overline{DA}$; $\triangle DBA$

Page 505, Algebra Activity

1.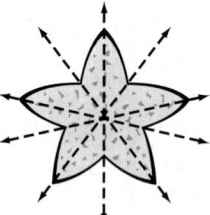

3.

Page 510, Lesson 10-3

11. $R'(-4, -3)$, $S'(0, -3)$, $T'(-4, 1)$

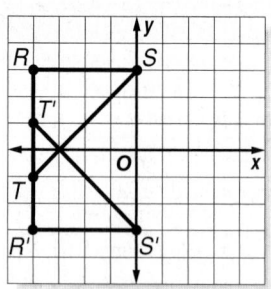

12. $A'(-1, 3)$, $B'(-4, 4)$, $C'(-4, 1)$, $D'(-2, -1)$

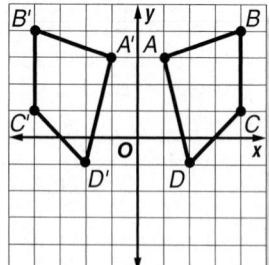

13. $M'(-1, -2)$, $N'(4, -4)$, $O'(3, -2)$, $P'(3, 0)$, $Q'(0, 0)$

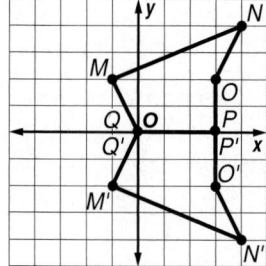

14.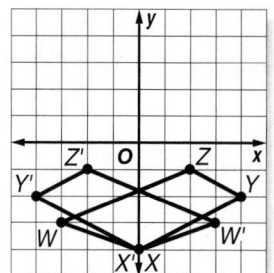

15.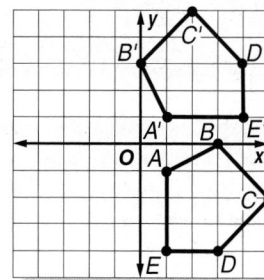

17.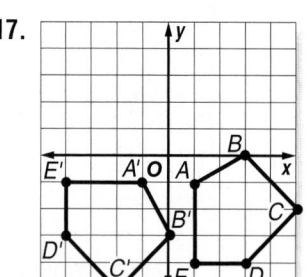

21. Sample answer:

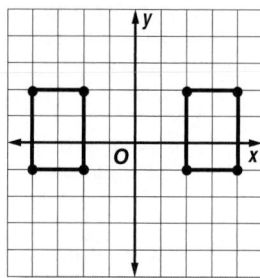

The image of the figure's reflection is the same as the image of its translation to the right 6 units.

Page 512, Algebra Activity

1. The corresponding angles have the same measure.

2. The lengths of the sides of the enlarged trapezoid are twice the length of the corresponding sides of the smaller trapezoid.

3. 2:1; The ratios are the same.

4. See students' work. The results are not the same. By multiplying the coordinates of trapezoid *ABCD* by a scale factor of one-half, the resulting figure is a trapezoid that has sides that are half the size of the original trapezoid.

5. If the scale factor is greater than 1, the image is an enlargement. If the scale factor is less than 1, the image is a reduction.

6. Whereas translations, reflections, and rotations produce congruent figures, dilations produce enlargements or reductions of the figure.

7. $M'(3, 6)$; $N'(6, 0)$

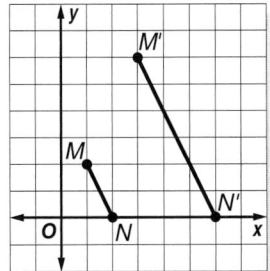

8. $A'(-1, 1)$; $B'(1, \frac{1}{2})$; $C'(1, 2)$

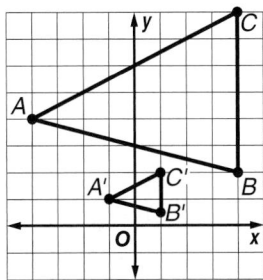

9. $D'(-6, -3)$; $E'(-7.5, -7.5)$; $F'(0, -6)$; $G'(-1.5, -1.5)$

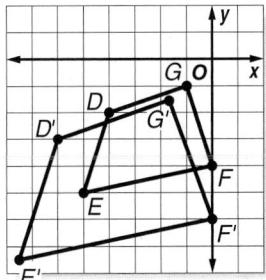

Page 526, Reading Mathematics

2. Sample answer: quad: quadrant— an arc of 90° that is one quarter of a circle.

pent: pentahedron— a three-dimensional solid with five faces.

hex: hexagram— a two-dimensional figure that has equilateral triangles on each side of a regular hexagon.

hept: heptagon— a two-dimensional, closed figure with seven sides.

oct: octal— a number system with a base of 8.

dec: decare— a metric unit of area equal to 0.2471 acre.

3. Sample answer: quad: quadricep— a muscle located on the front of the thigh that is divided into four parts.

pent: pentamerous— divided into or consisting of five parts.

hex: hexahydrate— a chemical compound with six molecules of water.

hept: heptameter— a line of verse consisting of seven metrical feet.

oct: octogenarian— a person whose age is in the eighties.

dec: decasyllabic— consisting of ten syllables or composed of verses of ten syllables.

Page 532, Algebra Activity

1.

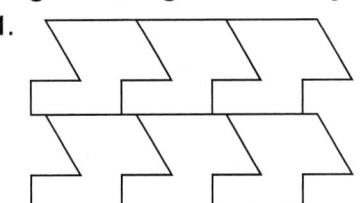

2.

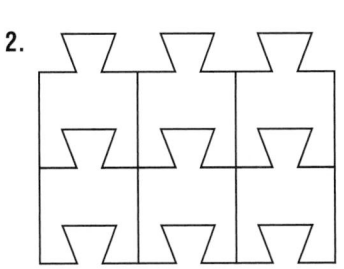

3.

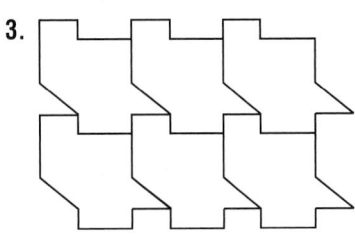

4.

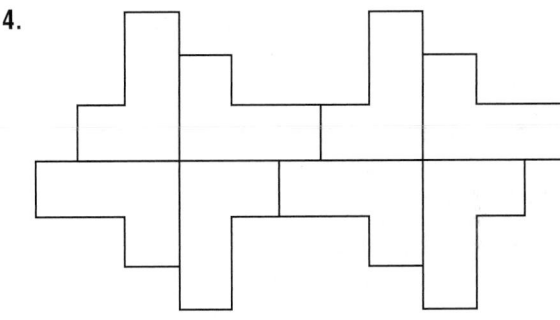

5.

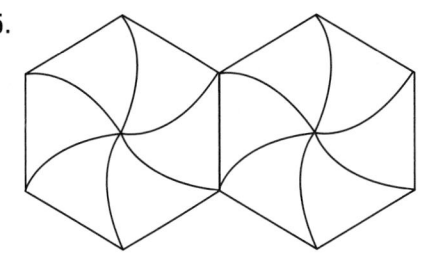

6.

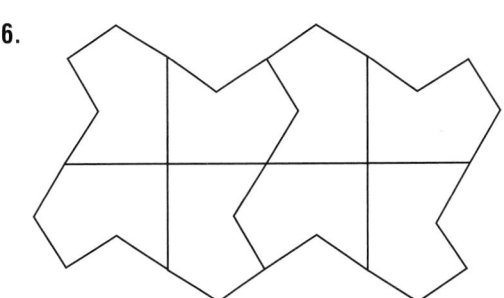

Chapter 11

Three-Dimensional Figures

Chapter Overview and Pacing

Year-long pacing: pages T20–T21.

LESSON OBJECTIVES	PACING (days)			
	Regular		Block	
	Basic/ Average	Advanced	Basic/ Average	Advanced
11-1 Three Dimensional Figures (pp. 554–561) *Preview:* Draw three-dimensional figures using different perspectives and create three-dimensional figures using nets. • Identify three-dimensional figures • Identify diagonals and skew lines.	2 (with 11-1 Preview)	1	1 (with 11-1 Preview)	0.5
11-2 Volume: Prisms and Cylinders (pp. 562–567) *Preview:* Investigate volume by creating and comparing containers of various shapes. • Find volumes of prisms. • Find volumes of circular cylinders.	2 (with 11-2 Preview)	1	1 (with 11-2 Preview)	0.5
11-3 Volume: Pyramids and Cones (pp. 568–572) • Find volumes of pyramids. • Find volumes of cones.	1	1	0.5	0.5
11-4 Surface Area: Prisms and Cylinders (pp. 573–577) • Find surface areas of prisms. • Find surface areas of cylinders.	1	1	0.5	0.5
11-5 Surface Area: Pyramids and Cones (pp. 578–582) • Find the surface areas of pyramids. • Find the surface areas of cones.	1	1	0.5	0.5
11-6 Similar Solids (pp. 583–588) *Preview:* Investigate similar solids using sugar cubes or centimeter cubes. • Identify similar solids. • Solve problems involving similar solids.	2 (with 11-6 Preview)	1	1 (with 11-6 Preview)	1
11-7 Precision and Significant Digits (pp. 590–594) • Describe measurements using precision and significant digits. • Apply precision and significant digits in problem-solving situations.	1	1	0.5	0.5
Study Guide and **Practice Test** (pp. 595–599) **Standardized Test Practice** (pp. 600–601)	1	1	0.5	0.5
Chapter Assessment	1	1	0.5	0.5
TOTAL	12	9	6	5

*An electronic version of this chapter is available on **StudentWorks™**. This backpack solution CD-ROM allows students instant access to the Student Edition, lesson worksheet pages, and web resources.*

Chapter Resource Manager

Timesaving Tools

TeacherWorks™

All-In-One Planner and Resource Center

See pages T5 and T21.

CHAPTER 11 RESOURCE MASTERS

Study Guide and Intervention	Practice (Skills and Average)	Reading to Learn Mathematics	Enrichment	Assessment	Prerequisite Skills Workbook	Applications*	Parent and Student Study Guide Workbook	5-Minute Check Transparencies	Interactive Chalkboard	Pre-AlgePASS: Tutorial Plus (lessons)	Materials
609	610–611	612	613				90	11-1	11-1		*Preview:* centimeter cubes, isometric dot paper, unlined paper, scissors, tape
614	615–616	617	618	659		SC 21 GCS 39	91	11-2	11-2		*Preview:* 5 × 8 index cards, tape, rice
619	620–621	622	623				92	11-3	11-3	35	
624	625–626	627	628	659, 661		SC 22 GCS 40	93	11-4	11-4		
629	630–631	632	633				94	11-5	11-5		
634	635–636	637	638	660			95	11-6	11-6	36	*Preview:* sugar cubes, centimeter cubes
639	640–641	642	643	660			96	11-7	11-7		
				645–658, 662–666							

Key to Abbreviations: GCS = Graphing Calculator and Spreadsheet Masters
SC = School-to-Career Masters
SM = Science and Mathematics Lab Manual

ELL Study Guide and Intervention, Skills Practice, Practice, and Parent and Student Study Guide Workbooks are also available in Spanish.

Mathematical Connections and Background

Continuity of Instruction

Prior Knowledge

In Chapter 10, students investigated intersecting lines and the relationships between the angles that are formed. Students identified properties of congruent triangles, drew transformations, and found angle measures of polygons. They learned to find the area of polygons and irregular figures. They explored properties of circles, including the relationships among diameter, circumference, area, and π.

This Chapter

Students will identify three-dimensional figures. They will find the surface area and volume of prisms, cylinders, pyramids, and cones. Students will also identify similar solids, noting that these figures have the same shape and their corresponding linear measures are proportional. Students will explore the concepts of precision and significant digits and apply precision and significant digits in problem-solving situations.

Future Connections

The study of three-dimensional figures, including surface area and volume, will be explored in analytical and solid geometry. Precision measurements and significant digits play important roles in engineering and the sciences.

11-1 Three-Dimensional Figures

A plane is a two-dimensional flat surface that extends in all directions. Intersecting planes can form the edges and vertices of three-dimensional figures or solids. A polyhedron is a solid with flat surfaces that are polygons. Polyhedrons are composed of faces, edges, and vertices and are differentiated by the shape and number of their bases. Skew lines are lines that lie in different planes. They are neither intersecting nor parallel.

11-2 Volume: Prisms and Cylinders

Volume is the measure of space occupied by a solid region. To find the volume of a prism, the area of the base is multiplied by the measure of the height, $V = Bh$. A solid containing several prisms can be broken down into its component prisms. Then the volume of each component can be found and the volumes added. The volume of a cylinder can be determined by finding the area of its circular base, πr^2, and then multiplying by the height of the cylinder.

11-3 Volume: Pyramids and Cones

A pyramid has one-third the volume of a prism with the same base and height. To find the volume of a pyramid, multiply the area of the base by the pyramid's height, and then divide by 3. Simply stated, the formula for the volume of a pyramid is $V = \frac{1}{3}bh$. A cone is a three-dimensional figure with one circular base and a curved surface connecting the base and the vertex. The volume of a cone is one-third the volume of a cylinder with the same base area and height. Like a pyramid, the formula for the volume of a cone is $V = \frac{1}{3}bh$. More specifically, the formula is $V = \frac{1}{3}\pi r^2 h$.

11-4 Surface Area: Prisms and Cylinders

The material needed to cover the surface of a figure is called its surface area. It can be calculated by finding the area of each face and adding them together. To find the surface area of a rectangular prism, for example, the formula $S = 2\ell w + 2\ell w + 2\ell w$ applies. A cylinder, on the other hand, may be unrolled to reveal two circles and a rectangle. Its surface area can be determined by finding the area of the two circles, $2\pi r^2$, and adding it to the area of the rectangle, $2\pi rh$ (the length of the rectangle is the circumference of one of the circles), or $S = 2\pi r^2 + 2\pi rh$.

11-5 Surface Area: Pyramids and Cones

The sides of a pyramid are triangles that intersect at the vertex. These sides are called lateral faces and the height of each is called the slant height. The sum of their areas is the lateral area of a pyramid. The surface area of a square pyramid is the lateral area $\frac{1}{2}bh$ (area of lateral face) times 4 (number of lateral faces), plus the area of the base. The surface area of a cone is the area of its circular base (πr^2) plus its lateral area ($\pi r \ell$, where ℓ is the slant height).

11-6 Similar Solids

Solid figures are considered to be similar if they have the same shape and their corresponding linear measures are proportional. Figures can be tested for similarity by comparing corresponding measures. If the compared ratios are proportional, then the figures are similar solids. Missing measures of similar solids can also be determined by using proportions. Proportional comparisons can be used to solve real-world problems involving relative size, scale models, and scale drawings.

11-7 Precision and Significant Digits

The precision of measurement is the exactness to which a measurement is made. Precision depends on the smallest unit of measure being used, or the precision unit. One way to record a measure is to estimate to the nearest precision unit. A more precise method is to include all of the digits that are actually measured, plus one estimated digit. The digits recorded, called significant digits, indicate the precision of the measurement. There are special rules for determining significant digits. If a number contains a decimal point, the number of significant digits is found by counting from left to right, starting with the first nonzero digit. If the number does not contain a decimal point, the number of significant digits is found by counting the digits from left to right, starting with the first digit and ending with the last nonzero digit.

Quick Review Math Handbook

Hot Words includes a glossary of terms while Hot Topics consists of explanations of key mathematical concepts with exercises to test comprehension. This valuable resource can be used as a reference in the classroom or for home study.

Lesson	Hot Topics Section	Lesson	Hot Topics Section
GS 11	7.2, 7.4	11-3	7.7
11-1P	7.6, 7.7	11-4	2.4, 2.6, 7.6
11-1	7.5, 7.6, 7.7	11-5	6.5, 7.6
11-2P	7.7	11-6P, 11-6	8.6
11-2	1.5, 2.4, 7.7	11-7	8.1

GS = Getting Started, P = Preview

 Additional mathematical information and teaching notes are available at www.pre-alg.com/key_concepts.

D A I L Y
INTERVENTION and Assessment

Key to Abbreviations:
TWE = Teacher Wraparound Edition; CRM = Chapter Resource Masters

	Type	Student Edition	Teacher Resources	Technology/Internet
INTERVENTION	Ongoing	Prerequisite Skills, pp. 553, 561, 567, 572, 577, 582, 588 Practice Quiz 1, p. 572 Practice Quiz 2, p. 588	5-Minute Check Transparencies Quizzes, *CRM,* pp. 659–660 Mid-Chapter Test, *CRM,* p. 661 Study Guide and Intervention, *CRM,* pp. 609, 614, 619, 624, 629, 634, 639	Pre-AlgePASS: Tutorial Plus, Lessons 35 and 36 www.pre-alg.com/ self_check_quiz www.pre-alg.com/ extra_examples
	Mixed Review	pp. 561, 567, 572, 577, 582, 588, 594	Cumulative Review, *CRM,* p. 662	
	Error Analysis	Find the Error, pp. 565, 592	Find the Error, *TWE,* pp. 565, 592 Unlocking Misconceptions, *TWE,* pp. 557, 579, 591	
ASSESSMENT	Standardized Test Practice	pp. 561, 564, 566, 567, 572, 577, 582, 588, 594, 600–601	*TWE,* pp. 600–601 Standardized Test Practice, *CRM,* pp. 663–664	Standardized Test Practice CD-ROM www.pre-alg.com/ standardized_test
	Open-Ended Assessment	Writing in Math, pp. 561, 567, 571, 577, 582, 588, 594 Open Ended, pp. 559, 565, 570, 575, 580, 586, 592 Standardized Test, p. 601	Speaking: *TWE,* pp. 567, 576 Writing: *TWE,* pp. 572, 588 Modeling: *TWE,* pp. 561, 582, 594 Open-Ended Assessment, *CRM,* p. 657	
	Chapter Assessment	Study Guide, pp. 595–598 Practice Test, p. 599	Multiple-Choice Tests (Forms 1, 2A, 2B), *CRM,* pp. 645–650 Free-Response Tests (Forms 2C, 2D, 3), *CRM,* pp. 651–656 Vocabulary Test/Review, *CRM,* p. 658	ExamView® Pro (see below) MindJogger Videoquizzes www.pre-alg.com/ vocabulary_review www.pre-alg.com/chapter_test

For more information on Yearly ProgressPro, see p. 432.

Pre-Algebra Lesson	Yearly ProgressPro Skill Lesson
11-1	Three-Dimensional Figures
11-2	Volume of Triangular Prisms
11-3	Volume of Pyramids and Cones
11-4	Surface Area of Triangular Prisms
11-5	Surface Area of Pyramids and Cones
11-6	Similar Figures
11-7	Precision and Measurement

ExamView® Pro

Use the networkable **ExamView® Pro** to:
- Create **multiple versions** of tests.
- Create **modified** tests for *Inclusion* students.
- **Edit** existing questions and **add** your own questions.
- Use built-in **state curriculum correlations** to create tests aligned with state standards.
- Change **English** tests to **Spanish** and vice versa.

For more information on Intervention and Assessment, see pp. T8–T11.

Reading and Writing in Mathematics

Glencoe Pre-Algebra provides numerous opportunities to incorporate reading and writing into the mathematics classroom.

Student Edition

- Foldables™ Study Organizer, p. 553
- Reading Mathematics, p. 589
- Concept Check questions require students to verbalize and write about what they have learned in the lesson. (pp. 557, 559, 565, 569, 570, 575, 580, 586, 592)
- Writing in Math questions in every lesson, pp. 561, 567, 571, 577, 582, 588, 594
- Reading Math, pp. 565, 569
- WebQuest, pp. 571, 594

Teacher Wraparound Edition

- Foldables™ Study Organizer, pp. 553, 595
- Study Notebook suggestions, pp. 555, 559, 562, 565, 570, 575, 580, 583, 586, 589, 592
- Modeling activities, pp. 561, 582, 594
- Speaking activities, pp. 567, 576
- Writing activities, pp. 572, 588
- **ELL** Resources, pp. 552, 556, 563, 568, 573, 578, 584, 589, 590, 595

Additional Resources

- Vocabulary Builder worksheets require students to define and give examples for key vocabulary terms as they progress through the chapter (*Chapter 4 Resource Masters,* pp. vii–viii)
- Reading to Learn Mathematics master for each lesson (*Chapter 4 Resource Masters,* pp. 612, 617, 622, 627, 632, 637, 642)
- *Vocabulary PuzzleMaker* software creates crossword, jumble, and word search puzzles using vocabulary lists that you can customize.
- *Teaching Mathematics with Foldables* provides suggestions for promoting cognition and language.
- *Reading and Writing in the Mathematics Classroom*
- *WebQuest and Project Resources*

For more information on Reading and Writing in Mathematics, see pp. T6–T7.

PROJECT CRISS℠ Study Skill

A content frame can help students understand mathematical relationships, especially when a number of new formulas are being learned.

The frame at the right shows a comparison of the formulas for the volumes of rectangular prisms and the volumes of cylinders. From the sketches, students should note that the volumes could both be written as $V = Bh$, where B is the area of the base. Have students include additional figures and formulas in their frame as they read through Chapter 11. Then, allow time for a class discussion so students can compare formulas.

Figure	Sketch	Volume Formula
rectangular prism		$V = \ell \cdot w \cdot h$
cylinder		$V = \pi r^2 h$

CReating **I**ndependence **T**hrough **S**tudent-Owned **S**trategies

What You'll Learn

Have students read over the list of objectives and make a list of any words with which they are not familiar.

Why It's Important

Point out to students that this is only one of many reasons why each objective is important. Others are provided in the introduction to each lesson.

What You'll Learn

- **Lesson 11-1**   Identify three-dimensional figures.
- **Lessons 11-2 and 11-3**   Find volumes of prisms, cylinders, pyramids, and cones.
- **Lessons 11-4 and 11-5**   Find surface areas of prisms, cylinders, pyramids, and cones.
- **Lesson 11-6**   Identify similar solids.
- **Lesson 11-7**   Use precision and significant digits to describe measurements.

Key Vocabulary

- polyhedron (p. 556)
- volume (p. 563)
- surface area (p. 573)
- similar solids (p. 584)
- precision (p. 590)

Why It's Important

Three-dimensional figures have special characteristics. These characteristics are important when architects are designing buildings and other three-dimensional structures. *You will investigate the characteristics of architectural structures in Lesson 11-1.*

552   Chapter 11   Three-Dimensional Figures

Lesson	NCTM Standards	Local Objectives
11-1 Preview	3, 10	
11-1	3, 6, 8, 9, 10	
11-2 Preview	3, 4, 6, 7, 9	
11-2	1, 2, 3, 4, 6, 8, 9, 10	
11-3	1, 2, 3, 4, 6, 8, 9, 10	
11-4	1, 2, 3, 4, 6, 8, 9, 10	
11-5	1, 2, 3, 4, 6, 8, 9, 10	
11-6 Preview	3, 4, 5, 6, 7, 8, 10	
11-6	1, 2, 3, 4, 6, 8, 9, 10	
11-7	1, 3, 4, 6, 8, 9, 10	

Key to NCTM Standards:

1=Number & Operations, 2=Algebra,
3=Geometry, 4=Measurement,
5=Data Analysis & Probability, 6=Problem Solving, 7=Reasoning & Proof,
8=Communication, 9=Connections,
10=Representation

Vocabulary Builder   ELL

The Key Vocabulary list introduces students to some of the main vocabulary terms included in this chapter. For a more thorough vocabulary list with pronunciations of new words, give students the Vocabulary Builder worksheets found on pages vii and viii of the *Chapter 11 Resource Masters*. Encourage them to complete the definition of each term as they progress through the chapter. You may suggest that they add these sheets to their study notebooks for future reference when studying for the Chapter 11 test.

▶ **Prerequisite Skills** To be successful in this chapter, you'll need to master these skills and be able to apply them in problem-solving situations. Review these skills before beginning Chapter 11.

For Lesson 11-1   Polygons

Determine whether each figure is a polygon. If it is, classify the polygon.

(For review, see Lesson 10-6.) **4. yes; quadrilateral**

1.  yes; triangle **2.** no **3.** no **4.**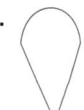

For Lessons 11-2 through 11-5   Multiplying Rational Numbers

Find each product. *(For review, see Lesson 5-3.)*

5. $8.5 \cdot 2$ **17**

6. $3.2(3.2)$**10 102.4**

7. $\frac{1}{2} \cdot 14$ **7**

8. $\frac{1}{2}(6.4)(5)$ **16**

9. $\frac{1}{3}(50)(9.3)$ **155**

10. $\frac{1}{3}\left(\frac{1}{2} \cdot 3 \cdot 8\right)$ **4**

For Lesson 11-6   Proportions

Determine whether each pair of ratios forms a proportion. *(For review, see Lesson 6-2.)*

11. $\frac{3}{8}, \frac{9}{24}$ **yes**

12. $\frac{7}{2}, \frac{14}{6}$ **no**

13. $\frac{18}{32}, \frac{9}{16}$ **yes**

14. $\frac{12}{15}, \frac{4}{5}$ **yes**

15. $\frac{1.2}{5}, \frac{6}{25}$ **yes**

16. $\frac{1.6}{2}, \frac{3.6}{6}$ **no**

Surface Area and Volume Make this Foldable to help you organize your notes. Begin with a plain piece of 11" × 17" paper.

Step 1 **Fold**

Fold the paper in thirds lengthwise.

Step 2 **Open and Fold**

Fold a 2" tab along the short side. Then fold the rest in fourths.

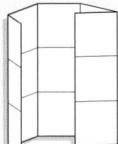

Step 3 **Label**

Draw lines along folds and label as shown.

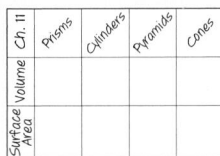

Reading and Writing As you read and study the chapter, write the formulas for surface area and volume and list the characteristics of each three-dimensional figure.

This section provides a review of the basic concepts needed before beginning Chapter 11. Page references are included for additional student help.

Prerequisite Skills in the Getting Ready for the Next Lesson section at the end of each lesson reviews a skill needed in the next lesson.

For Lesson	Prerequisite Skill
11-2	Areas of Triangles (p. 561)
11-3	Multiplying Fractions (p. 567)
11-4	Estimating Products (p. 572)
11-5	Multiplying Rational Numbers (p. 577)
11-6	Proportions (p. 582)
11-7	Rounding Decimals (p. 588)

Using Tables to Compare and Contrast In the grid of their table, students take notes, define terms, write formulas, and list characteristics of each three-dimensional figure. Use the data recorded to compare and contrast three-dimensional shapes. When making comparisons in mathematics, first determine what will be compared, then decide what standards will be used for comparison, and then use what is known to find similarities and differences.

For more information about Foldables, see *Teaching Mathematics with Foldables.*

A Preview of Lesson 11-1

Getting Started

Objective Draw three-dimensional figures using different perspectives and create three-dimensional figures using nets.

Materials
centimeter cubes, isometric dot paper, unlined paper, scissors, tape

Teaching Tip Use square building blocks to create a figure to demonstrate differing perspectives.

Teach

Activity 1

- Have students try to determine the number of blocks they need to build each figure before they begin. Discuss how they arrived at their answers.
- If students are having difficulty recognizing the different perspectives, encourage them to label their figures "top," "side," and "front."

Answers

1–3. Sample answers are given.

1.
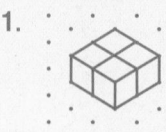

2.

3.
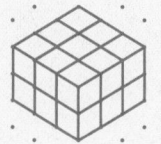

Building Three-Dimensional Figures

Activity 1

Different views of a stack of cubes are shown at the right. A point of view is called a **perspective**. You can build or draw a three-dimensional figure using different perspectives. When drawing figures, use isometric dot paper.

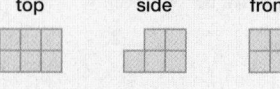

Step 1 Use the top view to build the base of the figure. The top view shows that the base is a 2-by-3 rectangle.

Step 2 Use the side view to complete the figure. The side view shows that the height of the first row is 1 unit, and the height of the second and third rows is 2 units.

Step 3 Use the front view to check the figure. The front view is a 2-by-2 square. This shows that the overall height and width of the figure is 2 units. So, the figure is correct.

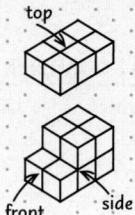

Model 1–9. See margin.

The top view, a side view, and the front view of three-dimensional figures are shown. Use cubes to build each figure. Draw your model on isometric dot paper.

1. top   side   front
2. top   side   front
3. top   side   front
4. top   side   front
5. top   side   front
6. top   side   front

Draw and label the top view, a side view, and the front view for each figure.

7.
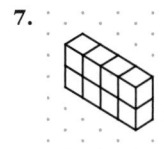

8.

9.

Resource Manager

Teaching Pre-Algebra with Manipulatives
- p. 143 (student recording sheet)
- p. 16 (master for isometric paper)

Glencoe Mathematics Classroom Manipulative Kit
- isometric dot grid stamp
- centimeter cubes

Activity 2

Suppose you cut a cardboard box along its edges, open it up, and lay it flat. The result is a two-dimensional figure called a net. **Nets** are two-dimensional patterns for three-dimensional figures.

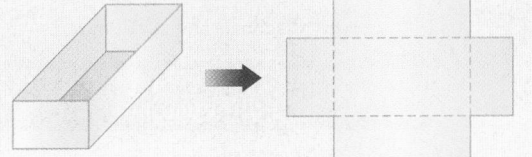

Nets can help you see the regions or *faces* that make up the surface of a figure. So, you can use a net to build a three-dimensional figure.

Step 1 Copy the net on a piece of paper, shading the base as shown.

Step 2 Use scissors to cut out the net.

Step 3 Fold on the dashed lines.

Step 4 Tape the sides together.

Different views of this figure are shown.

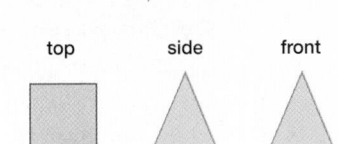

top   side   front

Model 10–15. See pp. 601A–601B.

Copy each net. Then cut out the net and fold on the dashed lines to make a 3-dimensional figure, using the purple areas as the bases. Sketch each figure, and draw and label the top view, a side view, and the front view.

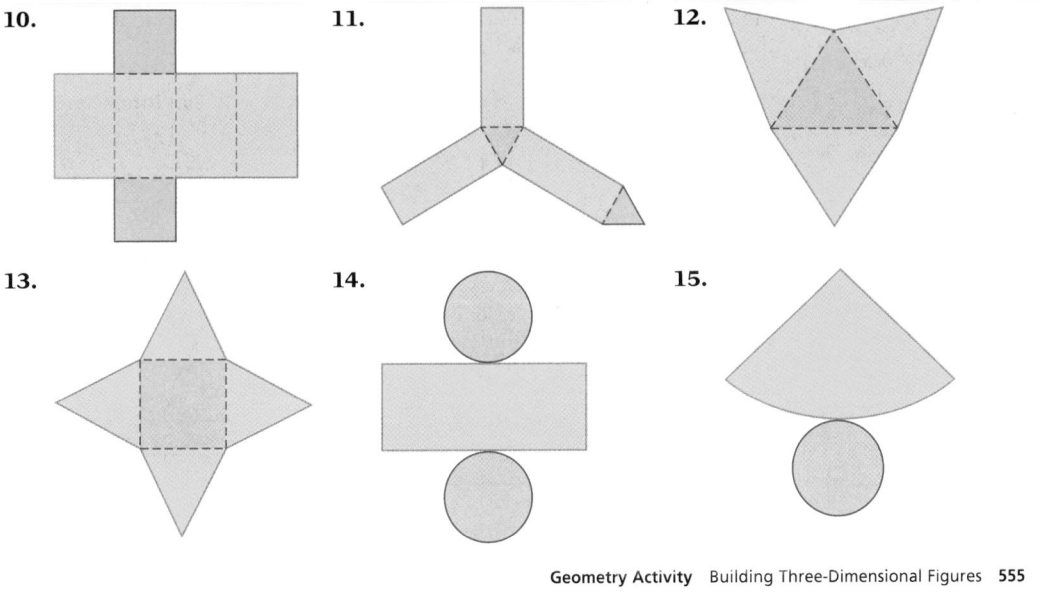

10.

11.

12.

13.

14.

15.

Answers

4–9. Sample answers are given.

4.

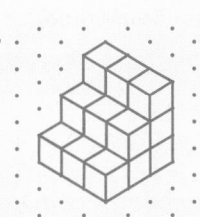

5.

6.

- Discuss with students how nets make the study of three-dimensional figures easier. Point out that nets allow for accurate measurements of the figure's faces, which cannot be done with the drawing of the entire figure.

- You may want to have advanced students attempt to make larger scale models of the figures in the exercises.

Assess

In **Exercises 1–9**, students should recognize and be able to build and draw various views of three-dimensional figures.

In **Exercises 10–15**, students should be able to construct three-dimensional figures from nets.

Study Notebook

Have students draw a three-dimensional figure, then draw and label its top, side, and front views in their notebooks.

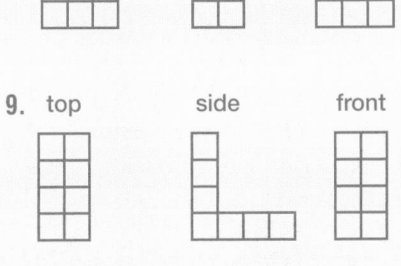

7.   top   side   front

8.   top   side   front

9.   top   side   front

11-1 Three-Dimensional Figures

1 Focus

5-Minute Check Transparency 11-1 Use as a quiz or review of Chapter 10.

Mathematical Background notes are available for this lesson on page 552C.

How are 2-dimensional figures related to 3-dimensional figures?

The opening activity questions are repeated on page 612 of the *Chapter 11 Resource Masters.*

Reading to Learn Mathematics, p. 612 — ELL

Pre-Activity How are 2-dimensional figures related to 3-dimensional figures?

Do the activity at the top of page 556 in your textbook. Write your answers below.

a. If you observed the Great Pyramid or the Inner Harbor and Trade Center from directly above, what geometric figure would you see?
square

b. If you stood directly in front of each structure, what geometric figure would you see? Pyramid, triangle; Trade Center, rectangle

c. Explain how you can see different polygons when looking at the same 3-dimensional figure. Sample answer: When a three-dimensional figure has faces that are different polygons, the polygon you see depends on your point of view.

Reading the Lesson 1–10. See students' work.

Write a definition and give an example of each new vocabulary word or phrase.

Vocabulary	Definition	Example
1. plane		
2. solid		
3. polyhedron		
4. edge		
5. vertex		
6. face		
7. prism		
8. base		
9. pyramid		
10. skew lines		

Vocabulary
- plane
- solid
- polyhedron
- edge
- vertex
- face
- prism
- base
- pyramid
- skew lines

c. Sample answer: When a three-dimensional figure has faces that are different polygons, the polygon you see depends on your point of view.

Study Tip

Dimensions
A two-dimensional figure has two dimensions, length and width. A three-dimensional figure has three dimensions, length, width, and depth (or height).

What You'll Learn
- Identify three-dimensional figures.
- Identify diagonals and skew lines.

How are 2-dimensional figures related to 3-dimensional figures?

Great Pyramid, Egypt

Inner Harbor & Trade Center, Baltimore

a. If you observed the Great Pyramid or the Inner Harbor & Trade Center from directly above, what geometric figure would you see? **square**

b. If you stood directly in front of each structure, what geometric figure would you see? **Pyramid, triangle; Trade Center, rectangle**

c. Explain how you can see different polygons when looking at a 3-dimensional figure.

IDENTIFY THREE-DIMENSIONAL FIGURES A **plane** is a two-dimensional flat surface that extends in all directions. There are different ways that planes may be related in space.

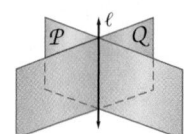
Intersect in a Line

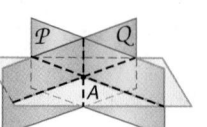
Intersect in a Point

No Intersection

These are called *parallel planes.*

Intersecting planes can also form three-dimensional figures or **solids**. A **polyhedron** is a solid with flat surfaces that are polygons.

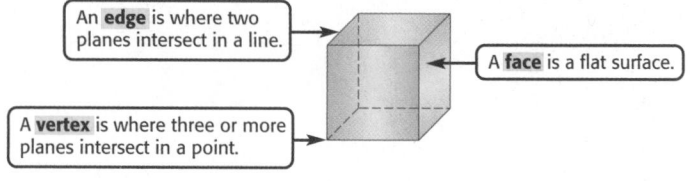

An **edge** is where two planes intersect in a line.

A **face** is a flat surface.

A **vertex** is where three or more planes intersect in a point.

Resource Manager

Workbooks and Reproducible Masters

Chapter 11 Resource Masters
- Study Guide and Intervention, p. 609
- Skills Practice, p. 610
- Practice, p. 611
- Reading to Learn Mathematics, p. 612
- Enrichment, p. 613

Parent and Student Study Guide Workbook, p. 90

Transparencies
5-Minute Check Transparency 11-1
Answer Key Transparencies

Technology
Interactive Chalkboard

A **prism** is a polyhedron with two parallel, congruent faces called **bases**. A **pyramid** is a polyhedron with one base that is any polygon. Its other faces are triangles.

Prisms and pyramids are named by the shape of their bases.

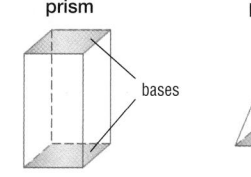
prism

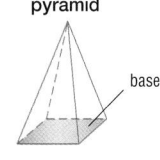
pyramid

bases

base

Key Concept — Polyhedrons

Polyhedron	triangular prism	rectangular prism	triangular pyramid	rectangular pyramid
Number of Bases	2	2	1	1
Polygon Base	triangle	rectangle	triangle	rectangle
Figure				

Use the labels on the vertices to name a base or a face of a solid.

Example 1 Identify Prisms and Pyramids

Identify each solid. Name the bases, faces, edges, and vertices.

a.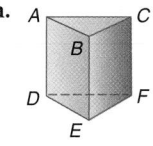

This figure has two parallel congruent bases that are triangles, *ABC* and *DEF*, so it is a triangular prism.

faces: *ABC, ADEB, BEFC, CFDA, DEF*

edges: $\overline{AB}, \overline{BC}, \overline{CA}, \overline{AD}, \overline{BE}, \overline{CF}, \overline{DE}, \overline{EF}, \overline{FD}$

vertices: *A, B, C, D, E, F*

b.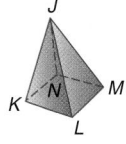

This figure has one rectangular base, *KLMN*, so it is a rectangular pyramid.

faces: *JKL, JLM, JMN, JNK, KLMN*

edges: $\overline{JK}, \overline{JL}, \overline{JM}, \overline{JN}, \overline{NK}, \overline{KL}, \overline{LM}, \overline{MN}$

vertices: *J, K, L, M, N*

✓**Concept Check** How many faces does a cube have? **6**

 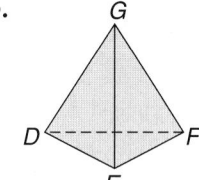

2 Identify a diagonal and name all segments that are skew to it.

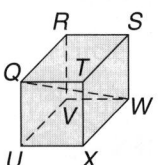

$\overline{QW}$; $\overline{UV}$, $\overline{UX}$, $\overline{RS}$, $\overline{ST}$, $\overline{TX}$, $\overline{RV}$

3 Refer to Example 3 to answer the following.

a. Find the area of the ground floor if each unit on the drawing represents 55 feet. **90,750 square feet**

b. How many floors are in the office building if each floor is 12 feet high? Assume each unit on the drawing represents 40 feet. **10 floors**

Teaching Tip Have students make a paper model of the figure, then draw the figure from the various angles.

DIAGONALS AND SKEW LINES

Skew lines are lines that are neither intersecting nor parallel. They lie in different planes. Line ℓ along the bridge below and line m along the river beneath it are skew.

The river is not parallel to the bridge and it does not touch the top of the bridge.

We can use rectangular prisms to show skew lines. $\overline{EC}$ is a *diagonal* of the prism at the right because it joins two vertices that have no faces in common. $\overline{EC}$ is skew to $\overline{AD}$.

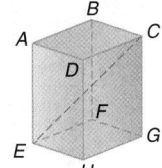

Study Tip

Diagonals
Three other diagonals could have been drawn in the prism at the right: $\overline{AG}$, $\overline{BH}$, and $\overline{DF}$.

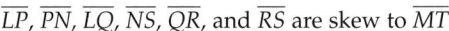

Example 2 *Identify Diagonals and Skew Lines*

Identify a diagonal and name all segments that are skew to it.

$\overline{MT}$ is a diagonal because vertex M and vertex T do not intersect any of the same faces.

$\overline{LP}$, $\overline{PN}$, $\overline{LQ}$, $\overline{NS}$, $\overline{QR}$, and $\overline{RS}$ are skew to $\overline{MT}$.

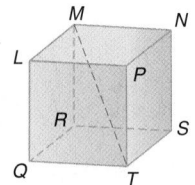

Example 3 *Analyze Real-World Drawings*

ARCHITECTURE An architect's sketch shows the plans for a new office building. Each unit on the drawing represents 40 feet.

a. Draw a top view and find the area of the ground floor.

The drawing is 6 × 5, so the actual dimensions are 6(40) × 5(40) or 240 feet by 200 feet.

$A = \ell \cdot w$ Formula for area

$A = 240 \cdot 200$ or 48,000

The area of the ground floor is 48,000 square feet.

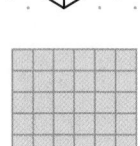

top view

b. How many floors are in the office building if each floor is 15 feet high?

You can see from the side view that the height of the building is 3 units.

total height: 3 units × 40 feet per unit = 120 feet

number of floors: 120 feet ÷ 15 feet per floor = 8 floors

There are 8 floors in the office building.

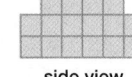

side view

DAILY INTERVENTION   **Differentiated Instruction**

- **Visual/Spatial** Provide students with scissors, cardboard or heavy paper, and tape. Have them make a rectangular prism, square pyramid, triangular prism, triangular pyramid, and intersecting planes. Have them assign letters to various points on the figures and identify skew lines.

Check for Understanding

1. Describe the number of planes that form a square pyramid and discuss how the planes form edges and vertices of the pyramid. **See margin.**

2. OPEN ENDED Choose a solid object from your home and give an example and a nonexample of edges that form skew lines. Include drawings of your example and nonexample. **See margin.**

Guided Practice

Identify each solid. Name the bases, faces, edges, and vertices.

GUIDED PRACTICE KEY	
Exercises	Examples
3, 4	1
5, 6	2
7, 8	3

3.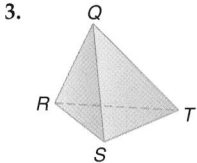

4.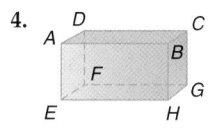

3–4. See margin.

For Exercises 5 and 6, use the rectangular pyramid shown at the right.

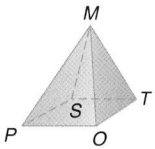

5. State whether $\overline{MP}$ and $\overline{TM}$ are *parallel, skew,* or *intersecting.* **intersecting**

6. Identify all lines skew to $\overline{PO}$. **$\overline{MS}$, $\overline{MT}$**

Application

BUILDING The sketch at the right shows the plans for porch steps.

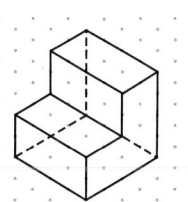

7. Draw and label the top, front, and side views. **See pp. 601A–601B.**

8. If each unit on the drawing represents 4 inches, what is the height of the steps in feet? $1\frac{1}{3}$ ft

Practice and Apply

Homework Help	
For Exercises	See Examples
9–12, 19–21	1
13–16, 22–25	2
17, 18	3
Extra Practice See page 750.	

Identify each solid. Name the bases, faces, edges, and vertices.

9.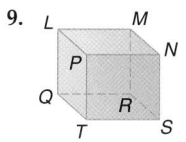

9–12. See pp. 601A–601B.

10.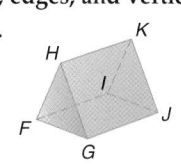

11.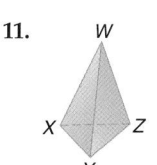

12.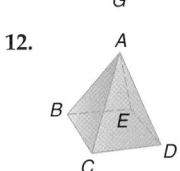

Lesson 11-1 Three-Dimensional Figures **559**

3 Practice/Apply

Study Notebook

Have students—
• add the definitions/examples of the vocabulary terms to their Vocabulary Builder worksheets for Chapter 11.
• write a paragraph describing the differences between prisms and pyramids.
• include any other item(s) that they find helpful in mastering the skills in this lesson.

About the Exercises . . .

Organization by Objective
• Identify Three-Dimensional Figures: 9–12
• Diagonals and Skew Lines: 13–16

Odd/Even Assignments
Exercises 9–12 are structured so that students practice the same concepts whether they are assigned odd or even problems.

Alert! Exercise 18 requires the Internet or other reference materials.

Assignment Guide

Basic: 9–17 odd, 19, 23, 25, 26–44

Average: 9–25 odd, 26–44

Advanced: 10–22 even, 24, 26–40 (Optional: 41–44)

Answers

1. Five planes form a square pyramid because the solid has five faces. An edge is formed when two planes intersect; a vertex is formed when three or four planes intersect.

2. Sample answer: On a television, the top front edge and a bottom side edge form skew lines. The top and bottom front edges do not form skew lines because they are parallel. See students' drawings.

3. triangular pyramid; any one of the following faces can be considered a base: RST, QRS, QST, QRT; $\overline{QR}$, $\overline{QS}$, $\overline{QT}$, $\overline{RT}$, $\overline{RS}$, $\overline{ST}$; Q, R, S, T

4. rectangular prism; $ABCD$, $EHGF$ or $ABHE$, $DCGF$ or $ADFE$, $BCGH$; $ABCD$, $EHGF$, $ABHE$, $DCGF$, $ADFE$, $BCGH$; $\overline{AB}$, $\overline{BC}$, $\overline{CD}$, $\overline{DA}$, $\overline{EF}$, $\overline{FG}$, $\overline{GH}$, $\overline{HE}$, $\overline{AE}$, $\overline{BH}$, $\overline{CG}$, $\overline{DF}$; A, B, C, D, E, F, G, H

Study Guide and Intervention, p. 609

Identifying Three-Dimensional Figures A prism is a polyhedron with two parallel bases. A pyramid is a polyhedron with one base. Prisms and pyramids are named by the shape of their bases, such as triangular or rectangular.

Example 1 Identify the solid. Name the bases, faces, edges, and vertices.

triangular pyramid

Any of the faces can be considered a base.

faces: *EFG, EGH, EFH, FGH*
edges: $\overline{EF}, \overline{EG}, \overline{EH}, \overline{FG}, \overline{FH}, \overline{GH}$
vertices: *E, F, G, H*

Diagonals and Skew Lines Skew lines are lines that lie in different planes and do not intersect. A diagonal of a figure joins two vertices that have no faces in common.

Example 2 Identify a diagonal and name all segments that are skew to it.

diagonal: $\overline{FM}$
skew segments: $\overline{EH}, \overline{HG}, \overline{JK}, \overline{KL}, \overline{EJ}, \overline{GL}$

Exercises

Identify each solid. Name the bases, faces, edges, and vertices.

1. 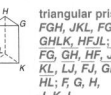 rectangular prism; any pair of parallel faces are the bases; *MNPQ, RSTU, MNSR, NPTS, PQUT, QMRU; MN, NP, PQ, QM, RS, ST, TU, UR, MR, NS, PT, QU; M, N, P, Q, R, S, T, U*

2. triangular prism; *FGH, JKL, FGKJ, GHLK, HFJL; FG, GH, HF, JK, KL, LJ, FJ, GK, HL; F, G, H, J, K, L*

For Exercises 3–4, use the rectangular prism in Example 2.

3. Identify a diagonal that could be drawn from point *E.* $\overline{EL}$

4. Name all segments that are skew to the new diagonal.
FG, GH, HM, KF, JK, JM

Skills Practice, p. 610 and Practice, p. 611 (shown)

Identify each solid. Name the bases, faces, edges, and vertices.

1.   square pyramid; *KLMN; KLMN, KLP, LMP, MNP, KNP; KL, LM, MN, NK, KP, LP, MP, NP; K, L, M, N, P*

2. rectangular prism; any pair of parallel faces are the bases; *ABCD, EFGH, ABFE, AEHD, DCGH, BCGF; AB, BC, CD, DA, EF, FG, GH, HE, AE, BF, CG, DH; A, B, C, D, E, F, G, H*

3. triangular prism; *RTS, UVW; RST, UVW, RSVU, STWV, TRUW; RS, ST, TR, UV, VW, WU, RU, SV, TW; R, S, T, U, V, W*

For Exercises 4–7, use the rectangular prism below.

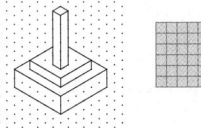

4. Identify a diagonal. $\overline{FH}$

5. Name four segments skew to $\overline{JK}$. Sample answer: $\overline{DH}, \overline{GL}, \overline{DE}, \overline{FG}$

6. State whether $\overline{HJ}$ and $\overline{FG}$ are *parallel, skew,* or *intersecting.* parallel

7. Name a segment that does *not* intersect plane *DGLH.* Sample answer: $\overline{JK}$

8. **ARCHITECTURE** A sketch shows the plans for a new observation tower at an amusement park. Each unit on the drawing represents 10 feet.

a. Draw a top view and find the area of the bottom section. 3600 ft²

b. At the center of the tower, there is a staircase landing every 15 feet. How many landings are in the tower? 6

Enrichment, p. 613

Perspective Drawings

To draw three-dimensional objects, artists make **perspective drawings** such as the ones shown below. To indicate depth in a perspective drawing, some parallel lines are drawn as converging lines. The dotted lines in the figures below each extend to a **vanishing point**, or spot where parallel lines appear to meet.

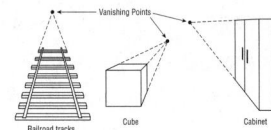

Draw lines to locate the vanishing point in each drawing of a box.

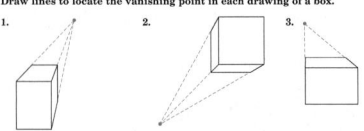

4. The fronts of two cubes are shown below. Using point *P* as the vanishing point for both cubes, complete the perspective drawings of the cubes.

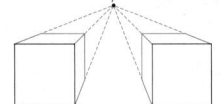

5. Find an example of a perspective drawing in a newspaper or magazine. Trace the drawing and locate a vanishing point. See students' work.

For Exercises 13–16, use the rectangular prism.

13. Identify a diagonal. $\overline{WR}$

14. $\overline{WP}, \overline{ZS}, \overline{WX}, \overline{ZY}$ 14. Name four segments skew to $\overline{QR}$.

15. State whether $\overline{WR}$ and $\overline{XY}$ are *parallel, skew,* or *intersecting.* skew

16. Name a segment that does *not* intersect the plane that contains *WXYZ.* Sample answer: $\overline{PS}$

COMICS For Exercises 17 and 18, use the comic below.

SHOE

17. Which view of the Washington Monument is shown? top

18. **RESEARCH** Use the Internet or another source to find a photograph of the Washington Monument. Draw and label the top, side, and front views. See pp. 601A–601B.

ART For Exercises 19 and 20, refer to Picasso's painting *The Factory, Horta de Ebro* shown at the right.

19. Describe the polyhedrons shown in the painting.

19. rectangular and pentagonal prisms

20. Explain how the artist portrayed three-dimensional objects on a flat canvas. See margin.

21. **RESEARCH** Find other examples of art in which polyhedrons are shown. Describe the polyhedrons. See students' work.

Determine whether each statement is *sometimes, always,* or *never* true. Explain. 22–25. See margin for explanations.

22. Any two planes intersect in a line. sometimes

23. Two planes intersect in a single point. never

24. A pyramid contains a diagonal. never

25. Three planes do not intersect in a point. sometimes

26. **CRITICAL THINKING** Use isometric dot paper to draw a three-dimensional figure in which the front and top views have a line of symmetry but the side view does not. Then discuss whether the figure has bilateral symmetry or rotational symmetry. See pp. 601A–601B.

More About. . .

Art

Pablo Picasso (1881–1973) was one of the developers of a movement in art called *Cubism.* Cubist paintings are characterized by their angular shapes and sharp edges.

Source: World Wide Arts Resources

Answers

20. Sample answer: using angles and shading to portray depth

22. Two planes may be parallel and not intersect at all.

23. Only three or more planes can intersect in a single point.

24. Every pair of vertices on a pyramid has a common edge.

25. Three planes may intersect in a line. Or, the planes may be parallel and not intersect at all.

27. WRITING IN MATH Answer the question that was posed at the beginning of the lesson. See margin.

How are 2-dimensional figures related to 3-dimensional figures?
Include the following in your answer:
- an explanation of the difference between 2-dimensional figures and 3-dimensional figures, and
- a description of how 2-dimensional figures can form a 3-dimensional figure.

Standardized Test Practice
Ⓐ Ⓑ Ⓒ Ⓓ

28. Determine the intersection of the three planes at the right. **A**

Ⓐ point
Ⓑ line
Ⓒ plane
Ⓓ no intersection

29. Which figure does *not* have the same dimensions as the other figures? **D**

Ⓐ 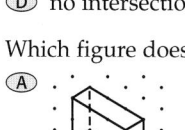   Ⓑ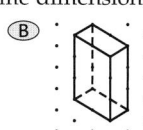

Ⓒ    Ⓓ

Maintain Your Skills

Mixed Review

30. Find the area of *ABCDEF* if each unit represents 1 square centimeter. *(Lesson 10-10)* **30 cm²**

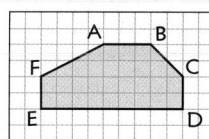

31. Find the circumference and the area of a circle whose radius is 6 centimeters. Round to the nearest tenth. *(Lesson 10-9)* **37.7 cm; 113.1 cm²**

Use a calculator to find each ratio to the nearest ten thousandth. *(Lesson 9-7)*
32. sin 35° **0.5736**   **33.** sin 30° **0.5000**   **34.** cos 280° **0.1736**

Solve each inequality. Check your solution. *(Lesson 7-4)* **37.** $n > -11$
35. $c + 4 < 12$ $c < 8$ **36.** $7 \geq t - 2$ $t \leq 9$ **37.** $-26 < n + (-15)$
38. $k + (-4) \geq 3.8$ $k \geq 7.8$ **39.** $y - \frac{1}{4} < 1\frac{1}{2}$ $y < 1\frac{3}{4}$ **40.** $3\frac{1}{5} > a - \frac{3}{10}$ $a < 3\frac{1}{2}$

Getting Ready for the Next Lesson

PREREQUISITE SKILL Find the area of each triangle described.
*(To review **areas of triangles**, see Lesson 10-5.)*
41. base, 4 in.; height, 7 in. **14 in²**   **42.** base, 10 ft; height, 9 ft **45 ft²**
43. base, 6.5 cm; height, 2 cm **6.5 cm²**   **44.** base, 0.4 m; height, 1.3 m **0.26 m²**

Lesson 11-1 Three-Dimensional Figures **561**

Teaching Tip For Exercise 26, explain to students that a three-dimensional figure has
- *bilateral symmetry* if a plane can divide the figure into matching halves, and
- *rotational symmetry* if the figure can be rotated less than 360° about a fixed axis and look exactly as it does in its original position.

4 Assess

Open-Ended Assessment
Modeling Have students draw a line on each of two pieces of paper. Then have them hold the papers to represent parallel lines and skew lines.

Tips for New Teachers

Motivating Students Demonstrate real-world uses of geometry by examining the shapes of objects created by humans, such as buildings, pencils, erasers, buses and other vehicles, walls, tiles, desks, elevators, and food containers.

Getting Ready for Lesson 11-2
PREREQUISITE SKILL Lesson 11-2 presents finding the volumes of prisms and cylinders. Exercises 41–44 should be used to determine your students' familiarity with finding the areas of triangles, a necessary step in finding the volume of triangular prisms.

Answer

27. Two-dimensional figures form three-dimensional figures. Answers should include the following.
- Two-dimensional figures have length and width and therefore lie in a single plane. Three-dimensional figures have length, width, and depth.
- Two-dimensional figures form the faces of three-dimensional figures.

A Preview of Lesson 11-2

Getting Started

Objective Investigate volume by creating and comparing containers of various shapes.

Materials
5 in. × 8 in. index cards
tape
rice

Teaching Tip Discuss with students the types and shapes of large storage containers they have seen, such as water towers, oil storage tanks, and grain silos.

Teach

• After students have completed their containers, have them use additional index cards to make nets of the figures. Discuss whether the nets make comparing the figures any easier.

Assess

In **Exercises 1–6**, students should successfully compare the relative volumes of the three containers and recognize the relationship between base area and volume.

Study Notebook

Have students draw the three containers in their notebooks, labeling the dimensions and including their estimations of the base areas. Students should include notes on the relative volumes of the three containers.

Volume

In this activity, you will investigate volume by making containers of different shapes and comparing how much each container holds.

Activity

Collect the Data

Step 1 Use three 5-inch × 8-inch index cards to make three different containers, as shown below.

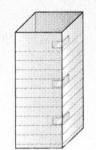   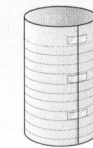   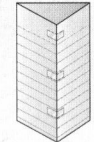

square base with   circular base with   triangular base
2-inch sides   8-inch circumference   with sides 2 inches,
                                                        3 inches, and 3 inches

Step 2 Tape one end of each container to another card as a bottom, but leave the top open, as shown at the right.

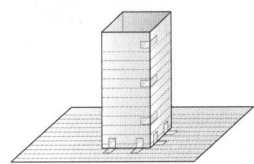

Step 3 Estimate which container would hold the most (have the greatest volume) and which would hold the least (have the least volume), or whether all the containers would hold the same amount.

Step 4 Use rice to fill the container that you believe holds the least amount. Then pour the rice from this container into another container. Does the rice fill the second container? Continue the process until you find out which container, if any, has the least volume and which has the greatest.

Analyze the Data 2. same height; 5 in.   4. circular: ≈ 5 in²; triangular: ≈ 3 in²; square:

1. Which container holds the greatest amount of rice? Which holds the least amount? **cylinder; triangular prism**

2. How do the heights of the three containers compare? What is each height?

3. Compare the perimeters of the bases of each container. What is each base perimeter? **same; 8 in.**

4. Trace the base of each container onto grid paper. Estimate the area of each base.

5. Which container has the greatest base area? **cylinder**

6. Does there appear to be a relationship between the area of the bases and the volume of the containers when the heights remain unchanged? Explain.
   Yes; the greater the base area, the greater the volume.

Resource Manager

📁 ***Teaching Pre-Algebra with Manipulatives***
• p. 144 (student recording sheet)

11-2 Volume: Prisms and Cylinders

What You'll Learn

- Find volumes of prisms.
- Find volumes of circular cylinders.

Vocabulary
- volume
- cylinder

How is volume related to area?

The rectangular prism is built from 24 cubes.

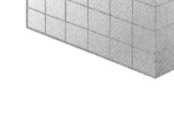

a. Build three more rectangular prisms using 24 cubes. Enter the dimensions and base areas in a table.

Prism	Length (units)	Width (units)	Height (units)	Area of Base (units²)
1	6	1	4	6
2	6	2	2	12
3	4	3	2	12
4	8	1	3	8

Sample dimensions are given.

b. *Volume* equals the number of cubes that fill a prism. How is the volume of each prism related to the product of the length, width, and height?

c. **Make a conjecture** about how the area of the base B and the height h are related to the volume V of a prism. $V = Bh$

Study Tip

Volume equals the product of the length, width, and height.

Measures of Volume
cubic centimeter (cm³) cube whose edges measure 1 centimeter.

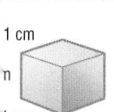
1 cm

VOLUMES OF PRISMS

The prism above has a volume of 24 cubic centimeters. **Volume** is the measure of space occupied by a solid region.

To find the volume of a prism, you can use the area of the base and the height, as given by the following formula.

Key Concept — Volume of a Prism

- **Words** The volume V of a prism is the area of the base B times the height h.

- **Models**

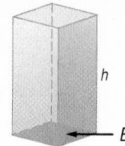
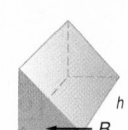

- **Symbols** $V = Bh$

Example 1 Volume of a Rectangular Prism

Find the volume of the prism.

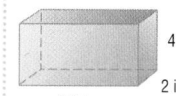
4 in.
2 in.
7.5 in.

$V = Bh$ — Formula for volume of a prism

$V = (\ell \cdot w)h$ — The base is a rectangle, so $B = \ell \cdot w$.

$V = (7.5 \cdot 2)4$ — $\ell = 7.5$, $w = 2$, $h = 4$

$V = 60$ — Simplify.

The volume is 60 cubic inches.

TEACHING TIP

An alternative method for finding the volume of a rectangular prism is using the formula $V = \ell wh$.

---

1 Focus

5-Minute Check Transparency 11-2 Use as a quiz or review of Lesson 11-1.

Mathematical Background notes are available for this lesson on page 552C.

How is volume related to area?

The opening activity questions are repeated on page 617 of the *Chapter 11 Resource Masters*.

Reading to Learn Mathematics, p. 617 — ELL

Pre-Activity *How is volume related to area?*

Do the activity at the top of page 563 in your textbook. Write your answers below.

a. Build three more rectangular prisms using 24 cubes. Enter the dimensions and base areas in a table.

Sample dimensions are given.

Prism	Length (units)	Width (units)	Height (units)	Area of Base (units²)
1	6	1	4	6
2	6	2	2	12
3	4	3	2	12
4	8	1	3	8

b. *Volume* equals the number of cubes that fill a prism. How is the volume of each prism related to the product of the length, width, and height? Volume equals the product of the length, width, and height.

c. **Make a conjecture** about how the area of the base B and the height h are related to the volume V of a prism. $V = Bh$

Reading the Lesson 1–2. See students' work.

Write a definition and give an example of each new vocabulary word or phrase.

Vocabulary	Definition	Example
1. volume		
2. cylinder		

Helping You Remember

3. For each figure below, write out the longer version showing how to determine the base area of the formula for volume.

$V = \ell wh$ — $V = \left(\frac{1}{2} \cdot b \cdot a\right)h$ — $V = \pi r^2 h$

Resource Manager

Workbooks and Reproducible Masters

Chapter 11 Resource Masters
- Study Guide and Intervention, p. 614
- Skills Practice, p. 615
- Practice, p. 616
- Reading to Learn Mathematics, p. 617
- Enrichment, p. 618
- Assessment, p. 659

Graphing Calculator and Spreadsheet Masters, p. 39
Parent and Student Study Guide Workbook, p. 91
School-to-Career Masters, p. 21

Transparencies
5-Minute Check Transparency 11-2
Answer Key Transparencies

Technology
Interactive Chalkboard

Building on Prior Knowledge

In Lesson 5-3, students multiplied rational numbers. In this lesson, students will use multiplication to find the volume of prisms and cylinders.

VOLUMES OF PRISMS

In-Class Examples

1 Find the volume of the prism.

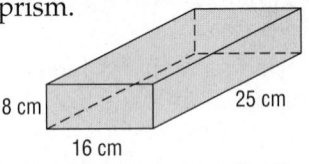

3200 cm³

2 Find the volume of the triangular prism.

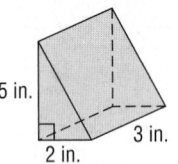

15 in³

3 **BAKING** Cake batter is poured into a pan that is a rectangular prism whose base is an 8 inch square. If the cake batter occupies 192 cubic inches, what will be the height of the batter?
3 in.

4 **Multiple-Choice Test Item**
Find the volume of the solid.
D

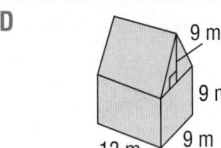

A 262 m³   **B** 918 m³

C 972 m³   **D** 1458 m³

Example 2 *Volume of a Triangular Prism*

Find the volume of the triangular prism.

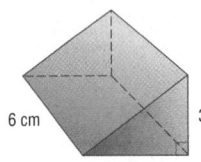

$V = Bh$ — Formula for volume of a prism

$V = \left(\frac{1}{2} \cdot 4 \cdot 3\right)h$ — B = area of base or $\frac{1}{2} \cdot 4 \cdot 3$

$V = \left(\frac{1}{2} \cdot 4 \cdot 3\right)6$ — The height of the prism is 6 cm.

$V = 36$ — Simplify.

The volume is 36 cubic centimeters.

Example 3 *Height of a Prism*

AQUARIUMS A wall is being constructed to enclose three sides of an aquarium that is a rectangular prism 8 feet long and 5 feet wide. If the aquarium is to contain 220 cubic feet of water, what is its height?

$V = Bh$ — Formula for volume of a prism

$V = \ell \cdot w \cdot h$ — Formula for volume of a rectangular prism

$220 = 8 \cdot 5 \cdot h$ — Replace V with 220, ℓ with 8, and w with 5.

$220 = 40h$ — Simplify.

$5.5 = h$ — Divide each side by 40.

The height of the aquarium is 5.5 feet.

To find the volume of a solid with several prisms, break it into parts.

Standardized Test Practice
Ⓐ Ⓑ Ⓒ Ⓓ

Example 4 *Volume of a Complex Solid*

Multiple-Choice Test Item

Find the volume of the solid at the right.

Ⓐ 180 ft³

Ⓑ 1320 ft³

Ⓒ 960 ft³

Ⓓ 1140 ft³

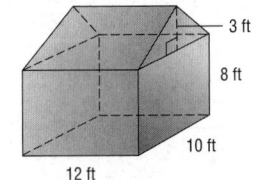

Read the Test Item

The solid is made up of a rectangular prism and a triangular prism. The *volume of the solid* is the sum of both volumes.

Solve the Test Item

Step 1 The volume of the rectangular prism is 12(10)(8) or 960 ft³.

Step 2 In the triangular prism, the area of the base is $\frac{1}{2}(10)(3)$, and the height is 12. Therefore, the volume is $\frac{1}{2}(10)(3)(12)$ or 180 ft³.

Step 3 Add the volumes.
960 ft³ + 180 ft³ = 1140 ft³

The answer is D.

Test-Taking Tip
Estimate You can eliminate A and C as answers because the volume of the rectangular prism is 960 ft³, so the volume of the whole solid must be greater.

Standardized Test Practice
Ⓐ Ⓑ Ⓒ Ⓓ

Example 4 Point out to students that another way to find the volume of the solid is to imagine the figure lying on a different base. For example, the figure could be lying on the right face. The height would then be 12. The area of that base is $(10)(8) + \frac{1}{2}(3)(10) = 80 + 15 = 95$. To find the volume, multiply that area by 12.

Reading Math

Cylinders

In this text, *cylinder* refers to a cylinder with a circular base.

VOLUMES OF CYLINDERS A **cylinder** is a solid whose bases are congruent, parallel circles, connected with a curved side. Like prisms, the volume of a cylinder is the product of the base area and the height.

Key Concept   **Volume of a Cylinder**

- **Words** The volume V of a cylinder with radius r is the area of the base B times the height h.

- **Model**

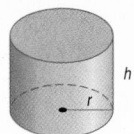

- **Symbols** $V = Bh$ or $V = \pi r^2 h$, where $B = \pi r^2$

Example 5 Volume of a Cylinder

Find the volume of each cylinder. Round to the nearest tenth.

TEACHING TIP
Unless specified otherwise, encourage students to use 2nd [π] on their calculators to evaluate expressions involving π. Then follow any instructions regarding rounding.

a.

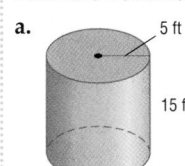

5 ft
15 ft

$V = \pi r^2 h$ Formula for volume of a cylinder
$V = \pi \cdot 5^2 \cdot 15$ Replace r with 5 and h with 15.
$V \approx 1178.1$ Simplify.

The volume is about 1178.1 cubic feet.

b. **diameter of base 16.4 mm, height 20 mm**

Since the diameter is 16.4 mm, the radius is 8.2 mm.

$V = \pi r^2 h$ Formula for volume of a cylinder
$V = \pi \cdot 8.2^2 \cdot 20$ Replace r with 8.2 and h with 20.
$V \approx 4224.8$ Simplify.

The volume is about 4224.8 cubic millimeters.

Check for Understanding

Concept Check

1. **OPEN ENDED** Describe a problem from an everyday situation in which you need to find the volume of a cylinder or a rectangular prism. Explain how to solve the problem. **See margin.**

2. **FIND THE ERROR** Eric says that doubling the length of each side of a cube doubles the volume. Marissa says the volume is eight times greater. Who is correct? Explain your reasoning. **See margin.**

Guided Practice

GUIDED PRACTICE KEY

Exercises	Examples
3, 6	1
4	2
5, 7	5
8, 9	3
10	4

Find the volume of each solid. If necessary, round to the nearest tenth.

3.   183.6 cm³   4.   5.

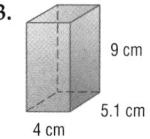
9 cm
5.1 cm
4 cm

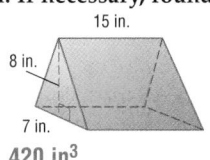
15 in.
8 in.
7 in.
420 in³

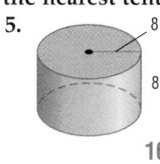
8 ft
8 ft
1608.5 ft³

6. rectangular prism: length 6 in., width 6 in., height 9 in. **324 in³**

7. cylinder: radius 3 yd, height 10 yd **282.7 yd³**

8. Find the height of a rectangular prism with a length of 3 meters, width of 1.5 meters, and a volume of 60.3 cubic meters. **13.4 m**

www.pre-alg.com/extra_examples   **Lesson 11-2** Volume: Prisms and Cylinders **565**

Answers

1. Sample answer: Finding how much sand is needed to fill a child's rectangular sandbox; measure the length, width, and height and then multiply to find the volume.

2. Marissa; a cube has three dimensions and when each dimension is multiplied by 2, the volume is multiplied by $2 \times 2 \times 2$ or 8.

In-Class Example   Power Point®

5 Find the volume of each cylinder. Round to the nearest tenth.

a.

7 ft
14 ft

2155.1 ft³

b. diameter of base 10 m, height 2 m   **157.1 m³**

Teaching Tip Have students measure various cereal boxes and cereal cylinders to see which dimensions have the greatest and least volume.

3 Practice/Apply

Study Notebook

Have students—
- add the definitions/examples of the vocabulary terms to their Vocabulary Builder worksheets for Chapter 11.
- write a paragraph that explains how to use the formula $V = Bh$ for both prisms and cylinders.
- include any other item(s) that they find helpful in mastering the skills in this lesson.

D A I L Y
INTERVENTION FIND THE ERROR
        If students are having difficulty with change in volume, have them find the volume of a $3 \times 4 \times 5$ rectangular prism. **60** Then have them compare volumes after doubling only one dimension **120**, two original dimensions **240**, and all original dimensions **480**.

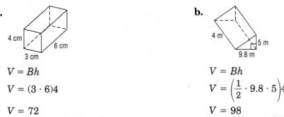
9. **ENGINEERING** A cylindrical storage tank is being manufactured to hold at least 1,000,000 cubic feet of natural gas and have a diameter of no more than 80 feet. What height should the tank be to the nearest tenth of a foot? **at least 198.9 ft**

10. Find the volume of the solid at the right. **D**
   Ⓐ 6 in³   Ⓑ 10 in³
   Ⓒ 13 in³   Ⓓ 16 in³

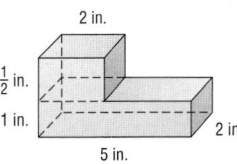

★ indicates increased difficulty

Practice and Apply

Find the volume of each solid shown or described. If necessary, round to the nearest tenth.

11. 512 cm³   12. 81.9 m³   13. 748 in³

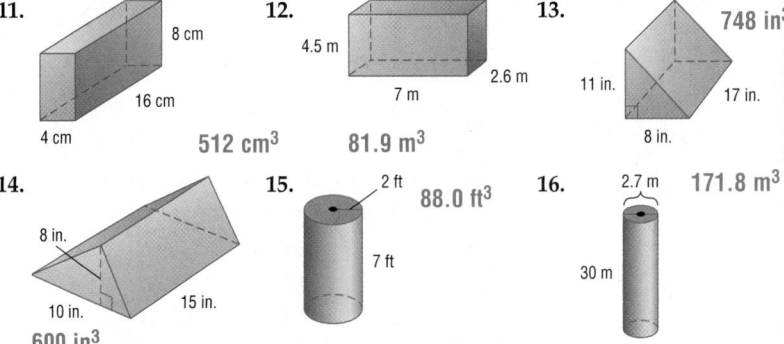

14. 600 in³   15. 88.0 ft³   16. 171.8 m³

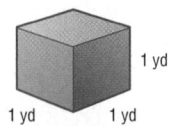 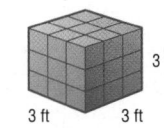

17. rectangular prism: length 3 mm, width 5 mm, height 15 mm **225 mm³**

18. triangular prism: base of triangle 8 in., altitude of triangle 15 in., height of prism $6\frac{1}{2}$ in. **390 in³**

19. cylinder: $d = 2.6$ m, $h = 3.5$ m **18.6 m³**

★ 20. octagonal prism: base area 25 m², height 1.5 m **37.5 m³**

21. Find the height of a rectangular prism with a length of 4.2 meters, width of 3.2 meters, and volume of 83.3 m³. **6.2 m**

22. Find the height of a cylinder with a radius of 2 feet and a volume of 28.3 ft³. **2.3 ft**

CONVERTING UNITS OF MEASURE

For Exercises 23–25, use the cubes at the right.
The volume of the left cube is 1 yd³. In the right cube, only the units have been changed. So, 1 yd³ = 3(3)(3) or 27 ft³. Use a similar process to convert each measurement.

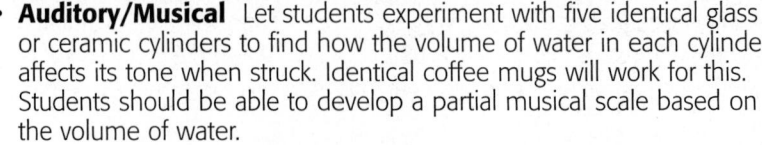

23. 1 ft³ = ■ in³ **1728**   24. 1 cm³ = ■ mm³ **1000**   25. 1 m³ = ■ cm³ **1,000,000**

26. **METALS** The *density* of gold is 19.29 grams per cubic centimeter. Find the mass in grams of a gold bar that is 2 centimeters by 3 centimeters by 2 centimeters. **231.48 g**

★ 27. MICROWAVES The inside of a microwave oven has a volume of 1.2 cubic feet and measures 18 inches wide and 10 inches long. To the nearest tenth, how deep is the inside of the microwave? (*Hint*: Convert 1.2 cubic feet to cubic inches.) **11.5 in.**

8. D 53.2 cm³;
25.5 cm³;
A 8.3 cm³;
AA 3.9 cm³

★ 28. BATTERIES The current of an alkaline battery corresponds to its volume. Find the volume of each cylinder-shaped battery shown in the table. Write each volume in cm³. (*Hint*: 1 cm³ = 1000 mm³)

Battery Size	Diameter (mm)	Height (mm)
D	33.3	61.1
C	25.5	50.0
AA	14.5	50.5
AAA	10.5	44.5

29. CRITICAL THINKING An $8\frac{1}{2}$-by-11-inch piece of paper is rolled to form a cylinder. Will the volume be greater if the height is $8\frac{1}{2}$ inches or 11 inches, or will the volumes be the same? Explain your reasoning. **See margin.**

30. WRITING IN MATH   Answer the question that was posed at the beginning of the lesson. **See margin.**

How is volume related to area?

Include the following in your answer:
- an explanation of why area is given in square units and volume is given in cubic units, and
- a description of why the formula for volume includes area.

31. Which is the best estimate for the volume of a cube whose sides measure 18.79 millimeters? **C**
- Ⓐ 80 mm³
- Ⓑ 800 mm³
- Ⓒ 8000 mm³
- Ⓓ 80,000 mm³

32. Find the volume of the figure at the right. **A**
- Ⓐ 24.5 ft³
- Ⓑ 20.5 ft³
- Ⓒ 48 ft³
- Ⓓ 49 ft³

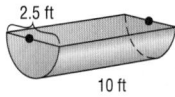
2.5 ft
10 ft

Maintain Your Skills

Mixed Review

33. Identify a pair of skew lines in the prism at the right. *(Lesson 11-1)*
Sample answer: $\overline{QT}$ and $\overline{YZ}$

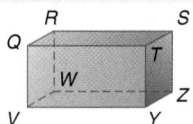

34. Estimate the area of the shaded figure to the nearest square unit. *(Lesson 10-8)*
Sample answer: 35 square units

Solve each inequality. Check your solution. *(Lesson 7-4)*

35. $x + 5 > -3$
$x > -8$

36. $k + (-9) \geq 1.8$
$k \geq 10.8$

Getting Ready for the Next Lesson

PREREQUISITE SKILL **Find each product.**
*(To review **multiplying fractions**, see Lesson 5-3.)*

37. $\frac{1}{3} \cdot 5 \cdot 15$ **25**

38. $\frac{1}{3} \cdot 4 \cdot 9$ **12**

39. $\frac{1}{3} \cdot 2 \cdot 2 \cdot 3$ **4**

40. $\frac{1}{3} \cdot 3 \cdot 4 \cdot 8$ **32**

41. $\frac{1}{3} \cdot 2^2 \cdot 21$ **28**

42. $\frac{1}{3} \cdot 3^2 \cdot 10$ **30**

Odd/Even Assignments
Exercises 11–28 are structured so that students practice the same concepts whether they are assigned odd or even problems.

Assignment Guide
Basic: 11–25 odd, 29–42
Average: 11–27 odd, 29–42
Advanced: 12–28 even, 29–36
(Optional: 37–42)

4 Assess

Open-Ended Assessment

Speaking Have students explain how finding the volume of a prism differs from finding the volume of a cylinder.

Getting Ready for Lesson 11-3

PREREQUISITE SKILL In Lesson 11-3, students will find the volume of pyramids and cones. The formulas for finding these volumes include multiplying by $\frac{1}{3}$. Use Exercises 37–42 to determine your students' familiarity with multiplying by $\frac{1}{3}$.

Assessment Options
Quiz (Lessons 11-1 and 11-2) is available on p. 659 of the *Chapter 11 Resource Masters.*

Answers

29. The volume will be greater if the height is $8\frac{1}{2}$ inches. By using the formula for circumference, you can find the radius and volume of each cylinder. If the height is $8\frac{1}{2}$ inches, the volume is 86.5 in³; if the height is 11 inches, the volume is 67.7 in³.

30. Volume of a solid equals the area of the solid's base times its height. Answers should include the following.
- Area is a measure of figures on a flat plane having two dimensions, length and width. Volume is a measure of objects in space having three dimensions, length, width, and height.
- The dimensions that are used to find area are also used to find volume, so the formula for volume includes the formula for area.

11-3 Volume: Pyramids and Cones

1 Focus

5-Minute Check Transparency 11-3 Use as a quiz or review of Lesson 11-2.

Mathematical Background notes are available for this lesson on page 552C.

How is the volume of a pyramid related to the volume of a prism?

The opening activity questions are repeated on page 622 of the *Chapter 11 Resource Masters*.

Reading to Learn Mathematics, p. 622 — ELL

Pre-Activity How is the volume of a pyramid related to the volume of a prism?

Do the activity at the top of page 568 in your textbook. Write your answers below.

a. Compare the base areas and compare the heights of the prism and the pyramid. The areas of the bases and the heights of both solids are the same.

b. How many times greater is the volume of the prism than the volume of one pyramid? 3 times

c. What fraction of the prism volume does one pyramid fill? $\frac{1}{3}$

Reading the Lesson

Write a definition and give an example of the new vocabulary word.

	Vocabulary	Definition	Example
1.	cone	See students' work.	

2. What is the relationship between the volume of a pyramid and the volume of a prism if both figures have the same base areas and heights? The volume of the pyramid is one-third that of the prism.

3. What is the relationship between the volume of a cone and the volume of a cylinder if both figures have the same base areas and heights? The volume of the cone is one-third that of the cylinder.

Helping You Remember

4. Write out in words an explanation for each step in finding the volume of the pyramid at the right.

$V = \frac{1}{3}Bh$ Formula for volume of a pyramid

$V = \frac{1}{3}\left(\frac{1}{2} \cdot 5 \cdot 8\right)h$ The base is a triangle, so $B = \frac{1}{2} \cdot 5 \cdot 8$.

$V = \frac{1}{3}\left(\frac{1}{2} \cdot 5 \cdot 8\right)27$ The height of the pyramid is 27 yd.

$V = 180$ Simplify.

What You'll Learn

- Find volumes of pyramids.
- Find volumes of cones.

Vocabulary

- cone

Study Tip

Height of Pyramid
The height of a pyramid is the distance from the vertex, perpendicular to the base.

How is the volume of a pyramid related to the volume of a prism?

You can see that the volume of the pyramid shown at the right is less than the volume of the prism in which it sits.

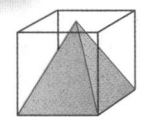

If the pyramid were made of sand, it would take three pyramids to fill a prism having the same base dimensions and height.

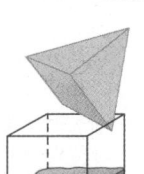 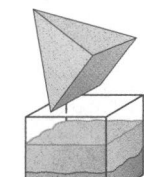

a. Compare the base areas and compare the heights of the prism and the pyramid.

b. How many times greater is the volume of the prism than the volume of one pyramid? **3 times**

c. What fraction of the prism volume does one pyramid fill? $\frac{1}{3}$

VOLUMES OF PYRAMIDS A pyramid has one-third the volume of a prism with the same base area and height.

Key Concept — Volume of a Pyramid

- **Words** The volume V of a pyramid is one-third the area of the base B times the height h.

- **Symbols** $V = \frac{1}{3}Bh$

- **Model**

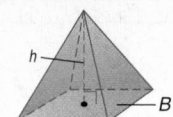

Example 1 Volumes of Pyramids

Find the volume of each pyramid. If necessary, round to the nearest tenth.

a.

$V = \frac{1}{3}Bh$ Formula for volume of a pyramid

$V = \frac{1}{3}\left(\frac{1}{2} \cdot 8 \cdot 6\right)h$ The base is a triangle, so $B = \frac{1}{2} \cdot 8 \cdot 6$.

$V = \frac{1}{3}\left(\frac{1}{2} \cdot 8 \cdot 6\right)20$ The height of the pyramid is 20 feet.

$V = 160$ Simplify.

The volume is 160 cubic feet.

Resource Manager

Workbooks and Reproducible Masters

Chapter 11 Resource Masters
- Study Guide and Intervention, p. 619
- Skills Practice, p. 620
- Practice, p. 621
- Reading to Learn Mathematics, p. 622
- Enrichment, p. 623

Parent and Student Study Guide Workbook, p. 92

Transparencies
5-Minute Check Transparency 11-3
Answer Key Transparencies

Technology
Interactive Chalkboard
Pre-AlgePASS: Tutorial Plus, Lesson 35

b. base area 125 cm², height 6.5 cm

$$V = \frac{1}{3}Bh \qquad \text{Formula for volume of a pyramid}$$

$$V = \frac{1}{3}(125)(6.5) \qquad \text{Replace } B \text{ with 125 and } h \text{ with 6.5.}$$

$$V \approx 270.8 \qquad \text{Simplify.}$$

The volume is about 270.8 cubic centimeters.

Reading Math

Cones
In this text, *cone* refers to a circular cone.

VOLUMES OF CONES A **cone** is a three-dimensional figure with one circular base. A curved surface connects the base and the vertex.

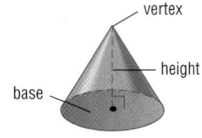

The volumes of a cone and a cylinder are related in the same way as the volumes of a pyramid and a prism are related.

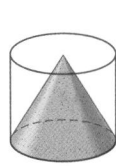 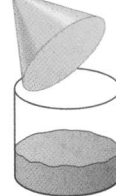 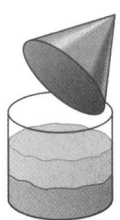

The volume of a cone is $\frac{1}{3}$ the volume of a cylinder with the same base area and height.

Key Concept — *Volume of a Cone*

- **Words** The volume V of a cone with radius r is one-third the area of the base B times the height h.

- **Model**

  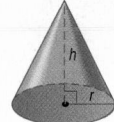

- **Symbols** $V = \frac{1}{3}Bh$ or $V = \frac{1}{3}\pi r^2 h$, where $B = \pi r^2$

Example 2 *Volume of a Cone*

Find the volume of the cone. Round to the nearest tenth.

$$V = \frac{1}{3}\pi r^2 h \qquad \text{Formula for volume of a cone}$$

$$V = \frac{1}{3} \cdot \pi \cdot 5^2 \cdot 12 \qquad \text{Replace } r \text{ with 5 and } h \text{ with 12.}$$

$$V \approx 314.2 \qquad \text{Simplify.}$$

The volume is about 314.2 cubic centimeters.

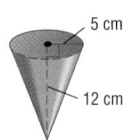

✓ **Concept Check** What is the volume of a cone whose base area is 86 meters squared and whose height is 3 meters? 86 m³

www.pre-alg.com/extra_examples

Lesson 11-3 Volume: Pyramids and Cones **569**

---

2 Teach

Teaching Tip To help students visualize the volume of a pyramid, pour water into a clear plastic cube until it is one-third full. Form a right pyramid with the water by tipping the container so the water comes to a point at one of the top corners, yet completely fills the face opposite the point.

VOLUMES OF PYRAMIDS

In-Class Example Power Point®

1 Find the volume of each pyramid. If necessary, round to the nearest tenth.

a.
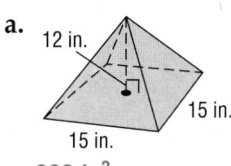
12 in.
15 in.
15 in.
900 in³

b. base area 19 cm², height 21 cm **133 cm³**

VOLUMES OF CONES

In-Class Example Power Point®

2 Find the volume of the cone. Round to the nearest tenth.

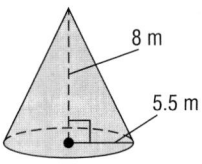
8 m
5.5 m

253.4 m³

Teaching Tip Watch for students who square the diameter rather than the radius.

Teacher to Teacher

Carol Malloy   University of North Carolina, Chapel Hill, NC

"I like to have my students to actually model the volume relationships shown on pages 568 and 569 by building cubes, pyramids, cylinders, and cones out of card stock and taping the edges for support. You can use snow-cone cups and cans to model cones and cylinders. You can also use rice, small beans, or even water to fill the models."

3 **LANDSCAPING** When mulch was dumped from a truck, it formed a cone-shaped mound with a diameter of 15 feet and a height of 8 feet.

a. What is the volume of the mulch? **about 471 ft³**

b. How many square feet can be covered with this mulch if 1 cubic foot covers 4 square feet of ground? **1884 ft²**

3 Practice/Apply

Study Notebook

Have students—

• add the definition/example of the vocabulary term to their Vocabulary Builder worksheets for Chapter 11.

• include any other item(s) that they find helpful in mastering the skills in this lesson.

About the Exercises . . .

Organization by Objective
• **Volumes of Pyramids:** 10–13, 16, 17, 20, 25, 27
• **Volumes of Cones:** 14, 15, 18, 19, 21–24, 26, 28

Odd/Even Assignments
Exercises 10–22 are structured so that students practice the same concepts whether they are assigned odd or even problems.

Assignment Guide

Basic: 11, 15, 17, 19, 23, 25–28, 32–38

Average: 11–23 odd, 25–28, 32–38 (Optional: 29–31)

Advanced: 10–24 even, 25–35 (Optional: 36–38)

All: Practice Quiz 1 (1–5)

Example 3 *Use Volume to Solve Problems*

HIGHWAY MAINTENANCE Salt and sand mixtures are often used on icy roads. When the mixture is dumped from a truck into the staging area, it forms a cone-shaped mound with a diameter of 10 feet and a height of 6 feet.

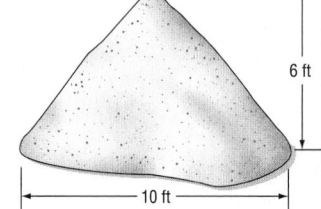

a. What is the volume of the salt-sand mixture?

Estimate: $\frac{1}{3} \cdot 3 \cdot 5^2 \cdot 6 = 150$

$V = \frac{1}{3}\pi r^2 h$ Formula for volume of a cone

$V = \frac{1}{3} \cdot \pi \cdot 5^2 \cdot 6$ Since $d = 10$, replace r with 5. Replace h with 6.

$V \approx 157$

The volume of the mixture is about 157 cubic feet.

b. How many square feet of roadway can be salted using the mixture in part a if 500 square feet can be covered by 1 cubic foot of salt?

$\text{ft}^2 \text{ of roadway} = 157 \text{ ft}^3 \text{ mixture} \times \dfrac{500 \text{ ft}^2 \text{ of roadway}}{1 \text{ ft}^3 \text{ mixture}}$

$= 78,500 \text{ ft}^2 \text{ of roadway}$

So, 78,500 square feet of roadway can be salted.

Study Tip

Look Back
To review **dimensional analysis**, see Lesson 5-3.

Check for Understanding

Concept Check

2–3. See pp. 601A–601B

1. **Explain** why you can use πr^2 to find the area of the base of a cone. **The base is a circle.**
2. **List** the formulas for volume that you have learned so far in this chapter. Tell what the variables represent and explain how you can remember which formula goes with which solid.
3. **OPEN ENDED** Draw and label a cone whose volume is between 100 cm³ and 1000 cm³.

Guided Practice

GUIDED PRACTICE KEY	
Exercises	Examples
4–8	1, 2
9	3

Find the volume of each solid. If necessary, round to the nearest tenth.

4. **100 m³**
[figure: pyramid with 15 m, 4 m, 5 m]

5. **37.7 cm³**
[figure: cone with 4 cm, 5 cm, 3 cm]

6. **160 in³**
[figure: pyramid with 10 in., $A = 48$ in²]

7. rectangular pyramid: length 9 ft, width 7 ft, height 18 ft **378 ft³**

8. cone: radius 4 mm, height 6.5 mm **108.9 mm³**

Application

9. **HISTORY** The Great Pyramid of Khufu in Egypt was originally 481 feet high and had a square base 756 feet on a side. What was its volume? Use an estimate to check your answer. **91,636,272 ft³**

570 Chapter 11 Three-Dimensional Figures

DAILY
INTERVENTION   **Differentiated Instruction**

• **Kinesthetic** Have groups of students use modeling clay to make a cube and a cylinder. Have them measure and record the height and volume of each solid. Then, without adding or removing any clay, have them reform each cube into a square pyramid and each cylinder into a cone, maintaining the same base areas. Have students record the height and volume of their pyramids and cones. Compare the volumes and the changes that occurred in the models.

Practice and Apply

Homework Help

For Exercises	See Examples
10–22	1, 2
23–25	3

Extra Practice
See page 751.

Find the volume of each solid. If necessary, round to the nearest tenth.

10. 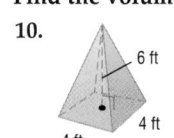 32 ft³

11. 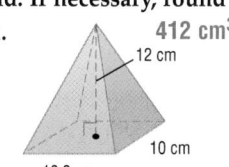 412 cm³

12. 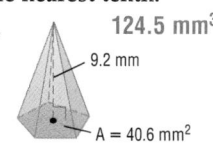 124.5 mm³

★ **13.** 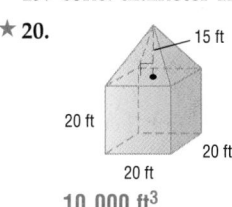 150 in³

14. 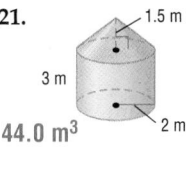 628.3 in³

15. 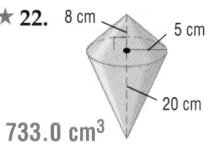 78.5 m³

16. square pyramid: length 5 in., height 6 in. **50 in³**

17. hexagonal pyramid: base area 125 cm², height 6.5 cm **270.8 cm³**

18. cone: radius 3 yd, height 14 yd **131.9 yd³**

19. cone: diameter 12 m, height 15 m **565.5 m³**

★ **20.** 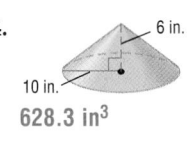 **10,000 ft³**

★ **21.** 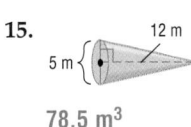 **44.0 m³**

★ **22.** 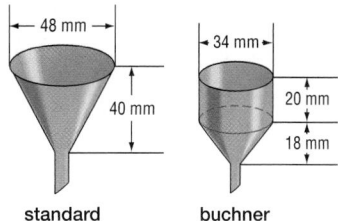 **733.0 cm³**

23. GEOLOGY A stalactite in the Endless Caverns in Virginia is cone-shaped. It is 4 feet long and has a diameter at its base of 1.5 feet.
 a. Find the volume of the stalactite to the nearest tenth. **2.4 ft³**
 b. The stalactite is made of calcium carbonate, which weighs 131 pounds per cubic foot. What is the weight of the stalactite? **314.4 lb**

WebQuest

Finding the volumes of three-dimensional figures will help you analyze structures. Visit www.pre-alg.com/webquest to continue work on your WebQuest project.

★ **24. SCIENCE** In science, a standard funnel is shaped like a cone, and a buchner funnel is shaped like a cone with a cylinder attached to the base. Which funnel has the greatest volume? **standard funnel**

25. **WRITING IN MATH** Answer the question that was posed at the beginning of the lesson. **See margin.**
How is the volume of a pyramid related to the volume of a prism?
Include the following in your answer:
• a discussion of the similarities between the dimensions and base area of the pyramid and prism shown at the beginning of the lesson, and
• a description of how the formulas for the volume of a pyramid and the volume of a prism are similar.

Answer

25. The volume of a pyramid is one-third the volume of a prism with the same base and height. Answers should include the following.
• The height of the pyramid and prism are equal. The bases of the pyramid and prism are squares with equal side lengths. Therefore, their base areas are equal.
• The formula for the volume of a pyramid is one-third times the formula for the volume of a prism.

Rounding Answers Students should learn to save all rounding for the very last step in their solution. To avoid rounding π before using it in the formula, you may want to have students use a scientific calculator to compute volumes of cylinders.

4 Assess

Open-Ended Assessment

Writing Have students write problems that involve a number of different-shaped but similar-sized solids. Students can exchange problems with partners and solve to find which solids have the greatest and least volumes.

Getting Ready for Lesson 11-4

PREREQUISITE SKILL In Lesson 11-4, students will find the surface area of prisms and cylinders. Exercises 36–38 review estimating products, a useful skill when determining surface area.

Assessment Options

Practice Quiz 1 The quiz provides students with a brief review of the concepts and skills in Lessons 11-1 through 11-3. Lesson numbers are given to the right of exercises or instruction lines so students can review concepts not yet mastered.

Answer

26b. The volume quadruples. The radius is squared when you find the volume, so when the radius is doubled, 2r, the squared value is 4r². So, the volume is 4 times greater.

---

26. CRITICAL THINKING a. The volume doubles.
  a. If you double the height of a cone, how does the volume change?
  b. If you double the radius of the base of a cone, how does the volume change? Explain. **See margin.**

27. Choose the best estimate for the volume of a rectangular pyramid 4.9 centimeters long, 3 centimeters wide, and 7 centimeters high. **B**
  (A) 7 cm³   (B) 35 cm³   (C) 70 cm³   (D) 105 cm³

28. The solids at the right have the same base area and height. If the cone is filled with water and poured into the cylinder, how much of the cylinder would be filled? **D**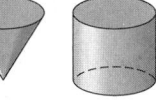
  (A) $\frac{3}{4}$ (B) $\frac{1}{2}$ (C) $\frac{2}{3}$ (D) $\frac{1}{3}$

Extending the Lesson The volume V of a sphere with radius r is given by the formula $V = \frac{4}{3}\pi r^3$. **Find the volume of each sphere to the nearest tenth. 31. 107.5 mm³**
  29. radius 6 cm **904.8 cm³** 30. radius 1.4 in. **11.5 in³** 31. diameter 5.9 mm

Maintain Your Skills

Mixed Review **Find the volume of each prism or cylinder. If necessary, round to the nearest tenth.** *(Lesson 11-2)*
  32. rectangular prism: length 4 cm, width 8 cm, height 2 cm **64 cm³**

34. triangular pyramid; any one of the following faces is a base: *DCG, DGF, DFC, CGF, $\overline{DC}$, $\overline{DG}$, $\overline{DF}$, $\overline{CG}$, $\overline{GF}$, $\overline{FC}$; C, D, F, G*

  33. cylinder: diameter 1.6 in., height 5 in. **10.1 in³**

  34. Identify the solid at the right. Name the bases, faces, edges, and vertices. *(Lesson 11-1)*

  35. Find the distance between $A(3, 7)$ and $B(-2, 1)$. Round to the nearest tenth, if necessary. *(Lesson 9-6)* **7.8**

Getting Ready for the Next Lesson **PREREQUISITE SKILL** Estimate each product.
  *(To review **estimating products**, see page 714.)* **36–38. Sample answers are given.**
  36. 4.9 · 5.1 · 3 **75**   37. 2 · 1.7 · 9 **36**   38. 2 · π · 6.8 **42**

Practice Quiz 1
Lessons 11-1 through 11-3

Identify each solid. *(Lesson 11-1)*
1. **triangular prism**
2. **rectangular pyramid**

Find the volume of each solid. If necessary, round to the nearest tenth. *(Lesson 11-2)* **4. 756 ft³**
3. cylinder: radius 2 cm, height 1 cm **12.6 cm³**   4. hexagonal prism: base area 42 ft², height 18 ft
5. **MINING** An open pit mine in the Elk mountain range is cone-shaped. The mine is 420 feet across and 250 feet deep. What volume of material was removed? *(Lesson 11-3)*
  ≈ 11,545,353 ft³

Surface Area: Prisms and Cylinders

What You'll Learn

- Find surface areas of prisms.
- Find surface areas of cylinders.

How is the surface area of a solid different from its volume?

The sizes and prices of shipping boxes are shown in the table.

a. For each box, find the area of each face and the sum of the areas.

b. Find the volume of each box. Are these values the same as the values you found in part **a**? Explain.

Box	Size (in.)	Price ($)
A	8 × 8 × 8	$1.50
B	15 × 10 × 12	$2.25
C	20 × 14 × 10	$3.00

SURFACE AREAS OF PRISMS

If you open up a box or prism to form a net, you can see all the surfaces. The sum of the areas of these surfaces is called the **surface area** of the prism.

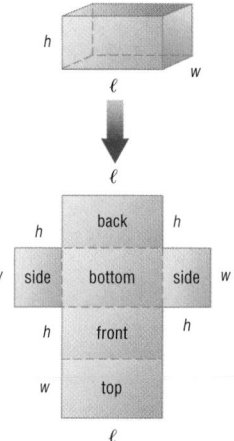

Faces	Area
top and bottom	$(\ell \cdot w) + (\ell \cdot w) = 2\ell w$
front and back	$(\ell \cdot h) + (\ell \cdot h) = 2\ell h$
two sides	$(w \cdot h) + (w \cdot h) = 2wh$
Sum of areas →	$2\ell w + 2\ell h + 2wh$ or
	$2(\ell w + \ell h + wh)$

Key Concept — Surface Area of Rectangular Prisms

- **Words** The surface area S of a rectangular prism with length ℓ, width w, and height h is the sum of the areas of the faces.

- **Model**

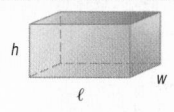

- **Symbols** $S = 2\ell w + 2\ell h + 2wh = 2(\ell w + \ell h + wh)$

Example 1 Surface Area of a Rectangular Prism

Find the surface area of the rectangular prism.

$S = 2\ell w + 2\ell h + 2wh$	Write the formula.
$S = 2(20)(14) + 2(20)(10) + 2(14)(10)$	Substitution
$S = 1240$	Simplify.

The surface area of the prism is 1240 square inches.

---

1 Focus

5-Minute Check Transparency 11-4 Use as a quiz or review of Lesson 11-3.

Mathematical Background notes are available for this lesson on page 552C.

How is the surface area of a solid different than its volume?

The opening activity questions are repeated on page 627 of the *Chapter 11 Resource Masters*.

Reading to Learn Mathematics, p. 627 ELL

Pre-Activity — How is the surface area of a solid different than its volume?
Do the activity at the top of page 573 in your textbook. Write your answers below.

a. For each box, find the area of each face and find the sum.
A, 384 in²; B, 900 in²; C, 1240 in²

b. Find the volume of each box. Are these values the same as the values you found in part a? Explain. A, 512 in³; B, 1800 in³; C, 2800 in³; No; for each box, the volume is greater.

Reading the Lesson
Write a definition and give an example of the new vocabulary phrase.

	Vocabulary	Definition	Example
1.	surface area	See students' work.	

2. How is finding the surface area of a prism or cylinder different from finding the figure's volume? The surface area is the sum of the areas of the faces of a solid figure, while the volume is the measure of space occupied by the figure.

Helping You Remember

3. How does drawing a net help you find the surface area of a prism or cylinder? Draw a prism or cylinder and its net to justify your answer. The net allows you to clearly see and measure all the faces of the figure. Students' drawings will vary.

Resource Manager

Workbooks and Reproducible Masters

Chapter 11 Resource Masters
- Study Guide and Intervention, p. 624
- Skills Practice, p. 625
- Practice, p. 626
- Reading to Learn Mathematics, p. 627
- Enrichment, p. 628
- Assessment, pp. 659, 661

Graphing Calculator and Spreadsheet Masters, p. 40
Parent and Student Study Guide Workbook, p. 93
School-to-Career Masters, p. 22

Transparencies

5-Minute Check Transparency 11-4
Answer Key Transparencies

Technology

Interactive Chalkboard
Multimedia Applications

Teaching Tip Have a number of actual different-sized shipping boxes, along with their prices, available to share with students. You may also be able to find shipping containers in the shape of triangular prisms to share. Discuss the relationship between surface area, volume, and price of the containers.

SURFACE AREAS OF PRISMS

In-Class Examples

1 Find the surface area of the rectangular prism.

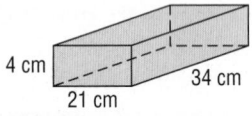

1868 cm²

2 Find the surface area of the triangular prism.

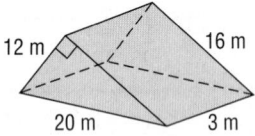

336 m²

Teaching Tip Have students use grid paper to create larger nets similar in shape to those on the student pages. Have students cut out and tape them together to form the solids. This will help them to see the surfaces that form the solids.

✓ Skills Check

Surface Areas of Prisms
A rectangular prism has a square base whose area is 25 ft². The height of the prism is 4 ft. Find the surface area.   **130 ft²**

Example 2 *Surface Area of a Triangular Prism*

Find the surface area of the triangular prism.

One way to easily see all of the surfaces of the prism is to draw a net on grid paper and label the dimensions of each face.

Find the area of each face.

$$
\left.
\begin{array}{ll}
\text{bottom} & 3 \cdot 6 = 18 \\
\text{left side} & 4 \cdot 6 = 24 \\
\text{right side} & 5 \cdot 6 = 30
\end{array}
\right\} \quad A = \ell w
$$

$$\text{two bases } 2\left(\frac{1}{2} \cdot 3 \cdot 4\right) = 12 \quad A = \frac{1}{2}bh$$

Add to find the total surface area.
$18 + 24 + 30 + 12 = 84$

The surface area of the triangular prism is 84 square centimeters.

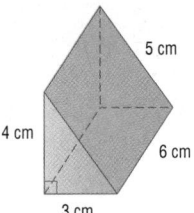

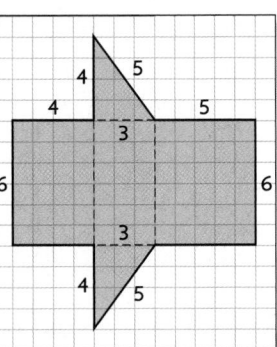

SURFACE AREAS OF CYLINDERS
You can also find surface areas of cylinders. If you unroll a cylinder, its net is a rectangle and two circles.

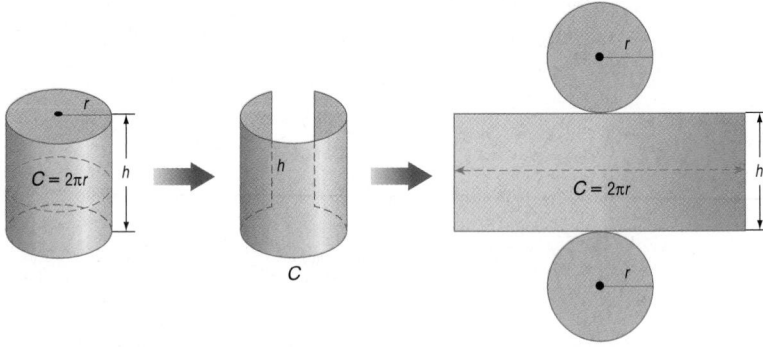

Model		Net
bases	▷	congruent circles
curved surface	▷	rectangle
height h	▷	width of rectangle
circumference C	▷	length of rectangle

The area of each circular base is πr^2. The area of the rectangular region is $\ell \cdot w$, or $2\pi r \cdot h$.

The surface area of a cylinder	equals	the area of two circular bases	plus	the area of the curved surface.
S	$=$	$2(\pi r^2)$	$+$	$2\pi rh$

DAILY INTERVENTION

Differentiated Instruction

- **Logical** Create the surface regions for a number of figures including rectangular prisms, triangular prisms, and cylinders. Cut apart or separate the surface regions for each figure, then shuffle all the pieces together. Have students, working alone or in groups, fit the pieces together again and either re-create the figures or make nets for the figures. Finally, have students find the surface areas for the figures they've put together.

Key Concept — Surface Area of Cylinders

- **Words** — The surface area S of a cylinder with height h and radius r is the area of the two bases plus the area of the curved surface.

- **Model**

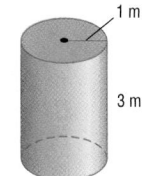

- **Symbols** — $S = 2\pi r^2 + 2\pi rh$

Example 3 — Surface Area of a Cylinder

Find the surface area of the cylinder. Round to the nearest tenth.

1 m
3 m

$S = 2\pi r^2 + 2\pi rh$ — Formula for surface area of a cylinder
$S = 2\pi(1)^2 + 2\pi(1)(3)$ — Replace r with 1 and h with 3.
$S \approx 25.1$ — Simplify.

The surface area is about 25.1 square meters.

You can compare surface areas of prisms and cylinders.

Example 4 — Compare Surface Areas

FRUIT DRINKS Both containers hold about the same amount of pineapple juice. Does the box or the can have a greater surface area?

7 cm
4 cm
9 cm
6 cm
9 cm

Surface area of box		
top/bottom	sides	front/back

$S = 2\ell w + 2\ell h + 2wh$
$\quad = 2(4 \cdot 7) + 2(4 \cdot 9) + 2(7 \cdot 9)$
$\quad = 254$

Surface area of can	
top/bottom	curved surface

$S = 2\pi r^2 + 2\pi rh$
$\quad = 2\pi(3)^2 + 2\pi(3)(9)$
$\quad \approx 226$

Since 254 cm^2 > 226 cm^2, the box has a greater surface area.

More About...

Fruit Drinks
A typical juice box is made of six layers of packaging. These layers include paper, foil, and special adhesives.
Source: www.dupont.com

Concept Check — Why might a company prefer to sell juice in cans?
Sample answer: less surface area to package, so less expensive to manufacture

Check for Understanding

Concept Check
1. **Explain** why surface area is given in square units rather than cubic units. See margin.
2. **OPEN ENDED** Find the surface areas of a rectangular prism and a cylinder found in your home. Sample answer: find the surface area of a cedar chest and a cylinder-shaped potato chip container.

www.pre-alg.com/extra_examples

Lesson 11-4 Surface Area: Prisms and Cylinders **575**

Answer

1. Sample answer: The surface of a solid is two-dimensional. Its area is the sum of the face areas, which are given in square units.

Tips for New Teachers

Modeling
Have students make and decorate cylinders, prisms, pyramids, and cones with a specific theme to display around the classroom.

SURFACE AREAS OF CYLINDERS

Teaching Tip Some students may confuse the volume formula with the surface area formula. Use models to help students visualize the derivation of each formula.

3 Find the surface area of the cylinder. Round to the nearest tenth.

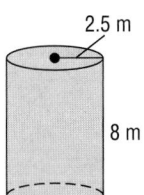

2.5 m
8 m

164.9 m^2

4 **CEREALS** A company packages its cereal in a rectangular prism that is 2.5 in. by 7 in. by 12 in. It is considering packaging it in a cylinder-shaped container having a 6-in. diameter and a height of 7.5 in. Which uses the least amount of packaging?
The cylinder has less packaging; 197.9 in^2 < 263 in^2.

3 Practice/Apply

Study Notebook

Have students—
- add the definition/example of the vocabulary term to their Vocabulary Builder worksheets for Chapter 11.
- write a paragraph describing the number of surface regions on a rectangular triangular prism, a triangular prism, and a cylinder.
- include any other item(s) that they find helpful in mastering the skills in this lesson.

4 Assess

Open-Ended Assessment

Speaking Have students explain in their own words how to find the surface areas of a rectangular prism, a triangular prism, and a cylinder.

Getting Ready for Lesson 11-5

PREREQUISITE SKILL In Lesson 11-5 students find the surface areas of pyramids and cones. Exercises 32–37 review multiplying rational numbers, a necessary step when finding surface area.

Assessment Options

Quiz (Lessons 11-3 and 11-4) is available on p. 659 of the *Chapter 11 Resource Masters.*

Mid-Chapter Test (Lessons 11-1 through 11-4) is available on p. 661 of the *Chapter 11 Resource Masters.*

Guided Practice **Find the surface area of each solid shown or described. If necessary, round to the nearest tenth.**

GUIDED PRACTICE KEY	
Exercises	Examples
3, 6	1
4	2
5, 7	3
8	4

3. 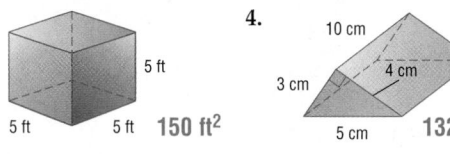 150 ft²

4. 132 cm²

5. 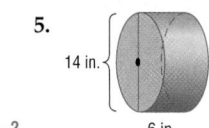 571.8 in²

6. rectangular prism: length 3 cm, width 2 cm, height 1 cm **22 cm²**

7. cylinder: radius 4 mm, height 1.6 mm **140.7 mm²**

Application
8. Box A;
166 in² > 145 in²

8. CRAFTS Brianna sews together pieces of plastic canvas to make tissue box covers. For which tissue box will she use more plastic canvas to cover the sides and the top? Explain.

Box	Length (in.)	Width (in.)	Height (in.)
A	9	4	5
B	5	5	6

★ indicates increased difficulty

Practice and Apply

Homework Help	
For Exercises	See Examples
9, 10, 15, 16	1
11, 12	2
13, 14, 17–19, 21, 22	3
20	4

Extra Practice See page 751.

Find the surface area of each solid shown or described. If necessary, round to the nearest tenth. **11. 264 m² 12. 211.2 cm²**

9. 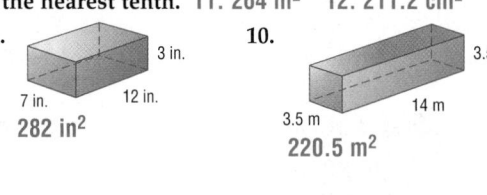 282 in²

10. 220.5 m²

11.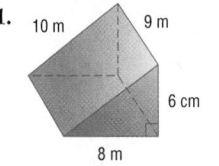

12.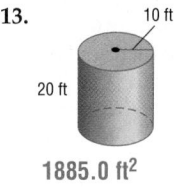

13. 1885.0 ft²

14. 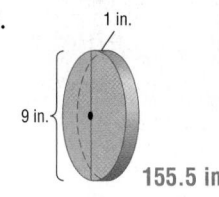 155.5 in²

15. cube: side length 7 ft **294 ft²**

16. rectangular prism: length 6.2 cm, width 4 cm, height 8.5 cm **223 cm²**

17. cylinder: radius 5 in., height 15 in. **628.3 in²**

18. cylinder: diameter 4 m, height 20 m **276.5 m²**

★ **19.** Find the surface area of the complex solid at the right. Use estimation to check the reasonableness of your answer. **264.0 in²**

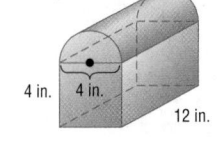

★ **20. AQUARIUMS** A standard 20-gallon aquarium tank is a rectangular prism that holds approximately 4600 cubic inches of water. The bottom glass needs to be 24 inches by 12 inches to fit on the stand. **b. 10 ft²**
  a. Find the height of the aquarium to the nearest inch. **16 in.**
  b. Find the total amount of glass needed in square feet for the five faces.
  c. An aquarium with an octagonal base has sides that are 9 inches wide and 16 inches high. The area of the base is 392.4 square inches. Do the bottom and sides of this tank have a greater surface area than the rectangular tank? Explain. **Yes; see margin for explanation.**

576 Chapter 11 Three-Dimensional Figures

Answer

20c. The sides of both tanks have the same surface area, 1152 in². However, the area of the octagon base is 392.4 in² and the area of the rectangular base is 288 in². So, the total surface area of the octagon-shaped tank is greater.

POOLS Vinyl liners cover the inside walls and bottom of the swimming pools whose top views are shown below. Find the area of the vinyl liner for each pool if they are 4 feet deep. Round to the nearest square foot.

★ **21.**   **754 ft²**

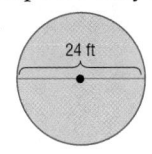
24 ft

★ **22.**   **690 ft²**

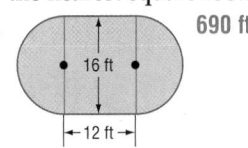
16 ft

←— 12 ft —→

23. CRITICAL THINKING Suppose you double the length of the sides of a cube. How is the surface area affected? **The surface area is 4 times greater.**

24. [WRITING IN MATH] Answer the question that was posed at the beginning of the lesson. **See margin.**

How is the surface area of a solid different than its volume?

Include the following in your answer:
- a comparison of formulas for surface area and volume, and
- an explanation of the difference between surface area and volume.

Standardized Test Practice
Ⓐ Ⓑ Ⓒ Ⓓ

25. Find the surface area of a cylinder with a diameter of 15 centimeters and height of 2 centimeters. **D**

   Ⓐ 30 cm²   Ⓑ 117.8 cm²   Ⓒ 353.4 cm²   Ⓓ 447.7 cm²

26. How many 2-inch squares will completely cover a rectangular prism 10 inches long, 4 inches wide, and 6 inches high? **B**

   Ⓐ 40   Ⓑ 62   Ⓒ 240   Ⓓ 248

Extending the Lesson
If you make cuts in a solid, different 2-dimensional cross sections result, as shown at the right. Describe the cross section of each figure cut below.

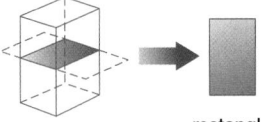
rectangle

27.

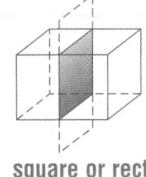
square or rectangle

28.

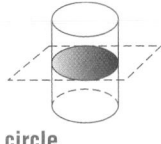
circle

29.

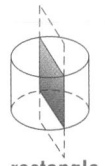
rectangle

Maintain Your Skills

Mixed Review
Find the volume of each solid. If necessary, round to the nearest tenth.
(Lessons 11-2 and 11-3)

30. rectangular pyramid: length 6 ft, width 5 ft, height 7 ft **70 ft³**

31. cylinder: diameter 6 in., height 20 in. **565.5 in³**

Getting Ready for the Next Lesson
PREREQUISITE SKILL Find each product.
*(To review **multiplying rational numbers**, see Lesson 5-3.)*

32. 10.3(8) **82.4**   **33.** 3.9(3.9) **15.21**   **34.** 12.3(9.2)(6) **678.96**

35. $\frac{1}{2} \cdot 2.6$ **1.3**   **36.** $\frac{1}{2} \cdot 82 \cdot 90$ **3690**   **37.** $\frac{1}{2}\left(6\frac{1}{2}\right)$ $3\frac{1}{4}$

Answer

24. Surface area is the boundary around a solid. Volume is the space inside a solid. Answers should include the following.

- The formula for surface area involves the product of two dimensions and is given in square units. The formula for volume involves the product of three dimensions and is given in cubic units.

- Surface area describes the size of the total surfaces of a solid. Volume describes the capacity or amount of space contained inside a solid.

1 Focus

5-Minute Check Transparency 11-5 Use as a quiz or review of Lesson 11-4.

Mathematical Background notes are available for this lesson on page 552D.

How is surface area important in architecture?

The opening activity questions are repeated on page 632 of the *Chapter 11 Resource Masters*.

Reading to Learn Mathematics, p. 632 ELL

Pre-Activity *How is surface area important in architecture?*
Do the activity at the top of page 578 in your textbook. Write your answers below.

a. The front triangle has a base of about 230 feet and height of about 120 feet. What is the area? 13,800 ft²

b. How could you find the total amount of glass used in the pyramid? Find the area of all the sides and add.

Reading the Lesson 1–3. See students' work.

Write a definition and give an example of each new vocabulary phrase.

Vocabulary	Definition	Example
1. lateral face		
2. slant height		
3. lateral area		

4. How does the slant height of a pyramid differ from the height of the pyramid? Include a drawing to help explain your answer. The slant height is the height of one of the lateral faces, while the height of the pyramid is the height from the vertex to the base.

Helping You Remember

5. Prepare the script for a short presentation on how to find the surface areas of pyramids and cones. Be sure to include any necessary vocabulary terms in your explanation. You may wish to include diagrams with your presentation. See students' work.

11-5 Surface Area: Pyramids and Cones

What You'll Learn

- Find surface areas of pyramids.
- Find surface areas of cones.

Vocabulary
- lateral face
- slant height
- lateral area

How is surface area important in architecture?

The front of the Rock and Roll Hall of Fame in Cleveland, Ohio, is a glass pyramid.

a. The front triangle has a base of about 230 feet and height of about 120 feet. What is the area? **13,800 ft²**

b. How could you find the total amount of glass used in the pyramid?

b. Find the area of all the sides and add.

SURFACE AREAS OF PYRAMIDS The sides of a pyramid are called **lateral faces**. They are triangles that intersect at the vertex. The altitude or height of each lateral face is called the **slant height**.

Square Pyramid   **Net of Square Pyramid**

vertex
lateral face
slant height
base

lateral face
base
slant height

The sum of the areas of the lateral faces is the **lateral area** of a pyramid. The surface area of a pyramid is the lateral area plus the area of the base.

Example 1 *Surface Area of a Pyramid*

Find the surface area of the square pyramid.

Find the lateral area and the base area.

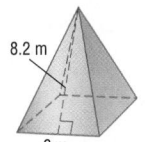

8.2 m

6 m

Area of each lateral face

$A = \frac{1}{2}bh$ Area of a triangle

$A = \frac{1}{2}(6)(8.2)$ Replace b with 6 and h with 8.2.

$A = 24.6$ Simplify.

There are 4 faces, so the lateral area is 4(24.6) or 98.4 square meters.

Resource Manager

 **Workbooks and Reproducible Masters**

Chapter 11 Resource Masters
- Study Guide and Intervention, p. 629
- Skills Practice, p. 630
- Practice, p. 631
- Reading to Learn Mathematics, p. 632
- Enrichment, p. 633

Parent and Student Study Guide Workbook, p. 94

 Transparencies
5-Minute Check Transparency 11-5
Answer Key Transparencies

 Technology
Interactive Chalkboard

Area of base

$A = s^2$ Area of a square

$A = 6^2$ or 36   Replace s with 6 and simplify.

The surface area of a pyramid	equals	the lateral area	plus	the area of the base.
S	$=$	98.4	$+$	36

The surface area of the pyramid is 134.4 square meters.

Example 2   Use Surface Area to Solve a Problem

ARCHITECTURE   The Louvre museum in Paris has a huge square glass pyramid at the entrance with a slant height of about 92 feet. Its square base is 116 feet on each side. How much glass did it take to cover the pyramid?

Find the lateral area only, since the bottom of the pyramid is not covered in glass.

$A = \frac{1}{2}bh$ Formula for area of a triangle

$A = \frac{1}{2}(116)(92)$ Replace b with 116 and h with 92.

$A = 5336$ Simplify.

One lateral face has an area of 5336 square feet. There are 4 lateral faces, so the lateral area is $4 \cdot 5336$ or 21,344 square feet.

It took 21,344 square feet of glass to cover the pyramid.

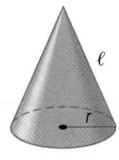
SURFACE AREAS OF CONES   You can also find surface areas of cones. The net of a cone shows the regions that make up the cone.

Model of Cone

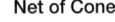

Net of Cone

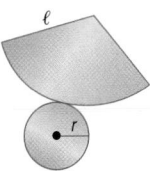

The lateral area of a cone with slant height ℓ is one-half the circumference of the base, $2\pi r$, times ℓ. So $A = \frac{1}{2} \cdot 2\pi r \cdot \ell$ or $A = \pi r\ell$. The base of the cone is a circle with area πr^2.

The surface area of a cone	equals	the lateral area	plus	the area of the base.
S	$=$	$\pi r \ell$	$+$	πr^2

Key Concept   **Surface Area of a Cone**

- **Words**   The surface area S of a cone with slant height ℓ and radius r is the lateral area plus the area of the base.

- **Model**

- **Symbols** $S = \pi r\ell + \pi r^2$

---

www.pre-alg.com/extra_examples   **Lesson 11-5**   Surface Area: Pyramids and Cones   **579**

SURFACE AREAS OF PYRAMIDS

In-Class Examples 

1   Find the surface area of the square pyramid.

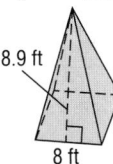

8.9 ft

8 ft

206.4 ft²

2   **CANOPIES**   A canopy is in the shape of a square pyramid that is 3.4 meters on each side. The slant height is 2 meters. How much canvas is used for the canopy? 13.6 m²

Teaching Tip   Have students explain the difference between height and the slant height of a pyramid. If necessary, demonstrate with a model of a pyramid.

DAILY
INTERVENTION   **Unlocking Misconceptions**

- **Surface Area of Pyramids and Cones**   Students may mistakenly assume that different types of solid figures with similar measures will have equal surface areas. For example, students may believe that a pyramid with a slant height of 6 and a base length of 6 would have a surface area equal to that of a cone with a slant height of 6 and a diameter of 6. Have students work a number of problems with measurements like those just given and discuss their answers.

3 Find the surface area of the cone. Round to the nearest tenth.

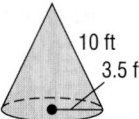
10 ft
3.5 ft

148.4 ft²

Example 3 **Surface Area of a Cone**

Find the surface area of the cone. Round to the nearest tenth.

$S = \pi r \ell + \pi r^2$ Formula for surface area of a cone

$S = \pi(10.6)(15) + \pi(10.6)^2$ Replace r with 10.6 and ℓ with 15.

$S \approx 852.5$ Simplify.

15 m
10.6 m

The surface area of the cone is about 852.5 square meters.

☑ **Concept Check**   What is the formula for the lateral area L of a cone? $L = \pi r \ell$

Check for Understanding

Concept Check   **1. Describe** the difference between slant height and height of a pyramid and a cone. **See margin.**

2. Explain how to find the lateral area of a pyramid. **See margin.**

3. OPEN ENDED Describe a situation in everyday life when a person might use the formulas for the surface area of a cone or a pyramid.
Sample answer: An architect might use the formulas to calculate the amount of materials needed for parts of a structure.

Guided Practice   **Find the surface area of each solid. If necessary, round to the nearest tenth.**

GUIDED PRACTICE KEY	
Exercises	Examples
4, 5	1
6	3
7	2

4. 66.4 ft²
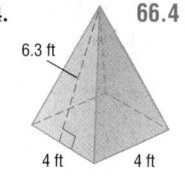
6.3 ft
4 ft   4 ft

5. 42.9 m²
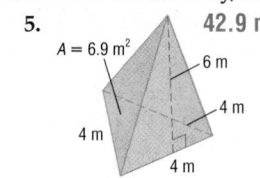
$A = 6.9$ m²
6 m
4 m
4 m
4 m

6.
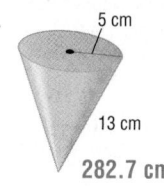
5 cm
13 cm
282.7 cm²

Application   **7. ARCHITECTURE** The small tower of a historic house is shaped like a regular hexagonal pyramid as shown at the right. How much roofing will be needed to cover this tower? (*Hint:* Do not include the base of the pyramid.) **336 ft²**

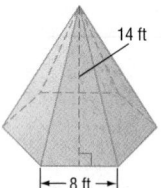
14 ft
←— 8 ft —→

★ indicates increased difficulty

Practice and Apply

Homework Help	
For Exercises	See Examples
8–11, 15, 16	1
12–14	3
17–19	2

Extra Practice
See page 751.

Find the surface area of each solid. If necessary, round to the nearest tenth.

8.
9 m
8 m   8 m
208 m²

9. 96.3 in²
6 in.
5½ in.
5½ in.

10.
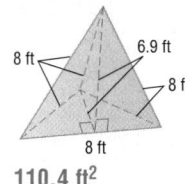
6.9 ft
8 ft
8 ft
8 ft
110.4 ft²

---

3 Practice/Apply

Study Notebook

Have students—
- add the definitions/examples of the vocabulary terms to their Vocabulary Builder worksheets for Chapter 11.
- include any other item(s) that they find helpful in mastering the skills in this lesson.

About the Exercises . . .
Organization by Objective
- **Surface Areas of Pyramids:** 8–11, 15, 16, 18, 25
- **Surface Areas of Cones:** 12–14, 17, 19–22, 24

Odd/Even Assignments
Exercises 18 and 20–21 are structured so that students practice the same concepts whether they are assigned odd or even problems.

Assignment Guide
Basic: 9, 11, 13, 17, 19, 21, 22–25, 29–39

Average: 9–21 odd, 22–25, 29–39 (Optional: 26–28)

Advanced: 8–20 even, 22–33 (Optional: 34–39)

DAILY
INTERVENTION

Differentiated Instruction

- **Intrapersonal** Have students write several paragraphs discussing the various formulas they have learned for surface area and volume in this chapter. They might answer questions such as: Which of the formulas are most difficult to work with? Why? What helps you remember the different formulas? Which examples proved most useful in learning the formulas?

Study Tip

Triangular Pyramids
Assume that when the base of a pyramid is an equilateral triangle, all the faces are congruent.

Find the surface area of each solid. If necessary, round to the nearest tenth.

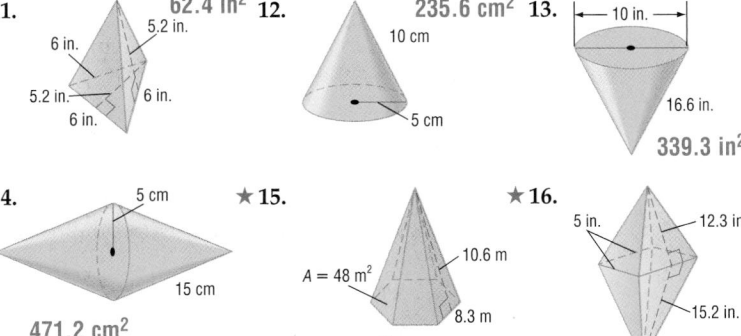

11. 6 in. 5.2 in. 5.2 in. 6 in. 6 in. **62.4 in²**

12. 10 cm **235.6 cm²**

13. ← 10 in. → 16.6 in. **339.3 in²**

14. 5 cm 15 cm **471.2 cm²**

15. $A = 48 \text{ m}^2$ 10.6 m 8.3 m **311.9 m²**

16. 5 in. 12.3 in. 15.2 in. **275 in²**

17. cone: radius 7.5 mm, slant height 14 mm **506.6 mm²**

18. square pyramid: base side length 9 yd, slant height 8 yd **225 yd²**

19. **FUND-RAISING** The cheerleaders are selling small megaphones decorated with the school mascot. There are two sizes, as shown at the right. What is the difference in the amount of plastic used in these two sizes? Round to the nearest square inch. (Note that a megaphone is open at the bottom.)
Style 8M has 29 in² more plastic.

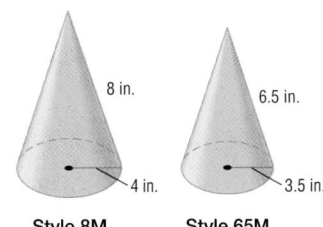

8 in. 4 in. **Style 8M**

6.5 in. 3.5 in. **Style 65M**

ARCHITECTURE For Exercises 20 and 21, use the following information.
A roofing company is preparing bids on two special jobs involving cone-shaped roofs. Roofing material is usually sold in 100-square-foot squares. For each roof, find the lateral surface area to the nearest square foot. Then determine the squares of roofing materials that would be needed to cover each surface.

20.

23 ft
8 ft
578 ft²; 6 squares

21.

12 ft
9 ft
339 ft²; 4 squares

22. Sinkers: about 251 in², original bar: 82 in²; the surface area is about tripled.

22. **CRITICAL THINKING** A bar of lead in the shape of a rectangular prism 13 inches by 2 inches by 1 inch is melted and recast into 100 conical fishing sinkers. The sinkers have a diameter of 1 inch, a height of 1 inch, and a slant height of about 1.1 inches. Compare the total surface area of all the sinkers to the surface area of the original lead bar.

Lesson 11-5 Surface Area: Pyramids and Cones **581**

Answers (p. 580)

1. Slant height is the altitude of a triangular face of a pyramid; it is the length from the vertex of a cone to the edge of its base. Height of a pyramid or cone is the altitude of the whole solid.

2. Use $A = \frac{1}{2}bh$ to find the area of each face. Then multiply by the number of faces.

Lesson 11-5 Surface Area: Pyramids and Cones **581**

Open-Ended Assessment

Modeling Have students make a net of a pyramid and a net of a cone out of heavy paper or cardboard. Have them label each face of the figures with the correct formula to determine its area, along with variables representing the needed measurements, such as slant height, base length, and radius. On a separate card, students should write the formula used to find the overall surface area of the solid and display the card with the net.

Getting Ready for Lesson 11-6

PREREQUISITE SKILL In Lesson 11-6, students will identify similar solids and solve problems involving similar solids. To determine whether solids are similar, a proportion comparing measurements of the solids must be written. Exercises 34–39 should be used to determine your students' familiarity with solving proportions.

---

23.  Answer the question that was posed at the beginning of the lesson. **See margin.**

    How is surface area important in architecture?

    Include the following in your answer:
    - examples of how surface area is used in architecture, and
    - an explanation of why building contractors and architects need to know surface areas.

Standardized Test Practice

24. Find the surface area of a cone with a radius of 7 centimeters and slant height of 11.4 centimeters. **D**

    Ⓐ 153.9 cm²   Ⓑ 250.7 cm²   Ⓒ 272.7 cm²   Ⓓ 404.6 cm²

25. What is the lateral area of the square pyramid at the right if the slant height is 7 inches? **C**

    Ⓐ 17.5 in²   Ⓑ 35 in²

    Ⓒ 70 in²   Ⓓ 95 in²

    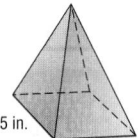
    5 in.

Extending the Lesson

The surface area S of a sphere with radius r is given by the formula $S = 4\pi r^2$. Find the surface area of each sphere to the nearest tenth.

26.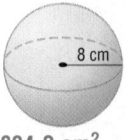
8 cm

804.2 cm²

27.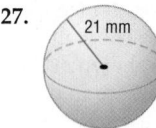
21 mm

5541.8 mm²

28.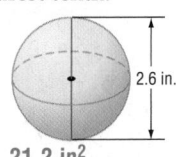
2.6 in.

21.2 in²

Maintain Your Skills

Mixed Review

Find the surface area of each solid. If necessary, round to the nearest tenth. *(Lesson 11-4)*

29. rectangular prism: length 2 ft, width 1 ft, height 0.5 ft   **7 ft²**

30. cylinder: radius 4 cm, height 13.8 cm   **447.4 cm²**

31. Find the volume of a cone that has a height of 6 inches and radius of 2 inches. Round to the nearest tenth.   *(Lesson 11-3)*   **25.1 in³**

State the solution of each system of equations.   *(Lesson 8-9)*

32.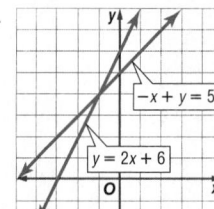
$-x + y = 5$
$y = 2x + 6$
(−1, 4)

33.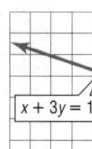
$y = -\frac{1}{3}x + 5$
$x + 3y = 15$

infinitely many solutions

Getting Ready for the Next Lesson

PREREQUISITE SKILL Solve each proportion.
*(To review **proportions**, see Lesson 6-2.)*

34. $\frac{1}{6} = \frac{x}{24}$ **4**

35. $\frac{9}{15} = \frac{n}{5}$ **3**

36. $\frac{t}{7} = \frac{40}{56}$ **5**

37. $\frac{1.6}{y} = \frac{9.6}{18}$ **3**

38. $\frac{4}{3.2} = \frac{w}{20}$ **25**

39. $\frac{18}{21} = \frac{2.7}{n}$ **3.15**

Answer

23. Many building materials are priced and purchased by square footage. Architects use surface area when designing buildings. Answers should include the following.
    - Surface area is used in covering building exteriors and in designing interiors.
    - It is important to know surface areas so the amounts and costs of building materials can be estimated.

Geometry Activity

A Preview of Lesson 11-6

Similar Solids

A model car is an exact replica of a real car, but much smaller. The dimensions of the model and the original are proportional. Therefore, these two objects are *similar solids*. The number of times that you increase or decrease the linear dimensions is called the scale factor.

You can use sugar cubes or centimeter blocks to investigate similar solids.

Activity 1
Collect the Data
- If each edge of a sugar cube is 1 unit long, then each face is 1 square unit and the volume of the cube is 1 cubic unit.
- Make a cube that has sides twice as long as the original cube.

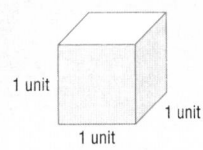

1 unit
1 unit
1 unit

Analyze the Data 3. 4 units²
1. How many small cubes did you use? **8**
2. What is the area of one face of the original cube? **1 unit²**
3. What is the area of one face of the cube that you built?
4. What is the volume of the original cube? **1 unit³**
5. What is the volume of the cube that you built? **8 units³**

Activity 2
Collect the Data
Build a cube that has sides three times longer than a sugar cube or centimeter block.

Analyze the Data 10. 4 times greater; 9 times greater
6. How many small cubes did you use? **27**
7. What is the area of one face of the cube? **9 units²**
8. What is the volume of the cube? **27 units³**
9. Complete the table at the right.
10. What happens to the area of a face when the length of a side is doubled? tripled?
11. Considering the unit cube, if the scale factor is x, what is the area of one face? the surface area? **x^2; $6x^2$**

Scale Factor	Side Length	Area of a Face	Volume
1	1	1	1
2	2	4	8
3	3	9	27

12. What happens to the volume of a cube when the length of a side is doubled? tripled? **2^3 or 8 times greater; 3^3 or 27 times greater**
13. Considering the unit cube, let the scale factor be x. Write an expression for the cube's volume. **x^3**
14. **Make a conjecture** about the surface area and the volume of a cube if the sides are 4 times longer than the original cube. **96 units²; 64 units³**
15. **RESEARCH** the scale factor of a model car. Use the scale factor to estimate the surface area and volume of the actual car. **See students' work.**

Geometry Activity   Similar Solids   **583**

Resource Manager

📁 ***Teaching Pre-Algebra with Manipulatives***
- p. 148 (student recording sheet)

Glencoe Mathematics Classroom Manipulative Kit
- centimeter cubes

1 Focus

5-Minute Check Transparency 11-6 Use as a quiz or review of Lesson 11-5.

Mathematical Background notes are available for this lesson on page 552D.

How **can linear dimensions be used to identify similar solids?**

The opening activity questions are repeated on page 637 of the *Chapter 11 Resource Masters*.

Reading to Learn Mathematics, p. 637 — ELL

Pre-Activity *How can linear dimensions be used to identify similar solids?*

Do the activity at the top of page 584 in your textbook. Write your answers below.

a. The model boxcar is shaped like a rectangular prism. If it is 8.5 inches long and 1 inch wide, what are the length and width of the original train boxcar to the nearest hundredth of a foot?
61.63 ft long, 7.25 ft wide

b. A model tank car is 7 inches long and is shaped like a cylinder. What is the length of the original tank car? 50.75 ft

c. Make a conjecture about the radius of the original tank car compared to the model. It is 87 times greater.

Reading the Lesson

Write a definition and give an example of the new vocabulary word.

Vocabulary	Definition	Example
1. similar solids	See students' work.	

2. If two cylinders are similar, then their __radii__ and __heights__ are proportional.

3. If two cubes are similar, then their __edge lengths__ are proportional.

Helping You Remember

4. For each pair of solids listed in the table below, describe what measurements you would need to determine if the pair is similar.

Pair of Solids	Measurements Needed
Rectangular Prisms	base measures, length
Cylinders	radius or diameter, height
Square Pyramids	base length, height or slant height
Triangular Prisms	base measures, length
Cones	radius or diameter, height or slant height

What You'll Learn

- Identify similar solids.
- Solve problems involving similar solids.

How **can linear dimensions be used to identify similar solids?**

Vocabulary
- similar solids

The model train below is $\frac{1}{87}$ the size of the original train.

a. The model boxcar is shaped like a rectangular prism. If it is 8.5 inches long and 1 inch wide, what are the length and width of the original train boxcar to the nearest hundredth of a foot? **61.63 ft long, 7.25 ft wide**

b. A model tank car is 7 inches long and is shaped like a cylinder. What is the length of the original tank car? **50.75 ft**

c. Make a conjecture about the radius of the original tank car compared to the model. **It is 87 times greater.**

IDENTIFY SIMILAR SOLIDS The cubes below have the same shape. The ratio of their corresponding edge lengths is $\frac{6}{2}$ or 3. We say that 3 is the scale factor.

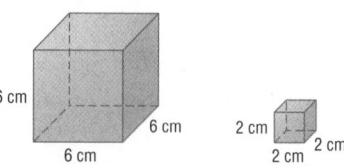

The cubes are **similar solids** because they have the same shape and their corresponding linear measures are proportional.

Study Tip

Look Back
To review **similar figures**, see Lesson 6-3.

TEACHING TIP

Point out that even though bases of cylinders have the same circular shape, if the corresponding lengths are not proportional, the cylinders are not similar.

Example 1 Identify Similar Solids

Determine whether each pair of solids is similar.

a.

$\frac{32}{1} \stackrel{?}{=} \frac{40}{1.25}$ Write a proportion comparing radii and heights.

$32(1.25) \stackrel{?}{=} 1(40)$ Find the cross products.

$40 = 40 \checkmark$ Simplify.

The radii and heights are proportional, so the cylinders are similar.

Resource Manager

Workbooks and Reproducible Masters

Chapter 11 Resource Masters
- Study Guide and Intervention, p. 634
- Skills Practice, p. 635
- Practice, p. 636
- Reading to Learn Mathematics, p. 637
- Enrichment, p. 638
- Assessment, p. 660

Parent and Student Study Guide Workbook, p. 95

Transparencies
5-Minute Check Transparency 11-6
Real-World Transparency 11
Answer Key Transparencies

Technology
Interactive Chalkboard
Pre-AlgePASS: Tutorial Plus, Lesson 36

b.

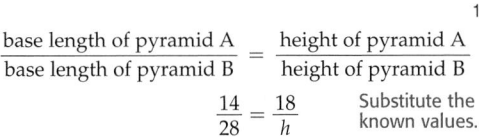

14 in. 20 in.
7 in. 12 in.

$\dfrac{14}{20} \overset{?}{=} \dfrac{7}{12}$ Write a proportion comparing corresponding edge lengths.

$14(12) \overset{?}{=} 20(7)$ Find the cross products.

$168 \neq 140$ Simplify.

The corresponding measures are not proportional, so the pyramids are not similar.

USE SIMILAR SOLIDS   You can find missing measures if you know solids are similar.

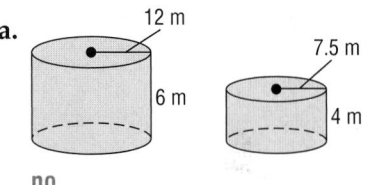

Pyramid A   Pyramid B

18 m
h
14 m
28 m

Example 2   *Find Missing Measures*

The square pyramids at the right are similar. Find the height of pyramid B.

$\dfrac{\text{base length of pyramid A}}{\text{base length of pyramid B}} = \dfrac{\text{height of pyramid A}}{\text{height of pyramid B}}$

$\dfrac{14}{28} = \dfrac{18}{h}$ Substitute the known values.

$14h = 28(18)$ Find the cross products.

$h = 36$ Simplify.

The height of pyramid B is 36 meters.

The prisms at the right are similar with a scale factor of $\dfrac{3}{2}$.

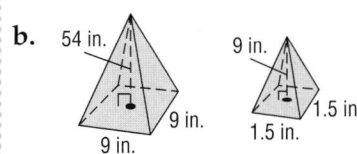

3 m
6 m
3 m
Prism X

2 m
4 m
2 m
Prism Y

Prism	Surface Area	Volume
X	90 m²	54 m³
Y	40 m²	16 m³

Notice the pattern in the following ratios.

$\dfrac{\text{surface area of prism X}}{\text{surface area of prism Y}} = \dfrac{90}{40} \text{ or } \dfrac{9}{4}$ ▷ $\dfrac{9}{4} = \dfrac{3^2}{2^2}$

$\dfrac{\text{volume of prism X}}{\text{volume of prism Y}} = \dfrac{54}{16} \text{ or } \dfrac{27}{8}$ ▷ $\dfrac{27}{8} = \dfrac{3^3}{2^3}$

This and other similar examples suggest that the following ratios are true for similar solids.

Key Concept   *Ratios of Similar Solids*

- **Words**   If two solids are similar with a scale factor of $\dfrac{a}{b}$, then the surface areas have a ratio of $\dfrac{a^2}{b^2}$ and the volumes have a ratio of $\dfrac{a^3}{b^3}$.

- **Model**

Solid A   Solid B
a   b

---

2 Teach

IDENTIFY SIMILAR SOLIDS

In-Class Example   Power Point®

1 Determine whether each pair of solids is similar.

a.

12 m
6 m
7.5 m
4 m

no

b.

54 in.
9 in.
9 in.
9 in.
1.5 in.
1.5 in.

yes

Teaching Tip   Make sure students write proportions using a measure from the base as well as a lateral side or height.

USE SIMILAR SOLIDS

In-Class Example   Power Point®

Teaching Tip   Watch for students who erroneously invert one of the ratios. Have these students write out the proportion in words first and then substitute the known values.

2 The cylinders below are similar. Find the radius of cylinder A.

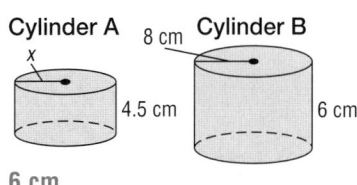

Cylinder A   Cylinder B
x
8 cm
4.5 cm
6 cm

6 cm

3 **DOLL HOUSES** Lita made a model of her fish tank for her doll house. The model is exactly $\frac{1}{25}$ the size of the original fish tank, whose dimensions are $120 \times 30 \times 38$ cm. What is the volume of the model?   **8.8 cm³**

3 Practice/Apply

Study Notebook

Have students—
- add the definition/example of the vocabulary term to their Vocabulary Builder worksheets for Chapter 11.
- include any other item(s) that they find helpful in mastering the skills in this lesson.

About the Exercises . . .

Organization by Objective
- **Identify Similar Solids:** 10–13, 16–19, 23, 24
- **Use Similar Solids:** 14, 15, 20–22, 25

Odd/Even Assignments
Exercises 10–19 are structured so that students practice the same concepts whether they are assigned odd or even problems.

Assignment Guide

Basic: 11, 13, 17, 19, 22–38
Average: 11–19 odd, 21–38
Advanced: 10–18 even, 20–32 (Optional: 33–38)
All: Practice Quiz 2 (1–5)

More About. . .

Space •·············
Engineers need to know the volume of the actual space capsules in order to estimate the air pressure.
Source: www.space.about.com

Example 3   Use Similar Solids to Solve a Problem

·······**SPACE TRAVEL**   A scale model of the NASA space capsule is a combination of a truncated cone and cylinder. The small model built by engineers on a scale of 1 cm to 20 cm has a volume of 155 cm³. What is the volume of the actual space capsule?

Explore   You know the scale factor $\frac{a}{b}$ is $\frac{1}{20}$ and the volume of the space capsule is 155 cm³.

Plan   Since the volumes have a ratio of $\frac{a^3}{b^3}$ and $\frac{a}{b} = \frac{1}{20}$, replace a with 1 and b with 20 in $\frac{a^3}{b^3}$.

Solve $\dfrac{\text{volume of model}}{\text{volume of capsule}} = \dfrac{a^3}{b^3}$ Write the ratio of volumes.

$= \dfrac{1^3}{20^3}$ Replace a with 1 and b with 20.

$= \dfrac{1}{8000}$ Simplify.

So, the volume of the capsule is 8000 times the volume of the model.

$8000 \cdot 155 \text{ cm}^3 = 1{,}240{,}000 \text{ cm}^3$

Examine   Use estimation to check the reasonableness of this answer. $8000 \cdot 100 = 800{,}000$ and $8000 \cdot 200 = 1{,}600{,}000$, so the answer must be between 800,000 and 1,600,000. The answer 1,240,000 cm³ is reasonable.

Check for Understanding

Concept Check   1. **OPEN ENDED**   Draw and label two cones that are similar. Explain why they are similar. **See pp. 601A–601B.**

2. **Explain** how you can find the surface area of a larger cylinder if you know the surface area of a smaller cylinder that is similar to it and the scale factor. **See margin.**

Guided Practice   Determine whether each pair of solids is similar.

GUIDED PRACTICE KEY	
Exercises	Examples
3, 4	1
5, 6	2
7–9	3

3.   **no**   **4.**   **yes**

1 in. 1 in. 3 in.   4 in.   4 in.   8 in.

4 m   6 m   2 m   3 m

Find the missing measure for each pair of similar solids.

5.   45 ft   6 ft $x = 33\frac{1}{3}$ ft   **6.**   30 cm   24 cm x 45 cm   75 cm y

250 ft x

$x = 50$ cm, $y = 36$ cm

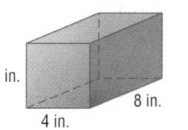

DAILY
INTERVENTION

Differentiated Instruction

- **Interpersonal**   Divide the class into small groups. Have each group draw a pair of similar solids with the appropriate dimensions labeled. The group should also determine the surface areas and volumes of their solids. Collect the groups' drawings, then present the dimensions of one of the pairs of similar solids to the class. Have the teams compete to see who can be the first to correctly give both the surface area and volume of each. Repeat several times.

Application **ARCHITECTURE** **For Exercises 7–9, use the following information.**
A model for an office building is 60 centimeters long, 42 centimeters wide, and 350 centimeters high. On the model, 1 centimeter represents 1.5 meters.

7. How tall is the actual building in meters? **525 m**

8. What is the scale factor between the model and the building? $\frac{1}{150}$

9. Determine the volume of the building in cubic meters. **2,976,750 m³**

★ indicates increased difficulty

Practice and Apply

Homework Help

For Exercises	See Examples
10–13, 16–19	1
14, 15	2
20, 21	3

Extra Practice
See page 752.

Determine whether each pair of solids is similar.

10. **no**
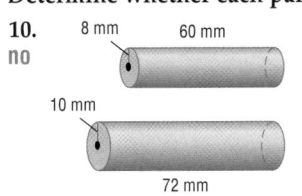
8 mm   60 mm
10 mm
72 mm

11. **yes**
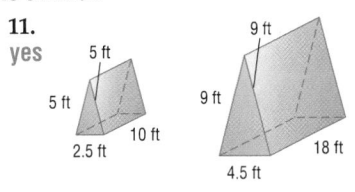
5 ft
5 ft   9 ft   9 ft
2.5 ft   10 ft
18 ft
4.5 ft

12. **no**
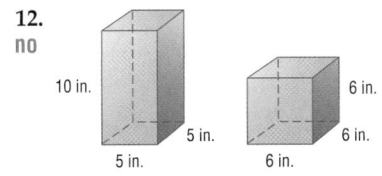
10 in.
5 in.
6 in.
6 in.
6 in.

13. **yes**
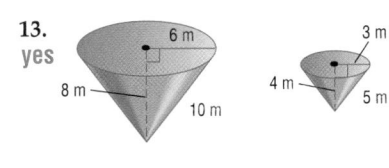
6 m
8 m   10 m
3 m
4 m   5 m

Find the missing measure for each pair of similar solids.

14. **$x = 5.1$ ft**
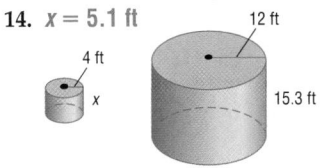
4 ft
x
12 ft
15.3 ft

★15. **$x = 7$ m, $y = 18$ m**
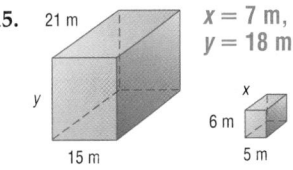
21 m
y
15 m
x
6 m
5 m

Determine whether each pair of solids is *sometimes*, *always*, or *never* similar. Explain. 16. **always; same shape, lengths are proportional**

16. two cubes

17. two prisms

18. a cone and a cylinder
never; different shapes

19. two spheres

HISTORY The *Mankaure* pyramid in Egypt has a square base that is 110 meters on each side, a height of 68.8 meters, and a slant height of 88.5 meters. Suppose you want to construct a scale model of the pyramid using a scale of 4 meters to 2 centimeters.

★20. How much material will you need to use? **7892.5 cm²**

★21. How much greater is the volume of the actual pyramid to the volume of the model? **200³ or 8,000,000 times greater**

 Online Research **Data Update** How have the dimensions of the Egyptian pyramids changed in thousands of years? Visit www.pre-alg.com/data_update to learn more.

22. **CRITICAL THINKING** The dimensions of a triangular prism are decreased so that the volume of the new prism is $\frac{1}{3}$ that of the original volume. Are the two prisms similar? Explain. **See margin.**

 www.pre-alg.com/self_check_quiz

17. Sometimes; bases must be the same polygon and the corresponding side lengths must be proportional.

19. always; same shape, diameters or radii are proportional

Lesson 11-6 Similar Solids **587**

Answers

2. Multiply the surface area of the smaller cylinder by the square of the scale factor.

22. Sample answer: The prisms are similar only if all the dimensions decreased proportionately.

Study Guide and Intervention, p. 634

Identify Similar Solids Solids are similar if they have the same shape and their corresponding linear measures are proportional.

Example 1 Determine whether each pair of solids is similar.
a.

$\frac{50}{6.25} \stackrel{?}{=} \frac{28}{3.5}$ Write a proportion comparing corresponding edge lengths.
$50(3.5) \stackrel{?}{=} 6.25(28)$ Find the cross products.
$175 = 175 ✓$ Simplify.
The corresponding measures are proportional, so the pyramids are similar.

b.

$\frac{8}{12} \stackrel{?}{=} \frac{10}{14}$ Write a proportion comparing radii and heights.
$8(14) \stackrel{?}{=} 12(10)$ Find the cross products.
$112 \neq 120$ Simplify.
The radii and heights are not proportional, so the cylinders are not similar.

Use Similar Solids You can find missing measures if you know solids are similar.

Example 2 Find the missing measure for the pair of similar solids.
$\frac{1}{0.8} = \frac{6}{x}$ Write a proportion.
$1x = 0.8(6)$ Find the cross products.
$x = 4.8$ Simplify.
The missing length is 4.8 ft.

Exercises
Determine whether each pair of solids is similar.
1.  yes   2.  yes

Find the missing measure for each pair of similar solids.
3. 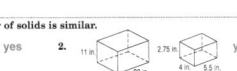 1.6 ft   4. 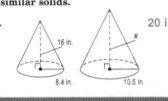 20 in.

Skills Practice, p. 635 and Practice, p. 636 (shown)

Determine whether each pair of solids is similar.
1. 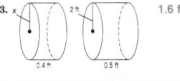   2.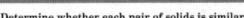
yes   yes
3.   4.
no   yes

Find the missing measure for each pair of similar solids.
5. 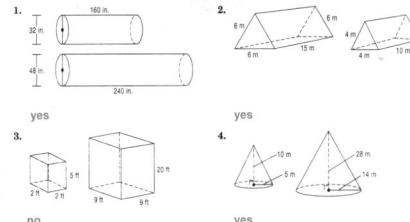   6.
27 cm   19.6 mm
7.   8.
48 in.   31.2 cm

PLAYGROUNDS For Exercises 9 and 10, use the following information.
In the miniature village at the playground, the model of the old school building is 6.6 feet long, 3.3 feet wide, and 4.6 feet high.
9. If the real building was 80 feet long and 40 feet wide, how high was it? **55.8 ft**
10. What was the volume of the old school building in cubic feet? **178,560 ft³**

Enrichment, p. 638

Reduced Triangle Principle
The following steps can be used to reduce the difficulty of a triangle problem by converting to easier side lengths.
Step 1 Multiply or divide the three lengths of the triangle by the same number.
Step 2 Solve for the missing side of the easier problem.
Step 3 Convert back to the original problem.

Example 1
33 and 55 are both multiples of 11. Reduce the problem to an easier problem by dividing the side lengths by 11. Let y represent $\frac{x}{11}$.
$3^2 + y^2 = 5^2$
$9 + y^2 = 25$
$y^2 = 16$
$y = 4$
Now convert back.
$\frac{x}{11} = y$
$x = 11y$
$x = 11(4)$ or 44

Example 2
Multiply each side by 2. Let x represent $2x$.
$8^2 + 15^2 = y^2$
$64 + 225 = y^2$
$289 = y^2$
$17 = y$
Now convert back.
$2x = y$
$x = \frac{y}{2}$
$x = \frac{17}{2}$ or $8\frac{1}{2}$

Use the reduced triangle method to find the value of x.
1.   2.   3.

Lesson 11-6 Similar Solids **587**

4 Assess

Open-Ended Assessment

Writing Have students describe in a short paragraph the use of proportions in identifying similar solids.

Getting Ready for Lesson 11-7

PREREQUISITE SKILL In Lesson 11-7, students will apply precision and significant digits to solving problems. Exercises 33–38 should be used to determine your students' familiarity with rounding decimals, which is an important step when determining significant digits.

Assessment Options

Practice Quiz 2 The quiz provides students with a brief review of the concepts and skills in Lessons 11-4 through 11-6. Lesson numbers are given to the right of exercises or instruction lines so students can review concepts not yet mastered.

Quiz (Lessons 11-5 and 11-6) is available on p. 660 of the *Chapter 11 Resource Masters.*

23. **WRITING IN MATH** Answer the question that was posed at the beginning of the lesson. **See margin.**

    How can linear dimensions be used to identify similar solids?

    Include the following in your answer:
    - a description of the ratios needed for two solids to be similar, and
    - an example of two solids that are *not* similar.

Standardized Test Practice

24. Which prism shown in the table is *not* similar to the other three? **C**

    Ⓐ prism A   Ⓑ prism B

    Ⓒ prism C   Ⓓ prism D

Prism	Length	Width	Height
A	4	3	2
B	6	4.5	3
C	5	4	2
D	28	21	14

25. If the dimensions of a cone are doubled, the surface area **C**

    Ⓐ stays the same.   Ⓑ is doubled.

    Ⓒ is quadrupled.   Ⓓ is 8 times greater.

Maintain Your Skills

Mixed Review Find the surface area of each solid. If necessary, round to the nearest tenth. *(Lessons 11-4 and 11-5)* **28. 3166.7 m²**

26.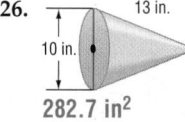
    13 in.
    10 in.
    282.7 in²

27.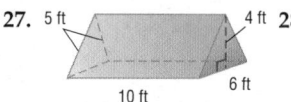
    5 ft
    4 ft
    10 ft
    6 ft
    184 ft²

28.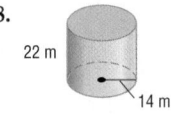
    22 m
    14 m

29. Angles *J* and *K* are complementary. Find $m\angle K$ if $m\angle J$ is 25°. *(Lesson 10-2)*
    65°

Solve each equation. Check your solution. *(Lesson 5-9)*

30. $r - 3.5 = 8$ **11.5**   31. $\frac{2}{3} + y = \frac{1}{9}$ $-\frac{5}{9}$ 32. $\frac{1}{4}a = 6$ **24**

Getting Ready for the Next Lesson **PREREQUISITE SKILL** Find the value of each expression to the nearest tenth. *(To review **rounding decimals**, see page 711.)*

33. $13.28 + 6.05$ **19.3**   34. $8.99 - 1.2$ **7.8**   35. $2.4 \cdot 2.5$ **6.0**

36. $55 \div 3.8$ **14.5**   37. $6 + 1.9 + 1.45$ **9.4**   38. $6.7(0.3)(1.8)$ **3.6**

Practice Quiz 2   Lessons 11-4 through 11-6

Find the surface area of each solid. If necessary, round to the nearest tenth. *(Lessons 11-4 and 11-5)*

1.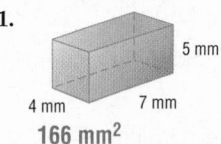
   5 mm
   4 mm   7 mm
   166 mm²

2.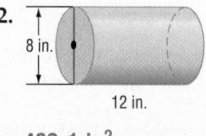
   8 in.
   12 in.
   402.1 in²

3.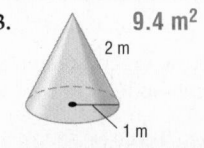
   9.4 m²
   2 m
   1 m

4.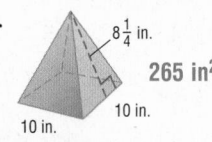
   $8\frac{1}{4}$ in.
   10 in.   10 in.
   265 in²

5. Are the cylinders described in the table similar? Explain your reasoning. *(Lesson 11-6)*
   Yes; their corresponding dimensions are proportional.

Cylinder	Diameter (mm)	Slant Height (mm)
A	24	21
B	16	14

Answer

23. If the ratios of corresponding linear dimensions are equal, the solids are similar. Answers should include the following.
    - For example, if the ratio comparing the heights of two cylinders equals the ratio comparing their radii, then the cylinders are similar.
    - A cone and a prism are not similar.

Reading Mathematics

Precision and Accuracy

In everyday language, *precision* and *accuracy* are used to mean the same thing. When measurement is involved, these two terms have different meanings.

Term	Definition	Example
precision	the degree of exactness in which a measurement is made	A measure of 12.355 grams is more precise than a measure of 12 grams.
accuracy	the degree of conformity of a measurement with the true value	Suppose the actual mass of an object is 12.355 grams. Then a measure of 12 grams is more accurate than a measure of 18 grams.

Reading to Learn
1. Sample answer: Accuracy is how close a measurement is to the true value. Precision is how exact a measurement is.

1. Describe in your own words the difference between accuracy and precision.

2. **RESEARCH** Use the Internet or other resources to find an instrument used in science that gives very precise measurements. Describe the precision of the instrument. **Sample answer: A certain analytical balance is precise to the nearest 0.01 milligram.**

3. Use at least two different measuring instruments to measure the length, width, height, or weight of two objects in your home. Describe the measuring instruments that you used and explain which measurement was most precise. **See students' work.**

8. Sample answer: Accuracy, because it is more important to have approximately the correct amount of cement than it is to have a very precise amount.

Choose the correct term or terms to determine the degree of precision needed in each measurement situation.

4. In a travel brochure, the length of a cruise ship is described in (millimeters, meters).

5. The weight of a bag of apples in a grocery store is given to the nearest (tenth of a pound, tenth of an ounce).

6. In a science experiment, the mass of one drop of solution is found to the nearest 0.01 (gram, kilogram).

7. A person making a jacket measures the fabric to the nearest (inch, eighth of an inch).

8. **CONSTRUCTION** A construction c ompany is ordering cement to complete all the sidewalks in a new neighborhood. Would the precision or accuracy be more important in the completion of their order? Explain.

Getting Started

Have students look up the words *precision* and *accuracy* in a dictionary and write two sentences, one for each word.

Teach

Provide students with a variety of instruments for measurement, for example, rulers, yardsticks, meter sticks, and tape measures with varying increments marked; thermometers; clocks, watches, and stopwatches; perhaps even a micrometer. Have students discuss which of the instruments are the most precise. Also discuss the accuracy of the instruments in a variety of situations.

Assess

Study Notebook

Have students pick a topic or field that interests them, such as sports or cooking, and discuss in several paragraphs how precision and accuracy relate to that topic. Students should provide several examples in their discussion.

ELL English Language Learners may benefit from writing key concepts from this activity in their Study Notebooks in their native language and then in English.

1 Focus

5-Minute Check Transparency 11-7 Use as a quiz or review of Lesson 11-6.

Mathematical Background notes are available for this lesson on page 552D.

Why are all measurements really approximations?

The opening activity questions are repeated on page 642 of the *Chapter 11 Resource Masters*.

Reading to Learn Mathematics, p. 642 **ELL**

Pre-Activity *Why are all measurements really approximations?*

Do the activity at the top of page 590 in your textbook. Write your answers below.

a. Measure several objects (book widths, paper clips, pens...) using each ruler. Use a table to keep track of your measurements. See students' work.

b. Analyze the measurements and determine which are most useful. Explain your reasoning. Sample answer: The third ruler; it gives the most exact measurements.

Reading the Lesson 1–2. See students' work.

Write a definition and give an example of each new vocabulary word or phrase.

Vocabulary	Definition	Example
1. precision		
2. significant digits		

3. When adding or subtracting measurements, the sum or difference should have the same precision as the least <u>precise measurement</u>.

4. When multiplying or dividing measurements, the product or quotient should have the same number of significant digits as the measurement with the least <u>number of significant digits</u>.

Helping You Remember

5. Provide two examples of each of the numbers described in the table below.

a. Write a number with four significant digits, two of which are zeros.	b. Write a number with three significant digits, no decimal point, and three zeros.	c. Write a number with two significant digits, a decimal point, and two zeros.
70.02	325,000	0.068
0.053	987,000	0.10

What You'll Learn

- Describe measurements using precision and significant digits.
- Apply precision and significant digits in problem-solving situations.

Vocabulary
- precision
- significant digits

b. Sample answer: The third ruler; it gives the most exact measurements.

Why are all measurements really approximations?

Use cardboard to make three rulers 20 centimeters long, labeling the increments as shown at the right.

Ruler	Scale (cm)
1	0, 5, 10, 15, 20
2	0, 1, 2, 3, ..., 18, 19, 20
3	0, 0.1, 0.2, 0.3, ..., 19.8, 19.9, 20.0

a. Measure several objects (book widths, paper clips, pens...) using each ruler. Use a table to keep track of your measurements. **See students' work.**

b. Analyze the measurements and determine which are most useful. Explain your reasoning.

PRECISION AND SIGNIFICANT DIGITS

The **precision** of a measurement is the exactness to which a measurement is made. Precision depends on the smallest unit of measure being used, or the *precision unit*. You can expect a measurement to be accurate to the nearest precision unit.

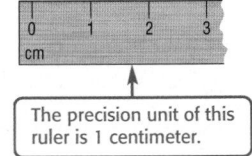

The precision unit of this ruler is 1 centimeter.

Example 1 Identify Precision Units

Identify the precision unit of the ruler at the right.

The precision unit is one tenth of a centimeter, or 1 millimeter.

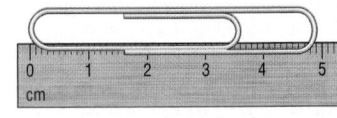

One way to record a measure is to estimate to the nearest precision unit. A more precise method is to include all of the digits that are actually measured, plus one *estimated* digit. The digits you record when you measure this way are called significant digits. **Significant digits** indicate the precision of the measurement.

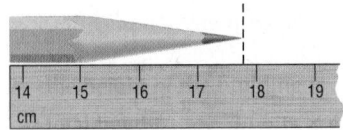

 estimated digit

17.7 cm ← 3 significant digits

 digits known for certain

Study Tip

Precision
The precision unit of the measuring instrument determines the number of significant digits.

precision unit: 1 cm
actual measure: 17–18 cm
estimated measure: 17.7 cm

590 Chapter 11 Three-Dimensional Figures

Resource Manager

📂 Workbooks and Reproducible Masters

Chapter 11 Resource Masters
- Study Guide and Intervention, p. 639
- Skills Practice, p. 640
- Practice, p. 641
- Reading to Learn Mathematics, p. 642
- Enrichment, p. 643
- Assessment, p. 660

Parent and Student Study Guide Workbook, p. 96

📺 Transparencies
5-Minute Check Transparency 11-7
Answer Key Transparencies

💿 Technology
Interactive Chalkboard

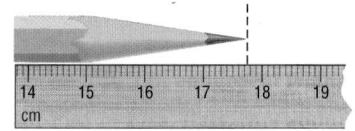

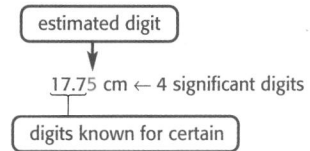

estimated digit

17.75 cm ← 4 significant digits

digits known for certain

precision unit: 0.1 cm
actual measure: 17.7–17.8 cm
estimated measure: 17.75 cm

There are special rules for determining significant digits in a given measurement. If a number contains a decimal point, the number of significant digits is found by counting the digits from left to right, starting with the first *nonzero* digit and ending with the last digit.

Number		Number of Significant Digits	
1.23	→	3	All nonzero digits are significant.
10.05	→	4	Zeros between two significant digits are significant.
0.072	→	2	Zeros used to show place value of the decimal are not significant.
50.00	→	4	In a number with a decimal point, all zeros to the right of a nonzero digit are significant.

If a number does *not* contain a decimal point, the number of significant digits is found by counting the digits from left to right, starting with the first digit and ending with the last *nonzero* digit. For example, 8400 contains 2 significant digits, 8 and 4.

Study Tip

Precision Units

Since 150 miles has only two significant digits, the measure is precise to the nearest 10 miles. Therefore, the precision unit is 10 miles, not 1 mile.

Example 2 *Identify Significant Digits*

Determine the number of significant digits in each measure.

a. 20.98 centimeters
4 significant digits

b. 150 miles
2 significant digits

c. 0.007 gram
1 significant digit

d. 6.40 feet
3 significant digits

COMPUTE USING SIGNIFICANT DIGITS   When adding or subtracting measurements, the sum or difference should have the *same precision* as the least precise measurement.

Example 3 *Add Measurements*

The sides of a triangle measure 14.35 meters, 8.6 meters, and 9.125 meters. Use the correct number of significant digits to find the perimeter.

```
  14.35   ← 2 decimal places
   8.6    ← 1 decimal place
+ 9.125   ← 3 decimal places
 32.075
```

The least precise measurement, 8.6 meters, has one decimal place. So, round 32.075 to one decimal place, 32.1. The perimeter of the triangle is about 32.1 meters.

Study Tip

Common Misconception

Calculators give answers with as many digits as the display can show. Be sure to use the correct number of significant digits in your answer.

www.pre-alg.com/extra_examples

Lesson 11-7 Precision and Significant Digits **591**

Lesson 11-7 Precision and Significant Digits **591**

---

2 Teach

PRECISION AND SIGNIFICANT DIGITS

In-Class Examples   Power Point®

1 Identify the precision unit of the thermometer shown below.   **5°F**

2 Determine the number of significant digits in each measure.

a. 1040 miles   **3**

b. 0.003 centimeter   **1**

c. 90.051 kilograms   **5**

d. 0.06300 liter   **4**

Teaching Tip   Ask students to describe measurements that require extreme precision and others that can be less precise. For example, a surgeon or dentist might require extremely precise measurements. A bulldozer operator's measurements would probably be less precise.

COMPUTE USING SIGNIFICANT DIGITS

In-Class Examples   Power Point®

3 The sides of a quadrilateral measure 0.6 m, 0.044 m, 0.024 m, and 0.103 m. Use the correct number of significant digits to find the perimeter.   **0.8 m**

4 Suppose the room in Example 4 was 12.25 ft wide and 14 ft long. What would be the area of the bedroom?   **170 ft²**

DAILY
INTERVENTION   **Unlocking Misconceptions**

• **Precision and Significant Digits**   Students may automatically look to the number of digits beyond the decimal point when determining significant digits in a multiplication or division problem. Remind them that the number of decimal places in the numbers being multiplied may be irrelevant when determining significant digits in the product. The number with least amount of significant digits, both before and after the decimal point, determines significance in the product.

Study Notebook

Have students—

• complete the definitions/examples for the remaining terms on the Vocabulary Builder worksheets for Chapter 11.

• include any other item(s) that they find helpful in mastering the skills in this lesson.

DAILY
INTERVENTION **FIND THE ERROR** If students are having difficulty determining significant digits with zeros, make a two-column table with the heads *Significant Zeros* and *Insignificant Zeros*. List several examples for each. Have students choose the correct column for each number.

About the Exercises . . .

Organization by Objective
• **Precision and Significant Digits:** 13–22, 35–37, 40–43
• **Compute Using Significant Digits:** 23–34

Odd/Even Assignments
Exercises 13–34 are structured so that students practice the same concepts whether they are assigned odd or even problems.

Assignment Guide

Basic: 13–31 odd, 33, 35–37, 39–42, 44–47
Average: 13–33 odd, 35–37, 39–42, 44–47 (Optional: 43)
Advanced: 14–34 even, 35–47

When multiplying or dividing measurements, the product or quotient should have the *same number of significant digits* as the measurement with the least number of significant digits.

Study Tip

Significant Digits
The least precise measure determines the number of significant digits in the sum or difference of measures. The measure with the fewest significant digits determines the number of significant digits in the product or quotient of measures.

Example 4 **Multiply Measurements**

What is the area of the bedroom shown at the right?

To find the area, multiply the length and the width.

$$
\begin{array}{r}
11.6 \quad \leftarrow \text{3 significant digits} \\
\times\ 8.2 \quad \leftarrow \text{2 significant digits} \\
\hline
95.12 \quad \leftarrow \text{4 significant digits}
\end{array}
$$

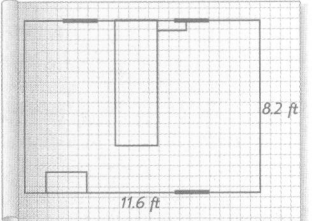

8.2 ft

11.6 ft

The answer cannot have more significant digits than the measurements of the length and width. So, round 95.12 ft² to 2 significant digits. The area of the bedroom is about 95 ft².

Check for Understanding

Concept Check

1. **FIND THE ERROR** A metal shelf is 0.0205 centimeter thick. Sierra says this measurement contains 2 significant digits. Josh says it contains 3 significant digits. Who is correct? Explain your reasoning. **See margin.**

2. **Choose** an instrument from the list at the right that is best for measuring each object.

   2b. surveyor's tools

   a. length of an envelope **cm ruler**
   b. distance between two stoplights
   c. width of a kitchen **12-ft tape measure**
   d. height of a small child **yardstick**

   | yardstick |
   | centimeter ruler |
   | surveyor's tools |
   | 12-foot tape measure |

3. **OPEN ENDED** Write a number that contains four digits, two of which are significant. **Sample answer: 0.012 or 2500**

Guided Practice

4. Identify the precision unit of the scale at the right. **1 oz**

GUIDED PRACTICE KEY	
Exercises	Examples
4	1
5–7	2
8–12	3, 4

Determine the number of significant digits in each measure.

5. 2.30 cm **3**   6. 50 yd **1**   7. 0.801 mm **3**

Calculate. Round to the correct number of significant digits.

8. 14.38 cm + 5.7 cm **20.1 cm**   9. 15.273 L − 8.2 L **7.1 L**

10. 3.147 mm · 1.8 mm **5.7 mm²**   11. 60.42 in. × 9.012 in. **544.5 in²**

Application

12. **MASONRY** A wall of bricks is 7.85 feet high and 13.0 feet wide. What is the area of the wall? Round to the correct number of significant digits.

102 ft²

592 Chapter 11 Three-Dimensional Figures

Answers

1. **Josh; the first two 0s are not significant because they are placeholders for the decimal point. The 0 between 2 and 5 is significant because it is between two significant digits and shows the actual value in the thousandths place.**

33. **b; The precision unit of ruler a is $\frac{1}{8}$ inch. The precision unit of ruler b is $\frac{1}{16}$ inch.**

Answers for Excercises 35 and 39 are on page 594.

Practice and Apply

Identify the precision unit of each measuring tool.

13.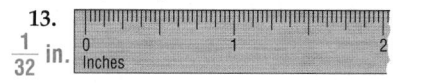
$\frac{1}{32}$ in.

14.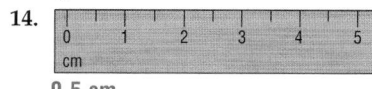
0.5 cm

Determine the number of significant digits in each measure.

15. 925 g **3**   **16.** 40 km **1**   **17.** 2200 ft **2**   **18.** 53.6 in. **3**

19. 0.01 mm **1**   **20.** 0.56 cm **2**   **21.** 18.50 m **4**   **22.** 4.0 L **2**

Calculate. Round to the correct number of significant digits. **27. 84.47 m**

23. 27 in. + 18.2 in. **45 in.**

24. 6.75 mm − 3.2 mm **3.6 mm**

25. 0.4 ft · 5.1 ft **2 ft^2**

26. 7.30 yd × 1.61 yd **11.8 yd^2**

27. 29.307 m + 4.23 m + 50.93 m

28. 127.2 g + 42.3 g − 5.7 g **163.8 g**

29. 50.2 cm − 0.75 cm **49.5 cm**

30. 18.160 L − 15 L **3 L**

31. 5.327 m · 4.8 m **26 m^2**

★ **32.** 4.397 cm · 2.01 cm **8.84 cm^2**

33. MEASUREMENT Choose the best ruler for measuring an object to the nearest sixteenth of an inch. Explain your reasoning. **See margin.**

a. 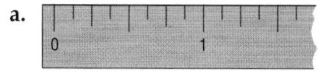   **b.**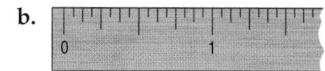

34. MEASUREMENT Order 0.40 mm, 40 mm, 0.4 mm, and 0.004 mm from most to least precise. **0.004 mm, 0.40 mm, 0.4 mm, 40 mm**

ORANGES For Exercises 35–37, refer to the graph at the right.

35. Are the numbers exact? Explain. **See margin.**

36. How many significant digits are used to describe orange production in 1992 and in 2001? **2; 3**

37. Write the number of tons of oranges produced in the United States in 2001 without using a decimal point. How many significant digits does this number have? **12,400,000; 3**

38. MEASUREMENT ERROR Mrs. Hernandez is covering the top of a kitchen shelf that is $26\frac{3}{8}$ inches long and $15\frac{1}{2}$ inches wide. She incorrectly measures the length to be 25 inches long. How will this error affect her calculations?

38. The error will cause her to underestimate the area of the shelf by about 21 square inches.

39. CRITICAL THINKING The sizes of Allen hex wrenches are 2.0 mm, 3.0 mm, 4.0 mm, and so on. Will they work with hexagonal bolts that are marked 2 mm, 3 mm, 4 mm, and so on? Explain. **See margin.**

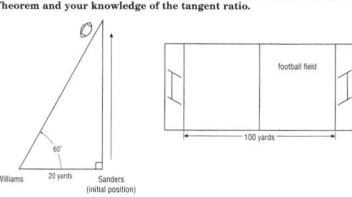

Open-Ended Assessment

Modeling create a table showing the rules for determining significant digits when adding, subtracting, and multiplying and include an example for each.

Assessment Options

Quiz (Lesson 7) is available on p. 660 of the *Chapter 11 Resource Masters*.

Answers (p. 593)

35. No, the numbers are estimated to the nearest 0.1 million.

39. Not necessarily, because the actual size of the 2.0 mm wrench can range from 1.95 mm to 2.05 mm and the actual size of the 2 mm bolt can range from 1.5 mm to 2.5 mm. So, the bolts could be larger than the corresponding wrenches.

Answer

40. Measurements are accurate to the nearest precision unit. A smaller precision unit gives a more accurate measure. Answers should include the following.

- The smallest unit of measure that is used determines the precision of a measurement.
- For example, when a pharmacist is determining the amount of medicine to put in a prescription, an exact solution is needed. When a landscaper is determining how much mulch is needed for a client's yard, an approximate solution is sufficient.

---

40. **WRITING IN MATH** Answer the question that was posed at the beginning of the lesson. **See margin.**

Why are all measurements really approximations?

Include the following in your answer:

- an explanation of what determines the precision of a measurement, and
- an example of a real-life situation in which an exact solution is needed and a situation in which an approximate solution is sufficient.

Standardized Test Practice
Ⓐ Ⓑ Ⓒ Ⓓ

41. Choose the measurement that is most precise. **A**
- Ⓐ 12 mm
- Ⓑ 12 cm
- Ⓒ 1.2 m
- Ⓓ 12 m

42. Which solution contains the correct number of significant digits for the product 2.80 mm · 0.1 mm? **D**
- Ⓐ 0.28 mm^2
- Ⓑ 0.280 mm^2
- Ⓒ 0.30 mm^2
- Ⓓ 0.3 mm^2

Extending the Lesson

The **greatest possible error** is one-half the precision unit. It can be used to describe the actual measure. Refer to the paper clip in Example 1. It appears to be 4.9 centimeters long.

$$\text{greatest possible error} = \frac{1}{2} \cdot \text{precision unit}$$

$$= \frac{1}{2} \cdot 0.1 \text{ cm or } 0.05 \text{ cm}$$

The possible actual length of the paper clip is 0.05 centimeter less than or 0.05 centimeter greater than 4.9 centimeters, or between 4.85 and 4.95 centimeters.

★ **43.** **TRAVEL** The odometer on a car shows 132.8 miles traveled. Find the greatest possible error of the measurement and use it to determine between which two values is the actual distance traveled.
0.05 mi; between 132.75 mi and 132.85 mi

Maintain Your Skills

Mixed Review

44. Determine whether a cone with a height 14 centimeters and radius 8 centimeters is similar to a cone with a height of 12 centimeters and a radius of 6 centimeters. *(Lesson 11-6)* **no**

Find the surface area of each solid. If necessary, round to the nearest tenth.
(Lesson 11-5)

45. 1.3 cm / 5.2 cm **26.5 cm^2**

46. 9 mm / 14 mm **351.9 mm^2**

47. 3.2 m / 1.8 m / 1.8 m **14.8 m^2**

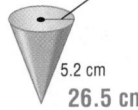

WebQuest **Internet Project**

Able to Leap Tall Buildings
It is time to complete your project. Use the information you have gathered about your building to prepare a report. Be sure to include information and facts about your building as well as a comparison of its size to some familiar item.

www.pre-alg.com/webquest

DAILY
INTERVENTION   **Differentiated Instruction**

- **Logical** Ask students if, when determining significant digits, the answer to 3.28 × 4 would equal the answer to 3.28 + 3.28 + 3.28 + 3.28. Have them explain their answer. **No; the answer to 3.28 × 4 would need to be adjusted to one significant digit, therefore the answer would be 10. The answer to 3.28 + 3.28 + 3.28 + 3.28 would be adjusted to two decimal places, 13.12.**

Vocabulary and Concept Check

base (p. 557)	plane (p. 556)	skew lines (p. 558)
cone (p. 569)	polyhedron (p. 556)	slant height (p. 578)
cylinder (p. 565)	precision (p. 590)	solid (p. 556)
edge (p. 556)	prism (p. 557)	surface area (p. 573)
face (p. 556)	pyramid (p. 557)	vertex (p. 556)
lateral area (p. 578)	significant digits (p. 590)	volume (p. 563)
lateral face (p. 578)	similar solids (p. 584)	

Determine whether each statement is *true* or *false*. If false, replace the underlined word or number to make a true statement.

1. The underlined surface area of a pyramid is the sum of the areas of its lateral faces. **false; lateral area**
2. underlined Volume is the amount of space that a solid contains. **true**
3. The underlined edge of a pyramid is the length of an altitude of one of its lateral faces. **false; slant height**
4. A triangular prism has two underlined bases. **true**
5. A solid with two bases that are parallel circles is called a underlined cone. **false; cylinder**
6. Prisms and pyramids are named by the shapes of their underlined bases. **true**
7. Figures that have the same shape and corresponding linear measures that are proportional are called underlined similar solids. **true**
8. Significant digits indicate the underlined precision of a measurement. **true**

Lesson-by-Lesson Review

11-1 Three-Dimensional Figures

See pages 556–561.

Concept Summary

- Prisms and pyramids are three-dimensional figures.

Example **Identify the solid. Name the bases, faces, edges, and vertices.**

There is one triangular base, so the solid is a triangular pyramid.

faces: JKL, JLM, JMK
edges: $\overline{JK}$, $\overline{JL}$, $\overline{JM}$, $\overline{KL}$, $\overline{LM}$, $\overline{MK}$
vertices: J, K, L, M

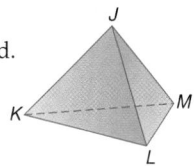

Exercises **Identify each solid. Name the bases, faces, edges, and vertices.**
See Example 1 on page 557. **9–11. See margin.**

9.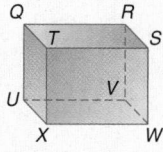

10.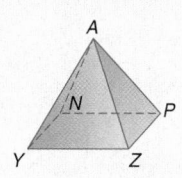

11.

FOLDABLES™
Study Organizer

For more information about Foldables, see *Teaching Mathematics with Foldables.*

Have students reexamine their Foldables to make sure the formulas and characteristics related to three-dimensional figures that they recorded are accurate.

Suggest that students refer to their Foldables if needed when working through the Study Guide exercises and studying for the chapter test.

Chapter
11 Study Guide and Review

Vocabulary and Concept Check

- This alphabetical list of vocabulary terms in Chapter 11 includes a page reference where each term was introduced.

- **Assessment** A vocabulary test/review for Chapter 11 is available on p. 658 of the *Chapter 11 Resource Masters.*

Lesson-by-Lesson Review

For each lesson,

- the main ideas are summarized,
- additional examples review concepts, and
- practice exercises are provided.

Vocabulary PuzzleMaker

ELL The Vocabulary PuzzleMaker software improves students' mathematics vocabulary using four puzzle formats—crossword, scramble, word search using a word list, and word search using clues. Students can work on a computer screen or from a printed handout.

MindJogger Videoquizzes

ELL MindJogger Videoquizzes provide an alternative review of concepts presented in this chapter. Students work in teams in a game show format to gain points for correct answers. The questions are presented in three rounds.

Round 1 Concepts (5 questions)
Round 2 Skills (4 questions)
Round 3 Problem Solving (4 questions)

Answers

See next page for Exercises 9–11.

9. rectangular prism; *QRST, UVWX* or *QTXU, RSWV* or *QRVU, TSWX*; *QRST, UVWX, QTXU, RSWV, QRVU, TSWX*; $\overline{QR}, \overline{RS}, \overline{ST}, \overline{TQ}, \overline{UV}, \overline{VW}, \overline{WX}, \overline{XU}, \overline{QU}, \overline{TX}, \overline{SW}, \overline{RV}$; Q, R, S, T, U, V, W, X

10. triangular prism; *GHJ, CDF*; *GHJ, CDF, CGJF, CGHD, FDHJ*; $\overline{CD}, \overline{DF}, \overline{FC}, \overline{GH}, \overline{HJ}, \overline{JG}, \overline{CG}, \overline{DH}, \overline{FJ}$; C, D, F, G, H, J

11. rectangular pyramid; *YNPZ*; *AYZ, AZP, ANP, ANY, YNPZ*; $\overline{AY}, \overline{AZ}, \overline{AP}, \overline{AN}, \overline{YZ}, \overline{ZP}, \overline{PN}, \overline{NY}$; A, Y, Z, P, N

11-2 *Volume: Prisms and Cylinders*

See pages 563–567.

Concept Summary

- Volume is the measure of space occupied by a solid region.
- The volume of a prism or a cylinder is the area of the base times the height.

Example   Find the volume of the cylinder. Round to the nearest tenth.

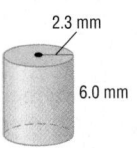

$V = \pi r^2 h$	Formula for volume of a cylinder
$V = \pi \cdot 2.3^2 \cdot 6.0$	Replace *r* with 2.3 and *h* with 6.0.
$V \approx 99.7$	Simplify.

The volume is about 99.7 cubic millimeters.

Exercises   Find the volume of each solid. If necessary, round to the nearest tenth.   *See Examples 1, 2, and 5 on pages 563–565.*

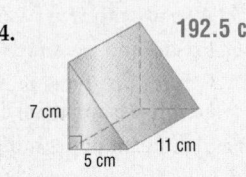

12. 217.9 m³   3.4 m   6 m

13. 0.8 mm³   1.9 mm   0.8 mm   0.5 mm

14. 192.5 cm³   7 cm   5 cm   11 cm

11-3 *Volume: Pyramids and Cones*

See pages 568–572.

Concept Summary

- The volume of a pyramid or a cone is one-third the area of the base times the height.

Example   Find the volume of the cone. Round to the nearest tenth.

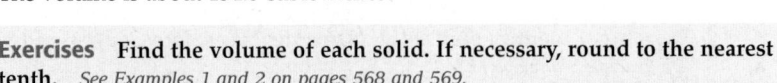

$$V = \frac{1}{3}\pi r^2 h \qquad \text{Formula for volume of a cone}$$

$$V = \frac{1}{3} \cdot \pi \cdot 4^2 \cdot 8 \quad \text{Replace } r \text{ with 4 and } h \text{ with 8.}$$

$$V \approx 134.0 \qquad \text{Simplify.}$$

The volume is about 134.0 cubic inches.

Exercises   Find the volume of each solid. If necessary, round to the nearest tenth.   *See Examples 1 and 2 on pages 568 and 569.*

15. 4 ft³   3 ft   2 ft   2 ft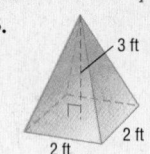

16. $A = 7.5$ m²   5.1 m   12.8 m³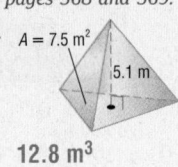

17. 20.3 cm   9 cm   1721.9 cm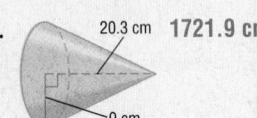

11-4 Surface Area: Prisms and Cylinders

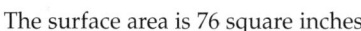

See pages
573–577.

Concept Summary

- The surface area of a prism is the sum of the areas of the faces.
- The surface area of a cylinder is the area of the two bases plus the product of the circumference and the height.

Example Find the surface area of the rectangular prism.

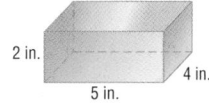

$S = 2\ell w + 2\ell h + 2wh$ Write the formula.

$S = 2(5)(4) + 2(5)(2) + 2(4)(2)$ Substitution

$S = 76$ Simplify.

The surface area is 76 square inches.

Exercises Find the surface area of each solid. If necessary, round to the nearest tenth. *See Examples 1–3 on pages 573–575.*

18.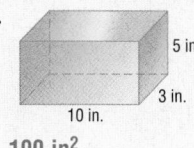

190 in²

19.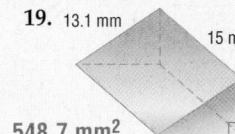

548.7 mm²

20.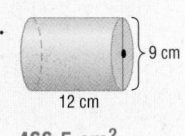

466.5 cm²

11-5 Surface Area: Pyramids and Cones

See pages
578–582.

Concept Summary

- The surface area of a pyramid or a cone is the sum of the lateral area and the base area.

Example Find the surface area of the cone. Round to the nearest tenth.

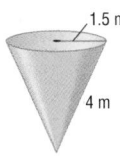

$S = \pi r \ell + \pi r^2$ Write the formula.

$S = \pi(1.5)(4) + \pi(1.5)^2$ Replace r with 1.5 and ℓ with 4.

$S \approx 25.9$ Simplify.

The surface area is about 25.9 square meters.

Exercises Find the surface area of each solid. If necessary, round to the nearest tenth. *See Examples 1 and 3 on pages 578 and 580.*

21. **45 in²**

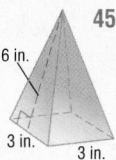

22.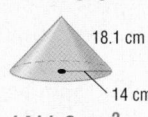

1411.8 cm²

23. **37.1 in²**

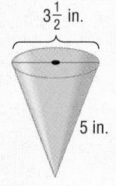

Chapter 11 For More ... • Extra Practice, see pages 750–752.
• Mixed Problem Solving, see page 768.

11-6 Similar Solids

See pages 584–588.

Concept Summary

• Similar solids have the same shape and their corresponding linear measures are proportional.

Example Determine whether the solids are similar.

$\frac{12}{6} \overset{?}{=} \frac{8}{3}$ Write a proportion comparing radii and heights.

$12(3) \overset{?}{=} 6(8)$ Find the cross products.

$36 \neq 48$ Simplify.

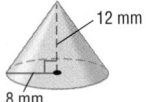

The radii and heights are not proportional, so the cones are not similar.

Exercises Determine whether each pair of solids is similar.
See Example 1 on pages 584 and 585.

24.
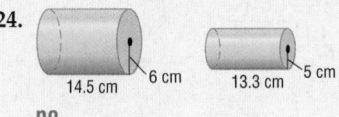
14.5 cm 6 cm   13.3 cm 5 cm

no

25. **yes**
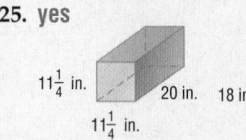
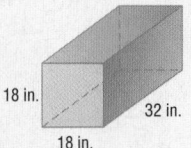
$11\frac{1}{4}$ in. 20 in. 18 in. 32 in. $11\frac{1}{4}$ in. 18 in.

26. Find the missing measure for the pair of similar solids at the right.
See Example 2 on page 585. $x = \textbf{16.8 in.}$

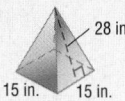
x 28 in. 9 in. 9 in. 15 in. 15 in.

11-7 Precision and Significant Digits

See pages 590–594.

Concept Summary

• The precision of a measurement depends on the smallest unit of measure being used.

• Significant digits indicate the precision of a measurement.

Example Find 0.5 m + 0.75 m. Round to the correct number of significant digits.

0.5 ← 1 decimal place
$+ 0.75$ ← 2 decimal places
1.25

The answer should have one decimal place. So, the sum is about 1.3 meters.

Calculate. Round to the correct number of significant digits.
See Examples 3 and 4 on pages 591 and 592. 27. **19.0 cm** 28. **14.5 kg** 30. **7.8 in²**

27. 10.3 cm + 8.7 cm   28. 25.71 kg − 11.2 kg   29. 0.04 m + 0.9 m **0.9 m**

30. 5.186 in. · 1.5 in.   31. 32.0 ft · 30.4 ft **973 ft²** 32. 80.51 g − 6.01 g **74.50 g**

Answers (p. 599)

1. A prism has two parallel congruent bases. A pyramid has one base.

2. Sample answer: Similar solids have the same shape and the corresponding linear measures are proportional.

4. rectangular prism; *ABCD*, *EFGH* or *ABFE*, *DCGH* or *ADHE*, *BCGF*; *ABCD*, *EFGH*, *ABFE*, *DCGH*, *ADHE*, *BCGF*; $\overline{AB}$, $\overline{BC}$, $\overline{CD}$, $\overline{DA}$, $\overline{EF}$, $\overline{FG}$, $\overline{GH}$, $\overline{HE}$, $\overline{AE}$, $\overline{BF}$, $\overline{CG}$, $\overline{DH}$; *A*, *B*, *C*, *D*, *E*, *F*, *G*, *H*

5. rectangular pyramid; *MNOP*; *LMN*, *LNO*, *LOP*, *LMP*, *MNOP*; $\overline{LM}$, $\overline{LN}$, $\overline{LO}$, $\overline{LP}$, $\overline{MN}$, $\overline{NO}$, $\overline{OP}$, $\overline{PM}$; *L*, *M*, *N*, *O*, *P*

Chapter 11 Practice Test

Vocabulary and Concepts

1. **Describe** the difference between a prism and a pyramid. **See margin.**
2. **Describe** the characteristics of similar solids. **See margin.**
3. **OPEN ENDED** Write a four-digit number that has three significant digits.
   Sample answer: 0.123 or 1230

Skills and Applications

Identify each solid. Name the bases, faces, edges, and vertices. 4–5. **See margin.**

4.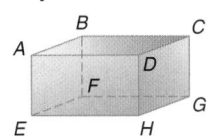

5.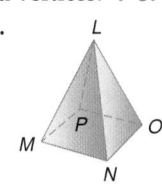

Find the volume of each solid. If necessary, round to the nearest tenth.

6. cylinder: radius 1.7 mm, height 8 mm **72.6 mm³**
7. rectangular pyramid: length 14 in., width 8 in., height 5 in. **186.7 in³**
8. cube: length 9.2 cm **778.7 cm³**
9. cone: diameter 26 ft, height 31 ft **5486.3 ft³**

Find the surface area of each solid. If necessary, round to the nearest tenth.

10. 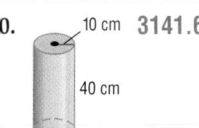 **3141.6 cm²**

11. 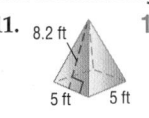 **107 ft²**

12. 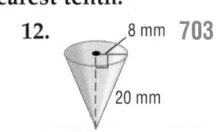 **703.7 mm²**

13. Determine whether the given pair of solids is similar. Explain. **No; the corresponding measures are not proportional.**

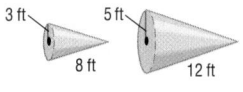

Find the missing measure for each pair of similar solids.

14. 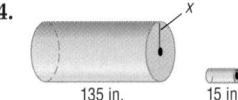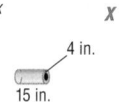 **x = 36 in.**

15. 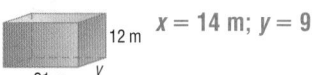 **x = 14 m; y = 9 m**

Determine the number of significant digits in each measure.

16. 4500 mm **2**

17. 0.036 in. **2**

Calculate. Round to the correct number of significant digits.

18. 37.65 cm – 12.9 cm **24.8 cm**

19. 6.8 ft × 3.875 ft **26 ft²**

20. **STANDARDIZED TEST PRACTICE** A model of a new grocery store is 15 inches long, 9 inches wide, and 7 inches high. The scale is 50 feet to 3 inches. Find the length of the actual store. **C**

   (A) 45 ft   (B) 150 ft   (C) 250 ft   (D) 750 ft

 www.pre-alg.com/chapter_test

Chapter 11 Practice Test **599**

Chapter 11 Practice Test

Assessment Options

Vocabulary Test A vocabulary test/review for Chapter 11 can be found on p. 658 of the *Chapter 11 Resource Masters.*

Chapter Tests There are six Chapter 11 Tests and an Open-Ended Assessment task available in the *Chapter 11 Resource Masters.*

Chapter 11 Tests			
Form	Type	Level	Pages
1	MC	basic	645–646
2A	MC	average	647–648
2B	MC	average	649–650
2C	FR	average	651–652
2D	FR	average	653–654
3	FR	advanced	655–656

MC = multiple-choice questions
FR = free-response questions

Open-Ended Assessment
Performance tasks for Chapter 11 can be found on p. 657 of the *Chapter 11 Resource Masters*, along with a sample scoring rubric for these tasks on p. A25.

Unit 4 Test A unit test/review can be found on pp. 665–666 of the *Chapter 11 Resource Masters.*

 ExamView® Pro

Use the networkable **ExamView® Pro** to:

- Create **multiple versions** of tests.
- Create **modified** tests for *Inclusion* students.
- **Edit** existing questions and **add** your own questions.
- Use built-in **state curriculum correlations** to create tests aligned with state standards.
- Change **English** tests to **Spanish** and vice versa.

Portfolio Suggestion

Introduction The study of three-dimensional figures and their properties is important for architects and others in design-related fields. It also serves as an introduction to a more detailed study of geometry in the future.

Ask Students to write a paragraph describing a number of real-life situations, such as architecture and packaging, in which the formulas for volume and surface area would be used.

Chapter 11 Practice Test **599**

These two pages contain practice questions in the various formats that can be found on the most frequently given standardized tests.

A practice answer sheet for these two pages can be found on page A1 of the *Chapter 11 Resource Masters*.

Standardized Test Practice
Student Recording Sheet, p. A1

Part 1 Multiple Choice

Select the best answer from the choices given and fill in the corresponding oval.

1 Ⓐ Ⓑ Ⓒ Ⓓ   4 Ⓐ Ⓑ Ⓒ Ⓓ   7 Ⓐ Ⓑ Ⓒ Ⓓ
2 Ⓐ Ⓑ Ⓒ Ⓓ   5 Ⓐ Ⓑ Ⓒ Ⓓ   8 Ⓐ Ⓑ Ⓒ Ⓓ
3 Ⓐ Ⓑ Ⓒ Ⓓ   6 Ⓐ Ⓑ Ⓒ Ⓓ

Part 2 Short Response/Grid In

Solve the problem and write your answer in the blank.

For Questions 11, 12, 14, 15, 19, and 20, also enter your answer by writing each number or symbol in a box. Then fill in the corresponding oval for that number or symbol.

9
10
11   (grid in)
12   (grid in)
13
14   (grid in)
15   (grid in)
16
17
18
19   (grid in)
20   (grid in)

11   12   14
15   19   20

Part 3 Extended Response

Record your answers for Question 21 on the back of this paper.

Additional Practice

See pp. 663–664 of the *Chapter 11 Resource Masters* for additional standardized test practice.

Part 1 Multiple Choice

Record your answers on the answer sheet provided by your teacher or on a sheet of paper.

1. If $-3x + 7 = -29$, then what is the value of x? (Lesson 3-5) **D**
- Ⓐ -12
- Ⓑ -6
- Ⓒ 6
- Ⓓ 12

2. Austin wants to buy a fish tank so that his fish get as much oxygen as possible. The pet shop has four different fish tanks. The dimensions below represent the length and width of each fish tank. Which tank has the greatest surface area at the top? (Lesson 3-7) **A**
- Ⓐ 22 in. × 18 in.
- Ⓑ 24 in. × 16 in.
- Ⓒ 26 in. × 14 in.
- Ⓓ 28 in. × 12 in.

3. The Hyde family's weekly food expenses for four consecutive weeks were $105.52, $98.26, $101.29, and $91.73. What is the mean of their weekly food expenses for those four weeks? (Lesson 5-7) **C**
- Ⓐ $98.63
- Ⓑ $98.75
- Ⓒ $99.20
- Ⓓ $99.78

4. Students taste-tested three brands of instant hot cereal and chose their favorite brand. Which of these statements is *not* supported by the data in the table? (Lesson 6-1) **D**

	Hot Cereal Brand		
	X	**Y**	**Z**
Girls	12	7	10
Boys	10	15	5

- Ⓐ Twice as many girls as boys chose Brand Z.
- Ⓑ The total number of students who chose Brand X is equal to the total number who chose Brand Y.
- Ⓒ Three times as many boys chose Brand Y as Brand Z.
- Ⓓ Half of the students who chose Brand Z were boys.

5. A sloppy-joe recipe for 12 servings calls for 2 pounds of ground beef. How many pounds of ground beef will be needed to make 30 servings? (Lesson 6-3) **C**
- Ⓐ 2.5 lb
- Ⓑ 4.5 lb
- Ⓒ 5 lb
- Ⓓ 6 lb

6. Three-fourths of a county's population is registered to vote. Only 50% of the registered voters in the county actually voted in the election. What fractional part of the county's population voted? (Lesson 6-4) **B**
- Ⓐ $\frac{1}{2}$
- Ⓑ $\frac{3}{8}$
- Ⓒ $\frac{2}{3}$
- Ⓓ $\frac{3}{4}$

7. Rod has $10 to spend at an arcade. Each bag of popcorn at the arcade costs $3.25, and each video game costs $1.00. Which expression represents the amount of money Rod will have left after he buys one bag of popcorn and plays n video games? (Lesson 7-2) **B**
- Ⓐ $10.00 + 3.25 + 1.00n$
- Ⓑ $10.00 - 3.25 - 1.00n$
- Ⓒ $3.25 - 1.00n - 10.00$
- Ⓓ $10.00 - 3.25n - 1.00n$

8. Cheyenne is 5 feet tall. She measures her shadow and a tree's shadow at the same time of day, as shown in the diagram below. How tall is the tree? (Lesson 9-7) **B**

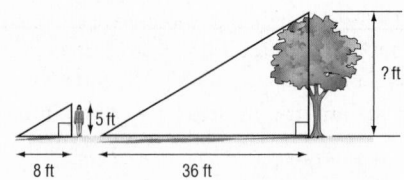

- Ⓐ 20 ft
- Ⓑ 22.5 ft
- Ⓒ 40 ft
- Ⓓ 57.6

Test-Taking Tip Ⓐ Ⓑ Ⓒ Ⓓ

Pace yourself. Do not spend too much time on any one question. If you're having difficulty answering a question, mark it in your test booklet and go on to the next question. Make sure that you also skip the question on your answer sheet. At the end of the test, go back and answer the questions that you skipped.

ExamView® Pro

Special banks of standardized test questions similar to those on the SAT, ACT, TIMSS 8, NAEP 8, and Pre-Algebra End-of-Course tests can be found on this CD-ROM.

Part 2 | Short Response/Grid In

Record your answers on the answer sheet provided by your teacher or on a sheet of paper.

9. Determine the range of the relation shown in the graph. (Lesson 1-6) **{1, 2, 8, 11}**

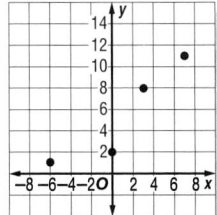

10. Simplify $-9s(4t)$. (Lesson 2-4) **$-36st$**

11. Thang is enclosing a rectangular area for his dog. He bought enough wire fencing to enclose 308 square feet of space. If he makes the length of the rectangle 22 feet, what is the width in feet? (Lesson 3-7) **14**

12. What is the value of x^{-2} for $x = 3$? (Lesson 4-7) **1/9**

13. Which number is greater, 3.45×10^3 or 5.87×10^2? (Lesson 4-8) **3.45×10^3**

14. Write the value of $\frac{5}{6} - \frac{1}{5} - \frac{1}{30}$ in simplest form. (Lesson 5-4) **3/5**

15. Mr. Vazquez budgeted $300 for his home's January heating bill. The actual bill was $240. What percent of the $300 was left after Mr. Vazquez paid the heating bill? (Lesson 6-4) **20**

16. What is the y-intercept of the graph of $y + 5 = 2x$? (Lesson 8-7) **-5**

17. Sarah is making a model house. The pitch of the roof is 35°. What is the measure, in degrees, of $\angle P$, the peak of the roof? (Lesson 10-3) **110**

18. What is the circumference of the circle? Use $\pi = 3.14$ and round to the nearest tenth, if necessary. (Lesson 10-9) **56.5 cm**

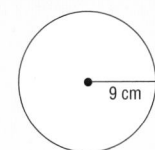

19. A concrete worker is making six cement steps. Each step is 4 inches high, 7 inches deep, and 20 inches wide. What volume of cement, in cubic inches, will be needed to make these steps? (Lesson 11-2) **3360**

20. The prisms below are similar. Find the height of the larger prism in centimeters. If necessary, round to the nearest tenth. (Lesson 11-6) **60.3**

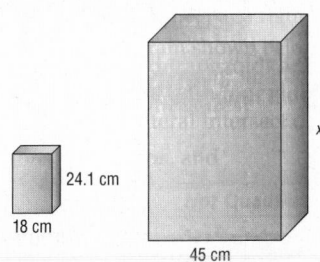

Part 3 | Extended Response

Record your answers on a sheet of paper. Show your work. **21c. 2560 cubic feet**

21. A manufacturer ships its product in boxes that are 3 feet × 2 feet × 2 feet. The company needs to store some products in a warehouse space that is 32 feet long by 8 feet wide by 10 feet high. (Lesson 11-2)

   a. What is the greatest number of boxes the company can store in this space? (All the boxes must be stored in the same position.) **200 boxes**

   b. What is the total volume of the stored boxes? **2400 cubic feet**

   c. What is the volume of the storage space?

   d. How much storage space is *not* filled with boxes? **160 cubic feet**

Chapter 11 Standardized Test Practice **601**

Evaluating Extended Response Questions

Extended Response questions are graded by using a multilevel rubric that guides you in assessing a student's knowledge of a particular concept.

Goal: Identify three-dimensional figures and determine their volumes and surface areas.

Sample Scoring Rubric: The following rubric is a sample scoring device. You may wish to add more detail to this sample to meet your individual scoring needs.

Score	Criteria
4	A correct solution that is supported by well-developed, accurate explanations
3	A generally correct solution, but may contain minor flaws in reasoning or computation
2	A partially correct interpretation and/or solution to the problem
1	A correct solution with no supporting evidence or explanation
0	An incorrect solution indicating no mathematical understanding of the concept or task, or no solution is given

Page 555, Geometry Activity

10–15. Sample answers are given.

10.
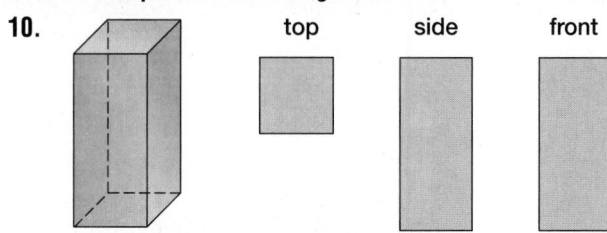
top   side   front

11.
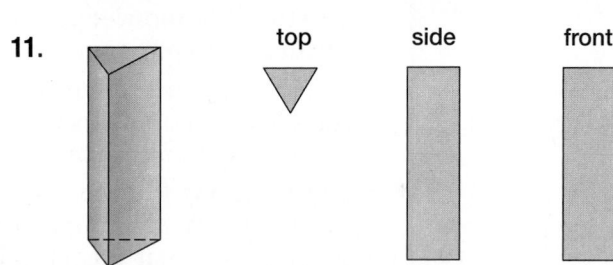
top   side   front

12.
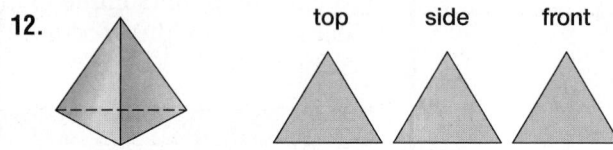
top   side   front

13.
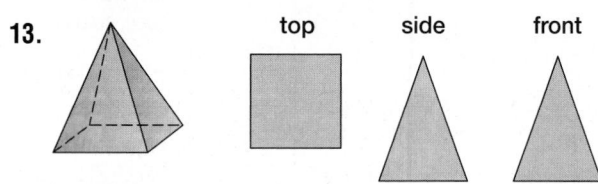
top   side   front

14.
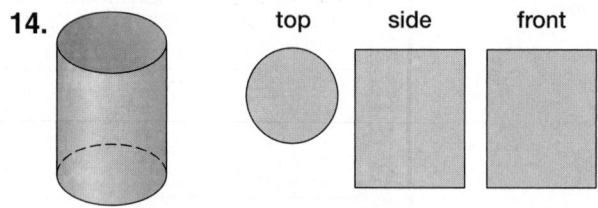
top   side   front

15.
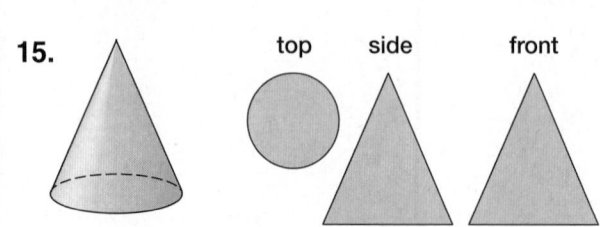
top   side   front

Pages 559–560, Lesson 11-1

7.
top   front   side
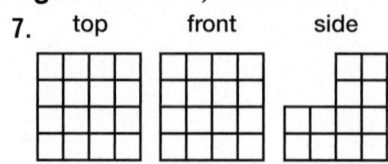

9. rectangular prism; *LMNP, QRST* or *LPTQ, MNSR* or *PNST, LMRQ; LMNP, QRST, LPTQ, MNSR, PNST, LMRQ;* $\overline{LM}$, $\overline{MN}$, $\overline{NP}$, $\overline{PL}$, $\overline{LQ}$, $\overline{MR}$, $\overline{NS}$, $\overline{PT}$, $\overline{QR}$, $\overline{RS}$, $\overline{ST}$, $\overline{TQ}$; *L, M, N, P, Q, R, S, T*

10. triangular prism; *FGH, IJK; FGH, IJK, HKIF, GHKJ, FGJI;* $\overline{FG}$, $\overline{GH}$, $\overline{HF}$, $\overline{IJ}$, $\overline{JK}$, $\overline{KI}$, $\overline{FI}$, $\overline{HK}$, $\overline{GJ}$; *F, G, H, I, J, K*

11. triangular pyramid; any one of the following faces can be considered a base: *WXY, WYZ, WZX, XYZ;* $\overline{WX}$, $\overline{WY}$, $\overline{WZ}$, $\overline{XZ}$, $\overline{XY}$, $\overline{YZ}$; *W, X, Y, Z*

12. rectangular pyramid; *BCDE; ABC, ACD, ADE, ABE, BCDE;* $\overline{AB}$, $\overline{AC}$, $\overline{AD}$, $\overline{AE}$, $\overline{BC}$, $\overline{CD}$, $\overline{DE}$, $\overline{EB}$; *A, B, C, D, E*

18.
top   side   front
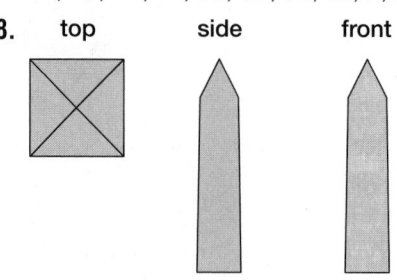

26. Sample answer:

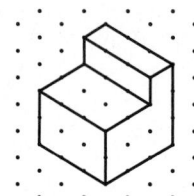

The figure has bilateral symmetry because it can be divided into two matching halves. It does not have rotational symmetry because when rotated less than 360°, it never looks exactly as it does in its original position.

Page 570, Lesson 11-3

2. Prism $V = Bh$; cylinder $V = \pi r^2 h$; pyramid $V = \frac{1}{3}Bh$; cone $V = \frac{1}{3}\pi r^2 h$; B = area of base, h = height, r = radius; the formula for the volume of a pyramid and a cone is one-third times the formula for the volume of a prism and a cylinder, respectively.

3. Sample answer:

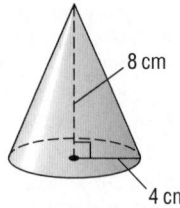
8 cm
4 cm

$V = 134.0$ cm³

Page 586, Lesson 11-6

1. Sample answer:

The cones are similar because the ratios comparing their radii and slant heights are equal: $\frac{2}{3} = \frac{5}{7.5}$.

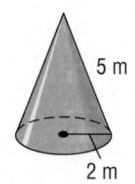
5 m
2 m

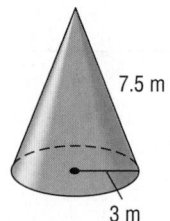
7.5 m
3 m

Notes

Extending Algebra to Statistics and Polynomials

Introduction

In this unit, students will display and interpret data in various plots and graphs, and use measures of variation to compare data. Students also will count outcomes and use permutations and combinations. Probability will be extended to using simulations, finding experimental probability, and finding the probability of multiple events.

Students also will identify and classify polynomials and find the degree of a polynomial. They will learn to use operations involving manomials and poynomials. Students will finish the unit with an examination of linear and nonlinear functions, extending to the graphing of quadratic and cubic functions.

In Unit 3, you learned about real-world data that can be represented by linear functions. In this unit, you will learn about real-world data that can be represented by nonlinear functions.

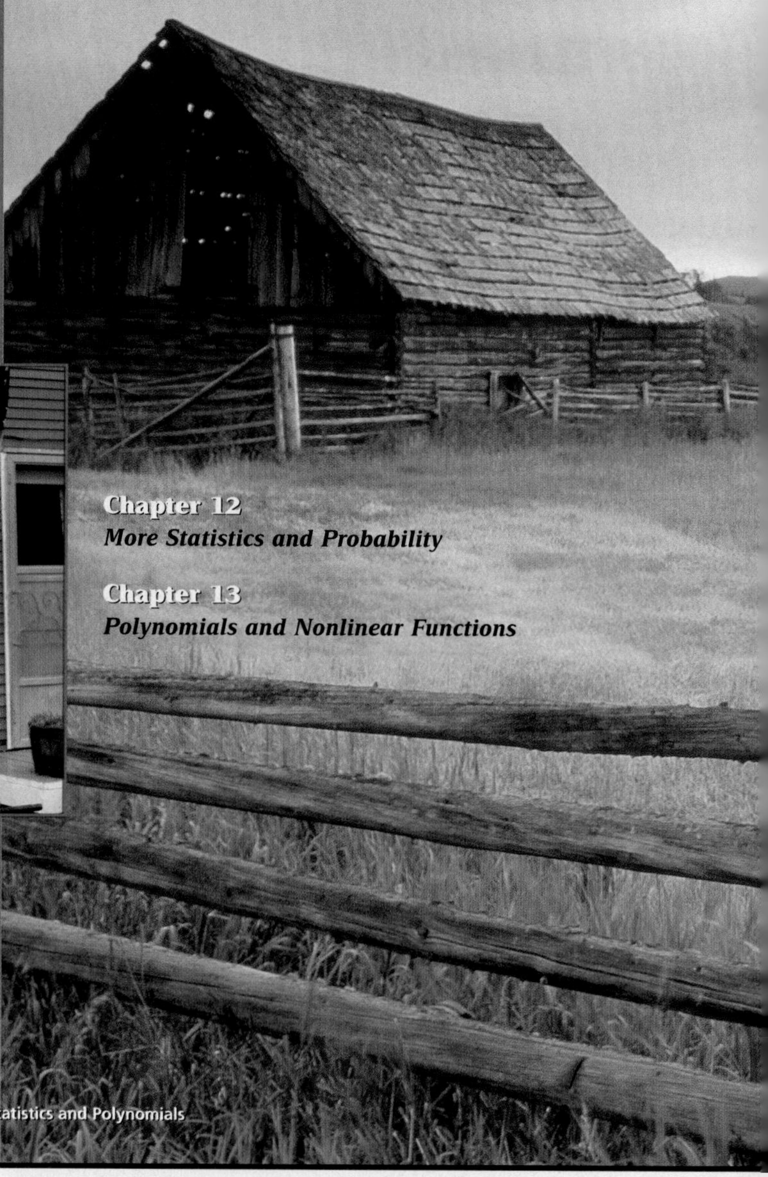

Assessment Options

 **Unit 5 Test** Pages 783–784 of the *Chapter 13 Resource Masters* may be used as a test or review for Unit 5. This assessment contains both multiple-choice and short answer items.

 **ExamView® Pro**
This CD-ROM can be used to create additional unit tests and review worksheets.

Yearly Progress Pro
An online, research-based instructional, assessment, and intervention tool that provides specific feedback on student mastery of state and national standards, instant remediation, and a data management system to track performance. For more information, contact

mhdigitallearning.com.

Chapter 12
More Statistics and Probability

Chapter 13
Polynomials and Nonlinear Functions

What's MATH Got To Do With It?

Real-Life Math Videos
What's Math Got to Do With It? Real-Life Math Videos engage students showing them how math is used in everyday situations. Use Video 4 with this unit.

WebQuest Internet Project

Will Family Farms Die Like Mom, Pop Stores?

"Once upon a time, in little towns … across the USA, every business was family owned. Mom and Pop ran the grocery store. Also the butcher shop. Drugstore, Movie house. Gas station. Most of their customers were area farm families."

Source: *USA TODAY*, November 1, 2000

In this project, you will be using statistics and functions to analyze farming or ranching in America.

 Log on to www.pre-alg.com/webquest. Begin your WebQuest by reading the Task.

Then continue working on your WebQuest as you study Unit 5.

Lesson	12-4	13-5
Page	626	690

USA TODAY Snapshots®

Long days on the farm

More than one in five agriculture workers put in at least 60 hours a week on the job in August. Percentage of workers putting in 40 hours or more:

- Agriculture
- Non-agriculture

- 40 hours: 39.6% / 27.8%
- 41 to 59 hours: 23.1% / 18%
- 60+ hours: 21.6% / 8.2%

Source: Bureau of Labor Statistics

By Mark Pearson and Web Bryant, USA TODAY

Unit 5 Extending Algebra to Statistics and Polynomials 603

WebQuest Internet Project

Problem-Based Learning A WebQuest is an online project in which students do research on the Internet, gather data, and make presentations using word processing, graphing, page-making, or presentation software. In each chapter, students advance to the next step in their WebQuest. At the end of Chapter 13, the project culminates with a presentation of their findings.

Teaching suggestions and sample answers are available in the *WebQuest and Project Resources*.

Year-long pacing: pages T20–T21.

LESSON OBJECTIVES	PACING (days)			
	Regular		Block	
	Basic/ Average	Advanced	Basic/ Average	Advanced
12-1 Stem-and-Leaf Plots *(pp. 606–611)* • Display data in stem-and-leaf plots. • Interpret data in stem-and-leaf plots.	1	1	0.5	0.5
12-2 Measures of Variation *(pp. 612–616)* • Find measures of variation. • Use measures of variation to interpret and compare data.	1	1	0.5	0.5
12-3 Box-and-Whisker Plots *(pp. 617–622)* • Display data in a box-and-whisker plot. • Interpret data in a box-and-whisker plot. *Follow-Up:* Use a graphing calculator to create box-and-whisker plots.	1	2 (with 12-3 Follow-Up)	0.5	1 (with 12-3 Follow-Up)
12-4 Histograms *(pp. 623–629)* • Display data in a histogram. • Interpret data in a histogram. *Follow-Up:* Use a graphing calculator to make a histogram.	1	2 (with 12-4 Follow-Up)	0.5	1 (with 12-4 Follow-Up)
12-5 Misleading Statistics *(pp. 630–633)* • Recognize when statistics are misleading.	1	1	0.5	0.5
12-6 Counting Outcomes *(pp. 635–640)* • Use tree diagrams or the Fundamental Counting Principle to count outcomes. • Use the Fundamental Counting Principle to find the probability of an event. *Follow-Up:* Explore the relationship between tossing coins and Pascal's triangle.	1	2 (with 12-6 Follow-Up)	0.5	1 (with 12-6 Follow-Up)
12-7 Permutations and Combinations *(pp. 641–645)* • Use permutations. • Use combinations.	1	1	1	0.5
12-8 Odds *(pp. 646–649)* • Find the odds of a simple event.	1	1	0.5	0.5
12-9 Probability of Compound Events *(pp. 650–657)* • Find the probability of independent and dependent events. • Find the probability of mutually exclusive events. *Follow-Up:* Use simulations to examine outcomes.	1	2 (with 12-9 Follow-Up)	0.5	1.5 (with 12-9 Follow-Up)
Study Guide and **Practice Test** *(pp. 658–663)* **Standardized Test Practice** *(pp. 664–665)*	1	1	0.5	0.5
Chapter Assessment	1	1	1	0.5
TOTAL	11	15	6.5	8

*An electronic version of this chapter is available on **StudentWorks**™. This backpack solution CD-ROM allows students instant access to the Student Edition, lesson worksheet pages, and web resources.*

Chapter Resource Manager

CHAPTER 12 RESOURCE MASTERS

Study Guide and Intervention	Practice (Skills and Average)	Reading to Learn Mathematics	Enrichment	Assessment	Prerequisite Skills Workbook	Applications*	Parent and Student Study Guide Workbook	5-Minute Check Transparencies	Interactive Chalkboard	Pre-AlgePASS: Tutorial Plus (lessons)	Materials
667	668–669	670	671		GCS 41		98	12-1	12-1		
672	673–674	675	676				99	12-2	12-2		
677	678–679	680	681	727	SM 22		100	12-3	12-3		*Follow-Up:* graphing calculator
682	683–684	685	686				101	12-4	12-4		*Follow-Up:* graphing calculator
687	688–689	690	691	727, 729			102	12-5	12-5	37	
692	693–694	695	696		SC 23		103	12-6	12-6		*Follow-Up:* penny, dime, nickel, quarter
697	698–699	700	701	728	SC 24		104	12-7	12-7		
702	703–704	705	706				105	12-8	12-8		
707	708–709	710	711	728	SM 6 GCS 42		106	12-9	12-9		*Follow-Up:* coin, number cube, red and white counters, blue and red marbles
				713–726, 730–732							

Key to Abbreviations: GCS = Graphing Calculator and Spreadsheet Masters,
SC = School-to-Career Masters,
SM = Science and Mathematics Lab Manual

 Study Guide and Intervention, Skills Practice, Practice, and Parent and Student Study Guide Workbooks are also available in Spanish.

Mathematical Connections and Background

Continuity of Instruction

Prior Knowledge

In Chapter 5, students learned how to find the mean, median, and mode, which are measures of central tendency. In Chapter 6, students discussed the difference between theoretical and experimental probability, learned how to calculate simple probabilities, and made predictions based on these calculations.

This Chapter

Students learn to display and interpret information in stem-and-leaf plots, box-and-whisker plots, and histograms. They also learn to recognize misleading displays and interpretations of data. Additionally, students calculate measures of variation for data sets. At the end of the chapter, students calculate more complex probabilities and odds, including probabilities of compound events.

Future Connections

This chapter forms a basis for further study in statistics, both in mathematics classes and applied in fields such as psychology and experimental science. Students' skill in understanding and interpreting data is vital in evaluating news broadcasts, advertisements, and political campaigns. An understanding of odds and probability will be useful in science and in interpreting weather data.

12-1 Stem-and-Leaf Plots

In a stem-and-leaf plot, numerical data are listed in ascending or descending order. The greatest place value of the data is used for the stems. The next greatest place value forms the leaves. For example, if the least number in a set of data is 32 and the greatest number is 56, draw a vertical line and write the stems from 3 to 5 to the left of the line. Write the leaves from 2 to 6 to the right of the line, with the corresponding stem. Next, rearrange the leaves so they are ordered from least to greatest. Then include a key or explanation, such as $3 \mid 2 = \$32$.

12-2 Measures of Variation

In statistics, measures of variation are used to describe how data are distributed. The range of a set of data is the difference between the greatest and the least values of the set. The quartiles are the values that divide the data into four equal parts. The median of a set of data separates the set in half. Similarly, the median of the lower half of a set of data is the lower quartile. The median of the upper half of a set of data is the upper quartile. The interquartile range is the difference between the upper quartile and the lower quartile.

12-3 Box-and-Whisker Plots

A box-and-whisker *plot* displays the measures of central tendency and variation. A box is drawn around the quartile values, and whiskers extend from each quartile to the extreme data points. To make a box-and-whisker plot for a set of data, draw a number line that covers the range of the data. Find the median, the extremes, and the upper and lower quartiles. Mark these points above the number line with bullets, then draw a box and the whiskers. The length of a whisker or box shows whether the values of the data in that part are concentrated or spread out.

12-4 Histograms

A histogram displays numerical data that have been organized into equal intervals with bars that have the same width and no space between them. While a histogram does not give exact data points, its shape shows the distribution of the data. Histograms also can be used to compare data.

12-5 Misleading Statistics

The way that statistics are displayed may sometimes be misleading. For example, expanding the vertical scale on a line graph can cause the line to flatten out, giving the appearance of slow, gradual change. Conversely, compressing the vertical scale emphasizes the variations, giving a more dramatic appearance. Similarly, breaking the vertical axis or not starting at zero changes the relative heights of the bars of a histogram. Other graph elements that may be misleading include the horizontal scale, the graph's title and labels, and the relative width of the bars in a bar graph.

12-6 Counting Outcomes

The Fundamental Counting Principle says that if event M can occur in m ways and is followed by event N that can occur in n ways, then the event M followed by N can occur in $m \cdot n$ ways. For example, if a shirt comes in 3 colors and 4 sizes, then there are $3 \cdot 4$ or 12 possible outcomes. If the number of possible outcomes is known, then the probability that an event will occur can be determined. For example, if 1 shirt is randomly selected from 12 shirts, the probability of randomly selecting a certain shirt is $\frac{1}{12}$.

12-7 Permutations and Combinations

An arrangement or listing in which order is important is called a permutation. The symbol $P(6, 3)$ represents the number of permutations of 6 things taken 3 at a time. For $P(6, 3)$, there are $6 \cdot 5 \cdot 4$ or 120 possible outcomes. An arrangement or listing where order is not important is called a combination. The symbol $C(10, 5)$ represents the number of combinations of 10 things taken 5 at a time. For $C(10, 5)$, there are

$$\frac{10 \cdot 9 \cdot 8 \cdot 7 \cdot 6}{5 \cdot 4 \cdot 3 \cdot 2 \cdot 1} \text{ or 252 possible outcomes.}$$

12-8 Odds

The odds in favor of an event is the ratio that compares the number of ways the event can occur to the ways that the event cannot occur. If the probability of an event occurring is $\frac{5}{7}$, then the odds of an event occurring are 5:2, or 5 to 2. The odds of the event *not* occurring are 2:5.

12-9 Probability of Compound Events

In independent events, the outcome of one event does *not* influence the outcome of a second. For example, if a bag contains 2 blue and 3 red marbles, then the probability of selecting a blue marble, replacing it, and then selecting a red marble is $P(A) \cdot P(B) = \frac{2}{5} \cdot \frac{3}{5}$ or $\frac{6}{25}$.

In dependent events, the outcome of one event affects the outcome of a second event. For example, if a bag contains 2 blue and 3 red marbles, then the probability of selecting a blue and then a red marble without replacing the first marble is $P(A) \cdot P(B \text{ following } A) = \frac{2}{5} \cdot \frac{3}{4}$ or $\frac{3}{10}$.

Two events that cannot happen at the same time are mutually exclusive. For example, when you roll two number cubes, you cannot roll a sum that is both 5 and even. So, $P(A \text{ or } B) = \frac{4}{36} + \frac{18}{36}$ or $\frac{11}{18}$.

Quick Review Math Handbook

Hot Words includes a glossary of terms while Hot Topics consists of explanations of key mathematical concepts with exercises to test comprehension. This valuable resource can be used as a reference in the classroom or for home study.

Lesson	Hot Topics Section	Lesson	Hot Topics Section
GS 12	2.3, 2.4, 4.4, 4.6	12-5	4.1, 4.2
12-1	1.5, 4.2	12-6	2.1, 4.5
12-2	4.3, 4.4	12-6F	4.6
12-3	4.2	12-7	4.5, 6.5
12-3F	4.2	12-8	2.4, 4.5
12-4	4.2	12-9	4.6
12-4F	4.2	12-9F	4.6

GS = Getting Started, F = Follow-Up

 Additional mathematical information and teaching notes are available at www.pre-alg.com/key_concepts.

D A I L Y
INTERVENTION and Assessment

Key to Abbreviations:
TWE = Teacher Wraparound Edition; CRM = Chapter Resource Masters

	Type	Student Edition	Teacher Resources	Technology/Internet
INTERVENTION	Ongoing	Prerequisite Skills, pp. 605, 611, 616, 621, 628, 633, 639, 645, 649 Practice Quiz 1, p. 628 Practice Quiz 2, p. 645	5-Minute Check Transparencies Quizzes, *CRM*, pp. 727, 728 Mid-Chapter Test, *CRM*, p. 729 Study Guide and Intervention, *CRM*, pp. 667, 672, 677, 682, 687, 692, 697, 702, 707	Pre-Alge*pass*: Tutorial Plus, Lesson 37 www.pre-alg.com/self_check_quiz www.pre-alg.com/extra_examples
	Mixed Review	pp. 611, 616, 621, 628, 633, 639, 645, 649, 655	Cumulative Review, *CRM*, p. 730	
	Error Analysis	Find the Error, pp. 643, 648	Find the Error, *TWE*, pp. 643, 648 Unlocking Misconceptions, *TWE*, pp. 616, 652	
ASSESSMENT	Standardized Test Practice	pp. 611, 616, 621, 627, 633, 639, 645, 647, 648, 649, 655, 664–665	*TWE*, pp. 664–665 Standardized Test Practice, *CRM*, pp. 731–732	Standardized Test Practice CD-ROM www.pre-alg.com/standardized_test
	Open-Ended Assessment	Writing in Math, pp. 610, 616, 621, 627, 633, 639, 645, 649, 654 Open Ended, pp. 608, 614, 619, 625, 631, 637, 643, 648, 653 Standardized Test, p. 665	Modeling: *TWE*, pp. 616, 633, 645 Speaking: *TWE*, pp. 611, 621, 655 Writing: *TWE*, pp. 628, 639, 649 Open-Ended Assessment, *CRM*, p. 725	
	Chapter Assessment	Study Guide, pp. 658–662 Practice Test, p. 663	Multiple-Choice Tests (Forms 1, 2A, 2B), *CRM*, pp. 713–718 Free-Response Tests (Forms 2C, 2D, 3), *CRM*, pp. 719–724 Vocabulary Test/Review, *CRM*, p. 726	ExamView® Pro (see below) MindJogger Videoquizzes www.pre-alg.com/vocabulary_review www.pre-alg.com/chapter_test

For more information on Yearly ProgressPro, see p. 602.

Pre-Algebra Lesson	Yearly ProgressPro Skill Lesson
12-1	Stem-and-Leaf Plots
12-2	Measures of Variation
12-3	Box-and-Whisker Plots
12-4	Histograms: Level 1
12-5	Misleading Statistics
12-6	Tree Diagrams and the Fundamental Counting Principal
12-7	Permutations; Combinations
12-8	Probability as Fractions: Level 2
12-9	Probability of Compound Events

ExamView® Pro
Use the networkable **ExamView® Pro** to:
- Create **multiple versions** of tests.
- Create **modified** tests for *Inclusion* students.
- **Edit** existing questions and **add** your own questions.
- Use built-in **state curriculum correlations** to create tests aligned with state standards.
- Change **English** tests to **Spanish** and vice versa.

For more information on Intervention and Assessment, see pp. T8–T11.

Reading and Writing in Mathematics

Glencoe Pre-Algebra provides numerous opportunities to incorporate reading and writing into the mathematics classroom.

Student Edition

- Foldables™ Study Organizer, p. 605
- Reading Mathematics, p. 634
- Concept Check questions require students to verbalize and write about what they have learned in the lesson. (pp. 607, 608, 613, 614, 618, 619, 625, 631, 636, 637, 643, 646, 647, 648, 651, 652, 653)
- Writing in Math questions in every lesson, pp. 610, 616, 621, 627, 633, 639, 645, 649, 654
- Reading Math, pp. 624, 641, 642, 643, 647, 650
- WebQuest, p. 626

Teacher Wraparound Edition

- Foldables™ Study Organizer, pp. 605, 658
- Study Notebook suggestions, pp. 608, 614, 619, 626, 633, 634, 637, 640, 643, 647, 653, 657
- Modeling activities, pp. 616, 633, 645
- Speaking activities, pp. 611, 621, 655
- Writing activities, pp. 628, 639, 649
- Differentiated Instruction (Verbal/Linguistic), p. 632
-  Resources, pp. 604, 606, 612, 617, 623, 630, 632, 634, 635, 641, 646, 650, 658

For more information on Reading and Writing in Mathematics, see pp. T6–T7.

Additional Resources

- Vocabulary Builder worksheets require students to define and give examples for key vocabulary terms as they progress through the chapter (*Chapter 12 Resource Masters,* pp. vii–viii)
- Reading to Learn Mathematics master for each lesson (*Chapter 12 Resource Masters,* pp. 670, 675, 680, 685, 690, 695, 700, 705, 710)
- *Vocabulary PuzzleMaker* software creates crossword, jumble, and word search puzzles using vocabulary lists that you can customize.
- *Teaching Mathematics with Foldables* provides suggestions for promoting cognition and language.
- *Reading and Writing in the Mathematics Classroom*
- *WebQuest and Project Resources*

ELL ENGLISH LANGUAGE LEARNERS

Lesson 12-1
Using Models

Make a connection to real life by drawing a tree with its branches and leaves so that students can make a connection between real life and a stem-and-leaf plot. Next, show them how the plot is drawn and how the numbers in the data set are plotted. To extend the analogy, you may also wish to draw a stem with a leaf attached and place the digit in the tens place on the stem and the digit in the ones place on the leaf.

Lesson 12-4
Using Applications

Have students go around the class and ask as many students as possible what their favorite candy is. Then students can return to their desks. Show students how they would make a frequency table from the information they have collected. Explain the vocabulary *statistics, data,* and *frequency table* based on the activity.

Lesson 12-7
Building on Prior Knowledge

Ask students how they would define *combination.* Have students give real-life examples of how and when they use combinations. For instance cooking, clothing, arranging a wardrobe or packing for a trip. Then relate their applications to the mathematical definition of *combination.*

What You'll Learn

Have students read over the list of objectives and make a list of any words with which they are not familiar.

Why It's Important

Point out to students that this is only one of many reasons why each objective is important. Others are provided in the introduction to each lesson.

Lesson	NCTM Standards	Local Objectives
12-1	5, 6, 10	
12-2	5, 6, 9	
12-3	5, 6, 9, 10	
12-3 Follow-Up	5, 10	
12-4	5, 6, 10	
12-4 Follow-Up	5, 10	
12-5	5, 8, 10	
12-6	5, 6, 7, 10	
12-6 Follow-Up	5, 7, 10	
12-7	1, 5, 6, 9	
12-8	1, 5, 6, 9	
12-9	1, 5, 6, 7, 9	
12-9 Follow-Up	1, 5, 6, 7, 8, 9	

Key to NCTM Standards:

1=Number & Operations, 2=Algebra, 3=Geometry, 4=Measurement, 5=Data Analysis & Probability, 6=Problem Solving, 7=Reasoning & Proof, 8=Communication, 9=Connections, 10=Representation

604   Chapter 12   More Statistics and Probability

More Statistics and Probability

What You'll Learn

- **Lessons 12-1, 12-3, and 12-4**   Display and interpret data in stem-and-leaf plots, box-and-whisker plots, and histograms.
- **Lesson 12-2**   Find measures of variation.
- **Lesson 12-5**   Recognize misleading statistics.
- **Lessons 12-6 and 12-7**   Count outcomes using tree diagrams, the Fundamental Counting Principle, permutations, or combinations.
- **Lessons 12-8 and 12-9**   Find probabilities and odds.

Key Vocabulary

- **stem-and-leaf plot** (p. 606)
- **measures of variation** (p. 612)
- **box-and-whisker plot** (p. 617)
- **histogram** (p. 623)
- **odds** (p. 646)

Why It's Important

Statistics is a branch of mathematics that involves the collection, presentation, and analysis of data. In statistics, graphs are usually used to present data. These graphs are important because they allow you to interpret the data easily. *You will display and interpret data about the United States government in Lesson 12-1.*

604   Chapter 12   More Statistics and Probability

Vocabulary Builder   **ELL**

The Key Vocabulary list introduces students to some of the main vocabulary terms included in this chapter. For a more thorough vocabulary list with pronunciations of new words, give students the Vocabulary Builder worksheets found on pages vii and viii of the *Chapter 12 Resource Masters*. Encourage them to complete the definition of each term as they progress through the chapter. You may suggest that they add these sheets to their study notebooks for future reference when studying for the Chapter 12 test.

▶ **Prerequisite Skills** To be successful in this chapter, you'll need to master these skills and be able to apply them in problem-solving situations. Review these skills before beginning Chapter 12.

For Lessons 12-1, 12-2, and 12-3   Measures of Central Tendency

Find the mean, median, and mode for each set of data. Round to the nearest tenth, if necessary. *(For review, see Lesson 5-8.)* **4. 5.0, 5.1, 5.4**

1. 10, 15, 23 **16; 15; none**

2. 21, 24, 24, 24, 42, 48 **30.5, 24, 24**

3. 3.2, 5.1, 6.5, 6.5 **5.3, 5.8, 6.5**

4. 2.2, 4.3, 5.4, 3.2, 4.8, 5.4, 6.2, 8.1

For Lesson 12-9   Simple Probability

The spinner at the right is spun. Find each probability.

(For review, see Lesson 6-9.)

5. $P(\text{green})$ $\frac{1}{3}$ **6.** $P(4)$ $\frac{1}{6}$ **7.** $P(\text{even})$ $\frac{1}{2}$

8. $P(\text{not blue})$ $\frac{2}{3}$ **9.** $P(\text{prime})$ $\frac{1}{2}$ **10.** $P(\text{composite})$ $\frac{1}{3}$

For Lesson 12-9   Compute with Fractions

Find each product, sum, or difference. *(For review, see Lessons 5-3 and 5-7.)*

11. $\frac{1}{6} + \frac{1}{3}$ $\frac{1}{2}$ **12.** $\frac{2}{3} - \frac{4}{9}$ $\frac{2}{9}$ **13.** $\frac{3}{4} \times \frac{1}{6}$ $\frac{1}{8}$ **14.** $\frac{5}{8} \times \frac{3}{4}$ $\frac{15}{32}$

15. $\frac{3}{8} \times \frac{4}{5} \times \frac{5}{9}$ $\frac{1}{6}$ **16.** $\frac{1}{2} \times \frac{5}{6} \times \frac{3}{4}$ $\frac{5}{16}$ **17.** $\frac{5}{12} + \frac{1}{12} - \frac{1}{3}$ $\frac{1}{6}$ **18.** $\frac{3}{8} + \frac{1}{2} - \frac{1}{4}$ $\frac{5}{8}$

Statistics and Probability Make this Foldable to help you organize your notes. Begin with a piece of notebook paper.

Step 1 Fold

Fold lengthwise to the holes.

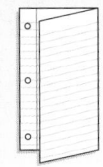

Step 2 Cut

Cut along the top line and then cut 9 tabs.

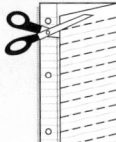

Step 3 Label

Label lesson numbers and titles as shown.

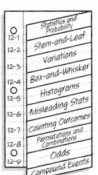

Reading and Writing As you read and study the chapter, you can write notes under the tabs.

This section provides a review of the basic concepts needed before beginning Chapter 12. Page references are included for additional student help.

Prerequisite Skills in the Getting Ready for the Next Lesson section at the end of each lesson reviews a skill needed in the next lesson.

For Lesson	Prerequisite Skill
12-2	Median (p. 611)
12-3	Ordering Decimals (p. 616)
12-4	Frequency Tables (p. 621)
12-5	Bar Graphs (p. 628)
12-6	Probability (p. 633)
12-7	Simplifying Fractions (p. 639)
12-8	Simplifying Ratios (p. 645)
12-9	Multiplying Fractions (p. 649)

Study Organizer

For more information about Foldables, see *Teaching Mathematics with Foldables.*

Vocabulary and Writing Definitions This Foldable helps students better understand statistics and probability by organizing what they learn in their own words. Have students write concepts on the front of each tab and definitions on the back. Ask students to include their own statistical examples. Students can use this self-checking study guide to review as they proceed through the chapter.

1 Focus

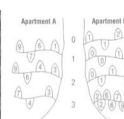

5-Minute Check Transparency 12-1 Use as a quiz or review of Chapter 11.

Mathematical Background notes are available for this lesson on page 604C.

How can stem-and-leaf plots help you understand an election?

The opening activity questions are repeated on page 670 of the *Chapter 12 Resource Masters.*

Reading to Learn Mathematics, p. 670   ELL

Pre-Activity *How can stem-and-leaf plots help you understand an election?*

Do the activity at the top of page 606 in your textbook. Write your answers below.

a. Is there an equal number of electors in each group? Explain.
   Sample answer: Even though the intervals are the same, the data are not distributed evenly as the number of pieces of data in each interval are not the same.

b. Name an advantage of displaying the data in groups.
   Sample answer: You can see how the data are distributed.

Reading the Lesson 1–4. See students' work.

Write a definition and give an example of each new vocabulary word or phrase.

Vocabulary	Definition	Example
1. stem-and-leaf plot		
2. stems		
3. leaves		
4. back-to-back stem-and-leaf plot		

Helping You Remember

5. How will you remember which numbers of a stem-and-leaf plot represent the greater place value? Using the data at right, draw a back-to-back stem-and-leaf plot to look like actual leaves on stems. Then to read the data, start from the tree trunk and move outward.

Ages of Persons	
Apartment Building A	Apartment Building B
33, 16, 19, 26, 23, 11, 34, 24, 37, 17, 29	39, 21, 20, 1, 10, 21, 36, 37, 32, 22, 11, 2, 10, 1, 32, 38, 12, 36, 39

Resource Manager

📂 **Workbooks and Reproducible Masters**

Chapter 12 Resource Masters
• Study Guide and Intervention, p. 667
• Skills Practice, p. 668
• Practice, p. 669
• Reading to Learn Mathematics, p. 670
• Enrichment, p. 671

Graphing Calculator and Spreadsheet Masters, p. 41
Parent and Student Study Guide Workbook, p. 98

🖥 **Transparencies**
5-Minute Check Transparency 12-1
Answer Key Transparencies

💿 **Technology**
Interactive Chalkboard

12-1 Stem-and-Leaf Plots

What You'll Learn

• Display data in stem-and-leaf plots.
• Interpret data in stem-and-leaf plots.

Vocabulary
• stem-and-leaf plot
• stems
• leaves
• back-to-back stem-and-leaf plot

a. Sample answer: Even though the intervals are the same, the data are not distributed evenly as the number of pieces of data in each interval are not the same.
b. Sample answer: You can see how the data are distributed.

How can stem-and-leaf plots help you understand an election?

The members of the Electoral College officially elect the President of the United States. These members are called electors. The number of electors for each state, including the District of Columbia, is shown.

Number of Electors								
AL: 9	DE: 3	IN: 12	MA: 12	NV: 4	OH: 21	TN: 11	WI: 11
AK: 3	DC: 3	IA: 7	MI: 18	NH: 4	OK: 8	TX: 32	WY: 3
AZ: 8	FL: 25	KS: 6	MN: 10	NJ: 15	OR: 7	UT: 5	
AR: 6	GA: 13	KY: 8	MS: 7	NM: 5	PA: 23	VT: 3	
CA: 54	HI: 4	LA: 9	MO: 11	NY: 33	RI: 4	VA: 13	
CO: 8	ID: 4	ME: 4	MT: 3	NC: 14	SC: 8	WA: 11	
CT: 8	IL: 22	MO: 10	NE: 5	ND: 3	SD: 3	WV: 5	

Source: *The World Almanac*

• Write each number on a self-stick note.
• Group the numbers: 0-9, 10-19, 20-29, 30-39, 40-49, 50-59.
• Organize the numbers in each group from least to greatest.

a. Is there an equal number of electors in each group? Explain.
b. Name an advantage of displaying the data in groups.

DISPLAY DATA   In a **stem-and-leaf plot**, numerical data are listed in ascending or descending order. The greatest place value of the data is used for the **stems**. The next greatest place value forms the **leaves**.

Example 1 *Draw a Stem-and-Leaf Plot*

ASTRONAUTS Display the data shown at the right in a stem-and-leaf plot.

Step 1 Find the least and the greatest number. Then identify the greatest place value digit in each number. In this case, tens.

54   77

The least number has 5 in the tens place.

The greatest number has 7 in the tens place.

Oldest U.S. Astronauts	
Astronaut	Age*
Roger K. Crouch	56
Don L. Lind	54
William G. Gregory	54
John H. Glenn	77
John E. Blaha	54
William E. Thornton	56
F. Story Musgrave	61
Karl G. Henize	58
Vance D. Brand	59
Henry W. Hartsfield	54

* At time of his last space shuttle flight
Source: *Top 10 of Everything,* 2001

Step 2 Draw a vertical line and write the stems from 5 to 7 to the left of the line.

Stem	
5	
6	
7	

Step 3 Write the leaves to the right of the line, with the corresponding stem. For example, for 56, write 6 to the right of 5.

Stem	Leaf
5	6 4 4 4 6 8 9 4
6	1
7	7

Step 4 Rearrange the leaves so they are ordered from least to greatest. Then include a key or an explanation.

Stem	Leaf
5	4 4 4 4 6 6 8 9
6	1
7	7

The key tells what the stems and leaves represent. → 5 | 6 = 56 years

✓ **Concept Check** Explain the difference between *stems* and *leaves*. See pp. 665A–665F.

INTERPRET STEM-AND-LEAF PLOTS It is often easier to interpret data when they are displayed in a stem-and-leaf plot instead of a table. You can "see" how the data are distributed.

Example 2 *Interpret Data*

PRESIDENTS The stem-and-leaf plot lists the ages of the U.S. Presidents at the time of their inauguration. **Source:** *The World Almanac*

Stem	Leaf
4	2 3 6 6 7 8 9 9
5	0 0 1 1 1 1 2 2 4 4 4 4 4 5 5 5 5 5 6 6 6 7 7 7 7 8
6	0 1 1 1 2 4 4 6 8 9

5 | 0 = 50 years

a. In which interval do most of the ages occur?

Most of the data occurs in the 50–59 interval.

b. What is the age difference between the youngest and oldest President?

The youngest age is 42. The oldest age is 69. The difference between these ages is 69 – 42 or 27.

c. What is the median age of a President at inauguration?

The median, or the number in the middle, is 55.

Two sets of data can be compared using a **back-to-back stem-and-leaf plot**. The back-to-back stem-and-leaf plot below shows the scores of two basketball teams for the games in one season.

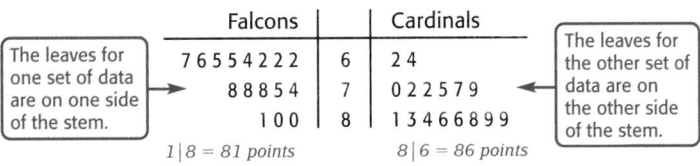

Falcons		Cardinals
7 6 5 5 4 2 2 2	6	2 4
8 8 8 5 4	7	0 2 2 5 7 9
1 0 0	8	1 3 4 6 6 8 9 9

The leaves for one set of data are on one side of the stem.
The leaves for the other set of data are on the other side of the stem.

1 | 8 = 81 points   8 | 6 = 86 points

 www.pre-alg.com/extra_examples

Lesson 12-1 Stem-and-Leaf Plots **607**

More About...

Presidents

The first President was George Washington. He was 57 years old at the time of his inauguration. He served as President from 1789 to 1797 and earned $25,000 per year.
Source: www.infoplease.com

Study Tip

Look Back
To review **mean, median,** and **mode,** see Lesson 5-8.

---

2 Teach

DISPLAY DATA

In-Class Example Power Point®

1 FOOD Display the data in a stem-and-leaf plot.

Peanuts Harvested, 2001	
State	**Amount (lb)**
Alabama	2400
Florida	2800
Georgia	2800
New Mexico	2400
North Carolina	2900
Oklahoma	2200
South Carolina	2900
Texas	2600
Virginia	3000

Source: USDA

Stem	Leaf
2	2 4 4 6 8 8 9 9
3	0

2 | 4 = 2400 lb

INTERPRET STEM-AND-LEAF PLOTS

In-Class Example Power Point®

2 VOTING The stem-and-leaf plot lists the percent of voters in each state that voted for U.S. representatives in 1998.
Source: U.S. Census Bureau

Stem	Leaf
1	1 0
2	2 5 5 8 8
3	0 0 0 2 2 2 3 3 3 4 4
3	5 5 6 6 7 7 7 8 8 9 9
4	0 0 0 1 1 3 3 3 4 4 4 4
4	5 6 7 9 9
5	0 1 4 9

3 | 4 = 34%

a. Which interval contains the most percentages? in the 30–39 interval

b. What is the greatest percent of voters that voted for U.S. representatives? 59%

c. What is the median percent of voters that voted for U.S. representatives? 37.5%

Lesson 12-1 Stem-and-Leaf Plots **607**

3 **AGRICULTURE** The yearly production of honey in California and Florida is shown for the years 1993 to 1997, in millions of pounds.
Source: USDA

California		Florida
	1	6 9
7 4	2	0 3 5
9 2	3	
5	4	

$9\,|\,3 = 39$ $2\,|\,5 = 25$

a. Which state produces more honey?   **California**

b. Which state has the most varied production? Explain.
California; the data are more spread out.

---

3 ## Practice/Apply

Study Notebook

Have students—

• add the definitions/examples of the vocabulary terms to their Vocabulary Builder Worksheets for Chapter 12.

• copy one stem-and-leaf plot from their homework and use colored highlighters and a legend to explain what each part of the plot represents.

• include any other item(s) that they find helpful in mastering the skills in this lesson.

Example 3 *Compare Two Sets of Data*

WEATHER The average monthly temperatures for Helena, Montana, and Seattle, Washington, are shown.
Source: *The World Almanac*

Seattle, WA		Helena, MT
	2	0 1 6
	3	2 4
7 6 4 2 1	4	3 5
6 4 0	5	3 5
6 5 1 1	6	2 7 9

$1\,|\,6 = 61°$ $4\,|\,5 = 45°$

a. Which city has lower monthly temperatures? Explain.

Helena; it experiences temperatures in the 20's and 30's.

b. Which city has more varied temperatures? Explain.

The data for Helena are spread out from the 20's to the 60's. The data for Seattle are clustered from the 40's to the 60's. So, Helena has the most varied temperatures.

Check for Understanding

Concept Check

1. OPEN ENDED Write a statement describing how the data in Example 2 on page 607 are distributed. **See margin.**

2. 3, 4, 5, 6

2. Identify the stems for the data set {48, 52, 46, 62, 51, 39, 41, 57, 68}.

Guided Practice

Display each set of data in a stem-and-leaf plot. 3–4. See pp. 665A–665F.

GUIDED PRACTICE KEY

Exercises	Examples
3, 4	1
5–7	2
8, 9	3

3.

Average Life Span					
Animal	Years	Animal	Years	Animal	Years
Asian Elephant	40	African Elephant	35	Lion	15
Horse	20	Red Fox	7	Chipmunk	6
Moose	12	Cow	15	Hippopotamus	41

Source: *The World Almanac*

4. **Summer Paralympic Games Participating Countries**

Year	'60	'64	'68	'72	'76	'80	'84	'88	'92	'96	'00
Countries	23	22	29	44	42	42	42	61	82	103	128

Source: www.paralympic.org

Applications

SCHOOL For Exercises 5–7, use the test score data shown at the right.

5. Find the lowest and highest scores. **50, 99**

6. What is the median score? **77.5**

7. Write a statement that describes the data.
See pp. 665A–665F.

Pre-Algebra Test Scores

Stem	Leaf
5	0 9
6	4 5 7 8
7	0 4 4 5 5 6 7 8 8
8	2 3 3 5 7 8
9	0 1 5 5 9

$5\,|\,9 = 59$

FOOD For Exercises 8 and 9, use the food data shown in the back-to-back stem-and-leaf plot.

8. What is the greatest number of fat grams in each sandwich? **20; 36**

9. Chicken; whereas chicken sandwiches have 8–20 grams of fat, burgers have 10–36 grams of fat.

9. In general, which type of sandwich has a lower amount of fat? Explain.

Fat (g) of Various Burgers and Chicken Sandwiches

Chicken		Burgers
8	0	
9 8 5 5 3 3	1	0 5 9
0	2	0 6
	3	0 3 6

$8\,|\,0 = 8\,g$ $2\,|\,6 = 26\,g$

Answer

1. Sample answer: The age of the youngest President at the time of his inauguration was 42 and the age of the oldest President to be inaugurated was 69. However, most of the Presidents were 50 to 59 years old at the time of their inauguration.

Practice and Apply

Homework Help

For Exercises	See Examples
10–15, 18	1
19–21	2
22–25	3

Extra Practice
See page 752.

Display each set of data in a stem-and-leaf plot. 10–12. See margin.

10.

State Representatives Northeast Region	
State	**Number**
Connecticut	6
Maine	2
Massachusetts	10
New Hampshire	2
Rhode Island	2
Vermont	1
New Jersey	13
New York	31
Pennsylvania	21

Source: *The World Almanac*

11.

Detroit Tigers Statistics, 2001	
Player	**Runs**
D. Cruz	39
Higginson	84
Encarnacion	52
Inge	13
Magee	26
T. Clark	67
Simon	28
Halter	53
Easley	77
Palmer	34
Macias	62
Fick	62
Cedeno	79

Source: www.tigers.mlb.com

12. **Percent of Young Adults (18–24) in U.S. Living at Home**

Year	1960	1970	1980	1985	1990	1991	1992
Percent	52	54	54	60	58	60	60
Year	1993	1994	1995	1996	1997	1998	
Percent	59	60	58	59	60	59	

Source: Bureau of the Census

13–15. See pp. 665A–665F.

13. **Approximate Number of Students per Computer in U.S. Public Schools**

Year	'85–'86	'86–'87	'87–'88	'88–'89	'89–'90	'90–'91	'91–'92
Number	50	37	32	25	22	20	18
Year	'92–'93	'93–'94	'94–'95	'95–'96	'96–'97	'97–'98	'98–'99
Number	16	14	11	10	8	6	6

Source: *The World Almanac*

TEACHING TIP
For Exercise 14, have students use stems from 46 to 57 to represent the whole number part of the data.

★ **14.** **Olympic Men's 400-m Hurdles Time(s), 1900–2000**

57.6	53.0	55.0	54.0	47.5	48.7
52.6	53.4	51.7	52.4	47.5	51.1
50.8	50.1	49.3	49.6	48.1	47.8
47.6	47.8	47.2	46.8		

Source: *The ESPN Sports Almanac*

★ **15.** **Heights (ft) of Tallest Buildings in Miami, Florida**

789	400	625	400	487	405
510	480	425	484	450	456
520	764				

Source: *The World Almanac*

Tell whether each statement is *sometimes*, *always*, or *never* true.

16. A back-to-back stem-and-leaf plot has two sets of data. **always**

17. A basic stem-and-leaf plot has two keys. **never**

About the Exercises . . .

Organization by Objective
- **Display Data:** 10–15, 18, 26
- **Interpret Stem-and-Leaf Plots:** 16–17, 19–25, 27

Odd/Even Assignments
Exercises 10–17 are structured so that students practice the same concepts whether they are assigned odd or even problems.

Alert! Exercises 26 and 27 involve research on the Internet or other reference materials.

Assignment Guide
Basic: 11–13 odd, 17, 18–21, 28–47
Average: 11–17 odd, 18–25, 28–47
Advanced: 10–16 even, 18–43 (Optional: 44–47)

Teaching Tip Students may make careless errors when completing stem-and-leaf plots. Remind them to check that the number of leaves is the same as the original number of data items.

Answers

10.

Stem	Leaf
0	1 2 2 2 6
1	0 3
2	1
3	1 2|1 = 21

11.

Stem	Leaf
1	3
2	6 8
3	4 9
4	
5	2 3
6	2 2 7
7	7 9
8	4

7\|7 = 77

12.

Stem	Leaf
5	2 4 4 8 8 9 9 9
6	0 0 0 0 0

5\|8 = 58

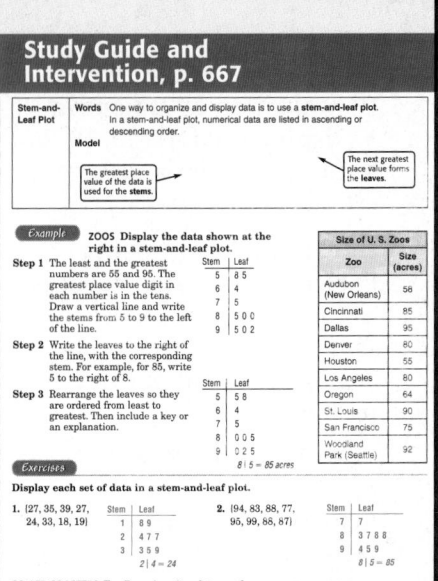

Study Guide and Intervention, p. 667

Stem-and-Leaf Plot	**Words** One way to organize and display data is to use a **stem-and-leaf plot**. In a stem-and-leaf plot, numerical data are listed in ascending or descending order. **Model**

The greatest place value of the data is used for the **stems**.

The next greatest place value forms the **leaves**.

Example **ZOOS** Display the data shown at the right in a stem-and-leaf plot.

Step 1 The least and the greatest numbers are 55 and 95. The greatest place value digit in each number is in the tens. Draw a vertical line and write the stems from 5 to 9 to the left of the line.

Stem	Leaf
5	8 5
6	4
7	5
8	5 0 0
9	5 0 2

Step 2 Write the leaves to the right of the line, with the corresponding stem. For example, for 85, write 5 to the right of 8.

Stem	Leaf
5	5
6	4
7	5
8	0 0 5
9	0 2 5

Step 3 Rearrange the leaves so they are ordered from least to greatest. Then include a key or an explanation.

8 | 5 = 85 acres

Size of U. S. Zoos	
Zoo	**Size (acres)**
Audubon (New Orleans)	58
Cincinnati	85
Dallas	95
Denver	80
Houston	55
Los Angeles	80
Oregon	64
St. Louis	90
San Francisco	75
Woodland Park (Seattle)	92

Exercises

Display each set of data in a stem-and-leaf plot.

1. {27, 35, 39, 27, 24, 33, 18, 19}

Stem	Leaf
1	8 9
2	4 7 7
3	3 5 9

2 | 4 = 24

2. {94, 83, 88, 77, 95, 99, 88, 87}

Stem	Leaf
7	7
8	3 7 8 8
9	4 5 9

8 | 5 = 85

ROLLER COASTERS For Exercises 3 and 4, use the stem-and-leaf plot shown.

The Fastest Roller Coasters

Stem	Leaf
8	3 5
9	2 5
10	0

8 | 3 = 83 mph

3. What is the speed of the fastest roller coaster? The slowest? **100 mph; 83 mph**

4. What is the median speed? **92 mph**

Skills Practice, p. 668 and Practice, p. 669 (shown)

Display each set of data in a stem-and-leaf plot.

1. {68, 63, 70, 59, 78, 64, 68, 73, 61, 66, 70}

Stem	Leaf
5	9
6	1 3 4 6 8 8
7	0 0 3 8

6 | 4 = 64

2. {27, 32, 42, 31, 36, 37, 47, 23, 39, 31, 41, 38, 30, 34, 29, 42, 37}

Stem	Leaf
2	3 7 9
3	0 1 1 2 4 6 7 7 8 9
4	1 2 2 7

3 | 6 = 36

3.
Major League Baseball Leading Pitchers, 2000	
Player and Team	**Wins**
T. Glavine, Atlanta	21
T. Hudson, Oakland	20
R. Johnson, Arizona	19
D. Kile, St. Louis	20
G. Maddux, Atlanta	19
P. Martinez, Boston	18
C. Park, Los Angeles	18
A. Pettite, New York Y.	19
A. Sele, Seattle	17
D. Wells, Toronto	20

Source: World Almanac

Stem	Leaf
1	7 8 8 9 9 9
2	0 0 0 1

2 | 0 = 20

4.
Average Prices Received by U.S. Farmers, 1999	
Commodity	**Price (dollars per 100 pounds)**
Beef Cattle	63
Hogs	30
Lambs	75
Milk	15
Sheep	31
Veal Calves	88

Source: World Almanac

Stem	Leaf
1	5
2	
3	0 1
4	
5	
6	3
7	5
8	8

6 | 3 = $63 per 100 lbs

RECREATION For Exercises 5–7, use the information in the back-to-back stem-and-leaf plot shown at the right.

Total U.S. Spending on Personal Recreation (by Category)

1992	Stem	1998
7 5 5	0	7 8 9
8 7 2 0	1	5 7
7 2	2	4 6
4 0	3	2
	4	
	5	
1	6	6 8
	7	
	8	
	9	3

7 | 2 = $27 billion   2 | 4 = $24 billion

5. The category with the lowest total expenditure in 1992 was motion pictures. What was its total? **$5 billion**

6. What is the median total recreational spending for 1992? For 1998? **$17.5 billion; $26 billion**

7. Compare the total spending on recreation in 1992 with that in 1998. In general, spending on recreation increases between 1992 and 1998.

Enrichment, p. 671

Statistical Graphs

Bar graphs and pictographs are used to compare quantities. Line graphs are used to show changes. Circle graphs compare parts to parts, or parts to the whole.

Solve. Use the pictograph.

Principal Languages of the World (to nearest fifty million)

English	☆☆☆☆
Hindi	☆☆⟨
Arabic	☆⟨
Portuguese	☆⟨
Chinese	☆☆☆☆☆☆☆⟨
Russian	☆☆⟨
Spanish	☆☆⟨
French	☆
Bengali	☆⟨

☆ = 100 million

1. How many people speak Portuguese? **150,000,000**

2. What is the ratio of people who speak Spanish to those who speak Russian? **1:1**

3. What three languages are each spoken by about 150 million people? **Arabic, Portuguese, Bengali**

4. How many fewer people speak Arabic than Hindi? **100,000,000**

Solve. Use the circle graph.

Population by Continent

Australia 0.3%, Europe 15.1%, North Am. 8.3%, South Am. 5.5%, Africa 10.9%, Asia 59.7%

5. Which continent has the smallest population? **Australia**

6. How does the population of South America compare to that of Africa? **South America has about half as many people.**

7. What is the population of Australia if the world's population is about 6 billion? **about 18,000,000**

Solve. Use the line graph.

Price Received by Farmers for One Dozen Eggs

8. During which ten-year period was the increase in the price of eggs greatest? **1940–1950**

9. What was the price of a dozen eggs in 1940? **16¢**

10. What was the percent of increase in the price of eggs from 1940 to 1950? **about 220–240%**

11. What was the increase in cents from 1930 to 1980? **about 32¢**

HEALTH For Exercises 18–21, use the graphic shown.

18. Display the data in a stem-and-leaf plot. **See margin.**

19. What is the greatest percent of people who exercise daily? **35%**

20. In how many of the cities do fewer than 30% of the people exercise daily? **5**

21. Write a sentence that describes the data. **See margin.**

BASKETBALL For Exercises 22–25, use the information shown in the back-to-back stem-and-leaf plot. **Source: USA TODAY**

NCAA Woman's Basketball Statistics
Overall Games Won, 2000–2001

Big Ten Conference		Big East Conference
8 4	0	5 8 9 9
9 8 8 7 7 6 4 0	1	2 2 3 5 6 9 9
4	2	0 4 5

8 | 1 = 18 wins   1 | 5 = 15 wins

22. What is the greatest number of games won by a Big Ten Conference team? **24**

23. What is the least number of games won by a Big East Conference team? **5**

24. How many teams are in the Big East Conference? **14**

25. Compare the average number of games won by each conference. **See margin.**

RESEARCH For Exercises 26 and 27, use the Internet, a newspaper, or another reference source to gather data about a topic that interests you.

26. Make a stem-and-leaf plot of the data. **26–27. See students' work.**

27. Write a sentence that describes the data.

28. **WRITING IN MATH** Answer the question that was posed at the beginning of the lesson. **See pp. 665A–665F.**

How can stem-and-leaf plots help you understand an election?

Include the following in your answer:

- a stem-and-leaf plot that displays the number of electors for each state and the District of Columbia,
- a statement describing how the data in the stem-and-leaf plot are distributed, and
- an explanation telling how a presidential candidate might use the display.

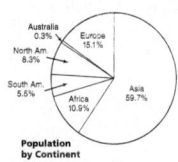

Answers

18.
Stem	Leaf
2	7 7 7 8 8
3	0 1 2 5

3 | 1 = 31

21. **Sample answer:** In the most populated U.S. cities, about 27 to 35% of the people exercise daily.

25. The average number of games won by the teams in the Big East Conference is less than the average number of games won by the teams in the Big Ten Conference.

29. CRITICAL THINKING Suppose you have a table and a stem-and-leaf plot that display the same data. **See margin.**

a. For which display is it easier to find the median? Explain.

b. For which display is it easier to find the mean? Explain.

c. For which display is it easier to find the mode? Explain.

Standardized Test Practice

30. What are the stems for the data {13, 34, 37, 25, 25, 35, 52, 28}? **B**

Ⓐ {2, 3, 4, 5, 7, 8}　　　Ⓑ {1, 2, 3, 4, 5}

Ⓒ {1, 2, 3, 5, 6}　　　Ⓓ {0, 1, 2, 3, 5}

31. The back-to-back stem-and-leaf plot shows the amount of protein in certain foods. Which of the following is a true statement? **C**

Amount of Protein (g)

Dairy Products		Legumes, Nuts, Seeds
9 8 8 7 7 5 2 2	0	5 6 9
0	1	4 5 8
6	2	
	3	9

6 | 2 = 26 grams　　　3 | 9 = 39 grams

Source: *The World Almanac*

Ⓐ The median amount of protein in dairy products is 9 grams.

Ⓑ The difference between the greatest and least amount of protein in dairy products is 28 grams.

Ⓒ The average amount of protein in legumes, nuts, and seeds is more than the average amount in dairy products.

Ⓓ The greatest amount of protein in legumes, nuts, and seeds is 93 grams.

Maintain Your Skills

Mixed Review **32.** A triangle has sides that measure 12.38 inches, 7.5 inches, and 6.185 inches. Find the perimeter of the triangle using the correct number of significant digits. *(Lesson 11-7)* **26.1 in.**

Determine whether each pair of solids is similar. *(Lesson 11-6)*

33.
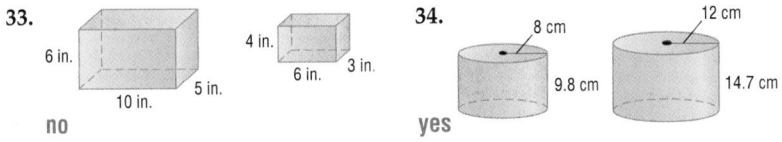
6 in. 10 in. 5 in.　4 in. 6 in. 3 in.
no

34. 8 cm 9.8 cm　12 cm 14.7 cm
yes

35. Find the circumference and area of a circle with a radius of 10 feet. Round to the nearest tenth. *(Lesson 10-7)* **62.8 ft; 314.2 ft²**

Express each decimal or fraction as a percent. Round to the nearest tenth percent, if necessary. *(Lesson 6-4)*

36. 0.36 **36%**　　**37.** 2.47 **247%**　　**38.** 0.019 **1.9%**　　**39.** 0.0065 **0.65%**

40. $\frac{6}{25}$ **24%**　　**41.** $\frac{4}{7}$ **57.1%**　　**42.** $\frac{15}{8}$ **187.5%**　　**43.** $\frac{24}{1500}$ **1.6%**

Getting Ready for the Next Lesson **PREREQUISITE SKILL** Find the median for each set of data. If necessary, round to the nearest tenth. *(To review median, see Lesson 5-8.)* **47. 1.1**

44. 23, 45, 21, 35, 28 **28**　　　**45.** 18, 9, 2, 4, 6, 15, 13, 6, 1 **6**

46. 78, 54, 50, 64, 39, 45 **52**　　　**47.** 0.4, 1.3, 0.8, 2.6, 0.3, 1.8, 0.2, 2.1

Open-Ended Assessment

Speaking Have students list the prices of various items sold in the school cafeteria. Ask them to describe what a stem-and-leaf plot of these data would look like and what the plot can tell them about cafeteria prices.

Getting Ready for Lesson 12-2

PREREQUISITE SKILL In Lesson 12-2, students will learn how to find the upper and lower quartiles of a set of data as well as the median. Use Exercises 44–47 to determine your students' familiarity with finding the median.

Answer

29a. Sample answer: It would be easier to find the median in a stem-and-leaf plot because the data are arranged in order from least to greatest.

29b. Sample answer: It would be easier to find the mean in a table because once you find the sum, it may be easier to count the number of items in a table.

29c. Sample answer: It would be easier to find the mode in a stem-and-leaf plot because the value or values that occur most often are grouped together.

DAILY INTERVENTION

Differentiated Instruction

• **Visual/Spatial** Have each student find the average daily temperatures of a city, rounded to the nearest degree. Tell students to write the last digit of each temperature on one side of an index card and the first digit(s) on the other in a different color. Have students sort cards by stem and then write each stem on the board. Have students complete the stem-and-leaf plot by taping each leaf into place.

12-2 Measures of Variation

1 Focus

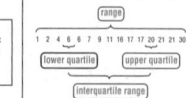

5-Minute Check Transparency 12-2 Use as a quiz or review of Lesson 12-1.

Mathematical Background notes are available for this lesson on page 604C.

Why are measures of variation important in interpreting data?

The opening activity questions are repeated on page 675 of the *Chapter 12 Resource Masters*.

Reading to Learn Mathematics, p. 675 — ELL

Pre-Activity *Why are measures of variation important in interpreting data?*

Do the activity at the top of page 612 in your textbook. Write your answers below.

a. What is the fastest speed? 173 mph
b. What is the slowest speed? 142 mph
c. Find the difference between these two speeds. 31 mph
d. Write a sentence comparing the fastest winning average speed and the slowest winning average speed. The fastest winning average speed and the slowest winning average speed are within 31 miles per hour of each other.

Reading the Lesson 1–6. See students' work.

Write a definition and give an example of each new vocabulary word or phrase.

Vocabulary	Definition	Example
1. measures of variation		
2. range		
3. quartiles		
4. lower quartile		
5. upper quartile		
6. interquartile range		

Helping You Remember

7. Complete the following diagram by filling in the boxes with the appropriate vocabulary words.

Diagram Title: Measures of Variation

range
1 2 4 6 9 11 16 17 20 21 30
lower quartile   upper quartile
interquartile range

12-2 Measures of Variation

What You'll Learn

* Find measures of variation.
* Use measures of variation to interpret and compare data.

Why are measures of variation important in interpreting data?

The race that attracts the largest audience in auto racing is the Daytona 500. The average speed of each winning car from 1990 to 2001 is shown.

Vocabulary
* measures of variation
* range
* quartiles
* lower quartile
* upper quartile
* interquartile range

Car Driver	Speed (mph)	Car Driver	Speed (mph)
Derrike Cope	166	Dale Jarrett	154
Ernie Irvan	148	Jeff Gordon	148
Davey Allison	160	Dale Earnhardt	173
Dale Jarrett	155	Jeff Gordon	162
Sterling Marlin	157	Dale Jarrett	156
Sterling Marlin	142	Michael Waltrip	162

Source: *The World Almanac*

a. What is the fastest speed? **173 mph**
b. What is the slowest speed? **142 mph**
c. Find the difference between these two speeds. **31 mph**
d. Write a sentence comparing the fastest winning average speed and the slowest winning average speed.

d. The fastest winning average speed and the slowest winning average speed are within 31 miles per hour of each other.

MEASURES OF VARIATION In statistics, **measures of variation** are used to describe the distribution of the data. One measure of variation is the range. The **range** of a set of data is the difference between the greatest and the least values of the set. It describes how a set of data varies.

Example 1 Range

Find the range of each set of data.

a. {5, 11, 16, 8, 4, 7, 15, 6}

The greatest value is 16, and the least value is 4.
So, the range is $16 - 4$ or 12.

b.
Stem	Leaf
5	4 4 4 4 6 6 8 9
6	1
7	7

$6 \mid 1 = 61$

The greatest value is 77, and the least value is 54.
So, the range is $77 - 54$ or 23.

Resource Manager

📂 Workbooks and Reproducible Masters

Chapter 12 Resource Masters
* Study Guide and Intervention, p. 672
* Skills Practice, p. 673
* Practice, p. 674
* Reading to Learn Mathematics, p. 675
* Enrichment, p. 676

Parent and Student Study Guide Workbook, p. 99

Transparencies

5-Minute Check Transparency 12-2
Answer Key Transparencies

Technology

Interactive Chalkboard

In a set of data, the **quartiles** are the values that divide the data into four equal parts. Recall that the median of a set of data separates the set in half.

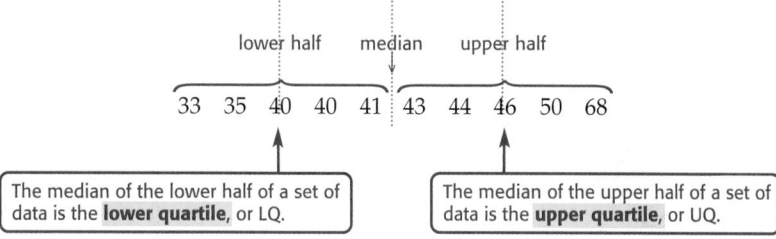

lower half   median   upper half

33   35   40   40   41   43   44   46   50   68

The median of the lower half of a set of data is the **lower quartile**, or LQ.

The median of the upper half of a set of data is the **upper quartile**, or UQ.

✓ **Concept Check**   Into how many parts do the quartiles divide a set of data?   **4**

The upper and lower quartiles can be used to find another measure of variation called the **interquartile range**.

Key Concept   Interquartile Range

- **Words**   The interquartile range is the range of the middle half of a set of data. It is the difference between the upper quartile and the lower quartile.

- **Symbols**   Interquartile range = UQ − LQ

Example 2   Interquartile Range

Find the interquartile range for each set of data.

a. {27, 37, 21, 54, 47, 35}

Step 1   List the data from least to greatest. Then find the median.

21   27   35   37   47   54

$$\text{median} = \frac{35 + 37}{2} \text{ or } 36$$

Step 2   Find the upper and lower quartiles.

lower half   upper half

21   27   35   37   47   54

LQ   median   UQ

The interquartile range is 47 − 27 or 20.

b. {7, 12, 3, 2, 11, 9, 6, 4, 8}

Step 1   List the data from least to greatest. Then find the median.

2   3   4   6   7   8   9   11   12

median

Step 2   Find the upper and lower quartiles.

lower half   upper half

2   3   4   6   7   8   9   11   12

median

The interquartile range is 10 − 3.5 or 6.5.

$$LQ = \frac{3 + 4}{2} \text{ or } 3.5 \qquad UQ = \frac{9 + 11}{2} \text{ or } 10$$

Lesson 12-2   Measures of Variation   **613**

2 Teach

MEASURES OF VARIATION

In-Class Examples   Power Point®

1 Find the range of each set of data.

a. {$79, $42, $38, $51, $63, $91}
$53

b.

Stem	Leaf	
3	3 3 5 7 7 8	**26**
4	0 3 3 4 9	
5	4 9	

3 | 5 = 35

2 Find the interquartile range for each set of data.

a. {38, 40, 32, 34, 36, 45, 33}   **7**

b. {2, 27, 17, 14, 14, 22, 15, 32, 24, 25}   **11**

Teaching Tip   Point out that with an odd number of data, the median is the middle number and should be excluded from both halves. With an even number of data, the median falls between the two middle values and no data point is eliminated.

Lesson 12-2   Measures of Variation   **613**

USE MEASURES OF VARIATION

Power Point®

3 **LAND USE** The urban land in certain western and eastern states is listed below as the percent of each state's total land, rounded to the nearest percent.

Western States		Eastern States
1 1 1 1 1 0 0	0	
3 2 2 2 1 1 1	0	3 3 4 5 6 6 8
5 4 4	0	8 9 9 9 9 9 9
	1	1 3 3 4 4 5
	2	3 6 7
2|0 = 2%	3	5 2|7 = 27%

Source: U.S. Census Bureau

a. What is the median percent of urban land use for each region?
western: 1%; eastern: 9%

b. Compare the range for each set of data.   **western: 5%; eastern: 32%; The percents of urban land use in the East vary more.**

3 Practice/Apply

Study Notebook

Have students—

• add the definitions/examples of the vocabulary terms to their Vocabulary Builder worksheets for Chapter 12.

• include any other item(s) that they find helpful in mastering the skills in this lesson.

More About . . .

SPEED LIMIT 75

Traffic Laws

In 1974, the national speed limit was 55 mph. Today, the speed limits for the 50 states range from 55 to 75 mph.
Source: www.infoplease.com

USE MEASURES OF VARIATION   You can use measures of variation to interpret and compare data.

Example 3 *Interpret and Compare Data*

TRAFFIC LAWS   The maximum allowable speed limits for certain western and eastern states are listed in the stem-and-leaf plot.

Western States		Eastern States
5	5	
5 5	6	5 5 5 5 5 5 5 5 5
5 5 5 5 5 5 5 5 0 0	7	0 0 0

0\|7 = 70 mph   6\|5 = 65 mph
Source: www.infoplease.com

a. What is the median speed limit for each region?
The median speed limit for the western states is 75.
The median speed limit for the eastern states is 65.

b. Compare the western states' range with the eastern states' range.
The range for the east is 70 − 65 or 5 mph, and the range for the west is 75 − 55 or 20 mph. So, the speed limits in the west vary more.

Check for Understanding

Concept Check

1. **Explain** how the range of a set of data differs from the interquartile range of a set of data. **1–3. See pp. 665A–665F.**

2. **Define** *upper quartile* and *lower quartile.*

3. **OPEN ENDED**   Write a list of at least 12 numbers that has an interquartile range of ten.

Guided Practice

Find the range and interquartile range for each set of data.

4. {26, 48, 12, 32, 41, 35} **36; 15**

5.
Stem	Leaf	**27; 6**
7	2 3 6 6 9	
8	0 0 1	
9	9	

GUIDED PRACTICE KEY	
Exercises	Examples
4, 5	1, 2
6–8	3

Application

SCIENCE   For Exercises 6–8, use the information in the table.

6. Which planet's day length divides the data in half? **Earth**

7. What is the median length of day for the planets? **24 h**

8. Write a sentence describing how the lengths of days vary. **See pp. 665A–665F.**

Planet	Length of Day* (Earth hours)
Mercury	1416
Venus	5832
Earth	24
Mars	25
Jupiter	10
Saturn	11
Uranus	17
Neptune	16
Pluto	154

*The lengths are approximate.
Source: *The World Almanac*

About the Exercises . . .

Organization by Objective
• Measures of Variation: 9–17, 19
• Use Measures of Variation: 17–20

Odd/Even Assignments
Exercises 9–16 are structured so that students practice the same concepts whether they are assigned odd or even problems.

Assignment Guide

Basic: 9–15 odd, 17, 18, 21–33

Average: 9–15 odd, 17–33

Advanced: 10–16 even, 17–29 (Optional: 30–33)

Practice and Apply

Homework Help

For Exercises	See Examples
9–16	1, 2
17–20	3

Extra Practice
See page 753.

Find the range and interquartile range for each set of data.

9. {65, 64, 73, 34, 15, 43, 92} **77; 39**   10. {9, 13, 25, 9, 1, 5, 6, 8} **24; 5.5**

11. {68°, 74°, 65°, 55°, 75°, 82°, 32°, 69°, 70°, 77°} **50; 10**

12. {$25, $21, $55, $43, $10, $89, $39, $91, $44, $76, $58} **81; 51**

13.

Stem	Leaf	**25; 15.5**
0	1 2 2 5	
1	3 4 7 8 9 9 9	
2	6 6	

2|6 = 26

14.

Stem	Leaf	**29; 11.5**
4	0	
5	0 1 1 5 7 7 7 8	
6	7 7 9	

5|7 = 57

15. Find the interquartile range for {213, 226, 204, 215, 210, 362, 119}. **22**

16. Determine the range of the middle half of the data set {30.2, 29.3, 35.3, 30.1, 28.5, 31.6, 27.5, 21.2}. **2.9**

WEATHER   For Exercises 17 and 18, use the data in the table.

Average Temperature (°F)					
City	Feb.	July	City	Feb.	July
Asheville, NC	39	73	Louisville, KY	36	77
Atlanta, GA	45	79	Oklahoma City, OK	41	82
Birmingham, AL	46	80	Portland, OR	44	68
Fresno, CA	51	82	Syracuse, NY	24	70
Houston, TX	54	83	Tampa, FL	62	82
Indianapolis, IN	30	75	Washington, DC	34	76
Little Rock, AR	44	82			

Source: *The World Almanac*

17. Find the interquartile range for each month's set of data. **Feb.: 13.5; July: 8**

18. Which month has more consistent temperatures? Justify your answer.
Sample answer: July; the temperatures are more tightly clustered around the median.

★ **BASEBALL**   For Exercises 19 and 20, use the data in the stem-and-leaf plot.

Home Runs Hit by League Leaders, 1960–2001

National League		American League
	2	2
9 9 8 8 8 7 7 7 6 6 6 5 1	3	2 2 2 2 3 6 6 7 9 9 9
4 4 4 3 1 0 0 0 0 0	4	0 0 0 0 1 2 3 3 4 4 4 4
9 9 9 8 8 8 7 7 7 6 6 5 5	4	5 5 6 6 7 8 8 9 9 9 9
2 2 0	5	0 1 2 2 6 6
5	6	1
3 0	7	

7|4 = 47 home runs   5|6 = 56 home runs

Source: *The World Almanac*

9. National League:
2, 44, 48, 38, 10
American League: 39,
4, 49, 39, 10

19. Find the range, median, upper quartile, lower quartile, and the interquartile range for each set of data.

20. Write a few sentences that compare the data. **See pp. 665A–665F.**

 www.pre-alg.com/self_check_quiz

---

Study Guide and Intervention, p. 672

The range and the interquartile range describe how a set of data varies.

Measures of Variation	
Term	Definition
range	The difference between the greatest and the least values of the set
median	The value that separates the data set in half
lower quartile	The median of the lower half of a set of data
upper quartile	The median of the upper half of a set of data
interquartile range	The difference between the upper quartile and the lower quartile

Example   Find the range and interquartile range for each set of data.

a. {3, 12, 17, 2, 21, 14, 14, 8}

Step 1 List the data from least to greatest. The range is 21 − 2 or 19. Then find the median.

2 3 8 12 14 14 17 21

median = (14 + 12)/2 or 13

Step 2 Find the upper and lower quartiles.

2 3 8 12 14 14 17 21

LQ = (3 + 8)/2   median = (14 + 17)/2
= 5.5   = 15.5

The interquartile range is 15.5 − 5.5 or 10.

b.

Stem	Leaf
2	2 6 9
3	1 1 3 4 9
4	0 2 5 5 7 7 8
5	3 4 6 6

3|4 = 34

The stem-and-leaf plot displays the data in order. The greatest value is 56. The least value is 22. So, the range is 56 − 22 or 34.

The median is 42. The LQ is 31 and the UQ is 48. So, the interquartile range is 48 − 31 or 17.

Exercises

WEATHER   For Exercises 1 and 2, use the data in the stem-and-leaf plot at the right.

1. Find the range, median, upper quartile, lower quartile, and the interquartile range for each set of data. July lows: range: 30°F; median: 73; UQ: 76; LQ: 59; interquartile range: 17°F; July highs: range: 43°F; median: 83; UQ: 91; LQ: 79; interquartile range: 12°F

2. Write a sentence that compares the data. July highs vary more widely than July lows.

Average Extreme July Temperatures in World Cities

Low Temps.		High Temps.
9 1 1 0	5	
	6	4 7 9
9 8 6 5 5 4 3 0 0	7	9
	8	1 1 3 3 4 8
	9	0 1 2 5
	10	7

0 | 8 = 80°F   7 | 9 = 79°F

Skills Practice, p. 673 and Practice, p. 674 (shown)

Find the range and interquartile range for each set of data.

1. {3, 9, 11, 8, 6, 12, 5, 4} **9; 5.5**   2. {8, 3, 9, 14, 12, 11, 20, 23, 5, 26} **18; 12**

3. {42, 50, 46, 47, 38, 41} **12; 6**   4. {10.3, 9.8, 10.1, 16.2, 18.0, 11.4, 16.0, 15.8} **8.2; 5.9**

5. {107, 82, 93, 112, 120, 95, 98, 86, 109, 110} **38; 17**   6. {106, 103, 112, 109, 115, 118, 113, 108} **15; 7**

7.
Stem	Leaf	**13; 7**
1	7 8	
2	3 5 6 8	
3	0	

19|2 = 192

8.
Stem	Leaf	**21; 12**
5	6 7	
6	0 1 1 4 8 8 9	
7	0 2 3 5 6 7	

6|1 = 61

9.
Stem	Leaf	**39; 26**
4	0 0 0 2 5 7	
5	2 6	
6	1 8 8	
7	0 1 9	

5|2 = 52

10.
Stem	Leaf	**31; 11**
6	4 7 9	
7	9	
8	1 1 3 3 4 6	
9	0 1 2 5	

7|9 = 79

11.
Stem	Leaf	**59; 39.5**
3	0 1 6 8	
4	4	
5	2	
6		
7	3 3	
8	9	

5|2 = 52

12.
Stem	Leaf	**52; 42**
4	3 3 5 7 9	
5	0 0 1	
6	2	
7	4 4 6 8	
8		
9	0 1 1 2 2 5	

5|1 = 51

POPULATION   For Exercises 13–15, use the data in the table at the right.

13. What is the range of populations shown? **13.8 million**

14. What is the interquartile range for the annual growth rate? **1.3%**

15. Where does the city with the fastest growth rate fall in terms of population? The city with the slowest growth rate? **near the median; at the LQ**

Populations of the World's Largest Cities 2000		
City	Population (millions)	Annual Growth Rate (%)
Tokyo, Japan	26.4	0.51
Mexico City, Mexico	18.1	1.81
Mumbai, India	18.1	3.54
Sao Paulo, Brazil	17.8	1.43
New York City, U.S.	16.6	0.37
Lagos, Nigeria	13.4	5.33
Los Angeles, U.S.	13.1	1.15
Calcutta, India	12.9	1.60
Shanghai, China	12.9	−0.35
Buenos Aires, Argentina	12.6	1.14

Source: *World Almanac*

Enrichment, p. 676

Variance

Another way to measure the variation of a set of data is by computing the **variance**. The higher the variance is for a group of numbers, the more "spread out" the data will be.

The table below shows the price of the stock for two companies during one week.

	Monday	Tuesday	Wednesday	Thursday	Friday
Acme Computer Systems	$10	$7	$3	$8	$12
Baker Pencil Company	$7	$8	$7	$9	$9

1. What is the mean average price for the week for each company? **$8 for both companies**

Computing the variance will show which company's stock has the greater variation. To compute the variance, follow these steps:

Step 1 Subtract the mean from each number in the set.
Step 2 Multiply each difference in step 1 by itself.
Step 3 Add these differences.
Step 4 Divide the total by the number of members of the set.

Example   Find the variance for Acme Computer Systems.

$(10 - 8) \times (10 - 8) + (7 - 8) \times (7 - 8) + (3 - 8) \times (3 - 8) + (8 - 8) \times (8 - 8) + (12 - 8) \times (12 - 8)$

4   +   1   +   25   +   0   +   16   = 46

The variance is 46 ÷ 5, or 9.2.

Solve.

2. Do you think the variance for Baker Pencil Company will be higher than the variance for Acme Computer Systems? Why? Compute the variance for Baker Pencil Company to see whether you are correct. **No; the prices are closer together; 0.8**

3. Consolidated Airlines also had an average price last week of $8 per share, but its variance was 10.8. Indicate five stock prices that could produce this variance. (*Hint:* Change only the Monday and Tuesday prices for Acme.) Answers may vary. Sample answer: **$11, $6, $3, $8, $12**

4. Sleepy Mattress Company's stock had an average price last week of $8 per share and a variance of 0. What was the price of shares each day last week? **$8 each day**

5. Are there any values that the variance cannot equal? If so, what are these values? **yes; values less than zero**

Teacher to Teacher

Diana L. Boyle   Judson M.S., Salem, OR

"To help my students understand how variations can affect data, I give them two sets of data (such as test scores for two students) that have the same range but very different scores. We use these two sets of data throughout the chapter to explore each of the various aspects of data analysis and finally display the data in a box-and-whisker plot to see the differences."

Open-Ended Assessment

Modeling Have students make a list of 27 randomly selected numbers and write them in numerical order in a column on notebook paper, one number per line. They should cut out the strip that contains the numbers, fold the strip in half to find the median, and in half again to find the lower and upper quartiles. Have them compare these results with the computed results for the data.

Getting Ready for Lesson 12-3

PREREQUISITE SKILL Lesson 12-3 presents box-and-whisker plots, for which they must organize data, often in decimal form. Exercises 30–33 should be used to determine your students' familiarity with ordering decimals.

Answers

21a–c. Sample answers are given.

21a. {43, 49, 50, 50, 58, 60, 60, 66, 70, 70, 71, 78}

21b. {15, 18, 20, 20, 44, 60, 60, 64, 70, 70, 75, 79}

21c. The first set of data has a smaller interquartile range, thus the data in the first set are more tightly clustered around the median and the data in the second are more spread out over the range.

22. They allow us to see how the data are distributed. Answers should include the following.
- 156.5; 31; 11
- The average speed was 156.5 miles per hour. The speeds varied by 31 miles per hour. The speeds of the cars in the middle of the data set are close in value.

21a–c. See margin.

21. CRITICAL THINKING Write a set of data that satisfies each condition.
   a. 12 pieces of data, a median of 60, an interquartile range of 20
   b. 12 pieces of data, a median of 60, an interquartile range of 50
   c. Compare the measures of variation for each set of data in parts **a** and **b**. What conclusions can be drawn about the sets of data?

22. WRITING IN MATH   Answer the question that was posed at the beginning of the lesson. **See margin.**

   Why are measures of variation important in interpreting data?

   Include the following in your answer:
   - the median, range, and interquartile range for the set of data, and
   - an explanation telling what the median, range, and interquartile range convey about the speeds of the winning cars.

Standardized Test Practice

23. Find the median for the set {43, 49, 91, 42, 94, 73, 93, 67, 55, 54, 78, 82}. **C**
   (A) 68   (B) 52   (C) 70   (D) 83

24. Which sentence best describes the data shown in the table? **B**

Height (ft) of Mountains in Alaska and Colorado					
Colorado			**Alaska**		
14,238	14,433	14,309	14,163	14,410	20,320
14,083	14,264	14,197	16,550	14,530	14,831
14,269	14,196	14,150	17,400	16,237	14,070
14,165	14,420	14,246	15,885	14,573	16,390
14,286	14,265	14,361	15,638	14,730	16,286

Source: The World Almanac

   (A) The heights of the mountains in Alaska vary by 6200 feet.
   (B) The heights of the mountains in Colorado are clustered around the median height.
   (C) The median height of a mountain in Alaska is 16,000 feet.
   (D) The heights of the mountains in Colorado tend to be less consistent than the heights of the mountains in Alaska.

Maintain Your Skills

Mixed Review

25. Display the data set {$12, $15, $18, $21, $14, $37, $27, $9} in a stem-and-leaf plot. *(Lesson 12-1)* **See pp. 665A–665F.**

26. Calculate 27.08 mm + 6.5 mm. Round to the correct number of significant digits. *(Lesson 11-7)* **33.6 mm**

Find the volume of each cone described. Round to the nearest tenth.
(Lesson 11-3) **28. 120.1 yd³**

27. radius 7 cm, height 9 cm **461.8 cm³**   **28.** diameter 8.4 yd, height 6.5 yd

29. The circumference of a circle is 9.82 feet. Find the radius of the circle to the nearest tenth. *(Lesson 10-7)* **1.6 ft**

Getting Ready for the Next Lesson

PREREQUISITE SKILL   Order each set of decimals from least to greatest.
(To review ordering decimals, see page 710.) **30–33. See pp. 665A–665F.**

30. 5.6, 5.3, 4.8, 4.3, 5.0, 4.9   **31.** 0.3, 1.4, 0.6, 1.5, 0.2, 0.8, 1.2

32. 45.2, 50.7, 46.0, 45.4, 40.6   **33.** 10.9, 11.4, 9.8, 10.5, 11.2, 9.9

DAILY INTERVENTION   **Unlocking Misconceptions**

- **Measures of Variation** Some students may mistakenly try to find the quartiles by dividing the range into four equal sections. Stress that *quartile* refers to quarters of the number of items, not quarters of the range.

What You'll Learn

- Display data in a box-and-whisker plot.
- Interpret data in a box-and-whisker plot.

How can box-and-whisker plots help you interpret data?

The table shows the average monthly temperatures for two cities.

Average Monthly Temperatures (°F)

	J	F	M	A	M	J	J	A	S	O	N	D
Tampa, FL	60	62	67	71	77	81	82	82	81	75	68	62
Caribou, ME	9	12	25	38	51	61	66	63	54	43	31	15

a. Find the low, high, and the median temperature, and the upper and lower quartile for each city.

b. Draw a number line extending from 0 to 85. Label every 5 units.

c. About one-half inch above the number line, plot the data found in part **a** for Tampa. About three-fourths inch above the number line, plot the data for Caribou.

d. Write a few sentences comparing the average monthly temperatures.

Vocabulary

- box-and-whisker plot

a. Tampa: 60, 82, 73, 81, 64.5; Caribou: 9, 66, 40.5, 57.5, 20
b–d. See margin.

Study Tip

Common Misconception
You may think that the median always divides the box in half. However, the median may not divide the box in half because the data may be clustered toward one quartile.

DISPLAY DATA A **box-and-whisker plot** divides a set of data into four parts using the median and quartiles. A *box* is drawn around the quartile values, and *whiskers* extend from each quartile to the extreme data points.

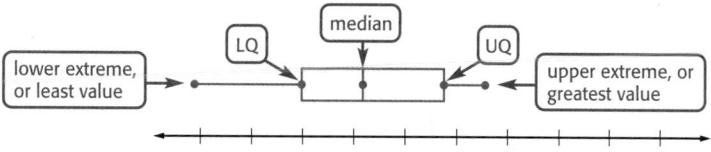

Example 1 Draw a Box-and-Whisker Plot

GEOGRAPHY The amount of coastline for states along the Atlantic Coast is shown. Display the data in a box-and-whisker plot.

Atlantic Coast Coastline

State	Amount (mi)	State	Amount (mi)
Delaware	28	New Jersey	130
Florida	580	New York	127
Georgia	100	North Carolina	301
Maine	228	Rhode Island	40
Maryland	31	South Carolina	187
Massachusetts	192	Virginia	112
New Hampshire	13		

Source: www.infoplease.com

(continued on the next page)

---

1 Focus

5-Minute Check Transparency 12-3 Use as a quiz or review of Lesson 12-2.

Mathematical Background notes are available for this lesson on page 604C.

How can box-and-whisker plots help you interpret data?

The opening activity questions are repeated on page 680 of the *Chapter 12 Resource Masters*.

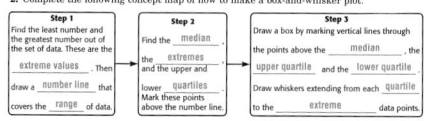

Reading to Learn Mathematics, p. 680 **ELL**

Pre-Activity How can box-and-whisker plots help you interpret data?

Do the activity at the top of page 617 in your textbook. Write your answers below.

a. Find the low, high, and the median temperature, and the upper and lower quartile for each city.

	Low	LQ	Median	UQ	High
Tampa, FL	60	64.5	73	81	82
Caribou, ME	9	20	40.5	57.5	66

b. Draw a number line extending from 0 to 85. Label every 5 units.

c. About one-half inch above the number line, plot the data found in part **a** for Tampa. About three-fourths inch above the number line, plot the data for Caribou.

d. Write a few sentences comparing the average monthly temperatures. Sample answer: The average monthly temperatures vary greatly in Caribou, ME, whereas the average monthly temperatures in Tampa, FL, are more consistent.

Reading the Lesson

Write a definition and give an example for the new vocabulary phrase.

Vocabulary	Definition	Example
1. box-and-whisker plot	See students' work.	

Helping You Remember

2. Complete the following concept map of how to make a box-and-whisker plot.

Step 1 Find the least number and the greatest number out of the set of data. These are the *extreme values*. Then draw a *number line* that covers the *range* of data.

Step 2 Find the *median*, the *extremes* and the upper and lower *quartiles*. Mark these points above the number line.

Step 3 Draw a box by marking vertical lines through the points above the *median*, the *upper quartile* and the *lower quartile*. Draw whiskers extending from each *quartile* to the *extreme* data points.

Resource Manager

Transparencies

5-Minute Check Transparency 12-3
Answer Key Transparencies

Technology

Interactive Chalkboard

DISPLAY DATA

In-Class Example Power Point®

1 **JOBS** The projected number of employees in 2008 in the fastest-growing occupations is shown in the table in the bottom margin. Display the data in a box-and-whisker plot.

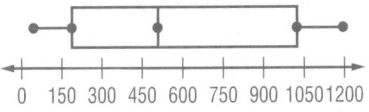

INTERPRET BOX-AND-WHISKER PLOTS

In-Class Example Power Point®

2 **WEATHER** The box-and-whisker plot below shows the average percent of sunny days per year for selected cities in each state.

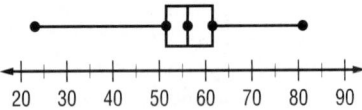

a. What is the smallest percent of sunny days in any state?
23%

b. Half of the selected cities have an average of sunny days under what percent?
56%

c. What does the length of the box in the box-and-whisker plot tell about the data? **The length of the box in the box-and-whisker plot is short. This tells us that the values of the data are clustered together.**

Step 1 Find the least and greatest number. Then draw a number line that covers the range of the data.

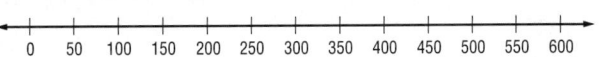

Step 2 Find the median, the extremes, and the upper and lower quartiles. Mark these points above the number line.

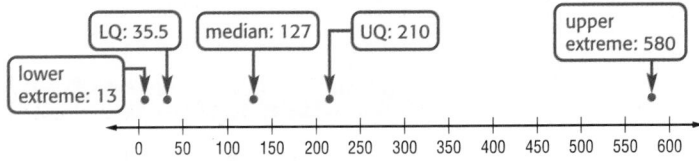

Step 3 Draw a box and the whiskers.

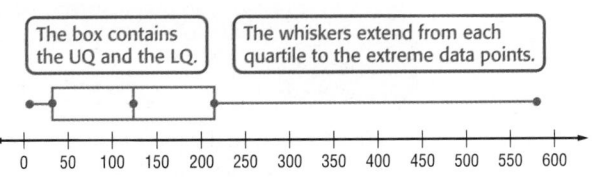

✓ **Concept Check** What are the extreme values of a set of data?
the highest and lowest values

INTERPRET BOX-AND-WHISKER PLOTS Box-and-whisker plots separate data into four parts. Even though the parts may differ in length, each part contains 25% of the data.

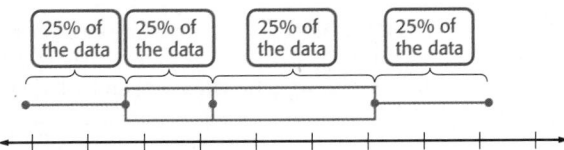

Data displayed in a box-and-whisker plot can be easily interpreted.

Example 2 *Interpret Data*

EDUCATION Refer to the information shown below.

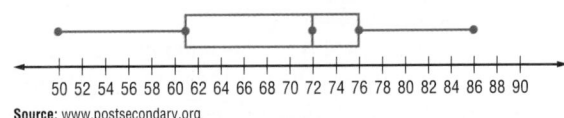

Source: www.postsecondary.org

a. **What is the smallest percent of students graduating in any state?**
The smallest percent of students graduating in any state is 50%.

b. **Half of the states have a graduation rate under what percent?**
Half of the states have graduation rates under 72%.

c. **What does the length of the box-and-whisker plot tell about the data?**
The length of the box-and-whisker plot is long. This tells us that the values of the data are spread out.

Study Tip

Box-and-Whisker Plots
If the length of the whisker or box is short, the values of the data in that part are concentrated. If the length of the whisker or box is long, the values of the data in that part are spread out.

Fastest-Growing Jobs			
Occupation	**Jobs (1000s)**	**Occupation**	**Jobs (1000s)**
Computer Engineer	622	Desktop Publishing	44
Computer Support	869	Paralegal/Legal Assistant	220
Systems Analyst	1194	Home Health Aide	1179
Database Administrator	155	Medical Assistant	398

Source: U.S. Census Bureau

Double box-and-whisker plots can be used to compare two sets of data. Notice that one number line is used to display both plots.

Example 3 Compare Two Sets of Data

ANIMALS The weight, in pounds, for Asiatic black bears and pandas is displayed below. How do the weights of Asiatic black bears compare to pandas?

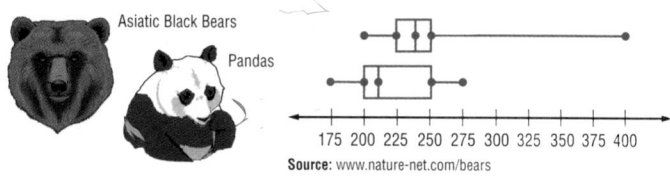

Asiatic Black Bears

Pandas

175 200 225 250 275 300 325 350 375 400

Source: www.nature-net.com/bears

Most Asiatic black bears weigh between 225 and 250 pounds. However, some weigh as much as 400 pounds. Most pandas weigh between 200 and 250 pounds. However, some weigh up to 275 pounds. Thus, the weights of the Asiatic black bears vary more than pandas.

Check for Understanding

Concept Check
–3. See margin.

1. **Tell** which points the two whiskers of a box plot connect.

2. **Explain** how a box-and-whisker plot separates a set of data.

3. **OPEN ENDED** Write a set of data that, when displayed in a box-and-whisker plot, will result in a long box and short whiskers.

Guided Practice Draw a box-and-whisker plot for each set of data. 4–5. See margin.

4. 25, 30, 27, 35, 19, 23, 25, 22, 40, 34, 20

5. $15, $22, $29, $30, $32, $50, $26, $22, $36, $31

Applications

OLYMPICS For Exercises 6 and 7, use the data shown in the table.

GUIDED PRACTICE KEY	
Exercises	Examples
4–6	1
7	2
8, 9	3

Summer Olympic Games 1924–2000
Winning Times for Men's Marathon

Year	1924	1928	1932	1936	1948	1952	1956	1960	1964
Time (min)	161	153	152	149	155	143	145	135	132
Year	1968	1972	1976	1980	1984	1988	1992	1996	2000
Time (min)	140	132	130	131	129	131	133	133	130

Source: *The ESPN Sports Almanac*

6. Make a box-and-whisker plot for the data. 6–7. See pp. 665A–665F.

7. Write a sentence describing what the length of the box-and-whisker plot tells about the winning times for the men's marathon.

www.pre-alg.com/extra_examples

Lesson 12-3 Box-and-Whisker Plots **619**

DAILY INTERVENTION

Differentiated Instruction

- **Logical** Have students work backward to better understand box-and-whisker plots. Have students create a data set for each plot described.
  - **a.** The box is very short.
  - **b.** The box is very long.
  - **c.** The whiskers are very short.
  - **d.** The whiskers are very long.
  - **e.** The box is very short, and the left whisker is longer than the right whisker.

  Have students compare their data.

In-Class Example Power Point®

3 TREES The average maximum height, in feet, for selected evergreen trees and deciduous trees is displayed. How do the heights of evergreen trees compare with the heights of deciduous trees?

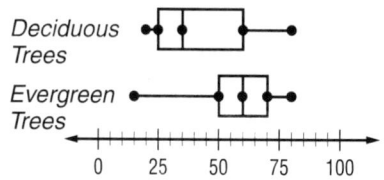

Deciduous Trees

Evergreen Trees

0 25 50 75 100

Source: ohioline.osu.edu

Most evergreen trees are taller than most deciduous trees.

3 Practice/Apply

Study Notebook

Have students—
- add the definition/example of the vocabulary term to their Vocabulary Builder Worksheets for Chapter 12.
- copy the box-and-whisker plot and its labels from p. 617 into their notebooks.
- include any other item(s) that they find helpful in mastering the skills in this lesson.

Answers

1. lower quartile, least value; upper quartile, greatest value

2. into fourths

3. Sample answer: {28, 30, 52, 68, 90, 92}

4.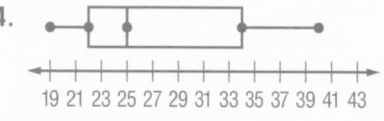

19 21 23 25 27 29 31 33 35 37 39 41 43

5.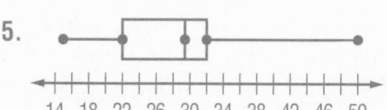

14 18 22 26 30 34 38 42 46 50

Study Guide and Intervention, p. 677

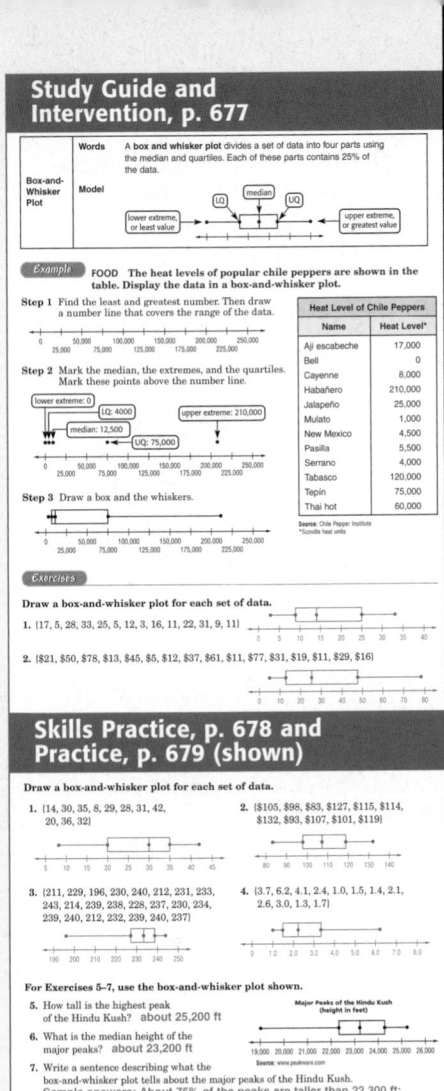

Words	A **box and whisker plot** divides a set of data into four parts using the median and quartiles. Each of these parts contains 25% of the data.

Box-and-Whisker Plot — Model

Example FOOD The heat levels of popular chile peppers are shown in the table. Display the data in a box-and-whisker plot.

Step 1 Find the least and greatest number. Then draw a number line that covers the range of the data.

Heat Level of Chile Peppers	
Name	**Heat Level***
Aji escabeche	17,000
Bell	0
Cayenne	8,000
Habañero	210,000
Jalapeño	25,000
Mulato	1,000
New Mexico	4,500
Pasilla	5,500
Serrano	4,000
Tabasco	120,000
Tepin	75,000
Thai hot	60,000

Source: Chile Pepper Institute
*Scoville heat units

Step 2 Mark the median, the extremes, and the quartiles. Mark these points above the number line.

Step 3 Draw a box and the whiskers.

Exercises

Draw a box-and-whisker plot for each set of data.

1. {17, 5, 28, 33, 25, 5, 12, 3, 16, 11, 22, 31, 9, 11}

2. {$21, $50, $78, $13, $45, $5, $12, $37, $61, $11, $77, $31, $19, $11, $29, $16}

Skills Practice, p. 678 and Practice, p. 679 (shown)

Draw a box-and-whisker plot for each set of data.

1. {14, 30, 35, 8, 29, 28, 31, 42, 20, 36, 32}

2. {$105, $98, $83, $127, $115, $114, $132, $93, $107, $101, $119}

3. {211, 229, 196, 230, 240, 212, 231, 233, 243, 214, 239, 238, 228, 237, 230, 234, 239, 240, 212, 232, 239, 240, 237}

4. {3.7, 6.2, 4.1, 2.4, 1.0, 1.5, 1.4, 2.1, 2.6, 3.0, 1.3, 1.7}

For Exercises 5–7, use the box-and-whisker plot shown.

Major Peaks of the Hindu Kush (height in feet)

5. How tall is the highest peak of the Hindu Kush? **about 25,200 ft**

6. What is the median height of the major peaks? **about 23,200 ft**

7. Write a sentence describing what the box-and-whisker plot tells about the major peaks of the Hindu Kush. **Sample answers: About 75% of the peaks are taller than 22,300 ft; most peaks are between 22,300 and 24,300 ft tall.**

For Exercises 8–10, use the box-and-whisker plot shown.

Corn Yield by State (bushels per acre)

8. In which year was the corn yield more varied? Explain. **1999; The range and the interquartile range are greater in 1999 than in 1997.**

9. How does the median yield in 1999 compare with the median yield in 1997? **The median yield is seven bushels per acre greater in 1999 than in 1997.**

10. Write a few sentences that compare the 1997 yields with the 1999 yields. **Sample answer: Yields are slightly higher in 1999 than in 1997. For example, 50% of the 1997 yields are between 122 and 146 bushels per acre, and 50% of the 1999 yields are between 129 and 150 bushels per acre. Both the range and the interquartile range are greater in 1999 than in 1997, meaning 1999 yields are more varied.**

Enrichment, p. 681

Mental Math: Compensation

To add or subtract in your head, work with multiples of 10 (20, 30, 40, . . .) or 100 (200, 300, 400, . . .) and then adjust your answer.

To add 52, first add 50, then add 2 more.
To subtract 74, first subtract 70, then subtract 4 more.
To subtract 38, first subtract 40, then add 2.
To add 296, first add 300, then subtract 4.

Write the second step you would use to do each of the following.

1. Add 83.
   1) Add 80.
   2) Add 3 more.

2. Add 304.
   1) Add 300.
   2) Add 4 more.

3. Subtract 62.
   1) Subtract 60.
   2) Subtract 2 more.

4. Add 27.
   1) Add 30.
   2) Subtract 3.

5. Subtract 79.
   1) Subtract 80.
   2) Add 1.

6. Subtract 103.
   1) Subtract 100.
   2) Subtract 3 more.

7. Add 499.
   1) Add 500.
   2) Subtract 1.

8. Add 294.
   1) Add 300.
   2) Subtract 6.

9. Subtract 590.
   1) Subtract 600.
   2) Add 10.

Use the method above to add 59 to each of the following.

10. 40
    40 + 60 − 1 = 99

11. 72
    72 + 60 − 1 = 131

12. 53
    53 + 60 − 1 = 112

13. 15
    15 + 60 − 1 = 74

Use the method above to subtract 18 from each of the following.

14. 96
    96 − 20 + 2 = 78

15. 45
    45 − 20 + 2 = 27

16. 71
    71 − 20 + 2 = 53

17. 67
    67 − 20 + 2 = 49

TRAVEL For Exercises 8 and 9, use the box-and-whisker plots shown.

Average Gas Mileage for Various Sedans and SUVs

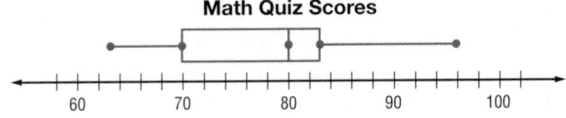

Source: www.classifieds2000.com

8. Which types of vehicles tend to be less fuel-efficient? **8–9. See pp. 665A–665F.**

9. Compare the most fuel-efficient SUV to the least fuel-efficient sedan.

★ indicates increased difficulty

Practice and Apply

Homework Help

For Exercises	See Examples
10–15	1
16–18	2
19	3

Extra Practice
See page 753.

Draw a box-and-whisker plot for each set of data. **10–15. See pp. 665A–665F.**

10. 65, 92, 74, 61, 55, 35, 88, 99, 97, 100, 96

11. 60, 60, 120, 80, 68, 90, 100, 69, 104, 99, 130

12. 80, 72, 42, 40, 63, 51, 55, 78, 81, 73, 77, 65, 67, 68, 59

13. $95, $105, $85, $122, $165, $55, $100, $158, $174, $162

★ 14.

Magnitudes of Recent Major Earthquakes		
6.8	6.2	6.2
5.9	6.1	6.8
6.9	6.5	6.7
6.1	6.9	7.4
7.5	6.3	5.9
6.1	5.8	7.6
7.3	7.8	7.9

Source: *The World Almanac*

★ 15.

Average Points Scored per Game for NBA Scoring Leaders		
33.1	37.1	29.8
30.7	35.0	29.3
32.3	32.5	30.4
28.4	33.6	29.6
30.6	31.5	28.7
32.9	30.1	26.8
30.3	32.6	29.7

Source: *The World Almanac*

SCHOOL For Exercises 16–18, use the box-and-whisker plot shown.

Math Quiz Scores

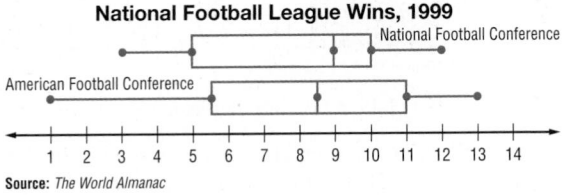

16. What was the highest quiz score? **96**

17. What percent of the students scored between 80 and 96? **50%**

18. Based on the plot, how did the students' scores vary? **See pp. 665A–665F.**

19. **SPORTS** The number of games won by the teams in each conference of the National Football League is displayed below. Write a few sentences that compare the data. **See pp. 665A–665F.**

National Football League Wins, 1999

Source: *The World Almanac*

Tips for New Teachers

Connections Explain to students that box-and-whisker plots have many applications in the business world. They make immediately clear the range and interquartile range of a set of data. For example, a bakery manager knows that her store typically sells from 130 to 210 blueberry muffins per week, and might sell up to 260 muffins in a week. This way she knows how many to bake in order to make enough for the customers without creating too much waste. Making box-and-whisker plots for each of the 200 items her store makes would be a visual way of arranging such data.

20. CRITICAL THINKING Write a set of data that contains 12 values for which the box-and-whisker plot has no whiskers. **See margin.**

21. **WRITING IN MATH** Answer the question that was posed at the beginning of the lesson. **See pp. 665A–665F.**

How can box-and-whisker plots help you interpret data?

Include the following in your answer:
- box-and-whisker plots that display the temperature data for each city,
- a description of the temperatures in Tampa and Caribou, and
- an advantage of displaying data in a box-and-whisker plot instead of in a table.

Standardized Test Practice
Ⓐ Ⓑ Ⓒ Ⓓ

For Exercises 22 and 23, use the box-and-whisker plot shown.

Highest Recorded Wind Speeds (mph) in the U.S.

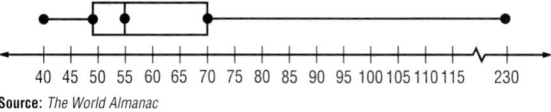

40 45 50 55 60 65 70 75 80 85 90 95 100 105 110 115   230

Source: *The World Almanac*

22. What is the least highest recorded wind speed? **A**
- Ⓐ 40 mph
- Ⓑ 55 mph
- Ⓒ 70 mph
- Ⓓ 230 mph

23. What percent of the wind speeds range from 40 to 70 mph? **C**
- Ⓐ 25%
- Ⓑ 50%
- Ⓒ 75%
- Ⓓ 100%

Extending the Lesson
Data that are more than 1.5 times the interquartile range from the quartiles are called **outliers**. Consider the data set shown.

15 22 22 26 27 29 30 31 32 36 50

The interquartile range is $32 - 22$ or 10. The outliers are the values more than $1.5(10)$ or 15 from the quartiles.

$$22 - 15 = 7 \qquad 32 + 15 = 47$$

The limits for the outliers are 7 and 47. So, there is one outlier, 50.

Determine whether any outliers exist for each data set.

24. 67, 75, 89, 72, 56, 65, 70 **none**

25. 27, 30, 36, 35, 37, 46, 31, 4, 29, 38, 30 **4**

Maintain Your Skills

Mixed Review
26. 3.4; 1.8

For Exercises 26 and 27, use the set of data {2.4, 2.1, 4.8, 2.7, 1.4, 3.9}.

26. What is the range and interquartile range for the data? *(Lesson 12-2)*

27. Display the data in a stem-and-leaf plot. *(Lesson 12-1)* **See margin.**

Getting Ready for the Next Lesson

PREREQUISITE SKILL For Exercises **28 and 29, refer to the table shown.**
*(To review **analyzing data**, see pages 722 and 723.)*

28. How many people were surveyed? **25**

29. How many people spend more than 7 hours a week on recreational activities? **14**

Weekly Recreation Time		
Time (h)	Tally	Frequency
0–3	III	3
4–7	IIII III	8
8–11	IIII IIII	9
12–15	IIII	5

Answers

20. Sample answer: {60, 60, 60, 60, 60, 70, 75, 80, 85, 85, 85, 85}

27.

Stem	Leaf
1	4
2	1 4 7
3	9
4	8

$2|4 = 2.4$

About the Exercises . . .
Organization by Objective
- **Display Data:** 10–15
- **Interpret Box-and-Whisker Plots:** 16–19

Odd/Even Assignments
Exercises 10–15 are structured so that students practice the same concepts whether they are assigned odd or even problems.

Assignment Guide
Basic: 11, 13, 16–23, 26–29
Average: 11–15 odd, 16–23, 26–29 (Optional: 24, 25)
Advanced: 10–14 even, 16–27 (Optional: 28, 29)

4 Assess

Open-Ended Assessment

Speaking Show students this plot. Ask students to state facts from the plot. For example, the median is 7, the interquartile range is 4, and so on.

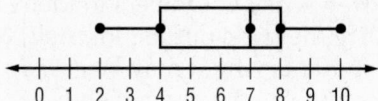

0 1 2 3 4 5 6 7 8 9 10

Getting Ready for Lesson 12-4

PREREQUISITE SKILL Lesson 12-4 presents histograms, which utilize frequency tables. Exercises 28 and 29 should be used to determine your students' familiarity with frequency tables.

Assessment Options

Quiz (Lessons 12-1 through 12-3) is available on p. 727 of the *Chapter 12 Resource Masters.*

Getting Started

Know Your Calculator There are two types of box-and-whisker plots. In Step 2, the keystrokes will select ModBoxPlot (modified box plot) rather than BoxPlot (regular box plot). ModBoxPlot will show outliers while BoxPlot will not.

Clearing Data If more than one column in students' calculators have data, have students enter the keystrokes `STAT` 4 to select ClrList function and then enter list names.

Teach

- Have students double-check their lists after entering the data and edit them if necessary.
- As students work through Step 3, ask volunteers to identify the parts of the plot. Ask students why it may be easier to display data using a box-and-whisker plot.
- Have students complete Exercises 1–5.

Assess

After students answer Exercises 1–5, ask them how box-and-whisker plots help them interpret data using medians, quartiles, and extreme values. Have students reset the **Xmin** and **Xmax** values to create a greater range. Ask them how this change affects the appearance of the graph and how this might be misleading.

Box-and-Whisker Plots

You can use a TI-83 Plus graphing calculator to create box-and-whisker plots.

Example

The table shows the ages of the students in two karate classes.

Class	Age (years)														
A	39	33	37	26	39	25	39	40	27	25	35	31	29	28	35
B	19	26	40	19	20	32	16	24	24	16	27	23	22	25	16

Make box-and-whisker plots for the ages in Class A and in Class B.

Step 1 *Enter the data.*
- Clear any existing data.
  KEYSTROKES: `STAT` `ENTER` `▲` `CLEAR` `ENTER`
- Enter the Class A ages in L1 and the Class B ages in L2.
  KEYSTROKES: *Review entering a list on page 45.*

Step 2 *Format the graph.*
- Turn on two statistical plots.
  KEYSTROKES: *Review statistical plots on page 45.*
- For Plot 1, select the box-and-whisker plot and L1 as the Xlist.
  KEYSTROKES: `▼` `▶` `▶` `▶` `ENTER` `▼` `2nd` L1 `ENTER`
- Repeat for Plot 2, using L2 as the Xlist, to make a box-and-whisker plot for Class B.

Step 3 *Graph the box-and-whisker plots.*
- Display the graph.
  KEYSTROKES: `ZOOM` 9

Press `TRACE`. Move from one plot to the other using the up and down arrow keys. The right and left arrow keys allow you to find the least value, greatest value, and quartiles.

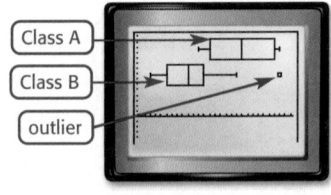

Exercises 1–5. See margin.

1. What are the least, greatest, quartile, and median values for Classes A and B?

2. What is the interquartile range for Class A? Class B?

3. Are there any outliers? How does the graphing calculator show them?

4. a. Estimate the percent of Class A members who are high school students.
   b. Estimate the percent of Class B members who are high school students.

5. If you were a high school student, which class would you join? Explain.

   www.pre-alg.com/other_calculator_keystrokes

Answers

1. Class A minimum: 25; Q1: 27; median: 33; Q3: 39; maximum: 40;
   Class B minimum: 16; Q1: 19; median: 23; Q3: 26; maximum: 40

2. Class A: 12; Class B: 7

3. Yes; a point is separated from the box-and-whisker plot.

4a. 0%

4b. 25%

5. Sample answer: Class B because there would be more members around my age.

What You'll Learn

- Display data in a histogram.
- Interpret data in a histogram.

Vocabulary

histogram

Study Tip

Frequency Distribution
A frequency distribution is the organizing of data in a table using classes or intervals, and frequencies.

b. the totals in the row of tally marks

How are histograms similar to frequency tables?

The number of counties for each state in the United States is displayed in the table shown. This table is a *frequency table*.

a. What does each tally mark represent? **a state**

b. What does the last column represent?

c. What do you notice about the intervals that represent the counties? **They are equal.**

Number of Counties in Each State		
Counties	Tally	Frequency
1–25	JHT JHT III	13
26–50	JHT II	7
51–75	JHT JHT II	12
76–100	JHT JHT II	12
101–125	IIII	4
126–150		0
151–175	I	1
176–200		0
201–225		0
226–250		0
251–275	I	1

Source: *The World Almanac*

DISPLAY DATA Another type of graph that can be used to display data is a histogram. A **histogram** uses bars to display numerical data that have been organized into equal intervals.

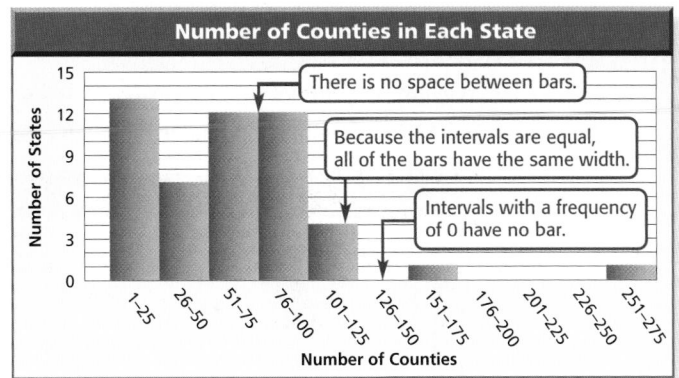

Number of Counties in Each State

- There is no space between bars.
- Because the intervals are equal, all of the bars have the same width.
- Intervals with a frequency of 0 have no bar.

Example 1 Draw a Histogram

WATER PARKS The frequency table shows certain water park admission costs. Display the data in a histogram.

Step 1 Draw and label a horizontal and vertical axis as shown. Include the title.

Water Park Admission		
Cost ($)	Tally	Frequency
8–15	JHT	5
16–23	JHT II	7
24–31	IIII	4
32–39		0
40–47	II	2

(continued on the next page)

1 Focus

5-Minute Check Transparency 12-4 Use as a quiz or review of Lesson 12-3.

Mathematical Background notes are available for this lesson on page 604D.

How are histograms similar to frequency tables?

The opening activity questions are repeated on page 685 of the *Chapter 12 Resource Masters*.

Reading to Learn Mathematics, p. 685 ELL

Pre-Activity *How are histograms similar to frequency tables?*
Do the activity at the top of page 623 in your textbook. Write your answers below.
a. What does each tally mark represent? a state
b. What does the last column represent?
the totals in the row of tally marks
c. What do you notice about the intervals that represent the counties?
They are equal.

Reading the Lesson
Write a definition and give an example of the new vocabulary word.

Vocabulary	Definition	Example
1. histogram	See students' work.	

Complete the following statements about frequency tables and histograms.

2. If the first frequency interval goes from 1 to 50, the next frequency interval goes from 51–100 .

3. Because the intervals in a histogram are equal , all of the bars have the same width .

4. In a histogram, there is no space between bars.

5. Intervals that have a frequency of 0 have no bar .

6. The height of a bar in a histogram corresponds to the frequency of the data for that interval .

Helping You Remember
7. Label the following in the histogram at right: interval, frequency, bar, and histogram. Then make a frequency table showing the same information as the histogram.

My Survey		
Age	Tally	Frequency
0–19	JHT IIII	9
20–39	JHT I	6
40–59	JHT JHT I	11
60–79	III	3

Resource Manager

Workbooks and Reproducible Masters

Chapter 12 Resource Masters
- Study Guide and Intervention, p. 682
- Skills Practice, p. 683
- Practice, p. 684
- Reading to Learn Mathematics, p. 685
- Enrichment, p. 686

Parent and Student Study Guide Workbook, p. 101

Transparencies
5-Minute Check Transparency 12-4
Answer Key Transparencies

Technology
Interactive Chalkboard

DISPLAY DATA

Teaching Tip Make sure that students know the difference between horizontal and vertical. Emphasize that a histogram is a type of bar graph.

1 **TOURISM** The frequency table shows the number of overseas visitors to certain U.S. cities in 1999. Display the data in a histogram.

Overseas Travelers		
Number of Visitors (1000s)	Tally	Frequency
0–1000	ЖЖ	5
1001–2000	III	3
2001–3000	ЖЖ	5
3001–4000	I	1
4001–5000		0
5001–6000	I	1

Source: U.S. Department of Commerce

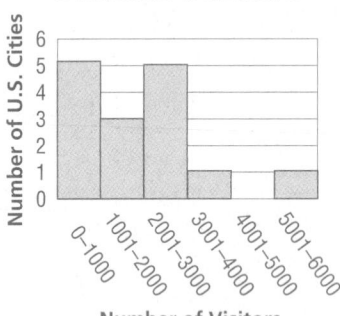

Overseas Travelers

Study Tip

Break in Scale
The symbol √ means there is a break in the scale. The scale from 0 to 7 has been omitted.

Reading Math

At Least
Recall that *at least* means *is greater than or equal to*.

Step 2 Show the intervals from the frequency table on the horizontal axis and an interval of 1 on the vertical axis.

Step 3 For each cost interval, draw a bar whose height is given by the frequency.

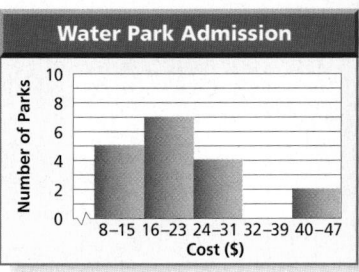

INTERPRET HISTOGRAMS A histogram gives a better visual display of data than a frequency table. Thus, it is easier to interpret data displayed in a histogram.

Example 2 *Interpret Data*

SCHOOL Refer to the histogram at the right.

a. How many students are at least 69 inches tall?

Since 30 students are 69–71 inches tall, and 10 students are 72–74 inches tall, 30 + 10 or 40 students are at least 69 inches tall.

b. Is it possible to tell the height of the tallest student?

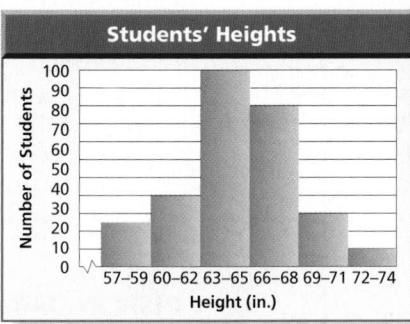

No, you can only tell that the tallest student is between 72 and 74 inches.

Histograms can also be used to compare data.

Example 3 *Compare Two Sets of Data*

OLYMPICS Use the histograms below to answer the question.

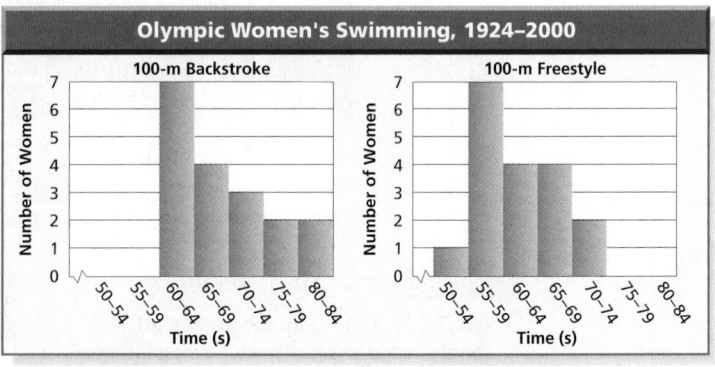

Source: *The World Almanac*

Which event has more winning times less than 1 minute?

The 100-meter freestyle has 1 + 7 or 8 athletes with a winning time less than 1 minute while the 100-meter backstroke has none.

DAILY INTERVENTION **Differentiated Instruction**

• **Auditory/Musical** Have students work in groups of four to compose a short piece of music inspired by the histograms in Example 3. Ask them to imagine that each bar on the histograms represents a range of notes in a musical scale. Have them assign musical intervals to each interval on the histograms and then "play" the graphs, using the heights of the bars as a guide for volume. Instruments such as the flute and the voice, which can play all of the notes in an interval in a sliding manner, lend themselves well to this activity.

Check for Understanding

Concept Check

1. **Explain** why there are no spaces between the bars of a histogram.

2. **OPEN ENDED** Tell how a histogram gives a better visual display than a frequency table. **1–2. See margin.**

Guided Practice

Display each set of data in a histogram. **3–4. See pp. 665A–665F.**

GUIDED PRACTICE KEY	
Exercises	Examples
3, 4	1
5–8	2
9, 10	3

3.

Pet Survey		
Pets	Tally	Frequency
1–3	ЖТ ЖТ ЖТ ЖТ I	21
4–6	ЖТ II	7
7–9	II	2
10–12		0
13–15	I	1

4.

Test Scores		
Score	Tally	Frequency
95–100	ЖТ	5
89–94	ЖТ ЖТ II	12
83–88	ЖТ IIII	9
77–82	ЖТ I	6
71–76	IIII	4

Applications

ROLLER COASTERS For Exercises 5–8, use the histogram shown.

5. Describe the data.

6. Which interval has the most roller coasters? **0–9**

7. Why is there a jagged line in the vertical axis?

8. How many states have no roller coasters? Explain.

5. the number of states that have a certain number of roller coasters
7. The numbers between 10 and 34 are omitted.
8. See pp. 665A–665F.

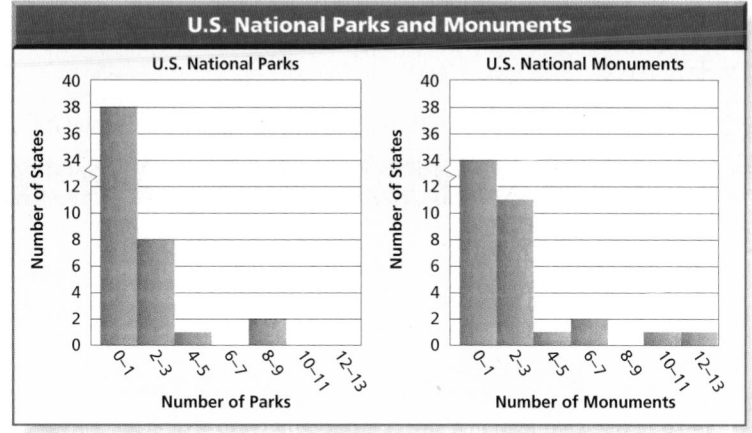

U.S. Roller Coasters

Source: The Roller Coaster Database

 Online Research **Data Update** How has the number of roller coasters in the United States changed since 2000? Visit www.pre-alg.com/data_update to learn more.

VACATIONS For Exercises 9 and 10, use the histograms below.

U.S. National Parks and Monuments

U.S. National Parks

U.S. National Monuments

Source: www.infoplease.com

9. Are there more states with two or more national parks or two or more national monuments? **2 or more national monuments**

10. How many more states have either one or no national parks than either one or no national monuments? **4**

   Lesson 12-4 Histograms **625**

Answers

1. Sample answer: Because the intervals are continuous.

2. Sample answer: By displaying the data in a histogram, it is much easier to see how the data in the intervals compare to each other.

In-Class Examples Power Point®

2 **ELEVATIONS** Use the histogram.

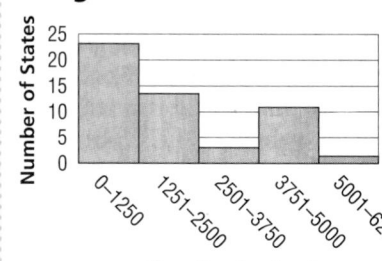

Highest Elevations in U.S.

Elevation (meters)

a. How many states have highest points with elevations at least 3751 meters? **12**

b. Is it possible to tell the height of the tallest point? **No, you can only tell that the highest point is between 5001 and 6250 meters.**

3 **EMPLOYMENT** Use the histograms.

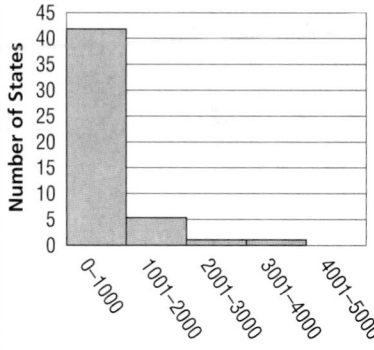

Trade

Number of Employees (thousands)

Services

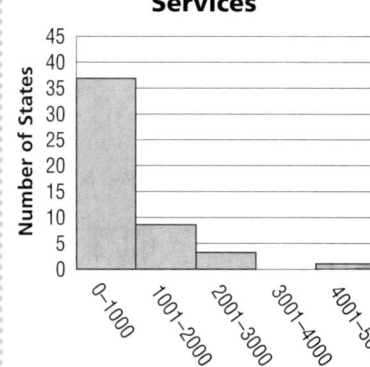

Number of Employees (thousands)

Which business sector has more states with between 1,001,000 and 3,000,000 employees? **services**

3 Practice/Apply

Study Notebook

Have students—
- add the definition/example of the vocabulary term to their Vocabulary Builder Worksheets for Chapter 12.
- include their histograms for Exercises 3 and 4.
- include any other item(s) that they find helpful in mastering the skills in this lesson.

About the Exercises . . .

Organization by Objective
- **Display Data:** 11–14
- **Interpret Histograms:** 15–20

Odd/Even Assignments
Exercises 11–14 are structured so that students practice the same concepts whether they are assigned odd or even problems.

Assignment Guide

Basic: 11, 13, 18–28, 32–35
Average: 11, 13, 15–17, 18–28, 32–35 (Optional: 29, 30)
Advanced: 12, 14, 15–33 (Optional: 34, 35)
All: Practice Quiz 1 (1–5)

Answers

11.

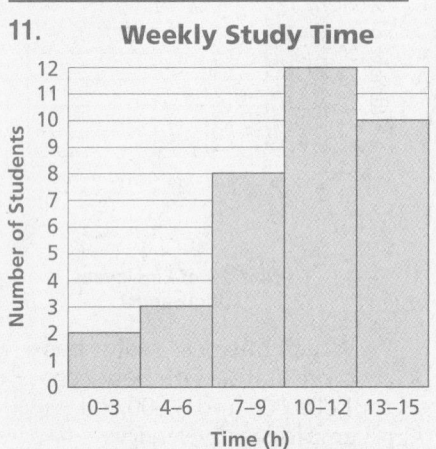
Weekly Study Time

Practice and Apply

Homework Help

For Exercises	See Examples
11–14	1
15–17	2
18–20	3

Extra Practice
See page 753.

Display each set of data in a histogram. **11. See margin.**

11.

Weekly Study Time		
Time (hr)	Tally	Frequency
0–3	II	2
4–6	III	3
7–9	JHT III	8
10–12	JHT JHT II	12
13–15	JHT JHT	10

12.

Weekly Allowance		
Amount	Tally	Frequency
$0–$5	JHT JHT I	11
$6–$11	JHT IIII	9
$12–$17	JHT III	8
$18–$23	III	3
$24–$29	JHT	5

12–14. See pp. 665A–665F.

13.

Touchdowns in a Season		
Amount	Tally	Frequency
80–96	JHT JHT	10
97–113	JHT	5
114–130	IIII	4
131–147	II	2
148–164		0
165–181	I	1

14.

Goals in a Season		
Amount	Tally	Frequency
65–69	JHT I	6
70–74	JHT II	7
75–79	III	3
80–84		0
85–89	III	3
90–94	I	1

FOOD   For Exercises 15–17, use the data in the histogram.

15. How many restaurants sell chicken sandwiches that cost under $3? **13**

16. How many restaurants were surveyed? **16**

★ **17.** What percent of the restaurants surveyed sell chicken sandwiches that cost between $2.00 and $2.49? **37.5%**

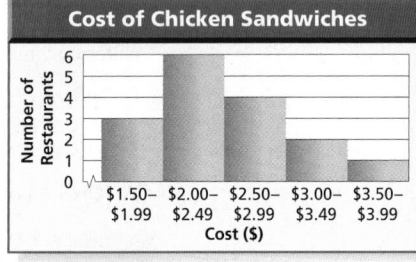

WebQuest

Frequency tables and histograms can help you analyze data. Visit www.pre-alg.com/webquest to continue work on your WebQuest project.

ARCHITECTURE   For Exercises 18–20, use the histograms below.

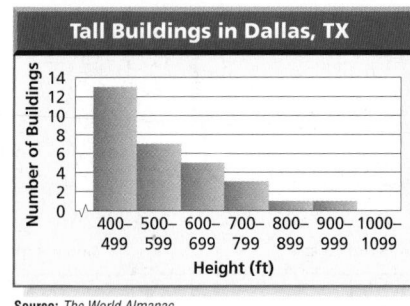

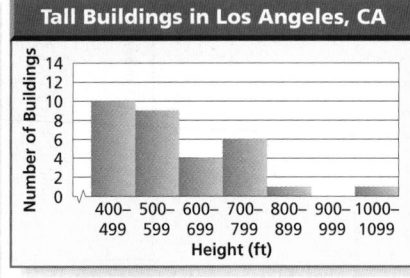

18. Which city has more tall buildings? **Los Angeles**

19. Which city has the fewer number of buildings over 600 feet? **Dallas**

20. Compare the heights of the tall buildings in the two cities. **See margin.**

20. Sample answer: Whereas Dallas, Texas, has more buildings with a height of 400–499 feet, Los Angeles, California, has more buildings classified as tall buildings.

CRITICAL THINKING For Exercises 21–25, determine whether each statement is *true* or *false*.

21. You can determine the median from a box-and-whisker plot. **true**

22. You can determine the range from a stem-and-leaf plot. **true**

23. You can reconstruct the original data from a histogram. **false**

24. You can reconstruct the original data from a box-and-whisker plot. **false**

25. You can determine the interval in which the median falls in a histogram. **true**

26.  Answer the question that was posed at the beginning of the lesson. **See pp. 665A–665F.**

How are histograms similar to frequency tables?

Include the following in your answer:
- examples of a histogram and a frequency table, and
- an explanation describing how data are displayed in each.

Standardized Test Practice
Ⓐ Ⓑ Ⓒ Ⓓ

The histogram shows the ages of the students in a drama club.

27. How old are the oldest students? **A**
 Ⓐ 18–19 Ⓑ 16–19
 Ⓒ 17–18 Ⓓ 16–18

28. What is the total number of students in the drama club? **C**
 Ⓐ 20 Ⓑ 22
 Ⓒ 24 Ⓓ 26

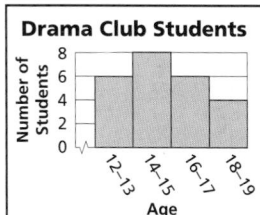
Drama Club Students
(Number of Students vs. Age: 12–13, 14–15, 16–17, 18–19)

Extending the Lesson

In the frequency table shown, the frequencies 5, 6, 4, 3, and 2 are called the **absolute frequencies**.

To find the **relative frequencies**, divide each absolute frequency by the total number of items. For the data shown, the relative frequencies are $\frac{5}{20}$ or $\frac{1}{4}$, $\frac{6}{20}$ or $\frac{3}{10}$, $\frac{4}{20}$ or $\frac{1}{5}$, $\frac{3}{20}$, and $\frac{2}{20}$ or $\frac{1}{10}$.

Quiz Scores		
Score	Tally	Frequency
23–25	JHT	5
20–22	JHT I	6
17–19	IIII	4
14–16	III	3
11–13	II	2

The **cumulative frequencies** are the sums of all preceding frequencies. For the data shown, the cumulative frequencies are 5, 5 + 6 or 11, 5 + 6 + 4 or 15, 5 + 6 + 4 + 3 or 18, and 5 + 6 + 4 + 3 + 2 or 20.

Find the absolute, relative, and cumulative frequency for each data set.

29–30. See margin.

29.
Record High Temperature (°F)		
Temp.	Tally	Frequency
100–104	II	2
105–109	JHT IIII	9
110–114	JHT JHT JHT II	17
115–119	JHT JHT II	12
120–124	JHT II	7
125–129	II	2

30.
Record Wind Speeds (mph)		
Speed	Tally	Frequency
30–36	JHT JHT I	11
37–43	JHT JHT JHT JHT	20
44–50	JHT JHT JHT JHT I	21
51–57	JHT JHT II	12
58–64	I	1
65–71	I	1

 www.pre-alg.com/self_check_quiz

Lesson 12-4 Histograms **627**

Answers

29. absolute frequency: 2, 9, 17, 12, 7, 2;
relative frequency: $\frac{2}{49}, \frac{9}{49}, \frac{17}{49}, \frac{12}{49}, \frac{1}{7}, \frac{2}{49}$; cumulative frequency: 2, 11, 28, 40, 47, 49

30. absolute frequency: 11, 20, 21, 12, 1, 1;
relative frequency: $\frac{1}{6}, \frac{10}{33}, \frac{7}{22}, \frac{2}{11}, \frac{1}{66}, \frac{1}{66}$; cumulative frequency: 11, 31, 52, 64, 65, 66

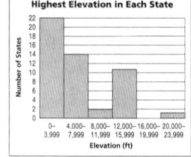
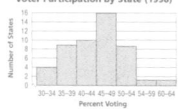
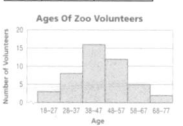 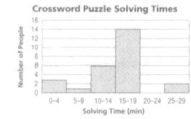
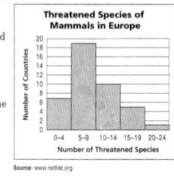
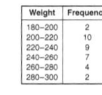
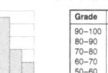
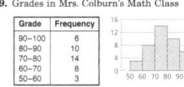
Lesson 12-4 Histograms **627**

Open-Ended Assessment

Writing Ask students to write a paragraph discussing the advantages of using a histogram to display data. Ask them to consider the types of information or statistics that could be depicted using a histogram.

Getting Ready for Lesson 12-5

PREREQUISITE SKILL Lesson 12-5 presents misleading line and bar graphs. Exercises 34 and 35 should be used to determine your students' familiarity with bar graphs.

Assessment Options

Practice Quiz 1 The quiz provides students with a brief review of the concepts and skills in Lessons 12-1 through 12-4. Lesson numbers are given to the right of exercises or instruction lines so students can review concepts not yet mastered.

Answers

31.

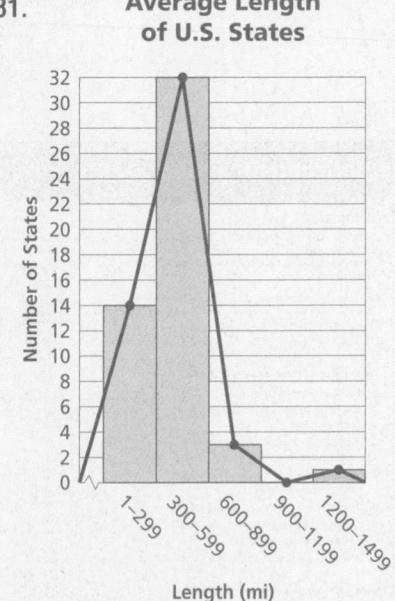

Average Length of U.S. States

Source: *The World Almanac*

35. Sample answer: Brand B costs one-third more than brand C.

When the middles of the intervals on a histogram are connected with line segments, a **frequency polygon** is formed. A frequency polygon is shown.

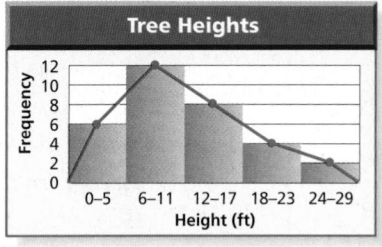

Tree Heights

31. Make a frequency polygon of the data shown below. **See margin.**

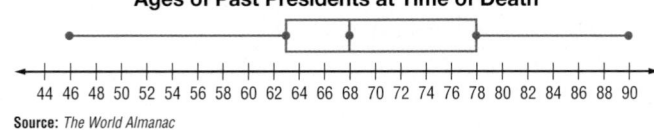

Average Length (mi) of U.S. States*									
330	1480	400	260	770	380	110	100	500	300
570	390	270	310	400	380	380	320	250	190
490	400	340	300	630	430	490	190	150	370
330	500	340	220	400	360	283	40	260	380
440	790	350	160	430	360	240	310	360	

Source: *The World Almanac* * Hawaii is not listed

Maintain Your Skills

Mixed Review **PRESIDENTS** For Exercises 32 and 33, use the data shown below.

Ages of Past Presidents at Time of Death

44 46 48 50 52 54 56 58 60 62 64 66 68 70 72 74 76 78 80 82 84 86 88 90

Source: *The World Almanac*

32. What percent of presidents died by the time they were 78 years old? *(Lesson 12-3)* **75%**

33. Find the range and interquartile range for the data. *(Lesson 12-2)* **44; 15**

Getting Ready for the Next Lesson **PREREQUISITE SKILL** For Exercises 34 and 35, use the graph shown.
*(To review **bar graphs**, see pages 722 and 723.)*

34. Which jeans cost the most? **Brand D**

35. How does the cost of Brand B compare to the cost of Brand C? **See margin.**

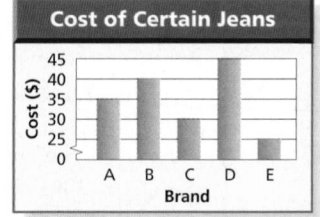

Cost of Certain Jeans

Practice Quiz 1 — *Lessons 12-1 through 12-4*

For Exercises 1–5, use the data in the table.

1. Display the data in a stem-and-leaf plot. *(Lesson 12-1)*

2. Find the range and interquartile range. *(Lesson 12-2)* **73; 22**

3. Display the data in a box-and-whisker plot. *(Lesson 12-3)*

4. What percent of the costs were less than $20? *(Lesson 12-3)* **25%**

5. Display the data in a histogram. *(Lesson 12-4)* **1, 3, 5. See pp. 665A–665F.**

$20	$28	$18	$89	$55	$28
$30	$86	$19	$42	$19	$16
$26	$43	$28	$22	$32	$40

Graphing Calculator Investigation

A Follow-Up of Lesson 12-4

Histograms

You can use a TI-83 Plus graphing calculator to make a histogram.

PRESIDENTS The list below shows the ages of the first 43 presidents at the time of inauguration.

57	61	57	57	58	57	61	54	68	51	49
64	50	48	65	52	56	46	54	49	50	47
55	55	54	42	51	56	55	51	54	51	60
62	43	55	56	61	52	69	64	46	54	

Make a histogram to show the age distribution.

Step 1 *Enter the data.*
- Clear any existing data in list L1.
  KEYSTROKES: [STAT] [ENTER] [▲] [CLEAR] [ENTER]

- Enter the ages in L1.
  KEYSTROKES: *Review entering a list on page 45.*

Step 2 *Format the graph.*
- Turn on the statistical plot.
  KEYSTROKES: [2nd] [STAT PLOT] [ENTER] [ENTER]

- Select the histogram and L1 as the Xlist.
  KEYSTROKES: [▼] [▶] [▶] [ENTER] [▼] [2nd] L1 [ENTER]

Step 3 *Graph the histogram.*

Set the viewing window so the *x*-axis goes from 40 to 75 in increments of 5, and the *y*-axis goes from −5 to 15 in increments of 1. So, [40, 75] scl: 5 by [−5, 15] scl: 1. Then graph.

KEYSTROKES: [WINDOW] 40 [ENTER] 75 [ENTER] 5 [ENTER] −5 [ENTER] 15 [ENTER] 1 [ENTER] [GRAPH]

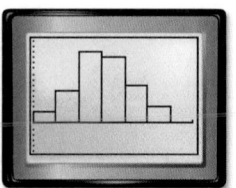

Exercises 1–7. See margin.

1. Press [Trace]. Find the frequency of each interval using the right and left arrow keys.

2. Discuss why the domain is from 40 to 75 for this data set.

3. How does the graphing calculator determine the size of the intervals?

4. At inauguration, how many presidents have been at least 45, but less than 65?

5. What percent of presidents falls in the interval of Exercise 4?

6. Can you tell from the histogram how many presidents were inaugurated at age 52? Explain.

7. Refer to Example 2 on page 607. How does the stem-and-leaf plot compare to the histogram you have graphed here? Which graph is easier to read?

www.pre-alg.com/other_calculator_keystrokes   **Graphing Calculator Investigation** Histograms **629**

Answers

1.

Interval	Frequency
40 up to 45	2
45 up to 50	6
50 up to 55	13
55 up to 60	12
60 up to 65	7
65 up to 70	3
70 up to 75	0

2. It contains all the possible ages.

3. It determines interval size by the scale factor of *x*.

4. 38

5. about 88%

6. No; the histogram shows the number of presidents for a range of ages, not the number of presidents for individual ages.

7. See students' work.

1 Focus

5-Minute Check
Transparency 12-5 Use as a quiz or review of Lesson 12-4.

Mathematical Background notes are available for this lesson on page 604D.

How can graphs be misleading?

The opening activity questions are repeated on page 690 of the *Chapter 12 Resource Masters.*

Reading to Learn Mathematics, p. 690

Pre-Activity *How can graphs be misleading?*
Do the activity at the top of page 630 in your textbook. Write your answers below.

a. Do both graphs show the same information? yes

b. Which graph suggests a dramatic increase in sales from May to June? Graph B

c. Which graph suggests steady sales? Graph A

d. How are the graphs similar? How are they different? Sample answer: The graphs differ in that Graph A shows a gradual increase and decrease over the year; Graph B shows a drastic increase and decrease. They are similar in that each graph contains labeled axes and a title.

Reading the Lesson
Complete the following statements by filling in the blanks with the following words.

| different | gradually | horizontal | interval(s) |
| label(s) | rapidly | title(s) | vertical |

1. If two graphs showing the same information have different vertical scales, that means that on the __vertical__ axis, the __intervals__ are different.

2. If two graphs showing the same information have different horizontal scales, that means that on the __horizontal__ axis, the intervals are __different__.

3. A graph can be misleading if it has no __title__ or if it has no __labels__ on the scales.

4. If a graph shows steady change, the plotted values should increase or decrease __gradually__.

5. If a graph shows dramatic change, the plotted values should increase or decrease __rapidly__.

Helping You Remember
6. Use a dictionary and a book of synonyms to rewrite the following sentence by replacing the underlined words with ones you are more familiar with.
__Statistics__ or statistical graphs can be __misleading__ when the same __data__ are __represented__ in different ways, so that each graph gives a different __visual impression__.
Sample answer: A collection of numerical information or statistical graphs can be deceptive when the same facts are shown in different ways, so that each graph gives a different effect to the eyes.

Teaching Tip Before starting the lesson, have students brainstorm ways in which groups may use partial data to mislead.

Resource Manager

Workbooks and Reproducible Masters

Chapter 12 Resource Masters
• Study Guide and Intervention, p. 687
• Skills Practice, p. 688
• Practice, p. 689
• Reading to Learn Mathematics, p. 690
• Enrichment, p. 691
• Assessment, pp. 727, 729

Parent and Student Study Guide Workbook, p. 102

Transparencies
5-Minute Check Transparency 12-5
Real-World Transparency 12
Answer Key Transparencies

Technology
Interactive Chalkboard
Pre-AlgePASS: Tutorial Plus, Lesson 37
Multimedia Applications

What You'll Learn
• Recognize when statistics are misleading.

How can graphs be misleading?

The graphs below show the monthly sales for one year for a company.

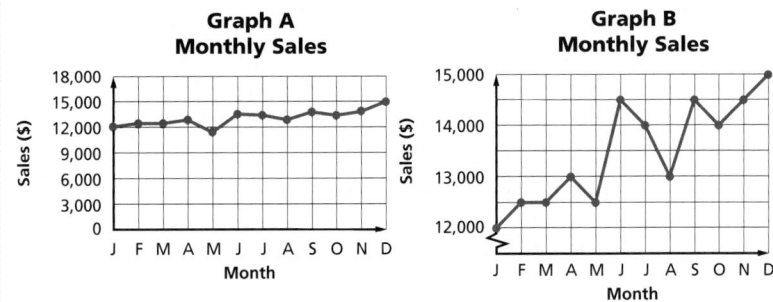

a. Do both graphs show the same information? yes

b. Graph B

b. Which graph suggests a dramatic increase in sales from May to June?

c. Which graph suggests steady sales? Graph A

d. How are the graphs similar? How are they different? See margin.

MISLEADING GRAPHS Two line graphs that represent the same data may look quite different. Consider the graphs above. Different vertical scales are used. So, each graph gives a different visual impression.

Study Tip

Statistics
A graph is also misleading if there is no title, there are no labels on either scale, and the vertical axis does not include zero.

Example 1 Misleading Graphs

TRAVEL The graphs show the growth of the cruise industry.

a. Why do the graphs look different?
The vertical scales differ.

b. Which graph appears to show a greater increase in the growth of the cruise industry? Explain.
Graph B; the size of the ship makes the increase appear more dramatic because both the height and width of the ship are increasing.

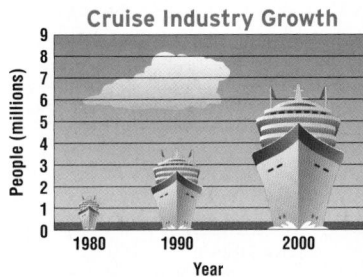

Bar graphs can also be misleading.

Example 2 Misleading Bar Graphs

Study Tip

Labels and Scales
When interpreting any graph, be sure to read the labels and the scales in addition to looking at the graph.

READING The graph shows the amount of time people spend reading the newspaper each day. Explain why the graph is misleading.

The inconsistent vertical scale and horizontal scale cause the data to be misleading.

The graph gives the impression that people aged 65 and up read the newspaper six times longer than those aged 18–24. By using the horizontal scale, you can see that it is only about 3.5 times longer.

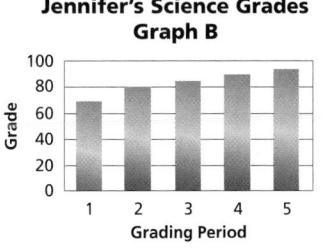

Time Spent Reading the Newspaper

Age	Time (min)
18–24	9
25–29	11
30–34	11
35–49	16
50–64	21
65–up	33

Check for Understanding

Concept Check
1. **Name** two ways a graph can be misleading. See margin.

2. **OPEN ENDED** Find an example of a misleading graph in a newspaper or magazine. Explain why it is misleading. See students' work.

Guided Practice **SCHOOL** For Exercises 3 and 4, refer to the graphs below.

GUIDED PRACTICE KEY	
Exercises	Examples
3–5	1, 2

Jennifer's Science Grades Graph A

Jennifer's Science Grades Graph B

3. Graph A has a break in the vertical scale.
4. Graph A because the increase appears more drastic.

3. Explain why the graphs look different.

4. Which graph appears to show Jennifer's grades improving more? Explain.

Application 5. **COMMUNICATION** The graph shows how the number of area codes in the U.S. have increased over the years. Tell why the graph is misleading. See margin.

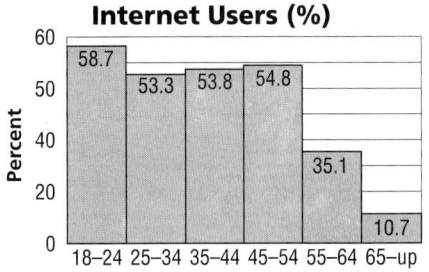

Increasing Area Codes

www.pre-alg.com/extra_examples

Answers

1. Sample answer: inconsistent vertical scale and break in vertical scale

5. From the vertical scale, you can see that the number of area codes in 1999 is about 1.5 times the number of area codes in 1996. The graph is misleading because the drawing of the phone for 1999 is about 3 times the size of the phone for 1996. Also, there is a break in the vertical scale.

MISLEADING GRAPHS

In-Class Examples Power Point®

1 FOOD The graphs show the increase in the price of lemons. **Source:** U.S. Bureau of Labor Statistics

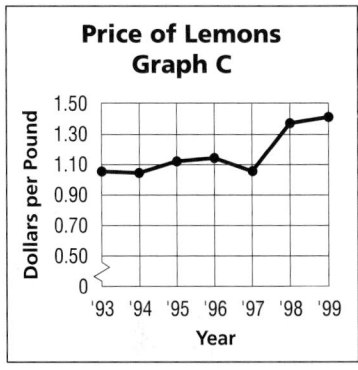

Price of Lemons Graph C

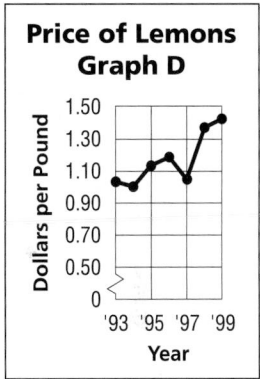

Price of Lemons Graph D

a. Why do the graphs look different? The horizontal scales differ.

b. Which graph appears to show a more rapid increase in the price of lemons after 1997? Explain. Graph D; the slope of the line from 1997 to 1998 is steeper in Graph D.

2 INTERNET Explain why the following graph is misleading.

Internet Users (%)

Age	Percent
18–24	58.7
25–34	53.3
35–44	53.8
45–54	54.8
55–64	35.1
65–up	10.7

The inconsistent horizontal and vertical scales cause the data to be misleading.

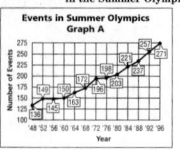 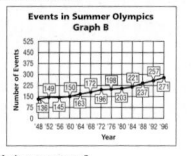
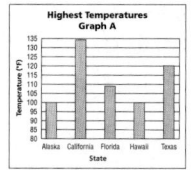 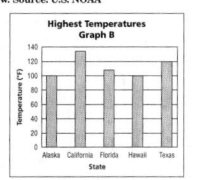
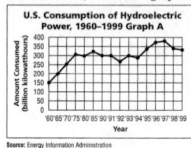 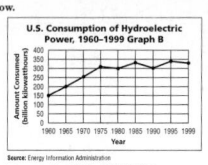
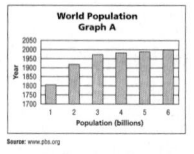 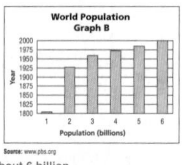
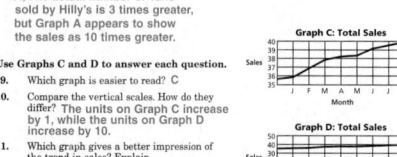
★ indicates increased difficulty

Practice and Apply

MOVIES For Exercises 6 and 7, refer to the graphs below.

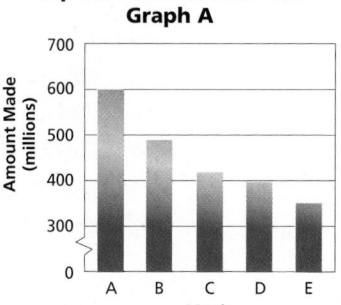 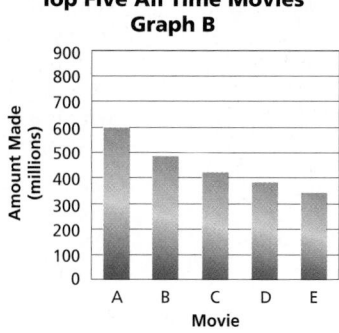

6. Which graph gives the impression that the top all-time movie made far more money than any other top all-time movie? **Graph A**

7. Which graph shows that movie C made nearly as much money as the other top movies? **Graph B**

JOBS For Exercises 8 and 9, use the graphs below.

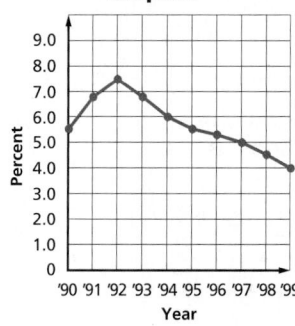 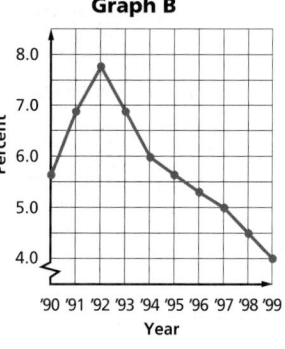

8. What causes the graphs to differ in their appearance? **8–9. See margin.**

9. Which graph appears to show that unemployment rates have decreased rapidly since 1992? Explain your reasoning.

10. **TRAVEL** The distance adults drive each week is shown in the graph at the right. Is the graph misleading? Explain your reasoning. **See margin.**

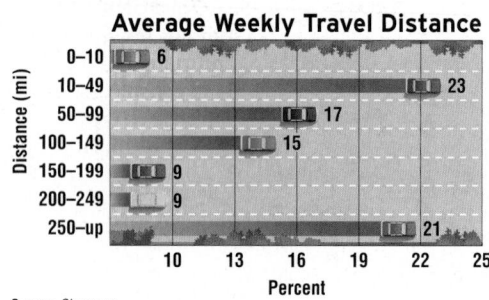

Source: *Simmons*

632 **Chapter 12** More Statistics and Probability

11. CRITICAL THINKING The table shows the number of yearly passengers on certain commuter trains.

Commuter Train Passengers

Year	Amount (millions)
1996	45.9
1997	48.5
1998	54.0
1999	58.3

Source: *Time Almanac*

a. Draw a graph that shows a slow increase in the number of passengers.

b. Redraw the graph so that it shows a rapid increase in the number of passengers. **a–b. See pp. 665A–665F.**

12. WRITING IN MATH Answer the question that was posed at the beginning of the lesson. **See pp. 665A–665F.**

How can graphs be misleading?

Include the following in your answer:

- an example of a graph that is misleading, and
- a discussion of how to redraw the graph so it is not misleading.

Standardized Test Practice
(A) (B) (C) (D)

13. Which sentence is a true statement about the data in the graph? **B**

(A) From 1995 to 1996, the amount spent on dining out doubled.

(B) The amount spent in 1998 was about 1.2 times the amount spent in 1994.

(C) The amount spent on dining out from 1995 to 1997 increased by three times.

(D) From 1997 to 1998 the amount spent on dining out increased by about 20%.

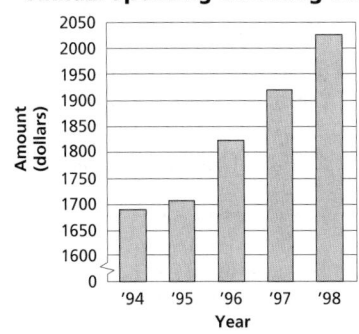

Annual Spending on Dining Out

Maintain Your Skills

Mixed Review

14. Display the data shown in a histogram. *(Lesson 12-4)*

15. Draw a box-and-whisker plot for {56°, 43°, 38°, 42°, 50°, 47°, 41°, 55°}. *(Lesson 12-3)* **14–15. See pp. 665A–665F.**

Book Survey

Books Read	Tally	Frequency
0–2	JHT III	8
3–5	IIII	4
6–8	JHT JHT	10
9–11	JHT	5
12–14	III	3

Find the area of each figure described. *(Lesson 10-5)*

16. triangle: base, 6 feet; height, 4.2 feet **12.6 ft²**

17. trapezoid: height, 5.8 meters; bases, 4 meters, 3 meters **20.3 m²**

Getting Ready for the Next Lesson

A bag contains 3 yellow marbles, 2 blue marbles, and 7 purple marbles. Suppose one marble is selected at random. Find the probability of each outcome. Express each probability as a fraction and as a percent.
*(To review **probability**, see Lesson 6-9)* **18–23. See pp. 665A–665F.**

18. $P(\text{yellow})$ **19.** $P(\text{blue})$ **20.** $P(\text{not purple})$

21. $P(\text{not blue})$ **22.** $P(\text{blue or purple})$ **23.** $P(\text{yellow or not blue})$

Answers (p. 632)

8. The vertical scale of graph A goes from 0 to 8.0 whereas the vertical scale of graph B goes from 4.0 to 8.0. In addition, the actual distance between vertical scales is less than the distance used in Graph B.

9. Graph B; the vertical scale used makes the decrease in the unemployment rates appear more drastic.

10. Yes; the intervals are inconsistent and the horizontal scale has a break in it.

---

3 **Practice/Apply**

Study Notebook

Have students—
- list all of the ways a graph can be misleading that have been mentioned in the lesson or in class.
- include any other item(s) that they find helpful in mastering the skills in this lesson.

Assignment Guide

Basic: 7, 9, 11–23
Average: 7, 9, 11–23
Advanced: 6, 8–17
(Optional: 18–23)

4 **Assess**

Open-Ended Assessment

Modeling Have students make a list of ways that graphs can be misleading. Then have each student choose one way and create a misleading graph.

Getting Ready for Lesson 12-6

PREREQUISITE SKILL Lesson 12-6 presents the Fundamental Counting Principle and applies it to probability. Exercises 18–23 should be used to determine your students' familiarity with probability.

Assessment Options

Quiz (Lessons 12-4 and 12-5) is available on p. 727 of the *Chapter 12 Resource Masters*.

Mid-Chapter Test (Lessons 12-1 through 12-5) is available on p. 729 of the *Chapter 12 Resource Masters*.

Getting Started

You may wish to have students review "Taking a Survey" on p. 309 before beginning this activity. In particular, review the terms *random, sample,* and *unbiased.*

Teach

Surveys Many survey-taking organizations now use the Internet as an efficient way to gather responses from people all over the country. You may wish to print out some Web surveys for the students to examine. How are the questions worded? How is the survey data to be compiled? How much time would it take for a respondent to complete the survey? Have students discuss in what ways surveys on the Web could create or reduce bias.

Assess

Study Notebook

Ask students to write down an example for each of the four types of bias covered in the activity.

ELL English Language Learners may benefit from writing key concepts from this activity in their Study Notebooks in their native language and then in English.

Dealing with Bias

In statistics, a sample is biased if it favors certain outcomes or parts of the population over others. While taking a random survey is the best way to eliminate bias or favoritism, there are still many ways in which a survey and its responses can be biased.

Voluntary Response
Consider a survey where people call or write in. Those who take the time to voluntarily respond usually have strong opinions on an issue. This may result in bias.

Response Bias
Some surveys are biased because either the people participating in the survey are influenced by the interviewer or the people do not give accurate responses.

Nonresponse
Consider a survey where the selected individuals cannot be contacted or they refuse to cooperate. Since the survey does not include a portion of the population, bias results.

Poorly Worded Questions
A survey is biased if it contains questions that are worded to influence people's responses.

Reading to Learn 1–4. See margin.
Tell whether each situation may result in bias. Explain your reasoning.

1. Suppose a bakery wants to know what percent of households makes baked goods from scratch. A sample is taken of 300 households. An interviewer goes from door to door between 9 A.M. and 4 P.M.

2. A telephone survey of 500 urban households is taken. The interviewer asks, "Does anyone in your household use public transportation?"

3. A radio station is conducting a survey as to whether people want a law that prohibits the use of computers for downloading music files. The radio announcer gives a number to call to answer *yes* or *no*. Of the responses, 85% said they do not want this law.

4. An interviewer states, "Due to heavy traffic, should another lane be added to Main Street?"

Sample Answers

1. This situation may result in bias. Many people may not be at home during these hours and thus, the survey will not include a portion of the population.

2. Since many cities offer public transportation, people living in urban households may be more apt to use public transportation. Thus, this may be biased.

3. The survey may be biased. It is a voluntary response and those who call in may have strong opinions.

4. This survey is biased due to the wording of the question.

12-6 Counting Outcomes

What You'll Learn

- Use tree diagrams or the Fundamental Counting Principle to count outcomes.
- Use the Fundamental Counting Principle to find the probability of an event.

Vocabulary
- tree diagram
- Fundamental Counting Principle

How can you count the number of skateboard designs that are available from a catalog?

The basic model of a skateboard has 5 choices for decks and 3 choices for wheel sets, as shown at the right. How many different skateboards are possible?

Decks	Wheel Sets
Alien	Eagle
Birdman	Cloud
Candy	Red Hot
Radical	
Trickster	

a. Write the names of each deck choice on 5 sticky notes of one color. Write the names of each type of wheel on 3 notes of another color.

b. Choose one deck note and one wheel note. One possible skateboard is Alien, Eagle. **a–b. See students' work.**

c. Make a list of all the possible skateboards. **See margin.**

d. How many different skateboard designs are possible? **15**

COUNTING OUTCOMES To solve the skateboard problem above, you can look at a simpler problem. Suppose there are only three deck choices, Birdman, Alien, or Candy, and only two wheel choices, Eagle or Cloud. You can draw a **tree diagram** to represent the possible outcomes.

Study Tip

Look Back
To review **outcomes**, see Lesson 6-9.

Example 1 Use a Tree Diagram to Count Outcomes

How many different skateboards can be made from three deck choices and two wheel choices?

You can draw a diagram to find the number of possible skateboards.

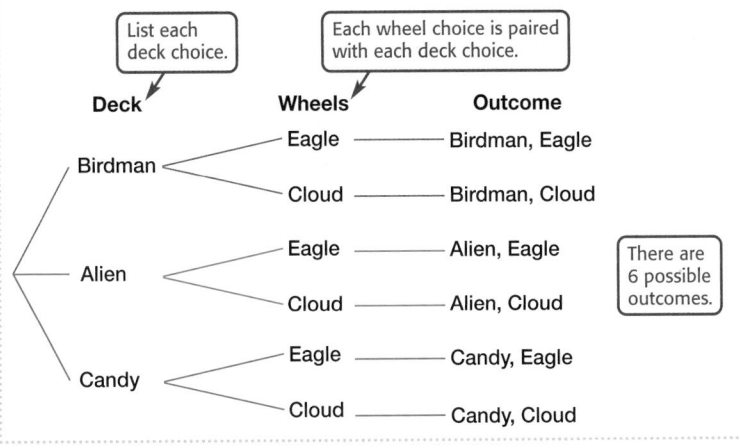

List each deck choice.

Each wheel choice is paired with each deck choice.

Deck	Wheels	Outcome
Birdman	Eagle	Birdman, Eagle
	Cloud	Birdman, Cloud
Alien	Eagle	Alien, Eagle
	Cloud	Alien, Cloud
Candy	Eagle	Candy, Eagle
	Cloud	Candy, Cloud

There are 6 possible outcomes.

---

1 Focus

5-Minute Check Transparency 12-6 Use as a quiz or review of Lesson 12-5.

Mathematical Background notes are available for this lesson on page 604D.

How can you count the number of skateboard designs that are available from a catalog?

The opening activity questions are repeated on page 695 of the *Chapter 12 Resource Masters*.

Reading to Learn Mathematics, p. 695 — ELL

Pre-Activity How can you count the number of skateboard designs that are available from a catalog?

Do the activity at the top of page 635 in your textbook. Write your answers below.

a. Write the names of each deck choice on 5 sticky notes of one color. Write the names of each type of wheel on 3 notes of another color. See students' work.

b. Choose one deck note and one wheel note. One possible skateboard is Alien, Eagle. See students' work.

c. Make a list of all the possible skateboards. alien-eagle, alien-cloud, alien-red hot, birdman-eagle, birdman-cloud, birdman-red hot, candy-eagle, candy-cloud, candy-red hot, radical-eagle, radical-cloud, radical-red hot, trickster-eagle, trickster-cloud, trickster-red hot

d. How many different skateboard designs are possible? 15

Reading the Lesson 1–2. See students' work.

Write a definition and give an example of each new vocabulary phrase.

Vocabulary	Definition	Example
1. tree diagram		
2. Fundamental Counting Principle		

Helping You Remember

3. Complete the two diagrams below by filling in each blank with one of the following words. Some words may be used more than once.

choices

favorable

outcomes

possible

Resource Manager

Workbooks and Reproducible Masters

Chapter 12 Resource Masters
- Study Guide and Intervention, p. 692
- Skills Practice, p. 693
- Practice, p. 694
- Reading to Learn Mathematics, p. 695
- Enrichment, p. 696

Parent and Student Study Guide Workbook, p. 103
School-to-Career Masters, p. 23

Transparencies
5-Minute Check Transparency 12-6
Answer Key Transparencies

Technology
Interactive Chalkboard

COUNTING OUTCOMES

1 **GREETING CARDS** A greeting-card maker offers four birthday greetings in five possible colors, as shown in the table below. How many different cards can be made from four greeting choices and five color choices?

Greeting	Color
Humorous	Blue
Traditional	Green
Romantic	Orange
"From the Group"	Purple, Red

20

2 **CELL PHONES** A cell phone company offers 3 payment plans, 4 styles of phones, and 6 decorative phone wraps. How many phone options are available? 72

FIND THE PROBABILITY OF AN EVENT

3 **a.** Henry rolls a number cube and tosses a coin. What is the probability that he will roll a 3 and toss heads? $\dfrac{1}{12}$

b. What is the probability of winning a multi-state lottery game where the winning number is made up of 6 numbers from 1 to 50 chosen at random? Assume all numbers are eligible each draw.

$\dfrac{1}{15,625,000,000}$

In Example 1, notice that the product of the number of decks and the number of types of wheels, 3 · 2, is the same as the number of outcomes, 6. The **Fundamental Counting Principle** relates the number of outcomes to the number of choices.

Key Concept *Fundamental Counting Principle*

- **Words** If event *M* can occur in *m* ways and is followed by event *N* that can occur in *n* ways, then the event *M* followed by *N* can occur in *m · n* ways.

- **Example** If there are 5 possible decks and 3 possible sets of wheels, then there are 5 · 3 or 15 possible skateboards.

☑ **Concept Check** How many outcomes are possible if you toss a coin and roll a 6-sided number cube? $2 \cdot 6 = 12$

You can also use the Fundamental Counting Principle when there are more than two events.

Example 2 *Use the Fundamental Counting Principle*

SKIING When you rent ski equipment at Bridger Peaks Ski Resort, you choose from 4 different types of ski boots, 5 lengths of skis, and 2 types of poles. How many different outfits are possible?

Use the Fundamental Counting Principle.

The number of types of boots	times	the number of lengths of skis	times	the number of types of poles	equals	the number of possible outcomes.
4	×	5	×	2	=	40

There are 40 possible different sets of boots, skis, and poles.

FIND THE PROBABILITY OF AN EVENT When you know the number of outcomes, you can find the probability that an event will occur.

Example 3 *Find Probabilities*

a. Jasmine is going to toss two coins. What is the probability that she will toss one head and one tail?

First find the number of outcomes.

First Coin		Heads			Tails	
Second Coin	Heads	Tails		Heads	Tails	
Outcomes	H, H	H, T		T, H	T, T	

There are four possible outcomes.

Study Tip

Multiplying More than Two Factors
Remember, when you multiply, you can change the order of the factors. For example, in 4 × 5 × 2 you can multiply 5 × 2 first, then multiply the product, 10, by 4 to get 40.

DAILY INTERVENTION **Differentiated Instruction**

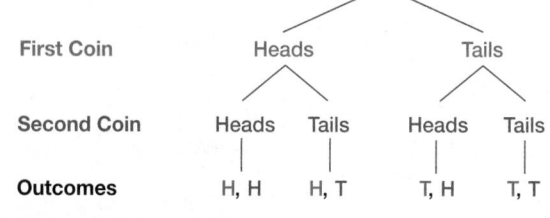

- **Kinesthetic** Have students work in groups of four or five to act out the number of different ways the students can be seated. Each student should have a chair. The students should keep a chart showing each of the arrangements of students and chairs. When each student in the group has sat in each of the chairs, the students should discuss their chart. They should then use the Fundamental Counting Principle to determine whether they recorded each possible arrangement once and only once.

Look at the tree diagram. There are two outcomes that have one head and one tail.

$$P(\text{one head, one tail}) = \frac{\text{number of favorable outcomes}}{\text{number of possible outcomes}}$$

$$= \frac{2}{4} \text{ or } \frac{1}{2}$$

The probability that Jasmine will toss one head and one tail is $\frac{1}{2}$.

b. **What is the probability of winning a state lottery game where the winning number is made up of four digits from 0 to 9 chosen at random?**

First, find the number of possible outcomes. Use the Fundamental Counting Principle.

choices for the 1st digit	times	choices for the 2nd digit	times	choices for the 3rd digit	times	choices for the 4th digit	equals	total number of outcomes
10	×	10	×	10	×	10	=	10,000

There are 10,000 possible outcomes. There is 1 winning number. So, the probability of winning with one ticket is $\frac{1}{10,000}$. This probability can also be written as a decimal, 0.0001, or a percent, 0.01%.

Check for Understanding

Concept Check

1. **Compare and contrast** using a tree diagram and using the Fundamental Counting Principle to find numbers of outcomes. **1–3. See margin.**

2. **OPEN ENDED** Give an example of a situation that would have 12 outcomes.

3. **Explain** how to find the probability of an order containing chicken filling from a choice of burrito or taco with chicken, beef, or bean filling.

Guided Practice

GUIDED PRACTICE KEY	
Exercises	Examples
4	1
5, 7	3
6, 8, 9	2

The spinner at the right is spun twice.

4. Draw a tree diagram to represent the situation. How many outcomes are possible? **See pp. 665A–665F.**

5. What is the probability of spinning two blues? $\frac{1}{16}$

A coin is tossed, and a six-sided number cube is rolled.

6. How many outcomes are possible? **12**

7. What is the probability of tails and an odd number? $\frac{1}{4}$

8. Four coins are tossed. How many outcomes are possible? **16**

Application

9. **FOOD SERVICE** Hastings Cafeteria serves toast, a muffin, or a bagel with coffee, milk, or orange juice. How many different breakfasts of one bread and one beverage are possible? **9**

www.pre-alg.com/extra_examples

Answers

1. Sample answer: Both methods find the number of outcomes. Using the Fundamental Counting Principle is faster and uses less space; using a tree diagram shows what each outcome is.

2. Sample answer: Choosing an outfit from 3 pairs of shorts and 4 T-shirts.

3. First find the number of outcomes possible. The possible outcomes are taco-chicken, taco-beef, taco-bean, burrito-chicken, burrito-beef, and burrito-bean, for a total of 6 outcomes. Two of the outcomes have chicken filling, so the probability of chicken filling is $\frac{2}{6}$ or $\frac{1}{3}$.

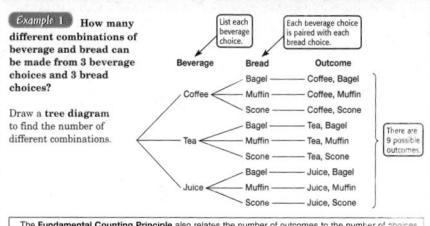
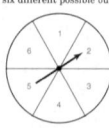

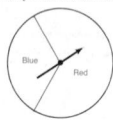
Practice and Apply

10–13. See pp. 665A–665F for tree diagrams.
12. 12 outcomes

25. Either; the probability of rolling either odd or even is one-half.

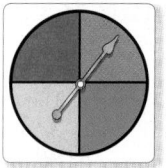
Draw a tree diagram to find the number of outcomes for each situation.

10. Each spinner shown at the right is spun once. **24 outcomes**

11. Three coins are tossed. **8 outcomes**
12. A restaurant offers three types of pasta with two types of sauce and a choice of meatball or sausage.
13. Andrew has a choice of a blue, yellow, white, or striped shirt with a choice of black, navy, or tan pants. **12 outcomes**

Find the number of possible outcomes for each situation.

14. School sweatshirts come in four sizes and four colors. **16 outcomes**
15. A number cube is rolled twice. **36 outcomes**
16. Two coins are tossed and a number cube is rolled. **24 outcomes**
17. A car comes with two or four doors, a four- or six-cylinder engine, and a choice of six exterior colors. **24 outcomes**
18. A quiz has five true-false questions. **32 outcomes**
19. There are four answer choices for each of five multiple-choice questions on a quiz. **1024 outcomes**

Find the probability of each event. 20. $\frac{3}{8}$ 23. $\frac{1}{100,000}$

20. Three coins are tossed. What is the probability of two heads and one tail?
21. Two six-sided number cubes are rolled. What is the probability of getting a 3 on exactly one of the number cubes? $\frac{5}{18}$
22. An 8-sided die is rolled three times. What is the probability of getting three 7s? $\frac{1}{512}$
23. What is the probability of winning a lottery game where the winning number is made up of five digits from 0 to 9 chosen at random?

24. **SKATEBOARDS** How many different deluxe skateboards are possible from 10 choices of decks, 8 choices of trucks (the axles that hold the wheels on), and 12 choices of wheels? **960**

25. **GAMES** Suppose you play a game where each player rolls two number cubes and records the sum. The first player chooses whether to win with an even or an odd sum. Should the player choose even or odd? Explain your reasoning.

26. **COMPUTERS** The table shows the features you can choose to customize a computer.

Processor	RAM	External Drive	Printer	Color
regular	64 MB	regular	basic	red
high-speed	128 MB	extra-capacity	standard	gray
	256 MB		deluxe	green
			fax edition	white
				lime

a. How many customized computers include the deluxe printer? **60**
b. How many customized computers include 256 MB of RAM and a high-speed processor? **40**

27. Sample answer: any two letters followed by any four digits

27. CRITICAL THINKING A certain state uses a system to design motor vehicle license plates that allows for 6,760,000 different plates using a total of six digits and letters. Find a way to use the digits 0–9 and letters A–Z to produce this exact number of arrangements.

28. WRITING IN MATH Answer the question that was posed at the beginning of the lesson. **See margin.**

How can you count the number of skateboard designs that are available from a catalog?

Include the following in your answer:

- the strategy you used to find all possible skateboard designs,
- the relationship of the number of designs to the number of wheels and decks, and
- how the number of skateboards would change if the number of types of decks was doubled.

Standardized Test Practice
Ⓐ Ⓑ Ⓒ Ⓓ

29. A 4-character password uses the letters of the alphabet. Each letter can be used more than once, but the letter I is not used at all. How many different passwords are possible? **D**

Ⓐ 100 Ⓑ 13,800
Ⓒ 303,600 Ⓓ 390,625

30. Elena has 6 sweaters, 4 pairs of pants, and 3 pairs of shoes. How many different outfits of one sweater, one pair of pants, and one pair of shoes can she make? **D**

Ⓐ 13 Ⓑ 24
Ⓒ 27 Ⓓ 72

Maintain Your Skills

Mixed Review

31. Sample answer: Vertical scale that does not start at zero.

31. STATISTICS Describe a situation that might cause a line graph to be misleading. *(Lesson 12-5)*

ANIMALS For Exercises 32–34, use the histogram. *(Lesson 12-4)*

32. How many years are there in each interval? **10 years**

33. Which interval has the greatest number of animals? **11–20**

34. How many of the animals have a life span more than 20 years? **3**

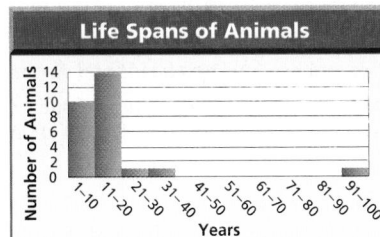

Life Spans of Animals

Source: *The World Almanac*

ALGEBRA Use the slope and the *y*-intercept to graph each equation. *(Lesson 8-3)* **35–38. See margin.**

35. $y = 3x + 1$ **36.** $y = \frac{1}{2}x - 2$ **37.** $y = 5$ **38.** $2x - y = 4$

Getting Ready for the Next Lesson

PREREQUISITE SKILL Simplify. *(To review simplifying fractions, see Lesson 4-5.)*

39. $\frac{6 \cdot 5}{2 \cdot 1}$ **15**   **40.** $\frac{5 \cdot 4 \cdot 3}{3 \cdot 2 \cdot 1}$ **10**   **41.** $\frac{8 \cdot 7}{2 \cdot 1}$ **28**   **42.** $\frac{6 \cdot 5 \cdot 4 \cdot 3}{4 \cdot 3 \cdot 2 \cdot 1}$ **15**

4 Assess

Open-Ended Assessment

Writing Have students write a paragraph comparing and contrasting tree diagrams and the Fundamental Counting Principle as methods for finding the number of outcomes of an event.

Getting Ready for Lesson 12-7

PREREQUISITE SKILL In Lesson 12-7, students will learn how to find the number of combinations of items by dividing the number of permutations of the set of items by the number of ways each smaller set can be arranged. Exercises 39–42 should be used to determine your students' familiarity with simplifying fractions.

Answers

28. Answers may include making a list pairing each deck choice with each wheel choice, making a tree diagram, multiplying the number of choices for deck times the number of choices for wheels. Answers should include the following.

- The strategy used by the student to count the possible designs is explained.
- The number of designs is the same as the product of the number of choices.
- The number of skateboards would double.

35.

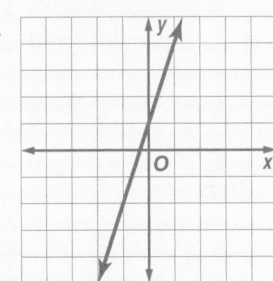

36.

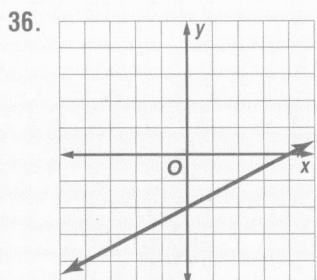

37.

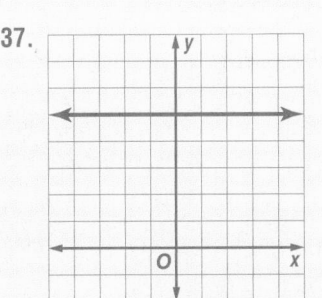

38.

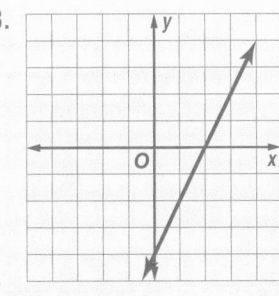

Getting Started

Objective Explore the relationship between tossing coins and Pascal's triangle.

Materials
penny
dime
nickel
quarter

Teach

- After students have completed their tree diagrams in Collect Data, have them quickly switch papers and proof the diagrams before proceeding to the rest of the activity.

Assess

In **Exercises 1–6**, students should be able to work quickly once they have done one or two of the exercises. Watch for students who are taking too much time as they may need some intervention.

In **Exercises 7 and 8,** students should demonstrate that they have found the connections between Pascal's triangle and tossing coins.

Use **Exercise 9** to determine whether students have discovered the patterns in the triangle and understand why the patterns exist.

Study Notebook

You may wish to have students summarize this activity and what they learned from it.

Algebra Activity

Probability and Pascal's Triangle

Collect Data

Step 1 Copy and complete the tree diagram shown below listing all possible outcomes if you toss a penny and a dime.

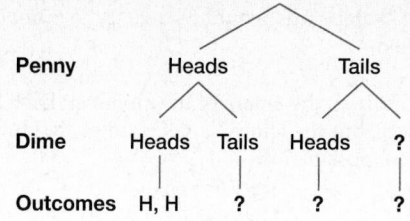

Penny	Heads		Tails	
Dime	Heads	Tails	Heads	?
Outcomes	H, H	?	?	?

Step 2 Make another tree diagram showing the possible outcomes if you toss a penny, a nickel, and a dime. **See pp. 665A–665F.**

Step 3 Make a third tree diagram to show the outcomes for tossing a penny, a nickel, a dime, and a quarter. **See pp. 665A–665F.**

Analyze the Data

1. For tossing two coins, how many outcomes are there? How many have one head and one tail? **4; 2**

2. Find P(two heads), P(one head, one tail) and P(two tails). Do not simplify. $\frac{1}{4}, \frac{2}{4}, \frac{1}{4}$

3. For tossing three coins, how many outcomes are there? How many have two heads and one tail? one head and two tails? **8; 3; 3**

4. Find P(three heads), P(two heads, one tail), P(one head, two tails), and P(three tails). Do not simplify. $\frac{1}{8}, \frac{3}{8}, \frac{3}{8}, \frac{1}{8}$

5. For tossing four coins, how many outcomes are there? How many have three heads and one tail? two heads and two tails? one head and three tails? **16; 4; 6; 4**

6. Find P(four heads), P(three heads, one tail), P(two heads, two tails), P(one head, three tails), and P(four tails). Do not simplify. $\frac{1}{16}, \frac{4}{16}, \frac{6}{16}, \frac{4}{16}, \frac{1}{16}$

Make a Conjecture

Pascal was a French mathematician who lived in the 1600s. He is known for the triangle of numbers at the right, called Pascal's triangle.

				1					Row 0
			1		1				Row 1
		1		2		1			Row 2
	1		3		3		1		Row 3
1		4		6		4		1	Row 4

7. Examine the rows of Pascal's triangle. Explain how the numbers in each row are related to tossing coins. (*Hint*: Row 2 relates to tossing two coins.) **See pp. 665A–665F.**

Extend the Activity

8. Use Pascal's triangle to find the probabilities for tossing five coins. **See pp. 665A–665F.**

9. Find other patterns in Pascal's triangle. **See students' work.**

Resource Manager

📁 *Teaching Pre-Algebra with Manipulatives*
- p. 151 (student recording sheet)

Permutations and Combinations

What You'll Learn

- Use permutations.
- Use combinations.

Vocabulary
- permutation
- factorial
- combination

Why is order sometimes important when determining outcomes?

Lenora, Michael, Ned, Olivia, and Patrick are running for president and treasurer of the class. How many pairs are possible for the two offices?

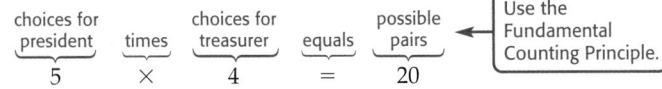

choices for president	times	choices for treasurer	equals	possible pairs
5	×	4	=	20

Use the Fundamental Counting Principle.

There are 20 possible pairs. How is the number of pairs different for five students running for two student council seats, where order is not important?

a. Make a list of all possible pairs for class offices. (*Note:* Lenora-Michael is different than Michael-Lenora.) **See margin.**

b. How does the Fundamental Counting Principle relate to the number of pairs you found? **The results are the same.**

c. Make another list for student council seats. (*Note:* For this list, Lenora-Michael is the same as Michael-Lenora.) **See margin.**

d. How does the answer in part **a** compare to the answer in part **c**?

d. The answer in part c equals the answer in part a divided by 2.

USE PERMUTATIONS An arrangement or listing in which order is important is called a **permutation**. The symbol $P(5, 2)$ represents the number of permutations of 5 things taken 2 at a time, as in 5 students running for 2 offices.

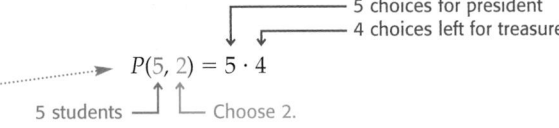

- 5 choices for president
- 4 choices left for treasurer

$$P(5, 2) = 5 \cdot 4$$

5 students — Choose 2.

Example 1 Use a Permutation

a. SWIMMING How many ways can six swimmers be arranged on a four-person relay team?

On a relay team, the order of the swimmers is important. This arrangement is a permutation.

6 swimmers — Choose 4.

$$P(6, 4) = 6 \cdot 5 \cdot 4 \cdot 3$$
$$= 360$$

- 6 choices for 1st person
- 5 choices for 2nd person
- 4 choices for 3rd person
- 3 choices for 4th person

There are 360 possible arrangements.

---

1 Focus

5-Minute Check Transparency 12-7 Use as a quiz or review of Lesson 12-6.

Mathematical Background notes are available for this lesson on page 604D.

Why is order sometimes important when determining outcomes?

The opening activity questions are repeated on page 700 of the *Chapter 12 Resource Masters*.

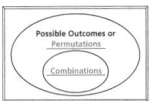

Possible Outcomes or Permutations / Combinations

Resource Manager

Workbooks and Reproducible Masters

Chapter 12 Resource Masters
- Study Guide and Intervention, p. 697
- Skills Practice, p. 698
- Practice, p. 699
- Reading to Learn Mathematics, p. 700
- Enrichment, p. 701
- Assessment, p. 728

Parent and Student Study Guide Workbook, p. 104
School-to-Career Masters, p. 24

 Transparencies

5-Minute Check Transparency 12-7
Answer Key Transparencies

 Technology

Interactive Chalkboard

2 Teach

USE PERMUTATIONS

In-Class Examples Power Point®

1 **a. TRAVEL** The Reyes family will visit a complex of theme parks during its summer vacation. They have a four-day pass good at one park per day; they can choose from seven parks. How many different ways can they arrange their vacation schedule? **840**

b. How many five-digit numbers can be made from the digits 2, 4, 5, 8, and 9 if each digit is used only once? **120**

2 Find the value of 12!. **479,001,600**

USE COMBINATIONS

In-Class Examples Power Point®

Teaching Tip Have students check that they have listed all possible permutations by calculating the permutations as they did in Example 1.

3 **HATS** How many ways can a window dresser choose two hats out of a fedora, a bowler, and a sombrero? **3**

4 **PENS** How many ways can a customer choose two pens from a purple, orange, green, red, or black pen? **10**

---

b. How many four-digit numbers can be made from the digits 1, 3, 5, and 2 if each digit is used only once?

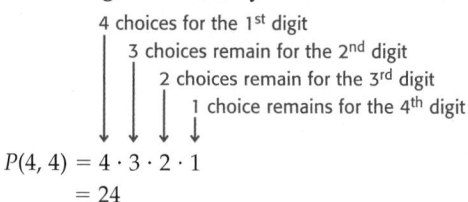

4 choices for the 1st digit
3 choices remain for the 2nd digit
2 choices remain for the 3rd digit
1 choice remains for the 4th digit

$P(4, 4) = 4 \cdot 3 \cdot 2 \cdot 1$
$= 24$

Reading Math

The Symbol !
Read 4! as *four factorial.*

The number of permutations in Example 1b can be written as 4!. It means $4 \cdot 3 \cdot 2 \cdot 1$. The notation n **factorial** means the product of all counting numbers beginning with n and counting backward to 1.

Example 2 **Factorial Notation**

Find the value of 5!.

$5! = 5 \cdot 4 \cdot 3 \cdot 2 \cdot 1$ Multiply 5 and all of the counting numbers less than 5.
$= 120$

USE COMBINATIONS   Sometimes order is not important. For example, *pepperoni, mushrooms,* and *onions* is the same as *onions, pepperoni,* and *mushrooms* when you order a pizza. An arrangement or listing where order is *not* important is called a **combination**.

Example 3 **Use a Combination**

SCHOOL COLORS How many ways can students choose two school colors from red, blue, white and gold?

Since order is not important, this arrangement is a combination.

First, list all of the permutations of red, blue, white, and gold taken two at a time. Then cross off arrangements that are the same as another one.

| RB | RW | RG | ~~BR~~ | BW | BG |
| ~~WR~~ | ~~WB~~ | WG | ~~GR~~ | ~~GB~~ | ~~GW~~ |

RB and BR are not different in this case, so cross off one of them.

There are only six *different* arrangements. So, there are six ways to choose two colors from a list of four colors.

Example 4 **Counting Arrangements**

FLOWERS How many ways can three flowers be chosen from tulips, daffodils, lilies, and roses?

The arrangement is a combination because order is not important.

TDL	TDR	TLR	~~TLD~~	~~TRD~~	~~TRL~~
DLR	~~DLT~~	~~DRT~~	~~DRL~~	~~DTL~~	~~DTR~~
LRT	~~LRD~~	~~LTD~~	~~LTR~~	~~LDR~~	~~LDT~~
~~RTD~~	~~RTL~~	~~RDL~~	~~RDT~~	~~RLT~~	~~RLD~~

First, list all of the permutations. Then cross off the arrangements that are the same.

There are 4 ways to choose three flowers from a list of four flowers.

D A I L Y
INTERVENTION   **Differentiated Instruction**

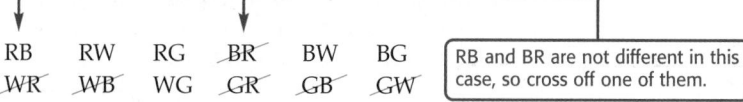

- **Visual/Spatial** Pascal's triangle can be used to answer questions involving combinations. Show students this table and ask them to find the number of combinations of 6 things taken 4 at a time. **15**

Number Taken at a Time	0	1	2	3	4	5	6
Row 6	1	6	15	20	15	6	1

You can find the number of combinations of items by dividing the number of permutations of the set of items by the number of ways each smaller set can be arranged.

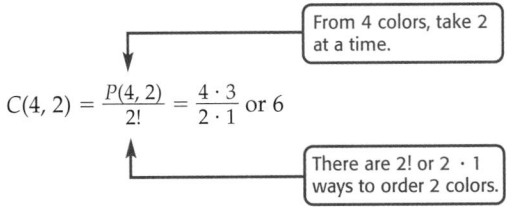

$$C(4, 2) = \frac{P(4, 2)}{2!} = \frac{4 \cdot 3}{2 \cdot 1} \text{ or } 6$$

From 4 colors, take 2 at a time.

There are 2! or $2 \cdot 1$ ways to order 2 colors.

Example 5 *Use a Combination to Solve a Problem*

GEOMETRY Find the number of line segments that can be drawn between any two vertices of an octagon.

Explore An octagon has 8 vertices.

Plan The segment connecting vertex A to vertex C is the same as the segment connecting C to A, so this is a *combination*. Find the combination of 8 vertices taken 2 at a time.

Solve $C(8, 2) = \dfrac{P(8, 2)}{2!}$

$= \dfrac{8 \cdot 7}{2 \cdot 1} \text{ or } 28$

Examine Draw an octagon and all the segments connecting any two vertices. Check to see that there are 28 segments.
Be sure to count the sides of the octagon.

Check for Understanding

Concept Check
1. **OPEN ENDED** Write a problem that can be solved by finding the value of $P(4, 3)$. **See margin.**

2. **Compare and contrast** $5 \cdot 4 \cdot 3$ and 5!. **See margin.**

3. **FIND THE ERROR** Sindu thinks choosing five CDs from a collection of 30 to take to a party is a permutation. Sarah thinks it is a combination. Who is correct? Explain your reasoning. **See margin.**

Guided Practice
4. Find the value of 6!. **720**

GUIDED PRACTICE KEY	
Exercises	Examples
4	2
5, 6	1
7, 8	3, 4
9	5

Tell whether each situation is a *permutation* or *combination*. Then solve.
5. How many ways can 5 people be arranged in a line? **P; 120 ways**

6. How many programs of 4 musical pieces can be made from 8 possible pieces? **P; 1680 programs**

7. How many ways can a 3-player team be chosen from 9 students? **C; 84 ways**

8. How many ways can 6 different flowers be chosen from 12 different flowers? **C; 924 ways**

Application
9. **FOOD** A pizza shop has 12 toppings to choose from. How many different 3-topping pizzas can be ordered? **220 pizzas**

5 GEOMETRY Find the number of line segments that can be drawn between any two vertices of a hexagon. **15**

3 Practice/Apply

Study Notebook

Have students—
• add the definitions/examples of the vocabulary terms to their Vocabulary Builder worksheets for Chapter 12.
• choose an example each of using a permutation and using a combination to label and add to their notebooks.
• include any other item(s) that they find helpful in mastering the skills in this lesson.

DAILY
INTERVENTION **FIND THE ERROR** Students may confuse combinations and permutations. Emphasize each definition, model various situations, and ask whether order is important. It may also be helpful to have students make up memory tools for each definition.

Answers

1. Sample answer: How many 3-digit numbers can be made from the digits 1, 2, 3, and 4 if no digit is repeated?

2. Both expressions have 5, 4, and 3 as factors; 5! also has factors of 2 and 1.

3. Sarah; five CDs from a collection of 30 is a combination because order is not important.

Teaching Tip Have students divide a sheet of paper into two columns. They should head one column "Permutation: order important" and the other "Combination: order not important." As students complete Exercises 5–8 and 10–17, have them write the number of the exercise under the proper column.

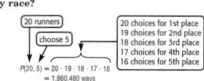
★ indicates increased difficulty

Practice and Apply

Homework Help

For Exercises	See Examples
10–17	1, 3, 4
18–21	2
22, 23	5

Extra Practice
See page 754.

12. C; 210 ways
16. C; 2,598,960 hands

Tell whether each situation is a *permutation* or combination. Then solve.

10. How many ways can 6 cars line up for a race? P; 720 ways

11. How many different flags can be made from the colors red, blue, green, and white if each flag has three vertical stripes? P; 24 flags

12. How many ways can 4 shirts be chosen from 10 shirts to take on a trip?

13. How many ways can you buy 2 DVDs from a display of 15? C; 105 ways

14. How many 3-digit numbers can you write using the digits 6, 7, and 8 exactly once in each number? P; 6 numbers

15. There are 12 paintings in a show. How many ways can the paintings take first, second, and third place? P; 1320 ways

16. How many 5-card hands can be dealt from a standard deck of 52 cards?

17. How many ways can you choose 3 flavors of ice cream from a choice of 14 flavors? C; 364 ways

Find each value.

18. 7! 5040
19. 8! 40,320
20. 10! 3,628,800
21. 11! 39,916,800

22. GEOMETRY Twelve points are marked on a circle. How many different line segments can be drawn between any two of the points?
66 line segments

23. HANDSHAKES Nine people gather for a meeting. Each person shakes hands with every other person exactly once. How many handshakes will take place? 36 handshakes

More About...

Amusement Parks

An amusement park in Ohio is known for its thrilling roller coasters. There are fourteen roller coasters at the park.

Source: www.cedarpoint.com

•AMUSEMENT PARKS For Exercises 24 and 25, use the information at the left.

24. Suppose you only have time to ride eight of the coasters. How many ways are there to ride eight coasters if order is important? 121,080,960 ways

25. How many ways are there to ride eight of the coasters if order is not important? 3003 ways

26. LICENSE PLATES North Carolina issues general license plates with three letters followed by four numbers. (The first number cannot be zero.) Numbers can repeat, but letters cannot. How many license plates can North Carolina generate with this format? 140,400,000 license plates

FLOWERS For Exercises 27–29, use the following information.

Three roses are to be placed in a vase. The color choices are red, pink, white, yellow, and orange. 27. 10 combinations

27. How many different 3-rose combinations can be made from the 5 roses?

28. What is the probability that 3 roses selected at random will include pink, white, and yellow? $\frac{1}{10}$

★ 29. What is the probability that 3 roses selected at random will *not* include red? $\frac{2}{5}$

30. CRITICAL THINKING Is the value of $P(x, y)$ *sometimes*, *always*, or *never* greater than the value of $C(x, y)$? (Assume neither x nor y equals 1 and $x \neq y$.) always

644 Chapter 12 More Statistics and Probability

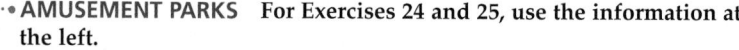

Answer (p. 645)

31. When order is not important, duplicate arrangements are not included in the number of arrangements. Answers should include the following.

- When order was not important there were half as many pairs.

- Order is important when you arrange things in a line; order is not important when you choose a group of things.

31. WRITING IN MATH Answer the question that was posed at the beginning of the lesson.

Why is order sometimes important when determining outcomes?

Include the following in your answer: **See margin.**
- how the number of pairs differed when order was not important, and
- an example of a situation where order is important and one where order is not important.

32. Refer to the table. How many different slates of officers could be made if a slate consists of one candidate for each office? **D**

President	Secretary	Treasurer
Tracy	Glenn	Ariel
Marta	Ling	Sherita
José		Wesley

   Ⓐ 3   Ⓑ 6

   Ⓒ 9   Ⓓ 18

33. Caitlyn knows a phone number begins with 444 and the last four digits are 3, 2, 1, and 0, but she does not remember in what order. What is the greatest number of calls she would have to make to get the right number?

   Ⓐ 4   Ⓑ 12   Ⓒ 24   Ⓓ 72   **C**

Maintain Your Skills

Mixed Review

34. Draw a tree diagram to find the number of outcomes for rolling two number cubes. *(Lesson 12-6)* **36 outcomes; see pp. 665A–665F for diagram.**

35. Is the graph at the right misleading? Explain your reasoning. *(Lesson 12-5)*

35. Yes; the vertical axis does not include zero.

Ticket Sales

Name all of the sets of numbers to which each real number belongs. Let N = natural numbers, W = whole numbers, Z = integers, Q = rational numbers, and I = irrational numbers. *(Lesson 9-2)*

36. 5 **N,W,Z,Q**   **37.** 0.262626… **Q**

38. −81 **Z, Q**   **39.** $\sqrt{20}$ **I**

Getting Ready for the Next Lesson

PREREQUISITE SKILL Write each ratio in simplest form.
*(To review **simplifying ratios**, see Lesson 6-1.)*

40. 16:14 **8:7**   **41.** 4:32 **1:8**   **42.** 4:48 **1:12**   **43.** 44:8 **11:2**   **44.** 45:55 **9:11**

Practice Quiz 2   Lessons 12-5 through 12-7

1. **STATISTICS** Describe a situation that might cause a bar graph to be misleading. *(Lesson 12-5)* **Sample answer: Bars are different widths.**

2. Draw a tree diagram to represent the possible combinations of blue or tan shorts with a red, white, or yellow shirt. *(Lesson 12-6)* **See margin.**

3. How many outcomes are possible for a quiz with 8 true-false questions? *(Lesson 12-6)* **256 outcomes**

4. How many ways can the letters of the word STUDY be arranged? *(Lesson 12-7)* **120 ways**

5. **GEOMETRY** Find the number of line segments that can be drawn between any two vertices of a hexagon. *(Lesson 12-7)* **15 segments**

Answer (Practice Quiz 2)

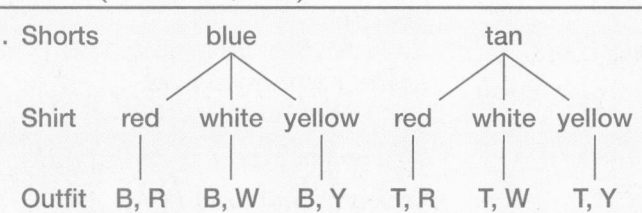

2.
Shorts	blue			tan		
Shirt	red	white	yellow	red	white	yellow
Outfit	B, R	B, W	B, Y	T, R	T, W	T, Y

Open-Ended Assessment

Modeling Have students work in small groups. Give each group seven different books. Have students model permutations and combinations if the books are used five at a time.

Getting Ready for Lesson 12-8

PREREQUISITE SKILL In Lesson 12-8, students learn how to find odds, for which they will need to simplify ratios. Exercises 40–44 should be used to determine your students' familiarity with simplifying ratios.

Assessment Options

Practice Quiz 2 The quiz provides students with a brief review of the concepts and skills in Lessons 12-5 through 12-7. Lesson numbers are given to the right of exercises or instruction lines so students can review concepts not yet mastered.

Quiz (Lessons 12-6 and 12-7) is available on p. 728 of the *Chapter 12 Resource Masters.*

About the Exercises . . .

Organization by Objective
- **Use Permutations:** 10–21
- **Use Combinations:** 10–17, 22, 23

Odd/Even Assignments

Exercises 10–23 are structured so that students practice the same concepts whether they are assigned odd or even problems.

Assignment Guide

Basic: 11–23 odd, 24, 25, 30–44

Average: 11–23 odd, 24–44

Advanced: 10–22 even, 24–39 (Optional: 40–44)

All: Practice Quiz 2 (1–5)

1 Focus

5-Minute Check Transparency 12-8 Use as a quiz or review of Lesson 12-7.

Mathematical Background notes are available for this lesson on page 604D.

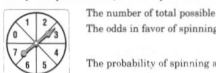 **are odds related to probability?**

The opening activity questions are repeated on page 705 of the *Chapter 12 Resource Masters*.

Reading to Learn Mathematics, p. 705   ELL

Pre-Activity *How are odds related to probability?*

Do the activity at the top of page 646 in your textbook. Write your answers below.

  a. Roll the number cubes 50 times. Record whether you win or lose each time. See students' work.

  b. What is the experimental probability of winning the game based on your results in part **a**? See students' work; theoretical probability is $\frac{5}{12}$.

  c. Write the ratio of wins to losses using your results in part a.
    See students' work; based on theoretical probability, the ratio is 5:7.

Reading the Lesson

Write a definition and give an example of the new vocabulary word.

	Vocabulary	Definition	Example
1.	odds	See students' work.	

2. The odds **in favor of** an outcome is the ratio of the number of successes to the number of failures.

3. The odds **against** an outcome is the ratio of the number of failures to the number of successes.

4. The number of successes added to the number of failures equals the number of **total possible** outcomes.

5. To find the **odds** of an outcome, compare the number of successes with the number of failures.

Helping You Remember

6. Study the spinner below, then complete the following.

  The number of total possible outcomes = **8**

  The odds in favor of spinning an even number = **1:1**

  The probability of spinning an even number = **$\frac{1}{2}$**

  The odds in favor of spinning a number less than 5 = **5:3**

  The odds against spinning a number less than 5 = **3:5**

What You'll Learn

- Find the odds of a simple event.

How are odds related to probability?

Vocabulary
- odds

a–b. See students' work; theoretical probability is $\frac{5}{12}$.

c. See students' work; based on theoretical probability, the ratio is 5:7.

Suppose you play the following game.
- Roll two number cubes.
- If the sum of the numbers you roll is 6 or less, you win. If the sum is *not* 6 or less, you lose.

Do you think you will win or lose more often? Play the game to find out.

  a. Roll the number cubes 50 times. Record whether you win or lose each time.

  b. What is the experimental probability of winning the game based on your results in part **a**?

  c. Write the ratio of wins to losses using your results in part **a**.

Study Tip

Rolling Number Cubes
There are 36 ways to roll two 6-sided number cubes. 15 of the results have a sum of 6 or less. 21 results have a sum greater than 6. See Lesson 6-9 for a table of possible outcomes.

FIND ODDS You can find theoretical probabilities for rolling a certain sum from two 6-sided number cubes.

$$P(6 \text{ or less}) = \frac{15}{36} \text{ or } \frac{5}{12} \qquad P(not\ 6 \text{ or less}) = \frac{21}{36} \text{ or } \frac{7}{12}$$

Another way to describe the chance of an event occurring is with odds. The **odds** in favor of an event is the ratio that compares the number of ways the event can occur to the ways that the event *cannot* occur.

ways to occur ⌐   ⌐ ways to not occur

odds of sum of 6 or less → 15:21 or 5:7

Read 15:21 as 15 to 21.

TEACHING TIP

Point out that the odds against an outcome is the reciprocal of the odds in favor of an outcome.

Key Concept — Definition of Odds

The odds in favor of an outcome is the ratio of the number of ways the outcome can occur to the number of ways the outcome cannot occur.

  Odds in favor = number of successes : number of failures

The odds against an outcome is the ratio of the number of ways the outcome cannot occur to the number of ways the outcome can occur.

  Odds against = number of failures : number of successes

 Concept Check   If the odds in favor of an outcome are 2:3, what are the odds *against* the same outcome? **3:2**

646   **Chapter 12**   More Statistics and Probability

Resource Manager

 Workbooks and Reproducible Masters

Chapter 12 Resource Masters
- Study Guide and Intervention, p. 702
- Skills Practice, p. 703
- Practice, p. 704
- Reading to Learn Mathematics, p. 705
- Enrichment, p. 706

Parent and Student Study Guide Workbook, p. 105

Transparencies
5-Minute Check Transparency 12-8
Answer Key Transparencies

Technology
Interactive Chalkboard

Example 1 Find Odds

a. **Find the odds of a sum less than 4 if a pair of number cubes are rolled.**

There are 6 · 6 or 36 sums possible for rolling a pair of number cubes.
There are 3 sums less than 4. They are (1, 1), (1, 2), and (2, 1).
There are 36 – 3 or 33 sums that are not less than 4.

Odds of rolling a sum less than 4

$$= \underbrace{\text{number of ways to roll a sum less than 4}} \quad \text{to} \quad \underbrace{\text{number of ways to roll any other sum}}$$

$$= \quad 3 \quad : \quad 33 \quad \text{or } 1{:}11$$

The odds of rolling a sum less than 4 are 1:11.

Reading Math

Odds Notation
Read 1:11 as *1 to 11*.

b. **A bag contains 6 red marbles, 4 blue marbles, and 2 gold marbles. What are the odds against drawing a blue marble from the bag?**

There are 12 – 4 or 8 marbles that are not blue.

Odds against drawing a blue marble

$$= \underbrace{\text{number of ways to draw a marble that is not blue}} \quad \text{to} \quad \underbrace{\text{number of ways to draw a blue marble}}$$

$$= \quad 8 \quad : \quad 4 \quad \text{or } 2{:}1$$

The odds *against* drawing a blue marble are 2:1.

Standardized Test Practice
Ⓐ Ⓑ Ⓒ Ⓓ

Example 2 Use Odds

Multiple-Choice Test Item

Enrico got positive results 6 out of the 18 times he conducted a science experiment. Based on these results, what are the odds that he will get a positive result the next time he conducts the experiment?

Ⓐ 3 to 9
Ⓑ 9 to 3
Ⓒ 1 to 2
Ⓓ 2 to 1

Test-Taking Tip

Preparing for Tests
As part of your preparation for a standardized test, review basic definitions such as *odds* and *probability*.

Read the Test Item

To find the odds, compare the number of success to the number of failures.

Solve the Test Item

The experiment was conducted 18 times.
6 results were positive.
18 – 6 or 12 results were not positive.

successes:failures = 6 to 12 or 1 to 2

The answer is C.

☑ Concept Check How do the number of successes and failures relate to the number of total possible outcomes?
successes + failures = total possible outcomes

FIND ODDS

In-Class Examples Power Point®

Teaching Tip To simplify finding the answer to In-Class Example 1a or to check it, have students find how many sums are less than or equal to 5, and subtract that number from the 36 possible sums.

1 **a.** Find the odds of a sum greater than 5 if a pair of number cubes are rolled. **13:5**

b. A bag contains 5 yellow marbles, 3 white marbles, and 1 black marble. What are the odds against drawing a white marble from the bag? **2:1**

2 **Multiple-Choice Test Item**
After 2 weeks, 8 out of 20 sunflower seeds that Tamara planted had sprouted. Based on these results, what are the odds that a sunflower seed will sprout under the same conditions? **C**

A	2 to 5	B	5 to 2
C	2 to 3	D	3 to 2

3 Practice/Apply

Study Notebook

Have students—
• add the definition/example of the vocabulary term to their Vocabulary Builder worksheets for Chapter 12.
• include any other item(s) that they find helpful in mastering the skills in this lesson.

DAILY INTERVENTION **Differentiated Instruction**

• **Naturalist** Have students find out the chance of precipitation for your town each day for a week. Then have students use the data to record the odds for and against precipitation each day onto one column of a chart. Then have students note what actually happened on another column of the chart and compare the actual results to the odds.

Study Guide and Intervention, p. 702

Odds	The **odds** in favor of an outcome is the ratio of the number of ways the outcome can occur to the number of ways the outcome cannot occur. Odds in favor = number of successes : number of failures The **odds** against an outcome is the ratio of the number of ways the outcome cannot occur to the number of ways the outcome can occur. Odds against = number of failures : number of successes

Example 1 Find the odds of a sum of 11 if a pair of number cubes are rolled.

There are 6 · 6 or 36 sums possible for rolling a pair of number cubes. There are 2 sums of 11. They are (5, 6) and (6, 5). There are 36 − 2 or 34 sums that are not 11.

Odds of rolling a sum of 11

$$= \frac{\text{numbers of ways to roll a sum of 11}}{2} : \frac{\text{numbers of ways to roll any other sum}}{34}$$

= 2:34 or 1:17

The odds of rolling an 11 are 1:17.

Example 2 In a bag of marbles, 30 are blue, 15 are orange, 20 are yellow, and 10 are green. What are the odds against drawing a green marble from the bag?

There are 75 − 10 marbles that are not green.

Odds against drawing a green marble

$$= \frac{\text{numbers of ways to draw a marble that is not green}}{65} : \frac{\text{numbers of ways to draw a green marble}}{10}$$

= 65:10 or 13:2

The odds against drawing a green marble are 13:2.

Exercises

Find the odds of each outcome if a pair of number cubes are rolled.

1. *not* a sum of 7 5:1
2. a sum less than 5 or greater than 9 1:2
3. a sum that is a multiple of 3 1:2
4. a double number 1:5
5. *not* a double number 5:1
6. double twos 35:1
7. A hockey team scores 3 goals for every 30 shots taken. What are the odds in favor of the next shot being a goal? 1:9
8. A bookshelf holds 12 mysteries, 3 history books, 4 how-to books, and 11 self-help books. What are the odds of randomly picking a how-to book? 2:13
9. A professional football team finished the season with a record of 10 wins and 6 losses. What were its odds that season of winning a game? 5:3
10. After many sessions of playing rock-paper-scissors with Joe, you discover that he throws "rock" 55 percent of the time. What are the odds in favor of his next throw being "rock"? 11:9

Skills Practice, p. 703 and Practice, p. 704 (shown)

Find the odds of each outcome if the spinner at the right is spun.

1. an odd number 1:1
2. a number less than 6 5:3
3. *not* 7 or 8 3:1
4. a number greater than 5 3:5

A card is selected from a standard deck of 52 cards.

5. What are the odds of selecting a red king? 1:25
6. What are the odds of selecting a 4 of diamonds? 1:51
7. What are the odds of *not* selecting an even club (not a face card)? 47:5
8. What are the odds of selecting a diamond or an 8 of spades? 7:19
9. What are the odds of *not* selecting a queen of hearts? 51:1
10. What are the odds of selecting a jack? 1:12
11. SURVEYS One opinion poll revealed that 41 percent of Americans are completely satisfied with their jobs and that 44 percent are somewhat satisfied. What are the odds of an American worker, chosen at random, being completely satisfied? Somewhat satisfied? Source: www.gallup.com 41:59; 44:56

SURVEYS For Exercises 12–14, use the information in the table at the right.

Gallup Poll, August 2001		
Sports Fan	Not a Fan	No Opinion
57%	42%	1%

Source: www.gallup.com

12. What are the odds against a randomly chosen respondent being a sports fan? 43:57
13. What are the odds against a person having no opinion? 99:1
14. Based on this poll, in a group of 1000 people, how many would you expect *not* to be sports fans? 420 people

SCIENCE For Exercises 15–18, use the information in the table at the right. Assume that one sample is drawn randomly from a bag containing one sample of each of the minerals in the table.

Mohs Scale of Mineral Hardness	
Mineral	Hardness (hardest rank is 10)
Diamond	10
Corundum	9
Topaz	8
Quartz	7
Orthoclase	6
Apatite	5
Fluorite	4
Calcite	3
Gypsum	2
Talc	1

Source: *The Sizesaurus*

15. What are the odds in favor of drawing a mineral harder than topaz? 1:4
16. What are the odds in favor of drawing quartz? 1:9
17. What are the odds against drawing a mineral softer than quartz? 2:3
18. What are the odds against drawing a mineral harder than apatite? 1:1

Enrichment, p. 706

Odds

The **odds** for an event can be found as follows.

odds *for* an event = number of ways that event can occur : number of ways that event cannot occur

If a number cube is rolled once, find the odds for a 4.

1 → A 4 can occur only in one way.
5 → The other events are 1, 2, 3, 5, and 6.

The odds of rolling a 4 are 1 to 5 or 1:5.

odds *against* an event = number of ways that event cannot occur : number of ways that event can occur

Find the odds for spinning each of the following.

1. for a 6 1:15
2. *not* for a 13 15:1
3. for a prime number 3:5
4. for a 4, 8, or 12 3:13
5. *not* for an odd number 1:1
6. for a 7 or 9 1:7
7. for an odd number less than 14 7:9
8. *not* for a number greater than 11 11:5

A pair of number cubes are rolled. Find the odds for each of the following.

9. for a sum of 6 5:31
10. for a sum of 2 or 10 1:8
11. *not* for a sum of 3 17:1
12. for matching numbers (doubles) 1:5
13. for a sum of 7, with a 2 on one die 1:17
14. for a sum of 10 with a 4 on one die 1:17
15. *not* for a sum greater than 9 5:1
16. for a sum greater than 9 1:5

Check for Understanding

Concept Check

1. **Explain** how to find the odds of an event occurring. 1–3. See margin.
2. **OPEN ENDED** Describe a situation in real life that uses odds.
3. **FIND THE ERROR** Hoshi says that the probability of getting a 2 on one roll of a number cube is 1 out of 6. Nashoba says that the odds of getting a 2 on one roll of a number cube are 1:6. Who is correct? Explain your reasoning.

GUIDED PRACTICE KEY

Exercises	Examples
4–7	1
8	2

Guided Practice

Find the odds of each outcome if a number cube is rolled.

4. a number less than 2 1:5
5. a multiple of 3 1:2
6. a number greater than 3 1:1
7. not a 5 5:1

Standardized Test Practice

8. Ramon found that 2 out of 8 promotional cards at a fast-food restaurant were instant winners. Based on these results, what are the odds against the next card being an instant winner? D

  (A) 1 to 4   (B) 4 to 1   (C) 1 to 3   (D) 3 to 1

★ indicates increased difficulty

Practice and Apply

Homework Help

For Exercises	See Examples
9–25	1
26–29	2

Extra Practice See page 755.

Find the odds of each outcome if the spinner at the right is spun.

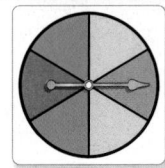

9. yellow 1:2
10. orange 0
11. not green 2:1
12. not red or green 1:1

Find the odds of each outcome if a pair of number cubes are rolled. 18. 7:5

13. an odd sum 1:1
14. an even sum 1:1
15. a sum that is a multiple of 4 1:3
16. a sum less than 2 0
17. a sum that is a prime number 5:7
18. a sum that is a composite number
19. *not* a sum of 8 31:5
20. not a sum of 9 or 10 29:7
★ 21. a sum of 6 with a 4 on one number cube 1:17
★ 22. an even sum or a sum greater than 6 5:1
★ 23. a sum that is *not* 6, 7, or 8 5:4

TEACHING TIP

To complete Exercises 24 and 25, students will need to be familiar with the contents of a *standard deck of cards*. In this text, a standard deck of cards always includes 52 cards in 4 suits of 13 cards each.

A card is selected from a standard deck of 52 cards.

24. What are the odds of selecting a red queen? 1:25
★ 25. What are the odds of *not* selecting a diamond *or* an ace? 9:4
26. The probability of having all girls in an eight-child family is $\frac{1}{256}$. What are the odds in favor of an eight-girl family? the odds against? 1:255; 255:1
27. A family had 13 children, and they were all boys. The odds in favor of this type of family are 1:8191. What is the probability of a 13-child family having all boys? $\frac{1}{8192}$

DAILY INTERVENTION FIND THE ERROR
Be sure that students do not confuse probability and odds. If the odds of an event happening are 1:1, the probability is $\frac{1}{2}$. For odds of 1:3, the probability is $\frac{1}{4}$.

Answers

1. Write a ratio comparing the ways the event can occur to the ways the event cannot occur.
2. Sample answer: Prize contests list the odds of winning the grand prize.
3. Hoshi; The probability of rolling a 2 is 1 out of 6. The odds of rolling a 2 are 1 in 5.

STATISTICS For Exercises 28–30, use the graphic shown below.

★ **28.** If you select a man at random from a group, what are the odds that he believes in aliens? **27:23**

★ **29.** If you select a woman at random from a group, what are the odds that she does *not* believe in aliens? **47:53**

30. In a group of 500 men, how many can be expected to believe in aliens? **270**

31. CRITICAL THINKING A carnival game consists of rolling three 8-sided dice. The odds for winning are listed as 8:512. Do you think the odds given are correct? Explain. **See margin.**

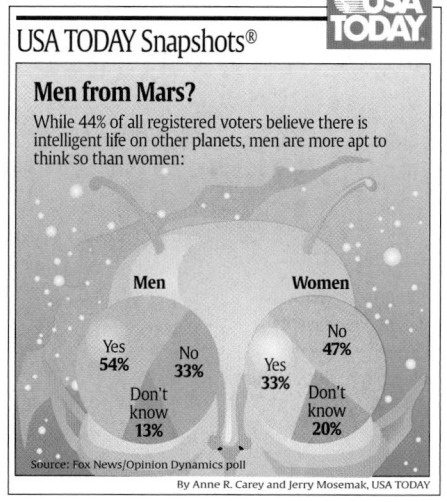

USA TODAY Snapshots®

Men from Mars?
While 44% of all registered voters believe there is intelligent life on other planets, men are more apt to think so than women:

Men
Yes 54%
No 33%
Don't know 13%

Women
No 47%
Yes 33%
Don't know 20%

Source: Fox News/Opinion Dynamics poll
By Anne R. Carey and Jerry Mosemak, USA TODAY

32. **WRITING IN MATH** Answer the question that was posed at the beginning of the lesson. **See margin.**

How are odds related to probability?

Include the following in your answer:
- a comparison of your results from parts **b** and **c** on page 646, and
- an explanation of how you can find the odds of an event if you know its probability.

Standardized Test Practice
Ⓐ Ⓑ Ⓒ Ⓓ

33. A set of cards is numbered 1 through 40. A card is drawn at random. What are the odds that the card drawn is greater than 25? **A**

    Ⓐ 3 to 5   Ⓑ 3 to 8   Ⓒ 5 to 3   Ⓓ 5 to 8

34. Judie made a basket 15 of the 25 times she shot the basketball. Based on this record, what would be the odds *against* Judie making a basket the next time she shoots the ball? **D**

    Ⓐ 3 to 5   Ⓑ 5 to 3   Ⓒ 3 to 2   Ⓓ 2 to 3

Maintain Your Skills

Mixed Review

35. How many ways can a family of four be seated in a row of four chairs at the theater if the father sits in the aisle seat? *(Lesson 12-7)* **6 ways**

36. How many outcomes are possible for rolling three number cubes? *(Lesson 12-6)* **216**

Solve each inequality. Then graph the solution on a number line. *(Lessons 7-5 and 7-6)* **37–39. See margin for graphs.**

37. $2a - 3 \geq 9$ $a \geq 6$ **38.** $4c + 4 > 32$ $c > 7$ **39.** $-2y + 3 < 9$ $y > -3$

Getting Ready for the Next Lesson

PREREQUISITE SKILL Find each product. *(To review **multiplying fractions**, see Lesson 5-3.)*

40. $\frac{1}{6} \cdot \frac{1}{3}$ $\frac{1}{18}$ **41.** $\frac{2}{3} \cdot \frac{3}{6}$ $\frac{1}{3}$ **42.** $\frac{1}{3} \cdot \frac{1}{3} \cdot \frac{1}{3}$ $\frac{1}{27}$ **43.** $\frac{3}{8} \cdot \frac{2}{7} \cdot \frac{1}{6}$ $\frac{1}{56}$

About the Exercises . . .

Odd/Even Assignments
Exercises 9–27 are structured so that students practice the same concepts whether they are assigned odd or even problems.

Assignment Guide
Basic: 9–19 odd, 27, 31–43
Average: 9–27 odd, 31–43
Advanced: 10–26 even, 28–39 (Optional: 40–43)

4 Assess

Open-Ended Assessment
Writing Have students write a paragraph comparing and contrasting odds and probability.

Getting Ready for Lesson 12-9
PREREQUISITE SKILL Lesson 12-9 presents finding the probability of compound events, which involves multiplying fractions. Use Exercises 40–43 to determine your students' familiarity with multiplying fractions.

Answers

37.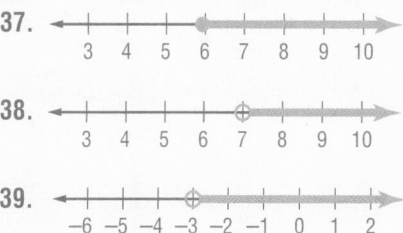
3 4 5 6 7 8 9 10

38.
3 4 5 6 7 8 9 10

39.
-6 -5 -4 -3 -2 -1 0 1 2

Answers

31. No; 512 is the total number of possible outcomes, so it could not be a number in the odds of winning.

32. Odds and probability both express the likelihood of an event happening. Answers should include the following.

- The sum of the numbers in the odds ratio is the total number of outcomes in the probability ratio; the first number in the odds ratio is the same as the numerator in the probability ratio.

- You can find the odds of an event by using the numerator of its probability as the first number in the odds ratio and subtracting that number from the denominator to find the second number in the odds ratio.

Lesson 12-8 Odds **649**

12-9 Lesson Notes

1 Focus

5-Minute Check Transparency 12-9 Use as a quiz or review of Lesson 12-8.

Mathematical Background notes are available for this lesson on page 604D.

How are compound events related to simple events?

The opening activity questions are repeated on page 710 of the *Chapter 12 Resource Masters*.

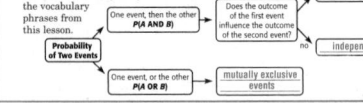

Reading to Learn Mathematics, p. 710 **ELL**

Pre-Activity *How are compound events related to simple events?*
Do the activity at the top of page 650 in your textbook. Write your answers below.
a. What was your experimental probability for the red then white outcome? See students' work; theoretical probability is $\frac{1}{4}$.
b. Would you expect the probability to be different if you did not place the first counter back in the bag? Explain your reasoning. Yes; by not replacing the first counter drawn, you affect the possibilities for the second draw.

Reading the Lesson 1–4. See students' work.
Write a definition and give an example of each new vocabulary phrase.

Vocabulary	Definition	Example
1. compound events		
2. independent events		
3. dependent events		
4. mutually exclusive events		

You are finding the probability of choosing the following arrangements of counters from a bag containing red, orange, and blue counters. Label each situation with *independent events*, *dependent events*, or *mutually exclusive events*.
5. a red counter, which is replaced, followed by a blue counter. independent events
6. an orange counter or a primary color mutually exclusive events
7. an orange counter, which is kept out of the bag, followed by a red counter dependent events

Helping You Remember
8. Complete the concept map below with the vocabulary phrases from this lesson.

Resource Manager

Workbooks and Reproducible Masters

Chapter 12 Resource Masters
- Study Guide and Intervention, p. 707
- Skills Practice, p. 708
- Practice, p. 709
- Reading to Learn Mathematics, p. 710
- Enrichment, p. 711
- Assessment, p. 728

Graphing Calculator and Spreadsheet Masters, p. 42
Parent and Student Study Guide Workbook, p. 106
Science and Mathematics Lab Manual, pp. 27–30

Transparencies
5-Minute Check Transparency 12-9
Answer Key Transparencies

Technology
Interactive Chalkboard

12-9 Probability of Compound Events

What You'll Learn

- Find the probability of independent and dependent events.
- Find the probability of mutually exclusive events.

Vocabulary
- compound events
- independent events
- dependent events
- mutually exclusive events

a. See students' work; theoretical probability is $\frac{1}{4}$.

b. Yes; by not replacing the first counter drawn, you affect the possibilities for the second draw.

How are compound events related to simple events?

Place two red counters and two white counters in a paper bag. Then complete the following activity.

Step 1 Without looking, remove a counter from the bag and record its color. Place the counter back in the bag.

Step 2 Without looking, remove a second counter and record its color. The two colors are one trial. Place the counter back in the bag.

Step 3 Repeat until you have 50 trials. Count and record the number of times you chose a red counter, followed by a white counter.

a. What was your experimental probability for the red then white outcome?

b. Would you expect the probability to be different if you did not place the first counter back in the bag? Explain your reasoning.

PROBABILITIES OF INDEPENDENT AND DEPENDENT EVENTS

A **compound event** consists of two or more simple events. The activity above finds *P*(red *and* white), the probability of choosing a red counter, followed by a white counter.

The results from the activity above are independent events. In **independent events**, the outcome of one event does *not* influence the outcome of a second event.

$$P(\text{red on 1st draw}) = \frac{2}{4} \text{ or } \frac{1}{2}$$ There are 4 counters and 2 of them are red.

$$P(\text{white on 2nd draw}) = \frac{2}{4} \text{ or } \frac{1}{2}$$ You replaced the first counter. There are still 4 counters and 2 are white.

The probability of two independent events can be found by using multiplication.

Reading Math

Probability Notation
Read *P(A and B)* as the probability of *A* followed by *B*.

Key Concept — Probability of Two Independent Events

- **Words** The probability of two independent events is found by multiplying the probability of the first event by the probability of the second event.
- **Symbols** $P(A \text{ and } B) = P(A) \cdot P(B)$
- **Example** $P(\text{red and white}) = \frac{1}{2} \cdot \frac{1}{2} \text{ or } \frac{1}{4}$

Example 1 *Probability of Independent Events*

• **GAMES** In some versions of the board game Parchisi, your piece returns to Start if you roll three doubles in a row. What is the probability of rolling three doubles in a row?

The events are independent since each roll of the number cubes does not affect the outcome of the next roll.

There are six ways to roll doubles, (1, 1), (2, 2), and so on, and there are 36 ways to roll two number cubes. So, the probability of rolling doubles on a toss of the number cubes is $\frac{6}{36}$ or $\frac{1}{6}$.

$P(\text{three doubles}) = P(\text{doubles on 1st roll}) \cdot P(\text{doubles on 2nd roll}) \cdot P(\text{doubles on 3rd roll})$

$$= \frac{1}{6} \cdot \frac{1}{6} \cdot \frac{1}{6}$$

$$= \frac{1}{216}$$

The probability of rolling three doubles in a row is $\frac{1}{216}$.

If the outcome of one event affects the outcome of a second event, the events are called **dependent events**. In the opening activity, if you do not replace the first counter, the events are dependent events.

$P(\text{red on 1st draw}) = \frac{1}{2}$

$P(\text{white on 2nd draw}) = \frac{2}{3}$ ← If you do not replace the counter, there are three counters left and two of them are white.

Key Concept	*Probability of Two Dependent Events*

- **Words** If two events, A and B, are dependent, then the probability of both events occurring is the product of the probability of A and the probability of B after A occurs.

- **Symbols** $P(A \text{ and } B) = P(A) \cdot P(B \text{ following } A)$

- **Example** $P(\text{red and white, without replacement}) = \frac{1}{2} \cdot \frac{2}{3}$ or $\frac{1}{3}$

✓ **Concept Check** How can you tell whether events are independent or dependent? **If the outcome of one event does not influence the outcome of a second event, the events are independent.**

Example 2 *Probability of Dependent Events*

Reiko takes two coins at random from the 3 quarters, 5 dimes, and 2 nickels in her pocket. What is the probability that she chooses a quarter followed by a dime?

$P(\text{quarter and dime}) = \frac{3}{10} \cdot \frac{5}{9}$ ← 3 of 10 coins are quarters.

$$= \frac{15}{90} \text{ or } \frac{1}{6}$$ ← 5 of 9 remaining coins are dimes.

www.pre-alg.com/extra_examples

Lesson 12-9 Probability of Compound Events **651**

Building on Prior Knowledge

In Chapter 6, students studied simple probability. In this lesson, they will add to this knowledge by learning about the probability of compound events.

PROBABILITIES OF INDEPENDENT AND DEPENDENT EVENTS

In-Class Examples

1 **GAMES** In a popular dice game, the highest possible score in a single turn is a roll of five of a kind. After rolling one five of a kind, every other five of a kind you roll earns 100 points. What is the probability of rolling two five of a kinds in a row?

$\dfrac{1}{1,679,616}$

Reading Tip Tell students that in dependent events, you always assume you were successful on the first event.

2 Charlie's clothes closet contains 3 blue shirts, 10 white shirts, and 7 striped shirts. What is the probability that Charlie will reach in and randomly select a white shirt followed by a striped shirt?

$\dfrac{7}{38}$

DAILY

INTERVENTION   **Differentiated Instruction**

- **Intrapersonal** Have each student give an example of one of the following: independent events, dependent events, or mutually exclusive events. Ask students to include a description of how that example helps them understand the selected concept.

Teaching Tip Show students that you can use Venn diagrams to show whether two events are mutually exclusive.

3 You draw a card from a standard deck of playing cards. What is the probability that the card will be a black nine or any heart? $\dfrac{15}{52}$

Teaching Tip Post a U.S. map. Have cooperative groups write probability problems relating independent information about the states. Trade and solve. For example, what is the probability that a state name begins with the letter "A" and that the state borders the Gulf of Mexico?

MUTUALLY EXCLUSIVE EVENTS If two events cannot happen at the same time, they are said to be **mutually exclusive**. For example, when you roll two number cubes, you cannot roll a sum that is both 5 and even.

Second Number Cube

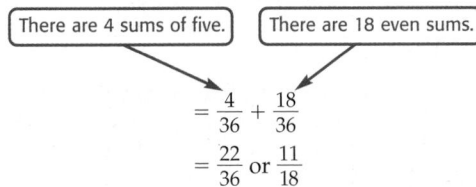

First Number Cube

+	1	2	3	4	5	6
1	2	3	4	5	6	7
2	3	4	5	6	7	8
3	4	5	6	7	8	9
4	5	6	7	8	9	10
5	6	7	8	9	10	11
6	7	8	9	10	11	12

The probability of two mutually exclusive events is found by adding.

$$P(5 \text{ or even}) = P(5) + P(\text{even})$$

There are 4 sums of five.   There are 18 even sums.

$$= \frac{4}{36} + \frac{18}{36}$$

$$= \frac{22}{36} \text{ or } \frac{11}{18}$$

Study Tip

Look Back
To review **adding fractions with like denominators**, see Lesson 5-5.

Key Concept   *Probability of Mutually Exclusive Events*

- **Words** The probability of one or the other of two mutually exclusive events can be found by adding the probability of the first event to the probability of the second event.

- **Symbols** $P(A \text{ or } B) = P(A) + P(B)$

- **Example** $P(5 \text{ or even}) = \dfrac{4}{36} + \dfrac{18}{36}$ or $\dfrac{11}{18}$

Example 3 *Probability of Mutually Exclusive Events*

The spinner at the right is spun. What is the probability that the spinner will stop on blue or an even number?

The events are mutually exclusive because the spinner cannot stop on both blue and an even number at the same time.

$P(\text{blue or even}) = P(\text{blue}) + P(\text{even})$

$$= \frac{1}{6} + \frac{1}{2}$$

$$= \frac{4}{6} \text{ or } \frac{2}{3}$$

The probability that the spinner will stop on blue or an even number is $\dfrac{2}{3}$.

✓ **Concept Check** Using the spinner in Example 3, are the events (green and even) mutually exclusive? Explain.
No; the spinner could land on 2, a space that is both green and even.

652   Chapter 12   More Statistics and Probability

DAILY INTERVENTION   **Unlocking Misconceptions**

- **Independent Events and Mutually Exclusive Events** Some students may think that all independent events are mutually exclusive events, or may mistake one term for the other. Reinforce that the results of a second independent event do not depend on the results of the first, and that these two events can occur at the same time. On the other hand, mutually exclusive events cannot happen at the same time.

Check for Understanding

Concept Check
See margin.

1. **Compare and contrast** independent and dependent events. **See margin.**

2. **OPEN ENDED** Write an example of two mutually exclusive events.

3. **Describe** how to find the probability of the second of two dependent events. **The result of the 1st event must be taken into account.**

Guided Practice

A number cube is rolled and the spinner is spun. Find each probability.

 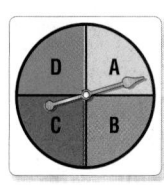

4. P(an odd number and a B) $\frac{1}{8}$

5. P(a composite number and a vowel) $\frac{1}{12}$

GUIDED PRACTICE KEY	
Exercises	Examples
4, 5	1
6, 7	2
8–10	3

A card is drawn from a deck of eight cards numbered from 1 to 8. The card is not replaced and a second card is drawn. Find each probability.

6. P(5 and 2) $\frac{1}{56}$

7. P(two odd numbers) $\frac{3}{14}$

8. A card is drawn from a standard deck of 52 cards. What is the probability that it is a diamond or a club? $\frac{1}{2}$

9. There are 3 books of poetry, 5 history books, and 4 books about animals on a shelf. If a book is chosen at random, what is the probability of choosing a book about history or animals? $\frac{3}{4}$

Application

10. **GAMES** Jack is playing a board game that involves rolling two number cubes. He needs to roll a sum of 5 or 8 to land on an open space. What is the probability that he will land on an open space? $\frac{1}{4}$

---

indicates increased difficulty

Practice and Apply

Homework Help	
For Exercises	See Examples
11–14	1
15–20	2
21–26	3

Extra Practice
See page 755.

A number cube is rolled and the spinner is spun. Find each probability.

 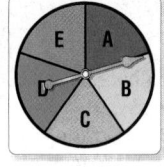

11. P(3 and E) $\frac{1}{30}$

12. P(an even number and A) $\frac{1}{10}$

13. P(a prime number and a vowel) $\frac{1}{5}$

14. P(an odd number and a consonant) $\frac{3}{10}$

There are 3 red marbles, 4 green marbles, 2 yellow marbles, and 5 blue marbles in a bag. Once a marble is drawn, it is not replaced. Find the probability of each outcome.

15. two yellow marbles in a row $\frac{1}{91}$

16. two blue marbles in a row $\frac{10}{91}$

17. a blue then a green marble $\frac{10}{91}$

18. a yellow then a red marble $\frac{3}{91}$

★ 19. a blue marble, a yellow marble, and then a red marble $\frac{5}{364}$

★ 20. three green marbles in a row $\frac{1}{91}$

Lesson 12-9 Probability of Compound Events **653**

Study Notebook

Have students—
• complete the definitions/examples for the remaining terms on the Vocabulary Builder worksheets for Chapter 12.
• draw models illustrating independent events, dependent events, and mutually exclusive events.
• include any other item(s) that they find helpful in mastering the skills in this lesson.

About the Exercises . . .

Organization by Objective
• **Probabilities of Independent and Dependent Events:** 11–20
• **Mutually Exclusive Events:** 21–26

Odd/Even Assignments
Exercises 11–30 are structured so that students practice the same concepts whether they are assigned odd or even problems.

Assignment Guide
Basic: 11–17 odd, 21–27 odd, 31–34, 36–50
Average: 11–29 odd, 31–34, 36–50 (Optional: 35)
Advanced: 12–28 even, 29–50

Answers

1. Independent and dependent events are similar because both are a connection of two or more simple events, and the probability of the compound event is found by multiplying the probabilities of each simple event. They are different because the second event in a dependent event is influenced by the outcome of the first event. Therefore, the probability of the second event used in calculating the probability of the compound event is dependent on the outcome of the first event.

2. Sample answer: choosing an odd or composite number when rolling a die

An eight-sided die is rolled. Find the probability of each outcome.

21. $P(3 \text{ or even})$ $\frac{5}{8}$
22. $P(6 \text{ or prime})$ $\frac{5}{8}$

A card is drawn from the cards shown. Find the probability of each outcome.

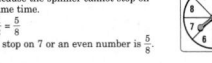

23. $P(3 \text{ or multiple of 2})$ $\frac{3}{7}$
24. $P(4 \text{ or greater than 5})$ $\frac{4}{7}$
25. $P(\text{odd or even})$ 1
26. $P(2 \text{ or } 6)$ $\frac{1}{7}$

27. A bag contains six blue marbles and three red marbles. A marble is drawn, it is replaced, and another marble is drawn. What is the probability of drawing a red marble and a blue marble in either order? $\frac{2}{9}$

28. **FAMILIES** Each time a baby is born, the chance for either a boy or a girl is one-half. Find the probability that a family of four children has four girls. $\frac{1}{16}$

INTERNET USE For Exercises 29 and 30, use the graphic.

★ 29. What is the probability that a teen chosen at random has used the Internet for both games and studying in the last 30 days? Write the probability as a decimal to the nearest hundredth. 0.16

★ 30. What is the probability that a teen chosen at random has used the Internet to both browse and use e-mail in the last 30 days? Write the probability as a percent to the nearest percent. 28%

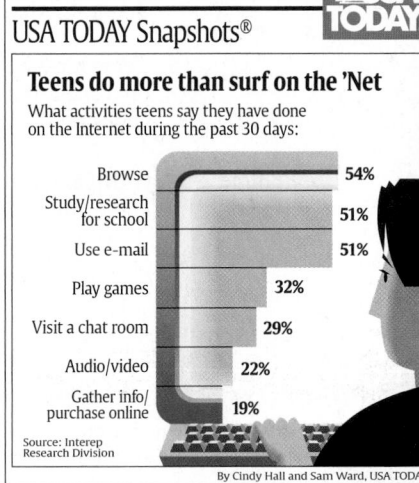

USA TODAY Snapshots®

Teens do more than surf on the 'Net

What activities teens say they have done on the Internet during the past 30 days:

Browse	54%
Study/research for school	51%
Use e-mail	51%
Play games	32%
Visit a chat room	29%
Audio/video	22%
Gather info/purchase online	19%

Source: Interep Research Division

By Cindy Hall and Sam Ward, USA TODAY

31. **CRITICAL THINKING** There are 9 marbles in a bag. Some are red, some are white, and some are blue. The probability of selecting a red marble, a white marble, and then a blue marble is $\frac{1}{21}$.

a. How many of each color are in the bag? **a–b. See margin.**

b. Explain why there is more than one correct answer to part **a**.

32. **WRITING IN MATH** Answer the question that was posed at the beginning of the lesson. **See margin.**

How are compound events related to simple events?

Include the following in your answer:

• an explanation of how the results of drawing two counters relate to the probability for drawing one counter, and
• the difference between independent and dependent events.

33. A bag contains three green balls, two blue balls, four pink balls, and one yellow ball, all the same size. Marcus chooses a ball at random, then without replacing it chooses a second ball. What is the probability that Marcus chooses a blue ball followed by a yellow ball? **B**

Ⓐ $\frac{1}{50}$ Ⓑ $\frac{1}{45}$ Ⓒ $\frac{2}{45}$ Ⓓ $\frac{3}{20}$

34. If a card is drawn at random from a standard deck of 52 cards, what is the probability that the card drawn is a jack, queen, or king? **D**

Ⓐ $\frac{1}{13}$ Ⓑ $\frac{1}{12}$ Ⓒ $\frac{3}{52}$ Ⓓ $\frac{3}{13}$

Extending ★ the Lesson
35. When two events are *inclusive*, they can happen at the same time. To find the probability of inclusive events, add the probabilities of the events and subtract the probability of both events happening. Find P(green or even) for the spinner shown at the right. $\frac{2}{3}$

Maintain Your Skills

Mixed Review
A card is drawn from a standard deck of 52 cards. *(Lesson 12-8)*

36. Find the odds of selecting a red card. **1:1**

37. Find the odds of selecting a jack, queen, or king. **3:10**

38. How many different teams of 3 players can be chosen from 8 players? *(Lesson 12-7)* **56**

39. How many license plates can be made from 3 letters (A–Z) and 3 numbers (0–9)? *(Lesson 12-7)* **17,576,000**

In the figure at the right, $a \parallel b$. Find the measure of each angle. *(Lesson 10-1)*

40. $\angle 1$ **25°**   **41.** $\angle 2$ **65°**

42. $\angle 3$ **115°**   **43.** $\angle 4$ **65°**

44. $\angle 5$ **115°**   **45.** $\angle 6$ **90°**

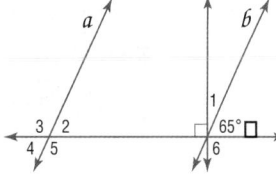

In a right triangle, if a and b are the measures of the legs and c is the measure of the hypotenuse, find each missing measure. Round to the nearest tenth. *(Lesson 9-5)*

46. $a = 6, b = 8$ **10**   **47.** $a = 7, b = 40$ **40.6**

48. $a = 8, c = 15$ **12.7**   **49.** $b = 63, c = 65$ **16**

50. BLOOD TYPES The distribution of blood types in a random survey is shown in the table. If there are 625 students at Ford Middle School, how many would you expect to have Type A blood? *(Lesson 6-7)* **250**

Distribution of Blood Types	
Type	Percent
A	40
B	9
AB	4
O	47

Lesson 12-9 Probability of Compound Events **655**

---

4 Assess

Open-Ended Assessment

Speaking Use a standard deck of playing cards and have students describe how to determine each outcome. Then find the probability of that outcome.

- Independent events, drawing a king and drawing a jack
  Draw a card. Replace it. Draw again. $\frac{1}{169}$

- Dependent events, drawing a king and drawing a jack Draw a card. Do not replace it. Draw again. $\frac{4}{663}$

- Mutually exclusive events, drawing a ten or drawing a face card
  Draw one card. $\frac{4}{13}$.

Assessment Options

Quiz (Lessons 12-8 and 12-9) is available on p. 728 of the *Chapter 12 Resource Masters*.

Answers (p. 654)

31a. Sample answer: 3 red, 2 white, and 4 blue

31b. Sample answer: The numerator must be 24. Any combination of 3, 2, and 4 will have a probability of $\frac{1}{21}$.

32. The probability of compound events is based on the probability of each simple event. Answers should include the following.

- The probability for two draws is the product of the probabilities of each single draw.

- Independent events do not affect one another; dependent events do.

Algebra Activity

A Follow-Up of Lesson 12-9

Objective Use simulations to examine outcomes.

Materials
coin
number cube
red and white counters
blue and red marbles

Teaching Tip Ask students which would take less time to do—roll a number cube 100 times or run a computer program that simulates rolling a die 100 times.

Teach

Activity 1
- Be sure that students understand the difference between tossing a coin as a good simulation and tossing a coin as a way to take the quiz.
- After students complete collecting the data for Activity 1, poll the class to see whether anyone rolled enough correct answers to pass the quiz. Discuss how the experimental probability compares with the theoretical probability for passing the quiz this way.

Activity 2
- You may wish to have students collect the data in pairs or small groups.
- Review the terms *experimental probability* and *theoretical probability* from Lesson 6-9, p. 311.

Simulations

You can use a **simulation** to act out a situation so that you can see outcomes. For many problems, you can conduct a simulation of the outcomes by using items such as a number cube, a coin, or a spinner. The items or combination of items used should have the same number of outcomes as the number of possible outcomes of the situation.

Activity 1

A quiz has 10 true-false questions. The correct answers are T, F, F, T, T, T, F, F, T, F. You need to correctly answer 7 or more questions to pass the quiz. Is tossing a coin to decide your answers a good strategy for taking the quiz?

Since two choices are available for each answer, tossing a coin is a reasonable activity to simulate guessing the answers.

Collect the Data

Step 1 Toss a coin and record the answer for each question. Write T(true) for tails and F(false) for heads.

Step 2 Repeat the simulation three times.

Step 3 Shade the cells with the correct answers. A sample for one simulation is shown in the table below.

Answers	T	F	F	T	T	T	F	F	T	F	Number Correct
Simulation 1	F	T	T	T	F	F	F	T	T	T	F	2
Simulation 2											
Simulation 3											

Analyze the Data

1. Based on the simulations, is tossing a coin a good way to take the quiz? Explain. **Sample answer: No; none of the simulations results in a passing grade.**

Extend the Activity

Use a simulation to act out the problem.

2. A restaurant includes prizes with children's meals. Six different prizes are available. There is an equally likely chance of getting each prize each time.

   a. Use a number cube to simulate this problem. Let each number represent one of the prizes. Conduct a simulation until you have one of each number. **See students' work.**

   b. Based on your simulation, how many meals must be purchased in order to get all six different prizes? **Sample answer: at least 6**

Resource Manager

📁 *Teaching Pre-Algebra with Manipulatives*
- p. 157 (student recording sheet)
- p. 20 (die patterns)

Glencoe Mathematics Classroom Manipulative Kit
- counters
- marbles
- dice

Activity 2

Logan usually makes three out of every four free throws he attempts during a basketball game. Conduct the following experiment to simulate the probability of Logan's making two free throws in a row.

Collect the Data

Step 1 Put 20 red and white counters in a bag. Use red to represent a basket and white to represent a miss. The probability Logan will make a free throw is $\frac{3}{4}$, or $\frac{15}{20}$. So, use 15 red counters and 5 white counters.

Step 2 Conduct a simulation for 25 free throws.

Step 3 Without looking, draw a counter from the bag and record its color. Replace the counter and draw a second counter.

Step 4 Repeat 25 times and record the results of the simulation in a chart like the one shown below.

Misses the first shot	Makes the first shot, misses the second	Makes both shots

Analyze the Data

3. Calculate the experimental probability that Logan makes two free throws in a row. **See students' work. The probability should be about 56%.**

4. How do the results in Activity 2 compare to the theoretical probability that Logan will make two free throws in a row? (*Hint*: These are independent events.) **See students' work.**

Model the Data **5. 0.64 or 64%   6. 40 red, 10 blue; red represents a basket; blue a miss**

5. Trevor usually makes four out of every five free throws he attempts. Calculate the theoretical probability that Trevor will make two free throws in a row.

6. To simulate the probability of Trevor making two free throws in a row, Drew puts 50 red and blue marbles in a bag. How many red and how many blue marbles should Drew use? Explain your reasoning.

7. Conduct a simulation for this situation. Compare the theoretical probability with the experimental probability. **See margin.**

Extend the Activity **8. No; the data suggests the number varies from machine to machine.**

8. There are three gumball machines numbered 1, 2, and 3 in a video arcade. Each machine contains an equal number of gumballs, some orange, some red, and some green. Ali thinks that her chance of getting a green gumball is the same from each machine. She conducted an experiment in which she bought 20 gumballs from each of the three machines. She got 4 green gumballs from machine 1, 8 from machine 2, and 12 from machine 3. Does this data support Ali's hypothesis? Explain why or why not.

Assess

In **Exercises 1–7**, watch for students who estimate results or use theoretical probabilities rather than experimental probabilities. Emphasize the need for systematically setting up the experiments and then completing them to find the experimental probabilities.

You may want to have students devise more than one way of simulating the situations.

Use **Exercise 8** to evaluate whether students understand how using a simulation can help solve problems involving outcomes.

Study Notebook

You may wish to have students summarize this activity and what they learned from it.

Answer

7. See students' work. The theoretical probability and the experimental probability should be about the same.

Chapter 12 · Study Guide and Review

Vocabulary and Concept Check

Vocabulary and Concept Check

- This alphabetical list of vocabulary terms in Chapter 12 includes a page reference where each term was introduced.

- **Assessment** A vocabulary review/test for Chapter 12 is available on p. 726 of the *Chapter 12 Resource Masters*.

Lesson-by-Lesson Review

For each lesson,
- the main ideas are summarized,
- additional examples review concepts, and
- practice exercises are provided.

Vocabulary PuzzleMaker

ELL The Vocabulary PuzzleMaker software improves students' mathematics vocabulary using four puzzle formats—crossword, scramble, word search using a word list, and word search using clues. Students can work on a computer screen or from a printed handout.

MindJogger Videoquizzes

ELL MindJogger Videoquizzes provide an alternative review of concepts presented in this chapter. Students work in teams in a game show format to gain points for correct answers. The questions are presented in three rounds.

Round 1 Concepts (5 questions)
Round 2 Skills (4 questions)
Round 3 Problem Solving (4 questions)

---

back-to-back stem-and-leaf plot (p. 607)
box-and-whisker plot (p. 617)
combination (p. 642)
compound events (p. 650)
dependent events (p. 651)
factorial (p. 642)
Fundamental Counting Principle (p. 636)
histogram (p. 623)

independent events (p. 650)
interquartile range (p. 613)
leaves (p. 606)
lower quartile (p. 613)
measures of variation (p. 612)
mutually exclusive events (p. 652)
odds (p. 646)
permutation (p. 641)

quartiles (p. 613)
range (p. 612)
simulation (p. 656)
stem-and-leaf plot (p. 606)
stems (p. 606)
tree diagram (p. 635)
upper quartile (p. 613)

Choose the letter of the term that best matches each statement or phrase.

1. an arrangement or listing in which order is important **b**

2. the ratio of the number of ways an event can occur to the ways that the event cannot occur **e**

3. two or more events that cannot occur at the same time **c**

4. an arrangement or listing in which order is not important **a**

5. the median of the lower half of a set of data **d**

a. combination
b. permutation
c. mutually exclusive events
d. lower quartile
e. odds

Lesson-by-Lesson Review

12-1 *Stem-and-Leaf Plots*

See pages 606–611.

Concept Summary
- A stem-and-leaf plot can be used to organize and display data.

Example **Display the data below in a stem-and-leaf plot.**

Lobster Length (mm)			
75	76	80	77
77	77	79	84
80	76	78	69
79	66	84	85

Stem	Leaf
6	6 9
7	5 6 6 7 7 7 8 9 9
8	0 0 4 4 5

7|6 = 76 mm

Exercises Display each set of data in a stem-and-leaf plot.
(See Example 1 on pages 606 and 607.) **6–8. See margin.**

6.
Height of Girls on Soccer Team (in.)			
58	62	59	60
61	65	57	56
55	59	62	61

7.
Price of Juice (¢)			
85	45	75	60
60	50	55	75
45	50	60	60
55	75	85	60

8.
Theater Attendance			
110	112	140	124
128	145	119	129
118	124	140	123
146	142	120	114

 www.pre-alg.com/vocabulary_review

Study Organizer

For more information about Foldables, see *Teaching Mathematics with Foldables.*

Have students review the statistical examples and vocabulary definitions on their Foldables for correctness.

Encourage students to refer to their Foldables while completing the Study Guide and Review and to use them in preparing for the Chapter Test.

12-2 Measures of Variation

See pages 612–616.

Concept Summary

- The range is the difference between the greatest and the least values of a data set.
- The interquartile range is the range of the middle half of a set of data.

Example Find the range and interquartile range for the set of data {18, 11, 26, 28, 15, 21, 20, 20, 15, 23, 19}.

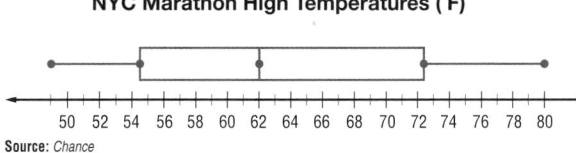

11, 15, 15, 18, 19, 20, 20, 21, 23, 26, 28   List the data from least to greatest.

The range is 28 − 11 or 17. The interquartile range is 23 − 15 or 8.

Exercises Find the range and interquartile range for each set of data.
(See Examples 1 and 2 on pages 612 and 613.)

9. {42, 45, 38, 27, 41, 39, 50} **23; 7**
10. {7, 6, 1, 3, 4, 4, 5, 8, 11, 8, 5} **10; 4**
11. {58°, 64°, 72°, 62°, 74°, 80°, 65°, 70°} **22; 10**

12.
Stem	Leaf
2	4 4 9
3	0 2 3 3 6 7
4	5 7 8 9 9 9

3|2 = 32

25; 18

12-3 Box-and-Whisker Plots

See pages 617–621.

Concept Summary

- A box-and-whisker plot separates data into four parts.

Example Use the box-and-whisker plot shown to find the percent of New York City marathons that were held on days that had a high temperature greater than 72.5°F.

Each of the four parts represents 25% of the data, so 25% of the marathons had a high temperature greater than 72.5°F.

NYC Marathon High Temperatures (°F)

50 52 54 56 58 60 62 64 66 68 70 72 74 76 78 80

Source: *Chance*

Exercises For Exercises 13–15, use the box-and-whisker plot shown above.
(See Example 2 on page 618.)

13. What was the highest temperature? **80°F**
14. Half the marathons were held on days having at least what high temperature? **62°F**
15. What percent of the marathons were held on days that had a high temperature between 54.5°F and 72.5°F? **50%**

Answers (p. 658)

6.
Stem	Leaf
5	5 6 7 8 9 9
6	0 1 1 2 2 5

6 |1 = 61 in.

7.
Stem	Leaf
4	5 5
5	0 0 5 5
6	0 0 0 0 0
7	5 5 5
8	5 5

7 |5 = 75¢

8.
Stem	Leaf
11	0 2 4 8 9
12	0 3 4 4 8 9
13	
14	0 0 2 5 6

12 |4 = 124

Study Guide and Review

Answers

16. Books Read in a Month

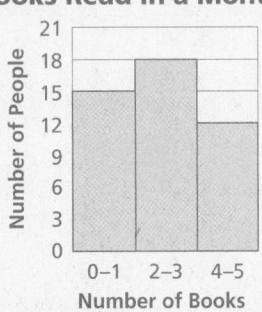

17. Graph A

18. Graph B

12-4 Histograms

See pages 623–628.

Concept Summary

- A histogram displays data that have been organized into equal intervals.

Example Display the set of data in a histogram.

Boys' 50-Yard Dash		
Time (s)	Tally	Frequency
6.0–6.4	III	3
6.5–6.9	JHT I	6
7.0–7.4	JHT III	8
7.5–7.9	JHT III	8
8.0–8.4	JHT	5

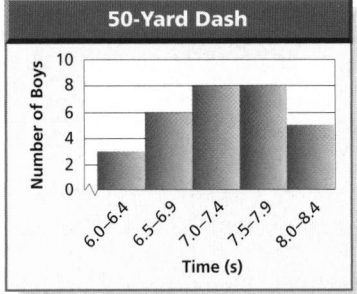

Exercises

16. The frequency table shows the results of a reading survey. Display the data in a histogram. *(See Example 1 on page 623.)* **See margin.**

Books Read in a Month		
Books	Tally	Frequency
0–1	JHT JHT JHT	15
2–3	JHT JHT JHT III	18
4–5	JHT JHT II	12

12-5 Misleading Statistics

See pages 630–633.

Concept Summary

- Graphs that do not have a title or labels on the scales may be misleading.
- Graphs that use different vertical scales may be misleading.

Example Explain why the graphs look different.

The vertical scales are different.

Weekly Allowance Graph A

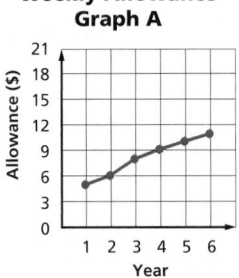

Weekly Allowance Graph B

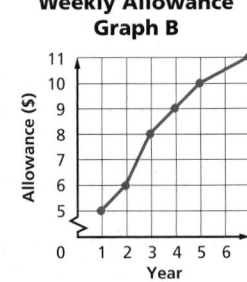

17–18. See margin.

Exercises Refer to the graphs shown. *(See Example 1 on page 630.)*

17. Which graph seems to show a slight increase in weekly allowances?

18. Which graph seems to show a dramatic increase in weekly allowance?

12-6 Counting

See pages 635–639.

Concept Summary

- The Fundamental Counting Principle relates the number of outcomes to the number of choices.

Example   A number cube is rolled three times. Find the number of possible outcomes.

Outcomes on the first roll	times	outcomes on the second roll	times	outcomes on the third roll	equals	possible outcomes.
6	×	6	×	6	=	216

There are 216 possible outcomes.

Exercises   Find the number of possible outcomes for each situation.
(See Example 2 on page 636.)

19. Four coins are tossed. **16 outcomes**

20. A tennis shoe comes in men's and women's sizes; cross training, walking, and running styles; blue, black, or white colors. **18 outcomes**

12-7 Permutations and Combinations

See pages 641–645.

Concept Summary

- Permutation: order is important.
- Combination: order is *not* important.

Examples

1 How many ways can 8 horses place first, second, and third in a race?

The order is important, so this is a permutation.

8 horses ⟶ ⌐ Choose 3.

$$P(8, 3) = 8 \cdot 7 \cdot 6$$

8 choices for first place
7 choices for second place
6 choices for third place

$$= 336$$

There are 336 ways for 8 horses to place first, second, and third.

2 An ice cream shop has 5 toppings from which to choose. How many different 2-topping sundaes are possible?

The order is not important, so this is a combination.

$$C(5, 2) = \frac{P(5, 2)}{2!} = \frac{5 \cdot 4}{2 \cdot 1} \text{ or } 10 \text{ different sundaes}$$

Exercises   Tell whether each situation is a *permutation* or *combination*.
Then solve.   *(See Examples 1 and 3 on pages 641 and 642.)*   **21. C; 364 ways**

21. How many ways can 3-person teams be chosen from 14 students?

22. How many 5-digit security codes are possible if each digit is a number from 0 to 9? **P; 100,000 codes**

C; 21 ways

23. How many ways can you choose 2 team colors from a total of 7 colors?

Chapter 12 For More ...
• Extra Practice, see pages 752–755.
• Mixed Problem Solving, see page 769

Answers (p. 663)

1. permutation: the number of ways 7 different plants can be planted in a row; combination: the number of ways 6 different candy bars can be chosen from 10 different candy bars.

2. They cannot happen at the same time.

3.
Stem	Leaf
5	8 9
6	0 2 4 7 8 9
7	0 3 4 5 5 6 8
8	1

$5 \mid 9 = 59$ in.

7. See below.

9.
Length of Bus Ride to School

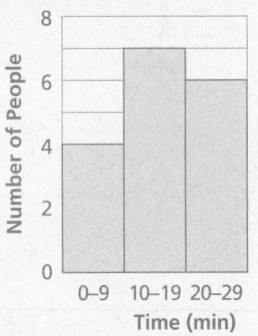

11. permutation; 5040 ways

12. combination; 220 ways

16. $\frac{4}{7}$

17. $\frac{4}{7}$

18. 1

19. $\frac{3}{7}$

12-8 Odds

See pages 646–649.

Concept Summary

• The odds in favor of an event is the ratio that compares the number of ways the event can occur to the ways that the event *cannot* occur.

Example Find the odds of spinning a red if the spinner at the right is spun.

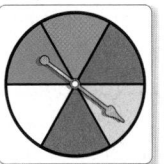

odds of spinning red

$= \underbrace{\text{number of ways to spin red}}$ to $\underbrace{\text{number of ways to spin any color other than red}}$

$= \quad 2 \quad : \quad 4$

$= 1:2$

The odds of spinning a red are 1:2.

Exercises Find the odds of each outcome if the spinner at the right is spun.
(See Example 1 on page 647.)

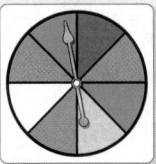

24. yellow **1:7**   25. blue **3:5**

26. not green **3:1**   27. white or red **1:3**

12-9 Probability of Compound Events

See pages 650–655.

Concept Summary

• A compound event consists of two or more simple events.

• When the outcome of one event does *not* affect the outcome of a second event, these are called independent events.

• When the outcome of one event *does* affect the outcome of a second event, these are called dependent events.

Example There are 3 red, 4 purple, and 2 green marbles in a bag. Find the probability of randomly drawing a purple marble and then a green marble without replacement.

$P(\text{purple, then green}) = P(\text{purple on 1st draw}) \cdot P(\text{green on 2nd draw})$

$= \frac{4}{9} \cdot \frac{2}{8}$ or $\frac{1}{9}$

The probability of drawing a purple marble and then a green marble is $\frac{1}{9}$.

Exercises A card is drawn from a deck of six cards numbered from 1 to 6. Find each probability. *(See Examples 1 and 3 on pages 651 and 652.)*

28. $P(\text{odd number or 2})$ $\frac{2}{3}$

29. The card is not replaced, and a second card is drawn. Find $P(3 \text{ and } 6)$. $\frac{1}{30}$

30. The card is replaced, and a second card is drawn. Find $P(4 \text{ and } 2)$. $\frac{1}{36}$

662 Chapter 12 More Statistics and Probability

7.

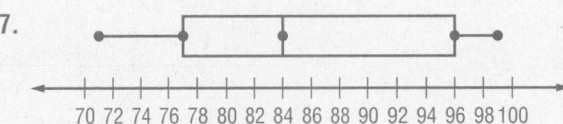

Vocabulary and Concepts

1. **OPEN ENDED** Describe a situation that involves a permutation and a situation that involves a combination. **1–2. See margin.**
2. **Explain** what it means when two events are mutually exclusive.

Skills and Applications

For Exercises 3–5, use the table shown.

Students' Heights (in.)							
70	81	59	69	78	68	75	73
76	62	67	74	75	64	60	58

3. Display the data in a stem-and-leaf plot. **3. See margin.**
4. What is the median height of the students? **4. 69.5 in.**
5. In which interval do most of the heights occur? **70 in.–79 in.**

For Exercises 6–8, use the stem-and-leaf plot shown.

Stem	Leaf
7	1 2 2 3 7
8	0 0 4 4 4 9
9	3 5 6 6 6 8 8 9

8|4 = $84

6. Find the range for the data. **$28**
7. Display the data in a box-and-whisker plot. **See margin.**
8. Find the interquartile range. **$19**

9. Display the data shown at the right in a histogram. **See margin.**

Length of Bus Ride to School		
Time (min)	Tally	Frequency
0–9	IIII	4
10–19	IIII II	7
20–29	IIII I	6

10. Find the number of possible outcomes for a choice of fish, chicken, pork, or beef and a choice of green beans, asparagus, or mixed vegetables. **12 outcomes**

Tell whether each situation is a *permutation* or *combination*. Then solve.

11. How many ways can 7 potted plants be arranged on a window sill? **11–12. See margin.**
12. A sand bucket contains 12 seashells. How many ways can you choose 3 of them?

13. Find the value of 4!. **24**

14. Find the odds of rolling a number greater than 4 if a ten-sided die is rolled. **3:2**

15. Four number cubes are tossed. What is the probability that all of them land on four? $\frac{1}{1296}$

A card is drawn from the cards shown. Find the probability of each outcome. 16–19. See margin.

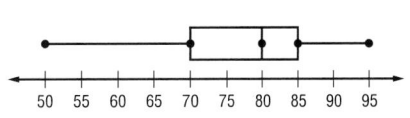

16. $P(5 \text{ or even})$
17. $P(\text{even or } 1)$
18. $P(\text{odd or even})$
19. $P(2 \text{ or greater than } 5)$

20. **STANDARDIZED TEST PRACTICE** Refer to the box-and-whisker plot shown. What percent of the daily high temperatures range from 70° to 95°? **C**

Daily High Temperatures (°F)

50 55 60 65 70 75 80 85 90 95

Ⓐ 25% Ⓑ 50%
Ⓒ 75% Ⓓ 100%

Assessment Options

Vocabulary Test A vocabulary review/test for Chapter 12 can be found on p. 726 of the *Chapter 12 Resource Masters*.

Chapter Tests There are six Chapter 12 Tests and an Open-Ended Assessment task available in the *Chapter 12 Resource Masters*.

Chapter 12 Tests			
Form	Type	Level	Pages
1	MC	basic	713–714
2A	MC	average	715–716
2B	MC	average	717–718
2C	FR	average	719–720
2D	FR	average	721–722
3	FR	advanced	723–724

MC = multiple-choice questions
FR = free-response questions

Open-Ended Assessment
Performance tasks for Chapter 12 can be found on p. 725 of the *Chapter 12 Resource Masters*, along with a sample scoring rubric for these tasks on p. A30.

ExamView® Pro

Use the networkable **ExamView® Pro** to:

- Create **multiple versions** of tests.
- Create **modified** tests for *Inclusion* students.
- **Edit** existing questions and **add** your own questions.
- Use built-in **state curriculum correlations** to create tests aligned with state standards.
- Change **English** tests to **Spanish** and vice versa.

Portfolio Suggestion

Introduction Statistical displays make the interpretation of data easier. Each type of display has particular advantages.

Ask Students to include a stem-and-leaf plot, a box-and-whisker plot, and a histogram from their homework answers. Next to each example, have them write a sentence or two stating in what ways that type of statistical display makes the data easier to understand.

These two pages contain practice questions in the various formats that can be found on the most frequently given standardized tests.

A practice answer sheet for these pages can be found on page A1 of the *Chapter 12 Resource Masters*.

**Standardized Test Practice
Student Recording Sheet, p. A1**

Part 1 *Multiple Choice*

Select the best answer from the choices given and fill in the corresponding oval.

1 Ⓐ Ⓑ Ⓒ Ⓓ   4 Ⓐ Ⓑ Ⓒ Ⓓ   7 Ⓐ Ⓑ Ⓒ Ⓓ   9 Ⓐ Ⓑ Ⓒ Ⓓ
2 Ⓐ Ⓑ Ⓒ Ⓓ   5 Ⓐ Ⓑ Ⓒ Ⓓ   8 Ⓐ Ⓑ Ⓒ Ⓓ   10 Ⓐ Ⓑ Ⓒ Ⓓ
8 Ⓐ Ⓑ Ⓒ Ⓓ   3 Ⓐ Ⓑ Ⓒ Ⓓ

Part 2 *Short Response/Grid In*

Solve the problem and write your answer in the blank.

For Questions 12 and 19, also enter your answer by writing each number or symbol in a box. Then fill in the corresponding oval for that number or symbol.

11
12   (grid in)
13
14
15
16
17
18
19   (grid in)

Part 3 *Extended Response*

Record your answers for Questions 20–21 on the back of this paper.

Additional Practice

- See pp. 731–732 of the *Chapter 12 Resource Masters* for additional standardized test practice.

Part 1 Multiple Choice

Record your answers on the answer sheet provided by your teacher or on a sheet of paper.

1. A package of 20 computer disks costs $18.40. How much does each individual disk cost? (Prerequisite Skill, p. 715) **B**

Ⓐ $0.46   Ⓑ $0.92
Ⓒ $1.60   Ⓓ $1.84

2. The point system for a basketball contest is shown below. **B**

basket made	basket missed
⬇	⬇
gain 3 points	lose 3 points

Suppose Shantelle made 8 baskets and missed 4 baskets, then what was her total score? (Lesson 1-2)

Ⓐ 4 points   Ⓑ 12 points
Ⓒ 24 points   Ⓓ 32 points

3. An office has 45 light fixtures. Each fixture uses two light bulbs and each bulb costs $0.89. Which expression could be used to find the total cost of replacing all of the bulbs in the office? (Lesson 1-2) **D**

Ⓐ $45(0.89)$ Ⓑ $2(45 + 0.89)$
Ⓒ $\frac{45}{2}(0.89)$ Ⓓ $2(45)(0.89)$

4. What is the value of m in the equation $\frac{5}{8} + m = \frac{3}{4}$? (Lesson 5-9) **D**

Ⓐ $\frac{1}{2}$ Ⓑ $\frac{2}{5}$
Ⓒ $\frac{3}{8}$ Ⓓ $\frac{1}{8}$

5. Rita makes $6.80 per hour. If she gets a 5% raise, what will be her new hourly rate? (Lessons 6-5 and 6-7) **C**

Ⓐ $0.34   Ⓑ $3.40
Ⓒ $7.14   Ⓓ $10.20

---

6. Juliet recorded the distance and the time she walked every day.

Day	Distance (mi)	Time (min)
1	2	28
2	3	42
3	4	?

What is the best estimate of how many minutes it will take her to walk 4 miles? (Lesson 8-1) **C**

Ⓐ 48 min   Ⓑ 52 min
Ⓒ 56 min   Ⓓ 64 min

7. A line passes through the points at (4, 0) and (8, 8). Which of the following points also lie on the line? (Lesson 8-7) **B**

Ⓐ $(2, -2)$ Ⓑ $(6, 4)$
Ⓒ $(6, 6)$ Ⓓ $(10, 6)$

8. What is the surface area of the cube? (Lesson 11-4) **C**

Ⓐ 9 in^2 Ⓑ 36 in^2
Ⓒ 54 in^2 Ⓓ 324 in^2

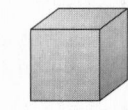

Volume: 27 in^3

9. How many different four-digit numbers can be formed using the digits 5, 6, 7, and 8 if each digit is used only once? (Lesson 12-7)

Ⓐ 26   Ⓑ 24
Ⓒ 12   Ⓓ 10

10. A bag contains 4 red marbles, 3 blue marbles, and 2 white marbles. One marble is chosen without replacement. Then another marble is chosen. What is the probability that the first marble is red and the second marble is blue? (Lesson 12-9) **C**

Ⓐ $\frac{7}{72}$ Ⓑ $\frac{4}{27}$
Ⓒ $\frac{1}{6}$ Ⓓ $\frac{4}{9}$

Test-Taking Tip

Questions 1–10
Eliminate the answer choices you know to be wrong. Then take your best guess from the choices that remain. If you can eliminate at least one answer choice, it is better to answer a question than to leave it blank.

 ExamView® Pro

Special banks of standardized test questions similar to those on the SAT, ACT, TIMSS 8, NAEP 8, and Pre-Algebra End-of-Course tests can be found on this CD-ROM.

Part 2 Short Response/Grid In

Record your answers on the answer sheet provided by your teacher or on a sheet of paper.

11. What is the value of $(0.3)^4$? (Lesson 4-2) **0.0081**

12. Sixteen pounds of ground beef will be divided into patties measuring one-quarter pound each. How many patties can be made? (Lesson 5-6) **64**

13. Suppose the segment shown is translated 3 units to the left. What are the coordinates of the endpoints of the resulting segment? (Lesson 10-3)

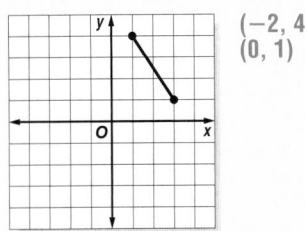

(−2, 4) and (0, 1)

14. What is the area of the trapezoid? (Lesson 10-5) **66 in²**

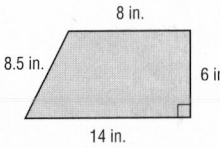

8 in.

8.5 in.

6 in.

14 in.

15. Use the formula $V = \frac{1}{3}\pi r^2 h$ to find the volume of a cone with a radius of 9 feet and a height of 12 feet. Round to the nearest tenth. (Lesson 11-3) **1017.9 ft³**

16. A can of soup is 12 cm high and has a diameter of 8 cm. A rectangular label is being designed for this can of soup. If the label will cover the surface of the can except for its top and bottom, what are the width and length of the label, to the nearest centimeter? (Lesson 11-4)

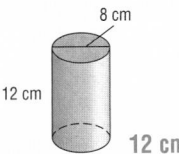

8 cm

12 cm

12 cm; 25 cm

www.pre-alg.com/standardized_test

For Exercises 17 and 18, use the following box-and-whisker plot.

Cost ($) of Various Scooters

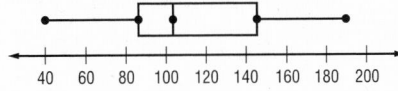

40 60 80 100 120 140 160 180 200

17. What is the median price of the scooters? (Lesson 12-3) **about $105**

18. About what percent of these scooters cost less than $90? (Lesson 12-3) **25%**

19. Only two of the five school newspaper editors can represent the school at the state awards banquet. How many different combinations of two editors can be selected to go to the banquet? (Lesson 12-7) **10**

Part 3 Extended Response

Record your answers on a sheet of paper. Show your work. **20a–b. See margin.**

20. The scores on a mathematics test are given in the frequency table. (Lesson 12-4)

Score	Tally	Frequency
60–69	I	1
70–79	IIII	4
80–89	ЖІ	5
90–99	II	2

a. Display the data in a histogram.

b. Which interval contains the greatest number of test scores?

21. If you order a "surprise pizza" special at a certain restaurant, the restaurant chooses two toppings at random. The available toppings are pepperoni, sausage, onions, green peppers, mushrooms, and black olives. (Lessons 12-6, 12-7, and 12-9)

a. List all of the possible "surprise pizzas."

b. How many different "surprise pizzas" are available at this restaurant?

c. If you order a "surprise pizza," what is the probability that it will have pepperoni or sausage on it?
a–c. See margin.

Answers

20b. 80—89

21a. PS, PO, PG, PM, PB, SO, SG, SM, SB, OG, OM, OB, GM, GB, MB

21b. 15

21c. $\frac{3}{5}$ or 60%

Evaluating Extended Response Questions

Extended Response questions are graded by using a multilevel rubric that guides you in assessing a student's knowledge of a particular concept.

Goal: Display and analyze data using a frequency table and a histogram, and explore the relationship between combinations and probability.

Sample Scoring Rubric: The following rubric is a sample scoring device. You may wish to add more detail to this sample to meet your individual scoring needs.

Score	Criteria
4	A correct solution that is supported by well-developed, accurate explanations
3	A generally correct solution, but may contain minor flaws in reasoning or computation
2	A partially correct interpretation and/or solution to the problem
1	A correct solution with no supporting evidence or explanation
0	An incorrect solution indicating no mathematical understanding of the concept or task, or no solution is given

Answer

20a. **Math Scores**

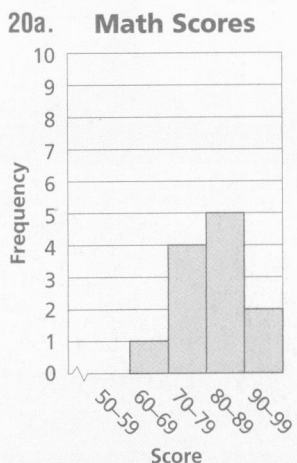

Page 607, Lesson 12-1

(Concept Check) The stems are the greatest common values of the data. The leaves are the numbers in the next place value position.

Page 608, Lesson 12-1

3.

Stem	Leaf
0	6 7
1	2 5 5
2	0
3	5
4	0 1

$2 \mid 0 = 20$

4.

Stem	Leaf
2	2 3 9
3	
4	2 2 2 4
5	
6	1
7	
8	2
9	
10	3
11	
12	8

$12 \mid 8 = 128$

7. Sample answer: The lowest score was 50. The highest score was 99. Most of the scores were in the 70–79 interval.

Page 609, Lesson 12-1

13.

Stem	Leaf
0	6 6 8
1	0 1 4 6 8
2	0 2 5
3	2 7
4	
5	0

$3 \mid 7 = 37$

14.

Stem	Leaf
46	8
47	2 5 5 6 8 8
48	1 7
49	3 6
50	1 8
51	1 7
52	4 6
53	0 4
54	0
55	0
56	
57	6

$53 \mid 4 = 53.4$

15.

Stem	Leaf
40	0 0 5
41	
42	5
43	
44	
45	0 6
46	
47	
48	0 4 7
49	
50	
51	0
52	0
•	
•	
•	
62	5
•	
•	
•	
76	4
77	
78	9

$76 \mid 4 = 764$

Page 610, Lesson 12-1

28. Stem-and-leaf plots can help you understand an election by allowing you to see how the number of electors in the U.S. is distributed. Answers should include the following.

- Most of the states in the U.S. have 0 to 10 electors. However, there are some states that have 10–19, 20–29, 30–39, and 50–59 electors.
- A presidential candidate might use the display to determine the importance of each state when campaigning.

Stem	Leaf
0	3 3 3 3 3 3 3 3
	4 4 4 4 4 4 5 5
	5 5 6 6 7 7 7 8
	8 8 8 8 8 9 9
1	0 0 1 1 1 1 2 2
	3 3 4 5 8
2	1 2 3 5
3	2 3
4	
5	4

$3 \setminus 2 = 32$

Page 614, Lesson 12-2

1. The range describes how the entire set of data is distributed, while the interquartile range describes how the middle half of the data is distributed.

2. The lower quartile is the median of the lower half of the set of data. The upper quartile is the median of the upper half of the set of data.

3. Sample answer: {8, 9, 13, 25, 26, 26, 26, 27, 28, 30, 35, 40}

8. Sample answer: Since the length of a day ranges from 5832 − 10 or 5822 hours, the lengths of days for the planets vary greatly.

Page 615, Lesson 12-2

20. Sample answer: Since the measures of variation are about the same, we can conclude that the number of home runs hit by the leaders in each league is consistent. That is, neither league exceeds the other.

Page 616, Lesson 12-2

25.

Stem	Leaf
0	9
1	2 4 5 8
2	1 7
3	7

3|7 = $37

30. {4.3, 4.8, 4.9, 5.0, 5.3, 5.6}

31. {0.2, 0.3, 0.6, 0.8, 1.2, 1.4, 1.5}

32. {40.6, 45.2, 45.4, 46.0, 50.7}

33. {9.8, 9.9, 10.5, 10.9, 11.2, 11.4}

Page 619, Lesson 12-3

6. Summer Olympic Games 1924–2000 Winning Times for Men's Marathon

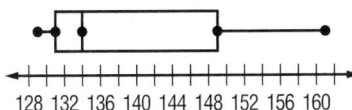

128 132 136 140 144 148 152 156 160

7. Sample answer: The length of the box-and-whisker plot shows that the winning times of the men's marathons are not concentrated around a certain time.

Page 620, Lesson 12-3

8. Since SUVs average the least miles per gallon, they tend to be less fuel-efficient.

9. The most fuel-efficient SUV and the least fuel-efficient sedan both average 22 miles per gallon.

10.

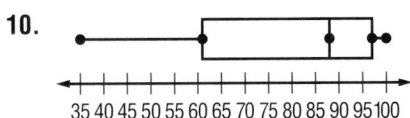

35 40 45 50 55 60 65 70 75 80 85 90 95 100

11.

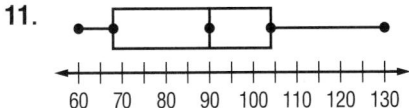

60 70 80 90 100 110 120 130

12.

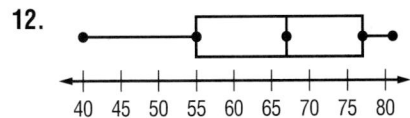

40 45 50 55 60 65 70 75 80

13.

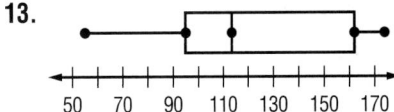

50 70 90 110 130 150 170

14.

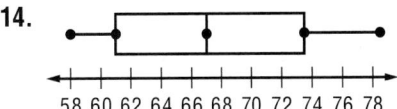

5.8 6.0 6.2 6.4 6.6 6.8 7.0 7.2 7.4 7.6 7.8

15.

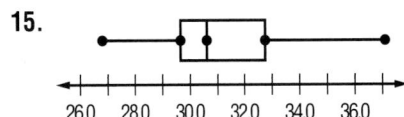

26.0 28.0 30.0 32.0 34.0 36.0

18. Sample answer: Based on the plot, the students' overall scores are between 63 and 96.

19. Sample answer: The least number of games won for the NFC is 3 and the least number of games won for the AFC is 1. The most number of games won for the NFC is 12 and the most number of games won for the AFC is 13. In addition, for both conferences, the median number of games won is about 9.

Page 621, Lesson 12-3

21. A box-and-whisker plot would clearly display any upper and lower extreme temperatures and the median temperature. Answers should include the following.

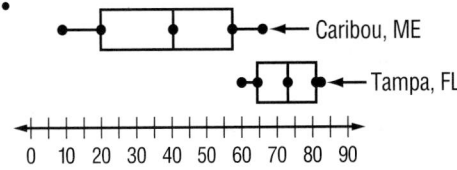

Caribou, ME

Tampa, FL

0 10 20 30 40 50 60 70 80 90

- Sample answer: Tampa has a median temperature of 73 and Caribou has a median temperature of 40.5. Whereas the highest average temperature for Tampa is 82, the highest average temperature for Caribou is 66.

- Sample answer: You can easily see how the temperatures vary.

Page 625, Lesson 12-4

3.

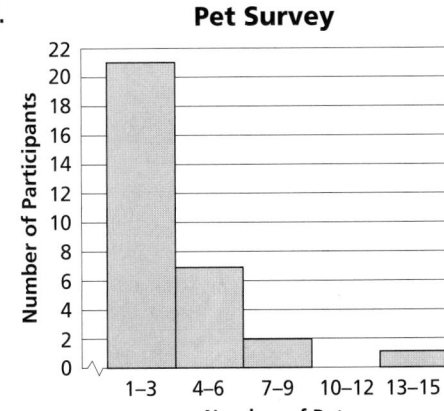

Pet Survey

Number of Participants

Number of Pets

4.

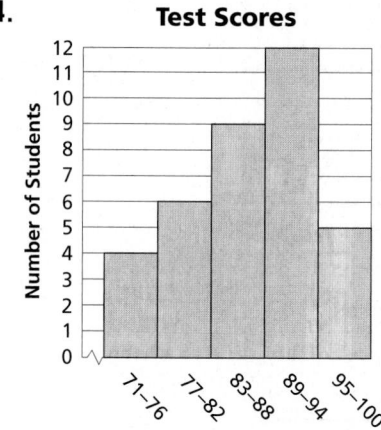

Test Scores

8. No; the graph shows that 34 states have anywhere from 0 to 9 roller coasters, but it does not indicate how many states have none.

Page 626, Lesson 12-4

12.

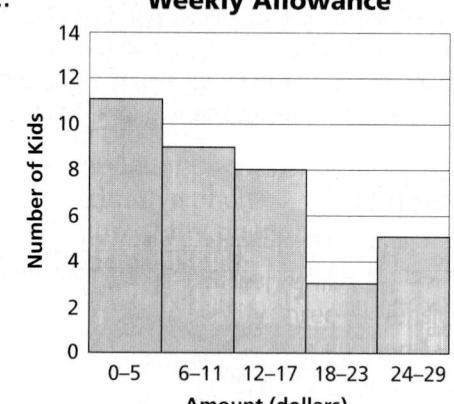

Weekly Allowance

13.

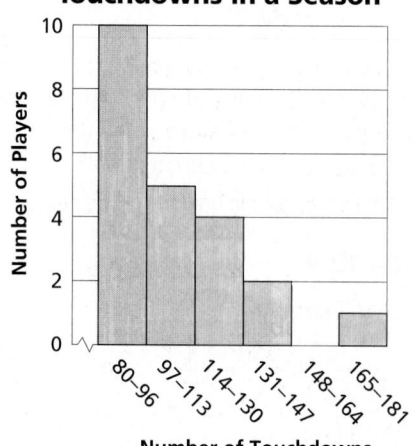

Touchdowns in a Season

14.

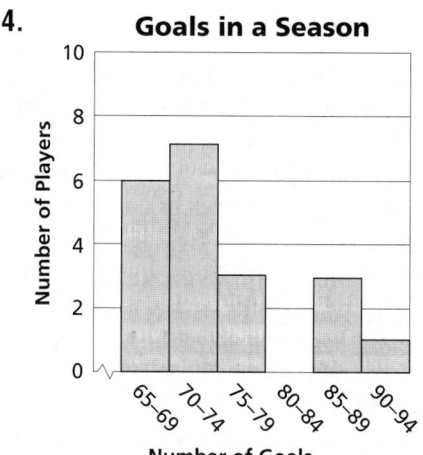

Goals in a Season

Page 627, Lesson 12-4

26. Histograms and frequency tables are similar in that they both categorize data using intervals. Answers should include the following.

•

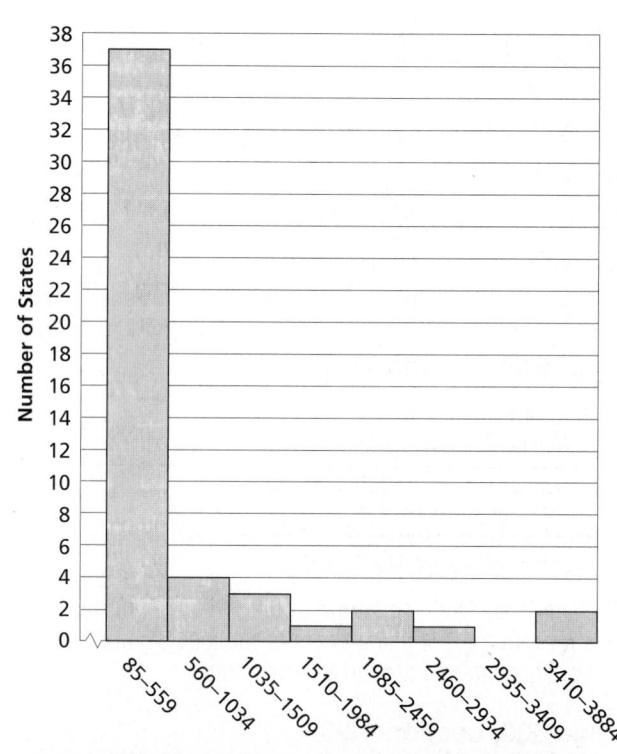

Size of U.S. Farms

Size of U.S. Farms		
Acres	**Tally**	**Frequency**
85–59	ЖЖ ЖЖ ЖЖ ЖЖ ЖЖ ЖЖ ЖЖ II	37
560–1034	IIII	4
1035–1509	III	3
1510–1984	I	1
1985–2459	II	2
2460–2934	I	1
2935–3409		0
3410–3884	II	2

- In the histogram, the size of the farm is shown on the horizontal axis and the number of states that contain a farm of that size is shown on the vertical axis. The bars are used to show the number of states that contain a farm of the given size. In the frequency table, the size of the farm is listed in the first column and the number of states that contain a farm of the given size is listed in the third column. The middle column is used for tallying the data.

Page 628, Lesson 12-4 (Practice Quiz)

1.

Stem	Leaf
1	6 8 9 9
2	0 2 6 8 8 8
3	0 2
4	0 2 3
5	5
6	
7	
8	6 9 5	5 = 55

3.

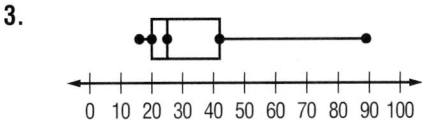

5.

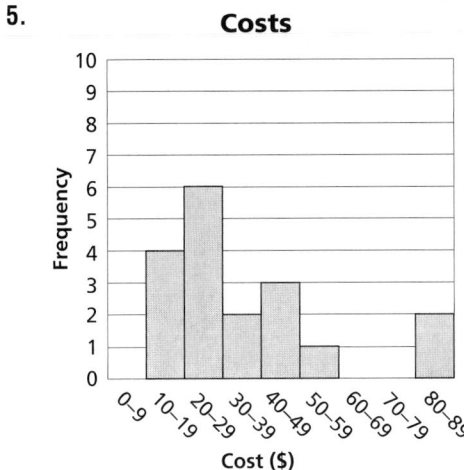

Costs

11a.

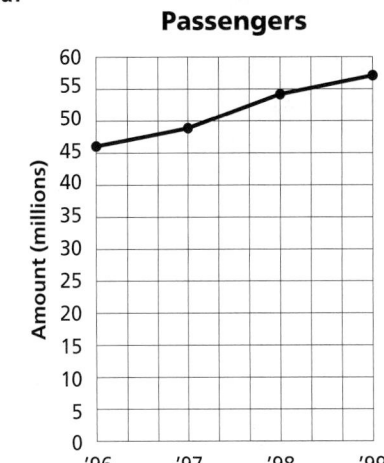

Commuter Train Passengers

11b.

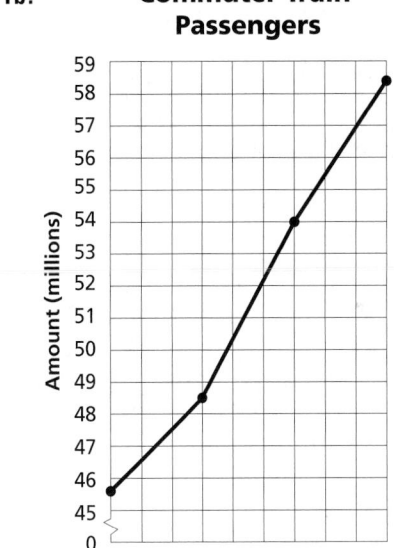

Commuter Train Passengers

12. The use of inconsistent scales, broken scales, expanded and shortened axes will make the graph misleading. Answers should include the following.

-
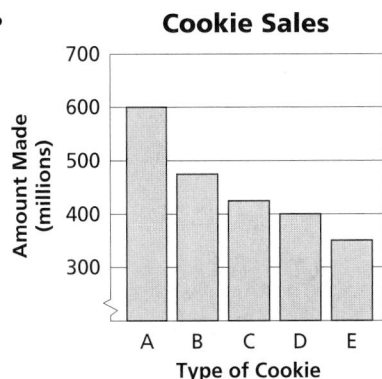

Cookie Sales

- This graph is misleading because the vertical axis does not start at zero. To redo the graph so that it is not misleading, you can redraw the vertical axis so that it does include zero and the intervals of the vertical axis are equal.

14.

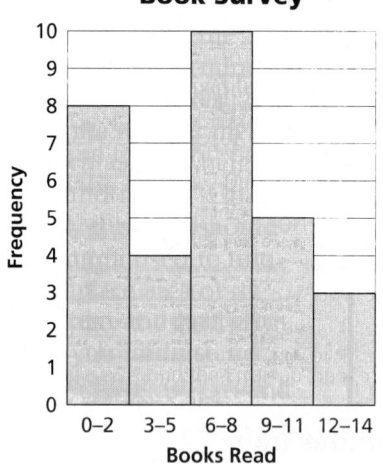

Book Survey

15.

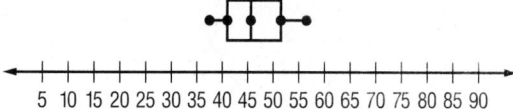

18. $\frac{1}{4}$ or 25%

19. $\frac{1}{6}$ or $16\frac{2}{3}$%

20. $\frac{5}{12}$ or $41\frac{2}{3}$%

21. $\frac{5}{6}$ or $83\frac{1}{3}$%

22. $\frac{3}{4}$ or 75%

23. $\frac{5}{6}$ or $83.\overline{3}$%

Page 637, Lesson 12-6

4.

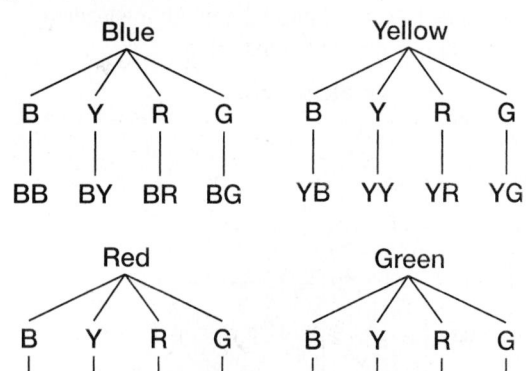

16 outcomes

Page 638, Lesson 12-6

10.

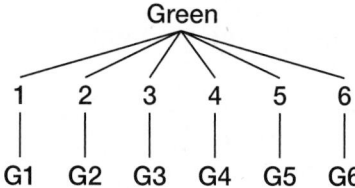

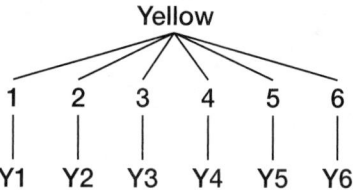

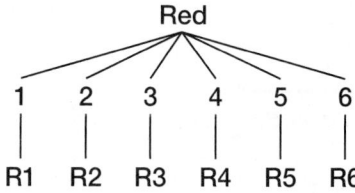

11.

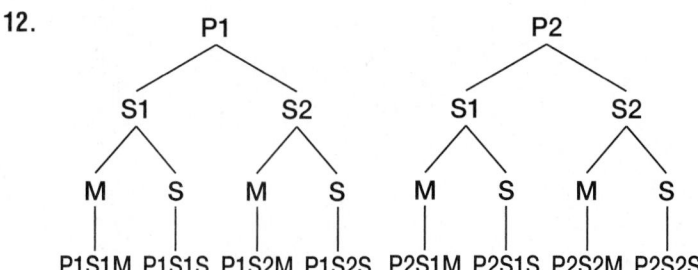

12.

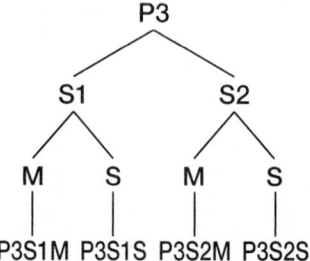

13.

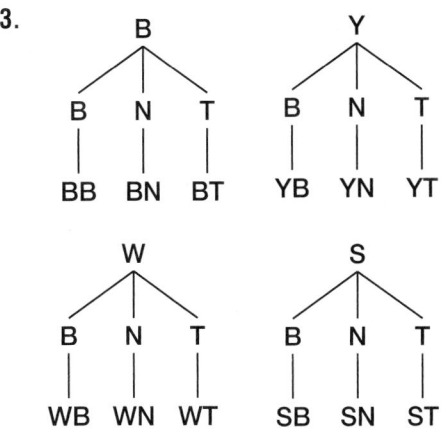

Page 640, Algebra Activity

Collect Data

Step 2.

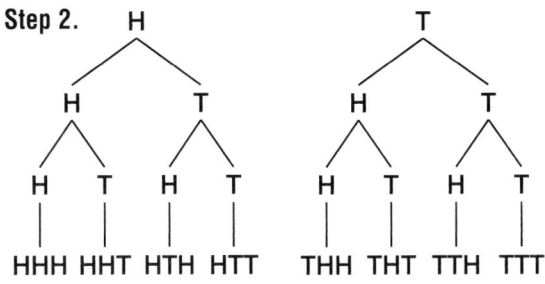

Step 3.

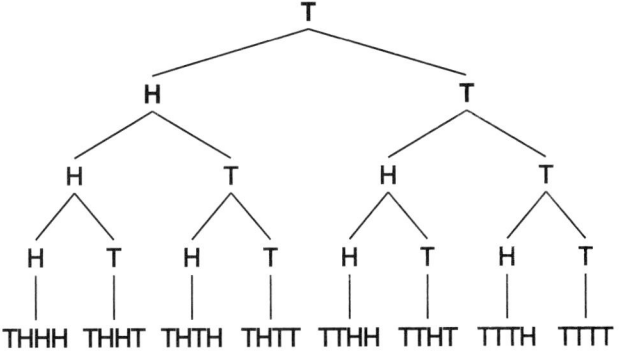

7. The sum of the numbers in each row is the number of outcomes for tossing a number of coins one less than the row number. The numbers in each row are the numerators for the probabilities for outcomes for the coin tossing connected with that row.

8. The numbers in the row are 1, 5, 10, 10, 5, 1. The number of outcomes is 32. The probabilities are:

$P(5 \text{ heads}) = \frac{1}{32}$, $P(4 \text{ heads}, 1 \text{ tail}) = \frac{5}{32}$, $P(3 \text{ heads}, 2 \text{ tails}) = \frac{10}{32}$, $P(2 \text{ heads}, 3 \text{ tails}) = \frac{10}{32}$, $P(1 \text{ head}, 4 \text{ tails}) = \frac{5}{32}$; $P(5 \text{ tails}) = \frac{1}{32}$.

Page 645, Lesson 12-7

34.

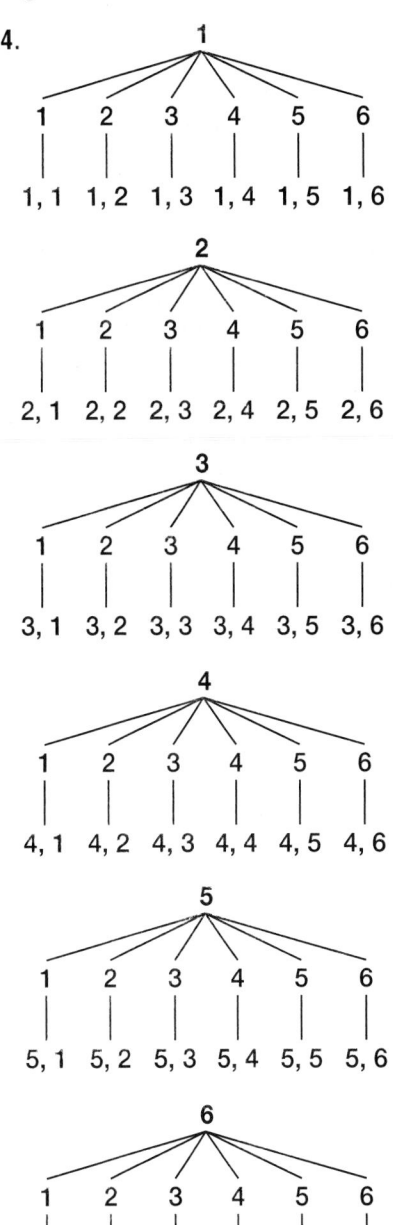

Polynomials and Nonlinear Functions
Chapter Overview and Pacing

Year-long pacing: pages T20–T21.

LESSON OBJECTIVES	PACING (days)			
	Regular		Block	
	Basic/ Average	Advanced	Basic/ Average	Advanced
13-1 Polynomials *(pp. 669–673)* • Identify and classify polynomials. • Find the degree of a polynomial. ***Follow-Up:*** Model polynomials with algebra tiles.	Optional	2 (with 13–1 Follow-Up)	Optional	1 (with 13–1 Follow-Up)
13-2 Adding Polynomials *(pp. 674–677)* • Add polynomials.	Optional	1	Optional	0.5
13-3 Subtracting Polynomials *(pp. 678–681)* • Subtract polynomials.	Optional	1	Optional	0.5
13-4 Multiplying a Polynomial by a Monomial *(pp. 682–686)* ***Preview:*** Model multiplication with algebra tiles. • Multiply a polynomial by a monomial.	Optional	2	Optional	1
13-5 Linear and Nonlinear Functions *(pp. 687–691)* • Determine whether a function is linear or nonlinear.	Optional	2	Optional	1
13-6 Graphing Quadratic and Cubic Functions *(pp. 692–697)* • Graph quadratic functions. • Graph cubic functions. ***Follow-Up:*** Graph families of quadratic functions.	Optional	3	Optional	1.5
Study Guide and **Practice Test** *(pp. 698–701)* **Standardized Test Practice** *(pp. 702–703)*	Optional	1	Optional	0.5
Chapter Assessment	Optional	1	Optional	0.5
TOTAL	**0**	**13**	**0**	**6.5**

Chapter Resource Manager

CHAPTER 13 RESOURCE MASTERS

Study Guide and Intervention	Practice (Skills and Average)	Reading to Learn Mathematics	Enrichment	Assessment	Prerequisite Skills Workbook	Applications*	Parent and Student Study Guide Workbook	5-Minute Check Transparencies	Interactive Chalkboard	Pre-AlgePASS: Tutorial Plus (lessons)	Materials
733	734–735	736	737				108	13-1	13-1		*Follow-Up:* algebra tiles
738	739–740	741	742	777			109	13-2	13-2		
743	744–745	746	747	777, 779		SC 25	110	13-3	13-3		
748	749–750	751	752			GCS 43	111	13-4	13-4	38	*Preview:* algebra tiles, product mat
753	754–755	756	757	778		SC 26	112	13-5	13-5		
758	759–760	761	762	778		GCS 44	113	13-6	13-6		*Follow-Up:* graphing calculator
				763–776 780–794							

* *Key to Abbreviations:* GCS = Graphing Calculator and Spreadsheet Masters
SC = School-to-Career Masters
SM = Science and Mathematics Lab Manual

 Study Guide and Intervention, Skills Practice, Practice, and Parent and Student Study Guide Workbooks are also available in Spanish.

Mathematical Connections and Background

Continuity of Instruction

Prior Knowledge

In Chapter 2, students learned to add integers, using the additive inverse when necessary. In Chapter 3, they studied the Distributive Property and its use in simplifying mathematical expressions. In Chapter 4, students learned about monomials. In addition, they studied functions and rate of change and graphed linear equations and inequalities in Chapter 8.

This Chapter

Students expand their knowledge of polynomials to include expressions with more than one term, such as binomials and trinomials, and they learn to add, subtract, and multiply polynomials. Students compare the rates of change of several functions. They compare linear and nonlinear functions, learn the shapes of some nonlinear functions, and graph quadratic and cubic functions.

Future Connections

The material covered in this chapter is fundamental for future mathematics courses, particularly calculus. Many formulas contain monomials and polynomials, and solving problems involving these formulas will be a necessary skill in higher level courses such as physics and engineering.

13-1 Polynomials

Recall that a monomial is a number, a variable, or a product of numbers and/or variables such as 3x4. An algebraic expression that contains one or more monomials is called a polynomial. In a polynomial, there are no terms with variables in the denominator and no terms with variables under a radical sign. Polynomials can be classified by the number of terms contained in the expression. Therefore, a polynomial with two terms is called a binomial ($z^2 - 1$), and a polynomial with three terms is called a trinomial ($2y^3 + 4y^2 - y$).

Polynomials also can be classified by their degrees. The degree of a monomial is the sum of the exponents of its variables. The degree of a nonzero constant such as 6 or 10 is 0. The constant 0 has no degree. For example, the monomial $4b^5c^2$ has a degree of 7. The degree of a polynomial is the same as that of the term with the greatest degree. For example, the polynomial $3x^4 - 2y^3 + 4y^2 - y$ has a degree of 4.

13-2 Adding Polynomials

Monomials that contain the same variables to the same power are like terms. Like terms differ only by their coefficients. Polynomials can be added by combining like terms. When a polynomial has a minus sign, the coefficient following is a negative number. There are two methods for adding polynomials. In one method, the polynomials are stacked vertically with like terms aligned, as shown below.

$$\begin{array}{r} 2ab - 3b^2 - 8 \\ (+) \quad ab + 6b^2 + 0 \\ \hline 3ab + 3b^2 - 8 \end{array}$$

When using the vertical method, it can be helpful to add zeros as placeholders when a term in one polynomial does not have a corresponding like term in another polynomial. In the other method, the polynomials are written horizontally and like terms are combined by using the Associative and Commutative Properties, as shown below.

$$(3xy + 4) + (xy - 2) = (3xy + xy) + (4 - 2)$$
$$= 4xy + 2$$

Polynomials often are used to represent measures of geometric figures. For example, a rectangle whose length is 3 times its width has the dimensions $x \times 3x$ and its perimeter is equal to $2x + 2(3x)$, or $8x$.

13-3 Subtracting Polynomials

Just as measurements are subtracted by subtracting like units, polynomials are subtracted by subtracting like terms. As with the addition of polynomials, polynomials can be subtracted vertically or horizontally. Recall that you can subtract a rational number by adding its additive inverse. Similarly, you can subtract a polynomial by adding its additive inverse. The additive inverse is found by multiplying the entire polynomial by –1. By the Distributive Property, this is done by multiplying each term of the polynomial by –1. For example, $-1(2a^2c + 4bc - 7) = -2a^2c - 4bc + 7$.

13-4 Multiplying a Polynomial by a Monomial

When multiplying a polynomial by a monomial, use the Distributive Property and then simplify, as shown below.

$$4y(2x^2y - 3x + 5) = 4y(2x^2y) + 4y(-3x) + 4y(5)$$
$$= 8x^2y^2 + (-12xy) + 20y$$

13-5 Linear and Nonlinear Functions

Linear functions have graphs that are straight lines. These graphs represent constant rates of change. In other words, the slope between any two points on the graph is the same. Nonlinear functions do not have constant rates of change. The slope changes along these graphs. Therefore, the graphs of nonlinear functions are *not* straight lines. Graphs of curves represent nonlinear functions. Recall that the equation for a linear function can be written in the form $y = mx + b$, where m represents the slope. Therefore, you can determine whether a function is linear by looking at its equation. For example, the equation $y = \frac{3}{x}$ is nonlinear because x is in the denominator and the equation cannot be written in the form $y = mx + b$. A nonlinear function does not increase or decrease at the same rate.

Some nonlinear functions are given special names. A quadratic function is a function that can be described by an equation of the form $y = ax^2 + bx + c$, where $a \neq 0$. The graph of a quadratic function has the shape of a parabola. A cubic function is a function that can be described by an equation of the form $y = ax^3 + bx^2 + cx + d$, where $a \neq 0$. Other nonlinear functions are exponential functions, such as $y = 4^x$, and inverse variation functions, such as $y = \frac{1}{x}$. See page 688 for examples of graphs of these four types of nonlinear functions.

13-6 Graphing Quadratic and Cubic Functions

Quadratic functions can be graphed using an equation or a table of values. For example, to graph $y = 3x^2 + 1$, substitute the values –1, –0.5, 0, 0.5, and 1 for x in the equation to yield the point coordinates (–1, 4), (–0.5, 1.75), (0, 1), (0.5, 1.75), and (1, 4). Plot these points on a coordinate grid and connect the points in the form of a parabola. Parabolas are symmetric with respect to a line drawn from the vertex to the focus of the parabola. Note that the graph of this example has a vertical line of reflection at $x = 0$. Parabolas with a horizontal line of reflection are not functions, since for every value x except the vertex, there are two values for y.

Cubic functions also can be graphed by making a table of values. Students sometimes will try to connect the points as a straight line. Note that the graph of any cubic function is a curve, and there is one point at which the curve changes from opening upward to opening downward, or vice versa. On the graph of the cubic function $y = 3x^3 + 1$, this point, called the point of inflection, is at (0, 1). At this point, the curve changes from being concave down to concave up.

Quick Review Math Handbook

Hot Words Hot Topics

Hot Words includes a glossary of terms while Hot Topics consists of explanations of key mathematical concepts with exercises to test comprehension. This valuable resource can be used as a reference in the classroom or for home study.

Lesson	Hot Topics Section	Lesson	Hot Topics Section
GS 13	1.4, 6.4	13-4	6.4, 6.7
13-1	6.2	13-5	6.4, 6.7, 6.8
13-3	6.2		

GS = Getting Started

 Additional mathematical information and teaching notes are available at www.pre-alg.com/key_concepts.

DAILY INTERVENTION and Assessment

Key to Abbreviations:
TWE = Teacher Wraparound Edition; CRM = Chapter Resource Masters

Type	Student Edition	Teacher Resources	Technology/Internet
INTERVENTION Ongoing	Prerequisite Skills, pp. 667, 672, 677, 681, 686, 691 Practice Quiz 1, p. 681 Practice Quiz 2, p. 691	5-Minute Check Transparencies *Prerequisite Skills Workbook,* pp. 1–2, 21–24, 27–28, 31–32, 47–62 Quizzes, *CRM,* pp. 777, 778 Mid-Chapter Test, *CRM,* p. 779 Study Guide and Intervention, *CRM,* p. 733, 738, 743, 748, 753, 758	Pre-AlgePASS: Tutorial Plus, Lesson 38 www.pre-alg.com/ self_check_quiz www.pre-alg.com/ extra_examples
Mixed Review	pp. 672, 677, 681, 686, 691, 696	Cumulative Review, *CRM,* p. 780	
Error Analysis	Find the Error, pp. 671, 676	Find the Error, *TWE,* pp. 671, 676 Unlocking Misconceptions, *TWE,* p. 693	
ASSESSMENT Standardized Test Practice	pp. 672, 677, 681, 686, 689, 691, 695, 702–703	*TWE,* pp. 702–703 Standardized Test Practice, *CRM,* pp. 781–872	Standardized Test Practice CD-ROM www.pre-alg.com/ standardized_test
Open-Ended Assessment	Writing in Math, pp. 672, 677, 681, 686, 691, 695 Open Ended, pp. 670, 676, 680, 684, 689,694 Standardized Test, p. 703	Speaking: *TWE,* pp. 680, 691 Writing: *TWE,* pp. 672, 695 Modeling: *TWE,* pp. 676, 685 Open-Ended Assessment, *CRM,* p. 775	
Chapter Assessment	Study Guide, pp. 698–700 Practice Test, p. 701	Multiple-Choice Tests (Forms 1, 2A, 2B), *CRM,* pp. 763–768 Free-Response Tests (Forms 2C, 2D, 3), *CRM,* pp. 769–774 Vocabulary Test/Review, *CRM,* p. 776	ExamView® Pro (see below) MindJogger Videoquizzes www.pre-alg.com/ vocabulary_review www.pre-alg.com/chapter_test

For more information on Yearly ProgressPro, see p. 602.

Pre-Algebra Lesson	Yearly ProgressPro Skill Lesson
13-1	Simplifying Polynomials
13-2	Adding polynomials
13-3	Subtracting Polynomials
13-4	Multiplying Monomials and Polynomials
13-5	Linear and Non-Linear Function
13-6	Graphing Quadratic Functions

ExamView® Pro

Use the networkable **ExamView® Pro** to:
- Create **multiple versions** of tests.
- Create **modified** tests for *Inclusion* students.
- **Edit** existing questions and **add** your own questions.
- Use built-in **state curriculum correlations** to create tests aligned with state standards.
- Change **English** tests to **Spanish** and vice versa.

For more information on Intervention and Assessment, see pp. T8–T11.

Reading and Writing in Mathematics

Glencoe Pre-Algebra provides numerous opportunities to incorporate reading and writing into the mathematics classroom.

Student Edition

- Foldables™ Study Organizer, p. 667
- Reading Mathematics, p. 668
- Concept Check questions require students to verbalize and write about what they have learned in the lesson. (pp. 669, 670, 675, 676, 679, 680, 684, 689, 694)
- Writing in Math questions in every lesson, pp. 672, 677, 681, 689, 691, 695
- Reading Math, p. 678, 684, 688
- WebQuest, pp. 690, 696

Teacher Wraparound Edition

- Foldables™ Study Organizer, pp. 667, 698
- Study Notebook suggestions, pp. 668, 671, 673, 675, 680, 682, 684, 689, 694
- Modeling activities, pp. 676, 685
- Speaking activities, pp. 680, 691
- Writing activities, pp. 672, 695
- Differentiated Instruction (Verbal/Linguistic), p. 694
- **ELL** Resources, pp. 666, 668, 669, 674, 678, 683, 687, 692, 694, 698

Additional Resources

- Vocabulary Builder worksheets require students to define and give examples for key vocabulary terms as they progress through the chapter (*Chapter 13 Resource Masters*, pp. vii–viii)
- Reading to Learn Mathematics master for each lesson (*Chapter 13 Resource Masters*, pp. 736, 741, 746, 751, 756, 761)
- *Vocabulary PuzzleMaker* software creates crossword, jumble, and word search puzzles using vocabulary lists that you can customize.
- *Teaching Mathematics with Foldables* provides suggestions for promoting cognition and language.
- *Reading and Writing in the Mathematics Classroom*
- *WebQuest and Project Resources*

For more information on Reading and Writing in Mathematics, see pp. T6–T7.

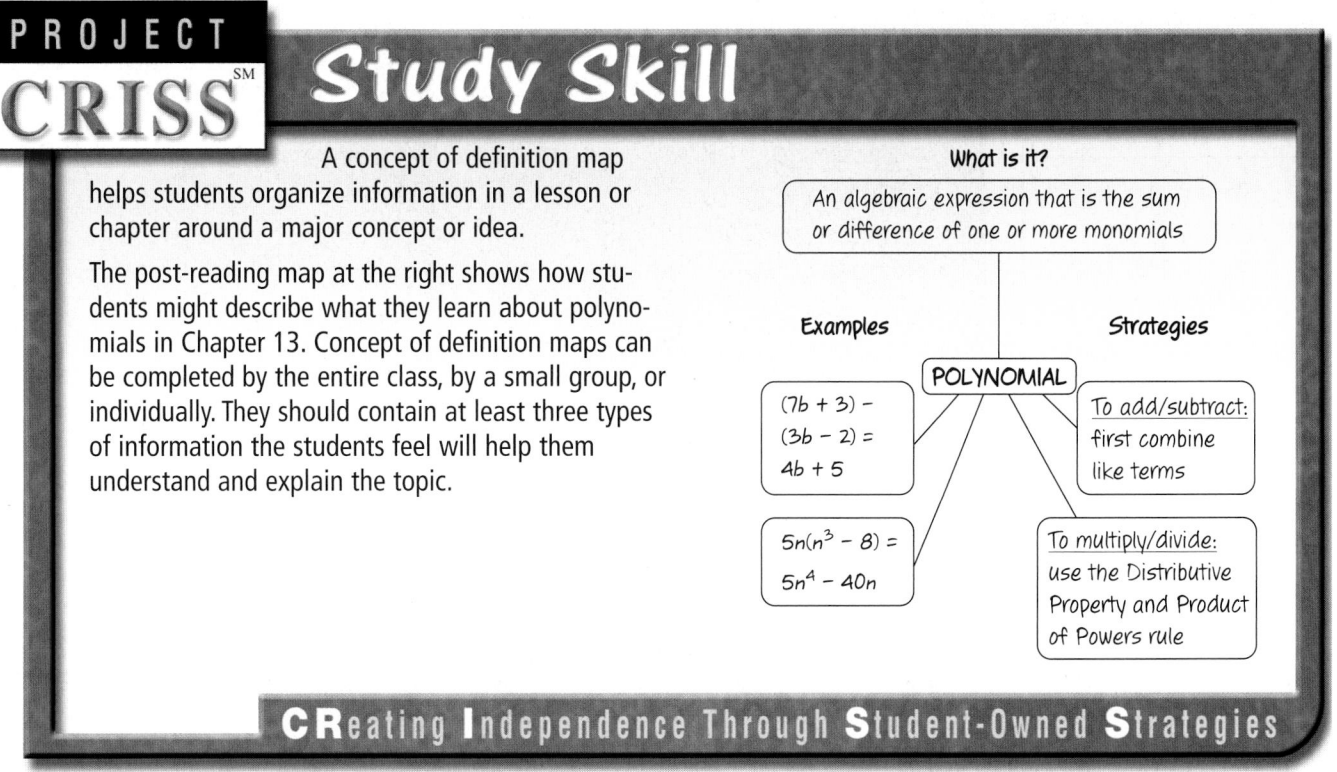

PROJECT CRISSsm **Study Skill**

A concept of definition map helps students organize information in a lesson or chapter around a major concept or idea.

The post-reading map at the right shows how students might describe what they learn about polynomials in Chapter 13. Concept of definition maps can be completed by the entire class, by a small group, or individually. They should contain at least three types of information the students feel will help them understand and explain the topic.

What is it?

An algebraic expression that is the sum or difference of one or more monomials

Examples

POLYNOMIAL

$(7b + 3) - (3b - 2) = 4b + 5$

$5n(n^3 - 8) = 5n^4 - 40n$

Strategies

To add/subtract: first combine like terms

To multiply/divide: use the Distributive Property and Product of Powers rule

CReating **I**ndependence **T**hrough **S**tudent-Owned **S**trategies

What You'll Learn

Have students read over the list of objectives and make a list of any words with which they are not familiar.

Why It's Important

Point out to students that this is only one of many reasons why each objective is important. Others are provided in the introduction to each lesson.

Lesson	NCTM Standards	Local Objectives
13-1 Preview	2, 8, 10	
13-1	2, 9, 10	
13-1 Follow-Up	2, 3, 4, 7, 9, 10	
13-2	1, 2, 9, 10	
13-3	1, 2, 9, 10	
13-4 Preview	1, 2, 3, 4, 8, 9, 10	
13-4	1, 2, 9, 10	
13-5	2, 3, 9, 10	
13-6	2, 3, 9, 10	
13-6 Follow-Up	2, 3, 6, 7, 9, 10	

Key to NCTM Standards:

1=Number & Operations, 2=Algebra,
3=Geometry, 4=Measurement,
5=Data Analysis & Probability, 6=Problem
Solving, 7=Reasoning & Proof,
8=Communication, 9=Connections,
10=Representation

Chapter
13 Polynomials and Nonlinear Functions

What You'll Learn

- **Lesson 13-1** Identify and classify polynomials.
- **Lessons 13-2 through 13-4** Add, subtract, and multiply polynomials.
- **Lesson 13-5** Determine whether functions are linear or nonlinear.
- **Lesson 13-6** Explore different representations of quadratic and cubic functions.

Key Vocabulary

- polynomial (p. 669)
- degree (p. 670)
- nonlinear function (p. 687)
- quadratic function (p. 688)
- cubic function (p. 688)

Why It's Important

You have studied situations that can be modeled by linear functions. Many real-life situations, however, are not linear. These can be modeled using nonlinear functions. *You will use a nonlinear function in Lesson 13-6 to determine how far a skydiver falls in 4.5 seconds.*

Vocabulary Builder   ELL

The Key Vocabulary list introduces students to some of the main vocabulary terms included in this chapter. For a more thorough vocabulary list with pronunciations of new words, give students the Vocabulary Builder worksheets found on pages vii and viii of the *Chapter 13 Resource Masters*. Encourage them to complete the definition of each term as they progress through the chapter. You may suggest that they add these sheets to their study notebooks for future reference when studying for the Chapter 13 test.

Getting Started

> **Prerequisite Skills** To be successful in this chapter, you'll need to master these skills and be able to apply them in problem-solving situations. Review these skills before beginning Chapter 13.

For Lesson 13-1   **Monomials**

Determine the number of monomials in each expression. *(For review, see Lesson 4-1.)*

1. $2x^3$ **1**   **2.** $a + 4$ **2**   **3.** $8s - 5t$ **2**

4. $x^2 + 3x - 1$ **3**   **5.** $\frac{1}{t}$ **0**   **6.** $9x^3 + 6x^2 + 8x - 7$ **4**

For Lesson 13-4   **Distributive Property**

Use the Distributive Property to write each expression as an equivalent algebraic expression. *(For review, see Lesson 3-1.)*

7. $5(a + 4)$ $5a + 20$ **8.** $2(3y - 8)$ $6y - 16$ **9.** $-4(1 + 8n)$ $-4 - 32n$

10. $6(x + 2y)$ $6x + 12y$ **11.** $(9b - 9c)3$ $27b - 27c$ **12.** $5(q - 2r + 3s)$
                                                                      $5q - 10r + 15s$

For Lesson 13-5   **Linear Functions**

Determine whether each equation is linear. *(For review, see Lesson 8-2.)*

13. $y = x - 2$ **yes**   **14.** $y = x^2$ **no**   **15.** $y = -\frac{1}{2}x$ **yes**

FOLDABLES™
Study Organizer

Polynomials Make this Foldable to help you organize your notes. Begin with a sheet of 11" by 17" paper.

Step 1 Fold

Fold the short sides toward the middle.

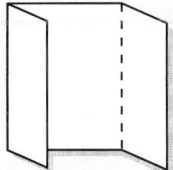

Step 2 Fold Again

Fold the top to the bottom.

Step 3 Cut

Open. Cut along the second fold to make four tabs.

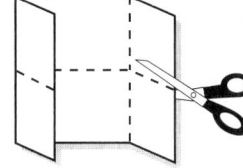

Step 4 Label

Label each of the tabs as shown.

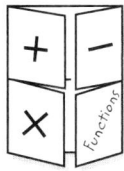

Reading and Writing As you read and study the chapter, write examples of each concept under each tab.

Chapter 13 Polynomials and Nonlinear Functions **667**

This section provides a review of the basic concepts needed before beginning Chapter 13. Page references are included for additional student help.

Prerequisite Skills, in the Getting Ready for the Next Lesson section at the end of each lesson, reviews a skill needed in the next lesson.

For Lesson	Prerequisite Skill
13-2	Properties of Addition (p. 672)
13-3	Additive Inverse (p. 677)
13-4	Multiplying Monomials (p. 681)
13-5	Using Tables to Find Ordered Pair Solutions (p. 686)
13-6	Graphing Equations (p. 691)

FOLDABLES™
Study Organizer

For more information about Foldables, see *Teaching Mathematics with Foldables.*

Expository Writing to Teach Others Under each tab of their Foldables, have students explain how to add, subtract, multiply, and divide polynomials and give several examples of each operation. Student expositions should be clear and concise so that someone who did not understand how to do these operations could read their explanations and learn from them. Encourage students to exchange and read their Foldables.

Chapter 13 Polynomials and Nonlinear Functions **667**

Reading Mathematics

Getting Started

Have students compare the list of *Monomials* to the list of *Not Monomials*. Ask what is different and the same about each list. Then ask which list $16jp^2r^3$ belongs in. Have them explain why.

Teaching Tip Point out to students that expressions like $\frac{1}{a}$ are not monomials.

Teach

Prefixes and Trinomials Have students think of as many words as they can that have the same prefix as *trinomial*. Write the words on the board as they say them. Examples include triad, triceps, tripod, trio, tricycle, trifocal, trimester, trinity, and triple. Have students discuss the meanings of the words and what they have in common.

Assess

Study Notebook

Have students copy their answers to Exercise 3 into their notebooks. Ask them to include at least one example for each definition.

ELL English Language Learners may benefit from writing key concepts from this activity in their Study Notebooks in their native language and then in English.

Prefixes and Polynomials

You can determine the meaning of many words used in mathematics if you know what the prefixes mean. In Lesson 4-1, you learned that the prefix *mono* means one and that a monomial is an algebraic expression with one term.

Monomials	Not Monomials
5	$x + y$
$2x$	$8n^2 - n + 1$
y^3	$a^3 + 4a^2 + a - 6$

The words in the table below are used in mathematics and in everyday life. They contain the prefixes *bi*, *tri*, and *poly*.

Prefix	Words	
bi	• bisect – to divide into two congruent parts • biannual – occurring twice a year • bicycle – a vehicle with two wheels	bisect
tri	• triangle – a figure with three sides • triathlon – an athletic contest with three phases • trilogy – a series of three related literary works, such as films or books	triangle
poly	• polyhedron – a solid with many flat surfaces • polychrome – having many colors • polygon – a figure with many sides	polyhedron

Reading to Learn 4. Sample answer: $x + y$; $a^2 + a + 1$; $x^3 + x^2 + x + 1$

1. How are the words in each group of the table related? **Each group has 2, 3, or many items.**

2. What do the prefixes *bi*, *tri*, and *poly* mean? **Bi means two, tri means three, poly means many.**

3. Write the definition of *binomial*, *trinomial*, and *polynomial*. **See margin.**

4. Give an example of a binomial, a trinomial, and a polynomial.

5. **RESEARCH** Use the Internet or a dictionary to make a list of other words that have the prefixes *bi*, *tri*, and *poly*. Give the definition of each word. **See margin.**

668 Chapter 13 Polynomials and Nonlinear Functions

Answers

3. Sample answer: binomial, an expression with two terms; trinomial, an expression with three terms; polynomial, an expression with many terms

5. Sample answer: bicolored means two-colored; a trident is a spear with three prongs; polysyllable means having many syllables.

13-1 Polynomials

What You'll Learn

- Identify and classify polynomials.
- Find the degree of a polynomial.

How are polynomials used to approximate real-world data?

Heat index is a way to describe how hot it feels outside with the temperature and humidity combined. Some examples are shown below.

	Temperature (°F)			
Humidity (%)	80	90	100	
40	79	93	110	Heat Index
45	80	95	115	
50	81	96	120	

To calculate heat index, meteorologists use an expression similar to the one below. In this expression, x is the percent humidity, and y is the temperature.

$$-42 + 2x + 10y - 0.2xy - 0.007x^2 - 0.05y^2 + 0.001x^2y + 0.009xy^2 - 0.000002x^2y^2$$

a. How many terms are in the expression for the heat index? 9

b. What separates the terms of the expression? plus and minus signs

CLASSIFY POLYNOMIALS Recall that a *monomial* is a number, a variable, or a product of numbers and/or variables. An algebraic expression that contains one or more monomials is called a **polynomial**. In a polynomial, there are no terms with variables in the denominator and no terms with variables under a radical sign.

A polynomial with two terms is called a **binomial**, and a polynomial with three terms is called a **trinomial**.

Polynomial	Number of Terms	Examples
monomial	1	4, x, $2y^3$
binomial	2	$x + 1$, $a - 5b$, $c^2 + d$
trinomial	3	$a + b + c$, $x^2 + 2x + 1$

The terms in a binomial or a trinomial may be added or subtracted.

Example 1 Classify Polynomials

Determine whether each expression is a polynomial. If it is, classify it as a *monomial*, *binomial*, or *trinomial*.

a. $2x^3 + 5x + 7$

This is a polynomial because it is the sum of three monomials. There are three terms, so it is a trinomial.

b. $t - \frac{1}{t^2}$

The expression is *not* a polynomial because $\frac{1}{t^2}$ has a variable in the denominator.

Concept Check Is $0.5x + 10$ a polynomial? Explain. Yes; it has two terms, so it is a binomial.

ocabulary

- polynomial
- binomial
- trinomial
- degree

tudy Tip

latrices

nother way to organize e data displayed in this ble is with a *matrix*. learn more about atrices, see page 705.

tudy Tip

lassifying olynomials

e sure expressions are ritten in simplest form. $x + x$ is the same as $2x$, so the expression is a monomial. $\sqrt{25}$ is the same as 5, so the expression is a monomial.

TEACHING TIP

xplain that in a nonomial, the exponent f a variable must be a vhole number. $\frac{1}{t^2}$ is not a monomial ecause $\frac{1}{t^2} = t^{-2}$.

www.pre-alg.com/extra_examples

13-1 Lesson Notes

1 Focus

5-Minute Check Transparency 13-1 Use as a quiz or review of Chapter 12.

Mathematical Background notes are available for this lesson on page 666C.

How are polynomials used to approximate real-world data?

The opening activity questions are repeated on page 736 of the *Chapter 13 Resource Masters.*

Reading to Learn Mathematics, p. 736 ELL

Pre-Activity *How are polynomials used to approximate real-world data?*

Do the activity at the top of page 669 in your textbook. Write your answers below.

a. How many terms are in the expression for the heat index? 9

b. What separates the terms of the expression? plus and minus signs

Reading the Lesson 1–4. See students' work.

Write a definition and give an example of each new vocabulary word.

Vocabulary	Definition	Example
1. polynomial		
2. binomial		
3. trinomial		
4. degree		

Helping You Remember

5. Notice that the words *binomial, trinomial,* and *polynomial* contain the same root—*nomial,* but have different prefixes.

   a. Find the definition of the prefix *bi-* in a dictionary. Write the definition. Explain how it can help you remember the meaning of *binomial*. Two; a binomial contains two terms.

   b. Find the definition of the prefix *tri-* in a dictionary. Write the definition. Explain how it can help you remember the meaning of *trinomial*. Three; a trinomial contains three terms.

   c. Find the definition of the prefix *poly-* in a dictionary. Write the definition. Explain how it can help you remember the meaning of *polynomial*. Many; a polynomial contains many terms.

Resource Manager

Workbooks and Reproducible Masters

Chapter 13 Resource Masters

- Study Guide and Intervention, p. 733
- Skills Practice, p. 734
- Practice, p. 735
- Reading to Learn Mathematics, p. 736
- Enrichment, p. 737

Parent and Student Study Guide Workbook, p. 108

Transparencies

5-Minute Check Transparency 13-1

Answer Key Transparencies

Technology

Interactive Chalkboard

2 Teach

CLASSIFY POLYNOMIALS

Teaching Tip Emphasize that when there is a variable in the denominator of a fraction, it cannot be a monomial. A variable can be in the numerator, such as $\frac{x}{2}$, because it can be written as $\frac{1}{2}x$.

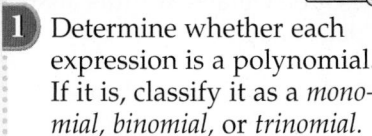

In-Class Example   **Power Point®**

1 Determine whether each expression is a polynomial. If it is, classify it as a *monomial, binomial,* or *trinomial.*

a. $\frac{-2}{x}$ not a polynomial

b. $x^2 - 12$ yes; binomial

DEGREES OF POLYNOMIALS

In-Class Examples   **Power Point®**

2 Find the degree of each monomial.

a. $-10w^4$ 4

b. $8x^3y^7z$ 11

3 Find the degree of each polynomial.

a. $a^2b^5 - 4$ 7

b. $2x^2y^2 + 7xy^6$ 7

4 **AREA** The formula for the surface area (A) of a cube is $A = 6s^2$, where s is the side length. Find the degree of the polynomial.   2

DEGREES OF POLYNOMIALS   The **degree** of a monomial is the sum of the exponents of its variables. The degree of a nonzero constant such as 6 or 10 is 0. The constant 0 has no degree.

Example 2 Degree of a Monomial

Find the degree of each monomial.

a. $5a$

The variable a has degree 1, so the degree of $5a$ is 1.

b. $-3x^2y$

x^2 has degree 2 and y has degree 1. The degree of $-3x^2y$ is $2 + 1$ or 3.

Study Tip

Degrees
The degree of a is 1 because $a = a^1$.

A polynomial also has a degree. The degree of a polynomial is the same as that of the term with the greatest degree.

Example 3 Degree of a Polynomial

Find the degree of each polynomial.

a. $x^2 + 3x - 2$

term	degree
x^2	2
$3x$	1
2	0

The greatest degree is 2. So the degree of $x^2 + 3x - 2$ is 2.

b. $a^2 + ab^2 + b^4$

term	degree
a^2	2
ab^2	1 + 2 or 3
b^4	4

The greatest degree is 4. So the degree of $a^2 + ab^2 + b^4$ is 4.

Career Choices

Ecologist
An ecologist studies the relationships between organisms and their environment.

Online Research
For more information about a career as an ecologist, visit: www.pre-alg.com/ careers

Example 4 Degree of a Real-World Polynomial

ECOLOGY In the early 1900s, the deer population of the Kaibab Plateau in Arizona was affected by hunters and by the food supply. The population from 1905 to 1930 can be approximated by the polynomial $-0.13x^5 + 3.13x^4 + 4000$, where x is the number of years since 1900. Find the degree of the polynomial.

$$\underbrace{-0.13x^5}_{\text{degree 5}} + \underbrace{3.13x^4}_{\text{degree 4}} + \underbrace{4000}_{\text{degree 0}}$$

So, $-0.13x^5 + 3.13x^4 + 4000$ has degree 5.

☑ **Concept Check**   Find the degree of the polynomial at the beginning of the lesson.   4

Check for Understanding

Concept Check   1. **Explain** how to find the degree of a monomial and the degree of a polynomial.
1–2. See margin.

2. **OPEN ENDED**   Write three binomial expressions. Explain why they are binomials.

Answers

1. The degree of a monomial is the sum of the exponents of its variables. The degree of a polynomial is the same as the degree of the term with the greatest degree.

2. Sample answer: $2x + 1$, $x - y$, $x^2 + x$; they are sums or differences of two monomials.

Interactive Chalkboard
PowerPoint® Presentations

This CD-ROM is a customizable Microsoft® Power-Point® presentation that includes:
• Step-by-step, dynamic solutions of each In-Class Example from the Teacher Wraparound Edition
• Additional, Your Turn exercises for each example
• The 5-Minute Check Transparencies
• Hot links to Glencoe Online Study Tools

3. Tanisha; the degree of a binomial is the degree of the term with the greater degree.

3. FIND THE ERROR Carlos and Tanisha are finding the degree of $5x + y^2$.

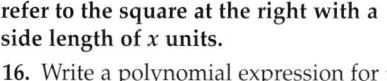

Carlos	Tanisha
$5x$ has degree 1.	$5x$ has degree 1.
y^2 has degree 2.	y^2 has degree 2.
$5x + y^2$ has degree 1 + 2 or 3.	$5x + y^2$ has degree 2.

Who is correct? Explain your reasoning.

Guided Practice

Determine whether each expression is a polynomial. If it is, classify it as a *monomial*, *binomial*, or *trinomial*.

4. -7 **yes; monomial**   **5.** $\frac{d}{2}$ **yes; monomial**   **6.** $\frac{1}{x} - x$ **no**

7. $a^5 + a^3$ **yes; binomial**   **8.** $y^2 - 4$ **yes; binomial**   **9.** $x^2 + xy^2 - y^2$ **yes; trinomial**

Find the degree of each polynomial.

10. $4b^2$ **2**   **11.** 121 **0**   **12.** $8x^3y^2$ **5**

13. $3x + 5$ **1**   **14.** $r^3 + 7r$ **3**   **15.** $d^2 + c^4$ **4**

Application

GEOMETRY For Exercises 16 and 17, refer to the square at the right with a side length of x units.

16. $x(x - y)$ or $x^2 - xy$

16. Write a polynomial expression for the area of the small blue rectangle.

17. What is the degree of the polynomial you wrote in Exercise 16? **2**

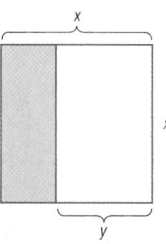

★ **indicates increased difficulty**

Practice and Apply

Determine whether each expression is a polynomial. If it is, classify it as a *monomial*, *binomial*, or *trinomial*. **20. yes; binomial   26. yes; trinomial**

18. 16 **yes; monomial**   **19.** $x^2 - 7x$ **yes; binomial**   **20.** $11a^2 + 4$

21. $-\frac{1}{3}w^2$ **yes; mono.**   **22.** $\sqrt{15c}$ **no**   **23.** $8 - \frac{2}{k}$ **no**

24. $r^4 + r^2s^2$ **yes; bi.**   **25.** $12 - n + n^4$ **yes; tri.**   **26.** $ab^2 + 3a - b^2$

27. $\sqrt{y} + y$ **no**   **28.** $\frac{ab}{c} - c$ **no**   **29.** $x^2 - \frac{1}{2}x + \frac{1}{3}$ **yes; trinomial**

Find the degree of each polynomial.

30. 3 **0**   **31.** 56 **0**   **32.** ab **2**

33. $12c^3$ **3**   **34.** xyz^2 **4**   **35.** $9s^4t$ **5**

36. $2 - 8n$ **1**   **37.** $g^5 + 5h$ **5**   **38.** $x^2 + 3x + 2$ **2**

39. $4y^3 + 6y^2 - 5y - 1$ **3** ★ **40.** $d^2 + c^4d^2$ **6**   ★ **41.** $x^3 - x^2y^3 + 8$ **5**

42. Sometimes; $x^3 + xy + 5$ has degree 3; $x + xy + 5$ has degree 2.

43. Always; any number is a monomial.

Tell whether each statement is *always*, *sometimes*, or *never* true. Explain.

42. A trinomial has a degree of 3.   **43.** An integer is a monomial.

44. MEDICINE Doctors can study a patient's heart by injecting dye in a vein near the heart. In a normal heart, the amount of dye in the bloodstream after t seconds is given by $-0.006t^4 + 0.140t^3 - 0.53t^2 + 1.79t$. Find the degree of the polynomial. **4**

DAILY
INTERVENTION   Differentiated Instruction

- **Interpersonal** Ask students to work in pairs. Have one of the pair write a binomial on a piece of paper. Then have the partner determine the degree of the binomial. Call on students to explain how they determined the degree of the binomial. Do the same for a monomial and a trinomial. Encourage students to discuss their answers and to clarify the procedure for those who are having difficulties.

---

3 Practice/Apply

Study Notebook

Have students—
- add the definitions/examples of the vocabulary terms to their Vocabulary Builder worksheets for Chapter 13.
- write an expression that is not a polynomial and explain why it is not.
- include any other item(s) that they find helpful in mastering the skills in this lesson.

DAILY
INTERVENTION **FIND THE ERROR**
If students are having difficulty determining which is correct, point out that the only time they add exponents to determine the degree is when the bases are being multiplied in the *same* term.

About the Exercises . . .
Organization by Objective
- **Classify Polynomials:** 18–29
- **Degrees of Polynomials:** 30–41

Odd/Even Assignments
Exercises 18–46 are structured so that students practice the same concepts whether they are assigned odd or even problems.

Alert! Exercise 47 involves research on the Internet or other reference materials.

Assignment Guide
Basic: 19–39 odd, 43, 45, 46, 48–62

Average: 19–43 odd, 45–62

Advanced: 18–44 even, 45–56 (Optional: 57–62)

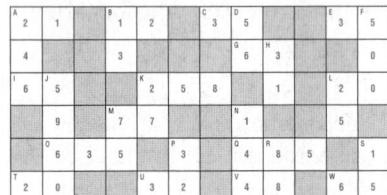
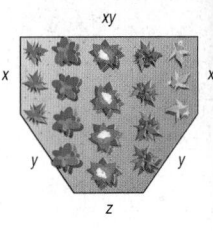

LANDSCAPING For Exercises 45 and 46, use the information below and the diagram at the right.
Lee wants to plant flowers along the perimeter of his vegetable garden.

45. Write a polynomial that represents the perimeter of the garden in feet. $2x + 2y + z + xy$

46. What is the degree of the polynomial? 2

★ 47. **RESEARCH** Suppose your grandparents deposited $100 in your savings account each year on your birthday. On your fifth birthday, there would have been approximately $100x^4 + 100x^3 + 100x^2 + 100x + 100$ dollars, where x is the annual interest rate plus 1. Research the current interest rate at your family's bank. Using that interest rate, how much money would you have on your next birthday? **See students' work.**

48. **CRITICAL THINKING** Find the degree of $a^x + 3 + x^x - 2b^3 + b^x + 2$. $x + 3$

49. **WRITING IN MATH** Answer the question that was posed at the beginning of the lesson. **See pp. 703A–703D.**

How are polynomials used to approximate real-world data?

Include the following in your answer:
- a description of how the value of heat index is found, and
- an explanation of why a linear equation cannot be used to approximate the heat index data.

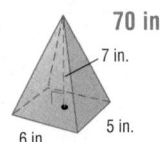
Standardized Test Practice
Ⓐ Ⓑ Ⓒ Ⓓ

50. Choose the expression that is *not* a binomial. **D**
   Ⓐ $x^2 - 1$
   Ⓑ $a + b$
   Ⓒ $m^3 + n^3$
   Ⓓ $7x + 2x$

51. State the degree of $4x^3 + xy - y^2$. **C**
   Ⓐ 1
   Ⓑ 2
   Ⓒ 3
   Ⓓ 4

Maintain Your Skills

Mixed Review

A number cube is rolled. Determine whether each event is *mutually exclusive* or *inclusive.* Then find the probability. *(Lesson 12-9)*

52. P(odd or greater than 3) **inclusive;** $\frac{5}{6}$
53. P(5 or even) **mut. exclusive;** $\frac{2}{3}$

54. A number cube is rolled. Find the odds that the number is greater than 2. *(Lesson 12-8)* **2:1**

Find the volume of each solid. If necessary, round to the nearest tenth. *(Lesson 11-3)*

55. **70 in³**
7 in.
5 in.
6 in.

56. **189.3 m³**
4 m
11.3 m

Getting Ready for the Next Lesson

PREREQUISITE SKILL Rewrite each expression using parentheses so that the terms having variables of the same power are grouped together.
(To review properties of addition, see Lesson 1-4.)

57–62. See pp. 703A–703D.

57. $(x + 4) + 2x$
58. $3x^2 - 1 + x^2$
59. $(6n + 2) + (3n + 5)$
60. $(a + 2b) + (3a + b)$
61. $(s + t) + (5s - 3t)$
62. $(x^2 + 4x) + (7x^2 - 3x)$

672 Chapter 13 Polynomials and Nonlinear Functions

Modeling Polynomials with Algebra Tiles

In a set of algebra tiles, $\boxed{1}$ represents the integer 1, x represents the variable x,

and represents x^2. Red tiles are used to represent -1, $-x$, and $-x^2$.

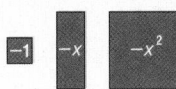

You can use these tiles to model monomials.

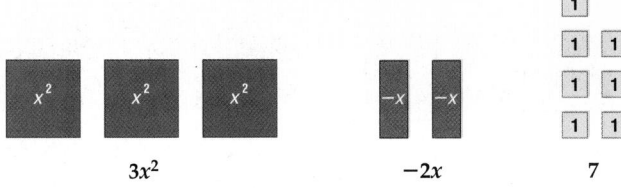

$$3x^2 \qquad\qquad -2x \qquad\qquad 7$$

You can also use algebra tiles to model polynomials. The polynomial $2x^2 - 3x + 4$ is modeled below.

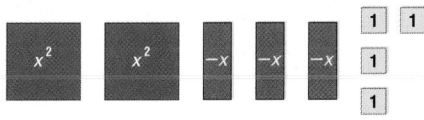

$$2x^2 - 3x + 4$$

Model and Analyze

Use algebra tiles to model each polynomial. 1–4. See pp. 703A–703D.

1. $-3x^2$ **2.** $5x + 3$ **3.** $4x^2 - x$ **4.** $2x^2 + 2x - 3$

5. Explain how you can tell whether an expression is a monomial, binomial, or trinomial by looking at the algebra tiles. **See pp. 703A–703D.**

6. Name the polynomial modeled below. $-x^2 + 3x - 5$

7. Explain how you would find the degree of a polynomial using algebra tiles.
The degree of a polynomial is determined by the size of the largest algebra tile.

Getting Started

Objective Model polynomials with algebra tiles.

Materials
algebra tiles

Teaching Tip Show students how to model 4 and -4 and $2x$ and $-2x$. Have students demonstrate other monomials.

Teach

- Ask students to model several binomials using x and x^2 tiles.
- Have students work Exercises 1–5 in small groups.

Assess

After working **Exercises 1–5**, students should understand how to use algebra tiles to model polynomials and to recognize the model of a monomial, binomial, and trinomial.

In **Exercises 6–7**, students should be able to name a polynomial and identify the degree of a polynomial using algebra tiles.

Study Notebook

Have students—
- draw algebra tiles to represent 5, -5, $3x$, $-3x$, $2x^2$, and $-2x^2$. Then have them draw algebra tiles to represent $-3x^2 + 5x - 1$.
- write how algebra tiles help them understand polynomials.

Resource Manager

📁 **Teaching Pre-Algebra with Manipulatives**
- pp. 7–8 (masters for algebra tiles)
- p. 160 (student recording sheet)

Glencoe Mathematics Classroom Manipulative Kit
- algebra tiles

13-2 **Adding Polynomials**

1 Focus

5-Minute Check Transparency 13-2 Use as a quiz or review of Lesson 13-1.

Mathematical Background notes are available for this lesson on page 666C.

How can you use algebra tiles to add polynomials?

The opening activity questions are repeated on page 741 of the *Chapter 13 Resource Masters*.

Reading to Learn Mathematics, p. 741   ELL

Pre-Activity   *How can you use algebra tiles to add polynomials?*

Do the activity at the top of page 674 in your textbook. Write your answers below.

a. Write the polynomial for the tiles that remain. $x^2 - 2x + 2$

b. Find the sum of $x^2 + 4x + 2$ and $7x^2 - 2x + 3$ by using algebra tiles. $8x^2 + 2x + 5$

c. Compare and contrast finding the sums of polynomials with finding the sum of integers. The concept of the zero pairs is the same, but there are tiles that represent different terms in polynomials.

Reading the Lesson

1. Draw a model that shows $(x^2 - 4x + 2) + (2x^2 + 2x - 3)$. Write the polynomial that shows the sum. $3x^2 - 2x - 1$

2. Show how to find the sum $(5x - 2) + (4x + 4)$ both vertically and horizontally.

Vertically	**Horizontally**
$5x - 2$	$(5x - 2) + (4x + 4)$
$(+)4x + 4$	$= (5x + 4x) + (-2 + 4)$
$9x + 2$	$= 9x + 2$

Helping You Remember

3. You have learned that you can combine like terms. On the left below, write three pairs of monomials that have like terms. On the right below, write three pairs of monomials that have unlike terms. Explain your answers. Sample answers are given.

Like Terms	**Unlike Terms**
1. $23a$ and $12a$	1. $2xy$ and $2x$
2. $4b^2c$ and b^2c	2. $3mn^2$ and $3m^2n$
3. xy^3 and $2xy^3$	3. $-8ab^3$ and $5ab^2$

---

b. $8x^2 + 2x + 5$

c. The concept of the zero pairs is the same, but there are tiles that represent different terms in polynomials.

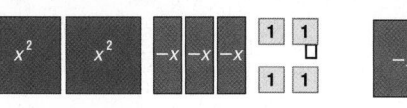

What You'll Learn

• Add polynomials.

How can you use algebra tiles to add polynomials?

Consider the polynomials $2x^2 - 3x + 4$ and $-x^2 + x - 2$ modeled below.

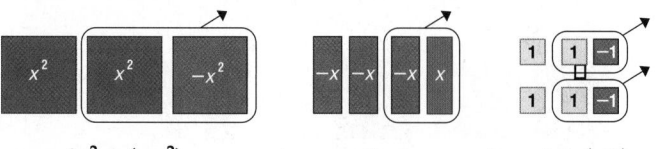

$2x^2 - 3x + 4$ $-x^2 + x - 2$

Follow these steps to add the polynomials.

Step 1   Combine the tiles that have the same shape.

Step 2   When a positive tile is paired with a negative tile that is the same shape, the result is called a *zero pair*. Remove any zero pairs.

$2x^2 + (-x^2)$ + $-3x + x$ + $4 + (-2)$

a. Write the polynomial for the tiles that remain. $x^2 - 2x + 2$

b. Find the sum of $x^2 + 4x + 2$ and $7x^2 - 2x + 3$ by using algebra tiles.

c. **Compare and contrast** finding the sums of polynomials with finding the sum of integers.

ADD POLYNOMIALS   Monomials that contain the same variables to the same power are *like terms*.   Terms that differ only by their coefficient are called like terms.

Like Terms	**Unlike Terms**
$2x$ and $7x$	$-6a$ and $7b$
$-x^2y$ and $5x^2y$	$4ab^2$ and $4a^2b$

You can add polynomials by combining like terms.

 Example 1 **Add Polynomials**

Find each sum.

a. $(3x + 5) + (2x + 1)$

Method 1   Add vertically.

$3x + 5$
$(+) \ 2x + 1$ Align like terms.
$5x + 6$ Add.

Method 2   Add horizontally.

$(3x + 5) + (2x + 1)$
$= (3x + 2x) + (5 + 1)$ Associative and Commutative Properties
$= 5x + 6$

The sum is $5x + 6$.

Resource Manager

 Workbooks and Reproducible Masters

Chapter 13 Resource Masters
• Study Guide and Intervention, p. 738
• Skills Practice, p. 739
• Practice, p. 740
• Reading to Learn Mathematics, p. 741
• Enrichment, p. 742
• Assessment, p. 777

Parent and Student Study Guide Workbook, p. 109

Transparencies
5-Minute Check Transparency 13-2
Answer Key Transparencies

Technology
Interactive Chalkboard

Study Tip

Negative Signs
When a monomial has a negative sign, the coefficient is a negative number.
$-4x \rightarrow$ coefficient is -4.
$-b \rightarrow$ coefficient is -1.
When a term in a polynomial is subtracted, "add its opposite" by making the coefficient negative.
$x - 2y \rightarrow x + (-2y)$

b. $(2x^2 + x - 7) + (x^2 + 3x + 5)$

Method 1

$$2x^2 + x - 7$$
$$\underline{(+) x^2 + 3x + 5} \qquad \text{Align like terms.}$$
$$3x^2 + 4x - 2 \qquad \text{Add.}$$

Method 2

$(2x^2 + x - 7) + (x^2 + 3x + 5)$ Write the expression.

$ = (2x^2 + x^2) + (x + 3x) + (-7 + 5)$ Group like terms.

$ = 3x^2 + 4x - 2$ Simplify.

The sum is $3x^2 + 4x - 2$.

c. $(9c^2 + 4c) + (-6c + 8)$

$(9c^2 + 4c) + (-6c + 8)$ Write the expression.

$ = 9c^2 + (4c - 6c) + 8$ Group like terms.

$ = 9c^2 - 2c + 8$ Simplify.

The sum is $9c^2 - 2c + 8$.

d. $(x^2 + xy + 2y^2) + (6x^2 - y^2)$

$$x^2 + xy + 2y^2$$
$$\underline{(+) 6x^2 - y^2}$$
$$7x^2 + xy + y^2$$

Leave a space because there is no other term like xy.

The sum is $7x^2 + xy + y^2$.

✓ **Concept Check**   Name the like terms in $b^2 + 5b - ab + 9b^2$. b^2 and $9b^2$

Polynomials are often used to represent measures of geometric figures.

Example 2   *Use Polynomials to Solve a Problem*

GEOMETRY   The lengths of the sides of golden rectangles are in the ratio 1:1.62. So, the length of a golden rectangle is approximately 1.62 times greater than the width.

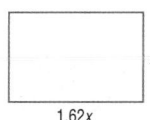

a. Find a formula for the perimeter of a golden rectangle.

$P = 2\ell + 2w$ Formula for the perimeter of a rectangle

$P = 2(1.62x) + 2x$ Replace ℓ with 1.62x and w with x.

$P = 3.24x + 2x$ or $5.24x$ Simplify.

A formula for the perimeter of a golden rectangle is $P = 5.24x$, where x is the measure of the width.

b. Find the length and the perimeter of a golden rectangle if its width is 8.3 centimeters.

length $= 1.62x$ Length of a golden rectangle

$ = 1.62(8.3)$ or 13.446   Replace x with 8.3 and simplify.

perimeter $= 5.24x$ Perimeter of a golden rectangle

$ = 5.24(8.3)$ or 43.492   Replace x with 8.3 and simplify.

The length of the golden rectangle is 13.446 centimeters, and the perimeter is 43.492 centimeters.

More About. . .

Geometry
The ancient Greeks often incorporated the golden ratio into their art and architecture.
Source: www.mcn.net

www.pre-alg.com/extra_examples   **Lesson 13-2**   Adding Polynomials   **675**

---

2 Teach

Teaching Tip Have students compare the *Like Terms* column to the *Unlike Terms* column. Ask them how like terms can differ from one another.   **sign, coefficient**
Ask what must be the same.
variable(s), exponent

ADD POLYNOMIALS

In-Class Examples   Power Point®

1   Find each sum.

a. $(9w - 4) + (w + 5)$ $10w + 1$

b. $(6x^2 - 3x + 1) + (x^2 + x - 1)$
$7x^2 - 2x$

c. $5a^3 + (2a - 4a) + 7$
$5a^3 - 2a + 7$

d. $(4x^2 - 3y^2) + (x^2 + 4xy + y^2)$
$5x^2 + 4xy - 2y^2$

Teaching Tip Some students may benefit from turning their ruled papers horizontally and using the lines to align like terms vertically so they can add.

2   **GEOMETRY**   The length of a rectangle is $3x^2 + 2x - 5$ units and the width is $8x - 1$ units.

a. Find the perimeter.
$6x^2 + 20x - 12$ units

b. Find the length of the rectangle if $x = -3$.   **16 units**

Study Notebook

Have students—
• choose a problem from the Practice to help them explain how to add two polynomials.
• include any other item(s) that they find helpful in mastering the skills in this lesson.

DAILY

INTERVENTION   **Differentiated Instruction**

• **Intrapersonal**   Have students find a question from the Practice exercises that they struggled with. In their math journals, have them determine or explain what made it difficult for them. Then ask them to write what they need to remember or do to overcome that difficulty.

If students are having difficulty determining whether the monomials are like terms, remind them that $2zyx = 2xyz$ by the Commutative Property of Multiplication. Review this rule, if necessary.

About the Exercises . . .

Odd/Even Assignments
Exercises 11–25 are structured so that students practice the same concepts whether they are assigned odd or even problems.

Assignment Guide

Basic: 11–21 odd, 26–28, 32–48

Average: 11–25 odd, 26–28, 32–48

Advanced: 12–24 even, 29–42 (Optional: 43–48)

4 Assess

Open-Ended Assessment

Modeling Use algebra tiles to find the sum of each of the following.

a. $(6) + (-2x^2)$ $-2x^2 + 6$

b. $(3x + 4) + (x^2 - 2x - 2)$
$x^2 + x + 2$

Getting Ready for Lesson 13-3

PREREQUISITE SKILL Lesson 13-3 presents subtracting polynomials. One method uses the additive inverse. Exercises 43–48 should be used to determine your students' familiarity with finding the additive inverse to subtract polynomials.

Assessment Options

Quiz (Lessons 13-1 and 13-2) is available on p. 777 of the *Chapter 13 Resource Masters*.

Check for Understanding

Concept Check
1. **Name** the like terms in $(x^2 + 5x + 2) + (2x^2 - 4x + 7)$.
x^2 and $2x^2$; $5x$ and $-4x$; 2 and 7

2. **OPEN ENDED** Write two binomials that share only one pair of like terms
Sample answer: $3x + 1$ and $4x + x^2$

3. **FIND THE ERROR** Hai says that $7xyz$ and $2zyx$ are like terms. Devin says they are not. Who is correct? Explain your reasoning.
Hai; the terms have the same variables in a different order.

Guided Practice Find each sum. 9. $4x^2 + 3x - 2$

GUIDED PRACTICE KEY	
Exercises	Examples
4–9	1
10	2

4.
$$\begin{array}{r} 4x + 5 \\ (+) -x - 3 \\ \hline 3x + 2 \end{array}$$

5.
$$\begin{array}{r} 3a^2 - 9a + 6 \\ (+) 4a^2 \qquad -2 \\ \hline 7a^2 - 9a + 4 \end{array}$$

6. $(x + 3) + (2x + 5)$ $3x + 8$

7. $(13x - 7y) + 3y$ $13x - 4y$

8. $(2x^2 + 5x) + (9 - 7x)$ $2x^2 - 2x + 9$

9. $(3x^2 - 2x + 1) + (x^2 + 5x - 3)$

Application
10. **GEOMETRY** Find the perimeter of the figure at the right.
$6x + 24$ units

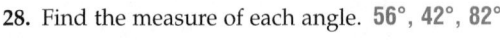

★ indicates increased difficulty

Practice and Apply

Homework Help	
For Exercises	See Examples
11–22	1
23–27	2

Extra Practice
See page 756.

20. $3a^2 + 2b^2 + 3a$

Find each sum.

11.
$$\begin{array}{r} -5x + 4 \\ (+) 8x - 1 \end{array}$$ $3x + 3$

12.
$$\begin{array}{r} 7b - 5 \\ (+) -9b + 8 \end{array}$$ $-2b + 3$

13.
$$\begin{array}{r} 10x^2 + 5xy + 7y^2 \\ (+) \quad x^2 \qquad -3y^2 \\ \hline 11x^2 + 5xy + 4y^2 \end{array}$$

14.
$$\begin{array}{r} 4a^3 + a^2 + 8a - 8 \\ (+) \quad 2a^2 \qquad + 6 \\ \hline 4a^3 + 3a^2 + 8a - 2 \end{array}$$

15. $(3x + 9) + (x + 5)$ $4x + 14$

16. $(4x + 3) + (x - 1)$ $5x + 2$

17. $(6y - 5r) + (2y + 7r)$ $8y + 2r$

18. $(8m - 2n) + (3m + n)$ $11m - n$

19. $(x^2 + y) + (4x^2 + xy)$ $5x^2 + xy + y$

20. $(3a^2 + b^2) + (3a + b^2)$

21. $(5x^2 + 6x + 4) + (2x^2 + 3x + 1)$
$7x^2 + 9x + 5$

22. $(-2x^2 + x - 5) + (x^2 - 3x + 2)$
$-x^2 - 2x - 3$

Find each sum. Then evaluate if $a = -3$, $b = 4$, and $c = 2$.

★ 23. $(3a + 5b) + (2a - 9b)$ $5a - 4b$; -31

★ 24. $(a^2 + 7b^2) + (5 - 3b^2) + (2a^2 - 7)$ $3a^2 + 4b^2 - 2$; 89

★ 25. $(3a + 5b - 4c) + (2a - 3b + 7c) + (-a + 4b - 2c)$ $4a + 6b + c$; 14

GEOMETRY For Exercises 26–28, refer to the triangle.

26. Find the sum of the measures of the angles. $(4x - 44)°$

27. The sum of the measures of the angles in any triangle is 180°. Find the value of x. 56

28. Find the measure of each angle. 56°, 42°, 82°

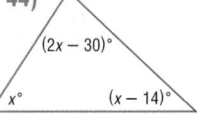

Answer (p. 677)

32.

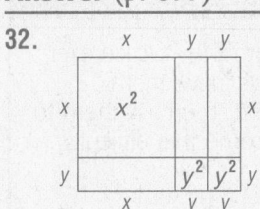

The length is $x + 2y$ and the width is $x + y$.
So, the perimeter is
$2(x + 2y) + 2(x + y)$
or $4x + 6y$.

FINANCE For Exercises 29–31, refer to the information below.

Jason and Will both work at the same supermarket and are paid the same hourly rate. At the end of the week, Jason's paycheck showed that he worked 23 hours and had $12 deducted for taxes. Will worked 19 hours during the same week and had $10 deducted for taxes. Let x represent the hourly pay.

29. $23x - 12$

30. $19x - 10$

★ 29. Write a polynomial expression to represent Jason's pay for the week.

★ 30. Write a polynomial expression to represent Will's pay for the week.

★ 31. Write a polynomial expression to represent the total weekly pay for Jason and Will. $42x - 22$

32. **CRITICAL THINKING** In the figure at the right, x^2 is the area of the larger square, and y^2 is the area of each of the two smaller squares. What is the perimeter of the whole rectangle? Explain.
$4x + 6y$; See margin for explanation.

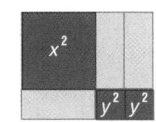

33. **WRITING IN MATH** Answer the question that was posed at the beginning of the lesson. **See margin.**

How can you use algebra tiles to add polynomials?

Include the following in your answer:
- a description of algebra tiles that represent like terms, and
- an explanation of how zero pairs are used in adding polynomials.

Standardized Test Practice
(A) (B) (C) (D)

34. Choose the pair of terms that are *not* like terms. **C**
(A) $6cd, 12cd$ (B) $\frac{x}{2}, 5x$ (C) a^2, b^2 (D) x^2y, yx^2

35. What is the sum of $11x + 2y$ and $x - 5y$? **B**
(A) $10x - 3y$ (B) $12x - 3y$ (C) $12x + 3y$ (D) $12x - 5y$

Maintain Your Skills

Mixed Review **Find the degree of each polynomial.** *(Lesson 13-1)*

36. a^3b **4**
37. $3x - 5y + z^2$ **2**
38. $c^2 - 7c^3y^4$ **7**

A card is drawn from a standard deck of 52 playing cards. Find each probability. *(Lesson 12-9)*

39. $P(2 \text{ or jack})$ $\frac{2}{13}$
40. $P(10 \text{ or red})$ $\frac{7}{13}$
41. $P(\text{ace or black } 7)$ $\frac{3}{26}$

42. Determine whether the prisms are similar. Explain. *(Lesson 11-6)*
Yes; the corresponding dimensions are proportional.

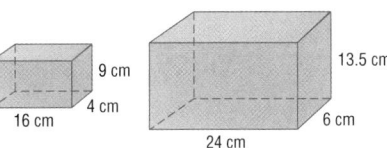

Getting Ready for the Next Lesson **PREREQUISITE SKILL** Rewrite each expression as an addition expression by using the additive inverse. *(To review **additive inverse**, see Lesson 2-3.)*

43. $15c - 26$ $15c + (-26)$
44. $x^2 - 7$ $x^2 + (-7)$
45. $1 - 2x$ $1 + (-2x)$
46. $6b - 3a^2$ $6b + (-3a^2)$
47. $(n + rt) - r^2$ $(n + rt) + (-r^2)$
48. $(s + t) - 2s$ $(s + t) + (-2s)$

www.pre-alg.com/self_check_quiz   **Lesson 13-2** Adding Polynomials   **677**

Answer

33. Use algebra tiles to model each polynomial and combine the tiles that have the same size and shape. Answers should include the following.

- Algebra tiles that represent like terms have the same size and shape.

- When adding polynomials, a red tile and a white tile that have the same size and shape are zero pairs and may be removed. The result is the sum of the polynomials.

Lesson 13-2 Adding Polynomials   **677**

Study Guide and Intervention, p. 738

Add polynomials by combining like terms, which are monomials that contain the same variables to the same power.

Example Find $(8x^2 - 7x + 1) + (x^2 + 5)$.

Method 1 Add vertically.
$$
\begin{aligned}
& 8x^2 - 7x + 1 \\
(+) & x^2 + 5 \\
\hline
& 9x^2 - 7x + 6
\end{aligned}
$$

Method 2 Add horizontally.
$(8x^2 - 7x + 1) + (x^2 + 5)$
$= (8x^2 + x^2) - 7x + (1 + 5)$
$= 9x^2 - 7x + 6$

Exercises
Find each sum.

1. $3x - 7$; $(+) \; x + 1$; $4x - 6$
2. $6d + 8$; $(+) \; -4d + 1$; $2d + 9$
3. $4w^2 - 6w + 3$; $(+) \; w^2 - 5$; $5w^2 - 6w - 2$
4. $5a^2 - a$; $(+) 2a - 5$; $5a^2 + a - 5$
5. $(-m + 3) + (7m - 1)$; $6m + 2$
6. $(9x^2 + 3x - 1) + (4x + 1)$; $9x^2 + 7x$
7. $(2k^2 - k) + (k - 1)$; $2k^2 - 1$
8. $(5a^2 + 6ab) + (-ab + b^2)$; $5a^2 + 5ab + b^2$
9. $(4c^2 - 7) + (c^2 - 3c + 6)$; $5c^2 - 3c - 1$
10. $(x^2 + y) + (xy + y)$; $x^2 + xy + 2y$
11. $(12h - 6) + (h^2 - 8h + 6)$; $h^2 + 4h$
12. $(10x^2 + x + 5) + (x - 10x^2)$; $2x + 5$
13. $(6y^2 - y + 1) + (y^2 - 3y - 6)$; $7y^2 - 4y - 5$
14. $(p^3 + 4) + (2p^2 - 2p + 3)$; $p^3 + 2p^2 - 2p + 7$
15. $(3g^2 + 3g + 5) + (5g^2 - 3)$; $8g^2 + 3g + 2$
16. $(5r^2 - 6) + (-r^2 - 4r + 7)$; $4r^2 - 4r + 1$

Skills Practice, p. 739 and Practice, p. 740 (shown)

Find each sum.

1. $8q + 3$; $(+) \; 4q - 2$; $12q + 1$
2. $9f - 3$; $(+) \; -f - 15$; $8f - 18$
3. $4r^2 + 11r$; $(+) \; 5r^2 - 3r - 7$; $9r^2 + 8r - 7$
4. $n^2 - 3n$; $(+) 3n - 10$; $n^2 - 10$
5. $6w^2 + 2w + 7$; $(+) \; 8w^2 + 3w - 9$; $14w^2 + 5w - 2$
6. $8c^2 - 3c + 15$; $(+) \; 3c^2 + 3c - 11$; $11c^2 + 4$
7. $-5p^2 - 2p + 4$; $(+) \; 5p^2 + 2p - 4$; 0
8. $7v^2 - 2v$; $(+) \; 7v^2 - v + 5$; $14v^2 - 3v + 5$
9. $5m^2 + 6m - 3$; $(-) \; 8m^2 + 9m - 2$; $13m^2 + 15m - 5$
10. $7d^2 + 8d - 3$; $(+) \; d^2 + d + 3$; $8d^2 + 9d$
11. $(r^2 + 9) + (-4r^2 + 6r + 10)$; $-3r^2 + 6r + 19$
12. $(g^2 + 3g - 6) + (6g^2 - 6g + 1)$; $7g^2 - 3g - 5$
13. $(-2m + 10) + (5m - 3)$; $3m + 7$
14. $(4x^2 - 7x) + (8x + 5)$; $4x^2 + x + 5$
15. $(3k^2 + 9k) + (k^2 - 2k - 4)$; $4k^2 + 7k - 4$
16. $(2a^2 - 3ab) + (4ab - 8b^2)$; $2a^2 + ab - 8b^2$
17. $(c + 4) + (c^2 - c + 6)$; $c^2 + 10$
18. $(5x^2 - 3xy) + (2xy + 9y^2)$; $5x^2 - xy + 9y^2$
19. $(2y^3 + y^2 + 5) + (2y^2 + 3y)$; $2y^3 + 3y^2 + 3y + 5$
20. $(-5p^2 + 6p - 7) + (p^2 - 2)$; $-4p^2 + 6p - 9$
21. $(3ab^2 - 2a - 1) + (a^2 + ab + 3)$; $3ab^2 + a^2 - 2a + ab + 2$
22. $(6rs^3 + 4r) + (5rs^3 + 7)$; $11rs^3 + 4r + 7$

23. **GEOMETRY** The lengths of the sides of a triangle are $(x^2 - 5)$, $(7x - 1)$, and x. Find the perimeter of the triangle. $x^2 + 8x - 6$

Enrichment, p. 742

Adding Polynomials

Can you make a sentence using these words?
A FRUIT TIME LIKE AN BUT FLIES BANANA ARROW LIKE FLIES

Add the polynomials. Then find the word in the table at the right that corresponds to the sum. Read the words in order down the column to discover the hidden saying.

		Word
1. $(2x^2 + 3x^2) + (5x^2 + x^2)$ $11x^2$		TIME
2. $(2x^2 + 3x^3) + (5x^2 + x^2)$ $3x^3 + 8x^2$		FLIES
3. $(2x^2 + x) + (xy + x)$ $2x^2 + 2x + xy$		LIKE
4. $(x^3 + 2x^2) + (5x^2 + x)$ $6x^3 + 2x^2 + x$		AN
5. $(x + xy) + (x^2 + xy)$ $x^2 + 2xy + x$		ARROW
6. $(5x^2 + x) + (x + 2x^4)$ $2x^4 + 5x^2 + 2x$		BUT
7. $(xy + y^2 + x^2) + (2xy + y^2)$ $2x^2 + 3xy + y^2$		FRUIT
8. $(3x^2 + 2x^3) + (x^3 + x)$ $3x^3 + 3x^2 + x$		FLIES
9. $(x + x^2) + x^3$ $x^3 + x^2 + x$		LIKE
10. $(x^3 + x^3) + (x^3 + x^3)$ $4x^3$		A
11. $2x^{12} + 2x^{12}$ $4x^{12}$		BANANA

$4x^3$	A
$2x^2 + 3xy + y^2$	FRUIT
$11x^2$	TIME
$x^3 + x^2 + x$	LIKE
$6x^3 + 2x^2 + x$	AN
$2x^4 + 5x^2 + 2x$	BUT
$3x^3 + 8x^2$	FLIES
$4x^{12}$	BANANA
$x^2 + 2xy + x$	ARROW
$2x^2 + 2x + xy$	LIKE
$3x^3 + 3x^2 + x$	FLIES

13-3 Lesson Notes

1 Focus

**5-Minute Check
Transparency 13-3** Use as
a quiz or review of Lesson 13-2.

Mathematical Background
notes are available for this lesson
on page 666D.

How is subtracting polynomials similar to subtracting
measurements?

The opening activity questions
are repeated on page 746 of the
Chapter 13 Resource Masters.

**Reading to Learn
Mathematics, p. 746** ELL

Pre-Activity *How is subtracting polynomials similar to subtracting measurements?*

Do the activity at the top of page 678 in your textbook. Write your answers below.

a. What is the difference in degrees and the difference in minutes between the two stations? 4 degrees, 8.1 minutes

b. Explain how you can find the difference in latitude between any two locations, given the degrees and minutes. Subtract the degrees and subtract the minutes.

c. The longitude of Station 1 is 162°16'36" and the longitude of Station 5 is 68°8'2". Find the difference in longitude between the two stations. 94°8'34"

Reading the Lesson

1. Show how to find the difference $(3x^2 + x + 2) - (2x^2 - 7)$ by aligning like terms and by adding the additive inverse.

Like Terms	Additive Inverse
$3x^2 + x + 2$	$3x^2 + x + 2$
$(-) 2x^2 \quad -7$	$(+)-2x^2 \quad +7$
$x^2 + x + 9$	$x^2 + x + 9$

2. Which method do you prefer? Why? Answers will vary.

Helping You Remember

3. a. You have learned to subtract polynomials by adding the additive inverse. Look up *inverse* in the dictionary. What is its definition? How does this help you remember how to find the additive inverse? Opposite; you change each sign to the opposite and then add instead of subtract.

b. Write the additive inverses of the polynomials in the table below.

Polynomial	Additive Inverse
$x^2 + 2x - 3$	$-x^2 - 2x + 3$
$6x - 8$	$-6x + 8$
$5x^2 + 8y^2 - 2xy$	$-5x^2 - 8y^2 + 2xy$

**b. Subtract the
degrees and subtract
the minutes.
c. 94° 8' 34"**

Reading Math

Symbols
The symbol " in 68° 8' 2" is read
as *seconds*.

13-3 Subtracting Polynomials

What You'll Learn

* Subtract polynomials.

How is subtracting polynomials similar
to subtracting measurements?

At the North Pole, buoy stations drift with the ice in the Arctic Ocean. The
table shows the latitudes of two North Pole buoys in April, 2000.

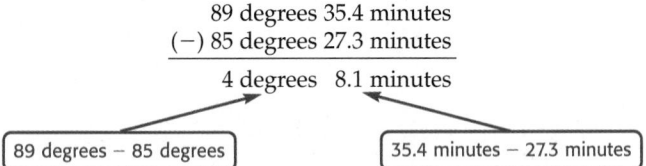

Station	Latitude
1	89° 35.4'N = 89 degrees 35.4 minutes
5	85° 27.3'N = 85 degrees 27.3 minutes

a. What is the difference in degrees and the difference in minutes between
the two stations? **4 degrees, 8.1 minutes**

b. Explain how you can find the difference in latitude between any two
locations, given the degrees and minutes.

c. The longitude of Station 1 is 162° 16' 36" and the longitude of Station 5
is 68° 8' 2". Find the difference in longitude between the two stations.

SUBTRACT POLYNOMIALS When you subtract measurements, you
subtract like units. Consider the subtraction of latitude measurements shown
below.

$$89 \text{ degrees } 35.4 \text{ minutes}$$
$$(-) \ 85 \text{ degrees } 27.3 \text{ minutes}$$
$$4 \text{ degrees } \quad 8.1 \text{ minutes}$$

| 89 degrees − 85 degrees | | 35.4 minutes − 27.3 minutes |

Similarly, when you subtract polynomials, you subtract like terms.

$$5x^2 + 14x - 9$$
$$(-) \ x^2 + 8x + 2$$
$$4x^2 + 6x - 11$$

$5x^2 - 1x^2 = 4x^2$ $-9 - 2 = -11$ $14x - 8x = 6x$

Example 1 Subtract Polynomials

Find each difference.

a. $(5x + 9) - (3x + 6)$

$$5x + 9$$
$$(-) \ 3x + 6 \quad \text{Align like terms.}$$
$$2x + 3 \quad \text{Subtract.}$$

The difference is $2x + 3$.

b. $(4a^2 + 7a + 4) - (3a^2 + 2)$

$$4a^2 + 7a + 4$$
$$(-) \ 3a^2 \quad\quad + 2 \quad \text{Align like terms.}$$
$$a^2 + 7a + 2 \quad \text{Subtract.}$$

The difference is $a^2 + 7a + 2$.

678 Chapter 13 Polynomials and Nonlinear Functions

Resource Manager

 Workbooks and Reproducible Masters

Chapter 13 Resource Masters
• Study Guide and Intervention, p. 743
• Skills Practice, p. 744
• Practice, p. 745
• Reading to Learn Mathematics, p. 746
• Enrichment, p. 747
• Assessment, pp. 777, 779

*Parent and Student Study Guide
Workbook,* p. 110
School-to-Career Masters, p. 25

 **Transparencies**
5-Minute Check Transparency 13-3
Answer Key Transparencies

Technology
Interactive Chalkboard
Multimedia Applications

Recall that you can subtract a rational number by adding its *additive inverse*.

$$10 - 8 = 10 + (-8)$$ The additive inverse of 8 is -8.

You can also subtract a polynomial by adding its additive inverse. To find the additive inverse of a polynomial, multiply the entire polynomial by -1.

Polynomial	Multiply by -1	Additive Inverse
t	$-1(t)$	$-t$
$x + 3$	$-1(x + 3)$	$-x - 3$
$-a^2 + b^2 - c$	$-1(-a^2 + b^2 - c)$	$a^2 - b^2 + c$

Example 2 *Subtract Using the Additive Inverse*

Find each difference.

a. $(3x + 8) - (5x + 1)$

The additive inverse of $5x + 1$ is $(-1)(5x + 1)$ or $-5x - 1$.

$(3x + 8) - (5x + 1)$
$= (3x + 8) + (-5x - 1)$ To subtract $(5x + 1)$, add $(-5x - 1)$.
$= (3x - 5x) + (8 - 1)$ Group the like terms.
$= -2x + 7$ Simplify.

The difference is $-2x + 7$.

b. $(4x^2 + y^2) - (-3xy + y^2)$

The additive inverse of $-3xy + y^2$ is $(-1)(-3xy + y^2)$ or $3xy - y^2$. Align the like terms and add the additive inverse.

$$
\begin{array}{r}
4x^2 \qquad + y^2 \\
(-)\quad -3xy + y^2 \\
\hline
\end{array}
\;\rightarrow\;
\begin{array}{r}
4x^2 \qquad + y^2 \\
(+)\quad 3xy - y^2 \\
\hline
4x^2 + 3xy + 0
\end{array}
$$

The difference is $4x^2 + 3xy$.

Study Tip

Zeros

It can be helpful to add zeros as placeholders when a term in one polynomial does not have a corresponding like term in another polynomial.

$4x^2 + 0xy + y^2$
$+) \ 0x^2 + 3xy - y^2$

✓ **Concept Check**   What is the additive inverse of $a^2 + 9a - 1$? $-a^2 - 9a + 1$

Example 3 *Subtract Polynomials to Solve a Problem*

SHIPPING   The cost for shipping a package that weighs x pounds from Dallas to Chicago is shown in the table at the right. How much more does the Atlas Service charge for shipping the package?

Shipping Company	Cost ($)
Atlas Service	$4x + 280$
Bell Service	$3x + 125$

difference in cost = cost of Atlas Service − cost of Bell Service
$= (4x + 280) - (3x + 125)$ Substitution
$= (4x + 280) + (-3x - 125)$ Add additive inverse.
$= (4x - 3x) + (280 - 125)$ Group like terms.
$= x + 155$ Simplify.

The Atlas Service charges $x + 155$ dollars more for shipping a package that weighs x pounds.

 www.pre-alg.com/extra_examples

---

2 Teach

Building on Prior Knowledge

In Lesson 2-3, students learned how to subtract an integer by adding its additive inverse. In this lesson, they will extend this knowledge to adding the additive inverse when subtracting polynomials.

SUBTRACT POLYNOMIALS

In-Class Examples Power Point®

1 Find each difference.

a. $(7a + 4) - (9a + 2)$ $-2a + 2$

b. $(8b^2 + 6) - (3b^2 + 6b + 1)$
$5b^2 - 6b + 5$

2 Find each difference.

a. $(4x - 8) - (3x + 9)$ $x - 17$

b. $(7ab + 2b^2) - (3a^2 + ab + b^2)$
$-3a^2 + 6ab + b^2$

3 **GEOMETRY**   The length of a rectangle is $x^2 - 9x + 10$ units. The width is $x^2 - x$ units. How much longer is the length than the width?
$-8x + 10$ units

✓ **Skills Check**

Subtract Polynomials   Have students subtract $(2x^3 - 4x + 2)$ from $(8x^4 - 6x^3 + 2x^2 - x)$.
$8x^4 - 8x^3 + 2x^2 + 3x - 2$

DAILY INTERVENTION

Differentiated Instruction

- **Kinesthetic**   To model $(2x^2 - 3x - 6) - (x^2 + 5x - 5)$, have students use algebra tiles to show $2x^2 - 3x - 6$. Remind them that subtracting is the same as adding the opposite. So, they should then add tiles to represent $-x^2 - 5x + 5$. Have them remove zero pairs, which results in $x^2 - 8x - 1$.

Study Notebook

Have students—
- write a paragraph comparing adding polynomials to subtracting them. Have them describe their similarities and differences.
- include any other item(s) that they find helpful in mastering the skills in this lesson.

About the Exercises . . .

Odd/Even Assignments
Exercises 10–25 are structured so that students practice the same concepts whether they are assigned odd or even problems.

Assignment Guide

Basic: 11–25 odd, 28–45
Average: 11–27 odd, 28–45
Advanced: 10–28 even, 29–39
(Optional: 40–45)
All: Practice Quiz 1 (1–10)

Open-Ended Assessment

Speaking Display a polynomial subtraction problem. Have students tell you everything you need to do to subtract. Be sure they mention aligning like terms and finding the additive inverse.

Getting Ready for Lesson 13-4

PREREQUISITE SKILL Lesson 13-4 presents using the Distributive Property to multiply a polynomial by a monomial. Exercises 40–45 should be used to determine your students' familiarity with multiplying monomials.

Check for Understanding

Concept Check

1. **Describe** how subtraction and addition of polynomials are related. See margin.
2. **OPEN ENDED** Write two polynomials whose difference is $x^2 + 2x - 4$. Sample answer: $2x^2 + 4x + 1$ and $x^2 + 2x + 5$

Guided Practice

Find each difference.

GUIDED PRACTICE KEY	
Exercises	Examples
3, 4	1
5–8	2
9	3

3. $\begin{array}{r} r^2 + 5r \\ (-)\ r^2 +\ \ r \\ \hline 4r \end{array}$

4. $\begin{array}{r} 3x^2 + 5x + 4 \\ (-)\ x^2 \qquad\ -1 \\ \hline 2x^2 + 5x + 5 \end{array}$

5. $(9x + 5) - (4x + 3)$ $5x + 2$

6. $(2x + 4) - (-x + 5)$ $3x - 1$

7. $(3x^2 + x) - (8 - 2x)$ $3x^2 + 3x - 8$

8. $(6a^2 - 3a + 9) - (7a^2 + 5a - 1)$ $-a^2 - 8a + 10$

Application

9. **GEOMETRY** The perimeter of the isosceles trapezoid shown is $16x + 1$ units. Find the length of the missing base of the trapezoid. $7x + 5$ units

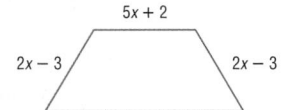

★ indicates increased difficulty

Practice and Apply

Find each difference.

Homework Help

For Exercises	See Examples
10–15	1
16–25	2
26, 27	3

Extra Practice
See page 756.

10. $\begin{array}{r} 8k + 9 \\ (-)\ k + 2 \\ \hline 7k + 7 \end{array}$

11. $\begin{array}{r} -n^2 + 1n \\ (-)\ \ n^2 - 5n \\ \hline -2n^2 + 6n \end{array}$

12. $\begin{array}{r} 5a^2 + 9a - 12 \\ (-) -3a^2 + 5a -\ \ 7 \\ \hline 8a^2 + 4a - 5 \end{array}$

13. $\begin{array}{r} 6y^2 - 5y + 3 \\ (-)\ 5y^2 + 2y - 7 \\ \hline y^2 - 7y + 10 \end{array}$

14. $\begin{array}{r} 5x^2 - 4xy \\ (-)\ \qquad - 3xy + 2y^2 \\ \hline 5x^2 - xy - 2y^2 \end{array}$

15. $\begin{array}{r} 9w^2 \qquad + 7 \\ (-) -6w^2 + 2w - 3 \\ \hline 15w^2 - 2w + 10 \end{array}$

16. $(3x + 4) - (x + 2)$ $2x + 2$

17. $(7x + 5) - (3x + 2)$ $4x + 3$

18. $(2y + 5) - (y + 8)$ $y - 3$

19. $(3t - 2) - (5t - 4)$ $-2t + 2$

21. $3a^2 + 2b^2$

20. $(2x + 3y) - (x - y)$ $x + 4y$

21. $(a^2 + 6b^2) - (-2a^2 + 4b^2)$

22. $(x^2 + 6x) - (3x^2 + 7)$ $-2x^2 + 6x - 7$

23. $(9n^2 - 8) - (n + 4)$ $9n^2 - n - 12$

24. $(6x^2 + 3x + 9) - (2x^2 + 8x + 1)$ $4x^2 - 5x + 8$

25. $(3x^2 - 5xy + 7y^2) - (x^2 - 3xy + 4y^2)$ $2x^2 - 2xy + 3y^2$

26. **GEOMETRY** Alyssa plans to trim a picture to fit into a frame. The area of the picture is $2x^2 + 11x + 12$ square units, but the area inside the frame is only $2x^2 + 5x + 2$ square units. How much of the picture will Alyssa have to trim so that it will fit into the frame? $6x + 10$ square units

★ 27. **TEMPERATURE** The highest recorded temperature in North Carolina occurred in 1983. The lowest recorded temperature in North Carolina occurred two years later. The difference between these two record temperatures is 68°F more than the sum of the temperatures. Write an equation to represent this situation. Then find the record low temperature in North Carolina. $x - y = 68 + (x + y)$; $-34°F$

28. **CRITICAL THINKING** Suppose A and B represent polynomials. If $A + B = 3x^2 + 2x - 2$ and $A - B = -x^2 + 4x - 8$, find A and B. $A = x^2 + 3x - 5$; $B = 2x^2 - x + 3$

680   Chapter 13   Polynomials and Nonlinear Functions

Answers

1. Subtracting one polynomial from another is the same as adding the additive inverse.

39.
Stem	Leaf
5	4 9
6	4 6 8
7	0 1 1 2
8	5 9
9	1

$5|4 = 54$

29. WRITING IN MATH Answer the question that was posed at the beginning of the lesson. **See pp. 703A–703D.**

How is subtracting polynomials similar to subtracting measurements?

Include the following in your answer:
- a comparison between subtracting measurements with two parts and subtracting polynomials with two terms, and
- an example of a subtraction problem involving measurements that have two parts, and an explanation of how to find the difference.

30. What is $(5x - 7) - (3x - 4)$? **A**

Ⓐ $2x - 3$ Ⓑ $2x + 3$ Ⓒ $2x - 11$ Ⓓ $2x + 11$

31. Write the additive inverse of $-4h^2 - hk - k^2$. **B**

Ⓐ $4h^2 - hk - k^2$ Ⓑ $4h^2 + hk + k^2$

Ⓒ $-4h^2 + hk + k^2$ Ⓓ $-4h^2 + hk - k^2$

Maintain Your Skills

Mixed Review **Find each sum.** *(Lesson 13-2)*

32. $(2x - 3) + (x - 1)$ **$3x - 4$**

33. $(11x + 2y) + (x - 5y)$ **$12x - 3y$**

34. $(5x^2 - 7x + 9) + (3x^2 + 4x - 6)$
$8x^2 - 3x + 3$

35. $(4t - t^2) + (8t + 2)$
$-t^2 + 12t + 2$

Determine whether each expression is a polynomial. If it is, classify it as a monomial, binomial, or trinomial. *(Lesson 13-1)* **38. yes; trinomial**

36. $\dfrac{1}{5a^2}$ **no**

37. $x^2 + 9$ **yes; binomial**

38. $c^2 - d^3 + cd$

39. Make a stem-and-leaf plot for the set of data shown below. *(Lesson 12-1)*
72, 64, 68, 66, 70, 89, 91, 54, 59, 71, 71, 85 **See margin.**

Getting Ready for the Next Lesson **PREREQUISITE SKILL Simplify each expression.**
*(To review **multiplying monomials**, see Lesson 4-2.)*

40. $x(3x)$ **$3x^2$**

41. $(2y)(4y)$ **$8y^2$**

42. $(t^2)(6t)$ **$6t^3$**

43. $(4m)(m^2)$ **$4m^3$**

44. $(w^2)(-3w)$ **$-3w^3$**

45. $(2r^2)(5r^3)$ **$10r^5$**

Practice Quiz 1 — *Lessons 13-1 through 13-3*

Find the degree of each polynomial. *(Lesson 13-1)*

1. cd^3 **4**

2. $a - 4a^2$ **2**

3. $x^2y + 7x^2 - 21$ **3**

Find each sum or difference. *(Lessons 13-2 and 13-3)*

4. $(2x - 8) + (x - 7)$ **$3x - 15$**

5. $(4x + 5) - (2x + 3)$ **$2x + 2$**

6. $(5d^2 - 3) - (2d^2 - 7)$ **$3d^2 + 4$**

7. $(3r + 6s) + (5r - 9s)$ **$8r - 3s$**

8. $(x^2 + 4x + 2) + (7x^2 - 2x + 3)$ **$8x^2 + 2x + 5$**

9. $(9x - 4y) - (12x - 9y)$ **$-3x + 5y$**

10. GEOMETRY The perimeter of the triangle is $8x + 3y$ centimeters. Find the length of the third side. *(Lessons 13-2 and 13-3)*
$3x + 2y$ cm

$4x - y$ cm $x + 2y$ cm

 www.pre-alg.com/self_check_quiz

---

Assessment Options

Practice Quiz 1 The quiz provides students with a brief review of the concepts and skills in Lessons 13-1 through 13-3. Lesson numbers are given to the right of exercises or instruction lines so students can review concepts not yet mastered.

Quiz (Lesson 13-3) is available on p. 777 of the *Chapter 13 Resource Masters*.

Mid-Chapter Test (Lessons 13-1 through 13-3) is available on p. 779 of the *Chapter 13 Resource Masters*.

Getting Started

Objective Model multiplication with algebra tiles.

Materials
algebra tiles
product mat

Teach

- Have students work in small groups, taking turns modeling and recording the results.
- Make sure students follow the format of placing the x^2 tiles in the upper left corner and the unit tiles in the lower right corner of the rectangle. Also, the short end of the x-tile faces the upper or left perimeter.
- Make sure students understand that the factors are read from uppermost and leftmost perimeter, and that the area is read from the interior of the rectangle.

Assess

In **Exercises 1–9**, students should
- use algebra tiles to multiply a monomial and a binomial.
- write an expression to represent a length and width and use it to solve a problem.

In **Exercise 10**, students write a multiplication problem represented by a model.

Study Notebook

Have students write a paragraph and show diagrams of algebra tiles explaining how to find $2x(x + 1)$.

Modeling Multiplication

Recall that algebra tiles are named based on their area. The area of each tile is the product of the width and length.

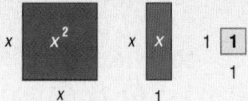

These algebra tiles can be placed together to form a rectangle whose length and width each represent a polynomial. The area of the rectangle is the product of the polynomials.

Use algebra tiles to find $x(x + 2)$.

Step 1 Make a rectangle with a width of x and a length of $x + 2$. Use algebra tiles to mark off the dimensions on a product mat.

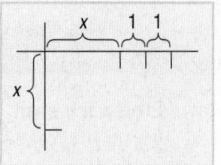

Step 2 Using the marks as a guide, fill in the rectangle with algebra tiles.

Step 3 The area of the rectangle is $x^2 + x + x$. In simplest form, the area is $x^2 + 2x$. Therefore, $x(x + 2) = x^2 + 2x$.

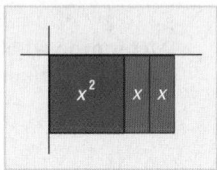

Model and Analyze 1–8. See pp. 703A–703D for models.

Use algebra tiles to determine whether each statement is *true* or *false*.

1. $x(x + 1) = x^2 + 1$ **false**
2. $x(2x + 3) = 2x^2 + 3x$ **true**
3. $(x + 2)2x = 2x^2 + 4x$ **true**
4. $2x(3x + 1) = 6x^2 + x$ **false**

Find each product using algebra tiles.

5. $x(x + 5)$ $x^2 + 5x$
6. $(2x + 1)x$ $2x^2 + x$
7. $(2x + 4)2x$ $4x^2 + 8x$
8. $3x(2x + 1)$ $6x^2 + 3x$

9. There is a square garden plot that measures x feet on a side.

   a. Suppose you double the length of the plot and increase the width by 3 feet. Write two expressions for the area of the new plot. $2x(x + 3)$; $2x^2 + 6x$

   b. If the original plot was 10 feet on a side, what is the area of the new plot? **260 ft²**

Extend the Activity $(x + 3)(2x + 3) = 2x^2 + 9x + 9$
10. Write a multiplication sentence that is represented by the model at the right.

Resource Manager

📁 ***Teaching Pre-Algebra with Manipulatives***
- pp. 7–8 (masters for algebra tiles)
- p. 14 (master for product mat)
- p. 161 (student recording sheet)

Glencoe Mathematics Classroom Manipulative Kit
- algebra tiles
- product mat

13-4 Multiplying a Polynomial by a Monomial

What You'll Learn

- Multiply a polynomial by a monomial.

How is the Distributive Property used to multiply a polynomial by a monomial?

The Grande Arche office building in Paris, France, looks like a hollowed-out prism, as shown in the photo at the right.

2w − 52

a. Write an expression that represents the area of the rectangular region outlined on the photo. $w(2w - 52)$ b. $2w^2 - 52w$

b. Recall that $2(4 + 1) = 2(4) + 2(1)$ by the Distributive Property. Use this property to simplify the expression you wrote in part **a**.

c. The Grande Arche is approximately w feet deep. Explain how you can write a polynomial to represent the volume of the hollowed-out region of the building. Then write the polynomial.

c. Use the Distributive Property to multiply $2w^2 - 52w$ by w; $2w^3 - 52w^2$.

MULTIPLY A POLYNOMIAL AND A MONOMIAL   You can model the multiplication of a polynomial and a monomial by using algebra tiles.

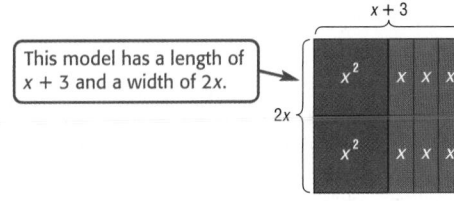
This model has a length of $x + 3$ and a width of $2x$.

Study Tip

Look Back
To review the **Distributive Property**, see Lesson 3-1.

The model shows the product of $2x$ and $x + 3$. The rectangular arrangement contains 2 x^2 tiles and 6 x tiles. So, the product of $2x$ and $x + 3$ is $2x^2 + 6x$. In general, the Distributive Property can be used to multiply a polynomial and a monomial.

Example 1 Products of a Monomial and a Polynomial

Find each product.

a. $4(5x + 1)$

$4(5x + 1) = 4(5x) + 4(1)$ Distributive Property
$\quad\quad\quad\quad = 20x + 4$ Simplify.

b. $(2x - 6)(3x)$

$(2x - 6)(3x) = 2x(3x) - 6(3x)$ Distributive Property
$\quad\quad\quad\quad\quad = 6x^2 - 18x$ Simplify.

 www.pre-alg.com/extra_examples

---

1 Focus

5-Minute Check Transparency 13-4 Use as a quiz or review of Lesson 13-3.

Mathematical Background notes are available for this lesson on page 666D.

How is the Distributive Property used to multiply a polynomial by a monomial?

The opening activity questions are repeated on page 751 of the *Chapter 13 Resource Masters*.

Reading to Learn Mathematics, p. 751   ELL

Pre-Activity   *How is the Distributive Property used to multiply a polynomial by a monomial?*

Do the activity at the top of page 683 in your textbook. Write your answers below.

a. Write an expression that represents the area of the rectangular region outlined on the photo. $w(2w - 52)$

b. Recall that $2(4 + 1) = 2(4) + 2(1)$ by the Distributive Property. Use this property to simplify the expression you wrote in part a. $2w^2 - 52w$

c. The Grande Arche is approximately w feet deep. Explain how you can write a polynomial to represent the volume of the hollowed-out region of the building. Then write the polynomial. Use the Distributive Property to multiply $2w^2 - 52w$ by w; $2w^3 - 52w^2$.

Reading the Lesson

1. Draw a model that shows the product $x(x + 2)$. Write the polynomial that shows the product. See students' work. $x^2 + 2x$

2. Explain the Distributive Property and give an example of how it is used to multiply a polynomial by a monomial. Sample answer: Multiply each number inside the parentheses by the number outside the parentheses.
$2(3y + 2) = 2(3y) + 2(2)$
$\quad\quad\quad\quad = 6y + 4$

Helping You Remember

3. *Distribute* is a common word in the English language.
   a. Find the definition of *distribute* in a dictionary. Write the definition that most closely relates to this lesson. to deliver to members of a group
   b. Explain how this definition can help you remember how to use the Distributive Property to multiply a polynomial by a monomial. The number outside the parentheses is "distributed" to each number inside.

Resource Manager

Workbooks and Reproducible Masters

Chapter 13 Resource Masters
- Study Guide and Intervention, p. 748
- Skills Practice, p. 749
- Practice, p. 750
- Reading to Learn Mathematics, p. 751
- Enrichment, p. 752

Graphing Calculator and Spreadsheet Masters, p. 43
Parent and Student Study Guide Workbook, p. 111

 Transparencies
5-Minute Check Transparency 13-4
Answer Key Transparencies

 Technology
Interactive Chalkboard
Pre-AlgePASS: Tutorial Plus, Lesson 38

Building on Prior Knowledge

In Lesson 3-1, students used the Distributive Property to write equivalent numerical and algebraic expressions. In this lesson, they will extend this knowledge to using the Distributive Property to multiply a polynomial by a monomial.

MULTIPLY A POLYNOMIAL AND A MONOMIAL

In-Class Examples

1 Find each product.

a. $-8(3x + 2)$ $-24x - 16$

b. $(6x - 1)(-2x)$ $-12x^2 + 2x$

2 Find $4b(-a^2 + 5ab + 2b^2)$.
$-4a^2b + 20ab^2 + 8b^3$

Teaching Tip If students are having trouble using the Distributive Property, have them write one polynomial below the other and multiply each monomial as they would with numerical multiplication.

3 **FENCES** The length of a dog run is 4 feet more than three times its width. The perimeter of the dog run is 56 feet. What are the dimensions of the dog run?   6 ft by 22 ft

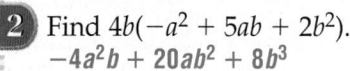
3 Practice/Apply

Study Notebook

Have students—
• write a paragraph explaining how to multiply a binomial and a monomial.
• include any other item(s) that they find helpful in mastering the skills in this lesson.

Example 2 Product of a Monomial and a Polynomial

Find $3a(a^2 + 2ab - 4b^2)$.

$3a(a^2 + 2ab - 4b^2)$
$= 3a(a^2) + 3a(2ab) - 3a(4b^2)$ Distributive Property
$= 3a^3 + 6a^2b - 12ab^2$ Simplify.

✓ **Concept Check**   What is the product of x^2 and $x + 1$? $x^3 + x^2$

Sometimes problems can be solved by simplifying polynomial expressions.

Example 3 Use a Polynomial to Solve a Problem

POOLS   The world's largest swimming pool is the Orthlieb Pool in Casablanca, Morocco. It is 30 meters longer than 6 times its width. If the perimeter of the pool is 1110 meters, what are the dimensions of the pool?

Explore   You know the perimeter of the pool. You want to find the dimensions of the pool.

Plan   Let w represent the width of the pool. Then $6w + 30$ represents the length. Write an equation.

Perimeter	equals	twice	the sum of the length and width.
P	$=$	2	$(\ell + w)$

Solve

$P = 2(\ell + w)$	Write the equation.
$1110 = 2(6w + 30 + w)$	Replace P with 1110 and ℓ with $6w + 30$.
$1110 = 2(7w + 30)$	Combine like terms.
$1110 = 14w + 60$	Distributive Property
$1050 = 14w$	Subtract 60 from each side.
$75 = w$	Divide each side by 14.

The width is 75 meters, and the length is $6w + 30$ or 480 meters.

Examine   Check the reasonableness of the results by estimating.

$P = 2(\ell + w)$ Formula for perimeter of a rectangle
$P \approx 2(500 + 80)$ Round 480 to 500 and 75 to 80.
$P \approx 2(580)$ or about 1160

Since 1160 is close to 1110, the answer is reasonable.

2. Multiply x^3 by $4x$ and multiply -7 by $4x$. Then add.

Check for Understanding

Concept Check   1. **Determine** whether the following statement is *true* or *false*.

If you change the order in which you multiply a polynomial and a monomial, the product will be different.

Explain your reasoning or give a counterexample. **See margin.**

GUIDED PRACTICE KEY	
Exercises	Examples
4–9	1, 2
10	3

2. **Explain** the steps you would take to find the product of $x^3 - 7$ and $4x$.

3. **OPEN ENDED**   Write a monomial and a polynomial, each having a degree no greater than 1. Then find their product. **Sample answer:**
$2x(x + 1) = 2x^2 + 2x$

DAILY
INTERVENTION   **Differentiated Instruction**

• **Visual/Spatial**   Have students work together in groups to draw diagrams of rectangles showing the lengths and widths in terms of x. Then have groups make up exercises involving their diagrams and the perimeters of the rectangles. After members of each group agree on the solutions to their own exercises, have them exchange diagrams and exercises with another group and solve that group's exercises. Encourage discussion of difficult problems.

Guided Practice Find each product. 9. $-15x^2 + 35x - 45$

4. $(5y - 4)3$ $15y - 12$ **5.** $a(a + 4)$ $a^2 + 4a$ **6.** $t(7t + 8)$ $7t^2 + 8t$

7. $(3x - 7)4x$ $12x^2 - 28x$ **8.** $a(2a + b)$ $2a^2 + ab$ **9.** $-5(3x^2 - 7x + 9)$

Application **10. TENNIS** The perimeter of a tennis court is 228 feet. The length of the court is 6 feet more than twice the width. What are the dimensions of the tennis court? **36 feet wide by 78 feet long**

★ indicates increased difficulty

Practice and Apply

Homework Help

For Exercises	See Examples
11–26	1, 2
27–30	3

Extra Practice
See page 756.

Find each product.

11. $7(2n + 5)$ $14n + 35$ **12.** $(1 + 4b)6$ $6 + 24b$

13. $t(t - 9)$ $t^2 - 9t$ **14.** $(x + 5)x$ $x^2 + 5x$

15. $-a(7a + 6)$ $-7a^2 - 6a$ **16.** $y(3 + 2y)$ $3y + 2y^2$

17. $4n(10 + 2n)$ $40n + 8n^2$ **18.** $-3x(6x - 4)$ $-18x^2 + 12x$

19. $3y(y^2 - 2)$ $3y^3 - 6y$ **20.** $ab(a^2 + 7)$ $a^3b + 7ab$

21. $5x(x + y)$ $5x^2 + 5xy$ **22.** $4m(m^2 - m)$ $4m^3 - 4m^2$

23. $-14x^2 + 35x - 77$ ★ **23.** $7(-2x^2 + 5x - 11)$ ★ **24.** $-3y(6 - 9y + 4y^2)$

24. $-18y + 27y^2 - 12y^3$

★ **25.** $4c(c^3 + 7c - 10)$ $4c^4 + 28c^2 - 40c$ ★ **26.** $6x^2(-2x^3 + 8x + 1)$
                                                  $-12x^5 + 48x^3 + 6x^2$

Solve each equation.

★ **27.** $30 = 6(-2w + 3)$ -1 ★ **28.** $-3(2a - 12) = 3a - 45$ 9

29. BASKETBALL The dimensions of high school basketball courts are different than the dimensions of college basketball courts, as shown in the table. Use the information in the table to find the length and width of each court.

Basketball Courts		
Measure	High School (ft)	College (ft)
Perimeter	268	288
Width	w	w
Length	$2w - 16$	$(2w - 16) + 10$

high school, 84 ft by 50 ft; college, 94 ft by 50 ft

★ 30. BOXES A box large enough to hold 43,000 liters of water was made from one large sheet of cardboard.

   a. Write a polynomial that represents the area of the cardboard used to make the box. Assume the top and bottom of the box are the same. (*Hint:* $(2x + 2y)(6x - 2y) = 12x^2 + 8xy - 4y^2$)

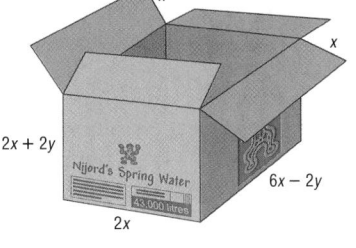
$2x + 2y$ $6x - 2y$ x $2x$

   b. If x is 1.2 meters and y is 0.1 meter, what is the total amount of cardboard in square meters used to make the box? **94 m²**   **30a.** $64x^2 + 16xy - 8y^2$

31. CRITICAL THINKING You have seen how algebra tiles can be used to connect multiplying a polynomial by a monomial and the Distributive Property. Draw a model and write a sentence to show how to multiply two binomials: $(a + b)(c + d)$. $(a + b)(c + d) = ac + ad + bc + bd$;
See margin for model.

Answers

1. False; the order in which numbers or terms are multiplied does not change the product, by the Commutative Property of Multiplication; $x(2x + 3) = 2x^2 + 3x$ and $(2x + 3)x = 2x^2 + 3x$.

31.

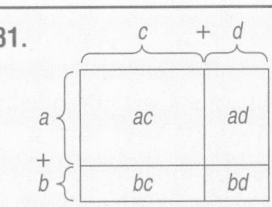

	c	$+$	d
a	ac		ad
$+$			
b	bc		bd

4 Assess

Open-Ended Assessment

Modeling Have students sketch algebra tiles that represent $4(3x + 2)$.

Getting Ready for Lesson 13-5

PREREQUISITE SKILL Lesson 13-5 presents determining whether a function is linear or nonlinear. One way to determine this is to complete a function table and compare the rates of change. Exercises 44–46 should be used to determine your students' familiarity with using tables to find ordered pair solutions of functions.

About the Exercises . . .
Odd/Even Assignments
Exercises 11–28 are structured so that students practice the same concepts whether they are assigned odd or even problems.

Assignment Guide
Basic: 11–21 odd, 29, 31–46
Average: 11–31 odd, 32–46
Advanced: 12–30 even, 31–43
(Optional: 44–46)

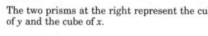
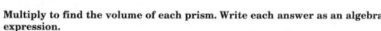
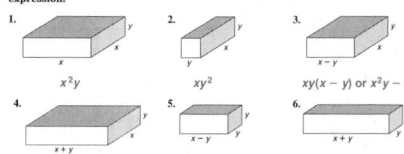
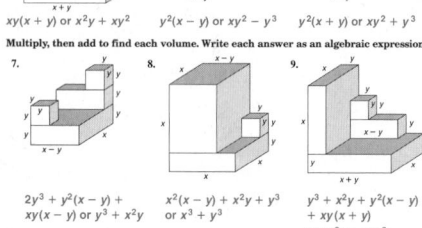
32. **WRITING IN MATH**  Answer the question that was posed at the beginning of the lesson. **See margin.**

How is the Distributive Property used to multiply a polynomial by a monomial?

Include the following in your answer:
- a description of the Distributive Property, and
- an example showing the steps used to multiply a polynomial and a monomial.

Standardized Test Practice

33. What is the product of $2x$ and $x - 8$? **D**
    (A) $2x - 8$ (B) $2x^2 - 8$ (C) $2x^2 - 16$ (D) $2x^2 - 16x$

34. The area of the rectangle is 252 square centimeters. Find the length of the longer side. **A**

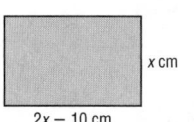

x cm

$2x - 10$ cm

    (A) 18 cm   (B) 16 cm
    (C) 14 cm   (D) 10 cm

Maintain Your Skills

Mixed Review

Find each sum or difference. *(Lessons 13-2 and 13-3)*

36. $10a + 3a^2 + 4$

35. $(2x - 1) + 5x$ $7x - 1$

36. $(9a + 3a^2) + (a + 4)$

37. $4y^2 - 2y + 14$

37. $(y^2 + 6y + 2) + (3y^2 - 8y + 12)$

38. $(4x - 7) - (2x + 2)$ $2x - 9$

40. $7n^2 + 6n$

39. $(9x + 8y) - (x - 3y)$ $8x + 11y$

40. $(13n^2 + 6n + 5) - (6n^2 + 5)$

41. **STATISTICS** Describe two ways that a graph of sales of several brands of cereal could be misleading. *(Lesson 12-5)* **See margin.**

State whether each transformation of the triangles is a *reflection*, *translation*, or *rotation*. *(Lesson 10-3)*

42. 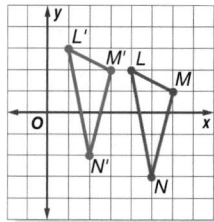 **translation**

43. 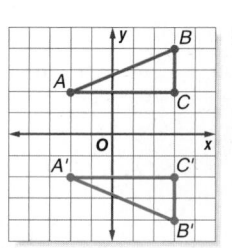 **reflection**

Getting Ready for the Next Lesson

PREREQUISITE SKILL Complete each table to find the coordinates of four points through which the graph of each function passes.

*(To review **using tables to find ordered pair solutions**, see Lesson 8-2.)*

44. $y = 4x$

x	$4x$	(x, y)
0	0	$(0, 0)$
1	4	$(1, 4)$
2	8	$(2, 8)$
3	12	$(3, 12)$

45. $y = 2x^2 - 3$

x	$2x^2 - 3$	(x, y)
0	-3	$(0, -3)$
1	-1	$(1, -1)$
2	5	$(2, 5)$
3	15	$(3, 15)$

46. $y = x^3 + 1$

x	$x^3 + 1$	(x, y)
0	1	$(0, 1)$
1	2	$(1, 2)$
2	9	$(2, 9)$
3	28	$(3, 28)$

Answers

32. To use the Distributive Property, multiply each term of the polynomial by the monomial. Answers should include the following.
    - The Distributive Property combines multiplication and addition when used to find the product of a polynomial and a monomial.
    - To find the product of $3x$ and $x + 2$, first find $3x \cdot x$. Then find $3x \cdot 2$. Finally, add the products, $3x^2 + 6x$.

41. Sample answer: The scales are labeled inconsistently or the bars on a bar graph are different widths.

Vocabulary
- nonlinear function
- quadratic function
- cubic function

a. $x(40 - 2x)$ or $40x - 2x^2$

b. 168 ft², 192 ft², 200 ft², 192 ft², 168 ft²

- Determine whether a function is linear or nonlinear.

The sum of the lengths of three sides of a new deck is 40 feet. Suppose x represents the width of the deck. Then the length of the deck is $40 - 2x$.

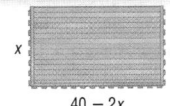

x x

$40 - 2x$

a. Write an expression to represent the area of the deck.

b. Find the area of the deck for widths of 6, 8, 10, 12, and 14 feet.

c. Graph the points whose ordered pairs are (width, area). Do the points fall along a straight line? Explain. **See margin.**

NONLINEAR FUNCTIONS In Lesson 8-2, you learned that linear functions have graphs that are straight lines. These graphs represent constant rates of change. **Nonlinear functions** do not have constant rates of change. Therefore, their graphs are *not* straight lines.

Example 1 Identify Functions Using Graphs

Determine whether each graph represents a *linear* or *nonlinear* function. Explain.

a.

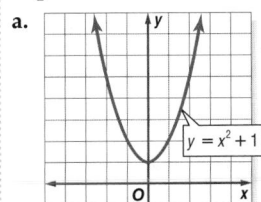

$y = x^2 + 1$

b.

$y = 2^x$

The graph is a curve, not a straight line, so it represents a nonlinear function.

This graph is also a curve, so it represents a nonlinear function.

Recall that the equation for a linear function can be written in the form $y = mx + b$, where m represents the constant rate of change. Therefore, you can determine whether a function is linear by looking at its equation.

Example 2 Identify Functions Using Equations

Determine whether each equation represents a *linear* or *nonlinear* function.

a. $y = 10x$

This is linear because it can be written as $y = 10x + 0$.

b. $y = \dfrac{3}{x}$

This is nonlinear because x is in the denominator and the equation cannot be written in the form $y = mx + b$.

---

1 Focus

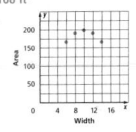

5-Minute Check Transparency 13-5 Use as a quiz or review of Lesson 13-4.

Mathematical Background notes are available for this lesson on page 666D.

How can you determine whether a function is linear?

The opening activity questions are repeated on page 756 of the *Chapter 13 Resource Masters*.

Reading to Learn Mathematics, p. 756   ELL

Pre-Activity *How can you determine whether a function is linear?*

Do the activity at the top of page 687 in your textbook. Write your answers below.

a. Write an expression to represent the area of the deck.
$x(40 - 2x)$ or $40x - 2x^2$

b. Find the area of the deck for widths of 6, 8, 10, 12, and 14 feet.
168 ft², 192 ft², 200 ft², 192 ft², 168 ft²

c. Graph the points whose ordered pairs are (width, area). Do the points fall along a straight line? Explain.
No; the connected points fall along a curve.

Reading the Lesson 1–3. See students' work.

Write a definition and give an example of each new vocabulary phrase.

Vocabulary	Definition	Example
1. nonlinear function		
2. quadratic function		
3. cubic function		

Helping You Remember

4. You have learned about linear and nonlinear functions. Nonlinear functions include quadratic functions and cubic functions. Below, write three equations that represent each type of function given. For the nonlinear functions, include at least one quadratic function and one cubic function. **Sample answers are given.**

Linear	Nonlinear
1. $y = x + 2$	1. $y = x^2 + 1$
2. $y = 2x + 1$	2. $y = 5x^3$
3. $y = \dfrac{x}{-5} - 5$	3. $y = x^2 + 2x - 1$

Resource Manager

📁 Workbooks and Reproducible Masters

Chapter 13 Resource Masters
- Study Guide and Intervention, p. 753
- Skills Practice, p. 754
- Practice, p. 755
- Reading to Learn Mathematics, p. 756
- Enrichment, p. 757
- Assessment, p. 778

Parent and Student Study Guide Workbook, p. 112
School-to-Career Masters, p. 26

Transparencies
5-Minute Check Transparency 13-5
Real-World Transparency 13
Answer Key Transparencies

💿 Technology
Interactive Chalkboard

2 Teach

NONLINEAR FUNCTIONS

In-Class Examples | Power Point®

1 Determine whether each graph represents a *linear* or *nonlinear* function.

a.

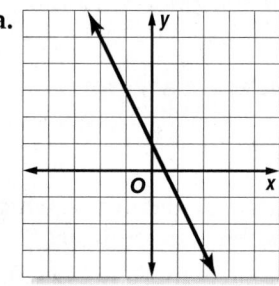

linear

b.

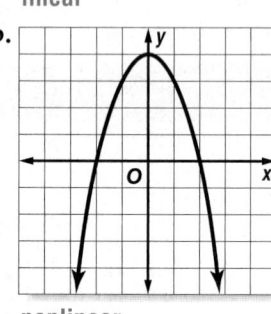

nonlinear

2 Determine whether each equation represents a *linear* or *nonlinear* function.

a. $y = -5x - 4$ linear

b. $y = 2x^2 + 3$ nonlinear

Teaching Tip Make sure students notice the degree of the equation in each case. Help them to discover that the degree of a linear equation must be 1.

3 Determine whether each table represents a *linear* or *nonlinear* function.

a.

x	y
2	25
4	17
6	9
8	1

linear

b.

x	y
5	2
8	4
11	8
14	16

nonlinear

The tables represent the functions in Example 2. Compare the rates of change.

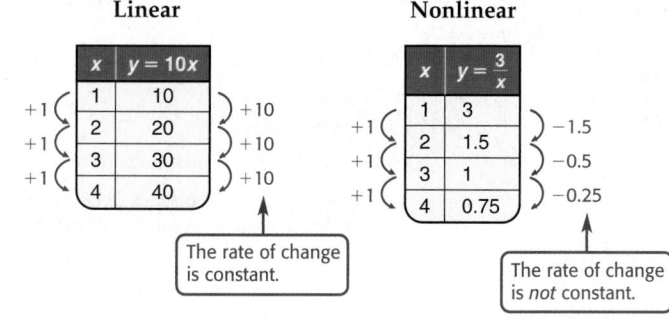

A nonlinear function does not increase or decrease at the same rate. You can check this by using a table.

Example 3 *Identify Functions Using Tables*

Determine whether each table represents a *linear* or *nonlinear* function.

a.

x	y
10	120
15	100
20	80
25	60

+5 → −20
+5 → −20
+5 → −20

As x increases by 5, y decreases by 20. So this is a linear function.

b.

x	y
2	4
4	16
6	36
8	64

+2 → +12
+2 → +20
+2 → +28

As x increases by 2, y increases by a greater amount each time. So this is a nonlinear function.

Some nonlinear functions are given special names.

Reading Math

Cubic

Cubic means three-dimensional. A cubic function has a variable to the third power.

Key Concept | *Quadratic and Cubic Functions*

A **quadratic function** is a function that can be described by an equation of the form $y = ax^2 + bx + c$, where $a \neq 0$.

A **cubic function** is a function that can be described by an equation of the form $y = ax^3 + bx^2 + cx + d$, where $a \neq 0$.

Examples of these and other nonlinear functions are shown below.

Concept Summary | *Nonlinear Functions*

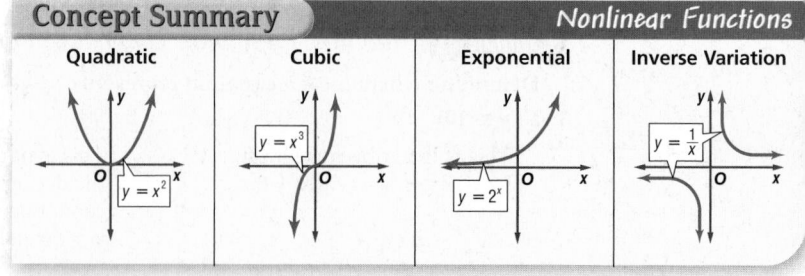

688   Chapter 13   Polynomials and Nonlinear Functions

DAILY INTERVENTION | **Differentiated Instruction**

- **Logical** Have students make a function table comparing altitude in feet (*x*) and temperature in °C (*y*). The altitudes are 0, 1500, 6000, and 9000 feet. The corresponding temperatures are 15, 5, −26, and −44°C. Have students graph the data and determine the altitude at which the temperature is −32°C.   **7000 ft**   Have them examine their graphs and discuss whether the function is linear or nonlinear.   **linear**

Example 4 *Describe a Linear Function*

Multiple-Choice Test Item

> Which rule describes a linear function?
> **A** $y = 7x^3 + 2$ **B** $y = (x - 1)5x$ **C** $4x + 3y = 12$ **D** $-2x^2 + 6y = 8$

Read the Test Item

A rule describes a relationship between variables. A rule that can be written in the form $y = mx + b$ describes a relationship that is linear.

Test-Taking Tip
Find out if there is a penalty for incorrect answers. If there is no penalty, making an educated guess can only increase your score, or at worst, leave your score the same.

Solve the Test Item

- $y = 7x^3 + 2 \rightarrow$ cubic equation   The variable has an exponent of 3.
  $-2x^2 + 6y = 8 \rightarrow$ quadratic equation   The variable has an exponent of 2.

  You can eliminate choices A and D.

- $y = (x - 1)5x$
  $y = 5x^2 - 5x$ This is a quadratic equation. Eliminate choice B.

The answer is C.

CHECK $4x + 3y = 12 \rightarrow y = -\dfrac{4}{3}x + 4$

This equation is in the form $y = mx + b$. ✓

Check for Understanding

Concept Check
1. See pp. 703A–703D.
2. Exponential; for the long term, growth of profits would occur at a faster rate.

1. **Describe** two methods for determining whether a function is linear.

2. **Explain** whether a company would prefer profits that showed linear growth or exponential growth.

3. **OPEN ENDED**   Use newspapers, magazines, or the Internet to find real-life examples of nonlinear situations.   Sample answer: population growth

Guided Practice

Determine whether each graph, equation, or table represents a *linear* or *nonlinear* function. Explain.

GUIDED PRACTICE KEY	
Exercises	Examples
4, 5	1
6, 7	2
8, 9	3
10	4

8. Nonlinear; rate of change is not constant.

4.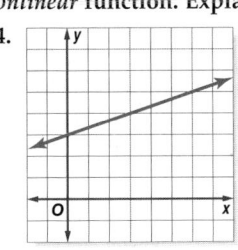
Linear; graph is a straight line.

5.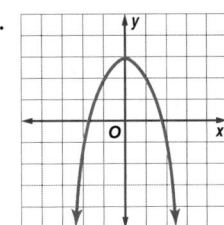
Nonlinear; graph is a curve.

6. $y = \dfrac{x}{5}$
Linear; equation can be written as $y = \dfrac{1}{5}x + 0$.

7. $xy = 12$
Nonlinear; equation cannot be written as $y = mx + b$.

8.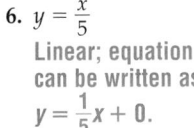

x	y
−4	13
−2	0
0	4
2	0

9.

x	y
8	19
9	22
10	25
11	28

Linear; rate of change is constant.

10. Which rule describes a nonlinear function? **B**
   A $x + y = 100$ **B** $y = \dfrac{8}{x}$ **C** $9 = 11x - y$ **D** $x = y$

www.pre-alg.com/extra_examples   **Lesson 13-5** Linear and Nonlinear Functions **689**

---

4 **Multiple-Choice Test Item**
Which rule describes a linear function?   **B**

A $y = \dfrac{1}{x} + 3$

B $y = -9x$

C $y = x(x - 5)$

D $32 = 2x^2 + 3y$

✓ Skills Check

Nonlinear Functions What is the degree of a nonlinear function?   **greater than 1**

3 Practice/Apply

Study Notebook

Have students—
- add the definitions/examples of the vocabulary terms to their Vocabulary Builder worksheets for Chapter 13.
- include any other item(s) that they find helpful in mastering the skills in this lesson.

About the Exercises . . .
Odd/Even Assignments
Exercises 11–26 are structured so that students practice the same concepts whether they are assigned odd or even problems.

Assignment Guide
Basic: 11–25 odd, 28, 30–43
Average: 11–27 odd, 28–43
Advanced: 12–28 even, 31–39
(Optional: 40–43)
All: Practice Quiz 2 (1–5)

Example 4   Point out to students that they might quickly spot either choice B or choice C as the correct answer since neither has an exponent and neither has a variable as a denominator. Even if they are certain of their choice, they should look over other choices.

★ indicates increased difficulty

Practice and Apply

Determine whether each graph, equation, or table represents a *linear* or *nonlinear* function. Explain. 11–16. See margin for explanations.

11.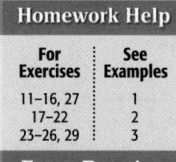

12.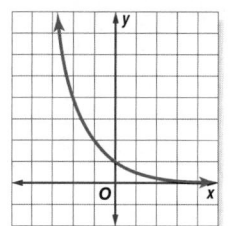

13.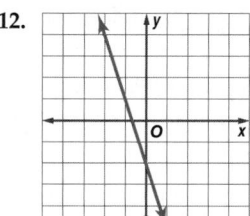

14.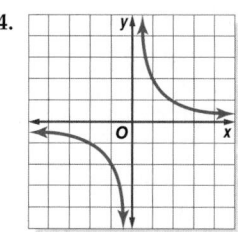

15.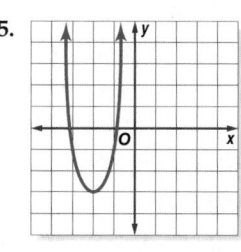

16.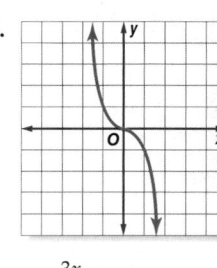

11. nonlinear
12. linear
13. linear
14. nonlinear
15. nonlinear
16. nonlinear

17–26. See pp. 703A–703D for explanations.

17. $y = 0.9x$ linear

18. $y = x^3 + 2$ nonlinear

19. $y = \frac{3x}{4}$ linear

20. $2x + 3y = 12$ linear

21. $y = 4^x$ nonlinear

22. $xy = -6$ nonlinear

23.

x	y
9	−2
11	−8
13	−14
15	−20

linear

24.

x	y
4	1
5	4
6	9
7	16

nonlinear

25.

x	y
−4	12
−2	0
0	4
2	0

nonlinear

26.

x	y
−10	20
−9	18
−8	16
−7	14

linear

27. Nonlinear; the points (year, applications) would lie on a curved line, not on a straight line. Or, the rate of change is not constant.

★ **27. TECHNOLOGY** The graph shows the increase of trademark applications for internet-related products or services. Would you describe this growth as linear or nonlinear? Explain.

 Online Research Data Update Is the growth of the Internet itself linear or nonlinear? Visit www.pre-alg.com/data_update to learn more.

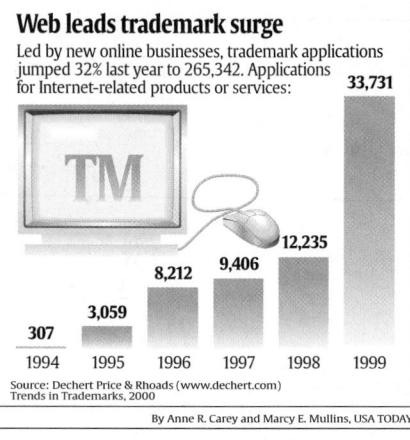

USA TODAY Snapshots®

Web leads trademark surge

Led by new online businesses, trademark applications jumped 32% last year to 265,342. Applications for Internet-related products or services:

1994: 307
1995: 3,059
1996: 8,212
1997: 9,406
1998: 12,235
1999: 33,731

Source: Dechert Price & Rhoads (www.dechert.com) Trends in Trademarks, 2000

By Anne R. Carey and Marcy E. Mullins, USA TODAY

28. CRITICAL THINKING Are all graphs of straight lines linear functions? Explain. See pp. 703A–703D.

Teaching Tip Have students determine which functions in Exercises 11–22 appear to be quadratic, cubic, exponential, and inverse variations.

Answers

11. Graph is a curve.

12. Graph is a straight line.

13. Graph is a straight line.

14. Graph is a curve.

15. Graph is a curve.

16. Graph is a curve.

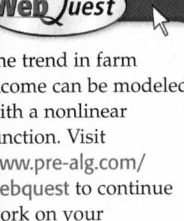
29. PATENTS The table shows the years in which the first six million patents were issued. Is the number of patents issued a linear function of time? Explain. **No, the difference between the years varies, so the change is not constant.**

Year	Number of Patents Issued
1911	1 million
1936	2 million
1961	3 million
1976	4 million
1991	5 million
1999	6 million

Source: *New York Times*

30. WRITING IN MATH Answer the question that was posed at the beginning of the lesson. **See margin.**

How can you determine whether a function is linear?

Include the following in your answer:

- a list of ways in which a function can be represented, and
- an explanation of how each representation can be used to identify the function as linear or nonlinear.

Standardized Test Practice

31. Which equation represents a linear function? **A**

Ⓐ $y = \frac{1}{2}x$ Ⓑ $3xy = 12$ Ⓒ $x^2 - 1 = y$ Ⓓ $y = x(x + 4)$

32. Determine which general rule represents a nonlinear function if $a > 1$. **C**

Ⓐ $y = ax$ Ⓑ $y = \frac{x}{a}$ Ⓒ $y = a^x$ Ⓓ $y = a + x$

Maintain Your Skills

Mixed Review   **Find each product.** *(Lesson 13-4)* **34.** $-5n + 15n^2$

33. $t(4 + 9t)$ $4t + 9t^2$ **34.** $5n(-1 + 3n)$ **35.** $(a - 2b)ab$ $a^2b - 2ab^2$

Find each difference. *(Lesson 13-3)* **36.** $x + 8$ **38.** $-2a - a^2 - 3$

36. $(2x + 7) - (x - 1)$ **37.** $(4x + y) - (5x + y)$ $-x$ **38.** $(6a - a^2) - (8a + 3)$

39. GEOMETRY Classify a 65° angle as *acute*, *obtuse*, *right*, or *straight*. *(Lesson 9-3)* **acute**

Getting Ready for the Next Lesson   **PREREQUISITE SKILL** Use a table to graph each line. *(To review **graphing equations**, see Lesson 8-3.)* **40–43. See pp. 703A–703D.**

40. $y = -x$ **41.** $y = x - 4$ **42.** $y = 2x + 2$ **43.** $y = -\frac{1}{2}x + 3$

Practice Quiz 2

Lessons 13-4 and 13-5

Find each product. *(Lesson 13-4)*

1. $c(2c^2 - 8)$ $2c^3 - 8c$ **2.** $(4x + 2)3x$ $12x^2 + 6x$ **3.** $a^2(5 + a + 2a^2)$ $5a^2 + a^3 + 2a^4$

Determine whether each equation represents a *linear* or *nonlinear* function. Explain. *(Lesson 13-5)*

4. $y = 9x$ Linear; equation can be written as $y = 9x + 0$.

5. $y = 0.25x^3$ Nonlinear; equation cannot be written as $y = mx + b$.

Answer

30. A function is linear if it has a constant rate of change. This can be determined from graphs, equations, or tables of values. Answers should include the following.

- Functions can be represented using graphs, equations, or tables.

- A graph that is a straight line represents a linear function. An equation that can be written in the form $y = mx + b$ is a linear function. If a table of values shows a constant rate of change, the function is linear.

4 Assess

Open-Ended Assessment

Speaking Have students read an equation to a partner and have the partner determine whether the equation is linear or nonlinear. Then have them switch roles.

Getting Ready for Lesson 13-6

PREREQUISITE SKILL Lesson 13-6 presents graphing nonlinear functions. Students will need to be able to make a table of values before graphing these functions. Exercises 40–43 should be used to determine your students' familiarity with using function tables to graph lines.

Assessment Options

Practice Quiz 2 The quiz provides students with a brief review of the concepts and skills in Lessons 13-4 and 13-5. Lesson numbers are given to the right of exercises or instruction lines so students can review concepts not yet mastered.

Quiz (Lessons 13-4 and 13-5) is available on p. 778 of the *Chapter 13 Resource Masters*.

13-6 Graphing Quadratic and Cubic Functions

1 Focus

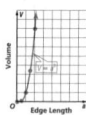

5-Minute Check Transparency 13-6 Use as a quiz or review of Lesson 13-5.

Mathematical Background notes are available for this lesson on page 666D.

How are functions, formulas, tables, and graphs related?

The opening activity questions are repeated on page 761 of the *Chapter 13 Resource Masters.*

Reading to Learn Mathematics, p. 761 **ELL**

Pre-Activity *How are functions, formulas, tables, and graphs related?*

Do the activity at the top of page 692 in your textbook. Write your answers below.

a. The volume of cube *V* equals the cube of the length of an edge *a.* Write a formula to represent the volume of a cube as a function of edge length. $V = a^3$

b. Graph the volume as a function of edge length. (*Hint:* Use values of *a* like 0, 0.5, 1, 1.5, 2, and so on.)

Reading the Lesson

1. Write a quadratic function. Explain what makes it a quadratic function and what its graph would look like. Sample answer: $y = 2x^2 + 5$; This is a quadratic function because it has the form $y = ax^2 + bx + c$, $a \neq 0$. It is a parabola.

2. Write a cubic function. Explain what makes it a cubic function and what its graph would look like. Sample answer: $y = 3x^3 + 2$; This is a cubic function because it has the form $y = ax^3 + bx^2 + cx$, $a \neq 0$. It is similar in appearance to $y = x^3$, only shifted up two units and increasing more rapidly.

Helping You Remember

3. You have learned to graph quadratic and cubic functions. Make a list of the steps you use to graph the two functions.

Make a table of values.

Plot the ordered pairs.

Connect the points with a curve.

Teaching Tip Discuss how to select "easy" values for *x* when making a function table. Suggest using numbers that will create whole numbers for *y* values.

Resource Manager

Workbooks and Reproducible Masters

Chapter 13 Resource Masters
• Study Guide and Intervention, p. 758
• Skills Practice, p. 759
• Practice, p. 760
• Reading to Learn Mathematics, p. 761
• Enrichment, p. 762
• Assessment, p. 778

Graphing Calculator and Spreadsheet Masters, p. 44
Parent and Student Study Guide Workbook, p. 113

Transparencies
5-Minute Check Transparency 13-6
Answer Key Transparencies

Technology
Interactive Chalkboard

Graphing Quadratic and Cubic Functions

What You'll Learn

• Graph quadratic functions.
• Graph cubic functions.

How are functions, formulas, tables, and graphs related?

You can find the area of a square *A* by squaring the length of a side *s*. This relationship can be represented in different ways.

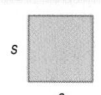

	Equation	
Area	equals	length of a side squared.
A	=	s^2

Table

s	s^2	(*s, A*)
0	$0^2 = 0$	(0, 0)
1	$1^2 = 1$	(1, 1)
2	$2^2 = 4$	(2, 4)

Graph

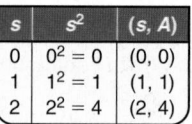

a. The volume of cube *V* equals the cube of the length of an edge *a.* Write a formula to represent the volume of a cube as a function of edge length. $V = a^3$

b. Graph the volume as a function of edge length. (*Hint:* Use values of *a* like 0, 0.5, 1, 1.5, 2, and so on.) **See margin.**

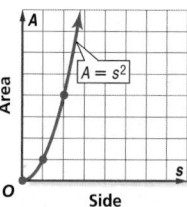

QUADRATIC FUNCTIONS In Lesson 13-5, you saw that functions can be represented using graphs, equations, and tables. This allows you to graph quadratic functions such as $A = s^2$ using an equation or a table of values.

Example 1 *Graph Quadratic Functions*

Graph each function.

a. $y = 2x^2$

Make a table of values, plot the ordered pairs, and connect the points with a curve.

Study Tip

Graphing
It is often helpful to substitute decimal values of *x* in order to graph points that are closer together.

x	$2x^2$	(*x, y*)
−1.5	$2(-1.5)^2 = 4.5$	(−1.5, 4.5)
−1	$2(-1)^2 = 2$	(−1, 2)
0	$2(0)^2 = 0$	(0, 0)
1	$2(1)^2 = 2$	(1, 2)
1.5	$2(1.5)^2 = 4.5$	(1.5, 4.5)

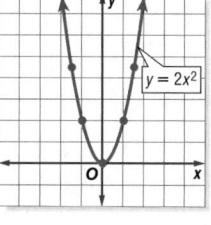

b. $y = x^2 - 1$

x	$x^2 - 1$	(x, y)
−2	$(-2)^2 - 1 = 3$	(−2, 3)
−1	$(-1)^2 - 1 = 0$	(−1, 0)
0	$(0)^2 - 1 = -1$	(0, −1)
1	$(1)^2 - 1 = 0$	(1, 0)
2	$(2)^2 - 1 = 3$	(2, 3)

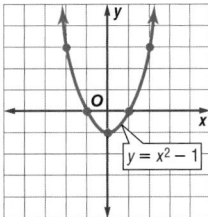

c. $y = -x^2 + 3$

x	$-x^2 + 3$	(x, y)
−2	$-(-2)^2 + 3 = -1$	(−2, −1)
−1	$-(-1)^2 + 3 = 2$	(−1, 2)
0	$-(0)^2 + 3 = 3$	(0, 3)
1	$-(1)^2 + 3 = 2$	(1, 2)
2	$-(2)^2 + 3 = -1$	(2, −1)

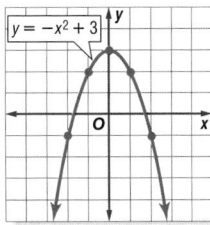

You can also write a rule from a verbal description of a function, and then graph.

Example 2 Use a Function to Solve a Problem

•**SKYDIVING** The distance in feet that a skydiver falls is equal to sixteen times the time squared, with the time given in seconds. Graph this function and estimate how far he will fall in 4.5 seconds.

Words   Distance is equal to sixteen times the time squared.

Variables   Let d = the distance in feet and t = the time in seconds.

Distance	is equal to	sixteen	times	the time squared.
d	$=$	16	$\cdot$	t^2

Equation

The equation is $d = 16t^2$. Since the variable t has an exponent of 2, this function is nonlinear. Now graph $d = 16t^2$. Since time cannot be negative, use only positive values of t.

t	$d = 16t^2$	(t, d)
0	$16(0)^2 = 0$	(0, 0)
1	$16(1)^2 = 16$	(1, 16)
2	$16(2)^2 = 64$	(2, 64)
3	$16(3)^2 = 144$	(3, 144)
4	$16(4)^2 = 256$	(4, 256)
5	$16(5)^2 = 400$	(5, 400)
6	$16(6)^2 = 576$	(6, 576)

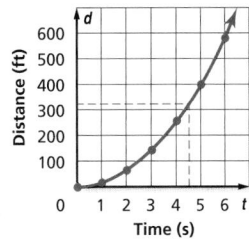

By looking at the graph, we find that in 4.5 seconds, the skydiver will fall approximately 320 feet.   You could find the exact distance by substituting 4.5 for t in the equation $d = 16t^2$.

 www.pre-alg.com/extra_examples

Lesson 13-6 Graphing Quadratic and Cubic Functions **693**

D A I L Y
INTERVENTION   **Unlocking Misconceptions**

- **Graphs of Quadratic Equations** Point out to students that not all quadratic equations have graphs that curve upward or downward. Equations like $x = y^2$ are quadratic but not quadratic functions. Their graphs open to the right or to the left.

---

2 Teach

QUADRATIC FUNCTIONS

In-Class Examples   Power Point®

1 Graph each function.

a. $y = -2x^2$

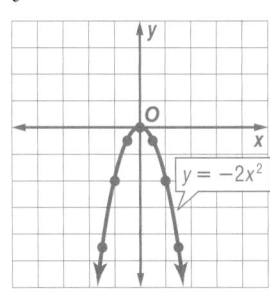

b. $y = \dfrac{x^2}{2} + 1$

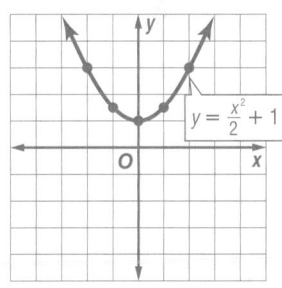

c. $y = -x^2 - 3$

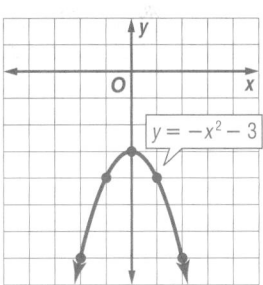

2 **GEOMETRY** The height of a triangle is 4 times its base. Write a formula for the area and graph it. Find the area of the triangle whose base is 3 units. $A = 2b^2$; 18 units²

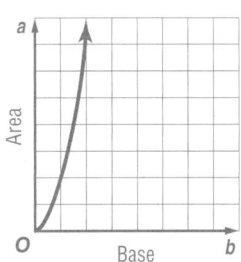

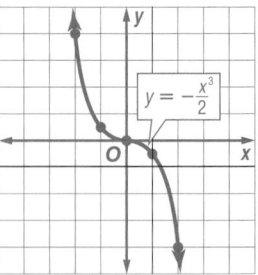
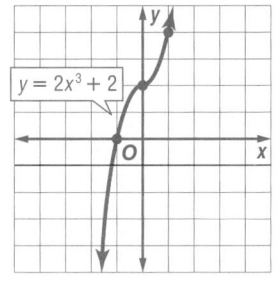
3 Practice/Apply

CUBIC FUNCTIONS

CUBIC FUNCTIONS You can also graph cubic functions such as the formula for the volume of a cube by making a table of values.

Example 3 Graph Cubic Functions

Graph each function.

a. $y = x^3$

x	$y = x^3$	(x, y)
−1.5	$(-1.5)^3 \approx -3.4$	$(-1.5, -3.4)$
−1	$(-1)^3 = -1$	$(-1, -1)$
0	$(0)^3 = 0$	$(0, 0)$
1	$(1)^3 = 1$	$(1, 1)$
1.5	$(1.5)^3 \approx 3.4$	$(1.5, 3.4)$

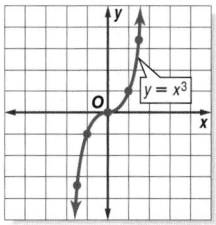

b. $y = x^3 - 1$

x	$y = x^3 - 1$	(x, y)
−1.5	$(-1.5)^3 - 1 \approx -4.4$	$(-1.5, -4.4)$
−1	$(-1)^3 - 1 = -2$	$(-1, -2)$
0	$(0)^3 - 1 = -1$	$(0, -1)$
1	$(1)^3 - 1 = 0$	$(1, 0)$
1.5	$(1.5)^3 - 1 \approx 2.4$	$(1.5, 2.4)$

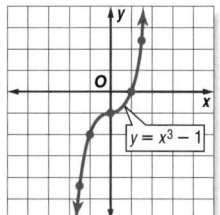

GUIDED PRACTICE KEY	
Exercises	Examples
4–9	1, 3
10	2

Check for Understanding

Concept Check

1. Sample answer: The graph of $y = nx^2$ has line symmetry and the graph of $y = nx^3$ does not.

1. **Describe** one difference between the graph of $y = nx^2$ and the graph of $y = nx^3$ for any rational number n.

2. **Explain** how to determine whether a function is quadratic. **See margin.**

3. **OPEN ENDED** Write a quadratic function and explain how to graph it.
   Sample answer: $y = x^2 + 3$; make a table of values and plot the points.

Guided Practice Graph each function. 4–5. See margin. 6–9. See pp. 703A–703D.

4. $y = x^2$ 5. $y = -2x^2$ 6. $y = x^2 + 1$

7. $y = -x^3$ 8. $y = 0.5x^3$ 9. $y = x^3 - 2$

Application 10. **GEOMETRY** A cube has edges measuring a units.
   a. Write a quadratic equation for the surface area S of the cube. $S = 6a^2$
   b. Graph the surface area as a function of a. (*Hint:* Use values of a like 0, 0.5, 1, 1.5, 2, and so on.) **See pp. 703A–703D.**

★ indicates increased difficulty

Practice and Apply

Graph each function. 11–22. See pp. 703A–703D.

11. $y = 3x^2$ 12. $y = 0.5x^2$ 13. $y = -x^2$

14. $y = 3x^3$ 15. $y = -2x^3$ 16. $y = -0.5x^2$

17. $y = 2x^3$ 18. $y = 0.1x^3$ 19. $y = x^3 + 1$

20. $y = x^2 - 3$ ★ 21. $y = \frac{1}{2}x^2 + 1$ ★ 22. $y = \frac{1}{3}x^3 + 2$

Answers

2. Sample answer: A function is quadratic if its equation contains one independent variable whose greatest exponent is 2.

4.
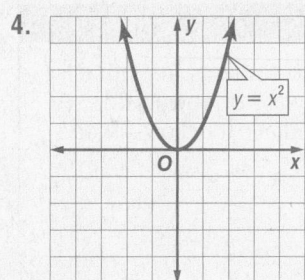

5.
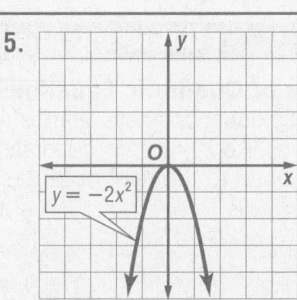

Homework Help

For Exercises	See Examples
11–22 31–33	1, 3 2

Extra Practice
See page 757.

23. See margin.

27. Similar shape; $y = 3x^2$ is more narrow.

28. Similar shape; $y = 2x^3$ is more narrow.

29. Same shape; $y = -2x^2$ is $y = 2x^2$ reflected over the x-axis.

30. Same shape; $y = x^3 - 3$ is translated 3 units down from $y = x^3$.

36. The solutions are the x-intercepts of the graph.

23. Graph $y = x^2 - 4$ and $y = -4x^3$. Are these equations functions? Explain.

24. Graph $y = x^2$ and $y = x^3$ in the first quadrant on the same coordinate plane. Explain which graph shows faster growth. **See margin for graph.** For $x > 1$, $y = x^3$ shows faster growth; the graph has a steeper upward slope.

The *maximum point* of a graph is the point with the greatest y value coordinate. The *minimum point* is the point with the least y value coordinate. Find the coordinates of each point.

25. the maximum point of the graph of $y = -x^2 + 7$ **(0, 7)**

26. the minimum point of the graph of $y = x^2 - 6$ **(0, -6)**

Graph each pair of equations on the same coordinate plane. Describe their similarities and differences. 27–30. See pp. 703A–703D for graphs.

27. $y = x^2$
    $y = 3x^2$

28. $y = 0.5x^3$
    $y = 2x^3$

29. $y = 2x^2$
    $y = -2x^2$

30. $y = x^3$
    $y = x^3 - 3$

CONSTRUCTION For Exercises 31–33, use the information below and the figure at the right.
A dog trainer is building a dog pen with a 100-foot roll of chain link fence.

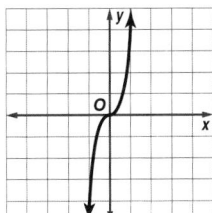

★ 31. Write an equation to represent the area A of the pen. $A = 50x - x^2$

★ 32. Graph the equation you wrote in Exercise 31. See pp. 703A–703D.

★ 33. What should the dimensions of the dog pen be to enclose the maximum area inside the fence? (*Hint:* Find the coordinates of the maximum point of the graph.) **25 ft by 25 ft**

GEOMETRY Write a function for each of the following. Then graph the function in the first quadrant. 34–35. See pp. 703A–703D for graphs.

★ 34. the volume V of a rectangular prism as a function of a fixed height of 2 units and a square base of varying lengths s $V = 2s^2$

★ 35. the volume V of a cylinder as a function of a fixed height of 0.2 unit and radius r $V = 0.2\pi r^2$ or $V \approx 0.6r^2$

36. **CRITICAL THINKING** Describe how you can find real number solutions of the quadratic equation $ax^2 + bx + c = 0$ from the graph of the quadratic function $y = ax^2 + bx + c$.

37. **WRITING IN MATH** Answer the question that was posed at the beginning of the lesson. See pp. 703A–703D.

How are functions, formulas, tables, and graphs related?

Include the following in your answer:
- an explanation of how to make a graph by using a rule, and
- an explanation of how to write a rule by using a graph.

Standardized Test Practice
Ⓐ Ⓑ Ⓒ Ⓓ

38. Which equation represents the graph at the right? **C**

Ⓐ $y = 4x^2$

Ⓑ $y = -4x^2$

Ⓒ $y = 4x^3$

Ⓓ $y = -4x^3$

Organization by Objective
- **Quadratic Functions:** 11–13, 16, 20, 21, 27, 29, 31–35
- **Cubic Functions:** 14, 15, 17–19, 22, 28, 30

Odd/Even Assignments
Exercises 11–30 are structured so that students practice the same concepts whether they are assigned odd or even problems.

Assignment Guide
Basic: 11–19 odd, 23–29 odd, 36–39, 42–48

Average: 11–29 odd, 36–39, 42–48 (Optional: 40, 41)

Advanced: 12–36 even, 37–48

Answers

23.

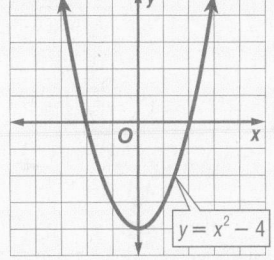

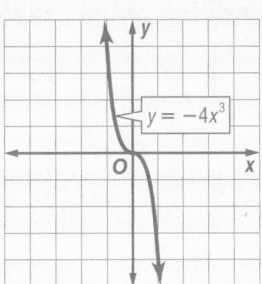

Both equations are functions because every value of x is paired with a unique value of y.

24.

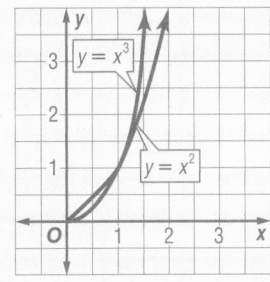

Study Guide and Intervention, p. 758

To graph a quadratic or cubic function, make a table of values and then plot the points.

Example Graph $y = 2x^3 - 1$.

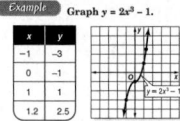

Exercises

Graph each function.

1. $y = x^2 + 2$

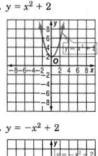

2. $y = x^3 + 2$

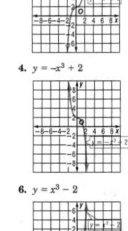

3. $y = -x^2 + 2$

4. $y = -x^3 + 2$

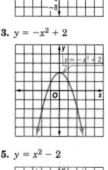
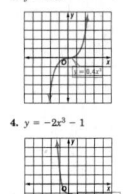

5. $y = x^2 - 2$

6. $y = x^3 - 2$

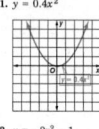
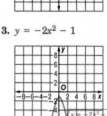
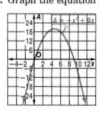

Skills Practice, p. 759 and Practice, p. 760 (shown)

Graph each function.

1. $y = 0.4x^2$

2. $y = 0.4x^3$

3. $y = -2x^2 - 1$

4. $y = -2x^3 - 1$

5. **WINDOWS** A window maker has 25 feet of wire to frame a window. One side of the window is x feet and the other side is $9 - x$ feet.

a. Write an equation to represent the area A of the window.
$A = -x^2 + 9x$

b. Graph the equation you wrote in part a.

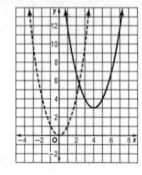

c. If the area of the window is 18 square feet, what are the two possible values of x?
$x = 3$ and $x = 6$

Enrichment, p. 762

Translating Quadratic Graphs

When a figure is moved to a new position without undergoing any rotation, then the figure is said to have been **translated** to the new position.

The graph of a quadratic equation in the form $y = (x - b)^2 + c$ is a translation of the graph of $y = x^2$.

Start with a graph of $y = x^2$.

Slide to the right 4 units.
$y = (x - 4)^2$

Then slide up 3 units.
$y = (x - 4)^2 + 3$

The following equations are in the form $y = x^2 + c$. Graph each equation.

1. $y = x^2 + 1$

2. $y = x^2 + 2$

3. $y = x^2 - 2$

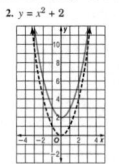
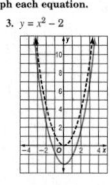

The following equations are in the form $y = (x - b)^2$. Graph each equation.

4. $y = (x - 1)^2$

5. $y = (x - 3)^2$

6. $y = (x + 2)^2$

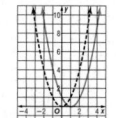
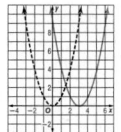
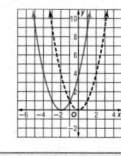

---

39. For a certain frozen pizza, as the cost goes from \$2 to \$4, the demand can be modeled by the formula $y = -10x^2 + 60x + 180$, where x represents the cost and y represents the number of pizzas sold. Estimate the cost that will result in the greatest demand. **C**

Ⓐ \$0   Ⓑ \$2
Ⓒ \$3   Ⓓ \$8

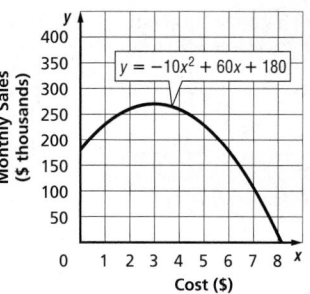

Extending the Lesson

Just as you can estimate the area of irregular figures, you can also estimate the area under a curve that is graphed on the coordinate plane. Estimate the shaded area under each curve to the nearest square unit.

40–41. Sample answers are given.

40. 15 units^2

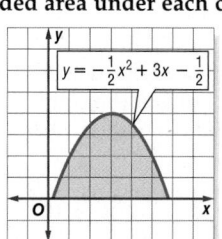

41. 18 units^2

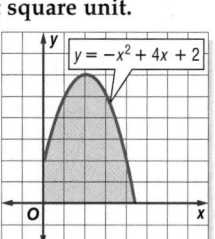

Maintain Your Skills

Mixed Review

42. **SCIENCE** The graph shows how water vapor pressure increases as the temperature increases. Is this relationship linear or nonlinear? Explain.
(Lesson 13-5)
Nonlinear; the points on the graph do not lie on a straight line.

Water Vapor Pressure

Find each product. (Lesson 13-4)

43. $(2x - 4)5$ $10x - 20$

44. $n(n + 6)$ $n^2 + 6n$

45. $3y(8 - 7y)$ $24y - 21y^2$

Write an equation in slope-intercept form for the line passing through each pair of points. (Lesson 8-7)

46. $(3, 6)$ and $(0, 9)$
$y = -x + 9$

47. $(2, 5)$ and $(-1, -7)$
$y = 4x - 3$

48. $(-4, -3)$ and $(8, 6)$
$y = \frac{3}{4}x$

WebQuest **Internet Project**

Family Farms
It is time to complete your project. Use the information and data you have gathered to prepare a Web page about farming or ranching in the United States. Be sure to include at least five graphs or tables that show statistics about farming or ranching and at least one scatter plot that shows a farming or ranching statistic over time, from which you can make predictions.

www.pre-alg.com/webquest

696 Chapter 13 Polynomials and Nonlinear Functions

4 Assess

Open-Ended Assessment

Writing Have students write a paragraph explaining how the shape of the graph of $y = x^2$ differs from the graph of $y = x^3$.

Assessment Options

Quiz (Lesson 13-6) is available on p. 778 of the *Chapter 13 Resource Masters*.

Graphing Calculator Investigation

A Follow-Up of Lesson 13-6

Families of Quadratic Functions

A quadratic function can be described by an equation of the form $ax^2 + bx + c$, where $a \neq 0$. The graph of a quadratic function is called a **parabola**. Recall that families of linear graphs share the same slope or y-intercept. Similarly, families of parabolas share the same maximum or minimum point, or have the same shape.

Graph $y = x^2$ and $y = x^2 + 4$ on the same screen and describe how they are related.

Step 1 *Enter the function $y = x^2$.*

- Enter $y = x^2$ as Y1.
  KEYSTROKES: [Y=] [X,T,θ,n] [x^2] [ENTER]

Step 2 *Enter the function $y = x^2 + 4$.*

- Enter $y = x^2 + 4$ as Y2.
  KEYSTROKES: [Y=] [X,T,θ,n] [x^2] [+] 4
  [ENTER]

Step 3 *Graph both quadratic functions on the same screen.*

- Display the graph.
  KEYSTROKES: [ZOOM] 6

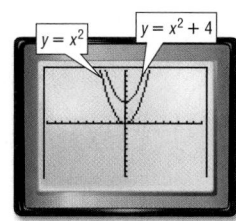

The first function graphed is Y1 or $y = x^2$. The second is Y2 or $y = x^2 + 4$. Press [TRACE] and move along each function by using the right and left arrow keys. Move from one function to another by using the up and down arrow keys.

The graphs are similar in that they are both parabolas. However, the graph of $y = x^2$ has its vertex at $(0, 0)$, whereas the graph of $y = x^2 + 4$ has its vertex at $(0, 4)$.

Exercises 3. $y = x^2 - 8$, $y = x^2 + 1$, $y = x^2 + 6$

1. Graph $y = x^2$, $y = x^2 - 5$, and $y = x^2 - 3$ on the same screen and draw the parabolas on grid paper. Compare and contrast the three parabolas. **See pp. 703A–703D.**

2. **Make a conjecture** about how adding or subtracting a constant c affects the graph of a quadratic function. **It shifts the graph vertically c units.**

3. The three parabolas at the right are graphed in the standard viewing window and have the same shape as the graph of $y = x^2$. Write an equation for each, beginning with the lowest parabola.

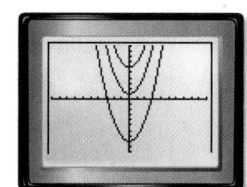

4. Clear all functions from the [Y=] menu. Enter $y = 0.4x^2$ as Y1, $y = x^2$ as Y2, and $y = 3x^2$ as Y3. Graph the functions in the standard viewing window on the same screen. Then draw the graphs on the same coodinate grid. How does the shape of the parabola change as the coefficient of x^2 increases? **See pp. 703A–703D for graphs.**
As the coefficient of x^2 increases, the parabola is narrower.

www.pre-alg.com/other_calculator_keystrokes

Graphing Calculator Investigation 697

Getting Started

Know Your Calculator In order for the graphs to display correctly, students may need to adjust the calculator settings. Have students use the arrow keys to place the cursor on any plot currently high-lighted, then press [ENTER].

Graph Modes The mode settings determine what type of graph will result. If students' displays do not match those shown on this page, check that their mode settings are the following, in order from top to bottom: **Normal, Float, Radian, Func, Connected, Sequential, Real,** and **Full.**

Teach

- Before beginning Step 1, and again before doing Exercise 1, students should clear all functions from the **Y=** list.

- As students work through Step 3, you may wish to show them the **TABLE** function. Have them key in [2nd] **TBLSET** and enter TblStart=0 and ΔTbl=.5. Then have them press [2nd] **TABLE** and use the up and down arrows to explore the points of the two graphs.

- Have students complete Exercises 1–4.

Assess

After students answer Exercises 1–4, ask how the shape of the parabola would change if the coefficient of x^2 were $\frac{1}{2}$. Have them make a generalization to describe this.

The parabola would become wider; as the coefficient of x^2 decreases, the parabola becomes wider.

Chapter 13 Study Guide and Review

Vocabulary and Concept Check

* This alphabetical list of vocabulary terms in Chapter 13 includes a page reference where each term was introduced.

* **Assessment** A vocabulary review/test for Chapter 13 is available on p. 776 of the *Chapter 13 Resource Masters.*

Lesson-by-Lesson Review

For each lesson,
* the main ideas are summarized,
* additional examples review concepts, and
* practice exercises are provided.

Vocabulary PuzzleMaker

ELL The Vocabulary PuzzleMaker software improves students' mathematics vocabulary using four puzzle formats—crossword, scramble, word search using a word list, and word search using clues. Students can work on a computer screen or from a printed handout.

MindJogger Videoquizzes

ELL MindJogger Videoquizzes provide an alternative review of concepts presented in this chapter. Students work in teams in a game show format to gain points for correct answers. The questions are presented in three rounds.

Round 1 Concepts (5 questions)
Round 2 Skills (4 questions)
Round 3 Problem Solving (4 questions)

Vocabulary and Concept Check

binomial (p. 669)	nonlinear function (p. 687)	quadratic function (p. 688)
cubic function (p. 688)	polynomial (p. 669)	trinomial (p. 669)
degree (p. 670)		

Choose the correct term to complete each sentence.

1. A (binomial, <u>trinomial</u>) is the sum or difference of three monomials.
2. Monomials that contain the same variables with the same (<u>power</u>, sign) are like terms.
3. The function $y = 2x^3$ is an example of a (<u>cubic</u>, quadratic) function.
4. The equation $y = x^2 + 5x + 1$ is an example of a (cubic, <u>quadratic</u>) function.
5. x^2 and $4x^2$ are examples of (binomials, <u>like terms</u>).
6. The equation $y = 4x^3 + x^2 + 2$ is an example of a (quadratic, <u>cubic</u>) function.
7. The graph of a quadratic function is a (straight line, <u>curve</u>).
8. To multiply a polynomial and a monomial, use the (<u>Distributive</u>, Commutative) Property.

Lesson-by-Lesson Review

13-1 Polynomials

See pages 669–672.

Concept Summary

* A polynomial is an algebraic expression that contains one or more monomials.
* A binomial has two terms and a trinomial has three terms.
* The degree of a monomial is the sum of the exponents of its variables.

Example State whether $x^3 - 2xy$ is a *monomial, binomial,* or *trinomial.* **Then find the degree.**

The expression is the difference of two monomials. So it is a binomial.
x^3 has degree 3, and $-2xy$ has degree $1 + 1$ or 2. So, the degree of $x^3 - 2xy$ is 3.

Exercises Determine whether each expression is a polynomial. If it is, classify it as a *monomial, binomial,* or *trinomial.* *See Example 1 on page 669.*

9. $c^2 + 3$ **yes; bi.**
10. -5 **yes; mono.**
11. $4t^4$ **yes; mono.**
12. $\frac{6}{a} + b$ **no**
13. $3x^2 + 4x - 2$ **yes; trinomial**
14. $x + y$ **yes; bi.**
15. $\sqrt{n}$ **no**
16. $1 + 3x + 5x^2$ **yes; trinomial**

Find the degree of each polynomial. *See Examples 2 and 3 on page 670.*

17. $2x$ **1**
18. $5xy$ **2**
19. $3a^2b$ **3**
20. $n^2 - 4$ **2**
21. $x^6 + y^6$ **6**
22. $2xy + 6yz^2$ **3**
23. $2x^5 + 9x + 1$ **5**
24. $x^2 + xy^2 - y^4$ **4**

 www.pre-alg.com/vocabulary_review

FOLDABLES™
Study Organizer

For more information about Foldables, see *Teaching Mathematics with Foldables.*

Have students refer to their Foldable journals for Chapter 13 to review concepts before beginning the Study Guide and Review or while preparing for the Chapter Test.

13-2 Adding Polynomials

See pages 674–677.

Concept Summary

- To add polynomials, add like terms.

Example   Find $(5x^2 - 8x + 2) + (x^2 + 6x)$.

$$
\begin{array}{l}
5x^2 - 8x + 2 \\
(+)\;\;\; x^2 + 6x \qquad \text{Align like terms.} \\
\hline
6x^2 - 2x + 2 \quad \text{Add.} \qquad \text{The sum is } 6x^2 - 2x + 2.
\end{array}
$$

Exercises   Find each sum.   *See Example 1 on pages 674 and 675.*

26. $8x^2 + 2x + 1$ 27. $5y^2 + 2y - 4$

25. $\begin{array}{l} 3b + 8 \quad \mathbf{8b + 3} \\ (+)\, 5b - 5 \end{array}$

26. $\begin{array}{l} 2x^2 + 3x - 4 \\ (+)\, 6x^2 - \;\; x + 5 \end{array}$

27. $\begin{array}{l} 4y^2 + 2y + 3 \\ (+)\;\; y^2 \qquad\; -7 \end{array}$

28. $(9m - 3n) + (10m + 4n)$ $\mathbf{19m + n}$ 29. $(-3y^2 + 2) + (4y^2 - y - 3)$ $\mathbf{y^2 - y - 1}$

13-3 Subtracting Polynomials

See pages 678–681.

Concept Summary

- To subtract polynomials, subtract like terms or add the additive inverse.

Example   Find $(4x^2 + 7x + 4) - (x^2 + 2x + 1)$.

$$
\begin{array}{l}
4x^2 + 7x + 4 \\
(-)\;\; x^2 + 2x + 1 \qquad \text{Align like terms.} \\
\hline
3x^2 + 5x + 3 \quad \text{Subtract.} \qquad \text{The difference is } 3x^2 + 5x + 3.
\end{array}
$$

30. $-2a^2 + 25$ 31. $3x^2 - 4x + 7$ 32. $16y^2 + 3y - 7$

Exercises   Find each difference.   *See Examples 1 and 2 on pages 678 and 679.*

30. $\begin{array}{l} a^2 + 15 \\ (-)\, 3a^2 - 10 \end{array}$

31. $\begin{array}{l} 4x^2 - 2x + 3 \\ (-)\;\; x^2 + 2x - 4 \end{array}$

32. $\begin{array}{l} 18y^2 + 3y - 1 \\ (-)\; 2y^2 + \quad\; + 6 \end{array}$

33. $(x + 8) - (2x + 7)$ $\mathbf{-x + 1}$ 34. $(3n^2 + 7) - (n^2 - n + 4)$ $\mathbf{2n^2 + n + 3}$

13-4 Multiplying a Polynomial by a Monomial

See pages 683–686.

Concept Summary

- To multiply a polynomial and a monomial, use the Distributive Property.

Example   Find $-3x(x + 8y)$.

$$
\begin{aligned}
-3x(x + 8y) &= -3x(x) + (-3x)(8y) \qquad \text{Distributive Property} \\
&= -3x^2 - 24xy \qquad\qquad\quad \text{Simplify.}
\end{aligned}
$$

Exercises   Find each product.   *See Example 1 on page 683.*

35. $5(4t - 2)$ $\mathbf{20t - 10}$ 36. $(2x + 3y)7$ $\mathbf{14x + 21y}$ 37. $k(6k + 3)$ $\mathbf{6k^2 + 3k}$

38. $4d(2d - 5)$ $\mathbf{8d^2 - 20d}$ 39. $-2a(9 - a^2)$ 40. $6(2x^2 + xy + 3y^2)$

39. $-18a + 2a^3$ 40. $12x^2 + 6xy + 18y^2$

Study Guide and Review

Chapter **13** For More ...
• Extra Practice, see pages 755–757.
• Mixed Problem Solving, see page 770.

Answers

44.

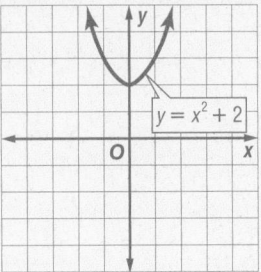

$y = x^2 + 2$

45.

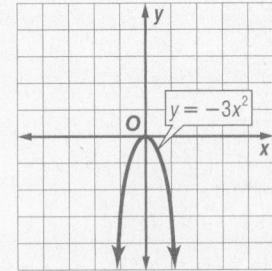

$y = -3x^2$

46.

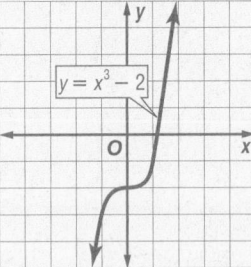

$y = x^3 - 2$

47.

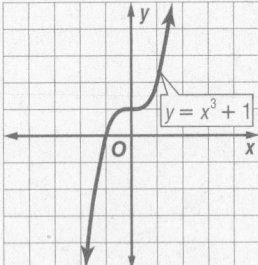

$y = x^3 + 1$

48.

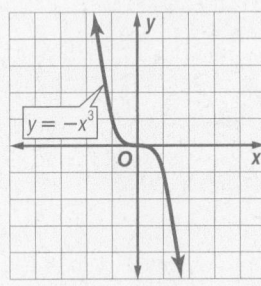

$y = -x^3$

13-5 ## Linear and Nonlinear Functions

See pages 687–691.

Concept Summary

• Nonlinear functions do not have constant rates of change.

Example Determine whether each graph, equation, or table represents a *linear* or *nonlinear* function. Explain.

a.

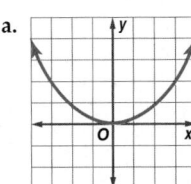

Nonlinear; graph is not a straight line.

b. $y = x + 12$

Linear; equation can be written as $y = mx + b$.

c.

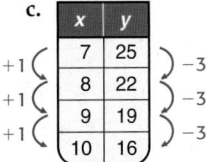

x	y
7	25
8	22
9	19
10	16

(+1, −3 pattern)

Linear; rate of change is constant.

Exercises Determine whether each graph, equation, or table represents a *linear* or *nonlinear* function. Explain. *See Examples 1–3 on pages 687 and 688.*

41.

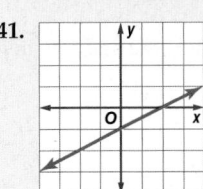

Linear; graph is a straight line.

42. $y = \dfrac{x}{2}$ Linear; equation can be written as $y = \dfrac{1}{2}x + 0$.

43.

x	y
−6	3
−4	4
−2	6
0	9

Nonlinear; rate of change is not constant.

13-6 ## Graphing Quadratic and Cubic Functions

See pages 692–696.

Concept Summary

• Quadratic and cubic functions can be graphed by plotting points.

Example Graph $y = -x^2 + 3$.

x	$y = -x^2 + 3$	(x, y)
−2	$-(-2)^2 + 3 = -1$	(−2, −1)
−1	$-(-1)^2 + 3 = 2$	(−1, 2)
0	$-(0)^2 + 3 = 3$	(0, 3)
1	$-(1)^2 + 3 = 2$	(1, 2)
2	$-(2)^2 + 3 = -1$	(2, −1)

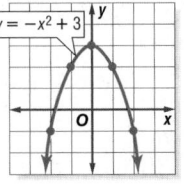

$y = -x^2 + 3$

Exercises Graph each function. *See Examples 1 and 3 on pages 692–694.*

44. $y = x^2 + 2$
45. $y = -3x^2$
46. $y = x^3 - 2$
47. $y = x^3 + 1$
48. $y = -x^3$
49. $y = 2x^2 + 4$

44–49. See margin.

49.

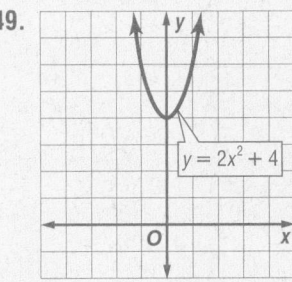

$y = 2x^2 + 4$

Vocabulary and Concepts

1. **Define** polynomial. **an algebraic expression that contains one or more monomials**
2. **Explain** how the degree of a monomial is found. **Add the exponents of the variables.**
3. **OPEN ENDED** Draw the graph of a linear and a nonlinear function. **See students' drawings; the linear function should be a straight line and the nonlinear function should be a curve.**

Skills and Applications

Determine whether each expression is a polynomial. If it is, classify it as a *monomial*, *binomial*, or *trinomial*.

4. $3x^3 - 2x + 7$ **yes; trinomial**   5. $6 + \dfrac{5}{m}$ **no**   6. $\dfrac{3}{5}p^4$ **yes; monomial**

Find the degree of each polynomial.

7. $5ab^3$ **4**

8. $w^5 - 3w^3y^4 + 1$ **7**

Find each sum or difference. **11. $4m^3 - 2m^2 + 5m - 5$**

9. $(5y + 8) + (-2y + 3)$ **$3y + 11$**
10. $(5a - 2b) + (-4a + 5b)$ **$a + 3b$**
11. $(-3m^3 + 5m - 9) + (7m^3 - 2m^2 + 4)$
12. $(6p + 5) - (3p - 8)$ **$3p + 13$**
13. $(5w - 3x) - (6w + 4x)$ **$-w - 7x$**
14. $(-2s^2 + 4s - 7) - (6s^2 - 7s - 9)$ **$-8s^2 + 11s + 2$**

Find each product.

15. $x(3x - 5)$ **$3x^2 - 5x$**
16. $-5a(a^2 - b^2)$ **$-5a^3 + 5ab^2$**
17. $6p(-2p^2 + 3p - 4)$ **$-12p^3 + 18p^2 - 24p$**

Determine whether each graph, equation, or table represents a *linear* or *nonlinear* function. Explain.

18.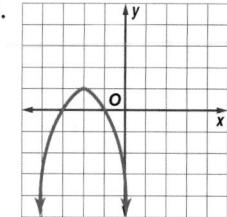

Nonlinear; graph is a curve.

19. $5x - 6y = 2$ **Linear; equation can be written as $y = \dfrac{5}{6}x - \dfrac{1}{3}$.**

20.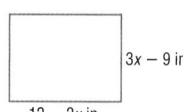

x	y
1	10
3	7
5	3
7	-2

Nonlinear; rate of change is not constant.

Graph each function. **21–23. See pp. 703A–703D.**

21. $y = 2x^2$
22. $y = \dfrac{1}{2}x^3$
23. $y = -x^2 + 3$

24. **GEOMETRY** Refer to the rectangle.
   a. Write an expression for the perimeter of the rectangle. **$2x + 6$ in.**
   b. Find the value of x if the perimeter is 14 inches. **4**

$3x - 9$ in.

$12 - 2x$ in.

25. **STANDARDIZED TEST PRACTICE** The length of a garden is equal to 5 less than four times its width. The perimeter of the garden is 40 feet. Find the length of the garden. **D**
   Ⓐ 1 ft   Ⓑ 5 ft   Ⓒ 10 ft   Ⓓ 15 ft

www.pre-alg.com/chapter_test

Portfolio Suggestion

Introduction Equations are used to solve many different types of problems. Sometimes special types of equations called formulas are used.

Ask Students to find a problem from their work in this chapter and explain how they used an equation or formula to solve it.

Assessment Options

Vocabulary Test A vocabulary review/test for Chapter 13 can be found on p. 776 of the *Chapter 13 Resource Masters*.

Chapter Tests There are six Chapter 13 Tests and an Open-Ended Assessment task available in the *Chapter 13 Resource Masters*.

Chapter 13 Tests			
Form	Type	Level	Pages
1	MC	basic	763–764
2A	MC	average	765–766
2B	MC	average	767–768
2C	FR	average	769–770
2D	FR	average	771–772
3	FR	advanced	773–774

MC = multiple-choice questions
FR = free-response questions

Open-Ended Assessment
Performance tasks for Chapter 13 can be found on p. 775 of the *Chapter 13 Resource Masters*, along with a sample scoring rubric for these tasks on p. A22.

Unit 5 Test A unit test/review can be found on pp. 783–784 of the *Chapter 13 Resource Masters*.

End-of-Year Tests A Second Semester Test for Chapters 6–13 and a Final Test for Chapters 1–13 can be found on pp. 785–794 of the *Chapter 13 Resource Masters*.

ExamView® Pro

Use the networkable **ExamView® Pro** to:

• Create **multiple tests.**
• Create **modified** tests for *Inclusion* students.
• **Edit** existing questions and **add** your own questions.
• Use built-in **state curriculum correlations** to create tests aligned with state standards.
• Change **English** tests to **Spanish** and vice versa.

These two pages contain practice questions in the various formats that can be found on the most frequently given standardized tests.

A practice answer sheet for these two pages can be found on page A1 of the *Chapter 13 Resource Masters*.

Standardized Test Practice
Student Recording Sheet, p. A1

Part 1 *Multiple Choice*

Select the best answer from the choices given and fill in the corresponding oval.

1. Ⓐ Ⓑ Ⓒ Ⓓ   4. Ⓐ Ⓑ Ⓒ Ⓓ   7. Ⓐ Ⓑ Ⓒ Ⓓ
2. Ⓐ Ⓑ Ⓒ Ⓓ   5. Ⓐ Ⓑ Ⓒ Ⓓ   8. Ⓐ Ⓑ Ⓒ Ⓓ
3. Ⓐ Ⓑ Ⓒ Ⓓ   6. Ⓐ Ⓑ Ⓒ Ⓓ   9. Ⓐ Ⓑ Ⓒ Ⓓ

Part 2 *Short Response/Grid In*

Solve the problem and write your answer in the blank.

For Questions 10 and 11, also enter your answer by writing each number or symbol in a box. Then fill in the corresponding oval for that number or symbol.

10 _____ (grid in)
11 _____ (grid in)
12 _____
13 _____
14 _____
15 _____
16 _____
17 _____
18 _____

Part 3 *Extended Response*

Record your answers for Questions 19–20 on the back of this paper.

Additional Practice

• Additional Standardized Test Practice is available on pp. 781–782 of the *Chapter 13 Resource Masters*.

Part 1 | **Multiple Choice**

Record your answers on the answer sheet provided by your teacher or on a sheet of paper.

1. If n represents a positive number, which of these expressions is equivalent to $n + n + n$? (Lesson 1-3) **B**
   Ⓐ n^3 Ⓑ $3n$
   Ⓒ $n + 3$ Ⓓ $3(n + 1)$

2. Connor sold 4 fewer tickets to the band concert than Miguel sold. Kylie sold 3 times as many tickets as Connor. If the number of tickets Miguel sold is represented by m, which of these expressions represents the number of tickets that Kylie sold? (Lesson 3-6) **D**
   Ⓐ $m - 4$
   Ⓑ $4 - 3m$
   Ⓒ $3m - 4$
   Ⓓ $3(m - 4)$

3. Melissa's family calculated that they drove an average of 400 miles per day during their three-day trip. They drove 460 miles on the first day and 360 miles on the second day. How many miles did they drive on the third day? (Lesson 5-7) **B**
   Ⓐ 340   Ⓑ 380
   Ⓒ 410   Ⓓ 420

4. What is the ratio of the length of a side of a square to its perimeter? (Lesson 6-1) **B**
   Ⓐ $\frac{1}{16}$ Ⓑ $\frac{1}{4}$
   Ⓒ $\frac{1}{3}$ Ⓓ $\frac{1}{2}$

Test-Taking Tip Ⓐ Ⓑ Ⓒ Ⓓ
Question 2
If you have time at the end of a test, go back to check your calculations and answers. If the test allows you to use a calculator, use it to check your calculations.

---

5. The table shows values of x and y, where x is proportional to y. What are the missing values, S and T? (Lesson 6-3) **B**

x	3	9	S
y	5	T	35

   Ⓐ $S = 36$ and $T = 3$
   Ⓑ $S = 21$ and $T = 15$
   Ⓒ $S = 15$ and $T = 21$
   Ⓓ $S = 3$ and $T = 36$

6. In the figure at the right, lines ℓ and m are parallel. Choose two angles whose measures have a sum of 180°. (Lesson 10-2) **C**
   Ⓐ $\angle 1$ and $\angle 5$
   Ⓑ $\angle 2$ and $\angle 8$
   Ⓒ $\angle 2$ and $\angle 5$
   Ⓓ $\angle 4$ and $\angle 8$

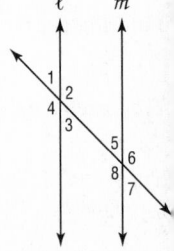

7. The point represented by coordinates $(4, -6)$ is reflected across the x-axis. What are the coordinates of the image? (Lesson 10-3) **D**
   Ⓐ $(-6, 4)$ Ⓑ $(-4, -6)$
   Ⓒ $(-4, 6)$ Ⓓ $(4, 6)$

8. If $2x^2 - 3x + 7$ is subtracted from $4x^2 + 6x - 3$, what is the difference? (Lesson 13-3) **A**
   Ⓐ $2x^2 + 9x - 10$
   Ⓑ $2x^2 + 3x + 4$
   Ⓒ $-2x^2 + 3x + 4$
   Ⓓ $-2x^2 - 9x + 10$

9. Which function includes all of the ordered pairs in the table? It may help you to sketch a graph of the points. (Lesson 13-6) **B**

x	-2	-1	1	2	3
y	4	2	-2	-4	-6

   Ⓐ $y = -x^2$ Ⓑ $y = -2x$
   Ⓒ $y = -x + 2$ Ⓓ $y = x^2$

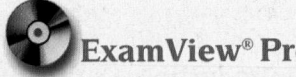
ExamView® Pro

Special banks of standardized test questions similar to those on the SAT, ACT, TIMSS 8, NAEP 8, and Pre-Algebra End-of-Course tests can be found on this CD-ROM.

Part 2 | Short Response/Grid In

Record your answers on the answer sheet provided by your teacher or on a sheet of paper.

9. The table shows the number of sandwiches sold during twenty lunchtimes. What is the mode? (Lesson 5-8) **9**

Number of Sandwiches Sold				
9	8	10	14	12
16	9	7	10	11
11	8	9	8	7
12	14	8	9	9

10. One machine makes plastic containers at a rate of 360 containers per hour. A newer machine makes the same containers at a rate of 10 containers per minute. If both machines are run for four hours, how many containers will they make? (Lesson 6-1) **3840**

11. What percent of 275 is 165? (Lesson 6-5) **60%**

12. Mrs. Rosales can spend $8200 on equipment for the computer lab. Each computer costs $850 and each printer costs $325. Mrs. Rosales buys 8 computers. Write an inequality that can be used to find p, the number of printers she could buy. (Lesson 7-6) **$8(850) + 325p \le 8200$**

13. What is the y-intercept of the graph shown at the right? Each square represents 1 unit. (Lesson 8-6) **−3**

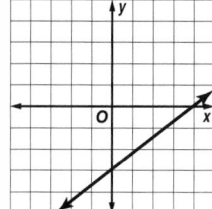

14. The area of a triangle is $\frac{1}{2}(b \times h)$. What is the area of the kite? (Lesson 10-5) **315 in²**

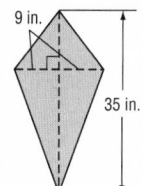

9 in.
35 in.

16. Brooke wants to fill her new aquarium two-thirds full of water. The aquarium dimensions are 20 inches by 20 inches by $8\frac{1}{2}$ inches. What volume of water, in cubic inches, is needed? (Lesson 11-2) **about 2267 in³**

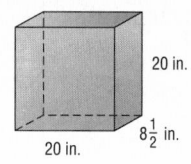

20 in.
20 in.
$8\frac{1}{2}$ in.

17. Let $s = 3x^2 - 2x - 1$ and $t = -2x^2 + x + 2$. Find $s + t$. (Lesson 13-2) **$x^2 - x + 1$**

18. The perimeter of a soccer field is 1040 feet. The length of the field is 40 feet more than 2 times the width. What is the length of the field? (Lesson 13-4) **360 ft**

Part 3 | Extended Response

Record your answers on a sheet of paper. Show your work.

19. An artist created a sculpture using five cylindrical posts. Each post has a diameter of 12 inches. The heights of the posts are 6 feet, 5 feet, 4 feet, 3 feet, and 2 feet. (Lesson 11-2)

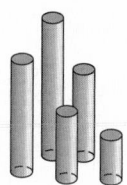

   a. What is the total volume of all five posts? $V = \pi r^2 h$ is the formula for the volume of a cylinder. Use $\pi = 3.14$. **15.7 ft³**

   b. The posts are made of a material whose density is 12 pounds per cubic foot. How much does the sculpture weigh? **188.4 lb**

20. Refer to the table below. (Lesson 13-6) **a–b. See margin.**

   a. Graph the ordered pairs in the table as coordinate points.

   b. Sketch a line or curve through the points.

   c. Write a quadratic function that includes all of the ordered pairs in the table. **$y = x^2 - 4$**

x	y
−2	0
−1	−3
0	−4
1	−3
2	0

Evaluating Extended Response Questions

Extended Response questions are graded by using a multilevel rubric that guides you in assessing a student's knowledge of a particular concept.

Goal: Find volume and weight of a sculpture/Use a table of ordered pairs to draw a graph and write a quadratic function.

Sample Scoring Rubric: The following rubric is a sample scoring device. You may wish to add more detail to this sample to meet your individual scoring needs.

Score	Criteria
4	A correct solution that is supported by well-developed, accurate explanations
3	A generally correct solution, but may contain minor flaws in reasoning or computation
2	A partially correct interpretation and/or solution to the problem
1	A correct solution with no supporting evidence or explanation
0	An incorrect solution indicating no mathematical understanding of the concept or task, or no solution is given

Answer

20a–b.

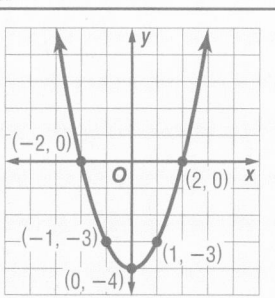

(−2, 0)
(2, 0)
(−1, −3)
(1, −3)
(0, −4)

Page 672, Lesson 13-1

49. Polynomials approximate real-world data by using variables to represent quantities that are related. Answers should include the following.

- Heat index is found by using a polynomial in which one variable represents the percent humidity and another variable represents the temperature.

- Heat index cannot be approximated using a linear equation because the values do not change at a constant rate.

57. $(x + 2x) + 4$

58. $(3x^2 + x^2) - 1$

59. $(6n + 3n) + (2 + 5)$

60. $(a + 3a) + (2b + b)$

61. $(s + 5s) + (t - 3t)$

62. $(x^2 + 7x^2) + (4x - 3x)$

Page 673, Algebra Activity

1.

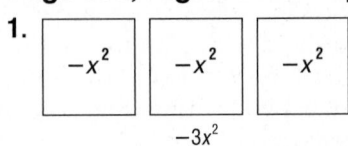

$-3x^2$

2.

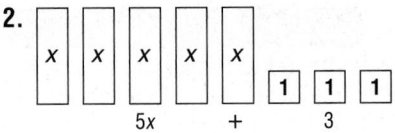

$5x \quad + \quad 3$

3.

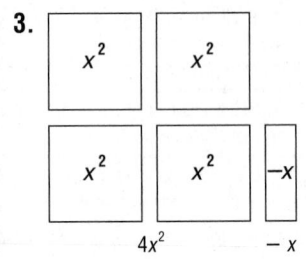

$4x^2 \qquad - x$

4.

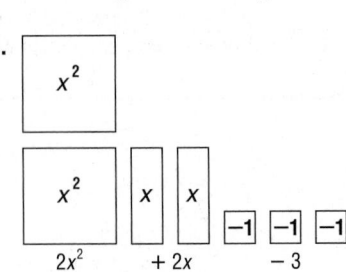

$2x^2 \qquad + 2x \qquad - 3$

5. A monomial has tiles of one size, a binomial has tiles of two sizes, and a trinomial has tiles of three sizes.

Page 681, Lesson 13-3

29. In subtracting polynomials and in subtracting measurements, like parts are subtracted. Answers should include the following.

- To subtract measurements with two or more units, subtract the like units. To subtract polynomials with two or more terms, subtract the like terms.

- For example, to subtract 1 foot 5 inches from 3 feet 8 inches, subtract the feet $3 - 1$ and subtract the inches $8 - 5$. The difference is 2 feet 3 inches.

Page 682, Algebra Activity

1.

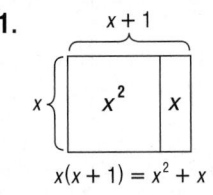

$x(x + 1) = x^2 + x$

2.

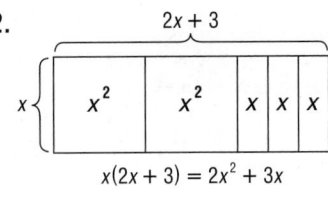

$x(2x + 3) = 2x^2 + 3x$

3.

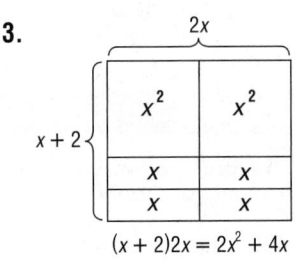

$(x + 2)2x = 2x^2 + 4x$

4.

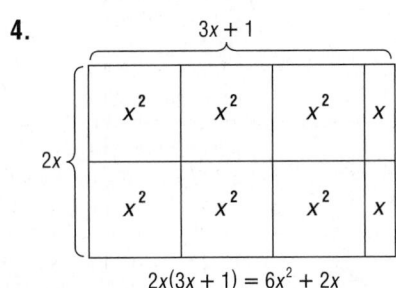

$2x(3x + 1) = 6x^2 + 2x$

5.

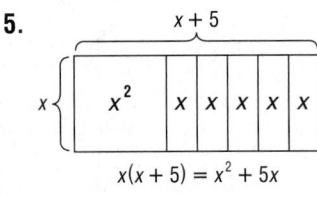

$x(x + 5) = x^2 + 5x$

6.

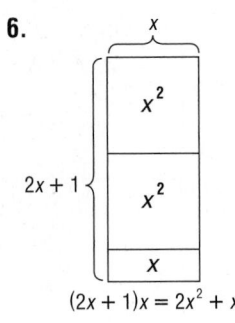

$(2x + 1)x = 2x^2 + x$

7.

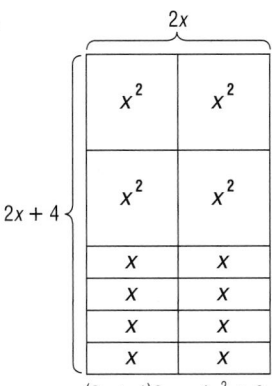

$(2x + 4)2x = 4x^2 + 8x$

8.

$3x(2x + 1) = 6x^2 + 3x$

Page 689, Lesson 13-5

1. Sample answer: Determine whether an equation can be written in the form $y = mx + b$ or look for a constant rate of change in a table of values.

Page 690, Lesson 13-5

17. Equation can be written as $y = 0.9x + 0$.

18. Equation cannot be written as $y = mx + b$.

19. Equation can be written as $y = \frac{3}{4}x + 0$.

20. Equation can be written as $y = -\frac{2}{3}x + 4$.

21. Equation cannot be written as $y = mx + b$.

22. Equation cannot be written as $y = mx + b$.

23. Rate of change is constant.

24. Rate of change is not constant.

25. Rate of change is not constant.

26. Rate of change is constant.

28. No, a vertical line based on a rule such as $x = 3$ is not a function because there is more than one y value for the x value 3.

Page 691, Lesson 13-5

40.

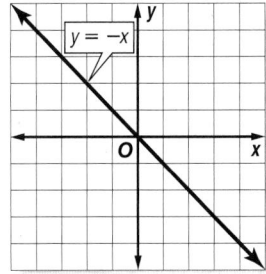

41.

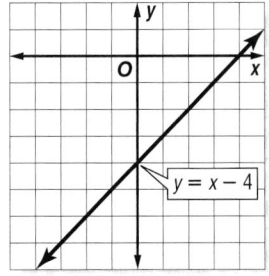

42.

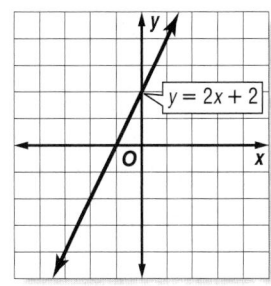

43.

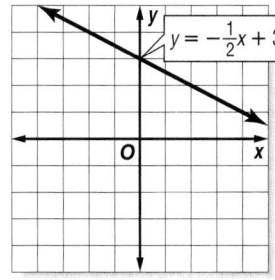

Page 694, Lesson 13-6

6.

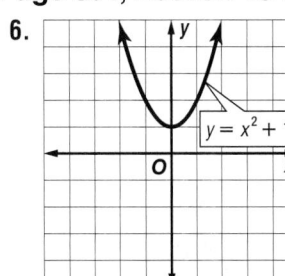

7.

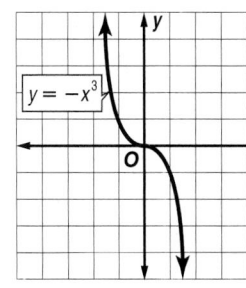

8.

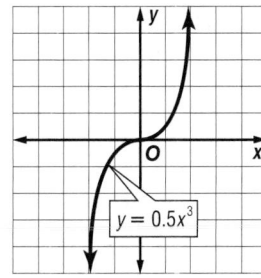

9.

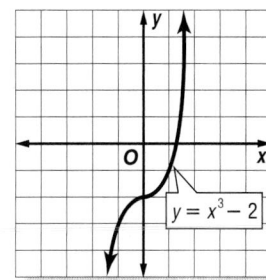

10b.

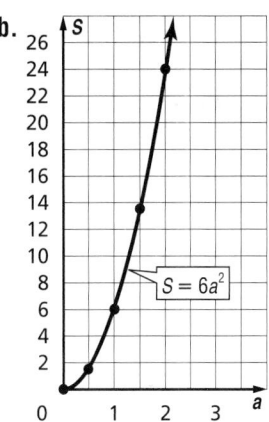

11.

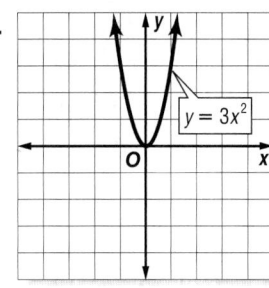

12.

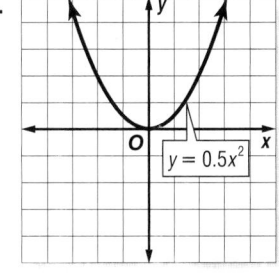

13.

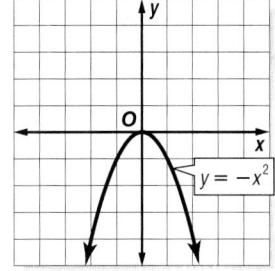

14.

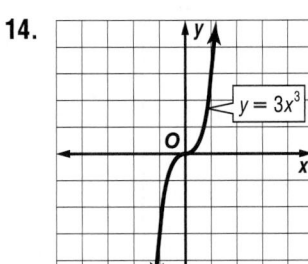

$y = 3x^3$

15.

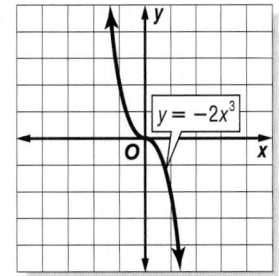

$y = -2x^3$

16.

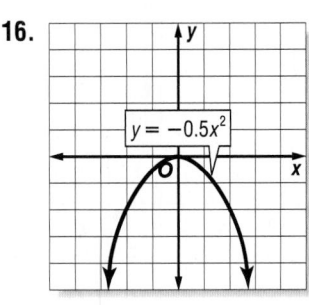

$y = -0.5x^2$

17.

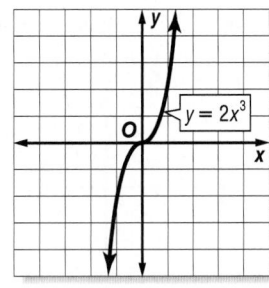

$y = 2x^3$

18.

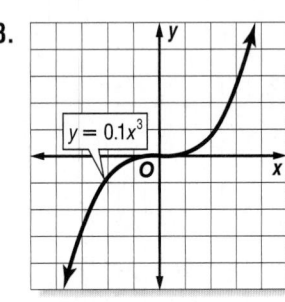

$y = 0.1x^3$

19.

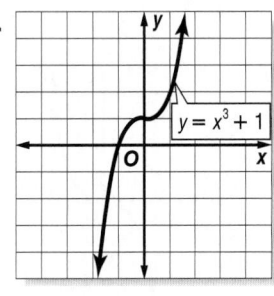

$y = x^3 + 1$

20.

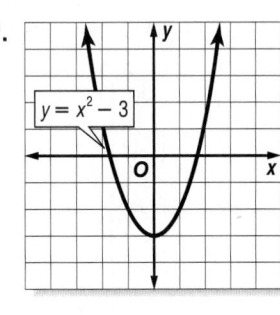

$y = x^2 - 3$

21.

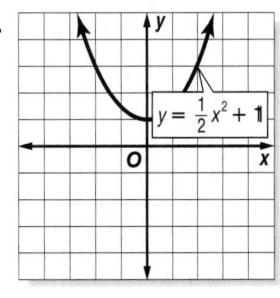

$y = \frac{1}{2}x^2 + 1$

22.

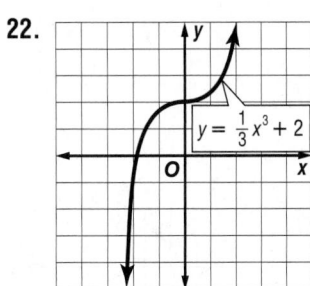

$y = \frac{1}{3}x^3 + 2$

27.

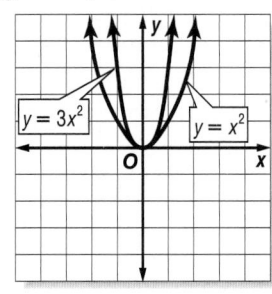

$y = 3x^2$ $y = x^2$

28.

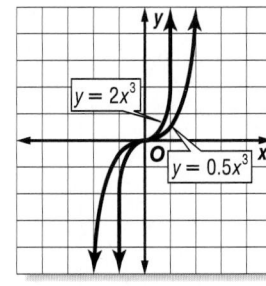

$y = 2x^3$ $y = 0.5x^3$

29.

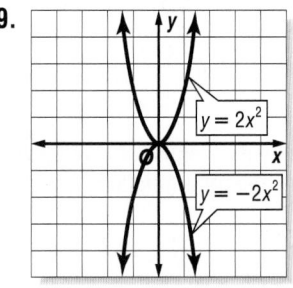

$y = 2x^2$ $y = -2x^2$

30.

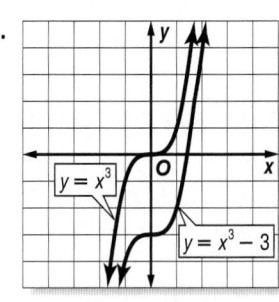

$y = x^3$ $y = x^3 - 3$

32.

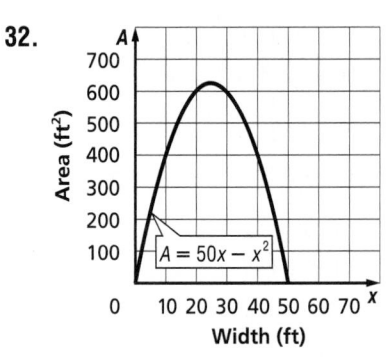

$A = 50x - x^2$

Area (ft²) vs. Width (ft)

34.

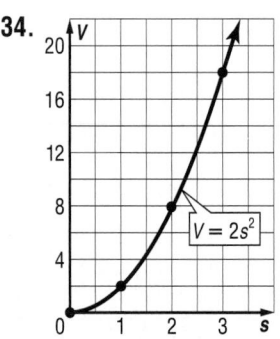

$V = 2s^2$

35.

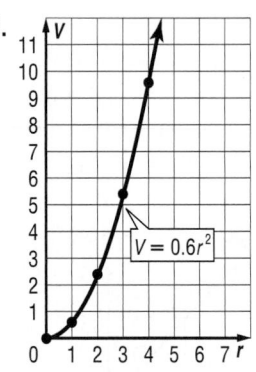

$V = 0.6r^2$

37. Formulas, tables, and graphs are interchangeable ways to represent functions. Answers should include the following.

- To make a graph, use a rule to make a table of values. Then plot the points and connect them to make a graph.

- To write a rule, find points that lie on a graph and make a table of values using the coordinates. Look for a pattern and write a rule that describes the pattern.

Page 697, Graphing Calculator Investigation

1.

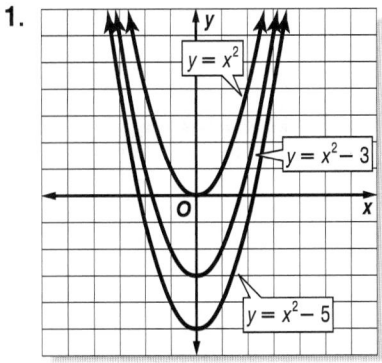

All the parabolas have the same shape. The graph of $y = x^2 - 5$ is shifted 5 units down from the graph of $y = x^2$. The graph of $y = x^2 - 3$ is shifted 3 units down from the graph of $y = x^2$.

4.

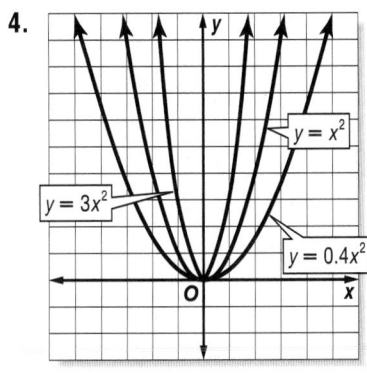

Page 701, Practice Test

21.

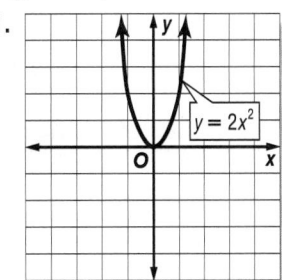

22.

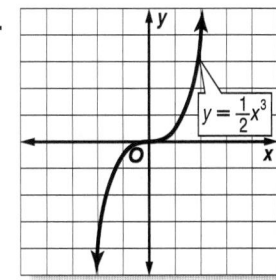

23.

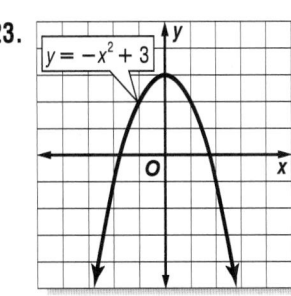

Student Handbook

Skills

Introduction to Matrices

A **matrix** is a rectangular arrangement of numerical data in **rows** (horizontal) and **columns** (vertical) enclosed with brackets that visually organizes the information. Each number in a matrix is called an **element**. *Matrices* are identified by their **dimensions**, or the number of rows and columns, with the number of rows stated first. To display a data set in matrix form, sort the data into categories and assign those categories appropriate labels.

Example Sue and Eva made a table of their science quiz grades during the grading period. Create a matrix organizing this information. Then state the dimensions of the matrix.

Sue	B	C	A	B	A	B	A	C	B	A	B	C
Eva	A	B	B	A	A	C	B	B	A	A	B	

Sue received 4 A's, 5 B's, and 3 C's.
Eva received 5 A's, 6 B's, and 1 C.
Label the rows of the matrix with each girl's name and the columns with each letter grade. The dimensions of the resulting matrix are 2 by 3.

This matrix has 3 columns.

This matrix has 2 rows.

$$\begin{array}{c} \\ \text{Sue} \\ \text{Eva} \end{array} \begin{array}{ccc} A & B & C \\ \left[\begin{array}{ccc} 4 & 5 & 3 \\ 5 & 6 & ① \end{array}\right] \end{array}$$

This element is in the second row and the third column.

State the dimensions of each matrix. Then identify the position of the circled element.

1. $\begin{bmatrix} 8 & 6 & 4 & ⑨-2 \\ -3 & 7 & 2 & 1 \end{bmatrix}$
2 by 4; first row, fourth column

2. $\begin{bmatrix} -6 & 2 \\ 0 & -3 \\ ⑤ & -8 \end{bmatrix}$
2. 3 by 2; third row, first column

3. $\begin{bmatrix} 14 & 10 & 11 \\ 9 & 7 & ⑮ \\ 16 & 4 & 10 \\ 21 & 17 & 13 \end{bmatrix}$
3. 4 by 3; second row, third column

4. $\begin{bmatrix} -5 & 8 & -1 & 4 & ② & 7 \end{bmatrix}$
1 by 6; first row, fifth column

Create a matrix organizing each set of data. 5–7. See margin.

5. Three clubs participated in a fund-raiser. Club 1 sold 114 plain and 57 chocolate doughnuts. Club B sold 75 plain and 89 chocolate doughnuts. Club C sold 50 plain and 35 chocolate doughnuts.

6. At the end of the 2003 NFL regular season, the Steelers had 275 first downs, 33 touchdowns, and 23 field goals. The Bears had 264 first downs, 29 touchdowns, and 26 field goals. The Ravens had 258 first downs, 41 touchdowns, and 34 field goals. The Browns had 267 first downs, 27 touchdowns, and 23 field goals.

7. Three teammates either won (W), lost (L), or tied (T) each of 10 chess matches they played. The table indicates the results.

Hector	W	L	L	W	W	T	W	W	L	W
Tim	T	L	L	L	W	W	W	L	W	W
Malik	L	W	W	W	T	T	W	T	L	W

Sample Answers:

	Plain	Chocolate
5. Club A	114	57
Club B	75	89
Club C	50	35

	FD	TD	FG
6. Steelers	275	33	23
Bears	264	29	26
Ravens	258	41	31
Browns	267	27	23

	W	L	T
7. Hector	6	3	1
Tim	5	4	1
Malik	5	2	3

Prerequisite Skills

 Problem-Solving Strategy: Solve a Simpler Problem

One of the strategies you can use to solve a problem is to **solve a simpler problem**. To use this strategy, first solve a simpler or more familiar case of the problem. Then use the same concepts and relationships to solve the original problem.

Example 1 **Find the sum of the numbers 1 through 500.**

Consider a simpler problem. Find the sum of the numbers 1 through 10. Notice that you can group the addends into partial sums as shown below.

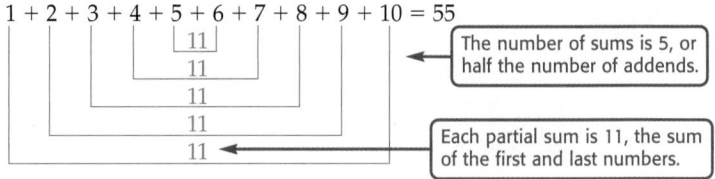

$1 + 2 + 3 + 4 + 5 + 6 + 7 + 8 + 9 + 10 = 55$

| 11 |
| 11 |
| 11 |
| 11 |
| 11 |

The number of sums is 5, or half the number of addends.

Each partial sum is 11, the sum of the first and last numbers.

The sum is 5×11 or 55.

Use the same concepts to find the sum of the numbers 1 through 500.

$1 + 2 + 3 + \ldots + 499 + 500 = 250 \times 501$
$= 125,250$

Multiply half the number of addends, 250, by the sum of the first and last numbers, 501.

A similar problem-solving strategy is to use subgoals.

Example 2 **Two workers can make two chairs in two days. How many chairs can 8 workers working at the same rate make in 20 days?**

First find how many chairs each worker can make in two days. Divide 2 chairs by 2 workers. ⟶ $2 \div 2 = 1$

So, each worker can make 1 chair in 2 days. To find how many chairs each worker can make in 20 days, divide 20 by 2. ⟶ $20 \div 2 = 1$

Now find how many chairs 8 workers can make by multiplying 8 by 10. ⟶ $8 \times 10 = 8$

So, 8 workers can make 80 chairs in 20 days.

Solve each problem by first solving a simpler problem.

1. Find the sum of the numbers 1 through 1000. **500,500**
2. Find the number of squares of any size in the game board shown at the right. **204 squares**
3. How many links are needed to join 30 pieces of chain into one long chain? **29 links**

Solve each problem by using subgoals.

4. Three people can pick six baskets of apples in one hour. How many baskets of apples can 12 people pick in one-half hour? **12 baskets**
5. A shirt shop has 112 orders for T-shirt designs. Three designers can make 12 shirts in 2 hours. How many designers are needed to complete the orders in 8 hours? **7 designers**

2 Problem-Solving Strategy: Work Backward

In most problems, a set of conditions or facts is given and an end result must be found. However, some problems start with the result and ask for something that happened earlier. The strategy of **working backward** can be used to solve problems like this. To use this strategy, start with the end result and *undo* each step.

Example Paco spent half of the money he had this morning on lunch. After lunch, he loaned his friend a dollar. Now he has $1.50. How much money did Paco start with?

Start with the end result, $1.50, and work backward to find the amount Paco started with.

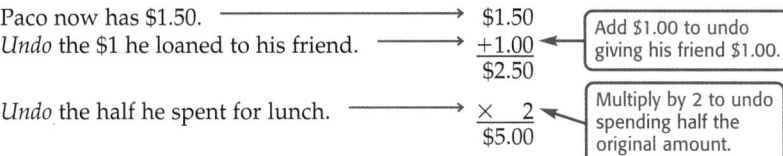

Paco now has $1.50. ————————→ $1.50
Undo the $1 he loaned to his friend. ———→ +1.00   ← Add $1.00 to undo giving his friend $1.00.
————
$2.50

Undo the half he spent for lunch. ———→ × 2   ← Multiply by 2 to undo spending half the original amount.
————
$5.00

The amount Paco started with was $5.00.

CHECK Paco started with $5.00. If he spent half of that, or $2.50, on lunch and loaned his friend $1.00, he would have $1.50 left. This matches the amount stated in the problem, so the solution is correct.

Solve each problem by working backward.

1. Katie used half of her allowance to buy a ticket to the class play. Then she spent $1.75 for an ice cream cone. Now she has $2.25 left. How much is her allowance? **$8**

2. Michele put $15 of her paycheck in savings. Then she spent one-half of what was left on clothes. She paid $24 for a concert ticket and later spent one-half of what was then left on a book. When she got home, she had $14 left. What was the amount of Michele's paycheck? **$119**

3. A certain number is multiplied by 3, and then 5 is added to the result. The final answer is 41. What is the number? **12**

4. Mr. and Mrs. Jackson each own an equal number of shares of a stock. Mr. Jackson sells one-third of his shares for $2700. What was the total value of Mr. and Mrs. Jackson's stock before the sale? **$16,200**

5. A certain bacteria doubles its population every 12 hours. After 3 full days, there are 1600 bacteria in a culture. How many bacteria were there at the beginning of the first day? **25 bacteria**

6. Masao had some pieces of bubble gum. He gave one-fourth of the gum to Bob. Bob then gave half of his gum to Lisa. Lisa gave a third of her gum to Maria. If Maria has 3 pieces of gum, how many pieces of gum did Masao have in the beginning? **72 pieces**

7. To catch a 7:30 A.M. bus, Carla needs 30 minutes to get dressed, 30 minutes for breakfast, and 15 minutes to walk to the bus stop. What time should she wake up? **6:15 A.M.**

8. Justin rented three times as many DVDs as Cole last month. Cole rented four fewer than Maria, but four more than Paloma. Maria rented 10 DVDs. How many DVDs did each person rent? **Justin, 18; Cole, 6; Maria, 10; Paloma, 2**

Problem-Solving Strategy: Make a Table or List

One strategy for solving problems is to **make a table**. A table allows you to organize information in an understandable way.

Example 1 A fruit machine accepts dollars, and each piece of fruit costs 65 cents. If the machine gives only nickels, dimes, and quarters, what combinations of those coins are possible as change for a dollar?

The machine will give back $1.00 − $0.65 or 35 cents in change in a combination of nickels, dimes, and quarters.

Make a table showing different combinations of nickels, dimes, and quarters that total 35 cents. Organize the table by starting with the combinations that include the most quarters.

The total for each combination of the coins is 35 cents. There are 6 combinations possible.

quarters	dimes	nickels
1	1	0
1	0	2
0	3	1
0	2	3
0	1	5
0	0	7

A similar strategy is to **list possibilities**. When you make a list, use an organized approach so you do not leave out important items.

Example 2 How many ways can you receive change for a quarter if at least one coin is a dime?

List the possibilities. Start with the ways that use the fewest number of coins.

1. dime, dime, nickel
2. dime, dime, 5 pennies
3. dime, nickel, nickel, nickel
4. dime, nickel, nickel, 5 pennies
5. dime, nickel, 10 pennies
6. dime, 15 pennies

There are 6 possibilities.

Solve each problem by making a table or list.

1. How many ways can you make change for a half-dollar using only nickels, dimes, and quarters? **10**
2. A number cube has faces numbered 1 to 6. If a red and a blue cube are tossed and the faces landing up are added, how many ways can you roll a sum less than 8? **21**
3. A penny, a nickel, a dime, and a quarter are in a purse. How many amounts of money are possible if you grab two coins at random? **6**
4. If the sides of a rectangular garden are whole numbers and the area of the garden is 48 square feet, how many combinations of side lengths are possible? **5**
5. Malcolm had 55 football cards. He traded 8 cards for 5 from Damon. He traded 6 more for 4 from Ines and 5 for 3 from Christopher. Finally, he traded 12 cards for 9 from Sam. How many cards does Malcolm have now? **45**

Problem-Solving Strategy: Guess and Check

To solve some problems, you can make a reasonable guess and then check it in the problem. You can then use the results to improve your guess until you find the solution. This strategy is called **guess and check**.

Example

The product of two consecutive even integers is 1088. What are the integers?

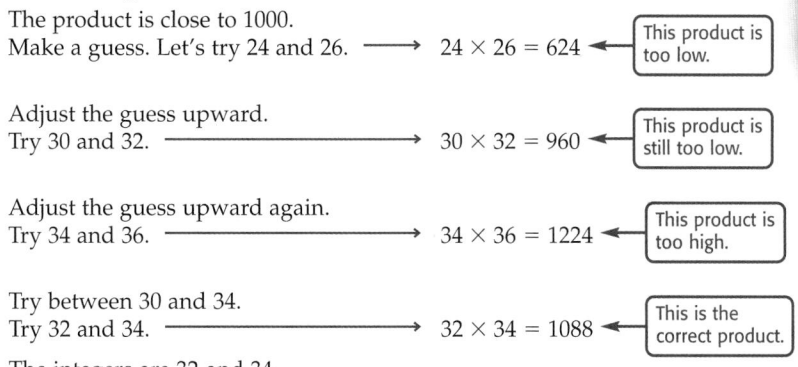

The product is close to 1000.
Make a guess. Let's try 24 and 26. ⟶ 24 × 26 = 624 ← This product is too low.

Adjust the guess upward.
Try 30 and 32. ⟶ 30 × 32 = 960 ← This product is still too low.

Adjust the guess upward again.
Try 34 and 36. ⟶ 34 × 36 = 1224 ← This product is too high.

Try between 30 and 34.
Try 32 and 34. ⟶ 32 × 34 = 1088 ← This is the correct product.

The integers are 32 and 34.

Use the guess-and-check strategy to solve each problem.

1. The product of two consecutive odd integers is 783. What are the integers? **27, 29**

2. Paula is three times as old as Courtney. Four years from now she will be just two times as old as Courtney. How old are Paula and Courtney now? **12 and 4**

3. The product of a number and its next two consecutive whole numbers is 120. What is the number? **4**

4. Stamps for postcards cost $0.21, and stamps for first-class letters cost $0.34. Diego wants to send postcards and letters to 10 friends. If he has $2.75 for stamps, how many postcards and how many letters can he send? **5 postcards, 5 letters**

5. Each hand in the human body has 27 bones. There are 6 more bones in the fingers than in the wrist. There are 3 fewer bones in the palm than in the wrist. How many bones are in each part of the hand? **f: 14, w: 8, p: 5**

6. The Science Club sold candy bars and soft pretzels to raise money for an animal shelter. They raised a total of $62.75. They made 25¢ profit on each candy bar and 30¢ profit on each pretzel sold. How many of each did they sell? **Sample answer: 125 candy bars and 105 pretzels**

7. Luis has the same number of quarters, dimes, and nickels. In all he has $4 in change. How many of each coin does he have? **10**

8. Kelsey sold tickets to the school musical. She had 12 bills worth $175 for the tickets she sold. If all the money was in $5 bills, $10 bills, and $20 bills, how many of each bill did she have? **Sample answer: 3 $5-bills, 2 $10-bills, and 7 $20-bills**

9. You can buy standard-sized postcards in packages of 5 and large-sized postcards in packages of 3. How many packages of each should you buy if you need exactly 16 postcards? **two 5-card packages and two 3-card packages**

⑤ Comparing and Ordering Decimals

To determine which of two decimals is greater, you can compare the digits in each place-value position, or you can use a number line.

Method 1 Use place value.

Line up the decimal points of the two numbers. Starting at the left, compare the digits in each place-value position. In the first position where the digits are different, the decimal with the greater digit is the greater decimal.

Method 2 Use a number line.

Graph each number on a number line. On a number line, numbers to the right are greater than numbers to the left.

Example 1 **Which is greater, 4.35 or 4.8?**

Method 1 Use place value.

4.35 Line up the decimal points.
4.8 The digits in the tenths place are not the same.

8 tenths > 3 tenths, so 4.8 > 4.35.

Method 2 Use a number line.

Compare the decimals on a number line.

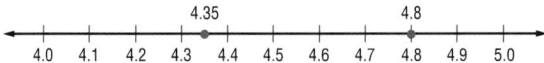

4.8 is to the right of 4.35. So 4.8 > 4.35.

Example 2 **Order 0.8, 1.52, and 1.01 from least to greatest.**

0.8 is less than both 1.52 and 1.01.
1.01 is less than 1.52.

Thus, the order from least to greatest is 0.8, 1.01, 1.52.

Replace each ● with < or > to make a true sentence.

1. 4.05 ● 4.45 $<$	**2.** 2.26 ● 2.28 $<$	**3.** 3.005 ● 3.05 $<$
4. 8.7 ● 82.1 $<$	**5.** 6.2 ● 6.008 $>$	**6.** 15.601 ● 16.9 $<$
7. 1.9 ● 1.96 $<$	**8.** 8.9 ● 7.99 $>$	**9.** 0.66 ● 0.582 $>$
10. 7.14 ● 7.2 $<$	**11.** 0.048 ● 0.11 $<$	**12.** 10.1 ● 1.01 $>$
13. 32.1 ● 3.215 $>$	**14.** 1.098 ● 2 $<$	**15.** 9.1 ● 9.005 $>$
16. 16.8 ● 16.791 $>$	**17.** 0.943 ● 0.4991 $>$	**18.** 0.117 ● 0.95 $<$

Order each set of decimals from least to greatest.

19. {0.2, 0.01, 0.6} **0.01, 0.2, 0.6**

20. {1.2, 2.4, 0.04, 2.2} **0.04, 1.2, 2.2, 2.4**

21. {3.5, 0.6, 2.06, 0.28} **0.28, 0.6, 2.06, 3.5**

22. {0.8, 0.07, 1.001, 0.392} **0.07, 0.392, 0.8**

23. {7.06, 7.026, 7.061, 7.009, 7.1}
7.009, 7.026, 7.06, 7.061, 7.1

24. {0.82, 0.98, 0.103, 0.625, 0.809}
0.103, 0.625, 0.809, 0.82, 0.98

6 Rounding Decimals

Rewriting a number to a certain place value is called **rounding**. Look at the digit to the right of the place being rounded.

- If the digit to the right is *less than or equal to* 4, the digit being rounded stays the same.

- If the digit to the right is *greater than or equal to* 5, the digit being rounded increases by one.

The place-value chart below shows how to round 3.81 to the nearest one (or whole number).

Tens	Ones	Tenths	Hundredths	Thousandths
	3 .	8	1	

- 3 is in the ones place

- 8 is to the right of 3

- 8 > 5

So, 3.81 rounded to the nearest one (or whole number) is 4.

Example 1 Round each number to the nearest one (or whole number).

a. **8.3**
8.3 rounds to 8.

b. **9.6**
9.6 rounds to 10.

Example 2 Round each number to the nearest tenth.

a. **16.08**
16.08 rounds to 16.1.

b. **29.54**
29.54 rounds to 29.5.

Example 3 Round each number to the nearest hundredth.

a. **50.345**
50.345 rounds to 50.35.

b. **19.998**
19.998 rounds to 20.00.

Round each number to the nearest whole number.

1. 3.2 3
2. 64.8 65
3. 50.57 51
4. 16.08 16
5. 41.29 41
6. 38.726 39
7. 74.455 74
8. 86.299 86
9. 79.603 80

Round each number to the nearest tenth.

10. 16.57 16.6
11. 1.05 1.1
12. 43.827 43.8
13. 53.865 53.9
14. 80.349 80.3
15. 24.731 24.7
16. 49.5463 49.5
17. 131.9884 132.0
18. 68.3553 68.4

Round each number to the nearest hundredth.

19. 62.624 62.62
20. 44.138 44.14
21. 85.5639 85.56
22. 105.3582 105.36
23. 99.9862 99.99
24. 24.8715 24.87
25. 458.7625 458.76
26. 206.6244 206.62
27. 153.2965 153.30

Round each number to the nearest dollar.

28. $40.29 $40
29. $72.50 $73
30. $36.82 $37

7 Estimating Sums and Differences of Decimals

Estimation is often used to provide a quick and easy answer when an exact answer is not necessary. It is also an excellent way to quickly see if your answer is reasonable or not.

Example 1 Estimate each sum or difference to the nearest whole number.

a. 16.9 + 5.4

$$
\begin{array}{r}
16.9 \\
+ \ 5.4
\end{array}
\quad \rightarrow \quad
\begin{array}{r}
17 \\
+ \ 5 \\
\hline
22
\end{array}
$$

> Round to the nearest whole number.

b. 200.35 − 174.82

$$
\begin{array}{r}
200.35 \\
-174.82
\end{array}
\quad \rightarrow \quad
\begin{array}{r}
200 \\
-175 \\
\hline
25
\end{array}
$$

> Round to the nearest whole number.

You can also use rounding to estimate answers involving money.

Example 2 Estimate each sum or difference to the nearest dollar.

a. $67.07 + $52.64 + $0.85

$$
\begin{array}{r}
\$67.07 \\
52.64 \\
+ \ 0.85
\end{array}
\quad \rightarrow \quad
\begin{array}{r}
\$67.00 \\
53.00 \\
+ \ 1.00 \\
\hline
\$121.00
\end{array}
$$

> Round to the nearest dollar.

b. $89.42 − $8.94

$$
\begin{array}{r}
\$89.42 \\
- \ 8.94
\end{array}
\quad \rightarrow \quad
\begin{array}{r}
\$89.00 \\
- \ 9.00 \\
\hline
\$80.00
\end{array}
$$

> Round to the nearest dollar.

Estimate each sum or difference to the nearest whole number.

1. 12.5 + 44.8 **58**
2. 8.6 + 11.9 **21**
3. 34.32 + 19.51 **54**
4. 15.9 + 20.32 **36**
5. 32 − 29.75 **2**
6. 125.8 − 22.4 **104**
7. 159.7 − 124.8 **35**
8. 8.890 + 15.98 **25**
9. 0.7 + 1.663 **3**
10. 52.4 − 21.01 **31**
11. 26.55 − 10 **17**
12. 2.79 + 5.9 + 0.02 **9**
13. 42.1 + 16.25 + 8.96 **67**
14. 209.5 − 110 **100**
15. 18 − 12.49 **6**

Estimate each sum or difference to the nearest dollar.

16. $6.89 + $1.20 **$8**
17. $5.72 + $4.35 **$10**
18. $1.68 − $0.99 **$1**
19. $5.00 − $2.56 **$2**
20. $20.00 − $15.34 **$5**
21. $12.86 + $3.33 **$16**
22. $4.99 + $3.29 **$8**
23. $50.00 − $39.89 **$10**
24. $92.30 − $40.00 **$52**
25. $16.39 − $11.80 **$4**
26. $84.99 + $5.52 **$91**
27. $132.62 − $45.81 **$87**
28. $20.19 + $3.60 + $5.08 **$29**
29. $4.80 + $7.65 + $2.59 **$16**
30. $325.44 + $125.10 **$450**

31. Annual precipitation in Seattle, Washington, is about 37.19 inches. The city of Spokane receives only about 16.49 inches annually. About how much more precipitation does Seattle receive than Spokane? **about 21 in.**

32. The Adventure Club holds monthly aluminum can recycling drives. During the last three months, they collected $45.45, $45.19, and $44.95 from the drives. About how much did the club collect altogether? **about $135**

8 Adding and Subtracting Decimals

To add or subtract decimals, write the numbers in a column and line up the decimal points. Then add or subtract as with whole numbers, and bring down the decimal point.

Example 1 Find each sum or difference.

a. $8.2 + 3.4$

$$
\begin{array}{r}
8.2 \\
+\ 3.4 \\
\hline
11.6
\end{array}
$$
Line up the decimal points. Then add.

b. $36.98 - 15.22$

$$
\begin{array}{r}
36.98 \\
-\ 15.22 \\
\hline
21.76
\end{array}
$$
Line up the decimal points. Then subtract.

In some cases, you may want to *annex*, or place zeros at the end of the decimals, to help align the columns. Then add or subtract.

Example 2 Find each sum or difference.

a. $21.43 + 5.2$

$$
\begin{array}{r}
21.43 \\
+\ 5.2 \\
\hline
\end{array}
\quad \rightarrow \quad
\begin{array}{r}
21.43 \\
+\ 5.20 \\
\hline
26.63
\end{array}
$$
Annex a zero to align the columns.

b. $7 - 1.75$

$$
\begin{array}{r}
7 \\
-\ 1.75 \\
\hline
\end{array}
\quad \rightarrow \quad
\begin{array}{r}
^{6\ 91} \\
7.00 \\
-\ 1.75 \\
\hline
5.25
\end{array}
$$
Annex two zeros to align the columns.

Find each sum or difference.

1. $\begin{array}{r} 42.3 \\ +\ 0.81 \end{array}$ **43.11**

2. $\begin{array}{r} 5.86 \\ -\ 1.51 \end{array}$ **4.35**

3. $\begin{array}{r} 13 \\ -\ 0.324 \end{array}$ **12.676**

4. $2.3 + 1.1$ **3.4**
5. $11.5 + 4.2$ **15.7**
6. $9.5 - 8.3$ **1.2**
7. $24.8 - 3.6$ **21.2**
8. $3.57 - 2.17$ **1.40**
9. $7.43 - 5.34$ **2.09**
10. $6.40 + 7.36$ **13.76**
11. $15.20 + 0.16$ **15.36**
12. $7.97 - 4.29$ **3.68**
13. $8.70 + 0.64$ **9.34**
14. $56.88 - 12.35$ **44.53**
15. $4.192 + 1.255$ **5.447**
16. $14.6 + 20.81$ **35.41**
17. $5.2 - 3.01$ **2.19**
18. $1.9 - 1.65$ **0.25**
19. $6.38 - 1.1$ **5.28**
20. $4.86 - 0.3$ **4.56**
21. $9.43 + 1.8$ **11.23**
22. $70.3 + 7.03$ **77.33**
23. $0.5 + 1.674$ **2.174**
24. $25 - 8.3$ **16.7**
25. $18 - 12.31$ **5.69**
26. $2.85 + 23.6$ **26.45**
27. $0.8 + 9.612$ **10.412**
28. $6.8 + 5.09 + 0.03$ **11.92**
29. $0.5 + 2.41 + 6.7$ **9.61**
30. $0.563 + 5.8 + 6.89$ **13.253**
31. $41.30 + 0.28 + 6.15$ **47.73**
32. $4.52 + 0.167 + 12.9$ **17.587**
33. $23.4 + 9.865 + 18.26$ **51.525**

34. Find the sum of 27.38 and 6.8. **34.18**

35. Add \$26.59, \$1.80, and \$13. **\$41.39**

36. Find the difference of 42.05 and 11.621. **30.429**

37. How much more than \$102.90 is \$115? **\$12.10**

38. Karen plans to buy a softball for \$6.50, a softball glove for \$37.99, and sliders for \$13.79. Find the cost of these items before tax is added. **\$58.28**

9 Estimating Products and Quotients of Decimals

You can use rounding to estimate products and quotients of decimals.

Example 1 Estimate each product or quotient to the nearest whole number.

a. **3.8 × 2.1**

$3.8 \times 2.1 \rightarrow 4 \times 2 = 8$ Round 3.8 to 4 and round 2.1 to 2.

3.8 × 2.1 is about 8.

b. **16.45 ÷ 3.92**

$16.45 \div 3.92 \rightarrow 16 \div 4 = 4$ Round 16.45 to 16 and round 3.92 to 4.

16.45 ÷ 3.92 is about 4.

You can use mental math and compatible numbers to estimate products and quotients of decimals. **Compatible numbers** are rounded so it is easy to compute with them mentally.

Example 2 Estimate each product or quotient to the nearest whole number.

a. **7 × 98.24**

$7 \times 98.24 \rightarrow 7 \times 100 = 700$ Even though 98.24 rounds to 98, 100 is a compatible number because it is easy to mentally compute 7 × 100.

7 × 98.24 is about 700.

b. **47.5 ÷ 5.23**

$47.5 \div 5.23 \rightarrow 48 \div 6 = 8$ Even though 5.23 rounds to 5, 6 is a compatible number because 48 is divisible by 6.

47.5 ÷ 5.23 is about 8.

Rewrite each expression using rounding and compatible numbers. Then estimate each product or quotient. 1–12. Sample answers are given.

1. 9.2 × 4.89 9 × 5 = 45
2. 6.75 × 5.25 7 × 5 = 35
3. 12.19 ÷ 3.8 12 ÷ 4 = 3
4. 39.79 ÷ 4.61 40 ÷ 5 = 8
5. 11.2 × 6.25 11 × 6 = 66
6. 15.2 ÷ 2.7 15 ÷ 3 = 5
7. 47.2 ÷ 5.1 45 ÷ 5 = 9
8. 16.53 ÷ 8.36 16 ÷ 8 = 2
9. 4.32(107.6) 4 × 100 =
10. 26 × 10.9 26 × 10 = 260
11. 73.2 ÷ 6.99 70 ÷ 7 = 10
12. 19.1(21.60) 20 × 20 =

Estimate each product or quotient. 13–34. Sample answers are given.

13. 4.6 × 8.3 5 × 8 = 40
14. 5.12 × 5.9 5 × 6 = 30
15. 7.5 ÷ 4.2 8 ÷ 4 = 2
16. 9.27 ÷ 3.31 9 ÷ 3 = 3
17. 19.8(2.6) 20 × 3 = 60
18. 41.75 ÷ 6 42 ÷ 6 = 7
19. 36.24 ÷ 8.7 36 ÷ 9 = 4
20. 5.85 × 7.55 6 × 8 = 48
21. 8.1 ÷ 2.2 8 ÷ 2 = 4
22. 7.9(9.12) 8 × 9 = 72
23. 6.1 ÷ 2.1 6 ÷ 2 = 3
24. 9 × 96.42 9 × 100 = 900
25. 13 × 9.1 13 × 10 = 130
26. 10.1 ÷ 4.7 10 ÷ 5 = 2
27. 28.6(5) 30 × 5 = 150
28. 21 ÷ 7.6 21 ÷ 7 = 3
29. 81 ÷ 10.5 80 ÷ 10 = 8
30. 52.7 ÷ 5.3 50 ÷ 5 = 10
31. 47.74 × 2 50 × 2 = 100
32. 204.5 × 3 200 × 3 = 600
33. 41.79 ÷ 7.23 42 ÷ 7 =

34. The speed of the spine-tailed swift has been measured at 106.25 miles per hour. At that rate, about how far can it travel in 1.8 hours? **about 200 miles**

10 Multiplying and Dividing Decimals

To multiply decimals, multiply as with whole numbers. Then add the total number of decimal places in the factors. Place the same number of decimal places in the product, counting from right to left.

Example 1 Find each product.

a. 6.3(2.1)

$$
\begin{array}{r}
6.3 \quad \leftarrow \text{1 decimal place} \\
\times\ 2.1 \quad \leftarrow \text{1 decimal place} \\
\hline
63 \\
12\ 6 \\
\hline
13.23 \quad \leftarrow \text{2 decimal places}
\end{array}
$$

The product is 13.23.

b. 9.47(0.5)

$$
\begin{array}{r}
9.47 \quad \leftarrow \text{2 decimal places} \\
\times\ 0.5 \quad \leftarrow \text{1 decimal place} \\
\hline
4.735 \quad \leftarrow \text{3 decimal places}
\end{array}
$$

The product is 4.735.

To divide decimals, move the decimal point in the divisor to the right, and then move the decimal point in the dividend the same number of places. Align the decimal point in the quotient with the decimal point in the dividend.

Example 2 Find each quotient.

a. 1.20 ÷ 0.8

$$
\begin{array}{r}
1.5 \\
0.8\overline{)1.2\,0} \\
\underline{8} \\
4\,0 \\
\underline{4\,0} \\
0
\end{array}
$$

Move each decimal point right 1 place.

The quotient is 1.5.

b. 32 ÷ 0.25

$$
\begin{array}{r}
128 \\
0.25\overline{)32.00} \\
\underline{25} \\
70 \\
\underline{50} \\
200 \\
\underline{200} \\
0
\end{array}
$$

Move each decimal point right 2 places.

The quotient is 128.

Find each product or quotient.

1. 1.2(3) **3.6**
2. 8(3.4) **27.2**
3. 0.2 × 7.2 **1.44**
4. 1.4(6.1) **8.54**
5. 0.63 ÷ 0.9 **0.7**
6. 8.4 ÷ 0.4 **21**
7. 0.06 × 3 **0.18**
8. 42 ÷ 0.8 **52.5**
9. 3.9(8.2) **31.98**
10. 0.2(3.1) **0.62**
11. 27 ÷ 0.3 **90**
12. 64 ÷ 0.4 **160**
13. 0.4 ÷ 2 **0.2**
14. 14.4 ÷ 0.16 **90**
15. 15.6 × 38 **592.8**
16. 0.51 ÷ 0.03 **17**
17. 5.7(3.8) **21.66**
18. 7.07(4) **28.28**
19. 1.25 × 12 **15**
20. 62.9 ÷ 100 **0.629**
21. 6.5(0.13) **0.845**
22. 14.9(0.56) **8.344**
23. 0.384 ÷ 1.2 **0.32**
24. 4.2 ÷ 1.05 **4**
25. 25.9 ÷ 2.8 **9.25**
26. 0.47 × 3.01 **1.4147**
27. 1.01(6.2) **6.262**
28. 9 ÷ 0.375 **24**
29. 50 ÷ 0.25 **200**
30. 500 ÷ 3.2 **156.25**
31. 0.001(7.09) **0.00709**
32. 6.32 × 0.81 **5.1192**
33. 2.92 ÷ 0.002 **1460**

34. Find the product of 13.6 and 9.15. **124.44**

35. What is the quotient of 72.05 and 0.11? **655**

36. If one United States dollar can be exchanged for 128.46 Spanish pesetas, how many pesetas would you receive for $50? **6423 pesetas**

11 Estimating Sums and Differences of Fractions and Mixed Numbers

You can use rounding to estimate sums and differences of fractions and mixed numbers. To estimate the sum or difference of proper fractions, round each fraction to 0, $\frac{1}{2}$, or 1.

Example 1 Estimate each sum or difference.

a. $\frac{5}{8} + \frac{9}{10}$

$$\frac{5}{8} + \frac{9}{10} \rightarrow \frac{1}{2} + 1 = 1\frac{1}{2}$$

The sum of $\frac{5}{8}$ and $\frac{9}{10}$ is about $1\frac{1}{2}$.

b. $\frac{5}{6} - \frac{3}{8}$

$$\frac{5}{6} - \frac{3}{8} \rightarrow 1 - \frac{1}{2} = \frac{1}{2}$$

$\frac{5}{6} - \frac{3}{8}$ is about $\frac{1}{2}$.

To estimate the sum or difference of mixed numbers, round each mixed number to the nearest whole number or to the nearest $\frac{1}{2}$.

Example 2 Estimate each sum or difference.

a. $3\frac{3}{8} + 15\frac{15}{16}$

$$3\frac{3}{8} + 15\frac{15}{16} \rightarrow 3\frac{1}{2} + 16 = 19\frac{1}{2}$$

The sum of $3\frac{3}{8}$ and $15\frac{15}{16}$ is about $19\frac{1}{2}$.

b. $10\frac{3}{4} - 4\frac{1}{6}$

$$10\frac{3}{4} - 4\frac{1}{6} \rightarrow 11 - 4 = 7$$

$10\frac{3}{4} - 4\frac{1}{6}$ is about 7.

Round each fraction to 0, $\frac{1}{2}$, or 1.

1. $\frac{9}{10}$ **1**

2. $\frac{1}{8}$ **0**

3. $\frac{13}{25}$ **$\frac{1}{2}$**

4. $\frac{3}{14}$ **0**

5. $\frac{9}{15}$ **$\frac{1}{2}$**

6. $\frac{78}{81}$ **1**

Estimate each sum or difference. 7–29. Sample answers given.

7. $\frac{8}{9} + \frac{1}{4}$ **$1 + 0 = 1$**

8. $\frac{14}{15} + \frac{5}{6}$ **$1 + 1 = 2$**

9. $\frac{47}{90} + \frac{3}{24}$ **$\frac{1}{2} + 0 = \frac{1}{2}$**

10. $\frac{11}{12} + \frac{4}{9}$ **$1 + \frac{1}{2} = 1\frac{1}{2}$**

11. $\frac{15}{16} + 9\frac{3}{4}$ **$1 + 10 = 11$**

12. $1\frac{5}{12} + \frac{7}{18}$ **$1\frac{1}{2} + \frac{1}{2} = 2$**

13. $5\frac{10}{11} + \frac{3}{5}$ **$6 + \frac{1}{2} = 6\frac{1}{2}$**

14. $21\frac{8}{9} + 6\frac{4}{25}$ **$22 + 6 = 28$**

15. $32\frac{3}{56} + 18\frac{2}{75}$ **$32 + 18 = $**

16. $\frac{4}{5} - \frac{1}{10}$ **$1 - 0 = 1$**

17. $\frac{7}{9} - \frac{13}{18}$ **$1 - 1 = 0$**

18. $\frac{9}{10} - \frac{3}{8}$ **$1 - \frac{1}{2} = \frac{1}{2}$**

19. $5\frac{1}{5} - 2\frac{3}{4}$ **$5 - 3 = 2$**

20. $8\frac{3}{5} - 2\frac{1}{8}$ **$8\frac{1}{2} - 2 = 6\frac{1}{2}$**

21. $16\frac{34}{35} - 3\frac{1}{6}$ **$17 - 3 = 14$**

22. $35\frac{7}{8} - 4\frac{1}{2}$ **$36 - 4\frac{1}{2} = 31\frac{1}{2}$**

23. $15\frac{4}{9} + 13\frac{9}{11}$ **$15\frac{1}{2} + 14 = 29\frac{1}{2}$**

24. $140\frac{4}{5} - 120\frac{2}{15}$ **$141 - 12$**

25. About how much longer than $\frac{5}{6}$ minute is $4\frac{1}{2}$ minutes? **$4\frac{1}{2}$ min $- 1$ min $= 3\frac{1}{2}$ min**

26. Estimate the sum $3\frac{3}{10} + 2\frac{4}{5} + 3\frac{1}{3}$. **$3 + 3 + 3 = 9$**

27. About how much more is $19\frac{3}{4}$ inches than $10\frac{7}{8}$ inches? **20 in. $- 11$ in. $= 9$ in.**

28. Estimate the sum of $7\frac{1}{3}$, $6\frac{4}{5}$, $6\frac{3}{4}$, $7\frac{1}{10}$, and $6\frac{15}{16}$. **$7 + 7 + 7 + 7 + 7 = 35$**

29. A board that is $63\frac{5}{8}$ inches long is about how much longer than a board that is $62\frac{1}{4}$ inches long? **$63\frac{1}{2}$ in. $- 62$ in. $= 1\frac{1}{2}$ in.**

2 Estimating Products and Quotients of Fractions and Mixed Numbers

You can estimate products and quotients of fractions and mixed numbers using rounding and compatible numbers. Compatible numbers are rounded to make it easy to compute with them mentally.

Example Estimate each product or quotient.

a. $\frac{5}{16} \times 30$

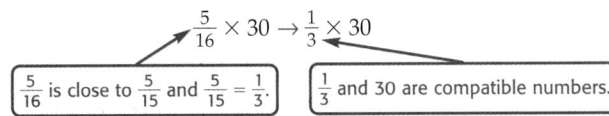

$$\frac{5}{16} \times 30 \rightarrow \frac{1}{3} \times 30$$

$\frac{5}{16}$ is close to $\frac{5}{15}$ and $\frac{5}{15} = \frac{1}{3}$. $\frac{1}{3}$ and 30 are compatible numbers.

Think: $\frac{1}{3} \times 30 = 10$

$\frac{5}{16} \times 30$ is about 10.

b. $9\frac{7}{8} \div 5$

$9\frac{7}{8} \div 5 \rightarrow 10 \div 5 = 2$ Round $9\frac{7}{8}$ to 10. 10 and 5 are compatible numbers.

$9\frac{7}{8} \div 5$ is about 2.

Estimate each product or quotient. 1–24. Sample answers given.

1. $\frac{1}{4} \cdot 11$ $\frac{1}{4} \cdot 12 = 3$

2. $\frac{1}{3}(20)$ $\frac{1}{3}(21) = 7$

3. $\frac{1}{3} \times 14$ $\frac{1}{3} \times 15 = 5$

4. $\frac{1}{4}(15)$ $\frac{1}{4}(16) = 4$

5. $\frac{7}{15} \times 120$ $\frac{1}{2} \times 120 = 60$

6. $\frac{11}{20}(62)$ $\frac{1}{2}(60) = 30$

7. $\frac{31}{40} \cdot 100$ $\frac{3}{4} \cdot 100 = 75$

8. $\frac{6}{13} \times 150$ $\frac{1}{2} \times 150 = 75$

9. $\frac{1}{5}(44)$ $\frac{1}{5}(45) = 9$

10. $1\frac{5}{6} \cdot 30$ $2 \cdot 30 = 60$

11. $2\frac{1}{4} \cdot 22$ $2 \times 22 = 44$

12. $4\frac{4}{5} \times 24$ $5 \times 25 = 125$

13. $5\frac{7}{8} \div 2$ $6 \div 2 = 3$

14. $8\frac{1}{4} \div 4$ $8 \div 4 = 2$

15. $14\frac{6}{7} \div 3$ $15 \div 3 = 5$

16. $50 \div 4\frac{7}{8}$ $50 \div 5 = 10$

17. $61 \div 2\frac{4}{5}$ $60 \div 3 = 20$

18. $148 \div 3\frac{1}{4}$ $150 \div 3 = 50$

19. $79 \div 1\frac{9}{10}$ $80 \div 2 = 40$

20. $75 \div 2\frac{11}{16}$ $75 \div 3 = 25$

21. $88 \div 2\frac{1}{8}$ $88 \div 2 = 44$

22. Kim needs $3\frac{1}{2}$ batches of cookies. If one recipe calls for $2\frac{1}{4}$ cups of flour, about how many cups of flour are needed? $4 \times 2 = 8$ cups

23. Mario wants to place photographs of people in one vertical row on a poster board that is $17\frac{1}{2}$ inches long. If each photograph is $2\frac{3}{4}$ inches long, about how many photographs can Mario place on the poster board? $18 \div 3 = 6$ photographs

24. A basketball hoop has a diameter of $18\frac{1}{2}$ inches. Estimate the circumference of the hoop. (*Hint:* To estimate the circumference of a circle, multiply the diameter by 3.) $18 \times 3 = 54$ in.

13 Converting Measurements within the Metric System

All units of length in the metric system are defined in terms of the meter (m). The diagram below shows the relationships between some common metric units.

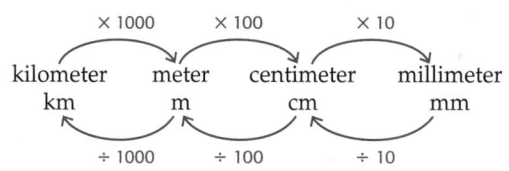

Comparing Metric and Customary Units of Length

1 mm ≈ 0.04 inch (height of a comma)
1 cm ≈ 0.4 inch (half the width of a penny)
1 m ≈ 1.1 yards (width of a doorway)
1 km ≈ 0.6 mile (length of a city block)

- To convert from larger units to smaller units, multiply.
- To convert from smaller units to larger units, divide.

There will be a greater number of smaller units than larger units.

Converting From Larger Units to Smaller Units	Converting From Smaller Units to Larger Units
1 km = 1 × 1000 = 1000 m	1 mm = 1 ÷ 10 = 0.1 cm
1 m = 1 × 100 = 100 cm	1 cm = 1 ÷ 100 = 0.01 m
1 cm = 1 × 10 = 10 mm	1 m = 1 ÷ 1000 = 0.001 km

There will be fewer larger units than smaller units.

Example 1 Complete each sentence.

a. 3 km = __?__ m

$3 \times 1000 = 3000$
$3 \text{ km} = 3000 \text{ m}$

To convert from kilometers to meters, multiply by 1000.

b. 9.75 cm = __?__ mm

$9.75 \times 10 = 97.5$
$9.75 \text{ cm} = 97.5 \text{ mm}$

To convert from centimeters to millimeters, multiply by 10.

c. 42 mm = __?__ cm

$42 \div 10 = 4.2$
$42 \text{ mm} = 4.2 \text{ cm}$

To convert from millimeters to centimeters, divide by 10.

The basic unit of capacity in the metric system is the liter (L). A liter and milliliter (mL) are related in a manner similar to meter and millimeter.

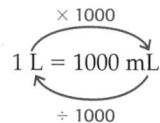

$1 \text{ L} = 1000 \text{ mL}$

Comparing Metric and Customary Units of Capacity

1 mL ≈ 0.03 ounce (drop of water)
1 L ≈ 1 quart (bottle of ketchup)

Example 2 Complete each sentence.

a. 2.5 L = __?__ mL

$2.5 \times 1000 = 2500$
$2.5 \text{ L} = 2500 \text{ mL}$

To convert from larger units to smaller units, multiply.

b. 860 mL = __?__ L

$860 \div 1000 = 0.86$
$860 \text{ mL} = 0.86 \text{ L}$

To convert from smaller units to larger units, divide.

The *mass* of an object is the amount of matter that it contains. The basic unit of mass in the metric system is the kilogram (kg). Kilogram, gram (g), and milligram (mg) are related in a manner similar to kilometer, meter, and millimeter.

Comparing Metric and Customary Units of Mass
1 g ≈ 0.04 ounce (one raisin)
1 kg ≈ 2.2 pounds (textbook)

$$1 \text{ kg} = 1000 \text{ g} \qquad 1 \text{ g} = 1000 \text{ mg}$$

Example 3 Complete each sentence.

a. 3400 mg = __?__ g

$3400 \div 1000 = 3.4$ To convert from smaller units
$3400 \text{ mg} = 3.4 \text{ g}$ to larger units, divide.

b. 74.2 kg = __?__ g

$74.2 \times 1000 = 74{,}200$ To convert from larger units
$74.2 \text{ kg} = 74{,}200 \text{ g}$ to smaller units, multiply.

State which metric unit you would probably use to measure each item. 4. milliliter

1. amount of water in a pitcher **liter**
2. distance between two cities **kilometer**
3. thickness of a coin **millimeter**
4. amount of water in a medicine dropper
5. length of a textbook **centimeter**
6. mass of a pencil **gram**
7. length of a football field **meter**
8. width of a quarter **centimeter**
9. thickness of a pencil **millimeter**
10. gas in the tank of a car **liter**
11. vanilla used in a cookie recipe **milliliter**
12. mass of a table tennis ball **milligram**
13. bag of sugar **kilogram**
14. mass of a horse **kilogram**

Complete each sentence.

15. 5 km = __?__ m **5000**
16. 3.5 cm = __?__ mm **35**
17. 6 L = __?__ mL **6000**
18. 370 mL = __?__ L **0.37**
19. 20 mm = __?__ cm **2**
20. 4000 g = __?__ kg **4**
21. 18 cm = __?__ mm **180**
22. 0.75 L = __?__ mL **750**
23. 935 cm = __?__ m **9.35**
24. 210 mm = __?__ cm **21**
25. 65 g = __?__ kg **0.065**
26. 2 m = __?__ cm **200**
27. 52.9 kg = __?__ g **52,900**
28. 800 m = __?__ km **0.8**
29. 9.05 kg = __?__ g **9050**
30. 0.62 km = __?__ m **620**
31. 1250 mL = __?__ L **1.25**
32. 20,000 mg = __?__ g **20**
33. 3100 m = __?__ km **3.1**
34. 2.6 m = __?__ cm **260**
35. 36 mg = __?__ g **0.036**
36. 7 mm = __?__ cm **0.7**
37. 0.085 L = __?__ mL **85**
38. 125.9 g = __?__ kg **0.1259**

39. The mass of a sample of rocks is 1.56 kilograms. How many grams are in 1.56 kilograms? **1560 g**

40. How many milliliters are in 0.09 liter? **90 mL**

41. Runners often participate in races that are 10 kilometers long. How many meters are in 10 kilometers? **10,000 m**

42. How many centimeters are in 0.58 meter? **58 cm**

43. A can holds 355 milliliters of soft drink. How many liters is this? **0.355 L**

The units of length in the customary system are inch, foot, yard, and mile. The table at the right shows the relationships among these units.

Customary Units of Length
1 foot (ft) = 12 inches (in.)
1 yard (yd) = 3 feet
1 mile (mi) = 5280 feet

- To convert from larger units to smaller units, multiply.

- To convert from smaller units to larger units, divide.

Larger Units		Smaller Units
5 ft $= 5 \times 12$		$= 60$ in.
4 yd $= 4 \times 3$		$= 12$ ft

There will be a greater number of smaller units than larger units.

Smaller Units		Larger Units
24 in. $= 24 \div 12$	$= 2$ ft
15 ft $= 15 \div 3$	$= 5$ yd

There will be fewer larger units than smaller units.

Example 1 Complete each sentence.

a. **6 yd = _?_ ft**

$6 \times 3 = 18$ To convert from yards to feet,
6 yd $= 18$ ft   multiply by 3.

b. **1.5 mi = _?_ ft**

$1.5 \times 5280 = 7920$ To convert from miles to feet,
1.5 mi $= 7920$ ft   multiply by 5280.

c. **120 in. = _?_ ft**

$120 \div 12 = 10$ To convert from inches to feet,
120 in. $= 10$ ft   divide by 12.

The units of weight in the customary system are ounce, pound, and ton. The table at the right shows the relationships among these units.

Customary Units of Weight
1 pound (lb) = 16 ounces (oz)
1 ton (T) = 2000 pounds

- To convert from larger units to smaller units, multiply.

- To convert from smaller units to larger units, divide.

Larger Units		Smaller Units
3 T $= 3 \times 2000 = 6000$ lb
2 lb $= 2 \times 16$ $= 32$ oz

Smaller Units		Larger Units
48 oz $= 48 \div 16$ $= 3$ lb
4000 lb $= 4000 \div 2000 = 2$ T

Example 2 Complete each sentence.

a. **120 oz = _?_ lb**

$120 \div 16 = 7.5$ To convert from smaller units
120 oz $= 7.5$ lb   to larger units, divide.

b. **4 T = _?_ lb**

$4 \times 2000 = 8000$ To convert from larger units
4 T $= 8000$ lb   to smaller units, multiply.

pacity is the amount of liquid or dry substance a
ntainer can hold. Customary units of capacity are
id ounce, cup, pint, quart, and gallon. The
lationships among these units are shown in the table.

with units of length and units of weight, to convert
m larger units to smaller units, multiply. To convert
m smaller units to larger units, divide.

Customary Units of Capacity
1 cup (c) = 8 fluid ounces (fl oz)
1 pint (pt) = 2 cups
1 quart (qt) = 2 pints
1 gallon (gal) = 4 quarts

Example 3 **Complete each sentence.**

a. 3 gal = __?__ qt

$3 \times 4 = 12$ larger unit → smaller unit
3 gal = 12 qt

b. 2 c = __?__ fl oz

$2 \times 8 = 16$ larger unit → smaller unit
2 c = 16 fl oz

c. 12 pt = __?__ qt

$12 \div 2 = 6$ smaller unit → larger unit
12 pt = 6 qt

d. 8 c = __?__ qt

$8 \div 2 = 4$ First, convert cups to pints.
8 c = 4 pt

$4 \div 2 = 2$ Next, convert pints to quarts.
4 pt = 2 qt
So, 8 c = 2 qt.

omplete each sentence.

. 5 ft = __?__ in. **60**

2. 2 gal = __?__ qt **8**

3. 96 oz = __?__ lb **6**

. 2 T = __?__ lb **4000**

5. 9 ft = __?__ yd **3**

6. 6 c = __?__ pt **3**

. 2 mi = __?__ ft **10,560**

8. 72 in. = __?__ ft **6**

9. 3 lb = __?__ oz **48**

. 7 yd = __?__ ft **21**

11. 32 fl oz = __?__ c **4**

12. 15,840 ft = __?__ mi **3**

. 2 qt = __?__ pt **4**

14. 5 pt = __?__ c **10**

15. 16 qt = __?__ gal **4**

. 3000 lb = __?__ T **1.5**

17. 6 pt = __?__ qt **3**

18. 8 pt = __?__ c **16**

. 14 pt = __?__ qt **7**

20. 8 yd = __?__ ft **24**

21. 5 gal = __?__ qt **20**

. 36 qt = __?__ gal **9**

23. 5 c = __?__ fl oz **40**

24. 120 in. = __?__ ft **10**

. 30 in. = __?__ ft **2.5**

26. 6.5 lb = __?__ oz **104**

27. 12 oz = __?__ lb **0.75**

olve each problem by breaking it into simpler parts.

. How many inches are in a yard? **36**

. How many ounces are in a ton? **32,000**

. How many cups are in a gallon? **16**

15 Displaying Data in Graphs

Statistics involves collecting, analyzing, and presenting information. The information that is collected is called data. Displaying **data** in graphs makes it easier to visualize the data.

- **Bar graphs** are used to compare the frequency of data. The bar graph below compares the amounts of recycled materials.

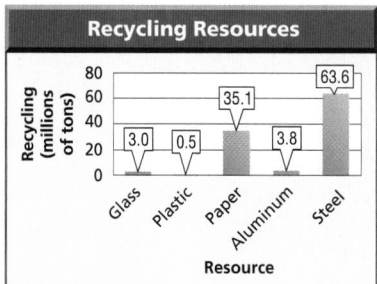

Source: Bureau of Mines

- **Double bar graphs** compare two sets of data. The double bar graph below shows movie preferences for men and women.

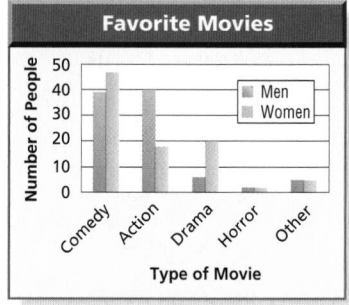

- **Line graphs** usually show how values change over a period of time. The line graph at the right shows the results of the women's Olympic high jump event from 1972 to 2000.

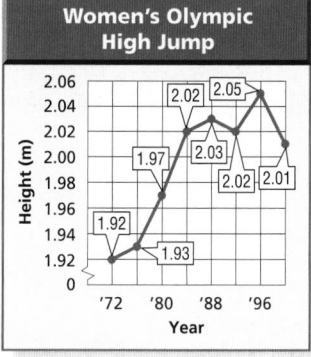

Source: *The World Almanac*

- **Double line graphs**, like double bar graphs, show two sets of data. The double line graph below compares the number of boys and the number of girls participating in high school athletics.

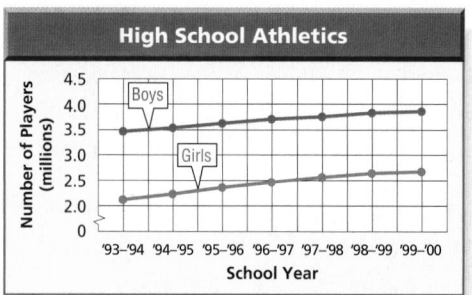

Source: Based on National Federation of State High School statistics

Circle graphs show how parts are related to the whole. The circle graph at the right shows how electricity is generated in the United States.

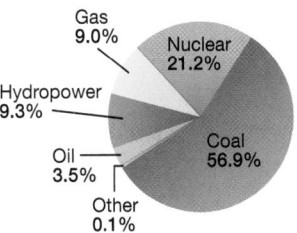

How America Powers Up

Gas 9.0%
Nuclear 21.2%
Hydropower 9.3%
Oil 3.5%
Coal 56.9%
Other 0.1%

Source: Energy Information Administration

Example

A newspaper wants to display the high temperature of the past week. Should they use a line graph, circle graph, or double bar graph?

Since the data would show how values change over a period of time, a line graph would give the reader a clear picture of what temperatures were and the changes in temperature.

–5. Sample answers are given. See margin for explanations.

Determine whether a bar graph, double bar graph, line graph, double line graph, or circle graph is the best way to display each of the following sets of data. Explain your reasoning.

the number of people who have different kinds of pets **bar graph**

the percent of students in class who have 0, 1, 2, 3, or more than 3 siblings **circle graph**

the number of teens who attended art museums, symphony concerts, rock concerts, and athletic events in 1990 compared to the number who attended the same events this year **double bar graph**

the minimum wage every year from 1980 to the present **line graph**

the number of boys and the number of girls participating in volunteer programs each year from 1995 to the present **double line graph**

The table below shows the number of events at recent Olympic games. Would the data be best displayed using a line graph, circle graph, or double bar graph? Explain your reasoning. **Line graph; it is easier to see the increase in events over time.**

Olympic Year	1968	1972	1976	1980	1984	1988	1992	1996	2000
Number of Events	172	196	199	200	223	237	257	271	300

It shows how each age group makes up the whole group of Internet users.

The graph at the right represents the age of Internet users.

Explain how the graph is useful in displaying the data.

Describe any advantages or disadvantages of using a different type of graph to display the data. **Sample answer: A bar graph would also compare the different age groups, but a circle graph is more useful in comparing the parts to the whole.**

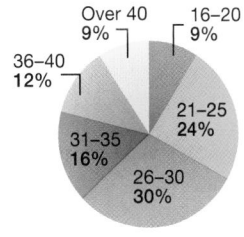

Age of Internet Users

Over 40 9%
16–20 9%
36–40 12%
21–25 24%
31–35 16%
26–30 30%

Source: *Time*

Answers

Sample Answers:

1. A bar graph would show the different frequencies of the data.

2. A circle graph would show how each category compares to the whole class.

3. A double bar graph would make a side-by-side comparison of the two sets of data.

4. A line graph would show the wage's increase during those years.

5. A double line graph would show the changes in boys' and girls' participation over time.

Extra Practice

Lesson 1-1

(pages 6–10)

Solve.

1. **POSTAL SERVICE** The U.S. Postal Service offers air mail service to other countries. The rates for International Air Mail letters and packages are shown in the table at the right. Determine the air mail rate for a package that weighs 5.5 ounces. **d. See students' work.**

   a. Write the *Explore* step. What do you know and what do you need to find? **know other rates, need to find rate for 5.5 oz**

   b. Write the *Plan* step. What strategy will you use? What do you estimate the answer to be? **sample answer: look for a pattern; $4.50**

   c. *Solve* the problem using your plan. What is your answer? **$4.46**

   d. *Examine* your solution. Is it reasonable? Does it answer the question?

Weight not over (ounces)	Rate
0.5	$0.50
1.0	$0.95
1.5	$1.34
2.0	$1.73
2.5	$2.12
3.0	$2.51
3.5	$2.90
4.0	$3.29

2. **POSTAL SERVICE** In 1995, the state of Florida celebrated the 150th anniversary of its statehood. The U.S. Postal Service issued a stamp, the first to bear the 32-cent price, to honor the occasion. Ninety million of the commemorative stamps were issued. About how much postage did the stamps represent? **b. about $30 million**

   a. Which method of computation do you think is most appropriate for this problem? Justify your choice. **sample answer: estimation since the problem says "about"**

   b. Solve the problem using the four-step plan. Be sure to examine your solution.

Find the next term in each list.

3. 3, 8, 13, 18, 23, … **28**   4. 32, 29, 26, 23, 20, … **17**   5. 6, 7, 9, 12, 16, … **21**

Lesson 1-2
(pages 12–16)

Find the value of each expression.

1. $8 + 7 + 12 \div 4$ **18**

2. $20 \div 4 - 5 + 12$ **12**

3. $(25 \cdot 3) + (10 \cdot 3)$ **105**

4. $36 \div 6 + 7 - 6$ **7**

5. $30 \cdot (6 - 4)$ **60**

6. $(40 \cdot 2) - (6 \cdot 11)$ **14**

7. $\frac{86 - 11}{11 + 4}$ **5**

8. $\frac{12 + 84}{11 + 13}$ **4**

9. $\frac{5 \cdot 5 + 5}{5 \cdot 5 - 15}$ **3**

10. $(19 - 8)4$ **44**

11. $75 - 5(2 \cdot 6)$ **15**

12. $81 \div 27 \times 6 - 2$ **16**

13. Find the value of *thirty-two divided by the product of four and two.* **4**

Write a numerical phrase for each verbal phrase.

14. three increased by nine $3 + 9$ 15. fifteen divided by three $15 \div 3$ 16. six less than ten $10 - 6$

Lesson 1-3
(pages 17–21)

ALGEBRA Evaluate each expression if $a = 2$, $b = 4$, and $c = 3$.

1. $ba - ac$ **2**

2. $4b + a \cdot a$ **20**

3. $11 \cdot c - ab$ **25**

4. $4b - (a + c)$ **11**

5. $7(a + b) - c$ **39**

6. $8a + 8b$ **48**

7. $\frac{8(a + b)}{4c}$ **4**

8. $36 - 12c$ **0**

9. $\frac{9(b + a)}{c - 1}$ **27**

10. $abc - bc$ **12**

11. $28 - bc + a$ **18**

12. $a(b - c)$ **2**

ALGEBRA Translate each phrase into an algebraic expression.

13. nine more than a $a + 9$

14. eleven less than k $k - 11$

15. three times p $3p$

16. the product of some number and five $5n$

17. twice Shelly's score decreased by 18 $2s - 18$

18. the quotient of 16 and n $16 \div n$

Lesson 1-4

(pages 23–27)

Name the property shown by each statement. **2. Associative (+)**

1. $1 \cdot 4 = 4$ **Mult. Identity**

2. $6 + (b + 2) = (6 + b) + 2$

3. $9(6n) = (9 \cdot 6)n$ **Associative (×)**

4. $8t \cdot 0 = 0 \cdot 8t$ **Commutative (×)**

5. $0(13n) = 0$ **Mult. Prop. of 0**

6. $7 + t = t + 7$ **Commutative (+)**

Find each sum or product mentally.

7. $6 + 8 + 14$ **28**

8. $5 \cdot 18 \cdot 2$ **180**

9. $0(13 \cdot 6)$ **0**

10. $8 + 4 + 12 + 16$ **40**

11. $8 \cdot 20 \cdot 10$ **1600**

12. $4 \cdot 14 \cdot 5$ **280**

ALGEBRA Simplify each expression.

13. $(12 + x) + 9$ **x + 21**

14. $2 \cdot (6 \cdot x)$ **12x**

15. $(5 \cdot m) \cdot 3$ **15m**

Lesson 1-5

(pages 28–32)

ALGEBRA Find the solution of each equation from the list given.

1. $16 - f = 11; 3, 5, 7$ **5**

2. $9 = \frac{72}{m}; 8, 9, 11$ **8**

3. $4b + 1 = 17; 3, 4, 5$ **4**

4. $17 + r = 25; 6, 7, 8$ **8**

5. $9 = 7n - 12; 3, 5, 7$ **3**

6. $67 = 98 - q; 21, 26, 31$ **31**

ALGEBRA Solve each equation mentally.

7. $13 - u = 7$ **6**

8. $23 = w + 6$ **17**

9. $88 + y = 96$ **8**

10. $9z = 45$ **5**

11. $88 = 11d$ **8**

12. $5t = 0$ **0**

13. $13g = 39$ **3**

14. $\frac{x}{2} = 8$ **16**

15. $\frac{84}{h} = 12$ **7**

ALGEBRA Define a variable. Then write an equation and solve.

16. The sum of a number and 8 is 14. **x + 8 = 14, 6**

17. Twelve less than a number is 50. **n − 12 = 50, 62**

18. The product of a number and ten is seventy. **10n = 70, 7**

19. A number divided by three is nine. **n ÷ 3 = 9, 27**

Lesson 1-6

(pages 33–38)

Use the grid at the right to name the point for each ordered pair.

1. $(9, 7)$ **P**

2. $(5, 5)$ **N**

3. $(3, 1)$ **Q**

4. $(2, 7)$ **B**

5. $(8, 4)$ **S**

6. $(4, 0)$ **T**

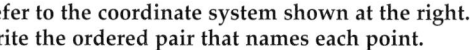
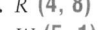

Refer to the coordinate system shown at the right. Write the ordered pair that names each point.

7. R **(4, 8)**

8. P **(9, 7)**

9. W **(5, 1)**

10. C **(0, 6)**

11. D **(0, 8)**

12. F **(3, 4)**

Express each relation as a table and as a graph. Then determine the domain and range. **13–14. See margin for tables and graphs.**

13. $\{(3, 6), (4, 9), (5, 1)\}$
D = {3, 4, 5}; R = {1, 6, 9}

14. $\{(2, 1), (4, 4), (6, 7), (4, 3)\}$
D = {2, 4, 6}; R = {1, 3, 4, 7}

Extra Practice **725**

13.

x	y
3	6
4	9
5	1

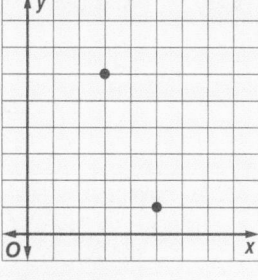

14.

x	y
2	1
4	4
6	7
4	3

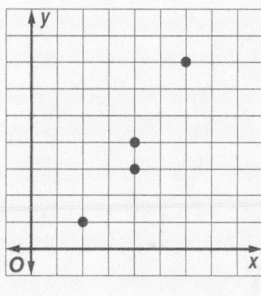

Answer Lesson 1-7

4. **Puzzle Completion**

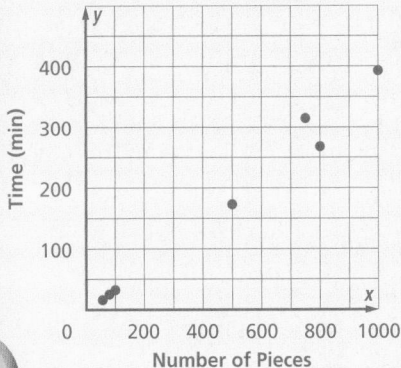

Lesson 1-7 *(pages 40–44)*

Determine whether a scatter plot of the data for the following might show a *positive*, *negative*, or *no* relationship. Explain your answer.

1. speed of airplane and miles traveled in three hours **positive**
2. weight and shoe size **no**
3. outside temperature and heating bill **negative**

GAMES For Exercises 4–6, use the following information. The number of pieces in a jigsaw puzzle and the number of minutes required for a person to complete it is shown below.

Number of Pieces	100	60	500	750	1000	800	75
Time (min)	35	20	175	315	395	270	25

4. Make a scatter plot of the data. **See margin.**
5. Does the scatter plot show any relationship? If so, is it positive or negative? Explain your reasoning. **Positive; as the number of pieces increases, the time increases.**
6. Suppose Dave purchases a puzzle having 650 pieces. Predict the length of time it will take him to complete the puzzle. **260 minutes**

Lesson 2-1 *(pages 56–61)*

Replace each ● with <, >, or = to make a true sentence.

1. $-4 ● -8$ **>**
2. $-6 ● 3$ **<**
3. $0 ● -5$ **>**
4. $-12 ● -9$ **<**
5. $12 ● -25$ **>**
6. $3 ● -7$ **>**
7. $0 ● -2$ **>**
8. $-15 ● 12$ **<**
9. $5 ● -7$ **>**
10. $|6| ● -2$ **>**
11. $-2 ● |-3|$ **<**
12. $|-7| ● |-4|$ **>**

Order the integers in each set from least to greatest. **16.** {−43, −40, −1, 8, 16, 27}

13. {−1, 2, −5} **{−5, −1, 2}**
14. {0, −2, 8, 5, −9} **{−9, −2, 0, 5, 8}**
15. {100, −34, −86, 21, 0} **{−86, −34, 0, 21, 100}**
16. {−1, 16, −43, 8, 27, −40}
17. {0, −23, 75, −15, 24} **{−23, −15, 0, 24, 75}**
18. {−6, 6, −5, 18} **{−6, −5, 6, 18}**

Evaluate each expression.

19. $|-3| + |9|$ **12**
20. $|-18| - |5|$ **13**
21. $|12 + 7|$ **19**
22. $-|6|$ **−6**
23. $|-8| + |4|$ **12**
24. $-|-20|$ **−20**
25. $|15 - 12|$ **3**
26. $|8 + 9|$ **17**
27. $-|4| \cdot |-5|$ **−20**
28. $|-6| \cdot |8|$ **48**
29. $-|12| \cdot |9|$ **−108**
30. $-\||-16| + |-22|\|$ **−38**

Lesson 2-2 *(pages 64–68)*

Find each sum.

1. $5 + (-6)$ **−1**
2. $-17 + 24$ **7**
3. $15 + (-29)$ **−14**
4. $-6 + 13$ **7**
5. $50 + (-14)$ **36**
6. $-21 + (-4)$ **−25**
7. $30 + (-7)$ **23**
8. $(-3) + (-10)$ **−13**
9. $-15 + 26$ **11**
10. $-17 + 4 + -2$ **−15**
11. $50 + (-16) + (-11)$ **23**
12. $-17 + 8 + (-14)$ **−23**
13. $-11 + 15 + -6$ **−2**
14. $23 + (-64)$ **−41**
15. $-1 + 14 + (-13)$ **0**
16. $33 + -18 + 7$ **22**
17. $-75 + (-13)$ **−88**
18. $26 + 14 + (-71)$ **−31**
19. $8 + (-9) + (-1)$ **−2**
20. $-16 + (-12) + 13$ **−15**
21. $35 + (-60)$ **−25**
22. $12 + -20 + 16$ **8**
23. $100 + (-54) + (-17)$ **29**
24. $11 + (-22) + (-33)$ **−44**

---

nd each difference.

8 − 17 **−9**   **2.** −15 − 3 **−18**   **3.** 10 − 21 **−11**
20 − (−5) **25**   **5.** 5 − (−9) **14**   **6.** −12 − (−7) **−5**
−19 − (−6) **−13**   **8.** −16 − (−23) **7**   **9.** −56 − 32 **−88**
−49 − (−52) **3**   **11.** −6 − 9 − (−7) **−8**   **12.** −6 − (−10) − 7 **−3**
17 − 33 **−16**   **14.** −21 − 19 **−40**   **15.** 12 − (−24) **36**
−35 − (−18) **−17**   **17.** −54 − 27 **−81**   **18.** 32 − (−18) **50**
−26 − (−41) **15**   **20.** 99 − (−1) **100**   **21.** −12 − (−25) **13**
18 − (−43) **61**   **23.** −66 − 13 **−79**   **24.** 54 − 100 **−46**

GEBRA   Evaluate each expression if $x = 6$, $y = -8$, $z = -3$, and $w = 4$.

$y - z$ **−5**   **26.** $3 - z$ **6**   **27.** $y - 5$ **−13**   **28.** $x - y$ **14**
$14 - y - x$ **16**   **30.** $6 + x - z$ **15**   **31.** $y + z + w$ **−7**   **32.** $w - z + 11$ **18**

nd each product.

−4(2) **−8**   **2.** −8(−5) **40**   **3.** 13(−4) **−52**
−5 · 6 · 10 **−300**   **5.** −6(−2)(−14) **−168**   **6.** 18(−3)(6) **−324**
4(−10)(−3) **120**   **8.** −9(3)(2) **−54**   **9.** 12(−8) **−96**

GEBRA   Simplify each expression.

−3 · 5x **−15x**   **11.** 7(−8m) **−56m**   **12.** −10(−3k) **30k**
−4y(−8z) **32yz**   **14.** (−2r)(−3s) **6rs**   **15.** 6(−2m)(3n) **−36mn**

GEBRA   Evaluate each expression.

−6t, if $t = 15$ **−90**   **17.** 7p, if $p = -9$ **−63**   **18.** −4k, if $k = -16$ **64**
aw, if $a = 0$ and $w = -72$ **0**   **20.** dk, if $d = -12$ and $k = 11$ **−132**   **21.** st, if $s = -8$ and $t = -10$ **80**
3hp, if $h = 9$ and $p = -3$ **−81**   **23.** −5bc, if $b = -6$ and $c = 2$ **60**   **24.** −4wx, if $w = -1$ and $x = -8$
                                                                                                                                −32

nd each quotient.

−36 ÷ 9 **−4**   **2.** 112 ÷ (−8) **−14**   **3.** −72 ÷ 2 **−36**
−26 ÷ (−13) **2**   **5.** −144 ÷ 6 **−24**   **6.** −180 ÷ (−10) **18**
304 ÷ (−8) **−38**   **8.** −216 ÷ (−9) **24**   **9.** 80 ÷ (−5) **−16**
−105 ÷ 15 **−7**   **11.** 120 ÷ (−30) **−4**   **12.** −200 ÷ (−8) **25**
42 ÷ (−6) **−7**   **14.** 144 ÷ (−12) **−12**   **15.** −360 ÷ 9 **−40**
−84 ÷ −6 **14**   **17.** 125 ÷ (−5) **−25**   **18.** 180 ÷ (−15) **−12**
−400 ÷ 20 **−20**   **20.** 72 ÷ (−9) **−8**   **21.** −156 ÷ (−2) **78**

GEBRA   Evaluate each expression if $x = -5$, $y = -3$, $z = 2$, and $w = 7$.

25 ÷ x **−5**   **23.** −42 ÷ w **−6**   **24.** 3 ÷ y **−1**   **25.** 2x ÷ z **−5**
−3x ÷ y **−5**   **27.** x ÷ (−1) **5**   **28.** xyz ÷ 10 **3**   **29.** yz ÷ 2 **−3**
$\dfrac{3y}{-3}$ **3**   **31.** $\dfrac{6 - y}{y}$ **−3**   **32.** $\dfrac{w}{-7}$ **−1**   **33.** $\dfrac{w - x}{y}$ **−4**

9.–14.

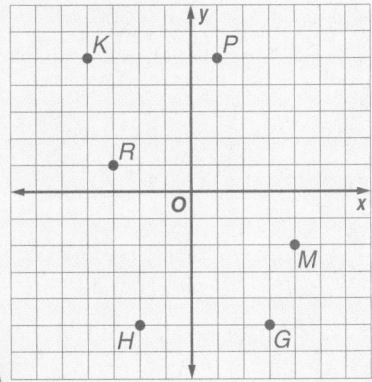

Extra Practice

Lesson 2-6
(pages 85–89)

Name the point for each ordered pair graphed at the right.

1. $(-6, 8)$ **D**
2. $(1, -2)$ **J**
3. $(9, 2)$ **C**
4. $(1, 4)$ **L**
5. $(-3, -4)$ **B**
6. $(2, 5)$ **N**
7. $(3, 0)$ **K**
8. $(5, -1)$ **M**

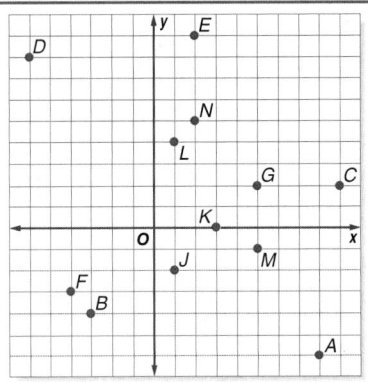

Graph and label each point on a coordinate plane. Name the quadrant in which each point is located. **9–14. See margin for graph.**

9. $H(-2, -5)$ **III**
10. $P(1, 5)$ **I**
11. $R(-3, 1)$ **II**
12. $M(4, -2)$ **IV**
13. $K(-4, 5)$ **II**
14. $G(3, -5)$ **IV**

Lesson 3-1
(pages 98–102)

Use the Distributive Property to write each expression as an equivalent expression. Then evaluate it.

1. $2(4 + 5)$ $2 \cdot 4 + 2 \cdot 5$, **18**
2. $4(5 + 3)$ $4 \cdot 5 + 4 \cdot 3$, **32**
3. $3(7 - 6)$ $3 \cdot 7 - 3 \cdot 6$, **3**
4. $(2 + 5)9$ $2 \cdot 9 + 5 \cdot 9$, **63**
5. $(10 - 4)3$ $10 \cdot 3 - 4 \cdot 3$, **18**
6. $-6(1 + 3)$ $-6 \cdot 1 - 6 \cdot 3$, **−24**

ALGEBRA Use the Distributive Property to write each expression as an equivalent algebraic expression.

7. $3(m + 4)$ $3m + 12$
8. $(y + 7)5$ $5y + 35$
9. $-6(x + 3)$ $-6x - 18$
10. $(p - 4)5$ $5p - 20$
11. $-3(s - 9)$ $-3s + 27$
12. $5(x + y)$ $5x + 5y$
13. $b(c + 3d)$ $bc + 3bd$
14. $(a - b)(-5)$ $-5a + 5b$
15. $-6(v - 3w)$ $-6v + 18w$
16. $5(x + 12)$ $5x + 60$
17. $(m - 6)(4)$ $4m - 24$
18. $-2(a - b)$ $-2a + 2b$
19. $(8 - m)(-3)$ $-24 + 3m$
20. $8(p - 3q)$ $8p - 24q$
21. $(2x + 3y)(4)$ $8x + 12y$
22. $-5(9 - z)$ $-45 + 5z$
23. $21(k - 3)$ $21k - 63$
24. $(7 - 2h)(-3)$ $-21 + 6h$

Lesson 3-2
(pages 103–107)

Identify the like terms in each expression.

1. $3 + 4x + x$ **4x, x**
2. $5n + 2 - 3n$ **5n, −3n**
3. $6 + 1 + 7y$ **6, 1**
4. $2c + c + 8d$ **2c, c**
5. $3a - 9 + b$ **none**
6. $2 + 6k + 7 - 5k$ **2, 7; 6k, −5k**

ALGEBRA Simplify each expression.

7. $8k + 2k + 7$ **10k + 7**
8. $3 + 2b + b$ **3 + 3b**
9. $t + 2t$ **3t**
10. $9(3 + 2x)$ **27 + 18x**
11. $4(y + 2) - 2$ **4y + 6**
12. $(6 + 3e)4$ **24 + 12e**
13. $4 + 9c + 3(c + 2)$ **12c + 10**
14. $5(7 + 2s) + 3(s + 4)$ **13s + 47**
15. $9(f + 2) + 14f$ **23f + 18**
16. $5a - 9a$ **−4a**
17. $-6 + 4x + 9 - 2x$ **2x + 3**
18. $6a + 11 + (-15) + 9a$ **15a − 4**
19. $2(8w - 7)$ **16w − 14**
20. $3(2d + 5) + 4d$ **10d + 15**
21. $2 + 4p - 6(p - 2)$ **−2p + 14**
22. $-3(b + 4)$ **−3b − 12**
23. $-6 + 3s + 11 - 5s$ **−2s + 5**
24. $3(x - 5) + 7(x + 2)$ **10x − 1**
25. $3q - r + q + 6r$ **4q + 5r**
26. $8(r + 1) + 7$ **8r + 15**
27. $3p - 2(p + 6q)$ **p − 12q**
28. $a + 2b + 4a$ **5a + 2b**
29. $9x - 12 + 12$ **9x**
30. $1 + g + 5g - 2$ **−1 + 6g**

GEBRA **Solve each equation. Check your solution.**

$y + 49 = 26$ **−23**

2. $d + 31 = -24$ **−55**

3. $q - 8 = 16$ **24**

$x - 16 = 32$ **48**

5. $40 = a + 12$ **28**

6. $b + 12 = -1$ **−13**

$21 = u + 6$ **15**

8. $-52 = p + 5$ **−57**

9. $-14 = 5 - g$ **19**

$121 = k + (-12)$ **133**

11. $-234 = m - 94$ **−140**

12. $110 = x + 25$ **85**

$f - 7 = 84$ **91**

14. $y - 864 = 652$ **1516**

15. $475 + z = -18$ **−493**

$x + 12 = -9$ **−21**

17. $15 - h = 11$ **4**

18. $16 = p + 21$ **−5**

$-13 + t = -2$ **11**

20. $86 = x + 43$ **43**

21. $y - 11 = -14$ **−3**

GEBRA **Write and solve an equation to find each number.**

The sum of −6 and a number is 8. **$-6 + x = 8$; 14**

When 3 is subtracted from a number, the result is −5. **$x - 3 = -5$; −2**

When 7 is added to a number, the result is −9. **$n + 7 = -9$; −16**

When a number is decreased by 8, the result is 5. **$w - 8 = 5$; 13**

GEBRA **Solve each equation. Check your solution.**

$-y = -32$ **32**

2. $7r = -56$ **−8**

3. $\frac{t}{-3} = 12$ **−36**

$4 = \frac{s}{-14}$ **−56**

5. $\frac{b}{47} = -2$ **−94**

6. $64 = -4n$ **−16**

$-144 = 12q$ **−12**

8. $\frac{r}{11} = -12$ **−132**

9. $-5g = -385$ **77**

$-16x = -176$ **11**

11. $-21 = \frac{y}{-4}$ **84**

12. $-372 = 31k$ **−12**

$84 = \frac{k}{5}$ **420**

14. $-b = 19$ **−19**

15. $\frac{v}{112} = -9$ **−1008**

$-3x = -27$ **9**

17. $\frac{p}{-12} = 4$ **−48**

18. $5q = -100$ **−20**

$\frac{d}{11} = -8$ **−88**

20. $-9n = -45$ **5**

21. $125 = -25z$ **−5**

GEBRA **Write and solve an equation for each sentence.**

The product of 8 and a number is −40. **$8m = -40$; −5**

The quotient of a number and −3 is 27. **$\frac{w}{-3} = 27$; −81**

When 6 is multiplied by a number, the result is −24. **$6e = -24$; −4**

GEBRA **Solve each equation. Check your solution.**

$3t - 13 = 2$ **5**

2. $-8j - 7 = 57$ **−8**

3. $9d - 5 = 4$ **1**

$6 - 3w = -27$ **11**

5. $\frac{k}{6} + 8 = 12$ **24**

6. $-4 = \frac{q}{8} - 19$ **120**

$15 - \frac{n}{7} = 13$ **14**

8. $44 = -4 + 8p$ **6**

9. $21 - h = -32$ **53**

$-19 = 11b - (-3)$ **−2**

11. $6 = 20 + \frac{x}{3}$ **−42**

12. $9 + 3a = -3$ **−4**

$2x - 8 = 10$ **9**

14. $\frac{m}{4} - 6 = 10$ **64**

15. $-12 + 3p = 3$ **5**

$-18 = 6a - 6$ **−2**

17. $\frac{t}{-3} + 11 = 23$ **−36**

18. $3 + 2v = 11$ **4**

$16 = \frac{k}{3} - 11$ **81**

20. $-6g - 12 = -60$ **8**

21. $15 - 4c = -21$ **9**

Lesson 3-6
(pages 126–130)

ALGEBRA   Write and solve an equation for each sentence.

1. Five less than three times a number is 13. $3x - 5 = 13$; 6
2. The product of 2 and a number is increased by 9. The result is 17. $2p + 9 = 17$; 4
3. Ten more than four times a number is 46. $4z + 10 = 46$; 9
4. The quotient of a number and -8, less 5 is -2. $\frac{a}{-8} - 5 = -2$; -24
5. Three more than two times a number is 11. $2n + 3 = 11$; 4
6. The quotient of a number and six, increased by 2 is -5. $\frac{w}{6} + 2 = -5$; -42
7. The product of -3 and a number, decreased by 9 is 27. $-3x - 9 = 27$; -12

Lesson 3-7
(pages 131–136)

ALGEBRA   Solve by replacing the variables with the given values.

1. $d = rt$, if $d = 366$ and $t = 3$. 122
2. $S = (n - 2) \cdot 180$, if $n = 8$. 1080
3. $A = bh$, if $A = 36$ and $h = 12$. 3
4. $P = 4s$, if $P = 108$. 27
5. $V = \ell wh$, if $\ell = 27$, $w = 5$, and $h = 2$. 270
6. $h = 69 + 2F$, if $F = 42$. 153

Find the perimeter and area of each rectangle.

7. a rectangle 23 centimeters long and 9 centimeters wide 64 cm, 207 cm²
8. a 16-foot by 14-foot rectangle 60 ft, 224 ft²
9. a rectangle with a length of 31 meters and a width of 3 meters 68 m, 93 m²
10. a square with sides 7 meters long 28 m, 49 m²

Find the missing dimension of each rectangle.

	Length	Width	Area	Perimeter
11.	9 ft	14 ft	126 ft²	46 ft
12.	6 in.	18 in.	108 in²	48 in.
13.	13 yd	21 yd	273 yd²	68 yd
14.	14 cm	12 cm	168 cm²	52 cm
15.	54 m	3 m	162 m²	114 m

16. The perimeter of a rectangle is 50 meters. Its width is 10 meters. Find the length. 15 m
17. The area of a rectangle is 96 square inches. Its length is 12 inches. Find the width. 8 in.

Lesson 4-1
(pages 148–152)

Use divisibility rules to determine whether each number is divisible by 2, 3, 5, 6, or 10.

1. 98 2
2. 243 3
3. 800 2, 5, 10
4. 252 2, 3, 6
5. 105 3, 5
6. 210 2, 3, 5, 6, 10
7. 225 3, 5
8. 180 2, 3, 5, 6, 10

List all the factors of each number.

9. 77 1, 7, 11, 77
10. 42 1, 2, 3, 6, 7, 14, 21, 42
11. 81 1, 3, 9, 27, 81
12. 132 1, 2, 3, 4, 6, 11, 12, 22, 33, 44, 66, 1

ALGEBRA   Determine whether each expression is a monomial. Explain why or why not. 13. yes; the product of a number and a variable   14. No; terms are subtracted.

13. $-6h$
14. $9 - v$
15. g yes; a variable
16. $3n + 9$ No; two terms are added.
17. 112 yes; a number
18. $2(x + 9)$ No; two terms are added.

ALGEBRA Write each expression using exponents.

1. $8 \cdot 8 \cdot 8 \cdot 8$ 8^4

2. 9 9^1

3. $(-6)(-6)(-6)(-6)(-6)$ $(-6)^5$

4. $(y \cdot y \cdot y) \cdot (y \cdot y \cdot y \cdot y)$ y^7

5. $a \cdot b \cdot b$ ab^2

6. $4 \cdot 4 \cdot 4 \cdot 4 \cdot x \cdot x \cdot x \cdot y$ $4^4 x^3 y$

7. $3q \cdot 3q \cdot 3q \cdot 3q \cdot 3q \cdot 3q$ $(3q)^6$

8. $\underbrace{n \cdot n \cdot n \cdot \ldots \cdot n}_{17 \text{ factors}}$ n^{17}

9. $(x + y)(x + y)$ $(x + y)^2$

Express each number in expanded form.

10. 56 $(5 \times 10^1) + (6 \times 10^0)$

11. 231 $(2 \times 10^2) + (3 \times 10^1) + (1 \times 10^0)$

12. 4075 $(4 \times 10^3) + (0 \times 10^2) + (7 \times 10^1) + (5 \times 10^0)$

ALGEBRA Evaluate each expression if $m = 3$, $n = 2$, and $p = -4$.

13. $3m^2$ 27

14. $n^0 + m$ 4

15. 7^4 2401

16. -5^3 -125

17. p^3 -64

18. $2(m - p)^2$ 98

19. $-2n^3 + m$ -13

20. $m - p^2$ -13

21. $(m + n + p)^3$ 1

22. $5p - m^2$ -29

23. $(n + p)^4$ 16

24. $(m - n)^8$ 1

Determine whether each number is *prime* or *composite*.

1. 57 composite

2. 369 composite

3. 116 composite

4. 125 composite

5. 83 prime

6. 99 composite

7. 91 composite

8. 79 prime

Write the prime factorization of each number. Use exponents for repeated factors.

9. 21 $3 \cdot 7$

10. 44 $2^2 \cdot 11$

11. 51 $3 \cdot 17$

12. 65 $5 \cdot 13$

13. 30 $2 \cdot 3 \cdot 5$

14. 28 $2^2 \cdot 7$

15. 117 $3^2 \cdot 13$

16. 88 $2^3 \cdot 11$

17. 54 $2 \cdot 3^3$

18. 32 2^5

19. 300 $2^2 \cdot 3 \cdot 5^2$

20. 210 $2 \cdot 3 \cdot 5 \cdot 7$

ALGEBRA Factor each number or monomial completely.

21. 40 $2 \cdot 2 \cdot 2 \cdot 5$

22. $630a$ $2 \cdot 3 \cdot 3 \cdot 5 \cdot 7 \cdot a$

23. 187 $11 \cdot 17$

24. 310 $2 \cdot 5 \cdot 31$

25. 510 $2 \cdot 3 \cdot 5 \cdot 17$

26. 1589 $7 \cdot 227$

27. $-18ab^2$ $-1 \cdot 2 \cdot 3 \cdot 3 \cdot a \cdot b \cdot b$

28. $-117x^3$ $-1 \cdot 3 \cdot 3 \cdot 13 \cdot x \cdot x \cdot x$

29. $105j^2k^5$ $3 \cdot 5 \cdot 7 \cdot j \cdot j \cdot k \cdot k \cdot k \cdot k \cdot k$

ALGEBRA Find the GCF of each set of numbers or monomials.

1. $27, 45$ 9

2. $30, 12$ 6

3. $16, 40, 28$ 4

4. $18, 17, 15$ 1

5. $112, 216$ 8

6. $120, 245$ 5

7. $84k, 108k^2$ $12k$

8. $135ab, 171b$ $9b$

9. $185fg, 74f^2g$ $37fg$

10. $44m, 60n$ 4

11. $90gh, 225k$ 45

12. $8, 28h$ 4

13. $16w, 28w^3$ $4w$

14. $24a, 30ab, 66a^2$ $6a$

15. $13z, 39yz, 52y$ 13

ALGEBRA Factor each expression.

16. $3m + 12$ $3(m + 4)$

17. $5x + 15$ $5(x + 3)$

18. $4 + 8b$ $4(1 + 2b)$

19. $7x + 21$ $7(x + 3)$

20. $2a + 100$ $2(a + 50)$

21. $42 - 14b$ $14(3 - b)$

22. $5f - 25$ $5(f - 5)$

23. $11p - 66$ $11(p - 6)$

24. $7y - 21$ $7(y - 3)$

25. $48 + 12s$ $12(4 + s)$

26. $18 - 2w$ $2(9 - w)$

27. $24k + 96$ $24(k + 4)$

28. $2y + 14$ $2(y + 7)$

29. $42 - 7b$ $7(6 - b)$

30. $13w + 39$ $13(w + 3)$

Lesson 4-5

(pages 169–173)

Write each fraction in simplest form. If the fraction is already in simplest form, write *simplified*.

1. $\frac{3}{54}$ $\frac{1}{18}$

2. $\frac{3}{16}$ **simplified**

3. $\frac{6}{58}$ $\frac{3}{29}$

4. $\frac{15}{55}$ $\frac{3}{11}$

5. $\frac{10}{90}$ $\frac{1}{9}$

6. $\frac{20}{49}$ **simplified**

7. $\frac{8}{20}$ $\frac{2}{5}$

8. $\frac{99}{9}$ **11**

9. $\frac{18}{54}$ $\frac{1}{3}$

10. $\frac{21}{64}$ **simplified**

11. $\frac{40}{76}$ $\frac{10}{19}$

12. $\frac{49}{56}$ $\frac{7}{8}$

13. $\frac{22}{66}$ $\frac{1}{3}$

14. $\frac{42}{49}$ $\frac{6}{7}$

15. $\frac{110}{200}$ $\frac{11}{20}$

16. $\frac{b}{b^4}$ $\frac{1}{b^3}$

17. $\frac{16p}{24p}$ $\frac{2}{3}$

18. $\frac{21x^2y}{81y}$ $\frac{7x^2}{27}$

19. $\frac{32d^2}{6d}$ $\frac{16d}{3}$

20. $\frac{72ab}{8b}$ $9a$

21. $\frac{120z^3x}{18zx}$ $\frac{20z^2}{3}$

22. Fourteen inches is what part of 1 yard? $\frac{7}{18}$

23. Nine hours is what part of one day? $\frac{3}{8}$

Lesson 4-6

(pages 175–179)

ALGEBRA Find each product or quotient. Express using exponents.

1. $r^4 \cdot r^2$ r^6

2. $\frac{2^9}{2^3}$ 2^6

3. $\frac{b^{18}}{b^5}$ b^{13}

4. $12^3 \cdot 12^8$ 12^{11}

5. $x \cdot x^9$ x^{10}

6. $(2s^6)(4s^2)$ $8s^8$

7. $w^3 \cdot w^4 \cdot w^2$ w^9

8. $(-2)^2(-2)^5(-2)$ $(-2)^8$

9. $\frac{4^7}{4^6}$ 4

10. $3(f^{17})(f^2)$ $3f^{19}$

11. $(5k)^2 \cdot k^7$ $25k^9$

12. $\frac{6m^8}{3m^2}$ $2m^6$

13. $(3x^4)(-6x)$ $-18x^5$

14. $(4k^4)(-3k)^3$ $-108k^7$

15. $\left(\frac{42}{-6}\right)\left(\frac{g^{10}}{g^3}\right)$ $-7g^7$

Lesson 4-7

(pages 181–185)

ALGEBRA Write each expression using a positive exponent.

1. y^{-9} $\frac{1}{y^9}$

2. m^{-4} $\frac{1}{m^4}$

3. 5^{-3} $\frac{1}{5^3}$

4. 2^{-7} $\frac{1}{2^7}$

5. 6^{-3} $\frac{1}{6^3}$

6. a^{-11} $\frac{1}{a^{11}}$

Write each fraction as an expression using a negative exponent other than −1.

7. $\frac{1}{p^4}$ p^{-4}

8. $\frac{1}{b^9}$ b^{-9}

9. $\frac{1}{5^3}$ 5^{-3}

10. $\frac{1}{7^4}$ 7^{-4}

11. $\frac{1}{15^2}$ 15^{-2}

12. $\frac{1}{25}$ 5^{-2}

13. $\frac{1}{c^7}$ c^{-7}

14. $\frac{1}{64}$ $4^{-3}, 8^{-2}$, or 2^{-6}

Write each decimal using a negative exponent.

15. 0.01 10^{-2}

16. 0.00001 10^{-5}

17. 0.0001 10^{-4} or 100^{-2}

18. 0.001 10^{-3}

19. 0.1 10^{-1}

20. 0.000001 10^{-6}

Evaluate each expression if $x = 3$ and $y = -2$.

21. x^{-2} $\frac{1}{9}$

22. 9^y $\frac{1}{81}$

23. y^{-3} $-\frac{1}{8}$

24. x^{-3} $\frac{1}{27}$

25. y^{-4} $\frac{1}{16}$

26. $(xy)^{-2}$ $\frac{1}{36}$

(pages 186–190)

Express each number in scientific notation.

1. 9040 9.04×10^3

2. 0.015 1.5×10^{-2}

3. 6,180,000 6.18×10^6

4. 27,210,000 2.721×10^7

5. 0.00004637 4.637×10^{-5}

6. 0.00546 5.46×10^{-3}

7. 500,300,100 5.003001×10^8

8. -0.0000032 -3.2×10^{-6}

Express each number in standard form.

9. -9.5×10^{-3} -0.0095

10. 8.245×10^{-4} 0.0008245

11. 8.2×10^4 $82,000$

12. -9.102040×10^2 -910.204

13. 4.02×10^3 4020

14. 1.6×10^{-2} 0.016

15. 2.41023×10^6 $2,410,230$

16. 4.21×10^{-5} 0.0000421

(pages 200–204)

Write each fraction or mixed number as a decimal. Use a bar to show a repeating decimal.

1. $\frac{6}{10}$ 0.6

2. $\frac{4}{25}$ 0.16

3. $-\frac{1}{8}$ -0.125

4. $1\frac{3}{4}$ 1.75

5. $\frac{5}{6}$ $0.8\overline{3}$

6. $\frac{9}{20}$ 0.45

7. $-4\frac{7}{12}$ $-4.58\overline{3}$

8. $\frac{8}{11}$ $0.\overline{72}$

9. $3\frac{4}{18}$ $3.\overline{2}$

10. $-\frac{3}{16}$ -0.1875

11. $8\frac{36}{44}$ $8.8\overline{1}$

12. $\frac{6}{15}$ 0.4

Replace each ● with <, >, or = to make a true sentence.

13. $\frac{7}{8}$ ● $\frac{5}{6}$ $>$

14. 0.04 ● $\frac{5}{9}$ $<$

15. $\frac{1}{3}$ ● $\frac{2}{7}$ $>$

16. $\frac{3}{5}$ ● $\frac{12}{20}$ $=$

17. $\frac{1}{2}$ ● 0.75 $<$

18. 0.3 ● $\frac{1}{3}$ $<$

19. $\frac{2}{3}$ ● 0.64 $>$

20. $\frac{2}{20}$ ● 0.10 $=$

21. $0.\overline{5}$ ● $\frac{5}{9}$ $=$

22. $2.\overline{1}$ ● $2\frac{1}{10}$ $>$

23. $3\frac{7}{8}$ ● 3.78 $>$

24. $-\frac{6}{7}$ ● $-\frac{5}{6}$ $<$

(pages 205–209)

Write each number as a fraction.

1. $3\frac{4}{5}$ $\frac{19}{5}$

2. $-1\frac{2}{9}$ $-\frac{11}{9}$

3. 15 $\frac{15}{1}$

4. $2\frac{3}{8}$ $\frac{19}{8}$

5. -13 $-\frac{13}{1}$

6. $2\frac{6}{7}$ $\frac{20}{7}$

7. 36 $\frac{36}{1}$

8. $-1\frac{3}{5}$ $-\frac{8}{5}$

Write each decimal as a fraction or mixed number in simplest form.

9. 0.6 $\frac{3}{5}$

10. 0.05 $\frac{1}{20}$

11. 0.38 $\frac{19}{50}$

12. 4.12 $4\frac{3}{25}$

13. 0.375 $\frac{3}{8}$

14. -3.24 $-3\frac{6}{25}$

15. $0.222\ldots$ $\frac{2}{9}$

16. $-0.\overline{4}$ $-\frac{4}{9}$

Identify all sets to which each number belongs.

17. $-4\frac{2}{5}$ Q

18. 6 N, W, I, Q

19. $3\frac{1}{3}$ Q

20. -10 I, Q

21. 5.9 Q

22. $-\frac{3}{1}$ I, Q

23. $\frac{16}{8}$ N, W, I, Q

24. $7.02002000\ldots$ not rational

Lesson 5-3

(pages 210–214)

Find each product. Write in simplest form.

1. $\frac{2}{5} \cdot \frac{3}{16}$ $\frac{3}{40}$

2. $3\frac{1}{4} \cdot \frac{2}{11}$ $\frac{13}{22}$

3. $\frac{3}{5}\left(-\frac{5}{12}\right)$ $-\frac{1}{4}$

4. $\frac{5}{8} \cdot \frac{2}{3}$ $\frac{5}{12}$

5. $-\frac{9}{10} \cdot \frac{5}{24}$ $-\frac{3}{16}$

6. $\frac{1}{7} \cdot \frac{21}{22}$ $\frac{3}{22}$

7. $\frac{4}{5} \cdot \frac{1}{8}$ $\frac{1}{10}$

8. $2\frac{2}{6} \cdot 6\frac{2}{7}$ $14\frac{2}{3}$

9. $2\left(-\frac{7}{12}\right)$ $-1\frac{1}{6}$

10. $1\frac{3}{7}\left(-9\frac{4}{5}\right)$ -14

11. $-\frac{6}{7}\left(-\frac{6}{7}\right)$ $\frac{36}{49}$

12. $\frac{6c}{10} \cdot \frac{2}{c}$ $\frac{6}{5}$

13. $\frac{p^3}{4} \cdot \frac{12}{p}$ $3p^2$

14. $\frac{ab}{9} \cdot \frac{3}{b^2}$ $\frac{a}{3b}$

15. $\frac{4x}{3y} \cdot \frac{12y^4}{x^2}$ $\frac{16y^3}{x}$

MEASUREMENT   Complete.

16. _?_ inches $= \frac{5}{12}$ yard **15**

17. _?_ minutes $= \frac{1}{5}$ hour **12**

18. $\frac{3}{4}$ pound $=$ _?_ ounces **12**

19. $\frac{7}{8}$ day $=$ _?_ hours **21**

Lesson 5-4

(pages 215–219)

Find the multiplicative inverse of each number.

1. $\frac{4}{7}$ $\frac{7}{4}$

2. $-\frac{5}{9}$ $-\frac{9}{5}$

3. $\frac{1}{4}$ 4

4. $5\frac{3}{8}$ $\frac{8}{43}$

5. 6 $\frac{1}{6}$

6. -18 $-\frac{1}{18}$

7. $\frac{7}{10}$ $\frac{10}{7}$

8. 2.35 $\frac{20}{47}$

Find each quotient. Write in simplest form.

9. $\frac{4}{5} \div \frac{2}{5}$ 2

10. $-\frac{1}{3} \div \frac{6}{7}$ $-\frac{7}{18}$

11. $\frac{4}{9} \div \frac{1}{5}$ $2\frac{2}{9}$

12. $\frac{2}{3} \div \frac{1}{9}$ 6

13. $\frac{4}{5} \div \left(-\frac{8}{15}\right)$ $-1\frac{1}{2}$

14. $\frac{1}{12} \div \frac{3}{4}$ $\frac{1}{9}$

15. $\frac{3}{4} \div \frac{15}{16}$ $\frac{4}{5}$

16. $16 \div 1\frac{7}{8}$ $8\frac{8}{15}$

17. $2\frac{1}{6} \div \left(-1\frac{1}{5}\right)$ $-1\frac{29}{36}$

18. $-11 \div 3\frac{1}{7}$ $-3\frac{1}{2}$

19. $\frac{8}{45} \div \frac{10}{27}$ $\frac{12}{25}$

20. $-22 \div \left(-5\frac{1}{2}\right)$ 4

21. $\frac{w}{5} \div \frac{w}{35}$ 7

22. $\frac{ab}{12} \div \frac{b}{16}$ $\frac{4a}{3}$

23. $\frac{21y}{8x^2} \div \frac{7y}{16x}$ $\frac{6}{x}$

Lesson 5-5

(pages 220–224)

Find each sum or difference. Write in simplest form.

1. $\frac{2}{7} + \frac{3}{7}$ $\frac{5}{7}$

2. $\frac{8}{15} - \frac{4}{15}$ $\frac{4}{15}$

3. $\frac{3}{7} + \frac{4}{7}$ 1

4. $-\frac{8}{9} + \frac{1}{9}$ $-\frac{7}{9}$

5. $\frac{5}{6} - \frac{1}{6}$ $\frac{2}{3}$

6. $\frac{7}{12} - \frac{5}{12}$ $\frac{1}{6}$

7. $\frac{5}{12} + \frac{11}{12}$ $1\frac{1}{3}$

8. $-\frac{3}{14} - \frac{5}{14}$ $-\frac{4}{7}$

9. $3\frac{1}{4} + \left(-\frac{3}{4}\right)$ $2\frac{1}{2}$

10. $\frac{3}{8} - \left(-1\frac{1}{8}\right)$ $1\frac{1}{2}$

11. $4\frac{9}{10} - 1\frac{1}{10}$ $3\frac{4}{5}$

12. $-5\frac{3}{5} + \left(-2\frac{1}{5}\right)$ $-7\frac{4}{5}$

ALGEBRA   Find each sum or difference. Write in simplest form.

13. $\frac{n}{5} + \frac{3n}{5}$ $\frac{4n}{5}$

14. $\frac{15}{k} - \frac{8}{k}, k \neq 0$ $\frac{7}{k}$

15. $12\frac{7}{8}s - 7\frac{3}{8}s$ $5\frac{1}{2}s$

16. $-6\frac{4}{9}t - 3\frac{2}{9}t$ $-9\frac{2}{3}t$

17. $6\frac{1}{4}g + \left(-6\frac{3}{4}g\right)$ $-\frac{1}{2}g$

18. $7\frac{2}{5}n - \left(-4\frac{2}{5}n\right)$ $11\frac{4}{5}n$

...d the least common multiple (LCM) of each set of numbers or monomials.

30, 18 **90**
2. 4, 16 **16**
3. $3m$, 12 **$12m$**

$6a$, $17a^5$ **$102a^5$**
5. 2, 5, 7 **70**
6. $9x^2y$, $12xy^3$ **$36x^2y^3$**

...d the least common denominator (LCD) of each pair of fractions.

$\frac{2}{5}, \frac{6}{25}$ **25**
8. $\frac{3}{12}, \frac{4}{5}$ **60**
9. $\frac{4}{6}, \frac{7}{9}$ **18**
10. $\frac{5}{9}, \frac{7}{12}$ **36**

$\frac{1}{4}, \frac{5}{6}$ **12**
12. $\frac{11}{20}, \frac{3}{8}$ **40**
13. $\frac{3}{10p}, \frac{7}{5p^3}$ **$10p^3$**
14. $\frac{1}{a^2}, \frac{2}{3a^4}$ **$3a^4$**

...place each ● with <, >, or = to make a true statement.

$\frac{2}{3}$ ● $\frac{3}{4}$ **<**
16. $-\frac{5}{8}$ ● $-\frac{3}{5}$ **<**
17. $\frac{4}{6}$ ● $\frac{7}{12}$ **>**

$\frac{11}{18}$ ● $\frac{33}{54}$ **=**
19. $\frac{4}{19}$ ● $\frac{8}{38}$ **=**
20. $\frac{9}{15}$ ● $\frac{1}{2}$ **>**

...d each sum or difference. Write in simplest form.

$\frac{1}{5} + \frac{2}{7}$ **$\frac{17}{35}$**
2. $\frac{4}{5} + \frac{7}{9}$ **$1\frac{26}{45}$**
3. $\frac{1}{9} - \frac{7}{12}$ **$-\frac{17}{36}$**

$\frac{8}{11} - \frac{4}{5}$ **$-\frac{4}{55}$**
5. $\frac{7}{12} - \left(-\frac{4}{11}\right)$ **$\frac{125}{132}$**
6. $-\frac{9}{14} + \frac{15}{16}$ **$\frac{33}{112}$**

$-\frac{3}{8} + \left(-1\frac{5}{12}\right)$ **$-1\frac{19}{24}$**
8. $-\frac{2}{15} - 3\frac{1}{5}$ **$-3\frac{1}{3}$**
9. $-5\frac{1}{3} + \left(-\frac{1}{6}\right)$ **$-5\frac{1}{2}$**

$3\frac{2}{5} + 2\frac{4}{7}$ **$5\frac{34}{35}$**
11. $-4\frac{1}{8} + 2\frac{5}{9}$ **$-1\frac{41}{72}$**
12. $-3\frac{3}{7} - 5\frac{1}{14}$ **$-8\frac{1}{2}$**

$11\frac{3}{5} - \left(-6\frac{5}{8}\right)$ **$18\frac{9}{40}$**
14. $\frac{5}{14} + \frac{2}{21}$ **$\frac{19}{42}$**
15. $2\frac{1}{7} - 3\frac{1}{3}$ **$-1\frac{4}{21}$**

...d the mean, median, and mode for each set of data. If necessary, round to the ...arest tenth.

82, 79, 93, 91, 95 **88; 91; none**
2. 88, 85, 76, 94, 85, 97 **87.5; 86.5; 85**

23, 32, 19, 27, 41, 21, 26, 32, 23 **27.1; 26; 23 and 32**
4. 7.4, 8.3, 6.1, 5.4, 6.8, 7.1, 8.0, 9.2 **7.3; 7.3; none**

0.57, 12.81, 12.6, 0.96, 6.1, 14.3, 4.1, 12.81, 0.96 **7.2; 6.1; 0.96 and 12.81**

11.7; 12; 11
7.

0.4; 0.4; 0.3

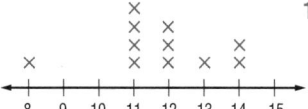

POPULATION The population of the Canadian provinces and territories in 2000 is shown in the table. Find the mean, median, and mode of the data. If necessary, round to the nearest tenth. **2365.4; 941.0; none**

Province/ Territory	Population (thousands)	Province/ Territory	Population (thousands)
Newfoundland	538.8	Saskatchewan	1023.6
Prince Edward Island	138.9	Northwest Territories	42.1
Nova Scotia	941.0	Alberta	2997.2
New Brunswick	756.6	Yukon	30.7
Quebec	7372.4	British Columbia	4063.8
Ontario	11,669.3	Nunavut	27.7
Manitoba	1147.9		

Lesson 5-9

(pages 244–248)

ALGEBRA Solve each equation. Check your solution.

1. $a - 4.86 = 7.2$ **12.06**
2. $n + 6.98 = 10.3$ **3.32**
3. $87.64 = f - (-8.5)$ **79.14**
4. $x - \frac{2}{5} = -\frac{8}{15}$ $-\frac{2}{15}$
5. $3\frac{3}{4} + m = 6\frac{5}{8}$ $2\frac{7}{8}$
6. $4\frac{1}{6} = r + 6\frac{1}{4}$ $-2\frac{1}{12}$
7. $7\frac{1}{3} = c - \frac{4}{5}$ $8\frac{2}{15}$
8. $-4.62 = h + (-9.4)$ **4.78**
9. $w - 1\frac{1}{5} = \frac{2}{9}$ $1\frac{19}{45}$
10. $\frac{2}{3}w = \frac{1}{6}$ $\frac{1}{4}$
11. $6 = -\frac{3}{4}x$ -8
12. $-0.5m = -10$ **20**
13. $-\frac{1}{9}t = 7$ -63
14. $5\frac{2}{3} = y - \frac{1}{8}$ $5\frac{19}{24}$
15. $-14.8 = -7.1 + t$ -7.7

Lesson 5-10

(pages 249–252)

State whether each sequence is *arithmetic*, *geometric*, or *neither*. If it is arithmetic or geometric, state the common difference or common ratio and write the next three terms of the sequence.

1. 3.5, 4.3, 5.1, … **arithmetic; 0.8; 5.9, 6.7, 7.5**
2. 125, 75, 45, … **geometric; 0.6; 27, 16.2, 9.72**
3. 5, 10, 20, … **geometric; 2; 40, 80, 160**
4. 2401, 49, 7, … **neither**
5. $\frac{1}{2}, \frac{5}{6}, 1\frac{1}{6}$ **arithmetic; $\frac{1}{3}$; $1\frac{1}{2}, 1\frac{5}{6}, 2\frac{1}{6}$**
6. geometric; $-\frac{5}{2}$; $-31\frac{1}{4}, 78\frac{1}{8}, -195\frac{5}{16}$
7. $\frac{1}{4}, \frac{1}{2}, 1, 2, …$ **geometric; 2; 4, 8, 16**
8. 23, 18, 13, … **arithmetic; −5; 8, 3, −2**
9. 45, 43, 39, 33, … **neither**
10. 2, 4, 8, 16, … **geometric; 2; 32, 64, 128**
11. 100, 75, 50, … **arithmetic; −25; 25, 0, −25**
12. $\frac{1}{5}, 1, 5, 25, …$ **geometric; 5; 125, 625, 3125**

6. $-\frac{4}{5}, 2, -5, 12\frac{1}{2}, …$

Lesson 6-1

(pages 264–268)

Express each ratio as a fraction in simplest form.

1. 15 vans out of 40 vehicles $\frac{3}{8}$
2. 6 pens to 14 pencils $\frac{3}{7}$
3. 12 dolls out of 18 toys $\frac{2}{3}$
4. 8 red crayons out of 36 crayons $\frac{2}{9}$
5. 18 boys out of 45 students $\frac{2}{5}$
6. 30 birds to 6 birds $\frac{5}{1}$
7. 98 ants to 14 ladybugs $\frac{7}{1}$
8. 140 dogs to 12 cats $\frac{35}{3}$
9. 321 pennies to 96 dimes $\frac{107}{32}$
10. 3 cups to 3 quarts $\frac{1}{4}$

Express each ratio as a unit rate. Round to the nearest tenth, if necessary.

11. 343.8 miles on 9 gallons **38.2 mi/gal**
12. $7.95 for 5 pounds **$1.60/lb**
13. $52 for 8 tickets **$6.50/ticket**
14. $43.92 for 4 CDs **$11/CD**
15. 450 miles in 8 hours **56.3 mi/h**
16. $3.96 for 12 cans of pop **$0.3/can**
17. $3.84 for 64 ounces **$0.06/oz**
18. 200 yards in 32.3 seconds **6.2 yd/s**

19. **MONEY** Which costs more per notebook, a 4-pack of notebooks for $3.98 or a 5-pack of notebooks for $4.99? Explain. **Since the 4-pack costs $0.995 per notebook and the 5-pack costs $0.998 per notebook, the 5-pack costs more per notebook.**
20. **ANIMALS** A cheetah can run 70 miles in 1 hour. How many feet is this per second? Round to the nearest whole number. **103 ft/s**

ALGEBRA Solve each proportion.

1. $\frac{7}{k} = \frac{49}{63}$ **9**

2. $\frac{s}{4.8} = \frac{30.6}{28.8}$ **5.1**

3. $\frac{6}{11} = \frac{19.2}{g}$ **35.2**

4. $\frac{8}{13} = \frac{b}{65}$ **40**

5. $\frac{x}{12} = \frac{26}{24}$ **13**

6. $\frac{21}{p} = \frac{3}{9}$ **63**

7. $\frac{6.5}{8} = \frac{w}{20}$ **16.25**

8. $\frac{10}{4.21} = \frac{7}{y}$ **2.947**

Write a proportion that could be used to solve for each variable.
Then solve.

9. 6 plums at \$1 $\frac{6}{\$1.00} = \frac{10}{d}$; **\$1.67**
   10 plums at d

10. 8 gallons at \$9.36 $\frac{8}{\$9.36} = \frac{f}{\$17.55}$; **15**
    f gallons at \$17.55

11. 3 packages at \$53.67 $\frac{3}{\$53.67} = \frac{7}{m}$; **\$125.23**
    7 packages at m

12. 10 cards at \$7.50 $\frac{10}{\$7.50} = \frac{p}{\$18.00}$; **24**
    p cards at \$18

13. 12 cookies at \$3.00 $\frac{12}{\$3.00} = \frac{16}{s}$; **\$4.00**
    16 cookies at s

14. 6 toy cars at \$4.50 $\frac{6}{\$4.50} = \frac{c}{\$6.75}$; **9**
    c toy cars at \$6.75

In a set of architectural drawings for a school, the scale is
$\frac{1}{2}$ inch = 4 feet. Find the actual length of each room.

Room	Drawing Distance	
1. Classroom	5 inches	**40 ft**
2. Principal's Office	1.75 inches	**14 ft**
3. Library	$7\frac{1}{2}$ inches	**60 ft**
4. Cafeteria	$9\frac{1}{4}$ inches	**74 ft**
5. Gymnasium	12.2 inches	**97.6 ft**
6. Nurse's Office	1.3 inches	**10.4 ft**

Express each decimal or fraction as a percent. Round to the nearest tenth percent,
if necessary.

1. 0.42 **42%**

2. 0.06 **6%**

3. 1.35 **135%**

4. 0.001 **0.1%**

5. 0.99 **99%**

6. 3.6 **360%**

7. 0.8 **80%**

8. 0.0052 **0.52%**

9. 0.00009 **0.009%**

10. $\frac{17}{50}$ **34%**

11. $\frac{9}{25}$ **36%**

12. $\frac{12}{8}$ **150%**

13. $\frac{7}{40}$ **17.5%**

14. $\frac{11}{33}$ **33.3%**

15. $\frac{36}{27}$ **133.3%**

Express each percent as a fraction or mixed number in simplest form and as a
decimal.

16. 32% $\frac{8}{25}$; **0.32**

17. 15% $\frac{3}{20}$; **0.15**

18. $88\frac{1}{2}\%$ $\frac{177}{200}$; **0.885**

19. 250% $\frac{5}{2}$; **2.5**

20. 21% $\frac{21}{100}$; **0.21**

21. 64% $\frac{16}{25}$; **0.64**

22. 25% $\frac{1}{4}$; **0.25**

23. 131% $\frac{131}{100}$; **1.31**

24. 72.5% $\frac{29}{40}$; **0.725**

25. $66\frac{2}{3}\%$ $\frac{2}{3}$; **0.$\overline{6}$**

26. 0.06% $\frac{3}{5000}$; **0.0006**

27. 315% $3\frac{3}{20}$; **3.15**

9. fraction method: $\frac{3}{5} \times 50$ or 30

10. fraction method: $\frac{1}{5} \times 40$ or 8

11. fraction method: $\frac{8}{10} \times 60$ or 48

12. meaning of percent method: 125% means about 125 for every 100 or about 13 for every 10. 81 has about 8 tens. $8 \times 13 = 104$. So, 125% of 81 is about 104.

13. 1% method: Since 1% of 502 is about 5, $\frac{1}{2}$% of 502 is about $\frac{1}{2}$ of 5 or 2.5.

14. fraction method: $\frac{3}{10} \times 20$ or 6

Extra Practice

Lesson 6-5 *(pages 288–292)*

Use the percent proportion to solve each problem. Round to the nearest tenth.

1. What is 81% of 134? **108.5**
2. 52.08 is 21% of what number? **248**
3. 11.18 is what percent of 86? **13%**
4. What is 120% of 312? **374.4**
5. 140 is what percent of 400? **35%**
6. 430.2 is 60% of what number? **717**
7. 32 is what percent of 80? **40%**
8. What is 15% of 125? **18.8**
9. 22 is what percent of 110? **20%**
10. 9.4 is 40% of what number? **23.5**
11. What is 41.5% of 95? **39.4**
12. 17.92 is what percent of 112? **16%**

13. **FOOD**   If 28 of the 50 soup cans on a shelf are chicken noodle soup, what percent of the cans are chicken noodle soup? **56%**

14. **SCHOOL**   Of the students in a classroom, 60% are boys. If there are 20 students, how many are boys? **12**

Lesson 6-6 *(pages 293–297)*

Find the percent of each number mentally.

1. 40% of 60 **24**
2. 25% of 72 **18**
3. 50% of 96 **48**
4. $33\frac{1}{3}$% of 24 **8**
5. 150% of 42 **63**
6. $37\frac{1}{2}$% of 80 **30**
7. 200% of 125 **250**
8. $66\frac{2}{3}$% of 45 **30**

Estimate. Explain which method you used to estimate.

9. 60% of 49 **30**
10. 19% of 41 **8**
11. 82% of 60 **48**
12. 125% of 81 **104**
13. $\frac{1}{2}$% of 502 **2.5**
14. 31% of 19 **6**

9–14. Sample answers are given. See margin for explanations.

Lesson 6-7 *(pages 298–302)*

Solve each problem using an equation.

1. 9.28 is what percent of 58? **16%**
2. What number is 43% of 110? **47.3**
3. 80% of what number is 90? **112.5**
4. What number is 61% of 524? **319.64**
5. 126 is what percent of 90? **140%**
6. 52% of what number is 109.2? **210**
7. 62% of what number is 29.76? **48**
8. 54 is what percent of 90? **60%**
9. Find 78% of 125. **97.5**
10. What is 0.2% of 12? **0.024**
11. 66% of what number is 49.5? **75**
12. 36.45 is what percent of 81? **45%**

Find the discount to the nearest cent.

13. $35 skirt, 20% off **$7**
14. $108 lamp, 25% off **$27**

Find the interest to the nearest cent.

15. $1585 at 6% for 5 years **$475.50**
16. $2934 at 5.75% for $3\frac{1}{2}$ years **$590.47**

17. **BOOKS**   A dictionary is on sale at a 15% discount. Find the sale price of the dictionary if it normally sells for $29.99. **$25.49**

ate whether each change is a *percent of increase* or a *percent of decrease*. Then
d the percent of change. Round to the nearest tenth, if necessary.

. from $56 to $42 **D; −25%**

2. from $26 to $29.64 **I; 14%**

. from $22 to $37.18 **I; 69%**

4. from $137.50 to $85.25 **D; −38%**

. from $455 to $955.50 **I; 110%**

6. from $3 to $15 **I; 400%**

. from $750.75 to $765.51 **I; 2%**

8. from $953 to $476.50 **D; −50%**

. from $101.25 to $379.69 **I; 275%**

10. from $836 to $842.27 **I; $\frac{3}{4}$%**

. from $18 to $24 **I; $33\frac{1}{3}$%**

12. from $250 to $100 **D; −60%**

. from $107.50 to $92 **D; −14.4%**

14. from $365 to $394.20 **I; 8%**

BASEBALL CARDS A baseball card collection contains 340 baseball cards. What is
the percent of change if 25 cards are removed from the collection? **−7.4%**

3. $\frac{6}{15}$; **40%** 4. $\frac{2}{15}$; **13%** 7. $\frac{10}{15}$; **67%** 8. $\frac{13}{15}$; **87%** 12. $\frac{9}{15}$; **60%**

ere are 4 blue marbles, 6 red marbles, 3 green marbles, and 2 yellow marbles in
ag. Suppose you select one marble at random. Find the probability of each
tcome. Express each probability as a fraction and as a percent. Round to the
arest percent.

. $P(\text{green})$ $\frac{3}{15}$; **20%**

2. $P(\text{blue})$ $\frac{4}{15}$; **27%**

. $P(\text{red})$

4. $P(\text{yellow})$

. $P(\text{not green})$ $\frac{12}{15}$; **80%**

6. $P(\text{white})$ **0; 0%**

. $P(\text{blue or red})$

8. $P(\text{not yellow})$

. $P(\text{neither red nor green})$ $\frac{6}{15}$; **40%**

10. $P(\text{red or yellow})$ $\frac{8}{15}$; **53%**

. $P(\text{not orange})$ **1; 100%**

12. $P(\text{neither blue nor yellow})$

. $P(\text{not red})$ $\frac{9}{15}$; **60%**

14. $P(\text{not green or yellow})$ $\frac{10}{15}$; **67%**

. Suppose two number cubes are rolled. What is the probability of rolling a sum greater
than 8? $\frac{5}{18}$ or about **28%**

COOKIES A sample from a package of assorted cookies revealed that 20% of the
cookies were sugar cookies. Suppose there are 45 cookies in the package. How many
can be expected to be sugar cookies? **9**

LGEBRA Solve each equation. Check your solution.

. $-7h - 5 = 4 - 4h$ **−3**

2. $5t - 8 = 3t + 12$ **10**

. $m + 2m + 1 = 7$ **2**

4. $2y + 5 = 6y + 25$ **−5**

. $3z - 1 = 23 - 3z$ **4**

6. $5a - 5 = 7a - 19$ **7**

. $5x + 12 = 3x - 6$ **−9**

8. $3x - 5 = 7x + 7$ **−3**

. $5c + 9 = 8c$ **3**

10. $3p = 4 - 9p$ $\frac{1}{3}$

. $6z + 5 = 4z - 7$ **−6**

12. $2a + 4.2 = 3a - 1.6$ **5.8**

. $3.21 - 7y = 10y - 1.89$ **0.3**

14. $1.9s + 6 = 3.1 - s$ **−1**

. $12b - 5 = 3b$ $\frac{5}{9}$

16. $9 + 11a = -5a + 21$ $\frac{3}{4}$

. $6 - x = -5$ **11**

18. $2.8 - 3w = 4.6 - w$ **−0.9**

. $2.9y + 1.7 = 3.5 + 2.3y$ **3**

20. $2.85a - 7 = 12.85a - 2$ $-\frac{1}{2}$

7.

8.

9.

10.

11.

12.

Extra Practice

Answers Lesson 8-1

1. Yes; each x value is paired with only one y value.

2. Yes; each x value is paired with only one y value.

3. No; 2 is paired with 9 and 36.

4. Yes; each x value is paired with only one y value.

5. No; 1 is paired with 0, 9, and 18.

6. Yes; each x value is paired with only one y value.

7. Yes; each x value is paired with only one y value.

8. No; -2 is paired with 4 and 8 and -1 is paired with 5 and 7.

9. Yes; each x value is paired with only one y value.

10. Yes; each x value is paired with only one y value.

Extra Practice

Lesson 7-2
(pages 334–338)

ALGEBRA Solve each equation. Check your solution.

1. $6(m - 2) = 12$ **4**
2. $4(x - 3) = 4$ **4**
3. $5(2d + 4) = 35$ **1.5**
4. $w + 6 = 2(w - 6)$ **18**
5. $3(b + 1) = 4b - 1$ **4**
6. $7w - 6 = 3(w + 6)$ **6**
7. $4(k - 6) = 6(k + 2)$ **-18**
8. $3x - 0.8 = 3x + 4$ **$\varnothing$**
9. $\frac{5}{9}g + 8 = \frac{1}{6}g + 1$ **-18**
10. $\frac{s - 3}{7} = \frac{s + 5}{9}$ **31**

11. **ALGEBRA** Find the solution of $3(3x + 4) - 2 = 9x + 10$. **all numbers**

12. **NUMBER THEORY** Four times the sum of three consecutive integers is 48.
    a. Write an equation that could be used to find the integers. $4[x + (x + 1) + (x + 2)] = 48$
    b. What are the integers? **3, 4, 5**

Lesson 7-3
(pages 340–344)

ALGEBRA For the given value, state whether each inequality is *true* or *false*.

1. $5 \geq 2t - 12$; $t = 11$ **false**
2. $7 + n < 25$; $n = 4$ **true**
3. $6r - 18 > 0$; $r = 3$ **false**
4. $3n + 2 < 26$; $n = 3$ **true**
5. $h - 19 < 13$; $h = 28$ **true**
6. $20m \geq 10$; $m = 0$ **false**

ALGEBRA Graph each inequality on a number line. **7–12. See margin.**

7. $b \geq 4$
8. $x < -2$
9. $y > 2$
10. $m \leq 0$
11. $p > -1$
12. $q \geq -3$

ALGEBRA Write an inequality for each sentence.

13. At least 295 students attend Greenville Elementary School. $s \geq 295$
14. An electric bill increased by \$15 is now more than \$80. $b + 15 > 80$
15. If 8 times a number is decreased by 2, the result is less than 15. $8n - 2 < 15$
16. Citizens who are 18 years of age or older can vote. $a \geq 18$
17. One dozen jumbo eggs must weigh at least 30 ounces. $w \geq 30$
18. A healthful breakfast cereal should contain no more than 5 grams of sugar. $s \leq 5$

Lesson 7-4
(pages 345–349)

ALGEBRA Solve each inequality and check your solution.

1. $m + 9 < 14$ $m < 5$
2. $k + (-5) < -12$ $k < -7$
3. $-15 < v - 1$ $-14 < v$
4. $-7 + f \geq 47$ $f \geq 54$
5. $r > -15 - 8$ $r > -23$
6. $18 \geq s - (-4)$ $14 \geq s$
7. $38 < r - (-6)$ $32 < r$
8. $z - 9 \leq -11$ $z \leq -2$
9. $-16 + c \geq 1$ $c \geq 17$
10. $d + 1.4 < 6.8$ $d < 5.4$
11. $-3 + x > 11.9$ $x > 14.9$
12. $-0.2 \geq 0.3 + y$ $y \leq -0.5$
13. $h + 5.7 > 21.3$ $h > 15.6$
14. $t - 8.5 > -4.2$ $t > 4.3$
15. $-13.2 > w - 4.87$ $w < -8.33$
16. $a + \frac{5}{12} \geq \frac{7}{18}$ $a \geq -\frac{1}{36}$
17. $7\frac{1}{2} < n - \left(-\frac{7}{8}\right)$ $6\frac{5}{8} < n$
18. $\frac{2}{3} \leq a - \frac{5}{6}$ $1\frac{1}{2} \leq a$
19. $-7.42 \leq d - 5.9$ $-1.52 \leq d$

Lesson 7-5 (pages 350–354)

ALGEBRA Solve each inequality and check your solution.

1. $6p < 78$ $p < 13$
2. $\frac{m}{-3} > 24$ $m < -72$
3. $-18 < 3b$ $b > -6$
4. $-5k \geq 125$ $k \leq -25$
5. $-75 > \frac{a}{5}$ $-375 > a$
6. $\frac{w}{6} < -5$ $w < -30$
7. $8 < \frac{2}{3}c$ $12 < c$
8. $\frac{m}{1.3} \geq 0.5$ $m \geq 0.65$
9. $0.4y > -2$ $y > -5$
10. $-\frac{1}{2}d \leq -5\frac{1}{2}$ $d \geq 11$
11. $\frac{2}{7}t < 4$ $t < 14$
12. $\frac{1}{5}m \geq 4\frac{3}{5}$ $m \geq 23$
13. $\frac{y}{-13} > -20$ $y < 260$
14. $14t < 266$ $t < 19$
15. $\frac{g}{-25} \geq 8$ $g \leq -200$

16. The product of a number and -4 is greater than or equal to -20. What is the number? $n \leq 5$

Lesson 7-6 (pages 355–359)

ALGEBRA Solve each inequality and check your solution.

1. $2m + 1 < 9$ $m < 4$
2. $-3k - 4 \leq -22$ $k \geq 6$
3. $-2 > 10 - 2x$ $6 < x$
4. $-6a + 2 \geq 14$ $a \leq -2$
5. $3y + 2 < -7$ $y < -3$
6. $\frac{d}{4} + 3 \geq -11$ $d \geq -56$
7. $\frac{x}{3} - 5 < 6$ $x < 33$
8. $-5g + 6 < 3g + 26$ $g > -2.5$
9. $-3(m - 2) > 12$ $m < -2$
10. $\frac{r}{5} - 6 \leq 3$ $r \leq 45$
11. $\frac{3(n + 1)}{7} \geq \frac{n + 4}{5}$ $n \geq 1.625$
12. $\frac{n + 10}{-3} \leq 6$ $n \geq -28$

13. Five plus three times a number is less than the difference of two times the same number and 4. What is the number? $x < -9$

Lesson 8-1 (pages 369–373)

Determine whether each relation is a function. Explain. **1–10. See margin for explanations.**

1. $\{(3, 6), (35, 64), (1, 1), (21, 7)\}$ **yes**
2. $\{(32, 24), (27, 24), (36, 24), (45, 24)\}$ **yes**
3. $\{(2, 9), (3, 18), (4, 27), (2, 36)\}$ **no**
4. $\left\{\left(\frac{1}{2}, 3\right), \left(\frac{1}{4}, 5\right), \left(\frac{1}{6}, 7\right), \left(\frac{1}{8}, 9\right), \left(\frac{1}{10}, 11\right)\right\}$ **yes**
5. $\{(1, 0), (1, 9), (1, 18)\}$ **no**
6. $\{(5, 5), (6, 6), (7, 7), (8, 7)\}$ **yes**

7. **yes**

x	y
8	8
15	8
22	51
29	22

8. **no**

x	y
-2	4
-1	5
0	6
-1	7
-2	8

9. 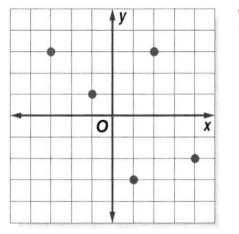 **yes**

10. 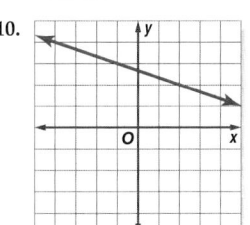 **yes**

13.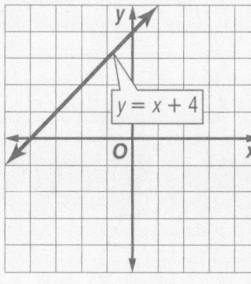
$y = x + 4$

14.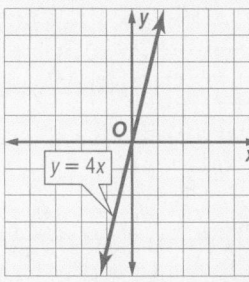
$y = 4x$

15.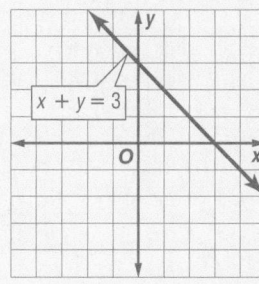
$x + y = 3$

16.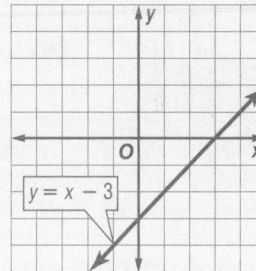
$y = x - 3$

17.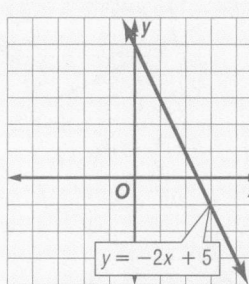
$y = -2x + 5$

18.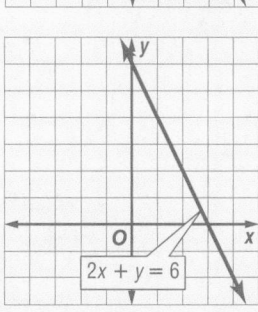
$2x + y = 6$

Extra Practice

7.

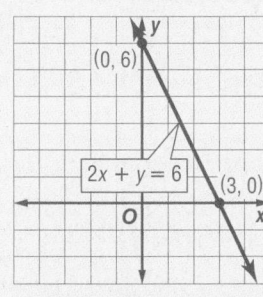

8.

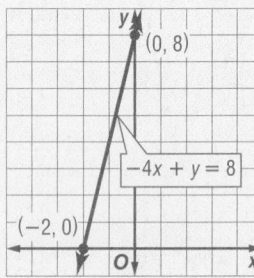

9.

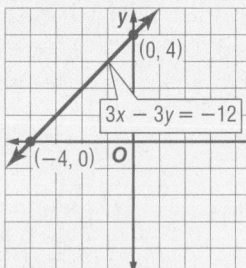

10.

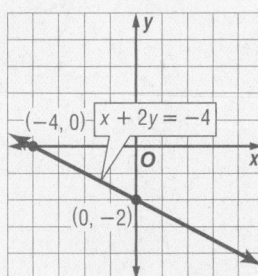

11.

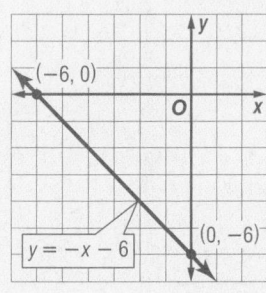

Extra Practice

Lesson 8-2

(pages 375–379)

Find four solutions of each equation. Write the solutions as ordered pairs.

1. $x = 4$ (4, 2), (4, 3), (4, 5), (4, 6)
2. $y = 0$ (1, 0), (5, 0), (6, 0), (0, 0)
3. $x + y = 2$ (2, 0), (1, 1), (0, 2), (−1, 3)
4. $y = 2x − 6$ (0, −6), (1, −4), (2, −2), (3, 0)
5. $x − y = 5$ (8, 3), (7, 2), (6, 1), (5, 0)
6. $3x − y = 8$ (3, 1), (4, 4), (0, −8), (2, −2)
7. $y = \frac{1}{2}x − 3$ (0, −3), (2, −2), (4, −1), (6, 0)
8. $y = \frac{1}{3}x + 1$ (0, 1), (3, 2), (−3, 0), (6, 3)
9. $2x + y = −2$ (1, −4), (0, −2), (−1, 0), (−2, 2)
10. $2x + 3y = 12$ (6, 0), (0, 4), (3, 2), (−3, 6)
11. $x + 2y = −4$ (0, −2), (2, −3), (−2, −1), (−4, 0)
12. $2x − 4y = 8$ (4, 0), (0, −2), (2, −1), (−2, −3)
1–12. Sample answers are given.

ALGEBRA Graph each equation by plotting ordered pairs. 13–18. See margin.

13. $y = x + 4$
14. $y = 4x$
15. $x + y = 3$
16. $y = x − 3$
17. $y = −2x + 5$
18. $2x + y = 6$

Lesson 8-3

(pages 381–385)

Find the x-intercept and the y-intercept for the graph of each equation.

1. $y = x + 7$ −7; 7
2. $y = 3x + 12$ −4; 12
3. $4x + 3y = 24$ 6; 8
4. $y = 8 − 2x$ 4; 8
5. $−5x + y = −10$ 2; −10
6. $y = \frac{2}{3}x − 7$ $\frac{21}{2}$; −7

ALGEBRA Graph each equation using the x- and y-intercepts. 7–12. See margin.

7. $2x + y = 6$
8. $−4x + y = 8$
9. $3x − 3y = −12$
10. $x + 2y = −4$
11. $y = −x − 6$
12. $y = −1$

Lesson 8-4

(pages 387–391)

Find the slope of each line.

1. 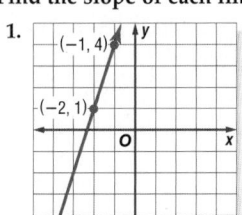 3

2. 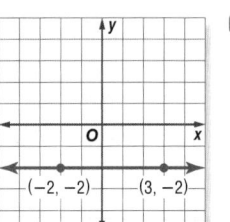 0

Find the slope of the line that passes through each pair of points.

3. $P(3, 8)$, $Q(4, −3)$ −11
4. $D(4, 5)$, $E(−3, −9)$ 2
5. $L(−1, 2)$, $M(0, 5)$ 3
6. $J(6, 2)$, $K(6, −4)$ undefined
7. $B(8, −3)$, $C(−4, 1)$ $−\frac{1}{3}$
8. $D(1, 5)$, $E(3, 10)$ $\frac{5}{2}$
9. $H(7, 2)$, $I(−2, −2)$ $\frac{4}{9}$
10. $K(2, −4)$, $L(5, −19)$ −5
11. $G(5, 6)$, $H(7, 6)$ 0
12. $A(−6, −3)$, $B(−9, 4)$ $−\frac{7}{3}$
13. $P(−1, −6)$, $Q(−5, −10)$ 1
14. $B(5, 9)$, $C(−4, −5)$ $\frac{14}{9}$

12.

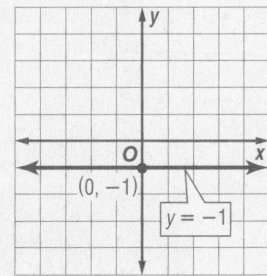

(pages 393–397)

LGEBRA   Find the rate of change for each linear function.

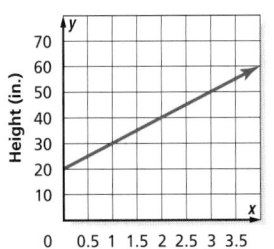

increase of
10 in. per year

2.

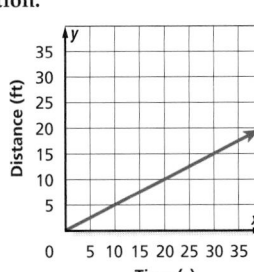

increase of
$\frac{1}{2}$ **ft per s**

Cookies Purchased	x	0	1	2	3
Balance ($)	y	6	5.6	5.2	4.8

decrease of $0.40 per cookie

uppose y varies directly with x. Write an equation relating x and y.

. $y = 12$ when $x = -3$ $y = -4x$

5. $y = 45$ when $x = 15$ $y = 3x$

. $y = 8$ when $x = 18$ $y = \frac{4}{9}x$

7. $y = 7.6$ when $x = 4$ $y = 1.9x$

(pages 398–401)

tate the slope and the y-intercept for the graph of each equation.

. $y = x + 9$ **1; 9**

2. $y = 2x - 5$ **2; −5**

3. $y = -6x$ **−6; 0**

. $y = \frac{3}{2}x$ $\frac{3}{2}$**; 0**

5. $y = \frac{1}{3}x + 8$ $\frac{1}{3}$**; 8**

6. $x + 2y = 12$ $-\frac{1}{2}$**; 6**

raph each equation using the slope and y-intercept.   7–14. See margin.

. $y = 3x - 2$

8. $x - 3y = 9$

. $y = \frac{1}{2}x + 4$

10. $y = -\frac{2}{3}x - 1$

. $x - y = -4$

12. $2x + 4y = -4$

. $y = x + 5$

14. $3x + y = 9$

(pages 404–408)

LGEBRA   Write an equation in slope-intercept form for each line.

. slope = 3, y-intercept = −4 $y = 3x - 4$

2. slope = $\frac{3}{4}$, y-intercept = 1 $y = \frac{3}{4}x + 1$

. slope = −7, y-intercept = −2 $y = -7x - 2$

4. slope = $\frac{5}{8}$, y-intercept = 9 $y = \frac{5}{8}x + 9$

. slope = $-\frac{1}{2}$, y-intercept = 0 $y = -\frac{1}{2}x$

6. slope = 0, y-intercept = −6 $y = -6$

LGEBRA   Write an equation in slope-intercept form for the line passing through ach pair of points.

. (4, 7) and (0, 3) $y = x + 3$

8. (3, −6) and (−1, 2) $y = -2x$

. (8, 7) and (0, 0) $y = \frac{7}{8}x$

10. (1, 4) and (3, −6) $y = -5x + 9$

. (−2, 5) and (3, 9) $y = \frac{4}{5}x + \frac{33}{5}$

12. (3, −1) and (5, −1) $y = -1$

13.

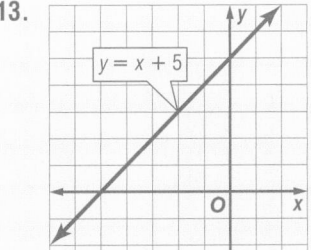

14.

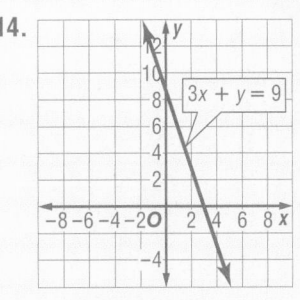

Answers Lesson 8-6

7.

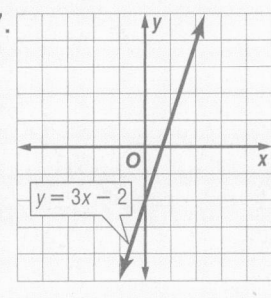

8.

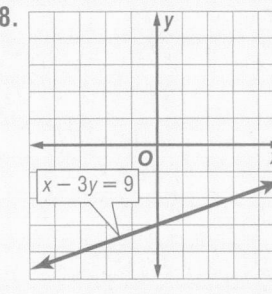

9.

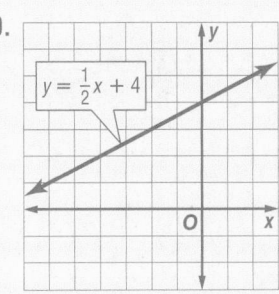

10.

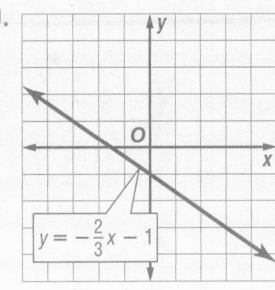

11.

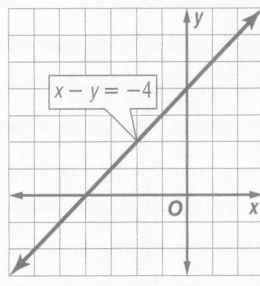

12.

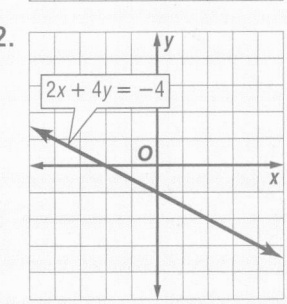

Extra Practice

Extra Practice

Answer Lesson 8-8

1.

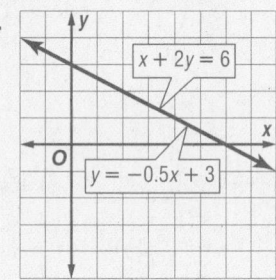

Answers Lesson 8-9

1.

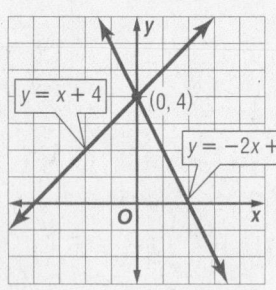

2.

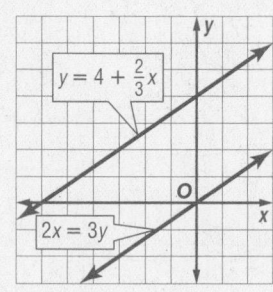

3.

4.

Lesson 8-8
(pages 409–413)

TECHNOLOGY For Exercises 1–3, use the table that shows the percent of U.S. households owning more than one television set.

Year	1955	1960	1965	1970	1975	1980	1985	1990	1995	2000
Percent	4	12	22	35	43	50	57	65	71	76

1. Make a scatter plot and draw a best-fit line. **See margin.**

2. Write an equation in slope-intercept form for the best-fit line. **Sample answer:** $y = 1.5x - 2925$

3. Use the equation to predict what percent of U.S. households will own more than one television set in 2010.
   Sample answer: 90%

Lesson 8-9
(pages 414–418)

Solve each system of equations by graphing. 1–6. See margin for graphs.

1. $x + 2y = 6$
   $y = -0.5x + 3$ **infinitely many**

2. $y = -2$
   $4x + 3y = 2$ **(2, −2)**

3. $y = x + 4$
   $y = -2x + 4$ **(0, 4)**

4. $y = 4 + \frac{2}{3}x$
   $2x = 3y$ **none**

5. $y = x - 2$
   $y = -\frac{1}{3}x + 2$ **(3, 1)**

6. $y = \frac{1}{2}x + 6$
   $2x + y = 1$ **(−2, 5)**

ALGEBRA Solve each system of equations by substitution.

7. $x + y = 4$
   $y = 2$ **(2, 2)**

8. $2x + y = 8$
   $x = 2$ **(2, 4)**

9. $y = x - 7$
   $x = 7$ **(7, 0)**

10. $x = 3$
    $y = 4$ **(3, 4)**

11. $y = 1$
    $2y + x = 1$ **(−1, 1)**

12. $y = 2x + 3$
    $y = 5$ **(1, 5)**

Lesson 8-10
(pages 419–422)

Graph each inequality. 1–9. See margin.

1. $y > 2x - 2$
2. $y \geq x$
3. $y < 1$
4. $x + y \leq -1$
5. $y + 3x \leq 0$
6. $x < -3$
7. $2x + 3y \geq 12$
8. $-2x + y > -1$
9. $y \geq -4$

WORK For Exercises 10–12, use the following information.
Seth can tutor students and volunteer at a soup kitchen no more than 9 evenings per month.

10. Write an inequality to represent this situation. $x + y \leq 9$

11. Graph the inequality. **See margin.**

12. Use the graph to determine how many days each month that Seth could tutor and volunteer. List two possibilities. **Sample answer: tutor 4 h, volunteer 5 h; tutor 6 h, volunteer 3 h**

5.

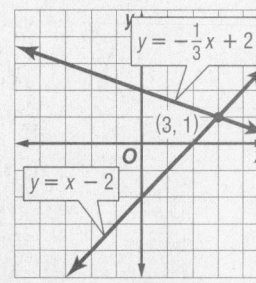

6.

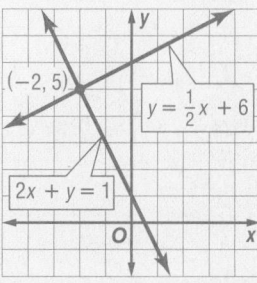

Lesson 9-1

(pages 436–440)

Find each square root, if possible.

1. $\sqrt{36}$ **6**
2. $-\sqrt{81}$ **−9**
3. $\sqrt{\frac{1}{4}}$ **$\frac{1}{2}$**

4. $-\sqrt{144}$ **−12**
5. $\sqrt{-25}$ **not possible**
6. $\sqrt{1.96}$ **1.4**

7. $\sqrt{-100}$ **not possible**
8. $-\sqrt{0.49}$ **−0.7**
9. $\sqrt{400}$ **20**

Use a calculator to find each square root to the nearest tenth.

10. $\sqrt{21}$ **4.6**
11. $\sqrt{99}$ **9.9**
12. $-\sqrt{60}$ **−7.7**

13. $\sqrt{124}$ **11.1**
14. $-\sqrt{350}$ **−18.7**
15. $\sqrt{18.6}$ **4.3**

16. $-\sqrt{42}$ **−6.5**
17. $-\sqrt{84.2}$ **−9.2**
18. $\sqrt{182}$ **13.5**

Estimate each square root to the nearest whole number. Do not use a calculator.

19. $\sqrt{21}$ **5**
20. $-\sqrt{85}$ **−9**
21. $\sqrt{7.3}$ **3**

22. $\sqrt{1.99}$ **1**
23. $-\sqrt{62}$ **−8**
24. $\sqrt{74.1}$ **9**

25. $\sqrt{810}$ **28**
26. $-\sqrt{88.8}$ **−9**
27. $\sqrt{1000}$ **32**

Lesson 9-2

(pages 441–445)

Name all of the sets of numbers to which each real number belongs. Let N = natural numbers, W = whole numbers, Z = integers, Q = rational numbers, and I = irrational numbers.

1. 15 **N, W, Z, Q**
2. 0 **W, Z, Q**
3. $\frac{3}{8}$ **Q**

4. 0.666… **Q**
5. 1.75 **Q**
6. $\sqrt{2}$ **I**

7. 5.14726… **I**
8. $-\sqrt{36}$ **Z, Q**
9. 0.3535… **Q**

Replace each ● with <, >, or = to make a true statement.

10. $3\frac{3}{4}$ ● $\sqrt{15}$ **<**
11. $-\sqrt{41}$ ● -6.8 **>**

12. 5.2 ● $\sqrt{27.04}$ **=**
13. $-\sqrt{110}$ ● -10.5 **>**

ALGEBRA Solve each equation. Round to the nearest tenth, if necessary.

14. $x^2 = 14$ **3.7, −3.7**
15. $y^2 = 25$ **5, −5**
16. $34 = p^2$ **5.8, −5.8**

17. $55 = h^2$ **7.4, −7.4**
18. $225 = k^2$ **15, −15**
19. $324 = m^2$ **18, −18**

20. $d^2 = 441$ **21, −21**
21. $r^2 = 25{,}000$ **158.1, −158.1**
22. $10{,}000 = x^2$ **100, −100**

Lesson 9-3

(pages 447–451)

Use a protractor to find the measure of each angle. Then classify each angle as *acute*, *right*, or *obtuse*.

1. $m\angle PQW$ **120°, obtuse**
2. $m\angle VQW$ **27°, acute**

3. $m\angle TQW$ **90°, right**
4. $m\angle SQW$ **140°, obtuse**

5. $m\angle SQR$ **40°, acute**
6. $m\angle VQR$ **153°, obtuse**

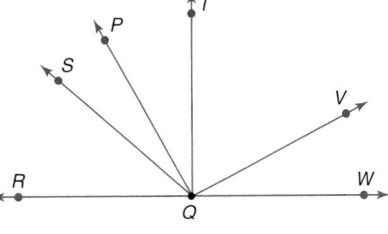

Use a protractor to draw an angle having each measurement. Then classify each angle as *acute*, *obtuse*, *right*, or *straight*. **7–12. See margin for drawings.**

7. 35° **acute**
8. 115° **obtuse**
9. 90° **right**

10. 160° **obtuse**
11. 180° **straight**
12. 18° **acute**

1. 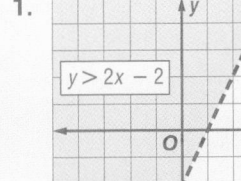 $y > 2x - 2$

2. 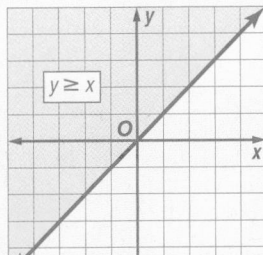 $y \geq x$

3. 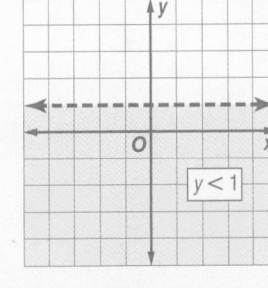 $y < 1$

4. 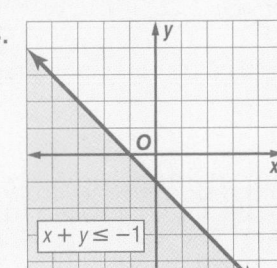 $x + y \leq -1$

5. 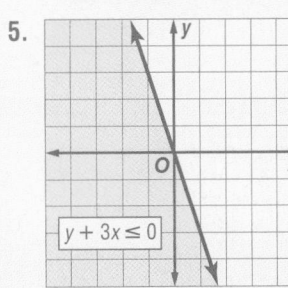 $y + 3x \leq 0$

6. 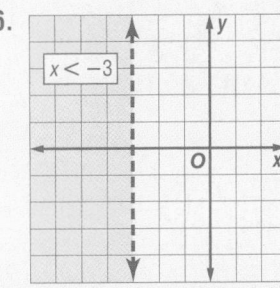 $x < -3$

7. 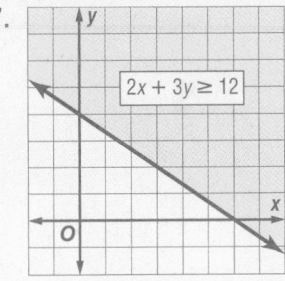 $2x + 3y \geq 12$

8. 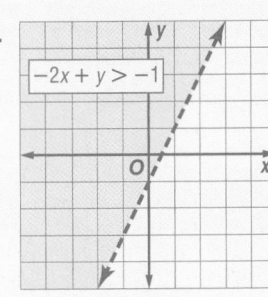 $-2x + y > -1$

9. 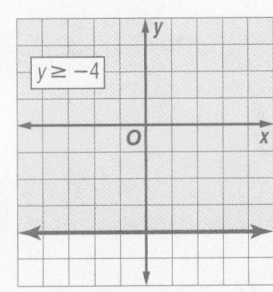 $y \geq -4$

Answers for Lessons 8-10 and 9-3 are continued on the next page.

Extra Practice

11.

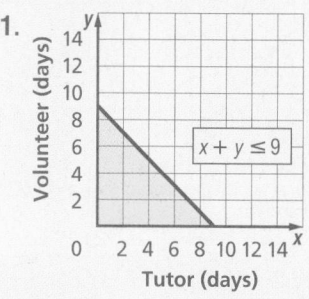

Answers Lesson 9-3

7.

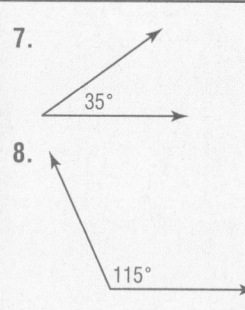

35°

8.

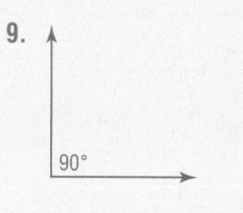

115°

9.

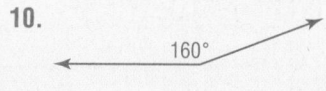

90°

10.

160°

11.

180°

12.

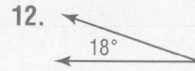

18°

Lesson 9-4   (*pages 453–457*)

Find the value of *x* in each triangle. Then classify each triangle as *acute*, *right*, or *obtuse*.

1. 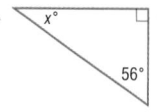 x° 56°   **34°; right**

2. 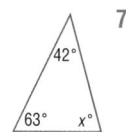 42° 63° x°   **75°; acute**

3. 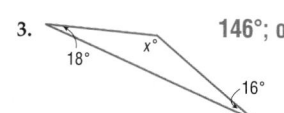 18° x° 16°   **146°; obtuse**

4. 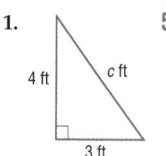 40° 95° x°   **45°; obtuse**

5. 31° x°   **59°; right**

6. 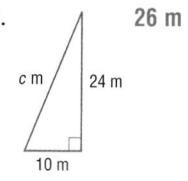 65° x° 65°   **50°; acute**

7. ALGEBRA   The measure of the angles of a triangle are in the ratio 1:2:3. What is the measure of each angle?   **30°; 60°; 90°**

8. ALGEBRA   Determine the measures of the angles of △*ABC* if the measures of the angles of a triangle are in the ratio 1:1:2.   **45°; 45°; 90°**

9. ALGEBRA   Suppose the measures of the angles of a triangle are in the ratio 1:9:26. What is the measure of each angle?   **5°; 45°; 130°**

Lesson 9-5   (*pages 460–464*)

Find the length of the hypotenuse in each right triangle. Round to the nearest tenth, if necessary.

1. 4 ft   c ft   3 ft   **5 ft**

2. 8 in.   6 in.   c in.   **10 in.**

3. c m   24 m   10 m   **26 m**

If *c* is the measurement of the hypotenuse, find each missing measure. Round to the nearest tenth, if necessary.

4. $a = 7$ m, $b = 24$ m   **25 m**
5. $a = 18$ in., $c = 30$ in.   **24 in.**
6. $b = 10$ ft, $c = 20$ ft   **17.3 ft**
7. $a = 3$ cm, $c = 9$ cm   **8.5 cm**
8. $b = 8$ m, $c = 32$ m   **31.0 m**
9. $a = 32$ yd, $c = 65$ yd   **56.6 yd**

Lesson 9-6   (*pages 466–470*)

Find the distance between each pair of points. Round to the nearest tenth, if necessary.

1. $A(2, 6)$, $B(-4, 2)$ **7.2**
2. $C(-3, 9)$, $D(2, 4)$ **7.1**
3. $E(6, -4)$, $F(1, -6)$ **5.4**
4. $G(0, -1)$, $H(9, -1)$ **9**
5. $I(-8, -3)$, $J(2, 2)$ **11.2**
6. $K(3, 0)$, $L(-7, -2)$ **10.2**

The coordinates of the endpoints of a segment are given. Find the coordinates of the midpoint of each segment.

7. $M(3, 5)$, $N(7, 1)$ **(5, 3)**
8. $O(-6, 2)$, $P(0, 8)$ **(−3, 5)**
9. $Q(4, -9)$, $R(-2, 7)$ **(1, −1)**
10. $S(13, -1)$, $T(-5, -3)$ **(4, −2)**

Lesson 9-7

(pages 471–475)

In Exercises 1–4, the triangles are similar. Write a proportion to find each missing measure. Then find the value of x.

1.

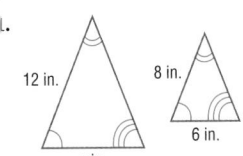

12 in.   8 in.
6 in.
x in.

$\dfrac{12}{8} = \dfrac{x}{6}$; 9 in.

2.

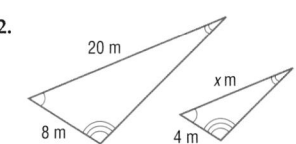

20 m
x m
8 m   4 m

$\dfrac{20}{x} = \dfrac{8}{4}$; 10 m

3.

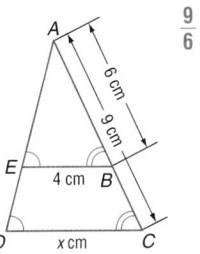

A
6 cm
9 cm
E   4 cm   B
D   x cm   C

$\dfrac{9}{6} = \dfrac{x}{4}$; 6 cm

4.

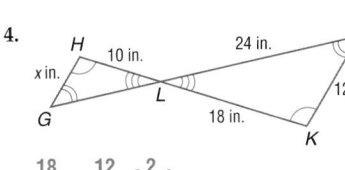

H   10 in.   24 in.   J
x in.
G   L   12 in.
18 in.   K

$\dfrac{18}{10} = \dfrac{12}{x}$; $6\dfrac{2}{3}$ in.

Lesson 9-8

(pages 477–481)

Find each sine, cosine, or tangent. Round to four decimal places, if necessary.

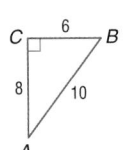
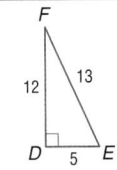

1. sin A **0.6**
2. sin B **0.8**
3. tan F **0.4167**
4. sin E **0.9231**
5. cos A **0.8**
6. tan A **0.75**

Use a calculator to find each value to the nearest ten thousandth.

7. sin 21° **0.3584**
8. tan 83° **8.1443**
9. cos 45° **0.7071**
10. tan 10° **0.1763**
11. sin 72° **0.9511**
12. cos 3° **0.9986**

Lesson 10-1

(pages 490–497)

In the figure at the right, ℓ is parallel to m and p is a transversal. If the measure of angle 2 is 38°, find the measure of each angle.

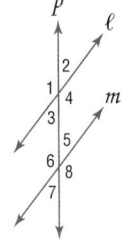

1. ∠1 **142°**
2. ∠4 **142°**
3. ∠3 **38°**
4. ∠6 **142°**
5. ∠5 **38°**
6. ∠8 **142°**

Find the value of x in each figure.

7.

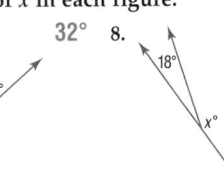

32°
x°

32°

8.

18°
x°

162°

9.

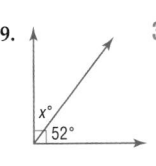

x°
52°

38°

10.

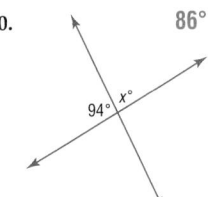

94°   x°

86°

Answers Lesson 10-2

1. $\angle A \cong \angle D$; $\angle B \cong \angle F$; $\angle C \cong \angle E$;
$\overline{AB} \cong \overline{DF}$, $\overline{BC} \cong \overline{FE}$; $\overline{AC} \cong \overline{DE}$;
$\triangle ABC \cong \triangle DFE$

2. $\angle G \cong \angle K$; $\angle H \cong \angle J$; $\angle I \cong \angle I$;
$\overline{GH} \cong \overline{KJ}$, $\overline{HI} \cong \overline{JI}$; $\overline{GI} \cong \overline{KI}$;
$\triangle GHI \cong \triangle KJI$

Answers Lesson 10-3

1. $A'(1, 1)$, $B'(5, -1)$, $C'(1, -3)$

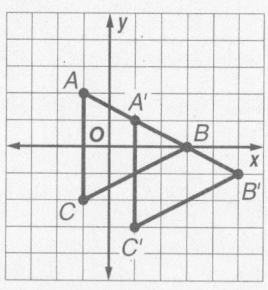

2. $K'(-3, 3)$, $L'(0, -2)$, $M'(-3, -4)$, $N'(-4, -2)$

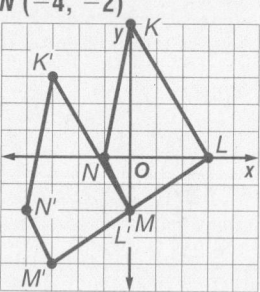

3. $J'(3, 3)$, $K'(1, 3)$, $I'(3, -3)$,

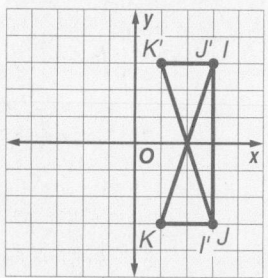

4. $D'(0, 4)$, $E'(-4, 2)$, $F'(-3, -4)$, $G'(0, 1)$

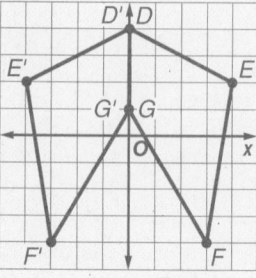

Lesson 10-2

(pages 500–504)

For each pair of congruent triangles, name the corresponding parts. Then complete the congruence statement. **1–2. See margin.**

1.
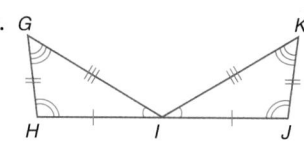

2.
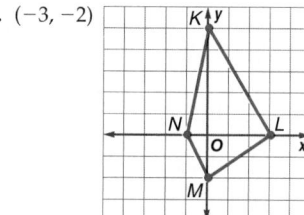

$\triangle ABC \cong \triangle$ __?__   DFE

$\triangle GHI \cong \triangle$ __?__   KJI

Complete each congruence statement if $\triangle JKL \cong \triangle DGW$.

3. $\angle K \cong$ __?__ $\angle G$

4. $\overline{WG} \cong$ __?__ $\overline{LK}$

5. $\angle D \cong$ __?__ $\angle J$

6. $\overline{KL} \cong$ __?__ $\overline{GW}$

7. $\overline{DG} \cong$ __?__ $\overline{JK}$

8. $\angle W \cong$ __?__ $\angle L$

Lesson 10-3

(pages 506–511)

Find the coordinates of the vertices of each figure after the given translation. Then graph the translation image. **1–4. See margin.**

1. $(2, -1)$

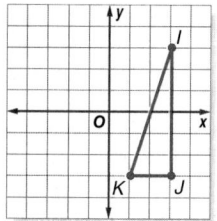

2. $(-3, -2)$

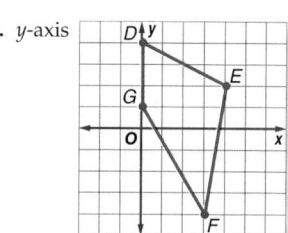

Find the coordinates of the vertices of each figure after a reflection over the given axis. Then graph the reflection image.

3. x-axis

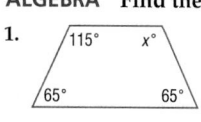

4. y-axis

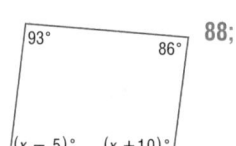

Lesson 10-4

(pages 513–517)

ALGEBRA   Find the value of x. Then find the missing angle measure.

1.
115; 115°

2.
110; 110°

3.
24; 48°

4.
88; 83°; 98°

nd the area of each figure.

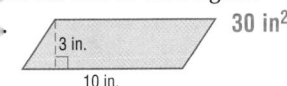 **30 in²**

2. **75.26 cm²**

10.6 cm

14.2 cm

 **18.125 ft²**

8.5 ft
2.5 ft
6 ft

4. **27 m²**

9 m

6 m

. What is the height of a parallelogram with a base of 3.4 inches and an area of 32.3 inches? **9.5 in.**

. The bases of a trapezoid measure 8 meters and 12 meters. Find the measure of the height if the trapezoid has an area of 70 square meters. **7 m**

lassify each polygon. Then determine whether it appears to be regular or not gular.

.  **hexagon; regular**

2. **11-gon; not regular**

nd the sum of the measures of the interior angles of each polygon.

. decagon **1440°**   4. pentagon **540°**   5. nonagon **1260°**
. hexagon **720°**   7. octagon **1080°**   8. 15-gon **2340°**

nd the circumference and area of each circle. Round to the nearest tenth.

. 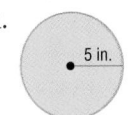 **31.4 in; 78.5 in²**

5 in.

2. **28.3 cm; 63.6 cm²**

9 cm

.  **113.1 ft; 1017.9 ft²**

18 ft

4. **22.9 cm; 41.9 cm²**

7.3 m

. The radius is 8.2 feet. **51.5 ft; 211.2 ft²**   6. The diameter is 1.3 yd. **4.1 yd; 1.3 yd²**
. The diameter is 5.2 yd. **16.3 yd; 21.2 yd²**   8. The radius is 4.8 cm. **30.2 cm; 72.4 cm²**

. Find the diameter of a circle if its circumference is 18.5 feet. Round to the nearest tenth. **5.9 ft**

. A circle has an area of 62.9 square inches. What is the radius of the circle? Round to the nearest tenth. **4.5 in.**

1. rectangular prism; bases: *ABCD*, *EFGH*, or *ADHE*, *BCGF*, or *ABFE*, *DCGH*; faces *ABCD*, *ADHF*, *DHGC*, *BCGF*, *ABFE*, *EFGH*; edges: $\overline{AB}$, $\overline{BC}$, $\overline{CD}$, $\overline{DA}$, $\overline{EF}$, $\overline{FG}$, $\overline{GH}$, $\overline{HE}$, $\overline{AE}$, $\overline{DH}$, $\overline{CG}$, $\overline{BF}$; vertices: *A, B, C, D, E, F, G, H*

2. triangular prism; bases: *HJK*, *LMN*; faces: *HJK*, *LMN*, *HJML*, *KJMN*, *HLNK*; edges: $\overline{HJ}$, $\overline{JK}$, $\overline{KH}$, $\overline{LM}$, $\overline{MN}$, $\overline{NL}$, $\overline{JM}$, $\overline{HL}$, $\overline{KN}$; vertices: *I, J, K, L, M, N*

Extra Practice

Lesson 10-8

(pages 539–543)

Find the area of each figure. Round to the nearest tenth.

1. 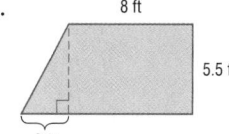 52.3 ft²

2. 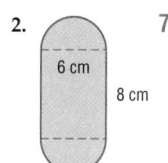 76.3 cm²

3. 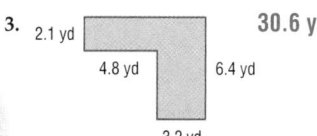 30.6 yd²

4. 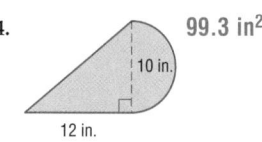 99.3 in²

Lesson 11-1

(pages 556–561)

Identify each solid. Name the bases, faces, edges, and vertices. 1–2. See margin.

1.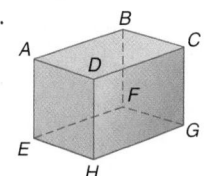

2.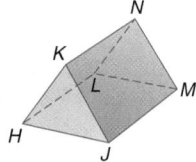

For Exercises 3–5, use the figure in Exercise 2.

3. State whether $\overline{HK}$ and $\overline{KN}$ are *parallel*, *skew*, or *intersecting*. **intersecting**
4. Name a segment that is skew to $\overline{JM}$. $\overline{HK}$ **or** $\overline{LN}$
5. Identify two planes that appear to be parallel. *HJK* **and** *LMN*

Lesson 11-2

(pages 563–567)

Find the volume of each solid. If necessary, round to the nearest tenth.

1. 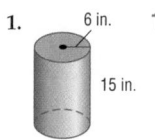 1696.5 in³

2. 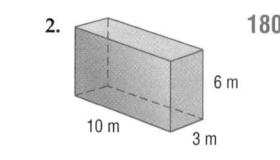 180 m³

3. 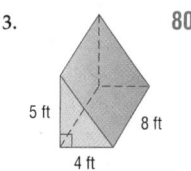 80 ft³

4. 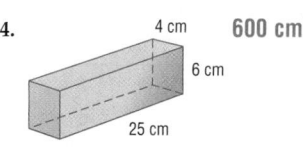 600 cm³

5. rectangular prism: length $2\frac{1}{2}$ yd, width 7 yd, height 12 yd **210 yd³**

6. cylinder: diameter 9.2 mm, height 16 mm **1063.6 mm³**

7. triangular prism: base of triangle 3.1 cm, altitude of triangle 1.7 cm, height of prism 5.0 cm **13.2 cm³**

8. Find the height of a rectangular prism with a length of 13 inches, width of 5 inches, and volume of 292.5 cubic inches. **4.5 in.**

Lesson 11-3
(pages 568–572)

Find the volume of each solid. If necessary, round to the nearest tenth.

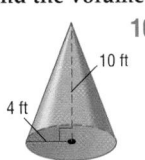

1. **167.6 ft³**

10 ft, 4 ft

2. **256 cm³**

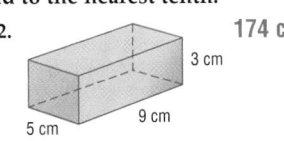

12 cm, 8 cm, 8 cm

3. cone: diameter 10 yd, height 7 yd   **183.3 yd³**

4. rectangular pyramid: length 6 in., width 6 in., height 9 in.   **108 in³**

5. square pyramid: length $3\frac{1}{4}$ ft, height 12 ft   **42.3 ft³**

6. cone: radius 3.6 cm, height 20 cm   **271.4 cm³**

7. hexagonal pyramid: base area 185 m², height 7 m   **431.7 m³**

Lesson 11-4
(pages 573–577)

Find the surface area of each solid. If necessary, round to the nearest tenth.

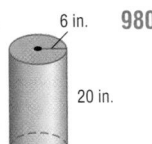

1. **980.2 in²**

6 in., 20 in.

2. **174 cm²**

3 cm, 5 cm, 9 cm

3. cube: side length 6 ft   **216 ft²**

4. cylinder: diameter 8 m, height 12 m   **402.1 m²**

5. cylinder: radius 2.5 cm, height 5 cm   **117.8 cm²**

6. cube: side length 4.9 m   **144.1 m²**

7. rectangular prism: length 7.6 mm, width 8.4 mm, height 7.0 mm   **351.7 mm²**

8. triangular prism: right triangle 3 in. by 4 in. by 5 in., height of prism 10 in.   **132 in²**

Lesson 11-5
(pages 578–582)

Find the surface area of each solid. If necessary, round to the nearest tenth.

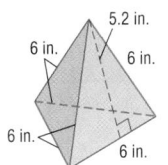

1. **62.4 in²**

5.2 in., 6 in., 6 in., 6 in., 6 in.

2. **578.1 cm²**

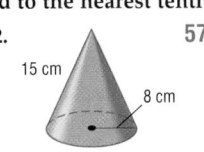

15 cm, 8 cm

3. **88 ft²**

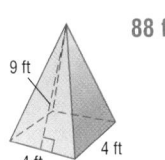

9 ft, 4 ft, 4 ft

4. **75.2 m²**

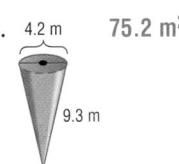

4.2 m, 9.3 m

5. square pyramid: base side length 1.8 mm, slant height 3.0 mm   **14.0 mm²**

6. cone: radius 4 in., slant height 7 in.   **138.2 in²**

7. cone: diameter 15.2 cm, slant height 12.3 cm   **475.1 cm²**

Answers Lesson 12-1

1.
Stem	Leaf
3	2 7
4	4 9
5	3 9
6	1 9

5|3 = 53

2.
Stem	Leaf
0	3 5 8
1	
2	1 4 6
3	0 5 5 8 9

2|1 = 21

3.
Stem	Leaf
0	5 6
⋮	
7	3 4 9
⋮	
15	3 7

7|3 = 7.3

1–3. See page 751.

4.

Stem	Leaf
17	1 2 9
18	1 1 2 6
19	3 8

$18|6 = 186$

5.

Stem	Leaf
5	5
6	2 7 9
7	1 4 5
8	0 1

$7|5 = 75$

6.

Stem	Leaf
9	8
10	6 9
11	1 7
12	1 5 6
13	2
14	2

$13|2 = 132$

7.

Stem	Leaf
1	7
2	1 4
3	7
4	
5	4
6	9
7	7
8	6
9	2

$8|6 = 86$

8.

Stem	Leaf
5	4 9
6	1 7
7	3 5
8	2 3 9
9	3
10	2

$6|7 = 6.7$

Lesson 11-6
(pages 584–588)

Determine whether each pair of solids is similar.

1. 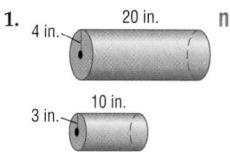 **no**

2. 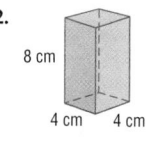 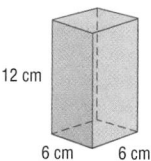 **yes**

Find the missing measure of each pair of similar solids.

3. 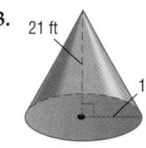 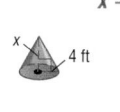 $x = 7$ ft

4. 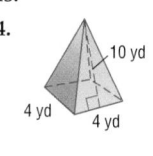 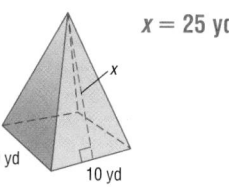 $x = 25$ yd

Determine whether each pair of solids is *sometimes*, *always*, or *never* similar. Explain.

5. two cylinders
   Sometimes; radii and heights must be proportional.

6. a square pyramid and a triangular pyramid
   never; different shapes

Lesson 11-7
(pages 590–594)

Determine the number of significant digits in each measure.

1. 625 ft **3**
2. 30 g **1**
3. 0.24 mm **2**
4. 36.83 L **4**
5. 6.0 in. **2**
6. 3900 ft **2**
7. 4.007 cm **4**
8. 0.0105 m **3**
9. 0.550 g **3**

Calculate. Round to the correct number of significant digits.

10. 32 yd + 16.9 yd **49 yd**
11. 14.36 in. − 9.4 in. **5.0 in.**
12. 20.86 cm − 0.375 cm **20.49 cm**
13. 9.600 m + 4.271 m **13.871 m**
14. 8 ft · 6.2 ft **50 ft²**
15. 7.50 m · 3.01 m **22.6 m²**
16. 41.61 in. + 18.4 in. − 3.65 in. + 7.371 in. **63.7 in.**

Lesson 12-1
(pages 606–611)

Display each set of data in a stem-and-leaf plot. 1–8. See margin.

1. 37, 44, 32, 53, 61, 59, 49, 69
2. 3, 26, 35, 8, 21, 24, 30, 39, 35, 5, 38
3. 15.7, 7.4, 0.6, 0.5, 15.3, 7.9, 7.3
4. 172, 198, 181, 182, 193, 171, 179, 186, 181
5. 55, 62, 81, 75, 71, 69, 74, 80, 67
6. 121, 142, 98, 106, 111, 125, 132, 109, 117, 126
7. 17, 54, 37, 86, 24, 69, 77, 92, 21
8. 7.3, 6.1, 8.9, 6.7, 8.2, 5.4, 9.3, 10.2, 5.9, 7.5, 8.3

For Exercises 9–11, use the stem-and-leaf plot shown at the right.

9. What is the greatest value? **98**
10. In which interval do most of the values occur? **80–89**
11. What is the median value? **82.5**

Stem	Leaf
7	2 2 3 5 9
8	0 1 1 4 6 6 8 9
9	3 4 8

$9|4 = 94$

Lesson 12-2

(pages 612–616)

Find the range and interquartile range for each set of data.

1. {44, 37, 23, 35, 61, 95, 49, 96} **73; 42**

2. {30, 62, 35, 80, 12, 24, 30, 39, 53, 38} **68; 23**

3. {7.15, 4.7, 6, 5.3, 30.1, 9.19, 3.2} **26.9; 4.49**

4. {271, 891, 181, 193, 711, 791, 861, 818} **710; 607.5**

5.
Stem	Leaf
2	0 1 1 2 4 7 9
3	3 3 6 8 8 8
4	2 4 5 7 9 9
5	2 9

39; 20.5

3 | 6 = 36

6.
Stem	Leaf
4	0 2 2 3 4 5 6 6 7 8
5	1 2 5 5 5 9
6	4 7 8 8
7	0 0 1 4 9 9 9
8	1 7 9
9	0 0 1 3 5

55; 32

8 | 7 = 87

Lesson 12-3

(pages 617–621)

Draw a box-and-whisker plot for each set of data. **1–4. See margin.**

1. 32, 54, 88, 17, 29, 73, 65, 52, 99, 103, 43, 13, 8, 59, 40, 37, 23

2. 42, 23, 31, 27, 32, 48, 37, 25, 19, 26, 30, 41, 32, 29

3. 124, 327, 215, 278, 109, 225, 186, 134, 251, 308, 179

4. 126, 432, 578, 312, 367, 400, 275, 315, 437, 299, 480, 365, 278

VOLLEYBALL   For Exercises 5–7, use the box-and-whisker plot shown.

Heights (in.) of Players on Volleyball Team

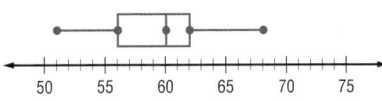

5. What is the height of the tallest player? **68 in.**

6. What percent of the players are between 56 and 68 inches tall? **75%**

7. Explain what the length of the box-and-whisker plot tells us about the data. **The values are spread out.**

Lesson 12-4

(pages 623–628)

Display each set of data in a histogram. **1–4. See margin.**

1.
Weekly Exercise Time		
Time (h)	Tally	Frequency
0–2	ЖΗΤ III	8
3–5	IIII	4
6–8	II	2
9–11	III	3

2.
Weekly Grocery Bill		
Amount ($)	Tally	Frequency
0–49	ЖΗΤ I	6
50–99	ЖΗΤ ЖΗΤ II	12
100–149	ЖΗΤ III	8
150–199	IIII	4
200–249	II	2

3.
Daily High Temperatures in August		
Temperature (°F)	Tally	Frequency
60–69	II	2
70–79	ЖΗΤ ЖΗΤ	10
80–89	ЖΗΤ I	6
90–99	III	3

4.
Score on Math Test		
Score	Tally	Frequency
50–59	II	2
60–69	I	1
70–79	ЖΗΤ III	8
80–89	ЖΗΤ ЖΗΤ IIII	14
90–99		0

Answers Lesson 12-4

1. **Weekly Exercise Time**

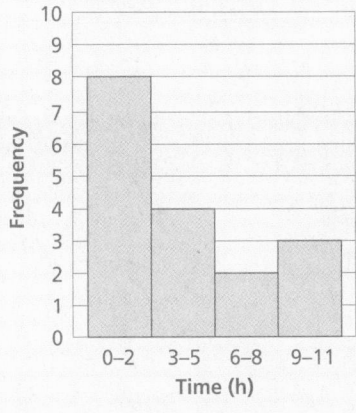

2. **Weekly Grocery Bill**

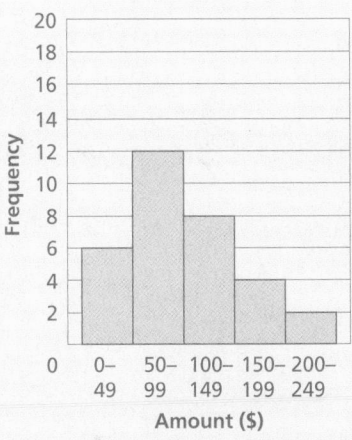

3. **Daily High Temperatures in August**

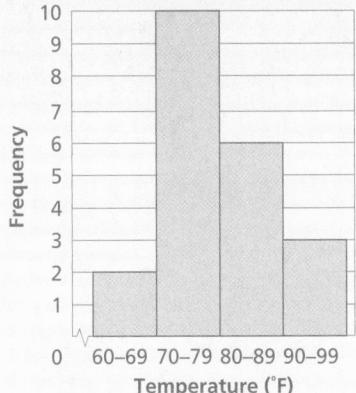

(continued on the next page)

Answers Lesson 12-3

1.
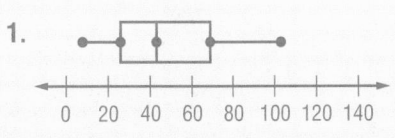

2.
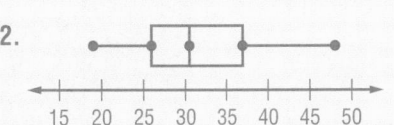

3.
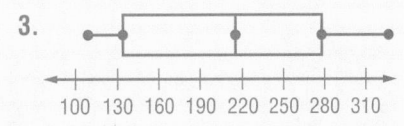

4.
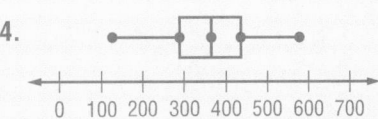

4. **Math Test Scores**

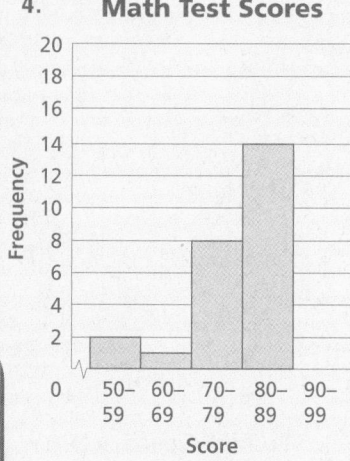

Lesson 12-5

(pages 630–633)

MONEY For Exercises 1–2, refer to the graphs below.

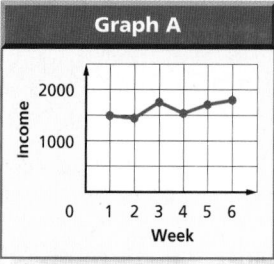
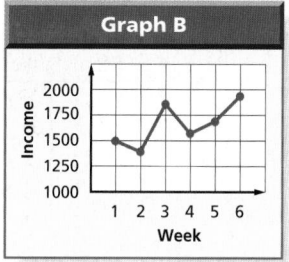

1. Explain why the graphs look different. **Different scales are used.**

2. Which graph appears to show that the income has been fairly consistent?
   Explain your reasoning. **Graph A; It shows a less dramatic increase and decrease.**

Lesson 12-6

(pages 635–639)

Find the number of possible outcomes for each situation.

1. Engagement rings come in silver, gold, and white gold. The diamond can weigh
   $\frac{1}{2}$ karat, $\frac{1}{3}$ karat, or $\frac{1}{4}$ karat. The diamond can have 4 possible shapes. **36**

2. A dress can be long, tea-length, knee-length, or mini. It comes in 2 colors and the dress
   can be worn on or off the shoulders. **16**

3. The first digit of a 7 digit phone number is a 2. The last digit is a 3. **100,000**

4. A chair can be a rocker, recliner, swivel, or straight back. It is available in fabric, vinyl,
   or leather. **12**

Find the probability of each event.

5. Three coins are tossed. What is the probability of three tails? $\frac{1}{8}$

6. Two six-sided number cubes are rolled. What is the probability of getting an
   odd sum? $\frac{1}{2}$

7. A ten-sided die is rolled and a coin is tossed. Find the probability of the coin landing
   on tails and the die landing on a number greater than 3. $\frac{7}{20}$

Lesson 12-7

(pages 641–645)

Tell whether each situation is a *permutation* or a *combination*. Then solve.

1. Seven people are running for four seats on student council. How many ways can the
   students be elected? **C; 35**

2. How many ways can the letters of the word ISLAND be arranged? **P; 720**

3. How many ways can five candles be arranged in three candlesticks? **C; 10**

4. How many ways can six students line up for a race? **P; 720**

5. How many ways can you select three books from a shelf containing 12 books? **C; 220**

6. **GEOMETRY** Determine the number of line segments that can be drawn between
   any two vertices of a pentagon. **10**

(pages 646–649)

Find the odds of each outcome if the spinner below is spun.

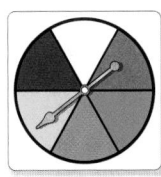

1. blue **1:5**
2. a color with less than 5 letters **1:2**
3. a color that begins with a consonant **5:1**
4. red, yellow, or blue **1:1**

Find the odds of each outcome if a 10-sided die is rolled.

5. number less than 7 **3:2**
6. odd number **1:1**
7. composite number **1:1**
8. number divisible by 3 **3:7**

Lesson 12-9   (pages 651–655)

A deck of Euchre cards consists of 4 nines, 4 tens, 4 jacks, 4 queens, 4 kings, and 4 aces. Suppose one card is selected and not replaced. Find the probability of each outcome.

1. 3 nines in a row $\frac{1}{506}$
2. a black jack and a red queen $\frac{1}{138}$
3. a nine of clubs, a black king, and a red ace $\frac{1}{3036}$
4. 4 face cards in a row $\frac{15}{322}$

A number from 6 to 19 is drawn. Find the probability.

5. P(13 or even) $\frac{4}{7}$
6. P(13 or less than 7) $\frac{1}{7}$
7. P(even or odd) **1**
8. P(14 or greater than 20) $\frac{1}{14}$
9. P(even or less than 10) $\frac{9}{14}$
10. P(odd or greater than 10) $\frac{11}{14}$

Lesson 13-1   (pages 669–672)

Determine whether each expression is a polynomial. If it is, classify it as a *monomial*, *binomial*, or *trinomial*.

1. $3x^2 + 5$ **yes; binomial**
2. $\frac{6}{x} + 9x$ **no**
3. $\frac{2}{3}p^4$ **yes; monomial**
4. $-6x^2 + 3x - 5$ **yes; trinomial**
5. $\sqrt{w} - 6$ **no**
6. $16 - 3m + m^3$ **yes; trinomial**
7. $\frac{d}{15}$ **yes; monomial**
8. $t^2 - 2$ **yes; binomial**
9. $\frac{x}{y} + z$ **no**

Find the degree of each polynomial.

10. 38 **0**
11. $4b + 9$ **1**
12. cd **2**
13. $4x$ **1**
14. $a^2 - 6$ **2**
15. $11r + 5s$ **1**
16. x^2y **3**
17. $n^2 - n$ **2**
18. $6a^2b^2$ **4**
19. $3y^2 - 2$ **2**
20. $9cd^3 - 5$ **4**
21. $-5p^3 + 8q^2$ **3**
22. $w^2 + 2x - 3y^3 - 7z$ **3**
23. $\frac{x^3}{6} - x$ **3**
24. $-17n^2p - 11np^3$ **4**

1. Nonlinear; the graph is a curve.

2. Linear; the graph is a straight line.

3. Nonlinear; the graph is a curve.

4. Linear; the graph is a straight line.

5. Linear; the graph is a straight line.

6. Nonlinear; the graph is a curve.

7. Linear; the graph is a straight line.

8. Linear; the graph is a straight line.

9. Nonlinear; the graph is a curve.

10. Nonlinear; the graph is a curve

11. Linear; as x increases by 2, y increases by 2.

12. Linear; as x increases by 5, y increases by 6.

Extra Practice

Lesson 13-2

(pages 674–677)

Find each sum.

1. $\begin{array}{r} -6m + 7 \\ (+)\ 9m - 2 \\ \hline 3m + 5 \end{array}$

2. $\begin{array}{r} 12y - 4 \\ (+)\ -8y + 9 \\ \hline 4y + 5 \end{array}$

3. $\begin{array}{r} 5x +\ y \\ (+)\ 9x - 2y \\ \hline 14x - y \end{array}$

4. $\begin{array}{r} 7c^2 - 10c + 5 \\ (+)\ 4c^2 -\ 4c - 8 \\ \hline 11c^2 - 14c - 3 \end{array}$

5. $\begin{array}{r} 2a^2 + 5ab + 6b^2 \\ (+)\ 3a^2 \quad\ -\ b^2 \\ \hline 5a^2 + 5ab + 5b^2 \end{array}$

6. $\begin{array}{r} 3d^3 + 2d^2 + 6d - 4 \\ (+)\quad -4d^2 \quad\ -\ 3 \\ \hline 3d^3 - 2d^2 + 6d - 7 \end{array}$

7. $(3a + 4) + (a + 2)$ **$4a + 6$**

8. $(8m - 3) + (4m + 1)$ **$12m - 2$**

9. $(5x - 3y) + (2x - y)$ **$7x - 4y$**

10. $(8p^2 - 2p + 3) + (-3p^2 - 2)$ **$5p^2 - 2p + 1$**

11. $(-11r^2 + 3s) + (5r^2 - s)$ **$-6r^2 + 2s$**

12. $(3a^2 + 5a + 1) + (2a^2 - 3a - 6)$ **$5a^2 + 2a - 5$**

Find each sum. Then evaluate if $m = -2$, $n = 4$, and $p = 3$.

13. $(3m - 5n) + (-6m + 8n)$ **$-3m + 3n$; 18**

14. $(m^2 + 2p^2) + (-4m^2 - 6p^2)$ **$-3m^2 - 4p^2$; -48**

15. $(-2m + 3n + 4p) + (5m - 6n - 8p)$ **$3m - 3n - 4p$; -30**

Lesson 13-3

(pages 678–681)

Find each difference.

1. $\begin{array}{r} 2a + 7 \\ (-)\ a + 3 \\ \hline a + 4 \end{array}$

2. $\begin{array}{r} -3k^2 + 6k \\ (-)\ 4k^2 +\ k \\ \hline -7k^2 + 5k \end{array}$

3. $\begin{array}{r} 6x^2 - 4x + 11 \\ (-)\ 5x^2 + 5x -\ 4 \\ \hline x^2 - 9x + 15 \end{array}$

4. $\begin{array}{r} 9r^2 \quad\ + 1 \\ (-)\ 2r^2 + 3r - 7 \\ \hline 7r^2 - 3r + 8 \end{array}$

5. $\begin{array}{r} 8n^2 + 3mn - 9 \\ (-)\ 4n^2 + 2mn \\ \hline 4n^2 + mn - 9 \end{array}$

6. $\begin{array}{r} -5b^2 -\ 2ab \\ (-)\quad - 10ab + 6a^2 \\ \hline -5b^2 + 8ab - 6a^2 \end{array}$

7. $(3n + 2) - (n + 1)$ **$2n + 1$**

8. $(-3c + 2d) - (7c - 6d)$ **$-10c + 8d$**

9. $(4x^2 + 1) - (3x^2 - 4)$ **$x^2 + 5$**

10. $(5a - 4b) - (-a + b)$ **$6a - 5b$**

11. $(-12a + 9b) - (3a - 7b)$ **$-15a + 16b$**

12. $(3w^3 + 5w - 6) - (5w^3 - 2w + 5)$ **$-2w^3 + 7w -$**

13. $(2t^2 - 5) - (t + 8)$ **$2t^2 - t - 13$**

14. $(x^2 + xy - 9y^2) - (3x^2 - xy + 3y^2)$
    $-2x^2 + 2xy - 12y^2$

Lesson 13-4

(pages 683–686)

Find each product. 19. **$-10x^3 + 15x^2 - 5x$**

1. $2(3a - 7)$ **$6a - 14$**

2. $(8c + 1)4$ **$32c + 4$**

3. $n(5n + 6)$ **$5n^2 + 6n$**

4. $t(2 - t)$ **$2t - t^2$**

5. $(3k - 5)k$ **$3k^2 - 5k$**

6. $(a + b)a$ **$a^2 + ab$**

7. $4n(5n - 3)$ **$20n^2 - 12n$**

8. $-3x(4 - x)$ **$-12x + 3x^2$**

9. $6m(-m^2 + 3)$ **$-6m^3 + 18m$**

10. $5(3x - 2)$ **$15x - 10$**

11. $(2p + 9)8$ **$16p + 72$**

12. $m(3m - 4)$ **$3m^2 - 4m$**

13. $-2w(6 - w)$ **$-12w + 2w^2$**

14. $ab(a + b)$ **$a^2b + ab^2$**

15. $7t(-3t + 4w)$ **$-21t^2 + 28tw$**

16. $4x(2x + y)$ **$8x^2 + 4xy$**

17. $(c^2 - 3d)2c$ **$2c^3 - 6cd$**

18. $-5z(z^2 - 9z)$ **$-5z^3 + 45z^2$**

19. $-5x(2x^2 - 3x + 1)$

20. $7r(r^2 - 3r + 7)$
    $7r^3 - 21r^2 + 49r$

21. $-3az(2z^2 + 4az + a^2)$
    $-6az^3 - 12a^2z^2 - 3a^3z$

Lesson 13-5

(pages 687–691)

Determine whether each graph, equation, or table represents a *linear* or a *nonlinear* function. Explain. **1–12. See margin.**

1.
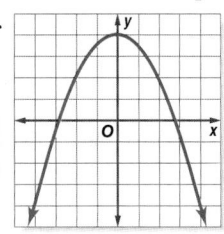

2.
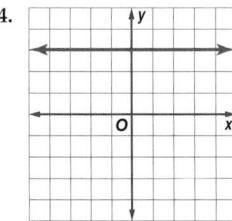

3.
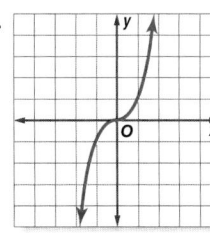

4.

5. $y = -3x$

6. $y = 2x^3 - 5$

7. $-2x + 5y = 10$

8. $x = 7y$

9. $y = (-2)^x$

10. $y = \dfrac{6}{x}$

11.

x	y
2	5
4	7
6	9
8	11

12.

x	y
5	7
10	13
15	19
20	25

Lesson 13-6

(pages 692–696)

Graph each function. **1–9. See margin.**

1. $y = 3x^2$

2. $y = -2x^2$

3. $y = \dfrac{1}{2}x^2$

4. $y = x^3$

5. $y = 0.3x^3$

6. $y = x^3 - 2$

7. $y = x^2 + 4$

8. $y = \dfrac{1}{3}x^2 - 3$

9. $y = -0.5x^2 + 1$

1.
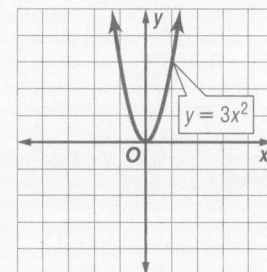
$y = 3x^2$

2.
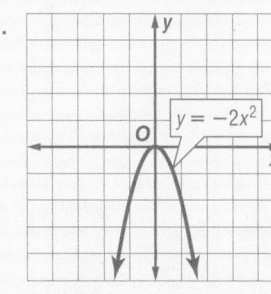
$y = -2x^2$

3.
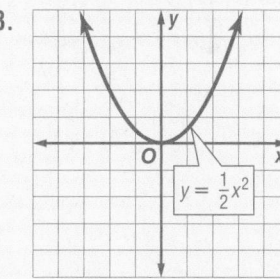
$y = \dfrac{1}{2}x^2$

4.
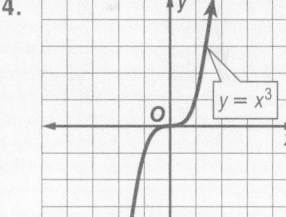
$y = x^3$

5.
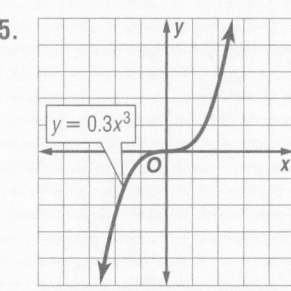
$y = 0.3x^3$

6.
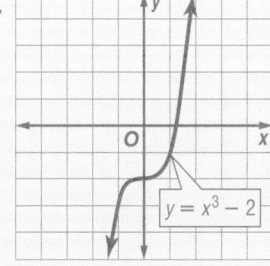
$y = x^3 - 2$

7.
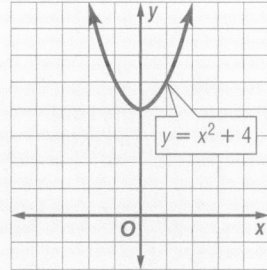
$y = x^2 + 4$

8.
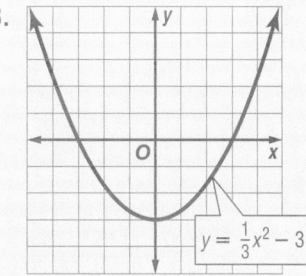
$y = \dfrac{1}{3}x^2 - 3$

9.
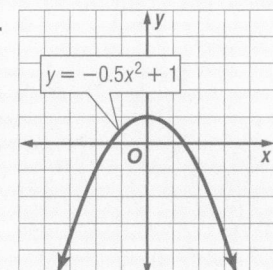
$y = -0.5x^2 + 1$

Answers

12.

Temperature (°C) vs Depth (km)

Points graphed at approximately (0, 20), (2, 90), (4, 160)

14.

Width (cm) vs Length (cm)

1. PATTERNS   How many cubes are in the tenth figure if the pattern below continues? *(Lesson 1-1)* **37 cubes**

  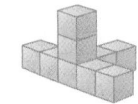

figure 1   figure 2   figure 3

2. SPACE EXPLORATION   On one flight, the space shuttle *Endeavour* traveled 6.9 million miles and circled Earth 262 times. About how many miles did the shuttle travel on each trip around Earth? *(Lesson 1-1)* **about 7 million ÷ 250 or 28,000 mi**

3. TREES   A conservation group collects seeds from trees at historic homes, grows them into saplings, and sells them to the public. Each sapling costs $35, and $7 is added to each order for shipping and handling. Write and then evaluate an expression for the total cost of one order of six saplings. *(Lesson 1-2)* **35(6) + 7; $217**

4. SALES   For a school fund-raiser, Sophia sold 15 white chocolate hearts at $4.25 each, 36 milk chocolate hearts at $3.75 each, and 22 milk chocolate assortments at $7.45 each. How much money did Sophia raise? *(Lesson 1-2)* **$362.65**

SPACE   For Exercises 5 and 6, use the following information.
Objects weigh six times more on Earth than they do on the moon because the force of gravity is greater. *(Lesson 1-3)*

5. Write an expression for the weight of an object on Earth if its weight on the moon is x. **6x**

6. A scientific instrument weighs 34 pounds on the moon. How much does the instrument weigh on Earth? **204 lb**

VOLLEYBALL   For Exercises 7 and 8, use the following information.
A volleyball net is 3 feet 3 inches tall. The bottom of the net is to be set 4 feet 8 inches from the floor. *(Lesson 1-4)*

7. Write an expression for the distance from the floor to the top of the net. **(3 ft + 3 in.) + (4 ft + 8 in.)**

8. Find the distance from the floor to the top of the net. **7 ft 11 in.**

9. NEWSPAPERS   Nick sold 86 newspapers on Monday, 79 on Tuesday, 68 on Wednesday, and [ ] on Friday. How many newspapers did Nick sell on Thursday if he sold a total of 391 in the five days? *(Lesson 1-5)* **75**

10. FOOD   Kristin is planning to buy twice as man[y] blueberry bagels as plain bagels for a staff meeting. Write a relation to show the different possibilities. *(Lesson 1-6)* **Sample answer: {(6, 3), (8, 4), (10, 5), (12, 6)}**

GEOLOGY   For Exercises 11 and 12, use the following information.
The underground temperature of rocks in degrees Celsius is estimated by the expression $35x + 20$, where x is the depth in kilometers. *(Lesson 1-6)*

11. Make a list of ordered pairs in which the x-coordinate represents the depth and the y-coordinate represents the temperature for depths of 0, 2, and 4 kilometers.

12. Graph the ordered pairs. **See margin.**
11. (0, 20), (2, 90), (4, 160)

13. EMPLOYMENT   The scatter plot shows the years of experience and salaries of twenty peopl[e]. Do the data show a *positive*, *negative*, or *no* relationship? Explain. *(Lesson 1-7)*

Salary ($ thousands) vs Years of Experience scatter plot

Positive; experien[ce] increases [as] salaries increase.

14. BIRDS   The table shows the average lengths an[d] widths of five bird eggs.

Bird	Length (cm)	Width (cm)
Canadian goose	8.6	5.8
robin	1.9	1.5
turtledove	3.1	2.3
hummingbird	1.0	1.0
raven	5.0	3.3

Source: *Animals as Our Companions*

Make a scatter plot of the data and predict the width of an egg 6 centimeters long. *(Lesson 1-7)*
See margin for graph, 4 cm.

Mixed Problem Solving

(pages 54–95)

ASTRONOMY   Mars is about 228 million kilometers from the Sun. Earth is about 150 million kilometers from the Sun. Write two inequalities that compare the two distances. *(Lesson 2-1)*
228 > 150, 150 < 228

GAMES   In a popular television game show, one contestant finished the regular round with a score of −200, and another contestant finished with a score of −500. Write two inequalities that compare their scores. *(Lesson 2-1)*
−200 > −500, −500 < −200

MONEY   Tino had $250 in his checking account at the beginning of April. During the month he wrote checks in the amounts of $72, $37, and $119. He also made one deposit of $45. Find Tino's account balance at the end of April. *(Lesson 2-2)* **$67**

ASTRONOMY   At noon, the average temperature on the moon is 112°C. During the night, the average temperature drops 252°C. What is the average temperature of the moon's surface during the night? *(Lesson 2-2)* **−140° C**

SUBMARINES   The research submarine *Alvin* is located at 1500 meters below sea level. It descends another 1250 meters to the ocean floor. How far below sea level is the ocean floor? *(Lesson 2-3)* **2750 m**

METEOROLOGY   Windchill factor is an estimate of the cooling effect the wind has on a person in cold weather. If the outside temperature is 10°F and the wind makes it feel like −25°F, what is the difference between the actual temperature and how cold it feels? *(Lesson 2-3)* **−35°F**

GEOGRAPHY   The highest point in Africa is Mount Kilimanjaro. Its altitude is 5895 meters. The lowest point on the continent is Lake Assal. Its altitude is −155 meters. Find the difference between these altitudes. *(Lesson 2-3)* **6050 m**

8. **GEOLOGY**   In December, 1994, geologists found that the Bering Glacier had come to a stop. The glacier had been retreating at a rate of about 2 feet per day. If the retreat resumes at the old rate, what integer represents how far the glacier will have advanced after 28 days? *(Lesson 2-4)* **−56**

9. **SPORTS**   The Wildcat football team was penalized the same amount of yardage four times during the third quarter. The total of the four penalties was 60 yards. If −60 represents a loss of 60 yards, write a division sentence to represent this situation. Then express the number of yards of each penalty as an integer. *(Lesson 2-5)*
$-60 \div 4 = y$; **−15**

10. **AEROSPACE**   To simulate space travel, NASA's Lewis Research Center in Cleveland, Ohio, uses a 430-foot shaft. If the free fall of an object in the shaft takes 5 seconds to travel the −430 feet, on average how far does the object travel in each second? *(Lesson 2-5)* **−86 feet per second**

11. **MAPS**   A map of a city can be created by placing the following buildings at the given coordinates: City Hall (1, 2), High School (−3, 6), Fire Department (4, −2), Recreation Center (0, 3). Draw and label the map. *(Lesson 2-6)*
See margin.

GEOMETRY   For Exercises 12 and 13, use the following information.
A vertex of a polygon is a point where two sides of the polygon intersect.

12. Identify the coordinates of the vertices in the triangle below. $A(2, 2)$, $B(-3, -1)$, $C(3, -3)$

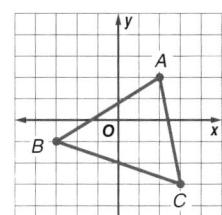

13. Add 2 to each *x*-coordinate. Graph the new ordered pairs. Describe how the position of the new triangle relates to the original triangle. *(Lesson 2-6)* **The triangle is moved two units right; see margin for graph.**

11.

13.

1. **BUSINESS**   A local newspaper can be ordered for delivery on weekdays or Sundays. A weekday paper is 35¢, and the Sunday edition is $1.50. The Stadlers ordered delivery of the weekday papers. The month of March had 23 weekdays and April had 20. How much should the carrier charge the Stadlers for those two months? *(Lesson 3-1)* **$15.05**

SHOPPING   For Exercises 2 and 3, use the following information.
One pair of jeans costs $23, and one T-shirt costs $15. *(Lesson 3-1)* **2. 3(23 + 15), 3 · 23 + 3 · 15**

2. Write two equivalent expressions for the total cost of 3 pairs of jeans and 3 T-shirts.

3. Find the total cost. **$114**

4. **ENTERTAINMENT**   Kyung bought 3 CDs that each cost x dollars, 2 tapes that each cost $10, and a video that cost $14. Write an expression in simplest form that represents the total amount that Kyung spent. *(Lesson 3-2)* **$3x + 34$**

TRANSPORTATION   For Exercises 5 and 6, use the following information.
A minivan is rated for maximum carrying capacity of 900 pounds.

5. If the luggage weighs 100 pounds, what is the maximum weight allowable for passengers? **800 lb**

6. What is the maximum average weight allowable for each of 5 passengers? *(Lesson 3-3)* **160 lb**

7. **GEOMETRY**   The perimeter of any square is 4 times the length of one of its sides. If the perimeter of a square is 72 centimeters, what is the length of each side of the square? *(Lesson 3-4)* **18 cm**

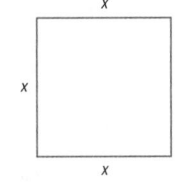

8. **PURCHASING**   Mr. Rockwell bought a television set. The price was $362. He paid $75 down and will pay the balance in 7 equal payments. How much is each payment? *(Lesson 3-5)* **$41**

9. **SPORTS**   Marcie paid $75 to join a tennis club for the summer. She will also pay $10 for each hour that she plays. If Marcie has budgeted $22 to play tennis this summer, how many hours ca she play tennis? *(Lesson 3-5)* **15 h**

FENCING   For Exercises 10 and 11, use the following information.
Wanda uses 130 feet of fence to enclose a rectangula flower garden. She also used the 50-foot wall of her house as one side of the garden. What is the width the garden? *(Lesson 3-6)* **10. $2w + 50 = 130$**

10. Write an equation that represents this situation.

11. Solve the equation to find the width of the garden. **40 ft**

WORKING   For Exercises 12 and 13, use the following information.
Kate worked a 40-hour week and was paid $410. Th amount included a $50 bonus. *(Lesson 3-6)*

12. Write an equation that represents this situation.

13. What was Kate paid per hour? **$9**
    12. $40x + 50 = 410$

14. **GEOMETRY**   The perimeter of the triangle below is 27 yards.

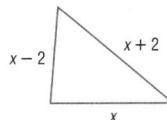

Find the lengths of the sides of the triangle. *(Lesson 3-7)* **7 yd, 9 yd, 11 yd**

15. **TRAVEL**   The Flynn family plans to drive 600 miles for their summer vacation. The speed limit on the highways they plan to use is 55 mi per hour. If they do not exceed the speed limit, how many hours of driving should it take them *(Lesson 3-7)* **10.9 h**

SCIENCE   For Exercises 16 and 17, use the following information.
Acceleration is the rate at which velocity is changin with respect to time. To find the acceleration, find t change in velocity by subtracting the starting veloci s from the final velocity, f. Then divide by the time, *(Lesson 3-7)*

16. Write the formula for acceleration, a. $a = \dfrac{f - s}{t}$

17. A motorcycle goes from 2 m/s to 14 m/s in 6 seconds. Find its acceleration. **2 m/s^2**

LUNCHTIME A group of 136 sixth graders needs to be seated in the cafeteria for lunch. If all of the tables need to be full, should the school use tables that seat 6, 8, or 10 students each? *(Lesson 4-1)* **8**

PATTERNS In a pattern, the number of colored tiles used in row x is 3^x. Find the number of tiles used in rows 4, 5, and 6 of the pattern. *(Lesson 4-2)* **81, 243, 729**

ELECTRICITY The amount of power lost in watts P can be found by using the formula $P = I^2R$, where I is current in amps, and R is resistance in ohms. The resistance of the wire leading from the source of power to a home is 2 ohms. If an electric stove causes a current of 41 amps to flow through the wire, find the power lost from the wire powering the stove. *(Lesson 4-2)* **3362 watts**

CODES Prime numbers are used to code and decode information. Suppose two prime numbers p and q are chosen so that $n = pq$. Then the key to the code is n. Find p and q if $n = 1073$. *(Lesson 4-3)* **29 and 37**

INTERIOR DESIGN Mrs. Garcia has two different fabrics to make square pillows for her living room. One fabric is 48 inches wide, and the other fabric is 60 inches wide. How long should each side of the pillows be if they are all the same size and no fabric is wasted? *(Lesson 4-4)* **12 in.**

ECONOMICS The graph below shows how each dollar spent by the Federal Government is used.

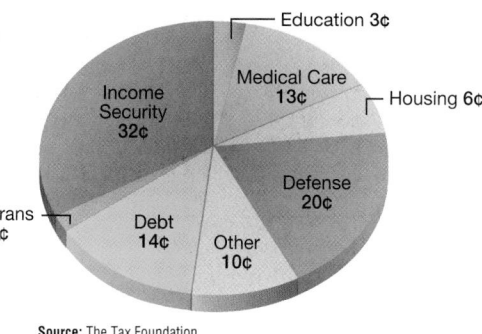

Government Spending

Education 3¢
Medical Care 13¢
Housing 6¢
Income Security 32¢
Defense 20¢
Debt 14¢
Other 10¢
rans ¢

Source: The Tax Foundation

Write a fraction in simplest form comparing the amount spent on housing assistance and the total amount spent. *(Lesson 4-5)* $\dfrac{3}{50}$

7. **BASKETBALL** Sydney made 8 out of 14 free throws in her last basketball game. Write her success as a fraction in simplest form. *(Lesson 4-5)* $\dfrac{4}{7}$

8. **TRANSPORTATION** Cameron spends 18 minutes traveling to work. What fraction of the day is this? *(Lesson 4-5)* $\dfrac{1}{80}$

9. **EARTHQUAKES** The table below describes different earthquake intensities.

Earthquake	Richter Scale	Intensity
A	8	10^7
B	4	10^3

Find $10^7 \div 10^3$ to determine how much more intense Earthquake A was than Earthquake B. *(Lesson 4-6)* 10^4 **or 10,000 times**

ASTRONOMY For Exercises 10 and 11, use the following information. **10.** $\dfrac{6.67}{10^{11}}$
Any two objects in space have an attraction that can be calculated by using a formula that includes the universal gravitational constant, 6.67×10^{-11} Nm²/kg². (N is newtons.) *(Lesson 4-7)*

10. Write the universal gravitational constant using positive exponents.

11. Write the constant as a decimal.
0.0000000000667   **12.** $\dfrac{1}{10^7}$ **m**

BIOLOGY For Exercises 12 and 13, use the following information.
Deoxyribonucleic acid, or DNA, contains the genetic code of an organism. The length of a DNA strand is about 10^{-7} meter. *(Lesson 4-7)*

12. Write the length of a DNA strand using positive exponents.

13. Write the length of a DNA strand as a decimal. **0.0000001 m**

14. **SCIENCE** Atoms are extremely small particles about two millionths of an inch in diameter. Write this measure in standard form and in scientific notation. *(Lesson 4-8)*
0.000002; 2.0 $\times$ 10^{-6}

15. **BUSINESS** A large corporation estimates its yearly revenue at 4.72×10^8. Write this number in standard form. *(Lesson 4-8)* **$472,000,000**

1. **FURNITURE**   A shelf $16\frac{5}{8}$ inches wide is to be placed in a space that is $16\frac{3}{4}$ inches wide. Will the shelf fit in the space? Explain. *(Lesson 5-1)*
yes; $16\frac{5}{8} < 16\frac{3}{4}$

2. **MEASUREMENT**   A piece of metal is 0.025 inch thick. What fraction of an inch is this? *(Lesson 5-2)*
$\frac{1}{40}$ in.

3. **HEALTH**   You can stay in the Sun 15 times longer than usual without burning by applying SPF number 15. If you usually burn after $\frac{1}{4}$ hour in the Sun, how long could you stay in the Sun using SPF 15 lotion? *(Lesson 5-3)* $3\frac{3}{4}$ h

4. **MONEY**   A dollar bill remains in circulation about $1\frac{1}{4}$ years. A coin lasts about $22\frac{1}{2}$ times longer. How long is a coin in circulation? *(Lesson 5-3)* $28\frac{1}{8}$ yr

5. **FOOD**   If each guest at a party eats two-thirds of a small pizza, how many guests would finish 12 small pizzas? *(Lesson 5-4)* **18 guests**

6. **PUBLISHING**   A magazine page is 8 inches wide. The articles are printed in three columns with $\frac{1}{4}$ inch of space in between and $\frac{3}{8}$-inch margins on each side, as shown below.

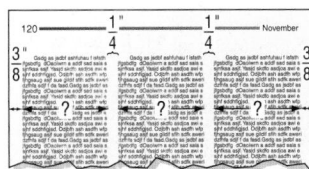

How wide should an author set the columns on her computer so that they are the same width as in the magazine? *(Lesson 5-4)* $2\frac{1}{4}$ in.

7. **REMODELING**   In their basement, the Jacksons installed $\frac{3}{8}$-inch thick paneling over a layer of dry wall that is $\frac{5}{8}$ inch thick. How thick are the wall coverings? *(Lesson 5-5)* **1 in.**

8. **COLLEGE**   In a college dormitory, $\frac{3}{8}$ of the residents are from Ohio, and $\frac{2}{5}$ of the residents are from New York. Which state has a greater representation? *(Lesson 5-6)* **New York**

9. **NUTRITION**   A survey found that $\frac{1}{6}$ of America households bought bottled water in 2000. Only of American households bought bottled water in 1993. What fraction of the population bought bottled water in 2000 that did not in 1993? *(Lesson 5-7)* $\frac{11}{102}$

10. **EMPLOYMENT**   The table below shows the earnings per woman for every \$100 earned by a man in the same occupation for two years. *(Lesson 5-8)*

Occupation	Earnings (\$)	
	Year 1	Year 2
Nurse	99.50	104.70
Teacher	88.60	90.30
Police Officer	91.20	94.20
Food Service	102.50	105.60
Postal Clerk	93.40	94.60

Find the mean, median, and mode of the earning for each year. **Year 1: 95.04; 93.40; none; Year 2: 97.88; 94.60; none**

11. **OIL PRODUCTION**   Texas and Alaska produce a total of 1372.2 million barrels of oil. Alaska produced 684.0 million barrels. How many barrels of oil were produced in Texas? *(Lesson 5-)* **688.2 million**

12. **ON-LINE SERVICE**   The cost of using an Intern service provider for 5, 6, 7, and 8 hours is given by the sequence \$9.95, \$12.90, \$15.85, and \$18.80 respectively. Is the cost an arithmetic or geometr sequence? Explain. *(Lesson 5-10)* **Arithmetic; the common difference is \$2.95.**

SHOPPING Best buys in grocery stores are generally found by comparing unit rates such as cents per ounce. Which bag of nachos shown in the table at the right is the better buy? *(Lesson 6-1)* **32-oz bag at $3.69**

Size	Price
16-oz	$2.49
32-oz	$3.69

COOKING A recipe that makes 72 cookies calls for $4\frac{1}{2}$ cups of flour. How many cups of flour would be needed to make 48 cookies? *(Lesson 6-2)* **3 c**

FERRIS WHEEL In a scale model of a Ferris wheel, the diameter of the wheel is 5 inches. If the actual height of the wheel is 55 feet, what is the scale of the model? *(Lesson 6-3)* **1 in. = 11 ft**

BUSINESS An executive of a marshmallow company said that marshmallows are 80% air. What fraction of a marshmallow is air? *(Lesson 6-4)* **$\frac{4}{5}$**

HEALTH Doctors estimate that 3 babies out of every 1000 are likely to get a cold during their first month. What percent is this? *(Lesson 6-4)* **0.3%**

NUTRITION Refer to the nutritional label from a bag of pretzels shown below.

Nutrition Facts
Serving Size 1 package (46.8g)
Servings per container 1

Amount per serving
Calories 190 Calories from Fat 15

	% Daily Value*
Total Fat 1.5g	3%
Saturated Fat 0g	0%
Cholesterol 0mg	0%
Sodium 760mg	32%
Total Carbohydrate 37g	12%

The 760 milligrams of sodium (salt) in one serving is 32% of the recommended daily value. What is the total recommended daily value of sodium? *(Lesson 6-5)* **about 2375 mg or 2.375 g**

7. **FAST FOOD** A certain hamburger has 560 Calories, and 288 of these are from fat. About what percent of the Calories are from fat? *(Lesson 6-6)* **about 50%**

8. **MONEY** If Simone wants to leave a tip of about 15% on a dinner check of $23.85, how much should she leave? *(Lesson 6-6)* **$3.60**

9. **BUSINESS** Many car dealers offer special interest rates as incentives to attract buyers. How much interest would a person pay for the first month of a $5500 car loan if the monthly interest rate is 0.24%? *(Lesson 6-7)* **$13.20**

10. **PETS** Hedgehogs are becoming so popular as pets that some breeders have reported a 250% increase in sales in recent years. If a breeder sold 50 hedgehogs one year before the increase, how many should he or she expect to sell a year from now? *(Lesson 6-8)* **175**

11. **BRAND NAMES** The graph below shows the results of a survey.

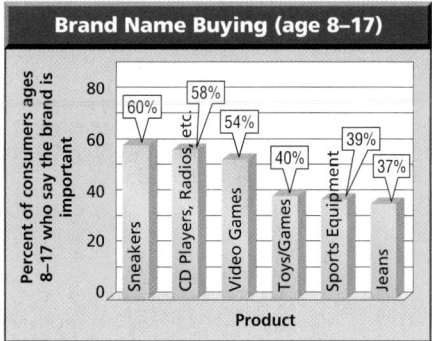

Brand Name Buying (age 8–17)

Source: International Mass Retail Association

How many of a class of 423 ninth grade students would you expect to say that they consider brand name when buying jeans? *(Lesson 6-9)* **157**

12. **CANDY** In a small bag of colored chocolate candies, there are 15 green, 23 red, and 18 yellow candies. What is the probability of selecting a red candy if one is taken from the bag at random? *(Lesson 6-9)* **$\frac{23}{56}$**

Mixed Problem Solving 763

CENSUS   For Exercises 1–3, use the following information.

The table below shows the 2000 populations and the average rates of change in population in the 1990s for Buffalo, New York, and Corpus Christi, Texas. Suppose the population of each city continued to increase or decrease at these rates. *(Lesson 7-1)*

City	Population in 2000	Yearly Rate of Change
Buffalo, NY	293,000	−3500
Corpus Christi, TX	277,000	+2000

1. Write an expression for the population of Buffalo after x years. **$293,000 - 3500x$**

2. Write an expression for the population of Corpus Christi after x years. **$277,000 + 2000x$**

3. In how many years would the population of the two cities be the same? **about 3 yr**

4. **INTERNET**   One Internet provider charges $19.95 a month plus $0.21 per minute, and a second provider charges $24.95 a month plus $0.16 per minute. For how many minutes is the cost of the plans the same? *(Lesson 7-1)* **100 min**

5. **GEOMETRY**   The length of a rectangle is three times the difference between its width and two. Find the width if the length is 15 inches. *(Lesson 7-2)* **7 in.**

6. **SPORTS**   More than 100,000 fans attended the opening football game of the season. Write an inequality for the number of people who attended. *(Lesson 7-3)* **$f > 100,000$**

7. **SCHOOL**   Julie has math and English homework tonight. She has no more than 90 minutes to spend on her homework. Suppose Julie spends 35 minutes completing her math homework. Write and solve an inequality to find how much time she can spend on her English homework. *(Lesson 7-4)* **$e + 35 \le 90$; at most 55 minutes**

8. **SAVINGS**   Curtis is saving money to buy a new mountain bike. The bikes that he likes start at $375, and he has already saved $285. Write and solve an inequality to find the amount he must still save. *(Lesson 7-4)* **$x + 285 \ge 375$; at least $90**

9. **STATISTICS**   The Boston Marathon had more than 2,600,000 spectators along its 26-mile route. Write and solve an inequality to find the average number of spectators per mile. *(Lesson 7-5)* **$26x > 2,600,000$; more than 100,000 spectators**

10. **GROCERY SHOPPING**   Mrs. Hiroshi spends at least twice as much on her weekly grocery shopping as she did one year ago. Last year, she spent $54 each week. How much is Mrs. Hiroshi now spending each week on groceries? *(Lesson 7-5)* **at least $108**

11. **GEOMETRY**   An *acute angle* has a measure less than 90°. If the measure of an acute angle is $2x$, write and solve an inequality to find the possible values of x. *(Lesson 7-5)* **$2x < 90$; less than 45**

12. **SHOPPING**   Luis plans to spend at most $85 on jeans and shirts. He bought 2 shirts for $15.30 each. How much can he spend on jeans? *(Lesson 7-6)* **at most $54.40**

13. **CAR SALES**   A car salesperson receives a monthly salary of $1000 plus a 3% commission on every car sold. For what amount of monthly sales will the salesperson earn more than $2500? *(Lesson 7-6)* **$s > $50,000**

14. **SCHOOL**   Dave has earned scores of 73, 85, 91, and 82 on the first four of five math tests for the grading period. He would like to finish the grading period with a test average of at least 82. What is the minimum score Dave needs to earn on the fifth test in order to achieve his goal? *(Lesson 7-6)* **79**

SHIPPING RATES For Exercises 1–3, use the following information.
The shipping costs for mail-order merchandise are given in the table below. (Lesson 8-1)

Total Price of Merchandise	Shipping Cost
$0–$30.00	$4.25
$30.01–$70.00	$5.75
$70.01 and over	$6.95

What is the shipping cost of merchandise totaling $75? **$6.95**

For what price of merchandise is the shipping cost $5.75? **$30.01–$70.00**

Does the table represent a function? Explain.
Yes, each price has a unique shipping cost.

PHYSICS For Exercises 4 and 5, use the following information.
As a thunderstorm approaches, you see lightning as it occurs, but you hear the accompanying thunder a short time afterward. The distance y in miles that sound travels in x seconds is given by $y = 0.21x$. (Lesson 8-2) **4. (1, 0.21), (2, 0.42), (3, 0.63)**

Find three ordered pairs that relate x and y.

How far away is lightning when thunder is heard 2.5 seconds after the lightning is seen?
about 0.525 mi

AVIATION For Exercises 6 and 7, use the following information.
The steady descent of a jetliner is represented by the equation $a = 24,000 - 1500t$, where t is the time in minutes and a is the altitude in feet. (Lesson 8-3) **6. 16**

Name the x-intercept of the graph of the equation.

What does the x-intercept represent? **Time when the altitude is zero and the jet has landed.**

KITES Drew is flying a kite in the park. The kite is a horizontal distance of 20 feet from Drew's position and a vertical distance of 70 feet. Find the slope of the kite string. (Lesson 8-4) $\frac{7}{2}$

FUEL The cost of gasoline varies directly as the number of gallons bought. If it costs $27.80 to fill a 20-gallon tank, what would it cost to fill a 12-gallon tank? (Lesson 8-5) **$16.68**

10. BUSINESS A company's monthly cost y is given by $y = 1500 + 12x$, where x represents the number of items produced. State the slope and y-intercept of the graph of the equation and describe what they represent. (Lesson 8-6)
12, cost per item; 1500, cost when no items are produced

CAR RENTAL For Exercises 11 and 12, use the following information.
It costs $59 per day plus $0.12 per mile driven to rent a minivan. (Lesson 8-7)

11. Write an equation in slope-intercept form that shows the cost y for renting a minivan for one day and driving x miles. $y = 59 + 0.12x$

12. Find the daily rental cost if 30 miles are driven.
$62.60

13. NUTRITION The graph below shows energy bar sales in the United States during the month of October.

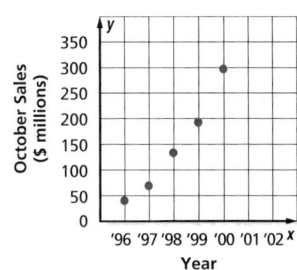

Source: ACNielsen

Use the graph to predict energy bar sales during October 2002. (Lesson 8-8)
Sample answer: $375 million

14. SCHOOL CONCERT Tickets for the fall concert cost $3 for students and $5 for nonstudents. If a total of 140 tickets were sold and $590 was collected, how many of each type of ticket was sold? (Lesson 8-9) **55 student, 85 nonstudent**

FINANCE For Exercises 15–17, use the following information. **15–17. See margin.**
Silvina earns $3.50 per hour for weeding the garden and $5.00 per hour for mowing the lawn. Suppose she wants to earn at least $35 this week. (Lesson 8-10)

15. Write an inequality to represent this situation. Let x represent the number of hours she weeds and let y represent the number of hours she mows.

16. Graph the inequality.

17. Determine two possible ways that she can earn at least $35 this week.

Answers

15. $3.5x + 5y \geq 35$

16.

17. Sample answer: weed 4 hours, mow 6 hours; weed 8 hours, mow 2 hours

Answer

5.

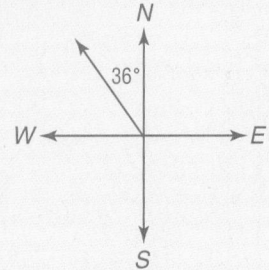

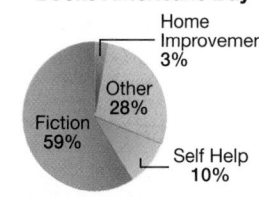

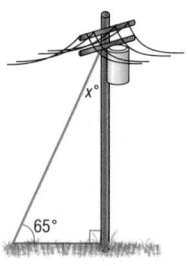

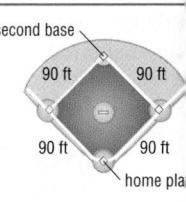

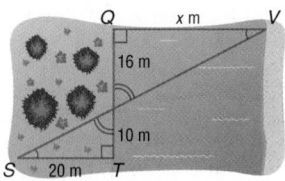

1. CONSTRUCTION   A banquet facility must allow at least 4 square feet for each person on the dance floor. Reston's Hotel is adding a square dance floor that will be large enough for 100 people. How long should it be on each side? *(Lesson 9-1)* **20 ft**

2. PHYSICS   The time t in seconds that it takes an object to fall d feet can be estimated by using $d = 0.5gt^2$. In this formula, g is acceleration due to gravity, 32 ft/s². If a ball is dropped from the top of a 55-foot building, how long does it take to hit the ground? *(Lesson 9-2)* **about 1.85 s**

BOOKS   For Exercises 3 and 4, use the following information.
The graph shows the results of a survey, which asked which types of books people buy the most. *(Lesson 9-3)*

Books Americans Buy

Home Improvement 3%
Other 28%
Fiction 59%
Self Help 10%

Source: *USA TODAY*

3. Classify the angle labeled Self Help as *acute, obtuse, right,* or *straight*. **acute**

4. Find the measure of the angle labeled Fiction. **212.4°**

5. AVIATION   Airplane flight paths can be described using angles and compass directions. The path of a particular airplane is described as 36° west of north. Draw a diagram that represents this path. *(Lesson 9-3)* **See margin.**

6. UTILITIES   A support cable is sometimes attached to give a utility pole stability. If the cable makes an angle of 65° with the ground, what is the measure of the angle formed by the cable and the pole? *(Lesson 9-4)* **25°**

7. BASEBALL   A baseball diamond is actually a square with 90 feet between the bases. What is the distance between home plate and second base? *(Lesson 9-5)* **about 127.3 ft**

8. SAILING   A rope from the top of a sailboat mast is attached to a point 6 feet from the base of the mast. If the rope is 24 feet long, how high is the mast? *(Lesson 9-5)* **about 23.2 ft**

9. TRAVEL   Matt's home is at $(-4, 9)$ on the map. His friend Carlos' home is at $(6, 3)$ on the same map. They want to meet halfway between their two homes. What are the coordinates on the map where they should plan to meet? *(Lesson 9-6)* **(1, 6)**

10. HISTORY   The largest known pyramid is Khufu's pyramid. At a certain time of day, a yardstick casts a shadow 1.5 feet long, and the pyramid casts a shadow 241 feet long. Use shadow reckoning to find the height of the pyramid. *(Lesson 9-7)* **482 ft**

11. SURVEYING   A surveyor needs to find the distance across a river and draws the sketch shown below.

Find the distance across the river. *(Lesson 9-7)* **32 m**

12. RECREATION   Maxine is flying a kite on a 75-yard string. The string is making a 45° angle with the ground. How high above the ground is the kite? *(Lesson 9-8)* **53 yd**

13. MAINTENANCE   A 15-foot ladder is propped against a house. The angle it forms with the ground is 60°. To the nearest foot, how far up the side of the house does the ladder reach? *(Lesson 9-8)* **13 ft**

TRANSPORTATION   The angle at the corner where two streets intersect is 125°. If a bus cannot make a turn at an angle of less than 70°, can bus service be provided on a route that includes turning that corner in both directions? Explain. *(Lesson 10-1)*

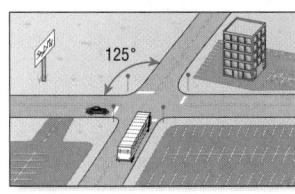

No; the corresponding angle has a measure of only 55°.

BRIDGES   For Exercises 2 and 3, use the following information.
The figure below shows part of the support structure of a bridge. Name a triangle that seems to be congruent to each triangle below. *(Lesson 10-2)*

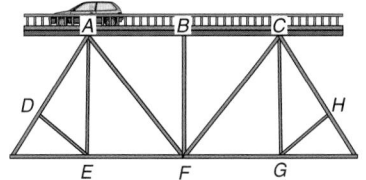

△AFB △CFB   **3.** △CHG △ADE

MOVING   A historic house in the shape of a rectangle has coordinates $A(-3, 5)$, $B(4, 5)$, $C(4, -3)$, and $D(-3, -3)$ on a map. The house is going to be moved to a new site 3 units east and two units north. Find the coordinates of the house once it reaches the new site. *(Lesson 10-3)*
$A'(0, 7)$, $B'(7, 7)$, $C'(7, -1)$, $D'(0, -1)$

SHAPES   Name three items in your room that are quadrilaterals. Classify the shapes. *(Lesson 10-4)*
See students' work.

6. GEOGRAPHY   The state of Indiana is shaped almost like a trapezoid. Estimate the area of the state. *(Lesson 10-5)*
about 33,600 mi²

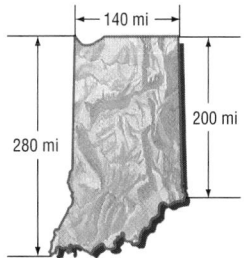

SIGNS   For Exercises 7 and 8, use the following information.
Part of a driver's license exam includes identifying road signs by color and by shape. Identify the shape of each road sign pictured below. *(Lesson 10-6)*

7.    8.

octagon   square

MANUFACTURING   For Exercises 9 and 10, use the following information.
Some cafeteria trays are designed so that four people can place their trays around a square table without bumping corners, as shown below. The top and bottom of the tray are parallel. *(Lesson 10-6)*

9. What is the shape of the tray? **trapezoid**

10. Find the measure of each angle of the tray so that the trays will fit side-to-side around the table.
45°, 45°, 135°, 135°

11. **PUBLIC SAFETY**   A tornado warning system can be heard for a 2-mile radius. Find the area that will benefit from the warning. *(Lesson 10-7)*
about 13 mi²

12. **CITY PLANNING**   The circular region inside the streets at DuPont Circle in Washington, D.C., is 250 feet across. What is the area of the region? *(Lesson 10-7)* **49,087.4 ft²**

13. **GEOMETRY**   Find the area of a figure that is formed using a rectangle having width equal to 8 feet and length equal to 5 feet and a half circle with a diameter of 6 feet. *(Lesson 10-8)* **54.14 ft²**

Mixed Problem Solving **767**

1. **PRESENTS**   Mateo received a gift wrapped in the shape of a rectangular pyramid. How many faces, edges, and vertices are on the gift box? *(Lesson 11-1)* **5; 8; 5**

2. **PET CARE**   Tina has an old fish tank in the shape of a circular cylinder. The tank is 2 feet in diameter and 6 feet high. How many cubic feet of water does it hold? Round to the nearest cubic foot. *(Lesson 11-2)* **19 ft³**

3. **CHEMISTRY**   A quartz crystal is a hexagonal prism. It has a base area of 1.41 square centimeters and a volume of 4.64 cubic centimeters. What is its height? If necessary, round to the nearest hundredth. *(Lesson 11-2)* **3.29 cm**

4. **BAKING**   A rectangular cake pan is 30 centimeters by 21 centimeters by 5 centimeters. A round cake pan has a diameter of 21 centimeters and a height of 4 centimeters. Which holds more batter, the rectangular pan or two round pans? *(Lesson 11-2)* **rectangular pan**

5. **MONUMENTS**   The top of the Washington Monument is a square pyramid 54 feet high and 34 feet long on each side. What is the volume of this top part of the monument? *(Lesson 11-3)* **20,808 ft³**

6. **MANUFACTURING**   A carton of canned fruit holds 24 cans. Each can has a diameter of 7.6 centimeters and a height of 10.8 centimeters. Approximately how much paper is needed to make the labels for the 24 cans? If necessary, round to the nearest tenth. *(Lesson 11-4)* **6188.7 cm²**

7. **CAMPING**   How much canvas was used to make the A-frame tent shown below? (*Hint:* Be sure to include the floor of the tent.) *(Lesson 11-4)* **94 ft²**

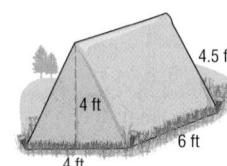

8. **HISTORY**   The Pyramid of Cestius is a monument in Rome. It is a square pyramid with the dimensions shown below.

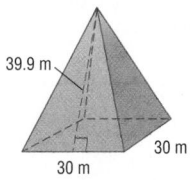

What is its lateral area? If necessary, round to the nearest tenth. *(Lesson 11-5)* **2394.0 m²**

9. **TEPEES**   The largest tepee in the United States in the shape of a cone with a diameter of 42 feet and a slant height of about 47.9 feet. How much canvas was used for the cover of the tepee? If necessary, round to the nearest tenth. *(Lesson 11)* **3160.1 ft²**

10. **SHIPPING**   Are the two packing tubes shown below similar solids? *(Lesson 11-6)* **yes**

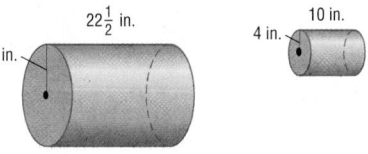

11. **MODELS**   A miniature greenhouse is a rectangular prism with a volume of 16 cubic fee The scale factor of this greenhouse to a larger greenhouse of the same shape is $\frac{1}{4}$. What is the volume of the larger greenhouse? $\left(Hint:\text{ scale factor} = \frac{a}{b}, \text{ ratio of volumes} = \frac{a^3}{b^3}\right)$ *(Lesson 11-6)* **1024 ft³**

12. **DECORATING**   Alicia is wallpapering a wall that is 8.25 feet high and 23.7 feet wide. What is the area of the wall? Round to the correct numb of significant digits. *(Lesson 11-7)* **195.5 ft²**

ARCHITECTURE   The *World Almanac* lists fifteen tall buildings in New Orleans, Louisiana. The number of floors in each of these buildings is listed below.

51	53	45	39	36
47	42	33	32	31
33	28	28	25	23

Make a stem-and-leaf plot of the data.
(Lesson 12-1) **See margin.**

WORLD CULTURES   Many North American Indians hold conferences called *powwows*, to celebrate their culture and heritage through various ceremonies and dances. The ages of participants and observers in a Menominee Indian powwow are shown in the chart below.

Participants	20, 18, 12, 13, 14, 72, 65, 23, 25, 43, 67, 35, 68, 13, 56
Observers	43, 55, 70, 63, 15, 41, 9, 42, 75, 25, 16, 18, 51, 80, 75, 39, 23, 55, 50, 54, 60, 43

Find the range and interquartile range for each group. *(Lesson 12-2)*
participants: 60, 51; observers: 71, 35

CONSUMERISM   The average retail price for one gallon of unleaded gasoline at a certain station are shown in the table below.

Year	1	2	3	4	5
Price ($)	1.21	1.20	0.92	0.95	0.95
Year	6	7	8	9	10
Price ($)	1.02	1.16	1.14	1.13	1.11

Make a box-and-whisker plot of the data.
(Lesson 12-3) **See margin.**

HOMEWORK   The frequency table below shows the amount of time students spend doing homework each week.

Weekly Homework Time		
Number of Hours	Tally	Frequency
0–3	IIII	5
4–7	JHT JHT IIII	14
8–11	JHT JHT JHT III	18
12–15	JHT JHT I	11

Display the data in a histogram. *(Lesson 12-4)*
See margin.

5. **ENTERTAINMENT**   The graph below displays data about movie attendance.

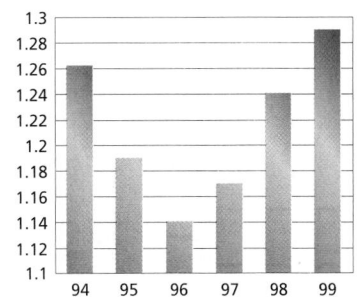

Tell why the graph appears to be misleading.
(Lesson 12-5) **See margin.**

6. **BUSINESS**   The Yogurt Oasis advertises that there are 1512 ways to enjoy a one-topping sundae. They offer six flavors of frozen yogurt, six different serving sizes, and several different toppings. How many toppings do they offer? *(Lesson 12-6)* **42 toppings**

7. **VOLLEYBALL**   How many different 6-player starting squads can be formed from a volleyball team of 15 players? *(Lesson 12-7)* **5005 teams**

8. **TELEVISION**   The odds in favor of a person in North America appearing on television sometime in their lifetime is 1:3. If there are 32 students in your class, predict how many will appear on television. *(Lesson 12-8)* **8 students**

9. **BUSINESS**   An auto dealer finds that of the cars coming in for service, 70% need a tune up and 50% need a new air filter. What is the probability that a car brought in for service needs both a tune up and a new air filter? *(Lesson 12-9)* **0.35**

10. **ECONOMICS**   Thirty-one percent of minimum-wage workers are between 16 and 19 years old. Twenty-two percent of the minimum-wage workers are between 20 and 24 years old. If a person who makes minimum wage is selected at random, what is the probability that he or she will be between 16 and 24 years old? *(Lesson 12-9)* **53%**

Mixed Problem Solving   769

Answers

1.

Stem	Leaf				
2	3	5	8	8	
3	1	2	3	3	6	9
4	2	5	7		
5	1	3			

$4 \mid 2 = 42$

3.
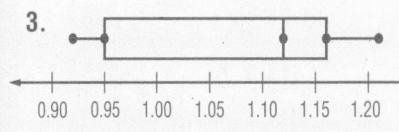

4. **Weekly Homework Time**
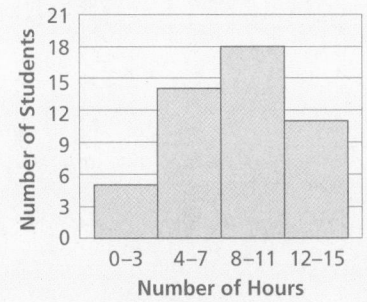

5. **There is no title or labels on either scale and the vertical axis does not include zero.**

Mixed Problem Solving

10.

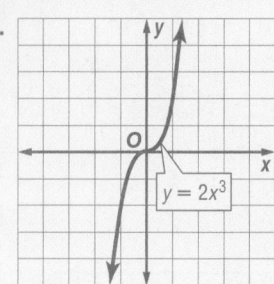

$y = 2x^3$

Mixed Problem Solving

Mixed Problem Solving

ARCHITECTURE   For Exercises 1 and 2, use the following information.
The polynomial $2xy + 2y^2 + 2yz$ represents the total area of the first floor shown in the plan below.   *(Lesson 13-1)*

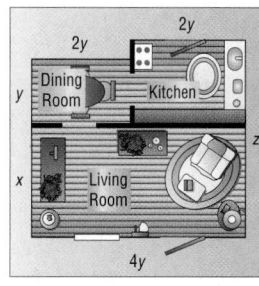

1. Find the degree of the polynomial. **2**

2. Find an expression to represent the area of the living room. Then classify the expression as a *monomial, binomial,* or *trinomial*. **4xy; monomial**

3. **CONSTRUCTION**   A standard unit of measurement for a window is the *united inch*. You can find the united inches of a window by adding the length and width of the window. If the length of a window is $3x - 5$ inches and the width is $x + 7$ inches, what is the size of the window in united inches? *(Lesson 13-2)* **4x + 2 united inches**

4. **GEOMETRY**   The perimeter of the triangle below is $4x + 4$ centimeters. Find the length of the hypotenuse of the triangle. *(Lesson 13-3)* **x + 5 cm**

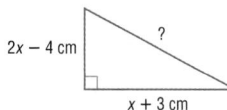

5. **GEOMETRY**   Find the area of the shaded region. Write in simplest form. *(Lesson 13-4)*
$3s^2 - 3s$ units²

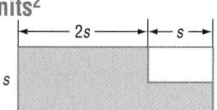

MANUFACTURING   For Exercises 6 and 7, use the following information.
The figure below shows a pattern for a cardboard box before it has been cut and folded. *(Lesson 13-4)*

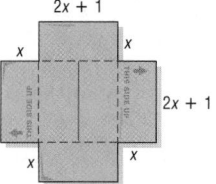

6. Find the area of each rectangular region and add to find a formula for the number of square inches of cardboard needed. **$12x^2 + 8x + 1$ units²**

7. Find the surface area if x is 2.5 inches. **96 in²**

8. **PRODUCTION**   The XYZ Production Company states that the cost y of producing x items is given by the equation $y = 2500 + 3.2x$. Does this equation represent a *linear* or *nonlinear* function? *(Lesson 13-5)* **linear**

9. **INTERNET**   The graph below shows the increase in electronic mailboxes in the United States.

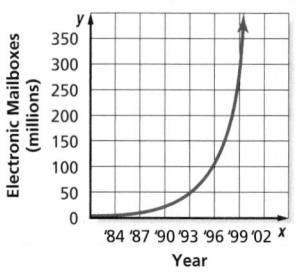

Source: Messaging Online

Does this graph represent a *linear* or *nonlinear* function? Explain. *(Lesson 13-5)*
Nonlinear; the graph is a curve.

10. **POPULATION**   The population growth of a particular species of insect is given by the equation $y = 2x^3$, where x represents time elapsed in days and y represents the population size. Graph this equation. *(Lesson 13-6)* **See margin.**

Becoming a Better Test-Taker

At some time in your life, you will probably have to take a standardized test. Sometimes this test may determine if you go on to the next grade level or course, or even if you will graduate from high school. This section of your textbook is dedicated to making you a better test-taker.

TYPES OF TEST QUESTIONS In the following pages, you will see examples of four types of questions commonly seen on standardized tests. A description of each type is shown in the table below.

Type of Question	Description	See Pages
multiple choice	Four or five possible answer choices are given from which you choose the best answer.	772–775
gridded response	You solve the problem. Then you enter the answer in a special grid and shade in the corresponding circles.	776–779
short response	You solve the problem, showing your work and/or explaining your reasoning.	780–783
extended response	You solve a multi-part problem, showing your work and/or explaining your reasoning.	784–788

PRACTICE After being introduced to each type of question, you can practice that type of question. Each set of practice questions is divided into five sections that represent the concepts most commonly assessed on standardized tests.

- Number and Operations
- Algebra
- Geometry
- Measurement
- Data Analysis and Probability

USING A CALCULATOR On some tests, you are permitted to use a calculator. You should check with your teacher to determine if calculator use is permitted on the test you will be taking, and if so, what type of calculator can be used.

TEST-TAKING TIPS In addition to the Test-Taking Tips like the one shown on the right, here are some additional thoughts that might help you.

- Get a good night's rest before the test. Cramming the night before does not improve your results.

- Budget your time when taking a test. Don't dwell on problems that you cannot solve. Just make sure to leave that question blank on your answer sheet.

- Watch for key words like NOT and EXCEPT. Also look for order words like LEAST, GREATEST, FIRST, and LAST.

> **Test-Taking Tip**
> If you are allowed to use a calculator, make sure you are familiar with how it works so that you won't waste time trying to figure out the calculator when taking the test.

Multiple-Choice Questions

Multiple-choice questions are the most common type of question on standardized tests. These questions are sometimes called *selected-response questions*. You are asked to choose the best answer from four or five possible answers.

To record a multiple-choice answer, you may be asked to shade in a bubble that is a circle or an oval or to just write the letter of your choice. Always make sure that your shading is dark enough and completely covers the bubble.

To make sure you have the correct solution, you must check to make sure that your answer satisfies the conditions of the original problem.

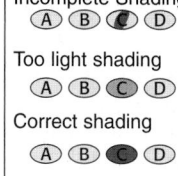

Incomplete Shading
Ⓐ Ⓑ Ⓒ Ⓓ
Too light shading
Ⓐ Ⓑ Ⓒ Ⓓ
Correct shading
Ⓐ Ⓑ Ⓒ Ⓓ

Example 1

Nathan wants to save $500 for a season ski pass. He has $200 and can save $25 per week. About how many months will he need to save in order to have enough money?

Ⓐ 20 months

Ⓑ 15 months

Ⓒ 12 months

Ⓓ 8 months

Ⓔ 3 months

Notice that the problem gives the amount that Nathan can save each *week*, but asks for the time it will take to save the money in *months*. Since Nathan can save $25 per week and there are about 4 weeks in a month, he can save about $4 \cdot \$25$ or $100 each month.

Let x represent the number of months. So, the amount he will have after x months is $200 + 100x$. Since Nathan wants to save $500, set the expression equal to 500. Write the equation $500 = 200 + 100x$.

Strategy
You can use backsolving to find the correct answer.

Next, test each value given in the answer choices.
$$500 = 200 + 100x$$
$$500 \stackrel{?}{=} 200 + 100(20) \quad \text{Replace } x \text{ with 20.}$$
$$500 \neq 2200$$

$$500 = 200 + 100x$$
$$500 \stackrel{?}{=} 200 + 100(15) \quad \text{Replace } x \text{ with 15.}$$
$$500 \neq 1700$$

$$500 = 200 + 100x$$
$$500 \stackrel{?}{=} 200 + 100(12) \quad \text{Replace } x \text{ with 12.}$$
$$500 \neq 1400$$

$$500 = 200 + 100x$$
$$500 \stackrel{?}{=} 200 + 100(8) \quad \text{Replace } x \text{ with 8.}$$
$$500 \neq 1000$$

$$500 = 200 + 100x$$
$$500 = 200 + 100(3) \quad \text{Replace } x \text{ with 3.}$$
$$500 = 500 \checkmark$$

The answer is E.

Many multiple-choice questions do not include a diagram. Drawing a diagram for the situation can help you to answer the question.

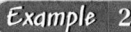 Example 2

Isabelle and Belinda take a hiking trip. They want to get to Otter's pond but cannot walk directly to it. They start from the beginning of the trail and follow the trail for 4 miles to the west. Then they turn south and walk 6 miles. How far is Otter's Pond from the start of the trail? Round to the nearest tenth of a mile.

Ⓐ 1.4 mi   Ⓑ 4.5 mi   Ⓒ 6.3 mi   Ⓓ 7.2 mi

Draw a diagram of the hiking trip. Isabelle and Belinda have walked in a path that creates a right triangle.

Looking at the diagram, you can eliminate 1.4 miles since it is too small.

The legs of the right triangle are 4 and 6. Use the Pythagorean Theorem to find the hypotenuse.

$c^2 = a^2 + b^2$ Pythagorean Theorem
$c^2 = 6^2 + 4^2$ Replace a with 6 and b with 4.
$c^2 = 36 + 16$ Evaluate $6^2 + 4^2$.
$c^2 = 52$ Add 36 and 16.
$\sqrt{c^2} = \sqrt{52}$ Take the square root of each side.
$c \approx 7.2$ Round to the nearest tenth.

The answer is D, 7.2 miles.

Often multiple-choice questions require you to convert measurements to solve. Pay careful attention to each unit of measure in the question and the answer choices.

Example 3

Malik is planning to draw a large map of his neighborhood for a school project. He wants the scale for the map to be 1 inch = 8800 feet. His house is 2.5 miles from school. How far on the map will his house be from the school?

Ⓐ 0.5 in.   Ⓑ 0.8 in.   Ⓒ 1.0 in.   Ⓓ 1.5 in.   Ⓔ 1.8 in.

The actual distance from Malik's house to the school is given in miles, and the scale is given in feet. You need to convert from miles to feet to solve the problem.

Since 1 mile is equal to 5280 feet, 2.5 miles = 2.5(5280) or 13,200 feet.

Now use the scale factor to find the distance.

$13{,}200 \text{ ft} \times \dfrac{1 \text{ in.}}{8800 \text{ ft}}$ or 1.5 inches

On the map, Malik's house will be 1.5 inches from the school. Choice D is the answer.

Multiple-Choice Practice

Choose the best answer.

Number and Operations

1. In 2001, the population of China was approximately 1,273,000,000. Write the population in scientific notation. **D**

   Ⓐ 12.73×10^1 Ⓑ 1273.0×10^6

   Ⓒ 1.27×10^9 Ⓓ 1.273×10^9

2. Tyler uses 4 gallons of stain to cover 120 square feet of fence. He still has 520 square feet left to cover. Which proportion could he use to calculate how many more gallons of stain he will need? **B**

   Ⓐ $\dfrac{120}{520} = \dfrac{x}{4}$ Ⓑ $\dfrac{4}{120} = \dfrac{x}{520}$

   Ⓒ $\dfrac{120}{x} = \dfrac{520}{4}$ Ⓓ $\dfrac{4}{520} = \dfrac{120}{x}$

3. If 1.5 cups of nuts are in a bag of trail mix that serves 6 people, how many cups of nuts will be needed for a trail mix that will serve 9 people? **C**

   Ⓐ 1 c   Ⓑ 1.5 c

   Ⓒ 2.25 c   Ⓓ 2.5 c

4. Hannah has a roll of ribbon for wrapping presents that is 10 yards long. If it takes $\dfrac{2}{3}$ yard of ribbon to wrap each present, how many presents can she wrap with the 10 yards? **C**

   Ⓐ 8   Ⓑ 10

   Ⓒ 15   Ⓓ 20

Algebra

5. Ms. Blackwell needs to rent a car for her family vacation. She has found a company that offers the following two options.

Plan	Flat Rate	Cost per Mile
Option A	$40	$0.25
Option B	$30	$0.35

   How many miles must the Blackwells drive for the plans to cost the same? **D**

   Ⓐ 0 mi   Ⓑ 10 mi   Ⓒ 25 mi   Ⓓ 100 mi

6. Six friends go to a movie and each buys a large container of popcorn. If a movie ticket costs $8.75 and a large popcorn costs $2.25, which expression can be used to find the total cost for all six people? **C**

   Ⓐ 2.25(8.75 + 5)   Ⓑ 2.25 + 8.75(6)

   Ⓒ 6(8.75 + 2.25)   Ⓓ 6(2.25) + 8.75

7. Midtown Printing Company charges $50 to design a flyer and $0.25 per flyer for printing. y is the total cost in dollars and x is the number of fliers, which equation describes the relationship between x and y? **C**

   Ⓐ $y = 50 - 0.25x$ Ⓑ $y = 50x + 0.25$

   Ⓒ $y = 50 + 0.25x$ Ⓓ $y = 0.25x - 50$

8. The simple interest formula, $I = Prt$, gives the interest I earned for an amount of money invested P at a given rate r for t years. If Nicholas invests $2100 at an annual interest rate of 7.5%, how long will it take him to earn $3000? Round to the nearest year. **B**

   Ⓐ 3 yr   Ⓑ 19 yr   Ⓒ 20 yr   Ⓓ 52 yr

Geometry

9. Alyssa wants to redecorate her room. She makes a scale diagram of her room on paper. She then cuts out scale pictures of her bed, dresser, and desk. If she slides her dresser along the wall, what type of transformation is this?

   Ⓐ reflection

   Ⓑ rotation

   Ⓒ dilation

   Ⓓ translation

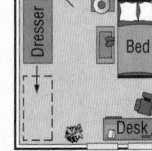

Test-Taking Tip

Question 8

Some multiple-choice questions have you use a formula to solve a problem. You can check your solution by replacing the variables with the given values and your answer. The answer choice that results in a true statement is the correct answer.

0. To get to work from her house, Amanda walks 6 blocks west then turns and walks 11 blocks south. If she could walk directly home from work, how many blocks would she need to walk? Round to the nearest block. **C**

Ⓐ 9 blocks

Ⓑ 12 blocks

Ⓒ 13 blocks

Ⓓ 15 blocks

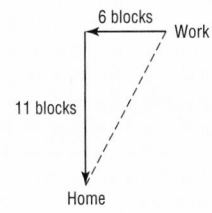

1. Andrés plans to lay sod in his yard. How many square feet of sod will he need? **B**

Ⓐ 5100 ft²

Ⓑ 8925 ft²

Ⓒ 9000 ft²

Ⓓ 9650 ft²

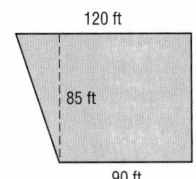

Measurement

2. The world's largest ball of Sisal Twine is located in Cawker City, Kansas. It consists of about 7,009,942 feet of twine. How many miles of twine is this? **B**

Ⓐ 586,080 mi   Ⓑ 1328 mi

Ⓒ 1402 mi   Ⓓ 37,012,493,760 mi

3. The world's largest pizza was made on October 11, 1987 by Lorenzo Amato and Louis Piancone. The pizza measured 140 feet across. If a regular size pizza at a local restaurant measures 12 inches across, how many times more area does the largest pizza cover than the regular pizza? **D**

Ⓐ about 12 times   Ⓑ about 136 times

Ⓒ 140 times   Ⓓ 19,600 times

4. A cookie recipe requires 6 cups of chocolate chips. The recipe serves 20 people. How many cups of chocolate chips would be needed to serve 35 people? **A**

Ⓐ 10.5 c   Ⓑ 11 c

Ⓒ 12 c   Ⓓ 15 c

15. Shopper's Mart sells two sizes of Corn Crunch cereal. The 16-ounce box costs $4.95. The 12-ounce box costs $3.55. What is true about these two cereals? **B**

Ⓐ The 16-ounce box is a better buy.

Ⓑ The 12-ounce box is a better buy.

Ⓒ They are the same cost per ounce.

Ⓓ None of these statements are true.

Test-Taking Tip Ⓐ Ⓑ Ⓒ Ⓓ

Question 15
Always read every answer choice, particularly in questions that ask what is true about a given situation.

Data Analysis and Probability

16. The graph below shows the number of hours that students in Mr. Cardona's math class watch television and the number of hours that they exercise in the same week. Based on the trend in the scatter plot, what number of hours of exercise would you expect a student to get that watches 15 hours of television each week? **A**

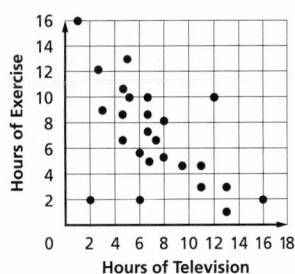

Exercise vs. Television

Ⓐ 2 h   Ⓑ 6 h

Ⓒ 10 h   Ⓓ 15 h

17. Mika received the following scores on 4 of his five social studies exams: 89, 75, 82, and 77. What score does he need on his fifth exam to ensure that he receives at least an average of 85? Note that a score cannot be over 100. **D**

Ⓐ 75   Ⓑ 85

Ⓒ 95   Ⓓ not possible

Gridded-Response Questions

Gridded-response questions are another type of question on standardized tests. These questions are sometimes called *student-produced response* or *grid in.*

For gridded response, you must mark your answer on a grid printed on an answer sheet. The grid contains a row of four or five boxes at the top, two rows of ovals or circles with decimal and fraction symbols, and four or five columns of ovals, numbered 0–9. At the right is an example of a grid from an answer sheet.

Example 1

Solve the equation $10 - 4a = -38$ for a.

What value do you need to find?

You need to find the value of a.

$$10 - 4a = -38 \qquad \text{Original equation}$$

$$10 - 4a - 10 = -38 - 10 \qquad \text{Subtract 10 from each side.}$$

$$-4a = -48 \qquad \text{Simplify.}$$

$$\frac{-4a}{-4} = \frac{-48}{-4} \qquad \text{Divide each side by } -4.$$

$$a = 12 \qquad \text{Simplify.}$$

How do you fill in the answer grid?

- Print your answer in the answer boxes.

- Print only one digit or symbol in each answer box.

- Do not write any digits or symbols outside the answer boxes.

- You may print your answer with the first digit in the left answer box, or with the last digit in the right answer box. You may leave blank any boxes you do not need on the right or the left side of your answer.

- Fill in only one bubble for every answer box that you have written in. Be sure not to fill in a bubble under a blank answer box.

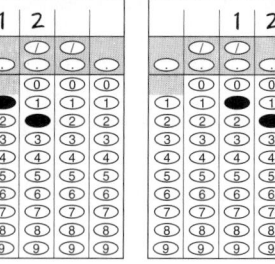

Many gridded-response questions result in an answer that is a fraction or a decimal. These values can also be filled in on the grid.

Example 2

A recipe for orange chicken calls for 1 cup of orange juice and serves 6 people. If Emily needs to serve 15 people, how many cups of orange juice will she need?

What value do you need to find?

You need to find the number of cups of orange juice Emily will need for 15 servings.

Write and solve a proportion for the problem. Let s represent the number of cups.

$$\frac{1 \text{ cup}}{6 \text{ servings}} = \frac{s \text{ cups}}{15 \text{ servings}}$$

$\dfrac{1}{6} = \dfrac{s}{15}$ Write the proportion.

$15 = 6s$ Find the cross products.

$\dfrac{15}{6} = \dfrac{6s}{6}$ Divide each side by 6.

$\dfrac{5}{2} = s$ Simplify.

How do you fill in the answer grid?

You can either grid the fraction $\dfrac{5}{2}$, or rewrite it as 2.5 and grid the decimal. Be sure to write the decimal point or fraction bar in the answer box. The following are acceptable answer responses that represent $\dfrac{5}{2}$ and 2.5.

Do not leave a blank answer box in the middle of an answer.

Some problems may result in an answer that is a mixed number. Before filling in the grid, change the mixed number to an equivalent improper fraction or decimal. For example, if the answer is $1\frac{1}{2}$, do not enter 11/2, as this will be interpreted as $\dfrac{11}{2}$. Instead, enter 3/2 or 1.5.

Example 3

The Corner Candy Store sells 16 chocolates in a gift box. For Mother's Day the store offers the chocolates in boxes of 20. What is the percent of change?

Write the ratio for percent of change.

percent of change $= \dfrac{\text{new amount} - \text{original amount}}{\text{original amount}}$

Remember percent of change has the original amount as the denominator.

$= \dfrac{20 - 16}{16}$ Substitution

$= \dfrac{4}{16}$ Subtraction

$= 0.25$ Rewrite as a decimal.

$= 25\%$

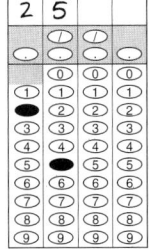

Since the question asks for the percent, be sure to grid 25, not 0.25.

Gridded-Response Practice

Solve each problem. Then copy and complete a grid like the one shown on page 776.

Number and Operations

1. The Downtown Department Store has a 75% markup on all clothing items. A certain sweater cost the store $20. What will be the selling price of the sweater in dollars? **35**

2. The following table shows the number of billionaires in the following countries in the year 2000.

Country	Number of Billionaires
USA	70
Germany	18
Japan	12
China	8
France/Mexico/Saudi Arabia	7

What percent of the billionaires were in the USA? Round to the nearest percent. **61**

3. Pepperoni is the most popular pizza topping. Each year approximately 251,770,000 pounds of pepperoni are eaten. If this number were written in scientific notation, what would be the power of 10? **8**

4. Dylan wants to buy an ice cream cone with three different flavors of ice cream. He has 18 flavors from which to choose. How many different ways can he have his cone? **4896**

5. Ignacio has $40 to spend at the mall. He spends half of it on a CD. He then spends $6 for lunch. Later he decides to go to a movie that costs $5.75. How much money does he have left in dollars? **8.25**

6. There are 264 tennis players and 31 coaches at a sports camp. What is the ratio of tennis players to coaches as a decimal rounded to the nearest tenth? **8.5**

Algebra

7. Find the x-intercept of the graph of the equation $2x + y = 5$. **2.5**

8. Solve $4x - 5 = 2x + 3$ for x. **4**

9. Ayana has $125 dollars to spend on CDs and DVDs. CDs cost $20. The equation $y = 125 - 20c$ represents the amount she has left to buy DVDs. If she buys 3 CDs, how much money in dollars will she have to buy DVDs? **65**

10. For her birthday, Allison and her five friends went out for pizza. They ate an entire pizza that was cut into 16 pieces. If two of her friends ate 4 pieces, one of her friends ate 3 pieces and two of her friends ate 1 piece, how many pieces did Allison eat? **3**

11. A parking garage has two different pay parking options. You can pay $11 for the day or $2 for the first hour and $0.75 for each additional half hour. How many hours would you need to stay for both rates to be the same? **7**

Geometry

12. The bridge over the Hoover Dam in Lake Mead, Nevada, stretches 1324 feet. A model is built that is 60 feet long. What is the scale factor of the model to the actual bridge? Round to the nearest hundredth. **0.05**

13. Use the figure to find the value of x. **55**

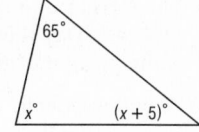

14. Quadrilateral $ABCD$ is translated 2 units to the right and 3 units down to get $A'B'C'D'$. What is the y-coordinate of A'? **0**

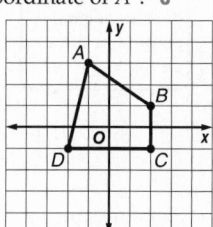

5. Toshiro swam across a river that was 20 feet wide. When he got across the river, the current had pushed him 40 feet farther down stream than when he had started. How far did he travel? Round to the nearest tenth of a foot. **44.7**

6. A building casts a shadow that is 210 feet long. If the angle of elevation from the end of the shadow to the top of the building is 40°, how tall is the building? Round to the nearest foot. **176**

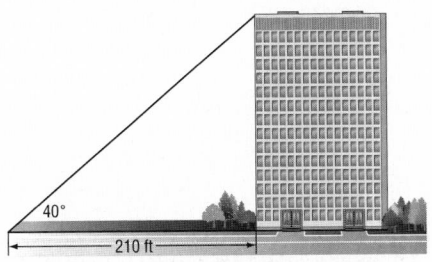

Measurement

7. The Student Council held a car wash for a fund-raiser. On Saturday, approximately 8 containers of car wash were used to wash 52 cars. Assuming the rate stayed the same, how many cars did they wash if they used 11 containers on Sunday? **72**

8. Ethan wants to know how much water his sister's swimming pool holds. If the pool is 1 foot high and 6 feet across, what is the volume in cubic feet? Use $\pi = 3.14$ and round to the nearest tenth of a cubic foot. **28.3**

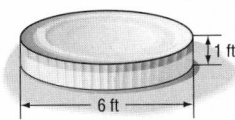

9. Marisa needs to make tablecloths for a wedding party. Each table is a rectangle measuring 8 feet by 3 feet. She wants the tablecloth to extend 1 foot on each of the four sides. In square feet, what will be the area of each tablecloth? **50**

20. Darnell's commute takes 1.5 hours. He drove at 20 miles per hour for 0.75 hour, and the rest of the time he drove at 50 miles per hour. In miles, how far is his work from his house? **52.5**

21. A juice company wants to make cylinder-shaped juice cans that hold approximately 196 cubic inches of juice. The base has to have a diameter of 5 inches. What will be the height of the can in inches? Use $\pi = 3.14$ and round to the nearest whole number. **10**

Data Analysis and Probability

22. The following table shows the average number of vacation days per year for people in selected countries. What is the mean number of vacation days per year for these countries? Round to the nearest whole day.

Average Number of Vacation Days per Year for 2000	
Country	Number of Days
Korea	25
Japan	25
United States	13
Brazil	34
Italy	42
France	37

Source: *The World Almanac*

29

23. Kaya and her family went on a vacation for spring break. The following table shows the distance traveled for each hour. What is the rate of change between hours 3 and 4?

Time (hours)	Distance (miles)
1	60
2	132
3	208
4	273
5	328

65

24. If a standard six-sided die is rolled, what is the probability of rolling a multiple of 2? **1/2**

Test-Taking Tip Ⓐ Ⓑ Ⓒ Ⓓ

Question 24
Fractions do not have to be written in simplest form. Any equivalent fraction that fits the grid is correct.

Short-Response Questions

Short-response questions require you to provide a solution to the problem, as well as any method, explanation, and/or justification you used to arrive at the solution. These are sometimes called *constructed-response, open-response, open-ended, free-response,* or *student-produced questions.*

The following is a sample **rubric**, or scoring guide, for scoring short-response questions.

Credit	Score	Criteria
Full	2	Full credit: The answer is correct and a full explanation is provided that shows each step in arriving at the final answer.
Partial	1	Partial credit: There are two different ways to receive partial credit. • The answer is correct, but the explanation provided is incomplete or incorrect. • The answer is incorrect, but the explanation and method of solving the problem is correct.
None	0	No credit: Either an answer is not provided or the answer does not make sense.

On some standardized tests, no credit is given for a correct answer if your work is not shown.

Example

In the first four events of a gymnastics competition, Nicole scored 7.6, 7.9, 8.5, and 8. Sandra scored 9.3, 7.4, 8.5, 7.9, and 8.1 after five events. If the entire competition consists of five events, what does Nicole need to get on her fifth event to score higher than Sandra?

Full Credit Solution

First find the total number of points that Nicole has scored so far.

$$7.6 + 7.9 + 8.5 + 8 = 32$$

Let x represent the score that Nicole will receive on her final event. Then Nicole's total score will be $32 + x$.

Next, find the total number of points that Sandra has scored.

$$9.3 + 7.4 + 8.5 + 7.9 + 8.1 = 41.2$$

The steps, calc and reasoning clearly stated.

Since Nicole needs to get a higher score than Sandra, we can write and solve an inequality.

Nicole's score > Sandra's score

$$32 + x > 41.2 \quad \text{Substitution}$$

$$x > 9.2 \quad \text{Subtract 32 from each side.}$$

The solution of the problem is clearly stated.

In order to score higher than Sandra in the competition, Nicole must score higher than a 9.2 on her fifth event.

Partial Credit Solution

In this sample solution, the answer is correct; however there is no justification for any of the calculations.

$$9.3 + 7.4 + 8.5 + 7.9 + 8.1 = 41.2$$

$$32 + x > 41.2$$

$$x > 9.2$$

Nicole will need to score higher than 9.2.

> There is not an explanation of how 32 was obtained.

Partial Credit Solution

In this sample solution, the answer is incorrect because the student added Nicole's points incorrectly. However, after this error, the calculations and reasoning are correct. An equation is used in this solution and the student reasons that the score must be greater than 9.7 in the final answer.

First find the total number of points that Nicole has scored so far.

$$7.6 + 7.9 + 8.5 + 8 = 31.5$$

Let x represent the score that Nicole will receive on her final event. Then Nicole's total score will be $32 + x$. Next, find the total number of points that Sandra has scored.

$$9.3 + 7.4 + 8.5 + 7.9 + 8.1 = 41.2$$

Now we can write an equation to solve.

$$31.5 + x = 41.2$$

$$x = 9.7$$

In order to score higher than Sandra in the competition, Nicole must score higher than a 9.7.

> The answer is incorrect, but the reasoning used to find the answer is correct.

No Credit Solution

$$7.6 + 7.9 + 8.5 + 8 = 32$$

$$9.3 + 7.4 + 8.5 + 7.9 + 8.1 = 41.2$$

$$\frac{41.2 + 32}{10} = 7.32$$

Nicole needs a 7.32.

> The student averaged all of the scores demonstrating no understanding of the problem.

Short-Response Practice

Solve each problem. Show all your work.

Number and Operations

1. Crispy Crunch cereal has a new box that says it is 25% larger than the original size. If the original box had 16 ounces, how many ounces does the new box have? **20 oz**

2. Austin has $\frac{1}{3}$ of a gallon of paint to paint his go cart. He knows that he will need $3\frac{1}{2}$ gallons to paint his entire cart. How many more gallons does he need? $3\frac{1}{6}$ **gal**

3. In 1999, the United States took in $\$6.206 \times 10^9$ from Canadian tourists. Express this value in standard notation. **\$6,206,000,000**

4. Prairie High School assigns every student a student identification code. The codes consist of one letter and five digits. What is the greatest number of students that can attend Prairie High School before codes will need to be reused? **2,600,000**

5. Jacob works at a computer factory making $8.50 per hour. The company has not been selling as many computers lately so they have decreased each employee's wage by 6%. What will Jacob's new hourly wage be? **$7.99**

Algebra

6. Francisca ran for 1.25 hours at an average rate of 5 miles per hour. What distance did Francisca run? (Use the formula $d = rt$, where d represents distance, r represents rate, and t represents time.) **6.25 mi**

7. Simplify the expression $-2(y + 4) - 3$. **$-2y - 11$**

8. Tariq plans to go to Raging Waters Water Park. The park charges a $12 admission and rents inner tubes for $1.50 per hour. If he has $15, for how many hours can he rent an inner tube? **2 h**

9. $m > -\frac{7}{2}$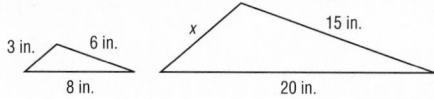
9. Solve and graph the inequality $6 - 2m < 13$.

10. Roller Way Amusement park closes the park for a day and allows only schools to visit. The schools must bring students in buses that carry 30 students. If 32 buses are at the park, write an equation to represent the total number of students S that are at the park that day. **$S = 30(32)$**

Geometry

11. Triangle RST is translated 3 units up and 1 unit to the left. Find the coordinates of translated $\triangle R'S'T'$. **$R'(3, 4)$, $S'(4, 1)$, $T'(1, 2)$**

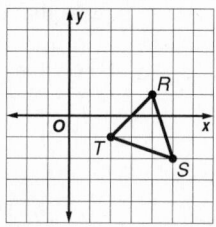

12. Chi-Yo wants to make a quilt pattern using similar triangles as shown. What is the length of the third side of the larger triangle? **7.5 in**

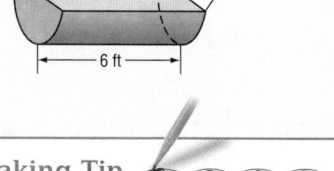

13. Lawana has a window planter in the shape of a cylinder cut in half. She needs to fill it with dirt before she can plant flowers. What is the volume of the planter? Use $\pi = 3.14$ and round to the nearest tenth of a cubic foot. **21.2 ft³**

Test-Taking Tip Ⓐ Ⓑ Ⓒ Ⓓ

Question 13
After finding the solution, always go back and read the problem again to make sure your solution answers what the problem is asking.

4. ∠KLM and ∠XYZ are complementary. If
$m\angle KLM = 3x - 1$ and $m\angle XYZ = x + 7$, find
the measure of each angle. **m∠KLM = 62,
m∠XYZ = 28**

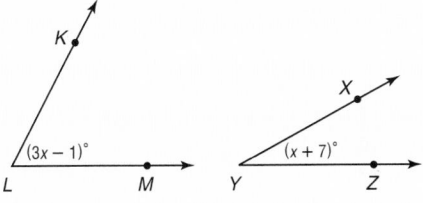

5. A cylindrical grain bin holds approximately
28,260 cubic feet of grain. If the bin has a
diameter of 50 feet, what is the bin's height?
Use π = 3.14 and round to the nearest tenth of
a foot. **14.4 ft**

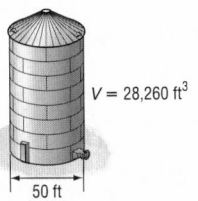

$V = 28,260 \text{ ft}^3$

50 ft

Measurement

6. One kilometer is equal to about 0.62 mile. Tito
is running a 10-kilometer race. How many
miles is this? **6.2 mi**

7. Jordan wants to make cone-shaped candles as
shown in the diagram. What is the volume of
one candle? Use π = 3.14 and round to the
nearest tenth of a cubic inch. **75.4 in³**

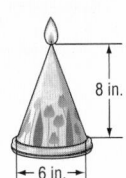

8 in.

6 in.

8. Abigail is planning a cookout at her house. She
wants to put trim around the edges of round
tables. If the diameter of each table is 8 feet,
how much trim will she need for each table?
Use π = 3.14 and round to the nearest tenth of
a cubic foot. **25.1 ft**

9. At Oakwood Lawncare Service, a lawn crew
can do 5 jobs in 3 days. At this rate, how many
days would it take the crew to do 20 jobs?
12 days

20. In a recent bicycle race, Kevin rode his bike at
a pace of 16 miles per hour. How many feet
per minute is this? **1408 ft/min**

21. Mateo wants to fill the cylindrical container
shown with water. How many pints of water
will he need? (*Hint:* One pint of liquid is
equivalent to 28.875 cubic inches.) Use π = 3.14
and round to the nearest pint. **2.4 pt**

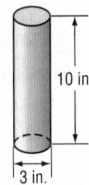

10 in.

3 in.

Data Analysis and Probability

22. Theo needs a four digit Personal Identification
Number (PIN) for his checking account. If he
can choose any digit from 0 to 9 for each of
the digits, how many different PIN numbers
are possible? **10,000**

23. Matthew is choosing some CDs to take on a
long car drive. He has 10 jazz CDs, 3 classical
CDs, and 9 soundtracks. If he chooses two
CDs without replacement, what is the
probability that the first CD is a soundtrack
and the second CD is a jazz CD? $\dfrac{15}{77}$

24. Nikki is playing a game in which you spin
the spinner below and then roll a six-sided
die labeled 1 through 6. Each section of the
spinner is equal in size. What is the probability
that the spinner lands on blue and the die
lands on an even number? $\dfrac{3}{16}$

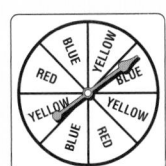

25. Two cards are drawn from a hand of eight
cards numbered 1 to 8. The first card is not
replaced after it is drawn. What is the
probability that a 2 and a 5 are drawn? $\dfrac{1}{28}$

Extended-Response Questions

Extended-response questions are often called *open-ended* or *constructed-response questions*. Most extended-response questions have multiple parts. You must answer all parts to receive full credit.

Extended-response questions are similar to short-response questions in that you must show all of your work in solving the problem and a rubric is used to determine whether you receive full, partial, or no credit. The following is a sample rubric for scoring extended-response questions.

Credit	Score	Criteria
Full	4	Full credit: A correct solution is given that is supported by well-developed, accurate explanations.
Partial	3, 2, 1	Partial credit: A generally correct solution is given that may contain minor flaws in reasoning or computation or an incomplete solution. The more correct the solution, the greater the score.
None	0	No credit: An incorrect solution is given indicating no mathematical understanding of the concept, or no solution is given.

On some standardiz[ed] tests, no credit is giv[en] for a correct answer [if] your work is not sho[wn].

Make sure that when the problem says to *Show your work,* you show every aspect of your solutio[n], including figures, sketches of graphing calculator screens, or reasoning behind computations.

Example

Northern Sofa Store's delivery charges depend upon the distance furniture is delivered. The graph shows the charge for deliveries according to the distance.

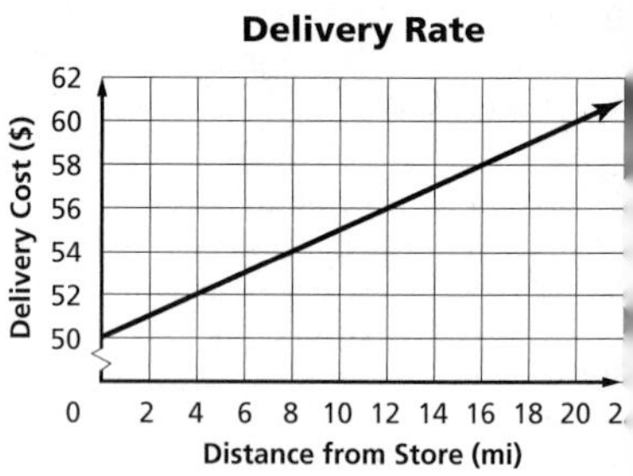

a. Write an equation to show the relationship between delivery cost y and distance from the store x.

b. Name the y-intercept and slope of the line that models the data. Explain what each means in this situation.

c. Suppose Mr. Hawkins wants a sofa delivered. His house is 21 miles from the store. What will be the cost of delivery?

Delivery Rate

Full Credit Solution

Part a   A complete solution for writing the equation shows all the computations needed and the reasoning behind those computations.

> To write the equation, first I need to find the slope. I will use the two points marked on the graph, (0, 50) and (10, 55).

$$m = \frac{y_2 - y_1}{x_2 - x_1} \qquad \text{slope formula}$$

$$= \frac{55 - 50}{10 - 0} \qquad (x_i, y_i) = (0, 50) \text{ and } (x_2, y_2) = (10, 55)$$

$$= \frac{5}{10} \text{ or } 0.5$$

The slope of the line is 0.5 and the y-intercept is 50.

$$y = mx + b \qquad \text{Slope-intercept form}$$
$$y = 0.5x + 50 \qquad m = 0.5 \text{ and } b = 50.$$

So an equation that fits the data is $y = 0.5x + 50$.

The calculations and reasoning are clearly stated. The solution of the problem is also clearly stated.

Part b In this sample answer, the student demonstrates clear understanding of the y-intercept and slope of the graph.

I can see from the graph that the y-intercept is 50 which means $50. This is the initial charge for any delivery and then additional money is charged for each mile. The slope of the line that I found in Part a is 0.5 which means $0.50. This is the additional charge per mile to deliver the furniture.

Part c In this sample answer, the student knows how to use the equation to find the delivery cost for a given distance.

I will substitute 21 for x into the equation since Mr. Hawkins lives 21 miles from the store.

$$y = 0.5x + 50$$
$$y = 0.5(21) + 50$$
$$y = 60.50$$

The cost of delivery will be $60.50.

Partial Credit Solution

Part a This sample answer includes no explanations for the calculations performed. However, partial credit is given for correct calculations and a correct answer.

$$m = \frac{y_2 - y_1}{x_2 - x_1} = \frac{55 - 50}{10 - 0} = \frac{1}{2}$$

$$y = \frac{1}{2}x + 50$$

More credit would have been given if an explanation had been given.

The equation is correct because $\frac{1}{2}$ is the same as 0.5.

Part b This part receives full credit because the student demonstrates understanding of the y intercept and slope.

> The y-intercept 50 is the charge for just making any delivery. It means $50. The slope $\frac{1}{2}$ is the charge per mile which is 50 cents.

Part c Partial credit is given for Part c because the student makes a calculation error.

> To get the delivery cost, substitute 21 miles into the equation.
>
> $y = \frac{1}{2}x + 50$
>
> $y = \frac{1}{2}(21) + 50$
>
> $y = 42 + 50 = 92$
>
> The cost is $92.

This sample answer might have received a score of 2, depending on the judgment of the scorer. Had the student gotten Part c correct, the score would probably have been a 3.

No Credit Solution

Part a The student demonstrates no understanding of how to write an equation for a line.

> If I use the points $(0, 50)$ and $(10, 55)$, an equation is $10y = 10x + 55$.

Part b The student does not understand the meaning of the y-intercept or the slope.

> The y-intercept is 0 because that is when the truck leaves the store. The slope is 10 because that is the distance from the store in miles when the truck makes its first stop.

Part c The student does not understand how to read the graph to find the cost or how to use an equation to find the cost.

> $21, because it is 21 miles from the store.

Extended-Response Practice

Solve each problem. Show all your work.

4a. Famous Photos: $C = 50 + 10p$
Picture Perfect: $C = 80 + 8p$
Timeless Portraits: $C = 45 + 15p$

Number and Operations

In a recent survey, Funtime Amusement Park found that 6 out of 8 of their customers had been to the park before. In one week, 4500 people attended the park.

a. What percent of customers have been to the park before? **75%**

b. How many of the park goers in that week had been there before? **3375**

c. If 3000 people were at the park the next week, how many would you expect had *not* been there before? **750**

The following table shows the number of people of each age living in the U.S. in the year 2000.

Age	Number of People
Under 15	60,253,375
15 to 24	39,183,891
25 to 34	39,891,724
35 to 44	44,148,527
45 to 64	61,952,636
65 and over	34,991,753

Source: U.S. Census Bureau

a. To the nearest million, how many people were under age 25? **99 million**

b. What percent of people were under 15? Round to the nearest percent. **21%**

c. What is the total population of the United States? Write in scientific notation. **2.80421906×10^8**

Algebra

Victoria needs to study for a math exam. The exam is in 18 days. She has decided to begin right away by studying 15 minutes the first night and increasing her study time by 5 minutes each day. **a. $T = 15 + 5d$**

a. Write an expression for the total number of minutes that Victoria will study T for a given time d days from today.

b. If she has 18 days to study, how many minutes will she study on the last day before the exam? **100 min**

c. Victoria begins to study on a Monday, 18 days before the exam. On what day will she study exactly one hour? **Wednesday**

4. Jasmine wants to get her portrait taken for her senior pictures. She finds that three different portrait studios charge a sitting fee and charge a separate fee for each ordered picture. The table below shows their prices.

Studio	Sitting Fee	Cost per Portrait
Famous Photos	$50	$10
Picture Perfect	$80	$8
Timeless Portraits	$45	$15

a. For each studio, write an equation that represents the total cost. In each of the three equations, use C to represent the total cost and p to represent the number of pictures. **See margin.**

b. If Jasmine wants to order 30 portraits, which studio would be the least expensive? **Picture Perfect**

c. How many portraits will she need to order for Famous Photos and Picture Perfect to cost the same? **15**

Geometry

5. Rodrigo stands 50 yards away from the base of a building. From his eye level of 5 feet, Rodrigo sees the top of the building at an angle of elevation of 25°.

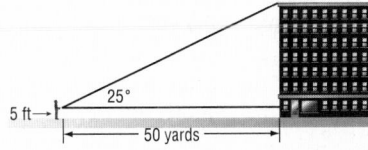

a. What is the height of the building? Round to the nearest tenth of a foot. **74.9 ft**

b. If Rodrigo moved back 15 more yards, how would the angle of elevation to the top of the building change? **smaller**

c. If the building were taller, would the angle of elevation be greater than or less than 25°? **greater**

Test-Taking Tip A B C D

Question 5
Be sure to use a trigonometric ratio that includes the measurement you are asked to find in order to solve the problem correctly.

6a. G' (-3, -4), H' (-1, -5), I' (-1, 1), J' (-3, -2)

6b.

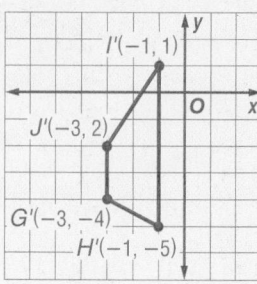

6. The diagram below shows polygon *GHIJ*.
6a–b. See margin.

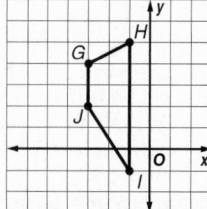

a. Find the coordinates of the vertices of quadrilateral $G'H'I'J'$ after a reflection of quadrilateral *GHIJ* in the *x*-axis.

b. Graph $G'H'I'J'$ after a reflection of quadrilateral *GHIJ* in the *x*-axis.

c. If *ABCD* is the image of *GHIJ* dilated by a scale factor of $\frac{1}{4}$ with respect to the origin, what are the coordinates of *C*? $\left(-\frac{1}{4}, -\frac{1}{4}\right)$

Measurement

7. The diagram shows a pattern for a garden that Marie plans to plant. Use $\pi = 3.14$.

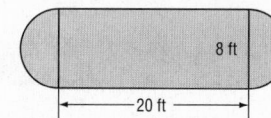

a. What is the area of the garden in square feet? **210.24 ft²**

b. What is the area of the garden in square yards? **23.36 yd²**

c. Marie wants to put a stone border around the outside of the garden. What is the perimeter of the garden? **65.12 ft**

8. The table below shows the speeds of several animals.

Animal	Speed (mph)
Cheetah	70
Zebra	40
Reindeer	32
Cat (domestic)	30
Wild Turkey	15

Source: *World Book*

a. What is the rate of the cat in feet per minute? **2640 feet per minute**

b. How many times faster is the cheetah than the wild turkey? Round to the nearest tenth. **4.7**

Data Analysis and Probability

9. The table shows the life expectancy in years of people in different countries. The figures are for the year 2000.

Country	Life Expectancy (yr)
Afghanistan	45.9
Australia	79.8
Brazil	62.9
Canada	79.4
France	78.8
Haiti	49.2
Japan	80.7
Madagascar	55.0
Mexico	71.5
United States	77.1

Source: U.S. Census Bureau **a. 74.3 yr**

a. What is the median life expectancy?

b. What is the mean life expectancy? **68.03 yr**

c. In 2000, Cambodians had a life expectancy of 56.5. If Cambodia was added to the table how would the mean be affected? **Sample answer: It would go down.**

10. The table shows the average cost for a year of higher education for all public institutions.

Year	Cost ($)
1997-1998	$6813
1998-1999	$7107
1999-2000	$7310
2000-2001	$7621

Source: *World Book*

a. What was the rate of change between the 1999-2000 year and the 2000-2001 school year? **$311 per year**

b. What was the rate of change in dollars per year between the 1997-1998 year and the 2000-2001 year? **$269.33 per year**

c. Between what two years was the rate of change the greatest? **1999-2000 and 2000-2001**

d. Find the mean annual increase in tuition cost between 1997 and 2001. Round to the nearest dollar. **$269**

e. Based on your answer in part d, what might you expect the cost of education to be in th 2009–2010 school year if the average increase remains constant? **$10,042**

Glossary/Glosario

Cómo usar el glosario en español:
1. Busca el término en inglés que desees encontrar.
2. El término en español, junto con la definición, se encuentran en la columna de la derecha.

English

Español

A

absolute value (58) The distance a number is from zero on the number line.

valor absoluto Distancia que un número dista de cero en la recta numérica.

accuracy (589) The degree of conformity of a measurement with the true value.

exactitud Grado de conformidad de una medida con el valor verdadero.

acute angle (449) An angle with a measure greater than 0° and less than 90°.

ángulo agudo Ángulo con una medida mayor que 0° y menor que 90°.

acute triangle (454) A triangle that has three acute angles.

triángulo acutángulo Triángulo que posee tres ángulos agudos.

adjacent angles (493) Two angles that have the same vertex, share a common side, and do *not* overlap.

ángulos adyacentes Dos ángulos que poseen el mismo vértice, comparten un lado y *no* se traslapan.

algebraic expression (17) An expression that contains sums and/or products of variables and numbers.

expresión algebraica Expresión que contiene sumas y/o productos de números y variables.

algebraic fraction (170) A fraction with one or more variables in the numerator or denominator.

fracción algebraica Fracción con una o más variables en el numerador o denominador.

alternate exterior angles (492) Nonadjacent exterior angles found on opposite sides of the transversal. In the figure below, ∠1 and ∠7, ∠2 and ∠8 are alternate exterior angles.

ángulos alternos externos Ángulos exteriores no adyacentes que se encuentran en lados opuestos de una transversal. En la siguiente figura, ∠1 y ∠7, ∠2 y ∠8 son ángulos alternos externos.

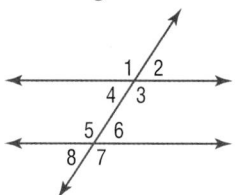

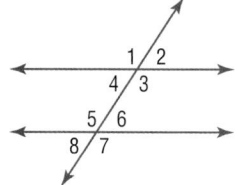

alternate interior angles (492) Nonadjacent interior angles found on opposite sides of the transversal. In the figure above, ∠4 and ∠6, ∠3 and ∠5 are alternate interior angles.

ángulos alternos internos Ángulos interiores no adyacentes que se encuentran en lados opuestos de una transversal. En la figura anterior, ∠4 y ∠6, ∠3 y ∠5 son ángulos alternos internos.

altitude (520) A line segment that is perpendicular to the base of a figure with endpoints on the base and the side opposite the base.

altura Segmento de recta perpendicular a la base de una figura y cuyos extremos yacen en la base y en el lado opuesto de la base.

angle (447) Two rays with a common endpoint form an angle. The rays and vertex are used to name an angle. The angle below is ∠ABC.

ángulo Dos rayos con un punto común forman un ángulo. Los rayos y el vértice se usan para identificar el ángulo. El siguiente ángulo es ∠ABC.

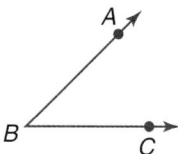

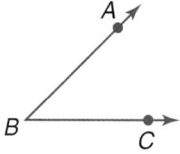

area (132) The measure of the surface enclosed by a geometric figure.

área Medida de la superficie que encierra una figura geométrica.

arithmetic sequence (249) A sequence in which the difference between any two consecutive terms is the same.

average (82) The sum of data divided by the number of items in the data set, also called the mean.

sucesión aritmética Sucesión en que la diferencia entre dos términos consecutivos cualesquiera es siempre la misma.

promedio Suma de los datos dividida entre el número de elementos en el conjunto de datos. También llamado media.

B

back-to-back stem-and-leaf plot (607) Used to compare two sets of data. The leaves for one set of data are on one side of the stem and the leaves for the other set of data are on the other side.

bar graph (722) A graphic form using bars to make comparisons of statistics.

bar notation (201) In repeating decimals the line or bar placed over the digits that repeat. For example, $2.\overline{63}$ indicates the digits 63 repeat.

base (153) In 2^4, the base is 2. The base is used as a factor as many times as given by the exponent (4). That is, $2^4 = 2 \times 2 \times 2 \times 2$.

base (288) In a percent proportion, the whole quantity, or the number to which the part is being compared.

$$\frac{part}{base} = \frac{percent}{100}$$

base (520, 521, 522) The base of a parallelogram or a triangle is any side of the figure. The bases of a trapezoid are the parallel sides.

base (557) The bases of a prism are any two parallel congruent faces.

best-fit line (409) On a scatter plot, a line drawn that is very close to most of the data points. The line that best fits the data.

binomial (669) A polynomial with exactly two terms.

boundary (419) A line that separates a graph into half planes.

box-and-whisker plot (617) A diagram that divides a set of data into four parts using the median and quartiles. A box is drawn around the quartile values and whiskers extend from each quartile to the extreme data points.

diagrama de tallo y hojas consecutivo Se usa para comparar dos conjuntos de datos. Las hojas de uno de los conjuntos de datos aparecen en un lado del tallo y las del otro al otro lado de éste.

gráfica de barras Tipo de gráfica que usa barras para comparar estadísticas.

notación de barra En decimales periódicos, la línea o barra que se escribe encima de los dígitos que se repiten. Por ejemplo, en $2.\overline{63}$ la barra encima del 63 indica que los dígitos 63 se repiten.

base En 2^4, la base es 2. La base se usa como factor las veces que indique el exponente (4). Es decir, $2^4 = 2 \times 2 \times 2 \times 2$.

base En una proporción porcentual, toda la cantidad o número al que se compara la parte.

$$\frac{parte}{base} = \frac{por\ ciento}{100}$$

base La base de un paralelogramo o de un triángulo es cualquier lado de la figura. Las bases de un trapecio son los lados paralelos.

base Las bases de un prisma son cualquier par de caras paralelas y congruentes.

recta de ajuste óptimo En una gráfica de dispersión, una recta que está muy cercana a la mayoría de los puntos de datos. La recta que mejor se ajusta a los datos.

binomio Polinomio con exactamente dos términos.

frontera Recta que divide una gráfica en semiplanos.

diagrama de caja y patillas Diagrama que divide un conjunto de datos en cuatro partes usando la mediana y los cuartiles. Se dibuja una caja alrededor de los cuartiles y se extienden patillas de cada uno de ellos a los valores extremos.

C

center (533) The given point from which all points on the circle are the same distance.

centro Punto dado del cual equidistan todos los puntos de un círculo.

circle (533) The set of all points in a plane that are the same distance from a given point called the center.

circle graph (723) A type of statistical graph used to compare parts of a whole.

circumference (533) The distance around a circle.

coefficient (103) The numerical part of a term that contains a variable.

combination (642) An arrangement or listing in which order is not important.

common difference (249) The difference between any two consecutive terms in an arithmetic sequence.

common multiples (226) Multiples that are shared by two or more numbers. For example, some common multiples of 4 and 6 are 0, 12, and 24.

common ratio (250) The ratio between any two consecutive terms in a geometric sequence.

compatible numbers (714) Numbers that have been rounded so when the numbers are divided by each other, the remainder is zero.

complementary (493) Two angles are complementary if the sum of their measures is 90°.

composite number (159) A whole number that has more than two factors.

compound event (650) Two or more simple events.

cone (569) A three-dimensional figure with one circular base. A curved surface connects the base and vertex.

congruent (455, 493, 500) Line segments that have the same length, or angles that have the same measure, or figures that have the same size and shape.

conjecture (7) An educated guess.

constant (103) A term without a variable.

constant of variation (394) The slope, or rate of change, in the equation $y = kx$, represented by k.

converse (462) The statement formed by reversing the phrases after *if* and *then* in an if-then statement.

círculo Conjunto de todos los puntos del plano que están a la misma distancia de un punto dado del plano llamado centro.

gráfica circular Tipo de gráfica estadística que se usa para comparar las partes de un todo.

circunferencia Longitud del contorno de un círculo.

coeficiente Parte numérica de un término que contiene una variable.

combinación Arreglo o lista en que el orden no es importante.

diferencia común Diferencia entre dos términos consecutivos cualesquiera de una sucesión aritmética.

múltiplos comunes Múltiplos compartidos por dos o más números. Por ejemplo, algunos múltiplos comunes de 4 y 6 son 0, 12 y 24.

razón común Razón entre dos términos consecutivos cualesquiera de una sucesión geométrica.

números compatibles Números redondeados de modo que cuando se dividen, el residuo es cero.

complementarios Dos ángulos son complementarios si la suma de sus medidas es 90°.

número compuesto Número entero que posee más de dos factores.

evento compuesto Dos o más eventos simples.

cono Figura tridimensional con una base circular, la cual posee una superficie curva que une la base con el vértice.

congruentes Segmentos de recta que tienen la misma longitud o ángulos que tienen la misma medida o figuras que poseen la misma forma y tamaño.

conjetura Suposición informada.

constante Término sin variables.

constante de variación La pendiente, o tasa de cambio, en la ecuación $y = kx$, representada por k.

recíproca Un enunciado que se forma intercambiando los enunciados que vienen a continuación de *si-entonces* en un enunciado *si-entonces*.

coordinate (57) A number that corresponds with a point on a number line.

coordinate plane (33) Another name for the coordinate system.

coordinate system (33) A coordinate system is formed by the intersection of two number lines that meet at right angles at their zero points, also called a coordinate plane.

corresponding angles (492) Angles that have the same position on two different parallel lines cut by a transversal. In the figure, $\angle 1$ and $\angle 5$, $\angle 2$ and $\angle 6$, $\angle 3$ and $\angle 7$, $\angle 4$ and $\angle 8$ are corresponding angles.

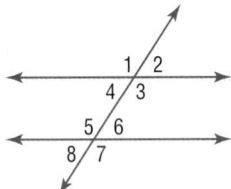

corresponding parts (500) Parts of congruent or similar figures that match.

cosine (477) If $\triangle ABC$ is a right triangle and A is an acute angle,

$$\text{cosine } \angle A = \frac{\text{measure of the leg adjacent to } \angle A}{\text{measure of the hypotenuse}}$$

counterexample (25) An example that shows a conjecture is not true.

cross products (270) If $\frac{a}{c} = \frac{b}{d}$, then $ad = bc$. If $ad = bc$, then $\frac{a}{c} = \frac{b}{d}$.

cubic function (688) A function that can be described by an equation of the form $y = ax^3 + bx^2 + cx + d$, where $a \neq 0$.

cylinder (565) A solid that has two parallel, congruent bases (usually circular) connected with a curved side.

coordenada Número que corresponde a un punto en la recta numérica.

plano de coordenadas Otro nombre para el sistema de coordenadas.

sistema de coordenadas Un sistema de coordenadas se forma de la intersección de dos rectas numéricas perpendiculares que se intersecan en sus puntos cero. También llamado plano de coordenadas.

ángulos correspondientes Ángulos que tienen la misma posición en dos rectas paralelas distintas cortadas por una transversal. En la figura, $\angle 1$ y $\angle 5$, $\angle 2$ y $\angle 6$, $\angle 3$ y $\angle 7$, $\angle 4$ y $\angle 8$ son ángulos correspondientes.

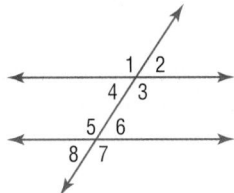

partes correspondientes Partes de figuras congruentes o semejantes que se corresponden mutuamente.

coseno Si $\triangle ABC$ es un ángulo rectángulo y A es uno de sus ángulos agudos,

$$\text{coseno } \angle A = \frac{\text{medida del cateto adyacente a } \angle A}{\text{medida de la hipotenusa}}$$

contraejemplo Ejemplo que muestra que una conjetura no es verdadera.

productos cruzados Si $\frac{a}{c} = \frac{b}{d}$, entonces $ad = bc$. Si $ad = bc$, entonces $\frac{a}{c} = \frac{b}{d}$.

función cúbica Función que puede describirse por una ecuación de la forma $y = ax^3 + bx^2 + cx + d$, donde $a \neq 0$.

cilindro Sólido que posee dos bases congruentes y paralelas (por lo general circulares) unidas por un lado curvo.

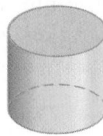

D

deductive reasoning (25) The process of using facts, properties, or rules to justify reasoning or reach valid conclusions.

defining a variable (18) Choosing a variable and a quantity for the variable to represent in an equation.

razonamiento deductivo Proceso de usar hechos, propiedades o reglas para justificar un razonamiento o para sacar conclusiones válidas.

definir una variable Seleccionar una variable y una cantidad para la variable psts representst en una ecuación.

degree (448) The most common unit of measure for angles.

grado La unidad de medida angular más común.

degree (670) The sum of the exponents of the variables of a monomial.

grado Suma de los exponentes de las variables de un monomio.

dependent events (651) Two or more events in which the outcome of one event does affect the outcome of the other event(s).

eventos dependientes Dos o más eventos en que el resultado de uno de ellos afecta el resultado del otro o de los otros eventos.

diagonal (528) A line segment that joins two nonconsecutive vertices of a polygon.

diagonal Segmento de recta que une dos vértices no consecutivos de un polígono.

diameter (533) The distance across a circle through its center.

diámetro Distancia de un lado a otro de un círculo medida a través de su centro.

dilation (512) A transformation that alters the size of a figure but not its shape.

dilatación Transformación que altera el tamaño de una figura, pero no su forma.

dimensional analysis (212) The process of including units of measurement when computing.

análisis dimensional Proceso que incorpora las unidades de medida al hacer cálculos.

direct variation (394) A special type of linear equation that describes rate of change. A relationship such that as x increases in value, y increases or decreases at a constant rate.

variación directa Tipo especial de ecuación lineal que describe tasas de cambio. Relación en que a medida que x aumenta de valor, y aumenta o disminuye a una tasa constante .

discount (299) The amount by which the regular price of an item is reduced.

descuento Cantidad por la que se reduce el precio normal de un artículo.

Distance Formula (466) The distance between two points, with coordinates (x_1, y_1) and (x_2, y_2), is given by $d = \sqrt{(x_2 - x_1)^2 + (y_2 - y_1)^2}$.

Fórmula de la distancia La distancia entre dos puntos, con coordenadas (x_1, y_1) y (x_2, y_2), se calcula con $d = \sqrt{(x_2 - x_1)^2 + (y_2 - y_1)^2}$.

divisible (148) A number is divisible by another if, upon division, the remainder is zero.

divisible Un número es divisible entre otro si, al dividirlos, el residuo es cero.

domain (35) The domain of a relation is the set of all x-coordinates from each pair.

dominio El dominio de una relación es el conjunto de coordenadas x de todos los pares .

E

edge (556) Where two planes intersect in a line.

arista Recta en donde se intersecan dos planos.

empty set (336) A set with no elements shown by the symbol { } or $\varnothing$.

conjunto vacío Conjunto que carece de elementos y que se denota con el símbolo { } o $\varnothing$.

equation (28) A mathematical sentence that contains an equals sign (=).

ecuación Enunciado matemático que contiene el signo de igualdad (=).

equilateral triangle (455) A triangle with all sides congruent.

triángulo equilátero Un triángulo cuyos lados son todos congruentes.

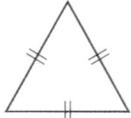

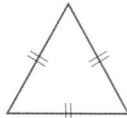

equivalent equations (111) Two or more equations with the same solution. For example, $x + 4 = 7$ and $x = 3$ are equivalent equations.

ecuaciones equivalentes Dos o más ecuaciones con las mismas soluciones. Por ejemplo, $x + 4 = 7$ y $x = 3$ son ecuaciones equivalentes.

equivalent expressions (98) Expressions that have the same value.

expresiones equivalentes Expresiones que tienen el mismo valor.

evaluate (12) Find the numerical value of an expression.

evaluar Calcular el valor numérico de una expresión.

expanded form (154) A number expressed using place value to write the value of each digit in the number.

forma desarrollada Número que se escribe usando el valor de posición para indicar el valor de cada dígito de un número.

experimental probability (311) What actually occurs in a probability experiment.

probabilidad experimental Lo que realmente sucede en un experimento probabilístico.

exponent (153) In 2^4, the exponent is 4. The exponent tells how many times the base, 2, is used as a factor. So, $2^4 = 2 \times 2 \times 2 \times 2$.

exponente En 2^4, el exponente es 4. El exponente indica cuántas veces se usa la base, 2, como factor. Así, $2^4 = 2 \times 2 \times 2 \times 2$.

exterior angles (492, 531) Four of the angles formed by the transversal and two parallel lines. Exterior angles lie outside the two parallel lines.

ángulos exteriores Cuatro de los ángulos formados por una transversal y dos rectas paralelas. Los ángulos exteriores yacen fuera de las dos rectas paralelas.

F

face (556) A flat surface, the side or base of a prism.

cara Superficie plana, el lado o la base de un prisma.

factorial (642) The expression *n factorial* (*n*!) is the product of all counting numbers beginning with *n* and counting backward to 1.

factorial La expresión *n factorial* (*n*!) es el producto de todos los números naturales, comenzando con *n* y contando al revés hasta llegar al 1.

factors (148) Two or more numbers that are multiplied to form a product.

factores Dos o más números que se multiplican para formar un producto.

factor tree (160) A way to find the prime factorization of a number. The factors branch out from the previous factors until all the factors are prime numbers.

árbol de factores Forma de encontrar la factorización prima de un número. Los factores se ramifican de los factores anteriores hasta que todos los factores son números primos.

formula (131) An equation that shows a relationship among certain quantities.

fórmula Ecuación que muestra la relación entre ciertas cantidades.

frequency table (623) A chart that indicates the number of values in each interval.

tabla de frecuencias Tabla que indica el número de valores en cada intervalo.

function (369) A function is a special relation in which each element of the domain is paired with exactly one element in the range.

función Una función es una relación especial en que a cada elemento del dominio le corresponde un único elemento del rango.

Fundamental Counting Principle (636) If event *M* can occur in *m* ways and is followed by event *N* that can occur in *n* ways, then the event *M* followed by event *N* can occur in $m \cdot n$ ways.

Principio fundamental de contar Si el evento *M* puede ocurrir de *m* maneras y lo sigue un evento *N* que puede ocurrir de *n* maneras, entonces el evento *M* seguido del evento *N* puede ocurrir de $m \cdot n$ maneras.

G

geometric sequence (250) A sequence in which the ratio between any two consecutive terms is the same.

sucesión geométrica Sucesión en que la razón entre dos términos consecutivos cualesquiera es siempre la misma.

graph (34) A dot at the point that corresponds to an ordered pair on a coordinate plane.

gráfica Marca puntual en el punto que corresponde a un par ordenado en un plano de coordenadas.

greatest common factor (GCF) (164) The greatest number that is a factor of two or more numbers.

greatest possible error (594) One-half the precision unit, used to describe the actual measure.

máximo común divisor (MCD) El número mayor que es factor de dos o más números.

error máximo posible La mitad de la unidad de precisión. Se usa para describir la medida exacta.

H

half plane (419) The region that contains the solution for an inequality.

histogram (623) A histogram uses bars to display numerical data that have been organized into equal intervals.

hypotenuse (460) The side opposite the right angle in a right triangle.

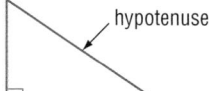

semiplano Región que contiene la solución de una desigualdad.

histograma Un histograma usa barras para exhibir datos numéricos que han sido organizados en intervalos iguales.

hipotenusa Lado opuesto al ángulo recto en un triángulo rectángulo.

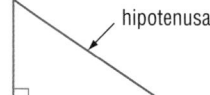

I

identity (336) An equation that is true for every value of the variable.

independent events (650) Two or more events in which the outcome of one event does *not* influence the outcome of the other event(s).

indirect measurement (472) Using the properties of similar triangles to find measurements that are difficult to measure directly.

inductive reasoning (7) Reasoning based on a pattern of examples or past events.

inequality (57, 340) A mathematical sentence that contains $<, >, \neq, \leq,$ or $\geq$.

integers (56) The whole numbers and their opposites.
$\ldots, -3, -2, -1, 0, 1, 2, 3, \ldots$

interior angles (492, 528) Four of the angles formed by the transversal and two parallel lines. Interior angles lie between the two parallel lines.

interquartile range (613) The range of the middle half of a set of data. It is the difference between the upper quartile and the lower quartile.

inverse operations (110) Operations that undo each other, such as addition and subtraction.

irrational number (441) A number that cannot be expressed as $\frac{a}{b}$, where a and b are integers and b does not equal 0.

identidad Ecuación que es verdadera para cada valor de la variable.

eventos independientes Dos o más eventos en que el resultado de uno de ellos *no* afecta el resultado del otro o de los otros eventos .

medición indirecta Uso de las propiedades de triángulos semejantes para hacer mediciones que son difíciles de realizar directamente.

razonamiento inductivo Rezonamiento basada en un patrón de ejemplos o de sucesos pasados.

desigualdad Enunciado matemático que contiene $<, >, \neq, \leq$ o $\geq$.

enteros Los números enteros y sus opuestos.
$\ldots, -3, -2, -1, 0, 1, 2, 3, \ldots$

ángulos interiores Cuatro de los ángulos formados por una transversal y dos rectas paralelas. Los ángulos interiores yacen entre las dos rectas paralelas.

amplitud intercuartílica Amplitud de la mitad central de un conjunto de datos. Es la diferencia entre el cuartil superior y el inferior.

operaciones inversas Operaciones que se anulan mutuamente, como la adición y la sustracción.

número irracional Número que no puede escribirse como $\frac{a}{b}$, donde a y b son enteros y b no es igual a 0.

isosceles triangle (455) A triangle that has at least two congruent sides.

triángulo isósceles Triángulo que posee por lo menos dos lados congruentes.

L

lateral area (578) The sum of the areas of the lateral faces of a solid.

área lateral Suma de las àreas de las caras laterales de un sólido.

lateral faces (578) The lateral faces of a prism, cylinder, pyramid, or cone are all the surface of the figure except the base or bases.

caras laterales Las caras laterales de un prisma, cilindro, pirámide o cono son todas las superficies de la figura, excluyendo la base o las bases.

least common denominator (LCD) (227) The least common multiple of the denominators of two or more fractions.

mínimo común denominador (mcd) El mínimo común múltiplo de los denominadores de dos o más fracciones.

least common multiple (LCM) (226) The least of the nonzero common multiples of two or more numbers. The LCM of 4 and 6 is 12.

mínimo común múltiplo (mcm) El menor de los múltiplos comunes no nulos de dos o más números. El MCM de 4 y 6 es 12.

leaves (606) In a stem-and-leaf plot, the next greatest place value of the data after the stem forms the leaves.

hojas En un diagrama de tallo y hojas, las hojas las forma el segundo valor de posición mayor después del tallo.

legs (460) The sides that are adjacent to the right angle of a right triangle.

catetos Lados adyacentes al ángulo recto de un triángulo rectángulo.

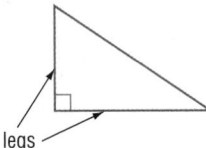

legs

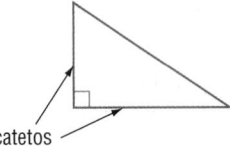

catetos

like terms (103, 674) Expressions that contain the same variables to the same power, such as $2n$ and $5n$ or $6xy^2$ and $4xy^2$.

términos semejantes Expresiones que tienen las mismas variables elevadas a los mismos exponentes, como $2n$ y $5n$ ó $6xy^2$ y $4xy^2$.

line (447) A never-ending straight path.

recta Trayectoria rectilínea interminable.

line graph (722) A type of statistical graph used to show how values change over a period of time.

gráfica lineal Tipo de gráfica estadística que se usa para mostrar cómo cambian los valores durante un período de tiempo.

line of symmetry (506) Each half of a figure is a mirror image of the other half when a line of symmetry is drawn.

eje de simetría Cuando se traza un eje de simetría, cada mitad de una figura es una imagen especular de la otra mitad.

line segment (453) Part of a line containing two endpoints and all the points between them.

segmento de recta Parte de una recta que contiene dos extremos y todos los puntos entre éstos.

linear equation (375) An equation in which the variables appear in separate terms and neither variable contains an exponent other than 1. The graph of a linear equation is a straight line.

ecuación lineal Ecuación en que las variables aparecen en términos separados y en la cual ninguna de ellas tiene un exponente distinto de 1. La gráfica de una ecuación lineal es una recta.

lower quartile (613) The median of the lower half of a set of data, indicated by LQ.

cuartil inferior Mediana de la mitad inferior de un conjunto de datos, se denota con CI.

mean (82, 238) The sum of data divided by the number of items in the data set, also called the average.

measures of central tendency (238) For a list of numerical data, numbers that can represent the whole set of data.

measures of variation (612) Used to describe the distribution of statistical data.

median (238) In a set of data, the middle number of the ordered data, or the mean of the two middle numbers.

midpoint (468) On a line segment, the point that is halfway between the endpoints.

Midpoint Formula (468) On a coordinate plane, the coordinates of the midpoint of a segment whose endpoints have coordinates at (x_1, y_1) and (x_2, y_2) are given by $\left(\frac{x_1 + x_2}{2}, \frac{y_1 + y_2}{2}\right)$.

mixed number (200) The indicated sum of a whole number and a fraction. For example, $3\frac{1}{2}$.

mode (238) The number or numbers that occurs most often in a set of data.

monomial (150) An expression that is a number, a variable, or a product of numbers and/or variables.

multiple (226) The product of a number and a whole number.

mutually exclusive events (652) Two or more events that cannot happen at the same time.

media Suma de los datos dividida entre el número de elementos en el conjunto de datos. También llamada promedio.

medidas de tendencia central Números que pueden representar todo el conjunto de datos en una lista de datos numéricos.

medidas de variación Se usan para describir la distribución de datos estadísticos.

mediana En un conjunto de datos, el número central de los datos ordenados numéricamente o la media de los dos números centrales.

punto medio En un segmento de recta, el punto que equidista de ambos extremos.

Fórmula del punto medio En el plano de coordenadas, el punto medio de un segmento cuyos extremos son (x_1, y_1) y (x_2, y_2) se calcula con la fórmula $\left(\frac{x_1 + x_2}{2}, \frac{y_1 + y_2}{2}\right)$.

número mixto Suma de un entero y una fracción. Por ejemplo, $3\frac{1}{2}$.

moda Número o números de un conjunto de datos que aparecen más frecuentemente.

monomio Expresión que es un número, una variable y/o un producto de números y variables.

múltiplo Producto de un número por un número entero.

eventos mutuamente exclusivos Dos o más eventos que no pueden ocurrir simultáneamente.

negative number (56) A number less than zero.

nonlinear function (687) A function with a graph that is not a straight line.

null set (336) A set with no elements shown by the symbol { } or ∅.

numerical expression (12) A combination of numbers and operations such as addition, subtraction, multiplication, and division.

número negativo Número menor que cero.

función no lineal Función cuya gráfica no es una recta.

conjunto vacío Conjunto que carece de elementos y que se denota con el símbolo { } o ∅.

expresión numérica Combinación de números y operaciones, como adición, sustracción, multiplicación y división.

obtuse angle (449) An angle with a measure greater than 90° but less than 180°.

ángulo obtuso Ángulo que mide más de 90°, pero menos de 180°.

obtuse triangle (454) A triangle with one obtuse angle.

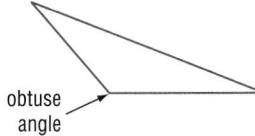

obtuse
angle

triángulo obtusángulo Triángulo que posee un ángulo obtuso.

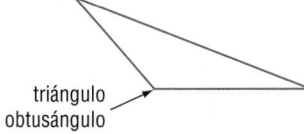

triángulo
obtusángulo

odds (646) A way to describe the chance of an event occurring.

posibilidades Una manera de describir la oportunidad de que ocurra un evento.

open sentence (28) An equation that contains a variable.

enunciado abierto Ecuación que contiene una variable.

opposites (66) Two numbers with the same absolute value but different signs.

opuestos Dos números que tienen el mismo valor absoluto, pero que tienen distintos signos.

ordered pair (33) A pair of numbers used to locate any point on a coordinate plane.

par ordenado Par de números que se usa para ubicar cualquier punto en un plano de coordenadas.

order of operations (12)

1. Simplify the expressions inside grouping symbols.
2. Evaluate all powers.
3. Do all multiplications and/or divisions from left to right.
4. Do all additions and/or subtractions from left to right.

orden de las operaciones

1. Reduce las expresiones dentro de símbolos de agrupamiento.
2. Evalúa todas las potencias.
3. Ejecuta todas las multiplicaciones y/o divisiones de izquierda a derecha.
4. Ejecuta todas las adiciones y/o sustracciones de izquierda a derecha.

origin (33) The point at which the number lines intersect in a coordinate system.

origen Punto de intersección de las rectas numéricas de un sistema de coordenadas.

outcomes (310) Possible results of a probability event.

resultado Resultados posibles de un experimento probabilístico.

outliers (621) Data that are more than 1.5 times the interquartile range from the quartiles.

valores atípicos Datos que distan de los cuartiles más de 1.5 veces la amplitud intercuartílica.

P

parallel lines (492) Two lines in the same plane that do not intersect.

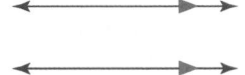

rectas paralelas Dos rectas en el mismo plano que no se intersecan.

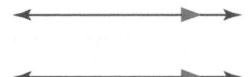

parallelogram (514) A quadrilateral with opposite sides parallel and congruent.

paralelogramo Cuadrilátero con lados opuestos congruentes y paralelos.

part (288) In a percent proportion, the number being compared to the whole quantity.

parte En una proporción porcentual, el número que se compara con la cantidad total.

percent (281) A ratio that compares a number to 100.

por ciento Razón que compara un número con 100.

percent equation (298) An equivalent form of percent proportion, where % is written as a decimal.

$$\text{Part} = \text{Percent} \times \text{Base}$$

ecuación porcentual Forma equivalente a la proporción porcentual en que el % se escribe como decimal.

$$\text{Parte} = \text{Por ciento} \times \text{Base}$$

percent of change (304) The ratio of the increase or decrease of an amount to the original amount.

porcentaje de cambio Razón del aumento o disminución de una cantidad a la cantidad original.

percent of decrease (306) The ratio of an amount of decrease to the previous amount, expressed as a percent. A negative percent of change.

percent of increase (305) The ratio of an amount of increase to the original amount, expressed as a percent.

percent proportion (288)

$$\frac{\text{part}}{\text{base}} = \frac{\text{percent}}{100} \text{ or } \frac{a}{b} = \frac{P}{100}$$

perfect squares (436) Rational numbers whose square roots are whole numbers. 25 is a perfect square because $\sqrt{25} = 5$.

perimeter (132) The distance around a geometric figure.

period (201) In a repeating decimal, the digit or digits that repeats. The period of $0.\overline{6}$ is 6.

permutation (641) An arrangement or listing in which order is important.

perpendicular lines (494) Lines that intersect to form a right angle.

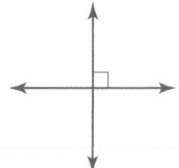

pi, π (533) The ratio of the circumference of a circle to the diameter of the circle. Approximations for π are 3.14 and $\frac{22}{7}$.

plane (556) A two-dimensional flat surface that extends in all directions and contains at least three noncollinear points.

point (447) A specific location in space with no size or shape.

polygon (527) A simple closed figure in a plane formed by three or more line segments.

polyhedron (556) A solid with flat surfaces that are polygons.

polynomial (669) An algebraic expression that contains the sums and/or products of one or more monomials.

power (153) A number that is expressed using an exponent.

precision (590) The exactness to which a measurement is made.

prime factorization (160) A composite number expressed as a product of prime factors. For example, the prime factorization of 63 is $3 \times 3 \times 7$.

porcentaje de disminución Razón de la cantidad de disminución a la cantidad original, escrita como por ciento. Un por ciento de cambio negativo.

porcentaje de aumento Razón de la cantidad de aumento a la cantidad original, escrita como por ciento.

proporción porcentual

$$\frac{\text{parte}}{\text{base}} = \frac{\text{por ciento}}{100} \text{ o } \frac{a}{b} = \frac{P}{100}$$

cuadrados perfectos Números racionales cuyas raíces cuadradas son números racionales. 25 es un cuadrado perfecto porque $\sqrt{25} = 5$.

perímetro Longitud alrededor de una figura geométrica.

período En un decimal periódico, el dígito o dígitos que se repiten. El período de $0.\overline{6}$ es 6.

permutación Arreglo o lista en que el orden es importante.

rectas perpendiculares Rectas que se intersecan formando un ángulo recto.

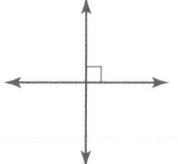

pi, π Razón de la circunferencia de un círculo al diámetro del mismo. 3.14 y $\frac{22}{7}$ son aproximaciones de π.

plano Superficie plana bidimensional que se extiende en todas direcciones y que contiene por lo menos tres puntos no colineales.

punto Ubicación específica en el espacio sin tamaño o forma.

polígono Figura simple y cerrada en el plano formada por tres o más segmentos de recta.

poliedro Sólido con superficies planas que son polígonos.

polinomio Expresión algebraica que contiene sumas y/o productos de uno o más monomios.

potencia Número que puede escribirse usando un exponente.

precisión Exactitud con que se realiza una medida.

factorización prima Número compuesto escrito como producto de factores primos. Por ejemplo, la factorización prima de 63 es $3 \times 3 \times 7$.

prime number (159) A whole number that has exactly two factors, 1 and itself.

número primo Número entero que sólo tiene dos factores, 1 y sí mismo.

principle (300) The amount of money in an account.

capital Cantidad de dinero en una cuenta.

prism (557) A polyhedron that has two parallel, congruent bases in the shape of polygons.

prisma Poliedro que posee dos bases congruentes y paralelas en forma de polígonos.

rectangular prism   triangular prism

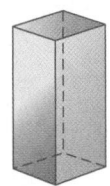 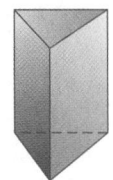

prisma rectangular   prisma triangular

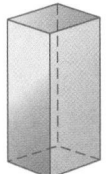 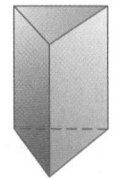

probability (310) The ratio of the number of ways a certain event can occur to the number of possible outcomes.

$$P(\text{event}) = \frac{\text{number of favorable outcomes}}{\text{number of possible outcomes}}$$

probabilidad La razón del número de maneras en que puede ocurrir el evento al número de resultados posibles.

$$P(\text{evento}) = \frac{\text{número de resultados favorables}}{\text{número de resultados posibles}}$$

properties (23) Statements that are true for any numbers.

propiedades Enunciados que son verdaderos para cualquier número.

proportion (270) A statement of equality of two or more ratios.

proporción Enunciado de la igualdad de dos o más razones.

protractor (448) An instrument used to measure angles.

transportador Instrumento que se usa para medir ángulos.

pyramid (557) A polyhedron that has a polygon for a base and triangles for sides.

pirámide Poliedro cuya base es un polígono y cuyos lados son triángulos.

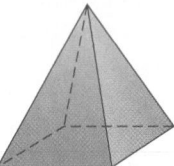

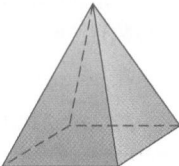

Pythagorean Theorem (460) If a triangle is a right triangle, then the square of the length of the hypotenuse is equal to the sum of the squares of the lengths of the legs or $c^2 = a^2 + b^2$.

Teorema de Pitágoras Si un triángulo es rectángulo, entonces el cuadrado de la longitud de la hipotenusa es igual a la suma de los cuadrados de las longitudes de los catetos, o $c^2 = a^2 + b^2$.

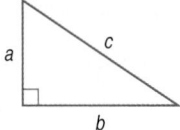

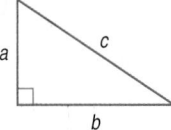

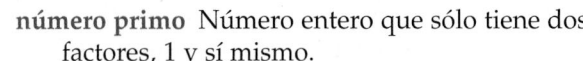

quadrants (86) The four regions into which the x-axis and y-axis separate the coordinate plane.

cuadrantes Las cuatro regiones en que los ejes x y y dividen el plano de coordenadas.

quadratic function (688) A function that can be described by an equation of the form $y = ax^2 + bx + c$, where $a \neq 0$.

función cuadrática Función que puede describirse por una ecuación de la forma $y = ax^2 + bx + c$, donde $a \neq 0$.

quadrilateral (513) A closed figure with four sides and four vertices, including squares, rectangles, and trapezoids.

cuadrilátero Figura cerrada de cuatro lados y cuatro vértices, incluyendo cuadrados, rectángulos y trapecios.

Glossary/Glosario

quartiles (613) The values that divide a set of data into four equal parts.

cuartiles Valores que dividen un conjunto de datos en cuatro partes iguales.

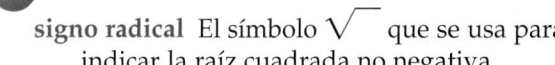

radical sign (436) The symbol $\sqrt{}$ used to indicate a nonnegative square root.

signo radical El símbolo $\sqrt{}$ que se usa para indicar la raíz cuadrada no negativa.

radius (533) The distance from the center to any point on the circle.

radio Distancia del centro a cualquier punto de un círculo.

range (35) The range of a relation is the set of all y-coordinates from each ordered pair.

rango El rango de una relación es el conjunto de coordenadas y de todos los pares.

range (612) A measure of variation that is the difference between the least and greatest values in a set of data.

amplitud Medida de variación que es la diferencia entre los valores máximo y mínimo de un conjunto de datos.

rate (265) A ratio of two measurements having different units.

tasa Razón de dos medidas que tienen unidades distintas.

rate of change (393) A change in one quantity with respect to another quantity.

tasa de cambio Cambio de una cantidad con respecto a otra.

ratio (264) A comparison of two numbers by division. The ratio of 2 to 4 can be stated as 2 out of 4, 2 to 4, 2:4, or $\frac{2}{4}$.

razón Comparación de dos números mediante división. La razón de 2 a 4 puede escribirse como 2 de cada 4, 2 a 4, 2:4 ó $\frac{2}{4}$.

rational number (205) A number that can be written as a fraction in the form $\frac{a}{b}$, where a and b are integers and $b \neq 0$.

número racional Número que puede escribirse como una fracción de la forma $\frac{a}{b}$ donde a y b son enteros y $b \neq 0$.

ray (447) A part of a line that extends indefinitely in one direction.

rayo Parte de una recta que se extiende indefinidamente en una dirección.

real numbers (441) The set of rational numbers together with the set of irrational numbers.

números reales El conjunto de los números racionales junto con el de números irracionales.

reciprocal (215) Another name for a multiplicative inverse.

recíproco Otro nombre del inverso multiplicativo.

rectangle (514) A parallelogram with four right angles.

rectángulo Paralelogramo con cuatro ángulos rectos.

reflection (506) A transformation where a figure is flipped over a line. Also called a flip.

reflexión Transformación en que una figura se voltea a través de una recta.

regular polygon (529) A polygon having all sides congruent and all angles congruent.

polígono regular Polígono cuyos lados son todos congruentes y cuyos ángulos son también todos congruentes.

relation (35) A set of ordered pairs.

relación Conjunto de pares ordenados.

repeating decimal (201) A decimal whose digits repeat in groups of one or more. Examples are 0.181818… and 0.8333… .

decimal periódico Decimal cuyos dígitos se repiten en grupos de uno o más. 0.181818… y 0.8333… son ejemplos de este tipo de decimales.

rhombus (514) A parallelogram with four congruent sides.

rombo Paralelogramo con cuatro lados congruentes.

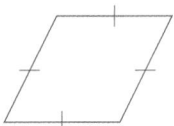

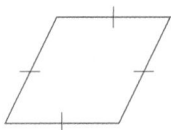

right angle (449) An angle that measures 90°.

right triangle (454) A triangle with one right angle.

rotation (506) A transformation where a figure is turned around a fixed point. Also called a turn.

ángulo recto Ángulo que mide 90°.

triángulo rectángulo Triángulo que tiene un ángulo recto.

rotación Transformación en que una figura se hace girar alrededor de un punto fijo. También se llama vuelta.

S

sample (309) A subgroup or subset of a population used to represent the whole population.

sample space (311) The set of all possible outcomes.

scale (276) The relationship between the measurements on a drawing or model and the measurements of the real object.

scale drawing (276) A drawing that is used to represent an object that is too large or too small to be drawn at actual size.

scale factor (277) The ratio of a length on a scale drawing or model to the corresponding length on the real object.

scale model (276) A model used to represent an object that is too large or too small to be built at actual size.

scalene triangle (455) A triangle with no congruent sides.

scatter plot (40) A graph that shows the relationship between two sets of data.

scientific notation (186) A number in scientific notation is expressed as $a \times 10^n$, where $1 \leq a < 10$ and n is an integer. For example, $5,000,000 = 5.0 \times 10^6$.

sequence (249) An ordered list of numbers, such as, 0, 1, 2, 3, or 2, 4, 6, 8.

sides (447) The two rays that make up an angle.

significant digits (590) The digits recorded from measurement, indicating the precision of the measurement.

similar solids (584) Solids that have the same shape but not necessarily the same size.

similar triangles (471) Triangles that have the same shape but not necessarily the same size.

muestra Subgrupo o subconjunto de una población que se usa para representarla.

espacio muestral Conjunto de todos los resultados posibles.

escala Relación entre las medidas de un dibujo o modelo y las medidas de la figura verdadera.

dibujo a escala Dibujo que se usa para representar una figura que es demasiado grande o pequeña como para ser dibujada de tamaño natural.

factor de escala Razón de la longitud en un dibujo a escala o modelo a la longitud correspondiente en la figura verdadera.

modelo a escala Modelo que se usa para representar una figura que es demasiado grande o pequeña como para ser construida de tamaño natural.

triángulo escaleno Triángulo que no tiene lados congruentes.

gráfica de dispersión Gráfica en que se muestra la relación entre dos conjuntos de datos.

notación científica Un número en notación científica se escribe como $a \times 10^n$, donde $1 \leq a < 10$ y n es un entero. Por ejemplo, $5,000,000 = 5.0 \times 10^6$.

sucesión Lista ordenada de números, como 0, 1, 2, 3 ó 2, 4, 6, 8.

lados Los dos rayos que forman un ángulo.

dígitos significativos Los dígitos de una medición que indican la precisión de la medición.

sólidos semejantes Sólidos que tienen la misma forma, pero no necesariamente el mismo tamaño.

triángulos semejantes Triángulos que tienen la misma forma, pero no necesariamente el mismo tamaño.

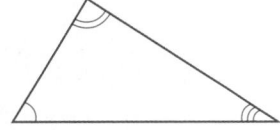 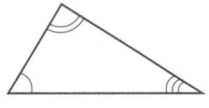

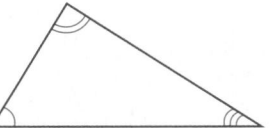

simple event (310) One outcome or a collection of outcomes.

simple interest (300) The amount of money paid or earned for the use of money.

$$I = prt \quad \text{(Interest = principal} \times \text{rate} \times \text{time)}$$

simplest form (104) An algebraic expression in simplest form has no like terms and no parentheses.

simplest form (169) A fraction is in simplest form when the GCF of the numerator and the denominator is 1.

simplify (25) To write an expression in a simpler form.

simulation (656) The process of acting out a situation to see possible outcomes.

sine (477) If $\triangle ABC$ is a right triangle and A is an acute angle,

$$\text{sine } \angle A = \frac{\text{measure of the leg opposite } \angle A}{\text{measure of the hypotenuse}}.$$

skew lines (558) Lines that are neither intersecting nor parallel. Skew lines lie in different planes.

slant height (578) The length of the altitude of a lateral face of a regular pyramid.

slope (387) The ratio of the rise, or vertical change, to the run, or horizontal change. The slope describes the steepness of a line.

$$\text{slope} = \frac{\text{rise}}{\text{run}}$$

slope-intercept form (398) A linear equation in the form $y = mx + b$, where m is the slope and b is the y-intercept.

solution (28) A value for the variable that makes an equation true. For $x + 7 = 19$, the solution is 12.

solving the equation (28) The process of finding a solution to an equation.

solving a right triangle (461) Using the Pythagorean Theorem to find the length of the third side of a right triangle, if the lengths of the other two sides are known.

square (514) A parallelogram with all sides congruent and four right angles.

square root (436) One of the two equal factors of a number. The square root of 25 is 5 since $5^2 = 25$.

standard form (154) A number is in standard form when it does not contain exponents. The standard form for seven hundred thirty-nine is 739.

evento simple Resultado o colección de resultados.

interés simple Cantidad que se paga o que se gana por usar el dinero.

$$I = crt \quad \text{(Interés = capital} \times \text{rédito} \times \text{tiempo)}$$

forma reducida Una expresión algebraica reducida no tiene ni términos semejantes ni paréntesis.

forma reducida Una fracción está reducida si el MCD de su numerador y denominador es 1.

reducir Escribir una expresión en forma más simple.

simulación Proceso de representación de una situación para averiguar los resultados posibles.

seno Si $\triangle ABC$ es un triángulo rectángulo y A es un ángulo agudo,

$$\text{seno } \angle A = \frac{\text{medida del cateto opuesto a } \angle A}{\text{medida de la hipotenusa}}.$$

rectas alabeadas Rectas que no se intersecan y que no son paralelas. Las rectas alabeadas yacen en distintos planos.

altura oblicua En una pirámide regular, la longitud de la altura de una cara lateral.

pendiente Razón de la elevación o cambio vertical al desplazamiento o cambio horizontal. La pendiente describe la inclinación de una recta.

$$\text{pendiente} = \frac{\text{elevación}}{\text{desplazamiento}}$$

forma pendiente-intersección Una ecuación lineal de la forma $y = mx + b$, donde m es la pendiente y b es la intersección y.

solución Valosss y que posee cuatro ángulos rectos.

resolver la ecuación (28) Proceso de hallar una solución a una ecuación.

resolver un triángulo rectángulo Uso del Teorema de Pitágoras para hallar la longitud de un tercer lado de un triángulo rectángulo, si se conocen las longitudes de los otros dos lados.

cuadrado Paralelogramo cuyos lados son todos congruentes y que posee cuatro ángulos rectos.

raíz cuadrada Uno de los dos factores iguales de un número. Una raíz cuadrada de 25 es 5 porque $5^2 = 25$.

forma estándar Un número está en forma estándar si no contiene exponentes. Por ejemplo, la forma estándar de setecientos treinta y nueve es 739.

stem-and-leaf plot (606) A system used to condense a set of data where the greatest place value of the data forms the stem and the next greatest place value forms the leaves.

stems (606) The greatest place value common to all the data values is used for the stem of a stem-and-leaf plot.

straight angle (449) An angle with a measure equal to 180°.

supplementary (494) Two angles are supplementary if the sum of their measures is 180°.

surface area (573) The sum of the areas of all the surfaces (faces) of a 3-dimensional figure.

system of equations (414) A set of equations with the same variables. The solution of the system is the ordered pair that is a solution for all of the equations.

diagrama de tallo y hojas Sistema que se usa para condensar un conjunto de datos, en que el valor de posición máximo de los datos forma el tallo y el segundo valor de posición máximo forma las hojas.

tallos Máximo valor de posición común a todos los datos que se usa como el tallo en un diagrama de tallo y hojas.

ángulo llano Ángulo que mide 180°.

suplementarios Dos ángulos son suplementarios si sus medidas suman 180°.

área de superficie Suma de las áreas de todas las superficies (caras) de una figura tridimensional.

sistema de ecuaciones Conjunto de ecuaciones con las mismas variables. La solución del sistema es el par ordenado que resuelve ambas ecuaciones.

T

tangent (477) If $\triangle ABC$ is a right triangle and A is an acute angle,

$$\text{tangent } \angle A = \frac{\text{measure of the leg opposite } \angle A}{\text{measure of the leg adjacent to } \angle A}$$

term (103) When plus or minus signs separate an algebraic expression into parts, each part is a term.

term (249) Each number within a sequence is called a term.

terminating decimal (200) A decimal whose digits end. Every terminating decimal can be written as a fraction with a denominator of 10, 100, 1000, and so on.

theoretical probability (311) What should occur in a probability experiment.

transformation (506) A movement of a geometric figure.

translation (506) A transformation where a figure is slid from one position to another without being turned. Also called a slide.

transversal (492) A line that intersects two parallel lines to form eight angles.

trapezoid (514) A quadrilateral with exactly one pair of parallel sides.

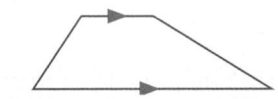

tree diagram (635) A diagram used to show the total number of possible outcomes.

tangente Si $\triangle ABC$ es un triángulo rectángulo y A es un ángulo agudo,

$$\text{tangente } \angle A = \frac{\text{medida del cateto opuesto al } \angle A}{\text{medida del cateto adyacente a } \angle A}$$

término Cada una de las partes de una expresión algebraica separadas por los signos de adición o sustracción.

término Cada número de una sucesión se llama término.

decimal terminal Decimal cuyos dígitos terminan. Todo decimal terminal puede escribirse como una fracción con un denominador de 10, 100, 1000, etc.

probabilidad teórica Lo que debería ocurrir en un experimento probabilístico.

transformación Desplazamiento de una figura geométrica.

translación Transformación en que una figura se desliza sin girar, de una posición a otra. También se llama deslizamiento.

transversal Recta que interseca dos rectas paralelas formando ocho ángulos.

trapecio Cuadrilátero con sólo un par de lados paralelos.

diagrama de árbol Diagrama que se usa para mostrar el número total de resultados posibles.

triangle (453) A polygon having three sides.

trigonometric ratio (477) A ratio of the lengths of two sides of a right triangle. The tangent, sine, and cosine ratios are three trigonometric ratios.

trigonometry (477) The study of the properties of triangles. Trigonometry means *angle measurement*.

trinomial (669) A polynomial with three terms.

two-step equation (120) An equation that contains two operations.

triángulo Polígono de tres lados.

razón trigonométrica Razón de las longitudes de dos lados de un triángulo rectángulo. La tangente, el seno y el coseno son tres razones trigonométricas.

trigonometría Estudio de las propiedades de los triángulos. La palabra significa *medida de ángulos*.

trinomio Polinomio de tres términos.

ecuación de dos pasos Ecuación que contiene dos operaciones.

U

unit rate (265) A rate simplified so that it has a denominator of 1.

upper quartile (613) The median of the upper half of a set of data, indicated by UQ.

tasa unitaria Tasa reducida que tiene denominador igual a 1.

cuartil superior Mediana de la mitad superior de un conjunto de datos, denotada por CS.

V

variable (17) A placeholder for any value.

Venn diagram (164) A diagram that is used to show the relationships among sets of numbers or objects by using overlapping circles in a rectangle.

vertex (447) The common endpoint of the rays forming an angle.

vertex (453) A vertex of a polygon is a point where two sides of the polygon intersect.

vertex (556) Where three or more planes intersect in a point.

vertical angles (493) Two pairs of opposite angles formed by two intersecting lines. The angles formed are congruent. In the figure, the vertical angles are $\angle 1$ and $\angle 3$, $\angle 2$ and $\angle 4$.

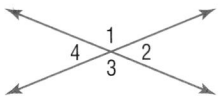

vertical line test (370) If any vertical line drawn on the graph of a relation passes through no more than one point on the graph for each value of x in the domain, then the relation is a function.

volume (563) The measure of space occupied by a solid region.

variable Marcador de posición para cualquier valor.

diagrama de Venn Diagrama que se usa para mostrar las relaciones entre conjuntos de números o elementos mediante círculos, que pueden traslaparse, dentro de un rectángulo.

vértice Extremo común de los dos rayos que forman un ángulo.

vértice El vértice de un polígono es un punto en que se intersecan dos lados del mismo.

vértice Punto en que se intersecan tres o más planos.

ángulos opuestos por el vértice Dos pares de ángulos opuestos formados por dos rectas que se intersecan. Los ángulos que resultan son congruentes. En la figura, los ángulos opuestos por el vértice son $\angle 1$ y $\angle 3$, $\angle 2$ y $\angle 4$.

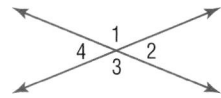

prueba de la recta vertical Si todas las rectas verticales trazadas en la gráfica de una relación no pasan por más un punto para cada valor de x en el dominio, entonces la relación es una función.

volumen Medida del espacio que ocupa un sólido.

X

x-axis (33) The horizontal number line which helps to form the coordinate system.

eje x Recta numérica horizontal que forma parte de un sistema de coordenadas.

***x*-coordinate** (33) The first number of an ordered pair.

***x*-intercept** (381) The *x*-coordinate of a point where a graph crosses the *x*-axis.

coordenada *x* El primer número de un par ordenado.

intersección *x* La coordenada *x* de un punto en que una gráfica interseca el eje *x*.

Y

***y*-axis** (33) The vertical number line which helps to form the coordinate system.

***y*-coordinate** (33) The second number of an ordered pair.

***y*-intercept** (381) The *y*-coordinate of a point where a graph crosses the *y*-axis.

eje *y* Recta numérica vertical que forma parte de un sistema de coordenadas.

coordenada *y* El segundo número en un par ordenado.

intersección *y* La coordenada *y* de un punto en que una gráfica interseca el eje *y*.

Glossary/Glosario

Selected Answers

Chapter 1 The Tools of Algebra

Page 5 Chapter 1 Getting Started
1. 14.8 **3.** 3.1 **5.** 2.95 **7.** 3.55 **9.** 7.88 **11.** Sample answer: 1200 **13.** Sample answer: 120 **15.** Sample answer: 20,000 **17.** Sample answer: 220 **19.** Sample answer: 14 **21.** Sample answer: $5 **23.** Sample answer: 120 **25.** Sample answer: 4 **27.** Sample answer: 10

Pages 9–10 Lesson 1-1
1. when an exact answer is not needed **3.** 1:33 P.M. **5.** 17 **7.** 3072 **9.** 178 beats per min **11.** 17 **13.** 25 **15.** 34 **17.** 27 **19.**

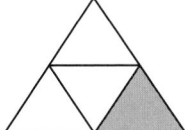

21. Since $68 + $15 + $20 + $16 = $119, Ryan does not have enough money for the ski trip. **23.** about 5 h **25.** Sample answer: about 21,800 transplants **27a.** There are more even products. Since any even number multiplied by any number is even, and only an odd number multiplied by an odd number is odd, there are more even products in the table. There are about 3 times as many evens as odds. **27b.** Yes; in the addition table, there is only one more even number than odd. **29.** B **31.** 3 **33.** 35 **35.** 109

Pages 14–16 Lesson 1-2
1. Sample answer: $(8 - 3) \cdot 2$ **3.** Emily; she followed the order of operations and divided first. **5.** ÷; 20 **7.** −; 66 **9.** ×; 15 **11.** 12 − 9 **13.** 4 **15.** 25 **17.** 38 **19.** 2 **21.** 55 **23.** 24 **25.** 64 **27.** 180 **29.** 50 **31.** 6 − 3 **33.** 9 × 5 **35.** 24 ÷ 6 **37.** 3 × $6 **39.** $(4 \times 2) + (2 \times 13)$ **41.** $(3 \times 57) + (2 \times 12)$ **43.** $61 - (15 + 3) = 43$ **45.** $56 ÷ (2 + 6) - 4 = 3$ **47.** $(50 \times 25) + (7 \times 24) + (4 \times 22) + (3 \times 16)$ **49.** 0-07-825200-8 **51.** Sample answer: $111 - (1 + 1 + 1) \times (11 + 1)$ **53.** C **55.** 64 **57.** 28 **59.** $275 **61.** Sample answer: about 26 compact cars **63.** 126 **65.** 563

Pages 19–21 Lesson 1-3
1. Sample answer: $7n$ and $3x - 1$; $2 + 3$ and 3×8 **3.** Sample answer: $4 \times c \times d$ **5.** 6 **7.** 17 **9.** $g - 5$ **11.** $7 + n ÷ 8$ **13.** 11 **15.** 38 **17.** 2 **19.** 9 **21.** 27 **23.** 56 **25.** 53 **27.** 44 **29.** 32 **31.** 71°F **33.** $s + 200 **35.** $h - 6$ **37.** $5q - 4$ **39.** $n ÷ 6 + 9$ **41.** $17 - 4w$ **43.** 10 **45.** $x + 3$ **47.** $p - 4$ **49.** $s = c + m - d$ **51.** 1 **53.** D **55.** 7 **57.** 9 **59.** 36 **61.** 22

Page 21 Practice Quiz 1
1. 14 **3.** 79 **5.** 22

Pages 26–27 Lesson 1-4
1. Sample answer: $3 \cdot 4 = 4 \cdot 3$ **3.** Kimberly; the Associative Property only holds true if all numbers are added or all numbers are multiplied, not a combination of the two. **5.** Additive Identity **7.** 28 **9.** 45 **11.** $n + 13$ **13.** $42; To find the total cost, add the three costs together.

Since the order in which the costs are added does not matter, the Commutative Property of Addition holds true and makes the addition easier. By adding 4 and 26, the result is 30, and 30 + 12 is 42. **15.** Multiplicative Identity **17.** Commutative Property of Multiplication **19.** Associative Property of Addition **21.** Additive Identity **23.** Associative Property of Multiplication **25.** Commutative Property of Addition **27.** 55 **29.** 40 **31.** 990 **33.** 0 **35.** false; $(100 ÷ 10) ÷ 2 \neq 100 ÷ (10 ÷ 2)$ **37.** false; $9 - 3 \neq 3 - 9$ **39.** $m + 12$ **41.** $a + 27$ **43.** $12y$ **45.** $48c$ **47.** $75s$
49. There are many real-life situations in which the order in which things are completed does not matter. Answers should include the following.
- Reading the sports page and then the comics, or reading the comics and then the sports page. No matter the order, both parts of the newspaper will be read.
- When washing clothes, you would add the detergent and then wash the clothes, not wash the clothes and then add the detergent. Order matters.

51. B **53.** 36 **55.** $w - 12$ **57.** 35 **59.** 15, 21 **61.** 296 **63.** 1050 **65.** 7493

Pages 30–32 Lesson 1-5
1. Sample answer: $b + 7 = 12$ and $8 - h = 3$ **3.** 6 **5.** 5 **7.** 6 **9.** Symmetric **11.** Let $n = $ the number; $n + 8 = 23$; 15 **13.** C **15.** 11 **17.** 12 **19.** 5 **21.** 15 **23.** 9 **25.** always **27.** 15 **29.** 0 **31.** 15 **33.** 17 **35.** 11 **37.** 9 **39.** 3 **41.** 4 **43.** Let $h = $ the number; $h - 10 = 27$; 37 **45.** Let $w = $ the number; $9 + w = 36$; 27 **47.** Let $x = $ the number; $3x = 45$; 15 **49.** $8 **51.** Symmetric Property of Equality **53.** Symmetric Property of Equality **55.** 3 **57.** Sample answer: Once the variable(s) are replaced in the open sentence, the order of operations is used to find the value of the expression. Answers should include the following.
- To evaluate an expression, replace the variable(s) with the given values, and then find the value of the expression.
- To solve an open sentence, find the value of the variable that makes the sentence true.

59. B **61.** $23 + d$ **63.** $10 - n$ **65.** 11 **67.** 42 **69.** 18 **71.** 50 **73.** 90

Page 32 Practice Quiz 2
1. Identity (×) **3.** $24h$ **5.** 8

Pages 36–38 Lesson 1-6
1. Sample answer: (3, 5); the x-coordinate is 3 and the y-coordinate is 5. **3.** The domain of a relation is the set of x-coordinates. The range is the set of y-coordinates. **5.** **7.** (6, 5)

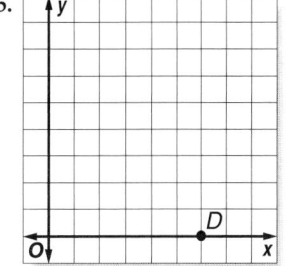

9.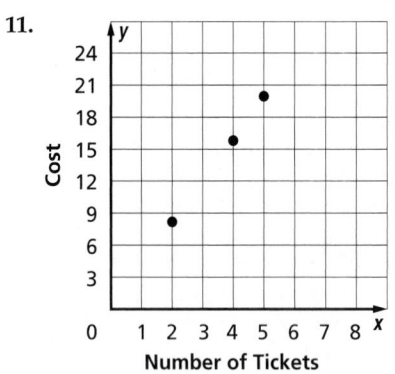

x	y
1	6
6	4
0	2
3	1

domain = {1, 6, 0, 3};
range = {6, 4, 2, 1}

11.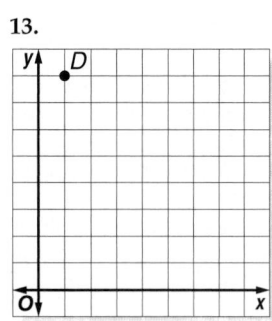

13. 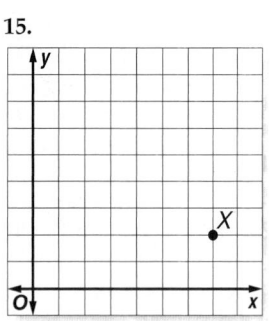   **15.**

17. 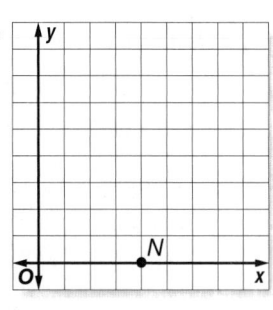   **19.** (7, 3)   **21.** (6, 6)
23. (3, 4)   **25.** on the *x*-axis;
on the *y*-axis

27.   Speed of a House Mouse
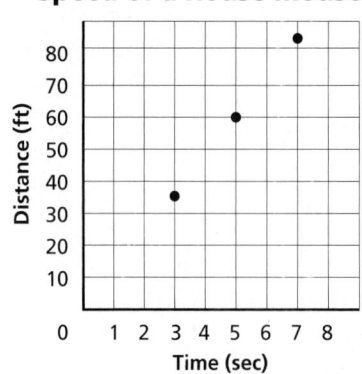

29. Science Experiment
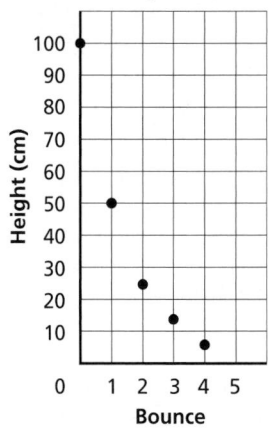

31.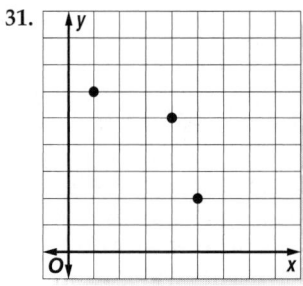

x	y
4	5
5	2
1	6

domain = {4, 5, 1};
range = {5, 2, 6}

33.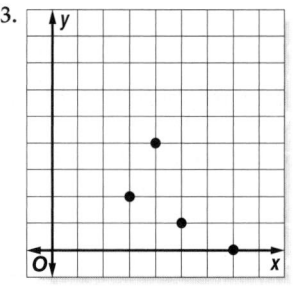

x	y
7	0
3	2
4	4
5	1

domain = {7, 3, 4, 5};
range = {0, 2, 4, 1}

35.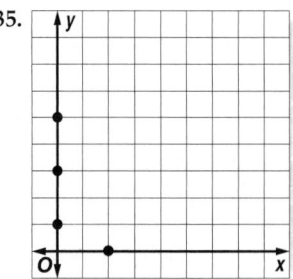

x	y
0	1
0	3
0	5
2	0

domain = {0, 2};
range = {1, 3, 5, 0}

37. (0, 14.7), (1, 10.2), (2, 6.4), (3, 4.3), (4, 2.7), (5, 1.6)
39. domain = {0, 1, 2, 3, 4, 5}; range = {14.7, 10.2, 6.4, 4.3, 2.7, 1.6}   **41.** {(0, 100), (1, 95), (2, 90), (3, 85), (4, 80), (5, 75)}
43. about 93°C; about 96°C   **45.** Ordered pairs can be used to graph real-life data by expressing the data as ordered pairs and then graphing the ordered pairs. Answers should include the following.
• The *x*- and *y*-coordinate of an ordered pair specifies the point on the graph.
• longitude and latitude lines.

47. D   **49a.**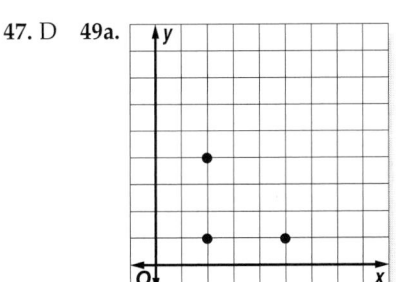

49b. triangle
49c. (4, 2), (4, 8), (10, 2)
49d. triangle
49e. The figures have the same shape but not the same size.

51. 6   **53.** Multiplicative Identity   **55.** 7   **57.** 10 · 30   **59.** 12
61. 28   **63.** 7   **65.** 9

Pages 42–44   Lesson 1-7

1. Sample answer: make predictions, draw conclusions, spot trends   **3.** negative, positive, and none   **5.** No; hair color is not related to height.   **7.** Since the points appear to be random, there is no relationship.   **9.** The number of songs on a CD usually does not affect the cost of the CD; no.   **11.** As speed increases, distance traveled increases; positive.   **13.** The size of a television screen and the number of channels it receives are not related; no.   **15.** The number decreases.

17.
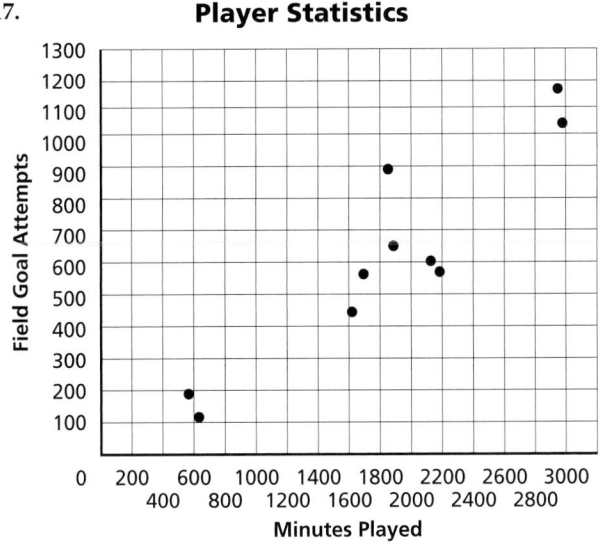

19. about 800   **21.** Sample answer: Yes; as more emphasis is placed on standardized tests, students will become more comfortable taking the tests, and the scores will increase.
23. C
25.   **27.**
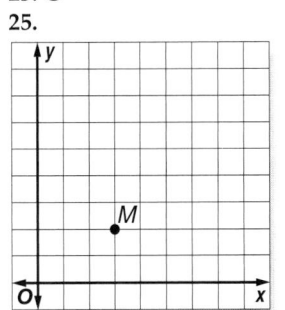

29. (0, 4)   **31.** domain = {0, 4, 2, 6}; range = {9, 8, 3, 1}
33. 7   **35.** $b + 18$ **37.** 31

Pages 47–50   Chapter 1 Study Guide and Review

1. d   **3.** e   **5.** c   **7.** 20   **9.** 22   **11.** 22   **13.** 16   **15.** 12
17. 14   **19.** 10   **21.** 25   **23.** Commutative Property of Addition   **25.** Multiplicative Property of Zero   **27.** 10
29. 17   **31.** 6
33.

x	y
2	3
6	1
7	5

domain: {2, 6, 7}; range: {3, 1, 5}

35. Positive; as the height increases, the circumference increases.

Chapter 2   Integers

Page 55   Chapter 2 Getting Started

1. 22   **3.** 42   **5.** 8   **7.** 4   **9.** T **11.** V **13.** Q

Pages 59–61   Lesson 2-1

1. Draw a number line. Draw a dot at −4.   **3.** The absolute value of a number is its distance from 0 on a number line.
5. +15
7. $-4 < 2; 2 > -4$ **9.** <   **11.** >   **13.** 10   **15.** 21   **17.** 3
19. −54, −52, −45, −37, −36, −34, −27, −27, −2
21. −6
23. +9
25. −5
27.
29.
31. $-5 > -10; -10 < -5$ **33.** $248 < 425; 425 > 248$
35. $212 > 32; 32 < 212$ **37.** >   **39.** >   **41.** >   **43.** >
45. {−15, −4, −2, −1}   **47.** {−60, −57, 38, 98, 188}   **49.** 46
51. −5   **53.** 7   **55.** 2   **57.** 9   **59.** −20   **61.** 4   **63.** 40   **65.** 3
67.
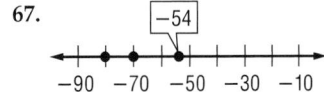

69. $-54 > -70$ **71.** 7   **73.** Sometimes; if A and B are both positive, both negative, or one is 0, it is true. If one number is negative and the other is positive, it is false.   **75.** B
77. Positive; as height increases, so does arm length.
79.

x	y
3	2
3	4
2	1
2	4

{(3, 2), (3, 4), (2, 1), (2, 4)}

81. Commutative Property of Multiplication
83. Commutative Property of Multiplication   **85.** 388
87. 17   **89.** 1049

Pages 67–68   Lesson 2-2
1a. Negative; both addends are negative.   **1b.** Positive;
$|12| > |-2|$.   **1c.** Negative; $|-11| > |9|$.   **1d.** Positive;
both addends are positive.   **3.** -6 **5.** 5   **7.** 3   **9.** 4
11. $4 + (-5) = -1$ **13.** -7 **15.** -11 **17.** -16 **19.** -21
21. -66 **23.** 2   **25.** -2 **27.** 6   **29.** -26 **31.** 21   **33.** -2
35. -6 **37.** -3 **39.** 0   **41.** -5 **43.** 8   **45.** 40
47. $+107,680$
49. To add integers on a number line, start at 0. Move right
to show positive integers and left to show negative
integers. Answers should include the following.
• Sample answer:

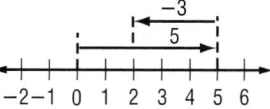

• Sample answer:

51. D   **53.** $\{-12, -9, -8, 0, 3, 14\}$ **55.** no relationship
57. 6   **59.** 20   **61.** 25   **63.** 42   **65.** 65

Pages 72–74   Lesson 2-3
1. Sample answer: $5, -5; -9, 9$ **3.** -3 **5.** 9   **7.** -2 **9.** 20
11. 21   **13.** Utah, Washington, Wisconsin, or Wyoming
15. -1 **17.** -3 **19.** -9 **21.** -12 **23.** 10   **25.** 12   **27.** 3
29. -9 **31.** -14 **33.** -28 **35.** 239   **37.** 1300   **39.** 14,776 ft
41. 24   **43.** -36 **45.** -9 **47.** -20 **49.** -23 **51.** -17
53. $-10,822$ **55a.** False; $3 - 4 \neq 4 - 3$ **55b.** False;
$(5 - 2) - 1 \neq 5 - (2 - 1)$ **57.** A   **59.** -2450 **61.** 3   **63.** 7
65. $\frac{x}{5}$ **67.** $\frac{86}{b}$ **69.** 20   **71.** 75   **73.** 120

Page 74   Practice Quiz 1
1. $-80, -70, -69$ **3.** 6   **5.** -7 **7.** 32   **9.** -9

Pages 77–79   Lesson 2-4
1. $3(-5) = -15$ **3.** Sample answer: $(-4)(9)(2)$ **5.** -40
7. 28   **9.** -540 **11.** $-21y$ **13.** 120   **15.** A   **17.** -42
19. -72 **21.** -70 **23.** 128   **25.** 45   **27.** 130   **29.** -308
31. 528   **33.** -1344 **35.** $-56°F$ **37.** $-96y$ **39.** $-55b$
41. $108mn$ **43.** $-135xy$ **45.** $-88bc$ **47.** $-90jk$ **49.** -99
51. 80   **53.** -216 **55.** 248 ft   **57a.** True; $3(-5) = -5(3)$
57b. True; $-2(3 \cdot 5) = (-2 \cdot 3)(5)$ **59.** B   **61.** -16 **63.** 4
65. 10   **67.** $126°F$ **69.** -14 **71.** $(6, 2)$ **73.** $(1, 5)$ **75.** $(5, 5)$
77. 480   **79.** 550   **81.** 6   **83.** 15   **85.** 4

Pages 83–84   Lesson 2-5
1. Sample answer: $-16 \div 4 = -4$ **3.** 11   **5.** -3 **7.** -10
9. -13 **11.** 0   **13.** 9   **15.** 8   **17.** 10   **19.** -50 **21.** -11
23. -11 **25.** 19   **27.** -12 **29.** -13 **31.** 16   **33.** 49 points
35. 61   **37.** Sample answer: $x = -144; y = 12; z = -12$
39. When the signs of the integers are the same, both a
product and a quotient are positive; when the signs are
different, the product and quotient are negative. Answers
should include the following.
• Sample answer: $4 \cdot (-6) = -24$ and $-24 \div 4 = -6$;
  $-3 \cdot 2 = -6$ and $-6 \div (-3) = 2$
• Sample answers: same sign: $-30 \div (-5) = 6, 30 \div 5 = 6$;
  different signs: $-24 \div 8 = -3, 24 \div (-8) = -3$
41. B   **43.** -39 **45.** $-50cd$ **47.** B   **49.** D

Page 84   Practice Quiz 2
1. -84 **3.** -126 **5.** -31 **7.** -25 **9.** $-20xy$

Pages 87–89   Lesson 2-6
1. Sample answer: $(3, 6)$ represents a point 3 units to the
right and 6 units up from the origin. $(6, 3)$ represents a
point 6 units to the right and 3 units up from the origin.
3. Keisha; a point in Quadrant I has two positive
coordinates. Interchanging the coordinates will still result
in two positive coordinates, and the point will be in
Quadrant I.   **5.** $(1, 3)$ **7.** $(5, -4)$ **9.** II   **11.** III   **13.** $(-2, 4)$
15. $(4, -2)$ **17.** $(2, 2)$ **19.** $(0, -2)$ **21.** $(-3, -5)$

23–34.

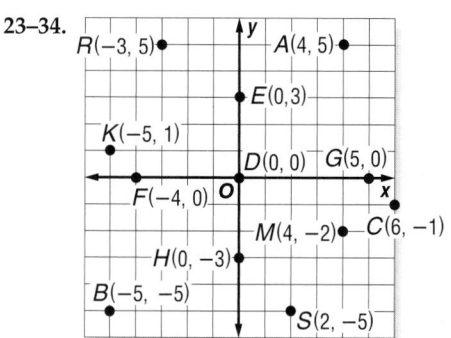

23. I   **25.** IV   **27.** IV   **29.** none   **31.** none   **33.** none

35. Sample answer:

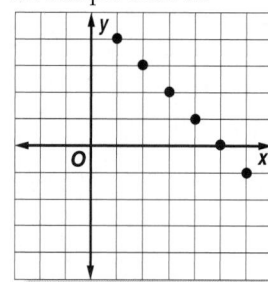

x	y
1	4
2	3
3	2
4	1
5	0
6	-1

The points are
along a line
slanting down to
the right,
crossing the
y-axis at 5 and
the x-axis at 5.

37. Sample answer:

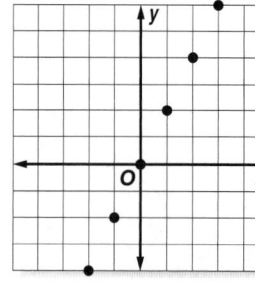

x	y
-2	-4
-1	-2
0	0
1	2
2	4
3	6

The points are
along a line
slanting up,
through the
origin.

39. Sample answer:

x	y
-3	-1
-2	0
-1	1
0	2
1	3
2	4

The points are
along a line
slanting up,
crossing the
y-axis at 2 and
the x-axis
at -2.

41. 5-point star

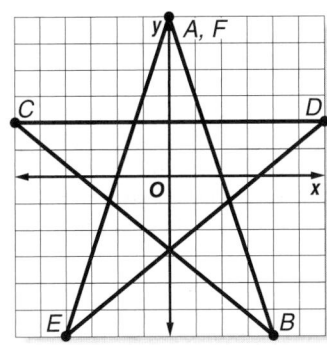

43. Sample answer:

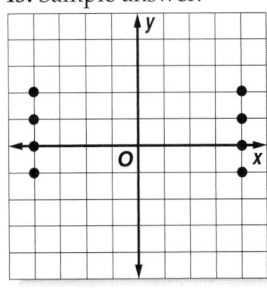

The graph can include any integer pairs where $x > 3$ or $x < -3$.

45. The new triangle is twice the size of the original triangle, and is moved to the right and up.

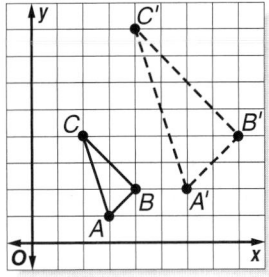

47. The new triangle is translated right 2 units and up 2 units; it is the same size as the original triangle.

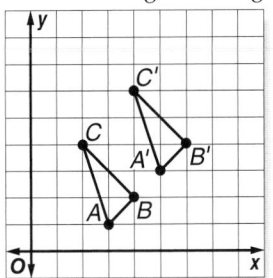

51. Sample answer:

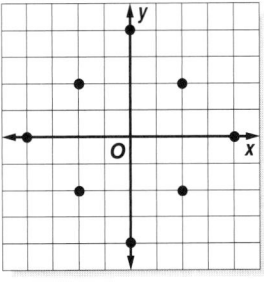

The points lie outside a rhombus defined by $(0, 4)$, $(4, 0)$, $(0, -4)$, and $(-4, 0)$.

53. D **55.** -3 **57.** 8 **59.** -96 **61.** 13°F **63.** $24h$ **65.** $45b$
67. 0

Pages 90–92 Chapter 2 Study Guide and Review
1. negative number **3.** coordinate **5.** integers
7. inequality **9.** = **11.** > **13.** 25 **15.** 22 **17.** -5 **19.** -4
21. -10 **23.** -8 **25.** 5 **27.** -4 **29.** 9 **31.** -66 **33.** 48
35. 7 **37.** -4 **39.** 2

40–43.

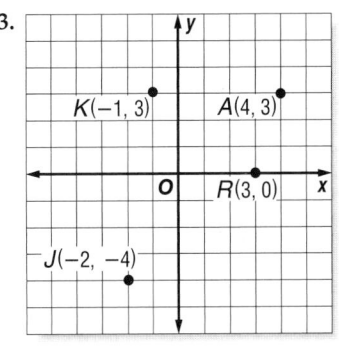

41. III **43.** None

Chapter 3 Equations

Page 97 Chapter 3 Getting Started
1. -6 **3.** 10 **5.** $5 + (-7)$ **7.** $-5 + (-9)$ **9.** -3 **11.** 0
13. $5 + 2n$ **15.** $n - 3$

Pages 100–102 Lesson 3-1
1. Sample answer: $2(3 + 4) = 2 \cdot 3 + 2 \cdot 4$ **3.** $5 \cdot 7 + 5 \cdot 8$,
75 **5.** $2 \cdot 6 + 4 \cdot 6$, 36 **7.** $3n + 6$ **9.** $-6x + 30$ **11.** \$56.25
13. $5 \cdot 7 + 5 \cdot 3$, 50 **15.** $4 \cdot 3 + 3 \cdot 3$, 21 **17.** $8 \cdot 2 + 8 \cdot 2$, 32
19. $6 \cdot 8 + 6(-5)$, 18 **21.** $-3 \cdot 9 + (-3)(-2)$, -21
23. $10(-5) - 3(-5)$, -35 **25.** $12(\$15 + \$10 + \$8)$,
$12(\$15) + 12(\$10) + 12(\$8)$; \$396 **27.** $5y + 30$ **29.** $7y + 56$
31. $10y + 20$ **33.** $10 + 5x$ **35.** $9m - 18$ **37.** $15s - 45$
39. $12x - 36$ **41.** $2w - 20$ **43.** $-5a - 50$ **45.** $-5w + 40$
47. $-5a + 30$ **49.** $3a + 3b$ **51.** \$488.75 **53.** No;
$3 + (4 \cdot 5) = 23$, $(3 + 4)(3 + 5) = 56$ **55.** C
57. $8(20 + 3) = 184$ **59.** $16(10 + 1) = 176$
61. $9(100 + 3) = 927$ **63.** $12(1000 + 4) = 12,048$ **65.** 6
67. 4 **69.** 21, 25, 29 **71.** 80, 160, 320 **73.** $-8 + (-4)$
75. $3 + (-9)$ **77.** $-7 + (-10)$

Pages 105–107 Lesson 3-2
1. terms that contain the same variable or are constants
3. Koko; $5x + x = 6x$, not $5x$. **5.** terms: $2m, -1n, 6m$; like
terms: $2m, 6m$; coefficients: $2, -1, 6$: constant: none **7.** $8a$
9. $7c + 12$ **11.** $9y$ **13.** $-3y - 16$ **15.** $4x + 12y$ **17.** terms:
$3, 7x, 3x, x$; like terms: $7x, 3x, x$; coefficients: 7, 3, 1;
constant: 3 **19.** terms $2a, 5c, -1a, 6a$; like terms: $2a, -1a, 6a$;
coefficients: 2, 5, -1, 6; constant: none **21.** terms: $6m, -2n$,
7; like terms: none; coefficients: 6, -2; constant: 7 **23.** $7x$
25. $11y$ **27.** $7a + 3$ **29.** $7y + 9$ **31.** $2x$ **33.** $-y$
35. $-4x + 8$ **37.** $8y$ **39.** $-x + 12$ **41.** $5b + 6$ **43.** $-4a - 6$
45. -8 **47.** $16m + 2n$ **49.** $-9c + 2d$ **51.** $3s + 80$
53. $5d - 2$ **55.** $6x + 2$ **57a.** Distributive Property
57b. Commutative Property **57c.** Substitution Property of
Equality **57d.** Distributive Property **59.** C **61.** $-2y - 16$
63. III **65.** 17 **67.** 2 **69.** -11 **71.** -5 **73.** -13

Page 107 Practice Quiz 1
1. $6x + 12$ **3.** $7y - 4$ **5.** $2m + 15$

Pages 113–114 Lesson 3-3
1. Addition Property of Equality **3.** 11 **5.** -4 **7.** 55
9.

$$-3\ -2\ -1\ \ 0\ \ 1\ \ 2\ \ 3\ \ 4$$

11. C **13.** 13 **15.** -8 **17.** -15 **19.** -1 **21.** 15 **23.** 24
25. 36 **27.** -4 **29.** -31 **31.** 118 **33.** $n + 9 = -2$; -11
35. $n - 3 = -6$; -3
37.

$$-6\ -5\ -4\ -3\ -2\ -1\ \ 0\ \ 1$$

39.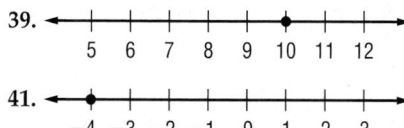

$$5 \quad 6 \quad 7 \quad 8 \quad 9 \quad 10 \quad 11 \quad 12$$

41.

$$-4 \quad -3 \quad -2 \quad -1 \quad 0 \quad 1 \quad 2 \quad 3$$

43. $12 = x - 20; 32$ **47.** 17 million   **49.** When you solve an equation, you perform the same operation on each side so that the two sides remain equal. Answers should include the following.

- In an equation, both sides are equal. In a balance scale, the weight of the items on both sides are equal.
- The Addition and Subtraction Properties of Equality allow you to add or subtract the same number from each side of an equation. The two sides of the equation remain equal.

51. C   **53.** $3t + 12$ **55.** $-4z + 4$ **57.** $-4m - 1$
59. Additive Inverse Property   **61.** 84   **63.** -25 **65.** -9
67. -4

Pages 117–119 Lesson 3-4

1. Multiplication Property of Equality   **3.** Sample answer: $-5x = -20$ **5.** -5 **7.** 27   **9.** 66   **11.** 7   **13.** -8
15. 8   **17.** 24   **19.** 14   **21.** -33 **23.** 9   **25.** -43 **27.** -135
29. 130   **31.** 29   **33.** -168 **35.** $6x = -42; -7$
37. $\frac{x}{-4} = 8; -32$

39.

$$-9 \quad -8 \quad -7 \quad -6 \quad -5 \quad -4 \quad -3 \quad -2$$

41.

$$-3 \quad -2 \quad -1 \quad 0 \quad 1 \quad 2 \quad 3 \quad 4$$

43.

$$30 \quad 31 \quad 32 \quad 33 \quad 34 \quad 35 \quad 36 \quad 37$$

45. $12,000 = 5x; 2400$ mi²   **47.** $6p = 24$, 4 painters
49a. True; one pyramid balances two cubes, so this is the same as adding one cube to each side.   **49b.** True; one pyramid and one cube balance three cubes, which balance one cylinder.   **49c.** False; one cylinder and one pyramid balance five cubes.   **51.** B   **53.** 13   **55.** -28 **57.** $7y + 6$
59. -36 **61.** 10   **63.** -2 **65.** 2   **67.** -19 **69.** -27

Pages 122–124 Lesson 3-5

1. You undo the operations in reverse order.   **3.** 8   **5.** -2
7. -40 **9.** -4 **11.** 10   **13.** 2   **15.** 4   **17.** 8   **19.** 13   **21.** 3
23. 28   **25.** 64   **27.** 65   **29.** 21   **31.** 11   **33.** 30   **35.** 33
37. -13 **39.** 5   **41.** 5   **43.** -2 **45.** 10   **47.** 3 h   **49.** 131 bikes
51. $5x - 2 = 8$ **53.** C   **55.** -7 **57.** -2 **59.** -2
61. $-5y - 15$ **63.** $-9y + 36$ **65.** $-8r + 40$ **67.** $(2, -3)$
69. $(-3, -4)$ **71.** $x \div 15$ **73.** $2x + 10$

Pages 128–130 Lesson 3-6

1. is, equals, is equal to   **3.** Ben; *Three less than* means that three is subtracted *from* a number.   **5.** $2n - 4 = -2, 1$
7. $2x + 5 = 37$, 21 yr   **9.** $3n + 20 = -4, -8$
11. $10n - 8 = 82, 9$ **13.** $\frac{n}{-4} - 8 = -42, 136$
15. $3n - 8 = -2, 2$ **17.** $17 - 2n = 5, 6$
19. $4n + 3n + 5 = 47, 6$ **21.** $8 - 5x = -7, 3$ h   **23.** $2x + 2 = 12$. 5 million people   **25.** Sample answer: By 2020, Texas is expected to have 10 thousand more people age 85 or older than New York will have. Together, they are expected to have 846 thousand people age 85 or older. Find the expected number of people age 85 or older in New York by 2020.   **27.** Two-step equations can be used when you start with a certain amount and increase or decrease at a certain rate. Answers should include the following.

- You've been running 15 minutes each day as part of a fitness program. You plan to increase your time by 5 minutes each week. After how many weeks do you plan to run 30 minutes each day? ($5w + 15 = 30$, 3 weeks)
- You are three years older than your sister is. Together the sum of your ages is 21. How old is your sister? ($2x + 3 = 21$, 9 years old)

29. D   **31.** 4   **33.** 5   **35.** -11 **37.** -4 **39.** -5 **41.** 6

Page 130 Practice Quiz 2

1. -13 **3.** -18 **5.** $3n + 20 = 32, 4$

Pages 133–136 Lesson 3-7

1. $d = rt$ **3.** Sample answer:

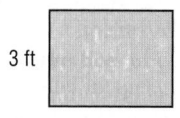

5 in.

4 in.

5. 34 km, 30 km²   **7.** 4 in.   **9.** 8 h   **11.** 15 mph   **13.** 54 cm, 162 cm²   **15.** 136 in., 900 in²   **17.** 48 m, 144 m²   **19.** 20 m, 25 m²   **21.** 11 yd   **23.** 5 m   **25.** 39 ft   **27.** 19 yd   **29.** 390 yd, 9000 yd²   **31.** $d = 2r$ **33.** 4300 ft²   **35.** ≈ 23.5 mph
37.   4 ft   **39.**   4 cm

3 ft

4 cm

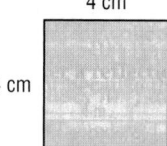

41. Sometimes; a 3-inch by 4-inch rectangle has a perimeter of 14 inches and an area of 12 square inches; a 6-inch by 8-inch rectangle has a perimeter of 28 inches and an area of 48 square inches.   **43.** Formulas are important in math and science because they summarize the relationships among quantities. Answers should include the following.

- Sample answer: The formula to find acceleration is $a = \dfrac{v_f - v_i}{t}$ where v_f is the final velocity and v_i is the initial velocity.
- You can find the acceleration of an automobile with this formula.

45. C   **47.** -9 **49.** -8 **51.** $-4x + 9$ **53a.** {(1870, 14), (1881, 600), (1910, 1000), (2000, 1500)}   **53b.** domain: {1870, 1881, 1910, 2000}, range: {14, 600, 1000, 1500}

Pages 138–140 Chapter 3 Study Guide and Review

1. like terms   **3.** Multiplication Property of Equality
5. Distributive Property   **7.** coordinate   **9.** constant
11. $3h + 18$ **13.** $-5k - 5$ **15.** $9t - 45$ **17.** $-2b + 8$
19. $9a$ **21.** $-2n - 8$ **23.** 3   **25.** 5   **27.** 8   **29.** -18
31. 1   **33.** -6 **35.** $2n + 3 = 53; 25$ **37.** 34 ft, 72 ft²

Chapter 4   Factors and Fractions

Page 147 Chapter 4 Getting Started

1. $2x + 2$ **3.** $-2k - 16$ **5.** $12c + 24$ **7.** $7a + 7b$ **9.** 14
11. 28   **13.** 63   **15.** 30   **17.** 45   **19.** 78   **21.** 0.39   **23.** 0.005

Pages 150–152 Lesson 4-1

1. Use the rules for divisibility to determine whether 18,450 is divisible by both 2 and 3. If it is, then the number is also divisible by 6 and there is no remainder.   **3a.** Sample

answer: 102   **3b.** Sample answer: 1035   **3c.** Sample answer: 343   **5.** 2   **7.** 2, 5, 10   **9.** 1, 2, 4, 5, 8, 10, 16, 20, 40, 80   **11.** yes; a number   **13.** No; two terms are added.   **15.** 2000, 2004, and 2032 are leap years.   **17.** 3, 5   **19.** 2, 3, 5, 6, 10   **21.** 2   **23.** 5   **25.** 2, 3, 6   **27.** 2, 5, 10   **29.** 1, 2, 3, 6, 19, 38, 57, 114   **31.** 1, 5, 13, 65   **33.** 1, 2, 4, 31, 62, 124   **35.** 1, 3, 5, 9, 15, 27, 45, 135   **37.** yes; a number   **39.** No; one term is subtracted from another term.   **41.** No; two terms are added.   **43.** No; one term is subtracted from another term.   **45.** yes; the product of a number and a variable   **47.** yes; the product of numbers and variables   **49.** 6 ways; 1×72, 2×36, 3×24, 4×18, 6×12, 8×9 **51.** Alternating rows of a flag contain 6 stars and 5 stars, respectively. Fifty is not divisible by a number that would make the arrangement of stars in an appropriate-sized rectangle.   **53.** Never; a number that has 10 as a factor is divisible by $2 \cdot 5$, so it is always divisible by 5.   **55a.** 24 cases   **55b.** 36 bags   **55c.** Sample answer: 12 cases, 18 bags; 14 cases, 15 bags; 16 cases, 12 bags   **57.** The side lengths or dimensions of a rectangle are factors of the number that is the area of the rectangle. Answers should include the following.
- A rectangle with dimensions and area labeled; for example, a 4×5 rectangle would have length 5 units, width 4 units, and area 20 square units.
- Factors are numbers that are multiplied to form a product. The dimensions of a rectangle are factor pairs of the area since they are multiplied to form the area.

59. C   **61.** 34 in., 60 in^2 **63.** $5n - 2 = 3$; 1   **65.** 2   **67.** 64   **69.** -27 **71.** 2304

Pages 155–157   Lesson 4-2
1. Sample answer: 2^5, x^5 **3.** When n is even, $1^n = (-1)^n = 1$. When n is odd, $1^n = 1$ and $(-1)^n = -1$.   **5.** 7^2 **7.** $(2 \times 10^3) + (6 \times 10^2) + (9 \times 10^1) + (5 \times 10^0)$ **9.** -11 **11.** 13^2 **13.** 6^1 **15.** $(-8)^4$ **17.** $(-t)^3$ **19.** m^4 **21.** $2x^2y^2$ **23.** $9(p+1)^2$ **25.** $(8 \times 10^2) + (0 \times 10^1) + (3 \times 10^0)$ **27.** $(2 \times 10^4) + (3 \times 10^3) + (7 \times 10^2) + (8 \times 10^1) + (1 \times 10^0)$ **29.** 1000   **31.** -32 **33.** 81   **35.** -54 **37.** 13   **39.** 9   **41.** 243   **43.** $81 = 9^2$ or 3^4, $64 = 8^2$ or 4^3 or 2^6 **45.** $(-8)^3$; $(-8)(-8)(-8)$; -512 **47.** Always; the product of two negative numbers is always positive.   **49.** 2^1, 2^2, 2^3, 2^4, 2^5 **51.** After 10 folds, the noodles are $5(2^{10}) = 5(1024)$ or 5120 feet long, which is slightly less than a mile. So, after 11 folds the length of the noodles will be greater than a mile.   **53.** $=$ **55.** $6 \cdot 3^2$ cm^2 **57.** No; the surface area is multiplied by 4. The volume is multiplied by 8.   **59.** As the capacity of computer memory increases, the factors of 2 in the number of megabytes increases. Answers should include the following.
- Computer data are measured in small units that are based on factors of 2.
- In describing the amount of memory in modern computers, it would be impractical to list all the factors of 2. Using exponents is a more efficient way to describe and compare computer data.

61. B   **63.** 2, 5, 10   **65.** 150 mph   **67.** 4   **69.** $3y + 8$ **71.** 1, 5   **73.** 1, 2, 4, 8, 16   **75.** 1, 5, 7, 35

Pages 161–163   Lesson 4-3
1. A prime number has exactly two factors: 1 and itself. A composite number has more than two factors.   **3.** Francisca; 4 is not prime.   **5.** prime   **7.** $2 \cdot 3^2$ **9.** $2 \cdot 5^2$ **11.** $5 \cdot a \cdot a \cdot b$ **13.** 3 and 5, 5 and 7, 11 and 13, 17 and 19, 29 and 31, 41 and 43   **15.** composite   **17.** composite   **19.** composite   **21.** prime   **23.** 3^4 **25.** $3^2 \cdot 7$ **27.** $2^2 \cdot 5^2$

29. $2 \cdot 5 \cdot 11$ **31.** $3 \cdot 3 \cdot t \cdot t$ **33.** $-1 \cdot 5 \cdot 5 \cdot z \cdot z \cdot z$ **35.** $-1 \cdot 2 \cdot 19 \cdot m \cdot n \cdot p$ **37.** $3 \cdot 7 \cdot g \cdot h \cdot h \cdot h$ **39.** $2 \cdot 2 \cdot 2 \cdot 2 \cdot 2 \cdot 2 \cdot n \cdot n \cdot n$ **41.** $-1 \cdot 2 \cdot 2 \cdot 2 \cdot 3 \cdot 5 \cdot r \cdot r \cdot s \cdot t \cdot t \cdot t$ **43.** Sample answer: $-25x$
45. The number of rectangles that can be modeled to represent a number indicate whether the number is prime or composite. Answers should include the following.
- If a number is prime, then only one rectangle can be drawn to represent the number. If a number is composite, then more than one rectangle can be drawn to represent the number.
- If a model has a length or width of 1, then the number may be prime or composite. If a model does not have a length or width of 1, then the number must be composite.

47. C   **49.** $(-5)^3 h^2 k$ **51.** yes   **53.** no   **55.** -9 **57.** -28 **59.** $5x - 35$ **61.** $10a + 60$ **63.** $72 - 8y$

Page 163   Practice Quiz 1
1. 3, 5   **3.** none   **5.** 37   **7.** $7 \cdot 11 \cdot x$ **9.** $-1 \cdot 23 \cdot n \cdot n \cdot n$

Pages 166–168   Lesson 4-4
1. Sample answer: Find the prime factorization of each number. Multiply the factors that are common to both.   **3.** Jack; the common prime factors of the expressions are 2 and 11, so the GCF is $2 \cdot 11$ or 22.   **5.** 3   **7.** 14   **9.** 36   **11.** $14n$ **13.** $3(n + 3)$ **15.** $5(3 + 4x)$ **17.** 4   **19.** 8   **21.** 10   **23.** 9   **25.** 8   **27.** 5   **29.** 4   **31.** 3   **33.** 4   **35.** $4x$ **37.** $2s$ **39.** $14b$ **41.** $4n$ **43.** Sample answer: $2x$, $6x^2$ **45.** $3(r + 4)$ **47.** $3(2 + y)$ **49.** $7(2 + 3c)$ **51.** $4(y - 4)$ **53a.** 7; Sample answer:

7	14	21	28	35
↓	↓	↓	↓	↓
7(1)	7(2)	7(3)	7(4)	7(5)

The terms increase by a factor of 7.   **53b.** 42, 49   **55a.** 6-in. squares   **55b.** 20 tiles   **57.** Yes; the GCF of 2 and 8 is 2.   **59.** D   **61.** yes   **63.** no   **65.** yes   **67.** $3 \cdot 3 \cdot n$ **69.** $-1 \cdot 5 \cdot j \cdot k$ **71.** 92   **73.** -6 **75.** -10 **77.** 36   **79.** 24   **81.** 1000

Pages 171–173   Lesson 4-5
1. The GCF of the numerator and denominator is 1.   **3.** $\frac{1}{7}$ **5.** simplified   **7.** $\frac{16}{17}$ **9.** $\frac{a}{2}$ **11.** simplified   **13.** B   **15.** $\frac{5}{6}$ **17.** $\frac{2}{9}$ **19.** $\frac{9}{22}$ **21.** simplified   **23.** $\frac{1}{3}$ **25.** $\frac{5}{12}$ **27.** $\frac{19}{20}$ **29.** $\frac{3}{92}$ **31.** $\frac{y^2}{1}$ or y^2 **33.** $\frac{20}{21}$ **35.** $\frac{1}{8t}$ **37.** $\frac{7z^2}{4}$ **39.** simplified   **41.** $\frac{gh}{3}$ **43.** $\frac{24}{25}$ **45a.** yes; $\frac{330}{440} = \frac{3}{4}$ **45b.** No; $\frac{294}{349}$ cannot be simplified.   **45c.** yes; $\frac{264}{528} = \frac{1}{2}$ **47.** $\frac{31}{50}$ **49.** $\frac{7}{10}$ **51.** Fractions represent parts of a whole. So, measurements that contain parts of units can be represented using fractions. Answers should include the following.
- Measurements can be given as parts of a whole because smaller units make up larger units. For example, inches make up feet.
- Twelve inches equals 1 foot. So, 3 inches equals $\frac{3}{12}$ or $\frac{1}{4}$ foot.

53. A   **55.** 2   **57.** 5   **59.** composite   **61.** prime   **63.** 27   **65.** $(6 \cdot 7)(k^3)$ **67.** $(3 \cdot -5)(x^4 \cdot x^2)$

Pages 177–179 Lesson 4-6
1. Neither; the factors have different bases. 3. Sample answer: $5 \cdot 5^2 = 5^3$ 5. a^6 7. $-12x^5$ 9. 10^2 11. a^4 13. 3^5 15. d^{10} 17. n^9 19. 9^9 21. $18y^5$ 23. $8a^3b^{10}$ 25. 5^3 27. b^3 29. m^{12} 31. $(-2)^1$ or -2 33. n^6 35. k^2m 37. 9^7 39. 7^9 41. 10^2 or 100 times 43. 3 45. 2 times 47. 8 49. 5
51. Each level on the Richter scale is 10 times greater than the previous level. So, powers of 10 can be used to compare earthquake magnitudes. Answers should include the following.
- On the Richter scale, each whole-number increase represents a 10-fold increase in the magnitude of seismic waves.
- An earthquake of magnitude 7 is 10^5 times greater than an earthquake of magnitude 2 because $10^7 \div 10^2 = 10^{7-2}$ or 10^5.

53. B 55. simplified 57. $\dfrac{3x}{2y}$ 59. 2 61. a 63. Positive; as the high temperature increases, the amount of electricity that is used also increases. 65. $-\dfrac{1}{10}$ 67. $-\dfrac{1}{20}$ 69. $\dfrac{1}{64}$

Pages 183–185 Lesson 4-7
1. To get each successive power, divide the previous power by 3. Therefore, $3^0 = 3 \div 3$ or 1. 3. $\dfrac{1}{5^2}$ 5. $\dfrac{1}{t^6}$ 7. 3^{-4}
9. 7^{-2} 11. $\dfrac{1}{32}$ 13. 10^{-3} 15. $\dfrac{1}{5^3}$ 17. $\dfrac{1}{(-3)^3}$ 19. $\dfrac{1}{10^4}$
21. $\dfrac{1}{a^{10}}$ 23. $\dfrac{1}{q^4}$ 25. x^2 27. $\dfrac{1}{5^4}$; 0.0016 29. 5^{-5} 31. 13^{-2}
33. 9^{-2} 35. 2^{-4} or 4^{-2} 37. 10^{-2} or 100^{-1} 39. 10^{-5}
41. $-\dfrac{1}{128}$ 43. $\dfrac{1}{729}$ 45. 128 times 47. x^{-5} 49. x^{-3}
51. a^3b^{-2} or $\dfrac{a^3}{b^2}$
53. Yes; $(x^3)^{-2} = \dfrac{1}{(x^3)^2}$
$$= \dfrac{1}{x^3 \cdot x^3} \text{ or } \dfrac{1}{x^6}$$
$$(x^{-2})^3 = (x^{-2})(x^{-2})(x^{-2})$$
$$= x^{-6} \text{ or } \dfrac{1}{x^6}$$
55. C 57. 9×10^{-1} 59. $(1 \times 10^{-1}) + (7 \times 10^{-2}) + (3 \times 10^{-3})$ 61. 3^7 63. 5^3 65. $8y + 48$ 67. $5n - 15$ 69. 720 71. 40.5 73. 0.0005

Page 185 Practice Quiz 2
1. 5 3. $2a$ 5. $\dfrac{2}{5}$ 7. $-2n^7$ 9. $\dfrac{1}{b^6}$

Pages 188–190 Lesson 4-8
1. Sample answer: Numbers that are greater than 1 can be expressed as the product of a factor and a positive power of 10. So, these numbers are written in scientific notation using positive exponents. Numbers between 0 and 1 cannot be expressed as the product of a factor and a whole number power of 10, so they are written in scientific notation using negative exponents. 3. 0.000308 5. 849,500 7. 6.97×10^5
9. 1.0×10^{-3} 11. Mars, Venus, Earth 13. 57,200
15. 0.005689 17. 0.0901 19. 2505 21. 2.0×10^6
23. 6.0×10^{-3} 25. 5.0×10^7 27. 5.894×10^6
29. 4.25×10^{-4} 31. 6.25×10^6 33. 7.53×10^{-7}
35. 2.3×10^5 37. 5000 39. Arctic, Indian, Atlantic, Pacific
41. 6.1×10^{-5}, 0.0061, 6.1×10^{-2}, 6100, 6.1×10^4
43. 48,396 45. 2.52×10^5; 252,000 47. Bezymianny; Santa Maria; Agung; Mount St. Helens tied with Hekla 1947; Hekla, 1970; Ngauruhoe 49. 3.14 51. B 53. $\dfrac{1}{81}$ 55. $\dfrac{1}{49}$
57. $15a^4$ 59. $c + \$2.50$

Pages 191–194 Chapter 4 Study Guide and Review
1. true 3. true 5. true 7. true 9. 3 11. 5 13. 2, 3, 6 15. 2, 5, 10 17. 27 19. 25 21. 90 23. 112 25. $3^2 \cdot 5$ 27. $2^2 \cdot 17$ 29. $7 \cdot 7 \cdot k$ 31. $2 \cdot 13 \cdot p \cdot p \cdot p$ 33. 6 35. n
37. $2(t + 10)$ 39. $2(15 + 2n)$ 41. $\dfrac{3}{5}$ 43. $\dfrac{10}{17}$ 45. simplified
47. $\dfrac{5c^2}{8b}$ 49. c^4 51. r^2 53. $\dfrac{1}{7^2}$ 55. $\dfrac{1}{b^4}$ 57. $\dfrac{1}{(-4)^3}$
59. 0.0029 61. 70,450 63. 8.0×10^{-3} 65. 4.571×10^7

Chapter 5 Rational Numbers

Page 199 Chapter 5 Getting Started
1. 0.6 3. 34 5. 0.2 7. -75 9. -1.7 11. $\dfrac{3}{5}$ 13. $\dfrac{18}{25}$ 15. 6
17. -13 19. 15 21. 9

Pages 202–204 Lesson 5-1
1. Sample answer: write the fractions as decimals and then compare. 3. Sample answer: $0.\overline{14}$ 5. 2.08 7. $0.2\overline{6}$ 9. $<$
11. $>$ 13. 0.2 15. 0.32 17. 7.3 19. 5.125 21. $0.\overline{1}$
23. $-0.\overline{45}$ 25. $0.1\overline{6}$ 27. 0.3125 29. 0.83 31. $\dfrac{7}{9}, 0.8, \dfrac{7}{8}$
33. $<$ 35. $<$ 37. $>$ 39. $=$ 41. $>$ 43. $>$ 45. Sample answer: 0.7 and $0.\overline{7}$; $\dfrac{1}{6} = 0.1\overline{6}$ and $\dfrac{8}{9} = 0.\overline{8}$; 0.7 and $0.\overline{7}$ are both greater than $0.1\overline{6}$ and less than $0.\overline{8}$. 47. This is greater than those who chose English in the survey because $\dfrac{1}{7} \approx 0.14$, and $0.14 > 0.13$. 49. All coins were made with a fraction of silver that was contained in a silver dollar. Answers should include the following.
- A quarter had one-fourth the amount of silver as a silver dollar, a dime had one-tenth the amount, and a nickel had one-twentieth the amount.
- It is easier to perform arithmetic operations using decimals rather than using fractions.

51. D 53. 7.7×10^{-2} 55. 9.25×10^5 57. $\dfrac{1}{(-2)^7}$ 59. $\dfrac{1}{y^3}$
61. 29 63. -32 65. 56 67. $\dfrac{1}{13}$ 69. $\dfrac{2}{3}$ 71. $\dfrac{4}{7}$ 73. $\dfrac{1}{8}$

Pages 207–209 Lesson 5-2
1. any number that can be written as a fraction 3. $-\dfrac{7}{3}$
5. $\dfrac{4}{5}$ 7. $-\dfrac{7}{9}$ 9. I, Q 11. $\dfrac{39}{1,000,000}$ 13. $-\dfrac{11}{7}$ 15. $\dfrac{60}{1}$
17. $\dfrac{9}{100}$ 19. $1\dfrac{17}{25}$ 21. $8\dfrac{1}{250}$ 23. $-\dfrac{1}{3}$ 25. $5\dfrac{2}{3}$ 27. $2\dfrac{25}{99}$
29. $\dfrac{3}{50}$ 31. $\dfrac{59}{200}$ 33. $\dfrac{4}{25}$ 35. I, Q 37. N, W, I, Q 39. Q
41. not rational 43. $200\dfrac{19}{100}$ 45. Sometimes; $\dfrac{1}{2}$ and 2 are both rational numbers, but only 2 is an integer. 47. $\dfrac{1}{1250}$ in.
49. Yes; $2\dfrac{3}{8} = 2.375$ and $2.375 > 2.37$. 51. The set of rational numbers includes the set of natural numbers, whole numbers, and integers. In the same way, natural numbers are part of the set of whole numbers and the set of whole numbers is part of the set of integers. Answers should include the following.
- The number 5 belongs to the set of natural numbers, whole numbers integers, and rational numbers.
- The number $\dfrac{1}{2}$ belongs only to the set of rational numbers.

53. C 55. -7.8 57. $2.\overline{5}$ 59. 3,050,000 61. 0.01681
63. $(4 \times 10^2) + (8 \times 10^1) + (3 \times 10^0)$ 65. 24 cm; 27 cm^2

67. $8 \cdot 2 + 1 \cdot 2$ **69.** $7x + 28$ **71.** Sample answer: $-5 \cdot 4 = -20$ **73.** Sample answer: $7 \cdot 2 = 14$ **75.** Sample answer: $16 \cdot 2 = 32$

Pages 212–214 Lesson 5-3

1. Sample answer: $\frac{1}{2}, \frac{1}{3}$ **3.** $\frac{3}{20}$ **5.** $\frac{5}{9}$ **7.** $\frac{13}{22}$ **9.** $\frac{6}{7}$ **11.** $\frac{8}{t}$
13. $\frac{12}{49}$ **15.** $-\frac{1}{40}$ **17.** $\frac{8}{45}$ **19.** $\frac{1}{3}$ **21.** $-\frac{1}{4}$ **23.** $\frac{3}{8}$ **25.** $1\frac{1}{6}$
27. $3\frac{1}{3}$ **29.** $14\frac{2}{3}$ **31.** 10 **33.** $-4\frac{4}{9}$ **35.** 6 **37.** 27 **39.** 27
41. $\frac{8c}{11}$ **43.** $\frac{xz^2}{3}$ **45.** $\frac{9}{25}$ **47.** $\frac{11}{60}$ **49.** 12.7 **51.** 10.257
53a. Sample answer: $\frac{8}{4} \times \frac{3}{5}$ **53b.** Sample answer: $\frac{3}{4} \times \frac{5}{6}$
55. A **57.** $\frac{5}{8}$ **59.** $\frac{13}{32}$ **61.** $-\frac{1}{5}$ **63.** $\frac{7}{9}$ **65.** $0.1\overline{6}$ **67.** -4.875
69. $8n$ **71.** $2t$ **73.** 9

Pages 217–219 Lesson 5-4

1. Dividing by a fraction is the same as multiplying by its reciprocal. **3.** $\frac{5}{4}$ **5.** $\frac{8}{25}$ **7.** $\frac{4}{5}$ **9.** $1\frac{7}{15}$ **11.** $-1\frac{29}{36}$ **13.** $\frac{3a}{2}$
15. 6 boards **17.** $-\frac{5}{1}$ or -5 **19.** $\frac{1}{24}$ **21.** $-\frac{9}{29}$ **23.** $\frac{8}{9}$
25. $-\frac{15}{22}$ **27.** $\frac{15}{16}$ **29.** -1 **31.** $1\frac{1}{2}$ **33.** -10 **35.** $1\frac{1}{3}$ **37.** 2
39. $-6\frac{1}{4}$ **41.** $\frac{4}{3}$ **43.** $\frac{5}{6r}$ **45.** $\frac{16}{t^5}$ **47.** 6 ribbons **49.** $\frac{81}{256}$
51. 8 days **53.** Dividing by a fraction is the same as multiplying by its reciprocal. Answers should include the following.
• For example, a model of two circles, each divided into four sections, represents $2 \div \frac{1}{4}$. Since there are 8 sections, $2 \div \frac{1}{4} = 8$.
• Division of fractions and multiplication of fractions are inverse operations. So, $2 \div \frac{1}{4}$ equals $2 \cdot 4$ or 8.
55. C **57.** $\frac{5}{24}$ **59.** $-\frac{10}{21}$ **61.** Q **63.** not rational **65.** 7
67. $1\frac{1}{7}$ **69.** $6\frac{1}{4}$ **71.** $3\frac{2}{3}$ **73.** $1\frac{2}{3}$

Pages 222–224 Lesson 5-5

1.
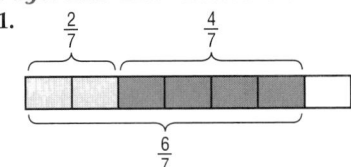

3. Kayla; Ethan incorrectly left out the negative sign on the first term. **5.** $\frac{4}{7}$ **7.** $-\frac{3}{4}$ **9.** $8\frac{1}{2}$ **11.** $\frac{8r}{11}$ **13.** $-\frac{1}{3x}$ **15.** $\frac{3}{5}$
17. $\frac{2}{3}$ **19.** $-\frac{1}{2}$ **21.** $-1\frac{1}{2}$ **23.** $-\frac{2}{9}$ **25.** $11\frac{4}{5}$ **27.** $9\frac{3}{3}$ **29.** $\frac{3}{4}$
31. $4\frac{6}{7}$ **33.** $8\frac{1}{8}$ **35.** $2\frac{3}{5}$ **37.** $\frac{1}{5}$ **39.** $\frac{5x}{8}$ **41.** $\frac{3}{m}$ **43.** $2\frac{3}{7}c$
45. $5\frac{3}{8}$ in. **47.** 38 ft **49.** When you use a ruler or a tape measure, measurements are usually a fraction of an inch. Answers should include the following.
• The marks on a ruler represent $\frac{1}{16}$ of an inch, $\frac{1}{8}$ of an inch, $\frac{1}{4}$ of an inch, and $\frac{1}{2}$ of an inch.
• Fractional measures are used in sewing and construction.
51. A **53.** $-1\frac{7}{8}$ **55.** $\frac{3}{10}$ **57.** $1\frac{1}{3}$ **59.** 42 cm; 90 cm^2
61. $5^2 \cdot 7$ **63.** $2^2 \cdot 3 \cdot n$ **65.** $2 \cdot 3 \cdot 7 \cdot a^2 \cdot b$

Page 224 Practice Quiz 1

1. 0.16 **3.** 3.125 **5.** $\frac{3}{25}$ **7.** $\frac{2}{27}$ **9.** $\frac{5}{12}$

Pages 228–230 Lesson 5-6

1. The LCM involves the common multiples of a set of numbers; the LCD is the LCM of the denominators of two or more fractions. **3.** 24 **5.** 70 **7.** 48 **9.** 8 **11.** $100x$
13. $=$ **15.** front gear: 5; back gear: 13 **17.** 60 **19.** 48
21. 84 **23.** 100 **25.** 96 **27.** 84 **29.** 630 **31.** $112a^2b$
33. $75n^4$ **35.** 15 **37.** 35 **39.** 24 **41.** $16c^2d$ **43.** 60 s **45.** $<$
47. $>$ **49.** $=$ **51.** $>$ **53.** amphibians **55.** 12 and 18
57. Never; sample answer: 5 and 6 do not contain any factors in common, and the LCM of 5 and 6 is 30. **59a.** If two numbers are relatively prime, then their LCM is the product of the two numbers. For example, the LCM of 4 and 5 is $2^2 \cdot 5$ or 20; the LCM of 6 and 25 is $2 \cdot 3 \cdot 5^2$ or 150.
59b. Always; the LCM contains all of the factors of both numbers. Therefore, it must contain any common factors.
61. B **63.** $\frac{1}{2}$ **65.** $1\frac{1}{7}$ **67.** 3 **69.** $\frac{ad}{5}$ **71.** $7 + 2n = 11$; 2
73. -20 **75.** Sample answer: $0 + 1 = 1$ **77.** Sample answer: $1 + 2 = 3$ **79.** Sample answer: $8 + 7 = 15$

Pages 234–236 Lesson 5-7

1. Find the least common denominator. **3.** José; he finds a common denominator by multiplying the denominators. Daniel incorrectly adds the numerators and the denominators of unlike fractions. **5.** $\frac{2}{9}$ **7.** $-\frac{5}{6}$ **9.** $-4\frac{1}{4}$
11. $\frac{9}{10}$ **13.** $\frac{5}{28}$ **15.** $1\frac{1}{16}$ **17.** $\frac{1}{8}$ **19.** $-\frac{1}{8}$ **21.** $1\frac{1}{15}$ **23.** $-7\frac{5}{9}$
25. $-11\frac{7}{9}$ **27.** $-14\frac{5}{8}$ **29.** $3\frac{11}{36}$ **31.** $5\frac{3}{5}$ lb **33.** $8\frac{3}{4}$ in.
35. Sample answer: Fill the $\frac{1}{2}$-cup. From the $\frac{1}{2}$-cup, fill the $\frac{1}{3}$-cup. $\frac{1}{6}$ cup will be left in the $\frac{1}{2}$-cup because $\frac{1}{2} - \frac{1}{3} = \frac{1}{6}$.
37. Find the LCM of the denominators. Then rename the fractions as like fractions with the LCM as the denominators. Answers should include the following.
• For example, the LCM of 4 and 6 is 12. So, $\frac{1}{4} + \frac{5}{6} = \frac{3}{12} + \frac{10}{12} = \frac{13}{12}$ or $1\frac{1}{12}$.
• Writing the prime factorization of the denominators is the first step in finding the LCM of the denominators, which is the LCD. Then the fractions can be added or subtracted.
39. B **41.** Sample answer: $\frac{1}{2} + \frac{1}{10}$ **43.** 36 **45.** $6n^3$ **47.** $9\frac{1}{2}$
49. $2\frac{4}{5}$ **51.** $1\frac{4}{5}$ **53.** 27 **55.** -9

Pages 241–242 Lesson 5-8

1. Mean; when an extreme value is added to the other data, it can raise or lower the sum, and therefore the mean.
3. 12.4; 8; none **5.** 3.6; 3.5; 4 **7.** Sample answer: 13 could be an extreme value because it is 12 less than the next value. It lowers the mean by 2.1. **9.** 98 **11.** 8.9; 8; 8
13. 7.6; 7.5; 7.1 and 7.4 **15.** 4.3; 4.2; 4.1 and 4.2 **17.** Sample answer: the median, 95, or the modes, 95 and 97, because most students scored higher than mean, which is 91.
19. Sample answer: The median home price would be useful because it is not affected by the cost of the very expensive homes. The cost of half the homes in the county would be greater than the median cost and half would be less. **21.** C **23.** $9\frac{5}{6}$ **25.** $-3\frac{7}{8}$ **27.** $>$ **29.** 18 **31.** -5
33. 7.9 **35.** 3

Pages 246–248 Lesson 5-9
1. Subtraction Property of Equality   **3.** Ling; dividing 0.3 by 3 does not isolate the variable on one side.   **5.** 18.7
7. $1\frac{13}{30}$ **9.** $-2\frac{1}{12}$ **11.** –90   **13.** 29.15 in.   **15.** –2.4   **17.** 12.24
19. 5.9   **21.** $-\frac{31}{36}$ **23.** $6\frac{7}{9}$ **25.** $-\frac{2}{15}$ **27.** $-2\frac{3}{10}$ **29.** 4
31. 5   **33.** –32   **35.** $1\frac{1}{4}$ **37.** $5\frac{3}{4}$ **39.** $2\frac{7}{8}$ **41.** $13\frac{1}{2}$ in. by $21\frac{1}{2}$ in.   **43.** $16.66   **45.** $2\frac{1}{4}$ ft   **47.** Equations with fractions can be written to represent the number of vibrations per second for different notes. To solve, multiply each side of the equation by the reciprocal of the fraction. Answers should include the following.
- For example, if n vibrations per second produce middle C, then $\frac{5}{4}n$ vibrations per second produce the note E above middle C.
- The equation $\frac{5}{3}n = 440$ represents the number of vibrations per second to produce middle C. To solve, multiply each side by the reciprocal of $\frac{5}{3}, \frac{3}{5}$.

49. D   **51.** 13; 12; 11 and 12   **53.** 70.8; 66; 60   **55.** $\frac{17}{24}$ **57.** $\frac{17}{36}$ **59.** $7\frac{11}{15}$ **61.** $\frac{3}{8}$ **63.** –6   **65.** –6   **67.** 5   **69.** $-\frac{1}{3}$

Page 248 Practice Quiz 2
1. 72   **3.** 10   **5.** $\frac{13}{16}$ **7.** $1\frac{2}{3}$ **9.** 32.4; 30.5; 29

Pages 251–252 Lesson 5-10
1. Arithmetic sequences have a common difference and the terms can be found by adding or subtracting. Geometric sequences have a common ratio and the terms can be found by multiplying or dividing.   **3.** A; 4; 19, 23, 27
5. neither   **7.** A; $-\frac{1}{3}, \frac{5}{3}, \frac{4}{3}, 1$ **9.** $11,027.36   **11.** A; 11; 38, 49, 60   **13.** G; 3; 162, 486, 1458   **15.** A; –3; 13, 10, 7
17. G; $-\frac{1}{5}$; $-\frac{1}{125}, \frac{1}{625}, -\frac{1}{3125}$ **19.** A; $\frac{1}{6}, \frac{2}{3}, \frac{5}{6}, 1$ **21.** A; –0.5, 2.5, 2, 1.5   **23.** neither   **25.** G; $-\frac{1}{3}, \frac{2}{9}, -\frac{2}{27}, \frac{2}{81}$
27. G; $\frac{1}{2}, \frac{1}{32}, \frac{1}{64}, \frac{1}{128}$ **29a.** Arithmetic; the common difference is $3.   **29b.** $48   **31.** Find the pattern, continue the sequence, and use the new values to make predictions. Answers should include the following.
- The difference between any two consecutive terms in an arithmetic sequence is the common difference. To find the next value in such a sequence, add the common difference to the last term. The ratio of any two consecutive terms in a geometric sequence is the common ratio. So, to find the next value in such a sequence, multiply the last term by the common ratio.
- Sequences occurring in nature include geysers spouting every few minutes, the arrangement of geese in migration patterns, and ocean tides.

33. A   **35.** 56   **37.** –5.28   **39.** 10   **41.** 3.3; 3.3; 3.6
43. $102\frac{7}{8}$ in.   **45.** b^3 **47.** 6   **49.** 15

Pages 254–258 Chapter 5 Study Guide and Review
1. rational   **3.** algebraic fraction   **5.** LCD   **7.** reciprocal
9. arithmetic   **11.** 0.45   **13.** $-0.4\overline{6}$ **15.** $6.\overline{36}$ **17.** $\frac{3}{5}$ **19.** $\frac{1}{8}$
21. $4\frac{11}{25}$ **23.** $\frac{5}{9}$ **25.** $1\frac{7}{9}$ **27.** $3\frac{4}{11}$ **29.** $-\frac{7}{27}$ **31.** $6\frac{2}{5}$ **33.** $1\frac{1}{3}$
35. –3   **37.** $9\frac{4}{9}$ **39.** x **41.** –6   **43.** $-3\frac{3}{4}$ **45.** $-4\frac{1}{5}$ **47.** $\frac{4}{21x}$

49. $\frac{5}{9}$ **51.** $1\frac{1}{3}$ **53.** $2\frac{3}{5}$ **55.** $\frac{4}{3x}$ **57.** 120   **59.** $21c^2$ **61.** <
63. >   **65.** $1\frac{2}{3}$ **67.** $2\frac{5}{6}$ **69.** $1\frac{11}{15}$ **71.** $3\frac{1}{6}$ **73.** 6.0; 6.5; 3.6 and 7.2   **75.** 3.25   **77.** $-2\frac{1}{2}$ **79.** G; 3; 81, 243, 729
81. neither

Chapter 6   Ratio, Proportion, and Percent

Page 263 Chapter 6 Getting Started
1. 24   **3.** 10,560   **5.** 480   **7.** 4000   **9.** 6   **11.** 580
13. 50   **15.** 15,000   **17.** 48.8   **19.** 13.44   **21.** 0.18
23. 3.04   **25.** $\frac{1}{3}$ **27.** simplified   **29.** simplified   **31.** $\frac{3}{4}$

Pages 266–268 Lesson 6-1
1. Sample answer:

3. Sample answer: $12 per person   **5.** $\frac{5}{8}$ **7.** $\frac{1}{3}$
9. 0.75 inch/hour   **11.** 24.2 miles/gallon   **13.** 576
15. No; the ratio will be 2 to 3.   **17.** $\frac{2}{5}$ **19.** $\frac{3}{7}$ **21.** $\frac{9}{32,000}$
23. $\frac{1760}{1}$ **25.** $\frac{17}{118}$ **27.** $\frac{3}{1}$ **29.** 0.10 cents/pencil
31. 4.5 m/sec   **33.** 7.8 ft/h   **35.** 39 pages/week   **37.** The 6-pack of soda costs $0.37 per can. The 12-pack of soda costs $0.35 per can. So, the 12-pack is less expensive.
39. 26.4   **41.** 19.2   **43.** 72   **45.** 105   **47.** about 579 mi/h
49. $9   **51.** C   **53b.** The ratios should be close in value.
53c. Sample answer: Pyramid of Khufu in Giza, Egypt; The Taj Mahal in India; The Lincoln Memorial in Washington, D.C.   **55.** arithmetic; 0.3; 13.3, 13.6, 13.9
57. $-\frac{1}{12}$ **59.** $13\frac{1}{3}$ **61.** 5.2×10^7 **63.** 3.8×10^{-2} **65.** 30
67. 40   **69.** 13

Pages 272–274 Lesson 6-2
1. A statement of equality of two ratios.   **3.** Yes   **5.** 15
7. 4.2   **9.** yes   **11.** no   **13.** yes   **15.** 4   **17.** 20   **19.** 15
21. 1.4   **23.** 7.5   **25.** 0.94   **27.** 0.8   **29.** 15   **31.** 26
33. $\frac{12}{3} = \frac{72}{m}$; 18   **35.** $\frac{5}{6.25} = \frac{d}{8.75}$; 7   **37.** about 360.8 ft
39. $22.47   **41.** chocolate pieces: 3 c; peanuts: $1\frac{1}{2}$ c
43. $\frac{a}{c} = \frac{b}{d}, \frac{b}{a} = \frac{d}{c}$, or $\frac{c}{a} = \frac{d}{b}$ **45.** C   **47.** 57.3 mph
49. 4   **51.** $\frac{4}{7y}$ **53.** 102   **55.** 6.5

Pages 278–280 Lesson 6-3
1. 1 unit   3 units   **3.** 40 mi   **5.** 1 in. = 5 ft

7.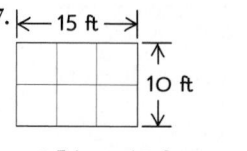
0.5 in. = 10 ft

9. 12 ft   **11.** 24.6 ft   **13.** 11.4 ft
15. $49\frac{1}{2}$ ft   **17.** $\frac{2}{3}$
19. 1 cm = 0.25 cm

21. A scale factor less than 1 means that the drawing or model is drawn smaller than actual size. A scale factor of 1 means that the drawing or model is drawn actual size. A

scale factor greater than 1 means the drawing or model is drawn larger than actual size. **23.** B **25a.** $\frac{1}{2}$ **25b.** $\frac{1}{4}$
25c. The perimeter of a 3-inch by 5-inch rectangle is 16 inches. The area is 15 square inches. For a 6-inch by 10-inch rectangle, the perimeter should be double the 3-inch by 5-inch rectangle. That is, 16×2 or 32 inches. The area should be 4 times the area of the 3-inch by 5-inch rectangle. That is, 4×15 or 60 square inches. Since the perimeter of the 6-inch by 10-inch rectangle is 32 and its area is 60, the conjecture is true. **27.** 3.5 **29.** 21.6 **31.** $6\frac{1}{12}$
33. $18t^5$ **35.** $\frac{4m^3}{3}$ **37.** $\frac{1}{20}$ **39.** $\frac{2}{5}$ **41.** $\frac{39}{50}$ **43.** $\frac{41}{50}$

Pages 283–285 Lesson 6-4
1. Sample answer: write an equivalent fraction with a denominator of 100 or express the fraction as a decimal and then express the decimal as a percent. A fraction is greater than 100% if it is greater than 1. It is less than 1% if it is less than $\frac{1}{100}$. **3.** $\frac{3}{10}$, 0.3 **5.** $1\frac{1}{4}$, 1.25 **7.** $1\frac{7}{20}$, 1.35 **9.** 45%
11. 0.8% **13.** 133.3% **15.** daily newspaper **17.** $\frac{22}{25}$, 0.88
19. $\frac{7}{8}$, 0.875 **21.** $3\frac{1}{2}$, 3.5 **23.** $\frac{61}{100}$, 0.61 **25.** $2\frac{23}{100}$, 2.23
27. $\frac{53}{10,000}$, 0.0053 **29.** 9% **31.** 270% **33.** 0.06% **35.** 22.5%
37. 175% **39.** 1.7% **41.** $\frac{37}{1000}$ **43.** 0.45 **45.** 19%
47. 61%, $\frac{2}{3}$, 0.69 **49.** 0.4 **51.** There are only two possibilities that satisfy the conditions, $\frac{1}{4}$ and $\frac{2}{5}$.
53. Percents are related to fractions and decimals because they can be expressed as them. Answers should include the following.

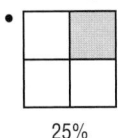 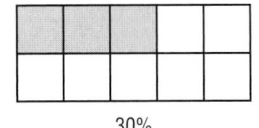

25%   30%

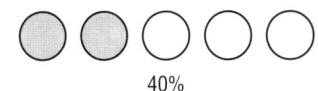

40%

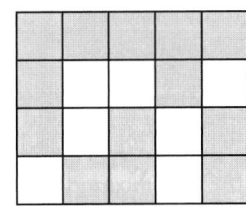

65%

• $25\% = \frac{1}{4} = 0.25$; $30\% = \frac{3}{10} = 0.3$; $40\% = \frac{2}{5} = 0.4$;
$65\% = \frac{13}{20} = 0.65$ **55.** A **57.** $\frac{1}{12}$ **59.** $\frac{11}{21}$ **61.** $1\frac{3}{13}$
63. composite **65.** composite **67.** 800 **69.** 0.94 **71.** 320

Pages 291–292 Lesson 6-5
1. $\frac{\text{number correct}}{50} = \frac{\%}{100}$ **3.** 40% **5.** 104 **7.** 60% **9.** 45%
11. 50 **13.** 77 **15.** 36% **17.** 112 **19.** 0.2% **21.** 16%
23. about 70% **25.** 26.8 lbs
27. In real-world situations, percents are important because they show how something compares to the whole. Answers should include the following.

• For example, the outer layer of the new state quarters is an alloy of 3 parts copper to 1 part nickel.
• Thus, there are 4 parts to the outer layer (copper, copper, copper, nickel). The outer layer is $\frac{3}{4}$ or 75% copper and $\frac{1}{4}$ or 25% nickel.
29. $\frac{21}{50}$ **31.** $1\frac{1}{5}$ **33.** $\frac{7}{9}$ **35.** $3\frac{1}{2}$ **37.** 8 **39.** 6 **41.** 25

Page 292 Practice Quiz 1
1. $0.14 per can **3.** 1 ft = 3069 ft **5.** 19.5

Pages 295–297 Lesson 6-6
1. 18% is about 20% or $\frac{1}{5}$. 216 is about 220. $\frac{1}{5}$ of 220 is 44. So, 18% of 216 is about 44. **5.** Sample answer: 13
7. Sample answer: 72 **9.** Sample answer: 8; fraction method: $\frac{1}{3} \times 24$ or 8 **11.** Sample answer: 21; meaning of percent method: 152% means about 150 for every 100 or about 15 for every 10. 14 has 1 tens. $1 \times 15 = 15$. So, 152% of 14 is about 21. **13.** Sample answer: 14 **15.** Sample answer: 33 **17.** Sample answer: 49 **19.** Sample answer: 4
21. Sample answer: 90 **23.** Sample answer: 375
25. Sample answer: $\frac{1}{4} \times 8$ or 2 billion **27.** Sample answer: 27; fraction method: $\frac{3}{10} \times 90$ or 27 **29.** Sample answer: 36; fraction method: $\frac{2}{5} \times 90$ or 36 **31.** Sample answer: 2; 1% method: Since 1% of 806 is about 8, $\frac{1}{4}$% of 806 is about $\frac{1}{4}$ of 8 or 2. **33.** Sample answer: 78; meaning of percent: 127% means about 130 for every 100 or about 13 for every 10. 64 has 6 tens. $6 \times 13 = 78$. So, 127% of 64 is about 78.
35. Sample answer: 450; meaning of percent: 295% means about 300 for every 100 or about 30 for every 10. 145 has one 100 and about 5 tens. $(300 \times 1) + (30 \times 5) = 300 + 150$ or 450. **37.** Sample answer: Pluto and Mars, or Neptune and Jupiter **39.** Sample answer: $\frac{1}{3} \times 90,000$ or 30,000 miles
41. about 10% **43.** 7 to 8 **45.** C **47.** 21 **49.** Maine: 31,813 sq mi; New Hampshire: 8238 sq mi; West Virginia: 18,779 sq mi; Vermont: 7279 sq mi; Alabama: 35,071 sq mi
51. 160% **53.** 0.77 **55.** 4.21 **57.** 8.9 **59.** −21 **61.** 0.5
63. 0.25 **65.** 0.07

Pages 300–302 Lesson 6-7
1. Use the percent equation in any situation where the rate and base are known. **3.** I = interest; p = principal; r = annual interest rate; t = time in years **5.** 50 **7.** 3%
9. $1680 **11.** 1.5 years **13.** 95% **15.** 50 **17.** 63 **19.** 37.5%
21. 14.52 **23.** 218% **25.** 0.9% **27.** 13.2 **29.** $25.49
31. $17 **33.** $18.50 **35.** $1113.75 **37.** $244.76 **39.** 16
41. $1.20 **43.** If you know two of the three values, you can use the percent proportion to solve for the missing value. Answers should include the following.
• To find the amount of tax on an item, you can use the percent proportion or the percent equation.
• For example, the following methods can be used to find 6% tax on $24.99.
Method 1: Percent Proportion
$$\frac{x}{24.99} = \frac{6}{100}$$
Method 2: Percent Equation
$$n = 0.06(24.99)$$
Using either method, $x = 1.50$. The amount of tax is $1.50.
45. B **47.** Sample answer: 250; meaning of percent method: 126% means about 125 for every 100 and 12.5 for every 10.

198 has about 2 one-hundreds. $125 \times 2 = 250$. So, 126% of 198 is about 250. **49.** 121 **51.** 41 **53.** 38 cm **55.** $8w - 24$ **57.** 89% **59.** 156% **61.** 22.4%

Pages 306–308 Lesson 6-8
1. If the amount increases, it is a percent of increase. If the amount decreases, it is a percent of decrease. **3.** Mark; he divided the difference of the new amount and the original amount by the original amount. **5.** -60%; D **7.** 10.1%; I **9.** A **11.** 170%; I **13.** -12%; D **15.** -5.4%; D **17.** 164%; I **19.** 10.1% **21.** -14.3% **23.** 150%

25. The amount by which a rectangle is increased or decreased can be represented by a percent. Answers should include the following.
- If the size of the new rectangle is greater than the size of the original rectangle, the percent of increase is greater than 100%.

- Original Rectangle   Less than 100%

Greater than 100%

27. D **29.** $149.85 **31.** $13.46 **33.** Sample answer: 63; fraction method: $\frac{9}{10} \times 70$ or 63 **35.** integer, rational

37. rational **39.** 20% **41.** $83\frac{1}{3}\%$

Page 308 Practice Quiz 2
1. Sample answer: 28; fraction method: $\frac{2}{5} \times 70$ or 28

3. $14.50 **5.** 158%

Pages 312–314 Lesson 6-9
1. The event will not happen.
3. Sample answer: Spinning the spinner shown and having it land on 4.

5. $\frac{1}{2}$; 50% **7.** $\frac{2}{5}$; 40% **9.** 1; 100% **11.** 75 **13.** $\frac{1}{4}$; 25%

15. $\frac{1}{2}$; 50% **17.** 0; 0% **19.** $\frac{7}{8}$; 87.5% **21.** $\frac{2}{9}$; 22.2%

23. $\frac{11}{18}$; 61.1% **25.** $\frac{1}{3}$; $33\frac{1}{3}\%$ **27.** 1; 100% **29.** $\frac{1}{6}$ **31.** $\frac{1}{16}$

33. $\frac{1}{4}$ **35.** 0.05; 5% **37.** 444

39. Once the probability or likeliness of something happening is known, then you can use the probability to make a prediction. For example, in football, if you know the number of field goals a player has made in the past, you can use the information to predict the number of field goals he/she will make in upcoming games. Answers should include the following.

- E: $\frac{12}{100}$ or 12%; A, I: $\frac{9}{100}$ or 9%; O: $\frac{8}{100}$ or 8%; N, R, T: $\frac{6}{100}$ or 6%; D, L, S, U: $\frac{4}{100}$ or 4%; G: $\frac{3}{100}$ or 3%; B, C, F, H, M, P, V, W, Y, blank: $\frac{2}{100}$ or 2%; J, K, Q, X, Z: $\frac{1}{100}$ or 1%

41. 146.9% **43.** 23.9 **45.** $2x^5$ **47.** $\frac{18n^2}{7}$

Pages 316–320 Chapter 6 Study Guide and Review
1. proportion **3.** scale factor **5.** experimental probability
7. $\frac{3}{4}$ **9.** $\frac{1}{4}$ **11.** $\frac{20}{9}$ **13.** 30 **15.** 0.9 **17.** 45.6 ft **19.** $\frac{7}{20}$; 0.35

21. $\frac{2}{25}$; 0.08 **23.** $1\frac{1}{5}$; 1.2 **25.** $\frac{5}{8}$; 0.625 **27.** 24% **29.** 45.2%

31. 40% **33.** 7.5% **35.** 40% **37.** 25 **39.** 50 **41.** 43 **43.** 9

45. 8 **47.** Sample answer: 16; fraction method: $\frac{1}{2} \times 32$ or 16

49. Sample answer: 10; fraction method: $\frac{1}{5} \times 50$ or 10

51. Sample answer: 1; 1% method: Since 1% of 304 is about 3, $\frac{1}{3}\%$ of 304 is about $\frac{1}{3}$ of 3 or 1. **53.** 48% **55.** 94.5

57. 200 **59.** D; -70% **61.** I; 86.2% **63.** $\frac{1}{3}$ **65.** $\frac{2}{3}$ **67.** 0

Chapter 7 Equations and Inequalities

Page 327 Chapter 7 Getting Started
1. 4 **3.** 24 **5.** -44 **7.** 11 **9.** -17 **11.** 16 **13.** -14
15. -15 **17.** 72 **19.** -5 **21.** 1

Pages 332–333 Lesson 7-1
1. Subtraction Property of Equality **3.** -8 **5.** 3 **7.** 0.3
9. 75 miles **11.** 13 **13.** -7 **15.** -0.5 **17.** -6 **19.** $\frac{4}{3}$
21. 3 **23.** 4.2 **25.** 0.3 **27.** 3.4 **29.** $3y - 14 = y$; 7 **31.** -16
33. 72 **35.** 70 min **37.** 29 **39.** A **41.** $-40°$ **43.** 12.5%
45. 6.48 **47.** 70 **49.** $6a + 27$ **51.** $2.4c + 28$ **53.** $\frac{1}{2}n - \frac{9}{2}$

Pages 336–338 Lesson 7-2
1. Multiply 4 times $(x - 1)$. Subtract $2x$ from each side. Add 4 to each side. Divide each side by 2. **3.** 11 **5.** 13 **7.** $\varnothing$
9. $\ell = 7$ ft; $w = 3$ ft; $A = 21$ ft² **11.** 6 **13.** 2.5 **15.** 18 **17.** 3
19. 35 **21.** $\varnothing$ **23.** all numbers **25.** 6 **27.** all numbers
29. 0 **31.** 70 yd by 150 yd **33.** w: 3 ft; ℓ: 13 ft; A: 39 ft²
35. triangle: 7, 8, 9; rectangle, 4, 8; perimeter: 24 **37.** 2 gal
39. Many equations include grouping symbols. You must use the Distributive Property to correctly solve the equation. Answers should include the following.
- The Distributive Property states that $a(b + c) = ab + ac$.
- You use the Distributive Property to remove the grouping symbols when you are solving equations.
41. D **43.** 0.4 **45.** 40% **47.** 0.375 **49.** 3.24 **51.** -7
53. -24 **55.** -8

Page 338 Practice Quiz 1
1. $2x = 5x - 150$; 50 **3.** $3.\overline{1}$ **5.** all numbers

Pages 342–344 Lesson 7-3
1. An inequality represents all numbers greater or less than a given number. A number line graph can represent all those numbers. **3.** $n + 14 \geq 25$ **5.** true
7.

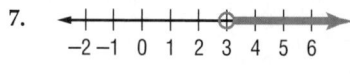

9.

11. $x \geq -20$ **13.** $f > 18,000$ **15.** $86 \geq 2w$ **17.** true
19. false **21.** true

23.

25.

27.

29.

31.

33.

35. $x > 13$ **37.** $x \le -3$ **39.** $x \ge -32$ **41.** $m \ge 6.4$
43. $b + 14{,}600 > 30{,}000$; $b > 15{,}400$ **45.** Symmetric: If $a < b$, then $b < a$; not true. Sample counterexample: $4 < 5$, but $5 \not< 4$. Transitive: If $a < b$ and $b < c$, then $a < c$; true.
47. B
49a.

49b.

51. 5 **53.** $4n - 6 = 3n + 2$; 8 **55.** G: $-16, 32, -64$ **57.** 13
59. -7 **61.** 19.8

Pages 347–349   Lesson 7-4
1. Use addition to undo subtraction; use subtraction to undo addition. **3.** Sample answer: Joanna works part-time at a clothing store. Part-time workers must work fewer than 30 hours a week. If Joanna has already worked 8 hours this week, how many hours can she still work? **5.** $y \ge -7$
7. $a > 11$ **9.** $t > -3$
11. $x \le 10$

13. $p < 2$ **15.** $b \le -22$ **17.** $y \le 5$ **19.** $r \le 7$ **21.** $j \le -4$
23. $w < 6$ **25.** $y \le 1.4$ **27.** $f \ge 5.4$ **29.** $b < 3\frac{1}{4}$
31. $n < 5$

33. $p > 2$

35. $x \le -5$

37. $m \ge 27$

39. $b < 1\frac{3}{4}$

41. $s \le 4\frac{2}{3}$

43. 980 lb **45.** $42 + x \ge 74$; $x \ge 32$; at least 32 mph
47. Always; subtracting x gives $-1 < 0$, which is always true. **49.** C **51.** F **53.** F **55.** 3 cm, 9 cm **57.** $8 + 32$
59. $5x - 17.5$ **61.** -3 **63.** -15 **65.** -2 **67.** -4 **69.** -48

Pages 353–354   Lesson 7-5
1. Multiply each side by -12 and reverse the inequality symbol. **3.** Tamika is correct. She divided each side of the inequality by 9. Since 9 is a positive number, she did not reverse the inequality symbol.
5. $x \ge -2$

7. $a > 50$

9. $m \ge -8.4$

11. $y \ge -72$

13. C
15. $y > 9$

17. $b \ge -3$

19. $t \le 5$

21. $h \le 98$

23. $z \ge 3$

25. $w \le 2$

27. $r > 4$

29. $k > -18$

31. $t \ge -16$

33. $n \le 4$

35. $y > 5.7$

37. $b < 72$

39a. $40m \ge 2000$ **39b.** at least 50 min **41.** Inequalities can be used to compare the weights of objects on different planets. Answers should include the following.
• Comparing the weight of an astronaut in a space suit on Mars to the same astronaut on the moon: $113 > 50$.
• If you multiply or divide the astronaut's weight by the same number, the inequality comparing the weights on different planets would still be true.

43. 40 **45.** $c \le -20$ **47.** $2n \le 14$ **49.** $-\dfrac{5}{21}$ **51.** $\dfrac{2a}{c}$ **53.** 4
55. -9 **57.** 32

Page 354 Practice Quiz 2

1. number line showing open circle at −1 with arrow pointing left
$$-4\ -3\ -2\ -1\ \ 0\ \ 1\ \ 2\ \ 3\ \ 4$$

3. $a \le 40$ **5.** $n \ge 124$ **7.** $r < -225$ **9.** $g \le 7$

Pages 357–359 Lesson 7-6

1. Check the solution by replacing the variable with a number in the solution. If the inequality is true, the solution checks.   **3.** Jerome is correct. By the Distributive Property $2(2y + 3) = 4y + 6$ not $4y + 3$.

5. $n > 2$
$$1\ \ 2\ \ 3\ \ 4\ \ 5\ \ 6\ \ 7\ \ 8\ \ 9$$

7. $c > 1$
$$-4\ -3\ -2\ -1\ \ 0\ \ 1\ \ 2\ \ 3\ \ 4$$

9. $x \ge 8$
$$1\ \ 2\ \ 3\ \ 4\ \ 5\ \ 6\ \ 7\ \ 8\ \ 9$$

11. $d < -9\frac{1}{2}$
$$-10\ \ -9\ \ -8\ \ -7\ \ -6$$

13. $x > 8$
$$1\ \ 2\ \ 3\ \ 4\ \ 5\ \ 6\ \ 7\ \ 8\ \ 9$$

15. $c > -4$
$$-4\ -3\ -2\ -1\ \ 0\ \ 1\ \ 2\ \ 3\ \ 4$$

17. $x > 3$
$$-4\ -3\ -2\ -1\ \ 0\ \ 1\ \ 2\ \ 3\ \ 4$$

19. $k \ge -5$
$$-7\ -6\ -5\ -4\ -3\ -2\ -1\ \ 0\ \ 1$$

21. $n < -5$
$$-7\ -6\ -5\ -4\ -3\ -2\ -1\ \ 0\ \ 1$$

23. $b \le 2$
$$-4\ -3\ -2\ -1\ \ 0\ \ 1\ \ 2\ \ 3\ \ 4$$

25. $y \ge 30$
$$10\ \ \ 30\ \ \ 50\ \ \ 70\ \ \ 90$$

27. $c < -4$
$$-10\ \ -8\ \ -6\ \ -4\ \ -2$$

29. $n > 7$

31. $n \le 4.5$
$$1\ \ 2\ \ 3\ \ 4\ \ 5\ \ 6\ \ 7\ \ 8\ \ 9$$

33. $t \le -1$
$$-4\ -3\ -2\ -1\ \ 0\ \ 1\ \ 2\ \ 3\ \ 4$$

35. $c < -4$
$$-10\ \ -8\ \ -6\ \ -4\ \ -2$$

37. $0.55c + 0.35 \le 2$; 3 candy bars   **39.** $2s + 10 \ge 40$, 15 subscriptions   **41.** $x < 200$; Sample explanation: The inequality finds at what mileage Able's charge is greater than Baker's charge.   **43.** more than 100 minutes   **45.** $k < 3$ and $k > -3$, or $k = \{-2, -1, 0, 1, 2\}$ **47.** D   **49.** $-5 < x < 1$
51. $y \ge 37$ **53.** $n \le 5$ **55.** $a < -18.6$ **57.** 0.5%
59. $16.\overline{6}$ mpg   **61.** $1.25 an issue   **63.** 6 m

Pages 360–362 Chapter 7 Study Guide and Review

1. true   **3.** false; identity   **5.** false; inequality   **7.** true
9. false; is greater than or equal to   **11.** 3   **13.** 4   **15.** 1
17. −1   **19.** −1.2   **21.** 9   **23.** 16   **25.** all numbers   **27.** true

29. $b \ge 17$
$$14\ \ \ 16\ \ \ 18\ \ \ 20\ \ \ 22\ \ \ 24$$

31. $t < 3\frac{1}{2}$
$$0\ \ \ 1\ \ \ 2\ \ \ 3\ \ \ 4\ \ \ 5$$

33. $k \le 5.1$
$$-1\ \ 0\ \ 1\ \ 2\ \ 3\ \ 4\ \ 5\ \ 6\ \ 7\ \ 8\ \ 9$$

35. $y \le -7$
$$-12\ \ -10\ \ -8\ \ \ -6\ \ \ -4$$

37. $a \ge -2\frac{2}{5}$
$$-4\ \ \ -2\ \ \ 0\ \ \ 2\ \ \ 4\ \ \ 6$$

39. $n \le 4$ **41.** $t > -12$ **43.** $b > -4\frac{1}{4}$

Chapter 8   Functions and Graphing

Page 367   Chapter 8 Getting Started

1.

x	y
0	4
−3	3

domain = $\{0, -3\}$; range = $\{4, 3\}$

3.

x	y
6	8
7	10
8	12

domain = $\{6, 7, 8\}$; range = $\{8, 10, 12\}$

5.

x	y
−8	5
7	−1
6	1
1	−2

domain = $\{-8, 7, 6, 1\}$; range = $\{5, -1, 1, -2\}$

7. E   **9.** A   **11.** F   **13.** true   **15.** true   **17.** true

Pages 371–373   Lesson 8-1

1. Sample answer: a set of ordered pairs: $\{(1, 2), (4, 3), (-2, -1), (-3, 3)\}$
a table: a graph:

x	y
1	2
4	3
−2	−1
−3	3

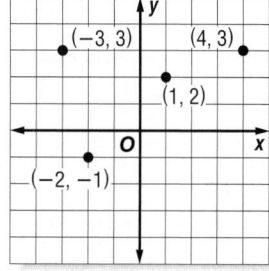

3. Sample answer: This graph does not represent a function because when x equals 1, there are two y values, 0 and 2.

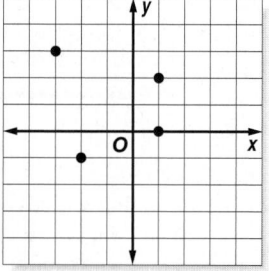

5. Yes; each x value is paired with only one y value. **7.** No; 5 is paired with 4 and 14. **9.** Yes; any vertical line passes through no more than one point of the graph. **11.** As wind speed increases, the windchill temperature decreases. **13.** Yes; each x value is paired with only one y value. **15.** No; 5 in the domain is paired with -4 and -1 in the range. **17.** No; -2 in the domain is paired with 5 and 1 in the range. **19.** Yes; each x value is paired with only one y value. **21.** No; a vertical line passes through more than one point. **23.** Yes; any vertical line passes through no more than one point of the graph. **25.** Generally, as the years progress, the number of farms decreases. An exception is in the year 2000. **27.** Generally, as the years progress, the size of farms increases. An exception is in the year 2000. **29.** Generally, as foot length increases, height increases. **31.** Sometimes; a relation that has a member of the domain paired with more than one member in the range is not a function. **33.** For a given wind speed, there is only one windchill temperature for each actual temperature. So, the relationship between actual temperatures and windchill temperatures is a function. Answers should include the following.

- For a given wind speed, as the actual temperature increases, the windchill temperature increases.
- Since the relationship between actual temperatures and windchill temperatures is a function, there cannot be two different windchill temperatures for the same actual temperature when the wind speed remains the same.

35. A **37.** $a < -21$ **39.** $x < 6$ **41.** $\varnothing$ **43.** 18 **45.** 75 **47.** 13 **49.** 5 **51.** 0

Pages 377–379 Lesson 8-2

1. Sample answer: Infinitely many values can be substituted for x, or the domain.
3.

x	$x + 5$	y
-3	$-3 + 5$	2
-1	$-1 + 5$	4
0	$0 + 5$	5
1	$1 + 5$	6

$(-3, 2)$, $(-1, 4)$, $(0, 5)$, $(1, 6)$

5. Sample answer: $(-1, -4)$, $(0, 0)$, $(1, 4)$, $(2, 8)$ **7.** Sample answer: $(-1, 1)$, $(0, 6)$, $(1, 11)$, $(2, 16)$
9.

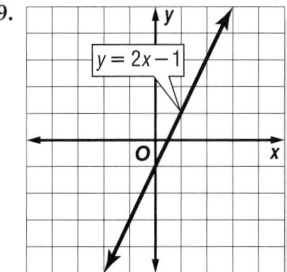

11. Sample answer: (1, 186,000) means that light travels 186,000 miles in 1 second. (2, 372,000) means that light travels 372,000 miles in 2 seconds.
13.

x	$2x + 6$	y
-4	$2(-4) + 6$	-2
0	$2(0) + 6$	6
2	$2(2) + 6$	10
4	$2(4) + 6$	14

$(-4, -2)$, $(0, 6)$, $(2, 10)$, $(4, 14)$

15. Sample answer: $(-1, -8)$, $(0, -7)$, $(1, -6)$, $(2, -5)$
17. Sample answer: $(-1, 5)$, $(0, 0)$, $(1, -5)$, $(2, -10)$
19. Sample answer: $(-1, -2)$, $(0, 1)$, $(1, 4)$, $(2, 7)$
21. Sample answer: $(-1, -5)$, $(0, -6)$, $(1, -7)$, $(2, -8)$
23. Sample answer: $(-1, -13)$, $(0, -10)$, $(1, -7)$, $(2, -4)$
25. Sample answer: $(-1, 0)$, $(-1, 1)$, $(-1, 2)$, $(-1, 3)$
27. 6.2 mi **29.** Quadrant I; a person cannot have a negative age or heart rate.
31.

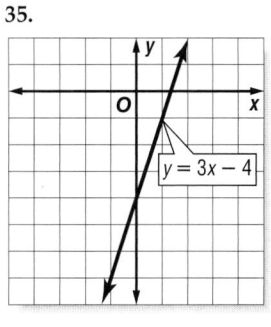

33.

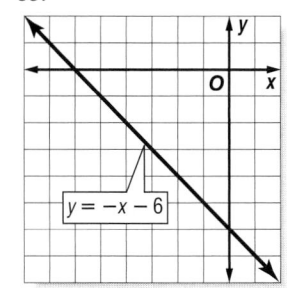

35.

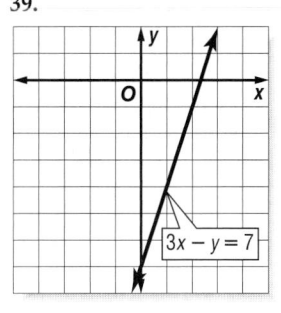

37.

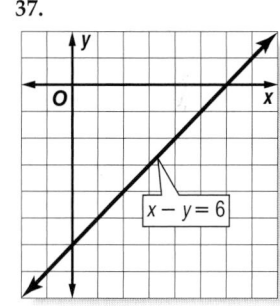

39.

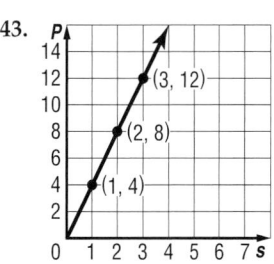

41.

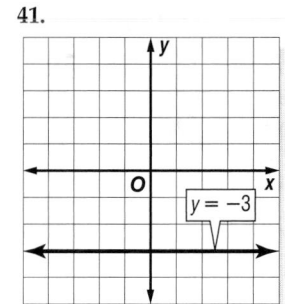

43.

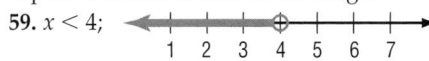

45. Yes; the points lie on a straight line. **47.** Yes; the points lie on a straight line. **49.** No; the exponent of x is not 1. **51.** Sample answer: In the first table, as the x values increase by 1, the y values increase by 2. In the second table, as the x values increase by 1, the y values do not change by a constant amount. **53.** B **55.** Yes; each x value is paired with only one y value. **57.** No; 11 in the domain is paired with 8 and 21 in the range.
59. $x < 4$;

61. $\frac{6}{7}$ **63.** 3 **65.** 4

Pages 384–385 **Lesson 8-3**

1. To find the *x*-intercept, let $y = 0$ and solve for *x*. To find the *y*-intercept, let $x = 0$ and solve for *y*. **3.** $-1; -3$
5. $-4; 4$ **7.** $3; 2$

9.

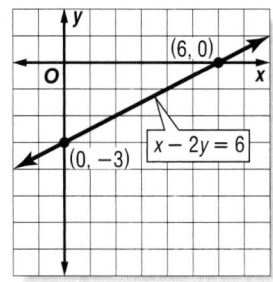

11.

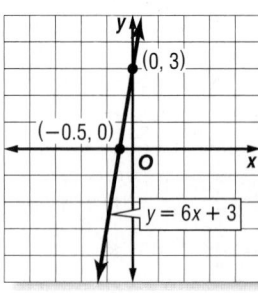

The *y*-intercept 3 represents the base fee of $3.

13. $1; 1$ **15.** none; -5 **17.** $-5; 5$ **19.** none; -4 **21.** $8; -4$
23. $5; 4$

25.

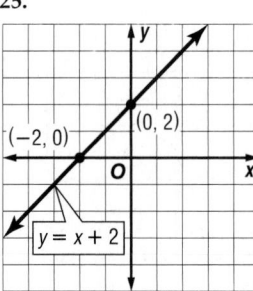

27.

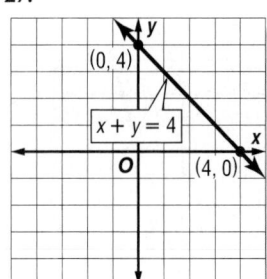

29.

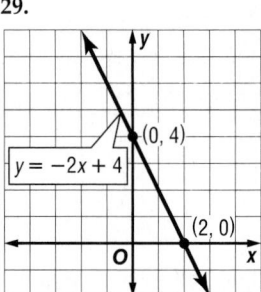

31.

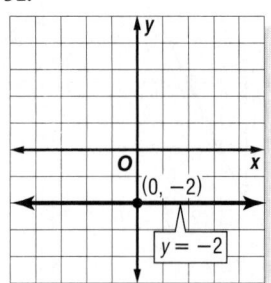

33.

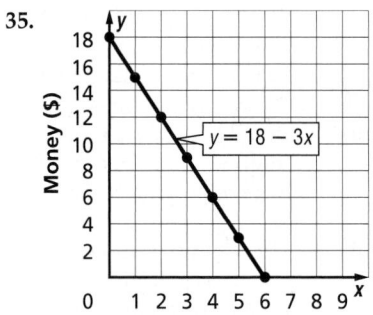

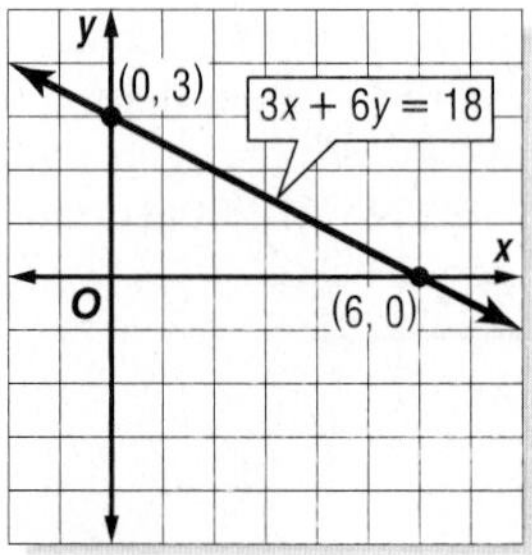

35.

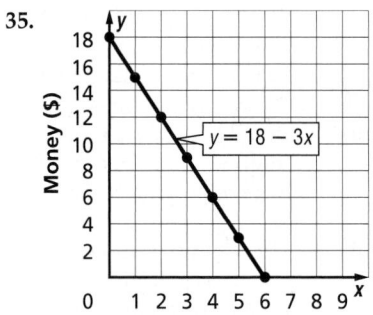

The *x*-intercept 6 represents the number of books that she can buy with no money left over. The *y*-intercept 18 represents the money she has before she buys any books.
37. The *x*- and *y*-intercept are both 0. Therefore, the line passes through the origin. Since two points are needed to graph a line, $y = 2x$ cannot be graphed using only the intercepts.

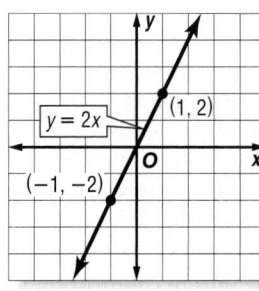

39. B **41.** Sample answer: $(-1, 5), (0, 7), (1, 9), (2, 11)$
43. Sample answer: $(-1, 1), (0, 5), (1, 9), (2, 13)$ **45.** no
47. $n > 12$ **49.** 2.8%
51. -16 **53.** 25

Pages 389–391 **Lesson 8-4**

1. Sample answer: horizontals do not rise, so
slope $= \dfrac{\text{rise}}{\text{run}} = \dfrac{0}{\text{run}}$ or 0. **3.** Mike; Chloe should have
subtracted -2 from 11 in the denominator. **5.** $-\dfrac{2}{3}$ **7.** 2
9. 0 **11.** B **13.** 4 **15.** $-\dfrac{3}{4}$ **17.** 0 **19.** 1 **21.** $-\dfrac{3}{2}$
23. undefined **25.** $-\dfrac{3}{4}$ **27.** It decreased; negative slope.
29. Slope can be used to describe the steepness of roller coaster hills. Answers should include the following.
• Slope is the steepness of a line or incline. It is the ratio of the rise to the run.
• An increase in rise with no change in run makes a roller coaster hill steeper. An increase in run with no change in rise makes a roller coaster less steep.
31. A **33.** $2; 6$ **35.** Sample answer: $(-1, 3), (0, 5), (1, 7), (2, 9)$ **37.** Sample answer: $(-1, 8), (0, 7), (1, 6), (2, 5)$
39. $y = -2x$ **41.** $y = \dfrac{1}{3}x$

Pages 395–397 **Lesson 8-5**

1. The slope is 60, the rate of change is 60 units for every 1 unit, and the constant of variation is 60. **3.** Justin; any linear function, including direct variations, has a rate of change. **5.** increase of $12 per hour **7.** $y = 6x$ **9.** increase of 12 in./ft **11.** decrease of $2°F/min
13. Sample answer: The population of wild condors decreased from 1966 to 1990. Then the population increased from 1990 to 1996. The population of condors in captivity

increased slowly from 1966 to 1982, then increased more rapidly from 1982 to 1996.

Interval	Rate of Change (number per year)	
	Condors in the Wild	Condors in Captivity
1966–1982	−2.25	0.1875
1982–1990	−3	4.625
1990–1992	0	8
1992–1994	1.5	14.5
1994–1996	12.5	3.5

15. $y = -5x$ **17.** $y = 0.75x$ **19.** $y = 2.54x$ **21.** A line representing the relationship between time and distance has a slope that is equal to the speed. Answers should include the following.

• Sample drawing:

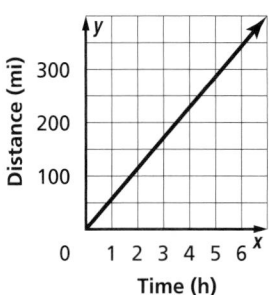

• As speed increases, the slope of the graph becomes steeper.

23. B   **25.** 2

27.

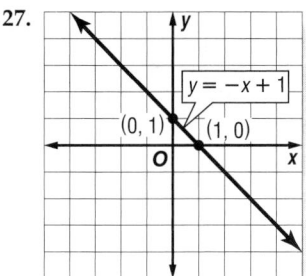

29. 14   **31.** $y = 1 - 3x$

Page 397   Practice Quiz 1

1. No; 1 is paired with 2 and −3.

3.

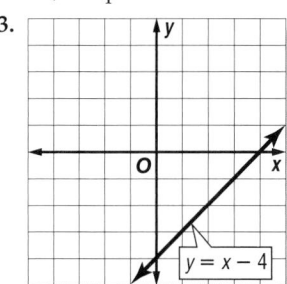

5. −9; 9   **7.** 5; −4   **9.** −2

Pages 400–401   Lesson 8-6

1. a **3.** Alex; the equation in slope-intercept form is $y = -\frac{1}{2}x + 4$.   **5.** −1; 0

7.

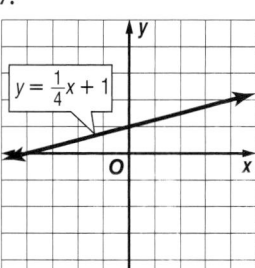

9.

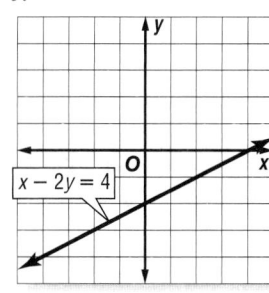

11. The y-intercept 25 represents the charge for a basic cake. Slope 1.5 represents the cost per additional slice.

13. 2; −4   **15.** −2; −3   **17.** 0; 4

19.

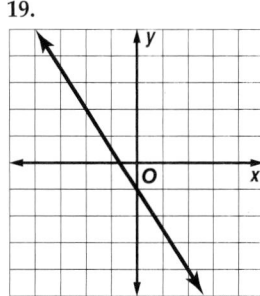

21.

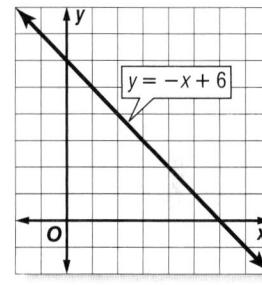

23.

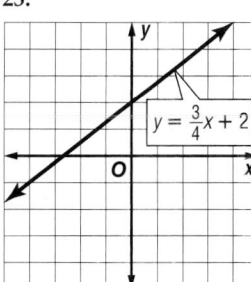

25.

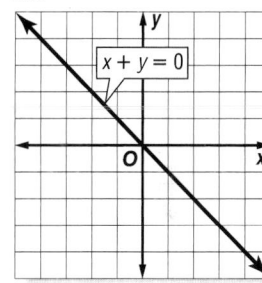

27.

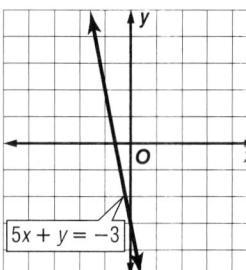

29.

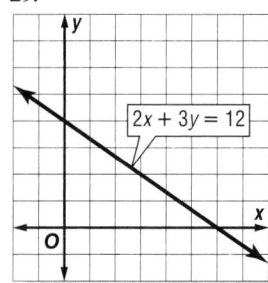

31.

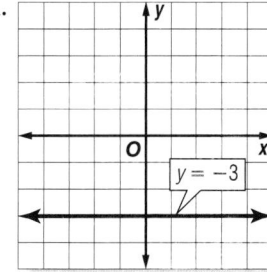

33. slope $= -50$, the descent in feet per minute; y-intercept $= 300$, initial altitude   **35.** $-\frac{b}{m}$. Replace y with 0

in $y = mx + b$ and solve for x. **37.** B **39.** $y = -4x$ **41.** 2
43. 4 **45.** $6x = 2x + 28; 7$ **47.** $-\dfrac{3}{5}$ **49.** 29 **51.** 11

Pages 407–408 Lesson 8-7
1. Sample answer: Find the y-intercept b and another point on the line. Use the points to determine the slope m. Then substitute these values in $y = mx + b$ and write the equation.
3. $y = \dfrac{1}{2}x + 1$ **5.** $y = -2x + 3$ **7.** $y = \dfrac{1}{2}x + 1$
9. $y = \dfrac{3}{4}x - 1$ **11.** $y = 2x + 6$ **13.** $y = 5$ **15.** $y = -\dfrac{1}{3}x + 8$
17. $y = 2x + 3$ **19.** $y = -2.5$ **21.** $y = -\dfrac{1}{2}x$ **23.** $y = x + 1$
25. $y = -x$ **27.** $y = 7$ **29.** $y = 4x - 3$ **31.** $y = 1088x$;
The speed of sound is 1088 feet per second.
33a. $d = 0.5(0.7c \times 1.06)$ or $d = 0.371c$ **33b.** \$18.55 **35.** C
37. 6; 7 **39.** 3; -2 **41.** positive

Pages 410–413 Lesson 8-8
1. Sample answer: Use a ruler to extend the line so that it passes through the x value for which you want to predict. Locate the x value on the line and determine the corresponding y value. Or, write an equation for the best-fit line and substitute the desired value of x to find the corresponding value of y.
3. Sample answer:

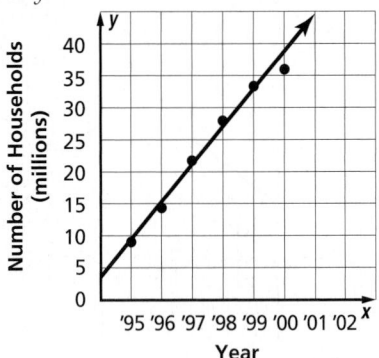

5. $y = 20x + 320$
7. Sample answer:

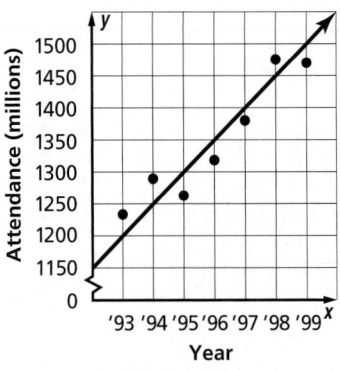

9. Sample answer:

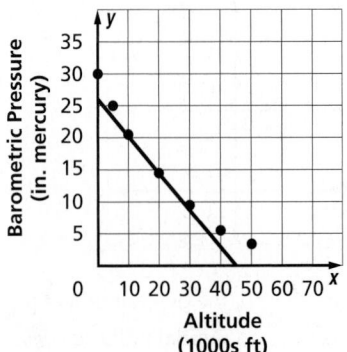

11. No, the equation gives a negative value for barometric pressure, which is not possible. Also, the data in the scatter plot do not appear to be linear. **13.** Sample answer: 238 in.
15. As latitude increases, temperature decreases.
17. Sample answer: 61.3°F **19.** The data describing the life expectancy for past generations can be displayed using a scatter plot. Then a line is drawn as close to as many of the points as possible. Then the line can be extended and used to predict the life expectancy for future generations. Answers should include the following.
• A best-fit line is a line drawn as close to as many of the data points as possible.
• Although the points may not be exactly linear, a best-fit line can be used to approximate the data set.
21. A **23.** $y = -2x + 2$ **25.** $y = -4$

27.

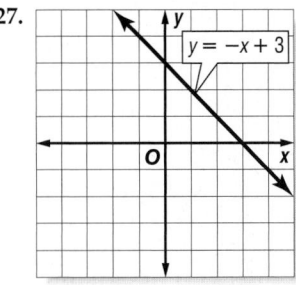

29. $n \le 7$ **31.** $d > -\dfrac{3}{2}$ **33.** 2 **35.** 4.5 **37.** 3 **39.** -1
41. -2

Pages 416–418 Lesson 8-9
1. Sample answer: A group of two or more equations form a system of equations. The solution is the ordered pair that satisfies all the equations in the system. If the equations are graphed, the solution is the coordinates of the point where the graphs intersect. The system has infinitely many solutions if the equations are the same and the graphs coincide. **3.** $(-5, -4)$

5. no solution

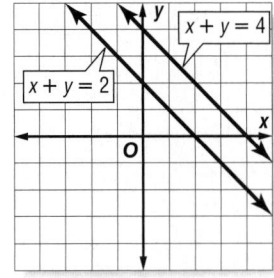

7. $(2, 6)$ **9.** $(3, -2)$ **11.** infinitely many

13. $(3, 3)$

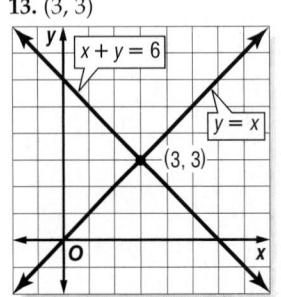

15. infinitely many

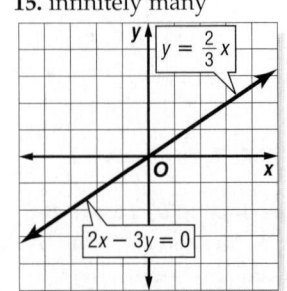

17. $(-2, 4)$

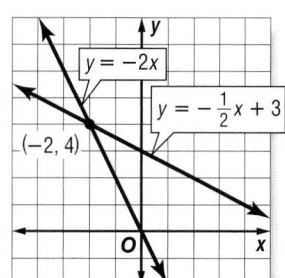

19. $(-2, 0)$ **21.** $(-4, 10)$ **23.** $(3, 6)$ **25.** $(6, 11)$; an order of 6 pounds will cost the same, $11.00, for both sites.

27a. Sample answer: No; since slope represents rate, the slopes of the graphs are the same. Therefore, the runners will never meet.

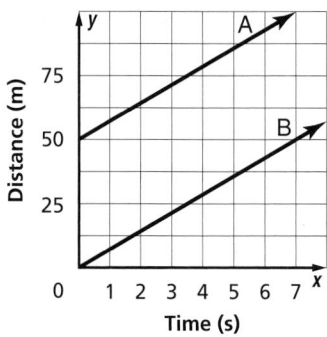

27b. Sample answer: The line representing runner B has a steeper slope than the line representing runner A. The intersection point represents the time and distance at which runner B catches up to runner A.

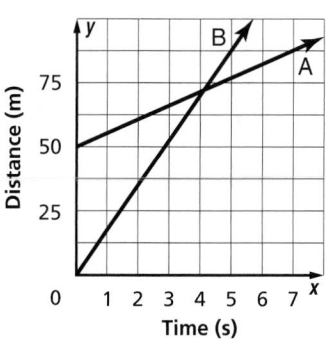

29. C   **31.** positive slope   **33.** $y = -3x$ **35.** yes   **37.** no
39. yes

Page 418   Practice Quiz 2
1. $-1; 8$ **3.** $-\frac{1}{2}; 3$ **5.** $y = 1$

7. Sample answer:

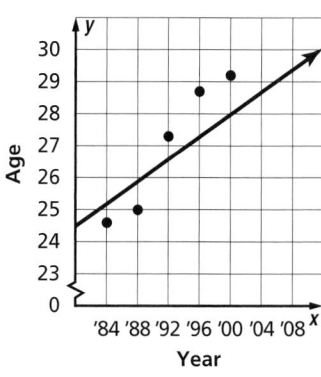

9. $(0, 5)$

Pages 421–422   Lesson 8-10
1. $y < -x + 3$ **3a.** Sample answer: $(0, -1), (1, 0), (2, 1)$
3b. Sample answer: $(0, 0), (1, 1), (2, 2)$

5.

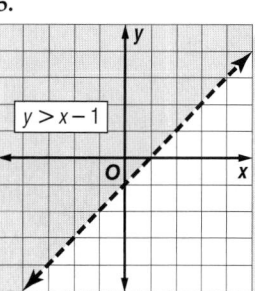

7.

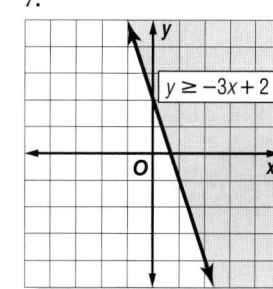

9.

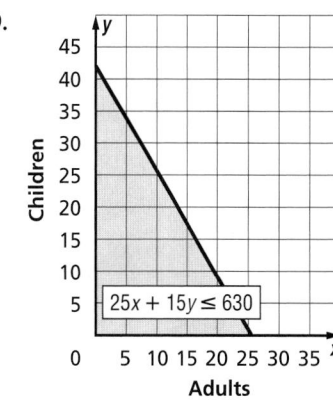

Sample answer:
5 adults, 30 children;
10 adults, 22 children;
15 adults, 15 children

11.

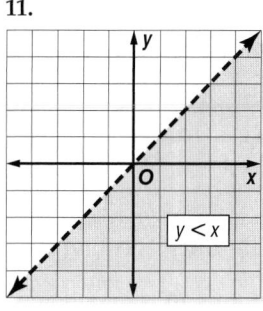

13.

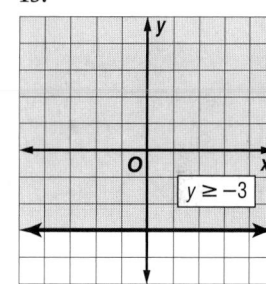

15.

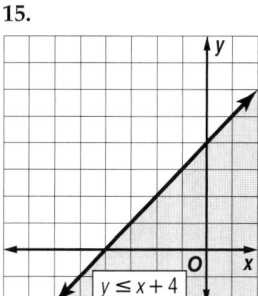

17.

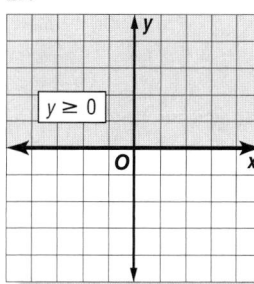

19.

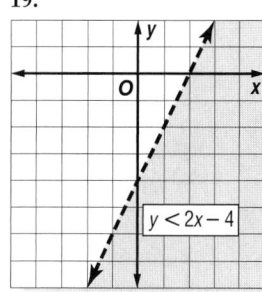

21.

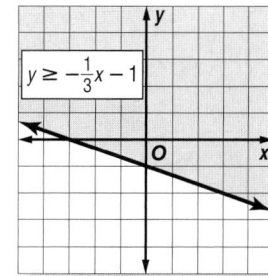

23.

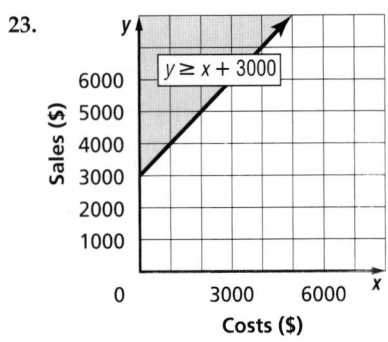

25. No; the number of sales and the costs cannot be negative. **27.** $10x + 25y \le 1440$ **29.** Sample answer: 25 small, 45 large; 50 small, 30 large; 100 small, 10 large

31.

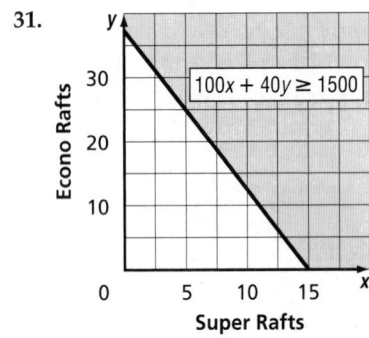

33a. $y > x - 1$, $y \le -\frac{3}{2}x + 2$
33b. Sample answers: $(0, 2)$, $(-1, 2)$, $(-3, -2)$ **35.** C

37. $(0, 3)$

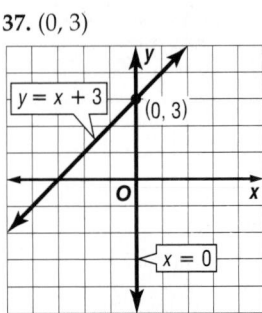

39. $(2, -5)$

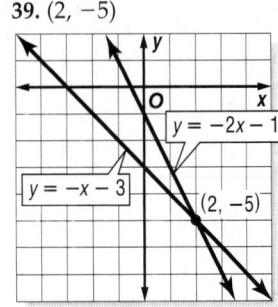

41. 0.4 **43.** $-0.\overline{5}$

Pages 424–428 Chapter 8 Study Guide and Review
1. d **3.** h **5.** a **7.** f **9.** c **11.** Yes; each x value is paired with only one y value. **13.** Yes; each x value is paired with only one y value.

15.

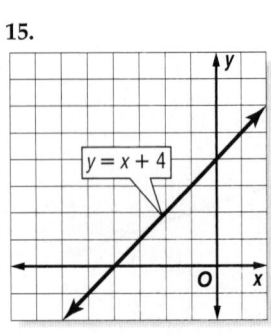

17.

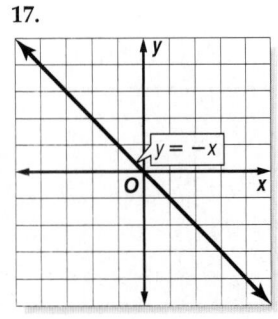

19.

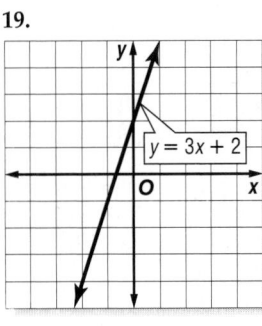

21.

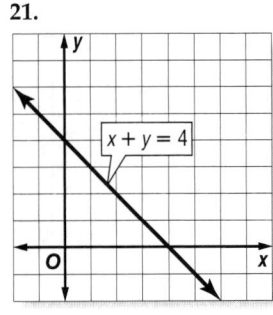

23.

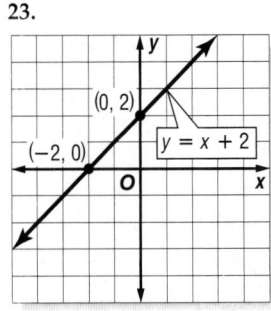

25.

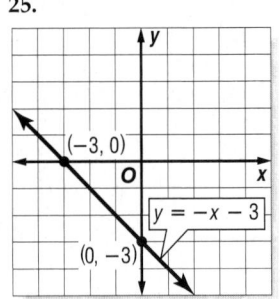

27.

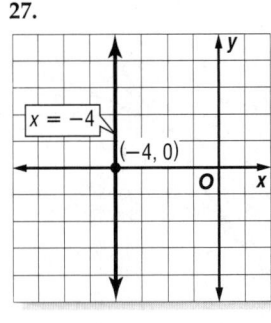

29.

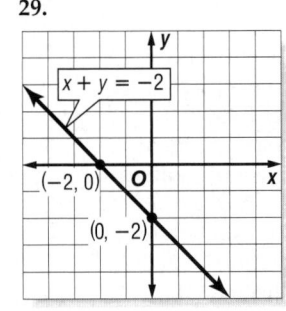

31. 1 **33.** $\frac{7}{8}$ **35.** undefined **37.** increase of 8 m/s

39.

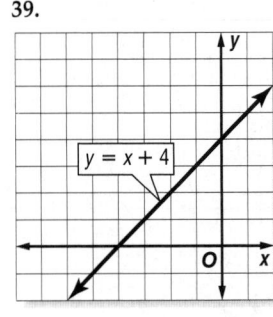

41.

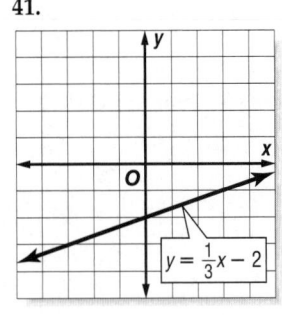

43. $y = -x + 3$

45. Sample answer:

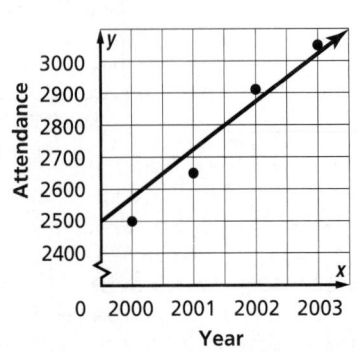

47. (3, 3)

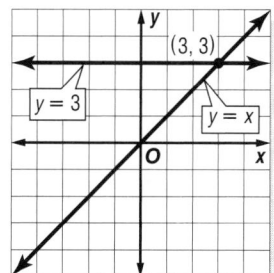

49. no solution

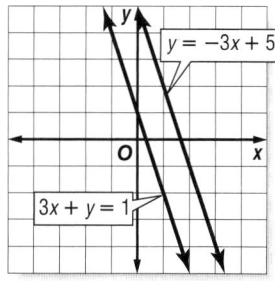

51. (4, 4)

53.

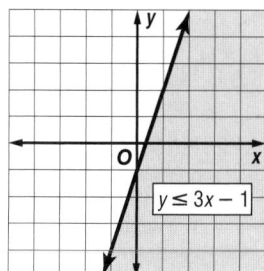

55.

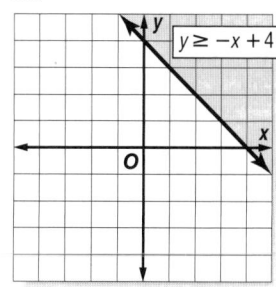

Chapter 9   Real Numbers and Right Triangles

Page 435   Chapter 9 Getting Started

1. <   **3.** <   **5.** >   **7.** <   **9.** 8   **11.** 60   **13.** 9   **15.** 11   **17.** 8
19. 34   **21.** 97

Pages 438–440   Lesson 9-1

1. A positive number squared results in a positive number, and a negative number squared results in a positive number.   **3.** Sample answer: $-\sqrt{1.69}$

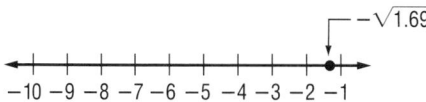

5. −8   **7.** 3.9   **9.** 8   **11.** 44.9 mi   **13.** 6   **15.** −5   **17.** not possible   **19.** 14   **21.** 18, −18   **23.** 1.5   **25.** 7.5   **27.** −9.3
29. 15.8   **31.** −1.7   **33.** 70.7   **35.** 9   **37.** −7   **39.** 14
41. −17   **43.** −2   **45.** 6   **47.** 14.8 mi   **49.** 9; Since
$64 < 65 < 81$, $\sqrt{64} < \sqrt{65} < \sqrt{81}$. Thus it follows that
$8 < \sqrt{65} < 9$. So, 9 is greater than $\sqrt{65}$.   **51a.** 10.4 in.;
41.6 in.   **51b.** 14.2 cm; 56.8 cm   **51c.** 8.4 m; 33.6 m
53. 10   **55.** 2   **57.** Sample answer: A number that has a rational square root will have an ending digit of 0, 1, 4, 5, 6, or 9. The last digit is the ending digit in one of the squares from 1–100. There are just six ending digits.   **59.** D
61. Sample answer: addition and subtraction   **63.** *a*

65.

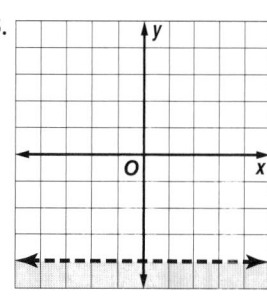

67. (5, 7)   **69.** (−4, −3)
71. $\frac{2}{3}$ **73.** 9   **75.** It can be written as a fraction.
77. It can be written as $\frac{3}{4}$.
79. It can be written as $\frac{6}{1}$.

Pages 443–445   Lesson 9-2

1. Whereas rational numbers can be expressed in the form $\frac{a}{b}$, where *a* and *b* are integers and *b* does not equal 0, irrational numbers cannot.   **3.** N, W, Z, Q   **5.** Q   **7.** <
9. $\frac{10}{3}$, $3\frac{3}{5}$, $\sqrt{13}$, $3.\overline{7}$ **11.** 8.6, −8.6   **13.** N, W, Z, Q   **15.** Q
17. Q   **19.** I   **21.** I   **23.** Z, Q   **25.** Q   **27.** Z, Q   **29.** always
31. always   **33.** >   **35.** <   **37.** =   **39.** $\frac{6}{5}$, $\sqrt{4}$, $2.\overline{1}$, $5\frac{1}{4}$
41. $-10\frac{1}{2}$, $-\sqrt{105}$, −10, −1.05   **43.** Sample answer: $\sqrt{4}$
and $\sqrt{49}$ **45.** 7, −7   **47.** 4.7, −4.7   **49.** 12, −12   **51.** 11.3,
−11.3   **53.** 1.3, −1.3   **55.** 1.9, −1.9   **57.** 12 or −12
59. 4 or −4   **61.** 36

63. If a square has an area that is not a perfect square, the lengths of the sides will be irrational. Answers should include the following.

-
 Area = 56 in²
 Area = 64 in²

65. B   **67.** 2621.2 ft²   **69.** 7   **71.** 3   **73.** Sample answer:
(0, 5), (1, 6), (−6, 2)   **75.** $x > 5$ **77.** $0.53/cupcake

79.

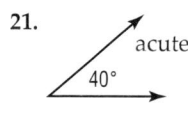 3:00

81. 10:00

83. 7:45

Pages 449–451   Lesson 9-3

1. N; $\overrightarrow{NM}$, $\overrightarrow{NP}$; ∠1, ∠MNP, ∠PNM, ∠N   **3.** 20°; acute
5. 70°; acute   **7.** acute   **9.** straight angle

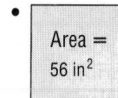 55°

11. 15°; acute   **13.** 85°; acute   **15.** 135°; obtuse
17. 60°; acute   **19.** 90°

21.

acute 40°

23.

acute 65°

25.

obtuse 95°

27.

obtuse 155°

29.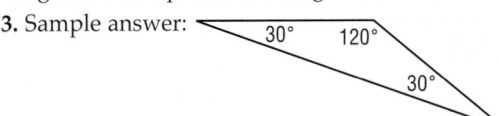
acute

31a. obtuse **31b.** right **31c.** acute
33. Intense: about 68°; Moderate: about 104°; Light: 72°; No standard routine: about 47°; Don't exercise regularly: about 68° **35.** 24
37. C **39.** Z, Q **41.** I **43.** 4 **45.** $x - 7 \geq 22$ **47.** 99
49. 60 **51.** 18

Page 451   Practice Quiz 2
1. 6 **3.** 8.2, −8.2 **5.** obtuse

Pages 455–457   Lesson 9-4
1. Whereas an isosceles triangle has at least two sides congruent, an equilateral triangle has three sides congruent.
3. Sample answer: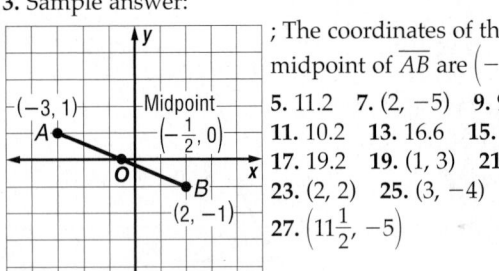
30° 120°
30°

5. 90; right **7.** right isosceles **9.** acute isosceles
11. 27; right **13.** 112; obtuse **15.** 90; right **17.** 20°, 60°, 100°
19. acute equilateral **21.** right scalene **23.** acute scalene
25. always **27.** obtuse **29.** acute **31.** not possible
33. not possible **35.** 45°; 50°; 85° **37.** 10, 15, 21 **39.** B
41. 180°; straight **43.** 145°; obtuse **45.** 9, −9 **47.** 9.2, −9.2
49. 144 **51.** 324 **53.** 729

Pages 462–464   Lesson 9-5
1. Sample answer: 8, 15, 17 **3.** 25 **5.** 15 **7.** no **9.** B
11. 26 **13.** 12.5 **15.** 18.9 **17.** 23 in. **19.** 12 **21.** 12.1
23. 37.3 **25.** 28 **27.** 33.5 **29.** yes **31.** no **33.** no
35. 32 in.
37. There is enough information to find the lengths of the legs. Since the right triangle is an isosceles right triangle, we know that the lengths of the legs are equal. So, in the Pythagorean Theorem, we can say that $a = b$. In addition, we know that $c = 8$.

$c^2 = a^2 + b^2$ *Pythagorean Theorem*
$8^2 = a^2 + a^2$ *$a = b$ and $c = 8$*
$8^2 = 2a^2$ *Add a^2 and a^2.*
$64 = 2a^2$ *Evaluate 8^2.*
$\dfrac{64}{2} = \dfrac{2a^2}{2}$ *Divide each side by 2.*
$32 = a^2$ *Simplify.*
$\sqrt{32} = a$ *Take the square root of each side.*

39. D **41.** 17 units **45.** 90; right **49.** $n \geq -9$ **51.** 5

Pages 468–470   Lesson 9-6
1. the point halfway between two endpoints
3. Sample answer:

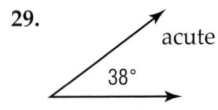

; The coordinates of the midpoint of $\overline{AB}$ are $\left(-\frac{1}{2}, 0\right)$.
5. 11.2 **7.** (2, −5) **9.** 9.2
11. 10.2 **13.** 16.6 **15.** 4.8
17. 19.2 **19.** (1, 3) **21.** (4, −2)
23. (2, 2) **25.** (3, −4)
27. $\left(11\frac{1}{2}, -5\right)$

29. Yes; $\overline{PM}$ and $\overline{MN}$ have equal measures. **31.** (−2, 3)
33. C **35.** 9.2 **37.** 35.1 **39.** 2, 1 **41.** −4, −6 **43.** 28
45. 21 **47.** 59

Page 470   Practice Quiz 2
1. obtuse isosceles **3.** Yes; $34^2 = 30^2 + 16^2$ **5.** (−1, 5)

Pages 473–475   Lesson 9-7
1. Sample answer:

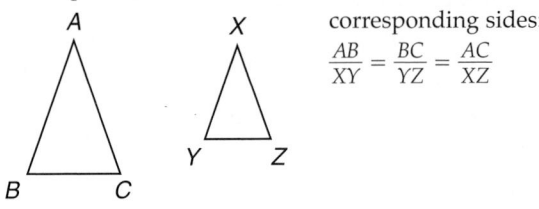

corresponding sides:
$$\frac{AB}{XY} = \frac{BC}{YZ} = \frac{AC}{XZ}$$

3. $\frac{x}{15} = \frac{6}{9}$; 10 **5.** 6 km **7.** $\frac{x}{4} = \frac{10}{5}$; 8 **9.** $\frac{x}{18} = \frac{20}{15}$; 24
11. $\frac{x}{3} = \frac{7}{4.2}$; 5 **13.** always **15.** 68 yd **17.** 6 ft
19. No, triangles *ABC* and *DEF* are not similar since the corresponding sides are not proportional. **21.** A **23.** 3.6
25. 7.1 **27.** 77.4 **29.** $\frac{1}{4}$ **31.** $1\frac{1}{2}$ **33.** 0.7143 **35.** 0.225

Pages 479–481   Lesson 9-8
1. The sine ratio compares the measure of the leg opposite the angle to the measure of the hypotenuse. The cosine ratio compares the measure of the leg adjacent to the angle to the measure of the hypotenuse. The tangent ratio compares the measure of the leg opposite the angle to the measure of the leg adjacent to the angle. **3.** 0.8824
5. 1.875 **7.** 0.9455 **9.** 25.6 **11.** 7.8 **13.** 0.9231 **15.** 0.7241
17. 2.4 **19.** 0.8944; 0.4472; 2.0 **21.** 0.1045 **23.** 0.8572
25. 0.2126 **27.** 6.8 **29.** 24.9 **31.** 97.6 **33.** about 21 m
35. about 44 m **37.** 24.0 **39.** 40.4 **41.** sin 45° = cos 45°;
sin 60° = cos 30°; sin 30° = cos 60° **43.** To find heights of buildings. Answers should include the following.
• If two of the three measures of the sides of a right triangle are known, you can use the Pythagorean Theorem to find the measure of the third side. If the measure of an acute angle and the length of one side of a right triangle are known, trigonometric ratios can be used to find the missing measures.

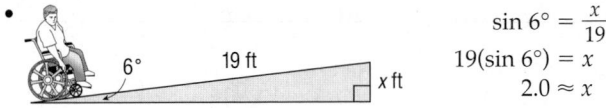

$\sin 6° = \frac{x}{19}$
$19(\sin 6°) = x$
$2.0 \approx x$

The height of the ramp is about 2 feet.
45. C **47.** $\left(1\frac{1}{2}, \frac{1}{2}\right)$ **49.** (−3, −4) **51.** $a < -6$

Pages 483–486   Chapter 9 Study Guide and Review
1. real numbers **3.** obtuse **5.** hypotenuse
7. trigonometric ratio **9.** 6 **11.** −9 **13.** not possible
15. 9, −9 **17.** 1.2, −1.2 **19.** 90°; right **21.** 35°; acute
23. obtuse isosceles **25.** 13.7 **27.** 15.9 **29.** 9.4 **31.** (3, 5)
33. (0, −2) **35.** $\frac{AB}{HJ} = \frac{BC}{JK}$; 10 **37.** 1.3333

Chapter 10   Two-Dimensional Figures

Page 491   Chapter 10 Getting Started
1. 44 **3.** 51 **5.** 28 **7.** 39 **9.** 44 **11.** 71.8 **13.** 12.5
15. 10.7 **17.** $10\frac{1}{6}$ **19.** $3\frac{7}{8}$ **21.** $5\frac{3}{8}$ **23.** $6\frac{2}{9}$

Pages 495–497   Lesson 10-1
1. Complementary angles have a sum of 90° and supplementary angles have a sum of 180°. **3.** 56° **5.** 124°
7. 28 **9.** D **11.** 127° **13.** 53° **15.** 127° **17.** 148 **19.** 175

21. 9 **23.** 41° **25.** 73° **27.** 112° **29.** 5 **31.** 9 **33.** They are supplementary. **35.** A **37.** Sample answer: Both graphs intersect to form right angles. **39.** Sample answer: The slopes of the graphs of perpendicular lines are negative reciprocals of each other. **41.** 0.8910 **43.** 7.5 **45.** $-9m$

47.

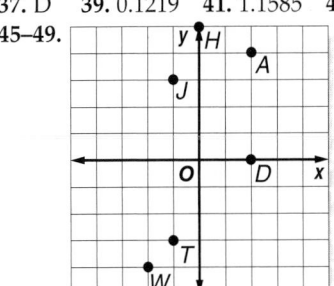

45°

49.

145°

Pages 502–504 Lesson 10-2
1. They have the same size and shape. **3.** $\angle J \cong \angle C$, $\angle K \cong \angle B$, $\angle M \cong \angle G$, $\overline{KM} \cong \overline{BG}$, $\overline{MJ} \cong \overline{GC}$, $\overline{KJ} \cong \overline{BC}$; $\triangle BGC$
5. $\angle M$ **7.** $\overline{MN}$ **9.** 15 ft **11.** $\angle K \cong \angle N$, $\angle J \cong \angle P$, $\angle M \cong \angle M$, $\overline{KJ} \cong \overline{NP}$, $\overline{JM} \cong \overline{PM}$, $\overline{KM} \cong \overline{NM}$; $\triangle NPM$
13. $\angle Z \cong \angle S$, $\angle W \cong \angle T$, $\angle Y \cong \angle R$, $\overline{ZW} \cong \overline{ST}$, $\overline{WY} \cong \overline{TR}$, $\overline{ZY} \cong \overline{SR}$; $\triangle STR$ **15.** sometimes **17.** 30° **19.** $\angle F$ **21.** $\angle A$
23. $\overline{HF}$ **25.** $\overline{DC}$ **27.** 20 **29.** 6 **31.** Sample answer: $\triangle ZQN$
33. Sample answer: $\triangle WQO$ **35.** Congruent triangles can be found on objects in nature like leaves and animals. Answers should include the following.
• Congruent triangles are triangles with the same angle measures and the same side lengths.
• Sample answer: A bird's wings when extended are an example of congruent angles. Another example of congruent angles would be the wings of a butterfly.
37. D **39.** 0.1219 **41.** 1.1585 **43.** -6
45–49.

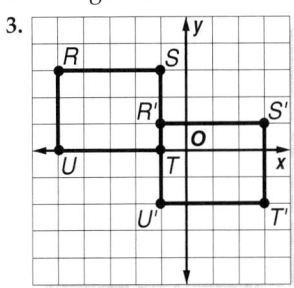

Pages 509–511 Lesson 10-3
1. The figure is moved 5 units to the right and 2 units down.
3.

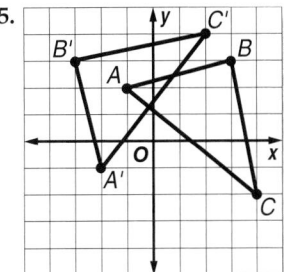

5.

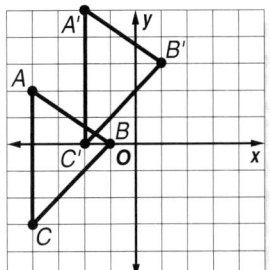

7. $A'(-2, 5)$, $B'(1, 3)$, $C'(-2, 0)$;

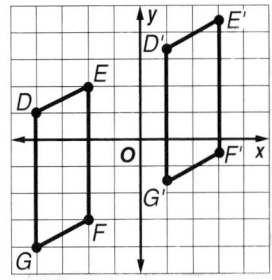

9. $D'\left(1, 3\frac{1}{2}\right)$, $E'\left(3, 4\frac{1}{2}\right)$, $G'\left(1, -1\frac{1}{2}\right)$, $F'\left(3, -\frac{1}{2}\right)$;

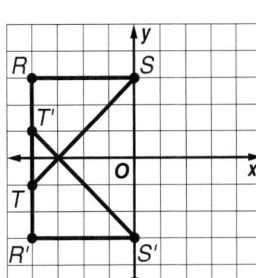

11. $R'(-4, -3)$, $S'(0, -3)$, $T'(-4, 1)$;

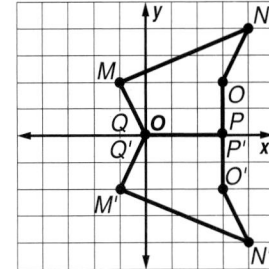

13. $M'(-1, -2)$, $N'(4, -4)$, $O'(3, -2)$, $P'(3, 0)$, $Q'(0, 0)$;

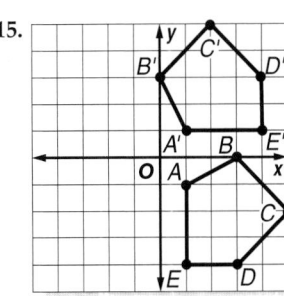

15.

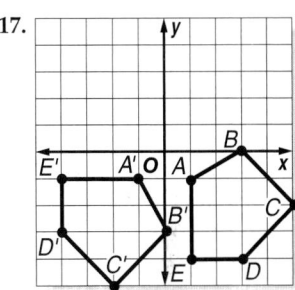

17.

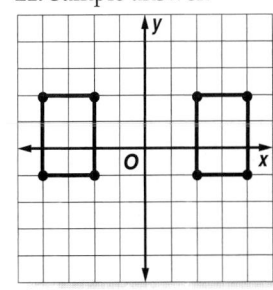

19. translation

21. Sample answer:

; The image of the figure's reflection is the same as the image of its translation to the right 6 units.

23. reflection **25.** Since many of the movements used in recreational activities involve rotating, sliding, and flipping, they are examples of transformations. Answers should include the following.
• a translation is a slide, a reflection is a mirror-image, and a rotation is a turn.
• sample answer: the swing represents a rotation, the scooter represents a translation, and the skateboard represents reflection.
27. C **29.** $\overline{DF}$ **31.** 110°

33. $x \geq 9.6$;

7.0 8.0 9.0 10.0

35. 113 **37.** 47 **39.** 106

Pages 515–517 Lesson 10-4
1. Sample answer: A textbook is an example of a quadrilateral; the tiles in a shuffleboard scoring region are examples of parallelograms; a "dead end" road sign is an example of a rhombus; and a floppy disk is an example of a square. **3.** 110; 110° **5.** rectangle **7.** trapezoids, parallelograms **9.** 102; 102° **11.** 60; 60°; 60°; 120° **13.** 70; 70°; 80°; 120° **15.** Sample answer: A chessboard; it is a square because it is a parallelogram with 4 congruent sides and 4 right angles. **17.** square **19.** parallelogram
21. rhombus **23.** always **25.** sometimes **27.** quadrilateral

29a. Yes; a rhombus is equilateral but may not be equiangular.

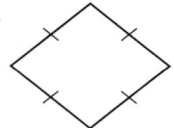

29b. Yes; a rectangle is equiangular but may not be equilateral.

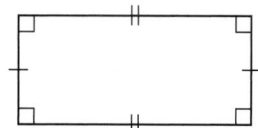

31. B   **33.**

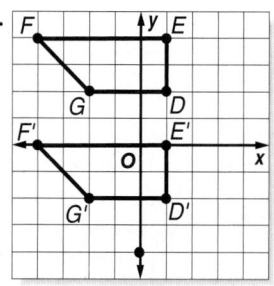

35. $\overline{MA}$ **37.** 14.4
39. 28.52

Page 517   Practice Quiz 1
1. 35°   **3.** $Q'(3, -3)$, $R'(5, -6)$, $S'(7, -3)$ **5.** 60; 60°; 120°

Pages 523–525   Lesson 10-5
1. Sample answer:

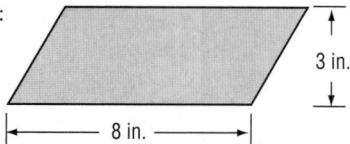

3. 8 ft²   **5.** 60 m²   **7.** 11 m²   **9.** 90 cm²   **11.** 43.99 cm²
13. 28 in²   **15.** 22.8 yd²   **17.** 36.75 m²   **19.** about 95,284 mi²
21. 147 km²   **23.** 57 ft²   **25.** 5 bags   **27.** 16 in.   **29.** 24.5%
31. The area of a parallelogram is found by multiplying the base and the height of the parallelogram. The area of a rectangle is found by multiplying the length and the width of the rectangle. Since in a parallelogram, the base is the length of the parallelogram, and the height is the width of the parallelogram, both areas are found by multiplying the length and the width. Answers should include the following.
• Parallelograms and rectangles are similar in that they are quadrilaterals with opposite sides parallel and opposite sides congruent. They are different in that rectangles always have 4 right angles.
•

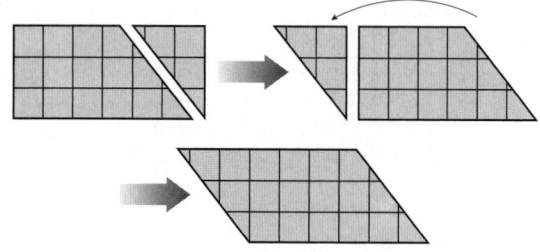

33. B   **35.** 24; 24°; 96°   **37.** 30   **39.** 26   **41.** 900   **43.** 1260

Pages 529–531   Lesson 10-6
1.

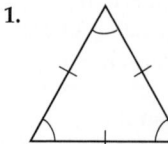

3. The number of triangles is 2 less than the number of sides.   **5.** octagon; regular   **7.** 128.6°   **9.** hexagon; regular **11.** nonagon; not regular   **13.** decagon, not regular   **15.** 540°   **17.** 1440°

19. 2880°   **21.** Sample answer: hexagon, triangle, decagon, quadrilateral, and pentagon   **23.** 140°   **25.** 135°   **27.** 150°
29. octagons, squares   **31.** 180 cm   **33.** 58.5 in.
35. In tessellations, polygons are fit together to create a pattern such that there are no gaps or spaces.
Answers should include the following.
• Sample answer:

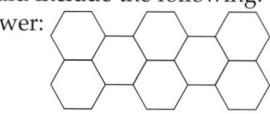

• Sample answer:

37. B   **39.** 120°   **41.** 60°   **43.** 30°   **45.** 18 cm²
47. quadrilateral   **49.** 16.4x   **51.** 33.9   **53.** 18.1

Pages 536–538   Lesson 10-7
1. Multiply 2 times π times the radius.   **3.** Mark; since the diameter of the circle is 7 units, its radius is 3.5 units. Thus, the area of the circle is π · (3.5)² or 38.5 square units.
5. 50.3 m; 201.1 m²   **7.** 8.2 km; 5.3 km²   **9.** about 9.1 mi²
11. 40.8 in.; 132.7 in²   **13.** 131.9 km; 1385.4 km²   **15.** 79.8 m;
506.7 m²   **17.** 22.9 cm; 41.9 cm²   **19.** 96.6 in; 742.6 in²
21. 1.5 m   **23.** 13 cm   **25.** about 3979 mi   **27.** d   **29.** a
31. about 26 times   **33.** are safe: 25.4 in²; are unsafe: 24.2 in²;
don't know: 14.0 in²   **35.** 4   **37.** C   **39.** 125°   **41.** 235°
43. 125°   **45.** 62.5°   **47.** Sample answer: $\overline{SP}$, $\overline{SQ}$, $\overline{RP}$
49. 144°   **51.** 38 m²   **53.** $x < -7$ **55.** 150.5

Page 538   Practice Quiz 2
1. 112.86 cm²   **3.** 32 m²   **5.** 29.5 in.; 69.4 in²

Pages 541–543   Lesson 10-8
1. Sample answer:

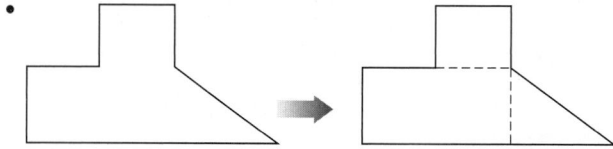

3. 49.5 yd²   **5.** 2   **7.** 72 ft²   **9.** 56.1 cm²   **11.** 18.3 in²
13. 45 ft²   **15.** 86.8 yd²   **17.** 85 units²   **19.** 6963.5 yd²
21. Sample answer: Separate the area into a rectangle and a trapezoid.   **23.** 68,679 mi²   **25.** You can use polygons to find the area of an irregular figure by finding the area of each individual polygon and then finding the total area of the irregular figure. Answers should include the following.
•

• To find the area of the irregular figure shown above, the figure can be separated into two rectangles and a triangle.
27. C   **29.** 44.0 cm, 153.9 cm²   **31.** 540°   **33.** 1080°
35. $-24xy$

Pages 544–548   Chapter 10 Study Guide and Review
1. supplementary   **3.** corresponding angles   **5.** equilateral
7. 109°   **9.** 71°   **11.** ∠H   **13.** $\overline{RS}$ **15.** $\overline{GF}$

17.

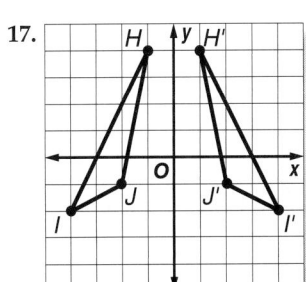

19. 112; 112° **21.** 70; 70°; 70° **23.** 11 yd² **25.** hexagon; 720° **27.** decagon; 1440° **29.** 13.2 m; 13.9 m² **31.** 118 in² **33.** 863.4 cm²

Chapter 11 Three-Dimensional Figures

Page 553 Chapter 11 Getting Started
1. yes; triangle **3.** no **5.** 17 **7.** 7 **9.** 155 **11.** yes **13.** yes **15.** yes

Pages 559–561 Lesson 11-1
1. Five planes form a square pyramid because the solid has five faces. An edge is formed when two planes intersect; a vertex is formed when three or four planes intersect.
3. triangular pyramid; any one of the following faces can be considered a base: RST, QRS, QST, QRT; $\overline{QR}$, $\overline{QS}$, $\overline{QT}$, $\overline{RT}$, $\overline{RS}$, $\overline{ST}$; Q, R, S, T **5.** intersecting
7.   top   front   side

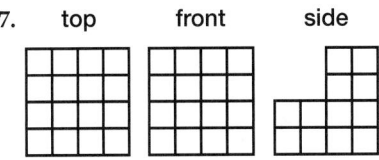

9. rectangular prism; $LMNP$, $QRST$ or $LPTQ$, $MNSR$ or $PNST$, $LMRQ$; $LMNP$, $QRST$, $LPTQ$, $MNSR$, $PNST$, $LMRQ$; $\overline{LM}$, $\overline{MN}$, $\overline{NP}$, $\overline{PL}$, $\overline{LQ}$, $\overline{MR}$, $\overline{NS}$, $\overline{PT}$, $\overline{QR}$, $\overline{RS}$, $\overline{ST}$, $\overline{TQ}$; L, M, N, P, Q, R, S, T **11.** triangular pyramid; any one of the following faces can be considered a base: WXY, WYZ, WZX, XYZ; $\overline{WX}$, $\overline{WY}$, $\overline{WZ}$, $\overline{XZ}$, $\overline{XY}$, $\overline{YZ}$; W, X, Y, Z **13.** $\overline{WR}$
15. skew **17.** top **19.** rectangular and pentagonal prisms
23. Never; only three or more planes can intersect in a single point. **25.** Sometimes; three planes may intersect in a line. Or, the planes may be parallel and not intersect at all.
27. Two-dimensional figures form three-dimensional figures. Answers should include the following.
- Two-dimensional figures have length and width and therefore lie in a single plane. Three-dimensional figures have length, width, and depth.
- Two-dimensional figures form the faces of three-dimensional figures.

29. D **31.** 37.7 cm; 113.1 cm² **33.** 0.5000 **35.** $c < 8$
37. $n > -11$ **39.** $y < 1\frac{3}{4}$ **41.** 14 in² **43.** 6.5 cm²

Pages 565–567 Lesson 11-2
1. Sample answer: Finding how much sand is needed to fill a child's rectangular sandbox; measure the length, width, and height, and then multiply to find the volume.
3. 183.6 cm³ **5.** 1608.5 ft³ **7.** 282.7 yd³ **9.** 198.9 ft
11. 512 cm³ **13.** 748 in³ **15.** 88.0 ft³ **17.** 225 mm³
19. 18.6 m³ **21.** 6.2 m **23.** 1728 **25.** 1,000,000 **27.** 11.5 in.
29. The volume will be greater if the height is $8\frac{1}{2}$ inches.

By using the formula for circumference, you can find the radius and volume of each cylinder. If the height is $8\frac{1}{2}$ inches, the volume is 86.5 in³; if the height is 11 inches, the volume is 67.7 in³. **31.** C **33.** Sample answer: $\overline{QT}$ and $\overline{YZ}$ **35.** $x > -8$ **37.** 25 **39.** 4 **41.** 28

Pages 570–572 Lesson 11-3
1. The base is a circle.
3. Sample answer:
$V = 134.0 \text{ cm}^3$

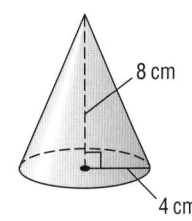

5. 37.7 cm³ **7.** 378 ft³ **9.** 91,636,272 ft³
11. 412 cm³ **13.** 150 in³ **15.** 78.5 m³
17. 270.8 cm³ **19.** 565.5 m³ **21.** 44.0 m³
23a. 2.4 ft³ **23b.** 314.4 lb

25. The volume of a pyramid is one-third the volume of a prism with the same base and height. Answers should include the following.
- The height of the pyramid and prism are equal. The bases of the pyramid and prism are squares with equal side lengths. Therefore, their base areas are equal.
- The formula for the volume of a pyramid is one-third times the formula for the volume of a prism.

27. B **29.** 904.8 cm³ **31.** 107.5 mm³ **33.** 10.1 in³
35. 7.8 **37.** 36

Page 572 Practice Quiz 1
1. triangular prism **3.** 12.6 cm³ **5.** ≈11,545,353 ft³

Pages 575–577 Lesson 11-4
1. Sample answer: The surface of a solid is two-dimensional. Its area is the sum of the face areas, which are given in square units. **3.** 150 ft² **5.** 571.8 in² **7.** 140.7 mm²
9. 282 in² **11.** 264 m² **13.** 1885.0 ft² **15.** 294 ft²
17. 628.3 in² **19.** 264.0 in² **21.** 754 ft² **23.** The surface area is 4 times greater. **25.** D **27.** square or rectangle
29. rectangle **31.** 565.5 in³ **33.** 15.21 **35.** 1.3 **37.** $3\frac{1}{4}$

Pages 580–582 Lesson 11-5
1. Slant height is the altitude of a triangular face of a pyramid; it is the length from the vertex of a cone to the edge of its base. Height of a pyramid or cone is the altitude of the whole solid. **3.** Sample answer: An architect might use the formulas to calculate the amount of materials needed for parts of a structure. **5.** 42.9 m² **7.** 336 ft²
9. 96.3 in² **11.** 62.4 in² **13.** 339.3 in² **15.** 311.9 m²
17. 506.6 mm² **19.** Style 8M has 29 in² more plastic.
21. 339 ft²; 4 squares **23.** Many building materials are priced and purchased by square footage. Architects use surface area when designing buildings. Answers should include the following.
- Surface area is used in covering building exteriors and in designing interiors.
- It is important to know surface areas so the amounts and costs of building materials can be estimated.

25. C **27.** 5541.8 mm² **29.** 7 ft² **31.** 25.1 in³ **33.** infinitely many solutions **35.** 3 **37.** 3 **39.** 3.15

Pages 586–588 Lesson 11-6
1. Sample answer:
The cones are similar because the ratios comparing their radii and slant heights are equal: $\frac{2}{3} = \frac{5}{7.5}$.

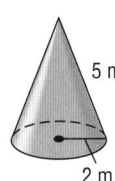
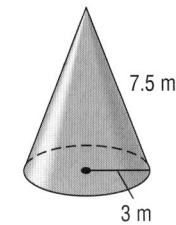

3. no **5.** $x = 33\frac{1}{3}$ ft **7.** 525 m **9.** 2,976,750 m^3 **11.** yes
13. yes **15.** $x = 7$ m, $y = 18$ m **17.** Sometimes; bases must be the same polygon and the corresponding side lengths must be proportional. **19.** always; same shape, diameters or radii are proportional **21.** 200^3 or 8,000,000 times greater **23.** If the ratios of corresponding linear dimensions are equal, the solids are similar. Answers should include the following.
- For example, if the ratio comparing the heights of two cylinders equals the ratio comparing their radii, then the cylinders are similar.
- A cone and a prism are not similar.

25. C **27.** 184 ft^2 **29.** 65° **31.** $-\frac{5}{9}$ **33.** 19.3 **35.** 6.0
37. 9.4

Page 588 Practice Quiz 2
1. 166 mm^2 **3.** 9.4 m^2 **5.** Yes; their corresponding dimensions are proportional.

Pages 592–594 Lesson 11-7
1. Josh; the first two 0s are not significant because they are placeholders for the decimal point. The 0 between 2 and 5 is significant because it is between two significant digits and shows the actual value in the thousandths place.
3. Sample answer: 0.012 or 2500 **5.** 3 **7.** 3 **9.** 7.1 L
11. 544.5 in^2 **13.** $\frac{1}{32}$ in. **15.** 3 **17.** 2 **19.** 1 **21.** 4
23. 45 in. **25.** 2 ft^2 **27.** 84.47 m **29.** 49.5 cm **31.** 26 m^2
33. b; The precision unit of ruler a is $\frac{1}{8}$ inch. The precision unit of ruler b is $\frac{1}{16}$ inch. **35.** No, the numbers are estimated to the nearest 0.1 million. **37.** 12,400,000; 3
39. Not necessarily, because the actual size of the 2.0 mm wrench can range from 1.95 mm to 2.05 mm and the actual size of the 2 mm bolt can range from 1.5 mm to 2.5 mm. So, the bolts could be larger than the corresponding wrenches.
41. A **43.** 0.05 mi; between 132.75 mi and 132.85 mi
45. 26.5 cm^2 **47.** 14.8 m^2

Pages 595–598 Chapter 11 Study Guide and Review
1. false; lateral area **3.** false; slant height **5.** false; cylinder
7. true **9.** rectangular prism; $QRST$, $UVWX$ or $QTXU$, $RSWV$ or $QRVU$, $TSWX$; $QRST$, $UVWX$, $QTXU$, $RSWV$, $QRVU$, $TSWX$; $\overline{QR}$, $\overline{RS}$, $\overline{ST}$, $\overline{TZ}$, $\overline{UV}$, $\overline{VW}$, $\overline{WX}$, $\overline{XU}$, $\overline{QU}$, $\overline{TX}$, $\overline{SW}$, $\overline{RV}$; Q, R, S, T, U, V, W, X **11.** rectangular pyramid; $YNPZ$; AYZ, AZP, ANP, ANY, $YNPZ$; $\overline{AY}$, $\overline{AZ}$, $\overline{AP}$, $\overline{AN}$, $\overline{YZ}$, $\overline{ZP}$, $\overline{PN}$, $\overline{NY}$; A, Y, Z, P, N **13.** 0.8 mm^3 **15.** 4 ft^3
17. 1721.9 cm^3 **19.** 548.7 mm^2 **21.** 45 in^2 **23.** 37.1 in^2
25. yes **27.** 19.0 cm **29.** 0.9 m **31.** 973 ft^2

Chapter 12 More Statistics and Probability

Page 605 Chapter 12 Getting Started
1. 16; 15; none **3.** 5.3, 5.8, 6.5 **5.** $\frac{1}{3}$ **7.** $\frac{1}{2}$ **9.** $\frac{1}{2}$ **11.** $\frac{1}{2}$
13. $\frac{1}{8}$ **15.** $\frac{1}{6}$ **17.** $\frac{1}{6}$

Pages 608–611 Lesson 12-1
1. Sample answer: The age of the youngest President at the time of his inauguration was 42 and the age of the oldest President to be inaugurated was 69. However, most of the Presidents were 50 to 59 years old at the time of their inauguration.

3.

Stem	Leaf
0	6 7
1	2 5 5
2	0
3	5
4	0 1 2|0 = 20

5. 50, 99 **7.** Sample answer: The lowest score was 50. The highest score was 99. Most of the scores were in the 70–79 interval.
9. Chicken; whereas chicken sandwiches have 8–20 grams of fat, burgers have 10–36 grams of fat.

11.

Stem	Leaf
1	3
2	6 8
3	4 9
4	
5	2 3
6	2 2 7
7	7 9
8	4 7|7 = 77

13.

Stem	Leaf
0	6 6 8
1	0 1 4 6 8
2	0 2 5
3	2 7
4	
5	0 3|7 = 37

15.

Stem	Leaf
40	0 0 5
41	
42	5
43	
44	
45	0 6
46	
47	
48	0 4 7
49	
50	
51	0
52	0
⋮	
62	5
⋮	
76	4
77	
78	9 76|4 = 764

17. never **19.** 35% **21.** Sample answer: In the most populated U.S. cities, about 27 to 35% of the people exercise daily. **23.** 5
25. The average number of games won by the teams in the Big East Conference is less than the average number of games won by the teams in the Big Ten Conference. **29a.** Sample answer: It would be easier to find the median in a stem-and-leaf plot because the data are arranged in order from least to greatest. **29b.** Sample answer: It would be easier to find the mean in a table because once you find the sum, it may be easier to count the number of items in a table.

29c. Sample answer: It would be easier to find the mode in a stem-and-leaf plot because the value or values that occur most often are grouped together. **31.** C **33.** no
35. 62.8 ft; 314.2 ft^2 **37.** 247% **39.** 0.65% **41.** 57.1%
43. 1.6% **45.** 6 **47.** 1.1

Pages 614–616 Lesson 12-2
1. The range describes how the entire set of data is distributed, while the interquartile range describes how the middle half of the data is distributed. **3.** Sample answer: {8, 9, 13, 25, 26, 26, 26, 27, 28, 30, 35, 40} **5.** 27; 6 **7.** 24 h
9. 77; 39 **11.** 50; 10 **13.** 25; 15.5 **15.** 22 **17.** Feb.: 13.5; July: 8 **19.** National League: 42, 44, 48, 38, 10; American League: 39, 44, 49, 39, 10 **21a.** Sample answer: {43, 49, 50, 50, 58, 60, 60, 66, 70, 70, 71, 78} **21b.** Sample answer: {15, 18, 20, 20, 44, 60, 60, 64, 70, 70, 75, 79} **21c.** Sample answer: The first set of data has a smaller interquartile range, thus the data in the first set are more tightly clustered around the median and the data in the second are more spread out over the range. **23.** C

25.

Stem	Leaf
0	9
1	2 4 5 8
2	1 7
3	7 3|7 = $37

27. 461.8 cm^3 **29.** 1.6 ft
31. {0.2, 0.3, 0.6, 0.8, 1.2, 1.4, 1.5}
33. {9.8, 9.9, 10.5, 10.9, 11.2, 11.4}

Pages 619–621   Lesson 12-3

1. lower quartile, least value; upper quartile, greatest value
3. Sample answer: {28, 30, 52, 68, 90, 92}

5.
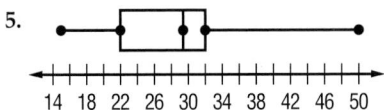

7. Sample answer: The length of the box-and-whisker plot shows that the winning times of the men's marathons are not concentrated around a certain time.   **9.** The most fuel-efficient SUV and the least fuel-efficient sedan both average 22 miles per gallon.

11.
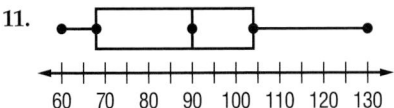

13.
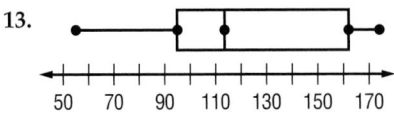

15.
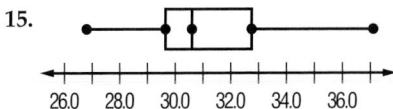

17. 50%   **19.** Sample answer: The least number of games won for NFC is 3 and the least number of games won for the AFC is 1. The most number of games won for the NFC is 12 and the most number of games won for the AFC is 13. In addition, for both conferences, the median number of games won is about 9.   **21.** A box-and-whisker plot would clearly display any upper and lower extreme temperatures and the median temperature. Answers should include the following.

•
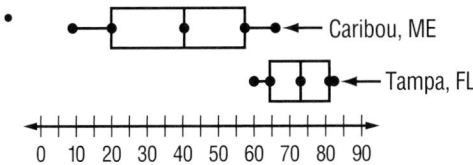

• Sample answer: Tampa has a median temperature of 73 and Caribou has a median temperature of 40.5. Whereas the highest average temperature for Tampa is 82, the highest average temperature for Caribou is 66.
• Sample answer: You can easily see how the temperatures vary.

23. C   **25.** 4

27.
Stem	Leaf
1	4
2	1 4 7
3	9
4	8 2|4 = 24

29. 14

Pages 625–628   Lesson 12-4

1. Sample answer: Because the intervals are continuous.

3.
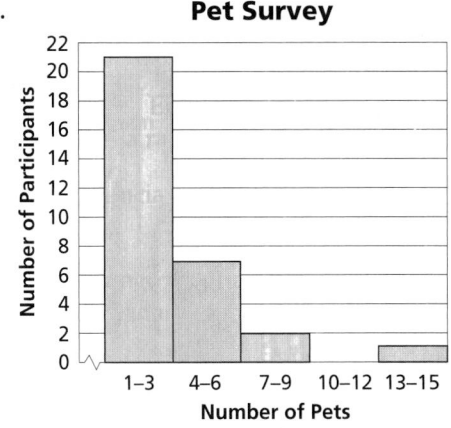

5. the number of states that have a certain number of roller coasters   **7.** The numbers between 10 and 34 are omitted.   **9.** 2 or more national monuments

11.
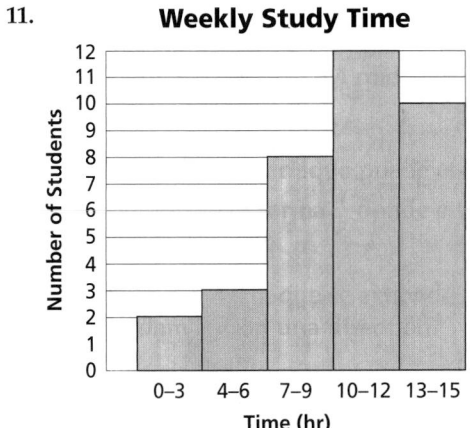

13.

Touchdowns in a Season

[bar graph with y-axis "Number of Players" and x-axis "Number of Touchdowns" with intervals 80–96, 97–113, 114–130, 131–147, 148–164, 165–181]

15. 13   **17.** 37.5%   **19.** Dallas   **21.** true   **23.** false   **25.** true   **27.** A   **29.** absolute frequency: 2, 9, 17, 12, 7, 2; relative frequency: $\frac{2}{49}, \frac{9}{49}, \frac{17}{49}, \frac{12}{49}, \frac{1}{7}, \frac{2}{49}$; cumulative frequency: 2, 11, 28, 40, 47, 49

31.

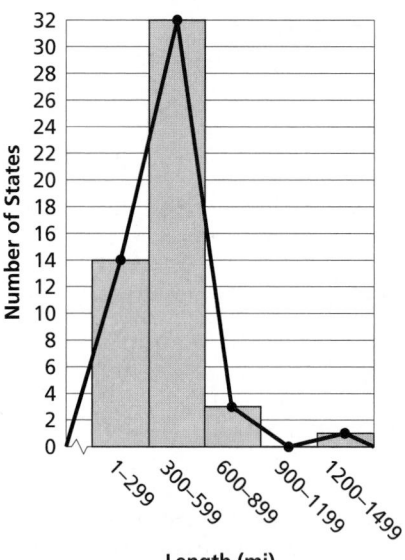

Average Length of U.S. States

(histogram: Number of States vs. Length (mi), with categories 1–299, 300–599, 600–899, 900–1199, 1200–1499)

Source: *The World Almanac*

33. 44; 15   **35.** Sample answer: Brand B costs one-third more than brand C.

Page 628   Practice Quiz 1

1.

Stem	Leaf
1	6 8 9 9
2	0 2 6 8 8 8
3	0 2
4	0 2 3
5	5
6	
7	
8	6 9

$5\,|\,5 = 55$

3.

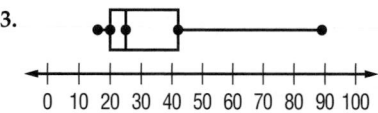

(box-and-whisker plot on scale 0 10 20 30 40 50 60 70 80 90 100)

5.

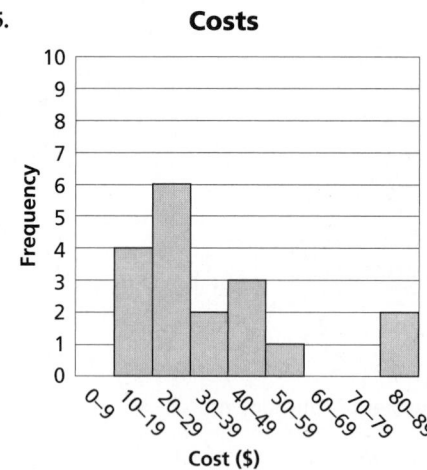

Costs

(histogram: Frequency vs. Cost ($), categories 0–9, 10–19, 20–29, 30–39, 40–49, 50–59, 60–69, 70–79, 80–89)

Pages 631–633   Lesson 12-5

1. Sample answer: inconsistent vertical scale and break in vertical scale   **3.** Graph A has a break in the vertical scale.
5. From the vertical scale, you can see that the number of

area codes in 1999 is about 1.5 times the number of area codes in 1996. The graph is misleading because the drawing of the phone for 1999 is about 3 times the size of the phone for 1996. Also, there is a break in the vertical scale.
7. Graph B   **9.** Graph B; the vertical scale used makes the decrease in the unemployment rates appear more drastic.

11a. Sample answer:

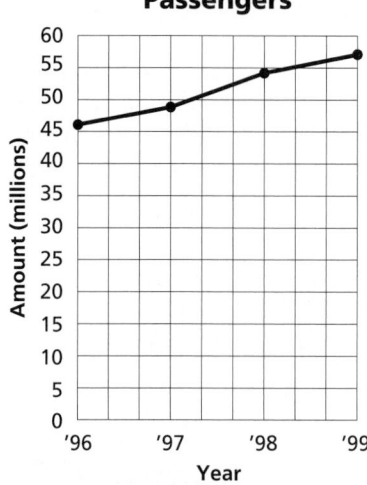

Commuter Train Passengers

(line graph: Amount (millions) vs. Year '96–'99, scale 0 to 60)

11b. Sample answer:

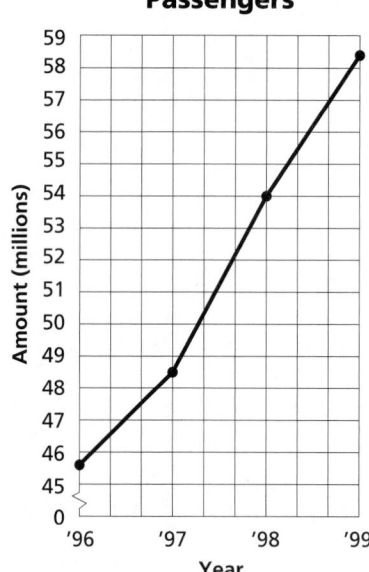

Commuter Train Passengers

(line graph: Amount (millions) vs. Year '96–'99, scale 45 to 59)

13. B

15.

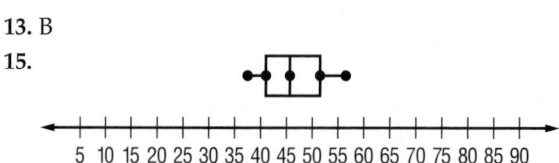

(box-and-whisker plot on scale 5 10 15 20 25 30 35 40 45 50 55 60 65 70 75 80 85 90)

17. 20.3 m²   **19.** $\frac{1}{6}$ or $16\frac{2}{3}$%   **21.** $\frac{5}{6}$ or $83\frac{1}{3}$%

23. $\frac{5}{6}$ or $83.\overline{3}$%

Pages 637–639   Lesson 12-6

1. Sample answer: Both methods find the number of outcomes. Using the Fundamental Counting Principle is faster and uses less space; using a tree diagram shows what each outcome is.   **3.** First find the number of outcomes possible. The possible outcomes are taco-chicken, taco-beef,

taco-bean, burrito-chicken, burrito-beef, and burrito-bean, for a total of 6 outcomes. Two of the outcomes have chicken filling, so the probability of chicken filling is $\frac{2}{6}$ or $\frac{1}{3}$. **5.** $\frac{1}{16}$
7. $\frac{1}{4}$ **9.** 9

11.

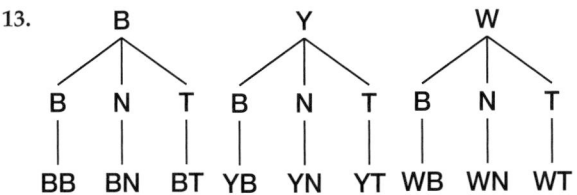

8 outcomes

13.

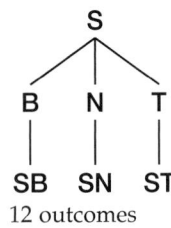

12 outcomes

15. 36 outcomes **17.** 24 outcomes
19. 1024 outcomes **21.** $\frac{5}{18}$ **23.** $\frac{1}{100,000}$
25. Either; the probability of rolling either odd or even is one-half.
27. Sample answer: any two letters followed by any four digits **29.** D
31. Sample answer: Vertical scale that does not start at zero. **33.** 11–20

35.

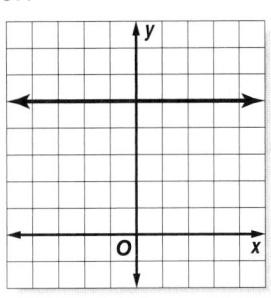

37.

39. 15 **41.** 28

Pages 643–645 Lesson 12-7
1. Sample answer: How many 3-digit numbers can be made from the digits 1, 2, 3, and 4 if no digit is repeated?
3. Sarah; five CDs from a collection of 30 is a combination because order is not important. **5.** P; 120 ways **7.** C; 84 ways **9.** 220 pizzas **11.** P; 24 flags **13.** C; 105 ways
15. P; 1320 ways **17.** C; 364 ways **19.** 40,320
21. 39,916,800 **23.** 36 handshakes **25.** 3003 ways
27. 10 combinations **29.** $\frac{2}{5}$ **31.** When order is not important, duplicate arrangements are not included in the number of arrangements. Answers should include the following.
• When order was not important there were half as many pairs.
• Order is important when you arrange things in a line; order is not important when you choose a group of things.

33. C **35.** Yes; the vertical axis does not include zero.
37. Q **39.** I **41.** 1:8 **43.** 11:2

Page 645 Practice Quiz 2
1. Sample answer: Bars are different widths.
3. 256 outcomes **5.** 15 segments

Pages 648–649 Lesson 12-8
1. Write a ratio comparing the ways the event can occur to the ways the event cannot occur. **3.** Hoshi; the probability of rolling a 2 is 1 out of 6. The odds of rolling a 2 are 1 in 5.
5. 1:2 **7.** 5:1 **9.** 1:2 **11.** 2:1 **13.** 1:1 **15.** 1:3 **17.** 5:7
19. 31:5 **21.** 1:17 **23.** 5:4 **25.** 9:4 **27.** $\frac{1}{8192}$ **29.** 47:53
31. No; 512 is the total number of possible outcomes, so it could not be a number in the odds of winning. **33.** A
35. 6 ways
37. ←——+——+——+——+——+——+——+——+——→ ; $a \geq 6$
      3   4   5   6   7   8   9   10
39. ←——+——+——+——+——+——+——+——+——→ ; $y > -3$
      −6 −5 −4 −3 −2 −1   0   1   2
41. $\frac{1}{3}$ **43.** $\frac{1}{56}$

Pages 653–655 Lesson 12-9
1. Independent and dependent events are similar because both are a connection of two or more simple events and the probability of the compound event is found by multiplying the probabilities of each simple event. They are different because the second event in a dependent event is influenced by the outcome of the first event. Therefore, the probability of the second event used in calculating the probability of the compound event is dependent on the outcome of the first event. **3.** The result of the 1st event must be taken into account. **5.** $\frac{1}{12}$ **7.** $\frac{3}{14}$ **9.** $\frac{3}{4}$ **11.** $\frac{1}{30}$
13. $\frac{1}{5}$ **15.** $\frac{1}{91}$ **17.** $\frac{10}{91}$ **19.** $\frac{5}{364}$ **21.** $\frac{5}{8}$ **23.** $\frac{3}{7}$ **25.** 1 **27.** $\frac{2}{9}$
29. 0.16 **31a.** Sample answer: 3 red, 2 white, and 4 blue
31b. Sample answer: The numerator must be 24. Any combination of 3, 2, and 4 will have a probability of $\frac{1}{21}$.
33. B **35.** $\frac{2}{3}$ **37.** 3:10 **39.** 17,576,000 **41.** 65° **43.** 65°
45. 90° **47.** 40.6 **49.** 16

Pages 658–662 Chapter 12 Study Guide and Review
1. b **3.** c **5.** d **7.**

Stem	Leaf
4	5 5
5	0 0 5 5
6	0 0 0 0 0
7	5 5 5
8	5 5 7|5 = 75¢

9. 23; 7 **11.** 22; 10 **13.** 80°F **15.** 50% **17.** Graph A
19. 16 outcomes **21.** C; 364 ways **23.** C; 21 ways **25.** 3:5
27. 1:3 **29.** $\frac{1}{30}$

Chapter 13 Polynomials and Nonlinear Functions

Page 667 Chapter 13 Getting Started
1. 1 **3.** 2 **5.** 0 **7.** $5a + 20$ **9.** $-4 - 32n$ **11.** $27b - 27c$
13. yes **15.** yes

Pages 670–672 Lesson 13-1

1. The degree of a monomial is the sum of the exponents of its variables. The degree of a polynomial is the same as the degree of the term with the greatest degree. **3.** Tanisha; the degree of a binomial is the degree of the term with the greater degree. **5.** yes; monomial **7.** yes; binomial **9.** yes; trinomial **11.** 0 **13.** 1 **15.** 4 **17.** 2 **19.** yes; binomial **21.** yes; monomial **23.** no **25.** yes; trinomial **27.** no **29.** yes; trinomial **31.** 0 **33.** 3 **35.** 5 **37.** 5 **39.** 3 **41.** 5 **43.** Always; any number is a monomial.
45. $2x + 2y + z + xy$ **49.** Polynomials approximate real-world data by using variables to represent quantities that are related. Answers should include the following.

• Heat index is found by using a polynomial in which one variable represents the percent humidity and another variable represents the temperature.
• Heat index cannot be approximated using a linear equation because the values do not change at a constant rate.

51. C **53.** mutually exclusive; $\frac{2}{3}$ **55.** 70 in^3
57. $(x + 2x) + 4$ **59.** $(6n + 3n) + (2 + 5)$
61. $(s + 5s) + (t - 3t)$

Pages 676–677 Lesson 13-2

1. x^2 and $2x^2$; $5x$ and $-4x$; 2 and 7 **3.** Hai; the terms have the same variables in a different order. **5.** $7a^2 - 9a + 4$
7. $13x - 4y$ **9.** $4x^2 + 3x - 2$ **11.** $3x + 3$
13. $11x^2 + 5xy + 4y^2$ **15.** $4x + 14$ **17.** $8y + 2r$
19. $5x^2 + xy + y$ **21.** $7x^2 + 9x + 5$ **23.** $5a - 4b$; -31
25. $4a + 6b + c$; 14 **27.** 56 **29.** $23x - 12$ **31.** $42x - 22$
33. Use algebra tiles to model each polynomial and combine the tiles that have the same size and shape. Answers should include the following.

• Algebra tiles that represent like terms have the same size and shape.
• When adding polynomials, a red tile and a white tile that have the same size and shape are zero pairs and may be removed. The result is the sum of the polynomials.

35. B **37.** 2 **39.** $\frac{2}{13}$ **41.** $\frac{3}{26}$ **43.** $15c + (-26)$
45. $1 + (-2x)$ **47.** $(n + rt) + (-r^2)$

Pages 680–681 Lesson 13-3

1. Subtracting one polynomial from another is the same as adding the additive inverse. **3.** $4r$ **5.** $5x + 2$
7. $3x^2 + 3x - 8$ **9.** $7x + 5$ units **11.** $-2n^2 + 6n$
13. $y^2 - 7y + 10$ **15.** $15w^2 - 2w + 10$ **17.** $4x + 3$
19. $-2t + 2$ **21.** $3a^2 + 2b^2$ **23.** $9n^2 - n - 12$
25. $2x^2 - 2xy + 3y^2$ **27.** $x - y = 68 + (x + y)$; $-34°$F
29. In subtracting polynomials and in subtracting measurements, like parts are subtracted. Answers should include the following.

• To subtract measurements with two or more units, subtract the like units. To subtract polynomials with two or more terms, subtract the like terms.
• For example, to subtract 1 foot 5 inches from 3 feet 8 inches, subtract the feet $3 - 1$ and subtract the inches $8 - 5$. The difference is 2 feet 3 inches.

31. B **33.** $12x - 3y$ **35.** $-t^2 + 12t + 2$ **37.** yes; binomial

39. Stem | Leaf

Stem	Leaf
5	4 9
6	4 6 8
7	0 1 1 2
8	5 9
9	1 $5\mid4 = 54$

41. $8y^2$ **43.** $4m^3$ **45.** $10r^5$

Page 681 Practice Quiz 1

1. 4 **3.** 3 **5.** $2x + 2$ **7.** $8r - 3s$ **9.** $-3x + 5y$

Pages 684–686 Lesson 13-4

1. False; the order in which numbers or terms are multiplied does not change the product, by the Commutative Property of Multiplication; $x(2x + 3) = 2x^2 + 3x$ and $(2x + 3)x = 2x^2 + 3x$. **3.** Sample answer: $2x(x + 1) = 2x^2 + 2x$ **5.** $a^2 + 4a$ **7.** $12x^2 - 28x$
9. $-15x^2 + 35x - 45$ **11.** $14n + 35$ **13.** $t^2 - 9t$
15. $-7a^2 - 6a$ **17.** $40n + 8n^2$ **19.** $3y^3 - 6y$ **21.** $5x^2 + 5xy$
23. $-14x^2 + 35x - 77$ **25.** $4c^4 + 28c^2 - 40c$ **27.** -1
29. high school, 84 ft by 50 ft; college, 94 ft by 50 ft

31.

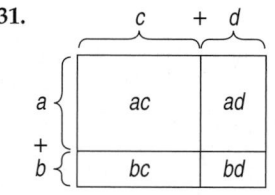

$(a + b)(c + d) = ac + ad + bc + bd$

33. D **35.** $7x - 1$
37. $4y^2 - 2y + 14$
39. $8x + 11y$

41. Sample answer: The scales are labeled inconsistently or the bars on a bar graph are different widths.
43. reflection

45.

x	$2x^2 - 3$	(x, y)
0	−3	(0, −3)
1	−1	(1, −1)
2	5	(2, 5)
3	15	(3, 15)

Pages 689–691 Lesson 13-5

1. Sample answer: Determine whether an equation can be written in the form $y = mx + b$ or look for a constant rate of change in a table of values. **3.** Sample answer: population growth **5.** Nonlinear; graph is a curve. **7.** Nonlinear; equation cannot be written as $y = mx + b$. **9.** Linear; rate of change is constant. **11.** Nonlinear; graph is a curve.
13. Linear; graph is a straight line. **15.** Nonlinear; graph is a curve. **17.** Linear; equation can be written as $y = 0.9x + 0$. **19.** Linear; equation can be written as $y = \frac{3}{4}x + 0$. **21.** Nonlinear; equation cannot be written as $y = mx + b$. **23.** Linear; rate of change is constant.
25. Nonlinear; rate of change is not constant.
27. Nonlinear; the points (year, applications) would lie on a curved line, not on a straight line. Or, the rate of change is not constant. **29.** No, the difference between the years varies, so the change is not constant. **31.** A **33.** $4t + 9t^2$
35. $a^2b - 2ab^2$ **37.** $-x$ **39.** acute

41.

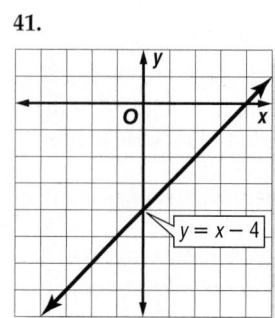

43.

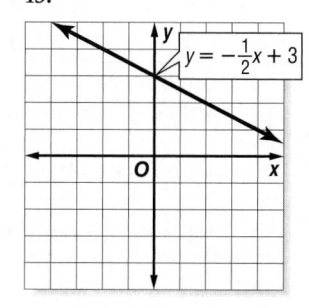

1. $2c^3 - 8c$ **3.** $5a^2 + a^3 + 2a^4$ **5.** Nonlinear; equation cannot be written as $y = mx + b$.

Pages 694–696   Lesson 13-6
1. Sample answer: The graph of $y = nx^2$ has line symmetry and the graph of $y = nx^3$ does not.   **3.** Sample answer: $y = x^2 + 3$; make a table of values and plot the points.

5.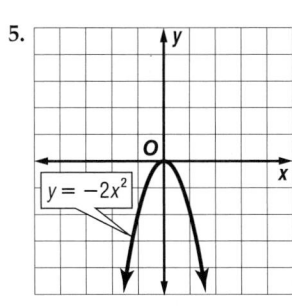

7.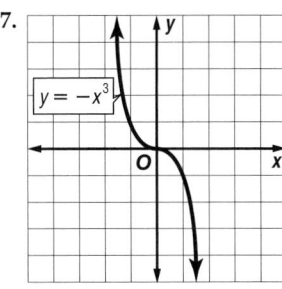

9.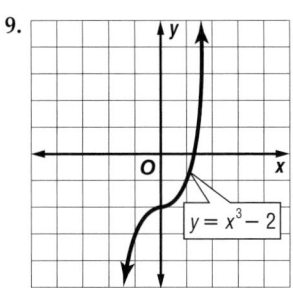

11.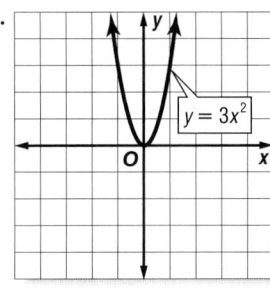

13.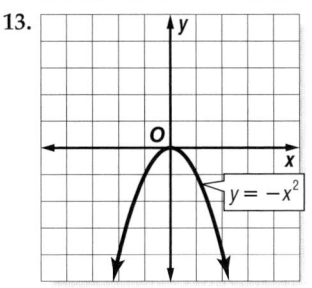

15.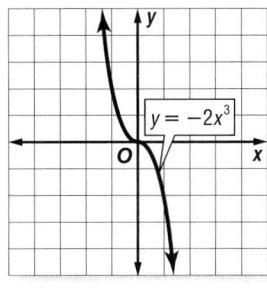

17.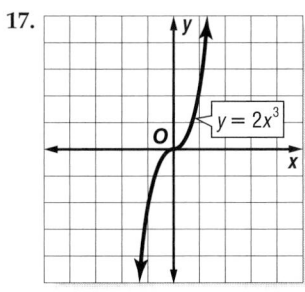

19.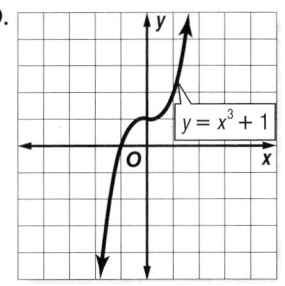

21.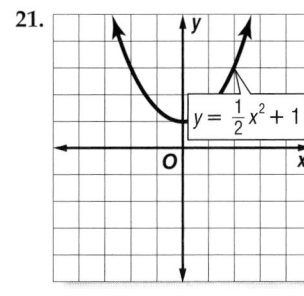

23.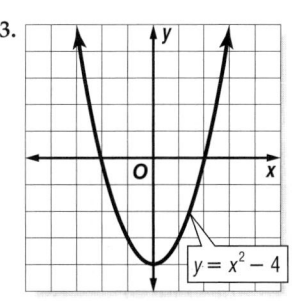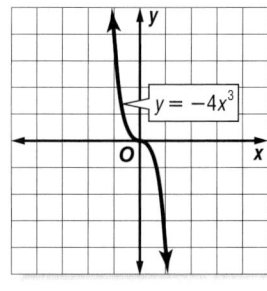

Both equations are functions because every value of x is paired with a unique value of y.

25. $(0, 7)$

27. 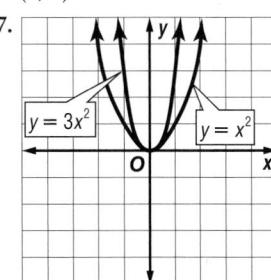   Similar shape; $y = 3x^2$ is more narrow.

29. 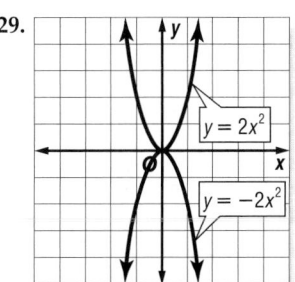   Same shape; $y = -2x^2$ is $y = 2x^2$ reflected over the x-axis.

31. $A = 50x - x^2$ **33.** 25 ft by 25 ft
35. $V = 0.2\pi r^2$ or $V \approx 0.6r^2$

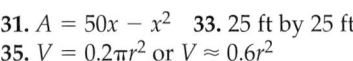
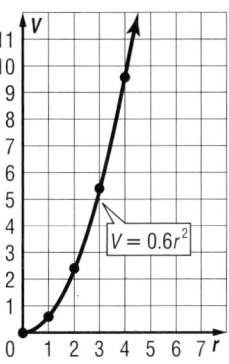

37. Formulas, tables, and graphs are interchangeable ways to represent functions. Answers should include the following.
- To make a graph, use a rule to make a table of values. Then plot the points and connect them to make a graph.
- To write a rule, find points that lie on a graph and make a table of values using the coordinates. Look for a pattern and write a rule that describes the pattern.

39. C   **41.** Sample answer: 18 units²   **43.** $10x - 20$
45. $24y - 21y^2$ **47.** $y = 4x - 3$

Pages 698–700   Chapter 13 Study Guide and Review
1. trinomial   **3.** cubic   **5.** like terms   **7.** curve   **9.** yes; binomial   **11.** yes; monomial   **13.** yes; trinomial   **15.** no

17. 1 **19.** 3 **21.** 6 **23.** 5 **25.** $8b + 3$ **27.** $5y^2 + 2y - 4$
29. $y^2 - y - 1$ **31.** $3x^2 - 4x + 7$ **33.** $-x + 1$ **35.** $20t - 10$
37. $6k^2 + 3k$ **39.** $-18a + 2a^3$ **41.** Linear; graph is a straight
line. **43.** Nonlinear; rate of change is not constant.

45.
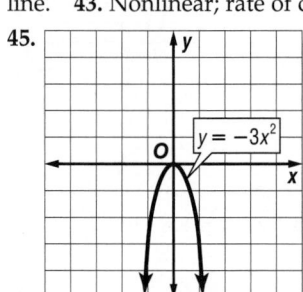

47.
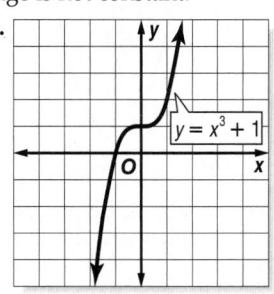

49.
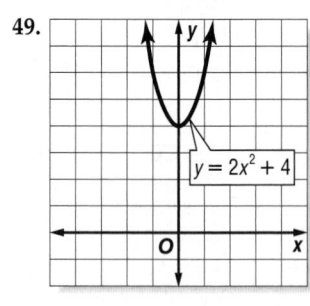

Photo Credits

About the Cover

The Great Bear at Hersheypark in Hershey, Pennsylvania, is an inverted coaster – that is, you ride below it, not above it. With four inversions, including loops, twists, and rolls, this ride reaches a speed of almost 60 miles per hour and at one point falls 124 feet. Roller coasters use math in their design and operation from beginning to end. Their designers want to make the tallest, fastest, most exciting coasters ever!

Cover Alan Schein/CORBIS Stock Market; **ix** Tom Pidgeon/ Getty Images, **x** Roy Ooms/Masterfile; **xi** David Young-Wolff/PhotoEdit; **xii** Robert Fried/Stock Boston; **xiii** Kay Chernush/Getty Images; **xiv** Tony Demin/ International Stock; **xv** Douglas Faulkner/Photo Researchers; **xvi** Chris Cole/DUOMO; **xvii** Adam Jones/ Photo Researchers; **xviii** SuperStock; **xix** Georgette Douwma/Getty Images; **xx** Matt Meadows; **xxi** Antonio M. Rosario/Getty Images; **1** Laura Sifferlin; **2–3** Ulf Sjostedt/ Getty Images, (bkgd)SuperStock; **4–5** Keren Su/CORBIS; **10** Doug Martin; **15** Tom Pidgeon/Getty Images, **19** TempSport/CORBIS; **27** Ken Eward/Photo Researchers; **31** Erik Dreyer/Getty Images; **35** Michael Boys/CORBIS; **37** Rhoda Sidney/Stock Boston; **42** Galen Rowell/CORBIS; **54–55** Jeff Hunter/Getty Images; **57** Jonathan Daniel/Getty Images; **66** NASA; **73** Doug Martin; **78** Mike Mazzaschi/ Stock Boston; **96–97** Jan Butchofsky-Houser/CORBIS; **99** AP/Wide World Photos; **105** Kit Kittle/CORBIS; **106** Mary Kate Denny/ PhotoEdit; **112** file photo; **116** Stuart Westmorland/ CORBIS; **123** Index Stock/Eric Kamp; **127** David Young-Wolff/PhotoEdit; **129** Dwayne Newton/ PhotoEdit; **131** PhotoDisc; **134** AFP/CORBIS; **144–145** David Young-Wolff/Getty Images, (bkgd)Jeffrey Myers/ Stock Boston/ PictureQuest; **146–147** Thomas Mangelsen/ Minden Pictures; **149** Elizabeth Whiting & Associates/ CORBIS; **151** Aaron Haupt; **156** Christophe Loviny/ CORBIS; **165** AP/Wide World Photos; **172** Geoff Butler; **178** Laura Sifferlin; **180** Latent Image; **182** Ralph A. Clevenger/ CORBIS; **184** VCG/Getty Images; **189** Robert Fried/Stock Boston; **198–199** SuperStock; **208** Lester Lefkowitz/CORBIS Stock Market; **214** JPL/ NASA; **217** Tony Anderson/Getty Images; **219** David Barnes/CORBIS Stock Market; **220** John Cancalosi/Stock Boston; **223** Tony Freeman/PhotoEdit; **229** NASA; **231 237** Geoff Butler; **247** Andy Caulfield/ Getty Images; **253** (t)Kay Chernush/Getty Images, (b)Geoff Butler; **262–263** SuperStock; **267** Chuck Pefley/ Stock Boston; **272** Louisville Slugger Museum, Louisville, KY; **275** Matt Meadows; **276** (t)Landscape plans provided by Greenscapes Landscape Architects and Contractors, Columbus, OH, (bl)Matt Meadows, (br)Ron Kimball/Ron Kimball Stock; **277** Kunio Owaki/CORBIS Stock Market; **278** Jeff Greenberg/Southern Stock/ PictureQuest; **284** Gary White Photography/StockFood; **288** Geoff Butler; **296** Frans Lanting/Minden Pictures; **299** Tony Demin/ International Stock; **306** Michael Paras/ International Stock; **324–325** Mark Richards/PhotoEdit, (bkgd)Marvin E. Newman/Getty Images; **326–327** Michael Melford/Getty Images; **331** SW Productions/Index Stock/Picturequest; **337** Matt Meadows; **344** Bob Daemmrich/Stock Boston;

347 Bob Daemmrich; **348** Douglas Faulkner/Photo Researchers; **356** SuperStock; **358** Doug Martin; **366–367** Allsport; **370** Peter/Stef Lamberti/Getty Images; **383** David Keaton/CORBIS Stock Market; **386** Matt Meadows; **387** Tony Freeman/PhotoEdit; **392** Doug Martin; **395** NASA/JSC; **399** Cris Haigh/Getty Images; **401** DUOMO; **408** Gail Shumway/Getty Images; **412** Michael Steele/Allsport; **417** Chris Cole/DUOMO; **422** Roy Ooms/Masterfile; **432–433** Index Stock/David Ball, (bkgd)David Zaitz/ Photonica; **434–435** Walter Bibikow/Getty Images; **438** Kunio Owaki/CORBIS Stock Market; **444** Kennan Ward/CORBIS Stock Market; **456** Garry Gay/ImageBank; **463** Steven E. Sutton/DUOMO; **472** Geoff Butler; **474** Adam Jones/Photo Researchers; **480** David Young-Wolff/ PhotoEdit; **490–491** J. David Andrews/Masterfile; **500** SuperStock; **503** Chuck Szymanski/International Stock; **511** Pete Saloutos/CORBIS Stock Market; **513** Richard Hamilton Smith/CORBIS; **515** (l)Pat LaCroix/Getty Images, (r)Irene Rica Pereira. Untitled, 1951. Oil on board, 101.5 × 61 cm (40 × 24 in.). Solomon R. Guggenheim Museum, New York, NY. Gift of Jerome B. Lurie, 1981; **516** Elizabeth Murray. Museum of Modern Art, New York, NY. Acquired through the Bernhill Fund. Gift of Agnes Gund; **524** SuperStock; **529** Papilio/ CORBIS; **530** Roy Lichtenstein. *Modern Painting with Clef*, 1967. Oil on synthetic polymer and pencil on canvas.

252.4 × 458.2 ($100\frac{1}{8} \times 180\frac{3}{8}$ in.)Hirshhorn Museum and Sculpture Garden, Smithsonian Institution; **537** Charles E. Rotkin/ CORBIS; **552–553** Rohan/Getty Images; **556** EyeWire, Yann Arthus-Bertrand/CORBIS; **558** Walter Bibikow/Getty Images; **560** (t)SHOE 8/31/94 ©Tribune Media Services. All Rights Reserved. Reprinted by permission, (bl)Roberto Otero/Black Star/PictureQuest, (br)Hermitage Museum, St. Petersburg, Russia/SuperStock; **575** Bob Mullenix; **578** SuperStock; **579** Bob Daemmrich; **581** (l)John Elk III/ Stock Boston, (r)John Elk III/Stock Boston; **583** Matt Meadows; **584** Aaron Haupt; **586** NASA; **602–603** Buddy Mays/CORBIS; **604–605** Larry Fisher/ Masterfile; **607 610** CORBIS; **614** Eastcott/Momatiuk/ Getty Images; **634** David Young-Wolff/PhotoEdit; **638** Michael Zito/ SportsChrome USA; **640** Aaron Haupt; **644** Mark Burnett; **649** Aaron Haupt; **651** Matt Meadows; **654** CORBIS; **656** Aaron Haupt; **666–667** (bkgd)Digital Stock, David Madison Sports Images; **670** Raymond Gehman/CORBIS; **675** Antonio M. Rosario/Getty Images; **683** Dallas & John Heaton/CORBIS; **685** Bettmann/ CORBIS; **693** Photri/Tom Sanders/CORBIS Stock Market.

Index

Index

Radical sign, 436, 437

Radius
circles, 443, 533, 536, 749
cones, 571

Range, 35, 36, 37, 44, 50, 51, 136, 367, 612–616, 618, 628, 659, 725, 753

Rate of change, 392, 393–397, 426, 743

Rates, 264–268, 316
converting, 266, 280

Rational numbers, 198–261, 440, 441, 443, 444, 451, 487, 745
division, 215–219, 256
identifying and classifying, 206
multiplication, 210–214, 255, 553, 577
solving equations, 244–248, 258
writing as fractions, 205–206

Ratios, 264–268, 273, 316, 321, 359, 386, 445, 454, 481, 553, 645, 736
common, 250, 251, 258
comparison, 269
writing as fractions, 264–265

Reading and Writing, 5, 55, 97, 147, 199, 263, 327, 367, 435, 491, 553, 605, 667

Reading Math, 17, 23, 24, 56, 57, 64, 75, 80, 88, 98, 103, 148, 149, 150, 159, 177, 200, 205, 206, 281, 300, 311, 341, 370, 381, 383, 437, 448, 453, 471, 472, 477, 493, 500, 508, 624, 641, 642, 643, 647, 650, 678, 688

Reading Mathematics
Dealing with Bias, 634
Factors and Multiples, 225
Language of Functions, 380
Learning Geometry Vocabulary, 446
Learning Mathematics Prefixes, 526
Learning Mathematics Vocabulary, 69
Making Comparisons, 269
Meanings of At Most and At Least, 339
Powers, 174
Precision and Accuracy, 589
Prefixes and Polynomials, 668
Translating Expressions into Words, 11
Translating Verbal Problems into Equations, 125

Real numbers, 441, 745

Real number system, 441–445, 484

Reasonableness, 7, 586

Reasoning. *See also* Critical Thinking
deductive, 25
inductive, 7, 25, 71

Reciprocals, 215, 247

Rectangles, 514, 546
area, 132, 133, 134, 135, 140, 141, 152, 214, 224, 349, 671, 730, 767
perimeter, 132, 133, 134, 135, 140, 141, 152, 224, 302, 335, 336, 349, 359, 363, 385, 417, 676, 701, 730

Rectangular prisms, 557, 560, 563, 565, 566, 575, 576, 582, 597

Rectangular pyramid, 557, 570, 572, 577

Reflections, 506, 508, 509, 510, 512, 686, 748

Regular polygon, 529

Regular tessellations, 527

Relations, 35, 50, 367
as tables and graphs, 35, 36, 37, 50

Relationships, types of, 41, 42, 43, 51 50, 68

Relative frequencies, 627

Relatively prime, 168

Repeating decimals, 201, 202, 203, 206, 214, 224, 254, 338, 733

Replacement set, 102

Research, 43, 46, 83, 113, 151, 225, 253, 268, 291, 308, 380, 446, 526, 530, 543, 560, 583, 589, 610, 668, 672. *See also* Online Research

Rhombus, 514, 546

Rotational symmetry, 505

Rotations, 506, 507, 508, 509, 510, 512, 532, 686
coordinate plane, 509

Rounding, 9, 10, 201, 242, 283, 284, 291, 314, 443, 445, 457, 462, 463, 468, 469, 475, 478, 480, 481, 482, 484, 486, 487, 491, 531, 534, 535, 536, 543, 548, 549, 565, 566, 568, 569, 570, 571, 572, 577, 580, 581, 582, 588, 592, 593, 596, 597, 598, 599, 605, 611, 672, 711, 735, 736, 737, 738, 745, 746, 747, 749, 750, 751, 752

Rows, 705

Sample space, 311

Scale, 276, 631, 737

Scale drawings, 276–280, 317

Scale factor, 277, 285, 583, 587

Scale model, 276

Index

Symbols and Properties

Symbols

$+$	plus or positive	$\circ$	degree
$-$	minus or negative	$!$	factorial
$\pm$	plus or minus	$\overline{AB}$	line segment AB
$\times$ or $\cdot$	times	AB	measure of $\overline{AB}$
$\div$	divided by	$-a$	opposite or additive inverse of a
$=$	is equal to	(a, b)	ordered pair a, b
$\neq$	is not equal to	O	origin
$>$	is greater than	$\%$	percent
$<$	is less than	π	pi
$\geq$	is greater than or equal to	$P(A)$	probability of A
$\leq$	is less than or equal to	$a{:}b$	ratio of a to b
$\approx$	is approximately equal to	$0.7\overline{5}$	repeating decimal $0.75555\ldots$
$|a|$	absolute value of a	$\sqrt{a}$	square root of a
$\angle$	angle	$\triangle$	triangle

Addition and Multiplication Properties

Additive Identity	For any number a, $a + 0 = 0 + a = a$.
Multiplicative Identity	For any number a, $a \cdot 1 = 1 \cdot a = a$.
Additive Inverse	For any number a, there is exactly one number $-a$ such that $a + (-a) = 0$.
Multiplicative Inverse	For any number $\frac{a}{b}$, where $a, b \neq 0$, there is exactly one number $\frac{b}{a}$ such that $\frac{a}{b} \cdot \frac{b}{a} = 1$.
Commutative (+)	For any numbers a and b, $a + b = b + a$.
Commutative (×)	For any numbers a and b, $a \cdot b = b \cdot a$.
Associative (+)	For any numbers a, b, and c, $(a + b) + c = a + (b + c)$.
Associative (×)	For any numbers a, b, and c, $(a \cdot b) \cdot c = a \cdot (b \cdot c)$.
Distributive	For any numbers a, b, and c, $a(b + c) = ab + ac$ and $a(b - c) = ab - ac$.

Formulas and Measures

Formulas

Midpoint on a coordinate plane		$M = \left(\dfrac{x_1 + x_2}{2}, \dfrac{y_1 + y_2}{2}\right)$
Distance on a coordinate plane		$d = \sqrt{(x_2 - x_1)^2 + (y_2 - y_1)^2}$
Perimeter of a rectangle		$P = 2\ell + 2w$ or $P = 2(\ell + w)$
Circumference of a circle		$C = 2\pi r$ or $C = \pi d$
Area	rectangle	$A = \ell w$
	parallelogram	$A = bh$
	triangle	$A = \frac{1}{2}bh$
	trapezoid	$A = \frac{1}{2}h(b_1 + b_2)$
	circle	$A = \pi r^2$
Surface Area	cube	$S = 6s^2$
	prism	$S = Ph + 2B$
	cylinder	$S = 2\pi rh + 2\pi r^2$
	regular pyramid	$S = \frac{1}{2}P\ell + B$
	cone	$S = \pi r\ell + \pi r^2$
Volume	cube	$V = s^3$
	prism	$V = Bh$
	cylinder	$V = \pi r^2 h$
	regular pyramid	$V = \frac{1}{3}Bh$
	cone	$V = \frac{1}{3}\pi r^2 h$

Measures

Measure	Metric	Customary
Length	kilometer (km) = 1000 meters (m) 1 meter = 100 centimeters (cm) 1 centimeter = 10 millimeters (mm)	1 mile (mi) = 1760 yards (yd) 1 mile = 5280 feet (ft) 1 yard = 3 feet 1 foot = 12 inches (in.) 1 yard = 36 inches
Volume and Capacity	1 liter (L) = 1000 milliliters (mL) 1 kiloliter (kL) = 1000 liters	1 gallon (gal) = 4 quarts (qt) 1 gallon = 128 fluid ounces (fl oz) 1 quart = 2 pints (pt) 1 pint = 2 cups (c) 1 cup = 8 fluid ounces
Weight and Mass	1 kilogram (kg) = 1000 grams (g) 1 gram = 1000 milligrams (mg) 1 metric ton (t) = 1000 kilograms	1 ton (T) = 2000 pounds (lb) 1 pound = 16 ounces (oz)